SHEPARD'S
ACTS AND CASES
BY
POPULAR NAMES

FEDERAL AND STATE

A compilation of popular names by which federal and
state acts and cases have been referred to or cited
together with an identification of each act
in terms of its constitutional or statutory
references and each case in terms of
the volume and page reference
where the text of the decision
may be found.

FIFTH EDITION - 1999, PART 2

SHEPARD'S
555 Middle Creek Parkway
Colorado Springs, CO 80921-3622
1-800-899-6000

0769833969

TABLE OF CONTENTS

PART 2

PREFACE

Shepard's Acts and Cases by Popular Names is a reference tool that provides citation information for statutes and cases that are commonly referred to by popular name.

Federal and state acts are listed alphabetically and can be located by name (e.g., Pine Creek Scenic Rivers Act or Pilot Records Improvement Act of 1996). Shepard's Acts and Cases by Popular Names also provides a quick indexing system for locating a citation or list of citations from several states–including federal statutes–dealing with a specific topic (e.g., Lemon Law or Water Conservation). These indexes also include citations to Constitutional provisions (e.g., Equal Suffrage Amendment).

Where a particular case is known only by its popular name, the alphabetical indexes found in these volumes can be used to locate the needed citation to the case (e.g., Miranda).

SUPPLEMENTATION

Shepard's Acts and Cases by Popular Names consists of the 1999 bound volume (Parts 1–3) and the current issue of the soft-covered cumulative supplement. Cumulative supplements are published bimonthly in February, April, June, August, October and December. Supplementation is cumulative, therefore, only the most recent supplement needs to be retained and used with the bound volume. From time to time, as the accumulation of citations necessitates, a cumulative supplement will be permanently bound. Each supplement-cover provides the necessary information as to "What Your Library Should Contain." Always consult these supplement covers before discarding any soft-covered supplements or bound volumes.

ORGANIZATION

Shepard's Acts and Cases by Popular Names contains two divisions. Acts, i.e., federal and state statutory and constitutional materials, are listed alphabetically by popular name in the first division. Cases are listed alphabetically by popular name in the second division. Please consult the tables of abbreviations used in the division for Federal and State cases cited by Popular Names to identify the citing references that appear in these bound volumes.

Citations to federal statutes include the United States Code title and section numbers wherever this information is available. Sometimes a law is merely cited by the date on which it was enacted. The citation format contained in these volumes for federal statutes includes a citation to the date a law was enacted, the Public sequential number and Congressional Session that enacted the law, a Statutes at Large citation, and the citation to the U.S. Code where this information is available.

Parallel citations, cases that are published in more than one reporter, are included for the widely available reports (e.g., U.S., S. Ct., and L. Ed. citations for the United States Supreme Court decisions; official and regional reporter citations for state-court decisions in jurisdictions that publish a separate state official report).

CITATIONS RESEARCH

After identifying a case or statute in Shepard's Acts and Cases by Popular Names, ascertain its status as authority and locate additional cases dealing with similar issues by consulting the pertinent Shepard's Citations.

SHEPARD'S

ABBREVIATIONS—ACTS

Adm.–Administrative
AG–Agriculture
Ala.–Alabama
Am.–Amended
Amend.–Amendment
Ann.–Annotated
Appx.–Appendix
Ariz.–Arizona
Ark.–Arkansas
Art.–Article
Aug.–August
BO–Business Occupations and
    Professions
BR–Business Regulation
CA–Corporations and Associations
Cal.–California
Ch[s].–Chapter[s]
Civ.–Civil
CJ–Courts and Judicial Proceedings
CL–Commercial Law
Cl[s].–Clause[s]
Colo.–Colorado
Comp.–Compiled
Conn.–Connecticut
Consol.–Consolidated
Const.–Constitution
Crim.–Criminal
C.S.–Called Session
D.C.–District of Columbia
Dec.–December
Del.–Delaware
Div.–Division
ED–Education
EN–Environment
ET–Estates and Trusts
Ex.–Extra
Ex. Sess.–Extra Session
Feb.–February
Fla.–Florida
FI–Financial Institutions
FL–Family Law

Ga.–Georgia
G.A.–General Assembly
Gen.–General
H.B.–House Bill
Haw.–Hawaii
HE–Health-Environmental
HG–Health-General
HO–Health-Occupation
H.R.–House Reports
Ida.–Idaho
Ill.–Illinois
IN–Insurance Law
Ind.–Indiana
Init. Meas.–Initiative Measure
Jan.–January
Kan.–Kansas
Ky.–Kentucky
La.–Louisiana
L.B.–Legislative Bill
LE–Labor and Employment
Leg.–Legislature
Mass.–Massachusetts
Md.–Maryland
Me.–Maine
Mich.–Michigan
Minn.–Minnesota
Miss.–Mississippi
Mo.–Missouri
Mont.–Montana
N.C.–North Carolina
N.D.–North Dakota
Neb.–Nebraska
Nev.–Nevada
N.H.–New Hampshire
N.J.–New Jersey
N.M.–New Mexico
No.–Number
Nov.–November
NR–Natural Resources
nt[s].–note[s]
N.Y.–New York

Oct.–October
Okla.–Oklahoma
Ore.–Oregon
p[p].–page[s]
Pa.–Pennsylvania
Pamph. Laws–Pamphlet Laws
P.L.–Public Law
PP–State Personnel and Pension
prec.–preceding
Proc.–Procedure
P.R.–Puerto Rico
Rev.–Revised
R.I.–Rhode Island
RP–Real Property
§[§]–Section[s]
S.B.–Senate Bill
S.C.–South Carolina
S.D.–South Dakota
SF–State Finance & Procurement
SG–State Government
Sept.–September
Sess.–Session

Sp.–Special
Sp. Sess.–Special Session
S.R.–Senate Reports
Stat.–Statutes or United States
      Statutes at Large
Subd.–Subdivision
Subsec.–Subsection
Supp.–Supplement
Tenn.–Tennessee
Tex.–Texas
TG–Tax-General
TP–Tax Property
TR–Transportation
Unconsol.–Unconsolidated
U.S.–United States
Va.–Virginia
Vol[s].–Volume[s]
Vt.–Vermont
Wash.–Washington
Wis.–Wisconsin
W. Va.–West Virginia
Wyo.–Wyoming

ABBREVIATIONS—CASES

The following abbreviations are used to identify the citing references that appear in this bound volume:

A.–Atlantic Reporter

A.2d–Atlantic Reporter, Second Series

Abb. N. Cas.–Abbott's New Cases, New York

Abb. Pr.–Abbott's Practice Reports, New York

Abb. Pr. (n.s.)–Abbott's Practice Reports, New Series, New York

Abs. (n.s.)–Abstracts, New Series (Treasury Decisions)

A.D.–Appellate Division Reports (New York Supreme Court)

A.D.2d–Appellate Division Reports, Second Series (New York Supreme Court)

Ala.–Alabama Reports

Ala. App.–Alabama Appellate Courts Reports

Alaska–Alaska Reports

Alaska Fed.–Alaska Federal Reports

Allen–Allen's Massachusetts Reports

Am. B.R. (n.s.)–American Bankruptcy Reports, New Series

A.M.C.–American Maritime Cases

App. D.C.–Appeal Cases, District of Columbia

Ariz.–Arizona Reports

Ariz. App.–Arizona Appeals Reports

Ark.–Arkansas Reports

Ark. App.–Arkansas Appellate Reports

Bailey–Bailey's South Carolina Law Reports

Barb.–Barbour's Supreme Court Reports, New York

Baxt.–Baxter's Tennessee Reports

B.C.R.–Baltimore City Reports

Bosw.–Bosworth's Superior Court Reports, New York

Boyce–Boyce's Reports, Delaware

B.R.–Bankruptcy Reporter

Bradf.–Bradford's Surrogate Reports, New York

Brewst.–Brewster's Reports, Pennsylvania

B.T.A.–Reports of the United States Board of Tax Appeals

Cal.–California Supreme Court Reports

Cal. 2d–California Supreme Court Reports, Second Series

Cal. 3d–California Supreme Court Reports, Third Series

Cal. 3d S.–California Supreme Court Reports, Third Series (Special Tribunal Supplement)

Cal. 4th–California Supreme Court Reports, Fourth Series

Cal. App.–California Appellate Reports

Cal. App. 2d–California Appellate Reports, Second Series

Cal. App. 3d–California Appellate Reports, Third Series

Cal. App. 3d S.–California Appellate Reports, Third Series Supplement

Cal. App. 4th–California Appellate Reports, Fourth Series

Cal. App. 4th S.–California Appellate Reports, Fourth Series Supplement

Cal. Comp. Cas.–California Compensation Cases

Cal. R. Com.–Opinions and Orders of the Railroad Commission of California

Cal. Rptr.–California Reporter

Cal. Rptr. 2d–California Reporter, Second Series

C.C.A.–Circuit Court of Appeals Reports

C.C.P.A.–United States Court of Customs and Patent Appeals Reports

C.D.–Decisions of the Commissioner of Patents

Civ. P. Rep.–Civil Procedure Reports, New York

Clark–Clark's Pennsylvania Law Journal Reports

Code Rep.–Code Reporter, New York

Colo.–Colorado Reports

Colo. App.–Colorado Court of Appeals Reports

Conn.–Connecticut Reports

Conn. App.–Connecticut Appellate Reports

Conn. Cir. Ct.–Connecticut Circuit Court Reports

Conn. Supp.–Connecticut Supplement

Cow.–Cowen's Common Law Reports, New York

Ct. Cl.–Court of Claims Reports, United States

Ct. Cust.–Court of Customs Appeals Reports, United States

Ct. Int'l Trade–United States Court of International Trade Reports

Cust. Ct.–Customs Court Reports, United States

Cush.–Cushing Massachusetts Reports

Dakota–Dakota Reports

Daly–Daly's Common Pleas Reports, New York

D.C.–District of Columbia Reports

D.C.H.–Reports of the United States District Court of Hawaii

Del.–Delaware Reports

Del. Ch.–Delaware Chancery Reports

Denio–Denio's Common Law Reports, New York

Dep't Rep.–State Department Reports, New York

Duer–Duer's Superior Court Reports, New York

E.D.R.–Education Department Reports, New York

Edm. Sel. Cas.–Edmond's Select Cases, New York

F.–Federal Reporter

F.2d–Federal Reporter, Second Series

F.3d–Federal Reporter, Third Series

F. Cas.–Federal Cases

F.C.C.–Federal Communications Commission Reports

F.C.C.2d–Federal Communications Commission Reports, Second Series

F. Supp.–Federal Supplement

F. Supp. 2d–Federal Supplement, Second Series

F.T.C.–Federal Trade Commission Decisions

Fla.–Florida Reports

Fla. Supp.–Florida Supplement

Fla. Supp. 2d–Florida Supplement, Second Series

F.P.C.–Federal Power Commission Reports

F.R.D.–Federal Rules Decisions

G. & J.–Gill and Johnson Reports, Maryland

Ga.–Georgia Reports

Ga. App.–Georgia Appeals Reports

Gen. Appraisers–United States General Appraisers

Gratt.–Grattan Virginia Reports

Gray–Gray Massachusetts Reports

Harr.–Harrington Delaware Reports

H.H.–Hayward and Hazleton's Reports, United States

Haw.–Hawaii Reports

Haw. App.–Hawaii Appellate Reports

Heisk.–Heiskell Tennessee Reports

Hill–Hill's Common Law Reports, New York

Hopk. Ch.–Hopkins' Chancery Reports

Houst.–Houston Reports, Delaware

How. Pr.–Howard's Practice Reports, New York

Hun–Hun's Supreme Court Reports, New York

I.C.–Interstate Commerce Reports

I.C.C.–Interstate Commerce Commission Reports

Idaho–Idaho Reports

Ill. Dec.–Illinois Decisions

Ill.–Illinois Reports

Ill. 2d–Illinois Reports, Second Series

Ill. App.–Illinois Appellate Court Reports

Ill. App. 2d–Illinois Appellate Court Reports, Second Series

Ill. App. 3d–Illinois Appellate Court Reports, Third Series

Ill. Cir. Ct.–Illinois Circuit Court Reports

Ill. Ct. Cl.–Illinois Court of Claims Reports

Ind.–Indiana Reports

Ind. App.–Indiana Court of Appeals Reports (Indiana Appellate Court Reports before 1972)

Interior Dec.–Decisions of the Department of the Interior

Iowa–Iowa Reports

Johns.–Johnson's Common Law Reports, New York

Johns. Ch.–Johnson's Chancery Reports, New York

Jones & S.–Jones and Spencer's Superior Court Reports, New York

Kan.–Kansas Reports

Kan. App.–Kansas Court of Appeals Reports

Kan. App. 2d–Kansas Court of Appeals Reports, Second Series

Keyes–Keyes' Reports, New York

Ky. Law Rep.–Kentucky Law Reporter

Ky.–Kentucky Reports

La.–Louisiana Reports

La. Ann.–Louisiana Annual Reports

La. App.–Louisiana Court of Appeals Reports

L. Ed.–Lawyer's Edition, United States Supreme Court Reports

L. Ed. 2d–Lawyer's Edition, United States Supreme Court Reports, Second Series

Leigh–Leigh Virginia Reports

Mart. (n.s.)–Martin Louisiana Reports, New Series (Louisiana Term Reports)

Mart. (o.s.)–Martin Louisiana Reports, Old Series (Louisiana Term Reports)

Marv.–Marvel Delaware Reports

Mass. App. Ct.–Massachusetts Appeals Court Reports

Mass. App. Div.–Appellate Division Reports Massachusetts

Mass.–Massachusetts Reports

McGrath–McGrath's Mandamus Cases, Michigan

M.C.C.–Interstate Commerce Commission Reports, Motor Carrier Cases

Md.–Maryland Reports

Md. App.–Maryland Appellate Reports

Me.–Maine Reports

Met.–Metcalf Massachusetts Reports

Mich.–Michigan Reports

Mich. App.–Michigan Appeals Reports

Mills–Mills' Surrogate's Court Reports, New York

Minn.–Minnesota Reports

Minor–Minor Alabama Reports

Misc.–New York Miscellaneous Reports

Misc. 2d–New York Miscellaneous Reports, Second Series

Miss.–Mississippi Reports

M.J.–Military Justice Reporter

Mo.–Missouri Reports

Mo. App.–Missouri Appeals Reports

Mont.–Montana Reports

N.C.–North Carolina Supreme Court Reports

N.C. App.–North Carolina Court of Appeals Reports

N.D.–North Dakota Reports

N.E.–North Eastern Reporter

N.E.2d–North Eastern Reporter, Second Series

Neb.–Nebraska Reports

Nev.–Nevada Reports

N.H.–New Hampshire Reports

N.J.–New Jersey Reports

N.J. Eq.–New Jersey Equity Reports

N.J.L.–New Jersey Law Reports

N.J. Misc.–New Jersey Miscellaneous Reports

N.J. Super.–New Jersey Superior Court Reports

N.L.R.B.–Decisions and Orders of the National Labor Relations Board

N.M.–New Mexico Reports

N.W.–North Western Reporter

N.W.2d–North Western Reporter, Second Series

N.Y.–New York Reports

N.Y.2d–New York Reports, Second Series

N.Y. Crim.–New York Criminal Reports

N.Y. St. Rep.–New York State Reporter

N.Y. Super. Ct.–New York Superior Court Reports

N.Y.S.–New York Supplement

N.Y.S.2d–New York Supplement, Second Series

Off. Gaz. Pat. Office–Official Gazette of the United States Patent Office

Ohio–Ohio Reports

Ohio Law Abs.–Ohio Law Abstract

Ohio App.–Ohio Appellate Reports

Ohio App. 2d–Ohio Appellate Reports, Second Series

Ohio App. 3d–Ohio Appellate Reports, Third Series

Ohio C.C. (n.s.)–Ohio Circuit Court Reports, New Series

Ohio Cir. Dec.–Ohio Circuit Decisions

Ohio Dec.–Ohio Decisions

Ohio Dec. Reprint–Ohio Decisions, Reprint

Ohio F. Des.–Ohio Federal Decisions

Ohio Law Rep.–Ohio Law Reporter

Ohio Misc.–Ohio Miscellaneous

Ohio Misc. 2d–Ohio Miscellaneous, Second Series

Ohio N.P. (n.s.)–Ohio Nisi Prius Reports, New Series

Ohio Op.–Ohio Opinions

Ohio Op. 2d–Ohio Opinions, Second Series

Ohio Op. 3d–Ohio Opinions, Third Series

Ohio St.–Ohio State Reports

Ohio St. 2d–Ohio State Reports, Second Series

Ohio St. 3d–Ohio State Reports, Third Series

Okla.–Oklahoma Reports

Okla. Crim.–Oklahoma Criminal Reports

Ore.–Oregon Reports

Ore. App.–Oregon Reports, Court of Appeals

P.–Pacific Reporter

P.2d–Pacific Reporter, Second Series

Pa.–Pennsylvania State Reports

Paige Ch.–Paige's Chancery Reports, New York

Park.–Parker's Criminal Reports, New York

Pa. Commw.–Pennsylvania Commonwealth Court Reports

Pa. D. & C.–Pennsylvania District and County Reports

Pa. D. & C.2d–Pennsylvania District and County Reports, Second Series

Pa. D. & C.3d–Pennsylvania District and County Reports, Third Series

Pa. D. & C.4th–Pennsylvania District and County Reports, Fourth Series

Pa. L.J. Rep.–Pennsylvania Law Journal Reports

Pa. Super.–Pennsylvania Superior Court Reports

Pelt.–Peltier's Decisions, Parish at Orleans, Louisiana

Penne.–Pennewill Delaware Reports

Phila.–Philadelphia Reports

Pick.–Pickering Massachusetts Reports

Pub. Lands Dec.–Public Lands Decisions

Quincy–Quincy's Massachusetts Reports

Reappr. Dec.–Reappraisement Decisions

Redf.–Redfield's Surrogates Reports, New York

R.I.–Rhode Island Reports

Sandf.–Sandford's Superior Court Reports, New York

Sandf. Ch.–Sandford's Chancery Reports, New York

S. Ct.–Supreme Court Reporter

S.C.–South Carolina Reports

S.C. Eq.–South Carolina Equity Reports

S.C.L.–South Carolina Law Reports

S.D.–South Dakota Reports

S.D.C. (n.s.)–Supreme Court, District of Columbia Reports, New Series

S.E.–South Eastern Reporter

S.E.2d–South Eastern Reporter, Second Series

S.E.C.–Securities and Exchange Commission Decisions and Reports

Serg. & Rawle–Sergeant and Rawle Pennsylvania State Reports

Silv.–Silvernail's Supreme Court Reports, New York

So.–Southern Reporter

So. 2d–Southern Reporter, Second Series

Stew.–Stewart Alabama Reports

S.W.–South Western Reporter

S.W.2d–South Western Reporter, Second Series

T.B. Mon.–Kentucky Reports, T.B. Monroe

T.C.–Tax Court Reports of the United States Tax Court

Tenn.–Tennessee Reports

Tenn. App.–Tennessee Appeals Reports

Tenn. Crim. App.–Tennessee Criminal Appeals Reports

Tex.–Texas Reports

Tex. Civ. App.–Texas Civil Appeals Reports

Tex. Crim.–Texas Criminal Reports

Thomp. & Cook's–Thompson and Cook's Supreme Court Reports, New York

Treas. Dec.–United States Treasury Decisions

U.S.–United States Reports

U.S. App. D.C.–United States Court of Appeals Reports

U.S.L.W.–United States Law Week

U.S.P.Q.–United States Patents Quarterly

Utah–Utah Reports

Utah 2d–Utah Reports, Second Series

Va.–Virginia Reports

Va. App.–Virginia Court of Appeals Reports

Va. Cir. Ct.–Virginia Circuit Court Opinions

Vt.–Vermont Reports

Wash.–Washington Reports

Wash. App.–Washing Appellate Reports

Wash. 2d–Washington Reports, Second Series

Wend.–Wendell's Common Law Reports, New York

Wheel. Crim. Cas.–Wheeler's Criminal Cases, New York

Wis.–Wisconsin Reports

Wis. 2d–Wisconsin Reports, Second Series

Wkly. L. Bull.–Weekly Law Bulletin, Ohio

W.L.J.–Western Law Journal, Ohio

W. Va.–West Virginia Reports

Wyo.–Wyoming Reports

Yates Sel. Cas.–Yates' Select Cases, New York

FEDERAL AND STATE ACTS
CITED BY POPULAR NAMES

H – R

H

Habeas Corpus Act
Ariz. Rev. Stat. Ann., § 13-4121 et seq.
Cal. Penal Code § 1473 et seq.
Colo. Rev. Stat., 13-45-101 et seq.
Conn. Gen. Stat. Ann., § 52-466 et seq.
Ga. Code Ann., 9-14-40 et seq.
Haw. Rev. Stat. Ann., § 660-1 et seq.
Ill. Rev. Stat. 1991, Ch. 110, § 10-101 et seq.
Iowa Code Ann., 663.1 et seq.
Kan. Stat. Ann., 60-1501 et seq.
Ky. Rev. Stat. 1971, 419.020 et seq.
Md. Ann. Code 1974,CJ, § 3-701 et seq.
Mich. Comp. Laws Ann., 600.4301 et seq.
Miss. Code Ann. 1972, § 11-43-1 et seq.
Mo. Rev. Stat., 532.010 et seq.
Mont. Code Ann., 46-22-101 et seq.
N.C. Gen. Stat. 1943, § 17-1 et seq.
Nev. Rev. Stat. 1979 Reprint, 34.360 et seq.
N.H. Rev. Stat. 1955, 534:1 et seq.
N.J. Stat. Ann., 2A:67-1 et seq.
N.Y. Civil Practice Law and Rules (Consol. Laws Ch. 8) § 7001 et seq.
Ohio Rev. Code 1953, 2725.01 et seq.
Okla. Stat. Ann., Title 12, § 1331 et seq.
Ore. Rev. Stat., 34.310 et seq.
Pa. Cons. Stat., Title 42, § 6501 et seq.
R.I. Gen. Laws 1956, 10-9-1 et seq.
S.C. Code Ann. 1976, § 17-17-10 et seq.
S.D. Codified Laws 1967, 21-27-1 et seq.
Tex. Code of Criminal Procedure, Art. 11.01 et seq.
Utah Rules of Civil Procedure 1950, Rule 65B et seq.
Va. Code 1950, § 8.01-654 et seq.
Vt. Stat. Ann., Title 12, § 3951 et seq.
Wash. Rev. Code Ann., 7.36.010 et seq.
W. Va. Code 1966, § 53-4-1 et seq.

Habeas Corpus Act (Civil War)
March 3, 1863, Ch. 81, 12 Stat. 755

Habeas Corpus Reform Act (Death Penalty)
Ga. Code Ann., 9-14-44 et seq., 15-1-9.1

Habeas Corpus Reimbursement Act
Ill. Rev. Stat. 1991, Ch. 65, § 36.9 et seq.

Habit Act (Alcoholics)
Pa. 1953 Pamph. Laws 1212, No. 338

Habit Forming Drug Act
Ore. Rev. Stat., 475.005 et seq.
Pa. 1917 Pamph. Laws 758, No. 282

Habitability Act (Warranty of)
N.Y. Real Property Law (Consol. Laws Ch. 50) § 235b

Habitat Enhancement Act (Fish and Wildlife)
Cal. Fish and Game Code 1957, § 2600 et seq.

Habitat Maintenance Funding Act
Cal. Fish and Game Code 1957, §§ 2900, 2901

Habitat Protection Act
N.M. Stat. Ann., 17-6-1 et seq.

Habitual and Serious Juvenile Offender Act
Okla. Stat. Ann., Title 10, § 1160.1 et seq.

Habitual Child Sex Offender Registration Act
Ark. Code Ann. 1987, 12-12-901 et seq.
Ill. Rev. Stat. 1991, Ch. 38, § 221 et seq.

Habitual Criminal Act
Alaska Stat. 1962, § 12.55.040 et seq.
Ariz. Rev. Stat. Ann., § 13-604
Ark. Code Ann. 1987, 16-90-201 et seq.
Cal. Penal Code §§ 644, 667 et seq.
Colo. Rev. Stat., 16-13-101 et seq.
Conn. Gen. Stat. Ann., § 53a-40
D.C. Code 1973, §§ 22-104
Del. Code of 1974, Title 11, § 4214
Fla. Stat. Ann., 775.084
Ga. Code Ann., 17-10-7
Ida. Code 1947, 19-2514
Ill. Rev. Stat. 1991, Ch. 38, § 1005-5-3 et seq.
Iowa Code Ann., 902.8
Kan. Stat. Ann., 21-4504
Continued

1

Ky. Rev. Stat. 1971, 523.080
Mass. Gen. Laws Ann., 279:25
Me. Rev. Stat. Ann. 1964, Title 15, § 1742
Mich. Comp. Laws Ann., 769.10 et seq.
Minn. Stat. 1978, 609.155, 609.16
Mo. Rev. Stat., 558.016 et seq.
Mont. Code Ann., 46-18-501 et seq.
N.D. Cent. Code, 12.1-32-09
Neb. Rev. Stat. 1943, 29-2221 et seq.
Nev. Rev. Stat. Ann., 207.010
N.H. Rev. Stat. 1955, 651:6
N.J. Stat. Ann., 2C:43-7, 2C:44-3
N.M. Stat. Ann., 31-18-17 et seq.
N.Y. Penal Law 1965 (Consol. Laws Ch. 40)
   § 70.10
Ohio Rev. Code 1953, 2929.11 et seq.
Okla. Stat. Ann., Title 21, § 51 et seq.
Ore. Rev. Stat. 1953, 168.015 et seq.
Pa. Cons. Stat., Title 18, § 1102 et seq.
R.I. Gen. Laws 1956, 12-19-21
S.C. Code Ann. 1976, § 17-25-40 et seq.
S.D. Codified Laws 1967, 22-7-1 et seq.
Tenn. Code Ann., 39-1-801 et seq.
Tex. Penal Code, §§ 12.42, 12.43
Utah Code Ann. 1953, 76-8-1001, 76-8-1002
Va. Code 1950, § 53-296
Vt. Stat. Ann., Title 13, § 11

**Habitual Criminal Act (Liquor Law
   Violators)**
Iowa Code Ann., 123.91

Habitual Criminal Act (Narcotic Drugs)
Md. Ann. Code 1957, Art. 27, § 293

Habitual Criminal Acts
N.C. Gen. Stat. 1943, § 14-7.1 et seq.
Neb. Rev. Stat. 1943, 29-2222

Habitual Criminal Sentencing Act
Kan. Stat. Ann., 21-4501 et seq.

Habitual Criminal Sterilization Act
Okla. Laws 1991, p. 94

Habitual Drunkard Act
Wash. Rev. Code Ann., 70.96A.010 et seq.

Habitual Felony Offender Act
Ala. Code 1975, § 13A-5-9

Habitual Offender Act
Ind. Code Ann., 35-50-2-8
La. Rev. Stat. Ann., 15:529.1
N.J. Stat. Ann., 2C:43-7, 2C:44-3, 2C:44-4
Va. Code 1950, § 46.1-387.1 et seq.

Habitual Offenders Act (Motor Vehicles)
La. Rev. Stat. Ann., 32:1471 et seq.
R.I. Gen. Laws 1956, 31-40-1 et seq.
Wash. Rev. Code Ann., 9.92.090
Wis. Stat. Ann., 939.62, 973.12
W. Va. Code 1966, § 61-11-18 et seq.
Wyo. Stat. Ann., § 6-10-201 et seq.

Habitual Sex Offender Act
Ohio Rev. Code 1953, 2950.01 et seq.

Habitual Sex Offender Registration Act
Kan. Laws 1994, Ch. 253, §§ 17 to 26

**Habitual Sexual Offenders Act (Civil
   Commitment of)**
Ida. Code 1947, 66-1401 et seq.

Habitual Traffic Offenders Act
Colo. Rev. Stat., 42-3-201 et seq.
N.C. Gen. Stat. 1943, § 20-16, a, Subd. 5
Ore. Laws 1983, Ch. 338, §§ 365 to 367, 397,
   398
Ore. Rev. Stat., 809.600 et seq.
Tenn. Code Ann., 55-10-601 et seq.
Tex. Rev. Civ. Stat., Art. 6687b, § 22
Wash. Rev. Code Ann., 46.65.010 et seq.

Habitual Violent Offender Incarceration Act
Haw. Session Laws 1999, S.B. 584

**Hackensack Meadowlands Food
   Distribution Center Commission Law**
N.J. Stat. Ann., 13:17A-1 et seq.

**Hackensack Meadowlands Reclamation and
   Development Act**
N.J. Stat. Ann., 13:17-1 et seq.

Hadley Rule
Mont. Code Ann., 27-1-311

Hagaman Zoning Regulations Law
N.Y. Local Laws 1968, Village of Hagaman, p. 3388

Hahira Telephone Authority Act
Ga. Laws 1977, p. 2585

Hahn, Nichols, Frymeier, Ashby, Hale, Render Act (Mosquito Control)
Ky. Rev. Stat. 1971, 249.510 et seq.

Haida Land Exchange Act of 1986
Nov. 17, 1986, P.L. 99-664, 100 Stat. p. 4308
Nov. 28, 1990, P.L. 101-626, 104 Stat. 4432
Oct. 14, 1992, P.L. 102-415, 106 Stat. 2122, 2125

Hail Associations Assessment Act
Neb. Rev. Stat. 1943, 44-813 et seq.

Hail Insurance Act
S.D. Code 1939, 31.3001 et seq.
S.D. Laws 1919, Ch. 244

Hailwood-Dunckel-Burns-Diggs Act (Civil Rights)
Mich. Comp. Laws Ann., 750.146 et seq.

Hair Seal Bounty Act
Alaska Stat. 1962, § 16.35.140 et seq.

Hairdressers Act
Mass. Gen. Laws Ann., 112:87T et seq.
Minn. Stat. Ann., 155.A01 et seq.
S.C. Code Ann. 1976, § 40-13-10 et seq.

Hairdressers and Barbers Act
Me. Rev. Stat. Ann. 1964, Title 32, § 351 et seq.

Hairdressers and Cosmetologists Act
N.J. Stat. Ann., 45:5B-1 et seq.
S.C. Code Ann. 1976, § 40-13-10 et seq.
Tex. Rev. Civ. Stat., Art. 8451a

Haitian Refugee Immigration Fairness Act of 1998
Oct. 21, 1998, P.L. 105-277, 101(h), Title IX, 112 Stat. 2681, 8 U.S. Code § 1101 nt.

Hal S. Marchman Alcohol and Other Drug Services Act
Fla. Stat. Ann., 397.301 et seq.

Hale, Nichols, Hahn, Frymeier, Ashby, Render Act (Mosquito Control)
Ky. Rev. Stat. 1971, 249.510 et seq.

Haleakala National Park Act
Sept. 13, 1960, P.L. 86-744, 74 Stat. 881, 16 U.S. Code § 396b

Half and Half Act (Descent and Distribution)
Ohio Rev. Code 1953, 2105.10
Okla. Stat. Ann., Title 84, § 213, Subd. 2

Half Blood Act (Inheritance)
Ky. Rev. Stat. 1971, 391.050
Neb. Rev. Stat. 1943, 30-2307

Halfmoon Local Law Restricting the Storage of Liquified Petroleum Gas
N.Y. Local Laws 1971, Town of Halfmoon, p. 2151

Halfmoon Zoning Law
N.Y. Local Laws 1969, Town of Halfmoon, p. 1283
N.Y. Local Laws 1973, Town of Halfmoon, p. 1893

Halifax County Law Enforcement Officers' Relief Act
N.C. Laws 1949, Ch. 1041

Hall County Civil Services System Act
Ga. Laws 1967, p. 2556

Hall County Commission for Children and Families Act
Ga. Laws 1999, H.B. 1003

Hall County Water and Sewerage Authority Act
Ga. Laws 1992, p. 6986

Hall Income Tax Law
Tenn. Code Ann., 67-2-101 et seq.

Hall-Mark Act
Feb. 21, 1905, Ch. 720, 33 Stat. 732, 15 U.S. Code §§ 291 to 293

Hall-Mark Act (Gold and Silver Articles)
See Jewelers' Liability Act (Gold And Silver Articles)

Hall Net Income Tax Law
Ark. Code Ann. 1987, 26-51-101 et seq.

Hall of Fame Act
Ga. Code Ann., 50-12-60 et seq.

Hall of Fame Authority Act (Golf)
Ga. Code Ann., 12-3-580 to 12-3-582

Hall of Fame Authority Act (Sports)
Ga. Code Ann., 12-3-561 et seq.

Hall of Fame Commission
Ga. Code Ann., 50-12-110, 50-12-111, 50-12-112

Halloween Curfew Law
N.Y. Local Laws 1971, Town of Rhinebeck, p. 3257

Hallucinogenic Drug, Barbiturate and Central Nervous System Stimulant Act
La. Acts 1952, No. 296

Halogeton Glomeratus Control Act
July 14, 1952, Ch. 721, 66 Stat. 597, 7 U.S. Code §§ 1651 to 1656

Haman Act (Oyster Grounds Lease)
Md. Ann. Code 1974, Art. NR, § 4-1101 et seq.

Hamburg Friendship Treaty (1848)
Haw. Statute Laws Supplement, p. 59, Jan. 8, 1848

Hamilton Charter
Nev. Statutes 1869, Ch. 99, p. 162
Nev. Statutes 1871, Ch. 41, p. 95

Hamilton County Anti-Rabies Law
Tenn. Private Acts 1967, Ch. 440

Hamilton County Council-Manager Act
Tenn. Private Acts 1941, Ch. 156

Hamilton County Jury Commission Law
Tenn. Private Acts 1931, Ch. 564

Hamilton County Liquid Waste Pumpers and Haulers Act
Tenn. Private Acts 1991, Ch. 84

Hamilton County Regional Disposal Authority Act
Tenn. Private Acts 1972, Ch. 420

Hamilton-Feld Career Act
N.Y. Civil Service Law 1958, (Consol. Laws Ch. 7) § 40 et seq.

Hamilton-Kircher Act (Pregnant Women Blood Test)
Mich. Comp.Laws 1970, 329.153

Hamilton Reservoir Loan Act
Mass. Acts 1956, Ch. 561

Hamilton-Roosevelt Act (Mortgage Moratorium)
Mich. Public Acts 1937, No. 1

Hamner Act (Milk Control Board)
Ala. Code 1975, § 2-13-40 et seq.

Hampden County Court House Loan Act
Mass. Acts 1961, Ch. 358
Mass. Acts 1962, Ch. 539

Hampden County Superior Court Building Elevator Loan Act
Mass. Acts 1953, Ch. 403

Hampton Act (Fire Platoon System)
N.Y. Laws 1941, Ch. 626

Hampton Act (Redevelopment Companies)
N.Y. Laws 1943, Ch. 234

Hampton Act (Veterans and Volunteer Firemen)
N.Y. Civil Service Law 1958 (Consol. Laws Ch. 7) § 85 et seq.

Hampton-Newport News Parking Authority Act
Va. Acts 1968, Ch. 20

Hand Book Act (Racing)
Ky. Rev. Stat. 1971, 528.020, 528.030

Hand Rail Act
Ohio Rev. Code 1953, 4107.14

Handgun Recordkeeping and Account-ability Act (Westchester County)
N.Y. Laws 1997, Ch. 446

Handicap Prevention Act
Fla. Stat. Ann., 411.101 et seq.

Handicapped Adults Act (Zollie M. Maunard, Sr., Education for)
Fla. Stat. Ann., 228.0727

Handicapped and Elderly Coordinated Public Transportation Assistance Act
Kan. Stat. Ann., 75-5032 et seq.

Handicapped and Elderly Security Assistance Act
Fla. Stat. Ann., 426.001 et seq.

Handicapped and Veterans Persons Employment Preference Act
Mont. Laws 1985, p. 1953

Handicapped Bill of Rights Act
S.C. Code Ann. 1976, § 43-33-510 et seq.

Handicapped Business Opportunity Act
Mich. Comp. Laws Ann., 450.791 et seq.

Handicapped Children Act (Mental)
Ill. Rev. Stat. 1991, Ch. 122, § 14-1.01 et seq.

Handicapped Children Transportation Act
Tenn. Code Ann., 49-6-2114

Handicapped Children's Act
Ark. Code Ann. 1987, 6-41-201 et seq.

Handicapped Children's Early Education Assistance Act
Sept. 30, 1968, P.L. 90-538, 82 Stat. 901, 20 U.S. Code §§ 621 to 624

Handicapped Children's Education Act
Colo. Rev. Stat., 22-20-101 et seq.
Ida. Code 1947, 33-2001 et seq.

Handicapped Children's Protection Act of 1986
Aug. 5, 1986, P.L. 99-372, 20 U.S. Code §§ 1400 nt., 1415, 1415 nt.

Handicapped Development Centers Act
Cal. Education Code 1976, § 56800 et seq.

Handicapped Drivers Law
Tenn. Code Ann., 55-21-101 et seq.

Handicapped Employment Act
N.M. Stat. Ann., 28-10-9 et seq.
Okla. Stat. Ann., Title 74, § 9.29 et seq.

Handicapped Employment Council Act
N.C. Gen. Stat. 1943, § 143-283.1 et seq.

Handicapped Exceptional Children's Act
La. Rev. Stat. Ann., 40:2121 et seq.

Handicapped Housing Authorization Act
Tenn. Code Ann., 13-23-201 et seq.

Handicapped Parking Act
Ark. Code Ann. 1987, 27-15-301 et seq.
Ga. Code Ann., 40-6-220 et seq.

Handicapped Persons and Veterans Employment Preference Act
Mont. Code Ann., 39-30-101 §§ 1 to 10

Handicapped Persons Civil Rights Act
La. Rev. Stat. Ann., 46:2251 et seq.

Handicapped Persons Protection Act
N.C. Gen. Stat. 1943, § 168A-1 et seq.

Handicapped Person's Recreational Opportunies Act
N.J. Stat. Ann., 52-27D-170 et seq.

Handicapped Products Procurement Act
R.I. Gen. Laws 1956, 37-2.2-1 et seq.

Handicapped Programs Technical Amendments Act of 1988
Nov. 7, 1988, P.L. 100-630, 20 U.S. Code § 1400 nt.

Handicapper Business Opportunity Act
Mich. Comp. Laws Ann., 450.791 et seq.

Handicappers' Civil Rights Act
Mich. Comp. Laws Ann., 37.1101 et seq.

Handicapping Conditions with Infants and Toddlers Act
S.C. Code Ann. 1976, § 44-7-2510 et seq.

Hanscom Field Improvement Loan Act
Mass. Acts 1955, Ch. 769

Hansen-Green Fire Safety Act
Cal. Health and Safety Code §§ 13143.2, 13143.5, 13146, 13869.7, 17958.5

Hansens Disease Act
Haw. Rev. Stat. Ann., § 326-1 et seq.

Hanson-Lloyd Act (Architects)
Ohio Rev. Code 1953, 4703.01 et seq.

Happy Canyon Law
Ore. Laws 1971, Ch. 669

Haralson County Family Connection Authority Act
Ga. Laws 1999, H.B. 920

Haralson County Water Authority Act
Ga. Laws 1971, p. 3258

Harassing and Obscene Communications Act
Ill. Comp. Stat. 1992, Ch. 720, § 135/0.01 et seq.

Harassment and Stalking Act
N.M. Stat. Ann., 30-3A-1 et seq.

Harbor Act
Ill. Rev. Stat. 1991, Ch. 24, § 11-123-1 et seq.
N.J. Stat. Ann., 40:179-6 to 40:179-20

Harbor Act (Lake Calumet)
Ill. Rev. Stat. 1991, Ch. 19, § 112.90 et seq.

Harbor Act (New York)
Me. Rev. Stat. Ann. 1964, Title 38, § 1 et seq.

Harbor and Dock Act
P.R. Laws Ann. 1954, Title 23, § 2101 et seq.

Harbor and River Improvements Act
Wash. Rev. Code Ann., 88.32.010 et seq.

Harbor Area Lands Act
Wash. Rev. Code Ann., 79.92.010 et seq.

Harbor Development Act
Mich. Comp. Laws Ann., 281.1251 et seq.

Harbor Development Bond Act
Cal. Harbors and Navigation Code § 3900 et seq.

Harbor District Act
Cal. Harbors and Navigation Code §§ 5800 et seq., 6000 et seq.

Harbor Improvement Loan Act (Dukes County)
Mass. Acts 1959, Ch. 488

Harbor Improvements Act
Me. Rev. Stat. Ann. 1964, Title 38, § 361 et seq.

Harbor Maintenance Revenue Act of 1986
Nov. 10, 1988, P.L. 100-647, 26 U.S. Code § 4461 nt.

Harbors Act (Small Craft)
Cal. Harbors and Navigation Code § 70 et seq.
Cal. Public Resources Code §§ 5823.5, 5865

Harbors and Beaches Bond Act
N.J. Laws 1977, Ch. 208

Harbors and Navigation Code
Cal. Statutes 1937, Ch. 368, p. 792

Hard of Hearing Services Act (Deaf and)
Minn. Stat. Ann., 256C.21 to 256C.27

Hard Road Tax Act
Ill. Rev. Stat. 1991, Ch. 121, § 6-601 et seq.

Hard Rock Mining Act
Mont. Code Ann., 82-4-30 et seq.

Hardee County Pollution Control Act
Fla. Special Laws 1967, Ch. 67-1436

Hardeman Act (Mechanics Liens)
Tex. Property Code, § 53.001 et seq.

Hardwoods Development Council Act
Pa. Purdon's Stat., Title 73, § 399.21 et seq.

Hardyston Township Charter (1985)
N.J. Laws 1985, Ch. 327, §§ 1-1 to 1-21

Hare Anti Cattle Rustling Act
Ala. Code 1975, § 12-15-40 et seq.

Hare-Hawes-Cutting Act
Jan. 17, 1933, Ch. 11, 47 Stat. 761

Harm Reduction Act
N.M. Stat. Ann., 24-2C-1 to 24-2C-6

Harmer-Greene Motor Vehicle Damage Control Act
Cal. Vehicle Code 1959, §§ 34700, 34710, 34715, 34725

Harmful Algal Bloom and Hypoxia Research and Control Act of 1998
Nov. 13, 1998, P.L. 105-383, Title VI, 112 Stat. 3447, 16 U.S. Code § 1451 nt.

Harmful Drug Act
Mass. Gen. Laws Ann., 94C:1 et seq.

Harmful Materials Act (Obscenity)
N.Y. Penal Law 1965 (Consol. Laws Ch. 40) § 235.20 et seq.

Harmful Plant Act
N.M. Stat. Ann., 76-7A-1 et seq.

Harmful Species Law (Ecologically)
Minn. Stat. Ann., 84.967 et seq.

Harmless Error Act
Fla. Stat. Ann., 59.041
Nev. Rev. Stat. 1979, Reprint, 178.598
Okla. Stat. Ann., Title 12, § 78
Tenn. Code Ann., 27-1-117
Wis. Stat. 1975, 817.37

Harmon Act (Narcotics)
Ala. Code 1958, Title 22, § 232 et seq.

Harmonized Tariff Schedule of the United States
Nov. 5, 1990, P.L. 101-508, 104 Stat. 1388-387, 1388-482
Dec. 4, 1991, P.L. 102-182, 105 Stat. 1236, 1243

Harness Racing Act
Ill. Rev. Stat. 1991, Ch. 8, § 37-1 et seq.
Me. Rev. Stat. Ann. 1964, Title 8, § 261 et seq.
N.Y. Laws 1954, Ch. 5
Pa. Purdon's Stat., Title 15, § 2601 et seq.

Harnett County Peace Officers' Relief Act
N.C. Laws 1961, Ch. 1132

Harrelson Road Law
Ark. Act 1923, Ex. Sess., p. 11, No. 5

Harriman Zoning Law
N.Y. Local Laws 1968, Village of Harriman, p. 3418

Harris Act (Veterans' Orphans)
Ga. Code 1933, 78-301 et seq.

Harris County Airport Authority Act
Ga. Laws 1984, p. 5239

Harris County Improvement District Act
Tex. Local Government Code, § 376.211 et seq.

Harris County Public Improvements Authority Act
Ga. Laws 1995, p. 4052

Harris County Road Act
Tex. Local and Special Laws 33rd Leg., 1913, p. 64, Ch. 17

Harris County Streets and Roads Authority Act
Ga. Laws 1995, p. 3752

Harris, Jr., Bert J., Private Property Rights Protection Act
Fla. Stat. Ann., 70.001

Harris-Katz California Taxpayers' Bill of Rights
Cal. Revenue and Taxation Code § 7080 et seq.

Harris-Katz Taxpayers' Bill of Rights Act
Cal. Revenue and Taxation Code § 21001 et seq.

Harrison Act (Restrictions on Territories)
See Special Laws Prohibition Act (Territories)

Harrison Acts (Narcotics)
Dec. 17, 1914, Ch. 1, 38 Stat. 785
Feb. 24, 1919, Ch. 18, 40 Stat. 1130
Nov. 23, 1921, Ch. 136, 42 Stat. 298

Harrison-Grogan Act (Dividends)
Ky. Rev. Stat. 1971, 287.350

Harrison Naval Stores Act
See Naval Stores Act

Harrisonburg Parking Authority Act
Va. Acts 1958, Ch. 517

Harry S. Truman Memorial Scholarship Act
Nov. 22, 1985, P.L. 99-159, 20 U.S. Code § 2007
Oct. 7, 1998, P.L. 105-244, 20 U.S. Code § 2002

Hart-Agnew Act (Bookmaking)
N.Y. Penal Law 1965 (Consol. Laws Ch. 40) § 225.05

Hart County Water and Sewer Utility Authority Act
Ga. Laws 1992, p. 6828

Hart-Hughes Educational Reform Act
Cal. Statutes 1983, Ch. 498

Hart-Morgan Class Size Reduction Act
Cal. Education Code 1976, § 52080 et seq.

Hart-Nejedly State, Urban and Coastal Park Bond Act
Cal. Public Resources Code § 5096.111 et seq.

Hart-Scott-Rodino Antitrust Improvements Act of 1976
Sept. 30, 1976, P.L. 94-435, 15 U.S. Code § 1311 et seq.

Harter Act (Carriage of Goods by Sea)
Feb. 13, 1893, Ch. 105, 27 Stat. 445, 46 U.S. Code §§ 190 to 195

Hartford Bridge Authority Act
Conn. Gen. Stat. Ann., §§ 13a-29, 13a-29a

Hartford Water Authority Act
Ga. Laws 1972, p. 2302

Hartwell Recreation Authority Act
Ga. Laws 1996, p. 3998

Harvesting Act (Forest)
Miss. Code Ann. 1972, § 49-19-53 et seq.

Harvesting Act (Ginseng)
Ill. Rev. Stat. 1991, Ch. 61, § 500 et seq.

Harvey and Melrose Park Civic Centers Act
Ill. Rev. Stat. 1991, Ch. 58, § 6701 et seq.

Harvey Clean Fuel and Campus Rideshare Act
Cal. Public Resources Code § 25620 et seq.

Harvey Water Act (Water Supply Districts)
Pa. Purdon's Stat., Title 53, § 3001 et seq.

Hasbrook Act (Gambling)
Ind. Code Ann., 35-25-1-1 et seq.

Haskell Indian Nations University and Southwestern Indian Polytechnic Institute Administrative Systems Act of 1998
Oct. 31, 1998, P.L. 105-337, 112 Stat. 3171, 25 U.S. Code § 3731 nt.

Haskell-Klaus Law (Indigents)
Iowa Laws 1919 (38th G. A.), Ch. 78

Hastings Amendment
June 30, 1919, Ch. 4, 41 Stat. 4, 18 U.S. Code § 1156

Hasty Boxing Act
Kan. Stat. Ann., 21-1801

Hatch Act (Flood Plains)
Mass. Gen. Laws Ann., 131:40

Hatch Act (Little, Politcial Activities)
N.Y. Civil Services Law (Consol. Laws Ch. 7) § 7

Hatch Act (Little)
N.M. Stat. Ann., 10-9-21
Tenn. Code Ann., 38-8-351

Hatch Act of 1887 (Agricultural Experiment Stations)
March 2, 1887, Ch. 314, 24 Stat. 440, 7 U.S. Code §§ 362, 363, 365, 368, 377 to 379
Aug. 11, 1955, Ch. 790, 69 Stat. 671, 7 U.S. Code §§ 361a to 361i
April 4, 1996, P.L. 104-127, 7 U.S. Code § 361c
June 23, 1998, P.L. 105-185, 7 U.S. Code §§ 361a, 361a nt., 361c, 361e, 361g
Oct. 21, 1998, P.L. 105-277, 7 U.S. Code § 361c

Hatch Act Reform Amendments of 1993
Oct. 6, 1993, P.L. 103-94, 5 U.S. Code §§ 1216, 2302, 3302, 3303, 5520a, 7301 nt., 7321 nt., 7321 et seq.; 18 U.S. Code §§ 602, 610; 39 U.S. Code §§ 410, 410 nt.; 42 U.S. Code §§ 1973d, 9904

Hatch-Metcalf Law (Animal Experiments)
N.Y. Public Health Law 1953 (Consol. Laws Ch. 45) §§ 504 et seq., 570 et seq.

Hatch Political Activity Act
Aug. 2, 1939, Ch. 410, 53 Stat. 1147 (See 5 U.S. Code §§ 1303, 3333, 7311, 7324, 7325; See 18 U.S. Code §§ 594, 595, 598, 600, 601, 604, 605, 1918)
July 19, 1940, Ch. 640, 54 Stat. 767 (See 1 U.S. Code § 1; See 5 U.S. Code §§ 1302, 1501 to 1508, 7324, 7326, 7327; See 18 U.S. Code §§ 595, 608, 609, 611)
March 27, 1942, Ch. 199, 56 Stat. 181 (See 5 U.S. Code § 7324)
Oct. 24, 1942, Ch. 620, 56 Stat. 986 (See 5 U.S. Code §§ 1501, 7324; See 18 U.S. Code § 595)
April 1, 1944, Ch. 150, 58 Stat. 136
Aug. 21, 1944, Ch. 404, 58 Stat. 727
Aug. 8, 1946, Ch. 904, 60 Stat. 937 (See 5 U.S. Code § 7327)
Oct. 5, 1962, P.L. 87-753, 76 Stat. 750 (See 5 U.S. Code § 7325)

Hatch-Sumners Act (Additional Judgeships)
May 31, 1938, Ch. 290, 52 Stat. 584 (See 28 U.S. Code §§ 44, 132)

Hate Crime Statistics Act
April 23, 1990, P.L. 101-275, 28 U.S. Code § 534 nt.
Sept. 13, 1994, P.L. 103-322, 28 U.S. Code § 534 nt.
July 3, 1996, P.L. 104-155, 28 U.S. Code § 534 nt.
Haw. Session Laws 1996, Act 176
Utah Code Ann. 1953, 77-76-3 et seq.

Hate Crimes Data Act
Mass. Gen. Laws Ann., 22C:32 et seq.

Hate Crimes Reporting Act
Fla. Stat. Ann., 877.19

Hatfield-Keller Railroad Retirement Act
June 28, 1934, Ch. 868, 48 Stat. 1284

Haulers Act (Oil and Gas Waste)
Tex. Water Code, § 29.001 et seq.

Hauser-Keene Safe Transport Law
Cal. Penal Code § 12026.2

Havana Regional Port District Act
Ill. Rev. Stat. 1991, Ch. 19, § 600 et seq.

Haverstraw Fire Prevention Code
N.Y. Local Laws 1973, Town of Haverstraw, p. 1979

Hawaii Omnibus Act
July 12, 1960, P.L. 86-624, 74 Stat. 411, 7 U.S. Code § 1837; 10 U.S. Code §§ 101, 802, 2662, 4744; 12 U.S. Code §§ 1422, 1466, 1706d, 1707, 1713, 1736, 1747l, 1748; 15 U.S. Code §§ 77b, 78c, 80a-2, 80a-6, 80b-2; 16 U.S. Code §§ 590h, 590q, 590r 669a, 758 to 758c, 777a; 18 U.S. Code §§ 1401, 5024; 20 U.S. Code §§ 12, 14, 15i, 15jj, 15ggg, 238, 244, 403, 442, 588, 645; 21 U.S. Code §§ 149, 188k; 22 U.S. Code § 2669; 23 U.S. Code §§ 101, 103, 105, 127; 26 U.S. Code §§ 2202, 3121, 3306, 4221, 4233, 4262, 4502, 4774, 7653, 7701; 28 U.S. Code § 91; 29 U.S. Code §§ 41, 49b, 213, 217, 302; 32 U.S. Code § 101; 33 U.S. Code §§ 466d, 466j, 875; 38 U.S. Code §§ 624, 903, 2007; 40 U.S. Code §§ 276a, 472, 491, 514, 522; 41 U.S. Code § 10c; 42 U.S. Code §§ 201, 255, 264, 291i, 402, 410, 418, 724, 1301, 1361; 43 U.S. Code § 4221; See 44 U.S. Code §§ 906, 1508; 46 U.S. Code §§ 18, 1155, 1176, 1192; 47 U.S. Code § 222; 48 U.S. Code prec. § 491 nt.; 50 U.S. Code Appx. §§ 466, 2285

Hawaii Prohibition Act
May 23, 1918, Ch. 84, 40 Stat. 560

Hawaii Statehood Bill
March 18, 1959, P.L. 86-3, 73 Stat. 4, 48 U.S. Code prec. § 491 nt.

Hawaii Territorial Act
See Hawaiian Organic Act

Hawaii Tropical Forest Recovery Act
Oct. 29, 1992, P.L. 102-574, 16 U.S. Code § 4501 nt.

Hawaii Volcanoes National Park Adjustment Act of 1998
Nov. 12, 1998, P.L. 105-380, 112 Stat. 3401, 16 U.S. Code § 391 nt.

Hawaiian Annexation Resolution
July 7, 1898, Res. No. 55, 30 Stat. 750

Hawaiian Citizens Declaration of Rights Act
Haw. Session Laws 1925, Act 222

Hawaiian Home Lands Recovery Act
Nov. 2, 1995, P.L. 104-42, Title II, 25 U.S. Code § 386a; 48 U.S. Code prec. § 491 nt.

Hawaiian Homes Commission Act, 1920
July 9, 1921, Ch. 42, 42 Stat. 108
July 10, 1937, Ch. 482, 50 Stat. 497
May 31, 1944, Ch. 216, 58 Stat. 260
June 3, 1948, Ch. 384, 62 Stat. 295
June 3, 1948, Ch. 397, 62 Stat. 303
June 14, 1948, Ch. 464, 62 Stat. 390
July 9, 1952, Ch. 614, 66 Stat. 511
July 9, 1952, Ch. 615, 66 Stat. 514
July 9, 1952, Ch. 618, 66 Stat. 515
Feb. 20, 1954, Ch. 10, 68 Stat. 16
June 18, 1954, Ch. 319, 68 Stat. 262
June 18, 1954, Ch. 321, 68 Stat. 263
Aug. 1, 1956, Ch. 855, 70 Stat. 915
Aug. 21, 1958, P.L. 85-708, 72 Stat. 705
Aug. 21, 1958, P.L. 85-710, 72 Stat. 706
Aug. 23, 1958, P.L. 85-733, 72 Stat. 822
Haw. Constitution, 1959 Amended 1978

Hawaiian Islands National Marine Sanctuary Act
Nov. 4, 1992, P.L. 102-587, 16 U.S. Code § 1433 nt.
Oct. 11, 1996, P.L. 104-283, 16 U.S. Code § 1433 nt.

Hawaiian Organic Act
April 30, 1900, Ch. 339, 31 Stat. 141
July 9, 1921, Ch. 42, 42 Stat. 115
June 12, 1940, Ch. 336, 54 Stat. 345
Oct. 26, 1949, Ch. 752, 63 Stat. 926

April 1, 1952, Ch. 127, 66 Stat. 32

July 9, 1952, Ch. 616, 66 Stat. 514

June 29, 1954, Ch. 418, 68 Stat. 323

April 6, 1956, Ch. 180, 70 Stat. 102

April 6, 1956, Ch. 185, 70 Stat. 104

May 9, 1956, Ch. 237, 70 Stat. 130

Aug. 1, 1956, Ch. 820, 70 Stat. 785

Aug. 1, 1956, Ch. 851, 70 Stat. 903

Aug. 1, 1956, Ch. 859, 70 Stat. 918

Aug. 1, 1956, Ch. 862, 70 Stat. 920

July 18, 1958, P.L. 85-534, 72 Stat. 379

Aug. 14, 1958, P.L. 85-650, 72 Stat. 606

Aug. 20, 1958, P.L. 85-690, 72 Stat. 684

Aug. 20, 1958, P.L. 85-691, 72 Stat. 685

Aug. 21, 1958, P.L. 85-714, 72 Stat. 707

Aug. 21, 1958, P.L. 85-714, 72 Stat. 709

Aug. 21, 1958, P.L. 85-719, 72 Stat. 709

Aug. 28, 1958, P.L. 85-793, 72 Stat. 957

Aug. 28, 1958, P.L. 85-803, 72 Stat. 971

Hawes Act (State Highway Department)
Mo. Laws 1917, p. 485

Hawes-Copper Act
Jan. 19, 1929, Ch. 79, 45 Stat. 1084, 49 U.S. Code § 60

Hawkers and Peddlers Act
Mass. Gen. Laws Ann., 101:13 et seq.
Md. Ann. Code 1957, Art. 56, § 21 et seq.
Me. Rev. Stat. Ann. 1964, Title 32, § 4688 et seq.
Mich. Comp. Laws 1948, 445.371 et seq.
N.H. Rev. Stat. 1955, 320:1 et seq.
N.Y. Local Laws 1972, Town of Cortlandt, p. 1188
N.Y. Local Laws 1973, Town of Big Flats, p. 1378
Okla. Stat. Ann., Title 72, § 1 et seq.
R.I. Gen. Laws 1956. 5-11-1 et seq.
S.C. Code Ann. 1976, § 40-41-10 et seq.

Hawkers and Vendors Act (Drug-Toilet Preparations)
Mich. Comp. Laws Ann., 446.301 et seq.

Hawkins Act (Housing Discrimination)
Cal. Health and Safety Code § 35700 et seq.

Hawley Act (Settlement of Claims against Germany)
June 5, 1930, Ch. 402, 46 Stat. 500

Hawley-Smoot Tariff Act
See Tariff Act Of 1930

Hay Brokers Act
Ariz. Rev. Stat. Ann., § 3-2712 et seq.

Hayden and Frusetta Witness Protection Act
Cal. Penal Code § 1054.2

Hayden-Cartwright Act
June 16, 1936, Ch. 582, 49 Stat. 1519 (See 23 U.S. Code §§ 101, 104 to 106, 109, 114, 118; 25 U.S. Code § 318b)

Hayden-Cartwright Federal Highway Act of 1938
See Federal Aid Highway Act

Hayden Planetarium Act
N.Y. Public Authorities Law (Consol. Laws Ch. 43A) § 1625 et seq.

Hayes, Cline, Lowman, Tayburn, Lyon Act (Workmen's Compensation)
Ky. Rev. Stat. 1971, 342.121, 342.185, 342.312, 342.316

Hayes-Mills Act (Use Fuel Tax)
Cal. Revenue and Taxation Code § 8655

Hays-McClain Act (Public Library Service)
Ky. Rev. Stat. 1971, 171.201 et seq.

Haywood County Employees Uniform Nepotism Policy Act
Tenn. Private Acts 1985, Ch. 27

Hazard Communication Act
Tex. Health and Safety Code, § 502.001 et seq.

Hazard Control Act (Environmental Lead)
Neb. Rev. Stat. 1943, 71-6318 et seq.

Hazard Mitigation and Relocation Assistance Act of 1993
Dec. 3, 1993, P.L. 103-181, 42 U.S. Code §§ 4601 nt., 5121 nt., 5170c, 5170c nt.

Hazardous Aerosol Act
La. Rev. Stat. Ann., 40:1057 et seq.

Hazardous and Solid Waste Act
N.M. Stat. Ann., 74-4A-1 et seq.
Utah Code Ann. 1953, 19-6-101 et seq.

Hazardous and Solid Waste Amendments of 1984
Nov. 8, 1984, P.L. 98-616, 42 U.S. Code § 6901 nt.

Hazardous and Solid Waste Recycling and Treatment Act
Ill. Rev. Stat. 1991, Ch. 127, § 2703-1 et seq.

Hazardous and Toxic Materials Emergency Notification Act
Ark. Acts 1991, No. 917

Hazardous Building Wall Anchorage Law
Cal. Government Code § 8893 et seq.

Hazardous Chemical Information Act
Del. Code of 1974, Title 16, § 2401 et seq.
Mont. Code Ann. 1987, 39-30-101 et seq.
N.M. Stat. Ann., 74-4E-1 et seq.

Hazardous Chemicals Right to Know Act
Ga. Code Ann., 45-22-1 et seq.
Iowa Code Ann., 455D.1 et seq.
N.C. Gen. Stat. 1943, § 95-173 et seq.
Tenn. Code Ann., 50-3-2001 et seq.

Hazardous Discharge Bond Act
N.J. Laws, Ch. 113
N.J. Laws 1981, Ch. 275

Hazardous Househld Substances Labeling Act
Colo. Rev. Stat., 25-5-501 et seq.

Hazardous Household Product Act
Ind. Code Ann., 16-6-9-1 et seq.

Hazardous Liquid Pipeline Law
La. Rev. Stat. Ann., 30:701 et seq.

Hazardous Liquid Pipeline Safety Act of 1979
Nov. 30, 1979, P.L. 96-129, 18 U.S. Code § 831 nt.; 49 U.S. Code Appx. §§ 1811, 2001, et seq., 2001 nt.
Jan. 14, 1983, P.L. 97-468, 96 Stat. 2543, 49 Appx. § 2005
Oct. 11, 1984, P.L. 98-464, 98 Stat. 1821, 49 U.S. Code Appx. §§ 2009, 2010, 2012, 2013
April 7, 1986, P.L. 99-272, 49 U.S. Code Appx. §§ 1682a, 2004, 2013
Oct. 22, 1986, P.L. 99-516, 49 U.S. Code Appx. §§ 2002, 2009, 2013
Oct. 31, 1988, P.L. 100-561, 49 U.S. Code Appx. §§ 2002, 2004, 2007, 2009 to 2011, 2013, 2015
Nov. 16, 1990, P.L. 101-599, 49 U.S. Code Appx. § 2002
Oct. 24, 1992, P.L. 102-508, 49 U.S. Code Appx. §§ 2001 to 2004, 2007 to 2010, 2012, 2013, 2016

Hazardous Liquid Transportation System Safety Act
Okla. Stat. Ann., Title 52, § 47.1 et seq.

Hazardous Machinery Act
Ill. Rev. Stat. 1937, Ch. 48, § 103 et seq.

Hazardous Material Emergency Planning and Response Act
Pa. Purdon's Stat., Title 35, § 6022.101 et seq.

Hazardous Material Emergency Response Reimbursement Act
Ill. Rev. Stat. 1991, Ch. 127 1/2, § 1001 et seq.

Hazardous Material Incidents Act (Response to)
Mont. Code Ann., 10-3-1201 et seq.

Hazardous Material Information Development, Preparedness, and Response Act
La. Rev. Stat. Ann., 30:2361 et seq.

Hazardous Materials Education Act
Cal. Education Code 1976, §§ 49340, 49341

Hazardous Materials Emergency Act
Ill. Rev. Stat. 1991, Ch. 127, § 1250 et seq.

Hazardous Materials Emergency Response and Community Right-to-Know Act
Fla. Stat. Ann., 252.81 et seq.

Hazardous Materials Highway Transportation Act
Ill. Laws 1976, p. 1390

Hazardous Materials Planning and Notification Act
Okla. Stat. Ann., Title 27A, § 4-2-101 et seq.

Hazardous Materials Polluters Pay Act
Mich. Comp. Laws Ann., 299.601 et seq.

Hazardous Materials Railroad Transportation Act
Ill. Rev. Stat. 1981, Ch. 114, § 501 et seq.

Hazardous Materials Transportation Act
Jan. 3, 1975, P.L. 93-633, 46 U.S. Code
§ 170, 49 U.S. Code Appx. §§ 1471, 1472, 1801 to 1812
July 19, 1975, P.L. 94-56, 49 U.S. Code
Appx. § 1812
Oct. 11, 1976, P.L. 94-474, 49 U.S. Code
Appx. §§ 1805, 1812
Sept. 30, 1978, P.L. 95-403, 49 U.S. Code
Appx. § 1812
Nov. 30, 1979, P.L. 96-129, 49 U.S. Code
Appx. § 1811
Oct. 30, 1984, P.L. 98-559, 49 U.S. Code
Appx. §§ 1812, 1813
Nov. 3, 1990, P.L. 101-500, 49 U.S. Code
Appx. § 2501 nt.
Nov. 16, 1990, P.L. 101-615, 49 U.S. Code
Appx. §§ 1801 nt., 1802, 1804 et seq.
Oct. 24, 1992, P.L. 102-508, 49 U.S. Code
Appx. §§ 1802, 1805, 1812, 1813, 1816, 1819
Ark. Code Ann. 1987, 27-2-101 et seq.
Colo. Rev. Stat., 40-2.1-101 et seq., 43-6-101 et seq.
Del. Code of 1974, Title 29, § 8223
Ill. Rev. Stat. 1991, Ch. 95 1/2, § 700-1 et seq.

N.M. Stat. Ann., 74-4F-1 to 74-4F-8
Pa. Cons. Stat., Title 75, § 8301 et seq.

Hazardous Materials Transportation Act Amendments of 1976
Oct. 11, 1976, P.L. 94-474, 49 U.S. Code
Appx. §§ 1801 nt., 1805, 1812

Hazardous Materials Transportation Act of 1994
Oct. 11, 1996, P.L. 104-287, 49 U.S. Code
§ 5116 nt.

Hazardous Materials Transportation Authorization Act of 1994
Aug. 26, 1994, P.L. 103-311, 49 U.S. Code
§ 5101 nt.
Oct. 31, 1994, P.L. 103-429, 49 U.S. Code
§ 5116 nt.
Nov. 28, 1995, P.L. 104-59, 23 U.S. Code
§ 307 nt.

Hazardous Materials Transportation Control Act of 1970
Oct. 16, 1970, P.L. 91-458, 84 Stat. 977, 49
U.S. Code Appx. §§ 1761, 1762
Aug. 11, 1973, P.L. 93-90, 87 Stat. 305, 49
U.S. Code Appx. § 1762
July 19, 1975, P.L. 94-56, 89 Stat. 264, 49
U.S. Code Appx. § 1812
Nov. 30, 1979, P.L. 96-129, 49 U.S. Code
Appx. § 1811

Hazardous Materials Transportation Uniform Safety Act of 1990
Nov. 16, 1990, P.L. 101-615, 29 U.S. Code
§ 655 nt.; 45 U.S. Code § 434 nt.; 49 U.S.
Code Appx. § 1801 nt.

Hazardous Materials/Hazardous Waste Transportation Enforcement Act of 1986
Ida. Code 1947, 49-2201 et seq.

Hazardous Occupations Act
Fla. Stat. Ann., 769.01 et seq.

Hazardous Radiation Control Act
Ga. Code Ann., 31-13-1 et seq.

Hazardous Site Reuse and Redevelopment Act
Ga. Code Ann., 12-8-200 et seq.

13

Hazardous Sites Cleanup Act
Del. Code of 1974, Title 7, § 9101 et seq.
Pa. Purdon's Stat., Title 35, § 6020.101 et seq.

Hazardous Substance Account Act
Cal. Health and Safety Code § 25300 et seq.

Hazardous Substance Account Act (Carpenter-Presley-Tanner)
Cal. Health and Safety Code § 25300 et seq.

Hazardous Substance Cleanup Act
Del. Code of 1974, Title 7, § 9101 et seq.

Hazardous Substance Mitigation Act
Utah Code Ann. 1953, 26-14d-101 et seq.

Hazardous Substance Response Revenue Act of 1980
Dec. 11, 1980, P.L. 96-510, 26 U.S. Code § 1 nt.
Oct. 17, 1986, P.L. 99-499, 42 U.S. Code §§ 9631 to 9633, 9641

Hazardous Substances Act
Cal. Health and Safety Code § 28740 et seq.
Colo. Rev. Stat., 25-5-501 et seq.
Fla. Stat. Ann., 501.061 et seq.
Ill. Rev. Stat. 1991, Ch. 111 1/2, § 251 et seq.
Ky. Rev. Stat. 1971, 217.650 et seq.
Md. Ann. Code 1974, Art. HE, § 7-101 et seq.
Me. Rev. Stat. Ann. 1964, Title 7, § 501 et seq.
Mich. Comp. Laws Ann., 286.451 et seq.
Minn. Stat. Ann., 24.32 et seq.
N.D. Cent. Code, 19-21-01 et seq.
N.J. Rev. Stat. 1937, 24:5A-1 et seq.
R.I. Gen. Laws 1956, 23-24-1 et seq.
S.C. Code Ann. 1962, § 32-1811 et seq.
S.C. Code Ann. 1976, § 23-39-10 et seq.
Tenn. Code Ann., 68-27-101 et seq.
Tex. Health and Safety Code § 501.001 et seq.
Vt. Stat. Ann., Title 18, § 4051 et seq.
Wis. Stat. Ann., 100.37

Hazardous Substances and Oil Pollution Control Act
Minn. Stat. Ann., 115E.01 et seq.
N.C. Gen. Stat. 1943, § 143-215,75 et seq.

Hazardous Substances and Oil Spill Prevention and Control Act
Tex. Water Code, § 26.261 et seq.

Hazardous Substances Bulk Storage Act
N.Y. Environmental Conservation Law 1972 (Consol. Laws Ch. 43B) § 40-0101 et seq.

Hazardous Substances Cleanup Bond Act
Cal. Health and Safety Code § 25385 et seq.

Hazardous Substances Cleanup Financing Authority Act
Cal. Health and Safety Code § 25392 et seq.

Hazardous Substances Community Right to Know Act
R.I. Gen. Laws 1956, 23-24.4-1 et seq.

Hazardous Substances Construction Disclosure Act
Ill. Rev. Stat. 1991, Ch. 29, §§ 1001, 1002

Hazardous Substances Emergency Response Law (City of New York)
N.Y. Adm. Code 1985, § 24-601 et seq.

Hazardous Substances Health Registry Act
Ill. Rev. Stat. 1991, Ch. 111 1/2, § 6701 et seq.

Hazardous Substances Highway Spill Containment and Abatement Act
Cal. Vehicle Code 1959, § 2450 et seq.

Hazardous Substances Information and Training Act
Cal. Labor Code § 6360 et seq.

Hazardous Substances Labeling Act
Fla. Stat. Ann., 501.071, 501.075 et seq.
Ill. Rev. Stat. 1991, Ch. 111 1/2, § 251 et seq.
Mass. Gen. Laws Ann., 94B:1 et seq.
Me. Rev. Stat. Ann. 1964, Title 7, § 501 et seq.
Mich. Comp. Laws. Ann., 286.451 et seq.
Minn. Stat. Ann., 24.32 et seq.

N.D. Cent. Code, 19-21-01 et seq.

N.H. Rev. Stat. 1955, 339-A:1 et seq.

Tenn. Code Ann., Superseded Vols., 53-3701 et seq.

Wis. Stat. Ann., 100.37

Hazardous Substances Mitigation Act
Utah Code Ann. 1953, 19-6-301 et seq.

Hazardous Substances Protection Act
Minn. Stat. Ann., 299F.091 et seq.

Hazardous Substances Response Act
Ida. Code 1947, 39-7101 et seq.

Hazardous Substances Response Action Contractors Indemnification Act
N.J. Stat. Ann., 58:10-23.11f8 et seq.

Hazardous Substances Right to Know Act
N.M. Stat. 50-9-2.1, 50-9-3, 50-9-5.1
R.I. Gen. Laws 1956, 28-21-1 et seq.

Hazardous Substances Risk Management Act
Del. Code of 1974, Title 7, § 7701 et seq.

Hazardous Substances Spill Prevention and Control Act
Ill. Rev. Stat. 1991, Ch. 111, § 7701 et seq.
Tex. Water Code, § 26.261 et seq.

Hazardous Substances Tax Act
Cal. Revenue and Taxation Code § 43001 et seq.

Hazardous Substances Tax Bill of Rights
Cal. Health and Safety Code § 43511 et seq.

Hazardous Substances Transportation Act
Pa. Cons. Stat., Title 75, § 8301 et seq.

Hazardous Waste Act
Cal. Health and Safety Code § 25100 et seq.
Mont. Code Ann., 75-10-401 et seq.
N.M. Stat. Ann., 74-4-1 et seq.
Tenn. Code Ann. 1955, 53-6301 et seq.

Hazardous Waste and Underground Storage Tank Act
Mont. Code Ann., 75-10-401 et seq.

Hazardous Waste Cleanup Good Samaritan Act
R.I. Gen. Laws 1956, 23-19.8-1 et seq.

Hazardous Waste Collection Program Act (Local)
Ill. Rev. Stat. 1991, Ch. 111 1/2, § 991-1 et seq.

Hazardous Waste Control Law
La. Rev. Stat. Ann., 30:1131 et seq.

Hazardous Waste Enforcement Act
Cal. Health and Safety Code § 25160

Hazardous Waste Equipment Operators and Laborers Act
Ill. Rev. Stat. 1991, Ch. 111, § 7700 et seq.

Hazardous Waste Facility Siting Act
Fla. Stat. Ann., 403.78 et seq.
Ida. Code 1947, 39-5801 et seq.
Mass. Gen. Laws Ann., 21D:1 et seq.
Miss. Code Ann. 1972, § 17-18-1 et seq.
N.J. Stat. Ann., 13:1E-49 et seq.
Utah Code Ann. 1953, 19-6-201 et seq.
Utah Code Ann. 1953, 26-14a-1 et seq.
Va. Code 1950, § 10-186.1 et seq.

Hazardous Waste Feasibility Study Act
N.M. Stat. Ann., 74-4C-1 et seq.

Hazardous Waste Fund Act
Okla. Stat. Ann., Title 27A, § 2-7-301 et seq.

Hazardous Waste Funding Act (Household)
Pa. Purdon's Stat., Title 35, § 6025.1 et seq.

Hazardous Waste Haulers Act
Cal. Health and Safety Code § 25167.1 et seq.

Hazardous Waste Incineration Siting Act
Colo. Rev. Stat., 25-15-501 et seq.

Hazardous Waste Laborers' Licensing Act
Ga. Laws 1986, p. 3609
Ill. Rev. Stat. 1991, Ch. 111, § 7801 et seq.

Hazardous Waste Management Act
Ala. Code 1975, § 22-30-1 et seq.
Ark. Code Ann. 1987, 8-7-201 et seq.
Cal. Health and Safety Code § 25179.1 et seq.
D.C. Code Ann., § 6-701 et seq.
Ga. Code Ann., 12-8-60 et seq.
Ida. Code 1947, 39-4401 et seq.
Mass. Gen. Laws Ann., 21C:1 et seq.
Mich. Comp. Laws. Ann., 324.11101 et seq.
Miss. Code Ann. 1972, § 17-17-101 et seq.
Mo. Rev. Stat., 260.350 et seq.
N.Y. Environmental Conservation Law 1972 (Consol. Laws Ch. 43B) §§ 27-0301 et seq., 27-0900 et seq., 27-1101 et seq., 71-2701 et seq.
N.Y. Public Authorities Law (Consol. Laws Ch. 43A) §§ 1281, 1285c
Okla. Stat. Ann., Title 27A, § 2-7-101 et seq.
R.I. Gen. Laws 1956, 23-19.1-1 et seq.
S.C. Code Ann. 1976, § 44-56-10 et seq.
Tenn. Code Ann., 68-212-101 et seq.
Wash. Rev. Code Ann., 70.05.020 et seq.
Wis. Stat. Ann., 144.60 et seq.
W. Va. Code 1966, § 22-18-1 et seq.

Hazardous Waste Management Authority Act
Ga. Code Ann., 12-8-100 et seq.

Hazardous Waste Management Facilities Act
R.I. Gen. Laws 1956, 23-19.7-1 et seq.

Hazardous Waste Management Facility Siting Act (Commercial)
W. Va. Code 1966, § 20-10-1 et seq.
W. Va. Code 1966, § 22C-5-1 et seq.

Hazardous Waste Management Reform Act
Cal. Statutes 1995, Ch. 638

Hazardous Waste Management Research Fund Act
S.C. Code Ann. 1976, § 44-56-810 et seq.

Hazardous Waste Reduction Act
Tenn. Code Ann., 68-212-101 et seq.

Hazardous Waste Reduction and Toxics Use Reduction Act
Ore. Rev. Stat., 465.003 et seq.

Hazardous Waste Reduction Program
Okla. Stat. Ann., Title 27A, § 2-11-201 et seq.

Hazardous Waste Reduction, Recycling, and Treatment Research and Demonstration Act
Cal. Health and Safety Code § 25244 et seq.
R.I. Gen. Laws 1956, 23-19.10-1 et seq.

Hazardous Waste Remedial Fund Act (State Superfund)
N.Y. Environmental Conservation Law 1972 (Consol. Laws Ch. 43B) §§ 27-0923, 27-1301 et seq.
N.Y. State Finance Law 1940 (Consol. Laws Ch. 56) § 97b

Hazardous Waste, Septage and Solid Waste Management Act
Me. Rev. Stat. Ann. 1964, Title 38, § 1301 et seq.

Hazardous Waste Source Reduction and Management Review Act
Cal. Health and Safety Code § 25244.12 et seq.

Hazardous Waste Technology Exchange Service Act
Ill. Rev. Stat. 1991, Ch. 111 1/2, § 6801 et seq.

Hazardous Waste Transporter Burden Reduction Act
Ark. Acts 1997, No. 1055

Hazardous Waste Treatment Permit Reform Act (Wright-Polanco-Lempert)
Cal. Statutes 1992, Ch. 1345

Hazardous Waste/Hazardous Materials Transportation Enforcement Act
Ida. Code 1947, 49-2201 et seq.

Hazardous Wastes Good Samaritan Law (Discharge of)
N.Y. Environmental Conservation Law 1972 (Consol. Laws Ch. 43B) § 27-1321

Hazardous Zoning and Air Safety Act
N.J. Stat. Ann., 6:1-80 et seq.

Hazel Law (Intoxicating Liquors)
Del. Laws Vol. 27, p. 340, Ch. 139

Hazing Act
Ill. Rev. Stat. 1991, Ch. 144, § 220.9 et seq.
R.I. Gen. Laws 1956, 11-21-1 et seq.
Tex. Education Code, § 4.51

Head and Spinal Cord Injury Act
Ill. Rev. Stat. 1991, Ch. 111 1/2, § 7850 et seq.

Head and Spinal Cord Injury Information System Act
S.C. Code Ann. 1976, § 44-38-10 et seq.

Head Injury Prevention Act
Wash. Rev. Code 1989, 43.70.400 et seq.

Head Shop Law (Drug-Related Paraphernalia)
N.Y. General Business Law (Consol. Laws Ch. 20) § 850 et seq.

Head Start Act
Aug. 13, 1981, P.L. 97-35, 42 U.S. Code § 9801 nt.
Sept. 30, 1986, P.L. 99-425, 42 U.S. Code §§ 9834, 9835, 9837, 9840
April 28, 1988, P.L. 100-297, 102 Stat. 330, 20 U.S. Code § 9833
Oct. 23, 1989, P.L. 101-120, 42 U.S. Code § 9834
Oct. 30, 1990, P.L. 101-476, 42 U.S. Code § 9835
Nov. 3, 1990, P.L. 101-501, 42 U.S. Code §§ 9831, 9832, 9834 to 9841, 9843 to 9848
Nov. 16, 1990, P.L. 101-597, 42 U.S. Code § 9840
Oct. 7, 1991, P.L. 102-119, 42 U.S. Code § 9835
Oct. 7, 1992, P.L. 102-401, 42 U.S. Code §§ 9835, 9835 nt., 9835a, 9836, 9836 nt., 9837, 9838, 9839, 9846, 9846a

Nov. 4, 1992, P.L. 102-586, 42 U.S. Code § 9843
March 9, 1994, P.L. 103-218, 42 U.S. Code § 9839
May 18, 1994, P.L. 103-252, 42 U.S. Code § 9832 et seq.
Aug. 22, 1996, P.L. 104-193, 42 U.S. Code § 9835
Oct. 7, 1998, P.L. 105-244, 42 U.S. Code § 9844
Oct. 27, 1998, P.L. 105-285, 42 U.S. Code §§ 9831 to 9836, 9836a, 9837, 9837a, 9838 to 9840, 9840a, 9843, 9843a, 9844, 9846, 9852a

Head Start Act Amendments of 1994
May 18, 1994, P.L. 103-252, 42 U.S. Code §§ 9801 nt., 9832 et seq.

Head Start Amendments of 1998
Oct. 27, 1998, P.L. 105-285, Title I, 112 Stat. 2703, 42 U.S. Code § 9801 nt.

Head Start Expansion and Quality Improvement Act
Nov. 3, 1990, P.L. 101-501, 42 U.S. Code § 9801 nt.

Head Start Improvement Act of 1992
Oct. 7, 1992, P.L. 102-401, 42 U.S. Code § 9801 nt.

Head Start Supplemental Authorization Act of 1989
Oct. 23, 1989, P.L. 101-120, 42 U.S. Code § 9801 nt.

Head Start Transition Project Act
Nov. 3, 1990, P.L. 101-501, 42 U.S. Code §§ 9801 nt., 9855 to 9855g
Oct. 7, 1991, P.L. 102-119, 42 U.S. Code § 9855d
May 18, 1994, P.L. 103-252, 42 U.S. Code § 9855a
Oct. 20, 1994, P.L. 103-382, 42 U.S. Code §§ 9855, 9855b, 9855c, 9855d
Oct. 27, 1998, P.L. 105-285, 42 U.S. Code §§ 9801 nt., 9855, 9855a to 9855g

Headgear Act (Motorcycles)
Mo. Rev. Stat., 1991 supp., 302.020 Subsec. 2

Headless Ballot Act
Colo. Rev. Stat., 1-6-406

Headlight Act (Motor Vehicles)
Ind. Code Ann., 9-8-6-1 et seq.

Headlight Act (Railroads)
Ark. Code Ann. 1987, 23-12-402
Ga. Code Ann., 46-8-170
Tex. Rev. Civ. Stat., Art. 6372

Headstart-Follow Through Act
See Follow Through Act

Healing Art Identification Act
Tex. Rev. Civ. Stat., Art. 4590e

Healing Arts Act
Ark. Stat. 1947, 72-141 et seq.
D.C. Code Ann., § 2-1301 et seq.
Kan. Stat. Ann., 65-2801 et seq.
Okla. Stat. Ann., Title 59, § 725.1 et seq.
Tenn. Code Ann., 63-1-101 et seq.

Health Access Corporation Act
Fla. Stat. Ann., 409.701

Health Access Improvement Act
Ga. Code Ann., 43-26-50 et seq.

Health, Accident and Life Guaranty Act
Tex. Insurance Code, Art. 21.28-E

Health Act
Ala. Code 1975, § 22-1-1 et seq.
Colo. Rev. Stat., 25-1-101 et seq.
Ga. Code Ann., 31-3-1 et seq., 31-5-1 et seq.
Ind. Code Ann., 16-1-36-1, 16-1-37-1 et seq.
Ky. Rev. Stat. 1971, 211.005 et seq.
Md. Ann. Code 1974, Art. HG, § 1-101 et seq.
Mich. Comp. Laws Ann., 327.1 et seq.
Mont. Code Ann., 50-1-101 et seq.
N.C. Gen. Stat. 1943, § 3130A-1 et seq.
N.J. Rev. Stat. 26:2-1 to 26:11-61
N.M. Stat. Ann., 24-1-1 et seq.
P.R. Laws Ann. 1954, Title 24, § 301 et seq.
R.I. Gen. Laws 1956, 23-1-1 et seq.
Utah Code Ann. 1953, 26-1-1 et seq.
Vt. Stat. Ann., Title 18, § 1 et seq.

W. Va. Code 1966, § 16-1-1 et seq.

Health Act (Community Mental)
Fla. Stat. Ann., 394.65 et seq.

Health Act (Hotels and Restaurants)
W. Va. Code 1966, § 16-6-1 et seq.

Health Act (Local Public)
Minn. Stat. Ann., 145A.01 et seq.

Health Act (Mental)
S.C. Code Ann. 1976, § 44-9-10 et seq.
Vt. Stat. Ann., Title 18, § 7101 et seq.

Health Administration Act
Ind. Laws 1953, Ch. 197, p. 730
Pa. Purdon's Stat., Title 16, § 12001 et seq.

Health Agencies for Home Care Act
S.C. Code Ann. 1976, § 44-69-10 et seq.

Health Agency Act (Community)
Tenn. Code Ann., 68-2-1101 et seq.

Health Agent Law
Fla. Stat. Ann., 626.826 et seq.

Health Aid Act
N.J. Stat. Ann., 26:2F-1 et seq.

Health Amendments Act of 1956
Aug. 2, 1956, Ch. 871, 70 Stat. 923, 20 U.S. Code §§ 15aa to 15jj; 42 U.S. Code §§ 242a, 242b 242d, 242e, 291d, 291s

Health and Accident Act
Fla. Stat. Ann., 627.501 et seq.

Health and Accident Insurance Act
Ark. Stat. 1947, 66-531 et seq.
La. Rev. Stat. Ann., 22:211 et seq.
Mich. Comp. Laws Ann., 500.3400 et seq.
Minn. Stat. Ann. 62A.01 et seq.
Okla. Stat. Ann., Title 36, § 4401 et seq.

Health and Accident Insurance Agents Act
Fla. Stat. Ann., 626.826 et seq.

Health and Accident Insurance Minimum Standards Act (Individual)
Iowa Code Ann., 514D.1 et seq.

Health and Accident Law (Insurance Policies)
Ark. Code Ann. 1987, 23-62-103 et seq.

Health and Educational Building Corporation Act
R.I. Gen. Laws 1956, 45-38.1-1 et seq.

Health and Educational Facilities Authority Act
Conn. Gen. Stat. Ann., § 10a-176 et seq.
Mass. Acts 1968, Ch. 614
Mass. Gen. Laws Ann., 53:1 et seq.
Mo. Rev. Stat., 360.010 et seq.
S.D. Codified Laws 1967, 1-16A-1 et seq.

Health and Environment Department Act
N.M. Stat. Ann., 9-7-1 et seq.

Health and Environment Department Education Act
N.M. Stat. Ann., 24-3B-1 et seq.

Health and Higher Educational Facilities Authority Act
Md. Ann. Code 1957, Art. 43C, § 1 et seq.
Me. Rev. Stat. Ann. 1964, Title 22, § 2051 et seq.
N.H. Rev. Stat. 1955, 195-D-1 et seq.

Health and Hospital Planning Act
La. Acts 1948, No. 65

Health and Hospitals Corporation Act
Ind. Code Ann., 16-12-21-1 et seq.
N.Y. Laws 1969, Ch. 1016
N.Y. Unconsolidated Laws, § 7381 et seq.

Health and Human Services Act (Partnership for)
Neb. Laws 1996, L.B. 1044

Health and Insurance Law (Group or Blanket)
Ky. Rev. Stat 1971, 304.18.010 et seq.

Health and Life Agent and Broker Law
Me. Rev. Stat. Ann. 1964, Title 22, § 2081 et seq.

Health and Life and Accident Insurance Policy Language Simplification Act
N.D. Cent. Code, 26-1.36-13 et seq.

Health and Life Insurance Code
N.J. Stat. Ann., 17B:17-1 et seq.

Health and Life Insurance Guaranty Association Act
See Life and Health Insurance Guaranty Association Act

Health and Life Insurance Policy Language Simplification Act
N.J. Stat. Ann., 17B:17-17 et seq.
Ore. Rev. Stat., 743.350 et seq.

Health and Life Insurance Protection Association Act
Colo. Rev. Stat., 10-20-101 et seq.

Health and Life Insurers Rehabilitation and Liquidation Act
N.J. Stat. Ann., 17B:32-31 et seq.

Health and Mental Hygiene Facilities Improvement Act
N.Y. Laws 1968, Ch. 359, § 1

Health and Rehabilitative Services Reorganization Act
Fla. Laws 1992, Ch. 58

Health and Safety Act
Alaska Stat. 1962, § 18.05.010 et seq.
Minn. Stat. Ann., 182. 65 et seq.

Health and Safety Act (Employee)
Ill. Rev. Stat. 1981, Ch. 48, § 137.1 et seq.
N.J. Stat. Ann., 34:6A-1 et seq.
Pa. Purdon's Stat., Title 43, § 25-1 et seq.

Health and Safety Act (Farm Occupational)
Pa. Purdon's Stat., Title 3, § 1901 et seq.

Health and Safety Act (Hotels and Multiple Dwellings)
N.J. Rev. Stat. 1937, 55:13A-1 et seq.

Health and Safety Act (Industrial)
Wash. Rev. Code Ann., 49.17.010

Health and Safety Act (Occupational)
Alaska Stat. 1962, § 18.60.010 et seq.
Md. Ann. Code 1974, Art. LE, § 5-101 et seq.
N.M. Stat, 1978, 50-9-1 et seq.
Okla. Stat. Ann., Title 40, § 401 et seq.

Health and Safety Act (Public)
Cal. Statutes 1939, Ch. 60, p. 482

Health and Safety Bond Act (School Facility)
N.Y. Laws 1997, Ch. 328

Health and Safety Fund Act
Mich. Comp. Laws Ann., 141.471

Health and Safety of Employees in Anthracite Coal Mines Act
Pa. 1891 Pamph. Laws 176, No. 177

Health and Safety of Employees in Bituminous Coal Mines Act
Pa. 1911 Pamph Laws 756

Health and Sanitation Law
N.Y. Local Laws 1972, Village of Greenwood Lake, p. 3431

Health and Social Welfare Facilities Act
P.R. Laws Ann. 1954, Title 24, § 331 et seq.

Health and Survival Education Act
Colo. Rev. Stat., 22-25-101 et seq.

Health and Welfare Act
Mass. Gen. Laws Ann., 23:10D et seq., 151D:1 et seq.
Me. Rev. Stat. Ann. 1964, Title 22, § 1 et seq.

Health and Welfare Agency Report on Long-Term Care
Cal. Health and Safety Code §§ 1001.45 to 1001.47

Health and Welfare Commission Act
Mass. Gen. Laws Ann., 6:125 et seq.

Health and Welfare Program Supervision Act (Rees-Doyle)
Cal. Insurance Code § 10640 et seq.

Health Appliance Law
Iowa Code 1971, 88.1 et seq.

Health Assistance Payments Act
Wis. Stat. 1975, 163.01 et seq.

Health Benefit Act (Small Employer)
Minn. Stat. 1986, 62L.01 et seq.

Health Benefit Agent Act
Mich. Comp. Laws Ann., 550.1001 et seq.

Health Benefits and Education Act (Omnibus)
S.C. Code Ann. 1976, §§ 38-33-325, 38-71-125, 38-71-130, 38-71-145

Health Benefits Program Act
N.J. Stat. Ann., 52:14-17.25 et seq.

Health Board Act (Cities and Towns)
Wash. Rev. Code Ann., 70.05.020 et seq.

Health Board Act (Counties)
Wash. Rev. Code Ann., 70.05.030 et seq.

Health Care Access Act
La. Rev. Stat. Ann., 40:1299.151 et seq.
Okla. Stat. Ann., Title 56, § 57 et seq.
Wash. Rev. Code 1989, 70.47.010 et seq.

Health Care Access Act (Employee)
Fla. Stat. Ann., 627.6699

Health Care Access Act (Medical Support)
Ala. Code 1975, § 27-21B-1 et seq.

Health Care Access Act (Office of)
Conn. Gen. Stat. 1983, § 19a-610

Health Care Act
Conn. Gen. Stat. Ann., § 38a-551 et seq.
Ga. Code Ann., 31-43-1 et seq.
Mo. Rev. Stat. 1978, 404.800

Health Care Act (Access to)
Fla. Stat. Ann., 776.1115

Health Care Act (Adult Day)
Cal. Health and Safety Code § 1570 et seq.

Health Care Act (Advance Directive for)
Pa. Cons. Stat., Title 20, § 5401 et seq.

Health Care Act (Advanced Directives)
N.J. Laws 1991, Ch. 201
N.J. Stat. Ann., 26:2H-53 et seq., 9:6-8.25

Health Care Act (Affordable Basic)
Cal. Labor Code § 2100 et seq.

Health Care Act (Children's Preventable)
Ark. Code 1987, 23-79-141

Health Care Act (Children's)
Pa. 1992 Pamph. Laws, No. 113

Health Care Act (Community)
Neb. Rev. Stat. 1943, 71-7501 et seq.

Health Care Act (Dental)
N.M. Stat. Ann., 61-5A-1 et seq.

Health Care Act (Durable Power of Attorney)
Ga. Code Ann., 31-36-1 et seq.
Miss. Code Ann. 1972, § 41-41-151 et seq.

Health Care Act (Fairness in)
Ga. Code Ann., 33-24-59.12 to 33-24-59.16

Health Care Act (Medicine Volunteers in)
Ga. Code Ann., 43-34-45.1

Health Care Act (Retiree)
N.M. Stat. Ann., 10-7C-1 et seq.

Health Care Act (Statewide)
N.M. Stat. Ann., 27-10-1 et seq.

Health Care Act (Universal)
Okla. Stat. Ann., Title 63, § 2521 et seq.

Health Care Act (Women's Right to)
Ga. Code Ann., 33-24-59.1

Health Care Act for Children and Pregnant Women
R.I. Gen. Laws 1956, 42-12.3-1 et seq.

Health Care Administrative Simplification Act
Minn. Stat. Ann., 62J.50 to 62J.61

Health Care Administrators Act (Long Term)
S.C. Code Ann. 1976, § 40-35-5 et seq.

Health Care Agent Act
Cal. Civil Code § 2500 et seq.

Health Care Agents and Proxies Act
N.Y. Public Health Law 1953 (Consol. Laws Ch. 45) § 2980 et seq.

Health Care and Insurance Reform Act
Fla. Stat. Ann., 20.42 et seq.

Health Care and State Veterans Homes Trust Funds Act
Miss. Laws 1999, H.B. 109

Health Care and Treatment Act (Indigent)
Tex. Health and Safety Code, § 61.001 et seq.

Health Care Arbitration Act
Ill. Rev. Stat. 1991, Ch. 10, § 201 et seq.

Health Care Assessment Act (Senior)
Cal. Welfare and Institutions Code § 9760 et seq.

Health Care Assistant Registration Act
Utah Code Ann. 1953, 58-60-101 et seq.

Health Care Authorities Act
Ala. Code 1975, § 22-21-310 et seq.

Health Care Authority Act
Okla. Stat. Ann., Title 63, § 5004 et seq.
W. Va. Code 1966, § 16-29B-1 et seq.

Health Care Availability Act
Colo. Rev. Stat., 13-64-101 et seq.

Health Care Benefits Jurisdiction Act
N.M. Stat. Ann., 59A-15-14

Health Care Certificate of Need Act
Ida. Code 1947, 39-4901 et seq.
Neb. Rev. Stat. 1943, 71-5801 et seq.
R.I. Gen. Laws 1956, 23-15-1 et seq.

Health Care Certificate of Need Act (Hospitals)
Neb. Rev. Stat. 1943, 71-5801 et seq.

Health Care Commission Act
Miss. Code Ann. 1972, § 41-7-171 et seq.

Health Care Community Antitrust Guidance Act
Fla. Stat. Ann., 455.277

Health Care Consent Act (Adult)
S.C. Code Ann. 1976, § 44-66-10 et seq.

Health Care Consent Law
Ind. Code Ann., 16-8-12-1 et seq.

Health Care Consumer Act
Ark. Acts 1997, Act 1196

Health Care Cooperation Act
S.C. Code Ann. 1976, § 44-7-500 et seq.

Health Care Cooperative Act
Minn. Stat. Ann., 62R.01 et seq.

Health Care Corporations Act
Mich. Comp. Laws Ann., 550.1101 et seq.

Health Care Corporations Act (Nassau)
N.Y. Public Authorities Law (Consol. Laws Ch. 43A) § 3400 et seq.

Health Care Corporations Act (Westchester County)
N.Y. Public Authorities Law (Consol. Laws Ch. 43A) § 3300 et seq.

Health Care Cost Containment Act
Fla. Stat. Ann., 407.001 et seq.
Pa. Purdon's Stat., Title 35, § 449.1 et seq.

Health Care Cost Information Act
Minn. Stat. Ann., 144.695 et seq.

Health Care Cost Reduction Act
N.J. Stat. Ann., 26:2H-18.24 et seq.

Health Care Cost Review Authority
W. Va. Code 1966 § 16-29B-1 et seq.

Health Care Coverage Act
Colo. Rev. Stat., 10-16-101 et seq.

Health Care Coverage Act (Expanded)
N.Y. Laws 1988, Ch. 703

Health Care Coverage Act (Tucker)
Cal. Labor Code § 2500 et seq.

Health Care Decisions Act
See also Uniform Health Care Decisions Act
Md. Ann. Code 1974, Art. HG, § 5-601 et seq.

Health Care Decisions Act (Adult)
Minn. Stat. Ann., 145B.01 et seq.

Health Care Delivery Act (Alternative)
Ill. Comp. Stat. 1992, Ch. 210, § 3/1 et seq.

Health Care Discrimination Act (Osteopathic and Allopathic)
Ill. Comp. Stat. 1992, Ch. 225, § 62/1

Health Care Expense Program (Catastrophic)
N.Y. Social Services Law (Consol. Laws Ch. 55) § 369a et seq.

Health Care Facilities Act
Pa. Purdon's Stat., Title 35, § 448.101 et seq.

Health Care Facilities Finance Act
N.C. Gen. Stat. 1943, § 131A-1 et seq.
N.J. Stat. Ann., 26:21-1 et seq.

Health Care Facilities Law
Iowa Code Ann., 135C.1 et seq.

Health Care Facilities Planning Act
N.J. Stat. Ann., 26:2H-1 et seq.

Health Care Facility Act (Long-Term)
Ga. Code Ann., 31-8-1 et seq.

Health Care Facility Licensing Act
N.C. Gen. Stat. 1943, § 131E-100 et seq.
R.I. Gen. Laws 1956, 23-17-1 et seq.

Health Care Facility Licensure and Inspection Act
Utah Code Ann. 1953, 26-21-1 et seq.

Health Care Facility Provider Assessment Act (Outpatient)
R.I. Gen. Laws 1956, 44-52-1 et seq.

Health Care Facility-Provider Cooperation Act
Neb. Rev. Stat. 1943, 71-7701 et seq.

Health Care False Charging Act
Conn. Gen. Stat. Ann., § 53-440 et seq.

Health Care False Claims Act
Conn. Gen. Stat. Ann., § 53-440 et seq.
Mich. Comp. Laws Ann., 752.1001 et seq.
Tenn. Code Ann., 56-26-401 et seq.
Wash. Rev. Code Ann., 48.80.010 et seq.

Health Care Financing Consolidation Act
N.Y. Public Authorities Law (Consol. Laws Ch. 43A) § 1699d et seq.

Health Care for the Medically Indigent Reform Act
Colo. Rev. Stat., 26-15-101 et seq.

Health Care Freedom of Access Act (Complementary and Alternative)
Ga. Code Ann., 31-43-1 et seq.

Health Care Freedom of Choice Act
Okla. Stat. Ann., Title 36, § 6053 et seq.

Health Care Information Act
See Uniform Health Care Information Act

Health Care Information Act (Government)
Mont. Code Ann., 50-16-601 et seq.

Health Care Information Confidentiality Act
R.I. Gen. Laws 1956, 5-37.3-1 et seq.

Health Care Information System Act
Okla. Stat. Ann., Title 63, § 1-115 et seq.

Health Care Insurance Plan Act
W. Va. Code 1966, § 5-16A-1 et seq.

Health Care Malpractice Act
Utah Code Ann. 1953, 78-14-1 et seq.

Health Care Options Act (Medicaid)
Okla. Stat. Ann., Title 56, § 1010.1 et seq.

Health Care Placement Decision Maker for an Adult Act (Temporary)
Ga. Code Ann., 31-36A-1 et seq.

Health Care Plan Act
Ala. Code 1975, § 27-21-1 et seq.
Ga. Code Ann., 33-20-1 et seq.

Health Care Plan Law (Nonprofit)
N.M. Stat. Ann., 59A-47-1 et seq.

Health Care Planning Commission Act
W. Va. Code 1966 § 16-1A-1 et seq.

Health Care Policy and Financing Act
Colo. Rev. Stat., 25.5-1-102 et seq.

Health Care Practice Act (Naturopathic)
Mont. Code Ann., 37-26-101 et seq.
Mont. Laws 1991, Ch. 306, §§ 1 to 8, 10 to 19

Health Care Practitioner Self-Referral Act
Me. Rev. Stat. Ann. 1964, Title 22, § 2081 et seq.

Health Care Practitioners Act (Primary)
Pa. Purdon's Stat., Title 62, § 5001.1301 et seq.

Health Care Practitioners Medicare Fee Control Act
Pa. Purdon's Stat., Title 35, § 449.31 et seq.

Health Care Professional Assistance Law (Allied)
Ill. Comp. Stat. 1992, Ch. 110, § 905/2001 et seq.
Ill. Rev. Stat. 1991, Ch. 144, § 1481 et seq.

Health Care Professional Compliance Act
S.C. Code Ann. 1976, § 44-30-10 et seq.

Health Care Professional Credentialing Verification Act
Neb. Rev. Stat. 1943, 58-701 to 58-711

Health Care Program (Community-based)
La. Rev. Stat. Ann., 40:2194 et seq.

Health Care Provider Act
Okla. Stat. Ann., Title 68, § 7001 et seq.

Health Care Provider Act (Impaired)
N.M. Stat. Ann., 61-7-1 et seq.

Health Care Provider Assessment Act
R.I. Gen. Laws 1956, 44-50-1 et seq.

Health Care Provider Cooperation Act
Kan. Stat. Ann., 65-4955 et seq.

Health Care Provider Income Tax Act
Neb. Rev. Stat. 1943, 77-4801 et seq.

Health Care Provider Insurance Availability Act
Kan. Stat. Ann., 40-3401 et seq.

Health Care Provider Medicaid Act
W. Va. Code 1966 § 9-4C-1 et seq.

Health Care Provider Medicaid Enhancement Tax Act
W. Va. Code 1966 § 11-26-1 et seq.

Health Care Provider Organization Act (Workers' Compensation)
Cal. Labor Code § 5150 et seq.

Health Care Provider Self-Referral Act
S.C. Code of 1976, § 44-113-30 et seq.

Health Care Provider Tax Act
W. Va. Code 1966 § 11-27-1 et seq.

Health Care Proxies Act
Mass. Gen. Laws Ann., 201D:1 et seq.

Health Care Purchasing Act
N.M. Stat. Ann., 13-7-1 to 13-7-4

Health Care Purchasing Cooperative Act
Fla. Stat. Ann., 408.001

Health Care Purchasing Group Act
Ill. Comp. Stat. 1992, Ch. 215, § 123/1 et seq.

Health Care Purchasing Pool Act
Neb. Rev. Stat. 1943, 44-6701, 44-6702

Health Care Quality Act
N.J. Stat. Ann., 26:25-1 et seq.

Health Care Quality Improvement Act
Haw. Rev. Stat. Ann., § 671D-1 et seq.

Health Care Quality Improvement Act of 1986
Nov. 14, 1986, P.L. 99-660, 42 U.S. Code § 11101 nt.
Dec. 1, 1987, P.L. 100-175, 42 U.S. Code §§ 11137, 1137 nt.

Health Care Reform Act
Fla. Stat. Ann., 408.0015 et seq.
Ky. Rev. Stat. 1971, 216.900 et seq.
N.J. Stat. Ann., 26:2H-18.51 et seq.
N.Y. Laws 1996, Ch. 639
Wash. Rev. Code Ann., 41.05.006 et seq.

Health Care Reimbursement Reform Act
Ill. Rev. Stat. 1991, Ch. 73, § 982f et seq.
Wyo. Stat. Ann., § 26-22-501 et seq.

Health Care Rescue Act
Tex. General and Special Laws 1991, p. 4128, Ch. 1027

Health Care Responsibility Act
Ala. Code 1975, § 22-21-290 et seq.
Fla. Stat. Ann., 154.301 et seq.

Health Care Right of Conscience Act
Ill. Comp. Stat. 1992, Ch. 745, § 70/1 et seq.

Health Care Savings Account Act
Wash. Rev. Code Ann., 48.68.005 et seq.

Health Care Service Plan
Cal. Health and Safety Code 340 et seq.

Health Care Service Plan Act (Non-Profit)
Ill. Rev. Stat. 1987, Ch. 32, § 551 et seq.

Health Care Service Utilization Review Act
Ala. Code 1975, § 27-3A-1 et seq.
Tenn. Public Acts 1992, Ch. 812

Health Care Services Act
Alaska Stat. 1962, Replaced Titles,
§ 21.20.140 et seq.
Wash. Rev. Code Ann., 48.44.010 et seq.

Health Care Services Act (Charitable)
Ky. Rev. Stat. 1971, 216.940 to 216.944

Health Care Services Act (Mobile)
Cal. Health and Safety Code § 1765.101 et
seq.

Health Care Services Act (Primary)
Tex. Health and Safety Code, § 31.001 et
seq.

Health Care Services in the Home Act of 1987
Nov. 29, 1987, P.L. 100-175, 42 U.S. Code
§§ 201 nt., 280c to 280c-5

Health Care Services Malpractice Act
Pa. Purdon's Stat., Title 40, § 1301.101 et
seq.

Health Care Surrogate Act
Fla. Stat. Ann., 765.201 et seq.
Ill. Rev. Stat. 1991, Ch. 110 1/2, § 851-1 et
seq.
Ky. Rev. Stat. 1971, 311.970
W. Va. Code 1966 § 16-30B-1 et seq.

Health Care System Affordability Act
R.I. Gen. Laws 1956, 23-15-2, 23-15-4,
23-15-6

Health Care Trust Fund Act (Children's)
Miss. Laws 1999, H.B. 69

Health Care Trust Fund Act (Indigent)
La. Rev. Stat. Ann., 40:2193 et seq.

Health Care Trust Fund Act (Public)
Miss. Laws 1999, H.B. 70

Health Care Worker Background Check Act
Ill. Comp. Stat. 1992, Ch. 225, § 46/1 et seq.

Health Care Worker Management Act (Infected)
Ala. Code 1975, § 22-11A-60 et seq.

Health Care Workers' Safety Act
Md. Ann. Code 1974, Art. LE, § 5-308.1

Health Center Finance Corporation Act (University of Connecticut)
Conn. Gen. Stat. 1983, § 10a-250 et seq.

Health Centers Consolidation Act of 1996
Oct. 11, 1996, P.L. 104-299, 42 U.S. Code
§ 201 nt.

Health Claim Form Act (Standardized)
Neb. Rev. Stat. 1943, 44-524

Health Clinic Act (Prepaid)
Fla. Stat. Ann., 641.40 et seq.

Health Club Act
Pa. Purdon's Stat., Title 73, § 2161

Health Compact (Mental)
Conn. Gen. Stat. Ann., § 17-258 et seq.
Fla. Stat. Ann., 394.479 et seq.
Me. Rev. Stat. Ann. 1964, Title 34-B, § 9001
et seq.

Health Coverage Incentive Act (Small Employer)
Cal. Revenue and Taxation Code
§§ 17053.20, 23615

Health Coverage Reform Act (Small Employer Group)
Tenn. Public Acts 1992, Ch. 808

Health Data and Advisory Council Consolidation Act
Cal. Health and Safety Code § 443 et seq.

Health Data Authority Act
Utah Code Ann. 1953, 26-33a-101 et seq.

Health Data Commission Act
Colo. Rev. Stat., 25-28-101 et seq.

Health, Dental and Life Insurance Act (State Employees)
Okla. Stat. Ann., Title 74, § 1301 et seq.

Health Department Act (Local)
Utah Code Ann. 1953, 26A-1-101 et seq.
Wash. Rev. Code Ann., 43.20.025 et seq.

Health Department Building and Local Grant Act
Ark. Code 1987, 20-7-201 et seq.

Health Department Reorganization Act
Colo. Rev. Stat., 25-1-101 et seq.

Health Districts Act
N.D. Cent. Code, 23-14-01 et seq.
Ohio Rev. Code 1953, 3709.01 et seq.
Utah Code Ann. 1953, 26A-1-101 et seq.
Wash. Rev. Code Ann., 70.46.020 et seq.

Health Education Act
Cal. Education Code 1976, § 51880 et seq.
Colo. Rev. Stat., 22-25-101 et seq.
Fla. Stat. Ann., 233.067
S.C. Code Ann. 1976, § 59-32-5 et seq.

Health Education Act (Dental)
Me. Rev. Stat. Ann. 1964, Title 22, § 2121 et seq.

Health Education Act (Department of)
N.M. Stat. Ann., 24-3B-1

Health Education and Academic Loan Act
Cal. Education Code 1976, § 69300 et seq.

Health Education and Critical Health Problems Act
Ill. Rev. Stat. 1991, Ch. 122, § 861 et seq.

Health Education and Substance Abuse Prevention Act
Fla. Stat. Ann., 233.067

Health Education Authority Act
La. Rev. Stat. Ann., 17:3051 et seq.

Health Educator Practice Act
Ark. Code 1987, 17-53-101 et seq.

Health Educators Regulation Act
P.R. Laws Ann. 1954, Title 20, § 2550 et seq.

Health, Employment and Industrial Resources Development Act
Tex. Rev. Civ. Stat., Art. 5190.1

Health Facilities Act
Del. Code of 1974, Title 16, § 9701 et seq.
Kan. Stat. Ann., 65-4801 et seq.
P.R. Laws Ann. 1954, Title 24, § 331 et seq.
Tenn. Code Ann., 68-11-201

Health Facilities and Health Services Planning Act
Fla. Stat. Ann., 154.201 et seq.

Health Facilities and Higher Educational Authority Act
N.H. Rev. Stat. 1955, 195-D:1 et seq.

Health Facilities and Services Administration Act
P.R. Laws Ann. 1954, Title 24, § 337 et seq.

Health Facilities Assistance Act
Nev. Rev. Stat. 1979 Reprint, 449.250 et seq.

Health Facilities Authority Act
Cal. Government Code § 15430 et seq.
Colo. Rev. Stat., 25-25-101 et seq.
Fla. Stat. Ann., 154.201 et seq.
Ida. Code 1947, 39-1441 et seq.
Ill. Rev. Stat. 1991, Ch. 111 1/2, § 1101 et seq.
Me. Rev. Stat. Ann. 1964, Title 22, § 2051 et seq.
Mont. Code Ann., 90-7-101 et seq.

Health Facilities Authority Act (Cape Coral)
Fla. Special Laws 1975, Ch. 75-354

Health Facilities Construction Act
Ida. Code 1947, 39-1401 et seq.
R.I. Gen. Laws 1956, 23-16-1 et seq.

Health Facilities Corporations Act (Municipal)
Mich. Comp. Laws Ann., 331.1101 et seq.

Health Facilities Development Act
Tex. Health and Safety Code, § 221.001 et seq.

Health Facilities Disclosure Act
Cal. Health and Safety Code § 440 et seq.

Health Facilities Financing Authority Act
Cal. Government Code § 15430 et seq.

Health Facilities Information Disclosure Act
Me. Rev. Stat. Ann. 1964, Title 22, § 381 et seq.

Health Facilities Planning Act
Ill. Rev. Stat. 1991, Ch. 111 1/2, § 1151 et seq.

Health Facility and Services Development Act
Fla. Stat. Ann., 408.031 et seq.

Health Facility Construction Loan Insurance Act
Cal. Health and Safety Code § 436 et seq.

Health Facility Licensing Act
Ind. Code Ann., 16-10-1-1 et seq.

Health Facility Licensure and State Certification of Need Act
S.C. Code Ann. 1976, § 44-7-320 et seq.

Health Finance Authority Act
Ill. Rev. Stat. 1981, Ch. 111 1/2, § 161 et seq.

Health Finance Reform Act
Ill. Rev. Stat. 1991, Ch. 111 1/2, § 6501-1 et seq.

Health Finance Transfer of Funds Act
Ill. Rev. Stat. 1991, Ch. 127, §§ 167f2.9, 167f3

Health Fitness and Education Act (State Employees)
Tex. Government Code, § 664.001 et seq.
Tex. Rev. Civ. Stat. 1974, Art. 6252-27

Health Hazard Abatement Law
Ore. Rev. Stat., 222.850 et seq.

Health Improvement Act (Minority)
Fla. Stat. Ann., 381.81

Health Improvement Act (Public)
Mont. Code Ann., 50-1-401 et seq.

Health Information, Health Promotion, and Vaccine Injury Compensation Amendments of 1991
Nov. 26, 1991, P.L. 102-167, 42 U.S. Code § 201 nt.

Health Information System Act
N.M. Stat. Ann., 24-14A-1 et seq.

Health Initiative Act (Rural)
W. Va. Code 1966 § 18B-16-1 et seq.

Health Initiative Act (Vietnam Veterans)
Pa. Purdon's Stat., Title 51, § 20201 et seq.

Health Insurance Access and Equity Act
Cal. Health and Safety Code § 1389.1 et seq.
Cal. Insurance Code §§ 799.03, 10112.5, 10291.5, 10350.2, 10364, 10380, 10384, 10508, 12683, 12684
Cal. Labor Code § 2808

Health Insurance Act
Mich. Comp. Laws Ann., 500.3400 et seq.

Health Insurance Act (Limited Mandate)
Mo. Rev. Stat., 376.995

Health Insurance Act (Newborn)
D.C. Code Ann., § 35-1101 et seq.

Health Insurance Act (Small Employer)
Neb. Rev. Stat. 1943, 44-5201 et seq.
Utah Code Ann. 1953, 31A-30-101 et seq.

Health Insurance Alliance Act
N.M. Stat. Ann., 59A-56-1 et seq.

Health Insurance Association Act
La. Rev. Stat. Ann., 22:1161 et seq.

Health Insurance Availability Act (Individual)
Ida. Code 1947, 41-5201 et seq.

Health Insurance Availability Act (Small Employer)
Colo. Rev. Stat., 10-8-601 et seq.
Ida. Code 1947, 41-4701 et seq.
Mont. Code Ann., 33-22-1801 to 33-22-1814
Neb. Rev. Stat. 1943, 44-5223 et seq.
R.I. Gen. Laws 1956, 27-50-1 et seq.
Wyo. Stat. Ann., § 26-19-301 et seq.

Health Insurance Claim Filing Act
Ill. Rev. Stat. 1991, Ch. 73, § 1350 et seq.

Health Insurance Code
Minn. Stat. Ann., 62E.01 et seq.

Health Insurance Coverage Access Act
Wash. Rev. Code Ann., 48.41.010 et seq.

Health Insurance Coverage Act (Catastrophic)
Colo. Rev. Stat., 10-16-114 to 10-16-117

Health Insurance Coverage Continuation Act
Fla. Stat. Ann., 627.6692

Health Insurance Disclosure Act
Cal. Insurance Code § 10600 et seq.

Health Insurance for the Aged Act
July 30, 1965, P.L. 89-97, 79 Stat. 290, 26 U.S. Code §§ 72, 79, 213, 401, 405, 1401, 3101, 3111, 3201, 3211, 3221, 6051; 42 U.S. Code §§ 303, 401, 401a, 402, 418, 426, 603, 907, 1203, 1301, 1306, 1309, 1315, 1353, 1383, 1395 to 1396d; 45 U.S. Code §§ 228e 228s-2

Health Insurance Guaranty Association Act
Pa. Purdon's Stat., Title 40, § 1801 et seq.

Health Insurance Guaranty Association Act (Life and)
Minn. Stat. Ann., 61B.18 to 61B.32

Health Insurance Initiative (Small Business)
W. Va. Code 1966 § 5-16A-1 et seq.

Health Insurance Law (Group or Blanket)
See Group or Blanket Health Insurance Law

Health Insurance, Life Insurance and Accident Act (Credit)
Mass. Gen. Laws Ann., 167F:2, 175:110, 175.117C, 175:133, 175:177, 175:184, 255:12G, 255B:10, 255C:14A, 255D:1 to 255D:11, 255D:26

Health Insurance Market Reform Act (Individual)
Iowa Code 1983, 513C.1 et seq.

Health Insurance Opportunities for Employed Uninsured Oklahomans Act
Okla. Stat. Ann., Title 36, § 6501 et seq.

Health Insurance Plan ("CHIP") Act (Catastrophic)
R.I. Gen. Laws 1956, 42-62-1 et seq.

Health Insurance Plan (Basic)
Ga. Code Ann., 33-47-1 et seq.

Health Insurance Plan (High Risk)
Ga. Code Ann., 33-44-1 et seq.

Health Insurance Plan Act (Comprehensive)
Ill. Comp. Stat. 1992, Ch. 215, § 105/1 et seq.

Health Insurance Plan Act (State Employees)
Ga. Code Ann., 45-18-1 et seq.

Health Insurance Plan Act (Uninsurable)
Colo. Rev. Stat., 10-8-501 et seq.

Health Insurance Policy Language Simplification Act
Okla. Stat. Ann., Title 36, § 3641 et seq.

Health Insurance Pool Act
Neb. Rev. Stat. 1943, 44-4201 et seq.
N.M. Stat. Ann., 59A-54-1 et seq.
S.C. Code Ann. 1976, § 38-74-10 et seq.
Utah Code Ann. 1953, 31A-29-101 et seq.

Health Insurance Pool Act (Comprehensive)
Ark. Code 1987, 23-60-101 et seq.
Tex. Insurance Code, Art. 26.01 et seq.

Health Insurance Portability Act
N.M. Stat. Ann., 59A-23E-1 et seq.

Health Insurance Portability and Account-ability Act
Ark. Code 1987, 23-86-301 et seq.

Health Insurance Portability and Account-ability Act of 1996
Aug. 21, 1996, P.L. 104-191, 42 U.S. Code § 201 nt.
Aug. 5, 1997, P.L. 105-33, 42 U.S. Code § 1395b-5
Aug. 5, 1997, P.L. 105-34, 26 U.S. Code § 264 nt.

Health Insurance Portability and Availability Act
Ill. Comp. Stat. 1992, Ch. 215, § 97/1 et seq.

Health Insurance Program
Colo. Rev. Stat., 10-21-101 et seq.

Health Insurance Program Act (Children's)
Ill. Comp. Stat. 1992, Ch. 215, § 106/1 et seq.
Miss. Code Ann. 1972, § 41-86-1 et seq.

Health Insurance Reform Act
Md. Ann. Code 1974, Art. IN, § 15-1201 et seq.

Health Insurance Reform Act (Child's)
Okla. Stat. Ann., Title 36, § 3201 et seq.

Health Insurance Reform Act (Individuals)
N.J. Stat. Ann., 17B:27A-2 et seq.

Health Insurance Reform Act (Small Employer)
Okla. Stat. Ann., Title 36, § 6511 et seq.

Health Insurance Reform Plan (Child)
Mo. Rev. Stat 1986, 376.801

Health Insurance Risk Pool Association Act (Comprehensive)
Miss. Code Ann. 1972, § 83-9-201 et seq.

Health Insurance Trust Commodities Act
N.C. Gen. Stat. 1943, § 58-68-1 et seq.

Health, Life and Accident Insurance Broker Act
Okla. Stat. Ann., Title 36, § 1461 et seq.

Health, Life, and Accident Insurance Guaranty Association Act
S.C. Code Ann. 1976, § 38-29-10 et seq.

Health Maintenance Organization Act
See also Managed Care Reform Act
Cal. Health and Safety Code § 1175 et seq.
Colo. Rev. Stat., 10-17-101 et seq.
Del. Code of 1974, Title 16, § 9101 et seq.
Fla. Stat. Ann., 641.17 et seq.
Ill. Rev. Stat. 1991, Ch. 111 1/2, § 1401 et seq.
Iowa Code Ann., 514B.1 et seq.
Kan. Stat. Ann., 40-3201 et seq.
Ky. Rev. Stat. 1971, 304.38-010 et seq.
La. Rev. Stat. Ann., 22:2001 et seq.
Mass. Gen. Laws Ann., 176G:1 et seq.
Md. Ann. Code 1974, Art. HG, § 19-701 et seq.
Me. Rev. Stat. Ann. 1964, Title 24-A, § 4201 et seq.
Mich. Comp. Laws Ann., 333.21001 et seq.
Minn. Stat. Ann., 62D.01 et seq.
Mo. Rev. Stat., 354.400 et seq.
Mont. Code Ann., 33-31-101 et seq.
N.C. Gen. Stat. 1943, § 58-67-1 et seq.
Neb. Rev. Stat. 1943, 44-3201 et seq.
Nev. Rev. Stat. 1979 Reprint, 695C.010 et seq.
N.J. Stat. Ann., 26:2J-1 et seq.
N.M. Stat. Ann., 59A-46-1 et seq.
Pa. Purdon's Stat., Title 40, § 1551 et seq.
R.I. Gen. Laws 1956, 27-41-1 et seq.
S.C. Code Ann. 1976, § 38-33-10 et seq.
S.D. Codified Laws 1967, 58-41-1 et seq.
Tenn. Code Ann., 56-32-101 et seq.
Tex. Health and Safety Code, § 534.101 et seq.
Tex. Insurance Code, Art. 20A.01 et seq.
Utah Code Ann. 1953, 31A-8-101 et seq.
Vt. Stat. Ann., Title 8, § 5101 et seq.
Wash. Rev. Code Ann., 48.46.010 et seq.
W. Va. Code 1966, § 33-25A-1 et seq.
Wyo. Stat. Ann., § 26-34-101 et seq.
Continued

Health Maintenance Organization Act of 1973

Dec. 29, 1973, P.L. 93-222, 87 Stat. 914, 12 U.S. Code § 1721; 42 U.S. Code §§ 201 nt., 280c, 300e to 300e-14, 2001

Nov. 10, 1978, P.L. 95-626, 42 U.S. Code § 300e-14a

Health Maintenance Organization Amendments of 1978

Nov. 1, 1978, P.L. 95-559, 42 U.S. Code §§ 201 nt., 300e et seq., 1320a-1, 1396a, 1396a nt., 1396b

July 10, 1979, P.L. 96-32, 42 U.S. Code §§ 300e, 300e-3, 1320a-1

Health Maintenance Organization Amendments of 1981

Aug. 13, 1981, P.L. 97-35, 42 U.S. Code § 201 nt.

Health Maintenance Organization Amendments of 1986

Nov. 14, 1986, P.L. 99-660, 42 U.S. Code § 201 nt.

Oct. 24, 1988, P.L. 100-517, 42 U.S. Code § 300e-1 nt.

Oct. 27, 1992, P.L. 102-531, 42 U.S. Code § 300e nt.

Health Maintenance Organization Amendments of 1988

Oct. 24, 1988, P.L. 100-517, 42 U.S. Code §§ 201 nt.

Health Maintenance Organization and Life and Health Insurance Form Approval Act

N.J. Stat. Ann., 17:48-8.1 et seq.

Health Maintenance Organization Consumer Assistance Plan

Fla. Stat. Ann., 631.811 et seq.

Health Maintenance Organization Guaranty Association Act

W. Va. Code 1966, § 33-26B-1 et seq.

Health Maintenance Organization Guaranty Association Law

Ill. Rev. Stat. 1991, Ch. 111 1/2, § 1418.1 et seq.

Wyo. Stat. Ann., § 26-34-101 et seq.

Health Maintenance Organization Non-Profit Medical Corporation Act

N.Y. Public Health Law 1953 (Consol. Laws Ch. 45) § 4400 et seq.

Health Maintenance Organization Preferred Provider and Other Prepaid Health Benefits Plans Protection Act

Miss. Code Ann. 1972, § 83-41-301 et seq.

Health Maintenance Organizations Act

Mass. Gen. Laws 1984, 176G:1 et seq.

Health Management Information System Act (Community)

Iowa Code Ann., 15E.81 et seq.

Health Manpower Act of 1968

Aug. 16, 1968, P.L. 90-490, 82 Stat. 773, 42 U.S. Code §§ 242d, 242g, 292b to 292e 293 to 293d, 294 to 294d, 294f, 295f to 295h-3, 295h-6, 295h-7 and others

Health Manpower Training Act of 1971

See Comprehensive Health Manpower Training Act of 1971

Health Medi-Cal Law (Adult Day)

Cal. Welfare and Institutions Code § 14520 et seq.

Health Omnibus Programs Extension of 1988

Nov. 4, 1988, P.L. 100-607, 42 U.S. Code § 201 nt.

Aug. 16, 1989, P.L. 101-93, 42 U.S. Code §§ 256, 290aa-3 nt., 290bb-2, 290cc-21, 290cc-28, 290cc-29, 290cc-35, 290cc-36, 290dd, 290ee, 290ee-1 292a, 295g-2, 295j, 300y-21 nt.

Nov. 16, 1990, P.L. 101-616, 42 U.S. Code §§ 273, 273 nt.

Oct. 27, 1992, P.L. 102-531, 42 U.S. Code §§ 241 nt., 300e-1, 300ee-2

Health Opportunities Loan Act (Rural)

Neb. Rev. Stat. 1943, 71-5671 et seq.

Health Personnel Support Act

N.C. Laws 1973, Ch. 574

Health Plan
Mont. Code Ann., 50-5-402 et seq.

Health Plan Act (Children's)
Colo. Rev. Stat., 26-17-101 et seq.

Health Plan Act (County Maternal and Child)
N.M. Stat. Ann., 24-1B-1

Health Plan Act (Group)
Mich. Comp. Laws Ann., 550.1801 et seq.

Health Plan Act (Knox-Mills)
Cal. Government Code § 12530 et seq.

Health Planning Act
Ida. Code 1947, 39-4901 et seq.
Ill. Rev. Stat. 1987, Ch. 111 1/2, § 1071 et seq.
Tenn. Code Ann., 68-11-101 et seq.

Health Planning Act (Kidney)
Okla. Stat. Ann., Title 63, § 1-2600 et seq.

Health Planning Agency Act (Comprehensive)
Md. Ann. Code 1974, Art. HG, § 19-101 et seq.
S.C. Code Ann. 1976, § 44-5-10 et seq.

Health Planning and Development Act
Ala. Code 1975, § 22-4-1 et seq.
Ga. Code Ann., 31-6-1 et seq.
Kan. Stat. Ann., 65-4701 et seq.
S.C. Code Ann. 1976, 44-5-10 et seq.
Tex. Health and Safety Code, § 104.001

Health Planning and Health Policy Development Act
Mich. Comp. Laws Ann., 325.2001

Health Planning and Health Service Research and Statistics Extension Act of 1977
Aug. 1, 1977, P.L. 95-83, 42 U.S. Code §§ 201 et seq.

Health Planning and Resources Development Act
Ga. Code Ann., 31-6-1 et seq.
Haw. Rev. Stat. Ann., § 323D-1 et seq.
Mich. Comp. Laws Ann., 325.2001 et seq.
N.C. Gen. Stat. 1943, § 131-170 et seq.
Tenn. Code Ann., 68-11-101 et seq.
Utah Code Ann. 1953, Miscellaneous Superseded Code Provisions, 26-33-1 et seq.
Va. Code 1950, § 32.1-117 et seq.
Wash. Rev. Code Ann., 70.38.015 et seq.

Health Planning and Resources Development Amendments of 1979
Oct. 4, 1979, P.L. 96-79, 21 U.S. Code § 1176; 42 U.S. Code §§ 201, 201 nt., 246, 300k-1 et seq., 300k-1 nt., 1396b, 2689t, 4573
Jan. 4, 1983, P.L. 97-414, 42 U.S. Code § 300t-11 nt.

Health Planning Authority Act
Ariz. Rev. Stat. Ann., § 36-103.01 et seq.

Health Policy Act
Miss. Code Ann. 1972, § 41-95-1 et seq.

Health Policy Provisions Law
Del. Code of 1974, Title 18, § 3301 et seq.
Ky. Rev. Stat. 1971, 304.17-010 et seq.
Me. Rev. Stat. Ann. 1964, Title 24-A, § 2701 et seq.
Nev. Rev. Stat. 1979 Reprint, 689A.010 et seq.

Health Problems Education Act
Mich. Comp. Laws Ann., 388.381 et seq.

Health Problems Reporting Act
Mich. Comp. Laws Ann., 325.71 et seq.

Health Problems Reporting Act (Critical)
N.H. Rev. Stat. 1955, 141-A:1 et seq.

Health Professional Loan Repayment Act
N.M. Stat. Ann., 21-22D-1 et seq.

Health Professions Act (Regulation of)
Wash. Rev. Code Ann., 18.120.010 et seq.

Health Professions Education Extension Amendments of 1992

Oct. 13, 1992, P.L. 102-408, 106 Stat. 1992

Oct. 27, 1992, P.L. 102-531, 42 U.S. Code § 295k nt.

Nov. 13, 1998, P.L. 105-392, 42 U.S. Code § 295k nt., 294o

Health Professions Education Partnerships Act of 1998

Nov. 13, 1998, P.L. 105-392, 112 Stat. 3524, 42 U.S. Code § 201 nt.

Health Professions Educational Assistance Act of 1963

Sept. 24, 1963, P.L. 88-129, 77 Stat. 164, 42 U.S. Code §§ 292 to 292b, 292d to 294e

Oct. 22, 1965, P.L. 89-290, 79 Stat. 1052, 42 U.S. Code §§ 293, 293a, 293d 294 to 294d 295f to 295f-4, 295g, 297b, 298b

Health Professions Educational Assistance Act of 1976

Oct. 12, 1976, P.L. 94-484, 42 U.S. Code §§ 201 et seq.

Aug. 1, 1977, P.L. 95-83, 8 U.S. Code § 1101 et seq.; 42 U.S. Code § 294t nt.

Nov. 9, 1978, P.L. 95-623, 42 U.S. Code §§ 292h nt., 295h-4 nt.

Health Professions Reauthorization Act of 1968

Nov. 4, 1988, P.L. 100-607, 42 U.S. Code § 201 nt.

Health Professions Regulation Act

Neb. Rev. Stat. 1943, 71-6201 et seq.

Wash. Rev. Code Ann., 18.120.010 et seq.

Health Professions Training Assistance Act of 1985

Oct. 22, 1985, P.L. 99-129, 42 U.S. Code §§ 201 nt., 2541, 292 et seq., 295 et seq., 296k to 296-m, 297a, 298b-5, 300aa-14

Health Programs Extension Act of 1973

June 18, 1973, P.L. 93-45, 87 Stat. 91, 42 U.S. Code §§ 242b, 242c, 242d 242g, 242h, 246 and others

July 12, 1974, P.L. 93-348, 88 Stat. 353, 42 U.S. Code § 300a-7

Sept. 29, 1979, P.L. 96-76, 42 U.S. Code § 300a-7

Health Programs Extension Act of 1980

Dec. 17, 1980, P.L. 96-538, 42 U.S. Code § 201 nt.

Health Promotion Act (Minority Populations)

R.I. Gen. Laws 1956, 23-64-1 et seq.

Health Promotion and Disease Prevention Amendments of 1984

Oct. 30, 1984, P.L. 98-551, 42 U.S. Code § 201 nt.

Health Protection Act

Tex. Health and Safety Code § 341.001 et seq.

Health Protection Act (Asbestos)

Tex. Rev. Civ. Stat., Art. 4477-3a

Health Protection and Cigarette and Tobacco Tax Act

Cal. Revenue and Taxation Code § 30121 et seq.

Health Protection Fund Act

Mass. Gen. Laws Ann., 29:2t

Health Provider Recruitment Strategy Act (Essential)

Mich. Comp. Laws Ann., 333.2701 et seq.

Health Reform Act (Mental)

Kan. Stat. Ann., 39-1601 et seq.

Health Research Act

Okla. Stat. Ann., Title 74, § 5046 et seq.

Health Research Extension Act of 1985

Nov. 20, 1985, P.L. 99-158, 42 U.S. Code §§ 201 nt., 217a, 218, 241, 275 et seq., 281 et seq., 285c nt., 285e-2 nt., 285j-1 nt., 287i, 289d, 290aa-5, 300c-12

Oct. 27, 1992, P.L. 102-531, 42 U.S. Code § 281 nt.

June 10, 1993, P.L. 103-43, 42 U.S. Code § 289d nt.

Health Research Facilities Act of 1956

July 30, 1956, Ch. 779, 70 Stat. 717, 31 U.S. Code §§ 72 nt., 711 nt.; 33 U.S. Code § 763c nt.; 42 U.S. Code §§ 2 nt., 16 nt., 98 nt., 201 nt., 201, 211a nt., 212a nt., 214 nt., 222 nt., 230 nt., 249 nt., 292 to 292i; 46 U.S. Code § 654 nt.; 49 U.S. Code §§ 177 nt., 181 nt.

Aug. 9, 1965, P.L. 89-115, 79 Stat. 448, 42 U.S. Code §§ 241, 292c, 292d

Health Research Fairness Act

Cal. Health and Safety Code § 439.900 et seq.

Health Resorts and Spas Act

Ind. Code 1971, 23-9-9-1 et seq.

Health Resources Development and Planning Act

Mich. Comp. Laws Ann., 325.2001 et seq.

Health, Safety and Comfort Act

Ill. Rev. Stat. 1937, Ch. 48, § 103 et seq.

Health Safety and Security Act (Nursing Homes, Long-Term Care)

Cal. Health and Safety Code § 1417 et seq.

Health Science Facilities Construction Program Bond Act

Cal. Statutes 1971, Ch. 665, p. 1315

Cal. Statutes 1972, Ch. 152, §§ 5 to 15, p. 199

Health Screening Act (Multiphasic)

Colo. Rev. Stat., 25-26-101 et seq.

Health Security Act

Me. Rev. Stat. Ann. 1964, Title 24, § 2501 et seq.

Health Service Act (Industrial)

Ark. Code Ann. 1987, 11-5-201, 11-5-202

Wyo. Stat. Ann., § 35-1-501 et seq.

Health Service Act (Radiology)

Tenn. Code Ann., 68-202-201 et seq.

Health Service Administrators Profession Regulation Act

P.R. Laws Ann. 1954, Title 20, § 2351 et seq.

Health Service Corporations Act

Mont. Code Ann., 33-30-101 et seq.

Health Service Corps Act

N.M. Stat. Ann., 24-1D-1 et seq.

Health Service Corps Program for Medically Underserved Areas Act

Tex. Health and Safety Code, §§ 106.101 to 106.106

Health Service for Public School Act

Ark. Code Ann. 1987, 6-1-205 et seq.

Health Service Organization Act (Limited)

Ill. Rev. Stat. 1991, Ch. 73, § 1501-1 et seq.

Health Service Plan Corporation Act

Minn. Stat. Ann., 62C.01 et seq.

Health Services Act

Wash. Laws 1993, Ch. 492

Health Services Act (Community Public)

Neb. Laws 1992, L.B. 1019, §§ 101 to 121

Health Services Act (Community)

Cal. Welfare and Institutions Code § 5000 et seq.

Minn. Stat. 1986, 145.911 et seq.

Health Services Act (Home)

Fla. Stat. Ann., 400.461 et seq.

Health Services Act (Juvenile Mental)

Wash. Rev. Code Ann., 71.34.010 et seq.

Health Services Act (Mental)

Mass. Gen. Laws Ann., 19:17 et seq.

Health Services Act (Voluntary Nonprofit)

Pa. Purdon's Stat., Title 40, § 1551 et seq.

Health Services Act (Volunteer)

Pa. Purdon's Stat., Title 35, § 449.41 et seq.

Tenn. Code Ann., 63-6-701 et seq.

Health Services Act (Women's Preventative)
Pa. Purdon's Stat., Title 40, § 1571 et seq.

Health Services Amendments Act of 1986
April 24, 1986, P.L. 99-280, 42 U.S. Code
§ 201 nt.

Health Services Amendments of 1985
Oct. 7, 1985, P.L. 99-117, 42 U.S. Code
§§ 201 nt., 207, 210, 213a, 241 nt., 242c,
242n, 243, 247b, 247e, 253, 300x-4,
300x-5, 300x-9

Health Services and Centers Amendments of 1978
Nov. 10, 1978, P.L. 95-626, 42 U.S. Code
§§ 201 nt., 218, 242p, 246, 247b et seq.,
254b et seq., 289d nt., 294t, 294u, 295h-1,
300a-21 et seq. 1396b July 10, 1979, P.L.
96-32, 42 U.S. Code §§ 246, 247b, 247b nt.,
247e, 254b 254c, 300u-6, 300u-7

Health Services and Facilities Compact (New England)
R.I. Gen. Laws 1956, 23-16.1-1 et seq.

Health Services Education Grants Act
Ill. Rev. Stat. 1985, Ch. 111 1/2, § 821 et seq.

Health Services Extension Act of 1977
Aug. 1, 1977, P.L. 95-83, 8 U.S. Code § 1101
et seq.; 21 U.S. Code §§ 1112, 1176; 25
U.S. Code § 1614; 42 U.S. Code §§ 201 nt.,
210 et seq.

Health Services Extension Act of 1978
Nov. 10, 1978, P.L. 95-626, 42 U.S. Code
§§ 201 nt., 246, 247a to 247c, 255, 289d nt.,
300b, 300b-3, 300b-6, 300c-21, 300c-22,
300d-2 et seq.

Health Services for Regional Districts Act
S.C. Code Ann. 1976, § 44-7-2010 et seq.

Health Services Integral Reform Act
P.R. Laws Ann. 1954, Title 24, § 3001 et seq.

Health Services Organizations Act
P.R. Laws Ann. 1954, Title 26, § 1901 et seq.

Health Services Plan Act
Ill. Rev. Stat. 1991, Ch. 32, § 595 et seq.

Health Services Rates Act
D.C. Code Ann., § 47-2713 et seq.

Health Services Reorganization Act
Miss. General Laws 1986, Ch. 437

Health Services Research, Health Statistics, and Health Care Technology Act of 1978
Nov. 9, 1978, P.L. 95-623, 42 U.S. Code
§§ 201 nt., 210, 229c, 242b et seq., 289k,
289l-1, 292e et seq., 4362a, 7411, 7412,
7417, 7617
July 10, 1979, P.L. 96-32, 42 U.S. Code
§§ 242b, 242n

Health Services Research, Health Statistics, and Medical Libraries Act of 1974
July 23, 1974, P.L. 93-353, 88 Stat. 362, 42
U.S. Code §§ 235, 236, 242b 242c, 242k to
242o, 244-1, 245a, 247d, 253b, 280b,
280b-1, 280b-2, 280b-4, 280b-5, 280b-7 to
280b-11

Health Services Revolving Fund Act (Rural)
Ark. Code 1987, 20-12-401 et seq.

Health Spa Act
Okla. Stat. Ann., Title 59, § 2000 et seq.
Tex. Rev. Civ. Stat., Art. 52211
Va. Code 1950, § 59.1-294 et seq.

Health Spa Consumer Protection Act
Ark. Code Ann. 1987, 4-94-101 et seq.
D.C. Code 1973, § 28-3817
Utah Code Ann. 1953, Miscellaneous
Superceded Code Provisions, 13-23-1 et
seq.

Health Start Support Services for Children Act
Cal. Education Code 1976, § 8800 et seq.

Health Statistics Act
Ill. Rev. Stat. 1991, Ch. 111 1/2, § 5601 et
seq.
N.D. Cent. Code, 23-02.1-01 et seq.

Health Studio Services Act
Cal. Civil Code § 1812.80 et seq.

Health Systems and Professional Incentive Act (Rural)
Neb. Rev. Stat. 1943, 71-5650 et seq.

Health Testing Center Act (Multiphasic)
Fla. Stat. Ann., 483.28 et seq.

Health Threat Act (Tuberculosis)
Minn. Stat. 1986, 144.4801 to 144.4813

Health Training Improvement Act of 1970
Nov. 2, 1970, P.L. 91-519, 84 Stat. 1342, 42
U.S. Code §§ 295f-1, 295f-2, 295h to
295h-2, 295h-3a to 295h-3d, 295h-7 to
295h-9

Health Warning Act (Cigarette)
Ill. Comp. Stat. 1992, Ch. 410, § 85/1 et seq.

Health, Welfare and Retirement Funds Act
Mass. Gen. Laws Ann., 151D:1 et seq.

Health Wellness Promotion Act
N.J. Stat. Ann., 26:1A-36.11 et seq.

Healthcare Protection Act (Minimum)
N.M. Stat. Ann., 59A-23B-1 et seq.

Healthy Communities and Healthy People Act
Fla. Stat. Ann., 408.601 et seq.

Healthy Kids Corporation Act
Fla. Stat. Ann., 624.91 et seq.
Tex. Health and Safety Code, § 109.001 et
seq.

Healthy Kids Program Act
Kan. Laws 1992, Ch. 168

Healthy Meals for Children Act
May 29, 1996, P.L. 104-149, 42 U.S. Code
§ 1751 nt.

Healthy Meals for Healthy Americans Act of 1994
Nov. 2, 1994, P.L. 103-448, 42 U.S. Code
§ 1751 nt.

Healthy Start Support Services for Children Act
Cal. Education Code 1976, § 8800 et seq.

Heard Acts
Aug. 13, 1894 Ch. 280, 28 Stat. 278
Feb. 24, 1905, Ch. 772, 33 Stat. 811

Hearing Aid Act
Fla. Stat. Ann., 484.0401
Kan. Stat. Ann., 74-5801 et seq.
La. Rev. Stat. Ann., 37:2441 et seq.
N.M. Stat. Ann., 61-24A-1 et seq.
Ore. Rev. Stat., 694.015 et seq.

Hearing Aid Assistance for the Aged and Disabled
N.J. Stat. Ann., 30:4D-36 et seq.

Hearing Aid Compatability Act of 1988
Aug. 16, 1988, P.L. 100-394, 102 Stat. 976,
47 U.S. Code §§ 609 nt., 610, 610 nt.

Hearing Aid Consumer Protection Act
Ill. Rev. Stat. 1991, Ch. 111, § 7401 et seq.

Hearing Aid Dealers Act
Colo. Rev. Stat., 12-65-101 et seq.
Md. Ann. Code 1974, Art. BO, § 8-101 et
seq.

Hearing Aid Dealers and Consumers Act
D.C. Code Ann., § 28-4001 et seq.

Hearing Aid Dealers and Dispensers Act
Ga. Code Ann., 43-20-1 et seq.

Hearing Aid Dealers and Fitters Act
N.D. Cent. Code, 43-33-01 et seq.
Okla. Stat. Ann., Title 59, § 1601 et seq.

Hearing Aid Dealers, Speech-Language Pathologists, and Audiologists Act
Md. Ann. Code 1974, Art. HO, § 2-101 et
seq.

Hearing Aid Dispensers Act
Ark. Code Ann. 1987, 17-83-201, 17-83-202
S.D. Codified Laws 1967, 36-24-1 et seq.

Hearing Aid Dispensers Licensing Law
Cal. Business and Professions Code § 3300 et seq.

Hearing Aid Sales Registration Law
Pa. Purdon's Stat., Title 35, § 6700-101 et seq.

Hearing Aid Specialist Licensure Act
Wyo. Stat. Ann., § 33-35-101 et seq.

Hearing Aid Specialists Act
Nev. Rev. Stat. 1979 Reprint, 637A.010 et seq.

Hearing Aid Specialists and Consumers Act
Utah Code Ann. 1953, 58-46-1 et seq.

Hearing Aids Fitting and Selling Act
S.C. Code Ann. 1976, § 40-25-10 et seq.

Hearing and Lung Act
Tenn. Code Ann., 7-51-201

Hearing-Ear Dogs Act
N.M. Stat. Ann., 28-11-1 et seq.

Hearing Impaired Act (Interpreter Services for the)
Utah Code Ann. 1953, 53A-26a-101 et seq.

Hearing-Impaired Act (Telecommunications)
Okla. Stat. Ann., Title 63, § 2416 et seq.

Hearing Impaired and Behavior Disordered Children Services Act
Ill. Rev. Stat. 1989, Ch. 23, §§ 3404.9, 3405

Hearing Impaired Services Act
Minn. Stat. Ann., 256C.21 et seq.

Hearing Impaired/Behavior Disordered Children Interagency Board Act
Ill. Rev. Stat. 1991, Ch. 23, § 6701 et seq.

Hearing Instrument Specialist Licensing Act
Utah Code Ann. 1953, 58-46a-102 et seq.

Hearing Loss Act
Iowa Code Ann., 85B.1 et seq.

Hearing Officer Act (Child Support)
N.M. Stat. Ann., 40-4B-1 et seq.

Hearing Test Act (Children)
Ill. Rev. Stat. 1991, Ch. 23, § 2331 et seq.

Hearings and Appeals Act (Insurance Code)
Ida. Code 1947, 41-231 et seq.

Hearsay Act
Mass. Gen. Laws Ann., 233:65
Okla. Stat. Ann., Title 12, § 2801

Hearsay Rule
Cal. Evidence Code § 1200

Heart Act (Line of Duty Presumption)
Mass. Gen. Laws Ann., 32:94

Heart Act (Retirement)
Mass. Gen. Laws Ann., 32:94

Heart Balm Act
Ala. Code 1975, §§ 6-5-330, 6-5-331
Cal. Civil Code § 43.5
Colo. Rev. Stat. 1963, 13-8-1 et seq.
Conn. Gen. Stat. Ann., § 52-572b
Fla. Stat. Ann., 771.01 et seq.
Ill. Rev. Stat. 1991, Ch. 40, § 1900 et seq.
Ind. Code Ann., 34-4-4-1 et seq.
Mass. Gen. Laws Ann., 207:47A
Md. Ann. Code 1974, Art. FL, § 3-101 et seq.
Me. Rev. Stat. Ann. 1964, Title 14, § 854
Mich. Comp. Laws Ann., 551.301 et seq.
Nev. Rev. Stat. 1979 Reprint, 41.370 et seq.
N.H. Rev. Stat. 1955, 508:11
N.J. Stat. Ann., 2A:23-1 et seq.
N.Y. Civil Rights Law (Consol. Laws Ch. 6) § 80a et seq.
Pa. Purdon's Stat., Title 48, § 170 et seq.
Wis. Stat. Ann., 768.01 et seq.
Wyo. Stat. Ann., § 1-23-101 et seq.

Heart Disease and Rheumatic Fever Medicine Act
Ill. Rev. Stat. 1991, Ch. 111 1/2, § 22.09 et seq.

Heart Disease, Cancer, and Stroke Act of 1965

Oct. 6, 1965, P.L. 89-239, 79 Stat. 926, 33 U.S. Code § 763c; 42 U.S. Code §§ 201 nts. 221a, 212a, 214 nt., 222 nt., 299 to 299i

Heart Disease, Cancer, Stroke, and Kidney Disease Amendments of 1970

Oct. 30, 1970, P.L. 91-515, 84 Stat. 1297, 42 U.S. Code §§ 299 to 299g, 299i, 299j

Heart Law (Presumption of Job Related Disability)

N.Y. General Municipal Law (Consol. Laws Ch. 24) § 204k

N.Y. Volunteer Fireman's Benefit Law (Consol. Laws Ch. 64A) § 61

Heart of Georgia Regional Airport Authority Act

Ga. Laws 1995, p. 4448

Hearth Baked Bread Act

Ill. Rev. Stat. 1991, Ch. 56 1/2, § 288.9 et seq.

Heath-Carroll-Goulette Act (Liquor Purchases by Minors)

Mich. Comp. Laws Ann., 750.141c

Heating Act (Municipal Plan) Cities of Primary, First and Second Classes and Villages

Neb. Rev. Stat. 1943, 19-1401 et seq.

Heating Assistance and Shut-Off Protection Act (Low Income)

Mich. Comp. Laws Ann., 400.1201 et seq.

Heating Cable Safety Act

Mich. Comp. Laws Ann., 125.2501 et seq.

Heating Contractors' License Act

N.C. Gen. Stat. 1943, § 87-16 et seq.

Heating Oil Pollution Liability Protection Act

Wash. Rev. Code Ann., 70.149.010 et seq.

Heating, Ventilation, Air Conditioning, and Refrigeration Contractors Act

Md. Ann. Code 1974, Art. BR, § 9A-101 et seq.

Heating, Ventilation, and Air Conditioning Act

Mont. Code Ann. 1979, 37-70-101 et seq.

Heating, Ventilation, and Air Conditioning Contractors' Act

Ky. Rev. Stat. 1971, 198B.650 to 198B.689

Heavy Equipment Dealer Act (Multiline)

Ga. Code Ann., 10-1-730 et seq.

Heavy Rescue Act (Urban)

Cal. Government Code §§ 8584, 8584.1

Heber Valley Historic Railroad Authority

Utah Code Ann. 1953, 9-3-301 et seq.

Hebert Act (Alcoholic Rehabilitation-District of Columbia)

D.C. Code Ann., § 24-521 et seq.

Hebert Act (Parole)

D.C. Code 1973, § 24-201a et seq.

Hedge and Weed Act

Kan. Stat. Ann., 29-419 et seq.

Hedge Fence Act

Kan. Stat. Ann., 29-410 et seq.

Heidis Law

Ga. Code Ann., 17-10-3.1, 17-16-1, 40-5-64, 40-5-121, 40-6-391, 40-6-393, 40-6-394, 42-8-111

Height of Buildings Act

Mich. Comp. Laws Ann., 700.183 et seq.

Heirship Acts

D.C. Code 1973, § 5-401 et seq.

N.J. Stat. Ann., 3B:22-39 et seq.

Ohio Rev. Code 1953, 2123.01 et seq.

Tex. Probate Code, § 48 et seq.

Helen Keller National Center Act
Feb. 21, 1984, P.L. 98-221, 29 U.S. Code §§ 1901, 1901 nt., 1902 et seq.
Oct. 21, 1986, P.L. 99-506, 29 U.S. Code § 1904
Nov. 7, 1988, P.L. 100-630, 29 U.S. Code § 1904
June 6, 1991, P.L. 102-52, 29 U.S. Code § 1904
Oct. 29, 1992, P.L. 102-569, 29 U.S. Code §§ 1901 to 1907
Aug. 7, 1998, P.L. 105-220, 29 U.S. Code §§ 1904, 1907, 1908

Helium Act
Sept. 13, 1960, P.L. 86-777, 74 Stat. 918, 50 U.S. Code §§ 167 to 167n
Nov. 10, 1998, P.L. 105-362, 50 U.S. Code sect167n

Helium Gas Act
See Helium Act
Sept. 1, 1937, Ch. 895, 50 Stat. 885, 50 U.S. Code §§ 161, 163 to 166
July 26, 1954, Ch. 596, 68 Stat. 530, 50 U.S. Code § 161

Helium Privatization Act of 1996
Oct. 9, 1996, P.L. 104-273, 50 U.S. Code § 167 nt.

Hell Gate Pilotage Act
N.Y. Laws 1847, Ch. 69

Helmet Law
Mass. Gen. Laws Ann., 90:7
Mich. Comp. Laws Ann., 257.658, Subd. d
Miss. Code Ann. 1972, § 63-7-64
Mo. Rev. Stat 1986, 302.020

Help Education Lead to Prosperity Act
Neb. Rev. Stat. 1943, 79-3501 et seq.

Help Our Wildlife Act
La. Rev. Stat. Ann., 56:70.1 et seq.

Helton-Golden Act (Attendance of Witnesses)
Ky. Rev. Stat. 1971, 421.230 et seq.

Hemodialysis Technician Training Act
Cal. Business and Professions Code §§ 1247 to 1247.9

Hemodialysis Technologists' Profession Act
P.R. Laws Ann. 1954, Title 20, § 2901 et seq.

Hemophilia Care Act
Ill. Rev. Stat. 1991, Ch. 111 1/2, § 2900 et seq.

Hemophilia Program Act
N.M. Stat. Ann., 24-2A-1 et seq.

Hempstead Dredging Act
N.Y. Local Laws 1964, Town of Hempstead, p. 1282

Hempstead Housing Authority Act
N.Y. Public Housing Law (Consol. Laws Ch. 44A) § 409

Hempstead Structures in Public Waterways Act
N.Y. Local Laws 1964, Town of Hempstead, p. 1279
N.Y. Local Laws 1967, Town of Hempstead, p. 1702

Hendel Act (Emergency Relief-Civil Service)
N.Y. Laws 1936, Ch. 822

Henderson Act (County Engineer)
Ala. Code 1975, § 11-6-1 et seq.

Henderson Act (Telephone Service)
Ohio Rev. Code 1953, 4905.241 et seq.

Henderson Charter
Nev. Statutes 1971, Ch. 266, p. 157

Hendley Act (Taxation)
Ohio Laws Vol. 94, p. 246

Hendry County Hospital Authority Act
Fla. Special Laws 1947, Ch. 24551

Hendry County Improvement Authority Act
Fla. Special Laws 1955, Ch. 30803

Hendry County Water District Management Act
Fla. Special Laws 1967, Ch. 67-1443

Henley-Van Ness Act (Elections)
Ind. Laws 1944, 1st Special Session, Ch. 3, p. 11

Hennessy Act (Municipalities)
N.J. Stat. Ann., 40:70-3

Henry County Community Improvement Districts Act
Ga. Laws 1985, p. 4946
Ga. Laws 1991, p. 4339

Henry County Development Authority Act
Ga. Laws 1967, p. 2291

Henry County Road Law
Tenn. Private Acts 1972, Ch. 326

Henry Hudson Parkway Authority Act
N.Y. Public Authorities Law (Consol. Laws Ch. 43A) § 225 et seq.

Hepatitis B Prevention Act
Pa. Purdon's Stat., Title 35, § 630.1 et seq.

Hepatitis C Education, Screening, and Treatment Act
Cal. Health and Safety Code § 12440 et seq.

Hepburn Act (Interstate Commerce)
June 29, 1906, Ch. 3591, 34 Stat. 584, 49 U.S. Code Appx. §§ 1, 6, 11, 14, 15, 16, 16a, 18, 20, 41

Herbert Act (Blue Sky Act)
Ohio Rev. Code 1953, 1707.01 et seq.

Herbert-Martin-Morgan Act (Elections)
Ohio Rev. Code 1953, 3501.01 et seq.

Herbicide Law
Ind. Code Ann., 15-3-1-1 et seq.
Tex. Agriculture Code, § 75.001 et seq.

Herbie Deskins - Kelsey Friend Tax Relief for Flood Victims Act
Ky. Rev. Stat. 1971, 141.011

Herd Acts
Kan. Stat. Ann., 47-301 et seq.
N.D. Cent. Code, 36-11-01 et seq.
Neb. Rev. Stat. 1943, 54-301 et seq.
N.M. Stat. Ann., 77-12-1 et seq.
Okla. Stat. Ann., Title 4, § 91 et seq.
S.D. Codified Laws 1967, 40-28-4 et seq.
Wash. Rev. Code Ann., 16.24.010 et seq.

Hereditary Disorders Act
N.J. Stat. Ann., 26:5B-1 et seq.

Herger-Feinstein Quincy Library Group Forest Recovery Act
Oct. 21, 1998, P.L. 105-277, 101(e), Title IV, § 401, 112 Stat. 2681, 16 U.S. Code § 2104 nt.

Heritage Act (Documentary)
N.Y. Education Law 1947 (Consol. Laws Ch. 16) § 140

Heritage Act (Preservation)
Utah Code Ann. 1953, 9-8-801 et seq.

Heritage Act (Wildlife)
Utah Code Ann. 1953, 23-26-1 et seq.

Heritage Affairs Act
Pa. Purdon's Stat., Title 71, § 1090.1 et seq.

Heritage Authority Act (Sapelo Island)
Ga. Code Ann., 12-3-440 et seq.

Heritage Museum Act (Farm and Ranch)
N.M. Stat. Ann., 18-11-1 et seq.

Heritage Network Act (Gene Chappie)
Cal. Vehicle Code 1959, § 5066

Heritage of Montana Enterprise Act
Mont. Code Ann., 20-26-1401 et seq.

Heritage Parkway Corridor Law (Alton Park)
Ill. Comp. Stat. 1992, Ch. 20, § 3905/1001 et seq.

Heritage Parkway Law (Alton Lake)
Ill. Rev. Stat. 1991, Ch. 105, § 901 et seq.

Heritage Preservation Act
Cal. Statutes 1963, Ch. 1938, p. 3991
Utah Code Ann. 1953, 63-77-1 et seq.

Heritage Trust Act
Ga. Code Ann., 12-3-70 et seq.
Mich. Comp. Laws Ann., 318.421 et seq.

Heritage Trust Program
S.C. Code Ann. 1976, § 51-17-10 et seq.

Herkimer County Act
N.Y. Laws 1852, Ch. 361

Hernando County Aviation Authority Act
Fla. Special Laws 1965, Ch. 65-1623

Hernando County Saltwater Fishing Law
Fla. Special Laws 1969, Ch. 69-1097

Herndon Parking Authority Act
Va. Acts 1991, Ch. 142

Hernia Act
Ariz. Rev. Stat. Ann., § 23-1043
Ark. Code Ann. 1987, 11-9-519 et seq.
Miss. Code Ann. 1972, § 71-3-23

Herrin, Jefferson County, and Quincy Civic Centers Act
Ill. Rev. Stat. 1991, Ch. 85, § 2700 et seq.

Hertel Law-T. Stopczynski Port Authority Act
Mich. Comp. Laws Ann., 120.101 et seq.

Hertzberg-Leslie Witness Protection Act
Cal. Penal Code § 14020 et seq.

Hewitt Act
Ky. Acts 1885-86 (Public) Ch. 1233

Hewitt Act (Public Utilities)
Cal. Statutes 1911 Ex. Sess., Ch. 40, p. 168

Heyburn Act (Pure Food and Drugs)
June 30, 1906, Ch. 3915, 34 Stat. 768

Hibbitts-Moss Act (Mine Disaster)
Ky. Acts 1948, Ch. 127

Hickenlooper Amendment
Oct. 7, 1964, P.L. 88-633, 78 Stat. 1013, 22
U.S. Code § 2370(e)(2)

Hickerson-Whitlock Act (Abandoned Cemeteries)
Ky. Rev. Stat. 1971, 381.720 et seq.

Hickey Act (Gambling)
Mont. Code Ann., 23-5-112 et seq.

Hidalgo County Hospital District Law
Tex. Rev. Civ. Stat. 1925, Art. 4494q-2

Hidden Gun Act
Miss. Code Ann. 1972, § 97-37-1 et seq.

Hide Amendment
Sept. 30, 1976, P.L. 94-439, 90 Stat. 1434
Dec. 9, 1977, P.L. 95-205, 91 Stat. 1460
Oct. 18, 1978, P.L. 95-480, 92 Stat. 1586
Nov. 20, 1979, P.L. 96-123, 93 Stat. 926
Oct. 1, 1980, P.L. 96-369, 94 Stat. 1352
Dec. 21, 1982, P.L. 97-377, 96 Stat. 1894

Hide and Brand Law
Cal. Food and Agricultural Code 1967,
§ 20001 et seq.

Higbie-Armstrong Act (County Highways)
N.Y. Laws 1898, Ch. 115

Higgins-Guggisberg-Nichols Act (Tax Exemptions)
Mich. Comp. Laws Ann., 211.7, 211.9

Higgins Road Retrocession Act
Ill. Rev. Stat. 1991, Ch. 1, §§ 4400, 4401

High Blood Pressure Control Act
Ill. Rev. Stat. 1991, Ch. 111 1/2, § 2601 et
seq.

High Capacity Well Act
Wis. Stat. Ann., 144.025, Subsec. 2, Subd. e

High Cost Transportation Funding Act
Ark. Code 1987, 6-20-1701 et seq.

High Level Radioactive Waste Act
N.H. Rev. Stat. 1955, 125-G:1 et seq.

High Performance Computing Act of 1991
Dec. 9, 1991, P.L. 102-194, 15 U.S. Code
§§ 5501 et seq., 5501 nt.
Dec. 21, 1995, P.L. 104-66, 15 U.S. Code
§§ 5511, 5523
Oct. 28, 1998, P.L. 105-305, 15 U.S. Code
§§ 5501, 5502, 5503, 5511, 5513

High Plains States Groundwater Demonstration Program Act of 1983
Sept. 28, 1984, P.L. 98-434, 98 Stat. 1675, 43
U.S. Code §§ 390g et seq., 390g nt.
Oct. 30, 1992, P.L. 102-575, 43 U.S. Code
§§ 390g-2, 390g-3, 390g-5
Dec. 21, 1995, P.L. 104-66, 43 U.S. Code
§ 390g-1

High Rise Safety Act
Okla. Stat. Ann., Title 19, § 863.44A et seq.

High Risk Health Insurance Plan
Ga. Code Ann., 33-44-1

High Risk Youth Career Development Act
Ill. Rev. Stat. 1991, Ch. 23, §§ 6550, 6551

High-Risk Youth Education and Public Safety Program
Cal. Education Code 1976, § 47750 et seq.

High School Academies for At-Risk Pupils
Cal. Education Code 1976, §§ 46800 to
46807

High School Act
Ill. Rev. Stat. 1991, Ch. 122, § 12-1 et seq.
Ore. Rev. Stat., 335.090 et seq.

High School Act (County and District)
Ore. Rev. Stat., 335.005 et seq.

High School Budget Act
Mont. Code Ann., 20-9-101 et seq.

High School Building Fund (County)
Fla. Laws 1947, Ch. 24224

High School Coaching Education and Training Program
Cal. Education Code 1976, § 35179.1 et seq.

High School Community Service Act
Fla. Stat. Ann., 228.0716

High School Districts Act (Interstate)
Vt. Acts 1959, No. 230

High School Education Technology Grant Act (Digital)
Cal. Education Code 1976, § 52250 et seq.

High School Free Textbook Act
Ark. Stat. 1947, 80-1701 et seq.

High School Fund Law (County)
Ore. Code 1930, §§ 35-4001 to 35-4008

High School Graduation Scholarship Program (Early)
Tex. Education Code, Art. 56.201 et seq.

High School Grounds Loan Act (Gloucester)
Mass. Acts 1953, Ch. 625

High School Inspector Act
Ind. Code 1971, 20-1-13-1 et seq.

High School Tuition Fund Law (County)
Ore. Code 1930, §§ 35-4101 to 35-4113

High Seas Driftnet Fisheries Enforcement Act
Nov. 2, 1992, P.L. 102-582, 16 U.S. Code
§ 1801 nt.
Oct. 14, 1998, P.L. 105-258, 46 U.S. Code
Appx. § 1707a

High Seas Driftnet Fishing Moratorium Protection Act
Nov. 3, 1995, P.L. 104-43, Title VI, 16 U.S.
Code §§ 1801 nt., 1826d et seq.

High Seas Fishing Compliance Act of 1995
Nov. 3, 1995, P.L. 104-43, Title I, 16 U.S.
Code § 5501 et seq.

High-Speed Ground Transportation Act
Sept. 30, 1965, P.L. 89-220, 79 Stat. 893, 49 U.S. Code Appx. §§ 1631 to 1642
July 24, 1968, P.L. 90-423, 82 Stat. 424, 49 U.S. Code Appx. §§ 1631, 1635, 1637, 1639, 1641, 1642

High Speed Intercity Rail Passenger Commission Act
Pa. Purdon's Stat., Title 55, § 681 et seq.

High Speed Rail Act
Tex. Rev. Civ. Stat., Art. 6674v-2

High Speed Rail Compact
Ind. Code Ann., 8-3-19-2

High Speed Rail Line Compact Act
Ill. Rev. Stat. 1991, Ch. 114, §§ 650, 651

High-Speed Rail Transportation Act
Fla. Stat. Ann., 341.3201 et seq.

High Tech Zone Act
Miss. Code Ann. 1972, § 57-53-1 et seq.

High Technology and Biotechnology Industry Promotion Act
N.J. Stat. Ann., 52:9X-9.1 et seq.

High-Technology Education and Training Act
Wash. Rev. Code Ann., 28B.65.010 et seq.

High Technology Theft Apprehension and Prosecution Program
Cal. Penal Code § 13848 et seq.

High-Voltage Line Safety Act (Overhead)
Me. Rev. Stat. Ann. 1964, Title 35-A, § 751 et seq.

High Voltage Lines Act
N.J. Stat. Ann., 34:6-47.1 et seq.

High Voltage Power Lines and Safety Restrictions Act
Wyo. Stat. Ann., § 37-3-301 et seq.

High-Voltage Proximity Act
N.Y. Labor Law (Consol. Laws Ch. 31) § 202h

High-Voltage Safety Act
Ga. Code Ann., 46-3-30 et seq.

Higher and Vocational Education Loan Guarantee Act
Colo. Rev. Stat., 23-3-101 et seq.

Higher Education Access 2000 Act
Fla. Laws 1995, Ch. 243, §§ 10 to 20

Higher Education Act
July 2, 1986, P.L. 99-349, 100 Stat. 740
Oct. 21, 1986, P.L. 99-509, 20 U.S. Code § 1063
N.J. Stat. Ann., 18A:3-1 et seq.
N.J. Stat. Ann., 18A:62-1 et seq.
Okla. Stat. Ann., Title 70, § 3101 et seq.
Tex. Education Code, § 62.001 et seq.
Utah Code Ann. 1953, Miscellaneous Superseded Code Provisions, 53-48-1 et seq.

Higher Education Act (Access to)
Mo. Rev. Stat 1986, 166.200 et seq., 173.053, 173.262

Higher Education Act (Board of)
Ill. Comp. Stat. 1992, Ch. 110, § 205/0.01 et seq.

Higher Education Act (Donahoe)
Cal. Education Code 1976, § 66000 et seq.

Higher Education Act (Endowment Trust Fund for)
Fla. Stat. Ann., 240.498

Higher Education Act (Senior Citizens)
Va. Code 1950, § 23-38.54 et seq.

Higher Education Act of 1965
Nov. 8, 1965, P.L. 89-329, 79 Stat. 1219, 20 U.S. Code §§ 403, 424, 425, 441, 443, 591, 711, 713 to 717, 731, 743, 751, 1001 to 1011, 1021 to 1028, 1031 to 1034 and others; 42 U.S. Code §§ 2751 to 2756, 2761
Oct. 29, 1966, P.L. 89-698, 80 Stat. 1072, 20 U.S. Code § 1085

Nov. 8, 1966, P.L. 89-794, 80 Stat. 1476, 20 U.S. Code § 1077

June 29, 1967, P.L. 90-35, 81 Stat. 82, 20 U.S. Code §§ 1091, 1091a to 1091f, 1092, 1101 to 1105, 1107, 1107a, 1108 to 1115, and others

Sept. 11, 1967, P.L. 90-83, 81 Stat. 223, 20 U.S. Code § 1105

Jan. 2, 1968, P.L. 90-247, 81 Stat. 820, 20 U.S. Code §§ 1111, 1112, 1118, 1119

Aug. 3, 1968, P.L. 90-460, 82 Stat. 634, 20 U.S. Code §§ 1071, 1074, 1077, 1078, 1081, 1082

Oct. 16, 1968, P.L. 90-575, 82 Stat. 1017, 20 U.S. Code §§ 403 424, 425, 441, 443, 591, 1001, 1005, 1006, 1021 to 1024 and others; 42 U.S. Code §§ 2741, 2751 to 2756

Oct. 16, 1968, P.L. 90-576, 82 Stat. 1091, 20 U.S. Code §§ 1119c to 1119c-4

Oct. 22, 1969, P.L. 91-95, 83 Stat. 143, 20 U.S. Code § 1061; 42 U.S. Code § 2751

April 13, 1970, P.L. 91-230, 84 Stat. 190, 20 U.S. Code §§ 1068, 1091a, 1101, 1103, 1104, 1119c-4, 1141

June 23, 1972, P.L. 92-318, 86 Stat. 236, 20 U.S. Code §§ 1001, 1003, 1005a, 1006 to 1011, 1021 to 1024, 1027, 1031, 1033, 1034, 1041, 1042, 1051 to 1056, 1061 and others

May 3, 1973, P.L. 93-29, 87 Stat. 59, 20 U.S. Code §§ 1008a, 1009 to 1011

April 18, 1974, P.L. 93-269, 88 Stat. 87, 20 U.S. Code § 1078

June 28, 1975, P.L. 94-43, 89 Stat. 233, 42 U.S. Code § 2756

June 15, 1977, P.L. 95-43, 20 U.S. Code § 1003 et seq.

Nov. 15, 1977, P.L. 95-180, 20 U.S. Code § 1088 et seq.

Aug. 4, 1978, P.L. 95-336, 20 U.S. Code §§ 1070e-1, 1070e-1 nt.

Nov. 1, 1978, P.L. 95-561, 20 U.S. Code §§ 1072, 1072 nt., 1087, 1088f-1, 1119, 1119a

Nov. 1, 1978, P.L. 95-566, 20 U.S. Code §§ 1070a, 1070a nt., 1070c-2, 1070d-1, 1075, 1077, 1078, 1087-ea, 1088, 1088f

Aug. 13, 1979, P.L. 96-49, 20 U.S. Code §§ 1001, 1001 nt., 1021, 1042, 1051, 1070a, 1070a nt., 1070b to 1070e-1, 1078, 1087-1, 1087-1 nt., 1087aa, 1087gg, 1087gg nt., 1088, 1101, 1119, 1121, 1132a to 1132c, 1132c-4, 1134, 1134e, 1134i, 1134n, 1134r-1, 1135a, 1136b, 1142b

Oct. 17, 1979, P.L. 96-88, 20 U.S. Code § 1102

Oct. 31, 1979, P.L. 96-96, 20 U.S. Code § 1003

Dec. 21, 1982, P.L. 97-375, 20 U.S. Code § 1125

Dec. 21, 1982, P.L. 97-377, 20 U.S. Code § 1070a nt.

June 12, 1984, P.L. 98-312, 20 U.S. Code § 1069c

Oct. 19, 1984, P.L. 98-524, 20 U.S. Code §§ 1013, 1014, 1205, 1135c-1

Oct. 30, 1984, P.L. 98-558, 20 U.S. Code §§ 1119d, 1119d-1 to 1119d-8, 1119e, 1119e-1 to 1119e-5

Nov. 8, 1985, P.L. 99-145, 10 U.S. Code § 2171; 20 U.S. Code §§ 1070d-31, 1070d-33, 1070d-35

Nov. 22, 1985, P.L. 99-159, 20 U.S. Code § 1134h

Aug. 22, 1986, P.L. 99-386, 20 U.S. Code §§ 1017, 1119, 1125

Oct. 17, 1986, P.L. 99-498, 100 Stat. 1268, 20 U.S. Code §§ 1001 et seq.; 42 U.S. Code §§ 2751 et seq., 2752 nt.

Nov. 6, 1986, P.L. 99-603, 20 U.S. Code §§ 1091, 1096

Dec. 22, 1987, P.L. 100-203, 20 U.S. Code §§ 1072, and nt., 1078, 1132i-2

April 28, 1988, P.L. 100-297, 102 Stat. 330, 20 U.S. Code §§ 1071, 1234

July 18, 1988, P.L. 100-369, 102 Stat. 835, 20 U.S. Code §§ 1058, 1062, 1070a-1 et seq., 1077, 1078, 1078-1, 1987-1, 1087dd, 1087ee, 1087nn, 1134m, 1091

Aug. 23, 1988, P.L. 100-418, 102 Stat. 1514, 20 U.S. Code §§ 1021, 1070d-1b, 1130a, 1130b, prec. 1132j, 1135d-6, 1145f

Oct. 24, 1988, P.L. 100-525, 20 U.S. Code § 1091

Dec. 12, 1989, P.L. 101-226, 20 U.S. Code §§ 1109, 1145g

Dec. 19, 1989, P.L. 101-239, 20 U.S. Code §§ 1077, 1078, 1078-1, 1078-6, 1078-7, 1082, 1085, 1087dd, 1087tt, 1088, 1092b, 1094

May 30, 1990, P.L. 101-305, 20 U.S. Code § 1018e

Oct. 30, 1990, P.L. 101-476, 20 U.S. Code § 1087ee

Nov. 5, 1990, P.L. 101-508, 20 U.S. Code §§ 1078, 1078-1, 1078-7, 1085, 1088, 1091

Continued

Nov. 8, 1990, P.L. 101-542, 20 U.S. Code §§ 1085, 1092, 1094

Nov. 16, 1990, P.L. 101-600, 20 U.S. Code § 1130b

Nov. 16, 1990, P.L. 101-610, 20 U.S. Code §§ 1018c, 1018e, 1070a- 6, 1087vv, 1092, 1092b

Nov. 29, 1990, P.L. 101-647, 20 U.S. Code §§ 1087ee, 1087ee nt.

April 9, 1991, P.L. 102-26, 20 U.S. Code §§ 1078-1, 1085, 1087ss, 1088, 1091, 1091a, 1094, 1141

June 13, 1991, P.L. 102-54, 20 U.S. Code §§ 1017, 1070a-2 to 1070a-4, 1070e-1

Oct. 7, 1991, P.L. 102-119, 20 U.S. Code § 1087ee

Nov. 15, 1991, P.L. 102-164, 20 U.S. Code §§ 1077, 1078, 1078-5, 1092, 1095a, 1096a

July 23, 1992, P.L. 102-325, 20 U.S. Code §§ 1001 nt., 1001 et seq., 1011 et seq., 1021 et seq., 1031 et seq., 1041 et seq., 1051 et seq., 1062 et seq., 1070 et seq., 1080 et seq., 1090 et seq., 1101 et seq., 1110 et seq., 1121 et seq., 1130 et seq., 1141, 1142, 1145, 1145d; 42 U.S. Code §§ prec. 2751, 2751 to 2753, 2755, 2756, 2756a, 2756b

Oct. 6, 1992, P.L. 102-394, 20 U.S. Code § 1141

Oct. 13, 1992, P.L. 102-408, 20 U.S. Code §§ 1078-3, 1078-3 nt.

Aug. 10, 1993, P.L. 103-66, 20 U.S. Code §§ 1072, 1077a, 1078, 1078-1, 1078-2, 1078-3, 1078-8, 1085, 1087-1, 1087-2, prec. 1087a, 1087a to 1087h

Sept. 21, 1993, P.L. 103-82, 20 U.S. Code §§ 1078, 1078-10, 1087ee, 1087vv, 1137a, 1141; 42 U.S. Code § 2751

Dec. 20, 1993, P.L. 103-208, 20 U.S. Code §§ 1003 et seq., 1047, 1051 et seq., 1062 et seq., 1070a et seq., 1087c et seq., 1091 et seq., 1102 et seq.; 42 U.S. Code 2752, 2753,

March 31, 1994, P.L. 103-227, 20 U.S. Code § 1107

Sept. 13, 1994, P.L. 103-322, 20 U.S. Code § 1070a

Oct. 20, 1994, P.L. 103-382, 20 U.S. Code §§ 1058, 1070a-27, 1078-3, 1085, 1087-2, 1087a, 1087e, 1087ee, 1087ii, 1088a, 1091, 1092, 1108d, 1111a, 1113, 1114, 1132c-2, 1135g, 1138c

July 27, 1995, P.L. 104-19, 20 U.S. Code § 1087h

Dec. 21, 1995, P.L. 104-66, 20 U.S. Code §§ 1082, 1089

Feb. 10, 1996, P.L. 104-106, 20 U.S. Code § 1087cc-1

April 26, 1996, P.L. 104-134, 20 U.S. Code §§ 1070a-23, 1078-8, 1087vv

May 6, 1996, P.L. 104-141, 20 U.S. Code § 1063b

Sept. 30, 1996, P.L. 104-208, 20 U.S. Code §§ 1069b, 1087-2, 1078-3, 1085, 1087-3, 1087-4, 1091, 1092, 1132f to 1132f-9

June 12, 1997, P.L. 105-18, 20 U.S. Code § 1092

Aug. 5, 1997, P.L. 105-33, 20 U.S. Code §§ 1072, 1074, 1078, 1078-3, 1087b, 1087h

Nov. 13, 1997, P.L. 105-78, 20 U.S. Code §§ 1078-3, 1087h, 1087oo, 1087pp, 1087qq, 1087vv

June 9, 1998, P.L. 105-178, 20 U.S. Code §§ 1077a, 1078-2, 1087-1

July 29, 1998, P.L. 105-216, 20 U.S. Code § 1088

Oct. 7, 1998, P.L. 105-244, 20 U.S. Code §§ 1001 to 1006, 1011, 1011a to 1011k, 1015, 1015a to 1015d, 1018, 1018a, 1018b, 1021 to 1030, 1051, 1057 to 1059, 1059a, 1059c, 1059d, 1062, 1063b, 1065, 1066, 1066a to 1066g, 1067, 1067a to 1067d, 1067g to 1067l, 1068, 1068a to 1068h, 1069, 1069b to 1069f, 1070a, 1070a-11 to 1070a-15, 1070a-17, 1070a-18, 1070a-21 to 1070a-28, 1070a-31 to 1070a-35, 1070a-41 to 1070a-43, 1070a-51 to 1070a-53, 1070a-61, 1070a-71, 1070a-81, 1070b, 1070b-2 to 1070b-4, 1070c, 1070c-1, 1070c-2, 1070c- 3a, 1070c-4, 1070d-2, 1070d-34, 1070d-41, 1070e, 1070f, 1070f-1 to 1070f-6, 1071, 1072, 1072a, 1072b, 1074, 1075, 1077a, 1078, 1078-1 to 1078-3, 1078-6 to 1078-8, 1078-10, 1078-11, 1080, 1082, 1083, 1085, 1087-0, 1087-1, 1087b, 1087c, 1087e, 1087f, 1087h, 1087i, 1087j, 1087aa to 1087gg, 1087ll to 1087tt, 1087vv, 1088 to 1091, 1091a, 1091b, 1092, 1092b, 1093, 1094, 1094a, 1095a, 1097a, 1098, 1098a, 1098c, 1098d, 1099a to 1099c, 1099c-1, 1099c-2, 1101, 1101a to 1101d, 1102, 1102a to 1102j, 1103, 1103a to 1103g, 1104, 1104a to 1104k, 1105, 1105a to 1105i, 1106, 1106a to 1106g, 1107, 1109, 1109a to 1109e, 1110, 1110a to 1110e, 1111, 1111a to 1111h, 1112, 1112a to 1112e, 1113, 1114, 1114a, 1115 to 1117, 1117a to 1117c, 1121 to 1124, 1124a, 1125, 1125a, 1125b, 1126 to 1128, 1128a, 1128b, 1130, 1130-1, 1130b, 1131, 1131-1, 1131a to 1131f, 1132, 1132-1, 1132a, 1132a-1, 1132b, 1132b-1 to 1132b-5, 1132c, 1132c-1 to 1132c-7, 1132d, 1132d-1 to 1132d-4, 1132f-10, 1132i, 1132i-1, 1132i-2, 1133 et seq., 1134 et seq., 1135 et seq., 1136 et seq., 1137 et seq., 1138 et seq., 1139, 1139a to 1139h, 1140, 1140a to 1140d, 1141 to 1144, 1144a, 1145, 1145a to 1145g, 1146a, 1152a, 1154, 1155; 42 U.S. Code §§ 2751 to 2753, 2755, 2756b

Oct. 21, 1998, P.L. 105-277, 20 U.S. Code §§ 1070d-2, 1087vv

Higher Education Administrative Procedure Act (State)
Wash. Rev. Code Ann., 28B.19.010 et seq.

Higher Education Affordability Act
Cal. Education Code 1976, §§ 17072, 17140, 17204

Higher Education Amendments
Nov. 3, 1966, P.L. 89-752, 80 Stat. 1240, 20 U.S. Code §§ 403, 421, 425, 441, 443, 711 to 715, 731, 743, 744, 751, 1022, 1051, 1071 nt., 1072, 1086, 1124
Oct. 16, 1968, P.L. 90-575, 82 Stat. 1014, 12 U.S. Code § 1464; 20 U.S. Code §§ 403, 421 to 426, 441 to 455, 462 to 464, 481, 483, 484, 511, 513, 562, 581, 582 and others 42 U.S. Code §§ 2741, 2751 to 2756, 2809

Higher Education Amendments of 1986
Oct. 17, 1986, P.L. 99-498, 20 U.S. Code § 1001 nt.
June 3, 1987, P.L. 100-50, 20 U.S. Code §§ 1011 nt., 1070b-3 nt., 1070d-1b nt., 1071 nt., 1087kk nt., 1087vv nt., 1091 nt., 1121 nt., 1221-1 nt., 1221e-1 nt., 42 U.S. Code §§ 2752 nt., 2753 nt.
Nov. 5, 1987, P.L. 100-153, 20 U.S. Code § 4421
April 28, 1988, P.L. 100-297, 102 Stat. 417, 20 U.S. Code §§ 4416, 4422, 4425, 4451
Sept. 27, 1988, P.L. 100-446, 20 U.S. Code § 4420
July 6, 1990, P.L. 101-324, 20 U.S. Code § 1221-1 nt.
Nov. 26, 1991, P.L. 102-170, 20 U.S. Code § 1221-1 nt.
Dec. 20, 1993, P.L. 103-208, 20 U.S. Code § 4414
May 4, 1994, P.L. 103-239, 20 U.S. Code § 4441
Oct. 20, 1994, P.L. 103-382, 20 U.S. Code §§ 4416, 4425
Sept. 30, 1996, P.L. 104-208, 20 U.S. Code § 1029 nt.
Oct. 31, 1998, P.L. 105-332, 20 U.S. Code §§ 1011 nt., 1029 nt., 1070a nt., 1071 nt., 1091 nt., 1121 nt., 1221-1 nt., 9003 nt.

Higher Education Amendments of 1988
April 28, 1988, P.L. 100-297, 102 Stat. 330, 20 U.S. Code §§ 4416 et seq.

Higher Education Amendments of 1992
July 23, 1992, P.L. 102-325, 20 U.S. Code § 1001 nt.
Oct. 6, 1992, P.L. 102-394, 20 U.S. Code § 1087dd nt.
Oct. 20, 1994, P.L. 103-382, 20 U.S. Code § 1088 nt.
Oct. 7, 1998, P.L. 105-244, 20 U.S. Code §§ 1001 nt., 1070 nt.; 25 U.S. Code § 3371
Oct. 31, 1998, P.L. 105-332, 20 U.S. Code §§ 1070 nt., 1070a-21 nt., 1071 nt., 1080 nt., 1101 nt., 1132a nt., 1134 nt., 1145h, 1221-1 nt., 1221e nt., 1452 nt., 9003 nt.; 25 U.S. Code §§ 3331 to 3338, 3351 to 3355, 3371; 29 U.S. Code §§ 2401 to 2405
Nov. 10, 1998, P.L. 105-362, 112 Stat. 3282

Higher Education Amendments of 1998
Oct. 7, 1998, P.L. 105-244, 112 Stat. 1581, 20 U.S. Code § 1001 nt.

Higher Education and Urban School Construction Program Bond Act
Cal. Education Code 1959, § 19250 et seq., § 17300

Higher Education Assistance Act for Senior Citizens
Ga. Code 1933, 32-175 et seq.

Higher Education Assistance Authority Act
N.J. Stat. Ann., 18A:72-1 et seq.
R.I. Gen. Laws 1956, 16-57-1 et seq.

Higher Education Assistance Corporation Act
Ga. Code Ann., 20-3-260 et seq.
Ill. Rev. Stat. 1965, Ch. 144, § 201 et seq.

Higher Education Authority Act
Ga. Laws 1979, p. 3288
Tex. Education Code, § 53.01 et seq.

Higher Education Award Act
Ind. Code Ann., 20-12-21-1 et seq.

Higher Education Buildings Construction Bond Act
N.J. Laws 1971, Ch. 164

Higher Education Children's Crusade Act
R.I. Gen. Laws 1956, 16-70-1 et seq.

Higher Education Commission Act
S.C. Code Ann. 1976, § 59-103-10 et seq.

Higher Education Compact (Midwestern)
Minn. Stat. Ann., 135A.20 et seq.
Neb. Rev. Stat. 1943, 85-1301, 85-1302

Higher Education Compact Act (New England)
Conn. Gen. Stat. Ann., § 10a-61 et seq.
Me. Rev. Stat. Ann. 1964, Title 20-A, § 11001 et seq.
N.H. Rev. Stat. 1955, 200-A:1 et seq.

Higher Education Construction Bond Act
N.J. Laws 1964, Ch. 142

Higher Education Construction Program Bond Act
Cal. Statutes 1966, 1st Ex. Sess., Ch. 156

Higher Education Cooperation Act
Ill. Rev. Stat. 1991, Ch. 144, § 281 et seq.

Higher Education Coordinating Act
Tex. Education Code, § 61.001 et seq.

Higher Education Council Act
Wyo. Stat. Ann., § 21-16-401 et seq.

Higher Education Employee Classification and Compensation Act
Ark. Code Ann. 1987, 6-63-201 et seq.

Higher Education Employer - Employee Relations Act
Cal. Government Code § 3560 et seq.

Higher Education Equal Opportunity Act
Pa. Purdon's Stat., Title 24, § 2510-301 et seq.

Higher Education Equipment Leasing Fund Act
N.J. Stat. Ann., 18A:72A-40 et seq.

Higher Education Equipment Loan Authority Act
Ala. Code 1975, § 16-18B-1 et seq.

Higher Education Excellence Act
R.I. Public Laws 1991, Ch. 596

Higher Education Expenditure Restriction Act
Ark. Code Ann. 1987, 6-63-301 et seq.

Higher Education Facilities Act
Me. Rev. Stat. Ann. 1964, Title 20A, §§ 10501, 10502

Higher Education Facilities Act (State Commission for)
Me. Rev. Stat. Ann. 1964, Title 20-A, § 10501 et seq.

Higher Education Facilities Act of 1963
Dec. 16, 1963, P.L. 88-204, 77 Stat. 363, 20 U.S. Code §§ 701, 711 to 721, 731 to 733, 741 to 744, 751 to 757
Nov. 8, 1965, P.L. 89-329, 79 Stat. 1266, 20 U.S. Code §§ 711, 713 to 717, 731, 743, 751
May 24, 1966, P.L. 89-429, 80 Stat. 166, 20 U.S. Code §§ 743, 745
Nov. 6, 1966, P.L. 89-769, 80 Stat. 1318, 20 U.S. Code § 758
May 29, 1967, P.L. 90-21, 81 Stat. 36, 20 U.S. Code § 758
Oct. 16, 1968, P.L. 90-575, 82 Stat. 1050, 20 U.S. Code §§ 711, 713 to 718, 731, 732, 746, 751, 758
Dec. 31, 1970, P.L. 91-606, 84 Stat. 1759, 20 U.S. Code § 758
May 22, 1974, P.L.93-288, 88 Stat. 164, 20 U.S. Code § 758

Higher Education Facilities Act of 1992
July 23, 1992, P.L. 102-325, 20 U.S. Code §§ 1132b to 1132b-5

Higher Education Facilities Authority Act
Fla. Stat. 1983, 243.18 et seq.
Md. Ann. Code 1957, Art. 43C, § 1 et seq.

Mich. Comp. Laws Ann., 390.921 et seq.

Pa. Purdon's Stat., Title 24, § 5501 et seq.

Higher Education Facilities Bond Act of 1986 to 1992

Cal. Education Code 1976, § 67330 et seq;n 67345 et seq.; 67350 et seq; 67358 et seq.

Higher Education Facilities Bond Act of 1994

Cal. Education Code 1976, § 67010

Higher Education Facilities Commission Act

Iowa Code Ann.,261.1 et seq.

Higher Education Facilities Construction Bond Act

N.J. Laws 1979, Ch. 206

Higher Education Facilities Revenue Bond Act

Cal. Education Code 1976, § 67359.6 et seq.

Higher Education Facilities Trust Fund Act

N.J. Stat. Ann., 18A:72A-49 et seq.

Higher Education Financial Control Act

Okla. Stat. Ann., Title 70, § 3906 et seq.

Higher Education Institutions Bond Act

Va. Acts 1991, Ch. 677

Higher Education Institutions Capital Improvement Voted Bond Act

N.C. Laws 1975, Ch. 854

Higher Education Loan Act

Ill. Rev. Stat. 1991, Ch. 144, § 1600 et seq.

Utah Code Ann. 1953, 53B-13-101 et seq.

Higher Education Loan Authority Act

Fla. Stat. Ann., 240.47 et seq.

Ill. Rev. Stat. 1985, Ch. 144, § 1600 et seq., 390.1151 et seq.

Iowa Code Ann., 261A.1 et seq.

Mich. Comp. Laws Ann., 390.1151 et seq.

Mo. Rev. Stat., 173.350 et seq.

Higher Education Loan Bond Program (Independent)

W. Va. Code 1966, § 18-27-1 et seq.

Higher Education Loan Program Guarantee Act

S.D. Codified Laws 1967, 13-56-1 et seq.

Higher Education Personnel Law

Wash. Rev. Code Ann., 28B.16.010 et seq.

Higher Education Restructuring Act

N.J. Stat. Ann., 18A:3B-1 et seq.

Higher Education Retirement Act

Wyo. Stat. Ann., § 21-19-101 et seq.

Higher Education Revenue Bond Act

S.C. Code Ann. 1976, § 59-147-10 et seq.

Higher Education Savings Program

Mo. Rev. Stat., 166.400 to 166.455

Higher Education Services for Visually Impaired, Auditorily Impaired and Hearing Disabled Students Act

N.J. Stat. Ann., 18A:72H-1 et seq.

Higher Education Student Assistance Act

Ill. Rev. Stat. 1991, Ch. 122, § 30-15 et seq.

Higher Education Student Loan Guarantee Act

Kan. Stat. Ann., 72-7401 et seq.

Higher Education Supplemental Loan Authority Act

Conn. Gen. Stat. Ann., § 10a-221 et seq.

Higher Education Talent Development Act

Cal. Education Code 1976, § 66910 et seq.

Higher Education Technical Amendments Act of 1987

June 3, 1987, P.L. 100-50, 20 U.S. Code §§ 1001 nt., 1057, 1058, 1059a, 1062, 1063a to 1063c, 1065 to 1067, 1069a, 1070a et seq., 1075, 1077, 1078 et seq., 1082, 1083, 1085, 1087 et seq., 1109 et seq.; 42 U.S. Code §§ 2752 nt., 2753 nt.

Aug. 23, 1988, P.L. 100-418, 102 Stat. 1523, 22 U.S. Code § 4604

Higher Education Technical Amendments of 1991

April 9, 1991, P.L. 102-26, 20 U.S. Code § 1001 nt.

July 23, 1992, P.L. 102-325, 20 U.S. Code § 1091a nt.

Higher Education Technical Amendments of 1993

Dec. 20, 1993, P.L. 103-208, 20 U.S. Code § 1001 nt.

Higher Education Technology Infrastructure Fund Act

N.J. Stat. Ann., 18A:72A-59 et seq.

Higher Education Tribal Grant Authorization Act

July 23, 1992, P.L. 102-325, 25 U.S. Code §§ 3301 to 3307

Higher Education Tuition Aid Act

N.J. Stat. Ann., 18A:71-41 et seq.

Okla. Stat. Ann., Title 70, § 626.1 et seq.

Higher Education Tuition Trust Act

W. Va. Code 1966 § 18-30-1 et seq.

Higher Educational and Health Facilities Authority Act

Me. Rev. Stat. Ann. 1964, Title 22, § 2051 et seq.

N.H. Rev. Stat. 1955, 195-D-1 et seq.

Higher Educational and Medical Facilities Bond Act

Va. Acts 1973, Ch. 206

Higher Educational Council Act

Wyo. Stat. Ann., § 21-16-401 et seq.

Higher Educational Facilities Authorities Act

Fla. Stat. Ann., 243.18 et seq.

Pa. Purdon's Stat., Title 24, § 5501 et seq.

Higher Educational Facilities Finance Act

N.C. Gen. Stat. 1943, § 115E-1 et seq.

N.C. Laws 1985, Ch. 794

Higher Educational Institutions Bond Act

Va. Acts 1968, Ch. 17

Va. Acts 1971, Ch. 147

Va. Acts 1973, Ch. 422

Va. Acts 1974, Ch. 307

Va. Acts 1975, Ch. 219

Va. Acts 1978, Ch. 809

Va. Acts 1981, Ch. 481

Va. Acts 1983, Ch. 81

Va. Acts 1983, Ch. 82

Va. Acts 1984, Ch. 250

Va. Acts 1986, Chs. 261, 262

Va. Acts 1988, Chs. 423, 617

Va. Acts 1991, Ch. 716

Va. Acts 1991, Chs. 32, 737

Va. Acts 1992, Ch. 616

Higher Educational Institutions Refunding Act

Va. Acts 1986, Ch. 262

Higher Educational Technical Amendments of 1979

Aug. 13, 1979, P.L. 96-49, 20 U.S. Code §§ 513, 1001, 1001 nt., 1021, 1042, 1051, 1070a, 1070a nt., 1070b to 1070d, 1070d-2, 1070e-1, 1078, 1087-1, 1087-1 nt., 1087aa, 1087gg, 1087gg nt., 1088, 1088 nt., 1101, 1119, 1121, 1132a to 1132c, 1132c-4, 1134, 1134e, 1134i, 1134n, 1134r-1, 1135, 1136, 1142b, 1221d, 1221e

Higher Learning Access Act

Okla. Stat. Ann., Title 70, § 2601 et seq.

Higher Learning English Fluency Act

S.C. Code Ann. 1976, § 59-103-160

Highland Park Municipal Court Act

Mich. Comp. Laws Ann., 730.101 et seq.

Highway Access Management Act (State)

N.J. Stat. Ann., 27:7-89 et seq.

Highway Accident Report Act

Iowa Code Ann., 321.266

Highway Act

Ala. Code 1975, § 23-1-1 et seq.

Alaska Stat. 1962, § 19.05.010 et seq.

Ariz. Rev. Stat. Ann., § 28-1801 et seq.

Colo. Rev. Stat., 43-1-201 et seq.
Fla. Stat. Ann., 334.01 et seq.
Fla. Stat. 334.01 et seq.
Ill. Rev. Stat. 1991, Ch. 121, § 1-101 et seq.
Ind. Code Ann., 8-11-1-1 et seq.
Kan. Stat. Ann., 68-401 et seq.
Ky. Rev. Stat. 1971, 176.010 et seq.
La. Rev. Stat. Ann., 48.1 et seq.
Mass. Gen. Laws Ann., 81:1 et seq.
Mich. Comp. Laws Ann., 220.1 et seq.
Minn. Stat. Ann., 160.01 et seq.
Miss. Code Ann. 1972, § 65-1-1 et seq.
Mo. Rev. Stat., 226-010 et seq.
Mont. Code Ann., 60-1-101 et seq.
Mont. Code Ann. 1947, 32-101 to 32-527
N.D. Cent. Code, 24-01-01 et seq.
N.H. Rev. Stat. 1955, 228:1 et seq.
N.J. Stat. Ann., 27:61-1 to 27:12-6
N.Y. Consol. Laws Ch. 25
Okla. Stat. Ann., Title 69, § 501 et seq.
Ore. Rev. Stat., 366.005 et seq.
Pa. Purdon's Stat., Title 36, § 670-101 et seq.
S.C. Code Ann. 1976, § 57-1-10 et seq.
Tenn. Code Ann., 54-1-101 et seq.
Vt. Stat. Ann., Title 19, § 1 et seq.
Wash. Rev. Code Ann., 47.01.011 et seq.
Wyo. Stat. Ann., § 24-2-101 et seq.

Highway Act (Burns-Collier)
Cal. Streets and Highways Code § 2000 et
   seq.

Highway Act (Capitol)
S.C. Acts 1927, p. 1023, No. 521

Highway Act (Coastal)
S.C. Acts 1926, p. 1492, No. 756

Highway Act (Condemnation)
Mich. Comp. Laws Ann., 23.171 et seq.

Highway Act (Controlled Access)
Miss. Code Ann. 1972, § 65-5-1 et seq.
Vt. Stat. Ann., Title 19, § 1701 et seq.

Highway Act (Covert)
Mich. Comp. Laws 1948, 247.415 et seq.

Highway Act (Dickson County)
Tenn. Private Acts 1919, Ch. 161

Highway Act (Dirksen Memorial)
Ill. Rev. Stat. 1991, Ch. 121, §§ 388, 389

Highway Act (Economic Development)
Miss. Code Ann. 1972, § 65-4-1 et seq.

Highway Act (Elwell)
Minn. Laws, 1911, Ch. 254

Highway Act (Industrial)
Tenn. Code Ann., 54-5-401 et seq.

Highway Act (Peerson Memorial)
Ill. Rev. Stat. 1989, Ch. 121, §§ 389.9, 390

Highway Act (Scenic and Recreational)
Wash. Rev. Code Ann., 47.39.010 et seq.

Highway Act (Scenic)
Pa. Cons. Stat., Title 74, § 8301

Highway Act (Stansel)
Miss. Code Ann. 1972, § 65-1-1 et seq.

Highway Act (State)
Del. Code of 1974, Title 17, § 101 et seq.
Kan. Stat. Ann., 68-401 et seq.
R.I. Gen. Laws 1956, 24-8-1 et seq.
Wash. Rev. Code Ann., 36.75.010 et seq.,
   47.08.080 et seq., 47.24.010 et seq.,
   36.77.010 et seq., 36.87.900 et seq.

Highway Act (Super)
Mich. Comp. Laws Ann., 252.1 et seq.

Highway Act (Towns)
R.I. Gen. Laws 1956, 24-1-1 et seq.

Highway Act (Township)
Mich. Comp. Laws 1948, 247.1 et seq.

Highway Act (Trunk Line)
Mich. Comp. Laws 1948, 250.31 et seq.

Highway Administration Act
Ida. Code 1947, 40-106 et seq.

Highway Advertising Control Act
Ill. Rev. Stat. 1991, Ch. 121, § 501 et seq.
Ind. Code Ann., 8-12-2-1 et seq.
Kan. Stat. Ann., 68-2231 et seq.
Mich. Comp. Laws Ann., 252.301 et seq.
N.D. Cent. Code, 24-17-01 et seq.
Okla. Stat. Ann., Title 69, § 1271 et seq.
R.I. Gen. Laws 1956, 24-10.1-1 et seq.
S.C. Code Ann. 1976, § 57-25-110 et seq.
Wash. Rev. Code Ann., 47.42.010 et seq.

Highway Aid Act
N.Y. Laws 1950, Ch. 824

Highway Aid Act (County)
Miss. Code Ann. 1972, § 65-11-1 et seq.

Highway and Bridge Authority Act
Pa. Purdon's Stat., Title 36, § 3601 et seq.

Highway and Bridge District Law
Cal. Streets and Highways Code § 27000 et seq.

Highway and Public Works Act
Alaska Stat. 1962, § 19.05.010 et seq.

Highway and Public Works Act of 1957
Alaska Laws 1957, Ch. 152

Highway and Street Revenue Bond Authority Act
Miss. Code Ann. 1972, § 65-13-1 et seq.

Highway and Traffic Safety Co-ordination Act
Ala. Code 1975, § 32-4-1 et seq.

Highway and Transportation Act
Ark. Code Ann. 1987, 27-1-101 et seq.

Highway Assessment Act (County)
Fla. Laws 1925, Ch. 10140

Highway Authority Act
Ala. Code 1975, § 23-1-150 et seq.
Colo. Rev. Stat., 43-4-501 et seq.
Fla. Special Laws 1963, Ch. 63-1643
Ga. Code Ann., 32-10-1 et seq.
Ill. Rev. Stat. 1957, Ch. 121, § 317 et seq.
Ky. Acts 1954, Ch. 39

Mont. Rev. Code 1947, 32-2201 et seq.
N.J. Stat. Ann., 27:12B-1 et seq.
P.R. Laws Ann. 1954, Title 9, § 2001 et seq.

Highway Beautification Act
Ark. Code Ann. 1987, 27-74-101 et seq.
Cal. Business and Professions Code § 5214 et seq., § 5208
Kan. Stat. Ann., 68-2201 et seq.
N.M. Stat. Ann., 67-12-1 et seq.
Tex. Rev. Civ. Stat., Art. 4477-9a, § 4.01 et seq.

Highway Beautification Act (Junkyard Control)
Ala. Code 1975, § 23-1-240 et seq.

Highway Beautification Act (Outdoor Advertising)
Ala. Code 1975, § 23-1-270 et seq.
Utah Code Ann. 1953, 27-12-136.1 et seq.

Highway Beautification Act (Scenic Enchancement)
Ala. Code 1975, § 23-1-220 et seq.

Highway Beautification Act of 1965
Oct. 22, 1965, P.L. 89-285, 79 Stat. 1028, 23 U.S. Code §§ 131, 135 nt., 136, 319

Highway Board Act
Ga. Code 1933, 95-1601 et seq.

Highway Bond Act
Colo. Rev. Stat., 43-4-101 et seq.
N.C. Laws 1943, Ch. 322
N.C. Laws 1965, Ch. 46
N.C. Laws 1977, Ch. 643
N.C. Public Laws 1927, Ch. 95
Neb. Rev. Stat. 1943, 39-2201 et seq.
Ore. Rev. Stat. 1953, 367.105 et seq.
S.C. Code Ann. 1962, § 33-251 et seq.

Highway Bond Assumption Act
Tex. Rev. Civ. Stat., Art. 6674q-1 et seq.

Highway Bond Guaranty Act
N.J. Stat. Ann., 27:12B-20 et seq.

Highway Bond Refunding Act
Ohio Laws Vol. 116, p. 561, §§ 1 to 12

Highway Bonding Authorization Act
Ariz. Rev. Stat. Ann., § 28-2001 et seq.

Highway Capital Budget Act
Pa. 1981 Pamph. Laws 352, No. 128
Pa. 1988 Pamph. Laws No. 114

Highway Capital Budget Project Itemization Act for 1996-1997
Pa. 1998 Pamph. Laws, No. 78

Highway Carriers Act
Cal. Public Utilities Code § 3501 et seq.

Highway Carriers' Licensing Tax Law
Cal. Revenue and Taxation Code § 9601 et seq.

Highway Carriers' Uniform Business License Tax Act
Cal. Public Utilities Code § 4301 et seq.

Highway Classification Act (State)
Cal. Streets and Highways Code § 230 et seq.

Highway Closing Act (New York City)
N.Y. Laws 1895, Ch. 1006

Highway Code
Mont. Code Ann., 60-1-101 et seq.
Okla. Stat. Ann., Title 69, §§ 101 et seq., 1904 et seq.
Ore. Rev. Stat., 367.105 et seq.
S.C. Code Ann. 1976, § 57-11-210 et seq.

Highway Commission Act
Ind. Code Ann., 8-13-1-1 et seq.
Kan. Stat. Ann., 75-5002 et seq.
Mont. Rev. Code 1947, 32-1601 et seq.
S.D. Codified Laws 1967, 31-2-2 et seq.
Wash. Rev. Code Ann., 47.01.010 et seq.

Highway Commission Law (County)
Cal. Streets and Highways Code § 1220 et seq.

Highway Commission Law (State)
Cal. Streets and Highways Code § 70 et seq.

Highway Competitive Bidding Act
Tex. Rev. Civ. Stat., Art. 6674h

Highway Condemnation Act
Ky. Rev. Stat. 1971, 177.081 et seq.
Mich. Comp. Laws Ann., 213.171 et seq.
N.Y. Highway Law (Consol. Laws Ch. 25) § 29 et seq.
S.C. Code Ann. 1976, § 57-5-370 et seq.
Va. Code 1950, § 33.1-89 et seq.
Vt. Stat. Ann., Title 19, § 221 et seq.

Highway Construction Act
Wash. Rev. Code Ann., 47.28.010 et seq.

Highway Construction Bond Account Act
N.Y. State Finance Law 1940 (Consol. Laws Ch. 56) § 90

Highway Construction Bond Act
Ark. Acts 1965, No. 23
N.Y. Laws 1955, Ch. 757
N.Y. Laws 1961, Ch. 761
Wash. Rev. Code Ann., 47.10.010 et seq.

Highway Construction Finance Act
Mich. Comp. Laws 1948, 207.251 et seq.

Highway Construction Information Act
Tenn. Code Ann., 54-1-115

Highway Construction Reimbursement Act
Tenn. Public Acts 1927, Ch. 23

Highway Construction Relocation Assistance Act
N.M. Stat. Ann., 42-3-1 et seq.

Highway Contractor Development Act
Kan. Stat. Ann., 68-440 et seq.

Highway Contractor Liability Act
Ill. Rev. Stat. 1991, Ch. 121, §§ 364.9, 365

Highway Corporation Act
Va. Code 1950, § 56-535 et seq.

Highway Courtesy Patrol Act
Colo. Rev. Stat., 43-5-101 et seq.

Highway Crossing Act
N.H. Rev. Stat. 1955, 265-30

Highway Crossing Act (Railroads)
N.J. Stat. Ann., 487:12-49 et seq.
Va. Code 1950, § 56-414 et seq.
Wash. Rev. Code Ann., 81.53.010 et seq.

Highway Defects Act
Mass. Gen. Laws Ann., 84:15 et seq.
Me. Rev. Stat. Ann. 1964, Title 23, § 3651 et
seq.
Wis. Stat. Ann., 81.15

Highway Department Act
Ind. Laws 1953, Ch. 225, p. 816
Nev. Rev. Stat. 1979 Reprint, 408.010
N.J. Stat. Ann., 27:1A-1 et seq.
Pa. 1911 Pamph. Laws 468

Highway Department Organization Act
Mich. Comp. Laws Ann., 247.801 et seq.
N.M. Stat. Ann., 67-1-1 et seq., 67-2-4,
67-3-7, 67-3-8, 67-3-23

**Highway Department Property Acquisition
Act**
Ga. Code Ann., 32-3-10

Highway District Act (Joint)
Cal. Streets and Highways Code § 25000 et
seq.

Highway Emergency Act
Del. Laws Vol. 44, p. 547, Ch. 187

Highway Eminent Domain Act
See Highway Condemnation Act

Highway Employees Retirement Act
Ark. Code Ann. 1987, 24-5-101 et seq.

Highway Excavation Local Law
N.Y. Local Laws 1970, Town of Farmington,
p. 1515

Highway Extension Act
D.C. Code Ann., § 7-107 et seq.

Highway Fencing Act
Miss. Code Ann. 1972, § 69-13-201 et seq.

Highway Finance Corporation Act
Ala. Code 1975, § 23-1-170 et seq.

Highway Flood Relief Loan Act
Mass. Acts 1955, Ch. 698

Highway Four Rod Act
Minn. Stat. Ann., 160.05

Highway Fuel Use Tax Law
N.C. Gen. Stat. 1943, § 105-449.1 et seq.

Highway Fund Act (Motor Vehicle)
Mich. Comp. Laws Ann., 247.660 et seq.

Highway Grade Separation Act
Mich. Comp. Laws Ann., 253.1 et seq.,
253.51 et seq.

Highway Improvement Act
Ohio Rev. Code 1953, 5501.11 et seq.

**Highway Improvement Act (Nassau, Suffolk
and Erie Counties)**
N.Y. Laws 1927, Ch. 190

Highway Improvement Act of 1982
Jan. 6, 1983, P.L. 97-424, 23 U.S. Code
§ 101 nt.
April 7, 1986, P.L. 99-272, 100 Stat. 112
April 2, 1987, P.L. 100-17, 23 U.S. Code
§§ 103 nt., 104 nt., 144 nt.
Sept. 30, 1988, P.L. 100-457, 102 Stat. 2156,
23 U.S. Code § 101 nt.

Highway Improvement Loan Act
Mass. Acts 1950, Ch. 685
Mass. Acts 1952, Ch. 556
Mass. Acts 1954, Ch. 403
Mass. Acts 1956, Ch. 718

Highway Junkyard Control Act
Ind. Code Ann., 8-12-1-1 et seq.
Pa. Purdon's Stat., Title 36, § 2719.1 et seq.

Highway Law (1921)
Colo. Stat. Ann. 1935, Ch. 143 § 92 et seq.
Mont. Code Ann. 1947, 32-101 to 32-527

Highway Law of Road Act
Tex. Penal Code 1925, Art. 801

Highway License Act
Wash. Rev. Code Ann., 46.16.006 et seq.

Highway Lighting District Act
Cal. Streets and Highways Code § 19000 et seq.

Highway Limited Access Facility Act
Wash. Rev. Code Ann., 47.52.001 et seq.

Highway Litigation Expenses Act
N.M. Stat. Ann., 42-3-9 et seq.

Highway Litter Act
Cal. Vehicle Code 1959, § 23111 et seq.

Highway Maintenance Act (Counties)
Ind. Code 1976, 8-17-3-1 et seq.

Highway Mining Act
Pa. Purdon's Stat., Title 52, § 1501 et seq.

Highway Note Act (35,000,000.00)
Okla. Laws 1937, p. 367

Highway Obstruction Act
S.C. Code Ann. 1976, § 57-7-210 et seq.

Highway Opening and Crossing Law of Putnam Valley
N.Y. Local Laws 1967, Town of Putnam Valley, p. 1886

Highway Paint Act
Ind. Code 1976, 8-11-4-1, 8-11-4-2

Highway Patrol Act
Cal. Vehicle Code 1959, § 2100 et seq.
Ga. Code Ann., 35-2-30 et seq.
Mo. Rev. Stat., 43.010 et seq.
Mont. Code Ann., 44-1-101 et seq.
N.C. Gen. Stat. 1943, § 20-184 et seq.
Tenn. Code Ann., 4-7-101 et seq.
Utah Code Ann. 1953, 53-8-101 et seq.

Highway Patrol Civil Service Act
Utah Code Ann. 1953, 67-19-1 et seq.

Highway Patrol Officers' Retirement Act
Mont. Code Ann., 19-6-106 et seq.

Highway Patrol Retirement and Pension Act
Ariz. Rev. Stat. Ann., § 38-765 et seq.
Kan. Laws 1947, Ch. 409
Mont. Code Ann., 19-6-101 et seq.
Ohio Rev. Code 1953, 5505.01 et seq.
Utah Code Ann. 1953, 67-19-1 et seq.
Wyo. Stat. Ann., § 9-3-601 et seq.

Highway Pay-As-You-Go Act
S.C. Acts 1924, p. 1193, No. 731

Highway Permit Law
Cal. Streets and Highways Code § 670 et seq.

Highway Post Office Service Act of 1955
Aug. 1, 1956, Ch. 813, 70 Stat. 781

Highway Protection Law (State)
Cal. Streets and Highways Code § 660 et seq.

Highway Protection Loan Act (Dukes County)
Mass. Acts 1954, Ch. 215

Highway-Rail Grade Crossing Safety and Consolidation Act
Neb. Laws 1997, L.B. 255

Highway-Railroad and Highway-Bridge Capital Budget Supplemental Act
Pa. 1992 Pamph. Laws, No. 143
Pa. 1994 Pamph. Laws, No. 147

Highway Referendum Act
N.Y. Laws 1912, Ch. 298

Highway Refunding Bonds Act
Ark. Acts 1965, No. 302
Colo. Stat. Ann. 1935, Ch. 153 § 135 et seq.

Highway Regulatory Act
La. Rev. Stat. Ann., 32:1 et seq.

Highway Reimbursement Act
S.C. Acts 1926, p. 1001, No. 559

Highway Relocation and Land Acquisition Policy Act
Ga. Code Ann., 32-8-1 et seq.

Highway Relocation Assistance Act
Cal. Government Code § 7260 et seq.
Cal. Streets and Highways § 156
Colo. Rev. Stat., 43-1-301 et seq.
Del. Code of 1953, Title 17, § 1901 et seq.
Ga. Code Ann., 32-8-1 et seq.
Ida. Code 1947, 40-2001 et seq.
Iowa Code Ann., 316.1 et seq.
N.C. Gen. Stat. 1943, § 133-5 et seq.
N.H. Rev. Stat. 1955, 230:33 et seq.
N.M. Stat. Ann. 1953, 55-12-1 et seq.
Utah Code Ann. 1953, Miscellaneous Superseded Code Provisions, 27-12-8 et seq.
Wyo. Stat. 1957, § 24-85.1 et seq.

Highway Reorganization Act (Counties)
Ida. Code 1947, 40-1701 et seq.

Highway Revenue Act of 1956
June 29, 1956, Ch. 462, 70 Stat. 387 (See 23 U.S. Code §§ 120 nt., 307 nt.; 26 U.S. Code §§ 4041, 4061, 4071 to 4073, 4084, 4226, 4227, 4481 to 4484, 6206, 6302, 6412, 6416, 6421, 6422, 6504, 6511, 6612, 6675, 7210, 7603 to 7605)
Aug. 28, 1958, P.L. 85-823, 72 Stat. 983, 23 U.S. Code § 304 nt.
Sept. 21, 1959, P.L. 86-342, Stat. 615, 23 U.S. Code § 120 nt.
Sept. 22, 1959, P.L. 86-346, 73 Stat. 622, 23 U.S. Code § 120 nt.
April 22, 1960, P.L. 86-440, 74 Stat. 81, 23 U.S. Code § 120 nt.
June 29, 1961, P.L. 87-61, 75 Stat. 128, 23 U.S. Code § 120 nt.
Sept. 3, 1964, P.L. 88-578, 78 Stat. 904, 23 U.S. Code § 120 nt.
June 21, 1965, P.L. 89-44, 79 Stat. 144, 23 U.S. Code § 120 nt.
May 21, 1970, P.L. 91-258, 84 Stat. 249, 23 U.S. Code § 120 nt.
Dec. 31, 1970, P.L. 91-605, 84 Stat. 1743, 23 U.S. Code § 120 nt.

Nov. 6, 1978, P.L. 95-599, 23 U.S. Code § 120 nt.
Nov. 9, 1978, P.L. 95-618, 23 U.S. Code § 120 nt.
Jan. 6, 1983, P.L. 97-424, 23 U.S. Code § 120 nt.

Highway Revenue Act of 1978
Nov. 6, 1978, P.L. 95-599, 16 U.S. Code § 460l-11; 23 U.S. Code § 101 nt., 120 nt., 307 nt.; 26 U.S. Code §§ 39, 4041, 4061, 4071, 4081, 4481, 4482, 6156, 6412, 6421, 6427, 7210, 7603 to 7605, 7609, 7610

Highway Revenue Act of 1982
Jan. 6, 1983, P.L. 97-424, 26 U.S. Code § 1 nt.
July 18, 1984, P.L. 98-369, 98 Stat. 976

Highway Revenue Act of 1987
April 2, 1987, P.L. 100-17, 26 U.S. Code § 1 nt.

Highway Revenue Bonds Act
Mont. Code Ann., 17-5-901 et seq.

Highway Revenue Distribution Law
Ark. Stat. 1947, 76-309.1 et seq.

Highway Right of Way Act
Tex. Rev. Civ. Stat., Art. 6701d, §§ 71 to 75

Highway, Road and Street Classification Act
Ark. Code Ann. 1987, 27-66-301 et seq.
Mich. Comp. Laws 1970, 247.651 et seq.

Highway Safety Act
Ariz. Rev. Stat. Ann., § 28-611
Haw. Rev. Stat. Ann., § 286-1 et seq.
La. Rev. Stat. Ann., 48:1351 et seq.
Mass. Gen. Laws Ann., 90A:1 et seq.
N.C. Gen. Stat. 1943, § 20-183.1 et seq.
N.J. Stat. Ann., 27:5F-18 et seq.
Okla. Stat. Ann., Title 47, § 1-101 et seq.

Highway Safety Act (Repairs)
Mich. Comp. Laws Ann., 247.841

Highway Safety Act of 1973
Nov. 6, 1978, P.L. 95-599, 23 U.S. Code § 130 nt.
Oct. 15, 1982, P.L. 97-327, 23 U.S. Code § 130 nt.

April 2, 1987, P.L. 100-17, 23 U.S. Code
§ 130 nt.

Highway Safety Act of 1976

May 5, 1976, P.L. 94-280, 49 U.S. Code
Appx. § 1605 et seq.

Highway Safety Act of 1978

Nov. 6, 1978, P.L. 95-599, 23 U.S. Code
§§ 130 nt., 154, 307 nt., 401 nt., 402, 403 nt.

Jan. 6, 1983, P.L. 97-424, 23 U.S. Code
§ 401 nt.

April 2, 1987, P.L. 100-17, 23 U.S. Code
§ 401 nt.

Highway Safety Act of 1982

Jan. 16, 1983, P.L. 97-424, 23 U.S. Code
§ 401 nt.

Highway Safety Act of 1987

April 2, 1987, P.L. 100-17, 23 U.S. Code
§ 401 nt.

Highway Safety Act of 1991

Dec. 18, 1991, P.L. 102-240, 23 U.S. Code
§ 401 nt.

Highway Safety Acts

Sept. 9, 1966, P.L. 89-564, 80 Stat. 731, 23
U.S. Code §§ 105, 303 nt., 307, 401 to 404

Oct. 15, 1966, P.L. 89-670, 80 Stat. 943, 23
U.S. Code § 401 nt.

Dec. 31, 1970, P.L. 91-605, 84 Stat. 1739, 23
U.S. Code §§ 144, 322, 401 nt., 402

Dec. 31, 1970, P.L. 91-605, 84 Stat. 1739, 23
U.S. Code § 401 nt.

Aug. 13, 1973, P.L. 93-87, 87 Stat. 284, 23
U.S. Code §§ 104, 144, 151 to 153, 401 to
405

Aug. 13, 1973, P.L. 93-87, 87 Stat. 292, 23
U.S. Code § 401 nt.

Highway Safety and Improvement Bond Act

N.J. Laws 1974, Ch. 112

Highway Safety Committee Act

R.I. Gen. Laws 1956, 22-7.2-1 et seq.

Highway Safety Coordination Act

Ga. Code Ann., 40-10-1 et seq.

Highway Safety Improvements Act (Federal-Aid)

Cal. Streets and Highways Code § 2330 et
seq.

Highway Safety Patrol and Driver's License Act

Miss. Code Ann. 1972, §§ 45-3-1 et seq.,
63-1-1 et seq.

Highway Safety Program Act

N.H. Rev. Stat. 1955, 238:1 et seq.

Highway Sign Act

Mich. Comp. Laws Ann., 247.275 et seq.

Highway Speed Act (Interstate)

Iowa Code Ann., 321.285, Subsec. 8

Highway Speed Act (Motor Vehicles)

Ga. Code Ann., 40-6-180 et seq.

Highway Spill Containment and Abatement Act (Hazardous Substances)

Cal. Vehicle Code 1959, § 2450 et seq.

Highway Superintendent Liability Act (County)

Ill. Rev. Stat. 1991, Ch. 121, § 380 et seq.

Highway Supplement to the Capital Budget Act

Pa. 1988 Pamph. Laws, No. 114
Pa. 1990 Pamph. Laws, No. 218
Pa. 1994 Pamph. Laws, No. 11

Highway System Access Management Act

Fla. Stat. Ann., 335.18 et seq.

Highway System Act

Colo. Rev. Stat., 43-2-101 et seq.
Ga. Code Ann., 40-6-180 et seq., 32-4-1 et
seq.
Mo. Rev. Stat. Stat. 1986, 227.010 et seq.

Highway Toll Bridge Act

Ky. Rev. Stat. 1962, 180.010 et seq.

Highway Traffic Act

See Traffic Act (Highways)
Ala. Code 1975, 32-1-1 et seq.
Alaska Stat. 1962, § 28.05.010 et seq.
Continued

Ariz. Rev. Stat. Ann., § 28-601 et seq.
Ark. Code Ann. 1987, 27-49-201 et seq.
Conn. Gen. Stat. Ann., § 14-212 et seq.
Ind. Code Ann., 9-4-1-1 et seq.
Kan. Stat. Ann., 8-1401 et seq.
Minn. Stat. Ann., 169.01 et seq.
Miss. Code Ann. 1972, § 63-3-1 et seq.
Mo. Rev. Stat., 227.010 et seq.
Mont. Code Ann., 61-8-101 et seq.
Neb. Rev. Stat. 1943, 39-601 et seq.
N.M. Stat. Ann. 1953, 64-14-1 et seq.
S.C. Code Ann. 1976, § 56-5-10 et seq.
Tex. Rev. Civ. Stat., Art. 6701d
Wyo. Stat. Ann., § 31-5-101 et seq.

Highway Traffic Regulation Act
See Uniform Highway Traffic Regulation
Act

**Highway Transportation Agency Act
(Collier-Burns)**
Cal. Government Code § 13975 et seq.

**Highway Transportation Agreement
(Interstate)**
Ariz. Rev. Stat. Ann., § 28-2301 et seq.

Highway Transportation Agreement Act
Ariz. Rev. Stat. Ann., § 28-2301 et seq.
Mont. Code Ann., 61-10-1101

**Highway Transportation Agreement Act
(Multistate)**
See Multistate Highway Transportation
Agreement Act

Highway Transportation License Tax Law
Cal. Revenue and Taxation Code § 9601 et
seq.

Highway Transportation Reform Act
Me. Rev. Stat. Ann. 1964, Title 29, § 2701 et
seq.

**Highway Treasury Anticipation Debenture
Acts**
Mont. Laws 1939, p. 743
Mont. Laws 1943, Ch. 217
Mont. Laws 1945, Ch. 39

Highway Trust Authority Act
Ill. Rev. Stat. 1971, Ch. 121, § 101.1 et seq.

Highway Use Tax Act
N.Y. Tax Law (Consol. Laws Ch. 60) § 501
et seq.
Ohio Rev. Code 1953, 5728.01 et seq.
Ore. Rev. Stat., 767.815

**Highway User Fee Apportionment Act
(Interstate)**
Nev. Rev. Stat. 1979 Reprint, 706.801 et seq.

Highway User Fuel Tax Act
Tenn. Code Ann., 67-3-701 et seq.

Highway Users Tax Fund Law
Colo. Rev. Stat., 43-4-201 et seq.

Highway Vegetation Control Act
Pa. Purdon's Stat., Title 36, § 2720.1 et seq.

Highway Warrants Act
Colo. Rev. Stat. 1963, 120-11-1 et seq.

Highway Weight Limitation Act
N.J. Stat. Ann., 39:3-84 et seq.

Highways
Aug. 27, 1958, P.L. 85-767, 72 Stat. 885, 23
U.S. Code §§ 101 to 131, 201 to 213, 301 to
320
May 29, 1959, P.L. 86-35, 73 Stat. 62, 23
U.S. Code § 108
June 25, 1959, P.L. 86-70, 73 Stat. 146, 23
U.S. Code §§ 103, 104, 116, 120
Sept. 21, 1959, P.L. 86-342, 73 Stat. 611, 23
U.S. Code §§ 101 nt., 104 nt., 120, 120 nt.,
125, 131, 320
July 12, 1960, P.L. 86-624, 74 Stat. 415, 23
U.S. Code §§ 101, 103, 105, 127
July 14, 1960, P.L. 86-657, 74 Stat. 522, 23
U.S. Code §§ 104, 114, 120, 129, 132, 203,
205, 210, 305
June 29, 1961, P.L. 87-61, 75 Stat. 122, 23
U.S. Code §§ 101 nt., 104 nt., 111, 120 nt.,
131, 210
Sept. 22, 1961, P.L. 87-282, 75 Stat. 584, 23
U.S. Code § 208
Oct. 4, 1961, P.L. 87-392, 75 Stat. 822, 23
U.S. Code § 303

Oct. 23, 1962, P.L. 87-866, 76 Stat. 1146, 23 U.S. Code §§ 101, 103, 104, 133, 134, 203, 214, 307

Oct. 24, 1963, P.L. 88-157, 77 Stat. 276, 23 U.S. Code §§ 104, 106, 109, 121, 131, 307

Aug. 13, 1964, P.L. 88-423, 78 Stat. 397, 23 U.S. Code §§ 101, 104, 205, 209, 320

Aug. 14, 1964, P.L. 88-426, 78 Stat. 425, 23 U.S. Code § 303

Oct. 13, 1964, P.L. 88-658, 78 Stat. 1090, 23 U.S. Code § 120

Aug. 28, 1965, P.L. 89-139, 79 Stat. 578, 23 U.S. Code § 135

Oct. 22, 1965, P.L. 89-285, 79 Stat. 1028, 23 U.S. Code §§ 131, 136, 319

Sept. 9, 1966, P.L. 89-564, 80 Stat. 731, 23 U.S. Code §§ 105, 307, 401 to 404

Sept. 13, 1966, P.L. 89-574, 80 Stat. 767, 23 U.S. Code §§ 101, 104, 106 nt., 109, 118, 120, 125, 131, 136 to 138, 302, 319

Jan. 2, 1968, P.L. 90-238, 81 Stat. 772, 23 U.S. Code § 103

Aug. 23, 1968, P.L. 90-495, 82 Stat. 816, 23 U.S. Code §§ 101, 103, 104, 108, 112, 113, 115, 116, 120, 125, 128, 129, 131, 135, 136, 139 to 141, 205, 319, 402, 501 to 511

Dec. 31, 1970, P.L. 91-605, 84 Stat. 1714, 23 U.S. Code §§ 101, 103 to 106, 109, 120, 125, 128, 129, 131, 134 to 137, 139, 140, 142 to 144, 215, 216 and others

Highways Administration Maintenance and Policing Act
P.R. Laws Ann. 1954, Title 9, § 2101 et seq.

Highways and Roads Law
Nev. Rev. Stat. 1979 Reprint, 408.010 et seq.

Highways Authority Act
P.R. Laws Ann. 1954, Title 9, § 2001 et seq.

Highways, Bridges and Ferries Act
S.C. Code Ann. 1976, § 57-1-10 et seq.

Highways Expropriation Act
La. Rev. Stat. Ann., 48:441 et seq.

Highways Protection Law (County)
Cal. Streets and Highways Code § 1480 et seq.

Highways Protection Law (State)
Cal. Streets and Highways Code § 660 et seq.

Highways Speed Act (Interstate)
Iowa Code Ann., 321.285, Subsec. 8

Hijacking Act (Anti-Motor Vehicle)
Ga. Laws 1994, p. 1625

Hill-Burton Act
See Hospital Survey And Construction Act

Hillcrest Sewer District Loan Act
Mass. Acts 1954, Ch. 612

Hillery Maximum Tax Rate Act
N.J. Laws 1906, p. 206, Ch. 116

Hillsborough County Assessment Bond Act
Fla. Special Laws 1927, Ch. 12867

Hillsborough County Aviation Authority Act
Fla. Special Laws 1945, Ch. 23339

Hillsborough County Charter
Fla. Special Laws 1972, Ch. 72-555

Hillsborough County Civil Service Act
Fla. Special Laws 1951, Ch. 27601

Hillsborough County Consumer Protection Act
Fla. Special Laws 1975, Ch. 75-394

Hillsborough County Environmental Protection Act
Fla. Special Laws 1967, Ch. 67-1504, 1972, Ch. 72563, 1975, Ch. 75-403, 412

Hillsborough County Local Government Comprehensive Planning Act
Fla. Special Laws 1975, Ch. 75-390

Hillsborough County Pollution Control Act
Fla. Special Laws 1967, Ch. 67-1504

Hillsborough County Port Authority Act
Fla. Special Laws 1945, Ch. 23338

Hillsborough County Port District Marine Construction Act
Fla. Special Laws 1978, Ch. 78-527

Hillsborough County Racing Act
Fla. Laws 1953, Ch. 28499

Hillsborough County Sanitary Sewer District Act
Fla. Special Laws 1927, Ch. 12868

Hillsborough County Solid Waste Disposal and Resource Act
Fla. Special Laws 1981, Ch. 81-387

Hillsborough County-Tampa Charter
Fla. Laws 1970, Ch. 70-724

Hillsborough County-Tampa Expressway Authority Act
Fla. Stat. 1977, 348.50 et seq.

Hillsborough County Teachers Professional Negotiations Law
Fla. Special Laws 1971, Ch. 71-686

Hilton-Cooper-Howard Act (Pari-Mutuel Betting)
Ky. Rev. Stat. 1971, 47.012, 137.190, 138.510 et seq.

Hilton-Warinner Act (Elections)
Ky. Rev. Stat. 1971, Superseded Vols., 118.040, 118.350, 118.370, 119.040
Ky. Rev. Stat. 1971, 117.275, 118.025, 118.035

Hinkle-Mobley-Newberry Act (School Term)
Ky. Rev. Stat. 1971, 158.070

Hinsdale Act (Nonsuit)
N.C. Gen. Stat. 1943, § 1-183

Hinsonton Water Authority Act
Ga. Laws 1974, p. 2997

Hire Act (Residents)
Alaska Stat. 1962, Replaced Titles, § 38.40.010 et seq.

Hispanic Cultural Center Act
N.M. Stat. Ann., 18-12-1 et seq.

Hispanic Interpreter Act (Mental Health)
Ill. Rev. Stat. 1991, Ch. 91 1/2, §§ 1750, 1751

Hispanic Women's Demonstration Resource Centers Act
N.J. Laws 1991, Ch. 378

Hiss Act (Pensions)
Sept. 1, 1954, Ch. 1214, 68 Stat. 1142 (See 5 U.S. Code §§ 2101, 8311, 8312, 8314 to 8319, 8321, 8322; See 18 U.S. Code § 3282)
Sept. 26, 1961, P.L. 87-299, 75 Stat. 640 (See 5 U.S. Code §§ 2101, 8311 to 8322; 18 U.S. Code § 3282)

Historian Act (Local)
Ill. Rev. Stat. 1991, Ch. 85, § 5700 et seq.

Historic Albemarle Tour Highway Act
N.C. Laws 1975, Ch. 567

Historic and Nature Preserve Dedication Act
N.C. Gen. Stat. 1943, § 143-260.6 et seq.

Historic and Prehistoric Sites Preservation Act
N.M. Stat. Ann., 18-8-1 et seq.

Historic Areas Zoning Act
Md. Ann. Code 1957, Art. 66B, § 8.01 et seq.

Historic Board of Trustees Act (Bradford County)
Fla. Special Laws 1973, Ch. 408

Historic Building Improvements Act
N.M. Stat. Ann., 4-55B-1 et seq.

Historic Building Preservation and Affordable Residential Housing Act of Pawtucket
R.I. Gen. Laws 1956, 44-4.2-1 et seq.

Historic Burial Places Preservation Act
Pa. Purdon's Stat., Title 9, § 211 et seq.

Historic Capitol Preservation Act
Fla. Stat. Ann., 272.128

Historic Cemeteries Act
N.J. Stat. Ann., 40:10B-1 et seq.

Historic Chattahoochee Compact
Ala. Acts 1993, No. 643

Historic Chattahoochee Compact Act
Ala. Code 1975, § 41-9-311
Ga. Code Ann., 12-10-80, 12-10-81

Historic Commission Act
N.J. Stat. Ann., 40:33B-1 et seq.

Historic District Act (Comstock)
Nev. Rev. Stat. 1979 Reprint, 384.010 et seq.

Historic District Act (Lowell)
Mass. Acts 1983, Ch. 566

Historic District and Landmark Act
N.M. Stat. Ann., 3-22-1 et seq.

Historic Districts Act
Ark. Code Ann. 1987, 14-172-201 et seq.
Mass. Gen. Laws Ann., 40C:1 et seq.
Mich. Comp. Laws Ann., 399.201 et seq.
Minn. Stat. Ann., 138.71 et seq.
Nev. Rev. Stat. 1979 Reprint, 384.010 et seq.
Pa. Purdon's Stat., Title 53, § 8001 et seq.
Utah Code Ann. 1953, 11-18-1 et seq.

Historic Districts Act (Local)
Mich. Comp. Laws. Ann., 399.201 et seq.

Historic Districts Enabling Act
Conn. Gen. Stat. Ann., § 7-147a et seq.

Historic Landmark and Historic District Protection Act
D.C. Code Ann., § 5-1001 et seq.

Historic Motor Vehicle Act
D.C. Code Ann., §§ 40-101, 40-104, 40-201

Historic Places Registration Act
Okla. Stat. Ann., Title 53, § 351 et seq.

Historic Preservation Act
Alaska Stat. 1962, § 41.35.010 et seq.
Ga. Code Ann., 44-10-20 et seq.
Miss. Code Ann. 1972, § 39-13-1 et seq.
Mo. Rev. Stat., 253.408
Mo. Rev. Stat., 253.415
Neb. Rev. Stat. 1943, 82-118
N.Y. General Municipal Law (Consol. Laws Ch. 24) § 119aa et seq.
N.Y. Parks and Recreation Law (Consol. Laws Ch. 36b) § 14.01 et seq.
N.Y. Parks, Recreation and Historic Preservation Law (Consol. Laws Ch. 36f) §§ 11.03, 11.05, 11.09, 14.01 et seq.
N.Y. Public Buildings Law (Consol. Laws Ch. 44) § 60 et seq.
Pa. Purdon's Stat., Title 71, § 1047.1a et seq.
Utah Code Ann. 1953, 63-18a-1 et seq.
Vt. Stat. Ann., Title 22, § 701 et seq.
W. Va. Acts 1972, Ch. 12
W. Va. Code 1966, § 29-1-1 et seq.

Historic Preservation Act (County)
Ill. Comp. Stat. 1992, Ch. 55, § 5/5-30001 et seq.

Historic Preservation Activities Act
S.D. Codified Laws 1967, 1-19B-1 et seq.

Historic Preservation Agency Act
Ill. Rev. Stat. 1991, Ch. 105 §§ 533a, 534a, 535a
Ill. Rev. Stat. 1991, Ch. 127, § 2701 et seq.

Historic Preservation and Conservation Agreements Act
N.C. Gen. Stat. 1943, § 121-34 et seq.

Historic Preservation Bond Act (Clean Acres, Clean Water, and Farmland)
N.J. Laws 1992, Ch. 88

Historic Preservation Easement Act
Mich. Comp. Laws Ann., 399.251 et seq.

Historic Preservation Loan Act
N.M. Stat. Ann., 18-6-18 et seq.

Historic Preservation Restriction Act
N.J. Stat. Ann., 13:8B-1 et seq.

Historic Preservation Revolving Fund Act
Mo. Rev. Stat. 1979, 253.400 et seq.

Historic Preservation Revolving Loan Fund
N.J. Stat. Ann., 13:1B-15.115a to
13:1B-15.115d

Historic Resources Preservation Act (State Agency)
Ill. Rev. Stat. 1991, Ch. 127, § 133c21 et seq.

Historic Rome Development Authority Act
N.Y. Public Authorities Law (Consol. Laws
Ch. 43A) § 1900 et seq.

Historic Sites Acts
Minn. Stat. Ann., 138.51 et seq.
Mont. Code Ann., 22-3-601 et seq.
N.D. Cent. Code, 55-10-01 et seq.
S.D. Codified Laws 1967, 1-19A-1 et seq.

Historic Sites, Buildings and Antiquities Act
Aug. 21, 1935, Ch. 593, 49 Stat. 666, 16 U.S.
Code §§ 461 to 467
Oct. 9, 1965, P.L. 89-249, 79 Stat. 971, 16
U.S. Code § 462

Historic Sites Council Act
N.J. Stat. Ann., 13:1B-15.108 et seq.

Historic Sites Subdivision Amendment of 1976
D.C. Laws 1976, No. 1-80

Historic St. Mary's City Commission Act
Md. Ann. Code 1974, Art. ED, § 24-501 et
seq.

Historic Structures and Landmarks Act
Conn. Gen. Stat. Ann., § 10-321a et seq.

Historic Zoning Law
N.Y. Local Laws 1973, Town of Charlton, p.
1450

Historical and Nature Preserve Act
N.Y. Environmental Conservation Law 1972
(Consol. Laws Ch. 43B) § 45-0101 et seq.

Historical Board of Trustees Act
Fla. Law 1973, Ch. 73-408

Historical Building Code
Cal. Health and Safety Code § 18950 et seq.

Historical Codes Act
N.M. Stat. Ann., 22-15-15 et seq.

Historical Commission Act
Mass. Gen. Laws Ann., 9:26 et seq.
Mich. Comp. Laws Ann., 399.1 et seq.
N.J. Stat. Ann., 40:33B-1 et seq.
Tenn. Code Ann., 4-11-101 et seq.

Historical Commission Act (County)
N.J. Stat. Ann., 40:33B-1 et seq.

Historical Commission Bicentennial Act
N.J. Laws 1973, Ch. 49

Historical District Loan Act
Alaska Stat. 1962, § 45.98.010 et seq.

Historical Document Preservation Act
Ill. Rev. Stat. 1991, Ch. 128, § 17.9 et seq.

Historical Library Act
Ill. Rev. Stat. 1991, Ch. 128, §§ 12.99, 13

Historical Museum Act
Cal. Public Resources Code § 5013
Ill. Rev. Stat. 1991, Ch. 105, §§ 325a, 325a.1

Historical Preservation Act
Ala. Code 1975, § 41-10-135 et seq.
Okla. Stat. Ann., Title 53, § 1.1 et seq.
Utah Code Ann. 1953, 9-8-501 et seq.

Historical Preserve and Nature Act
N.Y. Environmental Conservation Law 1972
(Consol. Laws Ch. 43B) § 45-0101 et seq.

Historical Records Act
S.D. Codified Laws 1967, 1-18B-1 et seq.

Historical Records and State Archives Act
R.I. Gen. Laws 1956, 42-8.1-1 et seq.

Historical Records Trust Act
R.I. Gen. Laws 1956, 42-8.1-20

Historical Rehabilitation Act (Marks)
Cal. Health and Safety Code § 37600 et seq.

Historical Research Act (County)
Ill. Comp. Stat. 1992, Ch. 55, § 95/0.01 et seq.

Historical Resources Act
Fla. Stat. Ann. 267.011 et seq.

Historical Sites Listing Act
Ill. Rev. Stat. 1991, Ch. 128, § 30 et seq.

Historical Society Act
Utah Code Ann. 1953, 63-18-1 et seq.

Historical Society Revolving Fund Act
Utah Code Ann. 1953, 63-18-7.5 et seq.

Historical Trust Act
Md. Ann. Code 1957, Art. 83B, § 5-611 et seq.

History and Archives Act
N.C. Gen. Stat. 1943, § 121-1 et seq.

History Code
Pa. Cons. Stat., Title 37, § 101 et seq.

History Record Information Act (Criminal)
Me. Rev. Stat. Ann. 1964, Title 16, § 611 et seq.

Hit and Run Act
Ala. Code 1975, § 32-10-1 et seq.
Ariz. Rev. Stat. Ann., § 28-661 et seq.
Cal. Vehicle Code 1959, § 20000 et seq.
Ga. Code Ann., 40-6-270
Haw. Rev. Stat. Ann., § 291-2
Ind. Code Ann., 9-4-1-40 et seq.
La. Rev. Stat. Ann., 14:100
Mich. Comp. Laws Ann., 257.617 et seq.
Miss. Code Ann. 1972, § 63-3-401 et seq.
Mo. Rev. Stat. 1969, 564.450
N.C. Gen. Stat. 1943, § 20-166
N.H. Rev. Stat. 1955, 264.25 et seq.
N.J. Rev. Stat. 1937, 39:4-129
N.Y. Vehicle and Traffic Law 1959 (Consol. Laws Ch. 71) § 600 et seq.
Ohio Rev. Code 1953, 4549.02

Ore. Rev. Stat., 483.602
Tenn. Code Ann., 55-10-101
Tex. Penal Code 1925, Art. 1150
Va. Code 1950, §§ 46.2-899, 46.2-900
W. Va. Code 1966, § 17C-4-1 et seq.

Hitchhiking Acts
Cal. Vehicle Code 1959, § 21957
Ill. Rev. Stat. 1991, Ch. 95 1/2, § 11-1006
Miss. Code Ann. 1972, § 63-3-1109
N.Y. Vehicle and Traffic Law 1959 (Consol. Laws Ch. 71) §§ 1157, 1642 subd. 8
Wash. Rev. Code Ann., 46.61.255

Hitler Act (Governor's Powers)
Mont. Laws 1937, Ch. 5

Hittle Act (Financing of Motor Vehicle Sales)
Mich. Comp. Laws Ann., 492.101 et seq.

Hittle-Burke-Rowell-Smith Martin Act (Occupational Disease)
Mich. Comp. Laws 1948, 417.1 et seq.

Hittle Juvenile Employment Act
Mich. Comp. Laws Ann., 409.1 et seq.

Hittle-Morley Act (Educational Aid to Children of Deceased Veterans)
Mich. Comp. Laws Ann., 35.111, 35.112

HIV-Related Information Act (Confidentiality)
Pa. Purdon's Stat. Title 35, § 7601 et seq.

HIV Testing for Insurance Act
Del. Code of 1974, Title 18, § 7301 et seq.

Hiwassee Solid Waste Utility District Act
Tenn. Public Acts 1969, Ch. 289

Hobart Act (Liquor-Local Enforcement)
N.J. Laws 1922, Ch. 255

Hobbs Act
July 3, 1946, Ch. 537, 18 U.S. Code § 1951
June 25, 1948, Ch. 645, 18 U.S. Code § 1951

Hobbs Administrative Orders Review Act
See Administrative Orders Review Act

Hobbs Anti-Racketeering Act
See Anti-Packeterring Act

Hobbs Bridge Act
June 21, 1940, Ch. 409, 54 Stat. 497, 33 U.S.
Code §§ 511 to 523

Hoch-Smith Resolution
Jan. 30, 1925, Ch. 120, 43 Stat. 801, 49 U.S.
Code § 55

Hodge Amendment (Tax Extension)
Ill. Rev. Stat. 1991, Ch. 120, § 643a

Hodson-Loughead Act (Dog Registration)
Ohio Rev. Code 1953, 955.01 et seq.

Hoffman Act (Equalization of Real Property Values)
Ohio Rev. Code 1953, 5715.01, 5715.29 et
seq.

Hoffman Act (State Employment)
Ohio Rev. Code 1953, 124.36

Hofstadter Act (Seabury Investigation)
N.Y. Laws 1931, Ex. Sess., Ch. 773

Hog Act
Kan. Stat. Ann., 47-112 et seq.

Hog Cholera Control Act
N.C. Gen. Stat. 1943, § 106-316.1 et seq.
Neb. Rev. Stat. 1943, 54-1513 et seq.
N.M. Stat. Ann., 77-7-1 et seq.
Tenn. Code Ann., 44-2-1101 et seq.

Hog-Cholera Serum Law
Iowa Code Ann., 166.1 et seq.

Hoisting Operations Safety Act
N.M. Stat. Ann., 60-15-1 et seq.

Holbeck-Moore Act (Delinquent Taxes)
Mich. Comp. Laws Ann., 211.301 et seq.

Holbeck-Smith-McNitt Act (Township Highways)
Mich. Comp. Laws 1948, 247.1 et seq.

Holbrook Sewerage Loan Act
Mass. Acts 1964, Ch. 74

Holden Act (Housing Financial Discrimination)
Cal. Health and Safety Code § 35800 et seq.

Holden Credit Denial Disclosure Act
Cal. Civil Code § 1787.1 et seq.

Holden-Moscone-Garamendi Genetically Handicapped Person's Program
Cal. Health and Safety Code § 340 et seq.

Holder in Due Course Act
Wash. Rev. Code Ann., 62A.3-302 et seq.

Holders of Low and Moderate Income Housing Restrictions Act
R.I. Gen. Laws 1956, 34-39.1-1 et seq.

Holding Company Act (Bank)
Ill. Comp. Stat. 1992, Ch. 205, § 10/1 et seq.
S.C. Code Ann. 1976, § 34-24-10 et seq.

Holding Company Act (Banks)
Ill. Rev. Stat. 1991, Ch. 17, § 2501 et seq.
La. Rev. Stat. Ann., 6:1001 et seq.
Me. Rev. Stat. Ann. 1964, Title 9-B, § 1011
et seq.
Nev. Rev. Stat. 1943, 8-1201 et seq.

Holding Company Act (County Buildings)
Ky. Rev. Stat. 1971, 67.450 et seq.

Holding Company Act (Insurance)
Kan. Stat. Ann., 40-3301 et seq.

Holding Company Act (Insurer)
Wash. Rev. Code Ann., 48.31B.900

Holding Company Act (Mutual Insurance)
Neb. Rev. Stat. 1943, 44-6122 to 44-6142

Holding Company Act (Public Utilities)
Kan. Stat. Ann., 66-1401 et seq.

Holding Company Dissolution Act (Boston Railroad)
Mass. Acts 1946, Ch. 518

Holding Company Law (Insurance)
Nev. Rev. Stat. Ann., 692C.010 et seq.

Holding Company or Foundation Act
Ind. Code 1971, 23-7-2-1 et seq.

Holding Company Regulation Act
See Public Utility Holding Company Act

Holding Company Regulatory Act (Insurance)
Ark. Code Ann. 1987, 23-63-501 et seq.

Holding Company Subsidiary Trust Formation Act (Bank)
Ark. Code Ann. 1987, 23-32-1901 et seq.

Holding Company System Act (Insurance)
Neb. Rev. Stat. 1943, 44-2120 et seq.

Holding Company System Regulatory Act
D.C. Code Ann., § 35-2001 et seq.

Holding Tank Act (Sewage)
Ga. Code Ann., 12-15-1 et seq.

Holdover Official Bond Act
Ill. Rev. Stat. 1991, Ch. 103, §§ 14.90, 15

Holiday Act (Columbus)
Ill. Comp. Stat. 1992, Ch. 5, § 490/35

Holiday Acts
Cal. Government Code § 6700 et seq.
La. Rev. Stat. Ann., 1:55
Mich. Comp. Laws Ann., 435.101 et seq.
N.Y. General Construction Law (Consol. Laws Ch. 22) §§ 24, 25
N.Y. Local Laws 1973, Village of Lancaster, p. 3449
S.C. Code Ann. 1976, § 53-5-10 et seq.
Wash. Rev. Code Ann., 1.16.050

Holiday or Sunday Burial Act
Ill. Rev. Stat. 1991, Ch. 21, § 100 et seq.

Holiday Pay Act
June 29, 1938, Ch. 818, 52 Stat. 1246 (See 5 U.S. Code §§ 6103, 6104)

Holland Law (Tax Sales)
Fla. Stat. 1967, 193.01 et seq., 194.01 et seq.

Hollinger-Mitchell Act (Employee Welfare Funds)
N.Y. Insurance Law (Consol. Laws Ch. 28) § 4401 et seq.

Hollywood Civil Service Act
Fla. Special Laws 1965, Ch. 65-1689

Holmdahl-Rains-Lockyer Economic Development Act
Cal. Government Code § 15310 et seq.

Holmes Beach Improvement Authority Act
Fla. Special Laws 1955, Ch. 30839

Holmes Youthful Trainee Act
Mich. Comp. Laws Ann., 762.11 et seq.

Holocaust Victim Compensation Relief Act
Cal. Revenue and Taxation Code § 17155

Holocaust Victims Insurance Act
Fla. Stat. Ann., 626.9543
N.Y. Insurance Law 1984 (Consol. Laws Ch. 28) § 2701 et seq.

Holocaust Victims Redress Act
Feb. 13, 1998, P.L. 105-158, 112 Stat. 15

Holyoke Gas and Electric Loan Act
Mass. Acts 1951, Ch. 436

Holyoke Public Parking Loan Act
Mass. Acts 1955, Ch. 663

Holyoke Water Loan Act
Mass. Acts 1953, Ch. 659

Home Act
Ky. Rev. Stat. 1971, Superseded Vol., 205.410 et seq.

Home Act (Nursing)
S.C. Code Ann. 1976, § 44-7-80 et seq.

Home Administration Act (Consolidated Farmers)
S.C. Code Ann. 1976, § 33-35-10 et seq.

Home and Community-Based Services and Home Health Act
Colo. Rev. Stat., 26-4.5-101 et seq.

Home and Community-Based Services for Mentally Ill Persons and Persons with Developmental Disabilities Act
Colo. Rev. Stat. 26-4.5-201 et seq.

Home and Community-Based Services for Persons with Developmental Disabilities Act
Colo. Rev. Stat., 26-4-621 et seq.

Home and Community-Based Services for Persons with Health Complexes Related to Acquired Immune Deficiency Syndrome Act
Colo. Rev. Stat., 26-4-641 et seq.

Home and Community-Based Services for Persons with Major Mental Illnesses Act
Colo. Rev. Stat., 26-4-671 et seq.

Home and Community-Based Services for the Elderly, Blind, and Disabled Act
Colo. Rev. Stat., 26-4-601 et seq.

Home and Family Advisory Council Act
Mass. Gen. Laws Ann., 6:151 et seq.

Home-Based Support Services Law for Mentally Disabled Adults
Ill. Rev. Stat. 1991, Ch. 91 1/2, § 1802-1 et seq.

Home Building Association Act
N.D. Laws 1919, Ch. 150

Home Building Law
S.D. Laws 1921, Ch. 254

Home Buyer Savings Account Act (First-Time)
Mont. Code Ann., 15-63-101 et seq.

Home Care Act
Okla. Stat. Ann., Title 63, § 1-1960 et seq.

Home Care and Board Licensing Law
La. Rev. Stat. Ann., 40:2151 et seq.

Home Care and Board Registration Law
Ill. Comp. Stat. 1992, Ch. 225, § 7/1 et seq.

Home Care Expansion Act
N.J. Stat. Ann., 30:4E-5 et seq.

Home Certification Act (Adult Companion)
Okla. Stat. Ann., Title 56, § 530.1 et seq.

Home Corporation Act
Miss. Code Ann. 1972, § 43-33-701 et seq.

Home-Delivered Meals Act
Cal. Welfare and Institutions Code § 9380 et seq.

Home Delivery Food Tax Act
D.C. Code Ann., § 47-2005, Subd. 18

Home Detention Act
S.C. Code Ann. 1976, § 24-13-1510 et seq.
W. Va. Code 1966 § 62-11B-1 et seq.

Home Detention Act (Electronic)
Ill. Rev. Stat. 1991, Ch. 38, § 1005-8A-1 et seq.
S.C. Code Ann. 1976, § 24-13-1510 et seq.

Home Energy Assistance Act of 1980
April 2, 1980, P.L. 96-223, 42 U.S. Code §§ 8601 et seq., 8601 nt.

Home Energy Fair Practices Act
N.Y. Public Service Law (Consol. Laws Ch. 48) § 30 et seq.

Home Environment Living Program
Ill. Rev. Stat. 1991, Ch. 91 1/2, § 2001 et seq.

Home Equity Assurance Act
Ill. Rev. Stat. 1991, Ch. 24, § 1601 et seq.

Home Equity Conversion Act
Fla. Stat. Ann., 697.20 et seq.

Home Equity Conversion Mortgage Act
Tenn. Code Ann., 47-30-101 et seq.

Home Equity Loan Consumer Protection Act of 1988
Nov. 23, 1988, P.L. 100-709, 15 U.S. Code § 1601 nt.

Home Equity Loan Disclosure Act
Cal. Civil Code §§ 2970, 2971

Home Exemption Act (Municipal)
Miss. Code Ann. 1972, § 27-33-501 et seq.

Home Exemption Acts
Miss. Code Ann. 1972, § 27-33- 1 et seq.

Home Finance Act
Md. Ann. Code 1974, Art. FI, § 13-301 et seq.

Home Food Establishments Law
Iowa Code Ann., 137D.1 et seq.

Home Food Service Plan Sales Act
Del. Code of 1974, Title 6, § 2590 et seq.

Home for Disabled Soldiers Land Cession Act
Ill. Rev. Stat. 1991, Ch. 1, § 3701

Home for the Aged and Nursing Home Licensing Law
Vt. Stat. Ann., Title 18, § 2001 et seq.

Home for the Aged Licensing Act
Mich. Comp. Laws Ann., 333.21301 et seq.

Home Furnishings and Thermal Insulation Act
Cal. Business and Professions Code § 19000 et seq.

Home Guard Act
Mont. Code Ann., 10-1-701 et seq.

Home Guard Act (Women)
Okla. Stat. Ann., Title 44, § 261 et seq.

Home Guards (State Police)
June 14, 1917, Ch. 28, 40 Stat. 181

Home Health Agencies Act
Miss. Code Ann. 1972, § 41-71-1 et seq.
S.C. Code Ann. 1976, § 44-69-10 et seq.

Home Health Agency Licensing Act
Ill. Rev. Stat. 1991, Ch. 111 1/2, § 2801 et seq.
Mo. Rev. Stat., 197.400 et seq.
N.C. Gen. Stat. 1943, § 131E-135 et seq.
S.C. Code Ann. 1976, § 44-69-10 et seq.
Va. Code 1950, § 32.1-157 et seq.

Home Health Agency Lien Act
Ill. Rev. Stat. 1991, Ch. 82, § 301 et seq.

Home Health Care and Alzheimer's Disease Amendments of 1990
Nov. 15, 1990, P.L. 101-557, 42 U.S. Code §§ 201 nt., 242q, 242q- 1 et seq.

Home Health Services Act
Fla. Stat. Ann., 400.461 et seq.

Home Heating Act (Emergency)
Me. Public Laws 1979, Ch. 574

Home Heating Oil Emergency Credit Act (Winter 1979-1980)
N.Y. Laws 1979, Ch. 728

Home Heating System Conversion Disclosure Act
N.Y. General Business Law (Consol. Laws Ch. 20) § 778aa

Home Improvement Act
Conn. Gen. Stat. Ann., § 20-418 et seq.
Md. Ann. Code 1974, Art. BR, §§ 8-101 et seq., 8-701 et seq.

Home Improvement Business Act
D.C. Code Ann., § 2-501 et seq.

Home Improvement Commission Act
Tenn. Code Ann., 62-37-101 et seq.

Home Improvement Contract Regulation Act
Ga. Code Ann., 10-1-910 to 10-1-914

Home Improvement Finance Act
Mich. Comp. Laws Ann., 445.1101 et seq.
Pa. Purdon's Stat., Title 73, § 500-101 et seq.

Home Improvement Law
Md. Ann. Code 1974, Art. BR, § 8-701 et seq.

Home Improvement Licensing Act
Tenn. Code Ann., 62-37-101 et seq.

Home Improvement Loan and Radon Gas Demonstration Project Act
Pa. Purdon's Stat., Title 35, § 7501 et seq.

Home Improvement Loans for Senior Citizens Act (Unfair)
R.I. Gen. Laws 1956, 6-28.1-1 et seq.

Home Improvement Partnership Act
Cal. Health and Safety Code § 50896 et seq.

Home Improvement Sales and Finance Act
Fla. Stat. Ann., 520.60 et seq.

Home Improvement Tax Cut Act
N.J. Stat. Ann., 54:4-3.72 et seq.

Home Incarceration Act
W. Va. Code 1966, § 62-11B-1 et seq.

Home Inspectors Licensing Act
Ind. Code 1982, 25-20.2-1-1 et seq.

Home Inspectors Registration Act
Ala. Code 1975, § 34-14B-1 et seq.
Ark. Code 1987, 17-52-101 to 17-52-106, 17-52-201 to 17-52-204, 19-5-1090

Home Insulation and Energy Conservation Act
N.Y. Public Service Law (Consol. Laws Ch. 48) § 135a et seq.

Home Invasion Act
Mass. Gen. Laws Ann., 265:18C

Home Investment Partnerships Act
Nov. 28, 1990, P.L. 101-625, 42 U.S. Code §§ 12701 nt., 12721 to 12725, 12741 to 12756, 12771 to 12774, 12781 to 12785, 12801 to 12809, 12821, 12831 to 12839
Cal. Health and Safety Code § 50896 et seq.

Home Loan Act
N.M. Stat. Ann., 56-8-22 et seq.

Home Loan Assistance and Protection Act
Minn. Stat. Ann., 47.20, 47.21

Home Loan Mortgage Act
Cal. Financial Code § 40000 et seq.

Home Loan Mortgage Corporation Act
Dec. 21, 1979, P.L. 96-153, 12 U.S. Code §§ 1451, 1452, 1455

Home-Made Trailer Act
Tenn. Code Ann., 55-4-101

Home Medical Equipment and Services Provider License Act
Ill. Comp. Stat. 1992, Ch. 225, § 51/1 et seq.

Home Mortgage Act
Tenn. Code Ann., 7-60-101 et seq.

Home Mortgage Credit Agency Act
Vt. Stat. Ann. 1959, Title 10, § 351 et seq.

Home Mortgage Disclosure Act
Nov. 7, 1988, P.L. 100-628, 12 U.S. Code §§ 2805, 2806
Conn. Gen. Stat. Ann., § 36-443 et seq.

Home Mortgage Disclosure Act of 1975
Dec. 31, 1975, P.L. 94-200, 12 U.S. Code § 2801 et seq.
Nov. 30, 1983, P.L. 98-181, 12 U.S. Code §§ 2803, 2807, 2809
Oct. 8, 1985, P.L. 99-120, 12 U.S. Code § 2811
Nov. 15, 1985, P.L. 99-156, 12 U.S. Code § 2811
Dec. 26, 1985, P.L. 99-219, 12 U.S. Code § 2811
March 27, 1986, P.L. 99-267, 12 U.S. Code § 2811
April 7, 1986, P.L. 99-272, 12 U.S. Code § 2811
Feb. 5, 1988, P.L. 100-242, 12 U.S. Code §§ 2802, 2803
Aug. 9, 1989, P.L. 101-73, 12 U.S. Code §§ 2802 to 2807, 2810
Dec. 19, 1991, P.L. 102-242, 12 U.S. Code §§ 2803, 2804, 2808

Oct. 28, 1992, P.L. 102-550, 12 U.S. Code § 2803

Sept. 30, 1996, P.L. 104-208, 12 U.S. Code §§ 2803, 2808

Home Mortgage Relief Act

May 28, 1935, Ch. 150, 49 Stat. 293 (12 U.S. Code generally distributed in 11 to 13)

Home of Florida Act (Veterans)

Fla. Stat. Ann., 296.01 et seq.

Home Owners' Loan Act of 1933

June 13, 1933, Ch. 64, 48 Stat. 128, 12 U.S. Code §§ 1461 to 1468

April 27, 1934, Ch. 168, 48 Stat. 643, 12 U.S. Code §§ 347, 355, 394, 1020c, 1430, 1463, 1463a, 1463b, 1464, 1465, 1467, 1468

June 27, 1934, Ch. 847, 48 Stat. 1263, 12 U.S. Code § 1463

May 28, 1935, Ch. 150, 49 Stat. 296, 12 U.S. Code §§ 1462 to 1465, 1467

Aug. 10, 1939, Ch. 666, 53 Stat. 1402, 12 U.S. Code § 1464

Aug. 11, 1939, Ch. 684, 53 Stat. 1403, 12 U.S. Code § 1463

Oct. 24, 1942, Ch. 621, 56 Stat. 1463., 12 U.S. Code § 1463

Aug. 6, 1947, Ch. 503, 61 Stat. 786, 12 U.S. Code § 1464

July 3, 1948, Ch. 825, 62 Stat. 1239, 12 U.S. Code § 1464

Oct. 20, 1951, Ch. 521, 65 Stat. 490, 12 U.S. Code § 1464

July 14, 1952, Ch. 723, 66 Stat. 604, 12 U.S. Code §§ 1464, 1466

June 30, 1953, Ch. 170, 67 Stat. 126, 12 U.S. Code § 1463 nt.

Aug. 2, 1954, Ch. 649, 68 Stat. 622, 12 U.S. Code § 1464

Aug. 7, 1956, Ch. 1029, 70 Stat. 1114, 12 U.S. Code § 1464

Aug. 11, 1956, Ch. 783, 70 Stat. 641, 12 U.S. Code § 1464

Sept. 2, 1958, P.L. 85-857, 72 Stat. 1264, 12 U.S. Code § 1464

June 25, 1959, P.L. 86-70, 73 Stat. 142, 12 U.S. Code § 1466

Sept. 23, 1959, P.L. 86-372, 73 Stat. 687, 12 U.S. Code § 1464

June 11, 1960, P.L. 86-507, 74 Stat. 200, 12 U.S. Code § 1464

July 12, 1960, P.L. 86-624, 74 Stat. 411, 12 U.S. Code § 1466

June 30, 1961, P.L. 87-70, 75 Stat. 189, 12 U.S. Code § 1464

Oct. 9, 1962, P.L. 87-779, 76 Stat. 778, 12 U.S. Code § 1464

Oct. 16, 1962, P.L. 87-834, 76 Stat. 984, 12 U.S. Code § 1464

Sept. 2, 1964, P.L. 88-560, 78 Stat. 804, 12 U.S. Code § 1464

Aug. 10, 1965, P.L. 89-117, 79 Stat. 465, 12 U.S. Code § 1464

Oct. 16, 1966, P.L. 89-695, 80 Stat. 1028, 12 U.S. Code § 1464

Aug. 1, 1968, P.L. 90-448, 82 Stat. 508, 12 U.S. Code § 1464

Sept. 21, 1968, P.L. 90-505, 82 Stat. 858, 12 U.S. Code § 1464

Oct. 16, 1968, P.L. 90-575, 82 Stat. 1026, 12 U.S. Code § 1464

Dec. 24, 1969, P.L. 91-152, 83 Stat. 401, 12 U.S. Code § 1464

July 24, 1970, P.L. 91-351, 84 Stat. 462, 12 U.S. Code § 1464

Dec. 31, 1970, P.L. 91-609, 84 Stat. 1803, 12 U.S. Code §§ 1464, 1466a

Aug. 16, 1973, P.L. 93-100, 87 Stat. 343, 12 U.S. Code § 1464

July 25, 1975, P.L. 94-60, 89 Stat. 301, 12 U.S. Code § 1464

Sept. 20, 1977, P.L. 95-109, 15 U.S. Code § 1692l

Oct. 12, 1977, P.L. 95-128, 12 U.S. Code § 1464

Oct. 28, 1977, P.L. 95-147, 12 U.S. Code § 1464

Nov. 10, 1978, P.L. 95-630, 12 U.S. Code §§ 1462, 1464

Dec. 21, 1979, P.L. 96-153, 12 U.S. Code §§ 1464

Dec. 28, 1979, P.L. 96-161, 12 U.S. Code § 1464

March 31, 1980, P.L. 96-221, 12 U.S. Code § 1464

Oct. 15, 1982, P.L. 97-320, 12 U.S. Code §§ 1462, 1464

Jan. 12, 1983, P.L. 97-457, 12 U.S. Code §§ 1464, 1464 nt.

Oct. 3, 1984, P.L. 98-440, 98 Stat. 1691, 12 U.S. Code § 1464

Oct. 27, 1986, P.L. 99-570, 12 U.S. Code § 1464

Continued

Aug. 10, 1987, P.L. 100-86, 12 U.S. Code §§ 1464, 1467, 1467a, 1468

Aug. 9, 1989, P.L. 101-73, 12 U.S. Code § 1461 et seq.

Dec. 19, 1991, P.L. 102-242, 12 U.S. Code §§ 1441a, 1464, 1467, 1467a

July 1, 1992, P.L. 102-310, 12 U.S. Code § 1464

Oct. 28, 1992, P.L. 102-550, 12 U.S. Code § 1464, 1467a

Sept. 23, 1994, P.L. 103-325, 12 U.S. Code §§ 1462a, 1464, 1468

Sept. 29, 1994, P.L. 103-328, 12 U.S. Code § 1462a

Sept. 23, 1996, P.L. 104-201, 12 U.S. Code § 1467a

Sept. 30, 1996, P.L. 104-208, 12 U.S. Code §§ 1464, 1467a

March 20, 1998, P.L. 105-164, 12 U.S. Code § 1464

Home Ownership and Equity Protection Act of 1994

Sept. 23, 1994, P.L. 103-325, 15 U.S. Code § 1601 nt.

Home Ownership Made Easy Act

Ill. Rev. Stat. 1991, Ch. 67 1/2, § 1101 et seq.

Home Port Act

Aug. 6, 1981, P.L. 97-31, 95 Stat. 155, 46 U.S. Code § 18

Home Protection Bill of Rights

Cal. Penal Code § 198.5

Home Protection Company Act

Va. Code 1950, § 38.2-2600 et seq.

Home Purchase Act (Veterans)

Miss. Code Ann. 1972, § 35-7-1 et seq.

Home Purchase Assistance Fund Act

D.C. Code Ann., § 45-2201 et seq.

Home Purchase Assistance Program

Cal. Health and Safety Code § 51341 et seq.

Home Purchase Assistance Program (Roberti-Greene)

Cal. Health and Safety Code § 51341 et seq.

Home Repair Financing Act

Me. Rev. Stat. Ann. 1964, Title 9, § 3721 et seq.

N.J. Stat. Ann., 17:16C-62 et seq.

Home Repair Fraud Act

Ga. Code Ann., 16-9-120 et seq.

Ill. Rev. Stat. 1991, Ch. 121 1/2, § 1601 et seq.

Okla. Stat. Ann., Title 15, § 765.1 et seq.

Home Repair Sales Act (Door to Door)

N.J. Stat. Ann., 17:16C-95 et seq.

Home Repair, Weatherization and Shutoff Protection Act (Public Assistance)

Mich. Comp. Laws Ann., 400.1151 et seq.

Home Rule Act

Ark. Code Ann. 1987, 14-43-602 et seq.

Colo. Rev. Stat., 31-2-201 et seq.

Conn. Gen. Stat. Ann., § 7-187 et seq.

D.C. Code Ann., § 1-201 et seq.

Del. Code of 1974, Title 22, § 801 et seq.

Ga. Code Ann., 36-35-1 et seq.

Iowa Code Ann., 561.1 et seq.

Ky. Rev. Stat. 1971, 83.410 et seq.

Md. Ann. Code 1957, Art. 23A, § 9 et seq.

Me. Rev. Stat. Ann. 1964, Title 30, § 1911 et seq.

Mich. Comp. Laws Ann., 45.501 et seq., 78.1 et seq., 117.1 et seq.

N.D. Cent. Code, 40-05.1-01 et seq.

N.J. Stat. Ann., 40A:2-1 et seq.

N.Y. General City Law (Consol. Laws Ch. 21) § 19 et seq.

N.Y. Municipal Home Rule Law (Consol. Laws Ch. 36A) § 1 et seq.

Ore. Rev. Stat., 221.410 et seq.

Pa. Purdon's Stat., Title 53, § 13101 et seq.

S.C. Code Ann. 1976, §§ 4-9-10 et seq., 5-5-10 et seq.

Tex. Rev. Civ. Stat., Art. 1165 et seq.

Wis. Stat. Ann., 59.001 et seq.

W. Va. Code 1966, § 8-1-1 et seq.

Home Rule Amendment

Mass. Const. 1780, Amendments Art. 8

N.Y. Const., 1894 as amended 1938, Art. 9 § 2

Pa. Const. 1968, Art. 9, § 2

Home Rule Amendment (Cities)
Tex. Const. 1876, Art. 11, § 5

Home Rule Charter Act
Mass. Acts 1991, Ch. 480

Home Rule Charter and Optional Plans Law
Pa. Cons. Stat., Title 53, § 2901 et seq.
Pa. Purdon's Stat., Title 53, § 1-101 et seq.

Home Rule Cigarette Tax Restriction Act
Ill. Comp. Stat. 1992, Ch. 35, § 140/1
Ill. Rev. Stat. 1991, Ch. 120, §§ 453.110, 453.111

Home Rule Cities Act
Mich. Comp. Laws Ann., 117.1 et seq.

Home Rule Cities Taxation Act
Mich. Comp. Laws Ann., 117.3, 117.5

Home Rule County Service Occupation Tax Act
Ill. Rev. Stat. 1987, Ch. 34, § 303a-2

Home Rule County Use Tax Act
Ill. Rev. Stat. 1987, Ch. 34, § 303a-3

Home Rule County Validation Act
N.M. Stat. Ann., 4-37-10 et seq.

Home Rule-Municipal Charters Act
N.H. Rev. Stat. 1955, 49-B:1 et seq.

Home Rule Municipal Retailers' Occupation Tax Act
Ill. Rev. Stat. 1991, Ch. 24, § 8-11-1

Home Rule Municipal Service Occupation Tax Act
Ill. Comp. Stat. 1992, Ch. 65, § 5/8-11-5

Home Rule Municipal Use Tax Act
Ill. Rev. Stat. 1991, Ch. 24, § 8-11-6

Home Rule Powers Act (County)
Colo. Rev. Stat., 30-35-101 et seq.

Home Rule Powers Act (Municipal)
Fla. Stat. 1983, 166.011 et seq.

Home Rule Procedure Act
Mass. Gen. Laws Ann., 43B:1 et seq.

Home Rule Tax Act
Pa. 1947 Pamph. Laws 1145, No. 481

Home Schooling Act
Colo. Rev. Stat., 22-33-104.5

Home Service Contracts Act
Me. Rev. Stat. Ann. 1964, Title 32, § 13221 et seq.

Home Solicitation and Referral Sales Act
Ariz. Rev. Stat. Ann., § 44-5001 et seq.

Home Solicitation of Aged Persons Act
La. Rev. Stat. Ann., 9:3541.21, 9:3541.22

Home Solicitation Sales Act
Conn. Gen. Stat. Ann., § 42-134a et seq.
Del. Code of 1974, Title 6, § 4401 et seq.
Ga. Code Ann., 10-1-1 et seq.
Md. Ann. Code 1974, Art. CL, § 14-301 et seq.
N.D. Cent. Code, 51-18-01 et seq.
N.Y. Personal Property Law (Consol. Laws Ch. 41) § 425 et seq.
R.I. Gen. Laws 1956, 6-28-1 et seq.
Tenn. Code Ann., 47-18-701
Tex. Rev. Civ. Stat. 1974, Art. 5069-13.01 et seq.
Va. Code 1950, § 59.1-21.1 et seq.
Wash. Rev. Code Ann., 63.14.154

Home Taxation Act (Manufactured)
N.J. Stat. Ann., 54:4-1.2 et seq.

Home Teacher Act
Cal. Education Code 1976, §§ 51800 et seq., 10100 et seq.

Home Warranty Act (New)
La. Rev. Stat. Ann., 9:2789.1 et seq.

Home Weatherization Act (Low Income Household)
Mich. Comp. Laws Ann., 400.1051 et seq.

Home Winterization Act (Emergency)
N.M. Laws 1977, Ch. 212

Home Work Act (Industrial)
Ill. Rev. Stat. 1991, Ch. 48, § 250.9 et seq.

Homebuilders Registration Act
Ark. Code Ann. 1987, 17-47-101 et seq.

Homebuyers Protection Act
Fla. Stat. Ann., 489.126, 489.1265

Homeless and Housing Bond Act
Cal. Health and Safety Code § 53150 et seq., 53180 et seq.

Homeless and Runaway Youth Act
N.Y. Executive Law 1951 (Consol. Laws Ch. 18) § 532 et seq.

Homeless and Runaway Youth Law
La. Rev. Stat. Ann., 46:1351 et seq.

Homeless Children Act (Education for)
Ill. Comp. Stat. 1992, Ch. 105, § 45/1-1

Homeless Children's Assistance Act of 1992
Oct. 24, 1992, P.L. 102-512, 42 U.S. Code § 1771 nt.

Homeless Eligibility Clarification Act
Oct. 27, 1986, P.L. 99-570, 7 U.S. Code 2011 nt.
Sept. 19, 1988, P.L. 100-435, 7 U.S. Code § 2012 nt.
Nov. 28, 1990, P.L. 101-624, 7 U.S. Code § 2012 nt.
Dec. 13, 1991, P.L. 102-237, 7 U.S. Code § 2012 nt.

Homeless Emergency Lease Program Act (California)
Cal. Government Code § 14670.25

Homeless Families Assistance Act
Haw. Rev. Stat. Ann., § 358D-1 et seq.

Homeless Family Placement Act
Ill. Comp. Stat. 1992, Ch. 310, § 85/1 et seq.

Homeless Housing Act of 1986
Oct. 18, 1986, P.L. 99-500, 100 Stat. 1783-242
Oct. 30, 1986, P.L. 99-591, 100 Stat. 3341-242
Dec. 22, 1987, P.L. 100-202, 101 Stat. 1329-433

Homeless Housing and Assistance Program
N.Y. Social Services Law (Consol. Laws Ch. 55) § 41 et seq.
N.Y. State Finance Law 1940 (Consol. Laws Ch. 56) § 921

Homeless Persons' Eye Care Program
Wash. Laws 1993, Ch. 96

Homeless Prevention Act
Ill. Rev. Stat. 1991, Ch. 67 1/2, § 1301 et seq.
Okla. Stat. Ann., Title 74, § 2900 et seq.

Homeless Relief Project
La. Rev. Stat. Ann., 46:581 et seq.

Homeless Shelter Assistance Trust Fund Act
Neb. Laws 1992, L.B. 1192, §§ 1 to 8

Homeless Veterans Comprehensive Service Programs Act of 1992
Nov. 4, 1992, P.L. 102-590, 38 U.S. Code § 101 nt.
Nov. 2, 1994, P.L. 103-446, 38 U.S. Code § 7721 nt.
Feb. 13, 1996, P.L. 104-110, 38 U.S. Code § 7721 nt.
Nov. 21, 1997, P.L. 105-114, 38 U.S. Code § 7721 nt.

Homeless Youth Act
Cal. Welfare and Institutions Code § 13700 et seq.
N.Y. Executive Law 1951 (Consol. Laws Ch. 18) § 532 et seq.

Homelessness Act (Prevention of)
N.J. Stat. Ann., 52:27D-280 et seq.

Homemaker Emergency Loan Act
Cal. Unemployment Insurance Code § 16000 et seq.

Homemaker Services Act
N.H. Rev. Stat. 1955, 161-F:58 et seq.

Homemakers Act (Displaced)
La. Rev. Stat. Ann., 46:1991 et seq.

Homeowner Protection Act
Ga. Code Ann., 8-3-340 et seq.

Homeowners and Renters Property Tax Assistance Law
Cal. Revenue and Taxation Code § 20501 et seq.

Homeowners Association Act
Md. Ann. Code 1974, Art. RP, § 11B-101 et seq.

Homeowners Income Security Act (Senior Citizens)
N.J. Stat. Ann., 46:10B-16 et seq.

Homeowners Property Tax Exemption Act
Cal. Const. Art. 13, § 3
Cal. Revenue and Taxation Code §§ 218, 218.5, 251 et seq.

Homeowners Property Tax Relief Act
Wash. Rev. Code Ann., 84.09.080, 84.33.040, 84.33.077, 84.33.078, 84.36.473, 84.36.475, 84.36.477, 84.40.405, 84.52.015, 84.55.005, 84.55.090

Homeowners Protection Act of 1998
July 29, 1998, P.L. 105-216, 12 U.S. Code § 4901 nt.

Homeowners Warranty Rights Act
Ga. Code Ann., 10-1-910 et seq.

Homeownership and Opportunity Through HOPE Act
Nov. 28, 1990, P.L. 101-625, 42 U.S. Code §§ 1437aa nt., 1437aaa nt., 12871 to 12880, 12891 to 12898

Homeownership Opportunity Act of 1979
Dec. 21, 1979, P.L. 96-153, 12 U.S. Code §§ 1701 nt., 1715z-10

Homes and Parks Law (Mobile)
Iowa Code Ann., 435.1 et seq.

Homes Commission Act, 1920
Haw. Constitution, 1959, Amended 1978

Homes for Disabled Persons Location Act
Tex. Human Resources Code, § 123.001 et seq.

Homes for the Aged Act
Cal. Welfare and Institutions Code § 16200 et seq.
Colo. Rev. Stat. 1963, 133-1-1 et seq.
Mich. Comp. Laws 1979, 333.21301 et seq.
Vt. Stat. Ann., Title 18, § 2001 et seq.

Homes for the Aged, Nursing Homes, and Sheltered Care Homes Act
Ill. Rev. Stat. 1991, Ch. 111 1/2, § 4151-101 et seq.

Homesite Land Act (Counties)
Wash. Rev. Code 1976, 36.59.300 et seq.

Homestead Act
Ark. Code Ann. 1987, 28-39-202 et seq.
Cal. Civil Code § 1237 et seq.
Cal. Probate Code § 660 et seq.
Colo. Rev. Stat., 38-41-201 et seq.
Ida. Code 1947, 55-1001 et seq.
Kan. Stat. Ann., 60-2301 et seq.
Ky. Rev. Stat. 1971, 427.060 et seq.
Miss. Code Ann. 1972, § 85-3-21 et seq.
Mont. Code Ann., 70-32-101 et seq.
N.C. Gen. Stat. 1943, § 1C-1601 et seq.
Neb. Rev. Stat. 1943, 40-101 et seq.
Nev. Rev. Stat. 1979 Reprint, 115.010 et seq.
N.H. Rev. Stat. 1955, 480:1 et seq.
Ohio Rev. Code 1953, 2329.661 et seq.
Okla. Stat. Ann., Title 31, § 1 et seq.
P.R. Laws Ann. 1954, Title 31, § 1851 et seq.
S.C. Code Ann. 1976, § 15-41-10 et seq.
S.D. Codified Laws 1967, 43-31-1 et seq.
Tenn. Public Acts 1985, Ch. 281
Vt. Stat. Ann., Title 27, § 101 et seq.
Wis. Stat. Ann., 815.20, 815.21
W. Va. Code 1966, § 38-9-1 et seq.
Wyo. Stat. 1957, § 36-45 et seq.
Continued

Homestead Act (Probate)
Ida. Code 1947, 15-2-401 et seq.
Okla. Stat. Ann., Title 58, § 311 et seq.

Homestead Act (Taxation)
Okla. Stat. Ann., Title 68, § 2801 et seq.

Homestead Act (Veterans)
Fla. Stat. 1969, 253.351 et seq.

Homestead Acts
May 20, 1862, Ch. 75, 12 Stat. 392
March 3, 1891, Ch. 561, 26 Stat. 1097, 43
   U.S. Code §§ 161, 162, 165, 173, 174, 185,
   202, 235, 254, 261, 277
Feb. 8, 1908, Ch. 19, 35 Stat. 6

Homestead Allowance Act
Wyo. Stat. Ann., § 2-7-504

**Homestead and Building Loan Association
   Act**
Ill. Rev. Stat. 1991, Ch. 17, § 3601 et seq.
La. Rev. Stat. Ann., 6:721 et seq.

Homestead and Other Exemptions Act
S.C. Code Ann. 1976, § 15-41-10 et seq.

Homestead Associations Act
Alaska Comp. Laws Ann. 1949, § 47-2-53 et
   seq.
La. Rev. Stat. Ann., 41:541 et seq.
Md. Ann. Code 1974, Art. CA, § 6-222

Homestead Exemption Act
Ala. Code 1975, §§ 6-10-2, 6-10-3
Alaska Stat. 1962, § 09.38.010 et seq.
Ariz. Rev. Stat. Ann., § 33-1101 et seq.
Ark. Code Ann. 1987, 16-66-210 et seq.
Ark. Code Ann. 1987, 28-39-202 et seq.
Cal. Civil Code § 1240 et seq.
Fla. Stat. 1967, 192.12
Fla. Stat. 1983, 222.01 et seq.
Ga. Code Ann., 44-13-1 et seq.
Ill. Rev. Stat. 1991, Ch. 110, § 12-901 et seq.
Iowa Code Ann., 561.1 et seq.
Kan. Stat. Ann., 60-2301 et seq.
La. Rev. Stat. Ann., 20:1 et seq.
Mass. Gen. Laws Ann., 188:1 et seq.
Mich. Comp. Laws Ann., 600.6023 et seq.

Minn. Stat. Ann., 510.01 et seq.
Miss. Code Ann. 1972, § 27-33-1 et seq.
Mo. Rev. Stat., 513.475 et seq.
N.D. Cent. Code, 30-16-01 et seq., 47-18-01
   et seq.
Neb. Rev. Stat. 1943, 77-3501 et seq.
Ore. Rev. Stat., 23.240 et seq.
S.C. Code Ann. 1976, § 15-41-10 et seq.
S.D. Codified Laws 1967, 43-31-1 et seq.
Tenn. Code Ann., 26-2-301 et seq.
Tex. Property Code, § 41.001 et seq.
Utah Code Ann. 1953, 78-23-3 et seq.
Va. Code 1950, § 34-4 et seq.
Wash. Rev. Code Ann., 6.13.010 et seq.
Wyo. Stat. Ann., § 1-20-101 et seq.

Homestead Exemption Act (Spouse)
Ala. Code 1975, § 6-10-60 et seq.

Homestead Exemption Act (Taxes)
Ala. Code 1975, § 40-9-19
Haw. Rev. Stat. Ann., § 246-27 et seq.

Homestead Option Sales and Use Tax Act
Ga. Code Ann., 48-8-100 to 48-8-109

Homestead Preservation Act
Mo. Rev. Stat., 137.102

Homestead Property Exclusion Program Act
Pa. Cons. Stat., Title 53, § 8581 et seq.

Homestead Property Tax Act
N.J. Stat. Ann., 54:4-8.57 et seq.

Homestead Property Tax Deferral Act
Fla. Stat. Ann., 197.242

Homestead Property Tax Refund Act
Kan. Stat. Ann., 79-4501 et seq.

Homestead Protection Act (Farm)
Neb. Rev. Stat. 1943, 76-1901 et seq.

Homestead Recording Act
Me. Rev. Stat. Ann. 1964, Title 14, § 4552

Homestead Settlement Act
Alaska Comp. Laws Ann. 1949, §§ 47-2-2,
   47-2-51 et seq.
Haw. Rev. Laws 1955, § 99-1 et seq.

Homestead Tax Credit Law
Iowa Code Ann., 425.1 et seq.

Homestead Tax Exemption Act (Veterans)
Mich. Comp. Laws Ann., 211.7b

Homestead Tax Relief Act
Kan. Stat. Ann., 79-4501 et seq.
Mont. Laws 1977, Ch. 457
N.J. Stat. Ann., 54A:3A-1 et seq.

Homesteaders' Relief Act
May 21, 1934, Ch. 320, 48 Stat. 787, 43 U.S.
Code § 237b

Homesteading Act (Urban)
N.J. Stat. Ann., 40A:12-31 et seq.

Homework Act
Cal. Labor Code § 2650 et seq.
N.J. Stat. Ann., 34:6-120 et seq.

Homicide Act
Ala. Code 1975, § 6-5-410
Cal. Penal Code § 187 et seq.
Colo. Rev. Stat., 18-3-101 et seq.
Ga. Code Ann., 16-5-1 et seq.
Kan. Stat. Ann., 21-3401 et seq.
N.Y. Penal Law 1965 (Consol. Laws Ch. 40)
§ 125.00 et seq.
Wash. Rev. Code Ann., 9A.32.010 et seq.

Homicide Act (Minors)
Ala. Code 1975, § 6-5-391

Homicide Act (Motor Vehicles)
See Motor Vehicle Homicide Act

Homicide Act (Negligent)
Wyo. Stat. Ann., § 6-2-106

Homicide Act (Vehicular)
N.Y. Penal Law 1965 (Consol. Laws Ch. 40)
§§ 125.10, 125.15 Subd. 1

Homicide Excuse Act
Wash. Rev. Code Ann., 9A.16.030

Homotransplantation Act
Va. Code 1950, § 32-31.9 et seq.

Honest Label Dog Food Law
Mo. Rev. Stat. 1959, 273.190 et seq.

Honest Mistake Act (Libel)
Okla. Stat. Ann., Title 12, § 1446a

Honey Act
Wash. Rev. Code Ann., 69.28.020 et seq.

Honey Certification and Honeybee Law
Fla. Stat. Ann., 586.01 et seq.

Honey Industry Act
Ida. Code 1947, 22-2801 et seq.

Honey Lake Valley Groundwater Basin Act
Cal. Water Code, Appendix § 129-101 et seq.

Honey Promotion Act
N.D. Cent. Code, 4-12.1-01 et seq.

Honey Research, Promotion, and Consumer Information Act
Oct. 30, 1984, P.L. 98-590, 7 U.S. Code §§ 4601 to 4612
Nov. 28, 1990, P.L. 101-624, 7 U.S. Code §§ 4602, 4606, 4608, 4610a, 4612
Dec. 13, 1991, P.L. 102-237, 7 U.S. Code §§ 4608, 4610a
April 4, 1996, P.L. 104-127, 7 U.S. Code § 4608
June 23, 1998, P.L. 105-185, 7 U.S. Code §§ 4601 to 4613
Oct. 21, 1998, P.L. 105-277, 7 U.S. Code § 4606

Honey Research, Promotion, and Consumer Information Act Amendments of 1990
Nov. 28, 1990, P.L. 101-624, 7 U.S. Code §§ 4601 nt., 4603 nt.

Honey Standardization Law
Cal. Food and Agricultural Code 1967, § 29401 et seq.

Honeybee Act
Aug. 31, 1922, Ch. 301, 42 Stat. 833, 7 U.S. Code §§ 281, 282
July 19, 1962, P.L. 87-539, 76 Stat. 169, 7 U.S. Code § 281
Dec. 8, 1993, P.L. 103-182, 7 U.S. Code § 281
Continued

Dec. 8, 1994, P.L. 103-465, 7 U.S. Code
§ 281
Fla. Stat. 1983, 586.01 et seq.

Hood Act (Intoxicating Liquor)
La. Acts 1921, Extra Session, No. 39

Hood Bay Land Exchange Act of 1997
Oct. 10, 1997, P.L. 105-60, 16 U.S. Code
§§ 431 nt., 1132 nt.

Hoods and Masks Act
Okla. Stat. Ann., Title 21, § 1301 et seq.

Hoopa Valley Reservation South Boundary Adjustment Act
Nov. 13, 1997, P.L. 105-79, 25 U.S. Code
§ 1300i-1
Oct. 14, 1998, P.L. 105-256, 25 U.S. Code
§ 1300i-1 nt.

Hoopa-Yorok Settlement Act
Oct. 31, 1988, P.L. 100-580, 25 U.S. Code
§ 407, prec. 1300i, 1300i
May 24, 1990, P.L. 101-301, 25 U.S. Code
§ 407, 1300i-4

Hoosic River Loan Act
Mass. Acts 1950, Ch. 649

Hoover Power Plant Act of 1984
Aug. 17, 1984, P.L. 98-381, 16 U.S. Code
§ 839b; 42 U.S. Code §§ 4133 nt., 7274,
7275; 43 U.S. Code §§ 617 nt., 617a, 617b,
618, 618a, 618e, 618k, 619, 619 nt., 619a,
619b, 1543
Oct. 24, 1992, P.L. 102-486, 42 U.S. Code
§§ 7275, 7276 to 7276c

Hop Industry Act
Ida. Code 1947, 22-3101 et seq.

Hop Marketing Act
See Agricultural Adjustment Act

Hopewell Mobile Home Law
N.Y. Local Laws 1971, Town of Hopewell,
p. 2373

Horizontal Property Act
See Condominium Act

Horizontal Property Amendment Act of 1975
D.C. Code Ann., §§ 45-1702, 45-1704,
45-1706, 45-1711, 45-1713 to 45-1716,
45-1721, 45-1722

Horizontal Property Regime Regulation Extention Act
D.C. Laws 1975, Nos. 1-10

Horizontal Property Regimes Act
Alaska Stat. 1962, § 34.07.010 et seq.
Wash. Rev. Code Ann., 64.32.010 et seq.

Horn of Africa Recovery and Food Security Act
April 21, 1992, P.L. 102-274, 22 U.S. Code
§ 2151 nt.

Horn Statute (Motor Vehicles)
Ky. Rev. Stat. 1971, 189.340

Hornell City Court Act
N.Y. Laws 1932, Ch. 434

Horologists Certification Act
Mich. Comp. Laws Ann., 338.1401 et seq.

Horse and Dog Lien Act
S.C. Code Ann. 1976, § 29-15-60

Horse and Dog Racing Act
Vt. Stat. Ann., Title 31, § 601 et seq.

Horse and Dog Racing Act (Simulcast Wagering)
Mass. Gen. Laws Ann., 128C:1 et seq.

Horse and Dummy Act
Ill. Rev. Stat. 1985, Ch. 131 1/4, § 0.01 et
seq.

Horse Control Law
N.Y. Local Laws 1969, Town of Pound
Ridge, p. 1989

Horse Development Board Act
Colo. Rev. Stat., 35-57.8-101 et seq.

Horse Meat Act
Cal. Food and Agricultural Code 1967,
§ 19200 et seq.
Cal. Health and Safety Code § 28000

D.C. Code Ann., § 33-401 et seq.
Ill. Rev. Stat. 1991, Ch. 56 1/2, § 240 et seq.
Ohio Rev. Code 1953, 919.01 et seq.

Horse Mutilation Act
Ill. Rev. Stat. 1991, Ch. 8, §§ 108m, 109

Horse Park and Agriculture Center Act
Fla. Stat. Ann., 570.952

Horse Protection Act of 1970
Dec. 9, 1970, P.L. 91-540, 15 U.S. Code
§§ 1821 to 1831
Dec. 21, 1995, P.L. 104-66, 15 U.S. Code
§ 1830

Horse Quarantine Act
Mich. Comp. Laws Ann., 287.101 et seq.

Horse Race Admissions Tax Law
N.Y. Laws 1926, Ch. 440, § 13a

Horse Racing Act
Ariz. Rev. Stat. Ann., § 5-101 et seq.
Ark. Code Ann. 1987, 23-110-101 et seq.
Cal. Business and Professions Code § 19400
et seq.
Fla. Stat. 1983, 550.011 et seq.
Ida. Code 1947, 54-2501 et seq.
Ill. Rev. Stat. 1991, Ch. 8, § 37-1 et seq.
Ind. Code 1976, 35-21-2-1 et seq.
Ky. Rev. Stat. 1971, 230.210 et seq.
La. Acts 1908, No. 57
Md. Ann. Code 1974, Art. BR, § 11-1101 et
seq.
Me. Rev. Stat. Ann. 1964, Title 8, §§ 261 et
seq., 321 et seq.
Mich. Comp. Laws Ann., 431.31 et seq.
Nev. Rev. Stat. 1979 Reprint, 466.010 et seq.
N.H. Rev. Stat. 1955, 284:1 et seq.
N.J. Stat. Ann., 5:5-22 et seq.
N.M. Stat. Ann., 60-1-1 et seq.
N.Y. Laws 1895, Ch. 570
N.Y. Laws 1926, Ch. 440
Ohio Rev. Code 1953, 3769.01 et seq.
Okla. Stat. Ann., Title 3A, § 200 et seq.
Pa. Purdon's Stat., Title 15, § 2651 et seq.
R.I. Gen. Laws 1956, 41-3-1 et seq.
Utah Code Ann. 1953, 4-38-1
Vt. Stat. Ann., Title 31, § 601 et seq.

Wash. Rev. Code Ann., 67.16.010 et seq.

Horse Racing Commission Act
Mont. Code Ann., 23-4-101 et seq.

Horse Racing Facility Bond Act
Neb. Rev. Stat. 1943, 23-389 et seq.

Horse Racing Facility Bond Act (County)
Neb. Rev. Stat. 1943, 23-389 et seq.

Horse Racing False Entries Act
Ill. Rev. Stat. 1991, Ch. 8, § 33.90 et seq.

Horse Racing Industry and Sport Act
P.R. Laws Ann. 1954, Title 15, § 198 et seq.

**Horse Racing Injury Compensation Board
Act**
N.J. Stat. Ann., 34:15-129 et seq.

Horse Racing Redevelopment Act
Del. Laws, Vol. 69, Ch. 446

Horse Regulation Act
Utah Code Ann. 1953, 4-38-1 et seq.

**Horse Theft Prevention and Investigation
Act**
Tex. Agriculture Code, § 151.001 et seq.

Horseheads Mass Gathering Law
N.Y. Local Laws 1972, Town of Horseheads,
p. 1869

Horseheads Mobile Home Law
N.Y. Local Laws 1968, Town of Horseheads,
p. 2603

Horsemeat and Pet Food Act
Cal. Food and Agricultural Code 1967,
§ 19200 et seq.

Horsemen Injury Compensation Fund Act
La. Rev. Stat. Ann., 4:250 et seq.

Horseneck Beach Reservation Act
Mass. Acts 1955, Ch. 583

Horseshoeing Act
Ill. Rev. Stat. 1991, Ch. 82, § 200 et seq.
Mich. Public Acts 1899, No. 229

Horseshoeing Lien Act
Mich. Comp. Laws Ann., 570.351 et seq.

Horseshoers' Lien Act
Ill. Rev. Stat. 1991, Ch. 82, § 200 et seq.

Horticultural and Quarantine Act
Ore. Rev. Stat., 570.005 et seq.

Horticultural Industry Law
Iowa Code Ann., 159.1 et seq.

Horticultural Pests and Diseases Act
Wash. Rev. Code Ann., 15.08.010 et seq.

Horticultural Protection District Act
Cal. Statutes 1935, p. 2123

Horticulture Growing Media Act
N.H. Rev. Stat. 1955, 433-A:1 et seq.

Horton Act (Gasoline Tax)
Mich. Comp. Laws 1948, 207.119 et seq.

Horton Act (Hunting on Private Property)
Mich. Comp. Laws Ann., 317.161 et seq.

Hospice Law
Ga. Code Ann., 31-7-170 et seq.
Miss. Code Ann. 1972, § 41-85-1 et seq.

Hospice Licensing Act
Ill. Rev. Stat. 1991, Ch. 111 1/2, § 6101 et
seq.
La. Rev. Stat. Ann., 40:2181 et seq.
N.C. Gen. Stat. 1943, § 131E-200 et seq.
Okla. Stat. Ann., Title 63, § 1-860.1 et seq.
S.C. Code Ann. 1976, § 44-71-10 et seq.
W. Va. Code 1966 § 16-5I-1 et seq.

Hospice Licensure Act
Neb. Rev. Stat. 1943, 71-7801 to 71-7806

Hospital Act (Indigent Hawaiians)
Haw. Session Laws 1858-59, p. 433, April
20, 1859

Hospital Act (State Charity)
Miss. Code Ann. 1972, § 41-11-1 et seq.

Hospital Act (Welfare)
Mich. Comp. Laws 1948, 404.100 et seq.

Hospital Act for Mentally Diseased Persons
Mich. Comp. Laws Ann., 330.11 et seq.

Hospital Acts
Alaska Stat. 1962, § 18.20.010 et seq.
Fla. Special Laws 1949, Ch. 25728
Fla. Stat. Ann., 395.102
Ill. Rev. Stat. 1985, Ch. 24, § 11-22-1 et seq.
Ill. Rev. Stat. 1989, Ch. 139, § 160.5h et seq.
Ill. Rev. Stat. 1991, Ch. 23, § 1370 et seq.
Ill. Rev. Stat. 1991, Ch. 139, § 160.01 et seq.
Ind. Code Ann., 16-12.1-1-1 et seq.
Md. Ann. Code 1974, Art. HG, § 19-301 et
seq.
Mich. Comp. Laws Ann., 331.1 et seq.,
331.151 et seq., 331.251 et seq.
Minn. Stat. Ann., 261.21 et seq.
Mo. Rev. Stat., 205.160 et seq.
N.C. Gen. Stat. 1943, §§ 131-28.1 et seq.,
131E-5 et seq.
Ohio Rev. Code 1953, 339.01 et seq.
Tenn. Code Ann., 68-11-101 et seq.
Tex. Health and Safety Code § 263.001 et
seq.
Wyo. Stat. Ann., § 18-8-101 et seq.

Hospital Adolescent Treatment Act
N.M. Stat. Ann., 23-9-1 et seq.

**Hospital and County Health Care Act
(Indigent)**
N.M. Stat. Ann., 27-5-1 et seq.

**Hospital and Emergency Medical Services
Act (Rural Primary Care)**
Okla. Stat. Ann., Title 63, § 1-706.1 et seq.

Hospital and Health Facility Licensing Act
Ind. Code Ann., 16-10-1-1 et seq.

**Hospital and Medical Care Act (State
Employees)**
Cal. Government Code § 22751 et seq.

Hospital and Medical Facilities Amendments of 1964

Aug. 18, 1964, P.L. 88-443, 78 Stat. 447, 42 U.S. Code §§ 247c 291 to 291o

June 30, 1970, P.L. 91-296, 84 Stat. 343, 42 U.S. Code § 291 nt.

Hospital and Medical Facilities Construction and Modernization Assistance Amendments of 1968

Oct. 15, 1968, P.L. 90-574, 82 Stat. 1011, 42 U.S. Code §§ 291a, 291b

Hospital and Medical Facilities Survey and Construction Act

Alaska Stat. 1962, § 18.20.140 et seq.

Haw. Rev. Stat. Ann., § 323-11 et seq.

Kan. Stat. Ann., 65-410 et seq.

N.M. Stat. Ann. 1953, 12-5-1 et seq.

Vt. Stat. Ann., Title 18, § 1801 et seq.

Wash. Rev. Code Ann., 70.40.005 et seq.

Wyo. Stat. Ann., § 35-2-301 et seq.

Hospital and Medical Malpractice Joint Underwriting Association Act

Me. Rev. Stat. Ann. 1964, Title 24, § 2401 et seq.

Hospital and Medical Nursing and Convalescent Home Act Citrus County (First Amendment)

Fla. Special Laws 1970, Ch. 70-1001

Hospital and Medical Services Utilization Review Act

Okla. Stat. Ann., Title 36, § 6551 et seq.

Hospital and Physicians Mutual Insurance Association Act

Neb. Rev. Stat. 1943, 44-2901 et seq.

Hospital and Public Welfare Facilities Construction Act

P.R. Laws Ann. 1954, Title 24, § 332 et seq.

Hospital Authorities Acts

Fla. Special Laws 1947, Ch. 24551

Ga. Code Ann., 31-7-70 et seq.

Ind. Code Ann., 5-1-4-1 et seq.

Mich. Comp. Laws Ann., 331.1 et seq.

N.C. Gen. Stat. 1943, § 131E-15 et seq.

Neb. Rev. Stat. 1943, 23-343.74 et seq.

Tenn. Code Ann., 7-57-101 et seq.

Tex. Health and Safety Code, §§ 262.001 et seq., 264.001 et seq.

Va. Code 1950, § 32-212 et seq.

Hospital Authorities Assistance Act (Rural)

Ga. Code Ann., 31-7-94.1

Hospital Bond Act

Miss. Code Ann. 1972, § 41-13-19

Hospital Building Authority Act

Ga. Code Ann., 31-7-20 et seq.

Hospital Capacity Reduction Corporation Act

Mich. Comp. Laws Ann., 331.701 et seq.

Hospital Care Associations Act

Ore. Rev. Stat., 750.005 et seq.

Hospital Claims Act (Indigents)

N.M. Stat. Ann., 27-5-1 et seq.

Hospital Commission Act

Mich. Comp. Laws Ann., 330.11 et seq.

Hospital Construction Act

Haw. Rev. Stat. Ann., § 323-11 et seq.

Ill. Rev. Stat. 1991, Ch. 23, § 1301 et seq.

Hospital Construction and Franchising Act

S.C. Code Ann. 1976, § 44-7-110 et seq.

Hospital Construction Loan Act

Md. Laws 1964, Ch. 138, §§ 1 to 6

Hospital Consumer Information Act

Neb. Rev. Stat. 1943, 71-2062 et seq.

Hospital Conversions Act

R.I. Gen. Laws 1956, 23-17.14-1 et seq.

Hospital Cooperation Act

Me. Rev. Stat. Ann. 1964, Title 22, § 1881 et seq.

Tenn. Code Ann., 68-11-1301 et seq.

Hospital Cost Containment Act
Cal. Health and Safety Code §§ 436.4, 436.490 to 436.492, 443.22, 15047.5, 15049.5, 15057, 15071
N.Y. Public Health Law 1953 (Consol. Laws Ch. 45) §§ 2803 Subd. 2, 2807 Subds. 2, 3
N.Y. Social Services Law (Consol. Laws Ch. 55) § 365a Subd. 2

Hospital Disclosure Act
Cal. Health and Safety Code § 440 et seq.

Hospital District Act
Ariz. Rev. Stat. Ann., § 48-1901 et seq.
Cal. Health and Safety Code § 32000 et seq.
Ill. Rev. Stat. 1991, Ch. 23, § 1251 et seq.
Mo. Rev. Stat., 206.010 et seq.
Mont. Code Ann., 7-34-2101 et seq.
N.C. Gen. Stat. 1943, § 131E-40 et seq.
Neb. Rev. Stat. 1943, 23-343.20 et seq.
N.M. Stat. Ann., 4-48A-1 et seq.
Okla. Stat. 1981 Title 19, § 1051 et seq.
Ore. Rev. Stat., 440.305 et seq.
S.D. Codified Laws 1967, 34-10-1 et seq.
Tex. Health and Safety Code, § 283.001 et seq.
Tex. Rev. Civ. Stat., Art. 4494o et seq.
Wash. Rev. Code Ann., 70.44.003 et seq.

Hospital District Immunity Act
Wash. Rev. Code Ann., 70.44.060, Subd. 8

Hospital District Revenue Bond Act (Marion County)
Fla. Special Laws 1971, Ch. 71-764

Hospital Divisions Act
Ark. Stat. 1947, 82-327 et seq.

Hospital Education Act (Community)
Fla. Stat. Ann., 381.001 et seq.

Hospital Efficiency and Cooperation Act
Colo. Rev. Stat., 24-32-2701 et seq.

Hospital Emergency Service Act
Ill. Rev. Stat. 1989, Ch. 111 1/2, § 85z et seq.

Hospital Equipment and Facilities Authority Act
Miss. Code Ann. 1972, § 41-73-1 et seq.

Hospital Equipment Financing Act
Tex. Health and Safety Code, § 224.001 et seq.

Hospital Equipment Financing Authority Act
Ga. Code Ann., 31-7-190 et seq.
Miss. Code Ann. 1972, § 41-73-1 et seq.
N.M. Stat. Ann., 58-23-1 et seq.

Hospital Facilities Acts
N.C. Gen. Stat. 1943, § 131E-1 et seq.
Okla. Stat. Ann., Title 17, § 111 et seq.

Hospital Facilities Finance Act
N.C. Gen. Stat. 1943, § 131-1 et seq.

Hospital Facility Seismic Safety Act (Alfred E. Alquist)
Cal. Health and Safety Code § 15000 et seq.

Hospital Finance Authority Act
Mich. Comp. Laws Ann., 331.31 et seq.
W. Va. Code 1966 § 16-29A-1 et seq.

Hospital Finance Corporation Act (John Dempsey)
Conn. Gen. Stat. Ann., § 10a-250 et seq.

Hospital Flexibility Act (Rural)
Miss. Code Ann. 1972, § 41-9-201 et seq.

Hospital Funding Act
N.M. Stat. Ann., 4-48B-1 et seq.

Hospital Gasoline Tax Act (Special County)
N.M. Stat. Ann., 7-24B-1 et seq.

Hospital Gross Receipts Tax Act (Local)
N.M. Stat. Ann., 7-20C-1 et seq.

Hospital Gross Receipts Tax Act (Special County)
N.M. Stat. Ann., 7-20-19 et seq.

Hospital Leasing Act (Township)
Ill. Rev. Stat. 1989, Ch. 139, § 160.28 et seq.

Hospital Levy Act
N.M. Stat. Ann. 1953, Superseded Vol., 14-33-7 et seq.

Hospital Liability Trust Act
Ida. Code 1947, 41-3701 et seq.

Hospital Licensing Act
Cal. Health and Safety Code § 1400 et seq.
Colo. Rev. Stat., 25-3-101 et seq.
Ill. Rev. Stat. 1991, Ch. 111 1/2, § 142 et seq.
Iowa Code Ann., 135B.1 et seq.
Kan. Stat. Ann., 65-425 et seq.
La. Rev. Stat. Ann., 40:2100 et seq.
Mich. Comp. Laws Ann., 333.21511 et seq.
Mo. Rev. Stat., 197.010 et seq.
Mont. Code Ann., 50-5-201 et seq.
N.C. Gen. Stat. 1943, § 131E-75 et seq.
N.H. Rev. Stat. 1955, 151:1 et seq.
Okla. Stat. Ann., Title 63, § 326.1 et seq.
P.R. Laws Ann. 1954, Title 24, § 10 et seq.
R.I. Gen. Laws 23-17-1 et seq.
S.C. Code Ann. 1976, § 44-7-310 et seq.
Tex. Health and Safety Code § 241.001 et seq.
Va. Code 1950, § 32-297 et seq.
Vt. Stat. Ann., Title 18, § 1901 et seq.
Wash. Rev. Code Ann., 70.41.005 et seq.
W. Va. Code 1966, § 16-5B-1 et seq.
Wyo. Stat. Ann., § 35-2-101 et seq.

Hospital Lien Act
Ala. Code 1975, § 35-11-370 et seq.
Conn. Gen. Stat. Ann., § 49-73
Del. Code of 1974, Title 25, § 4301 et seq.
Ga. Code Ann., 44-14-470 et seq.
Ill. Rev. Stat. 1991, Ch. 82, § 96.9 et seq.
Iowa Code Ann., 582.1 et seq.
Md. Ann. Code 1974, Art. CL, § 16-601 et seq.
Mont. Code Ann., 71-3-1111 et seq.
N.H. Rev. Stat. 1955, 448-A:1 et seq.
N.J. Stat. Ann., 2A:44-35 et seq.
N.Y. Lien Law (Consol. Laws Ch. 33) § 189
R.I. Gen. Laws 1956, 9-3-4 et seq.
Tenn. Code Ann., 29-22-101 et seq.
Tex. Property Code, § 55.001 et seq.

Hospital Liens for Money Due Act
D.C. Code 1973, § 38-301 et seq.

Hospital Loan Act (Cambridge)
Mass. Acts 1960, Ch. 292

Hospital Loan Act (Chelsea)
Mass. Acts 1958, Ch. 670

Hospital Loan Act (Plymouth County)
Mass. Acts 1939, Ch. 262

Hospital Malpractice Joint Underwriting Associations Act (Insurance Medical)
Me. Rev. Stat. Ann. 1964, Title 24, § 2401 et seq.

Hospital, Medical and Dental Service Corporation Law (Nonprofit)
Nev. Rev. Stat. 1979 Reprint, 695B.010 et seq.

Hospital, Medical and Dental Service Corporation Readable Insurance Certificate Act
N.C. Gen. Stat. 1943, § 58-66-1 et seq.

Hospital, Medical and Related Facility Survey and Construction Act
Mont. Rev. Code 1947, 69-5301 et seq.

Hospital-Medical Liability Act
Ida. Code 1947, 39-4201 et seq.
Neb. Rev. Stat. 1943, 44-2801 et seq.

Hospital Medical Liability Act (Malpractice Insurance)
Neb. Rev. Stat. 1943, 44-2801 et seq.

Hospital, Medical-Surgical, Dental and Health Service Corporation Act
Colo. Rev. Stat., 10-16-301 et seq.

Hospital Mortgage Loan Construction Law
N.Y. Public Health Law 1953 (Consol. Laws Ch. 45) § 2870 et seq.

Hospital Mutual Insurance Association Act
Neb. Rev. Stat. 1943, 44-2901 et seq.

Hospital Pharmacies Act
Ark. Code Ann. 1987, 17-91-601 et seq.

Hospital Plan Act (Nonprofit)
Pa. Cons. Stat., Title 40, § 6101 et seq.

Hospital Policy and Protocol for Organ and Tissue Donation
S.C. Code Ann. 1976, § 44-43-910 et seq.

Hospital Project Financing Act
Tex. Health and Safety Code, § 223.001 et seq.

Hospital Records Act
Ark. Code Ann. 1987, 16-46-301 et seq.

Hospital Records and Retention Act
La. Rev. Stat. Ann., 40:2144

Hospital Regulation Act
Ga. Code Ann., 31-7-1 et seq.

Hospital Regulation and Approval Act
Wis. Stat. Ann., 50.32 et seq.

Hospital Reimbursement Act
Ohio Rev. Code 1953, 3701.61 et seq.

Hospital Revenue Bond Act
S.C. Code Ann. 1976, § 44-7-1410 et seq.

Hospital Revenue Bond Act (Lakeland)
Fla. Special Laws 1970, Ch. 70-775

Hospital Sale Act (Nonprofit)
Neb. Rev. Stat. 1943, 71-20,102 to 71-20,113

Hospital Seismic Safety Act
Cal. Health and Safety Code § 15000 et seq.

Hospital Service Act
Mich. Comp. Laws Ann., 550.501 et seq.

Hospital Service Corporation Act
N.H. Rev. Stat. 1955, 419:1 et seq.
N.J. Stat. Ann., 17:48-1 et seq.
W. Va. Code 1966, § 33-24-1 et seq.

Hospital Service Corporation Act (Mutual Nonprofit)
Kan. Stat. Ann., 40-1801 et seq.

Hospital Service for the Indigent Act
Tenn. Code Ann., 14-22-101 et seq.

Hospital Service Nonprofit Corporation Act
Ga. Code Ann., 33-19-1 et seq.

Hospital Service Plan Law
S.D. Codified Laws 1967, 58-40-1 et seq.

Hospital Sinking Fund Act
Neb. Rev. Stat. 1943, 15-235.01 et seq.

Hospital Survey and Construction Act
Aug. 13, 1946, Ch. 958, 60 Stat. 1040, 24 U.S. Code § 219; 31 U.S. Code §§ 72, 583, 711; 33 U.S. Code § 763c; 42 U.S. Code §§ 2, 16, 98, 201 nts., 204 nt., 209, 214 nt., 222 nt., 230, 249 nt., 291, 291a to 291m; 46 U.S. Code § 654; 48 U.S. Code § 1011; 49 U.S. Code Appx. §§ 177, 181
Aug. 28, 1958, P.L. 85-791, 72 Stat. 950, 42 U.S. Code § 291j
Aug. 18, 1964, P.L. 88-443, 78 Stat. 447, 42 U.S. Code §§ 291 to 291o
Cal. Health and Safety Code § 430 et seq.
Conn. Gen. Stat. Ann., § 19a-34
Ida. Code 1947, 39-1401 et seq.
Iowa Code 1989, 135A.1 et seq.
Kan. Stat. Ann., 65-410 et seq.
Mass. Gen. Laws Ann., 111:55
Mich. Comp. Laws Ann., 331.501 et seq.
Mont. Code Ann. 1947, 69-5301 et seq.
Neb. Rev. Stat. 1943, 71-2001 et seq.
Nev. Rev. Stat. 1979 Reprint, 449.250 et seq.
N.H. Rev. Stat. 1955, 152:1 et seq.
N.M. Stat. Ann. 1953, 12-5-1 et seq.
Ore. Rev. Stat., 441.105 et seq.
Pa. 1947 Pamph. Laws 1335, No. 527
R.I. Gen. Laws 1956, 23-17-1 et seq.
S.D. Codified Laws 1967, 34-7-1 et seq.
Tenn. Code Ann., 68-11-202
Tex. Health and Safety Code, § 222.001 et seq.
Utah Code Ann. 1953, Miscellaneous Superseded Code Provisions, 26-11-1 et seq.

Utah Laws 1947, Ch. 52
Va. Code 1950, § 32-196 et seq.
Wash. Rev. Code Ann., 70.40.005 et seq.
Wis. Stat. 1981, 50.20 et seq.

Hospital Survey and Construction Amendments of 1949
Oct. 26, 1949, Ch. 722, 63 Stat. 898, 42 U.S. Code §§ 291, 291 nt., 291d 291f, 291g 291h, 291i, 291j, 291n
Dec. 31, 1970, P.L. 91-609, 84 Stat. 1776, 42 U.S. Code §§ 1453, 1456, 1458, 1460, 1465, 1471 and others

Hospital Treatment for Adolescents Act
N.M. Stat. Ann., 23-9-1 et seq.

Hospital Treatment for Drug Addicts
D.C. Code 1973, § 24-601 et seq.

Hospitality Act
Ky. Rev. Stat. 1971, 306.040

Hospitality and Visitor Travel Act
La. Rev. Stat. Ann., 51:1251 et seq.

Hospitality Cabinet Act
Ida. Code 1947, 23-1401 et seq.

Hospitality Tax Act (Local)
S.C. Code Ann. 1976, §§ 6-1-700 to 6-1-750

Hospitalization Act
March 3, 1919, Ch. 98, 40 Stat. 1302

Hospitalization and Commitment Act
Minn. Stat. Ann., 253B.01 et seq.

Hospitalization of the Mentally Ill Act
D.C. Code 1973, § 21-501 et seq.
Me. Rev. Stat. Ann. 1964, Title 34B, § 3201 et seq.
Mich. Comp. Laws Ann., 330.1001 et seq.
Mo. Rev. Stat. 1978, 202.843 et seq.
Nev. Rev. Stat. 1979 Reprint, Replaced Pages, 433.645 et seq.
Ohio Rev. Code 1953, 5122.01 et seq.

Hospitals and Institutions Department Act
N.M. Stat. Ann., 23-1-12 et seq.

Hostage Relief Act
Cal. Revenue and Taxation Code § 17165

Hostage Relief Act of 1980
Oct. 14, 1980, P.L. 96-449, 5 U.S. Code § 5561 nt.

Hostel Facilities Act (State)
Cal. Public Resources Code § 5050 et seq.

Hostile Witness Act
La. Rev. Stat. Ann., 15:487 et seq.

Hot Cargo Act
Cal. Labor Code § 1131 et seq.
Ore. Rev. Stat., 662.210 et seq.

Hot Check Act
Ark. Code Ann. 1987, 5-37-301 et seq.
Miss. Code Ann. 1972, §§ 11-7-12, 97-19-55 et seq.
Tex. Penal Code, §§ 31.06, 32.41

Hot Dog Tax Act
N.Y. Tax Law (Consol. Laws Ch. 60) § 1105

Hot-Oil Act
Feb. 22, 1935, Ch. 18, 49 Stat. 30, 15 U.S. Code §§ 715 to 715l
June 14, 1937, Ch. 335, 50 Stat. 257
June 29, 1939, Ch. 250, 53 Stat. 927
Oct. 13, 1966, P.L. 89-644, 80 Stat. 890, 15 U.S. Code § 715a "Hot Oil" Extension Act

Hot Pursuit Act
N.M. Stat. Ann., 31-2-1 et seq.
Wis. Stat. Ann., 976.04

Hot Spots Air Toxics Information and Assessment Act
Cal. Health and Safety Code §§ 44300 to 44304, 44306 to 44309, 44320 to 44325, 44340 to 44346, 44360 to 44366, 44380 to 44384

Hot Water Heater Efficiency Act
Ill. Rev. Stat. 1991, Ch. 96 1/2, §§ 9550, 9551

Hotel Act
Wash. Rev. Code Ann., 60.64.010 et seq.

Hotel and Food Service Establishment Act
Ky. Rev. Stat. 1971, 219.011 et seq.

Hotel and Motel Fire Safety Act of 1990
Sept. 25, 1990, P.L. 101-391, 15 U.S. Code § 2201 nt.
Sept. 23, 1996, P.L. 104-201, 5 U.S. Code § 5707 nt.
Oct. 19, 1996, P.L. 104-316, 5 U.S. Code § 5707 nt.

Hotel and Multiple Dwelling Act
N.J. Stat. Ann., 55:13A-1 et seq.

Hotel and Restaurant Act
Fla. Stat. Ann., 509.013 et seq.
Ky. Rev. Stat. 1971, 219.011 et seq.
Ohio Rev. Code 1953, 3731.01 et seq.
S.C. Code Ann. 1976, § 45-1-10 et seq.
Wis. Stat. Ann., 50.50 et seq.

Hotel and Restaurant Inspection Act
Ky. Rev. Stat. 1971, Superseded Vols., 219.010 et seq.
Tenn. Code Ann., 68-14-301 et seq.
W. Va. Code 1966, § 16-6-1 et seq.

Hotel and Restaurant Worker's Lien Law
Wash. Rev. Code Ann., 60.34.010 et seq.

Hotel Cafe and Restaurant Law
Iowa Code Ann., 137A.1 et seq.

Hotel Fire Safety Law
N.J. Stat. Ann., 55-13A-1 et seq.

Hotel Floor Plan Posting Act
Ill. Rev. Stat. 1991, Ch. 127 1/2, § 80 et seq.

Hotel Guest Registration Act
N.H. Rev. Stat. 1955, 353:3

Hotel Health Regulations Act
Wash. Rev. Code Ann., 70.62.200 et seq.

Hotel Inspection Act
Iowa Code Ann., 137A.12 et seq.
N.D. Cent. Code, 23-09-01 et seq.

Hotel License Law
S.D. Codified Laws 1967, 34-18-9 et seq.

Hotel Lien Act
Iowa Code Ann., 583.1 et seq.
Wash. Rev. Code Ann., 60.64.010 et seq.

Hotel Limited Liability Act
Tex. Rev. Civ. Stat., Art. 4592

Hotel Occupancy and Surtax on Corporations and Unincorporated Business Tax Act
D.C. Code Ann., §§ 47-1807.2, 47-3201 et seq.

Hotel Occupancy Tax Act
D.C. Code Ann., § 47-3201 et seq.
N.J. Stat. Ann., 40:48E-1 et seq.
Pa. 1955 Pamph. Laws 1256, No. 383
Pa. 1959 Pamph. Laws 2046, No. 748

Hotel Operators' Occupation Tax Act
Ill. Comp. Stat. 1992, Ch. 35, §§ 145/1 to 145/10
Ill. Rev. Stat. 1991, Ch. 120, § 481b.31 et seq.

Hotel Roanoke Conference Center Commission Act
Va. Acts 1991, Ch. 440

Hotel Room Occupancy Tax Law
N.Y. Local Laws 1971, County of Monroe, p. 696
N.Y. Local Laws 1973, City of Niagara Falls, p. 586

Hotel Safety Regulations Act
Wash. Rev. Code Ann., 70.62.200 et seq.

Hotel Sanitation Act
Cal. Health and Safety Code § 19400 et seq.
Iowa Code Ann., 137C.1 et seq.

Hotel Service Establishment and Public Swimming Pool Inspection Act
Tenn. Code Ann. 68-14-301 et seq.

Hotels Motels, Restaurants and Boarding-houses Act
S.C. Code Ann. 1976, § 45-1-10 et seq.

Hotels Sanitary Equipment Act
Ill. Rev. Stat. 1991, Ch. 56 1/2, § 66.90 et seq.

Hoult Act
Ore. Laws 1885, p. 38

Hoult Act (Railroad Rates)
Ore. Rev. Stat., 760.105 et seq.

Houlton Band of Malliseet Indians Supplementary Claims Settlement Act of 1986
Oct. 27, 1986, P.L. 99-566, 25 U.S. Code § 1724 nt.

Houma, Louisiana Redevelopment Agency Act
La. Acts 1968, No. 439

Hour and Wage Act
Md. Ann. Code 1974, Art. LE, § 3-401 et seq.
Mont. Code Ann., 39-3-401 et seq.
N.D. Cent. Code, 34-06-01 et seq.
N.J. Stat. Ann., 34:11-56a et seq.
S.D. Codified Laws 1967, 60-11-1 et seq.

Hours and Wages Law (Women and Minors)
Cal. Labor Code § 1171 et seq.

Hours of Labor (Wage and Hour) Act
Neb. Rev. Stat. 1943, 48-1201 et seq.

Hours of Labor Act
Cal. Labor Code § 510 et seq.
N.H. Stat. 1955, 275:15 et seq.
P.R. Laws Ann. 1954, Title 29, § 271 et seq.
Wash. Rev. Code Ann., 49.28.010 et seq.
Wis. Stat. Ann., 103.02

Hours of Service Act
June 22, 1988, P.L. 100-342, 102 Stat. 634, 45 U.S. Code §§ 61 to 64a
N.J. Stat. Ann., 39:9-1 to 39:9-4

Hours of Service Acts (Public Works)
See Contract Work Hours And Safety Standards Act
June 25, 1868, Ch. 72, 15 Stat. 77
Aug. 1, 1892, Ch. 352, 27 Stat. 340
March 3, 1901, Ch. 854, 31 Stat. 1334
June 19, 1912, Ch. 174, 37 Stat. 137
March 3, 1913, Ch. 106, 37 Stat. 726

Hours of Service Acts (Railroads)
Sept. 3, 5, 1916, Ch. 436, 39 Stat. 721, 45 U.S. Code §§ 65, 66
March 4, 1907, Ch. 2939, 34 Stat. 1415, 45 U.S. Code §§ 61 to 64
May 4, 1916, Ch. 109, 39 Stat. 61
Aug. 14, 1957, P.L. 85-135, 71 Stat. 352, 45 U.S. Code § 63
Dec. 26, 1969, P.L. 91-169, 83 Stat. 463
July 8, 1976, P.L. 94-348, 90 Stat. 818, 819
Nov. 2, 1978, P.L. 95-574, 92 Stat. 2459-2461
June 22, 1988, P.L. 100-342, 102 Stat. 634, 638
Sept. 3, 1992, P.L. 102-365, 45 U.S. Code § 64a

Hours of Work Act (Female)
D.C. Code 1973, § 36-301 et seq.
Ill. Rev. Stat. 1991, Ch. 48, § 8b et seq.
Tex. Rev. Civ. Stat., Art. 5172a

Hours Worked Act
Ida. Code 1947, 67-53-29 et seq.

House Employees Position Classification Act
Oct. 13, 1964, P.L. 88-652, 78 Stat. 1079, 2 U.S. Code §§ 88c, 123b, 291 to 303
Nov. 2, 1978, P.L. 95-574, 45 U.S. Code §§ 61, 63a
Nov. 19, 1995, P.L. 104-53, 2 U.S. Code §§ 292 et seq.
Aug. 20, 1996, P.L. 104-186, 2 U.S. Code §§ 293, 294, 300

House of Correction Act
Ill. Rev. Stat. 1991, Ch. 24, § 11-4-1 et seq.
Pa. Purdon's Stat., Title 61, § 671 et seq.
Tenn. Code Ann., 41-3-101 et seq.

House of Correction Loan Act (Barnstable)
Mass. Acts 1959, Ch. 482

House of Reform Act
Ky. Rev. Stat. 1948, 198.010 et seq.

House of Representatives Act
Wash. Rev. Code Ann., 44.12.010 et seq.

House of Representatives Administrative Reform Technical Corrections Act
Aug. 20, 1996, P.L. 104-186, 2 U.S. Code § 31 nt.
Oct. 7, 1997, P.L. 105-55, 2 U.S. Code §§ 72a, 92

House of Representatives Apportionment Act
Okla. Stat. Ann., Title 14, § 116 et seq.
S.C. Code Ann. 1976, § 2-1-10 et seq.

House of Representatives Reapportionment Act
S.C. Code of 1976, §§ 1-1-730 et seq., 2-1-10 et seq.

House of Representatives Redistricting Act
Okla. Stat. Ann., Title 14, § 121 et seq.

House Reapportionment Act (1982)
N.M. Stat. Ann., 2-7B-1 et seq.
N.M. Stat. Ann. 1953, 2-7-38 et seq., 2-7-119 et seq.

House Redistricting Act
N.M. Laws 1991, 1st Sp. Sess., Ch. 2

House Redistricting Act of 1991
N.M. Laws 1991, 1st Sp. Sess., Ch. 2

House Relocation Act
Ill. Rev. Stat. 1991, Ch. 67 1/2, § 102.9 et seq.

House Trailer Ad Valorem Tax Act
Miss. Code Ann. 1972, § 27-53-1 et seq.

House Trailer and/or Mobile Home Zoning Law
N.Y. Local Laws 1973, Town of Amenia, p. 1339

House Trailer Camps Act
Mich. Comp. Laws Ann., 125.1101 et seq.

House Trailers and Mobile Homes Regulations Law
N.Y. Local Laws 1972, Town of Pittstown, p. 2577

House Voting Device Act
Ill. Rev. Stat. 1991, Ch. 63, § 100.9 et seq.

Housebreaking, Robbery and Burglary Act
S.C. Code Ann. 1976, § 16-11-310 et seq.

Household and Small Business Pollution Prevention Program Act
Pa. Purdon's Stat., Title 35, § 6029.201 et seq.

Household Cleaners Act
N.C. Gen. Stat. 1943, § 66-85 et seq.

Household Goods Act
Ind. Laws 1961, Ch. 325, p. 959

Household Goods and Effects Storage Act
Nev. Rev. Stat. 1979 Reprint, 712.010 et seq.

Household Goods Carriers Act
Cal. Public Utilities Code § 5101 et seq.
Va. Code 1950, § 56-338.1 et seq.

Household Hazardous Waste Finding Act
Pa. Purdon's Stat., Title 35, § 6025.1 et seq.

Household Members Act (Crimes against)
N.M. Stat. Ann., 30-3-10 et seq.

Housekeeping Statute
Sept. 6, 1966, P.L. 89-554, 5 U.S. Code § 301

Houses of Prostitution Act
D.C. Code 1973, § 22-2713 et seq.

Housing Act
See also National Housing Act
May 16, 1918, Ch. 74, 40 Stat. 550
Cal. Health and Safety Code § 17910 et seq.
La. Rev. Stat. Ann., 51:2601 et seq.

Housing Act (Affordable)
Ill. Comp. Stat. 1992, Ch. 310, § 65/1 et seq.

Housing Act (AIDS)
Miss. Code Ann. 1972, § 43-33-717

Housing Act (Central Falls)
R.I. Public Laws 1958, Ch. 56

Housing Act (Cooperative)
Iowa Code Ann., 499A.1 et seq.

Housing Act (Defense)
Mich. Comp. Laws Ann., 125.711 et seq.
Pa. Purdon's Stat., Title 35, § 1595.1 et seq.

Housing Act (Disabled Veterans)
Ill. Rev. Stat. 1991, Ch. 126 1/2, § 57.90 et
seq.

Housing Act (Discrimination in)
Mass. Gen. Laws Ann., 151B:1 et seq.

Housing Act (East Providence)
R.I. Public Laws 1961, Ch. 66

Housing Act (Emergency)
Minn. Laws 1949, Ch. 733

Housing Act (Fair)
Ariz. Rev. Stat. Ann., § 41-1491 et seq.
Cal. Statutes 1992, Ch. 182
Fla. Stat. Ann., 760.20 et seq.
N.J. Stat. Ann., 52:27D-301 et seq.,
55:14A-7.5
Tex. Rev. Civ. Stat., Art. 1f

Housing Act (First Class Cities)
Kan. Stat. Ann., 17-2336

Housing Act (Health)
Ind. Code Ann., 16-1-25-1 et seq.

Housing Act (Insured Loans)
Okla. Stat. Ann., Title 6, §§ 421 et seq., 2041
et seq.

Housing Act (Limited Dividend)
S.C. Code Ann. 1976, § 31-1-110 et seq.

Housing Act (Low and Moderate Income)
R.I. Gen. Laws 1956, 45-53-1 et seq.

Housing Act (Manufactured)
Kan. Stat. Ann., 58-4201 et seq.

Housing Act (State Board)
Pa. 1937 Pamph. Laws 1705, No. 359

Housing Act (State)
Del. Code of 1953, Title 31, § 4101 et seq.
Kan. Laws 1933, Ch. 225

Housing Act (Temporary)
Miss. Code Ann. 1972, § 43-41-301 et seq.

Housing Act (Veterans)
Miss. Code 1942, § 7516.7-01 et seq.
Wis. Stat. Ann., 66.39, 66.92, 67.015

Housing Act (Warwick)
R.I. Public Laws 1958, Ch. 99

Housing Act (Woonsocket)
R.I. Public Laws 1961, Ch. 76

Housing Act of 1937
See United States Housing Act Of 1937

Housing Act of 1948
Aug. 10, 1948, Ch. 832, 62 Stat. 1268, 12
U.S. Code §§ 1437, 1701c to 1701g, 1702,
1703, 1706, 1709, 1710, 1713, 1716, 1738,
1743, 1744 to 1747, 1747 nt., 1747a to
1747l; 31 U.S. Code §§ 846, 850 nt., 866
nt.; See 38 U.S. Code §§ 1801 to 1803; 42
U.S. Code §§ 1403, 1404a, 1432
July 15, 1949, Ch. 338, 63 Stat. 431, 12 U.S.
Code §§ 1701e to 1701f-1
April 20, 1950, Ch. 94, 64 Stat. 80, 12 U.S.
Code § 1701c
Sept. 1, 1951, Ch. 378, 65 Stat. 311, 12 U.S.
Code §§ 1701g, 1701g-1, 1701g-2
July 14, 1952, Ch. 723, 66 Stat. 604, 12 U.S.
Code § 1701g-2
June 30, 1961, P.L. 87-70, 75 Stat. 192, 12
U.S. Code § 1701c
May 25, 1967, P.L. 90-19, 81 Stat. 20, 12
U.S. Code §§ 1701c, 1701e, 1701f; 42 U.S.
Code § 1404a
Aug. 12, 1970, P.L. 91-375, 84 Stat. 776, 12
U.S. Code § 1701e
Continued

February 5, 1988, P.L. 100-242, 42 U.S. Code §§ 1404a, 1701c

Housing Act of 1949

July 15, 1949, Ch. 338, 63 Stat. 413, 12 U.S. Code §§ 24, 84, 1701d-1, 1701e, 1701f, 1701f-1, 1701h, 1701i, 1703, 1709, 1738; 42 U.S. Code §§ 1401, 1409 to 1411, 1413 to 1416, 1420, 1421, 1421a to 1430, 1433, 1441 to 1445, 1451 to 1460, 1471 to 1483,

June 3, 1952, Ch. 362, 66 Stat. 98, 42 U.S. Code § 1456

July 14, 1952, Ch. 723, 66 Stat. 604, 42 U.S. Code §§ 1481 to 1483

June 30, 1953, Ch. 170, 67 Stat. 127, 42 U.S. Code §§ 1456, 1460

June 30, 1953, Ch. 174, 67 Stat. 132, 42 U.S. Code § 1477

June 29, 1954, Ch. 410, 68 Stat. 320, 42 U.S. Code §§ 1481, 1482, 1483

Aug. 2, 1954, Ch. 649, 68 Stat. 622, 42 U.S. Code §§ 1440, 1450 to 1454, 1456, 1457, 1459, 1460, 1481, 1483, 1701h

Aug. 11, 1955, Ch. 783, 69 Stat. 637, 42 U.S. Code § 1451, 1453, 1456, 1460, 1481 to 1483

Aug. 7, 1956, Ch. 1029, 70 Stat. 1097, 42 U.S. Code §§ 1452, 1454 to 1456, 1460, 1462, 1481 to 1483

July 12, 1957, P.L. 85-104, 71 Stat. 299, 42 U.S. Code §§ 1453, 1454, 1456, 1460

Sept. 23, 1959, P.L. 86-372, 73 Stat. 659, 42 U.S. Code §§ 1450 to 1453, 1455 to 1457, 1460, 1463

May 1, 1961, P.L. 87-27, 75 Stat. 57, 42 U.S. Code § 1464

June 30, 1961 P.L. 87-70, 42 U.S. Code §§ 1451, 1452, 1453 to 1455, 1456, 1457, 1460, 1463, 1471, 1472, 1476 to 1478, 1481 to 1484

Sept. 28, 1962, P.L. 87-723, 76 Stat. 670, 42 U.S. Code §§ 1471, 1472, 1474, 1476, 1481, 1485

June 30, 1964, P.L. 88-340, 78 Stat. 233, 42 U.S. Code § 1485

Sept. 2, 1964, P.L. 88-560, 78 Stat. 785, 42 U.S. Code §§ 1451, 1452, 1453, 1455 to 1457, 1460, 1465, 1476, 1481 to 1486

Aug. 10, 1965, P.L. 89-117, 79 Stat. 453, 42 U.S. Code §§ 1451 to 1453, 1455, 1456, 1460, 1465 to 1468, 1471, 1472, 1476, 1481 to 1483, 1485, 1487 to 1490

Sept. 9, 1965, P.L. 89-174, 79 Stat. 670, 42 U.S. Code § 1451

Nov. 3, 1966, P.L. 89-754, 80 Stat. 1260, 42 U.S. Code §§ 1453, 1455, 1456, 1460, 1463, 1471, 1472, 1474, 1485, 1487

May 25, 1967, P.L. 90-19, 81 Stat. 21, 12 U.S. Code §§ 1701h; 42 U.S. Code §§ 1441, 1451 to 1453, 1455, 1456 to 1460, 1462 to 1468

Aug. 1, 1968, P.L. 90-448, 82 Stat. 518, 42 U.S. Code §§ 1451, 1452, 1453, 1455 to 1457, 1460, 1462, 1465 to 1468, 1468a, 1469 to 1469c, 1483, 1484, 1490a to 1490c

Sept. 30, 1969, P.L. 91-78, 83 Stat. 125, 42 U.S. Code §§ 1483, 1485, 1487

Dec. 24, 1969, P.L. 91-152, 83 Stat. 385, 42 U.S. Code §§ 1451 to 1453, 1455, 1460, 1463, 1466 to 1468a, 1469b, 1483, 1485, 1487, 1489, 1490d

Oct. 2, 1973, P.L. 93-117, 87 Stat. 422, 42 U.S. Code §§ 1453, 1483, 1485, 1487, 1490c

April 30, 1977, P.L. 95-24, 42 U.S. Code § 1451

June 30, 1977, P.L. 95-60, 42 U.S. Code § 1483 et seq.

July 31, 1977, P.L. 95-80, 42 U.S. Code § 1483 et seq.

Oct. 12, 1977, P.L. 95-128, 42 U.S. Code §§ 1483, 1485 et seq.

Oct. 31, 1978, P.L. 95-557, 42 U.S. Code §§ 1476, 1480, 1483 et seq.

Nov. 6, 1978, P.L. 95-598, 42 U.S. Code § 1473

Nov. 9, 1978, P.L. 95-619, 12 U.S. Code 1735f-7; 42 U.S. Code 1471, §§ 1474, 1483, 1703

Sept. 28, 1979, P.L. 96-71, 42 U.S. Code §§ 1483, 1485, 1487, 1490c

Nov. 8, 1979, P.L. 96-105, 42 U.S. Code §§ 1483, 1485, 1487, 1490c

Dec. 21, 1979, P.L. 96-153, 42 U.S. Code §§ 1471, 1484 repealed, 1742, 1474, 1477, 1479, 1480, 1483, 1485 to 1487, 1487, 1490a, 1490c

Oct. 6, 1982, P.L. 97-289, 42 U.S. Code §§ 1485, 1487, 1490c

Nov. 30, 1983, P.L. 98-181, 42 U.S. Code §§ 1456, 1471, 1481 to 1487, 1490e to 1490g, 1490k to 1490o

Oct. 17, 1984, P.L. 98-479, 42 U.S. Code §§ 1471, 1472, 1472 nt., 1480, 1483, 1485, 1487, 1490, 1490a

Oct. 8, 1985, P.L. 99-120, 42 U.S. Code §§ 1485, 1490, 1490c

Nov. 15, 1985, P.L. 99-156, 42 U.S. Code §§ 1452b, 1485, 1490, 1490c

Dec. 26, 1985, P.L. 99-219, 42 U.S. Code §§ 1485, 1490, 1490c

March 27, 1986, P.L. 99-267, 42 U.S. Code §§ 1485, 1490, 1490c

April 7, 1986, P.L. 99-272, 42 U.S. Code §§ 1471, 1483, 1485, 1487, 1490, 1490c, 5302

July 2, 1986, P.L. 99-349, 100 Stat. 711

Feb. 5, 1988, P.L. 100-242, 42 U.S. Code §§ 1471, 1472, 1480, 1483 to 1487, 1490, 1490a-c, 1490f, 1490m, 1490n

Nov. 7, 1988, P.L. 100-628, 42 U.S. Code §§ 1472, 1480, 1484 to 1486, 1490o

Aug. 9, 1989, P.L. 101-73, 12 U.S. Code § 1701c

Nov. 3, 1989, P.L. 101-137, 42 U.S. Code §§ 1485, 1490, 1490c

Dec. 15, 1989, P.L. 101-235, 42 U.S. Code §§ 1472, 1485, 1490o, 1490p

Nov. 28, 1990, P.L. 101-625, 42 U.S. Code § 1471 et seq. generally, 1480 et seq. generally, 1490, 1490a, 1490m, 1490o to 1490q

June 13, 1991, P.L. 102-54, 42 U.S. Code § 1490o

Oct. 28, 1991, P.L. 102-142, 42 U.S. Code §§ 1472, 1485, 1490c

Dec. 12, 1991, P.L. 102-230, 42 U.S. Code § 1485

Oct. 28, 1992, P.L. 102-550, 42 U.S. Code §§ 1471, 1472, 1479, 1483, 1485, 1487, 1490, 1490a, 1490c, 1490d, 1490m, 1490o, 1490p-1, 1490q

Oct. 27, 1993, P.L. 103-120, 42 U.S. Code § 1490o

Dec. 19, 1995, P.L. 104-65, 42 U.S. Code § 1490p

Dec. 21, 1995, P.L. 104-66, 42 U.S. Code § 1476

March 28, 1996, P.L. 104-120, 42 U.S. Code §§ 1479, 1485, 1490p-2

Aug. 6, 1996, P.L. 104-180, 42 U.S. Code §§ 1472, 1479, 1484, 1485, 1490l

Aug. 22, 1996, P.L. 104-193, 42 U.S. Code § 1471

Nov. 18, 1997, P.L. 105-86, 42 U.S. Code §§ 1479, 1485, 1490p-2

Oct. 21, 1998, P.L. 105-276, 42 U.S. Code §§ 1472, 1479, 1483, 1484, 1485, 1490a, 1490j, 1490m, 1490p-2

Oct. 21, 1998, P.L. 105-277, 42 U.S. Code § 1474

Nov. 10, 1998, P.L. 105-362, 42 U.S. Code § 1490m

Housing Act of 1950

April 20, 1950, Ch. 94, 64 Stat. 48, 7 U.S. Code §§ 1001, 1001 nt., 1017; 12 U.S. Code §§ 371, 1430, 1701c, 1701j, 1701j nt., 1701k, 1701l, 1702, 1703, 1073 nt., 1705, 1706, 1706b, 1706c, 1707 to 1714, 1715c, 1715e, 1715f, 1716, 1717, 1720, 1721, 1736 to 1747l, 1749 to 1749c; 15 U.S. Code § 604; See 38 U.S. Code §§ 1801 to 1804, 1811, 1812, 1823; 42 U.S. Code §§ 1412, 1521 to 1524, 1541 to 1553, 1561 to 1564, 1571, 1572, 1574, 1575, 1581 to 1590

Sept. 1, 1951, Ch. 378, 65 Stat. 316, 12 U.S. Code § 1701j

June 30, 1953, Ch. 170, 67 Stat. 127, 12 U.S. Code §§ 1701, 1701j, 1749

March 10, 1954, Ch. 61, 68 Stat. 26, 42 U.S. Code § 1587

Aug. 2, 1954, Ch. 649, 68 Stat. 645, 12 U.S. Code § 1749

Aug. 11, 1955, Ch. 783, 69 Stat. 644, 12 U.S. Code §§ 1749, 1749c

Aug. 7, 1956, Ch. 1029, 70 Stat. 1113, 12 U.S. Code § 1749

July 12, 1957, P.L. 85-104, 71 Stat. 303, 12 U.S. Code §§ 1749, 1749c

Sept. 2, 1958, P.L. 85-857, 72 Stat. 1266, 12 U.S. Code § 1701k

Sept. 23, 1959, P.L. 86-372, 73 Stat. 681, 12 U.S. Code §§ 1749, 1749a, 1749c

Sept. 14, 1960, P.L. 86-788, 74 Stat. 1028, 12 U.S. Code § 1749

June 30, 1961, P.L. 87-70, 75 Stat. 172, 12 U.S. Code §§ 1749, 1749b, 1749c

Sept. 2, 1964, P.L. 88-560, 78 Stat. 806, 12 U.S. Code § 1749c

Aug. 10, 1965, P.L. 89-117, 79 Stat. 489, 12 U.S. Code §§ 149, 149a

May 24, 1966, P.L. 89-429, 80 Stat. 166, 12 U.S. Code § 1749

Nov. 3, 1966, P.L. 89-754, 80 Stat. 1292, 12 U.S. Code §§ 1749, 1749c

May 25, 1967, P.L. 90-19, 81 Stat. 22, 12 U.S. Code §§ 1701l, 1749, 1749a, 1749c

Aug. 1, 1968, P.L. 90-448, 82 Stat. 604, 12 U.S. Code §§ 1749, 1749b, 1749c

Dec. 24, 1969, P.L. 91-152, 83 Stat. 390, 12 U.S. Code § 1749
Continued

July 24, 1970, P.L. 91-351, 84 Stat. 463, 12 U.S. Code § 1749

Dec. 31, 1970, P.L. 91-609, 84 Stat. 1777, 12 U.S. Code § 1749

Oct. 31, 1983, P.L. 98-139, 12 U.S. Code § 1749a

Oct. 17, 1984, P.L. 98-479, 12 U.S. Code § 1749c

Dec. 12, 1985, P.L. 99-178, 12 U.S. Code § 1749

Oct. 17, 1986, P.L. 99-498, 12 U.S. Code §§ 1749 to 1749c

Housing Act of 1952

July 14, 1952, Ch. 723, 66 Stat. 601, 12 U.S. Code §§ 1422, 1423, 1464, 1466, 1701g-2, 1701m, 1706d, 1707, 1713, 1715d, 1715h, 1715i, 1716 and others; 42 U.S. Code §§ 1481 to 1483, 1589a, 1592a, 1592l, 1593

Housing Act of 1954

Aug. 2, 1954, Ch. 649, 68 Stat. 590, 12 U.S. Code §§ 24, 1430, 1431, 1436, 1440, 1464, 1701h, 1701j-1, 1701n to 1701p, 1702a, 1703, 1706c, 1709, 1710 and others; 18 U.S. Code § 709; 20 U.S. Code § 272; 31 U.S. Code § 846 nt.; See 38 U.S. Code § 1810; 40 U.S. Code §§ 459 to 462; 42 U.S. Code §§ 1407, 1410, 1411d, 1415, 1416, 1434, 1435, 1446, 1450 to 1454, 1455a, 1456 and others

Aug. 11, 1955, Ch. 783, 69 Stat. 641, 40 U.S. Code § 462

June 29, 1957, P.L. 85-66, 71 Stat. 209, 12 U.S. Code § 1750jj

July 12, 1957, P.L. 85-104, 71 Stat. 304, 12 U.S. Code § 1750jj; 40 U.S. Code § 461

Sept. 2, 1958, P.L. 85-857, 72 Stat. 1266, 12 U.S. Code §§ 1701j- 1, 1750bb, 1750gg

July 31, 1959, P.L. 86-119, 73 Stat. 266, 12 U.S. Code § 1750jj

Sept. 23, 1959, P.L. 86-372, 73 Stat. 678, 12 U.S. Code § 1750jj; 40 U.S. Code §§ 461, 462

June 11, 1960, P.L. 86-507, 74 Stat. 200, 12 U.S. Code § 1725

May 1, 1961, P.L. 87-27, 75 Stat. 58, 40 U.S. Code § 461

June 30, 1961, P.L. 87-70, 75 Stat. 170, 12 U.S. Code § 1750jj; 40 U.S. Code §§ 461, 462; 42 U.S. Code § 1434

Sept. 14, 1962, P.L. 87-658, 76 Stat. 544, 40 U.S. Code § 462

Sept. 2, 1964, P.L. 88-560, 78 Stat. 792, 40 U.S. Code §§ 461, 462; 42 U.S. Code § 1452a

March 9, 1965, P.L. 89-4, 79 Stat. 17, 40 U.S. Code § 461

Aug. 10, 1965, P.L. 89-117, 79 Stat. 502, 12 U.S. Code § 1701o; 40 U.S. Code §§ 461, 462

Nov. 3, 1966, P.L. 89-754, 80 Stat. 1273, 40 U.S. Code § 461

May 25, 1967, P.L. 90-19, 81 Stat. 22, 12 U.S. Code §§ 1701j-1, 1701n, 1701l, 1701p; 40 U.S. Code §§ 460, 461; 42 U.S. Code §§ 1434, 1435, 1452a

Oct. 11, 1967, P.L. 90-103, 81 Stat. 262, 40 U.S. Code § 461

Aug. 1, 1968, P.L. 90-448, 82 Stat. 526, 40 U.S. Code §§ 461, 462; 42 U.S. Code § 1452a

Dec. 24, 1969, P.L. 91-152, 83 Stat. 391, 40 U.S. Code § 461

Dec. 31, 1970, P.L. 91-606, 84 Stat. 1758, 40 U.S. Code § 461

Dec. 31, 1970, P.L. 91-609, 84 Stat. 1780, 40 U.S. Code § 461

July 1, 1972, P.L. 92-335, 86 Stat. 405, 40 U.S. Code § 461

Oct. 2, 1973, P.L. 93-117, 87 Stat. 423, 40 U.S. Code § 461

May 22, 1974, P.L. 93-288, 88 Stat. 163, 40 U.S. Code § 461

Oct. 12, 1977, P.L. 95-128, 40 U.S. Code § 461

Oct. 31, 1978, P.L. 95-557, 40 U.S. Code § 461

Dec. 21, 1979, P.L. 96-153, 40 U.S. Code § 461

Dec. 21, 1982, P.L. 97-375, 12 U.S. Code § 1701p

Feb. 5, 1988, P.L. 100-242, 40 U.S. Code §§ 1462, 1701o

Housing Act of 1956

Aug. 7, 1956, Ch. 1029, 70 Stat. 1091, 12 U.S. Code §§ 1701d-3, 1701h-1, 1703 nt., 1709, 1713, 1715e, 1715h, 1715k, 1715l, 1715r, 1717 to 1721, 1748, 1748b, 1749; See 38 U.S. Code § 1811; 40 U.S. Code § 461; 42 U.S. Code § 1402, 1410, 1412, 1415, 1421, 1451, 1452, 1460, 1462, 1481, 1483, 1496, 1589d and others

Sept. 23, 1959, P.L. 86-372, 73 Stat. 687, 42 U.S. Code § 1592c nt.

June 30, 1961, P.L. 87-70, 75 Stat. 191, 42 U.S. Code § 1592c nt.

May 25, 1967, P.L. 90-19, 81 Stat. 24, 12 U.S. Code §§ 1701d-3, 1701h-1

Aug. 12, 1970, P.L. 91-375, 84 Stat. 776, 12 U.S. Code § 1701d

Housing Act of 1957

July 12, 1957, P.L. 85-104, 71 Stat. 294, 12 U.S. Code §§ 1701d- 4, 1703, 1709, 1709a, 1709b, 1710, 1713, 1715e, 1715j, 1715k, 1715l, 1715m, 1715n, 1715q, 1718 to 1720, 1748b, 1749, 1749c, 1750jj; 40 U.S. Code § 461; 42 U.S. Code §§ 1402, 1415, 1453, 1454, 1456, 1460, 1476 nt., 1594a, 1594f

Sept. 23, 1959, P.L. 86-372, 73 Stat. 686, 42 U.S. Code § 1476 nt.

May 25, 1967, P.L. 90-19, 31 Stat. 24, 12 U.S. Code §§ 1701d-4, 1709a

Aug. 1, 1968, P.L. 90-448, 82 Stat. 606, 12 U.S. Code § 1701d-4

Housing Act of 1959

Sept. 23, 1959, P.L. 86-372, 73 Stat. 654, 12 U.S. Code §§ 24, 1464, 1701q, 1703, 1706c, 1709, 1710, 1713, 1715c to 1715e, 1715h, 1715k to 1715m and others; 40 U.S. Code §§ 461, 462; 42 U.S. Code §§ 1401, 1402, 1410, 1415, 1450 to 1453, 1455 to 1457, 1460, 1463, 1476 nt., 1586, 1592c nt., 1594a, 1594j

June 30, 1961, P.L. 87-70, 75 Stat. 162, 12 U.S. Code § 1701q

Sept. 28, 1962, P.L. 87-723, 76 Stat. 670, 12 U.S. Code § 1701q

Oct. 24, 1963, P.L. 88-158, 77 Stat. 278, 12 U.S. Code § 1701q

Sept. 2, 1964, P.L. 88-560, 78 Stat. 783, 12 U.S. Code § 1701q

Aug. 10, 1965, P.L. 89-117, 79 Stat. 457, 12 U.S. Code § 1701q

May 25, 1967, P.L. 90-19, 81 Stat. 25, 12 U.S. Code § 1701q

Aug. 1, 1968, P.L. 90-448, 82 Stat. 544, 12 U.S. Code §§ 1701q, 1721 nt.

Dec. 24, 1969, P.L. 91-152, 83 Stat. 390, 12 U.S. Code § 1701q

Oct. 12, 1977, P.L. 95-128, 12 U.S. Code §§ 1701q

Oct. 31, 1978, P.L. 95-557, 12 U.S. Code § 1701q

Nov. 30, 1983, P.L. 98-181, 12 U.S. Code § 1701q

Oct. 17, 1984, P.L. 98-479, 12 U.S. Code § 1701q

Feb. 5, 1988, P.L. 100-242, 12 U.S. Code § 1701q

Dec. 15, 1989, P.L. 101-235, 12 U.S. Code § 1701q-1

Nov. 28, 1990, P.L. 101-625, 12 U.S. Code § 1701q

Oct. 28, 1991, P.L. 102-139, 12 U.S. Code § 1701q

Dec. 19, 1991, P.L. 102-242, 12 U.S. Code § 1701q

Oct. 28, 1992, P.L. 102-550, 12 U.S. Code §§ 1701q, 5305 nt.

Housing Act of 1961

June 30, 1961, P.L. 87-70, 75 Stat. 149, 12 U.S. Code §§ 371, 1464, 1701c, 1701q, 1703, 1709, 1710, 1713, 1715, 1715c, 1715e, 1715h, 1715j to 1715l, 1715n, 1715o, 1715q, 1715r, 1715t, 1715v to 1715y, 1717 to 1721, 1723a, 1723b, 1748b and others; 15 U.S. Code §§ 631, 633, 636; 40 U.S. Code §§ 461, 462; 42 U.S. Code §§ 1402, 1410, 1415, 1421, 1421a, 1434, 1436, 1451, 1452 and others

Sept. 2, 1964, P.L. 88-560, 78 Stat. 784, 42 U.S. Code §§ 1436, 1500a

Aug. 10, 1965, P.L. 89-117, 79 Stat. 494, 42 U.S. Code §§ 1436, 1500 to 1500e

Nov. 3, 1966, P.L. 89-754, 80 Stat. 1279, 42 U.S. Code §§ 1500, 1500a, 1500c-2, 1500d, 1500d-1, 1500e

May 25, 1967, P.L. 90-19, 81 Stat. 25, 42 U.S. Code §§ 1436, 1500a to 1500e

Aug. 1, 1968, P.L. 90-448, 82 Stat. 534, 42 U.S. Code §§ 1436, 1500a, 1500d

Dec. 24, 1969, P.L. 91-152, 83 Stat. 391, 42 U.S. Code § 1500a

Dec. 31, 1970, P.L. 91-609, 84 Stat. 1781, 42 U.S. Code §§ 1500 to 1500b, 1500c to 1500c-3, 1500d, 1500d-1

July 1, 1972, P.L. 92-335, 86 Stat. 405, 42 U.S. Code § 1500d

Oct. 2, 1973, P.L. 93-117, 87 Stat. 422, 42 U.S. Code § 1500d

Nov. 30, 1983, P.L. 98-181, 42 U.S. Code §§ 1500c, 1500c-2

Housing Act of 1964

Sept. 2, 1964, P.L. 88-560, 78 Stat. 769, 12 U.S. Code §§ 24, 371, 1430, 1431, 1436, 1464, 1701q, 1703, 1709, 1710, 1713, 1715c, 1715e, 1715k to 1715n and others; 15 U.S. Code §§ 636, 637; 20 U.S. Code §§ 801 to 805, 811; 38 U.S. Code §§ 1820, 1823; 40 U.S. Code §§ 461, 462; 42 U.S. Code §§ 1402, 1410, 1415, 1436, 1451, 1452, 1453, 1455, 1456 and others

Aug. 10, 1965, P.L. 89-117, 79 Stat. 479, 20 U.S. Code §§ 802, 803; 42 U.S. Code § 1452b

May 25, 1967, P.L. 90-19, 81 Stat. 25, 20 U.S. Code §§ 802, 804, 805, 811; 42 U.S. Code § 1452b

Aug. 19, 1967, P.L. 90-66, 81 Stat. 167, 20 U.S. Code § 811

Aug. 1, 1968, P.L. 90-448, 82 Stat. 523, 20 U.S. Code §§ 801, 802, 805; 42 U.S. Code § 1452b

Dec. 24, 1969, P.L. 91-152, 83 Stat. 387, 20 U.S. Code §§ 801 to 807; 42 U.S. Code § 1452b

Dec. 31, 1970, P.L. 91-609, 84 Stat. 1809, 20 U.S. Code § 803

Aug. 10, 1973, P.L. 93-85, 87 Stat. 221, 42 U.S. Code § 1452b

Oct. 2, 1973, P.L. 93-117, 87 Stat. 423, 42 U.S. Code § 1452b

July 2, 1975, P.L. 94-50, 89 Stat. 256, 42 U.S. Code § 1452b

Oct. 12, 1977, P.L. 95-128, 42 U.S. Code § 1452b

Oct. 31, 1978, P.L. 95-557, 42 U.S. Code § 1452b

Sept. 28, 1979, P.L. 96-71, 42 U.S. Code § 1452b

Nov. 8, 1979, P.L. 96-105, 42 U.S. Code § 1452b

Dec. 21, 1979, P.L. 96-153, 42 U.S. Code § 1452b

Nov. 30, 1983, P.L. 98-181, 42 U.S. Code § 1452

Oct. 8, 1985, P.L. 99-120, 42 U.S. Code §§ 1452b

Nov. 15, 1985, P.L. 99-156, 42 U.S. Code § 1452b

Dec. 26, 1985, P.L. 99-219, 42 U.S. Code § 1452b

March 27, 1986, P.L. 99-267, 42 U.S. Code § 1452b

April 7, 1986, P.L. 99-272, 42 U.S. Code § 1452b

July 2, 1986, P.L. 99-349, 100 Stat. 728

Feb. 5, 1988, P.L. 100-242, 42 U.S. Code § 1452b

Housing Act of 1975

Haw. Rev. Stat. Ann., § 359-31 et seq.

Mont. Code Ann., 90-6-101 et seq.

Housing Affordability Impact Note Act

Ga. Code Ann., 28-5-140 et seq.

Housing Agency Act

Tex. Rev. Civ. Stat. 1974, Art. 1269L-6

Housing Agency Law

Pa. Purdon's Stat., Title 35, § 1680.101 et seq.

Housing Amendments of 1953

June 30, 1953, Ch. 170, 67 Stat. 121, 12 U.S. Code §§ 1463 nt., 1701j, 1706c, 1709, 1711, 1713, 1715d, 1715e, 1715h, 1715j, 1716, 1716-1, 1717, 1735, 1748b, 1749, 1750b, 1750g; 42 U.S. Code §§ 1402, 1456, 1460, 1591, 1591c, 1592d, 1592n, 48 U.S. Code §§ 1425, 1426; 50 U.S. Code Appx. § 2166

Housing Amendments of 1955

Aug. 11, 1955, Ch. 783, 69 Stat. 635, 12 U.S. Code §§ 1426, 1427, 1437, 1464, 1701d to 1703, 1710, 1713, 1715e, 1715h, 1715k, 1715l, 1715n, 1715r, 1720, 1726, 1729, 1739, 1748, 1748a to 1748g, 1749, 1749c; 40 U.S. Code § 46; 42 U.S. Code §§ 1410, 1451, 1453, 1456, 1460, 1481 to 1483, 1491 to 1495, 1585, 1591c, 1594, 1594a to 1594e; 48 U.S. Code §§ 910, 910a, 1408 nt., 1408b, 1408c

Aug. 3, 1956, Ch. 939, 70 Stat. 1019, 42 U.S. Code § 1594a

Aug. 7, 1956, Ch. 1029, 70 Stat. 1110, 42 U.S. Code §§ 1496, 1594, 1594a to 1594c, 1594f

July 12, 1957, P.L. 85-104, 71 Stat. 303, 42 U.S. Code §§ 1594a, 1594f

Aug. 20, 1958, P.L. 85-685, 72 Stat. 663, 42 U.S. Code § 1594a

Aug. 10, 1959, P.L. 86-149, 73 Stat. 323, 42 U.S. Code §§ 1594, 1594a

Sept. 23, 1959, P.L. 86-372, 73 Stat. 683, 42 U.S. Code §§ 1594a, 1594j

Sept. 14, 1960, P.L. 86-788, 74 Stat. 1028, 42 U.S. Code § 1493

June 30, 1961, P.L. 87-70, 75 Stat. 173, 42 U.S. Code §§ 1491 to 1493, 1497

July 27, 1962, P.L. 87-554, 76 Stat. 237, 42 U.S. Code § 1594a

Sept. 5, 1962, P.L. 87-634, 76 Stat. 435, 42 U.S. Code § 1492

Sept. 14, 1962, P.L. 87-658, 76 Stat. 543, 42 U.S. Code § 1492

Oct. 15, 1962, P.L. 87-808, 76 Stat. 920, 42 U.S. Code §§ 1491, 1492, 1497

Oct. 15, 1962, P.L. 87-809, 76 Stat. 920, 42 U.S. Code § 1492

Sept. 2, 1964, P.L. 88-560, 78 Stat. 798, 42 U.S. Code §§ 1492, 1594a

Aug. 10, 1965, P.L. 89-117, 79 Stat. 503, 42 U.S. Code § 1482

Nov. 3, 1966, P.L. 89-754, 80 Stat. 1273, 12 U.S. Code § 715e nt.; 42 U.S. Code § 1492

May 25, 1967, P.L. 90-19, 81 Stat. 23, 42 U.S. Code §§ 1492 to 1494, 1497, 1594, 1594a, 1594c, 1594e

Aug. 1, 1968, P.L. 90-448, 82 Stat. 518, 42 U.S. Code § 1492

Dec. 24, 1969, P.L. 91-152, 83 Stat. 395, 42 U.S. Code § 1496

Dec. 31, 1970, P.L. 91-609, 84 Stat. 1802, 42 U.S. Code § 1492

Housing and Community Development Act of 1974

Aug. 22, 1974, P.L. 93-383, 42 U.S. Code § 5301 et seq.

April 30, 1977, P.L. 95-24, 12 U.S. Code § 1706e

Oct. 12, 1977, P.L. 95-128, 12 U.S. Code § 1706e; 42 U.S. Code §§ 5301 et seq.

Oct. 31, 1978, P.L. 95-557, 12 U.S. Code §§ 1701j-2, 1706e; 42 U.S. Code §§ 5304, 5305, 5307, 5318, 5319

Dec. 21, 1979, P.L. 96-153, 12 U.S. Code § 1706e; 42 U.S. Code §§ 1439, 5302 to 5304, 5306, 5318

Oct. 6, 1982, P.L. 97-289, 42 U.S. Code § 5302(a)(4), (6)

Nov. 30, 1983, P.L. 98-181, 12 U.S. Code §§ 1701j-2, 1706e; 42 U.S. Code §§ 1439, 5301 et seq.

Oct. 17, 1984, P.L. 98-479, 12 U.S. Code § 1706e; 42 U.S. Code §§ 1438, 1439, 5302 to 5306, 5312, 5316 nt., 5318 nt.

Oct. 8, 1985, P.L. 99-120, 42 U.S. Code § 5302

Nov. 15, 1985, P.L. 99-156, 42 U.S. Code § 5302

Dec. 26, 1985, P.L. 99-219, 42 U.S. Code § 5302

March 27, 1986, P.L. 99-267, 42 U.S. Code § 5302

April 7, 1986, P.L. 99-272, 42 U.S. Code §§ 1471, 5302, 5308, 5318

Dec. 22, 1987, P.L. 100-202, 42 U.S. Code § 5302, 5318

Feb. 5, 1988, P.L. 100-242, 42 U.S. Code §§ 1439, 1701j-2, 1706e, 5301, 5302, 5304 to 5308, 5310, 5318 and nt.

Nov. 7, 1988, P.L. 100-628, 42 U.S. Code §§ 5302, 5304, 5306, 5318

Dec. 15, 1989, P.L. 101-235, 42 U.S. Code §§ 1439, 1706e, 5302, 5306, 5307

Oct. 31, 1990, P.L. 101-494, 42 U.S. Code § 1439

Nov. 5, 1990, P.L. 101-507, 42 U.S. Code § 5302

Oct. 6, 1992, P.L. 102-389, 42 U.S. Code § 1439

Oct. 28, 1992, P.L. 102-550, 12 U.S. Code §§ 1701j, 5403; 42 U.S. Code §§ 1438, 1439, 5302 to 5305, 5305 nt., 5306 to 5308

Dec. 14, 1993, P.L. 103-195, 42 U.S. Code § 5305

April 11, 1994, P.L. 103-233, 42 U.S. Code §§ 5301, 5403, 5305, 5308, 5318, 5321

March 28, 1996, P.L. 104-120, 42 U.S. Code § 5308

April 26, 1996, P.L. 104-134, 42 U.S. Code § 5305

Sept. 26, 1996, P.L. 104-204, 42 U.S. Code §§ 5302, 5305

Oct. 26, 1996, P.L. 104-330, 42 U.S. Code § 1439

Oct. 21, 1998, P.L. 105-276, 42 U.S. Code §§ 1438, 1439, 5305

Housing and Community Development Act of 1977

Oct. 12, 1977, P.L. 95-128, 12 U.S. Code §§ 1701q; 31 U.S. Code § 711; 40 U.S. Code § 461; 42 U.S. Code § 5301 et seq.

Housing and Community Development Act of 1980

Oct. 8, 1980, P.L. 96-399, 42 U.S. Code § 5301 nt.

Nov. 6, 1986, P.L. 99-603, 42 U.S. Code § 1436a

Feb. 5, 1988, P.L. 100-242, 42 U.S. Code § 1436a

Aug. 22, 1996, P.L. 104-193, 42 U.S. Code § 1436a

Sept. 30, 1996, P.L. 104-208, 42 U.S. Code § 1436a

Oct. 21, 1998, P.L. 105-276, 42 U.S. Code § 1436a

Housing and Community Development Act of 1987

Feb. 5, 1988, P.L. 100-242, 42 U.S. Code § 5301 nt.

Nov. 7, 1988, P.L. 100-628, 12 U.S. Code §§ 1709 nt., 1715l nt., 2802 nt., 42 U.S. Code §§ 1472 nt., 1490m nt., 11501

Nov. 3, 1989, P. L. 101-137, 12 U.S. Code § 1749bbb-10c; 42 U.S. Code §§ 1490m nt., 4015 nt.

Nov. 9, 1989, P.L. 101-144, 42 U.S. Code § 1490m nt.

Nov. 5, 1990, P.L. 101-508, 12 U.S. Code § 1749bbb-10c nt.; 42 U.S. Code § 4015 nt.

Nov. 28, 1990, P.L. 101-625, 12 U.S. Code § 1701z-11 nt.; 42 U.S. Code §§ 3536 nt., 3616

Oct. 28, 1991, P.L. 102-139, 12 U.S. Code § 1715l nt.

Oct. 28, 1992, P.L. 102-550, 12 U.S. Code §§ 1751l nt., 3616a, 4103, 4105 to 4112, 4116, 4119, 4121, 4122, 4124, 4141 to 4147, 11501

Oct. 28, 1992, P.L. 102-550, 42 U.S. Code § 5301 nt.

Oct. 27, 1993, P.L. 103-120, 42 U.S. Code § 1437f nt.

Dec. 14, 1993, P.L. 103-185, 42 U.S. Code § 8624 nt.

April 11, 1994, P.L. 103-233, 12 U.S. Code §§ 1707 nt., 1715z-1a nt., 42 U.S. Code 3545 nt., 4852

April 11, 1994, P.L. 103-233, 12 U.S. Code § 1701z-11 nt.

Dec. 21, 1995, P.L. 104-66, 42 U.S. Code §§ 3608a, 3616a

Jan. 26, 1996, P.L. 104-99, 42 U.S. Code §§ 12714, 13615

March 28, 1996, P.L. 104-120, 12 U.S. Code § 1707 nt.

April 26, 1996, P.L. 104-134, 12 U.S. Code §§ 1707 nt., 4516

Oct. 19, 1996, P.L. 104-316, 12 U.S. Code § 4524

Oct. 26, 1996, P.L. 104-330, 12 U.S. Code § 1715z-13a

June 12, 1997, P.L. 105-18, 12 U.S. Code § 1707

Oct. 27, 1997, P.L. 105-65, 12 U.S. Code § 1715z-4a

Oct. 21, 1998, P.L. 105-276, 12 U.S. Code § 1707 nt., 1715z-13a; 42 U.S. Code §§ 1437f nt., 13615

Oct. 21, 1998, P.L. 105-276, 12 U.S. Code § 4113; 42 U.S. Code sect1437f nt.

Nov. 10, 1998, P.L. 105-362, 42 U.S. Code §§ 1831m-1, 5318 nt., 11361 nt., 12705a nt.

Nov. 10, 1998, P.L. 105-362, 42 U.S. Code § 1490m nt.

Housing and Community Development Amendments of 1978

Oct. 31, 1978, P.L. 95-557, 12 U.S. Code §§ 1701j-2, 1701q, 1701z-1 et seq.; 15 U.S. Code § 1702; 40 U.S. Code §§ 461, 484b; 42 U.S. Code §§ 1437a et seq., 1441 nt., 1441c, 1452b, 1476, 1483 et seq., 3371, 3535, 3540, 4026, 4056, 4127, 4521, 5304 et seq., 8001 et seq.

Dec. 21, 1979, P.L. 96-153, 12 U.S. Code §§ 1715z-1a, 1715z-11; 42 U.S. Code §§ 3541, 8107, 8123, 8124, 8146

Nov. 30, 1983, P.L. 98-181, 12 U.S. Code § 1715z-1a

Feb. 5, 1988, P.L. 100-242, 12 U.S. Code §§ 1701z-11, 1715z-1a, 1715z-1b

Nov. 7, 1988, P.L. 100-628, 12 U.S. Code §§ 1701z-1, 1715z-1a

Dec. 15, 1989, P.L. 101-235, 12 U.S. Code §§ 1701z-11, 1715z-1a.

Nov. 28, 1990, P.L. 101-625, 12 U.S. Code §§ 1701z-11, 1715z-1a

June 13, 1991, P.L. 102-54, 42 U.S. Code § 3541

Oct. 28, 1992, P.L. 102-550, 12 U.S. Code § 1715z-1a

Oct. 27, 1993, P.L. 103-120, 12 U.S. Code § 1701z-11

April 11, 1994, P.L. 103-233, 12 U.S. Code
§§ 1701z-11, 1715z-1a

Oct. 21, 1998, P.L. 105-276, 12 U.S. Code
§§ 1715z-1a, 1715z-1b, 1701z-11

**Housing and Community Development
Amendments of 1979**

Dec. 21, 1979, P.L. 96-153, 5 U.S. Code
§ 5315; 12 U.S. Code §§ 901 et seq.; 15
U.S. Code § 1701 et seq.; 40 U.S. Code
§ 461; 42 U.S. Code § 1437a et seq.

**Housing and Community Development
Amendments of 1981**

Aug. 13, 1981, P.L. 97-35, 42 U.S. Code
§ 5301 nt.

Oct. 28, 1992, P.L. 102-550, 42 U.S. Code
§ 1437f nt.

Oct. 21, 1998, P.L. 105-276, 42 U.S. Code
§§ 1437f nt., 1437j-1

**Housing and Community Development
Authority Act**

Md. Laws 1969, Ch. 553, § 1, Subsec. 1 et
seq.

**Housing and Community Development
Technical Amendments Act of 1984**

Oct. 17, 1984, P.L. 98-479, 42 U.S. Code
§§ 5301 nt., 5301 et seq.

Housing and Conservation Trust Fund Act

R.I. Gen. Laws 1956, 42-113-1 et seq.

Vt. Stat. Ann., Title 10, § 301 et seq.

Housing and Development Act of 1965

Dec. 22, 1971, P.L. 92-213, 85 Stat. 776, 42
U.S. Code § 3102

July 1, 1972, P.L. 92-335, 86 Stat. 405, 42
U.S. Code §§ 3102, 3108

Oct. 2, 1973, P.L. 93-117, 87 Stat. 422, 42
U.S. Code §§ 3102, 3108

Housing and Development Act of 1968

Dec. 22, 1971, P.L. 92-213, 85 Stat. 775, 42
U.S. Code §§ 4012, 4013, 4021, 4056

Feb. 2, 1972, P.L. 93-4, 87 Stat. 4, 42 U.S.
Code § 4026

June 5, 1973, P.L. 93-38, 87 Stat. 73, 42 U.S.
Code § 4026

Housing and Finance Authority Act

Colo. Rev. Stat., 29-4-701 et seq.

Ga. Code Ann., 50-26-1 et seq.

Housing and Food Assistance Act

Ill. Rev. Stat. 1991, Ch. 23, § 6401 et seq.

Housing and Home Finance Act

Cal. Health and Safety Code § 50000 et seq.

**Housing and Home Finance Act (Zenovich-
Moscone-Chacon)**

Cal. Health and Safety Code § 50000 et seq.

Housing and Homeless Bond Act

Cal. Health and Safety Code §§ 53150 et
seq., 53180 et seq.

Housing and Jobs Investment Bond Act

Cal. Health and Safety Code § 52534 et seq.

Housing and Land Use Omnibus Act

Cal. Statutes 1995, Ch. 686

Cal. Statutes 1996, Ch. 799

Cal. Statutes 1997, Ch. 580

Housing and Local Redevelopment Law

N.J. Stat. Ann., 40A:12A-1 et seq.

Housing and Mobile Home Law

N.Y. Local Laws 1972, Town of Rensselaerville, p. 2690

Housing and Mortgage Finance Agency Law

N.J. Stat. Ann., 55:14K-1

**Housing and Mortgage Finance Corporation
Act**

N.J. Stat. Ann., 55:14K-1 et seq.

R.I. Gen. Laws 1956, 42-55-1 et seq.

Housing and Property Maintenance Code

N.Y. Local Laws 1973, Village of Ossining,
p. 3660

**Housing and Redevelopment Act (County
and Municipal)**

S.D. Codified Laws 1967, 11-7-1 et seq.

Housing and Redevelopment Act (Municipal)

Minn. Stat. 1986, 462.411 et seq.

Housing and Redevelopment Assistance Law

Pa. Purdon's Stat., Title 35, § 1661 et seq.

Housing and Redevelopment Cooperation Law

N.J. Stat. Ann., 55:14B-1 et seq.

S.D. Codified Laws 1967, 11-7A-1 et seq.

Housing and Rent Acts

June 30, 1947, Ch. 163, 61 Stat. 193

Feb. 27, 1948, Ch. 77, 62 Stat. 37

March 30, 1948, Ch. 161, 62 Stat. 93

March 30, 1949, Ch. 42, 63 Stat. 18

June 23, 1950, Ch. 354, 64 Stat. 255

Dec. 20, 1950, Ch. 1139, 64 Stat. 1113

March 23, 1951, Ch. 14, 65 Stat. 7

June 30, 1951, Ch. 198, 65 Stat. 110

July 31, 1951, Ch. 275, 65 Stat. 144

June 30, 1952, Ch. 530, 66 Stat. 306

July 15, 1952, Ch. 758, 66 Stat. 657

April 30, 1953, Ch. 31, 67 Stat. 24, 50 U.S. Code Appx. §§ 1884, 1894, 1898

Housing and Sanitation Act

Pa. Purdon's Stat., Title 53, § 14891 et seq.

Housing and Slum Clearance Act

Mich. Comp. Laws Ann., 125.651 et seq.

Housing and Urban Development Act of 1965

Aug. 10, 1965, P.L. 89-117, 79 Stat. 451, 12 U.S. Code §§ 371, 1464, 170d-3 nt., 1701h, 1701o, 1701q, 1701s, 1702, 1703, 1706c, 1709, 1710 and others; 15 U.S. Code §§ 633, 671, 692 to 694; 20 U.S. Code §§ 802, 803; 38 U.S. Code §§ 1804, 1816; 40 U.S. Code §§ 461, 462; 42 U.S. Code §§ 1402, 1410, 1412, 1415, 1421a, 1421b, 1422 and others; 49 U.S. Code §§ 1605, 1608

Nov. 3, 1966, P.L. 89-754, 80 Stat. 1284, 12 U.S. Code §§ 1701d-3 nt., 1701q nt., 1735g

May 25, 1967, P.L. 90-19, 81 Stat. 26, 12 U.S. Code § 1701s; 42 U.S. Code §§ 3071, 3072, 3074, 3102 to 3105

Oct. 31, 1967, P.L. 90-118, 81 Stat. 338, 42 U.S. Code § 1456 nt.

Aug. 1, 1968, P.L. 90-448, 82 Stat. 502, 12 U.S. Code § 1701s; 42 U.S. Code §§ 3101, 3102, 3104, 3108

Dec. 24, 1969, P.L. 91-152, 83 Stat. 383, 12 U.S. Code § 1701s; 42 U.S. Code §§ 3102, 3108

Oct. 6, 1970, P.L. 91-431, 84 Stat. 886, 42 U.S. Code §§ 3102, 3108

Dec. 31, 1970, P.L. 91-609, 84 Stat. 1771, 12 U.S. Code § 1701s; 42 U.S. Code § 3108

Dec. 21, 1979, P.L. 96-153, 12 U.S. Code § 1701s

Nov. 30, 1983, P.L. 98-181, 12 U.S. Code § 1701s; 42 U.S. Code § 3103

Oct. 17, 1984, P.L. 98-479, 12 U.S. Code § 1701s

July 2, 1986, P.L. 99-349, 100 Stat. 727

Feb. 5, 1988, P.L. 100-242, 12 U.S. Code § 1701s

June 13, 1991, P.L. 102-54, 12 U.S. Code § 1735g

Jan. 26, 1996, P.L. 104-99, 12 U.S. Code § 1701s

Oct. 21, 1998, P.L. 105-276, 12 U.S. Code § 1701s

Housing and Urban Development Act of 1968

Aug. 1, 1968, P.L. 90-448, 82 Stat. 476, 5 U.S. Code §§ 5315, 7313 nt.; 12 U.S. Code §§ 24, 371, 378, 1431, 1432, 1436, 1464, 1701c nt., 1701d-4 and others; 15 U.S. Code §§ 633, 636, 1701 to 1720; 18 U.S. Code § 709; 20 U.S. Code §§ 801, 805; 31 U.S. Code § 846; 38 U.S. Code § 1820; 40 U.S. Code §§ 461, 462, 612; 40 U.S. Code Appx. § 207; 42 U.S. Code §§ 1401 to 1403, 1410, 1415, 1417 nt., 1417a, 1420, 1421b, 1436, 1441a to 1441c, 1451 to 1453, 1455 to 1457 and others; 49 U.S. Code Appx. §§ 1603 to 1605, 1608

Dec. 24, 1969, P.L. 91-152, 83 Stat. 391, 12 U.S. Code § 1701u; 15 U.S. Code § 1702; 42 U.S. Code §§ 1441c, 3911, 4001, 4012, 4022, 4056, 4102, 4121

July 24, 1970, P.L. 91-351, 84 Stat. 462, 42 U.S. Code §§ 3906, 3941

Dec. 31, 1970, P.L. 91-609, 84 Stat. 1780, 12 U.S. Code § 1701x; 42 U.S. Code §§ 3906, 3907, 3911

Oct. 12, 1977, P.L. 95-128, 12 U.S. Code § 1701x

Oct. 31, 1978, P.L. 95-557, 42 U.S. Code § 1441c

Dec. 21, 1979, P.L. 96-153, 42 U.S. Code § 343a

Nov. 30, 1983, P.L. 98-181, 12 U.S. Code § 1701x; 42 U.S. Code § 3936

Oct. 17, 1984, P.L. 98-479, 42 U.S. Code §§ 3936, 3938

Feb. 5, 1988, P.L. 100-242, 12 U.S. Code § 1701x

Nov. 7, 1988, P.L. 100-628, 12 U.S. Code § 1701x

Nov. 3, 1989, P.L. 101-137, 12 U.S. Code § 1701x

Nov. 28, 1990, P.L. 101-625, 12 U.S. Code § 1701x

Oct. 28, 1992, P.L. 102-550, 12 U.S. Code §§ 1701u, 1701x

Dec. 21, 1995, P.L. 104-66, 12 U.S. Code § 1701y

Oct. 19, 1996, P.L. 104-316, 12 U.S. Code § 1701x

Oct. 21, 1998, P.L. 105-276, 12 U.S. Code § 1701x

Housing and Urban Development Act of 1969

Dec. 24, 1969, P.L. 91-152, 83 Stat. 379, 12 U.S. Code §§ 1425, 1464, 1701q, 1701s, 1701u, 1703, 1706d, 1707, 1709, 1709-1, 1713, 1715d, 1715e and others; 15 U.S. Code § 1702; 20 U.S. Code §§ 801 to 807; 40 U.S. Code §§ 461, 484b; 49 U.S. Code §§ 1603, 1604

Dec. 31, 1970, P.L. 91-609, 84 Stat. 1816, 40 U.S. Code § 484b

Oct. 31, 1978, P.L. 95-557, 40 U.S. Code § 484

Nov. 30, 1983, P.L. 98-181, 40 U.S. Code § 484b

Housing and Urban Development Act of 1970

Dec. 31, 1970, P.L. 91-609, 84 Stat. 1770, 12 U.S. Code §§ 371, 1431, 1432, 1464, 1466a, 1701c nt., 1701e nt., 1701s, 1701x, 1701z-1 to 1701z-4 and others; 15 U.S. Code §§ 692, 693, 694 to 694b, 1705; 16 U.S. Code § 617; 18 U.S. Code § 1014; 20 U.S. Code § 803; 40 U.S. Code §§ 461, 484b; 42 U.S. Code §§ 1401, 1402, 1410, 1415, 1421b, 1436 nt., 1453, 1456, 1458, 1460, 1465 and others

Dec. 22, 1971, P.L. 92-213, 85 Stat. 776, 42 U.S. Code § 4519

Oct. 2, 1973, P.L. 93-117, 87 Stat. 423, 42 U.S. Code § 4514

Oct. 12, 1977, P.L. 95-128, 12 U.S. Code § 1701z-1; 42 U.S. Code § 4521

Oct. 31, 1978, P.L. 95-557, 12 U.S. Code §§ 1701z-1, 1701z-9, 1701z-9 nt., 1701z-10; 42 U.S. Code § 4521

Dec. 21, 1979, P.L. 96-153, 12 U.S. Code § 1701z-1.

Nov. 30, 1983, P.L. 98-181, 12 U.S. Code §§ 1701z-1, 1701z-10a

Aug. 22, 1986, P.L. 99-386, 12 U.S. Code §§ 1701z-4, 1701z-5

February 5, 1988, P.L. 100-242, 12 U.S. Code §§ 1701z-1, 1709-2

Nov. 28, 1990, P.L. 101-625, 12 U.S. Code § 1701z-1

June 13, 1991, P.L. 102-54, 12 U.S. Code § 1709-2

Oct. 28, 1992, P.L. 102-550, 12 U.S. Code § 1701z-1; 42 U.S. Code §§ 4502, 4503

Housing and Urban Development Act of 1974

Nov. 28, 1990, P.L. 101-625, 42 U.S. Code § 5307

Housing and Urban Development, and Independent Agencies Appropriations Act, 1997

Sept. 26, 1996, P.L. 104-204, 110 Stat. 2874

Housing and Urban-Rural Recovery Act of 1983

Nov. 30, 1983, P.L. 98-181, 12 U.S. Code § 1701 nt.

Oct. 17, 1984, P.L. 98-479, 12 U.S. Code § 3612

Continued

Oct. 8, 1985, P.L. 99-120, 12 U.S. Code § 1701q nt.

Nov. 15, 1985, P.L. 99-156, 12 U.S. Code § 1701q nt.

Dec. 26, 1985, P.L. 99-219, 12 U.S. Code § 1701q nt.

March 27, 1986, P.L. 99-267, 12 U.S. Code § 1701q nt.

April 7, 1986, P.L. 99-272, 12 U.S. Code § 1701q nt.

Feb. 5, 1988, P.L. 100-242, 12 U.S. Code §§ 1701q nt., 1701z-6 nt., 5318 nt.

Nov. 7, 1988, P.L. 100-628, 12 U.S. Code § 1701z-6 nt.

Nov. 28, 1990, P.L. 101-625, 12 U.S. Code § 1701z-6 nt.; 42 U.S. Code § 5318

Oct. 28, 1992, P.L. 102-550, 12 U.S. Code § 1701z-6 nt.; 42 U.S. Code § 5318a

Oct. 21, 1998, P.L. 105-276, 12 U.S. Code § 1701z-6 nt.

Nov. 10, 1998, P.L. 105-362, 42 U.S. Code § 5318a

Housing Antidiscrimination Act
Mass. Gen. Laws Ann., 151B:1 et seq.
N.J. Stat. Ann., 10:5-4
Ore. Rev. Stat., 659.031, 659.033
Wash. Rev. Code Ann., 49.60.222 et seq.

Housing Assistance Act (Polanco-Ferguson)
Cal. Health and Safety Code §§ 33080.7, 33334.10, 33334.12, 34312.5

Housing Assistance Act (Senior Citizens)
Cal. Health and Safety Code § 51450 et seq.

Housing Assistance Bond Act
N.J. Laws 1968, Ch. 127
N.J. Laws 1974, Ch. 117
N.J. Laws 1975, Ch. 207

Housing Assistance Program (Local)
Iowa Code 1983, 15.351 to 15.354

Housing Authorities Act
Ala. Code 1975, §§ 24-1-20 et seq., 24-1-100 et seq.
Alaska Stat. 1962, § 18.55.010 et seq.
Ariz. Rev. Stat. Ann. 1956, § 36-1401 et seq.
Ark. Code Ann. 1987, 14-169-201 et seq.
Cal. Health and Safety Code § 34200 et seq.

Colo. Rev. Stat., 29-4-101 et seq., 29-4-201 et seq.

Conn. Gen. Stat. Ann., §§ 8-38 et seq., 8-119ZZ et seq.

Del. Code of 1974, Title 31, § 4301 et seq.

Fla. Stat. Ann., 421.01 et seq., 421.27 et seq.

Ga. Code Ann., 8-3-1 et seq., 8-3-100 et seq.

Ill. Rev. Stat. 1991, Ch. 67 1/2

Ind. Code Ann., 36-7-18-1 et seq.

La. Rev. Stat. Ann., 40:381 et seq.

Mass. Gen. Laws Ann., 121B:3 et seq.

Md. Ann. Code 1957, Art. 44A, § 1-101 et seq.

Me. Rev. Stat. Ann. 1964, Title 30-A, § 4701 et seq.

Miss. Code Ann. 1972, §§ 43-33-1 et seq.

Mo. Rev. Stat., 99.010 et seq.

Mont. Code Ann., 7-15-4401 et seq.

N.C. Gen. Stat. 1943, § 157-1 et seq.

N.D. Cent. Code, 23-11-01 et seq.

Neb. Laws 1937, Ch. 90

Neb. Rev. Stat. 1943, 71-1518 et seq.

Nev. Rev. Stat. 1973 Reprint, 315.140 et seq.

N.H. Rev. Stat. 1955, 203:1 et seq.

N.J. Stat. Ann., 55:14A-1 et seq., 55:14-1 to 55:14-13

N.M. Stat. Ann., 11-4-1 et seq.

Ohio Rev. Code 1953, 3735.27 et seq.

Okla. Stat. Ann., Title 63, § 1051 et seq.

Ore. Rev. Stat., 456.005 et seq.

Pa. Purdon's Stat., Title 35, § 1541 et seq.

P.R. Laws Ann. 1954, Title 17, § 31 et seq.

R.I. Gen. Laws 1956, 45-25-1 et seq.

S.C. Code Ann. 1976, §§ 31-3-110 et seq., 31-13-10 et seq., 31-13-160 et seq.

Tenn. Code Ann., 13-20-101 et seq.

Tex. Local Government Code, § 392.001 et seq.

Utah Code Ann. 1953, 55-18-1 et seq.

Va. Code 1950, § 36-1 et seq.

Vt. Stat. Ann., Title 24, § 4001 et seq.

Wash. Rev. Code Ann., 35.82.010 et seq.

Wis. Stat. 1981, 66.40 et seq.

Housing Authorities and Cooperation Law
Ida. Code 1947, 50-1901 et seq.

Housing Authorities and Cooperation Law (County)
Ida. Code 1947, 31-4201 et seq.

Housing Authority Act (Hempstead)
N.Y. Public Housing Law (Consol. Laws Ch. 44A) § 409

Housing Authority Act (New York City)
N.Y. Public Housing Law (Consol. Laws Ch. 44A) § 400 et seq.

Housing Authority Act (Oklahoma A. & M. College)
Okla. Stat. Ann., Title 70, § 3401 et seq.

Housing Authority Act (Veterans)
Pa. Purdon's Stat., Title 35, § 1590.1 et seq.

Housing Authority for Elderly Persons Law
Wis. Stat. Ann., 66.395

Housing Authority Law (Indian)
Me. Rev. Stat. Ann. 1964, Title 22, § 4731 et seq.

Housing Authorization Act of 1976
Aug. 3, 1976, 94-375, 12 U.S. Code § 1701 et seq.

Housing Bond Act
Cal. Health and Safety Code § 53500 et seq.

Housing Bond Allocation Act
Cal. Health and Safety Code § 50171 et seq.

Housing Bond Investment Law
Cal. Health and Safety Code § 34369 et seq.

Housing Code
N.Y. Local Laws 1967, Hudson, p. 296
N.Y. Local Laws 1967, Town of Southold, p. 1941
N.Y. Local Laws 1968, Town of Riverhead, p. 2955
N.Y. Local Laws 1970, Town of Rotterdam, p. 2604
N.Y. Local Laws 1971, Village of Canajoharie, p. 3842
N.Y. Local Laws 1972, Village of Great Neck Plaza, p. 3396

Housing Commission Act
Ky. Rev. Stat. 1971, 80.010 et seq.

Housing Commission Act (County and Regional)
Ky. Rev. Stat. 1971, 80.310 et seq.

Housing Companies Act (Limited Dividend)
N.Y. Private Housing Finance Law (Consol. Law Ch. 44B) § 70 et seq.

Housing Companies Act (Limited Profit)
N.Y. Private Housing Finance Law (Consol. Laws Ch. 44B) § 10 et seq.

Housing Companies Act (Limited-Profit)
N.Y. Private Housing Finance Law (Consol. Laws Ch. 44B) § 10 et seq.
Pa. 1937 Pamph. Laws 704, No. 181

Housing Cooperation Act
Cal. Health and Safety Code § 34500 et seq.
Fla. Stat. Ann., 422.001 et seq.
Ga. Code Ann., 8-3-150 et seq.
Ida. Code 1947, 50-1901 et seq.
Ill. Rev. Stat. 1991, Ch. 67 1/2, § 28 et seq.
Ind. Code 1976, 18-7-12-1 et seq.
Ky. Rev. Stat. 1971, 80.010, 80.270 et seq.
La. Rev. Stat. Ann., 40:531 et seq.
Md. Ann. Code 1957, Art. 44A, § 1-101 et seq.
Mich. Comp. Laws Ann., 125.601 et seq.
Neb. Rev. Stat. 1943, 71-1501 et seq.
N.J. Rev. Stat. 1937, 55:14B-1 et seq.
Ohio Rev. Code 1953, 3735.51 et seq.
Ore. Rev. Stat., 456.305 et seq.
Pa. Purdon's Stat., Title 35, § 1581 et seq.
P.R. Laws Ann. 1954, Title 17, § 1 et seq.
S.C. Code Ann. 1976, § 31-5-10 et seq.
Tenn. Code Ann., 13-20-111
Tex. Local Government Code, § 393.001 et seq.
Wash. Rev. Code Ann., 35.83.005 et seq.
W. Va. Code 1966, § 16-16-1 et seq.

Housing Cooperatives Act (Consumer)
Mich. Comp. Laws. Ann., 125.1471 et seq.

Housing Corporation Act
Ky. Rev. Stat. 1971, 198A.010 et seq.

Housing Corporation Act (Cooperative)
La. Rev. Stat. Ann., 12:499.1 et seq.
Mass. Gen. Laws Ann., 157B:1 et seq.

Housing Corporation Act (Limited Dividend)
Cal. Statutes 1933, p. 1426

Housing Corporations Act (Nonprofit)
Mich. Comp. Laws. Ann., 125.1401 et seq.

Housing Deficiency Act
March 4, 1939, Ch. 6, 53 Stat. 511

Housing Department Organic Act
P.R. Laws Ann. 1954, Title 3, § 441 et seq.

Housing Development Act
Ill. Rev. Stat. 1991, Ch. 67 1/2, § 52.9 et seq.

Housing Development Agency Act
Ark. Stat. 1947, 19-3080 et seq.

Housing Development Area Law
La. Rev. Stat. Ann., 40:582.1 et seq.

Housing Development Authority Act
Ga. Laws 1974, p. 2591
Ga. Laws 1975, p. 3053
Mich. Comp. Laws Ann., 125.1401 et seq.
S.D. Codified Laws 1967, 11-11-1 et seq.
Tenn. Code Ann., 13-23-101 et seq.
Va. Code 1950, § 36-55.24 et seq.

Housing Development Commission Act
Mo. Rev. Stat., 215.010 et seq.

Housing Development Corporation Act (New York City)
N.Y. Private Housing Finance Law (Consol. Laws Ch. 44B) § 650 et seq.

Housing Development Fund Act
W. Va. Code 1966, § 31-18-1 et seq.

Housing Development Fund Companies Law
N.Y. Private Housing Finance Law (Consol. Laws Ch. 44B) § 570 et seq.

Housing Discontinuance Regulation Act
D.C. Code Ann., § 5-835
D.C. Laws 1973, §§ 45-1699.6, 45-1699.19 to 45-1699.22

Housing Discrimination Act
Cal. Health and Safety Code § 35700 et seq.
Ill. Rev. Stat. 1991, Ch. 24, § 11-74.5-1 et seq.
N.Y. Civil Rights Law (Consol. Laws Ch. 6) § 18a et seq.
S.C. Code Ann. 1976, § 31-21-10 et seq.

Housing Finance Acts
La. Rev. Stat. Ann., 40:600.1 et seq.
Nev. Rev. Stat. 1979 Reprint, 319.010 et seq.

Housing Finance Agency Act
D.C. Code Ann., § 45-2101 et seq.
Fla. Stat. Ann., 420.501 et seq.
La. Rev. Stat. Ann., 40:600.1 et seq.
Mass. Acts 1966, Ch. 708
Minn. Stat. Ann., 462A.01 et seq.
N.C. Stat. 1943, § 122A-1 et seq.
N.J. Stat. Ann., 55:14K-1 et seq.
N.Y. Private Housing Finance Law (Consol. Laws Ch. 44B) § 40 et seq.
Pa. Purdon's Stat., Title 35, § 1680.101 et seq.
Utah Code Ann. 1953, 9-4-901 et seq.
Utah Code Ann. 1953, 63-44a-1 et seq.
Vt. Stat. Ann., Title 10, § 601 et seq.

Housing Finance Assistance Act (Municipal)
Conn. Gen. Stat. Ann., § 8-300 et seq.

Housing Finance Authority Act
Colo. Rev. Stat., 29-4-701 et seq.
Conn. Gen. Stat. Ann., § 8-241 et seq.
Fla. Stat. Ann., 159.601 et seq.

Housing Finance Bond Law of 1975
Cal. Health and Safety Code § 41800 et seq.

Housing Finance Corporations Act
Fla. Stat. Ann., 420.501 et seq.
Miss. Code Ann. 1972, § 43-33-501 et seq.
Tex. Local Government Code, § 394.001 et seq.

Housing Financial Discrimination Act
Cal. Health and Safety Code § 35800 et seq.

Housing for Older Persons Act of 1995
Dec. 28, 1995, P.L. 104-76, 42 U.S. Code § 3601 nt.

Housing for the Elderly (Security)
R.I. Gen. Laws 1956, 42-66.1-1 et seq.

Housing for the Elderly Act (Maintenance)
Fla. Stat. Ann., 420.901 et seq.

Housing for the Elderly Law
Cal. Health and Safety Code § 35800 et seq.

Housing Funds Act (Optional County Affordable)
Pa. 1992 Pamph. Laws, No. 137

Housing Incentive Finance Act
N.J. Stat. Ann., 55:4K-45 et seq.

Housing Incentive Partnership Act
Fla. Stat. Ann., 420.0001 et seq.

Housing Initiatives Partnership Act
Fla. Stat. Ann., 420.907 et seq.

Housing Integration Act
N.J. Stat. Ann., 10:5-1

Housing Land Acquisition and Site Development Act
Fla. Stat. 1983, 420.101 et seq.

Housing Law
Alaska Stat. 1962, § 18.55.010 et seq.
Ark. Pope's Digest 1937, § 12243 et seq.
Cal. Health and Safety Code § 17910 et seq.
Fla. Stat. Ann., 424.001 et seq.

Housing Law (Fair)
Ala. Code 1975, § 24-8-1
Colo. Rev. Stat., 24-32-701 et seq.

Fla. Stat. Ann., 420.001 et seq., 424.001 et seq.
Haw. Rev. Stat. Ann., §§ 171-84, 359-121 et seq., 359-141, 361-1 et seq.
Ill. Rev. Stat. 1991, Ch. 67 1/2, § 151 et seq.
Iowa Code 1979, 413.1 et seq.
Mich. Comp. Laws Ann., 125.401 et seq.
Mont. Code Ann., 90-6-101 et seq.
N.C. Public Laws 1933, Ch. 384
Nev. Rev. Stat. 1979 Reprint, Replaced Pages, 315.800 et seq.
N.J. Stat. Ann., 55:14H-1 et seq.
Ohio Rev. Code 1953, 3735.01 et seq.
S.C. Code Ann. 1976, § 31-1-10 et seq.
Tex. Rev. Civ. Stat., Art. 1528a
W. Va. Code 1966, § 16-15-1 et seq.

Housing Law (Municipal)
N.M. Stat. Ann., 3-45-1 et seq.

Housing Loan and Mortgage Act
Haw. Rev. Stat. Ann., § 356-201 et seq.

Housing Maintenance and Occupancy Code
R.I. Gen. Laws 1956, 45-24.3-1 et seq.

Housing Maintenance Code
N.Y. Adm. Code '85, § 27-2001 et seq.
N.Y. City Adm. Code 85, § 27-2001 et seq.

Housing Mortgage Insurance Act
Me. Rev. Stat. Ann. 1964, Title 30-A, § 4931 et seq.

Housing New York Program Act
Me. Rev. Stat. Ann. 1964, Title 30-A, § 4931 et seq.
N.Y. Laws 1986, Ch. 32, § 1
N.Y. Private Housing Finance Law (Consol. Laws Ch. 41) § 654c nt.

Housing Operations Act
Cal. Health and Safety Code § 34600 et seq.

Housing Opportunities for Maine Program
Me. Rev. Stat. Ann. 1964, Title 30-A, § 4851 et seq.

Housing Opportunity Act (Affordable)
R.I. Gen. Laws 1956, 42-11.2-1 et seq.

Housing Opportunity Program Extension Act of 1996
March 28, 1996, P.L. 104-120, 12 U.S. Code § 1701 nt.
Oct. 21, 1998, P.L. 105-276, 42 U.S. Code § 12805 nt.

Housing Ownership Act (Cooperative)
Vt. Stat. Ann., Title 11, § 1581 et seq.

Housing Partnership Act (Affordable)
Me. Rev. Stat. Ann. 1964, Title 30-A, § 5001 et seq.

Housing Policy Act
Wash. Rev. Code Ann., 43.185B.900

Housing Predevelopment and Elderly Homeowner Rehabilitation Assistance Act
Fla. Stat. Ann., 420.303 et seq.

Housing Preservation Act (Affordable)
R.I. Gen. Laws 1956, 34-45-1 et seq.

Housing Preservation Act (Assisted)
Md. Ann. Code 1957, Art. 83B, § 9-101 et seq.
Md. Ann. Code 1974, Department of Housing and Community Development, § 9-101 et seq.

Housing Preservation Act (Federally Subsidized)
Ill. Rev. Stat. 1991, Ch. 67 1/2, § 1151 et seq.

Housing Program Assistance Bond Act (Affordable)
N.J. Laws 1990, Ch. 81

Housing Project and Public Building Assistance Act
Alaska Stat. 1962, § 18.55.010 et seq.

Housing Prompt Processing Act
N.Y. Private Housing Finance Law (Consol. Laws Ch. 44B) §§ 1023, 1053

Housing Protection Act (Employee)
Cal. Statutes 1992, Ch. 1298

Housing Receivership Act
Ore. Rev. Stat., 105.420 et seq.

Housing Regulations Amendments (Security Deposits)
D.C. Laws 1975, No. 1-7 § 45-2527

Housing Rehabilitation Act
Tex. Government Code, § 2304.001 et seq.

Housing Rehabilitation Act (Abandoned)
Ill. Comp. Stat. 1992, Ch. 310, § 50/1 et seq.
Ill. Rev. Stat. 1991, Ch. 67 1/2, § 851 et seq.

Housing Rehabilitation Loan and Grant Act (Neighborhood Preservation)
N.J. Stat. Ann., 52:27D-152 et seq.

Housing Rent Act
N.Y. Laws 1950, Ch. 250
N.Y. Laws 1951, Ch. 443

Housing Rent Control Act
N.Y. Laws 1946, Ch. 274
N.Y. Laws 1949, Ch. 591
N.Y. Laws 1962, Ch. 21, § 1
N.Y. Local Laws 1947, New York City, Nos. 54, 66, 67, 68

Housing Rent Control Act (Local Emergency)
N.Y. Unconsolidated Law, § 8601 et seq.

Housing Rent Control Law (State)
N.Y. Unconsolidated Law § 8581 et seq.

Housing Replacement Authorization Act
Pa. Purdon's Stat., Title 35, § 1525 et seq.

Housing Restrictions Act (Low and Moderate Income)
R.I. Gen. Laws 1956, 34-39.1-1 et seq.

Housing Services Act (Neighborhood)
Pa. Purdon's Stat., Title 62, § 2090.11 et seq.

Housing Services Grant Fund Act
N.J. Stat. Ann., 52:27D-366 et seq.

Housing Standards Act (Manufactured)
Tex. Rev. Civ. Stat., Art. 5221f

Housing Standards Applicable to Mobile Homes and Mobile Home Courts
N.Y. Local Laws 1973, Village of Walden, p. 3999

Housing Standards Applicable to Mobile Homes Law (Town of Wallkill)
N.Y. Local Laws 1966, Town of Wallkill, p. 1762

Housing Standards Applicable to Residential Premises Act
N.Y. Local Laws 1966, Town of Wallkill, p. 1742
N.Y. Local Laws 1970, Town of New Paltz, p. 2164
N.Y. Local Laws 1973, Village of Walden, p. 3999

Housing Strategy Act (State)
Fla. Stat. Ann., 420.0001 et seq.

Housing Tax Credit Act (Affordable Neighborhood)
Ark. Code 1987, 15-5-1301 et seq.

Housing Trust Act (Low-Income)
N.M. Stat. Ann., 58-18B-1 et seq.

Housing Trust and Oil Overcharge Act
N.C. Gen. Stat. 1943, § 122E-1 et seq.

Housing Trust Fund Act
S.C. Code Ann. 1976, § 31-13-400 et seq.

Housing Trust Fund for the Homeless Act
Ga. Code Ann., 8-3-300 et seq.

Houston County Abandoned Automobile Act
Ala. Acts 1971, p. 3254

Houston County Commission on Children and Youth Act
Ga. Laws 1998, S.B. 373

Houston County Emergency Communications Service District Act
Ga. Laws 1990, p. 3517

Houston County School District Building Authority Act
Ga. Laws 1994, p. 3906

Houston-Perry County Airport Authority Act
Ga. Laws 1994, p. 3885

Houston Pilots Licensing and Regulatory Act
Tex. Laws 67th Leg., 1981, p. 441, Ch. 550
Tex. Transportation Code, § 66.001 et seq.

Hovering Vessels
Aug. 5, 1935, Ch. 438, 49 Stat. 521-529, 19 U.S. Code §§ 1401, 1432a, 1436, 1455, 1581, 1584, 1586, 1587, 1615, 1709; 46 U.S. Code § 91

Howard, Blake, Swope and Moore Act (Elections)
Ky. Acts 1944, Ch. 5

Howard County Airport Authority Act
Tex. Laws 60th Leg. 1967, p. 964, Ch. 425

Howard Development Corporation Act
R.I. Gen. Laws 1956, 37-19-1 et seq.

Howard-Hilton-Cooper Act (Pari-Mutuel Betting)
Ky. Rev. Stat. 1971, 47.012, 137.190, 138.510 et seq.

Howard Law
Ky. Acts 1924, Ch. 122

Howard M. Metzenbaum Multiethnic Placement Act of 1994
Oct. 20, 1994, P.L. 103-382, 42 U.S. Code § 5115a nt.
Aug. 20, 1996, P.L. 104-188, 42 U.S. Code § 5115a

Howard University Endowment Act
Oct. 17, 1984, P.L. 480, 20 U.S. Code §§ 130aa nt., 130aa et seq.

Howland Act (Insurers' Liability)
Ohio Rev. Code 1953, 3929.25 et seq.

Hoyt, William B., Memorial Children and Family Trust Fund Act
N.Y. Social Services Law (Consol. Laws Ch. 55) § 481a et seq.

HTS
See Harmonized Tariff Schedule of The United States

Hubbard Act (Sewage)
Ala. General Acts 1933, Ex. Sess., p. 29

Hubbard Act (Waterworks)
Ala. General Acts 1933, Ex. Sess., p. 22

Huber Act (Prison Labor)
Wis. Stat. 1987, 56.08 et seq.

Huber Act (Prisoner Employment)
Minn. Stat. Ann., 631.425

Huber Law
Wis. Stat. Ann., 303.08

Hubert H. Humphrey Institute of Public Affairs and the Everett McKinley Dirksen Congressional Leadership Research Center Assistance Act
April 27, 1978, P.L. 95-270, 20 U.S. Code §§ 2566 to 2569

HUBZone Act of 1997
Dec. 2, 1997, P.L. 105-135, Title VI, 15 U.S. Code § 631 nt.

Hucksters' License Act
Mont. Code Ann., 7-21-2501 et seq.

HUD Demonstration Act of 1993
Oct. 27, 1993, P.L. 103-120, 42 U.S. Code § 11301 nt.
Oct. 19, 1996, P.L. 104-316, 42 U.S. Code § 1437f nt.
Oct. 26, 1996, P.L. 104-330, 42 U.S. Code § 11301 nt.
June 12, 1997, P.L. 105-18, 42 U.S. Code § 9816 nt.

Hudson Act (Municipal Refunding)
Ohio Laws Vol. 116, p. 57

Hudson Electric Loan Act
Mass. Acts 1955, Ch. 19

Hudson-Mohawk Urban Cultural Park Commission Act
N.Y. Public Authorities Law (Consol. Laws Ch. 43A) § 2630 et seq.

Hudson Parking Authority Act
N.Y. Public Authorities Law (Consol. Laws Ch. 43A) § 1425a et seq.

Hudson River Estuary Management Act
N.Y. Environmental Conservation Law 1972 (Consol. Laws Ch. 43B) § 11-0306

Hudson River Fishery Management Program Act
N.Y. Environmental Conservation Law (Consol. Laws Ch. 43B) § 11-0306

Hudson River Park Act
N.Y. Laws 1998, Ch. 592

Hudson River Valley Greenway Act
N.Y. Environmental Conservation Law 1972 (Consol. Laws Ch. 43B) § 44-0101 et seq.

Hudson River Valley National Heritage Area Act of 1996
Nov. 12, 1996, P.L. 104-333, Division II, Title IX, 16 U.S. Code § 461 nt.

Hue and Cry Act (Escaped Felon)
Mo. Rev. Stat., 544.120

Huffman Act (Land Forfeiture)
W. Va. Code 1966, 11A-4-2

Hugh O'Conner Memorial Act
Fla. Stat. Ann., 772.12

Hughes Antisecrecy Act
Ind. Code Ann., 5-14-1.5-1 et seq.

Hughes Childrens Health Care Enforcement Act
Cal. Health and Safety Code § 324.3

Hughes Earthquake Safety Act
Cal. Education Code 1976, §§ 17701, 39141.4, 39250

Hughes-Greene School Building Lease-Purchase Bond Law
Cal. Education Code 1976, § 17696 et seq.

Hughes-Greene School Facilities Act
Cal. Statutes 1986, Ch. 886

Hughes-Griswold Act (Health Districts)
Ohio Rev. Code 1953, 3709.01 et seq., 3709.01 et seq.

Hughes-Hart Educational Reform Act
Cal. Education Code 1976, § 1296
Cal. Statutes 1983, Ch. 498

Hughes McGill, Georgia M. Davis, Mae Street Kidd Civil Rights Act
Ky. Rev. Stat. 1971, 344.010 et seq.

Hughes-Smith Act (State Board of Education)
Ohio Laws Vol. 107, p. 579

Hulette-Miller Act (Municipal Housing)
Ky. Rev. Stat. 1971, 80.020 et seq., 80.230

Human Affairs Act
S.C. Code Ann. 1976, § 1-13-10 et seq.

Human Burial Sites Preservation Act (Unmarked)
La. Rev. Stat. Ann., 8:671 et seq.

Human Cloning Act
Cal. Business and Professions Code §§ 2260.5, 16004, 16105
Cal. Health and Safety Code §§ 24185 to 24189

Human Immunodeficiency Virus Services Act
Tex. Health and Safety Code, § 85.001 et seq.

Human Immunodeficiency Virus Test Act
N.M. Stat. Ann., 24-2B-1 et seq.

Human Relations Act
Fla. Stat. Ann., 760.01 et seq.
Miss. Laws 1999, H.B. 361
Pa. Purdon's Stat., Title 43, § 951 et seq.
S.D. Codified Laws 1967, 20-13-1 et seq.

Human Resource Agency Act
Tenn. Code Ann., 13-26-101 et seq.

Human Resource Development Act
Fla. Laws 1994, Ch. 319, §§ 4 to 6

Human Resources Development Act
Cal. Unemployment Insurance Code § 9000 et seq.

Human Resources Hospital Facilities Finance Act
N.C. Gen. Stat. 1943, § 131-138 et seq.

Human Rights Act
Alaska Stat. 1962, § 18.80.010 et seq.
D.C. Code Ann., § 1-2501 et seq.
Fla. Stat. Ann., 760.01 et seq.
Ill. Rev. Stat. 1991, Ch. 68, § 1-101 et seq.
Me. Rev. Stat. Ann. 1964, Title 5, § 4551 et seq.
Minn. Stat. Ann., 363.01 et seq.
Mont. Code Ann., 49-2-101 et seq.
N.D. Cent. Code, 14-02.4-01 et seq.
N.M. Stat. Ann., 28-1-1 et seq.
N.Y. Executive Law 1951 (Consol. Laws Ch. 18) § 290 et seq.
Okla. Stat. Ann., Title 74, § 951 et seq.
Wis. Stat. Ann., 66.433
W. Va. Code 1966, § 5-11-1 et seq.

Human Rights Act (Broward County)
Fla. Laws 1991, Ch. 359

Human Rights and Opportunities Commission Act
Conn. Gen. Stat. Ann., § 46a-51 et seq.

Human Rights Commission Act
Ida. Code 1947, 67-5901 et seq.

Human Rights, Refugee, and Other Foreign Relations Provisions Act of 1996
Oct. 19, 1996, P.L. 104-319, 22 U.S. Code § 2151 nt.
Oct. 21, 1998, P.L. 105-277, 22 U.S. Code § 2151 nt.

Human Services Act
Minn. Stat. Ann., 402.01 et seq.
Wyo. Stat. Ann., § 35-1-611 et seq.

Human Services Amendments of 1994
May 18, 1994, P.L. 103-252, 42 U.S. Code § 9801 nt.

Human Services Code
Colo. Rev. Stat., 26-1-101 et seq.
Utah Code Ann. 1953, 62A-1-101 et seq.

Human Services Community Agency Accounting Practices Act
Me. Rev. Stat. Ann. 1964, Title 5, § 1651 et seq.

Human Services Demonstration Project Act
S.C. Code Ann. 1976, § 1-25-10 et seq.

Human Services Department Act
N.M. Stat. Ann., 9-8-1 et seq.

Human Services Development Fund Act
Pa. Purdon's Stat., Title 62, § 3101 et seq.

Human Services Facilities Construction Bond Act
N.J. Laws 1975, Ch. 203
N.J. Laws 1984, Ch. 157

Human Services Facilities Construction Bond and Developmental Disabilities Waiting List Reduction Act
N.J. Laws 1994, Ch. 108

Human Services Licensing Act
Minn. Stat. Ann., 245A.01 et seq.

Human Services Networking Program (Rural)
N.Y. Social Services Law (Consol. Laws Ch. 55) § 464 et seq.

Human Services Reauthorization Act of 1986
Oct. 30, 1984, P.L. 98-558, 42 U.S. Code §§ 9801 nt., 9832, 9834, 9835, 9836, 9840, 9843
Sept. 30, 1986, P.L. 99-425, 42 U.S. Code § 9801 nt.
Dec. 7, 1989, P.L. 101-204, 42 U.S. Code § 9910b
Nov. 3, 1990, P.L. 101-501, 42 U.S. Code § 9910b
Nov. 28, 1990, P.L. 101-625, 12 U.S. Code §§ 1701j-2, 1706e; 42 U.S. Code §§ 1439, 5301 to 5309, 5313
May 18, 1994, P.L. 103-252, 42 U.S. Code § 9910b
Oct. 27, 1998, P.L. 105-285, 42 U.S. Code § 9812a

Human Skeletal Remains and Burial Site Protection Act
Mont. Laws 1991, Ch. 748, §§ 1 to 10, 13

Human Skeletal Remains and Unmarked Human Burial Protection Act
N.C. Gen. Stat. 1943, § 70-26 et seq.

Human Skeletal Remains Protection Act
Ill. Rev. Stat. 1991, Ch. 127, § 2660 et seq.

Human Subjects Protection in Medical Experimentation Act
Cal. Health and Safety Code § 24170 et seq.

Humane Care for Animals Act
Ill. Rev. Stat. 1991, Ch. 8, § 701 et seq.

Humane Care for Equines Act
Ga. Code Ann., 4-13-1 et seq.

Humane Law
Vt. Stat. Ann., Title 20, § 3901 et seq.

Humane Methods of Slaughter Act
Oct. 10, 1978, P.L. 95-445, 92 Stat. 1069, 7 U.S. Code §§ 1902, 1904; 21 U.S. Code §§ 601 nt., 603, 610, 620

Humane Slaughter Act (Livestock)
Ill. Rev. Stat. 1991, Ch. 8, § 229.50 et seq.
N.H. Rev. Stat. 1955, 427:33 et seq.
Vt. Stat. Ann., Title 6, § 3131 et seq.
W. Va. Code 1966, § 19-2E-1 et seq.

Humane Slaughter and Meat and Poultry Inspection Act
Ind. Code Ann., 16-6-5-1 et seq.

Humane Slaughter of Livestock Act
Mich. Comp. Laws Ann., 287.551 et seq.

Humane Society Police Officer Enforcement Act
Pa. Purdon's Stat., Title 3, § 456.1 et seq.

Humanities and Arts Act
Okla. Stat. Ann., Title 53, § 161 et seq.

Humanities and Arts Commission Act
D.C. Code Ann., § 31-2001 et seq.

Humanities and Arts Council Act
Mass. Gen. Laws Ann., 15:40 et seq.

Humboldt Bay Harbor, Recreation, and Conservation District Act
Cal. Statutes 1970, Ch. 1283, p. 2343

Humbolt County Flood Control District Act
Cal. Water Code, Appendix, § 47-1 et seq.

Hump Law
Aug. 11, 1959, P.L. 86-155, 73 Stat. 333, 10 U.S. Code § 5701 nt., § 6387

Humphrey-Durham Act
See Federal Food, Drug, And Cosmetic Act

Humphrey-Durham Drug Prescriptions Act
Oct. 26, 1951, Ch. 578, 65 Stat. 648, 21 U.S. Code §§ 333, 353

Humphrey-Thye-Blatnik-Andresen Act
June 22, 1956, Ch. 425, 70 Stat. 326, 16 U.S. Code §§ 577d-1, 577g-1, 577h

Hundred Dollar Law (Justice of the Peace)
Pa. Cons. Stat., Title 42, § 1515

Hundred Million Dollar State Bond Issue Act
Ill. Rev. Stat. 1957, Ch. 121, § 281a et seq.

Hung Jury Act
Mich. Comp. Laws 1948, 691.701

Hungarian Declaration of War
June 5, 1942, Ch. 324, 56 Stat. 307, 50 U.S. Code Appx. nt. prec. § 1

Hunger Act
Tex. Human Resources § 333.001 et seq.

Hunger Act (Omnibus)
Tex. Human Resources Code, § 33.001

Hunger and Nutrition Interagency Council Act
S.C. Code Ann. 1976, § 44-85-10 et seq.
S.C. Code of 1976, § 44-85-10 et seq.

Hunger Prevention Act of 1988
Sept. 19, 1988, P.L. 100-435, 7 U.S. Code §§ 612c nt., 1731 nt., 2011 nt., 2012, 2012 nt., 2014 to 2017, 2020 to 2023, 2025, 2026; 15 U.S. Code § 713a-14; 42 U.S. Code §§ 1761, 1766, 1766 nt., 1773, 1786
Nov. 5, 1988, P.L. 100-619, 7 U.S. Code § 2012 nt.
Nov. 10, 1989, P.L. 101-147, 42 U.S. Code § 1766 nts.
Nov. 28, 1990, P.L. 101-624, 7 U.S. Code § 612c nt.
Dec. 13, 1991, P.L. 102-237, 7 U.S. Code § 612c nt.
April 4, 1996, P.L. 104-127, 7 U.S. Code § 612c nt.
Aug. 22, 1996, P.L. 104-193, 7 U.S. Code § 612c nt.

Hunger Relief Act
Ore. Laws 1991, 965
Ore. Rev. Stat., 411.851 et seq.,

Hunger Relief Act of 1988
Nov. 28, 1990, P.L. 101-624, 7 U.S. Code § 612c nt.

Hungerford Act (Firemen and Police Pensions)
Mich. Comp. Laws Ann., 38.551 et seq.

Hunnicutt Act (Employer-Employee Relations)
Ky. Rev. Stat. 1971, 336.010 et seq.

Hunt-Swope Act (State Theatre)
Ky. Rev. Stat. 1971, 153.110 et seq.

Hunter Interference Prohibition Act
Ill. Rev. Stat. 1991, Ch. 61, § 300 et seq.

Hunter Safety Act (Carlucci)
Fla. Stat. Ann., 372.5717

Hunter-Thompson Patient Protection Act
Cal. Statutes 1991, Ch. 1180

Hunter Training Act
N.M. Stat. Ann., 17-2-33 et seq.

Hunters Point Reclamation District Act
Cal. Statutes 1955, Ch. 1573, p. 2855

Hunting Act
Pa. Purdon's Stat., Title 43, § 1311.1 et seq.
Va. Code 1950, § 29-1 et seq.

Hunting and Fishing Act
Me. Rev. Stat. Ann. 1964, Title 12, § 7001 et seq.
Wis. Stat. Ann., 29.01 et seq.

Hunting and Fishing License Act
Cal. Fish and Game Code 1957, § 3007 et seq., § 7145 et seq.
Mich. Comp. Laws Ann., 316.101 et seq.

Hunting Season Act (Newberry County)
S.C. Acts 1933, p. 387, No. 282

Huntington Curb and Sidewalk Fund Law
N.Y. Local Laws 1971, Town of Huntington, p. 2417

Huron-Clinton Metropolitan Authority Act
Mich. Comp. Laws Ann., 119.51 et seq.

Huron Zoning Law
N.Y. Local Laws 1973, Town of Huron, p. 2214

Hurrel Act (Intoxicating Liquors)
Kan. Laws 1901, Ch. 232

Hurricane Barrier Loan Act (New Bedford)
Mass. Acts 1962, Ch. 565

Hurricane, Drought and Flood Disaster Act (Farmers)
Va. Code 1950, § 3.1-22.13 et seq.

Hurricane Relief Loan Act
Mass. Acts 1954, Ch. 689

Husband and Wife Act
Cal. Civil Code § 5100 et seq.
Ill. Rev. Stat. 1991, Ch. 40, § 1000 et seq.
Nev. Rev. Stat. 1979 Reprint, 123.010 et seq.
Ohio Rev. Code 1953, 3103.01 et seq.
W. Va. Code 1966, § 48-3-1 et seq.

Husky and Husky Plus Act
Conn. Acts 1997, No. 1, § 16, Oct. 29, Sp. Sess.
Conn. Gen. Stat. 1983, §§ 17b-289 to 17b-303;

Hutchcraft Law
Ky. Acts 1916, Ch. 14

Hutchinson Act (Strikes, Public Employees)
Mich. Comp. Laws Ann., 423.201 et seq.

Hybrid Seed Corn Act
Iowa Code Ann., 199.5
Minn. Stat. Ann., 21.90 et seq.

Hydration and Nutrition for Incompetent Patients Act
Okla. Stat. Ann., Title 63, § 3080.1 et seq.

Hydroelectric Power Act
Ore. Rev. Stat., 543.010 et seq.
S.D. Codified Laws 1967, 46A-2-34

Hydroelectric Power Development Revenue Bond Law (Municipalities and Counties)
Ark. Code Ann. 1987, 14-204-101 et seq.

Hydrogen Future Act of 1996
Oct. 9, 1996, P.L. 104-271, 42 U.S. Code § 12401 nt.

Hydrographic Services Improvement Act of 1998
Nov. 13, 1998, P.L. 105-383, 33 U.S. Code §§ 892c, 892d
Nov. 13, 1998, P.L. 105-384, Title III, 112 Stat. 3454, 33 U.S. Code § 951 nt.

Hygienists Act (Dentists and Dental)
Utah Code Ann. 1953, 58-7-1 et seq.

Hygienists Licensure Act (Industrial)
Ill. Comp. Stat. 1992, Ch. 225, § 52/1 et seq.

Hypnosis Law
Fla. Stat. Ann., 456.30 et seq.

Hypnotherapist Licensure Act
Ga. Code Ann., 43-21A-1 et seq.

Hypnotic Drug Act
Mich. Comp. Laws Ann., 335.101 et seq.
R.I. Gen. Laws 1956, 21-28-1.01 et seq.

Hypnotic, Somnifacient or Stimulating Drug Act
Kan. Stat. Ann., 65-4101 et seq.

Hypodermic Syringes and Needles Act
Ill. Rev. Stat. 1991, Ch. 38, § 22-49.9 et seq.

Hyre Act (Refunding Bonds)
Ohio Rev. Code 1953, 133.37

I

I Am an American Day Act
May 3, 1940, Ch. 183, 36 U.S. Code §§ 152, 391

IAP Air Reserve Station Retrocession Act (O'Hare)
Ill. Comp. Stat. 1992, Ch. 5, § 544/1 et seq.

ICC Termination Act of 1995
Dec. 29, 1995, P.L. 104-88, 49 U.S. Code § 101 nt.

Ice and Snow Act (Compulsory Removal)
Ind. Code 1971, 18-1-4-1, Subd. 31

Ice and Snow Act (Notice of Claim)
Ind. Code 1971, 18-2-2-1

Ice and Snow Removal Act
Ill. Rev. Stat. 1991, Ch. 70, § 200 et seq.

Ice Cream and Butterine Factories Law (Sanitary Standards)
Ill. Rev. Stat. 1971, Ch. 48, § 53 et seq.

Ice Cream and Frozen Food Act
Cal. Food and Agricultural Code 1967, § 36861 et seq.
Mich. Comp. Laws Ann., 288.321 et seq.
Mo. Rev. Stat., 198.851 et seq.
Pa. Purdon's Stat., Title 31, §§ 407 et seq., 417-1 et seq.

Ice-Cream Venders Act
D.C. Laws 1975, No. 1-9

Ice Milk Act
Cal. Food and Agricultural Code 1967, §§ 36921 et seq., 39151 et seq.
Kan. Stat. Ann., 65-720

Ice or Roller Skating Liability Immunity Act
S.C. Code Ann. 1976, § 52-19-10 et seq.

Ice Plant Act
Neb. Rev. Stat. 1943, 19-1401 et seq.

Ice-Skating Safety Act
Me. Rev. Stat. Ann. 1964, Title 8, § 621 et seq.

Iceboxes Act (Abandoned)
See Abandoned Iceboxes Act

Idaho Land Exchange Act of 1993
April 12, 1993, P.L. 103-17, 107 Stat. 50

Ideal Farms Drainage District Validating Act
Fla. Special Laws 1925, Ch. 10699

Identification Act (Criminal)
Ill. Rev. Stat. 1991, Ch. 38, § 206 et seq.
Utah Code Ann. 1953, 53-5-201 et seq., 210306

Identification Act (Minor)
Okla. Stat. Ann., Title 10, § 1629 et seq.

Identification Act (Missing Children)
La. Rev. Stat. Ann., 40:2511 et seq.
Neb. Rev. Stat. 1943, 43-2001 et seq.

Identification Card Act
Ill. Rev. Stat. 1991, Ch. 124, § 21 et seq.
Utah Code Ann. 1953, 53-3-801 et seq.

Identification Card Act (Firearm Owners)
Ill. Rev. Stat. 1991, Ch. 38, § 83-01 et seq.

Identification Cards for Nondrivers Act
N.J. Stat. Ann., 39:3-29.2 et seq.

Identification Cards for the Disabled Act
N.J. Stat. Ann., 39:3-29.2 et seq.

Identification Defacement Act (Construction Equipment)
Ill. Rev. Stat. 1991, Ch. 38, §§ 71, 71-1

Identification Profiling System Act (DNA)
Mich. Comp. Laws Ann., 28.171 et seq.

Identity Theft and Assumption Deterrence Act of 1998
Oct. 30, 1998, P.L. 105-318, 112 Stat. 3007, 18 U.S. Code § 1001 nt.

Ilfeld Act (Succession of Property)
N.M. Laws 1927, Ch. 163

Illegal Crude Oil Act
Cal. Business and Professions Code § 20740 et seq.

Illegal Drug Stamp Tax Act
Ida. Code 1947, 63-4201 et seq.
Utah Code Ann. 1953, 59-19-101 et seq.

Illegal Drugs Act (Trafficking)
Okla. Stat. Ann., Title 63, § 2-414 et seq.

Illegal Dumps Control Act
Ark. Code 1987, 8-6-501 to 8-6-507, 8-6-1002 to 8-6-1004

Illegal Firearm Confiscation Pilot Project
Cal. Political Code § 13760 et seq.

Illegal Immigration Reform and Immigrant Responsibility Act of 1996
Sept. 30, 1996, P.L. 104-208, Division C, 8 U.S. Code § 1101 nt.
Oct. 11, 1996, P.L. 104-302, 8 U.S. Code §§ 1101 nt., 1252 nt.
Aug. 5, 1997, P.L. 105-33, 8 U.S. Code § 1367
Oct. 6, 1997, P.L. 105-54, 8 U.S. Code § 1324a nt.
Nov. 19, 1997, P.L. 105-100, 8 U.S. Code § 1101 nt.
Dec. 2, 1997, P.L. 105-139, 8 U.S. Code § 1101 nt.
Oct. 21, 1998, P.L. 105-277, 8 U.S. Code §§ 1101 nt., 1221 nt., 1363b

Illegal Law Practice Act
Tex. Penal Code 338.12

Illegal Search Evidence Act (Bouse)
Md. Ann. Code 1957, Superseded Vol., Art. 35, § 5

Illegitimacy Act
Ga. Code Ann., 19-7-20 et seq.
Ind. Code Ann., 31-4-1-1 et seq.
Iowa Code Ann., 600B.1 et seq.
Iowa Code Ann., 675.1 et seq.
Kan. Stat. Ann., 38-1101 et seq.

N.C. Gen. Stat. 1943, § 49-10 et seq.
N.D. Cent. Code, 14-17-01 et seq.
Nev. Rev. Stat. 1979 Reprint, 126.010 et seq.
N.M. Stat. Ann., 40-11-1 et seq.
N.Y. Family Court Act § 511 et seq.
Ohio Rev. Code 1953, 3111.01 et seq.
S.D. Codified Laws 1967, 25-8-1 et seq.
W. Va. Code 1966, § 48A-7-1 et seq.
Wyo. Stat. Ann., § 14-2-101 et seq.

Illegitimacy Inheritance Act
Ala. Code 1975, § 43-8-48

Illegitimate Child Care Act
Cal. Penal Code § 270

Illegitimate Children's Legitimation Law
See Legitimation Act (Illegitimate Children)

Illinois Act on the Aging
Ill. Comp. Stat. 1992, Ch. 20, § 105/1 et seq.

Illinois and Des Plaines Rivers Act
Ill. Rev. Stat. 1991, Ch. 19, § 40.9 et seq.

Illinois and Michigan Canal Development Act
Ill. Rev. Stat. 1991, Ch. 19, § 37.10 et seq.

Illinois and Michigan Canal Land Use Act
Ill. Rev. Stat. 1991, Ch. 19, § 37.01 et seq.

Illinois and Michigan Canal Management Act
Ill. Rev. Stat. 1991, Ch. 19, § 0.01 et seq.

Illinois and Michigan Canal National Heritage Corridor Act of 1984
Aug. 24, 1984, P.L. 98-398, 16 U.S. Code §§ 450jj nt., 450jj-3 to 450jj-9, 461 nt.
Nov. 12, 1996, P.L. 104-333, 16 U.S. Code § 461 nt.
Nov. 6, 1998, P.L. 105-355, 16 U.S. Code § 461 nt.

Illinois and Michigan Canal Protection Act
Ill. Rev. Stat. 1991, Ch. 19, § 29.9 et seq.

Illinois and Michigan Canal State Park Act
Ill. Rev. Stat. 1991, Ch. 105, § 491.01 et seq.

Illinois and Mississippi Canal State Park Act
Ill. Rev. Stat. 1991, Ch. 105, § 482.9 et seq.

Illinois Central Railroad Company Charter Act
Ill. Private Laws 1851, p. 61

Illinois-Indiana Air Pollution Control Compact
Ind. Code Ann., 13-5-7-1 et seq.

Illinois-Indiana Bridge Commissioners Act
Ill. Rev. Stat. 1991, Ch. 121, § 420 et seq.

Illinois-Indiana Bridge Compact Act
Ill. Rev. Stat. 1991, Ch. 121, § 410 et seq.

Illinois International Port District Act
Ill. Rev. Stat. 1985, Ch. 19, § 152 et seq.

Illinois-Jefferson-Monroe-Missouri Bridge Commission Act
Ill. Rev. Stat. 1991, Ch. 127, § 63s-34.9 et seq.

Illinois-Jefferson-Monroe-Missouri Bridge Compact Act
Ill. Rev. Stat. 1991, Ch. 127, § 63s-30.9 et seq.

Illinois Land Conservation Act of 1995
Feb. 10, 1996, P.L. 104-106, Division B, Title XXIX, 16 U.S. Code § 1609 nt.

Illinois-Michigan Canal National Corridor Civic Center Authority of Cook County Act
Ill. Rev. Stat. 1991, Ch. 85, § 2601 et seq.

Illinois-Missouri Bridge Commission Act
Ill. Rev. Stat. 1991, Ch. 127, § 63s-24.9 et seq.

Illinois-Missouri Bridge Compact Act
Ill. Rev. Stat. 1991, Ch. 127, § 63s-20 et seq.

Illinois River Watershed Restoration Act
Ill. Comp. Stat. 1992, Ch. 20, § 3967/1 et seq.

Illinois State University Law
Ill. Comp. Stat. 1992, Ch. 110, § 675/20-1 et seq.

Illinois State University Name Change Act
Ill. Rev. Stat. 1991, Ch. 144, §§ 499, 500

Illinois State University Objects Act
Ill. Rev. Stat. 1991, Ch. 144, § 502.01 et seq.

Illinois State University Revenue Bond Law
Ill. Comp. Stat. 1992, Ch. 110, § 676/21-1 et seq.

Illinois University Act (Northeastern)
Ill. Rev. Stat. 1991, Ch. 144, § 1150 et seq.

Illinois Valley Civic Center Law
Ill. Rev. Stat. 1991, Ch. 85, § 7006-2 et seq.

Illinois Valley Regional Port District Act
Ill. Rev. Stat. 1991, Ch. 19, § 801 et seq.

Illinois Valley, Waukegan, Pontiac, Randolph County, Carbondale, Riverside, Matteson, and Ottawa Civic Centers Act
Ill. Rev. Stat. 1991, Ch. 85, § 7000-1 et seq.

Illinois Wilderness Act of 1990
Nov. 28, 1990, P.L. 101-633, 16 U.S. Code § 1132 nt.

Illiteracy Education Assistance Act (Employee)
Cal. Labor Code § 1040 et seq.

Illuminating Oil Test Act
Md. Ann. Code 1957, Art. 48, § 1 et seq.

Illuminating Oils Act
Ky. Acts 1873-74 (Public) Ch. 386
Vt. Stat. Ann., Title 9, § 3341 et seq.

Illusory Transfer Act
Ill. Rev. Stat. 1991, Ch. 110 1/2, § 600 et seq.

IMFA
See Immigration Marriage Fraud Amendments Of 1986

Imitation and Counterfeit Controlled Substances Act
Colo. Rev. Stat., 18-18-419 to 18-18-424
Iowa Code Ann., 124A.1 et seq.

Imitation Controlled Substances Act
Ala. Code 1975, § 20-2-140 et seq.
Alaska Stat. 1962, § 11.73.010 et seq.
Cal. Health and Safety Code § 11670 et seq.
Colo. Rev. Stat., 18-5-601 et seq.
N.M. Stat. Ann., 30-31A-1 et seq.
Utah Code Ann. 1953, 58-37b-1 et seq.

Imitation Dairy Products Act
Colo. Rev. Stat., 25-5.5-201 et seq.

Imitation Honey Act
N.M. Stat. Ann., 25-9-1 et seq.
W. Va. Code 1966, § 19-2D-1 et seq.

Imitation Milk Law
Cal. Food and Agricultural Code 1967, §§ 38931, 38901 et seq.

Immediate Possession Act
Ariz. Rev. Stat. Ann., § 12-1116

Immediate Transportation Act
June 10, 1880, Ch. 190, 21 Stat. 173

Immigrant Fund Act
Aug. 3, 1882, Ch. 376, 22 Stat. 214

Immigrant Workforce Preparation Act
Cal. Education Code 1976, § 52651 et seq.

Immigration Act (Chinese)
Haw. Session Laws 1887, Special Session, Ch. 28

Immigration Act of 1990
Nov. 29, 1990, P.L. 101-649, 8 U.S. Code § 1101 et seq. generally, 1201 et seq. generally, 1304 et seq. generally, 1421 et seq. generally; 29 U.S. Code § 1506
July 2, 1991, P.L. 102-65, 8 U.S. Code § 1254a
Oct. 1, 1991, P.L. 102-110, 8 U.S. Code §§ 1101 nt., 1153
Dec. 12, 1991, P.L. 102-232, 8 U.S. Code §§ 1101 nt., 1105a, 1105a nt., 1151 nt., 1153 nt., 1158 nt., 1182, 1184 nt., 1201 nt., 1229, 1251 nt., 1254, 1254a nt., 1421 nt., 1439, 1440, 1445, 1447, 1449, 1455

Oct. 25, 1994, P.L. 103-416, 8 U.S. Code §§ 1101 nt., 1153 nt., 1182 nt., 1884 nt., 1254a nt., 1255a nt., 1440 nt.
Sept. 30, 1996, P.L. 104-208, 8 U.S. Code §§ 1101 nt., 1159 nt., 1252b nt., 1254a nt., 1255a nt., 1182 nt.
Nov. 26, 1997, P.L. 105-119, 8 U.S. Code § 1440 nt.

Immigration Acts
July 4, 1864, Ch. 246, 13 Stat. 385
Aug. 2, 1882, Ch. 374, 22 Stat. 186, 46 U.S. Code §§ 151 to 162
March 3, 1891, Ch. 551, 26 Stat. 1084
March 3, 1903, Ch. 1012, 32 Stat. 1213
Feb. 20, 1907, Ch. 1134, 34 Stat. 898
Feb. 5, 1917, Ch. 29, 39 Stat. 874
June 29, 1918, Ch. 112, 40 Stat. 634
Oct. 16, 1918, Ch. 186, 40 Stat. 1012
Oct. 19, 1918, Ch. 190, 40 Stat. 1014
May 10, 1920, Ch. 174, 41 Stat. 593
June 5, 1920, Ch. 243, 41 Stat. 981
June 5, 1920, Ch. 251, 41 Stat. 1008
May 19, 1921, Ch. 8, 42 Stat. 5
May 26, 1924, Ch. 190, 43 Stat. 153
May 14, 1937, Ch. 181, 50 Stat. 164
May 14, 1937, Ch. 182, 50 Stat. 164
July 1, 1940, Ch. 502, 54 Stat. 711
June 20, 1942, Ch. 426, 56 Stat. 373
Dec. 8, 1942, Ch. 697, 56 Stat. 1044
Dec. 19, 1944, Ch. 608, 58 Stat. 816
Oct. 29, 1945, Ch. 437, 59 Stat. 551
Oct. 29, 1945, Ch. 438, 59 Stat. 551
Dec. 29, 1945, Ch. 652, 59 Stat. 672
Aug. 9, 1946, Ch. 945, 60 Stat. 975
July 30, 1947, Ch. 384, 61 Stat. 630
May 19, 1948, Ch. 311, 62 Stat. 241
May 25, 1948, Ch. 338, 62 Stat. 268
June 3, 1948, Ch. 403, 62 Stat. 335
July 1, 1948, Ch. 783, 62 Stat. 1206
Sept. 23, 1950, Ch. 1024, 64 Stat. 1010
March 20, 1952, Ch. 108, 66 Stat. 26
June 18, 1952, Ch. 442, 66 Stat. 138

Immigration Amendments of 1988
Nov. 15, 1988, P.L. 100-658, 8 U.S. Code § 1101 nt.

Immigration and Nationality Act

June 27, 1952, Ch. 477, 66 Stat. 163, 8 U.S. Code §§ 1101 to 1503; 18 U.S. Code §§ 1114, 1429, 1546; 22 U.S. Code §§ 618, 1446; 31 U.S. Code § 530; 49 U.S. Code §§ 1, 177; 50 U.S. Code Appx. §§ 1952 to 1955, 1961

Sept. 3, 1954, Ch. 1256, 68 Stat. 1146, 8 U.S. Code § 1481

Sept. 3, 1954, Ch. 1263, 68 Stat. 1232, 8 U.S. Code §§ 1252, 1451

June 4, 1956, Ch. 356, 70 Stat. 241, 22 U.S. Code § 1446

July 18, 1956, Ch. 629, 70 Stat. 575, 8 U.S. Code §§ 1182, 1251

Sept. 11, 1957, P.L. 85-316, 71 Stat. 639, 8 U.S. Code §§ 1101, 1153, 1434

July 7, 1958, P.L. 85-508, 72 Stat. 351, 8 U.S. Code §§ 1101, 1182, 1421, 1455

Aug. 8, 1958, P.L. 85-616, 72 Stat. 546, 8 U.S. Code § 1259

Aug. 20, 1958, P.L. 85-697, 72 Stat. 687, 8 U.S. Code § 1430

Aug. 21, 1958, P.L. 85-700, 72 Stat. 699, 8 U.S. Code § 1255

March 18, 1959, P.L. 86-3, 73 Stat. 13, 8 U.S. Code §§ 1101, 1182, 1421

Aug. 4, 1959, P.L. 86-129, 73 Stat. 274, 8 U.S. Code §§ 1485, 1486

Sept. 22, 1959, P.L. 86-363, 73 Stat. 644, 8 U.S. Code §§ 1153, 1155

July 14, 1960, P.L. 86-648, 74 Stat. 505, 8 U.S. Code §§ 1182, 1251, 1255

Sept. 21, 1961, P.L. 87-256, 75 Stat. 534, 8 U.S. Code §§ 1101, 1182, 1258

Sept. 26, 1961, P.L. 87-301, 75 Stat. 650, 8 U.S. Code §§ 1101, 1105a, 1152, 1155, 1182, 1201, 1202, 1251, 1421, 1440, 1451, 1481, 1486

June 28, 1962, P.L. 87-510, 76 Stat. 123, 8 U.S. Code § 1104

Oct. 24, 1962, P.L. 87-885, 76 Stat. 1247, 8 U.S. Code §§ 1154, 1254

Aug. 14, 1964, P.L. 880426, 78 Stat. 428, 8 U.S. Code § 1104

Oct. 3, 1965, P.L. 89-236, 79 Stat. 911, 8 U.S. Code §§ 1101, 1151 to 1156, 1181, 1182, 1201, 1202, 1204, 1251, 1253 to 1255, 1259, 1322, 1351

Nov. 2, 1966, P.L. 89-710, 80 Stat. 1104, 8 U.S. Code § 1101

Nov. 6, 1966, P.L. 89-770, 80 Stat. 1322, 8 U.S. Code § 1401

Dec. 18, 1967, P.L. 90-215, 81 Stat. 661, 8 U.S. Code § 1430

June 29, 1968, P.L. 90-369, 82 Stat. 279, 8 U.S. Code § 1430

Oct. 21, 1968, P.L. 90-609, 82 Stat. 1200, 8 U.S. Code §§ 1351, 1455

Oct. 24, 1968, P.L. 90-633, 82 Stat. 1343, 8 U.S. Code §§ 1429, 1439, 1440, 1440e

Dec. 5, 1969, P.L. 91-136, 83 Stat. 283, 8 U.S. Code § 1447

April 7, 1970, P.L. 91-225, 84 Stat. 116, 8 U.S. Code §§ 1101, 1182, 1184

July 10, 1970, P.L. 91-313, 84 Stat. 413, 8 U.S. Code §§ 1183, 1363

Oct. 27, 1972, P.L. 92-584, 86 Stat. 1289, 8 U.S. Code § 1401

Dec. 16, 1975, P.L. 94-155, 89 Stat. 824, 8 U.S. Code § 1101

Aug. 1, 1977, P.L. 95-83, 42 U.S. Code § 1101 et seq.

Aug. 17, 1977, P.L. 95-105, 8 U.S. Code § 1101 et seq.

Oct. 30, 1978, P.L. 95-549, 8 U.S. Code §§ 1182, 1251, 1253, 1254

Nov. 2, 1978, P.L. 95-579, 8 U.S. Code § 1423

Nov. 2, 1978, P.L. 95-582, 8 U.S. Code § 1324

Sept. 27, 1979, P.L. 96-70, 8 U.S. Code §§ 1101, 1101 nt., 1182, 1182 nt.

March 17, 1980, P.L. 96-212, 8 U.S. Code § 1151 et seq., 1521 et seq.

Oct. 22, 1982, P.L. 97-359, 8 U.S. Code § 1154

Oct. 25, 1982, P.L. 97-363, 8 U.S. Code §§ 1522 to 1524

Nov. 22, 1983, P.L. 98-164, 8 U.S. Code § 1522

Oct. 5, 1984, P.L. 98-454, 98 Stat. 1737, 8 U.S. Code §§ 1182, 1184

Oct. 12, 1984, P.L. 98-473, 8 U.S. Code §§ 1182, 1252, 1522

Dec. 4, 1985, P.L. 99-169, 8 U.S. Code § 1427

Aug. 27, 1986, P.L. 99-396, 8 U.S. Code §§ 1182, 1408, 1452

Oct. 18, 1986, P.L. 99-500, 8 U.S. Code § 1356

Oct. 21, 1986, P.L. 99-505, 8 U.S. Code § 1101

Oct. 27, 1986, P.L. 99-570, 8 U.S. Code §§ 1182, 1251, 1357

Oct. 30, 1986, P.L. 99-591, 8 U.S. Code § 1356 Nov. 6, 1986, P.L. 99-603, 100 Stat. 3359 et seq.; P.L. 99-605, 100 Stat. 3449, 8 U.S. Code §§ 1522, 1522 nt., 1524

Nov. 10, 1986, P.L. 99-639, 8 U.S. Code §§ 1154, 1154 nt., 1182, 1182 nt., 1184, 1186a, 1255

Nov. 14, 1986, P.L. 99-653, 8 U.S. Code § 1452

Dec. 22, 1987, P.L. 100-202, 8 U.S. Code § 1160; P.L. 100-204, 8 U.S. Code § 1182

Oct. 1, 1988, P.L. 100-459, 8 U.S. Code § 1101

Oct. 24, 1988, P.L. 100-525, 8 U.S. Code generally §§ 1101 et seq.

Nov. 18, 1988, P.L. 100-690, 102 Stat. 4468

Nov. 21, 1989, P.L. 101-162, 8 U.S. Code § 1101

Dec. 18, 1989, P.L. 101-238, 8 U.S. Code §§ 1101, 1182, 1160

Feb. 16, 1990, P.L. 101-246, 8 U.S. Code §§ 1101, 1182

March 6, 1990, P.L. 101-249, 8 U.S. Code § 1440-1

Nov. 5, 1990, P.L. 101-515, 8 U.S. Code §§ 1356, 1356 nt.

Nov. 29, 1990, P.L. 101-649, 8 U.S. Code §§ 1254a, 1254a nt., 1440 nt.

Oct. 1, 1991, P.L. 102-110, 8 U.S. Code §§ 1101, 1153, 1255, 1524

Oct. 28, 1991, P.L. 102-140, 8 U.S. Code § 1255a

Dec. 12, 1991, P.L. 102-232, 8 U.S. Code §§ 1101, 1101 nt., 1102, 1151 to 1154, 1157, 1159 to 1161, 1182, 1184, 1186a, 1186b, 1187, 1188, 1201, 1221, 1226, 1227, 1251 to 1252b, 1254a, 1255, 1255a, 1281, 1282, 1284, 1288, 1322, 1323, 1324a to 1325, 1356, 1357, 1421, 1423, 1424, 1433, 1441, 1443, 1445, 1446, 1448 to 1452, 1455

Oct. 6, 1992, P.L. 102-395, 8 U.S. Code § 1356

June 8, 1993, P.L. 103-37, 8 U.S. Code § 1524

June 10, 1993, P.L. 103-43, 8 U.S. Code §§ 1182, 1182 nt.

Oct. 27, 1993, P.L. 103-121, 8 U.S. Code § 1356

Dec. 8, 1993, P.L. 103-182, 8 U.S. Code § 1184

Dec. 17, 1993, P.L. 103-198, 8 U.S. Code § 1288

Dec. 20, 1993, P.L. 103-206, 8 U.S. Code § 1288

April 30, 1994, P.L. 103-236, 8 U.S. Code §§ 1101, 1104, 1521, 1522, 1523

Aug. 26, 1994, P.L. 103-317, 8 U.S. Code §§ 1182, 1255

Sept. 13, 1994, P.L. 103-322, 8 U.S. Code §§ 1101, 1105a, 1151 nt., 1154, 1158, 1182, 1184, 1186a, 1251, 1252, 1252a, 1254, 1255, 1258, 1324, 1326

Oct. 5, 1994, P.L. 103-337, 8 U.S. Code § 1101

Oct. 20, 1994, P.L. 103-382, 8 U.S. Code § 1255a

Oct. 25, 1994, P.L. 103-415, 108 Stat. 4301, 4303

Oct. 25, 1994, P.L. 103-416, 8 U.S. Code §§ 1101, 1105a, 1151, 1153, 1154, 1160, 1161, 1182, 1184, 1185, 1187, 1202, 1251, 1252, 1252a, 1252b, 1254a, 1255, 1255a, 1256, 1288, 1302, 1322, 1323, 1324a, 1324b, 1324c, 1330, 1356, 1401, 1421, 1423, 1424, 1433, 1435, 1444, 1449, 1451, 1452, 1483, 1501, 1504, 1522, 1524

Nov. 15, 1995, P.L. 104-51, 8 U.S. Code § 1101

April 24, 1996, P.L. 104-132, 8 U.S. Code §§ 1101, 1101 nt., 1105a, 1158, 1160, 1182, 1189, 1225, 1227, 1251, 1252, 1252a, 1253 to 1255, 1255a, 1259, 1326, prec. 1531, 1531 et seq.

Aug. 22, 1996, P.L. 104-193, 8 U.S. Code §§ 1160, 1183a, 1255a

Sept. 30, 1996, P.L. 104-208, 8 U.S. Code §§ 1103, 1225a, 1324d

Oct. 6, 1997, P.L. 105-54, 8 U.S. Code §§ 1101, 1351

Oct. 27, 1997, P.L. 105-65, 8 U.S. Code § 1184

Nov. 12, 1997, P.L. 105-73, 8 U.S. Code § 1182

Nov. 13, 1997, P.L. 105-78, 8 U.S. Code § 1524

Nov. 18, 1997, P.L. 105-85, 8 U.S. Code § 1440

Nov. 19, 1997, P.L. 105-100, 8 U.S. Code § 1229b

Nov. 26, 1997, P.L. 105-119, 8 U.S. Code §§ 1101, 1187, 1255

Dec. 2, 1997, P.L. 105-136, 8 U.S. Code § 1524

Continued

113

April 27, 1998, P.L. 105-173, 8 U.S. Code § 1187

Oct. 21, 1998, P.L. 105-277, 8 U.S. Code §§ 1101, 1182, 1184, 1255a, 1356

Oct. 27, 1998, P.L. 105-292, 8 U.S. Code §§ 1157, 1182

Oct. 30, 1998, P.L. 105-319, 8 U.S. Code § 1101

Oct. 31, 1998, P.L. 105-332, 8 U.S. Code § 1255a

Immigration and Nationality Act Amendments of 1981

Dec. 29, 1981, P.L. 97-116, 8 U.S. Code § 1101 nt.

Immigration and Nationality Act Amendments of 1986

Nov. 14, 1986, P.L. 99-653, 8 U.S. Code § 1101 nt.

Oct. 24, 1988, P.L. 100-525, 8 U.S. Code §§ 1101, 1152, 1182, 1356, 1431 to 1433, 1452, 1481; 22 U.S. Code § 4195

Immigration and Nationality Act of 1952

Nov. 26, 1997, P.L. 105-119, 8 U.S. Code § 1356

Immigration and Nationality Law Practice Act

Ariz. Rev. Stat. Ann., § 12-2701 et seq.

N.M. Stat. Ann., 36-3-1 et seq.

Immigration and Nationality Technical Corrections Act of 1994

Oct. 25, 1994, P.L. 103-416, 8 U.S. Code § 1101 nt.

Sept. 30, 1996, P.L. 104-208, 8 U.S. Code §§ 1101 nt., 1161 nt., 1182 nt., 1255a, 1255b, 1323, 1401 nt., 1433 nt.

Aug. 8, 1997, P.L. 105-38, 8 U.S. Code § 1433 nt.

Immigration Assistant Practices Act

Wash. Rev. Code Ann., 19.154.010 et seq.

Immigration Commission Act

See Immigration Acts

Immigration Marriage Fraud Amendments of 1986

Nov. 10, 1986, P.L. 99-639, 8 U.S. Code § 1101 nt.

Oct. 24, 1988, P.L. 100-525, 8 U.S. Code §§ 1182, 1186a, 1255

Immigration Nursing Relief Act of 1989

Dec. 18, 1989, P.L. 101-238, 8 U.S. Code § 1101 nt.

Nov. 29, 1990, P.L. 101-649, 8 U.S. Code §§ 1101, 1101 nt., 1182, 1255 nt.

Dec. 12, 1991, P.L. 102-232, 8 U.S. Code § 1255 nt.

Immigration Reform and Control Act of 1986

Nov. 6, 1986, P.L. 99-603, 8 U.S. Code § 1101 nt.

Oct. 24, 1988, P.L. 100-525, 8 U.S. Code § 1184, generally §§ 1254 et seq., 1324, 1357, 1546

Nov. 15, 1988, P.L. 100-658, 8 U.S. Code § 1153 nt.

Nov. 21, 1989, P.L. 101-166, 8 U.S. Code § 1255a nt.

Dec. 18, 1989, P.L. 101-238, 8 U.S. Code § 1255a nt.

Nov. 5, 1990, P.L. 101-517, 8 U.S. Code § 1255a nt.

Nov. 29, 1990, P.L. 101-649, 8 U.S. Code § 1160 nt.

Nov. 26, 1991, P.L. 102-170, 8 U.S. Code § 1255a nt.

Dec. 12, 1991, P.L. 102-232, 8 U.S. Code § 1160 nt.

Oct. 6, 1992, P.L. 102-394, 8 U.S. Code § 1255a nt.

Oct. 25, 1994, P.L. 103-416, 8 U.S. Code § 1255a nt.

Sept. 30, 1996, P.L. 104-208, 8 U.S. Code §§ 1253 nt., 1255a

Aug. 7, 1998, P.L. 105-220, 8 U.S. Code § 1255a nt.

Immigration Technical Corrections Act of 1988

Oct. 24, 1988, P.L. 100-525, 8 U.S. Code § 1101 nt.

Immigration Technical Corrections Act of 1991
Dec. 12, 1991, P.L. 102-232, 8 U.S. Code § 1101 nt.

Immokalee Water and Sewer District Act
Fla. Special Laws 1978, Ch. 78-494

Immoral Plays Act
N.Y. Penal Law 1965 (Consol. Laws Ch. 40) § 235.05, Subd. 2

Immoral Publications Sale to Children Act
Ill. Rev. Stat. 1991, Ch. 23, § 2362.9 et seq.

Immorality and Vice Act (Sunday Closing)
N.J. Stat. Ann., 2A:171-1 et seq.

Immunity Act
P.R. Laws Ann. 1954, Title 34 § 1476 et seq.
Vt. Stat. Ann., Title 12, § 1664

Immunity Act (Arson Reporting)
Me. Rev. Stat. Ann. 1964, Title 25, § 2411 et seq.
Neb. Rev. Stat. 1943, 81-5.115

Immunity Act (Charitable)
S.C. Code Ann. 1976, § 15-3-530 et seq.

Immunity Act (Charities)
N.J. Stat. Ann., 2A:53A-7 et seq.

Immunity Act (Governmental Torts)
Ill. Rev. Stat. 1991, Ch. 85, § 1-101 et seq.

Immunity Act (Governmental Units)
Cal. Civil Code § 22.3

Immunity Act (Governmental)
Colo. Rev. Stat., 24-10-101 et seq.
Utah Code Ann. 1953, 63-30-1 et seq.

Immunity Act (Hospital Districts)
Wash. Rev. Code Ann., 70.44.060, Subd. 8

Immunity Act (Insurance Fraud Reporting)
N.M. Stat. Ann., 59A-16A-1 et seq.

Immunity Act (Liquor Law)
Miss. Code Ann. 1972, § 97-31-51

Immunity Act (Municipalities)
N.J. Stat. Ann., 59:1-1

Immunity Act (Park District)
Ill. Rev. Stat. 1963, Ch. 105, § 333.2a

Immunity Act (Public Entities)
Cal. Government Code § 815

Immunity Act (Sovereign)
S.C. Code Ann. 1976, § 15-3-530 et seq.

Immunity Act (Sports Volunteer)
Ill. Rev. Stat. 1991, Ch. 70, §§ 700, 701

Immunity Act (Vote Corruption)
La. Rev. Stat. Ann., 15:468

Immunity Act (Witnesses)
See Witness Immunity Act

Immunity Act of 1954
Aug. 20, 1954, Ch. 769, 68 Stat. 745, 18 U.S. Code § 3486

Immunity Acts (Trusts and Interstate Commerce)
Feb. 11, 1893, Ch. 83, 27 Stat. 443, 49 U.S. Code § 46
June 30, 1906, Ch. 3920, 34 Stat. 798, 49 U.S. Code § 48

Immunity and Liability Act (Charitable)
Tex. Civil Practice and Remedies Code, § 84.001 et seq.

Immunity of Witnesses Act
Feb. 23, 1903, Ch. 755, 32 Stat. 904, 49 U.S. Code § 47
Oct. 15, 1970, P.L. 91-452, 84 Stat. 929, 18 U.S. Code §§ 6001 to 6005

Immunity Statute
Also known as Compulsion of Evidence Act
N.Y. Criminal Procedure Law (Consol. Laws Ch. 11A) §§ 50.10 et seq., 190.35 et seq.
Wash. Rev. Code Ann., 10.52.090

Immunity Statute (Arson Reporting)
Ark. Code Ann. 1987, 12-13-301

Immunization Act
La. Rev. Stat. Ann., 17:170
Mich. Comp. Laws Ann., 333.9201 et seq.
N.C. Gen. Stat. 1943, § 130-152a et seq.

Immunization Act (Child)
Miss. Code Ann. 1972, §§ 41-88-1, 41-88-3

Immunization Act (College Student)
Ill. Comp. Stat. 1992, Ch. 110, § 20/0.01 et seq.

Immunization Act (Infant)
Colo. Rev. Stat., 25-4-1701 et seq.

Immunization Act (Schools)
N.J. Stat. Ann., 18A:40-20

Immunization and Tuberculin Testing of Children Act
Mich. Comp. Laws Ann., 333.9201 et seq.

Immunization Insurance Act (Childhood)
Pa. 1992 Pamph. Laws, No. 35

Immunization of School Students Act
D.C. Code Ann., § 31-501 et seq.

Immuno-Augmentative Therapy Act
Okla. Stat. Ann., Title 63, § 2180 et seq.

Immunodeficiency Virus Services Act
N.M. Stat. Ann., 24-2B-1 et seq.
Tex. Health and Safety Code, § 85.001 et seq.

Impact Aid Act
Nov. 23, 1988, P.L. 100-707, 20 U.S. Code § 241-1

Impact Aid Reauthorization Act of 1988
April 28, 1988, P.L. 100-297, 102 Stat. 293, 20 U.S. Code § 236

Impact Fee Act (Development)
Ga. Code Ann., 36-71-1 et seq.

Impact Statement Act (Environmental)
N.Y. Environmental Conservation Law 1972 (Consol. Laws Ch. 43B) §§ 8-0105, 8-0109 et seq.

Impact Statement Act (Fiscal)
S.C. Code Ann. 1976, § 2-7-70 et seq.

Impact Statement Act (Victim)
Miss. Code Ann. 1972, § 99-19-151 et seq.
Tenn. Code Ann., 40-38-201 et seq.

Impacted Languages Act
Cal. Education Code 1976, § 52130 et seq.

Impacted Region Assistance Act (National Defense)
Tex. Rev. Stat. Art. 689a-4d

Impaired Dentist Act
N.M. Stat. Ann., 61-5-24 et seq.

Impaired Health Care Provider Act
N.M. Stat. Ann., 61-7-1 et seq.

Impaired Optometrist Treatment Program
Ark. Code 1987, 17-90-501 et seq.

Impaired Persons Licensing Act
Utah Code Ann. 1953, 53-3-301 et seq.

Impaired Pharmacists Act
N.M. Stat. Ann., 61-11A-1 et seq.

Impaired Physician Act
N.M. Stat. Ann., 61-7-1 et seq.

Impatient Interrers Act
W. Va. Code 1966, § 47-14-1 et seq.

Impeachment Act
Ind. Code Ann., 5-8-1-1 et seq.
Mich. Comp. Laws Ann., 6.1 et seq.
Mont. Code Ann., 5-5-401 et seq.

Imperial Valley College Barker Museum Land Transfer Act of 1988
Oct. 28, 1988, P.L. 100-535, 102 Stat. 2709

Impleader Act
Mass. Gen. Laws 1932, Ch. 231, § 4B

Implementation of Environmental Quality Bond Act
N.Y. Environmental Conservation Law 1972 (Consol. Laws Ch. 43B) § 52-0101 et seq.

Implied Consent Act
    N.M. Stat. Ann., 66-8-105 et seq.
    Ore. Rev. Stat. 1953, 801.010 et seq.
    Vt. Stat. Ann., Title 23, § 1202 et seq.

Implied Consent Act (Alcohol Tests)
    Ariz. Rev. Stat. Ann., § 28-691
    Ark. Code Ann. 1987, 75-1045, 75-1046
    Ark. Stat 1947, 5-65-202 et seq.
    Cal. Vehicle Code 1959 §§ 13353, 13354
    Colo. Rev. Stat., 42-4-1202
    Conn. Gen. Stat. 1983, § 14-227a et seq.
    D.C. Code Ann., § 40-501 et seq.
    Fla. Stat. Ann., 222.63
    Ga. Code Ann., 40-5-55
    Haw. Rev. Stat. Ann., § 286-151 et seq.
    Ida. Code 1947, 18-8002
    Ill. Rev. Stat. 1991, Ch. 95 1/2, § 11-501.1
    Iowa Code Ann., 321B.4
    Kan. Stat. Ann., 8-1001
    Ky. Rev. Stat. 1971, 186.565
    La. Rev. Stat. Ann., 32:661 et seq.
    Me. Rev. Stat. Ann. 1964, Title 29, § 1312
    Mich. Comp. Laws Ann., 257.625a et seq.
    Minn. Stat. Ann., 169.123
    Miss. Code Ann. 1972, § 63-11-1 et seq.
    Mo. Rev. Stat., 577.020 et seq.
    Mont. Code Ann., 61-8-402 et seq.
    N.C. Gen. Stat. 1943, § 20-16.2
    N.D. Cent. Code, 39-20-01 et seq.
    N.H. Rev. Stat. 1955, 265:84
    N.J. Stat. Ann., 39:4-50.2
    N.Y. Vehicle and Traffic Law 1959 (Consol. Laws Ch. 71) § 1194
    Okla. Stat. Ann., Title 47, § 7510 et seq.
    Ore. Rev. Stat., 487.805 et seq.
    R.I. Gen. Laws 1956, 31-27-2.1
    S.D. Codified Laws 1967, 32-23-10 et seq.
    Utah Code Ann. 1953, 41-6-44.10
    Va. Code 1950, § 18.2-268
    Vt. Stat. Ann., Title 23, § 1202
    Wash. Rev. Code Ann., 46.20.308

Implied Warranty Act
    Conn. Gen. Stat. Ann., §§ 42a-2-314, 42a-2-315

Implied Warranty Act (Personal Property)
    Ga. Code 1933, 96-307

Import Law (First)
    N.Y. Laws 1985, Ch. 44

Import Milk Act
    Feb. 15, 1927, Ch. 155, 44 Stat. 1101, 21 U.S. Code §§ 141 to 149
    July 12, 1943, Ch. 221, 57 Stat. 498

Import Tax Act (Liquor)
    Ky. Rev. Stat. 1962, 243.680, Subsec. 2

Importation Permit and Health Certificate Act of 1981
    Mont. Code Ann., 81-2-701 et seq.

Imported Butter Sales Regulation Law
    Cal. Food and Agricultural Code 1967, §§ 37261, 37262

Imported Meat Act
    N.M. Stat. Ann., 25-3-1 et seq.

Imported Vehicle Safety Compliance Act of 1988
    Oct. 31, 1988, P.L. 100-562, 15 U.S. Code § 1381 nt.

Importer Use Tax (Motor Vehicle)
    Okla. Stat. 1989, Title 68, § 601 et seq.

Importers for Use Tax Act
    N.D. Cent. Code, 57-43.1-01 et seq.

Importing and Distributing Corporation Act
    P.R. Laws Ann. 1954, Title 23, § 761 et seq.

Impound and Tow Truck Regulation Act
    Utah Code Ann. 1953, 41-6-187 et seq.

Impounding Act
    Haw. Rev. Stat. Ann., § 142-61 et seq.

Impoundment Authority Act (Conyers-Rockdale-Big Haynes)
    Ga. Laws 1991, p. 5053

Impoundment Control Act of 1974

July 12, 1974, P.L. 93-344, 88 Stat. 332, 31 U.S. Code §§ 665, 1401 to 1407

Nov. 8, 1984, P.L. 98-620, 2 U.S. Code § 687

Sept. 29, 1987, P.L. 100-119, 2 U.S. Code §§ 683, 684, 686 nt., 687

Impoundment Site Loan Act

Mass. Gen. Laws Ann., 21:9A

Impoundment Site Loan Act (Water Resources)

Mass. Gen. Laws Ann., 21:9A

Improper Practices Act (Labor)

N.Y. Labor Law (Consol. Laws Ch. 31) § 720 et seq.

Improper Supervision of Children Act

Ill. Rev. Stat. 1991, Ch. 23, § 2368.9 et seq.

Improved Penalty Administration and Compliance Tax Act

Dec. 19, 1989, P.L. 101-239, 26 U.S. Code § 1 nt.

Improved Student Learning Environment and Discipline Act

Ga. Laws 1999, H.B. 605

Improvement Act

Ariz. Rev. Stat. Ann., § 48-501 et seq.

Cal. Streets and Highways Code § 5000 et seq.

Improvement Act (Adjacent Property)

Tenn. Code Ann., 7-32-101 et seq.

Improvement Act (Consumer/Antitrust Protection)

Wash. Rev. Code Ann., 19.86.090 et seq.

Improvement Act (County Bridge)

Okla. Stat. Ann., Title 69, § 657

Improvement Act (County Road)

Okla. Stat. Ann., Title 69, § 685 et seq.

Improvement Act (Health Care Quality)

Haw. Rev. Stat. Ann., § 671D-1 et seq.

Improvement Act (Municipal)

Cal. Streets and Highways Code § 10000 et seq.

Improvement Act (Pre-K-16 Mathematics, Science, and Technology)

Colo. Rev. Stat., 22-81-101 et seq.

Improvement Act (Prison Facilities)

Pa. Purdon's Stat., Title 61, § 390.101 et seq.

Improvement Act (Rivers and Harbors)

Me. Rev. Stat. Ann. 1964, Title 38, §§ 1 et seq., 361 et seq.

Improvement Act Bonds (Refunding Act of 1984)

Cal. Streets and Highways Code § 9500 et seq.

Improvement and Accountability Act (Schools)

N.C. Laws 1991, Ch. 778

Improvement and Assessment Act

Haw. Rev. Stat. Ann., § 70-111

Kan. Stat. Ann., 12-6a01 et seq.

Improvement and Management Act (Surface Act)

Fla. Stat. Ann., 373.451 et seq.

Improvement and Management of Surface Water Act

Fla. Stat. Ann., 373.451 et seq.

Improvement and Service District Act

Wyo. Stat. Ann., § 18-12-101 et seq.

Improvement Assessment Act (Fulton County)

Ga. Laws 1949, p. 1423

Improvement Assessment Act (Real Property)

Ill. Comp. Stat. 1992, Ch. 35, §§ 210/1 to 210/4

Improvement Authorities Law

S.D. Code 1939, 52.1601 et seq.

Improvement Board Act (Belmont-De Villier)
Fla. Special Laws 1975, Ch. 75-483

Improvement Bond Act
Cal. Streets and Highways Code § 8500 et seq.

Improvement Bond Act (Municipal)
See Municipal Improvement Bond Act

Improvement Bond Act (Permanent)
N.C. Laws 1953, Ch. 1149

Improvement Bond Refunding Law
Cal. Streets and Highways Code § 9000 et seq.

Improvement Commission Law
Fla. Stat. 1953, 420.01 et seq.

Improvement Distribution Act (General)
Ark. Acts 1997, No. 1356

Improvement District Act
Ariz. Rev. Stat. Ann., § 11-701 et seq.
Ark. Code Ann. 1987, 14-88-202 et seq.
Colo. Rev. Stat., 31-25-501 et seq.
Nev. Rev. Stat. 1979 Reprint, 309.010 et seq.
Okla. Stat. Ann., Title 11, § 39-101 et seq.
Ore. Rev. Stat., 554.010 et seq.

Improvement District Act (Business)
Mont. Code Ann., 7-12-1100 et seq.
N.Y. General Municipal Law (Consol. Laws Ch. 23), § 980 et seq.
Pa. Cons. Stat., Title 53, § 5401 et seq.

Improvement District Act (Central Business)
See Central Business Improvement District Act

Improvement District Act (City Business)
Ga. Code Ann., 36-43-1 et seq.

Improvement District Act (County)
N.M. Stat. Ann., 4-55A-1 et seq.

Improvement District Act (Neighborhood)
Mo. Rev. Stat. 1978, 67.453

Improvement District Annexation Act
Ark. Code Ann. 1987, 14-88-503

Improvement District Law (Lake)
Minn. Stat. Ann., 103B.501 et seq.
Minn. Stat. 1986, 103B.501 et seq.

Improvement District Refinancing Act
Cal. Statutes 1937, p. 1876

Improvement Districts Act (Clayton County Community)
Ga. Laws 1992, p. 5698

Improvement Districts Act (Dahlonega)
Ga. Laws 1991, p. 4649

Improvement Districts Act (Rural)
Mont. Code Ann., 7-12-2101 et seq.

Improvement Districts Act (Special)
Colo. Rev. Stat., 31-25-501 et seq.

Improvement Districts Act (Water and Sewer)
Utah Code Ann. 1953, 17A-2-301 et seq.

Improvement Loan Act
R.I. Public Laws 1938, Ch. 2610

Improvement Loan Act (Fort Phoenix Beach)
Mass. Acts 1962, Ch. 637

Improvement Loan Act (Hanscom Field)
Mass. Acts 1955, Ch. 769

Improvement Loan Act (Highways)
Mass. Acts 1950, Ch. 685
Mass. Acts 1952, Ch. 556
Mass. Acts 1954, Ch. 403
Mass. Acts 1956, Ch. 718

Improvement Loan Act (Quequechan River)
Mass. Acts 1957, Ch. 607

Improvement of Deteriorating Real Property or Areas Tax Exemption
Pa. Purdon's Stat., Title 72, § 4711-101 et seq.

Improvements, Rents and Profits Act
Me. Rev. Stat. Ann. 1964, Title 14, § 6951 et seq.

Improver of Property Law (Good Faith)
Cal. Code of Civil Procedure § 8711 et seq.

Improving America's Schools Act of 1994
Oct. 20, 1994, P.L. 103-382, 20 U.S. Code § 6301 nt.
Sept. 17, 1997, P.L. 104-43, 15 U.S. Code § 1 nt.
Oct. 7, 1998, P.L. 105-244, 15 U.S. Code § 1 nt.

Impure Tea Importation Act
Neb. Rev. Stat. 1943, 43-801

Imputed Liability Act (Parents)
See Parental Liability Act

Imputed Negligence Act
Cal. Vehicle Code 1959, § 17150 et seq.

Imputed Negligence Act (Motor Vehicles)
Cal. Vehicle Code 1959, § 17150

In-Home Care Act (Adult)
N.H. Rev. Stat. 1955, 161-F:71 et seq.

In-Home Child Protection Act
Cal. Health and Safety Code § 1597.80 et seq.

In rem Act (Quiet Title)
Ala. Code 1975, § 6-6-560 et seq.

In rem Tax Deed Act
Cal. Revenue and Taxation Code § 3950 et seq.

In rem Tax Foreclosure Act
N.J. Stat. Ann., 54:5-104.29 et seq.

In rem Tax Foreclosure Act (Monroe County)
N.Y. Laws 1962, Ch. 905

In rem Tax Foreclosure Act (New York City)
N.Y. City Adm. Code '38, Ch. 17, § D17-1.0 et seq.

In-School Intervention Pilot Program
La. Rev. Stat. Ann., 17:201 to 17:205

In-School Suspension Act
Colo. Rev. Stat., 22-37-101 et seq.

In-Service Training Act
Wash. Rev. Code Ann., 28A.71.200 et seq.

In-State Investment Act
Mont. Code Ann., 17-6-301 et seq.
N.J. Stat. Ann., 17:16C-1 et seq.
P.R. Laws Ann. 1954, Title 10 § 731 et seq.
Utah Laws 1953, Ch. 24

In Transitu Act (Offenses)
Nev. Rev. Stat. 1979 Reprint, 171.040

INA
See Immigration And Nationality Act

INAA
See Immigration And Nationality Act Amendments Of 1986

Inactive and Abandoned Hazardous Waste Site Law
La. Rev. Stat. Ann., 30:1147.1 et seq.

Inc. Act
Kan. Stat. Ann., 74-8001 et seq.

Incarcerated Persons' Mental Treatment Act
Ill. Rev. Stat. 1991, Ch. 91 1/2, § 140 et seq.

Incarcerated Witness Fees Act of 1991
Oct. 14, 1992, P.L. 102-417, 28 U.S. Code §§ 1 nt., 1821, 1821 nt.

Incarceration Act (Boot Camp)
Del. Code of 1974, Title 11, § 6701 et seq.

Incarceration Law (Classification/ Alternatives to)

N.Y. Correction Law (Consol. Laws Ch. 43) §§ 485, 500, 500b, 500c, 500g

N.Y. Executive Law 1951 (Consol. Laws Ch. 18) § 261 et seq.

Incarceration Reimbursement Act

Mo. Rev. Stat. 1978, 217.825

Incentive Act (Military Careers)

Okla. Stat. Ann., Title 22, § 991a-5 et seq.

Incentive Aid Payments Act

Tex. Education Code, § 23.991 et seq.

Incentive and Productivity Act

Tex. General and Special Laws 1991, p. 3890, Ch. 888

Tex. Rev. Civ. Stat., Art. 6252-29a

Incentive Awards for State Employees Act

Okla. Stat. Ann., Title 74, § 4111 et seq.

Incentive Employment and Litter Control Program (Youth Corps)

La. Rev. Stat. Ann., 23:1821 et seq.

Incentive Employment Program (Youth)

La. Rev. Stat. Ann., 23:1821 et seq.

Incentive for Training and Employment Act (RIITE)

R.I. Gen. Laws 1956, 40-6.4-1 et seq.

Incentive Grants for Local Delinquency Prevention Programs Act

Nov. 4, 1992, P.L. 102-586, 42 U.S. Code § 5601 nt.

Incentive Guarantee Program (Rental Housing)

N.J. Stat. Ann., 55:14K-64 et seq.

Incentive Scholarship Program (Undergraduate and Vocational)

Va. Code 1950, § 23-38.19:3 et seq.

Incentive Tax Credit Act (New Coal Production)

Mont. Code Ann., 15-35-201 et seq.

Incentives for Budget Savings Act

Colo. Rev. Stat., 24-38-101 et seq.

Incentives for School Improvement Act

N.M. Stat. Ann., 22-13A-1 et seq.

Incentives Law (Local Government Service Sharing and Combination)

Minn. Stat. Ann., 465.80 et seq.

Incest Act

Md. Ann. Code 1957, Art. 27, § 335

Ohio Rev. Code 1953, 2907.03(A)(5)

Inchoate Crimes Act

Colo. Rev. Stat., 18-2-101

Incineration Siting Act (Hazardous Waste)

Colo. Rev. Stat., 25-15-501 et seq.

Incinerator Ash Disposal Act (Special)

Wash. Rev. Code Ann., 70.138.010 et seq.

Incinerator Authorities Law

N.J. Stat. Ann., 40:66A-1 et seq.

Incinerator Bond Act (Metropolitan Districts)

Mass. Gen. Laws Ann., 92:9A

Incinerator Loan Act (Boston, Brighton & Watertown)

Mass. Acts 1954, Ch. 523

Incinerator Loan Act (Waltham)

Mass. Acts 1958, Ch. 517

Incinerator Loan Act (Worcester)

Mass. Acts 1952, Ch. 164

Income Act

Md. Ann. Code 1974, Art. ET, § 14-201 et seq.

Income Act (Tenants and Remaindermen)

Cal. Civil Code § 730 et seq.

Income and Franchise Tax Act

D.C. Code 1973, § 47-1801.1 et seq.

Vt. Stat. Ann. 1959, Title 32, § 5811 et seq.

Income and Franchise Tax Act (Corporate)
N.M. Stat. Ann., 7-2A-1

Income and New Jobs Act
Iowa Code 1995, 15.326 et seq.

Income and Principal Act
See also Uniform Principal and Income Act
See Principal and Income Act
Fla. Stat. 1973, 690.01 et seq.
S.C. Code Ann. 1976, § 62-7-401 et seq.
Utah Code Ann. 1953, 22-3-1 et seq.

Income Division for Tax Purposes Act
See Uniform Division of Income for Tax
Purposes Act

Income Installment Act (Annualized)
Mass. Gen. Laws Ann., 62B:13, 62B:14

Income Producing Building or Improvement Bond Act (Educational Institutions)
N.M. Stat. Ann., 6-17-1 et seq.

Income Security Act for Aged, Blind, and Disabled Californians (Burton-Moscone-Bagley)
Cal. Welfare and Institutions Code § 12000 et seq.

Income Tax (Adjusted Gross)
Ind. Code Ann., 6-3-1-1 et seq.

Income Tax Act
Ariz. Laws 1933, 1st Sp. Sess., Ch. 8
Ariz. Laws 1954, Ch. 65
Ariz. Rev. Stat. Ann., § 43-101 et seq.
Ark. Code Ann. 1987, 26-51-804, 26-51-401 et seq.
Cal. Revenue and Taxation Code § 17001 et seq.
Ida. Code 1947, 63-300 et seq.
Ill. Comp. Stat. 1992, Ch. 35, § 5/101 et seq.
Mass. Gen. Laws Ann., 62:1 et seq.
Me. Rev. Stat. Ann. 1964, Title 36, § 5101 et seq.
Minn. Stat. Ann., 290.01 et seq.
Miss. Code Ann. 1972, § 27-7-1 et seq.
Mont. Code Ann., 15-30-101 et seq.
N.C. Gen. Stat. 1943, § 105-133 et seq.

N.Y. Tax Law (Consol Laws Ch. 60) § 601 et seq.
Okla. Stat. Ann., Title 68 § 2351 et eq.
Ore. Rev. Stat., 314.011 et seq.
Pa. Purdon's Stat., Title 72, § 3402-1 et seq.
Pa. Purdon's Stat., Title 72, § 7301 et seq.
P.R. Acts 1925, No. 74
R.I. Gen. Laws 1956, 44-30-1 et seq.
S.C. Code Ann. 1976, § 12-6-10 et seq.
Utah Code Ann. 1953, 59-10-101 et seq.
Wash. Rev. Code Ann., 82.30.010 et seq.
Wis. Stat. Ann., 71.01 et seq.

Income Tax Act (Banks)
S.D. Codified Laws 1967, 10-43-1 et seq.

Income Tax Act (Business Activities)
Mich. Comp. Laws 1948, 205.551 et seq.

Income Tax Act (C Corporation)
Colo. Rev. Stat., 39-22-301 et seq.

Income Tax Act (City)
See City Income Tax Act

Income Tax Act (Commuters)
N.J. Stat. Ann., 54:8A-1 et seq.

Income Tax Act (Cooperative Agricultural Associations)
N.C. Gen. Stat. 1943, § 105-133 et seq.
N.D. Cent. Code, 57-38-01 et seq.
Neb. Rev. Stat. 1943, 39-669.08
N.M. Stat. Ann., 7-2-1 et seq.
Okla. Stat. Ann., Title 68, § 2351 et seq.
Ore. Rev. Stat., 314.011 et seq.
Pa. Purdon's Stat., Title 72, § 3420-21 et seq.
P.R. Laws Ann. 1954, Title 13, § 3001 et seq.
S.C. Code Ann. 1976, § 12-7-10 et seq.
Vt. Stat. Ann., Title 32, § 5811 et seq.

Income Tax Act (Corporate)
Fla. Stat. Ann., 719.101 et seq.

Income Tax Act (Corporation)
Cal. Statutes 1937, p. 1284
Del. Code of 1974, Title 30, § 1901 et seq.
Haw. Rev. Stat. Ann., § 235-121 et seq.
La. Acts 1991, First Extra Session, No. 3
Mass. Gen. Laws Ann., 63C:1 et seq.

Mont. Code Ann., 15-30-101 et seq.
N.C. Gen. Stat. 1943, § 105.130 et seq.
N.J. Stat. Ann., 54:10E-1 et seq.
Ore. Rev. Stat., 318.010
Pa. Purdon's Stat., Title 72, § 7401 et seq.
W. Va. Code 1966, § 11-24-1 et seq.

Income Tax Act (First Class Cities and School Districts)
Pa. Purdon's Stat., Title 53, § 16111 et seq.

Income Tax Act (Gross)
Ind. Code Ann., 6-2.1-1-1 et seq.
S.D. Laws 1933, Ch. 184

Income Tax Act (Hall)
Ala. Code 1975, § 40-18-1 et seq.
Alaska Stat. 1962, § 43.20.010 et seq.
Ariz. Rev. Stat. Ann., § 43-101 et seq.
Ark. Code Ann. 1987, 26-51-101 et seq.
Colo. Rev. Stat., 39-22-101 et seq.
D.C. Code Ann., § 47-1801.1 et seq.
Fla. Stat. Ann., 220.01 et seq.
Ga. Code Ann., 48-7-1 et seq.
Haw. Rev. Stat. Ann., § 235-1 et seq.
Ida. Code 1947, 63-3001 et seq.
Ill. Rev. Stat. 1991, Ch. 120, § 1-101 et seq.
Iowa Code Ann., 422.1 et seq.
Kan. Stat. Ann., 79-3201 et seq.
Ky. Rev. Stat. 1971, 141.010 et seq.
La. Rev. Stat. Ann., 47:21 et seq.
Mass. Gen. Laws Ann., 62:1 et seq.
Md. Ann. Code 1974, Art. TG, § 10-101 et seq.
Me. Rev. Stat. Ann. 1964, Title 36, § 5101 et seq.
Mich. Comp. Laws Ann., 206.1 et seq.
Minn. Stat. Ann., 290.01 et seq.
Miss. Code Ann. 1972, § 27-7-1 et seq.
Mo. Rev. Stat., 143.005 et seq.
Mont. Code Ann., 15-30-101 et seq.
Neb. Rev. Stat. 1943, 77-2714 et seq.
N.H. Rev. Stat. 1955, 77:1 et seq.
Utah Code Ann. 1953, 59-10-101 et seq.
Va. Code 1950, § 58.1-301 et seq.
Wash. Laws 1933, Ch. 5
Wis. Stat. Ann., 71.01 et seq.
W. Va. Code 1966, § 11-21-1 et seq.

Income Tax Act (Health Care Provider)
Neb. Rev. Stat. 1943, 77-4801 et seq.

Income Tax Act (Municipal)
See Municipal Income Tax Act

Income Tax Act (New Castle County)
Del. Laws Vol. 40, p. 52, Ch. 12

Income Tax Act (S Corporation)
Colo. Rev. Stat., 39-22-320 et seq.
Haw. Rev. Stat. Ann., §§ 235-121 to 235-130
Miss. Code Ann. 1972, § 27-8-1 et seq.

Income Tax Act (Stocks and Bonds)
Tenn. Code Ann., 67-2-101 et seq.

Income Tax Act for Estates, Trusts and Beneficiaries
N.C. Gen. Stat. 1943, § 105-160 et seq.

Income Tax Acts
See also Internal Revenue Code Of 1939 And Internal Revenue Code Of 1954
Aug. 27, 1894, Ch. 349, 28 Stat. 509
Oct. 3, 1913, Ch. 16, 38 Stat. 114
Sept. 8, 1916, Ch. 463, 39 Stat. 756
Oct. 3, 1917, Ch. 63, 40 Stat. 300
Feb. 24, 1919, Ch. 18, 40 Stat. 1058
Nov. 23, 1921, Ch. 136, 42 Stat. 227
June 2, 1924, Ch. 234, 43 Stat. 254
May 29, 1928, Ch. 852, 45 Stat. 795
June 6, 1932, Ch. 209, 47 Stat. 173
May 10, 1934, Ch. 277, 48 Stat. 683
Aug. 30, 1935, Ch. 829, 49 Stat. 1014
May 28, 1938, Ch. 289, 52 Stat. 447

Income Tax Amendment Resolution
July 31, 1909, No. 40, 36 Stat. 184

Income Tax Apportionment Act
Kan. Stat. Ann., 79-3271 et seq.

Income Tax Check-off-Campaign Disclosure Act
Iowa Code Ann., 56.1 et seq.

Income Tax Conformity Act
Ala. Code 1975, §§ 40-18-1 et seq., 40-27-1

Income Tax Credit Act (Property Taxes)
N.C. Gen. Stat. 1943, § 105-163.01 et seq.

Income Tax Credit Law (Working Family)
Minn. Stat. Ann., 290.0671

Income Tax Fairness, Simplification and Conformity Act (Personal)
Cal. Revenue and Taxation Code §§ 16702, 16704, 16710, 17020.1 to 17020.4, 17020.9, 17020.11, 17021.5, 17024.5

Income Tax Federal Conforming Amendments
S.C. Acts 1985, p. 280, No. 101

Income Tax Federal Conformity Act
Kan. Stat. Ann., 79-32, 109 et seq.

Income Tax Law (Personal)
Cal. Revenue and Taxation Code § 17001 et seq.

Income Tax Lien Act
Iowa Code Ann., 422.26

Income Tax Payment Act
Ga. Code Ann., 48-7-100 et seq.

Income Tax Reform Act (Corporate)
Ala. Acts 1985, p. 517

Income Tax Return Act
April 10, 1936, Ch. 189, 49 Stat. 1199

Income Tax S Corporation Act
N.C. Gen. Stat. 1943, § 105-131 et seq.

Income Tax Setoff for Child Support Debt Act
Miss. Code Ann. 1972, § 27-7-501 et seq.

Income Tax Setoff for Student Loan Debt Act
Miss. Code Ann. 1972, § 27-7-701 et seq.

Income Tax Surcharge Act (City)
N.Y. Tax Law (Consol. Laws Ch. 60) § 1320 et seq.

Income Tax Surcharge Act (Yonkers)
N.Y. Laws 1987, Ch. 333, § 167

Income Tax Technical Revenue Act
Ark. Acts 1989, No. 826

Income Tax Withholding Act
Ark. Code Ann. 1987, 26-51-901 et seq.
Ky. Rev. Stat. 1971, 141.310 et seq.
Mass. Gen. Laws Ann., 62B:1 et seq.
Miss. Code Ann. 1972, § 27-7-301 et seq.
N.C. Gen. Stat. 1943, § 105-16 3.1 et seq.
N.M. Stat. Ann., 7-3-1 et seq.
Okla. Stat. Ann., Title 68, § 2385.1 et seq.

Income Trust Act
N.Y. Estates, Powers, and Trusts Law (Consol. Laws Ch. 17B) § 7-1.5

Income Withholding Act
Kan. Stat. Ann., 23-4,105 et seq.
Wyo. Stat. Ann., § 20-6-201 et seq.

Income Withholding Act (Interstate)
Kan. Stat. Ann., 23-4,125 et seq.
Mich. Comp. Laws Ann., 552.671 et seq.

Income Withholding Act (Model Interstate)
Tex. Family Code, § 14.61 et seq.

Income Withholding for Child Support Act
Neb. Rev. Stat. 1943, 43-1601 et seq.

Income Withholding for Support Act
Ill. Comp. Stat. 1992, Ch. 750, § 28/1 et seq.

Income Withholding to Enforce Support Obligations Act
S.C. Code Ann. 1976, § 20-7-1315 et seq.

Incompetency Act (Criminal Proceedings)
Mich. Comp. Laws Ann., 767.27 et seq.

Incompetency Act (Self Incrimination)
Ga. Code Ann., 24-9-20, 24-9-21

Incompetency-Irresponsibility Act
N.M. Stat. Ann., 31-9-1 et seq.

Incompetent Patients Act (Hydration and Nutrition)
Okla. Stat. Ann., Title 63, § 3080.1 et seq.

Incompetent Witness Acts
Kan. Stat. Ann., 60-417, 60-426 et seq.
Pa. Cons. Stat., Title 42, § 5930

Incompetents Commitment Act
Md. Ann. Code 1957, Superseded Volume, Art. 59, § 16 et seq.

Incompetents' Estates Act
Ill. Rev. Stat. 1991, Ch. 110 1/2, § 11-3 et seq.
Pa. Cons. Stat., Title 20, § 5501 et seq.

Incontestibility Act (Insurance)
Iowa Code Ann., 508.28
S.C. Code Ann. 1976, Superseded Vols., § 38-9-250
Wash. Rev. Code Ann., 48.23.050

Incorporated Act
Kan. Stat. Ann., 74-8001 et seq.

Incorporated Village Act
Wis. Stat. Ann., 61.187 et seq.

Incorporation Act (Cities and Towns)
Ind. Code 1976, 18-1-1-1 et seq.

Incorporation Act (Corporations)
Colo. Rev. Stat., 7-1-101 et seq.
Ore. Rev. Stat., 60.001 et seq.
Pa. 1874 Pamph. Laws 73, No. 32
S.D. Codified Laws 1967, 47-1-1 et seq.

Incorporation Act (Exposition Authority)
Ill. Rev. Stat. 1991, Ch. 32, § 503a90 et seq.

Incorporation Act (Municipal)
See Municipal Incorporation Act

Incorporation Act (Philadelphia)
Pa. Purdon's Stat., Title 53, § 16251 et seq.

Incorporation Act (Railroads)
See Railroad Incorporation Act

Incorporation Act (Village)
Alaska Stat. 1962, § 29.25.010 et seq.

Incorporation and Government of Towns Act
N.J. Rev. Stat. 1937, 40:123-1 et seq.

Increase of Public Assistance Payments Act
D.C. Code Ann., § 3-205.52

Increase Rate of Interest on Special Assessments Act
D.C. Code Ann., § 47-1205

Increased Penalty Act
Minn. Stat. 1961, 610.31

Increment Financing Act (Employment Tax)
Me. Rev. Stat. Ann. 1964, Title 36, § 6751 et seq.

Increment Financing Act (Tax)
Tex. Tax Code, § 311.001 et seq.

Incubator Enterprise Program Act (New Business)
Cal. Government Code § 15339.1 et seq.

Incubators Act (Small Business)
Cal. Statutes 1988, Ch. 634, § 1
Mo. Rev. Stat. 1978, 620.495
Okla. Stat. Ann., Title 74, § 5071 et seq.

Indecency Law
Iowa Code Ann., 728.1 et seq.

Indecent and Open Exposure Act
Mich. Comp. Laws Ann., 750.335 et seq.

Indecent Exposure Act
Cal. Penal Code § 314
Mich. Comp. Laws Ann., 750.335 et seq.
N.C. Gen. Stat. 1943, § 314-190.9

Indecent Liberties Act
Ala. Code 1975, §§ 13A-6-66, 13A-6-67
Colo. Rev. Stat., 18-2-301
Ill. Rev. Stat. 1983, Ch. 38, § 11-4
Mo. Rev. Stat. 1969, 559.360
Ohio Rev. Code 1953, 2907.04 et seq.

Indecent Liberties Act (Female Child)
Mich. Comp. Laws Ann.,750.336

Indecent Liberties Act (Male Child)
Mich. Comp. Laws Ann., 750.339, 750.340

Indefinite Reference to Mortgages Act
Okla. Stat. Ann., Title 46, § 201 et seq.

Indemnification Act (Corporate Officers)
N.C. Gen. Stat. 1943, § 355-8-57 et seq.

Indemnification Act (Corporations)
Del. Code of 1974, Title 8, § 145

Indemnification Act (Policemen)
Ill. Rev. Stat. 1991, Ch. 24, § 1-4-5
Mich. Comp. Laws 1948, 124.101 et seq.

Indemnification Act (State Employee)
Ill. Rev. Stat. 1991, Ch. 127, § 1300 et seq.

Indemnification for Negligence Act (Construction Contract)
Ill. Comp. Stat. 1992, Ch. 740, § 35/0.01 et seq.
Ill. Rev. Stat. 1991, Ch. 29, § 60.90 et seq.

Indemnification Trust Act (Nonprofit Risk)
La. Rev. Stat. Ann., 22:1521 et seq., 22:2001 et seq.
Minn. Stat. Ann., 60A.29

Indemnity Account Program (Commodity)
Ida. Code 1947, 69-255 et seq.

Indemnity Act
Mont. Code Ann., 28-11-301 et seq.

Indemnity Act (American Forces Abroad)
April 18, 1918, Ch. 57, 40 Stat. 532

Indemnity Act (Oil Field)
La. Rev. Stat. Ann., 9:2780

Indemnity Act (President's Orders and Proclamations, Civil War)
March 2, 1867, Ch. 155, 14 Stat. 432

Indemnity Act (State War Expenses, Civil War)
July 27, 1861, Ch. 21, 12 Stat. 276

Indemnity and Protection Club, and Commercial Fishermen's Hull Insurance Act
N.C. Gen. Stat. 1943, § 58-340.1 et seq.

Indemnity Fund Act (Livestock)
Cal. Food and Agricultural Code 1967, §§ 30651 et seq., 10401, 10421 et seq.

Indemnity Fund Act (Special)
Okla. Stat. Ann., Title 85, § 171 et seq.

Independent Administration of Estates Act
Cal. Probate Code § 591 et seq., § 10400 et seq.
S.D. Codified Laws 1967, 30-18A-1 et seq.

Independent Adoption Preplacement Program Act
Cal. Civil Code §§ 221.5, 226.5, 226.51
Cal. Health and Safety Code § 1522.4

Independent Advice Act (Wills)
Kan. Stat. Ann., 59-605

Independent Agencies Appropriation Act
July 9, 1971, P.L. 92-49, 85 Stat. 120, 26 U.S. Code § 7443 nt.
July 13, 1972, P.L. 92-351, 86 Stat. 478, 26 U.S. Code § 7443 nt.
Aug. 9, 1975, P.L. 94-91, 89 Stat. 448, 26 U.S. Code § 7443 nt.; 31 U.S. Code §§ 638c nt., 699b; 33 U.S. Code § 776; 40 U.S. Code § 490

Independent Agencies Appropriations Act, 1987
Oct. 18, 1986, P.L. 99-500, 26 U.S. Code § 7443 nt.
Oct. 30, 1986, P.L. 99-591, 26 U.S. Code § 7443 nt.

Independent Agencies Appropriations Act, 1988
Dec. 22, 1987, P.L. 100-202, 101 Stat. 1329
Nov. 16, 1989, P.L. 101-156, 103 Stat. 936

Independent Agencies Appropriations Act, 1989

Sept. 22, 1988, P.L. 100-440, 40 U.S. Code § 490c; 50 U.S. Code § 98h

Independent Agencies Appropriations Act, 1990

Nov. 3, 1989, P.L. 101-136, 103 Stat. 794

Independent Agencies Appropriations Act, 1991

Nov. 5, 1990, P.L. 101-509, 5 U.S. Code § 8902; 26 U.S. Code § 7443 nt.; 33 U.S. Code § 776; 40 U.S. Code § 490; 44 U.S. Code §§ 2102 nt., 2701 to 2706

Independent Agencies Appropriations Act, 1992

Oct. 28, 1991, P.L. 102-141, 105 Stat. 848

Independent Agencies Appropriations Act, 1993

Oct. 6, 1992, P.L. 102-393, 26 U.S. Code § 7443 nt.; 33 U.S. Code § 776; 40 U.S. Code §§ 490g, 490l

Independent Agencies Appropriations Act, 1994

Oct. 28, 1993, P.L. 103-123, 107 Stat. 1238

Independent Agencies Appropriations Act, 1995

Sept. 30, 1994, P.L. 103-329, 108 Stat. 2396

Independent Agencies Appropriations Act, 1996

Nov. 19, 1995, P.L. 104-52, Title IV, 109 Stat. 480

Independent Agencies Appropriations Act, 1998

Oct. 10, 1997, P.L. 105-61, Title IV, 111 Stat. 1295

Independent Agencies Appropriations Act, 1999

Oct. 21, 1998, P.L. 105-277, 101(h), Title IV, 112 Stat. 2681

Independent Agency Sunset Law

Fla. Special Laws 1977, Ch. 584

Independent Agricultural Crop Consultants Act

Ga. Official Code Ann., 43-21A-1 et seq.

Independent College and University Assistance Act

N.J. Stat. Ann., 18A:72B-15 et seq.

Independent Colleges and Universities Utilization Act

N.J. Laws 1972, Ch. 67

Independent Community College Act

N.M. Stat. Ann., 21-14A-1 et seq.

Independent Counsel Reauthorization Act of 1987

Dec. 15, 1987, P.L. 100-191, 5 U.S. Code Appx. 203, 205; 18 U.S. Code 202; 28 U.S. Code §§ 1 nt., 49, 591-599

Independent Counsel Reauthorization Act of 1994

June 30, 1994, P.L. 103-270, 3 U.S. Code § 113 nt., 28 U.S. Code §§ 1 nt., 591 et seq.

Independent Higher Education Loan Authority Act

Ill. Rev. Stat. 1991, Ch. 144, § 1600 et seq.

Independent Higher Education Loan Bond Program

W. Va. Code 1966, § 18-27-1 et seq.

Independent Liability Fund Act

Mont. Laws 1991, Ch. 564

Independent Living Services Act

Pa. Purdon's Stat., Title 62, § 3201 et seq.

Independent Offices Act of 1928

Feb. 11, 1927, Ch. 104, 44 Stat. 1069

Nov. 23, 1988, P.L. 100-710, 46 U.S. Code Appx. § 810a

Independent Offices Act of 1929

May 16, 1928, Ch. 580, 45 Stat. 573

Independent Offices and Department of Housing and Urban Development Appropriation Acts

Nov. 3, 1967, P.L. 90-121, 81 Stat. 341, 12 U.S. Code §§ 1428a nt., 1701g-5; 40 U.S. Code § 313-2 nt.; 42 U.S. Code § 1431; 49 U.S. Code § 305a

Oct. 4, 1968, P.L. 90-550, 82 Stat. 937, 12 U.S. Code §§ 1428a nt., 1701g-5; 40 USC § 313-2 nt.; 42 U.S. Code § 1431; 49 U.S. Code § 305a

Nov. 26, 1969, P.L. 91-126, 83 Stat. 221, 12 U.S. Code §§ 1428a nt., 1701g-5; 40 U.S. Code § 313-2 nt.; 42 U.S. Code § 1431

Dec. 17, 1970, P.L. 91-556, 84 Stat. 1448, 12 U.S. Code §§ 1428 nt., 1701g-5; 40 U.S. Code § 313-2 nt.; 42 U.S. Code § 1431

Independent Offices Appropriation Act of 1931

April 19, 1930, Ch. 201, 46 Stat. 229

Independent Offices Appropriation Act of 1932

Feb. 23, 1931, Ch. 281, 46 Stat. 1355

Independent Offices Appropriation Act of 1933

June 30, 1932, Ch. 330, 47 Stat. 452

Independent Offices Appropriation Act of 1934

June 16, 1933, Ch. 101, 48 Stat. 283, 15 U.S. Code § 46a; 40 U.S. Code § 315; 41 U.S. Code § 6b; 43 U.S. Code § 403; 46 U.S. Code § 891

Feb. 24, 1938, Ch. 34, 52 Stat. 81

Independent Offices Appropriation Act of 1935

March 28, 1934, Ch. 102, 48 Stat. 510

July 18, 1966, P.L. 89-504, 80 Stat. 298

Independent Offices Appropriation Act of 1938

June 28, 1937, Ch. 396, 50 Stat. 329, 19 U.S. Code § 1330 nt.; 49 U.S. Code § 350a

Independent Offices Appropriation Act of 1939

May 23, 1938, Ch. 259, 52 Stat. 410

Independent Offices Appropriation Act of 1940

March 16, 1939, Ch. 11, 53 Stat. 524, 49 U.S. Code § 305a

March 1, 1940, Ch. 31, 54 Stat. 37

Independent Offices Appropriation Act of 1941

April 18, 1940, Ch. 107, 54 Stat. 111, 49 U.S. Code § 305a

Independent Offices Appropriation Act of 1942

April 5, 1941, Ch. 40, 55 Stat. 92, 31 U.S. Code § 42 nt.; 49 U.S. Code § 305a

June 26, 1943, Ch. 145, 57 Stat. 180

Independent Offices Appropriation Act of 1943

June 27, 1942, Ch. 450, 56 Stat. 392, 36 U.S. Code § 121a; 49 U.S. Code § 305a

June 26, 1943, Ch. 145, 57 Stat. 180

Independent Offices Appropriation Act of 1944

June 26, 1943, Ch. 145, 57 Stat. 169, 12 U.S. Code §§ 1439a, 1463 nt.; 31 U.S. Code § 42 nt.; 49 U.S. Code § 305a

Sept. 30, 1961, P.L. 87-332, 75 Stat. 743

Independent Offices Appropriation Act of 1945

June 27, 1944, Ch. 286, 58 Stat. 361, 31 U.S. Code § 43a; 36 U.S. Code §§ 122, 135; 40 U.S. Code §§ 7a, 265a, 277a, 284; 49 U.S. Code § 305a

Independent Offices Appropriation Act of 1946

May 3, 1945, Ch. 106, 59 Stat. 106, 3 U.S. Code § 46; 15 U.S. Code § 712a nt.; 31 U.S. Code § 691; 40 U.S. Code §§ 7a, 265a, 277a, 284, 292, 293; 42 U.S. Code § 1431; 49 U.S. Code § 305a

Dec. 28, 1945, Ch. 589, 59 Stat. 632

Independent Offices Appropriation Act of 1947

March 28, 1946, Ch. 113, 60 Stat. 60, 3 U.S. Code § 46; 40 U.S. Code §§ 7a, 265a, 277a, 284, 292; 49 U.S. Code § 305a

Independent Offices Appropriation Act of 1948

July 30, 1947, Ch. 359, 61 Stat. 585, 3 U.S. Code § 107; 31 U.S. Code § 638c; 40 U.S. Code §§ 277a, 284, 292; 41 U.S. Code § 6a nt.; 49 U.S. Code §§ 246, 305a

Independent Offices Appropriation Act of 1949

April 20, 1948, Ch. 219, 62 Stat. 176, 3 U.S. Code § 46; 31 U.S. Code § 638c; 36 U.S. Code § 122; 40 U.S. Code §§ 277a, 284, 292; 49 U.S. Code § 305a; 50 U.S. Code § 157

June 30, 1948, Ch. 775, 62 Stat. 1205

Independent Offices Appropriation Act of 1950

Aug. 24, 1949, Ch. 506, 63 Stat. 631, 31 U.S. Code §§ 638c, 870; 36 U.S. Code § 122; 42 U.S. Code §§ 1431, 1576; 49 U.S. Code § 305a; 50 U.S. Code §§ 157, 160

Independent Offices Appropriation Act of 1951

Sept. 6, 1950, Ch. 896, 64 Stat. 697, 12 U.S. Code § 1749d; 22 U.S. Code § 1382; 24 U.S. Code § 290; 36 U.S. Code § 122; 41 U.S. Code § 219 nts.; 42 U.S. Code §§ 1431, 1576; 49 U.S. Code § 305a; 50 U.S. Code §§ 157, 160; 50 U.S. Code Appx. §§ 1738b, 2012a

Independent Offices Appropriation Act of 1952

Aug. 31, 1951, Ch. 376, 65 Stat. 268, 12 U.S. Code §§ 1701g-4, 1749d; 31 U.S. Code §§ 52a, 483a; 36 U.S. Code § 122; 42 U.S. Code §§ 1411a, 1431; 46 U.S. Code § 1242-1; 49 U.S. Code § 305a; 50 U.S. Code Appx. §§ 1738b, 2012a

Independent Offices Appropriation Act of 1953

July 5, 1953, Ch. 578, 66 Stat. 393, 12 U.S. Code §§ 1701g-4, 1749d; 36 U.S. Code § 122; 42 U.S. Code §§ 1411a to 1411c, 1431; 46 U.S. Code § 1242-1; 49 U.S. Code § 305a; 50 U.S. Code Appx. §§ 1738b, 2012a

Independent Offices Appropriation Act of 1955

June 24, 1954, Ch. 359, 69 Stat. 272, 12 U.S. Code §§ 1701c-1, 1701g-5, 1749d; 31 U.S. Code §§ 16b, 52a; 36 U.S. Code §§ 122, 122a, 125a; See 38 U.S. Code § 1665; 40 U.S. Code § 313-2; 42 U.S. Code §§ 1431, 1451a, 1461; 49 U.S. Code § 305a; 50 U.S. Code Appx. §§ 330, 2012a

Aug. 2, 1954, Ch. 649, 68 Stat. 629, 42 U.S. Code § 1452a

Independent Offices Appropriation Act of 1956

June 30, 1955, Ch. 244, 69 Stat. 199, 12 U.S. Code §§ 1428a nt., 1701g-5, 1749d; See 38 U.S. Code § 1665; 40 U.S. Code § 313-2; 42 U.S. Code § 1431; 49 U.S. Code § 305a; 50 U.S. Code Appx. § 330

May 19, 1956, Ch. 313, 70 Stat. 166, 12 U.S. Code §§ 1701g-5, 1749d nt.

Independent Offices Appropriation Act of 1957

June 27, 1956, Ch. 452, 70 Stat. 339; 12 U.S. Code §§ 1428a nt., 1701g-5, 1749d; See 38 U.S. Code § 1665; 40 U.S. Code §§ 313-2 nt., 459 nt., 462 nt.; 42 U.S. Code § 1431; 40 U.S. Code § 305a; 50 U.S. Code Appx. § 330

Independent Offices Appropriation Act of 1958

June 29, 1957, P.L. 85-69, 71 Stat. 227, 12 U.S. Code §§ 1428a nt., 1701g-5, 1749d; See 38 U.S. Code § 1665; 40 U.S. Code §§ 313-2 nt., 462 nt.; 42 U.S. Code § 1431; 49 U.S. Code § 305a; 50 U.S. Code Appx. § 330

Independent Offices Appropriation Act of 1959

Aug. 28, 1958, P.L. 85-844, 72 Stat. 1063, 12 U.S. Code §§ 1428a nt., 1701g-5, 1749d; See 38 U.S. Code § 1665; 40 U.S. Code §§ 313-2 nt., 356 nt., 462 nt.; 42 U.S. Code § 1431; 49 U.S. Code § 305a; 50 U.S. Code Appx. § 330

Independent Offices Appropriation Act of 1960

Sept. 14, 1959, P.L. 86-255, 73 Stat. 500, 12 U.S. Code §§ 1428a nt., 1701g-5, 1749d; 40 U.S. Code §§ 313-2 nt., 462 nt.; 42 U.S. Code § 1431; 49 U.S. Code § 305a; 50 U.S. Code § 98b nt.

Independent Offices Appropriation Act of 1961

July 12, 1960, P.L. 86-626, 74 Stat. 425, 12 U.S. Code §§ 1428a nt., 1438a, 1701g-5, 1749d; 16 U.S. Code § 793a; 40 U.S. Code §§ 313-2 nt., 462 nt., 484a; 42 U.S. Code § 1431; 49 U.S. Code § 305a

Independent Offices Appropriation Act of 1962

Aug. 17, 1961, P.L. 87-141, 75 Stat. 342, 12 U.S. Code §§ 1428a nt., 1701-5, 1749d; 40 U.S. Code §§ 313-2 nt., 462 nt.; 42 U.S. Code § 1431; 49 U.S. Code § 305a

Independent Offices Appropriation Act of 1963

Oct. 3, 1962, P.L. 87-741, 76 Stat. 716, 12 U.S. Code §§ 1428a nt., 1701g-5, 1749d; 40 U.S. Code §§ 313-2 nt., 462 nt.; 42 U.S. Code § 1431; 49 U.S. Code § 305a

Independent Offices Appropriation Act of 1964

Dec. 19, 1963, P.L. 88-215, 77 Stat. 425, 12 U.S. Code §§ 1428a nt., 1701g-5, 1749d; 40 U.S. Code §§ 313-2 nt., 462 nt.; 42 U.S. Code § 1431; 49 U.S. Code § 305a

Independent Offices Appropriation Act of 1965

Aug. 30, 1964, P.L. 88-507, 78 Stat. 640, 12 U.S. Code §§ 1428a nt., 1701g-5, 1749d. nt.; 40 U.S. Code §§ 313-2 nt., 462 nt., 484 nt.; 42 U.S. Code § 1431; 49 U.S. Code § 305a

Independent Offices Appropriation Act of 1966

Aug. 16, 1965, P.L. 89-128, 79 Stat. 543, 12 U.S. Code §§ 1428a nt., 1701g-5, 1749d nt.; 40 U.S. Code §§ 313-2 nt., 462 nt.; 42 U.S. Code § 1431; 49 U.S. Code § 305a

Independent Offices Appropriation Act of 1967

Sept. 6, 1966, P.L. 89-555, 80 Stat. 689, 12 U.S. Code §§ 1428a nt., 1701g-5, 1749d nt.; 38 U.S. Code § 1823 nt.; 40 U.S. Code § 313-2 nt.; 42 U.S. Code § 1431; 49 U.S. Code § 305a

Independent Review Act (Patient's Right to)

Ga. Official Code Ann., 33-20A-30 et seq.

Independent Safety Board Act Amendment of 1978

Sept. 11, 1978, P.L. 95-363, 49 U.S. Code §§ 1901 nt., 1907

Independent Safety Board Act Amendments of 1981

Nov. 3, 1981, P.L. 97-74, 49 U.S. Code § 1901 nt.

Independent Safety Board Act Amendments of 1990

Nov. 28, 1990, P.L. 101-641, 49 U.S. Code Appx. §§ 1657-1, 1801 nt., 1804 nt., 1901 nt.

Oct. 31, 1994, P.L. 103-429, 49 U.S. Code Appx. §§ 1804 nt., 1901 nt.

Independent Safety Board Act Amendments of 1994

Oct. 25, 1994, P.L. 103-411, 49 U.S. Code § 101 nt.

Independent Safety Board Act of 1974

Sept. 11, 1978, P.L. 95-363, 49 U.S. Code § 1907

Oct. 14, 1982, P.L. 97-309, 49 U.S. Code §§ 1902 nt., 1902, 1905

Oct. 19, 1984, P.L. 98-499, 49 U.S. Code Appx. § 1903

Dec. 30, 1987, P.L. 100-223, 49 U.S. Code Appx. §§ 1903, 1903 nt.

Nov. 28, 1990, P.L. 101-641, 49 U.S. Code Appx. §§ 1903, 1905, 1907

Oct. 24, 1992, P.L. 102-508, 49 U.S. Code Appx. § 1903

Independent School District Act

Ala. Code 1958, Title 52, § 197(1) et seq.

Independent Study Commissions and Committees Act
N.C. Laws 1985, Ch. 792

Independent Treasury Act
Aug. 6, 1846, Ch. 90, 9 Stat. 59
Ohio Rev. Code 1953, 113.05 et seq., 2921.41, 2945.64

Independent Wholesale Sales Representatives Contractual Relations Act
Cal. Civil Code § 1738.10

Indeterminate Sentence Act
Cal. Penal Code §§ 1168, 3020 et seq.
Colo. Rev. Stat., 16-12-101
Conn. Gen. Stat. Ann., § 53a-35
Fla. Stat. Ann., 921.18
Ga. Code 1933, 27-2501, 27-2502
Haw. Rev. Stat. 1968, § 711-76
Ida. Code 1947, 19-2513
Ill. Rev. Stat. 1991, Ch. 38, § 1005-8-1
Ind. Code Ann., 35-8-2-1 et seq.
Iowa Code 1977, 789.13
Kan. Stat. Ann., 21-4601 et seq.
Ky. Acts 1910, Ch. 4
Mass. Gen. Laws Ann., 279:24
Mich. Comp. Laws Ann., 769.8
Minn. Stat. Ann., 609.10 et seq.
N.C. Gen. Stat. 1943, § 148-42
Neb. Rev. Stat. 1943, 29-2204 et seq.
N.H. Rev. Stat. 1955, 651:2
N.J. Laws 1911, C 191
N.M. Stat. Ann., 31-18-1 et seq.
N.Y. Penal Law 1965 (Consol. Laws Ch. 40) § 70.00
Ohio Rev. Code 1953, 5145.01
Okla. Stat. Ann., Title 57, § 353 et seq.
Ore. Rev. Stat., 137.120
Pa. Cons. Stat., Title 42, § 9721 et seq.
P.R. Laws Ann. 1954, Title 34, §§ 1024, 1025
S.C. Code Ann. 1976, § 17-25-10 et seq.
S.D. Comp. Laws 1967, 23A-27-37 et seq.
Tenn. Code Ann., 40-20-107 et seq.
Tex. Code of Criminal Procedure, Art. 42.09
Utah Code Ann. 1953, Miscellaneous Superseded Code Provisions, 77-35-20
Wash. Rev. Code Ann., 9.95.005 et seq.

Wis. Stat. Ann., 973.01
W. Va. Code 1966, § 61-11-16
Wyo. Stat. Ann., § 7-13-201

Indeterminate Sentence and Parole Act
D.C. Code Ann., § 24-201c et seq.

Indexing Act (Recording)
Pa. Purdon's Stat., Title 16, § 9851 et seq.

India Emergency Food Aid Act of 1951
June 15, 1951, Ch. 138, 65 Stat. 70, 50 U.S. Code Appx. §§ 2311 to 2316

India-Pakistan Relief Act of 1998
Oct. 21, 1998, P.L. 105-277, 101(a), Title IX, 112 Stat. 2681, 22 U.S. Code § 2799aa-1 nt.

Indian Affairs Act
Wyo. Stat. Ann., § 9-2-1901 et seq.

Indian Affairs Administration Act
Aug. 8, 1946, Ch. 907, 60 Stat. 939, 25 U.S. Code § 1a

Indian Aid Law
Cal. Welfare and Institutional Code §§ 8000, 8001, 8025

Indian Alcohol and Substance Abuse Prevention and Treatment Act of 1986
Oct. 27, 1986, P.L. 99-570, 25 U.S. Code § 2401 nt.
Nov. 18, 1988, P.L. 100-690, 102 Stat. 4217
April 18, 1990, P.L. 101-272, 25 U.S. Code § 2433
Nov. 28, 1990, P.L. 101-630, 25 U.S. Code §§ 2415 nt., 2474
Oct. 29, 1992, P.L. 102-573, 25 U.S. Code §§ 2412, 2413, 2414a[2471], 2432, 2416, 2433, 2442, 2452, 2453, 2478[2472]

Indian Arts and Crafts Act
Aug. 27, 1935, Ch. 748, 49 Stat. 891, 25 U.S. Code §§ 305 to 305e
April 24, 1961, P.L. 87-23, 75 Stat. 45, 25 U.S. Code § 305

Indian Arts and Crafts Act of 1990
Nov. 29, 1990, P.L. 101-644, 18 U.S. Code §§ 162a, 1158, 1159; 25 U.S. Code §§ 305 nt., 305a et seq. generally, 483a

Indian Arts and Crafts Sales Act

Colo. Rev. Stat., 12-44.5-101 et seq.

N.M. Stat. Ann., 30-33-1 et seq.

Okla. Stat. Ann., Title 78, § 71 et seq.

Indian Child Protection and Family Violence Prevention Act

Nov. 28, 1990, P.L. 101-630, 25 U.S. Code §§ 3201 to 3211

June 21, 1995, P.L. 104-16, 25 U.S. Code §§ 3208, 3209, 3210

Nov. 10, 1998, P.L. 105-362, 25 U.S. Code § 3211

Indian Child Welfare Act

Neb. Rev. Stat. 1943, 43-1501 et seq.

Okla. Stat. Ann., Title 10, § 40 et seq.

Indian Child Welfare Act of 1978

Nov. 8, 1978, P.L. 95-608, 25 U.S. Code § 1901 et seq., 1901 nt.

Indian Civil Rights Act

See Civil Rights Act (Indians)

Indian Claims Commission Act

Aug. 13, 1946, Ch. 959, 60 Stat. 1049, 25 U.S. Code §§ 70 to 70v

July 24, 1956, Ch. 679, 70 Stat. 624, 25 U.S. Code § 70v

Sept. 8, 1960, P.L. 86-722, 74 Stat. 829, 25 U.S. Code § 70s

June 16, 1961, P.L. 87-48, 75 Stat. 92, 25 U.S. Code § 70v

April 10, 1967, P.L. 90-9, 81 Stat. 11, 25 U.S. Code §§ 70b, 70e, 70q, 70v, 70v-1

Indian Claims Limitation Act of 1982

Dec. 30, 1982, P.L. 97-394, 28 U.S. Code § 2415, 2415 nt.

Indian Claims Settlement Act (Catawba)

S.C. Code Ann. 1976, § 27-16-10 et seq.

Indian Claims Settlement Implementation Act

Me. Rev. Stat. Ann. 1964, Title 30, § 6201 et seq.

Indian Dams Safety Act of 1994

Aug. 23, 1994, P.L. 103-302, 25 U.S. Code §§ 3801 et seq., 3801 nt.

Feb. 12, 1996, P.L. 104-109, 25 U.S. Code § 3803

Oct. 12, 1996, P.L. 104-303, 25 U.S. Code § 3802

Indian Depredation Act

March 3, 1891, Ch. 538, 26 Stat. 851

Indian Education Act

June 28, 1972, P.L. 92-318, 86 Stat. 334, 20 U.S. Code §§ 240, 241a nt., 241c, 241aa to 241ff, 242 to 244, 821 nt., 822, 842, 880b-3a, 887c, 1091b, 1119a, 1211a, 1221f to 1221h, 1412

Nov. 1, 1978, P.L. 95-561, 20 U.S. Code §§ 887c-1, 887c-2, 1221g, 1221h

Oct. 19, 1984, P.L. 98-511, 20 U.S. Code §§ 3385a, 3385b

Oct. 27, 1986, P.L. 99-570, 20 U.S. Code § 2285b

Indian Education Act (American)

Minn. Stat. Ann., 126.45 et seq.

Indian Education Act of 1988

April 28, 1988, P.L. 100-297, 102 Stat. 395, 20 U.S. Code §§ 1221f to 1221h, 1411 nt., 3385a, 3385b, 25 U.S. Code §§ 2601 et seq., 2601 nt.

Sept. 9, 1988, P.L. 100-427, 25 U.S. Code §§ 2602, 2604, 2605, 2621, 2623, 2624, 2641, 2642, 2651

May 24, 1990, P.L. 101-301, 25 U.S. Code §§ 2604, 2624

Oct. 20, 1994, P.L. 103-382, 25 U.S. Code §§ 2601 to 2606, 2601 nt., 2621 to 2624, 2641 to 2643, 2651

Indian Education Amendments of 1988

April 28, 1988, P.L. 100-297, 102 Stat. 363, 25 U.S. Code § 2001 nt.

Sept. 9, 1988, P.L. 100-427, 20 U.S. Code §§ 1411 nt., 2011 nt.

Indian Education Assistance Act

Oct. 20, 1994, P.L. 103-382, 25 U.S. Code § 458e

Indian Education Technical Amendments Act of 1985

Aug. 15, 1985, P.L. 99-89, 25 U.S. Code §§ 2001, 2001 nt.

Indian Elementary and Secondary School Assistance Act

June 23, 1972, P.L. 92-318, 86 Stat. 235, 7 U.S. Code §§ 301, 326a, 326aa nt., 329, 331, 343, 349, 361a to 361i; 12 U.S. Code §§ 84, 1464, 1757; 16 U.S. Code §§ 582a-3, 582a-7, 1686; 20 U.S. Code §§ 1001 et seq.; 42 U.S. Code §§ 2000c, 2000c-6, 2000c-9, 2000h-2, 2751, 2752, 2754, 2756a, 3401 nt.

Nov. 1, 1978, P.L. 95-561, 20 U.S. Code §§ 241aa et seq.

Aug. 22, 1984, P.L. 98-396, 20 U.S. Code § 241ee

Oct. 19, 1984, P.L. 98-511, 20 U.S. Code §§ 241aa, 241bb, 241dd, 241ff, 1222a, 3385, 3385a, 3385b

Oct. 27, 1986, P.L. 99-570, 20 U.S. Code § 241cc

April 28, 1988, P.L. 100-297, 102 Stat. 404, 20 U.S. Code §§ 241aa, 241aa nt., 241bb, 241cc to 241ff

Indian Employment, Training and Related Services Demonstration Act of 1992

Oct. 23, 1992, P.L. 102-477, 25 U.S. Code §§ 3401, 3401 nt., 3402 to 3417

Nov. 2, 1994, P.L. 103-437, 25 U.S. Code §§ 3415, 3416

Indian Environmental General Assistance Program Act of 1992

Oct. 24, 1992, P.L. 102-497, 42 U.S. Code § 4368b

Nov. 24, 1993, P.L. 103-155, 42 U.S. Code § 4368b

Oct. 2, 1996, P.L. 104-233, 42 U.S. Code § 4368b

Indian Environmental Regulatory Enhancement Act of 1990

Oct. 4, 1990, P.L. 101-408, 42 U.S. Code § 2991 nt.

Indian Family Preservation Act

Minn. Stat. Ann., 257.35 et seq.

Indian Financing Act of 1974

April 12, 1974, P.L. 93-262, 88 Stat. 77, 25 U.S. Code §§ 1451 to 1453, 1461 to 1469, 1481 to 1498, 1511, 1512, 1521 to 1524, 1541 to 1543

July 20, 1977, P.L. 95-68, 25 U.S. Code § 1523

Oct. 4, 1984, P.L. 98-449, 98 Stat. 1725, 25 U.S. Code §§ 47a, 1461, 1465, 1481, 1484, 1491, 1497, 1512, 1522, 1523, 1541, 1543

Sept. 22, 1988, P.L. 100-442, 25 U.S. Code §§ 1452, 1484, 1485, 1496, 1497, 1497 nt., 1497a to 1499, 1544

Nov. 29, 1990, P.L. 101-644, 25 U.S. Code §§ 1461, 1484

Sept. 21, 1993, P.L. 103-82, 25 U.S. Code § 1542

Nov. 10, 1998, P.L. 105-362, 25 U.S. Code § 1497

Indian Gaming Regulatory Act

Oct. 17, 1988, P.L. 100-497, 102 Stat. 2467, 25 U.S. Code §§ 2701 nt., 2701 to 2721

Dec. 17, 1991, P.L. 102-238, 25 U.S. Code § 2703, 2718

Oct. 24, 1992, P.L. 102-497, 25 U.S. Code § 2703

Nov. 14, 1997, P.L. 105-83, 25 U.S. Code §§ 2717, 2718

Nov. 26, 1997, P.L. 105-119, 25 U.S. Code § 2718

Indian General Allotment Act

Feb. 8, 1887, Ch. 119, 24 Stat. 388, 25 U.S. Code §§ 331 to 334, 336, 339, 341, 342, 348, 349, 381

Feb. 21, 1931, Ch. 267, 46 Stat. 1202

Indian Health Care Amendments of 1980

Dec. 17, 1980, P.L. 96-537, 25 U.S. Code § 1601 nt.

Indian Health Care Amendments of 1988

Nov. 4, 1988, P.L. 100-607, 42 U.S. Code §§ 295j, 295j nt.

Nov. 23, 1988, P.L. 100-713, 25 U.S. Code §§ 1601 nt., 1601 et seq.

Aug. 16, 1989, P.L. 101-93, 42 U.S. Code § 295j

Indian Health Care Amendments of 1990

Nov. 28, 1990, P.L. 101-630, 25 U.S. Code §§ 1621h, 1621h nt., 1637, 1653, 1653 nt., 1657, 1659, 1660

Indian Health Care Amendments of 1992

Oct. 29, 1992, P.L. 102-573, 25 U.S. Code § 1601 nt.

Indian Health Care Improvement Act

Sept. 30, 1976, P.L. 94-437, 25 U.S. Code § 1601 et seq.

Aug. 1, 1977, P.L. 95-83, 25 U.S. Code § 1614

Oct. 31, 1988, P.L. 100-579, 25 U.S. Code § 1621d

Nov. 18, 1988, P.L. 100-690, 25 U.S. Code § 1621d

Nov. 28, 1990, P.L. 101-630, 25 U.S. Code § 1601 nt.

June 13, 1991, P.L. 102-54, 25 U.S. Code § 1680f

Oct. 29, 1992, P.L. 102-573, 25 U.S. Code §§ 1601 et seq., 1616e-1

Nov. 2, 1994, P.L. 103-435, 25 U.S. Code §§ 1616d, 1616k

Nov. 2, 1994, P.L. 103-437, 25 U.S. Code § 1621q

Oct. 19, 1996, P.L. 104-313, 25 U.S. Code § 1613a

April 30, 1997, P.L. 105-12, 25 U.S. Code § 1621x

Oct. 14, 1998, P.L. 105-256, 25 U.S. Code §§ 1660b, 1665j

Oct. 21, 1998, P.L. 105-277, 42 U.S. Code § 1645

Nov. 10, 1998, P.L. 105-362, 25 U.S. Code §§ 1645, 1660c

Indian Health Care Improvement Technical Corrections Act of 1996

Oct. 19, 1996, P.L. 104-313, 25 U.S. Code § 1601 nt.

Indian Housing Act of 1988

June 29, 1988, P.L. 100 to 358, 102 Stat. 676, 42 U.S. Code §§ 1437 nt., 1437a, 1437c, 1437aa nt., 1437aa to 1437ee

Indian Housing Authority Law

Ga. Laws 1977, p. 767

La. Rev. Stat. Ann., 40:581.1 et seq.

Me. Rev. Stat. Ann. 1964, Title 22, § 4731 et seq.

Indian Land Act (Sales)

Okla. Stat. Ann., Title 58, § 901 et seq.

Indian Land Consolidation Act

Jan. 12, 1983, P.L. 97-459, 25 U.S. Code §§ 2201 et seq., 2201 nt.

Nov. 29, 1990, P.L. 101-644, 25 U.S. Code § 2206

Dec. 17, 1991, P.L. 102-238, 25 U.S. Code § 2203

Indian Lands Open Dump Cleanup Act of 1994

Oct. 22, 1994, P.L. 103-399, 25 U.S. Code §§ 901 nt., 3901 et seq.

Feb. 12, 1996, P.L. 104-109, 25 U.S. Code § 3902

Indian Language and Culture Education Act

Minn. Stat. Ann., 126.45 et seq.

Indian Law

N.Y. Consol. Laws, Ch. 26

Indian Law Enforcement Reform Act

Aug. 18, 1990, P.L. 101-379, 25 U.S. Code §§ 2801, 2801 nt., 2802 to 2809, 42 U.S. Code § 2991a nt.

Indian Law Technical Amendments of 1987

Nov. 5, 1987, P.L. 100-159, 20 U.S. Code § 4221, 25 U.S. Code §§ 331 nt., 373, 1401, 2301

Nov. 2, 1994, P.L. 103-435, 108 Stat. 4569

Indian Lease Authority Act (Salamanca)

N.Y. Public Authorities Law (Consol. Laws Ch. 43A) § 1790 et seq.

Indian Long-Term Leasing Act

Aug. 9, 1955, Ch. 615, 69 Stat. 539, 25 U.S. Code §§ 415 to 415d

Sept. 21, 1959, P.L. 86-326, 73 Stat. 597, 25 U.S. Code § 415

June 11, 1960, P.L. 86-505, 74 Stat. 199, 25 U.S. Code § 415

Oct. 4, 1961, P.L. 87-375, 75 Stat. 804, 25 U.S. Code § 415

Oct. 10, 1962, P.L. 87-785, 76 Stat. 805, 25 U.S. Code § 415

Nov. 4, 1963, P.L. 88-167, 77 Stat. 301, 25 U.S. Code § 415

April 27, 1966, P.L. 89-408, 80 Stat. 132, 25 U.S. Code § 415

Indian Mineral Development Act of 1982

Dec. 22, 1982, P.L. 97-382, 25 U.S. Code § 2101 et seq.

Indian Nonintercourse Act

See Indian Intercourse Act

Indian Omnibus Law

May 29, 1908, Ch. 216, 35 Stat. 444, 25 U.S. Code § 404

Indian Reorganization Act

June 18, 1934, Ch. 216, 48 Stat. 984, 25 U.S. Code §§ 461 et seq.

Indian Reservation Criminal Jurisdiction Retrocession Act (Colville)

Wash. Rev. Code Ann., 37.12.100 et seq.

Indian Resources Development Act

N.M. Stat. Ann., 21-10-4 et seq.

Indian River County and Municipality Tax Collection Act

Fla. Special Laws 1967, Ch. 67-1517

Indian River County Permanent Registration Act

Fla. Laws 1949, Ch. 25154

Indian Self-Determination Act

Dec. 26, 1985, P.L. 99-221, 25 U.S. Code § 450i

Dec. 22, 1987, P.L. 100-202, 25 U.S. Code § 450g

Sept. 27, 1988, P.L. 100-446, 25 U.S. Code § 450g

Nov. 29, 1990, P.L. 101-644, 25 U.S. Code §§ 450f, 450h, 450h nt., 450j, 450j-1, 450k

Nov. 2, 1994, P.L. 103-435, 25 U.S. Code §§ 450f nt., 450k

Indian Self-Determination Act Amendments of 1994

Oct. 25, 1994, P.L. 103-413, 25 U.S. Code § 450 nt.

Indian Self-Determination and Education Assistance Act

Jan. 4, 1975, P.L. 93-638, 25 U.S. Code §§ 450 et seq.

Dec. 21, 1982, P.L. 97-375, 25 U.S. Code § 458d

Oct. 14, 1983, P.L. 98-129, 25 U.S. Code § 450i

April 3, 1984, P.L. 98-250, 25 U.S. Code § 450e-1

July 2, 1986, P.L. 99-349, 100 Stat. 737

April 28, 1988, P.L. 100-297, 102 Stat. 394, 25 U.S. Code §§ 2508 et seq.

Nov. 1, 1988, P.L. 100-581, 25 U.S. Code §§ 450b, 450c, 450f, 450m, 450m-1

May 24, 1990, P.L. 101-301, 25 U.S. Code §§ 450b, 450c, 450e-1, 450i, 450j, 450j-1, 450m, 450m-1

Nov. 29, 1990, P.L. 101-644, 25 U.S. Code §§ 450b, 450c

Dec. 4, 1991, P.L. 102-184, 25 U.S. Code § 450f nt.

Oct. 29, 1992, P.L. 102-573, 25 U.S. Code § 450f nt.

Oct. 25, 1994, P.L. 103-413, 25 U.S. Code §§ 450b, 450c, 450e, 450f, 450j, 450j-1, 450k, 450l, 450m, 450m-1, 458aa et seq.

Nov. 2, 1994, P.L. 103-437, 25 U.S. Code §§ 450f nt., 450k

Feb. 12, 1996, P.L. 104-109, 25 U.S. Code § 458cc

April 25, 1996, P.L. 104-133, 25 U.S. Code § 450k

Sept. 30, 1996, P.L. 104-208, 25 U.S. Code § 458bb

Oct. 11, 1996, P.L. 104-287, 25 U.S. Code § 450k nt.

Nov. 10, 1998, P.L. 105-362, 25 U.S. Code § 450j-1

Indian Self-Determination and Education Assistance Act Amendments of 1990

Nov. 29, 1990, P.L. 101-644, 25 U.S. Code § 450 nt.

Nov. 2, 1994, P.L. 103-435, 25 U.S. Code § 450a-1

Continued

Indian Self-Determination Contract Reform Act of 1994

Oct. 25, 1994, P.L. 103-413, 25 U.S. Code § 450 nt.

Feb. 12, 1996, P.L. 104-109, 25 U.S. Code § 450j

Indian Teacher-Training Act

Mont. Rev. Code 1947, 75-6133 et seq.

Indian Tribal Governmental Tax Status Act of 1982

Jan. 14, 1984, P.L. 97-473, 26 U.S. Code § 1 nt.

July 18, 1984, P.L. 98-369, 98 Stat. 1048, 26 U.S. Code § 7871 nt.

Indian Tribal Judgment Funds Use or Distribution Act

Nov. 5, 1987, P.L. 100-153, 25 U.S. Code § 1401

Nov. 2, 1994, P.L. 103-437, 25 U.S. Code § 1402

Indian Tribal Justice Act

Dec. 3, 1993, P.L. 103-176, 25 U.S. Code §§ 3601 nt., 3601 et seq., 3611 et seq., 3621 et seq., 3631 et seq.

Indian Tribal Tort Claims and Risk Management Act of 1998

Oct. 21, 1998, P.L. 105-277, 101(e), Title VII, 112 Stat. 2681, 25 U.S. Code § 450f nt.

Indian Vocational Training Act

See Adult Indian Vocational Training Act

Indian Voter Qualification Act (School Districts)

N.Y. Education Law 1947, (Consol. Laws Ch. 16) § 2012, Subd. 4

Indiana Dunes National Lakeshore Act

Nov. 5, 1966, P.L. 89- 761, 80 Stat. 1309, 16 U.S. Code §§ 460u to 460u-9

Oct. 23, 1992, P.L. 102-430, 16 U.S. Code §§ 460u, 460u nt., 460u-3, 460u-5, 460u-9, 460u-12, 460u-18, 460u-25, 460u-26

Indiana Economic Development Authority Act

Ind. Code Ann., 4-23-5-1 et seq.

Indiana-Illinois Air Pollution Control Compact

Ind. Code Ann., 13-5-7-1 et seq.

Indiana-Illinois Bridge Commissioners Act

Ill. Rev. Stat. 1991, Ch. 121, § 420 et seq.

Indiana-Illinois Bridge Compact Act

Ill. Rev. Stat. 1991, Ch. 121, § 410 et seq.

Indiana-Kentucky Boundary Compact

Ind. Code Ann., 13-5-6.5-1, 13-5-6.5-2

Indiana University of Pennsylvania Act

Pa. Purdon's Stat., Title 24, § 2510-101 et seq.

Indianapolis Public School Act

Ind. Code Ann., 20-3-11-1 et seq.

Indictment Act (Waiver)

S.C. Code Ann. 1976, § 17-23-120 et seq.

Indictment and Information Statute

Wash. Rev. Code Ann., 10.37.010 et seq.

Indigent Act

Cal. Welfare and Institutions Code §§ 17000 et seq., 2400

Indigent Afflicted Adults and Pregnant Women Act

Mich. Comp. Laws 1948, 404.101 et seq.

Indigent Care Act

W. Va. Code 1966 § 16-29C-1 et seq.

Indigent Catastrophic Illness Hospital Funding Act

N.M. Stat. Ann., 27-2-41 et seq.

Indigent Criminal Act

Kan. Stat. Ann., 22-4501 et seq.

Indigent Defendant Act

N.Y. County Law 1950 (Consol. Laws Ch. 11) § 722 et seq.

S.C. Code Ann. 1976, § 17-3-10 et seq.

Indigent Defense Act
Ga. Code Ann., 17-12-30 et seq.
N.M. Stat. Ann., 31-16-1 et seq.
Okla. Stat. Ann., Title 22, § 1355 et seq.

Indigent Hawaiians Hospital Act
Haw. Session Laws 1858-59, p. 433, April 20, 1859

Indigent Health Care Act
Okla. Stat. Ann., Title 56, § 57 et seq.

Indigent Health Care and Treatment Act
Tex. Health and Safety Code, § 61.001 et seq.

Indigent Health Care Trust Fund Act
La. Rev. Stat. Ann., 40:2193 et seq.

Indigent Hospital and County Health Care Act
N.M. Stat. Ann., 27-5-1 et seq.

Indigent Hospital Care Act
Miss. Code Ann. 1972, § 41-7-1 et seq.

Indigent Hospital Claims Act
N.M. Stat. Ann., 27-5-1 et seq.

Indigent Law (Medically)
Colo. Rev. Stat., 26-16-101 et seq.

Indigent, Medical Assistance Act
S.C. Code Ann. 1976, § 44-6-135 et seq.

Indigent Persons Transportation Act (Mental Hospital)
Conn. Gen. Stat. Ann., § 17-293

Indigent Prisoners Act
Ohio Rev. Code 1953, 2951.11

Indigent Relief Act
Alaska Comp. Laws Ann. 1949, § 35-1-51

Indigent Soldiers and Sailors Relief Act
Ore. Rev. Stat., 408.710 et seq.

Indigent Tuberculars Aid Act
Colo. Rev. Stat. 1963, 119-2-1 et seq.

Indigent Veterans Act (Assistance to)
Ill. Comp. Stat. 1992, Ch. 330, § 45/0.01 et seq.

Indigent Veterans Assistance Act
Ill. Rev. Stat. 1991, Ch. 23, § 3080 et seq.

Indigent Veterans' Relief Law
Cal. Military and Veterans Code § 920 et seq.

Indigent War Veterans Act
Ill. Rev. Stat. 1991, Ch. 23, § 3080 et seq.

Indigents Defense Act
S.C. Code Ann. 1976, § 17-3-10 et seq.

Indigents' Defense Services Act
Kan. Stat. Ann., 22-4501 et seq.

Indigents Support Act
Pa. Purdon's Stat., Title 62, § 1971 et seq.

Individual Accident Act
Mont. Code Ann., 39-71-101 et seq.

Individual Accident and Health Insurance Minimum Standards Act
Iowa Code Ann., 514D.1 et seq.

Individual Accident and Sickness Insurance Act
Iowa Code Ann., 514A.1 et seq.
Mo. Rev. Stat., 376.770 et seq.

Individual Accident and Sickness Insurance Minimum Standards Act
Pa. Purdon's Stat., Title 40, § 776.1 et seq.
Va. Code 1950, § 38.2-3516 et seq.
W. Va. Code 1966, § 33-28-1 et seq.

Individual Accident and Sickness Policy Provisions Act
Cal. Insurance Code § 10320 et seq.
Ind. Code Ann., 27-8-5-2
Md. Ann. Code 1957, Art. 48A, § 437 et seq.
N.J. Stat. Ann., 17B:26-2 et seq.

Individual Account Deposit Act (Financial Institution)
Wash. Rev. Code Ann., 30.22.010 et seq.

Individual and Family Services Act

Utah Code Ann. 1953, Miscellaneous Superseded Code Provisions, 55-15b-1 et seq.

Individual Deferred Annuities Standard Nonforfeiture Law

See Standard Nonforfeiture Law for Individual Deferred Annuities

Individual Development Account Act

Kan. Stat. Ann., 79-32,117h

Individual Family Disability Insurance Continuity of Coverage Act

Mont. Code Ann., 33-22-305 to 33-22-311

Individual Health Insurance Availability Act

Ida. Code 1947, 41-5201 et seq.

Individual Health Insurance Market Reform Act

Iowa Code 1983, 513C.1 et seq.

Individual Health Insurance Reform Act

N.J. Stat. Ann., 17B:27A-2 et seq.

Individual Income Tax Act

Mont. Code Ann., 15-30-101 et seq.

Individual Income Tax Act of 1944

May 29, 1944, Ch. 210, 58 Stat. 231

Individual Medical Account Act

Colo. Rev. Stat., 39-22-504.5 et seq.

Individual Medicare Supplement and Sickness and Accident Insurance Minimum Standards Act (Insurance)

Neb. Rev. Stat. 1943, 44-3611 et seq.

Individual Net Income Tax Act

Pa. Purdon's Stat., Title 72, § 3402-1 et seq.

Individual On-Site Wastewater Disposal System Act

Miss. Code Ann. 1972, § 41-67-1

Individual Onsite Wastewater Disposal System Act

Miss. Code Ann. 1972, § 41-67-1 et seq.

Individual Sewage Disposal Systems Act

Colo. Rev. Stat., 25-10-101 et seq.

Individual Surplus Return Act

Me. Rev. Stat. Ann. 1964, Title 36, § 6401 et seq.

Individual Surplus Return Act of 1988

Me. Rev. Stat. Ann. 1964, Title 36, § 6401 et seq.

Individuals with Disabilities Education Act

Oct. 30, 1990, P.L. 101-476, 20 U.S. Code §§ 1400 et seq. generally

June 6, 1991, P.L. 102-52, 20 U.S. Code § 1475

July 25, 1991, P.L. 102-73, 20 U.S. Code §§ 1401, 1411

Oct. 7, 1991, P.L. 102-119, 20 U.S. Code §§ 241, 241 nt., 1401, 1404, prec. 1411, 1411 to 1414, 1417, 1419, 1422 to 1425, 1431, 1434, 1435, 1442, 1461, 1471, 1472, 1475 to 1480, 1482, 1484, 1484 nt., 1484a, 1485

Oct. 16, 1992, P.L. 102-421, 20 U.S. Code §§ 1424a, 1424a nt. 1431, 1441

Oct. 19, 1992, P.L. 102-569, 20 U.S. Code § 1431

Aug. 11, 1993, P.L. 103-73, 20 U.S. Code § 1431

March 9, 1994, P.L. 103-218, 20 U.S. Code § 1431

Oct. 20, 1994, P.L. 103-382, 20 U.S. Code §§ 1401, 1411, 1413, 1414a, 1415, 1422, 1484, 1491, 1491a to 1491o

Nov. 2, 1994, P.L. 103-448, 20 U.S. Code § 1484a

June 4, 1997, P.L. 105-17, 20 U.S. Code §§ prec. 1400, 1400 to 406, prec. 1411, 1411 to 1419, 1421 to 1424a, 1425 to 1427, 1431 to 1445, prec. 1451, 1451 to 1456, prec. 1461, 1461, 1462, prec. 1471, 1471 to 1487, 1491 to 1491o

April 29, 1999, P.L. 106-25, 20 U.S. Code § 1415

Individuals with Disabilities Education Act Amendments of 1991

Oct. 7, 1991, P.L. 102-119, 20 U.S. Code § 1400 nt.

Individuals with Disabilities Education Act Amendments of 1997

June 4, 1997, P.L. 105-17, 20 U.S. Code § 1400 nt.

Indochina Migration and Refugee Assistance Act of 1975

May 23, 1975, P.L. 94-23, 89 Stat. 87, 22 U.S. Code § 2601 nt.

Oct. 28, 1977, P.L. 95-145, 22 U.S. Code § 2601 nt.

Oct. 30, 1978, P.L. 95-549, 22 U.S. Code § 2601 nt.

Nov. 13, 1979, 22 U.S. Code § 2601 nt.

March 17, 1980, P.L. 96-212, 22 U.S. Code § 2601 nt.

Indochina Refugee Children Assistance Act of 1976

Sept. 10, 1976, P.L. 94-405, 20 U.S. Code §§ 1211b et seq.

Nov. 1, 1978, P.L. 95-561, 20 U.S. Code §§ 1211b, 1211b nt.

Indochinese Refugee Resettlement and Protection Act of 1987

Dec. 22, 1987, P.L. 100-202, 101 Stat. 1329

Indoor Clean Air Act

Cal. Health and Safety Code § 25940 et seq.

Fla. Stat. Ann., 386.201 et seq.

Ill. Comp. Stat. 1992, Ch. 410, § 80/1 et seq.

Ind. Code Ann., 13-1-31-1 et seq.

Iowa Code Ann., 142B.1 et seq.

Me. Rev. Stat. Ann. 1964, Title 22, § 1578

Ore. Rev. Stat., 433.835 et seq.

Pa. Purdon's Stat., Title 35, § 1230.1

S.C. Code Ann. 1976, § 44-95-10 et seq.

Utah Code Ann. 1953, 26-38-1 et seq.

Wash. Rev. Code Ann., 70.160.010 et seq.

Indoor Clean Air Law (Office)

La. Rev. Stat. Ann., 40:1300.21 et seq.

Indorsement Act (Indictments)

W. Va. Code 1931, Ch. 62, Art. 9, § 1

Industrial Accident Act

Mont. Code Ann., 39-71-101 et seq.

Industrial Accident Board Act

Tex. Rev. Civ. Stat., Art. 8308-1.01 et seq.

Industrial Accident Commission Law

Ore. Rev. Stat., 656.712 et seq.

Industrial Act

Ariz. Rev. Stat. Ann., § 23-101 et seq.

Industrial Aid and Vocational Rehabilitation for the Blind Act

Ind. Code Ann., 16-7-9-1 et seq.

Industrial and Agricultural Board Act

Miss. Code Ann. 1972, § 57-1-1 et seq.

Industrial and Agricultural Development Commission Act

Tenn. Code Ann., 4-14-101 et seq.

Industrial and Agricultural Finance Authority Act

N.M. Stat. Ann., 58-24-1 et seq.

Industrial and Agricultural Relief Commission Act

Fla. Stat. Ann., 159.25 et seq.

Industrial and Agriculture Branch Rail Line Revitalization Act

Neb. Rev. Stat. 1943, 74-1401 et seq.

Industrial and Business Development Corporation Act

Conn. Public Acts 1993, No. 382, §§ 56 to 66

Ida. Code 1947, 26-2701 et seq.

La. Rev. Stat. Ann., 51:2386 et seq.

Industrial and Commercial Development Authority Law

Pa. Purdon's Stat., Title 73, § 371 et seq.

Industrial and Economic Development Corporations Act
Okla. Stat. Ann., Title 74, § 1351 et seq.

Industrial and Economic Development Revenue Bond Law
Ark. Code Ann. 1987, 14-164-501 et seq.

Industrial and Pollution Control Facilities Financing Act
N.C. Gen. Stat. 1943, § 159C-1 et seq.

Industrial and Pollution Control Facilities Pool Program Financing Act
N.C. Gen. Stat. 1943, § 159D-1 et seq.

Industrial Areas Act
Neb. Rev. Stat. 1943, 19-2501 et seq.

Industrial Areas Act (Cities of First and Second Class and Villages)
Neb. Rev. Stat. 1943, 19-2501 et seq.

Industrial Assistance Act
Conn. Gen. Stat. 1983, § 32-23c et seq.

Industrial Authority Act (Pearson)
Ga. Laws 1969, p. 2905

Industrial Authority Act (Valdosta-Lowndes County)
Ga. Laws 1960, P. 2786

Industrial Bank Act
Colo. Rev. Stat., 11-22-101 et seq.

Industrial Bank and Industrial Loan Company Act
W. Va. Code 1966, § 31-7-1 et seq.

Industrial Bank and Investment Company Regulatory Act
Tenn. Code Ann., 45-5-601 et seq.

Industrial Bank Savings Guaranty Act
Colo. Rev. Stat., 11-22-201 et seq.

Industrial Building Authority Act
Me. Rev. Stat. Ann. 1964, Title 10, § 701 et seq.
Va. Code 1950, § 2.1-64.4 et seq.
Vt. Stat. Ann., Title 10, § 251 et seq.

Industrial Building Bond Act
Tenn. Code Ann., 7-55-101 et seq.

Industrial Building Commission Act
Conn. Gen. Stat. 1958, § 32-11a et seq.

Industrial Building Revenue Bond Act
Tenn. Code Ann., 7-37-101 et seq.

Industrial City Study Act
Tenn. Public Acts 1972, Ch. 745

Industrial Cluster Act (Economic Development)
S.C. Code Ann. 1976, §§ 12-6-3480, 12-10-45, 12-20-105, 38-7-190

Industrial Code Commission Act
Wash. Laws 1919, Ch. 184

Industrial Commission Act
Ariz. Rev. Stat. 1956, § 23-101 et seq.
Colo. Rev. Stat., 8-1-101 et seq.
N.D. Cent. Code, 54-17-01 et seq.
Ohio Rev. Code 1953, 4121.01 et seq.
Tex. Government Code, § 481.001 et seq.
Wis. Stat. Ann., 101.01 et seq.

Industrial Commission Awards Act (State Employee)
Ill. Rev. Stat. 1991, Ch. 127, § 179.9 et seq.

Industrial Communities Action Program Act
Pa. Purdon's Stat., Title 73, § 399.51

Industrial Compensation Act
Alaska Stat. 1962, § 23.30.005 et seq.
Ariz. Rev. Stat. Ann., § 23-101 et seq.
Cal. Labor Code § 3201 et seq.
Ill. Rev. Stat. 1991, Ch. 48, § 138.1 et seq.
Utah Code Ann. 1953, 35-1-1 et seq.

Industrial Competitiveness and International Trade Act
N.Y. Economic Development Law (Consol. Laws Ch. 15) §§ 220 to 225
N.Y. Laws 1990, Ch. 291

Industrial, Construction and Farm Equipment Fair Dealership Law
Ill. Rev. Stat. 1991, Ch. 5, § 1501 et seq.

Industrial Control and Public Works Act
June 16, 1933, Ch. 90, 48 Stat. 195

Industrial Corporation Act
Wyo. Stat. Ann., § 17-11-101 et seq.

Industrial Development Act
Ark. Code Ammo. 1987, 15-14-101 et seq.
Minn. Stat. 1986, 474.01 et seq.
Okla. Stat. Ann., Title 62, § 651 et seq.

Industrial Development Act (Local)
Ind. Code 1976, 18-7-14-1 et seq.

Industrial Development Act (Rural)
Tex. Government Code, § 481.081 et seq.

Industrial Development Act (Tax Increment Financing)
Mont. Laws 1991, Ch. 712, § 1 et seq.

Industrial Development Agency Act
N.Y. General Municipal Law (Consol. Laws Ch. 24) § 850 et seq.

Industrial Development and Business Corporations Act
Mich. Comp. Laws Ann., 487.1101 et seq.

Industrial Development and Commercial Development Bond Act
W. Va. Code 1966, § 13-2C-1 et seq.

Industrial Development and Revenue Bond Act
Va. Code 1950, § 15.1-1373 et seq.

Industrial Development Assistance Law
Conn. Gen. Stat. Ann., § 32-23b et seq.
Ill. Rev. Stat. 1991, Ch. 85, § 891 et seq.
Pa. Purdon's Stat., Title 73, § 351 et seq.

Industrial Development Authority Act
Ala. Code 1975, § 41-10-20 et seq.
Ga. Code Ann., 36-62-1 et seq.
Ill. Rev. Stat. 1991, Ch. 48, § 850.01 et seq.
Mass. Gen. Laws Ann., 40E:1 et seq.

N.H. Rev. Stat. 1955, 162-A:1 et seq.
Pa. Purdon's Stat., Title 73, § 301 et seq.
Tenn. Code Ann., 13-16-101 et seq.
Vt. Stat. Ann., Title 10, § 211 et seq.
W. Va. Code 1966, § 31-15-1 et seq.

Industrial Development Authority Act (Auburn)
N.Y. Public Authorities Law (Consol. Laws Ch. 43A) § 2300 et seq.

Industrial Development Authority Act (Evans County)
Ga. Laws 1971, p. 2341

Industrial Development Authority Act (Local)
Ky. Rev. Stat. 1971, 152.810 et seq.

Industrial Development Authority Act (Sumter County)
Ga. Laws 1992, p. 5062

Industrial Development Authority Act (Thompson-McDuffie County)
Ga. Laws 1962, p. 2120

Industrial Development Authority Act (Troy)
N.Y. Public Authorities Law (Consol. Laws Ch. 43a) § 1950 et seq.

Industrial Development Boards Act
Ala. Code 1975, § 11-20-30 et seq.

Industrial Development Bond Act
S.C. Code Ann. 1976, § 4-29-10 et seq.

Industrial Development Bonds Act (Municipal and County)
Okla. Stat. Ann., Title 62, § 800 et seq.

Industrial Development Commission Loan Act (North Adams)
Mass. Acts 1953, Ch. 548

Industrial Development Corporation Act
Ala. Code 1975, § 11-54-80 et seq.
Cal. Financial Code § 31000 et seq.
Neb. Rev. Stat. 1943, 21-2301 et seq.
Tenn. Code Ann., 7-53-101 et seq.

Industrial Development Corporation Act (County)
Ark. Acts 1989, No. 660

Industrial Development Districts Act
Wash. Rev. Code Ann., 53.25.010 et seq.

Industrial Development Finance Act
Cal. Government Code § 91500 et seq.
Fla. Stat. Ann., 159.44 et seq.
Mass. Gen. Laws Ann., 40D:1 et seq.
Md. Ann. Code 1974, Art. FI, § 13-101 et seq.
Miss. Code Ann. 1972, § 57-4-1 et seq
Mo. Rev. Stat., 100.250 et seq.
N.C. Gen. Stat. 1943, § 123A-1 et seq.

Industrial Development Fund Act
Miss. Code Ann. 1972, § 57-4-1 et seq.

Industrial Development Guarantee Fund Act
P.R. Laws Ann. 1954, Title 7, § 1201 et seq.

Industrial Development Guaranty Bond Act
Ark. Code Ann. 1987, 15-4-7

Industrial Development Information and Siting Act
Wyo. Stat. Ann., § 35-12-101 et seq.

Industrial Development Law
Ark. Code Ann. 1987, 9-504 et seq.
Minn. Stat. 1986, 474.01 et seq.
N.D. Cent. Code, 54-34-01 et seq.
Neb. Rev. Stat. 1943, 18-1614 et seq.
Okla. Stat. Ann., Title 62, § 651 et seq.
P.R. Laws Ann. 1954, Title 23, § 271 et seq.
Wis. Stat. Ann., 59.071

Industrial Development Loan Program Act of 1981
Tenn. Code Ann., 4-31-301 et seq.

Industrial Development Plan Act (Municipalities and Counties)
Ariz. Rev. Stat. Ann., § 35-701 et seq.

Industrial Development Projects Act
Conn. Gen. Stat. Ann., § 8-186 et seq.
S.C. Code Ann. 1976, § 4-29-10 et seq.

Industrial Development Revenue Bond Act
Mich. Comp. Laws Ann., 125.1251 et seq.
Neb. Rev. Stat. 1943, 18-1614 et seq.

Industrial Disputes Act
Colo. Rev. Stat., 8-2-101 et seq.

Industrial Disputes Conciliation Act
S.C. Code Ann. 1976, § 41-17-10 et seq.

Industrial District Act (St. Landry Parish)
La. Rev. Stat. Ann., 33.130.31

Industrial, Employment and Health Resources Development Act
Tex. Rev. Civ. Stat., Art. 5190.1

Industrial Enterprise Projects Act (Financing)
Miss. Code Ann. 1972, § 57-41-1 et seq.

Industrial Equipment Franchise Act (Tractor, Lawn and Garden)
Ala. Code 1975, § 8-21A-1
Ala. Code 1975, § 8-21A-1 et seq.

Industrial Exhibit Authority Act
N.Y. Public Authorities Law (Consol. Laws Ch. 43A) § 1650 et seq.

Industrial Expansion Act
Mo. Rev. Stat., 100.300 et seq.

Industrial Facilities and Development Act
Utah Code Ann. 1953, 11-17-1 et seq.

Industrial Facilities Corporation Act
R.I. Gen. Laws 1956, 45-37.1-1 et seq.

Industrial Farm and Road Camp Act
Cal. Penal Code § 4100 et seq.

Industrial Farm, Workhouse and Reformatory Act (County)
Pa. 1917 Pamph. Laws 1151, No. 399

Industrial Feasibility Act
Miss. Code Ann. 1972, § 57-11-61 et seq.

Industrial Finance Act
Md. Ann. Code 1974, Art. CL, § 12-103

Industrial Finance Authority Act
Okla. Stat. Ann., Title 74, § 851 et seq.

Industrial Finance Corporation Act
Tenn. Code Ann., 4-17-401 et seq.

Industrial Ground Water Regulatory Act
Neb. Rev. Stat. 1943, 46-675 et seq.

Industrial Hazardous Waste Management Act
N.Y. Environmental Conservation Law 1972 (Consol. Laws Ch. 43B) §§ 27-0301, 27-0303, 27-0900 et seq, 27-1101 et seq., 71-2701 et seq.
N.Y. Public Authorities Law (Consol. Laws Ch. 43A) §§ 1281, 1285c, 1285d

Industrial Health Service Act
Ark. Code Ann. 1987, 11-5-201, 11-5-202 et seq.
Wyo. Stat. Ann., § 35-1-501 et seq.

Industrial Highway Act
Tenn. Code Ann., 54-5-401 et seq.

Industrial Homework Act
Cal. Labor Code § 2650 et seq.
Ill. Rev. Stat. 1991, Ch. 48, §§ 250.9, 251 et seq.
Mass. Gen. Laws Ann., 149:143 et seq.
N.Y. Labor Law (Consol. Laws Ch. 31) § 350 et seq.
Pa. Purdon's Stat., Title 43, § 491-1 et seq.
P.R. Laws Ann. 1954, Title 29, § 371 et seq.
Tex. Health and Safety Code, § 143.001 et seq.
W. Va. Code 1966, § 21-7-1 et seq.

Industrial Hygienist and Safety Professional Title Protection Act
Minn. Stat. 1986, 182A.01 et seq.

Industrial Hygienist Title Protection Act (Certified)
Neb. Rev. Stat. 1943, 71-8001 to 71-8008

Industrial Hygienists Licensure Act
Ill. Comp. Stat. 1992, Ch. 225, § 52/1 et seq.

Industrial Hygienists Truth in Advertising Act
N.J. Stat. Ann., 56:8-81 et seq.

Industrial Incentive Act
Alaska Stat. 1962, Replaced Titles § 43.25.010 et seq.
P.R. Laws Ann. 1954, Title 13, §§ 241 et seq., 252 et seq.

Industrial Insurance Act (Workmen's Compensation)
Mich. Comp. Laws Ann., 500.4200 et seq.
Nev. Rev. Stat. 1979 Reprint, 616.010 et seq.
Ohio Rev. Code 1953, 4123.01 et seq.
P.R. Laws Ann. 1954, Title 13, § 255 et seq.
Wash. Rev. Code Ann., 51.04.010 et seq.

Industrial Jobs Recovery Law
Ill. Comp. Stat. 1992, Ch. 65, § 5/11-74.6-1

Industrial Land Act
Md. Ann. Code 1957, Art. 41A, § 5-401 et seq.
Md. Ann. Code 1974, Department of Business and Economic Development, § 5-701 et seq.

Industrial Life Insurance Act
Mich. Comp. Laws Ann., 500.4200 et seq.
Tex. Insurance Code, Art. 3.52
Wash. Rev. Code Ann., 48.25.010 et seq.

Industrial Loan Act
Cal. Financial Code § 18000 et seq.
Ga. Code Ann., 7-3-1 et seq.
Iowa Code Ann., 536A.1 et seq.
Ky. Rev. Stat. 1971, 291.410 et seq.
N.M. Stat. Ann., 58-15-1 et seq.
Ore. Rev. Stat., 724.005 et seq.
Tex. Rev. Civ. Stat., § 5069-3.01 et seq.
Va. Code 1950, § 6.1-227 et seq.
Wash. Rev. Code Ann., 31.04.010 et seq.

Industrial Loan and Investment Act
Haw. Rev. Stat. Ann., § 408-1 et seq.
Ind. Code Ann., 28-5-1-1 et seq.
Neb. Rev. Stat. 1943, 8-401 et seq.
Tenn. Code Ann., 45-5-101 et seq.

Industrial Loan and Thrift Act
D.C. Code Ann., § 34-101 et seq.
Tenn. Code Ann., 45-5-101 et seq.

Industrial Loan Associations Act
Va. Code 1950, § 6.1-227 et seq.

Industrial Loan Company Act
Cal. Financial Code § 18000 et seq.
Minn. Stat. Ann., 53.01 et seq.
Utah Code Ann. 1953, 7-8-1 et seq.
W. Va. Code 1966, § 31-7-1 et seq.

Industrial Loan Company Guaranty Act
Haw. Rev. Stat. Ann., § 408A-1 et seq.

Industrial Loan Corporation Guaranty Act
Utah Code Ann. 1953, 7-8a-1 et seq.

Industrial Loan Corporation Thrift Guaranty Act
Iowa Code Ann., 536B.1 et seq.

Industrial Loan Investment Company Act
Neb. Rev. Stat. 1943, 8-401 et seq.

Industrial Loans Act
Jan. 22, 1932, Ch. 8, 47 Stat. 5, 15 U.S. Code §§ 601 to 617

Industrial Locations Bond Plan Enabling Act
Ala. Code 1975, § 11-54-20 et seq.

Industrial Materials Recycling Act
N.Y. Public Authorities Law (Consol. Laws Ch. 43A) § 1285g

Industrial, Medical, and Environmental Pollution Control Facilities Financing Authority Act
P.R. Laws Ann. 1954, Title 12, § 1251 et seq.

Industrial Mortgage Insurance Act
Pa. 1963 Pamph. Laws 1106, No. 471

Industrial New Jobs Training Act
Iowa Code Ann., 260E.1 et seq.

Industrial Parks Act
Ala. Code 1975, § 11-23-1 et seq.
Ala. Code 1975, § 11-92-1 et seq.

Miss. Code Ann. 1972, § 57-5-1 et seq.
Tenn. Code Ann., 13-16-201 et seq.
Vt. Stat. Ann., Title 10, § 301 et seq.

Industrial Parks Development Grant Fund Act
La. Rev. Stat. Ann., 33:130.58 et seq.

Industrial Pollution Control Financing Act
Ill. Rev. Stat. 1991, Ch. 127, § 721 et seq.
N.J. Stat. Ann., 40:37C-1 et seq.

Industrial Productivity and Labor Costs Act
June 7, 1940, Ch. 267, 54 Stat. 249, 29 U.S. Code § 2b
Aug. 30, 1954, Ch. 1076, 68 Stat. 968, 29 U.S. Code § 2b

Industrial Project Revenue Bond Act
Ill. Rev. Stat. 1991, Ch. 24, § 11-74-1 et seq.

Industrial Promotion Act
Ala. Code 1975, § 11-54-1 et seq.
Utah Code Ann. 1953, 63-31-1 et seq.

Industrial Recovery Act
Cal. Statutes 1933, Ch. 1037, p. 2632
Colo. Laws 1935, p. 298, Ch. 89
Nev. Statutes 1935, Ch. 114, p. 235
N.J. Laws 1933, C 372
Ohio Laws Vol. 115, p. 603
S.C. Acts 1934, p. 2281, No. 1213
Utah Laws 1935, Ch. 76
Wash. Laws 1935, Ch. 141
Wis. Laws 1933, Ch. 476
W. Va. Acts 1933, 2nd Ex. Sess., Ch. 86
Wyo. Session Laws 1935, Ch. 123

Industrial Recovery Act (Supplementary)
Cal. Statutes 1933, Ch. 1037, p. 2632
Cal. Statutes 1933, p. 2637

Industrial Rehabilitation Act
Ky. Statutes 1936, §§ 2175b-1 to 2175b-6

Industrial Relations Act
Ala. Code 1975, § 25-2-1 et seq.
Colo. Rev. Stat., 8-1-101 et seq.
Kan. Stat. Ann., 44-601 et seq.

Industrial Relations Commission Act
Aug. 23, 1912, Ch. 351, 37 Stat. 415

Industrial Relations Court Act
Kan. Stat. Ann., 44-601 et seq.
Neb. Rev. Stat. 1943, 48-801 et seq.

Industrial Revenue Bond Act
Kan. Stat. Ann., 12-3801 et seq.
N.M. Stat. Ann., 3-32-2 et seq.
S.C. Code Ann. 1976, § 4-29-10 et seq.

Industrial Revenue Bond Act (County)
N.M. Stat. Ann., 4-59-1 et seq.

Industrial Revenue Bond Guaranty Law
Ark. Code Ann. 1987, 15-4-601 et seq.

Industrial Road Program Act
Wyo. Stat. Ann., § 24-5-101 et seq.

Industrial Safety Act
Cal. Labor Code § 6300 et seq.
D.C. Code Ann., § 36-221 et seq.
Nev. Rev. Stat. 1967 Reprint, 618.010 et seq.

Industrial Safety and Health Act
Wash. Rev. Code Ann., 49.17.010 et seq.

Industrial School Act
Colo. Rev. Stat. 1963, 105-1-1 et seq.
Ill. Rev. Stat. 1991, Ch. 122, § 646 et seq.
Neb. Rev. Stat. 1943, 83-463 et seq.

Industrial School Building Loan Act (Worcester)
Mass. Acts 1952, Ch. 273

Industrial School for Girls Act
Alaska Comp. Laws Ann. 1949, §§ 37-8-4, 37-8-5
Ill. Rev. Stat. 1991, Ch. 122, § 645.9 et seq.

Industrial Selling Act
Okla. Stat. Ann., Title 15, § 651 et seq.

Industrial Service Program Act
Mass. Gen. Laws Ann., 23D:1 et seq.

Industrial Sites Environmental Assessment Act
Pa. Purdon's Stat., Title 35, § 6028.1 et seq.

Industrial Siting Act
Fla. Stat. Ann., 288.501 et seq.

Industrial Special Indemnity Fund Act
Ida. Code 1947, Superseded Vol., 72-314

Industrial Stabilization Act
Ind. Laws 1935, Ch. 177, p. 854

Industrial Tax Credit Act
Alaska Stat. 1962, Replaced Titles
§ 43.26.010 et seq.

Industrial Tax Exemption Act
N.D. Cent. Code, 40-57.1-01 et seq.
P.R. Laws Ann. 1954, Title 13, § 227 et seq.

Industrial Training Act
Miss. Code Ann. 1972, § 57-9-1 et seq.

Industrial Waste Disposal Act (Controlled)
Okla. Stat. Ann., Title 63, §§ 2262, 2751 et seq.

Industrial Welfare Commission Act
Cal. Labor Code § 70 et seq.
Ore. Code 1930, § 49-301 et seq.

Industrialized Building and Mobile Home Act
Md. Ann. Code 1957, Art. 83B, § 6-201 et seq.

Industrialized Building Safety Act
Va. Code 1950, § 36-70 et seq.

Industrialized Housing Act
Me. Rev. Stat. Ann. 1964, Title 30, § 4771 et seq.
Pa. Purdon's Stat., Title 35, § 1651.1 et seq.

Industrialized/Modular Buildings Interstate Compact
Minn. Stat. Ann., 16B.75

Industries Act
Mass. Gen. Laws Ann., 149:1 et seq.

Industries Act (Correctional)
Ga. Code Ann., 42-10-1 et seq.

Industries for the Blind Act
Ga. Code Ann., 30-2-1 et seq.

Industry Act (Motor Vehicle Rental)
Haw. Rev. Stat. Ann., § 437D-1 et seq.

Industry Act (Pecan)
N.M. Stat. Ann., 76-16-1 et seq.

Industry in Public Welfare Institutions Act
R.I. Gen. Laws 1956, 13-7-1 et seq.

**Industry Information Reporting Act
(Petroleum)**
Haw. Rev. Stat. Ann., § 486J-1 et seq.

**Industry Internship and Apprenticeship
Programs**
Cal. Education Code 1976, § 79140 et seq.

Industry Loan Guarantee Fund Act (Boat)
N.J. Stat. Ann., 34:1B-7.28 et seq.

Industry Promotion Act
La. Rev. Stat. Ann., 51:1201

Industry Sector Network Development Act
N.J. Stat. Ann., 34:1B-80 et seq.

Industry Task Force Act (Dry Cleaning)
Cal. Health and Safety Code § 42800 et seq.

Industry Training Act (Existing)
Colo. Rev. Stat., 23-60-307

Inebriates Act
N.H. Rev. Stat. 1955, 172:1 et seq.

Inedible Meat Rendering and Processing Act
Colo. Rev. Stat., 35-59-101 et seq.
Wyo. Stat. Ann., § 35-7-1201 et seq.

Infant and Fetal Experimentation Act
N.M. Stat. Ann., 24-9A-1 et seq.

Infant and Maternal Care Act
Okla. Stat. Ann., Title 63, § 1-231 et seq.

**Infant and Maternal Health Improvement
Act**
Tex. Health and Safety Code, § 32.001 et
seq.

Infant Crib Safety Act
Wash. Rev. Code Ann., 70.111.900 et seq.

Infant Eye Disease Act
Ill. Rev. Stat. 1991, Ch. 111 1/2, § 4700 et
seq.

Infant Formula Act of 1980
Sept. 26, 1980, P.L. 96-359, 21 U.S. Code
§ 301 nt.

Infant Immunization Act
Colo. Rev. Stat., 25-4-1701 et seq.

Infant Mortality Abatement Initiative Act
Mont. Laws 1991, Ch. 649

Infant Mortality Reduction Act
Ill. Rev. Stat. 1991, Ch. 111 1/2, § 7001 et
seq.

Infant Welfare Act
N.J. Stat. Ann., 9:5-1 et seq.

Infantile Blindness Prevention Act
Cal. Business and Professions Code § 550 et
seq.
Okla. Stat. Ann., Title 63, § 1-509 et seq.

Infants Act
Wash. Rev. Code Ann., 26.28.010 et seq.

Infants-Age of Majority Act
Ga. Code Ann., 39-1-1

Infants' and Mothers' Access Program
Cal. Insurance Code § 12695 et seq.

Infants and Toddlers Early Intervention Act
Miss. Code Ann. 1972, § 41-87-1 et seq.

Infants and Toddlers with Disabilities Act
S.C. Code Ann. 1976, § 44-7-2510 et seq.

Infants and Toddlers with Disabilities Act (Early Intervention for)
Ala. Code 1975, § 21-3A-1 et seq.

Infants and Toddlers with Handicapping Conditions Act
S.C. Code Ann. 1976, § 44-7-2510 et seq.

Infants Custody Act
Mich. Comp. Laws Ann., 722.21 et seq.

Infant's Protection Act
Mo. Rev. Stat., 565.300

Infected Health Care Worker Management Act
Ala. Code 1975, § 22-11A-60 et seq.

Infectious Diseases Act
S.C. Code Ann. 1976, § 44-29-10 et seq.

Infectious Waste Management Act
Minn. Stat. Ann., 116.75 et seq.
Mont. Laws 1991, Ch. 483
S.C. Code Ann. 1976, §§ 44-93-10 et seq., § 44-96-240

Inferior Criminal Court Act (City of New York)
N.Y. Laws 1910, Ch. 659

Inflation Act
May 12, 1933, Ch. 25, 48 Stat. 51, 12 U.S. Code § 462b; 31 U.S. Code §§ 462, 821 to 823

Informal Administration Act
Kan. Stat. Ann., 59-3301 et seq.

Information Access Montana Act
Mont. Laws 1989, Ch. 670

Information Act (Child Support)
Ill. Comp. Stat. 1992, Ch. 5, § 405/1 et seq.

Information Act (Criminal History Record)
Me. Rev. Stat. Ann. 1964, Title 16, § 611 et seq.

Information Act (Criminal Prosecution)
Colo. Rev. Stat., 16-4-101 et seq.
Me. Rev. Stat. Ann. 1964, Title 15, § 811

Ore. General Laws 1899, p. 99
Wash. Rev. Code Ann., 10.37.010 et seq.

Information Act (Food Stamp Program)
Cal. Welfare and Institutions Code §§ 18904.2, 18904.3, 18911

Information Act (Hazardous Chemicals)
N.M. Stat. Ann., 74-4E-1 et seq.

Information Act (Health Care)
See Uniform Health Care Information Act
Wash. Rev. Code Ann., 70.02.005 et seq.

Information Act (Missing Persons)
N.M. Stat. Ann., 29-15-1 et seq.

Information and Assessment Act (Air Toxics "Hot Spots")
Cal. Health and Safety Code §§ 44300 et seq., 44306 et seq., 44320 et seq., 44340 et seq., 44360 et seq., 44380 et seq.

Information and Assistance for the Agent Orange Act
S.C. Code Ann. 1976, § 44-40-10 et seq.

Information and Cable Television and Video Provider Customer Service Act
Cal. Government Code § 53054 et seq.

Information and Communication Management Act
N.M. Stat. Ann., 15-1-1 et seq.

Information and Data Technology Resources Act (Security)
Fla. Stat. Ann., 282.318

Information and Documentation Act (Bias Crimes)
Ga. Official Code Ann., 35-3-120 to 35-3-124

Information and State Energy Assistance Program Act
Md. Ann. Code 1957, Art. 41, § 6-401 et seq.

Information Center for Missing Person Act
S.C. Code Ann. 1976, § 23-3-200 et seq.

Information Coordination Act
Colo. Rev. Stat., 24-1-136

Information Freedom Act
See Freedom of Information Act

Information Law (DES)
Pa. Purdon's Stat., Title 35, § 6211 et seq.

Information Network of Kansas Act
Kan. Stat. Ann., 74-9301 et seq.

Information Practices Act
See also Freedom of Information Act
Cal. Civil Code § 1798 et seq.
Mass. Gen. Laws Ann., 66A:1 et seq.
Utah Code Ann. 1953, 63-50-1 et seq.

Information Practices Act (Fair)
Iowa Code Ann., 22.11

Information Practices Act (Modified)
See Uniform Information Practices Act
(Modified)

Information Practices and Records and Archives Services Act
Ark. Stat. 1947, 16-801 et seq.
Cal. Civil Code § 1798 et seq.
Utah Code Ann. 1953, 63-2-59 et seq.

Information Privacy Act (Genetic)
Ill. Comp. Stat. 1992, Ch. 410, § 513/1 et seq.

Information Program Act (Training)
Kan. Stat. Ann., 72-4450 et seq.

Information Reporting Act (Arson)
Colo. Rev. Stat., 10-4-1001 et seq.

Information Reporting Act (Oil and Gas)
Cal. Public Resources Code § 25350 et seq.

Information Reporting Act (Petroleum Industry)
Haw. Rev. Stat. Ann., § 486I-1 et seq.

Information Reporting Act (Public Securities)
Colo. Rev. Stat., 11-58-101 et seq.

Information Resources Management Act
Tex. General and Special Laws 1991, p. 3569, Ch. 788, § 2 et seq.
Tex. Government Code, § 2054.001 et seq.
Tex. Rev. Civ. Stat., Art. 4413(32j)

Information Resources Management and Paperwork Reduction Act
Fla. Stat. Ann., 282.003 et seq.

Information System Act (Criminal Offender Record)
Mass. Gen. Laws Ann., 6:167 et seq.

Information System Act (Legislative)
Ill. Rev. Stat. 1991, Ch. 63, § 42.10 et seq.

Information Systems Act
N.M. Stat. Ann., 15-1-1 et seq.

Information Systems Act (Health)
N.M. Stat. Ann., 24-14A-1 et seq.

Information Technology Access Act
Va. Code 1950, §§ 2.1-807 to 2.1-811

Information Technology Act (Judicial Committee on)
Tex. Government Code, § 77.001 et seq.

Information Technology and Planning Act
Fla. Stat. Ann., 282.301 et seq.

Information Technology Commission Act
Utah Code Ann. 1953, 63C-2-101 et seq.

Information Technology Education Act
Pa. Purdon's Stat., Title 24, § 6001 et seq.
Utah Code Ann. 1953, 63-2-59 et seq.

Information Technology Infrastructure Act
Neb. Rev. Stat. 1943, 81-1190 to 81-11,103

Information Technology Management Reform Act of 1996
Feb. 10, 1996, P.L. 104-106, Division E, 40 U.S. Code § 1401 nt.

Information Technology Policy Act
Ga. Official Code Ann., 50-29-1 et seq.

Informed Consent Act (Women's)
Ga. Official Code Ann., 16-12-150

Informer's Act
Dec. 23, 1943, Ch. 377, 57 Stat. 608, 31 U.S. Code § 232

Infrastructure Act (Rural)
N.M. Stat. Ann., 75-1-1 et seq.

Infrastructure Admissions Tax Act (Tourism)
S.C. Code Ann. 1976, §§ 12-21-6510 to 12-21-6580

Infrastructure and Economic Development Bank Act (Bergeson-Peace)
Cal. Government Code § 63000 et seq.

Infrastructure and Jobs Development Act
W. Va. Code 1966, § 31-15A-1 et seq.

Infrastructure Bank Act (Transportation)
S.C. Code Ann. 1976, § 11-40-10 et seq.
S.C. Code Ann. 1976, § 11-43-110 et seq.

Infrastructure Financing Authority Act
P.R. Laws Ann. 1954, Title 3, § 1901 et seq.

Infrastructure Gross Receipts Tax Act (Municipal)
N.M. Stat. Ann., 7-19C-1 et seq.

Infrastructure Improvement Act (Education Facilities)
Fla. Stat. Ann., 364.506 et seq.

Infrastructure Improvement Act (Sewage)
N.J. Stat. Ann., 58:25-23 et seq.

Infrastructure Improvement Act (Water Utility)
Cal. Public Utilities Code § 789 et seq.

Infrastructure Investment Authority Act
Pa. Purdon's Stat., Title 35, § 751.1 et seq.

Infrastructure Investment Authority Project Itemization Act
Pa. 1988 Pamph. Laws, No. 102

Infrastructure Redevelopment Fund Act (Municipal)
Neb. Rev. Stat. 1943, 18-2601 et seq.

Infrastructure Trust Act (Environmental)
N.J. Stat. Ann., 58:11B-1 et seq.

Ingalls Act (Aeronautics)
Ohio Rev. Code 1953, 4561.01 et seq.

Inhalation Therapy Act
Ark. Code Ann. 1987, 17-84-102 et seq.

Inheritance Act
Ark. Code Ann. 1987, 28-9-203 et seq.
Ga. Code Ann., 53-2-1 et seq.
Haw. Rev. Stat. Ann., § 532-1 et seq.
Md. Ann. Code 1974, Art. ET, § 3-101 et seq.
Me. Rev. Stat. Ann. 1964, Title 18A, § 2-102 et seq.
Ore. Rev. Stat., 111.005 et seq.
Pa. Cons. Stat., Title 20, § 2101 et seq.
S.C. Code Ann. 1976, Superseded Vols., § 21-3-20

Inheritance Act (Children Born Out of Wedlock)
Ind. Code Ann., 29-1-2-7

Inheritance Act (Foreign Benefit Rule)
See Iron Curtain Act (Nonresident Alien Beneficiary)
Ohio Rev. Code 1953, 2113.81

Inheritance and Estate Tax Act
Ark. Code Ann. 1987, 26-59-101 et seq.
Colo. Rev. Stat., 39-23-101 et seq.
Fla. Stat. Ann., 198.01 et seq.
Haw. Rev. Stat. Ann., § 236-1 et seq.
Ind. Code Ann., 6-4.1-1 et seq.
Kan. Stat. Ann., 79-1537 et seq.
Md. Ann. Code 1974, TC § 7-201 et seq.
Minn. Stat. Ann., 291.005 et seq.
Mo. Rev. Stat., 145.009 et seq.
Mont. Code Ann., 72-16-101 et seq.
N.D. Cent. Code, 57-37.1-01
Neb. Rev. Stat. 1943, 77-2001 et seq.
N.H. Rev. Stat. 1955, 86:6 et seq.
Pa. Cons. Stat., Title 72, § 1701 et seq.
S.C. Code Ann. 1976, § 12-15-10 et seq.
Continued

Tex. Tax Code, § 211.001 et seq.
Utah Code Ann. 1953, 59-11-101 et seq.
Wash. Rev. Code Ann., 83.100.010 et seq.
Wis. Stat. Ann., 72.11 et seq.

Inheritance and Estate Tax Revision Act

Alaska Stat. 1962, Replaced Titles § 43.30.011 et seq.
Ariz. Rev. Stat. Ann., § 42-1501 et seq.
Ark. Code Ann. 1987, 63-101 et seq.
Cal. Revenue and Taxation Code § 13301 et seq.
Conn. Gen. Stat. Ann., § 12-340 et seq.
D.C. Code Ann., § 47-3701 et seq.
Del. Code of 1974, Title 30, § 1301 et seq.
Ga. Code 1933, 92-3401 et seq.
Ida. Code 1947, 14-401 et seq.
Ill. Rev. Stat. 1991, Ch. 120, § 375 et seq.
Ind. Code Ann., 6-4.1-1-1 et seq.
Iowa Code Ann., 450.1 et seq.
Kan. Stat. Ann., 79-1501 et seq., 79-1537 et seq.
Ky. Rev. Stat. 1971, 140.010 et seq.
La. Rev. Stat. Ann., 47:2401 et seq., 47:2431 et seq.
Mass. Gen. Laws Ann., 65:1 et seq.
Md. Ann. Code 1974, Art. TG, § 7-201 et seq.
Me. Rev. Stat. Ann. 1964, Title 36, § 3401 et seq.
Mich. Comp. Laws Ann., 205.201 et seq.
Minn. Stat. Ann., 291.005 et seq.
Miss. Code Ann. 1972, § 27-9-1 et seq.
Mo. Rev. Stat., 145.010 et seq.
Mont. Code Ann., 72-16-101 et seq.
N.C. Gen. Stat. 1943, § 105-2 et seq.
N.D. Cent. Code, 57-37-01 et seq.
Neb. Rev. Stat. 1943, 77-2001 et seq.
Nev. Statutes 1913, Ch. 266, p. 411
N.H. Rev. Stat. 1955, 86:1 et seq.
N.J. Rev. Stat. 1937, 54:33-1 et seq.
N.Y. Tax Law (Consol. Laws Ch. 60) §§ 249m et seq., 951 et seq.
Ohio Rev. Code 1953, 5731.01 et seq.
Ore. Rev. Stat., 118.005 et seq.
P.R. Laws Ann. 1954, Title 13, § 881 et seq.
R.I. Gen. Laws 1956, 44-22-1 et seq.
S.C. Code Ann. 1976, § 12-15-10 et seq.
S.D. Codified Laws 1967, 10-40-1 et seq.

Tenn. Code Ann., 67-8-301 et seq.
Tex. Tax Code, § 211.001 et seq.
Utah Code Ann. 1953, 59-12-1 et seq.
Va. Code 1950, § 58-152 et seq.
Vt. Stat. Ann., Title 32, § 7441 et seq.
Wash. Rev. Code Ann., 83.100.010 et seq.
Wis. Stat. Ann., 72.01 et seq.
Wyo. Stat. Ann., § 39-6-801 et seq.

Inheritance and Successions Tax Law

Colo. Rev. Stat., 39-23-101 et seq.

Inheritance and Transfer Tax Act

Ill. Rev. Stat. 1991, Ch. 120, § 405A et seq.
W. Va. Code 1966, § 11-11-1 et seq.

Inheritance, Estate and Transfer Tax Act

Okla. Stat. Ann., Title 68, § 801 et seq.

Inheritance Tax Act

Me. Rev. Stat. Ann. 1964, Title 36, § 3461 et seq.

Inheritance Tax Act (Collateral Inheritance)

Pa. Purdon's Stat., Title 72, § 2302

Inheritance Tax Act (Direct Inheritance)

Pa. Purdon's Stat., Title 72, § 2301 et seq.

Inheritance Tax Act (Interstate Compromise and Arbitration)

Pa. Cons. Stat., Title 72, § 1756 et seq.

Inheritance Tax Act (Interstate Compromise)

Colo. Rev. Stat., 39-24-101 et seq.

Inheritance Tax Act (Joint Property)

Pa. Purdon's Stat., Title 72, § 2301

Inheritance Tax Act (Nonresident)

Pa. Purdon's Stat., Title 72, § 2303

Inheritance Tax Apportionment Act

Va. Code 1950, § 64.1-160 et seq.

Inheritance Tax Exemption Act

Mo. Rev. Stat., 145.090

Inheritance Tax Lien Act

Iowa Code Ann., 450.7

Inheritance Tax Rates Act
Wash. Rev. Code Ann., 83.100.030 et seq.

Inheritance Tax Valuation Law
Wash. Rev. Code 1981, 83.16.010 et seq.

Initiative and Referendum Act
Colo. Rev. Stat., 1-40-101 et seq.
D.C. Code Ann., § 1-281 et seq.
Mich. Comp. Laws Ann., 168.471 et seq.
Mont. Code Ann., 13-27-101 et seq.
Neb. Rev. Stat. 1943, 32-702 et seq.
Okla. Stat. Ann., Title 34, § 1 et seq.
Utah Code Ann. 1953, 20-11-1 et seq.
Wash. Rev. Code Ann., 29.79.010 et seq.

Initiative and Referendum Act (Municipal)
Iowa Laws 1907 (32d G. A.), Ch. 48, § 19
Kan. Laws 1925, Ch. 99
Ohio Rev. Code 1953, 731.28 et seq.
Wyo. Stat. Ann., § 22-24-101 et seq.

Initiative and Referendum Amendment
Ark. Const. 1874, Amend. No. 7

Initiative and Referendum Election Act (County)
Cal. Elections Code 1976, § 3700 et seq.

Initiative and Referendum Election Act (Municipal)
Cal. Elections Code 1976, § 4000 et seq.

Initiative and Referendum Election Act (State)
Cal. Elections Code 1976, § 3500 et seq.

Initiative and Referendum Enabling Act (County Measures)
Ark. Stat. 1947, 2-301 et seq.

Initiative and Referendum Implementation Act
Minn. Stat. 1980, 3B.01 et seq.

Initiative for Child Care Act
S.C. Acts 1989, p. 623, No. 189, Part 2, § 43

Initiative for the Abatement of Mortality in Infants (MIAMI) Act
Mont. Code Ann., 50-19-301 et seq.

Initiative Petitions Enabling Act
Ark. Code Ann. 1987, 7-9-108 et seq.

Initiative Procedure Act (Municipalities)
Ky. Rev. Stat. 1971, Superseded Vols., 89.260, 89.600 et seq.

Initiative, Referendum, and Recall Charter Amendments Act
D.C. Code 1988, §§ 1-281 et seq., 1-291 et seq.

Initiatives for Research and Academic Excellence Act
S.C. Code Ann. 1976, § 59-104-10 et seq.

Injection Well Act
Tex. Water Code, § 27.001 et seq.

Injunction Act
Ill. Rev. Stat. 1991, Ch. 110, § 11-101 et seq.
Kan. Stat. Ann., 60-901 et seq.
La. Rev. Stat. Ann., 13:4061 et seq.
Mass. Gen. Laws Ann., 214:1 et seq.
Mich. Comp. Laws 1948, 619.8 et seq.
Mo. Rev. Stat., 526.010 et seq.
Mont. Code Ann., 27-19-101 et seq.
N.C. Gen. Stat. 1943, § 1-485 et seq.
N.M. Stat. Ann., 50-3-1, 50-3-2
P.R. Laws Ann. 1954, Title 32, § 3521 et seq.
Wash. Rev. Code Ann., 7.40.010 et seq.
W. Va. Code 1966, § 53-5-1 et seq.

Injunction Act (Divorce)
Ill. Rev. Stat. 1991, Ch. 40, § 701

Injunction Act (Labor Disputes)
Me. Rev. Stat. Ann. 1964, Title 26, § 5
Mich. Comp. Laws Ann., 423.23
Minn. Stat. Ann., 185.01 et seq.
N.H. Laws 1935, Ch. 46
N.J. Stat. Ann., 2A:15-51 et seq.
N.Y. Labor Law (Consol. Laws Ch. 31) § 807
Ore. Rev. Stat., 662.010
R.I. Gen. Laws 1956, 28-10-1 et seq.

Injunction and Abatement Act (Prostitution)
Kan. Stat. Ann., 21-3512 et seq.

Injured Worker Reemployment Act
Utah Code Ann. 1953, 35-10-1 et seq.

Injuries Act
Ill. Rev. Stat. 1991, Ch. 70

Injuries to Employees, Liability Act
S.C. Code Ann. 1976, § 58-17-3710 et seq.

Injury Compensation Act
See Workmen's Compensation Acts

Injury Compensation Board Act (Horse Racing)
N.J. Stat. Ann., 34:15-129 et seq.

Injury Compensation Fund Act (Horsemen)
La. Rev. Stat. Ann., 4:250 et seq.

Injury Control Act of 1990
Nov. 15, 1990, P.L. 101-558, 42 U.S. Code § 201 nt.

Injury Fund Act (Second)
S.C. Code Ann. 1976, § 42-7-310 et seq.

Injury Information System Act (Head and Spinal Cord)
S.C. Code Ann. 1976, § 44-38-10 et seq.

Injury Law (Secondary)
N.Y. Worker's Compensation Law (Consol. Laws Ch. 67) § 15, Subd. 8

Injury Prevention Act (Head)
Wash. Rev. Code Ann., 43.70.400 et seq.

Injury Prevention Act of 1986
Nov. 10, 1986, P.L. 99-649, 42 U.S. Code § 201 nt.

Inland Bays' Watershed Enhancement Act
Del. Code of 1974, Title 7, § 7601 et seq.

Inland Definition Act (Nationwide)
Mont. Code Ann. 1987, 33-1-201 to 33-1-229

Inland Fish and Game Act
Me. Rev. Stat. Ann. 1964, Title 12, § 7001 et seq.

Inland Fish, Dog and Game Act
Va. Code 1950, § 29-1 et seq.

Inland Fishing Act
Mich. Comp. Laws Ann., 301.1 et seq.

Inland Gas Unit Operation Act
Mich. Comp. Laws Ann., 319.351 et seq.

Inland Lake Improvement Act
Mich. Comp. Laws Ann., 281.901 et seq.
Mich. Comp. Laws 1948, 281.701 et seq.

Inland Lake Level Act
Mich. Comp. Laws Ann., 281.61 et seq.

Inland Lakes and Streams Act
Mich. Comp. Laws Ann., 281.951 et seq.
Mich. Comp. Laws 1970, 281.731 et seq.

Inland Marine Definition Act
Mont. Code Ann., 33-1-221 et seq.

Inland Marine, Fire and Marine Rate Reglatory Act
Pa. Purdon's Stat., Title 40, § 1221 et seq.

Inland Navigation District Law
Fla. Stat. Ann., 374.980 et seq.

Inland Navigational Rules Act of 1980
Dec. 24, 1980, P.L. 96-591, 33 U.S. Code § 2001 nt.
Oct. 15, 1982, P.L. 97-322, 33 U.S. Code § 2073
Oct. 30, 1984, P.L. 98-557, 33 U.S. Code §§ 2014, 2024, 2073
Dec. 12, 1989, P.L. 101-225, 33 U.S. Code § 2073

Inland Ports Act
Miss. Code Ann. 1972, § 59-17-1 et seq.

Inland Rules
June 7, 1897, Ch. 4, 30 Stat. 96, 33 U.S. Code §§ 154 to 159, 171 to 183, 191, 192, 201 to 213, 221, 222, 231
Aug. 5, 1963, P.L. 88-84, 77 Stat. 116, 33 U.S. Code §§ 180, 191, 322, 331

Inland Waterways Revenue Act of 1978

Oct. 21, 1978, P.L. 95-502, 26 U.S. Code §§ 513, 513 nt., 527, 4042, 4042 nt., 4293; 33 U.S. Code § 1801 et seq.

Dec. 29, 1995, P.L. 104-88, 33 U.S. Code § 1803

Inland Wetlands Act

Mass. Gen. Laws Ann., 131:40A

Inland Wetlands and Water Courses Act

Conn. Gen. Stat. Ann., § 22a-36 et seq.

Inmate Community Reintegration under SIR Act

Ala. Acts 1983, 3d Sp., p. 62

Inmate Damages Act (Escaped)

Ill. Rev. Stat. 1991, Ch. 23, §§ 4040, 4041

Inmate Disciplinary Act

Cal. Penal Code § 2933

Inmate Forestry Work Camp Act

N.M. Stat. Ann., 33-13-1 to 33-13-8

Inmate Grievance Commission Act

Md. Ann. Code 1957, Art. 41, § 4-1104

Inmate Labor Act

N.C. Gen. Stat. 1943, §§ 148-26, Subsec. a, 148-26.1 et seq.

Inmate Literacy Act

N.M. Stat. Ann., 33-11-1 et seq.

Okla. Stat. Ann., Title 57, §§ 510.5 to 510.8

Inmate Reimbursement to County Act

Tenn. Code Ann., 41-11-101 to 41-11-112

Inmate Responsibility and Cost-Efficiency Omnibus Act

Wash. Rev. Code Ann., 72.09.450 et seq.

Innkeeper Protection Act

Ill. Rev. Stat. 1991, Ch. 71, § 0.01 et seq.

Innkeeper Rights Act

Okla. Stat. 1981, Title 15, § 504 et seq.

Pa. Purdon's Stat. Title 37, § 101 et seq.

Innkeepers' Act

Cal. Civil Code § 1859 et seq.

Colo. Rev. Stat., 12-44-101 et seq.

Ill. Rev. Stat. 1991, Ch. 71

Ind. Code Ann., 32-8-28-1 et seq.

Neb. Rev. Stat. 1943, 42-101 et seq.

Ohio Rev. Code 1953, 4721.01 et seq.

Okla. Stat. Ann., Title 15, § 501 et seq.

Pa. Purdon's Stat., Title 37, § 61 et seq.

P.R. Laws Ann. 1954, Title 10, § 711 et seq.

Wash. Rev. Code Ann., 19.48.010 et seq., 60.64.003 et seq.

Innkeepers Act (Loss by Fire)

N.Y. General Business Law (Consol. Laws Ch. 20) § 202 et seq.

Innkeepers' Liability Act

Ark. Code Ann. 1987, 20-26-302 et seq.

Cal. Civil Code § 1859 et seq.

D.C. Code Ann., § 34-101 et seq.

Del. Code of 1974, Title 24, § 1501

Fla. Stat. Ann., 509.111

Md. Ann. Code 1974, Art. BR, § 15-103 et seq.

Mich. Comp. Laws Ann., 427.101, 427.102

Mont. Code Ann., 70-6-501 et seq.

R.I. Gen. Laws 1956, 5-14-1, 5-14-2

Vt. Stat. Ann., Title 9, § 3141 et seq.

W. Va. Code 1966, § 16-6-22

Innkeepers' Liability Acts (Loss of Personal Property)

N.Y. General Business Law (Consol. Laws Ch. 20) §§ 200, 201, 203a

Innkeepers' Lien Act

Cal. Civil Code § 1861

D.C. Code Ann., § 34-102

Fla. Stat. Ann., 509.191

Ill. Rev. Stat. 1991, Ch. 71, § 2, Ch. 82, § 57, Ch. 141, § 3

Ill. Rev. Stat. 1991, Ch. 82, § 56.9 et seq.

Md. Ann. Code 1974, Art. CL, § 16-501 et seq.

Mich. Comp. Laws Ann., 427.201 et seq.

Miss. Code Ann. 1972, §§ 75-73-15, 75-73-17

Mont. Code Ann., 71-3-1401 et seq.

Continued

R.I. Gen. Laws 1956, 34-33-1, 34-33-2
Wash. Rev. Code Ann., 60.64.010 et seq.

Innocent Spouse Statute
Dec. 30, 1969, P.L. 91-172, 83 Stat. 675, 26
U.S. Code § 6013(e)

Innovation and Technology Act
Utah Code Ann. 1953, 63-60-1 et seq.

Innovation Capital Act
Conn. Gen. Stat. Ann., § 32-32 et seq.

Innovation Investment Program Act
Fla. Stat. Ann., 216.235 et seq.

Innovative Schools Act
Cal. Education Code 1959, §§ 32001 et seq.,
12002

Innovative Technology Authority Act
Va. Code 1950, § 9-250 et seq.

Inoculation Law for Pets
S.C. Code of Law 1976, § 47-5-60 et seq.

**Inpatient Mental Health Treatment of
    Children Act**
Okla. Stat. Ann., Title 43A, § 5-501 et seq.

Inpatient Support Act (Insane Persons)
Kan. Stat. Ann., 59-2006

Inquest Act
Mich. Comp. Laws Ann., 773.1 et seq.

Inquisition Act
Kan. Stat. Ann., 22-3101 et seq.

Insane and Mentally Ill Defendants Act
S.C. Code Ann. 1976, § 17-24-10 et seq.

Insane Hospitalization Act
Mich. Comp. Laws Ann., 330.11 et seq.

Insane Hospitals Act
Wash. Rev. Code Ann., 72.23.010 et seq.

**Insane Person Compulsory Commitment
    Act**
Colo. Rev. Stat., 27-10-101 et seq.

Insane Persons Act
Alaska Stat. 1962, Replaced Titles
    § 47.30.010 et seq.
R.I. Gen. Laws 1956, 40.1-5.1-1 et seq.
Wash. Rev. Code Ann., 71.05.010 et seq.

Insane Persons Commitment Act
Cal. Welfare and Institutions Code § 5000 et
    seq.
Va. Code 1950, § 37.1-63 et seq.

Insane Persons Support Act
Alaska Stat. 1962, Replaced Titles
    § 47.30.010 et seq.
Iowa Code Ann., 230.1 et seq.

Insane Persons Support Act (Inpatients)
Kan. Stat. Ann., 59-2006

Insane Private Institutions Act
Wash. Rev. Code Ann., 71.12.455 et seq.

Insane Screening Center Law
Iowa Code Ann., 229.13 et seq.

Insane Spouse Act
D.C. Code 1973, § 19-104

Insanitary Buildings Act
D.C. Code Ann., § 5-701 et seq.

Insanity Act
N.Y. Mental Hygiene Law (Consol. Laws
    Ch. 27)
S.D. Codified Laws 1967, 27A-1-1 et seq.

Insanity Act (Criminal Procedure)
Ohio Rev. Code 1953, 2945.37 et seq.

Insanity Act (Criminal)
See Criminal Insanity Act

Insanity Act (Defense)
Tex. Code of Criminal Procedure, Art. 46.02

Insanity Act (Habeas Corpus)
N.Y. Mental Hygiene Law 1977 (Consol.
    Laws Ch. 27) § 29.27, 33.15

Insanity Act (Marriage)
Kan. Laws 1903, Ch. 220, § 1

Insanity Defense Reform Act
N.Y. Criminal Procedure Law (Consol. Laws
Ch. 11A) §§ 60.55, 220.10, 220.15, 220.30,
220.60, 250.10, 300.10, 330.10, 330.20

Insanity Defense Reform Act of 1984
Oct. 12, 1984, P.L. 98-473, 18 U.S. Code
§ 4241

Insanity Plea Act
Colo. Rev. Stat. 16-8-101 et seq.

Insanity Proceedings Act
D.C. Code 1973, § 21-501 et seq.

Insanity Test Act (Reasonable)
Ala. Code 1975, § 13A-3-1

Insect Abatement Act (County)
Ore. Rev. Stat., 452.210 et seq.

Insect Act
Ill. Rev. Stat. 1991, Ch. 1, § 2901-15

Insect and Plant Disease Act
W. Va. Code 1966, § 19-12-1 et seq.

Insect Control Act
April 6, 1937, Ch. 69, 50 Stat. 57, 7 U.S.
Code § 148

Insect Infestation Emergency Control Act
Utah Code Ann. 1953, 4-35-1 et seq.

Insect Pest Act
June 13, 1939, Ch. 207, 53 Stat. 821
N.M. Stat. Ann. 1953, 45-8-1 et seq.

Insect Pest and Plant Disease Act
Ill. Rev. Stat. 1991, Ch. 5, § 61 et seq.
Mich. Comp. Laws Ann., 286.201 et seq.
Mo. Rev. Stat., 263.010 et seq.

Insect Sting Emergency Treatment Act
Ark. Code Ann. 1987, 20-13-401 et seq.
Fla. Stat. Ann., 402.60
Ill. Rev. Stat. 1983, Ch. 111 1/2, § 6401 et
seq.

S.C. Code Ann. 1976, § 44-99-10 et seq.

Insecticide Act
April 26, 1910, Ch. 191, 36 Stat. 331, 7 U.S.
Code §§ 121 to 134
June 25, 1947, Ch. 125, 61 Stat. 163, 7 U.S.
Code §§ 121, 135 nts.

Insecticide, Fungicide and Rodenticide Act
See also Federal Insecticide, Fungicide, and
Rodenticide Act
Colo. Rev. Stat., 35-9-101 et seq.
Iowa Code Ann., 206.1 et seq.
Mich. Comp. Laws Ann., 286.201 et seq.
Mont. Rev. Code 1947, 27-201 et seq.
N.C. Gen. Stat. 1943, § 143-434 et seq.
N.D. Cent. Code, 19-18-01 et seq.
P.R. Laws Ann. 1954, Title 10, § 976 et seq.
S.D. Codified Laws 1967, 38-20a-1 et seq.
Tenn. Code Ann., 43-8-101 et seq.
Tex. Agriculture Code, § 76.001 et seq.
Utah Code Ann. 1953, 4-14-1 et seq.
Va. Code 1950, § 3.1-189 et seq.
Vt. Stat. Ann., Title 6, § 911 et seq.

Insecticide, Fungicide and Rodenticide Act (Federal)
Miss. Code Ann. 1972, §§ 69-23-3,
69-23-107

Inservice Education Opportunities Act
Kan. Stat. Ann., 72-9601 et seq.

Insider Securities Trading Statute Act
S.C. Code Ann. 1976, § 38-23-10 et seq.

Insider Trading and Securities Fraud Enforcement Act of 1988
Nov. 19, 1988, P.L. 100-704, 15 U.S. Code
§ 78a nt.

Insider Trading Sanctions Act of 1984
Aug. 10, 1984, P.L. 98-376, 15 U.S. Code
§§ 78a nt., 78c, 78c nt., 78o, 78t, 78u, 78ff

Insider Trading Statute
S.C. Code Ann. 1976, § 38-23-10 et seq.

Insolvancy Fund Act (Insurers)
Mass. Gen. Laws Ann., 175D:1 et seq.

Insolvency Act
    Ark. Code Ann. 1987, 16-117-301, 16-117-302 et seq.
    Cal. Stat. 1880, Ch. 87, p. 82
    Cal. Stat. 1895, Ch. 143, p. 131
    Conn. Gen. Stat. 1983, § 45a-340 et seq.
    Del. Code of 1974, Title 10, § 7301 et seq.
    Mass. Gen. Laws 1932, Ch. 216
    Md. Ann. Code 1974, Art. CL, § 15-101 et seq.
    Me. Rev. Stat. Ann. 1964, Title 10, § 1351
    Minn. Laws, 1881, Ch. 148
    N.H. Rev. Stat. 1955, 568:1 et seq.
    N.Y. Debtor and Creditor Law (Consol. Laws Ch. 12) § 50 et seq.
    Ore. General Laws 1878, p. 36
    Pa. Purdon's Stat., Title 39, § 1 et seq.
    Tenn. Code Ann., 68-14-501 et seq.
    Wis. Stat. Ann., 128.01 et seq.

Insolvency Assignment Law
    S.C. Code Ann. 1976, § 27-25-10 et seq.

Insolvency Courts Act
    Vt. Acts 1876, No. 1

Insolvency Pool Act (Insurance)
    Ga. Code Ann., 33-36-1 et seq.

Insolvent Assessment Districts' Relief Act
    Cal. Statutes 1935, p. 63

Insolvent Corporation Act
    Ark. Code Ann. 1987, 4-25-104 et seq.

Insolvent Corporations Act (Preferences)
    Wash. Rev. Code Ann., 23.72.010 et seq.

Insolvent Debtors Act
    Ill. Rev. Stat. 1991, Ch. 110, § 12-1301 et seq.
    Ky. Rev. Stat. 1971, Superseded Vols., 426.400, 426.410, 426.420
    N.C. Gen. Stat. 1943, § 23-23 et seq.
    N.J. Stat. Ann., 2A:20-1 et seq.
    Ohio Rev. Code 1953, 1313.01 et seq.
    S.C. Code Ann. 1976, § 15-17-410 et seq.

Insolvent Estates Act (Secured Creditors Participation)
    N.Y. Debtor and Creditor Law (Consol. Laws Ch. 12) § 30 et seq.

Insolvent Prisoners Act
    Pa. Purdon's Stat., Title 61, § 377

Insolvent Prisoners Act (Discharge)
    Ohio Rev. Code 1953, 319.23

Insolvent Property Tax Law
    Tenn. Code Ann., 67-5-2601 et seq.

Insolvent Traders Act
    Ga. Code 1933, 28-401 et seq.

Inspection Act (Animal)
    N.Y. Agriculture and Markets Law (Consol. Laws Ch. 69) § 72 et seq.

Inspection Act (Boiler)
    Mass. Gen. Laws Ann., 146:5 et seq.

Inspection Act (Boilers)
    Minn. Stat. Ann., 183.375 et seq.
    Mont. Code Ann. 1947, 69-1501 et seq.

Inspection Act (Buildings)
    Vt. Stat. Ann., Title 24, § 3101 et seq.

Inspection Act (Dairy and Food)
    Mich. Comp. Laws Ann., 289.35 et seq.

Inspection Act (Documents)
    Cal. Code of Civil Procedure § 2031

Inspection Act (Elevator)
    Neb. Rev. Stat. 1943, 48-418 et seq.

Inspection Act (Factories)
    N.J. Stat. Ann., 34:6A-4
    Ore. Rev. Stat. 1953, 654.205 et seq.

Inspection Act (Factory)
    Colo. Rev. Stat., 8-11-105 et seq.

Inspection Act (Farm Products)
    Ill. Rev. Stat. 1991, Ch. 5, § 91.9 et seq.

Inspection Act (Fertilizer)
Mich. Comp. Laws Ann., 286.757 et seq.

Inspection Act (Kerosene)
Mich. Comp. Laws 1948, 28.301 et seq.

Inspection Act (Liquefied Compressed Gas Equipment)
Miss. Code Ann. 1972, § 75-57-1

Inspection Act (Liquified Petroleum Equipment)
Miss. Code Ann. 1972 § 75-57-1 et seq.

Inspection Act (Meat and Poultry)
Ga. Code Ann., 26-2-100 et seq.
Ill. Rev. Stat. 1991, Ch. 8, § 130.9 et seq.
Mass. Gen. Laws Ann., 94:146 et seq.
Mont. Code Ann., 46-401 et seq.
N.C. Gen. Stat. 1943, § 106.549.1 et seq.
Neb. Rev. Stat. 1943, 54-1901 et seq.

Inspection Act (Mines)
Minn. Stat. Ann., 180.01 et seq.

Inspection Act (Motor Vehicle Safety)
Utah Code Ann. 1953, 53-8-201 et seq.

Inspection Act (Motor Vehicles)
Neb. Rev. Stat. 1943, 60-1701 et seq.
W. Va. Code 1966, § 17C-16-1 et seq.

Inspection Act (Nursery Stock)
Mich. Comp. Laws Ann., 286.201 et seq.

Inspection Act (Oil)
Colo. Rev. Stat., 8-20-101 et seq.
Minn. Stat. 1986, 296.28 et seq.

Inspection Act (Petroleum Products)
Miss. Code Ann. 1972, § 75-55-1 et seq.

Inspection Act (Potato)
Neb. Rev. Stat. 1943, 2-1813 et seq.

Inspection Act (Poultry and Rabbits Products)
Ky. Rev. Stat. 1962, 217A.010 et seq.

Inspection Act (Public Records)
N.D. Cent. Code, 44-04-18

Inspection Act (Sardine Canning)
Me. Rev. Stat. Ann. 1964, Title 32, § 4151

Inspection Act (Tobacco)
Ky. Acts 1820, Ch. 96
Md. Ann. Code 1974, Art. AG, § 7-301 et seq.

Inspection and Insurance Act (Amusement Ride)
R.I. Gen. Laws 1956, 23-34-1 et seq.

Inspection Law (Grade A)
Iowa Code Ann., 192.101 et seq.

Inspection Law (Hotels and Restaurants)
Ky. Rev. Stat. 1971, 219.011 et seq.

Inspection Law (Oil and Gas)
Okla. Stat. Ann., Title 52, § 321 et seq.

Inspection Law (Petroleum Products)
Kan. Stat. Ann., 55-422 et seq.

Inspection of Bedding Act
Ohio Rev. Code 1953, 3713.01 et seq.

Inspection of Public Records Act
N.M. Stat. Ann., 14-2-4 et seq.

Inspection of Volative Oils Law
Tenn. Code Ann., 60-3-101 et seq.

Inspector General Act Amendments of 1988
Oct. 18, 1988, P.L. 100-504, 5 U.S. Code §§ 5315, 5316; generally 5 U.S. Code Appx. §§ 1 et seq.; 31 U.S. Code § 1105; 39 U.S. Code § 410; 42 U.S. Code §§ 3521 to 3527; 44 U.S. Code §§ 101 nt., 3901 to 3903, 3901 nt.; 45 U.S. Code § 231v

Inspector General Act of 1978
Oct. 12, 1978, P.L. 95-452, 5 U.S. Code Appx.
Oct. 17, 1979, P.L. 96-88, 5 U.S. Code Appx. §§ 2, 9, 11
Sept. 8, 1982, P.L. 97-252, 5 U.S. Code Appx. §§ 2, 5, 8, 9, 11
Aug. 16, 1985, P.L. 98-93, 5 U.S. Code Appx. §§ 2, 11
Continued

Aug. 27, 1986, P.L. 99-399, 5 U.S. Code
Appx. § 2

Oct. 18, 1988, P.L. 100-504, 102 Stat. 2515,
5 U.S. Code Appx. §§ 2, 4, 5, 6, 8, 8B to 8F,
9, 11

Aug. 9, 1989, P.L. 101-73, 5 U.S. Code
Appx. §§ 8E, 11

Dec. 12, 1991, P.L. 102-233, 5 U.S. Code
Appx. § 11

Sept. 21, 1993, P.L. 103-82, 5 U.S. Code
Appx. §§ 4, 8E, 8F, 8G, 9, 11

Dec. 17, 1993, P.L. 103-204, 5 U.S. Code
Appx. §§ 8C et seq., 11

Sept. 23, 1994, P.L. 103-325, 5 U.S. Code
Appx. §§ 11, 11 nt.

Dec. 29, 1995, P.L. 104-88, 5 U.S. Code
Appx. § 8G

Feb. 10, 1996, P.L. 104-106, 5 U.S. Code
Appx. §§ 8, 11

Sept. 30, 1996, P.L. 104-208, 5 U.S. Code
Appx. §§ 5, 8G, 8H

Dec. 2, 1997, P.L. 105-134, 5 U.S. Code
Appx. § 8G

July 22, 1998, P.L. 105-206, 5 U.S. Code
Appx. §§ 2, 8D, 8H, 9

Oct. 20, 1998, P.L. 105-272, 5 U.S. Code
Appx. §§ 8H, 8I

Oct. 21, 1998, P.L. 105-277, 5 U.S. Code
Appx. §§ 8A, 11

May 21, 1999, P.L. 106-31, 5 U.S. Code
Appx. § 8G

**Inspector General Improvement Act
(District of Columbia)**
D.C. Code Ann., § 1-6-0.6

Inspectors Act
Okla. Stat. Ann., Title 59, § 1031 et seq.

**Inspectors and Building Officials
Registration Act**
Mich. Comp. Laws Ann., 338.2301 et seq.

Installers Act (Water Well Pump)
Tex. Rev. Civ. Stat., Art. 8905

Installment Act (Redemption)
Pa. Purdon's Stat., Title 72, §§ 5573 et seq.,
6105.1 et seq.

Installment Finance Act
Fla. Stat. Ann., 520.50 et seq.

Installment Land Contracts Act
Fla. Stat. 1965, 478.011 et seq.
Ill. Rev. Stat. 1967, Ch. 30, § 351 et seq.
Md. Ann. Code 1974, Art. RP, § 10-101 et
seq.
Pa. Purdon's Stat., Title 68, § 901 et seq.

Installment Loan Act
Ark. Stat. 1947, 67-1301 et seq.
Del. Code of 1974, Title 5, § 2101 et seq.
Ind. Code 1971, 24-5-4-1 et seq.
Kan. Stat. Ann., 16-202
Neb. Rev. Stat. 1943, 45-114 et seq.
N.M. Stat. Ann., 58-7-1 et seq.
S.D. Codified Laws 1967, 54-5-1 et seq.

Installment Loan Act (Banks)
Iowa Code 1987, 524.906

Installment Loan Act (Consumer)
Ill. Comp. Stat. 1992, Ch. 205, § 670/1 et seq.

Installment Loan and Finance Act
Nev. Rev. Stat. 1979 Reprint, 675.010 et seq.

Installment Loan Rate Advertising Act
N.J. Stat. Ann., 17:13A-1 et seq.

Installment Loans Act
Tex. Rev. Civ. Stat., Art. 5069-4.01 et seq.

**Installment Repayment Small Loan
Consumer Finance Act**
S.D. Codified Laws 1967, 54-4-1 et seq.,
54-6-1 et seq.

Installment Sales Act
Alaska Stat. 1962, § 46.10.010 et seq.
Conn. Gen. Stat. Ann., § 42-83 et seq.
Fla. Stat. Ann., 520.30 et seq.
Ill. Rev. Stat. 1991, Ch. 121 1/2, § 501 et seq.
Ind. Code Ann., 24-5-2-26
Kan. Laws 1958, Ch. 9
Ky. Rev. Stat. 1971, 371.210 et seq.
Mass. Gen. Laws Ann., 255D:1 et seq.
Md. Ann. Code 1974, Art. CL, § 12-604 et
seq.

Mich. Comp. Laws Ann., 440.2612 et seq.
Neb. Rev. Stat. 1943, 45-334 et seq.
Pa. Purdon's Stat., Title 69, § 1101 et seq.
Tex. Rev. Civ. Stat., Art. 5069-6.01 et seq.

Installment Sales Act (Motor Vehicles)
See Motor Vehicle Installment Sales Act

Installment Sales Act (Personal Property)
Colo. Rev. Stat. 1963, 121-2-1 et seq.

Installment Sales Act (Retail)
See Retail Installment Sales Act

Installment Sales Finance Act
Fla. Stat. Ann., 520.50 et seq.

Installment Sales Finance Act (Motor Vehicle Retail)
Vt. Stat. Ann., Title 9, § 2351 et seq.

Installment Sales Revision Act of 1980
Oct. 19, 1980, P.L. 96-471, 26 U.S. Code § 1 nt.

Installment Savings and Investment Certificate Act
N.M. Stat. Ann. 1953, 48-16-1 et seq.

Installment Stock Sales Law
Iowa Code 1979, 501.1 et seq.

Instant Criminal Background Check System Act
Colo. Rev. Stat., 12-26.5-101 et seq.

Institute of Arts, Cinematographic and Television Industries Act
P.R. Laws Ann. 1954, Title 18, § 1301 et seq.

Institute of Food and Agricultural Sciences Supplemental Retirement Act
Fla. Stat. Ann., 121.40 et seq.

Institute of Forensic Sciences Act
P.R. Laws Ann. 1954, Title 34, § 3001 et seq.

Institute of Inter-American Affairs Act
Aug. 5, 1947, Ch. 498, 61 Stat. 780, 22 U.S. Code §§ 281, 281 nt., 281a to 281l

Institute of Phosphate Research Competitive Negotiation Act
Fla. Stat. Ann., 378.102

Institute of Technology Act
N.J. Stat. Ann., 18A:64E-12 et seq.

Institute on Superconductivity Act
N.Y. Laws 1987, Ch. 615, § 22 et seq.

Institute Transfer Act (Biologic Products)
Mich. Comp. Laws Ann., 333.26331 et seq.

Institutes for Juvenile Research and Developmental Disabilities Act (University of Illinois)
Ill. Rev. Stat. 1991, Ch. 144, § 2650 et seq.

Institution Bond Act
N.C. Public Laws 1937, Ch. 296
N.M. Stat. Ann., 6-13-1 et seq.

Institution District Law (County)
Pa. Purdon's Stat., Title 62, § 2201 et seq.

Institution for Tuberculosis Research Act
Ill. Rev. Stat. 1991, Ch. 111 1/2, § 121.990 et seq.

Institution of Higher Education Educational Loan Act
N.J. Stat. Ann., 18A:68-11.1 et seq.

Institution of Learning Powers Act
Ill. Rev. Stat. 1991, Ch. 144, § 0.01 et seq.

Institutional Assistance Grants Act
Pa. Purdon's Stat., Title 24, § 5181 et seq.

Institutional Building Bonds Act
Conn. Special Acts 1949, June Special Session, p. 1408, No. 9

Institutional Construction Bond Act
N.J. Laws 1978, Ch. 79

Institutional Funds Management Act
See also Uniform Management of Institutional Funds Act
N.Y. Not-For-Profit Corporation Law (Consol. Laws, Ch. 35), §§ 102, 512 et seq., 521, 522, 717
N.Y. Religious Corporations Law (Consol. Laws, Ch. 51) § 2b

Institutional Funds Management Law
Mass. Gen. Laws Ann., 180A:1 et seq.

Institutional Health Services Act (New)
Wyo. Stat. Ann., § 35-2-201 et seq.

Institutional Pension Act
N.M. Stat. Ann., 23-1-9 et seq.

Institutional Safe Meat Act
Pa. Purdon's Stat., Title 31, 491.1 et seq.

Institutional Service Act
Me. Rev. Stat. Ann. 1964, Title 34-A, § 1202 et seq.
Me. Rev. Stat. Ann. 1964, Title 34-B, § 1201 et seq.

Institutional Support Act
Conn. Gen. Stat. Ann., § 17-324

Institutionalized Elderly Ombudsman Act
Utah Code Ann. 1953, 63-26a-1 et seq.

Institutions and Agencies Act
N.J. Stat. Ann., 30:1-1 et seq.

Institutions Bond Act (Higher Educational)
Va. Acts 1992, Ch. 616

Institutions Construction Bond Act
N.J. Laws 1964, Ch. 144
N.J. Laws 1976, Ch. 93

Institutions Law (Educational)
Fla. Stat. Ann., 243.12

Institutions of Higher Learning Educational Facilities Authority Act (Private Non-profit)
Miss. Code Ann. 1972, § 37-104-21 et seq.

Instream Use Protection Act
Haw. Rev. Stat. Ann., § 176D-1 et seq.

Instructional Aide Act
Cal. Education Code 1976, §§ 45340 et seq., 88240 et seq.

Instructional Leadership Act
Ky. Rev. Stat. 1971, 156.101

Instructional Material Law
N.M. Stat. Ann., 22-15-1 et seq.

Instructional Technology Grant Act
Fla. Stat. Ann., 229.603

Instructional Television Act
Cal. Education Code 1976, § 51870 et seq.

Instructors' Tenure Act
Kan. Stat. Ann., 72-5410 et seq.

Instruments Recording and Registration Act
Tenn. Code Ann., 66-24-101 et seq.

Instruments Regarding Adopted Children Act
Ill. Rev. Stat. 1991, Ch. 40, §§ 1651.9, 1652

Insufficient Funds Act (Worthless Checks)
Ariz. Laws 1919, Ch. 33
Kan. Stat. Ann., 21-3707 et seq.

Insular Areas Drug Abuse Amendments of 1988
Nov. 18, 1988, P.L. 100-690, 48 U.S. Code § 1494 nt.

Insular Liquor Repeal Act
March 2, 1934, Ch. 37, 48 Stat. 361

Insular Supplies Act
P.R. Laws Ann. 1954, Title 23, § 731 et seq.

Insulting Words Act (Defamation)
Miss. Code Ann. 1972, § 95-1-1
Va. Code 1950, § 8.01-45

Insurable Interest Act
Mich. Comp. Laws Ann., 438.31 et seq.
N.C. Gen. Stat. 1943, § 358-58-10

Insurance (Consumer Credit Code)
Me. Rev. Stat. Ann. 1964, Title 9-A, § 4.101 et seq.

Insurance (Consumer Protection Code)
S.C. Code Ann. 1976, § 37-4-101 et seq.

Insurance (Revised Uniform Consumer Credit Code)
See Revised Uniform Consumer Credit Code—Insurance

Insurance (Uniform Commercial Code)
Colo. Rev. Stat., 5-4-101 et seq.

Insurance (Uniform Consumer Credit Code)
See Uniform Consumer Credit Code Insurance

Insurance Access and Equity Act (Health)
Cal. Health and Safety Code § 1389.1 et seq.

Insurance Accreditation Act
R.I. Gen. Laws 1956, 27-51-1 et seq.

Insurance Act
Ark. Stat. 1947, 66-2001 et seq.
Colo. Rev. Stat., 10-1-101 et seq.
Haw. Rev. Stat. Ann., § 431:1-100 et seq.
Ill. Rev. Stat. 1991, Ch. 73, § 613 et seq.
Ind. Code Ann., 27-1-2-1 et seq.
Me. Rev. Stat. Ann. 1964, Title 24-A, § 3 et seq.
Mich. Comp. Laws Ann., 500.100 et seq.
Miss. Code Ann. 1972, § 83-1-1 et seq.
Mont. Code Ann., 33-1-101 et seq.
N.D. Cent. Code, 26.1-01-01 et seq.
N.H. Rev. Stat. 1955, 400-A:1 et seq.
Okla. Stat. Ann., Title 36
S.C. Code Ann. 1976, § 38-1-10 et seq.
Utah Code Ann. 1953, 31A-1-101 et seq.
Wis. Stat. Ann., 424.101 et seq.

Insurance Act (Administration of)
Wis. Stat. Ann., 601.01 et seq.

Insurance Act (Bailment)
Ill. Comp. Stat. 1992, Ch. 765, § 1015/0.01 et seq.
Ill. Rev. Stat. 1991, Ch. 73, § 1091.9 et seq.

Insurance Act (Carnival Ride)
N.M. Stat. Ann., 57-25-1 et seq.

Insurance Act (Childhood Immunization)
Pa. 1992 Pamph. Laws, No. 35

Insurance Act (Credit)
See Credit Insurance Act

Insurance Act (Employers)
Mont. Code Ann., 39-71-101 et seq.

Insurance Act (Exchange or Reciprocal)
Tenn. Code Ann., 56-16-201 et seq.

Insurance Act (Family)
Ore. Laws 1991, Ch. 674

Insurance Act (Fire)
N.Y. Insurance Law 1984 (Consol. Laws Ch. 28) § 3404

Insurance Act (Group Life)
See Group Life Insurance Act

Insurance Act (Group Municipal Employees)
Mass. Gen. Laws Ann., 32B:1 et seq.

Insurance Act (Group State Employees)
Mass. Gen. Laws Ann., 32A:1 et seq.

Insurance Act (HIV Testing for)
Del. Code of 1974, Title 18, § 7301 et seq.

Insurance Act (Housing Mortgage)
Me. Rev. Stat. Ann. 1964, Title 30-1, § 4931 et seq.

Insurance Act (Industrial)
See Industrial Insurance Act

Insurance Act (Long-Term Care)
Ark. Code 1987, 23-97-201 et seq.
Cal. Insurance Code § 10230 et seq.
Colo. Rev. Stat., 10-19-101 et seq.
Del. Code of 1974, Title 18, § 7101 et seq.
Fla. Stat. Ann., 627.9401 et seq.
Iowa Code Ann., 514G.1 et seq.
Kan. Stat. Ann., 40-2225 et seq.
La. Rev. Stat. Ann., 22:3211 et seq.
Mo. Laws 1997, S.B. No. 765, §§ 1 to 8
Mont. Code Ann., 33-22-1101 et seq.
Neb. Rev. Stat. 1943, 44-4501 et seq.
N.H. Rev. Stat. 1955, 415-D:1 et seq.
N.M. Stat. Ann., 59A-23A-1 et seq.
Okla. Stat. Ann., Title 36, § 4421 et seq.
Continued

Ore. Rev. Stat., 743.650 et seq.
Pa. Purdon's Stat., Title 40, § 991.1101 et
  seq.
Wash. Rev. Code Ann., 48.84.010 et seq.
W. Va. Code 1966 § 33-15A-1 et seq.
Wyo. Stat. Ann., § 26-38-101 et seq.

Insurance Act (Medigap)
N.Y. Insurance Law 1984 (Consol. Laws Ch.
  28) §§ 3217, 3218, 3224

Insurance Act (Motor Vehicle Compulsory)
Mass. Gen. Laws Ann., 175:113A

Insurance Act (Motor Vehicle, No-Fault)
See No Fault Motor Vehicle Insurance Act

**Insurance Act (Motor Vehicle Service
  Contract Reimbursement)**
Neb. Rev. Stat. 1943, 44-3520 et seq.

Insurance Act (Motor Vehicles)
Mass. Gen. Laws Ann., 90:34A et seq.;
  175:113A et seq.
N.Y. Vehicle and Traffic Law 1959 (Consol.
  Laws Ch. 71) § 330 et seq.

Insurance Act (Mutual)
See Mutual Insurance Act

Insurance Act (No Fault Automobile)
N.Y. Insurance Law 1984 (Consol. Laws Ch.
  28) § 5101 et seq.

Insurance Act (No Fault)
Colo. Rev. Stat., 10-4-701 et seq.

Insurance Act (Product Liability)
Ill. Rev. Stat. 1991, Ch. 73, §§ 1200, 1201

Insurance Act (Public Employees)
See Public Employees Insurance Act

Insurance Act (School Busses)
Ga. Code Ann., 20-2-1090 et seq.
S.C. Code Ann. 1976, § 59-67-710 et seq.

Insurance Act (Service Warranty)
Okla. Stat. Ann., Title 36, § 6601 et seq.

Insurance Act (Standard Nonforfeiture)
See Standard Nonforfeiture Act (Insurance)

Insurance Act (Stipulated Premium Plan)
Mo. Rev. Stat., 377.199 et seq.

Insurance Act (Substituted Service)
Mo. Rev. Stat., 375.906, 375.911

Insurance Act (Suicide)
Mo. Rev. Stat., 376.620

Insurance Act (Surplus Lines)
See Surplus Line Insurance Act
Md. Ann. Code 1974, Art. IN, § 3-301 et seq.
Neb. Laws 1992, L.B. 1006, §§ 1 to 14

Insurance Act (Temporary Disability)
R.I. Gen. Laws 1956, 28-39-1 et seq.

Insurance Act (Title)
Conn. Gen. Stat. Ann., § 38a-400 et seq.
Ill. Rev. Stat. 1991, Ch. 73, § 1401 et seq.
Mo. Rev. Stat. 1978, 381.011 et seq.

Insurance Act (Titles)
See Title Insurance Act

Insurance Act (Unemployment)
See Unemployment Insurance Act

Insurance Act (Valuation)
See Valuation Act (Life Insurance)

Insurance Act (Veterans)
See Veterans' Insurance Act

Insurance Act (Vexatious Delay)
Mo. Rev. Stat., 375.420

Insurance Act of 1946
Aug. 1, 1946, Ch. 728, 60 Stat. 781 (See 38
  U.S. Code §§ 701 to 724, 781 to 784)

Insurance Act of 1951
April 25, 1951, Ch. 39, 65 Stat. 36 (See 38
  U.S. Code §§ 701 to 724, 781 to 784)
July 29, 1955, Ch. 431, 69 Stat. 395 (See 38
  U.S. Code § 724)

Insurance Adjusters Act
Cal. Insurance Code § 14000 et seq.
Fla. Stat. Ann., 626.851 et seq.
Me. Rev. Stat. Ann. 1964, Title 24-A, § 1851 et seq.
Nev. Rev. Stat. 1979 Reprint, 684A.010 et seq.
Wash. Rev. Code Ann., 48.17.010 et seq.

Insurance Adjusters Licensing Act
Okla. Stat. Ann., Title 36, § 6201 et seq.

Insurance Administrative Supervision Model Act
Minn. Stat. Ann., 60G.01 et seq.

Insurance Administrator Licensure Act
Pa. Purdon's Stat., Title 40, § 324.1 et seq.

Insurance Agent Act (Title)
Neb. Laws 1997, L.B. 53

Insurance Agents and Solicitors License Law
Fla. Stat. 1957, 627.71 et seq.

Insurance Agents Licensing Act
Fla. Stat. Ann., 626.011 et seq.
Okla. Stat. Ann., Title 36, § 1421 et seq.
Tenn. Code Ann., 56-6-131 et seq.
Tex. Insurance Code, Art. 21.07, 21.07A
Wash. Rev. Code Ann., 48.17.010 et seq.

Insurance and Annuity Act (Police)
S.C. Code Ann. 1962, § 61-302 et seq.

Insurance and Annuity Fund (Police Officers)
Fla. Laws 1941, Ch. 20916

Insurance and Health Care Reform Act
Fla. Stat. Ann., 20.42 et seq.

Insurance and Retirement Fund Act (Teachers')
N.D. Cent. Code, 15-39-01 et seq., 15-39.1-01 et seq.

Insurance and Safety Act
Ill. Rev. Stat. 1949, Ch. 48, § 138 et seq.

Insurance and Safety Inspection Act (Amusement Rides)
Tex. Insurance Code Art. 21.60

Insurance and Tort Reform Act
Fla. Laws 1977, Ch. 77-468
Fla. Stat. Ann., 57.105, 458.320, 459.0085, 624.460 et seq., 768.13

Insurance Anticompact Law
Wash. Rev. Code Ann., 48.30.020

Insurance as Security for Loans Act
Colo. Rev. Stat. 1963, 5-4-101 et seq.

Insurance Assistance Act
Iowa Code Ann., 507D.1 et seq.
Tenn. Code Ann., 68-1-115, 4-3-1404, 50-7-304

Insurance Assistance Plan
Mont. Code Ann. 1987, 33-8-201 et seq.
Mont. Laws 1986, Sp. Sess. Ch. 11, § 1 et seq.

Insurance Association Act
Neb. Rev. Stat. 1943, 44-2901 et seq.

Insurance Association Act (Health)
La. Rev. Stat. Ann., 22:1161 et seq.

Insurance Association Act (Windstorm)
Tex. Insurance Code, Art. 21.49 et seq.

Insurance Availability Act (Professional Liability)
Neb. Rev. Stat. 1943, 44-3001 et seq.

Insurance Availability Act (Property)
Md. Ann. Code 1974, Art. IN, § 25-401 et seq.

Insurance Benefits for College and University Employees Act
See Uniform Insurance Benefits Act for College and University Employees

Insurance Brokers Act
Wash. Rev. Code Ann., 48.17.010 et seq.

Insurance Cancellation Control Act (Automobile)
Me. Rev. Stat. Ann. 1964, Title 24-A, § 2911 et seq.

Insurance Cancellation Control Act (Property)
Me. Rev. Stat. Ann. 1964, Title 24-A, § 3048 et seq.

Insurance Claims for Excessive Charges Act
Ill. Rev. Stat. 1991, Ch. 73, § 1701 et seq.

Insurance Claims Resolution Act
Okla. Stat. Ann., Title 36, § 1251 et seq.

Insurance Code
Ala. Code 1975, § 27-1-1 et seq.
Alaska Stat. 1962, § 21.03.010 et seq.
Ariz. Rev. Stat. Ann., § 20-101 et seq.
Ark. Code Ann. 1987, 66-2001 et seq.
Cal. Statutes 1935, Ch. 145, p. 496
Colo. Rev. Stat., 10-1-101 et seq.
Conn. Gen. Stat. Ann., § 38-1 et seq.
Del. Code of 1974, Title 18, § 101 et seq.
Fla. Stat. Ann., 624.01 et seq.
Ga. Code Ann., 33-1-1 et seq.
Haw. Rev. Stat. Ann., § 431-1 et seq.
Ida. Code 1947, 41-101 et seq.
Ill. Rev. Stat. 1991, Ch. 73, § 613 et seq.
Kan. Stat. Ann., 40-101 et seq.
Ky. Rev. Stat. 1971, 304.1-010 et seq.
La. Rev. Stat. Ann., 22:1 et seq.
Mass. Gen. Laws Ann., 175:1 et seq.
Md. Ann. Code 1957, Art. 48A, § 1 et seq.
Me. Rev. Stat. Ann. 1964, Title 24-A, § 1 et seq.
Mich. Comp. Laws Ann., 500.100 et seq.
Minn. Stat. Ann., 60A.01 et seq.
Miss. Code Ann. 1972, § 83-1-1 et seq.
Mo. Rev. Stat., 374.010 et seq.
Mont. Code Ann., 33-1-101 et seq.
N.C. Gen. Stat. 1943, § 58-1-1 et seq.
N.D. Cent. Code, 26.1-01-01 et seq.
Neb. Rev. Stat. 1943, 44-101 et seq.
Nev. Rev. Stat. 1979 Reprint, 679A.010 et seq.
N.H. Rev. Stat. 1955, 400:1 et seq.
N.J. Stat. Ann., 17:1-1 et seq.
N.J. Stat. Ann., 17:46B-1 et seq.
N.M. Stat. Ann., 59A-1-1 et seq.
N.Y. Consol. Laws, Ch. 28
Ohio Rev. Code 1953, 3901.010 et seq.
Okla. Stat. Ann., Title 36, § 101 et seq.
Ore. Rev. Stat. 1953, 731.004 et seq.
P.R. Laws Ann. 1954, Title 26, § 101 et seq.
S.C. Code Ann. 1976, § 38-1-10 et seq.
S.D. Codified Laws 1967, 58-1-1 et seq.
Tenn. Code Ann., 56-1-101 et seq.
Tex. Insurance Code, 1.01 et seq.
Utah Code Ann. 1953, 31A-1-101 et seq.
Va. Code 1950, § 38.2-100 et seq.
Vt. Stat. Ann., Title 8, § 3301 et seq.
Wash. Rev. Code Ann., 48.01.010 et seq.
W. Va. Code 1966, § 33-1-1 et seq.
Wyo. Stat. Ann., § 26-1-101 et seq.

Insurance Code (Titles)
N.H. Rev. Stat. 1955, 416-A:1 et seq.

Insurance Code Commission Act
Ark. Acts 1957, No. 490

Insurance Code Hearings and Appeals Act
Ida. Code 1947, 41-231 et seq.

Insurance Companies Act
N.J. Stat. Ann., 17:20-1 to 17:20-5
Pa. Purdon's Stat., Title 40, § 341 et seq.
R.I. Gen. Laws 1956, 27-1-1 et seq.
Vt. Stat. Ann., Title 8, § 3301 et seq.

Insurance Companies Act (Foreign)
See Foreign Insurance Companies Act

Insurance Companies Anticompact Act
Mo. Rev. Stat. 1969, 416.290

Insurance Companies Deposits Act
Wash. Rev. Code Ann., 48.16.010 et seq.

Insurance Companies Fees Act
Wash. Rev. Code Ann., 48.14.010

Insurance Companies Insolvency and Liquidation Law
Cal. Insurance Code § 980 et seq.

Insurance Companies Investment Act
Ida. Code 1947, 41-701 et seq.
Mich. Comp. Laws Ann., 500.901 et seq.
Wash. Rev. Code Ann., 48.13.010 et seq.

Insurance Companies' Retaliatory Act
Ind. Code Ann., 27-1-20-12

Insurance Companies Tax Act
R.I. Gen. Laws 1956, 44-17-1 et seq.
Wash. Rev. Code Ann., 48.14.020 et seq.

Insurance Companies Unclaimed Funds Act
Pa. Purdon's Stat., Title 72, § 1301.29 et seq.

Insurance Company Act (Captive)
Colo. Rev. Stat., 10-6-101 et seq.

Insurance Company Assessment Act
Ind. Code Ann., 27-8-1-1 et seq.

Insurance Company Conversion, Reorganization and Merger Act (Mutual)
Miss. Code Ann. 1972, § 83-31-101 et seq.

Insurance Company Examination Law
Iowa Code Ann., 507.1 et seq.

Insurance Company Insider Trading and Proxy Regulation Act
Tex. Insurance Code, Art. 21.48

Insurance Company Insolvency Act
N.M. Stat. Ann., 59-6-31 et seq.

Insurance Company Investment Act
Cal. Insurance Code §§ 1211, 1212

Insurance Company Investments Act
Tex. Insurance Code, Art. 3.33

Insurance Company Loan Act
June 10, 1933, Ch. 55, 48 Stat. 119

Insurance Company Mutual-to-Stock Conversion Act
Pa. Purdon's Stat., Title 40, § 911-A et seq.

Insurance Company Plan of Exchange Act
Neb. Rev. Stat. 1943, 4-133.01 et seq.

Insurance Company Retaliatory Tax Act
Minn. Stat. 1965, 71.23

Insurance Consolidation Law
Iowa Code Ann., 521.1 et seq.

Insurance Consultant Law
Me. Rev. Stat. Ann. 1964, Title 24-A, § 1801 et seq.

Insurance Consultant Licensure Act
Mont. Code Ann., 33-17-501 et seq.

Insurance Consultation Services Exemption Act
Pa. Purdon's Stat., Title 40, § 1841 et seq.

Insurance Consumer Reform Act
Cal. Insurance Code §§ 675.5, 676, 676.2, 676.5, 677.2, 678.1

Insurance Contract Act
Ore. Rev. Stat., 742.016

Insurance Corporations Act
Wis. Stat. 1981, 610.00 et seq., 611.10 et seq.

Insurance Cost Containment Act
Ill. Rev. Stat. 1991, Ch. 73, § 1065.900 et seq.

Insurance Counselor Act
Mich. Comp. Laws 1970, 500.1468 et seq.

Insurance Counselor's Licensing Act
Tex. Insurance Code, Art. 21.07-2

Insurance Coverage Access Act (Health)
Wash. Rev. Code Ann., 48.41.010 et seq.

Insurance Coverage Act (Medical Food)
Pa. Purdon's Stat., Title 40, § 3901 et seq.

Insurance Coverage Act (Optional-Motor)
S.C. Code Ann. 1976, § 38-77-150 et seq.

Insurance Department Act
N.J. Stat. Ann., 17:1C-1 et seq.
Pa. Purdon's Stat., Title 40, § 1 et seq.

Insurance Deposit Act
N.M. Stat. Ann. 1953, 58-5-4

Insurance Direct Action Act
N.Y. Insurance Law 1984 (Consol. Laws Ch. 28) § 3420

Insurance Direct Action Statute
N.Y. Insurance Law (Consol. Laws Ch. 28) § 3420

Insurance Discrimination Law
Iowa Code Ann., 507B.4

Insurance Exemption Act
Wash. Rev. Code Ann., 48.18.400 et seq.

Insurance Fair Information Reporting Act
Minn. Stat. Ann., 72A.49 et seq.

Insurance Fair Practices Act
N.M. Stat. Ann. 1953, 58-9-9 et seq.

Insurance-Fictitious Groups Act
Okla. Stat. Ann., Title 36, § 6001.1

Insurance for Long Term Care Act
S.C. Code Ann. 1976, § 38-72-10 et seq.

Insurance Fraud Act
Iowa Code 1995, 507E.1 et seq.
Neb. Rev. Stat. 1943, 44-6601 et seq.
N.M. Stat. Ann., 59A-16C-1 to 59A-16C-16
Utah Code Ann. 1953, 31A-30-101 et seq.

Insurance Fraud and Motor Vehicle Theft Prevention Demonstration Program
N.Y. Executive Law 1951 (Consol. Laws Ch. 18) § 846i et seq.

Insurance Fraud and Reporting Immunity Act (Omnibus)
S.C. Code Ann. 1976, § 38-55-510 et seq.

Insurance Fraud and Theft Preparking Immunity Act (Motor Vehicle)
N.J. Stat. Ann., 17:23-8 et seq.

Insurance Fraud and Theft Reporting-Immunity Act (Motor Vehicles)
S.C. Code Ann. 1976, § 38-77-1110 et seq.

Insurance Fraud Protection Act
Mont. Code Ann., 33-1-1201 et seq.

Insurance Fraud Reporting Act (Workers' Compensation)
Cal. Insurance Code § 1877 et seq.

Insurance Fraud Reporting Immunity Act
N.M. Stat. Ann., 59A-16A-1 et seq.
Wash. Rev. Code Ann., 48.50.010 et seq.

Insurance Frauds Prevention Act
Cal. Insurance Code § 1871 et seq.
Del. Code of 1974, Title 18, § 2401 et seq.
N.J. Stat. Ann., 17:33A-1 et seq.
N.Y. Criminal Procedure Laws (Consol. Laws Ch. 11A) § 2.10
N.Y. Executive Law 1951 (Consol. Laws Ch. 18) § 835
N.Y. Insurance Law 1984 (Consol. Laws Ch. 28) § 401 et seq.
N.Y. Penal Law 1965 (Consol. Laws Ch. 40) § 176.00 et seq.
Pa. Purdon's Stat., Title 40, § 3501-101 et seq.

Insurance Fund Act
Mich. Comp. Laws Ann., 500.2500 et seq.
Okla. Stat. Ann., Title 85, § 131 et seq.
Pa. Purdon's Stat., Title 72, § 3731 et seq.

Insurance Fund Act (Major Medical)
Colo. Rev. Stat., 8-46-201 et seq., 8-66-101 et seq.

Insurance Fund Act (Worker's Compensation)
Tenn. Code Ann., 50-6-601 et seq.

Insurance Gross Receipts Tax Act
Tex. Rev. Civ. Stat. 1925, Art. 4769a

Insurance Guarantee Association Act (Life and Health)
Cal. Insurance Code § 1067 et seq.

Insurance Guaranty Act (Casualty and Property)
N.M. Stat. Ann., 59A-43-1 et seq.

Insurance Guaranty Act (Life)
N.M. Stat. Ann., 59A-42-1 et seq.

Insurance Guaranty Act (Property and Casualty)
See Property and Casualty Insurance Guaranty Act

Insurance Guaranty Association Act
Ala. Code 1975, § 27-42-1 et seq.
Alaska Stat. 1962, § 21.80.010 et seq.
Ariz. Rev. Stat. Ann., § 20-661 et seq.
Colo. Rev. Stat., 10-4-501 et seq.
Conn. Gen. Stat. 1983, § 38-273 et seq.
D.C. Code Ann., § 35-1901 et seq.
Del. Code of 1974, Title 18, § 4201 et seq.
Fla. Stat. Ann., 631.50 et seq.
Haw. Rev. Stat. Ann., §§ 431:16-101 et seq., 431D-1 et seq.
Ida. Code 1947, 41-3601 et seq.
Ind. Code Ann., 27-6-8-1 et seq.
Iowa Code Ann., 515B.1 et seq.
Kan. Stat. Ann., 40-2901 et seq.
Ky. Rev. Stat. 1971, 304.36-010 et seq.
La. Rev. Stat. Ann., 22:1375 et seq.
La. Rev. Stat. Ann., 22:5061 et seq.
Md. Ann. Code 1957, Art. 48A, § 504 et seq.
Me. Rev. Stat. Ann. 1964, Title 24-A, § 4601 et seq.
Minn. Stat. Ann., 60C.01 et seq.
Miss. Code Ann. 1972, § 83-23-101 et seq.
Mont. Code Ann., 33-10-1010 et seq.
N.C. Gen. Stat. 1943, § 58-155.41 et seq.
N.D. Cent. Code, 26.1-38.1-01 et seq.
Neb. Rev. Stat. 1943, 44-2401 et seq.
Nev. Rev. Stat. 1979 Reprint, 687A.010 et seq.
N.H. Rev. Stat. 1955, 404-B:1 et seq.
Okla. Stat. Ann., Title 36, § 2001 et seq.
Vt. Stat. Ann. Title 8, 4151 et seq.
Wash. Rev. Code Ann., 48.50.010 et seq.
W. Va. Code 1966, § 33-26-1 et seq.
Wyo. Stat. Ann., § 26-31-101 et seq.

Insurance Guaranty Association Act (Health and Life)
Conn. Gen. Stat. Ann., § 38a-858 et seq.
Iowa Code Ann., § 508C.1 et seq.
La. Rev. Stat. Ann., 22:1395.1 et seq.

Mo. Rev. Stat. 1978, 376.715 et seq.
N.C. Gen. Stat. 1943, § 58-62-2 et seq.
Nev. Rev. Stat. Ann., 686C.010 et seq.
N.H. Rev. Stat. 1955, 404-D:1 et seq.
Ohio Rev. Code 1953, 3956.01 et seq.
R.I. Gen. Laws 1956, 27-34.1-1 et seq.

Insurance Guaranty Association Act (Life, Accident and Sickness)
Va. Code 1950, § 38.2-1700 et seq.

Insurance Guaranty Association Act (Life, Accident, Health, and Hospital)
Tex. Insurance Code, Art. 21.28-D

Insurance Guaranty Association Act (Life and Disability)
Alaska Stat. 1962, § 21.79.010 et seq.
Ark. Code Ann. 1987, 23-96-101 et seq.
Haw. Rev. Stat. Ann., § 431:16-201 et seq.
Ore. Rev. Stat., 734.750
Pa. Purdon's Stat., Title 40, § 1701.101 et seq.
S.C. Code Ann. 1976, § 38-31-10 et seq.
S.D. Codified Laws 1967, 58-29A-1 et seq.
Tenn. Code Ann., 56-12-101 et seq.
Utah Code Ann. 1953, 31A-28-101 et seq.
Vt. Stat. Ann., Title 8, § 4151 et seq.
Wash. Rev. Code Ann., 48.32.010 et seq.
W. Va. Code 1966, § 33-26-1 et seq.
Wyo. Stat. Ann., § 26-31-101 et seq.

Insurance Guaranty Association Act (Life and Health)
Minn. Stat. 1994, 61B.18 to 61B.32
Mont. Code Ann., 33-10-201 et seq.

Insurance Guaranty Association Act (Property and Casualty)
Ohio Rev. Code 1953, 3955.01 et seq.
Vt. Stat. Ann., Title 8, § 3611 et seq.

Insurance Guaranty Association Act (Property-Liability)
Neb. Rev. Stat. 1943, 44-2401 et seq.
N.J. Stat. Ann., 17:30A-1 et seq.

Insurance Guaranty Association Act (Workers' Compensation)
Fla. Stat. Ann., 631.901 et seq.

Insurance Guaranty Association Bond Act
Tenn. Code Ann., 4-31-801 to 41-31-813

Insurance Guaranty Corporation Act (Life and Health)
Md. Ann. Code 1974, Art. IN, § 9-401 et seq.

Insurance Guaranty Fund Act (Surplus Lines)
N.J. Stat. Ann., 17:22-6.70 et seq.

Insurance Health Reform Act (Child)
Okla. Stat. Ann., Title 36, § 3201 et seq.

Insurance Holding Companies Registration Act
Del. Code of 1974, Title 18, § 5001 et seq.

Insurance Holding Company Act
Ga. Code Ann., 33-13-1 et seq.
Kan. Stat. Ann., 40-3301 et seq.
Mont. Code Ann. 1987, 33-2-1101 et seq.
Nev. Rev. Stat. 1979 Reprint, 692C.010 et seq.
N.M. Stat. Ann., 59A-37-1 et seq.
S.D. Codified Laws 1967, 58-5A-1 et seq., 58-5A-1 et seq.
W. Va. Code 1966, § 33-27-1 et seq.

Insurance Holding Company Regulatory Act
Ala. Code 1975, § 27-29-1 et seq., § 27-29-1 et seq.
Ark. Code Ann. 1987, 23-63-501 et seq.
N.J. Stat. Ann., 17:27A-1 et seq.
S.C. Code Ann. 1976, § 38-21-10 et seq.

Insurance Holding Company System Act
Neb. Rev. Stat. 1943, 44-2120 et seq.
Tenn. Public Acts 1986, Ch. 572

Insurance Holding Company System Regulatory Act
Cal. Insurance Code § 1215 et seq.
La. Rev. Stat. Ann., 22:1001 et seq.

Insurance Improvement and Medical Liability Act
Tex. Rev. Civ. Stat., Art. 4590i

Insurance Information and Privacy Protection Act
Cal. Insurance Code § 791 et seq.
Conn. Gen. Stat. Ann., § 38-500 et seq.
Mont. Code Ann., 33-19-101 et seq.
N.C. Gen. Stat. 1943, § 58-39-1 et seq.
Va. Code 1950, § 38.2-600 et seq.

Insurance Information Protection Act
Haw. Rev. Stat. Ann., § 431:17-101 et seq.

Insurance Insolvency Pool Act
Ga. Code Ann., 33-36-1 et seq.

Insurance Investments Act
Mich. Comp. Laws Ann., 500.901 et seq.

Insurance Law (Credit Life and Credit Disability)
Miss. Code Ann. 1972, § 83-53-1 et seq.

Insurance Law (Housing Mortgage)
Me. Rev. Stat. Ann. 1964, Title 30-A, § 4931 et seq.

Insurance Law (Surplus Lines)
Md. Ann. Code 1974, Art. IN, § 3-301 et seq.

Insurance Life Assessment Act
Iowa Code 1987, 510.1 et seq.

Insurance Limitation and Notification Act (Mortgage)
Ill. Comp. Stat. 1992, Ch. 765, § 930/1 et seq.

Insurance Liquidation Act
Tex. Insurance Code, Art. 21.28

Insurance Medical and Hospital Malpractice Joint Underwriting Associations Act
Me. Rev. Stat. Ann. 1964, Title 24, § 2401 et seq.

Insurance Model Act (Consumer Credit)
Del. Code of 1974, Title 18, § 3701 et seq.

Insurance Moratorium Act
See Insurance Regulation Act
Kan. Laws 1933, Ch. 203
Neb. Laws 1933, Ch. 78

Insurance Nondiscrimination Law (Auto)
Cal. Insurance Code § 11628

Insurance Nonforfeiture Act
See Nonforfeiture Act (Life Insurance)

Insurance Officers' Borrowing Law
Cal. Insurance Code § 1104 et seq.

Insurance on School Buses Act
S.C. Code Ann. 1976, § 59-67-710 et seq.

Insurance Opportunities for Employed Uninsured Oklahomans Act (Health)
Okla. Stat. Ann., Title 36, § 6501 et seq.

Insurance Payment to Registered Nurses Act
Pa. Purdon's Stat., Title 40, § 3021 et seq.

Insurance Penalty Law
La. Rev. Stat. Ann., 22:656 et seq.

Insurance Placement Act
D.C. Code Ann., § 35-1801 et seq.

Insurance Placement Facility Act (Urban Area)
Mass. Gen. Laws Ann., 175C:1 et seq.

Insurance Plain Language Act
Conn. Gen. Stat. Ann., § 38a-295 et seq.

Insurance Plan (Basic Health)
Ga. Code Ann., 33-51-1 et seq.

Insurance Plan (High Risk Health)
Ga. Code Ann., 33-44-1 et seq.

Insurance Plan (Safe Driver)
Mass. Gen. Laws Ann., 175:113D

Insurance Plan Act (Automobile)
Vt. Stat. Ann., Title 8, § 4241 et seq.

Insurance Plan Act (Health Care)
W. Va. Code 1966, § 5-16A-1 et seq.

Insurance Plan Act (Workers' Compensation)
Ark. Code 1987, 23-67-101 et seq.

Insurance Plans (Medicare Supplement)
Mass. Gen. Laws., 176K:1 et seq.

Insurance Policies and Contracts Act
Ohio Rev. Code 1953, 3902.01 et seq.

Insurance Policies Misrepresentation Law
Cal. Insurance Code § 780 et seq.

Insurance Policies Readability Act
Minn. Stat. Ann., 72C.01 et seq.

Insurance Policies Standard Provisions Act
Cal. Insurance Code § 10330 et seq.
Ore. Rev. Stat., 743.051

Insurance Policy Act (Standard)
Ore. Rev. Stat., 742.005

Insurance Policy Language Simplification Act
Ark. Stat. 1987, 23-80-201 et seq.
Me. Rev. Stat. Ann. 1964, Title 24-A, § 2438 et seq.
N.M. Stat. 1978, 59A-19-1 et seq.

Insurance Policy Language Simplification Act (Health)
Okla. Stat. Ann., Title 36, § 3641 et seq.

Insurance Policy Language Simplification Act (Life and Accident and Sickness)
W. Va. Code 1966, § 33-29-1 et seq.

Insurance Policy Readability Act (Life, Sickness and Accident)
Neb. Rev. Stat. 1943, 44-3401 et seq.

Insurance Pool Act (Health)
S.C. Code Ann. 1976, § 38-74-10 et seq.

Insurance Portability and Accountability Act (Health)
Ark. Code 1987, 23-86-301 et seq.

Insurance Powers Act (Bank and Trust Company)
Del. Laws, Vol. 67, Ch. 223

Insurance Premium Finance Company Act
Ga. Code Ann., 33-22-1 et seq.
Ill. Rev. Stat. 1991, Ch. 73, § 1065.60 et seq.
Continued

Kan. Stat. Ann., 40-2601 et seq.

Me. Rev. Stat. Ann. 1964, Title 9, § 4051 et seq.

Mich. Comp. Laws Ann., 500.1501 et seq.

Minn. Stat. Ann., 59A.01 et seq.

Mont. Code Ann., 33-14-101 et seq.

N.J. Stat. Ann., 17:16D-1 et seq.

Pa. Purdon's Stat., Title 40, § 3301 et seq.

Vt. Stat. Ann., Title 8, § 7001 et seq.

Wash. Rev. Code Ann., 48.56.010 et seq.

Insurance Premium Financing Act

N.M. Stat. Ann., 59A-45-1 et seq.

R.I. Gen. Laws 1956, 27-40-1 et seq.

Insurance Premium Service Act

S.C. Code Ann. 1976, § 38-39-10 et seq.

Insurance Premium Tax Act

Ariz. Rev. Stat. Ann., § 20-224 et seq.

Ind. Code Ann., 27-1-18-2

Neb. Rev. Stat. 1943, 77-907 et seq.

Wash. Rev. Code Ann., 48.14.020 et seq.

Insurance Premium Tax Reform Act

Ala. Code 1975, § 27-4A-1 et seq.

Insurance Premium Tax Retaliatory Law

Miss. Code Ann. 1972, § 27-15-121 et seq.

Insurance Pro Rata Act

Wis. Stat. Ann., 631.43

Insurance Producer and Consultant Continuing Education Act

Mont. Code Ann., 33-17-1201 to 33-17-1207

Insurance Producer Licensing Act

Neb. Laws 1984, L.B. 801, § 1 et seq.

N.J. Stat. Ann., 17:22A-1 et seq.

Insurance Producer Licensing Act (Single)

Colo. Rev. Stat., 10-2-101 et seq.

Insurance Protection Association Act (Life and Health)

Colo. Rev. Stat., 10-20-101 et seq.

Insurance-Public Health-Federal Portability and Accountability Act

N.Y. Laws 1997, Ch. 661

Insurance Rate and Form Act (Property and Casualty)

Neb. Rev. Stat. 1943, 44-5001 et seq.

Insurance Rate Initiative Measure

Cal. Insurance Code § 1861.01 et seq.

Insurance Rate Regulation Law

N.M. Stat. Ann., 59A-17-1 et seq.

Insurance Rate Review Procedures Act (Motor Vehicle)

Pa. Cons. Stat., Title 75, § 2001 et seq.

Insurance Rates Act

Ark. Code Ann. 1987, 23-67-101 et seq.

D.C. Code Ann., §§ 35-1601 et seq., 35-1701 et seq.

Ky. Acts 1912, Ch. 5

Wash. Rev. Code Ann., 48.19.010 et seq.

Insurance Rating Act

Okla. Stat. Ann., Title 36, § 900.1 et seq.

Insurance Rating Act (Other Than Life)

Mo. Rev. Stat., 379.316 et seq.

Insurance Rating Bureau Act

Ind. Code Ann., 27-1-22-1 et seq.

Insurance Rebate Act

Ark. Stat. 1947, 66-326 et seq.

N.C. Gen Stat. 1943, Miscellaneous Superceded Code Provisions, § 58-44.5

Wash. Rev. Code Ann., 48.30.140, 48.30.170

Insurance Reform Act (Automobile)

S.C. Acts 1989, p. 427, No. 148

Insurance Reform Act (Fair Automobile)

N.J. Stat. Ann., 17:33B-1 et seq.

Insurance Reform Act (Motor Vehicle)

Fla. Laws 1988, Ch. 370

Insurance Reform and Governmental Tort Claims Act

W. Va. Code 1966 § 29-12A-1 et seq.

Insurance Reform and Health Care Act

Fla. Stat. Ann., 20.42 et seq.

Insurance Regulation Act

March 9, 1945, Ch. 20, 59 Stat. 33, 15 U.S. Code § 1011 et seq.

Insurance Regulatory Act (McBride-Grunsky)

Cal. Insurance Code §§ 754, 1850 et seq.

Insurance Regulatory Reform Act

N.C. Gen. Stat. 1943, § 58-41-1 et seq.

Utah Laws 1981, Ch. 141

Insurance Rehabilitation and Liquidation Law

Me. Rev. Stat. Ann. 1964, Title 24-A, § 4351 et seq.

Insurance Reparations Act (Comprehensive Automobile)

N.Y. Insurance Law 1984 (Consol. Laws Ch. 28) § 5101 et seq.

Insurance Reparations Act (No-fault Automobile)

N.Y. Insurance Law 1984 (Consol. Laws Ch. 28) § 5101 et seq.

Insurance Requirements Fair Access Plan Act

Ga. Code Ann., 33-33-1 et seq.

Minn. Stat. Ann., 65A.31 et seq.

N.M. Stat. Ann., 59-10-1 et seq.

Insurance Sales Consumer Protection Act

Ark. Code 1987, 23-66-601 et seq.

Ida. Code 1947, 41-5701 et seq.

W. Va. Code 1966, § 33-11A-1 et seq.

Insurance Sales Law (Financial Institutions)

Ill. Comp. Stat. 1992, Ch. 215, §§ 5/1400 to 5/1416

Insurance Securities Act

Cal. Insurance Code § 820 et seq.

Tex. Rev. Civ. Stat., Art. 581-1 et seq.

Insurance Securities Exchange Act

Colo. Rev. Stat., 10-3-601 et seq.

Insurance Securities Sale Act

N.M. Stat. Ann., 59A-35-1 et seq.

Insurance Settlement Practices Act (Unfair Claims)

Neb. Rev. Stat. 1943, 44-1536 et seq.

Insurance Standard Nonforfeiture Law

Iowa Code Ann., 508.36

Minn. Stat. Ann., 61A.24

Insurance Standard Valuation Act

Iowa Code Ann., 508.36

Minn. Stat. Ann., 61A.25

Insurance State of Entry Act

Ga. Official Code Ann., 33-3A-1 et seq.

Insurance Tax Act

Pa. 1961 Pamph. Laws 33, No. 15

Insurance Tax Acts

Oct. 3, 1917, Ch. 63, 40 Stat. 315

Feb. 24, 1919, Ch. 18, 40 Stat. 1104

Nov. 23, 1921, Ch. 136, 42 Stat. 261

Insurance Tax Law (Nonadmitted)

Cal. Revenue and Taxation Code § 13201 et seq.

Insurance Trade Practices Act

Iowa Code Ann., 507B.1 et seq.

Vt. Stat. Ann., Title 8, § 4721 et seq.

Insurance Transactions Act (Disclosure of Material)

Neb. Rev. Stat. 1943, 44-6301 et seq.

Insurance Underwriting Association Act

Fla. Stat. Ann., 626.951 et seq.

Insurance Underwriting Association Act (Medical Liability)

Tex. Insurance Code, Art. 21.49-3

Insurance Underwriting Profits Act (Marine)
Pa. Purdon's Stat., Title 72, § 2281 et seq.

Insurance Unfair Trade Practices Act
Alaska Stat. 1962, Replaced Titles,
§ 21.10.865 et seq.
Fla. Stat. Ann., 626.951 et seq.
Ga. Code Ann., 33-6-1 et seq.
Ill. Rev. Stat. 1991, Ch. 73, § 1028 et seq.
Kan. Stat. Ann., 40-2401 et seq.
Ky. Rev. Stat. 1971, 304.12-010 et seq.
La. Rev. Stat. Ann., 22:1211 et seq.
Me. Rev. Stat. Ann. 1964, Title 24, § 2901 et seq.
Minn. Stat. Ann., 72A.17 et seq.
Pa. Purdon's Stat., Title 40, § 1171 et seq.
S.C. Code Ann. 1976, § 38-55-10 et seq.
S.D. Codified Laws 1967, 58-33-1 et seq.
Utah Code Ann. 1953, 31a-21-101 et seq.
Wash. Rev. Code Ann., 48.30.010 et seq.

Insurance Valuation Act
Me. Rev. Stat. Ann. 1964, Title 24-A, § 951 et seq.

Insurance Venue Act
Ky. Rev. Stat. 1971, 452.445

Insurance Warranty Association Act (General)
P.R. Laws Ann. 1954, Title 26, § 3801 et seq.

Insurance Warranty Association Act (Life, Disability and Health)
P.R. Laws Ann. 1954, Title 26, § 3901 et seq.

Insured Loans Housing Act
Okla. Stat. Ann., Title 6, § 2041 et seq.

Insurer Holding Company Act
Wash. Rev. Code Ann., 48.31B.900

Insurer Law (Broker Controlled)
N.M. Stat. Ann., 59A-12C-1 et seq.

Insurers (Unathorized) False Advertising Process Act
N.C. Gen. Stat. 1943, § 58-29-1 et seq.

Insurers Act
Ga. Code Ann., 33-17-1 et seq.

Insurers Act (Producer Controlled)
Miss. Code Ann. 1972, § 83-59-1 et seq.

Insurers Act (Reciprocal)
See Reciprocal Insurance Act

Insurers Act (Unauthorized)
See Unauthorized Insurers Act

Insurers Conservation, Rehabilitation and Liquidation Law
Nev. Rev. Stat. 1979 Reprint, 696B.010 et seq.
N.M. Stat. Ann., 59A-41-1 et seq.

Insurers Delay Penalty Act
Tenn. Code Ann., 56-7-105

Insurers Demutualization Act
Neb. Rev. Stat. 1943, 44-6101 et seq.

Insurers Examination act
Neb. Rev. Stat. 1943, 44-590 et seq.

Insurers False Advertising Process Act
See Unauthorized Insurers False Advertising Process Act

Insurers' Insolvency Fund Act
Mass. Gen. Laws Ann., 175D:1 et seq.
R.I. Gen. Laws 1956, 27-34-1 et seq.

Insurers' Insolvency Pool Act
Ga. Code Ann., 33-36-1 et seq.

Insurers Investment Act
Neb. Rev. Stat. 1943, 44-5101 et seq.

Insurers Law (Unauthorized)
Neb. Rev. Stat. 1943, 44-2001 to 44-2008
N.M. Stat. Ann., 59A-15-21 et seq.

Insurer's Liquidation Act
See also Uniform Insurer's Liquidation Act
Me. Rev. Stat. Ann. 1964, Title 24-A, § 4363 et seq.
Okla. Stat. Ann., Title 36, § 1901 et seq.

Insurers Liquidation, Rehabilitation and Supervision Act

Me. Rev. Stat. Ann. 1964, Title 24-A, § 4363 et seq.

Mo. Rev. Stat., 375.950 et seq.

Mont. Code Ann., 33-2-1301 et seq.

Ore. Rev. Stat., 734.330 et seq.

S.C. Code Ann. 1976, § 38-27-100 et seq.

Wis. Stat. Ann., 645.01 et seq.

Insurers Process Act (Authorized)

N.C. Gen. Stat. 1943, § 58-16-35

Insurers Rehabilitation and Liquidation Act

Cal. Insurance Code § 1064.1 et seq.

Conn. Gen. Stat. 1983, § 38a-903 to 38a-961

Fla. Stat. Ann., 631.001 et seq.

Ga. Code Ann., 33-37-1 et seq.

Ky. Rev. Stat. 1971, 304.33-010 et seq.

Me. Rev. Stat. Ann. 1964, Title 24-A, § 4351 et seq.

Minn. Stat. Ann., 60B.01 et seq.

Miss. Code Ann. 1972, § 83-24-1 et seq.

N.H. Rev. Stat. 1955, 402-C:1 et seq.

R.I. Gen. Laws 1956, 27-14.3-1 et seq.

Wis. Stat. Ann., 645.01 et seq.

Insurers Rehabilitation and Liquidation Act (Life and Health)

N.J. Stat. Ann., 17B:32-31 et seq.

Insurers Risk-Based Capital Act

Ida. Code 1947, 41-5401 et seq.

Mont. Code Ann., 33-2-1901 et seq.

Neb. Rev. Stat. 1943, 44-6001 et seq.

Insurers' Supervision, Rehabilitation and Liquidation Act

Conn. Gen. Stat. Ann., § 38a-903 et seq.

Ida. Code 1947, 41-3301 et seq.

Iowa Code Ann., 507C.1 et seq.

Kan. Stat. Ann., 40-3605 et seq.

Mo. Rev. Stat., 375.1150 et seq.

Mont. Code Ann., 33-2-1301 et seq.

Neb. Rev. Stat. 1943, 44-4801 et seq.

S.C. Code Ann. 1976, § 38-27-10 et seq.

Insurers' Tax Act

N.J. Stat. Ann., 54:18A-1 et seq.

Insurrection Act

Ga. Code Ann., 16-11-2, 16-11-3

Insurrection and Sedition Law

N.J. Stat. Ann., 2A:148-12 et seq.

Insurrection Ended Proclamation

April 2, 1866, No. 1, 14 Stat. 811

Intangible Property Tax Act

Ariz. Laws 1933, 1st Sp. Sess., Ch. 16

Fla. Stat. Ann., 199.012 et seq.

Ga. Code Ann., 48-20-60 et seq., 48-6-60 et seq.

Ind. Code Ann., 6-5.1-1-1 et seq.

Kan. Stat. Ann., 79-3109b et seq.

Mich. Comp. Laws Ann., 205.131 et seq.

Mo. Rev. Stat., 146.040 et seq.

Neb. Rev. Stat. 1943, 77-701 et seq.

Ohio Rev. Code 1953, 5725.01 et seq.

Okla. Stat. 1961, Title 68, §§ 1501 et seq., 2501 et seq.

Okla. Stat. 1961, Title 68, § 1501 et seq.

Ore. Code 1930, § 69-1401 et seq.

Tex. Rev. Civ. Stat. 1925, Art. 7098 et seq.

Intangible Tax Law

Ore. Code 1930, 69-1401 to 69-1417

Intangibles Classification Tax Act

Ga. Code Ann., 48-6-20 et seq.

Intangibles Income Tax Act

Ore. Laws 1931, Ch. 335

Integral Development and Regulation of Artisanry Act

P.R. Laws Ann. 1954, Title 18, § 1205 et seq.

Integrated Bar Act

Ala. Code 1975, § 34-3-40 et seq.

Alaska Stat. 1962, § 08.08.010 et seq.

Ida. Code 1947, 3-401 et seq.

Ky. Supreme Court Rules, Rule 3.010 et seq.

Mich. Comp. Laws Ann., 600.901 et seq.

Miss. Code Ann. 1972, § 73-3-101 et seq.

N.D. Cent. Code, 27-12-01 et seq.

Continued

Tex. Gov. Code, § 81.001 et seq.
Wash. Rev. Code Ann., 2.48.010 et seq.

Integrated Financing District Act
Cal. Government Code § 53175 et seq.

Integrated Health Care System Act
Tex. Health and Safety Code, § 281.0517

Integrated Least-Cost Resource Planning and Acquisition Act
Mont. Code Ann., 69-3-1201 et seq.

Integrated Living Arrangements Licensure and Certification Act (Community)
Ill. Comp. Stat. 1992, Ch. 210, § 135/1 et seq.

Integrated Local Planning Act
Cal. Government Code § 65420 et seq.

Integrated Pest and Pesticide Management Safety Program Act (Model School)
Mont. Code Ann., 80-8-401 et seq.

Integrated Service Network Act
Minn. Stat. 1994, 62N.01 to 62N.24

Integrated Solid Waste Management Act
Neb. Laws 1992, L.B. 1257, §§ 1 to 43

Integrated Waste Management Act
Cal. Public Resources Code § 40050 et seq.
Mont. Laws 1991, Ch. 222, § 1 et seq.

Integrated Waste Management Fee Law
Cal. Revenue and Taxation Code § 45001 et seq.

Integration Act (Social Security)
N.J. Stat. Ann., 43:15A-1 et seq.

Integration Act (Voluntary Pupil)
Cal. Education Code 1976, §§ 42248, 42249

Integration Development Program (Academic and Vocational)
Wash. Rev. Code Ann., 28A.630.880

Integration Finance Act (Long Term Care)
N.Y. Laws 1997, Ch. 659

Integrity Act (Law Enforcement)
Ga. Official Code Ann., 35-10-1 et seq.

Intelligence and Intelligence-Related Activities Authorization Act for Fiscal Year 1979
Sept. 17, 1978, P.L. 95-370, 8 U.S. Code § 1182 nt.

Intelligence and Intelligence-Related Activities Authorization Act for Fiscal Year 1980
Nov. 2, 1979, P.L. 96-100, 5 U.S. Code § 5924

Intelligence Authorization Act, Fiscal Year 1983
Dec. 2, 1987, P.L. 100-178, 10 U.S. Code §§ 1590, 1601, 1604, 1606, 1607; 22 U.S. Code § 254c-2; 50 U.S. Code §§ 403 nt., 403n

Intelligence Authorization Act, Fiscal Year 1984
Oct. 27, 1986, P.L. 99-569, 50 U.S. Code § 403e-1

Intelligence Authorization Act, Fiscal Year 1986
Dec. 4, 1985, P.L. 99-169, 5 U.S. Code §§ 9101, 9101 nt., 8 U.S. Code § 1427; 50 U.S. Code §§ 414, 414 nt.
Oct. 27, 1986, P.L. 99-569, 5 U.S. Code § 9101 nt.

Intelligence Authorization Act, Fiscal Year 1987
Oct. 27, 1986, P.L. 99-569, 100 Stat. 3190
Dec. 17, 1993, P.L. 103-199, 22 U.S. Code § 287 nt.

Intelligence Authorization Act, Fiscal Year 1989
Nov. 30, 1989, P.L. 101-193, 103 Stat. 1710

Intelligence Authorization Act, Fiscal Year 1990
Nov. 30, 1989, P.L. 101-193, 103 Stat. 1701
Dec. 3, 1993, P.L. 103-178. 50 U.S. Code § 403r-1
Dec. 17, 1993, P.L. 103-199, 107 Stat. 2325
Sept. 30, 1996, P.L. 104-208, 8 U.S. Code § 1430 nt.

Nov. 18, 1997, P.L. 105-85, 8 U.S. Code
§ 1430 nt.

**Intelligence Authorization Act, Fiscal Year
1991**

Aug. 14, 1991, P.L. 102-88, 105 Stat. 429

**Intelligence Authorization Act, Fiscal Year
1992**

Dec. 4, 1991, P.L. 102-183, 105 Stat. 1260

Oct. 21, 1998, P.L. 105-277, 50 U.S. Code
§ 1903

**Intelligence Authorization Act for Fiscal
Year 1988**

Dec. 17, 1993, P.L. 103-199, 22 U.S. Code
§ 254c-2

Oct. 14, 1994, P.L. 103-359, 22 U.S. Code
§ 5072a

**Intelligence Authorization Act for Fiscal
Year 1993**

Oct. 24, 1992, P.L. 102-496, 106 Stat. 3180

**Intelligence Authorization Act for Fiscal
Year 1994**

Dec. 3, 1993, P.L. 103-178, 107 Stat. 2024

**Intelligence Authorization Act for Fiscal
Year 1995**

Oct. 14, 1994, P.L. 103-359, 108 Stat. 3423

**Intelligence Authorization Act for Fiscal
Year 1996**

Jan. 6, 1996, P.L. 104-93, 109 Stat. 961

**Intelligence Authorization Act for Fiscal
Year 1997**

Oct. 11, 1996, P.L. 104-293, 110 Stat. 3461

**Intelligence Authorization Act for Fiscal
Year 1998**

Nov. 20, 1997, P.L. 105-107, 111 Stat. 2248

**Intelligence Authorization Act for Fiscal
Year 1999**

Oct. 20, 1998, P.L. 105-272, 112 Stat. 2396

**Intelligence Community Whistleblower
Protection Act of 1998**

Oct. 20, 1998, P.L. 105-272, 5 U.S. Code
Appx. § 1 nt.

Intelligence Identities Protection Act of 1982

June 23, 1982, P.L. 97-200, 50 U.S. Code
§§ 421 et seq.

Intelligence Organization Act of 1992

Oct. 24, 1992, P.L. 102-496, 50 U.S. Code
§ 401 nt.

**Intelligence Renewal and Reform Act of
1996**

Oct. 11, 1996, P.L. 104-293, Title VIII, 50
U.S. Code § 401 nt.

**Intelligent Transportation Systems Act of
1991**

Dec. 18, 1991, P.L. 102-240, 23 U.S. Code
§ 307 nt.

**Intelligent Transportation Systems Act of
1998**

June 9, 1998, P.L. 105-178, Title VI, Subtitle
C, 23 U.S. Code § 502 nt.

Inter-American Coffee Agreement Act

April 11, 1941, Ch. 59, 55 Stat. 133, 19 U.S.
Code §§ 1355 and nt., 1356

**Inter-American Cultural and Trade Center
Act**

Fla. Stat. 1973, 554.01 et seq.

Inter-American Development Bank Act

Aug. 7, 1959, P.L. 86-147, 73 Stat. 299, 12
U.S. Code § 24; 22 U.S. Code §§ 283 to
283i

Jan. 22, 1964, P.L. 88-259, 78 Stat. 3, 22 U.S.
Code § 283j

March 24, 1965, P.L. 89-6, 79 Stat. 23, 22
U.S. Code § 283l

Sept. 22, 1967, P.L. 90-88, 81 Stat. 226, 22
U.S. Code §§ 283j-1, 283l, 283m

June 4, 1968, P.L. 90-325, 82 Stat. 168, 22
U.S. Code § 238n

Dec. 30, 1970, P.L. 91-599, 84 Stat. 1658, 22
U.S. Code §§ 283a, 283o

March 10, 1972, P.L. 92-246, 86 Stat. 59, 22
U.S. Code §§ 283p to 283s

Oct. 3, 1977, P.L. 95-118, 22 U.S. Code
§§ 283y et seq.

June 3, 1980, P.L. 96-259, 22 U.S. Code
§ 283z-1

Nov. 30, 1983, P.L. 98-181, 22 U.S. Code
§ 283z-3
Continued

175

Dec. 22, 1987, P.L. 100-202, 22 U.S. Code § 283z-4

Dec. 19, 1989, P.L. 101-240, 22 U.S. Code §§ 283b, 283i, 283z-5 to 283z-8

Oct. 6, 1992, P.L. 102-391, 22 U.S. Code § 283z-9

Aug. 23, 1994, P.L. 103-306, 22 U.S. Code § 283z-10

Oct. 19, 1996, P.L. 104-316, 22 U.S. Code § 283j-1

Inter-American Foundation Act

Dec. 20, 1969, P.L. 91-175, 22 U.S. Code § 290f

Feb. 16, 1990, P.L. 101-246, 22 U.S. Code § 290f

Inter-American Investment Corporation Act

Dec. 19, 1989, P.L. 101-240, 22 U.S. Code § 283cc

Inter-American Statistical Institute Act

Jan. 27, 1942, Ch. 22, 56 Stat. 20, 22 U.S. Code § 269d

July 2, 1945, Ch. 218, 59 Stat. 311, 22 U.S. Code § 269d

Inter Indemnity Contract Act

Mo. Laws 1911, p. 301

Inter Party Agreements Act

Nev. Rev. Stat. Ann. 102.010 et seq.

Interagency Board for Hearing Impaired/ Behavior Disordered Children Act

Ill. Rev. Stat. 1991, Ch. 23, § 6701 et seq.

Interagency Children's Services Act

Cal. Welfare and Institutions Code § 18986 et seq.

Interagency Cooperation Act

Cal. Government Code § 65420 et seq.

Tex. Government Code, § 771.001 et seq.

Interagency Coordinating Council Act

Ill. Rev. Stat. 1991, Ch. 127, § 3831 et seq.

Interagency Council on Autism and Pervasive Developmental Disorders Act

Tex. Human Resources Code, § 114.001 et seq.

Interagency Council on Hunger and Nutrition Act

S.C. Code Ann. 1976, § 44-85-10 et seq.

Interagency Merit System of Personnel Administration Act (Grant-Aided Agencies)

S.C. Code Ann. 1976, § 8-19-10 et seq.

Interagency Pesticide Committee Act

W. Va. Code 1966, § 19-12C-1 et seq.

Interagency Provision of Services for Children, Adolescents and Families Act

Kan. Laws 1992, Ch. 264

Interagency School Safety Demonstration Act

Cal. Education Code 1976, § 32260 et seq.

Interagency Wetland Policy Act

Ill. Rev. Stat. 1991, Ch. 96 1/2, § 9701-1 et seq.

Interception of Communications Act

Utah Code Ann. 1953, 77-23a-1 et seq.

Interchange of Government Employees Act

Iowa Code Ann., 28D.1 et seq.

Me. Rev. Stat. Ann. 1964, Title 5, § 3001 et seq.

N.C. Gen. Stat. 1943, § 126-50 et seq.

Interchangeable Jury Act

Tex. Code of Criminal Procedure, Art. 33.09

Tex. Gov. Code, § 62.016 et seq.

Tex. Rules of Civil Procedure 1984, Rule 223

Intercity and Commuter Transit Right-of-Way Preservation Act

Cal. Government Code §§ 67410, 67421, 67460 et seq.

Cal. Streets and Highways Code § 164.57

Intercity and Commuter Transit Right of Way Preservation Act
Cal. Government Code § 67410 et seq.

Intercity and Rural Surface Transportation Assistance Act
Pa. Purdon's Stat., Title 55, § 651 et seq.

Intercity Passenger Rail Act
Cal. Government Code §§ 14031.8, 14070 et seq.

Intercity Rail Passenger Network Act
Pa. Purdon's Stat., Title 55, § 671

Intercoastal Shipping Act
March 3, 1933, Ch. 199, 47 Stat. 1425, 46 U.S. Code §§ 843 to 848
Aug. 28, 1958, P.L. 85-810, 72 Stat. 977, 46 U.S. Code § 844
July 9, 1965, P.L. 89-71, 79 Stat. 213, 46 U.S. Code § 844
Aug. 29, 1972, P.L. 92-416, 86 Stat. 653, 46 U.S. Code § 844
Oct. 18, 1978, P.L. 95-475, 46 U.S. Code §§ 843 to 845a
Aug. 16, 1989, P.L. 101-92, 46 U.S. Code Appx. § 844
Dec. 29, 1995, P.L. 104-88, 46 U.S. Code Appx. §§ 843 et seq.

Intercourse Act (Indian Tribes)
See Indian Intercourse Act
June 30, 1834, Ch. 161, 4 Stat. 729

Intercourse Act (Insurrectionary States)
July 2, 1864, Ch. 225, 13 Stat. 375

Interest Act
Fla. Stat. Ann., 687.01 et seq.
Ill. Rev. Stat. 1991, Ch. 17, § 6400 et seq.
Iowa Code Ann., 535.2 et seq.
Md. Ann. Code 1974, Art. CL, § 12-101 et seq.
Me. Rev. Stat. Ann. 1964, Title 9B, § 431 et seq.
Mich. Comp. Laws Ann., 438.31 et seq.
Miss. Code Ann. 1972, § 75-17-1 et seq.
Mont. Code Ann., 31-1-104 et seq.
N.C. Gen Stat. 1943, § 24-1 et seq.
Neb. Rev. Stat. 1943, 45-101.02 et seq.

N.H. Rev. Stat. 1955, 336:1
P.R. Laws Ann. 1954, Title 31, § 4591 et seq.
R.I. Gen. Laws 1956, 6-26-1 et seq.
Tenn. Code Ann., 47-14-101 et seq.
Vt. Stat. Ann., Title 9, § 41a et seq.
Wash. Rev. Code Ann., 19.52.005 et seq.

Interest Act (Condemnation)
Mo. Rev. Stat. 1978, 523.045

Interest Act (Security Deposit)
Ill. Rev. Stat. 1991, Ch. 80, § 120 et seq.

Interest and Dividend Tax Compliance Act of 1983
Aug. 5, 1983, P.L. 98-67, Title I, 97 Stat. 369
D.C. Code 1973, § 28-3301 et seq.
Utah Code Ann. 1953, 15-1-1 et seq.

Interest and Usury Act
D.C. Code Ann., § 28-3301 et seq.
N.Y. General Obligations Law (Consol. Laws Ch. 24A) 5-501 et seq.
Utah Code Ann. 1953, 15-1-1 et seq.

Interest Equalization Tax Act
Sept. 2, 1964, P.L. 88-563, 78 Stat. 809, 26 U.S. Code §§ 263, 1232, 4911 to 4920, 4931, 6011, 6076, 6103, 6680, 6681, 7241

Interest Equalization Tax Extension Act of 1965
Oct. 9, 1965, P.L. 89-243, 79 Stat. 954, 26 U.S. Code §§ 263, 4911, 4912, 4914, 4916, 4917, 4919, 4920, 6011 nt., 6076 nt.
July 31, 1967, P.L. 90-59, 81 Stat. 147, 26 U.S. Code §§ 4917, 4931

Interest Equalization Tax Extension Act of 1967
July 31, 1967, P.L. 90-59, 81 Stat. 145, 26 U.S. Code §§ 4911, 4912, 4914 to 4920, 4931, 6011, 6076, 6681, 7241

Interest Equalization Tax Extension Act of 1969
Nov. 26, 1969, P.L. 91-128, 83 Stat. 261, 26 U.S. Code §§ 4182, 4911, 4912, 4914, 4915, 4919, 4920, 6011, 6680

Interest Equalization Tax Extension Act of 1971
April 1, 1971, P.L. 92-9, 85 Stat. 13, 26 U.S. Code §§ 861, 4911, 4912, 4914 to 4916, 4919 to 4921, 6651, 6680, 6681

Interest for Life Act (Qualifying Income)
Mass. Gen. Laws Ann., 65A:5, 65A:5A

Interest on Lawyers' Trust Accounts Act
Pa. Purdon's Stat., Title 62, § 4021 et seq.

Interest on Offers of Settlement
Ida. Code 1947, 12-301 et seq.

Interest on Real Estate Brokers' Escrow Accounts Act (IREBEA)
Miss. Code Ann. 1972, § 73-35-101 et seq.

Interest Ownership Act (Common)
Conn. Gen. Stat. Ann., § 47-200

Interest Payment Act (Political Subdivision Procurement)
Pa. Purdon's Stat., Title 72, § 1601-C et seq.

Interest Rate Control Amendment of 1982
Ark. Const. 1874 Art. 19 § 13

Interest Rate Extension Act of 1976
D.C. Code Ann., § 28-3307

Interest Rates Act
Mo. Rev. Stat., 408.015 et seq.

Interested Party Act
Cal. Code of Civil Procedure § 387

Interests Act (Disclaimer of Property)
Me. Rev. Stat. Ann. 1964, Title 18-A, § 2-801 et seq.

Interference Act (Public Officer)
Wash. Rev. Code Ann., 9A.72.010 et seq.

Interference Act (Telephone Line)
Ill. Rev. Stat. 1991, Ch. 134, §§ 15a, 15a.1

Interference with Election Prohibition Act
Ill. Rev. Stat 1991, Ch. 46, § 101 et seq.

Interference with Utility Services Act
Ill. Rev. Stat. 1991, Ch. 111 2/3, § 1500 et seq.

Intergenerational Child Care Act
Cal. Education Code 1976, § 8475 et seq.

Intergenerational Education Act
Cal. Education Code 1976, § 33470 et seq.

Intergovernmental Antirecession Assistance Act of 1977
May 23, 1977, P.L. 95-30, 42 U.S. Code §§ 6721 nt., 6722

Intergovernmental Contracts Law
Colo. Rev. Stat., 29-1-201 et seq.

Intergovernmental Cooperation Act
Ill. Rev. Stat. 1991, Ch. 127, § 741 et seq.
Mont. Code Ann., 10-3-201 et seq.
S.D. Comp. Laws 1967, 1-15-10.1 et seq., 2-9-25 et seq.
Tex. Government Code, § 741.001 et seq.
Wis. Stat. Ann., 66.30

Intergovernmental Cooperation Act of 1968
Oct. 16, 1968, P.L. 90-577, 82 Stat. 1098, 40 U.S. Code §§ 531 to 535; 42 U.S. Code §§ 4201, 4211 to 4214, 4221 to 4225, 4231 to 4233, 4241 to 4244

Intergovernmental Cooperation Authority Act for Cities of the First Class
Pa. Purdon's Stat., Title 53, § 12720.101 et seq.

Intergovernmental Cooperation in Education Act
S.D. Codified Laws 1967, 13-15-1 et seq.

Intergovernmental Coordination Zone Act
Del. Code of 1974, Title 9, § 2675 et seq.

Intergovernmental Data Communication Act
Neb. Rev. Stat. 1943, 81-2301 et seq.

Intergovernmental Drug Enforcement Act
Me. Rev. Stat. Ann. 1964, Title 25, § 2951 et seq.

Intergovernmental Drug Laws Enforcement Act

Ill. Rev. Stat. 1991, Ch. 56 1/2, § 1701 et seq.

Intergovernmental Law Enforcement Officer's In-Service Training Act

Ill. Rev. Stat. 1991, Ch. 85, § 561 et seq.

Intergovernmental Missing Child Recovery Act

Ill. Rev. Stat. 1991, Ch. 23 § 2251 et seq.

Intergovernmental Personnel Act of 1970

Jan. 5, 1971, P.L. 91-648, 5 U.S. Code §§ 1304, 3371 to 3376; 42 U.S. Code §§ 4701, 4702, 4711 to 4713, 4721 to 4728, 4741 to 4746, 4761 to 4772

Intergovernmental Risk Management Act

Neb. Rev. Stat. 1943, 44-4301 et seq.

Intergovernmental Welfare Management and Information Systems Act

Cal. Welfare and Institutions Code § 11025 et seq.

Interim Children's Services Act

Me. Rev. Stat. Ann. 1964, Title 22, § 3711 et seq.

Interim Control Law (Liquors and Wines)

N.Y. Laws 1933, Ex. Sess., Ch. 819

Interim Executive and Judicial Succession Act

See Emergency Interim Executive and Judicial Succession Act

Interim Executive Succession Act

See also Emergency Interim Executive Succession Act

Ida. Code 1947, 56-413-et seq.

Ill. Rev. Stat. 1991, Ch. 102, § 101 et seq.

Kan. Stat. Ann., 48-1301 et seq.

N.H. Rev. Stat. 1955, 108-A:1 et seq.

N.J. Stat. Ann., 52:14A-1 et seq.

S.D. Codified Laws 1967, 2-3-1 et seq.

Tex. Government Code, § 401.021 et seq.

Tex. Rev. Civ. Stat., Art. 5429o

Interim Federal Aviation Administration Authorization Act

March 31, 1999, P.L. 106-6, 113 Stat. 10, 49 U.S. Code § 40101 nt.

Interim Legislative District and Apportionment Act

N.J. Rev. Stat. 1937, 52:10B-1 et seq.

Interim Legislative Succession Act

See Emergency Interim Legislative Succession Act

Interim Local Succession Act (Emergency)

Mich. Comp. Laws Ann., 31.101 et seq.

Interim Succession Act (Emergency)

Utah Code Ann. 1953, 63-5b-101 et seq.

Interinsurance Act

Wis. Stat. 1971, 201.39

Interinsurance Exchange Law

Cal. Insurance Code § 1280 et seq.

Interior and Related Agencies Appropriations Act, 1987

July 11, 1987, P.L. 100-71, 101 Stat. 418

Interior Department Appropriation Act of 1938

Aug. 9, 1937, Ch. 570, 50 Stat. 564, 24 U.S. Code § 169

Interior Department Appropriation Act of 1939

May 9, 1938, Ch. 187, 52 Stat. 291, 24 U.S. Code § 169; 25 U.S. Code § 123b; 30 U.S. Code § 11

Interior Department Appropriation Act of 1940

May 10, 1939, Ch. 119, 53 Stat. 685, 16 U.S. Code § 14a; 24 U.S. Code § 169; 25 USC §§ 305c-1, 480, 481; 42 U.S. Code §§ 1406a, 1406b

Interior Department Appropriation Act of 1941

June 18, 1940, Ch. 395, 54 Stat. 406, 16 U.S. Code § 17j-1; 24 U.S. Code § 169; 25 U.S. Code § 481; 43 U.S. Code §§ 611, 617u; 50 U.S. Code § 80 nt.

Interior Department Appropriation Act of 1942

June 28, 1941, Ch. 259, 55 Stat. 303, 16 U.S. Code §§ 14c, 590i-2, 752 to 754; 22 U.S. Code § 277f; 25 U.S. Code §§ 470a, 481, 561, 562; 41 U.S. Code § 6a; 43 U.S. Code § 611

Interior Department Appropriation Act of 1943

July 2, 1942, Ch. 473, 56 Stat. 506, 16 U.S. Code §§ 590i-2, 752 to 754; 25 U.S. Code § 481; 43 U.S. Code § 611

Interior Department Appropriation Act of 1944

July 12, 1943, Ch. 219, 57 Stat. 451, 43 U.S. Code § 611

Interior Department Appropriation Act of 1945

June 28, 1944, Ch. 298, 58 Stat. 463, 16 U.S. Code § 669c nt.; 41 U.S. Code § 6a nt.; 43 U.S. Code § 611

Interior Department Appropriation Act of 1946

July 3, 1945, Ch. 262, 59 Stat. 322, 43 U.S. Code § 611; 48 U.S. Code § 1405w-1

Interior Department Appropriation Act of 1947

July 1, 1946, Ch. 529, 60 Stat. 348, 43 U.S. Code § 611
June 26, 1947, Ch. 153, 61 Stat. 183

Interior Department Appropriation Act of 1948

July 25, 1947, Ch. 337, 61 Stat. 460

Interior Department Appropriation Act of 1949

June 29, 1948, Ch. 754, 62 Stat. 1112

Interior Department Appropriation Act of 1950

Oct. 5, 1949, Ch. 680, 63 Stat. 765, 16 U.S. Code § 825s-1

Interior Department Appropriation Act of 1951

Sept. 6, 1950, Ch. 896, 64 Stat. 769, 43 U.S. Code §§ 50, 377a, 1467; 48 U.S. Code §§ 1401f, 1423l

Interior Department Appropriation Act of 1952

Aug. 31, 1951, Ch. 375, 65 Stat. 248, 16 U.S. Code §§ 825s-1, 825s-2, 833a nt.; 43 USC §§ 50, 377a, 380b, 1423l, 1434; 48 U.S. Code §§ 1401f, 1409 nt.

Interior Department Appropriation Act of 1953

July 9, 1952, Ch. 597, 66 Stat. 445, 16 U.S. Code § 832a; 43 U.S. Code §§ 50, 377a, 380b, 390a, 775; 48 U.S. Code §§ 1401f, 1409 nt., 1423l, 1434 to 1438
Nov. 10, 1998, P.L. 105-362, 43 U.S. Code § 390a nt.

Interior Department Appropriation Act of 1954

July 31, 1953, Ch. 298, 67 Stat. 261, 16 U.S. Code §§ 17b-1, 460c nt.; 43 USC §§ 50, 377a, 390a, 775; 48 U.S. Code §§ 1401f, 1409 nt., 1423l, 1434 to 1437, 1439
July 14, 1956, Ch. 598, 70 Stat. 543, 16 U.S. Code § 17b-1
Nov. 10, 1998, P.L. 105-362, 43 U.S. Code § 390a

Interior Department Appropriation Act, 1955

July 1, 1954, Ch. 446, 68 Stat. 361, 43 U.S. Code §§ 50, 377a, 775; 48 U.S. Code §§ 1401f, 1423l, 1434, 1435, 1436

Interior Department Appropriations, Fiscal Year 1988

Nov. 30, 1989, P.L. 101-194, 18 U.S. Code § 208 nt.

Interior Design Profession Title Act

Ill. Rev. Stat. 1991, Ch. 111, § 8201 et seq.

Interior Designers Act

N.M. Stat. Ann., 61-24C-1 et seq.

Interior Designers Act (Certified)

Md. Ann. Code 1974, Art. BO, § 8-101 et seq.

Interjurisdictional Fisheries Act of 1986

Nov. 14, 1986, P.L. 99-659, 16 U.S. Code § 4101 nt.

Nov. 28, 1990, P.L. 101-627, 16 U.S. Code §§ 4103, 4107

Oct. 6, 1992, P.L. 102-396, 16 U.S. Code § 4107

Dec. 20, 1993, P.L. 103-206, 16 U.S. Code § 4107

April 30, 1994, P.L. 103-238, 16 U.S. Code § 4107

April 26, 1996, P.L. 104-134, 16 U.S. Code § 4107

Oct. 11, 1996, P.L. 104-297, 16 U.S. Code § 4107

Interlocal Agreements Act

Conn. Gen. Stat. Ann., § 7-339a et seq.

Interlocal Assistance Act

Tex. Rev. Civ. Stat., Art. 999b

Interlocal Cooperation Act

Ala. Code 1958, App., § 1059(14-bbbb) et seq.

Ark. Code Ann. 1987, 25-20-101 et seq.

Ind. Code Ann., 18-5-1-1 et seq.

Kan. Stat. Ann., 12-2901 et seq.

Ky. Rev. Stat. 1971, 65.210 et seq.

Miss. Code Ann. 1972, § 17-13-1 et seq.

Mont. Code Ann., 7-11-101 et seq.

Neb. Rev. Stat. 1943, 13-801 et seq.

Nev. Rev. Stat. 1979 Reprint, 277.080 et seq.

Okla. Stat. Ann., Title 74, § 1001 et seq.

R.I. Gen. Laws 1956, 45-40.1-1 et seq.

Tenn. Code Ann., 12-9-101 et seq.

Tex. Government Code, § 791.002 et seq.

Tex. Rev. Civ. Stat., Art. 4413(32c)

Utah Code Ann. 1953, 11-13-1 et seq.

Wash. Rev. Code Ann., 39.34.010 et seq.

Interlocal Cooperation Act (Public Agencies)

Fla. Stat. Ann., 163.01

Interlocal Financing Authority Act

Utah Code Ann. 1953, 11-13-1 et seq.

Interlocal Services Act

N.J. Stat. Ann., 40:8A-1 et seq.

Interlocal Services Aid Act

N.J. Stat. Ann., 40:8B-1 et seq.

Interlocutory Appeals Act

Miss. Code Ann. 1972, § 11-51-7

Intermeddling Act (Decedents' Property)

Ind. Code Ann., 29-1-13-10

Intermediary Reinsurance Act

Ala. Acts 1993, No. 673

Cal. Insurance Code § 1781.1 et seq.

Colo. Rev. Stat., 10-2-901 et seq.

Conn. Public Acts 1992, No. 112, §§ 22 to 31

Del. Code of 1974, Title 18, § 1601 et seq.

Fla. Stat. Ann., 626.7492

Ky. Rev. Stat. 1971, 304.9-700c et seq.

Mass. Gen. Laws Ann., 175:177M to 175:177W

Miss. Code Ann. 1972, § 83-19-201 et seq.

Mo. Rev. Stat., 375.1110 et seq.

Okla. Stat. Ann., Title 36, § 5102 et seq.

S.C. Code Ann. 1976, 38-46-10 et seq.

Tenn. Code Ann., 56-6-801 et seq.

Wash. Laws 1993, Ch. 462, §§ 22 to 33

W. Va. Code 1966 § 33-38-1 et seq.

Wyo. Stat. Ann., § 26-47-101 et seq.

Intermediate Care Facilities Act for the Mentally Retarded

Tex. Health and Safety Code, § 252.001 et seq.

Intermediate Offender Act (Nonviolent)

Okla. Stat. Ann., Title 22, § 995 et seq.

Intermediate Punishment Act (County)

Pa. 1990 Pamph. Laws, No. 193

Intermediate Sanctions for Medicaid Certified Nursing Home Act
S.C. Code Ann. 1976, § 44-6-400 et seq.

Intermodal Authority Port District Act (Mid-America)
Ill. Comp. Stat. 1992, Ch. 70, § 1832/1 et seq.

Intermodal Corridor of Economic Significance Act
Cal. Streets and Highways Code §§ 2190, 2191

Intermodal Facilities Act (Regional)
Ark. Code 1987, 14-143-101 et seq.

Intermodal Safe Container Transportation Act of 1992
Oct. 28, 1992, P.L. 102-548, 49 U.S. Code § 501 nt.

Intermodal Safe Container Transportation Amendments Act of 1996
Oct. 11, 1996, P.L. 104-291, Title II, 49 U.S. Code § 5101 nt.

Intermodal Surface Transportation Efficiency Act
Oct. 11, 1996, P.L. 104-287, 49 U.S. Code § 301 nt.

Intermodal Surface Transportation Efficiency Act of 1991
Dec. 18, 1991, P.L. 102-240, 49 U.S. Code § 101 nt.
Aug. 6, 1992, P.L. 102-334, 106 Stat. 858
Oct. 6, 1992, P.L. 102-388, 23 U.S. Code §§ 127 nt.
Oct. 24, 1992, P.L. 102-508, 106 Stat. 3314
Oct. 31, 1992, P.L. 102-580, 106 Stat. 4823
July 5, 1994, P.L. 103-272, 49 U.S. Code Appx. § 2302 nt.
Sept. 30, 1994, P.L. 103-331, 108 Stat. 2494
Nov. 28, 1995, P.L. 104-59, 16 U.S. Code §§ 1261, 1262; 23 U.S. Code §§ 101 nt., 104 nt., 109 nt., 112 nt., 127 nt., 149 nt., 307 nt.
Dec. 21, 1995, P.L. 104-66, 23 U.S. Code § 101 nt.
Oct. 19, 1996, P.L. 104-316, 45 U.S. Code § 831 nt.
Dec. 1, 1997, P.L. 105-130, 23 U.S. Code §§ 101 nt., 307 nt., 410; 49 U.S. Code §§ 111, 5309, 5337, 5338

June 9, 1998, P.L. 105-178, 16 U.S. Code §§ 1261, 1262; 23 U.S. Code §§ 101 nt., 127 nt., 129 nt., 149 nt., 307 nt.
Nov. 10, 1998, P.L. 105-362, 23 U.S. Code §§ 104 nt., 202 nt.

Intermodal Transportation Authority Act (Coachella Valley)
Cal. Public Utilities Code § 141000 et seq.

Intermountain Fixed Guideway Authority Act
Colo. Rev. Stat., 32-16-101 et seq.

Intermunicipal Commuter Rail Districts Act
Tex. Rev. Civ. Stat., Art. 6550c-1 et seq.

Intern Training Act (Law Enforcement)
Ill. Comp. Stat. 1992, Ch. 50, § 708/1 et seq.

Internal Auditing Act
Ill. Rev. Stat. 1987, Ch. 127, § 136.1 et seq.
Tex. Government Code, § 2102.001 et seq.

Internal Auditing and Fiscal Control Act
Ill. Rev. Stat. 1991, Ch. 15, § 1001 et seq.

Internal Improvement Act
Fla. Stat. 1983, 253.01 et seq.
Ky. Acts 1834-35, Ch. 837
Pa. 1827-1828 Pamph. Laws 221, No. 98
Tenn. Code Ann., 29-16-101 et seq., 29-17-101 et seq., 65-6-109 et seq.

Internal Improvement District Act
Colo. Rev. Stat., 31-25-501 et seq.

Internal Industrial Development Act
Miss. Code Ann. 1972, § 57-11-31 et seq.

Internal Revenue Act
See Income Tax Acts And War Revenue Acts
Colo. Stat. Ann. 1935, Ch. 142
P.R. Acts 1925, No. 85

Internal Revenue Code of 1939
Feb. 10, 1939, Ch. 2, 53 Stat. 1
Aug. 10, 1939, Ch. 666, 53 Stat. 1381
June 11, 1940, Ch. 307, 54 Stat. 264
June 24, 1940, Ch. 416, 54 Stat. 512
June 24, 1940, Ch. 417, 54 Stat. 513

July 2, 1940, Ch. 510, 54 Stat. 715

Oct. 8, 1940, Ch. 757, 54 Stat. 974

Oct. 10, 1940, Ch. 842, 54 Stat. 1101

Oct. 15, 1940, Ch. 887, 54 Stat. 1178

Jan. 31, 1941, Ch. 3, 55 Stat. 4

March 7, 1941, Ch. 10, 55 Stat. 27

April 11, 1941, Ch. 64, 55 Stat. 135

May 7, 1941, Ch. 96, 55 Stat. 184

Sept. 20, 1941, Ch. 412, 55 Stat. 687

Oct. 30, 1941, Ch. 464, 55 Stat. 757

Dec. 26, 1941, Ch. 638, 55 Stat. 873

Jan. 24, 1942, Ch. 17, 56 Stat. 17

March 27, 1942, Ch. 200, 56 Stat. 187

April 8, 1942, Ch. 226, 56 Stat. 201

April 8, 1942, Ch. 227, 56 Stat. 209

April 20, 1942, Ch. 244, 56 Stat. 218

July 23, 1942, Ch. 521, 56 Stat. 703

Sept. 29, 1942, Ch. 569, 56 Stat. 762

Oct. 21, 1942, Ch. 619, 56 Stat. 798

Dec. 17, 1942, Ch. 740, 56 Stat. 1054

March 23, 1943, Ch. 20, 57 Stat. 42

March 24, 1943, Ch. 26, 57 Stat. 46

March 31, 1943, Ch. 31, 57 Stat. 56

June 9, 1943, Ch. 120, 57 Stat. 126

Oct. 26, 1943, Ch. 279, 57 Stat. 575

Oct. 28, 1943, Ch. 290, 57 Stat. 584

Nov. 4, 1943, Ch. 294, 57 Stat. 585

Dec. 17, 1943, Ch. 346, 57 Stat. 601

Dec. 22, 1943, Ch. 375, 57 Stat. 607

Feb. 25, 1944, Ch. 63, 58 Stat. 26

May 29, 1944, Ch. 210, 58 Stat. 231

June 9, 1944, Ch. 240, 58 Stat. 272

June 20, 1944, Ch. 266, 58 Stat. 284

June 30, 1944, Ch. 332, 58 Stat. 647

July 1, 1944, Ch. 377, 58 Stat. 721

Dec. 16, 1944, Ch. 600, 58 Stat. 812

Dec. 20, 1944, Ch. 616, 58 Stat. 830

Dec. 22, 1944, Ch. 672, 58 Stat. 912

March 24, 1945, Ch. 36, 59 Stat. 38

June 30, 1945, Ch. 211, 59 Stat. 295

July 31, 1945, Ch. 340, 59 Stat. 517

Aug. 11, 1945, Ch. 364, 59 Stat. 531

Aug. 11, 1945, Ch. 367, 59 Stat. 532

Oct. 23, 1945, Ch. 433, 59 Stat. 548

Nov. 5, 1945, Ch. 446, 59 Stat. 555

Nov. 8, 1945, Ch. 453, 59 Stat. 556

Dec. 29, 1945, Ch. 652, 59 Stat. 670

March 8, 1946, Ch. 81, 60 Stat. 38

April 30, 1946, Ch. 244, 60 Stat. 157

May 29, 1946, Ch. 278, 60 Stat. 229

June 24, 1946, Ch. 459, 60 Stat. 300

June 24, 1946, Ch. 469, 60 Stat. 306

July 27, 1946, Ch. 685, 60 Stat. 707

July 31, 1946, Ch. 704, 60 Stat. 716

July 31, 1946, Ch. 709, 60 Stat. 722

July 31, 1946, Ch. 717, 60 Stat. 749

Aug. 10, 1946, Ch. 951, 60 Stat. 978

Aug. 13, 1946, Ch. 957, 60 Stat. 1032

Feb. 1, 1947, Ch. 2, 61 Stat. 4

Feb. 26, 1947, Ch. 7, 61 Stat. 6

March 11, 1947, Ch. 17, 61 Stat. 12

June 25, 1947, Ch. 143, 61 Stat. 178

June 25, 1947, Ch. 144, 61 Stat. 179

July 14, 1947, Ch. 245, 61 Stat. 319

July 14, 1947, Ch. 246, 61 Stat. 320

July 14, 1947, Ch. 247, 61 Stat. 320

July 24, 1947, Ch. 309, 61 Stat. 416

Aug. 1, 1947, Ch. 430, 61 Stat. 714

Aug. 5, 1947, Ch. 496, 61 Stat. 778

Aug. 6, 1947, Ch. 510, 61 Stat. 793

Aug. 8, 1947, Ch. 515, 61 Stat. 918

Aug. 8, 1947, Ch. 518, 61 Stat. 921

Aug. 8, 1947, Ch. 519, 61 Stat. 934

April 2, 1948, Ch. 168, 62 Stat. 110

April 20, 1948, Ch. 222, 62 Stat. 195

May 4, 1948, Ch. 257, 62 Stat. 210

June 12, 1948, Ch. 459, 62 Stat. 387

June 14, 1948, Ch. 468, 62 Stat. 438

June 19, 1948, Ch. 537, 62 Stat. 504

June 25, 1948, Ch. 646, 62 Stat. 991

June 30, 1948, Ch. 770, 62 Stat. 1171

July 1, 1948, Ch. 789, 62 Stat. 1214

July 3, 1948, Ch. 829, 62 Stat. 1259

March 31, 1949, Ch. 46, 63 Stat. 30

May 24, 1949, Ch. 139, 63 Stat. 107

Aug. 17, 1949, Ch. 453, 63 Stat. 611

Aug. 23, 1949, Ch. 498, 63 Stat. 624

Aug. 27, 1949, Ch. 518, 63 Stat. 675

Oct. 25, 1949, Ch. 720, 63 Stat. 891

Feb. 21, 1950, Ch. 36, 64 Stat. 6

March 16, 1950, Ch. 61, 64 Stat. 20

Aug. 9, 1950, Ch. 657, 64 Stat. 428

Aug. 18, 1950, Ch. 755, 64 Stat. 464

Aug. 28, 1950, Ch. 809, 64 Stat. 524
Continued

Sept. 1, 1950, Ch. 836, 64 Stat. 576
Sept. 5, 1950, Ch. 851, 64 Stat. 592
Sept. 21, 1950, Ch. 974, 64 Stat. 898
Sept. 23, 1950, Ch. 994, 64 Stat. 906
Sept. 27, 1950, Ch. 1061, 64 Stat. 1075
Dec. 15, 1950, Ch. 1137, 64 Stat. 1112
Jan. 2, 1951, Ch. 1195, 64 Stat. 1136
Jan. 2, 1951, Ch. 1196, 64 Stat. 1136
Jan. 11, 1951, Ch. 1226, 64 Stat. 1244
Jan. 11, 1951, Ch. 1227, 64 Stat. 1244
Feb. 28, 1951, Ch. 2, 65 Stat. 3
March 26, 1951, Ch. 19, 65 Stat. 26
May 12, 1951, Ch. 56, 65 Stat. 40
June 28, 1951, Ch. 165, 65 Stat. 91
June 30, 1951, Ch. 195, 65 Stat. 91
July 3, 1951, Ch. 208, 65 Stat. 115
July 5, 1951, Ch. 209, 65 Stat. 115
July 11, 1951, Ch. 221, 65 Stat. 116
July 12, 1951, Ch. 223, 65 Stat. 119
July 23, 1951, Ch. 238, 65 Stat. 124
Aug. 24, 1951, Ch. 345, 65 Stat. 198
Sept. 1, 1951, Ch. 379, 65 Stat. 320
Sept. 14, 1951, Ch. 400, 65 Stat. 321
Oct. 10, 1951, Ch. 458, 65 Stat. 371
Oct. 10, 1951, Ch. 480, 65 Stat. 387
Oct. 20, 1951, Ch. 521, 65 Stat. 452
Oct. 31, 1951, Ch. 661, 65 Stat. 733
Nov. 2, 1951, Ch. 666, 65 Stat. 768
May 21, 1952, Ch. 319, 66 Stat. 86
May 21, 1952, Ch. 320, 66 Stat. 88
May 22, 1952, Ch. 322, 66 Stat. 89
May 23, 1952, Ch. 329, 66 Stat. 93
June 12, 1952, Ch. 420, 66 Stat. 136
June 18, 1952, Ch. 442, 66 Stat. 138
July 8, 1952, Ch. 588, 66 Stat. 442
July 8, 1952, Ch. 592, 66 Stat. 444
July 9, 1952, Ch. 598, 66 Stat. 467
July 14, 1952, Ch. 741, 66 Stat. 629
July 16, 1952, Ch. 892, 66 Stat. 735
July 17, 1952, Ch. 924, 66 Stat. 752
July 17, 1952, Ch. 942, 66 Stat. 766
July 21, 1952, Ch. 951, 66 Stat. 818
July 16, 1953, Ch. 202, 67 Stat. 175
Aug. 5, 1953, Ch. 329, 67 Stat. 386
Aug. 7, 1953, Ch. 346, 67 Stat. 471
Aug. 7, 1953, Ch. 352, 67 Stat. 482
Aug. 8, 1953, Ch. 392, 67 Stat. 500

Aug. 8, 1953, Ch. 394, 67 Stat. 505
Aug. 15, 1953, Ch. 508, 67 Stat. 591
Aug. 15, 1953, Ch. 512, 67 Stat. 615
March 31, 1954, Ch. 126, 68 Stat. 37
June 30, 1954, Ch. 424, 68 Stat. 330
July 22, 1954, Ch. 558, 68 Stat. 508
Aug. 5, 1954, Ch. 657, 68 Stat. 672
Aug. 16, 1954, Ch. 736, 68A Stat. 929
Aug. 16, 1954, Ch. 740, 68 Stat. 731
Aug. 31, 1954, Ch. 1147, 68 Stat. 1001
Sept. 1, 1954, Ch. 1206, 68 Stat. 1089
Sept. 1, 1954, Ch. 1212, 68 Stat. 1135
Aug. 9, 1955, Ch. 663, 69 Stat. 594
Aug. 9, 1955, Ch. 693, 69 Stat. 625
Aug. 11, 1955, Ch. 808, 69 Stat. 693
Aug. 12, 1955, Ch. 870, 69 Stat. 716
Jan. 28, 1956, Ch. 16, 70 Stat. 7
Jan. 28, 1956, Ch. 18, 70 Stat. 8
Feb. 15, 1956, Ch. 36, 70 Stat. 15
Feb. 20, 1956, Ch. 66, 70 Stat. 26
June 29, 1956, Ch. 464, 70 Stat. 404
July 16, 1956, Ch. 624, 70 Stat. 554
Aug. 1, 1956, Ch. 836, 70 Stat. 855
Aug. 1, 1956, Ch. 857, 70 Stat. 917
March 29, 1957, P.L. 85-12, 71 Stat. 10
Feb. 11, 1958, P.L. 85-318, 72 Stat. 4
Aug. 27, 1958, P.L. 85-785, 72 Stat. 938
Sept. 2, 1958, P.L. 85-866, 72 Stat. 1657

Internal Revenue Code of 1954

Aug. 16, 1954, Ch. 736, 68A Stat. 3, 26 U.S. Code §§ 1 to 8023
Aug. 31, 1954, Ch. 1147, 68 Stat. 1003, 26 U.S. Code §§ 4704, 4705, 4724, 4773
Aug. 31, 1954, Ch. 1164, 68 Stat. 1040, 26 U.S. Code §§ 3201, 3202, 3211, 3221, 3231
Sept. 1, 1954, Ch. 1206, 68 Stat. 1087, 26 U.S. Code §§ 176, 1401, 1402, 3101, 3102, 3111, 3121, 3122, 6413
Sept. 1, 1954, Ch. 1212, 68 Stat. 1130, 26 U.S. Code §§ 3303, 3305, 3306, 6152
Jan. 20, 1955, Ch. 1, 69 Stat. 3, 26 U.S. Code § 7237
March 2, 1955, Ch. 9, 69 Stat. 10, 26 U.S. Code § 7443
June 15, 1955, Ch. 143, 69 Stat. 134, 26 U.S. Code § 381
Aug. 9, 1955, Ch. 659, 69 Stat. 591, 26 U.S. Code § 37

Aug. 9, 1955, Ch. 666, 69 Stat. 605, 26 U.S. Code § 3402

Aug. 9, 1955, Ch. 677, 69 Stat. 613, 26 U.S. Code §§ 4216, 4217

Aug. 9, 1955, Ch. 681, 69 Stat. 616, 26 U.S. Code § 3401

Aug. 9, 1955, Ch. 693, 69 Stat. 626, 26 U.S. Code § 152

Aug. 11, 1955, Ch. 792, 69 Stat. 675, 26 U.S. Code § 4233

Aug. 11, 1955, Ch. 793, 69 Stat. 676, 26 U.S. Code §§ 4091, 4092, 6416

Aug. 11, 1955, Ch. 804, 69 Stat. 688, 26 U.S. Code §§ 1304, 1305

Aug. 11, 1955, Ch. 805, 69 Stat. 689, 26 U.S. Code §§ 534, 4063, 4112, 4113, 4141, 4218, 4220, 6416

Aug. 12, 1955, Ch. 865, 69 Stat. 709, 26 U.S. Code § 4061

Aug. 12, 1955, Ch. 870, 69 Stat. 717, 26 U.S. Code § 1342

Aug. 12, 1955, Ch. 871, 69 Stat. 717, 26 U.S. Code §§ 542, 1233

Jan. 28, 1956, Ch. 15, 70 Stat. 7, 26 U.S. Code § 381

Jan. 28, 1956, Ch. 17, 70 Stat. 8, 26 U.S. Code § 37

Jan. 28, 1956, Ch. 19, 70 Stat. 9, 26 U.S. Code § 4332

Feb. 20, 1956, Ch. 63, 70 Stat. 23, 26 U.S. Code §§ 2011, 2053

March 13, 1956, Ch. 83, 70 Stat. 36, 26 U.S. Code §§ 316, 501, 594, 801 to 805, 811 to 813, 816 to 818, 821, 822, 832, 841 to 843, 891, 1201, 1504, 4371

March 29, 1956, Ch. 115, 70 Stat. 66, 26 U.S. Code §§ 11, 821, 4041, 4061, 4081, 5001, 5022, 5041, 5051, 5063, 5134, 5701, 5707, 6412

April 2, 1956, Ch. 160, 70 Stat. 87, 26 U.S. Code §§ 4041, 4084, 6206, 6207, 6416, 6420, 6421, 6504, 6511, 6612, 6675, 7210, 7603, 7604, 7605

April 27, 1956, Ch. 214, 70 Stat. 118, 26 U.S. Code § 1237

May 9, 1956, Ch. 240, 70 Stat. 139, 26 U.S. Code §§ 1101 to 1103

May 29, 1956, Ch. 342, 70 Stat. 221, 26 U.S. Code §§ 4501, 4502, 4504, 6412, 6418

June 29, 1956, Ch. 462, 70 Stat. 387, 26 U.S. Code §§ 4041, 4061, 4071 to 4073, 4081, 4084, 4226, 4227, 4481 to 4484, 6206, 6302, 6412, 6416, 6421, 6422, 6504, 6511, 6612, 6675, 7210, 7603 to 7605

June 29, 1956, Ch. 463, 70 Stat. 402, 26 U.S. Code §§ 108, 357, 373, 374

June 29, 1956, Ch. 464, 70 Stat. 406, 26 U.S. Code §§ 177, 1016, 1033

July 11, 1956, Ch. 573, 70 Stat. 530, 26 U.S. Code §§ 852, 5217

July 16, 1956, Ch. 624, 70 Stat. 554, 26 U.S. Code § 4541 nt.

July 18, 1956, Ch. 627, 70 Stat. 563, 26 U.S. Code § 1441

July 18, 1956, Ch. 629, 70 Stat. 567, 26 U.S. Code §§ 4744, 4755, 4774, 7237, 7607, 7608

July 24, 1956, Ch. 696, 70 Stat. 633, 26 U.S. Code §§ 802, 811

July 25, 1956, Ch. 725, 70 Stat. 644, 26 U.S. Code §§ 4261, 4262 to 4264, 4291, 6421

Aug. 1, 1956, Ch. 836, 70 Stat. 824, 26 U.S. Code §§ 1401, 1402, 3101, 3102, 3111, 3113, 3121

Aug. 1, 1956, Ch. 837, 70 Stat. 878, 26 U.S. Code §§ 121, 3121, 3122, 6051

Aug. 1, 1956, Ch. 852, 70 Stat. 909, 26 U.S. Code §§ 4705, 4716, 4735, 4774

Aug. 6, 1956, Ch. 1019, 70 Stat. 1074, 26 U.S. Code § 4231

Aug. 6, 1956, Ch. 1020, 70 Stat. 1075, 26 U.S. Code §§ 2055, 6503

Aug. 7, 1956, Ch. 1024, 70 Stat. 1077, 26 U.S. Code § 4262

Aug. 7, 1956, Ch. 1031, 70 Stat. 1117, 26 U.S. Code § 170

March 29, 1957, P.L. 85-12, 71 Stat. 9, 26 U.S. Code §§ 11, 821, 4061, 5001, 5022, 5041, 5051, 5063, 5134, 5701, 5707, 6412

June 17, 1957, P.L. 85-86, 71 Stat. 160, 26 U.S. Code § 121

June 29, 1957, P.L. 85-74, 71 Stat. 243, 26 U.S. Code § 4263

Aug. 14, 1957, P.L. 85-141, 71 Stat. 365, 26 U.S. Code § 1441

Aug. 26, 1957, P.L. 85-165, 71 Stat. 413, 26 U.S. Code §§ 168, 1305, 1306

Aug. 30, 1957, P.L. 85-235, 71 Stat. 516, 26 U.S. Code § 4511 nt.

Aug. 30, 1957, P.L. 85-239, 71 Stat. 521, 26 U.S. Code § 1402

Feb. 11, 1958, P.L. 85-320, 72 Stat. 4, 26 U.S. Code §§ 421, 1014

Feb. 11, 1958, P.L. 85-321, 72 Stat. 5, 26 U.S. Code §§ 7201, 7215, 7501, 7512

Feb. 11, 1958, P.L. 85-323, 72 Stat. 9, 26 U.S. Code §§ 6411, 6423

Continued

March 17, 1958, P.L. 85-345, 72 Stat. 36, 26 U.S. Code §§ 802, 811

April 7, 1958, P.L. 85-367, 72 Stat. 80, 26 U.S. Code § 512

April 16, 1958, P.L. 85-380, 72 Stat. 88, 26 U.S. Code § 4233

June 11, 1958, P.L. 85-453, 72 Stat. 184, 26 U.S. Code § 4541 nt.

June 30, 1958, P.L. 85-475, 72 Stat. 259, 26 U.S. Code §§ 11, 821, 4061, 4292, 5001, 5022, 5041, 5051, 5063, 5134, 5701, 5707, 6412, 6415, 6416, 7012, 7272

July 11, 1958, P.L. 85-517, 72 Stat. 357, 26 U.S. Code § 5217

Aug. 27, 1958, P.L. 85-785, 72 Stat. 938, 26 U.S. Code § 3121 nt.

Aug. 28, 1958, P.L. 85-840, 72 Stat. 1041, 26 U.S. Code §§ 1401, 1402, 3101, 3111, 3121, 3122, 6334, 6413

Sept. 2, 1958, P.L. 85-857, 72 Stat. 1266, 26 U.S. Code § 121

Sept. 2, 1958, P.L. 85-859, 72 Stat. 1275, 26 U.S. Code §§ 4001, 4003, 4031, 4041, 4053, 4057, 4058, 4121, 4141 to 4143, 4192, 4216 to 4218, 4221 to 4225 and others

Sept. 2, 1958, P.L. 85-866, 72 Stat. 1606, 26 U.S. Code §§ 35, 75, 101, 120 nt., 152, 162, 164 to 168, 170 to 172, 178, 179 and others

Sept. 2, 1958, P.L. 85-881, 72 Stat. 1704, 26 U.S. Code §§ 4818, 7303

May 19, 1959, P.L. 86-28, 73 Stat. 28, 26 U.S. Code §§ 3201, 3202, 3211, 3221

May 29, 1959, P.L. 86-37, 73 Stat. 64, 26 U.S. Code § 4511 nt.

June 25, 1959, P.L. 86-69, 73 Stat. 112, 26 U.S. Code §§ 34, 116, 381, 801, 802, 804 to 806, 809 to 812, 815, 817 to 820, 841, 842, 891, 1016, 1201, 1232, 1504, 4371, 6072 nt., 6501, 6655 nt.

June 25, 1959, P.L. 86-70, 73 Stat. 146, 26 U.S. Code §§ 2202, 3121, 3306, 4221, 4233, 4262, 4502, 4774, 7621, 7653, 7701

June 30, 1959, P.L. 86-75, 73 Stat. 157, 26 U.S. Code §§ 11, 821, 4061, 4251, 4261, 5001, 5022, 5041, 5051, 5063, 5701, 5707, 6412

Aug. 7, 1959, P.L. 86-141, 73 Stat. 288, 26 U.S. Code § 2038

Aug. 18, 1959, P.L. 86-168, 73 Stat. 389, 26 U.S. Code § 3121

Aug. 21, 1959, P.L. 86-175, 73 Stat. 396, 26 U.S. Code §§ 2011, 2014, 2053

Sept. 16, 1959, P.L. 86-280, 73 Stat. 563, 26 U.S. Code § 6511

Sept. 21, 1959, P.L. 86-319, 73 Stat. 590

Sept. 21, 1959, P.L. 86-344, 73 Stat. 617, 26 U.S. Code §§ 4001, 4057, 4221, 4233, 4241, 4243, 4253, 4294, 4321, 4323, 4461

Sept. 22, 1959, P.L. 86-346, 73 Stat. 621, 26 U.S. Code §§ 454, 1031, 1037

Sept. 22, 1959, P.L. 86-368, 73 Stat. 647, 26 U.S. Code §§ 7452, 7801, 8023

Sept. 23, 1959, P.L. 86-376, 73 Stat. 699, 26 U.S. Code §§ 152, 542, 1371, 1374, 1504

April 8, 1960, P.L. 86-413, 74 Stat. 31, 26 U.S. Code § 4021

April 8, 1960, P.L. 86-416, 74 Stat. 36, 26 U.S. Code § 4301

April 8, 1960, P.L. 86-418, 74 Stat. 38, 26 U.S. Code §§ 4218, 4221, 4223, 6416

April 8, 1960, P.L. 86-422, 74 Stat. 41, 26 U.S. Code § 4231

April 22, 1960, P.L. 86-428, 74 Stat. 54, 26 U.S. Code § 501

April 22, 1960, P.L. 86-429, 74 Stat. 57, 26 U.S. Code §§ 4702, 4731

April 22, 1960, P.L. 86-435, 74 Stat. 77, 26 U.S. Code §§ 543, 544, 553

April 22, 1960, P.L. 86-437, 74 Stat. 79, 26 U.S. Code §§ 402, 871

April 22, 1960, P.L. 86-440, 74 Stat. 80, 26 U.S. Code § 4071

May 14, 1960, P.L. 86-470, 74 Stat. 132, 26 U.S. Code §§ 213, 6659

June 1, 1960, P.L. 86-478, 74 Stat. 149, 26 U.S. Code §§ 5685, 5801, 5811, 5848

June 8, 1960, P.L. 86-496, 74 Stat. 164, 26 U.S. Code § 108

June 30, 1960, P.L. 86-564, 74 Stat. 290, 26 U.S. Code §§ 11, 162 nt., 613, 821, 4061, 4251, 4261, 5001, 5022, 5041, 5051, 5063, 5701, 5707, 6412

July 6, 1960, P.L. 86-592, 74 Stat. 330, 26 U.S. Code §§ 4501, 6412

July 6, 1960, P.L. 86-594, 74 Stat. 333, 26 U.S. Code § 615

July 12, 1960, P.L. 86-624, 74 Stat. 416, 26 U.S. Code §§ 2202, 3131, 3306, 4221, 4233, 4262, 4502, 4774, 7653, 7701

July 14, 1960, P.L. 86-667, 74 Stat. 534, 26 U.S. Code §§ 501, 503, 511, 513, 514

Sept. 6, 1960, P.L. 86-707, 74 Stat. 802, 26 U.S. Code § 912

Sept. 8, 1960, P.L. 86-723, 74 Stat. 847, 26 U.S. Code § 104

Sept. 13, 1960, P.L. 86-778, 74 Stat. 926, 26 U.S. Code §§ 1402, 1403, 3121, 3126, 3302, 3305, 3306, 3309, 6205, 6413, 7213, 7701

Sept. 14, 1960, P.L. 86-779, 74 Stat. 998, 26 U.S. Code §§ 11, 34, 116, 162, 170, 180, 243, 263, 318, 443, 852, 855 to 858, 861, 934, 1054, 1055, 1504, 2106, 2209, 2501, 4201, 5701, 6015

Sept. 14, 1960, P.L. 86-780, 74 Stat. 1010, 26 U.S. Code §§ 901, 902, 904, 1503, 6038, 6039, 6046, 6501

Sept. 14, 1960, P.L. 86-781, 74 Stat. 1017, 26 U.S. Code §§ 461, 5216, 6416

March 24, 1961, P.L. 87-6, 75 Stat. 16, 26 U.S. Code §§ 3301, 3302

March 31, 1961, P.L. 87-15, 75 Stat. 40, 26 U.S. Code §§ 4501, 6412

May 4, 1961, P.L. 87-29, 75 Stat. 64, 26 U.S. Code §§ 895, 1372

June 27, 1961, P.L. 87-59, 75 Stat. 120, 26 U.S. Code § 809

June 29, 1961, P.L. 87-61, 75 Stat. 123, 26 U.S. Code §§ 4041, 4061, 4071, 4081, 4218, 4221, 4226, 4481, 4482, 6156, 6157, 6412, 6416, 6421, 6601

June 30, 1961, P.L. 87-64, 75 Stat. 140, 26 U.S. Code §§ 1401, 1402, 3101, 3111

June 30, 1961, P.L. 87-72, 75 Stat. 193, 26 U.S. Code §§ 11, 821, 4061, 4251, 4261, 5001, 5022, 5041, 5051, 5063, 5701, 5707, 6412

July 26, 1961, P.L. 87-109, 75 Stat. 222, 26 U.S. Code § 456

Sept. 21, 1961, P.L. 87-256, 75 Stat. 535, 26 U.S. Code §§ 117, 871, 872, 1441, 3121, 3306, 3401, 3402

Sept. 22, 1961, P.L. 87-293, 75 Stat. 625, 26 U.S. Code §§ 912, 1303, 3121, 3122, 3401, 6051

Sept. 26, 1961, P.L. 87-321, 75 Stat. 683, 26 U.S. Code §§ 613 nt., 3302

Oct. 4, 1961, P.L. 87-370, 75 Stat. 796, 26 U.S. Code §§ 403, 7448

Oct. 5, 1961, P.L. 87-397, 75 Stat. 828, 26 U.S. Code §§ 6109, 6110, 6676

Feb. 2, 1962, P.L. 87-403, 76 Stat. 4, 26 U.S. Code §§ 301, 312, 535, 543, 545, 556, 561, 1111

March 31, 1962, P.L. 87-426, 76 Stat. 51, 26 U.S. Code § 165

May 24, 1962, P.L. 87-456, 76 Stat. 77, 26 U.S. Code §§ 4501, 6412, 6418

June 28, 1962, P.L. 87-508, 76 Stat. 114, 26 U.S. Code §§ 11, 821, 4061, 4251 to 4253, 4261 to 4264, 5001, 5022, 5041, 5051, 5063, 5701, 5707, 6412, 6416, 6421

July 13, 1962, P.L. 87-535, 76 Stat. 166, 26 U.S. Code §§ 4501, 6412

Sept. 25, 1962, P.L. 87-682, 76 Stat. 575, 26 U.S. Code §§ 6015, 6073, 6153, 6654

Sept. 27, 1962, P.L. 87-710, 76 Stat. 648, 26 U.S. Code § 172

Sept. 28, 1962, P.L. 87-722, 76 Stat. 670, 26 U.S. Code §§ 581, 584

Oct. 9, 1962, P.L. 87-768, 76 Stat. 766, 26 U.S. Code § 542

Oct. 9, 1962, P.L. 87-770, 76 Stat. 768, 26 U.S. Code § 4216

Oct. 10, 1962, P.L. 87-790, 76 Stat. 808, 26 U.S. Code §§ 809, 815

Oct. 10, 1962, P.L. 87-792, 76 Stat. 809, 26 U.S. Code §§ 37, 62, 72, 101, 104, 105, 172, 401 to 405, 503, 805, 1361, 2039, 2517, 3306, 3401, 6047, 7207

Oct. 11, 1962, P.L. 87-794, 76 Stat. 889, 26 U.S. Code §§ 172, 6501, 6511

Oct. 16, 1962, P.L. 87-834, 76 Stat. 962, 26 U.S. Code §§ 38, 39, 46 to 48, 72, 78, 162, 167, 170, 179, 181, 182, 216, 245, 263, 274, 301, 312, 318, 341 and others

Oct. 23, 1962, P.L. 87-858, 76 Stat. 1134, 26 U.S. Code §§ 170, 801, 802, 804, 809, 812, 815, 4216, 6501

Oct. 23, 1962, P.L. 87-863, 76 Stat. 1141, 26 U.S. Code §§ 213, 401, 404, 1341, 5113, 5123, 7608

Oct. 23, 1962, P.L. 87-870, 76 Stat. 1158, 26 U.S. Code §§ 281, 6512, 7515, 7516, 7701, 7809

Oct. 24, 1962, P.L. 87-876, 76 Stat. 1199, 26 U.S. Code §§ 37, 461

April 2, 1963, P.L. 88-4, 77 Stat. 4, 26 U.S. Code § 214

April 10, 1963, P.L. 88-9, 77 Stat. 6, 26 U.S. Code §§ 163, 1055, 1056

May 29, 1963, P.L. 88-31, 77 Stat. 51, 26 U.S. Code §§ 3301, 3302

June 4, 1963, P.L. 88-36, 77 Stat. 54, 26 U.S. Code §§ 6422, 6808

June 29, 1963, P.L. 88-52, 77 Stat. 72, 26 U.S. Code §§ 11, 821, 4061, 4251, 4261, 5001, 5022, 5041, 5051, 5063, 5701, 5707, 6412

Oct. 5, 1963, P.L. 88-133, 77 Stat. 221, 26 U.S. Code §§ 3201, 3202, 3211, 3221
Continued

Nov. 7, 1963, P.L. 88-173, 77 Stat. 305, 26 U.S. Code § 3302

Feb. 26, 1964, P.L. 88-272, 78 Stat. 19, 26 U.S. Code §§ 1 to 5, 11, 12, 21, 34, 35, 37, 38 nt., 46, 48, 62, 72, 79, 105, 116, 121, 122, 141, 144, 163 to 165 and others

June 30, 1964, P.L. 88-342, 78 Stat. 234, 26 U.S. Code § 5704

June 30, 1964, P.L. 88-348, 78 Stat. 237, 26 U.S. Code §§ 165, 4061, 4251, 4261, 5001, 5022, 5041, 5051, 5063, 5701, 5707, 6412

July 17, 1964, P.L. 88-380, 78 Stat. 333, 26 U.S. Code § 512

Aug. 14, 1964, P.L. 88-426, 78 Stat. 427, 26 U.S. Code §§ 7443, 7801

Aug. 22, 1964, P.L. 88-484, 78 Stat. 596, 26 U.S. Code §§ 301, 341, 453, 543

Aug. 31, 1964, P.L. 88-539, 78 Stat. 746, 26 U.S. Code § 453, 5062

Aug. 31, 1964, P.L. 88-554, 78 Stat. 761, 26 U.S. Code §§ 162 nt., 304, 318, 382, 856, 958, 6038

Sept. 2, 1964, P.L. 88-563, 78 Stat. 809, 26 U.S. Code §§ 263, 1232, 4911 to 4920, 4931, 6011, 6076, 6103, 6680, 6681, 7241

Sept. 2, 1964, P.L. 88-570, 78 Stat. 854, 26 U.S. Code §§ 691, 1038

Sept. 2, 1964, P.L. 88-571, 78 Stat. 857, 26 U.S. Code § 613, 805, 812, 815, 1212, 6501, 6511, 6601, 6611

Oct. 13, 1964, P.L. 88-650, 78 Stat. 1076, 26 U.S. Code §§ 1402, 3121, 3306

Oct. 13, 1964, P.L. 88-653, 78 Stat. 1085, 26 U.S. Code §§ 4062, 4063, 4142, 5382, 5511

June 21, 1965, P.L. 89-44, 79 Stat. 136, 26 U.S. Code §§ 39, 40, 72, 501 nt., 874, 1314, 1481, 4041, 4055, 4057, 4061, 4063, 4082, 4091, 4094, 4101 and others

July 30, 1965, P.L. 89-97, 79 Stat. 335, 26 U.S. Code §§ 72, 79, 213, 401, 405, 451, 1401, 1402, 3101, 3111, 3121, 3122, 3125, 3201, 3211, 3221, 3401, 3402, 6051, 6053, 6205, 6413, 6652, 6674

Sept. 29, 1965, P.L. 89-212, 79 Stat. 858, 26 U.S. Code §§ 3201, 3202, 3211, 3221, 3231, 3402, 6052, 6053

Nov. 8, 1965, P.L. 89-331, 79 Stat. 1278, 26 U.S. Code §§ 4501, 6418, 6511

Feb. 2, 1966, P.L. 89-352, 80 Stat. 4, 26 U.S. Code §§ 501, 511

Feb. 2, 1966, P.L. 89-354, 80 Stat. 5, 26 U.S. Code § 7447

March 8, 1966, P.L. 89-365, 80 Stat. 32, 26 U.S. Code §§ 72, 101, 122, 123, 2039, 2517

March 15, 1966, P.L. 89-368, 80 Stat. 38, 26 U.S. Code §§ 276, 1402, 1403, 3402, 4061, 4251, 4253, 6015, 6154, 6211, 6412, 6654, 6682, 7205, 7701

April 8, 1966, P.L. 89-384, 80 Stat. 99, 26 U.S. Code §§ 46, 80, 901, 1351, 6167, 6503, 6601

April 14, 1966, P.L. 89-389, 80 Stat. 111, 26 U.S. Code §§ 46, 1361, 1371 to 1373, 1375, 1378, 1504

July 5, 1966, P.L. 89-493, 80 Stat. 266, 26 U.S. Code § 6323

Aug. 1, 1966, P.L. 89-523, 80 Stat. 331, 26 U.S. Code §§ 4071, 4226

Sept. 12, 1966, P.L. 89-570, 80 Stat. 759, 26 U.S. Code §§ 170, 301, 312, 341, 453, 615, 617, 703, 751

Oct. 4, 1966, P.L. 89-621, 80 Stat. 872, 26 U.S. Code §§ 642, 2056

Oct. 30, 1966, P.L. 89-699, 80 Stat. 1078, 26 U.S. Code §§ 3201, 3211, 3221

Oct. 30, 1966, P.L. 89-700, 80 Stat. 1088, 26 U.S. Code §§ 3201, 3202, 3211, 3221

Nov. 2, 1966, P.L. 89-713, 80 Stat. 1107, 26 U.S. Code §§ 6091, 6151

Nov. 2, 1966, P.L. 89-719, 80 Stat. 1125, 26 U.S. Code §§ 545, 3505, 6322, 6323 to 6325, 6331 to 6335, 6337 to 6339, 6342, 6343, 6502, 6503, 6523 nt., 6532, 7402, 7403, 7421, 7505, 7506, 7809, 7810; 40 U.S. Code § 270a

Nov. 2, 1966, P.L. 89-721, 80 Stat. 1150, 26 U.S. Code §§ 6411, 6501, 6611

Nov. 2, 1966, P.L. 89-722, 80 Stat. 1151, 26 U.S. Code §§ 81, 166

Nov. 2, 1966, P.L. 89-739, 80 Stat. 1165, 26 U.S. Code § 112

Nov. 8, 1966, P.L. 89-800, 80 Stat. 1508, 26 U.S. Code §§ 46, 48, 167, 501

Nov. 13, 1966, P.L. 89-809, 80 Stat. 1541, 26 U.S. Code §§ 11, 154, 116, 245, 301, 512, 542, 543, 545, 821, 822, 831, 841, 842, 861, 864, 871 to 875, 877, 878, 881 and others

June 13, 1967, P.L. 90-26, 81 Stat. 57, 26 U.S. Code §§ 48, 167

July 31, 1967, P.L. 90-59, 81 Stat. 145, 26 U.S. Code §§ 4911, 4912, 4914 to 4920, 4931, 6011, 6076, 6681, 7241

Aug. 29, 1967, P.L. 90-73, 81 Stat. 175, 26 U.S. Code §§ 4918, 5362, 6681, 7241

Aug. 31, 1967, P.L. 90-78, 81 Stat. 191, 26 U.S. Code § 152

Dec. 27, 1967, P.L. 90-225, 81 Stat. 730, 26 U.S. Code §§ 46, 172, 815, 1102, 6411, 6501, 6511, 6601, 6611

Jan. 2, 1968, P.L. 90-240, 81 Stat. 776, 26 U.S. Code §§ 381, 832, 5701

Jan. 2, 1968, P.L. 90-248, 81 Stat. 385, 26 U.S. Code §§ 1401, 1402, 3101, 3111, 3121, 3122, 3125, 6413

April 12, 1968, P.L. 90-285, 82 Stat. 92, 26 U.S. Code §§ 4061, 4251, 6412

June 28, 1968, P.L. 90-364, 82 Stat. 251, 26 U.S. Code §§ 51, 103, 243, 276, 501, 963, 3402, 4061, 4251, 6020, 6154, 6412, 6425, 6651, 6655, 7203, 7502, 7701

Oct. 21, 1968, P.L. 90-615, 82 Stat. 1210, 26 U.S. Code § 5134

Oct. 22, 1968, P.L. 90-618, 82 Stat. 1227, 26 U.S. Code §§ 5801, 5802, 5811, 5812, 5821, 5822, 5841 to 5849, 5851 to 5854, 5871, 5872, 6806, 7273

Oct. 22, 1968, P.L. 90-619, 82 Stat. 1236, 26 U.S. Code §§ 5373, 5382 to 5387

Oct. 22, 1968, P.L. 90-621, 82 Stat. 1310, 26 U.S. Code §§ 358, 362, 368

Oct. 22, 1968, P.L. 90-622, 82 Stat. 1311, 26 U.S. Code § 883

Oct. 22, 1968, P.L. 90-624, 82 Stat. 1316, 26 U.S. Code § 3231

Oct. 22, 1968, P.L. 90-630, 82 Stat. 1328, 26 U.S. Code §§ 175, 504, 681, 5008, 5062, 5232

Oct. 24, 1968, P.L. 90-634, 82 Stat. 1349, 26 U.S. Code § 103

June 30, 1969, P.L. 91-36, 83 Stat. 42, 26 U.S. Code § 3402

Aug. 2, 1969, P.L. 91-50, 83 Stat. 86, 26 U.S. Code § 4911

Aug. 7, 1969, P.L. 91-53, 83 Stat. 91, 26 U.S. Code §§ 51, 963, 3306, 3402, 6157, 6201, 6317, 6513, 6601

Aug. 25, 1969, P.L. 91-65, 83 Stat. 105, 26 U.S. Code § 4911

Nov. 26, 1969, P.L. 91-128, 83 Stat. 261, 26 U.S. Code §§ 4182, 4911, 4912, 4914, 4915, 4919, 4920, 6011, 6680

Dec. 30, 1969, P.L. 91-172, 83 Stat. 487, 26 U.S. Code §§ 1 to 5, 11, 12, 21, 46 to 49, 51, 56 to 58, 62, 72, 82, 83, 101, 103, 123, 124, 141, 143, 151, 152 and others

March 17, 1970, P.L. 91-215, 84 Stat. 70, 26 U.S. Code §§ 3211, 3221

May 21, 1970, P.L. 91-258, 84 Stat. 237, 26 U.S. Code §§ 39, 874, 4041, 4082, 4261 to 4263, 4271, 4272, 4281 and others

Aug. 10, 1970, P.L. 91-373, 84 Stat. 695, 26 U.S. Code §§ 1563, 3301 to 3306, 3309 to 3311, 6157

Oct. 27, 1970, P.L. 91-513, 84 Stat. 1292, 26 U.S. Code §§ 4901, 4905, 6808, 7012, 7103, 7326, 7607, 7609, 7641, 7651, 7655

Oct. 30, 1970, P.L. 91-518, 84 Stat. 1341, 26 U.S. Code § 250

Dec. 31, 1970, P.L. 91-605, 84 Stat. 1743, 26 U.S. Code §§ 4041, 4061, 4071, 4081, 4481, 4482, 6156, 6412, 6421

Dec. 31, 1970, P.L. 91-606, 84 Stat. 1759, 26 U.S. Code §§ 165, 5064, 5708

Dec. 31, 1970, P.L. 91-614, 84 Stat. 1836, 26 U.S. Code §§ 56, 1015, 1223, 2012, 2032, 2055, 2204 and others

Dec. 31, 1970, P.L. 91-614, 84 Stat. 1836, 26 U.S. Code §§ 56, 1015, 1223, 2012, 2032, 2055, 2204, 2501 to 2504, 2512, 2513 and others

Dec. 31, 1970, P.L. 91-618, 84 Stat. 1855, 26 U.S. Code § 501

Jan. 8, 1971, P.L. 91-659, 84 Stat. 1964, 26 U.S. Code §§ 5008, 5066, 5067, 5173, 5178, 5215, 5232

Jan. 12, 1971, P.L. 91-673, 84 Stat. 2056, 26 U.S. Code §§ 5052, 5053, 5056, 5401, 5402, 5411, 5412, 5416, 5417

Jan. 12, 1971, P.L. 91-676, 84 Stat. 2060, 26 U.S. Code § 47

Jan. 12, 1971, P.L. 91-677, 84 Stat. 2061, 26 U.S. Code §§ 165, 172

Jan. 12, 1971, P.L. 91-679, 84 Stat. 2063, 26 U.S. Code §§ 6013, 6653

Jan. 12, 1971, P.L. 91-680, 84 Stat. 2064, 26 U.S. Code §§ 278, 7275

Jan. 12, 1971, P.L. 91-681, 84 Stat. 2065, 26 U.S. Code §§ 367, 1492

Jan. 12, 1971, P.L. 91-683, 84 Stat. 2067, 26 U.S. Code § 1372

Jan. 12, 1971, P.L. 91-684, 84 Stat. 2068, 26 U.S. Code § 902

Jan. 12, 1971, P.L. 91-686, 84 Stat. 2071, 26 U.S. Code § 1237

Jan. 12, 1971, P.L. 91-687, 84 Stat. 2071, 26 U.S. Code § 165

Jan. 12, 1971, P.L. 91-688, 84 Stat. 2072, 26 U.S. Code § 818

Jan. 12, 1971, P.L. 91-691, 84 Stat. 2074, 26 U.S. Code § 401

Continued

Jan. 12, 1971, P.L. 91-693, 84 Stat. 2077, 26 U.S. Code § 368

March 17, 1971, P.L. 92-5, 85 Stat. 11, 26 U.S. Code §§ 1402, 3101, 3111, 3121, 3122, 3125, 6413, 6654

April 1, 1971, P.L. 92-9, 85 Stat. 13, 26 U.S. Code §§ 861, 4911, 4912, 4914, 4915, 4919, 4920, 4921, 6651, 6680, 6681

July 1, 1971, P.L. 92-41, 85 Stat. 99, 26 U.S. Code §§ 7447, 7448

Oct. 14, 1971, P.L. 92-138, 85 Stat. 390, 26 U.S. Code § 4501(b)

Dec. 10, 1971, P.L. 92-178, 85 Stat. 498, 26 U.S. Code §§ 4, 21, 40 to 42, 46 to 49, 50, 50A, 50B, 56 to 58 and others

April 26, 1972, P.L. 92-279, 86 Stat. 124, 26 U.S. Code §§ 112, 3401

June 6, 1972, P.L. 92-310, 86 Stat. 209, 26 U.S. Code §§ 6803, 7101, 7103, 7402, 7803

June 30, 1972, P.L. 92-329, 86 Stat. 398, 26 U.S. Code §§ 3301, 6157

July 1, 1972, P.L. 92-336, 86 Stat. 406, 26 U.S. Code §§ 165, 1401, 1402, 3101, 3111, 3121, 3122, 3125, 6413, 6654

Aug. 29, 1972, P.L. 92-418, 86 Stat. 656, 26 U.S. Code §§ 165, 501, 512, 6405

Oct. 20, 1972, P.L. 92-512, 86 Stat. 935, 26 U.S. Code §§ 6017A, 6361 to 6365, 6405, 6687, 7463

Oct. 25, 1972, P.L. 92-558, 86 Stat. 1173, 26 U.S. Code § 4161

Oct. 27, 1972, P.L. 92-580, 86 Stat. 1276, 26 U.S. Code §§ 152, 164, 873, 2039

Oct. 30, 1972, P.L. 92-603, 86 Stat. 1341, 26 U.S. Code §§ 1401, 1402, 3101, 3111, 3121, 6051

Oct. 31, 1972, P.L. 92-606, 86 Stat. 1494, 26 U.S. Code §§ 881, 931, 932, 935, 1442, 6687, 7654, 7701

July 1, 1973, P.L. 93-53, 87 Stat. 138, 26 U.S. Code §§ 6096, 9003, 9006, 9007, 9012

July 9, 1973, P.L. 93-66, 87 Stat. 153, 26 U.S. Code §§ 1402, 3121, 3122, 3125, 6413, 6654

July 10, 1973, P.L. 93-69, 87 Stat. 162, 26 U.S. Code §§ 3201, 3202, 3211, 3221

Dec. 31, 1973, P.L. 93-233, 87 Stat. 953, 26 U.S. Code §§ 1401, 1402, 3101, 3111, 3121, 3122, 3125, 6413, 6654

May 22, 1974, P.L. 93-288, 88 Stat. 164, 26 U.S. Code §§ 165, 5064, 5708

Aug. 7, 1974, P.L. 93-368, 88 Stat. 422, 26 U.S. Code § 1402

March 29, 1975, P.L. 94-12, 89 Stat. 27, 26 U.S. Code §§ 3, 11, 12, 21, 42-48, 50A, 50B, 56, 141, 214, 243, 535, 613, 613A, 703, 851, 901, 902, 907, 951, 954, 955, 962, 993, 1034, 1551, 1561, 3402, 6012, 6201, 6401, 6428, 6611 nt.

June 30, 1975, P.L. 94-45, 89 Stat. 239, 26 U.S. Code §§ 44, 3302

Aug. 9, 1975, P.L. 94-81, 89 Stat. 417, 26 U.S. Code §§ 509, 1245, 1250

Aug. 9, 1975, P.L. 94-92, 89 Stat. 465, 26 U.S. Code §§ 3231, 1402

Dec. 23, 1975, P.L. 94-164, 89 Stat. 970, 26 U.S. Code §§ 1-nt., 11, 21, prec. 31, 42, 43, 103, 141, 883, 1561, 3402, 6012, 6153, 6154

Dec. 31, 1975, P.L. 94-182, 89 Stat. 1056, 26 U.S. Code § 103

Jan. 2, 1976, P.L. 94-202, 89 Stat. 1135, 26 U.S. Code §§ 6103, 7652

May 23, 1977, P.L. 95-30, 26 U.S. Code §§ 1 et seq.

Oct. 28, 1977, P.L. 95-147, 26 U.S. Code §§ 6302, 6302 nt., 7502

Nov. 12, 1977, P.L. 95-171, 26 U.S. Code §§ 50B et seq.

Nov. 14, 1977, P.L. 95-176, 26 U.S. Code §§ 506z et seq.

Dec. 20, 1977, P.L. 95-216, 26 U.S. Code § 3101 et seq.

Feb. 10, 1978, P.L. 95-227, 26 U.S. Code §§ 192, 501, 4121 nt., 4121 et seq., 4940 et seq., 6104 et seq.; 30 U.S. Code §§ 934, 934 nt.

Aug. 15, 1978, P.L. 95-345, 26 U.S. Code §§ 501, 509, 512, 514, 851, 1058, 1059, 1382, 4940

Oct. 20, 1978, P.L. 95-488, 26 U.S. Code §§ 192, 192 nt., 6104

Oct. 21, 1978, P.L. 95-502, 26 U.S. Code §§ 513, 513 nt., 527, 4042, 4042 nt., 4293

Nov. 6, 1978, P.L. 95-599, 26 U.S. Code §§ 39, 4041, 4061, 4071, 4081, 4481, 4482, 6156, 6412, 6421, 6427, 7210, 7603 to 7605, 7609, 7610

Nov. 6, 1978, P.L. 95-600, 26 U.S. Code §§ 1 et seq.

Nov. 8, 1978, P.L. 95-615, 26 U.S. Code §§ 1 nt., 43, 61 nt., 62, 117 nt., 119, 167, 217, 382 nt., 401 nt., 911, 913, 1302, 1304, 6011, 6012, 6091

Nov. 9, 1978, P.L. 95-618, 26 U.S. Code §§ 1 nt., 39, 44C, 46 to 48, 56, 57, 120 nt., 124, 167, 263, 465, 613, 613A, 614, 1016, 1254, 4041, 4061, 4063, 4064 nt., 4081, 4217, 4221, 4222, 4293, 4483, 6096, 6411, 6412, 6416, 6421, 6424, 6427, 6504, 6675

Nov. 10, 1978, P.L. 95-628, 26 U.S. Code §§ 267, 301, 312, 337, 1372, 6072, 6073, 6501, 6511, 6601, 6611, 6672, 7103, 7421

July 26, 1979, P.L. 96-39, 26 U.S. Code §§ 1 nt., 993, 5001 et seq.

Sept. 29, 1979, P.L. 96-72, 26 U.S. Code § 993

Oct. 10, 1979, P.L. 96-84, 26 U.S. Code § 3306, 3306 nt.

Jan. 2, 1980, P.L. 96-178, 26 U.S. Code §§ 50A, 50A nt., 50B, 50B nt., 162 nt., 280C

April 1, 1980, P.L. 96- 222, 26 U.S. Code §§ 1 et seq.

April 2, 1980, P.L. 96-223, 26 U.S. Code § 4986 et seq.

May 26, 1980, P.L. 96-249, 26 U.S. Code § 6103

July 1, 1980, P.L. 96-298, 26 U.S. Code § 4041

Oct. 24, 1983, P.L. 98-135, 26 U.S. Code § 3306

April 10, 1984, P.L. 98-259, 26 U.S. Code § 692

July 11, 1984, P.L. 98-355, 26 U.S. Code §§ 9008, 9008 nt.

July 18, 1984, P.L. 98-369, 98 Stat. 494

Aug. 16, 1984, P.L. 98-378, 26 U.S. Code §§ 6103, 6103 nt., 6402, 7213

Aug. 23, 1984, P.L. 98-397, 26 U.S. Code §§ 72, 401, 402, 410, 411, 414, 417, 1054, 6052, 6057

Oct. 4, 1984, P.L. 98-443, 98 Stat. 1708, 26 U.S. Code §§ 47, 7701

Oct. 12, 1984, P.L. 98-473, 26 U.S. Code § 5871

Oct. 30, 1984, P.L. 98-573, 26 U.S. Code §§ 162, 162 nt., 7607

Nov. 8, 1984, P.L. 98-620, 26 U.S. Code §§ 3310, 6110, 6363

May 24, 1985, P.L. 99-44, 26 U.S. Code §§ 274, 280F, 3402

Aug. 16, 1985, P.L. 99-92, 26 U.S. Code § 6103

Oct. 11, 1985, P.L. 99-121, 26 U.S. Code §§ 47, 48, 57, 168, 280G, 312, 483, 1245, 1274, 1274A, 7872

Dec. 26, 1985, P.L. 99-221, 26 U.S. Code § 3121

Jan. 2, 1986, P.L. 99-234, 26 U.S. Code § 4941

Apr 7, 1986, P.L. 99-272, 26 U.S. Code §§ 86, 106, 162, 404, 412, 501, 932, 3121, 3304, 3306, 3321

June 6, 1986, P.L. 99-335, 26 U.S. Code §§ 3121, 6103

Oct. 17, 1986, P.L. 99-499, 26 U.S. Code §§ prec. 1, prec. 59A, 164, 275, 936, 1561, 4041, 4042, 4081, 4611 nt., 4612, 4661 nt., 4661, 4662, 4671 nt., 95-2-9508

Oct. 21, 1986, P.L. 99-509, 26 U.S. Code §§ 42, 162, 410, 411, 469, 901, 3127, 4611, 5000, 5054, 5061, 5703, 5704, 6656, 6661, 9507, 9509

Oct. 22, 1986, P.L. 99-514, 26 U.S. Code §§ 1 et seq.

Oct. 31, 1986, P.L. 99-595, 26 U.S. Code § 3306

Nov. 10, 1988, P.L. 100-647, 26 U.S. Code § 103

Internal Revenue Code of 1986

Oct. 22, 1986, P.L. 99-514, 26 U.S. Code §§ 1 et seq.

April 2, 1987, P.L. 100-17, 26 U.S. Code §§ 4041, 4051, 4071, 4481, 6412, 9503

Dec. 22, 1987, P.L. 100-203, 26 U.S. Code §§ 401, 404, 411, 412, 414, 2057 and nt., 3121, 3201, 3221, 4061, 4131, 4221, 4971, 6416, 9510

Dec. 30, 1987, P.L. 100-223, 26 U.S. Code §§ 4041, 4041 nt., 4261, 4261 nt., 4271, 4283, 6427, 9502

July 1, 1988, P.L. 100-360, 102 Stat. 689, 26 U.S. Code §§ 59B, 59B nt., 6050F

Aug. 23, 1988, P.L. 100-418, 102 Stat. 1159, 26 U.S. Code §§ 164, 193, prec. 261, 280D prec. 4041, 4986 to 4998, prec. 6071, 6211, 6212, prec. 6221, 6302, prec. 6411, 6501, 6511, 6511 nt., 6611, 6654, 6655, 6724, 6862, prec. 7231, 7652, 9504

Oct. 13, 1988, P.L. 100-485, 102 Stat. 2378, 26 U.S. Code §§ 21, 51, 62, 62 nt., 129, 6103, 6103 nt., 6109, 7213

Nov. 10, 1988, P.L. 100-647, generally 26 U.S. Code §§ 1 et seq.

Nov. 18, 1988, P.L. 100-690, 26 U.S. Code §§ 6050I, 6103, 6721, 7203, 7608, prec. 7621, 7624, 7809

Nov. 23, 1988, P.L. 100-707, 26 U.S. Code § 165

Aug. 9, 1989, P.L. 101-73, 26 U.S. Code §§ 368, 382, 501, 593, 597

Nov. 8, 1989, P.L. 101-140, generally 26 U.S. Code §§ 1 et seq.

Nov. 30, 1989, P.L. 101-194, 26 U.S. Code §§ 1016, 1043, 1223, 7701

Continued

Dec. 12, 1989, P.L. 101-221, 26 U.S. Code § 4611

Dec. 19, 1989, P.L. 101-239, generally 26 U.S. Code §§ 1 et seq.

May 4, 1990, P.L. 101-280, 26 U.S. Code §§ 1043, 9509

Aug. 18, 1990, P.L. 101-380, 26 U.S. Code § 9509

Aug. 20, 1990, P.L. 101-382, 26 U.S. Code § 936

Nov. 5, 1990, P.L. 101-508, 26 U.S. Code § 1 et seq. generally

Nov. 28, 1990, P.L. 101-624, 26 U.S. Code § 6109

Nov. 29, 1990, P.L. 101-647, 26 U.S. Code § 7203

Nov. 29, 1990, P.L. 101-649, 26 U.S. Code § 3304

Jan. 30, 1991, P.L. 102-2, 26 U.S. Code § 7508

Aug. 14, 1991, P.L. 102-90, 26 U.S. Code § 7701

Nov. 15, 1991, P.L. 102-164, 26 U.S. Code §§ 3301, 3304, 6654

Dec. 11, 1991, P.L. 102-227, 26 U.S. Code §§ 25, 28, 41, 42, 48, 51, 57, 120, 127, 143, 144, 162, 864, 6655

Dec. 18, 1991, P.L. 102-240, 26 U.S. Code §§ 4041, 4051, 4071, 4081, 4091, 4221, 4481 to 4483, 6156, 6412, 6420, 6421, 6427, 9503, 9504, 9511

Feb. 7, 1992, P.L. 102-244, 26 U.S. Code § 6655

July 3, 1992, P.L. 102-318, 26 U.S. Code §§ 55, 62, 72, 151, 219, 401-404, 406-408, 411, 414, 415, 457, 691, 871, 877, 1441, 3121, 3302, not., 3304, 3306, 3405, 4973, 4980a, 6047, 6652, 6655, 7701

Oct. 24, 1992, P.L. 102-486, 26 U.S. Code § 4 prec. 27, 29, 30, prec. 38, 38, 39, 45, 48, 53, 55, 56, 57, 59A, 62, prec. 101, 132, 136, 137, 142, 146, prec. 161, 162, 179A, 192, 385, 468A, 501, 704, prec. 731, 731, 737, 1016, 2056, 2523, 3402, 3406, 4081, 4612, 4681, 4682, 4951, 6045, 6109, 6724, prec. 9701, 9701 to 9708, prec. 9711 to 9712, prec. 9721, 9721 to 9722

Oct. 29, 1992, P.L. 102-568, 26 U.S. Code § 6103

Oct. 31, 1992, P.L. 102-581, 26 U.S. Code § 9502

Nov. 23, 1993, P.L. 103-149, 26 U.S. Code § 901

Dec. 3, 1993, P.L. 103-178. 26 U.S. Code § 3121

Dec. 8, 1993, P.L. 103-182, 26 U.S. Code §§ 3306, 3306, 6103, 6302, 9505

May 26, 1994, P.L. 103-260, 26 U.S. Code § 9502

July 5, 1994, P.L. 103-272, 26 U.S. Code §§ 4064, 4261

Aug. 15, 1994, P.L. 103-296, 26 U.S. Code §§ 86, 871, 872, 1402, 1441, 3102, 3121, 3122, 3127, 3231, 3306, 6050F, 6057, 6103, 6109, 6402, 6511, 7701, 9704, 9706

Aug. 23, 1994, P.L. 103-305, 26 U.S. Code § 9502

Sept. 13, 1994, P.L. 103-322, 26 U.S. Code §§ 5802, 6050I, 6724

Oct. 22, 1994, P.L. 103-387, 26 U.S. Code §§ 3102, 3121, 3510

Oct. 31, 1994, P.L. 103-429, 26 U.S. Code § 9503

Dec. 8, 1994, P.L. 103-465, 26 U.S. Code §§ 32, 401, 402, 404, 408, 411, 412, 415, 417, 420, 731, 737, 871, 3304, 3306, 3402, 3507, 4971, 4972, 5001, 5002, 5005, 5007, 5061, 5131, 5132, 5134, 5703, 6051, 6109, 6302, 6621, 6654, 6655, 6662, 7652.2

April 11, 1995, P.L. 104-7, 26 U.S. Code §§ 32, 162, 1033, 1071, 1245, 1250

March 20, 1996, P.L. 104-117, 26 U.S. Code §§ 112, 3401

April 26, 1996, P.L. 104-134, 26 U.S. Code §§ 3701, 6050P, 6402

Aug. 20, 1996, P.L. 104-188, 26 U.S. Code §§ 871, 6109

Aug. 21, 1996, P.L. 104-191, 26 U.S. Code §§ prec. 1, 4980B, 4980D, prec. 9801, 9801 to 9806

Aug. 22, 1996, P.L. 104-193, 26 U.S. Code §§ 32, 51, 3304, 6103, 6305, 6334, 6402, 7523

Sept. 23, 1996, P.L. 104-201, 26 U.S. Code § 2055

Sept. 30, 1996, P.L. 104-208, 26 U.S. Code § 162 nt.

Oct. 9, 1996, P.L. 104-264, 26 U.S. Code § 9502

Oct. 12, 1996, P.L. 104-303, 26 U.S. Code § 9505

Oct. 19, 1996, P.L. 104-316, 26 U.S. Code § 7608

Feb. 28, 1997, P.L. 105-2, 26 U.S. Code §§ 4041, 4081, 4091, 4261, 4271, 9502

Aug. 5, 1997, P.L. 105-33, 26 U.S. Code
§§ 138, 139, 220, 501, 3306, 3309, 4973,
prec. 5001, prec. 5701, 5701, 5702, 5704,
prec. 5711, 5712, 5713, 5721, 5722, prec.
5751, 5754, 5761 to 5763, 6103, 7213

Aug. 5, 1997, P.L. 105-34, 26 U.S. Code
§§ prec. 1, 1, prec. 21, 23, 24, 25, 25A, 26,
prec. 27, 30A, 32, 39, 41, 45C, prec. 51, 51,
51A, 52, 55 to 57, 59, 62, 63, 72, prec. 101,
101, 108, 110, 121, 127, 130, 132, 135, 137,
143, 145, 148, prec. 161, 162, 163, 165,
167, 168, 170, 172, 198, prec. 211, 216, 219
to 222, 246, 263, 264, 265, 267, 274, 280A,
280F, 304, 312, 318, 351, 354, 355, 356,
358, 367, 368, prec. 401 to 404, 408, 408A,
409 to 412, 414, 415, 417, 447, 451, 457,
460, 464, 471, 475, prec. 501, 501, 512,
513, 528, prec. 529, 529, 530, 532, 542,
551, 552, 552a, 593, 613A, prec. 641, 641,
644 to 646, 653, 654a, 663 to 665, 674, 679,
prec. 681, 684, 685, 691, prec. 701, 704,
706, 721, 724, 731, 732, 735, 737, 751,
prec. 771, 771 to 777, 805, 807, 812, 814,
817, 832, 833, 851 to 853, 856, 857, 860L,
861, 863, 864, 877, 894, 901, 902, 904, 905,
911, 927, 951, 952, 954, 956, 960, 961, 964,
986, 988, 989, 1014, 1016, prec. 1031, 1033
to 1036, 1038, 1042, 1045, prec. 1051,
1057, 1059, 1092, 1201, 1223, prec. 1231,
1233, 1234A, 1239, 1245, 1250, 1259,
1271, 1272, 1274, prec. 1291, 1291, 1293,
prec. 1296, 1296, 1297, 1298, prec. 1301,
1301, 1361, 1374, prec. 1391, 1391, 1392,
1394, 1396, 1397A, 1397B, prec. 1397D,
1397D, 1397E, prec. 1397F, 1397F, prec.
1400, 1400, 1400A to 1400C, 1402, 1441,
1445, prec. 1491, 1491, 1492, 1494, 2001,
2010, 2013, prec. 2031, 2031, 2032A,
2033A, 2035, 2053, 2055, 2056, 2056A,
2102, 2105, 2107, 2207A, 2207B, 2501,
2503, 2504, 2505, 2523, 2612, 2631, 2651,
2652, 3301, 4001, 4003, 4041, 4051, 4052,
prec. 4081, 4081, 4082, 4083, 4091 to 4093,
4101, 4131, 4132, 4161, 4222, 4251, 4261,
4263, 4271, prec. 4461, prec. 4495, 4495 to
4498, 4681, 4682, 4947, 4962, 4972, 4973,
4975, 4978, 4979A, 4980A, 4980D, 4982,
5008, prec. 5041, 5041, 5044, 5053, 5055,
5056, prec. 5111, 5115, 5175, 5207, 5222,
prec. 5361, 5361, 5364, 5384, 5388, prec.
5411, 5418, 5517, 5681, 6011, 6012, 6018,
6019, prec. 6031, 6031, 6033, 6034A, 6038,
6038B, 6039D, 6039F, 6039G, prec. 6041,
6041A, 6045, 6046, 6046A, 6048, 6050Q to
6050S, 6103, 6111, 6166, prec. 6201, 6211
to 6213, prec. 6221, 6221, 6225 to 6227,
6229, 6230, 6231, 6234, prec. 6240, 6240 to
6242, prec. 6245, 6245 to 6248, prec. 6251,
6251, 6252, prec. 6255, 6255, 6311, 6331,
6334, 6416, 6421, 6422, 6427, 6501, 6503,
6504, 6511, 6512, 6601, 6611, 6621, 6652,
6654, 6655, 6662, prec. 6671, 6679, 6683,
6693, 6695, 6707, 6715, 6724, prec. 7421,
7421, 7430, 7436, 7437, 7453, 7459, 7481,
7482, 7485, prec. 7231, 7232, 7430, 7431,
prec. 7476, 7477, 7479, prec. 7501, 7508A,
7518, 7519, 7701, 7702B, 7704, 7872,
9502, 9503, 9508, prec. 9801, 9801, 9802,
9804 to 9806, prec. 9811, 9811, 9812, 9831
to 9833

Aug. 5, 1997, P.L. 105-35, 26 U.S. Code
§§ prec. 7201, 7213, 7213A, prec. 7421,
7431

Oct. 10, 1997, P.L. 105-61, 26 U.S. Code
§ 3121

Oct. 27, 1997, P.L. 105-65, 26 U.S. Code
§ 6103

Nov. 20, 1997, P.L. 105-102, 26 U.S. Code
§ 9503

Nov. 21, 1997, P.L. 105-115, 26 U.S. Code
§ 45C

Dec. 1, 1997, P.L. 105-130, 26 U.S. Code
§§ 9503, 9504, 9511

June 9, 1998, P.L. 105-178, 26 U.S. Code
§§ 40, 132, 4041, 4051, 4071, 4081, 4091,
4221, 4481, 4482, 4483, 6156, 6412, 6421,
6427, 9503, 9504, 9511

July 22, 1998, P.L. 105-206, 26 U.S. Code
§§ 1, 23, 24, 25, 26, 32, 34, 42, 45A, 49, 50,
55, 57, 59, 66, 72, 108, 119, 121, 135, 142,
162, 168, 170, 196, 219, 221, 264, 304, 351,
354, 355, 368, 402, 403, 403 nt., 404, 408,
408A, 475, 475 nt., 501, 512, 529, 530, 543,
641, 645, 646, 664, 672, 685, 751, 774, 853,
857, 871, 901, 991, 1017, 1045, 1059, 1223,
1235, 1250, 1259, 1291, 1296, 1297, 1298,
1361, 1397E, 1400, 1400A, 1400B, 1400C,
2001, 2031, prec. 2051, 2033A, 2057, 2501,
2631, 2652, 2654, 3121, 3401, 4041, 4052,
4082, 4083, 4091, 4092, 4101, 4221, 4222,
4251, 4946, prec. 4971, 4973, 4975, 5041,
5043, 5044, 5054, 5056, 5364, 6011, 6013,
6015, 6038, 6039, 6050R, 6050S, 6061,
6071, 6103, 6104, 6109, 6110, 6159, 6166,
6211 to 6213, 6230, 6231, 6304, 6311,
6320, 6323, 6325, 6330, 6331, 6334, 6335,
6340, 6343, 6344, 6401, 6402, 6404, 6416,
6421, 6427, 6501 to 6503, 6511, 6512,
6601, 6611, 6621, 6631, 6651, 6656, 6672,
6724, 6751, 7122, 7123, 7124, 7217, 7421,
7422, 7426, 7429, 7430, 7431, 7433, 7434,
7436, 7443, 7443A, 7463, 7479, 7491,
7502, 7525, 7526, 7602, 7603, 7608, 7609,
7612, 7613, 7702B, 7704, 7802, 7803,
7804, 7805, 7811, 7872, 8021, 8022, 9502,
9811

Aug. 12, 1998, P.L. 105-225, 26 U.S. Code
§ 9503

Oct. 21, 1998, P.L. 105-277, 26 U.S. Code
§§ 1, 24, 26, 41, 45C, 51, 56, 67, 68, 135,
146, 162, 163, 170, 172, 221, 264, 332, 334,
351, 368, 408A, 451, 873, 953, 954, 2001,
2031, 4132, 6033, 6103, 6104, 6159, 6213,
6311, 6404, 6652, 6654, 6685, 7207, 7421,
7491, 9503, 9510

Continued

June 25, 1999, P.L. 106-36, 26 U.S. Code
§§ 351, 357, 358, 362, 584, 1031

**Internal Revenue Service Restructuring and
Reform Act of 1998**

July 22, 1998, P.L. 105-206, 26 U.S. Code
§ 1 nt.

Oct. 21, 1998, P.L. 105-277, 26 U.S. Code
§§ 6601 nt., 7443A

Internal Revenue Tax Liens Act

Wis. Stat. Ann., 779.97

Internal Security Act of 1950

See Emergency Detention Act Of 1950;
Subversive Activities Control Act Of 1950

Internal Tax Act

Haw. Session Laws 1896, Act 51

**International Air Transportation
Competition Act of 1979**

Feb. 15, 1980, P.L. 96-192, 49 U.S. Code
§§ 1301 nt., 1371 et seq.

**International Air Transportation Fair
Competitive Practices Act of 1974**

Jan. 3, 1975, P.L. 93-623, 22 U.S. Code
§ 2122; 49 U.S. Code §§ 1151 nt., 1159a,
1159b, 1160, 1373, 1376, 1377, 1472, 1517

Feb. 15, 1980, P.L. 96-192, 49 U.S. Code
§ 1159b

Oct. 4, 1984, P.L. 98-443, 98 Stat. 1706, 49
U.S. Code Appx. § 1159b

Aug. 23, 1988, P.L. 100-418, 102 Stat. 1573,
49 U.S. Code Appx. § 1559b

International and Interstate Procedure Act

See also Uniform Interstate and International
Procedure Act

Mich. Comp. Laws Ann., 600.1852,
600.2114a, 600.2118a

Pa. Cons. Stat., Title 42, § 5321 et seq.

**International and Marine Trade Center
Authority Act**

Ga. Laws 1995, p. 4499

International Anti-Boycott Certification Act

Ill. Comp. Stat. 1992, Ch. 30, § 582/1

**International Anti-Bribery and Fair
Competition Act of 1998**

Nov. 10, 1998, P.L. 105-366, 112 Stat. 3302,
15 U.S. Code § 78a

**International Antitrust Enforcement
Assistance Act of 1994**

Nov. 2, 1994, P.L. 103-438, 15 U.S. Code
§§ 6201 nt., 6201 et seq.

International Arbitration Act

Fla. Stat. Ann., 684.01 et seq.

**International Arbitration, Mediation, and
Conciliation Act**

Haw. Rev. Stat. Ann., § 658D-1 et seq.

**International Atomic Energy Agency
Participation Act of 1957**

Aug. 28, 1957, P.L. 85-177, 71 Stat. 453, 22
U.S. Code §§ 2021 to 2026; 42 U.S. Code
§ 2074

Nov. 2, 1994, P.L. 103-437, 22 U.S. Code
§ 2022

International Aviation Facilities Act

June 16, 1948, Ch. 473, 62 Stat. 450, 49 U.S.
Code §§ 1151 to 1160

Aug. 23, 1958, P.L. 85-726, 72 Stat. 808, 49
U.S. Code §§ 1151, 1152, 1155, 1157, 1160

Oct. 4, 1984, P.L. 98-443, 98 Stat. 1706, 49
U.S. Code Appx. § 1159a

International Bank Act

Ida. Code 1947, 26-2601 et seq.

Miss. Code Ann. 1972, § 81-25-1 et seq.

N.H. Rev. Stat. 1955, 384-F:8

Okla. Stat. Ann., Title 6, § 1600 et seq.

International Bank Agency Act

Ga. Code Ann., 7-1-710 et seq.

International Banking Act

N.C. Gen. Stat. 1943, § 53-232.1 et seq.

International Banking Act of 1978

Sept. 17, 1978, P.L. 95-369, 12 U.S. Code
§§ 36 nt., 72, 247 nt., 347d, 378, 601 nt.,
611a, 611a nt., 614 et seq., 1813 et seq.,
3101 et seq., 3101 nt.

Nov. 10, 1978, P.L. 95-630, 12 U.S. Code
§§ 601 nt., 3106a

Sept. 14, 1979, P.L. 96-64, 12 U.S. Code § 3104

Oct. 15, 1982, P.L. 97-320, 12 U.S. Code § 3106

Aug. 10, 1987, P.L. 100-86, 12 U.S. Code § 3106

Dec. 19, 1991, P.L. 102-242, 12 U.S. Code §§ 1842, 3101, 3102, 3104 to 3111

Oct. 28, 1992, P.L. 102-550, 12 U.S. Code §§ 3104, 3105, 3107

Oct. 28, 1992, P.L. 102-558, 12 U.S. Code § 3104

Sept. 29, 1994, P.L. 103-328, 12 U.S. Code §§ 3103, 3104, 3105, 3106a

Sept. 30, 1996, P.L. 104-208, 12 U.S. Code § 3105

International Banking Center Regulatory Act

P.R. Acts 1989, No. 52

P.R. Laws Ann. 1954, Title 7 § 231 et seq.

International Banking Corporations and Bank Agencies Act

Ga. Code Ann., 7-1-710 et seq.

International Banking Development Act

Del. Code of 1974, Title 5, §§ 101, 907, 936, 1101

Del. Code of 1974, Title 6, § 2307

Del. Code of 1974, Title 30, § 1903

International Banking Facility Deposit Insurance Act

Dec. 26, 1981, P.L. 97-110, 12 U.S. Code § 1811 nt.

International Bridge Act of 1972

Sept. 26, 1972, P.L. 92-434, 86 Stat. 731, 33 U.S. Code §§ 535 to 535i

April 2, 1987, P.L. 100-17, 33 U.S. Code §§ 508, 535d

International Carriage of Perishable Foodstuff Act

Oct. 15, 1982, P.L. 97-325, 7 U.S. Code §§ 4401 et seq., 4401 nt.

International Center Act

Aug. 16, 1985, P.L. 99- 93, 99 Stat. 415

Feb. 16, 1990, P.L. 101-246, 104 Stat. 26

International Child Abduction Remedies Act

April 29, 1988, P.L. 100-300, 102 Stat. 437, 22 U.S. Code §§ 2701 nt.; 42 U.S. Code §§ 11601 et seq., 11601 nt.

Oct. 21, 1998, P.L. 105-277, 42 U.S. Code § 11606

International Children's Emergency Fund Assistance Act of 1948

April 3, 1948, Ch. 169, 62 Stat. 137

July 14, 1949, Ch. 336, 63 Stat. 412

International Claims Settlement Act of 1949

March 10, 1950, Ch. 54, 64 Stat. 12, 22 U.S. Code §§ 1621 to 1624, 1626, 1627

Aug. 8, 1953, Ch. 396, 67 Stat. 506

Aug. 9, 1955, Ch. 645, 69 Stat. 562, 22 U.S. Code §§ 1621 to 1624, 1626, 1631 to 1631n, 1641 to 1641q

Aug. 8, 1958, P.L. 85-604, 72 Stat. 527, 22 U.S. Code §§ 1641c, 1641j, 1642 to 1642p

Aug. 28, 1958, P.L. 85-791, 72 Stat. 951, 22 U.S. Code § 1631f

Oct. 16, 1964, P.L. 88-666, 78 Stat. 1110, 22 U.S. Code §§ 1643 to 1643k

Oct. 19, 1965, P.L. 89-262, 79 Stat. 988, 22 U.S. Code §§ 1643, 1643b, 1643d, 1643e, 1643j

Nov. 6, 1966, P.L. 89-780, 80 Stat. 1365, 22 U.S. Code §§ 1643 to 1643b, 1643d, 1643i

July 24, 1968, P.L. 90-421, 82 Stat. 420, 22 U.S. Code §§ 1623, 1626, 1627, 1631f, 1631o, 1641a to 1641c, 1641e, 1641i, 1641o

Dec. 24, 1969, P.L. 91-157, 83 Stat. 435, 22 U.S. Code § 1643i

Oct. 8, 1986, P.L. 99-451, 22 U.S. Code § 1623

Dec. 22, 1987, P.L. 100-204, 22 U.S. Code § 1627

June 27, 1988, P.L. 100-352, 102 Stat. 664, 22 U.S. Code § 1631e

March 12, 1996, P.L. 104-114, 22 U.S. Code §§ 1643l, 1643m

Oct. 19, 1996, P.L. 104-316, 22 U.S. Code § 1626

Oct. 21, 1998, P.L. 105-277, 22 U.S. Code § 1623

International Coffee Agreement Act of 1965

May 22, 1965, P.L. 89-23, 79 Stat. 112, 19 U.S. Code §§ 1356a to 1356e

March 24, 1972, P.L. 92-262, 86 Stat. 113, 19 U.S. Code § 1356f

International Coffee Agreement Act of 1968

Jan. 12, 1971, P.L. 91-694, 84 Stat. 2077, 19 U.S. Code § 1356f

International Coffee Agreement Act of 1980

Dec. 24, 1980, P.L. 96-599, 19 U.S. Code § 1356k nt.

Oct. 2, 1982, P.L. 97-276, 19 U.S. Code § 1356k

Jan. 12, 1983, P.L. 97-446, 19 U.S. Code § 1356k

Aug. 23, 1988, P.L. 100-418, 102 Stat. 1146, 19 U.S. Code § 1356k

Nov. 10, 1998, P.L. 105-362, 19 U.S. Code §§ 1356m, 1356n

International Commercial Arbitration Act

Ill. Comp. Stat. 1992, Ch. 710, § 30/1-1 et seq.

Md. Ann. Code 1974, Art. CJ, § 3-2B-01 et seq.

International Commercial Arbitration and Conciliation Act

Ore. Laws 1991, Ch. 405

International Commercial Arbitration Law (UNLITRAL)

Conn. Gen. Stat. Ann., § 50a-100 et seq.

Conn. Public Acts 1991, No. 179

International Commercial Dispute Arbitration and Conciliation Law

Cal. Code of Civil Procedure § 1297.11 et seq.

International Conciliation, Arbitration and Mediation Act

Haw. Rev. Stat. Ann., § 658D-1 et seq.

International Cooperation in Global Change Research Act of 1990

Nov. 16, 1990, P.L. 101-606, 15 U.S. Code § 2921 et seq.

International Cultural Exchange and Trade Fair Participation Act of 1956

Aug. 1, 1956, Ch. 811, 70 Stat. 778, 22 U.S. Code §§ 1991 to 2001

International Debt Management Act of 1988

Aug. 23, 1988, P.L. 100-418, 102 Stat. 1375, 22 U.S. Code § 5321

International Development and Finance Act of 1989

Dec. 19, 1989, P.L. 101-240, 22 U.S. Code § 2151 nt.

International Development and Food Assistance Act of 1975

Dec. 20, 1975, P.L. 94-161, 7 U.S. Code § 1691 et seq.

Dec. 20, 1975, P.L. 94-161, 89 Stat. 849, 7 U.S. Code §§ 1691, 1691a, 1703, 1704, 1706, 1709, 1711, 1721, 1726, 1736a, 1736b, 1736f; 22 U.S. Code §§ 2151 to 2151e, 2151h to 2151k, 2151n, 2169, 2174, 2181 to 2183, 2201, 2220a to 2220e, 2221, 2222, 2225, 2292 to 2292f, 2293, 2357, 2399-1a, 2399-1b, 2399h, 2421, 2425 to 2427

International Development and Food Assistance Act of 1977

Aug. 3, 1977, P.L. 95-88, 7 U.S. Code § 1427 et seq.

International Development and Food Assistance Act of 1978

Aug. 14, 1979, P.L. 96-53, 22 U.S. Code §§ 2385a, 2385a nt.

Sept. 21, 1979, P.L. 96-67, 22 U.S. Code § 2151 nt.

International Development Association Act

June 30, 1960, P.L. 86-565, 74 Stat. 293, 22 U.S. Code §§ 284 to 284g

May 26, 1964, P.L. 88-310, 78 Stat. 200, 22 U.S. Code § 284e

May 23, 1969, P.L. 91-14, 83 Stat. 10, 22 U.S. Code § 284h

March 10, 1972, P.L. 92-247, 86 Stat. 60, 22 UCS §§ 284i to 284k

Aug. 14, 1974, P.L. 93-373, 88 Stat. 445, 22 U.S. Code §§ 284l, 284m

Oct. 3, 1977, P.L. 95-118, 22 U.S. Code § 284n

Dec. 22, 1987, P.L. 100-202, 22 U.S. Code § 284r

Dec. 19, 1989, P.L. 101-240, 22 U.S. Code § 284b

Nov. 5, 1990, P.L. 101-513, 22 U.S. Code § 284s

International Development Authority Act

Ariz. Rev. Stat. Ann., § 41-1553 et seq.

International Development Cooperation Act of 1979

Aug. 14, 1979, P.L. 96-53, 5 U.S. Code §§ 5314 to 5316, 5924; 7 U.S. Code § 1703 et seq.; 22 U.S. Code §§ 2151 nt., 2151-1 et seq.

Nov. 22, 1983, P.L. 98-164, 22 U.S. Code § 3511

International Dispute Reduction Act

Colo. Rev. Stat., 13-22-501 et seq.

International Dolphin Conservation Act of 1992

Oct. 26, 1992, P.L. 102-523, 16 U.S. Code § 1361 nt.

International Dolphin Conservation Program Act

Aug. 15, 1997, P.L. 105-42, 16 U.S. Code § 1361 nt.

International Economic Policy Act of 1972

Aug. 29, 1972, P.L. 92-412, 86 Stat. 646, 22 U.S. Code §§ 2841 to 2849

Oct. 4, 1973, P.L. 93-121, 88 Stat. 447, 22 U.S. Code §§ 2844, 2846, 2848, 2849

June 22, 1974, P.L. 93-315, 88 Stat. 239, 22 U.S. Code § 2849

Aug. 9, 1975, P.L. 94-87, 89 Stat. 432, 22 U.S. Code §§ 2847 to 2849

International Education Act of 1966

Oct. 29, 1966, P.L. 89-698, 80 Stat. 1066, 20 U.S. Code §§ 511, 592, 601, 602, 1085, 1171 to 1177; 22 U.S. Code §§ 2452, 2454, 2455

Oct. 16, 1968, P.L. 90-575, 82 Stat. 1062, 20 U.S. Code § 1176

International Emergency Economic Powers Act

Dec. 28, 1977, P.L. 95-223, 50 U.S. Code §§ 1701 et seq., 1701 nt.

Oct. 6, 1992, P.L. 102-393, 50 U.S. Code § 1705

Oct. 6, 1992, P.L. 102-396, 50 U.S. Code § 1705

April 30, 1994, P.L. 103-236, 50 U.S. Code § 1702

Sept. 23, 1996, P.L. 104-201, 50 U.S. Code § 1705

International Environment Protection Act of 1983

Nov. 22, 1983, P.L. 98-164, 22 U.S. Code § 2151 nt.

International Finance Corporation Act

Aug. 11, 1955, Ch. 788, 69 Stat. 669, 22 U.S. Code §§ 282 to 282g

Aug. 30, 1961, P.L. 87-185, 75 Stat. 413, 22 U.S. Code § 282c

Aug. 14, 1965, P.L. 89-126, 79 Stat. 519, 22 U.S. Code § 282h

Oct. 3, 1977, P.L. 95-118, 22 U.S. Code § 282i

Dec. 19, 1989, P.L. 101-240, 22 U.S. Code § 282b

Nov. 5, 1990, P.L. 101-513, 22 U.S. Code § 282k

April 1, 1992, P.L. 102-266, 22 U.S. Code § 282l

Oct. 24, 1992, P.L. 102-511, 22 U.S. Code §§ 282m, 282n

International Financial Institutions Act

Aug. 13, 1981, P.L. 97-35, 22 U.S. Code § 262c nt.

Nov. 30, 1983, P.L. 98-181, 22 U.S. Code § 262d

Dec. 22, 1987, P.L. 100-202, 22 U.S. Code § 262m

Oct. 1, 1988, P.L. 100-461, 22 U.S. Code §§ 262p-4b to 262p-4f, 262p-5

Dec. 19, 1989, P.L. 101-240, 22 U.S. Code §§ 262d, 262g-2 nt., 262m-6, 262m-7, 262p-4g to 262p-4k, 262p-1, 262p-5, 262r to 262r-2, 262s to 262s-2, 262t

Nov. 5, 1990, P.L. 101-513, 22 U.S. Code §§ 262d, 262p-4l, 262p-4n, 262p-5, 262r

Continued

Oct. 24, 1992, P.L. 102-511, 22 U.S. Code
§ 262d

April 30, 1994, P.L. 103-236, 22 U.S. Code
§ 262d

Aug. 23, 1994, P.L. 103-306, 22 U.S. Code
§§ 262o-1, 262p-4o, 262p-4p, 262p-5

April 24, 1996, P.L. 104-132, 22 U.S. Code
§ 262p-4q

Aug. 20, 1996, P.L. 104-188, 22 U.S. Code
§ 262p-4p

Sept. 30, 1996, P.L. 104-208, 22 U.S. Code
§ 262r

Nov. 26, 1997, P.L. 105-118, 22 U.S. Code
§ 262m-7

Oct. 21, 1998, P.L. 105-277, 22 U.S. Code
§§ 262n-3, 262o-2, 262r, 262r-3, 262r-4,
262r-5

Oct. 27, 1998, P.L. 105-292, 22 U.S. Code
§ 262d.

May 21, 1999, P.L. 106-31, 22 U.S. Code
§ 262r-5

June 25, 1999, P.L. 106-36, 22 U.S. Code
§ 262n-2

International Forestry Cooperation Act of 1990

Nov. 5, 1990, P.L. 101-513, 16 U.S. Code
§§ 4501 nt., 4502 et seq.

Oct. 29, 1992, P.L. 102-574, 16 U.S. Code
§§ 1641, 1643, 2101, 2109, 4501, 4503,
4503a to 4503d, 4504, 4505

Nov. 2, 1994, P.L. 103-437, 16 U.S. Code
§ 4503a

International Health Research Act of 1960

July 12, 1960, P.L. 86-610, 74 Stat. 364, 22
U.S. Code §§ 2101 to 2104; 42 U.S. Code
§ 242f

Nov. 10, 1998, P.L. 105-362, 22 U.S. Code
§ 2103

International Investment and Trade in Services Survey Act

Oct. 11, 1976, P.L. 94-472, 22 U.S. Code
§ 3101 et seq.

Sept. 29, 1979, P.L. 96-72, 22 U.S. Code
§§ 3108, 3108 nt.

Oct. 30, 1984, P.L. 98-573, 22 U.S. Code
§ 3101 nt.

Nov. 7, 1990, P.L. 101-533, 22 U.S. Code
§§ 3101, 3103 to 3105

International Investment Survey Act of 1976

See International Investment And Trade In
Services Survey Act

Oct. 11, 1976, P.L. 94-472, 22 U.S. Code
§ 3101 et seq.

Sept. 29, 1979, P.L. 96-72, 22 U.S. Code
§ 3108, 3108 nt.

International Lending Supervisions Act of 1983

Nov. 30, 1983, P.L. 98-181, 12 U.S. Code
§ 3901 et seq., 3901 nt.

Aug. 23, 1988, P.L. 100-418, 102 Stat. 1379,
11 U.S. Code § 3912

Dec. 19, 1989, P.L. 101-240, 12 U.S. Code
§ 3904a

Sept. 30, 1996, P.L. 104-208, 12 U.S. Code
§ 3912

International Maritime and Port Security Act

Aug. 27, 1986, P.L. 99-399, 33 U.S. Code
§ 1226; 46 U.S. Code Appx. §§ 1801, 1801
nt., 1802 to 1809

Oct. 21, 1998, P.L. 105-277, 46 U.S. Code
Appx. § 1804

International Maritime Satellite Telecommunications Act

Nov. 1, 1978, P.L. 95-564, 47 U.S. Code
§§ 751 et seq., 751 nt.

International Narcotics Control Act of 1985

Aug. 8, 1985, P.L. 99-83, 22 U.S. Code
§§ 2151 nt., 2151x, 2291 et seq.

International Narcotics Control Act of 1986

Oct. 27, 1986, P.L. 99-570, 22 U.S. Code
§ 2151 nt.

Nov. 2, 1992, P.L. 102-583, 22 U.S. Code
§§ 2291 nt., 2291-1

Nov. 2, 1994, P.L. 103-447, 22 U.S. Code
§§ 2151 nt., 2291 nt.; 46 U.S. Code Appx.
§ 1902 nt.

International Narcotics Control Act of 1988

Nov. 18, 1988, P.L. 100-690, 22 U.S. Code
§ 2151 nt.

Nov, 2, 1992, P.L. 102-583, 22 U.S. Code
§§ 2291 nt., 2291-2

Nov. 2, 1994, P.L. 103-447, 22 U.S. Code
§§ 2151 nt., 2291-2; 31 U.S. Code § 5311
nt.; 41 U.S. Code § 701 nt.

International Narcotics Control Act of 1989

Dec. 13, 1989, P.L. 101-231, 22 U.S. Code § 2151 nt.

Nov. 21, 1990, P.L. 101-623, 104 Stat. 3355

International Narcotics Control Act of 1990

Nov. 21, 1990, P.L. 101-623, 18 U.S. Code § 3196; 22 U.S. Code §§ 2151 nt., 2291 nt., 2291h nt.

International Narcotics Control Act of 1992

Nov. 2, 1992, P.L. 102-583, 22 U.S. Code § 2151 nt.

Nov. 2, 1994, P.L. 103-447, 7 U.S. Code § 1736g-1; 12 U.S. Code § 635; 18 U.S. Code § 981; 19 U.S. Code §§ 1616a, 2492, 2494, 3203; 21 U.S. Code § 881; 22 U.S. Code §§ 2151 nt., 2151x-2, 2291, 2291e, 2291h nt., 2420 nt.

International Narcotics Control Corrections Act of 1994

Nov. 2, 1994, P.L. 103-447, 22 U.S. Code § 2151 nt.

International Navigational Rules Act of 1977

July 27, 1977, P.L. 95-75, 33 U.S. Code § 1601 et seq.

International Organizations Immunities Act

Dec. 29, 1945, Ch. 652, 59 Stat. 669, 22 U.S. Code §§ 288, 288a to 288f; 42 U.S. Code §§ 401 nt., 409, 1001 nt., 1011 nts.

Feb. 2, 1966, P.L. 89-353, 80 Stat. 5, 22 U.S. Code § 288f-1

Nov. 27, 1973, P.L. 93-161, 87 Stat. 635, 22 U.S. Code § 288f-2

Aug. 15, 1979, P.L. 96-60, 22 U.S. Code § 288f-2

Nov. 22, 1983, P.L. 98-164, 22 U.S. Code § 288f-1

Dec. 22, 1987, P.L. 100-204, 22 U.S. Code § 288f-3

April 30, 1994, P.L. 103-236, 22 U.S. Code § 288f-4

Oct. 21, 1998, P.L. 105-277, 22 U.S. Code § 288f-2

International Organizations Procurement Act of 1947

Aug. 4, 1947, Ch. 479, 61 Stat. 752, 22 U.S. Code § 288 nt.

International Parental Kidnapping Crime Act of 1993

Dec. 2, 1993, P.L. 103-173, 18 U.S. Code §§ 1201 nt., 1204, 1204 nt.

International Peace Garden Act

N.D. Cent. Code, 55-05-01 et seq.

International Peacekeeping Act of 1992

July 2, 1992, P.L. 102-311, 106 Stat. 277

International Port District Act (Chicago)

Ill. Rev. Stat. 1991, Ch. 19, § 152 et seq.

International Procedure Act

Okla. Stat. Ann., Title 12, § 1701.01 et seq.

International Regional Port District Act

Ill. Rev. Stat. 1991, Ch. 19, § 152 et seq.

International Regulations for Preventing Collisions at Sea

Sept. 24, 1963, P.L. 88-131, 77 Stat. 194, 33 U.S. Code §§ 1051 to 1053, 1061 to 1094

International Religious Freedom Act of 1998

Oct. 27, 1998, P.L. 105-292, 112 Stat. 2787, 22 U.S. Code § 6401 nt.

International Rules (Collisions at Sea)

Aug. 19, 1890, Ch. 802, 26 Stat. 320, 33 U.S. Code § 301

International Safe Container Act

Dec. 13, 1977, P.L. 95-208, 46 U.S. Code §§ 1501 et seq., 1501 nt.

Sept. 9, 1982, P.L. 97-249, 46 U.S. Code §§ 1502, 1502 nt., 1504

International Securities Enforcement Cooperation Act of 1990

Nov. 15, 1990, P.L. 101-550, 15 U.S. Code § 78a nt.

International Security and Development Assistance Authorizations Act of 1983

Nov. 14, 1983, P.L. 98-151, 22 U.S. Code § 2151 nt.

International Security and Development Cooperation Act of 1980

Dec. 16, 1980, P.L. 96-533, 22 U.S. Code § 2151 nt.

Aug. 8, 1985, P.L. 99-83, 22 U.S. Code § 2293 nt.

Oct. 1, 1988, P.L. 100-461, 22 U.S. Code § 290h-3

International Security and Development Cooperation Act of 1981

Dec. 29, 1981, P.L. 97-113, 22 U.S. Code § 2151 nt.

Aug. 8, 1985, P.L. 99-83, 22 U.S. Code § 2370 nt.

Nov. 21, 1989, P.L. 101-162, 22 U.S. Code § 2370 nt.

Nov. 5, 1990, P.L. 101-513, 22 U.S. Code § 2370 nt.

Dec. 17, 1993, P.L. 103-199, 107 Stat. 2328

April 30, 1994, P.L. 103-236, 108 Stat. 399

International Security and Development Cooperation Act of 1985

Aug. 8, 1985, P.L. 99-83, 15 U.S. Code § 4011 nt., 16 U.S. Code § 469j, 22 U.S. Code § 2151 nt.

Dec. 28, 1985, P.L. 99-230

Aug. 27, 1986, P.L. 99- 399, 22 U.S. Code § 2349aa-7

Oct. 18, 1986, P.L. 99-500, 100 Stat. 3582

Oct. 30, 1986, P.L. 99-591, 100 Stat. 3582

Feb. 16, 1990, P.L. 101-246, 22 U.S. Code § 2151 nt.

Nov. 23, 1993, P.L. 103-149, 107 Stat. 1505

Oct. 21, 1998, P.L. 105-277, 16 U.S. Code § 469j

International Security Assistance Act of 1977

Aug. 4, 1977 P.L. 95-92, 22 U.S. Code §§ 2151 nt., 2261 et seq.

International Security Assistance Act of 1978

Dec. 17, 1993, P.L. 103-199, 22 U.S. Code § 2151 nt.

International Security Assistance Act of 1979

Oct. 29, 1979, P.L. 96-92, 22 U.S. Code §§ 2151 nt., 2291, 2291a, 2312, 2318, 2321h to 2321j, 2346, 2346c, 2346c nt., 2346d, 2347a, 2348, 2348a, 2661, 2753, 2761, 2765, 2767, 2768, 2771, 2773, 2776, 2778, 2792, 2794

International Security Assistance and Arms Export Control Act of 1976

June 30, 1976, P.L. 94-329, 22 U.S. Code § 2151 et seq.

Dec. 17, 1993, P.L. 103-199, 22 U.S. Code § 2293 nt.

International Surface Transportation Efficiency Act of 1991

Dec. 29, 1995, P.L. 104-88, 109 Stat. 957

International Terrorism Act

Ill. Comp. Stat. 1992, Ch. 720, § 5/29C-5 et seq.

International Trade Act

Del. Code of 1974, Title 30, §§ 1902, 2301

International Trade and Export Development Act

Tenn. Code Ann., 13-27-201 et seq.

International Trade and Export Development for Agricultural Products Act

Tenn. Code Ann., 13-27-202 et seq.

International Trade and Industrial Competitiveness Act

N.Y. Agriculture and Markets Law (Consol. Laws Ch. 69) § 16

N.Y. Economic Development Law (Consol. Laws Ch. 15) §§ 220 to 225

N.Y. Laws 1990, Ch. 291

N.Y. Public Authorities Law (Consol. Laws Ch. 43A) §§ 3102, 3102a, 3102d

International Trade and Investment Act
Oct. 30, 1984, P.L. 98-573, 19 U.S. Code
§ 2101 nt.

International Trade Development Act
Okla. Stat. Ann., Title 2, § 3001 et seq.

International Trade Enhancement Act
Ore. Rev. Stat. 1953, 285.069 et seq.

International Tradeport Development Authority Act
Mich. Comp. Laws Ann., 125.2521 et seq.

International Travel Act of 1961
June 29, 1961, P.L. 87-63, 75 Stat. 129, 22
U.S. Code §§ 2121 to 2126
Aug. 14, 1964, P.L. 88-426, 78 Stat. 426, 22
U.S. Code § 2124
Oct. 21, 1970, P.L. 91-477, 84 Stat. 1071, 22
U.S. Code §§ 2123, 2124, 2126, 2127
Dec. 19, 1973, P.L. 93-193, 87 Stat. 765, 22
U.S. Code § 2126
Oct. 10, 1979, P.L. 96-85, 22 U.S. Code
§§ 2126, 2128
Oct. 16, 1981, P.L. 97-63, 22 U.S. Code
§ 2121 nt.
Nov. 5, 1990, P.L. 101-508, 22 U.S. Code
§§ 2128, 2129
Sept. 30, 1992, P.L. 102-372, 22 U.S. Code
§§ 2121, 2122, 2123, 2123a, 2123b, 2123c,
2123d, 2124, 2124a, 2124b, 2124c, 2126
Oct. 11, 1996, P.L. 104-288, 22 U.S. Code
§§ 2122, 2123, 2123a to 2123d, 2124,
2124a, 2124b, 2126 to 2129

International Treaties Act (Recognition of)
Fla. Stat. Ann., 260.011

International Voyage Load Line Act of 1973
Oct. 1, 1973, P.L. 93-115, 87 Stat. 418, 46
U.S. Code §§ 85 to 85g, 86 to 86i

International Waterways Act
June 13, 1902, Ch. 1079, 32 Stat. 373, 22
U.S. Code § 267b; 33 U.S. Code §§ 1, 4,
402, 418, 499, 541, 556, 558, 565, 602, 631

International Wheat Agreement Act of 1949
Oct. 27, 1949, Ch. 772, 63 Stat. 945, 7 U.S.
Code §§ 1641, 1642
Aug. 1, 1953, Ch. 306, 67 Stat. 358, 7 U.S.
Code § 1641

Aug. 3, 1956, Ch. 911, 70 Stat. 966, 7 U.S.
Code § 1641
Sept. 21, 1959, P.L. 86-336, 73 Stat. 600, 7
U.S. Code § 1641
Sept. 5, 1962, P.L. 87-632, 76 Stat. 434, 7
U.S. Code § 1641
Oct. 21, 1998, P.L. 105-277, Division C,
Title XI, 112 Stat. 2681, 47 U.S. Code
§ 151 nt.

International Wills Act
See Uniform International Wills Act

Interne Act
Pa. Purdon's Stat., Title 35, §§ 435, 436

Internet Privacy Act (Advisory Committee on)
Ill. Comp. Stat. 1992, Ch. 20, § 3902/1 et seq.

Internet Protection Act (Children's)
Cal. Education Code 1976, §§ 48980,
51870.5

Internship Act (Architecture-Engineering)
Ill. Comp. Stat. 1992, Ch. 110, § 910/1 et seq.

Interparliamentary Union Acts
June 28, 1935, Ch. 322, 49 Stat. 425, 22 U.S.
Code §§ 276, 276a
Aug. 25, 1937, Ch. 757, 50 Stat. 770, 22 U.S.
Code § 276b
Feb. 6, 1948, Ch. 48, 62 Stat. 19, 22 U.S.
Code § 276
June 20, 1958, P.L. 85-477, 72 Stat. 272, 22
U.S. Code § 276
June 30, 1958, P.L. 85-474, 72 Stat. 246, 22
U.S. Code § 276c
Sept. 4, 1961, P.L. 87-185, 75 Stat. 465, 22
U.S. Code § 276
Aug. 1, 1962, P.L. 87-565, 76 Stat. 263, 22
U.S. Code § 276
Oct. 7, 1964, P.L. 88-633, 78 Stat. 1014, 22
U.S. Code § 276
Nov. 14, 1967, Publ 90-137, 81 Stat. 463, 22
U.S. Code § 276
Feb. 7, 1972, P.L. 92-226, 86 Stat. 34, 22
U.S. Code § 276

Interparty Agreement Act
See Uniform Interparty Agreement Act

Interpleader Act

May 8, 1926, Ch. 273, 44 Stat. 416 (See 28 U.S. Code §§ 1335, 1397, 2361)

Ark. Stat. 1987, 16-61-113 et seq.

Cal. Code of Civil Procedure § 386

Haw. Rev. Stat. Ann., § 634-11 et seq.

Mo. Rev. Stat., 507.060

N.C. Gen. Stat. 1943, Rules of Civil Procedure, Rule 19

N.Y. Civil Practice Law and Rules (Consol. Laws Ch. 8) § 1006

Wis. Stat. Ann., 803.07

Wis. Stat. 1973, 260.19

Interpleader Act (Concursus)

La. Code of Civil Procedure 1960, Art. 4651 et seq.

Interpleader Act (Warehousemen)

Cal. Commercial Code § 7603

La. Rev. Stat. Ann., 10:7-603 et seq.

Interpleader Compact

Me. Rev. Stat. Ann. 1964, Title 14, § 6351 et seq.

Interpleader Compact Act

Me. Rev. Stat. Ann. 1964, Title 14, § 6351 et seq.

N.H. Rev. Stat. 1955, 5-A:1 et seq.

N.J. Stat. Ann., 2A:41A-1 et seq.

Pa. Cons. Stat., Title 42, § 7521 et seq.

Interposition Act

La. Rev. Stat. Ann., 49:801 et seq.

Interposition Resolution

Miss. General Laws 1956, Ch. 466, p. 741

Interpreter Act (Criminal Proceeding)

Ill. Rev. Stat. 1991, Ch. 38, § 165-10 et seq.

Interpreter for the Deaf Act

Okla. Stat. Ann., Title 63, § 2407 et seq.

Interpreter Privilege Act

Ill. Rev. Stat.1987, Ch. 110, § 51 et seq.

Interpreter Services for the Hearing Impaired Act

Utah Code Ann. 1953, 53A-26a-101 et seq.

Interpreters Act (Court)

N.M. Stat. Ann., 38-10-1 et seq.

Interpreters for the Deaf Act

Ill. Comp. Stat. 1992, Ch. 225, § 442/1 et seq.

W. Va. Code 1966, § 5-14A-1 et seq.

Interracial Cohabitation Act

Fla. Stat. 1967, 798.04, 798.05

Interracial Marriage Act

Fla. Stat. 1967, 741.11 et seq.

Interrogatory Act

Neb. Rev. Stat. 1943, 25-1267.28 et seq.

Va. Acts 1977, Ch. 617

Interscholastic Athletic Organization Act

Ill. Rev. Stat. 1991, Ch. 122, §§ 1820, 1821

Interscholastic Athletics Eligibility Act

Ill. Rev. Stat. 1987, Ch. 122, § 1801.01 et seq.

Interspousal Immunity Act

Ill. Rev. Stat. 1991, Ch. 40, § 1000 et seq.

La. Rev. Stat. Ann., 9:291

Interstate (Regional) Banking Act

Cal. Finance Code § 3770 et seq.

Interstate Act

Del. Code of 1974, Title 12, § 501 et seq.

Md. Ann. Code 1974, Art. ET, § 3-101 et seq.

Interstate Agreement in Qualifications of Educational Personnel Act

Iowa Code Ann., 272A.1 et seq.

Interstate Agreement on Detainers Act

Dec. 9, 1970, P.L. 91-538, 84 Stat. 1397

Nov. 18, 1988, P.L. 100-690, 18 U.S. Code Appx. § 9

Ala. Code 1975, § 15-9-80 et seq.

Alaska Stat. 1962, § 33.35.010 et seq.

Ariz. Rev. Stat. Ann., §§ 31-481, 31-482

Ark. Code Ann. 1987, 16-95-101 et seq.

Cal. Penal Code § 1389 et seq.

Colo. Rev. Stat., 24-60-501 et seq.

Conn. Gen. Stat. Ann., § 54-186 et seq.

D.C. Code 1973, § 24-701 et seq.

Fla. Stat. Ann., 941.45 et seq.

Ga. Code Ann., 42-6-20 et seq.

Haw. Rev. Stat. Ann., § 834-1 et seq.

Ida. Code 1947, 19-5001 et seq.

Ill. Comp. Stat. 1992, Ch. 750, § 5/3-8-9

Ind. Code Ann., 35-33-10-4 et seq.

Iowa Code Ann., 821.1 et seq.

Kan. Stat. Ann., 22-4401 et seq.

Kan. Stat. Ann., 727-60a 1 et seq.

Ky. Rev. Stat. 1971, 440.450 et seq.

Md. Ann. Code 1957, Art. 27, § 616A

Me. Rev. Stat. Ann. 1964, Title 34-A § 9601 et seq.

Mich. Comp. Laws Ann., 780.601 et seq.

Minn. Stat. Ann., 629.294

Mo. Rev. Stat., 217.450 et seq.

Mont. Code Ann., 46-31-101 et seq.

N.C. Gen. Stat. 1943, § 15A-761 et seq.

N.D. Cent. Code, 29-34-01 et seq.

Neb. Rev. Stat. 1943, 29-759 et seq.

Nev. Rev. Stat. 1979 Reprint, 178.620 et seq.

N.H. Rev. Stat. 1955, 606-A:1 et seq.

N.J. Stat. Ann., 2A:159A-1 et seq.

N.M. Stat. Ann., 31-5-12 et seq.

N.Y. Criminal Procedure Law (Consol. Laws Ch. 11A) § 580.20

Ohio Rev. Code 1953, 2963.30 et seq.

Okla. Stat. Ann., Title 22, § 1345 et seq.

Ore. Rev. Stat. 1953, 134.775 et seq.

Ore. Rev. Stat., 135.005 et seq.

Pa. Cons. Stat., Title 42, § 9101 et seq.

R.I. Gen. Laws 1956, 13-13-1 et seq.

S.C. Code Ann. 1976, § 17-11-10 et seq.

S.D. Codified Laws 1967, 23-24A-1 et seq.

Tenn. Code Ann., 40-31-101 et seq.

Tex. Code of Criminal Procedure, Art. 51.14

Utah Code Ann. 1953, 77-29-5 et seq.

Va. Code 1950, § 53.1-210 et seq.

Vt. Stat. Ann., Title 28, § 1501 et seq.

Wash. Rev. Code Ann., 9.100.010 et seq.

Wis. Stat. Ann., 976.05

W. Va. Code 1966, § 62-14-1 et seq.

Wyo. Stat. Ann., § 7-15-101 et seq.

Interstate Agreement on High Speed Intercity Rail Passenger Network

Mich. Comp. Laws Ann., 462.71 et seq.

Interstate Agreement on Qualification of Educational Personnel Act

Ala. Code 1975, § 16-23A-1 et seq.

Cal. Education Code 1976, §§ 12500, 12501

Conn. Gen. Stat. Ann., § 10-146c et seq.

D.C. Code Ann., § 31-1301 et seq.

Del. Code of 1974, Title 14, § 8211 et seq.

Fla. Stat. Ann., 244.09 et seq.

Haw. Rev. Stat. Ann., § 315-1 et seq.

Ida. Code 1947, 33-4104 et seq.

Ind. Code Ann., 20-1-17-1, 20-1-17-2

Kan. Stat. Ann., 72-60a01 et seq.

Ky. Rev. Stat. 1971, 161.124

Md. Ann. Code 1974, Art. ED, § 6-601 et seq.

Me. Rev. Stat. Ann. 1964, Title 20A, § 13901 et seq.

Mich. Comp. Laws Ann., 388.1371 et seq.

Mont. Code Ann., 20-4-121 et seq.

N.C. Gen. Stat. 1943, § 3115C-349 et seq.

N.H. Rev. Stat. 1955, 200-E:1 et seq.

N.J. Stat. Ann., 18A:26-11 et seq.

Okla. Stat. Ann., Title 70, § 508.1 et seq.

Pa. Purdon's Stat., Title 24, § 2401.1 et seq.

R.I. Gen. Laws 1956, 16-11-5 et seq.

S.C. Code Ann. 1976, § 59-27-10 et seq.

S.D. Codified Laws 1967, 13-42-18 et seq.

Va. Code 1950, § 22.1-316 et seq.

Vt. Stat. Ann., Title 16, § 2041 et seq.

Wis. Stat. Ann., 115.46 et seq.

W. Va. Code 1966, § 18-10E-1 et seq.

Interstate Agreements on Sexually Dangerous Persons Act

Ill. Rev. Stat. 1991, Ch. 38, §§ 205, 205-1

Interstate Agreements Records Act

Pa. Purdon's Stat., Title 71, § 808.1 et seq.

Interstate Air Pollution Agreements Act

Pa. Purdon's Stat., Title 35, § 4101 et seq.

Interstate Airport Authorities Act

Ill. Rev. Stat. 1991, Ch. 15 1/2, § 250 et seq.

Interstate and Foreign Highway Carriers' Registration Act
Cal. Public Utilities Code § 3901 et seq.

Interstate and International Banking Act
Ala. Code 1975, § 5-13B-1 et seq.

Interstate and International Procedure Act
See also Uniform Interstate and International Procedure Act
Ark. Code Ann. 1987, 16-4-108 et seq.
Mass. Gen. Laws Ann., 223A:1 et seq.
Mich. Comp. Laws Ann., 600.1852, 600.2114a, 600.2118a
Pa. Cons. Stat., Title 42, § 5321 et seq.

Interstate Arbitration and Compromise of Death Taxes Act
See also Uniform Interstate Arbitration and Compromise of Death Taxes Act
Neb. Rev. Stat. 1943, 77-3315 et seq.

Interstate Arbitration of Death Taxes Act
See Uniform Interstate Arbitration of Death Taxes
See Uniform Interstate Arbitration of Death Taxes Act

Interstate Bank Acquisition Act
N.M. Stat. Ann., 58-1B-1 to 58-1B-11

Interstate Bank Branching Act
N.M. Stat. Ann., 58-1C-1 to 58-1C-13

Interstate Banking Act
Cal. Revenue and Taxation Code § 13820
Conn. Gen. Stat. Ann., § 12-371 et seq.
Del. Code of 1974, Title 5, § 841 et seq.
Fla. Stat. Ann., 658.295
Md. Ann. Code 1974, Art. TG, § 7-104 et seq.
Minn. Stat. Ann., 48.91 et seq.
S.C. Code Ann. 1976, § 34-24-10 et seq.
Vt. Stat. Ann., Title 32, § 7101 et seq.
W. Va. Code 1966, § 11-11B-1 et seq.

Interstate Banking Act (Reciprocal)
N.C. Gen. Stat. 1943, § 53-209 et seq.

Interstate Banking and Branching Act (Caldera, Weggeland and Killea)
Cal. Statutes 1996, Ch. 799

Interstate Banking and Savings and Loan Association Act
Ariz. Rev. Stat. Ann., § 6-321 et seq.

Interstate Branch Act (Savings and Loan)
N.C. Gen. Stat. 1943, § 54B-265 et seq.

Interstate Branch Act (Savings Bank)
N.C. Gen. Stat. 1943, § 54C-199 et seq.

Interstate Branch Banking Act
Miss. Code Ann. 1972, § 81-23-1 et seq.
N.C. Gen. Stat. 1943, § 53-219 et seq.

Interstate Branching Act
Fla. Stat. Ann., 658.2953
Ida. Code 1947, 26-1601 et seq.

Interstate Branching by Merger Act
Neb. Rev. Stat. 1943, 8-2101 to 8-2108

Interstate Bridge Act
Iowa Code Ann., 313A.1 et seq.
Neb. Rev. Stat. 1943, 39-891 et seq.
Ore. Rev. Stat., 381.005 et seq.
Wis. Stat. Ann., 84.12

Interstate Bus Motor Fuel Tax Compact Act
N.H. Rev. Stat. 1955, 260:66

Interstate Buses Compact (Taxation of Motor Fuels Consumed by)
N.H. Rev. Stat. 1955, 260:66 et seq.

Interstate Certification Compact
Conn. Gen. Stat. Ann., § 10-146-C et seq.

Interstate Child Placement Compact
N.D. Cent. Code, 14-13-01 et seq.
Vt. Stat. Ann., Title 33, § 5901 et seq.

Interstate Civil Defense and Disaster Compact Act
Ark. Code Ann. 1987, 11-2001, 11-2002
Cal. Government Code, § 177 et seq.
Conn. Gen. Stat. Ann., § 28-23
Ga. Code Ann., 38-3-70 et seq.

Ind. Code Ann., 10-4-2-1 et seq.
Kan. Stat. Ann., 48-3201 et seq.
La. Rev. Stat. Ann., 29:715
Md. Ann. Code 1957, Art. 41, § 17-101 et seq.
Me. Rev. Stat. Ann. 1964, Title 37-B, § 902 et seq.
Mont. Code Ann. 1983, 10-3-206
Nev. Rev. Stat. Ann. 415.010
Tex. Rev. Civil Stat., Art. 6889-5
Wash. Rev. Code Ann., 38.52.090
W. Va. Code 1966, § 15-5-22

Interstate Civil Defense and Disaster Compacts Act
Me. Rev. Stat. Ann. 1964, Title 37-B, § 902 et seq.
Miss. Code Ann. 1972, § 33-15-101
S.C. Code Ann. 1976, § 25-9-20 et seq.

Interstate Civil Defense Compact Act
N.H. Rev. Stat. 1955, 108:1, 108:2
Vt. Stat. Ann., Title 20, § 81 et seq.

Interstate Co-operation Commission Act
Mass. Gen. Laws Ann., 9:21 et seq.

Interstate Commerce Acts
Feb. 4, 1887, Ch. 104, 24 Stat. 379, 49 U.S. Code §§ 1 to 22, 25 to 27, 153, 153 nt., 301 to 312, 314 to 327, 901 to 923, 1001 to 1022
March 2, 1889, Ch. 382, 25 Stat. 855, 49 U.S. Code §§ 6, 10, 12, 14, 16 to 18, 21, 22, 49
Feb. 10, 1891, Ch. 128, 26 Stat. 743, 49 U.S. Code § 12
Feb. 19, 1903, Ch. 708, 32 Stat. 847, 49 U.S. Code §§ 41 to 43
June 29, 1906, Ch. 3591, 34 Stat. 584, 49 U.S. Code §§ 1, 6, 11, 14 to 16, 18, 20, 41
April 13, 1908, Ch. 143, 35 Stat. 60, 49 U.S. Code § 1
June 18, 1910, Ch. 309, 36 Stat. 539, 49 U.S. Code §§ 1, 4, 6, 10, 13, 15, 16, 20, 50
Aug. 24, 1912, Ch. 390, 37 Stat. 566, 49 U.S. Code § 5
May 29, 1917, Ch. 23, 40 Stat. 101, 49 U.S. Code § 1
Feb. 28, 1920, Ch. 91, 41 Stat. 474, 49 U.S. Code §§ 1 to 6, 10 to 16, 17, 18, 19a to 20a, 26, 27
Aug. 9, 1935, Ch. 498, 49 Stat. 543, 49 U.S. Code §§ 1 to 13, 15 to 17, 19, 19a, 20, 20a, 22, 26, 27, 301 to 312, 314 to 327

July 5, 1937, Ch. 432, 50 Stat. 475, 49 U.S. Code § 22
Aug. 26, 1937, Ch. 818, 50 Stat. 835, 49 U.S. Code § 26
June 29, 1938, Ch. 811, 52 Stat. 1236, 15 U.S. Code § 77c; 49 U.S. Code §§ 303 to 306, 309, 310a, 312, 314, 316, 318, 324
Sept. 18, 1940, Ch. 722, 54 Stat. 899, 49 U.S. Code §§ 1, 3 to 6, 12, 13, 15, 15a, 16 to 17, 20, 22, 26, 27, 65 to 67, 301 to 306, 309 to 312, 314, 316 to 318, 320 to 322, 324a, 325, 326, 327, 901 to 923
March 27, 1942, Ch. 199, 56 Stat. 176, 49 U.S. Code §§ 304, 301a, 911
May 16, 1942, Ch. 318, 56 Stat. 284, 49 U.S. Code §§ 23, 302, 319, 1001 to 1022
Nov. 12, 1943, Ch. 299, 57 Stat. 590, 49 U.S. Code § 1009
Sept. 27, 1944, Ch. 423, 58 Stat. 751, 49 U.S. Code § 22
May 16, 1945, Ch. 128, 59 Stat. 169, 49 U.S. Code § 1009
Feb. 20, 1946, Ch. 32, 60 Stat. 21, 49 U.S. Code § 1009
April 9, 1948, Ch. 180, 62 Stat. 163, 49 U.S. Code § 20b
June 3, 1948, Ch. 386, 62 Stat. 295, 49 U.S. Code § 20
June 12, 1948, Ch. 457, 62 Stat. 386, 49 U.S. Code § 903
June 17, 1948, Ch. 491, 62 Stat. 472, 49 U.S. Code § 5b
June 24, 1948, Ch. 622, 62 Stat. 602, 49 U.S. Code § 1
May 24, 1949, Ch. 139, 63 Stat. 108, 49 U.S. Code § 305(g)
June 29, 1949, Ch. 272, 63 Stat. 280, 49 U.S. Code §§ 304a, 908, 1006a
July 26, 1949, Ch. 361, 63 Stat. 479, 49 U.S. Code § 305
Aug. 2, 1949, Ch. 379, 63 Stat. 485, 49 U.S. Code §§ 1, 3, 5, 6, 16, 20, 20a, 320 to 322, 913, 915, 1012
Sept. 1, 1950, Ch. 835, 64 Stat. 574, 49 U.S. Code §§ 303, 306, 309
Dec. 20, 1950, Ch. 1140, 64 Stat. 1113, 49 U.S. Code §§ 1002, 1009
July 9, 1952, Ch. 599, 66 Stat. 479, 49 U.S. Code § 303
July 10, 1952, Ch. 648, 66 Stat. 542, 49 U.S. Code § 314
July 16, 1952, Ch. 881, 66 Stat. 724, 49 U.S. Code § 20c
Continued

July 22, 1954, Ch. 563, 68 Stat. 526, 49 U.S. Code §§ 303, 315, 321

July 27, 1956, Ch. 759, 70 Stat. 702, 49 U.S. Code § 22

Aug. 3, 1956, Ch. 905, 70 Stat. 958, 49 U.S. Code §§ 303, 304

Aug. 3, 1956, Ch. 928, 70 Stat. 983, 49 U.S. Code § 304

July 11, 1957, P.L. 85-99, 71 Stat. 292, 49 U.S. Code § 4

Aug. 13, 1957, P.L. 85-124, 71 Stat. 343, 49 U.S. Code § 318

Aug. 14, 1957, P.L. 85-135, 71 Stat. 352, 49 U.S. Code § 322

Aug. 16, 1957, P.L. 85-150, 71 Stat. 369, 49 U.S. Code § 20b

Aug. 22, 1957, P.L. 85-163, 71 Stat. 411, 49 U.S. Code §§ 303, 309, 312

Aug. 28, 1957, P.L. 85-176, 71 Stat. 452, 49 U.S. Code § 1010

Aug. 31, 1957, P.L. 85-246, 71 Stat. 564, 49 U.S. Code § 22

Sept. 7, 1957, P.L. 85-309, 71 Stat. 631, 49 U.S. Code § 314

Aug. 12, 1958, P.L. 85-625, 72 Stat. 568, 49 U.S. Code §§ 1, 13, 13a, 15a, 303, 1231 to 1240

Aug. 23, 1958, P.L. 85-728, 72 Stat. 812, 49 U.S. Code § 313

Aug. 26, 1958, P.L. 85-762, 72 Stat. 859, 49 U.S. Code §§ 16, 304a, 908, 1006a

Sept. 2, 1958, P.L. 85-857, 72 Stat. 1264, 49 U.S. Code § 22

July 12, 1960, P.L. 86-615, 74 Stat. 382, 49 U.S. Code §§ 303, 306, 309, 903, 909, 1010, 1018

April 1, 1961, P.L. 87-16, 75 Stat. 41, 49 U.S. Code § 1240

Sept. 14, 1961, P.L. 87-247, 75 Stat. 517, 49 U.S. Code § 17

Aug. 24, 1962, P.L. 87-595, 76 Stat. 397, 49 U.S. Code §§ 316, 905

Sept. 27, 1962, P.L. 87-707, 76 Stat. 635, 49 U.S. Code § 4

Oct. 15, 1962, P.L. 87-805, 76 Stat. 911, 49 U.S. Code § 306

Dec. 17, 1963, P.L. 88-208, 77 Stat. 402, 49 U.S. Code § 303

July 24, 1965, P.L. 89-86, 79 Stat. 263, 49 U.S. Code §§ 20a, 314

July 27, 1965, P.L. 89-93, 79 Stat. 284, 49 U.S. Code §§ 5, 5 nt.

Sept. 6, 1965, P.L. 89-170, 79 Stat. 648, 49 U.S. Code §§ 302, 304a, 305, 322, 912a, 1006a, 1017

May 26, 1966, P.L. 89-430, 80 Stat. 168, 49 U.S. Code § 1

Oct. 15, 1966, P.L. 89-670, 80 Stat. 943, 49 U.S. Code Appx. § 312

Nov. 10, 1966, P.L. 89-804, 80 Stat. 1521, 49 U.S. Code § 308

July 26, 1968, P.L. 90-433, 82 Stat. 448, 49 U.S. Code §§ 303, 320

Oct. 17, 1968, P.L. 90-586, 82 Stat. 1149, 49 U.S. Code § 922a

Oct. 15, 1970, P.L. 91-452, 84 Stat. 931, 49 U.S. Code §§ 10301, 10302, 10321, 11703, 11705, 11913

Dec. 23, 1970, P.L. 91-569, 84 Stat. 1499, 49 U.S. Code §§ 26a, 27, 302, 325a, 922b

Dec. 28, 1970, P.L. 91-590, 84 Stat. 1687, 49 U.S. Code § 903

July 7, 1972, P.L. 92-338, 86 Stat. 423, 49 U.S. Code §§ 320, 326

July 13, 1972, P.L. 92-348, 86 Stat. 463, 49 U.S. Code §§ 1234, 1235, 1239a

Feb. 15, 1978, P.L. 95-231, 49 U.S. Code § 26b(6)

Nov. 2, 1978, P.L. 95-574, 49 U.S. Code § 26

Nov. 6, 1978, P.L. 95-598, 49 U.S. Code §§ 20c, 313, 922

Nov. 6, 1978, P.L. 95-599, 49 U.S. Code § 303

Nov. 8, 1978, P.L. 95-607, 49 U.S. Code §§ 1, 15

Nov. 8, 1978, P.L. 95-611, 49 U.S. Code § 17

Nov. 9, 1978, P.L. 95-620, 49 U.S. Code § 26b

June 22, 1988, P.L. 100-342, § 17, 102 Stat. 635

Sept. 3, 1992, P.L. 102-365, 49 U.S. Code Appx. § 26

Interstate Commerce Commission Dangerous Article Act

See Dangerous Cargo Act

Interstate Commission for Higher Education

Mont. Code Ann., 20-25-801 et seq.

Interstate Compact Act (Border State School)

Ill. Comp. Stat. 1992, Ch. 45, § 95/0.01 et seq.

Interstate Compact Act on Juveniles (Bendition Amendment)

Ala. Code 1975, 44-2-8

Pa. Purdon's Stat., Title 61, § 321 et seq.

Interstate Compact for Education Act

Ill. Rev. Stat. 1991, Ch. 122, § 100-0.1 et seq.

Minn. Stat. Ann., 121.81 et seq.

Mo. Rev. Stat., 173.300 et seq.

Ore. Laws 1967, Ch. 606

Pa. Purdon's Stat., Title 24, § 5401 et seq.

R.I. Gen. Laws 1956, 16-47-1

Vt. Stat. Ann., Title 16, § 1501 et seq.

Interstate Compact for Jurisdiction on the Colorado River

Ariz. Rev. Stat. Ann., § 37-620.11

Interstate Compact for Motor Vehicle Safety Equipment

Vt. Stat. Ann., Title 23, § 1801 et seq.

Interstate Compact for Mutual Military Aid in an Emergency Act

Conn. Gen. Stat. Ann., § 27-38

Pa. Cons. Stat., Title 51, § 4501

Interstate Compact for Protection of Resources

R.I. Gen. Laws 1956, 46-17-1 et seq.

Interstate Compact for Qualification of Educational Personnel Act

Utah Code Ann. 1953, 53A-6-201 et seq.

Interstate Compact for School Bus Safety Act

Wash. Rev. Code Ann., 46.39.010 et seq.

Interstate Compact for the Conservation and Utilization of Natural Energy and Water Resources Act

Tex. Natural Resource Code, § 142.001 et seq.

Interstate Compact for the Supervision of Parolees and Probationers Act

Ariz. Rev. Stat. Ann., § 31-461 et seq.

Mass. Gen. Laws 1984, 127:151A et seq.

Mo. Rev. Stat., 217.810

Mont. Code Ann., 46-23-1102

Pa. Purdon's Stat., Title 61, § 321 et seq.

Vt. Stat. Ann., Title 28, § 1301

Interstate Compact Mutual Military Aid in an Emergency

Conn. Gen. Stat. Ann., § 27-38

Interstate Compact on Adoption Act

Ill. Comp. Stat. 1992, Ch. 45, § 17/5-1 et seq.

Interstate Compact on Adoption and Medical Assistance

N.M. Stat. Ann., 40-7B-1 et seq.

Tenn. Code Ann., 36-1-201 et seq.

Interstate Compact on Adoption Assistance

Ind. Code Ann., 31-3-5-1 et seq.

Interstate Compact on Agricultural Grain Marketing Act

Colo. Rev. Stat., 24-60-2001 et seq.

Kan. Stat. Ann., 2-3101

Neb. Laws 1985, L.B. 628

S.D. Codified Laws 1967, 38-28-1

Interstate Compact on Air Pollution (Ohio-West Virginia)

See Air Pollution Compact Act (Ohio-West Virginia)

Interstate Compact on Air Pollution Act

Ky. Rev. Stat. 1971, 224.18-220

Ohio Rev. Code 1953, 3723.01 et seq.

W. Va. Code 1966, § 29-1G-1 et seq.

Interstate Compact on Arbitration of Death Taxes

Me. Rev. Stat. Ann. 1964, Title 36, § 3911 et seq.

Interstate Compact on Conservation Act

See Interstate Compact to Conserve Oil and Gas Act

Interstate Compact on Dairy Pricing (Northeast)
Conn. Public Acts 1993, p. 911, No. 320
Mass. Laws 1993, Ch. 370
N.H. Rev. Stat. 1955, 184-A:1
N.Y. Agriculture and Markets Law (Consol. Laws Ch. 69) §§ 258KK to 258NN
R.I. Gen. Laws 1956, 5-48.1-1 et seq.
Vt. Stat. Ann., Title 6, § 1801 et seq.

Interstate Compact on Detainers Act
Me. Rev. Stat. Ann. 1964, Title 34-A, § 9601 et seq.

Interstate Compact on Industrialized/ Modular Buildings
Minn. Stat. Ann., 16B.75

Interstate Compact on Interpleader
N.J. Stat. Ann., 2A:41A-1 et seq.

Interstate Compact on Juveniles
See Uniform Interstate Compact on Juveniles

Interstate Compact on Juveniles (Rendition Amendment)
Ala. Acts 1986, No. 419

Interstate Compact on Juveniles Act
Ala. Code 1975, § 44-2-1 et seq.
Ala. Code 1975, § 44-2-20 et seq.
Alaska Stat. 1962, § 47.15.010 et seq.
Ariz. Rev. Stat. Ann., § 8-361 et seq.
Cal. Welfare and Institutions Code § 1300
Conn. Gen. Stat. 1983, § 46b-151 et seq.
D.C. Code 1973, § 32-1101 et seq.
Del. Code of 1974, Title 31, § 5201 et seq.
Fla. Stat. Ann., 39.51 et seq.
Fla. Stat. Ann., 39.001 et seq.
Ga. Code Ann., 39-3-1 et seq.
Ida. Code 1947, 16-1901 et seq.
Ill. Rev. Stat. 1991, Ch. 23, § 2590 et seq.
Ind. Code Ann., 31-6-10-1 et seq.
Iowa Code Ann., 232.171, 232.172
Kan. Stat. Ann., 38-1001 et seq.
Ky. Rev. Stat. 1971, 615.010 et seq.
Md. Ann. Code 1957, Art. 83c, § 3-101 et seq.
Md. Ann. Code 1974, Art. HG, § 6-301 et seq.

Me. Rev. Stat. Ann. 1964, Title 34-A, § 9001 et seq.
Mich. Comp. Laws Ann., 3.701 et seq.
Minn. Stat. Ann., 260.51 et seq.
Miss. Code Ann. 1972, § 43-25-1 et seq.
Mont. Code Ann., 41-6-101 et seq.
N.C. Gen. Stat. 1943, § 110-58 et seq.
N.D. Cent. Code, 27-22-01 et seq.
Neb. Rev. Stat. 1943, 43-1001 et seq.
N.H. Rev. Stat. 1955, 169-A:1 et seq.
N.J. Stat. Ann., 9:23-1 et seq.
N.M. Stat. Ann., 32-3-1 et seq.
Okla. Stat. Ann., Title 10, § 531 et seq.
Ore. Rev. Stat., 417.010 et seq.
Pa. Purdon's Stat., Title 11, § 881 et seq.
Pa. Purdon's Stat., Title 62, § 731 et seq.
R.I. Gen. Laws 1956, 14-6-1 et seq.
S.C. Code Ann. 1976, § 20-7-2080
S.D. Codified Laws 1967, 26-12-1 et seq.
Tenn. Code Ann., 37-4-101 et seq.
Tex. Family Code, § 25.01 et seq.
Utah Code Ann. 1953, 55-12-1 et seq.
Utah Code Ann. 1953, 78-3a-1 et seq.
Va. Code 1950, § 16.1-323 et seq.
Vt. Stat. Ann., Title 33, §§ 551 et seq., 5701
Wyo. Stat. Ann., § 14-6-101 et seq.

Interstate Compact on Libraries
Mont. Code Ann., 22-1-601, 22-1-602

Interstate Compact on Low-Level Radioactive Waste (Rocky Mountain)
N.D. Cent. Code, 23-20.5-01 et seq.

Interstate Compact on Low-Level Radioactive Waste Act (Central)
Okla. Stat. Ann., Title 63, § 1-2101 et seq.

Interstate Compact on Low-Level Radioactive Waste Management Act (Northwest)
Ore. Rev. Stat., 469.930

Interstate Compact on Mental Health Act
April 26, 1972, P.L. 92-280, 86 Stat. 126
July 10, 1973, P.L. 93-69, 87 Stat. 166, 49 U.S. Code § 15a
Dec. 27, 1973, P.L. 93-201, 87 Stat. 838, 49 U.S. Code § 15a
Jan. 2, 1974, P.L. 93-236, 87 Stat. 1021, 49 U.S. Code § 1

Ala. Code 1975, § 22-55-1 et seq.

Ark. Code Ann. 1987, 20-50-101 et seq.

Conn. Gen. Stat. Ann., § 17-258 et seq.

Conn. Gen. Stat. 1983, § 17a-615 et seq.

D.C. Code Ann., § 6-1801 et seq.

Del. Code of 1974, Title 16, § 6101 et seq.

Fla. Stat. Ann., 394.479 et seq.

Ga. Code Ann., 37-10-1 et seq.

Haw. Rev. Stat. Ann., § 335-1 et seq.

Ida. Code 1947, 66-1201 et seq.

Ill. Rev. Stat. 1991, Ch. 91 1/2, § 50-0.1 et seq.

Ind. Code Ann., 16-13-8-1 et seq.

Iowa Code Ann., 221.1 et seq.

Ky. Rev. Stat. 1971, 210.520 et seq.

Md. Ann. Code 1974, Art. HG, § 11-101 et seq.

Me. Rev. Stat. Ann. 1964, Title 34-B, § 9001 et seq.

Mich. Comp. Laws Ann., 330.1920 et seq.

Minn. Stat. Ann., 245.51 et seq.

Mo. Rev. Stat., 630.810 et seq.

Mont. Code Ann., 53-22-101 et seq.

N.C. Gen. Stat. 1943, § 3122C-361 et seq.

N.D. Cent. Code, 25-11-01 et seq.

Neb. Rev. Stat. 1943, 83-801 et seq.

N.H. Rev. Stat. 1955, 135-A:1 et seq.

N.M. Stat. Ann., 11-7-1 et seq.

N.Y. Mental Hygiene Law 1977 (Consol. Laws Ch. 27) § 67.07

Ohio Rev. Code 1953, 5119.50

Okla. Stat. Ann., Title 43A, § 6-201 et seq.

Ore. Rev. Stat., 428.310, 428.320

R.I. Gen. Laws 1956, 40.1-9-1 et seq.

S.C. Code Ann. 1976, § 44-25-10 et seq.

S.D. Codified Laws 1967, 27A-6-1 et seq.

Tenn. Code Ann., 33-9-201 et seq.

Tex. Health and Safety Code, § 612.001 et seq.

Tex. Rev. Civ. Stat., Art. 5561f

Va. Acts 1976, Ch. 671, Va. Code 1950, § 37.1-1 et seq.

Vt. Stat. Ann., Title 18, § 9001 et seq.

Wyo. Stat. Ann., § 25-10-301 et seq.

Interstate Compact on Mentally Disordered Offender Act

Del. Code of 1974, Title 16, §§ 5201, 5202

Ill. Rev. Stat. 1991, Ch. 91 1/2, § 50-20 et seq.

Me. Rev. Stat. Ann. 1964, Title 15, § 2301 et seq.

Mo. Rev. Stat., 630.855

N.D. Cent. Code, 25-14-01, 25-14-02

N.H. Rev. Stat. 1955, 1126-C:1 et seq.

N.M. Stat. Ann., 31-5-10, 31-5-11

R.I. Gen. Laws 1956, 40.1-10-1 et seq.

W. Va. Code 1966, § 27-15-1 et seq.

Interstate Compact on Pest Control Act

Ore. Rev. Stat. 1953, 670.650 et seq.

Interstate Compact on Placement of Children Act

Ala. Code 1975, § 44-2-20 et seq.

Alaska Stat. 1962, § 47.70.010 et seq.

Ariz. Rev. Stat. Ann., § 8-548 et seq.

Ark. Code Ann. 1987, 9-29-201 et seq.

Cal. Civil Code § 264 et seq.

Colo. Rev. Stat., 24-60-1801 et seq.

Conn. Gen. Stat. Ann., § 17-81a et seq.

Del. Code of 1974, Title 31, § 381 et seq.

Fla. Stat. Ann., 409.401 et seq.

Ga. Code Ann., 39-4-1 et seq.

Haw. Rev. Stat. Ann., 350E-1 et seq.

Ida. Code 1947, 16-2101 et seq.

Ill. Rev. Stat. 1991, Ch. 23, § 2600 et seq.

Ind. Code Ann., 12-3-23-1 et seq.

Iowa Code Ann., 232.158 et seq.

Kan. Stat. Ann., 38-1201 et seq.

Ky. Rev. Stat. 1971, 600.010 et seq., 615.030, 615.040

La. Rev. Stat. Ann., 46:1700 et seq.

Md. Ann. Code 1974, Art. FL, § 5-601 et seq.

Me. Rev. Stat. Ann. 1964, Title 22, § 4191 et seq.

Mich. Comp. Laws Ann., 3.711 et seq.

Minn. Stat. Ann., 257.40 et seq.

Mo. Rev. Stat., 210.620 et seq.

Mont. Code Ann., 41-4-101 et seq.

N.C. Gen. Stat. 1943, § 110-57.1 et seq.

Neb. Rev. Stat. 1943, 43-1101

N.H. Rev. Stat. 1955, 170-A:1 et seq.

N.M. Stat. 1978, 32-4-1 et seq.

Ohio Rev. Code 1953, 5103.20 et seq.

Okla. Stat. Ann., Title 10, § 571 et seq.

Ore. Rev. Stat., 417.200 et seq.

Pa. Purdon's Stat., Title 62, § 746 et seq.

R.I. Gen. Laws 1956, 40-15-1 et seq.

Continued

S.C. Code Ann. 1976, § 20-7-1980 et seq.
S.D. Codified Laws 1967, 26-13-1 et seq.
Tenn. Code Ann., 37-4-101 et seq.
Tex. Human Resources Code, § 45.021 et seq.
Utah Code Ann. 1953, 62A-4-301 et seq.
Va. Code 1950, § 63.1-219.1 et seq.
Vt. Stat. Ann., Title 33, § 3151 et seq.
Vt. Stat. Ann., Title 33, § 5901 et seq.
Wash. Rev. Code Ann., 26.34.010 et seq.
Wis. Stat. Ann., 48.988, 48.989
W. Va. Code 1966, § 49-2A-1 et seq.
Wyo. Stat. Ann., § 14-5-101 et seq.

Interstate Compact on Qualifications of Educational Personnel Act
W. Va. Code 1966, § 18-10E-1 et seq.

Interstate Compact on the Mentally Disordered Offender
Me. Rev. Stat. Ann. 1964, Title 15, § 2301 et seq.
R.I. Gen. Laws 1956, 40.1-10-1 et seq.

Interstate Compact on Welfare Services Act
Conn. Gen. Stat. Ann., § 17-21a et seq.
Me. Rev. Stat. Ann. 1964, Title 22, § 4101 et seq.

Interstate Compact to Conserve Oil and Gas
July 7, 1943, Ch. 194, 57 Stat. 383

Interstate Compact to Conserve Oil and Gas Act
Cal. Public Resources Code § 3275 et seq.
Ill. Rev. Stat. 1991, Ch. 96 1/2, § 5300 et seq.
Kan. Stat. Ann., 55-803, 55-804 et seq.
Md. Ann. Code 1974, Art. NR, § 6-401 et seq.
Mich. Comp. Laws Ann., 319.301 et seq.
Mont. Code Ann., 82-11-301 et seq.
N.M. Laws 1935, Ch. 128
N.Y. Environmental Conservation Law 1972 (Consol. Laws Ch. 43B) § 23-2101
Pa. Purdon's Stat., Title 58, § 191 et seq.
S.C. Code Ann. 1976, § 48-41-10
S.D. Codified Laws 1967, 45-10-1 et seq.
Tenn. Code Ann., 60-2-101 et seq.
Tex. Natural Resources Code, § 90.007
Va. Code 1950, §§ 45.1-381, 45.1-382

Wyo. Stat. Ann., § 30-5-201 et seq.

Interstate Compromise and Arbitration of Death Taxes Act
See also Uniform Act of Interstate Compromise and Arbitration of Death
Md. Ann. Code 1974, Art. TG § 7-118 et seq.
Me. Rev. Stat Ann. 1964, Title 36, § 3981 et seq.
Va. Code 1950, § 58.1-920 et seq.
W. Va. Code 1966, § 11-11/A-1 et seq.

Interstate Compromise and Arbitration of Inheritance Taxes Act
Colo. Rev. Stat., 39-24-101 et seq.
Pa. Cons. Stat., Title 72, § 1756 et seq.

Interstate Compromise of Death Taxes Act
See Uniform Interstate Compromise of Death Taxes Act

Interstate Connecticut River Flood Control Compact Act
Vt. Stat. Ann., Title 10, § 1151 et seq.

Interstate Connecting Route Act
Tenn. Code Ann., 54-5-501 et seq.

Interstate Cooperation Act
Mass. Gen. Laws Ann., 9:21 et seq.
Okla. Stat. Ann., Title 74, § 423 et seq.

Interstate Cooperation Commission Act
Me. Rev. Stat. Ann. 1964, Title 3, § 201 et seq.
Mich. Comp. Laws Ann., 3.31 et seq.
Tex. Rev. Civ. Stat., Art. 4413b-1
Vt. Stat. Ann., Title 1, § 781 et seq.

Interstate Corrections Compact Act
Ala. Acts 1985, p. 1247
Ala. Code 1975, 14-13-1 et seq.
Alaska Stat. 1962, § 33.36.010 et seq.
Ariz. Rev. Stat. Ann., §§ 31-491, 31-492
Ark. Code Ann. 1987, 12-49-101 et seq.
Cal. Penal Code § 11189 et seq.
Colo. Rev. Stat., 24-60-801 et seq.
Conn. Gen. Stat. Ann., § 18-105 et seq.
Del. Code of 1974, Title 11, § 6570 et seq.
Fla. Stat. Ann., 941.55 et seq.
Ga. Code Ann., 42-11-1, 42-11-2, 42-11-3

Haw. Session Laws 1996, Act 57

Ida. Code 1947, 20-701 et seq.

Ill. Rev. Stat. 1991, Ch. 38, § 1003-4-4

Ind. Code Ann., 11-8-4-1 et seq.

Iowa Code Ann., 913.1 et seq.

Kan. Stat. Ann., 76-3001 et seq.

Md. Ann. Code 1957, Art. 41, § 4-1201 et seq.

Me. Rev. Stat. Ann. 1964, Title 34A § 9401 et seq.

Mich. Comp. Laws Ann., 3.981 et seq.

Minn. Stat. Ann., 241.28 et seq.

Mo. Rev. Stat., 217.525 et seq.

Mont. Code Ann., 46-19-401 et seq.

N.C. Gen. Stat. 1943, §§ 148-119, 148-120

Neb. Rev. Stat. 1943, 29-3401 et seq.

Nev. Rev. Stat. Ann., 78-450 et seq.

Nev. Rev. Stat. 1979 Reprint, 215A.010 et seq.

N.H. Rev. Stat. 1955, 622-B:1 et seq.

N.J. Stat. Ann., 30:7C-1 et seq.

N.M. Stat. Ann., 31-5-17 et seq.

N.Y. Correction Law (Consol. Laws Ch. 43) § 100 et seq.

Ohio Rev. Code 1953, 5120.50

Okla. Stat. Ann., Title 57, §§ 601, 602

Ore. Rev. Stat., 421.245 et seq.

Pa. Purdon's Stat., Title 61, § 1061 et seq.

S.C. Code Ann. 1976, § 24-11-10 et seq.

Tenn. Code Ann., 41-23-101 et seq.

Tex. Code of Criminal Procedure, Art. 42.19

Utah Code Ann. 1953, 77-63a-1 et seq.

Va. Code 1950, §§ 53.1-216, 53.1-217

Vt. Stat. Ann., Title 28, § 1601 et seq.

Wash. Rev. Code Ann., 72.74.010 et seq.

Wash. Rev. Code Ann., 72.76.005 et seq.

Wis. Stat. 1987, 53.25

Interstate Corrections Compact Act (New England)

See New England Interstate Corrections Compact Act

Interstate Corrections Compact Act (Western)

See Western Interstate Corrections Compact Act

Interstate Crime Compact Act

N.M. Stat. Ann. 1953, 41-20-1 et seq.

Wyo. Stat. Ann., § 7-3-530 et seq.

Interstate Depository Institutions Act

N.M. Stat. Ann., 58-26-1 et seq.

Interstate Disaster Compact Act

Alaska Stat. 1962, § 26.23.130

Ark. Code Ann. 1987, 11-2001, 11-2002

Cal. Government Code § 177 et seq.

Conn. Gen. Stat. Ann., § 28-23

Ga. Code Ann., 38-3-70, 38-3-71

Ill. Rev. Stat. 1987, Ch. 127, § 9131 et seq.

Ill. Rev. Stat. 1991, Ch. 127, § 1130 et seq.

Iowa Code Ann., 29C.21

Kan. Stat. Ann., 48-3201, 48-3202

La. Rev. Stat. Ann., 29:715

Md. Ann. Code 1957, Art. 41, § 17-101 et seq.

Mich. Comp. Laws Ann., 30.261

Mont. Code Ann., 10-3-206

Mont. Rev. Code 1983, 10-3-206 et seq.

Nev. Rev. Stat. 1979 Reprint, 415.010

S.C. Code Ann. 1976, § 25-9-20

Tenn. Code Ann., 58-2-401, 58-2-402

Tex. Rev. Civ. Stat. 1974, Art. 6889-5

Wash. Rev. Code Ann., 38.52.090

W. Va. Code 1966, § 15-5-22

Interstate Drainage Law

S.D. Codified Laws 1967, 46A-13-1 et seq.

Interstate Driver's License Compact Act

Iowa Code Ann., 321C.2

Tenn. Code Ann., 55-7-201 et seq.

Interstate Educational Personnel Contracts Act

Conn. Gen. Stat. 1983, § 10-146c et seq.

Interstate Educational Personnel Qualifications Act

Md. Ann. Code 1974, Art. ED, § 6-101 et seq.

Interstate Emergency Management and Disaster Compact Act

Ky. Rev. Stat. 1971, 39.450 et seq.

Interstate Emergency Management Assistance Compact
Minn. Stat. 1986, 192.89

Interstate Emergency Services Mutual Aid Act
Iowa Code Ann., 29C.21
Kan. Stat. Ann., 48-3201, 48-3202
La. Rev. Stat. Ann., 29:715
Md. Ann. Code 1957, Art. 41, § 17-101 et seq.
Mont. Code Ann., 10-3-206
Mont. Laws 1989, Ch. 5
Nev. Rev. Stat. 1979 Reprint, 415.010
S.C. Code Ann. 1976, § 25-9-20
Tenn. Code Ann., 58-2-401, 58-2-402
Tex. Rev. Civ. Stat. 1974, Art. 6889-5
Wash. Rev. Code Ann., 38.52.090
W. Va. Code 1966, § 15-5-22
Wyo. Stat. Ann., § 19-5-201 et seq.

Interstate Environmental Compact Act
Ark. Stat. 1987, 8-8-101 et seq.
Fla. Stat. Ann., 403.60
Ga. Code Ann., 12-10-40
Ky. Rev. Stat. 1971, 224.18-100
La. Rev. Stat. Ann., 40:2331
Md. Ann. Code 1974, Art. NR, § 3-501
Miss. Code Ann. 1972, §§ 49-21-1, 49,21-3
N.C. Gen. Stat. 1943, § 113A-21 et seq.
Tenn. Code Ann., 68-38-101

Interstate Extradition Compact Act
Iowa Code Ann., 818.1 et seq.

Interstate Extradition of Criminals Act
See also Uniform Extradition Act
Mich. Comp. Laws Ann., 780.1 et seq.

Interstate Extradition of Witnesses Act
Fla. Stat. Ann., 942.01 et seq.

Interstate Family Support Act
See also Uniform Interstate Family Support Act
Colo. Rev. Stat., 14-5-101 et seq.

Interstate Forest Fire Protection Compact Act
Pa. Purdon's Stat., Title 32, § 422 et seq.

Interstate Forest Fire Protection Compact Act (Middle Atlantic)
See Middle Atlantic Interstate Forest Fire Protection Compact Act

Interstate Forest Fire Protection Compact Act (Northeastern)
See Northeastern Interstate Forest Fire Protection Compact Act

Interstate Forest Fire Protection Compact Act (South Central)
See South Central Interstate Forest Fire Protection Compact Act

Interstate Forest Fire Protection Compact Act (Southeastern)
Ga. Code Ann., 12-10-60 et seq.
S.C. Code Ann. 1976, § 48-37-10 et seq.

Interstate Fresh Pursuit Act
See Uniform Act on Interstate Fresh Pursuit

Interstate Fuel Use Tax Act
Iowa Code Ann., 452A.50 et seq.

Interstate Fuel Use Tax Law
S.D. Codified Laws 1967, 10-49-1 et seq.

Interstate Furlough Compact Act
Tenn. Public Acts 1991, Ch. 231
Utah Code Ann. 1953, 77-34-1 et seq.

Interstate Gas Pipelines Act
Miss. Code Ann. 1972, § 77-11-301 et seq.

Interstate Great Lakes Basin Compact
Ind. Code Ann., 13-5-3-1 et seq.

Interstate High School Districts Act
Vt. Acts 1959, No. 230

Interstate High Speed Intercity Rail Passenger Network Compact Act
Ill. Rev. Stat. 1991, Ch. 114, § 601
Ohio Rev. Code 1953, 4981.35

Interstate High Speed Rail Compact
  Ind. Code Ann., 8-3-19-1, 8-13-19-2

Interstate Highway User Fee Apportionment Act
  Nev. Rev. Stat. 1979 Reprint, 706,801 et seq.

Interstate Highways Speed Act
  Iowa Code Ann., 321.285, Subsec.8

Interstate Horseracing Act of 1978
  Oct. 25, 1978, P.L. 95-515, 15 U.S. Code §§ 3001 et seq., 3001 nt.

Interstate Income Withholding Act
  Kan. Stat. Ann., 23-4,125 et seq.
  Mich. Comp. Laws Ann., 552.671 et seq.
  Pa. Purdon's Stat., Title 55, § 671

Interstate Income Withholding Act (Model)
  Tex. Family Code, § 14.61 et seq.

Interstate Juvenile Compact Act
  See Interstate Compact on Juveniles Act

Interstate Land Sales Full Disclosure Act
  Aug. 1, 1968, P.L. 90-448, 82 Stat. 590, 15 U.S. Code §§ 1701 to 1720
  Oct. 15, 1970, P.L. 91-452, 84 Stat. 929, 15 U.S. Code § 1714
  Dec. 31, 1970, P.L. 91-609, 84 Stat. 1811, 15 U.S. Code § 1705
  March 27, 1978, P.L. 95-251, 15 U.S. Code § 1715
  Oct. 31, 1978, P.L. 95-557, 15 U.S. Code § 1702
  Dec. 21, 1979, P.L. 96-153, 15 U.S. Code §§ 1701 to 1703, 1708, 1709, 1711, 1715, 1717, 1719a, 1720
  Nov. 7, 1988, P.L. 100-628, 15 U.S. Code §§ 1701, 1719
  Dec. 15, 1989, P.L. 101-235, 15 U.S. Code § 1717a
  Dec. 21, 1995, P.L. 104-66, 15 U.S. Code § 1719a

Interstate Law Enforcement Mutual Aid Act
  Mont. Code Ann., 44-11-301 et seq.

Interstate Library Compact
  Me. Rev. Stat. Ann. 1964, Title 27, § 141 et seq.

Interstate Library Compact Act
  Ala. Code 1975, § 41-8-20 et seq.
  Ark. Code Ann. 1987, 13-2-602 et seq.
  Colo. Rev. Stat., 24-60-1501 et seq.
  Conn. Gen. Stat. Ann., § 11-38 et seq.
  Fla. Stat. Ann., 257.28 et seq.
  Ga. Code Ann., 20-5-60, 20-5-61
  Ida. Code 1947, 33-2505 et seq.
  Ill. Rev. Stat. 1991, Ch. 81, § 100 et seq.
  Ind. Code Ann., 20-14-11-1 et seq.
  Iowa Code Ann., 303A.8 et seq.
  La. Rev. Stat. Ann., 25:631 et seq.
  Md. Ann. Code 1974, Art. ED, § 25-301 et seq.
  Me. Rev. Stat. Ann. 1964, Title 27, § 141 et seq.
  Minn. Stat. Ann., 134.21 et seq.
  Miss. Code Ann. 1972, § 39-3-201 et seq.
  Mont. Code Ann., 22-1-601, 22-1-602
  N.C. Gen. Stat. 1943, § 125-12 et seq.
  N.D. Cent. Code, 54-24.1-01 et seq.
  N.H. Rev. Stat. 1955, 201-B:1 et seq.
  N.M. Stat. Ann., 18-2-19 et seq.
  Ohio Rev. Code 1953, 3375.83 et seq.
  Okla. Stat. Ann., Title 65, § 6-101 et seq.
  Ore. Rev. Stat., 357.330 et seq.
  R.I. Gen. Laws 1956, 29-5-1 et seq.
  S.D. Codified Laws 1967, 14-7-12 et seq.
  Tenn. Code Ann., 10-6-101 et seq.
  Va. Code 1950, § 42.1-75
  Vt. Stat. Ann., Title 22, § 21 et seq.
  W. Va. Code 1966, § 10-1A-1 et seq.
  Wyo. Stat. Ann., § 9-2-1026.8 et seq.

Interstate Library Compact Enabling Act
  Vt. Stat. Ann., Title 22, § 21 et seq.

Interstate Low-Level Radioactive Waste Compact (Midwest)
  Ala. Code 1975, § 22-32-1 et seq.
  Ark. Code Ann. 1987, 82-4401 et seq.
  Fla. Stat. Ann., 404.30
  Ill. Rev. Stat. 1991, Ch. 127, § 63v et seq.
  Ind. Code Ann., 13-5-9-1 et seq.
Continued

Iowa Code Ann., 8C
Kan. Stat. Ann., 65-34a01
La. Rev. Stat. Ann., 30:1117 et seq.
Mich. Comp. Laws Ann., 3.751 et seq.
Minn. Stat. Ann., 116C.831 et seq.
Mo. Laws 1983, First Extra Session, S.B. No. 6
Neb. Laws 1983, L.B. 200
Ohio Rev. Code 1953, 3747.01 et seq.
Okla. Stat. Ann., Title 63, § 1-2101 et seq.
Utah Code Ann. 1953, 26-14c-1 et seq.
Va. Code 1950, § 32.1-238.1 et seq.
Wis. Stat. Ann., 16.10 et seq.

Interstate Low-Level Radioactive Waste Compact Act
Ark. Code Ann. 1987, 8-8-202 et seq.
Colo. Rev. Stat., 24-60-2201 et seq.
Fla. Stat. Ann., 404.30
Mo. Rev. Stat., 260.700 et seq.
Okla. Stat. Ann., Title 63, § 1-2101 et seq.
Tenn. Code Ann., 68-202-101
Wis. Stat. Ann., 16.10 et seq.

Interstate Low-Level Radioactive Waste Management Compact (Northeast)
Conn. Gen. Stat. Ann., § 22a-161

Interstate Low-Level Radioactive Waste Management Compact Act
Alaska Stat. 1962, §§ 46.45.010, 46.45.020
Conn. Gen. Stat. Ann., 22a-161 et seq.
Del. Code of 1974, Title 7, §§ 8001, 8002
Ga. Code Ann., 12-8-120 et seq.
Haw. Rev. Stat. Ann., § 339K-1 et seq.
Ida. Code 1947, 39-3025
Ky. Rev. Stat., 211.859
Md. Ann. Code 1974, Art. HE, § 7-301 et seq.
Miss. Code Ann. 1972, § 57-47-1 et seq.
Mont. Code Ann., 75-3-501, 75-3-502
N.C. Gen. Stat. 1943, § 104F-1 et seq.
N.D. Cent. Code, 23-20.5-01 et seq.
N.J. Stat. Ann., 32:31-1 et seq.
Ore. Rev. Stat., 469.930
S.C. Code Ann. 1976, § 48-47-10 et seq.
Va. Code 1950, § 32.1-238.6:1 et seq.
Wash. Rev. Code Ann., 43.145.010

Interstate Meat Packing Law
June 10, 1942, Ch. 403, 56 Stat. 351, 21 U.S. Code § 71 nt.

Interstate Mental Health Compact Act
Iowa Code Ann., 218A.1 et seq.

Interstate Metropolitan Authority Compact Act (Quad Cities)
Ill. Rev. Stat. 1991, Ch. 85, § 6241 et seq.

Interstate Mining Compact Act
Ill. Rev. Stat. 1991, Ch. 96 1/2, § 4701 et seq.
Ind. Code Ann., 14-4-2.2-1 et seq.
Ky. Rev. Stat. 1971, 350.300
Md. Ann. Code 1974, Art. NR, § 7-701 et seq.
Mo. Rev. Stat., 444.400 et seq.
N.C. Gen. Stat. 1943, §§ 74-37, 74-38
N.M. Stat. Ann., 11-11-1 et seq.
Ohio Rev. Code 1953, 1514.30 et seq.
Okla. Stat. Ann., Title 45, § 851 et seq.
Pa. Purdon's Stat., Title 52, § 3251 et seq.
S.C. Code Ann. 1976, § 48-21-10 et seq.
Tenn. Code Ann., 59-10-101 et seq.
Tex. Natural Resources Code, § 132.001 et seq.
W. Va. Code 1966, § 20-6B-1 et seq.

Interstate Motor Carrier Act
Neb. Rev. Stat. 1943, 75-348 et seq.

Interstate Motor Carriers Base State Fuel Tax Compact Act
Neb. Rev. Stat. 1943, 66-1401 et seq.

Interstate Motor Fuel Use Act
Kan. Stat. Ann., 79-34,108 et seq.

Interstate Multistate Tax Compact
Mont. Code Ann., 15-1-601

Interstate Mutual Aid Compact Act
Ida. Code 1947, 46-1018
Mont. Code Ann., 10-3-204, 10-3-207, 10-3-208

Interstate Nuclear Compact Act
Ala. Code 1975, 9-18-1 et seq.
Alaska Stat. 1962, §§ 46.45.010, 46.45.020

Ga. Code Ann., 12-10-1 et seq.

Mont. Code Ann. 1987, 90-5-201

S.C. Code Ann. 1976, § 13-7-410 et seq.

Wash. Rev. Code Ann., 38.52.090

Wyo. Stat. Ann., § 9-6-101 et seq.

Interstate Nuclear Compact Act (Southern)

See Southern Interstate Nuclear Compact Act

Miss. Code Ann. 1972, § 57-25-1

Interstate Nuclear Compact Act (Western)

See also Western Interstate Nuclear Compact Act

Alaska Stat. 1962, § 41.98.110 et seq.

Ariz. Rev. Stat. Ann., § 30-701 et seq.

N.M. Stat. Ann., 11-9-1 et seq.

Interstate Oil and Gas Compact Act

Md. Ann. Code 1974, Art. NR, § 6-401 et seq.

Interstate Oil and Gas Conservation Compact Act

See Interstate Compact To Conserve Oil and Gas Act

Interstate Oil Compact Act

Wyo. Stat. Ann., § 30-5-201 et seq.

Interstate Operating Authority Agreement Act

Neb. Rev. Stat. 1943, 75-372 et seq.

Interstate Ozone Transport Oversight Act

Ill. Comp. Stat. 1992, Ch. 415, § 130/1 et seq.

Interstate Parde Compact Law

N.Y. Executive Law (Consol. Laws, Ch. 18), § 259 et seq.

Interstate Parole Act

Okla. Stat. Ann., Title 57, § 347 et seq.

Interstate Parole and Probation Hearings Act

Va. Code 1950, § 53.1-168 et seq.

Interstate Parole Reciprocal Agreements Compact Act

Ill. Rev. Stat. 1991, Ch. 38, § 1003-3-11 et seq.

Interstate Parolee Supervision Act

See Uniform Act for Out of State Parolee Supervision

Interstate Pension Portability Act

Fla. Stat. Ann., 121.45 et seq.

Interstate Pest Control Compact Act

Minn. Stat. Ann., 18.62 et seq.

N.D. Cent. Code, 4-32-01 et seq.

Vt. Stat. Ann., Title 6, § 981 et seq.

Interstate Planning Compact Act

Me. Rev. Stat. Ann. 1964, Title 10, § 301 et seq.

Interstate Planning Compact Act (New England)

See New England Interstate Planning Compact Act

Interstate Pollution Phase-Out Compact (Mississippi River)

La. Rev. Stat. Ann., 30:1099.1 et seq.

Interstate Probation and Parole Compact Act

D.C. Code 1973, § 24-251 et seq.

Iowa Code 1985, 247.40

Interstate Public Water Supply Compact (New Hampshire-Vermont)

N.H. Rev. Stat. 1955, 485-D:1

Interstate Rail Compact Act

Ill. Rev. Stat. 1991, Ch. 114, §§ 600, 601

Interstate Rail Passenger Network Compact

Oct. 23, 1992, P.L. 102-452, 106 Stat. 2255

Interstate Reciprocal Banking Act

Minn. Stat. Ann., 48.90 et seq.

Interstate Regional Planning Compact Act

N.H. Rev. Stat. 1955, 36-B:1, 36-B:2

Interstate Rendition Act
Mass. Gen. Laws Ann., 276:11 et seq.

Interstate Sanitation Commission Tri-State Compact Act
Conn. Gen. Stat. Ann., § 22a-293 et seq.

Interstate School Compact Act
Me. Rev. Stat. Ann. 1964, Title 20-A, § 3601 et seq.

Interstate School Compact Act (Maine-New Hampshire)
See Maine-New Hampshire Interstate School Compact

Interstate School Compact Act (New Hampshire-Vermont)
See New Hampshire-Vermont Interstate School Compact Act

Interstate School Compact Act (New York-Vermont)
Vt. Stat. Ann., Title 16, § 791 et seq.

Interstate Sewage and Waste Disposal Facilities Compact Act (New Hampshire-Massachusetts)
See New Hampshire-Massachusetts Interstate Sewage and Waste Disposal Facilities Compact Act

Interstate Sewage and Waste Disposal Facilities Compact Act (New Hampshire-Vermont)
See New Hampshire-Vermont Interstate Sewage and Waste Disposal Facilities Compact Act

Interstate Solid Waste Compact Act
N.H. Rev. Stat. 1955, 53-D:1

Interstate Southern Nuclear Compact Act
S.C. Code Ann. 1976, § 13-7-420 et seq.

Interstate Stream Commission Act
N.M. Stat. Ann., 72-14-1 et seq.

Interstate Succession Act
N.C. Gen. Stat. 1943, § 29-1 et seq.

Interstate Supervision of Probationers and Parolees Act
Mass. Gen. Laws Ann., 127:151A et seq.

Interstate Telecommunications Gross Receipts Tax Act
N.M. Stat. Ann., 7-9C-1 et seq.

Interstate Toll Bridge Act
Ind. Code Ann., 8-126-2-1 et seq.

Interstate Transfer of Teacher Credentials Act
N.J. Stat. Ann., 18A:26-11 et seq.

Interstate Vehicle Equipment Safety Compact
S.D. Codified Laws 1967, 32-16-1 et seq.

Interstate Vehicle Equipment Safety Compact Act
See Vehicle Equipment Safety Compact Act

Interstate Water Pollution Control Commission Act
Also known as New England Interstate Water Pollution Control Compact
Me. Rev. Stat. Ann. 1964, Title 38, § 491 et seq.

Interstate Water Pollution Control Compact Act
Conn. Gen. Stat. Ann., § 22a-308 et seq.

Interstate Water Pollution Control Compact Act (New England)
See New England Interstate Water Pollution Control Compact Act

Interstate Watershed Cooperation Act
Ark. Stat. 1987, 14-115-104 et seq.

Interstate Wildlife Violator Compact
Mont. Laws 1995, Ch. 122

Interstate Yellowstone River Compact
Mont. Code Ann., 85-20-101

Interstate 90 Land Exchange Act of 1998
Oct. 21, 1998, P.L. 105-277, 101(e), Title VI, 112 Stat. 2681, 16 U.S. Code § 539k nt.

Intertrack Wagering Act
N.J. Stat. Ann., 5:5-62 et seq.

Interurban Railroad Act
Ind. Code Ann., 8-5-1-1 et seq.

Interurban Railroad Fare Act
Mich. Comp. Laws Ann., 468.31 et seq.

Interurban Railway Law
Iowa Code 1975, 484.1 et seq.

Interveners Law (Attachment)
Ark. Code Ann. 1987, 16-110-134

Intervenor and Reporting Immunity Law (Alcoholism and Drug Addiction)
Ill. Comp. Stat. 1992, Ch. 745, § 35/1 et seq.

Intervention Act (Civil Actions)
Ala. Code 1958, Title 7, § 247
Ill. Rev. Stat. 1991, Ch. 110, § 2-408
Mo. Rev. Stat., 507.090
N.Y. Civil Practice Law and Rules (Consol. Laws Ch. 8) § 1012 et seq.
P.R. Laws Ann. 1954, Title 32, § 1171 et seq.

Intervention Act for Infants and Toddlers (Early)
Miss. Code Ann. 1972, § 41-87-1 et seq.

Intervention on the High Seas Act
Feb. 5, 1974, P.L. 93-248, 88 Stat. 8, 33 U.S. Code §§ 1471 to 1487
June 26, 1978, P.L. 95-302, 33 U.S. Code § 1471 et seq.
Aug. 18, 1990, P.L. 101-380, 33 U.S. Code §§ 1481, 1486

Intervention Pilot Program (In-School)
La. Rev. Stat. Ann., 17:201 to 17:205

Intervention Services Act (Early Childhood)
Mass. Gen. Laws Ann., 111F:1 et seq., 111G:1 et seq.

Intervention Services System Act (Early)
Ill. Comp. Stat. 1992, Ch. 325, § 20/1 et seq.

Intestacy Act
Ala. Code 1975, § 43-8-40 et seq.
Alaska Stat. 1962, § 13.11.005 et seq.
Ariz. Rev. Stat. Ann., § 14-2101 et seq.
Cal. Probate Code § 200 et seq.
Colo. Rev. Stat., 15-11-101 et seq.
Del. Code of 1974, Title 12, § 501 et seq.
Ill. Rev. Stat. 1991, Ch. 110 1/2, § 2-1 et seq.
Ind. Code Ann., 29-1-2-1 et seq.
Iowa Code Ann., 633.210 et seq.
Kan. Stat. Ann., 59-501 et seq.
Ky. Rev. Stat. 1971, 391.010 et seq.
Mass. Gen. Laws Ann., 190:1 et seq.
Md. Ann. Code 1974, Art. ET, § 3-101 et seq.
Me. Rev. Stat. Ann. 1964, Title 18-A §§ 2-102 et seq., 1001 et seq.
Mich. Comp. Laws Ann., 700.104 et seq.
Minn. Stat. Ann., 525.13 et seq.
Miss. Code Ann. 1972, § 91-1-1 et seq.
Mo. Rev. Stat., 474.010 et seq.
Mont. Code Ann., 72-2-201 et seq., 72-11-101 et seq.
N.C. Gen. Stat. 1943, § 29-1 et seq.
N.D. Cent. Code, 30.1-04-01 et seq.
Neb. Rev. Stat. 1943, 30-2301 et seq.
Nev. Rev. Stat. 1979 Reprint, 134.010 et seq.
N.H. Rev. Stat. 1955, 561:1 et seq.
N.J. Stat. Ann., 3B:5-1 et seq.
Ohio Rev. Code 1953, 2105.01 et seq.
Okla. Stat. Ann., Title 84, § 213
Pa. Cons. Stat., Title 20, § 2101 et seq.
R.I. Gen. Laws 1956, 33-1-1 et seq.
S.C. Code Ann. 1976, Superseded Vols., § 21-3-20
S.D. Codified Laws 1967, 29-1-1 et seq.
Tenn. Code Ann., 31-1-101 et seq.
Utah Code Ann. 1953, 75-2-101 et seq.
Va. Code 1950, § 64.1-1 et seq.
Vt. Stat. Ann., Title 14, § 401 et seq.
Wash. Rev. Code Ann., 11.04.015 et seq.
Wis. Stat. Ann., 852.01 et seq.
W. Va. Code 1966, § 42-1-1 et seq.

Intoxicated Drivers Act
Kan. Stat. Ann., 8-1001 et seq.
N.H. Rev. Stat. 1955, 265:82
Tex. Rev. Civ. Stat., Art. 67011-1
Continued

Wash. Rev. Code Ann., 46.61.500 et seq.

Intoxicated Drivers Chemical Test Act
Ind. Code Ann., 9-4-1-39.1

Intoxicated Persons Transportation Act
N.M. Stat. Ann., 43-2-16 et seq.

Intoxicating Compounds Use Act
Ill. Rev. Stat. 1991, Ch. 38, § 81 et seq.

Intoxicating Liquor Act
Ark. Code Ann. 1987, 3-1-101 et seq.
Cal. Business and Professions Code § 23000 et seq.
Colo. Rev. Stat., 12-46-101 et seq.
D.C. Code 1973, § 25-101 et seq.
Ind. Code Ann., 7.1-1-1-1 et seq.
Kan. Stat. Ann., 41-101 et seq.
Mass. Gen. Laws Ann., 138:1 et seq.
Md. Ann. Code 1957, Art. 2B, § 1 et seq.
Me. Rev. Stat. Ann. 1964, Title 28A § 1 et seq.
Mich. Comp. Laws Ann., 436.1 et seq.
Minn. Stat. Ann., 340.069 et seq.
Miss. Code Ann. 1972, § 67-3-1 et seq.
Mo. Rev. Stat., 311.010 et seq.
Mont. Code Ann., 16-1-101 et seq.
N.C. Gen. Stat. 1943, § 18B-100 et seq.
Nev. Statutes 1923, Ch. 37, p. 43
N.H. Rev. Stat. 1955, 175:1 et seq.
N.J. Stat. Ann., 33:1-1 et seq.
Okla. Stat. Ann., Title 37, § 501 et seq.
Ore. Rev. Stat., 471.005 et seq.
R.I. Gen. Laws 1956, 3-1-1 et seq.
S.D. Codified Laws 1967, 35-1-1 et seq.
Tex. Alcoholic Beverage Code, § 1.01 et seq.
Vt. Stat. Ann., Title 7, § 1 et seq.
Wash. Rev. Code Ann., 66.04.010 et seq.

Intoxicating Liquor Act (Enforcement Tax)
Ind. Code 1971, 7-4-1-1

Intoxicating Liquor Act (Four Mile)
Tenn. Acts 1877, Ch. 23
Tenn. Acts 1885, Ch. 123
Tenn. Acts 1887, Ch. 167
Tenn. Acts 1905, Ch. 422
Tenn. Acts 1909, Ch. 1

Intoxicating Liquor Act (Griffin)
Tenn. Acts 1899, Ch. 221

Intoxicating Liquor Act (No Huckstering)
Ind. Code Ann., 7.1-5-10-10

Intoxicating Liquor Act (Pendelton)
Tenn. Acts 1907, Ch. 17

Intoxicating Liquor Act (Prohibition)
La. Acts 1921, Extra Session, No. 39

Intoxicating Liquor Act (Quart-a-Month)
S.C. Acts 1917, p. 69, No. 38 § 2

Intoxicating Liquor Act (Unlawful Sales Abatement)
Cal. Penal Code § 11200 et seq.

Intoxicating Liquor Bone Dry Law
Wash. Laws 1917, Ch. 19

Intoxicating Liquor Civil Damage Act
N.C. Gen. Stat. 1943, § 14-332
Wash. Rev. Code Ann., 71.08.080

Intoxicating Liquor Fair Trade Act
Minn. Stat. Ann., 340A.301 et seq.

Intoxicating Liquor License Act
Haw. Rev. Stat. Ann., § 281-31 et seq.
Wash. Rev. Code Ann., 66.24.010 et seq.

Intoxicating Liquor Local Option Act
Minn. Stat. Ann., 340.20 et seq.
Mo. Rev. Stat., 311.090 et seq.

Intoxicating Liquor Minimum Price Act
Conn. Gen. Stat. Ann., § 30-64 et seq.

Intoxicating Liquor Permit Act
Conn. Gen. Stat. Ann., § 30-14 et seq.

Intoxicating Liquor Price Posting Act
Conn. Gen. Stat. Ann., § 30-63 et seq.

Intoxicating Liquor Prohibition Act
See Prohibition Act (Liquor)

Intoxicating Liquor Quota Act
Wis. Stat. 1981, 125.51, Subsec. 4

Intoxicating Liquor Search and Seizure Act
N.C. Gen. Stat. 1943, § 18A-19 et seq.

Intoxicating Liquor Second Conviction Act
Miss. Code Ann. 1972, § 97-31-27

Intoxicating Liquor Trade Practices Act
N.M. Stat. Ann. 1953, 46-9-1 et seq.

Intoxicating Liquors Act (Forfeiture)
Tenn. Code Ann., 57-3-411

Intoxicating Liquors Act (Manufacture)
Tenn. Code Ann., 39-6-916 et seq.
Tenn. Code Ann., 39-17-706 et seq.

Intoxication and Alcoholism Treatment Act
See also Uniform Alcoholism and
Intoxication Treatment Act
Conn. Gen. Stat. Ann., § 17-155k et seq.
Del. Code of 1974, Title 16, § 2201 et seq.
Ill. Rev. Stat. 1983, Ch. 91 1/2, § 501 et seq.
Iowa Code Ann., 125.1 et seq.
Md. Ann. Code 1974, Art. HG, § 8-501 et
seq.
Mont. Code Ann., 53-24-101 et seq.
S.C. Code Ann. 1976, § 44-51-410 et seq.
S.D. Codified Laws 1967, 34-20A-1 et seq.

Intoxication, Chemical Test Act
See also Chemical Test for Intoxication of
Drivers Act
Ala. Code 1975, 32-5-190 et seq.
Ariz. Rev. Stat. Ann., § 28-692
Iowa Code 1985, 321B.3 et seq.
Mass. Gen. Laws Ann., 90:24
Md. Ann. Code 1974, Art. CJ, § 10-302 et
seq.
Me. Rev. Stat. Ann. 1964, Title 29, § 1312
Minn. Stat. Ann., 169.123 et seq.
Mo. Rev. Stat., 577.020 et seq.
Mont. Code Ann. 1987, 61-8-401 et seq.
N.C. Gen. Stat. 1943, § 20-139.1 et seq.
Okla. Stat. Ann., Title 47, § 751 et seq.
Ore. Rev. Stat., 813.140 et seq.
R.I. Gen. Laws 1956, 31-27-2.1, 3-27-3

S.C. Code Ann. 1976, § 56-5-2950
S.D. Codified Laws 1967, 32-23-7 et seq.

Intoxication Presumption Act (Drivers)
S.D. Codified Laws 1967, 32-23-7

Intoximeter Act
Pa. Cons. Stat., Title 75, § 1547 et seq.

Intractable Pain Treatment Act
Cal. Business and Professions Code § 2241.5
Mo. Rev. Stat., 334.105, 334.106
R.I. Gen. Laws 1956, 5-37.4-1 et seq.
Tex. Rev. Civ. Stat., Art. 4495c

Intrastate Aviation Act
Ark. Rev. Stat. 1971, 183.010 et seq.

Intrastate Bridge and Tunnel Revenue Bond Act
Pa. 1935 Pamph. Laws 735, No. 293

Intrastate Bridge Revenue Bond Act
Pa. 1931 Pamph. Laws 301, No. 139

Intrastate Corrections Compact
Wash. Rev. Code Ann., 72.76.010 et seq.

Intrastate Detainer Act (Prison Inmates)
Wis. Stat. Ann., 971.11

Intrastate Drainage Law
S.D. Codified Laws 1967, 46-20-1 et seq.

Intrastate Family Support Act
See Uniform Intrastate Family Support Act

Intrastate Financing Act
N.Y. General Business Law (Consol. Laws
Ch. 20), § 359ff

Intrastate Fresh Pursuit Act
See Uniform Act on Intrastate Fresh Pursuit

Intrastate Jurisdiction Act (Child Custody)
Ga. Code Ann., 19-9-20 et seq.

Intrastate Motor Carrier Act
Neb. Rev. Stat. 1943, 75-301 et seq.

Intrastate Pay-Per-Call Regulation Act
Neb. Laws 1993, L.B. 42

Intrastate Pipeline Act
Ga. Code Ann., 46-4-20 et seq.

Intrastate Regulatory Act (Natural Gas Transmission Pipeline)
Fla. Laws 1992, Ch. 284, § 2 et seq.

Intrastate Tunnel Revenue Bond Act
Pa. 1953 Pamph. Laws 1050, No. 271

Introduction and Duplication Act (Bill)
Ill. Comp. Stat. 1992, Ch. 25, § 35/0.01 et seq.

Intrusion Into Office Act
La. Rev. Stat. Ann., 42:76 et seq.

Invalid Pension Acts
June 27, 1890, Ch. 634, 26 Stat. 182
May 9, 1900, Ch. 385, 31 Stat. 170

Invalidity, Marriage, and Dissolution Records Act
Ill. Rev. Stat. 1991, Ch. 40, § 900 et seq.

Invasion Act (Home)
Mass. Gen. Laws Ann., 265:18C

Invasion of Privacy Act
Ga. Code Ann., 16-11-60 et seq.

Invention Development Fund Act
Haw. Rev. Stat. Ann., § 211E-1 et seq.

Invention Development Services Act
Iowa Code Ann., 523G.1 et seq.
Okla. Stat. Ann., Title 15, § 680 et seq.

Invention Development Services Disclosure Act
Neb. Rev. Stat. 1943, 87-601 et seq.

Invention Development Standards Act (Fair)
Ill. Comp. Stat. 1992, Ch. 815, § 620/10 et seq.

Invention Secrecy Act of 1951
Feb. 1, 1951, Ch. 4, 66 Stat. 3 (See 35 U.S. Code §§ 181 to 188)

Invention Services Act
Minn. Stat. Ann., 325A.01 et seq.

Inventors Assistance Act
Ark. Acts 1991, No. 707
Okla. Stat. Ann., Title 74, § 5061 et seq.

Inventory Chattel Mortgage Act
Colo. Rev. Stat. 1963, 21-2-1 et seq.

Inventory Lien Act
Cal. Civil Code § 3030 et seq.

Inventory Tax Act
Wyo. Stat. 1957, § 39-79 et seq.

Inverse Condemnation Act
Ind. Code Ann., 32-11-1-12
N.M. Stat. Ann., 42-1-1

Invested Capital Tax Act (Water Company)
Ill. Comp. Stat. 1992, Ch. 35, § 625/1 et seq.
Ill. Rev. Stat. 1991, Ch. 120, § 1411 et seq.

Investigating Committee Act (Legislative)
Utah Code Ann. 1953, 36-12-19 et seq.

Investigating Grand Jury Act
Pa. Cons. Stat., Title 42, § 4541 et seq.

Investigating Official of the Office of Disabled Persons Act
P.R. Laws Ann. 1954, Title 3, § 532 et seq.

Investigation Act (Commission of)
N.Y. Unconsolidated Laws § 7501 et seq.

Investigation Act (Labor Disputes)
Mass. Gen. Laws Ann., 150:3

Investigation and Prosecution of Organized Criminal Activity
Ohio Rev. Code 1953, 177.01 et seq.

Investigation and Registration Act (Charitable)
N.J. Stat. Ann., 45:17A-18 et seq.

Investigation Commission Act
N.Y. Laws 1958, Ch. 989
N.Y. Unconsolidated Law, § 7501 et seq.

Investigation Nomenclature Act (Bureau of)
Ga. Official Code Ann., 35-3-100 to
35-3-108

Investigations Act
Utah Code Ann. 1953, 53-4-101 et seq.

Investigations Act (County and Municipal)
N.J. Rev. Stat. 1937, 2A:67A-1 et seq.

Investigative Consumer Reporting Agencies Act
Cal. Civil Code § 1786 et seq.

Investigators Act (Private)
N.M. Stat. Ann., 61-27-1 et seq.

Investigators' and Private Detectives' Licensing Act
N.Y. General Business Law (Consol. Laws Ch. 20) § 70 et seq.

Investigatory Act (Criminal)
Wash. Rev. Code Ann., 10.27.010 et seq.

Investment Act
Mont. Code Ann., 30-10-101 et seq.

Investment Act (Business)
Miss. Code Ann. 1972, § 57-61-1 et seq.

Investment Act (Childrens Early)
Fla. Stat. Ann., 411.23

Investment Act (Fiduciaries)
See Fiduciaries Investment Act

Investment Act (Film and Television)
Fla. Laws 1992, Ch. 201

Investment Act (Franchise)
R.I. Gen. Laws 1956, 19-28.1-1 et seq.

Investment Act (Insurers)
Neb. Rev. Stat. 1943, 44-5101 et seq.

Investment Act (Job)
Mont. Code Ann., 17-6-501 et seq.

Investment Act (Non-Arbitrage)
Va. Code 1950, § 2.1-234.9:1 et seq.

Investment Act (Product)
Okla. Stat. Ann., Title 60, § 161

Investment Act (Public Funds)
Tex. Government Code, § 2256.001 et seq.
Tex. Rev. Civ. Stat., Art. 842a-2

Investment Act (Real Estate)
Ill. Rev. Stat. 1991, Ch. 85, § 900 et seq.
Tex. Rev. Civ. Stat., Art. 842a-1

Investment Act (Securities)
Mont. Code Ann., 30-8-101 et seq.
Pa. Cons. Stat., Title 13, § 8101 et seq.

Investment Act (State Funds)
Neb. Rev. Stat. 1943, 72-1237 et seq.

Investment Act (Telecommunications Technology)
Del. Laws, Vol. 69, Ch. 99

Investment Act (Venture Capital)
Iowa Code Ann., 28.111 et seq.
N.M. Stat. Ann., 7-2D-1 et seq.

Investment Advisers Act of 1940
Aug. 22, 1940, Ch. 686, 54 Stat. 847, 15 U.S. Code §§ 80b-1 to 80b-21
Aug. 28, 1958, P.L. 85-791, 72 Stat. 949, 15 U.S. Code § 80b-13
June 25, 1959, P.L. 86-70, 73 Stat. 143, 15 U.S. Code § 80b-2
June 11, 1960, P.L. 86-507, 74 Stat. 201, 15 U.S. Code § 80b-11
July 12, 1960, P.L. 86-624, 74 Stat. 412, 15 U.S. Code § 80b-2
Sept. 13, 1960, P.L. 86-750, 74 Stat. 885, 15 U.S. Code §§ 80b-2 to 80b-6, 80b-8 to 80b-11, 80b-17, 80b-18a
July 1, 1966, P.L. 89-485, 80 Stat. 243, 15 U.S. Code § 80b-2
Oct. 15, 1970, P.L. 91-452, 84 Stat. 929, 15 U.S. Code § 80b-9
Dec. 14, 1970, P.L. 91-547, 84 Stat. 1430, 15 U.S. Code §§ 80b-2, 80b-3, 80b-5, 80b-6a
Continued

Nov. 6, 1978, P.L. 95-598, 15 U.S. Code § 80b-2

Oct. 28, 1986, P.L. 99-571, 15 U.S. Code § 80b-3

Dec. 4, 1987, P.L. 100-181, 15 U.S. Code §§ 80b-2, 80b-3, 80b-5, 80b-9, 80b-11, 80b-13, 80b-14

Nov. 19, 1988, P.L. 100-704, 15 U.S. Code § 80b-4a

Oct. 15, 1990, P.L. 101-429, 15 U.S. Code §§ 80b-3, 80b-9, 80b-14

Nov. 15, 1990, P.L. 101-550, 15 U.S. Code §§ 80b-2, 80b-3, 80b-10, 80b-18

Dec. 8, 1995, P.L. 104-62, 15 U.S. Code § 80b-3

Oct. 11, 1996, P.L. 104-290, 15 U.S. Code §§ 80b-2, 80b-3, 80b-3a, 80b-5, 80b-18a

Nov. 3, 1998, P.L. 105-353, 15 U.S. Code §§ 80b-3, 80b-18a

Investment Advisers Supervision Coordination Act

Oct. 11, 1996, P.L. 104-290, Title III, 15 U.S. Code § 80b-20 nt.

March 31, 1997, P.L. 105-8, 15 U.S. Code § 80b-2 nt.

Investment Advisors Act

N.C. Gen. Stat. 1943, § 78c-1 et seq.

Investment Advisory Council Act

Wyo. Stat. Ann., § 9-1-411 et seq.

Investment and Employment Growth Act

Neb. Rev. Stat. 1943, 77-4101 et seq.

Investment and Financing Commission Act

Ga. Code Ann., 50-17-20 et seq.

Investment and Loan Companies Act

R.I. Gen. Laws 1956, 19-20-1 et seq.

Investment Authority Act (Infrastructure)

Pa. Purdon's Stat., Title 35, § 751.1 et seq.

Investment Bond Act

Cal. Government Code § 43760 et seq.

Investment Bond Act (Jobs and Housing)

Cal. Health and Safety Code § 52534 et seq.

Investment Capital Fund Act

P.R. Laws Ann. 1954, Title 7, § 1241 et seq.

Investment Certificate Act

Kan. Stat. Ann., 16-601 et seq.

N.M. Stat. Ann. 1953, 48-16-1 et seq.

Investment Certificate Guaranty Fund Act

Kan. Stat. Ann., 16-6a01 et seq.

Investment Companies Act

Cal. Corporations Code § 25000 et seq.

Minn. Stat. Ann., 59.01 et seq.

N.J. Stat. Ann., 17:16A-1 et seq.

P.R. Laws Ann. 1954, Title 10, § 661 et seq.

Tenn. Code Ann., 45-3-1201

Investment Company Act (Fiduciaries)

See Fiduciary Investment Company Act

Investment Company Act (Industrial Loans)

Neb. Rev. Stat. 1943, 8-401 et seq.

Investment Company Act Amendments of 1996

Oct. 11, 1996, P.L. 104-290, Title II, 15 U.S. Code § 80a-51 nt.

Investment Company Act of 1940

Aug. 22, 1940, Ch. 686, 54 Stat. 789, 11 U.S. Code §§ 72, 107; 15 U.S. Code §§ 80a-1 to 80a-52

Aug. 10, 1954, Ch. 667, 68 Stat. 689, 15 U.S. Code §§ 80a-2, 80a-24

Aug. 21, 1958, P.L. 85-699, 72 Stat. 694, 15 U.S. Code § 80a-18

Aug. 28, 1958, P.L. 85-791, 72 Stat. 949, 15 U.S. Code § 80a-42

June 25, 1959, P.L. 86-70, 73 Stat. 143, 15 U.S. Code §§ 80a-2, 80a-6

June 11, 1960, P.L. 86-507, 74 Stat. 201, 15 U.S. Code §§ 80a-8, 80a-39

July 12, 1960, P.L. 86-624, 74 Stat. 412, 15 U.S. Code §§ 80a-2, 80a-6

July 1, 1966, P.L. 89-485, 80 Stat. 243, 15 U.S. Code § 80a-3

Oct. 15, 1970, P.L. 91-452, 84 Stat. 929, 15 U.S. Code § 80a-41

Dec. 14, 1970, P.L. 91-547, 84 Stat. 1413, 15 U.S. Code §§ 80a-2, 80a-3, 80a-8, 80a-13, 80a-15, 80a-17, 80a-19, 80a-22, 80a-24, 80a-28, 80a-31, 80a-32, 80a-35, 80a-42, 80a-43

Nov. 23, 1971, P.L. 92-165, 85 Stat. 47, 15 U.S. Code § 80a-27

Oct. 27, 1972, P.L. 92-595, 86 Stat. 1316, 15 U.S. Code § 80a-18

Oct. 13, 1982, P.L. 97-303, 15 U.S. Code §§ 80a-2, 80b-2

Dec. 4, 1987, P.L. 100-181, 15 U.S. Code §§ 80a-2, 80a-3, 80a-5, 80a-6, 80a-9, 80a-12, 80a-15, 80a-17, 80a-18, 80a-20-80a-22, 80a-24, 80a-26, 80a-41, 80a-54, 80a-56

Oct. 15, 1990, P.L. 101-429, 15 U.S. Code §§ 80a-9, 80a-41

Nov. 15, 1990, P.L. 101-550, 15 U.S. Code §§ 80a-2, 80a-9, 80a-44, 80a-45

Dec. 8, 1995, P.L. 104-62, 15 U.S. Code §§ 80a-3, 80a-7

Oct. 11, 1996, P.L. 104-290, 15 U.S. Code §§ 80a-2, 80a-3, 80a-6, 80a-12, 80a-24, 80a-26, 80a-27, 80a-29, 80a-30, 80a-34, 80a-54, 80a-60, 80a-63

Nov. 3, 1998, P.L. 105-353, 15 U.S. Code §§ 80a-2, 80a-3, 80a-12, 80a-18, 80a-29, 80a-30

Investment Company Act of 1944
Nov. 6, 1978, P.L. 95-598, 15 U.S. Code §§ 80a-2, 80a-6, 80a-25

Investment Company Amendments Act of 1970
Dec. 14, 1970, P.L. 91-547, 84 Stat. 1413, 15 U.S. Code §§ 77b, 77c, 78c, 78l, 80a-2, 80a-3, 80a-8, 80a-13, 80a-15, 80a-17, 80a-19, 80a-22, 80a-24 and others

Investment Company and Industrial Bank Regulatory Act
Tenn. Code Ann., 45-5-601 et seq.

Investment Council Act
Neb. Rev. Stat. 1943, 72-1237 et seq.

Investment Credit Act
N.M. Stat. Ann., 7-9A-1 et seq.

Investment Credit Act (Insurance)
Tenn. Code Ann., 56-4-210

Investment Credit and Job Expansion Act
Colo. Rev. Stat., 39-22-508.1 et seq.
Kan. Stat. Ann., 79-32,153 et seq.

Investment Finance Authority Act
Neb. Rev. Stat. 1943, 58-201 et seq.

Investment Fund Program (Strategic)
Iowa Code Ann., 15.311 et seq.

Investment Incentive Act (Small Business)
Mont. Code Ann., 15-33-101 et seq.

Investment Incentive and Employment Expansion Act
Neb. Rev. Stat. 1943, 77-27,187 et seq.

Investment Management Act
W. Va. Code 1966, § 12-6-1 et seq.

Investment of Insurers Act
Minn. Stat. 1986, 60L.01 et seq.

Investment of Local Government Surplus Funds Act
Fla. Stat. Ann., 218.40 et seq.

Investment of Municipal Funds Act
Ill. Rev. Stat. 1991, Ch. 146 1/2, § 3.01 et seq.

Investment of Public Funds and Local Government Investment Pool Act
Va. Code 1950, § 2.1-234.1 et seq.

Investment of State Funds Act
Neb. Rev. Stat. 1943, 72-1237 et seq.
S.D. Codified Laws 1967, 4-5-12 et seq.
W. Va. Code 1966, § 12-6-1 et seq.

Investment of Trust Funds Act
Pa. 1917 Pamph. Laws 447, No. 193

Investment Partnership Act
Va. Code 1950, §§ 2.1-548.43:1 to 2.1-548.43:6

Investment Partnership Act (Home)
Cal. Health and Safety Code § 50896 et seq.

Investment Pool Act
Ga. Official Code Ann., 33-11A-1 et seq.

Investment Pool Act (Local Government)
Mich. Comp. Laws Ann., 129.141 et seq.

Investment Pool Act (Surplus Funds)
Mich. Comp. Laws Ann., 129.111 et seq.

Investment Pool Trust Fund Administration and Enforcement Act (Local Government)
Colo. Rev. Stat., 11-51-901 et seq.

Investment Program
Mont. Code Ann., 17-6-201 et seq.

Investment Program (Agriculture-Linked)
Pa. Purdon's Stat., Title 3, § 1721 et seq.

Investment Protection Act (Franchise)
Wash. Rev. Code Ann., 19.100.010 et seq.

Investment Recovery Act (Community)
Ill. Comp. Stat. 1992, Ch. 740, §§ 30/1, 30/5

Investment Regulations Act (Franchise and Distributorship)
R.I. Gen. Laws 1956, 19-28-1 et seq.

Investment Securities (Commercial Laws)
La. Rev. Stat. Ann., 10:8-101 et seq.

Investment Securities (Uniform Commercial Code)
See Uniform Commercial Code-Investment Securites

Investment Securities Act
Mass. Gen. Laws Ann., 106:8-101 et seq.

Investment Security Company Act
Mich. Comp. Laws 1948, 494.1 et seq.

Investment Tax Credit Act (Manufacturing Equipment and Employment)
N.J. Stat. Ann., 54:10A-5.16 et seq.

Investment Tax Credit Act (New Jobs)
N.J. Stat. Ann., 54:10A-5.4 et seq.

Investment Trust Act
N.H. Rev. Stat. 1955, 293-B:21

Investment Trust Act (Jobs)
W. Va. Code 1966 § 12-7-2 et seq.

Investment Trust Act (Real Estate)
Ala. Code 1975, § 10-13-1 et seq.
Ill. Rev. Stat. 1991, Ch. 30, § 250 et seq.
La. Rev. Stat. Ann., 12:491 et seq.

Investment Trust Law
Miss. Code Ann. 1972, § 79-15-1 et seq.

Investments Act (Securities)
Md. Ann. Code 1974, Art. ET, §§ 15-106, 15-401 et seq.
Mont. Code Ann., 30-8-101 et seq.

Investments for Tomorrow Act (Linked)
Iowa Code Ann., 12.31 et seq.

Investments in Lifelong Learning Act
Kan. Stat. Ann., 74-50,102 et seq.

Investments in Medium and Lower Quality Obligations Law
Mo. Rev. Stat., 375.1070 et seq.

Investments Prudent Man Rule
Kan. Stat. Ann., 17-5004 et seq.

Investor and Securities Protection Act
Fla. Stat. Ann., 517.011 et seq.

Investor-Owned Telephone Utility Act
Va. Code 1950, § 56-531 et seq.

Investor Protection Act
Cal. Corporation Code §§ 25210, 25213
Colo. Rev. Stat. 11-51.5-101 et seq.
Fla. Stat. Ann., 517.011 et seq.
Tenn. Code Ann., 48-35-101 et seq.

Investor Protection Take-Over Act
Ark. Code Ann. 1987, 23-43-101 et seq.

Invited Guest Law
See Guest Act (Motor Vehicles)

Involuntary Civil Commitment for Sexually Violent Predator's Treatment and Care Act (Jimmy Ryce)
Fla. Stat. Ann., 916.30 et seq.

Involuntary Dissolution and Receivership Act (Corporations)
Ill. Rev. Stat. 1991, Ch. 32, § 12.35 et seq.

Involuntary Manslaughter Act
Ark. Code Ann. 1987, 5-10-105
Cal. Penal Code § 192, Subd. 2
Colo. Rev. Stat. 1963, 40-2-7, 40-2-8
Ga. Code Ann., 16-5-3
Ill. Rev. Stat. 1991, Ch. 38, § 9-3 et seq.

Involuntary Wage Assignment Act
Ill. Rev. Stat. 1991, Ch. 40, § 706.1

Ionizing Radiation Control Act
Vt. Stat. Ann., Title 18, § 1651 et seq.

Iowa-Nebraska Boundary Compact
Iowa Laws 1943 (50th G. A.), Ch. 306
Neb. Laws 1943, Ch. 130
Neb. Laws 1943, p. 797

Ipswich River Improvement Loan Act (North Reading)
Mass. Acts 1961, Ch. 249

Ipswich Sewerage Loan Act
Mass. Acts 1946, Ch. 30

Iran and Libya Sanctions Act of 1996
Aug. 5, 1996, P.L. 104-172, 50 U.S. Code § 1701 nt.

Iran-Iraq Arms Non-Proliferation Act of 1992
Oct. 23, 1992, P.L. 102-484, 50 U.S. Code § 1701 nt.
Feb. 10, 1996, P.L. 104-106, 50 U.S. Code § 1701 nt.

Iraq Liberation Act of 1998
Oct. 31, 1998, P.L. 105- 338, 112 Stat. 3178, 22 U.S. Code § 2151 nt.

Iraq Sanctions Act of 1990
Nov. 5, 1990, P.L. 101-513, 50 U.S. Code § 1701 nt.

IRC Partnership/Ben Franklin Act
Pa. 1993 Pamph. Laws, No. 64

IRCA
See Immigration Reform And Control Act Of 1986

IREBEA (Interest on Real Estate Brokers' Escrow Accounts Act)
Miss. Code Ann. 1972, § 73-35-101 et seq.

Irish Peace Process Cultural and Training Program Act of 1998
Oct. 30, 1998, P.L. 105-319, 112 Stat. 3013, 8 U.S. Code § 1101 nt.

Irish Wilderness Act of 1984
May 21, 1984, P.L. 98-289, 16 U.S. Code § 1132 nt.

Iron Curtain Act (Nonresident Alien Beneficiary)
Conn. Gen. Stat. 1977, § 45a-449
Fla. Stat. Ann., 732.1101 et seq.
Mass. Gen. Laws Ann., 206:27B
Md. Ann. Code 1974, Art. ET, § 9-108
Mich. Comp. Laws Ann., 704.55a
N.J. Stat. Ann., 3B:23-22
N.Y. Surrogate's Court Procedure Act (Consol. Laws Ch. 59A) § 2218
Ohio Rev. Code 1953, 2113.81 et seq.
Ore. Rev. Stat. 1953, 111.070
Pa. 1953 Pamph. Laws 674, No. 209
Pa. 1955 Pamph. Laws 1084, No. 352, § 6
R.I. Gen. Laws 1956, 33-13-13
Wis. Stat. Ann., 879.03, Subsec. 3

Iron Industry Museum Advisory Board Act
Mich. Comp. Laws Ann., 399.71 et seq.

Iron Range Resources and Rehabilitation Act
Minn. Stat. Ann., 298.22

Irregular Government Personnel Act
P.R. Laws Ann. 1954, Title 3, § 711 et seq.

Irrigation Act
Colo. Rev. Stat., 37-81-101 et seq.
Kan. Stat. Ann., 42-106 et seq.
N.D. Cent. Code, 61-05-01 et seq.
Neb. Rev. Stat. 1943, 46-101 et seq.
P.R. Laws Ann. 1954, Title 22, § 251 et seq.
Continued

Tex. Water Code, §§ 1.003, 11.021 et seq.

Irrigation Acts
March 3, 1891, Ch. 561, 26 Stat. 1095, 16
U.S. Code §§ 471, 607, 611, 611a, 613; 25
USC § 426; 43 U.S. Code §§ 161, 162, 165,
173, 174, 185, 212, 262, 321, 323, 325, 327
to 329, 663, 671, 718, 728 and others
June 17, 1902, Ch. 1093, 32 Stat. 388, 43
U.S. Code §§ 372, 373, 381, 383, 391, 392,
411, 414, 416, 419, 421, 431, 432, 434, 439,
461, 476, 491, 498

**Irrigation and Agricultural Improvement
District Revenue Bond Act of 1951**
Ariz. Rev. Stat. Ann., § 48-141 et seq.

Irrigation and Water Act
Ore. Rev. Stat., 536.005 et seq.
Utah Code Ann. 1953, 73-1-1 et seq.

Irrigation District Act
Ariz. Rev. Stat. Ann., § 48-2901 et seq.
Cal. Water Code § 20500 et seq.
Colo. Rev. Stat., 37-41-101 et seq.
Ida. Code 1947, 43-101 et seq.
Mont. Code Ann., 85-7-101 et seq.
Neb. Rev. Stat. 1943, 70-601 et seq.
Nev. Rev. Stat. 1979 Reprint, 539.010 et seq.
N.M. Stat. Ann., 73-9-1 et seq.
Okla. Stat. Ann., Title 82, § 277.1 et seq.
Ore. Rev. Stat., 545.002 et seq.
S.D. Codified Laws 1967, 46A-4-1 et seq.
Utah Code Ann. 1953, 73-7-1 et seq.
Wash. Rev. Code Ann., 87.03.001 et seq.
Wyo. Stat. Ann., § 41-7-101 et seq.

Irrigation District Act (Consolidation)
Cal. Water Code § 27150 et seq.

Irrigation District Act (Debt Compromise)
Cal. Statutes 1933, Ch. 448, p. 1165

Irrigation District Act (Drainage)
Cal. Water Code § 22095 et seq.

**Irrigation District Act (Federal
Cooperation)**
Cal. Water Code § 23175 et seq.

Irrigation District Act (Formation)
Cal. Water Code § 20700 et seq.

Irrigation District Act (Improvement)
Cal. Water Code § 23600 et seq.

Irrigation District Act (Liability)
Cal. Water Code § 22725 et seq.

Irrigation District Act (Refinancing)
Cal. Statutes 1937, p. 92

Irrigation District Act (Validation of Bonds)
Cal. Statutes 1937, Ch. 119, p. 360

Irrigation District Assessments Act
Wash. Rev. Code Ann., 87.03.240 et seq.

Irrigation District Change of Name Law
Cal. Water Code §§ 20980, 20981

Irrigation District Codevelopment Law
Cal. Water Code § 22115 et seq.

Irrigation District Cooperation Law
Cal. Water Code § 23375 et seq.

Irrigation District Dissolution Act
Wash. Rev. Code Ann., 87.52.010 et seq.,
87.53.010 et seq., 87.56.010 et seq.

**Irrigation District Dissolution Law
(Involuntary)**
Cal. Water Code § 27700 et seq.

**Irrigation District Dissolution Law
(Voluntary)**
Cal. Water Code § 27400 et seq.

**Irrigation District Domestic Water System
Revenue Bond Act**
Ida. Code 1947, 43-1907 et seq.

Irrigation District Federal Cooperation Law
Cal. Water Code § 23175 et seq.

Irrigation District Joint Control Act
Wash. Rev. Code Ann., 87.80.010 et seq.

Irrigation District Law
Cal. Water Code § 20500 et seq.

Irrigation District Law (Drainage)
Cal. Water Code § 22095 et seq.

Irrigation District Power Development Law
Cal. Water Code § 22115 et seq.

Irrigation District Refunding Bond Act
Wash. Rev. Code Ann., 87.19.005 et seq.,
87.22.010 et seq.

Irrigation District Revenue Bond Act
Mont. Code Ann., 85-7-1401 et seq.
Wash. Rev. Code Ann., 87.28.005 et seq.

Irrigation District Salinity Control Act
Colo. Rev. Stat., 37-43-201 et seq.

**Irrigation Districts for Local Improvement
District Code**
Ida. Code 1947, 43-2501 et seq.

Irrigation Division Engineers Act
Colo. Rev. Stat. 1963, 148-12-1 et seq.

**Irrigation, Drainage and Watershed
Improvement District Act**
Ark. Code Ann. 1987, 14-117-101 et seq.

Irrigation Investigation Act
See Arid Land Act

Irrigation Law (Lajas Valley Public)
P.R. Laws Ann. 1954, Title 22, § 341 et seq.

Irrigation Law (Lajas Valley)
P.R. Laws Ann. 1954, Title 22, § 361 et seq.

Irrigation Map and Statement Act
Colo. Rev. Stat. 1963, 148-4-1 et seq.

**Irrigation Project Contract Extension Act of
1996**
Oct. 19, 1996, P.L. 104-326, 110 Stat. 4000

**Irrigation Project Contract Extension Act of
1998**
Oct. 27, 1998, P.L. 105-293, 112 Stat. 2816

Irrigator's Water Contract Law
Cal. Statutes 1901, Ch. 156, p. 331

Isaacs-Sharkey-Brown Act (Discrimination)
N.Y. City Adm. Code '38, Ch. 1, § D1-1.1 et
seq.

Isenberg-Costa Water Transfer Act
Cal. Water Code § 470 et seq.

**Isla Vista College Community Services
District Law**
Cal. Statutes 1972, Ch. 1420, p. 3083

Island Act
Ark. Code Ann. 1987, 22-6-201 et seq.

Islip Resource Recovery Agency Act
N.Y. Public Authorities Law (Consol. Laws
Ch. 43A) § 2046 et seq.

Isolated Act Statute (Foreign Corporations)
Minn. Stat. Ann., 303.13

Isolated Tract Act
March 28, 1912, Ch. 67, 37 Stat. 77, 43 U.S.
Code § 1171

Isthmian Canal Act
See Panama and Isthmian Canal Act
See Panama Canal Acts

Italian Friendship Treaty (1863)
Haw. Session Laws 1870, p. 73, Feb. 27,
1869

Item Pricing Act
Cal. Civil Code § 7100 et seq.
N.Y. Agriculture and Markets Law (Consol.
Laws Ch. 69) § 214i

**Itemization Act for 1990-1991 (Capital
Budget Project)**
Pa. 1990 Pamph. Laws, No. 223

Ithaca City Court Act
N.Y. Laws 1931, Ch. 415
N.Y. Laws 1973, Ch. 574

**Ithaca City School District Public
Construction Flexibility Demonstration
Project Act**
N.Y. Laws 1997, Ch. 500

Itinerant Merchants Act
Cal. Business and Professions Code § 16300 et seq.
Iowa Code 1979, 81.1 et seq.
Mont. Code Ann., 80-3-701 et seq.
Neb. Rev. Stat. 1943, 75-323 et seq.

Itinerant Vendors Act
Colo. Rev. Stat., 12-50-101 et seq.
Mich. Comp. Laws Ann., 445.371 et seq.
N.H. Rev. Stat. 1955, 321:1 et seq.
Ore. Rev. Stat. 1953, 689.350
R.I. Gen. Laws 1956, 5-15-1 et seq.
Vt. Stat. Ann., Title 32, § 9101 et seq.

Ives Pool Law
N.Y. Laws 1887, Ch. 479

Ives-Quinn Act (Anti-Discrimination)
N.Y. Executive Law 1951 (Consol. Laws Ch. 18) § 290 et seq.

Ives Teacher's Oath Act
N.Y. Education Law 1947 (Consol. Laws Ch. 16) § 3002

J

J. D. Smith Coal Research Act
Ky. Rev. Stat. 1971, 152A.210 et seq.

Jack and Stallion Pedigree Act
Ill. Rev. Stat. 1989, Ch. 8, §§ 32.9, 33

Jack and Stallion Service Lien Act
Ill. Rev. Stat. 1991, Ch. 8, § 50.9 et seq.

Jack Gordon Writing Skills Act
Fla. Stat. Ann., 236.1223

Jack Hagler Self-Defense Act
Fla. Stat. Ann., 790.06 et seq.

Jack Jones Act (Pleading Forms)
Ga. Laws 1847, p. 203

Jack O'Connell Beginning-Teacher Incentive Program
Cal. Education Code 1976, § 45023.4

Jack Stallion Act
Kan. Stat. Ann., 47-107 et seq.

Jack Trimble Act (Highways; Condemnation)
Ky. Rev. Stat. 1971, Superseded Vol., 177.084, 177.087
Ky. Rev. Stat. 1971, 416.540 et seq.

Jackass Act (Promissory Notes)
N.D. Laws 1921, Ch. 92

Jackson Civil Service Act
Tenn. Private Acts 1949, Ch. 156

Jackson-Conley-Kelly Act (Zoning and Planning)
Ky. Rev. Stat. 1962, 100.850 et seq.

Jackson County Airport Authority Act
Ga. Laws 1964 Ex. Sess., p. 2260

Jackson County Hospital District Act
Tex. Laws 66th Leg., 1979, p. 586, Ch. 275

Jackson County Water and Sewerage Authority Act
Ga. Laws 1986, p. 5473

Jackson, Jenkinsburg, Butts County, and Flovilla Water and Sewer Authority Act
Ga. Laws 1986, p. 5457

Jackson State University Main Campus Improvement Fund
Miss. General Laws 1995, Ch. 525

Jackson-Union Counties Regional Port District Act
Ill. Rev. Stat. 1991, Ch. 19, § 851 et seq.

Jackson-Vanik Amendment
Jan. 3, 1975, P.L. 93-618, 19 U.S. Code §§ 2192, 2193, 2432, 2437, 2439

Jacksonville City Charter
Fla. Special Laws 1967, Ch. 67-1320

Jacksonville Police Department Reorganization Law
Fla. Special Laws 1965, Ch. 65-1747

Jacksonville Transportation Authority Law
Fla. Stat. Ann., 349.01 et seq.

Jacob Battle Act (Quieting Title)
N.C. Gen. Stat. 1943, § 41-10

Jacob K. Javits Gifted and Talented Students Education Act of 1988
April 28, 1988, P.L. 100-297, 102 Stat. 237, 20 U.S. Code §§ 3061 et seq.

Jacobson Turner Act (Taxation)
Ark. Acts 1911, Ex. Sess., p. 495, No. 1

Jadwin Act
See Mississippi River Flood Control Act

Jai-a-Lai Act (Pelota)
Fla. Stat. Ann., 551.01 et seq.

Jail Act (County)
Ill. Rev. Stat. 1991, Ch. 75, § 100 et seq.

Jail and House of Correction Loan Act (Bristol County)
Mass. Acts 1953, Ch. 419

Jail and Prison Facility Authority Act (Regional)
W. Va. Code 1966, § 31-20-1 et seq.

Jail Authorities Act (Regional)
Ga. Code Ann., 42-4-90 to 42-4-105

Jail Authority Act (Regional)
Va. Acts 1990, Ch. 725

Jail Construction and Staffing Act
Ga. Code Ann., 15-21-90 et seq.

Jail Farm Barn Loan Act (Worcester County)
Mass. Acts 1970, Ch. 266

Jail Overcrowding Act (County)
Mich. Comp. Laws Ann., 801.51 et seq.

Jail Security Act
Tenn. Code Ann., 41-4-140

Jail Standards and Assistance Act
La. Rev. Stat. Ann., 15:1251 et seq.

Jail Time Act
Mo. Rev. Stat. 1969, 546.615

Jailbreak Act
Kan. Stat. Ann., 21-3809 et seq.

Jails Act (City and County)
Wash. Rev. Code Ann., 70.48.020 et seq., 70.48.170 et seq.

Jails and Jailers Act
Ill. Rev. Stat. 1991, Ch. 75, § 30 et seq.

Jamaica Center Mall Special Assessment Act
N.Y. Laws 1978, Ch. 665

James C. Ware Act (Exceptional Children)
Ky. Rev. Stat. 1971, 157.200 et seq.

James County Abolishment Act
Tenn. Private Acts 1919, Ch. 695

James Madison Bill of Rights Commemorative Coin Act
May 13, 1992, P.L. 102-281, 31 U.S. Code § 5112 nt.
Dec. 21, 1995, P.L. 104-66, 31 U.S. Code § 5112 nt.

James Madison Memorial Fellowship Act
Oct. 18, 1986, P.L. 99-500, 20 U.S. Code § 4501 nt.
Oct. 30, 1986, P.L. 99-591, 20 U.S. Code § 4501 nt.
Dec. 7, 1989, P.L. 101-208, 20 U.S. Code §§ 4502, 4512, 4513
Nov. 15, 1990, P.L. 101-557, 20 U.S. Code § 4512
Nov. 16, 1990, P.L. 101-589, 20 U.S. Code § 4512
Dec. 11, 1991, P.L. 102-221, 20 U.S. Code §§ 4502, 4510
Oct. 7, 1998, P.L. 105-244, 20 U.S. Code § 4514

Jamestown City Court Act
N.Y. Laws 1923, Ch. 666

Jamestown Parking Authority Act
N.Y. Public Authorities Law (Consol. Laws Ch. 43A) § 1599aaa et seq.

Janitors' Tenure Act
N.J. Stat. Ann., 18A:17-3

Japan-United States Friendship Act
Oct. 20, 1975, P.L. 94-118, 89 Stat. 603, 22 U.S. Code §§ 2901 et seq.
Aug. 24, 1982, P.L. 97-241, 22 U.S. Code §§ 2905, 2906
Oct. 28, 1991, P.L. 102-138, 22 U.S. Code § 2905
Oct. 21, 1998, P.L. 105-277, 22 U.S. Code §§ 2905, 2906

Japanese-American Evacuation Claims Act of 1948
July 2, 1948, Ch. 814, 62 Stat. 831, 50 U.S. Code Appx. §§ 1981 to 1987
Aug. 17, 1951, Ch. 327, 65 Stat. 192, 50 U.S. Code Appx. §§ 1984, 1987

July 9, 1956, Ch. 531, 70 Stat. 513, 50 U.S. Code Appx. §§ 1981 to 1984, 1987

Japanese American National Historic Landmark Theme Study Act
March 3, 1992, P.L. 102-248, 106 Stat. 42

Japanese Friendship Treaty (1871)
Haw. Session Laws 1871, p. 44, Sept. 27, 1871

Japanese Technical Literature Act of 1986
Aug. 14, 1986, P.L. 99-382, 15 U.S. Code §§ 3701 nt., 3704

Jar Games and Pull Tabs Act
Ill. Rev. Stat. 1991, Ch. 120, § 1051 et seq.

JARA Continuation Act
Pa. 1980 Pamph. Laws 693, No. 142
Pa. 1982 Pamph. Laws 1409, No. 326

Jarema Coudert Law (Demolition of Elevated Railroad)
N.Y. Laws 1942, Ch. 580

Jarema Law (Teachers)
N.Y. Education Law 1947 (Consol. Laws Ch. 16) § 3011 et seq.

Jarvis-Case Act (Home Rule Cities-Territorial Changes)
Mich. Comp. Laws Ann., 117.9

Jarvis-Gann Proposition 13 Initiative
Cal. Const. Art. 13A, § 1 et seq.

Jarvis Law (Criminal Costs)
Tenn. Code Ann., 40-25-129 et seq.

Jarvis-Mosier-Case-Root Act (Fresh Fruit)
Mich. Comp. Laws Ann., 286.341 et seq.

Jarvis-Root Act (Pari-Mutuel Horse Racing)
Mich. Comp. Laws 1948, 431.1 et seq.

Jasper Bingo Act
Ala. Acts 1992, No. 573

Jasper County, Brownstown Park District, Jo Davies County, Milford, Sheldon, Katherine Dunham, Oak Park, Aledo, Normal, and Mason County Civic Centers Act
Ill. Rev. Stat. 1991, Ch. 85, § 4500 et seq.

Jasper County Civic Center Law
Ill. Rev. Stat. 1991, Ch. 85, § 4801 et seq.

Jasper County Economic Development Authority Act
Ga. Laws 1991, p. 4524

Jasper County Water and Sewer Authority Act
Ga. Laws 1999, H.B. 972

Javits Wagner-O'Day Act
June 25, 1938, Ch. 617, 41 U.S. Code §§ 46 to 48
June 23, 1971, P.L. 92-28, 85 Stat. 77, 41 U.S. Code §§ 46 to 48c

Jaywalkers Act
Wis. Stat. Ann., 346.25

Jeanne Clery Disclosure of Campus Security Policy and Campus Crime Statistics Act
Oct. 7, 1998, P.L. 105-244, § 486(e), 20 U.S. Code § 1092

Jefferson City Court Act
Ga. Laws 1903, p. 138

Jefferson County Bingo Act
Ala. Acts 1980, p. 1027

Jefferson County Civil Service Act
Ala. Code 1958, App., § 645 et seq.

Jefferson County Law Library Tax Act
Ala. Code 1958, Title 62, § 138

Jefferson County Practice Act
Ala. General Acts 1888-89, p. 797

Jefferson County, Quincy, and Herrin Civic Centers Act
Ill. Rev. Stat. 1991, Ch. 85, § 2700 et seq.

Jefferson County Secret Venire Act
Ala. Code 1958, Title 62, § 196 et seq.

Jefferson-Monroe-Missouri-Illinois Bridge Commission Act
Ill. Rev. Stat. 1991, Ch. 127, § 63s-34.9 et seq.

Jefferson National Expansion Memorial Act
May 17, 1954, Ch. 204, 68 Stat. 98, 16 U.S. Code §§ 450jj to 450jj-2
Oct. 19, 1965, P.L. 89-269, 79 Stat. 991, 16 U.S. Code § 450jj nt.
Aug. 24, 1984, P.L. 98-398, 16 U.S. Code §§ 450jj-3-450jj-9

Jefferson National Expansion Memorial Amendments Act of 1984
Aug. 24, 1984, P.L. 98-398, 16 U.S. Code §§ 450jj nt., 450jj-3 to 450jj-9

Jefferson Public Building Authority
Ga. Laws 1999, H.B. 833

Jeffrey Tackett Law Enforcement and Safety Act
Fla. Stat. Ann., 166.049

Jekyll Island State Park Authority Act
Ga. Code Ann., 12-3-230 et seq.

Jencks Act
Sept. 2, 1957, P.L. 85-269, 71 Stat. 595, 18 U.S. Code § 3500
Aug. 26, 1992, P.L. 102-355, 16 U.S. Code §§ 450jj nt., 450jj-3, 450jj-8

Jencks Act (Witnesses' Statements and Reports)
Alaska Stat. 1962, § 12.45.060

Jenema-Deadman Act (Reforestation Fund)
Mich. Comp. Laws Ann., 320.71

Jenema-Milliken-Engstrom Act (Cherry Production)
Mich. Comp. Laws Ann., 290.501 et seq.

Jenkinsburg, Butts County, Flovilla, and Jackson Water and Sewer Authority Act
Ga. Laws 1986, p. 5457

Jennings Randolph Lake Project Compact
Md. Ann. Code 1974, Art. NR, § 8-4A-01 et seq.

Jeofails Act
Ill. Rev. Stat. 1985, Ch. 7, § 1 et seq.
Miss. Code Ann. 1972, § 11-7-167
Mo. Rev. Stat., 546.080

Jeopardy Act
Vt. Stat. Ann., Title 13, § 6556 et seq.
Wash. Rev. Code Ann., 10.43.020 et seq.

Jeopardy Act (Short)
La. Code of Civil Procedure, Art. 591 et seq.

Jersey City Medical Center Appropriations Act
N.J. Laws 1977, Ch. 7

Jerusalem Embassy Act of 1995
Nov. 8, 1995, P.L. 104-45, 109 Stat. 398

Jesse Mayo Disability Insurance Hospital Benefits Law
Cal. Unemployment Insurance Code § 2800 et seq.

Jessie Weiss Act (Admission Tax)
Fla. Stat. Ann., 212.04

Jewelers' Liability Act (Gold and Silver Articles)
June 13, 1906, Ch. 3289, 34 Stat. 260, 15 U.S. Code §§ 294 to 300

Jewelers' Lien Act
Mass. Gen. Laws Ann., 255:31C

Jewelry Appraisal Act
Pa. Purdon's Stat., Title 73, § 1981 et seq.

Jewish Law (Kosher Food)
See Kosher Food Act

Jicarilla Apache Tribe Water Rights Settlement Act
Oct. 23, 1992, P.L. 102-441, 106 Stat. 2237

Jim Crow Act (Common Carriers)
Ala. Code 1958, Title 48, §§ 196, 197, 464
Fla. Stat. 1967, 352.04 et seq.

Okla. Stat. Ann., Title 13, § 181 et seq.
Tenn. Code Ann., Superseded Vol., 65-1313, 65-1704 et seq.
Va. Code 1950, § 56-325 et seq.

Jim Davis Law
Tenn. Code Ann., Superseded Vol., 65-1508

Jim Smith Act (Tax Assessments)
Ga. Code 1933, 92-6701 et seq.

Jim Thorpe Memorial Commission Act
Okla. Stat. 1961, Title 53, § 61 et seq.

Jimmy Ryce Involuntary Civil Commitment for Sexually Violent Predator's Treatment and Care Act
Fla. Stat. Ann., 916.30 et seq.

Jingle Rule
Mont. Code Ann., 35-10-612

Jitney Bus Act
Conn. Gen. Stat. Ann., § 13b-80 et seq.
N.J. Rev. Stat. 1937, 48:4-1 to 48:4-11, 48:4-14 to 48:4-17

Jo Davies County Civic Center Law
Ill. Rev. Stat. 1991, Ch. 85, § 4801 et seq.

Jo Davies County, Milford, Sheldon, Katherine Dunham, Oak Park, Aledo, Normal, Mason County, Jasper County, and Brownstown Park District Civic Centers Act
Ill. Rev. Stat. 1991, Ch. 85, § 4500 et seq.

Job Creation and Development Act
Cal. Corporations Code § 14000 et seq.

Job Creation and Economic Development Act (East Kentucky)
Ky. Rev. Stat. 1971, 154B.100 et seq.

Job Creation Tax Credit Law
Pa. Purdon's Stat., Title 72, § 8801 et seq.

Job Development Act
Cal. Government Code § 15905 et seq.

Job Development Authority Act
Mich. Comp. Laws Ann., 125.1701 et seq.
N.Y. Public Authorities Law (Consol. Laws Ch. 43A) § 1800 et seq.

Job Development Zone Act
Vt. Stat. Ann., Title 10, § 691 et seq.

Job Evaluation Policy Act of 1970
March 17, 1970, P.L. 91-216, 84 Stat. 72, 5 U.S. Code § 5104 nt.

Job Expansion Act
Ida. Code 1947, 63-3029D et seq.

Job Expansion and Investment Credit Act
Colo. Rev. Stat., 39-22-508.1 et seq.
Kan. Stat. Ann., 79-32,153 et seq.

Job Increment Financing Program Act (Loring)
Me. Rev. Stat. Ann. 1964, Title 5, § 13080-O et seq.

Job Investment Act
Mont. Code Ann., 17-6-501 et seq.

Job Opportunities Act
Me. Rev. Stat. Ann. 1964, Title 22, § 3771 et seq.

Job Opportunity Zones Act
Me. Rev. Stat. Ann. 1964, Title 5, § 15131 et seq.

Job Protection Act
Conn. Gen. Stat. Ann., § 31-48a

Job Referral and Job Listing Services Consumer Protection Act
Ill. Rev. Stat. 1991, Ch. 121 1/2, § 2001 et seq.

Job Retention Act (Aerospace)
Cal. Statutes 1992, Ch. 1108

Job Retention Act (Garment Industry)
N.Y. Labor Law (Consol. Laws Ch. 31) § 358a
N.Y. Laws 1981, Ch. 624

Job Selling Act
Ohio Rev. Code 1953, 4143.26 et seq.

Job Sharing Act (State Employee)
Ill. Rev. Stat. 1991, Ch. 127, §§ 1350, 1351

Job Training Act
Neb. Laws 1984, L.B. 851
Neb. Rev. Stat. 1943, 48-1601 et seq.

Job Training Act (Alternative Sentencing)
Ill. Comp. Stat. 1992, Ch. 730, § 170/1 et seq.

Job Training and Economic Development Demonstration Grant Program
Ill. Comp. Stat. 1992, Ch. 20, § 605/46.19j

Job Training Center for Urban Women Act
N.J. Stat. Ann., 52:27D-288 et seq.

Job Training Coordinating Council Act
Ill. Rev. Stat. 1991, Ch. 48, § 2101 et seq.

Job Training Coordination Act
Utah Code Ann. 1953, 9-2-1101 et seq.
Utah Code Ann. 1953, 55-17-6 et seq.

Job Training Evaluation Act
Ill. Comp. Stat. 1992, Ch. 20, §§ 2220/5-1, 2220/5-5

Job Training Partnership Act
Oct. 13, 1982, P.L. 97-300, 29 U.S. Code § 1501 et seq.
Dec. 31, 1982, P.L. 97-404, 29 U.S. Code §§ 1513, 1532, 1551, 1591, 1603, 1658, 1671, 1734, 1753
Oct. 12, 1984, P.L. 98-473, 29 U.S. Code § 1695
Oct. 19, 1984, P.L. 98-524, 20 U.S. Code §§ 1503, 1532, 1535, 1697, 1753, 1754, 1772, 3223
Oct. 16, 1986, P.L. 99-496, 29 U.S. Code §§ 1511, 1533, 1602, 1630 to 1634, 1707
Oct. 27, 1986, P.L. 99-570, 29 U.S. Code §§ 1531, 1603
July 22, 1987, P.L. 100-77, 29 U.S. Code §§ 1503, 1551
Aug. 23, 1988, P.L. 100-418, 102 Stat. 1524, 29 U.S. Code §§ 1502, 1505, 1516, 1532, 1651
Oct. 17, 1988, P.L. 100-495, 29 U.S. Code §§ 1571, 1571 nt.
Nov. 7, 1988, P.L. 100-628, 29 U.S. Code generally §§ 49 et seq., 1502, 1514, 1516, 1583, 1791 et seq.
Sept. 25, 1990, P.L. 101-392, 29 U.S. Code §§ 1533, 1604, 1661c

Nov. 5, 1990, P.L. 101-510, 29 U.S. Code § 1662d
Nov. 15, 1990, P.L. 101-549, 29 U.S. Code §§ 1502, 1662e
Nov. 29, 1990, P.L. 101-645, 29 U.S. Code § 1703a
June 13, 1991, P.L. 102-54, 29 U.S. Code §§ 1503, 1531, 1721
Dec. 12, 1991, P.L. 102-235, 29 U.S. Code §§ 1503, 1514, 1531, 1532, 1533, 1604, 1737
Sept. 7, 1992, P.L. 102-367, 29 U.S. Code §§ 1501 nt., 1501 et seq., 1601 et seq., 1703 et seq.
Oct. 23, 1992, P.L. 102-484, 29 U.S. Code §§ 1551, 1661, 1661c, 1662d, 1662d-1
July 2, 1993, P.L. 103-50, 29 U.S. Code § 1782c
Nov. 30, 1993, P.L. 103-160, 29 U.S. Code §§ 1551, 1662d-1
March 31, 1994, P.L. 103-227, 29 U.S. Code § 1632
May 4, 1994, P.L. 103-239, 29 U.S. Code § 1699
Oct. 5, 1994, P.L. 103-337, 29 U.S. Code §§ 1662d, 1662d-1
Oct. 20, 1994, P.L. 103-382, 29 U.S. Code §§ 1503, 1643, 1645
Aug. 22, 1996, P.L. 104-193, 29 U.S. Code §§ 1503, 1516, 1531, 1533, 1603, 1604, 1605, 1632, 1644, 1645, 1699, 1734, 1735, 1791, 1791e, 1791g, 1792
Aug. 7, 1998, P.L. 105-220, 29 U.S. Code §§ 801 nt., 1501 to 1505, 1511 to 1519, 1531 to 1537, 1551 to 1555, 1571 to 1592, 1601 to 1606, 1630 to 1635, 1641 to 1646, 1651 to 1653, 1661, 1661a to 1661f, 1662, 1662a to 1662e, 1671 to 1673, 1691 to 1709, 1721, 1731 to 1735, 1737, 1751 to 1755, 1771 to 1775, 1781, 1782, 1782a to 1782h, 1783, 1784, 1784a, 1784b, 1791, 1791a to 1791h, 1792, 1792a, 1792b
Md. Ann. Code 1957, Art. 89, § 17 et seq.
Me. Rev. Stat. Ann. 1964, Title 26, § 2001 et seq.
Tex. Labor Code, § 301.001 et seq.

Job Training Partnership Act Amendments of 1986
Oct. 16, 1986, P.L. 99-496, 29 U.S. Code § 1501 nt.

Job Training Reform Amendments of 1992
Sept. 7, 1992, P.L. 102-367, 29 U.S. Code § 1501 nt.
Oct. 23, 1992, P.L. 102-484, 29 U.S. Code § 1551
Oct. 21, 1998, P.L. 105-277, 29 U.S. Code § 1501 nt.

Jobs Act (Environmental Restoration)
Wash. Laws 1993, Ch. 516

Jobs and Housing Investment Bond Act
Cal. Health and Safety Code § 52534 et seq.

Jobs and Training Law
Minn. Stat. Ann., 268.001 et seq.

Jobs, Clean Air, and Transportation Efficiency Act
Cal. Public Utilities Code §§ 99385 et seq., 99399 et seq.

Jobs Creation by Stimulating Small Business Growth Act
Ark. Code Ann. 1987, 15-4-401 et seq.

Jobs Development Act
R.I. Gen. Laws 1956, 42-64.5-1 et seq.

Jobs Development and Infrastructure Act
W. Va. Code 1966, § 31-15A-1 et seq.

Jobs-Economic Development Fund Act
S.C. Code Ann. 1976, § 41-43-10 et seq.

Jobs, Education, and Competitiveness Bond Act
N.J. Laws 1988, Ch. 78

Jobs for Employable Dependent Individuals Act
Nov. 7, 1988, P.L. 100-628, 29 U.S. Code § 1501 nt.

Jobs for Florida's Graduates Act
Fla. Stat. Ann., 446.609

Jobs for the New, New York Bond Act
N.Y. Laws 1992, Ch. 649

Jobs Investment Trust Act
W. Va. Code 1966 § 12-7-1 et seq.

Jobs Program Act (Quality)
Okla. Stat. Ann., Title 68, § 3601 et seq.

Jobs Protection Act (Revenue Bonding)
Wis. Stat. Ann., 66.521, 108.04

Jobs Recovery Law (Industrial)
Ill. Comp. Stat. 1992, Ch. 65, § 5/11-74.6-1

Jobs Retention Act (Natural Gas Industry)
W. Va. Code 1966, § 11-13L-1 et seq.

Jobs, Science and Technology Bond Act
N.J. Laws 1984, Ch. 99

Jobs Siting Act
Fla. Stat. Ann., 403.950 et seq.

Jobs Tax Credit Act
Cal. Revenue and Taxation Code §§ 17053.6, 23621
Cal. Statutes 1979, Ch. 1182
Cal. Statutes 1985, Ch. 1564

Jobs Through Exports Act of 1992
Oct. 28, 1992, P.L. 102-549, 22 U.S. Code § 2151 nt.
Dec. 21, 1995, P.L. 104-66, 15 U.S. Code § 4723a

Jobs Through Trade Expansion Act of 1994
Oct. 22, 1994, P.L. 103-392, 22 U.S. Code § 2151 nt.

Jobs Transportation Demonstration Act
N.J. Stat. Ann., 34:1A-70 et seq.

Joe Carlucci Uniform Firearms Act
Fla. Stat. Ann., 790.33

Joe Davis Law (Certificates of Convenience and Necessity)
Tenn. Code Ann. 1955, 65-1508

Joe Kershaw, Dempsey J. Barron and W.D. Childers Cane Pole Tax Repeal Act
Fla. Stat. Ann., 372.57

Joe Lang Kershaw Act (Tax Repeal)
Fla. Stat. Ann., 548.001 et seq.

Jogging Act
Tenn. Code Ann., 68-51-101 et seq.

John B. "Johnny" Johnson Act
Ala. Code 1975, § 40-20-2

John C. Hertel Toxic Substance Control Commission Act
Mich. Comp. Laws Ann., 286.181 et seq.

John C. Stennis Center for Public Service Training and Development Act
Oct. 1, 1988, P.L. 100-458, 102 Stat. 2172, 2 U.S. Code § 1101 nt., 1101 to 1110
Nov. 3, 1990, P.L. 101-520, 2 U.S. Code §§ 1105, 1106, 1108

John Dempsey Hospital Finance Corporation Act
Conn. Gen. Stat. Ann., § 10a-250 et seq.

John Doe Act (Investigations)
S.D. Codified Laws 1967, 23-20-10 et seq.
Wis. Stat. Ann., 968.26

John F. Kennedy Center Act
June 20, 1977, P.L. 95-50, 20 U.S. Code §§ 76l et seq.
June 29, 1978, P.L. 95-305, 20 U.S. Code § 76l
Dec. 2, 1983, P.L. 98-205, 20 U.S. Code § 76j
Oct. 22, 1990, P.L. 101-449, 20 U.S. Code §§ 76l to 76o
Oct. 24, 1992, P.L. 102-500, 20 U.S. Code § 76l
July 21, 1994, P.L. 103-270, 20 U.S. Code §§ 76h, 76h nt., 76j, 76k, 76l, 76p, 76r, 76s
Nov. 19, 1997, P.L. 105-95, 20 U.S. Code §§ 76i, 76j, 76k, 76s
Aug. 12, 1998, P.L. 105-226, 20 U.S. Code §§ 76j, 76l, 76r

John F. Kennedy Center Act Amendments of 1984
Oct. 12, 1984, P.L. 98-473, 20 U.S. Code § 76o

John F. Kennedy Center Act Amendments of 1994
July 21, 1994, P.L. 103-279, 20 U.S. Code 76h, 76h nt., 76j, 76k, 76l, 76p, 76r, 76s, 40 U.S. Code 193r, 193u, 193v

John F. Kennedy Center for the Performing Arts Authorization Act of 1998
Aug. 12, 1998, P.L. 105-226, 20 U.S. Code § 76h

John F. Kennedy Center Parking Improvement Act of 1997
Nov. 19, 1997, P.L. 105-95, 20 U.S. Code § 76h nt.

John J. Savage Memorial Act
Fla. Stat. Ann., 112.3191 et seq.

John L. Buskey Penny Trust Fund Matching Act
Ala. Code 1975, §§ 41-15A-10 to 41-15A-12

John Wallace Act
Ala. Code 1975, § 36-29-14

Johns Creek Community Improvement District Act
Ga. Laws 1990, p. 4665

Johnson Act (Gambling)
March 9, 1992, P.L. 102-251, 15 U.S. Code §§ 1172, 1175
Tenn. Code Ann., 39-6-607 et seq.

Johnson Act (Immigration)
May 26, 1924, Ch. 190, 43 Stat. 153 (See 8 U.S. Code §§ 1181 et seq., 1282, 1284, 1287, 1321, 1322)

Johnson Act (Injunctions Affecting Utility Rates)
May 14, 1934, Ch. 283, 48 Stat. 775, 28 U.S. Code §§ 1331, 1332, 1339, 1341, 1342, 1345, 1354

Johnson Act (Maritime Workers' Compensation)
Oct. 6, 1917, Ch. 97, 40 Stat. 395 (See 28 U.S. Code §§ 1251, 1333, 1338, 1351, 1355, 1356) 18 U.S. Code § 3231

Johnson Amendment

May 27, 1933, Ch. 38, 48 Stat. 92, 15 U.S. Code §§ 77bb to 77mm

Johnson City Downtown Development Authority Act

Tenn. Code Ann., 26-2-216, b, 1

Johnson City Parking Authority Act

N.Y. Public Authorities Law (Consol. Laws Ch. 43A) §§ 1421 et seq.

Johnson County Massage Registration Act

Tenn. Private Acts 1978, Ch. 282

Johnson County Road Act

Tenn. Private Acts 1949, Ch. 567

Johnson County Wholesale Water Supply Act

Kan. Stat. Ann., 19-3522 et seq.

Johnson Debt Default Act

April 13, 1934, Ch. 112, 48 Stat. 574 (See 18 U.S. Code § 955)

July 31, 1945, Ch. 339, 59 Stat. 516, 31 U.S. Code § 804b

Johnson-Dingell Enabling Act (Fish Restoration)

Mich. Comp. Laws Ann., 300.151

Johnson-Filante Hazardous Substance Cleanup Bond Act

Cal. Health and Safety Code § 25385 et seq.

Johnson Fish Restoration Act

See Fish Restoration And Management Projects Act

Johnson Grass Act

Ariz. Rev. Stat. Ann., § 48-320

Johnson Grass Act (Railroads)

Tex. Rev. Civ. Stat., Art. 6401

Johnson Grass Control and Eradication Act

Ark. Code Ann. 1987, 2-16-501 et seq.

Johnson-Marks Roos Property Tax Limitation Act

Cal. Revenue and Tax Code §§ 97.2, 97.65

Johnson-O'Malley Act

April 16, 1934, Ch. 147, 48 Stat. 596, 25 U.S. Code §§ 452 to 455

June 4, 1936, Ch. 490, 49 Stat. 1458, 25 U.S. Code §§ 452 to 455

Oct. 20, 1994, P.L. 103-382, 25 U.S. Code § 456

Johnston-Baker-Andal-Boatwright Delta Protection Act

Cal. Public Resources Code § 29700 et seq.

Johnston Charter Validation Act

R.I. Public Laws 1963, Ch. 187

Johnston County Peace Officers' Relief Association Act

N.C. Laws 1957, Ch. 861

Johnston Murray Turnpike Act

Okla. Laws 1953, p. 508

Johnston-Nielsen Boating Act

Cal. Statutes 1986, Ch. 877

Joinder Act (Husband and Wife)

Tex. Family Code, § 4.04

Joinder Act (Indictments)

Ark. Code Ann. 1987, 16-85-404 et seq.

Joinder Act (Insurers)

Wis. Stat. Ann., 803.04, Subsec. 2

Joinder of Actions Act

Wash. Rev. Code Ann., 4.36.150

Joinder of Claims Act

Kan. Stat. Ann., 60-218

N.C. Gen Stat. 1943, § 1-123

Wash. Rev. Code Ann., 4.36.150

Joinder of Offenses Act

N.Y. Criminal Procedure Law (Consol. Laws Ch. 11a) § 200.20

Joinder of Parties Act
Okla. Stat. Ann., Title 12, § 2017 et seq.

Joint Account Act (Statutory)
Mich. Comp. Laws 1979, 487.711 et seq.

Joint Airport Authorities Act
Ill. Rev. Stat. 1991, Ch. 15 1/2, § 600 et seq.
Neb. Rev. Stat. 1943, 3-701 et seq.

Joint Appropriation Review Committee (JARC) Act
S.C. Code Ann. 1976, § 2-65-10 et seq.

Joint Bank Account Act
Cal. Financial Code § 852
Conn. Gen. Stat. Ann., § 36-3
Ill. Rev. Stat. 1991, Ch. 76, § 2, Subd. A
N.H. Rev. Stat. 1955, 384.28 et seq.
N.J. Stat. Ann., 17:16I-1 et seq.
N.Y. Banking Law (Consol. Laws Ch. 2)
§§ 134, 171, 239,
Vt. Stat. Ann., Title 8, §§ 908, 909
Wis. Stat. Ann., 705.01 et seq.

Joint Bank Deposit Act
Cal. Financial Code § 852 et seq.

Joint Cemetary Act
Ill. Rev. Stat. 1991, Ch. 21, § 21.9 et seq.

Joint City-County Building Act
N.M. Stat. Ann., 5-5-1 et seq.

Joint Comprehensive Health Planning Agency Act
Md. Ann. Code 1974, Art. HG. § 19-101 et seq.

Joint Contribution Act (Tortfeasors)
Mich. Comp. Laws Ann., 600.2925 et seq.

Joint Cooperation Act (Local Governments)
Wis. Stat. Ann., 66.30

Joint County and Municipal Solid Waste Disposal Act
Ark. Code Ann. 1987, 14-233-101 et seq.

Joint County Flood Control Act
Wash. Rev. Code Ann., 86.13.010 et seq.

Joint County Infirmaries Act
Mich. Comp. Laws Ann., 404.1 et seq.

Joint County Jail Act
Cal. Penal Code § 4050 et seq.

Joint County Road Camp Act
Cal. Penal Code § 4200 et seq.

Joint Debtor Act
Cal. Education Code 1976, § 56875 et seq.
Mich. Comp. Laws 1948, 622.8 et seq.
N.D. Cent. Code, 32-30-01 et seq.
N.Y. Civil Practice Law and Rules (Consol. Laws Ch. 8) § 1501 et seq.
Wis. Stat. Ann., 113.11

Joint Debtor Act (Process)
Okla. Stat. Ann., Title 12, § 178

Joint Development Act (Water Quality)
Wash. Rev. Code Ann., 70.150.010 et seq.

Joint Exercise of Powers Act (Public Agencies)
Ariz. Rev. Stat. Ann., § 11-951 et seq.
Cal. Government Code § 6500 et seq.
Iowa Code Ann., 28e.1 et seq.
Mass. Gen. Laws Ann., 40:4A

Joint Flood and Drainage Planning Assessments Act
N.M. Stat. Ann., 73-24-1 et seq.

Joint Guardianship Act
Conn. Gen. Stat. Ann., § 45a-606

Joint Highway District Act
Cal. Streets and Highways Code § 2500 et seq.

Joint Hospital Act
Mich. Comp. Laws Ann., 331.1 et seq.

Joint Management Commission Act (State Capitol)
N.J. Stat. Ann., 52:31-34 et seq.

Joint Municipal Electric Power Act
Ill. Rev. Stat. 1981, Ch. 24, § 11-119.1-1 et seq.

Joint Municipal Electric Power and Energy Act
Miss. Code Ann. 1972, § 77-5-701 et seq.
N.C. Gen. Stat. 1943, § 159B-1 et seq.
S.C. Code Ann. 1976, § 6-23-10 et seq.

Joint Municipal Electric Power Generation Act
Ark. Code Ann. 1987, 14-202-101 et seq.

Joint Municipal Employee's Retirement System Act
Ga. Code Ann., 47-5-1 et seq.

Joint Municipal Natural Gas Act
Ill. Rev. Stat. 1989, Ch. 24, § 11-119.2-1 et seq.

Joint Municipal Sewage Disposal District Act
Cal. Health and Safety Code § 5700 et seq.

Joint Municipal Utility Commission Act
Mo. Rev. Stat., 393.700 et seq.

Joint Municipal Water Systems Act
S.C. Code Ann. 1976, § 6-25-10 et seq.

Joint Natural Guardian Act
Fla. Stat. Ann., 744.301

Joint Obligations Act
See Uniform Joint Obligations Act

Joint Ownership Act (Electricity and Gas)
Ill. Rev. Stat. 1991, Ch. 76, § 10 et seq.

Joint Planning Commission Act
Ga. Code 1933, 69-1201 et seq.

Joint Powers Act
Fla. Stat. Ann., 361.10 et seq.
Wyo. Stat. Ann., § 16-1-102 et seq.

Joint Powers Act (Public Agencies)
Cal. Government Code § 6500 et seq.
Wyo. Stat. Ann., § 16-1-102 et seq.

Joint Powers Agreements Act
N.M. Stat. Ann., 11-1-1 et seq.

Joint Public Power Authority Act
Neb. Rev. Stat. 1943, 70-1401 et seq.

Joint Purchase Act (Political Subdivisions)
Pa. Purdon's Stat., Title 72, § 6151.1 et seq.

Joint Purchasing Act
Ill. Rev. Stat. 1989, Ch. 85, § 1601 et seq.

Joint Purchasing Act (Governmental)
Ill. Rev. Stat. 1991, Ch. 85, § 1600 et seq.

Joint Rates Act (Railroads)
Minn. Stat. Ann., 218.031 et seq.

Joint Real Estate Holdings Act
Mich. Comp. Laws Ann., 557.51 et seq.

Joint Retirement Act
Tex. Rev. Civ. Stat., Art. 6228c

Joint Review Process Act
Colo. Rev. Stat., 34-10-101 et seq.

Joint Rights and Obligations Act
Ill. Rev. Stat. 1991, Ch. 76

Joint School Act
Pa. 1911 Pamph. Laws 309, § 1801 et seq.

Joint Service Pay Act
See Pay Readjustment Act (Army, Navy, Etc.)

Joint State and County Work Programs Act
Miss. Code Ann. 1972, § 47-5-451 et seq.

Joint Stock Company Act
Haw. Session Laws 1890, Ch. 43
N.Y. General Associations Laws (Consol. Laws Ch. 29) § 3 et seq.
Wis. General Laws 1853, Ch. 68

Joint Tenancy Act
Colo. Rev. Stat., 38-31-101 et seq.
Ill. Rev. Stat. 1991, Ch. 76, § 0.01 et seq.
Wash. Rev. Code Ann., 64.28.010 et seq.

Joint Tenancy Bank Deposits Act
Haw. Rev. Stat. Ann., § 403-134
Mich. Comp. Laws Ann., 487.703
Mo. Rev. Stat., 362.470
Wash. Rev. Code Ann., 30.22.050 et seq.

Joint Tortfeasors Contribution Act
See also Uniform Contribution Among
Tortfeasors Act
Ark. Code Ann. 1987, 16-61-201 et seq.
Cal. Code of Civil Procedure § 875 et seq.
Del. Code of 1974, Title 10, § 6301 et seq.
Ga. Code Ann., 51-12-31
Haw. Rev. Stat. Ann., § 663-11 et seq.
Mass. Gen. Laws Ann., 231B:1 et seq.
Md. Ann. Code 1957, Art. 50, § 16 et seq.
Miss. Code Ann. 1972, § 85-5-5
Mo. Rev. Stat., 537.060
N.J. Stat. Ann., 2A:53A-1 et seq.
N.M. Stat. Ann., 41-3-1 et seq.
Pa. Cons. Stat., Title 42, § 8322
R.I. Gen. Laws 1956, 10-6-1 et seq.
Tex. Civ. Prac and Rem. Code, § 32.001 et
seq.

Joint Township Hospital Districts Act
Ohio Rev. Code 1953, 513.07 et seq.

Joint Underwriting Association Act
Minn. Stat. Ann., 62I.01 et seq.
N.J. Stat. Ann., 17:30B-1 et seq.

**Joint Underwriting Association Act
(Insurance Medical and Hospital
Malpractice)**
Me. Rev. Stat. Ann. 1964, Title 24, § 2401 et
seq.

**Joint Underwriting Association Act
(Malpractice)**
Minn. Stat. Ann., 62F.01 et seq.

**Joint Underwriting Association Licensing
Act**
Tex. Insurance Code, Art. 21.49-3b

**Joint Wilkinson-McIntyre-Irwinton-
Toomsboro Water and Sewer Authority
Act**
Ga. Laws 1990, p. 4685

Jointure Act (Dower)
Va. Code 1950, § 64.1-19 et seq.

Joliet-Marquette Trail Act
Ill. Rev. Stat. 1991, Ch. 121, § 390.9 et seq.

Joliet Regional Port District Act
Ill. Rev. Stat. 1991, Ch. 19, § 251 et seq.

Jones A. A. A. Act of 1938
See Agricultural Adjustment Act Of 1938

Jones Act (Carriers for Hire)
N.J. Stat. Ann., 48:2-15

Jones Act (Intoxicating Liquors)
March 2, 1929, Ch. 473, 45 Stat. 1446

Jones Act (Merchant Marine)
See Merchant Marine Act, 1920

Jones Act (Philippine Government)
See Autonomy Act

Jones Act (Puerto Rico)
March 2, 1917, Ch. 145, 39 Stat. 951, 2 U.S.
Code § 46; 48 U.S. Code §§ 731, 733a, 734,
737, 741a, 742, 745, 747 to 749, 751, 752,
863 to 865, 868, 870 to 872, 874, 891 to 893
March 12, 1980, P.L. 96-205, 48 U.S. Code
§§ 747, 749

Jones Act (Taxation)
Mo. Rev. Stat., 140.080 et seq.
Ohio Rev. Code 1953, 5705.01 et seq.

Jones Amendment (Liquor Advertisements)
March 3, 1917, Ch. 162, 39 Stat. 1058

Jones Beach State Parkway Authority Act
N.Y. Public Authorities Law (Consol. Laws
Ch. 43A) § 150 et seq.

Jones-Connally Farm-Relief Act
April 7, 1934, Ch. 103, 48 Stat. 528, 7 U.S.
Code §§ 608, 608b, 609, 611 to 612a

Jones-Costigan Sugar Act
May 9, 1934, Ch. 263, 48 Stat. 670, 7 U.S. Code §§ 608 to 611, 613, 615 to 617, 620

Jones Farm Loan Act
See Emergency Farm Mortgage Act Of 1933

Jones-Marshall Act (Corporations)
Ohio Laws Vol. 113, p. 413

Jones-McCormack Act (Saturday Half Holidays)
March 3, 1931, Ch. 396, 46 Stat. 1482

Jones-Miller Act (Narcotics Import and Export)
May 26, 1922, Ch. 202, 42 Stat. 596, 21 U.S. Code §§ 171, 173, 174, 176, 177, 180, 182, 184, 185

Jones-Munger Act (Back Tax)
Mo. Rev. Stat., 140.080 et seq.

Jones-Reid Act
See Mississippi River Flood Control Act

Jones-White Act
May 22, 1928, Ch. 675, 45 Stat. 689, 46 U.S. Code §§ 866, 869, 880, 891, 891b, 891c, 891s, 891u to 891x

Jordan Animal Control Law
N.Y. Local Laws 1972, Village of Jordan, p. 3509

Jordan Electrical Code
N.Y. Local Laws 1973, Village of Jordan, p. 3441

Jordan Litter Law
N.Y. Local Laws 1973, Village of Jordan, p. 3444

Jordan Zoning Law
N.Y. Local Laws 1969, Village of Jordan, p. 2610

Joshua Tree National Monument Act
Sept. 25, 1950, Ch. 1030, 64 Stat. 1033, 16 U.S. Code §§ 450ii to 450ii-3
June 30, 1961, P.L. 87-80, 75 Stat. 197, 16 U.S. Code § 450ii

Journalism College Act (University of Illinois)
Ill. Rev. Stat. 1991, Ch. 144, § 61.90 et seq.

Journalists' Shield Act
Md. Ann. Code 1974, Art. CJ, § 9-112

Journeys Account Act
Del. Code of 1974, Title 10, § 8118

Joy Riding Act
Ariz. Rev. Stat. Ann., § 13-1803
Cal. Penal Code § 499b
Cal. Vehicle Code 1959, § 10851
Iowa Code Ann., 714.7
Mich. Comp. Laws Ann., 750.413
N.Y. Penal Law 1965 (Consol. Laws Ch. 40) §§ 165.05, 165.06, 165.08
Ore. Rev. Code 1953, 819.300
Tenn. Code Ann., 55-5-104
Utah Code Ann. 1953, 41-1-109
Wash. Rev. Code Ann., 9A.56.070
Wis. Stat. Ann., 943.23

Juan Bautista de Anza National Historic Trail Act
Aug. 15, 1990, P.L. 101-365, 16 U.S. Code § 1241 nt.

Judge Compensation Act (Election)
Ill. Rev. Stat. 1991, Ch. 46, § 900 et seq.

Judge-Jury Act
Mich. Comp. Laws Ann., 767.3 et seq.

Judge Sentencing Act
Tenn. Code Ann., 40-35-101

Judges Act (Associate)
Ill. Comp. Stat. 1992, Ch. 705, § 45/2

Judges Compulsory Retirement Act
Ill. Rev. Stat. 1991, Ch. 37, §§ 23.70, 23.71

Judges Disqualification Act
Ill. Rev. Stat. 1991, Ch. 37, §§ 160.10, 160.11
Mont. Code Ann., 3-1-801

Judges Pension Act
Conn. Gen. Stat. Ann., § 51-50 et seq.
Ky. Acts 1940, Ch. 131
Md. Ann. Code 1957, Art. 73B, § 55 et seq.
Nev. Rev. Stat. 1979 Reprint, 2.060, 3.090

Judges Retirement Act
Mich. Comp. Laws Ann., 38.2101 et seq.
Mont. Code Ann., 19-5-105 et seq.
Neb. Rev. Stat. 1943, 24-701 to 24-714

Judges' Retirement Act
Ariz. Rev. Stat. Ann., § 38-801 et seq.
Ark. Stat. 1947, 24-8-501, 24-8-201
Cal. Government Code § 75000 et seq.
D.C. Code Ann., § 11-1561 et seq.
Fla. Stat. Ann., 123.01 et seq.
Ida. Code 1947, 1-2001 et seq.
Ill. Rev. Stat. 1991, Ch. 108 1/2, § 18-101 et seq.
Ind. Code Ann., 33-13-8-1 et seq.
Iowa Code Ann., 602.9101 et seq.
Kan. Stat. Ann., 20-2601 et seq.
Ky. Rev. Stat. 1971, 21.345 et seq.
Minn. Stat. Ann., 490.025 et seq.
Mo. Rev. Stat., 476.450 et seq.
N.D. Cent. Code, 27-17-01 et seq.
Neb. Rev. Stat. 1943, 24-701 et seq.
Okla. Stat. Ann., Title 20, § 1101 et seq.
Ore. Rev. Stat., 1.310 et seq.
Pa. 1901 Pamph. Laws 165, No. 131
Pa. 1919 Pamph. Laws 461, No. 234
Pa. 1929 Pamph. Laws 844, No. 369
Tenn. Code Ann. 1955, 17-301 et seq.
Tex. Rev. Civ. Stat., Art. 6228b
Utah Code Ann. 1953, 49-6-101 et seq.
Wash. Rev. Code Ann., 2.12.0101 et seq.

Judges' Retirement Fund Act
Cal. Government Code § 75100 et seq.

Judges Retirement System II Law
Cal. Government Code § 75500 et seq.

Judges' Salary Act
Ind. Code Ann., 33-13-12-1 et seq.
Pa. 1903 Pamph. Laws 175, No. 134
Tex. Government Code, § 31.001 et seq.

Judges Salary Act (Assigned Appellate)
Ill. Comp. Stat. 1992, Ch. 5, § 295/0.01 et seq.
Ill. Rev. Stat. 1991, Ch. 53, § 5.10 et seq.

Judges Travel Expense Act (Circuit Court)
Ill. Comp. Stat. 1992, Ch. 5, §§ 300/0.01, 300/1 et seq.

Judgeship Act (Additional Judges)
May 31, 1938, Ch. 290, 52 Stat. 584 (See 28 U.S. Code §§ 44, 133)
May 24, 1940, Ch. 209, 54 Stat. 219, 48 U.S. Code § 1392a; See also, 28 U.S. Code §§ 44 nt., 133 nt.
Aug. 3, 1949, Ch. 387, 63 Stat. 493, 28 U.S. Code §§ 44, 133, 134

Judgeships Act
Ga. Code Ann., 9-11-56
Neb. Rev. Stat. 1943, 25-1515

Judgment Act (Dormant)
Neb. Rev. Stat. 1943, 25-1515

Judgment Act (Summary)
See Summary Judgment Act

Judgment Bond Act (Cities)
Mich. Comp. Laws Ann., 600.6097

Judgment by Confession Act
Wash. Rev. Code Ann., 4.60.010 et seq.

Judgment Certificate Act
Ohio Rev. Code 1953, 2329.02

Judgment Debtor Examination Act
La. Code of Civil Procedure Art. 2451 et seq.

Judgment Dormancy Act
Okla. Stat. Ann., Title 12, § 735

Judgment Interest Act (Torts)
Mass. Gen. Laws Ann., 231:6B

Judgment Interest Statute
Mich. Comp. Laws Ann., 600.6013

Judgment Lien Act
Alaska Stat. 1962, § 09.30.010
Cal. Code of Civil Procedure §§ 674, 674.5, 674.7

Iowa Code Ann., 624.23
Neb. Rev. Stat. 1943, 25-1303 et seq.
Ohio Rev. Code 1953, 2329.01 et seq.
Okla. Stat. Ann., Title 12, § 706 et seq.
Pa. Purdon's Stat., Title 12, § 877 et seq.
S.C. Code of 1976, § 15-35-810 et seq.
Utah Code Ann. 1953, 78-22-1 et seq.
Wash. Rev. Code Ann., 4.56.190 et seq.
Wis. Stat. Ann., 806.15

Judgment Notwithstanding Verdict Act
Ga. Code 1933, 110-113
Mich. Comp. Laws 1948, 691.691 et seq.

Judgment Refunding Act
Ill. Rev. Stat. 1977, Ch. 122, § 327.62 et seq.

Judgment Relief Act
Wis. Stat. Ann., 806.07

Judgment Satisfaction Act
Wash. Rev. Code Ann., 4.56.100

Judgment Tax Fund Act
Ill. Rev. Stat. 1991, Ch. 24, § 8-1-16

Judgment Vacation Act
Wash. Rev. Code Ann., 4.72.010 et seq.

Judgments Act
Ill. Rev. Stat. 1991, Ch. 110, § 12-101 et seq.
Wash. Rev. Code 1976, 4.56.010 et seq.

Judgments Act (Declaratory)
Ark. Code Ann. 1987, 16-11-1103 et seq.
La. Code of Civil Procedure, Art. 1871 et seq.
Me. Rev. Stat. Ann. 1964, Title 14, § 5951 et seq.
Ore. Rev. Stat., 28.160

Judgments Act (Dormant)
See Dormant Judgments Act

Judgments Act (Foreign)
Tex. Civil Practice and Remedies Code, § 35.002

Judgments Act (State Enforcement of Foreign)
Fla. Stat. Ann., 55.501 et seq.

Judgments Against Public Officers Act
Wis. Stat. Ann., 895.46

Judgments Conformity Act
N.C. Gen. Stat. 1943, § 1-237

Judgments, Decrees and Executions Act
Ill. Rev. Stat. 1991, Ch. 110, § 12-101 et seq.

Judgments Recognition-Uniform Foreign Money Act
See Uniform Foreign Money-Judgments Recognition Act

Judicature Act
Mich. Comp. Laws Ann., 600.101 et seq.

Judicial Administration Act
Ark. Code Ann. 1987, 16-10-101, 16-10-102
Ga. Code Ann., 15-5-1 et seq.
N.Y. Judiciary Law (Consol. Laws Ch. 30) § 210 et seq.
Ore. Rev. Stat., 2.310 et seq.
Utah Code Ann. 1953, 78-3-18 et seq.

Judicial Amendments Act of 1994
Oct. 25, 1994, P.L. 103-420, 28 U.S. Code § 1 nt.

Judicial and Executive Salary Act
Utah Code Ann. 1953, 67-8-1 et seq.

Judicial and Executive Succession Act
See Executive and Judicial Succession Act

Judicial and Fiducial Sales of Real Estate Act
Ky. Rev. Stat. 1971, 389A.010 et seq.

Judicial Arbitration Act
Cal. Code of Civil Procedure § 1141.10 et seq.

Judicial Article Implementation Act
Ala. Const. 1901, Art. 6, § 139 et seq.

Judicial Budget Administration Act
Ga. Laws 1998, H.B. 1617

Judicial Campaign Fairness Act
Tex. Election Code, 1985, § 253.151 et seq.

Judicial Code
Feb. 12, 1903, Ch. 547, 32 Stat. 825 (See 28 U.S. Code §§ 5, 135, 171, 173, 453)
March 3, 1911, Ch. 231, 36 Stat. 1087 (See 28 U.S. Code Judiciary and Judicial Procedure, Chs. 1 to 13)
Feb. 25, 1919, Ch. 29, 40 Stat. 1156 (See 28 U.S. Code §§ 44, 136, 171, 173, 201 to 213, 215, 293, 294, 296, 453)
April 17, 1940, Ch. 100, 54 Stat. 109 (See 28 U.S. Code § 83)
April 20, 1940, Ch. 117, 54 Stat. 143 (See 28 U.S. Code § 1331 et seq.)
April 22, 1940, Ch. 126, 54 Stat. 149 (See 28 U.S. Code § 456)
June 6, 1940, Ch. 247, 54 Stat. 237 (See 28 U.S. Code § 93)
June 11, 1940, Ch. 321, 54 Stat. 302 (See 28 U.S. Code § 83)
June 12, 1940, Ch. 341, 54 Stat. 348 (See 28 U.S. Code § 123)
Oct. 10, 1940, Ch. 843, 54 Stat. 1101 (See 28 U.S. Code §§ 251 to 254, 456, 1581, 2071, 2639, 2640)
March 6, 1942, Ch. 153, 56 Stat. 139 (See 28 U.S. Code § 90)
May 9, 1942, Ch. 295, 56 Stat. 271 (See 28 U.S. Code §§ 1291 to 1293)
July 7, 1942, Ch. 489, 56 Stat. 648 (See 28 U.S. Code § 132)
Dec. 29, 1942, Ch. 835, 56 Stat. 1094 (See 28 U.S. Code §§ 291, 292, 295, 296)
Jan. 20, 1944, Ch. 3, 58 Stat. 5 (See 28 U.S. Code §§ 753, 1915, 1920)
Dec. 7, 1944, Ch. 522, 58 Stat. 796 (See 28 U.S. Code §§ 9, 604, 755)
Dec. 13, 1944, Ch. 556, 58 Stat. 801 (See 28 U.S. Code § 121)
Dec. 16, 1944, Ch. 604, 58 Stat. 815 (See 28 U.S. Code § 114)
Dec. 23, 1944, Ch. 724, 58 Stat. 925 (See 28 U.S. Code § 42)
Oct. 29, 1945, Ch. 435, 59 Stat. 550 (See 28 U.S. Code § 90)
Oct. 31, 1945, Ch. 443, 59 Stat. 554 (See 28 U.S. Code § 127)
Nov. 6, 1945, Ch. 447, 59 Stat. 555 (See 28 U.S. Code § 117)
Nov. 15, 1945, Ch. 482, 59 Stat. 582 (See 28 U.S. Code § 108)
Dec. 28, 1945, Ch. 596, 59 Stat. 661 (See 28 U.S. Code § 128)
Dec. 28, 1945, Ch. 599, 59 Stat. 663 (See 28 U.S. Code § 86)
July 31, 1946, Ch. 704, 60 Stat. 716 (See 28 U.S. Code §§ 5, 44, 135, 171, 173, 201 to 213, 293, 296)
Utah Code Ann. 1953, 78-1-1 et seq.

Judicial Committee on Information Technology Act
Tex. Government Code, § 77.001 et seq.

Judicial Compensation Act
Colo. Rev. Stat., 13-30-101 et seq.

Judicial Conference Act
Mo. Rev. Stat., 476.320 et seq.
N.Y. Judiciary Law (Consol. Laws Ch. 30) § 214 et seq.

Judicial Confession Act
La. Civil Code, Art. 2291

Judicial Confirmation Law
Ida. Code 1947, 7-1301 et seq.
Nev. Rev. Stat. 1979 Reprint, 43.010 et seq.

Judicial Consolidated Retirement Act
N.C. Gen. Stat. 1943, § 135-50 et seq.

Judicial Council Act
Ga. Code Ann., 15-5-20 et seq.
Ida. Code 1947, 1-2101 et seq.
N.D. Cent. Code, 27-15-01 et seq.
N.H. Rev. Stat. 1955, 494:1 et seq.
Wash. Rev. Code Ann., 2.52.010 et seq.

Judicial Councils Reform and Judicial Conduct and Disability Act of 1980
Oct. 15, 1980, P.L. 96-458, 28 U.S. Code § 1 nt.

Judicial Department Act
Colo. Rev. Stat., 13-3-101 et seq.
Kan. Stat. Ann., 20-318 et seq.
N.C. Gen. Stat. 1943, § 7A-1 et seq.

Judicial Discipline Act
Pa. Cons. Stat., Title 42, § 1601 et seq.
Pa. Const. Art. 5, § 18

Judicial Discipline and Removal Reform Act of 1990
Dec. 1, 1990, P.L. 101-650, 28 U.S. Code §§ 1 nt., 332, 332 nt., 372, 2077
Dec. 9, 1991, P.L. 102-198, 105 Stat. 1626

Judicial Districts Act
Ill. Rev. Stat. 1991, Ch. 37, § 1.01 et seq.
Tex. Government Code, § 24.301 et seq.

Judicial Districts Act (Municipal and Justice Courts)
Cal. Government Code § 71040 et seq., § 71001

Judicial Efficiency and Improvement Act
D.C. Code Ann., § 11-1565, 11-1732

Judicial Election Act (Nonpartisan)
Miss. Code Ann. 1972, § 23-18-974 et seq.

Judicial Emancipation Act
La. Code of Civil Procedure Art. 3991 et seq.

Judicial Employees Labor Relations Act
Me. Rev. Stat. Ann. 1964, Title 26, § 1281 et seq.

Judicial Employees Unification Act
N.J. Stat. Ann., 2B:11-1 et seq.

Judicial Ethics Committee Act
Ark. Code Ann. 1987, 16-10-301 et seq.

Judicial Expense Act
Ky. Rev. Stat. 1971, Superseded Vol., 64.505

Judicial Extension Act (Real Estate Liens)
Tex. General Laws 43rd Leg., 1933, p. 225, Ch. 102

Judicial Housekeeping Act of 1986
Nov. 14, 1986, P.L. 99-657, 28 U.S. Code § 1 nt.

Judicial Impact Statement
N.Y. Judiciary Law (Consol. Laws Ch. 30) § 212, Subd. 1

Judicial Improvements Act of 1985
June 19, 1986, P.L. 99-336, 2 U.S. Code § 288d; 5 U.S. Code §§ 8706, 8714a to 8714c; 28 U.S. Code §§ 376, 620, 1364 to 1366, 1441, 1914, 2341

Judicial Improvements Act of 1990
Dec. 1, 1990, P.L. 101-650, 28 U.S. Code § 1 nt.
Dec. 9, 1991, P.L. 102-198, 18 U.S. Code § 3006A nt.
Oct. 29, 1992, P.L. 102-572, 28 U.S. Code § 620 nt.
Nov. 28, 1995, P.L. 104-60, 28 U.S. Code § 133 nt.
Oct. 19, 1996, P.L. 104-317, 28 U.S. Code § 133 nt.
Oct. 6, 1997, P.L. 105-53, 28 U.S. Code § 133 nt.
D.C. Code Ann., §§ 15-701 et seq., 15-709

Judicial Improvements and Access to Justice Act
Nov. 19, 1988, P.L. 100-702, 28 U.S. Code § 1 nt.
Nov. 21, 1989, P.L. 101-162, 42 U.S. Code § 10713
Oct. 30, 1990, P.L. 101-474, 28 U.S. Code § 604
Dec. 1, 1990, P.L. 101-650, 28 U.S. Code § 604
Dec. 14, 1993, P.L. 103-192, 28 U.S. Code § 651 nt.
Oct. 25, 1994, P.L. 103-420, 28 U.S. Code § 651 nt.
Oct. 30, 1998, P.L. 105-315, 28 U.S. Code § 652 nt.

Judicial Law Clerk and Staff Attorney Recruitment Law
Tex. Government Code, §§ 72.041, 72.042

Judicial Naturalization Ceremonies Amendments of 1991
Dec. 12, 1991, P.L. 102-232, 8 U.S. Code § 1101 nt.

Judicial Nominations and Appointments Act
Ill. Rev. Stat. 1969, Ch. 46, § 9-1 et seq.
Vt. Stat. Ann., Title 4, § 601 et seq.

Judicial Note Act
Ill. Rev. Stat. 1991, Ch. 63, § 42.60 et seq.

Judicial Notice Act
Cal. Evidence Code § 450 et seq.
Ill. Rev. Stat. 1991, Ch. 110, § 8-1001 et seq.
Mass. Gen. Laws Ann., 233:70
N.Y. Civil Practice Law and Rules (Consol. Laws Ch. 8) Rule 4511

Judicial Notice of Foreign Law Act
See Uniform Judicial Notice of Foreign Law Act

Judicial Officers' Election Law
Cal. Elections Code 1976, § 25300 et seq.

Judicial Plat Act
Ill. Rev. Stat. 1991, Ch. 109, § 10.9 et seq.

Judicial Primary Act of 1925
Ill. Laws 1925, p. 372, No. 2

Judicial Procedure Improvement Act (Medical)
Cal. Business and Professions Code §§ 802.5, 805
Cal. Government Code § 11371 et seq.

Judicial Qualification Commission Act
Ark. Code Ann. 1987, 16-10-120, 16-10-121

Judicial Redistricting Act
Ill. Comp. Stat. 1992, Ch. 705, § 21/1 et seq.
Kan. Stat. Ann., 20-325 et seq.
N.D. Cent. Code, 27-05-01 et seq.

Judicial Removal Act
Neb. Rev. Stat. 1943, 24-715 et seq.

Judicial Retirement Account Act
Wash. Rev. Code 1983, 2.14.010 et seq.

Judicial Retirement Act
Ala. Code 1975, § 12-18-1 et seq.
Ky. Rev. Stat. 1971, 21.345 et seq.
Mo. Rev. Stat., 476.450 et seq.

N.J. Stat. Ann., 43:6A-1 et seq.
N.M. Stat. Ann., 10-12B-1 et seq.
N.M. Stat. Ann., 10-12-1 et seq.
Tex. Public Retirement System, Title 110B, § 41.001 et seq.
Wash. Rev. Code Ann., 2.10.010 et seq.

Judicial Retirement Act (Consolidated)
N.C. Gen. Stat. 1943, § 135-50 et seq.

Judicial Retirement Reciprocity Act
N.M. Stat. Ann., 10-13-6 et seq.

Judicial Retirement System Law
Iowa Code Ann., 602.9101 et seq.
Wash. Rev. Code Ann., 2.10.010

Judicial Review Act (Administrative Agencies)
See also Administrative Agencies Judicial Review Act
Ariz. Rev. Stat. Ann., § 12-901 et seq.
Mich. Comp. Laws 1948, 24.101 et seq.
N.C. Gen. Stat. 1943, § 150B-43

Judicial Review and Civil Enforcement of Agency Actions Act
Kan. Stat. Ann., 77-601 et seq.

Judicial Review by Mandamus Act
Cal. Code of Civil Procedure § 1094.5

Judicial Salary Act
Ark. Code Ann. 1987, 16-11-114 et seq.

Judicial Selection and Tenure Act
Iowa Code Ann., 46.1 et seq.
Vt. Stat. Ann., Title 4, § 601 et seq.

Judicial Sentencing Disclosure Act
R.I. Gen. Laws 1956, 12-19.1-1 et seq.

Judicial Standards Commission Act
Tenn. Code Ann., 17-5-101 et seq.

Judicial Study Commission Act
Ind. Code Ann., 4-26-3-18.1

Judicial Succession Act
Ida. Code 1947, 59-1401 et seq.
Kan. Stat. Ann., 48-1201 et seq.
La. Rev. Stat. Ann., 13:2701 et seq.

Mich. Comp. Laws Ann., 691.971 et seq.
S.C. Code Ann. 1976, § 1-9-10 et seq.
S.D. Codified Laws 1967, 1-30-1 et seq.
W. Va. Code 1966, § 6A-1-1 et seq.

Judicial Succession Act (Emergency)
See Emergency Interim Executive and
Judicial Succession Act

Judicial Survivors Annuity Act, Amendment
Aug. 3, 1956, Ch. 944, 70 Stat. 1021, 28 U.S.
Code § 376
July 7, 1958, P.L. 85-508, 72 Stat. 348, 28
U.S. Code § 376
Aug. 8, 1968, P.L. 90-466, 82 Stat. 662, 28
U.S. Code § 376

Judicial Unification Act (State)
N.J. Stat. Ann., 2B:10-1 et seq.

Judicial Vacancies Act
Ill. Rev. Stat. 1989, Ch. 37, § 72.41-2 et seq.

Judiciary Act
Alaska Stat. 1962, § 22.05.010 et seq.
D.C. Code 1973, § 11-101 et seq.
Ga. Code Ann., 15-1-1 et seq.
N.Y. Consol. Laws, Ch. 30
Pa. Cons. Stat., Title 42, § 101 et seq.
P.R. Laws Ann. 1954, Title 4, § 1 et seq.

Judiciary Act (Nonpartisan Ballot)
Neb. Rev. Stat. 1943, 32-535 et seq.

Judiciary Act (Reorganization)
Haw. Session Laws 1892, Ch. 57

Judiciary Act Repealer Act
Pa. Cons. Stat., Title 42, § 20001 et seq.

Judiciary Acts
Sept. 24, 1789, Ch. 20, 1 Stat. 73
March 3, 1875, Ch. 137, 18 Stat. 470
March 3, 1887, Ch. 373, 24 Stat. 552
Aug. 13, 1888, Ch. 866, 25 Stat. 433

Judiciary and Judicial Procedure
June 25, 1948, Ch. 646, 62 Stat. 869, 28 U.S.
Code §§ 1 to 2680
April 25, 1949, Ch. 92, 63 Stat. 62, 28 U.S.
Code §§ 1346, 2401, 2672

May 10, 1949, Ch. 96, 63 Stat. 65, 28 U.S.
Code § 1821
May 24, 1949, Ch. 139, 63 Stat. 89, 28 U.S.
Code generally
July 14, 1949, Ch. 333, 63 Stat. 411, 28 U.S.
Code § 1871
July 16, 1949, Ch. 340, 63 Stat. 444, 28 U.S.
Code § 2680
July 18, 1949, Ch. 343, 63 Stat. 446, 28 U.S.
Code § 2072
Aug. 2, 1949, Ch. 383, 63 Stat. 491, 28 U.S.
Code §§ 604, 605, 756 nts.
Aug. 3, 1949, Ch. 387, 63 Stat. 493, 28 U.S.
Code §§ 44, 133, 134, 134 nt.
Aug. 16, 1949, Ch. 444, 63 Stat. 610, 28 U.S.
Code § 90
Aug. 27, 1949, Ch. 516, 63 Stat. 666, 28 U.S.
Code § 96
Oct. 5, 1949, Ch. 601, 63 Stat. 704, 28 U.S.
Code § 1823
Oct. 15, 1949, Ch. 695, 63 Stat. 881, 28 U.S.
Code § 603
Oct. 15, 1949, Ch. 695, 63 Stat. 881, 28 U.S.
Code § 792
May 10, 1950, Ch. 174, 64 Stat. 158, 28 U.S.
Code §§ 2072, 2073
Aug. 3, 1950, Ch. 514, 64 Stat. 393, 28 U.S.
Code § 117
Aug. 7, 1950, Ch. 601, 64 Stat. 415, 28 U.S.
Code § 104
Aug. 10, 1950, Ch. 675, 64 Stat. 438, 28 U.S.
Code §§ 93, 142 nt.
Aug. 14, 1950, Ch. 708, 64 Stat. 443, 28 U.S.
Code § 133
Aug. 29, 1950, Ch. 819, 64 Stat. 562, 28 U.S.
Code § 133
Sept. 5, 1950, Ch. 848, 64 Stat. 578, 28 U.S.
Code § 133
Sept. 9, 1950, Ch. 937, 64 Stat. 824, 28 U.S.
Code § 1921
Sept. 26, 1950, Ch. 1049, 64 Stat. 1038, 28
U.S. Code § 2680
Dec. 29, 1950, Ch. 1185, 64 Stat. 1128, 28
U.S. Code § 333
Aug. 28, 1951, Ch. 351, 65 Stat. 205, 28 U.S.
Code §§ 115, 1732
Oct. 31, 1951, Ch. 655, 65 Stat. 723, 28 U.S.
Code §§ 41, 45, 48, 90, 136, 333, 371, 373,
411, 460, 603, 610, 676, 753, 1252, 1291,
1292, 1294, 1346, 1498, 1821, 1915, 2253
July 3, 1952, Ch. 570, 66 Stat. 333, 28 U.S.
Code § 2680 nt.
Continued

July 7, 1952, Ch. 581, 66 Stat. 439, 28 U.S. Code § 1823

July 9, 1952, Ch. 609, 66 Stat. 509, 28 U.S. Code § 631

July 10, 1952, Ch. 632, 66 Stat. 540, 28 U.S. Code §§ 411 to 413

July 17, 1952, Ch. 929, 66 Stat. 757, 28 U.S. Code § 89

July 28, 1953, Ch. 253, 67 Stat. 226, 28 U.S. Code § 171

Aug. 8, 1953, Ch. 376, 67 Stat. 488, 28 U.S. Code § 456

Aug. 15, 1953, Ch. 505, 67 Stat. 589, 28 U.S. Code prec. § 1331

Feb. 10, 1954, Ch. 6, 68 Stat. 8, 28 U.S. Code §§ 44, 94, 102, 115, 124, 133, 134, 371, 372, 373

June 18, 1954, Ch. 304, 68 Stat. 253, 28 U.S. Code § 1923

July 27, 1954, Ch. 583, 68 Stat. 567, 28 U.S. Code § 2074

July 30, 1954, Ch. 648, 68 Stat. 648, 28 U.S. Code §§ 1346, 2402

Aug. 13, 1954, Ch. 728, 68 Stat. 703, 28 U.S. Code § 633

Aug. 23, 1954, Ch. 837, 68 Stat. 772, 28 U.S. Code § 1963

Aug. 24, 1954, Ch. 910, 68 Stat. 795, 28 U.S. Code § 1360

Aug. 28, 1954, Ch. 1033, 68 Stat. 890, 28 U.S. Code § 2201

Aug. 28, 1954, Ch. 1053, 68 Stat. 918, 28 U.S. Code § 375

Sept. 3, 1954, Ch. 1263, 68 Stat. 1240, 28 U.S. Code §§ 171, 291, 292, 295, 451 nt., 792, 1343, 1491, 1494, 1821, 2501, 2503, 2505, 2507, 2508, 2510, 2513, 2516, 2520, 2521

March 2, 1955, Ch. 9, 69 Stat. 9, 28 U.S. Code §§ 5, 44, 135, 173, 213, 252, 508

July 28, 1955, Ch. 424, 69 Stat. 394, 28 U.S. Code § 1823

Aug. 4, 1955, Ch. 550, 69 Stat. 492, 28 U.S. Code § 553

Aug. 9, 1955, Ch. 627, 69 Stat. 546, 28 U.S. Code § 107

June 20, 1956, Ch. 414, 70 Stat. 310, 28 U.S. Code § 604 nt.

July 9, 1956, Ch. 517, 70 Stat. 497, 28 U.S. Code §§ 291, 292, 294, 331, 605

July 14, 1956, Ch. 589, 70 Stat. 532, 28 U.S. Code §§ 251, 292, 293, 295

July 25, 1956, Ch. 722, 70 Stat. 642, 28 U.S. Code § 631

July 26, 1956, Ch. 740, 70 Stat. 658, 28 U.S. Code § 1332

Aug. 1, 1956, Ch. 826, 70 Stat. 798, 28 U.S. Code § 1821

Aug. 3, 1956, Ch. 944, 70 Stat. 1021, 28 U.S. Code §§ 375, 376, 604, 605

Aug. 10, 1956, Ch. 1041, 70A Stat. 626, 28 U.S. Code § 1442a

June 11, 1957, P.L. 85-49, 71 Stat. 65, 28 U.S. Code § 604 nt.

Aug. 28, 1957, P.L. 85-202, 71 Stat. 476, 28 U.S. Code § 331

Aug. 29, 1957, P.L. 85-219, 71 Stat. 495, 28 U.S. Code § 294

Sept. 2, 1957, P.L. 85-259, 71 Stat. 583, 28 U.S. Code § 1867

Sept. 2, 1957, P.L. 85-261, 71 Stat. 586, 28 U.S. Code § 372

Sept. 2, 1957, P.L. 85-276, 71 Stat. 600, 28 U.S. Code § 633

Sept. 4, 1957, P.L. 85-298, 71 Stat. 618, 28 U.S. Code § 124

Sept. 7, 1957, P.L. 85-299, 71 Stat. 618, 28 U.S. Code § 1871

Sept. 7, 1957, P.L. 85-310, 71 Stat. 631, 28 U.S. Code § 133

Sept. 9, 1957, P.L. 85-315, 71 Stat. 637, 28 U.S. Code §§ 1343, 1861

June 20, 1958, P.L. 85-462, 72 Stat. 207, 28 U.S. Code §§ 603 nt., 604 nt., 753

June 30, 1958, P.L. 85-474, 72 Stat. 254, 28 U.S. Code § 604 nt.

July 7, 1958, P.L. 85-508, 72 Stat. 348, 28 U.S. Code §§ 81A, 133, 333, 373, 376, 460, 610, 753, 1252, 1291, 1292, 1294, 1346, 1963, 2072, 2201, 2410

July 11, 1958, P.L. 85-513, 72 Stat. 356, 28 U.S. Code § 331

July 25, 1958, P.L. 85-554, 72 Stat. 415, 28 U.S. Code §§ 1331, 1332, 1445

Aug. 6, 1958, P.L. 85-593, 72 Stat. 497, 28 U.S. Code §§ 45, 136

Aug. 8, 1958, P.L. 85-615, 72 Stat. 545, 28 U.S. Code § 1360

Aug. 20, 1958, P.L. 85-689, 72 Stat. 683, 28 U.S. Code § 1964

Aug. 25, 1958, P.L. 85-752, 72 Stat. 845, 28 U.S. Code § 334

Aug. 25, 1958, P.L. 85-755, 72 Stat. 848, 28 U.S. Code §§ 211, 291 to 295

Aug. 28, 1958, P.L. 85-791, 72 Stat. 941, 28 U.S. Code § 2112

Sept. 2, 1958, P.L. 85-856, 72 Stat. 1104, 28 U.S. Code § 544

Sept. 2, 1958, P.L. 85-919, 72 Stat. 1770, 28 U.S. Code § 1292

Sept. 2, 1958, P.L. 85-920, 72 Stat. 1770, 28 U.S. Code § 1402

March 18, 1959, P.L. 86-3, 73 Stat. 8, 28 U.S. Code §§ 91, 133, 134, 371 nt., 373, 451, 501, 504, 541, 1252, 1293, 1294

June 25, 1959, P.L. 86-70, 73 Stat. 147, 28 U.S. Code § 81A

Aug. 7, 1959, P.L. 86-138, 73 Stat. 285, 28 U.S. Code § 456

Aug. 18, 1959, P.L. 86-168, 73 Stat. 389, 28 U.S. Code § 2680

Sept. 1, 1959, P.L. 86-221, 73 Stat. 452, 28 U.S. Code § 752

Sept. 8, 1959, P.L. 86-238, 73 Stat. 471, 28 U.S. Code §§ 2401, 2672

Sept. 9, 1959, P.L. 86-243, 73 Stat. 474, 28 U.S. Code §§ 253, 550, 871 to 873

Sept. 16, 1959, P.L. 86-282, 73 Stat. 565, 28 U.S. Code § 1870

Sept. 21, 1959, P.L. 86-312, 73 Stat. 587, 28 U.S. Code § 374

Sept. 21, 1959, P.L. 86-320, 73 Stat. 590, 28 U.S. Code § 1915

Sept. 23, 1959, P.L. 86-370, 73 Stat. 652, 28 U.S. Code §§ 601, 603, 606

June 11, 1960, P.L. 86-507, 74 Stat. 201, 28 U.S. Code §§ 2284 to 2410

July 1, 1960, P.L. 86-568, 74 Stat. 303, 28 U.S. Code §§ 603 nt., 604 nt., 753

July 12, 1960, P.L. 86-624, 74 Stat. 416, 28 U.S. Code § 91

Sept. 8, 1960, P.L. 86-726, 74 Stat. 885, 856, 28 U.S. Code § 1498.

Sept. 13, 1960, P.L. 86-770, 74 Stat. 912, 28 U.S. Code §§ 1406, 1506

May 19, 1961, P.L. 87-36, 75 Stat. 80, 28 U.S. Code §§ 44, 81, 83, 86, 89, 93, 98, 102, 123, 133, 134, 142 nt.

Aug. 14, 1961, P.L. 87-139, 75 Stat. 340, 28 U.S. Code § 553

Aug. 30, 1961, P.L. 87-183, 75 Stat. 413, 28 U.S. Code § 1732

Aug. 30, 1961, P.L. 87-187, 75 Stat. 415, 28 U.S. Code § 2414

Aug. 30, 1961, P.L. 87-189, 75 Stat. 417, 28 U.S. Code §§ 1258, 1294

Sept. 19, 1961, P.L. 87-253, 75 Stat. 521, 28 U.S. Code §§ 331, 605

Sept. 21, 1961, P.L. 87-258, 75 Stat. 539, 28 U.S. Code § 2679

Oct. 4, 1961, P.L. 87-352, 75 Stat. 772, 28 U.S. Code § 124

May 31, 1962, P.L. 87-461, 76 Stat. 85, 28 U.S. Code § 105

July 30, 1962, P.L. 87-562, 76 Stat. 247, 28 U.S. Code §§ 89, 133

Aug. 6, 1962, P.L. 87-573, 76 Stat. 307, 28 U.S. Code § 130

Aug. 13, 1962, P.L. 87-581, 76 Stat. 360, 28 U.S. Code § 1499

Aug. 31, 1962, P.L. 87-621, 76 Stat. 417, 28 U.S. Code § 1921

Sept. 19, 1962, P.L. 87-669, 76 Stat. 556, 28 U.S. Code § 2103

Sept. 25, 1962, P.L. 87-699, 76 Stat. 598, 28 U.S. Code § 128

Oct. 5, 1962, P.L. 87-748, 76 Stat. 744, 28 U.S. Code §§ 1361, 1391

Oct. 9, 1962, P.L. 87-764, 76 Stat. 762, 28 U.S. Code § 142

Oct. 11, 1962, P.L. 87-793, 76 Stat. 865, 28 U.S. Code § 508

Oct. 18, 1962, P.L. 87-845, 76A Stat. 699, 28 U.S. Code §§ 414, 547, 1404, 1406

Oct. 16, 1963, P.L. 88-139, 77 Stat. 248, 28 U.S. Code §§ 138 to 141, 452, 1869

Nov. 13, 1963, P.L. 88-176, 77 Stat. 331, 28 U.S. Code §§ 43, 46, 132, 332

Dec. 23, 1963, P.L. 88-234, 77 Stat. 473, 28 U.S. Code § 1391

March 10, 1964, P.L. 88-279, 78 Stat. 158, 28 U.S. Code §§ 671, 672

March 11, 1964, P.L. 88-282, 78 Stat. 163, 28 U.S. Code § 124

May 28, 1964, P.L. 88-312, 78 Stat. 201, 28 U.S. Code § 126

July 2, 1964, P.L. 88-352, 78 Stat. 266, 28 U.S. Code § 1447

Aug. 14, 1964, P.L. 88-426, 78 Stat. 428, 28 U.S. Code §§ 5, 44, 135, 173, 213, 252, 508, 603, 792

Aug. 14, 1964, P.L. 88-439, 78 Stat. 445, 28 U.S. Code § 1332

Aug. 30, 1964, P.L. 88-512, 78 Stat. 695, 28 U.S. Code § 124

Aug. 30, 1964, P.L. 88-513, 78 Stat. 695, 28 U.S. Code §§ 1336, 1398

Continued

Aug. 30, 1964, P.L. 88-519, 78 Stat. 699, 28 U.S. Code § 1346

Oct. 3, 1964, P.L. 88-619, 78 Stat. 995, 28 U.S. Code §§ 1696, 1741, 1745, 1781 to 1784

Oct. 3, 1964, P.L. 88-623, 78 Stat. 1001, 28 U.S. Code § 2075

Oct. 6, 1964, P.L. 88-627, 78 Stat. 1003, 28 U.S. Code § 102

Oct. 6, 1964, P.L. 88-631, 78 Stat. 1008, 28 U.S. Code § 508

Sept. 2, 1965, P.L. 89-162, 79 Stat. 618, 28 U.S. Code § 1825

Sept. 2, 1965, P.L. 89-163, 79 Stat. 619, 28 U.S. Code § 753

Sept. 2, 1965, P.L. 89-165, 79 Stat. 645, 28 U.S. Code § 1871

Sept. 2, 1965, P.L. 89-167, 79 Stat. 647, 28 U.S. Code § 753

Sept. 29, 1965, P.L. 89-215, 79 Stat. 887, 28 U.S. Code § 1446

Oct. 7, 1965, P.L. 89-242, 79 Stat. 951, 28 U.S. Code §§ 121, 133

Oct. 21, 1965, P.L. 89-281, 79 Stat. 1012, 28 U.S. Code § 755

Nov. 2, 1965, P.L. 89-319, 79 Stat. 1186, 28 U.S. Code § 113

March 18, 1966, P.L. 89-372, 80 Stat. 75, 28 U.S. Code §§ 44, 84, 133

May 11, 1966, P.L. 89-425, 80 Stat. 140, 28 U.S. Code §§ 171, 175

July 18, 1966, P.L. 89-505, 80 Stat. 304, 28 U.S. Code §§ 2415, 2416

July 18, 1966, P.L. 89-506, 80 Stat. 306, 28 U.S. Code §§ 2401, 2671, 2672, 2675, 2677 to 2679

July 18, 1966, P.L. 89-507, 80 Stat. 308, 28 U.S. Code §§ 2412, 2520

Aug. 4, 1966, P.L. 89-526, 80 Stat. 335, 28 U.S. Code § 116

Sept. 6, 1966, P.L. 89-554, 80 Stat. 611, 28 U.S. Code §§ 501 to 526, 531 to 537, 541 to 550, 561 to 575, 2341 to 2352

Sept. 7, 1966, P.L. 89-558, 80 Stat. 705, 28 U.S. Code § 86

Sept. 12, 1966, P.L. 89-571, 80 Stat. 764, 28 U.S. Code §§ 134, 373, 451

Sept. 19, 1966, P.L. 89-590, 80 Stat. 811, 28 U.S. Code § 2241

Oct. 10, 1966, P.L. 89-635, 80 Stat. 880, 28 U.S. Code § 1362

Oct. 10, 1966, P.L. 89-638, 80 Stat. 883, 28 U.S. Code § 122

Oct. 14, 1966, P.L. 89-651, 80 Stat. 901, 28 U.S. Code §§ 1544, 2602

Oct. 15, 1966, P.L. 89-681, 80 Stat. 958, 28 U.S. Code §§ 792, 1492, 2509

Nov. 2, 1966, P.L. 89-711, 80 Stat. 1104, 28 U.S. Code §§ 2244, 2254

Nov. 2, 1966, P.L. 89-713, 80 Stat. 1108, 28 U.S. Code § 2502

Nov. 2, 1966, P.L. 89-714, 80 Stat. 1111, 28 U.S. Code § 1391

Nov. 2, 1966, P.L. 89-719, 80 Stat. 1147, 28 U.S. Code §§ 1346, 1402, 2410

Nov. 6, 1966, P.L. 89-773, 80 Stat. 1323, 28 U.S. Code §§ 2072, 2112

Sept. 27, 1967, P.L. 90-92, 81 Stat. 229, 28 U.S. Code § 104

Dec. 16, 1967, P.L. 90-206, 81 Stat. 635, 28 U.S. Code §§ 603, 792

Dec. 18, 1967, P.L. 90-216, 81 Stat. 661, 28 U.S. Code § 124

Dec. 18, 1967, P.L. 90-217, 81 Stat. 662, 28 U.S. Code § 112

Dec. 20, 1967, P.L. 90-219, 81 Stat. 664, 28 U.S. Code §§ 376, 604, 611, 620 to 629

March 27, 1968, P.L. 90-274, 82 Stat. 53, 28 U.S. Code §§ 1821, 1861 to 1869, 1871

April 29, 1968, P.L. 90-296, 82 Stat. 109, 28 U.S. Code § 1407

June 18, 1968, P.L. 90-347, 82 Stat. 184, 28 U.S. Code § 44

July 5, 1968, P.L. 90-383, 82 Stat. 292, 28 U.S. Code § 127

Aug. 8, 1968, P.L. 90-466, 82 Stat. 662, 28 U.S. Code § 376

Oct. 17, 1968, P.L. 90-578, 82 Stat. 1107, 28 U.S. Code §§ 604, 631 to 639

Oct. 22, 1968, P.L. 90-623, 82 Stat. 1315, 28 U.S. Code prec. § 951

June 2, 1970, P.L. 91-271, 84 Stat. 274, 28 U.S. Code §§ 253 to 257, 1541, 1582, 2601, 2602, 2631 to 2639

June 2, 1970, P.L. 91-272, 84 Stat. 295, 28 U.S. Code § 133

July 23, 1970, P.L. 91-350, 84 Stat. 449, 28 U.S. Code §§ 1346, 1491

July 29, 1970, P.L. 91-358, 84 Stat. 590, 28 U.S. Code §§ 292, 1257, 1363, 1451, 1869, 2101, 2113

Oct. 15, 1970, P.L. 91-452, 84 Stat. 932, 28 U.S. Code § 1826

Oct. 27, 1970, P.L. 91-513, 84 Stat. 1293, 28 U.S. Code § 2901

Dec. 11, 1970, P.L. 91-543, 84 Stat. 1408, 28 U.S. Code § 1866

Dec. 11, 1970, P.L. 91-545, 84 Stat. 1412, 28 U.S. Code § 753

Dec. 14, 1970, P.L. 91-546, 84 Stat. 1412, 28 U.S. Code §§ 100, 104, 112

Dec. 24, 1970, P.L. 91-577, 84 Stat. 1558, 28 U.S. Code §§ 1338, 1498, 1545, 2353

Jan. 5, 1971, P.L. 91-647, 84 Stat. 1907, 28 U.S. Code § 332 March 1, 1972, P.L. 92-238, 86 Stat. 46, 28 U.S. Code § 677

March 1, 1972, P.L. 92-239, 86 Stat. 47, 28 U.S. Code § 636

April 6, 1972, P.L. 92-269, 86 Stat. 117, 28 U.S. Code §§ 1863, 1865

June 6, 1972, P.L. 92-310, 86 Stat. 203, 28 U.S. Code §§ 566, 671, 674, 954

July 18, 1972, P.L. 92-353, 86 Stat. 499, 28 U.S. Code § 2415 Aug. 10, 1972, P.L. 92-375, 86 Stat. 529, 28 U.S. Code § 797 Aug. 10, 1972, P.L. 92-376, 86 Stat. 529, 28 U.S. Code § 122 Aug. 22, 1972, P.L. 92-397, 86 Stat. 579, 28 U.S. Code §§ 375, 376, 604 Aug. 29, 1972, P.L. 92-415, 86 Stat. 652, 28 U.S. Code § 1491

Sept. 16, 1972, P.L. 92-420, 86 Stat. 677, 28 U.S. Code § 2901

Sept. 21, 1972, P.L. 92-428, 86 Stat. 721, 28 U.S. Code § 634

Sept. 29, 1972, P.L. 92-437, 86 Stat. 740, 28 U.S. Code § 1869

Oct. 13, 1972, P.L. 92-485, 86 Stat. 803, 28 U.S. Code § 2415

Oct. 25, 1972, P.L. 92-562, 86 Stat. 1176, 28 U.S. Code §§ 1346, 1402, 2409a

March 10, 1974, P.L. 93-253, 88 Stat. 50, 28 U.S. Code § 2680

Judiciary Appropriation Acts

May 14, 1940, Ch. 189, 54 Stat. 207

June 28, 1941, Ch. 258, 55 Stat. 298

June 28, 1943, Ch. 173, 57 Stat. 239

June 26, 1944, Ch. 277, 58 Stat. 354

May 21, 1945, Ch. 129, 59 Stat. 196

July 5, 1946, Ch. 541, 60 Stat. 475

July 9, 1947, Ch. 211, 61 Stat. 302

June 3, 1948, Ch. 400, 62 Stat. 329

July 20, 1949, Ch. 354, 63 Stat. 470

Sept. 6, 1950, Ch. 896, 64 Stat. 629

July 10, 1952, Ch. 651, 66 Stat. 567, 28 U.S. Code § 604 nt.

July 17, 1952, Ch. 930, 66 Stat. 757, 28 U.S. Code § 1498

Aug. 1, 1953, Ch. 304, 67 Stat. 334, 28 U.S. Code § 604 nt.

July 2, 1954, Ch. 455, 68 Stat. 410, 28 U.S. Code § 604 nt.

July 7, 1955, Ch. 729, 69 Stat. 276, 28 U.S. Code § 604 nt.

June 20, 1956, Ch. 414, 70 Stat. 310, 28 U.S. Code § 604 nt.

June 11, 1957, P.L. 85-49, 71 Stat. 64, 28 U.S. Code § 604 nt.

June 30, 1958, P.L. 85-474, 72 Stat. 253, 28 U.S. Code § 604 nt.

July 13, 1959, P.L. 86-84, 73 Stat. 190, 28 U.S. Code § 604 nt.

Aug. 31, 1960, P.L. 86-678, 74 Stat. 565, 28 U.S. Code § 604 nt.

Sept. 21, 1961, P.L. 87-264, 75 Stat. 554, 28 U.S. Code § 604 nt.

Oct. 18, 1962, P.L. 87-843, 76 Stat. 1097, 28 U.S. Code § 604 nt.

Dec. 30, 1963, P.L. 88-245, 77 Stat. 793, 28 U.S. Code § 604 nt.

Aug. 31, 1964, P.L. 88-527, 78 Stat. 728, 28 U.S. Code § 604 nt.

Sept. 2, 1965, P.L. 89-164, 79 Stat. 639, 28 U.S. Code § 604 nt.

Nov. 8, 1966, P.L. 89-797, 80 Stat. 1497, 28 U.S. Code § 604 nt.

Nov. 8, 1967, P.L. 90-133, 81 Stat. 426, 28 U.S. Code § 604 nt.

Aug. 9, 1968, P.L. 90-470, 82 Stat. 683, 28 U.S. Code § 604 nt.

Dec. 24, 1969, P.L. 91-153, 83 Stat. 418, 28 U.S. Code § 604 nt.

Oct. 21, 1970, P.L. 91-472, 84 Stat. 1055, 28 U.S. Code § 604 nt.

Aug. 10, 1971, P.L. 92-77, 85 Stat. 262, 28 U.S. Code § 604 nt.

Oct. 25, 1972, P.L. 92-544, 86 Stat. 1124, 28 U.S. Code § 604 nt.

Nov. 27, 1973, P.L. 93-162, 87 Stat. 651, 28 U.S. Code § 604 nt.

Oct. 21, 1975, P.L. 94-121, 89 Stat. 629, 28 U.S. Code § 604 nt.

Dec. 13, 1985, P.L. 99-180, 28 U.S. Code § 604 nt.

Oct. 18, 1986, P.L. 99-500, 100 Stat. 3406

Oct. 30, 1986, P.L. 99-591, 100 Stat. 3406

Dec. 22, 1987, P.L. 100-202, 101 Stat. 1329

Continued

Oct. 1, 1988, P.L. 100-459, 28 U.S. Code
§ 332

Nov. 21, 1989, P.L. 101-162, 103 Stat. 1010

Nov. 5, 1990, P.L. 101-515, 28 U.S. Code
§ 1913 nt.

Oct. 28, 1991, P.L. 102-140, 105 Stat. 807.

Oct. 6, 1992, P.L. 102-395, 106 Stat. 1856

Oct. 27, 1993, P.L. 103-121, 107 Stat. 1177

Aug. 26, 1994, P.L. 103-317, 108 Stat. 1749

April 26, 1996, P.L. 104-134, Title III, 110
Stat. 1321-32

Sept. 30, 1996, P.L. 104-208, Title III, 110
Stat. 3009

Oct. 19, 1996, P.L. 104-317, 28 U.S. Code
§ 1913 nt.

Nov. 26, 1997, P.L. 105-119, Title III, 111
Stat. 2488

Oct. 21, 1998, P.L. 105-277, 101(b), Title III,
112 Stat. 2681

Haw. Session Laws 1977, First Special
Session, Act 11

Haw. Session Laws 1979, Act 208

Haw. Session Laws 1981, First Sp. Sess., Act
2

Haw. Session Laws 1983, Act 291

Haw. Session Laws 1985, Act 169

Haw. Session Laws 1987, Act 375

Haw. Session Laws 1989, Act 315

Haw. Session Laws 1991, Act 299

Haw. Session Laws 1993, Act 277

Haw. Session Laws 1997, Act 155

Judiciary Article
Ind. Code Ann., 33-2.1-1-1 et seq.

Judiciary Branch Personnel Act
P.R. Laws Ann. 1954, Title 4, § 521 et seq.

**Judiciary Establishment Appropriation Act,
1943**
July 2, 1942, Ch. 472, 56 Stat. 503

Judiciary Office Building Development Act
Oct. 7, 1988, P.L. 100-480, 102 Stat. 2328,
40 U.S. Code §§ 1201 et seq.
Oct. 6, 1992, P.L. 102-392, 40 U.S. Code
§§ 1204, 1205, 1207

Judiciary Retirement Act
P.R. Laws Ann. 1954, Title 4, § 233 et seq.

Judiciary Supplemental Appropriations Act
Haw. Session Laws 1978, Act 246
Haw. Session Laws 1980, Act 301
Haw. Session Laws 1982, Act 267
Haw. Session Laws 1984, Act 286
Haw. Session Laws 1986, Act 348
Haw. Session Laws 1990, Act 30
Haw. Session Laws 1992, Act 301
Haw. Session Laws 1996, Act 244
Haw. Session Laws 1998, Act 126

**Judiciary Supplemental Appropriations Act
of 1976**
Haw. Session Laws 1976, Act 233

**Judiciary War Emergency Compensation
Act**
N.Y. Laws 1945, Ch. 303

Juett-Bach-Daniels Act (Counties-Leases)
Ky. Acts 1940, Ch. 44

Juke Box Licensing Act
Ark. Stat. 1947, 84-2633 et seq.

Julian Act (Use of Streets-Compensation)
Mo. Laws 1895, p. 53

Jumbling Act (Joinder)
S.C. Code Ann. 1976, §§ 15-13-780,
15-13-790

**Junction City, Louisiana Redevelopment
Agency Act**
La. Acts 1968, No. 439

June Act (Pensions)
June 27, 1890, Ch. 634, 26 Stat. 182

**Junior College Accreditation Amendment
Act**
D.C. Laws 1975, No. 1-15

Junior College Act
Ala. Code 1975, 16-60-1 et seq.
Cal. Education Code 1959, § 5701 et seq.
Ga. Code Ann., 20-3-130 et seq.
Ida. Code 1947, 33-2101 et seq.
Ill. Rev. Stat. 1991, Ch. 122, § 101-1 et seq.
N.M. Stat. Ann., 21-13-1 et seq.
Ore. Laws 1951, Ch. 640

Tex. Education Code, § 130.001 et seq.

Junior College Act (Community)
See Community Junior College Act

Junior College Construction Act
Cal. Education Code 1976, § 81800 et seq.

Junior College Construction Program Bond Act
Cal. Statutes 1967, Ch. 1555, p. 3728

Junior College Districts Act
Mo. Rev. Stat., 178.400 et seq.

Junior College Districts Bond Validation Laws
Cal. Statutes 1933, Ch. 19, p. 45
Cal. Statutes 1935, Ch. 13, p. 70
Cal. Statutes 1935, Ch. 21, p. 83
Cal. Statutes 1935, Ch. 114, p. 464

Junior College Facility Construction Act
Cal. Education Code 1976, § 82100 et seq.

Junior College Organization Act
Colo. Rev. Stat., 22-70-101 et seq.

Junior College Revenue Bond Act
Cal. Education Code 1976, § 81900 et seq.

Junior College Revenue Securities Law
Colo. Rev. Stat., 22-71-101 et seq.,
23-71-701 et seq.

Junior College Tax Relief Act
Cal. Education Code 1959, § 20001 et seq.

Junior College Vocational and Technical Training Act
Miss. Code Ann. 1972, § 37-29-161 et seq.

Junior Deputy Sheriff Act
Ill. Rev. Stat. 1991, Ch. 125, § 90 et seq.

Junior Duck Stamp Conservation and Design Program Act of 1994
Oct. 6, 1994, P.L. 103-340, 16 U.S. Code § 719 nt.

Juniper Butte Range Withdrawal Act
Oct. 17, 1998, P.L. 105-261, Title XXIX, 112 Stat. 2226

Junk Car Control Law of the Village of Baldwinsville
N.Y. Local Laws 1970, Village of Baldwinsville, p. 3048

Junk Car Disposal Law of the Town of Evans
N.Y. Local Laws 1967, Town of Evans, p. 1551

Junk Car Law
N.Y. Local Laws 1967, Town of Stanford, p. 1963
N.Y. Local Laws 1971, Town of Union, p. 3564
Vt. Stat. Ann., Title 19, § 1581 et seq.

Junk Dealers Act
Cal. Business and Professions Code § 21600 et seq.
Ind. Code Ann., 25-21-1-1 et seq.
Md. Ann. Code 1957, Art. 56, § 233 et seq.
Mich. Comp. Laws Ann., 445.401 et seq.
N.H. Rev. Stat. 1955, 322:1 et seq.

Junkin Anti-trust Act
Neb. Rev. Stat. 1943, 59-801 et seq.

Junkyard and Salvage Control Act
Kan. Stat. Ann., 68-2201 et seq.

Junkyard and Scrap Metal Processing Facility Control Act
Okla. Stat. Ann., Title 69, § 1251 et seq.

Junkyard Beautification and Billboard Control Act
Iowa Code Ann., 306C.1 et seq.

Junkyard Control Act
Ala. Code 1975, § 23-1-240 et seq.
Alaska Stat. 1962, § 19.27.010 et seq.
Cal. Streets and Highways Code § 745 et seq.
Conn. Gen. Stat. Ann., § 13a-123c et seq.
Fla. Stat. Ann., 339.241
Ga. Code Ann., 32-6-240 et seq.
Haw. Rev. Stat. Ann., § 264-81 et seq.
Continued

Ill. Rev. Stat. 1991, Ch. 121, § 460 et seq.

Ky. Rev. Stat. 1971, 177.905 et seq.

Mass. Gen. Laws Ann., 140B:1 et seq.

Minn. Stat. Ann., 161.242

Miss. Code Ann. 1972, § 49-25-1 et seq.

N.C. Gen. Stat. 1943, § 136-141 et seq.

N.H. Rev. Stat. 1955, 236:90 et seq.

N.J. Stat. Ann., 27:5e-1 et seq.

N.Y. Local Laws 1969, Town of Westfield, p. 2281

Ore. Rev. Stat., 109.700

P.R. Laws Ann. 1954, Title 10, § 971 et seq.

R.I. Gen. Laws 1956, 24-14-1 et seq.

S.C. Code Ann. 1976, § 57-27-10 et seq.

S.D. Codified Laws 1967, 31-30-1 et seq.

Tenn. Code Ann., 54-20-101 et seq.

Utah Code Ann. 1953, 27-12-137.1 et seq.

Wyo. Stat. Ann., § 33-19-101 et seq.

Junkyard Regulation Act

N.H. Rev. Stat. 1955, 236:111 et seq.

Jurisdiction Act (Child Custody)

See Uniform Child Custody Jurisdiction Act

Jurisdiction Over Nonresidents Act

La. Rev. Stat. Ann., 13:3201 et seq.

Jurisdiction Prosecution Act (Extended)

Mont. Laws 1995, Ch. 438

Jurisdiction to Determine Jurisdiction of Providers of Health Care Benefits Act

Mont. Code Ann., 33-1-1101 et seq.

Jurisdictional Act

Ore. Rev. Stat., 3.011 et seq.

Jurisdictional Act (Minor Judiciary)

Pa. Cons. Stat., Title 42, § 1515

Jurisdictional Strikes Act

Cal. Labor Code § 1115 et seq.

Jurisdictions Model Law (Conflict of)

Conn. Gen. Stat. 1983, § 50a-200 et seq.

Jurkiewicz-Reid Act (Home Rule Cities-Supervisors)

Mich. Comp. Laws 1948, 117.27

Juror Disqualification Act

Mo. Rev. Stat., 494.190

Jurors Certificates and Warrants Act

Ill. Rev. Stat. 1991, Ch. 146 1/2, § 0.01 et seq.

Jurors Fees in City Court Act

N.Y. Local Laws 1971, City of Gloversville, p. 101

Jury Act

Ala. Code 1975, § 12-16-1 et seq.

Alaska Stat. 1962, § 09.20.010 et seq.

Cal. Code of Civil Procedure § 190 et seq.

Fla. Stat. Ann., 40.01 et seq.

Haw. Rev. Stat. Ann., § 609-1 et seq.

Ill. Rev. Stat. 1991, Ch. 78, § 0.01 et seq.

Ky. Rev. Stat. 1971, 29A.010 et seq.

Md. Ann. Code 1974, Art. CJ, § 8-101 et seq.

Mich. Comp. Laws Ann., 600.1301 et seq.

Mont. Code Ann., 3-15-101 et seq.

N.H. Rev. Stat. 1955, 500-A:1 et seq.

N.J. Rev. Stat. 1937, 2A:68-1 et seq., 22A:1-1 to 22A:1-3

Ohio Rev. Code 1953, 2313.01 et seq.

R.I. Gen. Laws 1956, 9-9-1 et seq.

Wash. Rev. Code Ann., 2.36.010 et seq.

Jury Act (Counties Over One Million)

N.Y. Judiciary Law (Consol. Laws Ch. 30) § 500 et seq.

Jury Act (Cuyahoga County)

Ohio Laws Vol. 74, p. 218

Jury Act (Five-sixths)

Minn. Stat. Ann., 546.17

Jury Act (Kings County)

N.Y. Judiciary Law (Consol. Laws Ch. 30) § 680

Jury Act (Six-man)

Fla. Stat. Ann., 913.10

Jury Challenges Law (Civil)

Wash. Rev. Code Ann., 4.44.130 et seq.

Jury Challenges Law (Criminal)
Wash. Rev. Code Ann., 10.46.070 et seq.

Jury Code (Municipal Court)
Mich. Comp. Laws Ann., 725.101 et seq.

Jury Commission Act
Ill. Rev. Stat. 1991, Ch. 78, § 23.9 et seq.
Tenn. Code Ann., 22-2-201 et seq.
Vt. Stat. Ann., Title 4, § 951 et seq.

Jury Commission Act (Davidson County)
Tenn. Acts 1901, Ch. 124

Jury Commission Act (Hamilton County)
Tenn. Private Acts 1931, Ch. 564

Jury Commission Act (Robertson County)
Tenn. Private Acts 1925, Ch. 169

Jury Commission Act (Shelby County)
Tenn. Acts 1905, Ch. 230

Jury Commissioners Act
Colo. Rev. Stat. 1963, 78-3-1 et seq.
Ill. Rev. Stat. 1991, Ch. 78, § 23.9 et seq.
Mich. Comp. Laws 1948, 602.150 et seq.

Jury Exemption Act
Ariz. Rev. Stat. Ann., § 21-202
Cal. Code of Civil Procedure § 200
N.C. Gen. Stat. 1943, § 9-6

Jury Secrecy Act
Ill. Rev. Stat. 1991, Ch. 78, §§ 35.9, 36

Jury Selection Act
Miss. Code Ann. 1972, § 13-5-1 et seq.

Jury Selection Act (Second Class Counties)
Pa. Cons. Stat. Title 42, § 2121 et seq.

Jury Selection and Management Act (Trial)
Cal. Code of Civil Procedure § 190 et seq.

Jury Selection and Service Act
See also Uniform Jury Selection and Service Act
Ala. Code 1975, § 12-16-55 et seq.
Colo. Rev. Stat., 13-71-101 et seq.
Ida. Code 1947, 2-201 et seq.

Ind. Code Ann., 33-4-5.5-1 et seq.
Iowa Code 1983, 607A.21 et seq.
Me. Rev. Stat. Ann. 1964, Title 14, § 1211 et seq.
Miss. Code Ann. 1972 § 13-5-1 et seq.
N.D. Cent. Code, 27-09.1-01 et seq.
Utah Code Ann. 1953, 78-46-1 et seq.

Jury Selection and Service Act of 1968
March 27, 1968, P.L. 90-274, 82 Stat. 53, 28 U.S. Code §§ 1821, 1861 to 1869, 1871

Jury System Act
D.C. Code Ann., § 11-1901 et seq.

Jury System Improvements Act of 1978
Nov. 2, 1978, P.L. 95-572, 28 U.S. Code §§ 1363, 1364, 1861 nt., 1863 et seq.

Jury Trial Act
Kan. Stat. Ann., 60-238 et seq.

Jury Use and Management Act
Utah Laws 1992, Ch. 219

Jury View Act
Wash. Rev. Code Ann., 10.58.080

Jury Waiver Act
N.Y. Civil Practice Law and Rules (Consol. Laws Ch. 8), § 4102, Subd. c
Pa. Cons. Stat., Title 42, § 5104

Jury Wheel Act
Okla. Stat. Ann., Title 38, § 18 et seq.
Tex. Government Code, § 62.001 et seq.
Tex. Penal Code, § 39.01

Just Value Act (Assessments)
Fla. Stat. Ann., 193.011

Justice Act of 1970 (Criminal)
N.J. Stat. Ann., 52:17B-97 et seq.

Justice and Municipal Court Act
Cal. Government Code § 71001 et seq.

Justice Assistance Act of 1984
Oct. 12, 1984, P.L. 98-473, 42 U.S. Code § 3711 nt.
Nov. 10, 1998, P.L. 105-362, 42 U.S. Code § 10509
Continued

Justice Building Act
Ark. Code Ann. 1987, 22-3-901 et seq.

Justice Court Act
Cal. Welfare and Institutions Code §§ 200, 500 et seq.
Colo. Rev. Stat. 1963, 79-1-1 et seq.
Mich. Comp. Laws Ann., 730.1 et seq.
N.D. Cent. Code, 33-01-00.1 et seq.
N.J. Stat. Revised 1937, 2:33-1 to 2:33-180
N.Y. Uniform Justice Court Act, § 101 et seq.
Ore. Rev. Stat., 51.010 et seq.

Justice Court Act (Civil Procedure)
Mont. Code Ann. 1987, Title 25, Ch. 22
S.D. Codified Laws 1967, 15-33-1 et seq.
Wash. Rev. Code Ann., 12.04.010 et seq.

Justice Court Act (Criminal Procedure)
S.D. Codified Laws 1967, 23-54-1 et seq.

Justice Court Act (Port Chester)
N.Y. Laws 1949, Ch. 851

Justice Courts Training Council Act
Ga. Code Ann., 15-10-130 et seq.

Justice Department Organized Crime and Drug Enforcement Enhancement Act of 1988
Nov. 18, 1988, P.L. 100-690, 102 Stat. 4189

Justice Facilities Financing Act (San Diego County)
Cal. Revenue and Taxation Code § 7286.30 et seq.

Justice for Victims of Terrorism Act of 1996
April 24, 1996, P.L. 104-132, Title II, Subtitle C, 42 U.S. Code § 10601 nt.

Justice Information System Act (Comprehensive Criminal/Juvenile)
Mont. Code Ann. 1987, 44-5-101 et seq.
R.I. Gen. Laws 1956, 42-108-1 et seq.

Justice Reform Act (Juvenile)
N.Y. Education Law 1947 (Consol. Laws Ch. 16)
N.Y. Executive Law 1951 (Consol. Laws Ch. 18) §§ 515a, 516, 519, 523, 525

N.Y. Family Court Act §§ 254, 711, 712, 734, 746, 748 to 750, 752, 754, 764, 782a
N.Y. Mental Hygiene Law 1972 (Consol. Laws Ch. 27) § 7.05

Justice System Improvement Act of 1979
Dec. 27, 1979, P.L. 96-157, 5 U.S. Code §§ 5314, 5315; 18 U.S. Code §§ 1761, 1761 nt.; 42 U.S. Code §§ 3701 et seq., 3701 nt.

Justices Act (Village of Port Chest)
N.Y. Laws 1906, Ch. 106

Justices and Constables Act
Ill. Rev. Stat. 1963, Ch. 79
W. Va. Code 1931, Ch. 50, Art. 1, § 1 et seq.

Justices and Judges Retirement System Act
See also Uniform Retirement System for Justices and Judges Act
Okla. Stat. Ann., Title 20, § 1101 et seq.

Justices of the Peace Act
Ill. Rev. Stat. 1941, Ch. 79
Ind. Code 1971, 33-11-1-1 et seq.
Mich. Comp. Laws Ann., 600.6601 et seq.
N.C. Gen. Stat. 1943, § 7-112 et seq.
Ohio Rev. Code 1953, 1907.01 et seq.
Wash. Rev. Code Ann., 3.04.010 et seq., 3.30.010 et seq.

Justifiable Abortion Act
N.Y. Penal Law 1965 (Consol. Laws Ch. 40) § 125.05

Justifiable Homicide Act
Wash. Rev. Code Ann., 9A.16.040 et seq.

Justifiable Use of Deadly Force
Fla. Stat. Ann., 776.06 et seq.

Justification and State Government Evaluation Act
Also known as Justification of State Government Programs
Me. Rev. Stat. Ann. 1964, Title 3, § 921 et seq.

Juul Act
Ill. Rev. Stat. 1937, Ch. 120, §§ 329, 330

Juvenile Act
Alaska Stat. 1962, § 47.10.010 et seq.
Ariz. Rev. Stat. 1956, § 8-201 et seq.
Ark. Stat. 1947, 45-401 et seq.
Ida. Code 1947, 16-1801 et seq.
Ind. Code Ann., 31-6-1-1 et seq.
Kan. Stat. Ann., 38-801 et seq.
Ky. Rev. Stat. 1971, 600.010 et seq.
Mass. Gen. Laws Ann., 119:1 et seq., 120:1 et seq.
Me. Rev. Stat. Ann. 1964, Title 15, § 3001 et seq.
Mich. Comp. Laws Ann., 712A.1 et seq.
Neb. Rev. Stat. 1943, 43-245 et seq.
N.M. Stat. Ann., 32-1-1 et seq.
Okla. Stat. Ann., Title 10, § 1101 et seq.
Ore. Rev. Stat., 419.472 et seq.
Pa. Cons. Stat., Title 42, § 6301 et seq.
Tex. Family Code, § 51.01 et seq.

Juvenile Act (Polk County)
Ga. Laws 1947, p. 1245

Juvenile and Children's Facility Criminal Records Screening Act
N.J. Rev. Stat. 1937, 2A:4A-20 et seq.
N.M. Stat. Ann., 32-9-1 et seq.
S.C. Code Ann. 1976, § 14-21-10 et seq.

Juvenile and Domestic Relations Court Act
S.C. Code Ann. 1976, § 14-21-10 et seq.
Va. Code 1950, § 16.1-226 et seq.

Juvenile and Domestic Relations Court Act (Nashville)
Tenn. Private Acts 1947, Ch. 246, Art. 51

Juvenile Causes Act
Md. Ann. Code 1974, Art. CJ, § 3-801 et seq.

Juvenile Code
Me. Rev. Stat. Ann. 1964, Title 15, § 3001 et seq.
Neb. Rev. Stat. 1943, 43-2, 129 et seq.

Juvenile Commitment Law
Iowa Code Ann., 232.1 et seq.

Juvenile Community Corrections Act
Neb. Rev. Stat. 1943, 43-2.129 et seq.
N.M. Stat. Ann., 33-9A-1 et seq.

Juvenile Compact Act
See Interstate Compact on Juveniles Act
See Uniform Interstate Compact on Juveniles

Juvenile Correction Act
Ida. Code 1947, 20-501 et seq.

Juvenile Court Act
Ala. Code 1975, § 12-15-1 et seq.
Alaska Stat. 1962, § 47.10.010 et seq.
Ariz. Rev. Stat. Ann., § 8-201 et seq.
Ark. Code Ann. 1987, 45-401 et seq.
Cal. Welfare and Institutions Code § 500 et seq., § 200
Colo. Rev. Stat. 1963, 37-9-1 et seq.
Conn. Gen. Stat. Ann., § 46b-120 et seq.
D.C. Code Ann., § 16-2301 et seq.
Fla. Stat. Ann., 39.001 et seq.
Ga. Code Ann., 15-11-1 et seq.
Haw. Rev. Stat. Ann., § 571-1 et seq.
Ill. Rev. Stat. 1989, Ch. 37, § 801-1 et seq.
Ind. Code Ann., 33-12-2-1 et seq.
Iowa Code 1983, 231.1 et seq.
Kan. Stat. Ann., 38-806 et seq.
Ky. Rev. Stat. 1971, 208.010 et seq.
La. Rev. Stat. Ann., 13:1561 et seq.
Md. Ann. Code 1974, Art. CJ, § 3-801 et seq.
Me. Rev. Stat. Ann. 1964, Title 15, § 3002 et seq.
Mich. Comp. Laws Ann., 712A.1 et seq.
Minn. Stat. Ann., 260.011 et seq.
Miss. Code Ann. 1972, § 43-21-1 et seq.
Mo. Rev. Stat., 211.011 et seq.
Mont. Code Ann. 1947, 10-601 et seq.
N.C. Gen. Stat. 1943, § 7A-516 et seq.
N.D. Cent. Code, 27-20-01 et seq.
Neb. Rev. Stat. 1943, 43-201 et seq.
Nev. Rev. Stat. 1979 Reprint, 62.020 et seq.
N.M. Stat. Ann., 32-1-4 et seq.
N.Y. Laws 1962, Ch. 686, § 711 et seq.
Ohio Rev. Code 1953, 2151.01 et seq.
Okla. Stat. 1961, Title 10, § 1101 et seq.
Ore. Rev. Stat., 419.472 et seq.
Pa. Purdon's Stat., Title 11, § 243 et seq.

Continued

R.I. Gen. Laws 1956, 8-10-1 et seq., 14-1-1 et seq.

S.D. Codified Laws 1967, 26-7-1 et seq.

Tenn. Code Ann., 37-1-101 et seq.

Tex. Family Code, § 11.01 et seq.

Utah Code Ann. 1953, 78-3a-1 et seq.

Vt. Stat. Ann., Title 33, § 551 et seq.

Wash. Rev. Code Ann., 13.04.005 et seq.

Wis. Stat. Ann., 48.03 et seq.

Wyo. Stat. Ann., § 14-6-201 et seq.

Juvenile Court Act (Baltimore City)
Md. Laws 1943, Ch. 818, § 1

Juvenile Court Act (Kent and Sussex Counties)
Del. Code of 1953, Title 10, § 1101 et seq.

Juvenile Court Act Amendments
Ga. Code Ann., 15-11-1 et seq.

Juvenile Court Act in Cases Relating to Dependency of a Child and the Termination of a Parent and Child Relationship
Wash. Rev. Code Ann., 13.34.010 et seq.

Juvenile Court Act of Allegheny County
Pa. Purdon's Stat., Title 11, § 269-1 et seq.

Juvenile Court Act of the District of Columbia
June 1, 1938, Ch. 309, 52 Stat. 596
July 2, 1940, Ch. 525, 54 Stat. 735

Juvenile Court Advisory Board Act
Ga. Code 1933, 24-2434
Okla. Stat. 1961, Title 20, § 849
Va. Code 1950, § 16.1-240

Juvenile Court Procedure for Families in Conflict Act
Wash. Rev. Code Ann., 13.32A.010 et seq.

Juvenile Court Restructure Act
Tenn. Code Ann., 37-1-201 et seq.

Juvenile Crime Reduction and Education Academy Pilot Project
Cal. Welfare and Institutions Code § 749.5 et seq.

Juvenile Criminal Act
Ky. Rev. Stat. 1971, Superseded Vols., 208.010 et seq.

Juvenile Delinquency Act
Ark. Stat. 1947, 45-201 et seq.
Colo. Rev. Stat. 19-8-101 et seq.
Ill. Rev. Stat. 1991, Ch. 37 § 2001 et seq.
Mass. Gen. Laws Ann., 119:52 et seq.
Me. Rev. Stat. Ann. 1964, Title 15, § 3002 et seq.
Mont. Rev. Code 1947, 10-601 et seq.
P.R. Laws Ann. 1954, Title 34, § 2001 et seq.
Wash. Rev. Code Ann., 13.04.005 et seq.

Juvenile Delinquency and Gang Prevention Act
Fla. Stat. Ann., 39.025 et seq.
La. Rev. Stat. Ann., 15:1421 et seq.

Juvenile Delinquency and Youth Offenses Control Act of 1961
Sept. 22, 1961, P.L. 87-274, 75 Stat. 572, 42 U.S. Code §§ 2541 to 2546
July 9, 1964, P.L. 88-368, 78 Stat. 309, 42 U.S. Code §§ 2542, 2545, 2547, 2548
July 8, 1965, P.L. 89-69, 79 Stat. 212, 42 U.S. Code § 2545

Juvenile Delinquency Control Act
Ark. Stat. 1947, 45-201 et seq.
Colo. Rev. Stat., 19-8-101 et seq.
Ill. Rev. Stat. 1991, Ch. 37, § 801-1 et seq.
Md. Ann. Code 1974, Art. CJ, § 3-801 et seq.
Me. Rev. Stat. Ann. 1964, Title 15, § 3002 et seq.
Mont. Rev. Code 1947, 10-601 et seq.
N.J. Stat. Ann., 2A:14-14 et seq.
P.R. Laws Ann. 1954, Title 34, § 2001 et seq.
R.I. Gen. Laws 1956, 14-1-3 et seq.
Tex. Family Code, § 51.01 et seq.
Wash. Rev. Code Ann., 13.04.005 et seq.

Juvenile Delinquency Prevention Act
Aug. 14, 1972, P.L. 92-381, 86 Stat. 532, 42 U.S. Code §§ 3801, 3811 to 3814, 3861, 3862, 3871 to 3873, 3881 to 3891
Sept. 7, 1974, P.L. 93-415, 88 Stat. 1133, 42 U.S. Code §§ 3811 to 3814, 3821, 3882, 3883, 3888

Vt. Stat. Ann., Title 33, § 1051 et seq.

Juvenile Delinquency Prevention and Control Act of 1968

July 31, 1968, P.L. 90-445, 82 Stat. 462, 42 U.S. Code §§ 3801, 3811, 3812, 3821 to 3823, 3831 to 3833 and others

June 30, 1971, P.L. 92-31, 85 Stat. 84, 42 U.S. Code §§ 3822, 3823, 3882, 3887

Aug. 14, 1972, P.L. 92-381, 86 Stat. 532, 42 U.S. Code §§ 3801, 3811 to 3814, 3861, 3862, 3771 to 3873, 3881 to 3891

Juvenile Delinquent Law (Adult Contribution)

N.Y. Penal Law 1965 (Consol. Laws Ch. 40) 260.10

Juvenile Detention Act

La. Code Juvenile Procedure, Art. 25 et seq.

Juvenile Detention Facilities Cooperative Development and Operations Act

Ark. Code Ann. 1987, No. 486

Juvenile Detention Home, Group Home or Other Residential Care Facilities Act

Va. Code 1950, §§ 16.1-310 et seq., 16.1-202.1 et seq.

Juvenile Diversion Act

Mich. Comp. Laws Ann., 722.821 et seq.

Juvenile Drug Free Zone Act

Cal. Health and Safety Code § 11353

Juvenile Drug Trafficking Act of 1986

Oct. 27, 1986, P.L. 99-570, 21 U.S. Code § 801 nt.

Juvenile Drug Trafficking and Schoolyard Act

Cal. Health and Safety Code § 11353.6

Juvenile Employment Act

Mich. Comp. Laws 1970, 409.1 et seq.

Juvenile Facilities Act

Mich. Comp. Laws Ann., 803.221 et seq.

Juvenile Facility and County Correctional Facility Capital Expenditure Bond Act

Cal. Penal Code § 4496.50 et seq.

Juvenile Fraternal Act

D.C. Code Ann., § 35-1218 et seq.

Juvenile in Need of Supervision Act

Ark. Code Ann. 1987, 9-28-301 et seq.

Juvenile Institutions Administration Act (Organic)

P.R. Laws Ann. 1954, Title 8, § 551 et seq.

Juvenile Interstate Compact Act

See Interstate Compact on Juvenile Act

Juvenile Jurisdiction Act

Wis. Stat. Ann., 48.12 et seq.

Juvenile Justice Act

Fla. Stat. Ann., 39.001 et seq.

N.J. Stat. Ann., 2A:4A-20 et seq.

Wash. Rev. Code Ann., 13.40.010 et seq.

Juvenile Justice Amendments of 1977

Oct. 3, 1977, P.L. 95-115, 42 U.S. Code §§ 5601 nt., 5603 et seq.; 18 U.S. Code §§ 4351, 5038

Juvenile Justice Amendments of 1980

Dec. 8, 1980, P.L. 96-509, 42 U.S. Code § 5601 nt.

Juvenile Justice and Delinquency Prevention Act of 1974

Sept. 7, 1974, P.L. 93-415, 88 Stat. 1109, 18 U.S. Code §§ 4351 to 4353, 5031 to 5042; 42 U.S. Code §§ 3701, 3723, 3733, 3758, 3772 to 3774, 3811, 3814, 3821, 3882, 3883, 3888, 5601 to 5603, 5611 to 5619, 5631 to 5638, 5651 to 5661, 5671, 5672, 5701, 5702, 5711 to 5716, 5731, 5732, 5751

Oct. 3, 1977, P.L. 95-115, 42 U.S. Code §§ 5601 nt., 5603 et seq.

Oct. 12, 1984, P.L. 98-473, 42 U.S. Code § 5601

Nov. 18, 1988, P.L. 100-690, 42 U.S. Code §§ 5603, 5611, 5614, 5616, 5617, prec. 5631, 5631, 5632, 5633, 5651 to 5654, 5660, 5662, 5671, 5776

Continued

Dec. 7, 1989, P.L. 101-204, 42 U.S. Code § 5671

Nov. 4, 1992, P.L. 102-586, 42 U.S. Code §§ 5601, 5602, 5603, 5611, 5612, 5614, 5616, 5617, 5631 to 5633, 5651 to 5654, 5659, 5660, 5662, 5665, 5665a, 5667 et seq., 5671, 5701, 5711 to 5713, 5714-2, 5715, 5751, 5777, prec. 5781

Sept. 21, 1993, P.L. 103-82, 42 U.S. Code § 5616

Sept. 13, 1994, P.L. 103-322, 42 U.S. Code §§ 5633, 5667e-3, 5776a, 5777, 5778

Oct. 20, 1994, P.L. 103-382, 42 U.S. Code § 5667e-5

Oct. 11, 1996, P.L. 104-294, 42 U.S. Code § 5633

Oct. 21, 1998, P.L. 105-277, 42 U.S. Code §§ 5603, 5631, 5632, 5633, 5654, 5714b, 5784

Juvenile Justice and Delinquency Prevention Amendments of 1988

Nov. 18, 1988, P.L. 100-690, 42 U.S. Code § 5601 nt.

Juvenile Justice and Delinquency Prevention Program Act

P.R. Laws Ann. 1954, Title 3, § 1631 et seq.

Juvenile Justice Code

S.C. Code Ann. 1976, § 20-7-6600 et seq.

Tex. Family Code, § 51.01 et seq.

Juvenile Justice Reform Act

Fla. Stat. Ann., 39.0205 et seq.

Ida. Code 1947, 16-1801 et seq.

N.Y. Education Law 1947 (Consol. Laws Ch. 16) § 112

N.Y. Executive Law 1951 (Consol. Laws Ch. 18) §§ 515a, 516, 519, 523, 525

N.Y. Family Court Act §§ 254, 711, 712, 734, 746, 748 to 750, 752, 754, 764, 782a

N.Y. Laws 1976, Ch. 878

N.Y. Mental Hygiene Law 1972 (Consol. Laws Ch. 27) § 7.05

Juvenile Justice Reform Amendment

N.Y. Executive Law 1951 (Consol. Laws Ch. 18) §§ 515a, 519, 523 to 525

N.Y. Family Court Act §§ 712, 734, 750, 756

N.Y. Laws 1978, Ch. 478

Juvenile Justice Reform and School Safety Act

Ga. Laws 1994, p. 1012

Juvenile Justice, Runaway Youth, and Missing Children's Act Amendments of 1984

Oct. 12, 1984, P.L. 98-473, 42 U.S. Code § 5601 nt.

Juvenile Justice Services Act

Mich. Comp. Laws Ann., 722.801 et seq.

Juvenile Justice System Act (Community)

Fla. Stat. Ann., 39.025 et seq.

Juvenile Mental Health Services Act

Wash. Rev. Code 1983, 71.34.010 et seq.

Juvenile Obscenity Act

Minn. Stat. Ann., 617.294

Juvenile Offender Act

D.C. Code Ann., §§ 3-119, 3-120

Ill. Rev. Stat. 1971, Ch. 23, § 2501 et seq.

Kan. Stat. Ann., 38-1601 et seq.

Mass. Gen. Laws 1984, 119.74 et seq.

Mich. Comp. Laws Ann., 712A.1 et seq.

Okla. Stat. 1981, Title 10, § 1160.1 et seq.

Juvenile Offender Local Prevention and Corrections Act

Cal. Welfare and Institutions Code § 1820 et seq.

Juvenile Offender Rehabilitation Act

N.J. Stat. Ann., 30:8-61 et seq.

W. Va. Code 1966, § 49-5B-1 et seq.

Juvenile Offender Victim Restitution Work Program

Okla. Stat. Ann., Title 10, § 1404.1

Juvenile Parole Board Act

N.M. Stat. Ann., 32A-7-1 et seq.

N.M. Stat. Ann., 32-2-1 et seq.

Juvenile Post-Commitment Procedures Act

Tenn. Code Ann., 37-1-301 et seq.

Juvenile Probation Act
Ill. Rev. Stat. 1991, Ch. 37, § 801-1 et seq.

Juvenile Probation Relocation Procedure Act of 1986
Cal. Statutes 1986, Ch. 757

Juvenile Probation Revocation Procedural Act
Cal. Statutes 1986, Ch. 757

Juvenile Probation Services Act
N.M. Stat. Ann. 1953, 16-6-10 et seq.

Juvenile Procedure Act
La. Acts 1978, No. 172
Vt. Stat. Ann., Title 33, § 631 et seq.

Juvenile Reform Act
Okla. Laws 1995, Ch. 290

Juvenile Research and Developmental Disabilities Institutes Act (University of Illinois)
Ill. Rev. Stat. 1991, Ch. 144, § 2650 et seq.

Juvenile Services Act
N.C. Gen. Stat. 1943, § 7A-289.1 et seq.
Neb. Rev. Stat. 1943, 43-2401 et seq.

Juvenile Services Act (Community)
Ore. Rev. Stat., 417.400 et seq.

Juvenile Services Act (Regional)
N.M. Stat. Ann., 33-12-1 et seq.

Juvenile Sex Offender Registration Notification and Community Right-to-Know Act
Ida. Code 1947, 18-8401 et seq.

Juvenile Sex Offender Treatment Act
Cal. Penal Code § 13827 et seq.

Juvenile Substance Abuse Prevention Act
Fla. Stat. Ann., 396.1816, 397.215

Juvenile Terminal Illness Assistance Act
N.J. Stat. Ann., 26:2-93 et seq.

Juvenile Tobacco Access Prevention Act
Miss. General Laws 1997, Ch. 578

Juvenile Training Schools Act
Tex. Rev. Civ. Stat., Art. 5143a

Juvenile Transfer Act
D.C. Code Ann., § 16-2307
Ill. Rev. Stat. 1991, Ch. 37, § 805-4
Mont. Code Ann., 41-5-206

Juvenile Welfare Act
Kan. Stat. Ann., 38-101 et seq.

Juveniles Act (Interstate Compact)
See Interstate Compact on Juveniles Act

Juveniles Compact Act
See Interstate Compact on Juveniles Act

Juveniles Interstate Compact (Rendition Amendments)
Ala. Acts 1986, No. 419

Juveniles Interstate Compact Act
See Interstate Compact on Juveniles Act

K

K-Goal (Governmental Operations Accountability Law)
Kan. Stat. Ann., 74-7283 et seq.

K through 12 Mathematics, Science, and Computer Education Quality Improvement Act
Fla. Stat. Ann., 233.64 et seq.

K through 12 Mathematics, Science, and Technology Improvement Act
Colo. Rev. Stat., 22-81-101 et seq.

Kadlecek Amendment
Colo. Rev. Stat., 24-75-201.1, 24-75-201.2

Kalmia Woods Water District Loan Act
Mass. Acts 1953, Ch. 357

Kammer Recreational Land Trust Fund Act
Mich. Comp. Laws Ann., 318.401 et seq.

Kankakee River Valley Area Airport Authority Act
Ill. Rev. Stat. 1991, Ch. 15 1/2, § 701 et seq.

Kanner Act (Taxation)
Fla. Stat. 1955, 344.14

Kansas Act on the Aging
Kan. Stat. Ann., 72-5901 et seq.

Kansas and Missouri Metropolitan Culture and Recreation District Compact and Act
Mo. Rev. Stat. 1978, 70-445 et seq.

Kansas City Act
Kan. Stat. Ann., 74-8001 et seq.

Kansas City Court Act
Kan. Laws 1927, Ch. 180

Kansas City Enabling Act
Mo. Rev. Stat., 82.020

Kansas City Police Act
Mo. Rev. Stat., 84.350 et seq.

Kansas City Police Retirement System Act
Mo. Rev. Stat., 86.370 et seq.

Kansas-Missouri Air Quality Compact Act
Mo. Rev. Stat., 643.600 et seq.

Kansas-Missouri Flood Prevention and Control Compact Act
Mo. Rev. Stat., 70.327 et seq.

Kansas-Nebraska Act
May 30, 1854, Ch. 59, 10 Stat. 277

Kansas-Nebraska Big Blue River Compact Act
Kan. Stat. Ann., 82a-529
Neb. Laws 1971, L.B. 609

Kansas-Oklahoma-Arkansas River Basin Compact
Okla. Stat. Ann., Title 82, § 1401

KanWork Act
Kan. Stat. Ann., 39-7,101 et seq.

Kapiloff Acid Deposition Act
Cal. Health and Safety Code § 39900 et seq.

Kapiloff Land Bank Act
Cal. Public Resources Code § 8600 et seq.

Kapiloff-Z'berg Solid Waste Control Act
Cal. Government Code § 66795 et seq.

Karen Clarke and Leroy Brown, Jr. Witness Protection Program
Conn. Public Acts 1999, No. 240, §§ 6, 7

Kari Koskinen Manager Background Check Act
Minn. Stat. Ann., 299C.66 et seq.

Karnette Rental Purchase Act
Cal. Civil Code § 1812.620 et seq.

Kaskaskia Regional Port District Act
Ill. Comp. Stat. 1992, Ch. 70, § 1830/1.1 et seq.

Kaskaskia River Watershed and Basin Act
Ill. Rev. Stat. 1991, Ch. 19, §§ 41.09, 41.1

Kaskaskia River Watershed Operation and Maintenance Act
Ill. Rev. Stat. 1991, Ch. 105, §§ 540, 541

Kates Act (Auto Buses)
N.J. Stat. Ann., 48:4-1 to 48:4-11, 48:4-14 to 48:4-17

Katherine Dunham Metropolitan Exposition and Auditorium Authority Act
Ill. Rev. Stat. 1991, Ch. 85, § 1391 et seq.

Katherine Dunham, Oak Park, Aledo, Normal, Mason County, Jasper County, Brownstown Park District, Jo Daviess County, Milford, and Sheldon Civic Centers Act
Ill. Rev. Stat. 1991, Ch. 85, § 4500 et seq.

Kathy Fiscus Act (Abandoned Wells)
Mich. Comp. Laws Ann., 750.493b

Katz-Harris California Taxpayers' Bill of Rights
Cal. Revenue and Taxation Code § 7080 et seq., § 21001 et seq.

Katz-Kopp-Baker-Campbell Transportation Blueprint for Twenty-First Century
Cal. Statutes 1989, Ch. 106

Katz-Kopp-Baker Transportation Blueprint for Twenty-First Century
Cal. Statutes 1991, Ch. 105

Katz-Robbins Los Angeles Transportation Act
Cal. Statutes 1990, Ch. 95

Katz Safe Schoolbus and Clean Fuel Efficiency Demonstration Program
Cal. Education Code 1976, § 17910 et seq.

Kaufman Law (Railroad Electrification)
N.Y. Laws 1923, Ch. 901

Kaw Act (Indians)
July 1, 1902, Ch. 1361, 32 Stat. 636

Kaw City-Fairfax Authority Act
Okla. Stat. 1971, Title 82, § 951 et seq.

Keating Owen Act (Child Labor)
Sept. 1, 1916, Ch. 432, 39 Stat. 675

Keck Beauchamp-Montgomery Super Highway Act
Ky. Rev. Stat. 1971, 177.390 et seq.

Keeley Act (Public Improvement Bonds)
Ala. Code 1975, § 11-81-160 et seq.

Keene-Collier State Hostel Facilities Act
Cal. Public Resources Code § 5050 et seq.

Keene-Hauser Safe Transport Law
Cal. Penal Code § 12026.2

Keene Health Care Agent Act
Cal. Civil Code § 2500 et seq.

Keene-Knox Health Care Service Plan Act
Cal. Health and Safety Code § 1340 et seq.

Keene-Nejedly California Wetlands Preservation Act
Cal. Public Resources Code § 5810 et seq.

Keene-Nielson Fisheries Restoration Act
Cal. Fish and Game Code 1957, § 2760 et seq.

Keeping the Peace Law
Wash. Rev. Code Ann., 10.13.010 et seq.

Kelley-Mitchem Act (Housing Finance)
Ala. Acts 1980, p. 899

Kellogg Act (Advances for Agricultural Purposes)
Aug. 24, 1921, Ch. 80, 42 Stat. 181

Kellogg Act (Cable Companies)
May 27, 1921, Ch. 12, 42 Stat. 8, 47 U.S. Code §§ 34 to 39

Kelly-Abshire Salinity Control Barrier Act
Cal. Statutes 1953, Ch. 1104, p. 2601
Cal. Statutes 1957, Ch. 2092, p. 3717

Kelly-Jackson-Conley Act (Zoning and Planning)
Ky. Rev. Stat. 1962, 100.850 et seq.

Kelly Johnson Act
Fla. Laws 1998, Ch. 308

Kelp Act
Ore. Rev. Stat., 274.885 et seq.

Kelsey Friend-Herbie Deskins Tax Relief for Flood Victims Act
Ky. Rev. Stat. 1971, 141.011

Kenai Natives Association Equity Act Amendments of 1996
Nov. 12, 1996, P. L. 104-333, § 311, 43 U.S. Code § 1784 nt.

Keniston Act (Amendments to Federal Constitution)
Mass. Gen. Laws 1990, 53:18

Kennedy Center Act
Oct. 12, 1984, P. L. 98-473, 20 U.S. Code § 76o

Kennels Act
Ind. Laws 1925, Ch. 77, p. 236

Kennick-Arnold-Bee Act (Youth Authority)
Cal. Welfare and Institutions Code § 1821 et seq.

Kennick-Arnold Juvenile Court Law
Cal. Welfare and Institutions Code §§ 200, 500 et seq.

Kennick-McCarthy Nutrition Program for the Elderly Act
Cal. Welfare and Institutions Code § 18325 et seq.

Keno Licensing Act
La. Rev. Stat. Ann., 33:4861.1 et seq.

Kensington Act (Opening Streets)
Pa. Mar. 6, 1820, 7 Sm. L. 265, Ch. 4837

Kensington Water and Sewer Act
Ga. Laws 1972, p. 2025

Kent County Employees Retirement Act
Del. Code of 1974, Title 9, § 4301 et seq.

Kent County Redevelopment Urban Renewal Act
Md. Laws 1975, Ch. 380
Md. Laws 1976, Ch. 79
Md. Laws 1976, Ch. 80
Md. Laws 1976, Ch. 81
Md. Laws 1976, Ch. 410

Kent Town Code
N.Y. Local Laws 1973, Town of Kent, p. 2355

Kentucky Indiana Boundary Compact
Ind. Code Ann., 13-5-6.5-1, 13-5-6.5-2

Kentucky Ohio Interstate Compact on Air Pollution
Ohio Rev. Code 1953, 3723.04 et seq.

Kentucky Wilderness Act of 1985
Dec. 23, 1985, P. L. 99-197, 16 U.S. Code § 1132 nt.

Keogh Smathers Act
See Self-Employed Individuals Tax Retirement Act Of 1962
Oct. 10, 1962, P. L. 87-792, 76 Stat. 809

Kern County Vendor Payment Demonstration Project
Cal. Welfare and Institutions Code §§ 10830 to 10833

Kern County Water Agency Act
Cal. Water Code, Appendix, § 99-1 et seq.

Kern McGillicuddy Act (Federal Employees' Workmen's Compensation)
Sept. 7, 1916, Ch. 458, 39 Stat. 742 (See 5 U.S. Code § 8101 et seq.)

Kerosene and Motor Fuels Quality Inspection Act
Tenn. Code Ann., 47-18-1301 et seq.

Kerosene Inspection Act
Mich. Comp. Laws 1948, 28.301 et seq.

Kerr-Mills Social Security Act
See Social Security Amendments Of 1960

Kerr-Smith Tobacco Control Act
  See Anti-Kickback Act
  See Tobacco Control Act "Kick-Back" Racket Act

Kershaw County Road Superintendent Act
  S.C. Code Ann. 1962, § 33-1729 et seq.

Kershaw County Rural Police Act
  S.C. Code Ann. 1962, § 53-561 et seq.

Ketcham-Capper Act
  N.M. Stat. Ann., 76-2-3

Ketchum Act (Clyde Randolph)
  Wash. Rev. Code Ann., 43.20A.720

Ketchum Act (Grapes)
  Cal. Food and Agricultural Code 1967, § 65500 et seq.

Key in the Ignition Statute
  N.Y. Vehicle and Traffic Law 1959 (Consol. Laws Ch. 71) § 1210, Subd. a

Key West Urban Renewal Act
  Fla. Special Laws 1963, Ch. 63-1493
  Fla. Special Laws 1967, Ch. 67-1596

Keys Aqueduct Commission Act
  Fla. Special Laws 1941, Ch. 21230

Keys Aqueduct District Act
  Fla. Special Laws 1953, Ch. 29301

Keys Area Protection Act
  Fla. Stat. Ann., 380.0552

Keysor-Moscone Voter Registration Act
  Cal. Elections Code 1961, §§ 200 et seq., 310 et seq., 421 et seq., 14002, 14202, 14215.5, 14240, 14241, 14243, 14419, 14622, 17236, 18237

Keystone Recreation Park and Conservation Fund Act
  Pa. Purdon's Stat., Title 32, § 2011 et seq.

Keystone Recreation Park and Conservation Fund Current Revenue Project Itemization Act
  Pa. 1995 Pamph. Laws, No. 56

Keystone Shortway Act (Pennsylvania Turnpike)
  Pa. Purdon's Stat., Title 36, § 666.1 et seq.

Kick-Back of Wages Law
  N.Y. Labor Law (Consol. Laws Ch. 31) § 198b

Kickback Act
  Miss. Code Ann. 1972, § 97-11-53
  Okla. Stat. Ann., Title 74, § 3401 et seq.

Kickback Act (Wages)
  Cal. Labor Code §§ 221, 225
  N.Y. Labor Law (Consol. Laws Ch. 31) § 198b
  Pa. Purdon's Stat., Title 25, §§ 2374, 2375
  Wash. Rev. Code Ann., 49.52.050 et seq.

Kid Care Act
  Fla. Stat. Ann., 409.810 to 409.820

Kidnapping Act
  June 22, 1932, Ch. 271, 47 Stat. 326 (See 18 U.S. Code §§ 10, 1201, 1202)
  May 18, 1934, Ch. 301, 48 Stat. 781 (See 18 U.S. Code §§ 10, 1201)
  Jan. 24, 1936, Ch. 29, 49 Stat. 1099 (See 18 U.S. Code § 1202)
  Cal. Penal Code § 207 et seq.
  Colo. Rev. Stat., 18-3-301 et seq.
  Fla. Stat. Ann., 787.01
  Ga. Code Ann., 16-5-40
  Ill. Rev. Stat. 1991, Ch. 38, § 10-1 et seq.
  Ind. Code Ann., 35-42-3-2
  Kan. Stat. Ann., 21-3420, 21-3421
  Md. Ann. Code 1957, Art. 27, § 337 et seq.
  Mich. Comp. Laws Ann., 750.349, 750.350
  Mo. Rev. Stat., 565.110 et seq.
  Mont. Code Ann. 1991, 45-5-301 et seq.
  N.C. Gen. Stat. 1943, § 14-39 et seq.
  N.H. Rev. Stat. 1955, 633:1
  N.J. Stat. Ann., 2C:13-1
  N.Y. Penal Law 1965 (Consol. Laws Ch. 40) § 135.00 et seq.
  Continued

Pa. Cons. Stat., Title 18, § 2901 et seq.
R.I. Gen. Laws 1956, 11-26-1 et seq.
S.D. Codified Laws 1967, 22-19-1 et seq.
Tenn. Code Ann., 39-13-301 et seq.
Tex. Penal Code, § 20.04
Vt. Stat. Ann., Title 13, § 2401 et seq.
Wash. Rev. Code Ann., 9A.40.010 et seq.

Kidney Health Care Act
Tex. Health and Safety Code, § 42.001 et seq.

Kidney Health Planning Act
Okla. Stat. Ann., Title 63, § 1-2600 et seq.

Kids Voting Act (Ann Kravitz)
Fla. Laws 1992, Ch. 134

Kieran's Law
N.Y. Laws 1998, Ch. 3

Kilday Bill
May 20, 1958, P. L. 85-422, 72 Stat. 122, 10 U.S. Code §§ 1401, 1401 nt., 1405, 3888, 3927, 3991, 3991 nt., 5083, 5201, 5233, 6151, 6325, 6326, 6381, 6383, 6390, 6394, 6396, 6398 to 6400, 6483, 8888, 8927, 8991; 14 U.S. Code § 423; 33 U.S. Code § 853o

Kiley Act (Boxing Commission)
Mont. Rev. Code 1947, 82-301 et seq.

Killea-Thompson Limited Partner Protection Act
Cal. Corporations Code § 25014.5 et seq.

Killgrew-Byrne Act (Unemployment Insurance)
N.Y. Labor Law (Consol. Laws Ch. 31) § 500 et seq.

Kinchafoonee Lake Authority Act
Ga. Code Ann., 12-3-360 et seq.

Kindergarten Act
Okla. Stat. Ann., Title 70, § 1210.101 et seq.

Kinderhook Zoning Law
N.Y. Local Laws 1972, Village of Kinderhook, p. 3517

King Act (Building and Loan Associations)
Ohio Rev. Code 1953, 1151.02 et seq.

King Act (Insanity Proceedings)
D.C. Code 1961, § 21-308

King Act (Motor Vehicle Inspection)
D.C. Code 1973, § 40-201 et seq.

King Birthday Act
D.C. Code Ann., §§ 1-504,28-2701

King Crab Marketing and Quality Control Act
Alaska Stat. 1962, § 16.51.010 et seq.

King Holiday and Service Act of 1994
Aug. 23, 1994, P. L. 103-304, 36 U.S. Code §§ 169j nt., 169j-2 et seq.

King Road Act
Mo. Rev. Stat. 1969, 231.440 et seq.

King Thompson Act (Labor Relations)
Mo. Rev. Stat., 295.010 et seq.

Kingpin of Drugs Law
S.C. Code Ann. 1976, § 44-53-475

Kings County Jury Law
N.Y. Judiciary Law (Consol. Laws Ch. 30) § 680 et seq.

Kings River Conservation District Act
Cal. Water Code, Appendix, § 59-1 et seq.

Kingsland Area Convention and Visitors Bureau Authority Act
Ga. Laws 1991, p. 4101

Kingston City Charter
Tenn. Private Acts 1972, Ch. 298

Kingston City Court Act
N.Y. Laws 1952, Ch. 813

Kinkaid Act (Homestead Entries in Nebraska)
April 28, 1904, Ch. 1801, 33 Stat. 547, 43 U.S. Code § 224

Kiper-Tuthill Act (Taxation)
Ind. Laws 1920, Special Session, Ch. 45, p. 153

Kircher Hamilton Act (Pregnant Women Blood Test)
Mich. Comp. Laws 1970, 329.153

Kirkland Act (Town Law Revision)
N.Y. Town Law (Consol. Laws Ch. 62)

Kissimmee-St. Cloud Electric Revenue Bond Act
Fla. Special Laws 1970, Ch. 70-767

Kitchen and Table Wine Act (County Option)
Ida. Code 1947, 23-1301 et seq.

Kittery-Portsmouth Bridge Compact
N.H. Rev. Stat. 1955, 234:43 et seq.

Klair Act (Intoxicating Liquors)
Del. Laws Vol. 30, p. 635, Ch. 239

Klamath Indian Termination Act
See Klamath Termination Act

Klamath Indian Tribe Restoration Act
Aug. 27, 1986, P. L. 99-398, 25 U.S. Code §§ 566 nt., 566-566h

Klamath River Basin Fishery Resources Restoration Act
Oct. 29, 1992, P. L. 102-570, 16 U.S. Code § 460ss-3

Klamath River Fish and Game District Act
Cal. Fish and Game Code § 11036

Klamath Termination Act
Aug. 13, 1954, Ch. 732, 68 Stat. 718, 25 U.S. Code §§ 564 to 564w-1
Sept. 9, 1959, P. L. 86-247, 73 Stat. 477, 25 U.S. Code § 564w-1

Klamath Welfare Act
March 29, 1948, Ch. 160, 62 Stat. 92, 25 U.S. Code §§ 544, 544 nt., 545

Klaus-Haskell Law (Indigents)
Iowa Laws 1919 (38th G.A.), Ch. 78

Klehs-Alquist Tax Conformity Act
Cal. Health and Safety Code §§ 6051, 6201 et seq.

Kline Act (Municipal Improvements)
Wis. Laws 1931, Ch. 275

Kline Law
Wis. Stat. Ann., 32.50 et seq.

Knight Act (Termination of War Contracts)
N.Y. Laws 1919, Ch. 459

Knights' Landing Ridge Drainage District Act
Cal. Statutes 1913, Ch. 99, p. 109

Knives Act (Switch Blade)
See Switchblade Knives Act

Knock and Announce Rule
Iowa Code Ann., 808.6

Knock Knock Act
N.Y. Criminal Procedure Law (Consol. Laws Ch. 11A) § 690.35 et seq.

Knock Not Act (Searches and Seizures)
Neb. Rev. Stat. 1943, 29-411

Knox-Cortese Local Government Reorganization Act
Cal. Government Code § 56000 et seq.

Knox County Commission Form of Government Act
Tenn. Private Acts 1937, Ch. 183

Knox County Free Textbook Act
Tenn. Private Acts 1925, Ch. 625

Knox County Highway Act
Tenn. Private Acts 1925, Ch. 343

Knox County Teachers' Pension Act
Tenn. Private Acts 1925, Ch. 143

Knox County Teachers' Tenure Act
Tenn. Private Acts 1937, 3rd Ex. Sess., Ch. 18

Knox Keene Health Care Service Plan Act
Cal. Health and Safety Code § 1340 et seq.

Knox Law (Liquor Control)
Ore. Rev. Stat., 471.005 et seq.

Knox Mills Health Plan Act
Cal. Government Code § 12530 et seq.

Knox Moscone Professional Corporation Act
Cal. Corporations Code § 13400 et seq.

Knox Nisbet Act
Cal. Government Code § 54773 et seq.

Knoxville Local Improvement Act
Tenn. Private Acts 1925, Ch. 348

Knoxville Pension Act (City Employees)
Tenn. Private Acts 1947, Ch. 461

Knuckles and Lucas Act (Gas Procurement)
Ky. Acts 1958, Ch. 38

Knutson Vandenberg Act
June 9, 1930, Ch. 416, 16 U.S. Code §§ 576-576b
Oct. 22, 1976, P. L. 94-588, 16 U.S. Code § 576b

Kohler Act (Coal Mining)
Pa. Purdon's Stat., Title 52, § 661 et seq.

Koniag Lands Conveyance Amendments of 1991
Oct. 24, 1992, P. L. 102-489, 16 U.S. Code § 668dd nt.

Konohikis Act of 1852 (Land Titles)
Haw. Session Laws 1852, p. 28, June 19, 1852

Kopp-Katz-Baker-Campbell Transportation Blueprint for Twenty-First Century
Cal. Statutes 1991, Ch. 106

Kopp-Katz-Baker Transportation Blueprint for Twenty-First Century
Cal. Statutes 1991, Ch. 105

Korean Conflict Veterans Compensation Act
Pa. Cons. Stat., Unconsol. Stat., Title 51, § 20091 et seq.

Korean Conflict Veterans Compensation Bond Act
Pa. Cons. Stat., Unconsol. Stat., Title 51, § 20107 et seq.

Korean Veterans Bonus Act
Alaska Stat. 1962, § 26.15.160
Ind. Code Ann., 10-5-16-1 et seq.
Iowa Code 1977, 35B.1 et seq.
Mich. Comp. Laws Ann., 35.971 et seq.
Mont. Rev. Code 1947, 84-5606
N.D. Laws 1957, Ch. 242
Pa. Purdon's Stat., Title 51, § 458.1 et seq.
R.I. Public Laws 1955, Ch. 3608

Korean War Veterans Memorial Thirty-Eighth Anniversary Commemorative Coin Act
Oct. 31, 1990, P. L. 101-495, 31 U.S. Code § 5112 nt.
Oct. 6, 1992, P. L. 102-390, 31 U.S. Code § 5112 nt.

Kosher Food Act
Cal. Penal Code § 383b
D.C. Code 1973, § 22-3404 et seq.
Ill. Rev. Stat. 1991, Ch. 56 1/2, § 288.01 et seq.
N.Y. Agriculture and Markets Law (Consol. Laws Ch. 69) §§ 201a, 201b
N.Y. General Business Law (Consol. Laws, Ch. 20) § 392b
Wash. Rev. Code Ann., 69.90.010 et seq.

Kosher Food Consumer Protection Act
N.J. Stat. Ann., 56:8-61 et seq.

Kraft Geddis Child Care Center Act
Cal. Education Code 1959, §§ 8200, 16601 et seq.

Kramer Patent Act
Aug. 5, 1939, Ch. 450, 53 Stat. 1212 (See 35
U.S. Code §§ 101, 102, 119, 161, 171, 172,
282)

Kristin Smart Campus Safety Act
Cal. Education Code 1976, § 67381

Krueger Act (Bonds)
Ohio Laws Vol. 111, p. 335

Krueger Collister Act (Motor Transportation)
Ohio Rev. Code 1953, 4921.02, 4921.04,
4921.05

Ku Klux Klan Act
July 31, 1861, Ch. 33, 12 Stat. 284, 42 U.S.
Code § 1985
Feb. 28, 1871, Ch. 99, 16 Stat. 433
Ky. Rev. Stat. 1971, Superseded Vols.,
437.110 et seq.
Ky. Rev. Stat. 1971, 506.040 et seq.
Tenn. Code Ann., 39-14-112, 39-17-301 et
seq.

L

L P G Act
N.M. Stat. Ann., 70-5-1 et seq.
Tex. Natural Resources Code, § 113.001 et seq.

La Entrada al Pacifico Corridor Act
Tex. Transportation Code, § 225.034

La Follette Act (Seamen)
See Seamen's Act

La Follette-Barden Vocational Rehabilitation Act
See Vocational Rehabilitation Acts

La Follette-Bulwinkle Act (Venereal Diseases)
May 24, 1938, Ch. 267, 52 Stat. 439

La Follette Hours of Labor Act (Railroads)
March 4, 1907, Ch. 2939, 34 Stat. 1415, 45 U.S. Code §§ 61 to 64

La Follette-Young Self-Insurers Security Act
Cal. Labor Code § 3740 et seq.

La Guardia-McKeown Act
March 3, 1933, Ch. 204, 47 Stat. 1467, 11 U.S. Code §§ 101a, 205

La Guardia-Norris Act (Maryland)
Md. Ann. Code 1974, Art. LE, § 4-302 et seq.

La Plata River Compact
N.M. Stat. Ann., 72-15-16 et seq.

La Plata River Compact Act
Colo. Laws 1923, p. 696, Ch. 191

Label Act (Union)
See Union Label Act

Label Obliteration Act (Container)
Ill. Comp. Stat. 1992, Ch. 720, § 565/0.01 et seq.

Labeling Act
Iowa Code Ann., 189.1 et seq.
N.J. Rev. Stat. 56:3-13.3
Tenn. Public Acts 1965, Ch. 34

Labeling Act (Citrus Fruit)
Fla. Stat. Ann., 601.9905 et seq.

Labeling Act (Food)
Ariz. Rev. Stat. Ann., § 36-902,
Iowa Code Ann., 191.1 et seq.

Labeling Act (Fruits and Vegetables)
Ark. Code Ann. 1987, 2-20-301 et seq.

Labeling Act (Gasoline Receptacle)
Ill. Rev. Stat. 1991, Ch. 127 1/2, § 150 et seq.

Labeling Act (Hazardous Substances)
See Hazardous Substances Labeling Act
Me. Rev. Stat. Ann. 1964, Title 7, § 501 et seq.
Mich. Comp. Laws Ann., 286.451 et seq.

Labeling Act (Meat)
S.C. Code Ann. 1962, § 6-608

Labeling Act (Open Date)
Ore. Rev. Stat., 616.800 et seq.

Labeling Act (Plastic Container)
Okla. Stat. Ann., Title 27A, § 2-11-501 et seq.

Labeling Act (Seeds)
Fla. Stat. Ann., 578.011 et seq.

Labeling Act (State Institutions)
Cal. Penal Code § 2895 et seq.

Labeling and Marketing Act (Strawberries)
Ky. Rev. Stat. 1971, 260.010, 260.130 et seq., 260.990

Labeling and Packaging Act (Fair)
Me. Rev. Stat. Ann. 1964, Title 7, § 521 et seq.

Labels Act (Trademarks)
Pa. Purdon's Stat., Title 73, § 7 et seq.

Labor Act
Ala. Code 1975, § 25-3-1 et seq.
Cal. Statutes 1937, Ch. 90, p. 185
Ind. Code Ann., 22-2-1-1 et seq.
Mass. Gen.Laws 1990, 149:1 et seq.
Mo. Rev. Stat., 291.010 et seq.
N.J. Stat. Ann., 34:1-1 et seq.
N.Y. Consol. Laws Ch. 31
Okla. Stat. Ann., Title 40, § 101 et seq.
Pa. Purdon's Stat., Title 43, § 1 et seq.
S.C. Code Ann. 1976, § 41-1-10 et seq.

Labor Act (Child)
See Child Labor Act

Labor Act (Children)
Ark. Code Ann. 1987, 11-6-104 et seq.
Colo. Rev. Stat. 8-12-101 et seq.
Ga. Code Ann., 39-2-1 et seq.
Minn. Stat. Ann., 181A.01 et seq.

Labor Act (Convict)
N.H. Rev. Stat. 1955, 619:20 et seq.

Labor Act (Eight Hour)
Colo. Rev. Stat., 8-13-101 etseq.

Labor Act (Females)
See Female Labor Act

Labor Act (Lunch Hour)
Neb. Rev. Stat. 1943, 48-212, 48-213

Labor Act (Railways)
See Railway Labor Act

Labor Act (Union)
La. Rev. Stat. Ann., 51:211 et seq.

Labor Act (Wage and Hour)
Neb. Rev. Stat. 1943, 48-1201 et seq.

Labor Agency Act
Tex. Rev. Civ. Stat., Art. 5221a-5

Labor and Employer Campaign Finance Reform Act
Ga. Laws 1998, S.B. 497

Labor and Management Improper Practices Act
N.Y. Labor Law (Consol. Laws Ch. 31) § 720 et seq.

Labor and Storage Lien Act
Ill. Rev. Stat. 1991, Ch. 82, § 39.9 et seq.

Labor and Storage Lien Act (Small Amount)
Ill. Rev. Stat. 1991, Ch. 82, § 47.9 et seq.

Labor Anti-Coercion Act
Colo. Rev. Stat., 8-2-101 et seq.

Labor Anti-Injunction Act
See Anti-Injunction Act (Labor Disputes)

Labor Antiblacklisting Act
Wash. Rev. Code Ann., 49.44.010

Labor Arbitration Act
See Arbitration Act (Labor Disputes)

Labor Arbitration Services Act
Ill. Rev. Stat. 1991, Ch. 48, § 2300 et seq.

Labor Camp Act
Cal. Labor Code § 2410 et seq.

Labor Camp Act (Migrants)
See Migrant Labor Camp Act

Labor Compressed Air Safety Act
Wash. Rev. Code Ann., 49.24.010 et seq.

Labor Contract Act (Frauds)
Ga. Code 1933, 26-7408, 26-7409

Labor Controversies Act
Wis. Stat. Ann., 103.51 et seq.

Labor Controversies Act (Little Norris-La Guardia)
See Little Norris-La Guardia Act (Labor Injunctions)

Labor Day Act
June 28, 1894, Ch. 118, 28 Stat. 96

Labor Department Act
Ky. Rev. Stat. 1971, 336.010 et seq.
N.M. Stat. Ann., 9-18-1 et seq.
Continued

271

W. Va. Code 1966, § 21-1-1 et seq.

Labor Department Appropriation Act
See Department Of Labor Appropriation Acts

Labor Discrimination Act
Wis. Stat. Ann., 111.31 et seq.

Labor Dispute Act
Ill. Rev. Stat. 1991, Ch. 48, §§ 2a, 2a.1

Labor Dispute Election Act
Ore. Laws 1991, Ch. 355

Labor Dispute Injunctions Act
N.Y. Labor Law (Consol. Laws Ch. 31) § 807

Labor Disputes Act
See Norris-La Guardia Act
Conn. Gen. Stat. Ann., § 31-101 et seq.
La. Rev. Stat. Ann., 23:841 et seq.
Mass. Gen. Laws Ann., 150B:1 et seq.
Me. Rev. Stat. Ann. 1964, Title 26, § 5
Mich. Comp. Laws Ann., 423.1 et seq.
S.C. Code Ann. 1976, §§ 41-1, 7-10 et seq.

Labor Disputes Act (Anti-Injunction)
Wis. Stat. Ann., 103.51 et seq.

Labor Disputes Act (Arbitration)
Wash. Rev. Code Ann., 49.08.010 et seq.

Labor Disputes Act (Injunctions)
Wash. Rev. Code Ann., 49.32.011 et seq.

Labor Disputes Act (Public Utilities)
See Public Utilities Labor Disputes Act

Labor Disputes Arbitration Act
Md. Ann. Code 1974, Art. LE, § 4-101 et seq.
Mo. Rev. Stat., 295.080
N.C. Gen. Stat. 1943, § 95-36.1 et seq.

Labor Disputes Conciliation Act
Mass. Gen. Laws Ann., 150:1 et seq.

Labor-Disputes Joint Resolution
June 19, 1934, Ch. 677, 48 Stat. 1183

Labor Disputes Settlement Act
Ill. Rev. Stat. 1991, Ch. 10, § 20 et seq.

Labor Division Act (Migrant)
S.C. Code Ann. 1976, § 41-3-510 et seq.

Labor Education Center Act
Kan. Stat. Ann., 76-496 et seq.

Labor-Federal Security Appropriation Acts
June 26, 1940, Ch. 428, 54 Stat. 574, 29 U.S. Code § 31; 42 U.S. Code §§ 704a, 1301a
July 1, 1941, Ch. 269, 55 Stat. 466, 21 U.S. Code § 46a; 24 U.S. Code § 169; 42 U.S. Code § 704a
July 2, 1942, Ch. 475, 56 Stat. 565, 24 U.S. Code § 169; 41 U.S. Code § 6a nt.: 42 U.S. Code § 704a
July 12, 1943, Ch. 221, 57 Stat. 494, 21 U.S. Code § 372a; 24 U.S. Code § 169; 41 U.S. Code § 6a nt.; 42 U.S. Code § 704a
June 28, 1944, Ch. 302, 58 Stat. 547, 24 U.S. Code § 169; 41 U.S. Code § 6a nt.; 42 USC §§ 207 nt., 704a
July 3, 1945, Ch. 263, 59 Stat. 361, 24 U.S. Code § 169; 41 U.S. Code § 6a nt.; 42 U.S. Code §§ 209c 231, 703a, 704a
July 26, 1946, Ch. 672, 60 Stat. 679, 24 U.S. Code § 169; 29 U.S. Code §§ 49c nt., 49c-2 to 49c-5; 41 U.S. Code § 6a nts.; 42 U.S. Code §§ 703a, 704a, 1603
July 8, 1947, Ch. 210, 61 Stat. 260, 24 U.S. Code § 169; 41 U.S. Code § 6a nts.; 42 U.S. Code §§ 703a 704a, 1603, 1915, 1916
June 14, 1948, Ch. 465, 62 Stat. 394, 41 U.S. Code § 6a nt.
June 29, 1949, Ch. 275, 63 Stat. 283, 41 U.S. Code § 6a nt.; 42 U.S. Code §§ 703a, 704a, 1905 nt., 1917, 1918
Sept. 6, 1950, Ch. 896, 64 Stat. 642, 29 U.S. Code § 49d nt.; 42 U.S. Code §§ 703a, 704a
Aug. 31, 1951, Ch. 373, 65 Stat. 209, 42 U.S. Code §§ 703a, 704a
July 5, 1952, Ch. 575, 66 Stat. 358, 42 U.S. Code §§ 703a, 704a, 704b, 905

Labor Hours Act
Wash. Rev. Code Ann., 49.28.010 et seq.

Labor Injunction Act

See also Anti-Injunction Act (Labor Disputes) and Little Norris-La Guardia Act (Labor Injunctions)

Conn. Gen. Stat. Ann., § 31-112 et seq.

Kan. Stat. Ann., 60-904 et seq.

La. Rev. Stat. Ann., 23:841 et seq.

Mass. Gen. Laws Ann., 214:6

Me. Rev. Stat. Ann. 1964, Title 26, § 5

Mich. Comp. Laws 1948, 423.13a

Minn. Stat. Ann., 185.01 et seq.

N.H. Rev. Stat. 1955, Superseded Vols., 572.35 et seq.

N.J. Stat. Ann., 2A:15-51 et seq.

N.M. Stat. Ann., 50-3-1, 50-3-2

N.Y. Labor Law (Consol. Laws Ch. 31) § 807

Ore. Rev. Stat., 662.040 et seq.

P.R. Laws Ann. 1954, Title 29, § 101 et seq.

Wash. Rev. Code Ann., 49.32.011 et seq.

Labor Injunction Act (Cox-Phillips)

Mass. Gen. Laws Ann., 214:6

Labor Injunction Act (Hospital or Public Utility Employees)

Mich. Comp. Laws Ann., 423.23

Labor Injunction Relief Act

Ida. Code 1947, 44-701 et seq.

Labor Law (Eight-Hour Law)

See Contract Work Hours And Safety Standards Act

Labor Law (Trades Union Label)

Ark. Stat. 1947, 70-525 et seq.

Labor Laws (Child)

Miss. Code Ann. 1972, § 71-1-17 et seq.

Labor Lien Act

Ariz. Rev. Stat. Ann., § 33-981 et seq.

Labor Management Cooperation Act of 1978

Oct. 27, 1978, P.L. 95-524, 29 U.S. Code §§ 173, 175a, 175a nt., 186

Labor-Management Elections Act

Ore. Rev. Stat., 663.005 et seq.

Labor-Management Reform Act

N.M. Stat. Ann., 50-2-1 et seq.

Labor Management Relations Act of 1947

June 23, 1947, Ch. 120, 61 Stat. 136 (See 18 U.S. Code § 610) 29 U.S. Code §§ 141 to 144, 151, 151 nt., 152, 153, 153 nt., 154 to 158, 158 nt., 159, 159 nt., 160 to 167, 171 to 187

Aug. 10, 1948, Ch. 833, 62 Stat. 1286, 29 U.S. Code § 193

Oct. 22, 1951, Ch. 534, 65 Stat. 601, 29 U.S. Code §§ 158, 159, 168

Sept. 14, 1959, P.L. 86-257, 73 Stat. 537, 29 U.S. Code §§ 186, 187

Oct. 14, 1969, P.L. 91-86, 83 Stat. 133, 29 U.S. Code § 186

Oct. 15, 1970, P.L. 91-452, 84 Stat. 930, 29 U.S. Code § 161

Oct. 27, 1978, P.L. 95-524, 29 U.S. Code §§ 173, 175a, 186

Oct. 12, 1984, P.L. 98-473, 29 U.S. Code 186

April 18, 1990, P.L. 101-273, 29 U.S. Code § 186

Nov. 15, 1990, P.L. 101-552, 29 U.S. Code § 173

Aug. 26, 1992, P.L. 102-354, 29 U.S. Code § 173

Dec. 29, 1995, P.L. 104-88, 29 U.S. Code § 186

Oct. 19, 1996, P.L. 104-320, 29 U.S. Code § 173

Labor Management Relations Act, 1947

Kan. Stat. Ann., 44-801 et seq.

N.D. Cent. Code, 34-12-01 et seq.

Ore. Rev. Stat., 662.010 et seq.

Labor-Management Reporting and Disclosure Act of 1959

Sept. 14, 1959, P.L. 86-257, 73 Stat. 519, 29 U.S. Code §§ 153, 158, 159, 160, 164, 186, 187, 401, 402, 411 to 415, 431 to 440, 461 to 466, 481 to 483, 501 to 504, 521 to 531

Sept. 29, 1965 P.L. 89-216, 79 Stat. 888, 29 U.S. Code §§ 435, 437, 441, 502

Aug. 15, 1973, P.L. 93-95, 87 Stat. 314, 29 U.S. Code § 186

Continued

July 26, 1974, P.L. 93-360, 88 Stat. 396, 29 U.S. Code § 183

Nov. 6, 1978, P.L. 95-598, 29 U.S. Code § 402

Oct. 12, 1984, P.L. 98-473, 29 U.S. Code § 504

Dec. 7, 1987, P.L. 100-182, 20 U.S. Code § 504

Labor Mediation Act
La. Rev. Stat. Ann., 23:861 et seq.
Mich. Comp. Laws Ann., 423.1 et seq.
N.J. Stat. Ann., 34:13A-1 to 34:13A-13
Pa. Purdon's Stat., Title 43, § 211.31 et seq.
Wash. Rev. Code Ann., 49.08.010 et seq.

Labor Open Shop Law
Tex. Rev. Civ. Stat., Art. 5207a

Labor Organizations Act
Fla. Stat. Ann., 447.01 et seq.
Kan. Stat. Ann., 44-801 et seq.

Labor Organizations Liability Act
Tex. Rev. Civ. Stat., Art. 5154b

Labor Peace Act
Colo. Rev. Stat., 8-3-101 et seq.
Wis. Stat. Ann., 111.01 et seq.

Labor Picketing Act
Tex. Rev. Civ. Stat., Art. 5154d

Labor Pool Act
Fla. Stat. Ann., 448.20 et seq.

Labor Preference Law
Iowa Code Ann., 73.1 et seq.

Labor Recording Act
N.J. Stat. Ann., 34:15-96 et seq.

Labor Relations Act
See also National Labor Relations Act
Colo. Rev. Stat., 8-1-101 et seq.
Conn. Gen. Stat. Ann., § 31-101 et seq.
Del. Code of 1974, Title 19, § 110 et seq.
Haw. Rev. Stat. Ann., § 377-1 et seq.
Ida. Code 1947, 44-101 et seq.
Kan. Stat. Ann., 44-801 et seq.
Mass. Gen. Laws Ann., 150A:1 et seq.

Me. Rev. Stat. Ann. 1964, Title 26, § 891 et seq.
Mich. Comp. Laws Ann., 423.1 et seq.
Minn. Stat. Ann., 179.01 et seq.
Mo. Rev. Stat., 295.010 et seq.
N.H. Rev. Stat. 1955, 275:1 et seq.
N.Y. Labor Law (Consol. Laws Ch. 31) § 700 et seq.
Ore. Rev. Stat., 662.010 et seq.
Pa. Purdon's Stat., Title 43, § 211.1 et seq.
P.R. Laws Ann. 1954, Title 29, § 61 et seq.
R.I. Gen. Laws 1956, 28-7-1 et seq.
S.D. Codified Laws 1967, 60-9A-1 et seq.
Tex. Rev. Civ. Stat., Art. 5154a
Utah Code Ann. 1953, 34-19-1 et seq.
Vt. Stat. Ann., Title 21, § 1501 et seq.
Wis. Stat. Ann., 111.01 et seq.

Labor Relations Act (Agricultural)
Cal. Labor Code § 1140 et seq.

Labor Relations Act (Judicial Employees)
Me. Rev. Stat. Ann. 1964, Title 26, § 1281 et seq.

Labor Relations Act (Municipal Public Employees)
Me. Rev. Stat. Ann. 1964, Title 26, § 961 et seq.

Labor Relations Act (Municipal)
Vt. Stat. Ann. 1959, Title 21, § 1501 et seq.

Labor Relations Act (Public Employees)
See Public Employees Labor Relations Act

Labor Relations Act (Public Employment)
Minn. Stat. Ann., 179A.01 et seq.

Labor Relations Act (Public Utilities)
Va. Code 1950, § 40.1-52 et seq.

Labor Relations Act (State Employees)
Vt. Stat. Ann., Title 3, § 901 et seq.

Labor Relations Act (State Employment)
See State Employees Labor Relations Act

Labor Relations Act (University of Maine System)
Me. Rev. Stat. Ann. 1964, Title 26, § 1021 et seq.

Labor Safety Act
Wash. Rev. Code Ann., 49.17.010 et seq.

Labor Scrip Law
Ky. Rev. Stat. 1971, Supereded Vol., 337.040

Labor Secondary Strikes and Boycotts Act
Tex. Rev. Civ. Stat., Art. 5154f

Labor Underground Safety Act
Wash. Rev. Code Ann., 49.24.010 et seq.

Labor Union Control Act
S.D. Codified Laws 1967, 60-9-6 et seq.

Labor Union Democracy Act
Minn. Stat. Ann., 179.18 et seq.

Labor Union Dues Check-Off Law
Tex. Rev. Civ. Stat., Art. 5154e

Labor Union Officer Qualification Act
N.D. Cent. Code, 34-01-16

Labor Union Reporting Act
Conn. Gen. Stat. Ann., § 31-77

Labor Unions Act
Wash. Rev. Code Ann., 49.36.010 et seq.

Labor Unions and Corporations Campaign Finance Act
D.C. Code Ann., § 1-1441

Laboratories Act (Animal Disease)
Ill. Comp. Stat. 1992, Ch. 510, §§ 10/0.01, 10/1
Ill. Rev. Stat. 1991, Ch. 8, §§ 105.10, 105.11

Laboratories Certification Act (Clinical)
Neb. Rev. Stat. 1943, 71-6801 et seq.

Laboratory Act (Analytical-Biochemical-Biological)
Pa. Purdon's Stat., Title 35, § 2151 et seq.

Laboratory Act (Clinical)
Cal. Business and Professions Code § 1200 et seq.
Ill. Rev. Stat. 1989, Ch. 111 1/2, § 621-101 et seq.

Laboratory Act (Soil and Plant Analysis)
Neb. Rev. Stat. 1943, 2-3101 et seq.

Laboratory Animal Act of 1966
Aug. 24, 1966, P.L. 89-544, 80 Stat. 350, 7 U.S. Code §§ 2131 to 2154

Laboratory Certification Act (Water Quality)
Md. Ann. Code 1974, Art. HE, § 9-1001 et seq.

Laboratory Directors and Bio-analytical Laboratory Act
N.J. Rev. Stat. 1937, 45:9-42.1 et seq.

Laboratory Funding Act (Forensic)
Mich. Comp. Laws Ann., 12.201 et seq.

Laboratory Improvement Act (Environmental)
Cal. Health and Safety Code §§ 1010, 1029
Cal. Statutes 1988, Ch. 894

Laboratory Personnel Law (Clinical)
La. Rev. Stat. Ann., 37:1311 et seq.

Laboratory Review Board Act
Ill. Rev. Stat. 1991, Ch. 111 1/2, § 8001 et seq.

Laboratory Science Practice Act (Clinical)
Mont. Code Ann., 37-34-101 to 37-34-308
R.I. Gen. Laws 1956, 23-16.3-1 et seq.

Laborers Licensing Act (Hazardous Waste)
Cal. Penal Code §§ 311 to 313
Ga. Laws 1986, p. 3609
Ill. Rev. Stat. 1991, Ch. 111, § 7801 et seq.

Laborers' Lien Act
Ark. Code Ann. 1987, 18-43-101 et seq.
Ida. Code 1947, 45-606, 45-607
N.C. Gen. Stat. 1943, § 44A-1 et seq.
Okla. Stat. Ann., Title 42, § 92
Continued

Tenn. Code Ann., 66-13-101

Laborers' Lien Act (Mines and Wells)
Alaska Stat. 1962, § 34.35.125 et seq.

Laborers' Pension Act
Mass. Gen. Laws Ann., 32:77 et seq.

Lac Vieux Desert Band of Lake Superior Chippewa Indians Act
Sept. 8, 1988, P.L. 100-420, 25 U.S. Code §§ prec. 1300h, 1300h nt., 1300h-1-1300h-8
May 24, 1990, P.L. 101-301, 25 U.S. Code § 1300h-7
Feb. 12, 1996, P.L. 104-109, 25 U.S. Code § 1300h-3

Lacey Act (Game)
May 25, 1900, Ch. 553, 31 Stat. 187, 16 U.S. Code §§ 668d, 701

Lacey Act Amendments of 1981
Nov. 16, 1981, P.L. 97-79, 16 U.S. Code § 3371 nt.
June 25, 1984, P.L. 98-327, 16 U.S. Code § 1540
June 25, 1984, P.L. 98-327, 16 U.S. Code § 3375
Nov. 14, 1988, P.L. 100-653, 16 U.S. Code §§ 3372, 3373, 3375

Ladder Act
N.J. Stat. Ann., Superseded Vol., 34:5-93 et seq.

Lafayette Community Improvement Act
La. Acts 1968, No. 484

Lafayette County Recreation and Water Conservation and Control Act
Fla. Special Laws 1967, Ch. 67-1598

LaFramboise Carpenter MacKay Benzie Act (Game Bag Limit)
Mich. Comp. Laws Ann., 312.12

Lagomarsino Garrigus Act (Conservation Schools)
Cal. Education Code 1976, § 1790 et seq.

LaGuardia Economy Act
N.Y. Laws 1934, Ch. 178

Lajas Valley Public Irrigation Law
P.R. Laws Ann. 1954, Title 22, § 361 et seq.

Lake Andes-Wagner/Marty II Act of 1992
Oct. 30, 1992, P.L. 102-575, 106 Stat. 4677

Lake Arrowhead-Crestline Water Agency Act
Cal. Statutes 1962, 1st Ex. Sess., Ch. 40, p. 278

Lake Authority Act (Acworth)
Ga. Laws 1951, p. 265

Lake Bed Lease Act
Minn. Stat. Ann., 93.354

Lake Calumet Harbor Act
Ill. Rev. Stat. 1991, Ch. 19, § 112.90 et seq.

Lake Champlain Bridge Commission Act
N.Y. Laws 1927, Ch. 321

Lake Champlain Bridge Commission Compact
Vt. Acts 1927, No. 139
Vt. Stat. Ann., Title 19, § 1711 nt.

Lake Champlain Special Designation Act of 1990
Nov. 16, 1990, P.L.101-596, 33 U.S. Code § 1251 nt.
April 4, 1996, P.L. 104-127, 33 U.S. Code § 1270 nt.

Lake Charles Firemen's Pension and Relief Fund Act
La. Acts 1944, No. 186

Lake Charles, Louisiana Redevelopment Agency Act
La. Acts 1968, No. 272

Lake County Air and Water Pollution Control Act
Fla. Special Laws 1967, Ch. 67-1608

Lake County and Will County Metropolitan Exposition and Auditorium Authority Act
Ill. Rev. Stat. 1991, Ch. 85, § 1580-1 et seq.

Lake County Flood Control and Water Conservation District Act
Cal. Water Code, Appendix, § 62-1 et seq.

Lake County Land Cession Act
Ill. Rev. Stat. 1991, Ch. 1, §§ 4200, 4203

Lake County School Buildings Authority Act
Fla. Special Laws 1951, Ch. 27668

Lake Cuyamaca Recreation and Park District Act
Cal. Statutes 1961, Ch. 1654

Lake Erie and Ohio River Ship Canal Act
June 30, 1906, Ch. 3933, 34 Stat. 809

Lake Excavation Law
N.Y. Local Laws 1969, Town of Pound Ridge, p. 1982

Lake Front Act
Ill. Laws 1869, p. 245, No. 2

Lake George Anti-Litter Local Law
N.Y. Local Laws 1970, Town of Lake George, p. 2000

Lake George Environmental Preservation Law
N.Y. Local Laws 1972, Town of Lake George, p. 1964

Lake Improvement District Law
Minn. Stat. 1986, 103B.501 et seq.

Lake Lanier Islands Development Authority Act
Ga. Code Ann., 12-3-311 et seq.

Lake Level Act
Ind. Code Ann., 13-2-16-1 et seq.
Mich. Comp. Laws Ann., 281.61 et seq.

Lake Management Program Act
Ill. Rev. Stat. 1991, Ch. 19, § 1401 et seq.

Lake Michigan Shore Line Act
Ill. Rev. Stat. 1991, Ch. 19, § 1140 et seq.

Lake Project Compact (Jennings Randolph)
Md. Ann. Code 1974, Art. NR, § 8-4A-01 et seq.

Lake Providence and Rayville Louisiana Redevelopment Agency Act
La. Acts 1970, No. 525

Lake Quinsigamond State Park Loan Act
Mass. Acts 1955, Ch. 519

Lake Tahoe Acquisitions Bond Act
Cal. Government Code § 66950 et seq.

Lake Wales Sewer Revenue Act
Fla. Special Laws 1947, Ch. 24648

Lake Worth Downtown Development Authority Act
Fla. Special Laws 1972, Ch. 72-592

Lake Worth Municipal Courts of Record Act
Tex. Government Code, § 30.01251 et seq.

Lake Worth Urban Renewal Law
Fla. Special Laws 1965, Ch. 65-1793

Lakeland Downtown Development Authority Act
Fla. Special Laws 1977, Ch. 77-588

Lakeland Hospital Revenue Bond Act
Fla. Special Laws 1970, Ch. 70-775

Lakeland Lanier County Charter Commission Act
Ga. Laws 1986, p. 3609

Lakeland Urban Renewal Law
Fla. Special Laws 1961, Ch. 61-2382

Lakes and Streams Act
Mich. Comp. Laws Ann., 281.731 et seq.

Lakes, Streams, and Rivers Act
Ill. Rev. Stat. 1991, Ch. 19, § 51.9 et seq.

Lakeshores Protection Act
Mont. Code Ann., 75-7-201 et seq.

Lama Mitchell Law (Limited Profit Housing)
N.Y. Private Housing Finance Law. (Consol. Laws Ch. 44B) § 10 et seq.

Lamar County Court Act
Tex. Government Code, § 25.1411 et seq.

Lamar County Emergency Communications Service District Act
Ga. Laws 1990, p. 4871

Lamar County Livestock and Agricultural Exposition Authority Act
Ga. Laws 1996, p. 3703

Lamar County Water and Sewer Authority Act
Ga. Laws 1991, p. 3942

Lamprey River Study Act of 1991
Dec. 11, 1991, P.L. 102-214, 16 U.S. Code § 1271 nt.

Lancaster Demolition Law
N.Y. Local Laws 1972, Village of Lancaster, p. 3558

Lancaster Montoya Appraisal Act
Cal. Civil Code § 1922 et seq.

Lancaster Sewer District Sewerage Loan Act
Mass. Acts 1952, Ch. 43

Lance Fox-Crane Act (Urban Development)
N.J. Stat. Ann., 40:55C-40 et seq.

Lances Law Child Safety Reform Act
Cal. Penal Code §§ 11165.12, 11166.9, 11167.5, 11169, 11170, 11170.5

Land Acquisition Act (Bird Preserve)
Ill. Comp. Stat. 1992, Ch. 5, §§ 580/0.01, 580/1
Ill. Rev. Stat. 1991, Ch. 1, §§ 4050, 4051

Land Acquisition Act (Gathering Line)
N.M. Stat. Ann., 70-3A-1 et seq.

Land Acquisition Act (Particle Accelerator)
Ill. Rev. Stat. 1991, Ch. 127, § 47.20 et seq.

Land Acquisition Act (Upper Mississippi)
Ill. Rev. Stat. 1991, Ch. 1, §§ 4000, 4001

Land Acquisition and Borrowing Act (Project 70)
Pa. Purdon's Stat., Title 72, § 3946.1 et seq.

Land Acquisition and Recreation Opportunities Act (Green Acres)
N.J. Stat. Ann., 13:8A-35 et seq.

Land Acquisition Policy Act of 1960
July 14, 1960, P.L. 86-645, 74 Stat. 502, 33 U.S. Code §§ 596, 597

Land Acquisition Policy and Relocation Assistance Act
Ga. Code Ann., 22-4-1 et seq.

Land Act
Alaska Stat. 1962, § 38.05.005 et seq.
Ariz. Rev. Stat. Ann., § 37-101 et seq.
Haw. Session Laws 1895, Special Session, Act 26
P.R. Laws Ann. 1954, Title 28, § 241 et seq.

Land Act (Aliens)
Wis. Stat. Ann., 710.01 et seq.
Wyo. Stat. Ann., § 34-15-101

Land Act (County)
Ore. Rev. Stat., 275.020 et seq.

Land Act (Reclamation)
Mont. Rev. Code 1947, 81-2101 et seq.

Land Act (Survey Restoration and Perpetuation of Public)
Fla. Stat. Ann., 177.501 et seq.

Land Administration Act
P.R. Laws Ann. 1954, Title 23, § 311 et seq.

Land Administration and Management Act (County)

S.D. Codified Laws 1967, 7-31-1 et seq.

Land and Buildings Act (Local)

N.J. 40A:12-1 et seq.

Land and Water Act (Recreational Use of)

Pa. Purdon's Stat., Title 68, § 477-1 et seq.

Land and Water Areas Act (Recreational Use of)

Ill. Rev. Stat. 1989, Ch. 70, § 31 et seq.

Land and Water Conservation and Reclamation Act

Pa. Purdon's Stat., Title 32, § 5101 et seq.

Land and Water Conservation Fund Act of 1965

Sept. 8, 1080, P.L. 96-344, 16 U.S. Code § 46016a

Sept. 3, 1964, P.L. 88-578, 78 Stat. 897, 16 U.S. Code §§ 460d, 460l-4 to 460l-11; 23 U.S. Code § 120 nt.

July 9, 1965, P.L. 89-72, 79 Stat. 218, 16 U.S. Code § 460l-5

July 15, 1968, P.L. 90-401, 82 Stat. 354, 16 U.S. Code §§ 460l-5 460l-7, 460l-9, 460l-10a to 460l-10c

July 7, 1970, P.L. 91-308, 84 Stat. 410, 16 U.S. Code §§ 406l-5 406l-10a

Dec. 31, 1970, P.L. 91-605, 84 Stat. 1743, 16 U.S. Code § 460l-11

July 11, 1972, P.L. 92-347, 86 Stat. 459, 16 U.S. Code § 460l-6a

Aug. 1, 1973, P.L. 93-81, 87 Stat. 178, 16 U.S. Code § 460l-6a

Dec. 28, 1973, P.L. 93-205, 87 Stat. 902, 16 U.S. Code § 460l-9

June 7, 1974, P.L. 93-303, 88 Stat. 182, 16 U.S. Code §§ 460l-6a 460l-8, 460l-10

June 10, 1977, P.L. 95-42, 16 U.S. Code §§ 460l-5 et seq.

Nov. 10, 1978, P.L. 95-625, 16 U.S. Code § 460l-8

March 10, 1980, P.L. 96-203, 16 U.S. Code § 460l9

Jan. 6, 1983, P.L. 97-424, 16 U.S. Code § 460l-11

Oct. 12, 1984, P.L. 98-473

Oct. 22, 1986, P.L. 99-514, 16 U.S. Code § 460l-11(a)

Nov. 10, 1986, P.L. 99-645, 16 U.S. Code §§ 460l-8, 460l-9

Nov. 17, 1986, P.L. 99-663, 16 U.S. Code § 544g

Dec. 22, 1987, P.L. 100-203, 16 U.S. Code §§ 4601-5, 4601-6a

Nov. 5, 1990, P.L. 101-508, 16 U.S. Code § 460l-11

Dec. 18, 1991, P.L. 102-240, 16 U.S. Code § 460l-11

Aug. 10, 1993, P.L. 103-66, 16 U.S. Code § 460l-6a

Sept. 13, 1994, P.L. 103-322, 16 U.S. Code § 4601-8

Nov. 2, 1994, P.L. 103-437, 16 U.S. Code §§ 460l-6a, 460l-8, 460l-9

Dec. 21, 1995, P.L. 104-66, 16 U.S. Code § 460I-6a

Nov. 12, 1996, P.L. 104-333, 16 U.S. Code §§ 460l-9, 460l-10e

Nov. 14, 1997, 105-83, 16 U.S. Code § 460l-10e

Oct. 30, 1998, P.L. 105-327, 16 U.S. Code § 460l-6a

Land and Water Environmental Management Act

Fla. Stat. Ann., 380.012 et seq.

Land and Water Resources Compact Act (Northeastern)

N.H. Rev. Stat. 1955, 489-A:1

Land Assembly and Redevelopment Act

Mass. Gen. Laws Ann., 121A:1 et., 121B:1 et seq.

Land Bank Act

Cal. Public Resources Code § 8600 et seq.

Land Betterments Act

Me. Rev. Stat. Ann. 1964, Title 14, § 6956 et seq.

Land Between the Lakes Protection Act of 1998

Oct. 21, 1998, P.L. 105-277, 101(e), Title V, 112 Stat. 2681, 16 U.S. Code § 460lll nt.

Land Board Act
Wash. Rev. Code Ann., 79.01.048 et seq.

Land Cession Act (Champaign)
Ill. Comp. Stat. 1992, Ch. 5, §§ 525/0.01, 525/1

Land Cession Act (Chicago)
Ill. Comp. Stat. 1992, Ch. 5, §§ 515/0.01, 515/1

Land Cession Act (Home for Disabled Soldiers)
Ill. Rev. Stat. 1991, Ch. 1, § 3701

Land Cession Act (Lake County)
Ill. Rev. Stat. 1991, Ch. 1, § 4203

Land Cession Act (St. Clair)
Ill. Rev. Stat. 1991, Ch. 1, §§ 3800, 3801

Land Clearance Act
Ill. Rev. Stat. 1991, Ch. 67 1/2, § 63 et seq.

Land Clearance for Redevelopment Authority Law
Mo. Rev. Stat., 99.300 et seq.

Land Commissioners Act
Ark. Code Ann. 1987, 22-5-201 et seq.

Land Condemnation Act
D.C. Code Supp. 1966, § 16-1301 et seq.

Land Condemnation Act (Lincoln Park Commissioners)
Ill. Rev. Stat. 1991, Ch. 105, § 78.9 et seq.

Land Condemnation Act (Park Commissioners)
Ill. Rev. Stat. 1991, Ch. 105, § 53.9 et seq.

Land Conservation Act
Cal. Government Code § 51200 et seq.
Fla. Stat. Ann., 259.01 et seq.
Ind. Code Ann., 13-4-3-1 et seq.

Land Conservation and Bituminous Mine Subsidence Act
Pa. Purdon's Stat., Title 52, § 1406.1 et seq.

Land Conservation and Development Act
Ore. Rev. Stat., 197.005 et seq.

Land Conservation and Reclamation Act (Surface-Mining)
Kan. Stat. Ann., 49-601 et seq.
Pa. Purdon's Stat., Title 52, § 1396.1 et seq.

Land Conservation and Reclamation Act (Surface)
Ill. Rev. Stat. 1989, Ch. 96 1/2, § 7901.01 et seq.

Land Conservation Easement Act
Utah Code Ann. 1953, 57-18-1 et seq.

Land Contract Recording Act
Ohio Rev. Code 1953, 317.08, 5301.01, 5301.23, 5301.25, 5301.331

Land Contracts Act
Mich. Comp. Laws 1948, 565.351 et seq.

Land Contracts Moratorium Act
Mich. Public Acts 1933, No. 122, § 1, Subsec. 25a et seq.

Land Contracts Registration Act
N.C. Gen. Stat. 1943, § 47-17 et seq.

Land Conveyance Act (Park Commissioners)
Ill. Rev. Stat. 1991, Ch. 105, § 114.9 et seq.

Land Court Act
Haw. Rev. Stat. Ann., § 501-1 et seq.
Mass. Gen Laws 1990, 185:1 et seq.

Land Damage Act (Aeronautics)
S.C. Code Ann. 1976, § 55-3-60

Land Development Act
Mont. Code Ann. 1983, 15-24-1301 et seq.
Wash. Rev. Code Ann., 58.19.010 et seq.

Land Development Act (Real Estate)
Wash. Rev. Code Ann., 58.19.940

Land Development and Subdivision Review Enabling Act
R.I. Gen. Laws 1956, 45-23-25 et seq.

Land Development Consumer Protection Act
Ore. Rev. Stat., 91.501, 94.004 et seq.,
92.990, 696.301

Land Disposal Program Flexibility Act of 1996
March 26, 1996, P.L. 104-119, 42 U.S. Code
§ 6901 nt.

Land Districts Act
Alaska Comp. Laws Ann. 1949, § 47-2-12

Land Division Act
Mich. Comp. Laws Ann., 560.101 et seq.

Land Drainage Act
Wis. Stat. Ann., 88.01 et seq.

Land Exchange Facilitation Fund Act
Mich. Comp. Laws Ann., 322.461 et seq.

Land Fill Areas Act
Tenn. Code Ann., 68-213-101 et seq.

Land Fill Law
N.Y. Local Laws 1970, Town of Erwin, p.
1486
N.Y. Local Laws 1971, Town of Webster, p.
3680
N.Y. Local Laws 1973, Village of Ardsley, p.
3162

Land Fire Protection Law
Haw. Rev. Stat. Ann., § 185-1 et seq.

Land for Armories Act
Ill. Rev. Stat. 1991, Ch. 129, § 310.9 et seq.

Land for Cemeteries Act (City Sale or Lease)
Ill. Rev. Stat. 1991, Ch. 21, §§ 6h, 7

Land Forfeiture Act
Cal. Public Resources Code § 7771 et seq.
W. Va. Code 1966, § 11A-4-2

Land Grant Act
July 2, 1864, Ch. 217, 13 Stat. 365

Land Grant Act (Schools)
Alaska Comp. Laws Ann. 1949, § 47-2-21 et
seq.

Land Grant Adjustment Act
See Adjustment Act (Railroad Land Grants)

Land Installment Contracts Act
Md. Ann. Code 1974, Art. RP, § 10-101 et
seq.

Land Jurisdiction Act (Federal and State)
Ill. Rev. Stat. 1991, Ch. 1, § 7151 et seq.

Land Liability Act (Recreational)
Miss. Code Ann. 1972, § 89-2-21 et seq.

Land Management Act
Fla. Stat. Ann., 380.012 et seq.

Land Management Act (Coastal Public)
Tex. Natural Resources Code, § 33.001 et
seq.

Land Management Corporation Act
R.I. Gen. Laws 1956, 37-18-1 et seq.

Land Not Used for Burial Act (Cemetery Company)
Ill. Comp. Stat. 1992, Ch. 765, §§ 810/0.01,
810/1

Land Office Act
Tex. Natural Resources Code, § 31.001 et
seq.

Land Office Board Act
Mich. Comp. Laws 1948, 211.351 et seq.

Land Office Building Act
N.M. Stat. Ann., 19-12-1 et seq.

Land Offices Reorganization Act
Alaska Comp. Laws Ann. 1949, § 47-2-41 et
seq.

Land Owner Excavation Protection Act (Adjacent)
Ill. Comp. Stat. 1992, Ch. 765, §§ 140/0.01,
140/1

Land Ownership Act (Agricultural)
Ill. Comp. Stat. 1992, Ch. 765, § 55/0.01 et
seq.
Ill. Rev. Stat. 1991, Ch. 5, § 2100 et seq.

Land Ownership and Transfer Act (Cemetery)
Ill. Comp. Stat. 1992, Ch. 765, § 820/0.01 et seq.

Land Patent Act
Ill. Rev. Stat. 1991, Ch. 30, §§ 40.9, 41

Land Policy Act
N.C. Gen. Stat. 1943, § 113A-150 et seq.

Land Preservation Act
Mont. Code Ann., 75-7-101 et seq.

Land Protection Act
Del. Code of 1974, Title 7, § 7501 et seq.

Land Protection and Solid Waste Management Act
N.D. Cent. Code, 23-29-01 et seq.

Land Purchase Act (Alaska Trade Purposes)
Alaska Comp. Laws Ann. 1949, § 47-2-71 et seq.

Land Reclamation Act (Mined)
Ariz. Rev. Stat. Ann., § 49-1201 et seq.

Land Reclamation Act (Mining)
Colo. Rev. Stat., 34-32-101 et seq.

Land Reclamation Act (Open-Cut)
Ark. Acts 1991, No. 827

Land Reclamation Act (Open Cut)
See Open Cut Land Reclamation Act

Land Reclamation Act (Surface Mining)
Mo. Rev. Stat., 444. 760 et seq.
S.D. Codified Laws 1967, 45-6A-1 et seq.

Land Reclamation Act for the Extraction of Construction Materials
Colo. Rev. Stat., 34-32.5-101 et seq.

Land Reclamation and Improvement Authority Act
Mich. Comp. Laws Ann., 125.2451 et seq.

Land Recordation Act
Miss. Code Ann. 1972, § 89-5-1 et seq.

Land Recording Act
Mont. Code Ann., 70-21-201 et seq.

Land Recycling Act
Minn. Laws, 1992, Ch. 512

Land Recycling and Environmental Remediation Standards Act
Pa. Purdon's Stat., Title 35, § 6026.101 et seq.

Land Redevelopment Authority Act
Mo. Rev. Stat., 99.300 et seq.

Land Registration Act
Alaska Stat. 1962, § 34.10.010 et seq.
Ga. Code Ann., 44-2-40 et seq.
Ill. Rev. Stat. 1991, Ch. 30, § 44h et seq.
Mass. Gen. Laws Ann., 185:1 et seq.

Land Remediation Act
Ida. Code 1947, 39-7201 et seq.

Land Remote-Sensing Commercialization Act Amendments of 1987
Oct. 30, 1987, P.L. 100-147, 15 U.S. Code §§ 4201 nt., 4212, 4228, 4262, 4264, 4273

Land Remote-Sensing Commercialization Act of 1984
July 17, 1984, P.L. 98-365, 15 U.S. Code §§ 4201 et seq., 4211, et seq., 4221 et seq., 4241 et seq., 4261 et seq., 4271 et seq., 4291, 4292
Oct. 30, 1987, P.L. 100-147, 15 U.S. Code §§ 4212, 4228, 4262, 4264, 4273
Oct. 28, 1992, P.L. 102-555, 15 U.S. Code §§ 4201 et seq., 4201 nt.
Oct. 29, 1992, P.L. 102-567, 15 U.S. Code §§ 4242, 4272

Land Remote-Sensing Commercialization Act of 1985
July 11, 1985, P.L. 99-62, 15 U.S. Code § 4278

Land Remote Sensing Policy Act of 1992
Oct. 28, 1992, P.L. 102-555, 15 U.S. Code §§ 5601 et seq., 5601 nt.
Oct, 28, 1998, P.L. 105-303, 15 U.S. Code §§ 5621, 5622

Land Reutilization Act
Neb. Rev. Stat. 1943, 77-3201 et seq.
N.Y. Local Laws 1972, Town of Erwin, p. 1352

Land Reutilization Act (Municipal)
Mo. Rev. Stat., 92.700 et seq.

Land Sale Act (Park Commissioners)
Ill. Rev. Stat. 1991, Ch. 105, § 112.9 et seq.

Land Sales Act
Ga. Code Ann., 44-3-1 et seq.
Ill. Rev. Stat. 1987, Ch. 30, § 371 et seq.
Mich. Comp. Laws Ann., 565.801 et seq.

Land Sales Act (Installment)
See Installment Land Sales Act

Land Sales Act (Out of State)
Ga. Code Ann., 44-3-40 et seq.

Land Sales Act (Subdivisions)
Va. Code 1950, § 55-336 et seq.

Land Sales Full Disclosure Act
N.H. Rev. Stat. 1955, 489-A:1 et seq.
N.J. Stat. Ann., 45:15-16.3 et seq.

Land Sales Practices Act
See Uniform Land Sales Practices Act

Land Sales Practices Act (Out of State)
Mont. Code Ann., 76-4-1201 et seq.

Land Sales Registration Act
Ill. Rev. Stat. 1991, Ch. 30, § 1101 et seq.

Land Settlement Act
Cal. Government Code § 14705 et seq., § 13230
S.D. Laws 1919, Ch. 315
Wash. Rev. Code Ann., 89.04.005 et seq.

Land Stewardship Program Act (Agricultural)
Cal. Public Resources Code § 10200 et seq.

Land Subdivision Act
N.M. Stat. Ann., 47-5-1 et seq.
Va. Code 1950, § 15.1-465 et seq.

Land Subdivision Rules and Regulations
N.Y. Local Laws 1966, Town of Campbell, p. 819
N.Y. Local Laws 1970, Village of Cazenovia, pp. 1233, 3146
N.Y. Local Laws 1972, Town of Erwin, p. 1352
N.Y. Local Laws 1973, Village of Lewiston, p. 3455
Tenn. Code Ann. 1955, 62-1801 et seq.

Land Survey Monuments Act
Ill. Rev. Stat. 1991, Ch. 133, § 60-0.1 et seq.

Land Surveying and Engineering Act
N.C. Gen. Stat. 1943, § 89C-1 et seq.
N.M. Stat. 1978, 61-23-1 et seq.

Land Surveying and Engineering Practice Act
N.M. Stat. Ann., 61-23-1 et seq.

Land, Surveying, Architectural and Engineering Qualifications Based Selection Act
Ill. Rev. Stat. 1991, Ch. 127, § 4151-1 et seq.

Land Surveying, Architectural and Engineering Services Procurement Act
Wyo. Stat. Ann., § 9-2-1027 et seq.

Land Surveying Practice Act (Professional)
Tex. Rev. Civ. Stat. 1974, Art. 5282c

Land Surveying Registration Act
N.M. Stat. Ann., 61-23-4 et seq.

Land Surveyor Act (Professional)
Ill. Rev. Stat. 1989, Ch. 111, § 3251 et seq.

Land Surveyor, Engineer and Geologist Registration Law
Pa. 1992 Pamph. Laws, No. 151

Land Surveyors Act
Ark. Code Ann. 1987, 17-41-103 et seq.
Cal. Business and Professions Code § 8700 et seq.
Fla. Stat. Ann., 472.001 et seq.
Ill. Rev. Stat. 1991, Ch. 111, § 3201 et seq.
Ky. Rev. Stat. 1971, 322.010 et seq.
Continued

Md. Ann., Code 1974, BO, § 15-101 et seq.
Mich. Comp. Laws Ann., 338.551 et seq.
Nev. Rev. Stat. 1979 Reprint, 625.250 et seq.
N.H. Rev. Stat. 1955, 310-A:53 et seq.
Ore. Rev. Stat., 672.002 et seq.
Tenn. Code Ann., 62-18-101 et seq.
Tex. Rev. Civ. Stat., Art. 5282c
Vt. Stat. Ann., Title 26, § 2501 et seq.

Land Surveyors Act (Professional)
Cal. Business and Professions Code § 8700 et seq.

Land Surveyors and Engineers Registration Act
Pa. Purdon's Stat., Title 63, § 148 et seq.

Land Surveyors and Professional Engineers Licensing Act
Utah Code Ann. 1953, 58-22-101 et seq.

Land Surveyors, Architects and Engineers Registration Act
Alaska Stat. 1962, § 08.48.011 et seq.

Land Surveyor's Registration Act
Kan. Stat. Ann., 74-7001 et seq.

Land Tax Collection Act
Mo. Rev. Stat., 141.210 et seq.

Land Tax Credit Act (Agricultural)
Iowa Code Ann., 426.1 et seq.

Land Tenant Act
Tex. Property Code, § 54.001 et seq.

Land Title Registration Act
Alaska Stat. 1962, § 34.10.010 et seq.
Cal. Statutes 1915, p. 1932
Colo. Rev. Stat., 38-36-101 et seq.
Ga. Code Ann., 44-2-40 et seq.
Haw. Rev. Stat. Ann., § 501-1 et seq.
Ill. Rev. Stat. 1991, Ch. 30, § 44h et seq.
Mass. Gen. Laws Ann., 185:26 et seq.
Minn. Stat. Ann., 508.01 et seq.
Miss. Code Ann. 1972, 89-5-1 et seq.
Mont. Rev. Code 1947, 73-201 et seq.
N.C. Gen. Stat. 1943, § 43-1 et seq.
Neb. Laws 1915, Ch. 225
Ohio Rev. Code 1953, 5309.02 et seq.

Ore. Rev. Stat. 1953, 94.005 et seq.
S.D. Codified Laws 1967, 43-30-1 et seq.
Tenn. Private Acts 1917, Ch. 63
Utah Laws 1917, Ch. 28
Va. Code 1950, § 55-112
Wash. Rev. Code Ann., 65.12.005 et seq.

Land Title Simplification Act
Okla. Stat. Ann., Title 16, § 61 et seq.

Land Title Trust Fund Act
N.M. Stat. Ann., 58-28-1 to 58-28-8

Land Titles Act (Konohikis)
Haw. Session Laws 1852, p. 28, June 19, 1852

Land Titles Regulation Law
Cal. Public Resources Code §§ 6211, 6212

Land Transfer Act (State)
Ill. Laws 1994, P.A. 88-661

Land Transfer Act (University of Illinois at Chicago)
Ill. Rev. Stat. 1991, Ch. 144, § 70.01 et seq.

Land Trust Act
Fla. Stat. Ann., 689.071
Mo. Rev. Stat., 141.210 et seq.

Land Trust Act (Sale of Residential Property)
Ill. Rev. Stat. 1991, Ch. 29, § 8.30 et seq.

Land Trust Beneficial Interest Disclosure Act
Ill. Rev. Stat. 1991, Ch. 148, § 70 et seq.

Land Trust Recordation and Transfer Tax Act
Ill. Rev. Stat. 1987, Ch. 115 § 92a

Land Trust Successor Trustee Act
Ill. Rev. Stat. 1989, Ch. 148, § 60 et seq.

Land Trustee as Creditor Act
Ill. Rev. Stat. 1991, Ch. 148, § 80 et seq.

Land Use Act
Colo. Rev. Stat., 24-65-101 et seq.
Utah Code Ann. 1953, 63-28-1 et seq.

Land Use and Development Act
Vt. Stat. Ann., Title 10, § 6001 et seq.

Land Use and Environmental Dispute Resolution Act
Fla. Stat. Ann., 70.51

Land Use and Housing Omnibus Act of 1995
Cal. Statutes 1995, Ch. 686

Land Use and Housing Omnibus Act of 1996
Cal. Statutes 1996, Ch. 799

Land Use Control Enabling Act (Local Government)
Colo. Rev. Stat., 29-20-101 et seq.

Land Use Easement Act
N.M. Stat. Ann., 47-12-1 et seq.

Land Use Planning Act
Ore. Rev. Stat., 197.225 et seq.
Wyo. Stat. Ann., § 9-8-101 et seq.

Land Use Planning Act (Local)
Ida. Code 1947, 67-6501 et seq.

Land Use Regulation and Planning Act (Comprehensive)
Me. Rev. Stat. Ann. 1964, Title 30-A, § 4311 et seq.

Lander County Airport Authority Act
Nev. Statutes 1983, Ch. 458, p. 1208

Landfill Abatement Act (Metropolitan)
Minn. Stat. Ann., 473.841 et seq.

Landfill Site Closure, Remediation and Redevelopment Act (Municipal)
N.J. Stat. Ann., 13:1E-116.1 et seq.

Landing and Taking Off Restrictions Act (Aircraft)
Ill. Comp. Stat. 1992, Ch. 620, § 15/0.01 et seq.

Landing Field and General County Airport Act
Ill. Rev. Stat. 1991, Ch. 15 1/2, § 68.90 et seq.

Landlord and Tenant Act
See Uniform Residential Landlord and Tenant Act
D.C. Code Ann., § 45-1401 et seq.
Del. Code of 1974, Title 25, § 5101 et seq.
Fla. Stat. Ann., 83.001 et seq.
Ga. Code Ann., 44-7-1 et seq.
Haw. Rev. Stat. Ann., § 666-1 et seq.
Ill. Rev. Stat. 1991, Ch. 80
Kan. Stat. Ann., 58-2501 et seq.
Ky. Rev. Stat. 1971, 383.010 et seq.
Md. Ann. Code 1974, Art. RP, § 8-101 et seq.
Mo. Rev. Stat., 441. 010 et seq.
Mont. Rev. Code 1991, 70-24-101 et seq.
N.C. Gen. Stat. 1943, § 42-1 et seq.
N.H. Rev. Stat. 1955, 540:1 et seq.
N.J. Stat. Ann., 2A:42-1 et seq., 46:8-1 et seq.
N.M. Stat. Ann., 47-8-1 et seq.
Ohio Rev. Code 1953, 5321.01 et seq.
Okla. Stat. Ann., Title 41
Pa. Purdon's Stat., Title 68, § 250.101 et seq.
S.C. Code Ann. 1976, § 27-33-10 et seq.
Wash. Rev. Code Ann., 59.04.010 et seq., 59.18.010 et seq.
W. Va. Code 1966, § 37-6-1 et seq.

Landlord and Tenant Act (Disposition of Personal Property)
Fla. Stat. Ann., 715.10 et seq.
Neb. Rev. Stat. 1943, 69-2301 et seq.

Landlord and Tenant Act (Mini-self-storage)
Fla. Stat. Ann., 83.801 et seq.

Landlord and Tenant Act (Mobile Homes)
See Mobile Home Landlord and Tenant Act

Landlord and Tenant Act (Nonresidential)
Fla. Stat. Ann., 83.001 et seq.

Landlord and Tenant Act (Personal Property Disposition)
Neb. Rev. Stat. 1943, 69-2301 et seq.

Landlord and Tenant Act (Residential, Mobile Home Parks)
Ariz. Rev. Stat. Ann., § 33-1401 et seq.

Landlord and Tenant Act (Residential)
See also Uniform Residential Landlord and
Tenant Act
Miss. Code Ann. 1972, § 89-8-1 et seq.

**Landlord and Tenant Act (Summary
Proceedings)**
N.Y. Real Property Actions and Proceedings
Law (Consol. Laws Ch. 81) § 701 et seq.

**Landlord and Tenant Review Board Law
(Spring Valley)**
N.Y. Local Laws 1971, Village of Spring
Valley, p. 4599

Landlord and Tenant Security Deposit Act
Fla. Stat. Ann., 83.49

Landlord Eviction Remedies Act
N.C. Gen. Stat. 1943, § 42-25.6 et seq.

Landlord Tenant Act (Mobile Home)
Fla. Stat. Ann., 83.40 et seq.
Wash. Rev. Code Ann., 59.20.010 et seq.

Landlord Tenant Act (Residential)
Fla. Stat. Ann., 83.40 et seq.
Haw. Rev. Stat. Ann., § 521-1 et seq.
Wash. Rev. Code Ann., 59.18.010 et seq.

Landlord Tenant Review Board Law
N.Y. Local Laws 1973, Village of Suffern, p.
3802

Landlord's Crops Lien Act
Ill. Rev. Stat. 1991, Ch. 110, § 9-316

Landlord's Lien Act
Ark. Code Ann. 1987, 18-41-101 et seq.
Ind. Code Ann., 32-7-1-18
Iowa Code Ann., 570.1 et seq.
N.J. Rev. Stat. 1937, 2A:42-1 et seq.
N.M. Stat. Ann., 48-3-5
Tenn. Code Ann., 66-12-101 et seq.
Tex. Property Code, § 54.001 et seq.
Va. Code 1950, § 55-231
Wash. Rev. Code Ann., 60.72.010 et seq.

Landlords Lien Act (Apartment Houses)
Ore. Rev. Stat., 90.400

Landlords Preference Act
Pa. Purdon's Stat., Title 39, § 96

Landmark Destruction Act
Mo. Rev. Stat. 1969, 560.530

Landmark Preservation Act
N.Y. City Adm. Code 1985, § 25-301 et seq.

Landmarks and Historic District Act
N.M. Stat. Ann., 3-22-1 et seq.

Landmarks and Historic District Law
N.Y. Local Laws 1973, Town of Pound
Ridge, p. 2818

Landowner Notification Act (Mining)
Mont. Code Ann., 82-2-301 et seq.

Landowners' Bill of Rights
Minn. Stat. Ann., 84.0274

**Landowner's Liability (Recreational
Entrant Act)**
Wis. Stat. 1981, 29.68

Landrum-Griffin Act
See Labor Management Reporting And
Disclosure Act Of 1959

Landrum-Griffin Act (Labor Reform)
Mont. Code Ann., 82-2-301 et seq.

Lands Acquisition Act (Open Space)
See Open Space Lands Acquisition Act

Lands and Buildings Act (Local)
N.J. Stat. Ann., 40A:12-1 et seq.

Lands Cession Act (Federal)
S.C. Code Ann. 1976, § 3-1-110 et seq.

Lands Disposition Act (Subdivided)
See Subdivided Lands Disposition Act

Lands Management Act (Open)
N.J. Stat. Ann., 13:1B-15.131 et seq.

**Lands Management Act (State Wildlife and
Recreation)**
Wash. Rev. Code Ann., 43-98A-010 et seq.

Lands Protection Act (Geneva Freshwater)
Fla. Stat. Ann., 373.4597

Lands Protection Act (Natural)
N.M. Stat. Ann., 75-5-1 et seq.

Lands Protection Act (State Owned)
Mich. Comp. Laws Ann., 322.141 et seq.

Landscape Architect Act
Conn. Gen. Stat. Ann., § 20-367 et seq.
Ill. Rev. Stat. 1989, Ch. 111, § 8101 et seq.
Mich. Comp. Laws Ann., 338.1201 et seq.
Neb. Rev. Stat. 1943, 81-8, 184 et seq.

Landscape Architect Registration and Licensing Act
Ida. Code 1947, 54-3001 et seq.
Mont. Code Ann., 37-66-101 et seq.

Landscape Architects Act
Md. Ann. Code 1974, Art. BO, § 9-101 et seq.
N.M. Stat. Ann., 61-24B-1 et seq.
S.C. Code Ann. 1976, § 40-28-10 et seq.

Landscape Architects, Engineers, Land Surveyors and Architects Registration Act
Alaska Stat. 1962, § 08.48.011 et seq.

Landscape Architects Licensing Act
Utah Code Ann. 1953, 58-53-1 et seq.

Landscape Architects Registration and Licensing Article of the State Architectural Act
Okla. Stat. Ann., Title 59, § 45.25 et seq.

Landscape Architects Registration Law
Pa. Purdon's Stat., Title 63, § 901 et seq.

Landscape Architectural Practice Act
Miss. Code Ann. 1972, § 73-2-1 et seq.

Landscape Architectural Title Act
Ark. Code Ann. 1987, 17-29-101 et seq.

Landscape Architecture Act
Cal. Business and Professions Code § 5615 et seq.
Ill. Rev. Stat. 1991, Ch. 111, § 8101 et seq.

Landscape Contractors Law
Ore. Rev. Stat., 671.510 et seq.

Landscape Irrigation Contractor Certification Act
N.J. Stat. Ann., 45:5AA-1 to 45:5AA-3

Landscaping Act (Water Conservation)
Cal. Government Code § 65590 et seq.

Landscaping and Lighting Act
Cal. Streets and Highways Code § 22500 et seq.

Landslide Hazard Identification Act
Cal. Public Resources Code § 2670 et seq.

Lanesborough Garden Circle Sewerage Loan Act
Mass. Acts 1951, Ch. 133

Laney Act (Levee Improvement Districts)
Tex. Water Code, § 57.011 et seq.

Langley-Poole Act (Confederate Veterans)
Ala. Code 1975, § 31-8-1 et seq.

Language Act
P.R. Laws Ann. 1954, Title 1, § 51 et seq.

Language and Culture Education Act (American Indian)
Minn. Stat. Ann., 126.45 et seq.

Language Assistance Services Act
Ill. Comp. Stat. 1992, Ch. 210, §§ 87/1 to 87/15

Language Development Specialist Act
Cal. Education Code 1976, §§ 44475 et seq., 52163, 52171.6

Language Proficiency Act
Colo. Rev. Stat., 22-24-101 et seq.

Language Simplification Act (Health Insurance)
Okla. Stat. Ann., Title 36, § 3641 et seq.

Language Simplification Act (Insurance)
Ore. Rev. Stat., 743.100 et seq.

Language Simplification Act (Property and Casualty)
Mont. Code Ann., 33-15-333 et seq.

Language Simplification Law (Policy)
N.M. Stat. Ann., 59A-19-1 et seq.

Language Speech Pathology and Audiology Practice Act
Ill. Rev. Stat. 1991, Ch. 111, § 7901 et seq.

Lanham Patent Act
Aug. 5, 1939, Ch. 451, 53 Stat. 1212 (See 35 U.S. Code §§ 134, 135, 141, 145, 146)

Lanham Public War Housing Act
Oct. 14, 1940, Ch. 862, 54 Stat. 1125, 42 U.S. Code §§ 1521 to 1524, 1531 to 1535, 1541 to 1552, 1561 to 1564, 1571 to 1574
April 29, 1941, Ch. 80, 55 Stat. 147, 42 U.S. Code §§ 1521, 1523
June 28, 1941, Ch. 260, 55 Stat. 361, 42 U.S. Code §§ 1521, 1523, 1531 to 1534, 1541 to 1551
Jan. 21, 1942, Ch. 14, 56 Stat. 11, 42 U.S. Code §§ 1521 to 1524, 1534, 1544 to 1546, 1549, 1552
April 10, 1942, Ch. 239, 56 Stat. 212, 42 U.S. Code §§ 1541, 1544, 1546, 1547, 1561 to 1564
July 3, 1945, Ch. 264, 59 Stat. 383, 42 U.S. Code § 1534 and nt.
Dec. 31, 1945, Ch. 657, 59 Stat. 674, 42 U.S. Code § 1572
Feb. 18, 1946, Ch. 30, 60 Stat. 6, 42 U.S. Code § 1543
March 28, 1946, Ch. 118, 60 Stat. 85, 42 U.S. Code § 1572
June 26, 1946, Ch. 498, 60 Stat. 314, 42 U.S. Code § 1535
Aug. 8, 1946, Ch. 917, 60 Stat. 958, 42 U.S. Code §§ 1572, 1574
May 31, 1947, Ch. 91, 61 Stat. 128, 42 U.S. Code § 1572, 1572 nt.
June 19, 1948, Ch. 520, 62 Stat. 492, 42 U.S. Code § 1524

June 28, 1948, Ch. 688, 62 Stat. 1062, 42 U.S. Code §§ 1506, 1524, 1553, 1575, 1575 nt.
April 20, 1950, Ch. 94, 64 Stat. 59, 42 U.S. Code §§ 1521 to 1524, 1541 to 1553, 1561 to 1564, 1571, 1572, 1574, 1575, 1581 to 1590
June 30, 1951, Ch. 197, 65 Stat. 110, 42 U.S. Code § 1584
Sept. 1, 1951, Ch. 378, 65 Stat. 314, 42 U.S. Code §§ 1584, 1585, 1589a, 1589b
Oct. 26, 1951, Ch. 577, 65 Stat. 647, 42 U.S. Code §§ 1575, 1581, 1582
July 14, 1952, Ch. 723, 66 Stat. 603, 42 U.S. Code § 1589a
June 30, 1953, Ch. 174, 67 Stat. 132, 42 U.S. Code § 1573
March 10, 1954, Ch. 61, 68 Stat. 26, 42 U.S. Code § 1587
Feb. 15, 1956, Ch. 35, 70 Stat. 15, 42 U.S. Code § 1581
June 13, 1991, P.L. 102-54, 42 U.S. Code § 1581
Dec. 18, 1991, P.L. 102-240, 16 U.S. Code § 4601-11

Lanham Trade-Mark Act
See Trade-Mark Act Of 1946
Nov. 8, 1984, P.L. 98-620, 15 U.S. Code § 1064

Lanterman Developmental Disabilities Services Act
Cal. Welfare and Institutions Code § 4500 et seq.

Lanterman-Gibson-Waldie Act (Legislative Organization)
Cal. Government Code § 8900 et seq.

Lanterman Mental Retardation Services Act
Cal. Health and Safety Code § 38000 et seq.

Lanterman-Petris-Short Act (Community Mental Health)
Cal. Welfare and Institutions Code § 5000 et seq.

Lapse Act
Mass. Gen. Laws Ann., 191:22
S.D. Codifies Laws 1967, 29-6-8

Lapse Act (Estates)
Mich. Comp. Laws Ann., 700.134

Lapse Act (Legacies and Devises)
See Antilapse Act (Devises and Legacies)

Lapse Act (Wills)
R.I. Gen. Laws 1956, 33-6-19

Lapse Statute
Ill. Rev. Stat. 1991, Ch. 110 1/2, § 4-11

Lapsed Gift Act
Ohio Rev. Code 1953, 2107.52

Lapsed Legacy Act
N.C. Gen. Stat. 1943, § 31-42
Tex. Probate Code, § 68

Larceny Act
Ala. Code 1975, § 13A-8-3 et seq.
D.C. Code 1973, § 22-3811 to 22-3816
Fla. Stat. 1977, 812.021
Ga. Code Ann., 16-8-1 et seq.
Ill. Rev. Stat. 1991, Ch. 38, § 16-1 et seq.
Iowa Code Ann., 714.1 et seq.
Md. Ann. Code 1957, Art. 27, § 340 et seq.
Mich. Comp. Laws Ann., 750.356 et seq.
Minn. Stat. Ann., 609.52
Mont. Code Ann., 45-6-301 et seq.
N.H. Rev. Stat. 1955, 637:1 et seq.
N.Y. Penal Law 1965 (Consol. Laws Ch. 40)
§ 155.00 et seq.
Okla. Stat. Ann., Title 21, § 1701 et seq.
Ore. Rev. Stat., 164.015 et seq.
Pa. Cons. Stat., Title 18, § 3921 et seq.
R.I. Gen. Laws 1956, 11-41-1 et seq.
Vt. Stat. Ann., Title 13, § 2501 et seq.
Wash. Rev. Code Ann., 9A.56.010 et seq.

Larceny Act (Automobiles)
Wash. Rev. Code Ann., 9A.56.070

Larceny Act (Temporary)
N.C. Gen. Stat. 1943, § 14-72.2

Larceny by Fraud Act
Okla. Stat. Ann., Title 21, § 1701

Larceny by Trick Act
Ohio Rev. Code 1953, 2913.02, Subd. A, 3

Larchmont Unsafe Building Demolition Law
N.Y. Local Laws 1971, Village of
Larchmont, p. 4222

Large Business Development Act
Ill. Rev. Stat. 1987, Ch. 127, § 141.164

Large Employer Health Benefit Plans Act
Tex. Insurance Code, Art. 26.81 et seq.

Large Loan Act
Colo. Rev. Stat. 1963, 73-2-1 et seq.

**Large Municipalities for Urban Residential
Finance Authorities Act**
Ga. Code Ann., 36-41 1 et seq.

**Large Scale Metallic Minerals Mining Tax
Act of 1988**
S.D. Laws 1988, Ch. 102

**Large Scale Metallic Minerals Surface
Mining Reclamation Act**
S.D. Laws 1988, Ch. 359

Larger Counties Civil Service Law
Fla. Laws 1955, Ch. 30255

Larsen Elliott Civil Rights Act
Mich. Comp. Laws Ann., 37.2101 et seq.

Las Cruces Arroyo Flood Control Act
N.M. Stat. Ann., 72-17-1 et seq.

Las Vegas Charter
Nev. Statutes 1983, Ch. 517, p. 1391

Las Vegas Sewage District Act
Nev. Statutes 1947, Ch. 164, p. 534

LaSalle Veterans Home Act
Ill. Rev. Stat. 1991, Ch. 126 1/2, § 600 et seq.

Lascivious Carriage Act
Conn. Gen. Stat. Ann., § 53-219

Laser System Act
Ill. Comp. Stat. 1992, Ch. 420, § 56/1 et seq.
Ill. Rev. Stat. 1991, Ch. 111 1/2, § 700 et seq.
Continued

289

Lassen Modoc County Flood Control and Water Conservation District
Cal. Statutes 1959, Ch. 2127, p. 5009

Last Injurious Exposure Law
N.Y. Workmen's Compensation Law (Consol. Laws Ch. 67) § 44

Latchkey Children Act (After-School Child Care Programs)
N.Y. Education Law 1947 (Consol. Laws Ch. 16) § 414, Subd. 1
N.Y. Social Services Law (Consol. Laws Ch. 550 § 410c, Subd. 5

Lateral Railroad Act
Ind. Code Ann., 8-4-10-1 et seq.
Pa. Purdon's Stat., Title 15, § 4301 et seq.

Lateral Support Act
Ill. Rev. Stat. 1991, Ch. 111 1/2, § 3300, 3301
N.J. Stat. Ann., 46:10-1

Latin American Development Act
Dec. 16, 1963, P.L. 88-205, 77 Stat. 390, 22 U.S. Code §§ 1942 nt., 1943

Latino Community Development Act
D.C. Code Ann., § 1-2301 et seq.

Lattingtown General Fee and Deposit Law
N.Y. Local Laws 1972, Village of Lattingtown, p. 3561

Launch Services Purchase Act of 1990
Nov. 16, 1990 P.L. 101-611, 42 U.S. Code §§ 2451 nt., 2465b to 2465f
Oct. 28, 1998, P.L. 105-303, 42 U.S. Code §§ 2465b to 2465f

Laundering in Financial Institutions Act (Control of Money)
Fla. Stat. Ann., 655.50

Laundry and Dry Cleaning Industry Act
Fla. Laws 1937, Ch. 17894

Laundry License Tax Act
Mont. Code Ann. 1987, 7-21-2215

Laundry Supply Designations Act
Cal. Business and Professions Code § 14480 et seq.

Lauren Beth Rudolph Food Safety Act
Cal. Health and Safety Code § 113996 et seq.

Lava Hot Springs Foundation Act
Ida. Code 1947, 67-4401 et seq.

Law Abiding Citizens Self-Defense Act
S.C. Code Ann. 1976, § 23-31-205 et seq.

Law Against Discrimination
N.H. Rev. Stat. 1955, 354-A:1 et seq.
N.J. Stat. Ann., 10:5-1 et seq.

Law Against Discrimination in Employment
See Antidiscrimination Act (Employment)

Law and Equity Act
Me. Rev. Stat. 1954, Ch. 113, § 15 et seq.

Law Clerk and Secretary Act (Appellate Court)
Ill. Comp. Stat. 1992, Ch. 705, § 30/0.01 et seq.
Ill. Rev. Stat. 1991, Ch. 37, § 59.9 et seq.

Law Corporations Act
Cal. Business and Professions Code § 6160 et seq.
La. Rev. Stat. Ann., 12:801 et seq.

Law Enforcement Academy Act
Mont. Code Ann., 44-10-101 et seq.

Law Enforcement Academy and Council Act
Iowa Code Ann., 80B.1 et seq.

Law Enforcement Act
Fla. Stat. Ann., 775.0823
Kan. Stat. Ann., 19-4468 et seq.

Law Enforcement Act (Narcotics and Alcoholic Beverage)
Utah Code Ann. 1953, 53-4-201 et seq.

Law Enforcement and Emergency Service Solicitation of Funds Act
Fla. Stat. 1983, 496.20 et seq.

Law Enforcement and Fire Fighting Medal of Honor Act
Ill. Rev. Stat. 1991, Ch. 127, § 3851-1 et seq.

Law Enforcement and Technical Services Act
Utah Code Ann. 1953, 53-5-101 et seq.

Law Enforcement Assistance Act of 1965
Sept. 22, 1965, P.L. 89-197, 79 Stat. 828
Nov. 8, 1966, P.L. 89-798, 80 Stat. 1506

Law Enforcement Authority Act
Colo. Rev. Stat., 30-11-401 et seq.

Law Enforcement Availability Pay Act of 1994
Sept. 30, 1994, P.L. 103-329, 5 U.S. Code § 5547 nt.

Law Enforcement Council Act
N.J. Stat. Ann., 52:17B-43.1 et seq.

Law Enforcement Department Act
Fla. Stat. Ann., 943.01 et seq.

Law Enforcement Disposition of Property Act
Ill. Rev. Stat. 1991, Ch. 141, § 140 et seq.

Law Enforcement Emergency Care Act
Ill. Rev. Stat. 1991, Ch. 70, §§ 60, 61

Law Enforcement Funds Act
Fla. Stat. Ann., 943.25

Law Enforcement Information Network Policy Council Act
Mich. Comp. Laws Ann., 28.211 et seq.

Law Enforcement Integrity Act
Ga. Code Ann., 35-10-1 et seq.

Law Enforcement Intern Training Act
Ill. Comp. Stat. 1992, Ch. 50, § 708/1 et seq.

Law Enforcement Mutual Aid Act (Interstate)
Mont. Code Ann., 44-11-301 et seq.

Law Enforcement Mutual Assistance Act
W. Va. Code 1966 §§ 15-10-1 to 15-10-4

Law Enforcement Officer Immunity Act (Federal)
Ill. Comp. Stat. 1992, Ch. 745, § 22/1

Law Enforcement Officers Act (Special)
N.J. Stat. Ann., 40A:14-146.8 et seq.

Law Enforcement Officers and Firefighters Death Benefit Act
Fla. Stat. Ann., 112.191

Law Enforcement Officers' and Firefighters' Retirement System Act
Wash. Rev. Code Ann., 41.26.005 et seq.

Law Enforcement Officers' Association Act (Beaufort County)
N.C. Laws 1967, Ch. 627

Law Enforcement Officers, Civil Defense Workers, Civil Air Patrol Members, Paramedics and Firemen Compensation Act
Ill. Rev. Stat. 1991, Ch. 48, § 281 et seq.

Law Enforcement Officers' Death Benefit Act (State)
N.C. Gen. Stat. 1943, § 143-166.1 et seq.

Law Enforcement Officer's In-Service Training Act
Ill. Rev. Stat. 1991, Ch. 85, § 561 et seq.

Law Enforcement Officers, Paramedics, Civil Defense Workers, Civil Air Patrol Members and Firemen Compensation Act
Ill. Rev. Stat. 1989, Ch. 48, § 281 et seq.

Law Enforcement Officers' Relief Act (Bertie County)
N.C. Laws 1953, Ch. 897

Law Enforcement Officers' Relief Act (Dare County)
N.C. Laws 1963, Ch. 411

Law Enforcement Officers' Relief Act (Halifax County)
N.C. Laws 1949, Ch. 1041

Law Enforcement Officers' Relief Act (Northampton County)
N.C. Laws 1953, Ch. 1258

Law Enforcement Officers Retirement Act
N.C. Gen. Stat. 1943, § 143-166.1 et seq.
S.D. Codified Laws 1967, Superseded Vol.,
3-12-46 et seq.

Law Enforcement Officers' Training Academy Act
Miss. Code Ann. 1972, § 45-5-1 et seq.

Law Enforcement Officers Training Act
Neb. Rev. Stat. 1943, 81-1401 et seq.

Law Enforcement Officers Training Council Act
Mich. Comp. Laws Ann., 28.601 et seq.

Law Enforcement Planning Agency Act
Ala. Code 1975, § 41-8A-1 et seq.

Law Enforcement Planning Commission Act
Ida. Code 1947, 19-5101 et seq.

Law Enforcement Protection Act
Fla. Stat. Ann., 775.0823, 944.277(1)(h),(i)

Law Enforcement Protection Fund Act
N.M. Stat. Ann., 29-13-1 et seq.

Law Enforcement Response to Domestic Violence Act
Cal. Penal Code § 13700

Law Enforcement Safety Act (Officer Jeffrey Tackett)
Fla. Stat. Ann., 166.049

Law Enforcement Salary Grant Act
Ill. Rev. Stat. 1991, Ch. 85, § 520 et seq.

Law Enforcement Scholarships and Recruitment Act
Sept. 13, 1994, P.L. 103-322, 42 U.S. Code
§§ 13701 nt., 14111 et seq.
Oct. 7, 1998, P.L. 105-244, 42 U.S. Code
§ 14111

Law Enforcement Technology Advertisement Clarification Act of 1997
Nov. 21, 1997, P.L. 105-112, 18 U.S. Code
§ 2510 nt.

Law Enforcement Training Act
Kan. Stat. Ann., 74-5601 et seq.
Neb. Rev. Stat. 1943, 81-1401 et seq.
N.M. Stat. Ann., 29-7-1 et seq.

Law Enforcement Training Council Act
Vt. Stat. Ann., Title 20, § 2351 et seq.

Law Enforcement Youth Cadet Corps Act
N.M. Stat. Ann., 29-7B-1 et seq.

Law for Out-of-State Probation and Parole Supervision
See Uniform Law for Out-of-State Probation
and Parole Supervision

Law for Regulation of Credit Life Insurance and Credit Health Insurance
N.M. Stat. Ann., 59A-25-1 et seq.

Law for the Regulation of Mobile Homes and Mobile Home Camps
N.Y. Local Laws 1973, Town of
Shawangunk, p. 2934

Law for the Regulation of Mobile Homes and Mobile Home Parks
N.Y. Local Laws 1973, Town of Ellery, p.
1690

Law-Hertel-T. Slopczynski Port Authority Act
Mich. Comp. Laws Ann., 120.101 et seq.

Law Library Act
Okla. Stat. Ann., Title 20, § 1201 et seq.

Law Library Act (County)
See County Law Library Act

Law Library Act (Manatee County)
Fla. Special Laws 1961, Ch. 61-2455

Law Library Tax Act (Jefferson County)
Ala. Code 1958, Title 62, § 138

Law-McCauley-Traxler-Bowman-McNeely Lottery Act
Mich. Comp. Laws Ann., 432.1 et seq.

Law of Evidence Act
P.R. Laws Ann. 1954, Title 32, § 1621 et seq.

Law of the Road Act
Me. Rev. Stat. Ann. 1964, Title 29, § 941 et seq.
N.H. Rev. Stat. 1955, 265:1 et seq.

Law of Waters
P.R. Laws Ann. 1954, Title 12, § 1501 et seq.

Law on Fresh Pursuit
See Uniform Act on Fresh Pursuit

Law on Intrastate Pursuit
S.D. Codified Laws 1967, 23A-3-17 et seq.

Law on Notarial Acts
See also Uniform Law on Notarial Acts
Iowa Code Ann., 77A.1 et seq.

Law on Obscenity
Miss. Code Ann. 1972, § 99-33-1 et seq.

Law on the Protection of Minors from Harmful Materials
N.C. Gen. Stat. 1943, § 19-9 et seq.

Law Practice Act
R.I. Gen. Laws 1956, 11-27-1 et seq.

Law Revision Commission Act
D.C. Code 1973, § 49-401 et seq.
N.Y. Legislative Law (Consol. Laws Ch. 32) § 70 et seq.

Law Revision Commission Expansion Act
D.C. Code 1973, § 49-401

Law Scholarship Act (C. Clyde Ferguson)
N.J. Stat. Ann., 18A:71-40.1 et seq.

Law School Clinical Programs Funding Authorization Act
D.C. Code Ann., § 31-1901 et seq.

Law School Legal Aid Agency Act
Ga. Code Ann., 15-20-1 et seq.

Law School Public Prosecutor Act
Ga. Code Ann., 15-18-22

Law Student Limited Practice Act
Miss. Code Ann. 1972, § 73-3-201 et seq.

Law to Provide for the Filing of Vacancies in the Elective Office
N.Y. Local Laws 1973, County of Greene, p. 1075 (Member of the County Legislature)

Law-Traxler-McCauley-Bowman Bingo Act
Mich. Comp. Laws Ann., 432.102 et seq.

Lawery Act (Children's Emergency Relief)
Ohio Laws Vol. 114, p. 5

Lawful Fence Act
Cal. Food and Agricultural Code 1967, § 17121

Lawn and Garden Equipment Dealership Act
Kan. Stat. Ann., 16-1401 et seq.

Lawn Care Products Application and Notice Act
Ill. Rev. Stat. 1991, Ch. 5, § 851 et seq.

Lawn, Garden and Tractor and Light Industrial Equipment Franchise Act
Ala. Code 1975, § 8-21A-1

Lawrason Act (Local Government)
La. Rev. Stat. Ann., 33:321 et seq.

Lawrason Act (Municipal Incorporation)
La. Rev. Stat. Ann., 33:321 et seq.

Lawrence Act (New Rochelle Municipal Housing Authority)
N.Y. Public Housing Law (Consol. Laws, Ch. 44A) § 407

Lawrence G. Hanscom Field Improvement Loan Act
Mass. Acts 1955, Ch. 769

Lawrence Parking Facilities Loan Act
Mass. Acts 1963, Ch. 576

Laws of the Road Act
Iowa Code Ann., 321.1 et seq.

Lawsuit Immunity Act
Ill. Rev. Stat. 1991, Ch. 127, §§ 800, 801

Lawsuits Act (Frivolous)
N.J. Stat. Ann., 2A:15-59.1 et seq.

Lawyers Act
Md. Ann. Code 1974, Art. BO, § 10-101 et
seq.

Lawyers Corporation Act
S.D. Codified Laws 1967, 47-13A-1 et seq.

**Lawyers Referral Service Quality Assurance
Act**
Tex. Rev. Civ. Stat., Art. 320d

Lawyers Relief Act
D.C. Code Ann., § 1-201 et seq.

Lay Away Plan Act
Ill. Rev. Stat. 1991, Ch. 121 1/2, § 871 et seq.

Layaway Sales Act
Md. Ann. Code 1974, Art. CL, § 14-1101 et
seq.

**Layman Act (Prohibition of Intoxicating
Liquor)**
Va. Acts 1924, Ch. 407

Lazy Husband Act
Ind. Code 1976, 35-14-4-1 et seq.

Lazy Judge Act
Ind. Burns' 1933, 2-2102

Lazy Lawyer's Act
Ala. Code 1958, Title 7, § 372(1)
Minn. Stat. 1971, 547.03

Le Tort Spring Run Scenic River Act
Pa. Purdon's Stat., Title 32, § 820.101 et seq.

Lea Act (Radio-Coercive Practices)
April 16, 1946, Ch. 138, 60 Stat. 89, 47 U.S.
Code § 506

Lea-Brown Act (Natural Gas)
See Natural Gas Act

Lea-Wagner Act
See Investment Advisers Act Of 1940 And
Investment Company Act Of 1940

Lea Wheeler Transportation Act
See Transportation Act, 1940

**Lead-Acid Battery and Used Motor Oil
Recycling Act**
Okla. Stat. Ann., Title 27A, § 2001 et seq.

Lead and Zinc Mining Act
Okla. Stat. Ann., Title 45, § 411 et seq.

Lead-Based Paint Activities Act
Ida. Code 1947, 39-7701 et seq.

**Lead-Based Paint Activity Accreditation
and Certification Act**
Miss. Code Ann. 1972, § 49-17-501 et seq.

Lead-Based Paint Exposure Reduction Act
Oct. 28, 1992, P.L. 102-550, 15 U.S. Code
§ 2601 nt.

Lead-Based Paint Hazard Act
Ark. Code 1987, 8-4-401 et seq.

Lead-Based Paint Poisoning Prevention Act
Jan. 13, 1971, P.L. 91-695, 84 Stat. 2078, 42
U.S. Code §§ 4801, 4811, 4821, 4831, 4841
to 4843
Nov. 9, 1973, P.L. 93-151, 87 Stat. 565, 42
U.S. Code §§ 4801, 4811, 4821, 4822,
4831, 4841, 4843 to 4846
June 23, 1976, P.L. 94-317, 42 U.S. Code
§§ 4801, 4831, 4841 to 4843
Nov. 10, 1978, P.L. 95-626, 42 U.S. Code
§ 4844
Feb. 5, 1988, P.L. 100-242, 42 U.S. Code
§ 4822
Nov. 7, 1988, P.L. 100-628, 42 U.S. Code
§ 4822
Oct. 28, 1992, P.L. 102-550, 42 U.S. Code
§ 4822

Oct. 21, 1998, P.L. 105-276, 42 U.S. Code § 4822

Lead-Bases Paint Management Act
Okla. Stat. Ann., Title 27A, § 2-12-101 et seq.

Lead Certification Act
Pa. Purdon's Stat., Title 35, § 5901 et seq.

Lead Contamination Control Act of 1988
Oct. 31, 1988, P.L. 100-572, 42 U.S. Code § 201 nt.

Lead Manufacturers Act
Pa. Purdon's Stat., Title 43, § 471 et seq.

Lead Poisoning Act (Childhood)
Minn. Stat. 1986, 144.9501 et seq.

Lead Poisoning Control Act
Me. Rev. Stat. Ann. 1964, Title 22, § 1314 et seq.

Lead Poisoning Law
N.J. Stat. Ann., 34:6-48 to 34:6-57, 34:6A-1 et seq.

Lead Poisoning Prevention Act
Ga. Code Ann., 31-40-1 et seq.
Ill. Rev. Stat. 1991, Ch. 111 1/2, § 1301 et seq.
N.Y. Public Health Law 1953 (Consol. Laws Ch. 55) § 1370a et seq.
R.I. Gen. Laws 1956, 23-24.6-1 et seq.

Lead Poisoning Prevention Act (Childhood)
Cal. Health and Safety Code § 372 et seq.
Del. Code of 1974, Title 16, § 2601 et seq.
Neb. Rev. Stat. 1943, 71-2513 et seq.

Lead Poisoning Prevention and Control Act
S.C. Code Ann. 1976, § 44-53-1310 et seq.

Lead Protection Act (Occupational Health)
R.I. Gen. Laws 1956, 23-24.7-1 et seq.

Lead Reduction Act
Ala. Code 1975, § 22-37A-1 et seq.

Lead-Safe Schools Protection Act
Cal. Education Code 1976, § 32240 et seq.

Lead-Zinc Small Producers Stabilization Act of Oct. 3, 1961
Oct. 3, 1961, P.L. 87-347, 75 Stat. 766, 30 U.S. Code §§ 681 to 689
July 25, 1963, P.L. 88-75, 77 Stat. 92, 30 U.S. Code § 686
Oct. 5, 1965, P.L. 89-238, 79 Stat. 925, 30 U.S. Code §§ 682, 683, 686, 687, 689

Leadership Academy Act (Youth)
Neb. Rev. Stat. 1943, 50-1001 et seq.

Leadership Act (County)
Ga. Code Ann., 36-20-1 et seq.

Leadership and Revitalization Development Act (Rural)
Ore. Rev. Stat., 285.678

Leadership Development and Rural Revitalization Act
Ore. Laws 1991, Ch. 684

Leadership in Educational Administration Development Act of 1984
Oct. 30, 1984, P.L. 98-558, 20 U.S. Code §§ 4201 to 4206
Oct. 18, 1986, P.L. 99-500, 20 U.S. Code § 4206
Oct. 30, 1986, P.L. 99-591, 20 U.S. Code § 4206

Leadership Training Act (Rural)
Pa. 1992 Pamph. Laws, No. 65

Leaf Cutting Bee Management Act
Mont. Code Ann., 80-6-1101 et seq.

Leaking Petroleum Underground Storage Tank Cleanup Act
N.C. Gen. Stat. 1943, § 143-215.94A et seq.

Leaking Underground Storage Tank Act
Mich. Comp. Laws Ann., 299.831 et seq.
Mich. Comp. Laws Ann., 324.21301a et seq.

Learning Disabled, Visually Impaired, and Auditorily Impaired Students Act
N.J. Stat. Ann., 18A:72A-1 et seq.

Learning Powers Institution Act
Ill. Rev. Stat. 1991, Ch. 144, § 0.01 et seq.

Learning Resources Act
Miss. Code Ann. 1972, § 37-23-121 et seq.

Learning Zone Implementation Law (Chicago)
Ill. Comp. Stat. 1992, Ch. 105, § 5/34-8.6 et seq.

Learning/Language Disabilities Screening Act
Wash. Rev. Code Ann., 28A.03.300 et seq.

Lease Disclosure Act (Motor Vehicle)
Fla. Stat. Ann., 521.001 et seq.

Lease Lend Act
March 11, 1941, Ch. 11, 55 Stat. 31, 22 U.S. Code §§ 411 to 419
March 11, 1943, Ch. 15, 57 Stat. 20, 22 U.S. Code §§ 412, 415
May 17, 1944, Ch. 198, 58 Stat. 222, 22 U.S. Code §§ 412, 415
April 16, 1945, Ch. 61, 59 Stat. 52, 22 U.S. Code §§ 412, 415

Lease of Goods Act
Mich. Comp. Laws Ann., 440.2801 et seq.
Tex. Business and Commerce Code, Art. 2A.101 et seq.

Lease of Movables Act
La. Rev. Stat. Ann., 9:3301 et seq.

Lease or Sale of Land for Cemeteries Act (City)
Ill. Rev. Stat. 1991, Ch. 21, §§ 6h, 7

Lease Purchase Act (Local Government)
La. Rev. Stat. Ann., 38:2319 et seq.

Lease Purchase Act (State)
La. Rev. Stat. Ann., 39:1780 et seq.

Lease-Purchase Agreement Act
Ga. Code Ann., 10-1-680 et seq.
Ida. Code 1947, 28-36-101 et seq.
Wash. Laws 1992, Ch. 134

Lease-Purchase Agreement Act (Consumer)
Kan. Stat. Ann., 50-680 et seq.
Va. Code 1950, § 59.1-207.15 et seq.

Lease-Purchase Bond Law of 1976 (School Building)
Cal. Education Code 1976, 17700

Lease Recording Act
Pa. Purdon's Stat., Title 21, § 404 et seq.

Lease Release Act (Oil and Gas)
Ill. Rev. Stat. 1991, Ch. 80, § 38.9 et seq.

Lease Rental Act (School)
Ind. Code Ann., 21-5-11-1 et seq.

Leased Lands Act (University-Building Authority)
Ill. Rev. Stat. 1991, Ch. 144, § 70.10 et seq.

Leased Vehicle Gross Receipts Tax Act
N.M. Stat. Ann., 7-14A-1 et seq.

Leasehold Community Assistance Act
N.M. Stat. Ann., 6-6A-1 et seq.

Leasehold Management Bankruptcy Amendments Act of 1983
July 10, 1984, P.L. 98-353, 11 U.S. Code §§ 362, 365, 365 nt., 541

Leasehold Taxing Act
N.J. Stat. Ann., 54:4-2.3 et seq.

Leases (Uniform Commercial Code)
See also Uniform Commercial Code—Leases
Colo. Rev. Stat., 4-2.5-101 et seq.
Fla. Stat. Ann., 680.1011 et seq.
Ind. Code Ann., 26-1-2.1-101 et seq.
Ky. Rev. Stat. 1971, 355.2A-101 et seq.
Neb. Rev. Stat. 1943, UCC2A-101 et seq.
Utah Code Ann. 1953, 70A-2a-101 et seq.
Wyo. Stat. Ann., § 34.1-2A-101 et seq.

Leases-Uniform Commercial Code
See Uniform Commercial Code-Leases

Leasing Act (Consumer Protection)
N.J. Stat. Ann., 56:12-60 et seq.

Leasing Act (Governmental)
Ky. Rev. Stat. 1971, 65.940 et seq.

Leasing Act (Motor Vehicle)
Ill. Comp. Stat. 1992, Ch. 815, § 636/1 et seq.

Leasing Act (Public Lands)
Tex. Natural Resources Code, § 51.011 et seq.

Leasing Act (State Lands)
Cal. Public Resources Code § 6501 et seq.

Leasing Commission Act (Mineral)
Ga. Code 1933, 91-118 et seq.

Leasing Occupation Tax Act
Ill. Rev. Stat. 1965, Ch. 120, § 453.101 et seq.

Leasing Use Tax Act
Ill. Rev. Stat. 1965, Ch. 120, § 453.121 et seq.

Least Cost Resource Planning and Acquisition Act (Integrated)
Mont. Code Ann., 69-3-1201 et seq.

Leave Act (Family)
N.J. Stat. Ann., 34:11B-1 et seq.

Leave Act (State Employees)
Alaska Stat. 1962, § 39.20.200 et seq.

Leave Act of the United States
March 14, 1936, Ch. 140, 49 Stat. 1161
Dec. 17, 1942, Ch. 737, 56 Stat. 1052
Oct. 5, 1949, Ch. 598, 63 Stat. 703

Leave and Attendance Policy Act
Ark. Stat. 1987, 21-4-201 et seq.

Leave of Absence Act (Military)
Ill. Rev. Stat. 1991, Ch. 129, §§ 500, 501

Leavitt Act (Indians)
July 1, 1932, Ch. 369, 47 Stat. 564, 25 U.S. Code § 386a

Lechuguilla Cave Protection Act of 1993
Dec. 2, 1993, P.L. 103-169, 16 U.S. Code § 4301 nt.

Lee Act (Municipal Bonds)
Ala. Code 1975, § 11-81-140 et seq.

Lee Alexandria Hanley Act
Tex. Insurance Code, Art. 21.53F

Lee-Caraway-Gearhart Act (Cotton and Tobacco)
See Agricultural Adjustment Act, 1938

Lee County Code Enforcement Board Act
Fla. Special Laws 1982, Ch. 82-318

Lee County Peace Officers' Relief Association Act
N.C. Laws 1963, Ch. 526

Lee County Solid Waste Disposal and Resource Recovery Act
Fla. Laws 1985, Ch. 447

Lee County Utilities Authority Act
Ga. Laws 1992, p. 6419

Lee Metcalf Wilderness and Management Act of 1983
Oct. 31, 1983, P.L. 98-140, 16 U.S. Code §§ 460ll-3, 1132 nt.

Lee Uniform Water District Regulations
N.Y. Local Laws 1970, town of Lee, p. 2013

Left Turn Act (Motor Vehicles)
Ill. Rev. Stat. 1991, Ch. 95 1/2, § 11-701 et seq.
N.J. Stat. Ann., 39:4-123, Subsecs. b, c

Legacy and Seccession Tax Act
Kan. Stat. Ann., 79-1537 et seq.
N.H. Rev. Stat. 1955, 86:6 et seq.

Legacy Tax Acts
June 13, 1898, Ch. 448, 30 Stat. 464
April 12, 1902, Ch. 500, 32 Stat. 97
Continued

Legal Activities Law
N.Y. Labor Law (Consol. Laws Ch. 31)
§ 201d

Legal Advertising Act
Ind. Code Ann., 5-3-1-1 et seq.

Legal Advertising Rate Act
Ill. Rev. Stat. 1991, Ch. 100, §§ 10.9, 11

Legal Aid Act
D.C. Code Ann., § 1-2701 et seq.
Wash. Rev. Code Ann., 2.50.010 et seq.

Legal Aid Agency Act (Law Schools)
Ga. Code Ann., 15-20-1 et seq.

Legal Assistance Corporation Act
Mass. Gen. Laws Ann., 221A:1 et seq.

Legal Business Solicitation Act
Ill. Rev. Stat. 1991, Ch. 13, § 14.9 et seq.

Legal Estates Principal and Income Law
Cal. Civil Code § 731 et seq.

Legal Expense Insurance Act
Ala. Code 1975, § 27-43-1 et seq.
Fla. Stat. Ann., 642.011 et seq.

Legal Holidays Act
See Holidays Act (Legal)
S.C. Code Ann. 1976, § 53-5-10 et seq.

Legal Insurance Act
Ark. Code Ann. 1987, 23-91-201 et seq.

Legal Intern Limited Practice Act
Miss. Code Ann. 1972, § 73-3-201 et seq.

Legal List Act (Trust Funds)
Tenn. Code Ann., 35-3-101 et seq.
Wis. Stat. Ann., 881.01

Legal Newspaper Act
Wash. Rev. Code Ann., 65.16.010 et seq.

Legal Notice Act (Newspaper)
Ill. Rev. Stat. 1991, Ch. 100, § 9.9 et seq.

Legal Notices by Radio Act
Wash. Rev. Code Ann., 65.16.130 et seq.

Legal Notices Publication Act
Wash. Rev. Code Ann., 65.16.010 et seq.

Legal Panel Act (Chiropractic)
Mont. Code Ann., 27-12-101 et seq.

Legal Panel Act (Medical)
Mont. Code Ann., 27-6-101 et seq.

Legal Proceedings Against State Officers Act
Pa. Cons. Stat., Title 42, § 761

Legal Rate Act (Interest)
Colo. Rev. Stat. 5-3-201

Legal Relationship Termination Act (Parent-Child)
Colo. Rev. Stat., 19-3-601 et seq.
Mont. Code Ann., 41-3-601 et seq.

Legal Relationship Termination Act of 1977
Colo. Rev. Stat., 19-11-101 et seq.

Legal Remedies Act (Consumers)
Cal. Civil Code § 1750 et seq.

Legal Resources Act (Environmental)
Ill. Rev. Stat. 1991, Ch. 14, § 251 et seq.

Legal Responsibility Act
Tenn. Public Acts 1971, Ch. 162

Legal Separation Act
Conn. Gen. Stat. Ann., § 46b-40

Legal Service Plan Act
Minn. Stat. Ann., 62G.01 et seq.

Legal Services Corporation Act
Dec. 21, 1995, P.L. 104-66, 42 U.S. Code § 2996h
April 30, 1997, P.L. 105-12, 42 U.S. Code § 2996f
Md. Ann. Code 1957, Art. 10, § 45A et seq.

Legal Services Corporation Act Amendments of 1977
Dec. 28, 1977, P.L. 95-222, 42 U.S. Code §§ 2701 nt., 2996 et seq.

Legal Services Corporation Act of 1974
July 27, 1974, P.L. 93-355, 88 Stat. 378, 42 U.S. Code §§ 2809, 2971e, 2996 to 2996l

Legal Services Insurance Act
N.J. Stat. Ann., 17:46C-1 et seq.

Legal Services Liability Act
Ala. Code 1975, § 6-5-571

Legal Settlement Act
N.J. Laws 1933, C126
Wis. Stat. 1983, 49.10

Legal Tender Acts
Feb. 25, 1862, Ch. 33, 12 Stat. 345
July 11, 1862, Ch. 142, 12 Stat. 532
March 3, 1863, Ch. 72, 12 Stat. 709
May 12, 1933, Ch. 25, 48 Stat. 52, 31 U.S. Code § 462
June 5, 1933, Ch. 48, 48 Stat. 113, 31 U.S. Code §§ 314, 316, 462

Legalized Games of Chance Control Commission Law
N.J. Rev. Stat. 1937, 5:8-1 et seq.

Legalizing Act (Marriages)
S.C. Code Ann. 1976, § 20-1-30, 20-1-40

Legend Drug Act
Ind. Code Ann., 16-6-8-1 et seq.

Legend Drug and Controlled Substances Research Act
Tenn. Code Ann., 53-14-101 et seq.

Legislative Activities Disclosure Act
N.J. Stat. Ann., 52:13C-19

Legislative Actuarial Note Act
N.C. Gen. Stat. 1943, § 120-112 et seq.

Legislative Advisory Commission Act
Me. Rev. Stat. Ann. 1964, Title 3, § 221 et seq.

Legislative Agents Act
Mass. Gen. Laws Ann., 3:39 et seq.
Mich. Comp. Laws Ann., 4.411 et seq.

Legislative Apportionment Act
See Apportionment Act (Legislative)

Legislative Appropriations Act, 1954
Aug. 1, 1953, Ch. 304, 67 Stat. 318, 2 U.S. Code §§ 31c, 46a, 46b nt., 46c, 46c nt., 46d, 46d nt., 52, 65a, 122; 40 U.S. Code §§ 164a, 166a, 174b-1 nt. (See 44 U.S. Code §§ 309, 310, 1117)

Legislative Appropriations Act, 1955
July 2, 1954, Ch. 455, 68 Stat. 396, 2 U.S. Code §§ 38a, 42a, 42a-1, 42b, 46b, 46d 46f-1, 52, 53, 60g-1, 65a, 72a-3, 81, 119a, 122, 122a, 124, 125; 40 U.S. Code §§ 164a 166a
June 13, 1957, P.L. 85-54, 71 Stat. 82, 2 U.S. Code § 122a
Sept. 7, 1957, P.L. 85-301, 71 Stat. 622, 2 U.S. Code § 122
July 23, 1959, P.L. 86-102, 73 Stat. 224, 2 U.S. Code § 38a
Sept. 29, 1965, P.L. 89-211, 79 Stat. 857, 2 U.S. Code § 122
Aug. 20, 1996, P.L. 104-186, 2 U.S. Code § 46b

Legislative Appropriations Act, 1956
Aug. 3, 1956, Ch. 938, 70 Stat. 990, 2 U.S. Code §§ 60g-1, 92
Aug. 27, 1966, P.L. 89-545, 80 Stat. 357, 2 U.S. Code § 72a-1a
July 28, 1967, P.L. 90-57, 81 Stat. 144, 2 U.S. Code § 60a nts.
Sept. 29, 1969, P.L. 91-77, 83 Stat. 124, 40 U.S. Code § 166 nt.

Legislative Appropriations Act, 1978
Sept. 21, 1987, P.L. 100-137, 2 U.S. Code § 61-1 nt.
Oct. 21, 1987, P.L. 100-137, 2 U.S. Code § 61-1 nt.

Legislative Audit Act
Mont. Code Ann., 5-13-101 et seq.
N.M. Stat. Ann. 1953, 4-24-1 et seq.

Legislative Audit Commission Act

Ill. Rev. Stat. 1991, Ch. 63, § 103.9 et seq.

Legislative Branch Appropriations Act, 1936

July 8, 1935, Ch. 374, 49 Stat. 459

Aug. 11, 1993, P.L. 103-69, 2 U.S. Code § 43a

Legislative Branch Appropriations Act, 1938

May 18, 1937, Ch. 223, 50 Stat. 169, 2 U.S. Code § 121; 40 U.S. Code §§ 164a, 206

Legislative Branch Appropriations Act, 1939

May 17, 1983, Ch. 236, 52 Stat. 381, 40 U.S. Code §§ 164a, 206, 213a

Legislative Branch Appropriations Act, 1940

June 16, 1939, Ch. 208, 53 Stat. 822, 40 U.S. Code §§ 174b, 213a

Legislative Branch Appropriations Act, 1941

June 18, 1940, Ch. 396, 54 Stat. 462, 2 U.S. Code § 273; 40 U.S. Code §§ 164a, 174b, 206, 213a

Oct. 9, 1940, Ch. 780, 54 Stat. 1030

Legislative Branch Appropriations Act, 1942

July 1, 1941, Ch. 268, 55 Stat. 446, 2 U.S. Code §§ 42a, 46a, 60f, 117a; 40 U.S. Code §§ 164a 174b, 206, 213a

June 8, 1942, Ch. 396, 56 Stat. 333, 2 U.S. Code §§ 42a, 117a; See 2 U.S. Code § 61-1

June 28, 1943, Ch. 173, 57 Stat. 222, 2 U.S. Code § 117a; See 2 U.S. Code § 61-1

June 26, 1944, Ch. 277, 58 Stat. 337, 2 U.S. Code §§ 42a, 117a; See 2 U.S. Code § 61-1

Dec. 20, 1944, Ch. 617, 58 Stat. 832 (See 2 U.S. Code § 61-1)

June 13, 1945, Ch. 189, 58 Stat. 241, 2 U.S. Code §§ 42a, 46a, 117a; See 2 U.S. Code § 61-1

July 1, 1946, Ch. 530, 60 Stat. 390, 2 U.S. Code § 117a; See 2 U.S. Code 61-1

June 14, 1948, Ch. 467, 62 Stat. 425, 2 U.S. Code § 46a

Oct. 28, 1949, Ch. 783, 63 Stat. 974 (See 2 U.S. Code § 61-1)

Oct. 11, 1951, Ch. 485, 65 Stat. 391, 2 U.S. Code §§ 42a, 46a

Oct. 24, 1951, Ch. 554, 65 Stat. 614 (See 2 U.S. Code § 61-1)

Aug. 1, 1953, Ch. 304, 67 Stat. 320, 2 U.S. Code § 46a

July 2, 1954, Ch. 455, 68 Stat. 399, 2 U.S. Code § 42a

June 28, 1955, Ch. 189, 69 Stat. 177 (See 2 U.S. Code § 61-1)

Aug. 5, 1955, Ch. 568, 69 Stat. 503, 2 U.S. Code §§ 42a, 46a

May 19, 1956, Ch. 313, 70 Stat. 175 (See 2 U.S. Code § 61-1)

June 27, 1956, Ch. 453, 70 Stat. 359, 2 U.S. Code § 42a

July 31, 1958, P.L. 85-570, 72 Stat. 442, 2 U.S. Code § 42a

Sept. 1, 1959, P.L. 86-213, 73 Stat. 443 (See 2 U.S. Code § 61-1)

July 12, 1960, P.L. 86-628, 74 Stat. 449, 2 U.S. Code § 42a

Aug. 10, 1961, P.L. 87-130, 75 Stat. 323 (See 2 U.S. Code § 61-1)

Dec. 30, 1963, P.L. 88-248, 77 Stat. 805, 2 U.S. Code § 42a

Jan. 6, 1964, P.L. 88-258, 77 Stat. 864, 2 U.S. Code § 46a

July 27, 1965, P.L. 89-90, 79 Stat. 268, 2 U.S. Code § 42a

May 29, 1967, P.L. 90-21, 81 Stat. 38, 2 U.S. Code § 46a

Legislative Branch Appropriations Act, 1943

June 8, 1942, Ch. 396, 56 Stat. 330, 2 U.S. Code §§ 42a, 60f, 75a, 117a; 40 U.S. Code §§ 164a, 174c to 174e, 206, 213a

Aug. 20, 1996, P.L. 104-186, 2 U.S. Code § 75a

Legislative Branch Appropriations Act, 1944

Oct. 12, 1984, P.L. 98-473, 2 U.S. Code 92e

Legislative Branch Appropriations Act, 1945

Oct. 12, 1984, P.L. 98-473, 2 U.S. Code 92e

Legislative Branch Appropriations Act, 1946

June 13, 1945, Ch. 189, 59 Stat. 238, 2 U.S. Code §§ 31a, 42a, 46a, 46c, 46d, 60f, 67a, 92e, 117a; 40 U.S. Code §§ 164a, 166a, 213a

July 5, 1945, Ch. 271, 59 Stat. 412, 7 U.S. Code §§ 174, 176; 42 U.S. Code § 1523 nt.

Dec. 28, 1945, Ch. 589, 59 Stat. 632, 2 U.S. Code §§ 45 nt., 46a nt., 46b nt.

May 18, 1946, Ch. 263, 60 Stat. 184, 40 U.S. Code §§ 164a, 166b

Oct. 12, 1984, P.L. 98-473, 2 U.S. Code § 92e

Aug. 20, 1996, P.L. 104-186, 2 U.S. Code § 75a

Legislative Branch Appropriations Act, 1947

July 1, 1946, Ch. 530, 60 Stat. 386, 2 U.S. Code §§ 46c, 46d, 46e, 60f, 67a, 92e 117a; 40 U.S. Code §§ 164a, 166a, 166c, 213a

Aug. 8, 1946, Ch. 870, 60 Stat. 911

Feb. 19, 1947, Ch. 3, 61 Stat. 4

July 30, 1947, Ch. 361, 61 Stat. 610

Oct. 24, 1951, Ch. 554, 65 Stat. 614, 2 U.S. Code § 60f

May 19, 1956, Ch. 313, 70 Stat. 175, 2 U.S. Code § 60f

Sept. 1, 1959, P.L. 86-213, 73 Stat. 443, 2 U.S. Code § 60f

Aug. 10, 1961, P.L. 87-130, 75 Stat. 323, 2 U.S. Code § 60f

July 27, 1965, P.L. 89-90, 79 Stat. 268, 2 U.S. Code §§ 46c, 46d, 46d-2

Aug. 27, 1966, P.L. 89-545, 80 Stat. 356, 2 U.S. Code § 46c

Oct. 12, 1984, P.L. 98-473, 2 U.S. Code § 92e

Legislative Branch Appropriations Act, 1948

July 17, 1947, Ch. 262, 61 Stat. 361, 2 U.S. Code §§ 46b nt., 46b- 1, 72b, 72c, 84b; 40 U.S. Code §§ 164a, 166a

Aug. 20, 1996, P.L. 104-186, 2 U.S. Code §§ 72b, 72c

Legislative Branch Appropriations Act, 1949

June 14, 1948, Ch. 467, 62 Stat. 423, 2 U.S. Code §§ 46a, 46b nt., 52, 65a; 40 U.S. Code §§ 164a, 166a

Oct. 13, 1964, P.L. 88-652, 78 Stat. 1084, 2 U.S. Code § 88c

Legislative Branch Appropriations Act, 1950

June 22, 1949, Ch. 235, 63 Stat. 216, 2 U.S. Code §§ 42b, 46b nt., 52, 65a, 69, 162a; 40 U.S. Code §§ 164a, 166a

Legislative Branch Appropriations Act, 1951

Sept. 6, 1950, Ch. 896, 64 Stat. 595, 2 U.S. Code §§ 46b nt., 52, 65a; 40 U.S. Code §§ 164a, 166a

Legislative Branch Appropriations Act, 1952

Oct. 11, 1951, Ch. 485, 65 Stat. 387, 2 U.S. Code §§ 42a, 46a, 46b, 52, 65a; 40 U.S. Code §§ 164a 166a

Legislative Branch Appropriations Act, 1953

July 9, 1952, Ch. 598, 66 Stat. 464, 2 U.S. Code §§ 46b nt., 52, 65a, 122; 40 U.S. Code §§ 164a, 166a

Legislative Branch Appropriations Act, 1955

Aug. 20, 1996, P.L. 104-186, 2 U.S. Code §§ 38a, 125

Legislative Branch Appropriations Act, 1957

June 27, 1956, Ch. 453, 70 Stat. 356, 2 U.S. Code §§ 42a, 46c, 46c nt., 52, 53, 61a-1, 61b, 61c, 61c nt., 61f to 61h, 65a, 66a, 66b, 68c, 72a-3, 123b, 127; 5 U.S. Code 932c; 40 U.S. Code §§ 164a, 166a, 166b nt. (See 44 U.S. Code §§ 309, 1913)

July 12, 1960, P.L. 86-628, 74 Stat. 449, 2 U.S. Code § 127

March 31, 1961, P.L. 87-14, 75 Stat. 29, 2 U.S. Code § 127

Aug. 14, 1961, P.L. 87-139, 75 Stat. 340, 2 U.S. Code § 68b

Oct. 13, 1964, P.L. 88-652, 78 Stat. 1084, 2 U.S. Code § 123b

July 27, 1965, P.L. 89-90, 79 Stat. 269, 2 U.S. Code § 53

Continued

Sept. 29, 1965, P.L. 89-211, 79 Stat. 857, 2 U.S. Code § 52

Nov. 10, 1969, P.L. 91-114, 83 Stat. 190, 2 U.S. Code § 68b

Dec. 12, 1969, P.L. 91-145, 83 Stat. 342, 2 U.S. Code § 53

Aug. 5, 1977, P.L. 95-94, 2 U.S. Code § 68

Sept. 8, 1978, P.L. 95-355, 2 U.S. Code § 68b

Sept. 10, 1982, P.L. 97-257, 2 U.S. Code § 123b

Nov. 5, 1990, P.L. 101-520, 2 U.S. Code §§ 123b, 123b nt.

Aug. 20, 1996, P.L. 104-186, 2 U.S. Code § 123b

Legislative Branch Appropriations Act, 1958

July 1, 1957, P.L. 85-75, 71 Stat. 244, 2 U.S. Code §§ 61f, 72a- 3, 72a-4, 129, 273, 274 nt.; 40 U.S. Code §§ 164a, 166a, 166b-1; 41 U.S. Code § 6a

Legislative Branch Appropriations Act, 1959

July 31, 1958, P.L. 85-570, 72 Stat. 570, 2 U.S. Code §§ 43b, 46d, 60a nt., 61f, 65b 72a-3; 40 U.S. Code §§ 164a, 166a, 216a

Aug. 21, 1959, P.L. 86-176, 73 Stat. 401, 2 U.S. Code § 43b

July 19, 1963, P.L. 88-70, 77 Stat. 82, 2 U.S. Code § 43b

July 27, 1965, P.L. 89-90, 79 Stat. 269, 2 U.S. Code § 43b

Aug. 28, 1965, P.L. 89-147, 79 Stat. 583, 2 U.S. Code § 43b

Aug. 27, 1966, P.L. 89-545, 80 Stat. 358, 2 U.S. Code § 43b

Sept. 17, 1967, P.L. 90-86, 81 Stat. 226, 2 U.S. Code §§ 43b, 43b-1

Dec. 12, 1969, P.L. 91-145, 83 Stat. 343, 2 U.S. Code § 43b

July 9, 1971, P.L. 92-51, 85 Stat. 128, 2 U.S. Code § 43b

Aug. 20, 1996, P.L. 104-186, 2 U.S. Code § 43b

Legislative Branch Appropriations Act, 1960

Aug. 21, 1959, P.L. 86-176, 73 Stat. 398, 2 U.S. Code §§ 43b, 60a nt., 60f, 61c, 61f 61h, 72a-3; 40 U.S. Code §§ 164a, 166a

Oct. 31, 1965, P.L. 89-309, 79 Stat. 1147, 40 U.S. Code § 166b-3

Dec. 16, 1967, P.L. 90-206, 81 Stat. 638, 40 U.S. Code § 166b-3

Nov. 21, 1989, P.L. 101-163, 40 U.S. Code § 166b-3

Legislative Branch Appropriations Act, 1961

July 12, 1960, P.L. 86-628, 74 Stat. 446, 2 U.S. Code §§ 42a, 43c, 60a, nt., 61d 61f, 72a-3, 102, 126a, 127, 195a; 22 U.S. Code §§ 276c-1, 1754; 40 U.S. Code §§ 164a, 166a

Nov. 14, 1967, P.L. 90-137, 81 Stat. 463, 22 U.S. Code § 276c-1

Nov. 2, 1994, P.L. 103-437, 22 U.S. Code § 276c-1

Aug. 20, 1996, P.L. 104-186, 2 U.S. Code § 46b; 22 U.S. Code § 276c-1

Legislative Branch Appropriations Act, 1962

Aug. 10, 1961, P.L. 87-130, 75 Stat. 320, 2 U.S. Code §§ 60a nt., 60f, 61f, 61h 72a-3, 127; 5 U.S. Code §§ 2205, 2206 nts.; 40 U.S. Code §§ 164a, 166a, 166b-1

July 27, 1965, P.L. 89-90, 79 Stat. 269, 2 U.S. Code § 127

Dec. 12, 1969, P.L. 91-145, 83 Stat. 343, 2 U.S. Code § 127

Legislative Branch Appropriations Act, 1963

Oct. 2, 1962, P.L. 87-730, 76 Stat. 680, 2 U.S. Code §§ 60a nt., 60i nt., 60j 61b-1, 61f, 72a-3, 124; 40 U.S. Code §§ 164a, 166a

Aug. 20, 1964, P.L. 88-454, 78 Stat. 550, 2 U.S. Code § 60j

July 28, 1967, P.L. 90-57, 81 Stat. 143, 2 U.S. Code § 60j

Dec. 16, 1967, P.L. 90-206, 81 Stat. 637, 2 U.S. Code § 60j

March 7, 1978, P.L. 95-240, 2 U.S. Code §§ 60j

Aug. 20, 1996, P.L. 104-186, 2 U.S. Code § 124

Legislative Branch Appropriations Act, 1964

Dec. 30, 1963, P.L. 88-248, 77 Stat. 803, 2 U.S. Code §§ 42a, 60a nt., 61f, 72a-3, 274 nt.; 40 U.S. Code § 166a

Legislative Branch Appropriations Act, 1965

Aug. 20, 1964, P.L. 88-454, 78 Stat. 535, 2 U.S. Code §§ 60a nt., 60f nt., 60j 60j-1, 72a-3, 104a; 31 U.S. Code § 67; 40 U.S. Code §§ 162b, 166a, 185a

Oct. 13, 1964, P.L. 88-656, 78 Stat. 1088, 2 U.S. Code § 104a

Oct. 6, 1992, P.L. 102-392, 2 U.S. Code § 104a

July 22, 1994, P.L. 103-283, 2 U.S. Code § 104a

Aug. 20, 1996, P.L. 104-186, 2 U.S. Code § 104a

Legislative Branch Appropriations Act, 1966

July 27, 1965, P.L. 89-90, 79 Stat. 265, 2 U.S. Code §§ 42a, 43b, 46c, 46d-2, 53, 60a nt., 61c nt., 61h, 72a-3, 126b, 127 nt.; 40 U.S. Code § 166a; 41 U.S. Code § 6a-1

Legislative Branch Appropriations Act, 1967

Aug. 27, 1966, P.L. 89-545, 80 Stat. 370, 2 U.S. Code §§ 43b, 46a-2, 46c, 60a nt., 60f nt., 72a-1a, 72a-3, 126-2, 143a; 40 U.S. Code § 166a

Legislative Branch Appropriations Act, 1968

July 28, 1967, P.L. 90-57, 81 Stat. 127, 2 U.S. Code §§ 46d-4, 60a nts., 60f nt., 60j, 61-1, 72a-3, 143a; 5 U.S. Code § 5533; 40 U.S. Code § 166a (See 44 U.S. Code § 309)

Dec. 16, 1967, P.L. 90-206, 81 Stat. 637, 2 U.S. Code § 61-1

Dec. 12, 1969, P.L. 91-145, 83 Stat. 340, 2 U.S. Code §§ 60f nt., 61-1

Oct. 26, 1970, P.L. 91-510, 84 Stat. 1181, 2 U.S. Code § 61-1

Aug. 5, 1977, P.L. 95-94, 2 U.S. Code § 61-1

Oct. 18, 1978, P.L. 95-482, 2 U.S. Code § 61-1

July 8, 1980, P.L. 96-304, 2 U.S. Code §§ 61-1 et seq.

July 17, 1984, P.L. 98-367, 2 U.S. Code § 61-1

July 11, 1987, P.L. 100-71, 2 U.S. Code § 61-1

Oct. 21, 1987, P.L. 100-137, 2 U.S. Code § 61-1

Dec. 22, 1987, P.L. 100-202, 2 U.S. Code § 61-1

Aug. 20, 1996, P.L. 104-186, 2 U.S. Code § 61-1

June 12, 1997, P.L. 105-18, 2 U.S. Code § 61-1

Oct. 21, 1998, P.L. 105-275, 2 U.S. Code § 61-1

Legislative Branch Appropriations Act, 1969

July 23, 1968, P.L. 90-417, 82 Stat. 398, 2 U.S. Code §§ 42a, 46a-3, 60a nt., 72a-3, 143a; 40 U.S. Code §§ 166a, 167a nt.

Legislative Branch Appropriations Act, 1970

Dec. 12, 1969, P.L. 91-145, 83 Stat. 338, 2 U.S. Code §§ 42a, 43b, 46a, 46a-4, 53, 60a, 60f nt., 61-1, 61a-3, 61a-4, 61h-2, 61j, 72a-3, 127, 143a; 40 U.S. Code §§ 166a, 174b-1 nt.

Aug. 18, 1970, P.L. 91-382, 84 Stat. 807, 2 U.S. Code §§ 61a-4 to 61a-6, 61c-1, 61d, 61f-1

Dec. 22, 1987, P.L. 100-202, 2 U.S. Code § 61d-1

Nov. 21, 1989, P.L. 101-163, 2 U.S. Code § 61d-1

Legislative Branch Appropriations Act, 1971

Aug. 18, 1970, P.L. 91-382, 84 Stat. 807, 2 U.S. Code §§ 46d-5, 60a nt., 61a-4 to 61a-6, 61c-1, 61d, 61f-1, 64a, 143a nt., 72a-3 nt., 40 U.S. Code §§ 164a, 166a nt., 174b-1 nt.

Nov. 21, 1989, P.L. 101-163, 40 U.S. Code § 164a

Legislative Branch Appropriations Act, 1972

Nov. 5, 1990, P.L. 101-509, 40 U.S. Code § 174j-8

Legislative Branch Appropriations Act, 1973

July 10, 1972, P.L. 92-342, 86 Stat. 432, 2 U.S. Code §§ 61b-1a, 143a, 442; 40 U.S. Code §§ 166a, 174j-4

Oct. 31, 1972, P.L. 92-607, 86 Stat. 1508, 2 U.S. Code §§ 42a, 43b, 55

Legislative Branch Appropriations Act, 1974

Nov. 1, 1973, P.L. 93-145, 87 Stat. 527, 2 U.S. Code §§ 46a-3 nt., 58, 60a nt., 61-1, 61a-10, 61d, 61f-5, 64-1, 68-1, 143a, 208c; 5 U.S. Code § 5533; 40 U.S. Code §§ 166a, 175 nt., 206c; 44 U.S. Code § 906 nt.

Jan. 3, 1974, P.L. 93-245, 87 Stat. 1078, 2 U.S. Code §§ 61-1, 61f-6

March 27, 1974, P.L. 93-255, 88 Stat. 52, 2 U.S. Code § 61-1

July 25, 1974, P.L. 93-256, 88 Stat. 390, 41 U.S. Code § 6a-1

Aug. 13, 1974, P.L. 93-371, 88 Stat. 424, 2 U.S. Code §§ 58, 59, 60c-3, 60j, 61-1, 61a, 61a-3, 61b, 61d-1, 61e, 61g, 61h, 61h-1, 61j, 63a, 64a-1, 64b, 143a, 195b, 273, 274, 22 U.S. Code § 1734, 40 U.S. Code §§ 166a, 206c

May 19, 1975, P.L. 9422, 89 Stat. 86, 2 U.S. Code § 68b

July 25, 1975, P.L. 94-59, 89 Stat. 269, 2 U.S. Code §§ 59, 60a nt., 61-1, 61h-3; 22 U.S. Code § 276c-1; 40 U.S. Code § 174j-8

Oct. 12, 1984, P.L. 98-473, 2 U.S. Code § 68-1

Legislative Branch Appropriations Act, 1975

Aug. 5, 1977, P.L. 95-94, 2 U.S. Code § 59

July 8, 1980, P.L. 96-304, 2 U.S. Code § 59

Aug. 15, 1985, P.L. 99-88, 2 U.S. Code § 69

April 10, 1991, P.L. 102-27, 2 U.S. Code § 59

Aug. 14, 1991, P.L. 102-90, 2 U.S. Code § 59

Sept. 16, 1996, P.L. 104-197, 2 U.S. Code § 59

Legislative Branch Appropriations Act, 1976

Aug. 5, 1977, P.L. 95-94, 2 U.S. Code § 61a-9a

Sept. 8, 1978, P.L. 95-355, 2 U.S. Code § 61a-9

July 17, 1984, P.L. 98-367, 2 U.S. Code §§ 61a-9a, 61a-9a nt.

Legislative Branch Appropriations Act, 1977

Oct. 1, 1976, P.L. 94-440, 2 U.S. Code § 60c-2a

Oct. 1, 1988, P.L. 100-458, 2 U.S. Code §§ 121a, 121b

Legislative Branch Appropriations Act, 1978

Aug. 5, 1977, P.L. 95-94, 2 U.S. Code §§ 31a-1 et seq.; 17 U.S. Code §§ 203 et seq.; 17 U.S. Code Appx. § 805; 44 U.S. Code §§ 906 et seq.

Nov. 30, 1983, P.L. 98-191, 2 U.S. Code § 58a

Nov. 5, 1990, P.L. 101-509, 2 U.S. Code § 906

Oct. 6, 1992, P.L. 102-392, 2 U.S. Code § 61-1 nt.

Legislative Branch Appropriations Act, 1979

Oct. 2, 1982, P.L. 97-276, 2 U.S. Code §§ 60j-3, 60j-3 nt.

Oct. 16, 1986, P.L. 99-492, 2 U.S. Code § 72a nt.

April 3, 1987, P.L. 100-18, 2 U.S. Code § 72a nt.

Legislative Branch Appropriations Act, 1983

Oct. 2, 1982, P.L. 97-276, 2 U.S. Code § 60a nt.

Legislative Branch Appropriations Act, 1986

Nov. 13, 1985, P.L. 99-151, 22 U.S. Code § 2291 nt.

Legislative Branch Appropriations Act, 1987

July 11, 1987, P.L. 100-71, 101 Stat. 424

Nov. 21, 1989, P.L. 101-163, 2 U.S. Code § 117e, 40 U.S. Code §§ 84B, 184e, 184f

Aug. 14, 1991, P.L. 102-90, 40 U.S. Code §§ 184b-184f

Aug. 20, 1996, P.L. 104-186, 2 U.S. Code § 117e

Oct. 7, 1997, P.L. 105-55, 2 U.S. Code § 117e

Legislative Branch Appropriations Act, 1988

Dec. 22, 1987, P.L. 100-202, 101 Stat. 1329

Nov. 21, 1989, P.L. 101-163, 40 U.S. Code §§ 166b-3a, 166b-3a nt.

Nov. 5, 1990, P.L. 101-520, 2 U.S. Code § 60a-2a

Aug. 14, 1991, P.L. 102-90, 2 U.S. Code §§ 60a-1b, 60a-2a

Aug. 14, 1991, P.L. 102-90, 40 U.S. Code § 175 nt.

Dec. 12, 1991, P.L. 102-229, 40 U.S. Code § 216c

Aug. 20, 1996, P.L. 104-186, 2 U.S. Code § 60a-2a; 4 U.S. Code § 105 nt.

Legislative Branch Appropriations Act, 1989

Oct. 1, 1988, P.L. 100-458, 102 Stat. 2185

May 25, 1990, P.L. 101-302, 2 U.S. Code § 68-6

Nov. 19, 1995, P.L. 104-53, 40 U.S. Code § 216c

Aug. 20, 1996, P.L. 104-186, 2 U.S. Code § 117f; 40 U.S. Code § 175 nt.

Oct. 21, 1998, P.L. 105-275, 40 U.S. Code § 216c

Legislative Branch Appropriations Act, 1990

Nov. 21, 1989, P.L. 101-163, 103 Stat. 1041

Nov. 3, 1990, P.L. 101-520, 39 U.S. Code §§ 3210 nt., 3216, 3216 nt.

Aug. 14, 1991, P.L. 102-90, 2 U.S. Code § 121c

Oct. 6, 1992, P.L. 102-392, 39 U.S. Code § 3210 nt.

July 27, 1995, P.L. 104-19, 40 U.S. Code § 162-1

Nov. 19, 1995, P.L. 104-53, 2 U.S. Code § 130e

Legislative Branch Appropriations Act, 1991

Nov. 5, 1990, P.L. 101-520, 2 U.S. Code §§ 30a, 57 nt., 58a-4, 59e-59g, 60a nt., 60a-1b, 61g-6, 61g-6 nt., 61g-6a, 61g-8, 68-6a, 141, 141 nt., 142, 166 nt., 167j, 174b-1 nt., 605; 28 U.S. Code § 461 nt.; 31 U.S. Code § 782 nt.; 39 U.S. Code § 3210; 40 U.S. Code §§ 166 nt., 166a, 166b-2, 166b-3b, 188b-6, 206 nt., 212a, 216d; 44 U.S. Code §§ 303, 309, 501 nt., 1703, 1707

Aug. 14, 1991, P.L. 102-90, 40 U.S. Code § 166b-3b

Dec. 12, 1991, P.L. 102-229, 2 U.S. Code § 59e

Oct. 6, 1992, P.L. 102-392, 44 U.S. Code § 501 nt.

Oct. 23, 1992, P.L. 102-451, 2 U.S. Code § 141 nt.

July 22, 1994, P.L. 103-283, 2 U.S. Code § 59f

Aug. 20, 1996, P.L. 104-186, 2 U.S. Code § 59e

Oct. 7, 1997, P.L. 105-55, 40 U.S. Code § 166b-3b

Oct. 21, 1998, P.L. 105-275, 2 U.S. Code § 59e

April 8, 1999, P.L. 106-19, 2 U.S. Code § 59e

Legislative Branch Appropriations Act, 1992

Aug. 14, 1991, P.L. 102-90, 105 Stat. 471

Oct. 2, 1992, P.L. 102-378, 2 U.S. Code § 31-2

Oct. 6, 1992, P.L. 102-392, 40 U.S. Code § 184g

Aug. 20, 1996, P.L. 104-186, 40 U.S. Code §§ 184g

Legislative Branch Appropriations Act, 1993

Oct. 6, 1992, P.L. 102-392, 106 Stat. 1728

July 2, 1993, P.L. 103-50, 40 U.S. Code § 214d

July 22, 1994, P.L. 103-283, 44 U.S. Code § 501 nt.

Nov. 15, 1995, P.L. 104-49, 29 U.S. Code § 1854 nt.

Nov. 19, 1995, P.L. 104-53, 40 U.S. Code § 216c nt.

Sept. 23, 1996, P.L. 104-201, 44 U.S. Code § 501 nt.

Legislative Branch Appropriations Act, 1994

Aug. 11, 1993, P.L. 103-69, 107 Stat. 692

July 22, 1994, P.L. 103-283, 2 U.S. Code § 60-1 nt.

Aug. 20, 1996, P.L. 104-186, 2 U.S. Code § 96a

Oct. 19, 1996, P.L. 104-316, 2 U.S. Code § 60-1 nt.; 31 U.S. Code § 1105 nt.

Legislative Branch Appropriations Act, 1995

July 22, 1994, P.L. 103-283, 108 Stat. 1423

Aug. 20, 1996, P.L. 104-186, 2 U.S. Code § 74a-6

Legislative Branch Appropriations Act, 1996
Nov. 19, 1995, P.L. 104-53, 109 Stat. 514
Sept. 16, 1996, P.L. 104-197, 2 U.S. Code
§ 58a nt.; 40 U.S. Code § 174k nt.
Oct. 19, 1996, P.L. 104-316, 31 U.S. Code
§ 501 nt.
Oct. 7, 1997, P.L. 105-55, 2 U.S. Code § 60o

Legislative Branch Appropriations Act, 1997
Sept. 16, 1996, P.L. 104-197, 110 Stat. 2394

Legislative Branch Appropriations Act, 1998
Oct. 7, 1997, P.L. 105-55, 111 Stat. 1177
Oct. 21, 1998, P.L. 105-275, 40 U.S. Code
§ 174j-1 nt.

Legislative Branch Appropriations Act, 1999
Oct. 21, 1998, P.L. 105-275, 112 Stat. 2430

Legislative Budget Committee Act
Wash. Rev. Code Ann., 44. 28. 010 et seq.

Legislative Building Maintenance Appropriation Act
N.C. Laws 1963, Ch. 1051

Legislative Claims Commission Act
Minn. Stat. 1974, 3.66 et seq.

Legislative Code of Ethics
Pa. Purdon's Stat., Title 46, § 143.1 et seq.

Legislative Commission Hearing Act
Ill. Rev. Stat. 1991, Ch. 63, § 13.01 et seq.

Legislative Commission on Total Quality Government Act
Ala. Code 1975, § 41-9-940 et seq.

Legislative Commission Reorganization Act
Ill. Rev. Stat. 1991, Ch. 63, § 1001-1 et seq.

Legislative Commission to Preserve the Peace Act
Ala. Acts 1963, p. 380, No. 3

Legislative Construction Act
Pa. Cons. Stat., Title 1, § 1501 et seq.

Legislative Council Act
Md. Ann. Code 1974, Art. SG, § 2-402 et seq.
Mich. Comp. Laws Ann., 4.1101 et seq.
Mont. Code Ann., 5-11-101 et seq.
N.H. Rev. Stat. 1955, Superseded Volume, 17:1 et seq.
Wash. Rev. Code Ann., 44.24.010 et seq.

Legislative Council Committee Law
Tenn. Code Ann., Superseded Vol., 3-401 et seq.

Legislative Disaster Succession Act
N.M. Stat. Ann., 12-11-11 et seq.

Legislative Districting Act
Iowa Code Ann., 41.1, 41.2
N.M. Stat. Ann. 1953, 2-8-1 et seq.

Legislative Districts Act
Ill. Rev. Stat. 1991, Ch. 46, § 800 et seq.
Md. Ann. Code 1974, Art. SG, § 2-402 et seq.
Mich. Comp. Laws Ann., 4.1101 et seq.
Mont. Code Ann., 5-11-101 et seq.
N.H. Rev. Stat. 1955, Superseded Volume, 17:1 et seq.
Wash. Rev. Code 1981, 44.24.010 et seq.

Legislative Districts Apportionment Act
Wis. Stat. Ann., 4.001 et seq.

Legislative Districts Division Act
Ill. Rev. Stat. 1991, Ch. 46, § 810 et seq.

Legislative Emergency Succession and Procedures Act
Neb. Rev. Stat. 1943, 50-501 et seq.

Legislative Enabling Act
Alaska Stat. 1962, §§ 11.45.040, 37.10.085

Legislative Endowment Scholarship Act
N.M. Stat. Ann., 21-21J-1 et seq.

Legislative Finance Act
Mont. Code Ann., 5-12-101 et seq.

Legislative Findings and Declarations Act

Cal. Code of Civil Procedure § 116.120

Legislative Highway Relocation Assistance Act

See Highway Relocation Assistance Act

Legislative History Act

Mont. Code Ann., 5-4-401 et seq.

Legislative Information System Act

Ill. Rev. Stat. 1991, Ch. 63, § 42.10 et seq.

Legislative Inquiry Act

Wash. Rev. Code Ann., 44.16.010 et seq.

Legislative Intern Act

Mont. Code Ann., 5-6-101 et seq.

Legislative Investigating Commission Act

Ill. Rev. Stat. 1991, Ch. 127, § 146 et seq.

Legislative Investigations Rules Act

Me. Rev. Stat. Ann. 1964, Title 3, § 401 et seq.

Legislative-Judiciary Appropriation Act, 1944

June 28, 1943, Ch. 173, 57 Stat. 220, 2 U.S. Code §§ 60f, 92e, 117a; 40 U.S. Code §§ 164a 206, 213a

Legislative-Judiciary Appropriation Act, 1945

June 26, 1944, Ch. 277, 58 Stat. 277, 2 U.S. Code §§ 42a, 60f, 92e, 117a; 40 U.S. Code §§ 164a 213a

Legislative-Judiciary Appropriation Act, 1954

Aug. 1, 1953, Ch. 304, 67 Stat. 318, 2 U.S. Code §§ 31c, 46a, 46b nt., 46c, 46c nt., 46d, 46d nt., 52, 65a, 122; 28 U.S. Code § 604 nt.; 40 U.S. Code §§ 164a, 166a, 174b-1 nt. (See 44 U.S. Code §§ 309, 310, 1117)

Legislative-Judiciary Appropriation Act, 1955

July 2, 1954, Ch. 455, 68 Stat. 396, 2 U.S. Code §§ 38a, 42a, 42a- 1, 42b, 46b, 46d, 46f-1, 52, 53, 60g-1, 65a, 72a-3, 81, 119a, 122, 122a, 124, 125; 28 U.S. Code § 604 nt.; 40 U.S. Code §§ 164a, 166a

Legislative Law

N.Y. Consol. Laws Ch. 32

Legislative Lobbying Act

Ind. Code Ann., 2-7-1-1 et seq.

Legislative Materials Act (Copies)

Ill. Rev. Stat. 1991, Ch. 63, §§ 800, 801

Legislative Merit Award Program Act

Mich. Comp. Laws Ann., 390.1301 et seq.

Legislative Misconduct Act

Ill. Rev. Stat. 1991, Ch. 38, § 90-0.1 et seq.

Legislative Open Records Act

Cal. Government Code § 9070 et seq.

Legislative Pardons Act

Pa. Purdon's Stat., Title 19, § 893

Legislative Pay Act, 1929

June 20, 1929, Ch. 33, 46 Stat. 32

Legislative Policy Committee Act

Md. Ann. Code 1974, Art. SG, § 2-401 et seq.

Legislative Primary Act

Ill. Rev. Stat. 1991, Ch. 46, § 8-1 et seq.

Legislative Privilege Act

D.C. Code Ann., § 1-221 et seq.

Legislative Program Evaluation Act

Neb. Laws 1992, L.B. 988, §§ 1 to 15

Legislative Program Review and Evaluation Act

Va. Code 1950, § 30-64 et seq.

Legislative Reapportionment Act

See Reapportionment Act (Legislative)

N.M. Stat. Ann. 1953, 2-9-64 et seq.

Continued

Legislative Reapportionment Act (House)
N.M. Stat. Ann., 2-7B-1 et seq.

Legislative Reapportionment Act (Senate)
N.M. Stat. Ann., 2-8B-1 et seq.

Legislative Redistricting Act
Minn. Stat. 1957, 2.02 et seq.

Legislative Reference Bureau Act
Ill. Rev. Stat. 1991, Ch. 63, § 24m et seq.

Legislative Reference Library Act
Tex. Rev. Civ. Stat., Art. 5444a

Legislative Reform Act
Cal. Government Code § 9900 et seq.

Legislative Reorganization Act
Tex. Government Code, § 301.011 et seq.

Legislative Reorganization Act, 1946
Aug. 2, 1946, Ch. 753, 60 Stat. 812, 2 U.S. Code §§ 31, 31a, 72a, 72a nts., 74a, 74b, 74b nt., 88a, 132a, 132b, 166, 166 nt., 261, 261 nt., 262 to 270, 271 nt. (See 10 U.S. Code § 1552) 15 U.S. Code §§ 1022, 1024; 31 U.S. Code §§ 59, 60, 215 to 217 nt.; 33 U.S. Code §§ 525, 525 nts., 526 to 533, 541 nt., 542 nt., 701 nt.; 40 U.S. Code §§ 166 nt., 174d-1 (See 44 U.S. Code §§ 101, 905)
Jan. 31, 1947, Ch. 1, 61 Stat. 3
July 30, 1947, Ch. 361, 61 Stat. 611, 2 U.S. Code § 72a
Jan. 19, 1949, Ch. 2, 63 Stat. 4, 2 U.S. Code § 31
Feb. 24, 1949, Ch. 8, 63 Stat. 8, 2 U.S. Code § 72a
Aug. 5, 1953, Ch. 330, 67 Stat. 387, 2 U.S. Code § 75a-1
March 6, 1954, Ch. 59, 68 Stat. 21
March 2, 1955, Ch. 9, 69 Stat. 11, 2 U.S. Code § 31
June 20, 1958, P.L. 85-462, 72 Stat. 209, 2 U.S. Code § 72a
July 12, 1960, P.L. 86-622, 74 Stat. 410
Aug. 14, 1964, P.L. 88-426, 78 Stat. 414, 2 U.S. Code §§ 31, 72a
Oct. 29, 1965, P.L. 89-301, 79 Stat. 1120, 2 U.S. Code § 31
Sept. 15, 1969, P.L. 91-67, 83 Stat. 107, 2 U.S. Code § 31

Oct. 26, 1970, P.L. 91-510, 84 Stat. 1140, 2 U.S. Code §§ 72a, 166, 190a to 190d, 198
Dec. 16, 1970, P.L. 91-552, 84 Stat. 1440, 2 U.S. Code §§ 190a, 190b
July 9, 1971, P.L. 92-51, 85 Stat. 132, 2 U.S. Code §§ 282a, 282d
Oct. 11, 1971, P.L. 92-136, 85 Stat. 376, 2 U.S. Code §§ 72a, 190a, 190d; 31 §§ 1151 to 1154
July 12, 1974, P.L. 93-344, 88 Stat. 325, 2 U.S. Code §§ 190b, 190d
Dec. 19, 1985, P.L. 99-190, 2 U.S. Code § 166
Oct. 1, 1988, P.L.100-458, 2 U.S. Code § 72a
Nov. 30, 1989, P.L. 101-194, 2 U.S. Code § 31
Nov. 5, 1990, P.L. 101-509, 2 U.S. Code § 31
Oct. 13, 1994, P.L. 103-356, 2 U.S. Code § 31
Aug. 20, 1996, P.L. 104-186, 2 U.S. Code §§ 72a, 74b, 75a-1, 88a, 190d

Legislative Reorganization Act, 1970
Oct. 26, 1970, P.L. 91-510, 84 Stat. 1140, 2 U.S. Code §§ 28, 29, 60-1, 61-1, 72a, 88b-1, 166, 190a to 190d, 190f, 190h to 190k, 198, 281 to 281b, 282 to 282e, 331 to 336 411 to 417, 2107, 8332; 5 U.S. Code §§ 2107, 5533, 8332; 8 U.S. Code 1106 nt.; 31 U.S. Code §§ 11, 1151 to 1157, 1171 to 1176; 40 U.S. Code §§ 166 nt., 166b-1a to 166b-1f, 184a, 193m- 1, 851
Dec. 16, 1970, P.L. 91-552, 84 Stat. 1440
Sept. 20, 1977, P.L. 95-110, 2 U.S. Code § 190j
Nov. 13, 1985, 99-151, 2 U.S. Code § 166
Aug. 20, 1996, P.L. 104-186, 2 U.S. Code §§ 88b-1, 184a, 331, 332, 334, 335, 336, 411-417; 40 U.S. Code § 851
Oct. 9, 1996, P.L. 104-279, 40 U.S. Code § 851

Legislative Reorganization Act, 1971
July 9, 1971, P.L. 92-51, 85 Stat. 132, 2 U.S. Code §§ 282a, 282d

Legislative Research Unit Reports Act
Ill. Rev. Stat. 1991, Ch. 63, §§ 1050, 1051

Legislative Retirement System Act
Ga. Code Ann., 47-6-1 et seq.
Mich. Comp. Laws Ann., 38.1001 et seq.

Legislative Service and Governor's Pension Act
Utah Code Ann. 1953, 49-7-101 et seq.

Legislative Service Commission Act
Ohio Rev. Code 1953, 103.11 et seq.

Legislative Services Committee Law
Tenn. Code Ann., 3-10-101 et seq.

Legislative Services Law
N.J. Stat. Ann., 52:11-55 et seq.

Legislative Study Committee Act
N.H. Rev. Stat. 1955, 17-B:1 et seq.

Legislative Succession Act
Ida. Code 1947, 67-413 et seq.
Kan. Stat. Ann., 48-1301 et seq.
La. Rev. Stat. Ann., 24:61 et seq.
Okla. Stat. Ann., Title 63, § 686.1 et seq.
S.C. Code Ann. 1976, § 2-5-10 et seq.
S.D. Codified Laws 1967, 2-3-1 et seq.

Legislative Succession Act (Emergency)
See Emergency Interim Legislative Sucession Act
Tex. Government Code, § 304.001 et seq.

Legislative Succession and Procedures Act (Emergency)
Neb. Rev. Stat. 1943, 50-501 et seq.

Legislators' Retirement Act
Cal. Government Code § 9350 et seq.
Mo. Rev. Stat. 1969, 104.630 et seq.
Neb. Rev. Stat. 1943, 50-901 et seq.
Nev. Rev. Stat. 1979 Reprint, 218. 2371 et seq.

Legislature Act
Wash. Rev. Code Ann., 44.04.010 et seq.

Legislature Highway Relocation Assistance Act of 1968
Cal. Streets and Highways Code 156 et seq.

Legitimacy Act (Children)
Miss. Code Ann. 1972, § 93-7-5
N.Y. Domestic Relations Law (Consol. Laws Ch. 14) § 24

Va. Code 1950, §§ 20-31.1, 64.1-7

Legitimacy Law (Annulment)
N.Y. Domestic Relations Law (Consol. Laws Ch. 14) § 24

Legitimacy of Children Law
Miss. Code Ann. 1972, § 93-9-1 et seq.

Legitimation Act (Illegitimate Children)
Cal. Civil Code § 230
Ill. Rev. Stat. 1991, Ch. 40, § 303
La. Rev. Stat. Ann., 9:391
N.C. Gen. Stat. 1943, § 49-10 et seq.
Ohio Rev. Code 1953, 2105.18
Okla. Stat. Ann., Title 10, § 55
W. Va. Code 1966, § 42-1-6

Lehigh Scenic River Act
Pa. Purdon's Stat., Title 32, § 820.61

Leicester Water Supply District Improvement Loan Act
Mass. Acts 1954, Ch. 363

Leighton Act (New Counties)
Mont. Code Ann., 7-2-2201 et seq.

Lein Act (Surety)
Kan. Stat. Ann., 60-1111 et seq.

L.E.I.N. Policy Council Act
Mich. Comp. Laws Ann., 18.211 et seq.

Lemon Law
Ariz. Rev. Stat. Ann., § 44-1261 et seq.
Colo. Rev. Stat., 42-10-101 to 42-10-107
Fla. Stat. Ann., 681.10 et seq.
Iowa Code Ann., 322G.1 et seq.
Kan. Stat. Ann., 50-645 et seq.
La. Rev. Stat. Ann., 51:1941 et seq.
Mass. Gen. Laws Ann., 90:7N et seq.
Miss. Code Ann. 1972, § 63-17-151 et seq.
N.H. Rev. Stat. 1955, 357-D:1 et seq.
N.M. Stat. Ann., 57-16A-1 et seq.
S.C. Code Ann. 1976, § 56-28-10 et seq.
Tenn. Code Ann., 55-24-201
Tex. Rev. Civ. Stat., Art. 4413(36)
Wis. Stat. Ann., 218.015

Lemon Law (Automobile)
Cal. Civil Code § 1793.2
Fla. Stat. Ann., 681.10 et seq.
Ga. Code Ann., 10-1-640 et seq.
Mich. Comp. Laws Ann., 257.1401 et seq.
Mo. Rev. Stat. 1978, 407.560 et seq.
N.J. Stat. Ann., 56:12-29 et seq.
N.Y. General Business Law (Consol. Laws
   Ch. 20) § 198a
Okla. Stat. Ann., Title 15, § 901
Pa. Purdon's Stat., Title 73, § 1951 et seq.
P.R. Laws Ann. 1954, Title 10, § 2051 et seq.
Va. Code 1950, § 59.1-207.9 et seq.

Lemon Law (Dogs and Cats)
N.Y. General Business Law (Consol. Laws
   Ch. 20) § 740 et seq.

Lemon Law (Wheelchair)
N.Y. General Business Law (Consol. Laws
   Ch. 20) § 670

Lemon Law Buyback Act
Cal. Civil Code §§ 1793.23, 1793.24

Lemon Law II
Mont. Code Ann., 61-4-501 et seq.

**Lempert-Wright-Polanco Hazardous Waste
Treatment Permit Reform Act**
Cal. Statutes 1992, Ch. 1345

Lend-Lease Act
March 11, 1941, Ch. 11, 22 U.S. Code §§ 411
   to 419
March 11, 1943, Ch. 15, 22 U.S. Code
   §§ 412, 415
May 17, 1944, Ch. 198, 22 U.S. Code §§ 412,
   415
April 16, 1945, Ch. 61, 22 U.S. Code §§ 412,
   415

Lender Credit Card Act
Ga. Code Ann., 7-5-1 et seq.
Iowa Code Ann., 536C.1 et seq.

Lender Farmer Mediation Act
Minn. Stat. Ann., 583.20 et seq.

Lender Licensing Act
Colo. Rev. Stat. 1963, 5-3-101
Colo. Rev. Stat. 1963, 73-2-1 et seq.
D.C. Code Ann., § 26-701 et seq.
N.Y. Banking Law (Consol. Laws Ch. 2)
   § 340 et seq.

Lenders Act (Commercial Finance)
Cal. Financial Code § 26000 et seq.

Lenders of Money Act
See Money Lenders Act

Lending Act (Foreign Corporation)
Ill. Rev. Stat. 1991, Ch. 17, §§ 2900, 2901

Lending Act (Truth in)
Tenn. Code Ann., 47-14-125

Lending and Mortgage Brokerage Act
Fla. Laws 1991, Ch. 245, § 1 to 49
Fla. Stat. Ann., 494.001 et seq.

**Lenoir County Peace Officers' Benefit
Association Act**
N.C. Laws 1961, Ch. 1137

**Lenox Park Community Improvement
District Act**
Ga. Laws 1988, p. 4582

Lenox Water Loan Act
Mass. Acts 1958, Ch. 447

**Leominster Northwest School Construction
Act**
Mass. Acts 1956, Ch. 673

Leominster Sewerage Loan Act
Mass. Acts 1961, Ch. 337

**Leon County and Tallahassee Consolidated
Government Charter**
Fla. Special Laws 1971, Ch. 71-747, 1973,
   Ch. 73-628

**Leon County and Tallahassee Government
Charter**
Fla. Special Laws 1976, Ch. 76-492

Leprosy Act
March 3, 1905, Ch. 1443, 33 Stat. 1009
Haw. Rev. Stat. Ann., § 326-1 et seq.

Leroy Brown, Jr. and Karen Clarke Witness Protection Program
Conn. Public Acts 1999, No. 240, §§ 6, 7

Leroy F. Green School Facilities Act
Cal. Education Code 1976, § 17070.10 et seq.

Leroy F. Greene State School Building Lease-Purchase Law
Cal. Education Code 1976, § 17700 et seq.

Lesinski Pension Increase Act
June 6, 1940, Ch. 246, 54 Stat. 237

Lessor Liability Act (Motor Vehicle)
Conn. Gen. Stat. Ann., § 14-154a

Lessors Liability Act
Ill. Rev. Stat. 1991, Ch. 80, §§ 90, 91

Lethal Gas Chamber Act
Miss. Code Ann. 1972, § 99-19-51 et seq.

Lethal Weapons Training Act
Pa. Purdon's Stat., Title 22, § 41 et seq.

LeTort Spring Run Scenic River Act
Pa. Purdon's Stat., Title 32, § 820.101 et seq.

Letters of Credit (Commercial Laws)
La. Rev. Stat. Ann., 10:5-101 et seq.

Letters of Credit (Uniform Commercial Code)
See Uniform Commercial Code, Letters of Credit

Letters of Credit Act
See Uniform Commercial Code-Revised Article 5
Mass. Gen. Laws Ann., 106:5-101 et seq.
Mont. Code Ann. 1947, 30-601 et seq.

Letters of Credit Act of Puerto Rico
P.R. Laws Ann. 1954, Title 7, § 1601 et seq.

Levee Act
Ind. Code Ann., 13-2-19-1 et seq., 19-4-11-1 et seq.

Levee and Drainage Law
Tenn. Code Ann., 69-6-101 et seq.

Levee Authority Districts Act
Ind. Code Ann., 36-1-3.5-2 et seq.

Levee District Act
Ark. Code Ann. 1987, 14-123-201, 14-123-204
Cal. Water Code § 70000 et seq.
Ida. Code 1947, 42-4401 et seq.
Mo. Rev. Stat., 245.010 et seq.

Levee District Act (Bonds)
Cal. Statutes 1911, Ch. 139, p. 303

Levee District Act (Formation)
Cal. Statutes 1905, Ch. 310, p. 327

Levee District Act (Lower San Joaquin)
Cal. Statutes 1955, Ch. 1075, p. 2047

Levee Drainage Act
Ill. Rev. Stat. 1991, Ch. 42

Level of Lake Michigan Act
Ill. Rev. Stat. 1991, Ch. 19, § 119 et seq.

Lever Act (Food Control)
Aug. 10, 1917, Ch. 53, 40 Stat. 276
Oct. 22, 1919, Ch. 80, 41 Stat. 297

Levering Act (Public Employees Oath)
Cal. Government Code § 3100 et seq.

Levering Burton Act (Defense Production)
Cal. Statutes 1950, 3rd Ex. Sess., Ch. 33, p. 58, § 11
Cal. Statutes 1959, Ch. 99, p. 1951

Levering Reese Motor Vehicle Sales Finance Act
Cal. Civil Code § 2981 et seq.

Levitation Demonstration Project Act (Magnetic)
Fla. Stat. Ann., 341.401 et seq.

Levy Act (Elections)
N.Y. Laws 1911, Ch. 649

Levy and Tax Administration Act (Motor Carrier)
Tenn. Code Ann., 55-4-113

Lewd Invitation Act
D.C. Code 1973, § 22-2701

Lewdness Public Nuisance Act
Ill. Rev. Stat. 1991, Ch. 100 1/2, § 0.01 et seq.

Lewes-Cape May Ferry Act
N.J. Stat. Ann., 27:12B-27 et seq.

Lewis Air Quality Management Act
Cal. Health and Safety Code § 40400 et seq.

Lewis-Brown-Rodda-Moretti Child Development Act
Cal. Education Code 1976, § 8200 et seq.

Lewis County Tax Act
N.Y. Laws 1884, Ch. 153

Lewis-Pollock Act (Mining)
Ohio Laws Vol. 114, p. 603

Lewis-Presly Air Quality Management Act
Cal. Health and Safety Code § 40400 et seq.

Lewisboro Dog Control Law
N.Y. Local Laws 1967, Town of Lewisboro, p. 1716
N.Y. Local Laws 1972, Town of Lewisboro, p. 1980

Lewiston Dog Control Law
N.Y. Local Laws 1972, Town of Lewiston, p. 1983

Lewiston Recreational Vehicle Park and Camping Ground Law
N.Y. Local Laws 1971, Town of Lewiston, p. 2599

Lewiston Subdivision Regulation
N.Y. Local Laws 1973, Town of Lewiston, p. 2430

Lewisville Municipal Courts of Record Act
Tex. Government Code, § 30.01321 et seq.

Lexington Market Authority Act
Md. Laws 1945, Ch. 863

Lexington School Building Loan Act
Mass. Acts 1947, Ch. 186

Lexington School Remodeling Loan Act
Mass. Acts 1958, Ch. 4

Leyden Township Special Needs Law
Ill. Rev. Stat. 1991, Ch. 85, § 7701-1 et seq.

Liabilities Certification Act
Mass. Gen. Laws Ann., 78:22 et seq.

Liability Act (Civil Defense)
Colo. Rev. Stat., 24-32-2301 et seq.

Liability Act (Common Carrier)
Ill. Comp. Stat. 1992, Ch. 740, § 25/0.01 et seq.

Liability Act (Credit Card)
Ill. Rev. Stat. 1991, Ch. 17, § 6100 et seq.

Liability Act (Employers)
See Employers' Liability Act

Liability Act (Equine Activity)
Mich. Comp. Laws Ann., 691.1661 et seq.

Liability Act (Highway Contractor)
Ill. Rev. Stat. 1991, Ch. 121, §§ 364.9, 365

Liability Act (Hospital Medical)
Neb. Rev. Stat. 1943, 44-2801 et seq.

Liability Act (Innkeepers)
See Innkeepers Liability Act

Liability Act (Liquor)
Me. Rev. Stat. Ann. 1964, Title 28-A, § 2501 et seq.

Liability Act (Medicaid Third Party)
Fla. Stat. Ann., 409.910

Liability Act (Mobs and Riots)
N.Y. General Municipal Law (Consol. Laws Ch. 24) § 71

Liability Act (Motor Vehicle Owners)
See Motor Vehicle Owners Liability Act

Liability Act (Oil Spill Responder)
Pa. 1992 Pamph. Laws, No. 52
S.C. Code Ann. 1976, § 48-44-10 et seq.

Liability Act (Promises)
Ill. Rev. Stat. 1989, Ch. 80, § 301 et seq.

Liability Act (Public Entities)
Cal. Government Code § 815 et seq.

Liability Act (Railroad Employers)
See Employers' Liability Act (Railroads)
See Railroad Employers Liability Act

Liability Act (Railroads)
See Railroad Liability Act

Liability Act (Theft)
Tex. Civil Practice and Remedies Code, § 134.001 et seq.

Liability Act (Workmen's Compensation)
See Workmen's Compensation Act

Liability Acts (Inkeepers')
N.Y. General Business Law (Consol. Laws Ch. 20) §§ 200, 201, 203a

Liability and Property Insurance Guaranty Association Act
Neb. Rev. Stat. 1943, 44-2401 et seq.

Liability and Response Act (Environmental)
Minn. Stat. Ann., 115B.01 et seq.

Liability and Safety Act (Amusement Rider)
Pa. Purdon's Stat., Title 42, § 501 et seq.

Liability Company Act (Limited)
Fla. Stat. Ann., 608.401 et seq.
Mich. Comp. Laws Ann., 450.4101 et seq.
N.D. Cent. Code, 10-32-01 et seq.

Tex. Rev. Civ. Stat., Art. 1528n

Liability for causing Mental Anguish Act (Telegraph Companies)
S.C. Code Ann. 1976, § 58-9-1860

Liability for Forged or Raised Checks Act
Ill. Rev. Stat. 1991, Ch. 17, §§ 651, 652

Liability for Injuries to Employees Act
S.C. Code Ann. 1976, § 58-17-3710 et seq.

Liability Fund Act (Independent)
Mont. Laws 1987, Ch. 564

Liability Funds Law (Professional)
Ore. Rev. Stat., 752.055 et seq.

Liability Insurance Act (Motor Vehicles)
See Motor Vehicle Liability Insurance Act

Liability Insurance Direct Action Act
R.I. Gen. Laws 1956, 27-7-1

Liability Law (Employers)
Ore. Rev. Stat., 654.305 et seq.

Liability Limitation Act (Equine)
Utah Laws 1992, Ch. 126

Liability Liquidity Borrowing Act (Medicaid)
Ill. Comp. Stat. 1992, Ch. 30, § 342/1

Liability of Persons Responding to Oil Spills Act
Miss. Code Ann. 1972, § 49-18-1 et seq.

Liability of Schools Act (Tort)
Ill. Rev. Stat. 1991, Ch. 122, § 820 et seq.

Liability on Written Instruments Act (Fiduciaries)
Pa. Purdon's Stat., Title 20, §§ 1171, 1172

Liability Relief Act (Recreational Purposes)
Neb. Rev. Stat. 1943, 37-1001 et seq.

Liability Risk Retention Act
Ida. Code 1947, 41-4801 et seq.
Me. Rev. Stat. Ann. 1964, Title 24-A, § 6091 et seq.

Liability Risk Retention Act of 1986
Oct. 27, 1986, P.L. 99-563, 15 U.S. Code
§ 3901 nt.

Liability Security Act (Automobile)
Haw. Rev. Stat. Ann., § 287-1 et seq.

Liability Security Act (Automobiles)
Pa. 1933 Pamph. Laws 553, No. 110

Liability Security Fund Act (Motor Vehicle)
Md. Ann. Code 1974, Art. TR, § 17-105

Libel Act
Ga. Code Ann., 51-5-1 et seq.
La. Rev. Stat. Ann., 14:47 et seq.
Mich. Comp. Laws Ann., 750.370
Mont. Code Ann., 45-8-212
Ore. Rev. Stat., 30.150 et seq.
Pa. Purdon's Stat., Title 42, § 8341 et seq.
Tex. Civ. Prac. and Rem. Code, § 73.001 et
seq.

Libel Act (Criminal)
See Criminal Libel Act

Libel Act (Group)
See Group Libel Act

Libel Act (London)
See London Libel Act

Libel and Defamation Act
Ala. Code 1975, § 13A-11-160 et seq.

Libel and Slander Act
Ariz. Rev. Stat. Ann., § 12-651 et seq.
Cal. Civil Code § 44 et seq.
Cal. Code of Civil Procedure § 830 et seq.
Haw. Rev. Stat. 1968, § 751-1 et seq.
Ill. Rev. Stat. 1991, Ch. 126, § 0.01 et seq.
Mo. Rev. Stat., 537.110
N.C. Gen. Stat. 1943, § 99-1 et seq.
Ohio Rev. Code 1953, 2739.01 et seq.
P.R. Laws Ann. 1954, Title 32, § 3141 et seq.
Wash. Rev. Code Ann., 9.58.010 et seq.

Libel and Slander Act (Civil)
Mont. Rev. Code 1947, 64-201 et seq.
N.D. Cent. Code, 14-02-01 et seq.

Libel and Slander Act (Criminal)
N.D. Cent. Code, 12.1-15-01

Libel by Radio Act
Ill. Rev. Stat. 1991, Ch. 126, §§ 11, 2

Libel Law (London)
Fla. Stat. 770.01 et seq., 1991, 836.07 et seq.

Libel per Quod Act
Cal. Civil Code § 45a

Libel Retraction Act
See Retraction Act (Libel)

Liberty Airport Authority Act
N.Y. Public Authorities Law (Consol. Laws
Ch. 43A) § 1725 et seq.

Liberty Charter
N.C. Laws 1981, Ch. 579
N.C. Private Laws 1889, Ch. 16
N.C. Public Local Laws 1939, Ch. 514

Liberty Coin Act
July 9, 1985, P.L. 99-61, 31 U.S. Code
§§ 5112 nt., 5116, 5132

Liberty Loan Acts
April 24, 1917, Ch. 4, 40 Stat. 35, 31 U.S.
Code §§ 745, 746, 755, 755a, 759, 764, 768,
774, 804 (First)
Sept. 24, 1917, Ch. 56, 40 Stat. 288, 31 U.S.
Code §§ 745, 747, 752 to 754b, 757, 757b
to 757e, 758, 760, 764 to 766, 769, 771,
773, 774, 801 (Second)
April 4, 1918, Ch. 44, 40 Stat. 502, 31 U.S.
Code §§ 752, 752a, 754, 765, 766, 771, 774
(Third)
July 9, 1918, Ch. 142, 40 Stat. 844, 31 U.S.
Code §§ 750, 752, 772, 774 (Fourth)
Sept. 24, 1918, Ch. 176, 40 Stat. 965, 12 U.S.
Code §§ 84, 95a; 31 U.S. Code §§ 757, 774;
50 U.S. Code Appx. § 5 (Supplement to
Second)
March 3, 1919, Ch. 100, 40 Stat. 1309, 31
U.S. Code §§ 750, 753, 754, 763, 767, 774,
802, 803 (Victory)
March 2, 1923, Ch. 179, 42 Stat. 1427, 31
U.S. Code § 767

Liberty Memorial Act of 1993
Dec. 20, 1993, P.L. 103-206, 107 Stat. 2454

Liberty Prohibition of Topless Entertainment Law
N.Y. Local Laws 1972, Vallage of Liberty, p. 3571

Liberty Recreation and Parks Law
N.Y. Local Laws 1972, Village of Liberty, p. 3568

Librarians Certification Act
Mass. Gen. Laws Ann., 78:22 et seq.
N.M. Stat. Ann., 18-2-8 et seq.

Libraries Act
Wash. Rev. Code Ann., 27.12.010 et seq.

Libraries Act (County)
S.D. Codifies Laws 1967, 14-1-39 et seq.

Libraries Act (Schools)
S.D. Codifies Laws 1967, 14-5-1 et seq.

Libraries Act (Town)
N.H. Rev. Stat. 1955, 202-A:1 et seq.

Libraries in Parks Act
Ill. Rev. Stat. 1991, Ch. 81, § 40.9 et seq.

Library Act
Colo. Rev. Stat., 24-90-101 et seq.
D.C. Code 1973, § 37-101 et seq.
Md. Ann. Code 1974, Art. ED, § 23-101 et seq.
Me. Rev. Stat. Ann. 1964, Title 27, § 1 et seq.
Mich. Comp. Laws Ann., 397.11 et seq.
Okla. Stat. Ann., Title 65, § 1-101 et seq.
Pa. Purdon's Stat., Title 24, § 4101 et seq.
Wyo. Stat. Ann., § 9-2-401 et seq.

Library Act (City-County)
Okla. Stat. Ann., Title 65, § 151 et seq.

Library Act (County)
See County Libraries Act

Library Act (District Schools)
Mo. Rev. Stat. 1959, 160.180, 160.190, 165.107

Library Act (Legislative Research)
Mo. Rev. Stat., 23.030

Library Act (Local)
See Local Library Act

Library Act (Manatee County)
Fla. Special Laws 1971, Ch. 71-760

Library Act (Metropolitan Areas)
Okla. Stat. 1971, Title 65, § 551 et seq.

Library Act (Multi-County)
Okla. Stat. 1961, Title 65, § 62 et seq.

Library Act (Public)
See Public Library Act

Library Act (School)
See School Libraries Act

Library Act (State)
See State Library Act

Library Act (Supreme Court)
Mo. Rev. Stat., 180.030 et seq.

Library Act (Village)
Ill. Rev. Stat. 1991, Ch. 81, § 16b.9 et seq.

Library Aid Act
N.J. Stat. Ann., 18A:74-1 et seq.

Library and Gymnasium Tax Act (Village)
Ill. Rev. Stat. 1991, Ch. 81, § 73.9 et seq.

Library Board Act (Schools)
Mo. Rev. Stat. 1969, 170.181 et seq.

Library Bond Act (Township)
Ill. Rev. Stat. 1991, Ch. 81, § 45.9 et seq.

Library Bond Validation Act (1969)
Ill. Rev. Stat. 1991, Ch. 81, §§ 16.1h, 16.2, 16.3

Library Building Act
Ark. Acts 1969, p. 1011, No. 341

Library Certification Board Act
Ind. Code Ann., 20-14-12-1 et seq.

Library Code
Okla. Stat. Ann., Title 65, § 1-101 et seq.

Library Commission Act (Colleton County)
S.C. Code Ann. 1952, § 42-361 et seq.

Library Compact
Ind. Code Ann., 20-14-11,1
Minn. Stat. Ann., 134.21 et seq.
N.D. Cent. Code, 54-24.01-01 et seq.

Library Compact (Interstate)
Me. Rev. Stat. Ann. 1964, Title 27, § 141 et
seq.

Library Compact Act
See Interstate Library Compact Act

Library Compact Act (Interstate)
Colo. Rev. Stat., 24-60.1501 et seq.
Ill. Rev. Stat. 1991, Ch. 81, § 100 et seq.
Me. Rev. Stat. Ann. 1964, Title 27, § 141 et
seq.
N.M. Stat. Ann., 18-2-19 et seq.
R.I. Gen. Laws 1956, 29-5-1 et seq.

Library Compact Enabling Act (Interstate)
Vt. Stat. Ann., Title 22, § 21 et seq.

Library Consortium Act (Texshare)
Tex. Government Code, § 441.201 et seq.

**Library Construction and Renovation Bond
Act**
Cal. Education Code 1976, § 19950 et seq.

Library Construction Assistance Act
Del. Code of 1974, Title 29, § 6601A et seq.

Library Construction Incentive Act
N.J. Stat. Ann., 18A:74-14 et seq.

Library Conversion Act (Village)
Ill. Rev. Stat. 1991, Ch. 81, §§ 27.31h, 27.32

**Library Development System Act
(Statewide)**
Miss. Code Ann. 1972, §§ 39-3-307 et seq.,
39-3-351 et seq.

Library District Act
Cal. Education Code 1976, § 19400 et seq.
Ill. Rev. Stat. 1991, Ch. 81, § 1001-1 et seq.

Library District Act (County)
Ohio Rev. Code 1953, 3375.19 et seq.

Library District Act (Orange County)
Fla. Laws 1999, H.B. 1695

**Library District Act (Unincorporated Towns
and Villages)**
Cal. Education Code 1976, § 19600 et seq.

Library Establishment Act (District)
Mich. Comp. Laws Ann., 397.171 et seq.

**Library Facilities and Regional Services Act
(Shasta County)**
Cal. Government Code § 26170 et seq.

Library Financial Assistance Act
N.M. Stat. Ann. 1953, 4-11-19 et seq.

Library Financing Act (District)
Mich. Comp. Laws Ann., 397.281 et seq.

Library Incorporation Act
Ill. Rev. Stat. 1991, Ch. 81, § 31.9 et seq.

Library Law
Ind. Code Ann., 20-14-1-1 et seq.

Library Materials Security Law
Miss. Code Ann. 1972, § 39-3-301 et seq.

Library Network Act
Mich. Comp. Laws Ann., 397.131 et seq.
N.J. 18A: 73-35a et seq.

Library Network Law
N.J. Stat. Ann., 18A:73-35a et seq.

Library of Congress Bicentennial Commemorative Coin Act of 1998
Oct. 19, 1998, P.L. 105-268, 112 Stat. 2378, 31 U.S. Code § 5112 nt.

Library of Congress Police Act
Aug. 4, 1950, Ch. 561, 64 Stat. 411, 2 U.S. Code §§ 167 to 167j
June 17, 1970, P.L. 91-281, 84 Stat. 309, 2 U.S. Code § 167j

Library of Congress Trust Fund Board Act
March 3, 1925, Ch. 423, 43 Stat. 1107, 2 U.S. Code §§ 154 to 163

Library of Michigan Act
Mich. Comp. Laws Ann., 397.11 et seq.

Library Privacy Act
Mich. Comp. Laws Ann., 397.601 et seq.
N.C. Gen. Stat. 1943, §§ 125-18, 125-19
N.M. Stat. Ann., 18-9-1 et seq.

Library Property Sale Act
Ill. Rev. Stat. 1991, Ch. 81, § 27.99 et seq.

Library Protection Act (Public Schools)
Cal. Education Code 1976, § 18175

Library Records Confidentiality Act
Ill. Rev. Stat. 1991, Ch. 81, § 1201, 1202
Mont. Code Ann., 22-1-1101 et seq.

Library Services Act
See Library Services And Construction Act
June 19, 1956, Ch. 407, 70 Stat. 293, 20 U.S. Code §§ 351 to 358
Aug. 1, 1956, Ch. 852, 70 Stat. 911, 20 U.S. Code §§ 353, 355, 358
Aug. 31, 1960, P.L. 86-679, 74 Stat. 571, 20 U.S. Code §§ 352, 353, 355, 358
Sept. 25, 1962, P.L. 87-688, 76 Stat. 587, 20 U.S. Code §§ 353, 355, 358
Cal. Education Code 1976, § 18700 et seq.

Library Services Act (Bay Park)
N.Y. Laws 1998, Ch. 216

Library Services Act (Green Acres)
N.Y. Laws 1975, Ch. 593

Library Services Act (North Valley Stream)
N.Y. Laws 1975, Ch. 592

Library Services and Construction Act
Feb. 11, 1964, P.L. 88-269, 78 Stat. 11, 20 U.S. Code §§ 351 to 358
July 19, 1966, P.L. 89-511, 80 Stat. 313, 20 U.S. Code §§ 351 to 353, 355 to 355b, 355e to 355e-3, 355f to 355f-7, 356 to 358
Nov. 24, 1967, P.L. 90-154, 81 Stat. 509, 20 U.S. Code §§ 355e-2, 355f-2, 355f-3, 355f-6, 355f-7, 358
Dec. 30, 1970, P.L. 91-600, 84 Stat. 1660, 20 U.S. Code §§ 351 to 354, 355a to 355c, 355e to 355e-2
May 3, 1973, P.L. 93-29, 87 Stat. 57, 20 U.S. Code §§ 351b to 3511, 361 to 364
Oct. 19, 1973, P.L. 93-133, 87 Stat. 466, 20 U.S. Code § 351a
Oct. 7, 1977, P.L. 95-123, 20 U.S. Code §§ 351b, 351f et seq.
Nov. 22, 1985, P.L. 99-159, 20 U.S. Code §§ 351a, 351c, 351d, 351f nt., 353, 366
Oct. 31, 1988, P.L. 100-569, 20 U.S. Code § 351b
March 15, 1990, P.L. 101-254, generally, 20 U.S. Code §§ 351-386g
July 25, 1991, P.L. 102-73, 20 U.S. Code §§ 351a, 351c, 351e
Oct. 20, 1994, P.L. 103-382, 20 U.S. Code § 351b
Sept. 30, 1996, P.L. 104-208, 20 U.S. Code §§ 351 to 386g

Library Services and Construction Act Amendments of 1966
July 19, 1966, P.L. 89-511, 80 Stat. 313, 20 U.S. Code §§ 351 to 353, 355 to 355b, 355e to 355e-3, 355f to 355f-7, 356 to 358

Library Services and Construction Act Amendments of 1970
Dec. 30, 1970, P.L. 91-600, 84 Stat. 1660, 20 U.S. Code §§ 351 to 354, 355a to 355c, 355e to 355e-2, 1204, 1211

Library Services and Construction Act Amendments of 1977
Oct. 7, 1977, P.L. 95-123, 20 U.S. Code §§ 351 nt., 351b et seq.

Library Services and Construction Act Amendments of 1984
Oct. 17, 1984, P.L. 98-480, 20 U.S. Code §§ 351 et seq.

Library Services and Construction Act Amendments of 1990
March 15, 1990, P.L. 101-254, 20 U.S. Code § 351 nt.

Library Services Authority Act
Ind. Code Ann., 20-14-8-1 et seq.

Library System Act
Ill. Rev. Stat. 1991, Ch. 81, § 111 et seq.
Tex. Government Code, § 441.121 et seq.

Library Tax Act
Ala. Code 1958, Title 62, § 138
Okla. Stat. 1971, Title 11, § 31-101

License Act (Abstracters')
N.D. Cent. Code, 43-01-01 et seq.
S.D. Codified Laws 1967, 36-13-1 et seq.

License Act (Air)
Me. Rev. Stat. Ann. 1964, Title 6, § 44

License Act (Architects)
Cal. Business and Professions Code § 5550 et seq.

License Act (Automobile)
Me. Rev. Stat. Ann. 1964, Title 29, § 101 et seq.

License Act (Brokers)
Cal. Business and Professions Code § 10150

License Act (Businesses and Vocations)
Ala. Code 1975, § 40-12-40 et seq.

License Act (Chain Store)
Colo. Rev. Stat., 12-49-101 et seq.

License Act (Cigarette or Tobacco Products)
Vt. Stat. Ann., Title 32, § 7731 et seq.

License Act (Commercial Driver)
N.J. Stat. Ann., 39:3-10.9 et seq.
N.M. Stat. Ann., 66-5-52 et seq.
Wash. Rev. Code Ann., 46.25.001 et seq.

License Act (Contractors)
Cal. Business and Professions Code § 7065 et seq.

License Act (Detective)
Cal. Business and Professions Code § 7500 et seq.

License Act (Dog)
Me. Rev. Stat. Ann. 1964, Title 7, § 3921 et seq., § 3942 et seq.

License Act (Drivers)
See Uniform Drivers License Act
Ky. Rev. Stat. 1971, 186.400 et seq.
Miss. Code Ann. 1972, § 63-1-1 et seq.

License Act (Funeral Directors and Embalmers)
Ill. Rev. Stat. 1989, Ch. 111, § 2800 et seq.

License Act (Hospitals)
Colo. Rev. Stat., 25-3-101 et seq.
N.H. Rev. Stat. 1955, 419:1 et seq.

License Act (Liquor)
Minn. Stat. Ann., 340A.401 et seq.

License Act (Motor Vehicle Operators)
N.H. Rev. Stat. 1955, 263:1 et seq.

License Act (Motor Vehicles)
Minn. Stat. Ann., 168.09 et seq.

License Act (Nursing Home Administrators)
Ky. Rev. Stat. 1971, 216A.010 et seq.

License Act (Oleomargerine)
Vt. Stat. Ann., Title 9, § 3481 et seq.

License Act (Plumbing)
Ill. Rev. Stat. 1989, Ch. 111, § 1101 et seq.

License Act (Produce Wholesalers)
Mont. Code Ann. 1947, 84-3401 et seq.

License Act (Psychologists)
Colo. Rev. Stat., 12-42-101 et seq.

License Act (Vendors)
Colo. Rev. Stat., 12-51-101 et seq.

License Act (Wholesale Prescription Drug Distributors)
Pa. 1992 Pamph. Laws, No. 145

License and Registration Act (Motor Vehicles)
Okla. Stat. Ann., Title 47, § 22 et seq.

License and Tax Act (Bingo)
Ill. Comp. Stat. 1992, Ch. 230, § 25/1 et seq.

License, Certification, and Appraiser Registration for Real Estate Act
S.C. Code Ann. 1976, § 40-60-60 et seq.

License Compact (Driver)
Me. Rev. Stat. Ann. 1964, Title 29, § 631 et seq.
Minn. Stat. Ann., 171.50 et seq.
Vt. Stat. Ann., Title 23, § 601 et seq.
Wash. Rev. Code Ann., 46.21.010 et seq.

License Fee Act
Mich. Comp. Laws Ann., 338.2201 et seq.

License Fee Act (Chain Store)
Md. Ann. Code 1974, Art. BR, § 17-1805

License Fees and Charges Act
D.C. Laws 1976, No. 1-82

License Law (Dance Halls)
S.D. Codified Laws 1967, 42-4-1 et seq.

License Law (Establishments For Handicapped Persons)
Cal. Health and Safety Code § 1500 et seq.

License Law (Hospital)
Cal. Health and Safety Code 1400 et seq.

License Law (Hotels)
S.D. Codified Laws 1967, 34-18-9 et seq.

License Law (Peddlers)
S.D. Codified Laws 1967, 37-13-1 et seq.

License Law (Plumbing)
Okla. Stat. Ann., Title 59, § 1001 et seq.
Tex. Rev. Civ. Stat., Art. 6243-101

License Law for Agents of Legal Reserve Life Insurance Companies (Agents Qualifications)
Tex. Insurance Code, Art. 21.07-1

License Plate Act (Disabled Persons)
Ga. Code Ann., 40-2-74

License Plate Issuance Act (Motor Vehicles)
Ga. Code Ann., 40-2-20 et seq.

License Plates Act (Collegiate)
Mont. Laws 1989, Ch. 661

License Plates for the Arts Act (Polanco-Bates)
Cal. Vehicle Code 1959, § 5074

License Quota Act
Pa. 1939 Pamph. Laws 806, No. 358

License, Real Estate Appraiser Registration, and Certification Act
S.C. Code Ann. 1976, § 40-60-10 et seq.

License Revocation Procedure Act
N.C. Gen. Stat. 1943, § 150-9 et seq.

License Suspension Act
Neb. Laws 1997, L.B. 752

License Tax Act
Alaska Stat. 1962, § 43.70.020 et seq.
D.C. Code Ann., § 47-2801 et seq.
Ky. Rev. Stat. 1971, 137.010 et seq.
N.C. Gen. Stat. 1943, § 105-33 et seq.
Nev. Rev. Stat. 1979 Reprint, 364.010 et seq.

License Tax Act (Cement Producers)
Mont. Rev. Code 1947, 84-1201 et seq.

License Tax Act (Chain Stores)
See Chain Store License Tax Act

License Tax Act (Cigar and Cigarette)
Ga. Code 1933, 92-2201 et seq.

License Tax Act (Corporations)
See Corporation License Tax Act

License Tax Act (Express Companies)
Mont. Rev. Code 1947, 84-1701 et seq.

License Tax Act (Gasoline)
See Gasoline License Tax Act

License Tax Act (Highway Carriers)
Cal. Public Utilities Code § 4301 et seq.

License Tax Act (Laundry)
Mont. Rev. Code 1947, 84-3206

License Tax Act (Local Occupational)
Fla. Stat. Ann., 205.013 et seq.

License Tax Act (Municipalities)
P.R. Laws Ann. 1954, Title 21, § 651 et seq.

License Tax Act (Store)
Mont. Rev. Code 1947, 84-2401 et seq.

License Tax Refund Act (Gasoline)
Mont. Code Ann., 15-70-225 et seq.

Licensed Alcoholic Beverage Server Fair Liability Act
N.J. Stat. Ann., 2A:22A-1 et seq.

Licensed Carriage Act
Haw. Session Laws 1878, Ch. 27

Licensed Dietitian Act
Okla. Stat. Ann., Title 59, § 1721 et seq.
Tex. Rev. Civ. Stat. 1974, Art. 4512h

Licensed Dietitian/Nutritionist Act
R.I. Gen. Laws 1956, 5-64-1 et seq.

Licensed Lay Midwife Act
Ark. Code Ann. 1987, 17-85-101 et seq.

Licensed Lenders Act
Ariz. Laws 1919, Ch. 91
Colo. Rev. Stat. 1963, 5-3-101 et seq., 73-2-1 et seq.
N.J. Stat. Ann., 17:11C-1 et seq.
N.Y. Banking Law (Consol. Laws Ch. 2) § 340 et seq.

Licensed Marriage and Family Therapist Act
Tex. Rev. Civ. Stat., Art. 4512c-1

Licensed Midwifery Practice Act
Cal. Business and Professions Code § 2505 et seq.

Licensed Perfusionists Act
Tex. Rev. Civ. Stat., Art. 4529e

Licensed Physical Therapy Assistant Act
Nev. Rev. Stat. 1979 Reprint, 640.230 et seq.

Licensed Professional Counselor Act
Okla. Stat. Ann., Title 59, § 1901 et seq.
Tex. Rev. Civ. Stat. 1974, Art. 4512g

Licensed Professional Counselor's Lien Act
Mont. Code Ann., 71-3-1111 et seq.

Licensed Social Worker's Lien Act
Mont. Code Ann., 71-3-1111 et seq.

Licensed State Land Surveyors' Act
Tex. Rev. Civ. Stat., Art. 5282c

Licensee Agreement Act (Wholesale)
Me. Rev. Stat. Ann. 1964, Title 28-A, § 1451 et seq.

Licensee and Certificate of Approval Holder Agreement Act (Wholesale)
Me. Rev. Stat. Ann. 1964, Title 28-A, § 1451 et seq.

Licenses Department Act
Wash. Rev. Code Ann., 43.24.001 et seq.

Licensing Act
N.M. Stat. Ann., 61-1-1 et seq.

Licensing Act (Airports)
Fla. Stat. Ann., 330.27 et seq.

Licensing Act (Amusement Devices)
S.C. Code Ann. 1976, § 12-21-2720

Licensing Act (Auctioneer)
Ark. Code Ann. 1987, 17-15-101 et seq.
La. Rev. Stat. Ann., 37:3101 et seq.

Licensing Act (Automobile)
Ark. Code Ann. 1987, 27-14-1001 et seq.

Licensing Act (Bingo)
N.Y. General Municipal Law (Consol. Laws Ch. 24) § 475 et seq.

Licensing Act (Bird Dealers)
Ga. Code Ann., 4-10-1 et seq.

Licensing Act (Brokers, Lenders and Servicers)
Mich. Comp. Laws Ann., 445.1651 et seq.

Licensing Act (Check Cashiers)
Mass. Gen. Laws Ann., 169A:1 to 169A:13

Licensing Act (Child Care Center)
N.J. Stat. Ann., 30:5B-1 et seq.

Licensing Act (Child Care)
Miss. Code Ann. 1972, § 43-20-1 et seq.

Licensing Act (Commerical Fishing)
Alaska Stat. 1962, § 16.05.440 et seq.

Licensing Act (Construction Contractors)
Alaska Stat. 1962, § 08.18.010 et seq.

Licensing Act (Construction Trades)
Utah Code Ann. 1953, 58-55-101 et seq.

Licensing Act (Deception and Truth Examiners)
Neb. Rev. Stat. 1943, 81-1901

Licensing Act (Delayed Deposit Services)
Neb. Rev. Stat. 1943, 45-901 et seq.

Licensing Act (Dogs)
N.Y. Agriculture and Markets Law (Consol. Laws Ch. 69), § 106 et seq.

Licensing Act (Drivers)
Alaska Stat. 1962, § 28.15.011 et seq.

Licensing Act (Employee Leasing Company)
Utah Code Ann. 1953, 58-59-101 et seq.

Licensing Act (Employment Agencies)
N.Y. General Business Law (Consol. Laws Ch. 20) § 170 et seq.

Licensing Act (Fishing Guides)
Ark. Code Ann. 1987, 15-42-109 et seq., 15-14-239

Licensing Act (Frozen Dessert Manufacturer)
Tex. Health and Safety Code, § 440.001 et seq.

Licensing Act (Funeral Services)
Okla. Stat. Ann., Title 59, § 396 et seq.

Licensing Act (General Contractors)
Ark. Code Ann. 1987, 17-22-101, 17-22-102

Licensing Act (Hearing Instrument Specialist)
Utah Code Ann. 1953, 58-46a-102 et seq.

Licensing Act (Hospice Program)
Ill. Rev. Stat. 1989, Ch. 111 1/2, § 6101 et seq.

Licensing Act (Impaired Persons)
Utah Code Ann. 1953, 53-3-301 et seq.

Licensing Act (Joint Underwriting Association)
Tex. Insurance Code, Art. 21.49-3b

Licensing Act (Liquors and Narcotics)
Ore. Rev. Stat., 471.005 et seq.

Licensing Act (Livestock Dealer)
Neb. Rev. Stat. 1943, 54-1701 et seq.

Licensing Act (Livestock Dealers's)
Ill. Rev. Stat. 1989, Ch. 111, § 401 et seq.
W. Va. Code 1966, § 19-10B-1 et seq.

Licensing Act (Marriage and Family Therapist)
Utah Code Ann. 1953, 58-60-301 et seq.

Licensing Act (Meat Industry)
Tenn. Code Ann. 1955, 67-5601 et seq.

Licensing Act (Nursing Home Administrators)
Ark. Code Ann. 1987, 20-10-101 et seq.

Licensing Act (Occupational Therapy)
N.J. Stat. Ann., 45:9-37.51 et seq.

Licensing Act (Older Adult Daily Living Centers)
Pa. Purdon's Stat., Title 62, § 1511.1 et seq.

Licensing Act (Personal Care Facility)
Tex. Health and Safety Code, § 247.001 et seq.

Licensing Act (Physician)
Tex. Gen. and Spec. Laws 1993, Ch. 214

Licensing Act (Podiatrist)
Okla. Stat. Ann., Title 59, § 135.1 et seq.
Utah Code Ann. 1953, 58-5a-101 et seq.

Licensing Act (Pregnancy Birthing Center)
Tex. Rev. Civ. Stat., Art. 244.001 et seq.

Licensing Act (Private Detectives and Investigators)
N.Y. General Business Law (Consol. Laws, Ch. 20), § 70 et seq.

Licensing Act (Private Detectives' and Investigators')
N.Y. General Business Law (Consol. Laws Ch. 20) § 70 et seq.

Licensing Act (Professional Counselors)
N.J. Stat. Ann., 45:8B-34 et seq.
Utah Code Ann. 1953, 58-60-401 et seq.

Licensing Act (Psychologist)
Utah Code Ann. 1953, 58-61-101 et seq.

Licensing Act (Psychologists)
Okla. Stat. Ann., Title 59, § 1351 et seq.

Licensing Act (Public Adjusters')
N.J. Stat. Ann., 17:22B-1 et seq.

Licensing Act (Residential Care and Assisted Living Facility)
R.I. Gen. Laws 1956, 23-17.4-1 et seq.

Licensing Act (Respiratory Care Practitioner)
N.J. Stat. Ann., 45:14E-1 to 45:14E-15

Licensing Act (Roofing Industry)
Ill. Rev. Stat. 1989, Ch. 111, § 7501 et seq.

Licensing Act (Social Worker's)
Mass. Gen. Laws Ann., 112.130 et seq.
N.J. Stat. Ann., 45:15BB-1 et seq.
Okla. Stat. Ann., Title 59, § 1250 et seq.

Licensing Act (Social Workers)
Mass. Gen. Laws Ann., 112:130 et seq.
Okla. Stat. Ann., Title 59, § 1250 et seq.
R.I. Gen. Laws 1956, 5-39.1-1 et seq.
Utah Code Ann. 1953, 58-60-201 et seq.

Licensing Act (Special Care Facility)
Tex. Health and Safety Code, § 248.001 et seq.

Licensing Act (Supportive Residences)
Ill. Rev. Stat. 1991, Ch. 111 1/2, § 9001 et seq.

Licensing Act (Transient Merchant)
Kan. Stat. Ann., 19-2231 et seq.

Licensing Act (Vehicle Dealers and Manufacturers)
Kan. Stat. Ann., 8-2401 et seq.

Licensing Act (Veterinarians)
Fla. Stat. Ann., 474.201
Minn. Stat. Ann., 156.001 et seq.
N.Y. Education Law 1947 (Consol. Laws, Ch. 16), § 6701 et seq.
Tex. Rev. Civ. Stat., Art. 8890

Licensing Act (Wholesale Drug Distributor)
Minn. Stat. Ann., 151.42 et seq.

Licensing Acts (Dogs)
N.Y. Agriculture and Markets Law (Consol. Laws Ch. 69) § 106 et seq.

Licensing Acts (Employment Agencies)
N.Y. General Business Law (Consol. Laws Ch. 20) § 170 et seq.

Licensing Acts (Lenders)
N.Y. Banking Law (Consol. Laws Ch. 2) § 340 et seq.

Licensing Agencies Procedure Act
N.C. Gen. Stat. 1943, § 150A-23 et seq.

Licensing Agency Budget Act
La. Rev. Stat. Ann., 39:1331 et seq.

Licensing and Certification Act (Appraiser)
Tex. General and Special Laws 1991, Ch. 663
Tex. Rev. Civ. Stat., Art. 6573a.2

Licensing and Certification Act (Real Estate Appraiser)
Cal. Business and Professions Code § 11300 et seq.
Ga. Code Ann., 43-39A-1 et seq.
Mont. Laws 1991, Ch. 409, §§ 1, 2, 4 to 28
Neb. Rev. Stat. 1943, 76-2201 et seq.
W. Va. Code 1966 § 37-14-1 et seq.

Licensing and Certification Act (Real Estate)
Me. Rev. Stat. Ann. 1964, Title 32, § 3961 et seq.

Licensing and Certifying Act (State Appraiser)
Ariz. Rev. Stat. Ann., § 32-3601 et seq.

Licensing and Monitoring of Child Care Providers and Child Placing Agencies Act
R.I. Gen. Laws 1956, 42-72.1-1 et seq.

Licensing and Permitting Act (Underground Storage Tank Installer)
Mont. Laws 1989, Ch. 594

Licensing and Protection Law (Rental Horse)
N.Y. Adm. Code '85, § 17-326

Licensing and Registration Act (Motor Vehicles)
S.C. Code Ann. 1976, § 53-3-10 et seq.

Licensing and Registration Fees Act
D.C. Code 1973, §§ 1-346, 1-347

Licensing and Regulation Department Act
N.M. Stat. Ann., 9-16-1 et seq.

Licensing and Regulatory Act (Intoxicating Liquors)
Ind. Code Ann., 7. 1-1-1-1 et seq.

Licensing and Regulatory Act (Pilots)
Tex. Rev. Civ. Stat., Art. 8280c

Licensing and Regulatory Act (Private Investigators)
Tenn. Code Ann., 62-26-201 et seq.

Licensing and Safety Act (Fireworks)
N.M. Stat. Ann., 60-2C-1 et seq.

Licensing and Taxing Act (Merchants)
Tenn. Code Ann. 1955, 67-4701 et seq.

Licensing Boards Uniform Procedure Act
N.C. Gen. Stat. 1943, § 150A-23 et seq.

Licensing Coordination Act (Small Business)
Mont. Code Ann., 30-16-101 et seq.

Licensing Fees Act (Music)
Iowa Code Ann., 549.1 et seq.

Licensing for Alarm Systems Act
Ark. Code Ann. 1987, 17-13 101 et seq.

Licensing Law
See Uniform Licensing Law

Licensing Law (Hearing Aid Dispensers)
Cal. Business and Professions Code § 3310 et seq.

Licensing Law (Hospital)
La. Rev. Stat. Ann., 40:2100 et seq.

Licensing Law (Nursing Home and Home for the Aged)
Vt. Stat. Ann., Title 18, § 2001 et seq.

Licensing Law (Real Estate)
Fla. Stat. Ann., 475.001 et seq.

Licensing Law for Psychologists
Minn. Stat. Ann., 148.88 et seq.

Licensing of Amusement Games Law
N.D. Cent. Code, 53-04-1 et seq.

Licensing of Certificated Personnel Act
Cal. Education Code 1959, § 13200 et seq.

Licensing of Controlled Substances Act
Colo. Rev. Stat., 12-22-301 et seq.

Licensing of Places of Public Assembly Act
N.Y. Local Laws 1966, Town of Hempstead, p. 1081
N.Y. Local Laws 1970, Town of Olive, p. 2210

Licensing of Truth and Deception Examiners Act
Neb. Rev. Stat. 1943, 81-1901 et seq.

Licensing of Wholesale Drug Distribution Act
W. Va. Code 1966 § 60A-8-1 et seq.

Licensing Periods Act
D.C. Code Ann., §§ 1-351, 47-2805

Licensing Practices Act (Music)
N.J. Stat. Ann., 56:3A-1 et seq.

Licensing Procedures Law
Fla. Stat. Ann., 626.011 et seq.

Licensing Procedures Law (Insurance Agent)
Fla. Stat. Ann., 626.011 et seq.

Licensing Provisions (Consumer Loan Law)
Md. Ann. Code 1974, Art. FI, § 11-201 et seq.

Licensing Provisions (Secondary Mortgage Loan Law)
Md. Ann. Code 1974, Art. FI, § 12-301 et seq.

Licensing Provisions (Small Loan Law)
Md. Ann. Code 1974, Art. FI, § 11-201 et seq.

Licensure Act (Athletic Trainers)
Miss. Code Ann. 1972, § 73-55-1 et seq.

Licensure Act (Birth Center)
Fla. Stat. Ann., 383.30 et seq.

Licensure Act (Cholestrol Screening Center)
Fla. Stat. Ann., 483.601 et seq.

Licensure Act (Hospice)
W. Va. Code 1966 § 16-51-1 et seq.

Licensure Act (Industrial Hygienists)
Ill. Comp. Stat. 1992, Ch. 225, § 52/1 et seq.

Licensure Act (Insurance Administrator)
Pa. Purdon's Stat., Title 40, § 324.1 et seq.

Licensure Act (Nursing Home Administrators)
Ky. Rev. Stat. 1971, 216A.010 et seq.

Licensure Act (Nursing Pool)
N.C. Gen. Stat. 1943, § 131E-154.1 et seq.

Licensure Act for Commercial Driving Instruction
Me. Rev. Stat. Ann. 1964, Title 32, § 9501 et seq.

Licensure Act for Professional Speech Pathologists and Professional Clinical Audiologists
Me. Rev. Stat. Ann. 1964, Title 32, § 6001 et seq.
Mo. Rev. Stat., 345.010 et seq.

Licensure Act for Speech Pathologists and Audiologists
See Speech Pathologists and Audiologists Licensure Act

Licensure Law (Public Health)
Neb. Rev. Stat. 1943, 71-101 et seq.

Licensure of Home Health Agencies Act
See Home Health Agency Licensing Act

Lick Run Wild and Scenic River Act
Pa. Purdon's Stat., Title 32, § 820.71 et seq.

Lie Detection Prevention Procedures Act
D.C. Code Ann., § 36-801 et seq.

Lie Detector Licensing Act
N.D. Cent. Code, 43-31-01 et seq.
Neb. Rev. Stat. 1943, 81-1901 et seq.

Lien Act
Ala. Code 1975, § 35-11-1 et seq.
Alaska Stat. 1962, § 34.35.005 et seq.
Cal. Code of Civil Procedure § 1185.1, Subd. a
Colo. Rev. Stat., 38-20-101 et seq.
Fla. Stat. Ann., 726.776 et seq.
Ill. Rev. Stat. 1991, Ch. 82
Kan. Stat. Ann., 60-1101 et seq.
La. Rev. Stat. Ann., 9:4801 et seq.
Mass. Gen. Laws Ann., 254:1 et seq.
Minn. Stat. Ann., 514.01 et seq.
Miss. Code Ann. 1972, § 85-7-1 et seq.
Mont. Code Ann., 71-3-101 et seq.
N.C. Gen. Stat. 1943, § 44A-1 et seq.
N.D. Cent. Code, 35-01-01 et seq.
Nev. Rev. Stat. 1979 Reprint, 108.221 et seq.
N.Y. Consol. Laws, Ch. 33
Ore. Rev. Stat., 87.005 et seq.
S.C. Code Ann. 1976, § 15-35-810 et seq.
Wash. Rev. Code Ann., 60.04.010 et seq.
W. Va. Code 1966, § 38-3-1 et seq.

Lien Act (Agisters')
Miss. Code Ann. 1972, § 85-7-101 et seq.

Lien Act (Attorneys)
Ill. Comp. Stat. 1992, Ch. 770, §§ 5/0.01, 5/1

Lien Act (Boaters)
Cal. Harbors and Navigation § 500 et seq.

Lien Act (Commercial Real Estate Broker)
Ill. Rev. Stat. 1991, Ch. 82, § 651 et seq.

Lien Act (Cornsheller)
Iowa Code Ann., 571.1 et seq.

Lien Act (Cornshellers)
Iowa Code Ann., 571.1 et seq.

Lien Act (Corporation Employees)
Ind. Code Ann., 32-8-24-1 et seq.

Lien Act (Factors)
Ind. Code 1955, Ch. 167, p. 337
Me. Rev. Stat. Ann. 1964, Title 11, § 9-101 et seq.
N.Y. Uniform Commercial Code (Consol. Laws Ch. 38) § 9-101 et seq.
R.I. Public Laws 1938, Ch. 2568

Lien Act (Garageman)
La. Rev. Stat. Ann., 9:4501

Lien Act (Hospitals)
Conn. Gen. Stat 1983, § 49-73
Ga. Code Ann., 44-14-470 et seq.
Iowa Code Ann., 582.1 et seq.
N.H. Rev. Stat. 1955, 448-A:1 et seq.
R.I. Gen. Laws 1956, 9-3-4 et seq.

Lien Act (Inn Keepers)
Cal. Civil Code § 1861
R.I. Gen. Laws 1956, 34-33-1, 34-33-2

Lien Act (Judgments)
Cal. Code of Civil Procedure § 674, 674.5
Neb. Rev. Stat. 1943, 25-1303 et seq.
Pa. Purdon's Stat., Title 12, § 877 et seq.

Lien Act (Landlords)
N.J. Stat. Ann., 2A:42-1 et seq.

Lien Act (Materialmen and Mechanics)
Ark. Code Ann. 1987, 18-44-101 et seq.

Lien Act (Materialmen)
Haw. Rev. Stat. § 507-41 et seq.

Lien Act (Mechanics)
See Mechanics' Lien Act

Lien Act (Miners)
Alaska Stat. 1962, § 34.35.125 et seq.
Colo. Rev. Stat. 38-22-104 et seq.
Ill. Rev. Stat. 1989, Ch. 82, §§ 47m, 48

Lien Act (Motor Vehicles)
S.C. Code Ann. 1976, § 29-15-20
Wyo. Stat. 1957, § 29-102 et seq.

Lien Act (Municipal Taxes)
Conn. Gen. Stat. Ann., § 12-171 et seq.
Pa. Purdon's Stat., Title 53, § 7101 et seq.

Lien Act (Personalty)
Mo. Rev. Stat., 430.010 et seq.

Lien Act (Physical Therapist)
Ill. Rev. Stat. 1991, Ch. 82, § 601 et seq.

Lien Act (Producer's)
N.M. Stat. Ann., 48-5B-1 et seq.

Lien Act (Tax)
Me. Rev. Stat. Ann. 1964, Title 36, § 941 et seq.

Lien Act (Taxes)
Pa. Purdon's Stat., Title 72, § 5971a et seq.

Lien Act (Threshers)
Iowa Code Ann., 571.1 et seq.

Lien Act (Veterinarians)
Iowa Code Ann., 581.1 et seq.

Lien Act (Work and Materials)
Tenn. Code Ann., 66-11-102

Lien Claim Act
N.J. Stat. Ann., 2A:44-97 et seq.

Lien Date Act (Taxes)
Ohio Rev. Code 1953, 5719.01

Lien Enforcement Statute
Fla. Stat. Ann., 85.011 et seq.

Lien Foreclosure Act (Timeshare)
Fla. Stat. Ann., 721.80 to 721.86

Lien Law
N.C. Gen. Stat. 1943, § 44A-1 et seq.

Lien Law (Attorneys)
Colo. Rev. Stat., 12-5-119, 12-5-120

Lien Law (Construction)
Fla. Stat. 1986, 713.001 et seq.
Ore. Rev. Stat., 87.001 et seq.

Lien Law (Judgment)
Neb. Rev. Stat. 1943, 25-1303 et seq.

Lien Law (Loggers and Lumbermen)
Cal. Civil Code § 3065 et seq.

Lien Notation Act (Motor Vehicle)
Ky. Rev. Stat. 1962, 186.195

Lien Priority Law
Pa. Cons. Stat., Title 42, § 8141

Lien Recovery Fund and Residence Lien Restrictions Act
Utah Code Ann. 1953, 38-11-101 et seq.

Lien Registration Act
See Uniform Federal Lien Registration Act
La. Rev. Stat. Ann., 52:51 et seq.
Miss. Code Ann. 1972, § 85-8-1 et seq.
Mont. Code Ann., 71-3-201 et seq.
N.D. Cent. Code, 35-29-01 et seq.
N.H. Rev. Stat. 1955, 454-B:1 et seq.
Ore. Rev. Stat., 87.806 et seq.
Pa. Purdon's Stat., Title 74, § 157-1 et seq.

Lien Registration Act (Federal Tax)
See Uniform Federal Tax Lien Registration Act

Lien Registration Act (Uniform Federal)
See Uniform Federal Lien Registration Act

Liens Against Railroads Act
Ill. Rev. Stat. 1991, Ch. 82, § 48.9 et seq.

Liens on Animals Act
Tenn. Code Ann., 66-20-101 et seq.

Liens on Personal Property in Self-Service Storage Act
Minn. Stat. Ann., 514.970 et seq.

Liens on Vessels Act
June 23, 1910, Ch. 373, 36 Stat. 604

Lieu Land Title Validation Law
Cal. Statutes 1909, Ch. 716, p. 1091

Lieu Lands Act
Wash. Rev. Code Ann., 79.28.010 et seq.

Lieu Lands Act (Forest Reservations)
June 4, 1897, Ch. 2, 30 Stat. 36

Lieu Lands Act (Indian Reservations)
April 21, 1904, Ch. 1402, 33 Stat. 211, 16
U.S. Code § 152; 25 U.S. Code §§ 52a, 292;
43 U.S. Code § 149

Lieu Lands Act (Northern Pacific Railroad)
July 1, 1898, Ch. 546, 30 Stat. 620
March 2, 1901, Ch. 807, 31 Stat. 950
May 17, 1906, Ch. 2470, 34 Stat. 197
Feb. 27, 1917, Ch. 135, 39 Stat. 946

Lieutenant Generals Act
Aug. 5, 1939, Ch. 454, 53 Stat. 1214 (See 10
U.S. Code §§ 3036, 3212)

Life, Accident and Health Insurance Broker Act
Okla. Stat. Ann., Title 36, § 1461 et seq.

Life, Accident, and Health Insurance Guaranty Association Act
S.C. Code Ann. 1976, § 38-29-10 et seq.

Life, Accident, and Health Insurance Policy Language Simplification Act
Okla. Stat. Ann., Title 36, § 3641 et seq.

Life, Accident and Sickness Insurance Guaranty Association Act
Va. Code 1950, § 38.2-1700 et seq.

Life, Accident, Health, and Hospital Service Insurance Guaranty Association Act
Tex. Insurance Code, Art. 21.28-D

Life Act (Aquatic)
Tex. Health and Safety Code, § 436.001 et seq.

Life Agent and Broker Law
Me. Rev. Stat. Ann. 1964, Title 24-A, § 1671 et seq.

Life Agent Law
Fla. Stat. Ann., 626.776 et seq.

Life and Accident and Health Insurance Policy Language Simplification Act
N.D. Cent. Code, 26.1-36-13 et seq.

Life and Accident and Sickness Insurance Policy Language Simplification Act
W. Va. Code 1966, § 33-29-1 et seq.

Life and Disability Insurance Act (Credit)
Haw. Rev. Stat. Ann., § 431:10B-101 et seq.

Life and Disability Insurance Guaranty Association Act
Ala. Code 1975, § 27-44-1 et seq.
Alaska Stat. 1962, § 21.79.010 et seq.
Ark. Code Ann. 1987, 23-96-101 et seq.
Haw. Rev. Stat. Ann., § 431:16-201 et seq.
Utah Code Ann. 1953, 31A-28-101 et seq.
Wash. Rev. Code Ann., 48.32A.010 et seq.

Life and Disability Insurance Policy Language Simplification Act
Ark. Code Ann. 1987, 23-80-201 et seq.
Mont. Code Ann., 33-15-321 et seq.

Life and Health Agent and Broker Law
Me. Rev. Stat. Ann. 1964, Title 24-A, § 1671 et seq.

Life and Health Insurance and Health Maintenance Organization Form Approval Reform Act
N.J. Stat. Ann., 17:48-8.1 et seq.

Life and Health Insurance Code
N.J. Stat. Ann., 17B:17-1 et seq.

Life and Health Insurance Guaranty Association Act
Cal. Insurance Code § 1067 et seq.
Conn. Gen. Stat. Ann., § 38-301 et seq.
Del. Code of 1974, Title 18, § 4401 et seq.
Fla. Stat. Ann., 631.711 et seq.
Ida. Code 1947, 41-4301 et seq.
Ill. Rev. Stat. 1991, Ch. 73, § 1065, 80-1 et seq.
Ill. Rev. Stat. 1991, Ch. 82 § 401 et seq.
Iowa Code Ann., 508C.1 et seq.
Continued

Kan. Stat. Ann., 40-3001 et seq.

Ky. Rev. Stat. 1971, 304.42-010 et seq.

La. Rev. Stat. Ann., 22:1395.1 et seq.

Md. Ann. Code 1957, Art. 48A, § 520 et seq.

Me. Rev. Stat. Ann. 1964, Title 24-A, § 4601 et seq.

Mich. Comp. Laws Ann., 500.7701 et seq.

Minn. Stat. Ann., 61B.01 et seq.

Minn. Stat. Ann., 61B.18 to 61B.32

Miss. Code Ann. 1972, § 83-23-201 et seq.

Mo. Rev. Stat., 376.715 et seq.

Mont. Code Ann., 33-10-201 et seq.

N.C. Gen. Stat. 1943, § 58-62-2 et seq.

Neb. Rev. Stat. 1943, 44-2701 et seq.

Nev. Rev. Stat. 1979 Reprint, 686C.010 et seq.

N.H. Rev. Stat. 1955, 404-D:1 et seq.

N.H. Rev. Stat. 1955, 408:B-1 et seq.

N.J. Stat. Ann., 17B:32A-1 et seq.

N.M. Stat. Ann., 48-1-1 et seq.

Ohio Rev. Code 1953, 3956.01 et seq.

Okla. Stat. Ann., Title 36, § 2021 et seq.

Ore. Rev. Stat., 734.750 et seq.

Pa. Purdon's Stat., Title 40, § 1801 et seq.

R.I. Gen. Laws 1956, 27-34.3-1 et seq.

S.C. Code Ann. 1976, § 38-17-10 et seq.

Tenn. Code Ann., 56-12-201 et seq.

Utah Code Ann. 1953, 31A-28-101 et seq.

Vt. Stat. Ann., Title 8, § 4151 et seq.

W. Va. Code 1966, § 33-26A-1 et seq.

Wyo. Stat. Ann., § 29-6-201 et seq.

Life and Health Insurance Guaranty Corporation Act
Md. Ann. Code 1974, Art. IN, § 9-401 et seq.

Life and Health Insurance Guaranty Law
N.M. Stat. Ann., 59A-42-1 et seq.

Life and Health Insurance Policy Language Simplification Act
N.J. Stat. Ann., 17B:17-17 et seq.
Ore. Rev. Stat., 743.100 et seq.

Life and Health Insurance Protection Association Act
Colo. Rev. Stat., 10-20-101 et seq.

Life and Health Insurers Rehabilitation and Liquidation Act
N.J. Stat. Ann., 17B:32-31 et seq.

Life Care Facilities Act
Ill. Rev. Stat. 1991, Ch. 111 1/2, § 4160-1 et seq.

Life-Care Registration Act
Del. Code of 1974, Title 18, § 4601 et seq.

Life Check Act (Miners)
Ind. Code Ann., 22-10-11-6

Life-Cycle Cost and Procurement Act
Tenn. Code Ann., 12-3-601 et seq.

Life Estate Principal and Income Act
See Principal and Income Act

Life, Health and Accident Guaranty Act
Tex. Insurance Code, Art. 21.28-E

Life, Health and Dental Insurance Act (State Employees)
Okla. Stat. Ann., Title 74, § 1301 et seq.

Life Insurance, Accident and Health Insurance Act (Credit)
Mass. Gen. Laws Ann., 167F:2, 175:110, 175:117C, 175:133, 175:177, 175:184, 255:12G, 255B:10, 255C:14A, 255D:1 to 255D:11, 255D:26

Life Insurance Act
D.C. Code 1973, § 35-301 et seq.
Ill. Rev. Stat. 1935, Ch. 73, § 205 et seq.
La. Rev. Stat. Ann., 22:161 et seq.
Mo. Rev. Stat., 376.010 et seq.
Okla. Stat. Ann., Title 36, § 4001 et seq.
Wash. Rev. Code Ann., 48.23.010 et seq.

Life Insurance Act (Group)
See Group Life Insurance Act

Life Insurance Agent's License Act
Wis. Stat. Ann., 628.03 et seq.

Life Insurance and Annuity Policyholders Protection Act
Okla. Stat. Ann., Title 36, § 4031 et seq.

Life Insurance Association Act (Cooperative)
Utah Code Ann. 1953, 31-32-1 et seq.

Life Insurance Companies, General Agents, Managers and Agents Unclaimed Funds Act
P.R. Laws Ann. 1954, Title 26, § 2601 et seq.

Life Insurance Companies Unclaimed Funds Act
See Unclaimed Funds Act for Life Insurance Companies

Life Insurance Company Guaranty Corporation Act
N.Y. Insurance Law (Consol. Laws Ch. 28) § 7701 et seq.

Life Insurance Company Guaranty Corporation of New York Act
N.Y. Insurance Law 1984 (Consol. Laws Ch. 28) § 7701 et seq.

Life Insurance Company Income Tax Act of 1959
June 25, 1959, P.L. 86-69, 73 Stat. 112, 26 U.S. Code §§ 34, 116, 381, 801, 802, 804 to 806, 809 to 812, 815, 817 to 820, 841, 842, 891, 1016, 1201, 1232, 1504, 4371, 6072 nt., 6501, 6655 nt.

Life Insurance Company Investments Act
N.J. Stat. Ann., 17B:20-1 et seq.

Life Insurance Company Reorganization Act (Mutual)
Pa. Purdon's Stat., Title 40, § 1010.21 et seq.

Life Insurance Company Tax Act for 1955
March 13, 1956, Ch. 83, 70 Stat. 36, 26 U.S. Code §§ 316, 501, 594, 801 to 805, 811 to 813, 816 to 818, 821, 822, 832, 841 to 843, 891, 1201, 1504, 4371

Life Insurance Exemption Act
Fla. Stat. Ann., 222.13, 222.14
La. Rev. Stat. Ann., 22:647
N.Y. Insurance Law 1984 (Consol. Laws Ch. 28) § 3212
Pa. 1868 Pamph. Laws 103, No. 64
Wash. Rev. Code Ann., 48.18.410

Life Insurance Guaranty Association Act
Cal. Insurance Code § 1067 et seq.

Life Insurance Incontestability Law
Wash. Rev. Code Ann., 48.23.050

Life Insurance Law (Group)
Ky. Rev. Stat. 1971, 304.16-010 et seq.
Nev. Rev. Stat. Ann., 688B.010 et seq.
N.M. Stat. Ann., 59A-21-1 et seq.

Life Insurance Law (Savings Bank)
N.Y. Insurance Law 1984 (Consol. Laws Ch. 28) § 2201 et seq.

Life Insurance Nonforfeiture Act
See Nonforfeiture Act (Life Insurance)

Life Insurance Nonforfeiture Provisions Act
Va. Code 1950, § 38.2-3200 et seq.

Life Insurance Policy Act
Mich. Comp. Laws Ann., 500.4000 et seq.

Life Insurance Proceeds Exemption Act
Ind. Code Ann., 27-1-12-14

Life Insurance Standard Nonforfeiture Law
Minn. Stat. Ann., 61A.24
N.C. Gen. Stat. § 58-58-58
Ore. Rev. Stat., 743.204 et seq.
S.C. Code Ann. 1976, § 38-63-510 et seq.
Wash. Rev. Code 1983, 48.76.010 et seq.

Life Insurance Standard Valuation Act
Ky. Rev. Stat. 1971, 304.6-120 et seq.
Miss. Code Ann. 1972, § 83-7-23
N.C. Gen. Stat. 1943, § 58-58-55
N.H. Rev. Stat. 1955, 410:1 et seq.
Wash. Rev. Code Ann., 48.74.010 et seq.

Life Insurance Tax Act
Ark. Code Ann. 1987, 26-51-403, 26-51-432, 26-51-404, 26-51-411

Life Insurance Unclaimed Funds Act
P.R. Laws Ann. 1954, Title 26, § 2601

Life Insurer's Unclaimed Funds Act
Me. Rev. Stat. Ann. 1964, Title 24-A, § 4551 et seq.

Life or Health Threatening Conditions Summary Abatement Act
D.C. Code Ann., §§ 5-513, 5-604, 5-605, 45-1311

Life-Prolonging Procedure Act
Fla. Stat. Ann., 765.01 et seq.
Fla. Stat. Ann., 765.302 et seq.

Life-Saving Mechanisms Act (Withdrawal of)
Miss. Code Ann. 1972, § 41-41-101 et seq.

Life-Saving Service Act
March 26, 1908, Ch. 99, 35 Stat. 46

Life Sciences and Conservation Education Project
Cal. Education Code 1976, § 52760 et seq.

Life Sentence Parole Act
Mich. Comp. Laws Ann., 791.234
Tenn. Code Ann., 40-28-116

Life Settlement Act
Fla. Stat. Ann., 626.994 et seq.

Life, Sickness and Accident Insurance Policy Readability Act
Neb. Rev. Stat. 1943, 44-3401 et seq.

Life Skills Education and Alcohol and Drug Abuse Prevention Act
Okla. Stat. Ann., Title 70, § 1210.229-1 et seq.

Life Sustaining Procedures Act
Fla. Stat. Ann., 765.01 et seq.
Iowa Code Ann., 144A.1 et seq.

Lifeboat Maintenance Law
Cal. Health and Safety Code § 24000 et seq.

Lifeline Act
Colo. Rev. Stat., 40-3.4-101 et seq.

Lifelong Learning Investments Act
Kan. Stat. Ann., 74-50, 102 et seq.

Lifetime Supervision of Sex Offenders Act
Colo. Rev. Stat., 16-13-801 et seq.

Lifetime Transfer of Property Act
Ill. Rev. Stat. 1991, Ch. 110 1/2, § 600 et seq.

Light Act (Warning)
Neb. Rev. Stat. 1943, 39-6, 148

Light, Heat and Power Authority Act (Albany)
N.Y. Public Authorities Law (Consol. Laws Ch. 43A) § 1025 et seq.

Light Industrial Equipment, Tractor, Lawn and Garden Franchise Act
Ala. Code 1975, § 8-21A-1

Light Wine, Beer and Other Alcoholic Beverages Act
Miss. Code Ann. 1972, § 67-3-1 et seq.

Lighthouse Service Retirement Act
June 20, 1918, Ch. 103, 40 Stat. 608, 33 U.S. Code § 763
March 4, 1925, Ch. 523, 43 Stat. 1261, 33 U.S. Code § 765
Oct. 2, 1972, P.L. 92-455, 86 Stat. 761, 33 U.S. Code § 763

Lighting Act (Municipal Plan), Cities of Primary, First and Second Class and Villages
Neb. Rev. Stat. 1943, 19-1401 et seq.

Lighting Act (Municipal Plant)
Neb. Rev. Stat. 1943, 19-1401 et seq.

Lighting and Water Systems Act (Municipal)
N.H. Rev. Stat. 1955, 38:2 et seq.

Lighting District Act (Highways)
Cal. Streets and Highways Code § 19000 et seq.

Lighting Efficiency Code
Fla. Stat. Ann., 366.80

Lighting Efficiency Standards for Existing Public Buildings Act
N.Y. Energy Law (Consol. Laws Ch. 17A) § 8-101 et seq.

Lighting Energy Conservation Act
Okla. Stat. Ann., Title 61, § 151 et seq.

Lighting Installation Act (Outdoor)
Ill. Rev. Stat. 1991, Ch. 67 1/2, § 120 et seq.

Lime and Fertilizer Law
Vt. Stat. Ann., Title 6, § 411 et seq.

Lime, Avocado and Mango Sales Law
Fla. Stat. Ann., 570.55

Lime Grinding Act
Va. Code 1950, § 53-75.1 et seq.

Lime Research, Promotion, and Consumer Information Act of 1990
Nov. 28, 1990, P.L. 101-624, 7 U.S. Code §§ 6201 to 6212
Dec. 14, 1993, P.L. 103-194, 7 U.S. Code §§ 6201 nt., 6202, 6204, 6209

Liming Materials Act
See Agricultural Liming Materials Act

Liming Materials Act (Agricultural)
Me. Rev. Stat. Ann. 1964, Title 7, § 761 et seq.
Miss. Code Ann. 1972, § 69-39-1 et seq.
N.H. Rev. Stat. 1955, 431:22 et seq.

Limitation Act (Actions)
Colo. Rev. Stat., 13-80-101 et seq.

Limitation Act (Adopted Child Inheritance)
Mass. Gen. Laws Ann., 210:7

Limitation Act (Civil)
N.C. Gen. Stat. 1943, § 1-15 et seq.

Limitation Act (Colorado River)
Cal. Statutes 1929, Ch. 16, p. 38

Limitation Act (Criminal)
Ga. Code Ann., 17-3-1 et seq.

Limitation Act (Liquor Licenses)
Pa. 1939 Pamph. Laws 806, No. 358

Limitation Act (Misdemeanors)
N.C. Gen. Stat. 1943, § 15-1

Limitation of Action Act (Public Securities)
N.M. Stat. Ann., 1-14-4 et seq.

Limitation of Actions (Criminal)
Okla. Stat. Ann., Title 22, § 151 et seq.

Limitation of Actions Act
See Statute of Limitations

Limitation of Actions Act (Civil)
N.H. Rev. Stat. 1955, 508:1 et seq.
R.I. Gen. Laws 1956, 9-1-13 et seq.
Vt. Stat. Ann., Title 12, § 461 et seq.
Wash. Rev. Code Ann., 4.16.005 et seq.
Wyo. Stat. Ann., § 1-3-101 et seq.

Limitation of Actions Act (Criminal)
N.H. Rev. Stat. 1955, 625:8
Vt. Stat. Ann., Title 13, § 4501 et seq.
Wash. Rev. Code Ann., 9A.04.080

Limitation of Actions Act (Personnel)
Mich. Comp. Laws Ann., 600.5813 et seq.

Limitation of Actions Act (Real)
Mich. Comp. Laws Ann., 600.5801

Limitation of Actions - Contracts for Sale
D.C. Code § 28:2-725

Limitation of Actions Statute
Okla. Stat. Ann., Title 12, § 91 et seq.

Limitation of Armament Resolution
July 12, 1921, Ch. 44, 42 Stat. 141

Limitation of Levy Act (County Taxes)
Colo. Rev. Stat. 30-25-201 et seq.

Limitation of Property Tax Extension Act
Ill. Rev. Stat. 1989, Ch. 120, § 2501 et seq.

Limitation of Prosecutions
See Statute of Limitations

Limitation of Risk Act (Fire, Casualty and Surety Insurance)
Fla. Stat. Ann., 624.609

Limitation on Collection of Personal Property Tax Act
Ill. Comp. Stat. 1992, Ch. 35, §§ 225/1, 225/2
Ill. Rev. Stat. 1991, Ch. 120, §§ 2201, 2202

Limitation on Indebtedness Act (Local Government)
Ill. Rev. Stat. 1991, Ch. 85, § 851 et seq.

Limitations Act (Prosecutions)
La. Code of Criminal Procedure, Act. 571 et seq.

Limitations Act (Real Estate)
Ill. Rev. Stat. 1985, Ch. 110, § 13-101 et seq.

Limitations on Foreign Claims Act
Mich. Comp. Laws Ann., 600.5861
Pa. Cons. Stat., Title 42, § 5521 et seq.
W. Va. Code 1966, § 55-2A-1 et seq.

Limited Access Highway Act
Fla. Stat. Ann., 338.01 et seq.
Ga. Code Ann., 32-6-110 et seq.
Ind. Code Ann., 8-11-1-1 et seq.
Ky. Rev. Stat. 1971, 177.220 et seq., 177.990
Mass. Gen. Laws Ann., 81:7A et seq.
Mich. Comp. Laws Ann., 252.51 et seq.
N.H. Rev. Stat. 1955, 230:44 et seq.
Pa. Purdon's Stat., Title 36, § 2391.1 et seq.
Utah Code Ann. 1953, 27-12-111 et seq.
Vt. Stat. Ann., Title 19, § 1861 et seq.
Wash. Rev. Code Ann., 47.52.001 et seq.

Limited Actions Civil Procedure Act
Kan. Stat. Ann., 61-1601 et seq.

Limited Dividend Act (Public Housing)
N.Y. Private Housing Finance Law (Consol. Laws Ch. 44B) §§ 70 et seq.

Limited Dividend Act (Urban Redevelopment)
Mass. Gen. Laws Ann., 121A:9

Limited Dividend Housing Act
N.Y. Private Housing Finance Law (Consol. Laws, Ch. 44B) § 76
S.C. Code Ann. 1976, § 31-1-110 et seq.

Limited Dividend Housing Companies Act
N.Y. Private Housing Finance Law (Consol. Laws Ch. 44B) § 70 et seq.

Limited Dividend Housing Corporation Act
Cal. Health and Safety Code § 34800 et seq.
Pa. Purdon's Stat., Title 15, § 2801 et seq.
Wis. Stat. Ann., 66.405 et seq.

Limited Dividend Nonprofit Housing Corporation or Associations Law
N.J. Stat. Ann., 55:16-1 et seq.

Limited Electrical Energy Producers Act
N.H. Rev. Stat. 1955, 362-A:1 et seq.

Limited Franchise Act
N.J. Stat. Ann., 48:3-11 to 48:3-17

Limited Gaming Act
Colo. Rev. Stat., 12-47.1-101 et seq.

Limited Guardianship Act
Wyo. Stat. Ann., § 3-4-101 et seq.

Limited Guardianship Proceedings for Disabled Persons Law
Tenn. Code Ann., 34-4-101 et seq.

Limited Health Service Organization Act
Ill. Rev. Stat. 1991, Ch. 73, § 1501-1 et seq.

Limited Health Service Organization Act (Prepaid)
Fla. Stat. Ann., 636.002 et seq.
Neb. Rev. Stat. 1943, 44-4701 et seq.

Limited Liability Act
Alaska Stat. 1962, § 10.50.010 et seq.

Limited Liability Act (Fire Insurance Corporations)
Cal. Insurance Code § 3030 et seq.

Limited Liability Act (Hotels)
Tex. Rev. Civ. Stat., Art. 4592

Limited Liability Acts (Shipping)

March 3, 1851, Ch. 43, 9 Stat. 635
June 26, 1884, Ch. 121, 23 Stat. 57, 46 U.S. Code § 189
Feb. 13, 1893, Ch. 105, 27 Stat. 445, 46 U.S. Code §§ 190 to 196

Limited Liability Companies Act (Registration of Foreign)

Miss. Code Ann. 1972, § 79-6-1 et seq.

Limited Liability Company Act

See also Uniform Limited Liability Company Act
Ala. Code 1975, § 10-12-1 et seq.
Ariz. Rev. Stat. Ann., § 29-601 et seq.
Cal. Corporations Code § 17000
Colo. Rev. Stat., 7-80-101 et seq.
Conn. Public Acts 1993, p. 730, No. 267
D.C. Code Ann., § 29-1301 to 29-1375
Del. Code of 1974, Title 6, § 18-101 et seq.
Fla. Stat. Ann., 608.401 et seq.
Ga. Code Ann., 14-11-100 et seq.
Ill. Comp. Stat. 1992, Ch. 815, § 180/1-1 et seq.
Iowa Code Ann., 490A.100 et seq.
Kan. Stat. Ann., 17-7601 et seq.
Ky. Rev. Stat. 1971, 275.001 et seq.
La. Rev. Stat. Ann., 9:3431 et seq.
Mass. Gen. Laws Ann., 156C:1 et seq.
Md. Ann. Code 1974, Art. CA, § 4A-1101 et seq.
Me. Rev. Stat. Ann. 1964, Title 31, § 601 et seq.
Mich. Comp. Laws Ann., 450.4101 et seq.
Minn. Stat. 1986, 322B.01 et seq.
Mont. Code Ann., 35-8-101 et seq.
N.D. Cent. Code, 10-32-01 et seq.
N.J. Stat. Ann., 42:2B-1 et seq.
N.M. Stat. Ann., 53-19-1 et seq.
N.M. Stat. Ann., 53-19-1 to 53-19-74
N.Y. Limited Liability Company Law (Consol. Laws Ch. 34) § 101 et seq.
Okla. Stat. Ann., Title 18, § 2001 et seq.
Ore. Laws 1993, Ch. 173
Pa. 1994 Pamph. Laws, No. 106
R.I. Gen. Laws 1956, 7-16-1 et seq.
S.C. Code Ann. 1976, § 33-43-101 et seq.
Tex. General and Special Laws 1991, Ch. 901, § 46
Tex. Rev. Civ. Stat., Art. 1528n, § 1.01
Utah Code Ann. 1953, 48-2b-101 et seq.
Va. Code 1950, § 13.1-1000 et seq.
W. Va. Code 1966 § 31-1A-1 et seq.
Wyo. Stat. Ann., § 17-15-101 et seq.

Limited Liability Company and Professional Service Corporation Act

Fla. Stat. Ann., 621.02 et seq.

Limited Liability Partnership Act

Haw. Session Laws 1996, Act 93
Me. Rev. Stat. Ann. 1964, Title 31, § 801 et seq.
Okla. Stat. Ann., Title 54, § 401 et seq.
Utah Code Ann. 1953, 48-1-41 et seq.

Limited Liability Partnerships Act (Registered)

Ariz. Rev. Stat. Ann., § 29-244 et seq.

Limited Mandate Health Insurance Act

Mo. Rev. Stat., 376.995

Limited Obligation Bond Law

Cal. Government Code § 43648 et seq.

Limited Partner Protection Act (Thompson-Killea)

Cal. Corporation Code § 25014.5 et seq.

Limited Partnership Act

See also Revised Uniform Limited Partnership Act
See also Uniform Limited Partnership Act
Ala. Code 1975, § 10-9B-101 et seq.
Ariz. Rev. Stat. Ann., § 29-301 et seq.
Cal. Corporations Code § 25014.5 et seq.
Iowa Code Ann., 487.101 et seq.
Okla. Stat. Ann., Title 54, §§ 141 et seq., 301 et seq.

Limited Partnership Act (1985) (Modified)

See Uniform 1985 Modified Limited Partnership Act

Limited Partnership Act (Foreign)

N.Y. Partnership Law (Consol. Laws Ch. 39) § 120 et seq.

Limited Partnership Act (Revised)
See Revised Uniform Limited Partnership
Act
Cal. Corporations Code § 15611 et seq.

Limited Partnership Act, 1985
See also Uniform Limited Partnership Act
Ala. Code 1975, § 10-9-1 et seq.
Alaska Stat. 1962, § 32.10.010 et seq.
Ariz. Rev. Stat. Ann., § 29-301 et seq.
Ark. Code Ann. 1987, 4-44-101 et seq.
Haw. Rev. Stat. Ann., § 425D-101 et seq.
Ida. Code 1947, 53-201 et seq.
Me. Rev. Stat. Ann. 1964, Title 31, § 151 et
seq.
Nev. Rev. Stat. Ann., 88,010 et seq.
N.M. Stat. Ann., 54-2-1 et seq.
Pa. Cons. Stat., Title 59, § 501 et seq.
S.C. Code Ann. 1976, § 33-42-10 et seq.
S.D. Codified Laws 1967, 48-6-1 et seq.

Limited Partnership Association Act
Colo. Rev. Stat., 7-63-101 et seq.

Limited Partnership Rollup Reform Act of 1993
Dec. 17, 1993, P.L. 103-202, 15 U.S. Code
§ 78a nt.

Limited Practice Act (Law Student)
Miss. Code Ann. 1972, § 73-3-201 et seq.

Limited Practice Act (Medicine)
Ohio Rev. Code 1953, 4731.15 et seq.

Limited Prescriptive Authority Demonstration Act (Nursing)
Ga. Code Ann., 43-26-50 et seq.

Limited Profit Housing Companies Act
N.Y. Private Housing Finance Law (Consol.
Laws Ch. 44B) § 10 et seq.

Limited Profit Housing Companies Law
N.Y. Private Housing Finance Law (Consol.
Laws Ch. 44B), § 10 et seq.

Limited Purpose Trust Company Act
Del. Code of 1974, Title 5, § 773 et seq.

Limited Sales, Excise and Use Tax Act
Tex. Tax Code, § 151.001 et seq.

Limited Water District Law
Cal. Statutes 1959, Ch. 2136, p. 5048

Limited Winery Signage Act
Pa. Purdon's Stat., Title 73, § 411 et seq.

Limousine Transportation Act
Mich. Comp. Laws Ann., 257.1901 et seq.

Lincoln County Flood Control District Act
Nev. Statutes 1947, Ch. 174, p. 610

Lincoln County Funding Act
Nev. Statutes 1873, Ch. 13, p. 54

Lincoln County, Montana, Lands Transfer Act of 1994
Oct. 22, 1994, P.L. 103-398, 108 Stat. 4162

Lincoln County Pilot Land Development and Disposal Law
Nev. Rev. Stat. 1979 Reprint, 321. 540 et
seq.

Lincoln County Recreation Authority Act
Ga. Laws 1997, p. 4566

Lincoln Holiday Act
Ill. Rev. Stat. 1991, Ch. 1, § 3051-60

Lincoln Home Jurisdiction Act
Ill. Rev. Stat. 1991, Ch. 1, § 7000 et seq.

Lincoln Monument Act
Ill. Rev. Stat. 1991, Ch. 84, § 7.9 et seq.

Lincoln Park Commissioners Land Condemnation Act
Ill. Rev. Stat. 1991, Ch. 105, § 78.9 et seq.

Lincoln Park Submerged Lands Act
Ill. Rev. Stat. 1991, Ch. 105, § 437.9 et seq.

Lincoln Reservoir Act
Ill. Rev. Stat. 1991, Ch. 19, §§ 1110, 1111

Lincoln School Loan Act
Mass. Acts 1951, Ch. 356

Lincoln University Act
Mo. Rev. Stat., 175.010 et seq.

Lincoln University-Commonwealth Act
Pa. Purdon's Stat., Title 24, § 2510-401 et seq.

Lindbergh Act (Kidnapping)
N.J. Stat. Ann., 2C:13-1

Lindbergh Kidnapping Act
See Kidnapping Act

Linden Drainage and Flood Control Act
Mass. Acts 1955, Ch. 574

Lindsay Act (County Council)
Md. Ann. Code 1957, Art. 25A, § 2

Line Item Veto Act
April 9, 1996, P.L. 104-130, 2 U.S. Code §§ 681 nt., 692

Line of Duty Act
Va. Code 1950, § 15.1-136.1 et seq.

Line of Duty Presumption Act (Heart)
Mass. Gen. Laws Ann., 32:94

Line Tapping Act (Telecommunication)
Ill. Rev. Stat. 1991, Ch. 134, §§ 15m, 16

Lines Law (Surplus)
Me. Rev. Stat. Ann. 1964, Title 24-A, § 2001 et seq.
Mo. Rev. Stat. 1978, 384.011 et seq.

Linked Deposit Act
Iowa Code Ann., 12.31 et seq.

Linked Deposit Act (Excelsior)
N.Y. State Finance Law 1940 (Consol. Laws Ch. 56) § 212 et seq.

Linked Deposit Act (Small Business)
Okla. Stat. Ann., Title 62, § 88.1 et seq.

Linked Deposit Program Act
Ark. Acts 1991, Nos. 671, 682

Linked Investments for Tomorrow Act
Iowa Code Ann., 12.31 et seq.

Linseed Oil Act
Pa. Purdon's Stat., Title 3, § 141 et seq.

Linthicum-Moses Act
See Foreign Service Act

Linton-Dycus Act (Payments by Sheriff)
Ky. Rev. Stat. 1971, 134.300 et seq., 134.990

Lipp Act (Motor Vehicles)
Ohio Laws Vol. 111, p. 460

Liquefied Compressed Gas Equipment Inspection Act
Miss. Code Ann. 1972, § 75-57-1 et seq.

Liquefied Gas Tax Law
Tenn. Code Ann., 67-3-1101 et seq.

Liquefied Natural and Petroleum Gas Act
N.Y. Environmental Conservation Law 1972 (Consol. Laws Ch. 43B) § 23-1701 et seq.

Liquefied Natural Gas Terminal Act
Cal. Public Utilities Code § 5550 et seq.

Liquefied Petroleum Equipment Inspection Act of Mississippi
Miss. Code Ann. 1972, § 75-57-1 et seq.

Liquefied Petroleum Gas Act
Ala. Code 1958, Title 26, § 179(57) et seq.
Nev. Rev. Stat. 1979 Reprint, 590.465 et seq.
N.M. Stat. Ann., 70-5-1 et seq.
Okla. Stat. Ann., Title 52, § 420.1 et seq.
Ore. Rev. Stat., 480.410 et seq.
Pa. Purdon's Stat., Title 35, § 1321 et seq.
Tex. Natural Resources Code, § 113.001 et seq.
Utah Code Ann. 1953, 53-7-301 et seq.

Liquefied Petroleum Gas Board Act
Ark. Code Ann. 1987, 15-75-101 et seq.

Liquefied Petroleum Gas Container Act
Ill. Rev. Stat. 1991, Ch. 96 1/2, § 5700 et seq.
Minn. Stat. Ann., 299F.40

Liquefied Petroleum Gas Regulation Act
Ill. Rev. Stat. 1991, Ch. 96 1/2, § 5600 et seq.

Liquefied Petroleum Gas Research, Marketing and Safety Act
Okla. Stat. Ann., Title 52, § 420.20 et seq.

Liquefied Petroleum Gas Storage Law
N.Y. Local Laws 1971, Town of Halfmoon, p. 2151

Liquefied Petroleum Motor Fuel Tax Law
Kan. Stat. Ann., 79-3490 et seq.

Liquefied Petroleum Safety Act
Ga. Code Ann., 10-1-260 et seq.
Tenn. Code Ann., 68-26-101 et seq.

Liquid Fuel Act
Fla. Stat. Ann., 526.01 et seq.

Liquid Fuel Act (Transportation)
Kan. Stat. Ann., 55-501 et seq.

Liquid Fuels and Fuel Use Tax Enforcement Act
Pa. Cons. Stat., Title 75, § 9001 et seq.

Liquid Fuels Display Act (Prices)
Pa. Purdon's Stat., Title 72, §§ 2611y, 2611z

Liquid Fuels License Act
Pa. 1937 Pamph. Laws 1193, No. 307

Liquid Fuels Tax Act
Haw. Rev. Stat. Ann., § 243-1 et seq.
Pa. Purdon's Stat., Title 72, § 2611a et seq.

Liquid Waste Pumpers and Haulers Act (Hamilton County)
Tenn. Private Acts 1991, Ch. 84

Liquidation Act
See Uniform Liquidation Act

Liquidation Act (Insurers)
See also Uniform Insurers Liquidation Act
Ill. Rev. Stat. 1935, Ch. 73, § 495 et seq.
Mass. Gen. Laws Ann., 175:180A et seq.
Md. Ann. Code 1957, Art. 48A, § 74 et seq.
Me. Rev. Stat. Ann. 1964, Title 24-A, § 4363 et seq.

Minn. Stat. Ann., 60B.01 et seq.
N.C. Gen. Stat. 1943, § 58-155.10 et seq.
N.J. Stat. Ann., 17:30C-1, 17:30C-5, 17:30C-15 to 17:30C-23, 17B:3, 17:B:32-4, 17B:32-5, 17B:32-15 to 23
N.Y. Insurance Law 1984 (Consol. Laws Ch. 28) § 7408 et seq.
Ohio Rev. Code 1953, 3903.01 et seq.
Ore. Rev. Stat., 734.330
Tex. Insurance Code, Art. 21.28

Liquidation and Insurance Rehabilitation Law
Me. Rev. Stat. Ann. 1964, Title 24-A, § 4351 et seq.

Liquidation and Rehabilitation Act (Insurers Supervision)
Mo. Rev. Stat. 1978, 375.1150

Liquidation and Rehabilitation Act (Insurers)
Fla. Stat. Ann., 631.001 et seq.
Ga. Code Ann., 33-37-1 et seq.
Me. Rev. Stat. Ann. 1964, Title 24-A, 4351 et seq.
Miss. Code Ann. 1972, § 83-24-1 et seq.

Liquidation and Rehabilitation Act (Life and Health Insurers)
N.J. Stat. Ann., 17B:32-31 et seq.

Liquidation and Rehabilitation Law (Insurance)
See Insurers Rehabilitation and Liquidation Act

Liquidation, Insurers Supervision and Rehabilitation Act
Kan. Stat. Ann., 40-3605 et seq.
Neb. Rev. Stat. 1943, 44-4801 et seq.
S.C. Code Ann. 1976, § 38-27-10 et seq.

Liquidator for Sewer District Act
Mo. Rev. Stat., 249.670 et seq.

Liquor Act
Ala. Code 1975, § 28-3-1 et seq.
Ariz. Rev. Stat. Ann., § 4-101 et seq.
Ark. Code Ann. 1987, 3-8-205 et seq.
Colo. Rev. Stat., 12-47-101 et seq.
Fla. Stat. Ann., 561.01 et seq.

Ida. Code 1947, 23-101 et seq.
Mass. Gen. Laws Ann., 138:1 et seq.
Me. Rev. Stat. Ann. 1964, Title 28-A, § 1 et seq.
Minn. Stat. Ann., 340A.101 et seq.
N.H. Rev. Stat. 1955, 175:1 et seq.
N.J. Stat. Ann., 33:1-1 et seq.
Okla. Stat. Ann., Title 37, § 1
Pa. Purdon's Stat., Title 47, § 1-101 et seq.
S.C. Code Ann. 1976, § 61-3-10 et seq.
S.D. Codified Laws 1967, 35-1-1 et seq.
Tenn. Code Ann., 57-1-101 et seq.
Wash. Rev. Code Ann., 66.98.010 et seq.
Wis. Stat. 1979, 176.01 et seq.
Wyo. Stat. Ann., § 12-1-101 et seq.

Liquor Act (Inspection)
N.D. Laws 1909, Ch. 189

Liquor Administration Act
See Federal Alcohol Administration Act

Liquor Authority Law
N.Y. Laws 1933, 1st Ex. Sess., Ch. 819

Liquor, Beer and Wine Control Act
Iowa Code Ann., 123.1 et seq.

Liquor Bonding Act
Minn. Stat. Ann., 340A.412

Liquor by the Drink Act
Tenn. Code Ann., 57-4-101

Liquor by the Drink Law
Ore. Rev. Stat., 472.010 et seq.

Liquor Civil Damage Act
Conn. Gen. Stat. Ann., § 30-102

Liquor Club Regulation Act
Kan. Stat. Ann., 41-2601 et seq.

Liquor Control Act
Alaska Stat. 1962, § 04.06.010 et seq.
Cal. Business and Professions Code § 23000 et seq.
Conn. Gen. Stat. Ann., § 30-1 et seq.
Del. Code of 1974, Title 4, § 101 et seq.
Ga. Code Ann., 3-3-1 et seq.
Ill. Rev. Stat. 1991, Ch. 43, § 93.9 et seq.

Ind. Code Ann., 7.1-1-1-1 et seq.
Iowa Code Ann., 123.1 et seq.
Kan. Stat. Ann., 41-101 et seq.
Ky. Rev. Stat. 1971, 241.010 et seq.
La. Rev. Stat. Ann., 26:1 et seq.
Mich. Comp. Laws Ann., 436.1 et seq.
Minn. Stat. Ann., 340A.201 et seq.
Mo. Rev. Stat., 311.010 et seq.
Mont. Code Ann., 16-1-101 et seq.
N.D. Cent. Code, 5-01-01 et seq.
Neb. Rev. Stat. 1943, 53-101 et seq.
N.M. Stat. Ann., 60-3A-1 et seq.
N.Y. Alcoholic Beverage Control Law (Consol. Laws Ch. 3B)
Ohio Rev. Code 1953, 4301.01 et seq.
Okla. Stat. Ann., Title 37, § 501 et seq.
Ore. Rev. Stat., 471.005 et seq.
Pa. Purdon's Stat., Title 47, §§ 1-101 et seq., 2-201 et seq.
R.I. Gen. Laws 1956, 3-1-1 et seq.
S.D. Codified Laws 1967, 35-4-1 et seq.
Tex. Alcoholic Beverage Code, § 11.01 et seq.
Utah Code Ann. 1953, 32A-1-101 et seq.
Va. Code 1950, § 4-1 et seq.
Vt. Stat. Ann., Title 7, § 1 et seq.
Wash. Rev. Code Ann., 66.08.010 et seq.
W. Va. Code 1966, § 60-1-1 et seq.

Liquor Control Act (Distilled)
Ore. Rev. Stat., 472.010 et seq.

Liquor Enforcement Act
Ark. Code Ann. 1987, 3-2-301 et seq.
Okla. Stat. Ann., Title 37, § 501 et seq.

Liquor Enforcement Act of 1936
June 25, 1936, Ch. 815, 49 Stat. 1928 (See 18 U.S. Code §§ 1263 to 1265)

Liquor Excise Tax Act
N.M. Stat. Ann., 7-17-1 et seq.

Liquor Excise Tax Act (Local)
N.M. Stat. Ann., 7-24-8 et seq.

Liquor Floor Tax Law
Pa. 1933 Ex. Pamph. Laws 5, No. 1

Liquor Gallonage Tax Act
Ill. Rev. Stat. 1991, Ch. 43, § 158 et seq.

Liquor Law
N.C. Gen. Stat. 1943, § 18B-100 et seq.

Liquor Law Immunity Act
Miss. Code Ann. 1972, § 97-31-51

Liquor Law Repeal and Enforcement Act
Aug. 27, 1935, Ch. 740, 49 Stat. 872, 27 U.S. Code § 122

Liquor Liability Act
Me. Rev. Stat. Ann. 1964, Title 28-A, § 2501 et seq.
R.I. Gen. Laws 1956, 3-14-1 et seq.

Liquor License Act
Haw. Rev. Stat. Ann., § 281-31 et seq.
Minn. Stat. Ann., 340A.401 et seq.
Nev. Rev. Stat. 1979 Reprint, 369.010 et seq.
Ore. Rev. Stat., 471.205 et seq.
Pa. 1856 Pamph. Laws 200, No. 233
S.D. Codified Laws 1967, 35-2-1 et seq.
Tenn. Code Ann., 57-3-201 et seq.
Vt. Stat. Ann., Title 7, § 221 et seq.
Wash. Rev. Code Ann., 66.24.010 et seq.
Wis. Stat. Ann., 125.04 et seq.

Liquor License Act (Retail)
Mont. Rev. Code 1947, 4-101 et seq.
W. Va. Code 1966 § 60-3A-1 et seq.

Liquor License Quota Act
Mont. Code Ann., 16-4-201
Pa. 1939 Pamph. Laws 806, No. 358

Liquor Permit Act
Okla. Stat. Ann., Title 37, § 501 et seq.

Liquor Permits Act
Wash. Rev. Code Ann., 66.20.010 et seq.

Liquor Price Control Act
Kan. Stat. Ann., 41-1111 et seq.

Liquor Price Posting Act
Conn. Gen. Stat. Ann., § 30-63 et seq.

Liquor Prohibition Act
See Prohibition Act (Liquor)

Liquor Referendum Law
Miss. Code 1942, § 10208.7
Pa. 1933 Ex. Pamph. Laws 15, No. 4, § 501 et seq.

Liquor Repeal Act
Alaska Stat. 1962, § 04.06.010 et seq.

Liquor Revenue Act
Ore. Rev. Stat., 473.010 et seq.

Liquor Sale Abatement Law
Cal. Penal Code § 11200 et seq.

Liquor Sale Act (Civil Damage)
W. Va. Code 1931, Ch. 60, Art. 1, § 22

Liquor Sales Act (Black List)
Ohio Rev. Code 1953, 4399.01

Liquor Sales Liability Act (Black List)
Ohio Rev. Comp. 1953, 4399.01

Liquor Sales Tax Act (First Class School District)
Pa. Purdon's Stat., Title 53, § 16131 et seq.

Liquor Seizure and Confiscation Act
Tenn. Code Ann., 57-9-201 et seq.

Liquor Service License Act
Ore. Laws 1945, Ch. 271

Liquor Store Act (Mom and Pop)
S.C. Code Ann. 1976, § 61-3-460 et seq.

Liquor Stores Act
Wash. Rev. Code Ann., 66.16.010 et seq.

Liquor Tax Act
Haw. Rev. Stat. Ann., § 244D-1 et seq.
Minn. Stat. Ann., 340.47 et seq.
Nev. Rev. Stat. 1979 Reprint, 369.010 et seq.
N.Y. Laws 1909, Ch. 39
Pa. Purdon's Stat., Title 47, § 745 et seq.
Vt. Stat. Ann., Title 7, § 421 et seq.
Wis. Stat. Ann., 139.01 et seq.

Liquor Tax Administration Act
June 26, 1936, Ch. 830, 49 Stat. 1939 (See 18 U.S. Code §§ 1114, 2231) 19 U.S. Code §§ 1201, 1311, 1313; 27 U.S. Code § 205; 48 U.S. Code § 1402
June 15, 1938, Ch. 439, 52 Stat. 699

Liquor Tax Law (Spirituous and Vinous)
Pa. Purdon's Stat., Title 47, § 745 et seq.

Liquor Taxing Act of 1934
Jan. 11, 1934, Ch. 1, 48 Stat. 313

Liquor Transportation Act
Ala. Code 1975, § 28-4-120 et seq.

Liquor Warehouse Act
Wyo. Stat. 1957, § 9-652 et seq.

Lis Pendens Act
Ala. Code 1975, § 35-4-130 et seq.
Ga. Code Ann., 44-14-610 et seq.
Ind. Code Ann., 34-1-4-1 et seq.
La. Code of Civil Procedure Art. 3751 et seq.
Mich. Comp. Laws Ann., 600.2701 et seq.
Miss. Code Ann. 1972, § 11-47-1 et seq.
Mont. Code Ann., 70-28-213
N.C. Gen. Stat. 1943, § 1-116 et seq.
N.J. Rev. Stat. 1937, 2A:15-6 et seq.
N.Y. Civil Practice Law and Rules (Consol. Laws Ch. 8) § 6501 et seq.
Ohio Rev. Code 1953, 2703.26, 2703.27
Okla. Stat. Ann., Title 12, § 180
R.I. Gen. Laws 1956, 9-4-9
Tex. Property Code, §§ 12.007, 13.004
Wash. Rev. Code Ann., 4.28.320 et seq.

Lis Pendens Act (Notices)
Ark. Code Ann. 1987, 16-59-101 et seq.

Literacy Act (Basic)
Colo. Rev. Stat., 22-53-601 et seq.

Literacy Act (Braille)
N.M. Stat. Ann., 22-15-21 et seq.

Literacy Act (Inmate)
Okla. Stat. Ann., Title 57, §§ 510.5 to 510.8

Literacy Act (Prison)
Cal. Penal Code § 2053

Literacy Corps Act
Fla. Stat. Ann., 228.0716

Literacy for Children at Risk Act
N.M. Stat. Ann., 22A-1-1 et seq.

Literacy Rights and Education Act (Blind Persons')
Apr. 26, 1996, P.L. 104-134, 110 Stat. 1321-66, Title 8
Fla. Stat. Ann., 233.0561
Ga. Code Ann., 30-7-1 et seq.
Ga. Code Ann., 42-12-1 et seq.
La. Rev. Stat. Ann., 17:1981 et seq.
S.C. Code Ann. 1976, § 59-34-10 et seq.
Utah Code Ann. 1953, 53A-25a-101 et seq.

Literary Fund Act
Va. Code 1950, § 22.1-142 et seq.

Literature Commission Act
Ga. Code 1933, 40-3101 et seq.

Literature Commission Act (Obscenity)
Okla. Stat. 1961, Title 21, § 1040.1 et seq.

Litigation Accountability Act
Ala. Acts 1987, p. 254, No. 186
Miss. Code Ann. 1972, § 11-55-1 et seq.

Litter Abatement Act
Ore. Rev. Stat. 1953, 279.510 et seq.
Tex. Health and Safety Code, § 365.001 et seq.

Litter Act
Fla. Stat. Ann., 403.413
N.Y. Local Laws 1971, Town of Ogden, p. 2974
N.Y. Local Laws 1973, Village of Jordan, p. 3444
N.Y. Local Laws 1973, Village of Schuyler-ville, p. 3772

Litter and Plastic Recycling Act
R.I. Gen. Laws 1956, 21-27.1-1 et seq.

Litter Bugs Act
> Tex. Rev. Civ. Stat., Art. 4477-9a,
> §§ 2.04, 4.01 et seq.

Litter Control Act
> Ark. Code Ann. 1987, 8-6-401, 8-6-402
> Colo. Rev. Stat., 24-32-1001 et seq.
> Del. Code of 1974, Title 16, § 1601 et seq.
> Ga. Code Ann., 16-7-40 et seq.
> Haw. Rev. Stat. Ann., § 339-1 et seq.
> Ill. Rev. Stat. 1991, Ch. 38, § 86-1 et seq.
> Ky. Rev. Stat. 1971, Superseded Vols.
>   224.905 et seq.
> Md. Ann. Code 1957, Art. 27, § 468
> Me. Rev. Stat. Ann. 1964, Title 17, § 2261 et
>   seq.
> Mont. Laws 1971, Ch. 323
> N.H. Rev. Stat. 1955, 163-B:1 et seq.
> S.C. Code Ann. 1976, § 44-67-10 et seq.
> Tenn. Code Ann., 39-3-1001 et seq.
> Va. Code 1950, § 10-197 et seq.
> Wash. Rev. Code Ann., 70.93.010 et seq.

Litter Control and Beautification Act
> N.M. Stat. Ann., 67-16-1 et seq.

Litter Control and Incentive Employment Program (Youth Corps)
> La. Rev. Stat. Ann., 23:1821 et seq.

Litter Control and Recycling Chapter
> R.I. Gen. Laws 1956, 37-15-1 et seq.

Litter Control, Recycling, and Resource Recovery Act
> Cal. Government Code § 68000 et seq.

Litter Control, Recycling, and Resource Recovery Assessment Act
> Cal. Revenue and Taxation Code § 42000 et
>   seq.

Litter Law
> N.Y. Vehicle and Traffic Law 1959 (Consol.
>   Laws Ch. 71) §§ 1219, 1220, 1642, Subd.
>   19

Litter Law (Marine)
> Miss. Code Ann. 1972, § 51-2-1 et seq.

Litter Prevention and Control Law
> Tenn. Code Ann., 4-7-301 et seq.

Litter Reduction and Recycling Act
> Neb. Rev. Stat. 1943, 81-1534 et seq.

Litter Tax Act
> Va. Code 1950, § 58.1-1706 et seq.

Littering Laws
> Miss. Code Ann. 1972, §§ 49-1-13, 49-1-44,
>   97-15-21, 97-15-29, 97-27-9

Little Arkansas River Watershed District Act
> Kan. Laws 1957, Ch. 227

Little Byrd Commission Act (State Economies)
> N.Y. Laws 1942, Ch. 917

Little Calument River Flood Control Coordinating Commission Act
> Ill. Rev. Stat. 1979, Ch. 19, § 112.11 et seq.

Little Cigar Act of 1973
> Sept. 21, 1973, P.L. 93-109, 87 Stat. 352, 15
>   U.S. Code §§ 1332, 1335

Little Clayton Act (Domestic Insurance Companies)
> Pa. Purdon's Stat., Title 40, § 459.1 et seq.

Little Comstock Act (Obscenity)
> Conn. Gen. Stat. Ann., § 53a-193 et seq.

Little Davis-Bacon Act
> Mont. Code Ann., 18-2-401 et seq.
> N.M. Stat. Ann., 13-4-11 et seq.

Little Falls City Court Act
> N.Y. Laws 1945, Ch. 544

Little FTC Act
> Fla. Stat. Ann., 501.201 et seq.
> Ill. Rev. Stat. 1991, Ch. 121 1/2, § 261 et seq.

Little Habitual Criminal Act
> Colo. Rev. Stat., 16-13-101

Little Hatch Act (Political Activities)
Cal. Statutes 1940, 1st Ex. Sess., Ch. 45, § 18, p. 122
N.M. Stat. Ann., 10-9-21
N.Y. Civil Services Law (Consol. Laws Ch. 7) § 107
N.Y. Election Law 1976 (Consol. Laws Ch. 17) § 17-154
Tenn. Code Ann., 38-8-351

Little Jencks Act
See also Jencks Act (Witnesses Statements and Reports)
Kan. Stat. Ann., 22-3213

Little League Bill
Mass. Gen. Laws Ann., 231.85

Little Lindberg Act
Cal. Penal Code § 209

Little McCarran Act (Subversive Activities)
Ala. Code 1958, Title 14, § 97(1) et seq.
La. Rev. Stat. Ann., 14:358 et seq.
Mich. Comp. Laws Ann., 752.321 et seq.
Tex. Rev. Civ. Stat., Art. 6889-3

Little Miller Act (Public Contracts)
Alaska Stat. 1962, §§ 36.25.010, 36.25.020
Ariz. Rev. Stat. Ann., § 34-221 et seq.
Fla. Stat. Ann., 255.05
Md. Ann. Code 1974, Art. SF, § 17-101 et seq.
N.M. Stat. Ann., 13-4-1 et seq.

Little Missouri State Scenic River Act
N.D. Cent. Code, 61-29-01 et seq.

Little Norris-La Guardia Act (Labor Injunctions)
See also Labor Injunction Act
Ariz. Rev. Stat. Ann., § 12-1808
Colo. Rev. Stat., 8-3-118
Conn. Gen. Stat. Ann., § 31-112 et seq.
Haw. Rev. Stat. Ann., § 380-1 et seq.
Ida. Code 1947, 44-701 et seq.
Ill. Rev. Stat. 1991, Ch. 48, § 2a
Ind. Code Ann., 22-6-1-4
Kan. Stat. Ann., 60-904 et seq.
La. Rev. Stat. Ann., 23:841 et seq.
Mass. Gen. Laws Ann., 214:6
Md. Ann. Code 1974, Art. LE, § 4-302 et seq.
Me. Rev. Stat. Ann. 1964, Title 26, § 5
Minn. Stat. Ann., 185.01 et seq.
N.D. Cent. Code, 34-08-01 et seq.
N.J. Rev. Stat. 1937, 2A:15-51 et seq.
N.M. Stat. Ann., 50-3-1, 50-3-2
N.Y. Labor Law (Consol. Laws Ch. 31) § 807
Ore. Rev. Stat., 662.010 et seq.
Pa. Purdon's Stat., Title 43, § 206a et seq.
P.R. Laws Ann. 1954, Title 29, § 101 et seq.
R.I. Gen. Laws 1956, 28-10-1 et seq.
Utah Code Ann. 1953, 34-19-1 et seq.
Wash. Rev. Code Ann., 49.32.011 et seq.
Wis. Stat. Ann., 103.51 et seq.
Wyo. Stat. Ann., § 27-7-103

Little Randolph Sheppard Act
Fla. Stat. Ann., 413.051
Pa. Purdon's Stat., Title 62, § 2151 et seq.

Little RICO (Organized Crime Control Act)
N.Y. Civil Practice Laws and Rules (Consol. Laws Ch. 8) § 1353 et seq.
N.Y. Criminal Procedure Law (Consol. Laws Ch. 11A) §§ 40.20, 40.50, 200.40, 200.65, 210.40, 300.10, 310.50, 450.10, 450.20
N.Y. Penal Law 1965 (Consol. Laws Ch. 40) §§ 105.35, 460.00 et seq.

Little Right to Work Act
Mont. Code Ann., 39-33-101 et seq.

Little River Canyon National Preserve Act of 1992
Oct. 12, 1992, P.L. 102-427, 16 U.S. Code §§ 698q to 698t
Nov. 2, 1994, P.L. 103-437, 16 U.S. Code § 698s

Little River Canyon Preservation Act
Ala. Acts 1976, Nos. 227, 524

Little Robinson-Patman Act
Ida. Code 1947, 48-401 et seq.
Utah Code Ann. 1953, 13-5-1 et seq.

Little Rock Civil Service Act
Ark. Code Ann. 1987, 14-49-102 et seq.

Little Sherman Act (Antitrust)
Colo. Rev. Stat., 6-4-101 et seq.

Little Smith Act (Subversive Activities)
Mich. Comp. Laws Ann., 752.311 et seq.
N.C. Gen. Stat. 1943, § 14-11, et seq.

Little Taft-Hartley Act (Labor Disputes)
Del. Laws Vol. 46, p. 528, Ch. 196
Mass. Gen. Laws Ann., 150A:1 et seq.,
    150B:1 et seq., 214:6A

**Little Traverse Bands of Odawa Indians and
    the Little River Band of Ottawa Indians
    Act**
Sept. 21, 1994, P.L. 103-324, 25 U.S. Code
    §§ 1300k nt., 1300k et seq.
Nov. 2, 1994, P.L. 103-435, 25 U.S. Code
    § 1300k-7

**Little Traverse Bay Bands of Odawa Indians
    and the Little River Band of Ottawa
    Indians Act**
Feb. 12, 1996, P.L. 104-109, 25 U.S. Code
    §§ 1300k-3, 1300k-7

Little TVA Act (Municipal Utilities)
Wis. Stat. Ann., 66.065 et seq.

Little Wagner Act (Labor Relations)
Conn. Gen. Stat. Ann., § 31-101 et seq.
Fla. Stat. 1983, 447.01 et seq.
Kan. Stat. Ann., 44-801 et seq.
Mass. Gen. Laws Ann., 150A:1 et seq.
N.Y. Labor Law (Consol. Laws Ch. 31)
    § 700 et seq.
Pa. Purdon's Stat., Title 43, § 211.1 et seq.
R.I. Gen. Laws 1956, 28-9-1 et seq.
Utah Code Ann. 1953, 34-1-1 et seq.
Wis. Stat. Ann., 111.01 et seq.

**Little Williams Act (Security Takeover
    Disclosure Act)**
N.Y. Business Corporations Law 1961
    (Consol. Laws Ch. 4) § 1600 et seq.

Livable Cities Act of 1978
Oct. 31, 1978, P.L. 95-557, 42 U.S. Code
    §§ 8141 et seq., 8141 nt.

Livable Communities Act (Metropolitan)
Minn. Stat. Ann., 473.25 et seq.

Live Oak Revenue Bond Act
Fla. Special Laws 1949, Ch. 25987

Live Oak Urban Renewal Act
Fla. Special Laws 1965, Ch. 65-1860
Fla. Special Laws 1967, Ch. 67-1650

Live Poultry Law
Colo. Rev. Stat., 35-20-101 et seq.

Live stock Bankruptcy Act
May 15, 1935, Ch. 114, 49 Stat. 246, 11 U.S.
    Code § 22

Live Stock Contagious Diseases Acts
See Cattle Contagious Diseases Acts

Live Stock Transportation Act
June 29, 1906, Ch. 3594, 34 Stat. 607, 45
    U.S. Code §§ 71 to 74

Livery and Charter Boat Safety Act
Mich. Comp. Laws Ann., 281.571 et seq.

Livestock Act
Ariz. Rev. Stat. Ann., § 24-101 et seq.
Colo. Rev. Stat., 35-41-101 et seq.
La. Rev. Stat. Ann., 3:2801 et seq.
Miss. Code Ann. 1972, § 69-13-1 et seq.
S.C. Code Ann. 1976, § 47-7-110 et seq.

Livestock Act (Humane Slaughter)
Ill. Rev. Stat. 1991, Ch. 8, § 229.50 et seq.

Livestock Act (Running at Large)
Mo. Rev. Stat., 270.010 et seq.

**Livestock and Agricultural Exposition
    Authority Act (Lamar County)**
Ga. Laws 1996, p. 3703

Livestock and Poultry Act
Md. Ann. Code 1974, Art. AG, § 3-101 et
    seq.

Livestock and Poultry Disease Control Board Act
Ga. Code Ann., 4-4-1.1 et seq.
Ga. Code 1933, 62-1801, 62-1802

Livestock and Poultry Raising Law (Cooperative)
Miss. Code Ann. 1972, § 79-19-1 et seq.

Livestock Auction Agency Act
S.D. Codified Laws 1967, 40-15-1 et seq.

Livestock Auction Market Act
Ill. Rev. Stat. 1991, Ch. 121 1/2, § 208 et seq.
Okla. Stat. Ann., Title 2, § 9-130 et seq.
Ore. Rev. Stat., 599.205 et seq.

Livestock Auction Market Development Act
Neb. Rev. Stat. 1943, 54-1157 et seq.

Livestock Auction Sales Act
Okla. Stat. Ann., Title 2, § 9-131 et seq.

Livestock Biologics and Drug Act
Miss. Code Ann. 1972, § 69-17-1 et seq.

Livestock Board Act
N.M. Stat. Ann., 77-2-1 et seq.

Livestock Brand Act
Kan. Stat. Ann., 47-414 et seq.

Livestock Brand and Anti-theft Act
Utah Code Ann. 1953, 4-24-1 et seq.

Livestock Brands Act
Mont. Code Ann., 81-3-101 et seq.
S.D. Codified Laws 1967, 40-18-1 et seq.

Livestock Brands and Marks Act
Wash. Rev. Code Ann., 16.57.010 et seq.

Livestock Commission Act
Okla. Stat. 1961, Title 2, § 9-201 et seq.

Livestock Commission Merchants Act
Tex. Agriculture Code, § 147.001 et seq.

Livestock Crimestoppers Act
Mont. Code Ann., 81-6-301 et seq.

Livestock Dealer Act
Mo. Rev. Stat., 276.600 et seq.
N.D. Cent. Code, 36-04-01 et seq.
Ohio Rev. Code 1953, 943.01 et seq.
Okla. Stat. Ann., Title 2, § 1751 et seq.
Tenn. Code Ann., 44-10-201 et seq.

Livestock Dealers Financial Responsibility Act
Ala. Code 1975, § 2-15-130 et seq.

Livestock Dealers License Act
Ill. Rev. Stat. 1991, Ch. 111, § 401 et seq.
Ind. Code Ann., 15-2.1-14-1 et seq.
Mich. Comp. Laws Ann., 287.121 et seq.
Mont. Code Ann., 81-8-211 et seq.
N.C. Gen. Stat. 1943, § 106-418.8 et seq.
Neb. Rev. Stat. 1943, 54-1701 et seq.
W. Va. Code 1966 § 19-10B-1 et seq.

Livestock Development Authority Act
Ga. Code Ann., 50-10-1 et seq.

Livestock Disease Control Act
Mo. Rev. Stat., 267.560 et seq.

Livestock Disease Eradication Act
Tex. Agriculture Code, § 161.001 et seq.

Livestock Disease Prevention Act
Ga. Code Ann., 4-4-1 et seq.

Livestock Diseases Act
Mich. Comp. Laws Ann., 287.2 et seq.
Wash. Rev. Code Ann., 16.36.005 et seq.

Livestock District Act
Ill. Rev. Stat. 1981, Ch. 111, § 401 et seq.
Wyo. Stat. Ann., § 11-33-101 et seq.

Livestock Fraud Protection Act
Oct. 12, 1984, P.L. 98-473, 18 U.S. Code § 641 nt.

Livestock Grazing Act
Alaska Stat. 1962, § 03.35.010 et seq.

Livestock Identification Act
Ore. Rev. Stat. 1953, 604.005 et seq.
Wash. Rev. Code Ann., 16.57.010 et seq.
Continued

Livestock Indemnity Fund Act
Cal. Food and Agricultural Code 1967,
§ 30651 et seq. § 10401, 10421 et seq.

Livestock Inspection Act
Alaska Stat. 1962, § 03.45.010 et seq.

Livestock Law
N.C. Gen. Stat. 1943, § 68-15 et seq.

Livestock Local Option Law
Tex. Agriculture Code, § 143.021 et seq.

Livestock Management Facilities Act
Ill. Comp. Stat. 1992, Ch. 510, § 77/1 et seq.

Livestock Market Act
Neb. Rev. Stat. 1943, 54-2001 et seq.

Livestock Market Agency and DealerLicensing Act
Minn. Stat. Ann., 17A.01 et seq.

Livestock Market Charter Act
See Public Livestock Market Charter Act

Livestock Market Development Act
Ida. Code 1947, 25-1719 et seq.

Livestock Market Development Act (Auction)
Neb. Rev. Stat. 1943, 54-1157 et seq.

Livestock Marketing Act
Mo. Rev. Stat., 277.010 et seq.
Mont. Code Ann., 81-8-211 et seq.

Livestock Marketing Business Act (Public)
Ala. Code 1975, § 2-15-115 et seq.

Livestock Medicine Act
N.D. Cent. Code, 19-14-01 et seq.

Livestock Ownership Inspection Act
S.D. Codified Laws 1967, 40-20-1 et seq.

Livestock, Poultry and Egg Production Assistance Act
Miss. Code 1942, § 4435-51 et seq.

Livestock Products Inspection Act (Exotic)
Okla. Stat. Ann., Title 2, § 6-290.1 et seq.

Livestock Prompt Pay Law
N.C. Gen. Stat. 1943, § 106-418.1 et seq.

Livestock Protection Act
Ky. Rev. Stat. 1971, 258.095 et seq.
Va. Code 1950, §§ 1-22.53 to 1-22.57

Livestock Quarantine Act
La. Rev. Stat. Ann., 3:2091 et seq.
Wash. Rev. Code Ann., 16.36.005 et seq.

Livestock Raisers' Disaster Relief Act
Cal. Statutes 1977, Ch. 476

Livestock Record Act
Ill. Rev. Stat. 1991, Ch. 8, § 108.9 et seq.

Livestock Remedy Act
Ohio Rev. Code 1953, 923.21 et seq.
Tex. Rev. Civ. Stat., Art. 192-1
Wash. Rev. Code Ann., 15.52.010 et seq.

Livestock Sales Act
Tenn. Code Ann., 44-11-101 et seq.

Livestock Sales Auction Act
Ore. Rev. Stat., 599.205 et seq.

Livestock Sales Ring Act
Colo. Rev. Stat., 35-55-101 et seq.

Livestock Sanitary Board Act
Pa. 1895 Pamph. Laws 91, No. 66

Livestock Sanitation Act
Ind. Code 1971, 15-2-1-1 et seq.

Livestock Scabies Eradication Act
Tex. Agriculture Code, § 164.001 et seq.

Livestock Sellers Custodial Account Act
Ga. Code Ann., 4-6-20 et seq.

Livestock Sellers Protective Act
Neb. Rev. Stat. 1943, 54-1801 et seq.

Livestock Slaughter Act
Wash. Rev. Code Ann., 16.48.120 et seq., 16.49.430 et seq.

Livestock Tax Act
Mont. Code Ann., 15-24-901 et seq.

Livestock Tax Reform Act
Mont. Code Ann., 15-6-207, 15-8-201, 15-24-903, 15-24-904

Livestock Taxation Act
Cal. Revenue and Taxation Code § 5501 et seq.

Livestock Theft Act
La. Rev. Stat. Ann., 14:67.1

Livestock Theft Prevention Act (Meat Dealers)
Ore. Rev. Stat., 603.010 et seq.

Livestock Tick Eradication Act
Tex. Agriculture Code, § 167.001 et seq.

Livestock Transportation Act
Wash. Rev. Code Ann., 16.48.120, 81.56.120

Livestock Warranty Exemption Act
Iowa Code Ann., 554A.1

Livestock Water Tank Act
Colo. Rev. Stat., 35-49-101 et seq.

Living Apart Divorce Act
Ala. Code 1975, § 30-2-2
Ark. Code Ann. 1987, 9-12-301
La. Rev. Stat. Ann., 9:301
Minn. Stat. Ann., 518.06
N.D. Cent. Code, 14-06-05
Tex. Family Code, § 3.06
Wyo. Stat. 1957, § 20-47

Living Arrangements Licensure and Certification Act (Community-Integrated)
Ill. Rev. Stat. 1991, Ch. 91 1/2, § 1701 et seq.

Living Care Disclosure Act
Mich. Comp. Laws Ann., 554.801 et seq.

Living Centers Act (Specialized)
Ill. Rev. Stat. 1991, Ch. 91 1/2, § 601 et seq.

Living Facilities Licensing Act (Community)
Ill. Comp. Stat. 1992, Ch. 210, § 35/1 et seq.

Living Services Act (Independent)
Pa. Purdon's Stat., Title 62, § 3201 et seq.

Living Trust Act
Mont. Code Ann., 30-10-901 et seq.

Living War Memorial Act
Ill. Rev. Stat. 1991, Ch. 105, § 255.26h et seq.

Living Will Act
Colo. Rev. Stat., 15-18-101 et seq.
Fla. Stat. Ann., 765.301 et seq.
Ga. Code Ann., 31-32-1 et seq.
Ill. Rev. Stat. 1991, Ch. 110 1/2, § 701 et seq.
Kan. Stat. Ann., 65-28,101 et seq.
Ky. Rev. Stat. 1971, 311.622 et seq.
La. Rev. Stat. Ann., 40:1299.58.1 et seq.
Mass. Gen. Laws Ann., 201B:1 et seq.
Minn. Stat. Ann., 145B.01 et seq.
N.M. Stat. Ann., 24-7-1 et seq.
Pa. Cons. Stat., Title 20, § 5401 et seq.
S.C. Code Ann. 1976, § 44-77-10 et seq.
Tex. Health and Safety Code, § 672.001 et seq.

Living Will and Personal Choice Act
Utah Code Ann. 1953, 75-2-1101 et seq.

Living Will Directive Act
Ky. Rev. Stat. 1971, 311.621 to 311.643

Living Wills Acts (Health Care Proxies)
Mass. Gen. Laws Ann., 201D:1 et seq.

Livingston Act (Emergency Relief)
N.Y. Laws 1937, Ch. 358

Livingston Piper Act (Savings Bank Life Insurance)
N.Y. Insurance Law (Consol. Laws Ch. 28) § 2201 et seq.

Livingston Wadsworth Act (Emergency Relief)
N.Y. Laws 1937, Ch. 358

Lloyd Hanson Act (Architects)
Ohio Rev. Code 1953, 4703.01 et seq.

Lloyd La Follette Act
Aug. 24, 1912, Ch. 389, 37 Stat. 555 (See 5 U.S. Code §§ 5595, 7101, 7102, 7501)
June 10, 1948, Ch. 447, 62 Stat. 354 (See 5 U.S. Code §§ 5595, 7101, 7102, 7501)

Load Limit Act (Motor Vehicles)
W. Va. Code 1966, § 17C-17-1 et seq.

Load Line Act
May 26, 1939, Ch. 151, 53 Stat. 783, 46 U.S. Code §§ 85, 85g

Load Size and Weight Regulations
Miss. Code Ann. 1972, § 63-5-1

Loan Act
Colo. Rev. Stat. 1963, 73-2-1 et seq.
Mich. Comp. Laws Ann., 493.1 et seq.
Mont. Code Ann., 70-7-101 et seq.
Tex. Rev. Civ. Stat., Art. 5069-2.01 et seq.

Loan Act (Chattle)
Neb. Rev. Stat. 1943, 45-159 et seq.

Loan Act (Consumer)
N.J. Stat. Ann., 17:10-1 et seq.
Wash. Rev. Code Ann., 31.04.005 et seq.

Loan Act (Health Education and Academic)
Cal. Education Code 1976, § 69300 et seq.

Loan Act (Higher Education)
Ill. Rev. Stat. 1991, Ch. 144, § 1600 et seq.

Loan Act (Impoundment Site)
Mass. Gen. Laws Ann., 21:9A

Loan Act (Refund Anticipation)
N.C. Gen. Stat. 1943, § 53-245 et seq.

Loan Act (Residential Improvement)
Ill. Rev. Stat. 1991, Ch. 17, § 5800 et seq.

Loan Act (School District)
N.M. Stat. Ann., 22-18A-1 et seq.

Loan Act (Small)
See Small Loan Act

Loan Act (Student)
Okla. Stat. Ann., Title 70, § 695.1 et seq.

Loan Act (Usury Injunction)
Tex. Rev. Civ. Stat., Art. 4646b

Loan Advertising to Bankrupts Act
Ill. Rev. Stat. 1991, Ch. 121 1/2, § 157.24 et seq.

Loan Agencies Act
N.C. Gen. Stat. 1943, § 53-164 et seq.

Loan Agency Law (Nursing Home)
Pa. Purdon's Stat., Title 62, § 1521.101 et seq.

Loan and Building Association Act
See Building and Loan Association Act

Loan and Grant Program Act (Public Infrastructure)
Ill. Rev. Stat. 1991, Ch. 127, § 2708-1 et seq.

Loan and Investment Act (Industrial)
Haw. Rev. Stat. Ann., § 408-1 et seq.

Loan and Investment Companies Act
Mo. Rev. Stat., 368.010 et seq.
R.I. Gen. Laws 1956, 19-20-1 et seq.

Loan and Mortgage Housing Act
Haw. Rev. Stat. Ann., § 356-201 et seq.

Loan and Savings Code
Kan. Stat. Ann., 17-5101 et seq.

Loan Associations and Building Act
Ind. Code Ann., 28-1-12-1 et seq.

Loan Authority Act (Agricultural)
Mont. Code Ann., 80-12-101 et seq.

Loan Authority Act (Educational)
Me. Rev. Stat. Ann. 1964, Title 20-A, § 11411

Loan Authority Act (Higher Education Equipment)
Ala. Code 1975, § 16-18B-1 et seq.

Loan Authority Act (Student)
Mass. Gen. Laws Ann., 15C:1 et seq.

Loan Bond Program (Independent Higher Education)
W. Va. Code 1966 § 18-27-1 et seq.

Loan Broker Act (Consumer)
Miss. Code Ann. 1972, § 81-19-1 et seq.

Loan Broker and Mortgage Loan Company Act
N.M. Stat. Ann., 58-21-1 et seq.

Loan Brokers Act
Iowa Code Ann., 535C.1 et seq.
Neb. Rev. Stat. 1943, 45-189 et seq.
Tex. Penal Code 1925, Art. 1129a
Tex. Rev. Civ. Stat., Art. 5069-1.01

Loan Brokers Registration Requirements Act (Mortgage)
S.C. Code Ann. 1976, § 40-58-10 et seq.

Loan, Building and Homestead Associations Act
Ill. Rev. Stat. 1991, Ch. 17, § 3600 et seq.

Loan Business Act
R.I. Gen. Laws 1956, 19-25.3-1 et seq.

Loan Companies Act (Financial Services)
Haw. Rev. Stat. Ann., § 408-1 et seq.

Loan Forgiveness Act (Agriculture Education)
Pa. 1992 Pamph. Laws, No. 64

Loan Foundation Act (Student)
Conn. Gen. Stat. Ann., § 10a-201 et seq.

Loan Fund Act (Local Government Capital Project)
Pa. Purdon's Stat., Title 53, § 6781-1 et seq.

Loan Guarantee for Developmental Disability Programs (Small Facility)
Cal. Health and Safety Code § 436.40 et seq.

Loan Guarantee Fund Act (Boat Industry)
N.J. Stat. Ann., 34:1B-7.28 et seq.

Loan Guaranty Act
Colo. Rev. Stat., 11-47.5-101 et seq.

Loan Holding and Mutual Savings Company Act
Tenn. Code Ann., 45-3-1501 et seq.

Loan Insurance Law (Community Health Center Facilities)
Cal. Health and safety Code § 436.70 et seq.

Loan or Scholarship Act (Omnibus)
Miss. Code Ann. 1972, § 37-143-1 et seq.

Loan Program Act (Opportunity)
Miss. Code Ann. 1972, § 37-145-1

Loan Purchase Program Law (Education)
Ill. Rev. Stat. 1989, Ch. 122, § 30-51.14a et seq.

Loan Redemption Program and Minority Faculty Advancement Act
N.J. Stat. Ann., 18A:72F-1 et seq.

Loan Repayment Act (Health Professional)
N.M. Stat. Ann., 21-22D-1 et seq.

Loan Repayment Act (Rural Physician Education)
Utah Code Ann. 1953, 26-9a-101 et seq.

Loan Shark Act
Colo. Rev. Stat. 1963, 73-2-1 et seq.
D.C. Code Ann., § 26-701 et seq.
Ill. Rev. Stat. 1991, Ch. 17, § 5401 et seq.
N.M. Stat. Ann., 30-43-1 et seq.
Okla. Stat. 1961, Title 15, § 280.1 et seq.
Pa. 1913 Pamph. Laws 429, No. 285
Tenn. Code Ann., Superseded Vol., 45-2101 et seq.
Continued

Tex. Rev. Civ. Stat., Art. 4646b

Loans (Consumer Protection Code)
S.C. Code Ann. 1976, § 37-3-101 et seq.

Loans (Uniform Consumer Credit Code)
See Uniform Consumer Credit Code—Loans

Loans Insurance Act
Colo. Rev. Stat. 1963, 73-4-1 et seq.

Loans to Eligible Businesses Act (Funding)
P.R. Laws Ann. 1954, Title 23, § 263 et seq.

Loans to Lenders Program
N.Y. Public Authorities Law (Consol. Laws
Ch. 43) § 1835 et seq.

Lobby Registration Act
N.Y. Legislative Law (Consol. Laws, Ch.
32), § 66a et seq.

Lobbying Act
Cal. Government Code § 86100 et seq.
D.C. Code Ann., § 1-1451 et seq.
Kan. Stat. Ann., 46-215 et seq.
Ky. Rev. Stat. 1971, 6.250 et seq.
La. Rev. Stat. Ann., 24:51 et seq.
Mass. Gen. Laws Ann., 3:39 et seq.
Miss. Code Ann. 1972, § 5-7-1 et seq.
Mo. Rev. Stat., 21.420
Mont. Code Ann., 5-7-101 et seq.
N.H. Rev. Stat. 1955, 15: et seq.
N.Y. Legislative Law (Consol. Laws Ch. 32)
§ 1 nt.
R.I. Gen. Laws 1956, 22-10-1 et seq.
Tex. Government Code, § 305.001
Tex. Rev. Civ. Stat., Art. 6252-9c
Va. Code 1950, § 30-28.01 et seq.
Wis. Stat. Ann., 13.60 et seq.

Lobbying Amendments of 1976
D.C. Code 1973, §§ 1-1451 to 1-1457

Lobbying Disclosure Act
Nev. Rev. Stat. 1979 Reprint, 218.900 et seq.

Lobbying Disclosure Technical Amendments Act of 1998
April 6, 1998, P.L. 105-166, 2 U.S. Code
§ 1601 nt.

Lobbying Ethics Act
Tenn. Public Acts 1991, Ch. 589

Lobbying Law Reform Act
Miss. Code Ann. 1972, § 5-8-1 et seq.
Tenn. Code Ann., 3-6-102, 3-6-103, 3-6-106,
3-6-110, 3-6-114

Lobbying Registration and Regulation Act
Pa. Purdon's Stat., Title 46, § 148.1 et seq.

Lobbying Regulation Act
Alaska Stat. 1962, § 24.45.011 et seq.

Lobbyist Disclosure and Public Officials Conduct Act
Ga. Laws 1992, p. 1075

Lobbyist Disclosure Regulation Act
Utah Code Ann. 1953, 36-11-101 et seq.

Lobbyist Registration Act
Ill. Rev. Stat. 1991, Ch. 63, § 171 et seq.
Neb. Rev. Stat. 1943, 49-1480 et seq.
S.C. Code Ann. 1976, § 2-17-10 et seq.
Vt. Stat. Ann., Title 2, § 251 et seq.

Lobbyist Registration Act (Constitutional Convention)
Ill. Comp. Stat. 1992, Ch. 5, § 30/1 et seq.

Lobbyist Registration and Disclosure Act
Tenn. Code Ann., 3-6-101 et seq.

Lobbyist Regulation Act
N.M. Stat. Ann., 2-11-1 et seq.

Loble Law
Mont. Code Ann., 41-5-521, 41-5-601

Local Accommodations Tax Act
S.C. Code Ann. 1976, §§ 6-1-500 to 6-1-560

Local Affairs Department Act
N.C. Gen. Stat. 1943, § 143-319 et seq.

Local Agency Allocation Law
Cal. Government Code § 15500 et seq.

Local Agency Infrastructure Incentive Act
Cal. Health and Safety Code § 52580

Local Agency Law
Pa. Cons. Stat., Title 2, § 101 et seq.

Local Agency Military Base Recovery Area Act
Cal. Government Code § 7105 et seq.

Local Agency Public Construction Act
Cal. Public Contract Code § 20100 et seq.
La. Rev. Stat. Ann., 49:213.1 et seq.

Local Agency Reduced Worktime Act
Cal. Government Code § 53300 et seq.

Local Agricultural and Forestal Districts Act
Va. Code 1950, § 15.1-1513.1 et seq.

Local and Regional Capital Improvement Planning Process Act
Okla. Stat. Ann., Title 62, § 910 et seq.

Local and State Government Convention, Sports Facility, Meeting, and Tourism Act
Mo. Laws 1991, S.B. Nos. 295, 312, §§ 21 to 31

Local and State Government Revenue Bond Act
N.C. Gen. Stat. 1943, § 159-80 et seq.

Local Appointive List Act
Cal. Government Code § 54970 et seq.

Local Authorities Fiscal Control Law
N.J. Stat. Ann., 40:5A-1 et seq.

Local Bond Law
N.J. Stat. Ann., 40A:2-1 et seq.

Local Bond Pooling Act
Cal. Government Code § 6584 et seq.

Local Bonds Registration Act
Mo. Rev. Stat., 108.240 et seq.

Local Budget Act
Iowa Code Ann., 24.1 et seq.
N.J. Stat. Ann., 40A:4-1 et seq.
Ore. Rev. Stat., 294.305 et seq.

Local Citizen Review Board Pilot Program Act
Mont. Code Ann., 41-3-1001 et seq.

Local Development Act
Okla. Stat. Ann., Title 62, § 850 et seq.

Local Development Authority Act
Tenn. Code Ann., 4-31-101 et seq.

Local Development Authority Capital Projects Loan Act
Tenn. Code Ann., 4-31-401 et seq.

Local Development Authority Mental Health and Mental Retardation Facilities Act
Tenn. Code Ann., 4-31-701 et seq.

Local Development Authority Rural Fire Protection Equipment Act
Tenn. Code Ann., 4-31-501 et seq.

Local Development Corporation Program
La. Rev. Stat. Ann., 51:2381 et seq.

Local Development District Act
Pa. Purdon's Stat., Title 73, § 801 et seq.

Local Development Financing Act
Mich. Comp. Laws Ann., 125.2151 et seq.

Local Development Financing Fund Act
N.J. Stat. Ann., 34:1B-36 et seq.

Local Drinking Water Protection Act
Cal. Health and Safety Code §§ 116610, 116612

Local Drug Abuse Services Act
N.Y. Mental Hygiene Law 1972 (Consol. Laws Ch. 27) § 83.01 et seq.

Local DWI Grant Program Act
N.M. Stat. Ann., 11-6A-1 et seq.

Local Economic Adjustment Act
Tenn. Code Ann., 4-31-101

Local Economic Development Act
Ida. Laws 1988, Ch. 210
N.M. Stat. Ann., 5-10-1 et seq.

Local Economic Revitalization Tax Assistance Act
Pa. Purdon's Stat., Title 72, § 4722 et seq.

Local Emergency Aid Act
N.J. Laws 1969, Ch. 94

Local Emergency Housing Rent Control Act
N.Y. Laws 1962, Ch. 21, § 1 et seq.
N.Y. Unconsolidated Law, § 8601 et seq.

Local Energy Conservation Programs Act
Cal. Public Resources Code § 25390 et seq.

Local Environmental Protection Act
N.Y. Environmental Conservation Law 1972
(Consol. Laws Ch. 43B) § 47-0101 et seq.

Local Executive Succession Act
La. Rev. Stat. Ann., 33:1401 et seq.

Local Fairs Act
Ky. Rev. Stat. 1971, 247.220

Local Finance Law
N.Y. Consol. Laws, Ch. 33A

Local Fire District Law (Protection Zones)
Cal. Health and Safety Code § 14301 et seq.

Local Fire Fighters Retirement Act
Tex. Rev. Civ. Stat., Art. 6243e

Local Fiscal Affairs Law
N.J. Stat. Ann., 40A:5-1 et seq.

Local Fiscal Management Responsibility Act
Ark. Acts 1991, No. 724

Local Fish and Game Law
N.J. Stat. Ann., 23:9-1 et seq.

Local Government Accounting Systems Act
Ill. Rev. Stat. 1991, Ch. 15, § 600 et seq.

Local Government Act (Lawrason)
La. Rev. Stat. Ann., 33:321 et seq.

Local Government Air Rights Act
Ill. Rev. Stat. 1991, Ch. 85, § 1060 et seq.

Local Government Antitrust Act of 1984
Oct. 24, 1984, P.L. 98-544, 15 U.S. Code
§§ 1 nt., 34, 34 nt., 35, 36

Local Government Antitrust Exemption Act
Ill. Rev. Stat. 1991, Ch. 85, §§ 2900, 2901

Local Government Assistance Corporation Act
N.Y. Public Authorities Law (Consol. Laws
Ch. 43A) § 3231 et seq.

Local Government Audit Act
Colo. Rev. Stat., 29-1-601 et seq.

Local Government Authorities Registration Act
Ga. Code Ann., 36-80-16

Local Government Bond Act
Ark. Code Ann. 1987, 14-164-301 et seq.
N.C. Gen. Stat. 1943, § 159-43 et seq.

Local Government Bond Validity Act
Ill. Rev. Stat. 1991, Ch. 85, §§ 860, 861

Local Government Budget Act
Colo. Rev. Stat., 29-1-101 et seq.
La. Rev. Stat. Ann., 39:1301 et seq.
Nev. Rev. Stat. 1979 Reprint, 354.470 et seq.

Local Government Budget and Fiscal Control Act
N.C. Gen. Stat. 1943, § 159-7 et seq.

Local Government Cable Fair Competition Act
Ga. Code Ann., 36-89-1 et seq.

Local Government Capital Improvement Revenue Bond Act
Ark. Code Ann. 1987, 14-164-401 et seq.

Local Government Capital Project Loan Fund Act
Pa. Purdon's Stat., Title 53, § 6781-1 et seq.

Local Government Code
Mont. Code Ann., 7-3-101 et seq.

Local Government Code (General)
Pa. Cons. Stat., Title 53, § 101 et seq.

Local Government Code Enforcement Board Act
Ky. Rev. Stat. 1971, 65.8801 to 65.8839

Local Government Code Enforcement Boards Act
Fla. Stat. Ann., 162.01 et seq.

Local Government Compliance Act
Ark. Code Ann. 1987, 10-4-301 et seq.

Local Government Comprehensive Planning Act
Fla. Stat. Ann., 163.3161 et seq.

Local Government Comprehensive Planning Act (Hillsborough County)
Fla. Special Laws 1975, Ch. 390

Local Government Comprehensive Planning and Land Development Regulation Act
Fla. Stat. Ann., 163.3161 et seq.

Local Government Comprehensive Planning Enabling Act
S.C. Code Ann. 1976, § 6-29-310 et seq.

Local Government Credit Enhancement Act
Ill. Rev. Stat. 1991, Ch. 85, § 4301 et seq.

Local Government Debt Limitation Act
Ill. Rev. Stat. 1991, Ch. 85, § 850 et seq.

Local Government Debt Offering Act
Ill. Rev. Stat. 1991, Ch. 85, § 840 et seq.

Local Government Debt Reform Act
Ill. Rev. Stat. 1989, Ch. 17, § 6901 et seq.

Local Government Defeasance of Debt Law
Ill. Rev. Stat. 1991, Ch. 85, § 4400 et seq.

Local Government Development Agreement Act
Fla. Stat. Ann., 163.3220 et seq.
S.C. Code Ann. 1976, § 6-31-10 et seq.

Local Government Emergency Assistance Act
N.J. Laws 1979, Ch. 34
Tenn. Public Acts 1991, Ch. 155

Local Government Employee-Management Relations Act
Nev. Rev. Stat. 1979 Reprint, 288.010 et seq.

Local Government Employees Retirement System Act
N.C. Gen. Stat. 1943, § 128-21 et seq.

Local Government Environmental Facilities Authority Act
La. Rev. Stat. Ann., 33:4548.1 et seq.

Local Government Equipment Lease Purchase Act
La. Rev. Stat. Ann., 38:2319 et seq.

Local Government Ethics Law
N.J. Stat. Ann., 40A:9-22.1 to 40A:9-22.25

Local Government Executive Succession Act
N.C. Gen. Stat. 1943, § 162B-5 et seq.

Local Government Finance Act
N.C. Gen. Stat. 1943, § 159-1 et seq.

Local Government Financial Emergencies Act
Fla. Stat. Ann., 218.50 et seq.

Local Government Financial Emergency and Accountability Act
Fla. Stat. Ann., 11.45, 75.05, 112.61, 112.625 to 112.665, 121.135, 165.091, 189.001 to 189.009, 218.31, 218.32, 218.37, 218.38, 218.50 to 218.504

Local Government Financial Management and Reporting Act
See Uniform Local Government Financial Management and Reporting Act

Local Government Financial Planning and Supervision Act
Ill. Rev. Stat. 1991, Ch. 85, § 7201 et seq.

Local Government Financial Statement Act
Ill. Rev. Stat. 1991, Ch. 85, §§ 600, 601

Local Government Fiscal Assistance Amendments of 1983
Nov. 30, 1983, P.L. 98-185, 31 U.S. Code § 6701 nt.

Local Government Fiscal Information Act
N.C. Gen. Stat. 1943, § 120-30.41 et seq.

Local Government Fiscal Responsibility Act
La. Rev. Stat. Ann., 38:2319 et seq.
Mich. Comp. Laws Ann., 141.1101 et seq.

Local Government Formation Act
Fla. Stat. Ann., 165.011 et seq.

Local Government Historic Preservation Act
Miss. Code Ann. 1972, § 39-13-1 et seq.

Local Government Impact Fiscal Notes Act
Ga. Code Ann., 28-5-47 et seq.

Local Government Infrastructure Commitment Act
Fla. Laws 1991, Ch. 239

Local Government Investment Pool Act
Ga. Code Ann., 36-83-1 et seq.
Mich. Comp. Laws Ann., 129.141 et seq.

Local Government Investment Pool and Investment of Public Funds Act
Va. Code 1950, § 2.1-234.1 et seq.

Local Government Investment Pool Trust Fund Administration and Enforcement Act
Colo. Rev. Stat., 11-51-901 et seq.

Local Government Land Use Control Enabling Act
Colo. Rev. Stat., 29-20-101 et seq.

Local Government Miscellaneous Expenditure Act
Neb. Rev. Stat. 1943, 13-2201 et seq.

Local Government Non-Arbitrage Investment Act
Va. Code 1950, §§ 2.1-234.9:1 to 2.1-234.9:7

Local Government Nuisance Code Enforcement Act
Ky. Rev. Stat. 1971, 82.700c et seq.

Local Government Omnibus Act
Cal. Statutes 1991, Ch. 1226

Local Government Omnibus Act of 1992
Cal. Statutes 1992, Ch. 1020

Local Government Omnibus Act of 1995
Cal. Statutes 1995, Ch. 579

Local Government Omnibus Act of 1996
Cal. Government Code §§ 12467, 23101
Cal. Streets and Highways Code § 11011
Cal. Water Code §§ 32551, 50707

Local Government Omnibus Act of 1997
Cal. Government Code § 25332 et seq.

Local Government Parking Citation Enforcement Act
Ky. Rev. Stat. 1971, 82.600 et seq.

Local Government Planning Act
S.C. Code Ann. 1976, § 6-7-10 et seq.

Local Government Privatization Act
Cal. Government Code § 54250 et seq.

Local Government Professional Services Selection Act
Ill. Rev. Stat. 1991, Ch. 85, § 6400 et seq.

Local Government Prompt Payment Act
Ill. Rev. Stat. 1991, Ch. 85, § 4301 et seq.

Local Government Property Transfer Act
Ill. Rev. Stat. 1991, Ch. 30, § 155h et seq.

Local Government Public Obligations Act
Tenn. Public Acts 1986, Ch. 770

Local Government Purchasing Act
Nev. Rev. Stat. 1979 Reprint, 332.005 et seq.

Local Government Reapportionment Law
Nev. Rev. Stat. 1979 Reprint, 237.015 et seq.

Local Government Records Act
Me. Rev. Stat. Ann. 1964, Title 30-A, § 1701 et seq.
N.Y. Arts and Cultural Affairs Law (Consol. Laws Ch. 11C) § 57.13 et seq.
Tex. Local Government Code, § 201.001 et seq.

Local Government Records Law
Me. Rev. Stat. Ann. 1964, Title 30-A, § 1701 et seq.

Local Government Reorganization Act (Cortese-Knox)
Cal. Government Code § 56000 et seq.

Local Government Revenue Bond Election Act
Ark. Code Ann. 1987, 14-72-601 et seq.

Local Government Risk Pool Act
N.C. Gen. Stat. 1943, § 58-23-1 et seq.

Local Government Sales and Use Tax Act
Colo. Rev. Stat., 29-1-501 et seq.
N.C. Gen. Stat. 1943, § 105-463 et seq.

Local Government Securities Act
Nev. Rev. Stat. 1979 Reprint, 350.500 et seq.

Local Government Service Sharing and Combination Incentives Law
Minn. Stat. Ann., 465.80 et seq.

Local Government Solid Waste Collection and Disposal Assistance Act
Miss. Laws 1994, Ch. 624

Local Government Study Commission of the Halifax Area Act
Fla. Special Laws 1983, Ch. 83-531

Local Government Supervision Act
N.J. Stat. Ann., 52:27BB-1 et seq.

Local Government Surplus Funds Investment Act
Fla. Stat. Ann., 218.40 et seq.

Local Government Tax Collection Act
Ill. Rev. Stat. 1989, Ch. 120, § 1801 et seq.

Local Government Training Act
Ala. Code 1975, § 11-3-40 et seq.

Local Government Transportation Assistance Act
Fla. Stat. Ann., 335.20

Local Government Uniform Accounting Act
Colo. Rev. Stat., 29-1-501 et seq.

Local Government Unit Debt Act
Pa. Cons. Stat., Title 53, § 8001 et seq.

Local Government Volunteers Act
Ark. Code Ann. 1987, 21-13-101 et seq.

Local Governmental Acceptance of Credit Cards Act
Ill. Comp. Stat. 1992, Ch. 50, § 345/1 et seq.

Local Governmental and Governmental Employees Tort Immunity Act
Ill. Rev. Stat. 1991, Ch. 85, § 1-101 et seq.

Local Governmental Cooperation Act
Wis. Stat. Ann., 66.30

Local Governmental Employees Political Rights Act
Ill. Rev. Stat. 1991, Ch. 85, § 7601 et seq.

Local Governmental Subdivision Self-Insurance Act
La. Rev. Stat. Ann., 33:1341 et seq.

Local Governmental Subdivision Self Insurance Act of 1979
La. Rev. Stat. Ann., 33:1341 et seq.

Local Governmental Tax Collection Act
Ill. Comp. Stat. 1992, Ch. 35, § 715/1 et seq.
Ill. Rev. Stat. 1991, Ch. 120, § 1801 et seq.

Local Governments Formation Act
Fla. Stat. Ann., 165.011 et seq.

Local Grant and Health Department Building Act
Ark. Code 1987, 20-7-201 et seq.

Local Hazardous Waste Program Act
Ill. Rev. Stat. 1991, Ch. 111 1/2, § 991-1 et seq.

Local Health Act
Iowa Code Ann., 137.1 et seq.

Local Health Administration Law
Pa. Purdon's Stat., Title 16, § 12001 et seq.

Local Health Department Act
Utah Code Ann. 1953, 26A-1-101 et seq.

Local Health District Act
Cal. Health and Safety Code § 880 et seq.

Local Health Regulation Act
R.I. Gen. Laws 1956, 23-19.2-1 et seq.

Local Health Service Stabilization Act
Tenn. Code Ann., 68-2-401 et seq.

Local Health Services Act
N.J. Stat. Ann., 26:3A2-1 et seq.

Local Historian Act
Ill. Rev. Stat. 1991, Ch. 85, § 5700 et seq.

Local Historians Enabling Act
N.J. Stat. Ann., 40-10A-1 et seq.

Local Historic Districts Act
Mich. Comp. Laws Ann., 399.201 et seq.

Local Historic Preservation Act
Mo. Rev. Stat., 253.415

Local Hospital District Act
Cal. Health and Safety Code § 32000 et seq.
Neb. Rev. Stat. 1943, 23-3528 et seq.

Local Hospital Gross Receipts Tax Act
N.M. Stat. Ann., 7-20C-1 et seq.

Local Hospitality Tax Act
S.C. Code Ann. 1976, §§ 6-1-700 to 6-1-750

Local Housing Assistance Program
Iowa Code 1983, 15.351 to 15.354

Local Housing Authorities Law
N.J. Stat. Ann., 55:14A-1 et seq.

Local Housing Authority Self Insurance Act
La. Rev. Stat. Ann., 33:1351 et seq.

Local Improvement Act
Colo. Rev. Stat., 31-25-501 et seq.
Ill. Rev. Stat. 1981, Ch. 24, § 9-2-1 et seq.
Minn. Stat. Ann., 429.011 et seq.

Local Improvement Act (Coral Gables)
Fla. Special Laws 1949, Ch. 25742

Local Improvement Act (Daytona Beach)
Fla. Special Laws 1945, Ch. 23236
Fla. Special Laws 1967, Ch. 67-1277

Local Improvement Act (Limitation of Actions, Contest of Assesments)
Cal. Code of Civil Procedure § 349

Local Improvement Act (Miami Village)
Fla. Special Laws 1947, Ch. 24716

Local Improvement Act (Municipal)
N.C. Gen. Stat. 1943, § 160A-216 et seq.
Wash. Rev. Code Ann., 35.43.010 et seq.

Local Improvement Act (Sarasota)
Fla. Special Laws 1967, Ch. 67-2031, § 5

Local Improvement Act (Tampa)
Fla. Special Laws 1925, Ch. 11232

Local Improvement Assessment Law (Fulton County)
Ga. Laws 1949, p. 1423

Local Improvement District Code
Ida. Code 1947, 50-1701 et seq.

Local Improvement District Code for Irrigation Districts
Ida. Code 1947, 43-2501 et seq.

Local Improvement Guarantee Act
Ida. Code 1947, 50-1762 et seq.
Wash. Rev. Code Ann., 35.54.010 et seq.

Local Industrial Development Act
Ind. Code 1976, 18-7-14-1 et seq.
Ky. Rev. Stat. 1971, 152.810 et seq.
Okla. Stat. Ann., Title 62, § 651 et seq.

Local Interim Emergency Succession Act
Minn. Stat. Ann., 1.27

Local Interstate Connecting Route Act
Tenn. Code Ann., 54-5-501 et seq.

Local Land Resource Management Planning Act
Ill. Rev. Stat. 1991, Ch. 85, § 5801 et seq.

Local Land Use Planning Act
Ida. Code 1947, 67-6501 et seq.

Local Lands and Buildings Law
N.J. Stat. Ann., 40A:12-1 et seq.

Local Law Certificate Procedure Act (Federal Court)
Wash. Rev. Code Ann., 2.60.010 et seq.

Local Law Relating to Zoning
N.Y. Local Laws 1973, Town of Halfmoon, p. 1893

Local Legislative Meetings Act (Anti-Secrecy)
Cal. Government Code § 54950 et seq.

Local Library Act
Ill. Rev. Stat. 1991, Ch. 81, § 1-0.1 et seq.

Local Liquor Excise Tax Act
N.M. Stat. Ann., 7-24-8 et seq.

Local Management Act
La. Rev. Stat. Ann., 49:213.1 et seq.

Local Management of Historic Sites and Buildings Act
Mont. Code Ann., 22-3-601 et seq.

Local Marketing District Act
Colo. Rev. Stat., 29-25-101 et seq.

Local Mass Transit District Act
Ill. Rev. Stat. 1991, Ch. 111 2/3, § 351 et seq.

Local Neighborhood Model Development Corporation Act
Tenn. Public Acts 1991, Ch. 343

Local Nonemergency Telephone System Pilot Program
Cal. Government Code § 53125 et seq.

Local Nonproperty Tax Law
N.Y. Laws 1947, Ch. 278

Local Occupational License Tax Act
Fla. Stat. Ann., 205.013 et seq.

Local Offender Advisory Council Act
Pa. Purdon's Stat., Title 10, § 311 et seq.

Local Option Alcoholic Beverage Control Law
Miss. Code Ann. 1972, § 67-1-1 et seq.

Local Option Budgeting Law
Tenn. Code Ann., 5-12-201 et seq.

Local Option City Charters, Enabling Act
N.H. Rev. Stat. 1955, 49-B:1 et seq.

Local Option Election Law
Ark. Code Ann. 1987, 3-8-309, 3-8-310

Local Option Gross Receipts Taxes Act (County)
N.M. Stat. Ann., 7-20E-2 et seq.

Local Option Gross Receipts Taxes Act (Municipal)
N.M. Stat. Ann., 7-19D-1 et seq.

Local Option Law
N.Y. Alcoholic Beverage Control Law (Consol. Laws Ch. 3B) § 140 et seq.

Local Option Law (Livestock)
Tex. Agriculture Code, § 143.01 et seq.

Local Option Municipal Economic Development Act
Neb. Rev. Stat. 1943, 18-2701 to 18-2723

Local Option Revenue Act
Neb. Rev. Stat. 1943, 77-27, 142 et seq.
Tenn. Code Ann., 67-6-701 et seq.

Local Option Sales Tax Act
Ga. Code Ann., 48-8-80 et seq.
S.C. Code Ann. 1976, §§ 4-10-10 to 4-10-100

Local Option Single Member Representation Law (School District)
Fla. Stat. Ann., 230.105

Local Option Small Games of Chance Act
Pa. Purdon's Stat., Title 10, § 311 et seq.

Local Option Stock Law for the State of Alabama with the County as the Unit
Ala. Code 1975, § 3-5-1 et seq.

Local Option Tax Control Act
Neb. Rev. Stat. 1943, 77-3401 et seq.

Local Option Tax Control Act (Political Subdivisions)
Neb. Rev. Stat. 1943, 77-3401 et seq.
Tenn. Code Ann., 67-6-701 et seq.

Local Option Tourist Development Act
Fla. Stat. Ann., 125.0104

Local or State Employee Grievance Procedure Act
S.C. Code Ann. 1976, § 8-17-110 et seq.

Local Partnership Act (School Districts)
Minn. Stat. Ann., 124C.10 et seq.

Local Personnel Program Assistance Act
Ill. Rev. Stat. 1991, Ch. 127, §§ 63b119, 63b119.1

Local Planning Act
Ida. Code 1947, 67-6501 et seq.
S.C. Code Ann. 1976, § 6-7-310 et seq.

Local Planning Act (Integrated)
Cal. Government Code § 65420 et seq.

Local Planning-Commissions Act
S.C. Code Ann. 1976, § 6-7-310 et seq.

Local Police and Fire Retirement System Act
Ark. Code Ann. 1987, 24-10-101 et seq.

Local Powers Act
W. Va. Code 1966 § 7-20-1 et seq.

Local Prevention and Corrections Act (Juvenile Offender)
Cal. Welfare and Institutions Code § 1820 et seq.

Local Privilege Tax Law
Miss. Code Ann. 1972, § 27-17-1 et seq.

Local Public Contracts Law
N.J. Stat. Ann., 40A:11-1 et seq.

Local Public Health Act
Minn. Stat. Ann., 145A.01 et seq.

Local Public Health Reorganization Act
Tex. Health and Safety Code, § 121.001 et seq.

Local Public Works Capital Development and Investment Act of 1976
July 22, 1976, P.L. 94-369, 42 U.S. Code § 6701 et seq.
May 13, 1977, P.L. 95-28, 42 U.S. Code § 6701 et seq.
Nov. 2, 1994, P.L. 103-446, 42 U.S. Code § 6706

Local Rail Service Assistance Act of 1978
Nov. 8, 1978, P.L. 95-607, 49 U.S. Code § 1651 nt., 1954

Local Rail Service Reauthorization Act
Dec. 11, 1989, P.L. 101-213, 49 U.S. Code Appx. § 1651 nt.

Local Records Act
Ill. Rev. Stat. 1991, Ch. 116, § 43.101 et seq.

Local Redevelopment and Housing Law
N.J. Stat. Ann., 40A:12A-1 et seq.

Local Referendum Act
Nev. Rev. Stat. 1957 Ed., 302.150 et seq.
Nev. Statutes 1915, Ch. 137, p. 157

Local Residential Housing Finance Law
Kan. Stat. Ann., 12-5219 et seq.

Local River Management Act
Mich. Comp. Laws Ann., 323.301 et seq.

Local Road Improvements and Operations Revenue Act
Mich. Comp. Laws Ann., 247.521 et seq.

Local Sales and Use Tax Act
Ga. Code Ann., 16-8-1 et seq.
Iowa Code Ann., 422B.8 et seq.
Tex. Tax Code, § 321.001 et seq.
Utah Code Ann. 1953, 11-9-1 et seq.

Local Sales and Use Tax Law (Burns-Bradley)
Cal. Revenue and Taxation Code § 7200 et seq.

Local Scenic Easement Act
Ky. Rev. Stat. 1971, 65.410 et seq.

Local School Board Member Recall Act
N.M. Stat. Ann., 22-7-1 et seq.

Local School Support Tax Act
Nev. Rev. Stat. 1979 Reprint, 374.010 et seq.

Local Services Law
La. Rev. Stat. Ann., 33:1321 et seq.

Local Services Tax Act (Mobile Home)
Ill. Comp. Stat. 1992, Ch. 35, § 515/1 et seq.

Local Solid Waste Disposal Act
Ill. Rev. Stat. 1991, Ch. 85, § 5901 et seq.

Local State Financial Coordination Act
Cal. Government Code §§ 53980 et seq., 65591 et seq.

Local Tax Abatement Act (New Home Construction)
Pa. Purdon's Stat., Title 72, § 4754-1 et seq.

Local Tax Anything Act
Pa. 1947 Pamph. Laws 1145, No. 481

Local Tax Authorization Act
N.J. Stat. Ann., 40:48C-1 et seq.

Local Tax Collection Act
Ill. Comp. Stat. 1992, Ch. 35, § 720/1
Ill. Rev. Stat. 1991, Ch. 120, §§ 1900, 1901
Pa. Purdon's Stat., Title 72, § 5511.1 et seq.

Local Tax Enabling Act
Pa. Purdon's Stat., Title 53, § 6901 et seq.

Local Tax Law (Pistols or Other Firearms)
Mich. Comp. Laws Ann., 123.1101 et seq.

Local Tax Procedures Act
Ala. Code 1975, § 40-2A-5 et seq.

Local Tax Reform Act
Pa. Purdon's Stat., Title 72, § 4750.101 et seq.

Local Tax Reimbursement Act
Ill. Comp. Stat. 1992, Ch. 35, § 740/1 et seq.
Ill. Rev. Stat. 1991, Ch. 85, § 751-1 et seq.

Local Tax Simplification Act
Ala. Acts 1998, No. 192

Local Taxpayers Bill of Rights
Pa. Cons. Stat., Title 53, § 8421 et seq.

Local Tourism and Convention Act
Tenn. Public Acts 1982, Ch. 922

Local Toxics Enforcement and Training Act
Cal. Penal Code § 14300 et seq.

Local Transportation Act
Ill. Laws 1935, p. 283
Wash. Rev. Code Ann., 39.92.010 et seq.

Local Transportation Authority and Improvement Act
Cal. Public Utilities Code § 18000 et seq.

Local Transportation Development Act (Collier-Unruh)
Cal. Statutes 1963, Ch. 1852, p. 3805

Local Transportation Funding Act
Tenn. Code Ann., 67-3-1001 et seq.

Local Union Autonomy Act
Alaska Stat. 1962, § 23.40.045 et seq.

Local Units Permissive Consolidation Act
N.J. Stat. Ann., 40:43-66.1 to 40:43-66.34

Local Water and Sewer Authority Act (New York State)
N.Y. Public Authorities Law (Consol. Laws Ch. 43A) § 1196a et seq.

Local Water Management Act
Minn. Stat. Ann., 103B.301 et seq.
Minn. Stat. 1986, 103B.301 et seq.

Local Water Resources Protection and Management Program
Minn. Stat. Ann., 103B.3361 et seq.

Location Act (Mining Claims)
Colo. Rev. Stat., 34-43-101 et seq.

Location Act for Community Homes for Developmentally Disabled Persons
Ark. Code Ann. 1987, 20-48-601 et seq.

Location of Development Law (Site)
Me. Rev. Stat. Ann. 1964, Title 38, § 481 et seq.

Lock Act (Motor Vehicles)
La. Rev. Stat. Ann., 32:145

Locke Act (Horse Race Gambling)
La. Acts 1908, No. 57

Locker Law (Refrigerated Storage)
Colo. Rev. Stat., 35-33-101 et seq.

Locker Plant Act (Frozen Food)
See Frozen Food Locker Plant Act

Lockwood-Donohue Law (Teachers' Salaries)
N.Y. Education Law 1947 (Consol. Laws Ch. 16) § 3102 et seq.

Lockwood Law (Rapid Transit Construction)
N.Y. Laws 1918, Ch. 586

Lockwood Primary Act (Cities)
Ore. General Laws 1901, p. 317

Lockyer-Isenberg Trial Court Funding Act
Cal. Statutes 1997, Ch. 850

Lockyer-Polanco-Farr Pet Protection Act
Cal. Health and Safety Code § 25995 et seq.

Lockyer-Polanco Pet Breeder Warranty Act
Cal. Health and Safety Code § 25989.500 et seq.

Locomotive Act
Mo. Rev. Stat., 389.790 et seq.

Locomotive Automatic Bell-Ringer Act
Ind. Code 1971, 8-8-6-1, 8-8-6-2

Locomotive Bell Ringing Device Law
Cal. Public Utilities Code § 7605

Locomotive Boiler Acts
See Boiler Inspection Acts (Railroads)

Locomotive Headlight Act
Ala. Code 1975, §§ 37-2-90, 37-8-117
Cal. Public Utilities Code § 7607
Ga. Code Ann., 46-8-170

Locomotive Inspection Act
Feb. 17, 1911, Ch. 103, 36 Stat. 913, 45 U.S. Code §§ 22-29, 30- 34
March 4, 1915, Ch. 169, 38 Stat. 1192, 45 U.S. Code § 30
Sept. 3, 1992, P.L. 102-365, 45 U.S. Code § 34

Locomotive Water Glass Law
Cal. Public Utilities Code § 7606

Lode Claim Act
Colo. Rev. Stat., 34-43-101 et seq.
Wyo. Stat. Ann., § 30-1-101 et seq.

Lodge Act (Consular Reorganization)
April 5, 1906, Ch. 1366, 34 Stat. 99, 19 U.S.
Code §§ 338, 341; 22 U.S. Code §§ 1180,
1181, 1188, 1190, 1191, 1195, 1196, 1199,
1200, 1201, 1203; 31 U.S. Code § 603; 46
U.S. Code §§ 98, 570, 571, 657, 659, 676 to
678

Lodge Act (Philippine Organic Act)
July 1, 1902, Ch. 1369, 32 Stat. 691

Lodge Copyright Act
See Copyright Acts

Lodgers' Tax Act
N.M. Stat. Ann., 3-38-13 et seq.

Lodgers Tax Law (Douglas County)
Nev. Statutes 1969, Ch. 639, p. 1250

Lodging Establishment Act
S.C. Code Ann. 1976, § 45-2-10 et seq.

Lodging Home and Board Registration Act
Tex. Human Resources Code, § 105.001 et
seq.

Lodging House Act
Mass. Gen. Laws Ann., 140:22 et seq.

Loft Act
N.J. Stat. Ann., 2A:44-65 et seq.

Loft Conversion Law
N.Y. Multiple Dwelling Law 1946 (Consol.
Laws Ch. 61A) § 280 et seq.

Loft Law (Residential Occupancy of Lofts etc.)
N.Y. Multiple Dwelling Law 1946 (Consol.
Laws Ch. 61A) § 275 et seq.

Log Binding Act (Motor Vehicles)
Mich. Comp. Laws Ann., 257.720

Log Driving Companies Act
Wash. Rev. Code Ann., 76.32.010 et seq.

Log Patrol Act
Ore. Rev. Stat., 532.510 et seq.
Wash. Rev. Code Ann., 76.40.010 et seq.

Log Rule Act (Log Measurement)
Pa. Purdon's Stat., Title 76, § 435

Logan Act (Foreign Relations)
Jan. 30, 1799, Ch. 1, 1 Stat. 613
March 4, 1909, Ch. 321, 35 Stat. 1088 (See
18 U.S. Code § 953)
April 22, 1932, Ch. 126, 47 Stat. 132 (See 18
U.S. Code § 953)

Logan Airport Improvement Loan Act
Mass. Acts 1951, Ch. 733
Mass. Acts 1957, Ch. 484
Mass. Acts 1957, Ch. 712

Loggers Lien Act
Cal. Civil Code § 3065 et seq.
Ida. Code 1947, 45-401 et seq.
Mich. Comp. Laws Ann., 426.1 et seq.
Minn. Stat. Ann., 514.40 et seq.
Mont. Code Ann., 71-3-601 et seq.
N.C. Gen. Stat. 1943, § 44-3
Wash. Rev. Code Ann., 60.24.020 et seq.

Logging Boom Act
W. Va. Code 1966, § 31-3-1 et seq.

Logging Franchise Act
Ore. Rev. Stat. 1953, 768.110 et seq.

Logging Roads Act
Wash. Rev. Code Ann., 76.24.010 et seq.

Logging Sediment Control Act
W. Va. Code 1966 § 19-1B-1 et seq.

Logging Trucks Act (Christensen-Belloti)
Cal. Vehicle Code 1959, § 35552

Logo Signing Act (Traveler Information)
Okla. Stat. Ann., Title 69, § 4021 et seq.

Loitering Act
Cal. Penal Code § 647, Subd. e
N.Y. Penal Law 1965 (Consol. Laws Ch. 40) § 240.35

Loma Prieta Earthquake-Cypress Neighborhood Relief Act
Cal. Streets and Highways Code §§ 227, 227.1

London Libel Act
Fla. Stat. Ann., 770.01 et seq., 836.07 et seq.
N.C. Gen. Stat. 1943, § 99-1 et seq.
Vt. Stat. Ann., Title 12, § 851 et seq.
W. Va. Code 1966, § 31-1-15

Long and Short Haul Act
Cal. Public Utilities Code § 461.5
Fla. Stat. 1983, 350.56
Ky. Rev. Stat. 1971, 276.230
Minn. Stat. Ann., 218.021
Wash. Rev. Code Ann., 81.28.200

Long Arm Act
Ariz. Rules of Civil Procedure 1955, Rule 4
Colo. Rev. Stat., 13-1-124, 13-1-125
Ida. Code 1947, 5-514 et seq.
Kan. Stat. Ann., 8-401 et seq.
Kan. Stat. Ann., 60-308
Mass. Gen. Laws Ann., 223A:1 et seq.
Mo. Rev. Stat., 506.500 et seq.
Okla. Stat. Ann., Title 12, § 187
Vt. Stat. Ann., Title 12, § 851 et seq.

Long Arm Act (Nonresident Motorist)
Colo. Rev. Stat. 1963, 13-8-1 et seq.
Ill. Rev. Stat. 1991, Ch. 45 1/2, § 10-301
Iowa Code Ann., 321.498 et seq.
Minn. Stat. Ann., 170.55

Long Arm Act (Nonresidents)
Ga. Code Ann., 9-10-90 et seq.

Long Arm Act (Products Liability)
Nev. Rev. Stat. 1979 Reprint, 14.080

Long Arm Service Act (Nonresident Motorists)
Miss. Code Ann. 1972, § 11-11-13

Long Arm Service of Process Act (Civil Actions)
Ala. Code 1958, Title 7, § 193 et seq.
Ark. Code Ann. 1987, 16-58-119 et seq.
Cal. Code of Civil Procedure §§ 415.40, 415.50
Colo. Rev. Stat., 13-1-124, 13-1-125
Ga. Code Ann., 40-12-1 et seq.
Haw. Rev. Stat. Ann., § 634-35
Ill. Rev. Stat. 1991, Ch. 110, § 2-208
Iowa Code Ann., 617.3
Kan. Stat. Ann., 60-307, et seq.
Ky. Rev. Stat. 1971, 454.210
Mass. Gen. Laws Ann., 90:3A et seq.
Me. Rev. Stat. Ann. 1964, Title 14, § 704-A
Mich. Comp. Laws Ann., 600.701 et seq.
Miss. Code Ann. 1972, §§ 11-11-11, 13-3-57, 13-3-59, 13-3-61
N.C. Gen. Stat. 1943, § 1-105 et seq.
N.M. Stat. Ann., 38-1-16
N.Y. Civil Practice Law and Rules (Consol. Laws Ch. 8) § 302
Ohio Rev. Code 1953, 2307.381 et seq.
Okla. Stat. Ann., Title 12, §§ 187, 1701.03
Ore. Rules of Civil Procedure, Rule 4
Tenn. Code Ann., 20-2-201 et seq.
Tex. Civ. Prac. and Rem. Code, 317.001 et seq.
Utah Code Ann. 1953, 78-27-22 et seq.
Va. Code 1950, § 8.01-328 et seq.
Wash. Rev. Code Ann., 4.28.180 et seq.
Wis. Stat. Ann., 801.05
Wyo. Stat. 1957, § 5-4.1 et seq.

Long Arm Service of Process Act (Corporations)
Conn. Gen. Stat. 1983, § 33-411
Fla. Stat. 1983, 48.181
Ill. Rev. Stat. 1981, Ch. 32, § 5.25, 5.26
Ind. Code Ann., 23-1-24-4
Kan. Stat. Ann., 8-401 et seq.
Minn. Stat. Ann., 303.13
S.D. Codified Laws 1967, 47-8-17
Vt. Stat. Ann., Title 2, § 421 et seq.

Long Arm Service of Process Act (Nonresident Motorists)

See Nonresident Motorists Substituted Service Act

Long Arm Statute

S.C. Code Ann. 1976, §§ 15-3-30, 15-9-201 et seq., 36-2-801 et seq.

Wis. Stat. Ann., 801.05

Long Arm Statutes

N.Y. General Business Law (Consol. Laws Ch. 20) § 250 (Aircraft)

N.Y. Navigation Law 1941 (Consol. Laws Ch. 37) § 74 (Vessels)

N.Y. Parks, Recreation and Historic Preservation Law (Consol. Laws Ch. 36b) § 25.27 (Snowmobiles)

N.Y. Vehicle and Traffic Law 1959 (Consol. Laws Ch. 71) § 253 (Vehicles)

Long Beach Parking Authority Act

N.Y. Public Authorities Law (Consol. Laws Ch. 43A) § 1599aaaa et seq.

Long Bridge Act

Wis. Stat. Ann., 84.11

Long Distance Telecommunications Consumer Choice Act

Cal. Public Utilities Code § 709.2

Long Island Job Development Authority Act

N.Y. Public Authorities Law (Consol. Laws Ch. 43A) § 1840 et seq.

Long Island Pine Barrens Maritime Reserve Act

N.Y. Environmental Conservation Law (Consol. Laws Ch. 43B) § 57-0101 et seq.

Long Island Pine Barrens Protection Act

N.Y. Environmental Conservation Law 1972 (Consol. Laws Ch. 43B) § 57-0103 et seq.

N.Y. Public Officers Law (Consol. Laws Ch. 47) § 17

N.Y. State Finance Law 1940 (Consol. Laws Ch. 56) § 97o

Long Island Power Authority Act

N.Y. Public Authorities Law (Consol. Laws Ch. 43A) § 1020 et seq.

Long Island Sound Improvement Act of 1990

Nov. 16, 1990, P.L. 101-596, 33 U.S. Code § 1251 nt.

Long Island South Shore Estuary Reserve Act

N.Y. Executive Law 1951 (Consol. Laws Ch. 18) § 960 et seq.

Long Island State Park Act

N.Y. Laws 1924, Ch. 112

Long-Term Birth Defects Treatment Program Act

Del. Code of 1974, Title 16, § 201 et seq.

Long-Term Care Act (Public Employees')

Cal. Government Code, § 21410 et seq.

Long-Term Care Aide Training Act

Ark. Code Ann. 1987, 20-10-701 et seq.

Long-Term Care Certificate of Need Act

Okla. Stat. Ann., Title 63, § 1-850 et seq.

Long Term Care Choice Act

Ga. Code Ann., 30-7-1 et seq.

Long-Term Care Community Diversion Pilot Project Act

Fla. Stat. Ann., 430.702

Long-Term Care Facilities Ombudsman Act

Miss. Code Ann. 1972, § 43-7-51 et seq.

Long-Term Care Facilities Residents Bill of Rights

Ga. Code Ann., 31-8-100 et seq.

S.C. Code Ann. 1976, § 44-81-10 et seq.

Long-Term Care Facility Receivership Law

Ark. Code 1987, 20-10-901 et seq.

Long-Term Care Facility Resident Abuse Reporting Act

Ga. Code Ann., 31-8-80 et seq.

Long-Term Care Facility Residents Reporting Act (Abused and Neglected)
Ill. Comp. Stat. 1992, Ch. 210, § 30/1 et seq.

Long-Term Care Group Insurance Act
Cal. Government Code §§ 31696.1 to 31696.5

Long Term Care, Health, Safety and Security Act
Cal. Health and Safety Code § 1417 et seq.

Long-Term Care Insurance Act
Ark. Code 1987, 23-97-201 et seq.
Cal. Insurance Code § 10230 et seq.
Colo. Rev. Stat., 10-19-101 et seq.
Del. Code of 1974, Title 18, § 7101 et seq.
Fla. Stat. Ann., 627.9401 et seq.
Iowa Code Ann., 514G.1 et seq.
Kan. Stat. Ann., 40-2225 et seq.
Ky. Rev. Stat. 1971, 304.14-600 to 304.14-625
La. Rev. Stat. Ann., 22:1731 et seq.
Mont. Code Ann., 33-22-1101 et seq.
N.C. Gen. Stat. 1943, § 58-55-1 et seq.
Neb. Rev. Stat. 1943, 44-4501 et seq.
N.H. Rev. Stat. 1955, 415-D:1 et seq.
N.M. Stat. Ann., 59A-23A-1 et seq.
Okla. Stat. Ann., Title 36, § 4421 et seq.
Ore. Rev. Stat., 743.650 et seq.
Pa. Purdon's Stat., Title 40, § 991.101 et seq.
S.C. Code Ann. 1976, § 38-72-10 et seq.
Tenn. Code Ann., 56-42-101 et seq.
Wash. Rev. Code Ann., 48.84.010 et seq.
W. Va. Code 1966, § 33-15A-1 et seq.
Wyo. Stat. Ann., § 26-38-101 et seq.

Long Term Care Integration and Finance Act
N.Y. Laws 1997, Ch. 659

Long-Term Care Ombudsman Act
Ark. Code Ann. 1987, 20-10-601 et seq.
Colo. Rev. Stat., 26-11.5-101 et seq.
Kan. Stat. Ann., 75-5916 et seq.
Mass. Gen. Laws Ann., 19A:27 et seq.
Neb. Laws 1992, L.B. 677, §§ 1 to 28
N.M. Stat. Ann., 28-17-1 et seq.
Okla. Stat. Ann., Title 63, § 1-2211 et seq.

R.I. Gen. Laws 1956, 42-66.7-1 et seq.
W. Va. Code 1966 § 16-51-1 et seq.
Wyo. Stat. Ann., § 9-2-1301 et seq.

Long Term Care Partnership Act
Ill. Rev. Stat. 1991, Ch. 23, § 6801-1 et seq.

Long-Term Care Peer Review Protection Act
Ill. Rev. Stat. 1991, Ch. 111 1/2, § 4141 et seq.

Long-Term Care Plan Act (Employee)
Fla. Laws 1998, Ch. 400

Long Term Care Planning Act
N.M. Laws 1985, Ch. 96

Long-Term Care Reform Act
Cal. Statutes 1982, Ch. 1453
Mont. Code Ann., 53-6-601 et seq.

Long-Term Care Reform Act (Omnibus)
Ark. Code 1987, 20-10-1001 et seq.

Long Term Care Reimbursement Act (Medi-Cal)
Cal. Welfare and Institutions Code § 14126 et seq.

Long Term Care Residents' Bill of Rights
Mont. Code Ann., 50-5-1101 to 50-5-1107
Mont. Laws 1987, Ch. 582

Long-Term Care Services Act
N.M. Stat. Ann., 24-17A-1 to 24-17A-5

Long-Term Foster Care Custody Act
N.J. Stat. Ann., 30:4C-26.10 et seq.

Long Term Health Care Administrators Act
S.C. Code Ann. 1976, § 40-35-5 et seq.

Long Term Health Care Facility Act
Ga. Code Ann., 31-8-1 et seq.

Long Term Medicaid Takeover Act
N.Y. Social Services Law (Consol. Laws Ch. 55) § 368a, Subd. 1

Long-Term Policy Act (Rose-Blanford)
Ky. Rev. Stat. 1971, 7B.010c et seq.

Long Term Quality Health Care Act
Ala. Code 1975, § 22-6-20 et seq.

Long-Term Residential Health Care Recipient Ombudsman Act
Ala. Acts 1985, p. 1029

Long Term Tax Exemption Law
N.J. Stat. Ann., 40A:20-1 et seq.

Longevity Pay Act
March 3, 1883, Ch. 97, 22 Stat. 472
Jan. 29, 1927, Ch. 62, 44 Stat. 1054

Longmeadow Sewerage Loan Act
Mass. Acts 1955, Ch. 178

Longshore and Harbor Workers' Compensation Act
March 4, 1927, Ch. 509, 44 Stat. 1424, 33 U.S. Code §§ 901 to 945, 947 to 950
June 24, 1948, Ch. 623, 62 Stat. 602, 33 U.S. Code §§ 906, 908, 909, 910, 914
July 26, 1956, Ch. 735, 70 Stat. 654, 33 U.S. Code §§ 906, 908, 909, 914, 918, 939, 944
Aug. 23, 1958, P.L. 85-742, 72 Stat. 835, 33 U.S. Code § 941
Aug. 18, 1959, P.L. 86-171, 73 Stat. 391, 33 U.S. Code § 933
June 11, 1960, P.L. 86-507, 74 Stat. 202, 33 U.S. Code § 919
Sept. 13, 1960, P.L. 86-757, 74 Stat. 900, 33 U.S. Code § 907
July 14, 1961, P.L. 87-87, 75 Stat. 203, 33 U.S. Code §§ 906, 909, 914
Oct. 27, 1972, P.L. 92-576, 86 Stat. 1251, 33 U.S. Code §§ 902, 903, 905 to 910, 912 to 914, 917
March 27, 1978, P.L. 95-251, 33 U.S. Code §§ 919, 921
Dec. 21, 1982, P.L. 97-375, 33 U.S. Code § 941
Sept. 28, 1984, P.L. 98-426, 33 U.S. Code §§ 901 nt., 902 to 910, 912 to 914, 917, 918, 921, 922, 928, 930 to 933, 938, 939, 942, 944 to 947, 948a
Dec. 21, 1995, P.L. 104-66, 33 U.S. Code § 942

Oct. 19, 1996, P.L. 104-324, 33 U.S. Code § 903

Longshore and Harbor Worker's Compensation Act Amendments of 1984
Sept. 28, 1984, P.L. 98-426, 30 U.S. Code § 932; 33 U.S. Code §§ 901 nt., 902 to 910, 912 to 914, 917, 918, 921, 922, 928, 930 to 933, 938, 939, 942, 944 to 947, 948a

Longshore Emergency Act
Haw. Session Laws 1951, Act. 209

Longworth Act (Municipal Bonds)
Ohio Laws Vol. 95, p. 318

Lookout Act (Railroads)
Ark. Code Ann. 1987, 23-12-907
Tenn. Code Ann., 65-12-108

Lookout Mountain CARTA Privilege Tax Act
Tenn. Private Acts 1988, Ch. 170

Looreen—Brookhart Law (Sinking Fund)
Iowa Code Ann., 453.9

Loose Law (Intoxicating Liquors)
Del. Rev. Code 1935, § 6202

Lorbach Act (Jury Code)
Ohio Rev. Code 1953, 2313.01 et seq.

Lord Campbell's Act
Ala. Code 1975, 6-5-410
Colo. Rev. Stat., 13-21-202
Conn. Gen. Stat. Ann., § 52-555
Kan. Stat. Ann., 60-1901 et seq.
La. Civil Code 1972, Art. 2315
Mass. Gen. Laws Ann., 229:1 et seq.
Md. Ann. Code 1974, Art. CJ § 3-901 et seq.
Me. Rev. Stat. Ann. 1964, Title 18-A, § 2-804 et seq.
Minn. Stat. Ann., 573.02
Mont. Code Ann., 27-1-501
Neb. Rev. Stat. 1943, 30-809, 30-810
N.M. Stat. Ann., 41-2-3
Ohio Rev. Code 1953, 2125.01 et seq.
Vt. Stat. Ann., Title 14, § 1491 et seq.

Lord Campbell's Act (Wrongful Death)
See Wrongful Death Act

Lord Tenterden's Act (Limitation of Actions)
Minn. Stat. Ann., 541.17

Lords Day Act
Mass. Gen. Laws Ann., 136:1 et seq.
N.Y. General Business Law (Consol. Laws Ch. 20) § 2 et seq.
Pa. Apr. 22, 1794, 3 Sm. L. 177, Ch. 1746
Pa. 1705, 1 Sm. L.25, Ch. 119

Loring Constitutional Amendment
Mass. Const. 1780, Amendments Art. 48

Loring Job Increment Financing Program Act
Me. Rev. Stat. Ann. 1964, Title 5, § 13080-O et seq.

Lorton Technical Corrections Act of 1998
Oct. 21, 1998, P.L. 105-277, Division C, § 141, 112 Stat. 2681

Los Angeles County Court Act
Cal. Statutes 1980, Ch. 578

Los Angeles County Flood Control District Act
Cal. Water Code, Appendix, § 28-1 et seq.

Los Angeles County Metropolitan Transportation Authority Reform Act
Cal. Statutes 1992, Ch. 60

Los Angeles County Municipal Court Judges Law
Cal. Government Code § 72620

Los Angeles County Toll Tunnel Authority Act
Cal. Streets and Highways Code § 31300 et seq.

Los Angeles County Transportation Commission Revenue Bond Act
Cal. Public Utilities Code § 130500 et seq.

Los Angeles Transportation Act (Katz-Robbins)
Cal. Statutes 1990, Ch. 95

Los Padres Condor Range and River Protection Act
June 19, 1992, P.L. 102-301, 16 U.S. Code § 1132 nt.

Loss Claimant's Priorities Act
Tex. Insurance Code, 21.28B

Loss Leader Act (Unfair Sales)
La. Rev. Stat. Ann., 51:422 et seq.
Wis. Stat. Ann., 100.30

Lost and Found Property Act
N.Y. Personal Property Law (Consol. Laws Ch. 41) § 251 et seq.
Wash. Rev. Code Ann., 63.21.010 et seq.

Lost and Unclaimed Property Act
Conn. Gen. Stat. Ann., § 50-1 et seq.

Lost Bond Act
April 9, 1934, Ch. 105, 48 Stat. 571

Lost Boundary Act
Wash. Rev. Code Ann., 58.04.020

Lost, Damaged and Destroyed Records and Documents Act
Cal. Evidence Code § 1601

Lost Deed Act
Mo. Rev. Stat., 527.190 et seq.

Lost Money and Goods Law
Cal. Civil Code § 2080 et seq.

Lost or Destroyed Tax Records Act
Cal. Revenue and Taxation Code § 4838

Lost or Destroyed Wills Act
N.Y. Surrogates Court Procedure Act (Consol. Laws Ch. 59A) § 1407

Lost Property Act
Mich. Comp. Laws Ann., 434.1 et seq.
Mo. Rev. Stat., 447.010 et seq.
Mont. Code Ann., 70-5-101 et seq.
N.H. Rev. Stat. 1955, 471:1 et seq.

Vt. Stat. Ann., Title 27, § 1101 et seq.

Lost Property Act (Military Service)
March 3, 1885, Ch. 335, 23 Stat. 350

Lost Property and Estrays Act
Ill. Rev. Stat. 1991, Ch. 50, § 0.01 et seq.

Lost State Archives Act
Ill. Rev. Stat. 1991, Ch. 124, §§ 10.9, 11

Lost Will Statute
R.I. Gen. Laws 1956, 33-7-24

Lot and Property Maintenance Law
N.Y. Local Laws 1972, Village of Sloan, p. 3860

Lot Clearing Act (Sarasota County)
Fla. Laws 1963, Ch. 63-1922

Lot Control Law
N.Y. Local Laws 1969, Town of Sodus, p. 2094

Lot Rental Act (Mobile Home)
Va. Code 1950, § 55-248.41 et seq.

Lottery Act
Ala. Code 1975, § 13A-12-20 et seq.
Ariz. Rev. Stat. Ann., § 5-501 et seq.
Ark. Code Ann. 1987, 5-66-118 et seq.
Cal. Penal Code § 319 et seq.
Conn. Gen. Stat. Ann., § 53-290 et seq.
D.C. Code 1973, § 22-1501 et seq.
Del. Code of 1974, Title 29, § 4801 et seq.
Fla. Stat. Ann., 849.09 et seq.
Ga. Code Ann., 16-12-27
Haw. Rev. Stat. 1968, § 746-1 et seq.
Ill. Rev. Stat. 1991, Ch. 120, § 1151 et seq.
Ind. Code Ann., 35-1-104-1 et seq.
Iowa Code Ann., 99E.1 et seq.
Kan. Stat. Ann., 21-4302 et seq.
Mass. Gen. Laws Ann., 271:1 et seq.
Md. Ann. Code 1974, Art. SG, § 9-101
Me. Rev. Stat. Ann. 1964, Title 17, § 2304
Me. Rev. Stat. Ann. 1964, Title 17, § 2304 et seq.
Minn. Stat. Ann., 609.755 et seq.
Mo. Rev. Stat., 313.200 et seq.
Mont. Code Ann. 1987, 23-5-201 et seq.

Mont. Laws 1985, Ch. 669
N.C. Gen. Stat. 1943, § 14-289 et seq.
N.H. Rev. Stat. 1955, 647:1
N.J. Stat. Ann., 2C:37-2 et seq., 5:9-1 et seq.
N.M. Stat. Ann., 6-24-1 et seq.
Ohio Rev. Code 1953, 2915.01 et seq.
Ore. Laws 1985, Ch. 2
Ore. Rev. Stat., 461.010
Pa. Cons. Stat., Title 18, § 5512 et seq.
P.R. Laws Ann. 1954, Title 15, § 111 et seq.
R.I. Gen. Laws 1956, 11-19-1 et seq.
Tenn. Code Ann., 39-17-506
Va. Code 1950, §§ 18.2-242, 18.2-325 et seq.
Vt. Stat. Ann., Title 13, § 2101 et seq.
Vt. Stat. Ann., Title 31, § 651 et seq.
Wash. Rev. Code Ann., 67.70.010 et seq.
Wis. Stat. Ann., 945.01 et seq.
W. Va. Code 1966 § 29-22-1 et seq., § 61-10-11 et seq.

Lottery Act (County and City)
Neb. Rev. Stat. 1943, 9-601 et seq.

Lottery Act (Gambling)
Neb. Rev. Stat. 1943, 28-1101 et seq.

Lottery Act (McCauley-Traxler-Law-Bowman-McNeely)
Mich. Comp. Laws Ann., 432.1 et seq.

Lottery Act (Municipal)
P.R. Laws Ann. 1954, Title 15, § 601 et seq.

Lottery Act (Pickle Card)
Neb. Rev. Stat. 1943, 9-301 et seq.

Lottery Act (Public Education)
Fla. Stat. Ann., 24.101 et seq.

Lottery Act (State)
Tex. Government Code, § 466.001 et seq.

Lottery and Bingo Control Act
Neb. Rev. Stat. 1943, 9-1.101 et seq.
N.Y. Executive Law 1951 (Consol Laws, Ch. 18) § 430 et seq.

Lottery and Raffle Act
Neb. Rev. Stat. 1943, 9-401 et seq.

Lottery and Raffle Act (Small)
Neb. Rev. Stat. 1943, 9-501 et seq.

Lottery Control Act
N.Y. Executive Law 1951 (Consol. Laws Ch. 18) § 430 et seq.

Lottery Corporation Law
La. Rev. Stat. Ann., 47:9000 et seq.

Lottery for Education Act
Ga. Code Ann., 50-27-1 et seq.

Lottery for Education Act (New York State)
N.Y. Tax Law (Consol. Laws Ch. 60) § 1600 et seq.

Lottery for Education Law
N.Y. Tax Law (Consol Laws Ch. 60) § 1600 et seq.

Lottery Fund Preservation Act
Pa. Purdon's Stat., Title 72, § 3762-101 et seq.

Lottery Law (State)
Mo. Rev. Stat. 1978, 313.200 et seq.

Lotto Compact Act (Tri-State)
Me. Rev. Stat. Ann. 1964, Title 8, § 401 et seq.
N.H. Rev. Stat. 1955, 287-F:1 et seq.
Vt. Stat. Ann., Title 31, § 671 et seq.

Loughead Hodson Act (Dog Registration)
Ohio Rev. Code 1953, 955.01 et seq.

Louis Friend Memorial Act
Cal. Vehicle Code § 23109

Louisiana-Alabama-Georgia-Mississippi Rapid Rail Transit Compact Act
Ga. Code Ann., 46-9-300

Louisiana-Mississippi Bridge Construction Compact Act
See Mississippi-Louisiana Bridge Construction Compact Act

Louisiana-Mississippi Rapid Rail Transit Compact Act
Miss. Code Ann. 1972, § 57-45-1

Louisville City Government Act
Ky. Rev. Stat. 1971, 83.410 et seq.

Louisville Housing Act
Ky. Acts 1920, Ch. 68

Louisville Zoning Regulation
N.Y. Local Laws 1972, Town of Louisville, p. 2001

Love Field Amendment
Feb. 15, 1980, P.L. 96-192, 94 Stat. 48

Love, Williamson, Beatty Act (Trucks)
Ky. Rev. Stat. 1971, 189.340

Low and Moderate Income Housing Act
R.I. Gen. Laws 1956, 45-53-1 et seq.

Low and Moderate Income Housing Restrictions Act
R.I. Gen. Laws 1956, 34-39.1-1 et seq.

Low Bid Statute
La. Rev. Stat. Ann., 38:2211 et seq.

Low Cost Housing Act (Miami Beach)
Fla. Special Laws 1949, Ch. 26033

Low-Income Heating Assistance and Shut-Off Protection Act
Mich. Comp. Laws Ann., 400.1201 et seq.

Low-Income Home Energy Assistance Act of 1981
Aug. 13, 1981, P.L. 97-35, 42 U.S. Code §§ 8601 to 8612, 8621 to 8629
Oct. 30, 1984, P.L. 98-558, 42 U.S. Code §§ 8621 to 8629
Sept. 30, 1986, P.L. 99-425, 42 U.S. Code §§ 8621, 8623 et seq.

Low-Income Home Energy Assistance Amendments of 1994
May 18, 1994, P.L. 103-252, 42 U.S. Code § 8621 nt., 8621 et seq.

Low-Income Home Energy Assistance Amendments of 1998

Oct. 27, 1998, P.L. 105-285, Title III, 112 Stat. 2756, 42 U.S. Code § 8621 nt.

Low Income Household Home Weatherization Act

Mich. Comp. Laws Ann., 400.1051 et seq.

Low-Income Housing Preservation and Resident Homeownership Act of 1990

Feb. 5, 1988, P.L. 100-242, 101 Stat. 1877, 12 U.S. Code §§ 4101 et seq.

Dec. 15, 1989, P.L. 101-235, 103 Stat. 2037, 2038

Oct. 1, 1990 P.L. 101-402, 12 U.S. Code § 1715l nt.

Oct. 31, 1990, P.L. 101-494, 12 U.S. Code §§ 1709, 1715l nts.

Nov. 28, 1990, P.L. 101-625, 12 U.S. Code §§ 1715z-6, 1715z-15, 4101 to 4124; 42 U.S. Code §§ 1437t, 1485

Sept. 28, 1994, P.L. 103-327, Title II LS 2881, Title VI § 601, 108 Stat. 2316

Oct. 21, 1998, P.L. 105-276, 12 U.S. Code § 4116

Low Income Housing Tax Credit Program

Tex. Government Code, § 2306.671 et seq.

Low-Income Housing Tax Credit Program Act (Federal)

Miss. Code Ann. 1972, § 7-1-255

Low-Income Housing Trust Act

N.M. Stat. Ann., 58-18B-1 et seq.

Low Income Telephone Service Assistance Act

N.M. Stat. Ann., 63-9C-1

Low Income Utility Assistance Act

N.M. Stat. Ann., 27-6-11 et seq.

Low Income Water, Sewer and Solid Waste Service Assistance Act

N.M. Stat. Ann., 27-6A-1 et seq.

Low-Level Radioactive Waste Authority Act

Me. Rev. Stat. Ann. 1964, Title 38, § 1501 et seq.

Mich. Comp. Laws Ann., 333.26201 et seq.

Low-Level Radioactive Waste Compact Act

Ala. Code 1975, § 22-32-1 et seq.

Ark. Code Ann. 1987, 8-8-202 et seq.

Colo. Rev. Stat., 24-60-2201 et seq.

Fla. Stat. Ann., 404.30

Iowa Code Ann., 8c

Iowa Laws 1983, S.F. 195

Kan. Stat. Ann., 65-34a01

La. Rev. Stat. Ann., 30:1117 et seq.

Mich. Comp. Laws Ann., 3.751 et seq.

Mo. Rev. Stat., 260.700 et seq.

Mont. Code Ann. 1987, 75-3-501, 75-3-502

N.D. Cent. Code, 23-20.5-01 et seq.

Ohio Rev. Code 1953, 3747.01 et seq.

Tenn. Code Ann., 68-202-101 et seq.

Wis. Stat. Ann., 16.10 et seq.

Low-Level Radioactive Waste Compact Act (Appalacian States)

W. Va. Code 1966 § 29-1H-1 et seq.

Low-Level Radioactive Waste Compact Act (Central Interstate)

Neb. Laws 1983, L.B. 200

Low Level Radioactive Waste Compact Act (Central Midwest Interstate)

Ill. Rev. Stat. 1991, Ch. 127, § 63v-1 et seq.

Ind. Code Ann., 13-5-9-1 et seq.

Minn. Stat. Ann., 116C.831 et seq.

Mo. Rev. Stat., 260.700 et seq.

Nev. Rev. Stat. 1979 Reprint, 459.007, 459.008

N.M. Stat. 1978, 11-9A-1 et seq.

Ohio Rev. Code 1953, 3747.01 et seq.

Okla. Stat. Ann., Title 63, § 1-2101 et seq.

Utah Code Ann. 1953, 26-14c-1 et seq.

Va. Code 1950, § 32.1-238.1 et seq.

Wyo. Stat. Ann., § 9-6-201 et seq.

Low-Level Radioactive Waste Compact Act (Rocky Mountain)

N.D. Cent. Code, 23-20.5-01 et seq.

N.M. Stat. Ann., 11-9A-1 et seq.

Low-Level Radioactive Waste Disposal Act

Me. Rev. Stat. Ann. 1964, Title 38, § 1481 et seq.

Neb. Rev. Stat. 1943, 81-1578 et seq.

Continued

Pa. Purdon's Stat., Title 35, § 7130.101 et seq.

Low-Level Radioactive Waste Disposal Authority Act

Tex. Health and Safety Code, § 402.001 et seq.

Low-Level Radioactive Waste Disposal Facility Siting Act (Regional)

N.J. Stat. Ann., 13:1E-177 et seq.

Pa. Purdon's Stat., Title 35, § 7131.101 et seq.

Low-Level Radioactive Waste Interstate Compact (Rocky Mountain)

N.D. Laws 1985, Ch. 298

Low-Level Radioactive Waste Management Act

Mass. Gen. Laws Ann., 111H:1 to 111H:48

N.Y. Environmental Conservation Law 1972 (Consol. Laws Ch. 43B) § 29-0101 et seq.

N.Y. Laws 1986, Ch. 673

N.Y. Public Authorities Law (Consol. Laws Ch. 43A) §§ 1851, 1854b et seq.

N.Y. Public Health Law 1953 (Consol. Laws Ch. 45) § 2485

Low-Level Radioactive Waste Management Authority Act

N.C. Gen. Stat. 1943, § 104G-1 et seq.

Low-Level Radioactive Waste Management Compact (Northeast Interstate)

Conn. Gen. Stat. Ann., § 22a-161

Low-Level Radioactive Waste Management Compact Act

Miss. Code Ann. 1972, § 57-47-1 et seq.

Low-Level Radioactive Waste Management Compact Act (Southeast Interstate)

Alaska Stat. 1962, §§ 46.45.010, 46.45.020

Conn. Gen. Stat. 1983, 22a-161 et seq.

Del. Code of 1974, Title 7, §§ 8001, 8002

Ga. Code Ann., 12-8-120 et seq.

Haw. Rev. Stat. Ann., § 339K-1 et seq.

Ida. Code 1947, 39-3025

Ill. Rev. Stat. 1991, Ch. 111 1/2, § 241-1 et seq.

Md. Ann. Code 1974, Art. HE, § 7-301 et seq.

Miss. Code Ann. 1972, § 57-47-1 et seq.

Mont. Code Ann., 75-3-501, 75-3-502

N.C. Gen. Stat. 1943, § 104G-1 et seq.

N.J. Stat. Ann., 32:31-1 et seq.

Ore. Rev. Stat., 469.930

S.C. Code Ann. 1976, § 48-47-10 et seq.

Va. Code 1950, § 32.1-238.6:1 et seq.

Wash. Rev. Code Ann., 43.145.010

Low-Level Radioactive Waste Policy Act

Dec. 22, 1980, P.L. 96-573, 42 U.S. Code §§ 2021b to 2021d, 2021b nt.

Jan. 15, 1986, P.L. 99-240, 42 U.S. Code §§ 2021b et seq., 2021b nt.

May 19, 1988, P.L. 100-319, 42 U.S. Code § 2021d

Low-Level Radioactive Waste Policy Amendments Act of 1985

Jan. 15, 1986, P.L. 99-240, 42 U.S. Code §§ 2021b et seq., 2021b nt.

Nov. 3, 1990, P.L. 101-501, 42 U.S. Code §§ 8621, 8623, 8624, 8626, 8626a, 8627

June 10, 1993, P.L. 103-43, 42 U.S. Code § 8621

Dec. 21, 1995, P.L. 104-66, 42 U.S. Code § 8624

Aug. 22, 1996, P.L. 104-193, 42 U.S. Code § 8624

Oct. 27, 1998, P.L. 105-285, 42 U.S. Code §§ 8621 to 8624, 8626, 8626b, 8628a

Low-Level Waste Disposal Compact Act (Western)

Ariz. Rev. Stat. Ann., §§ 30-721, 30-722

Low-Rent Housing Act

See United States Housing Act Of 1937

Low Rental Housing Act

Conn. Gen. Stat. 1983, § 8-38 et seq.

Lowden Act (Purchase of Embassy Buildings, etc.)

Feb. 17, 1911, Ch. 105, 36 Stat. 917

Lowell Historic District Act

Mass. Acts 1983, Ch. 566

Lowell Public Parking Loan Act

Mass. Acts 1955, Ch. 362

Lower Brandywine Scenic Rivers Act
Pa. Purdon's Stat., Title 32, § 820.121

Lower Colorado River Authority Act
Tex. General and Special Laws 43rd Leg., 1934, 4th C.S., p. 19, Ch. 7

Lower Colorado River Basin Project Act
Oct. 30, 1984, P.L. 569, 43 U.S. Code §§ 1543, 1595

Lower Concho River Water and Soil Conservation Authority Act
Tex. Special Laws 46th Leg., 1939, p. 1053

Lower Court Reorganization Act
Mich. Comp. Laws Ann., 600.8101 et seq.

Lower Fairfield County Convention Center Authority Act
Conn. Gen. Stat. Ann., § 32-200 et seq.

Lower Hudson Regional Market Authority Act
N.Y. Public Authorities Law (Consol. Laws Ch. 43A) § 800 et seq.

Lower Niobrara River and Ponca Creek Compact Act
S.D. Codified Laws 1967, 46-32-1, 46-32-2

Lower Rio Grande Valley Health Center Act
Tex. Education Code, §§ 74.611 to 74.615

Lower Saint Croix River Act of 1972
Oct. 25, 1972, P.L. 92-560, 86 Stat. 1174, 16 U.S. Code § 1274

Lower San Joaquin Levee Water District Act
Cal. Water Code, Appendix, § 75-1 et seq.

Lower St. Croix Wild and Scenic River Act
Minn. Stat. Ann., 103F.301 et seq.

Lowman, Rayburn, Lyon, Hayes, Cline Act (Workmen' Compensation)
Ky. Rev. Stat. 1971, 342.121, 342.185, 342.315, 342.316

Lowman Rayburn-Ray-Fitzpatrick Act (Teachers' Retirement)
Ky. Rev. Stat. 1971, 161.220, 161.260, 161.290, 161.340, 161.400, 161.410, 161.430, 161.470, 161.515, 161.540, 161.550, 161.600, 161.620

Lowndes County Enhanced 911 Service District Act
Ga. Laws 1991, p. 4842

Lowndes County Utilities Authority Act
Ga. Laws 1970, p. 3112

Lowndes County-Valdosta Industrial Authority Act
Ga. Laws 1960, p. 2786

Lowndes County Water and Sewerage Authority Act
Ga. Laws 1973, p. 3285
Ga. Laws 1974, p. 2678

Lowville Demolition Law
N.Y. Local Laws 1972, Village of Lowville, p. 3573

Loxahatchee River Environmental Control Act
Fla. Special Laws 1971, Ch. 71-822

Loyalty Act
Pa. Purdon's Stat., Title 65, § 211 et seq.

Loyalty Oath Act (Officers and Employees)
Ariz. Rev. Stat. Ann., § 38-231 et seq.
Cal. Government Code § 3100 et seq.
Fla. Stat. Ann., 876.05
Ida. Code 1947, 59-401
Md. Ann. Code 1957, Art. 85A, § 10 et seq.
Okla. Stat. Ann., Title 51, § 36.1 et seq.
Wash. Rev. Code Ann., 9.81.070

Loyalty Oath Act (Public Employees)
N.H. Rev. Stat. 1955, 648:13

Loyalty Oath Act (Teacher)
See Teachers Oath Act (Loyalty)

Lubock Reese Redevelopment Authority Act
Tex. Government Code, § 2311.001 et seq.

Lubricant Act (Used)
Ill. Rev. Stat. 1991, Ch. 96 1/2, § 5800 et seq.

Lubricating Oils Tax Act
La. Rev. Stat. Ann., 47:731 et seq.

Lucas Act
Aug. 7, 1946, Ch. 864, 60 Stat. 902, 41 U.S. Code § 106 nt.
June 25, 1948, Ch. 646, 62 Stat. 992, 41 U.S. Code § 106 nt.

Lucas and Knuckles Act (Gas Procurement)
Ky. Acts 1958, Ch. 38

Luce Patent Act
Aug. 9, 1939, Ch. 619, 53 Stat. 1293 (See 35 U.S. Code §§ 12, 13, 41, 151)

Luciano Act (Indictment; Separate Counts)
N.Y. Criminal Procedure Law (Consol. Laws, Ch. 11A) § 200.20, 290.10 et seq.

Luckel Act (Public Employees; Refusal to Answer)
Cal. Government Code § 1028.1

Ludlow Act (Probation)
Pa. Cons. Stat., Title 42, § 9721 et seq.

Lumber Laborers' Lunch-hour Law
Cal. Labor Code §§ 800, 801

Lumber Lien Law
Wash. Rev. Code Ann., 60.24.020 et seq.

Lumbermens Lien Law
Cal. Civil Code § 3065 et seq.

Lump Sum Judgment Act (Workmen's Compensation)
Kan. Stat. Ann., 44-512a

Lumpkin County Water and Sewerage Authority Act
Ga. Laws 1984, p. 4500

Lunacy Act
Ill. Rev. Stat. 1991, Ch. 91 1/2
Me. Rev. Stat. Ann. 1964, Title 34-B § 3801 et seq.
Okla. Stat. Ann., Title 43A, § 1-101 et seq.
Pa. 1835-36 Pamph. Laws 589, No. 171
Tex. Rev. Civ. Stat., Art. 5550 et seq.

Lunch Hour Labor Act
Neb. Rev. Stat. 1943, 48-212, 48-213

Lunenberg School Building Loan Act
Mass. Acts 1949, Ch. 283

Lung and Hearing Act
Tenn. Code Ann., 7-51-201

Lusk Law (School Teachers' Loyalty)
N.Y. Laws 1921, Ch. 666

Lusk Law (War Relief)
N.Y. Laws 1919, Ch. 404

Luxury Tax Act
Ariz. Rev. Stat. Ann., § 42-1201 et seq.

Luxury Tax and Omnibus Act
Ky. Acts 1936, 3rd. Sp. Sess., Ch. 3

Lybrand Timmons-Taylor Insurance Code
Ala. Code 1975, § 27-1-1 et seq.

Lynch Act
Cal. Penal Code §§ 405a, 405b
Ind. Code Ann., 35-1-77-3 et seq., 35-27-1-1 et seq.
Va. Code 1950, § 18.2-38 et seq.

Lynchburg Parking Authority Act
Va. Acts 1974, Ch. 76

Lynn Public Parking Loan Act
Mass. Acts 1956, Ch. 655

Lynn Remodeling and Reconstruction Loan Act
Mass. Acts 1951, Ch. 359

Lynn School Loan Act
Mass. Acts 1951, Ch. 358
Mass. Acts 1959, Ch. 420

Lynnfield School Building Loan Act
Mass. Acts 1951, Ch. 723

Lynnfield Water District Loan Act
Mass. Acts 1956, Ch. 616

Lyon Davis Act (Merger or Consolidation of Cities)
Ky. Rev. Stat. 1971, 81.410 et seq.

Lyon, Hayes, Cline, Lowman, Rayburn Act (Workmen's Compensation)
Ky. Rev. Stat. 1971, 342.121, 342.185, 342.315, 342.316

Lyons Dental Practice Act
Ky. Rev. Stat. 1971, 313.010 et seq.

Lyons Residence Law
N.Y. Local Laws 1937, New York City, No. 40, p. 289

Lyric Loan Act
Md. Laws 1983, Ch. 325

M

Macaroni Act
Wash. Rev. Code Ann., 69.16.010 et seq.

MacGregor Act (Contractors' Bonds)
Tex. Rev. Civ. Stat. 1948, Art. 5160

Machine Guarding Act
Mo. Rev. Stat., 292.020 et seq.

Machine Gun Act
Ark. Code Ann. 1987, 5-73-201 et seq.
Cal. Penal Code § 12200 et seq.
Conn. Gen. Stat. Ann., § 53-202
Md. Ann. Code 1957, Art. 27, § 372 et seq.
Mont. Code Ann., 45-8-301 et seq.
Ohio Rev. Code 1953, 2923.03 et seq.
S.D. Codified Laws 1967, 23-7-26 et seq.
Va. Code 1950, § 18.2-288 et seq.
Wis. Stat. Ann., 941.25 et seq.

Machine Law (Pinball)
Vt. Stat. Ann., Title 13, § 2135 et seq.

Machinery Act (Taxes)
N.C. Gen. Stat. 1943, § 105-271 et seq.

Machinery and Equipment Loan Fund Act
Pa. Purdon's Stat., Title 73, § 399.31 et seq.

MacKay-Benzie-LaFramboise-Carpenter Act (Game Bag Limit)
Mich. Comp. Laws Ann., 312.12

MacKay-Vander Werp Act (Hunting)
Mich. Comp. Laws Ann., 312.11, 314.19a, 314.26

Mackinac Bridge Authority Act
Mich. Comp. Laws Ann., 254.301 et seq.

Macon-Bibb County Transit Authority Act of 1980
Ga. Laws 1980, p. 4313, §§ 1.1 to 5.1

Macon-Bibb County Water and Sewerage Authority Act
Ga. Laws 1966, p. 2757
Ga. Laws 1973, p. 2603

Macon County Road Act
Tenn. Private Acts 1947, Ch. 249

Macon Firemen and Police Pension Fund Act
Ga. Laws 1939, p. 1149

Macon Transit Authority Act
Ga. Laws 1973, p. 2914

Macon Water Authority Act
Ga. Laws 1992, p. 4991

Macon's Law
May 1, 1810, Ch. 39, 2 Stat. 605

Maddy Appointive Registry Act
Cal. Government Code §§ 1750.5, 12033 et seq.

Maddy-Dixon-Zenovich California Arts Act
Cal. Government Code § 8750 et seq.

Maddy Local Appointive List Act
Cal. Government Code § 54970 et seq.

Madera County Flood Control and Water Conservation Agency Act
Cal. Water Code Appendix, § 110-100 et seq.

Madera Transactions and Use Tax Act
Cal. Revenue and Taxation Code § 7286.65

Madera Water District Act
Cal. Statutes 1991, Ch. 735

Madison Act (Labor Relations)
Mo. Laws 1947, Vol. I, p. 351

Madison and Sullivan Resolution (World Government)
Ala. General Acts 1943, p. 117, No. 117

Madison-Morgan County Airport Authority Act
Ga. Laws 1965, p. 2687

Mae Street Kidd, Hughes McGill, Georgia M. Davis Civil Rights Act
Ky. Rev. Stat. 1971, 344.010 et seq.

Mae Street Kidd Kentucky Housing Corporation Act
Ky. Rev. Stat. 1971, 198A.010 et seq.

Magisterial District Reform Act
Pa. Purdon's Stat., Title 42, § 2101 et seq.

Magisterial Districts Act
Pa. Purdon's Stat., Title 42, § 1301 et seq.

Magisterial Districts Act for Counties of the Second Class
Pa. Purdon's Stat., Title 42, § 1401 et seq.

Magistrate Courts Training Council Act
Ga. Code Ann., 15-10-130 et seq.

Magistrate Retirement Act
N.M. Stat. Ann., 10-12A-1 et seq.
N.M. Stat. Ann., 10-12C-1 et seq.

Magistrates Act (Assignments)
Ill. Rev. Stat. 1969, Ch. 37, § 621 et seq.

Magistrates Act (Family Support)
Conn. Gen. Stat. Ann., § 46b-231

Magistrates' Collections Act
Pa. Purdon's Stat., Title 42, § 1107

Magistrates' Court Act
Ind. Code 1971, 33-7-1-1 et seq.
Mo. Rev. Stat. 1969, 482.010 et seq.
Pa. Purdon's Stat., Title 42, §§ 1041 et seq., 1101 et seq.
S.D. Codified Laws 1967, 16-12A-1 et seq.

Magistrates' Fee Bill of Cities of the First Class
Pa. Purdon's Stat., Title 42, § 231 et seq.

Magistrates' Pay Act
Ky. Rev. Stat. 1971, Superseded Vols., 64.255

Magistrates' Retirement Parity Act of 1987
June 18, 1987, P.L. 100-53,5 U.S. Code §§ 8331, 8331 nt., 8334, 8336, 8339

Magnet School for Mathematics, Science and Technology Act
Colo. Rev. Stat., 22-84-101 et seq.

Magnetic Fusion Energy Engineering Act of 1980
Oct. 7, 1980, P.L. 96-386, 42 U.S. Code § 9301 nt.
Nov. 13, 1995, P.L. 104-46, 42 U.S. Code § 9306
Dec. 21, 1995, P.L. 104-66, 42 U.S. Code § 9311

Magnetic Levitation Demonstration Project Act
Fla. Stat. Ann., 341.401 et seq.

Magnuson Fishery Conservation and Management Act
April 13, 1976, P.L. 94-265, 16 U.S. Code § 1801 et seq.
Aug. 28, 1978, P.L. 95-354, 16 U.S. Code § 1801 et seq.
Aug. 15, 1979, P.L. 96-61, 16 U.S. Code §§ 1821, 1882
Nov. 16, 1979, P.L. 96-118, 16 U.S. Code § 1821
June 1, 1982, P.L. 97-191, 16 U.S. Code §§ 1856, 1857
Dec. 29, 1982, P.L. 97-389, 16 U.S. Code § 1823 nt.
Nov. 8, 1984, P.L. 98-623, 16 U.S. Code § 1821
April 7, 1986, P.L. 99-272, 16 U.S. Code § 1824
Aug. 22, 1986, P.L. 99-386, 16 U.S. Code § 1821
Nov. 14, 1986, P.L. 99-659, 16 U.S. Code § 1802
Jan. 11, 1988, P.L. 100-239, 16 U.S. Code § 1802
Nov. 7, 1988, P.L. 100-629, 16 U.S. Code § 1857
Dec. 12, 1989, P.L. 101-224, 16 U.S. Code § 1857
Nov. 28, 1990, P.L. 101-627, 16 U.S. Code §§ 1801, 1802, 1811, 1812, 1812 nt., 1821, 1822, 1824, 1825, 1825 nt., 1852 to 1854, 1854 nt., 1855 to 1862, 1882
March 9, 1992, P.L. 102-251, 16 U.S. Code § 4, 1801, 1802, 1811, 1821, 1822, 1824, 1853, 1857, 1861

Continued

Oct. 29, 1992, P.L. 102-567, 16 U.S. Code
§§ 1854, 1861, 1863

Nov. 2, 1992, P.L. 102-582, 16 U.S. Code
§§ 1852, 1862

Dec. 20, 1993, P.L. 103-206, 16 U.S. Code
§ 1854

Nov. 2, 1994, P.L. 103-437, 16 U.S. Code
§ 1823

Magnuson-Moss Warranty—Federal Trade Commission Improvement Act

Jan. 4, 1975, P.L. 93-637, 15 U.S. Code
§ 2301 nt.

Mahaffie Act

April 9, 1948, Ch. 180, 62 Stat. 163, 49 U.S.
Code § 20b

Aug. 16, 1957, P.L. 85-150, 71 Stat. 369, 49
U.S. Code § 20b

Mahin Act (Intoxicating Liquors)

Kan. Laws 1913, Ch. 248

Mahoney Law (Anti-Discrimination)

N.Y. Civil Rights Law (Consol. Laws Ch. 6)
§ 44

Mahoney Law (Home Relief)

N.Y. Social Services Law (Consol. Laws Ch.
55) § 139a

Mail and Telephone Consumer Product Promotion Fair Practices Act

Ark. Acts 1991, No. 680

Mail Ballot Election Act

Colo. Rev. Stat., 1-7.5-101 et seq.

Fla. Stat. Ann., 101.6101 et seq.

Kan. Stat. Ann., 25-431 et seq.

Mo. Rev. Stat., 115.650 et seq.

N.M. Stat. Ann., 1-23-1 et seq.

Mail Carriers' Free Ride Law

Cal. Public Utilities Code § 6041

Mail Fraud Act

March 4, 1909, Ch. 321, 35 Stat. 1130 (See
18 U.S. Code §§ 1341, 1342)

Mail-in Voting Act

Mo. Rev. Stat., 115.650 et seq.

Mail Order Address Disclosure Act

R.I. Gen. Laws 1956, 6-40-1 et seq.

Mail Order Consumer Protection Amendments of 1983

Nov. 30, 1983, P.L. 98-186, 39 U.S. Code
§ 3001 nt.

Dec. 21, 1995, P.L. 104-66, 39 U.S. Code
§ 3005 nt.

Mail Order Drug Paraphernalia Control Act

Oct. 27, 1986, P.L. 99-570, 21 U.S. Code
§§ 801 nt., 857, 857 nt.

Mail Service Law

S.C. Code Ann. 1976, § 15-9-930

Mail Service Pharmacy Licensing Act

Ida. Code 1947, 54-1740 et seq.

Mail Service Prescription Drug Act

Neb. Rev. Stat. 1943, 71-2406 et seq.

Maiming Act

Ohio Rev. Code 1953, 2903.11

Va. Code 1950, § 18.2-51

W. Va. Code 1966, § 61-2-9

Main Arteries and Full Stop Streets Law (Castleton-on-Hudson)

N.Y. Local Laws 1966, Village of Castleton-
on-Hudson, p. 1916

Main Party in Interest Act (Civil Actions)

Wash. Rev. Code Ann., 4.08.030 et seq.

Main Street Act

N.M. Stat. Ann., 3-60B-1 et seq.

Main Street Program Act

Mo. Rev. Stat., 251.470 et seq.

Utah Code Ann. 1953, 9-8-901 et seq.

Maine Acadian Culture Preservation Act

Nov. 8, 1990, P.L. 101-543, 16 U.S. Code
§ 461 nt.

Maine-Canadian Legislative Advisory Commission Act

Me. Rev. Stat. Ann. 1964, Title 3, § 221 et
seq.

Maine Dam Registration, Abandonment and Water Level Act
Me. Rev. Stat. Ann. 1964, Title 38, § 815 et seq.

Maine Indian Claims Settlement Act of 1980
Oct. 10, 1980, P.L. 96-420, 25 U.S. Code §§ 1721 et seq., 1721 nt.
Jan. 8, 1983, P.L. 97-428, 25 U.S. Code § 1725

Maine-New Hampshire Commission on Oceanography Act
N.H. Rev. Stat. 1955, 12-C:1 et seq.

Maine-New Hampshire Interstate School Compact Act
Me. Rev. Stat. Ann. 1964, Title 20A, § 3601 et seq.
N.H. Rev. Stat. 1955, 200-F:1

Maine Separation Act
Mass. Acts 1819-20, January Session, Ch. 287
Mass. Acts 1819-20, May Session, Ch. 161

Maine Wilderness Act of 1990
Sept. 28, 1990, P.L. 101-401, 104 Stat. 863

Maintained Cemeteries Act (Perpetually)
Mont. Code Ann., 37-19-801 et seq.

Maintenance Act (Resale Price)
Mass. Gen. Laws Ann., 93:14E et seq.

Maintenance and Champerty Act
Miss. Code Ann. 1972, § 97-9-11 et seq.

Maintenance and Emission Inspection Act (Motor Vehicle)
Ga. Code Ann., 12-9-40 et seq.

Maintenance and Emission Inspection Program Act (Motor Vehicle)
Mich. Comp. Laws Ann., 257.2051 et seq.

Maintenance Code (Housing)
N.Y. Adm. Code '85, § 27-2001 et seq.

Maintenance District Act (Cemetery)
Ill. Rev. Stat. 1991, Ch. 21, § 64.24a1 et seq.

Maintenance Funding Act (Habitat)
Cal. Fish and Game Code 1957, §§ 2900, 2901

Maintenance of Housing for the Elderly Act
Fla. Stat. Ann., 420.901 et seq.

Maintenance of Viable Neighborhoods Act
N.J. Stat. Ann., 52:27D-142 et seq.

Major Crimes Act (Indians)
See Indian Major Crimes Act

Major Economic Impact Act
Miss. Code Ann. 1972, §§ 57-75-11, 57-75-15

Major Energy Project Act
Tenn. Code Ann., 13-18-101 et seq., 59-8-205, 59-8-208, 59-8-306, 59-8-307, 59-8-310, 59-8-313, 68-7-102, 68-25-105, 68-25-108, 68-25-115, 68-25-202, 68-31-105 et seq., 68-46-107, 68-46-108, 68-46-116, 69-3-108, 69-3-110

Major Facility Siting Act
Mont. Code Ann., 75-20-101 et seq.

Major Fraud Act Amendments of 1989
Oct. 23, 1989, P.L. 101-123, 18 U.S. Code § 1001 nt.

Major Fraud Act of 1988
Nov. 19, 1988, P.L. 100-700, 18 U.S. Code § 10001 nt.
Oct. 23, 1989, P.L. 101-123, 18 U.S. Code §§ 293, 293 nt.

Major General Peter C. Harris Act (Veterans' Orphans)
Ga. Code 1933, 78-301 et seq.

Major Hazardous Waste Facilities Siting Act
N.J. Stat. Ann., 13:1E-49 et seq.

Major League Baseball Stadium District Act (Denver Metropolitan)
Colo. Rev. Stat., 32-14-101 et seq.

Major Medical Insurance Fund Act
Colo. Rev. Stat., 8-46-201 et seq., 8-66-101 et seq.

Major Narcotic Vendors Persecution Law
Cal. Penal Code § 13880 et seq.

Major Street Improvement Act
Ky. Rev. Stat. 1971, Superseded Vols., 93.880 et seq.

Majority Age Act
Ala. Code 1975, § 26-1-1
Mich. Comp. Laws Ann., 722.51 et seq.

Majority Card Act (Liquor)
Conn. Gen. Stat. Ann., § 30-88

Majority Protest Act (Special Assessments)
Cal. Streets and Highways Code § 2800 et seq.

Make It Easy on the Family and Small Business Act
Cal. Unemployment Insurance Code § 1118

Make-My-Day Act
Colo. Rev. Stat., 18-1-704.5
Okla. Stat. 1981, Title 21, § 1289.25

Make My Day Law
Okla. Stat. Ann., Title 21, § 1289.25

Malcolm Baldrige National Quality Improvement Act of 1987
Aug. 20, 1987, P.L. 100-107, 15 U.S. Code §§ 3701 nt., 3708, 3711a, 3711a nt., 3712 to 3714

Malden Funding Loan Act
Mass. Acts 1956, Ch. 25
Mass. Acts 1958, Ch. 451
Mass. Acts 1960, Ch. 280

Malden Public Parking Loan Act
Mass. Acts 1954, Ch. 600

Malfeasance in Office Act
La. Rev. Stat. Ann., 14:134

Malicious Injury Act (Animals)
Ala. Code 1975, §§ 3-1-10, 3-1-11

Malicious Injury Act (Property)
Ala. Code 1975, § 13A-7-20 et seq.

Malicious Mischief Act
Ala. Code 1975, § 13A-7-20 et seq.
Colo. Rev. Stat. 18-4-501 et seq.
Okla. Stat. Ann., Title 21, § 1751 et seq.
Wash. Rev. Code Ann., 9.61.140 et seq.

Malicious Prosecution Act
Mich. Comp. Laws Ann., 600.2907
Tex. Penal Code, § 38.12
Wash. Rev. Code Ann., 9.62.010 et seq.

Malicious Telephone Call Act
N.Y. Penal Law 1965 (Consol. Laws Ch. 40) § 240.30, Subd. 1 et seq.

Malicious Trespass Act
Ind. Code Ann., 35-1-66-1

Malone Bill (City Boundaries)
Tex. Local Government Code, § 43.031

Maloney-Bauer Act (Taxation)
Ky. Rev. Stat. 1971, 132.200

Maloney-John McCarthy-Murdy-J. Howard Williams-Abshire Bill (Average Annual Earnings)
Cal. Labor Code §§ 4452, 4453, 4455, 4460, 4702

Malpractice Act
Ark. Code Ann. 1987, 17-93-409, 17-93-410
Mich. Comp. Laws Ann., 600.2912

Malpractice Act (Health Care Services)
Pa. Purdon's Stat., Title 40, § 1301.101 et seq.

Malpractice Act (Limitation of Action)
Ind. Code Ann., 34-4-19-1
N.H. Rev. Stat. 1955, 508:4

Malpractice Act (Medical)
Ind. Code Ann., 16-9.5-1-1 et seq.
N.M. Stat. Ann., 41-5-1 et seq.

Malpractice Arbitration Act
Ill. Rev. Stat. 1991, Ch. 10, § 201 et seq.
Mich. Comp. Laws Ann., 600.5040 et seq.

Malpractice Claims Act
N.H. Rev. Stat. 1955, 519-A:1 et seq.

Malpractice Evidentiary Act
Mass. Gen Laws 1990, 233:79C

Malpractice Joint Underwriting Association Act (Medical and Hospital)
Me. Rev. Stat. Ann. 1964, Title 24, § 2401 et seq.

Malpractice Liability Insurance Act (Medical)
N.J. Stat. Ann., 14:30D-1 et seq.

Malpractice Limitation Act
Ohio Rev. Code 1953, 2305.11

Malpractice Reform Act (Medical)
Fla. Stat. Ann., 95.11, 627.351, 627.357, 725.01, 768.042, 768.41, 768.46, 768.47, 768.54

Malpractice Review Board and Claims Act (Medical)
Tenn. Code Ann., 29-26-101 et seq.

Malpractice Statute of Limitations
N.Y. Civil Practice Law and Rules (Consol. Laws, Ch. 8), §§ 214 Subd. 6, 214a

Malt and Vinous Beverage Act
Ill. Laws 1933, p. 518, No. 2

Malt Beverage Tax Law
Pa. Purdon's Stat., Title 47, § 103 et seq.

Malt Liquor Act
Ga. Code Ann., 3-5-1 et seq.
Minn. Stat. Ann., 340.001 et seq.
Tex. Alcoholic Beverage Code, § 12.01 et seq.

Malt Liquor License Law
Pa. 1933 Ex. Pamph. Laws 75, No. 14

Malt Products Tax Act
Kan. Stat. Ann., 79-3817 et seq.

Malt Tax Act
Mich. Public Acts 1929, No. 304
Ohio Rev. Code 1953, 4309.01 et seq.

Mamakatin Snowmobiles Operation Law
N.Y. Local Laws 1972, Town of Mamakatin, p. 2043

Mammogram Quality Assurance Act
Utah Code Ann. 1953, 26-21a-201

Mammography Quality Assurance Act
Pa. Purdon's Stat., Title 35, § 5651 et seq.

Mammography Quality Standards Act of 1992
Oct. 27, 1992, P.L. 102-539, 42 U.S. Code § 201 nt.

Mammography Quality Standards Reauthorization Act of 1998
Oct. 9, 1998, P.L. 105-248, 112 Stat. 1864, 42 U.S. Code § 201 nt.

Man in the Home Act
Cal. Welfare and Institutions Code § 11351.5, § 1508

Man-Power Act
Aug. 31, 1918, Ch. 166, 40 Stat. 955, 43 U.S. Code § 183

Managed Audit Program
Cal. Revenue and Taxation Code §§ 7076.1 to 7076.7

Managed Care and Publicly Funded Primary Care Program Coordination Act
Fla. Stat. Ann., 381.0407

Managed Care Contract Compliance Act
Tex. General and Special Laws 1997, Ch. 692

Managed Care Delivery System Law (Medicaid)
Tex. Government Code, § 532.001 et seq.

Managed Care Information and Training Act
Tex. General and Special Laws 1997, Ch. 618

Managed Care Patient Protection Act
Neb. Laws 1997, L.B. 279

Managed Care Plan Act
Neb. Rev. Stat. 1943, 68-1048 et seq.

Managed Care Plan Network Adequacy Act
Neb. Rev. Stat. 1943, 44-7101 to 44-7112

Managed Care Plan Network Adequacy and Quality Assurance Act
Mont. Code Ann., 33-36-101 et seq.

Managed Care Program Law (Medicaid)
Tex. Government Code, § 533.001 et seq.

Managed Care Reform Act
See also Health Maintenance Organization Act
Ida. Code 1947, 41-3901 et seq.

Managed Care Responsibility Act
Ga. Code Ann., 33-24-59.1

Management Act (Archives and Records)
Me. Rev. Stat. Ann. 1964, Title 5, § 91 et seq.

Management Act (Boll Weevil)
Miss. Code Ann. 1972, § 69-37-1 et seq.

Management Act (Civil Defense and Emergency Resources)
Okla. Stat. 1981, Title 63, § 683.1 et seq.

Management Act (Coastal Public Land)
Tex. Natural Resources Code, § 33.001 et seq.

Management Act (Equal)
La. Civil Code 1972, Art. 2325 et seq.

Management Act (Grant and Contract)
Tex. Government Code, § 783.001

Management Act (Hazardous Waste)
Mass. Gen. Laws Ann., 21C:1 et seq.
Okla. Stat. Ann., Title 27A, § 2-7-101 et seq.

Management Act (Information Resources)
Tex. Rev. Civ. Stat., Art. 4413(32j)

Management Act (Jury Use)
Utah Laws 1992, Ch. 219

Management Act (Local Water)
Minn. Stat. Ann., 103B.301 et seq.

Management Act (Nutrient)
Pa. Purdon's Stat., Title 3, § 1701 et seq.

Management Act (Ocean Resources)
Wash. Rev. Code Ann., 43.143.005 et seq.

Management Act (Open Lands)
N.J. Stat. Ann., 13:1B-15.131 et seq.

Management Act (Radiation)
Okla. Stat. Ann., Title 27A, § 2-9-101 et seq.

Management Act (Smith River)
Mont. Laws 1989, Ch. 512

Management Act (Solid Waste)
Conn. Gen. Stat. Ann., § 22a-207 et seq.

Management Act (Southern Illinois University)
Ill. Rev. Stat. 1991, Ch. 144, § 650 et seq.

Management Act (Water)
Mass. Gen. Laws Ann., 21G:1 et seq.

Management and Budget Act
Mich. Comp. Laws Ann., 18.1101 et seq.

Management and Improvement Act (Surface Water)
Fla. Stat. Ann., 373.451 et seq.

Management and Labor Improper Practices Act
N.Y. Labor Law (Consol. Laws Ch. 31) § 720 et seq.

Management and Maintenance Law of Parking, Accessory and Other Areas
N.Y. Local Laws 1969, Town of Ramapo, p. 2013

Management and Trial Jury Selection Act
Cal. Code of Civil Procedure, § 190 et seq.

Management Assistance Compact (Emergency)
Ark. Code 1987, 12-49-401, 12-49-402
Del. Code of 1974, Title 20, § 3401 et seq.
Fla. Stat. Ann., 252.921 et seq.
Tenn. Code Ann., 58-2-403
Tex. Health and Safety Code, § 778.001 et seq.

Management, Collection, and Recycling of Used Oil Act
Tex. Health and Safety Code, § 371.001 et seq.

Management Compact (Northeast Interstate Low-Level Radioactive e) Waste)
Conn. Gen. Stat. Ann., § 22a-161

Management for Infectious Waste Act
S.C. Code Ann. 1976, § 44-96-240

Management Information Services
Utah Code Ann. 1953, 53-1-301 et seq.

Management Information System Act (Community Health)
Iowa Code Ann., 144C.1 et seq.

Management Interlocks Revision Act of 1988
Nov. 10, 1988, P.L. 100-650, 12 U.S. Code § 3201 nt.

Management-Labor Reform Act
See Labor-Management Reform Act

Management-Labor Relations Act
See Labor Management Relations Act

Management Law (Archives and Records)
Me. Rev. Stat. Ann. 1964, Title 5, § 91 et seq.

Management Law (Equal)
La. Civil Code 1972, Art. 2325 et seq.

Management Law (Floodplain)
Minn. Stat. Ann., 103F.101 et seq.

Management of Educational Institutional Funds Act
See Uniform Management of Educational Institutional Funds Act

Management of Institutional Funds Act
See also Uniform Management of Institutional Funds Act
N.Y. Religious Corporation Law (Consol. Laws Ch. 51) § 26
S.C. Code Ann. 1976, § 34-6-10 et seq.

Management of Wildlife Habitat Areas Act
Ill. Rev. Stat. 1991, Ch. 61, § 217.9 et seq.

Management Planning Act (Watershed)
Cal. Statutes 1996, Ch. 166

Management Research Fund for Hazardous Waste Act
S.C. Code Ann. 1976, § 44-56-810 et seq.

Management Responsibility Act (Local Fiscal)
Ark. Acts 1991, No. 724

Management Services Act (Solid Waste)
Conn. Gen. Stat. Ann., § 20-7a

Management Services Code (Emergency)
Pa. Cons. Stat., Title 35, § 7101 et seq.

Management Stability Act
Wyo. Stat. Ann., § 17-18-101 et seq.

Management Training Act (Education)
Fla. Stat. Ann., 231.087

Manager Act (County)
Neb. Laws 1933, Ch. 35

Manager Background Check Act (Kari Koskinen)
Minn. Stat. Ann., 299C.66 et seq.

Manager-Council Act
Ala. Code 1975, § 11-43A-70

Managerial Form of Municipal Government Act
Ill. Rev. Stat. 1991, Ch. 24, § 5-1-1 et seq.

Managing General Agents Act

Cal. Insurance Code § 769.80 et seq.

Colo. Rev. Stat., 10-2-401 et seq., 10-2-1001 et seq.

Del. Code of 1974, Title 18, § 1801 et seq.

Ga. Code Ann., 33-47-1 et seq.

Ida. Code 1947, 41-1501 et seq.

Iowa Code Ann., 510.1A et seq.

La. Rev. Stat. Ann., 22:1201 et seq.

Mass. Gen. Laws Ann., 175:177F to 175:177L

Me. Rev. Stat. Ann. 1964, Title 24-A, § 1881 et seq.

Minn. Stat. Ann., 60H.01 et seq.

Miss. Code Ann. 1972, § 83-18-101 et seq.

Mo. Rev. Stat. 1986, 375.147 et seq.

Neb. Rev. Stat. 1943, 44-4901 et seq.

N.M. Stat. Ann., 59A-12B-1 et seq.

Okla. Stat. Ann., Title 36, § 1471 et seq.

S.C. Code Ann. 1976, § 38-44-10 et seq.

Wash. Rev. Code Ann., 48.98.900

Managing General Agents' Licensing Act

Tex. Insurance Code, Art. 21.07-3

Manasota Key Conservation District Act

Fla. Special Laws 1971, Ch. 71-904

Manassas National Battlefield Park Amendments of 1980

Oct. 13, 1980, P.L. 96-442, 16 U.S. Code § 429b nt.

Manassas National Battlefield Park Amendments of 1988

Nov. 10, 1988, P.L. 100-647, 16 U.S. Code § 429b nt.

Manatee County Environmental Protection Act

Fla. Laws 1991, Ch. 412

Manatee County Free Public Library Act

Fla. Special Laws 1971, Ch. 71-760

Manatee County Law Library Act

Fla. Special Laws 1961, Ch. 61-2455

Manatee County Pollution Control Act

Fla. Special Laws 1967, Ch. 67-1671

Manatee County Port Authority Act

Fla. Special Laws 1967, Ch. 67-1681

Manatee County Transportation Authority Act

Fla. Special Laws 1980, Ch. 80-533

Manatee County Utility Bond Act

Fla. Special Laws 1963, Ch. 63-1598

Manatee Sanctuary Act

Fla. Stat. Ann., 370.12, Subsec. 2

Manatee-Sarasota Airport Authority Act

Fla. Laws 1991, Ch. 358

Fla. Special Laws 1977, Ch. 77-651

Manatee-Sarasota Airport Traffic Control Act

Fla. Special Laws 1967, Ch. 67-2053

Manchester Partial Exemption From Taxation of Certain Real Property Owned by Persons Sixty-five Years of Age or Over Local Law

N.Y. Local Laws 1971, Town of Manchester, p. 2647

Manchester School Building Enlargement Loan Act

Mass. Acts 1951, Ch. 348

Mancos Project Private Power Development Authorization Act of 1994

Oct. 31, 1994, P.L. 103-434, 108 Stat. 4549

Mandamus Act

Oct. 5, 1962, P.L. 87-748, 28 U.S. Code § 1361

Haw. Rev. Stat. 1968, § 659-1 et seq.

Ill. Rev. Stat. 1991, Ch. 110, § 14-101 et seq.

Md. Rules of Procedure, Rule BE 40

Mich. Comp. Laws Ann., 600.4401 et seq.

Mont. Code Ann., 27-26-101 et seq.

N.J. Stat. Revised 1937 Ann., Superseded Vol., 2:83-1 to 2:83-15

N.M. Stat. Ann., 44-2-1 et seq.

Vt. Acts 1876, No. 74

Wash. Rev. Code Ann., 7.16.010, 7.16.020, 7.16.150 et seq., 7.16.330 et seq.

Mandate Relief and Reform Act (Ayala-Monteith-Johannesson)
Cal. Government Code §§ 17526, 17553 et seq.
Cal. Revenue and Taxation Code § 2246

Mandated Services Act
N.Y. Laws 1970, Ch. 138

Mandates Act (Federal)
Mont. Code Ann., 2-1-401 et seq.

Mandatory Arbitration Act
Colo. Rev. Stat., 13-22-401 et seq.

Mandatory Automobile Insurance Act
Alaska Stat. 1962, § 28.22.011 et seq.

Mandatory Borough Act
Alaska Laws 1963, Ch. 52

Mandatory Bureau Act (Insurance Rates)
Miss. Code Ann. 1972, § 83-3-1 et seq.

Mandatory Confinement Act (Criminal Insane)
Nev. Rev. Stat. Ann., 175.521

Mandatory Confinement Act (Insanity Plea)
Wis. Stat. Ann., 971.14, Subsec. 6, Subd. 6

Mandatory Continuance Act
Tex. Civil Prac. and Rem. Code, § 30.003

Mandatory Detention for Offenders Convicted of Serious Crimes Act
Nov. 29, 1990, P.L. 101-647, 18 U.S. Code §§ 3141 nt., 3143, 3145

Mandatory Disposition of Detainers Act
See also Uniform Mandatory Disposition of Detainers Act
Ida. Laws 1969, Ch. 131
Neb. Rev. Stat. 1943, 30-2201 et seq.
N.H. Rev. Stat. 1955, 606-A:1 et seq.

Mandatory Divorce Investigation Act
Ohio Civ. Rule 75(D)

Mandatory Fair Trade Law (Liquor Control)
Ill. Rev. Stat. 1977, Ch. 43, § 196 et seq.

Mandatory Financial Responsibility Act
N.M. Stat. Ann., 66-5-201 et seq.

Mandatory Indemnification Act (Corporations)
Wis. Stat. Ann., 180.0851

Mandatory Item Pricing Law
N.Y. Agriculture and Markets Law (Consol. Laws Ch. 69) § 214i

Mandatory Joinder Act (Prosecutions)
Ill. Rev. Stat. 1991, Ch. 38, § 3-3

Mandatory Life Imprisonment or Death Penalty for Murder in the District of Columbia
Oct. 5, 1992, P.L. 102-382, 106 Stat. 1436

Mandatory Medical Support Act
N.M. Stat. Ann., 40-4C-1 et seq.

Mandatory Park Board Act
Iowa Code 1973, 371.1 et seq.

Mandatory Reporting Act (Child Abuse)
Ohio Rev. Code 1953, 2151.421

Mandatory Sanitary Disposal Act
Iowa Code 1971, 406.1 et seq.

Mandatory Seat Belt Use Act
Okla. Stat. Ann., Title 47, § 12-416 et seq.

Mandatory Sentencing Act
Kan. Stat. Ann., 21-4601 et seq.

Mandatory Sine Die Act
S.C. Code Ann. 1976, § 2-1-180 et seq.

Mandatory Source Separation and Recycling Act (Statewide)
N.J. Stat. Ann., 13:1E-99.11 et seq.

Mandatory Supervision and Parole Act (Adult)
Tex. Code of Criminal Procedure, Art. 42.18

Mandatory Supervision and Parole Law (Adult)
Tex. Code of Criminal Procedure 1965, Art. 42.18

Mandatory Treatment Act
Ala. Acts 1990, No. 390

Mandatory Victims Restitution Act of 1996
April 24, 1996, P.L. 104-132, Title II, Subtitle A, 18 U.S. Code § 3551 nt.

Mandelbaum Act (Emergency Relief)
N.Y. Laws 1933, 1st Ex. Sess., Ch. 782

Manderson Act (Printing and Binding)
See also Printing and Binding Acts
Jan. 12, 1895, Ch. 23, 28 Stat. 601

Manford Labor Act
Tex. Rev. Civ. Stat., Art. 5154a

Mango, Avocado, and Lime Sales Law
Fla. Stat. Ann., 570.55

Mangrove Trimming and Preservation Act
Fla. Stat. Ann., 403.9321 et seq.

Manicurists, Cosmetologists, and Barbers Act
Wash. Rev. Code Ann., 18.16.010 et seq.

Mann Acts
See White-Slave Laws

Mann-Elkins Act
June 18, 1910, Ch. 309, 36 Stat. 539, 49 U.S. Code §§ 1, 4, 6, 10, 13, 15, 16, 20, 50

Manomin Act
Minn. Stat. Ann., 116J.645

Manpower Act of 1965
April 26, 1965, P.L. 89-15, 79 Stat. 75, 42 U.S. Code §§ 2513 nt., 2571 to 2574, 2582, 2583, 2601, 2610a to 2612, 2614 to 2616, 2619, 2620

Manpower Council Act
N.C. Gen. Stat. 1943, § 143-283.41 et seq.

Manpower Development and Training Act
Miss. Code Ann. 1972, § 37-31-101 et seq.

Manpower Development and Training Act of 1962
March 15, 1962, P.L. 87-415, 76 Stat. 23, 42 U.S. Code §§ 2571 to 2574, 2581 to 2587, 2601, 2602, 2611 to 2620
Oct. 1, 1962, P.L. 87-729, 76 Stat. 679, 42 U.S. Code § 2583
Dec. 19, 1963, P.L. 88-214, 77 Stat. 422, 42 U.S. Code §§ 2571, 2582, 2583, 2585, 2588, 2601, 2614, 2615, 2619, 2620
April 26, 1965, P.L. 89-15, 79 Stat. 75 to 80, 42 U.S. Code §§ 2571 to 2574, 2582, 2583, 2601, 2610a to 2612, 2614 to 2616, 2619, 2620
Nov. 7, 1966, P.L. 89-792, 80 Stat. 1434, 42 U.S. Code §§ 2572b, 2572c, 2582, 2583, 2601, 2603, 2610b, 2611, 2614
Nov. 8, 1966, P.L. 89-794, 80 Stat. 1475, 42 U.S. Code §§ 2581, 2583, 2610
Oct. 24, 1968, P.L. 90-636, 82 Stat. 1352, 42 U.S. Code §§ 2572b, 2572c, 2573, 2582 to 2584, 2601, 2610b, 2611, 2614, 2618 to 2628
March 19, 1969, P.L. 91-4, 83 Stat. 6, 42 U.S. Code § 2611

Manpower Development and Training Amendments of 1966
Nov. 7, 1966, P.L. 89-792, 80 Stat. 1434, 42 U.S. Code §§ 2572b, 2572c, 2582, 2583, 2601, 2603, 2610b, 2611, 2614
April 24, 1972, P.L. 92-277, 86 Stat. 124, 42 U.S. Code § 2620

Manpower Employment Assistance and Training Act
Pa. Purdon's Stat., Title 43, § 690.1 et seq.

Manpower Planning Act
Fla. Stat. 1981, 13.998 et seq.

Manpower Planning and Analysis Act
Ill. Rev. Stat. 1991, Ch. 144, § 178 et seq.

Manpower Services Act
Minn. Stat. Ann., 268.03 et seq.

Manpower Services Act (Rural)
Fla. Stat. Ann., 446.40 et seq.

Manpower Training and Career Education Advisory Act
Nev. Rev. Stat. 1973 Reprint, Replaced Pages, 399.010 et seq.

Manpower Training and Retraining Act
N.J. Stat. Ann., 34:15A-1 et seq.

Mansfield Sewerage Loan Act
Mass. Acts 1929, Ch. 348

Manslaughter Act
Ark. Code Ann. 1987, 41-1504
Cal. Penal Code § 192 et seq.
D.C. Code 1973, § 22-2405
Fla. Stat. Ann., 776.06
Iowa Code Ann., 707.4, 707.5
La. Rev. Stat. Ann., 14:31
Md. Ann. Code 1957, Art. 27, § 387
Mo. Rev. Stat., 565.023 et seq.
Mont. Code Ann., 45-5-103, 45-5-104
Neb. Rev. Stat. 1943, 28-305
N.H. Rev. Stat. 1955, 630:2
N.M. Stat. Ann., 30-2-3
Ohio Rev. Code 1953, 2903.03 et seq.
Ore. Rev. Stat. 1953, 163.118, 163.125
R.I. Gen. Laws 1956, 11-23-3
Wash. Rev. Code Ann., 9A.32.060 et seq.
Wis. Stat. Ann., 940.05 et seq.
Wyo. Stat. Ann., § 6-4-105

Manslaughter Act (Involuntary)
See Involuntary Manslaughter Act

Manslaughter Act (Motor Vehicle)
Md. Ann. Code 1957, Art. 27, § 388
Ohio Rev. Code 1953, 2903.06 et seq.

Manslaughter by Abortion Act
Ore. Rev. Stat. 1953, 163.060

Manslaughter Short Form Indictment Act
Wyo. Stat. Ann., § 7-6-204

Manteno Veterans Home Act
Ill. Rev. Stat. 1991, Ch. 126 1/2, § 500 et seq.

Manual and Mechanical Laborers Preference Law
Ind. Laws 1885, Ch. 21, p. 36

Manufactured Building Act
Fla. Stat. Ann., 553.35 et seq.

Manufactured Building and Factory Built Housing Act
Nev. Rev. Stat. 1979 Reprint, 461.020 et seq.

Manufactured Dairy Products Act
Mont. Code Ann., 81-22-101 et seq.

Manufactured Home Anchoring Act
Tenn. Code Ann., 68-45-101 et seq.

Manufactured Home Installers Act
Ill. Comp. Stat. 1992, Ch. 430, § 120/1 et seq.

Manufactured Home Park Tenancy Act
S.C. Code Ann. 1976, § 27-47-10 et seq.

Manufactured Home Property Act
La. Rev. Stat. Ann., 9:1149.1 et seq.

Manufactured Home Property Tax Law
Cal. Revenue and Taxation Code § 5800 et seq.

Manufactured Home Real Property Act
Wash. Rev. Code Ann., 65.20.010 et seq.

Manufactured Home Recovery Act
Ark. Code Ann. 1987, 20-29-101 et seq.

Manufactured Home Repossession Security Act
Minn. Stat. Ann., 327.61 et seq.

Manufactured Home Taxation Act
N.J. Stat. Ann., 54:4-1.2 et seq.

Manufactured Homes and Recreational Vehicles Uniform Standard Code
Neb. Rev. Stat. 1943, 71-4601 et seq.

Manufactured Homes Standards Act
Ark. Code Ann. 1987, 20-25-101 et seq.
Ga. Code Ann., 8-2-130 et seq.
N.Y. Executive Law 1951 (Consol. Laws Ch. 18) § 400a et seq.
Continued

Manufactured Homes Titles Act
Colo. Rev. Stat., 38-29-101 et seq.

Manufactured Housing Act
Kan. Stat. Ann., 58-4201 et seq.
Me. Rev. Stat. Ann. 1964, Title 10, § 9001 et seq.
N.M. Stat. Ann., 60-14-1 et seq.

Manufactured Housing and Mobile Home Safety Act
Ill. Rev. Stat. 1991, Ch. 67 1/2, § 501 et seq.

Manufactured Housing and Zoning Act
N.M. Stat. Ann., 3-21A-1 et seq.

Manufactured Housing Assistance Act
Cal. Health and Safety Code § 50003 et seq.

Manufactured Housing Construction and Safety Standards Act
S.C. Code Ann. 1976, Superseded Vols., § 31-17-10 et seq.
Tex. Rev. Civ. Stat. 1974, Art. 5221f
Va. Code 1950, § 36-85.2 et seq.
W. Va. Code 1966, §§ 21-9-1 et seq., 29-1H-1 et seq.

Manufactured Housing Construction and Safety Standards Act of 1974
Oct. 21, 1998, P.L. 105-276, 42 U.S. Code § 5402

Manufactured Housing Construction and Safety Standards Authorization Act
Pa. Purdon's Stat., Title 35, § 1656.1 et seq.

Manufactured Housing Production Act
Cal. Government Code § 65852.1 et seq.

Manufactured Housing Sales and Use Tax Act
Tex. Tax Code, § 158.001 et seq.

Manufactured Housing Standards Act
Tex. Rev. Civ. Stat., Art. 5221f

Manufactured Housing Uniform Standards Code
N.C. Gen. Stat. 1943, § 143-144 et seq.
S.C. Code Ann. 1976, § 40-29-10 et seq.

Manufactured Housing Units Standards Act
Neb. Rev. Stat. 1943, 71-1555 et seq.

Manufacturer-Dealer Licensing Act (Motor Vehicles)
Tenn. Code Ann., 55-17-101 et seq.

Manufacturer Recycling Incentive Act
Okla. Stat. Ann., Title 68, § 2357.51 et seq.

Manufacturers Act (Intoxicating Liquors)
Tenn. Code Ann., 39-17-701 et seq.

Manufacturers and Dealers Act (Farm Equipment)
Fla. Stat. Ann., 686.40 et seq.

Manufacturers and Vehicle Dealers Licensing Act
Kan. Stat. Ann., 8-2401 et seq.

Manufacturer's Income Tax Credit Act
N.C. Gen. Stat. 1943, § 105-163.01 et seq.

Manufacturer's Investment Sales and Use Tax Credit Act
Ark. Code Ann. 1987, 26-52-701 et seq.

Manufacturers or Dealers Registration Act (Motor Vehicles)
Kan. Stat. Ann., 8-2401 et seq.

Manufacturing and Business Corporation Act
Mo. Rev. Stat., 351.010 et seq.

Manufacturing and Economic Development Assistance Act
Conn. Public Acts 1991, No. 270

Manufacturing Corporation Act
N.Y. Laws 1811, Ch. 67
N.Y. Laws 1848, Ch. 40

Manufacturing Equipment and Employment Investment Tax Credit Act
N.J. Stat. Ann., 54:10A-5.16 et seq.

Manufacturing Facilities Community Right-to-Know Act
Tex. Health and Safety Code, § 505.001 et seq.

Manufacturing Milk Act
Mich. Comp. Laws Ann., 288.101 et seq.
Neb. Rev. Stat. 1943, 2-3913 et seq.

Manufacturing Milk and Dairy Market Testing Law
Mo. Rev. Stat., 196.520 et seq.

Manufacturing Production Property Valuation Act (Specialized)
W. Va. Code 1966, § 11-6E-1 et seq.

Manufacturing Site Act
Alaska Comp. Laws Ann. 1949, § 47-2-71

Manufacturing Technology Alliance Act
Ill. Rev. Stat. 1991, Ch. 48, § 2601 et seq.

Manure Digesters Act (Anaerobic)
Pa. Purdon's Stat., Title 3, § 2001 et seq.

Map Act
Cal. Public Resources Code §§ 8001 et seq., 8002 et seq.
N.J. Rev. Stat. 1937, 46:23-1 et seq.
N.Y. General City Law (Consol. Laws Ch. 21) § 26 et seq.

Map Act (Cities)
Wis. Stat. Ann., 62.23, Subsec. 6

Map and Deed Validation Law
Cal. Statutes 1929, Ch. 380, p. 700

Map and Plat Restoration Law
Cal. Code of Civil Procedure § 1855b

Map and Statement Act (Irrigation)
Colo. Rev. Stat. 1963, 148-4-1 et seq.

Map Filing Law
N.J. Stat. Ann., 46:23-9.9 et seq.

Maple Products Act
Pa. Cons. Stat., Title 3, § 6101 et seq.

Mapp Act (Intoxicating Liquor)
Va. Acts 1922, Ch. 345

Mapping Act (Seismic Hazards)
Cal. Public Resources Code § 2690 et seq.

Maps Sale Act
Ill. Rev. Stat. 1991, Ch. 124, § 200 et seq.

Marchman Alcohol and Other Drug Services Act
Fla. Stat. Ann., 397.301 et seq.

Marengo Civic Center Law
Ill. Rev. Stat. 1991, Ch. 85, § 6251 et seq.

Marengo, Crystal Lake, and Bowdre Township Civic Centers Act
Ill. Rev. Stat. 1991, Ch. 85, § 6250 et seq.

Margarine Tax Act
S.D. Codified Laws 1967, 10-51-1 et seq.

Marginal Wells Act (Oil)
Tex. Natural Resources Code, § 85.121 et seq.

Margolin-Bill Greene Workers' Compensation Reform Act
Cal. Statutes 1991, Ch. 892

Marianna Downtown Development Authority Act
Fla. Special Laws 1973, Ch. 73-548

Marietta Civil Service Act
Ga. Laws 1952, p. 2246, § 7 et seq.

Marietta-Cobb County Anti-Drug Commission Act
Ga. Laws 1991, p. 4233

Marietta-Cobb County Water Authority Act
Ga. Laws 1951, p. 497

Marijuana Act
N.M. Stat. Ann. 1953, 54-9-1 et seq.

Marijuana and Controlled Substances Tax Act
S.C. Code Ann. 1976, § 12-21-5010 et seq.

Marijuana and Controlled Substances Taxation Act
R.I. Gen. Laws 1956, 4-49-1 et seq.

Marijuana and Health Reporting Act
June 30, 1970, P.L. 91-296, 84 Stat. 352, 42 U.S. Code § 242 nt.
Oct. 14, 1978, P.L. 95-461, 92 Stat. 1268, 42 U.S. Code § 242 nt.

Marijuana Control Act
Cal. Health and Safety Code § 11530 et seq.
Me. Rev. Stat. Ann. 1964, Title 22, § 2381 et seq.

Marijuana Possession Act
Cal. Health and Safety Code § 11530 et seq.

Marijuana Reform Act
N.Y. Penal Law 1965 (Consol. Laws Ch. 40) §§ 221.00 et seq.,2411

Marijuana Tax Act of 1937
Aug. 2, 1937, Ch. 553, 50 Stat. 551

Marijuana Therapeutic Research and Use Act
Me. Rev. Stat. Ann. 1964, Title 22, §§ 2401 et seq., 2411 et seq.
S.C. Code Ann. 1976, § 44-53-610 et seq.

Marin County Flood Control and Water Conservation District Act
Cal. Water Code Appendix, § 68-1 et seq.

Marin County Transit District Act
Cal. Public Utilities Code § 70000 et seq.

Marina and Boatyard Storage Act
Me. Rev. Stat. Ann. 1964, Title 10, § 1381 et seq.

Marine and Fire Insurance Act
Ill. Rev. Stat. 1991, Ch. 73, § 1005 et seq.

Marine Conservation Law of the Town of Huntington
N.Y. Local Laws 1970, Town of Huntington, p. 1875

Marine Corps Personnel Act
May 29, 1934, Ch. 367, 48 Stat. 809

Marine Fisheries Act
N.C. Gen. Stat. 1943, § 143B-289.1 et seq.

Marine Fisheries Compact (Atlantic States)
Me. Rev. Stat. Ann. 1964, Title 12, § 4601 et seq.

Marine Fisheries Compact Act
Wash. Rev. Code Ann., 75.40.030

Marine Fisheries Compact Act (Atlantic States)
See Atlantic States Marine Fisheries Compact Act

Marine Fisheries Compact Act (Gulf States)
See Gulf States Marine Fisheries Compact Act

Marine Fisheries Compact Act (Pacific)
See Pacific Marine Fisheries Compact Act

Marine Fisheries Management and Commercial Fisheries Act
N.J. Stat. Ann., 23:2B-1 et seq.

Marine Fuel Tax Act
Ind. Code Ann., 6-6-1.1-101 et seq.
Mich. Comp. Laws Ann., 281.509

Marine Highway Authority Act
Alaska Stat. 1962, § 19.55.010 et seq.

Marine, Inland Marine and Fire Rate Regulatory Act
Pa. Purdon's Stat., Title 40, § 1221 et seq.

Marine Insurance Act
D.C. Code Ann., § 35-1401 et seq.

Marine Insurance Act (District of Columbia)
March 4, 1922, Ch. 93, 42 Stat. 401

Marine Insurance Underwriting Profits Tax Act
Pa. Purdon's Stat., Title 72, § 2281 et seq.

Marine Law of the Town of Brookhaven

N.Y. Local Laws 1967, Brookhaven, p. 1317

Marine Litter Act

Miss. Code Ann. 1972, § 51-2-1 et seq.

Marine Mammal Health and Screening Response Act

Nov. 4, 1992, P.L. 102-587, 16 U.S. Code § 1361 nt.

Marine Mammal Protection Act

Oct. 11, 1996, P.L. 104-297, 16 U.S. Code § 1362

Oct. 21, 1998, P.L. 105-277, 16 U.S. Code § 1374

Ala. Code 1975, § 9-11-390 et seq.

Marine Mammal Protection Act Amendments of 1988

Nov. 23, 1988, P.L. 100-711, 16 U.S. Code § 1361 nt.

Marine Mammal Protection Act Amendments of 1994

April 30, 1994, P.L. 103-238, 16 U.S. Code § 1361 nt.

Jan. 6, 1996, P.L. 104-91, 110 Stat. 8

Marine Mammal Protection Act of 1972

Oct. 21, 1972, P.L. 92-522, 86 Stat. 1027, 16 U.S. Code §§ 1361, 1362, 1371 to 1384, 1401 to 1407

Dec. 28, 1973, P.L. 93-205, 87 Stat. 902, 16 U.S. Code §§ 1362, 1371, 1372, 1402

Oct. 18, 1977, P.L. 95-136, 16 U.S. Code § 1380 et seq.

July 10, 1978, P.L. 95-316, 16 U.S. Code § 1379 et seq.

July 17, 1984, P.L. 98-364, 16 U.S. Code §§ 1371, 1374, 1401, 1406

Nov. 14, 1986, P.L. 99-659, 16 U.S. Code § 1371

Nov. 23, 1988, P.L. 100-711, 16 U.S. Code §§ 1371, 1372, 1374, 1378 to 1380, 1383a, 1383b, 1384, 1384 nt., 1407

Nov. 28, 1990, P.L. 101-627, 16 U.S. Code § 1371

March 9, 1992, P.L. 102-251, 16 U.S. Code § 1362

Oct. 26, 1992, P.L. 102-523, 16 U.S. Code §§ 1362, 1411 to 1418

Nov. 2, 1992, P.L. 102-582, 16 U.S. Code §§ 1362, 1371

Nov. 4, 1992, P.L. 102-587, 16 U.S. Code §§ 1362, 1372, 1379, 1382, prec. 1421, 1421 to 1421h

Sept. 21, 1993, P.L. 103-86, 16 U.S. Code § 1383a

March 31, 1994, P.L. 103-228, 16 U.S. Code § 1383a

April 30, 1994, P.L. 103-238, 16 U.S. Code §§ 1361 et seq., 1407, 1421 et seq.

June 12, 1997, P.L. 105-18, 16 U.S. Code §§ 1371, 1374

Aug. 15, 1997, P.L. 105-42, 16 U.S. Code §§ 1362, 1371, 1374, 1378, 1380, 1411 to 1414, 1414a, 1415 to 1418

Marine Mineral Resources Research Act of 1996

Oct. 19, 1996, P.L. 104-325, 30 U.S. Code § 1901 nt.

Marine Parkway Authority Act

N.Y. Public Authorities Law (Consol. Laws Ch. 43A) § 250 et seq.

Marine Pilotage Act

Alaska Stat. 1962, § 08.62.010 et seq.

Marine Plastic Pollution Research and Control Act of 1987

Dec. 29, 1987, P.L. 100-220, 33 U.S. Code §§ 1901 nt., 1901 et seq.

Nov. 11, 1988, P.L. 100-688, 33 U.S. Code § 2267 nt.

Dec. 21, 1995, P.L. 104-66, 33 U.S. Code § 1902 nt.

Oct. 19, 1996, P.L. 104-324, 33 U.S. Code §§ 1902 nt., 1914; 42 U.S. Code § 6981 nt.

Marine Protection, Research, and Sanctuaries Act of 1972

Oct. 23, 1972, P.L. 92-532, 86 Stat. 1052, 16 U.S. Code §§ 1431 to 1434; 33 U.S. Code §§ 1401, 1402, 1411 to 1421, 1441 to 1444

March 22, 1974, P.L. 93-254, 88 Stat. 56, 33 U.S. Code §§ 1401, 1402, 1411, 1412

Nov. 4, 1977, P.L. 95-153, 33 U.S. Code §§ 1420, 1444 et seq.

Aug. 29, 1980, P.L. 96-332, 16 U.S. Code § 1431 et seq.

Dec. 21, 1982, P.L. 97-375, 16 U.S. Code § 1432

Continued

Jan. 6, 1983, P.L. 97-424, 33 U.S. Code
§ 1414

Oct. 19, 1984, P.L. 98-498, 16 U.S. Code
§§ 1431 to 1439

April 7, 1986, P.L. 99-272, 33 U.S. Code
§§ 1441 to 1445

Oct. 17, 1986, P.L. 99-499, 33 U.S. Code
§ 1416

April 2, 1987, P.L. 100-4, 33 U.S. Code
§ 1414

Oct. 28, 1988, P.L. 100-536, 33 U.S. Code
§ 1420

Nov. 7, 1988, P.L. 100-627, 16 U.S. Code
§§ 1432, 1434, 1437 to 1445; 33 U.S. Code
§§ 1442, 1444, 1445

Nov. 11, 1988, P.L. 100-688, 33 U.S. Code
§§ 1402, 1412, 1414a to 1414c, 1415

Nov. 16, 1990, P.L. 101-593, 16 U.S. Code
§§ 1447 to 1447f, prec. 1450

Nov. 16, 1990, P.L. 101-596, 33 U.S. Code
§ 1416

Nov. 16, 1990, P.L. 101-605, 16 U.S. Code
§ 1444

Oct. 29, 1992, P.L. 102-567, 33 U.S. Code
§§ prec. 2801, 2801 to 2805

Oct. 31, 1992, P.L. 102-580, 33 U.S. Code
§§ 1412 to 1416, 1420, 1421

Nov. 4, 1992, P.L. 102-587, 16 U.S. Code
§§ 1431 to 1437, 1440, 1442 to 1444, 1445a

Oct. 12, 1996, P.L. 104-303, 33 U.S. Code
§ 1412

Marine Recreation Land Act
Wash. Rev. Code Ann., 43.99.010 et seq.

**Marine Resources and Engineering
Development Act of 1966**
June 17, 1966, P.L. 89-454, 80 Stat. 203, 33
U.S. Code §§ 1101 to 1108

Oct. 15, 1966, P.L. 89-670, 80 Stat. 943, 33
U.S. Code § 1102

Oct. 15, 1966, P.L. 89-688, 80 Stat. 998, 33
U.S. Code §§ 1101 nt., 1103, 1104, 1107,
1108, 1121 to 1124

Jan. 2, 1968, P.L. 90-242, 81 Stat. 780, 33
U.S. Code §§ 1102, 1104

Aug. 11, 1968, P.L. 90-477, 82 Stat. 704, 33
U.S. Code §§ 1122, 1123

May 23, 1969, P.L. 91-15, 83 Stat. 10, 33
U.S. Code §§ 1102, 1108

Sept. 25, 1970, P.L. 91-414, 84 Stat. 865, 33
U.S. Code § 1102

Aug. 22, 1986, P.L. 99-386, 33 U.S. Code
§ 1106

**Marine Resources Conservation and
Development Act**
Cal. Government Code § 8800 et seq.

Marine Resources Protection Act
Cal. Const. 1879, Art. 10B, § 1 et seq.

Marine Safety Act
Mich. Comp. Laws Ann., 281.1001 et seq.

Marine Sanctuaries Amendments of 1984
Oct. 19, 1984, P.L. 98-498, 16 U.S. Code
§ 1431 nt.

**Marine Science, Technology, and Policy
Development Act of 1987**
Dec. 29, 1987, P.L. 100-220, 33 U.S. Code
§§ 883a nt., 1121 to 1131

**Marine Seafood Processing Revolving Loan
Fund Act**
Mass. Gen. Laws Ann., 23A:29, 23A:30,
23A:38A to 23A:38C

Marine Turtle Protection Act
Fla. Stat. Ann., 370.12

Marine War-Risk Insurance Act
See Merchant Maring Act, 1936

**Marion County Hospital District Revenue
Bond Act**
Fla. Special Laws 1971, Ch. 71-764

Marion duPont Scott Memorial Act
S.C. Code Ann. 1976, § 52-5-100 et seq.

**Marion National Fish Hatchery and Claude
Harris National Aquacultural Research
Center Conveyance Act**
Sept. 23, 1998, P.L. 105-239, 112 Stat. 1564

**Mariposa County Municipal Court District
Act**
Cal. Government Code § 73783.1 et seq.

Mariposa County Water Agency Act
Cal. Statutes 1959, Ch. 2036, p. 4685
Cal. Water Code Appendix, § 85-1 et seq.

MARIS (Mississippi Automated Resource Information System)
Miss. Code Ann. 1972, § 57-13-23

Marital Agreement Act
Colo. Rev. Stat., 14-2-301 et seq.

Marital and Family Therapist Licensure Act
N.C. Gen. Stat. 1943, § 90-270.45 et seq.
Okla. Stat. Ann., Title 59, § 1925.1 et seq.
S.C. Code Ann. 1976, § 40-75-10 et seq.

Marital or Parent and Child Long-Arm Jurisdiction and Uniform Child Custody Jurisdiction Amendments Act
D.C. Code Ann., § 16-4501 et seq.

Marital Privilege Act (Evidence)
Cal. Evidence Code § 970 et seq.
Colo. Code of Civil Procedure § 1881

Marital Property Act
Ida. Code 1947, 32-901 et seq.

Marital Property Equitable Distribution Law
N.Y. Domestic Relations Law (Consol. Laws Ch. 14) § 236
N.Y. General Obligations Law (Consol. Laws Ch. 24A) § 5-311
N.Y. Laws 1980, Ch. 281

Marital Relations Act
Ala. Code 1975, § 30-1-3 et seq.

Maritime Academy Act of 1958
Aug. 18, 1958, P.L. 85-672, 72 Stat. 622, 46 U.S. Code §§ 1381 to 1388
July 9, 1971, P.L. 92-53, 85 Stat. 146, 46 U.S. Code § 1382
Nov. 12, 1977, P.L. 95-173, 46 U.S. Code § 1383 et seq.
June 26, 1978, P.L. 95-298, 46 U.S. Code § 1382

Maritime Act of 1981
Aug. 6, 1981, P.L. 97-31, 46 U.S. Code § 1601 nt.
Nov. 23, 1988, P.L. 100-710, 46 U.S. Code Appx. § 1606

Maritime and Airport Plant Quarantine, Inspection and Protection Act
Cal. Statutes 1990, Ch. 1612

Maritime Appropriation Authorization Act for Fiscal Year 1980
Nov. 16, 1979, P.L. 96-112, 46 U.S. Code §§ 833, 922

Maritime Appropriation Authorization Act of 1975
Nov. 13, 1975, P.L. 94-127, 89 Stat. 680, 46 U.S. Code §§ 1213(a), 1273(f)

Maritime Appropriation Authorization Act of 1978
Nov. 12, 1977, P.L. 95-173, 46 U.S. Code § 1383 et seq.

Maritime Drug Law Enforcement Act
Sept. 15, 1980, P.L. 99-350, 46 U.S. Code Appx. §§ 1901 to 1903
Nov. 29, 1990, P.L. 101-647, 46 U.S. Code Appx. § 1903
Oct. 19, 1996, P.L. 104-324, 46 U.S. Code Appx. § 1903

Maritime Drug Law Enforcement Prosecution Improvements Act of 1986
Oct. 27, 1986, P.L. 99-570, 46 U.S. Code Appx. § 1901 nt.

Maritime Education and Training Act of 1980
Oct. 15, 1980, P.L. 96-453, 46 U.S. Code § 1295 nt.

Maritime Labor Agreements Act of 1980
Aug. 8, 1980, P.L. 96-325, 46 U.S. Code §§ 801 et seq.

Maritime Labor Board Act
See Merchant Marine Act

Maritime Lien Act
Miss. Code Ann. 1972, § 85-7-7

Maritime Reserve Act (Long Island Pine Barrens)
N.Y. Environmental Conservation Law (Consol. Law Ch. 43B) § 57-0101 et seq.

Maritime Safety Act of 1984
   Oct. 19, 1984, P.L. 98-498, 46 U.S. Code § 3301 nt.

Maritime Security Act of 1996
   Oct. 8, 1996, P.L. 104-239, 46 U.S. Code Appx. § 1245 nt.

Maritime Shipping Authority Act
   P.R. Laws Ann. 1954, Title 23, § 3051 et seq.

Marjory Stoneman Douglas Everglades Protection Act
   Fla. Stat. Ann., 373.4592

Marjory Stoneman Douglas Wilderness and Ernest F. Coe Visitor Center Designation Act
   Nov. 13, 1997, P.L. 105-82, 16 U.S. Code § 410r-5 nt.

Market Act
   Ga. Code Ann., 2-10-50

Market Agent Act
   Ore. Code 1991, §§ 18-2201 to 18-2213

Market Assistance Association Act (Insurance)
   Okla. Stat. 1981, Title 36, § 6411

Market Assistance Association Act (Surety)
   Okla. Stat. Ann., Title 36, § 6423 et seq.

Market Authority Act
   Mich. Comp. Laws Ann., 123.671 et seq.

Market Authority Act (Farmer's)
   Ga. Code Ann., 2-10-1 et seq.

Market Based Medicaid Reform Act
   Ga. Code Ann., 49-4-152.4

Market Commission Act
   Cal. Food and Agricultural Code § 58001 et seq.

Market Demand Act (Oil and Gas)
   Tex. Natural Resources Code, § 85.001 et seq.

Market Development Act (Alligators)
   La. Rev. Stat. Ann., 3:599 et seq.

Market Development Act (Beef)
   Ill. Comp. Stat. 1992, Ch. 505, § 25/1 et seq.

Market Development Act (Livestock Auction)
   Neb. Rev. Stat. 1943, 54-1157 et seq.

Market Rate Consumer Loan Act
   N.J. Stat. Ann., 17:3B-4 et seq.

Market Reform Act of 1990
   Oct. 16, 1990, P.L. 101-432, 15 U.S. Code § 78a nt.

Market Road Act
   Ore. Rev. Stat., 369.020, 369.025

Market Sharing Act (Natural Gas)
   Okla. Stat. Ann., Title 52, § 581.1 et seq.

Marketable Record Title Act
   Kan. Stat. Ann., 58-3401 et seq.

Marketable Title Act
   Conn. Gen. Stat. Ann., § 47-33b et seq.
   Fla. Stat. Ann., 712.01 et seq.
   Ill. Rev. Stat. 1991, Ch. 110, § 13-101 et seq.
   Ind. Code Ann., 32-1-5-1 et seq.
   Iowa Code Ann., 614.17 et seq.
   Mass. Gen Laws 1990, 184:26 et seq.
   Mich. Comp. Laws Ann., 565.101 et seq.
   Minn. Stat. Ann., 541.023
   N.C. Gen. Stat. 1943, § 47B-1 et seq.
   N.D. Cent. Code, 447-19.1-01 et seq.
   Neb. Rev. Stat. 1943, 76-288 et seq.
   N.Y. Real Property Law (Consol. Laws, Ch. 50), §§ 250 et seq., 345
   Ohio Rev. Code 1953, 5301.47 et seq.
   Okla. Stat. Ann., Title 16, § 71 et seq.
   S.D. Codified Laws 1967, 43-30-1 et seq.
   Utah Code Ann. 1953, 57-9-1 et seq.
   Wis. Stat. Ann., 893.15

Marketable Title Act (Forty Years)
   Iowa Code 1983, 614.17 et seq.
   Mich. Comp. Laws Ann., 565.101 et seq.

Marketing Act (Agricultural Commodities)
S.C. Code Ann. 1976, § 46-17-10 et seq.

Marketing Act (Agricultural Cooperative)
Haw. Rev. Stat. Ann., § 421-1 et seq.

Marketing Act (Agricultural)
Ala. Code 1975, § 2-10-20 et seq.
Cal. Food and Agricultural Code 1967,
§ 58601 et seq.
Colo. Rev. Stat., 7-56-101 et seq., 35-28-101
et seq.
Haw. Rev. Stat. Ann., § 163-1 et seq.
Mich. Comp. Laws Ann., 290.651 et seq.
Okla. Stat. Ann., Title 2, § 5-1 et seq.
Ore. Rev. Stat., 576.006 et seq.
Tex. Agriculture Code, § 52.001 et seq.
Va. Code 1950, § 3.1-47 et seq.
Wis. Stat. Ann., 96.01 et seq.
Wyo. Stat. Ann., § 11-35-101 et seq.

Marketing Act (Apple and Peach)
Ill. Comp. Stat. 1992, Ch. 505, § 20/1 et seq.

Marketing Act (Apples)
Me. Rev. Stat. Ann. 1964, Title 7, § 531 et
seq.

Marketing Act (Celery and Sweet Corn)
Fla. Stat. Ann., 573.101 et seq.

Marketing Act (Citrus)
Fla. Stat. Ann., 600.011 et seq.

Marketing Act (Cooperative)
See Cooperative Marketing Act

Marketing Act (Dairy)
Wyo. Stat. Ann., § 11-36-101 et seq.

Marketing Act (Farm Products)
Ill. Rev. Stat. 1991, Ch. 5, §§ 90z, 91

Marketing Act (Fish)
Me. Rev. Stat. Ann. 1964, Title 13, § 2001 et
seq.

Marketing Act (Flue-Cured Tobacco)
Fla. Stat. Ann., 573.857 et seq.

Marketing Act (Foliage Plants)
Fla. Stat. Ann., 573.50 et seq.

Marketing Act (Fresh Fruit and Vegetable)
Ill. Rev. Stat. 1991, Ch. 5, § 138.2 et seq.

Marketing Act (Motor Fuel)
Ala. Acts 1984, p. 433
N.C. Gen. Stat. 1943, § 75-80 et seq.

Marketing Act (Peanuts)
Fla. Stat. Ann., 573.883 et seq.

Marketing Act (Potatoes)
Me. Rev. Stat. Ann. 1964, Title 7, § 991 et
seq.

Marketing Act (Regional Tourism)
Mich. Comp. Laws Ann., 141.891 et seq.

Marketing Act (Soybeans)
Fla. Stat. Ann., 573.830 et seq.

Marketing Act (Telecommunications)
Ga. Code Ann., 46-5-180 et seq.

Marketing Act (Watermelons)
Fla. Stat. Ann., 573.801 et seq.

Marketing and Business Act (Public Livestock)
Ala. Code 1975, § 2-15-115

Marketing and Development Act (Salmon)
Cal. Food and Agricultural Code 1967,
§ 76501 et seq.

Marketing and Distribution Act (Motor and Special Fuel)
Iowa Code Ann., 323.1 et seq.

Marketing and Energy Education Act
Okla. Stat. Ann., Title 52, § 288.1 et seq.

Marketing and Fair Practices Act (Agricultural)
Wash. Rev. Code Ann., 15.83.005 et seq.

Marketing and Labeling Act (Strawberries)
Ky. Rev. Stat. 1971, 260.010, 260.090 et
seq., 260.130

Marketing and Stabilization of Fluid Milk and Cream Act
Cal. Food and Agricultural Code 1967, § 61801 et seq. § 62730 et seq.

Marketing Associations Law (Agricultural Cooperative)
Miss. Code Ann. 1972, § 79-19-1 et seq.

Marketing Authority Law
Wis. Stat. Ann., 100.01 et seq.

Marketing Bureau Act (Agriculture)
Mo. Rev. Stat., 261.030 et seq.

Marketing Cooperative Act
Mont. Code Ann., 35-17-101 et seq.

Marketing District Act (Local)
Colo. Rev. Stat., 29-25-101 et seq.

Marketing for Milk and Milk Products Act
S.C. Code Ann. 1976, § 39-33-1710 et seq.

Marketing Fresh Fruits and Vegetables Act
Ill. Rev. Stat. 1991, Ch. 5, § 139 et seq.

Marketing Law (Agricultural Commodities)
Fla. Stat. Ann., 573.101 et seq.

Marketing Law (Milk)
N.Y. Agriculture and Markets Law (Consol. Laws Ch. 69) § 258c

Marketing of Agricultural Products and Industry Program Act
Miss. Code Ann. 1972, § 69-1-101 et seq.

Marketing Practice Act
Tex. Health and Safety Code, § 164.001 et seq.

Marketing Quotas Act
See Agricultural Adjustment Act of 1938

Marketing Research Act (Agricultural)
Ind. Code Ann., 15-4-2-1 et seq.

Marketing Seller-Assisted Plan Act
Neb. Rev. Stat. 1943, 59-1701 to 59-1761

Marketing Unfair Practices Act (Agricultural)
Wash. Rev. Code Ann., 15.83.005 et seq.

Markets Act
Ala. Code 1975, § 2-11-1 et seq.

Markets Act (Public)
See Public Markets Act

Markets Board Act
Ala. Code 1975, § 2-3-20 et seq.

Marks and Brands Act
Wash. Rev. Code Ann., 9.16.010 et seq., 16.57.010 et seq, 19.76.100 et seq.

Marks and Brands Act (Forest Products)
Wash. Rev. Code Ann., 76.36.010 et seq.

Marks and Serial Numbers Act
Ill. Rev. Stat. 1991, Ch. 121 1/2, §§ 157.13, 157.13a

Marks-Badham Environmental Protection and Research Act
Cal. Health and Safety Code § 39069 et seq.
Cal. Vehicle Code 1959, § 5100 et seq.

Marks-Foran Residential Rehabilitation Act
Cal. Health and Safety Code § 37910 et seq.

Marks Historical Rehabilitation Act
Cal. Health and Safety Code § 37600 et seq.

Marks-Mello-Vasconcellos Service Credit Act
Cal. Welfare and Institutions Code § 9500 et seq.

Marks-Roos-Johnson Property Tax Limitation Act
Cal. Revenue and Tax Code §§ 97.2, 97.65

Marks-Roose Local Bond Pooling Act
Cal. Government Code § 6584 et seq.

Marks-Slater Act (Monroe County Taxes)
N.Y. Laws 1933, Ch. 833

Marland Act (Income Tax Refund)
Okla. Laws 1937, p. 461

Marlborough Sewerage Loan Act
Mass. Acts 1962, Ch. 355

Marlborough Water Loan Act
Mass. Acts 1959, Ch. 518

Marler-Johnson Highway-Park Act
Cal. Government Code § 14012

Marler-Quimby Instructional Television Act
Cal. Education Code 1976, § 51870 et seq.

Marquette-Jolliet Trail Act
Ill. Rev. Stat. 1991, Ch. 121, § 390.9 et seq.

Marriage Act (Three Day)
Mass. Gen. Laws Ann., 207:19 et seq.

Marriage and Dissolution of Marriage Act
Ill. Rev. Stat. 1991, Ch. 40, § 101 et seq.

Marriage and Divorce Act
See also Uniform Marriage and Divorce Act
Ala. Code 1975, § 30-1-3 et seq.
Alaska Stat. 1962, § 25.05.011 et seq.
Ark. Code Ann. 1987, 9-11-101 et seq.
Cal. Civil Code § 4100 et seq.
Colo. Rev. Stat., 14-2-101 et seq.
D.C. Laws 1977, No. 1-107
Fla. Stat. Ann., 741.01 et seq.
Ga. Code Ann., 19-3-1 et seq.
Ind. Code Ann., 31-7-1-1 et seq.
Kan. Stat. Ann., 23-101 et seq.
Ky. Rev. Stat. 1971, 403.110 et seq.
La. Civil Code, Art. 86 et seq.
Md. Ann. Code 1974, Art. FL, § 2-101 et seq.
Mich. Comp. Laws Ann., 551.2 et seq.
Miss. Code Ann. 1972, § 93-1-1 et seq.
Nev. Rev. Stat. 1979 Reprint, 122.010 et seq.
N.H. Rev. Stat. 1955, 457:1 et seq.
N.J. Stat. Ann., 2A:34-1 et seq.
N.Y. Domestic Relations Law (Consol. Laws Ch. 14) § 5 et seq.
Ohio Rev. Code 1953, 3101.01 et seq.
Okla. Stat. Ann., Title 43, § 1 et seq.
Pa. Cons. Stat., Title 23, § 1101 et seq.

R.I. Gen. Laws 1956, 15-1-1 et seq.
S.C. Code Ann. 1976, § 20-1-30 et seq.
Tenn. Code Ann., 36-3-101 et seq.
Tex. Family Code, § 1.01 et seq.
Vt. Stat. Ann., Title 15, § 1 et seq.
Wash. Rev. Code Ann., 26.04.010 et seq.
Wis. Stat. Ann., 765.001 et seq.
Wyo. Stat. Ann., § 20-1-101 et seq.

Marriage and Divorce Act (Uniform)
Ariz. Rev. Stat. Ann., § 25-311 et seq.

Marriage and Family Counselor Licensing Act
Utah Code Ann. 1953, 58-39-1 et seq.

Marriage and Family Therapist Licensing Act
Ga. Code Ann., 43-10A-1 et seq.
Ill. Rev. Stat. 1991, Ch. 111, § 8351-1 et seq.
Kan. Stat. Ann., 65-6401 et seq.
Tex. Rev. Civ. Stat., Art. 4512c-1
Utah Code Ann. 1953, 58-60-301 et seq.

Marriage and Family Therapists Registration Act
Kan. Stat. Ann., 65-6401 et seq.

Marriage and Family Therapy Licensure Act
Ala. Code 1975, § 34-17A-1 et seq.
Miss. Code Ann. 1972, § 73-54-1 et seq.

Marriage Annulment Act
See Annulment Act (Marriage)

Marriage Blood Test Act
Colo. Rev. Stat., 14-2-106

Marriage Counseling Act
N.J. Stat. Ann., 45:8B-1 et seq.
Utah Code Ann. 1953, 30-3-12 et seq.

Marriage Counseling Certification Act
Mich. Comp. Laws Ann., 338.1031 et seq.

Marriage Counseling Service Act
Mich. Comp. Laws Ann., 551.331 et seq.

Marriage Dissolution Act
Colo. Rev. Stat., 14-10-101 et seq.
Fla. Stat. Ann., 61.001 et seq.
Ill. Rev. Stat. 1991, Ch. 40, § 101 et seq.
Ind. Code Ann., 31-1-11.5-1 et seq.
Iowa Code Ann., 598.1 et seq.
Ky. Rev. Stat. 1971, 403.010, 403.110 et seq.
Mo. Rev. Stat., 452.300 et seq.
Wash. Rev. Code Ann., 26.09.010 et seq.

Marriage, Dissolution, and Invalidity Records Act
Ill. Rev. Stat. 1991, Ch. 40, § 900 et seq.

Marriage Evasion Act
D.C. Code 1973, § 30-105
Ill. Rev. Stat. 1991, Ch. 40, § 216 et seq.
La. Rev. Stat. Ann., 9:221 et seq.
Mass. Gen Laws 1990, 207:10 et seq.
Miss. Code Ann. 1972, § 93-1-3
Vt. Stat. Ann., Title 15, §§ 5, 6
Wis. Stat. Ann., 765.04

Marriage, Family, and Child Counselors Act
Cal. Business and Professions Code §§ 4980, 17801 et seq.

Marriage Legalizing Act
S.C. Code Ann. 1976, §§ 20-1-30, 20-1-40

Marriage License Act
Cal. Civil Code § 4201
Ga. Code Ann., 19-3-30 et seq.
Mich. Comp. Laws Ann., 551.101 et seq.
N.Y. Domestic Relations Law (Consol. Laws Ch. 14) § 13 et seq.
Pa. 1885 Pamph. Laws 146, No. 115
Pa. 1939 Pamph. Laws 148, No. 76
Wis. Stat. Ann., 765.12 et seq.

Marriage License Application Act
Okla. Stat. Ann., Title 43, § 4 et seq.

Marriage Penalty Repeal Act
Ga. Code Ann., 48-7-20

Marriage Preparation and Preservation Act
Fla. Laws 1998, Ch. 403, §§ 1 to 16

Marriage Protection Act
Ala. Laws 1998, S.B. 71

Marriage Registry Act
Ill. Rev. Stat. 1991, Ch. 40, § 900

Marriage Relationship Act
Tex. Family Code, § 1.001 et seq.

Marriage Statistics Act
La. Rev. Stat. Ann., 9:261 et seq.

Married Persons Act
N.J. Stat. Ann., 37:2-1 et seq.

Married Person's Property Act
Pa. 1887 Pamph. Laws 332, No. 224

Married Woman's Enabling Act
Ark. Code Ann. 1987, 9-11-502 et seq.

Married Woman's Scheduling Act
Ark. Code Ann. 1987, 9-11-509 et seq.

Married Women Enabling Act
N.Y. Domestic Relations Law (Consol. Laws Ch. 14) § 50 et seq.

Married Women's Act
Ala. Code 1975, § 30-4-1 et seq.
Alaska Stat. 1962, § 25.15.010 et seq.
Ariz. Rev. Stat. Ann., § 25-214
Cal. Civil Code § 5100 et seq.
Colo. Rev. Stat., 14-2-201 et seq.
Conn. Gen. Stat. Ann., § 46b-36
D.C. Code Ann., § 30-201
Del. Code of 1974, Title 13, § 311 et seq.
Fla. Stat. Ann., 708.08 et seq.
Ga. Code Ann., 19-3-9
Haw. Rev. Stat. Ann., § 573-1 et seq.
Ida. Code 1947, 32-903 et seq.
Ill. Rev. Stat. 1991, Ch. 40, §§ 1000 et seq., 1009
Ind. Code Ann., 31-7-10-1 et seq.
Iowa Code Ann., 597.1 et seq.
Kan. Stat. Ann., 23-201 et seq.
Ky. Rev. Stat. 1971, 404.010 et seq.
La. Rev. Stat. Ann., 9:103 et seq.
Mass. Gen Laws 1990, 209:1 et seq.
Md. Ann. Code 1974, Art. FL, § 4-101 et seq.

Me. Rev. Stat. Ann. 1964, Title 19, § 161 et seq.

Mich. Comp. Laws Ann., 557.1 et seq.

Minn. Stat. Ann., 519.01 et seq.

Miss. Code Ann. 1972, § 93-3-1 et seq.

Mo. Rev. Stat., 451.250 et seq.

Mont. Code Ann., 40-2-201 et seq.

N.C. Gen. Stat. 1943, § 52-1 et seq.

N.D. Cent. Code, 14-07-04 et seq.

Neb. Rev. Stat. 1943, 42-201 et seq.

Nev. Rev. Stat. 1979 Reprint, 123.010 et seq.

N.H. Rev. Stat. 1955, 460:1 et seq.

N.J. Stat. Ann., 37:2-1 et seq.

N.M. Stat. Ann., 38-4-6

N.Y. Domestic Relations Law (Consol. Laws Ch. 14) § 50 et seq.

Okla. Stat. Ann., Title 43, § 214

Ore. Rev. Stat., 108.010 et seq.

Pa. Purdon's Stat., Title 48, § 32.1 et seq.

R.I. Gen. Laws 1956, 15-4-1 et seq.

S.C. Code Ann. 1976, § 20-5-10 et seq.

S.D. Codified Laws 1967, 25-2-7, 25-2-15

Tenn. Code Ann., 36-3-504

Tex. Family Code, § 5.01 et seq.

Utah Code Ann. 1953, 30-2-1 et seq.

Va. Code 1950, § 55-35 et seq.

Vt. Stat. Ann., Title 15, § 61 et seq.

Wash. Rev. Code 1971, 26.16.150 et seq.

W. Va. Code 1966, § 48-3-1 et seq.

Wyo. Stat. Ann., § 20-1-201 et seq.

Married Women's Citizenship Act
Sept. 22, 1922, Ch. 411, 42 Stat. 1021

Married Women's Emancipation Act
Ark. Code Ann. 1987, 9-11-502 et seq.

Fla. Stat. Ann., 708.08 et seq.

La. Rev. Stat. Ann., 9:101 et seq.

N.C. Gen. Stat. 1943, § 52-2

Ohio Rev. Code 1953, 3103.01 et seq.

Tenn. Code Ann., 36-3-501 et seq.

Tex. Family Code, § 4.03

Married Women's Life Insurance Act
Ill. Rev. Stat. 1935, Ch. 73, § 231

N.H. Rev. Stat. 1955, 408:1

Married Women's Rights Act
D.C. Code 1973, § 30-201 et seq.

Ill. Rev. Stat. 1991, Ch. 40, § 1000 et seq.

Wis. Stat. Ann., 766.001 et seq.

Married Women's Rights Act (District of Columbia)
June 1, 1896, Ch. 303, 29 Stat. 193

Marsh and Tidelands Quiet Title Act
Cal. Statutes 1941, Ch. 1262, p. 3208

Marsh-Billings National Historical Park Establishment Act
Aug. 26, 1992, P.L. 102-350, 16 U.S. Code § 410vv nt.

Nov. 2, 1994, P.L. 103-437, 16 U.S. Code § 410vv-7

Marshall Act (Arbitration)
Ohio Rev. Code 1953, 2711.01 et seq.

Marshall Act (Fees)
Ohio Laws Vol. 112, p. 269

Marshall Act (Loans)
Ohio Laws Vol. 113, p. 43

Marshall Act (Motor Vehicles)
Ohio Laws Vol. 114, p. 815

Marshall-Jones Act (Corporations)
Ohio Laws Vol. 113, p. 413

Marshall Plan
See Foreign Assistance Act of 1948

Marshfield Riprap Loan Act
Mass. Acts 1957, Ch. 341

Marshfield Sea Wall Loan Act
Mass. Acts 1957, Ch. 340

Marshfield Tide Gate Loan Act
Mass. Acts 1962, Ch. 464

Marshlands Protection Act (Coastal)
Ga. Code Ann., 12-5-280 et seq.

Martha's Vineyard Act (Land Use)
Mass. Acts 1974, Ch. 637

Martin (Joseph F.)-Brown Act (Agricultural Research)
Mich. Comp. Laws Ann., 390.161

Martin Act (Conspiracy)
Ky. Rev. Stat. 1971, Superseded Vol., 437.110 et seq.

Martin Act (Conversion of Rental Status to Cooperative or Condominium Ownership)
N.Y. General Business Law (Consol. Laws Ch. 20) § 352eeee

Martin Act (Fraudulent Securities Practices)
N.Y. General Business Law (Consol. Laws Ch. 20) § 352 et seq.

Martin Act (Married Women's Contracts)
N.C. Gen. Stat. 1943, § 52-2

Martin Act (Tax Arrears)
N.J. Stat. Ann., 54:6-1 to 54:6-3

Martin and Washington Counties Peace Officers' Relief Act
N.C. Laws 1953, Ch. 402

Martin-Baer Act (Alcoholic Study Commission)
Ky. Acts 1952, Ch. 32

Martin County Environmental Control Act
Fla. Special Laws 1978, Ch. 78-560

Martin-Estes-Campbell Act
Ala. Code 1975, §§ 32-6-150, 32-6-156

Martin-Herbert-Morgan Act (Elections)
Ohio Rev. Code 1953, 3501.01 et seq.

Martin J. Duffy, Jr.Installment Sales Act
Ky. Rev. Stat. 1971, 371.210 et seq.

Martin Luther King, Jr. Federal Holiday Commission Extension Act
May 17, 1989, P.L. 101-30, 36 U.S. Code §§ 169j et seq., 169j nt.

Martin Luther King, Jr. Holiday Act
Ill. Comp Stat. 1992, Ch. 5, § 490/65

Martin Luther King, Jr. Institute for Nonviolence
N.Y. Executive Law 1951 (Consol. Laws Ch. 18) § 320 et seq.

Martin Luther King, Jr. Physician-Dentist Scholarship Act
N.J. Stat. Ann., 18A:72J-1 et seq.

Martin-Webb Act (Fraudulent Practices with Securities)
N.Y. General Business Law (Consol. Laws Ch. 20) § 352 et seq.

Martineau Road Law
Ark. Acts 1927, p. 17, No. 11

Martinsville Parking Authority Act
Va. Acts 1968, Ch. 365

Mary E. Burnett Act (Marriage Licenses)
Ky. Rev. Stat. 1971, 402.080

Maryland and Virginia Compact of 1785
Md. Laws 1785-86, Ch. 1

Maryland Home Improvement Law
Md. Ann. Code 1957, Art. 56, § 245 et seq.
Md. Ann. Code 1974, Art. BR, § 8-701 et seq.

Maryland-National Capital Park and Planning Commission Act
Md. Laws 1959, Ch. 780

Maryland-Washington Metropolitan District Act
Md. Laws 1943, Ch. 1008

Maryland-Washington Regional District Act
Md. Laws 1943, Ch. 992

MASAWPA
See Migrant and Seasonal Agricultural Worker Protection Act

Mascotte Revenue Bond Act
Fla. Special Laws 1955, Ch. 30977

Mashantucket Pequot Indian Claims Settlement Act

Oct. 18, 1983, P.L. 98-134, 25 U.S. Code § 1751 et seq.

Mask and Identity Concealment Laws

Cal. Penal Code § 185

Masked Gunman Act

Ill. Rev. Stat. 1991, Ch. 38, § 24-1, Subd. a

Masked Persons Act

Wash. Rev. Code 1974, 9.27.090, 9.27.100

Masks and Hoods Act

Okla. Stat. Ann., Title 21, § 1301 et seq.

Mason Act (Nonsuit)

N.C. Gen. Stat. 1943, § 15-173

Mason Act (Sale of Skin of Endangered Species)

N.Y. Environmental Conservation Law 1972 (Consol. Laws Ch. 43B) § 11-0536

Mason County Civic Center Law

Ill. Rev. Stat. 1991, Ch. 85, § 4701 et seq.

Mason County, Jasper County, Brownstown Park District, Jo Davies County, Milford, Sheldon, Katherine Dunham, Oak Park, Aledo, and Normal Civic Centers Act

Ill. Rev. Stat. 1991, Ch. 85, § 4500 et seq.

Mass Gathering Licensing Law

Ind. Code Ann., 16-1-42-1 et seq.

Mass Gatherings Act

N.Y. Local Laws 1972, Town of Horseheads, p. 1869

Tex. Health and Safety Code, § 751.001 et seq.

Mass Picketing Act (Labor)

Tex. Rev. Civ. Stat., Art. 5154d

Mass Transit Authorities Act

Vt. Stat. Ann., Title 24, § 5101 et seq.

Mass Transit Authority Act (Terrebonne Parish)

La. Rev. Stat. Ann., 48:1501 et seq.

Mass Transit District Act

Ill. Rev. Stat. 1991, Ch. 111 2/3, § 351 et seq.

Mass Transportation Act

Ind. Code Ann., 36-3-7-2 et seq.
N.M. Stat. Ann., 67-3-67 et seq.

Mass Transportation Assistance Law

Pa. Purdon's Stat., Title 74, § 1101 et seq.

Mass Transportation Authority Act

Ind. Code Ann., 36-3-1-9 et seq.

Mass Transportation Commission Act

Tex. Rev. Civ. Stat., Arts. 6663b, 6663c

Mass Transportation Financing Act

Ore. Rev. Stat., 267.227, 391.500 et seq.

Mass Transportation Study Commission Act

Ind. Code Ann., 4-23-13-1 et seq.

Massachusetts Bay Protection Act of 1988

Nov. 14, 1988, P.L. 100-653, 33 U.S. Code § 1251 nt.

Massachusetts Bay Transportation Authority Act

Mass. Gen. Laws Ann., 161A:1 et seq.

Massachusetts-New Hampshire Interstate Sewage and Waste Disposal Facilities Compact Act

N.H. Rev. Stat. 1955, 149-K:1

Massachusetts Trust Act

Tenn. Code Ann., 48-3-201 et seq.
Wash. Rev. Code Ann., 23.90.010 et seq.

Massage Act

N.M. Stat. Ann., 61-25-1 et seq.
S.D. Codified Laws 1967, 36-10A-1 et seq.

Massage Parlor Code

Colo. Rev. Stat., 12-48.5-101 et seq.

Massage Practice Act
Fla. Stat. Ann., 480.031 et seq.
Utah Code Ann. 1953, 58-47a-1 et seq.

Massage Registration Act
N.D. Cent. Code, 43-25-01 et seq.
Tenn. Code Ann., 63-18-101 et seq.
Tenn. Private Acts 1977, Ch. 20 (Unicoi County)
Tenn. Private Acts 1978, Ch. 276 (Carter County)
Tenn. Private Acts 1978, Ch. 282 (Johnson County)
Tenn. Private Acts 1979, Ch. 56

Massage Therapists and Massage Establishments Act
La. Rev. Stat. Ann., 37:3501 et seq.

Massage Therapy Act
Ark. Code Ann. 1987, 17-98-101 et seq.

Massage Therapy Licensure Act
Ala. Code 1975, § 34-43-1 et seq.
Tenn. Code Ann., 63-18-201 et seq.

Massage Therapy Practice Act
N.M. Stat. Ann., 61-12C-1 et seq.

Massage/Bodywork Practice Act
S.C. Code Ann. 1976, § 40-30-10 et seq.

Massage/Bodywork Practitioner Act (Professional)
Del. Code of 1974, Title 24, § 5301 et seq.

Massive Resistance Act (Schools)
Va. Code 1950, § 22-188.3 et seq.

Mastectomy Patient Care Act
Also known as Breast Cancer Patient Care Act
Ga. Code Ann., 33-24-70 et seq.

Master and Apprentice Act
Minn. Stat. Ann., 178.01 et seq.

Master and Servant Act
Haw. Session Laws 1850, p. 170, June 21, 1850

Master and Servant Liability Act
Ark. Code Ann. 1987, 11-8-103 et seq.

Master Electricians Act
Md. Ann. Code 1974, Art. BO, § 6-101 et seq.

Master Form Mortgage Act
Wyo. Stat. Ann., § 34-2-109 et seq.

Master Mortgage Act
Pa. Purdon's Stat., Title 21, § 629 et seq.

Master Mortgage or Deed of Trust Recording Act
Ark. Code Ann. 1987, 14-15-405 et seq.

Master Mortgage Recording Act
Conn. Gen. Stat. Ann., § 49-5a
Me. Rev. Stat. Ann. 1964, Title 33, § 207 et seq.

Master Plan Act (Capital Complex)
Mont. Code Ann., 2-17-801 et seq.

Master Plan Act (City-County)
Mont. Code Ann., 76-1-101 et seq.

Master Plan Act (Municipal Planning)
Mich. Comp. Laws Ann., 125.31 et seq.
Wis. Stat. Ann., 62.23, Subsec. 3

Master Settlement Agreement Plan (Tobacco)
Ida. Code 1947, 39-7801 et seq.

Master Teacher Act (Ryan)
Cal. Education Code 1976, § 44490 et seq.

Master Water Management District Act
Miss. Code Ann. 1972, § 51-7-1 et seq.

Masters in Chancery Act
Ill. Rev. Stat. 1963, Ch. 90, § 1 et seq.

Mastery Learning through Individualized Learning Plans Act
Minn. Stat. 1986, 129B.62 et seq.

Mastick Amendment (Grade Crossings)
N.Y. Const. 1894, Art. 7 § 14

Matching Assistance Act (Financially Disadvantaged Municipalities)
Pa. Purdon's Stat, Title 73, § 398.1 et seq.

Matching Grants for Scholarships Act
Ill. Rev. Stat. 1991, Ch. 144, § 270 et seq.

Material Transactions Disclosure Act
Mont. Code Ann., 33-3-701 et seq.

Material Witness Act
Tenn. Code Ann., 40-17-101 et seq.

Materialman's Act (Public Works)
See Mechanics' Lien Acts (Public Works)

Materialmen's Act
D.C. Code Ann., § 1-1104 et seq.

Materialmen's Lien Act
See Mechanics' Lien Act

Materials Act of 1947
July 31, 1947, Ch. 406, 61 Stat. 681, 30 U.S. Code §§ 601 to 604
Aug. 31, 1950, Ch. 830, 64 Stat. 572
July 23, 1955, Ch. 375, 69 Stat. 367
Sept. 25, 1962, P.L. 87-689, 76 Stat. 587
April 21, 1976, P.L. 94-273, 90 Stat. 379
Oct. 19, 1980, P.L. 96-470, 94 Stat. 2237

Maternal and Child Health and Mental Retardation Planning Amendments of 1963
Oct. 24, 1963, P.L. 88-156, 77 Stat. 273, 42 U.S. Code §§ 701, 702, 711, 712, 729, 729a, 1391 to 1394

Maternal and Child Health Plan Act (County)
N.M. Stat. Ann., 24-1B-1 et seq.

Maternal and Child Health Services Block Grant Act
Aug. 13, 1981, P.L. 97-35, 42 U.S. Code § 1305 nt.

Maternal and Child Nutrition Act
Minn. Stat. Ann., 145.891 et seq.

Maternal and Infant Care Act
Okla. Stat. Ann., Title 63, § 1-231 et seq.

Maternal and Infant Health Improvement Act
Tex. Health and Safety Code, § 32.001 et seq.

Maternal, Fetal and Infant Experimentation Act
N.M. Stat. Ann., 24-9A-1 et seq.

Maternal Infant and Child Health Council Act
S.C. Code Ann. 1976, § 20-7-5410 et seq.

Maternity Act
Nov. 23, 1921, Ch. 135, 42 Stat. 224

Maternity Care Access Act
Wash. Rev. Code Ann., 74.09.760 et seq.

Maternity Hospital Act
Ind. Code 1982, 12-5-5-1 et seq.
R.I. Gen. Laws 1956, 23-15-1 et seq.
R.I. Public Laws 1949, Ch. 2378

Maternity Law (Child Care)
Colo. Rev. Stat., 22-1-8

Mathematics and Science Academy Law
Ill. Rev. Stat. 1991, Ch. 122, § 1503 et seq.

Mathematics and Science Teacher Tuition Assistance Act
Neb. Laws 1984, L.B. 931
Neb. Rev. Stat. 1943, 79-12, 142 et seq., 89-182.01 et seq.

Mathematics and Science Teaching Student Assistance Act
Neb. Rev. Stat. 1943, 79-12,122 et seq.

Mathematics, Engineering and Science Achievement Program Act
Cal. Education Code 1976, § 8600 et seq.

Mathematics Program Act (Abstract, Conceptually Oriented)
Cal. Education Code 1976, § 54680 et seq.

Mathematics, Science and Computer Education Quality Improvement Act (K through 12)
Fla. Stat. Ann., 233.64 et seq.

Mathematics, Science and Technology Improvement Act (K through 12)
Colo. Rev. Stat., 22-81-101 et seq.

Mathematics, Science, Technology Act (Magnet School)
Colo. Rev. Stat., 22-84-101 et seq.

Mathematics Staff Development Act (Standard-Based)
Cal. Education Code 1976, § 44695 et seq.

Matriculation Act
Cal. Education Code 1976, § 78210 et seq.

Matrimonial Causes Act
Ill. Rev. Stat. 1991, Ch. 40, § 101 et seq.

Matrimonial Property Act
Tex. Family Code, § 5.01 et seq.

Matrimonial Property Reform Act
N.Y. Laws 1980, Ch. 281

Matt McNeely Boulevard Act
Mich. Comp. Laws Ann., 250.431 et seq.

Mattapoisett Water Loan Act
Mass. Acts 1952, Ch. 331

Matteson Civic Center Law
Ill. Rev. Stat. 1991, Ch. 85, § 7004-1 et seq.

Matteson, Ottawa, Illinois Valley, Waukegan, Pontiac, Randolph County, Carbondale, and Riverside Civic Centers Act
Ill. Rev. Stat. 1991, Ch. 85, § 7000-1 et seq.

Matthews Act (St. Joseph Superior Court)
Ind. Code Ann., 33-5-40-1 et seq.

Matthews-Palmer Act (Public Libraries Appropriation)
Mich. Comp. Laws 1948, 397.102 et seq.

Mattoon Act (Public Ways Improvements)
Cal. Statutes 1925, Ch. 419, p. 849

Mattress Act
D.C. Code Ann., § 6-801 et seq.
Ind. Code Ann., 16-1-33-1, 16-9-4-1 et seq.
Mo. Rev. Stat., 421.010 et seq.

Mattress Manufacturing Law
Ky. Rev. Stat. 1971, 214.280 et seq.

Mature Defensive Driving Act
Mont. Code Ann., 33-16-221 et seq.

Mature Driving Program
Mont. Code Ann., 33-16-203, 33-16-221 to 33-16-225

Mature Minors Emancipation Act
Ill. Rev. Stat. 1991, Ch. 40, § 2201 et seq.

Maturity Act (Citrus Fruits)
Fla. Stat. Ann., 601.9910

Maury County Budget Law
Tenn. Private Acts 1963, Ch. 233

Mausoleum and Columbarium Act
Cal. Health and Safety Code § 9501 et seq.
Mont. Code Ann., 35-21-101 et seq.

Mausoleum Construction Act
Cal. Health and Safety Code §§ 9501 et seq., 9600 et seq.

Maximum Class Size Study Act
Fla. Laws 1998, Ch. 211, § 1

Maximum Effort School Aid Law
Minn. Stat. Ann., 124.36 et seq.

Maximum Fare Law
Ill. Rev. Stat. 1983, Ch. 114, § 154 et seq.

Maximum Fee Bill
Tex. Local Government Code, § 152.904

Maximum Freight Rate Act
Mo. Laws 1905, p. 102, No. 2

Maximum Freight Weight Act
Mo. Laws 1907, p. 171

Maximum Hour Act
Haw. Rev. Stat. Ann., § 387-3
Mass. Gen Laws 1990, 149:30 et seq.
Mont. Rev. Code 1947, 41-1101 et seq.
N.C. Gen. Stat. 1943, § 95-25.1 et seq.
Ore. Rev. Stat., 652.010 et seq.

Maximum Hour Act (Women and Minors)
Cal. Labor Code § 1350 et seq.

Maximum Hour Act (Women)
Me. Rev. Stat. Ann. 1964, Title 26, § 731 et seq.
Neb. Laws 1889, Ch. 107
N.J. Rev. Stat. 1937, 34:2-28
N.M. Stat. Ann., 50-5-1
Va. Code 1950, § 40.1-35 et seq.

Maximum Hours Act (Minors)
Ark. Code Ann. 1987, 11-6-108, 11-6-102, 11-6-110
Ohio Rev. Code 1953, 4109.22

Maximum Hours Act (Restaurants)
N.M. Stat. Ann., 50-4-13

Maximum Load and Wide Tire Law
Ky. Rev. Stat. 1971, 189.200 et seq.

Maximum Passenger Rate Act (Railroads)
Ala. General Acts 1907, p. 104
Kan. Stat. Ann., 66-167

Maximum Prices Act
P.R. Laws Ann. 1954, Title 23, § 731 et seq.

Maximum Salary Act (County Officers and Clerks)
Tenn. Code Ann., 8-24-102

Maximum Sentence Act
Tenn. Code Ann., 40-20-107 et seq.

Maximum Weight Act
Tenn. Code Ann., 55-7-203

Maximum Weight Act (Motor Vehicles)
Conn. Gen. Stat. Ann., § 14-266 et seq.
Fla. Stat. Ann., 316.535
Ill. Rev. Stat. 1991, Ch. 95 1/2, § 15-100 et seq.
Pa. 1929 Pamph. Laws 905, No. 403, § 903

Maximum Weight Act (Truck Axles)
Tenn. Code Ann., 55-7-203

Maxine Waters Child Abuse Prevention Training Act
Cal. Education Code 1976, § 94316 et seq.

Maxine Waters School Reform and Student Protection Act
Cal. Education Code 1976, § 94840 et seq.

May Army Officer Strength Act
April 13, 1938, Ch. 146, 52 Stat. 216

May Defense Expediting Act
See Army Reorganization Acts

May-Goff Act (Jefferson Davis Day)
Ky. Rev. Stat. 1971, 2.110

May, Overbey, Davidson and Travis Act (State Colleges)
Ky. Rev. Stat. 1971, 164.290, 164.310

Mayaguez Port Commission Act
P.R. Laws Ann. 1954, Title 23, § 551 et seq.

Mayer-Garnett Act
Ky. Acts 1936, Ch. 19

Mayfield Act
March 4, 1927, Ch. 510, 44 Stat. 1446, 49
U.S. Code §§ 3, 15, 20, 22, 73, 74, 102

Mayhem Statute
Ill. Rev. Stat. 1991, Ch. 38, § 12-4

Mayor-Council Act of 1955-1977
Ala. Acts 1977, p. 150
Ala. Code 1958, App., § 1123 (38c) et seq.
Ala. Code 1958, App., § 1247 (216a) et seq.
Ala. Code 1958, App., § 1514 et seq.

Mayor Economic Impact Act
Miss. Code Ann. 1972, § 57-75-1 et seq.

Mayoral Election Validation Act
Ill. Rev. Stat. 1991, Ch. 24, §§ 808d.01, 808d.1

Maywood Civic Center Law
Ill. Rev. Stat. 1991, Ch. 85, § 6905.1 et seq.

McAlister-Duffy-Greene Unemployment Benefit Pension Offset Refund Act
Cal. Unemployment Insurance Code § 1255.3

McAlister-Mello Restricted Employment Driving Privilege Act
Cal. Vehicle Code 1959, § 16076

McAlister-Robbins Financial Responsibility Act
Cal. Statutes 1991, Ch. 946

McAllister Act
Fla. Stat. Ann., 721.50 et seq.

McAllister Drug Treatment Program Act
Tex. Health and Safety Code, § 465.001 et seq.

McAteer Act (Educational Programs)
Cal. Education Code 1976, § 54400 et seq.

McAteer Alcoholism Act
Cal. Health and Safety Code § 11750 et seq.

McAteer-Petris Act (San Francisco Bay)
Cal. Government Code § 66600 et seq.

McBrayer-Strange Act
Ky. Acts 1930, Ch. 152

McBride Act (Child Care Centers)
Cal. Education Code 1959, §§ 16645.9, 16645.11, 8200 et seq.

McBride-Grunsky Insurance Regulatory Act
Cal. Insurance Code §§ 754, 1850 et seq.

MCCA
See Medicare Catastrophic Coverage Act of 1988

McCaffrey Act (Wage Assignments)
N.Y. Personal Property Law (Consol. Laws Ch. 41) § 46 et seq.

McCain Law
Ky. Acts 1891-93, Ch. 19

McCall Act (Greater New York Charter)
N.Y. Laws 1933, Ch. 764

McCallum Act (Normal School Gifts)
Mich. Comp. Laws 1948, 390.419

McCallum, Burnley and Morgan Act (Circuit Court Districts)
Ky. Rev. Stat. 1971, 23A.020

McCallum-Rawson Act (Statute of Limitations)
Mich. Comp. Laws 1948, 609.13

McCann Act (Vehicle Equipment-Television)
Ky. Rev. Stat. 1971, Superseded Vols., 189.025

McCann-Burnley Act (Pay of Election Officers)
Ky. Rev. Stat. 1971, Superseded Vols., 116.140

McCarran Act
See Immigration and Nationality Act

McCarran Act (Carrying Concealed Weapons)
D.C. Code Ann., § 22-3204

McCarran Amendment (Department of Justice Appropriation Act, 1953)
July 10, 1952, Ch. 651, 43 U.S. Code § 666

McCarran-Ferguson Act
March 9, 1945, Ch. 20, 15 U.S. Code §§ 1011 to 1015
July 25, 1947, Ch. 326, 15 U.S. Code §§ 1012, 1013
Aug. 1, 1956, Ch. 852, 15 U.S. Code § 1015

McCarran-Lea Civil Aeronautics Authority Act

See Civil Aeronautics Act of 1938

McCarran-Walter Act

See Immigration and Nationality Act

McCarter Act (Taxation)

N.J. Laws 1908, c. 6

McCarthy Bill (Salary Increments)

N.Y. City Adm. Code 1938, Ch. 40, § B40-6.0

McCarthy, John-Murdy-J. Howard Williams-Abshire-Maloney Bill (Average Annual Earnings)

Cal. Labor Code §§ 4452, 4453, 4455, 4460, 4702

McCarthy-Kennick Nutrition Program for the Elderly Act

Cal. Welfare and Institutions Code § 18325 et seq.

McCarthy-Ramey Old Age Assistance Act

Ky. Rev. Stat. 1971, 205.010 et seq.

McCauley-Traxler-Law-Bowman Bingo Act

Mich. Comp. Laws Ann., 432.102 et seq.

McCauley-Traxler-Law-Bowman Lottery Act

Mich. Comp. Laws 1948, 432.1 et seq.

McChord Act (Railroad Commission)

Ky. Rev. Stat. 1971, 276.100, 276.310 et seq.

McClain-Hays Act (Public Library Service)

Ky. Rev. Stat. 1971, 171.201 et seq.

McClintock Firearm Act

Cal. Penal Code §§ 1170.1, 1192.7, 12021, 12021.1, 12022.5

McClintock-Mello-Condit Tax Rebate Act

Cal. Revenue and Taxation Code § 17070 et seq.

McCollough-Sheridan Primary Reimbursement Act

Mich. Comp. Laws Ann., 168.624F

McCormick Act (Budget)

See Budget and Accounting Act, 1921

McCorquodale-Neilson-Hauser Rural Economic Development Act

Cal. Government Code § 15372.5 et seq.

McCorquodale-Nielsen-Hauser Rural Renaissance Act

Cal. Government Code § 15373 et seq.

McCorquodale, Wright, and Bronzan Act

Cal. Welfare and Institutions Code § 5800 et seq.

McCray-Abrams Act (Insurance)

Ind. Code Ann., 27-2-4-1

McCreary Act (Chinese Exclusion)

Nov. 3, 1893, Ch. 14, 28 Stat. 7

McCullough-Morgan Act (Highways)

Mo. Laws 1917, p. 485

Mo. Laws 1919, p. 650

McCumber Act (Pensions)

Feb. 6, 1907, Ch. 468, 34 Stat. 879

McCumber Act (Transportation)

April 28, 1904, Ch. 1766, 33 Stat. 518 (See 10 U.S. Code § 2631)

Aug. 10, 1956, Ch. 1041, 70A Stat. 146, 10 U.S. Code § 2631

McCurdy-Thomas Act

Ala. Acts 1990, No. 339

McDermott Act (Intoxicating Liquors)

Ohio Laws Vol. 106, p. 560

McDonald Act (Taxation)

Ohio Rev. Code 1953, 5713.01

McDonald-Stone Act (Recreational Corporations)

Ala. Code 1975, § 11-60-1 et seq.

McDuffie County-Thomson Industrial Development Authority Act
Ga. Laws 1962, p. 2120

McDuffie-Tydings Acts
Jan. 17, 1933, Ch. 11, 47 Stat. 761 (See 5 U.S. Code § 2102)
March 24, 1934, Ch. 84, 48 Stat. 456, 2 U.S. Code § 31; See 5 U.S. Code § 2102

McElhanon-Dudley Consolidation and Coordination Law (Revenue Commission)
Ark. Stat. 1947, 84-1701 et seq.

McEnerney Act (Lost or Destroyed Records)
Cal. Code of Civil Procedure § 751.01 et seq.

McFadden Act (Branch Banks)
Feb. 25, 1927, Ch. 191, 44 Stat. 1224, 12 U.S. Code §§ 24, 29, 34a, 36, 51, 52, 57, 72, 76, 81, 82, 84, 161, 321, 341, 371, 501, 521, 591, 593

McFadden-Pepper Act
See Mcfadden Act (Branch Banks)

McGehee Act (Unemployment Compensation)
D.C. Code Ann., § 46-101 et seq.

McGillicuddy Act
See Federal Employees' Compensation Act

McGrath-Feld Tenure Law
N.Y. Education Law 1947 (Consol. Laws Ch. 16) § 6206 et seq.

McGregor Act
See Lanham Act (Public War Housing)

McGuire Bill
July 14, 1952, c 745, 66 Stat. 632, 15 U.S. Code §§ 45, 45 nt.

McHenry County Dam Act
Ill. Rev. Stat. 1991, Ch. 19, § 1350 et seq.

McIntire-Stennis Act of 1962
Oct. 10, 1962, P.L. 87-788, 16 U.S. Code §§ 582a to 582a-7
June 23, 1972, P.L. 92-318, 16 U.S. Code § 582a-3

Dec. 22, 1981, P.L. 97-98, 16 U.S. Code §§ 582a, 582a-1, 582a-3 to 582a-5

McIntyre Act (Banking)
Ohio Rev. Code 1953, 1113.06

McKellar-Mead 40-Hour Mail Act
Aug. 14, 1935, Ch. 535, 49 Stat. 650

McKeown Act (Corporate Bankruptcy)
June 7, 1934, Ch. 424, 48 Stat. 911, 11 U.S. Code §§ 76a, 103, 107

McKinley Act (Tariff)
Oct. 1, 1890, Ch. 1244, 26 Stat. 567

McKool-Stroud Primary Financing Law
Tex. Election Code § 173.001 et seq.

McLaughlin Act (Religious Observance)
N.Y. Education Law 1947 (Consol. Laws Ch. 16) § 3210

McLaughlin Bankruptcy Act
See Bankruptcy Acts

McLinn-Bates Reciprocal Tax Act
Ind. Code 1976, 6-2-2-1 et seq.

McMahon Atomic Energy Act
See Atomic Energy Act of 1946

McMillan-Merrill Adult Rights Act
Ala. Acts 1975, p. 600, No. 126

McNaboe Law (Kickback of Wages)
N.Y. Labor Law (Consol. Laws Ch. 31) § 198b

McNamara-O'Hara Service Contract Act
See Service Contract Act of 1965

McNamee Art in Public Places Act
Mich. Comp. Laws Ann., 18.71 et seq.

McNary-Mapes Amendment (Pure Foods)
July 8, 1930, Ch. 874, 46 Stat. 1019

McNeely Boulevard Act (Matt)
Mich. Comp. Laws Ann., 250.431 et seq.

McNeely-Geake-R. Hood Malpractice Arbitration Act
Mich. Comp. Laws Ann., 600.5040 et seq.

McNeely-McCauley-Traxler-Law-Bowman Lottery Act
Mich. Comp. Laws Ann., 423.1 et seq.

McNitt-Creen Act (Emergency Banking)
Mich. Public Acts 1933, No. 32

McNitt-Holbeck-Smith Act (Township Highways)
Mich. Comp. Laws 1948, 247.1 et seq.

Mead Air Mail Extension Act
Jan. 14, 1938, Ch. 9, 52 Stat. 6

Mead Two-Cent Postal Rate Act
June 24, 1940, Ch. 414, 54 Stat. 505

Meadow Act (Irrigation)
Colo. Rev. Stat., 37-86-113

Meal Tax Statute
Mass. Gen. Laws Ann., 64B:1 et seq.

Meals and Rooms Tax Act
N.H. Rev. Stat. 1955, 78-A:1 et seq.
Vt. Stat. Ann., Title 32, § 9201 et seq.

Means of Egress for Building Act
D.C. Code Ann., § 5-518 et seq.

Measurement Standards Act
Colo. Rev. Stat., 35-14-101 et seq.

Measures Act
Alaska Stat. 1962 §§ 45.75.010, 45.75.20
Md. Ann. Code 1974, Art. AG, § 11-101 et seq.
Mont. Code Ann. 1987, 30-12-101 et seq.
R.I. Gen. Laws 1956, 47-4-1

Measures and Weights Act
See Weights and Measures Act
N.D. Cent. Code, 64-01-01 et seq.
Neb. Rev. Stat. 1943, 89-182.01 et seq.
N.H. Rev. Stat. 1955, 438:1 et seq.
Wash. Rev. Code Ann., 19.94.010 et seq.

Measures and Weights Law
Miss. Code Ann. 1972, § 75-27-1 et seq.

Measures Law
Me. Rev. Stat. Ann. 1964, Title 10, § 2301 et seq.

Measures, Public Initiatives and Referendums Referred to Voters by the General Assembly Disclosure Act
Ark. Code 1987, 7-9-401 et seq.

Meat Act (Imported)
See Imported Meat Act

Meat Act (Wholesome)
P.R. Laws Ann. 1954, Title 24 § 771 et seq.

Meat and Food Laws (Kosher)
N.Y. Agriculture and Markets Law (Consol. Laws Ch. 69) §§ 201a, 201b

Meat and Meat Food Regulations and Inspection Act
S.C. Code Ann. 1976, § 47-17-10 et seq.

Meat and Meat Products Certification Act
Ark. Code Ann. 1987, 20-60-301 et seq.

Meat and Meat Products Inspection Act
Ark. Code Ann. 1987, 20-60-201 et seq.

Meat and Poultry Hygiene Law
Pa. Purdon's Stat., Title 31, § 483.1 et seq.

Meat and Poultry Inspection Act
Ala. Code 1975, 2-17-1 et seq.
Cal. Food and Agricultural Code 1967, § 18650 et seq.
Ill. Rev. Stat. 1991, Ch. 56 1/2, § 301 et seq.
Iowa Code Ann., 189A.1 et seq.
Kan. Stat. Ann., 65-6a18 et seq.
La. Rev. Stat. Ann., 40:2271 et seq.
Mass. Gen. Laws Ann., 94:146 et seq.
Mont. Laws 1991, Ch. 577, §§ 1 to 16
Neb. Rev. Stat. 1943, 54-1901 et seq.
N.J. Stat. Ann., 24:16B-1 et seq.
Tenn. Code Ann., 53-7-201 et seq.
Tex. Health and Safety Code, § 433.001 et seq.
Vt. Stat. Ann., Title 6, § 3191 et seq.
Continued

Meat and Poultry Inspection and Humane Slaughter Act
Ind. Code Ann., 16-6-5-1 et seq.

Meat and Poultry Products Inspection Act
Conn. Gen. Stat. Ann., § 22-392 et seq.
Del. Code of 1974, Title 3, § 8701 et seq.
Okla. Stat. Ann., Title 2, § 6-161 et seq.
Va. Code 1950, § 3.1-844.17 et seq.

Meat and Poultry Products Inspection and Licensing Act
Utah Code Ann. 1953, 4-32-1 et seq.

Meat and Poultry Supplemental Inspection Act
Cal. Food and Agriculture Code 1967, §§ 18940 et seq., 18950 et seq.

Meat Grading Law
N.C. Gen. Stat. 1943, § 106-17 3.1 et seq.

Meat Hygiene Law
Pa. Purdon's Stat., Title 31, § 483.1 et seq.

Meat Import Act of 1979
Dec. 31, 1979, P.L. 96-177, 19 U.S. Code § 1202 nt.
Aug. 23, 1988, P.L. 100-418, 102 Stat. 1162
Dec. 8, 1993, P.L. 103-182, 19 U.S. Code § 2253 nt.
Dec. 8, 1994, P.L. 103-465, 19 U.S. Code § 2253 nt.

Meat Inspection Act
See also Wholesome Meat Act And Federal Meat Inspection Act
Ariz. Rev. Stat. Ann., § 3-2041 et seq.
Ga. Code Ann., 26-2-100 et seq.
Haw. Rev. Stat. Ann., § 159-1 et seq.
Ida. Code 1947, 37-1901 et seq.
Ky. Rev. Stat. 1971, Superseded Vols., 217.800 et seq.
Md. Ann. Code 1974, Art. AG, § 4-101 et seq.
Me. Rev. Stat. Ann. 1964, Title 22, § 2541 et seq.
Minn. Stat. Ann., 31A.01 et seq.
Miss. Code Ann. 1972, § 75-35-1 et seq.

Mont. Code Ann., 81-9-111 et seq.
N.C. Gen. Stat. 1943, § 106-549.15 et seq.
N.D. Cent. Code, 36-23.1-01 et seq.
N.M. Stat. Ann., 25-3-6 et seq.
Okla. Stat. Ann., Title 2, § 6-181 et seq.
Ore. Rev. Stat., 619.010 et seq.
Pa. 1907 Pamph. Laws 234, No. 187
S.D. Codified Laws 1967, 39-5-6 et seq.
Tex. Health and Safety Code, § 433.001 et seq.
Wash. Rev. Code Ann., 16.49A.010 et seq.

Meat Labeling Act
S.C. Code Ann. 1962, § 6-608

Meat Marketing Act
P.R. Laws Ann. 1954, Title 10, § 241 et seq.

Meat, Meat-Food and Poultry Regulation and Inspection Act
Miss. Code Ann. 1972, § 75-33-1 et seq.

Meat Packers Licensing Act
Pa. Purdon's Stat., Title 31, § 483.1 et seq.

Meat Packing Plants Inspection Act
N.C. Gen. Stat. 1943, § 106-169 et seq.

Meat Sale Regulation Act
Ore. Rev. Stat., 603.010 et seq.

Meat Sellers Fair Competition Act
Cal. Statutes 1935, p. 1333

Mechanical Amusement Device Tax Act
Neb. Rev. Stat. 1943, 77-3001 et seq.

Mechanical Contractors Act
Mich. Comp. Laws Ann., 338.971 et seq.

Mechanical Licensing Act
Okla. Stat. Ann., Title 59, § 1850.1 et seq.

Mechanics Act (Scale)
N.C. Gen. Stat. 1943, § 81A-70 et seq.

Mechanics' and Furnishers' Lien Law
Tenn. Code Ann. 1955, 64-112 et seq.

Mechanics' Lien Act

See also Materialmen's Lien Act and
Mechanics' and Materialmen's Lien Act

Ala. Code 1975, § 35-11-110 et seq.

Alaska Stat. 1962, § 34.35.050 et seq.

Ariz. Rev. Stat. Ann., § 33-981 et seq.

Ark. Code Ann. 1987, 18-44-101 et seq.

Cal. Civil Code § 3109 et seq.

Colo. Rev. Stat., 38-22-101 et seq.

Conn. Gen. Stat. Ann. 1983, § 49-33

D.C. Code Ann., § 38-101 et seq.

Del. Code of 1974, Title 25, § 2701 et seq.

Fla. Stat. Ann., 713.01 et seq.

Ga. Code Ann., 44-14-360 et seq.

Haw. Rev. Stat. Ann., § 507-41 et seq.

Ida. Code 1947, 45-501 et seq.

Ill. Rev. Stat. 1991, Ch. 82, §§ 0.01 et seq., 1
et seq.

Ind. Code Ann., 32-8-3-1 et seq.

Iowa Code Ann., 572.1 et seq.

Kan. Stat. Ann., 60-1101 et seq.

Ky. Rev. Stat. 1971, 376.010 et seq.

La. Rev. Stat. Ann., 9:4801 et seq.

Mass. Gen. Laws Ann., 254:1 et seq.

Md. Ann. Code 1974, Art. RP, § 9-101 et seq.

Md. Rule of Procedure, Rule BG 71

Me. Rev. Stat. Ann. 1964, Title 10, § 3251 et
seq.

Mich. Comp. Laws Ann., 570.1 et seq.

Minn. Stat. Ann., 514.01 et seq.

Miss. Code Ann. 1972, §§ 85-7-101,
85-7-105, 85-7-131 et seq.

Mo. Rev. Stat., § 429.010 et seq.

Mont. Code Ann. 1985, 71-3-501 et seq.

N.C. Gen. Stat. 1943, § 44A-7 et seq.

N.D. Cent. Code, 35-27-01 et seq.

Neb. Rev. Stat. 1943, 52-101 et seq.

Nev. Rev. Stat. 1979 Reprint, 108.221 et seq.

N.H. Rev. Stat. 1955, 447:1 et seq.

N.J. Stat. Ann., 2A:44-64 et seq.

N.M. Stat. Ann., 48-2-1 et seq.

N.Y. Lien Law (Consol. Laws Ch. 33) § 3 et
seq.

Ohio Rev. Code 1953, 1311.01 et seq.

Okla. Stat. Ann., Title 42, § 141 et seq.

Ore. Rev. Stat., 87.005 et seq.

Pa. Purdon's Stat., Title 49, § 1101 et seq.

R.I. Gen. Laws 1956, 34-28-1 et seq.

S.C. Code Ann. 1976, § 29-5-10 et seq.

S.D. Codified Laws 1967, 44-9-1 et seq.,
44-11-1 et seq.

Tenn. Code Ann., 66-11-101 et seq.

Tex. Property Code, § 53.001 et seq.

Utah Code Ann. 1953, 38-1-1 et seq.

Va. Code 1950, § 43-1 et seq.

Vt. Stat. Ann., Title 9, § 1921 et seq.

Wash. Rev. Code Ann., 60.04.010 et seq.

Wis. Stat. Ann., 289.01 et seq., 779.41 et seq.

Wyo. Stat. Ann., § 29-2-101 et seq.

Mechanics' Lien Act (Mines and Wells)

Alaska Stat. 1962, § 34.35.125 et seq.

Mechanics' Lien Act (Municipal)

N.J. Stat. Ann., 2A:44-125 et seq.

Mechanics' Lien Acts (Public Works)

See also Miller Act

Aug. 13, 1894, Ch. 280, 28 Stat. 278

Feb. 24, 1905, Ch. 778, 33 Stat. 811

Mechanicville City Court Act

N.Y. Laws 1955, Ch. 798

Mecklenburg County Distress Merchandise Sales Act

N.C. Laws 1955, Ch. 1375

Medal of Honor Act (Law Enforcement and Fire Fighting)

Ill. Rev. Stat. 1991, Ch. 127, § 3851-1 et seq.

Medal of Honor Winners' License Plates Act

Ga. Code Ann., 40-2-67

Medal of Valor

Mont. Code Ann., 1-1-515

Medals of Honor Act (Railroads and Motor Vehicles)

Feb. 23, 1905, Ch. 744, 33 Stat. 743, 49 U.S.
Code §§ 1201 to 1203

June 13, 1957, P.L. 85-50, 71 Stat. 69, 49
U.S. Code §§ 1201, 1203

Medi-Cal Act

Cal. Welfare and Institutions Code § 14000
et seq.

Medi-Cal Conflict of Interest Law
Cal. Welfare and Institutions Code §§ 14022, 14030 et seq.

Medi-Cal Long Term Care Reimbursement Act
Cal. Welfare and Institutions Code § 14126 et seq.

Media Confidentiality Act
Mont. Code Ann., 26-1-901 et seq.

Mediation Act (Domestic Relations)
N.M. Stat. Ann., 40-12-1 et seq.

Mediation Act (Farm)
Ark. Code 1987, 2-7-101 et seq.

Mediation Act (Farmer-Lender)
Minn. Stat. Ann., 583.20 et seq.

Mediation Act (Firefighters)
Ga. Code Ann., 25-5-1 et seq.

Mediation Act (Labor)
See Labor Mediation Act

Mediation Act (Public Utilities)
Mo. Rev. Stat., 295.010 et seq.

Mediation Act (Public Works)
N.M. Stat. Ann., 13-14C-1 et seq.

Mediation and Arbitration Labor Act
Conn. Gen. Stat. Ann., § 31-91 et seq.
La. Rev. Stat. Ann., 23:861 et seq.
Nev. Rev. Stat. 1979 Reprint, 614.010 et seq.
Wash. Rev. Code Ann., 49.08.010 et seq.

Mediation and Conciliation Labor Act
Fla. Stat. Ann., 448.06

Mediation and Conciliation Service Non-Disclosure Act
Ark. Code Ann. 1987, 11-2-201 et seq.

Mediation Center Act (Victim-Offender)
Tenn. Code Ann., 16-20-101 et seq.

Mediation, Conciliation and Arbitration Act (International)
Haw. Rev. Stat. Ann., § 658D-1 et seq.

Medicaid Act
Miss. Code Ann. 1972, § 43-13-101 et seq.
N.Y. Social Services Law (Consol. Laws Ch. 55) § 363 et seq.

Medicaid Act (Health Care Provider)
W. Va. Code 1966 § 9-4C-1 et seq.

Medicaid Certified Nursing Home Intermediate Sanctions Act
S.C. Code Ann. 1976, § 44-6-400 et seq.

Medicaid Disciplinary Act
S.C. Code Ann. 1976, § 40-47-200 et seq.

Medicaid Estate Recovery Act
N.M. Stat. Ann., 27-2A-1 to 27-2A-9

Medicaid False Claim Act
Mass. Gen. Laws Ann., 118E:21A et seq.
Mich. Comp. Laws Ann., 400.601 et seq.
Neb. Rev. Stat. 1943, 68-1037.01 to 68-1037.05
Tenn. Code Ann., 71-5-181 et seq.

Medicaid Fraud Act
Ark. Code Ann. 1987, 5-55-101 et seq.
Mich. Comp. Laws Ann., 400.601 et seq.
N.M. Stat. Ann., 30-44-1 et seq.

Medicaid Fraud Control Act
Miss. Code Ann. 1972, § 43-13-201 et seq.

Medicaid Gross Receipts Tax Act
Ark. Code 1987, 26-52-1101 et seq.

Medicaid Health Care Options Act
Okla. Stat. Ann., Title 56, § 1010.1 et seq.

Medicaid Hospital Provider Temporary Assessment Act
Utah Code Ann. 1953, 26-36-101 et seq.

Medicaid Law
Ind. Code Ann., 12-1-7-14.1 et seq.

Medicaid Liability Liquidity Borrowing Act
Ill. Comp. Stat. 1992, Ch. 30, § 342/1

Medicaid Managed Care Delivery System Law
Tex. Government Code, § 532.001 et seq.

Medicaid Managed Care Program Law
Tex. Government Code, § 533.001 et seq.

Medicaid Mills Act (Shared Health Facilities)
N.Y. Public Health Law 1953 (Consol. Laws Ch. 55) § 4700 et seq.

Medicaid New Drug Review Act
Va. Code 1950, § 32.1-331.1 et seq.

Medicaid Nursing Home Permits Act
S.C. Code Ann. 1976, § 44-7-80 et seq.

Medicaid Program Integrity Act
Okla. Stat. Ann., Title 56, § 1001 et seq.

Medicaid Provider Act
N.M. Stat. Ann., 27-11-1 to 27-11-5

Medicaid Provider Fraud Law
Ind. Code Ann., 12-1-7-15.1 et seq.

Medicaid Reform Act (Market Based)
Ga. Code Ann., 49-4-152.4

Medicaid Takeover Act (Long Term)
N.Y. Social Services Law (Consol. Laws 55) § 368a Subd. 1

Medicaid Third Party Liability Act
Fla. Stat. Ann., 409.910

Medicaid Voluntary Contribution and Provider-Specific Tax Amendments of 1991
Dec. 12, 1991, P.L. 102-234, 42 U.S. Code § 1305 nt.

Medical Access Program (Rural)
Me. Rev. Stat. Ann. 1964, Title 24-A, § 6301 et seq.

Medical Account Act (Individual)
Colo. Rev. Stat., 39-22-504.5 et seq.

Medical Act
Ind. Code Ann., 25-22.5-1-1 et seq.
Ky. Rev. Stat. 1971, 311.250 et seq.
Nev. Rev. Stat. 1979 Reprint, 630.003 et seq.

Medical Advisory Board Act
La. Rev. Stat. Ann., 40:1351 et seq.

Medical Aid Act (Workmen)
Wash. Rev. Code Ann., 51.36.010 et seq.

Medical Aid Contracts Act (Workmen)
Wash. Rev. Code Ann., 51.04.010 et seq.

Medical and Adoption Assistance Compact Act
See Interstate Compact on Adoption and Medical Assistance

Medical and Dental College Act
N.J. Stat. Ann., 18A:64C-1 et seq.

Medical and Dental Education Act
N.J. Stat. Ann., 18A:64G-1 et seq.

Medical and Dental Manpower Act
D.C. Code Ann., § 31-1711 et seq.

Medical and Dental Service Corporation Act (Nonprofit)
Pa. Cons. Stat., Title 40, § 6101 et seq.

Medical and Higher Education Facilities Bond Act
Va. Acts 1973, Ch. 206

Medical and Hospital Care Act (State Employees)
Cal. Government Code § 22751 et seq.

Medical and Hospital Malpractice Joint Underwriting Association Act
Me. Rev. Stat. Ann. 1964, Title 24, § 2401 et seq.

Medical and Hospital Service Corporation Act (Nonprofit)
Kan. Stat. Ann., 40-1801 et seq.

Medical and Hospital Services Utilization Review Act
Okla. Stat. Ann., Title 36, § 6551 et seq.

Medical and Osteopathic Practice Act
Ky. Rev. Stat. 1971, 311.550 et seq.

Medical and Osteopathic Service Corporation Act (Nonprofit)
Pa. Cons. Stat., Title 40, § 6101 et seq.

Medical and Surgical Licensure and Supervision Act (Allopathic)
Okla. Stat. Ann., Title 59, § 480 et seq.

Medical and Surgical Plan Law
S.D. Codified Laws 1967, 58-38-1 et seq.

Medical Arts Building Act
Tenn. Code Ann., 68-11-601 et seq.

Medical Assistance Act
Colo. Rev. Stat., 26-4-101 et seq.
Ga. Code Ann., 49-4-140 et seq.
Iowa Code Ann., 249A.1 et seq.
Ky. Rev. Stat. 1971, 205.510 et seq.
Mass. Gen. Laws Ann., 118E:1 et seq.
Miss. Code Ann. 1972, § 43-13-101 et seq.
R.I. Gen. Laws 1956, 40-8-1 et seq.
Tenn. Code Ann., 71-5-101 et seq.

Medical Assistance and Adoption Compact
Okla. Stat. Ann., Title 10, § 61 et seq.
Tex. Human Resources Code, § 32.001 et seq.
Utah Code Ann. 1953, 26-18-1 et seq.
Vt. Stat. Ann., Title 33, § 2901 et seq.

Medical Assistance and Adoption Interstate Compact
N.M. Stat. Ann., 40-7B-1 et seq.

Medical Assistance and Health Services Act
N.J. Stat. Ann., 30:4D-1 et seq.

Medical Assistance and Services Act
Wyo. Stat. Ann., § 42-4-101 et seq.

Medical Assistance for Needy Persons Act
N.Y. Social Services Law (Consol. Laws Ch. 55), § 363 et seq.

Medical Assistance for the Aged Act
Cal. Welfare and Institutions Code § 4700 et seq.
Colo. Rev. Stat., 26-11-101 et seq.
Ga. Code Ann., 49-4-120 et seq.
Mich. Comp. Laws 1948, 400.361 et seq.
Miss. Code Ann. 1972, § 43-13-1 et seq.
Wyo. Stat. 1957, § 42-47 et seq.

Medical Assistance Fraud Law
R.I. Gen. Laws 1956, 40-8.2-1 et seq.

Medical Benefits Recovery Act
Utah Code Ann. 1953, 26-19-1 et seq.

Medical Care Act
R.I. Gen. Laws 1956, Superseded Vol., 40-18-1 et seq.

Medical Care and Assistance Act
Mass. Gen. Laws Ann., 118E:1 et seq.

Medical Care and Treatment Act (Consent to)
Tex. Health and Safety Code, § 313.001

Medical Care Commission Hospital Facilities Finance Act
N.C. Gen. Stat. 1943, § 131-138 et seq.

Medical Care Corporation Act
Mich. Comp. Laws Ann., 550.301 et seq.

Medical Care Facilities Certificate of Public Need Law
Va. Code 1950, § 32.1-102.1 et seq.

Medical Care Facilities Finance Agency Act
N.Y. Laws 1973, Ch. 392

Medical Care Facilities Finance Agency Act (New York State)
N.Y. Unconsolidated Laws, § 7411 et seq.

Medical Care for the Aged Act
Tenn. Code Ann., 71-2-301 et seq.

Medical Care Recovery Act
Sept. 25, 1962, P.L. 87-693, 76 Stat. 593, 42 U.S. Code §§ 2651 to 2653
D.C. Code Ann., § 4-501 et seq.

Medical Care Savings Account Act
Ga. Code Ann., 33-20B-1 et seq.
Ida. Code 1947, 41-5301 et seq.
Ill. Comp. Stat. 1992, Ch. 820, § 152/1
Mich. Comp. Laws Ann., 550.981 et seq.
Mont. Laws 1995, Ch. 295
N.M. Stat. Ann., 59A-23D-1 et seq.
Pa. Purdon's Stat., Title 72, § 3402a.2 et seq.

Medical Center Act
P.R. Laws Ann. 1954, Title 24, § 49a et seq.

Medical Center Act (Chicago)
Ill. Rev. Stat. 1991, Ch. 111 1/2 § 5000 et seq.

Medical Center District Act
Ill. Rev. Stat. 1991, Ch. 111 1/2, § 5000 et seq.

Medical Center Quota Act
Ark. Code Ann. 1987, 6-64-505 et seq.

Medical Clinic Act
Ala. Code 1975, § 11-58-1 et seq.

Medical College Act
Mo. Rev. Stat., 334.160

Medical Conduct Reform Act (Professional)
N.J. Stat. Ann., 45:9-19.4 et seq.

Medical Consent Law
Fla. Stat. Ann., 766.103

Medical Contribution Act (Employee)
Ga. Code Ann., 31-9-1 et seq.
Ill. Rev. Stat. 1991, Ch. 48, § 35a et seq.
La. Rev. Stat. Ann., 40:1299.50 et seq.

Medical Corporation Act
Ark. Code Ann. 1987, 4-29-301 et seq.
Cal. Business and Professions Code § 2500 et seq.
Ill. Rev. Stat. 1991, Ch. 32, § 631 et seq.
La. Rev. Stat. Ann., 12:901 et seq.

Minn. Stat. Ann., 319A.01 et seq.
N.Y. Public Health Law 1953 (Consol. Laws Ch. 45), § 4400 et seq.
S.D. Codified Laws 1967, 47-11-1 et seq.

Medical Corporation Act (Non-Profit Health Maintenance Organization)
N.Y. Public Health Law 1953 (Consol. Laws Ch. 45), § 4400 et seq.

Medical Cost Advisory Committee Act
Ill. Rev. Stat. 1991, Ch. 23, § 5090 et seq.

Medical Database Commission Act
N.C. Gen. Stat. 1943, § 131E-210 et seq.

Medical, Dental and Hospital Service Corporation Readable Insurance Certificate Act
N.C. Gen. Stat. 1943, § 58-66-1 et seq.

Medical, Dental, Optometric and Hospital Service Corporation Act
Ariz. Rev. Stat. 1956, § 20-821 et seq.

Medical Device Amendments of 1992
June 16, 1992, P.L. 102-300, 21 U.S. Code § 301 nt.

Medical Disaster Insurance Fund Act
Colo. Rev. Stat., 8-46-301 et seq., 8-65-101 et seq.

Medical Disciplinary Act
S.C. Code Ann. 1976, § 40-47-200 et seq.

Medical Disciplinary Board Act
Wash. Rev. Code Ann., 18.72.010 et seq.

Medical Education and Tertiary Care Act
Fla. Stat. Ann., 395.60 et seq., 395.801 et seq.

Medical Education Facilities Bond Act
N.J. Laws 1977, Ch. 235

Medical Emergencies Act (Coal Mine)
Ill. Comp. Stat. 1992, Ch. 410, § 15/1 et seq.

Medical Emergency Services Act
Tex. Health and Safety Code, § 773.001 et seq.

Medical Employee Protection Act
D.C. Code Ann., §§ 1-1211, 1-1215

Medical Enhancement Tax Act (Health Care Provider)
W. Va. Code 1966, § 11-26-2 et seq.

Medical Estate Recovery Act
N.M. Stat. Ann., 27A-2A-1 et seq. '

Medical Examination Act (Premarital)
See Premarital Medical Examination Act (Venereal Disease)

Medical Examination of Employees Act
Ill. Rev. Stat. 1991, Ch. 48, § 172c.9 et seq.

Medical Examiners Act
Fla. Stat. Ann., 406.01 et seq.
Iowa Code Ann., 331.801 et seq.
Me. Rev. Stat. Ann. 1964, Title 22, § 3021 et seq.
Mich. Comp. Laws Ann., 52.201 et seq.
Miss. Code Ann. 1972, §§ 41-61-1, 41-61-51 et seq.
N.C. Gen. Stat. 1943, § 130A-377 et seq.
N.J. Stat. Ann., 52:17B-78 et seq.
N.Y. Local Laws 1971, County of Rensselaer, p. 792
R.I. Gen. Laws 1956, 23-4-1 et seq.
Utah Code Ann. 1953, 26-4-1 et seq.

Medical Examiners' Tax Refund Law
Cal. Business and Professions Code § 2457

Medical Expense Act (Workmen's Compensation)
Mo. Rev. Stat., 287.140

Medical Facilities Construction and Modernization Amendments of 1970
June 30, 1970, P.L. 91-296, 84 Stat. 336, 12 U.S. Code § 1717; 21 U.S. Code §§ 186, 187; 42 U.S. Code §§ 201 nt., 229b, 242b, 242g, 246, 291a to 291f, 291i, 291j-1 to 291j-10, 291o, 291o-1, 299a, 2661 nt.
June 18, 1973, P.L. 93-45, 87 Stat. 95, 42 U.S. Code § 300a-7
July 28, 1974, P.L. 93-352, 88 Stat. 360, 42 U.S. Code § 201 nt.

Medical Facilities Survey and Construction Act
See Hospital and Medical Facilities Survey and Construction Act
Kan. Stat. Ann., 65-411 et seq.

Medical Facilities Survey and Construction Act of 1954
July 12, 1954, Ch. 471, 68 Stat. 461, 42 U.S. Code §§ 291, 291h, 291i, 291j, 291m, 291o, 291p, 291q, 291r, 291s, 291t, 291u, 291v

Medical Facility Plan
Mont. Code Ann., 50-5-402 et seq.

Medical Fees of State Inmate Escapees Act
Ill. Rev. Stat. 1991, Ch. 37, §§ 439.25, 439.26

Medical Foods Insurance Coverage Act
Pa. Purdon's Stat., Title 40, § 3901 et seq.

Medical Group Clinic Corporation Act
Conn. Gen. Stat. Ann., § 33-180 et seq.

Medical-Hospital Liability Act
Ida. Code 1947, 39-4201 et seq.
Neb. Rev. Stat. 1943, 44-2801 et seq.

Medical Information Confidentiality Act
Cal. Civil Code § 56 et seq.

Medical Injury Compensation Reform Act
Cal. Business and Professions Code § 800 et seq.
Cal. Statutes 1975, 2d Ex. Sess., Ch. 1

Medical Insurance Fund Act (Major)
Colo. Rev. Stat., 8-46-201 et seq., 8-66-101 et seq.

Medical Judicial Procedure Improvement Act
Cal. Business and Professions Code §§ 802.5, 805
Cal. Government Code § 11371 et seq.

Medical Laboratory Act
Ky. Rev. Stat. 1971, 333.010 et seq.
Me. Rev. Stat. Ann. 1964, Title 22, § 2011 et seq.
Tenn. Code Ann., 68-29-101 et seq.

Medical Laboratory Certification and Improvement Act
Nev. Rev. Stat. 1979 Reprint, 652.010 et seq.

Medical Legal Panel Act
Mont. Code Ann., 27-6-101 et seq.

Medical Liability Act
Ala. Code 1975, §§ 6-5-548 to 6-5-549.1

Medical Liability and Insurance Improvement Act
Tex. Rev. Civ. Stat., Art. 4590i

Medical Liability Insurance Underwriting Association Act
Tex. Insurance Code, Art. 21.49-3

Medical Library Act
Cal. Business and Professions Code § 525 et seq.

Medical Library Assistance Act of 1965
Oct. 22, 1965, P.L. 89-291, 79 Stat. 1059, 42 U.S. Code §§ 277, 280a-1, 280b to 280b-11

Medical Library Assistance Extension Act of 1970
March 13, 1970, P.L. 91-212, 84 Stat. 63, 42 U.S. Code §§ 201, 275 to 280a-1, 280b to 280b-12

Medical Licensure Act
Minn. Stat. Ann., 147.01 et seq.

Medical Lien Law
Wash. Rev. Code Ann., 60.44.010 et seq.

Medical Malpractice Act
Ariz. Rev. Stat. Ann., § 12-561 et seq.
Ind. Code Ann., 16-9.5-1-1 et seq.
N.M. Stat. Ann., 41-5-1 et seq.

Medical Malpractice Arbitration Act
Mich. Comp. Laws Ann., 600.5040 et seq.

Medical Malpractice Insurance Act
S.C. Code Ann. 1976, § 38-79-10 et seq.

Medical Malpractice Insurance and Claims Act
Ky. Rev. Stat. 1971, 304.40-250 et seq.

Medical Malpractice Liability Insurance Act
N.J. Stat. Ann., 17:30D-1 et seq.

Medical Malpractice Reform Act
Fla. Laws 1991, 95.11
Fla. Stat. Ann., 95.11, 627.351, 627.357, 725.01, 768.042, 768.41, 768.46, 768.47
Ga. Code Ann., 9-3-73, 9-11-9.1, 51-1-29.1
Ill. Rev. Stat. 1991, Ch. 110, § 2-1113 et seq.
R.I. Public Laws 1976, Ch. 244

Medical Malpractice Review Board and Claims Act
Tenn. Code Ann., 29-26-101 et seq.

Medical Needs Act (Special)
N.M. Stat. Ann., 27-4-1 et seq.

Medical Needs Compact Act (Northern New England)
Vt. Acts 1957, No. 154

Medical, Nursing and Hospital Lien Act
Ark. Code Ann. 1987, 18-46-101 et seq.

Medical Patient Rights Act
Ill. Rev. Stat. 1991, Ch. 111 1/2, § 5400 et seq.

Medical Physicists Act
Fla. Stat. Ann., 483.901

Medical Physics Practice Act
Tex. Rev. Civ. Stat., Art. 4512n

Medical Power of Attorney Act
W. Va. Code 1966 § 16-30A-1 et seq.

Medical Practice Act
Ala. Code 1975, § 34-24-50 et seq.
Alaska Stat. 1962, § 08.64.010 et seq.
Ariz. Rev. Stat. Ann., § 32-1401 et seq.
Ark. Code Ann. 1987, 17-93-201 et seq.
Cal. Business and Professions Code § 2000 et seq.
Colo. Rev. Stat., 12-36-101 et seq.
Conn. Gen. Stat. Ann., § 20-8 et seq.
Continued

D.C. Code Ann., § 2-1301 et seq.

Del. Code of 1974, Title 24, § 1701 et seq.

Fla. Stat. Ann., 458.301 et seq.

Ga. Code Ann., 43-34-1 et seq.

Haw. Rev. Stat. Ann., § 453-1 et seq.

Ida. Code 1947, 54-1801 et seq.

Ill. Rev. Stat. 1991, Ch. 111, § 4400-1 et seq.

Iowa Code Ann., 148.1 et seq.

Kan. Stat. Ann., 65-2801 et seq.

La. Rev. Stat. Ann., 37:1261 et seq.

Mass. Gen Laws 1990, 112:2 et seq.

Md. Ann. Code 1974, Art. HO, § 14-101 et seq.

Me. Rev. Stat. Ann. 1964, Title 32, § 3263 et seq.

Mich. Comp. Laws Ann., 338.1801 et seq.

Miss. Code Ann. 1972, § 73-25-1 et seq.

Mo. Rev. Stat., 334.010 et seq.

Mont. Code Ann., 37-3-101 et seq.

N.C. Gen. Stat. 1943, § 90-1 et seq.

N.D. Cent. Code, 43-17-01 et seq.

Neb. Rev. Stat. 1943, 71-1-102 et seq.

N.H. Rev. Stat. 1955, 329:1 et seq.

N.J. Stat. Ann., 45:9-1 et seq.

N.M. Stat. Ann., 61-6-1 et seq.

N.Y. Education Law 1947 (Consol. Laws Ch. 16), §§ 6509a, 6510a, 6520 et seq.

N.Y. Public Health Law 1953 (Consol. Laws Ch. 45), § 230

Ohio Rev. Code 1953, 4731.01 et seq.

Okla. Stat. Ann., Title 59, § 481 et seq.

Ore. Rev. Stat., 677.010 et seq.

Pa. Purdon's Stat., Title 63, §§ 401 et seq., 421.1 et seq., 422.1 et seq.

S.C. Code Ann. 1976, § 40-47-5 et seq.

S.D. Codified Laws 1967, 36-4-1 et seq.

Tenn. Code Ann., 63-6-101 et seq.

Tex. Rev. Civ. Stat., Art. 4495b

Utah Code Ann. 1953, 58-12-26 et seq.

Va. Code 1950, § 54.1-2900 et seq.

Vt. Stat. Ann., Title 26, § 1311 et seq.

Wis. Stat. Ann., 448.01 et seq.

W. Va. Code 1966, § 30-3-1 et seq.

Wyo. Stat. Ann., § 33-26-101 et seq.

Medical Practice Act (Podiatric)

Ill. Rev. Stat. 1991, Ch. 111, § 4801 et seq.

Medical Practice Act (Veterinary)

Okla. Stat. Ann., Title 59, § 698.1 et seq.

Pa. Purdon's Stat., Title 63, § 485.1 et seq.

Medical Practice Act for Osteopathic Physicians and Surgeons

See Osteopathy Act

Medical Practices Act

N.Y. Education Law 1947 (Consol. Laws Ch. 16), §§ 6501 et seq., 6509 Subd. 10, 6527 Subd. 5

Medical Practitioner/Physician Provider Medicaid Act

W. Va. Code 1966 § 9-4B-1 et seq.

Medical Privilege Act (Evidence)

See Physician-Patient Privileged Communication Act

Medical Procedures Act (Consent by Minors to)

Ill. Comp. Stat. 1992, Ch. 410, § 210/0.01 et seq.

Medical Profession Law (General)

N.Y. Education Law 1947 (Consol. Laws Ch. 16), § 6520

Medical Professional Act (Volunteer)

Ala. Acts 1998, No. 297

Medical Professional Conduct Reform Act

N.J. Stat. Ann., 2A:84A-22.10, 2C:21-4.1, 2C:21-20, 2C:43-12, 2C:52-2, 17:30D-17, 26:2H-12.2, 26:2H-12.2a, 45:1-2.5, 45:5-8, 45:9-1, 45:9-16, 45:9-19.3 to 45:9-19.15 et seq.

Medical Professional Corporation Act

Ind. Code Ann., 23-1.5-1-1 et seq.

Minn. Stat. Ann., 319A.01 et seq.

Okla. Stat. Ann., Title 18, § 801 et seq.

Medical Radiation Health and Safety Act

La. Rev. Stat. Ann., 37-3171 et seq.

Me. Rev. Stat. Ann. 1964, Title 32, § 9851 et seq.

N.M. Stat. Ann., 61-14E-1 et seq.

Medical Radiation Inspection Safety Act
Tenn. Code Ann., 68-202-101 et seq.

Medical Radiologic Technologist Certification Act
Tex. Rev. Civ. Stat., Art. 4512m, §§ 2.01 to 2.14

Medical Records Act
D.C. Code Ann., § 32-501 et seq.
Tenn. Code Ann., 68-11-301 et seq.

Medical Registration Act
Md. Ann. Code 1974, Art. HG, § 4-101 et seq.

Medical Review Panel Act
Wyo. Stat. Ann., § 9-2-1501 et seq.

Medical Savings Account Act
Colo. Rev. Stat., 39-22-504.5 to 39-22-504.7
Miss. Laws 1994, Ch. 468

Medical Scholarship Agreement Act (Private)
Ill. Rev. Stat. 1991, Ch. 144, § 2700 et seq.

Medical Scholarship Fund Act (Rural)
Ky. Rev. Stat. 1971, Superseded Vols., 211.290 et seq.

Medical School Curriculum Act
Ill. Rev. Stat. 1991, Ch. 144, § 54.10 et seq.

Medical School License Act
N.J. Stat. Ann., 18A:68-12 et seq.

Medical Service Act
Mich. Comp. Laws Ann., 550.301 et seq.

Medical Service Act (Nonprofit)
Ga. Code Ann., 33-18-1 et seq.

Medical Service Corporation Act
Ariz. Rev. Stat. Ann., § 20-821 et seq.
Kan. Stat. Ann., 40-1901 et seq.
N.D. Cent. Code, 26.1-17-01 et seq.
N.H. Rev. Stat. 1955, 420:1 et seq.
N.J. Stat. Ann., 17:48A-1 et seq.

Medical Service Corporation Act (Nonprofit)
See Nonprofit Medical Service Corporation Act

Medical Service Facility Act
Ill. Rev. Stat. 1991, Ch. 85, § 921 et seq.

Medical Service Facility Revenue Bond Act
Ill. Rev. Stat. 1991, Ch. 85, § 2401 et seq.

Medical Service Plan Act
Ill. Rev. Stat. 1987, Ch. 32, § 563 et seq.
Tenn. Code Ann., 56-27-101 et seq.

Medical Services Act (Emergency and Nonemergency)
Fla. Stat. 1919, 401.101 et seq.

Medical Services Act (Emergency)
See Emergency Medical Services Act
Me. Rev. Stat. Ann. 1964, Title 32, § 81 et seq.
Neb. Laws 1997, L.B. 138, §§ 1 to 30
W. Va. Code 1966, § 16-4C-1 et seq.

Medical Services Act (Prison)
Pa. Purdon's Stat., Title 61, § 1011 et seq.

Medical Services Administration Act
P.R. Laws Ann. 1954, Title 24, § 342 et seq.

Medical Services and Care Systems Act (Emergency)
Okla. Stat. 1981, Title 63, § 330.90 et seq.

Medical Services Do Not Resuscitate Order Act (Emergency)
S.C. Code Ann. 1976, § 44-78-10 et seq.

Medical Services for Children Act
Fla. Stat. 1983, 391.011 et seq.

Medical Services for Children Resource Center Act (Emergency)
Okla. Stat. Ann., Title 63, § 1-706.10 et seq.

Medical Services Fund Act (Emergency)
N.M. Stat. 1978, 24-10A-1 et seq.

Medical Services Grant Act (Emergency)
Fla. Stat. Ann., 401.101 et seq.

Medical Services Law (Emergency)
Nev. Rev. Stat. Ann. 450B.015 et seq.

Medical Services Personnel Training Act (Emergency)
N.Y. Public Health Law 1953 (Consol. Laws Ch. 45) § 3050 et seq.

Medical Services System Support Act (Emergency)
Minn. Stat. Ann., 144.8093

Medical Services Systems Act (Emergency)
See Emergency Medical Services Systems Act
Ill. Comp. Stat. 1992, Ch. 210, § 50/1 et seq.

Medical Solicitations Act
Va. Code 1950, § 32-168 et seq.

Medical Student Assistance Act
Neb. Rev. Stat. 1943, 71-5613 et seq.

Medical Student Loan Act
Kan. Stat. Ann.,76-380 et seq.
N.M. Stat. Ann., 21-22-1 et seq.

Medical Student Loan Act (Osteopathic)
N.M. Stat. Ann., 21-22A-1 et seq.

Medical Supplies and Drugs Manufacturers Act
Pa. 1945 Pamph. Laws 615, No. 261

Medical Support Act (Child)
Ariz. Rev. Stat. Ann., § 12-2481 et seq.

Medical Support Health Care Access Act
Ala. Code 1975, § 27-21B-1 et seq.

Medical Support Reform Act
Mont. Code Ann., 40-5-801 et seq.

Medical Technician-Paramedic Act (Emergency)
Neb. Rev. Stat. 1943, 71-5501 et seq.

Medical Technician Practices Act (Advanced Emergency)
Mich. Comp. Laws Ann., 338.1901 et seq.

Medical Technician Training Fund Act (Emergency)
N.J. Stat. Ann., 26:2K-54 et seq.

Medical Technicians Liability Act
Ill. Rev. Stat. 1979, Ch. 111 1/2, §§ 87a, 87b

Medical Technologists College Act
P.R. Laws Ann. 1954, Title 20, § 2151 et seq.

Medical Technology in Puerto Rico Act (Regulating the Profession of)
P.R. Laws Ann. 1954, Title 20, § 281 et seq.

Medical Titles Act
Ky. Rev. Stat. 1971, 311.375, 311.376

Medical Training Act
Tex. Education Code, § 73.051 et seq.

Medical Treatment Act
Tex. Health and Safety Code, § 313.001 et seq.

Medical Treatment Act (Access to)
Ga. Code Ann., 43-34-42.1

Medical Treatment Act (Emergency)
Ill. Rev. Stat. 1991, Ch. 111 1/2, §§ 85z, 6150, 6151 et seq.

Medical Treatment Decision Act
Colo. Rev. Stat., 15-18-101 et seq.

Medical Unity Bill
N.Y. Laws 1907, Ch. 344

Medical Waste Act
W. Va. Code 1966, § 20-5J-1 et seq.

Medical Waste Management Act
Cal. Health and Safety Code § 25015 et seq.
N.J. Stat. Ann., 13:1E-48.1 et seq.

Medical Waste Regulatory Act
Mich. Comp. Laws Ann., 333.13801 et seq.

Medical Waste Tracking Act of 1988
Nov. 1, 1988, P.L. 100-582, 42 U.S. Code § 6901 nt.

Medically Indigent Act
Colo. Rev. Stat., 26-15-101 et seq.

Medically Indigent Assistance Act
S.C. Code Ann. 1976, § 44-6-135 et seq.

Medically Indigent Law
Cal. Welfare & Institutions Code § 14000 et seq.
Colo. Rev. Stat., 26-16-101 et seq.

Medically Underserved Community-State Matching Incentive Program
Tex. Health and Safety Code, § 106.101 et seq.

Medicare Act
See Health Insurance For the Aged Act

Medicare and Medicaid Amendments of 1980
Dec. 5, 1980, P.L. 96-499, 42 U.S. Code § 1305 nt.

Medicare and Medicaid Amendments of 1981
Aug. 13, 1981, P.L. 97-35, 42 U.S. Code § 1301 nt.

Medicare and Medicaid Budget Reconciliation Amendments of 1985
April 7, 1986, P.L. 99-272, 42 U.S. Code § 1305 nt.

Medicare and Medicaid Patient and Program Protection Act of 1987
Aug. 18, 1987, P.L. 100-93, 21 U.S. Code § 824; 42 U.S. Code §§ 704, 1305 nt., 1320a-3, 1320a-5, 1320a-7, 1320a-7 nt., 1320a-7a, 1320a-7b, 1320a-7b nt., 1320c-5, 1395u, 1395y, 1395cc et seq., 1396a et seq.

Medicare Catastrophic Coverage Act of 1988
July 1, 1988, P.L. 100-360, 102 Stat. 683, 26 U.S. Code § 59B; 42 U.S. Code §§ 300aa-12, 300aa-15, 300aa-21, 1305 nt., 1320a et seq., 1382 et seq., 1395 et seq., 1396 et seq.
Oct. 13, 1988, P.L. 100-485, generally 42 U.S. Code §§ 1230a-2, 1320c-3, 1320c-5 nt., 1320c-7, 1320c-7a, 1395 et seq., 1396r-1, 1396r-4

Nov. 10, 1988, P.L. 100-647, 42 U.S. Code §§ 1395b nt., 1395b-1 nt.
Dec. 13, 1989, P.L. 101-234, 5 U.S. Code § 8902 nt.; 26 U.S. Code §§ 59B, 6050F; 42 U.S. Code §§ 401, 1320a-7a nt.; generally 42 U.S. Code §§ 1395c et seq.
Dec. 19, 1989, P.L. 101-239, 42 U.S. Code § 1396b nt.
Oct. 30, 1990, P.L. 101-476, 20 U.S. Code § 1400 nt.

Medicare Catastrophic Coverage Repeal Act of 1989
Dec. 13, 1989, P.L. 101-234, 42 U.S. Code § 1305 nt.
Nov. 5, 1990, P.L. 101-508, 42 U.S. Code § 1395e nt.

Medicare Fee Control Act (Health Care Practitioners)
Pa. Purdon's Stat., Title 35, § 449.31 et seq.

Medicare-Medicaid Anti-Fraud and Abuse Amendments
Oct. 25, 1977, P.L. 95-142, 42 U.S. Code §§ 1305 nt., 1395u et seq.

Medicare Supplement Act
Cal. Health and Safety Code § 1358 et seq.
Cal. Insurance Code § 10193 et seq.
Md. Ann. Code 1974, Art. IN, § 15-901 et seq.
N.M. Stat. Ann., 59A-24A-1 et seq.

Medicare Supplement and Sickness and Accident Insurance Minimum Standards Act
Neb. Rev. Stat. 1943, 44-3611 et seq.

Medicare Supplement and Specified Disease Act
Md. Ann. Code 1957, Art. 48A, §§ 468B to 468H

Medicare Supplement Health Insurance Act
Wash. Rev. Code Ann., 48.66.010 et seq.

Medicare Supplement Insurance Act
Mo. Rev. Stat., 376.850 et seq.
Pa. Purdon's Stat., Title 40, § 3101 et seq.

Medicare Supplement Insurance Minimum Standards Act
Ala. Code 1975, § 27-19-50 et seq.
Del. Code of 1974, Title 18, §§ 2502, 3401 et seq., 6309
Mont. Code Ann., 33-22-901 et seq.

Medicare Supplement Insurance Plans
Mass. Gen. Laws Ann., 176K:1 et seq.

Medicare Supplement Reform Act
Fla. Stat. Ann., 627.671 et seq.

Medicare Supplemental Insurance Protection Act
Tenn. Public Acts 1988, Ch. 989

Medication Administration by Unlicensed Personnel Act
W. Va. Code 1966, § 16-5O-1 et seq.

Medicinal Liquor Act
N.J. Laws 1920, Ch. 293

Medicine and Dentistry Flexibility Act (University)
N.J. Stat. Ann., 18A:64G-1 et seq.

Medicine and Surgery Act
Ky. Rev. Stat. 1971, 311.250 et seq.
Wash. Rev. Code Ann., 18.71.005 et seq.

Medicolegal Investigations Act
Conn. Gen. Stat. Ann., § 19a-400 et seq.

Medigap Insurance Law
N.Y. Insurance Law 1984 (Consol. Laws Ch. 28), §§ 3217, 3218, 3224

Meditation in Public Schools Act
N.M. Stat. Ann., 22-27-1 et seq.

Meeting, Convention, Sports Facility and Tourism Act (State and Local Government)
Mo. Rev. Stat. 1978, 70.840 et seq.

Meeting Law (Public)
La. Rev. Stat. Ann., 44:4 et seq.

Meeting the National Education Goals: Schools for Arkansas' Future Act
Ark. Code 1987, 6-15-1001 et seq.

Meetings Act (Open)
Colo. Rev. Stat., 24-6-402
La. Rev. Stat. Ann., 42:4.1 et seq.

Meetings of Public Agencies Act
Ill. Rev. Stat. 1991, Ch. 102, § 41 et seq.

Megalandfill Siting Act
Mont. Laws 1991, Ch. 468

Megan's Law
May 17, 1996, P.L. 104-145, 42 U.S. Code § 14701, Subsec. d
Ala. Code 1975, §§ 13A-11-200 to 13A-11-203
Alaska Stat. 1962, §§ 11.56.840, 12.63.010 to 12.63.100, 18.65.087, 28.05.048, 33.30.035
Ariz. Rev. Stat. Ann., §§ 13-3821 to 13-3825
Ark. Code 1987, 12-12-901 to 12-12-909
Cal. Penal Code §§ 290 to 290.4
Colo. Rev. Stat., 18-3-412.5
Conn. Gen. Stat. 1983, §§ 54-102a to 54-102r
Del. Code of 1974, Title 11, § 4120
Fla. Stat. Ann., 775.13, 775.22
Ga. Code Ann., 42-9-44.1
Haw. Session Laws 1995, Act 160
Ida. Code 1947, 9-340, Subd. 11, Para. f; 18-8301 to 18-8311
Ill. Comp. Stat. 1992, Ch. 730, §§ 150/1 to 150/10
Ind. Code 1982, 5-2-12-1 to 5-2-12-13
Kan. Stat. Ann., 22-4901 to 22-4910
Ky. Rev. Stat. 1971, 17.500 to 17.540
La. Rev. Stat. Ann., 15:540 to 15:549
Md. Laws 1995, Ch. 142
Me. Rev. Stat. Ann. 1964, Title 34-A, §§ 11001 to 11004
Mich. Public Acts 1994, No. 295
Minn. Stat. 1986, 243.166
Miss. Code Ann. 1972, §§ 45-33-1 to 45-33-19
Mo. Rev. Stat. 1986, 566.600 to 566.625
Mont. Code Ann., 46-23-501 to 46-23-507

N.C. Gen. Stat. 1943, §§ 14-208.5 to
14-208.10

N.D. Cent. Code, 12.1-32-15

Nev. Rev. Stat. Ann., 207.080, 207.151 to
207.157

N.H. Rev. Stat. 1955, 632-A:11 to 632-A:19

N.J. Stat. Ann., 2C:7-1 to 2C:7-11

N.M. Stat. Ann., 29-11A-1 to 29-11A-8

N.Y. Correction Law (Consol. Laws Ch. 43)
§§ 168 to 168V

Ohio Rev. Code 1953, 2950.01 to 2950.08

Okla. Stat. Ann., Title 57, §§ 581 to 587

Ore. Rev. Stat., 181.507 to 181.519

Pa. 1995 Pamph. Laws, No. 24

R.I. Gen. Laws 1956, 11-37-16

S.D. Codified Laws 1967, 22-22-30 to
22-22-41

Tenn. Code Ann., 40-39-101 to 40-39-108

Tex. Rev. Civ. Stat., Art. 6252-13c-1

Utah Code Ann. 1953, 53-5-212.5,
77-27-21.5

Va. Code 1950, §§ 19.2-298.1 to 19.2-390.1

Wash. Rev. Code Ann., 4.24.550, 9A.44.130,
9A.44.140, 10.01.200, 70.48.470,
72.09.330

Wis. Stat. Ann., 175.45

W. Va. Code 1966, §§ 61-8F-1 to 61-8F-8

Wyo. Stat. Ann., §§ 7-19-301 to 7-19-306

Meigs Field Airport Act
Ill. Comp. Stat. 1992, Ch. 620, § 60/1 et seq.

Melbourne Urban Renewal Act
Fla. Special Laws 1961, Ch. 61-2486

Mello-Condit-McClintock Tax Rebate Act
Cal. Revenue and Taxation Code § 17070 et
seq.

Mello-Drink Products Act
Okla. Stat. Ann., Title 63, § 1-1301.30 et seq.

**Mello-McAlister Restricted Employment
Driving Act**
Cal. Vehicle Code 1959, § 16076

Mello-Roos Community Facilities Act
Cal. Government Code § 53311 et seq.

Mellon Art Gallery Act
March 24, 1937, Ch. 50, 50 Stat. 51, 20 U.S.
Code §§ 71 to 75

Melon Inspection Act
Colo. Laws 1925, p. 246, Ch. 95

**Melrose Park and Chicago South Civic
Center Act**
Ill. Comp. Stat. 1992, Ch. 70, § 245/0.01 et
seq.

Melrose Park and Harvey Civic Centers Act
Ill. Rev. Stat. 1991, Ch. 85, § 6701 et seq.

Melrose Park Civic Center Law
Ill. Rev. Stat. 1991, Ch. 85, § 6702-1 et seq.

Melton-Cleveland Act (Horticulture)
Ky. Rev. Stat. 1971, 247.060

Melville Artesian Well Law
S.D. Code 1939, 61.0701 et seq.

Membership Campground Act
Fla. Stat. Ann., 509.501 et seq.
Ill. Rev. Stat. 1991, Ch. 29, § 901 et seq.
Neb. Rev. Stat. 1943, 76-2101 et seq.
N.Y. General Business Law (Consol. Laws
Ch. 20) § 650 et seq.

Membership Camping Act
N.C. Gen. Stat. 1943, § 66-220 et seq.
Tenn. Code Ann., 47-18-401 et seq.
Va. Code 1950, § 59.1-311 et seq.

Membership Camping Practices Act
Minn. Stat. Ann., 82A.01 et seq.

Membership Camping Resort Act
Tex. Property Code, § 222.001 et seq.

Membership Corporations Law
N.Y. Consol. Laws, Ch. 35

Membership Resort Act (Camping)
Tex. Property Code, § 222.001

Membership Sales Law
Iowa Code Ann., 503.1 et seq.

Membrane Processes Research Act of 1992
Oct. 24, 1992, P.L. 102-490, 42 U.S. Code §§ 10341 to 10345, 10341 nt.

Memorial Act
Ind. Code Ann., 10-7-1-1 et seq.

Memorial Act (Ron Ennis)
Fla. Stat. Ann., 553.64 et seq.

Memorial Association Act (Stone Mountain)
Ga. Code Ann., 12-3-190 et seq.

Memorial Auditorium Authority Act (Upper Mohawk Valley)
N.Y. Public Authorities Law (Consol. Laws Ch. 43A) § 1940 et seq.

Memorial Commission Act
Ky. Rev. Stat. 1971, 97.630 et seq.

Memorial Commission Act (Florence County)
S.C. Acts 1946, p. 2102, No. 711

Memorial Commission Act (Veterans)
Pa. Cons. Stat., Title 71, § 1901 et seq.

Memorial Day Act (Coal Miners)
Ill. Comp. Stat. 1992, Ch. 5, § 490/30

Memorial District Act
Ill. Rev. Stat. 1989, Ch. 1, § 3051-30

Memorial for Marion DuPont Act
S.C. Code Ann. 1976, § 52-5-100 et seq.

Memorial Hall Act (Soldiers)
Ill. Rev. Stat. 1991, Ch. 23, § 3050 et seq.

Memorial Monument Permanent Trust Act (First Special Service Force)
Mont. Code Ann., 35-21-901 to 35-21-903

Memorial Stadium Act
Miss. Code Ann. 1972, § 55-23-1 et seq.

Memphis Housing Authority Law
Tenn. Private Acts 1935, Ch. 615

Memphis Plan Act
Tenn. Code Ann., 56-7-2001 et seq.

Mendocino County Flood Control and Water Conservation District Act
Cal. Water Code Appendix, § 54-1 et seq.

Mendocino Woodlands Outdoor Center Act
Cal. Public Resources Code § 5820 et seq.

Mendon Abandoned and Junk Vehicles Law
N.Y. Local Laws 1973, Town of Mendon, p. 2538

Menominee Restoration Act
Dec. 22, 1973, P.L. 93-197, 87 Stat. 770, 25 U.S. Code § 903 to 903f

Mens Rea Act
Cal. Penal Code § 20

Men's Reformatory Act
Me. Rev. Stat. Ann. 1964, Title 34A, § 3401 et seq.

Men's Reformatory Sentence Act
Me. Rev. Stat. Ann. 1964, Title 17A, § 1250 et seq.

Mental Anguish Act
Ark. Code Ann. 1987, 23-17-112 et seq.
Fla. Stat. Ann., 363.06, 363.07
S.C. Code Ann. 1976, § 58-9-1860

Mental Care and Treatment Act
Kan. Stat. Ann., 59-2901 et seq.

Mental Defectives Act
Mich. Comp. Laws Ann., 720.301 et seq.
N.J. Stat. Ann., 39:3-10.4 et seq.

Mental Deficiency Act
Ill. Rev. Stat. 1951, Ch. 91 1/2, § 51-1 et seq.
Tenn. Code Ann., 33-1-101 et seq.

Mental Disability and Developmental Disability Services Act
Ill. Rev. Stat. 1991, Ch. 91 1/2, § 1801-1 et seq.

Mental Disease Act
Mich. Comp. Laws Ann., 330.1001 et seq.

Mental Examination Act (Criminal Procedure)
Wis. Stat. Ann., 971.13

Mental Health Act (Children's Community)
N.C. Laws 1973, Ch. 584

Mental Health Act (Community)
See Community Mental Health Services Act
Fla. Stat. Ann., 394.65 et seq.
Ill. Comp. Stat. 1992, Ch. 405, § 20/0.01 et seq.

Mental Health Act (Comprehensive Adult)
Minn. Stat. Ann., 245.461 et seq.

Mental Health Act of the Unified Juvenile Code
Ky. Rev. Stat. 1971, 645.010

Mental Health, Alcohol, and Drug Abuse Services Act
Fla. Stat. Ann., 394.65 et seq.

Mental Health, Alcohol, Drug Abuse and Developmental Disabilities Act
Wis. Stat. Ann., 51.001 et seq.

Mental Health Amendments of 1967
June 24, 1967, P.L. 90-31, 81 Stat. 79, 42 U.S. Code §§ 225a, 2681, 2684, 2687, 2688a, 2688d, 2691

Mental Health Amendments of 1990
Nov. 28, 1990, P.L. 101-639, 42 U.S. Code § 201 nt.

Mental Health and Chemical Dependency Insurance Act
Mo. Rev. Stat. 1994, 376.825 to 376.833

Mental Health and Developmental Disabilities Act (Children's)
N.M. Stat. Ann., 32A-6-1 et seq.

Mental Health and Developmental Disabilities Administrative Act
Ill. Laws 1997, P.A. 90-423

Mental Health and Developmental Disabilities Code
Ill. Rev. Stat. 1991, Ch. 91 1/2, § 1-100 et seq.
N.M. Stat. Ann., 43-1-2 et seq.

Mental Health and Developmental Disabilities Commission Act
Ill. Rev. Stat. 1983, Ch. 91 1/2, § 100-101 et seq.

Mental Health and Developmental Disabilities Confidentiality Act
Ill. Rev. Stat. 1991, Ch. 91 1/2, § 801 et seq.

Mental Health and Developmental Disabilities Department Act
Ill. Rev. Stat. 1991, Ch. 91 1/2, § 100-0.1 et seq.

Mental Health and Mental Retardation Act
Nev. Rev. Stat. 1979 Reprint, 433.003 et seq.
Pa. Purdon's Stat., Title 50, § 4101 et seq.
Tex. Health and Safety Code, § 531.001 et seq.

Mental Health and Mental Retardation Licensure Law
Tenn. Code Ann., 33-2-501 et seq.

Mental Health and Substance Abuse Act
N.C. Gen. Stat. 1943, § 122C-1 et seq.

Mental Health Authority Act
Iowa Code Ann., 225C.1 et seq.

Mental Health Center Assistance Act
Kan. Stat. Ann., 65-6401 et seq.

Mental Health Centers Act
Ida. Code 1947, 39-3101 et seq.

Mental Health Clinic Act (County)
Ind. Code Ann., 16-16-4-1 et seq.

Mental Health Code
Alaska Stat. 1962, § 47.30.660 et seq.
Ariz. Rev. Stat. Ann., § 36-501 et seq.
Cal. Welfare and Institutions Code § 5000 et seq.
Colo. Rev. Stat., 27-10-101 et seq.
Conn. Gen. Stat. Ann., § 17a-495 et seq.
Continued

D.C. Code 1973, § 21-501 et seq.
Fla. Stat. Ann., 394.451 et seq.
Ga. Code Ann., 37-1-1 et seq.
Ida. Code 1947, 66-317 et seq.
Ill. Rev. Stat. 1991, Ch. 91 1/2, § 1-100 et seq.
Ind. Code Ann., 16-13-1-1 et seq.
La. Rev. Stat. Ann., 28:1 et seq.
Mich. Comp. Laws Ann., 330.1001 et seq.
N.D. Cent. Code, 25-01-01 et seq.
N.Y. Mental Hygiene Law 1977 (Consol. Laws Ch. 27) § 7.01 et seq.
Ohio Rev. Code 1953, 5122.01 et seq.
Okla. Stat. Ann., Title 43A, § 1-101 et seq.
Pa. 1923 Pamph. Laws 998, No. 414
Pa. 1951 Pamph. Laws 533, No. 141
P.R. Laws Ann. 1954, Title 24 § 4001 et seq.
R.I. Gen. Laws 1956, 40.1-5-1 et seq.
S.C. Code Ann. 1976, § 44-25-10 et seq.
Tenn. Code Ann., 33-1-101 et seq.
Tex. Health and Safety Code, § 571.001 et seq.
Vt. Stat. Ann., Title 18, § 7101 et seq.
Wis. Stat. Ann., 51.001 et seq.
Wyo. Stat. Ann., § 25-10-101 et seq.

Mental Health Commitment Act
Neb. Rev. Stat. 1943, 83-1001 et seq.

Mental Health Compact (Interstate)
Fla. Stat. Ann., 394.479 et seq.
Ind. Code Ann., 16-13-8-1 et seq.
Iowa Code Ann., 221.1 et seq.
Me. Rev. Stat. Ann. 1964, Title 34-B, § 9001 et seq.
N.M. Stat. Ann., 11-7-1 et seq.
R.I. Gen. Laws 1956, 40.1-9-1 et seq.

Mental Health Compact Act
Conn. Gen. Stat. Ann., § 17-258 et seq.
Fla. Stat. Ann., 394.479 et seq.
Haw. Rev. Stat. Ann., § 335-1 et seq.
Ill. Rev. Stat. 1991, Ch. 91 1/2, § 50-0.1 et seq.
Iowa Code Ann., 218A.1 et seq.
Md. Ann. Code 1974, Art. HG, § 11-101 et seq.
Me. Rev. Stat. Ann. 1964, Title 34-B, § 9001 et seq.

Minn. Stat. Ann., 245.51 et seq.
Mont. Code Ann., 53-22-101 et seq.
N.D. Cent. Code, 25-11-01 et seq.
Neb. Rev. Stat. 1943, 83-801 et seq.
Ohio Rev. Code 1953, 5119.50
Okla. Stat. 1981, Title 43A, § 6-201 et seq.
S.C. Code Ann. 1976, § 44-25-10 et seq.
S.D. Codified Laws 1967, 27A-6-1 et seq.
Vt. Stat. Ann., Title 18, 9001 et seq.
Wyo. Stat. Ann., §§ 16-4-101 et seq., 25-10-301 et seq.

Mental Health Construction Bond Act
N.Y. Laws 1954, Ch. 8

Mental Health Consumers' Rights Act
Ala. Code 1975, § 22-56-1 et seq.

Mental Health Counselor Licensing Act
La. Rev. Stat. Ann., 37:1101 et seq.

Mental Health Department Act
Mich. Comp. Laws Ann., 330.1100 et seq.

Mental Health Detention Law
Mo. Rev. Stat., 632.300 et seq.

Mental Health Education Act
Ill. Rev. Stat. 1987, Ch. 91 1/2, § 1201 et seq.

Mental Health Enabling Act
Alaska Comp. Laws Ann. 1949, Supp. 1957, § 51-4-16 et seq.

Mental Health Equity Funding Act (Community)
Ill. Comp. Stat. 1992, Ch. 405, § 70/1 et seq.

Mental Health Facilities Act
Tenn. Code Ann., 33-2-101 et seq.

Mental Health Facilities Bond Act
Va. Acts 1977, Ch. 652
Va. Acts 1992, Ch. 892

Mental Health Facilities Loan Insurance Law
Cal. Health and Safety Code § 436.30 et seq.

Mental Health Hispanic Interpreter Act
Ill. Rev. Stat. 1991, Ch. 91 1/2, §§ 1750, 1751

Mental Health Hospitalization Act
Ky. Rev. Stat. 1971, 202A.006 et seq.

Mental Health Information Act
D.C. Code Ann., § 6-2001 et seq.

Mental Health Institution Bond Act
Ill. Rev. Stat. 1991, Ch. 127, § 313.9 et seq.

Mental Health Integrated Fund (Children's)
Minn. Stat. Ann., 245.492 to 245.496

Mental Health Interstate Compact Act
See Interstate Compact on Mental Health Act

Mental Health Law (Planning Council)
Ill. Rev. Stat. 1991, Ch. 91 1/2, § 1901 et seq.

Mental Health Master Plan Development Act
Cal. Welfare and Institutions Code § 5730 et seq.

Mental Health Parity Act
Ark. Code 1987, 23-99-501 et seq.

Mental Health Parity Act of 1996
Sept. 26, 1996, P.L. 104-204, Title VII, 42 U.S. Code § 201 nt.

Mental Health Patient Travel Act
Ill. Rev. Stat. 1991, Ch. 91 1/2, §§ 1450, 1451

Mental Health Procedures Act
Pa. Purdon's Stat., Title 50, § 7101 et seq.

Mental Health Professional Practice Act
Utah Code Ann. 1953, 58-60-101 et seq.

Mental Health Professions Practices Act
Wyo. Stat. Ann., § 33-38-101 et seq.

Mental Health Program Assistance Act
D.C. Code Ann., §§ 32-619, 32-621, 32-623, 32-627

Mental Health Programs Act
Alaska Stat. 1962, § 47.30.010 et seq.
Mich. Comp. Laws Ann., 330.1200 et seq.

Mental Health Reform Act
Kan. Stat. Ann., 39-1601 et seq.
Miss. General Laws 1997, Ch. 587

Mental Health Research Foundation Act
Pa. 1955 Pamph. Laws 1642, No. 551

Mental Health Service Act (Regional)
Ida. Code 1947, 39-3123 et seq.

Mental Health Service System Act
Ill. Rev. Stat. 1991, Ch. 91 1/2, § 1601 et seq.

Mental Health Services Act
Conn. Gen. Stat. 1983, § 17-476 et seq.
Mass. Gen. Laws Ann., 19:1 et seq., 19:17 et seq.
Minn. Stat. Ann., 245.61 et seq.
Okla. Stat. Ann., Title 43A, § 2-101 et seq.

Mental Health Services Act (Children's)
Cal. Welfare and Institutions Code §§ 5565.10 et seq.,5850 et seq.

Mental Health Services Act (Community)
See Community Mental Health Services Act
Cal. Welfare and Institutions Code § 5000 et seq.

Mental Health Services Act (Comprehensive Child and Adolescent)
Fla. Stat. Ann., 394.490 to 394.497

Mental Health Services Act (Juvenile)
Wash. Rev. Code Ann., 71.34.010 et seq.

Mental Health Services Act (Unified Community)
Okla. Stat. 1981, Title 43A, § 3-301 et seq.

Mental Health Services for the Deaf and Hearing Impaired Act (Comprehensive)
Okla. Stat. 1981, Title 43A, § 3-501 et seq.

Mental Health Services Incentive Act (Rehabilitation and Support)
Neb. Rev. Stat. 1943, 71-5042 to 71-5052

Mental Health Services Reform Act
Cal. Statutes 1985, Ch. 1286

Mental Health Study Act of 1955
July 28, 1955, Ch. 417, 69 Stat. 382, 42 U.S. Code § 242b

Mental Health Systems Act
Oct. 7, 1980, P.L. 96-398, 42 U.S. Code § 9401 nt. Nov. 10, 1986, P.L. 99-646, 42 U.S. Code §§ prec. 9511, 9511,
Nov. 14, 1986, P.L. 99-654, 42 U.S. Code §§ prec. 9511, 9511

Mental Health Task Force Act (Community)
Ill. Comp. Stat. 1992, Ch. 405, § 60/0.01 et seq.

Mental Health Technicians Licensure Act
Kan. Stat. Ann., 65-4201 et seq.

Mental Health Therapist Grant and Scholarship Program
Utah Code Ann. 1953, 62A-13-101 et seq.

Mental Health Treatment Act (Declarations for)
Ida. Code 1947, 66-601 et seq.

Mental Health Treatment and Civil Commitment Act (Children's)
Cal. Welfare and Institutions Code § 5585 et seq.

Mental Health Treatment Facilities Marketing Practices Act
Tex. Health and Safety Code, § 164.001

Mental Health Treatment of Children Act (Inpatient)
Okla. Stat. Ann., Title 43B, § 5-501 et seq.

Mental Hospital Act
Pa. Purdon's Stat., Title 50, § 1051
Tenn. Code Ann., 33-2-101 et seq.

Mental Hospital Voluntary Admission Procedures Act
Okla. Stat. Ann., Title 43A, § 551 et seq.

Mental Hospitals and Institutions Bond Act
Va. Acts 1968, Ch. 16

Mental Hygiene Act
Md. Ann. Code 1974, Art. HG, § 10-1101
N.Y. Consol. Laws. Ch. 27

Mental Illness Act
Kan. Stat. Ann., 59-2901 et seq.

Mental Illness Hospitalization Act
D.C. Code 1973, § 21-501 et seq.
Wash. Rev. Code Ann., 71.02.010 et seq.

Mental Illness Services Pilot Project Act
Ill. Rev. Stat. 1991, Ch. 91 1/2, § 1400 et seq.

Mental Institution Act
Cal. Statutes 1950, 1st Ex. Sess., Ch. 29, p. 471

Mental Institutions Bond Act
N.C. Laws 1953, Ch. 1148

Mental Offenders Act
Ohio Rev. Code 1953, 2947.24 et seq.

Mental Patient's Bill of Rights
N.Y. Mental Hygiene Law (Consol. Laws 1972 Ch. 27) § 33.02

Mental Patients Convalescent Act
N.M. Stat. Ann. 1953, 34-2-11

Mental Private Institutions Act
Wash. Rev. Code Ann., 71.12.455 et seq.

Mental Responsibility Act (Criminal Proceedings)
Mo. Rev. Stat., 552.010 et seq.

Mental Retardation Act
Ariz. Rev. Stat. Ann., § 36-551 et seq.
Ark. Code Ann. 1987, 20-48-201 et seq.
La. Rev. Stat. Ann., 28:380 et seq.
Md. Ann. Code 1974, Art. HG, § 16-101 et seq.

S.C. Code Ann. 1976, § 44-19-10 et seq.

Tenn. Code Ann., 33-5-301 et seq.

Tex. Health and Safety Code, § 591.001 et seq.

Mental Retardation Amendments of 1967

Dec. 4, 1967, P.L. 90-170, 81 Stat. 527, 20 U.S. Code § 617; 42 U.S. Code §§ 2661, 2665, 2671, 2672, 2674, 2677 to 2678d, 2698 to 2698b

Mental Retardation and Developmental Disabilities Act

La. Rev. Stat. Ann., 28:380 et seq.

Md. Ann. Code 1974, Art. HG, § 7-101 et seq.

N.Y. Mental Hygiene Law 1977 (Consol. Laws Ch. 27) § 13.01 et seq.

Mental Retardation and Mental Health Licensure Law

Tenn. Code Ann., 33-2-501 et seq.

Mental Retardation and Related Disabilities Act

S.C. Code Ann. 1976, § 44-20-10 et seq.

Mental Retardation Center Act

Ariz. Laws 1967, Ch. 121

Mental Retardation Facilities and Community Mental Health Centers Act

Iowa Code 1987, 135.43, 135.44

Mental Retardation Facilities and Community Mental Health Centers Construction Act

Aug. 4, 1965, P.L. 89-105, 79 Stat. 427, 20 U.S. Code § 618; 42 U.S. Code §§ 2672, 2682 to 2688d, 2692, 2697

Wis. Stat. Ann., 140.65 et seq.

Mental Retardation Facilities and Community Mental Health Centers Construction Act Amendments of 1965

Aug. 4, 1965, P.L. 89-105, 79 Stat. 427, 20 U.S. Code §§ 615, 617, 618; 31 U.S. Code § 553; 42 U.S. Code §§ 2672, 2682 to 2688d, 2692, 2697

Mental Retardation Facilities and Community Mental Health Centers Construction Act of 1963

Oct. 31, 1963, P.L. 88-164, 77 Stat. 282, 20 U.S. Code §§ 611, 612, 613, 617, 618, 676; 42 U.S. Code §§ 291k, 295 to 295e, 2661 to 2665, 2671 to 2677, 2681 to 2687, 2691 to 2696

June 24, 1967, P.L. 90-31, 81 Stat. 79, 42 U.S. Code §§ 2684, 2691

Dec. 4, 1967, P.L. 90-170, 81 Stat. 530, 531, 42 U.S. Code §§ 2698 to 2698b

Oct. 15, 1968, P.L. 90-574, 82 Stat. 1011, 42 U.S. Code §§ 2693, 2697a

March 13, 1970, P.L. 91-211, 84 Stat. 55, 42 U.S. Code §§ 2691, 2693

Oct. 30, 1970, P.L. 91-517, 84 Stat. 1324, 42 U.S. Code §§ 2691, 2693 to 2696

Mental Retardation Facilities and Local Development Authority Mental Health Act

Tenn. Code Ann., 4-31-701 et seq.

Mental Retardation Facilities Assistance Act (Community)

Kan. Stat. Ann., 65-4411 et seq.

Mental Retardation Facilities Construction Act

See also Developmental Disabilities Services and Facilities Construction Act

Wis. Stat., 140.65 et seq.

Mental Retardation Hospitalization Act

Ky. Rev. Stat. 1971, 202B.010 et seq.

Mental Retardation Protection Act

Minn. Stat. Ann., 252A.01 et seq.

Mental Retardation Services Companies Law

N.Y. Mental Hygiene Law 1977 (Consol. Laws Ch. 27) § 75.01 et seq.

Mental Retardation, Substance Abuse and Mental Health Act

N.C. Gen. Stat. 1943, § 122C-1 et seq.

Mental Treatment for Incarcerated Persons Act
Ill. Rev. Stat. 1991, Ch. 91 1/2, § 140 et seq.

Mentally Disabled Adults Support Services Law (Home Based)
Ill. Rev. Stat. 1991, Ch. 91 1/2, § 1802-1 et seq.

Mentally Disabled Children's Family Assistance Law
Ill. Rev. Stat. 1991, Ch. 91 1/2, § 1803-1 et seq.

Mentally Diseased Persons Hospital Act
Mich. Comp. Laws Ann., 330.1135 et seq.

Mentally Disordered Offenders Compact
See Interstate Compact on the Mentally Disordered Offenders Act

Mentally Disordered Offenders Interstate Compact Act
Ill. Rev. Stat. 1991, Ch. 91 1/2, § 50-20 et seq.

Mentally Disordered Sex Offenders Act
Cal. Welfare and Institutions Code § 6300 et seq.
Fla. Stat. Ann., 917.011 et seq.

Mentally Disturbed Children Family Assistance Law
Ill. Comp. Stat. 1992, Ch. 405, § 80/3-1 et seq.

Mentally Ill Act
D.C. Code Ann., § 21-501 et seq.

Mentally Ill Act (Hospitalization)
Me. Rev. Stat. Ann. 1964, Title 34B, § 3201 et seq.
Mo. Rev. Stat. 1978, 202.843 et seq.

Mentally Ill and Developmentally Disabled Long-term Nursing Home Care Alternatives Act
Colo. Rev. Stat., 26-4.5-201 et seq.

Mentally Ill Commitment Act
N.M. Stat. Ann. 1953, 34-2-1 et seq.

Mentally Ill or Insane Defendants Act
S.C. Code Ann. 1976, § 17-24-10 et seq.

Mentally Ill Persons and Persons with Developmental Disabilities Home and Community-Based Services Act
Colo. Rev. Stat., 26-4.5-201 et seq.

Mentally Ill Persons Home and Community Based Services Act
Colo. Rev. Stat., 26-4-671 et seq.

Mentally Ill Persons' Protection and Advocacy Act
Ill. Rev. Stat. 1991, Ch. 91 1/2, § 1350 et seq.

Mentally Retarded and Developmentally Disabled Persons Act
Ill. Comp. Stat. 1992, Ch. 55, § 105/0.01 et seq.

Mentally Retarded Citizens Constitutional Rights and Dignity Act
D.C. Code Ann., § 6-1901 et seq.

Mentally Retarded Client Rights in Community Residences Act
R.I. Gen. Laws 1956, 40.1-22.1-1 et seq.

Mentally Retarded Community Services Act
Ga. Code Ann., 37-5-1 et seq.

Mentally Retarded Offender Act
Ga. Laws 1975, p. 567

Mentally Retarded Persons Act
Iowa Code Ann., 222.1 et seq.
Neb. Rev. Stat. 1943, 83-381 et seq.
S.C. Code Ann. 1976, § 44-21-10 et seq.
Tex. Health and Safety Code, § 591.001 et seq.

Mentally Retarded Persons Act (Protective Services for)
Vt. Stat. Ann., Title 33, § 3601 et seq.

Mentor and Volunteer Service Act (Academic)
Cal. Government Code § 96100 et seq.

Mentor-Protege Program (Polanco)
Cal. Government Code § 14136

Mentor Teacher Program Act
Cal. Education Code 1976, § 4490 et seq.

Mentoring Services Act (Youth)
Colo. Rev. Stat., 24-32-2801, 24-32-2805

Mercantile Act (Banking)
N.M. Stat. Ann. 1953, 48-14-1 et seq.

Mercantile Act (Children)
N.J. Stat. Ann., 34:2-21.1 et seq.

Mercantile Act (Women)
N.J. Stat. Ann., 34:2-1 to 34:2-28.2

Mercantile and Trading Act (Feme Sole)
Tex. Family Code, § 4.04

Mercantile License Act
Del. Code of 1974, Title 30, § 2101 et seq.

Mercantile License Tax Act
Pa. Purdon's Stat., Title 72, § 2641 et seq.

Mercantile License Tax Ordinance
Pa. Philadelphia Code § 19-1000 et seq.

Mercantile Partnerships and Assumed Business Names Act
Me. Rev. Stat. Ann. 1964, Title 31, § 1 et seq.

Mercantile Registration Act
N.Y. Local Laws 1973, Village of Valley Stream, p. 3854

Mercantile Tax Act
Pa. 1846 Pamph. Laws 486, No. 390

Merced County Flood Control District Act
Cal. Water Code Appendix, § 122-1 et seq.

Merchandising Act
Ky. Rev. Stat. 1971, Superseded Vols., 436.360, 528.020, 528.050, 528.060

Merchandising Practices Act
Mo. Rev. Stat., 407.010 et seq.

Merchant Act (Transient)
See Transient Merchants Act

Merchant Detention Act
La. Code of Crim. Proc. 1966, Art. 215

Merchant Licensing Act (Transient)
Kan. Stat. Ann., 19-2231 et seq.
Okla. Stat. Ann., Title 19, § 1601 et seq.
W. Va. Code 1966, § 47-11E-1 et seq., § 11-12-20 et seq.

Merchant Marine Act
Oct. 29, 1992, P.L. 102-567, 46 U.S. Code Appx. § 1271
Oct. 19, 1996, P.L. 104-324, 46 U.S. Code Appx. §§ 883, 883 nt., 883-1

Merchant Marine Act of 1970
Oct. 21, 1970, P.L. 91-469, 84 Stat. 1018, 5 U.S. Code § 5315, 5 U.S. Code Appx.; 15 U.S. Code § 1507a; 33 U.S. Code §§ 985, 988; 40 U.S. Code § 270f; 46 U.S. Code §§ 1101, 1111, 1119 to 1121, 1151 to 1155, 1159, 1160 and others

Merchant Marine Act, 1920
June 5, 1920, Ch. 250, 41 Stat. 988, 46 U.S. Code §§ 13, 597, 599, 688, 802, 803, 808, 812, 813, 861, 864 to 869, 871, 872, 875 to 877, 880 to 885, 887 to 889, 911, 921 to 927, 941, 951 to 954, 961, 971 to 975, 981 to 984
July 14, 1956, Ch. 600, 70 Stat. 544, 46 U.S. Code § 883
July 7, 1958, P.L. 85-508, 72 Stat. 351, 46 U.S. Code § 883
Sept. 2, 1958, P.L. 85-902, 72 Stat. 1736, 46 U.S. Code § 883-1
Sept. 21, 1959, P.L. 86-327, 73 Stat. 597, 46 U.S. Code § 888
July 5, 1960, P.L. 86-583, 74 Stat. 321, 46 U.S. Code § 883
Sept. 21, 1965, P.L. 89-194, 79 Stat. 823, 46 U.S. Code § 883
Aug. 11, 1968, P.L. 90-474, 82 Stat. 700, 46 U.S. Code § 883
Nov. 16, 1979, P.L. 96-112, 46 U.S. Code §§ 833, 922
Dec. 29, 1982, P.L. 97-389, 46 U.S. Code § 883
March 20, 1984, P.L. 98-224, 46 U.S. Code Appx. §§ 812, 813
Continued

Oct. 21, 1986, P.L. 99-509, 46 U.S. Code Appx. § 952

Jan. 11, 1988, P.L. 100-239, 46 U.S. Code Appx. §§ 883, 883 nt.

June 7, 1988, P.L. 100-329, 102 Stat. 588, 46 U.S. Code Appx. §§ 316, 883, 883 nt.

Nov. 23, 1988, P.L. 100-710, 46 U.S. Code Appx., §§ 13, 862 to 864, 874, 878, 879, 911, 921 to 927, 941, 951 to 954, 961, 971 to 975, 981 to 984

Dec. 12, 1989, P.L. 101-225, 103 Stat. 1925

Nov. 16, 1990, P.L. 101-595, 46 U.S. Code Appx. § 876

Nov. 4, 1992, P.L. 102-587, 46 U.S. Code Appx. §§ 876, 883

Dec. 29, 1995, P.L. 104-88, 46 U.S. Code Appx. §§ 867, 883-1, 884

Oct. 14, 1998, P.L. 105-258, 46 U.S. Code Appx. § 876

Oct. 17, 1998, P.L. 105-261, 46 U.S. Code Appx. § 1295b

Merchant Marine Act, 1928

May 22, 1928, Ch. 675, 45 Stat. 689, 46 U.S. Code §§ 866, 869, 880, 891, 891b, 891c, 891s, 891u to 891x

Dec. 12, 1989, P.L. 101-225, 46 U.S. Code Appx. § 891s

Merchant Marine Act, 1936

June 29, 1936, Ch. 858, 49 Stat. 1985

April 1, 1937, Ch. 64, 50 Stat. 57, 46 U.S. Code § 1194

Aug. 26, 1937, Ch. 822, 50 Stat. 839, 46 U.S. Code §§ 871, 1112, 1116, 1119

May 18, 1938, Ch. 253, 52 Stat. 408, 46 U.S. Code § 1113

June 1, 1938, Ch. 311, 52 Stat. 606, 46 U.S. Code § 1142

June 23, 1938, Ch. 600, 52 Stat. 965, 46 U.S. Code §§ 1271 to 1279

May 14, 1940, Ch. 201, 54 Stat. 216, 46 U.S. Code §§ 1160, 1194 nts.

June 11, 1940, Ch. 327, 54 Stat. 306

June 29, 1940, Ch. 447, 54 Stat. 689, 46 U.S. Code §§ 1128 to 1128g

Oct. 10, 1940, Ch. 849, 54 Stat. 1106, 46 U.S. Code § 1161

June 23, 1941, Ch. 228, 55 Stat. 259, 46 U.S. Code §§ 1254, 1256, 1258, 1259, 1260 nts., 1262

March 6, 1942, Ch. 154, 56 Stat. 140, 46 U.S. Code §§ 1128a, 1128g nt.

March 14, 1942, Ch. 186, 56 Stat. 171, 46 U.S. Code § 1127

April 11, 1942, Ch. 240, 56 Stat. 214, 46 U.S. Code §§ 1128 to 1128g

March 24, 1943, Ch. 26, 57 Stat. 47, 49 to 51, 46 U.S. Code §§ 1128a, 1128b, 1128c, 1128d, 1128e, 1128h, 1242

June 17, 1943, Ch. 130, 57 Stat. 157, 46 U.S. Code § 1161

April 24, 1944, Ch. 178, 58 Stat. 216, 46 U.S. Code §§ 1128-e, 1128e-1

Dec. 23, 1944, Ch. 714, 58 Stat. 920, 46 U.S. Code § 1161

Sept. 7, 1950, Ch. 906, 64 Stat. 773, 46 U.S. Code §§ 1281 to 1294

July 17, 1952, Ch. 939, 66 Stat. 760, 46 U.S. Code §§ 1151, 1153, 1154, 1157, 1159, 1160, 1161, 1175, 1176, 1177, 1223, 1244

Aug. 15, 1953, Ch. 513, 67 Stat. 626, 46 U.S. Code § 1273

Aug. 10, 1954, Ch. 664, 68 Stat. 680, 46 U.S. Code § 1160

Aug. 26, 1954, Ch. 936, 68 Stat. 832, 46 U.S. Code § 1241

Aug. 30, 1954, Ch. 1076, 68 Stat. 967, 46 U.S. Code § 1127

Sept. 3, 1954, Ch. 1265, 68 Stat. 1267, 46 U.S. Code §§ 1271 to 1279

Aug. 3, 1955, Ch. 492, 69 Stat. 440, 46 U.S. Code § 1294

Feb. 20, 1956, Ch. 64, 70 Stat. 25, 46 U.S. Code § 1126

May 10, 1956, Ch. 247, 70 Stat. 148, 46 U.S. Code § 1176

May 28, 1956, Ch. 325, 70 Stat. 187, 46 U.S. Code § 1241

June 25, 1956, Ch. 437, 70 Stat. 332, 46 U.S. Code § 1122a

June 25, 1956, Ch. 438, 70 Stat. 332, 46 U.S. Code § 1273

July 11, 1956, Ch. 574, 70 Stat. 531, 46 U.S. Code § 1205

July 26, 1956, Ch. 737, 70 Stat. 657, 46 U.S. Code § 1152

July 30, 1956, Ch. 792, 70 Stat. 731, 46 U.S. Code § 1206

Aug. 3, 1956, Ch. 929, 70 Stat. 984, 46 U.S. Code §§ 1242, 1286, 1289

Aug. 7, 1956, Ch. 1026, 70 Stat. 1087, 46 U.S. Code §§ 1271, 1273, 1275

Aug. 28, 1957, P.L. 85-191, 71 Stat. 471, 46 U.S. Code § 1192

Feb. 20, 1958, P.L. 85-331, 72 Stat. 16, 46 U.S. Code § 1126

Feb. 20, 1958, P.L. 85-332, 72 Stat. 17, 46 U.S. Code § 1160

July 7, 1958, P.L. 85-507, 72 Stat. 337, 46 U.S. Code § 1111

July 15, 1958, P.L. 85-520, 72 Stat. 358, 46 U.S. Code § 1275

Aug. 14, 1958, P.L. 85-637, 72 Stat. 592, 46 U.S. Code § 1177

Aug. 28, 1958, P.L. 85-791, 72 Stat. 947, 46 U.S. Code § 1181

March 18, 1959, P.L. 86-3, 73 Stat. 12, 46 U.S. Code §§ 883 nt., 1156, 1175, 1204

July 31, 1959, P.L. 86-120, 73 Stat. 266, 46 U.S. Code § 1294

July 31, 1959, P.L. 86-123, 73 Stat. 269, 46 U.S. Code §§ 1272, 1274, 1276, 1276a, 1277 to 1279

July 31, 1959, P.L. 86-127, 73 Stat. 272, 46 U.S. Code §§ 1271, 1274, 1279a

Sept. 8, 1959, P.L. 86-237, 73 Stat. 471, 46 U.S. Code § 1161

Sept. 21, 1959, P.L. 86-327, 73 Stat. 597, 46 U.S. Code § 1244

June 12, 1960, P.L. 86-518, 74 Stat. 216, 46 U.S. Code §§ 1125, 1152, 1153, 1156, 1157, 1159, 1160, 1175, 1177, 1181, 1195, 1204, 1274, 1276, 1276a

July 5, 1960, P.L. 86-575, 74 Stat. 312, 46 U.S. Code § 1160

July 7, 1960, P.L. 86-607, 74 Stat. 362, 46 U.S. Code § 1152

July 12, 1960, P.L. 86-624, 74 Stat. 421, 46 U.S. Code §§ 1155, 1176, 1192

Sept. 2, 1960, P.L. 86-685, 74 Stat. 733, 46 U.S. Code §§ 1271, 1274

May 27, 1961, P.L. 87-45, 75 Stat. 89, 46 U.S. Code §§ 1171 to 1173, 1176, 1177, 1183

July 20, 1961, P.L. 87-93, 75 Stat. 212, 46 U.S. Code § 1126

Sept. 6, 1961, P.L. 87-199, 75 Stat. 468, 46 U.S. Code § 1126

Sept. 6, 1961, P.L. 87-208, 75 Stat. 480, 46 U.S. Code § 1126

Sept. 14, 1961, P.L. 87-243, 75 Stat. 513, 46 U.S. Code § 1173

Sept. 21, 1961, P.L. 87-266, 75 Stat. 565, 46 U.S. Code § 1241

Sept. 21, 1961, P.L. 87-271, 75 Stat. 570, 46 U.S. Code § 1177

Sept. 26, 1961, P.L. 87-303, 75 Stat. 661, 46 U.S. Code §§ 1161, 1271

Oct. 5, 1961, P.L. 87-401, 75 Stat. 833, 46 U.S. Code § 1160

Oct. 3, 1962, P.L. 87-743, 76 Stat. 740, 46 U.S. Code § 1288

Oct. 5, 1962, P.L. 87-755, 76 Stat. 751, 46 U.S. Code § 1160

Oct. 10, 1962, P.L. 87-782, 76 Stat. 796, 46 U.S. Code § 1161

Oct. 18, 1962, P.L. 87-839, 76 Stat. 1074, 46 U.S. Code § 1122b

Oct. 24, 1962, P.L. 87-877, 76 Stat. 1200, 46 U.S. Code §§ 1123, 1152, 1159

Dec. 23, 1963, P.L. 88-227, 77 Stat. 470, 46 U.S. Code § 1161

July 11, 1964, P.L. 88-370, 78 Stat. 313, 46 U.S. Code § 1152

Aug. 10, 1964, P.L. 88-410, 78 Stat. 385, 46 U.S. Code § 1152

Aug. 22, 1964, P.L. 88-478, 78 Stat. 587, 46 U.S. Code § 1289

Sept. 12, 1964, P.L. 88-595, 78 Stat. 943, 46 U.S. Code § 1161

July 7, 1965, P.L. 89-66, 79 Stat. 211, 46 U.S. Code § 1122b

July 27, 1965, P.L. 89-89, 79 Stat. 264, 46 U.S. Code § 1294

Aug. 14, 1965, P.L. 89-127, 79 Stat. 519, 46 U.S. Code § 1152

Oct. 10, 1965, P.L. 89-254, 79 Stat. 980, 46 U.S. Code § 1160

Sept. 19, 1966, P.L. 89-589, 80 Stat. 811, 46 U.S. Code § 1152

Sept. 5, 1967, P.L. 90-81, 81 Stat. 193, 46 U.S. Code § 1119

Dec. 10, 1967, P.L. 90-183, 81 Stat. 559, 46 U.S. Code § 1159

Dec. 14, 1967, P.L. 90-194, 81 Stat. 580, 46 U.S. Code § 1279b

Dec. 18, 1967, P.L. 90-214, 81 Stat. 660, 46 U.S. Code § 1159

March 16, 1968, P.L. 90-268, 82 Stat. 49, 46 U.S. Code § 1122

June 15, 1968, P.L. 90-341, 82 Stat. 180, 46 U.S. Code § 1274

June 22, 1968, P.L. 90-358, 82 Stat. 248, 46 U.S. Code § 1183

July 27, 1968, P.L. 90-434, 82 Stat. 449, 46 U.S. Code § 1122b

Oct. 12, 1968, P.L. 90-572, 82 Stat. 1004, 46 U.S. Code § 1152

Continued

July 8, 1969, P.L. 91-40, 83 Stat. 44, 46 U.S. Code § 1152

May 14, 1970, P.L. 91-250, 84 Stat. 215, 46 U.S. Code § 1183

Oct. 15, 1970, P.L. 91-452, 84 Stat. 930, 46 U.S. Code § 1124

Oct. 21, 1970, P.L. 91-469, 84 Stat. 1018, 46 U.S. Code §§ 1101, 1111, 1119 to 1121, 1151 to 1155, 1159, 1160, 1171, 1173, 1175 to 1177, 1204, 1213, 1222, 1223, 1241, 1244, 1271, 1273 to 1275, 1294

Dec. 31, 1970, P.L. 91-603, 84 Stat. 1675, 46 U.S. Code §§ 1151, 1152, 1171

Dec. 31, 1970, Pub 91-603, 84 Stat. 1675, 46 U.S. Code §§ 1151, 1152, 1171, 1223

Nov. 12, 1977, P.L. 95-173, 46 U.S. Code § 1119 et seq.

Nov. 15, 1977, P.L. 95-177, 46 U.S. Code § 1160

April 7, 1978, P.L. 95-257, 46 U.S. Code § 1274

June 26, 1978, P.L. 95-298, 46 U.S. Code § 1273

July 28, 1978, P.L. 95-323, 46 U.S. Code § 1126

Oct. 24, 1978, P.L. 95-505, 46 UCS § 1159

Nov. 6, 1978, P.L. 95-598, 46 U.S. Code § 1247

Feb. 25, 1980, P.L. 96-195, 46 U.S. Code § 1294

March 17, 1980, P.L. 96-210, 46 U.S. Code § 1152

Aug. 3, 1980, P.L. 96-320, 46 U.S. Code § 1271 et seq.

Jan. 6, 1983, P.L. 97-424, 46 U.S. Code § 1273

March 20, 1984, P.L. 98-224, 46 U.S. Code Appx. § 1122

Oct. 30, 1984, P.L. 98-595, 46 U.S. Code Appx. §§ 1124, 1273 to 1275

July 3, 1985, P.L. 99-59, 46 U.S. Code Appx. § 1294

Dec. 23, 1985, P.L. 99-198, 46 U.S. Code Appx. §§ 241e to 1241o

Aug. 1, 1986, P.L. 99-368, 46 Appx. § 1295b

Oct. 22, 1986, P.L. 99-514, 46 U.S. Code Appx. § 1177

Aug. 23, 1988, P.L. 100-418, 102 Stat. 1572, 46 U.S. Code Appx. § 1122b

Nov. 10, 1988, P.L. 100-647, 46 U.S. Code Appx. § 1177

Nov. 23, 1988, P.L. 100-710, 46 U.S. Code Appx. §§ 1113, 1141 et seq., 1206, 1242 et seq., 1251 et seq., 1260 et seq., 1271

Oct. 13, 1989, P.L. 101-115, 46 U.S. Code Appx. §§ 1282, 1294, 1295c

Dec. 12, 1989, P.L. 101-225, 46 U.S. Code Appx. §§ 1111, 1160, 1182, 1222 to 1225, 1276, 1279, 1279b

Aug. 18, 1990, P.L. 101-380, 46 U.S. Code Appx. §§ 1274, 1274a

Nov. 5, 1990, P.L. 101-508, 46 U.S. Code Appx. § 1177

Nov. 16, 1990, P.L. 101-595, 46 U.S. Code Appx. §§ 1160, 1295b, 1295b nt., 1295d

Nov. 28, 1990, P.L. 101-624, 46 U.S. Code Appx. § 1241f

Nov. 4, 1992, P.L. 102-587, 46 U.S. Code Appx. §§ 1271, 1274a, 1295c

Nov. 30, 1993, P.L. 103-160, 46 U.S. Code Appx. §§ 1271 et seq., 1279d, 1279e

Dec. 29, 1995, P.L. 104-88, 46 U.S. Code Appx. § 1114a

Feb. 10, 1996, P.L. 104-106, 46 U.S. Code Appx. § 1294

Oct. 8, 1996, P.L. 104-239, 46 U.S. Code Appx. §§ 1132, 1162, prec. 1171, 1175, 1185a, 1185e, prec. 1187, 1187, 1187a to 1187d, 1222, 1223, 1241f, 1271, 1273, 1274, 1279, 1279f, 1294

Oct. 19, 1996, P.L. 104-316, 46 U.S. Code Appx. § 1241

Oct. 19, 1996, P.L. 104-324, 46 U.S. Code Appx. § 1295a

Aug. 5, 1997, P.L. 105-34, 46 U.S. Code Appx. § 1177

Nov. 18, 1997, P.L. 105-85, 46 U.S. Code Appx. §§ 1123, 1187a, 1187b, 1187e

Oct. 17, 1998, P.L. 105-261, 46 U.S. Code Appx. § 1285

Nov. 13, 1998, P.L. 105-385, 46 U.S. Code Appx. § 1241f

Merchant Marine Acts

Sept. 7, 1916, Ch. 451, 39 Stat. 728, 31 U.S. Code § 745; 46 U.S. Code §§ 801-806, 808-842

July 15, 1918, Ch. 152, 40 Stat. 900, 46 U.S. Code §§ 801-803, 808, 811-840, 842

July 31, 1976, P.L. 94-372, 46 U.S. Code § 1152 et seq.

Merchant Marine Decorations and Medals Act
May 30, 1988, P.L. 100-324, 102 Stat. 576, 49 U.S. Code Appx. §§ 2001 et seq., 2001 nt.

Merchant Marine Emergency Act
June 16, 1942, Ch. 416, 56 Stat. 370, 40 U.S. Code § 326 nt.

Merchant Mariner Memorial Act of 1990
Nov. 16, 1990, P.L. 101-595, 104 Stat. 2996

Merchant Ship Priorities Act
July 14, 1941, Ch. 297, 55 Stat. 591

Merchant Ship Sales Act of 1946
March 8, 1946, Ch. 82, 60 Stat. 41, 50 U.S. Code Appx. §§ 1735 to 1746
June 28, 1947, Ch. 161, 61 Stat. 190, 50 U.S. Code Appx. §§ 1735 nt., 1738, 1744
Feb. 27, 1948, Ch. 78, 62 Stat. 38, 46 U.S. Code prec. § 1 nt.; 50 U.S. Code Appx. §§ 1735, 1739 nts., 1744
Feb. 28, 1949, Ch. 12, 63 Stat. 9, 46 U.S. Code prec. § 1 nt.; 50 U.S. Code Appx. §§ 1735 nt., 1739 nt., 1744
June 29, 1949, Ch. 281, 63 Stat. 349, 46 U.S. Code prec. § 1 nt., § 864b; 50 U.S. Code Appx. §§ 1735 nt., 1739 nt., 1744
June 30, 1950, Ch. 427, 64 Stat. 308, 46 U.S. Code §§ prec. § 1 nt., 883 nt.; 50 U.S. Code Appx. §§ 1735 nt., 1738, 1744
Aug. 17, 1950, Ch. 725, 64 Stat. 452, 50 U.S. Code Appx. § 1735 nt.
Sept. 28, 1950, Ch. 1093, 64 Stat. 1078, 46 U.S. Code § 1274; 50 U.S. Code Appx. § 1745
Aug. 3, 1954, Ch. 1175, 68 Stat. 1050, 50 U.S. Code Appx. § 1738
Aug. 6, 1956, Ch. 1013, 70 Stat. 1068, 50 U.S. Code Appx. § 1742
June 12, 1960, P.L. 86-518, 74 Stat. 216, 50 U.S. Code Appx. § 1737
Aug. 22, 1986, P.L. 99-386, 50 U.S. Code Appx. § 1746
Oct. 13, 1989, P.L. 101-115, 50 U.S. Code Appx. § 1744
Dec. 19, 1991, P.L. 102-241, 50 U.S. Code Appx. § 1744
Nov. 4, 1992, P.L. 102-587, 50 U.S. Code Appx. §§ 1744, 1744 nt.
Feb. 10, 1996, P.L. 104-106, 50 U.S. Code Appx. § 1744
Oct. 8, 1996, P.L. 104-239, 50 U.S. Code Appx. § 1744

Merchant Truckmen Act
N.Y. Agriculture and Markets Law (Consol. Laws Ch. 69) § 223 et seq.

Merchantability of Title Act
See Marketable Title Act

Merchants Act (Farm Produce Commission)
Ill. Rev. Stat. 1991, Ch. 111, § 100 et seq.

Merchants Act (Itinerant)
See Itinerant Merchants Act

Merchants' Licensing Act
Mo. Rev. Stat., 150.010 et seq.

Merchants' Taxing and Licensing Act
Tenn. Code Ann., Superseded Vol., 67-4701 et seq.

Mercury-Containing and Rechargeable Battery Management Act
May 13, 1996, P.L. 104-142, 42 U.S. Code § 14301 nt.

Mercury-Containing Battery Management Act
May 13, 1996, P.L. 104-142, Title II, 42 U.S. Code § 14301 nt.

Mercury Emissions Consumer Information Act
Minn. Stat. Ann., 116. 925

Mercy Act (Murder)
Mass. Gen Laws 1990, 265:2

Merger Act (Authorization)
Pa. 1876 Pamph. Laws 30, No. 25, § 5
Pa. 1909 Pamph. Laws 408, No. 229

Merger Act (Banks)
See Bank Merger Act

Merger Act (City of Bristol)
Tenn. Private Acts 1921, Ch. 967

Merger Act (Corporations)
See Corporation Merger Act

Merger Act (Nonstock Corporations)
Wis. Stat. Ann., 181.42 et seq.

Merger Act (Stock Corporations)
N.Y. Business Corporations Law (Consol. Laws, Ch. 4) § 901 et seq.

Merger Act (Street Railways)
D.C. Code 1973, § 43-801 et seq.

Merger Act (Utilities)
D.C. Code Ann., § 43-801 et seq.

Merger Acts
N.Y. Banking Law (Consol. Laws Ch. 2) § 600 et seq.
N.Y. Business Corporations Law 1961 (Consol. Laws Ch. 4) § 901 et seq.

Merger and Consolidation Act (Corporations)
Mo. Rev. Stat., 351.410 et seq.

Merger of Contiguous Cities Act
Ky. Rev. Stat. 1971, 81.410 et seq.

Merger of Not for Profit Corporations Act
Ill. Rev. Stat 1991, Ch. 32, § 188.90 et seq.

Merger or Municipal Consolidation Act
Pa. Cons. Stat., Title 53, § 731 et seq.

Merger or Surrender of Reversion Act
Ill. Rev. Stat. 1991, Ch. 30, §§ 38.9, 39

Merit Act (Montgomery County)
Ala. Code 1958, App., § 523(32) et seq.

Merit Award Program Act (Legislative)
Mich. Comp. Laws Ann., 390.1301 et seq.

Merit Employment Code (Comptrollers)
Ill. Comp. Stat. 1992, Ch. 30, § 725/1 et seq.

Merit Employment Code (Secretary of State)
Ill. Rev. Stat. 1991, Ch. 124, § 101 et seq.

Merit Personnel Act (Government)
D.C. Code Ann., § 1-601.1 et seq.

Merit Rating Act
Mass. Gen. Laws 1932, Ch. 90A, § 5 et seq.

Merit Selection of P.S.C. Act
S.C. Code Ann. 1976, § 58-3-21 et seq.

Merit System Act
Ala. Code 1975, § 36-26-1 et seq.
Fla. Stat. Ann., 110.1245 et seq.
Ky. Rev. Stat. 1971, Superseded Vols., 18.110 et seq.
Md. Ann. Code 1957, Art. 64A
Mo. Rev. Stat., 36.010 et seq.
N.C. Gen. Stat. 1943, § 126-1 et seq.
Neb. Rev. Stat. 1943, 81-1301 et seq.
Ore. Rev. Stat., 240.005 et seq.
R.I. Gen. Laws 1956, 36-3-1 et seq.
Tenn. Public Acts 1937, Ch. 54
Vt. Stat. Ann., Title 3, § 301 et seq.

Merit System Act (Americus)
Ga. Laws 1951, p. 2007

Merit System Act (City of Lilburn)
Ga. Laws 1975, p. 4819

Merit System Act (Civil Service)
Ala. Code 1958, Title 12, § 133 et seq.
Ky. Rev. Stat. 1971, Superseded Vols., 18.110 et seq.
Okla. Stat. Ann., Title 74, § 840.2 et seq.

Merit System Act (DeKalb County)
Ga. Laws 1956, p. 3111

Merit System Act (Floyd County)
Ga. Laws 1967, p. 2253
Ga. Laws 1969, p. 2505

Merit System Act (Jefferson County)
Ala. Code 1958, App. § 645 et seq.

Merit System Act (Municipal Employees)
Conn. Gen. Stat. Ann., § 7-407 et seq.

Merit System Act (State Employees)
Conn. Gen. Stat. Ann., § 5-193 et seq.
Ga. Code Ann., 45-20-1 et seq.

Merit System Extension Act (Highway Employees)
Ga. Laws 1949, p. 504

Meriwether County Airport Authority Act
Ga. Laws 1997, p. 3640

Meriwether County Public Facilities Authority Act
Ga. Laws 1977, p. 3820

Meriwether County Water and Sewerage Authority Act
Ga. Laws 1975, p. 3194

Merrill-McMillan Adult Rights Act
Ala. Acts 1975, p. 600, No. 126

Merrimack River Flood Control Compact Act
N.H. Rev. Stat. 1955, 484:7 et seq.

Merrimack River Study Act of 1990
Aug. 10, 1990, P.L. 101-356, 16 U.S. Code § 1271 nt.

Merritt Parkway Act
Conn. Gen. Stat. Ann., § 13a-26 et seq.

Merritt-Quinlan Act (Marriage Licenses)
Mich. Comp. Laws Ann., 551.103a

Mervyn M. Dymally Aid for the Adoption of Children Act
Cal. Statutes 1971, Ch. 1724, p. 3669

Mesa Consolidated Water District Law
Cal. Water Code § 33200 et seq.

Mesa Verde National Park Acts
June 29, 1906, Ch. 3607, 34 Stat. 616, 16 U.S. Code §§ 111, 112 to 115
June 30, 1913, Ch. 4, 38 Stat. 83, 16 U.S. Code §§ 111, 112
June 12, 1917, Ch. 27, 40 Stat. 152 (See 16 U.S. Code § 6)
April 25, 1928, Ch. 434, 45 Stat. 458, 16 U.S. Code §§ 117, 117c, 117d; See, also 18 U.S. Code §§ 13, 3041, 3053, 3141; Fed. Rules Crim. Proc. Rules 4, 5(c) 9; 28 U.S. Code §§ 85, 604, 631, 632, 634; Fed Rules Civ. Proc. Rule 4

May 14, 1930, Ch. 273, 46 Stat. 315, 16 U.S. Code § 118
Jan. 26, 1931, Ch. 47, 46 Stat. 1043, 16 U.S. Code § 115a
Feb. 26, 1931, Ch. 308, 46 Stat. 1422, 16 U.S. Code §§ 111a, 111b
Dec. 23, 1963, P.L. 88-235, 77 Stat. 473, 16 U.S. Code §§ 111c to 111e

Messages Tax Act
Ill. Comp. Stat. 1992, Ch. 35, § 610/1 et seq.
Ill. Rev. Stat. 1991, Ch. 120, § 467.1 et seq.

Metallic Minerals Conservation Act
Iowa Code Ann., 458A.1 et seq.

Metallic Minerals Mining Tax Act
S.D. Codified Laws 1988, Ch. 102

Metallic Minerals Surface Mining Reclamation Act
S.D. Codified Laws 1988, Ch. 359

Metallic Minerals Waste Management Act
Mo. Laws 1989, H.B. No. 321
Mo. Rev. Stat., 444.352 et seq.

Metallic Mining Reclamation Act
Wis. Stat. Ann., 144.80 et seq.

Metalliferous Mining Securities Act
Wash. Laws 1937, Ch. 178

Metals Recyclers and Second-Hand Dealers
Fla. Stat. Ann., 538.03 et seq.

Metcalf-Baker Act (Discrimination in Housing Accommodations)
N.Y. Executive Law 1951 (Consol. Laws Ch. 18) §§ 292, Subd. 12; 296, Subd. 5

Metcalf-Baker Act (Public Housing)
N.Y. Civil Rights Law (Consol. Laws Ch. 6) § 18b, Subd. 3

Metcalf-Hatch Law (Animal Experiments)
N.Y. Public Health Law 1953 (Consol. Laws Ch. 45) § 504 et seq.

Metcalf-Pomeroy Act (Laboratory)
N.Y. Public Health Law 1953 (Consol. Laws Ch. 45) § 570 et seq.

Metcalf-Volker Act (Drug Addiction)
N.Y. Mental Hygiene Law 1972 (Consol. Laws Ch. 27) § 19.01 et seq.

Metering Act (Water)
Colo. Rev. Stat., 37-97-101 et seq.

Methamphetamine Trafficking Penalty Enhancement Act of 1998
Oct. 21, 1998, P.L. 105-277, Division E, 112 Stat. 2681, 21 U.S. Code § 801 nt.

Methane Gas Hazards Reduction Act
Cal. Public Resources Code § 3850 et seq.

Methane Gas Well Plugging Fund Act (Coalbed)
Ala. Code 1975, § 9-17-130 et seq.

Methane Transportation Research, Development, and Demonstration Act of 1980
Dec. 12, 1980, P.L. 96-512, 15 U.S. Code §§ 3801 et seq., 3801 nt.
Dec. 21, 1982. P.L. 97-375, 15 U.S. Code § 3803
Nov. 2, 1994, P.L. 103-437, 15 U.S. Code § 3803
Dec. 21, 1995, P.L. 104-66, 15 U.S. Code § 3808

Metric Conversion Act of 1975
Dec. 23, 1975, P.L. 94-168, 89 Stat. 1007, 15 U.S. Code § 205a et seq.
Aug. 23, 1988, P.L. 100-418, 102 Stat. 1451, 15 U.S. Code §§ 205a, 205k
Dec. 21, 1995, P.L. 104-66, 15 U.S. Code § 205j-1
Oct. 11, 1996, P.L. 104-289, 15 U.S. Code §§ 205c, 205l

Metric Implementation and Standards Act
Minn. Stat. Ann., 239.001 et seq.

Metric System Act
July 28, 1866, Ch. 301, 14 Stat. 339
S.C. Code Ann. 1976, § 39-9-230 et seq.

Metro-East Exposition and Performing Arts Authority Act
Ill. Rev. Stat. 1977, Ch. 85, § 1501 et seq.

Metro-East Sanitary District Act
Ill. Rev. Stat. 1991, Ch. 42, § 501-1 et seq.

Metro East Solid Waste Disposal and Energy Producing Service Act
Ill. Rev. Stat. 1991, Ch. 111 1/2, § 7101 et seq.

Metro Sheriff's Restitution Act
Tenn. Code Ann., 7-3-401 et seq.

Metro Transit Police Force Act
D.C. Laws 1976, Nos. 1-67

Metrobus Commercial Advertising Act
D.C. Laws 1977, Nos. 1-91

Metroplex Development Authority Act (Schenectady)
N.Y. Public Authorities Law (Consol. Laws Ch. 43A) § 2650 et seq.

Metropolitan Agricultural Preserves Act
Minn. Stat. Ann., 473H.01 et seq.

Metropolitan Airport Authority Act
Tenn. Code Ann., 42-4-101 et seq.

Metropolitan Airport Authority Act (Missouri-St. Louis)
Mo. Rev. Stat. 1969, 305.500 et seq.

Metropolitan Airports Commission Act
Minn. Stat. Ann., 473.601 et seq.

Metropolitan and Regional Planning Act (Southwestern Illinois)
Ill. Rev. Stat. 1985, Ch. 85, § 1151 et seq.

Metropolitan Area Aircraft Noise Attenuation Act
Minn. Stat. Ann., 473.192

Metropolitan Area Airport Authority Act (St. Louis)
Ill. Rev. Stat. 1983, Ch. 15 1/2, § 301 et seq.

Metropolitan Area Development Act
Ind. Code Ann., 18-7-2-1 et seq.

Metropolitan Area Planning Act
Minn. Stat. 1986, 472.01 et seq.

Metropolitan Area Planning Act (Southwestern Illinois)
Ill. Rev. Stat. 1985, sect. 1151 et seq.

Metropolitan Area Planning Commission Act
Okla. Stat. Ann., Title 19, § 863.1 et seq.

Metropolitan Area Transit Authority Compact Act
Md. Ann. Code 1974, Art. TR, § 10-204

Metropolitan Area Transit Regulation Compact Act
Md. Ann. Code 1974, Art. TR, § 10-203

Metropolitan Area Waste Disposal Act
Miss. Code Ann. 1972, § 21-27-161 et seq.

Metropolitan Area Water Quality Control Commission Act
Ga. Laws 1966, p. 3346

Metropolitan Area Water Supply Act
Miss. Code Ann. 1972, § 51-9-189 et seq.

Metropolitan Atlanta Rapid Transit Authority Act of 1965
Ga. Laws 1965, p. 2243

Metropolitan Authority Act (Huron-Clinton)
Mich. Comp. Laws 1970, 119.51 et seq.

Metropolitan Boundary Act for Class A Counties
N.M. Stat. Ann., 3-57-1 et seq.

Metropolitan Bus Authority Act
P.R. Laws Ann. 1954, Title 23, § 601 et seq.

Metropolitan Celebration Authority Act
Tenn. Code Ann., 7-6-101 et seq.

Metropolitan Cities Incorporation Law
Nev. Rev. Stat. 1973 Reprint, Replaced Pages, 266A.005 et seq.

Metropolitan Civic Center Act
Ill. Rev. Stat. 1991, Ch. 85, § 1361 et seq.

Metropolitan Civic Center Support Act
Ill. Rev. Stat. 1991, Ch. 85, § 1391 et seq.

Metropolitan Class Cities Zoning Act
Neb. Rev. Stat. 1943, 14-401 et seq.

Metropolitan Council Act
Mich. Comp. Laws Ann., 124.651 et seq.
Wash. Rev. Code Ann., 35.58.010 et seq.

Metropolitan Council Service Improvement Act
Minn. Stat. 1986, 473.1295

Metropolitan Culture and Recreation District Compact Act (Missouri-Kansas)
Mo. Laws 1987, S.B. No. 14
Mo. Rev. Stat., 70.445 et seq.

Metropolitan District Act
Conn. Gen. Stat. Ann., § 7-333 et seq.
Mich. Comp. Laws Ann., 119.1 et seq.

Metropolitan District Act (Maryland-Washington)
Md. Laws 1943, Ch. 1008

Metropolitan District Beach Erosion Loan Act
Mass. Acts 1956, Ch. 736

Metropolitan District Commission Recreational Loan Act
Mass. Acts 1957, Ch. 627
Mass. Acts 1959, Ch. 549

Metropolitan District Incinerator Bond Act
Mass. Gen Laws 1990, 92:9A

Metropolitan District Mystic River Water Tunnel Loan Act
Mass. Acts 1950, Ch. 741

Metropolitan District Park Loan Act
Mass. Acts 1961, Ch. 517

Metropolitan District Recreational Loan Act
Mass. Acts 1955, Ch. 731

Metropolitan District Sewerage Relief Loan Act
Mass. Acts 1962, Ch. 655

Metropolitan District Water Loan Act
Mass. Acts 1950, Ch. 660
Mass. Acts 1952, Ch. 619
Mass. Acts 1956, Ch. 685

Metropolitan District Water Main Loan Act
Mass. Acts 1954, Ch. 278
Mass. Acts 1957, Ch. 711
Mass. Acts 1959, Ch. 590

Metropolitan Elections District Law
N.Y. Election Law 1976 (Consol. Laws Ch. 17) § 4-100

Metropolitan Exposition and Auditorium Authority Act
Ill. Rev. Stat. 1991, Ch. 85 § 1391 et seq.

Metropolitan Exposition and Auditorium Authority Act (Lake County and Will County)
Ill. Rev. Stat. 1991, Ch. 85, § 1580-1 et seq.

Metropolitan Fiscal Disparities Act
Minn. Stat. Ann., 473.01 et seq.

Metropolitan Flood Control Act (Fresno)
Cal. Statutes 1955, Ch. 503, p. 971

Metropolitan Football Stadium District Act
Colo. Rev. Stat., 32-15-101 et seq.

Metropolitan Government Act
Tenn. Code Ann., 7-1-101 et seq.

Metropolitan Governments' Port Authority Act
Tenn. Code Ann., 7-5-101 et seq.

Metropolitan Hearing Officer Act
Tenn. Code Ann., 7-7-101 et seq.

Metropolitan Hospital Authority Act
Tenn. Code Ann., 7-57-101 et seq.

Metropolitan Improvement Act (Chattanooga)
Tenn. Private Acts 1927, Ch. 457

Metropolitan Landfill Abatement Act
Minn. Stat. Ann., 473.841 et seq.

Metropolitan Library Act
Okla. Stat. Ann., Title 65, § 551 et seq.

Metropolitan Livable Communities Act
Minn. Stat. Ann., 473.25 et seq.

Metropolitan Municipal Corporations Act
Wash. Rev. Code Ann., 35.58.010 et seq.

Metropolitan Park District Act
Wash. Rev. Code Ann., 35.61.010 et seq.

Metropolitan Pier and Exposition Authority Act
Ill. Rev. Stat. 1991, Ch. 85, § 1221 et seq.

Metropolitan Planning Commission Act
Ind. Code Ann., 18-7-2-1 et seq., 18-7-3-1 et seq.
Iowa Code Ann., 473A.1 et seq.
Iowa Code 1983, 28I.1 et seq.

Metropolitan Police Act
Ind. Code Ann., 36-8-2-1 et seq.
Kan. Laws 1887, Ch. 100
Ky. Rev. Stat. 1971, 95.160 et seq.
Mont. Code Ann., 7-32-4101 et seq.

Metropolitan Police Act (Kansas City)
Mo. Rev. Stat., 84.350 et seq.

Metropolitan Police Act (St. Louis)
Mo. Rev. Stat., 84.010 et seq.

Metropolitan Police Officer Civil Rights Act
D.C. Laws 1978, Nos. 2-71

Metropolitan Port Authority Act
Ark. Code Ann. 1987, 14-185-101 et seq.

Metropolitan Rapid Transit Authority Act (Los Angeles)
Cal. Statutes 1957, Ch. 547, p. 1609

Metropolitan Rapid Transit District Act (San Francisco Bay Area)
Cal. Statutes 1949, Ch. 1239, p. 2173

Metropolitan Recreation District Act
Colo. Rev. Stat., 32-2-101 et seq.

Metropolitan Redevelopment Code
N.M. Stat. Ann., 3-60A-1 et seq.

Metropolitan Reorganization Act
Minn. Laws 1974, Ch. 422

Metropolitan River Protection Act
Ga. Code Ann., 12-5-440 et seq.

Metropolitan Sanitary and Storm Sewer Districts Act
Mont. Code Ann., 7-13-101 et seq.

Metropolitan School District Act
Ind. Code Ann., 20-4-8-12 et seq.

Metropolitan Service District Act
Ore. Rev. Stat., 268.010 et seq.

Metropolitan Sewage Disposal District Act
Colo. Rev. Stat., 32-4-501 et seq.

Metropolitan Sewerage District Act
Ky. Rev. Stat. 1971, 76.010 et seq.
N.C. Gen. Stat. 1943, § 162A-64 et seq.
Wis. Stat. Ann., 66.20 et seq.

Metropolitan Sewerage Loan Act
Mass. Acts 1951, Ch. 645
Mass. Acts 1954, Ch. 580
Mass. Acts 1955, Ch. 551
Mass. Acts 1957, Ch. 710
Mass. Acts 1962, Ch. 658

Metropolitan Sewerage Loan Act (North District)
Mass. Acts 1951, Ch. 757
Mass. Acts 1954, Ch. 452
Mass. Acts 1955, Ch. 682

Metropolitan Stadium Act
Colo. Rev. Stat., 89-10-1 et seq.

Metropolitan Thoroughfare Authority Act
Ind. Code Ann., 19-5-4-1 et seq.

Metropolitan Transit Authority Act
Ill. Rev. Stat. 1991, Ch. 111 2/3, § 301 et seq.
Kan. Stat. Ann., 12-2801 et seq.
Mass. Acts 1947, Ch. 544
Neb. Rev. Stat. 1943, 14-1801 et seq.
Pa. Purdon's Stat., Title 66, § 2001 et seq.

Metropolitan Transit Authority Act (Los Angeles)
Cal. Statutes 1957, Ch. 547, p. 1609

Metropolitan Transit Commission Act
Minn. Stat. Ann., 473.404 et seq.

Metropolitan Transit District Act (Fresno)
Cal. Statutes 1961, Ch. 1932

Metropolitan Transit District Act (Greater Bakersfield)
Cal. Public Utilities Code § 101000 et seq.

Metropolitan Transit District Act (Stockton)
Cal. Public Utilities Code § 50000 et seq.

Metropolitan Transit District Compact (New York—New Jersey)
N.Y. Laws 1958, Ch. 965

Metropolitan Transportation Authorities Act
Mich. Comp. Laws Ann., 124.401 et seq.
N.Y. Public Authorities Law (Consol. Laws Ch. 43A) § 1260 et seq.

Metropolitan Transportation Authority Act
Fla. Stat. Ann., 163.801 et seq.

Metropolitan Transportation Authority Reform Act (Los Angeles County)
Cal. Statutes 1992, Ch. 60

Metropolitan Transportation Commission Act
Cal. Government Code § 66500 et seq.

Metropolitan Transportation Planning Act (Federal Aid)
Cal. Streets and Highways Code § 2230 et seq.

Metropolitan Washington Airports Act Amendments of 1991
Dec. 18, 1991, P.L. 102-240, 49 U.S. Code Appx. §§ 2451 nt., 2456

Metropolitan Washington Airports Act of 1986
Oct. 18, 1986, P.L. 99-500, 49 U.S. Code Appx. §§ 2451 nt., 2451 to 2461
Oct. 30, 1986, P.L. 99-591, 49 U.S. Code Appx. §§ 2451 nt., 2451 to 2461

Metropolitan Washington Airports Amendments Act of 1996
Oct. 9, 1996, P.L. 104-264, Title IX, 110 Stat. 3274

Metropolitan Washington Waste Management Study Act
Oct. 6, 1992, P.L. 102-386, 106 Stat. 1517

Metropolitan Water Authority Law (Washoe County)
Nev. Stat. 1983, Ch. 487, p. 1309

Metropolitan Water District Act
Cal. Water Code Appendix, § 109-1 et seq.
Mo. Rev. Stat., 247.230 et seq.
N.C. Gen. Stat. 1943, § 162A-31 et seq.
Utah Code Ann. 1953, 73-8-1 et seq.

Metropolitan Water District Additional Loan Act
Mass. Acts 1962, Ch. 654

Metropolitan Water Reclamation District Act
Ill. Rev. Stat. 1991, Ch. 42, § 3245 et seq.

Metropolitan Water Supply Act
Cal. Water Code Appendix, § 109-1 et seq.
Mass. Gen. Laws 1990, 92:1 et seq.

Metzenbaum Act (Retail Installment Sales)
Ohio Rev. Code 1953, 1317.01 et seq.

Metzger Act (Railroads)
Ohio Rev. Code 1953, 4973.02 et seq.

Meussdorffer Act
Ore. Laws 1891, p. 633

Mexican Agricultural Workers Importation Act
July 12, 1951, Ch. 223, 65 Stat. 119, 7 U.S. Code §§ 1461 to 1468, 1461 nt.
Aug. 8, 1953, Ch. 391, 67 Stat. 500, 7 U.S. Code § 1461 nt.
March 16, 1954, Ch. 98, 68 Stat. 28, 7 U.S. Code § 1461
Aug. 9, 1955, Ch. 679, 69 Stat. 615, 7 U.S. Code §§ 1461 nt., 1462, 1463
Aug. 27, 1958, P.L. 85-779, 72 Stat. 934, 7 U.S. Code § 1461 nt.
Sept. 14, 1960, P.L. 86-783, 74 Stat. 1021, 7 U.S. Code § 1461 nt.
Oct. 3, 1961, P.L. 87-345, 75 Stat. 761, 7 U.S. Code §§ 1461 nt., 1462 to 1468
Dec. 13, 1963, P.L. 88-203, 77 Stat. 363, 7 U.S. Code § 1461 nt.

Mexican Border Act
Jan. 31, 1942, Ch. 31, 56 Stat. 40, 7 U.S. Code § 149
May 23, 1957, P.L. 85-36, 71 Stat. 34, 7 U.S. Code § 149

Mexican Debt Disclosure Act of 1995
April 10, 1995, P.L. 104-6, Title IV, 31 U.S. Code § 5302 nt.

Mexican Fruit Fly Control and Eradication Act
Tex. Agriculture Code, § 72.001 et seq.

Mexican War Act
May 13, 1846, Ch. 16, 9 Stat. 9

Mexico-United States Interparliamentary Group Act
April 9, 1960, P.L. 86-420, 74 Stat. 40, 22 U.S. Code §§ 276h to 276k

Meyers-Geddes State Employees' Medical and Hospital Care Act
Cal. Government Code § 22751 et seq.

Meyers-Milias-Brown Act (Public Employees Organizations)
Cal. Government Code § 3500 et seq.

MIAMI Act (Montana Initiative for the Abatement of Infant Mortality)
Mont. Laws 1989, Ch. 649

Miami Beach Civil Service Act
Fla. Special Laws 1937, Ch. 18696

Miami Beach Low-Cost Housing Act
Fla. Special Laws 1949, Ch. 26033

Miami Port Facilities Financing Act
Fla. Special Laws 1957, Ch. 57-1584

Miami Sanitary Sewer Financing Act
Fla. Special Laws 1945, Ch. 23407

Miami Shores Village Local Improvement Act
Fla. Special Laws 1947, Ch. 24716

Miami Shores Village Sewer Financing Act
Fla. Special Laws 1947, Ch. 24715

Miccosukee Reserved Area Act
Oct. 30, 1998, P.L. 105-313, 112 Stat. 2964, 16 U.S. Code § 410 nt.

Miccosukee Settlement Act of 1997
Nov. 14, 1997, P.L. 105-83, Title VII, 25 U.S. Code § 1750 nt.

Michael Scott "Spike" Speicher Act
Fla. Stat. Ann., 295.0195

Michelle Montoya School Safety Act
Cal. Education Code 1976, §§ 44237, 45125, 45125.1

Michigan and Illinois Canal Development Act
Ill. Rev. Stat. 1991, Ch. 19, § 37.10 et seq.

Michigan and Illinois Canal Land Use Act
Ill. Rev. Stat. 1991, Ch. 19, § 37.10 et seq.

Michigan and Illinois Canal Management Act
Ill. Rev. Stat. 1991, Ch. 19, § 0.01 et seq.

Michigan and Illinois Canal Protection Act
Ill. Rev. Stat. 1991, Ch. 19, § 29.9 et seq.

Michigan and Illinois Canal State Park Act
Ill. Rev. Stat. 1991, Ch. 105, § 491.01 et seq.

Michigan Indian Land Claims Settlement Act
Dec. 15, 1997, P.L. 105-143, 111 Stat. 2652

Michigan Public Lands Improvement Act of 1988
Oct. 29, 1988, P.L. 100-537, 102 Stat. 2711
Oct. 18, 1990, P.L. 101-442, 104 Stat. 1026

Michigan Scenic Rivers Act of 1991
March 3, 1992, P.L. 102-249, 16 U.S. Code § 1271 nt.

Michigan Wilderness Act of 1987
Dec. 8, 1987, P.L. 100-184, 16 U.S. Code § 1132 nt.

Mickey Leland Childhood Hunger Relief Act
Aug. 10, 1993, P.L. 103-66, 7 U.S. Code § 2011 nt.

Mickey Leland Food for Peace Act
Nov. 28, 1990, P.L. 101-624, 7 U.S. Code §§ 1691 nt., 1706

Mickey Leland Memorial Domestic Hunger Relief Act
Nov. 28, 1990, P.L. 101-624, 7 U.S. Code § 2011 nt.

Micmac Settlement Act
Me. Rev. Stat. Ann. 1964, Title 30, § 7201 et seq.

Micro-Business Development and Assistance Act

N.J. Stat. Ann., 34:1B-70 et seq.

Microbusiness Development Act

Mont. Laws 1991, Ch. 602, §§ 1 to 9

Microenterprise Development Act

Neb. Rev. Stat. 1943, 81-1295 to 81-12,105

Microfilm Act (County)

Kan. Stat. Ann., 19-250 et seq.

Microfilm and Photographic Records Act

Tex. Local Government Code, §§ 181.001 et seq., 201.001 et seq.

Microfilm and Reproduction of Documents Act

Ariz. Laws 1947, Ch. 119

Microfilm Evidence Act

Minn. Stat. Ann., 600.135

Microlending Expansion Act of 1992

Sept. 4, 1992, P.L. 102-366, 15 U.S. Code § 631 nt.

Microloan Program Technical Corrections Act of 1999

April 27, 1999, P.L. 106-22, 113 Stat. 36, 15 U.S. Code § 631 nt.

Micronesian Claims Act of 1971

July 1, 1971, P.L. 92-39, 85 Stat. 92, 50 U.S. Code Appx. §§ 2018 to 2020b

Oct. 19, 1973, P.L. 93-131, 87 Stat. 460, 50 U.S. Code Appx. §§ 2019, 2019c

Mid-America Intermodal Authority Port District Act

Ill. Comp. Stat. 1992, Ch. 70, § 1832/1 et seq.

Mid-Atlantic Interstate Low-Level Radioactive Waste Compact Act

Va. Code 1950, § 32.1-238.1 et seq.

Mid-Atlantic State Police Compact Act

N.J. Stat. Ann., 53:6-1 et seq.

Mid-Atlantic States Air Pollution Control Compact

N.Y. Environmental Conservation Law 1972 (Consol. Laws Ch. 43B) § 21-1501 et seq.

Mid-Atlantic States Air Pollution Control Compact Act

Conn. Gen. Stat. Ann., §§ 22a-166, 22a-167

N.J. Stat. Ann., 32:29-1 et seq.

Mid-Carolina Commission for Higher Education

S.C. Code Ann. 1976, § 59-108-10 et seq.

Mid-Dakota Rural Water System Act of 1992

Oct. 30, 1992, P.L. 102-575, 106 Stat. 4673

Middle Atlantic Interstate Forest Fire Protection Compact Act

Del. Code of 1974, Title 7, § 2961 et seq.

Md. Ann. Code 1974, Art. NR, § 5-801

N.J. Stat. Ann., 32:24-1 et seq.

Pa. Purdon's Stat., Title 32, § 422 et seq.

Middle East Peace and Stability Act

March 9, 1957, P.L. 85-7, 71 Stat. 5, 22 U.S. Code §§ 1961 to 1965

Middle East Peace Facilitation Act of 1993

Oct. 28, 1993, P.L. 103-125, 107 Stat. 1309

Dec. 2, 1993, P.L. 103-166, 107 Stat. 1978

Aug. 23, 1994, P.L. 103-306, 108 Stat. 1650

Middle East Peace Facilitation Act of 1995

Feb. 12, 1996, P.L. 104-107, Title VI, 110 Stat. 755

Middle Georgia Surface and Air Transportation Commission Act

Ga. Laws 1990, p. 5170

Middle Income Student Assistance Act

Nov. 1, 1978, P.L. 95-566, 20 U.S. Code §§ 1070a, 1070a nt., 1070c-2, 1070d-1, 1075, 1077, 1078, 1087-3a, 1088, 1088f

Aug. 13, 1979, P.L. 96-49, 20 U.S. Code § 1070a nt.

Middleport Trailer Local Law
N.Y. Local Laws 1972, Village of
Middleport, p. 3606

Middlesex County Court House Loan Act
Mass. Acts 1952, Ch. 491
Mass. Acts 1967, Ch. 542

Middleton Parking Authority Act
N.Y. Public Authorities Law (Consol. Laws
Ch. 43A) § 1621a et seq.

Middletown City Court Act
N.Y. Laws 1955, Ch. 730

Middletown Parking Authority Act
N.Y. Public Authorities Law (Consol. Laws
Ch. 43A) § 1621a et seq.

**Midnight Basketball League Training and
Partnership Act**
March 31, 1994, P.L. 103-227, 20 U.S. Code
§ 11901 nt.

Midnight Deadline Act (Bank Posting)
Ind. Code Ann., 26-1-4-301

Midshipmen Increase Act
Sept. 4, 1940, Ch. 706, 54 Stat. 867
Jan. 30, 1941, Ch. 2, 55 Stat. 3

Midwest Education Compact Act
Iowa Code Ann., 272B.1 et seq.
Minn. Stat. 1988, 121.843 et seq.
Neb. Laws 1979, L.B., 291
Neb. Laws 1979, p. 867
Ohio Rev. Code 1953, 3301.60 et seq.
S.D. Codified Laws 1967, 13-53A-1 et seq.

**Midwest Interstate Compact Low-Level
Radioactive Waste**
Ind. Code Ann., 13-5-9-1 et seq.

**Midwest Interstate Low-Level Radioactive
Waste Compact Act**
Ill. Rev. Stat. 1991, Ch. 127, § 63v et seq.
Iowa Laws 1991 8C
Mich. Comp. Laws Ann., 3.751 et seq.
Minn. Stat. Ann., 116C.831 et seq.
Mo. Rev. Stat., 260.700 et seq.
Ohio Rev. Code 1953, 3747.01 et seq.

Wis. Stat. Ann., 16.10 et seq.

**Midwest Interstate Low-Level Radioactive
Waste Management Compact**
Jan. 15, 1986, P.L. 99-240, 99 Stat. 1892

Midwest Nuclear Compact Act
Ill. Rev. Stat. 1991, Ch. 127, § 63t-11 et seq.
Ind. Code Ann., 13-5-8-1 et seq.
Iowa Code Ann., 15D.1 et seq.
Kan. Stat. Ann., 48-2001 et seq.
Neb. Laws 1972, L.B. 1085
Ohio Rev. Code 1953, 122.13

Midwestern Higher Education Compact
Mich. Comp. Laws Ann., 390.1531,
390.1532
Minn. Stat. Ann., 135A.20 et seq.
Neb. Rev. Stat. 1943, 85-1301, 85-1302

Midwife Nurse Practice Act
Utah Code Ann. 1953, 58-44a-101 et seq.

Midwife Practitioners Act
La. Rev. Stat. Ann., 37:3240 et seq.

Midwifery Act
Ark. Code Ann. 1987, 17-86-501 et seq.
La. Rev. Stat. Ann., 37:3171 et seq.
Md. Ann. Code 1974, Art. HO, § 8-601 et
seq.
N.C. Gen. Stat. 1943, § 90-178.1 et seq.
Neb. Laws 1984, L.B. 761, §§ 1 to 28
Pa. Purdon's Stat., Title 63, § 171 et seq.
Tex. Rev. Civ. Stat., Art. 4512i
Wash. Rev. Code Ann., 18.50.003 et seq.

Midwifery Act (Certified Professional)
Ga. Code Ann., 31-26-1 et seq.

Midwifery Licensing Act (Direct-Entry)
Fla. Stat. Ann., 467.001 et seq.
Mont. Code Ann., 37-27-101 et seq.
Mont. Laws 1991, Ch. 550, §§ 1 to 4, 6 to 23

Midwifery Practice Act
Neb. Rev. Stat. 1943, 71-1738 et seq.

Midwifery Practice Act (Licensed)
Cal. Business and Professions Code § 2505 et seq.

Midwifery Practice Act (Professional)
N.Y. Education Law 1947 (Consol. Laws Ch. 16) § 6950 et seq.

Migrant and Community Health Centers Amendments of 1978
Nov. 10, 1978, P.L. 95-626, 42 U.S. Code §§ 201 nt., 218, 247d, 247e, 254b, 254c, 255, 256, 256a, 300e-12, 300e-14a, 1396b

Migrant and Seasonal Agricultural Worker Protection Act
Jan. 14, 1983, P.L. 97-470, 29 U.S. Code §§ 1801 et seq., 1801 nt.
Nov. 6, 1986, P.L. 99-603, 29 U.S. Code §§ 1802, 1802 nt., 1813, 1816, 1851
Oct. 6, 1992, P.L. 102-392, 29 U.S. Code § 1854
Nov. 15, 1995, P.L. 104-49, 29 U.S. Code §§ 1821, 1831, 1841, 1854
Dec. 29, 1995, P.L. 104-88, 29 U.S. Code § 1841

Migrant Children Educational Act
Colo. Rev. Stat., 22-23-101 et seq.

Migrant Housing Act
N.C. Gen. Stat. 1943, § 95-222 et seq.

Migrant Labor Act
N.J. Stat. Ann., 34:9A-1 et seq.

Migrant Labor Camp Act
Fla. Stat. 1983, 381.422 et seq.
Ill. Rev. Stat. 1991, Ch. 111 1/2, § 185.1 et seq.

Migrant Labor Division Act
S.C. Code Ann. 1976, § 41-3-510 et seq.

Migrant Registration Act
N.Y. Labor Law (Consol. Laws Ch. 31) § 212a

Migrant Workers Act
Kan. Stat. Ann., 44-125 et seq.

Migration and Refugee Assistance Act of 1962
June 28, 1962, P.L. 87-510, 76 Stat. 121, 8 U.S. Code §§ 1104, 1182 nt.; 22 U.S. Code §§ 2601 to 2605
Oct. 7, 1964, P.L. 88-634, 78 Stat. 1021, 22 U.S. Code § 2601
March 17, 1980, P.L. 96-212, 22 U.S. Code § 2601
Aug. 16, 1985, P.L. 99-93, 22 U.S. Code §§ 2601, 2605, 2606
Feb. 16, 1990, P.L. 101-246, 22 U.S. Code § 2606
Dec. 21, 1995, P.L. 104-66, 22 U.S. Code § 2606

Migratory Bird Act
Vt. Stat. Ann., Title 10, § 4901 et seq.

Migratory Bird Conservation Act
Feb. 18, 1929, Ch. 257, 45 Stat. 1222, 16 U.S. Code §§ 715 to 715r
Oct. 15, 1962, P.L. 87-812, 76 Stat. 922, 16 U.S. Code § 715q
Oct. 15, 1966, P.L. 89-669, 80 Stat. 929, 16 U.S. Code §§ 715c, 715i to 715k
March 2, 1968, P.L. 90-261, 82 Stat. 39, 16 U.S. Code § 715a
Dec. 28, 1973, P.L. 93-205, 87 Stat. 902, 16 U.S. Code §§ 715i, 715s
Oct. 30, 1978, P.L. 95-552, 16 U.S. Code § 715c
Nov. 8, 1978, P.L. 95-616, 16 U.S. Code § 715d, 715i, 715j
Oct. 31, 1994, P.L. 103-434, 16 U.S. Code § 715f

Migratory Bird Hunting and Conservation Stamp Act
Nov. 8, 1978, P.L. 95-616, 16 U.S. Code §§ 718b, 718c

Migratory Bird Hunting and Conservation Stamp Promotion Act
Oct. 19, 1998, P.L. 105-269, 112 Stat. 2381, 16 U.S. Code § 718 nt.

Migratory Bird Hunting Stamp Act
March 16, 1934, Ch. 71, 48 Stat. 452, 16 U.S. Code §§ 718 to 718h
Aug. 12, 1949, Ch. 421, 63 Stat. 599, 16 U.S. Code §§ 718b, 718b nt., 718d

Oct. 20, 1951, Ch. 520, 65 Stat. 451, 16 U.S. Code § 718d

July 30, 1956, Ch. 782, 70 Stat. 722, 16 U.S. Code §§ 718a, 718b

Aug. 1, 1958, P.L. 85-585, 72 Stat. 486, 16 U.S. Code §§ 718b, 718d

Oct. 15, 1966, P.L. 89-669, 80 Stat. 929, 16 U.S. Code § 718d

Dec. 22, 1971, P.L. 92-214, 85 Stat. 777, 16 U.S. Code §§ 718b, 718d

July 18, 1984, P.L. 98-369, 98 Stat. 1054, 16 U.S. Code § 718e

Oct. 19, 1998, P.L. 105-269, 16 U.S. Code § 718d

Migratory Bird Treaty Act

July 3, 1918, Ch. 128, 40 Stat. 755, 16 U.S. Code §§ 703 to 708, 709a, 710, 711

Sept. 8, 1960, P.L. 86-732, 74 Stat. 866, 16 U.S. Code § 707

Dec. 5, 1969, P.L. 91-135, 83 Stat. 282, 16 U.S. Code §§ 668aa, 668bb, 668cc-1, 705

June 1, 1974, P.L. 93-300, 88 Stat. 190, 16 U.S. Code § 703

Nov. 8, 1978, P.L. 95-616, 16 U.S. Code § 706

Oct. 30, 1998, P.L. 105-312, 16 U.S. Code §§ 704, 707

Migratory Bird Treaty Reform Act of 1998

Oct. 30, 1998, P.L. 105-312, Title I, 112 Stat. 2956, 16 U.S. Code § 710 nt.

Migratory Chattel Act

Ore. Rev. Stat., 86.350 et seq.

Migratory Game Birds Act

Tex. Parks and Wildlife Code, § 64.021 et seq.

Migratory Livestock Act

Colo. Laws 1923, p. 599, Ch. 174

Mike Mansfield Fellowship Act

April 30, 1994, P.L. 103-236, 22 U.S. Code §§ 6101 nt., 6101 et seq.

Milan Zoning Law

N.Y. Local Laws 1969, Town of Milan, p. 1617

Mileage Act

Ky. Rev. Stat. 1971, 64.070

Mileage and Per Diem Act

N.M. Stat. Ann., 10-8-1 et seq.

Mileage Book Act

N.Y. Railroad Law (Consol. Laws Ch. 49) § 60

Mileage Tax Act (Motor Vehicles)

Ala. Code 1975, § 40-19-1 et seq.
Mich. Comp. Laws 1948, 478.2 et seq.

Miles Land Exchange Act of 1998

Oct. 27, 1998, P.L. 105-288, 112 Stat. 2778

Milford Civic Center Act

Ill. Rev. Stat. 1991, Ch. 85, § 5101 et seq.

Milford, Sheldon, Katherine Dunham, Oak Park, Aledo, Normal, Mason County, Jasper County, Brownstown Park District, and Jo Daviess County Civic Centers Act

Ill. Rev. Stat. 1991, Ch. 85, § 4500 et seq.

Milford Swimming Facilities Loan Act

Mass. Acts 1953, Ch. 360

Milias-Meyers-Brown Act (Public Employees Organizations)

Cal. Government Code § 3500 et seq.

Military Act

Mich. Comp. Laws Ann., 32.501 et seq.

Military Active Duty Act (Municipal Employees)

Ill. Rev. Stat. 1991, Ch. 24 1/2, § 149m et seq.

Military Affairs Act

N.M. Stat. Ann., 9-9-1 et seq.

Military Affairs and Veterans Act

Alaska Stat. 1962, § 26.03.010 et seq.

Military Aid Act

Mass. Gen Laws 1990, 115:1 et seq.

443

Military Aid Compact Act
Pa. Cons. Stat., Title 51, § 4501

Military and Naval Code
Ill. Rev. Stat. 1991, Ch. 129, § 220.001 et
seq.

Military and Veterans Code
Cal. Statutes 1935, Ch. 389, p. 1339
N.J. Stat. Ann., 38A:1-1 et seq.
Pa. Cons. Stat., Title 51, § 101 et seq.

Military Appropriation Acts
July 1, 1937, Ch. 423, 50 Stat. 442, 31 U.S.
Code §§ 448, 493a, 650a
June 11, 1938, Ch. 347, 52 Stat. 642, 31 U.S.
Code §§ 493a, 650a
April 26, 1939, Ch. 88, 53 Stat. 592, 31 U.S.
Code §§ 493a, 650a
June 13, 1940, Ch. 343, 54 Stat. 350, 31 U.S.
Code §§ 493a, 650a
June 26, 1940, Ch. 430, 54 Stat. 601
Sept. 9, 1940, Ch. 717, 54 Stat. 872
April 5, 1941, Ch. 41, 55 Stat. 123
June 30, 1941, Ch. 262, 55 Stat. 366, 31 U.S.
Code §§ 493a, 640a; 50 U.S. Code Appx.
§ 1171 nt.
Aug. 25, 1941, Ch. 409, 55 Stat. 669
Dec. 17, 1941, Ch. 591, 55 Stat. 810, 22 U.S.
Code § 412 nt.; 31 U.S. Code § 649a
March 5, 1942, Ch. 141, 56 Stat. 128
April 28, 1942, Ch. 247, 56 Stat. 226
July 2, 1942, Ch. 477, 56 Stat. 612, 31 U.S.
Code §§ 493a, 649a, 650a
July 1, 1943, Ch. 185, 57 Stat. 347, 31 U.S.
Code §§ 493a, 649a, 650a; 50 U.S. Code
Appx. § 1191
June 28, 1944, Ch. 303, 58 Stat. 573, 31 U.S.
Code §§ 493a, 649a, 650a; 37 U.S. Code
§ 412
July 3, 1945, Ch. 265, 59 Stat. 384, 31 U.S.
Code §§ 493a, 649a, 650a
July 16, 1946, Ch. 583, 60 Stat. 541, 31 U.S.
Code §§ 493a, 649a, 650a; 37 U.S. Code
§ 412
July 30, 1947, Ch. 357, 61 Stat. 551, 31 U.S.
Code §§ 493a, 649a, 650a; 37 U.S. Code
§ 412

Military Ballot Act
Pa. 1944 Ex. Pamph. Laws 1439, No. 1

Military Base Conversion Authority Act
Mich. Comp. Laws Ann., 3.571 et seq.

**Military Base Recovery Area Act (Local
Agency)**
Cal. Government Code § 7105 et seq.

Military Base Reuse Advisory Board Act
Ill. Rev. Stat. 1991, Ch. 127, § 3630 et seq.

Military Base Reuse Authority Act
Cal. Government Code § 67800 et seq.

Military Child Care Act of 1989
Nov. 29, 1989, P.L. 101-189, 10 U.S. Code
§ 113 nt.
Feb. 10, 1996, P.L. 104-106, 10 U.S. Code
§ 113 nt.

Military Code
Ala. Code 1975, § 31-2-1 et seq.
Alaska Stat. 1962, § 26.05.010 et seq.
Ariz. Rev. Stat. Ann., § 26-121 et seq.
Ark. Code Ann. 1987, 12-60-101 et seq.
Fla. Stat. Ann., 250.01 et seq.
Ind. Code Ann., 10-2-1-1 et seq.
Iowa Code 1983, 29A.1 et seq.
Me. Rev. Stat. Ann. 1964, Title 37-B, § 1 et
seq.
Minn. Stat. Ann., 190.01 et seq.
Mo. Rev. Stat., 41.010 et seq.
Mont. Code Ann., 10-1-101 et seq.
Neb. Rev. Stat. 1943, 55-101 et seq.
N.Y. Consol. Laws, Ch. 36
Okla. Stat. Ann., Title 44, § 1 et seq.
P.R. Laws Ann. 1954, Title 25 § 2001 et seq.
R.I. Gen. Laws 1956, 30-1-1 et seq.
S.C. Code Ann. 1976, § 25-1-10 et seq.
Tenn. Code Ann., 58-1-101 et seq.
Va. Code 1950, § 44-1 et seq.

Military Code of the State of Washington
Wash. Rev. Code Ann., 38.04.010 et seq.

Military Compensation Records Act
Ill. Rev. Stat. 1991, Ch. 126 1/2, §§ 61m, 62

Military Construction Act of 1958

Aug. 20, 1958, P.L. 85-685, 72 Stat. 636, 10 U.S. Code §§ 2674, 9331 nt.; 42 U.S. Code §§ 1502a nt., 1594a, 1594i, 1594j; 50 U.S. Code § 171b

Aug. 10, 1959, P.L. 86-149, 73 Stat. 322

Military Construction Act of 1959

July 12, 1982, P.L. 97-214, 7 U.S. Code § 1704b

Military Construction Act of 1981

Dec. 21, 1982, P.L. 97-375, 31 U.S. Code § 1114 nt.

Military Construction Act, 1983

Nov. 5, 1990, P.L. 101-510, 104 Stat. 1807

Military Construction Appropriations Act of 1959

Aug. 28, 1958, P.L. 85-852, 72 Stat. 1098, 31 U.S. Code §§ 638f, 700b

Aug. 10, 1959, P.L. 86-149, 73 Stat. 302

Nov. 19, 1969, P.L. 91-121, 83 Stat. 207, 10 U.S. Code § 133 nt.

Military Construction Appropriations Act of 1960

Sept. 16, 1959, P.L. 86-275, 73 Stat. 558, 31 U.S. Code §§ 638f, 700b

June 8, 1960, P.L. 86-500, 74 Stat. 166, 7 U.S. Code § 1704b nt.; 10 U.S. Code § 2662; 12 U.S. Code § 1748b; 42 U.S. Code §§ 1594i, 1594j; 50 U.S. Code Appx. § 2285

Military Construction Appropriations Act of 1961

July 12, 1960, P.L. 86-630, 74 Stat. 463, 31 U.S. Code §§ 638f, 700b

June 27, 1961, P.L. 87-57, 75 Stat. 108, 10 U.S. Code §§ 2674, 9331 nts.; 12 U.S. Code § 1748b; 42 U.S. Code § 1594j

Military Construction Appropriations Act of 1962

Sept. 26, 1961, P.L. 87-302, 75 Stat. 658, 31 U.S. Code §§ 638f, 700b

Military Construction Appropriations Act of 1963

Sept. 25, 1962, P.L. 87-684, 76 Stat. 576, 31 U.S. Code §§ 638f, 700b

Military Construction Appropriations Act of 1964

Dec. 21, 1963, P.L. 88-220, 77 Stat. 463, 31 U.S. Code §§ 638f, 700b

Military Construction Appropriations Act of 1965

Sept. 2, 1964, P.L. 88-576, 78 Stat. 887, 31 U.S. Code §§ 638f, 700b

Military Construction Appropriations Act of 1966

Sept. 25, 1965, P.L. 89-202, 79 Stat. 837, 31 U.S. Code §§ 638f, 700b

Military Construction Appropriations Act of 1967

Nov. 2, 1966, P.L. 89-744, 80 Stat. 1176, 31 U.S. Code §§ 638f, 700b

Military Construction Appropriations Act of 1968

Dec. 8, 1967, P.L. 90-180, 81 Stat. 550, 31 U.S. Code §§ 638f, 700b

Military Construction Appropriations Act of 1969

Sept. 26, 1968, P.L. 90-513, 82 Stat. 864, 31 U.S. Code §§ 638f, 700b, 700c

Military Construction Appropriations Act of 1970

Dec. 29, 1969, P.L. 91-170, 83 Stat. 465, 31 U.S. Code §§ 638f, 700b, 700c

Military Construction Appropriations Act of 1971

Dec. 11, 1970, P.L. 91-544, 84 Stat. 1409, 31 U.S. Code §§ 638f, 700b

Military Construction Appropriations Act of 1984

Oct. 11, 1983, P.L. 98-116, 97 Stat. 795

Aug. 22, 1984, P.L. 98-396

Military Construction Appropriations Act of 1985

Oct. 12, 1984, P.L. 98-473, 22 U.S. Code § 1928 nt.

Military Construction Appropriations Act of 1988 and 1989

Dec. 4, 1987, P.L. 100-180, 101 Stat. 1179

Dec. 27, 1987, P.L. 100-202, 101 Stat. 1329

Military Construction Appropriations Act of 1990

Nov. 10, 1989, P.L. 101-148, 103 Stat. 920

Military Construction Appropriations Act of 1991

Nov. 5, 1990, P.L. 101-519, 10 U.S. Code § 2860 nt.; 50 U.S. Code § 1701 nt.

April 6, 1991, P.L. 102-25, 105 Stat. 109

April 10, 1991, P.L. 102-27, 18 U.S. Code §§ prec. 1, prec. 2331, 2331 to 2338, 2331 nt.; 50 U.S. Code § 1701 nt.

Military Construction Appropriations Act of 1992

Oct. 25, 1991, P.L. 102-136, 105 Stat. 645

Military Construction Appropriations Act of 1993

Oct. 5, 1992, P.L. 102-380, 106 Stat. 1366

Military Construction Appropriations Act of 1994

Oct. 21, 1993, P.L. 103-110, 107 Stat. 1037

Military Construction Appropriations Act of 1995

Aug. 23, 1994, P.L. 103-307, 108 Stat. 1659

Military Construction Appropriations Act of 1996

Oct. 3, 1995, P.L. 104-32, 109 Stat. 283

Military Construction Appropriations Act of 1997

Sept. 16, 1996, P.L. 104-196, 110 Stat. 2385

Military Construction Appropriations Act of 1998

Sept. 30, 1997, P.L. 105-45, 111 Stat. 1142

Military Construction Appropriations Act of 1999

Sept. 20, 1998, P.L. 105-237, 112 Stat. 1553

Military Construction Appropriations Act, 1978

Aug. 15, 1977, P.L. 95-101, 31 U.S. Code §§ 638f, 700b

Military Construction Appropriations Act, 1980

Nov. 30, 1979, P.L. 96-130, 31 U.S. Code § 628-3

Military Construction Appropriations Act, 1986

Dec. 10, 1985, P.L. 99-173, 10 U.S. Code §§ 2860, 2860 nt.

July 1, 1986, P.L. 99-348, 100 Stat. 707

Dec. 4, 1987, P.L. 100-180, 101 Stat. 1227

Military Construction Appropriations Act, 1987

Oct. 18, 1986, P.L. 99-500, 100 Stat. 3637

Oct. 30, 1986, P.L. 99-591, 100 Stat. 3637

Nov. 14, 1986, P.L. 99-661, 10 U.S. Code § 114 nt.

July 11, 1987, P.L. 100-71, 101 Stat. 409

Dec. 4, 1987, P.L. 100-180, 101 Stat. 1192, 1193, 1204

Oct. 25, 1991, P.L. 102-136, 10 U.S. Code § 2860 nt.

Military Construction Authorization Act for Fiscal Year 1991

Nov. 5, 1990, P.L. 101-510, 104 Stat. 1758

Dec. 5, 1991, P.L. 102-190, 10 U.S. Code § 2391 nt.

Oct. 23, 1992, P.L. 102-484, 106 Stat. 2598

Nov. 30, 1993, P.L. 103-160, 106 Stat. 1865, 1872, 1879, 1896

Oct. 5, 1994, P.L. 103-337, 10 U.S. Code § 2687 nt.

Feb. 10, 1996, P.L. 104-106, 10 U.S. Code § 2687 nt.

Military Construction Authorization Act for Fiscal Year 1992

Dec. 5, 1991, P.L. 102-190, 105 Stat. 1508

Oct. 23, 1992, P.L. 102-484, 106 Stat. 2597

Nov. 30, 1993, P.L. 103-160, 106 Stat. 1871, 1872, 1877, 1879, 1895

Oct. 5, 1994, P.L. 103-337, 108 Stat. 3030, 3047

Military Construction Authorization Act for Fiscal Year 1993

Oct. 23, 1992, P.L. 102-484, 106 Stat. 2586

Nov. 30, 1993, P.L. 103-160, 106 Stat. 1859, 1864, 1870, 1878, 1895, 1896

Oct. 5, 1994, P.L. 103-337, 108 Stat. 3057

Military Construction Authorization Act for Fiscal Year 1994

Nov. 30, 1993, P.L. 103-160, 106 Stat. 1856

Oct. 5, 1994, P.L. 103-337, 108 Stat. 3045, 3058, 3059, 3072

Military Construction Authorization Act for Fiscal Year 1995

Oct. 5, 1994, P.L. 103-337, 108 Stat. 3027

Military Construction Authorization Act for Fiscal Year 1996

Feb. 10, 1996, P.L. 104-106, Division B, 110 Stat. 523

Military Construction Authorization Act for Fiscal Year 1997

Sept. 23, 1996, P.L. 104-201, Division B, 110 Stat. 2763

Military Construction Authorization Act for Fiscal Year 1999

Oct. 17, 1998, P.L. 105-261, Division B, 112 Stat. 2182; 10 U.S. Code § 2805 nt.

Military Construction Authorization Act of 1964

Nov. 7, 1963, P.L. 88-174, 77 Stat. 307, 10 U.S. Code §§ 2674, 2681, 2682, 4774, 7574, 9774; 42 U.S. Code §§ 1594h-1 nt., 1594i to 1594k

Sept. 16, 1965, P.L. 89-188, 79 Stat. 814, 42 U.S. Code § 1594k

Oct. 21, 1967, P.L. 90-110, 81 Stat. 304, 10 U.S. Code § 2674 nt.; 42 U.S. Code §§ 1594a-1, 1594j, 1594k

July 21, 1968, P.L. 90-408, 82 Stat. 388, 42 U.S. Code § 1594k

Dec. 5, 1969, P.L. 91-142, 83 Stat. 312, 42 U.S. Code § 1594k

Oct. 26, 1970, P.L. 91-511, 84 Stat. 1220, 42 U.S. Code § 1594k

July 12, 1982, P.L. 97-214, 42 U.S. Code § 1594k

Military Construction Authorization Act of 1965

Aug. 1, 1964, P.L. 88-390, 78 Stat. 341, 10 U.S. Code §§ 2674 nt., 9331 nt.

Military Construction Authorization Act of 1966

Sept. 16, 1965, P.L. 89-188, 79 Stat. 819, 10 U.S. Code §§ 1077 nt., 2662 nt., 2674, 9503 nt.; 42 U.S. Code §§ 1594h-1, 1594k; 50 U.S. Code Appx. § 2281 nt.

Sept. 12, 1966, P.L. 89-568, 80 Stat. 757, 10 U.S. Code § 2662 nt.

May 25, 1967, P.L. 90-19, 81 Stat. 27

July 12, 1982, P.L. 97-214, 10 U.S. Code §§ 1077, 2662 nts.

Military Construction Authorization Act of 1967

Sept. 12, 1966, P.L. 89-568, 80 Stat. 739, 10 U.S. Code §§ 2662 nt., 2674; 31 U.S. Code § 723a; 42 U.S. Code § 1594j; 50 U.S. Code Appx. § 2287

Oct. 21, 1967, P.L. 90-110, 81 Stat. 308, 50 U.S. Code Appx. § 2287

July 12, 1982, P.L. 97-214, 31 U.S. Code § 723a, 50 U.S. Code Appx. § 2287

Military Construction Authorization Act of 1968

Oct. 21, 1967, P.L. 90-110, 81 Stat. 279, 10 U.S. Code § 2674 nt.; 42 U.S. Code §§ 1594a-1, 1594j, 1594k; 50 U.S. Code Appx. § 2287

Sept. 8, 1978, P.L. 95-356, 42 U.S. Code § 1594h-2

July 12, 1982, P.L. 97-214, 42 U.S. Code § 1594h-2

Military Construction Authorization Act of 1969

July 21, 1968, P.L. 90-408, 82 Stat. 367, 10 U.S. Code §§ 2674 nt., 9331 nt.; 42 U.S. Code § 1594k

Military Construction Authorization Act of 1970

Dec. 5, 1969, P.L. 91-142, 83 Stat. 293, 10 U.S. Code §§ 2674 nt., 4774, 7574, 9774; 42 U.S. Code §§ 1594a-1, 1594k, 3374

Military Construction Authorization Act of 1971

Oct. 26, 1970, P.L. 91-511, 84 Stat. 1204, 10 U.S. Code §§ 2674, 2675, 2683; 42 U.S. Code §§ 1594k, 3374

Military Construction Authorization Act of 1973

July 12, 1982, P.L. 97-214, 42 U.S. Code § 1594j-1

Military Construction Authorization Act of 1978

Aug. 1, 1977, P.L. 95-82, 10 U.S. Code § 2662 et seq.

Military Construction Authorization Act of 1979

Sept. 8, 1978, P.L. 95-356, 10 U.S. Code §§ 2674, 2674 nt., 2675, 2686; 42 U.S. Code § 1594h-2

Nov. 26, 1979, P.L. 96-125, 42 U.S. Code § 5504a, § repealed

July 12, 1982, P.L. 97-214, 30 U.S. Code §§ 1002a, 1002a nt.

Sept. 29, 1988, P.L. 100-456, 102 Stat. 2123

Military Construction Authorization Act of 1980

Nov. 26, 1979, P.L. 96-125, 10 U.S. Code §§ 2233, 2632, 2674, 2675, 2686, 2688; 30 U.S. Code § 1002a

Military Construction Authorization Act of 1981

July 12, 1982, P.L. 97-214, 42 U.S. Code § 1594h-3

Nov. 5, 1990, P.L. 101-510, 10 U.S. Code § 2431 nt.

Military Construction Authorization Act of 1982

July 12, 1982, P.L. 97-214, 10 U.S. Code 140 nt.

Oct. 30, 1984, P.L. 98-557, 42 U.S. Code § 248c

Sept. 23, 1996, P.L. 104-201, 42 U.S. Code § 248c

Military Construction Authorization Act of 1983

Dec. 23, 1981, P.L. 97-99, 10 U.S. Code § 139 nt., 140 nt., 2233, 2675; 31 U.S. Code § 723; 42 U.S. Code § 248c

Oct. 15, 1982, P.L. 97-321, 10 U.S. Code §§ 2239, 2394, 2394a, 2394a nt., 2652, 2667, 2685, 2806, 2828, 2857

Dec. 3, 1985, P.L. 99-167, 99 Stat. 985, 988

Military Construction Authorization Act of 1984

Aug. 28, 1984, P.L. 98-406, 10 U.S. Code § 2821 nt.

Dec. 3, 1985, P.L. 99-167, 10 U.S. Code §§ 2667a nt., 2821 nt.

Nov. 14, 1986, P.L. 99-661, 100 Stat. 4042

Nov. 29, 1989, P.L. 101-189, 103 Stat. 1646

Nov. 5, 1990, P.L. 101-510, 10 U.S. Code § 2821 nt.

Dec. 5, 1991, P.L. 102-190, 10 U.S. Code § 2821 nt.

Military Construction Authorization Act of 1985

Aug. 28, 1984, P.L. 98-407, 10 U.S. Code §§ 2233, 2233a, 2483, 2665, 2676, 2677, 2691, 2692, 2775, 2821 nt., 2828, 2853, 2855; 31 U.S. Code §§ 1348, 1348 nt.

Dec. 3, 1985, P.L. 99-167, 99 Stat. 966, 994

Nov. 14, 1986, P.L. 99-661, 100 Stat. 4037

Oct. 23, 1992, P.L. 102-484, 106 Stat. 2611

Military Construction Authorization Act of 1986

Dec. 3, 1985, P.L. 99-167, 10 U.S. Code §§ 2233, 2236, 2546, 2571, 2667a nt., 2672, 2775, 2805, 2809, 2821, 2828, 2833, 2834, 2860, 2862; 20 U.S. Code § 241 nt.

Nov. 14, 1986, P.L. 99-661, 100 Stat. 4026

Military Construction Authorization Act of 1987

Nov. 14, 1986, P.L. 99-661, 100 Stat. 4012

Sept. 29, 1988, P.L. 100-456, 102 Stat. 2111, 2117

Nov. 29, 1989, P.L. 101-189, 103 Stat. 1641

Nov. 5, 1990, P.L. 101-510, 104 Stat. 1778

Military Construction Authorization Act of 1990 and 1991

Nov. 29, 1989, P.L. 101-189, 103 Stat. 1614

Nov. 5, 1990, P.L. 101-510, 104 Stat. 1774, 1780, 1866

Dec. 5, 1991, P.L. 102-190, 105 Stat. 1513, 1520, 1521, 1528, 1535

Nov. 30, 1993, P.L. 103-160, 106 Stat. 1872

Oct. 5, 1994, P.L. 103-337, 108 Stat. 3059

Military Construction Authorization Act, 1988 and 1989

Sept. 29, 1988, P.L. 100-456, 102 Stat. 2112, 2118

Oct. 1, 1988, P.L. 100-463, 102 Stat. 2270-47

Nov. 29, 1989, P.L. 101-189, 103 Stat. 1653

Military Construction Authorization Act, 1989

Sept. 29, 1988, P.L. 100-456, 102 Stat. 2087

Nov. 29, 1989, P.L. 101-189, 103 Stat. 1628

Nov. 5, 1990, P.L. 101-510, 104 Stat. 1762

Military Construction Codification Act

July 12, 1982, P.L. 97-214, 10 U.S. Code § 2801 et seq.

Military Divorce Statute

N.M. Stat. Ann., 40-4-5

Military Emergency Aircraft Restriction Act

Ill. Rev. Stat. 1991, Ch. 15 1/2, § 178.9 et seq.

Military Establishment Act

N.M. Stat. Ann., 20-6-2, 20-9-8

N.M. Stat. Ann. 1953, 9-1-4 et seq., 9-2-16, 9-2-25, 9-3-1

Military Establishment Supply Act

See Military Appropriation Acts

Military Facility Development Act (Former)

Okla. Stat. Ann., Title 68, § 3801 et seq.

Military Family Act of 1985

Nov. 8, 1985, P.L. 99-145, 5 U.S. Code § 5911; 10 U.S. Code § 133 nt., 37 U.S. Code §§ 403, 1011

Nov. 14, 1986, P.L. 99-661, 10 U.S. Code § 113 nt.

Sept. 29, 1988, P.L. 100-456, 102 Stat. 1975, 10 U.S. Code § 113 nt.

Feb. 10, 1996, P.L. 104-106, 10 U.S. Code § 113 nt.

Military Force Structure Review Act of 1996

Sept. 23, 1996, P.L. 104-201, Title IX, Subtitle B, 10 U.S. Code § 111 nt.

Military Forces Act

Mo. Rev. Stat., 41.010 et seq.

Military Forces Fresh Pursuit Act

N.J. Stat. Ann., 38A:16-1, 38A:16-2

Military Forces Reorganization Act

Ga. Code Ann., 38-2-1 et seq.

Military Functions Appropriation Act of 1949

June 24, 1948, Ch. 652, 62 Stat. 1016, 31 U.S. Code §§ 493a, 649a, 650a; 37 U.S. Code § 412; 50 U.S. Code § 406

Military Housing Assistance Act of 1995

Feb. 10, 1996, P.L. 104-106, Division B, Title XXVIII, Subtitle B, Section 2822, 38 U.S. Code § 101 nt.

Military Incentive Program Act

W. Va. Acts 1991, Ch. 170

Military Inspection Act (University)

Ill. Rev. Stat. 1991, Ch. 144, § 17p et seq.

Military Justice Act

See also Uniform Code of Military Justice

Iowa Code Ann., 29B.1 et seq.

Mich. Comp. Laws Ann., 32.1001 et seq.

Military Justice Act of 1968

Oct. 24, 1968, P.L. 90-632, 82 Stat. 1335, 10 U.S. Code §§ 801, 806, 816, 818 to 820, 825 to 827, 829, 835, 837 to 842, 845, 849, 851, 852, 854, 857, 865 to 871, 873, 936

Military Justice Act of 1983

Dec. 6, 1983, P.L. 98-209, 10 U.S. Code § 801 nt.

Oct. 19, 1984, P.L. 98-525, 10 U.S. Code § 867 nt.

Military Justice Amendments of 1981
Nov. 20, 1981, P.L. 97-81, 10 U.S. Code § 801 nt.
Dec. 6, 1983, P.L. 98-209, 10 U.S. Code § 706 nt.

Military Justice Amendments of 1986
Nov. 14, 1986, P.L. 99-661, 10 U.S. Code § 801 nt.

Military Justice Amendments of 1995
Feb. 10, 1996, P.L. 104-106, Division A, Title XI, 10 U.S. Code § 801 nt.

Military Justice Code
See Code of Military Justice

Military Lands Withdrawal Act of 1986
Nov. 6, 1986, P.L. 99-606, 100 Stat. 3468
June 17, 1988, P.L. 100-338, 102 Stat. 619
June 20, 1989, P.L. 101-40, 103 Stat. 81

Military Leave of Absence Act
Ill. Rev. Stat. 1991, Ch. 129, §§ 500, 501

Military Medical Benefits Amendments of 1966
Sept. 30, 1966, P.L. 89-614, 80 Stat. 862, 10 U.S. Code §§ 1071 to 1074, 1076 to 1079, 1082, 1084, 1086, 1087

Military Member Power of Attorney Act
Ariz. Rev. Stat. Ann., § 14-5104.01 et seq.

Military Missing Persons Record Act
Cal. Evidence Code § 1282 et seq.

Military Pay Act (Veterans)
See Veterans' Military Pay Act

Military Pay and Allowances Benefits Act of 1980
Dec. 23, 1980, P.L. 96-579, 37 U.S. Code § 101 nt.

Military Personnel and Civilian Employees' Claims Act of 1964
Aug. 31, 1964, P.L. 88-558, 78 Stat. 767, 10 U.S. Code §§ 2732 nt., 2735 nt.; 14 U.S. Code § 490 nt.; 31 U.S. Code §§ 240 to 242
Sept. 15, 1965, P.L. 89-185, 79 Stat. 789, 31 U.S. Code §§ 240, 241, 243

Oct. 12, 1968, P.L. 90-561, 82 Stat. 998, 31 U.S. Code § 241
July 8, 1970, P.L. 91-311, 84 Stat. 412, 31 U.S. Code § 241
July 13, 1972, P.L. 92-352, 86 Stat. 491, 31 U.S. Code § 241
July 28, 1982, P.L. 97-226, 31 U.S. Code §§ 241, 241 nt.

Military Personnel and Compensation Amendments of 1980
Sept. 8, 1980, P.L. 96-343, 37 U.S. Code § 101 nt.

Military Personnel Claims Act of 1945
May 29, 1945, Ch. 135, 59 Stat. 225
June 7, 1956, Ch. 376, 70 Stat. 255, 31 U.S. Code § 222c

Military Property Act
Ill. Rev. Stat. 1991, Ch. 129, § 222a et seq.

Military Public Works Appropriation Acts
Nov. 1, 1951, Ch. 665, 65 Stat. 764
July 15, 1952, Ch. 758, 66 Stat. 646

Military Reservation Act
July 26, 1939, Ch. 373, 53 Stat. 1123

Military Reserve Act
Cal. Military and Veterans Code § 550 et seq.

Military Reservist Relief Act
Cal. Statutes 1991, Ch. 49

Military Retirement Reform Act of 1986
July 1, 1986, P.L. 99-348, 5 USC §§ 5313, 5314; 10 U.S. Code §§ 101, 131 et seq., 716, 1040, 1331 et seq., 1401 to 1412, 1447 to 1452, 2830, 3925, 3991, 3992, 5083, 5201, 6151, 6321 to 6330, 6333, 6383, 8925, 8991, 8992; 14 U.S. Code §§ 46 to 51, 288, 291 to 293, 327, 334, 353 to 357, 362, 421 to 424; 33 U.S. Code § 853o; 42 U.S. Code §§ 211, 212
Oct. 18, 1986, P.L. 99-500, 10 U.S. Code § 2327 nt.
Oct. 30, 1986, P.L. 99-591, 10 U.S. Code § 2327 nt.
Nov. 14, 1986, P.L. 99-661, 100 Stat. 3945

Military Scholarship Act (North Georgia College)
Ga. Code Ann., 20-3-420 et seq.

Military School Scholarship Act
Ill. Rev. Stat. 1991, Ch. 144, § 21a et seq.

Military Secretary Act
March 28, 1939, Ch. 19, 53 Stat. 551

Military Selective Service Act
Oct. 12, 1984, P.L. 98-473, 50 U.S. Code Appx. § 460
Oct. 19, 1984, P.L. 98-525, 50 U.S. Code Appx. § 456
Nov. 14, 1986, P.L. 99-661, 50 U.S. Code Appx. § 462
Nov. 5, 1990, P.L. 101-510, 50 U.S. Code Appx. § 468
June 13, 1991, P.L. 102-54, 50 U.S. Code Appx. § 461
Dec. 5, 1991, P.L. 102-190, 50 U.S. Code Appx. § 460
Sept. 23, 1996, P.L. 104-201, 50 U.S. Code Appx. § 460
Nov. 18, 1997, P.L. 105-85, 50 U.S. Code Appx. § 454

Military Selective Service Act of 1967
June 30, 1967, P.L. 90-40, 81 Stat. 100, 10 U.S. Code §§ 673a, 3201 nt.; 37 U.S. Code §§ 302, 303; 50 U.S. Code Appx. §§ 451, 454 to 456, 460, 462, 467, 2216
Aug. 17, 1968, P.L. 90-491, 82 Stat. 790, 50 U.S. Code Appx. § 459
Nov. 26, 1969, P.L. 91-124, 83 Stat. 220, 50 U.S. Code Appx. § 455
Dec. 31, 1970, P.L. 91-604, 84 Stat. 1712, 50 U.S. Code Appx. § 456
Nov. 16, 1973, P.L. 93-155, 87 Stat. 616, 50 U.S. Code Appx. § 468
Dec. 5, 1973, P.L. 93-176, 87 Stat. 693, 50 U.S. Code Appx. § 460
Oct. 7, 1975, P.L. 94-106, 89 Stat. 537, 50 Appx. U.S. Code §§ 4054, 4056
Nov. 9, 1979, P.L. 96-107, 50 U.S. Code Appx. § 451
Sept. 8, 1982, P.L. 97-252, 50 U.S. Code Appx. §§ 462, 462 nt.
Nov. 8, 1984, P.L. 98-620, 50 U.S. Code Appx. §§ 462, 1984

Military Service Button Act
Ill. Rev. Stat. 1991, Ch. 126 1/2, §§ 44.9, 45

Military Service Overseas Act
Mass. Acts 1970, Ch. 174

Military Service Relief Act
La. Rev. Stat. Ann., 29:401 et seq.

Military Service Tax Credit Act
Iowa Code Ann., 426A.1 et seq.

Military Services Registration and Voting of Electors Act
Utah Code Ann. 1953, 20-17-1 et seq.

Military Survivor Benefits Improvement Act of 1989
Nov. 29, 1989, P.L. 101-189, 10 U.S. Code § 1447 nt.
Nov. 5, 1990, P.L. 101-510, 10 U.S. Code §§ 1331 nt., 1431 nt., 1448 nt., 1456 nt.
Dec. 5, 1991, P.L. 102-190, 10 U.S. Code § 1448 nt.
Oct. 23, 1992, P.L. 102-484, 10 U.S. Code § 1448 nt.

Military Terms Act (Business Use of)
Ill. Comp. Stat. 1992, Ch. 720, § 230/0.01 et seq.
Ill. Rev. Stat. 1991, Ch. 96, § 8m et seq.

Military Veterans Assistance Act
Ill. Rev. Stat. 1991, Ch. 23, § 3080 et seq.

Militia Act
Alaska Stat. 1962, § 26.05.010 et seq.
Cal. Military and Veterans Code § 100 et seq.
Ga. Code Ann., 38-2-1 et seq.
Ill. Rev. Stat. 1991, Ch. 129, § 220.001 et seq.
Ind. Burns' 1933, 45-101 et seq.
Ky. Rev. Stat. 1971, 37.170 et seq.
Mass. Gen Laws 1990, 33:1 et seq.
Md. Ann. Code 1957, Art. 65
Mich. Comp. Laws 1948, 32.1 et seq.
N.H. Rev. Stat. 1955, 110-B:1 et seq.
N.J. Stat. Ann., 38A:4-1 et seq.
Pa. Apr. 9, 1807, 4 Sm. L. 413, Ch. 2842
Wyo. Stat. Ann., § 19-2-101 et seq.
Continued

Militia Act (Naval)
See Naval Militia Act

Militia Acts
Feb. 28, 1795, Ch. 36, 1 Stat. 424
July 29, 1861, Ch. 25, 12 Stat. 281
July 17, 1862, Ch. 201, 12 Stat. 597
Jan. 21, 1903, Ch. 196, 32 Stat. 775
May 27, 1908, Ch. 204, 35 Stat. 399

Milk Act
Me. Rev. Stat. Ann. 1964, Title 7, § 3101 et seq.
Mich. Comp. Laws Ann., 288.21 et seq.
Neb. Rev. Stat. 1943, 2-3913 et seq.
S.C. Code Ann. 1976, § 39-33-10 et seq.
Wash. Rev. Code Ann., 15.36.005 et seq.

Milk Act (Manufacturing)
Mich. Comp. Laws Ann., 288.101 et seq.
Neb. Rev. Stat. 1943, 2-3913 et seq.

Milk Act (Pasteurized)
Neb. Rev. Stat. 1943, 2-3901 et seq.

Milk Adulteration Act
P.R. Laws Ann. 1954, Title 24, § 791 et seq.

Milk and Cream Act
Kan. Stat. Ann., 65-701 et seq.
N.J. Rev. Stat. 1937, 4:12-1 et seq.

Milk and Ice Cream Container Act
Fla. Stat. Ann., 506.29 et seq.

Milk and Milk Products Act
Cal. Food and Agricultural Code 1967, § 32501 et seq.
Fla. Stat. Ann., 502.012 et seq.
Ill. Rev. Stat. 1991, Ch. 56 1/2, § 2201 et seq.
Ky. Rev. Stat. 1971, 217C.010 et seq.
Md. Ann. Code 1974, Art. HG, § 21-401 et seq.
Okla. Stat. Ann., Title 63, § 1-1301.1 et seq.
S.D. Codified Laws 1967, 39-6-1 et seq.
Tenn. Code Ann., 53-3-101 et seq.

Milk and Milk Products Act (Grade A)
Ill. Laws 1983, P.A. 83-102
Mich. Comp. Laws Ann., 288.21 et seq.

Okla. Stat. Ann., Title 63, § 1-301.1 et seq.

Milk and Milk Products Marketing Act
S.C. Code Ann. 1976, § 39-33-1710 et seq.

Milk Audit Act
La. Rev. Stat. Ann., 40:931 et seq.
Miss. Code 1942, § 4560-21 et seq.

Milk Audit and Stabilization Act
Ore. Rev. Stat., 583.001 et seq.

Milk Bottle Act
D.C. Code 1973, § 48-201 et seq.
Mich. Comp. Laws 1948, 288.351 et seq.

Milk Case Recovery Act
N.J. Stat. Ann., 4:12A-63 et seq.

Milk Commission Act
Me. Rev. Stat. Ann. 1964, Title 7, § 2951 et seq.
Miss. Code 1942, § 4560-141 et seq.
N.C. Gen. Stat. 1943, § 106-266.6 et seq.

Milk Commissioner Act
La. Rev. Stat. Ann., 40:881 et seq.

Milk Container Act
Ore. Rev. Stat., 621.656 et seq.

Milk Control Act
Ala. Code 1975, § 2-13-40 et seq.
Cal. Food and Agricultural Code 1967, § 61801 et seq.
Fla. Stat. 1967, 501.01 et seq.
Ga. Code Ann., 26-2-230 et seq.
Haw. Rev. Stat. Ann., § 157-1 et seq.
Ind. Laws 1935, Ch. 281, p. 1365
Mass. Gen Laws 1990, 94A:1 et seq.
Miss. Code 1942, § 4560-141 et seq.
Mont. Rev. Code 1947, 27-401 et seq.
N.H. Rev. Stat. 1955, Superseded Vols., 183:1 et seq.
N.J. Gen. Stat. 1943 § 106-266.6 et seq.
N.J. Stat. Ann., 4:12A-1 et seq.
N.Y. Agriculture and Markets Law (Consol. Laws Ch. 69) § 252 et seq.
Ore. Rev. Stat., 621.055 et seq.
Pa. Purdon's Stat., Title 31, § 700j-101 et seq.

R.I. Gen. Laws 1956, 21-4-1 et seq.
S.C. Code Ann. 1976, § 39-33-1710 et seq.
Utah Code Ann. 1953, 4-3-1 et seq.
Va. Code 1950, § 3.1-425 et seq.
Wis. Stat. Ann., 97.01 et seq.

Milk Control Act (Emergency)

N.J. Stat. Ann., Superseded Vol., 4:12A-59 et seq.

Milk Control and Milk Producer Security Reform Act

N.Y. Agriculture and Markets Law (Consol. Laws Ch. 69) §§ 256b, 258a to 258c, 258e, 258k, 258n, 258p to 258r
N.Y. Laws 1991, Ch. 540

Milk Control Board Act

Pa. 1933 Ex. Pamph. Laws 174, No. 37
Vt. Acts 1937, No. 99

Milk Control Law (State)

N.J. Stat. Ann., App. A:8-1 to App. A:8-49

Milk Dam Act

Fla. Stat. Ann., 361.02
Kan. Stat. Ann., 82a-101 et seq.
Me. Rev. Stat. Ann. 1964, Title 38, § 651 et seq.
Mo. Rev. Stat. 1969, 236.010 et seq.
Pa. Purdon's Stat., Title 32, § 693.1 et seq.
R.I. Gen. Laws 1956, 46-18-1 et seq.
S.D. Code 1939, 37.4101 et seq.
Wis. Stat. Ann., 31.01 et seq.

Milk Dealers Act

Ohio Rev. Code 1953, 917.01 et seq.

Milk Dealers' Bonding Act

Me. Rev. Stat. Ann. 1964, Title 7, §§ 2901, 2955 et seq.

Milk Fat Test Law

Mich. Comp. Laws Ann., 288.51 et seq.

Milk Filled Act

See Filled Milk Act

Milk Grading and Pasteurization Act

Tex. Rev. Civ. Stat., Art. 165-3

Milk Importation Act

See Import Milk Act

Milk Industry Regulation Act

P.R. Laws Ann. 1954, Title 5, § 1092 et seq.

Milk Inspection Act

N.H. Rev. Stat. 1955, 184:1 et seq.

Milk Inspection Law (Grade "A")

Iowa Code 1977, 192.1 et seq.

Milk Manufacturing and Dairy Market Testing Law

Mo. Rev. Stat., 196.520 et seq.

Milk Marketing Act

Conn. Gen. Stat. Ann., § 22-204 et seq.
Ky. Rev. Stat. 1971, 260.675 et seq.
La. Rev. Stat. Ann., 40:940.1 et seq.
Mich. Public Acts 1941, No. 369
Ohio Rev. Code 1953, 917.01 et seq.
Ore. Rev. Stat., 583.001 et seq.
Wash. Rev. Code 1951, 15.42.010 et seq.

Milk Marketing Fee Act

Pa. Purdon's Stat., Title 31, § 700k-1 et seq.

Milk Marketing Law

N.Y. Agriculture and Markets Law (Consol. Laws Ch. 69) § 258c
Pa. Purdon's Stat., Title 31, § 700j-101 et seq.

Milk Minimum Price Act

N.J. Stat. Ann., 4:12A-29

Milk Pasteurization Act

Ill. Rev. Stat. 1991, Ch. 56 1/2, § 2208

Milk Permit Act

Pa. Purdon's Stat., Title 31, § 645 et seq.

Milk Pooling Act

Cal. Food and Agricultural Code 1967, § 62700 et seq.
Wash. Rev. Code Ann., 15.35.010 et seq.

Milk Price Control Act

Mont. Code Ann., 81-23-101 et seq.
R.I. Gen. Laws 1956, 21-4-1 et seq.
Continued

Milk Price Fixing Act
Pa. Purdon's Stat., Title 31, § 700j-801 et seq.

Milk Processor's Regulation Act
Miss. Code Ann. 1972, § 75-31-501 et seq.

Milk Producers' and Cooperative Security Funds Act
Pa. Purdon's Stat., Title 31, § 626.1 et seq.

Milk Producers Security Act
Cal. Food and Agriculture 1967, § 62500 et seq.
Pa. Purdon's Stat., Title 31, § 626.1 et seq.

Milk Products Act
Mich. Comp. Laws Ann., 288.21 et seq.

Milk Products Container Act
Mass. Gen Laws 1990, 110:21

Milk Products Sales Act
Miss. Code Ann. 1972, § 75-31-301 et seq.

Milk Program Act
Ark. Code Ann. 1987, 20-59-101 et seq.

Milk Promotion Act
Ill. Rev. Stat. 1991, Ch. 5, § 1901 et seq.

Milk Regulation Act
D.C. Code 1973, § 33-301 et seq.

Milk River Moratorium
Mont. Code Ann., 85-2-321 to 85-2-323

Milk Sales Practices Act
See Unfair Milk Sales Act

Milk Sanitation Act
Pa. Purdon's Stat., Title 31, § 645 et seq.
R.I. Gen. Laws 1956, 21-2-1 et seq.
Tex. Rev. Civ. Stat., Art. 165-3a

Milk Stabilization and Marketing Act
Cal. Food and Agricultural Code 1967, §§ 61801, 61825

Milk Standards Act
Mich. Comp. Laws Ann., 288.101 et seq.

Milk Tax Act
Me. Rev. Stat. Ann. 1964, Title 36, § 4501 et seq.

Milk Testing Law
Ky. Rev. Stat. 1971, Superseded Vols., 260.170 et seq.
Ky. Rev. Stat. 1971, 260.775 et seq.
La. Rev. Stat. Ann., 40:881 et seq.

Mill Act
Ill. Rev. Stat. 1939, Ch. 92, § 1 et seq.
Mass. Gen Laws 1990, 253:1 et seq.
Me. Rev. Stat. Ann. 1964, Title 38, § 611 et seq.
N.H. Rev. Stat. 1955, 355:1 et seq.

Mill and Elevator Association Act
N.D. Cent. Code, 54-18-01 et seq.

Mill and Elevator Association Bond Act
N.D. Cent. Code, 54-31-01 et seq.

Mill Tailings Licensing and Perpetual Care Act
Wash. Rev. Code Ann., 70.121.010 et seq.

Millage Rollback Act
Fla. Stat. 1973, 236.251

Miller Act
Aug. 24, 1935, Ch. 642, 49 Stat. 793, 40 U.S. Code §§ 270a to 270d
Aug. 4, 1959, P.L. 86-135, 73 Stat. 279, 40 U.S. Code §§ 270b, 270c
Oct. 13, 1994, P.L. 103-355, 40 U.S. Code §§ 270a, 270a nt., 270d-1
Feb. 10, 1996, P.L. 104-106, 40 U.S. Code § 270a nt.

Miller Act (Horizontal Property)
Ky. Rev. Stat. 1971, 381.805 et seq.

Miller Act (Prohibition Enforcement)
Ohio Laws Vol. 109, p. 4

Miller Act (Railroads)
Ohio Rev. Code 1953, 4905.20, 4905.21

Miller Act (Sexual Psychopaths)
D.C. Code 1973, § 22-3501 et seq.

Miller Act (Teacher Retirement)
Ill. Rev. Stat. 1961, Ch. 122, § 25-1 et seq.

Miller Antipollution Act
Cal. Harbors and Navigation Code § 293

Miller-Burton Act (Needy Children)
Cal. Welfare and Institutions Code § 11200 et seq.

Miller Child Care Services Act
Cal. Welfare and Institutions Code § 10811

Miller-Collier Act
Cal. Unemployment Insurance Code § 3501 et seq.

Miller County Salary Act
Ark. 1948 Initiated Act No. 2 of Miller County

Miller-Hulette Act (Municipal Housing)
Ky. Rev. Stat. 1971, 80.020, 80.230 et seq.

Miller-O. Johnson Act (Sewer Districts)
Ky. Acts 1962, Ch. 14

Miller-Tydings Fair Trade Act
See fair Trade Act

Miller-Unruh Basic Reading Act
Cal. Education Code 1976, § 54100 et seq.

Miller-Warren Energy Lifeline Act
Cal. Public Utilities Code § 739

Milliken-Bullard Worker Safety Act
Mich. Comp. Laws Ann., 408.1002 et seq.

Milliken-Engstrom-Jenema Act (Cherry Production)
Mich. Comp. Laws 1970, 290.501 et seq.

Mills Act (Customs Reorganization)
March 4, 1923, Ch. 251, 42 Stat. 1453, 19 U.S. Code §§ 4, 6 to 10, 13, 16, 29, 33, 36, 48, 51, 52

Mills Act (Public Transit)
Cal. Public Utilities Code § 99000 et seq.

Mills-Alquist-Deddeh Act
Cal. Public Utilities Code § 99200 et seq.

Mills-Deddeh Transit Development Act
Cal. Public Utilities Code § 120000 et seq.

Mills-Hayes Act (Use Fuel Tax)
Cal. Revenue and Taxation Code § 8655

Mills-Knox Health Plan Act
Cal. Government Code § 12530 et seq.

Millspaugh Act (Banking)
D.C. Code 1973, § 26-103

Millspaugh Act (D. C. Banks)
April 26, 1922, Ch. 147, 42 Stat. 500

Milrite Act (Economic Development)
Pa. Purdon's Stat., Title 73, § 391.1 et seq.

Milton Marks Postgovernment Employment Restrictions Act
Cal. Government Code § 87406

Milwaukee County Civil Court Act
Wis. Laws 1951, Ch. 168

Milwaukee District Court Act
Wis. Laws 1899, Ch. 218

Milwaukee Municipal Court Act
Wis. Laws 1879, Ch. 256
Wis. Laws 1951, Ch. 384

Milwaukee Railroad Restructuring Act
Nov. 4, 1979, P.L. 96-101, 45 U.S. Code §§ 231f, 662, 721, 821, 825, 901, 901 nt., 902 et seq.
May 30, 1980, P.L. 96-254, 45 U.S. Code §§ 902, 913, 916
April 7, 1986, P.L. 99-272, 45 U.S. Code § 797b nt.
Dec. 29, 1995, P.L. 104-88, 45 U.S. Code § 916

Milwaukee Teachers Retirement Act
Wis. Stat. Ann., 40.20 et seq.

Milwaukee Teachers Tenure Act
Wis. Stat. Ann., 119.42

Minden, Louisiana Redevelopment Agency Act
La. Acts 1968, No. 439

Mine Act (Anthracite Coal)
Pa. Purdon's Stat., Title 52, § 70-101 et seq.

Mine and Tunnel Safety Act (Tom Carrell Memorial)
Cal. Labor Code § 7950 et seq.

Mine Claim Recording Act
Me. Rev. Stat. Ann. 1964, Title 12, § 547, Subsec. 4

Mine Dewatering Act
See also Anthracite Mine Water Control Act
N.M. Stat. 1978, 72-12A-1 et seq.

Mine Inspection Act
Ill. Rev. Stat. 1991, Ch. 96 1/2, § 401 et seq.
Minn. Stat. Ann., 180.01 et seq.
Wash. Rev. Code Ann., 43.22.200 et seq.

Mine Location Act
Utah Code Ann. 1953, 40-1-1 et seq.

Mine Managers Act, 1891
Ill. Laws 1891, p. 168

Mine Occupation Tax Act
Utah Code Ann. 1953, 59-5-101 et seq.

Mine Reclamation Act
Mont. Code Ann., 82-4-201 et seq.

Mine Reclamation Act (Abandoned Hardrock)
Ida. Code 1947, 47-1702 et seq.

Mine Reclamation Act (Abandoned)
Ida. Code 1947, 47-1701 et seq.
N.M. Stat. Ann., 69-25B-1 et seq.
Okla. Stat. Ann., Title 45, § 740.1 et seq.

Mine Safety Act
Ill. Rev. Stat. 1991, Ch. 96 1/2, § 251 et seq.
Mich. Comp. Laws Ann., 425.131 et seq.

N.J. Stat. Ann., 34:6-98.1 et seq.
S.D. Codified Laws 1967, 45-6-1 et seq.
Tex. Rev. Civ. Stat., Art. 5901 et seq.
Va. Code 1950, § 45.1.1 et seq.

Mine Safety Act (Anthracite Coal)
Pa. 1891 Pamph. Laws 176, No. 177

Mine Safety and Health Act
N.C. Gen. Stat. 1943, § 74-24.1 et seq.

Mine Sealing Act
Pa. Purdon's Stat., Title 52, § 28.1 et seq.

Mine Seizure Act
Va. Code 1950, § 45.1-145 et seq.

Mine Siting Act
Mont. Code Ann., 82-4-101 et seq.

Mine Subsidence and Land Conservation Act (Bituminous)
Pa. Purdon's Stat., Title 52, § 1406.1 et seq.

Mine Subsidence Disclosure Act
Ill. Rev. Stat. 1991, Ch. 30, § 1001 et seq.

Mine Telephone Law
Cal. Labor Code §§ 7500, 7501

Mine Ventilation Act
Pa. 1870 Pamph. Laws 3, No. 1, § 7

Mine Waste Act
Fla. Stat. Ann., 533.01 et seq.

Mined Coal Act
Ill. Rev. Stat. 1991, Ch. 29, § 35.9 et seq.

Mined-Land Conservation and Reclamation Act
Kan. Stat. Ann., 49-401 et seq.

Mined Land Reclamation Act
Ariz. Rev. Stat. Ann., § 49-1201 et seq.

Mined Land Reclamation Law
Colo. Rev. Stat., 34-32-101 et seq.
N.Y. Environmental Conservation Law 1972 (Consol. Laws Ch. 43B) § 23-2701 et seq.
S.D. Codified Laws 1967, 45-6B-1 et seq.
Utah Code Ann. 1953, 40-8-1 et seq.

Mined Lands and Water Reclamation Act (Abandoned)
Ill. Comp. Stat. 1992, Ch. 20, § 1920/1.01

Mined Lands Reclamation Act (Abandoned)
Ill. Rev. Stat. 1979, Ch. 96 1/2, § 4601 et seq.

Mined Underground Space Development Act
Minn. Stat. 1986, 472B.01 et seq.

Miner Training, Education and Certification Act
W. Va. Code 1966, § 22A-7-1 et seq.

Mineral Act
Ill. Rev. Stat. 1991, Ch. 1, § 2901-25

Mineral Board Act
La. Rev. Stat. Ann., 30:121 et seq.

Mineral Claims Act
Alaska Stat. 1962, § 27.10.010 et seq.

Mineral Code
La. Rev. Stat. Ann., 31:1 et seq.

Mineral Conservation Act
Miss. Code Ann. 1972, § 53-1-1 et seq.

Mineral County Power System Revenue Bond Law
Nev. Statutes 1961, Ch. 169, p. 537

Mineral Documentary Tax Act
Miss. Code Ann. 1972, § 27-31-71 et seq.

Mineral Exploration Act
S.D. Codified Laws 1967, 45-6C-1 et seq.

Mineral Interest Pooling Act
Tex. Natural Resources Code, § 102.001 et seq.

Mineral Interests Act (Dormant)
Conn. Gen. Stat. Ann., 47-33m et seq.

Mineral Land Free Timber Act
June 3, 1878, Ch. 150, 20 Stat. 88, 16 U.S. Code §§ 604 to 606

Mineral Lands Leasing Act
Wash. Rev. Code Ann., 78.16.010 et seq.

Mineral Lands Leasing Act (Public Lands)
Wash. Rev. Code Ann., 79.01.616 et seq.

Mineral Lands Leasing Act of 1920
Feb. 25, 1920, Ch. 85, 41 Stat. 437, 30 U.S. Code §§ 22, 48, 49, 171, 181 to 194, 201 to 209, 211 to 214, 221, 223 to 229, 229a, 241, 251, 261 to 263
Aug. 8, 1946, Ch. 916, 60 Stat. 950, 30 U.S. Code §§ 181, 184, 187a, 187b, 188, 209, 225, 226, 226d, 226e
May 27, 1947, Ch. 83, 61 Stat. 119, 30 U.S. Code § 191
June 1, 1948, Ch. 365, 62 Stat. 285, 30 U.S. Code § 184
June 3, 1948, Ch. 379, 62 Stat. 289, 30 U.S. Code §§ 184, 201, 202, 209, 211 to 214
Aug. 3, 1950, Ch. 527, 64 Stat. 402, 30 U.S. Code § 191
July 29, 1954, Ch. 644, 68 Stat. 583, 30 U.S. Code §§ 187a, 188, 226, 226e
July 10, 1957, P.L. 85-88, 71 Stat. 282, 30 U.S. Code § 191
Aug. 13, 1957, P.L. 85-122, 71 Stat. 341, 30 U.S. Code § 184
Aug. 21, 1958, P.L. 85-698, 72 Stat. 688, 30 U.S. Code § 184
Sept. 21, 1959, P.L. 86-294, 73 Stat. 571, 30 U.S. Code § 184
March 18, 1960, P.L. 86-391, 74 Stat. 7, 30 U.S. Code §§ 184, 211, 214
June 11, 1960, P.L. 86-507, 74 Stat. 201, 30 U.S. Code § 226
Oct. 15, 1962, P.L. 87-822, 76 Stat. 943, 30 U.S. Code § 188
Aug. 31, 1964, P.L. 88-526, 78 Stat. 710, 30 U.S. Code §§ 184, 201, 201-1
Aug. 31, 1964, P.L. 88-548, 78 Stat. 754, 30 U.S. Code § 184
May 12, 1970, P.L. 91-245, 84 Stat. 206, 30 U.S. Code § 188
Continued

Nov. 16, 1973, P.L. 93-153, 87 Stat. 576, 30 U.S. Code § 185

Aug. 4, 1976, P.L. 94-377, 30 U.S. Code § 181 et seq.

Oct. 30, 1978, P.L. 95-554, 30 U.S. Code §§ 187, 193, 201, 203

Dec. 12, 1982, P.L. 97-394, 30 U.S. Code § 241

Jan. 12, 1983, P.L. 97-451, 30 U.S. Code §§ 188, 191

July 12, 1985, P.L. 99-64, 30 U.S. Code § 185

Dec. 19, 1985, P.L. 99-190, 30 U.S. Code § 201 nt.

Mineral Law (Conservation)
La. Rev. Stat. Ann., 30:1 et seq.

Mineral Lease Release of Record Act
Ill. Rev. Stat. 1991, Ch. 96 1/2, § 4400 et seq.

Mineral Leasing Act
Feb. 25, 1920, Ch. 85, 30 U.S. Code §§ 181 nt., 183 et seq., 201 et seq.

Dec. 22, 1987, P.L. 100-203, 30 U.S. Code § 181 nt.

Sept. 22, 1988, P.L. 100-442, 102 Stat. 1768, 30 U.S. Code §§ 191, 226-3

Oct. 30, 1990, P.L. 101-475, 30 U.S. Code § 185

Nov. 15, 1990, P.L. 101-567, 30 U.S. Code § 188

Oct. 24, 1992, P.L. 102-486, 30 U.S. Code § 226

Aug. 10, 1993, P.L. 103-66, 30 U.S. Code § 191

Nov. 2, 1994, P.L. 103-437, 30 U.S. Code §§ 185, 188, 226

Nov. 28, 1995, P.L. 104-58, 30 U.S. Code § 185

Dec. 21, 1995, P.L. 104-66, 30 U.S. Code §§ 185, 208-2, 226

Mineral Leasing Act for Acquired Lands
Aug. 7, 1947, Ch. 513, 61 Stat. 913, 30 U.S. Code §§ 351, 352 to 359

Oct. 24, 1992, P.L. 102-486, 30 U.S. Code §§ 355, 360

Aug. 10, 1993, P.L. 103-66, 30 U.S. Code § 355

Mineral Leasing Act Revision of 1960
Sept. 2, 1960, P.L. 86-705, 74 Stat. 781, 30 U.S. Code §§ 181, 182, 184, 187a, 226, 226-1, 226-2, 241

Mineral Leasing Commission Act
Ga. Code 1933, 91-118 et seq.

Mineral Leasing Laws
Cal. Public Resources Code § 6890 et seq.

Mineral Leasing Laws (State Lands) Oil and Gas
Cal. Public Resources Code §§ 6826 et seq., 8626

Mineral Permit and Lease Act
Tex. Natural Resources Code, § 53.011 et seq.

Mineral Reservation Law (State Lands)
Cal. Public Resources Code §§ 6401, 6402

Mineral Resources Development Act
N.M. Stat. Ann., 69-10-1 et seq.
P.R. Laws Ann. 1954, Title 28, § 91 et seq.

Mineral Servitude Act
La. Civil Code, Art. 741 et seq.

Mineral Surface Mining Law
Tenn. Code Ann., 59-8-201 et seq.

Mineral Test Hole Regulatory Act
Tenn. Code Ann., 60-1-501 et seq.

Mineral Waters Law
Cal. Public Resources Code § 6961 et seq.

Mineral Well Act
Mich. Comp. Laws Ann., 319.211 et seq.

Minerals Conservation Act
Miss. Code Ann. 1972, § 53-1-1 et seq.

Minerals, Energy and Natural Resources Department Act
N.M. Stat. Ann., 9-5A-1 et seq.

Minerals Severance Tax Act
Wyo. Stat. Ann., § 39-6-302 et seq.

Miners' Certificate of Competency Act
Okla. Stat. Ann., Title 45, § 391 et seq.

Miners' Compensation Act
Alaska Laws 1915, Ch. 71

Miners' Eight Hour Day Law
Cal. Labor Code § 750 et seq.

Miners' Health and Safety Act
Ind. Code Ann., 22-10-4-1 et seq.

Miner's Inch Law
Cal. Water Code § 24

Miner's Labor Lien Act (Alaska)
June 25, 1910, Ch. 422, 36 Stat. 848

Miners' Lien Act
Alaska Stat. 1962, § 34.35.125 et seq.
Ark. Code Ann. 1987, 18-44-202 et seq.
Ill. Rev. Stat. 1991, Ch. 82, §§ 47m, 48
Minn. Stat. Ann., 514.17
S.D. Codified Laws 1967, 44-9-1 et seq.

Miners' Life Check Act
Ind. Code Ann., 22-10-11-6

Miners' Wage Payment Act
Ark. Code Ann. 1987, 11-7-319

Miners' Wages Law
Cal. Labor Code § 270

Miners' Washroom Act
Ill. Laws 1903, p. 252, No. 2
Ind. Code Ann., 22-10-11-13

Mines and Mining Act
Ky. Rev. Stat. 1971, 351.010 et seq., 352.010 et seq.
Wash. Rev. Code Ann., 78.04.010 et seq.

Mines License Tax Act
Ida. Code 1947, 47-1201 et seq.

Mines Net Proceeds Tax Act
Mont. Code Ann., 15-23-501 et seq.

Mini-Code (Consumer Finance)
Ala. Code 1975, § 5-19-1 et seq.

Mini-Self-Storage Landlord and Tenant Act
Fla. Stat. Ann., 83.801 et seq.

Minimum Consumer Resale Price Act
Mass. Gen. Laws 1932, Ch. 93, §§ 14A to 14D

Minimum Crew Act (Railroad)
Ind. Code Ann., 8-9-2-1 et seq.

Minimum Criminal Penalties (Obune Act)
Md. Ann. Code 1957, Art. 27, § 643

Minimum Educational Program Act
Colo. Rev. Stat., 123-6-1 et seq.

Minimum Fair Wage Act
Conn. Gen. Stat. Ann., § 31-58 et seq.
Mass. Gen Laws 1990, 151:1 et seq.
N.J. Stat. Ann., 34:11-56a1 et seq.

Minimum Fair Wage Standards Act
Ohio Rev. Code 1953, 4111.01 et seq.

Minimum Foundation Program Act (Education)
Ark. Code Ann. 1987, 80-853 et seq.
Fla. Stat. 1971, 236.012 et seq.
Ga. Code 1933, 32-601 et seq.
Ky. Rev. Stat. 1971, 157.310 et seq.
S.D. Codified Laws 1967, 13-13-10 et seq.

Minimum Foundation Program for Local Law Enforcement Officers
Fla. Stat. 1971, 163.550 et seq.

Minimum Health Care Protection Act
N.M. Stat. Ann., 59A-23B-1 et seq.

Minimum Housing Code (Newport)
R.I. Public Laws 1962, Ch. 55

Minimum Housing Code (Ocala)
Fla. Special Laws 1967, Ch. 67-1782, § 14.01 et seq.

Minimum Housing Code Act
Fla. Special Laws 1978, Ch. 624, Art. 12

Minimum Kindergarten Program Law
Tenn. Code Ann., 49-6-201

Minimum Markup Act (Retail Sales)
Utah Code Ann. 1953, 13-5-7

Minimum Nonresidential Standards Act (East Providence)
R.I. Public Laws 1968, Ch. 208

Minimum Nonresidential Standards Act (Pawtucket)
R.I. Public Laws 1968, Ch. 70

Minimum Nonresidential Standards Act (Westerly)
R.I. Public Laws 1968, Ch. 67

Minimum Nonresidential Standards Act (Woonsocket)
R.I. Public Laws 1970, Ch. 40

Minimum Penalties Act
Cal. Penal Code § 3024

Minimum Price Act (Alcoholic Liquors)
Conn. Gen. Stat. Ann., § 30-64 et seq.

Minimum Price Act (Milk)
N.J. Stat. Ann., 4:12A-29
Va. Code 1950, § 3.1-437

Minimum Rating Act (Insurance)
Cal. Insurance Code § 11730 et seq.

Minimum Salary Act (County Judges)
Tenn. Code Ann., Superseded Vol., 8-2414 et seq.

Minimum Salary Act (County Officers and Clerks of Courts)
Tenn. Code Ann., 8-24-104

Minimum Salary Act (State Police)
Del. Code of 1974, Title 11, § 8303

Minimum Salary Act (Teachers)
See Teachers' Minimum Salary Act

Minimum Salary Apportionment Act
Ida. Code 1947, 33-1219

Minimum School Budget Law
Ark. Stat. 1947, 80-843 et seq.

Minimum School Finance Act
Utah Code Ann. 1953, 53A-17-101 et seq.

Minimum School Program Act
Utah Code Ann. 1953, 53A-17a-101 et seq.

Minimum Severance Tax Act
W. Va. Code 1966, § 11-12B-1 et seq.

Minimum Speed Act
Ohio Rev. Code 1953, 4511.22

Minimum Standards Housing Act (Central Falls)
R.I. Public Laws 1958, Ch. 56

Minimum Standards Housing Act (East Providence)
R.I. Public Laws 1961, Ch. 66

Minimum Standards Housing Act (Pawtucket)
R.I. Public Laws 1956, Ch. 3783

Minimum Standards Housing Act (Providence)
R.I. Public Laws 1956, Ch. 3715

Minimum Standards Housing Act (Warwick)
R.I. Public Laws 1958, Ch. 99

Minimum Standards Housing Act (Woonsocket)
R.I. Public Laws 1961, Ch. 76

Minimum Wage Act
Alaska Stat. 1962, § 23.10.050 et seq.
Ark. Code Ann. 1987, 11-4-201 et seq.
Colo. Rev. Stat., 8-6-101 et seq.
Conn. Gen. Stat. 1983, § 31-58 et seq.
D.C. Code Ann., § 36-201 et seq.
Del. Code of 1974, Title 19, § 901 et seq.
Ga. Code Ann., 34-4-1 et seq.
Haw. Rev. Stat. Ann., § 387-2

Ida. Code 1947, 44-1501 et seq.

Ill. Rev. Stat. 1991, Ch. 48, § 1001 et seq.

Ky. Rev. Stat. 1971, Superseded Vols., 337.210 et seq.

Md. Ann. Code 1974, Art. LE, § 3-413 et seq.

Me. Rev. Stat. Ann. 1964, Title 26, § 661 et seq.

Mich. Comp. Laws Ann., 408.381 et seq.

Minn. Stat. Ann., 177.22 et seq.

Mo. Rev. Stat. 1978, 290.500 et seq.

N.C. Gen. Stat. 1943, § 95-25.1 et seq.

Neb. Rev. Stat. 1943, 48-1201 et seq.

Nev. Rev. Stat. 1979 Reprint, 608.250 et seq.

N.H. Rev. Stat. 1955, 279:1 et seq.

N.J. Stat. Ann., 34:11-56a

N.M. Stat. Ann., 50-4-19 et seq.

N.Y. Labor Law (Consol. Laws Ch. 31) § 650 et seq.

Ohio Rev. Code 1953, 4111.01 et seq.

Okla. Stat. Ann., Title 40, § 197.1 et seq.

Ore. Rev. Stat., 653.010 et seq.

Pa. Purdon's Stat., Title 43, § 333.101 et seq.

P.R. Laws Ann. 1954, Title 29, § 245 et seq.

R.I. Gen. Laws 1956, 28-12-1 et seq.

Tex. Labor Code, § 62.001 et seq.

Utah Code Ann. 1953, 34-40-101 et seq.

Va. Code 1950, § 40.1-28.8 et seq.

Vt. Stat. Ann., Title 21, § 381 et seq.

Wash. Rev. Code Ann., 49.46.005 et seq.

Wis. Stat. Ann., 104.01 et seq.

Wyo. Stat. Ann., § 24-4-201 et seq.

Minimum Wage Act (Minors')

Ariz. Rev. Stat. Ann., § 23-311 et seq.

Wash. Rev. Code Ann., 49.12.121 et seq.

Minimum Wage Act (Public Works)

Ind. Code Ann., 5-16-7-1 et seq.

Kan. Stat. Ann., 44-201 et seq.

N.M. Stat. Ann., 13-4-11 et seq.

Minimum Wage Act (Teachers')

See Teachers' Minimum Salary Act

Ind. Code Ann., 20-6.1-5-1 et seq.

Iowa Laws 1945, Ch. 135

Minimum Wage Act (Women and Minors)

Cal. Labor Code § 1171 et seq.

Ill. Rev. Stat. 1991, Ch. 48, § 198 et seq.

La. Rev. Stat. Ann., 23:351 et seq.

Minimum Wage Act (Women)

Ark. Code Ann. 1987, 11-4-201 et seq.

Wash. Rev. Code Ann., 49.12.005 et seq.

Minimum Wage Amendments Act of 1966-1975

D.C. Code 1973, § 36-201 et seq.

Minimum Wage and Hour Act

See also Fair Labor Standards Act of 1938

Mont. Code Ann., 39-3-401 et seq.

N.D. Cent. Code, 34-06-01 et seq.

Neb. Rev. Stat. 1943, 48-1201 et seq.

Wash. Rev. Code Ann., 49.46.005

Minimum Wage and Longevity Act (Firemen and Policemen)

Tex. Local Government Code, § 141.031 et seq.

Minimum Wage and Maximum Hours Law

Kan. Stat. Ann., 44-1201 et seq.

Minimum Wage for State Employees Act

S.C. Code Ann. 1976, § 8-11-140 et seq.

Minimum Wage Increase Act of 1996

Aug. 20, 1996, P.L. 104-188, 29 U.S. Code § 201 nt.

Minimum Wage Law

Ind. Code Ann., 22-2-2-1 et seq.

Minimum Wage Law (District of Columbia)

Sept. 19, 1918, Ch. 174, 40 Stat. 960

Minimum Wage Law (New York City)

N.Y. City Adm. Code '38, Ch. 42, § B42-1.0 et seq.

Mining Act

Ala. Code 1975, § 9-16-1 et seq.

Alaska Stat. 1962, § 27.05.010 et seq.

Colo. Rev. Stat., 34-20-101 et seq.

Ill. Rev. Stat. 1991, Ch. 96 1/2, §§ 150 et seq., 251 et seq.

Ind. Code Ann., 22-10-1.5-1 et seq.

Kan. Stat. Ann., 49-101 et seq.

Md. Ann. Code 1974, Art. NR, § 7-101 et seq.

Continued

Me. Rev. Stat. Ann. 1964, Title 12, § 545 et seq.

Mo. Rev. Stat., 444.010 et seq.

N.C. Gen. Stat. 1943, § 74-46 et seq.

N.M. Stat. Ann., 69-36-1 et seq.

Ohio Rev. Code 1953, 4151.01 et seq.

Okla. Stat. Ann., Title 45

Ore. Rev. Stat., 517.010 et seq.

P.R. Laws Ann. 1954, Title 28, § 111 et seq.

S.C. Code Ann. 1976, § 48-20-10 et seq.

Wyo. Stat. Ann., § 30-1-101 et seq.

Mining Act (Anthracite Coal)
Pa. Purdon's Stat., Title 52, § 70-101 et seq.

Mining Act (Bituminous Coal)
Pa. Purdon's Stat., Title 52, § 70-101 et seq.

Mining Act (Child Labor)
Pa. Purdon's Stat., Title 52, § 31 et seq.

Mining Act (Coal)
See Coal Mining Act

Mining Act (Strip)
See Strip Mining Act

Mining Act (Surface)
Ga. Code Ann., 12-4-70 et seq.

Mining and Mineral Resources Institutes Act
Oct. 19, 1996, P.L. 104-312, 30 U.S. Code § 1201 nt.

Mining and Mineral Resources Research Institute Act of 1984
Nov. 2, 1990, P.L. 101-498, 30 U.S. Code § 1230a

Oct. 19, 1996, P.L. 104-312, 30 U.S. Code § 1222

Mining and Minerals Policy Act of 1970
Dec. 31, 1970, P.L. 91-631, 84 Stat. 1876, 30 U.S. Code § 21a

Dec. 21, 1995, P.L. 104-66, 30 U.S. Code § 21a

Oct. 19, 1996, P.L. 104-325, 30 U.S. Code §§ 21a, PRO 1901, 1901 to 1905

Mining Assessments Work Act
Alaska Comp. Laws Ann. 1949, §§ 47-3-52, 47-3-54

Mining Claims Act
Alaska Comp. Laws Ann. 1949, § 47-3-21 et seq.

Wash. Rev. Code Ann., 78.08.005 et seq.

Mining Claims Location Law
Colo. Rev. Stat., 34-43-101 et seq.

Mining Claims Recording Act
Alaska Stat. 1962, §§ 27.10.050, 27.10.060

Mining Claims Rights Restoration Act of 1955
June 11, 1960, P.L. 86-507, 74 Stat. 202, 30 U.S. Code § 621

Mining Compact (Interstate)
Mo. Rev. Stat., 444.400 et seq.

Mining Compact Act
Ky. Rev. Stat. 1971, 350. 300

N.C. Gen. Stat. 1943, §§ 74-37, 74-38

Pa. Purdon's Stat., Title 52, § 3251 et seq.

S.C. Code Ann. 1976, § 48-21-10 et seq.

Mining Compact Act (Interstate)
See Interstate Mining Compact Act

Mining Engineering Act (University of Illinois)
Ill. Rev. Stat. 1991, Ch. 144, § 54.90 et seq.

Mining Fee Act (Surface Coal Mining)
Ill. Rev. Stat. 1991, Ch. 96 1/2, § 7500 et seq.

Mining Lands Reclamation Act
Colo. Rev. Stat., 34-32-101 et seq.

Mont. Code Ann., 82-4-301 et seq.

Okla. Stat. Ann., Title 45, § 721 et seq.

Mining Law
P.R. Laws Ann. 1954, Title 28, § 111 et seq.

Mining Law (Oil, Gas and Solution)
N.Y. Environmental Conservative Law 1972 (Consol. Laws Ch. 43B) § 23-0101 et seq.

Mining Leases Act
Ore. Rev. Stat., 517.420 et seq.
Wash. Laws 1939, Ch. 110

Mining License Act
Alaska Stat. 1962, § 43.65.010 et seq.

Mining Lien Law
Colo. Rev. Stat., 38-22-104 et seq.

Mining Occupation Tax Act
Minn. Stat. Ann., 298.01 et seq.
Utah Code Ann. 1953, 59-5-101 et seq.

Mining Registration Act
N.C. Gen. Stat. 1943, § 74-39 et seq.

Mining Royalties Tax Act
Minn. Stat. 1986, 299.01 et seq.

Mining Safety Act
N.M. Stat. Ann., 69-8-1 et seq.

Mining Securities Act
Wash. Laws 1937, Ch. 178

Mining Tax Act
S.D. Codified Laws 1988, Ch. 102

Minkoff Law (Unlawful Occupation)
N.Y. Multiple Dwelling Law 1946 (Consol. Laws Ch. 61A) § 302

Minneapolis Municipal Court Act
Minn. Stat. Ann., 488A.01 et seq.

Minneapolis-St. Paul Sanitary District Act
Minn. Stat. Ann., 115.18 et seq.

Minnesota Family Investment Program-Statewide (MFIP-S)
Minn. Stat. 1986, 256J.01 et seq., 256K.01 et seq.

Minnesota Public Lands Improvement Act of 1990
Oct. 18, 1990, P.L. 101-442, 104 Stat. 1020

Minnesota Reinvest in Resources Law
Minn. Stat. Ann., 103F.501 et seq.

Minnesota Valley National Wildlife Refuge Act
Oct. 8, 1976, P.L. 94-466, 16 U.S. Code § 1132 nt.
June 25, 1984, P.L. 98-327

Minnow Dealers Act (Wholesale)
Miss. Code Ann. 1972, § 49-7-29

Minor and Technical Criminal Law Amendments Act of 1988
Nov. 18, 1988, P.L. 100-690, 18 U.S. Code § 1 nt.

Minor Children Support Act
Ga. Code Ann., 19-6-17

Minor Court Act
Conn. Gen. Stat. Ann., § 51-127 et seq.

Minor Courts Accounting Law
Ark. Code Ann. 1987, 16-10-201 et seq.

Minor Employment Act
Fla. Stat. Ann., 450.01 et seq.

Minor Homicide Act
Ala. Code 1975, § 6-5-391

Minor Identification Act
Okla. Stat. 1981, Title 10, § 1629 et seq.

Minor Identification and Protection Act
Ill. Rev. Stat. 1991, Ch. 23, § 2451 et seq.

Minor Judiciary Court Appeals Act
Pa. Purdon's Stat., Title 42, § 3001 et seq.

Minor Judiciary Education Act
Pa. Purdon's Stat., Title 42, § 1211 et seq.

Minor Judiciary Fee Bill
Pa. Purdon's Stat., Title 42, § 216 et seq.

Minor Judiciary Jurisdictional Act
Pa. Cons. Stat., Title 42, § 1515

Minor Motor Vehicle Operator's Responsibility Act
Ohio Rev. Code 1953, 450.07

Minor Operators' Liability Act
Ohio Rev. Code 1953, 4507.07

Minor Veterans Enabling Act
N.C. Gen. Stat. 1943, § 165-12 et seq.

Minorities, Females and Persons with Disabilities Act (Business Enterprise for)
Ill. Comp. Stat. 1992, Ch. 30, § 575/0.01 et seq.

Minority and At-Risk Student Scholarship Act
Ida. Code 1947, 33-4601 et seq.

Minority and Female Business Enterprise Act
Ill. Rev. Stat. 1991, Ch. 127, § 132.600

Minority and Female Small Business Procurement Act
Iowa Laws 1985, H.F. 225

Minority and Small Business Assistance Act
Fla. Stat. Ann., 288.701 et seq.

Minority and Women-Owned Business Assistance Act (Omnibus)
Wash. Rev. Code Ann., 43.172.900

Minority and Women's Business Assistance Act
Ore. Rev. Stat., 200.005 et seq.

Minority and Women's Business Enterprise Act
La. Rev. Stat. Ann., 36:1951 et seq.

Minority Assistance Program for Certified Public Accountant Education
Fla. Stat. Ann., 473.3065

Minority Business Development Act
La. Rev. Stat. Ann., 51:1751 et seq.

Minority Business Development Authority Act
Pa. Purdon's Stat., Title 73, § 390.1 et seq.

Minority Business Development Compliance Act
R.I. Gen. Laws 1956, 37-21-1 et seq.

Minority Business Economic Development Act
Ark. Acts 1991, No. 698

Minority Business Enterprise Act
La. Rev. Stat. Ann., 39:1951 et seq.
Miss. Code Ann. 1972, § 57-69-1 et seq.

Minority Business Enterprise Assistance Act
Okla. Stat. Ann., Title 74, § 85.45 et seq.

Minority Business Enterprises Systems Act
Okla. Stat. Ann., Title 74, § 85.45 et seq.

Minority Business, Small Business and Female Business Set Aside Act
N.J. Stat. Ann., 52:35-17 et seq.

Minority Contracting Act
D.C. Code Ann., § 1-1141 et seq.

Minority Doctoral Assistance Act
N.M. Stat. Ann., 21-21I-1 et seq.

Minority Doctoral Assistance Loan for Service Program Act
N.M. Stat. Ann., 21-21I-1

Minority Faculty Advancement Loan and Loan Redemption Program Act
N.J. Stat. Ann., 18A:72F-1 et seq.

Minority Fellowship Program (Ethnic)
Kan. Laws 1993, Ch. 47

Minority-Focused Civics Education Act of 1994
March 31, 1994, P.L. 103-227, 20 U.S. Code § 5981 et seq.

Minority Health Improvement Act
Fla. Stat. Ann., 381.81

Minority Males Act
Ill. Rev. Stat. 1991, Ch. 127, § 132.631 et seq.

Minority Populations Health Promotion Act
R.I. Gen. Laws 1956, 23-64-1 et seq.

Minority Representation Act (Boards)
Conn. Gen. Stat. Ann., § 9-167a

Minority Stockholders Act
Me. Rev. Stat. Ann. 1964, Title 13-A, § 908 et seq.

Minority Teacher Act
Ore. Laws 1991, Ch. 434

Minors Act
N.J. Stat. Ann., 9:2-1 et seq.
P.R. Laws Ann. 1954, Title 34, § 2201 et seq.

Minors Act (Conditions of Employment)
Pa. Purdon's Stat., Title 43, § 41 et seq.

Minors Act (Gifts of Securities)
R.I. Gen. Laws 1956, 18-7-1 et seq.

Minors Act (Sale or Pledge of Goods)
Ill. Rev. Stat. 1991, Ch. 23, § 2365.9 et seq.

Minors Act (Sentencing)
Ind. Code 1976, 35-8-3-1

Minors Act (Transfers to)
Wis. Stat. Ann., 880.61 et seq.

Minors Act (Wayward)
N.Y. Family Court Act § 711 et seq.

Minors and Womens Ten Hour Act
N.H. Rev. Stat. 1955, 275:15

Minors' and Women's Wages Act
Ill. Rev. Stat. 1991, Ch. 48, 198 et seq.

Minors' Baseball Contracts Act
Wash. Rev. Code Ann., 67.04.090 et seq.

Minors' Birth Control Services Act
Ill. Rev. Stat. 1991, Ch. 111 1/2, §§ 4650, 4651

Minors' Consent to Medical Procedures Act
Ill. Rev. Stat. 1991, Ch. 111, § 4500 et seq.

Minors' Contracts Act (Artistic)
Ill. Rev. Stat. 1991, Ch. 48, § 31.80 et seq.

Minors Emancipation Act
N.M. Stat 1978, 28-6-1 et seq.

Minors Emergency War Employment Act
Cal. Statutes 1943, Ch. 771, p. 2547

Minors Firearm Safety Act
Minn. Stat. Ann., 97B.021

Minors' Gift Act
See Uniform Gifts to Minors Act

Minors' Gift of Securities Act
Ga. Code Ann., 44-5-110 et seq.

Minors' Hours and Wages Law
Cal. Labor Code § 1171 et seq.

Minors' Life Check Act
Ind. Code Ann., 22-10-11-6

Minors' Minimum Wage Act
Wash. Rev. Code Ann., 49.12.121, 49.46.020

Minors Protection Act
D.C. Code Ann., § 22-2011 et seq.

Minors Residency for Tuition Act
Ill. Rev. Stat. 1991, Ch. 144, § 40a.9 et seq.

Minors Securities Ownership Act
See Uniform Securities Ownership by Minors Act

Minors Wrongful Death Act
See Wrongful Death of Minors Act

Mint Industry Act
Ida. Code 1947, 22-3801 et seq.

Minute Man National Historical Park Amendments of 1991
Oct. 24, 1992, P.L. 102-488, 16 U.S. Code §§ 410s, 410s nt., 410t, 410x-410x-2

MIP Law
Mont. Code Ann., 41-5-601

Misbranding Act
Mass. Gen Laws 1990, 94:186 et seq.

Misbranding Act (Foods, Drugs and Cosmetics)
Wash. Rev. Code Ann., 69.04.001 et seq.

Miscegenation Act
Ala. Code 1958, Title 14, §§ 360, 361
Ark. Stat. 1947, 55-104
Cal. Civil Code §§ 60, 69
Del. Code of 1974, Title 13, § 101, Subd. a
Fla. Stat. 1967, 741.11 et seq.
Ga. Code 1933, 53-106
Ind. Burns' 1933, 44-104
Ky. Rev. Stat. 1971, 402.020
La. Rev. Stat. Ann., 9:201, 14:79
Md. Ann. Code 1957, Art. 27, § 398
Miss. Code Ann. 1972, § 93-1-3
Mo. Rev. Stat., 451.020
Mont. Laws 1909, Ch. 49
N.C. Gen. Stat. 1943, §§ 14-181, 51-3
N.D. Cent. Code, Superseded Vol., 12-22-13
Nev. Rev. Stat. 1957, 122.180
Okla. Stat. Ann., Title 43, §§ 12, 13
S.C. Code Ann. 1962, § 20-7
Tenn. Code Ann., Superseded Vol., 36-402, 36-403
Tex. Penal Code 1925, Art. 492
Utah Code Ann. 1953, Superseded Vol., 30-1-2, Subds. 5, 6
Va. Code 1950, § 20-54
Wyo. Stat. 1957, §§ 20-18, 20-19

Miscegenation Laws
La. Rev. Stat. Ann., 9:201, 14:79

Miscellaneous and Mutual Corporation Act
Wash. Rev. Code Ann., 24.06.005 et seq.

Miscellaneous and Technical Immigration and Naturalization Amendments of 1991
Dec. 12, 1991, P.L. 102-232, 8 U.S. Code § 1101 nt.
Oct. 25, 1994, P.L. 103-416, 8 U.S. Code §§ 1101 nt., 1182, 1160, 1188, 1254a, 1324a, 1356 nt., 1449
Sept. 30, 1996, P.L. 104-208, 8 U.S. Code § 1254a nt.

Miscellaneous and Technical Social Security Act Amendments of 1989
Dec. 19, 1989, P.L. 101-239, 42 U.S. Code § 1305 nt.

Miscellaneous Appropriation Act
Tenn. Public Acts 1941, Ch. 87
Tenn. Public Acts 1947, Ch. 237
Tenn. Public Acts 1949, Ch. 287
Tenn. Public Acts 1951, Ch. 268
Tenn. Public Acts 1953, Ch. 251
Tenn. Public Acts 1967, Ch. 344

Miscellaneous Corporation Laws Act
Tex. Rev. Civ. Stat., Art. 1302-1.01 et seq.

Miscellaneous Federal Grant Act
Ark. Code Ann. 1987, 19-7-501 et seq.

Miscellaneous Revenue Act of 1980
Dec. 28, 1980, P.L. 95-605, 26 U.S. Code § 1 nt.

Miscellaneous Revenue Act of 1982
Oct. 25, 1982, P.L. 97-362, 26 U.S. Code § 1 nt.

Miscellaneous Trade and Technical Corrections Act of 1996
Oct. 11, 1996, P.L. 105-295, 19 U.S. Code § 1654 nt.
June 25, 1999, P.L. 106-36, 19 U.S. Code § 1631

Miscellaneous Trade and Technical Corrections Act of 1999
June 25, 1999, P.L. 106-36, 113 Stat. 127, 19 U.S. Code § 1654 nt.

Misconduct Act (Legislative)
Ill. Rev. Stat. 1991, Ch. 38 § 90-0.1 et seq.

Misconduct Act (Traditional Housing Participant)
Cal. Health and Safety Code § 50580 et seq.

Misdemeanor Adult Probation and Supervision Law
Tex. Code of Criminal Procedure 1965, Art. 42.13

Misdemeanor and Quasi-criminal Bail Act
Ill. Rev. Stat. 1991, Ch. 16, § 80 et seq.

Misdemeanor in Office Act
La. Rev. Stat. Ann., 14:134

Misdemeanor Trial Law
N.Y. Criminal Procedure Law (Consol. Laws Ch. 11A) §§ 340.40 Subd. 2, 400.22
N.Y. Penal Law 1965 (Consol. Law Ch. 40) § 70.15 Subd. 1

Mishandled or Adulterated Foods Act
Tenn. Code Ann., 53-1-101 et seq.

Misrepresentation Act (Insurance)
Mo. Rev. Stat., 376.580

Missile Defense Act of 1991
Dec. 5, 1991, P.L. 102-190, 10 U.S. Code § 2431 nt.
Oct. 23, 1992, P.L. 102-484, 10 U.S. Code § 2431 nt.
Oct. 24, 1992, P.L. 102-486, 15 U.S. Code §§ 2001, 2002, 2006, 2013
Nov. 30, 1993, P.L. 103-160, 10 U.S. Code § 2431 nt.
Oct. 5, 1994, P.L. 103-337, 10 U.S. Code § 2431 nt.
Feb. 10, 1996, P.L. 104-106, 10 U.S. Code § 2431 nt.

Missing Child Recovery Act (Intergovernmental)
Ill. Rev. Stat. 1991, Ch. 23 § 2251 et seq.

Missing Child Reporting Act
Ida. Code 1947, 18-4507 et seq.
N.M. Stat. Ann., 32A-14-1 to 32A-14-4

Missing Children (Control Register)
Mass. Gen. Laws Ann., 22A:1 et seq.

Missing Children Act
Oct. 12, 1982, P.L. 97-292, 28 U.S. Code § 1 nt.

Missing Children Act (Davis-Grisham)
Cal. Education Code 1976, § 40048

Missing Children Identification Act
La. Rev. Stat. Ann., 40:2511 et seq.
Neb. Rev. Stat. 1943, 43-2001 et seq.

Missing Children Information Act
W. Va. Code 1966, § 49-9-1 et seq.

Missing Children Records Act
Ill. Rev. Stat. 1991, Ch. 23, § 2280 et seq.

Missing Children Recovery Act
Tenn. Code Ann., 37-10-201 et seq.

Missing Children Registration Law
Ill. Rev. Stat. 1991, Ch. 23, § 2270 et seq.
Pa. Purdon's Stat., Title 35, § 450.401-A et seq.

Missing Children's Act
Minn. Stat. Ann., 299C.51 et seq.
Mont. Laws 1985, Ch. 559

Missing Children's Assistance Act
Oct. 12, 1984, P.L. 98-473, 42 U.S. Code § 5601 nt.
Nov. 18, 1988, P.L. 100-690, 42 U.S. Code §§ 5773 to 5778
Dec. 8, 1989, P.L. 101-204, 42 U.S. Code §§ 5601 nt., 5773, 5775
Oct. 3, 1996, P.L. 104-235, 42 U.S. Code §§ 5777, 5778

Missing Person Act
Mich. Comp. Laws Ann., 720.501 et seq.

Missing Person Information Center Act
S.C. Code Ann. 1976, § 23-3-200 et seq.

Missing Persons Act
March 7, 1942, Ch. 166, 56 Stat. 143 (See 5 U.S. Code §§ 5561 to 5568; See 37 U.S. Code §§ 551 to 558)
Dec. 24, 1942, Ch. 828, 56 Stat. 1093 (See 5 U.S. Code §§ 5562, 5563, 5565; See 37 U.S. Code §§ 552, 553, 555)
July 1, 1944, Ch. 371, 58 Stat. 679 (See 5 U.S. Code §§ 5561 to 5563, 5566, 5567; See 37 U.S. Code §§ 551 to 553, 556, 557)
Feb. 12, 1946, Ch. 6, § 1, 60 Stat. 5 (See 5 U.S. Code § 5564; See 37 U.S. Code § 554)
May 16, 1947, Ch. 70, 61 Stat. 96 (See 5 U.S. Code § 5561)
Continued

Aug. 8, 1947, Ch. 515, 61 Stat. 918 (See 5 U.S. Code § 5568; See 37 U.S. Code § 558)

Aug. 29, 1951, Ch. 356, 65 Stat. 207 (See 5 U.S. Code § 5564; See 37 U.S. Code § 554)

April 4, 1953, Ch. 17, 67 Stat. 21 (See 5 U.S. Code §§ 5561 to 5566; See 37 U.S. Code §§ 551 to 556)

Jan. 30, 1954, Ch. 3, 68 Stat. 7

June 30, 1955, Ch. 254, 69 Stat. 238

July 20, 1956, Ch. 658, 70 Stat. 595

Aug. 7, 1957, P.L. 85-121, 71 Stat. 341

Aug. 29, 1957, P.L. 85-217, 71 Stat. 491 (See 5 U.S. Code §§ 5561, 5562, 5564 to 5567; See 37 U.S. Code §§ 551, 552, 554 to 557)

Aug. 14, 1964, P.L. 88-428, 78 Stat. 437 (See 5 U.S. Code §§ 5561 to 5566, 5568; See 37 U.S. Code §§ 551 to 556, 558)

Oct. 19, 1965, P.L. 89-271, 79 Stat. 992 (See 5 U.S. Code § 5564; See 37 U.S. Code § 554)

Missing Persons Act (Probate)

Ill. Rev. Stat. 1991, Ch. 110 1/2, §§ 5-1, 5-2, 10-1 to 10-5

Mich. Comp. Laws Ann., 720.501 et seq.

Ore. Rev. Stat., 127.010 et seq.

Missing Persons Information Act

N.M. Stat. Ann., 29-15-1 et seq.

Missing Persons Presumed Dead Act (Evidence)

Pa. 1945 Pamph. Laws 187, No. 88

Mississippi-Alabama Railroad Authority Compact

Miss. Code Ann. 1972, § 77-9-531 et seq.

Mississippi and Illinois Canal State Park Act

Ill. Rev. Stat. 1991, Ch. 105, § 482.9 et seq.

Mississippi-Arkansas Great River Bridge Construction Compact

Miss. Code Ann. 1972, § 65-25-121 et seq.

Mississippi-Louisiana-Alabama-Georgia Rapid Rail Transit Compact Act

Ga. Code Ann., 46-9-300

Miss. Code Ann. 1972, § 57-45-1

Mississippi-Louisiana Bridge Construction Compact Act

La. Rev. Stat. Ann., 48:1107

Mississippi River Bridge Revenue Bond Law

Miss. Code Ann. 1972, § 65-25-1 et seq.

Mississippi River Corridor Study Commission Act of 1989

Sept. 28, 1990, P.L. 101-398, 104 Stat. 855

Mississippi River Flood Control Act

May 15, 1928, Ch. 569, 45 Stat. 534, 33 U.S. Code §§ 702a to 702m, 704

June 15, 1936, Ch. 548, 49 Stat. 1508, 33 U.S. Code §§ 702a-1 to 702a-11, 702g-1, 702j-1, 702j-2, 702k-1, 702k-2

Mississippi River Interstate Pollution Phase-Out Compact

La. Rev. Stat. Ann., 30:1099.1 et seq.

Mississippi River Parkway Act

Mo. Rev. Stat., 226.280 et seq.

Mississippi River Timberlands Control Act

Miss. Code Ann. 1972, § 49-20-1 et seq.

Mississippi Sioux Tribes Judgment Fund Distribution Act of 1998

Nov. 13, 1998, P.L. 105-387, 112 Stat. 3471, 25 U.S. Code § 1300d nt.

Mississippi University Research Authority Act

Miss. Code Ann. 1972, § 37-147-1 et seq.

Missouri and Kansas Metropolitan Culture and Recreation District Compact and Act

Mo. Rev. Stat. 1978, 70.445 et seq.

Missouri Compromise

March 6, 1820, Ch. 22, 3 Stat. 545

March 2, 1821, No. 1, 3 Stat. 645

Missouri Enabling Acts

See Missouri Compromise

Missouri-Illinois Bridge Commission Act
Ill. Rev. Stat. 1991, Ch. 127, § 63s-24.9 et seq.

Missouri-Illinois Bridge Compact Act
Ill. Rev. Stat. 1991, Ch. 127, § 63s-20 et seq.

Missouri-Illinois-Jefferson-Monroe Bridge Commission Act
Ill. Rev. Stat. 1991, Ch. 127, § 63s-34.9 et seq.

Missouri-Illinois-Jefferson-Monroe Bridge Compact Act
Ill. Rev. Stat. 1991, Ch. 127, § 63s-30.9 et seq.

Missouri-Kansas Air Quality Compact
Mo. Rev. Stat., 643.600 et seq.

Missouri-Kansas Flood Prevention and Control Compact Act
Mo. Rev. Stat., 70.327 et seq.

Missouri-Kansas Metropolitan Culture and Recreation District Compact Act
Mo. Rev. Stat., 70.327 et seq.

Missouri-Nebraska Boundary Compact
Neb. Laws 1971, L. B. 1034

Missouri River Barge Compact Act
Iowa Code Ann., 307C.1 et seq.

Missouri-St. Louis Metropolitan Airport Authority Law
Mo. Rev. Stat., 305.500 et seq.

Mitchell Act (Columbia River Basin Fishery Development)
May 11, 1938, Ch. 193, 16 U.S. Code §§ 755-757
Aug. 8, 1946, Ch. 883, 16 U.S. Code §§ 756, 757

Mitchell Act (Railroad Right of Way)
N.Y. Railroad Law (Consol. Laws Ch. 49) § 52b

Mitchell-Coudert Laws (Action for Corporate Misconduct)
N.Y. Business Corporations Law 1961 (Consol. Laws Ch. 4) §§ 626, 706, 720

Mitchell-Coudert Laws (Security for Expenses in Derivative Action)
N.Y. Business Corporations Law 1961 (Consol. Laws Ch. 4) §§ 627, 720

Mitchell-Hollinger Act (Employee Welfare Funds)
N.Y. Insurance Law 1984 (Consol. Laws Ch. 28) § 4401 et seq.

Mitchell-Lama Law (Limited Profit Housing)
N.Y. Private Housing Finance Law (Consol. Laws, Ch. 44B) § 10 et seq.

Mitchem-Kelley Act (Housing Finance)
Ala. Acts 1980, p. 899

Mitigation Act (Radon)
Ill. Rev. Stat. 1991, Ch. 111 1/2, § 243-1 et seq.

Mitigation Bank Act (Wetlands)
Ore. Rev. Stat., 196.600 et seq.

Mitigation Banking Act (Resource)
Colo. Rev. Stat., 37-85.5-101 et seq.

Mixed Flour Act
June 13, 1898, Ch. 448, 30 Stat. 466, 31 U.S. Code § 756

Mixed Funding Pilot Program
Mont. Laws 1995, Ch. 584

Mni Wiconi Act Amendments of 1994
Oct. 31, 1994, P.L. 103-434, 108 Stat. 4539

Mni Wiconi Project Act of 1988
Oct. 24, 1988, P.L. 100-516, 43 U.S. Code § 615 llll-6

MNJOBS Program
Minn. Stat. 1986, 256.7381 to 256.7387

Mob Action Act (Damages)
N.Y. General Municipal Law (Consol. Laws Ch. 24) § 71

Mob and Riot Act
Ill. Rev. Stat. 1991, Ch. 38, § 25-1

Ind. Code 1976, 35-1-77-1 et seq., 35-27-1-1 et seq.

Wis. Stat. Ann., 66.091

Mob Violence Act (Liability)
Cal. Government Code § 50140 et seq.

Kan. Laws 1862, Ch. 77

Mobile Act (Fraternal Beneficiary Associations)
Mo. Rev. Stat., 378.010 et seq.

Mobile Business Practices Act (Personal Sports)
Me. Rev. Stat. Ann. 1964, Title 10, § 1241 et seq.

Mobile County Bingo Act
Ala. Acts 1983, p. 1184

Mobile County Civil Service Act
Ala. Local Acts 1939, p. 298

Mobile County Litter Control Act
Ala. Acts 1981, p. 792

Mobile Health Care Services Act
Cal. Health and Safety Code § 1765.101 et seq.

Mobile Home Act
Cal. Health and Safety Code § 18000 et seq.

Fla. Stat. Ann., 723.001 et seq.

Mobile Home Act (Abandoned)
Ill. Comp. Stat. 1992, Ch. 210, § 117/5

Mobile Home Ad Valorem Tax Act
Miss. Code Ann. 1972, § 27-53-1 et seq.

Mobile Home Anchoring Act
Tenn. Code Ann., 68-45-101 et seq.

Mobile Home and Manufactured Housing Safety Act
Ill. Rev. Stat. 1991, Ch. 67 1/2, § 501 et seq.

Mobile Home and Mobile Home Camps Law
N.Y. Local Laws 1973, Town of Shawangunk, p. 2934

Mobile Home and Recreational Vehicle Park Act
Ky. Rev. Stat. 1971, 219.310 et seq.

Mobile Home Commission Act
Mich. Comp. Laws Ann., 125.1101 et seq.

Mobile Home Dealer Regulation Act
N.D. Cent. Code, 39-18-01 et seq.

Mobile Home Health, Sanitation and Safety Act
Ind. Code Ann., 13-1-7-1 et seq.

Mobile Home Landlord and Tenant Rights Act
Fla. Stat. Ann., 83.40 et seq.

Ida. Code 1947, 55-2001 et seq.

Ill. Rev. Stat. 1991, Ch. 80, § 201 et seq.

Iowa Code 1983, 562B.1 et seq.

Neb. Laws 1984, L.B. 916, §§ 1 to 62

Wash. Rev. Code Ann., 59.20.010 et seq.

Mobile Home Local Services Tax Act
Ill. Comp. Stat. 1992, Ch. 35, § 515/1 et seq.

Ill. Rev. Stat. 1991, Ch. 120, § 1201 et seq.

Mobile Home Lot Rental Act
Va. Code 1950, § 55-248.41 et seq.

Mobile Home Manufactured Housing Act
Cal. Health and Safety Code § 18000 et seq.

Mobile Home Park Residency Act
Utah Code Ann. 1953, 57-16-1 et seq.

Mobile Home Park Rights Act
Pa. Purdon's Stat., Title 68, § 398.1 et seq.

Mobile Home Parks Act
Cal. Health and Safety Code § 18200 et seq.

Colo. Rev. Stat., 38-12-200.1 et seq.

Ida. Code 1947, 55-2001 et seq.

Ill. Rev. Stat. 1991, Ch. 111 1/2, § 711 et seq.

Mobile Home Parks Residential Landlord and Tenant Act

Ariz. Rev. Stat. Ann., § 33-1401 et seq.

Ill. Rev. Stat. 1991, Ch. 111 1/2, § 711 et seq.

Ind. Code Ann., 13-1-7-1 et seq.

Iowa Code 1983, 562B.1 et seq.

Kan. Laws 1992, Ch. 306

Mass. Gen. Laws Ann., 140:32F et seq.

Md. Ann. Code 1974, Art. RP, § 8A-101 et seq.

N.M. Stat. 1978, 47-10-1 et seq.

Mobile Home Parks Standards Act

Neb. Rev. Stat. 1943, 71-4621 et seq.

Mobile Home Property Tax Law

Cal. Revenue and Taxation Code § 5800 et seq.

Mobile Home Property Tax Postponement Law (Senior Citizens)

Cal. Revenue and Taxation Code § 20639 et seq.

Mobile Home Relocation Site Acquisition and Development Act

Fla. Stat. Ann., 420.701 et seq.

Mobile Home Repossession Security Act

Minn. Stat. Ann., 327.61 et seq.

Mobile Home Safety Act

Del. Code of 1974, Title 31, § 4600 et seq.

S.D. Codified Laws 1967, 34-34A-1 et seq.

Va. Code 1950, § 36-70 et seq.

Mobile Home Sales Act

Ky. Rev. Stat. 1971, 367.710 et seq.

Mobile Home Standards Act

Nev. Rev. Stat. 1979 Reprint, 489.021 et seq.

Mobile Home Standards Code (Factory Manufactured)

Okla. Stat. Ann., Title 63, § 2451 et seq.

Mobile Home Tenant Bill of Rights

N.Y. Real Property Law (Consol. Laws Ch. 50) § 233

Mobile Home Tiedown Act

Ill. Rev. Stat. 1991, Ch. 111 1/2, § 4401 et seq.

Mobile Home Titling Act

Pa. Purdon's Stat., Title 68, § 1001 et seq.

Mobile Homes and Manufactured Housing Uniform Standards Code

La. Rev. Stat. Ann., 51:911.21 et seq.

Mobile Homes and Parks Law

Iowa Code Ann., 435.1 et seq.

Mobile Homes and Recreational Vehicles Standards Act

See Uniform Mobile Homes and Recreational Vehicles Standards Act

Mobile Homes and Recreational Vehicles Uniform Standards Code

See Uniform Standards Code for Mobile Homes and Recreational Vehicles

Mobile Homes Code

Tex. Rev. Civ. Stat., Art. 5221f

Mobile Homes Construction and Installation Standards Code

N.Y. Executive Law 1951 (Consol. Laws Ch. 18) § 400aa et seq.

Mobile Homes HUD Construction and Safety Standards Act

Ark. Code Ann. 1987, 20-25-101 et seq.

Mobile Homes-Manufactured Housing Act

Cal. Health and Safety Code § 18000 et seq.

Mobile Homes Standards Code

Fla. Stat. Ann., 553.35 et seq.

N.D. Cent. Code, 54-21.1-01 et seq.

Pa. Purdon's Stat., Title 35, § 1656.1 et seq.

Mobile Homes Tax Act

Ariz. Rev. Stat. Ann., § 42-640 et seq.

Ind. Code Ann., 6-1.1-7-1 et seq.

N.D. Cent. Code, 57-55-01 et seq.

S.D. Codified Laws 1967, 10-9-1 et seq.

Mobile Homes Uniform Standards Code
See Uniform Standards Code for Mobile Homes

Mobile Homes Warranty Act
Mich. Comp. Laws Ann., 125.991 et seq.
Wyo. Stat. Ann., § 35-18-101 et seq.

Mobile Housing Act
N.M. Stat. Ann., 60-14-1 et seq.

Mobile Paramedic Act
Utah Code Ann. 1953, 26-8-1 et seq.

Mobile Sales Business Regulation Act
P.R. Laws Ann. 1954, Title 10, § 2001 et seq.

Mobilehome Residency Law
Cal. Civil Code § 798 et seq.

Mobilehomes-Manufactured Housing Act
Cal. Health and Safety Code § 18000

Mobilization Act (Fire Defense)
See Fire Defense Mobilization Act

Mobley California Youth Conservation Corps Act
Cal. Public Resources Code § 14000 et seq.

Mobley-Nejedly Delta Levees Act
Cal. Water Code § 12225 et seq.

Mobley-Newberry-Hinkle Act (School Term)
Ky. Rev. Stat. 1971, 158.070

Mock Auction Act
Mont. Rev. Code 1947, 94-1809

Model Act Concerning the Administration of Charitable Trusts, Devises and Bequests
Vt. Stat. Ann., Title 14, § 2328

Model Act for the Regulation of Credit Accident and Health Insurance
R.I. Gen. Laws 1956, 27-31-1 et seq.

Model Act for the Regulation of Credit Life Insurance
R.I. Gen. Laws 1956, 27-30-1 et seq.

Model Act for the Regulation of Credit Life Insurance and Credit Health Insurance Act
See Credit Life Insurance and Credit Accident and Health Insurance Act Act
S.D. Codified Laws 1967, 58-19-1 et seq.

Model Act for the Regulation of Reserves Ceded to Nonadmitted Reinsurers
Ark. Code Ann. 1987, 23-62-302 et seq.

Model Act Providing Remedies for the Unauthorized Practice of Law
N.H. Rev. Stat. 1955, 311:7a et seq.

Model Act to Provide for the Appointment of Commissioners (Uniform State Laws)
Okla. Stat. Ann., Title 74, § 471 et seq.
Ore. Rev. Stat., 172.010, 172.020

Model Act to Simplify Security Transfers by Fiduciaries
Ill. Rev. Stat. 1991, Ch. 32, § 439.49 et seq.

Model Airport Zoning Act
Alaska Comp. Law Ann. 1949, § 32-5-1 et seq.
N.C. Gen. Stat. 1943, § 63-30 et seq.
N.H. Rev. Stat. 1955, 424:1 et seq.
S.D. Codified Laws 1967, 50-10-1 et seq.

Model Arson Law
Mont. Rev. Code 1947, 94-501 et seq.

Model Business Corporation Act
Ky. Rev. Stat. 1971, 271b.1-010
Neb. Rev. Stat. 1943, 21-2001 et seq.

Model Business Records Act
Ala. Code 1975, § 12-21-44

Model Cities Act
Cal. Health and Safety Code § 36100 et seq.

Model Consumer Credit Insurance Act
Del. Code of 1974, Title 18, § 3701 et seq.

Model Credit Insurance Act
See Credit Life Insurance and Credit Accident and Health Insurance Act

Model Defender Act
Del. Code of 1974, Title 29, § 4601 et seq.

Model Drug Paraphernalia Act
Mont. Code Ann., 45-10-101 et seq.

Model Execution of Wills Act
Tenn. Code Ann., 32-1-101 et seq.

Model Expedited Eviction of Drug Traffickers Act
Pa. Purdon's Stat., Title 35, § 780-151 et seq.

Model Expert Testimony Act
S.D. Codified Laws 1967, 19-15-1 et seq.

Model Foreign Bank Loan Act
Alaska Stat. 1962, § 06.10.010 et seq.

Model Group Life Insurance Act
N.M. Stat. Ann., 59A-21-1 et seq.

Model Health Maintenance Organization Act
Neb. Rev. Stat. 1943, 44-3201 et seq.

Model Insurers Supervision, Rehabilitation, and Liquidation Act
Mont. Code Ann., 33-2-1301 et seq.

Model Interparty Agreement Act
Nev. Rev. Stat. 1979 Reprint, 102.010 et seq.
Utah Code Ann. 1953, 15-3-1 et seq.

Model Interstate Income Withholding Act
Tex. Family Code, § 14.61 et seq.

Model Interstate Parole and Probation Hearings Act
Va. Code 1950, § 53.1-168 et seq.

Model Joint Obligations Act
See Uniform Joint Obligations Act
See Uniform Model Joint Obligations Act

Model Law for the Regulation of Credit Life Insurance and Credit Disability Insurance
Ida. Code 1947, 41-2301 et seq.

Model Law on International Commercial Arbitration (UNCITRAL)
Conn. Gen. Stat. Ann., § 50a-100 et seq.
Conn. Gen. Stat. 1983, § 50a-101 et seq.

Model Life and Health Insurance Guaranty Association Act
Mont. Rev. Code 1947, 40-5801 et seq.

Model Litter Control Act
Wash. Rev. Code Ann., 70.93.010 et seq.

Model Procurement Code
Ky. Rev. Stat. 1971, 45A.005 et seq.

Model Prudent Person Investment Act
Iowa Code Ann., 633.123

Model Public Obligations Registration Act
Mont. Code Ann., 17-5-1101 et seq.

Model Quality Replacement Parts Act
Colo. Rev. Stat., 10-3-1301 et seq.

Model Real Estate Time-Share Act
Wis. Stat. Ann., 707.02 et seq.

Model Registration Act (Voters)
Ky. Rev. Stat. 1971, Superseded Vol., 117.600 et seq.

Model Relocation Assistance Act
N.D. Cent. Code, 54-01.1-01 et seq.

Model Risk Retention Act
Colo. Rev. Stat., 10-3-1401 et seq.

Model Rule Against Perpetuities Act
Cal. Civil Code § 715.2
Wyo. Stat. Ann., §§ 34-1-138, 34-1-139

Model School Consortia Act
Fla. Stat. Ann., 228.0855

Model School Integrated Pest and Pesticide Management Safety Program Act
Mont. Code Ann., 80-8-401 et seq.

Model Small Group Rating Law
Iowa Code Ann., 513B.1

Model State Administrative Procedure Act
See Uniform Model State Administrative Procedure Act

Model State Civil Defense Act
Mont. Code Ann., 10-3-101 et seq.

Model State Commodity Code
Iowa Code Ann., 502A.1 et seq.

Model State Community Code
N.M. Stat. Ann., 58-13A-1 et seq.

Model State Public Weigher Law
Conn. Gen. Stat. Ann., § 43-16a et seq.

Model State Trademark Act
N.H. Rev. Stat. 1955, 350-A:1 et seq.

Model Toxics Control Act
Wash. Rev. Code Ann., 70.105D.010 et seq.

Model Trademark Act
Tenn. Code Ann., 47-25-501 et seq.

Model Traffic Ordinance Act
Fla. Stat. 1969, 186.01 et seq.
Wash. Rev. Code Ann., 46.90.005 et seq.

Model Unfair Competition Trade Practices Act (Insurance)
Neb. Rev. Stat. 1943, 44-1522 et seq.

Model Uniform Choice of Forum Act
Neb. Rev. Stat. 1943, 25-413 et seq.

Model Water and Sewer Reorganization Act
Mass. Gen. Laws Ann., 40N:2

Moderate and Low Income Housing Act
R.I. Gen. Laws 1956, 45-53-1 et seq.

Moderate and Low Income Housing Restrictions Act
R.I. Gen. Laws 1956, 34-39.1-1 et seq.

Moderate Rental Housing Act
Conn. Gen. Stat. Ann., § 8-69 et seq.

Modern Secondary School for the Deaf Act
Aug. 4, 1986, P.L. 99-371, 20 U.S. Code §§ 693, 693 nt., 693a, 693b

Modernization Act (Uniform Commercial Code)
See Uniform Commercial Code Modernization Act

Modification of Alimony Act
Ga. Code Ann., 19-6-18 et seq.

Modoc-Lassen County Flood Control and Water Conservation District Act
Cal. Statutes 1959, Ch. 2127, p. 5009

Modular Buildings Construction Act
S.C. Code Ann. 1976, § 23-43-10 et seq.

Modular/Industrialized Buildings Interstate Compact
Minn. Stat. Ann., 16B.75

Moffat Act (Fare on Unified Subway)
N.Y. Laws 1940, Ch. 560

Moffat Bill (Transit Control)
N.Y. Public Service Law (Consol. Laws Ch. 48) §§ 135, 137

Moffat Tunnel Act
Colo. Rev. Stat., 32-8-101 et seq.

Moffat Work or Don't Eat Act
N.Y. Labor Law (Consol. Laws Ch. 31) § 21c
N.Y. Social Services Law (Consol. Laws Ch. 55) § 158a

Moffett Antipicketing Act
Va. Code 1950, § 40.1-53

Mohegan Nation of Connecticut Land Claims Settlement Act of 1994
Oct. 19, 1994, P.L. 103-377, 25 U.S. Code § 1775 nt.

Moiety Act (Informers)
See Anti-Moiety Act (Informers)

Mojave Water Agency Act
Cal. Statutes 1959, Ch. 2146, p. 5114, §§ 1-48

Mojonnier-Ayala Electronic Home Detention Act
Cal. Penal Code § 1203.016

Mojonnier-Bronzan Act (Mental Health)
Cal. Statutes 1985, Ch. 1286

Mold Lien and Retention Act
S.C. Code Ann. 1976, § 39-69-10 et seq.

Molestation Act (Minor)
Mo. Rev. Stat. 1969, 563.160

Molesting and Indecent Liberties Act
Mo. Rev. Stat. 1969, 559.360

Mom and Pop Liquor Store Act
S.C. Code Ann. 1976, § 61-3-460 et seq.

Monetary Act
July 6, 1939, Ch. 260, 53 Stat. 998, 31 U.S. Code §§ 314, 316, 316c, 821, 822a

Monetary Control Act of 1980
March 31, 1980, P.L. 96-221, 12 U.S. Code §§ 226 nt., 248, 461

Money Act (Transmitters of)
Ill. Comp. Stat. 1992, Ch. 205, § 657/1

Money and Credits Act
Iowa Code 1966, 429.1 et seq.
N.D. Laws 1917, Ch. 230

Money and Credits Tax Act
Minn. Stat. 1978, 285.01 et seq.

Money and Other Liquid Assets Act (Abandoned or Unclaimed)
P.R. Acts 1989, No. 36

Money and Rates of Interest Act
Wis. Stat. Ann., 138.01 et seq.

Money Brokers Act
N.D. Cent. Code, 13-04.1-01 et seq.

Money Forwarders Act
Conn. Gen. Stat. Ann., § 36-244a et seq.

Money Judgment Act (Foreign Country)
N.Y. Civil Practice Laws and Rules (Consol. Laws Ch. 8) § 5301 et seq.

Money-Judgments Recognition Act (Foreign Country)
See also Uniform Foreign Money-Judgments Recognition Act
Va. Code 1950, § 8.01-465.6 et seq.

Money Judgments Recognition Act (Foreign)
Mass. Gen. Laws Ann., 235:23A
N.C. Gen. Stat. 1943, § 1C-1800 et seq.

Money Laundering Act
N.M. Stat. Ann., 30-51-1 to 30-51-5

Money Laundering and Currency Transaction Reporting Act
Utah Code Ann. 1953, 76-10-1901 et seq.

Money Laundering and Financial Crimes Strategy Act of 1998
Oct. 30, 1998, P.L. 105-310, 112 Stat. 2941, 31 U.S. Code § 5301 nt.

Money Laundering Control Act
Fla. Stat. Ann., 896.101 et seq.

Money Laundering Control Act of 1986
Oct. 27, 1986, P.L. 99-570, 18 U.S. Code § 981

Money Laundering Control in Financial Institutions Act
Fla. Stat. Ann., 655.50

Money Laundering Control in Money Transmitters Act
Fla. Stat. Ann., 560.123

Money Laundering in Financial Institutions Act (Control of)
Fla. Stat. Ann., 655.50

Money Laundering Prosecution Improvements Act of 1988
Nov. 18, 1988, P.L. 100-690, 18 U.S. Code § 981 nt.

Money Laundering Suppression Act of 1994
Sept. 23, 1994, P.L. 103-325, 31 U.S. Code § 5301 nt.

Money Lenders Act
Ariz. Law 1919, Ch. 91
Colo. Rev. Stat., 73-2-1 et seq.
D.C. Code Ann., § 26-701 et seq.
Haw. Rev. Stat. Ann., § 409-1 et seq.
Tenn. Code Ann., Superseded Vol., 45-2101 et seq.

Money Management Act (State Treasury)
Ark. Code 1987, 11-9-301, 19-3-601 et seq.

Money Management Act (State)
Utah Code Ann. 1953, 51-7-1 et seq.

Money Order Act
Colo. Rev. Stat., 12-52-101 et seq.

Money Order and Travelers Check Licensees Act
Conn. Gen. Stat. Ann., § 36-530 et seq.

Money Transmitters Act
N.C. Gen. Stat. 1943, § 53-192 et seq.

Money Transmitters' Act
Fla. Stat. Ann., 560.101 to 560.128
Ida. Code 1947, 26-2901 et seq.
Me. Rev. Stat. Ann. 1964, Title 32, § 6101 et seq.
N.J. Stat. Ann., 17:15C-1 et seq.

Moneyed Capital Tax Law
N.Y. Tax Law (Consol. Laws Ch. 60) § 219p et seq.

Monition Law (New Castle County)
Del. Code of 1974, Title 9, § 8721 et seq.

Monition Tax Statute
Del. Laws, Vol. 36, p. 411, Ch. 143

Monkey Law
Ark. Code Ann. 1987, 80-1627, 80-1628
Tenn. Code Ann. 1955, Superseded Vol., 49-1922

Mono County Public Utility District Act
Cal. Statutes 1957, Ch. 1413, p. 2747

Mono County Tri-Valley Groundwater Management District Act
Cal. Water Code Appendix, § 128-1 et seq.

Monopolies Act
N.C. Gen. Stat. 1943, § 75-1 et seq.

Monopolies and Unfair Trade Practices Anti-Trust Act
Ariz. Rev. Stat. Ann., § 44-1401 et seq.

Monopoly Act
Ind. Code Ann., 24-1-1-1 et seq.
Iowa Code Ann., 553.1 et seq.
Kan. Stat. Ann., 50-101 et seq.
La. Rev. Stat. Ann., 51:121 et seq.
Mass. Gen. Laws Ann., 93:1 et seq.
Mich. Comp. Laws Ann., 445.701 et seq., 445.761 et seq.
Mont. Code Ann., 30-14-101 et seq.
N.H. Rev. Stat. 1955, 356:1 et seq.
N.Y. General Business Law (Consol. Laws Ch. 20) § 340 et seq.
Ohio Rev. Code 1953, 1331.01 et seq.
P.R. Laws Ann. 1954, Title 10, § 257 et seq.
Tex. Business and Commerce Code, § 15.01 et seq.
Wash. Const. 1889, Art. 12, § 22

Monopoly Appropriation Act
April 26, 1939, Ch. 104, 53 Stat. 624

Monopoly or Restraint of Trade Act
N.Y. General Business Law (Consol. Laws
Ch. 20) § 340 et seq.

Monroe County Airport Authority Act
N.Y. Public Authorities Law (Consol. Laws
Ch. 43A) § 2750 et seq.

Monroe County Development Authority Act
Fla. Special Laws 1963, Ch. 63-1658

Monroe County Highway Authority Act
Fla. Special Laws 1963, Ch. 63-1643

**Monroe County In Rem Tax Foreclosure
Act**
N.Y. Laws 1962, Ch. 905

**Monroe County Public Safety Financial
Sharing Act**
N.Y. Laws 1983, Ch. 833

Monroe County Public Safety Services Act
N.Y. Laws 1983, Ch. 835

**Monroe County Quadrennial
Re-registration Act**
Fla. Laws 1945, Ch. 22708

Monroe County Right-of-Way Naming Act
N.Y. Laws 1991, Ch. 769

Monroe County Sales Tax Adjustment Act
N.Y. Laws 1984, Ch. 359

Monroe County Tax Act
N.Y. Laws 1938, Ch. 441

Monroe County Tax Foreclosure Act
N.Y. Laws 1938, Ch. 440
N.Y. Laws 1962, Ch. 905

Monroe County Water Authority Act
N.Y. Public Authorities Law (Consol. Laws
Ch. 43A) § 1093 et seq.

**Monroe County Waterways Development
Authority Act**
Fla. Special Laws 1963, Ch. 63-1657

Monroe Doctrine Act
April 10, 1941, Ch. 49, 55 Stat. 133, 22 U.S.
Code § 504, 504 nt.

**Monroe, Louisiana Redevelopment Agency
Act**
La. Acts 1968, No. 215

Monroe Regional Parking Authority Act
N.Y. Public Authorities Law (Consol. Laws
Ch. 43A) § 1420a et seq.

Monroe Sewer District Loan Act
Mass. Acts 1963, Ch. 559

Montague Center Water District Loan Act
Mass. Acts 1953, Ch. 107

Montague Sewerage Loan Act
Mass. Acts 1960, Ch. 440

**Montalvo Municipal Improvement District
Act**
Cal. Statutes 1955, Ch. 549, p. 1016

**Montana Initiative for the Abatement of
Mortality in Infants Act (MIAMI)**
Mont. Laws 1991, Ch. 649

Montana Wilderness Study Act of 1977
Nov. 1, 1977, P.L. 95-150, 16 U.S. Code
§ 1132 nt.

**Monterey County Flood Control and Water
Conservation District Act**
Cal. Statutes 1947, Ch. 699, p. 1739

**Monterey County Special Health Care
Authority Act**
Cal. Health and Safety Code § 1170 et seq.

**Monterey County Water Resources Agency
Act**
Cal. Water Code Appendix, § 52-3 et seq.

Monterey Peninsula Airport District Act
Cal. Statutes 1941, p. 684

**Monterey Peninsula Water Management
District Law**
Cal. Water Code Appendix, § 118-1 et seq.

Montgomery County Bingo Act
Ala. Acts 1982, p. 1067

Montgomery County Merit Act
Ala. Code 1958, App., § 523 (32) et seq.

Montgomery GI Bill Act of 1984
Oct. 19, 1984, P.L. 98-525, 38 U.S. Code §§ 101 nt., prec. 1401, 1401 to 1436
Oct. 28, 1986, P.L. 99-576, 38 U.S. Code § 1621 nt.
June 1, 1987, P.L. 100-48, 38 U.S. Code § 101 nt.

Montgomery-Keck-Beauchamp Super Highway Act
Ky. Rev. Stat. 1971, 177.390 et seq.

Montgomery, Otsego, Schoharie Solid Waste Management Authority Act
N.Y. Public Authorities Law (Consol. Laws Ch. 43A) § 2041 et seq.

Montgomery-Romano-Cihak Act (Charter Townships)
Mich. Comp. Laws Ann., 42.1 et seq.

Montoya-Lancaster Appraisal Act
Cal. Civil Code § 1922 et seq.

Montoya-Rodda Act (Education)
Cal. Statutes 1976, Ch. 323

Montoya Structural Pest Control Act
Cal. Business and Professions Code § 8516

Monument Act (Township)
Ill. Rev. Stat. 1991, Ch. 139, §§ 150.9, 151

Monuments Act (Land Survey)
Ill. Rev. Stat. 1991, Ch. 133, § 60-0.1 et seq.

Moonwalker Safety Act
Utah Code Ann. 1953, 53-5-601 et seq.

Moore, Blake, Swope and Howard Act (Elections)
Ky. Acts 1944, Ch. 5

Moore-Brown-Roberti Family Rights Act
Cal. Government Code §§ 12945.1, 12945.2, 19702.3

Moore County Peace Officers' Relief Act
N.C. Laws 1961, Ch. 920

Moore-Holbeck Act (Delinquent Taxes)
Mich. Comp. Laws Ann., 211.301 et seq.

Moore Universal Telephone Service Act
Cal. Public Utilities Code § 871 et seq.

Moorman-Williams Anti Daylight Saving Time Act
Ky. Rev. Stat. 1962, 2.160

Moratorium Act
See also Soldiers' and Sailors' Civil Relief Acts
N.Y. Civil Practice Act §§ 1077a to 1077g, 1083a to 1083c

Moratorium Act (Bank Holiday)
Minn. Laws 1933, Ch. 56

Moratorium Act (Chattel Mortgages)
Cal. Statutes 1939, Ch. 86, p. 1045
Cal. Statutes 1941, Ch. 204, p. 1263

Moratorium Act (Contracts to Purchase Real Estate)
Cal. Statutes 1939, Ch. 86, p. 1045
Cal. Statutes 1941, Ch. 204, p. 1263

Moratorium Act (Deeds of Trust)
Cal. Statutes 1933, Ch. 1057, p. 2717
Cal. Statutes 1939, Ch. 86, p. 1045
Cal. Statutes 1941, Ch. 204, p. 1263

Moratorium Act (Foreclosures)
Iowa Code Ann., 654.15
Neb. Laws 1933, Ch. 65
Neb. Laws 1935, Ch. 41
Neb. Laws 1937, Ch. 42

Moratorium Act (Land Contracts)
Mich. Public Acts 1933, No. 122, § 1, Subsec. 25a et seq.

Moratorium Act (Military Service)
N.D. Laws 1918 Spec. Sess., Ch. 10

Moratorium Act (Mortgages)
Ala. General Acts 1935, p. 184, No. 146
Kan. Laws 1933, Ch. 232
Kan. Laws 1934, Sp. Sess., Ch. 3
Kan. Laws 1935, Ch. 226
Mich. Public Acts 1933, No. 98
Minn. Laws 1933, Ch. 339
Minn. Laws 1941, Ch. 682
N.D. Laws 1935, Ch. 242
N.D. Laws 1937, Ch. 161
N.D. Laws 1939, Ch. 165
S.D. Laws 1937, Ch. 207

Moratorium Act (Public Liability)
Cal. Civil Code § 22.3

Moratorium Act (Real Estate Liens)
Tex. General & Special Laws 43rd Leg.,
1934, 2nd C. S., p. 2, Ch. 2, p. 42, Ch. 16
Tex. General Laws 43rd Leg., 1933, p. 225,
Ch. 102

Moratorium Act (Real Estate Mortgages)
Cal. Statutes 1933, Ch. 1057, p. 2717
Cal. Statutes 1939, p. 1045
Cal. Statutes 1941, p. 1263

Moratorium Act (School Lands)
Cal. Statutes 1935, Ch. 8, p. 61
Cal. Statutes 1937, Ch. 10, p. 69
Cal. Statutes 1939, Ch. 609, p. 2030

Moratorium Act (Servicemen)
Ore. Rev. Stat., 408.440

Moratorium Act (Special Assessment Bond Liens)
Cal. Statutes 1939, Ch. 969, p. 2720

Moratorium Act (Special Assessment Guaranties)
Cal. Statutes 1935, Ch. 400, p. 1446

Moratorium Act (Tax Deeds)
Ida. Code 1947, 63-1128 et seq.

Moratorium Act (Taxes)
See Tax Moratorium Act

Moratorium Act (War Service)
S.D. Laws 1918, Spec. Sess. Ch. 55

Moratorium on Private Correctional Facility Act
Ill. Rev. Stat. 1991, Ch. 38, § 1581 et seq.

Morbid Obesity Anti-Discrimination Act
Ga. Code Ann., 33-24-59.1

More Oklahoma Science and Technology (MOST) Eminent Scholars and Research Equipment Act
Okla. Stat. Ann., Title 74, §§ 2013 to 2016

Moreau Town Code
N.Y. Local Laws 1973, Town of Moreau, p. 2574

Moreland Act (Examination and Inspection by the Governor)
N.Y. Executive Law 1951 (Consol. Laws Ch. 18) § 6

Moretti-Deukmejian Act (Crime Council)
Cal. Penal Code § 13800 et seq.

Moretti-Deukmejian-Campbell Drug Abuse Treatment Act
Cal. Statutes 1972, Ch. 1255, p. 2464

Moretti-Lewis-Brown-Rodda Child Development Act
Cal. Education Code 1976, § 8200 et seq.

Morgan Act (Repealer)
Ohio Laws Vol. 113, p. 685

Morgan, Burnley and McCallum Act (Circuit Court Districts)
Ky. Rev. Stat. 1971, Superseded Vols., 23.040 et seq.
Ky. Rev. Stat. 1971, 23A.020 et seq.

Morgan City Community Improvement Act
La. Acts 1970, No. 238

Morgan County Court House Commission Act
Ala. Local Acts 1927, p. 249

Morgan County-Madison Airport Authority Act
Ga. Laws 1965, p. 2687

Morgan County Water Authority Act
Ga. Laws 1991, p. 4670

Morgan-Farr-Quackenbush Educational Technology Act
Cal. Education Code 1976, § 51870 et seq.

Morgan-Hart Class Size Reduction Act
Cal. Education Code 1976, § 52080 et seq.

Morgan-Herbert-Martin Act (Elections)
Ohio Rev. Code 1953, 3501.01 et seq.

Morgan-McCullough Act (Highways)
Mo. Laws 1917, p. 485 Laws 1919, p. 650

Morgan P. Hardiman Task Force on Missing and Exploited Children Act
Sept. 13, 1994, P.L. 103-322, 42 U.S. Code §§ 5601 nt., 5776a nt., 5777, 5778

Morgan Primary Act (Counties)
Ore. General Laws 1901, p. 400

Morgan Property Taxpayers Bill of Rights
Cal. Revenue and Taxation Code § 5900 et seq.

Morgue Act
Pa. Purdon's Stat., Title 16, §§ 9521, 9522

Morley-Fitzgerald-Fehling Act (Holidays)
Mich. Comp. Laws Ann., 435.101 et seq.

Morley-Hittle Act (Educational Aid to Children of Deceased Veterans)
Mich. Comp. Laws Ann., 35.111, 35.112

Moroni L. Jensen State House Fellows Program Act
Utah Code Ann. 1953, 63-39-1 et seq.

Morrill Act (Tariff)
March 2, 1861, Ch. 68, 12 Stat. 178

Morrill Acts (Agricultural Colleges)
July 2, 1862, Ch. 130, 12 Stat. 503, 7 U.S. Code §§ 301 to 305, 307, 308
March 3, 1883, Ch. 102, 22 Stat. 484, 7 U.S. Code § 304
Aug. 30, 1890, Ch. 841, 26 Stat. 417, 7 U.S. Code §§ 321 to 326, 328

Morrill Hall Act (Interference with Use of Public Property)
Minn. Stat. Ann., 624.72

Morris Act (Chippewa Indians of Minnesota)
June 27, 1902, Ch. 1157, 32 Stat. 400, 25 U.S. Code § 197

Morris Act (Intoxicating Liquor)
N.J. Laws 1908, C 146

Morris Bill
Ky. Stat. 1936, § 4019-1 et seq.

Morris K. Udall Parkinson's Disease Research Act of 1997
Nov. 13, 1997, P.L. 105-78, § 603, 42 U.S. Code § 201 nt.

Morris K. Udall Scholarship and Excellence in National Environmental and Native American Public Policy Act of 1992
March 19, 1992, P.L. 102-259, 20 U.S. Code §§ 5601 et seq., 5601 nt.
Feb. 11, 1998, P.L. 105-156, 20 U.S. Code §§ 5602 to 5608, 5608a, 5608b, 5609
Oct. 7, 1998, P.L. 105-244, 20 U.S. Code § 5602
Oct. 21, 1998, P.L. 105-277, 20 U.S. Code §§ 5608 to 5610

Morris K. Udall Scholarship and Excellence in National Environmental Policy Act
March 19, 1992, P.L. 102-259, 20 U.S. Code § 5601 nt.

Morris Plan Act (Industrial Loan Company)
Minn. Stat. 1949, 53.01 et seq.

Morrison Act (Tariff)
March 3, 1883, Ch. 121, 22 Stat. 488, 12 U.S.
Code §§ 541, 544, 545

Morrison Creek Flood Control District Act
Cal. Statutes 1953, Ch. 1771, p. 3528

**Morrissey Retirement Income Protection
Act**
Cal. Revenue and Taxation Code § 17952.5

Mortgage Act
Ark. Code Ann. 1987, 18-40-101 et seq.
Fla. Stat. Ann., 697.01 et seq.
Ill. Rev. Stat. 1991, Ch. 95, § 50 et seq.
La. Rev. Stat. Ann., 31:203 et seq.
Md. Ann. Code 1974, Art. RP, § 7-101 et seq.
Mont. Code Ann., 71-1-101 et seq.
N.C. Gen. Stat. 1943, § 45-4 et seq.
N.H. Rev. Stat. 1955, 479:1 et seq.
N.J. Stat. Ann., 2A:50-1 et seq.
P.R. Laws Ann. 1954, Title 30, § 2051 et seq.
R.I. Gen. Laws 1956, 34-23-1 et seq.
Wash. Rev. Code Ann., 61.12.020 et seq.

Mortgage Act (Bulk Secured Transactions)
N.Y. Uniform Commercial Code (Consol.
Laws Ch. 38) § 9-101 et seq.

Mortgage Act (Chattel)
See Chattel Mortgage Act

Mortgage Act (Dealers' Chattel)
N.Y. Uniform Commercial Code (Consol.
Laws Ch. 38) § 9-101 et seq.

Mortgage Act (Estates)
N.H. Rev. Stat. 1955, 554:30 et seq.

Mortgage Act (Realty)
Colo. Rev. Stat., 38-40-101 et seq.

Mortgage Act (Reverse)
Mo. Laws 1995, H.B. 63, §§ 1 to 5
N.C. Gen. Stat. 1943, § 53-255 et seq.
S.C. Code Ann. 1976, § 29-4-20 et seq.

Mortgage Agency Act
N.Y. Public Authorities Law (Consol. Laws
Ch. 43A) § 2400 et seq.

Mortgage and Bond Relief Act (Emergency)
N.Y. Civil Practice Act §§ 1083a to 1083c

**Mortgage and Housing Finance Corporation
Act**
R.I. Gen. Laws 1956, 42-55-1 et seq.

Mortgage and Loan Housing Act
Haw. Rev. Stat. Ann., § 356-201 et seq.

Mortgage and Property Registry Act
P.R. Laws Ann. 1954, Title 30, § 2001 et seq.

Mortgage and Trust Deed Recording Act
Cal. Government Code § 27320 et seq.

Mortgage Assignment Act
Wash. Rev. Code Ann., 61.16.010

Mortgage Assistance Bond Act
N.J. Laws 1976, Ch. 94

Mortgage Authority Act
Conn. Gen. Stat. Ann., § 8-241 et seq.
R.I. Gen. Laws 1956, 42-55-1 et seq.

Mortgage Bankers and Brokers Act
Pa. Purdon's Stat., Title 63, § 456.01

Mortgage Broker Practices Act
Wash. Rev. Code Ann., 19.146.005 et seq.

**Mortgage Brokerage and Mortgage Lenders
Act**
Fla. Stat. Ann., 494.001 et seq.

Mortgage Brokers and Lenders Act
La. Rev. Stat. Ann., 6:1081 et seq.

**Mortgage Brokers, Lenders, and Servicers
Licensing Act**
Mich. Comp. Laws Ann., 445.1651 et seq.

Mortgage Commission Act
N.Y. Laws 1935, Ch. 19

Mortgage Company Act
Ida. Code 1947, 26-2801 et seq.

Mortgage Deficiency Judgments Act
Pa. Cons. Stat., Title 42, § 8103

Mortgage Disclosure Act (Home)
Conn. Gen. Stat. 1983, § 36-443 et seq.

Mortgage Enabling Act (Reverse)
W. Va. Code 1966, § 47-24-1 et seq.

Mortgage Escrow Account Act
Ill. Rev. Stat. 1991, Ch. 17, § 4901 et seq.

Mortgage Facilities Corporation Law
N.Y. Private Housing Finance Law (Consol. Laws Ch. 44B) § 300 et seq.

Mortgage Finance Act (Municipal)
N.M. Stat. Ann., 58-18A-1 et seq.

Mortgage Finance Agency Law
N.J. Stat. Ann., 17:1B-4 et seq.

Mortgage Finance Authority Act
N.M. Stat. Ann., 58-18-1 et seq.

Mortgage Finance Fund Act
Neb. Rev. Stat. 1943, 76-1601 et seq.

Mortgage Foreclosure Act
Haw. Rev. Stat. Ann., § 667-1 et seq.
Ill. Rev. Stat. 1991, Ch. 110, § 15-1101 et seq.
Mich. Comp. Laws Ann., 600.3101 et seq., 600.3201 et seq.
Pa. Cons. Stat., Title 42, § 8103

Mortgage Foreclosure Act (Fifty Year Limitation)
Ill. Rev. Stat. 1991, Ch. 110, § 15-1101 et seq.
Mass. Gen Laws 1990, 260:33 et seq.

Mortgage Foreclosure Act (Limitation)
Mass. Gen. Laws Ann., 26:33 et seq.

Mortgage Foreclosure Act (Power of Sale)
Okla. Stat. Ann., Title 46, § 40 et seq.

Mortgage Foreclosure Curative Act
Minn. Laws 1947, Ch. 345
Minn. Laws 1949, Ch. 205

Mortgage Foreclosure Delay Emergency Act
Iowa Code Ann., 654.15

Mortgage Foreclosure Moratorium Act
Neb. Laws 1933, Ch. 65
Neb. Laws 1935, Ch. 41
Neb. Laws 1937, Ch. 42

Mortgage Foreclosure Procedure Act
S.C. Acts 1934, p. 2286, No. 1214

Mortgage Fund Act (Veterans')
W. Va. Code 1966, § 31-18c-1 et seq.

Mortgage Guaranty Corporation Rehabilitation Law
N.J. Stat. Ann., 17:46A-1 et seq.

Mortgage Guaranty Insurance Act
Cal. Insurance Code § 12640.01 et seq.
Ida. Code 1947, 41-2650 et seq.
Kan. Stat. Ann., 40-3501 et seq.
N.J. Stat. Ann., 17:46A-1 et seq.

Mortgage Institutions Act
P.R. Laws Ann. 1954, Title 7, § 1051 et seq.

Mortgage Insurance Act (Housing)
Me. Rev. Stat. Ann. 1964, Title 30-A, § 4931 et seq.

Mortgage Insurance Fund Act
Ill. Rev. Stat. 1991, Ch. 67 1/2, § 801 et seq.

Mortgage Insurance Law (Housing)
Me. Rev. Stat. Ann. 1964, Title 30-A, § 4931

Mortgage Insurance Limitation and Notification Act
Ill. Comp. Stat. 1992, Ch. 765, § 930/1 et seq.

Mortgage Law (Ship)
See Ship Mortgage Act

Mortgage Lender Law
Md. Ann. Code 1974, Art. FI, § 11-501 et seq.

Mortgage Lending Act
Fla. Stat. Ann., 521.201 et seq.

Mortgage Lending and Servicing Act
Utah Code Ann. 1953, 70D-1-2 et seq.

Mortgage License Act (Residential)
Ill. Rev. Stat. 1991, Ch. 17, § 2321-1 et seq.

Mortgage Lien Act (Motor Vehicle)
Neb. Rev. Stat. 1943, 60-110

Mortgage Limitation Act
Ill. Rev. Stat. 1991, Ch. 110, § 13-115 et seq.

Mortgage Loan Act (Reverse Annuity)
Mont. Code Ann., 90-6-501 et seq.

Mortgage Loan Act (Secondary)
See Secondary Mortgage Loan Act

Mortgage Loan Brokers Registration Requirements Act
S.C. Code Ann. 1976, § 40-58-10 et seq.

Mortgage Loan Company and Loan Broker Act
Ark. Code Ann. 1987, 23-39-101 et seq.
Ky. Rev. Stat. 1971, 294.010 et seq.
N.M. Stat. Ann., 58-21-1 et seq.

Mortgage Loan Extension Act (Veterans)
N.H. Rev. Stat. 1955, 479:18-a et seq.

Mortgage Loans Act (Secondary)
Mich. Comp. Laws Ann., 493.51 to 493.80
Tex. Rev. Civ. Stat., Art. 5069-5.01 et seq.

Mortgage Loans Insurance Act
P.R. Laws Ann. 1954, Title 26, § 2301 et seq.

Mortgage Moratorium Act
Ark. Code Ann. 1987, 51-1115 et seq.
Kan. Laws 1933, Ch. 232
Kan. Laws 1934, Sp. Sess., Ch. 3
Kan. Laws 1935, Ch. 226
Mich. Public Acts 1933, No. 98
Minn. Laws 1933, Ch. 339
Minn. Laws 1941, Ch. 682
Miss. General Laws 1934, Ch. 247, p. 518
N.D. Laws 1935, Ch. 242
N.Y. Civil Practice Act §§ 1077a to 1077g, 1083a to 1073c
Ohio Laws Vol. 115, p. 227

Okla. Laws 1991, Title 12, § 686
S.D. Laws 1937, Ch. 207

Mortgage Originator and Servicer Licensing Act (Residential)
Minn. Stat. 1986, 58.01 et seq.

Mortgage Payment Statement Act
Ill. Rev. Stat. 1991, Ch. 95, § 70 et seq.

Mortgage Practices Act (Residential)
Ida. Code 1947, 26-3101 et seq.

Mortgage Purchase Amendments of 1981
Dec. 26, 1981, P.L. 97-110, 12 U.S. Code § 1451 nt.

Mortgage Recording Act
Me. Rev. Stat. Ann. 1964, Title 33, § 207 et seq.

Mortgage Recording Act (Master)
Conn. Gen. Stat. Ann., § 49-5a

Mortgage Recording Tax Law
N.Y. Tax Law (Consol. Laws Ch. 60) § 253

Mortgage Redemption Act
Kan. Stat. Ann., 60-2410 et seq.

Mortgage Redemption Act (One Hundred Eighty Day)
S.D. Codified Laws 1967, 21-49-11 et seq.

Mortgage Redemption Emergency Act
Iowa Laws 1933 (45th G. A.), Ch. 179

Mortgage Registration Act
Kan. Stat. Ann., 79-3101 et seq.
Ky. Rev. Stat. 1971, 382.290 et seq.
Minn. Stat. Ann., 507.32 et seq.
N.J. Stat. Ann., 46:17-1 et seq.

Mortgage Registration Act (Chattel)
See Chattel Mortgage Registration Act

Mortgage Registration Tax Act
S.D. Laws 1919, Ch. 113
Tex. General & Special Laws 44th Leg., 1936, 3rd C. S., p. 2040, Ch. 495, Art. IV, § 9

Mortgage Regulations
P.R. Laws Ann. 1954, Title 30, § 2005 et seq.

Mortgage Release Act (Building and Loan)
Ill. Comp. Stat. 1992, Ch. 765, § 105/0.01 et seq.
Ill. Rev. Stat. 1991, Ch. 17, § 3630 et seq.

Mortgage Satisfaction Act
Utah Code Ann. 1953, 57-1-16
Wash. Rev. Code Ann., 61.16.010 et seq.

Mortgage Subsidy Bond Tax Act of 1980
Dec. 5, 1980, P.L. 96-499, 26 U.S. Code § 1 nt.
July 18, 1984, P.L. 98-369, 98 Stat. 914, 26 U.S. Code § 103A nt.
Oct. 22, 1986, P.L. 99-514, 26 U.S. Code §§ 103A nt., 141 nt.
Nov. 10, 1988, P.L. 100-647, 102 Stat. 3550

Mortgage Tax Act
Mich. Comp. Laws Ann., 205.131 et seq.
Neb. Rev. Stat. 1943, 77-1401 et seq.
N.Y. Tax Law (Consol. Laws Ch. 60) § 250 et seq.
Ore. Rev. Stat., 307.010

Mortgage Tax Act (Real Estate)
Okla. Stat. Ann., Title 68, § 1901 et seq.

Mortgage Tax Escrow Act
Ill. Rev. Stat. 1991, Ch. 17, §§ 5000, 5001

Mortgages Act (Chattel)
Wyo. Stat. 1957, § 32-242 et seq.

Mortgages and Lien Act
Conn. Gen. Stat. Ann., § 49-1 et seq.

Mortgages and Trust Receipts Act
Wash. Rev. Code Ann., 62A.9-203(1) et seq.

Mortgages No Waiver Act
Cal. Civil Code § 2953

Morticians Act
See Embalmers and Funeral Directors Act

Mortmain Act (Charitable Devises)
Fla. Stat. Ann., 732.803
Iowa Code 1981, 633.266
Miss. Code Ann. 1972, § 91-5-31
N.Y. Estates, Powers and Trusts Law (Consol. Laws Ch. 17B) § 5-3.3
Ohio Rev. Code 1953, 2107.06
Pa. Purdon's Stat., Title 10, §§ 31 et seq., 81
Pa. Purdon's Stat., Title 27, §§ 162, 212
Pa. Purdon's Stat., Title 68, § 21

Mortmain Act (Real Estates)
Ky. Rev. Stat. 1971, Superseded Vols., 271.145, 273.090

Mortuary Act
Mich. Comp. Laws Ann., 338.861 et seq.

Mortuary Act (Tables)
S.C. Code Ann. 1976, § 19-1-150

Mortuary Science Act
Colo. Rev. Stat., 12-54-101 et seq.
N.J. Stat. Ann., 45:7-32 to 45:7-81

Moscone-Burton-Bagley Citizens' Income Security Act for Aged, Blind, and Disabled Californians
Cal. Welfare and Institutions Code § 12000 et seq.

Moscone-Chacon Bilingual-Bicultural Education Act
Cal. Education Code 1959, §§ 5767, 52160

Moscone-Chacon-Zenovich Housing and Home Finance Act
Cal. Health and Safety Code § 50000 et seq.

Moscone-Duffy Family Nutrition Education and Service Act
Cal. Education Code 1976, § 49510 et seq.

Moscone Governmental Conflict of Interests and Disclosure Act
Cal. Government Code § 3601 et seq.

Moscone-Keysor Voter Registration Act
Cal. Elections Code 1961, §§ 200 et seq., 310 et seq., 421 et seq., 14002, 14202, 14215.5, 14240, 14241, 14243, 14419, 14622, 17236, 18237

Moscone-Knox Professional Corporation Act
Cal. Corporations Code § 13400 et seq.

Moses Agreement (Indian Land Patents)
July 4, 1884, Ch. 180, 23 Stat. 79

Moses Grade Crossing Elimination Act
N.Y. Laws 1939, Ch. 289

Mosier-Case-Root-Jarvis Act (Fresh Fruit)
Mich. Comp. Laws Ann., 286.341 et seq.

Mosquito Abatement Act
R.I. Gen. Laws 1956, 23-7-1 et seq.

Mosquito Abatement District Act
Cal. Health and Safety Code § 2200 et seq.
Ill. Rev. Stat. 1991, Ch. 111 1/2, § 73.990 et seq.
Utah Code Ann. 1953, 17A-2-901 et seq.

Mosquito Abatement Funding Act (Emergency)
Cal. Statutes 1983, Ch. 1055

Mosquito Control Act
Ky. Rev. Stat. 1971, 249.510 et seq.
N.Y. Public Health Law 1953 (Consol. Laws Ch. 45) § 1500 et seq.

Mosquito Control Act (Counties)
Fla. Stat. Ann., 388.011 et seq.

Mosquito Control Districts Act
Mont. Code Ann., 7-22-2401 et seq.

Mosquito Craft Base Act
June 24, 1941, Ch. 234, 55 Stat. 262

Mosquito Extermination Act
N.J. Stat. Ann., 26:9-1 to 26:9-31

Moss-Hibbitts Act (Mine Disaster)
Ky. Acts 1948, Ch. 127

Motel, Resort and Auto Court Act
Cal. Health and Safety Code § 18500 et seq.

Motel Signs Act
Nev. Rev. Stat. 1979 Reprint, 651.040

Motels, Hotels, Restaurants and Boardinghouses Act
S.C. Code Ann. 1976, § 45-1-10 et seq.

Mother and Newborn Baby Protection Act
Ga. Code Ann., 33-24-58 to 33-24-60

Mother Hubbard Act (Taxes Payment Under Protest)
Okla. Stat. Ann., Title 68, § 2469

Mothers' and Infants' Access Program
Cal. Insurance Code § 12695 et seq.

Mothers' Assistance Act
Pa. 1919 Pamph. Laws 893, No. 354

Mothers' Compensation Act
Colo. Rev. Stat. 19-1-101

Mother's Day Act
May 8, 1914, No. 13, 38 Stat. 770, 36 U.S. Code §§ 141, 142

Mothers' Day Act (Gold Star)
Ill. Rev. Stat. 1991, Ch. 1, § 3051-50

Mothers Day and Fathers Day Act
Ill. Rev. Stat. 1991, Ch. 1, § 3051-40, 3051-70

Mothers' Milk Act
Cal. Welfare and Institutions Code § 14132.34

Mothers' Pension Act
Ark. Code Ann. 1987, 83-401 et seq.
Del. Code of 1953, Title 31, § 321 et seq.
Ill. Rev. Stat. 1965, Ch. 23, § 322 et seq.
Minn. Stat. Ann., 256.72 et seq.
N.D. Laws 1915, Ch. 185
Neb. Laws 1919, Ch. 221
Ore. Code 1930, §§ 27-1301 to 27-1321
S.D. Code 1939, 43.0201 et seq.
Tenn. Code Ann., Superseded Vol., 14-1101 et seq.
Continued

Wis. Stat. Ann., 49.19

Motion Picture Act
N.M. Stat. Ann., 57-5-1 et seq.

Motion Picture and Television Development Act
N.J. Stat. Ann., 34:1B-22 et seq.

Motion Picture Censorship Act
See Censorship Act (Motion Pictures)

Motion Picture Classification Board Act
R.I. Gen. Laws 1956, 42-43-1 et seq.

Motion Picture Control Act
Pa. Cons. Stat., Title 18, § 5903

Motion Picture Fair Bidding Act
Ida. Code 1947, 18-7701 et seq.
Utah Code Ann. 1953, 13-13-1 et seq.

Motion Picture Fair Business Practices Law
Pa. Purdon's Stat., Title 73, § 203-1 et seq.

Motion Picture Fair Competition Act
Ala. Code 1975, § 8-18-1 et seq.
Ga. Code Ann., 10-1-290 et seq.
La. Rev. Stat. Ann., 37:2901 et seq.
N.M. Stat. Ann., 57-5A-1 et seq.
Tenn. Code Ann., 47-25-701 et seq.
Va. Code 1950, § 59.1-255 et seq.
Wash. Rev. Code Ann., 19.58.010 et seq.

Motion Picture Fair Trade Practices Act
Mont. Code Ann., 30-14-301 et seq.

Motion Picture Incentive Act
Ark. Code Ann. 1987, 26-4-201 et seq.
La. Rev. Stat. Ann., 47:1121 et seq.

Motion Picture Marketing Act (Rosenthal-Farr)
Cal. Government Code § 15335.22

Motion Picture Referendum Act (Sunday Exhibitions)
Pa. Purdon's Stat., Title 4, § 61 et seq.

Motion Picture, Television, and Commercial Industries Act
Cal. Government Code § 14998 et seq.

Motion Picture Theater Competition Act
Wash. Rev. Code Ann., 19.58.010 et seq.

Motion to Dismiss Act
Ind. Code Ann., 4-6-4-1 et seq.

Motivational Boot Camp Act
Pa. Purdon's Stat., Title 61, § 1121 et seq.

Motive Power Act (Reimbursement under Federal Control)
Utah Code Ann. 1953, 59-13-101 et seq.

Motor and Vessel Excise Tax Act
Okla. Stat. 1981, Title 63, § 4101 et seq.

Motor and Vessel Registration Act
Okla. Stat. 1981, Title 63, § 4001 et seq.

Motor Boat Law
Pa. Cons. Stat., Title 30, § 5101 et seq.

Motor Boat Regulations Act
June 9, 1910, Ch. 268, 36 Stat. 462

Motor Boats Regulation Act
Wash. Rev. Code Ann., 88.12.010 et seq.

Motor Bus Act
Conn. Gen. Stat. Ann., § 13b-80 et seq.
Ky. Rev. Stat. 1971, 281.010 et seq.
N.C. Gen. Stat. 1943, § 62-259 et seq.
N.C. Gen. Stat. 1943, Superseded Vol., § 62-121.43 et seq.
S.C. Code Ann. 1976, § 58-23-10 et seq.

Motor Bus Act (Franchise)
Ky. Rev. Stat. 1971, 281.635

Motor Bus and Truck Act
Mo. Rev. Stat., 390.011 et seq.

Motor Bus Segregation Act
Tex. Penal Code 1925, Art. 1661.1

Motor Bus Ticket Brokers Act
Tex. Rev. Civ. Stat., Art. 911d

Motor Bus Transportation Act
Mich. Comp. Laws Ann., 474.101 et seq.
Tex. Rev. Civ. Stat., Art. 911a

Motor Carrier Act
Aug. 9, 1935, Ch. 498, 49 Stat. 543, 15 U.S. Code § 77c; 49 U.S. Code §§ 1 to 5, 6 to 13, 15 to 17, 19 to 20a, 22, 26, 27, 301 to 327
Ala. Code 1975, § 37-3-1 et seq.
Alaska Stat. 1962, Replaced Titles, § 42.10.010 et seq.
Ariz. Rev. Stat. Ann., § 28-2401 et seq.
Ark. Code Ann. 1987, 23-13-201 et seq.
Cal. Public Utilities Code § 3501 et seq.
Colo. Rev. Stat., 40-10-101 et seq.
Ga. Code Ann., 46-7-50 et seq.
Haw. Rev. Stat. Ann., § 271-1 et seq.
Ida. Code 1947, 61-801 et seq.
Ind. Code Ann., 8-2-7-1 et seq.
Iowa Code Ann., 325.1 et seq.
Kan. Stat. Ann., 66-1, 108 et seq.
Ky. Rev. Stat. 1971, 281.010 et seq.
La. Rev. Stat. Ann., 45:161 et seq.
Mass. Gen Laws 1990, 159B:1 et seq.
Me. Rev. Stat. Ann. 1964, Title 35, § 1501 et seq.
Mich. Comp. Laws Ann., 475.1 et seq.
Minn. Stat. Ann., 221.011 et seq.
Mo. Rev. Stat., 390.011 et seq.
Mont. Code Ann., 69-12-101 et seq.
N.C. Gen. Stat. 1943, § 62-259 et seq.
N.D. Cent. Code, 49-18-01 et seq.
Nev. Rev. Stat. 1979 Reprint, 706.011 et seq.
N.M. Stat. Ann., 65-2-80 et seq.
N.Y. Transportation Law (Consol. Laws Ch. 61a) § 160 et seq.
Ohio Rev. Code 1953, 4921.01 et seq.
Okla. Stat. Ann., Title 47, §§ 161 et seq.,240.1 et seq.
Ore. Rev. Stat., 767.005 et seq.
S.D. Codified Laws 1967, 49-28-1 et seq.
Tenn. Code Ann., 65-15-101 et seq.
Tex. Rev. Civ. Stat., Art. 911b
Utah Code Ann. 1953, 54-6-1 et seq.
Va. Code 1950, § 56-273 et seq.

Wash. Rev. Code Ann., 81.68.010 et seq., 81.80.010 et seq.
Wis. Stat. Ann., 194.01 et seq.
Wyo. Stat. Ann., § 37-8-101 et seq.

Motor Carrier Act (Grandfather Clause)
Neb. Laws 1937, Ch. 142, § 7(a)

Motor Carrier Act (Interstate)
Neb. Rev. Stat. 1943, 75-348 et seq.

Motor Carrier Act (Intrastate)
Neb. Rev. Stat. 1943, 75-301 et seq.

Motor Carrier Act of 1980
July 1, 1980, P.L. 96-296, 49 U.S. Code § 10101 nt.
Sept. 20, 1982, P.L. 97-261, 49 U.S. Code § 10706 nt.
Jan. 6, 1983, P.L. 97-424, 49 U.S. Code § 10927 nt.
Oct. 30, 1984, P.L. 98-554, 49 U.S. Code § 10927 nt.
Nov. 18, 1988, P.L. 100-690, 49 U.S. Code § 10927 nt.
Nov. 16, 1990, P.L. 101-615, 49 U.S. Code § 10927 nt.

Motor Carrier Act of 1991
Dec. 18, 1991, P.L. 102-240, 49 U.S. Code Appx. § 2301 nt.

Motor Carrier Certification Act
S.C. Code Ann. 1976, § 58-23-10 et seq.

Motor Carrier Fuel Tax Act
Mich. Comp. Laws Ann., 207.211 et seq.

Motor Carrier Funding and Tax Administration Act
Tenn. Code Ann., 55-4-113

Motor Carrier Mileage Tax Act
Ala. Code 1975, § 40-19-1 et seq.

Motor Carrier of Property Act
Ill. Rev. Stat. 1983, Ch. 95 1/2, § 18-100 et seq.
N.H. Rev. Stat. 1955, 375-B:1 et seq.

Motor Carrier Regulatory Act
Miss. Code Ann. 1972, § 77-7-1 et seq.

Motor Carrier Road Tax Act
Pa. Cons. Stat., Title 75, § 9601 et seq.
Pa. Purdon's Stat., Title 72, § 2617.1 et seq.
W. Va. Code 1966, § 11-14A-1 et seq.

Motor Carrier Safety Act of 1984
Oct. 30, 1984, P.L. 98-554, 49 U.S. Code
Appx. §§ 2501, nt., 2501 et seq.
Nov. 18, 1988, P.L. 100-690, 49 U.S. Code
Appx. §§ 2505, 2507, 2521
Nov. 16, 1990, P.L. 101-615, 49 U.S. Code
Appx. § 2509

Motor Carrier Safety Act of 1990
Nov. 3, 1990, P.L. 101-500, 49 U.S. Code
Appx. § 2501 nt.

Motor Carrier Safety Acts of 1984-1990
Mich. Comp. Laws Ann., 480.11 et seq.

Motor Carrier Safety and Hazardous Materials Transportation Act
Okla. Stat. Ann., Title 47, §§ 230.1 to 230.14

Motor Carrier Tax Act
Kan. Stat. Ann., 79-6a01 et seq.

Motor Carrier Transportation Agent Act
Cal. Statutes 1933, Ch. 390, p. 1011
N.M. Stat. Ann., 65-4-1 et seq.
Wash. Rev. Code 1951, 81.76.010 et seq.

Motor Carrier Truck Act
S.C. Code Ann. 1976, § 56-5-4010 et seq.
Tex. Rev. Civ. Stat., Art. 6701d-11

Motor Carrier Vehicle Registration Act
Okla. Stat. Ann., Title 47, § 180 et seq.

Motor Carriers Act
Miss. Code 1942, § 9352 et seq.

Motor Carriers Base State Fuel Tax Compact Act
Neb. Rev. Stat. 1943, 66-1401 et seq.

Motor Carriers' City Tax Exemption Act
Cal. Public Utilities Code § 4301 et seq.

Motor Carriers Fuel Purchase Act
Del. Code of 1974, Title 30, § 5201 et seq.

Motor Carriers Road Tax Act
Md. Ann. Code 1974, Art. TP, § 6-103
N.J. Stat. Ann., 54:39A-1 et seq.
Pa. Cons. Stat., Title 75, § 9601 et seq.

Motor Club Act
Nev. Rev. Stat. 1979 Reprint, 696A.010 et seq.
N.M. Stat. Ann., 59A-50-1 et seq.

Motor Club Licensing Act
Colo. Rev. Stat., 12-53-101 et seq.

Motor Club Service Act
Cal. Insurance Code § 12142 et seq.
Neb. Rev. Stat. 1943, 44-3701 et seq.
Ore. Rev. Stat., 751.005 et seq.
S.C. Code Ann. 1976, § 39-61-10 et seq.
Wis. Stat. Ann., 616.71 et seq.
Wyo. Stat. Ann., § 31-14-101 et seq.

Motor Common Carriers Act
Ala. Code 1975, § 8-17-150 et seq.
Ga. Code Ann., 46-7-1 et seq.
R.I. Gen. Laws 1956, 39-12-1 et seq.
Wash. Rev. Code Ann., 81.80.010 et seq.

Motor Fuel Act (Retail Sales)
N.J. Stat. Ann., 56:6-1 et seq.

Motor Fuel and Diesel Fuel Use Tax Act
Fla. Stat. Ann., 207.001 et seq.

Motor Fuel and Petroleum Standards Act
Ill. Rev. Stat. 1991, Ch. 5, § 1701 et seq.

Motor Fuel and Special Fuel Marketing and Distribution Act
Iowa Code Ann., 323.1 et seq.

Motor Fuel and Special Fuel Tax Act
Va. Code 1950, § 58.1-2100 et seq.

Motor Fuel and Special Fuel Tax Law
Iowa Code 1983, 452A.1 et seq.

Motor Fuel Distribution Act
Mich. Comp. Laws Ann., 445.1801 et seq.

Motor Fuel Distribution and Sales Act
Me. Rev. Stat. Ann. 1964, Title 10, § 1451 et seq.
R.I. Gen. Laws 1956, 5-55-1 et seq.

Motor Fuel Excise Tax Act
Colo. Rev. Stat., 39-27-101 et seq.
Okla. Stat. Ann., Title 68, § 501 et seq.

Motor Fuel First Importation Tax Law
N.Y. Laws 1985, Ch. 44

Motor Fuel Importer for Use Tax Code
Okla. Stat. Ann., Title 68, § 601 et seq.

Motor Fuel Inspection Act
Utah Code Ann. 1953, 4-33-1 et seq.

Motor Fuel License Tax Act
Cal. Revenue and Taxation Code § 7301 et seq.

Motor Fuel Marketing Act
Ala. Acts 1984, p. 433
Mo. Rev. Stat. 1986, 416.600 et seq.
N.C. Gen. Stat. 1943, § 75-80 et seq.
Utah Code Ann. 1953, 13-16-1 et seq.

Motor Fuel Marketing Act (Retail)
Mont. Laws 1991, Ch. 499

Motor Fuel Marketing Practices Act
Fla. Stat. Ann., 526.301 et seq.

Motor Fuel Quality Act
Wash. Rev. Code Ann., 19.112.005 et seq.

Motor Fuel Sales Act
Ill. Rev. Stat. 1991, Ch. 121 1/2, § 1500 et seq.
Mass. Gen Laws 1990, 94:295A et seq.

Motor Fuel Standards Act
Ill. Rev. Stat. 1991, Ch. 5, § 1701 et seq.

Motor Fuel Tax Act
See also Motor Vehicle Fuel Tax Act
Alaska Stat. 1962, § 43.40.010 et seq.
Colo. Rev. Stat., 39-27-101 et seq.
Del. Code of 1974, Title 30, § 5101 et seq.
Ga. Code Ann., 48-9-1 et seq.
Ida. Code 1947, 63-2401 et seq.
Ill. Comp. Stat. 1992, Ch. 35, § 505/1 et seq.
Ill. Rev. Stat. 1991, Ch. 120, § 417 et seq.
Iowa Code Ann., 324.1 et seq., 452A.1 et seq.
Kan. Stat. Ann., 79-3401 et seq.
La. Rev. Stat. Ann., 47:711 et seq.
Md. Ann. Code 1974, Art. BR, § 10-101 et seq.
N.M. Stat. Ann., 7-13-1 et seq.
Okla. Stat. Ann., Title 68, § 501 et seq.
Tex. Tax Code, § 153.001 et seq.
Utah Code Ann. 1953, 59-13-101 et seq.
Vt. Stat. Ann., Title 32, § 8801 et seq.
Wis. Stat. Ann., 78.01 et seq.

Motor Fuel Tax Fund Bond Act
Ill. Rev. Stat. 1991, Ch. 121, § 101-90 et seq.

Motor Fuel Tax Law
Ind. Code Ann., 6-6-1.1-101 et seq.

Motor Fuel Tax Note Act
Ill. Rev. Stat. 1951, Ch. 146 1/2, § 28 et seq.

Motor Fuel Tax Refund Act
Tex. Taxation-General 1959, Arts. 10.14, 10.15

Motor Fuel Use Act (Interstate)
Kan. Stat. Ann., 79-34,108 et seq.

Motor Fuel Use Tax Act
Ark. Code Ann. 1987, 75-1223 et seq.
N.J. Stat. Ann., 54:39A-1 et seq.

Motor Fuel/Diesel Fuel Importer for Use Tax Code
Okla. Stat. Ann., Title 68, § 601 et seq.

Motor Fuels and Kerosene Quality Inspection Act
Tenn. Code Ann., 47-18-1301 et seq.

Motor Fuels Consumed by Interstate Buses Act (Taxation of)
Me. Rev. Stat. Ann. 1964, Title 36, § 3091 et seq.

Motor Fuels Consumed by Interstate Buses Compact (Taxation of)
N.H. Rev. Stat. 1955, 260:66 et seq.

Motor Fuels Quality Act
Mich. Comp. Laws Ann., 290.641 et seq.

Motor Insurance Coverage Act (Optional)
S.C. Code Ann. 1976, § 38-77-150 et seq.

Motor License Fund Appropriation Act
Pa. 1983 Pamph. Laws 599, No. 6-A
Pa. 1984 Pamph. Laws 1479, No. 8A
Pa. 1985 Pamph. Laws 715, No. 6A

Motor License Fund Supplement to the General Appropriation Acts
Pa. 1971 Pamph. Laws 805, No. 2-A
Pa. 1972 Pamph. Laws 1891, No. 19-A
Pa. 1973 Pamph. Laws 483, No. 9-A
Pa. 1974 Pamph. Laws 1412, No. 23-A
Pa. 1975 Pamph. Laws 687, No. 9A
Pa. 1976 Pamph. Laws 1378, No. 15A
Pa. 1977 Pamph. Laws 403, No. 7-A
Pa. 1978 Pamph. Laws 1594, No. 55-A
Pa. 1979 Pamph. Laws 714, No. 11A
Pa. 1980 Pamph. Laws 1441, No. 22A
Pa. 1981 Pamph. Laws 621, No. 2A

Motor Oil Recycling Act
Ill. Rev. Stat. 1991, Ch. 96 1/2, § 7751 et seq.

Motor Passenger Carrier Act
N.H. Rev. Stat. 1955, 376:1 et seq.
R.I. Gen. Laws 1956, 39-13-1 et seq.
Wash. Rev. Code Ann., 81.68.010 et seq.

Motor Pool Act
N.M. Laws 1994, Ch. 119

Motor Registration Act
Mont. Code Ann., 61-3-301 et seq.

Motor Sales Act
N.J. Stat. Ann., 39:10-1 et seq.

Motor Traffic Law
N.C. Gen. Stat. 1943, § 20-138.1 et seq.

Motor Transportation Act
Ala. Code 1975, § 37-3-1 et seq.
Fla. Stat. Ann., 323.01 et seq.
N.M. Stat. Ann., 65-1-1 et seq.
Ohio Rev. Code 1953, 4921.01 et seq.
Ore. Rev. Stat., 767.005 et seq.
S.C. Code Ann. 1976, § 58-23-10 et seq.
Tex. Rev. Civ. Stat., Art. 911b
Utah Code Ann. 1953, 54-6-1 et seq.

Motor Transportation Brokers Act
Cal. Public Utilities Code § 4801 et seq.
Tex. Transportation Code, § 646.001 et seq.

Motor Transportation License Tax Lien Act
Cal. Revenue and Taxation Code § 10096 et seq.

Motor Vehicle Accident Act
R.I. Gen. Laws 1956, 31-26-1 et seq.

Motor Vehicle Accident Act (Government Liability)
Wis. Stat. Ann., 345.05

Motor Vehicle Accident Act (Venue)
Wash. Rev. Code Ann., 4.12.020, Subd. 3

Motor Vehicle Accident Claims Act
Mich. Comp. Laws Ann., 257.1101 et seq.

Motor Vehicle Accident Indemnification Corporation Act
N.Y. Insurance Law (Consol. Laws Ch. 28) § 5201 et seq.

Motor Vehicle Accident Reparations Act
Ga. Code Ann., 33-34-1 et seq.
Haw. Rev. Stat. Ann., § 294-1 et seq.

Motor Vehicle Accident Reporting Act
See Accident Reporting Act (Motor Vehicles)

Motor Vehicle Act

See also Motor Vehicle Law

Ala. Code 1975, § 32-1-1 et seq.

Alaska Stat. 1962, § 28.10.011 et seq.

Ariz. Rev. Stat. Ann., § 28-101 et seq.

Ark. Code Ann. 1987, 27-14-201 et seq.

Cal. Vehicle Code 1959, § 1 et seq.

Colo. Rev. Stat., 42-1-101 et seq.

Conn. Gen. Stat. Ann., § 14-1 et seq.

D.C. Code Ann., § 40-101 et seq.

Del. Code of 1974, Title 21, § 101 et seq.

Fla. Stat. Ann., 316.001 et seq.

Ga. Code Ann., 40-1-1 et seq.

Haw. Rev. Stat. Ann., § 286-1 et seq.

Ill. Rev. Stat. 1991, Ch. 95 1/2, § 1-100 et seq.

Ind. Code Ann., 9-1-1-1 et seq.

Iowa Code Ann., 321.1 et seq.

Ky. Rev. Stat. 1971, 186.005 et seq., 189.010 et seq.

Mass. Gen Laws 1990, 90:1 et seq.

Md. Ann. Code 1974, Art. TR, § 11-101 et seq.

Me. Rev. Stat. Ann. 1964, Title 29, § 1 et seq.

Mich. Comp. Laws Ann., 257.1 et seq.

Minn. Stat. Ann., 168.011 et seq.

Miss. Code Ann. 1972, § 63-1-1 et seq.

Mo. Rev. Stat., 301.010 et seq.

Mont. Code Ann., 61-1-101 et seq.

N.C. Gen. Stat. 1943, § 20-39 et seq.

N.D. Cent. Code, 39-01-01 et seq.

N.H. Rev. Stat. 1955, 259:1 et seq.

N.J. Stat. Ann., 39:1-1 et seq.

N.M. Stat. Ann., 66-1-1

N.Y. Vehicle and Traffic Law 1959 (Consol. Laws Ch. 71) § 300 et seq.

Ohio Rev. Code 1953, 4501.01 et seq.

Okla. Stat. Ann., Title 47

Ore. Rev. Stat. 1953, 801.010 et seq.

Pa. Cons. Stat., Title 75

R.I. Gen. Laws 1956, 31-1-1 et seq.

S.C. Code Ann. 1976, § 56-5-10 et seq.

Tenn. Code Ann., 55-1-101

Utah Code Ann. 1953, 41-1-1 et seq., 41-1A-101 et seq.

Va. Code 1950, § 46.2-100 et seq.

Vt. Stat. Ann., Title 23, § 1 et seq.

Wash. Rev. Code Ann., 46.01.011 et seq.

Wis. Stat. Ann., 340.01 et seq.

Wyo. Stat. Ann., § 31-4-101 et seq.

Motor Vehicle Act (Buy-American)

Pa. Purdon's Stat., Title 73, § 1891 et seq.

Motor Vehicle Act (Commercial)

Wyo. Stat. Ann., § 37-8-101 et seq.

Motor Vehicle Act (One-Bite)

N.Y. Vehicle and Traffic Law 1959 (Consol. Laws Ch. 71) § 330 et seq.

Motor Vehicle Act (Speed Regulation)

Ind. Code Ann., 9-4-1-57 et seq.

Motor Vehicle Act-Salvage Vehicles

Utah Code Ann. 1953, 41-1-36.1 et seq.

Motor Vehicle Ad Valorem Tax Act

Miss. Code Ann. 1972, § 27-55-1 et seq.

Motor Vehicle Administration, Certificate of Title and Anti-Theft Act

Ark. Code Ann. 1987, 27-14-101 et seq.

Motor Vehicle Air Pollution Control Act

Oct. 20, 1965, P.L. 89-272, 79 Stat. 992, 42 U.S. Code §§ 1857f-1 to 1857f-8

Motor Vehicle, Aircraft, Boat or Boat Motor Theft Act

Fla. Stat. 1973, 814.01 et seq.

Motor Vehicle Anti-Bushing Act

Wis. Stat. Ann., 218.01, Subsec. 3, Subd. a

Motor Vehicle Anti-Theft Act

See Antitheft Act (Motor Vehicles)

Motor Vehicle Antifreeze Act

Iowa Code 1966, 208A.1 et seq.

Motor Vehicle Assigned Risks Law

N.M. Stat. Ann., 59A-32-1 et seq.

Motor Vehicle Attachment Act

S.C. Code Ann. 1976, § 29-15-20

Motor Vehicle Automated Registration Code Act
Ky. Rev. Stat. 1971, 186A.010, 186A.020

Motor Vehicle Bailor Responsibility Act
Conn. Gen. Stat. Ann., § 14-15a

Motor Vehicle Bill of Sale Act
N.J. Stat. Ann., 39:10-1 et seq.
Ohio Rev. Code 1953, 4505.01 et seq.

Motor Vehicle Business Regulation Act
Utah Code Ann. 1953, 41-3-101 et seq.

Motor Vehicle Buyback Disclosure Act
Utah Code Ann. 1953, 41-3-406 et seq.

Motor Vehicle Buyers Protection Act
P.R. Laws Ann. 1954, Title 23, § 1021 et seq.

Motor Vehicle Caravan Tax Act
N.M. Stat. Ann., 66-6-2

Motor Vehicle Caravaning Act
Ida. Code 1947, 49-1101 et seq.
Wash. Rev. Code Ann., 46.76.010 et seq.

Motor Vehicle Carrier Safety Act
N.M. Stat. Ann., 65-3-1 et seq.

Motor Vehicle Carriers Act
Va. Code 1950, § 56-273 et seq.

Motor Vehicle Certificate of Title Act
See also Motor Vehicle Title Act
Ariz. Rev. Stat. Ann., § 28-301 et seq.
Ark. Code Ann. 1987, 27-14-101 et seq.,
    27-14-201 et seq.
Colo. Rev. Stat., 42-6-101 et seq.
Conn. Gen. Stat. Ann., § 14-165 et seq.
Del. Code of 1974, Title 21, § 2301 et seq.
Fla. Stat. 1981, 319.001 et seq.
Ga. Code Ann., 40-3-1 et seq.
Ill. Rev. Stat. 1991, Ch. 95 1/2, § 3-100 et
    seq.
Ind. Code Ann., 9-1-2-1 et seq.
Iowa Code Ann., 321.17 et seq.
Kan. Stat. Ann., 8-126 et seq.
La. Rev. Stat. Ann., 32:701 et seq.
Mass. Gen Laws 1984, 90:1 et seq.

Mass. Gen Laws 1990, 90D:1 et seq.
Md. Ann. Code 1974, Art. TR, § 13-101 et
    seq.
Me. Stat. Ann. 1978, 66-3-1 et seq.
Mich. Comp. Laws Ann., 257.201 et seq.
N.C. Gen. Stat. 1943, § 20-50 et seq.
Neb. Rev. Stat. 1943, 60-101 et seq.
N.H. Rev. Stat. 1955, 26:1 et seq.
N.J. Stat. Ann., 39:10-1 et seq.
N.M. Stat. Ann., 66-3-1 et seq.
N.Y. Vehicle and Traffic Law 1959 (Consol.
    Laws Ch. 71) § 2101 et seq.
Ohio Rev. Code 1953, 4505.01 et seq.
Okla. Stat. Ann., Title 47, § 23 et seq.
Ore. Rev. Stat., 481.110 et seq.
Pa. Cons. Stat., Title 75, § 1101 et seq.
R.I. Gen. Laws 1956, 31-3.1-1 et seq.
S.C. Code of Law 1976, § 56-19-210 et seq.
S.D. Codified Laws 1967, 32-3-1 et seq.
Tenn. Code Ann., 55-3-101 et seq.
Tex. Rev. Civ. Stat., Art. 6687-1
Utah Code Ann. 1953, 41-1-18 et seq.
Va. Code 1950, § 46.1-68 et seq.
Wash. Rev. Code Ann., 46.12.005 et seq.
W. Va. Code 1966, § 17A-3-1 et seq.
Wyo. Stat. Ann., § 31-2-101 et seq.

Motor Vehicle Certificate of Title and Anti-Theft Act
See also Uniform Motor Vehicle Certificate
    of Title and Antitheft Act
Ala. Code 1975, 32-8-1 et seq.
Mass. Gen. Laws Ann., 90D:1 et seq.
Me. Rev. Stat. Ann. 1964, Title 29, § 2350 et
    seq.
Minn. Stat. Ann., 168A.01 et seq.
N.H. Rev. Stat. 1955, 261:1 et seq.
S.C. Code Ann. 1976, § 56-19-10 et seq.
Vt. Stat. Ann., Title 23, § 2001 et seq.

Motor Vehicle Certificate of Title Transfer Act
Mich. Comp. Laws Ann., 257.233 et seq.

Motor Vehicle Chop Shop, Stolen and Altered Property Act
Ga. Code Ann., 16-8-80 et seq.
Miss. Code Ann. 1972, § 63-25-1 et seq.
Okla. Stat. Ann., Title 47, § 1501 et seq.

S.C. Code Ann. 1976, § 56-29-10 et seq.

Motor Vehicle Chop Shop Stolen and Altered Property Act

R.I. Gen. Laws 1956, 31-48-1 et seq.

Motor Vehicle Civil Liability Act

Mich. Comp. Laws Ann., 257.401 et seq.

Motor Vehicle Claim and Judgment Fund Act

Md. Ann. Code 1957, Superseded Vol., Art. 66 1/2, § 7-601 et seq.

Motor Vehicle Commission Act

Ark. Code Ann. 1987, 23-112-101 et seq.
La. Rev. Stat. Ann., 32:1251 et seq.
Miss. Code Ann. 1972, § 63-17-51 et seq.
Okla. Stat. Ann., Title 47, § 561 et seq.
Tenn. Code Ann., 55-17-101 et seq., 3(36)
Tex. Rev. Civ. Stat., Art. 4413(36)

Motor Vehicle Comptroller's Act

Miss. Code Ann. 1972, § 27-5-1 et seq.

Motor Vehicle Compulsory Inspection Act

N.Y. Vehicle and Traffic Law 1959 (Consol. Laws Ch. 71) § 301 et seq.

Motor Vehicle Compulsory Insurance Act

Conn. Gen. Stat. Ann., § 14-112 et seq.
Mass. Gen Laws 1990, 90:34A et seq., 175:113A et seq.
N.Y. Vehicle and Traffic Law 1959 (Consol. Laws Ch. 71) § 310 et seq.

Motor Vehicle Construction or Agricultural Machinery Junk Yard Act

Minn. Stat. Ann., 161.242

Motor Vehicle Consumer Lease Act

Wis. Stat. Ann., 429.101 et seq.

Motor Vehicle Damage Control Act

Cal. Vehicle Code 1959, §§ 34700, 34710, 3415, 34725

Motor Vehicle Damage Disclosure Act

S.C. Code Ann. 1976, §§ 56-32-10, 56-32-20

Motor Vehicle Dealer Act (Franchised)

N.Y. Vehicle and Traffic Law 1959 (Consol. Laws Ch. 71) § 460 et seq.

Motor Vehicle Dealers and Distributors Franchising Practices Act

Vt. Stat. Ann., Title 9, § 4083 et seq.

Motor Vehicle Dealers and Used Motor Vehicle Parts Dealers' Registration Act

Ga. Code Ann., 43-47-1 et seq.

Motor Vehicle Dealers' Commission Law

Pa. 1937 Pamph. Laws 2465, No. 461

Motor Vehicle Dealer's Day in Court Act

Ga. Code Ann., 10-1-630, 10-1-631

Motor Vehicle Dealers License Act

Cal. Vehicle Code 1959, § 11700 et seq.
Colo. Rev. Stat., 12-6-101 et seq.
Iowa Code Ann., 322.1 et seq.
La. Rev. Stat. Ann., 32:1251 et seq.
N.C. Gen. Stat. 1943, § 20-285 et seq.
N.D. Cent. Code, 39-22-01 et seq.
Neb. Rev. Stat. 1943, 60-1401.01 et seq.
Va. Code 1950, § 46.1-515 et seq.
Wash. Rev. Code Ann., 46.70.005 et seq.

Motor Vehicle Dealers Sunday Closing Act

Colo. Rev. Stat., 12-6-301 et seq.

Motor Vehicle Dealers Tag Permit Act

Miss. Code Ann. 1972, § 27-19-301 et seq.

Motor Vehicle Dealers Unlawful Practices Act

Wash. Rev. Code Ann., 46.70.180 et seq.

Motor Vehicle Dealership Act

La. Rev. Stat. Ann., 32:1251

Motor Vehicle Distribution and Sales Act

Okla. Stat. Ann., Title 47, § 561 et seq.

Motor Vehicle Drivers' License Act

See Drivers' License Act

Motor Vehicle Driver's License Compact

Cal. Vehicle Code § 15000 et seq.

Motor Vehicle Drivers' Licensing Act
Cal. Vehicle Code § 12500 et seq.

Motor Vehicle Emission Inspection and Maintenance Act
Ga. Code Ann., 12-9-40 et seq., 40-8-150 et seq.

Motor Vehicle Emissions Inspection and Maintenance Program Act
Mich. Comp. Laws Ann., 257.2051 et seq.

Motor Vehicle Emissions Testing Program Act
Mich. Comp. Laws Ann., 257.2001 et seq.

Motor Vehicle Enforcement Fund Act
Okla. Stat. Ann., Title 47, § 161 et seq.

Motor Vehicle Equipment Law
Wash. Rev. Code Ann., 46.37.005 et seq.

Motor Vehicle Excise Act
Mass. Gen. Laws 1984, 60A:1 et seq.

Motor Vehicle Excise Tax Act
Ind. Code Ann., 6-6-5-1 et seq.
Mass. Gen. Laws Ann., 60A:1 et seq.
N.D. Cent. Code, 57-40.3-01 et seq.
N.M. Stat. Ann., 7-14-1 et seq.
Okla. Stat. Ann., Title 47, § 52 et seq.
Wash. Rev. Code Ann., 82.44.010 et seq.

Motor Vehicle Fair Practices Act
Ga. Code Ann., 10-1-660 et seq.

Motor Vehicle Fair Trade Act
Kan. Stat. Ann., 8-601 et seq.

Motor Vehicle, Farm Machinery and Construction Equipment Franchise Practices Act
Ga. Code 1933, 84-6601 et seq.

Motor Vehicle Finance Act
Ore. Laws 1931, Ch. 377

Motor Vehicle Financial Responsibility Act
See Financial Responsibility Act (Motor Vehicles)
Cal. Vehicle Code § 16000 et seq.

Mass. Gen. Laws Ann., 90:34A et seq., 175:113A et seq.
Me. Rev. Stat. Ann. 1964, Title 29, § 781 et seq.
Ore. Rev. Stat., 806.010 et seq.

Motor Vehicle Financial Responsibility and Safety Act
Iowa Code Ann., 321A.1 et seq.

Motor Vehicle Financial Responsibility Law
Ohio Rev. Code 1953, 4509.01 et seq.
S.C. Code Ann. 1976, § 56-9-10 et seq.

Motor Vehicle Financial Security Act
N.Y. Vehicle and Traffic Law 1959 (Consol. Laws Ch. 71) § 310 et seq.

Motor Vehicle Financing Act
D.C. Code 1973, § 40-1101 et seq.

Motor Vehicle Flare Act
Ind. Code Ann., 9-8-6-41, 9-8-6-42
Minn. Stat. Ann., 169.75

Motor Vehicle Forfeiture Law (Intoxicating Liquors)
Tenn. Code Ann., 57-3-411

Motor Vehicle Franchise Act
Ala. Code 1975, § 8-20-1 et seq.
Del. Code of 1974, Title 6, § 4901 et seq.
Ill. Rev. Stat. 1991, Ch. 121 1/2, § 751 et seq.
Wyo. Stat. Ann., § 40-15-101 et seq.

Motor Vehicle Franchise Continuation and Succession Act
Ga. Code Ann., 10-1-650 et seq.

Motor Vehicle Franchise Practices Act
Ga. Code Ann., 10-1-620 et seq.
Mo. Rev. Stat., 407.810 et seq.

Motor Vehicle Franchise Protection Act
S.D. Codified Laws 1967, 36-6A-1 et seq.

Motor Vehicle Fuel Conservation Act
Cal. Public Resources Code § 25370 et seq.

Motor Vehicle Fuel Importer Use Tax Act
Wash. Rev. Code Ann., 82.37.010 et seq.

Motor Vehicle Fuel License Tax Law
See also Motor Fuel Tax Act
Ariz. Rev. Stat. Ann., § 28-1501 et seq.
Ark. Code Ann. 1987, 75-1101 et seq.
Cal. Revenue and Taxation Code § 7301 et seq.
D.C. Code Ann., § 47-2301 et seq.
Ky. Rev. Stat. 1971, 138.210 et seq.
Md. Ann. Code 1957, Art. 56, § 135 et seq.
Mich. Comp. Laws Ann., 207.101 et seq.
Mo. Rev. Stat., 142.010 et seq.
N.D. Cent. Code, 57-43.1-01 et seq.
Neb. Rev. Stat. 1943, 66-401 et seq.
Nev. Rev. Stat. 1979 Reprint, 365.010 et seq.
N.J. Stat. Ann., 54:39-1 et seq.
Ohio Rev. Code 1953, 5735.01 et seq.
Ore. Rev. Stat. 1989, 319.010 et seq.
Pa. Purdon's Stat., Title 72, § 2614.1 et seq.
S.D. Codified Laws 1967, 10-47-1 et seq.
Wash. Rev. Code Ann., 82.36.010 et seq.

Motor Vehicle Fuel Tax Act
Ark. Code Ann. 1987, 26-55-201, 26-55-203 et seq.
Ky. Rev. Stat. 1971, 138.210 et seq.
Md. Ann. Code 1974, Art. BR, § 10-101 et seq.
Mich. Comp. Laws Ann., 207.101 et seq.
Ore. Rev. Stat. 1989, 319.010 et seq.

Motor Vehicle Fuel Tax Act (County)
Nev. Rev. Stat. 1979 Reprint, 373.010 et seq.

Motor Vehicle Fuel Use Tax Law
Tenn. Code Ann., 67-3-801 et seq.

Motor Vehicle Fuels Carriers' License Act
Kan. Stat. Ann., 55-501 et seq.

Motor Vehicle Fund Law
Wash. Rev. Code Ann., 46.68.070 et seq.

Motor Vehicle Guest Act
Ala. Code 1975, 32-1-2
Conn. Public Acts 1991, p. 4404, Ch. 308
Del. Code of 1974, Title 21, § 6101
Fla. Stat. 1971, 320.59
Ga. Code 1933, 68-301
Ill. Rev. Stat. 1991, Ch. 95 1/2, §§ 10-201, 10-202

Ind. Code Ann., 9-3-3-1, 9-3-3-2
Iowa Code Ann., 321.494
Mich. Comp. Laws Ann., 257.401
Mont. Rev. Code 1947, 32-1113 et seq.
Neb. Rev. Stat. 1943, 39-6191
Nev. Rev. Stat. 1979 Reprint, Replaced Pages, 41.180
N.M. Stat. Ann., 1953, 64-24-1
Ore. Rev. Stat., 30.115 et seq.
Wash. Rev. Code Ann., 46.08.070

Motor Vehicle Habitual Offender Act
Cal. Vehicle Code 1959, § 17158
R.I. Gen. Laws 1956, 31-40-1 et seq.
Tenn. Code Ann., 55-10-601 et seq.

Motor Vehicle Highway Account Act
Ind. Code Ann., 8-14-1-1 et seq.

Motor Vehicle Highway Fund Act
Mich. Comp. Laws Ann., 247.660 et seq.

Motor Vehicle Highway Safety Act
N.C. Gen. Stat. 1943, § 20-183.1 et seq.

Motor Vehicle Hit and Run Act
See Hit and Run Act

Motor Vehicle Homicide Act
Mich. Comp. Laws Ann., 750.324 et seq.
Neb. Rev. Stat. 1943, 28-306
N.Y. Penal Law 1965 (Consol. Laws Ch. 40) § 125.12 et seq.
Wyo. Stat. Ann., § 6-2-106

Motor Vehicle Importer Use Tax
Okla. Stat. 1981, Title 68, § 601 et seq.

Motor Vehicle Improvement Act
Tenn. Code Ann., 55-17-102 et seq.

Motor Vehicle Imputed Negligence Act
Cal. Vehicle Code 1959, § 17150

Motor Vehicle Indigent Accident Act
Ore. Rev. Stat., 455.010 et seq.

Motor Vehicle Industry Licensing Act
Haw. Rev. Stat. Ann., § 437-1 et seq.
Neb. Rev. Stat. 1943, 60-1401.01 et seq.

Motor Vehicle Information and Cost Saving Act

Oct. 20, 1972, P.L. 92-513, 86 Stat. 947, 15 U.S. Code §§ 1901, 1911 to 1922, 1941 to 1949, 1961 to 1964, 1981 to 1991

Dec. 22, 1975, P.L. 94-163, 89 Stat. 871, 15 U.S. Code §§ 2001 et seq.

Nov. 9, 1978, P.L. 95-619, 15 U.S. Code §§ 2006, 2008

Jan. 7, 1980, P.L. 96-185, 15 U.S. Code § 2003

Oct. 25, 1984, P.L. 98-547, 15 U.S. Code § 1901, 2021 to 2034

Nov. 8, 1984, P.L. 98-620, 15 U.S. Code § 2003

Oct. 28, 1986, P.L. 99-579, 15 U.S. Code §§ 1982, 1988, 1990b, 1990c

Oct. 14, 1988, P.L. 100-494, 102 Stat. 2448, 15 U.S. Code §§ 2001, 2002, 2006, 2013, 2006 nt.

Oct. 31, 1988, P.L. 100-561, 15 U.S. Code § 1988

Nov. 28, 1990, P.L. 101-641, 15 U.S. Code §§ 1988, 1988 nt.

Oct. 6, 1992, P.L. 102-388, 15 U.S. Code § 1950

Oct. 25, 1992, P.L. 102-519, 15 U.S. Code §§ 2021 to 2023, 2025, 2026a, 2026b, 2027 to 2034

Dec. 8, 1993, P.L. 103-182, 15 U.S. Code § 2003

Motor Vehicle Inspection Act

D.C. Code 1973, § 40-201 et seq.
La. Rev. Stat. Ann., 32:1301 et seq.
N.C. Gen. Stat. 1943, § 20-183.2 et seq.
Neb. Rev. Stat. 1943, 60-1701 et seq.
N.J. Rev. Stat. 1937, 39:8-1 et seq.
N.Y. Vehicle and Traffic Law 1959 (Consol. Laws Ch. 71) § 301 et seq.
Wash. Rev. Code Ann., 46.32.010 et seq.
Wyo. Stat. 1957, § 31-214.1 et seq.

Motor Vehicle Inspectors' and State Police Retirement Act

Vt. Stat. Ann., Title 3, § 501 et seq.

Motor Vehicle Installment Sales Act

Cal. Civil Code § 2981 et seq.
Colo. Rev. Stat., 13-16-1 et seq., 42-6-101 et seq.

Conn. Gen. Stat. Ann., § 42-83 et seq.
D.C. Code Ann., § 40-1101 et seq.
Fla. Stat. Ann., 520.01 et seq.
Iowa Code Ann., 322.17 et seq.
Ky. Rev. Stat. 1971, 190.090 et seq.
Mass. Gen. Laws Ann., 255B:1 et seq.
Me. Rev. Stat. Ann. 1964, Title 9, § 3401 et seq.
Mich. Comp. Laws Ann., 566.301 et seq.
Minn. Stat. Ann., 168.66 et seq.
N.H. Rev. Stat. 1955, 361-A:1 et seq.
N.Y. Personal Property Law (Consol. Laws Ch. 41) § 301 et seq.
Ore. Rev. Stat., 83.510 et seq.
Tex. Rev. Civ. Stat., Art. 5069-7.01 et seq.
Vt. Stat. Ann., Title 9, § 2351 et seq.
Wis. Stat. Ann., 218.01 et seq.

Motor Vehicle Insurance Act

Nev. Rev. Stat. 1979 Reprint, 698.010 et seq.

Motor Vehicle Insurance Act (Compulsory/No-Fault)

D.C. Code Ann., § 35-2101 et seq.

Motor Vehicle Insurance Act (No Fault)

See No Fault Motor Vehicle Insurance Act

Motor Vehicle Insurance Assigned Risk Plan

N.Y. Insurance Law (Consol. Laws Ch. 29) § 5301 et seq.

Motor Vehicle Insurance Fraud and Motor Vehicle Theft Reporting Act

Cal. Vehicle Code 1959, § 10900 et seq.

Motor Vehicle Insurance Law

Haw. Rev. Stat. Ann., § 431:10C-101 et seq.

Motor Vehicle Insurance Rate Review Procedures Act

Pa. Cons. Stat., Title 75, § 2001 et seq.

Motor Vehicle Insurance Reform Act

Fla. Laws 1988, Ch. 370

Motor Vehicle Junk Law

N.J. Stat. Ann., 39:11-1 et seq.

Motor Vehicle Lease Disclosure Act
Fla. Stat. Ann., 521.001 et seq.
Haw. Rev. Stat. Ann., § 481L-1 et seq.

Motor Vehicle Leasing Act
Ill. Comp. Stat. 1992, Ch. 815, § 636/1 et seq.

Motor Vehicle Lemon Law
Ariz. Rev. Stat. Ann., § 44-1261 et seq.
Mo. Rev. Stat. 1978, 407.560 et seq.
Tex. Rev. Civ. Stat., Art. 4413(36)

Motor Vehicle Lemon Law II
Mont. Code Ann., 61-4-501 et seq.

Motor Vehicle Lessor Liability Act
Conn. Gen. Stat. Ann., § 14-154a

Motor Vehicle Liability Act
La. Rev. Stat. Ann., 32:891 et seq.

Motor Vehicle Liability Act (Financial Responsibility)
See Financial Responsibility Act (Motor Vehicles)

Motor Vehicle Liability Insurance Act
Mass. Gen Laws 1990, 90:34A et seq.
N.H. Rev. Stat. 1955, 264:1 et seq.

Motor Vehicle Liability Security Act
Wash. Rev. Code Ann., 46.29.010 et seq.

Motor Vehicle Liability Security Fund Act
Md. Ann. Code 1974, Art. TR, § 17-101
N.J. Stat. Ann., 39:6-92 et seq.

Motor Vehicle License Act
Ga. Code Ann., 40-2-20 et seq.
Minn. Stat. Ann., 168.09 et seq.
S.D. Codified Laws 1967, 32-5-1 et seq.
Wash. Rev. Code Ann., 46.16.006 et seq.

Motor Vehicle License Fee Law
Cal. Revenue and Taxation Code § 10701 et seq.

Motor Vehicle License Plate Issuance Act
Ga. Code Ann., 40-2-20 et seq.

Motor Vehicle License Tax Act
Ala. Code 1975, § 40-12-240 et seq.
Cal. Revenue and Taxation Code § 10701 et seq.
Fla. Stat. Ann., 320.01 et seq.
Ohio Rev. Code 1953, 4504.01 et seq.

Motor Vehicle Lien Act
D.C. Code Ann., § 40-1001 et seq.
Fla. Stat. 1981, 319.151 et seq.
Ky. Rev. Stat. 1971, 382.675
Minn. Stat. 1949, 514.35 et seq.
Neb. Rev. Stat. 1943, 60-110
S.C. Code Ann. 1976, § 29-15-20 et seq.
Wyo. Stat. 1957, § 29-102 et seq.

Motor Vehicle Lien Filing Act
Ark. Code Ann. 1987, 27-14-801, 27-14-804 et seq.

Motor Vehicle Lighting Act
Conn. Gen. Stat. Ann., § 14-96a et seq.

Motor Vehicle Management Act
S.C. Code Ann. 1976, § 1-11-220 et seq.

Motor Vehicle Manufacturer's, Dealer's, and Salesmen's Licensing Act
Pa. Purdon's Stat., Title 63, § 818.1 et seq.

Motor Vehicle Manufacturers, Distributors and Dealers Franchising Practices Act
Vt. Stat. Ann., Title 9, § 4083 et seq.

Motor Vehicle Manufacturers License Act
N.C. Gen. Stat. 1943, § 20-285 et seq.

Motor Vehicle Manufacturers or Dealers Registration Act
Kan. Stat. Ann., 8-2401 et seq.

Motor Vehicle Maximum Weight Act
See Maximum Weight Act (Motor Vehicles)

Motor Vehicle Mileage Tax Act
Mich. Comp. Laws 1948, 478.2 et seq.

Motor Vehicle Minimum Speed Act
Ohio Rev. Code 1953, 4511.22

Motor Vehicle Mortgage Lien Act
Neb. Rev. Stat. 1943, 60-110

Motor Vehicle Muffler Act
See Muffler Act (Motor Vehicles)

Motor Vehicle Negligent Homicide Act
See Negligent Homicide Act (Motor Vehicles)
Wash. Rev. Code Ann., 46.61.520

Motor Vehicle No-Fault Law
Fla. Stat. Ann., 627.730 et seq.

Motor Vehicle Noise Prevention and Control Act
Fla. Stat. Ann., 316.293, 403.415, 403.4151

Motor Vehicle Nonresident Service Act
See Nonresident Motorist Substituted Service Act

Motor Vehicle Operation Act
Mich. Comp. Laws Ann., 257.601 et seq.
S.D. Codified Laws 1967, 32-26-1 et seq.
Tex. Rev. Civ. Stat., Art. 6701d-11

Motor Vehicle Operators' and Chauffeurs' Licensing Act
Ariz. Rev. Stat. Ann., § 28-401 et seq.
Ark. Code Ann. 1987, 27-16-201 et seq.
Del. Code of 1974, Title 21, § 2701 et seq.
Ida. Code 1947, 49-301 et seq.
Ind. Code Ann., 9-1-4-26
Iowa Code Ann., 321.174 et seq.
Kan. Stat. Ann., 8-234a et seq.
Ky. Rev. Stat. 1971, 186.400 et seq.
Mich. Comp. Laws Ann., 257.301 et seq.
Mo. Rev. Stat., 302.010 et seq.
Mont. Code Ann., 61-5-101 et seq.
Nev. Rev. Stat. 1979 Reprint, 483.010 et seq.
N.M. Stat. Ann. 1953, 64-13-38 et seq.
Okla. Stat. Ann., Title 47, § 6-101 et seq.
Ore. Rev. Stat., 807.010 et seq.
R.I. Gen. Laws 1956, 31-10-1 et seq.
Tenn. Code Ann., 55-7-101 et seq.
Tex. Rev. Civ. Stat., Art. 6687b
Utah Code Ann. 1953, 41-2-102 et seq.
Va. Code 1950, § 46.1-348 et seq.

W. Va. Code 1966, § 17B-1-1 et seq.

Motor Vehicle Operators' Financial Responsibility Act
See Financial Responsibility Act (Motor Vehicles)

Motor Vehicle Operators' License Act (Uniform)
Md. Ann. Code 1974, Art. TR, § 16-101 et seq.
Mont. Code Ann., 61-5-101 et seq.
N.D. Cent. Code, 39-06-01 et seq.
Neb. Rev. Stat. 1943, 60-401 et seq.
N.H. Rev. Stat. 1955, 263:1 et seq.
R.I. Gen. Laws 1956, 31-10-1 et seq.
Utah Code Ann. 1953, 41-2-101 et seq.
Vt. Stat. Ann., Title 23, § 601 et seq.
Wash. Rev. Code Ann., 46.20.011 et seq.
Wis. Stat. Ann., 343.01 et seq.

Motor Vehicle Operators' Responsibility Act (Minors)
Ohio Rev. Code 1953, 4507.07

Motor Vehicle Owner Liability Act
Minn. Stat. Ann., 170.54

Motor Vehicle Owners and Operators Financial Responsibility Act
Utah Code Ann. 1953, 41-12A-101 et seq.

Motor Vehicle Owners' Liability Act
See Owners' Liability Act (Motor Vehicles)

Motor Vehicle Ownership Act
Mich. Comp. Laws Ann., 257.401

Motor Vehicle Parental Responsibility Law
Del. Code of 1974, Title 21 § 6105

Motor Vehicle Parking Act
See Parking Act (Motor Vehicles)

Motor Vehicle Parking Facilities Act
D.C. Code 1973, § 40-801 et seq.
Ore. Rev. Stat., 223.805 et seq.

Motor Vehicle Parking Law
Wash. Rev. Code Ann., 46.61.560 et seq.

Motor Vehicle Passing Act
Ill. Rev. Stat. 1991, Ch. 95 1/2, § 11-702 et seq.

Motor Vehicle Physical Damage Appraiser Act
Pa. Purdon's Stat., Title 63, § 851 et seq.

Motor Vehicle Point System Act
See Point System Act (Drivers of Motor Vehicles)

Motor Vehicle Pollution Control Act
Cal. Health and Safety Code § 43000 et seq.

Motor Vehicle Private Passenger Safety Act
Cal. Vehicle Code 1959, § 27315

Motor Vehicle Procurement Act
Pa. Cons. Stat., Title 62, § 3731 et seq.
Pa. Purdon's Stat., Title 73, § 1891 et seq.

Motor Vehicle Public Parking Areas Regulation Act
P.R. Laws Ann. 1954, Title 23, § 805 et seq.

Motor Vehicle Quality Assurance Act
N.M. Stat. Ann., 57-16A-1 et seq.

Motor Vehicle Racing Act (City)
Mich. Comp. Laws Ann., 257.1701 et seq.
Vt. Stat. Ann., Title 31, § 301 et seq.

Motor Vehicle Racing Act (Municipal)
Fla. Stat. Ann., 549.01

Motor Vehicle Reciprocity Act
See Reciprocity Act (Motor Vehicles)

Motor Vehicle Records Disclosure Act
See Uniform Motor Vehicle Records Disclosure Act

Motor Vehicle Recreation Act (Off-Highway)
Cal. Public Resources Code § 5090.01 et seq.

Motor Vehicle Registration Act
Ariz. Rev. Stat. Ann., § 28-301 et seq.
Cal. Vehicle Code 1959, § 4000 et seq.
Conn. Gen. Stat. Ann., § 14-12 et seq.
Del. Code of 1974, Title 21, § 2101 et seq.
Fla. Stat. Ann., 320.01 et seq.
Ga. Code Ann., 40-2-1 et seq.
Ida. Code 1947, 49-401 et seq.
Iowa Code Ann., 321.17 et seq.
Kan. Stat. Ann., 8-126 et seq.
Ky. Rev. Stat. 1971, 186.005 et seq.
La. Rev. Stat. Ann., 32:701 et seq.
Mass. Gen Laws 1990, 90:1 et seq.
Mich. Comp. Laws Ann., 257.201 et seq.
Minn. Stat. Ann., 168.09 et seq.
Mo. Rev. Stat., 301.010 et seq.
Mont. Code Ann., 61-3-301 et seq.
N.C. Gen. Stat. 1943, § 20-50 et seq.
N.D. Cent. Code, 39-04-01 et seq.
Neb. Rev. Stat. 1943, 60-301 et seq.
Nev. Rev. Stat. 1979 Reprint, 482.010 et seq.
N.H. Rev. Stat. 1955, 261:52 et seq.
Ohio Rev. Code 1953, 4503.01 et seq.
R.I. Gen. Laws 1956, 31-3-1 et seq.
Tex. Rev. Civ. Stat., Art. 6675a-1 et seq.
Utah Code Ann. 1953, 41-1-18 et seq.
Va. Code 1950, § 46.2-600 et seq.
Vt. Stat. Ann., Title 23, § 301 et seq.
Wash. Rev. Code Ann., 46.12.005 et seq.
Wis. Stat. Ann., 341.01 et seq.

Motor Vehicle Registration and Licensing Act
Ind. Code Ann., 9-1-4-1 et seq.
Okla. Stat. Ann., Title 47, § 7-335 et seq.
S.C. Code Ann. 1976, § 56-3-10 et seq.
S.D. Codified Laws 1967, 32-5-1 et seq.

Motor Vehicle Registration Code
Haw. Rev. Stat. Ann., § 286-41 et seq.
Ky. Rev. Stat. 1971, 186A.010, 186A.020

Motor Vehicle Registration Date Act
D.C. Code Ann., § 40-102

Motor Vehicle Registration Law
N.Y. Vehicle and Traffic Law 1959 (Consol. Laws Ch. 71) §§ 400 et seq., 500 et seq.

Motor Vehicle Regulatory Act
La. Rev. Stat. Ann., 32:1 et seq.

Motor Vehicle Rental Industry Act
Haw. Rev. Stat. Ann., § 437D-1 et seq.

Motor Vehicle Rental Statute
  N.J. Stat. Ann., 45:21-1 et seq.

Motor Vehicle Repair Act
  Colo. Rev. Stat., 42-11-101 et seq.
  Fla. Stat. Ann., 559.901 et seq.

Motor Vehicle Repair Shop Registration Act
  N.Y. Vehicle and Traffic Law 1959 (Consol. Laws Ch. 71) § 398 et seq.

Motor Vehicle Reparation Act
  R.I. Gen. Laws 1956, 31-47-1 et seq.

Motor Vehicle Reparations Act
  Ky. Rev. Stat. 1971, 107.770

Motor Vehicle Reporting Act (Theft and Insurance Fraud)
  Cal. Vehicle Code 1959, § 10900 et seq.

Motor Vehicle Responsibility Act (Public Passenger)
  La. Rev. Stat. Ann., 45:200.1 et seq.

Motor Vehicle Retail Installment Sales Act
  Ill. Rev. Stat. 1991, Ch. 121 1/2, § 561 et seq.
  Mich. Comp. Laws Ann., 566.301 et seq.
  Minn. Stat. Ann., 168.66 et seq.
  N.Y. Personal Property Law (Consol. Laws Ch. 41) § 301 et seq.
  S.D. Codified Laws 1967, 54-7-1 et seq.

Motor Vehicle Retail Installment Sales Finance Act
  Vt. Stat. Ann., Title 9, § 2351 et seq.

Motor Vehicle Retail Leasing Act
  N.Y. Personal Property Law (Consol. Laws Ch. 41) § 330 et seq.

Motor Vehicle Retail Sales and Use Tax Act
  Tex. Tax Code, § 152.021 et seq.

Motor Vehicle Revenues Distribution Act
  Ohio Rev. Code 1953, 4501.04

Motor Vehicle Right of Way Act
  See Right of Way Act (Motor Vehicles)

Motor Vehicle Road Toll Law
  N.H. Rev. Stat. 1955, 260:30 et seq.

Motor Vehicle Rolling Store Tax Act
  Ga. Code 1933, 92-2950 et seq.

Motor Vehicle Rules of the Road Act
  See Rules of the Road Act (Motor Vehicles)

Motor Vehicle Safe Driver Discount Act
  S.C. Code Ann. 1976, § 38-73-760 et seq.

Motor Vehicle Safety Act
  S.C. Code Ann. 1976, § 56-5-4410 et seq.

Motor Vehicle Safety Act (Commercial)
  Cal. Public Utilities Code § 3557

Motor Vehicle Safety Act (Private Passenger)
  Cal. Vehicle Code 1959, § 27315

Motor Vehicle Safety and Cost Savings Authorization Act of 1982
  Oct. 15, 1982, P.L. 97-331, 15 U.S. Code §§ 1381 nt., 1392, 1409, 1413, 1418, 1921, 1949, 1990g

Motor Vehicle Safety Equipment (Interstate Compact)
  Vt. Stat. Ann., Title 23, § 1801 et seq.

Motor Vehicle Safety Equipment Compact Act
  See Vehicle Equipment Safety Compact Act

Motor Vehicle Safety Glass Act
  Ind. Code Ann., 9-8-6-40

Motor Vehicle Safety Inspection Act
  Fla. Stat. Ann., 316.610
  Ga. Code Ann., 40-8-220 et seq.
  Miss. Code Ann. 1972, § 63-13-1 et seq.
  Utah Code Ann. 1953, 53-8-201 et seq.

Motor Vehicle Safety Responsibility Act
  Ala. Code 1975, § 32-7-1 et seq.
  Alaska Stat. 1962, § 28.20.010 et seq.
  Ariz. Rev. Stat. Ann., § 28-1101 et seq.
  Ark. Code Ann. 1987, 27-19-201 et seq.
  Colo. Rev. Stat., 42-7-101 et seq.

D.C. Code Ann., § 40-401 et seq.

Del. Code of 1974, Title 21, § 2901 et seq.

Fla. Stat. Ann., 324.011 et seq.

Ga. Code Ann., 40-9-1 et seq.

Haw. Rev. Stat. Ann., § 287-1 et seq.

Ida. Code 1947, 49-1201 et seq.

Ill. Rev. Stat. 1991, Ch. 95 1/2, § 7-100 et seq.

Iowa Code Ann., 321A.1 et seq.

Kan. Laws 1957, Ch. 68

Ky. Rev. Stat. 1971, 187.290 et seq.

La. Rev. Stat. Ann., 32:851 et seq.

Md. Ann. Code 1974, Art. TR, § 2-401 et seq.

Minn. Stat. 1971, 170.21 et seq.

Miss. Code Ann. 1972, § 63-15-1 et seq.

Mo. Rev. Stat., 303.010 et seq.

Mont. Code Ann., 61-6-101 et seq.

N.C. Gen. Stat. 1943, § 20-279t1 et seq.

N.D. Cent. Code, 39-16-01 et seq.

Neb. Rev. Stat. 1943, 60-501 et seq.

Nev. Rev. Stat. 1979 Reprint, 485.010 et seq.

N.M. Stat. Ann. 1953, 64-24-5 et seq.

N.Y. Vehicle and Traffic Law 1959 (Consol. Laws Ch. 71) § 330 et seq.

Ohio Rev. Code 1953, 4509.01 et seq.

Okla. Stat. Ann., Title 47, § 7-216 et seq.

Ore. Rev. Stat. 1953, 486.011 et seq.

Pa. Cons. Stat., Title 75, § 1701 et seq.

R.I. Gen. Laws 1956, 31-31-1 et seq.

S.C. Code Ann. 1976, § 56-9-10 et seq.

S.D. Codified Laws 1967, 32-35-1 et seq.

Tex. Rev. Civ. Stat., Art. 6701h

Utah Code Ann. 1953, 41-12A-101 et seq.

Va. Code 1950, § 46.1-388 et seq.

Wash. Rev. Code Ann., 46.29.020 et seq.

Wis. Stat. Ann., 344.01 et seq.

Wyo. Stat. Ann., § 31-9-101 et seq.

Motor Vehicle Safety-Responsibility Act
Mont. Code Ann. 1987, 61-6-101 et seq.

Motor Vehicle Safety Responsibility and Driver Improvement Act
Ind. Code Ann., 9-2-1-1 et seq.

Motor Vehicle Sales and Use Tax Act
Va. Code 1950, § 58.1-2400 et seq.

Motor Vehicle Sales Finance Act
Cal. Civil Code § 2981 et seq.

Del. Code of 1974, Title 5, § 2901 et seq.

Fla. Stat. Ann., 520.01 et seq.

Ga. Code Ann., 10-1-30 et seq.

La. Rev. Stat. Ann., 6:951 et seq.

Mass. Gen Laws 1990, 255B:1 et seq.

Me. Rev. Stat. Ann. 1964, Title 9, § 3401 et seq.

Mich. Comp. Laws Ann., 492.101 et seq.

Miss. Code Ann. 1972, § 63-19-1 et seq.

Nev. Rev. Stat. 1987, 97.297 et seq.

N.M. Stat. Ann., 58-19-1 et seq., 57-11-1 et seq.

Pa. Purdon's Stat., Title 69, § 601 et seq.

S.C. Code Ann. 1976, Superseded Vols., § 56-17-10 et seq.

Wis. Stat. Ann., 218.01

Motor Vehicle Salesmen Unlawful Practices Act
Wash. Rev. Code Ann., 46.70.180 et seq.

Motor Vehicle Salesmen's License Act
N.C. Gen. Stat. 1943, § 20-285 et seq.

Pa. Purdon's Stat., Title 63, § 818.1 et seq.

Wash. Rev. Code Ann., 46.70.005 et seq.

Motor Vehicle Seat Belt Usage Act
Utah Code Ann. 1953, 41-6-181

Motor Vehicle Security Recording Act
Miss. Code Ann. 1972, § 63-19-5

Motor Vehicle Security-Responsibility Law
N.J. Rev. Stat. 1937, 39:6-23 et seq.

Motor Vehicle Self-Insurance Act (School)
Ark. Acts 1991, No. 824

Motor Vehicle Service and Repair Act
Mich. Comp. Laws Ann., 257.1301 et seq.

Motor Vehicle Service Contract Act
Ida. Code 1947, 49-2801 et seq.

Motor Vehicle Service Contract Reimbursement Insurance Act
Neb. Rev. Stat. 1943, 44-3520 et seq.

Motor Vehicle Service Trade Practices Act
Iowa Code Ann., 537B.1 et seq.

Motor Vehicle Size and Weight Law
Ore. Rev. Stat. 1953, 483.502 et seq.

Motor Vehicle Special Fuel Use Tax Act
Mo. Rev. Stat., 142.010 et seq.

Motor Vehicle Speed Act
See Speed Act (Motor Vehicles)

Motor Vehicle Stop Act
N.C. Gen. Stat. 1943, § 20-158

Motor Vehicle Storage Act
Tenn. Code Ann., 55-23-101 et seq.

Motor Vehicle Tax Act
Minn. Stat. Ann., 168.012 et seq.

Motor Vehicle Theft Act
Cal. Statutes 1991, Ch. 930
D.C. Code 1973, § 22-2204
Mich. Comp. Laws Ann., 257.252 et seq.

Motor Vehicle Theft Act (Omnibus)
Cal. Penal Code § 186.2

Motor Vehicle Theft and Insurance Fraud Prevention Demonstration Program
N.Y. Executive Law 1951 (Consol. Laws Ch. 18) § 846i et seq.

Motor Vehicle Theft and Motor Vehicle Insurance Fraud Reporting Act
Cal. Insurance Code § 1874 et seq.
Cal. Vehicle Code 1959, § 10900 et seq.

Motor Vehicle Theft and Motor Vehicle Insurance Fraud Reporting— Immunity Act
N.J. Stat. Ann., 17:23-8 et seq.

Motor Vehicle Theft and Motor Vehicle Insurance Fraud Reporting—Immunity Act
S.C. Code Ann. 1976, § 38-77-1110 et seq.

Motor Vehicle Theft Law Enforcement Act of 1984
Oct. 25, 1984, P.L. 98-547, 15 U.S. Code §§ 1901 nt., 2021

Motor Vehicle Theft Prevention Act
Sept. 13, 1994, P.L. 103-322, 18 U.S. Code §§ 511, 511A; 42 U.S. Code §§ 13701 nt., 14171
Fla. Stat. Ann., 860.151 et seq.
Ill. Rev. Stat. 1991, Ch. 95 1/2, § 1301 et seq.

Motor Vehicle Theft Reporting Act
Ill. Comp. Stat. 1992, Ch. 625, § 10/1

Motor Vehicle Time Sales Act
Mo. Rev. Stat., 365.010 et seq.

Motor Vehicle Time Sales Disclosure Act
Ariz. Rev. Stat. Ann., § 44-294 et seq.

Motor Vehicle Title Act
See also Motor Vehicle Certificate of Title Act
Ariz. Rev. Stat. Ann., § 28-301 et seq.
Ida. Code 1947, 49-501 et seq.
Ind. Code Ann., 9-1-2-1 et seq.
Mich. Comp. Laws Ann., 257.201 et seq.
Miss. Code Ann. 1972, § 63-21-1 et seq.
Mont. Code Ann., 61-3-101 et seq.
Ohio Rev. Code 1953, 4505.01 et seq.
Okla. Stat. Ann., Title 47, § 23 et seq.

Motor Vehicle Title and Registration Act
Ark. Code Ann. 1987, 27-14-201 et seq.
Fla. Stat. Ann., 320.01 et seq.
Ga. Code Ann., 40-3-1 et seq.
Kan. Stat. Ann., 8-126 et seq.
Ohio Rev. Code 1953, 4505.01 et seq.
Tenn. Code Ann., 55-1-101 et seq.
Wash. Rev. Code Ann., 46.12.010 et seq.

Motor Vehicle Title Registration Act
Kan. Stat. Ann., 8-126 et seq.

Motor Vehicle Traffic Act
D.C. Code Ann., § 40-701 et seq.
La. Rev. Stat. Ann., 32:1 et seq.
N.J. Stat. Ann., 39:4-1 et seq.
N.M. Stat. Ann. 1953, 64-14-3 et seq.

Ore. Rev. Stat., 483.002 et seq., 811.010 et seq.

Wyo. Stat. Ann., § 31-5-101 et seq.

Motor Vehicle Transfer Act
La. Rev. Stat. Ann., 32:701 et seq.
Mich. Comp. Laws Ann., 257.233

Motor Vehicle Transportation Act
Minn. Stat. Ann., 221.011 et seq.
Ore. Rev. Stat., 481.005 et seq.
Utah Code Ann. 1953, 54-6-1 et seq.
Wis. Stat. Ann., 194.01 et seq.

Motor Vehicle Transportation License Tax Law
Cal. Revenue and Taxation Code § 9601 et seq.

Motor Vehicle Unloading Act
Tex. Rev. Civ. Stat., Art. 6701d-11 § 6

Motor Vehicle Use Tax Act
Ill. Rev. Stat. 1991, Ch. 95 1/2 § 3-1001 et seq.
Ky. Rev. Stat. 1971, 138.450 et seq.
Mo. Rev. Stat., 144.440 et seq.

Motor Vehicle Venue Act
Ohio Rev. Code 1953, 4515.01

Motor Vehicle Warranty Act
Cal. Civil Code § 1793.2, Subd. e
Colo. Rev. Stat., 42-12-101 et seq.
P.R. Laws Ann. 1954, Title 10, § 2051 et seq.

Motor Vehicle Warranty Enforcement Act
Fla. Stat. Ann., 681.110 et seq.
Miss. Code Ann. 1972, § 63-17-151 et seq.
Va. Code 1950, § 59.1-207.9 et seq.

Motor Vehicle Warranty Practices Act
Ga. Code Ann., 10-1-640 et seq.

Motor Vehicle Warranty Rights Act
Ga. Code Ann., 10-1-780 et seq.

Motor Vehicle Weight-Distance Tax Act
N.Y. Tax Law (Consol. Laws Ch. 60) § 501 et seq.

Motor Vehicle Weight Tax Act
Mich. Comp. Laws Ann., 257.801

Motor Vehicles Compulsory Financial Responsibilities Act
Cal. Vehicle Code 1959, § 16000 et seq.

Motor Vehicles Criminal Recklessness Act
Minn. Stat. Ann., 169.13

Motor Vehicles Long-Arm Law
Kan. Stat. Ann., 8-401 et seq.

Motor Vehicles No-Fault Law
Fla. Stat. Ann., 627.730

Motor Vehicles Nonresident Violator Compact
N.J. Stat. Ann., 39:5F-1 et seq.

Motor Vehicles Racing Act
N.C. Gen. Stat. 1943, § 20-141.3
Vt. Stat. Ann., Title 31, § 301 et seq.

Motor Vehicles Racing Act (Municipal)
Fla. Laws 1984, Ch. 214

Motor Vehicles Radar Act
Ohio Rev. Code 1953, 4511.091

Motor Vehicles Security Following Accident Act
Cal. Vehicle Code 1959, § 16000 et seq.

Motor Vehicles Warehouse Endorsement Act
Minn. Stat. Ann., 168.81

Motor Vehicles Warranties Act (New)
Utah Code Ann. 1953, 13-20-1 et seq.

Motor Vehicles Wreckers Act
Wash. Rev. Code 1973, 46.80.005 et seq.

Motor Vehicles Wrecking Act
Ore. Rev. Stat. 1953, 481.345 et seq.

Motor-Voter Act
Alaska Stat. 1962, § 28.05.045

Motor Voter Act
See National Voter Registration Act of 1993

Motorbike Recreation Fund Act
Ida. Code 1947, 67-71-22 et seq.

Motorboat Act
Mass. Gen Laws 1990, 90B:1 et seq.
Mich. Comp. Laws Ann., 281.1001 et seq.
Pa. Purdon's Stat., Title 55, § 483 et seq.
Vt. Stat. Ann., Title 25, § 301 et seq.

Motorboat Act of 1940
April 25, 1940, Ch. 155, 54 Stat. 163, 46 U.S.
Code §§ 526 to 526t
Sept. 2, 1958, P.L. 85-911, 72 Stat. 1756, 46
U.S. Code §§ 526l, 526o, 526u
March 28, 1960, P.L. 86-396, 74 Stat. 10, 46
U.S. Code § 526u

Motorboat Fuel Revenue Bond Act
N.M. Laws 1964, 1st Sp. Sess., Ch. 10

Motorboat Guest Act
Cal. Harbors and Navigation Code § 661.1

Motorboat Muffler Act
Mich. Comp. Laws Ann., 281.1114

Motorboat Numbering Act
Ga. Code Ann., 52-7-1 et seq.

**Motorboat Registration and Certification
Act**
Fla. Stat. Ann., 327.01 et seq., 328.01 et seq.

Motorbus Act
N.C. Gen. Stat. 1943, § 62-259 et seq.

Motorbus Road Tax Act
Pa. Cons. Stat., Title 75, § 9801 et seq.

Motorcoach Carrier Incentive Act
Ark. Acts 1997, No. 1187

Motorcycle Act (Off-Highway)
N.M. Stat. Ann., 66-3-1001 et seq.

Motorcycle Dealers' Franchise Act
Wash. Rev. Code Ann., 46.94.001 et seq.

Motorcycle Headgear Act
Mo. Rev. Stat., 1991 Supp., 302.020, Subsec.
2

Motorcycle Helmet Act
Fla. Stat. Ann., 316.211
Mich. Comp. Laws Ann., 257.658, Subd. d

Motorcycle Operators' License Act
Conn. Gen. Stat. Ann., § 14-40a

Motorcycle Racing Regulation Act
Vt. Stat. Ann., Title 31

Motorcycle Rider Education Act
Utah Code Ann. 1953, 41-26-101 et seq.

Motorcycle Rider Safety Act
Va. Code 1950, § 46.1-564 et seq.

Motorcycle Safety Act
Pa. Cons. Stat., Title 75, § 7901 et seq.

Motorcycle Safety Education Act
Neb. Rev. Stat. 1943, 60-2120 et seq.

Motorcycle Safety Program Act
Md. Ann. Code 1974, Art. TR, § 16-606 et
seq.

Motorist Act (Nonresident)
See Nonresident Motorist Act

Motorist Coverage Act (Underinsured)
S.C. Code Ann. 1976, § 38-77-160 et seq.

**Motorist Identification Data Base Program
(Uninsured)**
Utah Code Ann. 1953, 41-12a-801 et seq.

Motorist Implied Consent Law
N.H. Rev. Stat. 1955, 260:67 et seq.
Ore. Laws 1983, Ch. 338, §§ 358, 591, 593 to
596
Ore. Rev. Stat., 813.440 et seq.

Motorist Information Act
Ore. Rev. Stat., 377.700 et seq.

Motorist Law (Uninsured)
See Uninsured Motorist Act

Motorist Protection Act
Del. Code of 1974, Title 21, § 2118

Motorist Service Act (Nonresident)
See Nonresident Motorists Substituted Service Act

Motorist Violator Compact Act (Nonresident)
Mo. Rev. Stat., 544.046

Motorists' Financial Responsibility Act
See Financial Responsibility Act (Motor Vehicles)

Motorists Protection Act
Del. Code of 1974, Title 21, § 2118

Motorized Bicycle Act
D.C. Code Ann., 40-104, 40-201, 40-301

Motorized Wheelchair Warranty Act
Md. Ann. Code 1974, Art. CL, § 14-2701 et seq.
Pa. Purdon's Stat., Title 73, § 2231 et seq.

Mount Carmel Regional Port District Act
Ill. Rev. Stat. 1991, Ch. 19, § 701 et seq.

Mount Kisco Parking Authority Act
N.Y. Public Authorities Law (Consol. Laws Ch. 43A) § 1599aaa et seq.

Mount Pleasant Sewerage Loan Act
Mass. Acts 1955, Ch. 671

Mount Pleasant Water District Loan Act
Mass. Acts 1955, Ch. 664

Mount Rogers National Recreation Area Act
May 31, 1966, P.L. 89-438, 80 Stat. 190, 16 U.S. Code §§ 460r to 460r-5

Mount Rushmore Commemorative Coin Act
July 16, 1990, P.L. 101-332, 31 U.S. Code § 5112 nt.
Oct. 6, 1992, P.L. 102-390, 31 U.S. Code § 5112 nt.
Sept. 29, 1994, P.L. 103-328, 31 U.S. Code § 5112 nt.

Mount Rushmore Memorial Act of 1938
June 15, 1938, Ch. 402, 52 Stat. 694
May 22, 1940, Ch. 205, 54 Stat. 218

Mount San Jacinto Winter Park Authority Act
Cal. Statutes 1945, p. 2007

Mount St. Helens National Volcanic Monument Completion Act
Oct. 23, 1998, P.L. 105-279, 112 Stat. 2690, 16 U.S. Code § 431 nt.

Mount Vernon and Herrin Civic Center Act
Ill. Rev. Stat. 1991, Ch. 85, § 2701 et seq.

Mount Vernon City Court Act
N.Y. Laws 1922, Ch. 490, § 173 et seq.

Mount Vernon Parking Authority Act
N.Y. Public Authorities Law (Consol. Laws Ch. 43A) § 1599a et seq.

Mount Vernon Water Act
N.Y. Laws 1911, Ch. 127

Mountain Fair Authority of Towns County Act
Ga. Laws 1980, p. 3134

Mountain Park Project Act
Oct. 31, 1994, P.L. 103-434, 108 Stat. 4536

Mountain Resorts Airport Authority Act
Me. Rev. Stat. Ann. 1964, Title 10, § 7001 et seq.

Mountain Ridge Protection Act
N.C. Gen. Stat. 1943, § 113A-205 et seq.
S.C. Code Ann. 1976, § 48-49-10 et seq.

Mountains Commission Act (North Georgia)
Ga. Code 1933, 99-2701 et seq.

Mountville Water Authority Act
Ga. Laws 1982, p. 4452

Movie Act (Sunday Exhibitions)
Pa. Purdon's Stat., Title 4, § 59 et seq.

Movie Censorship Act
See Censorship Act (Motion Pictures)

Moving Cost Act (Condemnation)
Tenn. Code Ann., 29-16-114

Moving Permit Act
N.J. Stat. Ann., 40:52A-1 et seq.

Moving Picture Theater Act
Mich. Comp. Laws Ann., 29.81 et seq.

Mrs. Murphy (Civil Rights Act) Exemption
April 11, 1968, P.L. 90-284, 42 U.S. Code § 3603(b)(2)

Mrs. Ruth Q. de Prida Pension Protection Act
Cal. Education Code 1976, § 22951.5 et seq.

MTBE Public Health and Environmental Protection Act
Cal. Health and Safety Code §§ 116366; 25299.37.1
Cal. Water Code § 13285

Mudguard Act
Ill. Rev. Stat. 1991, Ch. 95 1/2, § 12-710

Mueller Act
Ill. Rev. Stat. 1939, Ch. 24, § 564 et seq.

Muffler Act (Motor Vehicles)
N.Y. Vehicle and Traffic Law 1959 (Consol. Laws Ch. 71) § 375, Subd. 31
Tex. Penal Code 1925, Arts. 797 to 797b
Tex. Rev. Civ. Stat., Art., 6701d, § 134, Subd. a

Mulcahy-White Act (Highways)
Ohio Laws, 107, p. 69

Mulct Law
Iowa Code 1971, 128.38

Mule Quarantine Act
Mich. Comp. Laws Ann., 287.101 et seq.

Mulford Act (Criminal Trespass)
Cal. Penal Code § 602.7

Mulford-Carrell Air Resources Act
Cal. Health and Safety Code § 39000 et seq.

Mullan-Gage Act (Prohibition Enforcement)
N.Y. Laws 1921, Chs. 155, 156

Multi-City Water and Sewerage Authority Act
Ga. Laws 1975, p. 3033

Multi-County Fire Protection District Act
Cal. Health and Safety Code § 14600 et seq.

Multi-County Library Act
Okla. Stat. 1961, Title 65, § 62 et seq.

Multi-Jurisdictional Tourism, Sports and Entertainment Special District Act
Fla. Laws 1994, Ch. 338

Multi-Party Accounts Act
Cal. Probate Code §§ 5100 to 5407
Minn. Stat. Ann., 528.01 et seq.

Multi-State Life and Health Insurance Resolution Facility Act
Iowa Code Ann., 508D.1 et seq.

Multi-Town Solid Waste Management Authority Act
N.Y. Public Authorities Law (Consol. Laws Ch. 43A) § 2040a et seq.

Multicounty Airport and Riverport Financing Act
Ark. Acts 1991, No. 738

Multicounty Grand Jury Act
Okla. Stat. Ann., Title 22, § 350 et seq.

Multiemployer Pension Plan Amendments Act of 1980
Sept. 26, 1980, P.L. 96-364, 29 U.S. Code § 1001 nt.
July 18, 1984, P.L. 98-369, 29 U.S. Code § 1385 nt.

Multifamily Assisted Housing Reform and Affordability Act of 1997
Oct. 27, 1997, P.L. 105-65, Title V, 12 U.S. Code § 1701 nt.
Oct. 21, 1998, P.L. 105-276, 42 U.S. Code § 1437f nt.

Multifamily Dwelling Code
Wis. Stat., 101.971 et seq.

Multifamily Housing Finance Improvement Act
Oct. 28, 1992, P.L. 102-550, 12 U.S. Code § 1707 nt.

Multifamily Housing Property Disposition Reform Act of 1994
April 11, 1994, P.L. 103-233, 12 U.S. Code § 1701 nt.

Multifamily Mortgage Foreclosure Act of 1981
Aug. 13, 1981, P.L. 97-35, 12 U.S. Code § 3701 et seq.
Nov. 30, 1983, P.L. 98-181, 12 U.S. Code § 3703
Oct. 28, 1992, P.L. 102-550, 12 U.S. Code §§ 3701, 3702, 3705, 3706

Multilateral Development Banks Procurement Act of 1988
Aug. 23, 1988, P.L. 100-418, 102 Stat. 1382, 22 U.S. Code § 262q nt.

Multilateral Export Control Enhancement Amendments Act
Aug. 23, 1988, P.L. 100-418, 102 Stat. 1364, 50 U.S. Code Appx. §§ 2401 nt., 2404, 2410a, 2413

Multilateral Investment Guarantee Agency Act
Dec. 22, 1987, P.L. 100-202, 22 U.S. Code § 290k
Dec. 19, 1989, P.L. 101-240, 22 U.S. Code § 290k-5

Multilevel and Pyramid Distributorship Act
Wyo. Stat. Ann., § 40-3-101 et seq.

Multilevel Distribution Plan Act
S.D. Codified Laws 1967, 37-254 et seq.

Multilevel or Pyramid Sales Act
N.M. Stat. Ann., 57-13-1 et seq.

Multiline Heavy Equipment Dealer Act
Ga. Code Ann., 10-1-730

Multilingual Election Materials Act
D.C. Code Ann., § 1-1309

Multimedia Waste Minimization Act (Comprehensive)
Also known as Multimedia Pollution Prevention Act
Miss. Code Ann. 1972, § 49-31-1 et seq.

Multinational Force and Observers Participation Resolution
Dec. 29, 1981, P.L. 97-132, 22 U.S. Code § 3401 nt.

Multiphasic Health Screening Act
Colo. Rev. Stat., 25-26-101 et seq.

Multiphasic Health Testing Center Act
Fla. Stat. Ann., 483.28 et seq.

Multiple Art Sales Act
Mich. Comp. Laws Ann., 442.351 et seq.

Multiple Count Act (Prosecutions)
Mont. Code Ann., 46-11-501 et seq.

Multiple County Public Health Department Act
Ill. Rev. Stat. 1987, Ch. 111 1/2, § 20c et seq.

Multiple Dwelling and Hotel Act
N.J. Stat. Ann., 55:13A-1 et seq.

Multiple Dwelling Code (New York City)
N.Y. Adm. Code 38, Ch. 26, § D26-1.0 et seq.

Multiple Dwelling Law
N.J. Stat. Ann., 55:13A-1 et seq.
N.Y. Consol. Laws, Ch. 61A

Multiple Employer Welfare Arrangement Act
Fla. Stat. Ann., 624.436 et seq.

Multiple Employer Welfare Arrangement Act (Self-Funded)
Mont. Code Ann., 33-35-101 et seq.

Multiple Lines Insurance Act
Wis. Stat. Ann., 627.06

Multiple Mineral Development Act
Dec. 24, 1970, P.L. 91-581, 84 Stat. 1573, 30 U.S. Code § 530

Multiple Offender Act
Conn. Gen. Stat. Ann., § 53a-40
Fla. Stat. Ann., 775.084
La. Rev. Stat. Ann., 15:529.1
Mass. Gen Laws 1990, 279:25
N.J. Stat. Ann., 2C:43-7, 2C:44-3
N.Y. Penal Law 1965 (Consol. Laws, Ch. 40) § 70.10
Pa. Cons. Stat., Title 18, § 1103 et seq.
Va. Code 1950, § 53-296

Multiple Party Accounts Act
Cal. Probate Code §§ 5100 to 5407
Va. Code 1950, § 6.1-125.1 et seq.

Multiple-Party Deposit Account Act
N.J. Stat. Ann., 17:16I-1 et seq.

Multiple-Person Accounts Act
See Uniform Multiple-Person Accounts Act

Multiple Residence Law
N.Y. Consol. Laws, Ch. 61B

Multiple Sentences Act
Kan. Stat. Ann., 21-4608

Multiple Textbook Act
Ind. Code Ann., 20-10.1-9-1 et seq.

Multiple Use Law
Aug. 13, 1954, Ch. 730, 68 Stat. 708, 30 U.S. Code §§ 521 et seq.
Dec. 24, 1970, P.L. 91-581, 84 Stat. 1573, 30 U.S. Code § 530

Multiple Use Rivers Act
Conn. Public Acts 1995, No. 333

Multiple-Use Sustained-Yield Act of 1960
June 12, 1960, P.L. 86-517, 74 Stat. 215, 16 U.S. Code §§ 528 to 531

Multipurpose Hazardous Waste Facility Siting Act
Fla. Stat. Ann., 403.78 et seq.

Multipurpose Small Lakes Program Act
Kan. Stat. Ann., 82a-1601 et seq.

Multistate Highway Transportation Agreement
Ariz. Rev. Stat. Ann., § 28-2301 et seq.

Multistate Highway Transportation Agreement Act
Cal. Vehicle Code 1959, § 35900 et seq.
Colo. Rev. Stat., 24-60-2501, 24-60-2502
Ida. Code 1947, 49-1901 et seq.

Multistate Motor Fuel Tax Agreement Act
Wash. Rev. Code Ann., 82.41.010 et seq.

Multistate Tax Compact
Me. Rev. Stat. Ann. 1964, Title 10, § 7101 et seq.

Multistate Tax Compact Act
Ala. Code 1975, § 40-27-1 et seq.
Alaska Stat. 1962, § 43.19.010 et seq.
Ark. Code Ann. 1987, 26-5-101 et seq.
Cal. Revenue and Taxation Code § 38001 et seq.
Colo. Rev. Stat., 24-60-1301 et seq.
D.C. Code Ann., § 47-441 et seq.
Fla. Stat. 1975, 213.15 et seq.
Haw. Rev. Stat. Ann., 255-1 et seq.
Ida. Code 1947, 63-3701 et seq.
Ill. Rev. Stat. 1973, Ch. 120, § 871 et seq.
Ind. Code Ann., 6-8-9-101 et seq.
Kan. Stat. Ann., 79-4301
Mich. Comp. Laws Ann., 205.581 et seq.
Minn. Stat. Ann., 290.171
Mo. Rev. Stat., 32.200 et seq.
Mont. Code Ann., 15-1-601 et seq.
N.D. Cent. Code, 57-59-01 et seq.
Neb. Rev. Stat. 1943, 77-2901
Nev. Rev. Stat. 1973 Reprint, 376.010 et seq.
N.M. Stat. Ann., 7-5-1 et seq.
Ore. Rev. Stat., 314.710
S.D. Codified Laws 1967, 10-54-1 et seq.
Tex. Tax Code, § 141.001 et seq.
Utah Code Ann. 1953, 59-1-801 et seq.
Wash. Rev. Code Ann., 82.56.010 et seq.
Wyo. Stat. 1957, §§ 39-375, 39-376

Muncy Act (State Industrial Home for Women)
Pa. Purdon's Stat., Title 61, § 551 et seq.

Munger-Jones Act (Back Tax)
Mo. Rev. Stat., 140.080 et seq.

Municipal Accounting Law
Ark. Code Ann. 1987, 14-59-101 et seq.

Municipal Adjustment of Assets and Liabilities Act
Wis. Stat. Ann., 66.03

Municipal Administration Act
Ore. Rev. Stat., 221.110 et seq.

Municipal Administration Act (Optional Forms)
Mass. Gen. Laws 1984, 43C:1 et seq.

Municipal Adoption of Codes and Records Act
Ill. Rev. Stat. 1991, Ch. 85, § 1000 et seq.

Municipal Aid Act
N.J. Stat. Ann., 52:27D-118.24 et seq.
N.Y. Laws 1982, Ch. 431

Municipal Airport Act
Miss. Code Ann. 1972, § 61-5-1 et seq.

Municipal Airport Authorities Act
Ill. Rev. Stat. 1991, Ch. 15 1/2, § 68.01 et seq.

Municipal Airport Loan Act
Mass. Acts 1941, Ch. 24

Municipal Airport Zoning Law
N.M. Stat. Ann., 3-39-16 et seq.

Municipal Airports Act
Alaska Stat. 1962, Replaced Titles, § 29.60.010 et seq.
Ark. Code Ann. 1987, 14-361-101 et seq.
Fla. Stat. Ann., 332.003 et seq.
Mont. Code Ann., 67-10-101 et seq.
Nev. Rev. Stat. 1973 Reprint, 496.010 et seq.
N.H. Rev. Stat. 1955, 423:1 et seq.
N.J. Stat. Ann., 40:8-1 et seq.
N.M. Stat. Ann., 3-39-1 et seq.
Okla. Stat. Ann., Title 3, § 65.1 et seq.
Tenn. Code Ann., 42-5-101 et seq.
Tex. Rev. Civ. Stat., Art. 46d-1 et seq.
Vt. Stat. Ann., Title 5, § 601 et seq.
Wash. Rev. Code Ann., 14.08.010 et seq.

Municipal Ambulance Licensing Act
Ark. Code Ann. 1987, 14-266-101 et seq.

Municipal and County Airport Law
Cal. Government Code § 50470 et seq.

Municipal and County Barrett Law
Ind. Code Ann., 36-9-18-1 et seq.

Municipal and County Flood Control Financing Act
N.J. Stat. Ann., 40A:27-1 et seq.

Municipal and County Home Rule Act
S.C. Code Ann. 1976, §§ 4-9-10 et seq., 5-5-10 et seq.

Municipal and County Industrial Development Bonds Act
Okla. Stat. Ann., Title 62, § 800 et seq.

Municipal and County Planning for Future Development Act
Fla. Stat. Ann., 163.160 et seq.

Municipal and County Police Departments Nomenclature Act
Ga. Code Ann., 35-10-1 et seq.

Municipal and County Police Pension Plan Act
Del. Code of 1974, Title 11, § 8801 et seq.

Municipal and County Sewerage Act
N.J. Stat. Ann., 40A:26A-1 et seq.

Municipal and County Solid Waste Disposal Act
Ark. Stat. 1987, 14-233-101 et seq.

Municipal and County Water Supply Act
N.J. Stat. Ann., 40A:31-1 et seq.

Municipal and Domestic Water and Wastewater System Operator Certification Act
Miss. Code Ann. 1972, § 21-27-201 et seq.

Municipal and Justice Court Act
Cal. Government Code § 71001 et seq.

Municipal and Parish Fire and Police Civil Service Law
La. Rev. Stat. Ann., 33:2531 et seq.

Municipal and Rural Domestic Ground Water Transfers Permit Act
Neb. Rev. Stat. 1943, 46-638 et seq.

Municipal and Rural Electrification Cooperative Agency Act
Me. Rev. Stat. Ann. 1964, Title 35-A, § 4101 et seq.

Municipal and School Tax Levy Validation Act
Ill. Rev. Stat. 1991, Ch. 122, §§ 407.41h, 407.42

Municipal and State Court Compact
R.I. Gen. Laws 1956, 8-18-1 et seq.

Municipal Annexation Act
See Annexation Act
Colo. Rev. Stat., 31-12-101 et seq.
N.D. Cent. Code, 40-51.2-01 et seq.

Municipal Annexation Law
N.Y. General Municipal Law (Consol. Laws, Ch. 24), § 700 et seq.

Municipal Annexation or Contraction Act
Fla. Stat. Ann., 171.011 et seq.

Municipal Assistance Corporation Act (State)
N.Y. Public Authorities Law (Consol. Laws Ch. 43A) § 3001 et seq.

Municipal Assistance Corporation for the City of New York Act
N.Y. Public Authorities Law (Consol. Laws Ch. 43A) § 3030 et seq.

Municipal Assistance Corporation for the City of Troy Act
N.Y. Public Authorities Law (Consol. Laws Ch. 43A) § 3050 et seq.

Municipal Audit Law
Ore. Rev. Stat., 297.010 et seq.

Municipal Auditing Act
Conn. Gen. Stat. Ann., § 7-391 et seq.
Ill. Rev. Stat. 1991, Ch. 24, § 8-8-1 et seq.
Ore. Rev. Stat., 297.405 et seq.

Municipal Auditing Law
Neb. Rev. Stat. 1943, 19-2901 et seq.

Municipal Auditorium Act
N.M. Stat. Ann., 5-3-1 et seq.

Municipal Auditorium Loan Act (Boston)
Mass. Acts 1957, Ch. 718

Municipal Authorities Act
Pa. Purdon's Stat., Title 53, § 301 et seq.

Municipal Automobile Renting Occupation Tax Act
Ill. Rev. Stat. 1991, Ch. 24, § 8-11-7

Municipal Automobile Renting Use Tax Act
Ill. Rev. Stat. 1991, Ch. 24, § 8-11-8

Municipal Bankruptcy Act
May 24, 1934, Ch. 345, 48 Stat. 798
Aug. 16, 1937, Ch. 657, 50 Stat. 653, 11 U.S. Code §§ 401 to 403

Municipal Bankruptcy Extension Act
April 10, 1936, Ch. 186, 49 Stat. 1198, 11 U.S. Code § 302

Municipal Biennial Budget Act
Wash. Rev. Code 1983, 35A.34.020 et seq.

Municipal Bond Act
Ala. Code 1975, § 11-81-1 et seq.
Cal. Government Code § 43600 et seq.
Ida. Code 1947, 57-201 et seq.
Mich. Comp. Laws Ann., 131.1 et seq.
Minn. Stat. Ann., 475.51 et seq.
Miss. Code Ann. 1972, § 21-33-301 et seq.

Nev. Rev. Stat. 1979 Reprint, 350.010 et seq.

N.H. Rev. Stat. 1955, 33:1 et seq.

N.J. Stat. Ann., 40:1-1 et seq.

S.C. Code Ann. 1976, § 5-21-210 et seq.

Utah Code Ann. 1953, 11-14-1 et seq.

Vt. Stat. Ann., Title 24, § 1751 et seq.

Municipal Bond Act (Industrial Building)

Tenn. Code Ann., 7-37-101 et seq., 7-55-101 et seq.

Municipal Bond Bank Act

Me. Rev. Stat. Ann. 1964, Title 30-A, § 5901 et seq.

N.D. Cent. Code, 6-09.4-01 et seq.

N.H. Rev. Stat. 1955, 35-A:1 et seq.

Vt. Stat. Ann., Title 24 § 4551 et seq.

Municipal Bond Bank Agency Act

N.Y. Public Authorities Law (Consol. Laws Ch. 43A) § 2430 et seq.

Municipal Bond Bank Authority Act

Alaska Stat. 1962, § 44.85.005 et seq.

Municipal Bond Bank Educational Institutions Bond Financing Act

N.H. Rev. Stat. 1955, 195-F:1 et seq.

Municipal Bond Bank Small Scale Power Facility Act

N.H. Rev. Stat. 1955, 374E:1 et seq.

Municipal Bond Compromise Law

Cal. Government Code § 43850 et seq.

Municipal Bond Reform Act

Ill. Rev. Stat. 1991, Ch. 24, § 8-4.1-1 et seq.

Municipal Bond Refunding Trust Act

Conn. Gen. Stat. Ann., § 3-76a et seq.

Municipal Bond Registration Act

Kan. Stat. Ann., 10-601 et seq.

N.C. Gen. Stat. 1943, § 160-40t et seq.

Vt. Stat. Ann., Title 24, § 1881 et seq.

Municipal Bond Supervision Act

Colo. Rev. Stat., 11-59-101 et seq.

Municipal Bond Validation Laws

Cal. Statutes 1911, Ch. 83, p. 95

Cal. Statutes 1913, Ch. 183, p. 329

Cal. Statutes 1915, Ch. 33, p. 41

Cal. Statutes 1921, Ch. 146, p. 146

Cal. Statutes 1927, Ch. 9, p. 6

Cal. Statutes 1929, Ch. 10, p. 16

Cal. Statutes 1931, Ch. 429, p. 983

Cal. Statutes 1933, Ch. 18, p. 44

Cal. Statutes 1935, Ch. 93, p. 444

Cal. Statutes 1935, Ch. 422, p. 1477

Municipal Borrowing Act

Minn. Stat. Ann., 475.51 et seq.

Pa. 1941 Pamph. Laws 159, No. 87

P.R. Laws Ann. 1954, Title 21, § 921 et seq.

Wis. Stat. Ann., 67.01 et seq.

Municipal Boundary Zoning Approval Act

N.Y. General Municipal Law (Consol. Laws Ch. 24) § 239m

Municipal Budget Act

Ill. Rev. Stat. 1991, Ch. 85, § 801 et seq.

Ind. Code Ann., 6-1-1-24 et seq.

Miss. Code Ann. 1972, § 21-35-1 et seq.

Mont. Code Ann., 7-6-4201 et seq.

N.D. Cent. Code, 40-40-01 et seq.

Neb. Rev. Stat. 1943, 13-502 et seq., 23-921 et seq.

N.H. Rev. Stat. 1955, 32:1 et seq.

Okla. Stat. Ann., Title 11, § 17-201 et seq.

Tenn. Code Ann., 6-56-201 et seq.

Wash. Rev. Code Ann., 35.32A.010 et seq.

Wis. Stat. Ann., 65.01 et seq.

Wyo. Stat. Ann., § 16-4-101 et seq.

Municipal Building Authority Act

Utah Code Ann. 1953, 11-29-1 et seq.

Municipal Building Commission Act

Cal. Statutes 1940, 1st Ex. Sess. Ch. 38, p. 99

Municipal Cable Television Act

N.M. Stat. Ann., 3-23A-1 et seq.

Municipal Capital Improvement Law
Pa. Purdon's Stat., Title 53, § 10501-A et seq.

Municipal Capital Reserve Act
N.C. Gen. Stat. 1943, § 160-40 et seq.

Municipal Census Act
Ala. Code 1975, § 11-47-90 et seq.

Municipal Center Act
D.C. Code 1973, § 9-201

Municipal Charter Act
N.M. Stat. Ann., 3-15-1 et seq.
Ohio Rev. Code 1953, 705.01 et seq.

Municipal Charter Amendments Law (Paramus)
N.J. Laws 1977, Ch. 100

Municipal Charter Law (Optional)
N.J. Stat. Ann., 40:69A-1 et seq.

Municipal Civil Service Act
Ark. Code Ann. 1987, 19-1301 et seq.
Cal. Government Code § 45000 et seq.
Minn. Stat. Ann., 44.01 et seq.
Miss. Code Ann. 1972, § 21-31-51 et seq.
Pa. Purdon's Stat., Title 53, § 23431 et seq.

Municipal Claims and Liens Act (Taxation)
Pa. Purdon's Stat., Title 53, § 7101 et seq.

Municipal Clerk Training Act
Ill. Rev. Stat. 1991, Ch. 144, § 61.50 et seq.

Municipal Code
Ill. Rev. Stat. 1991, Ch. 24, § 1-1-1 et seq.
Miss. Code Ann. 1972, § 21-1-1 et seq.
N.M. Stat. Ann., 3-1-1 et seq.
Okla. Stat. Ann., Title 11, § 1-101 et seq.
P.R. Laws Ann. 1954, Title 21, § 2051 et seq.
Utah Code Ann. 1953, 10-1-101 et seq.
W. Va. Code 1966, § 8-1-1 et seq.

Municipal Code Enforcement Boards Act
Fla. Stat. Ann., 162.01 et seq.

Municipal Commission Act
Minn. Stat. 1974, 414.01 et seq.

Municipal Commission Act (Herkimer)
N.Y. Laws 1910, Ch. 162

Municipal Compositions Act
See Bankruptcy Act

Municipal Condemnation Law
Tenn. Code Ann., 7-31-107 et seq.

Municipal Connecting Links Act
Ark. Code Ann. 1987, 16-17-701 et seq.

Municipal Consolidation Act
Cal. Government Code §§ 3570 et seq., 35800 et seq.
N.J. Stat. Ann., 40:43-66.35 et seq.

Municipal Consolidation or Merger Act
Pa. Cons. Stat., Title 53, § 731 et seq.

Municipal Contracting Law
Minn. Stat. Ann., 471.345

Municipal Contracts Act
N.J. Stat. Ann., 40A:11-4 et seq.

Municipal Cooperative Financing Act
Neb. Rev. Stat. 1943, 18-2401 et seq.

Municipal Corporation Bankruptcy Act
Neb. Rev. Stat. 1943, 18-2401 et seq.
Tex. Local Government Code, §§ 140.001, 140.002

Municipal Corporation, City and Village Ground Water Permit Act
Neb. Rev. Stat. 1943, 46-638 et seq.

Municipal Corporation Tunnel Act
Cal. Statutes 1951, Ch. 1347, p. 3248

Municipal Corporations Act
Ala. Code 1975, § 11-40-1 et seq.
Alaska Stat. 1962, § 29.03.010 et seq.
Cal. Government Code §§ 34000, 34301 et seq.
Ind. Code Ann., 18-1-1-1 et seq.
Kan. Stat. Ann., 12-101 et seq.

N.C. Gen. Stat. 1943, § 160A-1 et seq.
Ohio Rev. Code 1953, 701.01 et seq.

Municipal Corporations Bond Act
Wash. Rev. Code Ann., 39.44.070 et seq.

Municipal Corporations Charter Act
Md. Ann. Code 1957, Art. 23B

Municipal Corporations Classification Act
Cal. Government Code § 34100 et seq.
Pa. Purdon's Stat., Title 53, § 181 et seq.

Municipal Corporations Debt Limit Act
Wash. Rev. Code Ann., 39.36.010 et seq.

Municipal Corporations Debt Readjustment Act
Wash. Rev. Code Ann., 39.64.005 et seq.

Municipal Corporations Deposit Law
Cal. Government Code § 53630 et seq.

Municipal Corporations Funding Bond Act
Wash. Rev. Code Ann., 39.52.010 et seq.

Municipal, County, and Volunteer Fire Departments Nomenclature Act
Ga. Code Ann., 25-13-1 et seq.

Municipal-County Court Act
N.C. Gen. Stat. 1943, § 7-240 et seq.

Municipal County Court Act (Greensboro)
N.C. Laws 1949, Ch. 693
N.C. Public Laws 1909, Ch. 651

Municipal-County Court Act (Guilford)
N.C. Laws 1955, Ch. 971
N.C. Public Laws 1909, Ch. 651

Municipal Court Act
Ark. Code Ann. 1987, 16-17-201, 16-17-204 et seq.
Cal. Government Code § 71080 et seq.
Conn. Gen. Stat. Ann., § 51-127 et seq.
D.C. Code 1961, § 11-704 et set.
Mich. Comp. Laws Ann., 725.1 et seq.
Mich. Comp. Laws Ann., 730.101 et seq.
Mich. Comp. Laws Ann., 730.501 et seq.
Minn. Stat. Ann., 488.01 et seq.
Mont. Code Ann., 3-6-101 et seq.

N.H. Rev. Stat. 1955, 502:1 et seq.
Ohio Rev. Code 1953, 1901.01 et seq.
S.C. Code Ann. 1976, § 14-25-10 et seq.
Wash. Rev. Code Ann., 35.20.010 et seq.

Municipal Court Act (Atlanta)
Ga. Laws 1913, p. 145

Municipal Court Act (Brown)
Wis. Laws 1951, Ch. 383

Municipal Court Act (Chicago)
Ill. Rev. Stat. 1963, Ch. 37, § 356 et seq.

Municipal Court Act (County Seat)
Ark. Code Ann. 1987, 16-17-301 et seq.

Municipal Court Act (Highland Park)
Mich. Comp. Laws Ann., 730.101 et seq.

Municipal Court Act (Milwaukee)
Wis. Laws 1879, Ch. 256
Wis. Laws 1951, Ch. 384

Municipal Court Act (Minneapolis)
Minn. Stat. Ann., 488A.01 et seq.

Municipal Court Act (New York City)
N.Y. Laws 1902, Ch. 580

Municipal Court Act (Philadelphia)
Pa. Cons. Stat., Title 42, § 1121 et seq.

Municipal Court Act (Racine)
Wis. Laws 1951, Ch. 177

Municipal Court Act (Ripon)
Wis. Laws 1951, Ch. 179

Municipal Court Act (Shawano)
Wis. Laws 1957, Ch. 682

Municipal Court Act (St. Paul)
Minn. Stat. Ann., 488A.18 et seq.

Municipal Court and Law Department Employees' Annuity and Benefit Fund Act
Ill. Rev. Stat. 1961, Ch. 37, § 505 et seq.

Municipal Court Code (Syracuse)
N.Y. Laws 1937, Ch. 742

Municipal Court Judges Act (Los Angeles County)
Cal. Statutes 1953, Ch. 1165, p. 2664

Municipal Court Jury Code
Mich. Comp. Laws Ann., 600.1301 et seq.

Municipal Court Procedure Act
S.D. Codified Laws 1967, 15-32-1 et seq.

Municipal Courts Appeal Bond Act
Colo. Rev. Stat., 139-36-1 et seq.

Municipal Courts Code of Procedure Act
Kan. Stat. Ann., 12-4101 et seq.

Municipal Courts, Police Courts, City Courts, Mayors Courts and Justice of the Peace Courts Accounting Law
Ark. Code Ann. 1987, 16-10-201 et seq.

Municipal Courts Training Council Act
Ga. Code Ann., 36-32-20 et seq.

Municipal Criminal Court of Record Act
Okla. Stat. Ann., Title 11, § 28-101 et seq.

Municipal Debt Service Aid Law
Minn. Stat. Ann., 475A.01 et seq.

Municipal Depository Act
Mont. Code Ann., 7-6-201 et seq.

Municipal Development Act
Fla. Stat. Ann., 163.160

Municipal Development Authority Act
Tenn. Public Acts 1986, Ch. 820

Municipal Development Projects Act
Conn. Gen. Stat. Ann., § 8-186 et seq.

Municipal Distributable Aid Bond Act
Mich. Comp. Laws Ann., 141.1021 et seq.

Municipal Drainage Utility Systems Act
Tex. Local Government Code, § 402.041 et seq.

Municipal Economic Development Act
Ind. Code 1976, 18-6-4.5-1 et seq.
Vt. Stat. Ann., Title 24, § 2741 et seq.

Municipal Economic Development Act (Local Option)
Neb. Rev. Stat. 1943, 18-2701 to 18-2723

Municipal Election Act
See also Uniform Election Law
Ala. Code 1975, § 11-46-20 et seq.
Cal. Elections Code 1976, § 22600 et seq.
Colo. Rev. Stat., 31-10-101 et seq, 49-22-1 et seq.
Ga. Code Ann., 21-3-1 et seq.
Ida. Code 1947, 50-401 et seq.
N.C. Gen. Stat. 1943, § 163-279 et seq.
Neb. Rev. Stat. 1943, 19-3001 et seq.
N.M. Stat. Ann., 3-8-1 et seq.
S.C. Code Ann. 1976, § 5-15-10 et seq.
Utah Code Ann. 1953, 20-5-1 et seq., 20-5-101 et seq.

Municipal Electric Company Act
Wis. Stat. Ann., 66.073

Municipal Electric District Enabling Act
Me. Rev. Stat. Ann. 1964, Title 35-A, § 3901 et seq.

Municipal Electric Generation Act
N.M. Stat. Ann., 3-24-11 et seq.

Municipal Electric Plant Act
Miss. Code Ann. 1972, § 77-5-401 et seq.

Municipal Electric Power and Energy Act
S.C. Code Ann. 1976, § 6-23-10 et seq.

Municipal Electric Power and Energy Act (Joint)
N.C. Gen. Stat. 1943, § 159B-1 et seq.
Tenn. Code Ann., 7-52-101 et seq.

Municipal Electric Power Generation Act
Ark. Code Ann. 1987, 14-202-101 et seq.

Municipal Electric Refunding Revenue Bond Act
Ill. Rev. Stat. 1991, Ch. 111 2/3, § 110 et seq.

Municipal Electric System Financing Act
Ark. Code Ann. 1987, 14-203-101 et seq.

Municipal Electric System Tax Equivalent Law
Tenn. Public Acts 1991, Ch. 84

Municipal Emergency Procedure Act
Ore. Laws 1935, Ch. 348
Pa. 1937 Pamph. Laws 1604, No. 329
S.D. Laws 1935, Ch. 161
Tenn. Public Acts 1935, Ex. Sess., Ch. 30

Municipal Employee Relations Act
Mass. Gen Laws 1990, 150E:1 et seq.
Mich. Comp. Laws Ann., 423.201 et seq.
Vt. Stat. Ann., Title 21, § 1721 et seq.

Municipal Employees' Arbitration Act
R.I. Gen. Laws 1956, 28-9.4-1 et seq.

Municipal Employees Civil Service Enabling Act
Cal. Government Code § 45000 et seq.

Municipal Employees Collective Bargaining Act
Conn. Gen. Stat. Ann., § 7-467 et seq.

Municipal Employees Group Insurance Act
Mass. Gen. Laws 1984, 32B:1 et seq.

Municipal Employees Inducted into Land or Naval Forces Act
Ill. Rev. Stat. 1991, Ch. 24 1/2, § 149m et seq.

Municipal Employees Military Active Duty Act
Ill. Rev. Stat. 1991, Ch. 24 1/2, § 149m et seq.

Municipal Employees', Officers', and Officials' Annuity and Benefit Fund Act
Ill. Rev. Stat. 1991, Ch. 108 1/2, § 8-101 et seq.

Municipal Employees Pension Fund Act
Ill. Rev. Stat. 1961, Ch. 24, § 1008 et seq.

Municipal Employees Relations Act
Mass. Gen. Laws 1984, 150E:1 et seq.

Municipal Employees' Retirement Act
Conn. Gen. Stat. Ann., § 7-425 et seq.
Ga. Laws 1927, p. 265
Mich. Comp. Laws Ann., 38.601 et seq., 38.1501 et seq.
Miss. Code Ann. 1972, § 21-29-1 et seq.
N.C. Gen. Stat. 1943, § 128-21 et seq.
N.J. Stat. Ann., 43:13-1 et seq.
Pa. Purdon's Stat., Title 53, § 881.101 et seq.
R.I. Gen. Laws 1956, 45-21-1 et seq.
Tex. Rev. Civ. Stat., Art. 6228n
Vt. Stat. Ann., Title 24, § 5051

Municipal Employees' Retirement Act (Trust Funds)
N.J. Stat. Ann., 43:12-1.12 et seq.

Municipal Employment Relations Act
Wis. Stat. Ann., 111.70 et seq.

Municipal Energy Finance Authorities Act
Colo. Rev. Stat., 35-25-901 et seq.

Municipal Environmental Services Gross Receipts Tax Act
N.M. Stat. Ann., 7-19B-1 et seq.

Municipal Facilities Act (Revenue Producing)
Me. Rev. Stat. Ann. 1964, Title 30-A, § 5401 et seq.

Municipal Federal Grant Tax and Bond Act
Ill. Rev. Stat. 1991, Ch. 24, § 808.01 et seq.

Municipal Federal Surplus Property Authority Law
Cal. Government Code § 40500 et seq.

Municipal Finance Act
Mass. Gen Laws 1990, 44:1 et seq.
Mich. Comp. Laws 1970, 131.1 et seq.
N.H. Rev. Stat. 1955, 33:1 et seq.
N.J. Stat. Ann., 52:27-1 et seq.

Municipal Finance Agency Act
P.R. Laws Ann. 1954, Title 21, § 681 et seq.

Municipal Finance Board Act (Emergency)
Me. Rev. Stat. Ann. 1964, Title 30, § 5301 et seq.

Municipal Finance Commission Act
N.J. Stat. Ann., 52:27-1 et seq.

Municipal Finance Consolidation Act
Mont. Code Ann., 17-5-1601 et seq.

Municipal Financing Act
Ill. Laws 1983, P.A. 83-651

Municipal Fire and Police Civil Service Law
La. Rev. Stat. Ann., 33:2471 et seq.

Municipal Fire Defense Mobilization Act
Fla. Laws 1943, Ch. 27163

Municipal Fiscal Agency Act
N.C. Gen. Stat. 1943, §§ 160-404, 160-405

Municipal Fiscal Control Act
N.C. Gen. Stat. 1943, § 159-7 et seq.

Municipal Fiscal Procedures Act
Utah Code Ann. 1953, 10-6-101 et seq.
Wyo. Stat. Ann., § 16-4-101 et seq.

Municipal Forest Act
Mich. Comp. Laws Ann., 320.201 et seq.

Municipal Franchise Act
Ind. Code 1976, 18-1-21-5 et seq., 18-5-4-1 et seq.

Municipal Free Library Law
Cal. Education Code 1959, 18960 et seq.

Municipal Funding Bond Act
Okla. Stat. Ann., Title 62, §§ 391 et seq., 411 et seq.

Municipal Funds Investment Act
Ill. Rev. Stat. 1991, Ch. 146 1/2, § 3.01 et seq.

Municipal Gas Authority Law
Miss. Code Ann. 1972, § 77-6-1

Municipal Gas Distribution Act
Minn. Stat. Ann., 453A.01 et seq.

Municipal Gas System Tax Equivalent Law
Tenn. Public Acts 1991, Ch. 220

Municipal Gasoline Tax Act
N.M. Stat. Ann., 7-24A-1 et seq.

Municipal General Election Act
Ala. Code 1975, 11-46-20 et seq.

Municipal Gift Acceptance Law
Cal. Government Code §§ 37354, 37355

Municipal Governing Body Vacancy Law
N.J. Stat. Ann., 40A:16-1

Municipal Government Act
Cal. Government Code §§ 34000, 34301
N.C. Gen. Stat. 1943, § 160A-1 et seq.
S.C. Code Ann. 1976, § 5-1-10 et seq.
S.D. Codified Laws 1967, 9-1-1 et seq.

Municipal Government Act (Commission Form)
Ill. Rev. Stat. 1991, Ch. 24, § 4-1-1 et seq.

Municipal Government Act (Council-Manager Form)
S.C. Code Ann. 1976, § 5-13-10 et seq.

Municipal Government Act (Walsh)
N.J. Stat. Ann., 40:72-1 et seq.

Municipal Government Capital Improvement Act
Ala. Acts 1986, No. 234

Municipal Government Code (Uniform)
Minn. Stat. Ann., 412.015 et seq.

Municipal Government Optional Forms Act
Utah Code Ann. 1953, 10-3-1201 et seq.

Municipal Gross Receipts Tax Act
N.M. Stat. Ann., 7-19-1 et seq.

Municipal Gross Receipts Tax Act (Special)
N.M. Stat. Ann., 7-19A-1 et seq.

Municipal Gross Receipts Tax Act (Supplemental)
N.M. Stat. Ann., 7-19-10 et seq.

Municipal Group-Funded Pool Act
Kan. Stat. Ann., 12-2616 et seq.

Municipal Guard Act
P.R. Laws Ann. 1954, Title 21 § 1061 et seq.

Municipal Health and Hospitals Corporations Act
Ind. Code Ann., 16-12-21-1 et seq.

Municipal Health Facilities Corporations Act
Mich. Comp. Laws Ann., 331.1101 et seq.

Municipal Home Exemption Act
Miss. Code Ann. 1972, § 27-33-501 et seq.

Municipal Home Rule
N.J. Stat. Ann., 40:42-1 to 40:69-4

Municipal Home Rule Act
Colo. Rev. Stat., 31-2-201 et seq.
Conn. Gen. Stat. Ann., § 7-187 et seq.
Del. Code of 1974, Title 22, § 801 et seq.
Ga. Code Ann., 36-35-1 et seq.
Iowa Code Ann., 362.1 et seq.
Md. Ann. Code 1957, Art. 23A, § 9 et seq.
Me. Rev. Stat. Ann. 1964, Title 30, § 1911 et seq.
Mich. Comp. Laws 1970, 117.1 et seq.
N.D. Cent. Code, 40-05.1-01 et seq.
N.J. Stat. Ann., 40:42-1 et seq.
N.Y. Municipal Home Rule Laws (Consol. Laws, Ch. 36A) § 1 et seq.
Pa. Purdon's Stat., Title 53, § 13101 et seq.
Tex. Local Government Code, § 9.001 et seq.

Municipal Home Rule Powers Act
Fla. Stat. Ann., 166.011 et seq.

Municipal Hospital Facilities Act
N.C. Gen. Stat. 1943, § 131E-5 et seq.

Municipal Housing Act
Ariz. Rev. Stat. Ann., § 36-1401 et seq.
Iowa Code Ann., 403A.1 et seq.
Kan. Stat. Ann., 17-2337 et seq.
Mich. Comp. Laws Ann., 125.651 et seq.
Mo. Rev. Stat., 99.010 et seq.
N.J. Stat. Ann., 55:14F-1 et seq.
N.M. Stat. Ann., 3-45-1 et seq.

Municipal Housing and Redevelopment Act
Minn. Stat. 1986, 462.411 et seq.
S.D. Codified Laws 1967, 11-7-1 et seq.

Municipal Housing Authorities Act
Ala. Code 1975, § 24-1-20 et seq.
Conn. Gen. Stat. Ann., § 8-38 et seq.
Ky. Rev. Stat. 1971, 80.010 et seq.
Mont. Code Ann., 7-15-4401 et seq.
N.Y. Public Housing Law (Consol. Laws Ch. 44A) § 30 et seq.

Municipal Housing Authority Act (Buffalo)
N.Y. Public Housing Law (Consol. Laws Ch. 44A) § 403

Municipal Housing Authority Act (New Rochelle)
N.Y. Public Housing Law (Consol. Laws Ch. 44A) § 407

Municipal Housing Authority Act (Schenectady)
N.Y. Public Housing Law (Consol. Laws Ch. 44A) § 405

Municipal Housing Finance Act
Ill. Rev. Stat. 1991, Ch. 24, § 11-74.5-1 et seq.

Municipal Housing Finance Assistance Act
Conn. Gen. Stat. Ann., § 8-300 et seq.

Municipal Improvement Act
Ala. Code 1975, § 11-48-1 et seq.
Ariz. Rev. Stat. 1956, § 9-601 et seq.
Cal. Streets and Highways Code §§ 5000 et seq., 10000 et seq., 43600 et seq.
N.C. Gen. Stat. 1943, § 160-78 et seq.
S.C. Code Ann. 1976, § 5-37-10 et seq.

Municipal Improvement Bond Act
Cal. Government Code §§ 8500, 43600 et seq.
Nev. Rev. Stat. 1967 Reprint, Replaced Pages, 350.260 et seq.
Ore. Rev. Stat., 223.205 et seq.
Continued

S.D. Codified Laws 1967, 9-44-1 et seq.

Municipal Improvement District Act
Ark. Code Ann. 1987, 14-88-202 et seq.
Cal. Statutes 1927, Ch. 731, p. 1351
Kan. Stat. Ann., 12-1794 et seq.
Utah Code Ann. 1953, 11-16-1 et seq.

Municipal Improvement District Act (Bethel Island)
Cal. Statutes 1960, 1st Ex. Sess., Ch. 22

Municipal Improvement District Act (Embarcadero)
Cal. Statutes 1960, 1st Ex. Sess., Ch. 81

Municipal Improvement District Act (Estero)
Cal. Statutes 1960, 1st Ex. Sess., Ch. 82

Municipal Improvement District Act (Guadalupe Valley)
Cal. Statutes 1959, Ch. 2037, p. 4703

Municipal Improvement District Act (Montalvo)
Cal. Statutes 1955, Ch. 549, p. 1016

Municipal Improvement District Act (Solvang)
Cal. Statutes 1951, Ch. 1635, p. 3676

Municipal Improvements Act (Kline)
Wis. Laws 1931, Ch. 275

Municipal Income Tax Act
Del. Code of 1974, Title 22, § 901 et seq.
Ohio Rev. Code 1953, 718.01 et seq.

Municipal Incorporation Act
Colo. Rev. Stat., 31-1-101 et seq.
Ill. Rev. Stat. 1991, Ch. 24, § 2-2-1 et seq.
La. Rev. Stat. Ann., 33:51 et seq.
N.J. Rev. Stat. 1937, 40:123-1 et seq.

Municipal Incorporation Act (Fourth Class Cities)
Minn. Stat. 1971, 411.01 et seq.

Municipal Indebtedness Act (Public Works and Improvements)
Cal. Government Code § 43600 et seq.

Municipal Industrial and Recreational Obligations Act
Me. Rev. Stat. Ann. 1964, Title 30, § 5325 et seq.

Municipal Industrial Development Act
Ala. Code 1975, § 11-54-80 et seq.
Minn. Stat. 1986, 474.01 et seq.
N.D. Cent. Code, 40-57-01 et seq.

Municipal Infrastructure Gross Receipts Tax Act
N.M. Stat. Ann., 7-19C-1 et seq.

Municipal Infrastructure Maintenance Fee Act (Telecommunications)
Ill. Comp. Stat. 1992, Ch. 35, § 635/1 et seq.

Municipal Infrastructure Redevelopment Fund Act
Neb. Rev. Stat. 1943, 18-2601 et seq.

Municipal Initiative and Referendum Act
See Initiative and Referendum Act (Municipal)

Municipal Investigation Law
N.J. Stat. Ann., 2A:67A-1 et seq.

Municipal Investment Act
S.C. Code Ann. 1976, § 6-5-10 et seq.

Municipal Key Positions Law (Optional)
N.J. Stat. Ann., 40:46-39 et seq.

Municipal Labor Relations Act
Vt. Stat. Ann. 1959, Title 21, § 1721 et seq.

Municipal Land Reutilization Law
Mo. Rev. Stat., 92.700 et seq.

Municipal Land Use Development and Management Act
Utah Code Ann. 1953, 10-9-101 et seq.

Municipal Land Use Law
N.J. Stat. Ann., 40:55D-1 et seq.

Municipal Landfill Site Closure, Remediation and Redevelopment Act
N.J. Stat. Ann., 13:1E-116.1 et seq.

Municipal Lands Disconnection Act
Ill. Rev. Stat. 1991, Ch. 24, § 7-3-1 et seq.

Municipal Law
P.R. Laws Ann. 1954, Title 21, § 1101 et seq.

Municipal Liability Act
Mich. Comp. Laws Ann., 691.1401 et seq.
N.Y. General Municipal Law (Consol. Laws Ch. 24) § 71

Municipal Library Act
Cal. Education Code 1976, §§ 18900, 18960 et seq.

Municipal License Tax Act
P.R. Laws Ann. 1954, Title 21, § 651 et seq.

Municipal Lien Act
N.J. Stat. Ann., 2A:44-125 et seq.
N.Y. Lien Law (Consol. Laws Ch. 33) § 21

Municipal Lighting and Water Systems Act
Neb. Rev. Stat. 1943, 19-1401 et seq.
N.H. Rev. Stat. 1955, 38:2 et seq.

Municipal Lighting Maintenance District Act
Cal. Streets and Highways Code § 18600 et seq.

Municipal Loan Act (Emergency)
Mich. Comp. Laws Ann., 141.931 et seq.

Municipal Local Improvements Act
N.C. Gen. Stat. 1943, § 160A-216 et seq.

Municipal Local Option Gross Receipts Taxes Act
N.M. Stat. Ann., 7-19D-1 et seq.

Municipal Lottery Act
P.R. Laws Ann. 1954, Title 15, § 601 et seq.

Municipal Manager Form of Government Law
N.J. Stat. Ann., 40:79-1 et seq.

Municipal Mechanics' Lien Act
N.J. Stat. Ann., 2A:44-125 et seq.

Municipal Mortgage Finance Act
N.M. Stat. Ann., 58-18A-1 et seq.

Municipal Motor Vehicle Racing Act
Fla. Stat. Ann., 549.08

Municipal Natural Gas Purchasing and Distribution Act
La. Rev. Stat. Ann., 33:4546.1 et seq.

Municipal Natural Gas Regulation Act
Neb. Rev. Stat. 1943, 19-4601 et seq.

Municipal Non-Ad Valorem Tax Act
S.D. Codified Laws 1967, 10-52-1 et seq.

Municipal Officers and Employees Disclosure Act
Utah Code Ann. 1953, 67-1-1 et seq.

Municipal Officers' and Employees' Ethics Act
Utah Code Ann. 1953, 10-3-1305

Municipal Officers' Recall Law
Cal. Elections Code 1976, § 27200 et seq.

Municipal Ordinance Applicable to State Agencies - Zoning Act
S.C. Code Ann. 1976, § 6-7-830 et seq.

Municipal Ordinance Validation Act
Cal. Statutes 1947, Ch. 1199, p. 2709

Municipal Organization Act
Cal. Government Code § 35000 et seq.

Municipal Ownership Act (Public Utilities)
Ill. Rev. Stat. 1991, Ch. 24, § 11-117-1 et seq.

Municipal Park Abandonment Law
Cal. Government Code § 38501 et seq.

Municipal Park and Playground Act
Cal. Government Code § 38000 et seq.

Municipal Parking Authority Act
Kan. Stat. Ann., 13-1301 et seq.
N.D. Cent. Code, 40-61-01 et seq.

Municipal Parking Law
N.M. Stat. Ann., 3-50-1 et seq.

Municipal Parking Revenue Bond Law
Cal. Streets and Highways Code § 33800 et seq.

Municipal Parking Station Act
Okla. Stat. Ann., Title 11, § 32-101 et seq.

Municipal Pension Act
Conn. Gen. Stat. Ann., § 7-425 et seq.
Md. Ann. Code 1957, Art. 73B, § 21 et seq.
N.J. Rev. Stat., 43:13-2

Municipal Pension Act (Minneapolis)
Minn. Stat. 1971, 422.01 et seq.

Municipal Pension Plan Funding Standard and Recovery Act
Pa. Purdon's Stat., Title 53, § 895.101 et seq.

Municipal Plan and Art Commission Act
N.J. Laws 1915, p. 350, Ch. 188

Municipal Planned Unit Development Act
N.J. Stat. Ann., 40:55-54 et seq.

Municipal Planning Act
La. Rev. Stat. Ann., 33:101 et seq.
Mass. Gen Laws 1990, 41:70 et seq.
Mich. Comp. Laws Ann., 125.31 et seq.
Minn. Stat. 1949, 462.351 et seq.
N.J. Stat. Ann., 40:55-1.1 et seq.
Vt. Stat. Ann., Title 24, § 4301 et seq.
Wyo. Stat. 1957, § 15.1-71 et seq.

Municipal Planning and Enabling Act
Utah Code Ann. 1953, 10-9-19 et seq.
Wyo. Stat. Ann., § 15-1-601 et seq.

Municipal Planning and Zoning Act
Md. Ann. Code 1957, Art. 66B, §§ 1.00 et seq., 3.01 et seq.
S.D. Codified Laws 1967, 11-4-1 et seq.

Municipal Planning Commission Act
Ark. Code Ann. 1987, 14-56-402, 14-56-404, 14-56-410
Vt. Stat. Ann., Title 24, § 4321 et seq.

Municipal Plant Enabling Act
Vt. Stat. Ann., Title 30, § 2901 et seq.

Municipal Plant Lighting Act
Neb. Rev. Stat. 1943, 19-1401 et seq.

Municipal Police and Firefighter Postretirement Adjustment Act (Special Ad Hoc)
Pa. Purdon's Stat., Title 53, § 896.101 et seq.

Municipal Police Officers' Retirement Act
Mont. Code Ann., 19-9-101 et seq.
Pa. Purdon's Stat., Title 53, § 881.101 et seq.
S.D. Laws 1961, Ch. 255

Municipal Police Officers Retirement Trust Fund
Fla. Stat. Ann., 185.01 et seq.

Municipal Police Pension Fund Act
Ill. Rev. Stat. 1991, Ch. 108 1/2, § 3-101 et seq.

Municipal Poor Relief Act
Vt. Acts 1957, No. 299 et seq.

Municipal Port Authority Act
Alaska Stat. 1962, § 29.35.600 et seq.
Conn. Gen. Stat. Ann., § 7-329a et seq.
N.J. Stat. Ann., 40:68A-29 et seq.

Municipal Port District Law
Cal. Harbors and Navigation Code § 5000 et seq.

Municipal Post-War Reserve Fund and Planning Act
Fla. Laws 1943, Ch. 21893

Municipal Power Authority Act
Okla. Stat. Ann., Title 11, § 24-101 et seq.

Municipal Power District Enabling Act
Me. Rev. Stat. Ann. 1964, Title 35A, § 3901 et seq.

Municipal Powers Act
Iowa Code Ann., 364.1 et seq.

Municipal Powers and Duties Act
Alaska Stat. 1962, § 29.35.010 et seq.

Municipal Property Owner's Improvement District Law
Ark. Code Ann. 1987, 14-94-101 et seq.

Municipal Property Tax Relief Act (Supplemental)
N.J. Stat. Ann., 52:27D-118.32 et seq.

Municipal Property Tax Stabilization Act (Pinelands)
N.J. Stat. Ann., 54:1-68 et seq.

Municipal Proprietary Function Act
Neb. Rev. Stat. 1943, 18-2801 et seq.

Municipal Public Buildings Authorities Law
R.I. Gen. Laws 1956, 45-50-1 et seq.

Municipal Public Employees Labor Act
Wis. Stat. Ann., 111.70 et seq.

Municipal Public Employees Labor Relations Law
Me. Rev. Stat. Ann. 1964, Title 26, § 961 et seq.

Municipal Public Improvement Act
Ala. Code 1975, 11-48-1 et seq.

Municipal Public Liability Act
Cal. Government Code § 53051

Municipal Public Safety Act
N.J. Laws 1991, Ch. 78

Municipal Public Works Act
S.C. Code Ann. 1976, § 5-31-10 et seq.

Municipal Purchasing Act (over 500,000)
Ill. Rev. Stat. 1991, Ch. 24, § 8-10-1 et seq.

Municipal Purchasing Law
Tenn. Code Ann., 6-56-301 et seq.

Municipal Purposes Tax Assistance Act
N.J. Stat. Ann., 54:1-46 et seq.

Municipal Qualified Bond Act
N.J. Stat. Ann., 40A:3-1 et seq.

Municipal Reapportionment Act
Pa. Cons. Stat., Title 53, § 901 et seq.
Pa. Purdon's Stat., Title 53, § 11601 et seq.

Municipal Recorder's Court Act
N.C. Gen. Stat. 1943, §§ 7-109 et seq., 7A-185 et seq.

Municipal Records Act
Me. Rev. Stat. Ann. 1964, Title 30, §§ 2211, 2751 et seq.
Pa. Cons. Stat., Title 53, § 1381 et seq.

Municipal Recovery and Post War Aid Act
Tenn. Code Ann., 7-36-101 et seq.

Municipal Recreation Act
Minn. Stat. Ann., 471.15 et seq.

Municipal Redevelopment Law
N.Y. General Municipal Law (Consol. Laws Ch. 24) § 960a et seq.

Municipal Redevelopment Law (Tax Increment Financing)
N.Y. General Municipal Law (Consol. Laws Ch. 24) § 970a et seq.

Municipal Refunding Act
Mich. Comp. Laws Ann., 136.1 et seq.
Neb. Rev. Stat. 1943, 18-1101, 18-1102
Ohio Laws Vol. 116, p. 57

Municipal Refunding Bond Act
Okla. Stat. Ann., Title 62, § 421 et seq.

Municipal Reimbursement Act
N.J. Stat. Ann., 27:10-1 et seq.

Municipal Relief Loan Act
Mass. Acts 1943, Ch. 44
Mass. Acts 1951, Ch. 108
Mass. Acts 1955, Ch. 18
Mass. Acts 1959, Ch. 329
Mass. Acts 1962, Ch. 502
Continued

Municipal Rent Control Enabling Act
N.J. Stat. Ann., 2A:42-14 et seq.

Municipal Retailers Occupation Tax Act
Ill. Rev. Stat. 1991, Ch. 24, § 8-11-1.3; Ch. 120, § 440 et seq.

Municipal Retailers Occupation Tax Act (Home Rule)
Ill. Rev. Stat. 1991, Ch. 24, § 8-11-1

Municipal Retirement Act
Pa. Purdon's Stat., Title 53, § 881.101 et seq.
S.D. Codified Laws 1967, 9-16-1 et seq.

Municipal Retirement Fund Act
Ill. Rev. Stat. 1991, Ch. 108 1/2, § 7-101 et seq.
Wis. Stat. Ann., 40.20 et seq.

Municipal Retirement Law (Special Cities)
Tex. Rev. Civ. Stat., Art. 6235a-1

Municipal Retirement System Act
Neb. Laws 1945, Ch. 37
Tex. Rev. Civ. Stat., Art. 6243h

Municipal Revenue Act
Iowa Code Ann., 384.80 et seq.

Municipal Revenue Bonds Act
Ala. Code 1975, § 11-81-140 et seq.
Alaska Stat. 1962, § 29.47.240 et seq.
Ariz. Rev. Stat. Ann., § 9-521 et seq.
Mont. Code Ann., 7-7-4401 et seq.
Wash. Rev. Code Ann., 35.41.010 et seq.

Municipal Sales and Use Tax Act
Tex. Tax Code, § 321.001 et seq.

Municipal Sanitation and Sewerage Enterprise Contract Act
Cal. Government Code § 54725 et seq.

Municipal Securities Act
Tenn. Code Ann., Superseded Vol., 9-1401 et seq.

Municipal Securities Approval Act
Me. Rev. Stat. Ann. 1964, Title 30, § 5325 et seq.

Municipal Securities Recording Act
N.C. Gen. Stat. 1943, § 160-406 et seq.

Municipal Service Administration Act
P.R. Laws Ann. 1954, Title 21, § 1031 et seq.

Municipal Service District Act
N.C. Gen. Stat. 1943, § 160A-535 et seq.

Municipal Service Occupation Tax Act
Ill. Rev. Stat. 1991, Ch. 24, § 8-11-5

Municipal Service Occupation Tax Act (Home Rule)
Ill. Comp. Stat. 1992, Ch. 65, § 5/8-11-5

Municipal Sewage Disposal District Act
Cal. Health and Safety Code § 5700 et seq.

Municipal Sewer and Water Facilities Law
Cal. Health and Safety Code § 4600 et seq.

Municipal Sewer District Act
Cal. Health and Safety Code § 4659 et seq.
Cal. Statutes 1939, Ch. 24, p. 37

Municipal Slum Clearance Act
Ill. Rev. Stat. 1991, Ch. 24, § 11-11-1

Municipal Solid Waste Management, Resource Recovery, and Conservation Act
Tex. Health and Safety Code, § 363.001 et seq.

Municipal Street and Parking Revenue Bond Act
Ark. Code Ann. 1987, 14-302-101 et seq.

Municipal Street Railway Bonds Act
Wash. Rev. Code 1951, 35.93.010 et seq.

Municipal Subdivision Control Act
N.C. Gen. Stat. 1943, § 160A-371 et seq.

Municipal Surplus Funds Investment Law
Cal. Government Code § 53600 et seq.

Municipal Tax Authorization Act (Video Programming)
Pa. Purdon's Stat., Title 72, § 6171 et seq.

Municipal Tax Claims Act
Pa. Purdon's Stat., Title 53, § 7101 et seq.

Municipal Tax Compliance Act
Ill. Rev. Stat. 1991, Ch. 24, § 1551 et seq.

Municipal Tax Exemption Reimbursement Act (Enterprise Zone)
Pa. Purdon's Stat., Title 72, § 4729-1

Municipal Tax Lien Act
Conn. Gen. Stat. Ann., § 12-171 et seq.
Pa. Purdon's Stat., Title 53, § 7101 et seq.

Municipal Tax Validation Act
Ill. Rev. Stat. 1991, Ch. 24, §§ 1650, 1651

Municipal Tollway Authority Act
Ark. Code Ann. 1987, 14-303-101 et seq.

Municipal Tort Claims Act
Iowa Code Ann., 613A.1 et seq.

Municipal Traffic Bail Bond Procedure Act
Okla. Stat. Ann., Title 22, §§ 1115 to 1115.5

Municipal Training Act
Ga. Code Ann., 36-45-1 et seq.

Municipal Transit Law
N.M. Stat. Ann., 3-52-1 et seq.

Municipal Transportation Authority Act
Ill. Rev. Stat. 1991, Ch. 111 2/3, § 301 et seq.

Municipal Tuberculosis Sanitarium Act
Ill. Rev. Stat. 1991, Ch. 24, § 11-29-1 et seq.

Municipal Tunnel Authority Act
Cal. Statutes 1951, Ch. 1347, p. 3248

Municipal Unclaimed Moneys Act
Pa. Purdon's Stat., Title 27, § 491 et seq.

Municipal Use Tax Act
Ill. Rev. Stat. 1991, Ch. 24, § 8-11-6
N.Y. City Adm. Code 1938, Ch. 46, § M46-15.0 et seq.

Municipal Use Tax Act (Home Rule)
Ill. Rev. Stat. 1991, Ch. 24, § 8-11-6

Municipal User Tax Act (Income)
Del. Code of 1974, Title 22, § 901 et seq.

Municipal Usufruct for Passive Recreation Parks Act
P.R. Laws Ann. 1954, Title 21 § 1093 et seq.

Municipal Utilities Act
Ind. Code Ann., 8-1-11.1-3 et seq.
Wash. Rev. Code Ann., 35.92.010 et seq.

Municipal Utilities Authorities Law
N.J. Stat. Ann., 40:14B-1 et seq.

Municipal Utilities Lease Act
Wash. Rev. Code Ann., 35.94.010 et seq.

Municipal Utilities Sale Act
Wash. Rev. Code Ann., 35.94.010 et seq.

Municipal Utility District Act
Cal. Public Utilities Code § 11501 et seq.

Municipal Utility Revenue Bond Act
Okla. Stat. Ann., Title 11, § 22-150 et seq.

Municipal Vacancy Law
N.J. Stat. Ann., 40A:16-1 et seq.

Municipal Ward Law
N.J. Stat. Ann., 40:44-9 et seq.

Municipal Waste Planning, Recycling and Waste Reduction Act
Pa. Purdon's Stat., Title 53, § 4000.101 et seq.

Municipal Wastewater Disposal Zones Act
Ill. Rev. Stat. 1991, Ch. 24, § 1400 et seq.

Municipal Wastewater Treatment Construction Grant Amendments of 1981
Dec. 29, 1981, P.L. 97-117, 33 U.S. Code § 1251 nt.

Municipal Water and Sewer Department Accounting Law
Ark. Code Ann. 1987, 14-237-101 et seq.

Municipal Water and Sewer Facilities Act
Wash. Rev. Code Ann., 35.91.010 et seq.

Municipal Water District Act
Cal. Statutes 1935, Ch. 78, p. 423
Cal. Water Code § 71000 et seq.
Cal. Water Code Appendix, § 41-1 et seq.
Wis. Stat. Ann., 198.22

Municipal Water Finance Authority Act (Albany)
N.Y. Public Authorities Law (Consol. Laws, Ch. 43A), § 1115a et seq.

Municipal Water Finance Authority Act (New York City)
N.Y. Public Authorities Law (Consol. Laws, Ch. 43A), § 1045a et seq.

Municipal Water Supply Authorities Act
Mich. Comp. Laws Ann., 124.251 et seq.

Municipal Water Systems Act (Joint)
S.C. Code Ann. 1976, § 6-25-10 et seq.

Municipal Waterfront Development Act
Ohio Rev. Code 1953, 721.11

Municipal Waterworks Act
S.C. Code Ann. 1976, § 5-31-10 et seq.

Municipal Weed Abatement Act
Cal. Government Code §§ 39501, 39560 et seq.

Municipal Workhouse Law
Tenn. Code Ann., 41-3-101 et seq.

Municipal Youth Guidance Council Act
N.J. Stat. Ann., 9:22-1 et seq.

Municipal Zoning Act
Conn. Gen. Stat. 1983, § 8-2 et seq.
Ind. Code Ann., 36-7-1-1 et seq.
Kan. Stat. Ann., 12-715b et seq.
Mass. Gen. Laws Ann., 40A:1 et seq.
Me. Rev. Stat. Ann. 1964, Title 30, § 4951 et seq.
Mont. Code Ann., 76-2-301 et seq.
N.C. Stat. 1943, § 160A-381 et seq.
Okla. Stat. Ann., Title 19, § 866.2
S.D. Codified Laws 1967, 11-4-1 et seq.

Municipal Zoning and Planning Act
Ga. Code 1933, 69-801 et seq.

Municipal Zoning Enabling Act
Ala. Code 1975, § 11-52-70 et seq.
Ariz. Rev. Stat. Ann., § 9-461 et seq.
Colo. Rev. Stat., 31-23-301 et seq.
Conn. Gen. Stat. Ann., § 8-1 et seq.
Del. Code of 1974, Title 22, § 301 et seq.
Fla. Stat. 1971, 163.160 et seq.
Ill. Rev. Stat. 1991, Ch. 24, § 11-13-1 et seq.
Ind. Code Ann., 36-7-1-1 et seq.
Iowa Code Ann., 414.1 et seq.
La. Rev. Stat. Ann., 33:4721 et seq.
Mass. Gen Laws 1990, 40A:1 et seq.
Me. Rev. Stat. Ann. 1964, Title 30, §§ 2411, 4961 et seq.
Mont. Code Ann., 76-2-301 et seq.
N.C. Gen. Stat. 1943, § 160A-381 et seq.
N.D. Cent. Code, 40-47-01 et seq.
N.J. Rev. Stat. 1937, 40:55D-62 et seq.
Ohio Rev. Code 1953, 713.06 et seq.
Okla. Stat. Ann., Title 11, § 43-101 et seq.
Ore. Rev. Stat., 227.010 et seq.
S.D. Codified Laws 1967, 11-4-1 et seq.
Tenn. Code Ann., 13-7-201 et seq.
Tex. Local Government Code, § 211.001 et seq.
Utah Code Ann. 1953, 10-9-1 et seq.
Vt. Stat. Ann., Title 24
Wash. Rev. Code Ann., 35.63.010 et seq.

Municipalities Act
N.J. Stat. Ann., 40:42-1 et seq.

Municipalities Act (Financially Distressed)
Pa. Purdon's Stat., Title 53, § 11701.101 et seq.

Municipalities and Counties Hydroelectric Power Development Revenue Bond Law
Ark. Code Ann. 1987, 14-204-101 et seq.

Municipalities and Counties Industrial Development Revenue Bond Law
Ark. Code Ann. 1987, 14-164-201 et seq.

Municipalities Budget Act
Okla. Stat. 1981, Title 2, § 17-201 et seq.

Municipalities, Counties, Utility Districts and Education Agencies Act (Financially Distressed)
Tenn. Code Ann., 9-13-301 et seq.

Municipalities Financial Recovery Act
Pa. Purdon's Stat., Title 53, § 11701.101 et seq.

Municipalities for Urban Residential Finance Authorities Act (Large)
Ga. Code Ann., 36-41-1 et seq.

Municipalities Official Map Act
Me. Rev. Stat. 1964, Title 30, § 4964

Municipalities Planning Code
Pa. Purdon's Stat., Title 53, § 10101 et seq.

Municipalities Public Improvement Act
Ind. Code 1976, 19-8-16-1 et seq.

Municipalities-Sales and Use Tax Act
Tex. Tax Code, § 321.001 et seq.

Municipalities, Sales and Use Taxes, Local Option Revenue Act
Neb. Rev. Stat. 1943, 77-27, 142 et seq.

Municipalities Traffic Engineering Act
Ind. Code Ann., 18-4-19-1 et seq.

Municipality and Sanitary District Mutual Expenditure Act
Ill. Rev. Stat. 1991, Ch. 85, § 1620 et seq.

Municipality Authorities Act
Pa. Purdon's Stat., Title 53, § 301 et seq.

Municipality Tax Collection Act (Brevard County)
Fla. Laws 1961, Ch. 61-1917

Municipality Tax Collection Act (St. Lucie County)
Fla. Laws 1963, Ch. 63-1858

Munition Manufacturer's Tax Act of 1916
Sept. 8, 1916, Ch. 463, 39 Stat. 780

Munshaw-Bischoff Act (Emergency Foreclosure)
Mich. Public Acts 1933, No. 98

Munshaw-Frey Act (Prison Industries)
Mich. Comp. Laws 1948, 800.301 et seq.

Murder Act
Cal. Penal Code § 189
Colo. Rev. Stat., 18-3-101 et seq.
Ill. Rev. Stat. 1991, Ch. 38, § 9-1
Kan. Stat. Ann., 21-3401
Md. Ann. Code 1957, Art. 27, § 407 et seq.
Mich. Comp. Laws Ann., 750.316 et seq.
Mont. Code Ann., 45-5-101 et seq.
N.H. Rev. Stat. 1955, 630:1 et seq.
N.M. Stat. Ann., 30-2-1
Pa. Cons. Stat., Title 18, § 2502 et seq.
R.I. Gen. Laws 1956, 11-23-1 et seq.
Tex. Penal Code, § 19.01 et seq.
Vt. Stat. Ann., Title 13, § 2301 et seq.
Wash. Rev. Code Ann., 9A.32.010 et seq.

Murder by Poison Act
Cal. Penal Code § 189

Murder Statute (Probate)
Fla. Stat. Ann., 732.802

Murder Without Malice Act
Tex. Penal Code, § 19.04, 19.05

Murderers Act (Out of State Arrest and Conviction)
Ill. Rev. Stat. 1991, Ch. 60, §§ 50, 51

Murdy-J. Howard Williams-Abshire-Maloney-John McCarthy Bill (Average Annual Earnings)
Cal. Statutes 1955, Ch. 956, p. 1851

Murphy Act (Highway Bridges)
Ky. Rev. Stat. 1971, 180.010 et seq.

Murphy Act (Prohibition Amendment Repeal)
N.C. Public Laws 1933, Ch. 403

Murphy Act (State Tax Certificates)
Fla. Stat. 1983, 197.366 et seq.

Murphy Toll Bridge Act
Ky. Rev. Stat. 1971, 180.020 et seq.

Murrah Crime Victims Compensation Act
Okla. Stat. Ann., Title 21, § 142.31 et seq.

Murrah Federal Building Commemorative Flag Act (Alfred P.)
Okla. Stat. Ann., Title 25, § 93.2

Murray-Beverly Small Business Bridge Loan Program
Cal. Statutes 1992, Ch. 61

Murray-Chatsworth Water and Sewage Authority Act
Ga. Laws 1981, p. 3779

Murray County Water and Sewer Authority Act
Ga. Laws 1980, p. 3447

Murray H. Dubbin Act (Educational Facilities Construction)
Fla. Stat. 1977, 235.001 et seq.

Murray Prior Lien Law
N.Y. Multiple Dwelling Law 1946 (Consol. Laws Ch. 61A) § 307

Murtagh-Jackson Law (Workman's Compensation)
N.Y. Laws 1913, Ch. 816
N.Y. Laws 1914, Ch. 41

Muscle Shoals Act
See Tennessee Valley Authority Act of 1933

Muscogee County Building Code Authority Act
Ga. Laws 1951, p. 2729

Muscogee County Charter Commission Act
Ga. Laws 1969, p. 3571

Muscogee County Pension Fund Act
Ga. Laws 1945, p. 1100

Museum Act
Mich. Comp. Laws Ann., 399.301 et seq.
Mo. Rev. Stat. 1969, 184.020 et seq.
N.M. Stat. Ann., 18-3-1 et seq.

Museum Advisory Board Act (Iron Industry)
Mich. Comp. Laws Ann., 399.71 et seq.

Museum and Aquarium Act (Park District)
Ill. Rev. Stat. 1991, Ch. 105, § 325h et seq.

Museum and Cultural Center Act
Ark. Code Ann. 1987, 13-5-301 et seq.

Museum and Library Services Act
Dec. 1, 1997, P.L. 105-128, 20 U.S. Code §§ 9105, 9122, 9131, 9133, 9161, 9162

Museum and Library Services Act of 1996
Sept. 30, 1996, P.L. 104-208, 20 U.S. Code § 9101 nt.

Museum and Library Services Technical and Conforming Amendments of 1997
Dec. 1, 1997, P.L. 105-128, 20 U.S. Code § 9101 nt.

Museum Construction Act
Ill. Rev. Stat. 1991, Ch. 127, §§ 59.01, 59.1

Museum Development and Educational Research Act
N.J. Stat. Ann., 18A:73-44 et seq.

Museum Disposition of Property Act
Ill. Comp. Stat. 1992, Ch. 765, § 1033/1 et seq.

Museum District Act
Ill. Rev. Stat. 1991, Ch. 85, § 6800 et seq.

Museum Districts Act
Wyo. Stat. Ann., § 18-10-201 et seq.

Museum Donation Act
Tenn. Code Ann., 4-12-301 et seq.

Museum Inventory Act
Tenn. Code Ann., 4-12-201 et seq.

Museum Loan Act
Mont. Code Ann., 22-3-501 et seq.

Museum Planetarium Act
N.Y. Arts and Cultural Affairs Law (Consol. Laws Ch. 11C) § 59.01 et seq.
N.Y. Public Authorities Law (Consol. Laws Ch. 43A) § 1625 et seq.

Museum Property Act
Iowa Code Ann., 305B.1 et seq.
Kan. Stat. Ann., 58-4001 et seq.
Mo. Laws 1991, S.B. No. 344
Mo. Rev. Stat., 184.101 et seq.
Neb. Rev. Stat. 1943, 51-701 to 51-712
N.H. Rev. Stat. 1955, 201-E:1 et seq.

Museum Services Act
Oct. 8, 1976, P.L. 94-462, 90 Stat. 1975, 20 U.S. Code §§ 958, 961-968
May 31, 1984, P.L. 98-306, 20 U.S. Code §§ 962 to 964
Dec. 20, 1985, P.L. 99-194, 20 U.S. Code §§ 963, 964, 967
Nov. 5, 1990, P.L. 101-512, 20 U.S. Code §§ 963-965, 967, 969
Sept. 30, 1996, P.L. 104-208, 20 U.S. Code §§ 961, 961 nt., 962 to 969, 9101 nt., 9101 to 9106, prec. 9121, 9121 to 9123, prec. 9131, 9131 to 9134, prec. 9141, 9141, prec. 9151, 9151, prec. 9161, 9161 to 9163, prec. 9171, 9171 to 9176

Museum Unclaimed Property Act
Miss. Code Ann. 1972, § 39-19-1 et seq.

Mushroom Promotion, Research, and Consumer Information Act of 1990
Nov. 28, 1990, P.L. 101-624, 7 U.S. Code §§ 6101 to 6112

Music Hall of Fame Authority Act
Ga. Code Ann., 12-3-520 et seq.

Music Licensing and Copyright Enforcement Act
Ida. Code 1947, 48-1301 et seq.

Music Licensing Fees Act
Iowa Code Ann., 549.1 et seq.

Music Licensing Practices Act
N.J. Stat. Ann., 56:3A-1 et seq.

Musical Arts Corporation Act
P.R. Laws Ann. 1954, Title 18, § 1165 et seq.

Musician Booking Agency Act
Cal. Business and Professions Code § 9999 et seq.

Muskrat Farm Licensing Act
Wis. Stat. Ann., 29.575

Musmanno Law (Revolutionary Organizations)
Pa. Purdon's Stat., Title 18, § 3811

Mussels Law
Iowa Code 1985, 109.99 et seq.

Mustering-Out Payment Act of 1944
Feb. 3, 1944, Ch. 9, 58 Stat. 8 (See 38 U.S. Code §§ 101, 2101 to 2104)
Dec. 16, 1944, Ch. 599, 58 Stat. 812 (See 38 U.S. Code § 2104)
Oct. 6, 1945, Ch. 393, 59 Stat. 540 (See 38 U.S. Code §§ 2102, 2104)
June 28, 1947, Ch. 162, 61 Stat. 192 (See 38 U.S. Code § 2101)
May 19, 1948, Ch. 312, 62 Stat. 241 (See 38 U.S. Code § 2104)

Mutilated Evidence of Indebtedness Act
Ill. Rev. Stat. 1991, Ch. 130, §§ 42.9, 43

Muttontown Utility Tax Law
N.Y. Local Laws 1971, Village of Muttontown, p. 4255

Mutual Aid Act
Fla. Stat. Ann., 23.12 et seq.
Ga. Code Ann., 36-69-1 et seq.
N.M. Stat. Ann., 29-8-1 et seq.

Mutual Aid Compact (Interstate)
Mont. Code Ann. 1987, 10-3-204, 10-3-207, 10-3-208

Mutual Aid Fire Protection Act
Vt. Stat. Ann., Title 20, § 2981 et seq.

Mutual Aid Peace Officer Powers Act
Wash. Rev. Code Ann., 10.93.001 et seq.

Mutual Aid Resources Pact Act
Ga. Code Ann., 25-6-1 et seq.

Mutual and Miscellaneous Corporation Act (Nonprofit)
Wash. Rev. Code 1983, 24.06.900

Mutual Assessment Act of 1893
Ill. Rev. Stat. 1935, Ch. 73, § 302 et seq.

Mutual Assistance Act (Law Enforcement)
W. Va. Code 1966 §§ 15-10-1 to 15-10-4

Mutual Assistance Compact Act (National Guard)
See National Guard Mutual Assistance Compact Act

Mutual Assistance Counter-Drug Activities Compact Law (National Guard)
Ala. Code 1975, §§ 31-11-1, 31-11-2
Miss. Code Ann. 1972, §§ 33-7-501, 33-7-503
S.C. Code Ann. 1976, §§ 1-3-490, 1-3-491
Va. Code 1950, § 44-75.1:1

Mutual Benefit Association Act
Colo. Rev. Stat., 10-12-301 et seq.

Mutual Benefit Association Act (Insurance)
Ill. Rev. Stat. 1935, Ch. 73, § 505 et seq.
Okla. Stat. Ann., Title 36, § 2401 et seq.

Mutual Benefit Corporation Act (Nonprofit)
Cal. Corporation Code § 7110 et seq.

Mutual Building, Loan and Homestead Associations Act
Ill. Rev. Stat. 1991, Ch. 17, § 3600 et seq.

Mutual Company Act (Employers)
N.M. Stat. Ann., 52-9-1 et seq.

Mutual Corporation Act
Wash. Rev. Code Ann., 24.06.005 et seq.

Mutual Defense Assistance Act
Oct. 6, 1949, Ch. 626, 63 Stat. 714
July 26, 1950, Ch. 491, 64 Stat. 373
June 20, 1952, Ch. 449, 66 Stat. 148
July 16, 1953, Ch. 195, 67 Stat. 160

Mutual Defense Assistance Control Act of 1951
Oct. 26, 1951, Ch. 575, 65 Stat. 644
Sept. 4, 1961, P.L. 87-195, 75 Stat. 463, 22 U.S. Code § 1613d

Mutual Demurrage Act
Kan. Stat. Ann., 66-168, 66-201 et seq.

Mutual Deposit Guaranty Associations Act
N.C. Gen. Stat. 1943, § 54B-236 et seq.

Mutual Domestic Water Consumers Act
N.M. Stat. Ann. 1953, Superseded Vol., 14-40-58 et seq.

Mutual Drainage Act
Ill. Rev. Stat. 1955, Ch. 42, § 193 et seq.

Mutual Educational and Cultural Exchange Act of 1961
Sept. 21, 1961, P.L. 87-256, 75 Stat. 527, 8 U.S. Code §§ 1101, 1182, 1258; 22 U.S. Code §§ 1431, 1434 nt., 1439 nt., 1440 nt., 1448 nt., 1466 nt., 1467 nt., 1468 nt., 2451 to 2458; 26 U.S. Code §§ 117, 871, 872, 1441, 3121, 3306, 3401, 3402; 42 U.S. Code § 410; 50 U.S. Code Appx. § 1641
Aug. 1, 1962, P.L. 87-565, 76 Stat. 253, 22 U.S. Code § 2452
Oct. 11, 1962, P.L. 87-793, 76 Stat. 865, 22 U.S. Code § 2454
Oct. 29, 1966, P.L. 89-698, 80 Stat. 1071, 22 U.S. Code §§ 2452, 2454, 2455
Aug. 15, 1979, P.L. 96-60, 22 U.S. Code §§ 2454 repealed, 2456, 2456 nt., 2458, 2458a
Nov. 22, 1983, P.L. 98-164, 22 U.S. Code §§ 2452, 2460
Dec. 22, 1987, P.L. 100-204, 22 U.S. Code § 2460
Feb. 16, 1990, P.L. 101-246, 22 U.S. Code §§ 2456, 2460, 2461
June 13, 1991, P.L. 102-54, 22 U.S. Code § 2456

Dec. 17, 1993, P.L. 103-199, 22 U.S. Code
§§ 2460, 2461

April 30, 1994, P.L. 103-236, 22 U.S. Code
§§ 2454, 2460

Oct. 7, 1998, P.L. 105-244, 22 U.S. Code
§ 2460

Oct. 21, 1998, P.L. 105-277, 22 U.S. Code
§§ 2456, 2460

Oct. 27, 1998, P.L. 105-292, 22 U.S. Code
§ 2452

Mutual Expenditure Act (Municipality and Sanitary District)

Ill. Rev. Stat. 1991, Ch. 85, § 1620 et seq.

Mutual Insurance Act

Ill. Rev. Stat. 1935, Ch. 73, § 376 et seq.

Mich. Comp. Laws Ann., 500.5400 et seq.

Mo. Rev. Stat. 1983, 379.205 et seq.

Ohio Rev. Code 1953, 3913.01 et seq.

Okla. Stat. Ann., Title 36, § 201 et seq.

S.D. Codified Laws 1967, 58-36-1 et seq.

Wash. Rev. Code Ann., 48.09.010 et seq.

Mutual Insurance Company Act (County, Town, Farm)

Mo. Rev. Stat., 380.011 et seq.

Mutual Insurance Company Act (Farm)

Ill. Rev. Stat. 1991, Ch. 73, §§ 1251 to 1267

Mutual Insurance Company Act (Professional Association)

Neb. Rev. Stat. 1943, 4-3101 et seq.

Mutual Insurance Company Conversion, Reorganization and Merger Act

Miss. Code Ann. 1972, § 83-31-101 et seq.

Mutual Insurance Holding Company Act

Neb. Rev. Stat. 1943, 44-6122 to 44-6142

Mutual Life Insurance Company Reorganization Act

Pa. Purdon's Stat., Title 40, § 1010.21 et seq.

Mutual Military Aid Compact Act

Pa. Cons. Stat., Title 51, § 4501

Mutual Military Aid in an Emergency (Interstate Compact)

Conn. Gen. Stat. Ann., § 27-38

Mutual Nonprofit Hospital Service Corporation Act

Kan. Stat. Ann., 40-1801 et seq.

Mutual Participation Program Act

Fla. Stat. Ann., 947.135

Mutual Savings and Loan Holding Company Act

Tenn. Code Ann., 45-3-1501 et seq.

Mutual Savings Bank Act

Alaska Stat. 1962, § 06.15.010 et seq.

Ohio Rev. Code 1953, 1123.01 et seq.

P.R. Laws Ann. 1954, Title 7 § 1001 et seq.

Wash. Rev. Code Ann., 32.04.010 et seq.

Mutual Security Act of 1951

Oct. 10, 1951, Ch. 479, 65 Stat. 373

April 5, 1952, Ch. 159, 66 Stat. 43, 22 U.S.
Code §§ 272b, 281b, 290a, 1434

June 20, 1952, Ch. 449, 66 Stat. 141, 7 U.S.
Code § 612c; 22 U.S. Code § 286b

July 16, 1953, Ch. 195, 67 Stat. 152

Mutual Security Act of 1952

June 20, 1952, Ch. 449, 66 Stat. 141, 7 U.S.
Code § 612c; 22 U.S. Code § 266b; 50 U.S.
Code Appx. § 1641

Mutual Security Act of 1953

July 16, 1953, Ch. 195, 67 Stat. 152

Mutual Security Act of 1954

Aug. 26, 1954, Ch. 937, 68 Stat. 832

Sept. 3, 1954, Ch. 1262, 68 Stat. 1223

July 8, 1955, Ch. 301, 69 Stat. 283

July 18, 1956, Ch. 627, 70 Stat. 555

July 31, 1956, Ch. 804, 70 Stat. 740

Aug. 14, 1957, P.L. 85-141, 71 Stat. 355

June 30, 1958, P.L. 85-477, 72 Stat. 261

Aug. 27, 1958, P.L. 85-766, 72 Stat. 880

July 24, 1959, P.L. 86-108, 73 Stat. 246

May 14, 1960, P.L. 86-472, 74 Stat. 134

July 12, 1960, P.L. 86-628, 74 Stat. 460

Sept. 8, 1960, P.L. 86-735, 74 Stat. 870

Continued

Sept. 4, 1961, P.L. 87-195, 75 Stat. 464, 22 U.S. Code § 1783

Oct. 18, 1962, P.L. 87-845, 76A Stat. 698, 22 U.S. Code § 1934

Oct. 7, 1964, P.L. 88-633, 78 Stat. 1015, 22 U.S. Code § 1754

Nov. 14, 1967, P.L. 90-137, 81 Stat. 463, 22 U.S. Code § 1934

Oct. 18, 1973, P.L. 93-126, 87 Stat. 452, 22 U.S. Code § 1754

Dec. 17, 1973, P.L. 93-189, 87 Stat. 732, 22 U.S. Code § 1934

Aug. 13, 1974, P.L. 93-371, 88 Stat. 444, 22 U.S. Code § 1754

Nov. 29, 1975, P.L. 94-141, 89 Stat. 760, 22 U.S. Code § 1934

April 4, 1996, P.L. 104-127, 22 U.S. Code § 1922

Aug. 20, 1996, P.L. 104-186, 22 U.S. Code § 1754

Mutual Security Act of 1955
July 8, 1955, Ch. 301, 69 Stat. 283

Mutual Security Act of 1956
July 18, 1956, Ch. 627, 70 Stat. 555

Mutual Security Act of 1957
Aug. 14, 1957, P.L. 85-141, 71 Stat. 355

Mutual Security Act of 1958
June 30, 1958, P.L. 85-477, 72 Stat. 261

Mutual Security Act of 1959
July 24, 1959, P.L. 86-108, 73 Stat. 246
May 14, 1960, P.L. 86-472, 74 Stat. 141

Mutual Security Act of 1960
May 14, 1960, P.L. 86-472, 74 Stat. 134

Mutual Security and Related Agencies Appropriation Act of 1961
Sept. 2, 1960, P.L. 86-704, 74 Stat. 776, 22 U.S. Code § 1811 nt.

Mutual Security Appropriation Acts
Oct. 31, 1951, Ch. 656, 65 Stat. 730
July 15, 1952, Ch. 758, 66 Stat. 649
Sept. 3, 1954, Ch. 1262, 68 Stat. 1221
Aug. 2, 1955, Ch. 491, 69 Stat. 435
July 31, 1956, Ch. 803, 70 Stat. 735
Sept. 3, 1957, P.L. 85-279, 71 Stat. 601

Aug. 28, 1958, P.L. 85-853, 72 Stat. 1100

Sept. 28, 1959, P.L. 86-383, 73 Stat. 717, 22 U.S. Code § 1811 nt.; 42 U.S. Code § 1975c

Oct. 31, 1977, P.L. 95-148, 22 U.S. Code §§ 1819, 1819 nt.

Mutual Thrift Institutions Tax Act
Pa. Purdon's Stat., Title 72, § 8501 et seq.

Mutual-to-Stock Conversion Act (Insurance Company)
Pa. Purdon's Stat., Title 40, § 911-A et seq.

Mutual Trust Investment Company Act
Fla. Stat. 1979, 660.15 et seq.
Me. Rev. Stat. Ann. 1964, Title 9, § 1271 et seq.
N.C. Gen. Stat. 1943, § 36A-90 et seq.
Tex. Rev. Civ. Stat. 1974, Art. 1528i

Mutualization Act (Insurance)
Ohio Rev. Code 1953, 3913.01 et seq.

Muzzicato Act (Transit Fare Referendum)
N.Y. Rapid Transit Law (Consol. Laws Ch. 48A) § 36 et seq.

MVAIC Act
N.Y. Insurance Law 1984 (Consol. Laws Ch. 28) § 5201 et seq.

Myakka River Wild and Scenic Designation and Preservation Act
Fla. Stat. Ann., 258.501

Myer-Anderson State Aid Act
Ky. Rev. Stat. 1962, 166.160, 166.170

Myers-Gains Compulsory Primary Law
Ky. Acts 1935 (Ex. Sess.) Ch. 1

Myers Patent Act
Aug. 5, 1939, Ch. 452, 53 Stat. 1213 (See 35 U.S. Code §§ 132, 135)

Mystic River Dam Loan Act
Mass. Acts 1957, Ch. 647
Mass. Acts 1963, Ch. 547

**Mystic River Water Tunnel Loan Act
  (Metropolitan District)**
  Mas. Acts 1950 Ch. 741

N

NAFTA
See North American Free Trade Agreement Implementation Act

NAFTA (North American Free Trade Agreement Act)

NAFTA Conformity Act
Cal. Vehicle Code 1959, §§ 2418, 2418.1

NAFTA Worker Security Act
Dec. 8, 1993, P.L. 103-182, 19 U.S. Code § 2101 nt.

Name Act (Business)
Me. Rev. Stat. Ann. 1964, Title 31, § 1 et seq.

Name Act (True)
Me. Rev. Stat. Ann. 1964, Title 30, § 2801 et seq.

Name Change Act
Ill. Rev. Stat. 1991, Ch. 96, § 1 et seq.
Ohio Rev. Code 1953, 2717.01
Wash. Rev. Code Ann., 4.24.130
W. Va. Code 1966, § 48-5-1 et seq.

Name Change Act (Eastern Illinois University)
Ill. Rev. Stat. 1991, Ch. 144, §§ 699, 700

Name Change Act (Illinois State University)
Ill. Rev. Stat. 1991, Ch. 144, §§ 499, 500

Name Change Act (Northern Illinois University)
Ill. Rev. Stat. 1991, Ch. 144, §§ 799, 800

Name Change Act (Southern Illinois University)
Ill. Rev. Stat. 1991, Ch. 144, §§ 599, 600

Name Change Act (University of Illinois)
Ill. Rev. Stat. 1991, Ch. 144, §§ 47m, 48

Name Change Act (Western Illinois University)
Ill. Rev. Stat. 1991, Ch. 144, §§ 899, 900

Name Protection Act
Neb. Rev. Stat. 1943, 21-2502 et seq.

Naming of Public Places Act
D.C. Code Ann. § 1-337, Subd f, 7-454, 7-451

Nantucket Park and Recreation Loan Act
Mass. Acts 1962, Ch. 15

Nantucket Sewer Reconstruction Loan Act
Mass. Acts 1959, Ch. 275

Napa County Flood Control and Water Conservation District Act
Cal. Water Code, Appendix, § 61-1 et seq.

Naphtha Container Act
Mich. Comp. Laws Ann., 750.502

Naples Airport Authority Act
Fla. Special Laws 1969, Ch. 69-1326

Naples Zoning Act
N.Y. Local Laws 1973, Village of Naples, p. 3593

Narcotic Addict Rehabilitation Act of 1966
Nov. 8, 1966, P.L. 89-793, 80 Stat. 1438, 18 U.S. Code §§ 4251 to 4255; 28 U.S. Code §§ 2901 to 2906; 42 U.S. Code §§ 3411 to 3426, 3441, 3442
Oct. 27, 1970, P.L. 91-513, 84 Stat. 1293, 42 U.S. Code § 3411
Sept. 16, 1972, P.L. 92-420, 86 Stat. 677, 42 U.S. Code § 3411

Narcotic Addict Treatment Act of 1974
May 14, 1974, P.L. 93-281, 88 Stat. 124, 21 U.S. Code §§ 802, 823 , 824, 827

Narcotic and Drug Abuse Control Act
Cal. Health and Safety Code § 11000 et seq.
N.J. Stat. Ann., 26:2G-1 et seq.
N.Y. Mental Hygiene Law 1977 (Consol. Laws Ch. 27) § 23.01 et seq.
Utah Laws 1957, Ch. 168

Narcotic Anti-Addiction Act
Ky. Rav. Stat. 1971, Superseded Vols. 218A.010 et seq.

Narcotic Commitment Act (Addicts)
Cal. Penal Code § 6399 et seq.
Cal. Welfare and Institutions Code § 3000 et seq.
N.Y. Mental Hygiene Law 1977 (Consol. Laws Ch. 27) § 23.09 et seq.

Narcotic Control Act of 1956
July 18, 1956, Ch. 629, 70 Stat. 567, 8 U.S. Code §§ 1182, 1251; 18 U.S. Code §§ 1401 to 1407; 21 U.S. Code §§ 174, 176a, 176b, 184a, 198; 26 U.S. Code §§ 4744, 4755, 4774, 7237, 7607, 7608

Narcotic Control Division Abolition Act
Ill. Rev. Stat. 1991, Ch. 127, § 55c.9 et seq.

Narcotic Drug Act
See also Uniform Controlled Substances Act
Vt. Stat. Ann., Title 18, § 4201 et seq.

Narcotic Drug Addicts Treatment Act
D.C. Code 1973, § 24-601 et seq.
Mich. Comp. Laws Ann., 330.1116 et seq.
Wash. Rev. Code Ann., 69.32.010 et seq.
Wis. Stat. 1969, 161.02, Subsec 3

Narcotic Drug Control Act
N.Y. Public Health Law 1953 (Consol. Laws, Ch. 45), § 3300 et seq.

Narcotic Drug Illegitimate Traffic Suppression Act
Mich. Comp. Laws 1970, 335.151 et seq.

Narcotic Drugs Act
See also Uniform Narcotic Drug Act
D.C. Code Ann., § 33-501 et seq.
Pa. Purdon's Stat., Title 35, § 780-101 et seq.
P.R. Laws Ann. 1954, Title 24 § 2101 et seq.

Narcotic Drugs Import and Export Acts
Feb. 9, 1909, Ch. 100, 35 Stat. 614, 21 U.S. Code §§ 171, 173, 174 to 184, 185
Jan. 17, 1914, Ch. 9, 38 Stat. 275, 21 U.S. Code §§ 171, 173, 174- -184
May 26, 1922, Ch. 202, 42 Stat. 596, 21 U.S. Code §§ 171, 173, 174 to 177, 180, 182, 184, 185
July 1, 1944, Ch. 377, 58 Stat. 721, 21 U.S. Code §§ 171, 200, 200a

March 8, 1946, Ch. 81, 60 Stat. 39, 21 U.S. Code § 171
July 18, 1956, Ch. 629, 70 Stat. 570, 21 U.S. Code §§ 174, 176a, 176b

Narcotic Enforcement Act
Cal. Health and Safety Code § 11100 et seq.

Narcotic Nuisance Abatement Act
Cal. Health and Safety Code § 11570 et seq.

Narcotic Rehabilitation Act
Cal. Welfare and Institutions Code § 5350 et seq.
La. Rev. Stat. Ann., 40:1051 et seq.

Narcotics Act (Possession and Sale)
Cal. Health and Safety Code §§ 11350 et seq., 11500

Narcotics Acts
Dec. 17, 1914, Ch. 1, 38 Stat. 789
Feb. 24, 1919, Ch. 18, 40 Stat. 1130
Nov. 23, 1921, Ch. 136, 42 Stat. 298
June 2, 1924, Ch. 234, 43 Stat. 328
Feb. 26, 1926, Ch. 27, 44 Stat. 9, 6 U.S. Code § 15; 48 U.S. Code § 845
Utah Laws 1957, Ch. 168

Narcotics and Alcoholic Beverage Law Enforcement Act
Utah Code Ann. 1953, 53-4-201 et seq.

Narcotics Control Trade Act
Oct. 27, 1986, P.L. 99-570, 19 U.S. Code § 2491 et seq.
Dec. 13, 1989, P.L. 101-231, 19 U.S. Code § 2492

Narcotics Detention and Rehabilitation Act
Cal. Health and Safety Code §§ 11560 et seq., 11750

Narcotics Manufacturing Act of 1960
April 22, 1960, P.L. 86-429, 74 Stat. 55, 21 U.S. Code §§ 182, 501 to 517; 26 U.S. Code §§ 4702, 4731

Narcotics Penalties and Enforcement Act of 1986
Oct. 27, 1986, P.L. 99-570, 21 U.S. Code § 801 nt.

Narcotics Profit Forfeiture Act
Ill. Rev. Stat. 1991, Ch. 56 1/2, § 1651 et seq.

Narcotics Rehabilitation Act
La. Rev. Stat. Ann., 40:1051 et seq.

Narcotics Secrecy Act
Fla. Stat. 1969, 398.18, Subsec. 1

Narcotics Use Act
N.J. Stat. Ann., 2A:170-8

Narragansett Bay Water Quality Management District Commission Act
R.I. Gen. Laws 1956, 46-25-1 et seq.

Narragansett Indian Land Management Corporation Act
R.I. Gen. Laws 1956, 37-18-1 et seq.

NASA Authorization Act of 1970
July 2, 1970, P.L. 91-303, 84 Stat. 372, 42 U.S. Code § 2462

Nashville Charter Act
Tenn. Private Acts 1947, Ch. 246

Nashville Juvenile and Domestic Relations Court Act
Tenn. Private Acts 1947, Ch. 246, Art. 51

Nashville Parking Board Act
Tenn. Private Acts 1949, Ch. 429

Nassau and Suffolk Counties Improvement Act
N.Y. Laws 1939, Ch. 276

Nassau County Act (Election)
N.Y. Laws 1898, Ch. 588

Nassau County Administrative Code
N.Y. Laws 1939, Ch. 272

Nassau County Bridge Authority Act
N.Y. Public Authorities Law (Consol. Laws Ch. 43A) § 651 et seq.

Nassau County Charter
N.Y. Laws 1935, Ch. 938

Nassau County Civil Divisions Act
N.Y. Laws 1939, Ch. 273

Nassau County District Court Act
N.Y. Laws 1939, Ch. 274

Nassau County Government Act
N.Y. Laws 1936, Ch. 879

Nassau County Police Act
N.Y. Laws 1925, Ch. 451

Nassau County Recreation and Water Conservation and Control Act
Fla. Special Laws 1961, Ch. 61-2525

Nassau County Sanitation Act
N.Y. Laws 1936, Ch. 162

Nassau County Tax Act
N.Y. Laws 1916, Ch. 541

Nassau Health Care Corporation Act
N.Y. Public Authorities Law (Consol. Laws Ch. 43A) § 3400 et seq.

Nassau Street Mall Special Assessment Act
N.Y. Laws 1977, Ch. 806

Nassau, Suffolk and Erie Counties Highway Improvement Act
N.Y. Laws 1927, Ch. 190

Natick School Loan Act
Mass. Acts 1952, Ch. 1

National Advisory Commission on Multiple Sclerosis Act
Oct. 25, 1972, P.L. 92-563, 86 Stat. 1177, 42 U.S. Code § 289a nt.

National Advisory Committee on Oceans and Atmosphere Act of 1977

July 5, 1977, P.L. 95-63, 33 U.S. Code §§ 857-13 et seq.

June 29, 1978, P.L. 95-304, 33 U.S. Code §§ 857-14, 857-18

June 21, 1979, P.L. 96-26, 33 U.S. Code § 857-18

National Advisory Committee on Semiconductor Research and Development Act of 1988

Aug. 23, 1988, P.L. 100-418, 15 U.S. Code § 4632

National Advisory Council on the Public Service Act of 1990

Aug. 14, 1990, P.L. 101-363, 5 USC § 3301 nt.

National Aeronautics and Space Act of 1958

July 29, 1958, P.L. 85-568, 72 Stat. 426, 10 U.S. Code §§ 2302, 2303; 18 U.S. Code §§ 799, 1114; 42 U.S. Code §§ 2451 to 2459, 2471 to 2476; 50 U.S. Code §§ 511 to 513, 515

May 13, 1959, P.L. 86-20, 73 Stat. 21, 42 U.S. Code § 2473

June 1, 1960, P.L. 86-481, 74 Stat. 153, 42 U.S. Code § 2473

April 25, 1961, P.L. 87-26, 75 Stat. 46, 42 U.S. Code § 2471

Oct. 4, 1961, P.L. 87-367, 75 Stat. 791, 42 U.S. Code §§ 2471, 2473

Aug. 14, 1962, P.L. 87-584, 76 Stat. 384, 42 U.S. Code §§ 2471, 2473

Oct. 11, 1962, P.L. 87-793, 76 Stat. 864, 42 U.S. Code § 2473

Sept. 6, 1963, P.L. 88-113, 77 Stat. 144, 42 U.S. Code § 2459

Aug. 14, 1964, P.L. 88-426, 78 Stat. 423, 42 U.S. Code §§ 2471 to 2474

Aug. 19, 1964, P.L. 88-448, 78 Stat. 490, 42 U.S. Code §§ 2473, 2474

Sept. 23, 1970, P.L. 91-406, 84 Stat. 855, 42 U.S. Code § 2471

Aug. 6, 1971, P.L. 92-68, 85 Stat. 177, 42 U.S. Code § 2476

June 22, 1974, P.L. 93-316, 88 Stat. 243, 42 U.S. Code § 2473

Sept. 3, 1974, P.L. 93-409, 88 Stat. 1070, 42 U.S. Code § 2473

Feb. 25, 1978, P.L. 95-238, 42 U.S. Code § 2451

July 16, 1984, P.L. 98-361, 42 U.S. Code § 2451

Nov. 8, 1984, P.L. 98-620, 42 U.S. Code § 2457

Oct. 30, 1987, P.L. 100-147, 42 U.S. Code §§ 2476b, 2459c

Nov. 27, 1988, P.L. 100-685, 42 U.S. Code §§ 2451, 2456a

Nov. 16, 1990, P.L. 101-611, 42 U.S. Code § 2473

Nov. 4, 1992, P.L. 102-588, 42 U.S. Code § 2454

Nov. 2, 1994, P.L. 103-437, 42 U.S. Code § 2476a

National Aeronautics and Space Administration Authorization Act, 1968

Oct. 30, 1987, P.L. 100-147, 15 U.S. Code §§ 4201 nt., 4212, 4228 , 4262, 4264, 4273; 42 U.S. Code § 2451 nt., 2459 nt., 2459a, 2459c, 2476b, 2486 et seq.

National Aeronautics and Space Administration Authorization Act, 1978

Nov. 2, 1994, P.L. 103-437, 42 U.S. Code § 2463

National Aeronautics and Space Administration Authorization Act, 1980

Aug. 8, 1979, P.L. 96-48, 42 U.S. Code §§ 2458b and nt., 2459, 2473

National Aeronautics and Space Administration Authorization Act, 1984

Nov. 10, 1998, P.L. 105-362, 42 U.S. Code § 2465

National Aeronautics and Space Administration Authorization Act, 1985

July 16, 1984, P.L. 98-361, 15 U.S. Code § 4261 nt.; 42 U.S. Code §§ 2451, 2451 nt., 2459 nt., 2459a

Dec. 5, 1985, P.L. 99-170, 42 U.S. Code § 2451 nt.

National Aeronautics and Space Administration Authorization Act, 1986

Dec. 5, 1985, P.L. 99-170, 42 U.S. Code §§ 2451 nt., 2459 nt., 2459a, 2466 to 2466c, 2466c nt., 49 U.S. Code Appx. § 2623

Nov. 2, 1994, P.L. 103-437, 42 U.S. Code § 2466c

Continued

National Aeronautics and Space Administration Authorization Act, 1988

Dec. 9, 1991, P.L. 102-195, 42 U.S. Code § 2451 nt.

Nov. 10, 1998, P.L. 105-362, 42 U.S. Code § 2451 nt.

National Aeronautics and Space Administration Authorization Act, 1989

Nov. 17, 1988, P.L. 100-685, 102 Stat. 4083

Oct. 29, 1992, P.L. 102-567, 15 U.S. Code § 313 nt.

National Aeronautics and Space Administration Authorization Act, 1991

Nov. 16, 1990, P.L. 101-611, 15 U.S. Code § 1535, 42 U.S. Code §§ 2451 nt., 2459 nt., 2459a, 2465a, 2471 nt., 2471a

Dec. 9, 1991, P.L. 102-195, 105 Stat. 1610

Nov. 4, 1992, P.L. 102-588, 106 Stat. 5116

National Aeronautics and Space Administration Authorization Act, 1992

Dec. 9, 1991, P.L. 102-195, 105 Stat. 1605

Nov. 4, 1992, P.L. 102-588, 106 Stat. 5107

National Aeronautics and Space Administration Authorization Act, 1993

Oct. 28, 1998, P.L. 105-303, 15 U.S. Code § 5803

Nov. 10, 1998, P.L. 105-362, 42 U.S. Code § 2487d

National Aeronautics and Space Administration Authorization Acts

Aug. 14, 1962, P.L. 87-584, 76 Stat. 382, 31 U.S. Code § 699; 42 U.S. Code §§ 2471, 2473

Sept. 6, 1963, P.L. 88-113, 77 Stat. 141, 31 U.S. Code § 699; 42 U.S. Code § 2459

July 11, 1964, P.L. 88-369, 78 Stat. 310, 31 U.S. Code § 699

June 28, 1965, P.L. 89-53, 79 Stat. 192, 31 U.S. Code § 699; 42 U.S. Code § 2459 nt.

Aug. 5, 1966, P.L. 89-528, 80 Stat. 339, 31 U.S. Code § 699; 42 U.S. Code § 2459 nt.

Aug. 21, 1967, P.L. 90-67, 81 Stat. 168, 31 U.S. Code § 699; 42 U.S. Code §§ 2459 nt., 2477

Nov. 8, 1967, P.L. 90-131, 81 Stat. 384

July 3, 1968, P.L. 90-373, 82 Stat. 280, 31 U.S. Code § 699; 42 U.S. Code § 2459 nt.

Nov. 18, 1969, P. L . 91-119, 83 Stat. 196, 31 U.S. Code § 699; 42 U.S. Code §§ 2459 nt., 2462

July 2, 1970, P.L. 91-303, 84 Stat. 368, 31 U.S. Code § 699; 42 U.S. Code § 2462

Aug. 6, 1971, P.L. 92-68, 85 Stat. 174, 31 U.S. Code § 699; 42 U.S. Code §§ 2459 nts., 2476

May 19, 1972, P.L. 92-304, 86 Stat. 157, 31 U.S. Code § 699; 42 U.S. Code § 2459

July 23, 1973, P.L. 93-74, 87 Stat. 171, 5 U.S. Code § 5316; 42 U.S. Code §§ 2473, 2476a

June 22, 1974, P. L, 93-316, 88 Stat. 240, 42 U.S. Code §§ 2459 nt., 2463, 2473

June 19, 1975, P.L. 94-39, 89 Stat. 218, 42 U.S. Code §§ 2459 nt. , 2463, 2481 to 2484

National Affordable Housing Act

See Cranston-Gonzalez National Affordable Housing Act

National Agricultural Policy Commission Act of 1985

Dec. 23, 1985, P.L. 99-198, 7 U.S. Code § 5001 et seq.

National Agricultural Research, Extension, and Teaching Policy Act Amendments of 1981

Dec. 22, 1981, P.L. 97-98, 7 U.S. Code § 3101 nt.

Dec. 23, 1985, P.L. 99-198, 7 U.S. Code §§ 2281 nt., 3222 nt., 3223

Nov. 28, 1990, P.L. 101-624, 7 U.S. Code § 3222 nt.

June 23, 1998, P.L. 105-185, 7 U.S. Code § 3222 nt.

National Agricultural Research, Extension, and Teaching Policy Act Amendments of 1985

Dec. 23, 1985, P.L. 99-198, 7 U.S. Code §§ 343, 390 et seq., 450I , 3101, 3121 et seq., 3151, 3152, 3174, 3177, 3194 to 3196, 4701 et seq.

June 17, 1988, P.L. 100-339, 102 Stat. 620

Nov. 28, 1990, P.L. 101-624, 7 U.S. Code §§ 4701 to 4710

National Agricultural Research, Extension, and Teaching Policy Act of 1977

Sept. 29, 1977, P.L. 95-113, 7 U.S. Code §§ 3101 et seq., 3101 nt.; 42 U.S. Code § 6651

June 30, 1980, P.L. 96-294, 7 U.S. Code § 3154 et seq.; 7 U.S. Code § 3129

Dec. 23, 1985, P.L. 99-198, 7 U.S. Code §§ 3101 to 3336

Dec. 12, 1989, P.L. 101-220, 7 U.S. Code § 3319e

Nov. 28, 1990, P.L. 101-624, 7 U.S. Code §§ 3101 et seq. generally

Dec. 13, 1991, P.L. 102-237, 7 U.S. Code §§ 3103, 3122, 3123, 3123a, 3127, 3152, 3154, 3194, 3222a, 3291, 3311, 3319, 3319e

Oct. 13, 1994, P.L. 103-354, 7 U.S. Code § 3128

Dec. 21, 1995, P.L. 104-66, 7 U.S. Code §§ 3122, 3123, 3322

April 4, 1996, P.L. 104-127, 7 U.S. Code §§ 3101, 3103, 3121 to 3123, 3123a, 3124a, 3125, 3127 to 3129, 3129a, 3152, 3154, 3155, 3174, 3174a, 3175 , 3191, 3194 to 3196, 3221, 3222a to 3222c, prec. 3241, 3291, 3292, 3311, 3312, 3319d, 3322 to 3324, 3334 to 3336

June 23, 1998, P.L. 105-185, 7 U.S. Code §§ 3103, 3123, 3127, 3128, 3152, 3154, 3155, 3174, 3174a, 3175, 3192, 3195, 3196, 3221, 3222, 3222b, 3222c, 3222d, 3241, 3291, 3292a, 3292b, 3310, 3311, 3312, 3314, 3315, 3319a, 3319d, 3323, 3324, 3336

Oct. 7, 1998, P.L. 105-244, 7 U.S. Code § 3152

Nov. 10, 1998, P.L. 105-362, 7 U.S. Code § 3222

National Agricultural Research, Extension, and Teaching Policy Act of 1981

April 4, 1996, P.L. 104-127, 7 U.S. Code § 3222 nt.

National Agricultural Research, Extension, and Teaching Policy Act of 1985

April 4, 1996, P.L. 104-127, 7 U.S. Code §§ 3173 nt., 3224

National Agriculture Weather Information System Act

Nov. 28, 1990, P.L. 101-624, 7 U.S. Code §§ 5851 to 5855

National Air Museum Amendments Act of 1965

July 19, 1966, P.L. 89-509, 80 Stat. 310, 20 U.S. Code §§ 77, 77a , 77b nt., 77c, 77d

National and Community Service Act (Commission on)

Utah Code Ann. 1953, 9-1-801 et seq.

National and Community Service Act of 1990

See Nov. 16, 1990, P.L. 101-610, 42 U.S. Code §§ 12501 nt.

Sept. 21, 1993, P.L. 103-82, 42 U.S. Code §§ 12501 et seq.

Nov. 30, 1993, P.L. 103-160, 42 U.S. Code § 12639

Oct. 5, 1994, P.L. 103-337, 42 U.S. Code § 12619

Oct. 20, 1994, P.L. 103-382, 42 U.S. Code §§ 12511, 12524, 12528

Feb. 10, 1996, P.L. 104-106, 42 U.S. Code § 12639

Oct. 1, 1996, P.L. 104-210, 42 U.S. Code §§ prec. 12671, 12671- 12673

Aug. 7, 1998, P.L. 105-220, 42 U.S. Code § 12511

Oct. 7, 1998, P.L. 105-244, 42 U.S. Code §§ 12511, 12604, 12626

Oct. 21, 1998, P.L. 105-277, 22 U.S. Code § 2452a; 42 U.S. Code §§ 12637, 12653c, 12655m

Nov. 3, 1998, P.L. 105-354, 42 U.S. Code § 12653

National and Community Service Technical Amendment Act of 1992

Oct. 5, 1992, P.L. 102-384, 42 U.S. Code §§ 12501 nt., 12511 et seq.

National and Community Service Technical Amendments Act of 1991

March 12, 1991, P.L. 102-10, 42 U.S. Code § 12501 nt.

National and Community Service Trust Act of 1993

Sept. 21, 1993, P.L. 103-82, 42 U.S. Code § 12501 nt.

National and State Defense Act

Del. Code of 1974 Title 20, § 3101 et seq.

National Antidrug Reorganization and Coordination Act

Oct. 27, 1986, P.L. 99-570, 100 Stat. 3367

National Appliance Energy Conservation Act of 1987

March 3, 1987, P.L. 100-12, 42 U.S. Code § 6201 nt.

National Appliance Energy Conservation Amendments of 1988

June 28, 1988, P.L. 100-357, 102 Stat. 671, 42 U.S. Code §§ 6201 nt., 6291 to 6295, 6297

National Apprenticeship Act

Aug. 16, 1937, Ch. 663, 50 Stat. 664, 29 U.S. Code §§ 50, 50a, 50b

National Aquaculture Act of 1980

Sept. 26, 1980, P.L. 96-362, 16 U.S. Code § 2801 nt.

Nov. 8, 1984, P.L. 98-623, 16 U.S. Code § 2809

Dec. 23, 1985, P.L. 99-198, 16 U.S. Code §§ 2801 to 2805, 2809

Nov. 28, 1990, P.L. 101-624, 16 U.S. Code § 2809

June 23, 1998, P.L. 105-185, 16 U.S. Code § 2809

National Aquaculture Improvement Act of 1985

Dec. 23, 1985, P.L. 98-198, 16 U.S. Code §§ 2801 et seq., 2801 nt.

National Archives Act

See Federal Records Act of 1950

June 19, 1934, Ch. 668, 48 Stat. 1122

National Archives and Records Administration Act of 1984

Oct. 19, 1984, P.L. 98-497, 44 U.S. Code §§ 101 nt., 2102 et seq.

National Archives Trust Fund Board Act

July 9, 1941, Ch. 284, 55 Stat. 581 (See 44 U.S. Code §§ 2301 to 2308)

National Arts and Cultural Development Act of 1964

Sept. 3, 1964, P.L. 88-579, 78 Stat. 905, 20 U.S. Code §§ 781 to 790

Aug. 13, 1965, P.L. 89-125, 79 Stat. 518, 20 U.S. Code § 789

Sept. 29, 1965, P.L. 89-209, 79 Stat. 847, 20 U.S. Code §§ 784 to 786

Sept. 11, 1967, P.L. 90-83, 81 Stat. 223, 20 U.S. Code § 785

National Assessment of Chapter 1 Act, 1992

May 30, 1990, P.L. 101-305, 20 U.S. Code §§ 236 nt., 237, 237 nt. 238, 238 nt., 240, 244, 1018e, 2882 nt.

National Assessment of Educational Progress Improvement Act

April 28, 1988, P.L. 100-297, 102 Stat. 344, 20 U.S. Code §§ 1221 nt., 1221e, 1221e-1

National Aviation Day Act

May 11, 1939, Ch. 123, 53 Stat. 739, 36 U.S. Code § 151

National Bank Acts

Feb. 25, 1791, Ch. 10, 1 Stat. 191

April 10, 1816, Ch. 44, 3 Stat. 266

June 3, 1864, Ch. 106, 13 Stat. 99, 12 U.S. Code § 165

June 30, 1874, Ch. 343, 18 Stat. 123

June 29, 1949, Ch. 276, 63 Stat. 298, 12 U.S. Code § 24

July 28, 1959, P.L. 86-114, 73 Stat. 263, 12 U.S. Code § 141 nt.

Sept. 8, 1959, P.L. 86-230, 73 Stat. 457, 12 U.S. Code § 24

National Bank Consolidation and Merger Act

Nov. 7, 1918, Ch. 209, 12 U.S. Code §§ 215 et seq.

National Bank Receivership Act
June 30, 1876, Ch. 156, 12 U.S. Code § 191
Oct. 28, 1992, P.L. 102-550, 12 U.S. Code § 191 nt.

National Bank Tax Act
March 4, 1923, Ch. 267, 42 Stat. 1499, 12 U.S. Code § 548

National Bankruptcy Act
See Bankruptcy Act

National Bankruptcy Review Commission Act
Oct. 22, 1994, P.L. 103-394, 11 U.S. Code prec. . 101 nt.

National Banks Extension Act
See Currency Acts

National Bicentennial Celebration Commission
Ga. Code Ann., 50-12-1 et seq.

National Bone Marrow Registry Reauthor- ization Act of 1998
July 16, 1998, P.L. 105-196, 42 U.S. Code § 201 nt.

National Bureau of Standards
Sept. 2, 1958, P.L. 85-890, 72 Stat. 1711, 15 U.S. Code §§ 278a, 278c to 278e
March 1, 1968, P.L. 90-259, 82 Stat. 35, 15 U.S. Code §§ 278f, 278g

National Bureau of Standards Act
See National Institute of Standards and Technology Act
March 3, 1901, Ch. 872, 15 U.S. Code § 271 nt.

National Bureau of Standards Authorization Act for Fiscal Year 1983
Oct. 6, 1982, P.L. 97-286, 15 U.S. Code § 275b

National Bureau of Standards Authorization Act for Fiscal Year 1986
July 29, 1985, P.L. 99-73, 5 U.S. Code § 5316, 15 U.S. Code §§ 274, 275c, 278b, 281a
Sept. 30, 1985, P.L. 99-105, 99 Stat. 476

National Bureau of Standards Authorization Act for Fiscal Year 1987
Oct. 28, 1986, P.L. 99-574, 100 Stat. 3236

National Cancer Act of 1971
Dec. 23, 1971, P.L. 92-218, 85 Stat. 778, 42 U.S. Code § 286a nt.

National Cancer Institute Act
Aug. 5, 1937, Ch. 565, 50 Stat. 559
July 1, 1944, Ch. 373, 58 Stat. 707, 42 U.S. Code § 281 et seq.

National Capital Area Interest Arbitration Standards Act of 1995
Nov. 15, 1995, P.L. 104-50, Title IV, 40 U.S. Code §§ 1301 et seq.

National Capital Area Transit Act
D.C. Code Ann., § 1-2471 et seq.

National Capital Area Transit Act of 1972
Oct. 21, 1972, P.L. 92-517, 86 Stat. 999

National Capital Park and Planning Commission Act
D.C. Code Ann., § 1-2001 et seq.
Md. Laws 1959, Ch. 780

National Capital Planning Act of 1952
July 19, 1952, Ch. 949, 66 Stat. 781, 20 U.S. Code § 76 nt.; 40 U.S. Code §§ 71 to 71i, 72, 72a, 72b, 72c, 73, 74, 74a, 122, 125, 126, 128
Sept. 25, 1962, P.L. 87-683, 76 Stat. 575, 40 U.S. Code § 71a

National Capital Revitalization and Self-Government Improvement Act of 1997
Aug. 5, 1997, P.L. 105-33, Title XI, 111 Stat. 712

National Capital Transportation Act
D.C. Code Ann., § 1-2451 et seq.

National Capital Transportation Act of 1960
July 14, 1960, P.L. 86-669, 74 Stat. 537, 40 U.S. Code §§ 651, 652, 661 to 665, 671
Oct. 4, 1961, P.L. 87-367, 75 Stat. 787, 40 U.S. Code § 665
Aug. 14, 1964, P.L. 88-426, 78 Stat. 426, 40 U.S. Code § 661
Continued

539

Sept. 8, 1965, P.L. 89-173, 79 Stat. 666, 40 U.S. Code § 662

National Capital Transportation Act of 1965

Sept. 8, 1965, P.L. 89-173, 79 Stat. 663, 40 U.S. Code §§ 681 to 685

Dec. 20, 1967, P.L. 90-220, 81 Stat. 670, 40 U.S. Code § 682

Dec. 9, 1969, P.L. 91-143, 83 Stat. 323, 40 U.S. Code § 684

National Capital Transportation Act of 1969

Dec. 9, 1969, P.L. 91-143, 83 Stat. 320, 40 U.S. Code § 684

National Capital Transportation Amendments of 1990

Nov. 15, 1990, P.L. 101-551, 104 Stat. 2733

National Capital Transportation Amendments 1979-1990

D.C. Code Ann., § 1-2451 et seq.

National Cattle Theft Act

Aug. 18, 1941, Ch. 366, 55 Stat. 631, (See 18 U.S. Code §§ 10, 2311, 2316, 2317, 3237)

National Cave and Karst Research Institute Act of 1998

Oct. 30, 1998, P.L. 105-325, 112 Stat. 3038, 16 U.S. Code § 4310 nt.

National Cemeteries Act

Ill. Rev. Stat. 1991, Ch. 21, §§ 64.90, 65

National Center for The Study of Afro-American History and Culture Act

Oct. 10, 1980, P.L. 95-430, 20 U.S. Code § 3701 nt.

National Child Protection Act of 1993

Dec. 20, 1993, P.L. 103-209, 5 U.S. Code §§ 5101 nt., 5119 et seq.

Sept. 13, 1994, P.L. 103-322, 42 U.S. Code §§ 5119, 5119a et seq. .

Oct. 9, 1998, P.L. 105-251, 42 U.S. Code §§ 5119a, 5119b

National Childhood Vaccine Injury Act of 1986

Nov. 14, 1986, P.L. 99-660, 42 U.S. Code § 201 nt.

Dec. 22, 1987, P.L. 100-203, 42 U.S. Code § 300aa-1

Dec. 19, 1989, P.L. 101-239, 42 U.S. Code § 300aa-1 nt.

Nov. 3, 1990, P.L. 101-502, 42 U.S. Code §§ 300aa-1 nt., 300aa- 11 nt., 300aa-12 nt.

Nov. 26, 1991, P.L. 102-168, 42 U.S. Code § 300aa-1 nt.

National Children's Island Act of 1995

July 19, 1996, P.L. 104-163, 110 Stat. 1416

National Climate Program Act

Sept. 17, 1978, P.L. 95-367, 15 U.S. Code §§ 2901 et seq., 2901 nt.

Dec. 21, 1982, P.L. 97-375, 15 U.S. Code § 2906

April 7, 1986, P.L. 99-272, 15 U.S. Code §§ 2903 to 2905

National Coal Heritage Area Act of 1996

Nov. 12, 1996, P.L. 104-333, Division II, Title I, 16 U.S. Code § 461 nt.

National Coal Imports Reporting Act of 1985

July 2, 1985, P.L. 99-58, 42 U.S. Code §§ 7277, 7277 nt.

National Commission on Acquired Immune Deficiency Syndrome Act

Nov. 4, 1988, P.L. 100-607, 42 U.S. Code § 300cc nt.

National Commission on Judicial Discipline and Removal Act

Dec. 1, 1990, P.L. 101-650, 28 U.S. Code § 372 nt.

Dec. 9, 1991, P.L. 102-198, 28 U.S. Code § 372 nt.

National Commission on Libraries and Information Science Act

July 20, 1970, P.L. 91-345, 84 Stat. 440, 20 U.S. Code §§ 1501 to 1506

May 3, 1973, P.L. 93-29, 87 Stat. 59, 20 U.S. Code §§ 1504, 1505

Aug. 14, 1991, P.L. 102-95, 105 Stat. 479

Sept. 30, 1996, P.L. 104-208, 20 U.S. Code §§ 1504, 1505

National Commission on Libraries and Information Science Act Amendments of 1991

Aug. 14, 1991, P.L. 102-95, 20 U.S. Code § 1501 nt.

National Commission on Measured Responses to Achieve a Drug-Free America by 1995 Authorization Act

Nov. 18, 1988, P.L. 100-690, 21 U.S. Code § 1502 nt.

National Commission on Product Safety Act

Nov. 20, 1967, P.L. 90-146, 81 Stat. 466, 15 U.S. Code § 1262 nt.

Aug. 4, 1969, P.L. 91-51, 83 Stat. 86, 15 U.S. Code § 1262 nt.

National Commission on Supplies and Shortage Act of 1974

Sept. 30, 1974, P.L. 93-426, 88 Stat. 1167, 50 U.S. Code Appx. § 2169

National Commission to Prevent Infant Mortality Act of 1986

Nov. 14, 1986, P.L. 99-660, 42 U.S. Code § 286g nt.

National Commission to Support Law Enforcement Act

Nov. 5, 1990, P.L. 101-515, 42 U.S. Code §§ 3721 nt., 3721(b) nt.

National Community Economic Partnership Act of 1994

Sept. 13, 1994, P.L. 103-322, 42 U.S. Code §§ 13701 nt., 13821 et seq., 13841 et seq., 13851 et seq.

National Community Service Act of 1990

Aug. 23, 1994, P.L. 103-304, 42 U.S. Code §§ 121591, 12602, 12615, 12619, 12622, 12651d, 12653, 12655n

National Competitiveness Technology Transfer Act of 1989

Nov. 29, 1989, P.L. 101-189, 15 U.S. Code § 3701 nt.

National Conference of State Legislatures Act

Ill. Rev. Stat. 1991, Ch. 63, §§ 122.9, 123

National Conscription Act

See Conscription Act

See Selective Draft Acts

National Consumer Cooperative Bank Act

Aug. 20, 1978, P.L. 95-351, 12 U.S. Code §§ 3001, 3001 nt., 3011 et seq.

Dec. 16, 1979, P.L. 96-149, 12 U.S. Code § 3013

Dec. 7, 1989, P.L. 101-206, 12 U.S. Code § 3014

National Consumer Cooperative Bank Act Amendments of 1981

Aug. 13, 1981, P.L. 97-35, 12 U.S. Code § 3001 nt.

National Consumer Cooperative Bank Amendments of 1989

Dec. 7, 1989, P.L. 101-206, 12 U.S. Code § 3001 nt.

National Consumer Health Information and Health Promotion Act of 1976

June 23, 1976, P.L. 94-317, 42 U.S. Code §§ 201 et seq.

National Contaminated Sediment Assessment and Management Act

Oct. 31, 1992, P.L. 102-580, 33 U.S. Code § 1271 nt.

National Cooley's Anemia Control Act

Aug. 29, 1972, P.L. 92-414, 86 Stat. 650, 42 U.S. Code §§ 300b, 300b-2, 300b-3, 300b-5, 300c to 300c-4

National Cooperative Production Amendments of 1993

June 10, 1993, P.L. 102-42, 15 U.S. Code §§ 4301, 4301 nt., 4302, 4303, 4304, 4305, 4305 nt., 4306

National Cooperative Research Act of 1984

See National Cooperative Research and Production Act of 1993

National Cooperative Research and Production Act of 1993

Oct. 11, 1984, P.L. 98-462, 98 Stat. 1815, 15 U.S. Code §§ 4301 et seq., 4301 nt.

National Council on Education Standards and Testing Act

June 27, 1991, P.L. 101-62, 20 U.S. Code § 1221-1

National Credit Union Central Liquidity Facility Act

Nov. 10, 1978, P.L. 95-630, 12 U.S. Code §§ 1751 nt., 1795 et seq.

National Crime Prevention and Privacy Compact Act of 1998

Oct. 9, 1998, P.L. 105-251, Title II, Subtitle A, 112 Stat. 1874, 42 U.S. Code § 14601 nt.

National Criminal History Access and Child Protection Act

Oct. 9, 1998, P.L. 105-251, Title II, 112 Stat. 1874, 42 U.S. Code § 14601 nt.

National Critical Materials Act of 1984

July 31, 1984, P.L. 98-373, 30 U.S. Code §§ 1801 et seq., 1801 nt.

Aug. 23, 1988, P.L. 10-418, 102 Stat. 1454, 30 U.S. Code §§ 1809, 1810

June 10, 1993, P.L. 103-42, 15 U.S. Code §§ 4301, 4301 nt., 4302 , 4303, 4304, 4305, 4306

National Currency Association Acts

May 30, 1908, Ch. 229, 35 Stat. 546, 12 U.S. Code § 104

Dec. 23, 1913, Ch. 6, 38 Stat. 274

National Deafness and Other Communication Disorders Act of 1988

Oct. 28, 1988, P.L. 100-553, 42 U.S. Code § 201 nt.

National Defense Act

Oct. 31, 1951, Ch. 655, 65 Stat. 728 (See 10 U.S. Code §§ 771 to 774, 3612, 6297, 8612)

July 9, 1952, Ch. 608, 66 Stat. 506 (See 32 U.S. Code §§ 302, 304)

May 27, 1953, Ch. 69, 67 Stat. 35 (See 10 U.S. Code § 5864)

July 6, 1954, Ch. 462, 68 Stat. 451 (See 32 U.S. Code § 708)

Aug. 28, 1954, Ch. 1039, 68 Stat. 896 (See 10 U.S. Code §§ 772, 6016, 6325, 6381, 6383, 6394, 6400)

Sept. 3, 1954, Ch. 1257, 68 Stat. 1188 (See 10 U.S. Code §§ 3571, 8571)

Aug. 11, 1955, Ch. 802, 69 Stat. 686 (See 32 U.S. Code § 109)

Fla. Stat. Ann., 250.01 et seq.

National Defense Acts

See Army Reorganization Acts

National Defense Authorization Act, Fiscal Years 1988 and 1989

Dec. 4, 1987, P.L. 100-180, 5 U.S. Code § 3328; 10 U.S. Code §§ 301c, 305a, 308 et seq., 401 to 406, 517, 524, 525, 774, 775, 1071 nt., 2120 et seq., 2400, 2632, 2801 et seq., 3359, 3964, 4315, 4415, 4621, 5517, 5721, 6334, 7299a, 7312, 8964 to 8966; 15 U.S. Code §§ 644, 4601 to 4606; 16 U.S. Code §§ 281, 283; 37 U.S. Code §§ 407, 411b, 411g, 411h 419 to 421; 50 U.S. Code §§ 98 nt., 1513 nt., 1521 nt.

Dec. 30, 1987, P.L. 100-224, 10 U.S. Code § 2437

Sept. 29, 1988, P.L. 100-456, 102 Stat. 1963, 10 U.S. Code §§ 261 nt., 521 nt., 978 nt., 2366, 2366 nt., 2411, 2435, 8855; 37 U.S. Code § 301c

Oct. 1, 1988, P.L. 100-463, 102 Stat. 2270-14

Nov. 29, 1989, P.L. 101-189, 10 U.S. Code § 113 nt.

Nov. 5, 1990, P.L. 101-510, 104 Stat. 1669

Feb. 14, 1992, P.L. 102-245, 15 U.S. Code § 4603

Oct. 23, 1992, P.L. 102-484, 10 U.S. Code §§ 2301 nt., 2432 nt.

Nov. 30, 1993, P.L. 103-160, 15 U.S. Code §§ 4601, 4602, 4603, 4603 nt.

Dec. 17, 1993, P.L. 103-199, 10 U.S. Code § 2431 nt.

Oct. 5, 1994, P.L. 103-337, 15 U.S. Code § 4603

Nov. 2, 1994, P.L. 103-437, 15 U.S. Code § 4631

Dec. 21, 1995, P.L. 104-66, 15 U.S. Code § 4604

Feb. 10, 1996, P.L. 104-106, 10 U.S. Code §§ 167 nt., 2431 nt., 2432 nt.

Nov. 18, 1997, P.L. 105-85, 10 U.S. Code § 113 nt.

National Defense Authorization Act, Fiscal Years 1990 and 1991

Nov. 21, 1989, P.L. 101-165, 103 Stat. 1152

Nov. 29, 1989, P.L. 101-189, 103 Stat. 1352

Nov. 5, 1990, P.L. 101-510, 10 U.S. Code §§ 113 nt., 2114 nt., 2701 nt.; 15 U.S. Code § 3710a nt.; 19 U.S. Code § 2242 nt.; 22 U.S. Code § 1928 nt.

April 6, 1991, P.L. 102-25, 18 U.S. Code § 207; 37 U.S. Code § 302 nt.

Dec. 5, 1991, P.L. 102-190, 10 U.S. Code §§ 1101, 2701 nt.; 15 U.S. Code § 636 nt.; 20 U.S. Code § 1101 nt.

Oct. 23, 1992, P.L. 102-484, 10 U.S. Code §§ 372 nt., 1592 nt., 2301 nt., 2323a; 15 U.S. Code § 637 nt.

May 31, 1993, P.L. 103-35, 37 U.S. Code §§ 301a, 301a nt.

Nov. 30, 1993, P.L. 103-160, 10 U.S. Code § 2431 nt.; 32 U.S. Code § 709

Oct. 13, 1994, P.L. 103-355, 15 U.S. Code § 637 nt.

Feb. 10, 1996, P.L. 104-106, 10 U.S. Code §§ 113 nt., 942 nt.; 15 U.S. Code § 637 nt.

Sept. 23, 1996, P.L. 104-201, 10 U.S. Code §§ 372 nt., 942 nt., 2431 nt.

Nov. 18, 1997, P.L. 105-85, 10 U.S. Code § 1746 nt., 2687 nt.; 15 U.S . Code § 637 nt.; 42 U.S. Code §§ 7271a, 7274a

National Defense Authorization Act for Fiscal Year 1986

Nov. 18, 1997, P.L. 105-85, 50 U.S. Code § 1521

National Defense Authorization Act for Fiscal Year 1987

Nov. 14, 1986, P.L. 99-661, 100 Stat. 3816

Dec. 4, 1987, P.L. 100-180, 101 Stat. 1036, 1066, 1121, 10 U.S. Code § 2301 nt.

Sept. 29, 1988, P.L. 100-456, 10 U.S. Code §§ 521 nt., 2301 nt., 22 U.S. Code § 2767a

Nov. 10, 1989, P.L. 101-147, 42 U.S. Code §§ 1758, 1760, 1762a, 1772, 1773, 1786

Nov. 29, 1989, P.L. 101-189, 10 U.S. Code §§ 510 nt., 2301 nt., 2407 nt.; 22 U.S. Code § 2767a

Nov. 5, 1990, P.L. 101-510, 10 U.S. Code § 2301 nt.

Dec. 5, 1991, P.L. 102-190, 105 Stat. 1404

Oct. 23, 1992, P.L. 102-484, 10 U.S. Code §§ 2301 nt., 2323

Dec. 17, 1993, P.L. 103-199, 107 Stat. 2327

Feb. 10, 1996, P.L. 104-106, 10 U.S. Code § 114 nt.

National Defense Authorization Act for Fiscal Year 1989

Sept. 29, 1988, P.L. 100-456, 102 Stat. 1918

Oct. 1, 1988, P.L. 100-463, 102 Stat. 2270-59

Oct. 24, 1988, P.L. 100-526, 10 U.S. Code §§ 1095a, 2324, 2324 nt., 2683, 4415

Nov. 19, 1988, P.L. 100-700, 10 U.S. Code § 2324 nt.

Nov. 29, 1989, P.L. 101-189, 10 U.S. Code §§ 113 nt., 374 nt., 2505 nt.; 37 U.S. Code §§ 301b nt., 302 nt.; 42 U.S. Code § 8287 nt.

Nov. 5, 1990, P.L. 101-510, 10 U.S. Code § 2391 nt., 37 U.S. Code § 302 nt.

Nov. 15, 1990, P.L. 101-574, 44 U.S. Code § 502 nt.

Dec. 5, 1991, P.L. 102-190, 5 U.S. Code § 5316 nt.

Oct. 23, 1992, P.L. 102-484, 10 U.S. Code § 113 nt.; 44 U.S. Code § 502 nt.

Nov. 30, 1993, P.L. 103-160, 32 U.S. Code § 709

Dec. 17, 1993, P.L. 103-199, 10 U.S. Code § 2592b

Oct. 5, 1994, P.L. 103-337, 37 U.S. Code § 302 nt.

Feb. 10, 1996, P.L. 104-106, 10 U.S. Code § 2341 nt.; 37 U.S. Code § 302 nt.

Nov. 18, 1997, P.L. 105-85, 10 U.S. Code § 2431 nt.; 42 U.S. Code § 2121 nt.

Oct. 17, 1998, P.L. 105-261, 10 U.S. Code § 2391 nt.

National Defense Authorization Act for Fiscal Year 1991

Nov. 5, 1990, P.L. 101-510, 104-1485

April 6, 1991, P.L. 102-25, 10 U.S. Code §§ 115 nt., 687, 690, 690 nt., 1035 nt., 1079 nt., 2301 nt., 2306a nt., 2432 nt., 3074; 22 U.S. Code § 1928 nt.; 37 U.S. Code §§ 403a nt., 501 nt.; 42 U.S. Code § 6686

Nov. 26, 1991, P.L. 102-172, 10 U.S. Code § 2301 nt.

Dec. 5, 1991, P.L. 102-190, 10 U.S. Code §§ 115 nt., 261 nt., 374 nt., 1408 nt., 1721 nt., 2301 nt., 2341 nt., 2687 nt., 4342 nt.; 15 U.S. Code § 3075 nt.; 22 U.S. Code § 2797 nt.; 24 U.S. Code §§ 415, 417; 42 U.S. Code § 6686

Oct. 23, 1992, P.L. 102-484, 10 U.S. Code §§ 114a nt., 374 nt., 1074 nt., 2301 nt., 2341 nt., 2430 nt., 2687 nt.; 15 U.S. Code 637 nt.; 31 U.S. Code § 1551 nt.

Continued

543

Nov. 30, 1993, P.L. 103-160, 10 U.S. Code §§ 261 nt., 374 nt., 2301 nt., 2341 nt., 2430 nt., 2687 nt., 3074 nt.; 32 U.S. Code § 406 nt.; 42 U.S. Code §§ 248c nt., 6686

Oct. 5, 1994, P.L. 103-337, 10 U.S. Code §§ 374 nt., 2687 nt., 7291 nt.

Dec. 21, 1995, P.L. 104-66, 10 U.S. Code § 1701 nt.

Feb. 10, 1996, P.L. 104-106, 10 U.S. Code §§ 115 nt., 1701 nt., 2302 nt., 2687 nt.; 42 U.S. Code § 248c nt.; 50 U.S. Code §§ 404b, 404c

Sept. 23, 1996, P.L. 104-201, 10 U.S. Code §§ 2302 nt., 2391 nt. , 3074 nt.; 42 U.S. Code § 248c nt.

Nov. 18, 1997, P.L. 105-85, 10 U.S. Code § 2302 nt.

July 29, 1998, P.L. 105-209, 42 U.S. Code § 6686

Oct. 17, 1998, P.L. 105-261, 10 U.S. Code § 374 nt.

Oct. 21, 1998, P.L. 105-277, 10 U.S. Code § 2391 nt.

National Defense Authorization Act for Fiscal Year 1993

Oct. 23, 1992, P.L. 102-484, 106 Stat. 2315

May 31, 1993, P.L. 103-35, 10 U.S. Code §§ 155, 155 nt., 664 nt., 1079, 1086a, 1162 nt., 1174a, 1463, 2323, 2347, 2350a nt., prec. 2381, 2391, 2410d, 2431 nt., 2501 nt., 2505 nt., 3077; 15 U.S. Code § 5611 nt.; 36 U.S. Code §§ 5013, 5113

Sept. 21, 1993, P.L. 103-82, 32 U.S. Code § 501 nt.; 42 U.S. Code § 12612 nt.

Nov. 30, 1993, P.L. 103-160, 10 U.S. Code §§ 113 nt., 664 nt., 1073 nt., 1079 nt., 1143a nt., 1162 nt., 1293 nt., 2208 nt., 2341 nt., 2687 nt., 2778 nt., 5859a; 20 U.S. Code § 238 nt.; 32 U.S. Code § 501 nt.; 50 U.S. Code § 98d nt., 1521 nt.

Oct. 5, 1994, P.L. 103-337, 10 U.S. Code §§ 113 nt., 261 nt., 1071 nt., 1079 nt., 2350a nt.; 22 U.S. Code § 5859a; 32 U.S. Code § 501 nt.; 50 U.S. Code § 98d nt.

Oct. 20, 1994, P.L. 103-382, 20 U.S. Code § 238 nt.; 32 U.S. Code § 501 nt.

Feb. 10, 1996, P.L. 104-106, 5 U.S. Code §§ prec. 3301, 3329, 3330; 10 U.S. Code §§ 113 nt., 115 nt., 410 nt., 1059 nt., 1293 nt., 2208 nt., 2301 nt., 2302 nt., 5859a, 10105 nt., 12001 nt., 12681 nt.; 20 U.S. Code § 7703 nt.; 42 U.S. Code § 7274j

Sept. 23, 1996, P.L. 104-201, 10 U.S. Code §§ 2505 nt., 2506 nt. ; 50 U.S. Code § 1521 nt.

Sept. 30, 1996, P.L. 104-208, 22 U.S. Code § 2778 nt.

Nov. 18, 1997, P.L. 105-85, 10 U.S. Code §§ 1448 nt., 1723 nt.; 2501 nt.; 20 U.S. Code § 7703 nt.; 32 U.S. Code § 501 nt.

Oct. 17, 1998, P.L. 105-261, 10 U.S. Code §§ 1143a nt., 1293 nt. , 12681 nt.

Oct. 21, 1998, P.L. 105-277, 10 U.S. Code §§ 1143 nt., 2501 nt.; 42 U.S. Code § 7274h

National Defense Authorization Act for Fiscal Year 1994

Nov. 30, 1993, P.L. 103-160, 107 Stat. 1547

Feb. 12, 1994, P.L. 103-211, 108 Stat. 41

Oct. 5, 1994, P.L. 103-337, 10 U.S. Code §§ 111 nt., 523 nt., 1073 nt., 1086 nt., 5013 nt., 7604 nt.; 22 U.S. Code § 2751 nt.; 42 U.S. Code § 7274k

Oct. 13, 1994, P.L. 103-355, 10 U.S. Code § 2430 nt.

Feb. 10, 1996, P.L. 104-106, 10 U.S. Code §§ 1059 nt., 1073 nt., 2208 nt., 2358 nt., 2401 nt., 2431 nt., 2687 nt., 4331 nt., 7604 nt.; 22 U.S. Code § 2751 nt.

Sept. 23, 1996, P.L. 104-201, 10 U.S. Code §§ 523 nt., 2358 nt., 2371 nt.; 22 U.S. Code § 2751 nt.; 42 U.S. Code § 7274k; 50 U.S. Code § 1522

Nov. 18, 1997, P.L. 105-85, 42 U.S. Code §§ 2121 nt., 7274k; 50 U.S. Code § 1523

Oct. 7, 1998, P.L. 105-244, 10 U.S. Code §§ 2324 nt., 2371 nt., 2701 nt.

Oct. 21, 1998, P.L. 105-277, 10 U.S. Code § 2701 nt.

National Defense Authorization Act for Fiscal Year 1995

Oct. 5, 1994, P.L. 103-337, 108 Stat. 2663

Feb. 10, 1996, P.L. 104-106, 10 U.S. Code §§ prec. 121, 221 nt., 401 nt., 571 nt., prec. 1031, 1074 nt., 2112 nt., 2153 nt., 2208 nt., 2358 nt., 2466 nt., 2687 nt., 2701, prec. 6951, 6975, 10501 nt.; 22 U.S. Code § 5956

Sept. 23, 1996, P.L. 104-201, 10 U.S. Code §§ 523 nt., 2112 nt., 2358 nt., 4411 nt.; 22 U.S. Code § 2751 nt.; 42 U.S. Code § 2153 nt.

Oct. 19, 1996, P.L. 104-324, 10 U.S. Code § 503 nt.

Nov. 13, 1997, P.L. 105-78, 10 U.S. Code § 176 nt.

Nov. 18, 1997, P.L. 105-85, 10 U.S. Code §§ 1092 nt., 2324 nt., 2358 nt.; 42 U.S. Code § 7231 nt.

Oct. 17, 1998, P.L. 105-261, 42 U.S. Code § 7231 nt.

National Defense Authorization Act for Fiscal Year 1996

Feb. 10, 1996, P.L. 104-106, 110 Stat. 186

April 26, 1996, P.L. 104-134, 10 U.S. Code § 1177 nt.

Sept. 23, 1996, P.L. 104-201, 10 U.S. Code §§ 129a nt., 131, 131 nt., 133a, 134a, 137, 138, 142, 167 nt., 176, 1056, 1076b nt., 1216, 1401 nt., 1405, 1587, 2112 nt., 2410b, 2305, 10201; 22 U.S. Code § 5955 nt.; 41 U.S. Code §§ 253b, 427; 42 U.S. Code §§ 248c nt., 2121 nt.; 50 U.S. Code §§ 523 nt., 1521 nt.

Nov. 18, 1997, P.L. 105-85, 10 U.S. Code §§ 1076, 1130 nt., 1701 nt., prec. 2460, 2461 nt., 2464 nt., 2466, 2469, 2501 nt., 2701 nt., 6975, 10001, 10154; 42 U.S. Code §§ 2121, 7271b; 50 U.S. Code § 1521

Oct. 17, 1998, P.L. 105-261, 10 U.S. Code § 221 nt.; 37 U.S. Code §§ 301a, 301a nt., 402 nt.

National Defense Authorization Act for Fiscal Year 1997

Sept. 23, 1996, P.L. 104-201, 110 Stat. 2422

Sept. 30, 1996, P.L. 104-208, 10 U.S. Code § 1073 nt.

Nov. 18, 1997, P.L. 105-85, 10 U.S. Code §§ 131 nt., 441 nt., 1073 nt., 1076c nt., 2302 nt., 2430 nt., 2502, prec. 2541, 2554, 2702 nt., 2706 nt., 4411 nt., 7902 nt., 7903 nt., 12733; 20 U.S. Code §§ 901, 903; 37 U.S . Code § 302c; 41 U.S. Code § 10b-3; 42 U.S. Code §§ 7257b, 7271c, 7274k nt., 7274o

Oct. 17, 1998, P.L. 105-261, 41 U.S. Code § 10b-3

National Defense Authorization Act for Fiscal Year 1998

Nov. 18, 1997, P.L. 105-85, 111 Stat. 1629

Dec. 1, 1997, P.L. 105-129, 10 U.S. Code § 113 nt.

Oct. 17, 1998, P.L. 105-261, 10 U.S. Code §§ 113 nt., 2461 nt.; 22 U.S. Code § 1928 nt.; 31 U.S. Code § 1113 nt.; 41 U.S. Code § 435 nt.; 42 U.S. Code §§ 2121 nt., 7273; 50 U.S. Code Appx. § 2404 nt.

Oct. 21, 1998, P.L. 105-277, 10 U.S. Code § 2687 nt.

National Defense Authorization Act for Fiscal Years 1992 and 1993

Dec. 5, 1991, P.L. 102-190, 105 Stat. 1290

Oct. 23, 1992, P.L. 102-484, 10 U.S. Code §§ 113 nt., 115a nt., 261 nt., 663 nt., 1071 nt., 1079, 1086 nt., 2208 nt., 2301 nt., 2320 nt., 2321j nt., 2352, 2431 nt., 2466 nt., 2687 nt., 2803; 50 U.S. Code § 98d nt.

Nov. 4, 1992, P.L. 102-585, 10 U.S. Code § 1074 nt.; 38 U.S. Code § 527 nt.

May 31, 1993, P.L. 103-35, 10 U.S. Code §§ 591 nt., 1086, 2431 nt.; 42 U.S. Code §§ 2123, 7142

Nov. 30, 1993, P.L. 103-160, 10 U.S. Code §§ 261 nt., 1928 nt., 2208 nt., 2372 nt., 2680 nt., 2687 nt.

Oct. 5, 1994, P.L. 103-337, 10 U.S. Code §§ 555 nt., 2208 nt., 12001 nt.; 42 U.S. Code § 7274g; 50 U.S. Code § 401 nt.

Oct. 13, 1994, P.L. 103-355, 10 U.S. Code § 2301 nt.

Feb. 10, 1996, P.L. 104-106, 10 U.S. Code §§ 115 nt., 2192 nt., 2208 nt., 2680 nt., 2687 nt., 12001 nt., 12321 nt.; 22 U.S. Code § 2751 nt.; 50 U.S. Code § 435 nt.

Sept. 23, 1996, P.L. 104-201, 10 U.S. Code §§ 2687 nt., 12001 nt.

Nov. 18, 1997, P.L. 105-85, 10 U.S. Code § 2320 nt.

Oct. 7, 1998, P.L. 105-244, 42 U.S. Code § 7274e

National Defense Authorization Act, 1985

Oct. 23, 1992, P.L. 102-484, 22 U.S. Code § 1928 nt.

National Defense Cooperation Act

Mo. Rev. Stat., 91.620 et seq.

National Defense Education Act Amendments of 1964

Oct. 16, 1964, P.L. 88-665, 78 Stat. 1100, 20 U.S. Code §§ 237- 239, 242 nt., 244, 401, 403, 421-426, 441-445, 462-464, 481, 483-485, 491, 511, 513, 563, 584, 589, 591, 592, 633, 644, 645

National Defense Education Act of 1958

Sept. 2, 1958, P.L. 85-864, 72 Stat. 1580, 20 U.S. Code §§ 15aaa--15ggg, 401 to 403, 421 to 429, 441 to 445, 461 to 465, 481 to 484, 491, 511 to 513, 521 and others; 42 U.S. Code §§ 1876 to 1879

June 25, 1959, P.L. 86-70, 73 Stat. 144, 20 U.S. Code §§ 403, 442 , 588

July 12, 1960, P.L. 86-624, 74 Stat. 413, 20 U.S. Code §§ 403, 442, 588

Sept. 22, 1961, P.L. 87-293, 75 Stat. 623, 20 U.S. Code § 425

Oct. 3, 1961, P.L. 87-344, 75 Stat. 759, 20 U.S. Code §§ 421, 422 , 426, 441, 442, 444, 462, 481, 484, 491, 511, 521, 563, 589

Oct. 5, 1961, P.L. 87-400, 75 Stat. 832, 20 U.S. Code § 425

Oct. 16, 1962, P.L. 87-835, 76 Stat. 1070, 20 U.S. Code § 581

Dec. 18, 1963, P.L. 88-210, 77 Stat. 415, 20 U.S. Code §§ 403, 421 to 423, 425, 426, 441 to 444, 462, 464, 481 to 484, 491, 511, 521, 541, 551, 561, 563, 588, 589

Oct. 16, 1964, P.L. 88-665, 78 Stat. 1100, 20 U.S. Code §§ 401, 403, 421 to 426, 441 to 445, 462 to 464, 481, 483 to 485, 491, 511, 513, 563, 584, 589, 591, 592

Oct. 9, 1965, P.L. 89-253, 79 Stat. 979, 20 U.S. Code § 425

Nov. 8, 1965, P.L. 89-329, 79 Stat. 1228, 20 U.S. Code §§ 403, 424, 425, 441, 591, 591 nt.

Oct. 29, 1966, P.L. 89-698, 80 Stat. 1069, 20 U.S. Code §§ 511, 592, 601, 602

Nov. 3, 1966, P.L. 89-752, 80 Stat. 1245, 20 U.S. Code §§ 403, 421, 425, 441, 443

Nov. 8, 1966, P.L. 89-794, 80 Stat. 1476, 20 U.S. Code § 425

Jan. 2, 1968, P.L. 90-247, 81 Stat. 820, 20 U.S. Code § 591

July 18, 1968, P.L. 90-407, 82 Stat. 367, 42 U.S. Code § 1877

Oct. 16, 1968, P.L. 90-575, 82 Stat. 1034, 20 U.S. Code §§ 403, 421 to 426, 441 to 455, 462 to 464, 481, 483, 484, 511, 513, 562, 581, 584, 588

Oct. 22, 1969, P.L. 91-95, 83 Stat. 143, 20 U.S. Code § 421

April 13, 1970, P.L. 91-230, 84 Stat. 174, 20 U.S. Code §§ 425, 441, 443

June 23, 1972, P.L. 92-318, 86 Stat. 272, 20 U.S. Code §§ 421, 511, 513

Sept. 24, 1977, P.L. 95-112, 20 U.S. Code § 441

Aug. 12, 1979, P.L. 96-49, 20 U.S. Code § 513

National Defense Education Act of 1959

Aug. 21, 1986, P.L. 99-383, 42 U.S. Code §§ 1876 to 1879

National Defense Emergency Appropriation Act

Dec. 23, 1941, Ch. 621, 55 Stat. 855, 42 U.S. Code § 1523 nt.

National Defense Facilities Act of 1950

Sept. 11, 1950, Ch. 945, 64 Stat. 829 (See 10 U.S. Code §§ 2231 to 2233, 2236 to 2238)

Aug. 9, 1955, Ch. 662, 69 Stat. 593 (See 10 U.S. Code §§ 2232, 2233, 2236 to 2238)

Aug. 3, 1956, Ch. 939, 70 Stat. 1018 (See 10 U.S. Code § 2233)

Aug. 29, 1957, P.L. 85-215, 71 Stat. 490 (See 10 U.S. Code § 2233)

Aug. 20, 1958, P.L. 85-685, 72 Stat. 665, 10 U.S. Code § 2233 nt.

National Defense Housing Act

See Lahham Act (Public War Housing)
Pa. Purdon's Stat., Title 35, § 1595.1 et seq.
W. Va. Code 1966, § 16-17-1 et seq.

National Defense Housing Projects Act

N.J. Stat. Ann., 55:14C-1 et seq.

National Defense Impacted Region Assistance Act of 1985

Tex. Laws 69th Leg., 1985, p.263, Ch. 69, Art. 1, §§ 1 to 4
Tex. Rev. Civ. Stat., Art. 689a-4d

National Defense Patents Act

Aug. 21, 1941, Ch. 393, 55 Stat. 657

National Defense Ship Radio Act

Dec. 17, 1941, Ch. 588, 55 Stat. 808

National Defense Stockpile Amendments of 1987

Dec. 4, 1987, P.L. 100-180, 50 U.S. Code §§ 98 nt., 98a, 98b, 98d , 98e-1, 98h, 98h-2, 98h-4, 98h-5

National Dental Research Act

June 24, 1948, Ch. 621, 62 Stat. 598, 42 U.S. Code §§ 201, 210, 218, 241, 288 to 288e, 291k

National Diabetes Mellitus Research and Education Act

July 23, 1974, P.L. 93-354, 88 Stat. 373, 42 U.S. Code §§ 247b, 289c-1, 289c-1a, 289c-2, 4121

National Driver Register Act

Dec. 18, 1991, P.L. 102-240, 23 U.S. Code § 401 nt.

Oct. 31, 1994, P.L. 103-429, 23 U.S. Code § 401 nt.

National Driver Register Act of 1982

Oct. 25, 1982, P.L. 97-364, 23 U.S. Code § 401 nt.

Dec. 30, 1987, P.L. 100-223, 23 U.S. Code § 401 nt.

June 22, 1988, P.L. 100-342, 102 Stat. 624, 23 U.S. Code § 401 nt.

Aug. 18, 1990, P.L. 101-380, 23 U.S. Code § 401 nt.

National Dropout Prevention Act of 1991

Aug. 17, 1991, P.L. 102-103, 20 U.S. Code § 3241 nt.

National Drought Policy Act of 1998

July 16, 1998, P.L. 105-199, 42 U.S. Code § 5121 nt.

National Drug Interdiction Act of 1986

Dec. 21, 1995, P.L. 104-66, 21 U.S. Code § 801 nt.

National Drug Interdiction Improvement Act of 1986

Oct. 27, 1986, P.L. 99-570, 21 U.S. Code § 801 nt.

National Earthquake Hazards Reduction Program Reauthorization Act

Nov. 16, 1990, P.L. 101-614, 42 U.S. Code §§ 7701 nt., 7704 nt.

National Education Commission on Time and Learning Act

June 27, 1991, P.L. 102-62, 20 U.S. Code § 1221-1 nt.

Aug. 1, 1994, P.L. 103-290, 20 U.S. Code § 1221-1 nt.

National Education Statistics Act of 1994

Oct. 20, 1994, P.L. 103-382, 20 U.S. Code §§ 9001 nt., 9001 et seq.

Oct. 7, 1998, P.L. 105-244, 20 U.S. Code § 9001

National Emergencies Act

Sept. 14, 1976, P.L. 94-412, 50 U.S. Code § 1601 et seq.

Dec. 28, 1977, P.L. 95-223, 50 U.S. Code § 1651

Aug. 16, 1985, P.L. 99-93, 50 U.S. Code § 1622

Nov. 10, 1998, P.L. 105-362, 50 U.S. Code § 1651

National Emission Standards Act

Nov. 21, 1967, P.L. 90-148, 81 Stat. 499, 42 U.S. Code §§ 1857f-1 to 1857f-7

National Employment Service Act

June 6, 1933, Ch. 49, 48 Stat. 113, 29 U.S. Code §§ 49 to 49c, 49d, 49g, 49h, 49j, 49k, 557

National Endowment for Children's Educational Television Act of 1990

Oct. 18, 1990, P.L. 101-437, 47 U.S. Code § 609 nt.

National Endowment for Democracy Act

Nov. 22, 1983, P.L. 98-164, 22 U.S. Code §§ 4411 and nt., 4413

Aug. 16, 1985, P.L. 99-93, 22 U.S. Code §§ 4413 to 4415

Oct. 8, 1985, P.L. 99-120, 42 U.S. Code §§ 4026, 4056, 4101

Dec. 22, 1987, P.L. 100-204, 22 U.S. Code §§ 4412, 4413

Oct. 28, 1991, P.L. 102-138, 22 U.S. Code § 4413

April 30, 1994, P.L. 103-236, 22 U.S. Code § 4413

National Energy Conservation Policy Act

Nov. 9, 1978, P.L. 95-619, 12 U.S. Code §§ 1451, 1471, 1703, 1709 , 1713, 1715z-6, 1717, 1723f to 1723h, 1735f-4, 1735f-7; 15 U.S. Code §§ 2006, 2008; 42 U.S. Code §§ 300h-2, 300n-1, 1437c, 1474, 1483, 6211, 6215, 6233 et seq., 6245, 6272 to 6274, 6291 et seq., 6862 et seq., 7141, 8231 et seq.

June 30, 1980, P.L. 96-294, 42 U.S. Code § 8211 et seq.

April 7, 1986, P.L. 99-272, 42 U.S. Code § 8287

Aug. 28, 1986, P.L. 99-412, 42 U.S. Code §§ 8201, 8216 to 8218, 8226 to 8229, 8281 to 8284

Nov. 5, 1988, P.L. 100-615, 42 U.S. Code §§ prec. 8251, 8251 et seq.

Dec. 11, 1989, P.L. 101-218, 42 U.S. Code § 8243

June 13, 1991, P.L. 102-54, 42 U.S. Code § 8232

Oct. 24, 1992, P.L. 102-486, 42 U.S. Code §§ prec. 8236, 8236 to 8236b, 8252 to 8256, 8258, 8258a, 8258b, 8259, prec. 8287, 8287, 8287c

Dec. 21, 1995, P.L. 104-66, 42 U.S. Code §§ 8253, 8258

Feb. 10, 1996, P.L. 104-106, 42 U.S. Code § 8287

Oct. 19, 1996, P.L. 104-316, 42 U.S. Code § 8287

Oct. 21, 1998, P.L. 105-277, 42 U.S. Code § 6873

Nov. 13, 1998, P.L. 105-388, 42 U.S. Code §§ 8217, 8231, 8235e, 8259, 8287, 8287c

National Energy Extension Service Act

June 3, 1977, P.L. 95-39, 42 U.S. Code § 5813 et seq.

Oct. 5, 1984, P.L. 98-454, 98 Stat. 1736, 42 U.S. Code § 7011

Oct. 24, 1992, P.L. 102-486, 42 U.S. Code §§ 7001 to 7011, 7001 nt.

National Environmental Education Act

Nov. 16, 1990, P.L. 101- 619, 20 U.S. Code § 5501 et seq.

Oct. 20, 1994, P.L. 103-382, 20 U.S. Code § 5502

National Environmental Policy Act of 1969

Jan. 1, 1970, P.L. 91-190, 83 Stat. 852, 42 U.S. Code §§ 4321, 4331 to 4335, 4341 to 4347

July 3, 1975, P.L. 94-52, 89 Stat. 258, 42 U.S. Code §§ 4343, 4346a, 4346b, 4347

Aug. 9, 1975, P.L. 94-83, 89 Stat. 424, 42 U.S. Code § 4332

Nov. 9, 1978, P.L. 95-620, 42 U.S. Code § 8473

Nov. 8, 1985, P.L. 99-145

National Fallen Firefighters Foundation Act

Oct. 26, 1992, P.L. 102-522, 36 U.S. Code § 5201 nt.

Oct. 21, 1998, P.L. 105-276, 36 U.S. Code §§ 151302 nt., 151304 nt., 151307 nt.

National Film Preservation Act of 1988

Sept. 27, 1988, P.L. 100-446, 2 U.S. Code § 178 nt.

June 26, 1992, P.L. 102-307, 2 U.S. Code §§ 178-1781

National Film Preservation Act of 1992

June 26, 1992, P.L. 102-307, 2 U.S. Code §§ 179 nt., 179-179k

Oct. 11, 1996, P.L. 104-285, 2 U.S. Code §§ 179-179k, 179 nt.

National Film Preservation Act of 1996

Oct. 11, 1996, P.L. 104-285, 2 U.S. Code § 179l nt.

National Film Preservation Foundation Act

Oct. 11, 1996, P.L. 104-285, 36 U.S. Code § 5701 nt.

National Firearms Act

June 26, 1934, Ch. 757, 48 Stat. 1236

Aug. 16, 1954, Ch. 736, 68A Stat. 721, 26 U.S. Code §§ 5801 to 5803, 5811 to 5814, 5821, 5831, 5841 to 5848, 5851 to 5853, 5861, 5862

Sept. 2, 1958, P.L. 85-859, 72 Stat. 1427, 26 U.S. Code §§ 5801, 5811, 5814, 5821, 5843, 5848, 5849, 5851, 5854, 5855

June 1, 1960, P.L. 86-478, 74 Stat. 149, 26 U.S. Code §§ 5801, 5811, 5848

Oct. 22, 1968, P.L. 90-618, 82 Stat. 1227, 26 U.S. Code §§ 5801, 5802, 5811, 5812, 5821, 5822, 5841 to 5849, 5851 to 5854, 5861, 5871, 5872

May 19, 1986, P.L. 99-308, 26 U.S. Code
§ 5845

National Firearms Act Amendments of 1968

Oct. 22, 1968, P.L. 90-618, 82 Stat. 1227, 26
U.S. Code §§ 5801, 5802, 5811, 5812,
5821, 5822, 5841 to 5849, 5871, 5872,
6806, 7273

National Fish and Wildlife Foundation Establishment Act

March 26, 1984, P.L. 98-244, 16 U.S. Code
§§ 3701 et seq., 3701 nt.

Jan. 11, 1988, P.L. 100-240m, 16 U.S. Code
§§ 3701, 3703, 3704, 3706, 3709

Nov. 14, 1988, P.L. 100-653, 16 U.S. Code
§ 3704

Nov. 16, 1990, P.L. 101-593, 16 U.S. Code
§§ 3702, 3709

April 11, 1994, P.L. 103-232, 16 U.S. Code
§§ 3701, 3702, 3709

National Fish and Wildlife Foundation Establishment Act Amendments of 1990

Nov. 16, 1990, P.L. 101-593, 16 U.S. Code
§ 3701

National Fish and Wildlife Foundation Improvement Act of 1994

April 11, 1994, P.L. 103-232, 16 U.S. Code
§ 3701 nt.

National Flag Week Act

June 9, 1966, P.L. 89-443, 80 Stat. 194, 36
U.S. Code § 157a

National Flood Insurance Act

Oct. 21, 1998, P.L. 105-276, 42 U.S. Code
§ 4016

National Flood Insurance Act of 1968

Aug. 1, 1968, P.L. 90-448, 82 Stat. 572, 42
U.S. Code §§ 1401, 2414, 4001 nt., 4011 to
4027, 4041, 4051 to 4055, 4071, 4072,
4081 to 4084, 4101 to 4103, 4121 to 4127

Dec. 31, 1973, P.L. 93-234, 87 Stat. 977, 42
U.S. Code §§ 4012a, 4013 to 4016, 4026,
4054, 4056, 4101, 4104, 4121

Dec. 23, 1975, P.L. 94-173, 89 Stat. 1028, 42
U.S. Code § 4056

June 30, 1977, P.L. 95-60, 42 U.S. Code
§ 4026

July 31, 1977, P.L. 95-80, 42 U.S. Code
§ 4026

Oct. 12, 1977, P.L. 95-128, 42 U.S. Code
§ 4026 et seq.

Oct. 31, 1978, P.L. 95-557, 42 U.S. Code
§§ 4026, 4056, 4127

Dec. 21, 1979, P.L. 96-153, 42 U.S. Code
§§ 4026, 4056, 4127

Oct. 6, 1982, P.L. 97-289, 42 U.S. Code
§§ 4026, 4056(a)

Oct. 18, 1982, P.L. 97-348, 42 U.S. Code
§ 4028

Nov. 30, 1983, P.L. 98-181, 42 U.S. Code
§§ 4011 to 4027, 4101 to 4104a

Oct. 17, 1984, P.L. 98-479, 42 U.S. Code
§§ 4017, 4101, 4124

Oct. 8, 1985, P.L. 99-120, 42 U.S. Code
§§ 4026, 4056, 4101

Nov. 15, 1985, P.L. 99-156, 42 U.S. Code
§§ 4026, 4056, 4101

Dec. 26, 1985, P.L. 99-219, 42 U.S. Code
§§ 4026, 4056, 4101

March 27, 1986, P.L. 99-267, 42 U.S. Code
§§ 4026, 4056, 4101

April 7, 1986, P.L. 99-272, 42 U.S. Code
§§ 4026, 4056, 4101

Feb. 5, 1988, P.L. 100-242, 40 U.S. Code
§§ 4013, 4026, 4029, 4056, 4101, 4127

Nov. 7, 1988, P.L. 100-628, 42 U.S. Code
§§ 4013, 4121

Nov. 23, 1988, P.L. 100-707, 42 U.S. Code
§ 4013

Nov. 3, 1989, P.L. 101-137, 42 U.S. Code
§§ 4013, 4026, 4056, 4071, 4101, 4127

Nov. 5, 1990, P.L. 101-508, 42 U.S. Code
§§ 4013 to 4015, 4017, 4026, 4056, 4126

Nov. 16, 1990, P.L. 101-591, 42 U.S. Code
§ 4028

Oct. 28, 1992, P.L. 102-550, 42 U.S. Code
§ 4014

Sept. 23, 1994, P.L. 103-325, 42 U.S. Code
§§ 4001, 4011, 4013, 4015, 4017, 4022,
4026, 4027, 4029, 4056, 4081, 4101, 4103,
4104a et seq., 4121

Sept. 26, 1996, P.L. 104-204, 42 U.S. Code
§§ 4026, 4127

Sept. 30, 1996, P.L. 104-208, 42 U.S. Code
§ 4016

Sept. 30, 1997, P.L. 105-46, 42 U.S. Code
§§ 4026, 4056

Oct. 27, 1997, P.L. 105-65, 42 U.S. Code
§§ 4016, 4026, 4056, 4127

Oct. 21, 1998, P.L. 105-276, 42 U.S. Code
§§ 4026, 4056, 4127

Continued

549

National Flood Insurance Reform Act of 1994

Sept. 23, 1994, P.L. 103-325, 42 U.S. Code § 4001 nt.

National Forest and Public Lands of Nevada Enhancement Act of 1988

Oct. 28, 1988, P.L. 100-550, 102 Stat. 2749

National Forest-Dependent Rural Communities Economic Diversification Act of 1990

Nov. 28, 1990, P.L. 101-624, 7 U.S. Code §§ 6601 nt., 6611 to 6617

National Forest Foundation Act

Nov. 16, 1990, P.L. 101-593, 16 U.S. Code §§ 583j nt., 583j to 583j-8

Oct. 12, 1993, P.L. 103-106, 16 U.S. Code §§ 583j-3, 583j-8

National Forest Foundation Act Amendment Act of 1993

Oct. 12, 1993, P.L. 103-106, 16 U.S. Code §§ 583j nt., 583j-3, 583j-3 nt., 583j-8

National Forest Land Act

Ill. Rev. Stat. 1991, Ch. 1, §§ 4100, 4101

National Forest Management Act of 1976

Oct. 22, 1976, P.L. 94-588, 16 U.S. Code § 1600 et seq.

Feb. 20, 1978, P.L. 95-233, 16 U.S. Code § 472a(e)

Aug. 20, 1988, P.L. 100-409, 102 Stat. 1090, 16 U.S. Code § 521b

Nov. 28, 1990, P.L. 101-626, 16 U.S. Code § 472a nt.

Nov. 2, 1994, P.L. 103-437, 16 U.S. Code § 521b

National Forest Ski Area Permit Act of 1986

Oct. 22, 1986, P.L. 99-522, 16 U.S. Code § 497b nt.

National Forest System Drug Control Act of 1986

Oct. 27, 1986, P.L. 99-570, 16 U.S. Code § 559b

Nov. 18, 1988, P.L. 100-690, 16 U.S. Code §§ 559c, 559d, 559g

National Forests Act of 1972

June 5, 1978, P.L. 95-289, 16 U.S. Code § 558d

Sept. 21, 1993, P.L. 103-82, 16 U.S. Code § 558a

National Foundation on the Arts and the Humanities Act Amendments of 1983

May 31, 1984, P.L. 98-306, 20 U.S. Code § 951 nt.

National Foundation on the Arts and the Humanities Act of 1965

Sept. 29, 1965, P.L. 89-209, 79 Stat. 845, 20 U.S. Code §§ 784 to 786, 951 to 963

Sept. 11, 1967, P.L. 90-83, 81 Stat. 223, 20 U.S. Code §§ 954, 956

June 18, 1968, P.L. 90-348, 82 Stat. 184, 20 U.S. Code §§ 952, 954, 955, 957, 959, 960

Oct. 16, 1968, P.L. 90-575, 82 Stat. 1061, 20 U.S. Code § 961

July 20, 1970, P.L. 91-346, 84 Stat. 443, 20 U.S. Code §§ 951, 952, 954 to 960

Oct. 19, 1973, P.L. 93-133, 87 Stat. 461, 20 U.S. Code §§ 951, 952, 954-960

May 31, 1984, P.L. 98-306, 20 U.S. Code §§ 951 nt., 953, 955, 957 , 960

Dec. 20, 1985, P.L. 99-194, 20 U.S. Code §§ 951 et seq.

July 9, 1986, P.L. 99-362, 20 U.S. Code § 960

Nov. 5, 1990, P.L. 101-512, 20 U.S. Code §§ 951, 952, 954, 954 nt., 954a, 955, 956, 958-960

Dec. 2, 1993, P.L. 103-171, 20 U.S. Code § 958

Oct. 20, 1994, P.L. 103-382, 20 U.S. Code § 960

Nov. 14, 1997, P.L. 105-83, 20 U.S. Code § 955

Nov. 26, 1997, P.L. 105-119, 20 U.S. Code § 955

Oct. 21, 1998, P.L. 105-277, 20 U.S. Code § 955

National Fund for the Financing of Cultural Endeavors Act

P.R. Laws Ann. 1954, Title 18, § 1701 et seq.

National Gallery of Art Act

March 24, 1937, Ch. 50, 50 Stat. 51, 20 U.S. Code §§ 71 to 75

April 13, 1939, Ch. 61, 53 Stat. 577, 20 U.S. Code § 74

July 5, 1968, P.L. 90-376, 82 Stat. 286, 20 U.S. Code §§ 71a, 71b

National Gambling Impact Study Commission Act

Aug. 3, 1996, P.L. 104-169, 18 U.S. Code § 1955 nt.

July 25, 1997, P.L. 105-30, 18 U.S. Code § 1955 nt.

National Gas Pipeline Safety Act of 1968

Aug. 12, 1968, P.L. 90-481, 82 Stat. 720, 49 U.S. Code Appx. §§ 1671 et seq.

Aug. 30, 1974, P.L. 93-403, 88 Stat. 802, 49 U.S. Code §§ 1674, 1684

Oct. 11, 1984, P.L. 98-464, 98 Stat. 1821, 49 U.S. Code Appx. §§ 1681, 1683, 1684

National Geography Studies Centers Act

Oct. 31, 1988, P.L. 100-569, 20 U.S. Code § 2701 nt.

National Geologic Mapping Act of 1992

May 18, 1992, P.L. 102-285, 43 U.S. Code §§ 31a-31h, 31a nt.

Nov. 2, 1994, P.L. 103-437, 43 U.S. Code §§ 31c, 31g

Aug. 5, 1997, P.L. 105-36, 43 U.S. Code §§ 31b to 31h

Nov. 10, 1998, P.L. 105-362, 43 U.S. Code § 31g

National Geologic Mapping Reauthorization Act of 1997

Aug. 5, 1997, P.L. 105-36, 43 U.S. Code § 31a nt.

National Gold and Silver Stamping Act of 1906

June 13, 1906, Ch. 3289, 34 Stat. 260, 15 U.S. Code §§ 294 to 300

National Guard

Aug. 10, 1956, Ch. 1041, 70A Stat. 596, 32 U.S. Code §§ 1 to 713

Sept. 2, 1958, P.L. 85-861, 72 Stat. 1542, 32 U.S. Code §§ 101, 109, 111, 305, 307, 309, 310, 313, 318, 321, 323, 710, 714

Sept. 2, 1958, P.L. 85-894, 72 Stat. 1713, 32 U.S. Code § 314

June 25, 1959, P.L. 86-70, 73 Stat. 148, 32 U.S. Code § 101

July 7, 1960, P.L. 86-601, 74 Stat. 343, 32 U.S. Code § 709 nts.

July 12, 1960, P.L. 86-624, 74 Stat. 417, 32 U.S. Code § 101

Sept. 13, 1960, P.L. 86-740, 74 Stat. 878, 32 U.S. Code § 715

June 16, 1961, P.L. 87-46, 75 Stat. 92, 32 U.S. Code § 714

Sept. 13, 1961, P.L. 87-224, 75 Stat. 496, 32 U.S. Code § 709

Oct. 4, 1961, P.L. 87-378, 75 Stat. 808, 32 U.S. Code § 302

Sept. 7, 1962, P.L. 87-649, 76 Stat. 495, 32 U.S. Code §§ 303, 318, 321, 715

Oct. 5, 1962, P.L. 87-751, 76 Stat. 748, 32 U.S. Code § 304

Oct. 3, 1964, P.L. 88-621, 78 Stat. 999, 32 U.S. Code §§ 502, 504

Sept. 11, 1967, P.L. 90-83, 81 Stat. 220, 32 U.S. Code § 107

Nov. 8, 1967, P.L. 90-130, 81 Stat. 383, 32 U.S. Code §§ 305, 313

Dec. 1, 1967, P.L. 90-168, 81 Stat. 526, 10 U.S. Code §§ 133 nt., 136 nt., 8212 nt.; 32 U.S. Code § 502

Aug. 13, 1968, P.L. 90-486, 82 Stat. 755, 32 U.S. Code §§ 709, 715

Sept. 26, 1968, P.L. 90-525, 82 Stat. 878, 32 U.S. Code § 715

July 8, 1970, P.L. 91-312, 84 Stat. 412, 32 U.S. Code § 715

Aug. 13, 1971, P.L. 92-119, 85 Stat. 340, 32 U.S. Code §§ 107, 709

June 6, 1972, P.L. 92-310, 86 Stat. 203, 32 U.S. Code § 708

Sept. 29, 1972, P.L. 92-445, 86 Stat. 745, 32 U.S. Code § 715

Oct. 2, 1972, P.L. 92-453, 86 Stat. 759, 32 U.S. Code § 716

Oct. 13, 1972, P.L. 92-492, 86 Stat. 810, 32 U.S. Code §§ 101, 307

July 8, 1974, P.L. 93-336, 88 Stat. 292, 32 U.S. Code § 715

National Guard Act

Alaska Stat. 1962, § 26.05.010 et seq.

D.C. Code 1973, § 39-101 et seq.

Continued

Del. Code of 1974, Title 20, § 101 et seq.

Ill. Rev. Stat. 1991, Ch. 129

Md. Ann. Code 1957, Art. 65, § 1 et seq.

N.H. Rev. Stat. 1955, 110-B:1 et seq.

Ore. Rev. Stat. 1953, 397.005 et seq.

Pa. Cons. Stat., Title 51, § 1101 et seq.

R.I. Gen. Laws 1956, 30-3-1 et seq.

Vt. Stat. Ann., Title 20, § 361 et seq.

W. Va. Code 1966, § 15-1B-1 et seq.

Wyo. Stat. Ann., § 19-2-101 et seq.

National Guard Act of 1933

June 15, 1933, Ch. 87, 48 Stat. 153 (See 10 U.S. Code §§ 101, 591 to 593, 3015, 3033, 3034, 3063 to 3065, 3075, 3355, 3395, 3445, 3447, 3496, 3541, 3820 and others; 31 U.S. Code § 698; 32 U.S. Code §§ 101, 104, 107, 302 to 304, 307, 312, 313, 322 to 324, 506, 701, 705; 37 U.S. Code §§ 231 et seq.)

National Guard Armory and Robert F. Kennedy Memorial Stadium Public Safety Act

D.C. Code Ann., § 2-341 et seq.

National Guard Armory Board Act

Tex. Government Code, § 435.001 et seq.

National Guard Court-Martial Act

Ark. Code Ann. 1987, 12-60-102 et seq.

National Guard Educational Assistance Act

Ala. Acts 1984, p. 498

Miss. Code Ann. 1972, § 33-7-401 et seq.

N.H. Rev. Stat. 1955, 110-B:63a et seq.

National Guard Facilities Construction Act

Ky. Rev. Stat. 1971, 36.082

National Guard Members' Farm and Home Purchase Act of 1978

Cal. Military and Veterans Code § 270 et seq.

National Guard Members' Revenue Bond Act of 1978

Cal. Military and Veterans Code § 480 et seq.

National Guard Mobilization Act of 1940

Aug. 27, 1940, Ch. 689, 54 Stat. 858

July 28, 1942, Ch. 529, 56 Stat. 723

National Guard Mutual Assistance Compact

Alaska Stat. 1962, § 26.25.010 et seq.

Kan. Stat. Ann., 48-1701 et seq.

N.C. Gen. Stat. 1943, § 127A-175 et seq.

S.D. Codified Laws 1967, 33-9-12 et seq.

Va. Code 1950, § 44-54.1 et seq.

National Guard Mutual Assistance Counter-Drug Activities Compact Law

Ala. Code 1975, §§ 31-11-1, 31-11-2

Miss. Code Ann. 1972, §§ 33-7-501, 33-7-503

S.C. Code Ann. 1976, §§ 1-3-490, 1-3-491

Va. Code 1950, § 44-75.1:1

National Guard Officers' Act

June 19, 1935, Ch. 277, 49 Stat. 391, 10 U.S. Code § 3015; See 32 U.S. Code §§ 304, 324, 709

National Guard Reenlistment or Extension Act of 1981

Mont. Code Ann., 1991, 10-1-801 et seq.

National Guard Reserve Act

Cal. Military and Veterans Code § 550 et seq.

National Guard Scholarship Act

Ark. Code Ann. 1987, 6-82-801 et seq.

Ill. Rev. Stat. 1991, Ch. 129, § 421 et seq.

N.C. Gen. Stat. 1943, § 127A-190 et seq.

S.C. Code Ann. 1976, § 59-114-10 et seq.

National Guard Technicians Act of 1968

Aug. 13, 1968, P.L. 90-486, 82 Stat. 755, 5 U.S. Code §§ 2105, 8332, 8334, 8339; 10 U.S. Code §§ 3848, 3851, 8848, 8851; 32 U.S. Code §§ 709, 715; 42 U.S. Code § 418

Nov. 6, 1990, P.L. 101-530, 32 U.S. Code § 709 nt.

National Guard Tuition Waiver Act

N.D. Cent. Code 37-07.1-01 et seq.

National Guardsman's and Naval Militia-man's Compensation Act

Ill. Rev. Stat. 1991, Ch. 129, § 401 et seq.

National Guardsman's Compensation Act

Ill. Rev. Stat. 1989, Ch. 129, § 401 et seq.

National Health Museum Development Act

Nov. 13, 1997, P.L. 105-78, Title VII, 20 U.S. Code § 50 nt.

National Health Service Corps Revitalization Amendments of 1990

Nov. 16, 1990, P.L. 101-597, 42 U.S. Code § 201 nt.

National Health Survey Act

July 3, 1956, Ch. 510, 70 Stat. 489, 42 U.S. Code §§ 241, 242c

National Heart Act

June 16, 1948, Ch. 481, 62 Stat. 464, 42 U.S. Code §§ 201, 203, 206, 210, 218, 219, 241, 246 and others

National Heart, Blood Vessel, Lung and Blood Act of 1972

Sept. 19, 1972, P.L. 92-423, 86 Stat. 679, 42 U.S. Code §§ 218, 241, 287, 287a to 287i

National Highway System Designation Act of 1995

Nov. 28, 1995, P.L. 104-59, 23 U.S. Code § 101 nt.

Dec. 29, 1995, P.L. 104-88, 16 U.S. Code § 1261; 23 U.S. Code §§ 127, 149

June 9, 1998, P.L. 105-178, 23 U.S. Code § 109 nt.; 49 U.S. Code § 31136 nt.

National Highway Traffic Safety Administration Authorization Act of 1991

Dec. 18, 1991, P.L. 102-240, 15 U.S. Code § 1392 nt.

National Highway Traffic Safety Administration Reauthorization Act of 1998

June 9, 1998, P.L. 105-178, Title VII, Subtitle A, 49 U.S. Code § 30101 nt.

National Historic Preservation Act

Oct. 15, 1966, P.L. 89-665, 80 Stat. 915, 16 U.S. Code §§ 470 to 470n

Oct. 17, 1984, P.L. 98-483, 16 U.S. Code § 470t

Oct. 9, 1987, P.L. 100-127, 16 U.S. Code § 470h

Oct. 30, 1992, P.L. 102-575, 16 U.S. Code §§ 470-1, 470a, 470b, 470c, 470h, 470h-2, 470h-3, 470h-4, 470h-5, 470i, 470t, 470s, 470w, 470w-3, 470x et seq.

Nov. 2, 1994, P.L. 103-437, 16 U.S. Code §§ 470a, 470t, 470w-6

Nov. 12, 1996, P.L. 104-333, 16 U.S. Code §§ 470a, 470i, 470t, 470v-1, 470w-6

National Historic Preservation Act Amendments of 1980

Dec. 12, 1980, P.L. 96-515, 16 U.S. Code § 470 nt.

Nov. 2, 1994, P.L. 103-437, 16 U.S. Code §§ 469c-2, 470a-1

National Historic Preservation Act Amendments of 1992

Oct. 30, 1992, P.L. 102-575, 16 U.S. Code § 470 nt.

National Historic Publications and Records Commission Amendments of 1988

July 13, 1988, P.L. 100-365, 102 Stat. 823, 44 U.S. Code §§ 101 nt., 2501 to 2504

National Historical Park Act of 1974

Nov. 12, 1996, P.L. 104-333, 16 U.S. Code § 410z-1

National Homeownership Trust Act

Nov. 28, 1990, P.L. 101-625, 42 U.S. Code §§ 12701 nt., 12851- 12859

National Housing Act

June 27, 1934, Ch. 847, 48 Stat. 1246, 12 U.S. Code §§ 371, 1131g- 1, 1422, 1426, 1430, 1431, 1462, 1463, 1701 to 1703, 1705 to 1742; 41 U.S. Code § 22; 49 U.S. Code § 22

Feb. 19, 1937, Ch. 12, 50 Stat. 20, 12 U.S. Code § 1710

April 22, 1937, Ch. 121, 50 Stat. 70, 12 U.S. Code § 1703

Feb. 3, 1938, Ch. 13, 52 Stat. 8, 12 U.S. Code §§ 24, 1703, 1707 to 1715, 1715b, 1716 to 1718, 1722, 1731, 1733

March 28, 1941, Ch. 31, 55 Stat. 55, 12 U.S. Code §§ 371, 1430, 1702, 1706, 1707, 1713, 1715 to 1717, 1736 to 1742; 15 U.S. Code § 609k

June 28, 1941, Ch. 261, 55 Stat. 364, 12 U.S. Code §§ 1702, 1703, 1706b, 1709, 1710, 1731

Sept. 2, 1941, Ch. 410, 55 Stat. 686, 12 U.S. Code § 1738 (a)

May 26, 1942, Ch. 319, 56 Stat. 301, 12 U.S. Code §§ 1701b, 1703, 1715c, 1737 to 1740, 1743, 1743 nt.

Continued

March 23, 1943, Ch. 21, 57 Stat. 42, 12 U.S. Code §§ 1703, 1738

Oct. 14, 1943, Ch. 258, 57 Stat. 570, 12 U.S. Code §§ 1710, 1739

Oct. 15, 1943, Ch. 259, 57 Stat. 571, 12 U.S. Code §§ 1703, 1709, 1738

June 30, 1944, Ch. 334, 58 Stat. 648, 12 U.S. Code § 1738

March 31, 1945, Ch. 48, 59 Stat. 47, 12 U.S. Code §§ 1738, 1743

May 22, 1946, Ch. 268, 60 Stat. 212, 12 U.S. Code §§ 1738, 1739, 1743; 50 U.S. Code Appx. § 1830

July 1, 1946, Ch. 531, 60 Stat. 408, 12 U.S. Code § 1709

June 26, 1947, Ch. 152, 61 Stat. 182, 12 U.S. Code § 1703

June 30, 1947, Ch. 163, 61 Stat. 193, 12 U.S. Code § 1744; 50 U.S. Code Appx. § 1883

Aug. 5, 1947, Ch. 495, 61 Stat. 777, 12 U.S. Code §§ 1738, 1745

Dec. 27, 1947, Ch. 525, 61 Stat. 945, 12 U.S. Code § 1738

March 31, 1948, Ch. 165, 62 Stat. 101, 12 U.S. Code §§ 1738, 1739

July 1, 1948, Ch. 784, 62 Stat. 1206, 12 U.S. Code §§ 1713, 1716 to 1721

July 3, 1948, Ch. 825, 62 Stat. 1240, 12 U.S. Code § 1725

Aug. 10, 1948, Ch. 832, 62 Stat. 1268, 12 U.S. Code §§ 1702, 1703, 1706, 1709, 1710, 1713, 1716, 1738, 1743 to 1747l

March 30, 1949, Ch. 42; 63 Stat. 29, 12 U.S. Code § 1738; 50 U.S. Code Appx. § 1909

April 23, 1949, Ch. 89, 63 Stat. 57, 12 U.S. Code § 1715d; 48 U.S. Code §§ 484 to 484e

July 15, 1949, Ch. 338, 63 Stat. 421, 12 U.S. Code §§ 1703, 1709, 1738

July 19, 1949, Ch. 351, 63 Stat. 446, 12 U.S. Code § 1717

Aug. 30, 1949, Ch. 524, 63 Stat. 681, 12 U.S. Code §§ 1703, 1709, 1738

Oct. 25, 1949, Ch. 729, 63 Stat. 905, 12 U.S. Code §§ 1702, 1703, 1709, 1716, 1716 nt., 1717, 1734, 1738

April 20, 1950, Ch. 94, 64 Stat. 48, 12 U.S. Code §§ 1702, 1703, 1703 nt., 1705, 1706, 1706b, 1706c, 1707 to 1714, 1715c, 1715e, 1715f, 1716, 1717, 1720, 1721, 1736 to 1747l

May 2, 1950, Ch. 151, 64 Stat. 97, 12 U.S. Code § 1748h

June 27, 1950, Ch. 369, 64 Stat. 258, 12 U.S. Code §§ 1725, 1727, 1728, 1728 nt., 1730

Sept. 21, 1950, Ch. 967, 64 Stat. 894, 12 U.S. Code § 1728

Aug. 3, 1951, Ch. 293, 65 Stat. 173, 12 U.S. Code § 1706c

Sept. 1, 1951, Ch. 378, 65 Stat. 295, 12 U.S. Code §§ 1702, 1706, 1710, 1713, 1715c, 1715d, 1715f, 1715g, 1715h, 1716, 1743, 1747a, 1747f, 1747l, 1748b, 1748b nt., 1748g-1, 1750 to 1750g

Oct. 26, 1951, Ch. 577, 65 Stat. 647, 12 U.S. Code § 1715e

April 9, 1952, Ch. 173, 66 Stat. 51, 12 U.S. Code § 1716

July 14, 1952, Ch. 723, 66 Stat. 601, 12 U.S. Code §§ 1706d, 1707, 1713, 1715d, 1715h, 1715i, 1716, 1717, 1726, 1736, 1745, 1747l, 1748, 1750b

July 16, 1952, Ch. 883, 66 Stat. 727, 12 U.S. Code § 1724

June 30, 1953, Ch. 170, 67 Stat. 121, 12 U.S. Code §§ 1706c, 1709, 1711, 1713, 1715d, 1715e, 1715h, 1715j, 1716, 1717, 1735, 1748b, 1750b, 1750g; 48 U.S. Code §§ 723, 724, 1425, 1426

Aug. 8, 1953, Ch. 398, 67 Stat. 521 (See 10 U.S. Code § 4387)

June 29, 1954, Ch. 410, 68 Stat. 320, 12 U.S. Code §§ 1716, 1748

Aug. 2, 1954, Ch. 649, 68 Stat. 590, 12 U.S. Code §§ 1702a, 1703, 1706c, 1709 to 1711, 1713, 1715c, 1715e, 1715h and others

March 11, 1955, Ch. 10, 69 Stat. 11, 12 U.S. Code § 1715h

June 30, 1955, Ch. 251, 69 Stat. 225, 12 U.S. Code §§ 1703, 1748b

Aug. 4, 1955, Ch. 543, 69 Stat. 484, 12 U.S. Code § 1715n

Aug. 11, 1955, Ch. 783, 70 Stat. 635, 12 U.S. Code §§ 1703, 1710, 1713, 1715e, 1715h, 1715k, 1715l, 1715n, 1715r, 1720, 1726, 1729, 1739, 1748 1748a to 1748g; 42 U.S. Code §§ 1594, 1594a to 1594e

Feb. 10, 1956, Ch. 33, 70 Stat. 11, 12 U.S. Code § 1703

June 13, 1956, Ch. 381, 70 Stat. 273, 12 U.S. Code § 1748h-1

Aug. 7, 1956, Ch. 1029, 70 Stat. 1091, 12 U.S. Code §§ 1701h-1, 1703, 1709, 1713, 1715e, 1715h, 1715k, 1715l, 1715r, 1717, 1718, 1719, 1720, 1721, 1748, 1748b, 1749

March 27, 1957, P.L. 85-10, 71 Stat. 7, 12 U.S. Code §§ 1715k, 1718 to 1720

July 12, 1957, P.L. 85-104, 71 Stat. 294, 12 U.S. Code §§ 1703, 1709, 1710, 1713, 1715e, 1715j, 1715k, 1715l, 1715m, 1715n, 1715q, 1718, 1719, 1720, 1748b

April 1, 1958, P.L. 85-364, 72 Stat. 73, 12 U.S. Code §§ 1709, 1715h, 1720, 1748b

June 4, 1958, P.L. 85-442, 72 Stat. 176, 12 U.S. Code § 1715h

Sept. 2, 1958, P.L. 85-857, 72 Stat. 1265, 12 U.S. Code § 1731a

June 25, 1959, P.L. 86-70, 73 Stat. 142, 12 U.S. Code §§ 1706d, 1707, 1713, 1715d, 1736, 1747l, 1748, 1748e

July 28, 1959, P.L. 86-112, 73 Stat. 262, 12 U.S. Code § 1724

Aug. 10, 1959, P.L. 86-149, 73 Stat. 322, 12 U.S. Code § 1748b

Sept. 23, 1959, P.L. 86-372, 73 Stat. 654, 12 U.S. Code §§ 1703, 1706c, 1709, 1710, 1713, 1715c to 1715e, 1715h, 1715k to 1715m, 1715r, 1715t to 1715w and others

Sept. 23, 1959, P.L. 86-374, 73 Stat. 691, 12 U.S. Code § 1730a

June 8, 1960, P.L. 86-500, 74 Stat. 185, 12 U.S. Code § 1748b

June 11, 1960, P.L. 86-507, 74 Stat. 200, 12 U.S. Code § 1725

July 5, 1960, P.L. 86-578, 74 Stat. 314, 12 U.S. Code § 1748h-1

July 12, 1960, P.L. 86-624, 74 Stat. 411, 12 U.S. Code §§ 1706d, 1707, 1713, 1736, 1747l, 1748

Sept. 13, 1960, P.L. 86-746, 74 Stat. 883, 12 U.S. Code § 1730a

Sept. 13, 1960, P.L. 86-774, 74 Stat. 915, 12 U.S. Code § 1748h-1

Sept. 14, 1960, P.L. 86-788, 74 Stat. 1028, 12 U.S. Code § 1703

May 25, 1961, P.L. 87-38, 75 Stat. 85, 12 U.S. Code § 1715h

June 27, 1961, P.L. 87-57, 75 Stat. 111, 12 U.S. Code § 1748b

June 30, 1961, P.L. 87-70, 75 Stat. 175, 12 U.S. Code §§ 1703, 1709, 1710, 1713, 1715, 1715c, 1715e, 1715h, 1715j, 1715k, 1715l, 1715n, 1715o, 1715q and others; 42 U.S. Code § 1594i

Sept. 8, 1961, P.L. 87-210, 75 Stat. 483, 12 U.S. Code § 1727

Aug. 31, 1962, P.L. 87-623, 76 Stat. 418, 12 U.S. Code §§ 1748b, 1748h-1, 1748h-2

Oct. 5, 1962, P.L. 87-756, 76 Stat. 751, 12 U.S. Code § 1748h-3

June 29, 1963, P.L. 88-54, 77 Stat. 73, 12 U.S. Code § 1715l

Sept. 23, 1963, P.L. 88-127, 77 Stat. 163, 12 U.S. Code §§ 1748h- 1, 1748h-2

July 2, 1964, P.L. 88-349, 78 Stat. 239, 12 U.S. Code § 1715c

Sept. 2, 1964, P.L. 88-560, 78 Stat. 769, 12 U.S. Code § 1703, 1709, 1710, 1713, 1715c, 1715e, 1715k to 1715n, 1715r, 1715u to 1715y, 1717, 1719 to 1721, 1723b, 1723c and others

Aug. 10, 1965, P.L. 89-117, 79 Stat. 454, 12 U.S. Code §§ 1702, 1703, 1706c, 1709, 1710, 1713, 1715, 1715c, 1715e, 1715h, 1715k, 1715l to 1715n, 1715t, 1715v to 1715y, 1717 and others

Sept. 10, 1966, P.L. 89-566, 80 Stat. 738, 12 U.S. Code §§ 1718 to 1720

Oct. 16, 1966, P.L. 89-695, 80 Stat. 1036, 12 U.S. Code §§ 1724, 1728, 1730, 1730a

Nov. 3, 1966, P.L. 89-754, 80 Stat. 1267, 12 U.S. Code §§ 1702, 1709, 1715c, 1715e, 1715k, 1715l, 1715n, 1715r, 1717, 1719, 1720, 1723, 1731a and others

Nov. 6, 1966, P.L. 89-769, 80 Stat. 1317, 12 U.S. Code § 1715l; 42 U.S. Code § 1855a

May 25, 1967, P.L. 90-19, 81 Stat. 17, 12 U.S. Code §§ 1702, 1703 , 1705, 1706b, 1706c, 1707 to 1709, 1710 to 1715 and others

Dec. 15, 1967, P.L. 90-203, 81 Stat. 611, 12 U.S. Code § 1730c

Feb. 14, 1968, P.L. 90-255, 82 Stat. 5, 12 U.S. Code § 1730a

May 7, 1968, P.L. 90-301, 82 Stat. 114, 12 U.S. Code §§ 1713, 1715e, 1715v, 1715y

July 5, 1968, P.L. 90-389, 82 Stat. 295, 12 U.S. Code § 1729

Aug. 1, 1968, P.L. 90-448, 82 Stat. 477, 12 U.S. Code §§ 1701w, 1703, 1709, 1709-1, 1715c, 1715e, 1715k to 1715o, 1715q, 1715r, 1715w to 1715z- 7 and others

Sept. 21, 1968, P.L. 90-505, 82 Stat. 858, 12 U.S. Code § 1727

Oct. 21, 1968, P.L. 90-608, 82 Stat. 1194, 12 U.S. Code § 1730a

Sept. 30, 1969, P.L. 91-78, 83 Stat. 125, 12 U.S. Code §§ 1703, 1715h, 1715l, 1748h-1, 1748h-2, 1749bb, 1749aaa

Dec. 23, 1969, P.L. 91-151, 83 Stat. 375, 12 U.S. Code §§ 1724, 1727, 1728
Continued

Dec. 24, 1969, P.L. 91-152, 83 Stat. 379, 12 U.S. Code §§ 1703, 1706d, 1707, 1709, 1713, 1715d, 1715e, 1715h, 1715k to 1715n, 1715v, 1715w, 1715y, 1715z to 1715z-3 and others

July 24, 1970, P.L. 91-351, 84 Stat. 450, 12 U.S. Code §§ 82, 1709-1, 1710 nt., 1715z-3, 1715z-8, 1717, 1720, 1726, 1730a

Oct. 2, 1970, P.L. 91-432, 84 Stat. 886, 12 U.S. Code §§ 1703, 1715h, 1715l, 1748h-1, 1748h-2, 1749bb, 1749aaa

Oct. 21, 1970, P.L. 91-473, 84 Stat. 1064, 12 U.S. Code §§ 1703, 1715h, 1715l, 1748h-1, 1748h-2, 1749bb, 1749aaa

Oct. 26, 1970, P.L. 91-508, 84 Stat. 1116, 12 U.S. Code § 1730d

Dec. 1, 1970, P.L. 91-525, 84 Stat. 1384, 12 U.S. Code §§ 1703, 1715h, 1715l, 1748h-1, 1748h-2, 1749bb, 1749aaa

Dec. 31, 1970, P.L. 91-606, 84 Stat. 1758, 12 U.S. Code §§ 1706c, 1709, 1715l

Dec. 31, 1970, P.L. 91-609, 84 Stat. 1770, 12 U.S. Code §§ 1703, 1712, 1715c, 1715e, 1715h, 1715l, 1715z, 1715z-1, 1715z-3, 1715z-6, 1715z-7, 1717, 1718, 1735b to 1735d, 1735f-2 and others

Dec. 31, 1970, P.L. 91-621, 84 Stat. 1865, 12 U.S. Code §§ 1715g, 1715m

Dec. 22, 1971, P.L. 92-213, 85 Stat. 776, 12 U.S. Code § 1727

June 6, 1972, P.L. 92-310, 86 Stat. 206, 12 U.S. Code § 1723a

Oct. 18, 1972, P.L. 92-503, 86 Stat. 906, 12 U.S. Code §§ 1703, 1715h, 1715l, 1715z, 1715z-1, 1748h-1, 1748h-2, 1749bb, 1749aaa

Aug. 6, 1973, P.L. 93-84, 87 Stat. 220, 12 U.S. Code §§ 1703, 1715h, 1715l, 1715z, 1715z-1, 1748h-1, 1748h-2, 1749bb, 1749aaa

Aug. 16, 1973, P.L. 93-100, 87 Stat. 343, 12 U.S. Code §§ 1725, 1727

Dec. 28, 1973, P.L. 93-204, 87 Stat. 883, 12 U.S. Code § 1715w

May 22, 1974, P.L. 93-288, 88 Stat. 163, 12 U.S. Code §§ 1706c, 1709, 1715l

April 8, 1975, P.L. 94-13, 89 Stat. 69, 12 U.S. Code § 1749bbb

July 2, 1975, P.L. 94-50, 89 Stat. 254, 12 U.S. Code §§ 1723e, 1735b

Dec. 23, 1975, P.L. 94-173, 89 Stat. 1027, 12 U.S. Code §§ 1703, 1713, 1715e, 1715k, 1715l, 1715v, 1715y, 1715z-1

April 30, 1977, P.L. 95-24, 12 U.S. Code § 1715k et seq.

June 30, 1977, P.L. 95-60, 12 U.S. Code § 1703 et seq.

July 31, 1977, P.L. 95-80, 12 U.S. Code § 1703 et seq.

Sept. 20, 1977, P.L. 95-109, 15 U.S. Code § 1692l

Oct. 12, 1977, P.L. 95-128, 12 U.S. Code §§ 1715z, 1715z-1 et seq. .

Oct. 28, 1977, P.L. 95-147, 12 U.S. Code § 1725

Oct. 31, 1978, P.L. 95-557, 42 U.S. Code § 1703 et seq.

Nov. 9, 1978, P.L. 95-619, 12 U.S. Code §§ 1709, 1713, 1715z-6, 1735f-4

Nov. 10, 1978, P.L. 95-630, 12 U.S. Code §§ 1715z-10, 1726, 1728, 1729, 1730, 1730a

Sept. 28, 1979, P.L. 96-71, 12 U.S. Code §§ 1703, 1715h, 1715l, 1715z et seq., 1748h-1, 1748h-2, 1749b, 1749aaa

Nov. 5, 1979, P.L. 96-104, 12 U.S. Code § 1730e

Nov. 8, 1979, P.L. 96-105, 12 U.S. Code §§ 1703, 1715h, 1715l, 1715z, 1715z-1, 1715z-9, 1715z-10, 1748h-2, 1749bb, 1749aaa

Dec. 21, 1979, P.L. 96-153, 12 U.S. Code §§ 1703, 1709, 1713, 1715e, 1715h, 1715k to 1715m, 1715v, 1715y to 1715z-1, 1715z-6, 1715z-7, 1715z-9, 1715z-10, 1717, 1728, 1735c, 1735f-7, 1748h-1, 1748h-2, 1749bb, 1749aaa, 1749bbb

Dec. 28, 1979, P.L. 96-161, 12 U.S. Code § 1730e

March 31, 1980, P.L. 96-221, 12 U.S. Code §§ 1724, 1728, 1730g

May 24, 1982, P.L. 97-185, 12 U.S. Code § 1715z(h)(1)

Sept. 8, 1982, P.L. 97-253, 12 U.S. Code §§ 1709, 1709 nt., 1715e , 1715l, 1715y, 1715z

Oct. 6, 1982, P.L. 97-289, 12 U.S. Code §§ 1703, 1709-1, 1715h, 1715l, 1715z, 17152-1, 1715z-9, 1748h-1, 1749bb

Oct. 15, 1982, P.L. 97-320, 12 U.S. Code §§ 1725, 1726, 1728 to 1730a

Dec. 21, 1982, P.L. 97-377, 12 U.S. Code §§ 1713, 1715e, 1715k, 1715l, 1715y

Jan. 12, 1983, P.L. 97-457, 12 U.S. Code §§ 1729, 1729 nt., 1730, 1730g

Nov. 30, 1983, P.L. 98-181, 12 U.S. Code §§ 1703, 1706d, 1709, 1715h, 1715z-1, 1715z-12 to 1715z-18, 1735c, 1735f-4, 1748h-1, 1749bb, 1749aaa

Oct. 12, 1984, P.L. 98-473, 12 U.S. Code § 1749bb

Oct. 17, 1984, P.L. 98-479, 12 U.S. Code §§ 1715z, 1715z-1

Oct. 8, 1985, P.L. 99-120, 12 U.S. Code §§ 1703, 1715, 1715l, 1715z, 1715z-9, 1715z-10, 1715z-14, 1748h-1, 1748h-2, 1749bb, 1749aaa, 1749bbb

Nov. 15, 1985, P.L. 99-156, 12 U.S. Code §§ 1703, 1715h, 1715l, 1715z, 1715z-9, 1715z-10, 1715z-14, 1748h-1, 1748h-2, 1749bb, 1749aaa, 1749bbb

Dec. 26, 1985, P.L. 99-219, 12 U.S. Code §§ 1703, 1715a, 1715h, 1715l, 1715z, 1715z-9, 1715z-10, 1715z-14, 1748h-1, 1748h-2, 1749bb, 1749aaa, 1749bbb

March 27, 1986, P.L. 99-267, 12 U.S. Code §§ 1703, 1715h, 1715l, 1715z, 1715z-9, 1715z-10, 1748h-2, 1749bb, 1749aaa, 1749bbb

April 7, 1986, P.L. 99-272, 12 U.S. Code §§ 1703, 1715h, 1715l, 1715z, 1715z-9, 1715z-10, 1715z-13, 1715z-14, 1748h-1, 1748h-2, 1749bb, 1749aaa, 1749bbb

July 2, 1986, P.L. 99-349, 100 Stat. 727, 728

Oct. 27, 1986, P.L. 99-570, 12 U.S. Code § 1730

Nov. 5, 1986, P.L. 99-601, 12 U.S. Code § 1709

March 3, 1987, P.L. 100-14, 12 U.S. Code § 1721

Aug. 10, 1987, P.L. 100-86, 12 U.S. Code §§ 1725, 1727, 1729- 1730a, 1730h, 1730i

Sept. 30, 1987, P.L. 100-122, 12 U.S. Code § 1735f-9

Dec. 22, 1987, P.L. 100-202, 12 U.S. Code § 1715z-12

Feb. 5, 1988, P.L. 100-242, generally 12 U.S. Code §§ 1701 et seq.

Nov. 7, 1988, P.L. 100-628, 12 U.S. Code §§ 1709, 1710, 1715z-20

Nov. 18, 1988, P.L. 100-690, 12 U.S. Code § 1730d

Nov. 23, 1988, P.L. 100-707, 12 U.S. Code §§ 1706c, 1709, 1715l

Aug. 9, 1989, P.L. 101-73, 12 U.S. Code § 1724 et seq.

Nov. 3, 1989, P.L. 101-137, 12 U.S. Code §§ 1749bbb, 1749bbb-10d

Nov. 9, 1989, P.L. 101-144, 12 U.S. Code §§ 1709, 1715z

Dec. 15, 1989, P.L. 101-235, 12 U.S. Code §§ 1702, 1703, 1708- 1710, 1715e, 1715z, 1723i, 1731a, 1735f, 1735f-8, 1715t, 1715z-1, 1715z-6, 1715z -9, 1715z-15, 1735f-14 to 1735f-16, 1742aa to 1749ll

Oct. 1, 1990, P.L. 101-402, 12 U.S. Code § 1709

Nov. 5, 1990, P.L. 101-507, 12 U.S. Code § 1709

Nov. 5, 1990, P.L. 101-508, 12 U.S. Code §§ 1709, 1711, 1715l, 1715z-20, 1749bbb

Nov. 28, 1990, P.L. 101-625, 12 U.S. Code §§ 1701j-2, 1703, et seq. generally, 1715d, 1715l, 1715z-1, 1715z-6, 1715z-20, 1735f-9, 1735f-17 to 1735f-18 nt.

June 13, 1991, P.L. 102-54, 12 U.S. Code §§ 1717, 1731a

Oct. 6, 1992, P.L. 102-389, 12 U.S. Code §§ 1703, 1709, 1715z-20

Oct. 28, 1992, P.L. 102-550, 12 U.S. Code §§ 1703, 1708 to 1711, 1711 nt., 1713, 1715e, 1715k, 1715l, 1715n, 1715v, 1715w, 1715y, 1715z-1, 1715z -6, 1735b, 1735c, 1735f-9, 1735f-12, 1748h-1

Aug. 10, 1993, P.L. 103-66, 12 U.S. Code § 1721

Feb. 12, 1994, P.L. 103-211, 12 U.S. Code §§ 1709, 1709 nt., 1715y

April 11, 1994, P.L. 103-233, 42 U.S. Code §§ 1713, 1715e, 1715k, 1715y, 1715z-3, 1735c, 1735f-19, 1735f-20

Sept. 28, 1994, P.L. 103-327, 12 U.S. Code §§ 1709, 1715n

Jan. 26, 1996, P.L. 104-99, 12 U.S. Code §§ 1710, 1715u, 1715z-1, 1715z-20

March 28, 1996, P.L. 104-120, 12 U.S. Code § 1715z-20

April 26, 1996, P.L. 104-134, 12 U.S. Code §§ 1710, 1715l, 1715u, 1715z-1

Sept. 26, 1996, P.L. 104-204, 12 U.S. Code §§ 1707, 1709, 1715z-1, 1715z-21

Sept. 30, 1996, P.L. 104-208, 12 U.S. Code §§ 1723i, 1735f-14

June 12, 1997, P.L. 105-18, 12 U.S. Code § 1715y

Oct. 27, 1997, P.L. 105-65, 12 U.S. Code §§ 1708, 1709, 1715w, 1715z-1, 1715z-19, 1735f-14, 1735f-15, 1735f-19

Oct. 7, 1998, P.L. 105-244, 12 U.S. Code § 1721

Continued

557

Oct. 21, 1998, P.L. 105-276, 12 U.S. Code §§ 1709, 1710, 1715l, 1715n, 1715u, 1715z-1, 1715z-2, 1715z-20, 1717, 1735f-14

National Housing Act of 1953

June 30, 1953, Ch. 170, 67 Stat. 121, 12 U.S. Code §§ 1706, 1709, 1711, 1713, 1715, 1735, 1748, 1750, 1716, 1717

National Housing Act of 1959

Dec. 21, 1979, P.L. 96-153, 12 U.S. Code § 1701q

National Housing Census Act

Aug. 11, 1939, Ch. 688, 53 Stat. 1406 (See 13 U.S. Code § 142)

National Imagery and Mapping Agency Act of 1996

Sept. 23, 1996, P.L. 104-201, Title XI, 10 U.S. Code § 441 nt.

National Independent Colleges and Universities Discovery Act

July 23, 1992, P.L. 102-325, 20 U.S. Code § 1221-1 nt.

National Indian Forest Resources Management Act

Nov. 28, 1990, P.L. 101-630, 18 U.S. Code prec. § 1151, 25 U.S. Code §§ 3101 to 3120

Nov. 2, 1994, P.L. 103-437, 25 U.S. Code § 3111

National Industrial Recovery Act

June 16, 1933, Ch. 90, 48 Stat. 195

June 29, 1956, Ch. 462, 70 Stat. 384

National Industrial Recovery Extension Act

June 14, 1935, Ch. 246, 49 Stat. 375

National Industrial Reserve Act of 1948

July 2, 1948, Ch. 811, 62 Stat. 1225, 50 U.S. Code §§ 451 to 462

Nov. 16, 1973, P.L. 93-155, 87 Stat. 617, 50 U.S. Code §§ 451 to 455

National Institute of Standards and Technology Act

Feb. 14, 1992, P.L. 102-245, 15 U.S. Code §§ 272, 278d, 278g, 278g-1, 278k, 278n

Feb. 10, 1996, P.L. 104-106, 15 U.S. Code § 278g-3

March 7, 1996, P.L. 104-113, 15 U.S. Code §§ 272, 278, 278e, 278g-2

Nov. 18, 1997, P.L. 105-85, 15 U.S. Code § 278g-3

Oct. 30, 1998, P.L. 105-309, 15 U.S. Code §§ 271 nt., 278g-2a, 278k, 278p

National Institute of Standards and Technology Authorization Act of Fiscal Year 1989

Oct. 24, 1988, P.L. 100-519, 102 Stat. 2589

Nov. 17, 1988, P.L. 100-685, 15 U.S. Code § 3704 nt.

National Institute on Deafness and Other Communication Disorders and Health Research Extension Act of 1988

Nov. 4, 1988, P.L. 100-607, 42 U.S. Code § 201 nt.

National Institutes of Health Amendments of 1990

Nov. 16, 1990, P.L. 101-613, 42 U.S. Code § 201 nt.

National Institutes of Health Revitalization Act of 1993

June 10, 1993, P.L. 103-43, 8 U.S. Code §§ 1182, 1182 nt.; 21 U.S. Code §§ 394, 395; 42 U.S. Code §§ 201 nt., 201 et seq., 8621

National Insurance Development Act of 1975

April 8, 1975, P.L. 94-13, 89 Stat. 68, 12 U.S. Code § 1749bbb

National Interstate Corrections Compact Act

N.H. Rev. Stat. 1955, 622-B:1 et seq.

National Invasive Species Act of 1996

Oct. 26, 1996, P.L. 104-332, 16 U.S. Code § 4701 nt.

National Irrigation Act

See Irrigation and Reclamation Act

See Reclamation Act (Irrigation of Arid Lands)

National Kiwifruit Research, Promotion, and Consumer Information Act

April 4, 1996, P.L. 104-127, Title V, Subtitle D, 7 U.S. Code § 7401 nt.

June 23, 1998, P.L. 105-185, 7 U.S. Code §§ 7463, 7464

National Labor Relations Act

See also Labor Management Relations Act of 1947

July 5, 1935, Ch. 372, 49 Stat. 449, 29 U.S. Code §§ 151 to 166

June 23, 1947, Ch. 120, 61 Stat. 136, 29 U.S. Code §§ 151 to 167

Oct. 22, 1951, Ch. 534, 65 Stat. 601, 29 U.S. Code §§ 158, 159, 168

Aug. 28, 1958, P.L. 85-791, 72 Stat. 945, 29 U.S. Code § 160

Sept. 14, 1959, P.L. 86-257, 73 Stat. 525, 29 U.S. Code §§ 153, 159, 160, 164

July 26, 1974, P.L. 93-360, 88 Stat. 395, 29 U.S. Code §§ 152, 158, 169

Nov. 6, 1978, P.L. 95-598, 29 U.S. Code § 152

May 21, 1980, P.L. 96-245, 29 U.S. Code § 161

Dec. 21, 1982, P.L. 97-375, 29 U.S. Code § 153

Nov. 8, 1984, P.L. 98-620, 29 U.S. Code § 160

National Labor Relations Board Appropriation Acts

June 26, 1940, Ch. 428, 54 Stat. 595

July 1, 1941, Ch. 269, 55 Stat. 495

July 2, 1942, Ch. 475, 56 Stat. 590

July 12, 1943, Ch. 221, 57 Stat. 515

June 28, 1944, Ch. 302, 58 Stat. 567

July 3, 1945, Ch. 263, 59 Stat. 377

July 26, 1946, Ch. 672, 60 Stat. 698

July 8, 1947, Ch. 210, 61 Stat. 276

June 14, 1948, Ch. 465, 62 Stat. 404

Sept. 6, 1950, Ch. 896, 64 Stat. 655

Aug. 31, 1951, Ch. 373, 65 Stat. 221

July 5, 1952, Ch. 575, 66 Stat. 370

July 31, 1953, Ch. 296, 67 Stat. 259

National Law Enforcement Cooperation Act of 1990

Nov. 29, 1990, P.L. 101-647, 28 U.S. Code § 534 nt.

National Library of Medicine Act

Aug. 3, 1956, Ch. 907, 70 Stat. 960, 42 U.S. Code §§ 275 to 281

National Literacy Act of 1991

July 25, 1991, P.L. 102-73, 20 U.S. Code § 1201 nt.

Aug. 17, 1991, P.L. 102-103, 20 U.S. Code § 1211-2

Sept. 13, 1994, P.L. 103-322, 20 U.S. Code § 1211-2

Aug. 7, 1998, P.L. 105-220, 20 U.S. Code §§ 1201 nt., 1211-1, 1211-2, 1213c nt., 2963 nt., 2966 nt.

National Loan Acts (Civil War)

July 17, 1861, Ch. 5, 12 Stat. 259

Aug. 5, 1861, Ch. 46, 12 Stat. 313

National Manufactured Housing Construction and Safety Standards Act of 1974

Oct. 17, 1984, P.L. 98-479, 42 U.S. Code § 5403

Feb. 5, 1988, P.L. 100-242, 42 U.S. Code § 5403

National Marine Sanctuaries Act

Nov. 4, 1992, P.L. 102-587, 16 U.S. Code § 1431 nt.

National Marine Sanctuaries Preservation Act

Oct. 11, 1996, 104-283, 16 U.S. Code §§ 1431, 1431 nt., 1432, 1437

National Marine Sanctuaries Program Amendments Act of 1992

Nov. 4, 1992, P.L. 102-587, 16 U.S. Code § 1431 nt.

Oct. 11, 1996, P.L. 104-283, 16 U.S. Code §§ 1442, 1443, 1443 nt., 1434

National Maritime Heritage Act of 1994

Nov. 2, 1994, P.L. 103-451, 16 U.S. Code §§ 5401 nt., 5401 et seq.

Nov. 18, 1997, P.L. 105-85, 16 U.S. Code § 5405

Continued

National Mass Transportation Assistance Act of 1974

Jan. 6, 1983, P.L. 97-424, 49 U.S. Code 1604a

National Materials and Minerals Policy, Research and Development Act of 1980

Oct. 21, 1980, P.L. 96-479, 30 U.S. Code § 1601 nt.

National Materials Policy Act of 1970

Oct. 26, 1970, P.L. 91-512, 84 Stat. 1234, 42 U.S. Code § 3251 nt.

National Mediation Board Appropriation Acts

June 26, 1940, Ch. 428, 54 Stat. 595

July 1, 1941, Ch. 269, 55 Stat. 495

July 2, 1942, Ch. 475, 56 Stat. 590

July 12, 1943, Ch. 221, 57 Stat. 515

June 28, 1944, Ch. 302, 58 Stat. 568

July 3, 1945, Ch. 263, 59 Stat. 378

July 26, 1946, Ch. 672, 60 Stat. 699

July 8, 1947, Ch. 210, 61 Stat. 277

June 14, 1948, Ch. 465, 62 Stat. 405

June 29, 1949, Ch. 275, 63 Stat. 296

Sept. 6, 1950, Ch. 896, 64 Stat. 655

Aug. 31, 1951, Ch. 373, 65 Stat. 221

July 5, 1952, Ch. 575, 66 Stat. 370

July 31, 1953, Ch. 296, 67 Stat. 258

National Mental Health Act

July 3, 1946, Ch. 538, 60 Stat. 421, 42 U.S. Code §§ 201, 209, 210, 215, 218, 219, 232, 241, 242a, 244, 246

National Military Establishment Appropriation Act of 1950

Oct. 29, 1949, Ch. 787, 63 Stat. 987

National Military Establishment Lands Act of 1950

July 11, 1950, Ch. 456, 64 Stat. 325

National Mimbres Culture Study Act of 1988

Oct. 28, 1988, P.L. 100-559, 102 Stat. 2798

National Missile Defense Act of 1999

July 22, 1999, P.L. 106-38, 113 Stat. 205, 10 U. S. Code § 101 nt.

National Mobile Home Construction and Safety Standards Act of 1974

Oct. 31, 1978, P.L. 95-557, 42 U.S. Code § 5425

Dec. 21, 1979, P.L. 96-153, 42 U.S. Code § 5419

National Monument Act (Preservation of Antiquities)

June 8, 1906, Ch. 3060, 34 Stat. 225, 16 U.S. Code §§ 431 to 433

National Monument Establishment Act of 1990

Nov. 12, 1996, P.L. 104-333, 16 U.S. Code § 431 nt.

National Motor Vehicle Theft Act

Oct. 29, 1919, Ch. 89, 41 Stat. 324 (See 18 U.S. Code §§ 10, 2311 to 2313)

Sept. 24, 1945, Ch. 383, 59 Stat. 536 (See 18 U.S. Code §§ 10, 2311 to 2313)

National Museum Act of 1966

Oct. 15, 1966, P.L. 89-674, 80 Stat. 953, 20 U.S. Code § 65a, 65a nt.

Dec. 31, 1970, P.L. 91-629, 84 Stat. 1875, 20 U.S. Code § 65a

July 12, 1974, P.L. 93-345, 88 Stat. 339, 20 U.S. Code § 65a

National Museum of the American Indian Act

Nov. 28, 1989, P.L. 101-185, 20 U.S. Code §§ 80q nt., 80q et seq.

Oct. 9, 1996, P.L. 104-278, 20 U.S. Code § 80q-9a

National Museum of the American Indian Act Amendments of 1996

Oct. 9, 1996, P.L. 104-278, 20 U.S. Code § 80q nt.

National Narcotics Act of 1984

Oct. 12, 1984, P.L. 98-473, 21 U.S. Code § 1201 nt.

Nov. 18, 1988, P.L. 100-690, 21 U.S. Code §§ 1201, 1201 nt., 1202 to 1204

National Narcotics Leadership Act of 1988

Nov. 18, 1988, P.L. 100-690, 21 U.S. Code § 1501 nt.

Dec. 12, 1989, P.L. 101-226, 42 U.S. Code § 11841

Sept. 13, 1994, P.L. 103-322, 21 U.S. Code §§ 1502, 1504 et seq.

June 27, 1997, P.L. 105-20, 21 U.S. Code §§ prec. 1501, prec. 1521, 1521 to 1524, prec. 1531, 1531 to 1534, prec. 1541, 1541 to 1548

National Natural Resources Conservation Foundation Act

April 4, 1996, P.L. 104-127, Title III, Subtitle F, 16 U.S. Code § 5801 nt.

National Neighborhood Policy Act

April 30, 1977, P.L. 95-24, 42 U.S. Code § 1441 nt.

Oct. 31, 1978, P.L. 95-557, 42 U.S. Code § 1441 nt.

National Nutrition Monitoring and Related Research Act of 1990

Oct. 22, 1990, P.L. 101-445, 7 U.S. Code §§ 5301, 5301 nt., 5302 , 5311 to 5316, 5331, 5332, 5341, 5342

National Ocean Pollution Planning Act of 1978

May 8, 1978, P.L. 95-273, 33 U.S. Code § 1701 et seq.

April 7, 1986, P.L. 99-272, 33 U.S. Code §§ 1701, 1702, 1702a, 1703, 1707, 1709

Nov. 8, 1988, P.L. 100-636, 33 U.S. Code § 1702 et seq.

Oct. 29, 1992, P.L. 102-567, 33 U.S. Code §§ 1701, 1701 nt., 1702, 1702A, 1703 to 1709

National Ocean Pollution Research and Development and Monitoring Planning Act of 1978

May 8, 1978, P.L. 95-273, 33 U.S. Code §§ 1701 et seq., 1701 nt.

June 4, 1979, P.L. 96-17, 33 U.S. Code § 1709

May 30, 1980, P.L. 96-255, 33 U.S. Code §§ 1701, 1701 nt., 1703, 1709

Dec. 21, 1982, P.L. 97-375, 33 U.S. Code § 1703

National Oceanic and Atmospheric Administration Authorization Act of 1992

Oct. 29, 1992, P.L. 102-567, 106 Stat. 4270

Nov. 10, 1998, P.L. 105-362, 33 U.S. Code § 1251 nt.

National Oceanic and Atmospheric Administration Marine Fisheries Program Authorization Act

Nov. 10, 1986, P.L. 99-659, 100 Stat. 3739

Oct. 29, 1992, P.L. 102-567, 106 Stat. 4282

National Oceanic and Atmospheric Administration Ocean and Coastal Programs Authorization Act of 1989

Dec. 12, 1989, P.L. 101-224, 103 Stat. 1905

National Organ Transplant Act

Oct. 19, 1984, P.L. 98-507, 42 U.S. Code §§ 201 nt., 273 nt.

Nov. 4, 1988, P.L. 100-607, 42 U.S. Code § 274e

National Park Act

Ky. Rev. Stat. 1971, 148.111 et seq.

National Park Foundation Act

Dec. 18, 1967, P.L. 90-209, 81 Stat. 656, 16 U.S. Code §§ 19e to 19n

Nov. 13, 1998, P.L. 105-391, 16 U.S. Code § 19o

National Park Police Drug Enforcement Supplemental Authority Act

Oct. 27, 1986, P.L. 99-570, 16 U.S. Code § 1 nt.

National Park Service Concessions Management Improvement Act of 1998

Nov. 13, 1998, P.L. 105-391, Title IV, 112 Stat. 3503, 16 U.S. Code § 5901 nt.

National Park Service Concessions Policy Act

Nov. 13, 1998, P.L. 105-391, 16 U.S. Code §§ 20, 20a-20g

National Park Service Organic Act

Aug. 25, 1916, Ch. 408, 39 Stat. 535

National Park System General Authorities Act
Nov. 13, 1998, P.L. 105-391, 16 U.S. Code §§ 1a-2, 1a-5, 1a-7

National Park System New Areas Studies Act
Nov. 13, 1998, P.L. 105-391, Title III, 112 Stat. 3501, 16 U.S. Code § 1 nt.

National Park System Visitor Facilities Fund Act
Jan. 8, 1983, P.L. 97-433, 16 U.S. Code §§ 19aa et seq., 19aa nt.
Nov. 13, 1998, P.L. 105-391, 16 U.S. Code § 3

National Parks and Recreation Act of 1978
Nov. 10, 1978, P.L. 95-625, 16 U.S. Code §§ 1 nt., 1a-5, 1a-7, 45a-1, 45a-3, 45f, 230 et seq., 241g, 273f, 282c, 283e, 396d, 397 et seq., 410y-la, 410y-6, 410z, 430mm et seq., 441e-1, 450bb nt.
Oct. 12, 1979, P.L. 96-87, 16 U.S. Code §§ 230a, 230c, 230f, 396d , 431 nt., 450dd nt., 460ff-1, 460kk, 461 nt., 1244, 1246, 1274, 1274 nt.
March 5, 1980, P.L. 96-199, 16 U.S. Code §§ 459 c-1 et seq.
Oct. 30, 1984, P.L. 98-572, 16 U.S. Code § 460kkk
Oct. 18, 1986, P.L. 99-500, 16 U.S. Code § 460m-16
Oct. 30, 1986, P.L. 99-590, 16 U.S. Code § 460m-16
Oct. 30, 1986, P.L. 99-591, 16 U.S. Code § 460m-16
Feb. 16, 1988, P.L. 100-250, 102 Stat. 16, 16 U.S. Code §§ 230, 230a, 230f
Aug. 22, 1988, P.L. 100-412, 102 Stat. 1100, 16 U.S. Code § 1274 nt.
Oct. 13, 1988, P.L. 100-486, 16 U.S. Code § 471i
Oct. 25, 1988, P.L. 100-528, 16 U.S. Code §§ 430nn nt., 430oo nt.
Oct. 26, 1988, P.L. 100-534, 16 U.S. Code §§ 460m-15, 460m-26 to 460m-29
Nov. 2, 1994, P.L. 103-437, 16 U.S. Code §§ 45f, 460kk
Nov. 12, 1996, P.L. 104-333, 16 U.S. Code §§ 460m-15, 460m-20, 460m-30
Nov. 13, 1997, P.L. 105-82, 16 U.S. Code § 1132 nt.

Nov. 2, 1998, P.L. 105-342, 112 Stat. 3202

National Parks Omnibus Management Act of 1998
Nov. 13, 1998, P.L. 105-391, 112 Stat. 3497, 16 U.S. Code § 5901 nt.

National Portrait Gallery Act
April 27, 1962, P.L. 87-443, 76 Stat. 62, 20 U.S. Code §§ 75a to 75g

National Productivity and Quality of Working Life Act of 1975
Nov. 28, 1975, P.L. 94-136, 89 Stat. 733, 15 U.S. Code §§ 2401 et seq.

National Productivity and Quality of Working Life Act of 1976
Nov. 28, 1976, P.L. 94-136, 15 U.S. Code § 2401 et seq.

National Prohibition Acts
Oct. 28, 1919, Ch. 85, 41 Stat. 305
Nov. 23, 1921, Ch. 134, 42 Stat. 222

National Reclamation Law
See Reclamation Acts (Irrigation of Arid Lands)

National Research Act
July 12, 1974, P.L. 93-348, 88 Stat. 342, 42 U.S. Code §§ 218, 241, 242a, 282, 286a, 286b, 287a, 287b, 287d, 288a, 288c, 288c-1, 289g, 289k, 289l, 289l-1 to 289l-3, 295f-2, 295f-3, 295h-9, 300a-7
Nov. 23, 1977, P.L. 95-203, 42 U.S. Code § 289l-1 nt.

National School Lunch Act
June 4, 1946, Ch. 281, 60 Stat. 230, 42 U.S. Code §§ 1751 to 1760
April 5, 1952, Ch. 159, 66 Stat. 43, 42 U.S. Code § 1874
July 12, 1952, Ch. 699, 66 Stat. 591, 42 U.S. Code §§ 1753, 1754, 1760
Sept. 25, 1962, P.L. 87-688, 76 Stat. 587, 42 U.S. Code §§ 1753, 1754, 1760
Oct. 15, 1962, P.L. 87-823, 76 Stat. 944, 42 U.S. Code §§ 1752 to 1755, 1759, 1759a, 1760
May 8, 1968, P.L. 90-302, 82 Stat. 117, 42 U.S. Code §§ 1752, 1755, 1758, 1761
March 12, 1970, P.L. 91-207, 84 Stat. 51, 42 U.S. Code § 1762

May 14, 1970, P.L. 91-248, 84 Stat. 208, 42 U.S. Code §§ 1752, 1755, 1756, 1758, 1759, 1759a, 1760, 1761, 1763

June 30, 1971, P.L. 92-32, 85 Stat. 85, 42 U.S. Code §§ 1761, 1764

Nov. 5, 1971, P.L. 92-153, 85 Stat. 420, 42 U.S. Code §§ 1758, 1759a

Sept. 26, 1972, P.L. 92-433, 86 Stat. 724, 42 U.S. Code §§ 1756 to 1759, 1761

March 30, 1973, P.L. 93-13, 87 Stat. 10, 42 U.S. Code § 1755

Nov. 7, 1973, P.L. 93-150, 87 Stat. 560, 42 U.S. Code §§ 1753, 1755, 1757, 1758, 1763

June 30, 1974, P.L. 93-326, 88 Stat. 286, 42 U.S. Code §§ 1752, 1755, 1758, 1762a, 1763

May 2, 1975, P.L. 94-20, 89 Stat. 82, 42 U.S. Code § 1761

Nov. 10, 1977, P.L. 95-166, 42 U.S. Code §§ 1754 to 1756, 1761

Nov. 1, 1978, P.L. 95-561, 42 U.S. Code § 1769b

Nov. 10, 1978, P.L. 95-627, 42 U.S. Code §§ 1755, 1758 et seq., 1769, 1769c

Oct. 9, 1984, P.L. 98-459, 98 Stat. 1792, 42 U.S. Code § 1762a

Oct. 18, 1986, P.L. 99-500, 42 U.S. Code §§ 1752, 1755, 1758, 1758 nt., 1760 to 1762a, 1766 to 1769, 1769a to 1769c

Oct. 30, 1986, P.L. 99-591, 42 U.S. Code §§ 1752, 1755, 1758, 1758 nt., 1760 to 1762a, 1766 to 1769, 1769a to 1769c

Nov. 14, 1986, P.L. 99-661, 42 U.S. Code §§ 1752, 1755, 1758, 1758 nt., 1760, 1761, 1762a, 1766 nt., 1766 to 1769c

July 11, 1987, P.L. 100-71, 42 U.S. Code § 1760

Jan. 8, 1988, P.L. 100-237, 42 U.S. Code §§ 1755, 1769

June 28, 1988, P.L. 100-356, 42 U.S. Code §§ 1758, 1762a

Sept. 19, 1988, P.L. 100-435, 42 U.S. Code §§ 1761, 1766

Oct. 1, 1988, P.L. 100-460, 42 U.S. Code § 1766

Nov. 10, 1989, P.L. 101-147, 42 U.S. Code § 1751 et seq.

Aug. 7, 1992, P.L. 102-337, 42 U.S. Code § 1769b-1

Aug. 14, 1992, P.L. 102-342, 42 U.S. Code §§ 1766, 1769

Sept. 30, 1992, P.L. 102-375, 42 U.S. Code § 1766

Oct. 24, 1992, P.L. 102-512, 42 U.S. Code § 1769

Dec. 2, 1993, P.L. 103-171, 42 U.S. Code § 1766

Nov. 2, 1994, P.L. 103-448, 42 U.S. Code §§ 1755, 1756, 1758, 1759a, 1760, 1761, 1762a, 1766, 1766b, 1769 et seq.

May 29, 1996, P.L. 104-149, 42 U.S. Code § 1758

Aug. 22, 1996, P.L. 104-193, 42 U.S. Code §§ 1757, 1758, 1759a, 1760, 1761, 1762a, 1766, 1769, 1769a, 1769d, 1769e

Aug. 7, 1998, P.L. 105-220, 42 U.S. Code § 1769h

Oct. 31, 1998, P.L. 105-336, 42 U.S. Code §§ 1755, 1758, 1759a, 1760, 1761, 1762a, 1765, 1766, 1766a, 1766b, 1769, 1769b-1, 1769c, 1769f to 1769h

National School Lunch Act and Child Nutrition Amendments of 1977

Nov. 10, 1977, P.L. 95-166, 42 U.S. Code §§ 1751 nt., 1754 to 1756.

National Science and Technology Policy, Organization, and Priorities Act of 1976

May 11, 1976, P.L. 94-282, 42 U.S. Code § 6601 et seq.

Sept. 29, 1977, P.L. 95-113, 42 U.S. Code § 6651(h)

Dec. 21, 1982, P.L. 97-375, 42 U.S. Code §§ 6614, 6615, 6618

Nov. 29, 1989, P.L. 101-189, 42 U.S. Code § 6681 et seq.

June 13, 1991, P.L. 102-54, 42 U.S. Code § 6651

Feb. 14, 1992, P.L. 102-245, 42 U.S. Code §§ 6618, 6683

April 4, 1996, P.L. 104-127, 42 U.S. Code § 6651

National Science, Engineering, and Mathematics Authorization Act of 1986

Nov. 22, 1985, P.L. 99-159, 20 U.S. Code §§ 3901 nt., 3902, 3911 et seq.; 29 U.S. Code §§ 1503, 1753; 42 U.S. Code §§ 1861 to 1864, 1868 to 1874, 1882, 1884 to 1886

National Science Foundation Act of 1950

May 10, 1950, Ch. 171, 64 Stat. 149, 42 U.S. Code §§ 1861 to 1875

Aug. 8, 1953, Ch. 377, 67 Stat. 488, 42 U.S. Code § 1875

Continued

July 11, 1958, P.L. 85-510, 72 Stat. 353, 42 U.S. Code §§ 1862, 1872a, 1873 to 1875

Sept. 8, 1959, P.L. 86-232, 73 Stat. 467, 42 U.S. Code §§ 1862 to 1865, 1869, 1870, 1872, 1873

June 11, 1960, P.L. 86-507, 74 Stat. 202, 42 U.S. Code § 1863

June 29, 1960, P.L. 86-550, 74 Stat. 256, 42 U.S. Code § 1869

Oct. 16, 1962, P.L. 87-835, 76 Stat. 1069, 42 U.S. Code §§ 1869, 1874

July 18, 1968, P.L. 90-407, 82 Stat. 360, 42 U.S. Code §§ 1862 to 1870, 1872 to 1875

Nov. 18, 1969, P.L. 91-120, 83 Stat. 203, 42 U.S. Code § 1873

Aug. 10, 1972, P.L. 92-372, 86 Stat. 526, 42 U.S. Code § 1862

Aug. 10, 1972, P.L. 92-372, 86 Stat. 528, 42 U.S. Code § 1862

Oct. 13, 1972, P.L. 92-484, 86 Stat. 802, 42 U.S. Code § 1862

Aug. 16, 1973, P.L. 93-96, 87 Stat. 315, 42 U.S. Code §§ 1862 nt. , 1882

Sept. 4, 1974, P.L. 93-413, 88 Stat. 1095, 42 U.S. Code § 1882

Aug. 9, 1975, P.L. 94-86, 89 Stat. 427, 42 U.S. Code §§ 1864 nt., 1869a, 1881a, 1882, 5820 nt.

Dec. 21, 1982, P.L. 97-375, 42 U.S. Code § 1863

Nov. 22, 1985, P.L. 99-159, 42 U.S. Code §§ 1862 to 1864, 1868 to 1874

Aug. 21, 1986, P.L. 99-383, 5 U.S. Code § 5316; 42 U.S. Code §§ 1862, 1864a, 1869, 1870

Oct. 31, 1988, P.L. 100-570, 42 U.S. Code §§ 1863, 1873, 1874

Nov. 16, 1990, P.L. 101-589, 42 U.S. Code §§ 1869, 1873

Oct. 28, 1991, P.L. 102-139, 42 U.S. Code § 1873

Oct. 23, 1992, P.L. 102-476, 42 U.S. Code § 1862

Nov. 4, 1992, P.L. 102-588, 42 U.S. Code § 1862

Nov. 2, 1994, P.L. 103-437, 42 U.S. Code § 1864

Dec. 21, 1995, P.L. 104-66, 42 U.S. Code § 1873

July 29, 1998, P.L. 105-207, 42 U.S. Code §§ 1862, 1863, 1864, 1873, 1874

National Science Foundation Authorization Act, Fiscal Year 1978

Aug. 15, 1977, P.L. 95-99, 42 U.S. Code §§ 1861 nt., 1862 et seq.

Nov. 22, 1985, P.L. 99-159, 42 U.S. Code §§ 1862, 1863, 1869b, 1873, 1873a, 1882 nt., 1884

National Science Foundation Authorization Act for Fiscal Year 1980

Aug. 2, 1979, P.L. 96-44, 42 U.S. Code §§ 1862 nt., 1882

Nov. 22, 1985, P.L. 99-159, 42 U.S. Code § 1882

Nov. 2, 1994, P.L. 103-437, 42 U.S. Code § 1882

National Science Foundation Authorization Act for Fiscal Year 1986

Nov. 22, 1985, P.L. 99-159, 42 U.S. Code §§ 1861 nt., 1861 to 1864, 1868 to 1874, 1882, 1884 to 1886

National Science Foundation Authorization Act for Fiscal Year 1987

Aug. 21, 1986, P.L. 99-383, 42 U.S. Code §§ 1861 nt., 1862

National Science Foundation Authorization Act of 1971

July 24, 1970, P.L. 91-356, 84 Stat. 471

National Science Foundation Authorization Act of 1972

Aug. 11, 1971, P.L. 92-86, 85 Stat. 308, 42 U.S. Code § 1862 nt.

National Science Foundation Authorization Act of 1998

July 29, 1998, P.L. 105-207, 42 U.S. Code § 1861 nt.

National Science Foundation Authorization Act, 1970

Nov. 18, 1969, P.L. 91-120, 83 Stat. 203, 42 U.S. Code §§ 1873, 1882

National Science Foundation Authorization Act, 1976

Nov. 22, 1985, P.L. 99-159, 42 U.S. Code §§ 1869a, 1881a

July 29, 1998, P.L. 105-207, 42 U.S. Code § 1881a

National Science Foundation Authorization Act, 1977

Oct. 11, 1976, P.L. 94-471, 42 U.S. Code § 1861 et seq.

Aug. 22, 1986, P.L. 99-386, 42 U.S. Code § 1883

National Science Foundation Authorization Act, 1988

Oct. 31, 1988, P.L. 100-570, 42 U.S. Code § 1861 nt.

July 29, 1998, P.L. 105-207, 42 U.S. Code § 1881b

National Science Foundation Authorization and Science and Engineering Equal Opportunities Act

Dec. 12, 1980, P.L. 96-516, 42 U.S. Code § 1861 nt.

Nov. 22, 1985, P.L. 99-159, 42 U.S. Code §§ 1861 nt., 1885, 1885 nt., 1885a to 1885d

National Science Foundation Authorization and Science and Technology Equal Opportunities Act

See National Science Foundation Authorization and Science and Engineering Equal Opportunities Act

Dec. 12, 1980, P.L. 96-516, 42 U.S. Code § 1861 nt.

National Science Foundation University Infrastructure Act of 1988

Aug. 23, 1988, P.L. 100-418, 102 Stat. 1542, 42 U.S. Code § 1861 nt.

National Sea Grant College and Program Act of 1966

Oct. 15, 1966, P.L. 89-688, 80 Stat. 998, 33 U.S. Code §§ 1121 to 1124

July 23, 1970, P.L. 91-349, 84 Stat. 448, 33 U.S. Code § 1122

July 10, 1973, P.L. 93-73, 87 Stat. 170, 33 U.S. Code §§ 1122 to 1124

Oct. 8, 1976, P.L. 94-461, 33 U.S. Code § 1121 et seq.

June 29, 1977, P.L. 95-58, 33 U.S. Code §§ 1125, 1131

June 28, 1980, P.L. 96-289, 33 U.S. Code § 1121 et seq.

Dec. 29, 1987, P.L. 100-220, 33 U.S. Code §§ 1121 to 1123, 1126, 1128, 1129

National Sea Grant College Program Act

Dec. 4, 1991, P.L. 102-186, 33 U.S. Code §§ 1122 to 1125, 1127, 1128, 1130, 1131

March 9, 1992, P.L. 102-251, 33 U.S. Code § 1122

March 6, 1998, P.L. 105-160, 33 U.S. Code §§ 1121 to 1123, 1124a, 1126 to 1128, 1131

May 1, 1998, P.L. 105-174, 33 U.S. Code § 1122

National Sea Grant College Program Authorization Act of 1987

Dec. 29, 1987, P.L. 100-220, 33 U.S. Code §§ 1121 to 1131

National Sea Grant College Program Authorization Act of 1991

Dec. 4, 1991, P.L. 102-186, 33 U.S. Code § 1121 nt.

National Sea Grant College Program Reauthorization Act of 1998

March 6, 1998, P.L. 105-160, 33 U.S. Code § 1121 nt.

National Securities Markets Improvement Act of 1996

Oct. 11, 1996, P.L. 104-290, 15 U.S. Code § 78a nt.

National Security Act of 1947

July 26, 1947, Ch. 343, 61 Stat. 495

April 2, 1949, Ch. 47, 63 Stat. 30

Aug. 10, 1949, Ch. 412, 63 Stat. 578

Sept. 9, 1950, Ch. 939, 64 Stat. 828

Sept. 19, 1951, Ch. 407, 65 Stat. 333

June 28, 1952, Ch. 479, 66 Stat. 282

April 4, 1953, Ch. 16, 67 Stat. 20

Aug. 3, 1954, Ch. 652, 68 Stat. 649

Sept. 3, 1954, Ch. 1263, 68 Stat. 1228

Aug. 10, 1956, Ch. 1041, 70A Stat. 629

Aug. 6, 1958, P.L. 85-599, 72 Stat. 514

Aug. 14, 1964, P.L. 88-426, 78 Stat. 425

June 23, 1982, P.L. 97-200, 50 U.S. Code §§ 421 et seq.

Dec. 9, 1983, P.L. 98-215, 50 U.S. Code § 403-1

Oct. 15, 1984, P.L. 98-477, 50 U.S. Code §§ 431, 432

Dec. 4, 1985, P.L. 99-169, 50 U.S. Code § 414

Continued

Oct. 1, 1986, P.L. 99-433, 50 U.S. Code §§ 402, 404a

Oct. 18, 1986, P.L. 99-500, 50 U.S. Code § 402

Oct. 27, 1986, P.L. 99-569, 50 U.S. Code § 415

Oct. 30, 1986, P.L. 99-591, 50 U.S. Code § 402

Nov. 14, 1986, P.L. 99-661, 50 U.S. Code § 402

Nov. 18, 1988, P.L. 100-690, 50 U.S. Code § 402

Aug. 14, 1991, P.L. 102-88, 50 U.S. Code §§ 413, 413a, 413b, 414, 415

Oct. 24, 1992, P.L. 102-496, 50 U.S. Code §§ 401a, 402, 403, 403-1, 403-3 to 403-6, 404, 404a

Dec. 3, 1993, P.L. 103-178. 50 U.S. Code §§ 403-3, 404d, 411

Oct. 14, 1994, P.L. 103-359, 50 U.S. Code §§ 401a, 403-5, 435 et seq.

Jan. 6, 1996, P.L. 104-93, 50 U.S. Code §§ 403, 431, 441, 441a et seq.

Feb. 10, 1996, P.L. 104-106, 50 U.S. Code §§ 403, 403-4

Sept. 23, 1996, P.L. 104-201, 50 U.S. Code §§ 401a, 403-5, 404e, 404f

Oct. 11, 1996, P.L. 104-293, 50 U.S. Code §§ 402, 403, 403-1, 403-3, 403-4, 403-5, 403-5a, 403-6, 404d, 404d-1, 441d

Nov. 20, 1997, P.L. 105-107, 50 U.S. Code §§ 403, 404d-1, 404e, 404f, 404h, 441d

Oct. 20, 1998, P.L. 105-272, 50 U.S. Code §§ 403, 404i, 441d

Oct. 21, 1998, P.L. 105-277, 50 U.S. Code § 402

Oct. 27, 1998, P.L. 105-292, 50 U.S. Code § 402

National Security Act of 1950

Sept. 23, 1996, P.L. 104-201, 50 U.S. Code § 402 nt.

National Security Act of 1959

Oct. 27, 1986, P.L. 99-569, 50 U.S. Code § 402 nt.

National Security Agency Act of 1959

June 6, 1986, P.L. 99-335, 50 U.S. Code § 402 nt.

Nov. 30, 1989, P.L. 101-193, 50 U.S. Code § 402 nt.

Nov. 30, 1989, P.L. 101-194, 50 U.S. Code § 402 nt.

Aug. 14, 1991, P.L. 102-88, 50 U.S. Code § 402 nt.

Dec. 4, 1991, P.L. 102-183, 50 U.S. Code § 402 nt.

Oct. 24, 1992, P.L. 102-496, 50 U.S. Code § 402 nt.

Oct. 14, 1994, P.L. 103-359, 50 U.S. Code § 402 nt.

Feb. 10, 1996, P.L. 104-106, 50 U.S. Code § 402 nt.

National Security Education Act of 1991

See David L. Boreb National Security Education Act of 1991

National Service Life Insurance Act of 1940

Oct. 8, 1940, Ch. 757, 54 Stat. 1008 (See 38 U.S. Code §§ 701 to 724, 781 to 788)

Dec. 20, 1941, Ch. 602, 55 Stat. 844

Feb. 11, 1942, Ch. 69, 56 Stat. 88

July 11, 1942, Ch. 504, 56 Stat. 657

April 12, 1943, Ch. 56, 57 Stat. 64

Sept. 30, 1944, Ch. 454, 58 Stat. 762

Sept. 30, 1944, Ch. 455, 58 Stat. 764

Aug. 1, 1946, Ch. 728, 60 Stat. 781

Feb. 21, 1947, Ch. 5, 61 Stat. 5

March 3, 1948, Ch. 90, 62 Stat. 59

June 29, 1948, Ch. 736, 62 Stat. 1109

May 23, 1949, Ch. 135, 63 Stat. 74

April 25, 1951, Ch. 39, 65 Stat. 38

May 18, 1951, Ch. 94, 65 Stat. 44

Aug. 2, 1951, Ch. 289, 65 Stat. 153

July 23, 1953, Ch. 240, 67 Stat. 186 (See 38 U.S. Code §§ 701 to 710, 712 to 714, 716 to 719, 721, 723)

March 16, 1954, Ch. 97, 68 Stat. 28 (See 38 U.S. Code §§ 701 to 717, 719, 721)

July 29, 1955, Ch. 431, 69 Stat. 395 (See 38 U.S. Code § 724)

Aug. 1, 1956, Ch. 837, 70 Stat. 880 (See 38 U.S. Code §§ 722 to 724, 781)

June 17, 1957, P.L. 85-56, 71 Stat. 159 (See 38 U.S. Code §§ 718, 784)

Aug. 18, 1958, P.L. 85-678, 72 Stat. 630 (See 38 U.S. Code §§ 701 to 710, 712 to 714, 716 to 719, 721)

National Shipbuilding and Shipyard Conversion Act of 1993

Nov. 30, 1993, P.L. 103-160, 10 U.S. Code § 2501 nt.

National Sickle Cell Anemia Control Act

May 16, 1972, P.L. 92-294, 86 Stat. 136, 33 U.S. Code § 763c nt.; 42 U.S. Code §§ 201 nt., 211a nt., 212a nt., 222 nt., 300b to 300b-5

National Sickle Cell Anemia, Cooley's Anemia, Tay-Sachs, and Genetic Diseases Act

Nov. 10, 1978, P.L. 95-626, 42 U.S. Code § 300b nt.

National Skill Standards Act of 1994

March 31, 1994, P.L. 103-227, 20 U.S. Code § 5931 et seq.

Oct. 21, 1998, P.L. 105-277, 20 U.S. Code §§ 5934, 5938

National Soldiers' Home Acts

March 3, 1865, Ch. 91, 13 Stat. 509

March 21, 1866, Ch. 21, 14 Stat. 10

National Space Council Authorization Act of 1990

July 8, 1990, P.L. 101-328, 42 U.S. Code § 2471 nt.

National Space Grant College and Fellowship Act

Oct. 30, 1987, P.L. 100-147, 42 U.S. Code §§ 2486 et seq., 2486 nt.

Nov. 10, 1998, P.L. 105-362, 42 U.S. Code § 2486j

National Stolen Property Act

May 22, 1934, Ch. 333, 48 Stat. 794 (See 18 U.S. Code §§ 10, 2311, 2314, 2315, 3237)

National Superconductivity and Competitiveness Act of 1988

Nov. 19, 1988, P.L. 100-697, 15 U.S. Code § 5201 nt.

National Teachers Exam Act

S.C. Code Ann. 1976, § 59-26-10 et seq.

National Technical Information Act of 1988

Oct. 24, 1988, P.L. 100-519, 15 U.S. Code § 3701 nt.

Feb. 14, 1992, P.L. 102-245,15 U.S. Code § 3704b

National Technical Institute for the Deaf Act

June 8, 1965, P.L. 89-36, 79 Stat. 125, 20 U.S. Code §§ 681 to 685

Aug. 4, 1986, P.L. 99-371, 20 U.S. Code §§ 681, 681 nt., 682 to 685

National Technology Transfer and Advancement Act of 1995

March 7, 1996, P.L. 104-113, 15 U.S. Code § 3701 nt.

National Telecommunications and Information Administration Organization Act

Oct. 27, 1992, P.L. 102-538, 47 U.S. Code § 901 nt.

Aug. 10, 1993, P.L. 103-66, 42 U.S. Code § 254r nt.; 47 U.S. Code §§ 394, prec. 901, 903, 921 to 927

Aug. 5, 1997, P.L. 105-33, 47 U.S. Code §§ 923 to 925

Oct. 17, 1998, P.L. 105-261, 47 U.S. Code § 923

National Tourism Policy Act

Oct. 16, 1981, P.L. 97-63, 22 U.S. Code § 2121 nt.

National Traffic and Motor Vehicle Safety Act of 1966

Sept. 9, 1966, P.L. 89-563, 80 Stat. 718, 15 U.S. Code §§ 1381 nt., 1391 to 1409, 1421 to 1425; 23 U.S. Code § 313 nt.

Oct. 15, 1966, P.L. 89-670, 80 Stat. 943, 15 U.S. Code § 1404

April 10, 1968, P.L. 98-283, 82 Stat. 72, 15 U.S. Code § 1410

May 22, 1970, P.L. 91-265, 84 Stat. 262, 15 U.S. Code §§ 1391, 1401, 1402, 1408, 1409, 1426, 1431

Oct. 25, 1972, P.L. 92-548, 86 Stat. 1159, 15 U.S. Code §§ 1409, 1410

Nov. 6, 1978, P.L. 95-599, 15 U.S. Code § 1418

Nov. 8, 1984, P.L. 98-620, 15 U.S. Code § 1415

Continued

Dec. 18, 1991, P.L. 102-240, 15 U.S. Code §§ 1392, 1413, 1414

National Trails System Act

Oct. 2, 1968, P.L. 90-543, 82 Stat. 919, 16 U.S. Code §§ 1241 to 1249

March 21, 1978, P.L. 95-248, 16 U.S. Code § 1244 et seq.

Nov. 10, 1978, P.L. 95-625, 16 U.S. Code § 1241 et seq.

Sept. 8, 1980, P.L. 96-344, 16 U.S. Code § 1244

Aug. 28, 1984, P.L. 98-405, 16 U.S. Code § 1244

Oct. 6, 1986, P.L. 99-445, 16 U.S. Code § 1244

May 8, 1987, P.L. 100-35, 16 U.S. Code §§ 1244, 1249

Dec. 11, 1987, P.L. 100-187, 16 U.S. Code § 1244

Dec. 16, 1987, P.L. 100-192, 16 U.S. Code §§ 1244, 1249

Oct. 4, 1988, P.L. 100-470, 102 Stat. 2281, 16 U.S. Code §§ 1244, 1248

Oct. 28, 1988, P.L. 100-559, 16 U.S. Code § 1244

July 3, 1990, P.L. 101-321, 16 U.S. Code § 1244

Aug. 15, 1990, P.L. 101-365, 16 U.S. Code §§ 1244, 1249

Aug. 3, 1992, P.L. 102-328, 16 U.S. Code § 1244

Oct. 23, 1992, P.L. 102-461, 16 U.S. Code § 1244

Nov. 17, 1993, P.L. 103-144, 16 U.S. Code § 1244

Nov. 17, 1993, P.L. 103-145, 16 U.S. Code § 1244

Nov. 2, 1994, P.L. 103-437, 16 U.S. Code §§ 1244, 1249

Dec. 29, 1995, P.L. 104-88, 16 U.S. Code §§ 1247, 1248

Nov. 12, 1996, P.L. 104-333, 16 U.S. Code §§ 1242, 1244, 1249

National Trails System Improvement Act of 1988

Oct. 4, 1988, P.L. 100-470, 102 Stat. 2281, 16 U.S. Code §§ 1241 nt., 1244, 1248 nt., 1248

National Transportation Policy

Sept. 18, 1940, Ch. 722, 54 Stat. 899, 15 U.S. Code § 605

National Transportation Safety Board Amendments of 1996

Oct. 11, 1996, 104-291, Title I, 49 U.S. Code § 1101 nt.

National Underground Railroad Network to Freedom Act of 1998

July 21, 1998, P.L. 105-203, 16 U.S. Code § 461 nt.

National Urban Policy and New Community Development Act of 1970

Oct. 17, 1984, P.L. 98-479, 42 U.S. Code § 4502

National Venereal Disease Prevention and Control Act

Sept. 30, 1972, P.L. 92-449, 86 Stat. 750, 42 U.S. Code § 247c nt.

National Visitor Center Emergency Repair Act of 1980

Dec. 28, 1980, P.L. 96-610, 40 U.S. Code § 801 nt.

National Visitor Center Facilities Act of 1968

March 12, 1968, P.L. 90-264, 82 Stat. 43, 40 U.S. Code §§ 801 to 808, 821 to 823, 831

July 6, 1973, P.L. 93-62, 87 Stat. 146, 40 U.S. Code §§ 802, 804

Aug. 20, 1996, P.L. 104-186, 40 U.S. Code § 831

Nov. 12, 1996, P.L. 104-333, 40 U.S. Code § 805

June 9, 1998, P.L. 105-178, 40 U.S. Code § 819a

National Vocational Student Loan Insurance Act of 1965

Oct. 22, 1965, P.L. 89-287, 79 Stat. 1037, 20 U.S. Code §§ 981 to 996

Aug. 3, 1968, P.L. 90-460, 82 Stat. 634, 20 U.S. Code §§ 981, 984 , 987 to 989

Oct. 16, 1968, P.L. 90-575, 82 Stat. 1023, 20 U.S. Code §§ 1077, 1078, 1084 to 1086

National Voter Registration Act of 1993

May 20, 1993, P.L. 103-31, 39 U.S. Code §§ 2401, 3627, 3629; 42 U.S. Code §§ 1973gg et seq.

National War Agencies Appropriation Acts

July 12, 1943, Ch. 228, 57 Stat. 522, 31 U.S. Code §§ 487a, 665 nt.; 41 U.S. Code § 6a nt.

June 28, 1944, Ch. 301, 58 Stat. 533

July 17, 1945, Ch. 319, 59 Stat. 743

Dec. 28, 1945, Ch. 589, 59 Stat. 632

National Water Commission Act

Sept. 26, 1968, P.L. 90-515, 82 Stat. 868, 42 U.S. Code § 1962a nt.

National Weather Modification Policy Act of 1976

Oct. 13, 1976, P.L. 94-490, 15 U.S. Code §§ 330 et seq.

National Whale Conservation Fund Act of 1998

Oct. 21, 1998, P.L. 105-277, 101(b) Title IX, 112 Stat. 2681, 16 U.S. Code § 3701 nt.

National Wildlife Refuge Designation Act

Ga. Laws 1988, p. 4498

National Wildlife Refuge System Administration Act of 1966

Dec. 5, 1969, P.L. 91-135, 83 Stat. 283, 16 U.S. Code §§ 668dd, 668ee

Dec. 28, 1973, P.L. 93-205, 87 Stat. 902, 16 U.S. Code § 668dd

Nov. 8, 1978, P.L. 95-616, 16 U.S. Code § 668dd

Dec. 31, 1987, P.L. 100-226, 16 U.S. Code § 668dd

Nov. 14, 1988, P.L. 100-653, 16 U.S. Code § 668dd

Oct. 9, 1997, P.L. 105-57, 16 U.S. Code §§ 668dd, 668ee

National Wildlife Refuge System Administration Act of 1996

Oct. 30, 1998, P.L. 105-312, 16 U.S. Code § 668dd

National Wildlife Refuge System Improvement Act of 1997

Oct. 9, 1997, P.L. 105-57, 16 U.S. Code § 668dd nt.

National Wildlife Refuge System Improvement Act of 1998

Oct. 30, 1998, P.L. 105-312, Title II, 112 Stat. 2957, 16 U.S. Code § 668dd nt.

National Wildlife Refuge System Volunteer and Community Partnership Enhancement Act of 1998

Oct. 5, 1998, P.L. 105-242, 112 Stat. 1574, 16 U.S. Code § 742a nt.

National Wool Act of 1954

Aug. 28, 1954, Ch. 1041, 68 Stat. 910, 7 U.S. Code §§ 1781, 1787

Aug. 28, 1958, P.L. 85-835, 72 Stat. 994, 7 U.S. Code §§ 1782 to 1784

Aug. 8, 1961, P.L. 87-128, 75 Stat. 306, 7 U.S. Code § 1782

Nov. 3, 1965, P.L. 89-321, 79 Stat. 1188, 7 U.S. Code § 1782

Nov. 30, 1970, P.L. 91-524, 84 Stat. 1362, 7 U.S. Code § 1782

Sept. 29, 1977, P.L. 95-113, 7 U.S. Code §§ 1781, 1782

Dec. 23, 1985, P.L. 99-198, 7 U.S. Code §§ 1782, 1787

Dec. 22, 1987, P.L. 100-203, 7 U.S. Code § 1782

Aug. 23, 1988, P.L. 100-418, 102 Stat. 1162, 7 U.S. Code §§ 1783, 1784

Nov. 5, 1990, P.L. 101-508, 7 U.S. Code § 1783

Nov. 28, 1990, P.L. 101-624, 7 U.S. Code §§ 1782, 1783, 1787

Dec. 13, 1991, P.L. 102-237, 7 U.S. Code §§ 1783, 1787

Aug. 10, 1993, P.L. 103-66, 7 U.S. Code §§ 1782, 1783, 1785

Nov. 1, 1993, P.L. 103-130, 7 U.S. Code § 1781 et seq.

National Youth Administration Appropriation Acts

June 26, 1940, Ch. 428, 54 Stat. 580

July 1, 1941, Ch. 269, 55 Stat. 471

July 2, 1942, Ch. 475, 56 Stat. 569

Continued

Nationality Act of 1940

Oct. 14, 1940, Ch. 876, 54 Stat. 1137 (See 8 U.S. Code §§ 1101 et seq.)

Oct. 16, 1941, Ch. 446, 55 Stat. 743

March 27, 1942, Ch. 199, 56 Stat. 182

April 2, 1942, Ch. 208, 56 Stat. 198

Oct. 9, 1942, Ch. 585, 56 Stat. 779

Dec. 7, 1942, Ch. 690, 56 Stat. 1041

Dec. 8, 1942, Ch. 696, 56 Stat. 1043

Dec. 24, 1942, Ch. 819, 56 Stat. 1085

Dec. 17, 1943, Ch. 344, 57 Stat. 601

Jan. 20, 1944, Ch. 2, 58 Stat. 4

July 1, 1944, Ch. 368, 58 Stat. 677

Sept. 27, 1944, Ch. 415, 58 Stat. 745

Sept. 27, 1944, Ch. 418, 58 Stat. 746

Sept. 27, 1944, Ch. 419, 58 Stat. 747

Sept. 28, 1944, Ch. 446, 58 Stat. 755

Dec. 22, 1944, Ch. 662, 58 Stat. 886

Oct. 11, 1945, Ch. 410, 59 Stat. 544

Nov. 21, 1945, Ch. 490, 59 Stat. 658

Dec. 28, 1945, Ch. 590, 59 Stat. 658

July 2, 1946, Ch. 534, 60 Stat. 416

July 31, 1946, Ch. 708, 60 Stat. 721

Aug. 7, 1946, Ch. 769, 60 Stat. 865

May 16, 1947, Ch. 72, 61 Stat. 97

May 31, 1947, Ch. 87, 61 Stat. 121

July 1, 1947, Ch. 194, 61 Stat. 240

July 23, 1947, Ch. 304, 61 Stat. 414

June 1, 1948, Ch. 360, 62 Stat. 281

June 25, 1948, Ch. 656, 62 Stat. 1026

June 29, 1949, Ch. 274, 63 Stat. 282

Aug. 1, 1950, Ch. 512, 64 Stat. 384

Sept. 23, 1950, Ch. 1024, 64 Stat. 1013

Sept. 26, 1950, Ch. 1049, 64 Stat. 1038

Nationality and Immigration Law Practice Act

N.M. Stat. Ann., 36-3-1 et seq.

Nationality Law and Immigration Practice Act

Ariz. Rev. Stat. Ann., § 12-2701 et seq.

Nation's Capital Religious Liberty and Academic Freedom Act

Oct. 1, 1988, P.L. 100-462, 102 Stat. 2269-14

Nov. 21, 1989, P.L. 101-168, 103 Stat. 1284

D.C. Code Ann., § 1-2520

Nationwide Inland Marine Definition Act

Mont. Code Ann., 1991, 33-1-221 et seq.

Native American Counseling Act

N.M. Stat. Ann., 33-10-1, 33-10-2

Native American Grave Protection and Repatriation Act

Utah Code Ann. 1953, 9-9-401 et seq.

Native American Graves Protection and Repatriation Act

Nov. 16, 1990, P.L. 101-601, 18 U.S. Code §§ 1170, 25 U.S. Code §§ 3001 nt., 3001 to 3013

Native American Housing Assistance and Self-Determination Act of 1996

Oct. 26, 1996, P.L. 104-330, 25 U.S. Code § 4101 nt.

Oct. 14, 1998, P.L. 105-256, 25 U.S. Code § 4103

Oct. 21, 1998, P.L. 105-276, 25 U.S. Code §§ 4103, 4111 to 4113, 4135 to 4139, 4168

Native American Languages Act

Oct. 30, 1990, P.L. 101-477, 25 U.S. Code §§ 2901 to 2906

Feb. 12, 1996, P.L. 104-109, 25 U.S. Code § 2902

Native American Languages Act of 1992

Sept. 30, 1992, P.L. 102-375, 42 U.S. Code § 2991 nt.

Oct. 26, 1992, P.L. 102-524, 42 U.S. Code § 2991 nt.

Native American Programs Act Amendments of 1984

Oct. 30, 1984, P.L. 98-558, 42 U.S. Code §§ 2991b, 2992b, 2992c, 2992d

Native American Programs Act Amendments of 1987

Nov. 29, 1987, P.L. 100-175, 42 U.S. Code §§ 2991 nt., 2991a to 2991h, 2992 to 2992d

Native American Programs Act Amendments of 1998

Nov. 10, 1998, P.L. 105-361, 112 Stat. 3278, 42 U.S. Code § 2991 nt.

Native American Programs Act of 1974

Aug. 20, 1964, P.L. 88-452, 42 U.S. Code §§ 2991, 2991a to 2991h, 2992, 2992a to 2992d

Jan. 4, 1975, P.L. 93-644, 42 U.S. Code §§ 2991, 2991a to 2991h, 2992, 2992a to 2992d

Nov. 29, 1987, P.L. 100-175, 42 U.S. Code §§ 2991 nt., 2991a to 2991h, 2992 to 2992d

Nov. 1, 1988, P.L. 100-581, 42 U.S. Code § 2992d

Oct. 4, 1990, P.L. 101-408, 42 U.S. Code §§ 2991b, 2992d

Sept. 30, 1992, P.L. 102-375, 42 U.S. Code §§ 2991a, 2991b, 2991b-1, 2991b-2, 2991c, 2991d, 2991d-1, 2991e, 2991f, 2991g, 2991h, 2992, 2992 -1, 2992a-1, 2992b, 2992c, 2992d

Oct. 24, 1992, P.L. 102-497, 42 U.S. Code §§ 2991b, 2992c, 2992d

Oct. 26, 1992, P.L. 102-524, 42 U.S. Code §§ 2991b-3, 2992d

Dec. 2, 1993, P.L. 103-171, 42 U.S. Code §§ 2991a, 2991b, 2991b-1, 2991b-2, 2991d-1, 2992c, 2992d

Nov. 2, 1994, P.L. 103-437, 42 U.S. Code § 2991d-1

Nov. 10, 1998, P.L. 105-361, 42 U.S. Code §§ 2991b-1, 2992d

Native American Public Health Act

Neb. Rev. Stat. 1943, 71-7615 to 71-7622

Native American Veterans' Memorial Establishment Act of 1994

Oct. 22, 1994, P.L. 103-384, 20 U.S. Code § 80q-5 nt.

Native Americans Educational Assistance Act

Oct. 26, 1992, P.L. 102-524, 25 U.S. Code § 2001 nt.

Nov. 10, 1998, P.L. 105-362, 25 U.S. Code § 2001 nt.

Native Brandy Act

Ark. Code Ann. 1987, 3-6-101 et seq.

Native Claims Settlement Act (Alaska)

Alaska Stat. 1962, Replaced Titles, § 38.30.010 et seq.

Native Hawaiian Health Care Act of 1988

Oct. 31, 1988, P.L. 100-579, 42 U.S. Code § 11701 nt.

Nov. 18, 1988, P.L. 100-690, 42 U.S. Code § 11701 nt.

Native Hawaiian Health Care Improvement Act

Oct. 14, 1998, P.L. 105-256, 42 U.S. Code § 11709

Native Hawaiians Study Commission Act

Dec. 22, 1980, P.L. 96-565, 42 U.S. Code § 2991a nt.

Native Latex Commercialization and Economic Development Act of 1978

Nov. 4, 1978, P.L. 95-592, 7 U.S. Code §§ 178, 178 nt., 178a et seq., 1314f

Native Plant Act

Ariz. Rev. Stat. Ann., § 3-901 et seq.

Cal. Food and Agricultural Code 1967, § 80000 et seq.

N.H. Rev. Stat. 1955, 217-A:1 et seq.

Native Plants Act (Desert)

Cal. Food and Agricultural Code 1967, § 80001 et seq.

Native Species Conservation and Enhancement Act

Cal. Fish and Game Code 1957, § 1750 et seq.

Native Townsite Act of 1926

See Alaskan Native Townsite Act of 1926

Native Wine Act

La. Rev. Stat. Ann., 26:321 et seq.

Miss. Code Ann. 1972, § 67-5-1 et seq.

Native Wine Industry Disaster Relief Act

Ark. Code Ann. 1987, 3-5-801 et seq.

NATO Enlargement Facilitation Act of 1996

Sept. 30, 1996, P.L. 104-208, Title VI, 22 U.S. Code § 1928 nt.

NATO Participation Act of 1994
   Nov. 2, 1994, P.L. 103-447, 22 U.S. Code § 1928 nt.
   Feb. 12, 1996, P.L. 104-107, 22 U.S. Code § 1928 nt.
   Sept. 30, 1996, P.L. 104-208, 22 U.S. Code § 1928 nt.
   Oct. 21, 1998, P.L. 105-277, 22 U.S. Code § 1928 nt.

Natural and Scenic Rivers Act
   Ark. Code Ann. 1987, 15-23-301 et seq.
   N.C. Gen. Stat. 1943, § 113A-30 et seq.

Natural and Scientific Areas Preservation Act
   Kan. Stat. Ann., 74-6601 et seq.

Natural and Wilderness Areas Act
   Colo. Rev. Stat., 33-33-101 et seq.
   Ga. Code Ann., 12-3-90 et seq.
   Haw. Rev. Stat. Ann., § 195-1 et seq.
   Ill. Rev. Stat. 1991, Ch. 105, § 701 et seq.
   La. Rev. Stat. Ann., 56:1861 et seq.
   Mich. Comp. Laws Ann., 322.751 et seq.
   Mont. Code Ann., 1991, 76-12-101 et seq.
   N.J. Stat. Ann., 13:1B-15.12a et seq.
   Tenn. Code Ann., 11-14-101 et seq.

Natural Areas Act
   Colo. Rev. Stat., 33-33-101 et seq.

Natural Areas Protection Act
   R.I. Gen. Laws 1956, 42-122-1 et seq.

Natural Children Act (Adoption)
   Ky. Rev. Stat. 1971, 199.520

Natural Community Conservation Planning Act
   Cal. Fish and Game Code 1957, § 2800 et seq.

Natural Death Act
   Ala. Code 1975, § 22-8A-1 et seq.
   Ark. Code Ann. 1987, 20-17-201 et seq.
   Cal. Health and Safety Code § 7185 et seq.
   D.C. Code Ann., § 6-2421 et seq.
   Ida. Code 1947, 39-4501 et seq.
   Kan. Stat. Ann., 65-28, 101 et seq.

   N.C. Gen. Stat. 1943, § 90-320 et seq.
   Nev. Rev. Stat. 1979 Reprint, 449.540 et seq.
   N.M. Stat. Ann., 24-7-1 et seq.
   Okla. Stat. Ann., Title 63, § 3101 et seq.
   Ore. Rev. Stat. 1953, 97.050 et seq.
   Tex. Health and Safety Code, § 672.001 et seq.
   Va. Code 1950, § 54.1-2981 et seq.
   Wash. Rev. Code Ann., 70.122.010 et seq.
   W. Va. Code 1966, § 16-30-1 et seq.

Natural Disaster Assistance Act
   Cal. Government Code § 8680 et seq.

Natural Disaster Assistance Act Amendments (Campbell-Torres-Cortese)
   Cal. Statutes 1988, Ch. 1507

Natural Energy and Water Resources Compact Act
   Tex. Natural Resources Code, § 142.001 et seq.

Natural Fund for the Financing of Cultural Endeavors Act
   P.R. Laws Ann. 1954, Title 18, § 1701 et seq.

Natural Gas Act
   June 21, 1938, Ch. 556, 52 Stat. 821, 15 U.S. Code §§ 717 to 717w
   Feb. 7, 1942, Ch. 49, 56 Stat. 83, 15 U.S. Code § 717f
   July 25, 1947, Ch. 333, 61 Stat. 459, 15 U.S. Code § 717f
   March 27, 1954, Ch. 115, 68 Stat. 36, 15 U.S. Code § 717
   Aug. 28, 1958, P.L. 85-791, 72 Stat. 947, 15 U.S. Code § 717r
   May 21, 1962, P.L. 87-454, 76 Stat. 72, 15 U.S. Code § 717c
   Oct. 15, 1970, P.L. 91-452, 84 Stat. 929, 15 U.S. Code § 717m
   Nov. 9, 1978, P.L. 95-617, Title VI, § 608, 15 U.S. Code § 717f
   Oct. 24, 1992, P.L. 102-486, 15 U.S. Code §§ 717, 717 nt., 717a, 717b, 717b nt.
   Kan. Stat. Ann., 55-701 et seq.
   Okla. Stat. Ann., Title 52, § 260 to 272

Natural Gas and Crude Oil Production Incentive Act
N.M. Stat. Ann., 7-29B-1 et seq.

Natural Gas and Oil Conservation Act
Vt. Stat. Ann., Title 29, § 501 et seq.

Natural Gas and Oil Production Tax Act
Mont. Code Ann., 15-36-301 et seq.

Natural Gas and Propane Act
Me. Rev. Stat. Ann. 1964, Title 32, § 14801 et seq.

Natural Gas Authority Act (Catawba Valley)
N.C. Laws 1955, Ch. 1267

Natural Gas Authority Act (Clinton-Newberry)
S.C. Acts 1952, p. 1958, No. 789

Natural Gas Company Act
Pa. Purdon's Stat., Title 15, § 3541 et seq.

Natural Gas Competition and Deregulation Act
Ga. Code Ann., 46-4-150 et seq.

Natural Gas Condemnation Act
Ark. Code Ann. 1987, 15-72-601 et seq.

Natural Gas Conservation Act
See Oil and Gas Conservation Act

Natural Gas Industry Jobs Retention Act
W. Va. Code 1966, § 11-13L-1 et seq.

Natural Gas Market Sharing Act
Okla. Stat. 1991, Title 52, § 581.1 et seq.

Natural Gas Marketing Act
Ga. Code Ann., 46-4-170 et seq.
Miss. Code Ann. 1972, § 75-58-1 et seq.

Natural Gas Odor Injection Act
Ill. Rev. Stat. 1991, Ch. 111, 1/2, § 3600 et seq.

Natural Gas Pipe Line Act
Conn. Gen. Stat. Ann., § 16-263 et seq.
Mich. Comp. Laws Ann., 483.101 et seq.

Natural Gas Pipeline Safety Act
Ark. Code Ann. 1987, 23-15-201 et seq.
Neb. Rev. Stat. 1943, 81-542 et seq.
S.D. Codified Laws 1967, Miscellaneous Superseded Code 34-41-1 et seq.

Natural Gas Pipeline Safety Act of 1968
Aug. 12, 1968, P.L. 90-481, 82 Stat. 720, 49 U.S. Code §§ 1671 to 1684
Aug. 22, 1972, P.L. 92-401, 86 Stat. 616, 49 U.S. Code §§ 1674, 1682, 1684
Nov. 30, 1979, P.L. 96-129, 49 U.S. Code §§ 1671, 1671 nt., 1672 et seq., 1678, 1679 repealed
April 7, 1986, P.L. 99-272, 49 U.S. Code Appx. § 1684
Oct. 22, 1986, P.L. 99-516, 49 U.S. Code Appx. §§ 1672, 1680, 1684
Oct. 31, 1988, P.L. 100-561, 49 U.S. Code Appx. §§ 1672, 1674, 1676, 1679a, 1680, 1681, 1684, 1687
Nov. 16, 1990, P.L. 101-599, 49 U.S. Code Appx. § 1672
Oct. 24, 1992, P.L. 102-508, 49 U.S. Code Appx. §§ 1671 to 1674, 1679a, 1679b, 1680, 1681, 1683 to 1685, 1687, 1688

Natural Gas Policy Act of 1978
Nov. 9, 1978, P.L. 95-621, 15 U.S. Code §§ 3301, 3301 nt., 3311 et seq.; 42 U.S. Code § 7255
May 21, 1987, P.L. 100-42, 15 U.S. Code §§ 3341 to 3348, 3341 nt.
Sept. 22, 1988, P.L. 100-439, 15 U.S. Code § 3375
July 26, 1989, P.L. 101-60, 15 U.S. Code §§ 3311 to 3333, 3372, 3373 , 3375, 3411 to 3417, 3431, 3432
Oct. 29, 1992, P.L. 102-572, 15 U.S. Code § 3416

Natural Gas Price Control Act
Kan. Stat. Ann., 55-1416 et seq.
La. Rev. Stat. Ann., 30:1001 et seq.
N.M. Stat. Ann., 62-7-1 et seq.
Okla. Stat. Ann., Title 52, § 260.1 et seq.

Natural Gas Price Protection Act
Kan. Stat. Ann., 55-1401 et seq.

Natural Gas Processors/Producers Tax Act
N.M. Stat. Ann., 7-33-1 et seq.
Tex. Tax Code, § 201.001 et seq.

Natural Gas Purchasing and Distribution Act
La. Rev. Stat. Ann., 33:4546.1 et seq.
Neb. Rev. Stat. 1943, 19-4601 et seq.
Tex. Natural Resources Code, § 86.001 et seq.

Natural Gas Safety Act
N.J. Stat. Ann., 48:10-2 et seq.

Natural Gas Storage Act
Ill. Rev. Stat. 1991, Ch. 96 1/2, § 5500 et seq.
Wash. Rev. Code Ann., 80.40.010 et seq.

Natural Gas Storage Act (Underground)
Wash. Rev. Code Ann., 80.40.010 et seq.

Natural Gas Transmission Pipeline Intrastate Regulatory Act
Fla. Stat. Ann., 368.101 et seq.

Natural Gas Transmission Pipeline Siting Act
Fla. Stat. Ann., 403.9401 et seq.

Natural Gas Utilities Act
Fla. Special Laws 1967, Ch. 67-1103
Tex. Rev. Civ. Stat., Art. 6050 et seq.

Natural Gas Utility Restructuring and Customer Choice Act
Mont. Code Ann., 69-3-1401 et seq.

Natural Gas Wellhead Decontrol Act of 1989
July 26, 1989, P.L. 101-60, 15 U.S. Code § 3301 nt.

Natural Guardian Act (Joint)
Fla. Stat. Ann., 744.301
Va. Code 1950, § 31-1

Natural Heritage Act
Miss. Code Ann. 1972, § 49-5-141 et seq.

Natural Heritage Endowment Trust Fund Act
Ill. Rev. Stat. 1985, Ch. 105, § 73 et seq.

Natural Heritage Trust Act
Mont. Code Ann., 90-15-101 et seq.
N.Y. Arts and Cultural Affairs Law (Consol. Laws Ch. 11C) § 55.01 et seq.
N.Y. Public Authorities Law (Consol. Laws Ch. 43A) § 2000 et seq
R.I. Gen. Laws 1956, 42-17.5-1 et seq.

Natural History and Science Museum Act
N.M. Stat. Ann., 18-3A-1 et seq.

Natural Lakes Drainage or Diversion Act
Neb. Rev. Stat. 1943, 46-801 et seq.

Natural Lands Protection Act
N.M. Stat. Ann., 75-5-1 et seq.

Natural Patrimony Act
P.R. Laws Ann. 1954, Title 12, § 1225 et seq.

Natural Resources Act
Ga. Code Ann., 12-2-20 et seq.
Ind. Code Ann., 14-3-3-1 et seq.
Iowa Code 1983, 455B.261 et seq.
La. Rev. Stat. Ann., 30:501 et seq.
Ohio Rev. Code 1953, 1501.01 et seq.
Tex. Rev. Civ. Stat., Art. 4413 (48)
Utah Code Ann. 1953, 63-34-1 et seq.

Natural Resources Act (Department of)
Ill. Comp. Stat. 1992, Ch. 20, § 801/1-1 et seq.

Natural Resources and Conservation Act
Pa. Purdon's Stat., Title 71, § 1340.101 et seq.

Natural Resources and Environmental Management Council Law
N.D. Laws 1961, Ch. 326

Natural Resources and Environmental Protection Act
Mich. Comp. Laws Ann., 324.101 et seq.

Natural Resources and Recreation Act
Minn. Stat. 1986, 86.01 et seq.

Natural Resources Bond Act
N.J. Laws 1980, Ch. 70

Natural Resources Conservation District Act
N.M. Stat. Ann., 73-20-25 et seq.

Natural Resources Department Act
N.M. Stat. Ann., 9-5A-1 et seq.
P.R. Laws Ann. 1954, Title 3, § 151 et seq.

Natural Resources Development Board Act
Ill. Rev. Stat. 1985, Ch. 19, § 1071 et seq.

Natural Resources Development Bond Act
Ill. Laws 1968, p.10

Natural Resources, Energy and Minerals Department Act
N.M. Stat. Ann., 9-5A-1 et seq.

Natural Resources Protection Act (Broward County)
Fla. Laws 1991, Ch. 355

Natural Resources Rangers of the Department of Natural Resources Act
P.R. Laws Ann. 1954, Title 12, § 1201 et seq.

Natural Resources Research Act (Renewable)
Miss. Code Ann. 1972, § 57-18-1 et seq.

Natural Resources Trust Fund Act
Mich. Comp. Laws Ann., 318.501 et seq.
Tenn. Code Ann., 11-14-301 et seq.

Natural Resources Trustee Act
N.M. Stat. Ann., 75-7-1 et seq.

Natural River Act
Mich. Comp. Laws Ann., 281.761 et seq.

Natural Streambed and Land Preservation Act
Mont. Code Ann., 1991, 75-7-101 et seq.

Natural Streams Preservation Act
W. Va. Code 1966, § 22-13-1 et seq.

Natural Wild Rice Preservation Act
Minn. Stat. Ann., 116J.645

Naturalization Acts
See Immigration and Nationality Act
Jan. 29, 1795, Ch. 20, 1 Stat. 414
June 18, 1798, Ch. 54, 1 Stat. 566
April 14, 1802, Ch. 28, 2 Stat. 153
March 26, 1804, Ch. 186, 4 Stat. 69
May 24, 1824, Ch. 138, 4 Stat. 31
July 14, 1870, Ch. 254, 16 Stat. 254
June 29, 1906, Ch. 3592, 34 Stat. 596
March 26, 1970, Ch. 3, 1 Stat. 103

Nature and Historical Preserve Act
N.Y. Environmental Conservation Law 1972 (Consol. Laws Ch. 43B) § 45-0101 et seq.

Nature Preserves Act
Ill. Rev. Stat. 1979, Ch. 105, § 501 et seq.
Ky. Rev. Stat. 1971, 146.410 et seq.
N.C. Gen. Stat. 1943, §§ 113A-164.1 et seq., 143-260.6 et seq.
N.Y. Environmental Conservation Law 1972 (Consol. Laws Ch. 43B) § 45-0101 et seq.

Naturopathic Health Care Practice Act
Mont. Code Ann., 37-26-101 et seq.

Naturopathy Act
Ariz. Rev. Stat. Ann., § 32-1501 et seq.
Fla. Stat. Ann., 462.01 et seq.
Mont. Laws 1991, Ch. 306, §§ 1 et seq., 10 et seq.
S.C. Code Ann. 1976, §§ 40-31-10, 40-31-20
Tex. Rev. Civ. Stat., Art. 4590d

Nautical Education Act
Aug. 4, 1939, Ch. 416, 53 Stat. 1181 (See 14 U.S. Code § 148)

Nautical Schools Act
Cal. Education Code 1976, § 70000 et seq.

Navajo and Hopi Indian Relocation Amendments Act of 1980
July 8, 1980, P.L. 96-305, 25 U.S. Code §§ 640d et seq., 640d nt.

Navajo and Hopi Indian Relocation Amendments of 1988

Nov. 16, 1988, P.L. 100-666, 25 U.S. Code § 640d nt.

Navajo Community College Act

Dec. 15, 1971, P.L. 92-189, 85 Stat. 646, 25 U.S. Code § 640a nt.

Dec. 1, 1983, P.L. 98-192, 25 U.S. Code § 640c-1

Sept. 30, 1986, P.L. 99-428, 25 U.S. Code § 640c-1

April 28, 1988, P.L. 100-297, 102 Stat. 414, 25 U.S. Code §§ 640c -1, 640c-3

Oct. 30, 1990, P.L. 101-477, 25 U.S. Code §§ 640c, 640c-1

July 23, 1992, P.L. 102-325, 25 U.S. Code § 640c-1

Oct. 7, 1998, P.L. 105-244, 25 U.S. Code § 640c-1

Navajo-Hopi Land Dispute Settlement Act of 1996

Oct. 11, 1996, P.L. 104-301, 25 U.S. Code § 640d nt.

Oct. 14, 1998, P.L. 105-256, 25 U.S. Code § 640d nt.

Navajo-Hopi Land Settlement Act of 1974

Dec. 22, 1974, P.L. 93-531, 25 U.S. Code §§ 640d-640d-24

Navajo-Hopi Rehabilitation Act

April 19, 1950, Ch. 92, 64 Stat. 44, 25 U.S. Code §§ 631 to 640

Dec. 31, 1973, P.L. 93-233, 87 Stat. 974, 25 U.S. Code § 639

Navajo-Hopi Relocation Housing Program Reauthorization Act of 1991

Dec. 2, 1991, P.L. 102-180, 25 U.S. Code § 640d nt.

Naval Academy Act

June 3, 1941, Ch. 162, 55 Stat. 238

Naval Academy Age Limit Act

Sept. 24, 1940, Ch. 729, 54 Stat. 959

Naval Air Base Act

April 25, 1939, Ch. 87, 53 Stat. 590 (See 10 U.S. Code § 7212)

Naval Air Station Act

Aug. 16, 1941, Ch. 359, 55 Stat. 624

Naval Air Station Tax Exemption Act (Glenview)

Ill. Comp. Stat. 1992, Ch. 35, § 805/1

Naval Aircraft-Public Works Act

June 15, 1940, Ch. 375, 54 Stat. 400 (See 10 U.S. Code § 6022)

Naval Appropriation Act, 1946

June 13, 1991, P.L. 102-54, 24 U.S. Code § 16a

Naval Appropriation Acts

April 26, 1938, Ch. 175, 52 Stat. 223, 31 U.S. Code § 495a

May 25, 1939, Ch. 149, 53 Stat. 757, 31 U.S. Code § 495a

June 11, 1940, Ch. 313, 54 Stat. 265

June 26, 1940, Ch. 430, 54 Stat. 604

Sept. 9, 1940, Ch. 717, 54 Stat. 875, 50 U.S. Code Appx. § 1152

April 5, 1941, Ch. 41, 55 Stat. 128

May 6, 1941, Ch. 86, 55 Stat. 151, 31 U.S. Code § 495a

July 3, 1941, Ch. 273, 55 Stat. 541

Aug. 25, 1941, Ch. 409, 55 Stat. 670

Oct. 28, 1941, Ch. 460, 55 Stat. 747

Dec. 17, 1941, Ch. 591, 55 Stat. 816

Feb. 7, 1942, Ch. 46, 56 Stat. 54

April 28, 1942, Ch. 247, 56 Stat. 233, 22 U.S. Code § 412 nt.

June 23, 1942, Ch. 444, 56 Stat. 389

Oct. 26, 1942, Ch. 629, 56 Stat. 990, 22 U.S. Code § 412 nt.

March 31, 1943, Ch. 30, 57 Stat. 52, 42 U.S. Code § 70

June 26, 1943, Ch. 147, 57 Stat. 197, 22 U.S. Code § 412 nt.; 31 U.S. Code § 495

June 22, 1944, Ch. 269, 58 Stat. 301, 22 U.S. Code § 412 nt.; 24 U.S. Code § 16a; 31 U.S. Code § 495a

May 29, 1945, Ch. 130, 59 Stat. 201, 22 U.S. Code § 412 nt.; 24 U.S. Code § 16a; 31 U.S. Code § 495

July 8, 1946, Ch. 543, 60 Stat. 481, 31 U.S. Code § 495a; 50 U.S. Code Appx. § 1291 nt.

July 18, 1947, Ch. 268, 61 Stat. 382

Naval Auxiliary Vessel Acts
April 26, 1939, Ch. 89, 53 Stat. 618 (See 10 U.S. Code § 7296)
May 24, 1941, Ch. 131, 55 Stat. 197

Naval Aviation Cadet Act
April 15, 1935, Ch. 71, 49 Stat. 156

Naval Aviation Cadet Act of 1942
Aug. 4, 1942, Ch. 547, 56 Stat. 737 (See 10 U.S. Code §§ 6911, 6915; 14 U.S. Code §§ 758a, 759a)
Oct. 21, 1943, Ch. 269, 57 Stat. 573
Oct. 25, 1943, Ch. 275, 57 Stat. 574
June 11, 1946, Ch. 325, 60 Stat. 245
July 25, 1947, Ch. 323, 61 Stat. 424
March 31, 1955, Ch. 20, 69 Stat. 22 (See 10 U.S. Code § 6912)

Naval Aviation Personnel Act of 1940
Aug. 27, 1940, Ch. 694, 54 Stat. 864 (See 10 U.S. Code §§ 5942, 6023 to 6025, 6148, 6914)
June 20, 1949, Ch. 225, 63 Stat. 201 (See 10 U.S. Code § 6148)

Naval Aviation Reserve Act
June 13, 1939, Ch. 205, 53 Stat. 819 (See 10 U.S. Code § 6148)

Naval Code
Ill. Rev. Stat. 1991, Ch. 129, § 220.001 et seq.

Naval Drydock Act
Sept. 18, 1940, Ch. 723, 54 Stat. 956

Naval Expansion Acts
May 17, 1938, Ch. 243, 52 Stat. 401 (See 10 U.S. Code §§ 7294, 7302, 7344)
June 14, 1940, Ch. 364, 54 Stat. 394 (See 10 U.S. Code §§ 7295, 7299)
June 15, 1940, Ch. 375, 54 Stat. 400 (See 10 U.S. Code § 6022)
July 19, 1940, Ch. 644, 54 Stat. 779 (See 10 U.S. Code §§ 7341, 7342)
Dec. 23, 1941, Ch. 619, 55 Stat. 853

July 9, 1942, Ch. 503, 56 Stat. 655

Naval Facilities Act
July 29, 1941, Ch. 328, 55 Stat. 608

Naval Line-Officer Act
July 22, 1935, Ch. 402, 49 Stat. 487 (See 10 U.S. Code §§ 5404, 5572, 5582, 6021)

Naval Militia Act
Feb. 16, 1914, Ch. 21, 38 Stat. 283
Mich. Comp. Laws 1970, 33.1 et seq.
Ore. Laws 1911, Ch. 269, § 4 et seq.
Ore. Laws 1917, Ch. 129

Naval Militiaman's Compensation Act
Ill. Rev. Stat. 1991, Ch. 129, § 401 et seq.

Naval Museum Authority Act
Va. Code 1950, § 9-106.6 et seq.

Naval Parity Act
March 27, 1934, Ch. 95, 48 Stat. 503 (See 10 U.S. Code §§ 2382, 7300, 7342, 7343; 40 U.S. Code § 474)

Naval Petroleum Reserve Production Act of 1976
April 5, 1976, P.L. 94-258, 42 U.S. Code § 6501 et seq.
July 17, 1984, P.L. 98-366, 42 U.S. Code §§ 6502, 6504, 6504 nt.
Nov. 2, 1994, P.L. 103-437, 42 U.S. Code § 6504

Naval Plant-Protection Force Act
Aug. 11, 1941, Ch. 352, 55 Stat. 616

Naval Public Works Act
June 2, 1939, Ch. 169, 53 Stat. 798
Aug. 6, 1942, Ch. 549, 56 Stat. 742

Naval R. O. T. C. Act
Sept. 11, 1940, Ch. 718, 54 Stat. 884 (See 10 U.S. Code § 6901)
Oct. 8, 1940, Ch. 765, 54 Stat. 1023 (See 10 U.S. Code § 6902)

Naval Reserve Act of 1938

June 25, 1938, Ch. 690, 52 Stat. 1175 (See 10 U.S. Code §§ 261 et seq., 683 et seq., 1201 et seq., 6115, 6330, 6332, 6521)

April 25, 1940, Ch. 153, 54 Stat. 162 (See 10 U.S. Code §§ 6331, 6485)

Jan. 30, 1941, Ch. 2, 55 Stat. 3

May 4, 1942, Ch. 282, 56 Stat. 266

July 30, 1942, Ch. 538, 56 Stat. 730

Aug. 4, 1942, Ch. 547, 56 Stat. 739 (See 10 U.S. Code § 671 et seq.; 37 U.S. Code §§ 231 et seq.)

Oct. 25, 1943, Ch. 277, 57 Stat. 575

Nov. 8, 1943, Ch. 297, 57 Stat. 586

Sept. 27, 1944, Ch. 428, 58 Stat. 754

Aug. 7, 1946, Ch. 796, 60 Stat. 892 (See 10 U.S. Code § 6148)

Aug. 10, 1946, Ch. 952, 60 Stat. 993 (See 10 U.S. Code §§ 261 et seq., 6330, 6331)

July 1, 1947, Ch. 192, 61 Stat. 239

June 12, 1948, Ch. 449, 62 Stat. 363

July 9, 1952, Ch. 608, 66 Stat. 508 (See 10 U.S. Code §§ 6485, 6486)

Aug. 1, 1956, Ch. 837, 70 Stat. 883 (See 10 U.S. Code § 6148)

Naval Ship Alteration Act

Jan. 29, 1941, Ch. 1, 55 Stat. 3

Naval Special Duty Act

July 17, 1941, Ch. 304, 55 Stat. 598 (See 10 U.S. Code §§ 5231, 5501)

Naval Staff Corps Act

Aug. 5, 1935, Ch. 439, 49 Stat. 530 (See 10 U.S. Code § 5571 et seq.)

Naval Station Tax Exemption Act (Great Lakes)

Ill. Comp. Stat. 1992, Ch. 35, § 810/1

Naval Stores Act

March 3, 1923, Ch. 217, 42 Stat. 1435, 7 U.S. Code §§ 91 to 99

Ga. Code 1933, 5-1601 et seq.

Navigable Stream Thirty Foot Act

Tex. Natural Resources Code, § 21.001 et seq.

Navigable Waters Act (Removal of Sand)

Ala. Code 1975, § 33-17-1 et seq.

Ill. Rev. Stat. 1989, Ch. 42, § 350m et seq.

N.Y. Local Laws 1971, Village of Dering Harbor, p. 4060

S.D. Codified Laws 1967, 5-2-4 et seq.

Wis. Stat. Ann., 144.26

Navigable Waters Obstruction Act

Ill. Rev. Stat. 1991, Ch. 19, § 47a.1 et seq.

Navigation Acts

March 3, 1899, Ch. 425, 30 Stat. 1152, 33 U.S. Code §§ 401, 403, 404, 406 to 409, 411 to 416, 418, 502, 549, 686, 687

May 28, 1908, Ch. 212, 35 Stat. 424, 19 U.S. Code § 289; 33 U.S. Code §§ 152, 153, 443 to 448; 46 U.S. Code §§ 49, 104, 112, 124, 224, 395 to 398, 460, 461

N.Y. Consol. Laws Ch. 37

Navigation Commission Act (Chautauqua)

N.Y. Laws 1950, Ch. 780

Navigation Rules Act (Charter Boat)

Iowa Code Ann., 106.1 et seq.

Mich. Comp. Laws Ann., 281.1071

Wash. Rev. Code Ann., 88.04.005 et seq.

Navy and Marine Corps Officer Augmentation Act of 1955

Aug. 9, 1955, Ch. 668, 769 Stat. 606 (See 10 U.S. Code § 5572 nt.)

July 20, 1956, Ch. 646, 70 Stat. 588 (See 10 U.S. Code §§ 3212, 3284 to 3288, 3295, 3574, 4353, 8284 to 8288, 8574, 9353)

Navy Construction Act

May 17, 1938, Ch. 243, 52 Stat. 401

Navy Department Reorganization Act

June 20, 1940, Ch. 400, 54 Stat. 492

Navy Enlisted Strength Act

April 22, 1941, Ch. 74, 55 Stat. 145

Navy Enlistment Acts

Aug. 18, 1941, Ch. 364, 55 Stat. 629

Dec. 13, 1941, Ch. 570, 55 Stat. 799

Navy Local Defense Ship Act
Nov. 21, 1941, Ch. 502, 55 Stat. 782

Navy Marine Advancement Act
Feb. 23, 1942, Ch. 110, 56 Stat. 120 (See 10 U.S. Code §§ 6150, 6483)

Navy Marine Corps Enlisted Strength Act
Jan. 12, 1942, Ch. 1, 56 Stat. 3 (See 10 U.S. Code § 5401)

Navy Ordnance Act
March 17, 1942, Ch. 187, 56 Stat. 172

Navy Personnel Act
March 3, 1899, Ch. 413, 30 Stat. 1004

Navy Promotion Act
May 29, 1934, Ch. 368, 48 Stat. 814

Navy Public Works Act
March 23, 1941, Ch. 25, 55 Stat. 47
March 23, 1941, Ch. 26, 55 Stat. 49, 40 U.S. Code § 276a-7
July 14, 1941, Ch. 298, 55 Stat. 592
Aug. 21, 1941, Ch. 395, 55 Stat. 658, 40 U.S. Code § 276a-7
Feb. 6, 1942, Ch. 43, 56 Stat. 51 (See 10 U.S. Code § 7213)
April 28, 1942, Ch. 250, 56 Stat. 248

Navy Reorganization Acts
March 3, 1915, Ch. 83, 38 Stat. 928
Aug. 29, 1916, Ch. 417, 39 Stat. 556
June 4, 1920, Ch. 228, 41 Stat. 812

Navy Shipbuilding and Repair Act
Jan. 29, 1942, Ch. 25, 56 Stat. 23

Navy Shipbuilding Facilities Act
Jan. 31, 1941, Ch. 4, 55 Stat. 5

Navy Shipbuilding Program Act
Feb. 6, 1942, Ch. 45, 56 Stat. 53

Navy Warship Construction Act
See Naval Expansion Acts

Navy Yard Tracks Act
May 27, 1908, Ch. 203, 35 Stat. 397

Nazi War Crimes Disclosure Act
Oct. 8, 1998, P.L. 105-246, 112 Stat. 1859, 5 U.S. Code § 552 nt.

Ne Exeat Act
Ill. Rev. Stat. 1991, Ch. 110, § 16-101 et seq.
Wash. Rev. Code Ann., 7.44.010 et seq.

Nearshore Gill and Trammel Net Fishery Mitigation Act
Cal. Statutes 1986, Ch. 910

Neat Cattle Act
Ore. Rev. Stat., 607.344 et seq.

Nebraska Iowa Boundary Line Compact
Iowa Laws 1943 (50th G. A.), Ch. 306
Neb. Laws 1943, Ch. 130, p. 797

Nebraska Kansas Act
May 30, 1854, Ch. 59, 10 Stat. 277

Nebraska Kansas Big Blue River Compact
Kan. Stat. Ann., 82a-529
Neb. Laws 1971, L.B. 609

Nebraska Missouri Boundary Compact
Neb. Laws 1971, L. B. 1034

Nebraska Redevelopment Act
Neb. Rev. Stat. 1943, 58-501 to 58-533

Nebraska Wilderness Act of 1985
Oct. 22, 1986, P.L. 99-504, 100 Stat. p. 1802

Necessary Expense Reserve Fund Act of 1967
N.C. Laws 1967, Ch. 649

Necessitous Borrowers Act
Cal. Business and Professions Code § 10240 et seq.

Need Based Educational Aid Antitrust Protection Act of 1997
Sept. 17, 1997, P.L. 105-43, 15 U.S. Code § 1 nt.

Needles and Hypodermic Syringes Act
Ill. Rev. Stat. 1991, Ch. 38, § 22-49.9 et seq.

Needy Blind Act
Iowa Code 1973, 241.1 et seq.

Needy Children Aid Act
Cal. Welfare and Institutions Code §§ 1500, 11200 et seq.

Needy Disabled Aid Act
Colo. Rev. Stat. 26-2-101 et seq.

Neel Act (Pleading)
Ga. Code 1933, 81-103

Neglect and Abuse Child Prevention Act
Ala. Code 1975, § 26-16-1 et seq.
Ark. Code Ann. 1987, 9-30-101 et seq.
Wash. Rev. Code Ann., 26.44.010 et seq.

Neglect and Child Abuse Task Force Act
N.J. Stat. Ann., 9:6-8.74 et seq.

Neglect and Exploitation Act (Adult Abuse)
Ida. Code 1947, 39-5301 et seq.

Neglect Proceedings Amendment Act
D.C. Laws 1977, No. 2-22, § 401

Neglected, Abused, or Exploited Disabled Adult Protection Act
N.C. Gen. Stat. 1943, § 108A-99 et seq.

Neglected and Abused Child Reporting Act
D.C. Code Ann., §§ 6-2126, 6-2127
Ill. Rev. Stat. 1991, Ch. 23, § 2051 et seq.

Neglected and Abused Long Term Care Facility Residents Reporting Act
Ill. Rev. Stat. 1991, Ch. 111 1/2, § 4162 et seq.

Neglected Children Offense Act
Ill. Rev. Stat. 1991, Ch. 23, § 2359.9 et seq.

Neglected, Delinquent and Dependent Children Acts
Ill. Rev. Stat. 1991, Ch. 37, § 701-1 et seq., § 801-1 et seq.
Ind. Code Ann., 31-6-11-1 et seq.
Iowa Code Ann., 232.1 et seq.
Kan. Stat. Ann., 38-824
Ky. Rev. Stat. 1971, 620.010 et seq.

Mo. Rev. Stat., 211.011 et seq.
N.H. Rev. Stat. 1955, 169:1 et seq.
N.M. Stat. Ann., 32-1-1 et seq.
Ohio Rev. Code 1953, 2151.03
Tex. Family Code, Art. 15.01 et seq.
Utah Code Ann. 1953, 62A-11-301 et seq.

Negligence Act (Comparative)
See Comparative Negligence Act

Negligence Act (Construction Contract Indemnification)
Ill. Rev. Stat. 1991, Ch. 29, § 60.90 et seq.

Negligence Act (Contributory)
See Contributory Negligence Act

Negligence Act (Culpable)
Miss. Code Ann. 1972, § 97-3-47

Negligence Causing Death Act
D.C. Code 1973, § 16-2701 et seq.

Negligence Statute of Limitations
N.Y. Civil Practice Laws and Rules (Consol. Laws Ch. 8) § 214

Negligent Driving Act
Wash. Rev. Code Ann., 46.61.525

Negligent Homicide Act
Wyo. Stat. Ann., § 6-2-106

Negligent Homicide Act (Motor Vehicles)
Ariz. Rev. Stat. Ann., § 13-1102
Colo. Rev. Stat., 18-3-106
D.C. Code Ann., § 40-713
Haw. Rev. Stat. Ann., §§ 707-703, 707-704
Ky. Rev. Stat. 1971, 507.040, 507.050
Me. Rev. Stat. Ann. 1964, Title 29, §§ 1315, 1316
Mich. Comp. Laws Ann., 750.324
N.M. Stat. Ann. 1953, 64-22-1
Ore. Rev. Stat., 163.145
Wash. Rev. Code Ann., 46.61.520
Wis. Stat. Ann., 940.08
Wyo. Stat. Ann., § 6-2-106

Negligent Parent Act
W. Va. Code 1966, § 55-7A-1 et seq.

Negotiable Instruments
See Uniform Commercial Code-Negotiable Instruments

Negotiable Instruments (Uniform Commercial Code)
See Uniform Commercial Code-Negotiable Instruments

Negotiable Instruments Act
See Uniform Negotiable Instruments Act

Negotiable Instruments Deferred Posting Act
Ark. Stat. 1947, 67-544 et seq.

Negotiable Warehouse Receipts Act
Ark. Stat. 1947, 68-1201 et seq.

Negotiated Rate Act
Minn. Stat. Ann., 256I.01 et seq.

Negotiated Rates Act of 1993
Dec. 3, 1993, P.L. 103-180, 49 U.S. Code §§ 10101 nt., 10701, 10701 nt., 10702, 10762, 10767, 11101, 11706, 11712, 11901, 11909

Negotiated Rulemaking Act
Mont. Code Ann., 2-5-101 et seq.
Neb. Rev. Stat. 1943, 84-921 et seq.
Tex. Government Code, § 2008.001 et seq.

Negotiated Rulemaking Act of 1990
Nov. 29, 1990, P.L. 101-648, 5 U.S. Code §§ 500, 581 to 590
Aug. 26, 1992, P.L. 102-354, 5 U.S. Code § 561 nt.
Oct. 19, 1996, P.L. 104-320, 5 U.S. Code §§ prec. 500, prec. 561, 561 nt., 561 to 570

Negotiated Shipbuilding Contracting Act of 1976
July 31, 1976, P.L. 94-372, 46 U.S. Code § 1152 et seq.

Negotiation Act (Consultants' Competitive)
Fla. Stat. Ann., 287.055

Negotiation Act (Professional Consultants Competitive)
Fla. Stat. Ann., 287.055
Neb. Rev. Stat. 1943, 81-1701

Negro Exclusion Act (Primaries)
Tex. Rev. Civ. Stat. 1925, Art. 3107

Negro Segregation Act (Cities)
Tex. Rev. Civ. Stat., Art. 1015b

Negro Segregation Act (Transportation)
Tex. Penal Code 1925, Arts. 1659, 1660, 1661.1
Tex. Rev. Civ. Stat., Art. 6417

Neighborhood Assistance Act
Del. Code of 1974, Title 30, § 2001 et seq.
Mo. Rev. Stat., 32.100 et seq.
Pa. Purdon's Stat., Title 62, § 2081 et seq.
Pa. Purdon's Stat., Title 72, § 8901-A et seq.
Va. Code 1950, § 63.1-320 et seq.

Neighborhood Assistance Act (R.E. Van Norstrand)
Conn. Gen. Stat. 1983, § 12-631 et seq.

Neighborhood Assistance and Participation Act
Mich. Comp. Laws Ann., 125.801 et seq.

Neighborhood Based Initiatives Act (New York State)
N.Y. Executive Law 1951 (Consol. Laws Ch. 18) § 548a

Neighborhood Corps Act of 1983
Ill. Rev. Stat. 1991, Ch. 48, § 1901 et seq.

Neighborhood Crime Prevention Act
R.I. Gen. Laws 1956, 42-96-1 et seq.

Neighborhood Development Act
Utah Code Ann. 1953, 11-19-1 et seq.

Neighborhood Education Center Act
N.J. Stat. Ann., 18A:54A-1 et seq.

Neighborhood Enterprise Zone Act
Mich. Comp. Laws Ann., 207.771 et seq.

Neighborhood Housing Services Act
Fla. Stat. Ann., 420.421 et seq.
Pa. Purdon's Stat., Title 62, § 2090.11 et seq.

Neighborhood Housing Services Grant Fund Act
N.J. Stat. Ann., 52:27D-366 et seq.

Neighborhood Improvement and Youth Employment Act
Kan. Laws 1994, Ch. 264, §§ 1 to 8

Neighborhood Improvement District Act
Mo. Rev. Stat., 67.453 et seq.
Pa. Purdon's Stat., Title 62, § 2090.11 et seq.

Neighborhood Investment Program Act
W. Va. Code 1966, § 11-13J-1 et seq.

Neighborhood Preservation Crime Prevention Act
N.Y. Executive Law 1951 (Consol. Laws, Ch. 18), § 846a et seq.

Neighborhood Preservation Housing Rehabilitation Loan and Grant Act
N.J. Stat. Ann., 52:27D-152 et seq.

Neighborhood Redevelopment Act
Ky. Rev. Stat. 1971, 99A.005 et seq.

Neighborhood Redevelopment Corporation Act
Ill. Rev. Stat. 1985, Ch. 67, § 251 et seq.
Minn. Laws 1945, Ch. 493

Neighborhood Reinvestment Corporation Act
Oct. 31, 1978, P.L. 95-557, 42 U.S. Code §§ 8101, 8101 nt., 8102 et seq.
Oct. 15, 1982, P.L. 97-320, 42 U.S. Code §§ 8103, 8105
Nov. 30, 1983, P.L. 98-181, 42 U.S. Code § 8107
Oct. 17, 1984, P.L. 98-479, 42 U.S. Code § 8107
February 5, 1988, P.L. 100-242, 42 U.S. Code § 8103
Nov. 7, 1988, P.L. 100-628, 42 U.S. Code § 8103
Nov. 28, 1990, P.L. 101-625, 42 U.S. Code § 8107

Oct. 28, 1992, P.L. 102-550, 42 U.S. Code § 8107
Dec. 21, 1995, P.L. 104-66, 42 U.S. Code § 8106

Neighborhood Restorative Justice Act
Fla. Stat. Ann., 39.0361

Neighborhood Revitalization Act
Kan. Stat. Ann., 12-17,114 et seq.

Neighborhood Self-Help Development Act of 1978
Oct. 31, 1978, P.L. 95-557, 42 U.S. Code §§ 8121, 8121 nt., 8122 et seq.

Neikirk Act (Schools Moral Instructions)
Ky. Rev. Stat. 1971, 158.200 et seq.

Neill Act (State Aid Roads)
Ga. Code 1933, 95-1711 et seq.

Neill Primary Act (County Unit Vote)
Ga. Code 1933, 34-3212 et seq.

Nejedly-Bagley-Z'berg Suisun Marsh Preservation Act
Cal. Fish and Game Code 1957, § 1850 et seq.

Nejedly-Hart State, Urban and Coastal Park Bond Act
Cal. Public Resources Code § 5096.111 et seq.

Nejedly-Keene California Wetlands Preservation Act
Cal. Public Resources Code § 5810 et seq.

Nejedly-Mobley Delta Levees Act
Cal. Water Code § 12225 et seq.

Nejedly-Z'berg-Dills Solid Waste Management and Resource Recovery Act
Cal. Government Code § 66700 et seq.

Nejedly-Z'berg Forest Practice Act
Cal. Public Resources Code § 4511 et seq.

Neligence Statute of Limitations

N.Y. Civil Practice Law and Rules (Consol. Laws, Ch. 8), § 214 et seq.

Nelsen Bill

Sept. 22, 1970, P.L. 91-405, 84 Stat. 3752, 5 U.S. Code § 2106; 10 U.S. Code §§ 4342, 6954, 9342; 18 U.S. Code §§ 201, 203, 204, 591, 594, 595; 42 U.S. Code § 1973i

Nelson Act (Alaska Roads, Schools, and Insane)

Jan. 27, 1905, Ch. 277, 33 Stat. 616

Nelson Act (Bankruptcy Act of 1898)

July 1, 1898, Ch. 541, 30 Stat. 544

Nelson Act (Chippewa Indians of Minnesota)

Jan. 14, 1889, Ch. 24, 25 Stat. 642

Nelson Act (Criminal Appeals Act)

See Criminal Appeals Act

Nelson Act (Department of Commerce and Labor)

See Department of Commerce and Labor Act

Nelson Amendment (Agricultural Colleges)

March 4, 1907, Ch. 2907, 34 Stat. 1256, 7 U.S. Code §§ 322, 2219, 2221, 2227, 2243, 2245; 15 U.S. Code § 320; 16 U.S. Code §§ 471, 496, 499; 21 U.S. Code §§ 71 to 91; 43 U.S. Code § 203, 420, 956, 957

Nelson Tax Act (Taxed Property)

Ky. Rev. Stat. 1971, 132.200 et seq.

Nematocide, Plant Regulator, Defoliant, and Desiccant Amendment of 1959

Aug. 7, 1959, P.L. 86-139, 73 Stat. 286, 7 U.S. Code § 135

March 29, 1961, P.L. 87-10, 75 Stat. 18, 7 U.S. Code § 135 nt.

April 7, 1961, P.L. 87-19, 75 Stat. 42, 7 U.S. Code § 135 nt.

Oct. 3, 1964, P.L. 88-625, 78 Stat. 1002, 7 U.S. Code § 135 nt.

Neponset River Drainage and Flood Control Act

Mass. Acts 1955, Ch. 743

Nepotism Act

Ala. General Acts 1931, p. 247, No. 173

Fla. Stat. Ann., 112.3135

Ida. Code 1947, 59-701, 59-702

Iowa Code Ann., 71.1, 71.2

Mont. Code Ann., 1991, 2-2-301 et seq.

Neb. Rev. Stat. 1943, 81-108

Nev. Rev. Stat. 1979 Reprint, 281.210

N.M. Stat. Ann., 10-1-10

Okla. Stat. Ann., Title 21, § 481 et seq.

S.C. Code Ann. 1976, § 8-5-10

Tenn. Code Ann., 8-31-101 et seq.

Tex. Rev. Civ. Stat., Art. 5996a et seq.

Utah Code Ann. 1953, 52-3-1 et seq.

Nepotism Policy Act (Haywood County Employees)

See Uniform Nepotism Policy Act (Haywood County Employees)

NESHAP Act (Asbestos)

Va. Code 1950, § 40.1-51.20 et seq.

Net Container Act

Cal. Business and Professions Code § 12601 et seq.

Net Earnings Tax Act

Pa. 1889 Pamph. Laws 420, No. 332, § 27

Net Income Tax Act

Alaska Stat. 1962, § 43.20.010 et seq.

Ark. Code Ann. 1987, 26-51-101 et seq.

Ga. Code Ann., 48-7-1 et seq.

Okla. Stat. Ann., Title 68, § 2351 et seq.

S.D. Codified Laws 1967, 10-43-1 et seq.

Wash. Rev. Code Ann., 82.30.010 et seq.

Net Income Tax Act (Corporation)

W. Va. Code 1966, § 11-24-1 et seq.

Net Proceeds Tax Act (Mines)

Mont. Code Ann., 1991, 15-23-502, 15-23-503

Net Weight Container Act
N.J. Stat. Ann., 51:1-29

Net Worth Certificate Act
Oct. 15, 1982, P.L. 97-320, Title II, 12 U.S. Code § 1811 nt.

Network Development Act (Industry Sector)
N.J. Stat. Ann., 34:1B-80 et seq.

Network for Opportunity Act
Ill. Rev. Stat. 1991, Ch. 127, § 2201 et seq.

Network Law (Library)
N.J. Stat. Ann., 18A:73-35a et seq.

Network Law (Venture Capital)
La. Rev. Stat. Ann., 51:1141 et seq.

Neurological Injury Compensation Act (Birth-Related)
Va. Code 1950, § 38.2-5000 et seq.

Neustein-Doyle State Labor Relations Act
N.Y. Labor Law (Consol. Laws Ch. 31) § 700 et seq.

Neustein-Quinn Act (Labor Injunctions)
N.Y. Labor Law (Consol. Laws Ch. 31) § 807

Neutrality Acts
Aug. 31, 1935, Ch. 837, 49 Stat. 1081
May 1, 1937, Ch. 146, 50 Stat. 121
Nov. 4, 1939, Ch. 2, 54 Stat. 4, 22 U.S. Code §§ 441, 444, 445, 447 to 451, 453 to 457
June 26, 1940, Ch. 431, 54 Stat. 611, 22 U.S. Code § 444
Aug. 27, 1940, Ch. 695, 54 Stat. 866, 22 U.S. Code § 444
Nov. 17, 1941, Ch. 473, 55 Stat. 764
Feb. 21, 1942, Ch. 104, 56 Stat. 95, 22 U.S. Code § 447

Neutrality Proclamations
April 22, 1793, No. 3, 11 Stat. 753
Jan. 5, 1838, No. 32, 11 Stat. 784
Nov. 21, 1838, No. 33, 11 Stat. 785
Sept. 25, 1841, No. 35, 11 Stat. 786
Aug. 22, 1870, No. 12, 16 Stat. 1132
June 12, 1895, No. 4, 29 Stat. 870

July 27, 1896, No. 14, 29 Stat. 881
Feb. 11, 1904, 33 Stat. 2332
Oct. 24, 1911, 37 Stat. 1719
Aug. 4, 1914, 38 Stat. 1999
Aug. 5, 1914, 38 Stat. 2002
Aug. 7, 1914, 38 Stat. 2005
Aug. 13, 1914, 38 Stat. 2008
Aug. 14, 1914, 38 Stat. 2011
Aug. 18, 1914, 38 Stat. 2015
Aug. 24, 1914, 38 Stat. 2018
Aug. 27, 1914, 38 Stat. 2021
Sept. 1, 1914, 38 Stat. 2025
Nov. 6, 1914, 38 Stat. 2036
May 24, 1915, 39 Stat. 1729
Aug. 23, 1915, 39 Stat. 1743
Nov. 11, 1915, 39 Stat. 1757
March 13, 1916, 39 Stat. 1770
Aug. 30, 1916, 39 Stat. 1798
Sept. 18, 1916, 39 Stat. 1805
Sept. 5, 1939, No. 2348, 54 Stat. 2629, 50 U.S. Code Appx. prec. § 1 nt.
Sept. 8, 1939, No. 2353, 54 Stat. 2643, 50 U.S. Code Appx. prec. § 1 nt.
Sept. 10, 1939, No. 2359, 54 Stat. 2652, 50 U.S. Code Appx. prec. § 1 nt.
April 25, 1940, No. 2399, 54 Stat. 2699, 50 U.S. Code Appx. prec. § 1 nt.
May 11, 1940, No. 2405, 54 Stat. 2704, 50 U.S. Code Appx. prec. § 1 nt.
June 10, 1940, No. 2408, 54 Stat. 2707, 50 U.S. Code Appx. prec. § 1 nt.
Nov. 15, 1940, No. 2444, 54 Stat. 2764, 50 U.S. Code Appx. prec. § 1 nt.

Nevada Arizona Boundary Compact
Ariz. Laws 1960, Ch. 69

Nevada California Interstate Compact Act (Water Apportionment)
Cal. Water Code §§ 5975, 5976
Nev. Rev. Stat. 1979 Reprint, 538.600 et seq.

Nevada California Super Speed Ground Transportation Act
Cal. Statutes 1988, Ch. 149
Cal. Statutes 1992, Ch. 27

Nevada Compact Act
Cal. Government Code §§ 8100, 8101

Nevada County Water Agency Act
Cal. Statutes 1959, Ch. 2122, p. 4966
Cal. Water Code, Appendix, § 90-1 et seq.

Nevada Florida Land Exchange Authorization Act
March 31, 1988, P.L. 100-275, 102 Stat. 52, 16 U.S. Code § 670g nt.

Nevada Publicity Act
Nev. Statutes 1937, Ch. 177, p. 382

Nevada Wilderness Protection Act of 1989
Dec. 5, 1989, P.L. 101-195, 16 U.S. Code § 1132 nt.

New and Further Disability Act
Cal. Labor Code § 5410

New Assistive Devices Warranty Act
La. Rev. Stat. Ann., 51:2761 et seq.

New Bank Tax Credit Law
Pa. Purdon's Stat. Title 72, § 4754 et seq.
Pa. 1971 Pamph. Laws, No. 2, § 1901 et seq.

New Bedford Development and Industrial Loan Act
Mass. Acts 1949, Ch. 736

New Bedford Hurricane Barrier Loan Act
Mass. Acts 1962, Ch. 565

New Bedford Public Parking Loan Act
Mass. Acts 1958, Ch. 242

New Bedford Public Welfare Loan Act
Mass. Acts 1952, Ch. 547

New Bedford Steamship Authority Funding Loan Act
Mass. Acts 1961, Ch. 470

New Braintree School Building Loan Act
Mass. Acts 1950, Ch. 675

New Business Incubator Enterprise Program Act
Cal. Government Code § 15339.1 et seq.

New Capital Sources Partnership Act
N.J. Stat. Ann., 34:1B-107 et seq.

New Car Lemon Laws
Ill. Rev. Stat. 1991, Ch. 121 1/2, § 1201 et seq.
N.Y. General Business Law (Consol. Laws Ch. 20) § 198a

New Careers in Education Act
Cal. Education Code 1976, § 44520 et seq.

New Castle County Building Code Act
Del. Code of 1974, Title 16, § 8301 et seq.

New Castle County Employees' Retirement Act
Del. Code of 1953, Title 9, § 1701 et seq.

New Castle County Family Court Act
Del. Code of 1953, Title 10, § 901 et seq.

New Castle County Income Tax Act
Del. Laws Vol. 40, p. 52, Ch. 12

New Castle County Monition Act
Del. Code of 1974, Title 9, § 8721 et seq.

New Castle County Plumbing Code Act
Del. Code of 1974, Title 16, § 8101 et seq.

New Castle County Sewer Act
Del. Code of 1974, Title 9, § 2201 et seq.

New Castle County Zoning Act
Del. Code of 1974, Title 9, § 2601 et seq.

New Castle Refuse Collection Act
N.Y. Local Laws 1969, Town of New Castle, p. 1693

New Castle Traffic Act
N.Y. Local Laws 1964, Town of New Castle, p. 1326

New Castle Traffic Exclusion Act
N.Y. Local Laws 1969, Town of New Castle, p. 1710

New Castle Watercourse Protection Act
N.Y. Local Laws 1971, Town of New Castle,
p. 2881

New Center Corporation of San Juan Act
P.R. Laws Ann. 1954, Title 23, § 141 et seq.

**New Coal Production Incentive Tax Credit
Act**
Mont. Code Ann., 15-35-201 et seq.

New Cockfighting Act
P.R. Laws Ann. 1954, Title 15, § 292 et seq.

New Communities Act of 1968
Aug. 1, 1968, P.L. 90-448, 82 Stat. 513, 42
U.S. Code §§ 3901 to 3914

New Community Development Act
Fla. Stat. Ann., 163.601 et seq.
La. Rev. Stat. Ann., 33:7601 et seq.
Tenn. Code Ann., 13-15-101 et seq.

New Counties Act
Mont. Code Ann., 1991, 7-2-2201 et seq.

New Dog Act
Ky. Rev. Stat. 1971, 258.005 et seq.

New Drug Review Act (Medicaid)
Va. Code 1950, § 32.1-331.1 et seq.

New Ellenton Public Service District Act
S.C. Acts 1951, p. 854, No. 452

**New England Compact on Radiological
Health Protection**
Conn. Gen. Stat. Ann., §§ 22a-159, 22a-160
Mass. Acts 1967, Ch. 801
Me. Rev. Stat. Ann. 1964, Title 22, § 751 et
seq.
N.H. Rev. Stat. 1955, 125-B:1 et seq.
R.I. Gen Laws 1956, 23-12.5-1 et seq.
Vt. Stat. Ann., Title 18, § 1601 et seq.

**New England Fishery Resources Restoration
Act of 1990**
Nov. 16, 1990, P.L. 101-593, 16 U.S. Code
§ 777e-1

**New England Health Services and Facilities
Compact**
R.I. Gen. Laws 1956, 23-16.1-1 et seq.

New England Higher Education Compact
Conn. Gen. Stat. Ann., § 10a-61 et seq.
Mass. Acts 1954, Ch. 589, § 1
Me. Rev. Stat. Ann. 1964, Title 20A, § 11001
et seq.
N.H. Rev. Stat. 1955, 200-A:1 et seq.
R.I. General Laws 1956, 16-41-1 et seq.
Vt. Stat. Ann., Title 16, § 2691 et seq.

**New England Interstate Corrections
Compact**
Me. Rev. Stat. Ann. 1964, Title 34-A, § 9201
et seq.

**New England Interstate Corrections
Compact Act**
Conn. Gen. Stat. Ann., § 18-102 et seq.
Me. Rev. Stat. Ann. 1964, Title 34-A, § 9201
et seq.
N.H. Rev. Stat. 1955, 622-A:1 et seq.
R.I. Gen. Laws 1956, 13-11-1 et seq.
Vt. Stat. Ann., Title 28, § 1401 et seq.

**New England Interstate Planning Compact
Act**
Conn. Gen. Stat. Ann., § 8-37c et seq.
Me. Rev. Stat. Ann. 1964, Title 10, § 301 et
seq.
N.H. Rev. Stat. 1955, 163-A:1 et seq.

**New England Interstate Water Pollution
Control Compact**
Me. Rev. Stat. Ann. 1964, Title 38, § 491 et
seq.

**New England Interstate Water Pollution
Control Compact Act**
Conn. Gen. Stat. Ann., § 22a-308 et seq.
Me. Rev. Stat. Ann. 1964, Title 38, § 491 et
seq.
N.H. Rev. Stat. 1955, 488:1 et seq.
R.I. Gen. Laws 1956, 46-16-1 et seq.
Vt. Stat. Ann., Title 10, § 1331 et seq.

New England State Police Compact Act
Conn. Gen. Stat. Ann., § 29-162 et seq.
Me. Rev. Stat. Ann. 1964, Title 25, § 1665 et
seq.

N.H. Rev. Stat. 1955, 106-D:1 et seq.

Vt. Stat. Ann. 1959, Title 20, § 1951 et seq.

New England Truckers Compact Act

N.H. Rev. Stat. 1955, 267:1

New England Welfare Compact

Me. Rev. Stat. Ann. 1964, Title 22, § 4151 et seq.

R.I. Gen. Laws 1956, 40-7-1 et seq.

Vt. Acts 1965, No. 12

New GI Bill Continuation Act

June 1, 1987, P.L. 100-48, 10 U.S. Code § 2132; 38 U.S. Code §§ 101 nt., 1401, 1411, 1412

New Goods Public Auction Act

Kan. Stat. Ann., 58-1014 et seq.

New Hampshire Forest Management Initiatives Act of 1988

Sept. 27, 1988, P.L. 100-446, 102 Stat. 1805

New Hampshire-Maine Commission on Oceanography Act

N.H. Rev. Stat. 1955, 12-C:1 et seq.

New Hampshire-Maine Interstate School Compact Act

Me. Rev. Stat. Ann. 1964, Title 20A, § 3601 et seq.

N.H. Rev. Stat. 1955, 200-F:1

New Hampshire-Marine Interstate School Compact

Oct. 24, 1992, P.L. 102-494, 106 Stat. 3153

New Hampshire-Massachusetts Interstate Sewage and Waste Disposal Facilities Compact Act

N.H. Rev. Stat. 1955, 149-K:1

New Hampshire-Vermont Interstate Public Water Supply Compact

N.H. Rev. Stat. 1955, 485-D:1

New Hampshire-Vermont Interstate School Compact Act

N.H. Rev. Stat. 1955, 200-B:1

Vt. Stat. Ann., Title 16, § 771 et seq.

New Hampshire-Vermont Interstate Sewage and Waste Disposal Facilities Compact Act

N.H. Rev. Stat. 1955, 149-Kal

N.H. Rev. Stat. 1955, 149-4:1

Vt. Stat. Ann., Title 10, § 1201 et seq.

New Hampshire-Vermont Interstate Solid Waste Compact Act

N.H. Rev. Stat. 1955, 53-D:1

Vt. Stat. Ann., Title 10, § 1222 et seq.

New Hampshire Wilderness Act of 1984

June 19, 1984, P.L. 98-323, 16 U.S. Code §§ 132 nt., 1276

New Hanover-Brunswick Maritime Commission Act

N.C. Laws 1965, Ch. 1097

New Hire Act

Ala. Code 1975, § 25-2-40 et seq.

New Hire Reporting Act

Ill. Comp. Stat. 1992, Ch. 20, § 1020/1 et seq.

Neb. Rev. Stat. 1943, 48-2301 to 48-2308

New Home Construction Local Tax Abatement Act

Pa. Purdon's Stat., Title 72, § 4754-1 et seq.

New Home Warranty Act

La. Rev. Stat. Ann., 9:3141 et seq.

Miss. Code Ann. 1972, § 83-58-1 et seq.

N.J. Stat. Ann. 46:3B-1 et seq.

New Horizons Act

Mont. Laws 1987, Ch. 579

New Horizons Development Authority Act

S.C. Code Ann. 1976, § 13-11-10 et seq.

New Iberia and Zachary Community Improvement Act

La. Acts 1972, No. 32

New Industries Act

Okla. Stat. Ann., Title 68, § 1571 et seq.

New Industries Tax Exemption Act
N.D. Cent. Code 40-57.1-01 et seq.

New Institutional Health Services Act
Wyo. Stat. Ann., § 35-2-201 et seq.

New Jersey Battleship Commission Act
N.J. Stat. Ann. 13:15A-1 et seq.

New Jersey Better Educational Savings Trust Act (NJBEST)
N.J. Stat. Ann., 18A:72-34 et seq.

New Jersey-Delaware Compact Act
Del. Code of 1974, Title 17, § 1701 et seq.
N.J. Stat. Ann., 32:11E-1 et seq.

New Jersey-New York Clean Ocean and Shore Trust Committee Act (COAST)
N.J. Stat. Ann., 32:34-1 et seq.

New Jersey-New York Metropolitan Transit District Compact
N.J. Rev. Stat. 1937, 32:22A-1 et seq.
N.Y. Laws 1958, Ch. 965

New Jersey-New York Transportation Agency Compact Act
N.J. Rev. Stat. 1937, 32:22A-1 et seq.
N.Y. Laws 1959, Ch. 420

New Jersey-New York Waterfront Commission Compact Act
N.J. Rev. Stat. 1937, 32:23-1 et seq.

New Jobs and Income Act
Iowa Code 1995, 15.326 et seq.

New Jobs Investment Tax Credit Act
N.J. Stat. Ann., 54:10A-5.4 et seq.

New Jobs Training Act (Industrial)
Iowa Code Ann., 260E.1 et seq.

New Lebanon Vehicle Parking Act
N.Y. Local Laws 1972, Town of New Lebanon, p. 2161

New Marsh Wholesale Produce Market Authority Act
Md. Laws 1955, Ch. 662

New Mexico Statehood and Enabling Act Amendments of 1997
Aug. 7, 1997, P.L. 105-37, 111 Stat. 1113

New Mexico-Texas State Line School District Compact Act
N.M. Laws 1933, Ch. 110

New Mexico Works Act
N.M. Stat. Ann., 27-2B-1 to 27-2B-20

New Motor Vehicles Warranties Act
Utah Code Ann. 1953, 13-20-1 et seq.

New Orleans Community Improvement Act
La. Acts 1968, No. 170

New Orleans Firemen's Pension Act
La. Rev. Stat. Ann., 33:2101 et seq.

New Orleans Food Center Act
La. Rev. Stat. Ann., 3:431 et seq.

New Orleans Jazz National Historical Park Act of 1994
Oct. 31, 1994, P.L. 103-433, 16 U.S. Code §§ 410bbb nt., 410bbb et seq.

New Paltz Zoning Act
La. Rev. Stat. Ann., 3:431 et seq.
N.Y. Local Laws 1973, Town of New Paltz, p. 2603

New Parks Act
N.Y. Laws 1884, Ch. 522

New Prison Construction Bond Act
Cal. Penal Code §§ 7100 et seq., 7200 et seq., 7300 et seq., 7400 et seq.

New Prison Construction Bond Act of 1990
Cal. Penal Code, § 7420 et seq.

New Prison Construction Bond Act of 1990-B
Cal. Penal Code, § 7440 et seq.

New Products, New Jobs Act
N.J. Stat. Ann. 34:1A-69.3

New Residents Voting Act
Neb. Rev. Stat. 1943, 32-1301.01 et seq.

New Residents Voting Act (Presidential Elections)
See Uniform Act for Voting by New Residents in Presidential Elections

New Rochelle City Court Act
N.Y. Laws 1931, Ch. 499

New Rochelle Municipal Housing Authority Act
N.Y. Public Housing Law (Consol. Laws Ch. 44A) § 407

New Rochelle Parking Authority Act
N.Y. Public Authorities Law (Consol. Laws Ch. 43A) § 1597a et seq.

New Rochelle Police Pension Fund Act
N.Y. Laws 1904, Ch. 268

New Schools Relief Act
Cal. Education Code 1976, § 39050 et seq.

New Trial Act (Civil)
Wash. Rev. Code Ann., 4.76.010 et seq.

New Trial Act (Criminal)
Wash. Rev. Code Ann., 10.67.010 et seq.

New Trials and Appeals Act
Nev. Statutes 1935, Ch. 90, p. 195
Nev. Statutes 1937, Ch. 32, p. 53

New Vehicle Buyer Protection Act
Ill. Rev. Stat. 1991, Ch. 121 1/2, § 1201 et seq.

New Windsor Anti-Dumping Act
N.Y. Local Laws 1967, Town of New Windsor, p. 1764

New Windsor Mobile Home Act
N.Y. Local Laws 1971, Town of New Windsor, p. 2902

New World School of the Arts Act
Fla. Stat. Ann., 240.535

New York and New Jersey Port Authority Act
N.Y. Unconsol. Laws § 6401 et seq.

New York Bight Wood Debris Study Act
N.J. Stat. Ann., 58:10A-46

New York City Administrative Code
N.Y. Adm. Code '85, § 1-101 et seq.
N.Y. Laws 1937, Ex. Sess., Ch. 929

New York City Air Pollution Control Code
N.Y. City Adm. Code '85, § 24-101 et seq.

New York City Airport Authority Act
N.Y. Public Authorities Law (Consol. Laws Ch. 43A) § 1444 et seq.

New York City Aqueduct Act
N.Y. Laws 1883, Ch. 490

New York City Bingo Licensing Act
N.Y. City Adm. Code '38, Ch. 32, § B32-274.0 et seq.

New York City Bingo Licensing Law
N.Y. Adm. Code '85, § 20-338 et seq.

New York City Building Code
N.Y. Adm. Code '85, § 27-101 et seq.
N.Y. City Adm. Code '38, Ch. 26, § C26-1.0 et seq.

New York City Campaign Finance Act
N.Y. Adm. Code '85, § 3-701 et seq.

New York City Children's Court Act
N.Y. Laws 1924, Ch. 254

New York City Civil Court Act
N.Y. Laws 1962, Ch. 693

New York City Collective Bargaining Act
N.Y. City Adm. Code '38, Ch. 54, § 1173-1.0 et seq.

New York City Commercial Rent or Occupancy Tax Act
N.Y. Laws 1963, Ch. 257

New York City Consolidation Act
N.Y. Laws 1882, Ch. 410

New York City Court Act
N.Y. Laws 1926, Ch. 539

New York City Criminal Court Act
N.Y. Laws 1962, Ch. 697

New York City Domestic Relations Court Act
N.Y. Laws 1933, Ch. 482

New York City Economy Act
N.Y. Laws 1932, Ex. Sess., Ch. 637
N.Y. Laws 1934, Ch. 178

New York City Education Construction Fund Act
N.Y. Education Law 1947 (Consol. Laws Ch. 16) § 450 et seq.

New York City Emergency Moratorium Act
N.Y. Laws 1975, Ex. Sess., Ch. 874

New York City Employees Retirement Act
N.Y. City Adm. Code '85, § 13-101 et seq.

New York City Eviction Act
N.Y. City Adm. Code '38, Ch. 51, § Y51-6.0

New York City Games of Chance Licensing Law
N.Y. Adm. Code '85, § 20-433 et seq.

New York City General Business and Financial Tax Act
N.Y. City Adm. Code '38, Ch. 46, § B46-1.0 et seq.

New York City Government Reorganization Act
N.Y. Laws 1870, Ch. 137

New York City Grade Crossing Elimination Act
N.Y. Laws 1928, Ch. 677

New York City Gun Control Act
N.Y. City Adm. Code '85, § 10-301 et seq.

New York City Hazardous Substances Emergency Response Law
N.Y. Adm. Code '85, § 24-601 et seq.

New York City Health and Hospitals Corporation Act
N.Y. Laws 1969, Ch. 1016
N.Y. Unconsolidated Laws, § 7381 et seq.

New York City Highway Closing Act
N.Y. Laws 1895, Ch. 1006

New York City Housing Authority Act
N.Y. Public Housing Law (Consol. Laws Ch. 44A) § 400 et seq.

New York City Housing Development Corporation Act
N.Y. Private Housing Finance Law (Consol. Laws Ch. 44B) § 650 et seq.

New York City In Rem Tax Foreclosure Act
N.Y. City Adm. Code '85, § 11-401 et seq. .

New York City Inferior Criminal Court Act
N.Y. Laws 1910, Ch. 659

New York City Landmark Preservation Act
N.Y. City Adm. Code '85, § 25-301 et seq.

New York City Loan Guarantee Act of 1978
Aug. 8, 1978, P.L. 95-339, 31 U.S. Code §§ 1521, 1521 nt., 1522 et seq.

New York City Milk Compact Act
Pa. Purdon's Stat. Title 31, § 700.1 et seq.

New York City Minimum Wage Act
N.Y. City Adm. Code '38, Ch. 42, § B42-1.0 et seq.

New York City Multiple Dwelling Code
N.Y. City Adm. Code '85, § 27-2001 et seq.

New York City Municipal Assistance Corporation Act
N.Y. Public Authorities Law (Consol. Laws Ch. 43A) § 3030 et seq.

New York City Municipal Court Act
N.Y. Laws 1902, Ch. 580
N.Y. Laws 1915, Ch. 279

New York City Municipal Water Finance Authority Act

N.Y. Public Authorities Law (Consol. Laws Ch. 43A) § 1045a et seq.

New York City Noise Control Code

N.Y. City Adm. Code '85, § 24-201 et seq.

New York City Off-Track Betting Corporation Act

N.Y. Laws 1970, Ch. 144, § 1

New York City Parking Authority Act

N.Y. Public Authorities Law (Consol. Laws Ch. 43A) § 1600 et seq.

New York City Parkway Authority Act

N.Y. Public Authorities Law (Consol. Laws Ch. 43A) § 275 et seq.

New York City Price Control Act

N.Y. Local Laws 1945, New York City, No. 34

New York City Private Dwelling Discrimination and Segregation Act

N.Y. City Adm. Code '38, Ch. 1, § D1-1.0

New York City Recycling Law

N.Y. Adm. Code '85, § 16-301 et seq.

New York City Rehabilitation Mortgage Insurance Corporation Act

N.Y. Private Housing Finance Law (Consol. Laws Ch. 44B)

New York City Rent and Rehabilitation Act

N.Y. City Adm. Code '38, Ch. 51, § Y51-1.0 et seq.

New York City Rent and Rehabilitation Law

N.Y. Unconsolidated Laws, § 26-401 et seq.

New York City Rent Control Act (Housing)

N.Y. Local Laws 1947, New York City, No. 54, 66 et seq.

New York City Rent Stabilization Law

N.Y. Unconsolidated Laws, § 26-501 et seq.

New York City Retail Sales Tax Act

N.Y. City Adm. Code '38, Ch. 46, § M46-15.0 et seq.

New York City Sales Tax Act

N.Y. City Adm. Code '38, Ch. 46, § N46-1.0 et seq.

New York City School Construction Authority Act

N.Y. Public Authorities Law (Consol. Laws Ch. 43A) § 1725 et seq.

New York City Seasonal Financing Act of 1975

Dec. 9, 1975, P.L. 94-143, 31 U.S. Code § 1501 et seq.

New York City Solid Fuel Act

N.Y. City Adm. Code '85, § 20-611 et seq.

New York City Sports Authority Act

N.Y. Public Authorities Law (Consol. Laws Ch. 43A) § 2500 et seq.

New York City Stabilization Reserve Corporation Act

N.Y. Public Authorities Law (Consol. Laws Ch. 43A) § 2530 et seq.

New York City Tax Lien Foreclosure Act

N.Y. City Adm. Code '85, § 11-401 et seq.

New York City Tax Reduction and Tax Reform Technical Corrections Act

N.Y. Laws 1987, Ch. 333

New York City Taxicab Tax Act

N.Y. City Adm. Code '85, § 11-801 et seq.

New York City Transit Authority Act

N.Y. Public Law (Consol. Laws Ch. 43A) § 1200 et seq.

New York City Transitional Finance Authority Act

N.Y. Public Authorities Law (Consol. Laws Ch. 43A) § 2799aa et seq.

New York City Tunnel Authority Act

N.Y. Public Authorities Law (Consol. Laws Ch. 43A) § 625 et seq

New York City Utility Excise Tax Act
N.Y. City Adm. Code '38, Ch. 46, § Q46-1.0 et seq.

New York City World's Fair Act
N.Y. Laws 1936, Chs. 543, 544, 866
N.Y. Laws 1937, Chs. 40, 58, 125, 686, 727, 786

New York-Connecticut Railroad Passenger Transportation Compact Act
Conn. Gen. Stat. Ann., § 16-343 et seq.

New York Convention Center Operating Corporation Act
N.Y. Public Authorities Law (Consol. Laws Ch. 43A) § 2560 et seq.

New York Local Government Assistance Corporation Act
N.Y. Public Authorities Law (Consol. Laws Ch. 43A) § 3231 et seq.

New York Management of Institutional Funds Act
N.Y. Not-for-Profit Corporations Law (Consol. Laws, Ch. 35), §§ 102, 512 to 514, 521, 522, 717
N.Y. Religious Law (Consol. Laws, Ch. 51), § 2b

New York-New Jersey Metropolitan Transit District Compact
N.J. Rev. Stat. 1937, 32:22A-1 et seq.
N.Y. Laws 1958, Ch. 965

New York-New Jersey Transportation Agency Compact
N.J. Rev. Stat. 1937, 32:22A-1 et seq.
N.Y. Laws 1959, Ch. 420

New York-New Jersey Waterfront Commission Compact Act
N.J. Rev. Stat. 1937, 32:23-1 et seq.

New York Program Act (Housing)
N.Y. Private Housing Finance Law (Consol. Laws Ch. 41) § 654c nt.

New York Soldiers' and Sailors' Civil Relief Act
N.Y. Military Law (Consol. Laws, Ch. 36), § 300 et seq.

New York State Archives Partnership Trust Act
N.Y. Arts and Cultural Affairs Law (Consol. Laws Ch. 11C) § 57.05 nt.

New York State Atomic Research and Development
N.Y. Public Authorities Law (Consol. Laws, Ch. 43a), § 1850 et seq.

New York State Bridge Authority Act
N.Y. Public Authorities Law (Consol. Laws, Ch. 43A), § 525 et seq.

New York State Campaigns, Elections and Procedure Law
N.Y. Election Law 1949 (Consol. Laws, Ch. 17), § 465 et seq.

New York State Civil Defense Law
N.Y. Executive Law 1982 (Consol. Laws, Ch. 18), § 20 et seq.

New York State College Choice Tuition Savings Program Act
N.Y. Education Law 1947 (Consol. Laws Ch. 16) § 695 et seq.

New York State Cultural Resources Act
N.Y. General Municipal Law (Consol. Laws, Ch. 24), § 301 et seq.

New York State Defense Emergency Act
N.Y. Unconsolidated Laws, § 9101 et seq.

New York State Economic Development Zones Act
N.Y. General Municipal Law (Consol. Laws Ch. 24) § 955 et seq.

New York State Emerging Industry Jobs Act
N.Y. Laws 1998, Ch. 56, Part A, § 29

New York State Employees' Retirement Act
N.Y. Retirement and Social Security Law (Consol. Laws Ch. 51A) § 2 et seq.

New York State Energy Research and Development Authority Act

N.Y. Public Authorities Law (Consol. Laws Ch. 43A) § 1850 et seq.

New York State Export Finance Awareness Program Act

N.Y. Banking Law (Consol. Laws Ch. 2) § 45

N.Y. Education Law 1947 (Consol. Laws Ch. 16) § 305, Subd. 18

New York State Freedom Trail Program Act

N.Y. Laws 1997, Ch. 574

New York State Governmental Account-ability, Audit and Internal Control Act

N.Y. Executive Law 1951 (Consol. Laws Ch. 18) § 950

N.Y. Judiciary Law (Consol. Laws Ch. 30) § 211, 249 et seq.

N.Y. Legislative Law (Consol. Laws Ch. 32) § 89 et seq.

N.Y. Public Authorities Law (Consol. Laws Ch. 43A) §§ 2930 to 2932

N.Y. Public Officers Law (Consol. Laws Ch. 47) §§ 87, 88

N.Y. State Finance Law 1940 (Consol. Laws Ch. 56) §§ 2a, 8,

New York State Historic Preservation Act

N.Y. General Municipal Law (Consol. Laws Ch. 24) § 119aa et seq.

N.Y. Parks, Recreation and Historic Preservation Law (Consol. Laws Ch. 36f) §§ 11.03, 11.05, 11.09, 14.01 et seq.

N.Y. Public Buildings Law (Consol. Laws Ch. 44) § 60 et seq.

New York State Institute on Superconduc-tivity Act

N.Y. Laws 1987, Ch. 615, § 22 et seq.

New York State Local Water and Sewer Authority Act

N.Y. Public Authorities Law (Consol. Laws Ch. 43A) § 1196a et seq.

New York State Lottery for Education Act

N.Y. Tax Law (Consol. Laws Ch. 60) § 1600 et seq.

New York State Martin Luther King, Jr. Institute for Nonviolence Act

N.Y. Executive Law 1951 (Consol. Laws Ch. 18) § 320 et seq.

New York State Medical Care Facilities Finance Agency Act

N.Y. Unconsolidated Laws, § 7411 et seq.

New York State Neighborhood Based Initiatives Act

N.Y. Executive Law 1951 (Consol. Laws Ch. 18) § 548a

New York State Poison Control Network Act

N.Y. Laws 1986, Ch. 70, § 1

N.Y. Public Health Law 1953 (Consol. Laws Ch. 45) § 2500d

New York State Prohibition of Female Genital Mutilation Act

N.Y. Laws 1997, Ch. 618

New York State Project Finance Agency Act (Urban Development Corporation)

N.Y. Unconsolidated Laws § 6361 et seq.

New York State Public Retirement System Reporting and Disclosure Act

N.Y. Retirement and Social Security Law (Consol. Laws Ch. 51A) § 150 et seq.

New York State Residential Telephone Equipment Consumer Protection Act

N.Y. General Business Law (Consol. Laws Ch. 20) § 349b

New York State Resource Recovery Policy Act

N.Y. Environmental Conservation Law 1972 (Consol. Laws Ch. 43B) § 27-0101 et seq.

New York State Support Enforcement Act

N.Y. Civil Practice Laws and Rules (Consol. Laws Ch. 8) §§ 211, 5241, 5242, 5252

N.Y. Domestic Relations Law (Consol. Laws Ch. 14) §§ 34, 35, 37, 37a, 236, 237, 240, 241, 244, 245

N.Y. Executive Law 1951 (Consol. Laws Ch. 18) § 256

N.Y. Family Court Act, §§ 171a, 117, 421, 424, 424a, 425, 426, 433, 434, 435, 438, 439, 439a, 440, 448, 451, 454, 460, 471, 475, 513, 516a, 517, 522, 536, 545, 571

Continued

N.Y. Laws 1986, Ch. 892

N.Y. Social Services Law (Consol. Laws Ch. 55) §§ 111b, 111c, 111f, 111g, 111h, 111k, 111m, 111n

N.Y. Tax Law (Consol. Laws Ch. 60), § 171c

N.Y. Worker's Compensation Law (Consol. Laws Ch. 67) §§ 33, 218

New York State Teacher Tenure Act
N.Y. Education Law 1947 (Consol. LAws Ch. 16) §§ 3012a, 3014 et seq., 6212

New York State Urban Development and Research Corporations Act
N.Y. Unconsolidated Law, §§ 6251 et seq., 6301 et seq.

New York State Veterans Bill of Rights for Employment and Training Services
N.Y. Laws 1994, Ch. 553

New York State Waste Management Institute at Cornell University Act
N.Y. Environmental Conservation Law 1972 (Consol. Laws Ch. 43B) § 27-0403 nt.

New York-Vermont Interstate School Compact
Vt. Stat. Ann., Title 16, § 791 et seq.

Newberry-Clinton Natural Gas Authority Act
S.C. Acts 1952, p. 1958, No. 789

Newberry County Fishing Season Act
S.C. Acts 1933, p. 387, No. 282

Newberry County Hunting Season Act
S.C. Acts 1933, p. 387, No. 282

Newberry-Hinkle-Mobley Act (School Term)
Ky. Rev. Stat. 1971, 158.070

Newborn and Prenatal Care Act
Ill. Rev. Stat. 1991, Ch. 111 1/2, § 7021 et seq.

Newborn Baby and Mother Protection Act
Ga. Code Ann., 33-24-58 to 33-24-60

Newborn Child Testing Act
Pa. Purdon's Stat., Title 35, § 621 et seq.

Newborn Health Insurance Act
D.C. Code Ann., § 35-1101 et seq.

Newborn Screening and Genetic Counseling and Education Act
Colo. Rev. Stat. 25-4-1001 et seq.

Newborns' and Mothers' Health Act
Cal. Health and Safety Code § 1367.62
Cal. Insurance Code § 10123.87

Newborns' and Mothers' Health Protection Act of 1996
Sept. 26, 1996, P.L. 104-204, Title VI, 42 U.S. Code § 201 nt.

Newburgh City Court Act
N.Y. Laws 1948, Ch. 569

Newburgh Fire Protection Act
N.Y. Local Laws 1971, Town of Newburgh, p. 2875

Newburgh Peddling, Hawking and Soliciting Act
N.Y. Local Laws 1972, Town of Newburgh, p. 2128

Newburgh Police Pension Fund Act
N.Y. Laws 1907, Ch. 205

Newburyport Sewerage Loan Act
Mass. Acts 1963, Ch. 261

Newlands Act (Irrigation)
June 17, 1902, Ch. 1093, 32 Stat. 388, 43 U.S. Code §§ 372, 373, 381, 383, 391, 392, 411, 414, 419, 421, 431, 432, 434, 439, 461, 476, 491, 498, 1457

Newlands Act (Railroad Mediation)
See Arbitration Act (Labor Disputes)

Newlands Resolution (Annexation of Hawaii)
July 7, 1898, No. 55, 30 Stat. 750

Newman Act (Appeals)
N.D. Cent. Code 28-27-32 et seq.

Newman Convention Authority Act
Ga. Laws 1999, H.B. 599

Newman Coweta County Airport Authority Act
Ga. Laws 1965, p. 2041

Newport Minimum Housing Code
R.I. Public Laws 1962, Ch. 55

Newport News and Hampton Parking Authority Act
Va. Acts 1968, Ch. 200

Newsmans Privilege Act (Disclosure)
Ala. Code 1975, § 12-21-142
Ariz. Rev. Stat. Ann., § 12-2237
Ark. Code Ann. 1987, 16-85-510
Cal. Evidence Code § 1070
Md. Ann. Code 1974, Art. CJ, § 9-112
Mont. Code Ann., 1983, 26-1-901 et seq.
N.J. Stat. Ann., 2A:84A-21
Ohio Rev. Code 1953, 2739.12
Pa. Cons. Stat., Title 42, § 5942
R.I. Gen. Laws 1956, 9-19.1-1 et seq.

Newspaper Advertising Act
Pa. Cons. Stat., Title 45, § 101 et seq.

Newspaper Legal Notice Act
Ill. Rev. Stat. 1991, Ch. 100, § 9.9 et seq.
Wash. Rev. Code Ann., 65.16.010 et seq.

Newspaper Libel Act
Ind. Code Ann., 34-4-15-1 et seq.
Pa. Cons. Stat., Title 42, § 8342 et seq.

Newspaper Preservation Act
July 24, 1970, P.L. 91-353, 84 Stat. 466, 15 U.S. Code §§ 1801 to 1804

Newsprint Use Act (Recycled)
Ill. Rev. Stat. 1991, Ch. 96 1/2, § 9751 et seq.

Newton Amendment to the Carmack Amendment
April 23, 1930, Ch. 208, 46 Stat. 251, 49 U.S. Code § 20(11)

Newton County Water and Sewerage Authority Act
Ga. Laws 1970, p. 2449

Newton Retirement Act
Mass. Acts 1928, Ch. 355

Next Friend Act (Minors)
Va. Code 1950, § 8.01-8

Next Generation Internet Research Act of 1998
Oct. 28, 1998, P.L. 105-305, 112 Stat. 2919, 15 U.S. Code § 5501 nt.

Nez Perce National Historical Park Act
May 15, 1965, P.L. 89-19, 79 Stat. 110, 16 U.S. Code §§ 281 to 281f

Nez Perce National Historical Park Additions Act of 1991
Oct. 30, 1992, P.L. 102-576, 16 U.S. Code § 281 nt.

Niagara Bridge Act
N.Y. Laws 1853, Ch. 622

Niagara County Tax Act
N.Y. Laws 1904, Ch. 744

Niagara Falls City Court Act
N.Y. Laws 1957, Ch. 994

Niagara Falls Parking Authority Act
N.Y. Public Authorities Law (Consol. Laws Ch. 43A) § 1599 et seq.

Niagara Frontier Authority Act
N.Y. Public Authorities Law (Consol. Laws Ch. 43A) § 500 et seq.

Niagara Frontier Bridge Commission Act
N.Y. Public Authorities Law (Consol. Laws Ch. 43A) § 500 et seq.

Niagara Frontier Port Authority Act
N.Y. Public Authorities Law (Consol. Laws Ch. 43A) § 1300 et seq.

Niagara Frontier Transportation Act
N.Y. Public Authorities Law (Consol. Laws Ch. 43A) § 1299 et seq.

Niagara Power Project Act
Aug. 21, 1957, P.L. 85-159, 71 Stat. 401, 16 U.S. Code §§ 836, 836a

Nicaraguan Adjustment and Central American Relief Act
Nov. 19, 1997, P.L. 105-100, Title II, 8 U.S. Code § 1101 nt.
Dec. 2, 1997, P.L. 105-139, 8 U.S. Code §§ 1255 nt., 1151 nt., 1153 nt.

Niceville Urban Renewal Act
Fla. Special Laws 1967, Ch. 67-1767

Nichols Act (Public Utilities)
Ohio Rev. Code 1953, 5727.14 et seq.

Nichols Act (Revenue)
D.C. Code Ann., §§ 47-1504, 47-3701 et seq., 47-2501 et seq., 47-3302 et seq., 47-3401 et seq.

Nichols, Hahn, Frymeier, Ashby, Hale, Render Act (Mosquito Law)
Ky. Rev. Stat. 1971, 249.510 et seq.

Nichols-Higgins-Guggisberg Act (Tax Exemptions)
Mich. Comp. Laws Ann., 211.7, 211.9

Nicholson Water Authority Act
Ga. Laws 1972, p. 3964

Nickell Shields Governmental Reorganization Act
Ky. Rev. Stat. 1971, Superseded Vols., 12.025
Ky. Rev. Stat. 1971, 12.027

Nickels Act (State Insurance Fund)
Ohio Rev. Code 1953, 4123.38 et seq.

Nicole Hadley, Jessica James and Kayce Steger Act
Ky. Rev. Stat. 1971, 158.181 to 158.187

Nielsen-Johnston Boating Act
Cal. Statutes 1986, Ch. 877

Nielson-Bergeson-Costa-Robbins County Revenue Stabilization Act
Cal. Government Code, § 16265 et seq.

Night Court Act
Wash. Rev. Code Ann., 3.24.010 et seq.

Night Herd Act
Kan. Stat. Ann., 47-301 et seq.

Night Rider Act
Tenn. Code Ann., 39-17-309 et seq.

Night Work Act (Females)
Ind. Burns' 1933, 40-903

Nimble Dividend Act
Ark. Stat. 4-26-617, 4-26-619, Subd. II, Cl. 3
Cal. Corporations Code § 1500, Subd. b.
Del. Code of 1974, Title 8. § 170, Subd. a
Ga. Code 1933, 22-511
Kan. Stat. Ann., 17-6420, Subd. a
Minn. Stat. 1980, 301.22, Subd. 2
Mont. Rev. Code 1947, 15-2240, Subsec. a
N.C. Gen. Stat. 1943, § 55-6-40
Nev. Rev. Stat. 1979 Reprint, 78.290, Subsec. 1
Okla. Stat. Ann., Title 18, § 1.132, Subd. a
Wyo. Stat. Ann., § 17-1-139

Nine Eight Act (Congressional Representatives)
Ala. Code 1958, Title 17, § 426(1) et seq.

Nine Hour Act (Labor-Women and Children)
Mass. Gen. Laws Ann., 149:56

Nine Hour Day Act
Haw. Session Laws 1876, Ch. 47

Nine Hour Law (Railroads)
See Hours of Service Acts (Railroads)

Nine Juror Verdict Law
Miss. Code Ann. 1972, § 13-5-93

Nine Jury Verdict Act
Miss. Code Ann. 1972, § 13-5-93

Nineteen-Hundred-Eighty-Four Act to Combat International Terrorism (1984)
Oct. 19, 1984, P.L. 98-533, 18 U.S. Code § 3071 nt.

Nineteen-Hundred-Fifty Act (1950)
June 9, 1998, P.L. 105-178, 16 U.S. Code §§ 777a, 777c, 777g, 777g-1

Nineteen-Hundred-Fifty Amendment to Public Law 88 (1950)
Aug. 5, 1950, Ch. 592, 64 Stat. 414, 12 U.S. Code §§ 1148a-1, 1148a-1 nt.
July 14, 1953, Ch. 192, 67 Stat. 149, 12 U.S. Code §§ 1148a-2, 1148a-4

Nineteen-Hundred-Fifty-Five Amendments to the Universal Military Training and Service Act (1955)
June 30, 1955, Ch. 250, 69 Stat. 223, 37 U.S. Code § 234; 50 U.S. Code Appx. §§ 454, 454a, 454a nt., 456, 467, 2216,

Nineteen-Hundred-Fifty-Nine Amendment to the Texas City Disaster Relief Act (1959)
Sept. 25, 1959, P.L. 86-381, 73 Stat. 706

Nineteen-Hundred-Fifty-One Amendment to the Universal Military Training and Service Act (1951)
June 19, 1951, Ch. 144, 65 Stat. 75, 50 U.S. Code Appx. §§ 451, 451 nt., 452, 453, 454, 454 nt., 455, 456, 459, 460, 463, 466, 467, 471 to 473
Nov. 8, 1985, P.L. 99-145, 50 U.S. Code Appx. § 473

Nineteen-Hundred-Ninety-Eight Supplemental Appropriations and Rescissions Act (1998)
May 1, 1998, P.L. 105-174, 112 Stat. 58,

Nineteen-Hundred-Ninety-Nine Emergency Supplemental Appropriations Act (1999)
May 21, 1999, P.L. 106-31, 113 Stat. 57

Nineteen-Hundred-Ninety-Seven Emergency Supplemental Appropriations Act for Recovery from Natural disasters, and for Overseas Peacekeeping Efforts, Including Those in Bosnia (bfe Natural Disasters, and for Overseas Peacekeeping Efforts, Including Those in Bosnia
June 12, 1997, P.L. 105-18, 111 Stat. 158,

Nineteen-Hundred-Ninety-Two White House Commemorative Coin Act (1992)
May 13, 1992, P.L. 102-281, 31 U.S. Code § 5112 nt.
Oct. 6, 1992, P.L. 102-390, 31 U.S. Code § 5112 nt.

Nineteen-Hundred-Sixty-Four Amendments to the Alaska Omnibus Act (1964)
Aug. 19, 1964, P.L. 88-451, 78 Stat. 505, 48 U.S. Code prec. § 21 nt.

Nineteenth Amendment.
June 5, 1919, 41 Stat. 362,

Nineties Bond Act (Accelerated Capacity and Transportation Improvements)
N.Y. Transportation Law (Consol. Laws Ch. 61a) § 450 et seq.

Ninety Day Act (Rejected Claims)
Tex. Probate Code, § 313

Ninety Day Divorce Act
Ark. Code Ann. 1987, 9-12-307
Ida. Code 1947, 32-701

Ninety Nine Year Act
Ill. Private Laws 1865, Vol. 1, p. 597

Ninteen-Hundred-Eighty-Eight Olympic Commemorative Coin Act (1988)
Oct. 28, 1987, P.L. 100-141, 31 U.S. Code § 5112 nt.

Ninteen-Hundred-Ninety-Three White House Conference on Children, Youth and Families (1993)
Nov. 3, 1990, P.L. 101-501, 42 U.S. Code §§ 12301 nt., 12371 to 12377
Oct. 6, 1992, P.L. 102-390, 31 U.S. Code § 5112 nt.

Niobrara Scenic River Designation Act of 1991
May 24, 1991, P.L. 102-50, 16 U.S. Code
§ 1271 nt.
Nov. 10, 1998, P.L. 105-362, 16 U.S. Code
§§ 1a-5 nt., 1274 nt.

Nisbet Knox Act
Cal. Government Code § 54773 et seq.

Nissequogue Highway Act
N.Y. Local Laws 1972, Village of
Nissequogue, p. 3640

Nitroglycerin Transportation Act
Ill. Rev. Stat. 1991, Ch. 127 1/2, §§ 50, 51

NJBEST Act (New Jersey Better Educational Savings Trust)
N.J. Stat. Ann., 18A:72-43 et seq.

No Action Act
Tex. Bus & Com Code, §§ 24.01, 26.01

No Administration Necessary Act
Fla. Stat. Ann., 735.101 et seq.

No Concession Act (Fair Trade Evasions)
Del. Code of 1974, Title 6, § 1903
N.C. Gen. Stat. 1943, § 66-53, Subsec. 2

No Covenant Act (Conveyances)
Mich. Comp. Laws Ann., 565.5, 565.6

No Early Release Act
N.J. Stat. Ann., 2C:43-7.2

No Electronic Theft (NET) Act
Dec. 16, 1997, P.L. 105-147, 18 U.S. Code
§ 2311 nt.

No Fault Divorce Act
Fla. Stat. Ann., 61.001 et seq.
Ida. Code 1947, 32-616
Iowa Code 1983, 598.1 et seq.
Ky. Rev. Stat. 1971, 403.010 et seq.
Mich. Comp. Laws Ann., 552.6 et seq.
Minn. Stat. Ann., 518.002 et seq.
N.Y. Domestic Relations Law (Consol. Laws
Ch. 14) §§ 8, 170, 173, 210 et seq., 230, 235
N.Y. General Obligations Law (Consol.
Laws Ch. 24A) § 5-311

Va. Code 1950, § 20-91, Subsec. 9

No Fault Motor Vehicle Insurance Act
Colo. Rev. Stat., 10-4-701 et seq.
Conn. Gen. Stat. Ann., § 38-319 et seq.
D.C. Code Ann., § 35-2101 et seq.
Fla. Stat. 1983, 627.730 et seq.
Ga. Code Ann., 33-34-1 et seq.
Haw. Rev. Stat. Ann., § 294-1 et seq.
Kan. Stat. Ann., 40-3101 et seq.
Mass. Gen. Laws Ann., 90:34M
Minn. Stat. Ann., 65B.41 et seq.
N.Y. Insurance Law (Consol. Laws Ch. 28)
§ 5101 et seq.
Pa. Cons. Stat., Title 75, § 1701 et seq.
Utah Code Ann. 1953, 31A-22-301 et seq.

No Fence Act
Cal. Food and Agriculture Code 1967,
§§ 17041, 17121 et seq.
Ga. Code Ann., 4-3-1
Ga. Code 1933, 62-405, 62-501 et seq.,
62-601, 62-602, 62-603, 62-9905
Tenn. Acts 1895, Ch. 182
Tenn. Acts 1899, Ch. 23
Va. Code 1950, § 55-310 et seq.

No Frills Prison Act
Alaska Stat. 1962, § 33.30.011 et seq.

No Fund Check Act
Kan. Stat. Ann., 21-3707 et seq.

No Huckstering Act (Intoxicating Liquors)
Ind. Code Ann., 7.1-5-10-10

No Knock Act (Search Warrants)
N.Y. Criminal Procedure Law (Consol. Laws
Ch. 11A) § 690.50
Utah Code Ann. 1953, Miscellaneous
Superseded Code Provisions 77-54-9

No Net Cost Tobacco Program Act of 1982
July 20, 1982, P.L. 97-218, 7 U.S. Code
§§ 1281 nt., 1301, 1314, 1314 nt., 1314-1,
1314b, 1314b-1, 1314b-2, 1314c, 1314e,
1314f, 1316, 1445, 1445 nt., 1445-1,
1445-1 nt., 1445-2, 1445-2 nt., 16 U.S.
Code § 590h nt.

No par Value Stock Act
N.C. Gen. Stat. 1943, Superseded Vol.,
§ 55-73 et seq.
Pa. 1919 Pamph. Laws 914, No. 363
R.I. Public Laws 1921, Ch. 116

No Sock Act (Resisting Arrest)
N.Y. Penal Law 1965 (Consol. Laws Ch. 40)
§ 35.27

No Strike Act (Public Employees)
N.Y. Laws 1967, Ch. 392, § 210

No Waiver Act (Mortgages)
Cal. Civil Code § 2953

No Work on Sunday Act
S.C. Code Ann. 1976, § 53-1-40

NOAA Fleet Modernization Act
Oct. 29, 1992, P.L. 102-567, 33 U.S. Code
§§ 851 nt., 891 to 891h
June 25, 1999, P.L. 106-36, 33 U. S. Code
§ 891e

Nodding Thistle Act
La. Rev. Stat. Ann., 3:1801 et seq.

Noise Attenuation Act (Metropolitan Area Aircraft)
Minn. Stat. Ann., 473.192

Noise Control Act
Cal. Health and Safety Code § 46000 et seq.
D.C. Code Ann. § 1-315
Del. Code of 1974, Title 7, § 7101 et seq.
Ga. Code 1933, 99-4201 et seq.
Haw. Rev. Stat. Ann., § 342-41 et seq.
Ky. Rev. Stat. 1971, 224.30-100 et seq.
N.J. Stat. Ann., 13:1G-1 et seq.
N.Y. City Adm. Code '38, Ch. 57,
§ 1403.3-1.01 et seq.
N.Y. Local Laws 1973, County of Orange, p.
1160
N.Y. Local Laws 1973, Town of Camillus, p.
1427
Wash. Rev. Code Ann., 70.107.010 et seq.

Noise Control Act (Power Vessel)
N.J. Stat. Ann., 12:7-23.1 et seq.

Noise Control Act of 1972
Oct. 27, 1972, P.L. 92-574, 86 Stat. 1234, 42
U.S. Code §§ 4901 to 4918; 49 U.S. Code
§ 1431
Nov. 8, 1978, P.L. 95-609, 42 U.S. Code
§§ 4905, 4910, 4913, 4918
Oct. 31, 1994, P.L. 103-429, 49 U.S. Code
Appx. § 1431 nt.
Dec. 29, 1995, P.L. 104-88, 42 U.S. Code
§ 4917
Oct. 11, 1996, P.L. 104-287, 42 U.S. Code
§ 4916

Noise Control Code
N.Y. Adm. Code '85, § 24-201 et seq.

Noise Monitoring Act (Permanent)
Ill. Rev. Stat. 1991, Ch. 15 1/2, § 751 et seq.

Noise Pollution and Abatement Act of 1970
Dec. 31, 1970, P.L. 91-604, 84 Stat. 1709, 42
U.S. Code §§ 1858, 1858a

Noise Prevention and Control Act (Motor Vehicle)
Fla. Stat. Ann., 316.293, 403.415, 403.4151

Noise Reduction Reimbursement Act of 1989
Aug. 4, 1989, P.L. 101-71, 49 U.S. Code
Appx. §§ 2201 nt., 2212, 2212 nt.

Nolan Act (Minimum Wage)
D.C. Code Ann., § 36-201 et seq.

Nolan Act (Patents)
March 3, 1921, Ch. 126, 41 Stat. 1313

Nolan Minimum Wage Law (District of Columbia)
Sept. 19, 1918, Ch. 174, 40 Stat. 960

Nominal Condition Act (Defeasible Estates)
Minn. Stat. Ann., 500.20

Nominations and Appointments Act (Judicial)
Vt. Stat. Ann., Title 4, § 601 et seq.

Nominee Act (Trusts)
Ill. Rev. Stat. 1991, Ch. 17, § 2050

Nominee Registration Act (Fiduciaries)
Ida. Code 1947, 68-601 et seq.

Non-Arbitrage Investment Act
Va. Code 1950, § 2.1-234.9:1 et seq.

Non-High School District Act
Ore. Rev. Stat., 335.605 et seq.

Non-Home Rule Municipal Retailer's Occupation Tax Act
Ill. Rev. Stat. 1991, Ch. 24, § 8-11-1.3

Non-Home Rule Municipal Service Occupation Tax Act
Ill. Rev. Stat. 1991, Ch. 24, § 8-11-1.4

Non-Home Rule Municipal Use Tax Act
Ill. Rev. Stat. 1991, Ch. 24, § 8-11-1.5

Non-Intercourse Act (Foreign Relations)
March 1, 1809, Ch. 24, 2 Stat. 528

Non-Profit Medical Corporation Act (Health Maintenance Organization)
N.Y. Public Health Law 1953 (Consol. Laws Ch. 45) § 4400 et seq.

Non-Profit Medical Corporation Act (Health Maintenance Organizations)
N.Y. Public Health Law 1953 (Consol. Laws Ch. 45) § 4400 et seq.

Non-Sectarian Hospital Act (Township)
Ill. Rev. Stat. 1991, Ch. 139, § 160.01 et seq.

Non-Vessel-Operating Common Carrier Act of 1991
March 9, 1992, P.L. 102-251, 46 Appx. § 1701 nt.

Non-Vessel-Operating Common Carrier Amendments of 1990
Nov. 16, 1990, P.L. 101-595, 46 U.S. Code Appx. § 1701 nt.

Nonabatement Act
Del. Code of 1974, Title 10, § 3701 et seq.
La. Code of Civil Procedure Art. 428

Nonadmitted Carriers Act (Insurance)
Fla. Stat. 1957, 645.01 et seq.

Nonadmitted Insurance Act
Vt. Stat. Ann., Title 8, § 5021 et seq.

Nonadmitted Insurance Tax Law
Cal. Revenue and Taxation Code § 13201 et seq.

Nonalcoholic Beverage Act
Ore. Rev. Stat., 635.010 et seq.
Pa. Purdon's Stat., Title 31, § 790.1 et seq.

Nonalcoholic Beverage Plant Act
Ore. Rev. Stat., 635.015 et seq.

Nonappropriated Fund Instrumentalities Employees' Retirement Credit Act of 1986
Nov. 10, 1986, P.L. 99-638, 5 U.S. Code § 8331 nt.

Nonbeverage Liquor Act
N.J. Laws 1921, C 150

Nonbusiness Corporation Act
R.I. Gen. Laws 1956, 7-6-1 et seq.

Noncitizen Benefit Clarification and Other Technical Amendments Act of 1998
Oct. 28, 1998, P.L. 105-306, 112 Stat. 2926, 42 U.S. Code § 1305 nt.

Nonclaim Act (Administrators)
N.H. Rev. Stat. 1955, 556:1 et seq.

Nonclaim Act (Estates)
Ala. Code 1975, § 43-2-350 et seq.
Ariz. Rev. Stat. Ann., § 14-3803
Ark. Code Ann. 1987, 28-50-101
Cal. Probate Code § 707
Colo. Rev. Stat., 15-12-801 et seq.
Conn. Gen. Stat. Ann., § 45a-395
Del. Code of 1974, Title 12, § 2102
Fla. Stat. Ann., 733.702
Fla. Stat. 1973, 733.16
Haw. Rev. Stat. Ann., § 560:3-801 et seq.
Ill. Rev. Stat. 1991, Ch. 110 1/2, § 18-12
Ind. Code Ann., 29-1-14-1
Kan. Stat. Ann., 59-2239

Miss. Code Ann. 1972, § 91-7-151

Mont. Code Ann., 1991, 72-3-803

N.D. Cent. Code 30.1-19-03

Neb. Rev. Stat. 1943, 30-2485, 30-2486

N.M. Stat. Ann., 45-3-803 et seq.

Ohio Rev. Code 1953, 2117.06 et seq.

Okla. Stat. Ann., Title 58, § 333

Ore. Rev. Stat. 1953, 116.510

S.C. Code Ann. 1976, Superseded Vols., § 21-15-640 et seq.

S.D. Codified Laws 1967, 30-21-17

Utah Code Ann. 1953, 75-3-803

Wash. Rev. Code Ann., 11.40.010

Wis. Stat. Ann., 859.05, et seq.

Nonclaim Act (Insolvent Banks)

Wash. Rev. Code Ann., 30.44.060

Nonclaim Act (Insolvent Estates)

Conn. Gen. Stat. Ann., § 45a-410

Nonclaim Act (Probate)

Ariz. Rev. Stat. Ann., § 14-3803

Conn. Gen. Stat. Ann., § 45-205

Iowa Code 1983, 633.410

Md. Ann. Code 1974, Art. ET, § 10-103

Mo. Rev. Stat., 473.360

N.J. Stat. Ann. 3B:22-9

N.M. Stat. Ann., 45-3-803

Ohio Rev. Code 1953, 2117.06, 2117.07

Ore. Rev. Stat., 115.005

Tenn. Code Ann., 30-2-310

Tex. Probate Code, § 298

Va. Code 1950, § 64.1-179

Noncoal Surface Mining Conservation and Reclamation Act

Pa. Purdon's Stat., Title 52, § 3301 et seq.

Noncoal Surface Mining Law

La. Rev. Stat. Ann., 30:961 et seq.

Noncontributory Pension Act (Schools)

N.J. Stat. Ann., 43:8B-1 et seq.

Noncontrolled Substances Reporting & Registration Act

Pa. Purdon's Stat., Title 35, § 881 et seq.

Nondisclosure Act (Public Assistance Records)

Alaska Stat. 1962, § 47.05.030

Nondiscrimination in Health Insurance Act (Genetic Information)

Miss. Laws 1999, H.B. 347

Nondiscrimination Law (Auto Insurance)

Cal. Insurance Code § 11628

Nondomiciliaries Jurisdiction Act

N.Y. Civil Practice Law and Rules (Consol. Laws Ch. 8) § 302

Nondrivers Identification Cards Act

N.J. Stat. Ann., 39:3-29.2 et seq.

Nonemblem Law

Ky. Acts 1922, Ch. 137

Nonemergency Telephone System Pilot Program (Local)

Cal. Government Code § 53125 et seq.

Nonforfeiture Act (Life Insurance)

Ala. Code 1975, § 27-15-28

Cal. Insurance Code § 10159.1 et seq.

D.C. Code Ann., § 35-507

Fla. Stat. Ann., 627.476

Haw. Rev. Stat. Ann., § 431-561

Ida. Code 1947, 41-1927

Iowa Code 1983, 508.37

Md. Ann. Code 1957, Art. 48A, § 414

Me. Rev. Stat. Ann. 1964, Title 24-A, § 2528 et seq.

Mich. Comp. Laws Ann., 500.4060

Minn. Stat. Ann., 61A.24

Miss. Code Ann. 1972, § 83-7-25

Mo. Rev. Stat., 376.630

Mont. Rev. Code 1947, 40-3831 et seq.

N.C. Gen. Stat. 1943, § 58-58-55

Neb. Rev. Stat. 1943, 44-407

Nev. Rev. Stat. 1979 Reprint, 688A.290 et seq.

N.H. Rev. Stat. 1955, 409:1 et seq.

N.J. Stat. Ann., 17B:25-19

N.Y. Insurance Law (Consol. Laws Ch. 28) § 4221

Pa. Purdon's Stat., Title 40, § 510.1
Continued

S.C. Code Ann. 1976, § 38-63-510 et seq.
S.D. Codified Laws 1967, 58-15-31 et seq.
Tex. Insurance Code, Art. 3.44a
Utah Code Ann. 1953, 31A-22-408
Va. Code 1950, § 38.2-3200 et seq.
Vt. Stat. Ann., Title 8, § 3741 et seq.
Wash. Rev. Code Ann., 48.76.010 et seq.
W. Va. Code 1966, § 33-13-30

Nonforfeiture Act for Individual Deferred Annuities

See Standard Nonforfeiture Law for Individual Deferred Annuities

Nonforfeiture and Valuation Act

Colo. Rev. Stat., 10-7-301 et seq.
Conn. Gen. Stat. Ann., § 38a-438 et seq.

Nonforfeiture and Valuation Amendments Act

D.C. Code Ann., §§ 35-501, 35-503, 35-505, 35-507, 35-508, 35-526

Nonforfeiture Law (Standard Life Insurance)

Ore. Rev. Stat., 743.204 et seq.
Wash. Rev. Code 1983, 48.76.010

Nonforfeiture Law (Standard)

Conn. Gen. Stat. Ann., § 38a-438 et seq.
Neb. Rev. Stat. 1943, 44-407 et seq.
N.Y. Insurance Law 1984 (Consol. Laws Ch. 28) § 4221

Nonforfeiture Law for Individual Deferred Annuities (Standard)

La. Rev. Stat. Ann., 22:173.1

Nonforfeiture Law for Individual Deferred Annuities Act (Standard)

Md. Ann. Code 1974, Art. IN, § 16-501 et seq.
R.I. Gen. Laws 1956, 27-4.4-1 et seq.

Nonforfeiture Law for Life Insurance (Standard)

Md. Ann. Code 1974, Art. IN, § 16-301 et seq.
Pa. Purdon's Stat., Title 40, § 510.1
R.I. Gen. Laws 1956, 27-4.3-1 et seq.

Nongame and Endangered or Threatened Species Conservation Act

Colo. Rev. Stat., 33-2-101 et seq.
Ill. Rev. Stat. 1991, Ch. 61, § 401 et seq.
Kan. Stat. Ann., 32-957 et seq., 32-1009 et seq., 32-1033
Md. Ann. Code 1974, Art. NR, § 10-2A01 et seq.
Miss. Code Ann. 1972, § 49-5-101 et seq.
Mont. Code Ann., 1991, 87-5-101 et seq.
Neb. Rev. Stat. 1943, 37-430 et seq.
N.H. Rev. Stat. 1955, 212-B:1 et seq.
N.J. Stat. Ann., 23:2A-1 et seq.
S.C. Code Ann. 1976, § 50-15-10 et seq.
Tenn. Code Ann., 70-8-101 et seq.
Vt. Stat. Ann., Title 10, § 4048

Nongame and Endangered Species Conservation Act

Kan. Stat. Ann., 32-957

Nongame Fish and Wildlife Trust Fund Act

Mich. Comp. Laws Ann., 299.151 et seq.

Nonhazardous Solid Waste Planning Act

Miss. Code Ann. 1972, § 17-17-201 et seq.

Nonimprisonment Act

N.Y. Civil Rights Law (Consol. Laws Ch. 6) § 20 et seq.

Nonindigenous Aquatic Nuisance Prevention and Control Act of 1990

Nov. 29, 1990, P.L. 101-646, 16 U.S. Code §§ 777c, 4701 et seq. generally, 18 U.S. Code § 42
Dec. 4, 1991, P.L. 102-186, 16 U.S. Code § 4741
Oct. 31, 1992, P.L. 102-580, 16 U.S. Code § 4711
Nov. 4, 1992, P.L. 102-587, 16 U.S. Code § 4711
Aug. 6, 1996, P.L. 104-182, 16 U.S. Code §§ 4701, 4721
Nov. 10, 1998, P.L. 105-362, 16 U.S. Code § 4712

Nonindigenous Aquatic Plant Control Act

Ala. Code 1975, § 9-20-1 et seq.
Fla. Stat. 1983, 369.22

Nonintercourse Act (Indians)
See Indian Nonintercourse Act

Nonintervention Will Act
Wash. Rev. Code Ann., 11.68.010 et seq.

Nonintoxicating Beer Act
Mo. Rev. Stat., 312.010 et seq.
Okla. Stat. Ann., Title 37, § 163.1 et seq.
W. Va. Code 1966, 11-16-1 et seq.

Nonintoxicating Beverage Act
Okla. Stat. Ann., Title 37, § 163.1 et seq.

Nonintoxicating Beverage Distribution Act
Okla. Stat. Ann., Title 37, § 163.18A et seq.

Nonintoxicating Malt Liquor Act
Minn. Stat. Ann., 340.001 et seq.
Tex. Penal Code 1911, Art. 157 et seq.
Tex. Rev. Civ. Stat. 1911, Art. 7476 et seq.

Nonjudicial Court Personnel Compensation Act
N.Y. Laws 1961, Ch. 492
N.Y. Laws 1962, Ch. 640

Nonlapse Act
Fla. Stat. Ann., 732.603

Nonliability for Valuables Not Deposited in Safe Act
Pa. Purdon's Stat., Title 37, § 61 et seq.

Nonmanufacturing Facility Community Right-to-Know Act
Tex. Health and Safety Code, § 507.001

Nonmineral Land Leasing Act
Cal. Public Resources Code § 6501 etseq.

Nonnotice Act (Mechanics' Lien)
Colo. Rev. Stat., 38-22-102, 38-22-105

Nonoccupational Disability Act
N.J. Stat. Ann., 43:21-25 et seq.
R.I. Gen. Laws 1956, 28-39-1 et seq.

Nonpar Corporations Act
Tex. Business Corporation Act, Art. 2.15 et seq.

Nonpartisan Election Act
Ill. Rev. Stat. 1991, Ch. 24, § 21-24 et seq.
N.J. Stat. Ann. 40:45-5 et seq.
Pa. 1913 Pamph. Laws 1001, No. 457

Nonpartisan Judicial Primary Act
Ky. Rev. Stat. 1971, 118A.060
Neb. Rev. Stat. 1943, 32-535 et seq.

Nonpartisan Judiciary Act
Mo. Laws 1913, p. 334
Ore. Rev. Stat., 252.010 et seq.

Nonpartisan Offices Act
Nev. Rev. Stat. 1957 Ed., 294.010, 394.040, 294.015

Nonpartisan School Committee Act (Glocester)
R.I. Public Laws 1976, Ch. 101

Nonpoint Financial Assistance Act (Agricultural)
Ala. Code 1975, § 22-38-1 et seq.

Nonpoint Source Pollution Management and Control Act
Haw. Session Laws 1993, Act 345

Nonprobate Transfers Act
Ind. Code Ann., 32-4-1.5-1 et seq.
Mo. Rev. Stat. 461.003 et seq.

Nonprobate Transfers on Death Act
See Uniform Nonprobate Transfers on Death Act

Nonprofit Associations Act (Unincorporated)
See also Uniform Unincorporated Nonprofit Associations Act
Ala. Code 1975, § 10-3B-1 et seq.
Wyo. Stat. 1977, § 17-21-101 et seq.

Nonprofit Associations Real Estate Holding Act
Cal. Corporations Code § 20001 et seq., 21200

Nonprofit Cooperative Agricultural Marketing Associations Act
Cal. Corporations Code § 14550 et seq.

Nonprofit Cooperative Associations Act
Ga. Code Ann., 20-10-80 et seq.

Nonprofit Cooperative Marketing Act
Mo. Rev. Stat., 274.010 et seq.

Nonprofit Corporation Act
Ala. Code 1975, § 10-3A-1 et seq.
Alaska Stat. 1962, § 10.20.005 et seq.
Ariz. Rev. Stat. Ann., § 10-3101 et seq.
Ark. Code Ann. 1987, 4-28-201 et seq.
Cal. Corporations Code, §§ 5000 et seq., 9000 et seq.
Colo. Rev. Stat., 7-20-101 et seq.
D.C. Code Ann., § 29-501 et seq.
Fla. Stat. Ann., 617.001 et seq., 617.01011 et seq.
Ga. Code Ann., 14-3-1 et seq.
Haw. Rev. Stat.Ann., § 415B-1 et seq.
Ida. Code 1947, 30-3-1 et seq.
Ill. Rev. Stat. 1991, Ch. 32, § 101.01 et seq.
Ind. Code 1982, 23-17-1-1 et seq.
Iowa Code 1983, 504A.1 et seq.
Ky. Rev. Stat. 1971, 273.161 et seq.
La. Rev. Stat. Ann., 12:201 et seq.
Me. Rev. Stat. Ann. 1964, Title 13-B, § 101 et seq.
Mich. Comp. Laws Ann., 450.2101 et seq.
Minn. Stat. Ann., 317A.001 et seq.
Miss. Code Ann. 1972, 79-11-101 et seq.
Mo. Rev. Stat., 355.010 et seq.
Mont. Code Ann., 1991, 35-2-113 et seq.
N.C. Gen. Stat. 1943, § 55A-1 et seq.
N.D. Cent. Code 10-24-01 et seq.
Neb. Rev. Stat. 1943, 21-1901 et seq.
Nev. Rev. Stat. 1979 Reprint, 81.010 et seq.
N.J. Stat. Ann. 15A:1-1 et seq.
N.M. Stat. Ann., 53-8-1 et seq.
Ohio Rev. Code 1953, 1702.01 et seq.
Okla. Stat. Ann., Title 18, § 1001 et seq.
Ore. Rev. Stat. 1953, 61.005 et seq.
Ore. Rev. Stat., 65.011 et seq.
Pa. Cons. Stat., Title 15, § 5101 et seq.
Pa. Cons. Stat., Title 15, § 7101 et seq.
R.I. Gen. Laws 1956, 7-6-1 et seq.
S.C. Code Ann. 1976, § 33-31-10 et seq.
S.C. Code Ann. 1976, § 33-31-101 et seq.
S.D. Codified Laws 1967, 47-22-1 et seq.
Tenn. Code Ann., 48-56-101 et seq.
Tenn. Public Acts 1991, Ch. 242
Tex. Rev. Civ. Stat., Art. 1396-1.01 et seq.
Utah Code Ann. 1953, 16-6-18 et seq.
Vt. Stat. Ann., Title 11, § 2301 et seq.
Wash. Rev. Code Ann., 24.03.005 et seq.
Wyo. Stat. Ann., § 17-6-101 et seq.
Wyo. Stat. 1977, § 17-19-101 et seq.

Nonprofit Corporation Act (Hospital Service)
Ga. Code Ann., 33-19-1 et seq.

Nonprofit Corporation-Keys Amendment Facility Insurance Pooling Act
N.J. Stat. Ann., 17:49A-1 et seq.

Nonprofit Corporation Revival Act
Mich. Comp. Laws Ann., 450.441

Nonprofit Dental Service Corporation Act
Kan. Stat. Ann., 40-19a01 et seq.
Miss. Code Ann. 1972, § 83-43-1 et seq.
N.D. Cent. Code 26.1-17-01 et seq.
Okla. Stat. Ann., Title 36, § 2671 et seq.
Pa. Cons. Stat., Title 40, § 6101 et seq.

Nonprofit Funeral Service Association Act
La. Rev. Stat. Ann., 22:331 et seq.

Nonprofit Health Care Corporation Reform Act
Mich. Comp. Laws Ann., 550.1101 et seq.

Nonprofit Health Care Plan Act
Ill. Rev. Stat. 1985, Ch. 32, § 551 et seq.
N.M. Stat. Ann., 59A-47-1 et seq.

Nonprofit Health Service Act (Voluntary)
Pa. Purdon's Stat., Title 40, § 1551 et seq.

Nonprofit Health Service Plan Corporation Act

Ariz. Rev. Stat. Ann., § 20-821 et seq.

Colo. Rev. Stat., 10-16-101 et seq.

Ga. Code Ann., 33-18-1 et seq.

Kan. Stat. Ann., 40-1801 et seq.

Kan. Stat. Ann., 40-1901 et seq.

Ky. Rev. Stat. 1971, 304.32-010 et seq.

Minn. Stat. Ann., 62C.01 et seq.

N.D. Cent. Code 26.1-17-01 et seq.

N.Y. Public Health Law 1953 (Consol. Laws Ch. 45) § 4400

Pa. Cons. Stat., Title 40, §§ 6101, 6301 et seq.

Utah Code Ann. 1953, 31A-7-101 et seq.

Nonprofit Hospital, Medical-Surgical, Dental and Health Service Corporation Act

Colo. Rev. Stat., 10-16-301 et seq.

Ky. Rev. Stat. 1971, 304.32-010 et seq.

Nev. Rev. Stat. 1979 Reprint, 695B.010 et seq.

Nonprofit Hospital Plan Act

Pa. Cons. Stat., Title 40, § 6101 et seq.

Nonprofit Hospital Sale Act

Neb. Rev. Stat. 1943, 71-20,102 to 71-20,113

Nonprofit Hospital Service and Indemnity Plan

N.M. Stat. Ann. 1953, 58-15-12 et seq.

Nonprofit Housing Corporations Act

Mich. Comp. Laws Ann., 125.1401 et seq.

N.J. Stat. Ann., 55:16-1 et seq.

N.Y. Private Housing Finance Law (Consol. Laws Ch. 44B) § 570 et seq.

Nonprofit Housing Developments' Water and Sanitary Sewer Service Rate Charges Reduction and the Consumer Credit Interest Rate Amendments Clarification Act

D.C. Code Ann., § 43-1522 et seq.

Nonprofit Legal Service Plan Act

Minn. Stat. Ann., 62G.01 et seq.

Nonprofit Medical, Osteopathic, Dental and Podiatry Service Corporation Act

Pa. Cons. Stat., Title 40, § 6101 et seq.

Nonprofit Miscellaneous and Mutual Corporation Act

Wash. Rev. Code Ann., 24.06.005 et seq.

Nonprofit Multiple Employer Welfare Arrangement Act

Fla. Stat. Ann., 624.436 et seq.

Nonprofit Mutual Benefit Corporation Act

Cal. Corporations Code, § 7110 et seq.

Nonprofit Optometric Service Corporation Act

Kan. Stat. Ann., 40-19b01 et seq.

Nonprofit Pharmacy Service Corporation Act

Kan. Stat. Ann., 40-19d01 et seq.

Nonprofit Public Benefit Corporation Act

Cal. Corporations Code, § 5110 et seq.

Nonprofit Religious Corporation Act

Cal. Corporations Code, § 9110 et seq.

Nonprofit Risk Indemnification Trust Act

La. Rev. Stat. Ann., 22:2001 et seq.

Minn. Stat. Ann., 60A.29

Nonprofit School Building Corporation Act

Ind. Code Ann., 21-5-11-1 et seq.

Nonprofit Service Organizations Preferred Provider Arrangement Act

Me. Rev. Stat. Ann. 1964, Title 24, § 2333 et seq.; Title 24-A, § 201 et seq.

Nonpublic Elementary and Secondary Education Act

N.J. Stat. Ann., 18A:58-59 et seq.

Pa. Purdon's Stat., Title 24, § 5701 et seq.

Nonpublic Institutions of Higher Learning Financial Assistance Act

Ill. Rev. Stat. 1991, Ch. 144, § 1331 et seq.

Nonpublic Post-Secondary Institution License Act

S.C. Code Ann. 1976, § 59-58-10 et seq.

Nonpublic Postsecondary Educational Institutions Act

Ga. Code Ann., 20-3-250.1 et seq.

Nonpublic School Aid, Equal Opportunity Education Assistance Act

La. Rev. Stat. Ann., 17:2990.1 et seq.

Nonpublic School Secular Education Act

Conn. Gen. Stat. Ann., § 10-281a et seq.

Nonpublic School Teachers Salary Supplement Act

R.I. Gen. Laws 1956, 16-51-1 et seq.

Nonpublic State Parental Grant Plan for Children of Low Income Families Act

Ill. Rev. Stat. 1973, Ch. 122, §§ 1001 et seq., 1021 et seq.

Nonpublication Local Law (Village of Greenwood Lake)

N.Y. Local Laws 1964, Village of Greenwood Lake, p. 911

Nonresident Aircraft and Watercraft Act

Ill. Rev. Stat. 1981, Ch. 110, § 263a et seq.

Nonresident Aircraft Service Act

Pa. Cons. Stat., Title 42, § 5322 et seq.

Nonresident Alien Beneficiary Act

Fla. Stat. Ann., 732.1101

Nonresident Attachment Act

Conn. Gen. Stat. Ann., § 52-284
Md. Ann. Code 1974, Art. CJ, § 3-301 et seq.
Miss. Code Ann. 1972, §§ 11-33-7, 11-33-9, 11-33-19, 11-33-39

Nonresident Automobile Act

Wash. Rev. Code Ann., 46.08.070, 46.64.040

Nonresident Boating Act

Ky. Rev. Stat. 1971, 454.260 et seq.

Nonresident Brokers and Agents Process Act (Unauthorized)

See Unauthorized Nonresident Brokers and Agents Process Act

Nonresident Brokers and Agents Process Act (Unlicensed)

Va. Code 1950, § 38.2-808 et seq.

Nonresident College Trustees Act

Ill. Rev. Stat. 1991, Ch. 144, § 6.9 et seq.

Nonresident Commercial Fishermen License Act

Tex. Penal Code 1925, Art. 934b-1

Nonresident Contact Lens Seller Registration Act

Cal. Business and Professions Code § 2546 et seq.

Nonresident Corporation Act (Process)

La. Rev. Stat. Ann., 13:3471

Nonresident Direct Service Act

Wash. Rev. Code Ann., 4.28.185

Nonresident Inheritance Tax Act

Pa. Purdon's Stat., Title 72, § 2303

Nonresident Liquor Seller's Permit Act

Tenn. Code Ann., 57-3-601 et seq.

Nonresident Motorist Act

Ariz. Rev. Stat. Ann., §§ 28-502, 28-503
Ga. Code Ann., 40-12-1 et seq.
Ill. Rev. Stat. 1991, Ch. 951/2, § 1-150
Kan. Stat. Ann., 8-401, et seq.
Mass. Gen. Laws Ann., 90:3
Neb. Rev. Stat. 1943, 25-530, 25-530.01
N.H. Rev. Stat. 1955, 260:67 et seq.
Wash. Rev. Code 1983, 46.08.070, 46.64.040

Nonresident Motorist Process Act

N.D. Cent. Code, 39-01-11 et seq.

Nonresident Motorist Substituted Service Act

Ala. Code 1958, Title 7, § 199
Alaska Stat. 1962, § 09.05.020 et seq.

Ariz. Rev. Stat. Ann. §§ 2-502, 28-503
Ark. Code Ann. 1987, 16-58-121, 27-342.2
Cal. Vehicle Code 1959, § 17450 et seq.
Colo. Rev. Stat. 1963, 13-8-1 et seq.
Conn. Gen. Stat. Ann., § 52-62
D.C. Code Ann., § 40-407
Del. Code of 1974, Title 10, § 3112
Del. Code of 1974, Title 21, § 2927
Fla. Stat. Ann., 48.171
Ga. Code 1933, 68-801 et seq.
Haw. Rev. Stat. Ann., § 634-33
Ida. Code 1947, 49-2420 et seq.
Ill. Rev. Stat. 1991, Ch. 95 1/2, § 10-301
Ind. Code 1971, 9-3-2-1
Iowa Code Ann., 321.498 et seq.
Ky. Rev. Stat. 1971, 188.010 et seq.
La. Rev. Stat. Ann., 13:3474 et seq.
Mass. Gen. Laws Ann., 90:3A et seq.
Md. Ann. Code 1957, Superseded Volume, Art. 66 1/2, § 9-301
Md. Ann. Code 1974, Art. CJ, § 6-103
Me. Rev. Stat. Ann. 1964, Title 29, § 1911 et seq.
Mich. Comp. Laws Ann., 257.403
Minn. Stat. Ann., 170.55
Miss. Code Ann. 1972, §§ 11-11-13, 13-3-63
Mo. Rev. Stat., 506.200 et seq.
Mont. Code Ann., 1991, 25-3-601 et seq.
N.C. Gen. Stat. 1943, §§ 1-105, 1-105.1
N.D. Cent. Code 39-01-11 et seq.
Neb. Rev. Stat. 1943, 25-530, 25-535
Nev. Rev. Stat. 1979 Reprint, 14.070
N.H. Rev. Stat. 1955, 264:1 et seq.
N.J. Stat. Ann., 39:71 et seq.
N.M. Stat. Ann., 66-5-103
N.Y. Vehicle & Traffic Law 1959 (Consol. Laws Ch. 71) § 253
Ohio Rev. Code 1953, 2703.20
Okla. Stat. Ann., Title 47, § 391 et seq.
Ore. Rules of Civil Procedure, Rule 7
Pa. Cons. Stat., Title 42, § 5322 et seq.
R.I. Gen. Laws 1956, 31-7-6, 31-7-7
S.C. Code Ann. 1976, § 15-9-350
S.D. Codified Laws 1967, 15-7-6 et seq.
Tenn. Code Ann., 20-2-203
Tex. Civ. Prac. and Rem. Code, § 17.061 et seq.
Tex. Rev. Civ. Stat., Art. 2039a

Utah Code Ann. 1953, 41-12A-505
Va. Code 1950, § 8.01-307 et seq.
Vt. Stat. Ann., Title 12, § 891 et seq.
Wis. Stat. Ann., 345.09
W. Va. Code 1966, § 56-3-31
Wyo. Stat. Ann., § 1-6-301

Nonresident Property Owners Service Act
Pa. Cons. Stat., Title 42, § 5322 et seq.

Nonresident Real Estate Brokers' License Act
Ind. Burns' 1933, 42-1001 et seq.

Nonresident Service of Process Act
Ala. Code 1958, Title 7, § 199(1)
N.M. Stat. Ann., 38-1-16
Wash. Rev. Code Ann., 4.28.185

Nonresident Tax Foreclosure Act
Tex. Rev. Civ. Stat., Art. 7342
Tex. Rules of Civil Procedure as am. 1984, Rule 117a

Nonresident Traffic Violator Compact
Miss. Code Ann. 1972, § 63-1-1 et seq.
S.C. Code Ann. 1976, § 56-25-10 et seq.

Nonresident Tuition Act
D.C. Code Ann., § 31-602 et seq.

Nonresident Vessel Owner Substituted Service Act
Pa. Purdon's Stat., Title 42, § 5322

Nonresident Violator Compact
Tex. Transportation Code, § 703.001 et seq.
Utah Code Ann. 1953, 53-3-701 et seq.

Nonresident Violator Compact (Motor Vehicles)
N.J. Stat. Ann., 39:5F-1 et seq.

Nonresident Violator Compact Act
Colo. Rev. Stat. 24-60-2101 et seq.
Fla. Stat. Ann., 322.50
Ill. Rev. Stat. 1991, Ch. 95 1/2, § 6-800 et seq.
Kan. Stat. Ann., 8-1219
Miss. Code Ann. 1972, § 63-10-1 et seq.
Mo. Rev. Stat., 544.046

Continued

Neb. Rev. Stat. 1943, 60-426
N.H. Rev. Stat. 1955, 262:29, 262:30
N.J. Stat. Ann. 39:5F-1 et seq.
N.M. Stat. Ann., 66-8-137.1 et seq.
Vt. Stat. Ann., Title 23, § 3551 et seq.
Wash. Rev. Code Ann., 46.23.010 et seq.
W. Va. Code 1966, § 17B-1C-1 et seq.

Nonresident Watercraft Operator Substituted Service Act
Fla. Stat. 1977, 48.19
La. Rev. Stat. Ann., 13:3479 et seq.

Nonresident Witness Attendance Act
W. Va. Code 1966, § 62-6A-1 et seq.

Nonresidential Landlord and Tenant Act
Fla. Stat. Ann., 83.001 et seq.

Nonresidents Traffic Violators Act
S.C. Code Ann. 1976, § 56-25-10 et seq.

Nonsectarian Hospital Act
Ill. Rev. Stat. 1991, Ch. 34, § 5-7001 et seq.

Nonsigner Act (Fair Trade Law)
Mass. Gen. Laws Ann., 93:14E et seq.
N.J. Stat. Ann., 56:4-6

Nonstock Act (Livestock)
La. Rev. Stat. Ann., 3:2801 et seq.

Nonstock Cooperative Marketing Act
Neb. Rev. Stat. 1943, 21-1401 et seq.

Nonstock Corporation Act
Conn. Gen. Stat. Ann., § 33-419 et seq.
Va. Code 1950, § 13.1-801 et seq.
Wis. Stat. Ann., 181.01 et seq.

Nonsuit Act (Civil)
Ark. Code Ann. 1987, 16-56-126
Fla. Stat. 1965, 54.09
N.C. Gen. Stat. 1943, § 1-183

Nonsuit Act (Criminal)
N.C. Gen. Stat. 1943, § 15-173

Nonsuit Act (Foreign Corporations)
Wyo. Stat. 1957, § 17-32

Nonsuit and Dismissal Act
Wash. Rev. Code Ann., 4.56.120

Nonsuit Saving Act
Mo. Rev. Stat., 516.230

Nonsupport Act (Reciprocal)
See Uniform Reciprocal Enforcement of Support Act

Nonsupport and Abandonment Act
See Abandonment and Nonsupport Act

Nonsupport and Desertion Act
See Desertion and Nonsupport Act
See Uniform Nonsupport and Desertion Act

Nontax Reserve Fund Act of 1967
N.C. Laws 1967, Ch. 648

Nontestamentary Instrument Disclaimer Act
Ill. Rev. Stat. 1991, Ch. 30, §§ 210, 211

Nontidal Waters Act (Boat Regulation)
N.J. Stat. Ann., 12:7-34.1 et seq.

Nontraditional Employment for Women Act
Dec. 12, 1991, P.L. 102-235, 29 U.S. Code § 1501 nt.

Nontraditional Occupation Act
Me. Rev. Stat. Ann. 1964, Title 26, § 2021 et seq.

Nonvested Pension Benefits Protection Tax Act (Private)
N.J. Laws 1973, Ch. 124
R.I. Gen. Laws 1956, 28-46-1 et seq.

Nonviolent Intermediate Offender Act
Okla. Stat. Ann., Title 22, § 995 et seq.

Nonwaivable Deficiency Act
Cal. Code of Civil Procedure § 580a et seq.

Norfolk County Agricultural School Loan Act
Mass. Acts 1956, Ch. 372

Norfolk County Court House Loan Act
Mass. Acts 1949, Ch. 590

Norfolk County Probate Court and Registry of Deeds Loan Act
Mass. Acts 1959, Ch. 472

Norfolk County Reconciliation Act
Mass. Acts 1961, Ch. 620

Normal Civic Center Law
Ill. Rev. Stat. 1991, Ch. 85, § 4601 et seq.

Normal, Mason County, Jasper County, Brownstown Park District, Jo Davies County, Milford, Sheldon, Katherine Dunham, Oak Park, and Aledo Civic Centers Act
Ill. Rev. Stat. 1991, Ch. 85, § 4500 et seq.

Normal, Mason County, Jasper County, Jo Davies County, Milford, Sheldon, Katherine Dunham, and Oak Park Civic Centers Act
Dec. 8, 1993, P.L. 103-182, 107 Stat. 2057
Ill. Comp. Stat. 1992, Ch. 70, § 220/1 et seq.

Normal School Act (State)
Ky. Rev. Stat. 1971, 164.290 et seq.

Norman S. Waters-Ruben S. Ayala Milk Producers Security Act
Cal. Food and Agriculture Code 1967, § 62500 et seq.

Norman-Walden Act (Local Option Stock)
Ala. Code 1975, § 3-5-1 et seq.

Norris Act (Conveyances by Union Pacific Ry. Co.)
June 24, 1912, Ch. 181, 37 Stat. 138

Norris Act (Labor)
Ohio Rev. Code 1953, 4113.03 et seq.

Norris and Cope Act
Ala. Acts 1987, p. 1479

Norris-La Guardia Act (Labor Disputes)
March 23, 1932, Ch. 90, 47 Stat. 70, 29 U.S. Code §§ 101 to 115
Nov. 8, 1984, P.L. 98-620, 29 U.S. Code § 110

Norris-La Guardia Act (Maryland)
Md. Ann. Code 1974, Art. LE, § 4-302 et seq.

Norris-La Guardia Act (Oregon)
Ore. Rev. Stat., 662.010 et seq.

Norris Muscle Shoals Act
See Tennessee Valley Authority Act of 1933

Norris-Rayburn Rural Electrification Act
See Rural Electrification Act of 1936

North Adams Industrial Development Commission Loan Act
Mass. Acts 1953, Ch. 548

North Adams Park and Recreation Improvement Loan Act
Mass. Acts 1964, Ch. 87

North Adams Police Station Loan Act
Mass. Acts 1954, Ch. 571

North American Free Trade Agreement Implementation Act
Dec. 8, 1993, P.L. 103-182, 19 U.S. Code § 3301 nt.
Aug. 20, 1996, P.L. 104-188, 19 U.S. Code § 3331
Oct. 11, 1996, P.L. 104-295, 19 U.S. Code §§ 1592, 2541, 2543, 2545 to 2547, 2552, 2553, 2561, 2573, 3358, 3432, 3437, 3451, 3381
July 22, 1998, P.L. 105-206, 19 U.S. Code § 3332
Oct. 28, 1998, P.L. 105-306, 26 U.S. Code § 3306 nt.
June 25, 1999, P.L. 106-36, 19 U. S. Code § 1592

North American Wetlands Conservation Act
Nov. 16, 1990, P.L. 101-593, 16 U.S. Code §§ 4403, 4404
Oct. 19, 1994, P.L. 103-375, 16 U.S. Code §§ 4406, 4407, 4409, 4414
Oct. 30, 1998, P.L. 105-312, 16 U.S. Code § 4406

North American Wetlands Conservation Act Amendments of 1994
Oct. 19, 1994, P.L. 103-375, 16 U.S. Code § 4401 nt.

North Atlantic Treaty Organization Mutual Support Act of 1979
Aug. 4, 1980, P.L. 96-323, 10 U.S. Code § 2321 et seq., 2321 nt.

North Attleborough School Loan Act
Mass. Acts 1952, Ch. 57

North Beach Community Development Act
Md. Laws 1978, Ch. 709

North Brookfield School Building Loan Act
Mass. Acts 1950, Ch. 677

North Brookfield Water Loan Act
Mass. Acts 1951, Ch. 140

North Carolina Wilderness Act of 1984
June 19, 1984, P.L. 98-324, 11 U.S. Code § 1132 nt.

North Casey Key Conservation District Act
Fla. Special Laws 1970, Ch. 70-937

North Central Texas Airport Authority Act of 1967
Tex. Laws 60th Leg., 1967, p. 6, Ch. 6

North Coast Railroad Authority Act
Cal. Government Code, § 93000 et seq.

North Country Development Authority Act
N.Y. Public Authorities Law (Consol. Laws Ch. 43A) §§ 2700, 2701 et seq.

North Delta Water Agency Act
Cal. Water Code, Appendix, § 115-1.1

North Georgia Mountains Authority Act
Ga. Code Ann., 12-3-290 et seq.
Ga. Code 1933, 99-2701 et seq.

North Hempstead Solid Waste Management Authority Act
N.Y. Public Authorities Law (Consol. Laws Ch. 43A) § 2049a et seq.

North Lake Tahoe Transportation Authority Act
Cal. Government Code § 67960 et seq.

North Lake Tahoe-Truckee River Sanitation Agency Act
Cal. Statutes 1967, Ch. 1503, p. 3511

North Orange and South Seminole County Wastewater Transmission Authority Act
Fla. Special Laws 1978, Ch. 617

North Pacific Anadromous Stocks Act of 1992
Oct. 29, 1992, P.L. 102-567, 16 U.S. Code §§ 5001 nt., 5001 to 5012
Nov. 4, 1992, P.L. 102-587, 16 U.S. Code §§ 5001 nt., 5001 et seq.

North Pacific Fisheries Act of 1954
Aug. 12, 1954, Ch. 669, 68 Stat. 698, 16 U.S. Code §§ 1021 to 1032
July 24, 1957, P.L. 85-114, 71 Stat. 310, 16 U.S. Code § 1031
Oct. 9, 1972, P.L. 92-471, 86 Stat. 784, 16 U.S. Code §§ 1022, 1023, 1025a, 1026, 1027, 1029, 1030, 1031, 1032
July 28, 1978, P.L. 95-326, 16 U.S. Code §§ 1021, 1021 nt., 1022, 1022 nt., 1023 et seq.
Oct. 30, 1978, P.L. 95-553, 16 U.S. Code §§ 1030, 1034
Dec. 29, 1982, P.L. 97-389, 16 U.S. Code § 1034

North Reading Ipswich River Improvement Loan Act
Mass. Acts 1961, Ch. 249

North San Diego County Transit Development Board Act
Cal. Public Utilities Code § 125000 et seq.

North Shore Community Public Library Act
N.Y. Laws 1968, Ch. 856

North Shore Sanitary District Act
Ill. Rev. Stat. 1991, Ch. 42, § 276.99 et seq.

North Shore Sanitary District Extension (1st) Act
Ill. Rev. Stat. 1991, Ch. 42, §§ 297h, 298

North Shore Sanitary District Extension (2nd) Act
Ill. Rev. Stat. 1991, Ch. 42, §§ 298a, 298a1

North Smithfield Water Authority Act
R.I. Public Laws 1993, Ch. 218

North South Center Act
P.R. Laws Ann. 1954, Title 3, § 67 et seq.

North South Center Act of 1991
See Dante B. Fascell North-South Center Act of 1991
Oct. 28, 1991, P.L. 102-138, 22 U.S. Code § 2075

North Tarrytown Parking Authority Act
N.Y. Public Authorities Law (Consol. Laws Ch. 43A) § 1600aa et seq.

North Tonawanda City Court Act
N.Y. Laws 1942, Ch. 907

North Tonawanda Parking Authority Act
N.Y. Public Authorities Law (Consol. Laws Ch. 43A) § 1601 et seq.

North Valley Stream Library Services Act
N.Y. Laws 1975, Ch. 592

Northampton County Law Enforcement Officers' Relief Act
N.C. Laws 1953, Ch. 1258

Northampton Public Works Building Loan Act
Mass. Acts 1953, Ch. 598

Northampton Sewerage Treatment Loan Act
Mass. Acts 1955, Ch. 462

Northeast Georgia Surface and Air Transportation Commission Act
Ga. Laws 1991, p. 4596

Northeast Interstate Compact on Dairy Pricing
Conn. Public Acts 1993, p. 911, No. 320
Mass. Laws 1993, Ch. 370
N.H. Rev. Stat. 1955, 184-A:1
N.Y. Agriculture and Markets Law (Consol. Laws Ch. 69) §§ 258KK to 258NN
R.I. Gen. Laws 1956, 5-48.1-1 et seq.
Vt. Stat. Ann., Title 6, § 1801 et seq.

Northeast Interstate Low-level Radioactive Waste Management Compact
Jan. 15, 1986, P.L. 99-240, 99 Stat. 1909

Northeast Interstate Low-Level Radioactive Waste Management Compact Act
Conn. Gen. Stat. Ann., 22a-161 et seq.
Del. Code of 1974, Title 7, §§ 8001, 8002
Md. Ann. Code 1974, Art. HE, § 7-301 et seq.
N.J. Stat. Ann. 32:31-1 et seq.

Northeast Maryland Waste Disposal Authority Act
Md. Ann. Code 1974, Art. NR, § 3-901 et seq.

Northeast Minnesota Economic Protection Fund Act
Minn. Stat. Ann., 298.291 et seq.

Northeast Rail Service Act of 1981
Aug. 13, 1981, P.L. 97-35, 45 U.S. Code § 1101 et seq.
Dec. 21, 1982, P.L. 97-377, 45 U.S. Code § 591 nt.
April 7, 1986, P.L. 99-272, 45 U.S. Code §§ 1111, 1111 nt.
Oct. 21, 1986, P.L. 99-509, 45 U.S. Code §§ 1105, 1107, 1110, 1114 to 1116
Dec. 29, 1995, P.L. 104-88, 45 U.S. Code § 1112
Oct. 19, 1996, P.L. 104-317, 45 U.S. Code §§ 1104, 1105
Dec. 2, 1997, P.L. 105-134, 45 U.S. Code § 1111

Northeastern Expressway Act
Md. Laws 1956, Ex. Sess., Ch. 437

Northeastern Extension Act (Pennsylvania Turnpike)

Pa. Purdon's Stat., Title 36, § 660.1 et seq.

Northeastern Forest Fire Protection Compact

Vt. Stat. Ann., Title 10, § 2501 et seq.

Northeastern Illinois Metropolitan Area Planning Act

Ill. Rev. Stat. 1991, Ch. 85, § 1101 et seq.

Northeastern Illinois University Law

Ill. Comp. Stat. 1992, Ch. 110, § 680/25-1 et seq.

Northeastern Illinois University Revenue Bond Law

Ill. Comp. Stat. 1992, Ch. 110, § 681/26-1 et seq.

Northeastern Interstate Forest Fire Protection Compact Act

Conn. Gen. Stat. Ann., § 23-53 et seq.

N.H. Rev. Stat. 1955, 226:1 et seq.

Vt. Stat. Ann., Title 10, § 2501 et seq.

Northeastern Land and Water Resources Compact Act

N.H. Rev. Stat. 1955, 489-A:1

Northeastern Oklahoma Pasture Improvement Act

Okla. Stat. Ann., Title 70, § 3417

Northeastern Resources Compact Act

N.H. Rev. Stat. 1955, 489-A:1 et seq.

Northeastern Water and Land Interstate Forest Fire Protection Compact Act

N.H. Rev. Stat. 1955, 226:1 et seq.

Northeastern Water and Related Land Resources Compact

Conn. Gen. Stat. Ann., § 25-120 et seq.

R.I. Gen. Laws 1956, 46-17-2 et seq.

Northern Cheyenne Indian Reserved Water Rights Settlement Act of 1992

Sept. 30, 1992, P.L. 102-374, 106 Stat. 1186

May 31, 1994, P.L. 103-263, 108 Stat. 707

Northern Great Plains Rural Development Act

Aug. 26, 1994, P.L. 103-318, 7 U.S. Code § 2661 nt.

Oct. 19, 1996, P.L. 104-327, 7 U.S. Code § 2661 nt.

Northern Illinois University Law

Ill. Comp. Stat. 1992, Ch. 110, § 685/30-1 et seq.

Northern Illinois University Name Change Act

Ill. Rev. Stat. 1991, Ch. 144, §§ 799, 800

Northern Illinois University Objects Act

Ill. Rev. Stat. 1991, Ch. 144, § 802.01 et seq.

Northern Illinois University Revenue Bond Law

Ill. Comp. Stat. 1992, Ch. 110, § 686/31-1 et seq.

Northern Indiana Hospital Act

Ind. Code Ann., 16-14-20-1 et seq.

Northern New England Medical Needs Compact Act

Vt. Acts 1957, No. 154

Northern Pacific Adjustment Acts

July 1, 1898, Ch. 546, 30 Stat. 597

March 2, 1901, Ch. 807, 31 Stat. 950

May 17, 1906, Ch. 2470, 34 Stat. 197

Feb. 27, 1917, Ch. 135, 39 Stat. 946

Northern Pacific Halibut Act of 1937

June 7, 1924, Ch. 345, 43 Stat. 648

May 2, 1932, Ch. 154, 47 Stat. 142

June 28, 1937, Ch. 392, 50 Stat. 325, 16 U.S. Code §§ 772 to 772i

Aug. 8, 1953, Ch. 382, 67 Stat. 494, 16 U.S. Code § 777a, 772a nt.

Oct. 1, 1965, P.L. 89-233, 79 Stat. 902, 16 U.S. Code § 772j

May 17, 1982, P.L. 97-196, 16 U.S. Code §§ 772 et seq.

Northern Pacific Halibut Act of 1982

   May 17, 1982, P.L. 97-176, 16 U.S. Code §§ 773 et seq.

   March 9, 1992, P.L. 102-251, 16 U.S. Code §§ 773, 773e

Northern Virginia Recreation and Cultural Authority Act

   Va. Acts 1968, Ch. 676

Northern Worcester County Welfare District Loan Act

   Mass. Acts 1958, Ch. 653

Northwest Atlantic Fisheries Act of 1950

   Sept. 27, 1950, Ch. 1054, 64 Stat. 1067, 16 U.S. Code §§ 981 to 991

   July 24, 1968, P.L. 90-420, 82 Stat. 419, 16 U.S. Code §§ 981, 983

   Aug. 11, 1971, P.L. 92-87, 85 Stat. 310, 16 U.S. Code §§ 981, 982 , 984 to 986, 988 to 991

   July 10, 1974, P.L. 93-339, 88 Stat. 293, 16 U.S. Code §§ 981, 986, 983, 988

Northwest Atlantic Fisheries Convention Act of 1995

   Nov. 3, 1995, P.L. 104-43, Title II, 16 U.S. Code § 5601 et seq.

   Nov. 13, 1998, P.L. 105-384, 16 U.S. Code §§ 5606, 5608 to 5612

Northwest Interstate Compact on Low-Level Radioactive Waste Management

   Jan. 15, 1986, P.L. 99-240, 99 Stat. 1860

Northwest Interstate Compact on Low-Level Radioactive Waste Management Act

   Alaska Stat. 1962, §§ 46.45.010, 46.45.020

   Haw. Rev. Stat. Ann., § 339K-1 et seq.

   Ida. Code 1947, 39-3025

   Mont. Code Ann., 1991, 75-3-501, 75-3-502

   Ore. Rev. Stat., 469.930

   Wash. Rev. Code Ann., 43.145.010

Northwest Pacific Electric Power Planning and Conservation Act

   Sept. 30, 1996, P.L. 104-206, 16 U.S. Code § 839b

Northwest School Construction Loan Act (Leominster)

   Mass. Acts 1956, Ch. 673

Northwest Straits Marine Conservation Initiative Act

   Nov. 13, 1998, P.L. 105-384, Title IV, 112 Stat. 3458

Northwest Territory Ordinance of 1787

   July 13, 1787, 1 Stat. 51

Northwestern Extension Act (Pennsylvania Turnpike)

   Pa. Purdon's Stat., Title 36, § 668.1 et seq.

Norton Act (Juvenile Court)

   D.C. Code 1961, § 11-902 et seq.

Norton Edwards Act (Highway Code)

   Ohio Rev. Code 1953, 5501.02 et seq.

Norwegian and Swedish Friendship Treaty (1852)

   Haw. Session Laws 1855, p. 64, April 5, 1855

Norwich City Court Act

   N.Y. Laws 1952, Ch. 812

Norwood Act (Indeterminate Sentences)

   Ohio Rev. Code 1953, 5145.01

Not a Drop Law

   Tex. Alcoholic Beverage Code, § 106.04

Not for Profit Corporation Act

   Fla. Stat. Ann., 617.001 et seq.

   Mo. Rev. Stat., 355.010 et seq.

Not for Profit Corporation Act (General)

   Ill. Rev. Stat. 1991, Ch. 32, § 101.01 et seq.

Not-for-Profit Corporation Law

   See also Nonprofit Corporation Act

   Fla. Stat. Ann., 617.001 et seq.

   N.Y. Consol. Laws Ch. 35

Not-for-Profit Corporations Merger Act

   Ill. Rev. Stat. 1991, Ch. 32, § 188.90 et seq.

Not-for-Profit Corporations Special Charter Act
Ill. Rev. Stat. 1991, Ch. 32, § 197.9 et seq.

Not-For-Profit Dispute Resolution Center Act
Ill. Rev. Stat. 1991, Ch. 37, § 851 et seq.

Notaries Public Act
See also Uniform Law on Notarial Acts
See also Uniform Notary Act
See Uniform Notary Act
N.Y. Executive Law 1951 (Consol. Laws Ch. 18) § 130 et seq.

Notaries Public Expense Act of 1955
July 11, 1956, Ch. 554, 70 Stat. 519 (See 5 U.S. Code § 5945)

Notaries Public Reform Act
Utah Code Ann. 1953, 46-1-1 et seq.

Note Stamp Act
Tex. General & Special Laws 44th Leg., 1936, 3rd C.S., p. 2040, Ch. 495, Art. 4, § 9

Notice Act (Claims against Municipality)
Pa. Cons. Stat., Title 42, § 5522

Notice Act (Public Conveyance)
Ill. Rev. Stat. 1991, Ch. 100, §§ 30, 31

Notice Act (Transfer of Vehicles)
Cal. Vehicle Code 1959, § 5900 et seq.

Notice by Publication Act
Ill. Rev. Stat. 1991, Ch. 100, § 0.01 et seq.

Notice Filing Act (Assignment of Accounts Receivable)
La. Rev. Stat. Ann., 9:3101 et seq.
N.C. Gen. Stat. 1943, § 44-78 et seq.
Ohio Rev. Code 1953, 1309.21, 1309.38, 1309.40
Tenn. Public Acts 1959, Ch. 114, § 2

Notice of Abortion Act (Parental)
Del. Code of 1974, Title 24, § 1780 et seq.
Ill. Rev. Stat. 1991, Ch. 38, § 81-61 et seq.
Mont. Code Ann., 50-20-201 et seq.

Notice of Claim Act (Ice and Snow)
Ind. Code 1971, 18-2-2-1

Notice of Claim Act (Municipalities)
Minn. Stat. Ann., 466.01 et seq.

Notice of Injury Act (Railroads)
Wis. Stat. 1977, 839.19, Subsec. 8

Notice of Prepayment of Federally Subsidized Mortgage Act
Ill. Rev. Stat. 1991, Ch. 67 1/2, § 901 et seq.

Notice to Lessees Numbered 5 Gas Royalty Act of 1987
Jan. 6, 1987, P.L. 100-234, 101 Stat. 1719

Notice to Parents Act
Fla. Stat. Ann., 925.07

Notices Act
Ill. Rev. Stat. 1991, Ch. 100

Notification Act (Convicted Persons)
N.J. Stat. Ann., 2A:169A-6

Notification Act (Emergency Response)
Okla. Stat. Ann., Title 63, § 689 et seq.

Notification Act (Parental)
Ga. Code Ann., 15-11 110 et seq.

Notification Act (Trial of Minor)
Fla. Stat. Ann., 925.07

Notification System Act (One-Call)
Neb. Rev. Stat. 1943, 76-2301 et seq.

Notla Water Authority Act
Ga. Laws 1972, p. 3385

N.O.V. (Non obstante veredicto)
Pa. Cons. Stat., Title 42, § 5105

Noxious Weed Control Act
Ark. Acts 1925, p. 786, No. 262
Colo. Rev. Stat., 35-5.5-101 et seq.
Ill. Rev. Stat. 1991, Ch. 5, § 951 et seq.
Minn. Stat. Ann., 18.171 et seq.
Minn. Stat. 1986, 18.76 to 18.88
N.D. Cent. Code 63-01.1-01 et seq.

Neb. Rev. Stat. 1943, 2-945.01 et seq.
N.M. Stat. Ann., 76-7-1 et seq.
Pa. Purdon's Stat., Title 3, § 255.1 et seq.
S.C. Code Ann. 1976, § 46-23-10 et seq.
S.D. Codified Laws 1967, 31-31-1 et seq.
Utah Code Ann. 1953, 4-17-1 et seq.
Va. Code 1950, § 3.1-296.11 et seq.
W. Va. Code 1966, § 19-12D-1 et seq.

Noxious Weed Management Act
N.M. Stat. Ann., 76-7D-1 to 76-7D-6

Noxious Weed Seed Free Forage Act
Mont. Code Ann., 80-7-901 et seq.

Nuclear Act
Fla. Stat. Ann., 377.71 et seq.

Nuclear Activity Consent Law
Me. Rev. Stat. Ann. 1964, Title 38, § 1451 et
seq.

Nuclear Advisory Commission Act
Ga. Code 1933, 43-1001 et seq.

Nuclear Advisory Council Act
S.C. Code Ann. 1976, § 13-7-810 et seq.

Nuclear and Space Authority Act
La. Rev. Stat. Ann., 51:1351 et seq.

Nuclear Compact Act
Mont. Code Ann., 1991, 90-5-201
S.C. Code Ann. 1976, § 13-7-410 et seq.

Nuclear Compact Act (Interstate)
Alaska Stat. 1962, §§ 46.45.010, 46.45.020

Nuclear Compact Act (Midwest)
See Midwest Nuclear Compact Act
Ind. Code 1976, 13-5-8-1 et seq.
Iowa Code Ann., 8B.1 et seq.
Iowa Code Ann., 15D.1 et seq.
Kan. Stat. Ann., 48-2001 et seq.
Neb. Laws. 1972, p. 567
Ohio Rev. Code 1953, 122.13

Nuclear Compact Act (Southern Interstate)
See Southern Interstate Nuclear Compact
Act

Nuclear Compact Act (Western Interstate)
See Western Interstate Nuclear Compact Act

Nuclear Decommissioning Financing Act
Me. Rev. Stat. Ann. 1964, Title 135-A,
§ 4351 et seq.

Nuclear Emergency Planning Act
Me. Rev. Stat. Ann. 1964, Title 37-B, § 951
et seq.

Nuclear Energy Acts
Kan. Stat. Ann., 48-1601 et seq.
Ky. Rev. Stat. 1971, 278.600 et seq.
La. Rev. Stat. Ann., 30:1101 et seq.

Nuclear Energy Development and Radiation Control Act
Kan. Stat. Ann., 48-1601 et seq.

Nuclear Energy Education Act
Ill. Rev. Stat. 1991, Ch. 122, § 27-25 et seq.

Nuclear Facility Decommissioning Act
Cal. Public Utilites Code, § 8321 et seq.

Nuclear Facility Safety Act
Ill. Rev. Stat. 1991, Ch. 111 1/2, § 4351 et
seq.

Nuclear Fuel Act (Spent)
Ill. Rev. Stat. 1991, Ch. 111 1/2, § 230.20 et
seq.

Nuclear Materials Transportation Act
Colo. Rev. Stat., 40-2.2-101 et seq.

Nuclear Non-proliferation Act of 1978
March 10, 1978, P.L. 95-242, 22 U.S. Code
§§ 3201 et seq., 3201 nt.; 42 U.S. Code
§ 2074 et seq.
Nov. 14, 1986, P.L. 99-661, 22 U.S. Code
§ 3282
April 30, 1994, P.L. 103-236, 22 U.S. Code
§ 3281; 42 U.S. Code § 2139a
Nov. 2, 1994, P.L. 103-437, 22 U.S. Code
§ 3282; 42 U.S. Code § 2153c
Oct. 21, 1998, P.L. 105-277, 22 U.S. Code
§§ 3203, 3222, 3282; 42 U.S. Code
§§ 2139a, 2156a, 2160a

Nuclear Pharmacy Law
Ga. Code Ann., 26-4-130 et seq.

Nuclear Power and Waste Disposal Voter Approval and Legislative Certification Act
Mass. Acts 1982, Ch. 503, § 1 et seq.

Nuclear Powerplant Communities Information Act
Cal. Public Utilities Code, § 8301 et seq.

Nuclear Proliferation Prevention Act of 1994
April 30, 1994, P.L. 103-236, 22 U.S. Code § 3201 nt.
July 21, 1996, P.L. 104-164, 22 U.S. Code § 3201 nt.

Nuclear Regulation Act
Mont. Code Ann., 1991, 75-3-101 et seq.

Nuclear Regulatory Commission Authorization Act for Fiscal Year 1979
June 30, 1980, P.L. 96-295, 42 U.S. Code § 2051 nt.

Nuclear Safety Education Assistance Act
Ill. Rev. Stat. 1991, Ch. 144, § 2501 et seq.

Nuclear Safety Emergency Preparedness Act
Kan. Stat. Ann., 48-1601 et seq.

Nuclear Safety Preparedness Act
Ill. Rev. Stat. 1991, Ch. 111 1/2, § 4301 et seq.

Nuclear Safety Research, Development, and Demonstration Act of 1980
Dec. 22, 1980, P.L. 96-567, 42 U.S. Code § 9701 nt.
Dec. 21, 1995, P.L. 104-66, 42 U.S. Code § 9707

Nuclear Waste Activity Law
Me. Rev. Stat. Ann. 1964, Title 38, § 1451 et seq.

Nuclear Waste Interstate Compact Act
Ill. Rev. Stat. 1991, Ch. 111 1/2, § 230.50 et seq.

Nuclear Waste Policy Act of 1982
Jan. 7, 1983, P.L. 97-425, 42 U.S. Code §§ 10101 et seq., 10101 nt.
Oct. 18, 1988, P.L. 100-507, 42 U.S. Code §§ 10163, 10242
Oct. 24, 1992, P.L. 102-486, 42 U.S. Code §§ 10241, 10250
Nov. 2, 1994, P.L. 103-437, 42 U.S. Code § 10198
Dec. 21, 1995, P.L. 104-66, 42 U.S. Code §§ 10137, 10204, 10224
Oct. 7, 1998, P.L. 105-245, 42 U.S. Code § 10204

Nuclear Waste Policy Amendments Act of 1987
Dec. 22, 1987, P.L. 100-203, as Incorporated in Act Dec. 22, 1987, P.L. 100 -202, 42 U.S. Code § 10101 nt.

Nuclear Weapons Freeze Act
D.C. Code Ann., § 6-1511 et seq.

Nudism Act
Tenn. Code Ann., Superseded Vol., 39-3009

Nudist Colony Act
Ky. Rev. Stat. 1971, 232.010 et seq.

Nuisance Abatement Act
Mich. Comp. Laws Ann., 600.3801 et seq., 600.2940
N.H. Rev. Stat. 1955, 544:1 et seq.
N.Y. Adm. Code '85, § 7-702
R.I. Gen. Laws 1956, 10-1-1 et seq.
Tenn. Code Ann., 29-3-101 et seq.
Wash. Rev. Code Ann., 7.48.010 et seq.

Nuisance Act
Cal. Civil Code § 3479 et seq.
Me. Rev. Stat. Ann. 1964, Title 17, § 2741 et seq.
Mont. Code Ann., 1991, 27-30-101 et seq.

Nuisance Act (Criminal)
Cal. Penal Code § 370 et seq.
N.J. Rev. Ann. 2C:33-12 et seq.
N.J. Rev. Stat. 1937, 2A:130-1 et seq.
Ohio Rev. Code 1953, 3767.01 et seq.
Ore. Rev. Stat., 161.310
R.I. Gen. Laws 1956, 11-30-1 et seq.

Tenn. Code Ann., 39-17-301 et seq.

Wash. Rev. Code Ann., 9.66.010 et seq.

Nuisance Act (Public Health)

N.J. Stat. Ann., 26:3B-1 et seq.

Ohio Rev. Code 1953, 3707.01 et seq.

Nuisance Act (Public)

Colo. Rev. Stat., 16-13-301 et seq.

Nuisance Act (Sarasota County)

Fla. Special Laws 1953, Ch. 29527

Nuisance Act (Streets)

Ohio Rev. Code 1953, 723.01

Nuisance Bird Act

Md. Ann. Code 1974, Art. AG, § 5-801 et seq.

Va. Code 1950, § 3.1-1011 et seq.

Nuisance Code Enforcement Act (Local Government)

Ky. Rev. Stat. 1971, 82.700c et seq.

Nuisance Debt Act (Forest Fires)

N.M. Stat. Ann., 30-32-1 et seq.

Nuisance Elimination Act

D.C. Code Ann., §§ 5-604, 5-606, 6-1102

Nuisance Law (Drugs)

Pa. Cons. Stat., Title 42, § 8381 et seq.

Nuisance Species Prevention and Control Act (Aquatic)

Cal. Fish and Game Code 1957, § 6430 et seq.

Nuisance Tax Extension Act

June 29, 1937, Ch. 402, 50 Stat. 358

Numbering Act (Motorboats)

Ga. Code Ann., 52-7-1 et seq.

Nunan Allen Act (Milk Control)

N.Y. Agriculture and Markets Law (Consol. Laws Ch. 69) § 258k, 258m

Nurse Agency Licensing Act

Ill. Rev. Stat. 1991, Ch. 111, § 951 et seq.

Nurse Aid Resident Abuse Prevention Training Act

Pa. Purdon's Stat., Title 63, § 671 et seq.

Nurse Anesthetists Act

Cal. Business and Professions Code § 2825 et seq.

Nurse Education Amendments of 1985

Aug. 16, 1985, P.L. 99-92, 15 U.S. Code § 1333, 42 U.S. Code §§ 201 nt., 296k to 296m, 297 to 297e, 298, 298b-5

Nurse Education and Practice Improvement Amendments of 1992

Oct. 6, 1992, P.L. 102-391, 22 U.S. Code § 2796

Oct. 13, 1992, P.L. 102-408, 42 U.S. Code § 201 nt.

Nurse Good Samaritan Law

N.Y. Education Law 1947 (Consol. Laws Ch. 16, § 6909, Subd. 1

Nurse Midwife Practice Act

Utah Code Ann. 1953, 58-44a-101 et seq.

Nurse Midwifery Act

Ark. Code Ann. 1987, 17-86-501 et seq.

Okla. Stat. Ann., Title 59, § 577.1 et seq.

Nurse Practice Act

Colo. Rev. Stat., 12-38-101 et seq.

Fla. Stat. Ann., 464.001 et seq.

Ga. Code Ann., 43-26-1 et seq.

Md. Ann. Code 1974, Art. HO, § 8-101 et seq.

Minn. Stat. Ann., 148.171 et seq.

Neb. Laws 1995, L.B. 563

N.M. Stat. Ann., 61-23-1

Utah Code Ann. 1953, 58-31-1 et seq.

Nurse Practitioner Act

Neb. Rev. Stat. 1943, 71-1704 et seq.

Nurse Practitioner Prescriptive Practice Act

Utah Code Ann. 1953 Miscellaneous Superseded Code Provisions, 58-31a-1 et seq.

Nurse Practitioner/Clinical Nurse Specialist Certification Act
N.J. Stat. Ann., 40:20-10 et seq.

Nurse Practitioners Pilot Project Act
Utah Laws 1979, Ch. 20

Nurse Training Act of 1964
Sept. 4, 1964, P.L. 88-581, 78 Stat. 908, 33 U.S. Code § 763c nt.; 42 U.S. Code §§ 201 nt., 211a nt., 212a nt., 222 nt., 291c, 291o, 293, 293a, 293e, 293h, 296 to 298b

Nurse Training Act of 1971
Nov. 18, 1971, P.L. 92-158, 85 Stat. 465, 42 U.S. Code § 296 nt.

Nurse Training Act of 1975
Nov. 9, 1978, P.L. 95-623, 42 U.S. Code § 296 nt.

Nurse Training Amendments of 1979
Sept. 29, 1979, P.L. 96-76, 42 U.S. Code §§ 201 nt., 296, 296 nt. , 296d, 296e, 296k to 296m, 297 to 297c, 297e, 297j, 297j nt., 297-1

Nursery Act
Cal. Public Resources Code §§ 4351,4681 et seq.
Colo. Rev. Stat., 35-26-101 et seq.
Fla. Stat. Ann., 581.011 et seq.
Ky. Rev. Stat. 1971, 249.010 et seq.
Mich. Comp. Laws Ann., 286.201 et seq.
Minn. Stat. Ann., 89.35 et seq.
N.D. Cent. Code 4-21.1-01 et seq.
Ore. Rev. Stat. 1989, 571.005 et seq.
R.I. Gen. Laws 1956, 2-18.1-1 et seq.
Utah Code Ann. 1953, 4-15-1 et seq.
Wash. Rev. Code Ann., 15.13.250 et seq.

Nursery Fraud Act
Ark. Code Ann. 1987, 2-21-101 et seq.

Nursery Stock Inspection Act
Ohio Rev. Code 1953, 927.59 et seq.
Wash. Rev. Code Ann., 15.14.010 et seq.

Nursery Stock Law
Colo. Rev. Stat. 35-26-101 et seq.

Nursery Stock Lien Act
Ore. Rev. Stat., 87.358
Wash. Rev. Code Ann., 60.20.010 et seq.

Nursery Stock Quarantine Act
Aug. 20, 1912, Ch. 308, 37 Stat. 315, 7 U.S. Code §§ 151 to 154, 156 to 164a, 167; 46 U.S. Code §§ 103, 106
Jan. 8, 1983, P.L. 97-432, 7 U.S. Code §§ 159 to 160

Nurses Act
Mich. Comp. Laws Ann., 333.17201 et seq.

Nurses Licensing Act
Md. Ann. Code 1974, Art. HO, § 8-301 et seq.

Nurses Licensing Act (Practical)
D.C. Code Ann., § 2-1702.1 et seq.
Pa. Purdon's Stat., Title 63, § 651 et seq.
Wash. Rev. Code 1976, 18.78.003 et seq.
W. Va. Code 1966, § 30-7A-1 et seq.

Nurse's Lien Act
Mont. Code Ann., 1991, 71-3-1111 et seq.

Nurses Practice Act
Cal. Business and Professions Code § 2700 et seq.
Colo. Rev. Stat. 12-38-101 et seq.
Fla. Stat. Ann., 464.001 et seq.
Ga. Code Ann., 43-26-1 et seq.
Haw. Rev. Stat. Ann., § 457-1 et seq.
Ill. Rev. Stat. 1991, Ch. 111, § 3501 et seq.
Ind. Code Ann., 25-23-1-1 et seq.
Iowa Code 1983, 152.1 et seq.
Kan. Stat. Ann., 65-1130 et seq.
Md. Ann. Code 1974, Art. HO, § 8-101 et seq.
Mich. Comp. Laws 1970, 338.1151 et seq.
Miss. Code Ann. 1972, § 73-15-1 et seq.
Mo. Rev. Stat., 335.011 et seq.
Mont. Code Ann., 1991, 37-8-101 et seq.
N.D. Cent. Code 43-12.1-01 et seq.
Neb. Rev. Stat. 1943, 71-1, 132.04 et seq.
Nev. Rev. Stat. 1979 Reprint, 632.010 et seq.
N.H. Rev. Stat. 1955, 326B:1 et seq.
N.M. Stat. Ann., 61-3-1 et seq.

N.Y. Education Law 1947 (Consol. Laws Ch. 16) § 6900 et seq.

Okla. Stat. Ann., Title 59, § 567.1 et seq.

R.I. Gen. Laws 1956, 5-34-1 et seq.

S.C. Code Ann. 1976, § 40-33-10 et seq.

S.D. Codified Laws 1967, 36-9-1 et seq.

Utah Code Ann. 1953, 58-31-1 et seq.

Vt. Stat. Ann. Title 26, § 1551 et seq.

Wis. Stat. Ann., 441.01 et seq.

Wyo. Stat. Ann., § 33-21-119 et seq.

Nurses Registration Act

D.C. Code Ann., § 2-1701.1 et seq.

Mass. Gen. Laws Ann., 112:74 et seq.

Md. Ann. Code 1974, Art. HO, § 8-101 et seq.

N.Y. Education Law 1947 (Consol. Laws Ch. 16) § 690 et seq.

Pa. Purdon's Stat., Title 63, § 211 et seq.

Wash. Rev. Code Ann., 18.88.005 et seq.

W. Va. Code 1966, § 30-7-1 et seq.

Nurses' Registry Act

Cal. Business and Professions Code § 9890 et seq.

Nurses Training Act

June 15, 1943, Ch. 126, 57 Stat. 153

Nursing and Convalescent Homes Licensing Act

Tex. Health and Safety Code, § 242.001 et seq.

Nursing Corporations Act

La. Rev. Stat. Ann., 12:1071 et seq.

Nursing Dispensing Act

S.C. Code Ann. 1976, § 40-33-30 et seq.

Nursing Education Act

Neb. Rev. Stat. 1943, 71-1, 132.43 et seq.

Nursing Education and Practice Improvement Act of 1998

Nov. 13, 1998, P.L. 105-392, Subtitle B, 112 Stat. 3562, 42 U.S. Code § 201 nt.

Nursing Education Scholarship Law

Ill. Rev. Stat. 1991, Ch. 144, § 2751 et seq.

Nursing Facilities Administrators Licensure Act

Tex. Rev. Civ. Stat., Art. 4512q

Nursing Facility Assessment Act

Utah Code Ann. 1953, 26-35-101 et seq.

Nursing Facility Provider Assessment Act

R.I. Gen. Laws 1956, 44-51-1 et seq.

Nursing Home Act

Del. Code of 1974, Title 24, § 5200 et seq.

Fla. Stat. Ann., 400.011 et seq.

Ky. Rev. Stat. 1971, 216.750 et seq.

Mo. Rev. Stat., 198.003 et seq.

Neb. Rev. Stat. 1943, 71-6008 et seq.

S.C. Code Ann. 1976, § 44-7-80 et seq.

Nursing Home Act (State and Veterans)

Colo. Rev. Stat., 26-12-101 et seq.

Nursing Home Act (Veterans')

Fla. Stat. Ann., 296.31 et seq.

Nursing Home Administration Act

S.D. Codified Laws 1967, 36-28-13 et seq.

Nursing Home Administration Licensing and Disciplinary Act

Ill. Rev. Stat. 1991, Ch. 111, § 3651 et seq.

Nursing Home Administration Registration Act

Mass. Gen. Laws Ann., 112:108 et seq.

Nursing Home Administrators Act

Ark. Code Ann. 1987, 20-10-101 et seq.

Cal. Business and Professions Code § 3901 et seq.

Del. Code of 1974, Title 16, § 1201 et seq.

Ga. Code Ann., 43-27-1 et seq.

Haw. Rev. Stat. Ann., § 457B-1 et seq.

Ill. Rev. Stat. 1991, Ch. 111, § 3651 et seq.

Ky. Rev. Stat. 1971, 216A.010 et seq.

Md. Ann. Code 1974, Art. HO, § 9-101 et seq.

Miss. Code Ann. 1972, § 73-17-1 et seq.

N.C. Gen. Stat. 1943, § 90-275.1 et seq.

N.D. Cent. Code 43-34-01 et seq.

N.M. Stat. Ann., 61-13-1 et seq.

Continued

S.C. Code Ann. 1976, § 40-35-10 et seq.

Wash. Rev. Code Ann., 18.52.010 et seq.

Nursing Home Administrators Licensure Act

Pa. Purdon's Stat., Title 63, § 1101 et seq.

Tex. Rev. Civ. Stat., Art. 4442d

Nursing Home Advisory Council Act

Neb. Rev. Stat. 1943, 71-6043 et seq.

Nursing Home Auditing and Cost Reimbursement Act

Wash. Rev. Code Ann., 74.46.010 et seq.

Nursing Home Care Act

Ill. Rev. Stat. 1991, Ch. 1111/2, § 4151-101 et seq.

Okla. Stat. Ann., Title 63, § 1-1901 et seq.

Nursing Home Companies Act

N.Y. Public Health Law 1953 (Consol. Laws Ch. 45) § 2850 et seq.

Nursing Home District Act

Mo. Rev. Stat., 198.200 et seq.

Nursing Home Licensing Act

Ind. Code Ann., 16-10-2.5-1 et seq.

Mich. Comp. Laws Ann., 333.21701 et seq., 333.21301 et seq.

Vt. Stat. Ann., Title 18, § 2001 et seq.

Wis. Stat. 1981, 50.01 et seq.

Nursing Home Loan Agency Law

Pa. Purdon's Stat., Title 62, § 1521.101 et seq.

Nursing Home Patients' Bill of Rights

N.Y. Public Health Law 1953 (Consol. Laws Ch. 45) § 2803c

Nursing Home Permits-Medicaid Act

S.C. Code Ann. 1976, § 44-7-80 et seq.

Nursing Home Reform Act

Fla. Stat. Ann., 233.0671, 400.22, 400.071, 400.17 to 400.191, 400.23, 400.29, 400.504, 400.268, 400.601 to 413.605

Nursing Home Resident Protection Amendments of 1999

March 25, 1999, P.L. 106-4, 113 Stat. 7, 42 U. S. Code § 1305 nt.

Nursing Home Residents Act (Ombudsman for)

N.Y. Public Health Law 1953 (Consol. Laws Ch. 45) § 2803c, Subd. 3

N.Y. Social Services Law (Consol. Laws Ch. 55) § 461a, Subd. 3

Nursing Home without Walls Program

N.Y. Public Health Law 1953 (Consol. Laws Ch. 45) § 3600 et seq.

Nursing Homes, Long-Term Care, Health, Safety, and Security Act

Cal. Health and Safety Code § 1417 et seq.

Nursing in Expanded Roles Act

Neb. Rev. Stat. 1943, 71-1704 et seq.

Nursing Incentive Act

Neb. Rev. Stat. 1943, 71-1766 et seq.

Nursing Law (Professional)

Pa. Purdon's Stat., Title 63, § 211 et seq.

Nursing License Revocation Act

N.Y. Education Law 1971 (Consol. Laws Ch. 16) § 6510

Nursing Limited Prescriptive Authority Demonstration Act

Ga. Code Ann., 43-26-50 et seq.

Nursing or Personal Care Home Accountability Act

R.I. Gen. Laws, 1956, 23-17.2-1 et seq.

Nursing Pool Licensure Act

N.C. Gen. Stat. 1943, § 131E-154.1 et seq.

Nursing Practice Act

Cal. Business and Professions Code § 2700 et seq.

Md. Ann. Code 1974, Art. HO, § 8-101 et seq.

Miss. Code Ann. 1972, § 73-15-1 et seq.

Mo. Rev. Stat., 335.011 et seq.

Okla. Stat. Ann., Title 59, § 567.1 et seq.

Tex. Rev. Civ. Stat., Art. 4513 et seq.

Nursing Practice Regulation Act
P.R. Laws Ann. 1954, Title 20, § 203 et seq.

Nursing Shortage Reduction and Education Extension Act of 1988
Nov. 4, 1988, P.L. 100-607, 42 U.S. Code § 201 nt.

Nursing Student Loan Act
N.M. Stat. Ann., 21-22B-1 et seq.

Nursing Student Scholarship Program Act
Kan. Stat. Ann., 74-3291 et seq.

Nursing Training Facilities Construction Act
Va. Code 1950, § 32-391 et seq.

Nutrient Management Act
Pa. Purdon's Stat., Title 3, § 1701 et seq.

Nutrition Act
Mich. Comp. Laws Ann., 325.871 et seq.

Nutrition and Dietetics Practice Act
Fla. Stat. Ann., 468.501 et seq.
Ill. Rev. Stat. 1991, Ch. 111, § 8401-5 et seq.
La. Rev. Stat. Ann., 37:3081 et seq.
N.M. Stat. Ann., 61-7A-1 et seq.

Nutrition and Hydration for Incompetent Patients Act
Okla. Stat. Ann., Title 63, § 3080.1 et seq.

Nutrition Assistance Contingency Fund Act (Supplemental)
N.J. Stat. Ann., 26:1A-36.1 et seq.

Nutrition Improvement Act (Women's, Infants and Children)
Pa. Purdon's Stat., Title 62, § 2951 et seq.

Nutrition Labeling and Education Act Amendments of 1993
Aug. 13, 1993, P.L. 103-80, 21 U.S. Code § 301 nt.

Nutrition Labeling and Education Act of 1990
Nov. 8, 1990, P.L. 101-535, 21 U.S. Code § 301 nt.
Aug. 17, 1991, P.L. 102-108, 21 U.S. Code §§ 343, 343 nt.
Oct. 29, 1992, P.L. 102-571, 21 U.S. Code §§ 343 nt., 343-1 nt.

Nutrition Monitoring Development Act
Cal. Health and Safety Code, § 235 et seq.

Nutrition Program for the Elderly Act (McCarthy-Kennick)
Cal. Welfare and Institutions Code § 18325 et seq.

Nutrition/Dietetics Practice Act
Ala. Code 1975, § 34-34A-1 et seq.
La. Rev. Stat. Ann., 37:3081 et seq.
N.C. Gen. Stat. 1943, § 90-350 et seq.
R.I. Gen. Laws 1956, 5-64-1 et seq.

Nyack Parking Authority Act
N.Y. Public Authorities Law (Consol. Laws Ch. 43A) § 1622a et seq.

Nyberg Act (Beer Consumers Sales Tax)
Ark. Acts 1939, p. 758, No. 310

O

O and P Nonimmigrant Amendments of 1991
See Omnibus Budget Reconciliation Act
Dec. 12, 1991, P.L. 102-232, 8 U.S. Code
§ 1101 nt.

O'Brien Economy Act
N.Y. Laws 1932, Ex. Sess., Ch. 637

O'Dunne Act (Minimum Criminal Penalties)
Md. Ann. Code 1957, Art. 27, § 643

O'Hara Act (Athletic Contests Bribery)
D.C. Code 1973, § 22-1513

O'Hare IAP Air Reserve Station Retrocession Act
Ill. Comp. Stat. 1992, Ch. 5, § 544/1 et seq.

O'Johnson-Miller Act (Sewer Districts)
Ky. Acts 1962, Ch. 14

O'Mahoney-Ramspeck Act (Civil Service)
June 25, 1938, Ch. 678, 52 Stat. 1076

Oahu Railway Act
Haw. Session Laws 1888, Ch. 62

Oak Creek Act
Wis. Stat. Ann., 60.81

Oak Park, Aledo, Normal, Mason County, Jasper County, Brownstown Park District, Jo Davies County, Milford, Sheldon, and Katherine Dunham Civic Centers Act
Ill. Rev. Stat. 1991, Ch. 85, § 4500 et seq.

Oak Park Civic Center Law
Ill. Rev. Stat. 1991, Ch. 85 § 5401 et seq.

Oak Ridge Water and Sewage Authority Act
Ga. Laws 1991, p. 4310

Oakham School Building Loan Act
Mass. Acts 1950, Ch. 701

Oakland-San Francisco Bay Bridge Act
Cal. Streets and Highways Code § 30600 et seq.

Oath Act (Gubernatorial Appointee)
Ill. Rev. Stat. 1991, Ch. 101, §§ 100, 101

Oath of Allegiance Act (Teachers)
Mich. Comp. Laws Ann., 388.401 et seq.
Wash. Rev. Code 1951, Replaced Pages, 28A.67.020 et seq.

Oath of Office Acts
July 2, 1862, Ch. 128, 12 Stat. 502
July 11, 1868, Ch. 139, 15 Stat. 85

Oaths and Affirmations Act
Ill. Rev. Stat. 1991, Ch. 101, § 0.01 et seq.
Vt. Stat. Ann. 1959, Title 12, § 5801 et seq.
Wash. Rev. Code Ann., 5.28.010 et seq.

Ober Act (Subversive Activities)
Md. Ann. Code 1957, Superseded Vol., Art. 85A

Objective Parole Guidelines Act
Fla. Stat. Ann., 947.001 et seq.

Objects Act (Eastern Illinois University)
Ill. Rev. Stat. 1991, Ch. 144, § 702-01 et seq.

Objects Act (Illinois State University)
Ill. Rev. Stat. 1991, Ch. 144, § 502-01 et seq.

Objects Act (Northern Illinois University)
Ill. Rev. Stat. 1991, Ch. 144, § 802-01 et seq.

Objects Act (Southern Illinois University)
Ill. Rev. Stat. 1991, Ch. 144, § 601-9 et seq.

Objects Act (Western Illinois University)
Ill. Rev. Stat. 1989, Ch. 144, § 902-01 et seq.

Obligation Bonds for Refunding Act (Special)
S.C. Code Ann. 1976, § 11-15-600 et seq.

Obligations Act
N.Y. General Obligations Law (Consol. Laws, Ch. 24A)

Obscene and Harassing Communications Act
Ill. Comp. Stat. 1992, Ch. 720, § 135/0.01 et seq.

Obscene Literature Act
Mass. Gen. Laws. Ann., 272:28 et seq.
Mich. Comp. Laws Ann., 750.343 et seq.

Obscene Literature Commission Act
Okla. Stat. Ann., Title 21, § 1040.1 et seq.

Obscenity Act
S.C. Code Ann. 1976, § 16-15-250 et seq.

Obscenity Act (Comstock)
N.Y. Penal Law 1965 (Consol. Laws Ch. 40) §§ 235.05, 235.10

Obscenity Act (Minors)
Minn. Stat. Ann., 617.293, 617.294
N.Y. Penal Law 1965 (Consol. Laws Ch. 40) § 235.20 et seq.

Obscenity Act (Motion Pictures)
Md. Ann. Code 1957, Art. 66A, § 15

Obscenity Act (Telephone)
Miss. Code Ann. 1972, § 97-29-45

Obscenity Enforcement and Child Protection Act
Fla. Stat. Ann., 847.001, 847.012, 847.013, 847.0145, 847.0147

Obscenity Publications Act
Ala. Code 1975, § 13A-12-150 et seq.
Ariz. Rev. Stat. Ann., § 13-3501 et seq.
Ark. Stat. 1947, 41-3501 et seq.
Cal. Penal Code § 311 et seq.
Colo. Rev. Stat., 18-7-101 et seq.
Conn. Gen. Stat. Ann., § 53a-193 et seq.
Fla. Stat. Ann., 847.011 et seq.
Ida. Code 1947, 18-1513 et seq.
Ill. Rev. Stat. 1991, Ch. 38, § 11-20
Ind. Code Ann., 35-49-1-1 et seq.
Iowa Code Ann., 728.1 et seq.
Ky. Rev. Stat. 1971, 531.010 et seq.
La. Rev. Stat. Ann., 14:106
Md. Ann. Code 1957, Art. 27, § 417 et seq.

Miss. Code Ann. 1972, § 97-29-33 et seq., § 99-31-1 et seq.
Mo. Rev. Stat., 542.281 et seq.
Neb. Rev. Stat. 1943, 28-807 et seq.
N.J. Stat. Ann., 2C:14-4 et seq.
N.Y. Penal Law 1965 (Consol. Laws Ch. 40) § 235.00 et seq.
Ohio Rev. Code 1953, 2907.01 et seq.
Okla. Stat. Ann., Title 21, § 1040.11 et seq.
Ore. Rev. Stat., 167.060 et seq.
Pa. Cons. Stat., Title 18, § 5903
R.I. Gen. Laws 1956, 11-31-1 et seq.
S.C. Code Ann. 1976, § 16-15-250 et seq.
S.D. Codified Laws 1967, 22-24-1 et seq.
Tenn. Code Ann., 39-17-901 et seq.
Tex. Penal Code, § 43.21 et seq.
Utah Code Ann. 1953, 76-10-1201 et seq.
Va. Code 1950, § 18.2-372 et seq.
Wash. Rev. Code Ann., 9.68.015 et seq.
Wis. Stat. Ann., 944.20 et seq.

Observant Consumer Protection Law (Jewish Religious Articles)
N.Y. General Business Law (Consol. Laws Ch. 20) § 349a

Obstructed Crossing Act (Railroads)
Ind. Burns' 1933, 55-2016 et seq.

Obstructing Justice Act
Wash. Rev. Code Ann., 9.69.100 et seq.

Obstructing Public Passages Act
La. Rev. Stat. Ann., 14:100.1

Obstruction Act (Navigable Waters)
Ill. Rev. Stat. 1989, Ch. 19, § 47a et seq.

Obstruction and Resistance Act (Public Officers)
Ariz. Rev. Stat. Ann. § 13-2402
Okla. Stat. Ann., Title 21, § 540

Obstruction of Interstate Commerce Act
Aug. 10, 1917, Ch. 51, 40 Stat. 272

Obstruction Removal Act (Chicago Sanitary District)
Ill. Rev. Stat. 1989, Ch. 42, § 372-9 et seq.

Obstruction to Air Navigation Control Act
 Tex. Rev. Civ. Stat. 1974, Arts. 46i-1 et seq.

Obstructions and Drainage Act (Highway)
 S.C. Code Ann. 1976, § 57-7-210 et seq.

Ocala Minimum Housing Code
 Fla. Special Laws 1967, Ch. 67-1782

Occupancy Law (Recreational Vehicle Park)
 Cal. Civil Code § 799.20 et seq.

Occupant Act
 Ohio Rev. Code 1953, 5303.07 et seq.
 Tenn. Acts 1839-40, Ch. 62

Occupation Accreditation and Certification Act (Asbestos)
 Pa. 1990 Pamph. Laws, No. 194

Occupation Act (Nontraditional)
 Me. Rev. Stat. Ann. 1964, Title 26, § 2021 et seq.

Occupation and Use Tax Act (Automobile Renting)
 Ill. Comp. Stat. 1992, Ch. 35, §§ 155/1 to 155/4
 Ill. Rev. Stat. 1991, Ch. 120, § 1701 et seq.

Occupation Privilege Sales Tax Act
 Ga. Laws 1929, p. 103

Occupation Tax Act
 Alaska Stat. 1962, § 43.70.010 et seq.
 Ariz. Rev. Stat. Ann., § 23-401 et seq.
 Ind. Code Ann., 6-3.5-3-1 et seq.
 N.M. Stat. Ann., 3-38-3 et seq.

Occupation Tax Act (County Automobile Renting)
 Ill. Rev. Stat. 1991, Ch. 34, § 5-1032

Occupation Tax Act (Home Rule County Retailer's)
 Ill. Rev. Stat. 1989, Ch. 34, § 5-1006

Occupation Tax Act (Home Rule County Service)
 Ill. Rev. Stat. 1989, Ch. 34, § 5-1007

Occupation Tax Act (Hotel Operators')
 Ill. Comp. Stat. 1992, Ch. 35, §§ 145/1 to 145/10

Occupation Tax Act (Hotel Operators)
 Ill. Rev. Stat. 1991, Ch. 120, § 481b-31 et seq.

Occupation Tax Act (Municipal Automobile Renting)
 Ill. Rev. Stat. 1991, Ch. 24, § 8-11-8

Occupation Tax Act (Municipalities)
 Okla. Stat. Ann., Title 11, § 22-106

Occupation Tax Act (Ores)
 Minn. Stat. Ann., 298.01 et seq.

Occupation Tax Act (Retailers)
 Ill. Rev. Stat. 1991, Ch. 120, § 440 et seq.

Occupation Tax Act (Retailers')
 Ill. Comp. Stat. 1992, Ch. 35, § 120/1 et seq.

Occupation Tax Act (Service)
 Ill. Comp. Stat. 1992, Ch. 35, § 115/1 et seq.
 Ill. Rev. Stat. 1991, Ch. 120, § 439-101 et seq.

Occupation Tax Lien Act
 Neb. Rev. Stat. 1943, 21-312, 21-323

Occupational Accreditation and Certification Act (Asbestos)
 Pa. 1990 Pamph. Laws, No. 194

Occupational and Physical Therapy Practice Act
 Tenn. Code Ann., 63-13-101 et seq.

Occupational and Professional Licensing Act
 Utah Code Ann. 1953, 58-1-1 et seq.

Occupational and Professional Licensing Act (Division of)
 Utah Code Ann. 1953, 53-1-101 et seq.

Occupational Carcinogens Control Act
 Cal. Health and Safety Code § 24200 et seq.
 Cal. Labor Code, § 9000 et seq.

Occupational Certification Act (Private)
Conn. Gen. Stat. Ann., § 10-7a et seq.

Occupational Code
Mich. Comp. Laws Ann., 339.101 et seq.

Occupational Condition Reporting Act
Tex. Health and Safety Code, § 84.001 et seq.

Occupational Disease Act
Ala. Code 1975, § 25-5-140 et seq.
Ariz. Laws 1943, Ch. 26
Colo. Rev. Stat., 8-60-101 et seq.
Conn. Public Acts 1991, p. 1735, Ch. 138
Fla. Stat. Ann., 440.151
Ga. Code Ann., 34-9-280 et seq.
Ida. Code 1947, 72-437 et seq.
Ill. Rev. Stat. 1991, Ch. 48, § 172-36 et seq.
Ind. Code Ann., 22-3-7-1 et seq.
Iowa Code 1983, 85A.1 et seq.
Kan. Stat. Ann., 44-5a01 et seq.
Ky. Rev. Stat. 1971, 342.316
La. Rev. Stat. Ann., 23:1031.1
Md. Ann. Code 1974, Art. LE, § 9-502 et seq.
Me. Rev. Stat. Ann. 1964, Title 39, § 181 et seq.
Me. Rev. Stat. Ann. 1964, Title 39-A, §§ 601 to 615
Mich. Comp. Laws Ann., 418.401 et seq.
Minn. Stat. Ann., 176.66 et seq.
Mo. Rev. Stat., 292.010 et seq.
Mont. Code Ann., 1991, 39-72-101 et seq.
N.C. Gen. Stat. 1943, §§ 97-52 to 97-76
Nev. Rev. Stat. 1979 Reprint, 617.010 et seq.
N.J. Stat. Ann., 34:15-30 to 34:15-35
N.M. Stat. Ann., 52-3-1 et seq.
N.Y. Workmen's Compensation Law (Consol. Laws Ch. 67) § 37 et seq.
Ohio Rev. Code 1953, 4123.68 et seq.
Okla. Stat. Ann., Title 85, § 1.1 et seq.
Ore. Rev. Stat., 656.802 et seq.
Pa. Purdon's Stat., Title 77, § 1201 et seq.
R.I. Gen. Laws 1956, 28-34-1 et seq.
S.C. Code Ann. 1976, § 42-11-10 et seq., § 42-11-60 et seq.
S.D. Codified Laws 1967, 62-8-1 et seq.
Tenn. Code Ann., 50-6-301 et seq.
Tex. Rev. Civ. Stat.,Art. 8306 § 20 et seq.
Utah Code Ann. 1953, 35-2-1 et seq.
Utah Code Ann. 1953, 35-2-101 et seq.
Va. Code 1950, § 65.1-46 et seq.
Vt. Stat. Ann., Title 21, § 1001 et seq.
Wash. Rev. Code Ann., 51.08.140, 51.16.040, 51.32.180
W. Va. Acts 1949, Ch. 136, Art. 4 § 8d et seq.
Wyo. Stat. 1957, § 27-288 et seq.

Occupational Diseases or Workers Compensation Insurance for Rejected Employers Act
Ill. Rev. Stat. 1991, Ch. 73, § 1081 et seq.

Occupational Education Act
Colo. Rev. Stat., 23-60-101 et seq.

Occupational Education Act (Private)
Colo. Rev. Stat. 12-59-101 et seq.

Occupational Health and Safety Act
Alaska Stat. 1962, § 18.60.010 et seq.
Fla. Stat. Ann., 442.001 et seq.
Mont. Code Ann., 1991, 50-70-101 et seq.
Okla. Stat. Ann., Title 63, § 691 et seq.

Occupational Health and Safety Act (Farm)
Pa. Purdon's Stat., Title 3, § 1901 et seq.

Occupational Health Lead Protection Act
R.I. Gen. Laws 1956, 23-24.7-1 et seq.

Occupational Hearing Loss Act
Iowa Code Ann., 85B.1 et seq.

Occupational License Tax Act
Fla. Stat. Ann., 205.013 et seq.
La. Rev. Stat. Ann., 47:341 et seq.
N.C. Gen. Stat. 1943, § 105-33 et seq.

Occupational Regulation Review Law
Ga. Code Ann., 43-1A-1 et seq.

Occupational Retraining and Reemployment Act
N.Y. Labor Law (Consol. Laws Ch. 31) § 820 et seq.

Occupational Safety and Health Act
Ariz. Rev. Stat. Ann., § 23-401 et seq.
Cal. Labor Code § 6300 et seq.
Continued

Colo. Rev. Stat., 8-11-100.1 et seq.
Conn. Gen. Stat. Ann., § 31-367 et seq.
Fla. Stat. Ann., 442.001 et seq.
Haw. Rev. Stat. Ann., § 396-1 et seq.
Ind. Code Ann., 22-8-1.1-1 et seq.
Iowa Code Ann., 88.1 et seq.
Ky. Rev. Stat. 1971, 338.011 et seq.
Md. Ann. Code 1974, Art. LE, § 5-101 et seq.
Mich. Comp. Laws Ann., 408.1001 et seq., 408.851 et seq.
Minn. Stat. Ann., 182.65 et seq.
N.C. Gen. Stat. 1943, § 95-126 et seq.
Nev. Rev. Stat. 1979 Reprint, 618.005 et seq.
N.M. Stat. Ann., 50-9-1 et seq.
Okla. Stat. Ann., Title 40, § 401 et seq.
P.R. Laws Ann. 1954, Title 29, § 361 et seq.
Tenn. Code Ann., 50-3-101 et seq.
Utah Code Ann. 1953, 35-9-1 et seq.
Va. Code 1950, § 40.1-49.3 et seq.
W. Va. Code 1966, § 21-3A-1 et seq.
Wyo. Stat. Ann., § 27-11-101 et seq.

Occupational Safety and Health Act (Public Employees)
N.J. Stat. Ann., 34:6A-25 et seq.

Occupational Safety and Health Act for State Employees
N.Y. Labor Law (Consol. Laws Ch. 31) §§ 27, 27a, 213

Occupational Safety and Health Act of 1970
Dec. 29, 1970, P.L. 91-596, 84 Stat. 1590, 5 U.S. Code §§ 5108, 5314, 5315, 7902; 15 U.S. Code §§ 633, 636; 18 U.S. Code § 1114; 29 U.S. Code §§ 553, 651 to 678; 42 U.S. Code § 3142-1; 49 U.S. Code § 1421
Jan. 2, 1974, P.L. 93-237, 87 Stat. 1024, 42 U.S. Code § 3142-1
March 27, 1978, P.L. 95-251, 29 U.S. Code § 661
Dec. 21, 1982, P.L. 97-375, 29 U.S. Code § 668
Nov. 8, 1984, P.L. 98-620, 29 U.S. Code § 660
Nov. 5, 1990, P.L. 101-508, 29 U.S. Code § 666
July 16, 1998, P.L. 105-197, 29 U.S. Code § 670
July 16, 1998, P.L. 105-198, 29 U.S. Code § 657

Sept. 28, 1998, P.L. 105-241, 29 U.S. Code §§ 652, 668

Occupational Safety and Health Administration Compliance Assistance Authorization Act of 1998
July 16, 1998, P.L. 105-197, 29 U.S. Code § 651 nt.

Occupational Therapist's Lien Act
Mont. Code Ann., 71-3-1111 et seq.

Occupational Therapy Act
N.M. Stat. Ann., 61-12A-1 to 61-12A-24
Wash. Rev. Code 1983, 18.59.010 et seq.

Occupational Therapy Corporations Act
La. Rev. Stat. Ann., 12:1190 et seq.

Occupational Therapy Licensing Act
N.J. Stat. Ann., 45:9-37.51 et seq.

Occupational Therapy Practice Act
Ala. Code 1975, § 34-39-1
Ark. Code Ann. 1987, 17-87-101 et seq.
D.C. Code Ann., § 2-1705.1 et seq.
Fla. Stat. Ann., 468.201 et seq.
Ga. Code Ann., 42-28-1 et seq.
Haw. Rev. Stat. Ann., § 457G-1 et seq.
Ill. Rev. Stat. 1991, Ch. 111, § 3701 et seq.
Iowa Code Ann., 148B.1 et seq.
Kan. Stat. Ann., 65-5401 et seq.
La. Rev. Stat. Ann., 37:3001 et seq.
Md. Ann.Code 1974, HO, § 10-101 et seq.
Miss. Code Ann. 1972, § 73-24-1 et seq.
Mo. Laws 1997, S.B. No. 141, §§ 1 to 14
Mont. Code Ann. 1983, 37-24-101 et seq.
N.C. Gen. Stat. 1943, § 90-270.65 et seq.
Neb. Rev. Stat. 1943, 71-6101 et seq.
N.H. Rev. Stat. 1955, 326-C:1 et seq.
N.M. Stat. Ann., 61-12A-1 et seq.
Okla. Stat. Ann., Title 59, § 888.1 et seq.
Pa. Purdon's Stat., Title 63, § 1501 et seq.
R.I. Gen. Laws 1956, 5-40.1-1 et seq.
S.C. Code Ann. 1976, § 40-36-10 et seq.
Tenn. Code Ann., 63-13-101 et seq.
Tex. Rev. Civ. Stat., Art. 851 et seq.
Utah Code Ann. 1953, 58-42-1 et seq., 58-42a-101 et seq.
Wash. Rev. Code Ann., 18.59.010 et seq.

W. Va. Code 1966, § 30-28-1 et seq.

Wyo. Stat. Ann., § 33-40-101 et seq.

Occupational Therapy Title Act

Tex. Rev. Civ. Stat. 1974, Art. 8851

Occupations Act

W. Va. Code 1966, § 30-1-1 et seq.

Occupations and Business Tax Act

Wash. Rev. Code Ann., 82.04.010 et seq.

W. Va. Code 1966, § 11-13-1 et seq.

Occupations Tax Act (Miscellaneous)

Tex. Tax Code, § 191.001 et seq.

Occupier's Liability Act

Ga. Code Ann., 51-3-1, 51-3-2

Occupying Claimants Act (Ejectment)

Ill. Rev. Stat. 1991, Ch. 110, § 6-101 et seq.

Ind. Code Ann., 34-1-49-1 et seq.

Iowa Code Ann., 560.1 et seq.

Kan. Stat. Ann., 60-1004

Ky. Rev. Stat. 1971, 381.460 et seq.

Minn. Stat. Ann., 559.10 et seq.

Mo. Rev. Stat., 524.160

Neb. Rev. Stat. 1943, 76-301 et seq.

Ohio Rev. Code 1953, 5303.07 et seq.

Okla. Stat. Ann., Title 12, § 1481 et seq.

Pa. Purdon's Stat., Title 72, § 5875

Utah Code Ann. 1953, 57-6-1 et seq.

Ocean and Submerged Lands Leasing Act

Haw. Stat. § 190D-1 et seq.

Ocean County Oyster Act of 1886

N.J. Laws 1886, C 237

Ocean Dumping Ban Act of 1988

Nov. 18, 1988, P.L. 100-688, 33 U.S. Code § 1401 nt.

Ocean Dumping Enforcement Act

N.J. Stat. Ann., 58:10A-47 et seq.

Ocean Education Act (Clean)

N.J. Stat. Ann., 58:10A-52 et seq.

Ocean Mail Acts

March 3, 1891, Ch. 519, 26 Stat. 830

May 10, 1892, Ch. 63, 27 Stat. 27

Ocean Pollution Reduction Act

Oct. 31, 1994, P.L. 103-431, 33 U.S. Code § 1251 nt.

Ocean Resources Management Act

Cal. Public Resources Code, § 36000 et seq.

Ore. Rev. Stat., 196.410 et seq.

Wash. Rev. Code Ann., 43.143.005 et seq., 43.143.901

Ocean Sanctuaries Act

Mass. Gen. Laws. Ann., 132A:12A to 16E, 18

Ocean Science Center Act

Ga. Code Ann., 20-12-1 et seq.

Ocean Shipping Act of 1978

Oct. 18, 1978, P.L. 95-483, 46 U.S. Code §§ 801, 817, 842 nt.

Ocean Shipping Reform Act of 1998

Oct. 14, 1998, P.L. 105-258, 112 Stat. 1902, 46 U.S. Code Appx. § 1701 nt.

Ocean Sludge Dumping Elimination Act

N.J. Stat. Ann., 58:10A-44 et seq., 58:10A-45

Ocean Solid Waste Dumping Elimination Act

Del. Code of 1974, Title 7, § 6070 et seq.

Ocean Thermal Energy Conversion Act of 1980

Aug. 3, 1980, P.L. 96-320, 42 U.S. Code §§ 9101 et seq., 9101 nt.

Ocean Thermal Energy Conversion Research, Development, and Demonstration Act

July 17, 1980, P.L. 96-310, 42 U.S. Code §§ 9001 et seq., 9001 nt.

Dec. 21, 1995, P.L. 104-66, 42 U.S. Code § 9002

Oceanographic Commission Act
N.H. Rev. Stat. 1955, 12-C:1 et seq.

Oceans Act of 1992
Nov. 4, 1992, P.L. 102-587, 16 U.S. Code § 1431 nt.
Nov. 13, 1998, P.L. 105-383, 46 U.S. Code § 2101 nt.

Oconee County Public Utility Authority Act
Ga. Laws 1980, p. 3429

Oconee Utility Authority Act
Ga. Laws 1986, p. 4123

OCS Paperwork and Reporting Act
July 2, 1986, P.L. 99-349, 100 Stat. 748
July 7, 1986, P.L. 99-367, 43 U.S. Code § 1301 nt.

Octorara Creek Scenic Rivers Act
Pa. Purdon's Stat., Title 32, § 820.81 et seq.

Oden Act (Franklin County Revenue Board)
Ala. General Acts 1951, p. 1288, No. 735

Odessa Water District Act
Cal. Statutes 1991, Ch. 533

Odometer Fraud Prevention and Detection Act
Fla. Stat. Ann., 319.001 et seq.

Odometer Rollback and Disclosure Act
Ohio Rev. Code 1953, 4549.41 et seq.

Odometer Setting Act
Okla. Stat. Ann., Title 47, § 12-501 et seq.

Off-Campus Instruction Act
N.M. Stat. Ann., 21-14A-1 et seq.

Off-Highway Gas Tax Act
Cal. Statutes 1972, Ch. 1382, p. 2870
Cal. Statutes 1972, Ch. 1405, p. 2928

Off-Highway Motor Vehicle Recreation Act
Cal. Public Resources Code § 5090.01 et seq.

Off-Highway Motorcycle Act
N.M. Stat. Ann., 63-3-1001 et seq.

Off-Road Vehicle Act
Ga. Code Ann., 40-7-1 et seq.

Off-Street Parking Act (First Class Cities)
Ind. Code Ann., 36-1-3.5-2 et seq.

Off-Street Parking Act (Second to Fifth Class Cities)
Ind. Code Ann., 19-5-11-1 et seq.

Off-Street Parking Facilities Act
Ala. Code 1975, § 11-47-240 et seq.
Alaska Stat. 1962, Replaced Title, § 29.55.010 et seq.
Haw. Rev. Stat. Ann., § 56-1 et seq.
Neb. Rev. Stat. 1943, 19-3301 et seq.
N.Y. Local Laws 1971, Village of Old Brookville, p. 4302
S.C. Code Ann. 1976, § 5-29-10 et seq.

Off-Street Parking Facilities Loan Act (Pittsfield)
Mass. Acts 1955, Ch. 694

Off-Street Parking Facilities Loan Act (Worcester)
Mass. Acts 1955, Ch. 365

Off-Street Parking Garage Act (Fitchburg)
Mass. Acts 1954, Ch. 608

Off Street Parking in Rockford Act
Ill. Rev. Stat. 1991, Ch. 127, §§ 3470, 3471

Off-Street Parking Loan Act (Woburn)
Mass. Acts 1956, Ch. 276

Off-System Roads Act (Federal Aid)
Cal. Streets and Highways Code § 2520 et seq.

Off-track Betting Corporation Law
N.Y. Laws 1970, Ch. 144, § 1
N.Y. Laws 1973, Ch. 346, § 5

Off-track Parimutuel Betting Laws
N.Y. Laws 1970, Ch. 143, § 1
N.Y. Laws 1973, Ch. 346, § 4
N.Y. Local Laws 1971, City of Gloversville, p. 102

Offender Act (Multiple)
Conn. Gen. Stat. Ann., § 53a-40

Offender Act (Youthful)
Ga. Code Ann., 42-7-1 et seq.

Offender Management System Act
S.C. Code Ann. 1976, § 24-22-10 et seq.

Offenders Act (Habitual)
La. Rev. Stat. Ann., 32:1471 et seq.

Offenses Against Children Disclosure Act
Ill. Rev. Stat. 1989, Ch. 23, §§ 2240, 2241

Offenses Against Property Act
Ind. Code Ann., 35-17-5-1 et seq.

Offensive Sexual Material Law (Public Display)
N.Y. Penal Law 1965 (Consol. Laws Ch. 40) §§ 245.10, 245.11

Offers of Settlement (Interest)
Ida. Code 1947, 12-301 et seq.

Office Building Authority Act
Ga. Code Ann., 50-9-1 et seq.
N.J. Stat. Ann., 52:18A-50 et seq.

Office Building Commission Act
Kan. Laws 1945, Ch. 314

Office Building Loan Act
Mass. Acts 1960, Ch. 635

Office Building Loan Act (State)
Mass. Acts 1955, Ch. 625

Office for the Affairs of the Elderly Act
P.R. Laws Ann. 1954, Title 3, § 1951 et seq.

Office Hour Act (County Officers)
Nev. Rev. Stat. 1979 Reprint, 245.040

Office Indoor Clean Air Law
La. Rev. Stat. Ann., 40:1300.21 et seq.

Office of Alcoholism and Substance Abuse Services Consolidation Act
N.Y. Laws 1992, Ch. 223

Office of Banks and Real Estate Act
Ill. Comp. Stat. 1992, Ch. 20, § 3205/0.1 et seq.

Office of Child Support Act
Mich. Comp. Laws Ann., 400.231 et seq.

Office of Consumer Services Information Act
Ill. Rev. Stat. 1991, Ch. 127, § 1600 et seq.

Office of Correctional Education Act of 1990
Sept. 25, 1990, P.L. 101-392, 20 U.S. Code § 3401 nt.

Office of Cultural Affairs Act
N.M. Stat. Ann., 9-6-7 et seq.

Office of Disabled Persons Investigating Official Act
P.R. Laws Ann. 1954, Title 3, § 532 et seq.

Office of Education and Related Agencies Appropriation Act 1972
July 9, 1971, P.L. 92-48, 85 Stat. 103

Office of Education Appropriation Act of 1971
Aug. 18, 1970, P.L. 91-380, 84 Stat. 800

Office of Federal Procurement Policy Act
Aug. 30, 1974, P.L. 93-400, 88 Stat. 796, 5 U.S. Code § 5315; 40 U.S. Code §§ 474, 481, 487; 41 U.S. Code §§ 401 to 412
Oct. 10, 1979, P.L. 96-83, 41 U.S. Code §§ 401, 403, 405, 405 nt. , 407, 409 to 412
July 18, 1984, P.L. 98-369, 98 Stat. 1195, 41 U.S. Code §§ 403, 405, 414, 416 et seq.
Nov. 8, 1985, P.L. 99-145, 10 U.S. Code § 2324 nt.; 40 U.S. Code § 759; 41 U.S. Code § 759; 41 U.S. Code § 418a
Jan. 2, 1986, P.L. 99-234, 41 U.S. Code § 420
Oct. 18, 1986, P.L. 99-500, 41 U.S. Code § 416
Oct. 30, 1986, P.L. 99-591, 41 U.S. Code § 416
Nov. 14, 1986, P.L. 99-661, 41 U.S. Code § 416
Nov. 17, 1988, P.L. 100-679, 41 U.S. Code §§ 401-403, 405, 410, 420-424
Nov. 29, 1989, P.L. 101-189, 10 U.S. Code § 423
Continued

Nov. 5, 1990, P.L. 101-510, 41 U.S. Code §§ 403, 403 nt., 416, 421, 423, 423 nt.

April 6, 1991, P.L. 102-25, 41 U.S. Code § 423

Oct. 13, 1994, P.L. 103-355, 41 U.S. Code §§ 401, 403, 405, 415 et seq.

Feb. 10, 1996, P.L. 104-106, 41 U.S. Code §§ 401 et seq.

Sept. 23, 1996, P.L. 104-201, 41 U.S. Code §§ 405, 413, 421, 434

Nov. 18, 1997, P.L. 105-85, 41 U.S. Code §§ 405, 416, 421, 426, 426a, 427, 431, 435

Dec. 2, 1997, P.L. 105-135, 41 U.S. Code § 405

Oct. 17, 1998, P.L. 105-261, 41 U.S. Code §§ 416, 435

Oct. 21, 1998, P.L. 105-277, 41 U.S. Code § 436

Office of Federal Procurement Policy Act Amendments of 1979

Oct. 10, 1979, P.L. 96-83, 40 U.S. Code §§ 481, 487; 41 U.S. Code §§ 401, 401 nt., 403, 405, 405 nt., 407, 409 to 412

Office of Federal Procurement Policy Act Amendments of 1983

Dec. 1, 1983, P.L. 98-191, 41 U.S. Code §§ 401 nt., 413 to 415

Office of Federal Procurement Policy Act Amendments of 1988

Nov. 17, 1988, P.L. 100-679, 41 U.S. Code § 401 nt.

Office of Fiscal Affairs Act

N.J. Laws 1971, Ch. 211

Office of Government Ethics Amendment of 1992

Oct. 24, 1992, P.L. 102-506, 5 U.S. Code Appx. §§ 101 nt., 405

Office of Government Ethics Authorization Act of 1996

Aug. 6, 1996, P.L. 104-179, 5 U.S. Code Appx. § 101 nt.

Office of Government Reports Act

June 9, 1941, Ch. 189, 55 Stat. 247

Office of Hawaiian Affairs Supplemental Appropriations Act

Haw. Session Laws 1996, Act 176

Office of Health Care Access Act

Conn. Gen. Stat. 1983, § 19a-610

Office of National Drug Control Policy Reauthorization Act of 1998

Oct. 21, 1998, P.L. 105-277, Division C, Title VII, 112 Stat. 2681, 21 U.S . Code § 1701 nt.

Office of the Town Clerk Act

N.Y. Local Laws 1972 Town of Oyster Bay, p. 2471

Office of Volunteerism Act

Colo. Rev. Stat., 24-32-1501 et seq.

Office Paper Recovery Act, Recycling Makes Cents

Mich. Comp. Laws Ann., 299.461 et seq.

Office Records Act (Shop Rule)

Md. Ann. Code 1974, Art. CJ, § 10-101

Office Shops Act (Railroads)

Tex. Rev. Civ. Stat., Arts. 6275 to 6277

Officer Grade Limitation Act of 1954

May 5, 1954, Ch. 180, 68 Stat. 65 (See 10 U.S. Code §§ 686, 3202, 5442 to 5445, 5451, 5454, 5504, 5505, 5703, 5705 to 5711, 5751, 5755 to 5757, 5759, 5765 and others)

Officer Jeffrey Tackett Law Enforcement Safety Act

Fla. Stat. Ann., 166.049

Officer Personnel Act of 1947

Aug. 7, 1947, Ch. 512, 62 Stat. 489 (See 10 U.S. Code § 5701 nt.)

June 12, 1948, Ch. 449, 62 Stat. 358

June 25, 1949, Ch. 248, 63 Stat. 277

Aug. 5, 1949, Ch. 402, 63 Stat. 567

June 23, 1950, Ch. 344, 64 Stat. 250

July 10, 1950, Ch. 454, 64 Stat. 322

June 30, 1951, Ch. 196, 65 Stat. 108

May 5, 1954, Ch. 189, 68 Stat. 66

June 18, 1954, Ch. 311, 68 Stat. 256

June 30, 1954, Ch. 433, 68 Stat. 357

April 30, 1956, Ch. 223, 70 Stat. 121

June 15, 1956, Ch. 389, 70 Stat. 283

July 20, 1956, Ch. 646, 70 Stat. 587

Aug. 10, 1956, Ch. 1041, 70A Stat. 639

Sept. 2, 1958, P.L. 85-861, 72 Stat. 1556

June 28, 1962, P.L. 87-509, 76 Stat. 121, 10 U.S. Code § 5701 nt.

Feb. 10, 1996, P.L. 104-106, 10 U.S. Code § prec. 5401 nt.

Officers and Employees Absent on Military Duty Act

N.Y. Military Law (Consol. Laws Ch. 36) § 242, Subd. 2, 243, Subd. 2

Officers and Employees Group Insurance Act

Minn. Stat. Ann., 471.61

Officers and Employees Money Disposition Act (State)

Ill. Rev. Stat. 1989, Ch. 127, § 170 et seq.

Officers and Employees Retirement Act (County)

Fla. Stat. 1953, 134.01 et seq.

Officers' and Employees' Retirement and Benefit Act (Banks)

N.J. Stat. Ann., 17:9A-25.1 et seq.

Officers and Employees Saving Bank Life Insurance Law

N.Y. Insurance Law 1984 (Consol. Laws Ch. 28) § 2201 et seq.

Officers' and Employees' Tenure Act (Augusta)

Ga. Laws 1937-38 Ex. Sess., p. 938

Officers Competency Certificates Act

July 17, 1939, Ch. 316, 53 Stat. 1049, 46 U.S. Code § 224a

Officers' Corrupt Practices Act

Ill. Rev. Stat. 1991, Ch. 102, § 0-01 et seq.

Officers' Facsimile Signature Act

Cal. Government Code § 11100 et seq.

Officers' Fees and Salaries Act (County)

Ind. Code Ann., 36-3-6-2 et seq.

Officers, Officials and State Employees' Code of Conduct

Del. Code of 1974, Title 29, § 5801 et seq.

Officers Protection Act (Undercover)

Ala. Code 1975, § 13A-5-40

Officers Salary Act

Tex. Rev. Civ. Stat., Art. 3912e

Officers Salary Act (County)

Mich. Comp. Laws Ann., 45.401 et seq.

Officers Salary Act (Eighth Class Counties)

Pa. Purdon's Stat., Title 16, § 1555

Officers Salary Act (State)

Ga. Code 1933, 89-707 et seq.

Official and Penal Bonds

July 30, 1947, Ch. 390, 61 Stat. 646, 6 U.S. Code §§ 1 to 15

Oct. 31, 1951, Ch. 655, 65 Stat. 715, 6 U.S. Code § 1.

Sept. 3, 1954, Ch. 1263, 68 Stat. 1231, 6 U.S. Code § 3

Aug. 9, 1955, Ch. 683, 69 Stat. 618, 6 U.S. Code prec. §§ 6, 14

Official Ballot Act

Ill. Rev. Stat. 1991, Ch. 46, § 16-1 et seq.

Official Bond Act

Ill. Rev. Stat. 1991, Ch. 103, § 0-01 et seq.

Official Bond Approval Act (County)

Ill. Rev. Stat. 1991, Ch. 103, §§ 16-9, 17

Official Bond Payment Act

Ill. Rev. Stat. 1989, Ch. 103, § 16

Official Correspondence Regulations Act

D.C. Code Ann., § 1-1701 et seq.

Official Court Reports Act

Ill. Rev. Stat. 1991, Ch. 37, § 640 et seq.

Official Court Stenographer's Act
Tex. Government Code, § 51.601

Official Language Act
Ill. Rev. Stat. 1991, Ch. 1, § 2901-20

Official Lottery Act
P.R. Laws Ann. 1954, Title 15, § 111 et seq.

Official Map Act (Municipalities)
Me. Rev. Stat. Ann. 1964, Title 30, § 4964
N.Y. General City Law (Consol. Laws Ch. 21) § 26 et seq.
Wis. Stat. Ann., 62.23, Subsec. 6

Official Map and Building Permit Act
N.J. Stat. Ann., 40:55-1.30 et seq.

Official Meetings Time Off Act
Ill. Rev. Stat. 1991, Ch. 102, §§ 250, 251

Official Oppression Act
Tenn. Code Ann., 39-16-4

Official Purpose Funds Act
D.C. Code Ann., §§ 1-356, 31-2215

Official Reports as Evidence Act
See Uniform Official Reports as Evidence Act

Official Salary Act (Anti-Fee)
Tenn. Code Ann., 8-22-101 et seq., 8-24-101 et seq.

Official State Wild Game Bird Act (Wild Turkey)
S.C. Code Ann. 1976, § 1-1-635

Official Visitation of Prisons Act
Pa. Purdon's Stat., Title 61, § 1091 et seq.

Officials Convicted of Infamous Crimes Act
Ill. Rev. Stat. 1991, Ch. 102, §§ 119, 120

Officials' Parking Lot Act
N.Y. Local Laws 1972, County of Schenectady, p. 821

Officials Salaries and Fees Act (State)
Ind. Code Ann., 4-2-1-1, 4-2-1-2

Offshore Oil and Gas Act
Ore. Rev. Stat., 274.705 et seq.

Offshore Shrimp Fisheries Act of 1973
Jan. 2, 1974, P.L. 93-242, 87 Stat. 1061, 16 U.S. Code §§ 1085, 1100b to 1100b-10
July 24, 1975, P.L. 94-58, 89 Stat. 266, 16 U.S. Code §§ 1100b et seq.

Ogden Littering Law
N.Y. Local Laws 1971, Town of Ogden, p. 2974

Ogden Parks Law
N.Y. Local Laws 1971, Town of Ogden, p. 2970

Ogdensburg Bridge and Port Authority Act
N.Y. Public Authorities Law (Consol. Laws Ch. 43A) § 725 et seq.

Ogdensburg Bridge Authority Act
N.Y. Public Authorities Law (Consol. Laws Ch. 43A) § 700 et seq.

Ogdensburg Port Authority Act
N.Y. Public Authorities Law (Consol. Laws Ch. 43A) § 1375 et seq.

Oglethorpe County Water Authority Act
Ga. Laws 1991, p. 3605

Oglethorpe Housing Development Authority Act (De Kalb County)
Ga. Laws 1974, p. 2591
Ga. Laws 1975, p. 3053

Ogonowski Scoliosis Screening Act
Mich. Comp. Laws Ann., 333.9152

Ogrin Act (Refund of Penalties)
Ohio Laws Vol. 116, p. 468

Oh! Grab Me Act (Embargo 1807)
Dec. 22, 1807, Ch. 5, 2 Stat. 451

Ohio & Erie Canal National Heritage Corridor Act of 1996
Nov. 12, 1996, P.L. 104-333, Division II, Title VIII, 16 U.S. Code § 461 nt.

Ohio and Wabash Rivers Improvement Act
Ill. Rev. Stat. 1991, Ch. 1, § 3550 et seq.

Ohio-Kentucky Interstate Compact on Air Pollution
Ohio Rev. Code 1953, 3723.04 et seq.

Ohio River Valley Water Sanitation Compact Act
Ill. Rev. Stat. 1991, Ch. 111 1/2, § 116-990 et seq.
Ind. Code Ann., 13-5-5-1 et seq.
Ky. Rev. Stat. 1971, 224.18-760
N.Y. Laws 1939, Ch. 945
Pa. Purdon's Stat., Title 32, § 816.1 et seq.
Va. Code 1950, § 62.1-70 et seq.

Ohio Valley Compact
Ind. Code Ann., 13-5-6-1 et seq.

Ohio-West Virginia Interstate Compact on Air Pollution
Ohio Rev. Code 1953, 3723.01 et seq.

Oil and Gas Accounting Commission Act
N.M. Stat. Ann., 7-28-1 et seq.

Oil and Gas Act
Ill. Rev. Stat. 1989, Ch. 96 1/2, § 5401a et seq.
Md. Ann. Code 1974, Art. NR, § 6-101 et seq.
N.M. Stat. Ann., 70-2-1 et seq.
Pa. Purdon's Stat., Title 58, § 601.101
Va. Code 1950, § 45.1-286 et seq.

Oil and Gas Ad Valorem Production Act
N.M. Stat. Ann., 7-32-1 et seq.

Oil and Gas and Deep Drilling Act
Ga. Code Ann., 12-4-40 et seq.
Ga. Code 1933, 43-701 et seq.

Oil and Gas Compact Act
Mont. Code Ann., 1947, 60-601 et seq.
N.Y. Environmental Conservation Law 1972 (Consol. Laws Ch. 43B) § 23-2101

Oil and Gas Compact Act (Extension)
Md. Ann. Code 1974, Art. NR, § 36-401 et seq.

Oil and Gas Compact Act (Interstate)
See Interstate Compact to Conserve Oil and Gas Act

Oil and Gas Compulsory Pooling Act
Miss. Code Ann. 1972, § 53-3-7

Oil and Gas Compulsory Unitization Act
Ark. Code Ann. 1987, 15-72-301 et seq.
Ohio Rev. Code 1953, 1509.27, 1509.28, 15-72-323

Oil and Gas Conservation Act
Ala. Code 1975, § 9-17-1 et seq.
Alaska Stat. 1962, § 31.05.010 et seq.
Ariz. Rev. Stat. Ann., § 27-501 et seq.
Ark. Code Ann. 1987, 15-72-101 et seq.
Ark. Stat. 15-72-101 et seq.
Cal. Public Resources Code § 3000 et seq., § 3275
Colo. Rev. Stat., 34-60-101 et seq.
Ida. Code 1947, 47-315 et seq.
Ill. Rev. Stat. 1985, Ch. 96 1/2, § 7101 et seq.
Iowa Code Ann., 84.1 et seq.
Kan. Stat. Ann., 55-601 et seq.
Ky. Rev. Stat. 1971, 353.500 et seq.
La. Rev. Stat.Ann., 30:1 et seq.
Mich. Comp. Laws Ann., 319.1 et seq.
Miss. Code Ann. 1972, § 53-1-1 et seq.
Mont. Code Ann., 1947, 60.124 et seq.
Mont. Code Ann., 1991, 82-11-301 et seq.
N.C. Gen. Stat. 1943, § 113-381 et seq.
N.D. Cent. Code 38-08-01 et seq.
Neb. Rev. Stat. 1943, 57-901 et seq.
Ohio Rev. Code 1953, 1509.01 et seq.
Okla. Stat. Ann., Title 52, § 81 et seq., § 292 et seq.
Pa. Purdon's Stat., Title 58, § 401 et seq.
S.D. Codified Laws 1967, 45-9-1 et seq.
Tex. Natural Resources Code § 85.001 et seq.
Utah Code Ann. 1953, 40-6-1 et seq.
Wash. Rev. Code Ann., 78.52.001 et seq.
Wyo. Stat. Ann., § 30-5-101 et seq.

Oil and Gas Conservation and Development Control Act
Me. Rev. Stat. Ann. 1964, Title 10, § 2151 et seq.

Oil and Gas Conservation Compact Act
See Interstate Compact to Conserve Oil and Gas Act

Oil and Gas Conservation Compact Act (Extension)
See Interstate Compact to Conserve Oil and Gas (Extension)

Oil and Gas Conservation Tax Act
N.M. Stat. Ann., 6-30-1 et seq.

Oil and Gas Economic Units
N.Y. Real Property Tax Law (Consol. Laws, Ch. 50A), § 590 et seq.

Oil and Gas Emergency School Tax Act
N.M. Stat. Ann., 7-31-1 et seq.

Oil and Gas Information Reporting Act
Cal. Public Resources Code, § 25350 et seq.

Oil and Gas Inspection Act
Colo. Rev. Stat., 8-20-101 et seq.
Ill. Rev. Stat. 1991, Ch. 96 1/2, § 5411, § 5412
Ind. Code Ann., 16-6-11-1 et seq.
Kan. Stat. Ann., 55-422 et seq.
Minn. Stat. Ann., 296.04
N.C. Gen. Stat. 1943, § 119-14 et seq.
N.D. Cent. Code 19-10-01 et seq.
Ohio Rev. Code 1953, 4159.21 et seq.
Okla. Stat. Ann., Title 52, § 321 et seq.
S.D. Laws 1897, Ch. 68
Wash. Laws 1907, Ch. 192
Wis. Stat. Ann., 168.01 et seq.

Oil and Gas Lands Leasing Act (Statelands)
Ariz. Rev. Stat. Ann., § 27-551 et seq.
Wash. Rev. Code Ann., 79.14.010 et seq.
Wash. Rev. Code 1983, 78.16.010 et seq.

Oil and Gas Lease Release Act
Ill. Rev. Stat. 1991, Ch. 80, § 38-9 et seq.

Oil and Gas Lien Act
Cal. Code of Civil Procedure § 1203.50 et seq.
Ill. Rev. Stat. 1987, Ch. 82, § 71 et seq.
Ill. Rev. Stat. 1991, Ch. 82, § 501 et seq.
Kan. Stat. Ann., 55-207 et seq.
Mich. Comp. Laws Ann., 570.251 et seq.
Neb. Rev. Stat. 1943, 57-801 et seq.
N.M. Stat. Ann., 70-4-1 et seq.
Okla. Stat. Ann., Title 42, § 144 et seq.
Okla. Stat. Ann., Title 52, § 548 et seq.

Oil and Gas Manufacturers Privilege Tax Act
N.M. Stat. Ann., 7-33-1 et seq.

Oil and Gas Market Demand Act
Tex. Natural Resources Code, § 85.001 et seq.

Oil and Gas Owners' Lien Act
Okla. Stat. Ann., Title 52, § 548 et seq.

Oil and Gas Permit and Lease Act
Tex. Natural Resources Code, § 52.221 et seq.

Oil and Gas Pooling Act
Okla. Stat. Ann., Title 52, § 87.1

Oil and Gas Proceeds Payment Act
N.M. Stat. Ann., 70-10-1 et seq.

Oil and Gas Production Act
Tex. Natural Resources Code, § 88.051 et seq.

Oil and Gas Production Equipment Ad Valorem Tax Act
N.M. Stat. Ann., 7-34-1 et seq.

Oil and Gas Production Tax Act
Ill. Rev. Stat. 1943, Ch. 120, § 416-1 et seq.

Oil and Gas Products Lien Act
N.M. Stat. Ann., 48-9-1 et seq.

Oil and Gas Prospecting Act
Aug. 21, 1935, Ch. 599, 49 Stat. 678, 30 U.S. Code §§ 185, 221, 223, 226, 236a

Oil and Gas Recovery Act
Ill. Rev. Stat. 1991, Ch. 96 1/2, § 5100 et seq.

Oil and Gas Rights Act
Ill. Rev. Stat. 1991, Ch. 96 1/2, § 4900 et seq.

Oil and Gas Severance Tax Act
Kan. Laws 1957, Ch. 516
Mich. Comp. Laws Ann., 205.301 et seq.
Mont. Code Ann., 1991, 15-36-101 et seq.
N.M. Stat. Ann., 7-29-1 et seq.

Oil and Gas Surface Owners Compensation Act
Tenn. Code Ann., 60-1-601 et seq.

Oil and Gas Unitization Act
See Unitization Act (Oil and Gas)

Oil and Gas Waste Haulers Act
Tex. Water Code, § 29.001 et seq.

Oil and Gas Well Safety Regulation Act
W. Va. Code 1966, § 22B-1-1 et seq.

Oil and Gas Well Spacing Act
Cal. Public Resources Code, § 3600 et seq.

Oil and Gas Wells on Public Lands Act
Ill. Rev. Stat. 1991, Ch. 96 1/2, § 5000 et seq.

Oil and Hazardous Material Release Prevention Act
Mass. Gen. Laws. Ann., 21E:1 et seq.

Oil and Hazardous Material Release Prevention and Response Act
Mass. Gen. Laws. Ann., 21E:1 et seq.

Oil and Hazardous Substances Discharge Law
Minn. Stat. Ann., 115E.01 et seq.

Oil and Hazardous Substances Spill Prevention and Control Act
Tex. Water Code, § 26.261 et seq.

Oil and Mining Leases Act
Wash. Laws 1939, Ch. 110

Oil and Natural Gas Production Tax Act
Mont. Code Ann., 15-36-301 et seq.

Oil Compact Act
Wyo. Stat. Ann., § 30-5-201 et seq.

Oil Company Excise Tax Act
Va. Code 1950, § 58.1-2300 et seq.

Oil Conservation Act
N.M. Stat. Ann., 70-2-1 et seq.

Oil Curtailment Act
Okla. Stat. Ann., Title 52, § 271 et seq.
Vt. Stat. Ann., Title 29, § 501 et seq.

Oil Discharge Prevention and Pollution Control Act
Alaska Stat. 1962, Replaced Titles, § 30.25.010 et seq.
Me. Rev. Stat. Ann. 1964, Title 38, § 541 et seq.

Oil, Gas and Solution Mining Law
N.Y. Environmental Conservation Law 1972 (Consol. Laws Ch. 43B) § 23-0101 et seq.

Oil, Gas, and Water Well Act
La. Rev. Stat. Ann., 9:4861 et seq.

Oil Heat Commission Act
Ore. Rev. Stat., 469.228 et seq.

Oil Heating System Act
Mich. Comp. Laws Ann., 125.551 et seq.

Oil Inspection Act
Minn. Stat. 1986, 296.28 et seq.
Wis. Stat. Ann., 168.01 et seq.

Oil Lands Leasing Act
See Mineral Lands Leasing Act

Oil Occupation Tax Act
Tex. Tax Code, § 202.001 et seq.

Oil Overcharge and Housing Trust Act
N.C. Gen. Stat. 1943, § 122E-1 et seq.

Oil Overcharge Restitutionary Act
Tex. Government Code, § 2305.001 et seq.

Oil Petroleum Severance Tax Act
Ind. Code Ann., 6-8-1-1 et seq.

Oil Pipe Line Act
May 21, 1896, Ch. 212, 29 Stat. 127, 43 U.S.
Code §§ 962 to 965
Iowa Code Ann., 479.1 et seq.
Mich. Comp. Laws Ann., 483.1 et seq.

Oil Pipeline Environmental Responsibility Act
Cal. Civil Code § 3333.4

Oil Pollution Act of 1924
June 7, 1924, Ch. 316, 43 Stat. 604, 33 U.S.
Code §§ 431 to 437
Nov. 3, 1966, P.L. 89-753, 80 Stat. 1252, 33
U.S. Code §§ 431 to 437
Oct. 4, 1973, P.L. 93-119, 87 Stat. 424, 33
U.S. Code §§ 1001 to 1010, 1013, 1014

Oil Pollution Act of 1961
Aug. 30, 1961, P.L. 87-167, 75 Stat. 402, 33
U.S. Code §§ 1001 to 1015
Sept. 1, 1966, P.L. 89-551, 80 Stat. 372, 33
U.S. Code §§ 1001 to 1004, 1008, 1009,
1011, 1015

Oil Pollution Act of 1990
Aug. 18, 1990, P.L. 101-380, 33 U.S. Code
§ 2701 nt.
Nov. 8, 1990, P.L. 101-537, 33 U.S. Code
§ 2761
Nov. 29, 1990, P.L. 101-646, 33 U.S. Code
§ 2761
Oct. 6, 1992, P.L. 102-388, 33 U.S. Code
§ 2735
Nov. 20, 1995, P.L. 104-55, 33 U.S. Code
§§ 2704, 2716
Oct. 19, 1996, P.L. 104-324, 33 U.S. Code
§§ 2705, 2713 to 2716, 2731, 2736, 2752,
2761
Nov. 13, 1998, P.L. 105-383, 33 U.S. Code
§§ 2701, 2704, 3703 nt.

Oil Pollution and Hazardous Substances Control Act
N.C. Gen. Stat. 1943, § 143-215.75 et seq.

Oil Pollution Control Act
R.I. Gen. Laws 1956, 46-12.5-1 et seq.

Oil Production Allotment Act
Okla. Stat. Ann., Title 52, § 271 et seq.

Oil Production Tax Act
Ill. Rev. Stat. 1943, Ch. 120, § 416.1 et seq.
Ky. Rev. Stat. 1971, 137.120 et seq.

Oil Recovery Act (Enhanced)
N.M. Stat. Ann., 7-29A-1 et seq.

Oil Recycling Act (Used)
Mich. Comp. Laws Ann., 319.311 et seq.
Wash. Rev. Code Ann., 70.951.005 et seq.

Oil Recycling Enhancement Act
Cal. Public Resources Code, § 48600 et seq.

Oil Refinement Act
Utah Code Ann. 1953, 40-9-1 et seq.

Oil Refinery and Chemical Plant Safety Preparedness Act
Cal. Government Code, § 51020 et seq.

Oil Severance Tax Act
Cal. Revenue and Taxation Code § 42002 et
seq.
Miss. Code Ann. 1972, § 27-25-501 et seq.

Oil Spacing Act
Cal. Public Resources Code § 3600 et seq.

Oil Spill Cleanup and Environmental Preservation Act
Tenn. Code Ann., 68-216-101 et seq.

Oil Spill Prevention and Contingency Act
N.Y. Navigation Law 1941 (Consol. Laws
Ch. 37) §§ 70, 71, 172, 174a, 174b, 177,
177b, 179

Oil Spill Prevention and Pollution Control Act
Fla. Stat. Ann., 376.011 et seq.

Oil Spill Prevention and Response Act
Cal. Government Code §§ 8574.1 et seq.,
8670.1 et seq.
Cal. Public Resources Code § 8750 et seq.

La. Rev. Stat. Ann., 30:2451 et seq.
Tex. Natural Resources Code, § 40.001 et seq.

Oil Spill Responders Liability Act
Ala. Code 1975, § 6-5-332.2
Ill. Comp. Stat. 1992, Ch. 740, § 113/1
Pa. Purdon's Stat., Title 35, § 6023.1 et seq.
S.C. Code Ann. 1976, § 48-44-10 et seq.

Oil Spill Response Liability Act
Ala. Acts 1991, p. 852, No. 470

Oil Spill Response, Prevention, and Administration Fees Law
Cal. Revenue and Taxation Code, § 46001 et seq.

Oil Spills Act (Regarding Liability for Persons Responding to)
Ala. Code 1975, § 6-5-332.2

Oil Storage and Pipe Line Utility Act
Tex. Natural Resources Code, § 111.001 et seq.

Oil Terminal and Oil Tanker Environmental Oversight and Monitoring Act of 1990
Aug. 18, 1990, P.L.101-380, 33 U.S. Code § 2732

Oil Test Act (Illuminating)
Md. Ann. Code 1957, Art. 48, § 1 et seq.

Oil Transportation Act
Tex. Rev. Civ. Stat., Art. 6066a

Oil Well Act
Iowa Code Ann., 84.1 et seq.
Mich. Comp. Laws Ann., 319.1 et seq.

Oil Well Mechanics' Lien Act
N.Y. Laws 1880, Ch. 440

Oil Well Pollution Act
Kan. Stat. Ann., 55-121, et seq.

Oil Well Spacing Act
Okla. Stat. Ann., Title 52, § 87.1

Oilfield Indemnity Act
La. Rev. Stat. Ann., 9:2780

Oilfield Site Restoration Law
La. Rev. Stat. Ann., 30:80 et seq.

Oilfield Waste Site Law (Abandoned)
La. Rev. Stat. Ann., 30:71 et seq.

Ojai Basin Groundwater Management Agency Act
Cal. Water Code, Appendix, § 131-101 et seq.

Oklahoma A. & M. College Housing Authority Act
Okla. Stat. Ann., Title 70, § 1371.1 et seq.

Oklahoma City Bombing Remembrance Day Act
Okla. Stat. Ann., Title 25, § 90.9

Oklahoma City National Memorial Act of 1997
Oct. 9, 1997, P.L. 105-58, 16 U.S. Code § 450ss nt.

Oklahoma-Kansas-Arkansas River Basin Compact
Okla. Stat. Ann., Title 82, § 1401

Oklahoma State Paper Recycling Act
Okla. Stat. Ann., Title 74, § 85.50 et seq.

Oklahoma State Regent's Academic Scholars Act
Okla. Stat. Ann., Title 70, §§ 2401 to 2407

Old Age and Survivor Insurance Act
N.D. Cent. Code, 52-09-01 et seq.

Old Age and Survivors' Insurance Act (Public Employees)
Ind. Code Ann., 5-10.1-1-1 et seq.
N.D. Cent. Code 52-09-01 et seq.
R.I. Gen. Laws 1956, 36-7-1 et seq.

Old Age Assistance Act
Alaska Stat. 1962, § 47.25.430 et seq.
Ariz. Rev. Stat. Ann., § 46-251 et seq.
Colo. Rev. Stat., 26-2-101 et seq.
Conn. Gen. Stat. Ann., § 17-109 et seq.
Continued

D.C. Code 1973, § 3-201 et seq.

Del. Code of 1974, Title 31, § 501 et seq.

Fla. Stat. Ann., 410.021 et seq.

Ga. Code Ann., 49-4-30 et seq.

Ill. Rev. Stat. 1991, Ch. 23, § 6101 et seq.

Ind. Code Ann., 12-1-5-1 et seq.

Iowa Code Ann., 249.1 et seq.

Ky. Rev. Stat. 1971, 205.010 et seq.

Mass. Gen. Laws. Ann., 118A:1 et seq.

Md. Ann. Code 1957, Art. 88A, § 63 et seq.

Me. Rev. Stat. Ann. 1964, Title 22, § 3172 et seq.

Mich. Comp. Laws Ann., 400.24 et seq.

Minn. Stat. 1971, 256.11 et seq.

Miss. Code Ann. 1972, § 43-9-1 et seq.

Mo. Rev. Stat., 208.010 et seq.

N.C. Gen. Stat. 1943, § 108-25 et seq.

Neb. Rev. Stat. 1943, 68-201 et seq., 68-214 et seq.

Nev. Rev. Stat. 1979 Reprint Replaced Pages, 427.020 et seq.

N.J. Stat. Ann., 44:7-1 et seq.

N.Y. Social Service Law (Consol. Laws Ch. 55) § 131 et seq.

Ohio Rev. Code 1953, 5105.01 et seq.

Ore. Rev. Stat., 413.005 et seq.

Pa. Purdon's Stat., Title 62, § 431 et seq.

R.I. Gen. Laws 1956, 40-6-6 et seq.

S.C. Code Ann. 1976, § 43-21-10 et seq.

Tenn. Code Ann., 71-2-201 et seq.

Tex. Human Resources Code, § 101.001 et seq.

Wash. Rev. Code Ann., 74.08.025 et seq.

Wis. Stat. Ann., 49.20 et seq.

Old Age Assistance Claims Settlement Act

Oct. 19, 1984, P.L. 98-500, 25 U.S. Code §§ 2301 nt., 2301 et seq.

Nov. 5, 1987, P.L. 100-153, 25 U.S. Code § 2301

Nov. 1, 1988, P.L. 100-581, 25 U.S. Code § 2302

Old Age Assistance Law (Blind and Disabled)

N.Y. Social Services Law (Consol. Laws Ch. 55) § 207 et seq.

Old Age Assistance Lien Act

N.C. Gen. Stat. 1943, § 108-30.1, et seq.

Old Age Medical Assistance Act

Mich. Comp. Laws Ann., 400.105 et seq.

Wyo. Stat. 1957, § 42-47 et seq.

Old Age Pension Act

See Service Pension Acts; See Social Security Act

Colo. Rev. Stat. 26-2-101 et seq.

Minn. Stat. 1971, 256.11 et seq.

Old Age Pensions Act

Wash. Laws 1933, Ch. 29

Old Age Security Act

Cal. Welfare and Institutions Code § 12000 et seq.

Ill. Rev. Stat. 1935, Ch. 23, § 410 et seq.

Miss. Code Ann. 1972, § 43-9-1 et seq.

Old-Age, Survivors, and Disability Insurance Amendments of 1965

July 30, 1965, P.L. 89-97, 79 Stat. 361, 26 U.S. Code §§ 451, 1401, 1402, 3101, 3102, 3111, 3121, 3122, 3125, 3401, 3402, 6051, 6053, 6205, 6413, 6652, 6674; 42 U.S. Code §§ 401, 402 to 406, 409, 410, 411, 413, 415 to 418, 422, 423, 424a, 425, 427, 1306; 45 U.S. Code §§ 228a 228e

Old Age Tax Abatement Act

Mass. Gen. Laws. Ann., 59:5, Cl. 41

Old Age Welfare Act

Del. Code of 1953, Title 31, § 501 et seq.

Old and Historic Marblehead Districts Act

Mass. Acts 1965, Ch. 101

Old Galveston Quarter Act

Tex. Rev. Civ. Stat., Art. 6145-4

Old Georgetown Act

D.C. Code Ann., § 5-1101 et seq.

Old Map Act

N.J. Stat. Ann., 46:23-1 et seq.

Old Series Currency Adjustment Act
June 30, 1961, P.L. 87-66, 75 Stat. 146, 12 U.S. Code §§ 415, 416; 31 U.S. Code §§ 404, 911 to 917

Old Soldiers Act
Minn. Stat. Ann., 197.46

Minn. Stat. 1974, 197.45

Old South Pass Historical Preserve Act
Wyo. Session Laws 1967, Ch. 86

Old State Capitol Act
Ill. Rev. Stat. 1991, Ch. 123, § 51-9 et seq.

Older Adult Daily Living Centers Licensing Act
Pa. Purdon's Stat., Title 62, § 1511.1 et seq.

Older Adults Protective Services Act
Pa. Purdon's Stat., Title 35, § 10211 et seq.

Pa. Purdon's Stat., Title 35, § 10225.101 et seq.

Older American Community Service Employment Act
May 3, 1973, P.L. 93-29, 87 Stat. 60, 42 U.S. Code §§ 3061 to 3067

Oct. 1, 1973, P.L. 93-113, 87 Stat. 417, 42 U.S. Code § 3067

Nov. 28, 1975, P.L. 94-135, 42 U.S. Code §§ 3001 et seq., 3056

Sept. 30, 1992, P.L. 102-375, 42 U.S. Code §§ 3056, 3056a, 3056c , 3056d, 3056e, 3056f, 3056h, 3056i

Older Americans Act
Ariz. Rev. Stat. Ann., § 46-137, § 46-182

Ind. Laws 1969, Ch. 489

Mont. Code Ann., 52-3-501 et seq.

Older Americans Act Amendments of 1981
Dec. 29, 1981, P.L. 97-115, 42 U.S. Code § 3001 nt.

Older Americans Act Amendments of 1984
Oct. 9, 1984, P.L. 98-459, 98 Stat. 1767, 42 U.S. Code §§ 3001 et seq., 3001 nt.

Older Americans Act Amendments of 1986
April 1, 1986, P.L. 99-269, 42 U.S. Code § 3001 nt.

Older Americans Act Amendments of 1987
Nov. 29, 1987, P.L. 100-175, 42 U.S. Code §§ 3001 et seq., 3001 nt.

Sept. 30, 1992, P.L. 102-375, 42 U.S. Code § 3001 nts.

Dec. 2, 1993, P.L. 103-171, 42 U.S. Code § 3001 nt.

Older Americans Act Amendments of 1992
Sept. 30, 1992, P.L. 102-375, 42 U.S. Code § 3001 nt.

Dec. 2, 1993, P.L. 103-171, 42 U.S. Code §§ 3001 nt., 3056

Older Americans Act of 1965
July 14, 1965, P.L. 89-73, 79 Stat. 218, 42 U.S. Code §§ 3001, 3002, 3011, 3012, 3021 to 3025, 3031, 3032, 3041, 3042, 3051 to 3053

July 1, 1967, P.L. 90-42, 81 Stat. 106, 42 U.S. Code §§ 3002, 3021, 3022, 3024, 3031, 3043, 3051 to 3053

Sept. 17, 1969, P.L. 91-69, 83 Stat. 108, 42 U.S. Code §§ 3002, 3021 to 3025, 3031, 3041, 3044 to 3044e, 3051 to 3055

March 22, 1972, P.L. 92-258, 86 Stat. 88, 42 U.S. Code §§ 3045 to 3045i, 3051 to 3055

Sept. 19, 1972, P.L. 92-424, 86 Stat. 705, 42 U.S. Code § 3044

Nov. 28, 1975, P.L. 94-135, 89 Stat. 713, 20 U.S. Code §§ 1008a, 1208a, 1341; 42 U.S. Code §§ 289k-5, 2809 nt., 3002, 3012, 3014, 3015, 3020a, 3022, 3023, 3024, 3025, 3026, 3028, 3033, 3034, 3037, 3037a, 3041f, 2045b, 2045d, 2045e, 3045f, 3045g, 3056 to 3056f, 3061 to 3067, 5011, 5012, 5082, 6101 to 6107

July 11, 1977, P.L. 95-65, 42 U.S. Code § 3045

Oct. 18, 1978, P.L. 95-478, 42 U.S. Code §§ 3001, 3001 nt., 3002 et seq.

Oct. 9, 1984, P.L. 98-459, 98 Stat. 1767, 42 U.S. Code §§ 3001 et seq.

April 1, 1986, P.L. 99-269, 42 U.S. Code § 3030a

Nov. 29, 1987, P.L. 100-175, 42 U.S. Code §§ 3001 et seq., 3001 nt., 3030h to 3030p, 3035g, 3056g, 3057 to 3057n

Continued

Nov. 7, 1988, P.L. 100-628, 42 U.S. Code §§ 3002, 3015, 3021, 3025 to 3026, 3031, 3035a, 3056e

Nov. 23, 1988, P.L. 100-707, 42 U.S. Code § 3030

June 13, 1991, P.L. 102-54, 42 U.S. Code §§ 3018, 3021, 3030bb

July 10, 1992, P.L. 102-321, 42 U.S. Code §§ 3012, 3021, 3030bb

Sept. 30, 1992, P.L. 102-375, 42 U.S. Code §§ 3001, 3001 nt., 3002, 3011 et seq., 3020b, 3021 et seq., 3030aa, 3030bb, 3030jj, 3034 et seq., 3037 et seq., 3057 et seq., prec. 3058, 3058 et seq., prec. 3058aa, 3058aa, prec. 3058bb, 3058bb, 3058cc, 3058dd, 3058ee

Sept. 21, 1993, P.L. 103-82, 42 U.S. Code §§ 3012, 3013, 3035a

Dec. 2, 1993, P.L. 103-171, 42 U.S. Code §§ 3001 et seq.

Oct. 20, 1994, P.L. 103-382, 42 U.S. Code §§ 3030g-12, 3030o

Nov. 2, 1994, P.L. 103-437, 42 U.S. Code § 3018

Aug. 7, 1998, P.L. 105-220, 42 U.S. Code §§ 3013, 3056

Oct. 7, 1998, P.L. 105-244, 42 U.S. Code § 3002

Oct. 21, 1998, P.L. 105-277, 42 U.S. Code §§ 3013, 3056, 3056a, 3056h

Oct. 27, 1998, P.L. 105-285, 42 U.S. Code § 3026

Oct. 30, 1998, P.L. 105-332, 42 U.S. Code §§ 3056, 3056c

Older Americans Act Technical Amendments of 1993

Dec. 2, 1993, P.L. 103-171, 42 U.S. Code § 3001 nt.

Older Americans Amendments of 1975

Sept. 21, 1993, P.L. 103-82, 42 U.S. Code § 5001 nt.

Older Americans Comprehensive Services Amendments of 1973

May 3, 1973, P.L. 93-29, 87 Stat. 30, 20 U.S. Code §§ 351b to 351e, 361 to 364, 1008a, 1009 to 1011, 1209 to 1211, 1504, 1505, 2809; 42 U.S. Code §§ 3001, 3003, 3011 to 3028, 3031 to 3037a, 3041 to 3044b, 3045a to 3045e, 3051 to 3055, 3061 to 3067

Older Americans Personal Health Education and Training Act

Oct. 9, 1984, P.L. 98-459, 98 Stat. 1788, 42 U.S. Code §§ 3058 et seq., 3058 nt.

Older Californians Act

Cal. Welfare and Institutions Code § 9000 et seq.

Cal. Welfare and Institutions Code, § 9000 et seq.

Older Californians Training and Employment Programs Act

Cal. Unemployment Insurance Code § 16000 et seq.

Older Citizens Electric Service Policy

Me. Rev. Stat. Ann. 1964, Title 35-A, §§ 3171, 3172

Older Citizens Lifeline Electrical Service Act

Me. Rev. Stat. Ann. 1964, Title 35, § 81 et seq.

Older Coloradans Act

Colo. Rev. Stat., 26-11-100.1, 26-11-100.3

Older Housing Preservation Act

Colo. Rev. Stat. 1973, 7-49-101 et seq.

Older Michiganians Act

Mich. Comp. Laws Ann., 400.581 et seq.

Older Nebraskans Act

Neb. Rev. Stat. 1943, 68-1301 et seq.

Older Worker Community Service Employment Act

Ark. Stat. 1947, 81-1501 et seq.

Older Workers Benefit Protection Act

Oct. 16, 1990, P.L. 101-433, 29 U.S. Code § 621 nt.

Dec. 12, 1991, P.L. 102-236, 29 U.S. Code § 623 nt.

Oldham Act (State Capitol)

Ark. Acts 1909, p. 727, No. 238

Olean Parking Authority Act
N.Y. Public Authority Law (Consol. Laws Ch. 43A) § 1599 et seq.

Oleomargarine Act
Ky. Stat. 1936, § 4224d-1 et seq.
Mass. Gen. Laws. Ann., 94:49 et seq.
Mich. Comp. Laws Ann., 288.251 et seq.
Mo. Rev. Stat., 196.695 et seq.
Mont. Rev. Code 1947, 27-501 et seq.
N.H. Rev. Stat. 1955, 184:48 et seq.
N.J. Stat. Ann., 24:13-1 et seq.
Ohio Rev. Code 1953, 3717.14 et seq.
Okla. Laws 1937, p. 89, S. B. 217
Ore. Rev. Stat., 621.440, 621.445
Pa. Purdon's Stat., Title 31, § 800-1 et seq.
R.I. Gen. Laws 1956, 21-10-5 et seq.
Tex. Rev. Civ. Stat., Art. 4476-2
Vt. Stat. Ann., Title 9, §§ 3441 et seq., 3481 et seq.
Wash. Rev. Code Ann., 15.40.010 et seq.
Wis. Stat. Ann., 97.18

Oleomargarine Acts
May 9, 1902, Ch. 784, 21 U.S. Code § 25

Oleomargarine Fortification Act
Ala. Code 1975, § 20-1-110 et seq.

Oleomargarine Tax Act
Iowa Laws 1931, (44th G. A.), Ch. 63
Tex. Rev. Civ. Stat., Art. 7057c
Wyo. Session Laws 1931, Ch. 137

Olive Oil Act
Cal. Health and Safety Code § 28475 et seq.

Olive Planning Board Regulations Act (Enforcement Procedures)
N.Y. Local Laws 1972, Town of Olive, p. 2249

Olivehurst Public Utility District Act
Cal. Statutes 1950, 1st Ex. Sess., Ch. 12, p. 446
Cal. Water Code, Appendix, § 56-1 et seq.

Olympians Assistance Act
Ill. Rev. Stat. 1991, Ch. 1, §§ 7061, 7062

Olympic And Amateur Sports Act Amendments of 1998
Oct. 21, 1998, P.L. 105-277, Division C, § 142, 36 U.S. Code § 101 nt.

Olympic Commemorative Coin Act
July 22, 1982, P.L. 97-220, 31 U.S. Code § 324 nt.

Olympic Commemorative Coin Act of 1992
Oct. 3, 1990, P.L. 101-406, 31 U.S. Code § 5112 nt.

Olympic Committee Act
Ill. Rev. Stat. 1987, Ch. 1 § 7051 et seq.

Olympic Movement Insignia Protection and Olympic Committee Exclusive Rights Granting Act
P.R. Acts 1987, No. 71

Olympic Regional Development Authority Act
N.Y. Public Authorities Law (Consol. Laws Ch. 43A) § 2605 et seq.

Ombudsman Act (Children's)
Mich. Comp. Laws. Ann., 722.921 et seq.

Ombudsman Act (Citizen's Aide)
Alaska Stat. 1962, § 24.55.010 et seq.
Haw. Rev. Stat. Ann., § 96-1 et seq.
Iowa Code 1983, 601G.1 et seq.
P.R. Laws Ann. 1954, Title 3, § 531 et seq.

Ombudsman Act (Crime Victim)
Minn. Stat. Ann., 611A.72 et seq.

Ombudsman Act (Long-Term Care Facilities)
Miss. Code Ann. 1972, § 43-7-51 et seq.

Ombudsman Act (Long-Term Care Program)
Colo. Rev. Stat., 26-11.5-101 et seq.
Kan. Stat. Ann., 75-5916 et seq.
Mass. Gen. Laws. Ann., 19A:27 et seq.
N.M. Stat. Ann., 28-17-1 et seq.
Okla. Stat. Ann., Title 63, § 1-2211 et seq.
W. Va. Code 1966, § 16-5L-1 et seq.

Ombudsman Act (Long Term Care)
Neb. Laws 1997, L.B. 677, §§ 1 to 28
R.I. Gen. Laws 1956, 42-66.7-1 et seq.

Ombudsman for Institutionalized Elderly Act
Utah Code Ann. 1953, 62A-3-201 et seq.

Ombudsman for Nursing Home Residents
N.Y. Public Health Law 1945 (Consol. Laws Ch. 45) § 2803c, Subd. 3
N.Y. Social Services Law (Consol. Laws Ch. 55) § 461a, Subd. 3

Ombudsman for Private Property Rights Act
Ariz. Rev. Stat. Ann., § 41-1311 et seq.

Ombudsman for the Protection of Children Act (State)
Ga. Code Ann., 15-11-120 et seq.

Ombudsman Public Counsel Act
Neb. Rev. Stat. 1943, 81-8, 240 et seq.

Omitted Assessments Act
N.J. Stat. Ann., 54:4-63.12 et seq.

Omitted Child Act (Wills)
Mass. Gen. Laws. Ann., 191:20

Omitted Property Act (Taxation)
Ore. Rev. Stat., 311.207 et seq.

Omnibus Act (Jurisdiction)
Ill. Rev. Stat. 1991, Ch. 110, § 2-201 et seq.

Omnibus Act (Local Government)
Cal. Statutes 1991, Ch. 1226
Cal. Statutes 1992, Ch. 1020

Omnibus Act (Statehood)
Feb. 22, 1889, Ch. 180, 25 Stat. 676

Omnibus Acts of 1850
Sept. 9, 1850, Ch. 49, 9 Stat. 446
Sept. 9, 1850, Ch. 50, 9 Stat. 452
Sept. 9, 1850, Ch. 51, 9 Stat. 453
Sept. 18, 1850, Ch. 60, 9 Stat. 462
Sept. 20, 1850, Ch. 62, 9 Stat. 467

Omnibus Adjustment Act of May 25, 1926
May 25, 1926, Ch. 383, 44 Stat. 649, 43 U.S. Code § 423e
July 11, 1956, Ch. 563, 70 Stat. 524, 43 U.S. Code § 423e

Omnibus Adult Protection Act
S.C. Code Ann. 1976, § 43-35-5 et seq.

Omnibus Appropriations Act (Big Bill)
Vt. Acts 1991, No. 50

Omnibus Banking Law
N.Y. Laws 1984, Ch. 360

Omnibus Bond Authorization Act
La. Acts 1981, No. 859
La. Acts 1982, No. 707
La. Acts 1992, No. 1137
La. Acts 1994, No. 16

Omnibus Budget Reconciliation Act of 1981
Aug. 13, 1981, P.L. 97-35, 7 U.S. Code §§ 2012 et seq.
Jan. 6, 1983, P.L. 97-424, 23 U.S. Code § 104 nt.
Nov. 30, 1983, P.L. 98-181, 42 U.S. Code § 1437a nt.
Dec. 2, 1983, P.L. 98-199, 20 U.S. Code §§ 101 nt., 681 nt., 1411 , 1411 nt.
June 12, 1984, P.L. 98-312, 20 U.S. Code § 3488 nt.
July 18, 1984, P.L. 98-369, 98 Stat. 1061, 39 U.S. Code § 403 nt.
Oct. 11, 1984, P.L. 98-469, 7 U.S. Code § 79 nt.
Oct. 30, 1984, P.L. 98-558, 42 U.S. Code §§ 9871 to 9877
Oct. 7, 1985, P.L. 99-117, 42 U.S. Code § 247b
Sept. 30, 1986, P.L. 99-425, 42 U.S. Code §§ 9871, 9874
Oct. 21, 1986, P.L. 99-509, 42 U.S. Code § 1396a
April 28, 1988, P.L. 100-297, 102 Stat. 325, 42 U.S. Code §§ 9801 et seq.
June 27, 1988, P.L. 100-352, 102 Stat. 664, 45 U.S. Code § 1105
May 18, 1994, P.L. 103-252, 42 U.S. Code §§ 9881 to 9887
Oct. 20, 1994, P.L. 103-382, 20 U.S. Code § 241 nt.

Oct. 25, 1994, P.L. 103-414, 108 Stat. 4296

Omnibus Budget Reconciliation Act of 1982

Oct. 14, 1982, P.L. 97-306, 38 U.S. Code §§ 314, 314 nt., 315, 362, 411, 413, 414

Oct. 15, 1982, P.L. 97-320, 38 U.S. Code §§ 314, 314 nt., 315, 362, 411, 413, 414

Oct. 15, 1982, P.L. 97-346, 5 U.S. Code §§ 5504 nt., 5532 nt., 5728 nt., 8831 nt., 8832, 8832 nt., 8337, 8342, 8906 nt.

April 18, 1984, P.L. 98-270, 5 U.S. Code § 8340 nt.

July 18, 1984, P.L. 98-369, 98 Stat. 1059, 5 U.S. Code §§ 5532 nt., 8331 nt.

Aug. 22, 1984, P.L. 98-396, 5 U.S. Code § 8340 nt.

Nov. 8, 1984, P.L. 98-623, 7 U.S. Code § 1707a nt.

Omnibus Budget Reconciliation Act of 1983

April 18, 1984, P.L. 98-270, 5 U.S. Code §§ 5343 nt., 8340, 8340 nt.; 15 U.S. Code §§ 631 nt., 632, 632 nt., 633, 636, 636 nt., 647

Omnibus Budget Reconciliation Act of 1986

Oct. 21, 1986, P.L. 99-509, 100 Stat. 1874

May 15, 1987, P.L. 100-40, 31 U.S. Code § 3101 nt.

Aug. 18, 1987, P.L. 100-93, 42 U.S. Code § 1320a-7a

Sept. 29, 1987, P.L. 100-119, 42 U.S. Code § 1320b-8 nt.

Dec. 22, 1987, P.L. 100-203, 42 U.S. Code §§ 1320a-7a nt., 1395u nts. 1395mm nt., 1395rr nt., 1396a nt., 1396d nt.

Jan. 6, 1988, P.L. 100-233, 7 U.S. Code § 1929a nt.

July 1, 1988, P.L. 100-360, 102 Stat. 772, 42 U.S. Code §§ 1320c- 3 nt., 1395y nts., 1395mm nt., 1395pp nt., 1395ww nt.

Oct. 13, 1988, P.L. 100-485, 42 U.S. Code §§ 1395k nt., 1320a-7a

Dec. 12, 1989, P.L. 101-220, 7 U.S. Code § 1929a

Dec. 19, 1989, P.L. 101-239, 42 U.S. Code §§ 1320a-7a nt., 1395k nt., 1395mm nt., 1395rr nt.

Nov. 5, 1990, P.L. 101-508, 42 U.S. Code §§ 1395b-1 nt., 1395l nt., 1395x nt., 1385y nt., 1395pp nt., 1395rr nt., 1395yy nt., 1396a nt.

Omnibus Budget Reconciliation Act of 1987

Dec. 22, 1987, P.L. 100-203, 101 Stat. 1330

July 1, 1988, P.L. 100-360, 102 Stat. 768, generally 42 U.S. Code §§ 1320a et seq., 1396 et seq.

Nov. 7, 1988, P.L. 100-628, 102 Stat. 3257

Nov. 10, 1988, P.L. 100-647, 45 U.S. Code §§ 231n nt., 3121 nt., 3304 nt.

Sept. 30, 1989, p. l. 101-103, 5 U.S. Code § 8343a nt.

Dec. 19, 1989, P.L. 101-239, 42 U.S. Code §§ 1395f nt., 1395 m nt., 1395ww nt.

Dec. 19, 1989, P.L. 101-239, 103 Stat. 2106

Nov. 5, 1990, P.L. 101-508, 5 U.S. Code § 8343a nt., 42 U.S. Code §§ 1395f nt., 1395l nt., 1395m nt., 1395u nt., 1395w-1 nt., 1396a nt. , 1396r nt.

Dec. 8, 1993, P.L. 103-182, 19 U.S. Code § 3 nt.

Oct. 31, 1994, P.L. 103-432, 42 U.S. Code § 1395ww nt.

Dec. 21, 1995, P.L. 104-66, 42 U.S. Code § 1383 nt.

Aug. 22, 1996, P.L. 104-193, 42 U.S. Code § 602 nt.

Nov. 10, 1998, P.L. 105-362, 42 U.S. Code § 1395l nt.

Omnibus Budget Reconciliation Act of 1989

Dec. 19, 1989, P.L. 101-239, 103 Stat. 2106

Nov. 3, 1990, P.L. 101-502, 104 Stat. 1285

Nov. 5, 1990, P.L. 101-508, 5 U.S. Code §§ 8343a nt., 8348 nt., 20 U.S. Code § 1078-1 nt., 42 U.S. Code §§ 602 nt., 606 nt., 627 nt., 1395l nt., 1395m nt., 1395u nt., 1395w-4 nt., 1395x nt., 1395nn nt., 1395ww nt., 1396a, 1396d

Nov. 26, 1991, P.L. 102-168, 42 U.S. Code § 300aa-1 nt.

July 2, 1992, P.L. 102-317, 106 Stat. 289

Aug. 10, 1993, P.L. 103-66, 42 U.S. Code § 674 nt.

Aug. 20, 1996, P.L. 104-188, 26 U.S. Code §§ 381, 401 nt., 461, 954, 4979A, 4980B, 6050H

Oct. 19, 1996, P.L. 104-316, 42 U.S. Code § 1395nn nt.

Nov. 10, 1998, P.L. 105-362, 42 U.S. Code §§ 1395w-4 nt., 1395ww nt.

Omnibus Budget Reconciliation Act of 1990

Nov. 5, 1990, P.L. 101-508, 104 Stat. 1388

April 9, 1991, P.L. 102-26, 20 U.S. Code §§ 1088, 1088 nt., 1091

Oct. 28, 1991, P.L. 102-139, 38 U.S. Code § 1710 nt.

Dec. 10, 1991, P.L. 102-204, 35 U.S. Code § 41 nt.

July 23, 1992, P.L. 102-325, 11 U.S. Code § 362 nt.

Oct. 2, 1992, P.L. 102-378, 5 U.S. Code §§ 2105 nt., 8348 nt.

Oct. 7, 1992, P.L. 102-401, 42 U.S. Code prec. § 9858

Oct. 24, 1992, P.L. 102-486, 42 U.S. Code § 2214

Oct. 28, 1992, P.L. 102-550, 12 U.S. Code § 1709 nt.

Oct. 29, 1992, P.L. 102-568, 38 U.S. Code § 1710 nt.

Nov. 4, 1992, P.L. 102-586, 42 U.S. Code §§ 9801 nt., prec. 9858, 9858 et seq.

Aug. 10, 1993, P.L. 103-66, 7 U.S. Code §§ 1421 nt., 1445b-3a nt.; 35 U.S. Code § 41 nt.; 38 U.S. Code § 1710 nt.; 42 U.S. Code §§ 1382a nt., 2214; 46 U.S. Code Appx. § 121

Oct. 31, 1994, P.L. 103-432, 42 U.S. Code §§ 254b nt., 1320a-7a, 1320b-9, 1320c-3, 1382a, 1395b-2, 1395b-4, 1395m, 1395u, 1395x, 1395w-4, 1395aa, 1395dd, 1395hh nt., 1395mm nt., 1395nn, 1395pp, 1395rr, 1395ss, 1395ww, 1395bbb, 1396bbb nt.

Nov. 2, 1994, P.L. 103-437, 42 U.S. Code § 1395b-4

July 7, 1995, P.L. 104-18, 42 U.S. Code § 1320c-3 nt.

April 4, 1996, P.L. 104-127, 7 U.S. Code § 1421 nt.

Oct. 19, 1996, P.L. 104-316, 42 U.S. Code § 1396r-8 nt.

Oct. 19, 1996, P.L. 104-324, 46 U.S. Code § 2110

Aug. 5, 1997, P.L. 105-33, 38 U.S. Code § 1710 nt.

Oct. 7, 1998, P.L. 105-245, 42 U.S. Code § 2214

Nov. 10, 1998, P.L. 105-362, 42 U.S. Code §§ 1395b-4, 1395x nt., 1396r nt.

Omnibus Budget Reconciliation Act of 1993

Aug. 10, 1993, P.L. 103-66, 107 Stat. 312

Nov. 2, 1994, P.L. 103-443, 16 U.S. Code §§ 500 nt., 1181f nt.

April 4, 1996, P.L. 104-127, 7 U.S. Code § 5623 nt.

Aug. 22, 1996, P.L. 104-193, 42 U.S. Code § 674 nt.

Aug. 5, 1997, P.L. 105-33, 47 U.S. Code § 309 nt.

Nov. 19, 1997, P.L. 105-89, 42 U.S. Code § 670 nt.

July 16, 1998, P.L. 105-200, 29 U.S. Code § 1144

Omnibus Claims Act

March 4, 1915, Ch. 140, 38 Stat. 996 (See 28 U.S. Code §§ 121, 2501)

Omnibus Clause Act (Insurance)

Neb. Rev. Stat. 1943, 60-534

Omnibus Consolidated and Emergency Supplemental Appropriations Act, 1999

Oct. 21, 1998, P.L. 105-277, 112 Stat. 2681

Omnibus Consolidated Appropriations Act, 1997

Sept. 30, 1996, P.L. 104-208, 110 Stat. 3009

Omnibus Consolidated Rescissions and Appropriations Act of 1996

Sept. 30, 1996, P.L. 104-208, 16 U.S. Code § 460l-6a nt.

Omnibus Consumer Protection and Banking Deregulation Act

N.Y. General Business Law (Consol. Laws Ch. 20) § 520c

Omnibus Coverage Act (Accident Insurance)

Wis. Stat. Ann., 632.32

Omnibus Credentialing Act for Counselors

Wash. Rev. Code Ann., 18.19.010 et seq.

Omnibus Crime Classification Act

S.C. Code Ann. 1976, § 16-1-10 et seq.

Omnibus Crime Control Act of 1970

Jan. 2, 1971, P.L. 91-644, 84 Stat. 1880, 5 U.S. Code §§ 5108, 5313 to 5316; 18 U.S. Code §§ 351, 924, 1752, 2516, 3056, 3731; 42 U.S. Code §§ 3711, 3723, 3724, and others

Omnibus Crime Control and Safe Streets Act of 1968

June 19, 1968, P.L. 90-351, 82 Stat. 197, 5 U.S. Code §§ 5315, 5316, 7313; 18 U.S. Code §§ 921 to 928, 2510 to 2520, 3103a, 3501, 3502, 3731; 18 U.S. Code Appx. §§ 1201 to 1203; 28 U.S. Code § 532 nt.; 42 U.S. Code §§ 3334, 3701, 3711, 3721 to 3725, 3731 to 3737, 3741 to 3746, 3751 to 3769, 3781; 47 U.S. Code § 605

Aug. 8, 1968, P.L. 90-462, 82 Stat. 638, 42 U.S. Code § 3768

Oct. 22, 1968, P.L. 90-618, 82 Stat. 1236, 18 U.S. Code Appx.

Jan. 2, 1971, P.L. 91-644, 84 Stat. 1881, 5 U.S. Code §§ 5314 to 5316; 18 U.S. Code § 2510 nt.; 42 U.S. Code §§ 3711, 3723, 3724, 3731, 3733, 3735 and others

Aug. 6, 1973, P.L. 93-83, 87 Stat. 197, 5 U.S. Code §§ 5108, 5314 to 5316; 40 U.S. Code § 484; 42 U.S. Code §§ 3334, 3701, 3711, 3721 to 3725, 3731 to 3738, 3741 to 3747, 3750

Sept. 7, 1974, P.L. 93-415, 88 Stat. 1142, 42 U.S. Code §§ 3701, 3723, 3733, 3768, 3772 to 3774

Dec. 23, 1975, P.L. 94-176, 89 Stat. 1031, 18 U.S. Code § 2510 nt.

Oct. 3, 1977, P.L. 95-115, 42 U.S. Code §§ 3767, 3723

Dec. 27, 1979, P.L. 96-157, 5 U.S. Code §§ 5314, 5315; 18 U.S. Code § 1761, 1761 nt.; 42 U.S. Code §§ 3701, 3701 nt., 3702 to 3797

Jan. 2, 1980, P.L. 96-181, 42 U.S. Code § 3733

Aug. 30, 1984, P.L. 98-411, 42 U.S. Code §§ 3796, 3796 nt., 3796a , 3796b

Oct. 12, 1984, P.L. 98-473, 18 U.S. Code Appx. § 1202, 3701

May 19, 1986, P.L. 99-308, 18 U.S. Code §§ 1201 to 1203

Oct. 18, 1986, P.L. 99-500, 42 U.S. Code § 3796b

Oct. 27, 1986, P.L. 99-570, 42 U.S. Code §§ 3741; 3782, 3783, 3789, 3793, prec. 3797

Oct. 30, 1986, P.L. 99-591, 42 U.S. Code § 3796b

Nov. 18, 1988, P.L. 100-690, 42 U.S. Code §§ 3732, 3741 to 3748, 3751, 3761 to 3768, 3791, 3793

Nov. 21, 1989, P.L. 101-162, 42 U.S. Code §§ 3754, 3756

May 25, 1990, P.L. 101-302, 42 U.S. Code § 3756.

Nov. 5, 1990, P.L. 101-515, 42 U.S. Code § 3754

Nov. 29, 1990, P.L. 101-647, 42 U.S. Code §§ 3342, 3751, 3754, 3756, 3759 to 3761, 3762a, 3762b, 3763, 3764, 3766, 3782, 3783, 3789, 3791, 3793, 3796, 3796 nt., 3796a, 3796b, 3796aa to 3796aa-8, 3796bb, 3796bb-1, 3797

Nov. 29, 1990, P.L. 101-649, 42 U.S. Code §§ 3753, 3653 nt.

Oct. 28, 1991, P.L. 102-140, 42 U.S. Code § 3754

Dec. 12, 1991, P.L. 102-232, 42 U.S. Code § 3753

Oct. 25, 1992, P.L. 102-520, 42 U.S. Code § 3796

Oct. 25, 1992, P.L. 102-521, 42 U.S. Code §§ prec. 3796cc, 3796cc , 3796cc-1 to 3796cc-6, 3793, prec. 3797, 3797

Oct. 27, 1992, P.L. 102-534, 42 U.S. Code § 3793

Nov. 11, 1993, P.L. 103-159, 42 U.S. Code § 3759

Sept. 13, 1994, P.L. 103-322, 42 U.S. Code §§ 3722, 3732, 3751, 3753, 3754, 3756, 3762a, 3762b, 3769a, 3782, 3783, 3785, 3789, 3789d, 3789f, 3791, 3793, 3796, 3796aa et seq., 3796bb, 3796dd et seq., 3796ee et seq., 3796ff et seq., 3796gg et seq., 3796hh et seq., 3796ii et seq., 3796jj et seq., 3796kk et seq., 3797

April 24, 1996, P.L. 104-132, 42 U.S. Code § 3751

April 26, 1996, P.L. 104-134, 42 U.S. Code §§ 3793, prec. 3796ii, 3796ii-3796ii-8

Oct. 3, 1996, P.L. 104-238, 42 U.S. Code §§ prec. 3796, prec. 3796d, 3796d, 3796d-1 to 3796d-7

Nov. 26, 1997, P.L. 105-119, 42 U.S. Code § 3796dd

June 16, 1998, P.L. 105-180, 42 U.S. Code §§ 3793, 3796a-1, 3796c, prec. 3796ll, 3796ll, 3796ll-1, 3796ll-2, prec. 3797, 3797

Continued

Oct. 7, 1998, P.L. 105-244, 42 U.S. Code § 3791

Oct. 21, 1998, P.L. 105-277, 42 U.S. Code §§ 3760, 3791, 3796ee

Oct. 27, 1998, P.L. 105-302, 42 U.S. Code §§ 3796dd, 3796dd-8

Nov. 13, 1998, P.L. 105-390, 42 U.S. Code §§ 3796d, 3796d-1, 3796d-3, 3796d-5, 3796d-6

Omnibus Criminal Forfeiture Act

Haw. Rev. Stat. Ann., § 712A-1 et seq.

Omnibus Criminal Justice Improvements Act

S.C. Acts 1986, p. 2955, No. 462

Omnibus Diplomatic Security and Antiterrorism Act of 1986

Aug. 27, 1986, P.L. 99-399, 22 U.S. Code § 4801 nt.

Oct. 24, 1986, P.L. 99-529, 22 U.S. Code § 3229

Dec. 22, 1987, P.L. 100-202, 22 U.S. Code § 4802

Oct. 1, 1988, P.L. 100-461, 22 U.S. Code § 4802

Feb. 16, 1990, P.L. 101-246, 22 U.S. Code § 4863

Oct. 28, 1991, P.L. 102-138, 22 U.S. Code § 4852

Oct. 24, 1992, P.L. 102-511, 22 U.S. Code § 4903

April 30, 1994, P.L. 103-236, 22 U.S. Code §§ 4801, 4802, et seq., 4821 et seq., 4851, 4851 nt., 4852, 4858

Oct. 25, 1994, P.L. 103-415, 22 U.S. Code § 4802

Oct. 21, 1998, P.L. 105-277, 22 U.S. Code § 4824

Omnibus Direct Service Act

Me. Rev. Stat. Ann. 1964, Title 14, § 701 et seq.

N.M. Stat. Ann., 38-1-16

Omnibus Drug Act

N.C. Laws 1990, Ch. 1039

Omnibus Drug Supplemental Appropriations Act of 1986

Oct. 18, 1986, P.L. 99-500, 100 Stat. 3341-362

Oct. 30, 1986, P.L. 99-591, 100 Stat. p. 3341-362

Omnibus Drunk Driving Act

Wash. Laws 1994, Ch. 275

Omnibus Drunk Driving Act of 1994

Wash. Laws 1994, Ch. 275

Omnibus DWI Act

Ark. Code Ann. 1987, 5-65-101 et seq.

Omnibus Economic Development Act

N.Y. Education Law 1947 (Consol. Laws Ch. 16) § 3032

N.Y. Environmental Conservation Law 1972 (Consol. Laws Ch. 43B) § 1 et seq.

N.Y. Laws 1987, Ch. 839

N.Y. Public Authorities Law (Consol. Laws Ch. 43A) §§ 1803a, 3102

N.Y. Unconsolidated Laws §§ 6253, 6259a et seq., 6260, 6266a, 6268

Omnibus Education Act of 1994

Sept. 30, 1996, P.L. 104-208, 20 U.S. Code § 3489

Omnibus Education Reconciliation Act of 1981

Aug. 13, 1981, P.L. 97-35, 20 U.S. Code § 3489 nt.

Sept. 8, 1982, P.L. 97-252, 10 U.S. Code § 1448 nt.; 42 U.S. Code §§ 295g-4, 300, 4577, 4588

Sept. 8, 1982, P.L. 97-253, 7 U.S. Code §§ 2014, 2020, 2026

Oct. 18, 1982, P.L. 97-348, 42 U.S. Code § 4028 nt.

May 31, 1984, P.L. 98-306, 20 U.S. Code §§ 960 nt., 967 nt.

Oct. 19, 1984, P.L. 98-511, 20 U.S. Code §§ 237 nt., 238 nt., 631 nt.

Omnibus Flood Control Act

Aug. 11, 1939, Ch. 699, 53 Stat. 1414, 33 U.S. Code §§ 558b-1, 701b-3, 701b-4, 701c-1, 701f nt., 701g, 707

Omnibus Health Benefits and Education Act

S.C. Code Ann. 1976, §§ 38-33-325, 38-71-125, 38-71-130, 38-71-145

Omnibus Health Care Rescue Act

Tex. General and Special Laws 1991, p. 4128, Ch. 1027

Omnibus Housing Act

Haw. Rev. Stat. Ann., §§ 171-84, 359-121 et seq., 359-141, 361-1 et seq.

N.Y. Laws 1985, Ch. 668

N.Y. Private Housing Finance Law (Consol. Laws Ch. 44B) §§ 44, 47, 59c, 654, 656, 902 to 904, 907, 1002 et seq., 1006, 1007, 1010

N.Y. Public Authorities Law (Consol. Laws Ch. 43A) §§ 2402, 2404, 2406, 2407

N.Y. Real Property Law (Consol. Laws Ch. 50) § 235f

Omnibus Housing and Land Use Act

Cal. Statutes 1997, Ch. 580

Omnibus Hunger Act

Tex. Human Resources Code, § 33.001

Omnibus Hunger Act of 1985

Tex. Laws 69th Leg., 1985, p. 785, Ch. 150, § 1

Omnibus Implementation Act (Proposition 218)

Cal. Statutes 1997, Ch. 38

Omnibus Insular Areas Act of 1992

Feb. 24, 1992, P.L. 102-247, 16 U.S. Code § 410tt nt.

Nov. 2, 1994, P.L. 103-437, 16 U.S. Code § 410tt-3; 42 U.S. Code § 5204b

Omnibus Insurance Fraud and Reporting Immunity Act

S.C. Code Ann. 1976, § 38-55-510 et seq.

Omnibus Judgeship Act

Aug. 28, 1935, Ch. 793, 49 Stat. 945 (See 28 U.S. Code § 132)

May 19, 1961, P.L. 87-36, 75 Stat. 80, 28 U.S. Code §§ 44, 81, 83 , 86, 89, 93, 98, 102, 123, 133, 134, 142 nt.

Omnibus Judgeship Act of 1978

Oct. 20, 1978, P.L. 95-486, 5 U.S. Code § 5108; 28 U.S. Code §§ 41 nt., 44, 45 nt., 46, 133, 1337, 1445

Omnibus Liability Insurance Act

N.Y. Civil Practice Laws and Rules (Consol. Laws Ch. 8) §§ 3016 Subd. h, 3211 Subd. a, 4545 Subd. c, 8303a Subd. a

N.Y. Court of Claims Act, § 27

N.Y. General Municipal Law (Consol. Laws Ch. 24) § 50f, 99p

N.Y. Insurance Law 1984 (Consol. Laws Ch. 28) §§ 107 Subd. a, 218, 334, 2305, Subds. b, d, 2305 Subd. f, 2329, 2342, 2344, 2402, 3426, 3435, 4402, 5405 Subd. f, 5412, 6102 Subd. a, 6102 Subd. b, 6102 Subds. g, h, j, k, 6104 Subd. a, 6106 Subd. a, 6106 Subd. c, 6108 Subd. d, 7602 Subd. c

N.Y. Local Finance Law (Consol. Laws Ch. 33A) 11.00 Subd. a

N.Y. State Administrative Procedure Act (Consol. Laws Ch. 82) § 101 Subd. 2

Omnibus Loan or Scholarship Act

Miss. Code Ann. 1972, § 37-143-1 et seq.

Omnibus Local Government Act of 1995

Cal. Statutes 1995, Ch. 579

Omnibus Local Government Act of 1996

Cal. Government Code §§ 12467, 23101

Cal. Streets and Highways Code § 11011

Cal. Water Code §§ 32551, 50707

Omnibus Long-Term Care Reform Act

Ark. Code Ann. 1987, 20-10-1001 et seq.

Omnibus Low-level Radioactive Waste Interstate Compact Consent Act

Jan. 15, 1986, P.L. 99-240, 42 U.S. Code § 2021d nt.

Omnibus Minority and Women-Owned Businesses Assistance Act

Wash. Laws 1993, Ch. 512

Omnibus Mortgage Foreclosure Curative Act

Minn. Laws 1947, Ch. 345

Minn. Laws 1949, Ch. 205

Omnibus Motor Vehicle Theft Act
Cal. Penal Code § 186.2

Omnibus Natural Resources and Recreation Act
Minn. Stat. 1986, 86.01 et seq.

Omnibus Nursing Home Act
Fla. Stat. Ann., 233.0671, 400.022, 400.071, 400.17 to 400.191, 400.23, 400.29, 400.504, 409.268, 413.601 et seq.
Mo. Rev. Stat., 198.003 et seq.

Omnibus Oregon Wild and Scenic Rivers Act of 1988
Oct. 28, 1988, P.L. 100-557, 16 U.S. Code § 1271 nt.

Omnibus Parks and Public Lands Management Act of 1996
Nov. 12, 1996, P.L. 104-333, 16 U.S. Code § 1 nt.
Oct. 7, 1998, P.L. 105-244, 16 U.S. Code § 698u-5
Nov. 2, 1998, P.L. 105-345, 40 U.S. Code § 1003 nt.
Nov. 6, 1998, P.L. 105-355, 16 U.S. Code § 460kkk

Omnibus Privacy Act
Ark. Stat. 1947, 16-801 et seq.
Conn. Gen. Stat. Ann., § 4-190 et seq.
Ind. Code Ann., 4-1-6-1 et seq.
Mass. Gen. Laws. Ann., 66A:1 et seq.
Minn. Stat. Ann., 13.01 et seq.
Ohio Rev. Code 1953, 1347.01 et seq.
Va. Code 1950, § 2.1-377 et seq.

Omnibus Procedure Act
N.Y. Economic Development Law (Consol. Laws Ch. 15) §§ 100, 141, 142
N.Y. Public Authorities Law (Consol. Laws Ch. 46) § 2879
N.Y. State Finance Law 1940 (Consol. Laws Ch. 56) §§ 139i, 164a, 174b

Omnibus Property Tax Relief and Replacement Act
R.I. Gen. Laws 1956, 44-45-1, 44-45-2

Omnibus Public Lands and National Forests Adjustments Act of 1988
Nov. 19, 1988, P.L. 100-699, 102 Stat. 4624

Omnibus Reconciliation Act of 1980
June 13, 1991, P.L. 102-54, 42 U.S. Code § 632a

Omnibus Reconciliation Act of 1981
Nov. 30, 1983, P.L. 98-181, 12 U.S. Code § 3620 nt.

Omnibus Small Business Capital Formation Act of 1980
Oct. 21, 1980, P.L. 96-477, 15 U.S. Code § 80c nt.

Omnibus State Reorganization Act
Mo. Rev. Stat., Appendix B

Omnibus Substance Abuse Prevention Act
R.I. Gen. Laws 1956, 42-109-1 et seq.

Omnibus Tax Act
Ky. Acts 1936 (3rd Sp. Sess.) Ch. 3
Pa. 1947 Pamph. Laws 1145, No. 481
Tex. General & Special Laws 44th Leg., 1936, 3rd C. S., p. 2040, Ch. 495
Tex. General & Special Laws 47th Leg., 1941, p. 269, Ch. 184

Omnibus Tax Equity and Enforcement Act
N.Y. Civil Practice Laws and Rules (Consol. Laws Ch. 8) § 1328
N.Y. Criminal Procedure Law (Consol. Laws Ch. 11A) §§ 1.20 Subd. 34, 2.10 Subd. 4, 30.10 Subd. 3
N.Y. General City Law (Consol. Laws Ch. 21) § 25m
N.Y. Laws 1985, Ch. 65

Omnibus Taxpayer Bill of Rights
Nov. 10, 1988, P.L. 100-647, 26 U.S. Code § 1 nt.

Omnibus Trade and Competitiveness Act of 1988

Aug. 23, 1988, P.L. 100-418, 102 Stat. 1107, 7 U.S. Code generally §§ 1421 et seq.; 15 U.S. Code generally §§ 271 et seq.; 19 U.S. Code § 2901 et seq.; 19 U.S. Code § 2901 nt., generally §§ 1201 et seq.; 20 U.S. Code generally §§ 5001 et seq.; 22 U.S. Code generally §§ 2151 et seq.

Oct. 31, 1988, P.L. 100-570, 42 U.S. Code §§ 1861 nt., 1892a, 1826b

Nov. 10, 1988, P.L. 100-647, 19 U.S. Code §§ 58c, 1337, 1671 nt. 2253, 2703

Dec. 19, 1989, P.L. 101-240, 15 U.S. Code § 4722; 22 U.S. Code § 262q

Aug. 20, 1990, P.L. 101-382, 15 U.S. Code §§ 4804 to 4806, 4808; 19 U.S. Code § 2902

Oct. 30, 1990, P.L. 101-476, 20 U.S. Code § 1400 nt.

Nov. 28, 1990, P.L. 101-624, 7 U.S. Code §§ 1691 nt., 1736t nt., 5211, 5212, 5215, 5216, 5231 to 5233

Feb. 14, 1992, P.L. 102-245, 15 U.S. Code §§ 2781 nt., 4603a, 4632

July 2, 1993, P.L. 103-49, 19 U.S. Code § 2902

Dec. 17, 1993, P.L. 103-199, 19 U.S. Code § 1307 nt.

Dec. 8, 1994, P.L. 103-465, 19 U.S. Code §§ 1677k, 2905, 2906, 3107, 3111

April 4, 1996, P.L. 104-127, 7 U.S. Code § 1446 nt.

Aug. 20, 1996, P.L. 104-188, 19 U.S. Code § 3011

Oct. 11, 1996, P.L. 104-295, 19 U.S. Code §§ 2905, 3007, 3010

Omnibus Traffic Safety Act

Cal. Vehicle Code 1959, § 27315 et seq.

Omnibus Transportation Act

Cal. Education Code 1976, §§ 17912.3 et seq., 39005 et seq.

Cal. Statutes 1993, Ch. 272

Cal. Statutes 1996, Ch. 10

Omnibus Transportation Act (Second)

Cal. Government Code § 14524.15

Omnibus Transportation Employee Testing Act of 1991

Oct. 28, 1991, P.L. 102-143, 49 U.S. Code Appx. § 1301 nt.

Omnibus Validating Act

Conn. Public Acts 1991, p. 4744, Ch. 289

Omnibus Water Development Act

S.D. Laws 1982, Ch. 316

S.D. Laws 1983, Ch. 315

Onderdonk-Foshee Act

Ala. Code 1975, §§ 40-20-1, 40-20-2

One Act Act (Jurisdiction)

Wis. Stat. Ann., 801.05

One Act Act (Service of Process)

Ala. Code 1958, Title 7, § 199(1)

Minn. Stat. Ann., 303.13, Subd. 1

Mo. Rev. Stat., 351.633

Vt. Stat. Ann., Title 12, § 855 et seq.

One Action Act (Foreclosure)

Nev. Rev. Stat. 1979 Reprint, 40.430

One Bank Holding Company Act

Neb. Rev. Stat. 1943, 8-1201 et seq.

One Bite Act (Motor Vehicles)

N.Y. Vehicle and Traffic Law 1959 (Consol. Laws Ch. 71) § 330 et seq.

One-Call Notification System Act

Neb. Rev. Stat. 1943, 76-2301 et seq.

One Church, One Child of Florida Corporation Act

Fla. Stat. Ann., 409.1755

One Day of Rest In Seven Act (Labor)

Cal. Labor Code § 551 et seq.

Ill. Rev. Stat. 1991, Ch. 48, § 8a et seq.

Mass. Gen. Laws 1984, 149:47 et seq.

N.Y. Labor Law (Consol. Laws Ch. 31) § 161

One Day Rest in Seven Act

Ill. Rev. Stat. 1991, Ch. 48, § 8a et seq.

One Gallon Act
Okla. Laws 1910-11, p. 154, § 5

One-Hundred-and-Sixty Acre Act
Tex. Rev. Civ. Stat., Art. 5510

One-Hundred-and-Sixty Acre Homestead Act
See Homestead Acts

One-Hundred-Eighty Day Redemption Mortgage Act
S.D. Codified Laws 1967, 21-49-11 et seq.

One-Hundred Million Dollar Bond Issue Act
Ill. Rev. Stat. 1957, Ch. 121, § 281a et seq.

One-Hundred-Sixty-Fifth Street Mall Special Assessment Act
N.Y. Laws 1976, Ch. 910

One-Hundred-Twenty-Hour Rule
Mont. Code Ann., 70-1-309, 72-2-205, 72-2-511, 72-2-512

One Man Car Act
Tenn. Public Acts 1925, Ch. 129

One-Man Grand Jury Act
Mich. Comp. Laws Ann., 767.3 et seq.

One Man, One Vote Act
Mich. Comp. Laws Ann., 46.401 et seq.

One Mile Pike Act
Ohio Laws Vol. 73, p. 96

One Mill State Tax Act (Personal Property)
Pa. Purdon's Stat., Title 72, § 3242 et seq.

One Per Cent Act
Minn. Laws, 1931, Ch. 439

One Per Cent Act (Taxation)
Ohio Rev. Code 1953, 5705.02

One Percent Fund Act
N.J. Stat. Ann., 34:15-94

One Year After Notice Act (Relief from Judgments)
Wis. Stat. 1973, 269.46, Subsec. 1

One Year and Thirty Day Act (Limitations)
N.Y. Public Authorities Law (Consol. Laws, Ch. 43A), § 1212, Subds. 1, 2, 4

One Year Property Tax Extension Limitation Law
Ill. Comp. Stat. 1992, Ch. 35, §§ 200/18-246 to 200/18-249.5

One Year Separation Act
N.C. Gen. Stat. 1943, § 50-6
Nev. Rev. Stat. Ann., 125.010

One Year Statute of Limitations
Ala. Code 1975, 6-2-39
Cal. Code of Civil Procedure, § 340
Colo. Rev. Stat. 13-80-102
Fla. Stat. 95.11
Ga. Code Ann., 34-9-82
Kan. Stat. Ann., 60-514
La. Civil Code Art. 3534 et seq.
Miss. Code Ann. 1972, § 91-7-235

One Year Statute of Limitations (Compensation Cases)
Okla. Stat. Ann., Title 85, § 43

One Year Statute of Limitations (Interpleader)
N.Y. Civil Practice Law and Rules (Consol. Laws, Ch. 8), § 216a

One Year Statute of Limitations (Misdemeanors)
Cal. Penal Code § 801

One Year Statute of Limitations (Personal Actions)
N.Y. Civil Practice Law and Rules (Consol. Laws, Ch. 8), § 215
Tex. Civ. Proc & Rem. Code, § 16.002

One Year Statute of Limitations (Slander and Libel)
Ill. Rev. Stat. 1991, Ch. 110, sect. 13-201
R.I. Gen. Laws 1956, 9-1-14

One Year Statute of Limitations (Workmen's Compensation)
S.C. Code Ann. 1976, § 42-15-40 et seq.

Oneida County Administrative Code
N.Y. Local Laws 1962, Oneida County, No. 5

Oneida County Airport Motor Vehicle Operations Act
N.Y. Local Laws 1955, Oneida County, No. 2

Oneida County Charter
N.Y. Local Laws 1961, Oneida County, No. 3, p. 658

Oneida County Sports Facility Authority Act
N.Y. Public Authorities Law (Consol. Laws Ch. 43A), § 2052a et seq.

Oneida County Tax Act
N.Y. Laws 1902, Ch. 559

Oneida County Welfare Act
N.Y. Laws 1921, Ch. 646

Oneida-Herkimer Solid Waste Management Authority Act
N.Y. Public Authorities Law (Consol. Laws Ch. 43A) § 2049aa et seq.

Oneonta City Court Act
N.Y. Laws 1976, Ch. 835

Oneword-Mobilehome Dealers Licensing Act
Iowa Code Ann., 322B.1 et seq.

ONGARD System Development Act
N.M. Stat. Ann., 19-10B-1 et seq.

Onion Act (Vidalia)
Ga. Code Ann., 2-14-130 et seq.

Onion Futures Act
Aug. 28, 1958, P.L. 85-839, 72 Stat. 1013, 7 U.S. Code § 13-1

Online Copyright Infringement Liability Limitations Act
Oct. 28, 1998, P.L. 105-304, Title II, 112 Stat. 2877, 17 U.S. Code § 101 nt.

Online Disclosure Act
Cal. Government Code §§ 84600 to 84610

Onondaga Act (Mechanics' Liens)
N.Y. Laws 1864, Ch. 366

Onondaga City Act
N.Y. Laws 1864, Ch. 366

Onondaga County Administrative Code
N.Y. Local Laws 1961, Onondaga County, No. 2, p. 723

Onondaga County Public Works Act
N.Y. Laws 1949, Ch. 816

Onondaga County Purchasing Agent Act
N.Y. Laws 1906, Ch. 20

Onondaga County Resource Recovery Agency Act
N.Y. Public Authorities Law (Consol. Laws Ch. 43A) § 2045a et seq.

Onondaga County Right of Way Designation Act
N.Y. Local Laws 1972, County of Onondaga, p. 755

Onondaga County Sanitary Sewer and Public Works Act
N.Y. Laws 1933, Ch. 568

Onondaga County Solid Waste Disposal Authority Act
N.Y. Public Authorities Law (Consol. Laws Ch. 43A) § 2015 et seq.

Onondaga County Tax Act
N.Y. Laws 1937, Ch. 690

Onondaga County Water Authority Act
N.Y. Public Authorities Law (Consol. Laws Ch. 43A) § 1150

Onondaga Public Works Act
N.Y. Laws 1949, Ch. 816

Onsite Wastewater Disposal System Law (Individual)
Miss. Code Ann. 1972, § 41-67-1 et seq.

Opal Creek Wilderness and Opal Creek Scenic Recreation Area Act of 1996
Sept. 30, 1996, P.L. 104-208, 16 U.S. Code § 545b nt.

Opelousas, Louisiana Redevelopment Agency Act
La. Acts 1968, No. 439
La. Acts 1979, No. 372

Open and Farm Space Tax Law
Me. Rev. Stat. Ann. 1964, Title 36, § 1101 et seq.

Open and Public Meeting Act
Utah Code Ann. 1953, 52-4-1 et seq.

Open Appointments Act
Tenn. Public Acts 1992, Ch. 766

Open Beaches Act
Tex. Natural Resources Code, § 61.001 et seq.

Open Bottle Act
Ill. Rev. Stat. 1989, Ch. 95 1/2, § 11-502
Minn. Stat. Ann., 169.122

Open Cut Land Reclamation Act
Ark. Code Ann. 1987, 15-57-301 et seq.
Colo. Rev. Stat., 34-32-101 et seq.
Ill. Rev. Stat. 1991, Ch. 96 1/2, § 7901-01 et seq.
Mont. Rev. Code 1947, 50-1034 et seq.
Okla. Stat. Ann., Title 45, § 701 et seq.
Wyo. Session Laws 1969, Ch.192

Open-Cut Land Reclamation Act
Ark. Acts 1991, No. 827

Open Cut Mining Act
Ill. Rev. Stat. 1947, Ch. 93, § 162 et seq.
Mont. Code Ann. 1983, 82-4-401 et seq.

Open Date Labeling Act
Ore. Rev. Stat., 616.800 et seq.

Open Door Law (Public Meetings)
Ind. Code Ann., 5-14-1.5-1 et seq.

Open Formula Fertilizer Act
S.C. Code Ann. 1976, Superseded Vols. 46-25-220 et seq.

Open Gambling Act
Nev. Statutes 1931, Ch. 99, p. 165

Open Government Amendments Act
Fla. Stat. Ann., 119.14

Open Government Sunset Review Act
Fla. Stat. Ann., 119.14, 119.15

Open Housing Act
La. Rev. Stat. Ann., 40:597.1 et seq., 51:2501 et seq.

Open Land Taxation Act
Ore. Laws 1961, Ch. 695

Open Lands Management Act
N.J. Stat. Ann., 13:1B-15.131 et seq.

Open Meeting Law (Local Agencies)
Cal. Government Code, § 54950 et seq.

Open Meeting Law (State Agencies)
Cal. Government Code, § 11120 et seq.

Open Meetings Act
Ark. Code Ann. 1987, 25-19-106
Cal. Government Code § 9027 et seq.
Colo. Rev. Stat., 24-6-402
Ill. Rev. Stat. 1991, Ch. 102, § 41-01 et seq.
Iowa Code 1977, 21.1 et seq.
Kan. Stat. Ann., 75-4317 et seq.
Ky. Rev. Stat. 1971, 61.805 et seq.
La. Rev. Stat. Ann., 42:4.1 et seq.
Mass. Acts 1958, Ch. 626
Md. Ann. Code 1974, Art. SG, § 10-501 et seq.
Me. Rev. Stat. Ann. 1964, Title 1, § 401 et seq.
Mich. Comp. Laws 1970, 15.261 et seq.
Minn. Stat. Ann., 471.705

Mont. Code Ann., 1991, 2-3-201 et seq.

N.C. Gen. Stat. 1943, § 143-318.9 et seq.

N.H. Rev. Stat. 1955, 91-A:1 et seq.

N.J. Stat. Ann., 10:4-6 et seq.

N.M. Stat. 1978, 10-15-1 et seq.

N.Y. Public Officers Law (Consol. Laws Ch. 47) § 100 et seq.

Okla. Stat. Ann., Title 25, § 301 et seq.

R.I. Gen. Laws 1956, 42-46-1 et seq.

Tenn. Code Ann., 8-44-101 et seq.

Tex. Rev. Civ. Stat., Art. 6252-17

Vt. Stat. Ann., Title 1, § 311 et seq.

Wis. Stat. Ann., 19.81 et seq.

W. Va. Code 1966, § 6-9A-1 et seq.

Open Meetings Act (Common Interest Development)

Cal. Civil Code § 1363.05

Open Meetings Act (St. Mary's County)

Md. Ann. Code 1957, Art. 24, § 4-201 et seq.

Open Mining Land Reclamation Act

Colo. Rev. Stat., 34-32-101 et seq.

Open Parole Hearings Act

Tenn. Code Ann., 40-28-501 et seq.

Open Pit Mines Reclamation Act

Pa. Purdon's Stat., Title 52, § 1396.1 et seq.

Open Pit Mining Conservation Act (Bituminous Coal)

Pa. Purdon's Stat., Title 52, § 1396.1 et seq.

Open Port Act (Commerce)

Tex. Rev. Civ. Stat., Art. 907 et seq.

Open Presidential Primary Act (Alquist)

Cal. Elections Code 1961, § 6300 et seq.

Open Public Meetings Act

Ill. Rev. Stat.1991, Ch. 102, § 41-01 et seq.

Minn. Stat. Ann., 471.705

Neb. Rev. Stat. 1943, 84-1408 et seq.

N.J. Stat. Ann., 10:4-6 et seq.

Utah Code Ann. 1953, 52-4-1 et seq.

Wash. Rev. Code Ann., 42.30.010 et seq.

Open Public Meetings, Sunshine Law

S.C. Code Ann. 1976, § 30-4-70 et seq.

Open Range Act

Colo. Rev. Stat., 35-46-101 et seq.

Fla. Stat. 1947, 588.02

Mo. Rev. Stat., 272.010 et seq.

Open Records Act

Colo. Rev. Stat., 24-72-201 et seq.

Ga. Code Ann., 50-18-70 et seq.

Iowa Code 1983, 22.1 et seq.

Kan. Stat. Ann., 45-215 et seq.

Ky. Rev. Stat. 1971, 61.870 et seq.

Okla. Stat. Ann., Title 51, § 24A.1 et seq.

Pa. Purdon's Stat., Title 65, § 66.1 et seq.

Tex. Rev. Civ. Stat. 1974, Art. 6252.17a

Open Records Act (Legislative)

Cal. Government Code § 9070 et seq.

Open Shop Act (Labor)

Ariz. Rev. Stat. Ann., § 23-1302

Tenn. Code Ann., 50-1-201 et seq.

Tex. Rev. Civ. Stat., Art. 5207a

Open Space Act

Cal. Government Code § 6950 et seq.

N.Y. General Municipal Law (Consol. Laws Ch. 24) § 247

N.Y. Local Laws 1973, Town of Monroe, p. 2548

Open Space Act (Township)

Ill. Rev. Stat. 1991, Ch. 139, § 321 et seq.

Open Space, Agricultural and Forest Land Act

Tenn. Code Ann., 11-14-201, 11-15-107, 11-15-108, 67-5-101 et seq.

Open Space and Farmland Preservation Act

Mich. Comp. Laws Ann., 554.701 et seq.

Open Space and Park Act

Colo. Rev. Stat. 1973, 29-7.5-101 et seq.

Open-Space Authority Act (Santa Clara County)

Cal. Public Resources Code, § 35100 et seq.

Open Space Easement Act
Cal. Government Code §§ 51050 et seq., 51070 et seq.

Open Space Land Act
June 30, 1961, P.L. 87-70 §§ 701 to 706, 75 Stat. 149, 45 U.S. Code §§ 1500 to 1500e
Me. Rev. Stat. Ann. 1964, Title 36, § 1101 et seq.
Pa. Purdon's Stat., Title 32, § 5001 et seq.
Va. Code 1950, § 10.1-1700 et seq.

Open-Space Land and Voluntary Conservation Easement Act
Mont. Code Ann., 1991, 76-6-101 et seq.

Open Space Lands Acquisition Act
Ill. Rev. Stat. 1991, Ch. 85, § 2101 et seq.
N.Y. Local Laws 1973, Town of Chester, p. 1458

Open Space Maintenance Act
Cal. Government Code § 50575 et seq.

Open Space Preservation Bond Act
N.J. Laws 1991, Ch. 183

Open Space Program Act
Md. Ann. Code 1974, Art. NR, § 5-901 et seq.

Open Space Property Tax Act
Minn. Stat. Ann., 273.112

Open Space Tax Act
Wash. Rev. Code Ann., 84.34.010 et seq.

Operating Authority Agreement Act (Interstate)
Neb. Rev. Stat. 75-372 et seq.

Operation Desert Shield/Desert Storm Supplemental Appropriations Act, 1991
April 10, 1991, P.L. 102-28, 105 Stat. 168

Operation of Commercial Motor Vehicles Act
See Uniform Operation of Commercial Motor Vehicles Act

Operational Plan for the Federal Program for the Donation of Surplus Property Act
P.R. Laws Ann. 1954, Title 3, § 1651 et seq.

Operations Act (General Assembly)
Ill. Rev. Stat. 1991, Ch. 63, § 23-01 et seq.

Operations of Business Establishments Act (Regulations)
P.R. Acts 1989, First Special Session, No. 1

Operator and Chauffeur License Examiners Civil Service Act
Utah Code Ann. 1953, 67-14-1 et seq.

Operator Certification Act (Wastewater Treatment)
Neb. Rev. Stat. 1943, 81-15, 128 et seq.

Operator Certification Law (Solid Waste Site)
Ill. Rev. Stat. 1991, Ch. 111, § 7851 et seq.

Operator License Act
See Uniform Operator License Act

Operators and Chauffers' License Act
Ind. Code Ann., 9-1-4-26
Iowa Code Ann., 321.174 et seq.
Mich. Comp. Laws Ann., 257.301 et seq.
Okla. Stat. Ann., Title 47, § 6-101 et seq.
Ore. Rev. Stat., § 807.010
Va. Code 1950, § 46.1-348 et seq.
W. Va. Code 1966, § 17B-1-1 et seq.

Operators and Chauffeurs' License Act (Motor Vehicles)
See Motor Vehicle Operators' and Chauffeurs License Act

Operators Certification Act (Utility)
N.M. Stat. Ann., 61-33-1 et seq.

Operators Certification Act (Water and Wastewater)
Fla. Stat. Ann., 468.540 et seq.

Operators License Act (Motor Vehicles)
See Motor Vehicle Operators' License Act

Operators Responsibility Act (Motor Vehicles, Minors)
Ohio Rev. Code 1953, 4507.07

Ophthalmic Dispensing Act
Ark. Code Ann. 1987, 17-88-101 et seq.

Opium Act
Haw. Session Laws 1860, p. 22, Aug. 21, 1860

Opium Acts
Feb. 23, 1887, Ch. 210, 24 Stat. 409, 21 U.S. Code §§ 191 to 193
Oct. 1, 1890, Ch. 1244, 26 Stat. 620
Feb. 9, 1909, Ch. 100, 35 Stat. 614, 21 U.S. Code §§ 171, 173, 174 to 185
Jan. 17, 1914, Ch. 9, 38 Stat. 275, 21 U.S. Code §§ 171, 173, 174 to 184
Jan. 17, 1914, Ch. 10, 38 Stat. 277
Dec. 17, 1914, Ch. 1, 38 Stat. 785
Feb. 24, 1919, Ch. 18, 40 Stat. 1130

Opium Poppy Control Act of 1942
Dec. 11, 1942, Ch. 720, 56 Stat. 1045, 21 U.S. Code §§ 188 to 188n
June 25, 1959, P.L. 86-70, 73 Stat. 145, 21 U.S. Code § 188k
July 12, 1960, P.L. 86-624, 74 Stat. 415, 21 U.S. Code § 188k

Opportunities Act (Inservice Education)
Kan. Stat. Ann., 72-9601

Opportunities Act (Job)
Me. Rev. Stat. Ann. 1964, Title 22, § 3771 et seq.

Opportunities Industrialization Centers Assistance Act
Ala. Acts 1977, No. 590

Opportunities Loan Act (Rural Health)
Neb. Rev. Stat. 1943, 71-5671 et seq.

Opportunity Act (College)
Ga. Code Ann., 20-3-600 et seq.
Tex. Rev. Civ. Stat., Art. 6687b-2

Opportunity Act (Economic)
Ill. Rev. Stat. 1989, Ch. 127, § 2601 et seq.

Opportunity Act (State Network)
Ill. Rev. Stat. 1989, Ch. 127, § 2201 et seq.

Opportunity and Development Act (Corridors of)
Ill. Comp. Stat. 1992, Ch. 20, § 610/1 et seq.

Opportunity and Skills Training Program Act
Mich. Public Acts 1983, No. 259, §§ 12 to 23

Opportunity Loan Program Act
Miss. Code Ann. 1972, § 37-145-1

Opportunity Program Act (Youth)
N.Y. Laws 1990, Ch. 174

Opportunity Sales Act (Business)
Ill. Comp. Stat. 1992, Ch. 815, § 602/5-1 et seq.

Opportunity Scholarship Act
Ark. Code Ann. 1987, 6-82-901 et seq.

Opportunity Zones Act (Job)
Me. Rev. Stat. Ann. 1964, Title 5, § 15131 et seq.

Opposite Party Act
Mich. Comp. Laws Ann., 600.2166

Opposite Party Cross Examination Act
Mich. Comp. Laws Ann., 600.2161

Opthalmic Advertising Act
Ill. Rev. Stat. 1991, Ch. 121 1/2, § 349 et seq.

Optical Goods Act
Okla. Stat. Ann., Title 59, § 941 et seq.

Opticians Act
Cal. Business and Professions Code § 2550 et seq.
Conn. Gen. Stat. Ann., § 20-139 et seq.
Me. Rev. Stat. Ann. 1964, title 20-A, § 4751 et seq.

Opticians Registry Act
Tex. Rev. Civ. Stat., Art. 4551-1

Option to Retain Elective Assessors Act (Dover)
N.Y. Local Laws 1971. Town of Dover, p. 1578

Optional Blue Law
Tex. Rev. Civ. Stat., Art. 9001

Optional City Government Act
N.Y. Laws 1914, Ch. 444

Optional County Affordable Housing Funds Act
Pa. Purdon's Stat., Title 35, § 1690.1 et seq.

Optional County Charter Act
Fla. Stat. Ann., 125.80 et seq.
N.J. Stat. Ann., 40:41A-1 et seq.

Optional County Government Act
N.Y. Consol. Laws, Ch. 11a

Optional County Road Act
Tex. Rev. Civ. Stat., Art. 6716-1

Optional Forms Act (Counties)
Va. Code 1950, § 15.1-582

Optional Forms of County Government Act
Ida. Code 1947, 31-5001 et seq.

Optional Forms of Municipal Administration Act
Mass. Gen. Laws. Ann., 43C:1 et seq.

Optional Forms of Municipal Government Act
Utah Code Ann., 1953, 10-3-1201 et seq.

Optional Hospital District Law
Tex. Health and Safety Code, § 283.001 et seq.

Optional Motor Insurance Coverage Act
S.C. Code Ann. 1976, § 38-77-150 et seq.

Optional Municipal Charter Act
N.J. Stat. Ann., 40:69A-1

Optional Municipal Code
Wash. Rev. Code Ann., 35A.01.010 et seq.

Optional Municipal Key Positions Act
N.J. Stat. Ann., 40:46-39 et seq.

Optional Performance Incentive Program
Ariz. Rev. Stat. Ann., § 15-920

Optional Registration Act
N.M. Stat. Ann., 1-5-1 et seq.

Optional Rent Control Act
N.J. 2A:42-74

Optional Retirement Act (Schools)
Mich. Comp. Laws Ann., 38.381 et seq.

Optional Road Act
Tex. Rev. Civ. Stat., Art. 6702-1, § 3.001 et seq.

Optional Stock Act
W. Va. Code 1931, § 19-19-1 et seq.

Optional Tax Act (Western Oregon)
Ore. Rev. Stat., 321.705 et seq.

Optional Third Class City Charter Act
Pa. Purdon's Stat., Title 53, § 41101 et seq.

Options Pilot Program Act of 1990
Nov. 28, 1990, P.L. 101-624, 7 U.S. Code § 1421 nt.
April 4, 1996, P.L. 104-127, 7 U.S. Code § 1421 nt.

Options, Stock, or Commodity Transaction Tax Exemption Act
Ill. Rev. Stat. 1991, Ch. 121 1/2, § 1000 et seq.

Optometric Corporations Act
S.D. Codified Laws 1967, 47-11B-1 et seq.

Optometric Practice and Licensure Act
Pa. Purdon's Stat., Title 63, § 244.1 et seq.

Optometric Service Corporation Act (Nonprofit)
Kan. Stat. Ann., 40-19b01 et seq.

Optometrist Treatment Program (Impaired)
Ark. Code Ann. 1987, 17-90-501 et seq.

Optometrists' Licensing Act
N.M. Stat. Ann. 1953, 67-1-1

Optometrists Lien Act
Ill. Comp. Stat. 1992, Ch. 770, § 72/1 et seq.

Optometrists' Professional Corporation Act
Minn. Stat. Ann., 319A.01 et seq.

Optometry Act
Ala. Code 1975, § 34-22-1 et seq.
Alaska Stat. 1962, § 08.72.010 et seq.
Ariz. Rev. Stat. Ann., § 32-1701 et seq.
Ark. Code Ann. 1987, 17-89-101, 17-89-103, 17-89-401 et seq.
Cal. Business and Professions Code § 3000 et seq.
Colo. Rev. Stat., 12-40-101 et seq.
D.C. Code Ann., § 2-1801 et seq.
Del. Code of 1974, Title 24, § 2101 et seq.
Fla. Stat. Ann., 463.001 et seq.
Ga. Code Ann., 43-30-1 et seq.
Ill. Rev. Stat. 1991, Ch. 111, § 3901 et seq.
Ind. Code Ann., 25-24-1-1 et seq.
Kan. Stat. Ann., 65-1501 et seq., 74-1501 et seq.
Ky. Rev. Stat. 1971, 320.200 et seq.
La. Rev. Stat. Ann., 37:1041 et seq.
Mass. Gen. Laws. Ann., 112:66 et seq.
Md. Ann. Code 1974, Art. HO, § 11-101 et seq.
Me. Rev. Stat. Ann. 1964, Title 32, § 2415 et seq.
Mich. Comp. Laws Ann., 333.17401 et seq.
Minn. Stat. Ann., 148.52 et seq.
Miss. Code Ann. 1972, § 73-19-1 et seq.
Mont. Code Ann., 1991, 37-10-101 et seq.
N.C. Gen. Stat. 1943, § 90-114 et seq.
N.D. Cent. Code 43-13-01 et seq.
N.H. Rev. Stat. 1955, 327:1 et seq.
N.J. Stat. Ann., 45:12-1 et seq.
N.M. Stat. Ann., 61-2-1 et seq.
Ohio Rev. Code 1953, 4725.01 et seq.
Ore. Rev. Stat., 683.010 et seq.
Pa. Purdon's Stat., Title 63, § 244.1 et seq.
R.I. Gen. Laws 1956, 5-35-1 et seq.
S.C. Code Ann. 1976, § 40-37-10 et seq.
S.D. Codified Laws 1967, 36-7-1 et seq.
Tenn. Code Ann., 63-8-101 et seq.
Tex. Rev. Civ. Stat., Art. 4552-1.01 et seq.
Va. Code 1950, § 54.1-3200 et seq.
Vt. Stat. Ann., Title 26, § 1701 et seq.
Wash. Rev. Code Ann.,18.53.003 et seq.
Wis. Stat. Ann., 449.01 et seq.
W. Va. Code 1966 § 30-8-1 et seq.

Optometry Board Act
Wash. Rev. Code Ann., 18.54.010 et seq.

Optometry Corporations Law
La. Rev. Stat. Ann., 12:1110 et seq.

Optometry Practice Act
Utah Code Ann. 1953, 58-16a-101 et seq.

Oral Fire Insurance Contracts Act
N.Y. Insurance Law (Consol. Laws Ch. 28) § 168, Subd. 3

Oral Health Improvement Act
Tex. Health and Safety Code, § 43.001 et seq.

Orange Advertising Act
Fla. Stat. Ann., 601.15

Orange County Administrative Code
N.Y. Local Laws 1969, Orange County, p. 741

Orange County Air and Water Pollution Control Act
Fla. Special Laws 1967, Ch. 67-1830

Orange County Airport Authority Act
Tex. Laws 60th Leg., 1967, p. 1993, Ch. 739

Orange County Charter
N.Y. Local Laws 1968, Orange County, p. 1945

Orange County Flood Control Act
Cal. Water Code, Appendix, § 36-1 et seq.

Orange County Library District Act
Fla. Laws 1999, H.B. 1695
Fla. Special Laws 1980, Ch. 80-555

Orange County Noise Control Act
N.Y. Local Laws 1973, County of Orange, p. 1160

Orange County-Orlando Expressway Authority Act
Fla. Stat. Ann., 348.751 et seq.

Orange County Regional Justice Facilities Act
Cal. Government Code, § 26295 et seq.

Orange County Teachers' Tenure Act
Fla. Special Laws 1937, Ch. 18743

Orange County Transit District Act
Cal. Public Utilities Code § 40000 et seq.

Orange County Utility Bond Act
Fla. Special Laws 1971, Ch. 71-804

Orange County Waste Collection and Disposal System Act
Fla. Special Laws 1969, Ch. 69-1371

Orange County Water Authority Act
N.Y. Public Authorities Law (Consol. Laws Ch. 43A) § 1199aa et seq.

Orange County Water Conservation and Control Act
Fla. Special Laws 1961, Ch. 61-2581

Orange County Water District Act
Cal. Statutes 1933, Ch. 924, p. 2400
Cal. Water Code, Appendix, § 40-1 et seq.

Orange Rust Act
Neb. Laws 1929, Ch. 2

Orange Stabilization Act
Fla. Stat. Ann., 601.154

Orangetown Consumer Protection Act
N.Y. Local Laws 1973, Town of Orangetown, p. 2709

Orangetown Public Drinking Act
N.Y. Local Laws 1971, Town of Orangetown, p. 3020

Orangetown Zoning Act
N.Y. Local Laws 1969, Town of Orangetown, p. 1841

Orchard and Nursery Inspection Act
Tex. Agriculture Code, § 71.041 et seq.

Orchard Lien Act
Wash. Rev. Code Ann., 60.16.010 et seq.

Orderly Milk Marketing Act
La. Acts 1958, No. 193

Orderly School Termination Procedures Act
Utah Code Ann. 1953, 53-51-1 et seq.

Ordinance Publications Act
N.Y. Local Laws 1970, Village of Spring Valley, p. 4179
N.Y. Local Laws 1971, Town of North Castle, p. 2934

Ordinance Violation Incarceration Act (Park)
Ill. Rev. Stat. 1991, Ch. 105, § 327z et seq.

Ordinance Violation Procedure Act (Park)
Ill. Rev. Stat. 1991, Ch. 105, §§ 330h, 331

Ordinaries Retirement Act
Ga. Code Ann., 47-11-20 et seq.

Ordnance Tool Act
May 11, 1939, Ch. 122, 53 Stat. 739

Ore Processor's License Act
Cal. Public Resources Code § 2250 et seq.

Oregon Public Lands Transfer and Protection Act of 1998
Oct. 30, 1998, P.L. 105-321, 112 Stat. 3020, 43 U.S. Code § 390h nt.

Oregon Resource Conservation Act of 1996
Sept. 30, 1996, P.L. 104-208, 110 Stat. 3009

Oregon Wilderness Act of 1984
June 26, 1984, P.L. 98-328, 16 U.S. Code §§ 460oo, 460oo nt., 1132 nt.

Organ and Blood Transaction Liability Act
Ill. Comp. Stat. 1992, Ch. 745, § 40/0.01 et seq.
Ill. Rev. Stat. 1991, Ch. 111 1/2, § 5100 et seq.

Organ and Tissue Donation Protocol and Hospital Policy Act
S.C. Code Ann. 1976, § 44-43-910 et seq.

Organ and Tissue Procurement Act (Gift of Life)
S.C. Code Ann. 1976, §§ 12-6-5065, 44-13-1310 et seq.

Organ Donation Request Act
Ill. Rev. Stat. 1991, Ch. 110 1/2, § 751 et seq.

Organ Donor Act
Va. Code 1950, § 32.1-289 et seq.

Organ Donor Identification Act
D.C. Laws 1975, No. 1-8

Organ Transplant Amendments Act of 1988
Nov. 4, 1988, P.L. 100-607, 42 U.S. Code § 201 nt.
April 23, 1990, P.L. 101-274, 42 U.S. Code § 273. nt.

Organ Transplant Fund
Mass. Gen. Laws. Ann., 10:35E

Organ Transplantation Procedures Act
Ill. Rev. Stat. 1991, Ch. 111 1/2, § 6601 et seq.

Organic Act
Alaska Comp. Laws Ann. 1949, §§ 1-1-1 et seq., 66-3-1 et seq.
D.C. Code 1-101, 1-102, 1-103

Organic Act of Alaska
Nov. 13, 1942, Ch. 637, 56 Stat. 1016
July 28, 1956, Ch. 772, 70 Stat. 713

Organic Act of Guam
Aug. 1, 1950, Ch. 512, 64 Stat. 384 (See 8 U.S. Code §§ 1407, 1422; 48 U.S. Code §§ 1421 to 1424b)
Oct. 31, 1951, Ch. 655, 65 Stat. 728, 48 U.S. Code § 1424b

Aug. 27, 1954, Ch. 1017, 68 Stat. 882, 48 U.S. Code § 1424

Aug. 1, 1956, Ch. 852, 70 Stat. 911, 48 U.S. Code § 1421d

June 4, 1958, P.L. 85-444, 72 Stat. 178, 48 U.S. Code §§ 1424, 1424b

Aug. 20, 1958, P.L. 85-688, 72 Stat. 681, 48 U.S. Code § 1421i

Sept. 21, 1959, P.L. 86-316, 73 Stat. 588, 48 U.S. Code § 1421a

Sept. 13, 1960, P.L. 86-778, 74 Stat. 941, 48 U.S. Code § 1421h

March 16, 1962, P.L. 87-419, 76 Stat. 34, 48 U.S. Code § 1422b

June 30, 1965, P.L. 89-100, 79 Stat. 424, 48 U.S. Code § 1421d

Sept. 2, 1966, P.L. 89-552, 80 Stat. 375, 48 U.S. Code § 1423

Sept. 11, 1968, P.L. 90-497, 82 Stat. 842, 48 U.S. Code §§ 1421a to 1421d, 1421f, 1422 to 1422d, 1423b, 1423h, 1423i

Oct. 31, 1972, P.L. 92-606, 86 Stat. 1497, 48 U.S. Code § 1421i

May 27, 1975, P.L. 94-26, 89 Stat. 94, 48 U.S. Code § 1421

Oct. 15, 1977, P.L. 95-134, 48 U.S. Code § 1422d

Aug. 18, 1978, P.L. 95-348, 48 U.S. Code § 1421h

Nov. 6, 1978, P.L. 95-598, 48 U.S. Code § 1424

March 12, 1980, P.L. 96-205, 48 U.S. Code § 1423a

Oct. 19, 1982, P.L. 97-357, 48 U.S. Code §§ 1422, 1422a, 1422d

Dec. 8, 1983, P.L. 98-213, 48 U.S. Code § 1423

Oct. 5, 1984, P.L. 98-454, 98 Stat. 1733, 1741, 48 U.S. Code §§ 1421h, 1423a, 1424 et seq., 1424b

Aug. 27, 1986, P.L. 99-396, 48 U.S. Code §§ 1421g, 1422c

Nov. 2, 1994, P.L. 103-437, 48 U.S. Code § 1424-2

Aug. 20, 1996, P.L. 104-186, 48 U.S. Code § 1421k-1

Oct. 27, 1998, P.L. 105-291, 48 U.S. Code §§ 1421g, 1423a, 1423b

Nov. 10, 1998, P.L. 105-362, 48 U.S. Code § 1422

Organic Act of Puerto Rico
March 2, 1917, Ch. 145, 39 Stat. 951, 2 U.S. Code § 46; 48 U.S. Code Ch. 4
Aug. 5, 1947, Ch. 490, 61 Stat. 770
June 24, 1948, Ch. 610, 62 Stat. 579
June 25, 1948, Ch. 649, 62 Stat. 1015
Sept. 7, 1949, Ch. 544, 63 Stat. 692
Aug. 17, 1950, Ch. 731, 64 Stat. 458

Organic Act of the Bureau of the Budget
P.R. Laws Ann. 1954, Title 23, § 1 et seq.

Organic Act of the Correctional Administration
P.R. Laws Ann. 1954, Title 4, § 1101 et seq.

Organic Act of the Department of Addiction Services
P.R. Laws Ann. 1954, Title 3, § 401 et seq.

Organic Act of the Department of Commerce
P.R. Laws Ann. 1954, Title 3, § 431 et seq.

Organic Act of the Department of Housing
P.R. Laws Ann. 1954, Title 3, § 441 et seq.

Organic Act of the Department of Labor
P.R. Laws Ann. 1954, Title 3, § 304 et seq.

Organic Act of the Department of Natural Resources
P.R. Laws Ann. 1954, Title 3, § 151 et seq.

Organic Act of the Department of Puerto Rican Community Affairs in the United States
P.R. Acts 1989, No. 58

Organic Act of the Department of Social Services
P.R. Laws Ann. 1954, Title 3, § 211 et seq.

Organic Act of the Judiciary
P.R. Act 1950, No. 432

Organic Act of the Juvenile Institutions Administration
P.R. Laws Ann. 1954, Title 8, § 551 et seq.

Organic Act of the Municipalities
P.R. Laws Ann. 1954, Title 21 § 2001 et seq.

Organic Act of the Quality Control Center
P.R. Laws Ann. 1954, Title 23, § 248 et seq.

Organic Act of the Virgin Islands
June 22, 1936, Ch. 699, 49 Stat. 1807, 48 U.S. Code §§ 1405 to 405z, 1406 to 1406m
Feb. 10, 1954, Ch. 6, 68 Stat. 12, 48 U.S. Code § 1405y
Oct. 19, 1982, P.L. 97-357, 48 U.S. Code §§ 1405, 1405a to 1405g, 1405j to 1405p, 1405r, 1405u to 1405x, 1405z to 1406e, 1406g, 1406k

Organic Acts
D.C. Code Ann., 1-101, 1-102, 1-103

Organic Certification Act
Colo. Rev. Stat., 35-11.5-101 et seq.

Organic Commodity Act
N.M. Stat. Ann., 76-22-1 et seq.

Organic Farming and Food Law
Fla. Stat. Ann., 504.21 et seq.

Organic Food Products Standards Act
Pa. Cons. Stat., Title 3, § 5901 et seq.

Organic Foods Act
Cal. Health and Safety Code, § 26569.20 et seq.
Okla. Stat. Ann., Title 2 § 5-301 et seq.

Organic Foods Production Act of 1990
Nov. 28, 1990, P.L. 101-624, 7 U.S. Code §§ 6501, 6501 nt., 6502 -6522
June 23, 1998, P.L. 105-185, 7 U.S. Code § 6506

Organic Foods Truth in Labeling Act
Mont. Code Ann., 50-31-221 et seq.

Organization Valuation Act (Conservation District)
Ill. Comp. Stat. 1992, Ch. 70, §§ 415/0.01, 415/1

Organizational Affidavit Act (Teachers')
Ark. Stat. 1947, 80-1229

Organizations, Groups and Professional Employers Licensing Act
Mont. Code Ann., 39-8-101 et seq.

Organizations of Forest Fire Control Act
S.C. Code Ann. 1976, § 48-25-10 et seq.

Organizations Registration Act
Ark. Stat. 1947, 6-817 et seq.

Organized Crime Act
N.M. Stat. Ann., 29-9-1 et seq.

Organized Crime Control Act
Colo. Rev. Stat. 1973, 18-17-101 et seq.
N.Y. Civil Practice Laws and Rules (Consol. Laws Ch. 8) § 1353 et seq.
N.Y. Criminal Procedure Law (Consol. Laws Ch. 11A) §§ 40.20, 40.50, 200.40, 200.65, 210.40, 300.10, 310.50, 450.10, 450.20
N.Y. Penal Law 1965 (Consol. Laws Ch. 40) §§ 105.35, 460.00 et seq.
Wis. Stat. Ann., 946.80 et seq.

Organized Crime Control Act of 1970
Oct. 15, 1970, P.L. 91-452, 84 Stat. 922, 7 U.S. Code §§ 15, 87f, 135c, 499m, 2115; 11 U.S. Code § 25; 12 U.S. Code § 1820; 15 U.S. Code §§ 49, 77v, 78u, 79r, 80a-41, 80b-9, 155, 717m, 1271, 1714; 16 U.S. Code § 825f; 18 U.S. Code §§ 835, 841 to 848, 1505, 1511, 1954, 1955, 1961 to 1968, 2424, 2510 nt., 2516 and others; 19 U.S. Code § 1333; 21 U.S. Code § 373; 28 U.S. Code §§ 1073, 1623, 1826; 29 U.S. Code § 161; 33 U.S. Code § 506; 42 U.S. Code § 2201; 45 U.S. Code §§ 157, 352; 46 U.S. Code § 1124; 47 U.S. Code § 409; 49 U.S. Code §§ 9, 43, 46, 916, 1017, 1484; 50 U.S. Code § 792; 50 U.S. Code Appx. §§ 643a, 1152, 2026, 2155
Oct. 12, 1984, P.L. 98-473, 18 U.S. Code § prec. 3481 nt.

Organized Crime Profits Act (Control)
Cal. Penal Code § 186 et seq.

Organized Criminal Activity Investigation and Prosecution
Ohio Rev. Code 1953, 177.01 et seq.

Organotin Antifouling Paint Control Act of 1988
June 16, 1988, P.L. 100-333, 102 Stat. 605, 33 U.S. Code §§ 2401 nt., 2401 to 2410
Feb. 10, 1996, P.L. 104-106, 33 U.S. Code § 2406

Oriental Medicine and Acupuncture Practice Act
N.M. Stat. Ann., 61-14A-1 et seq.

Original Packages Act (Intoxicating Liquors)
Aug. 8, 1890, Ch. 728, 26 Stat. 313, 27 U.S. Code § 121

Orland Park, Centre East, Schaumburg, DuPage County, Sterling, and Elgin Civic Centers Act
Ill. Rev. Stat. 1991, Ch. 85, § 3400 et seq.

Orland Park Civic Center Act
Ill. Rev. Stat. 1991, Ch. 85, sect. 3701 et seq.

Orlando Central City Neighborhood Development Board Act
Fla. Special Laws 1971, Ch. 71-810

Orlando Downtown Development Board Act
Fla. Special Laws 1969, Ch. 69-1390

Orlando-Orange County Expressway Authority Act
Fla. Stat. Ann., 348.751 et seq.

Orlando Urban Renewal Act
Fla. Special Laws 1961, Ch. 61-2603

Orleans Water Loan Act
Mass. Acts 1953, Ch. 418

Oroville-Tonasket Claim Settlement and Conveyance Act
April 14, 1997, P.L. 105-9, 111 Stat. 16

Orphan Drug Act
Jan. 4, 1983, P.L. 97-414, 21 U.S. Code §§ 301 nt., 360aa et seq.
Oct. 30, 1984, P.L. 98-551, 21 U.S. Code § 360ee
Aug. 15, 1985, P.L. 99-91, 21 U.S. Code § 360ee
Nov. 20, 1985, P.L. 99-158, 42 U.S. Code § 287i nt.
April 18, 1988, P.L. 100-290, 21 U.S. Code §§ 360aa nt., 360ee

Orphan Drug Amendments of 1985
Aug. 15, 1985, P.L. 99-91, 21 U.S. Code §§ 301 nt., 360aa-360cc, 360ee; 42 U.S. Code §§ 236 nt., 295g-1, 6022
April 18, 1988, P.L. 100-290, 42 U.S. Code § 236 nt.
July 10, 1992, P.L. 102-321, 42 U.S. Code § 236 nt.

Orphan Drug Amendments of 1988
April 18, 1988, P.L. 100-290, 21 U.S. Code § 301 nt.

Orphan Well Fund Act
Mich. Comp. Laws. Ann., 319.41 et seq.

Orphans' Court Act
N.J. Stat. Ann., Superseded 2A:5-1, 3A:6-27
Pa. Cons. Stat., Title 20, § 2080.101 et seq.

Orphans' Court Partition Act
Pa. 1917 Pamph. Laws 337, No. 187

Orphan's Educational Act
Iowa Code Ann., 35.7 et seq.

Orphans' Trust Fund Act
Ore. Rev. Stat., 418.675 et seq.

Orthodontics and Prosthetics Act
Tex. Rev. Civ. Stat., Art. 8920

Orthotists Practice Act
Ga. Code Ann., 43-34-60 et seq.

Osage Act (Indians)
June 28, 1906, Ch. 3572, 34 Stat. 539

Osborn Act (Area of State)
Mich. Comp. Laws Ann., 2.1, 2.2

Ossining Housing and Property Maintenance Code
N.Y. Local Laws 1973, Village of Ossining, p. 3660

Osteopathic Act
Cal. Business and Professions Code § 3600 et seq.

Osteopathic and Allopathic Health Care Discrimination Act
Ill. Comp. Stat. 1992, Ch. 225, § 62/1

Osteopathic and Medical Practice Act
Ky. Rev. Stat. 1971, 311.530 et seq.
Pa. Purdon's Stat., Title 63, § 271.1 et seq.

Osteopathic and Medical Service Corporation Act (Nonprofit)
Pa. Cons. Stat., Title 40, § 6101 et seq.

Osteopathic Intern Act
N.M. Stat. Ann., 21-26-1 et seq.

Osteopathic Medical Student Loan Act
N.M. Stat. Ann., 21-22A-1 et seq.

Osteopathic Medicine Act
Okla. Stat. Ann., Title 59, § 640 et seq.

Osteopathic Physicians Assistants Act
N.M. Stat. Ann., 61-10A-1 et seq.

Osteopathy Act
Ariz. Rev. Stat. Ann., § 32-1801 et seq.
Cal. Business and Professions Code Appendix 2, § 3600 et seq.
Fla. Stat. Ann., 459.01 et seq.
Iowa Code Ann., 150.1 et seq.
Ky. Rev. Stat. 1971, 311.530 et seq.
Md. Ann. Code 1974, Art. HO, § 14-321 et seq.
Mich. Comp. Laws Ann., 333.17501 et seq.
Mont. Code Ann., 1991, 37-5-101 et seq.
N.D. Cent. Code, Superseded Volume, 43-14-01 et seq.
N.M. Stat. Ann., 61-10-1 et seq.
Okla. Stat. Ann., Title 59, § 620 et seq.

Ore. Rev. Stat., 677.010 et seq.

Pa. Purdon's Stat., Title 63, § 271.1 et seq.

R.I. Gen. Laws 1956, 5-36-1 et seq.

Utah Code Ann. 1953, 58-12-1 et seq.

Vt. Stat. Ann., Title 26, § 1751 et seq.

Wash. Rev. Code Ann., 18.57.001 et seq.

W. Va. Code 1966, § 30-14-1 et seq.

Osteoporosis Bone Mass Measurement Coverage Act

Ga. Code Ann., 31-15A-1 et seq.

Osteoporosis Prevention and Education Program Act

N.J. Stat. Ann., 26:2R-1 et seq.

Osteoporosis Prevention and Treatment Act

Ala. Code 1975, § 22-13A-1 et seq.

Ga. Code Ann., 31-42-1 to 31-42-3

Miss. Code Ann. 1972, § 41-93-1 et seq.

S.C. Code Ann. 1976, § 44-125-10 et seq.

Tenn. Code Ann., 68-1-1501 et seq.

Osteoporosis Prevention Education Act

Ark. Code Ann. 1987, 20-15-1401 et seq.

W. Va. Code 1966, § 16-5M-1 et seq.

Ostrander Amendment (Reservoirs)

N.Y. Const. 1894, Art. 14, § 2

Oswego City Court Act

N.Y. Laws 1933, Ch. 747

Oswego Port Authority Act

N.Y. Public Authorities Law (Consol. Laws, Ch. 43A), § 1825 et seq.

Otego Snowmobile Act

N.Y. Local Laws 1972, Town of Otego, p. 2458

Other Exemptions and Homestead Act

S.C. Code Ann. 1976, § 15-41-10 et seq.

Other Minerals

Cal. Public Resources Code § 6890 et seq.

Otis Act

Ill. Rev. Stat. 1941, Ch. 122, § 151 et seq., 186

Otsego, Montgomery, Schoharie Solid Waste Management Authority Act

N.Y. Public Authorities Law (Consol. Laws Ch. 43A) § 2401 et seq.

Ottawa Civic Center Law

Ill. Rev. Stat. 1991, Ch. 85, § 7005-1 et seq.

Ottawa, Illinois Valley, Waukegan, Pontiac, Randolph County, Carbondale, Riverside, and Matteson Civic Centers Act

Ill. Rev. Stat. 1991, Ch. 85, § 7000-1 et seq.

Otterbacher-Symons Renal Disease Act

Mich. Comp. Laws Ann., 333.5401 et seq.

Ouster Act (Public Officers)

Kan. Stat. Ann., 60-1205 et seq.

Tenn. Code Ann., 8-47-101 et seq.

Va. Code 1950, § 24.1-79.1 et seq.

Out-of-Country Foreign Money-Judgment Recognition Act

See Uniform Out-of-Country Foreign Money-Judgment Recognition Act

Out of Home Placement and Foster Care Act

Okla. Stat. Ann., Title 10, § 7201 et seq.

Out of State Attendance of Witnesses Act (Criminal Proceedings)

See Uniform Act to Secure Attendance of Witnesses from Without the State in Criminal Proceedings

Out of State Dumping Act

Me. Rev. Stat. Ann. 1964, Title 17, § 2253

Out of State Incarceration Act

Colo. Rev. Stat., 24-60-304

N.J. Stat. Ann., 2A:168-18 et seq.

Out of-State Incarceration Amendment

Ida. Code 1947, 20-301

Out of State Land Sales Practices Act

Ga. Code Ann., 44-3-40 et seq.

Mont. Code Ann., 1991, 76-4-1201 et seq.

Out-of-State Mail Service Pharmacy Licensing Act
Ida. Code 1947, 54-1740 et seq.

Out-of-State Murderers Act (Arrest and Conviction)
Ill. Comp. Stat. 1992, Ch. 725, §§ 110/0.01, 110/1
Ill. Rev. Stat. 1991, Ch. 60, §§ 50, 51

Out of State Parolee Supervision Act
See also Uniform Act for Out of State Parolee Supervision
Cal. Penal Code § 11175 et seq.
Colo. Rev. Stat., 24-60-301 et seq.
Conn. Gen. Stat. Ann., § 54-133 et seq.
Del. Code of 1974, Title 11, §§ 4358, 4359
Fla. Stat. Ann., 949.07 et seq.
Ga. Code Ann., 42-9-70, 42-9-71
Ida. Code 1947, 20-301, 20-302
Ind. Code Ann., 11-13-4-1, 11-13-4-2
Iowa Code 1977, 247.10
Kan. Stat. Ann., 22-4101 et seq.
Ky. Rev. Stat. 1971, 439.560
La. Rev. Stat. Ann., 15:574.14
Mass. Gen. Laws. Ann., 127:151A et seq.
Md. Ann. Code 1957, Art. 41, § 4-801 et seq.
Me. Rev. Stat. Ann. 1964, Title 34-A, § 9801 et seq.
Minn. Stat. Ann., 243.16 et seq.
Miss. Code Ann. 1972, § 47-7-71
Mont. Code Ann., 1991, 46-23-1101 et seq.
N.C. Gen. Stat. 1943, § 148-65.1 et seq.
N.D. Cent. Code, 12-56-01, 12-56-02
Neb. Rev. Stat. 1943, 29-2638
N.H. Rev. Stat. 1955, 651-A:25
N.M. Stat. Ann., 31-5-1, 31-5-2
N.Y. Executive Law 1951 (Consol. Laws, Ch. 18) § 259m
Ore. Rev. Stat., 144.610
Pa. Purdon's Stat., Title 61, § 321 et seq.
R.I. Gen Laws 1956, 13-9-1 et seq.
S.C. Code Ann. 1976, § 24-21-810 et seq.
S.D. Codified Laws 1967, 24-16-1 et seq.
Tex. Code of Crim Proc, Art. 42.11
Va. Code 1950, §§ 53.1-166, 53.1-167
Wash. Rev. Code Ann., 9.95.270
Wis. Stat. Ann., 304.13

Out-of-State Pharmacy Registration Act
La. Rev. Stat. Ann., 44:2701 et seq.

Out of State Proprietary School Act
N.M. Stat. Ann., 21-24-1 et seq.

Out-of-State Proprietary School Act
N.M. Stat. Ann., 21-24-2

Out of State Scholarship Act
Md. Ann. Code 1974, Art. ED, § 18-307

Out-of-State Service Credit Act
Cal. Education Code 1976, §§ 22820 to 22825

Out of State Service of Process Act
Tex. Rev. Civ. Stat., Art. 2031b
Wash. Rev. Code Ann., 4.28.180 et seq.

Out of-State Teacher Recruitment and Retention Act (Credentialed)
Cal. Education Code 1976, §§ 44205, 44205.5

Out of State Witnesses Act
Ind. Code Ann., 35-7-5-1 et seq.
Kan. Stat. Ann., 22-4201 et seq.

Out Patient Clinic Act (Chicago)
Ill. Comp. Stat. 1992, Ch. 20, §§ 2315/0.01, 2315/1

Outdoor Advertising Act
Cal. Business and Professions Code § 5200 et seq.
Colo. Rev. Stat., 43-1-401 et seq.
Ga. Code Ann., 32-6-70 et seq.
Iowa Code Ann., 306B.1 et seq.
Mass. Gen. Laws. Ann., 93:29 et seq.
Md. Ann. Code 1974, Art. TR, § 8-701 et seq.
Me. Rev. Stat. Ann. 1964, Title 23, § 1901 et seq.
Minn. Stat. Ann., 173.01 et seq.
Mont. Code Ann., 1991, 75-15-101 et seq.
N.C. Gen. Stat. 1943, § 136-126 et seq.
N.H. Rev. Stat. 1955, 236:69 et seq.
N.J. Laws 1991, Ch. 413
N.J. Stat. Ann., 54:40-50 et seq.
Pa. Purdon's Stat., Title 36, § 2718.101 et seq.

R.I. Gen. Laws 1956, 5-18-1 et seq.
Utah Code Ann. 1953, 27-12-136.1 et seq.
Vt. Stat. Ann., Title 9, § 3621 et seq.
Vt. Stat. Ann., Title 10, § 481 et seq.
Wyo. Stat. Ann., § 24-10-101 et seq.

Outdoor Advertising Act (Alcoholic Beverages)
Tex. Alcoholic Beverage Code, § 108.51 et seq.

Outdoor Advertising Act (Smokeless Tobacco)
Ill. Rev. Stat. 1991, Ch. 23, § 2358-30 et seq.

Outdoor Lighting Installation Act
Ill. Rev. Stat. 1991, Ch. 67 1/2, § 120 et seq.

Outdoor Power Equipment Dealership Act
Kan. Stat. Ann., 16-1301 et seq.

Outdoor Power Equipment Manufacturers, Distributors, Wholesalers, and Servicing Dealers Act
Fla. Stat. Ann., 686.601 to 686.614

Outdoor Recreation Act
Fla. Stat. Ann., 375.011 et seq.
Minn. Stat. 1988, 86A.01 et seq.
N.M. Stat. Ann., 16-1-1 et seq.

Outdoor Recreation and Resource Development Act
Neb. Rev. Stat. 1943, 37-1301 et seq.
N.Y. Laws 1965, Ch. 558, §§ 3, 4
Wis. Stat. Ann., 23.30, 23.31

Outdoor Recreation and Resources Plan Act
Cal. Public Resources Code, § 5099 et seq.

Outdoor Recreation Development Act
N.Y. Navigation Law 1941 (Consol. Laws Ch. 37) § 140 et seq.
N.Y. State Finance Law 1940 (Consol. Laws Ch. 56) § 61
N.Y. Tax Law (Consol. Laws Ch. 60) § 289c

Outdoor Recreation Land Loan Act
Md. Laws 1968, Ch. 492
Md. Laws 1969, Ch. 403

Outdoor Recreation Plan Act
Cal. Public Resources Code § 8750 et seq.

Outdoor Recreation Resources Act
Ill. Rev. Stat. 1991, Ch. 105, § 530 et seq.

Outdoor Recreation Resources Review Act
June 28, 1958, P.L. 85-470, 72 Stat. 238, 16 U.S. Code § 17k nt.
March 25, 1959, P.L. 86-6, 73 Stat. 14, 16 U.S. Code § 17k nt.
March 29, 1961, P.L. 87-12, 75 Stat. 19, 16 U.S. Code § 17k nt.

Outdoor Sidewalk Cafe Act
D.C. Laws 1977, No. 2-7

Outer Banks Protection Act
Aug. 18, 1990, P.L. 101-380, 33 U.S. Code § 2753

Outer Continental Shelf Deep Water Royalty Relief Act
Nov. 28, 1995, P.L. 104-58, Title III, 43 U.S. Code § 1301 nt.

Outer Continental Shelf Lands Act
Aug. 7, 1953, Ch. 345, 67 Stat. 462 (See 10 U.S. Code §§ 7421 to 7426, 7428 to 7438) 43 U.S. Code §§ 1331 nt., 1331 to 1343
Sept. 18, 1978, P.L. 95-372, 43 U.S. Code §§ 1331 et seq.
Nov. 8, 1984, P.L. 98-620, 43 U.S. Code § 1349
April 7, 1986, P.L. 99-272, 43 U.S. Code §§ 1332, 1337
July 31, 1986, P.L. 99-367, 43 U.S. Code § 1343
Dec. 22, 1987, P.L. 100-202, 43 U.S. Code § 1337
Aug. 18, 1990, P.L. 101-380, 43 U.S. Code §§ 1334, 1334 nt., 1350
Oct. 31, 1994, P.L. 103-426, 43 U.S. Code §§ 1337, 1346
Nov. 28, 1995, P.L. 104-58, 43 U.S. Code § 1337
Dec. 21, 1995, P.L. 104-66, 43 U.S. Code § 1346
Aug. 13, 1996, P.L. 104-185, 43 U.S. Code § 1339
Nov. 10, 1998, P.L. 105-362, 43 U.S. Code §§ 1337, 1343, 1348

Outer Continental Shelf Lands Act Amendments of 1978

Sept. 18, 1978, P.L. 95-372, 16 U.S. Code §§ 1456, 1456a, 1464, 30 U.S. Code § 237; 42 U.S. Code § 6213, 43 U.S. Code §§ 1331 et seq., 1801, 1801 nt., 1802 et seq.

June 30, 1982, P.L. 97-212, 43 U.S. Code §§ 1841 et seq.

Oct. 19, 1984, P.L. 98-498, 43 U.S. Code §§ 1843, 1845

July 31, 1986, P.L. 99-367, 43 U.S. Code §§ 1861, 1865

Nov. 5, 1988, P.L. 100-610, 43 U.S. Code § 1815

Dec. 19, 1989, P.L. 101-239, 43 U.S. Code § 1812

Aug. 18, 1990, P.L. 101-380, 26 U.S. Code § 9509 nt.; 43 U.S. Code §§ 1811, 1811 nt., 1812 to 1824

Dec. 21, 1995, P.L. 104-66, 43 U.S. Code § 1846

Outer Continental Shelf Lands Act Amendments of 1985

April 7, 1986, P.L. 99-272, 43 U.S. Code § 1301 nt.

Outer Continental Shelf Operations Indemnification Clarification Act of 1988

Nov. 5, 1988, P.L. 100-610, 43 U.S. Code § 1801 nt.

Outfitters and Guides Act

Colo. Rev. Stat. 1963, 62-22-1 et seq.

Mont. Code Ann., 1987, 87-4-101 et seq.

Outlawry Act

N.Y. Code of Criminal Procedure § 814 et seq.

Outlawry Act (Eavesdropping Warrents)

N.Y. Criminal Procedure Law (Consol. Laws, Ch. 11A), § 700.05 et seq.

Outlet-Sewer Act

Ill. Rev. Stat. 1991, Ch. 24, § 11-140-1 et seq.

Outpatient Health Care Facility Provider Assessment Act

R.I. Gen. Laws 1956, 44-52-1 et seq.

Outreach for Pregnant Women Act (Targeted)

Fla. Stat. Ann., 381.0045

Outstanding Schools Act

Mo. Laws 1993, S.B. No. 380

Over-the-Counter Market Act

June 25, 1938, Ch. 677, 52 Stat. 1070, 15 U.S. Code §§ 78cc, 78ff, 78o, 78o-3, 78q

Overbey, Davidson, Travis and May Act (State Colleges)

Ky. Rev. Stat. 1971, 164.290, 164.310

Overcharge Fund Act (Exxon)

Ill. Rev. Stat. 1991, Ch. 127, § 167m et seq.

Overcharge Restitution Act (Petroleum)

N.Y. Laws 1994, Ch. 722

Overcrowding Act (Motor Vehicle Passengers)

Minn. Stat. Ann., 169.37

Overdraft Act

Ark. Code Ann. 1987, 5-37-301 et seq.

Overdue Tax Act

Ark. Code Ann. 1987, 26-36-301 et seq.

Overflow District Act

Cal. Statutes 1911, Ch. 718, p. 1397

Overflow Land Act

Ark. Code Ann. 1987, 22-6-401 et seq.

Overhead Bridge Act (Railroad)

N.J. Stat. Ann., 27:5G-5 et seq.

Overhead High-Voltage Line Safety Act

Me. Rev. Stat. Ann. 1964, Title 35-A, § 751 et seq.

Overhead High Voltage Line Safety Act

Va. Code 1950, § 59.1-406 et seq.

Overhead Power Line Accident Prevention Act

Kan. Stat. Ann., 66-1701 et seq.

Kan. Stat. Ann., 66-1709 et seq.

Overhead Power Line and Safety Act
Mo. Rev. Stat. 1978, 319.075

Overload Act (Motor Vehicles)
Utah Code Ann. 1953, 62A-11-201 et seq.

Overman Act
May 20, 1918, Ch. 78, 40 Stat. 556

Overseas Citizens Voting Registration Act
Va. Code 1950, § 24.1-72.10 et seq.

Overseas Citizens Voting Rights Act of 1975
Jan. 2, 1976, P.L. 94-203, 89 Stat. 1142, 42 U.S. Code §§ 1973dd et seq.
Nov. 4, 1978, P.L. 95-593, 42 U.S. Code §§ 1973dd et seq.
Aug. 28, 1986, P.L. 99-410, 42 U.S. Code §§ 1973dd et seq.

Overseas Differentials and Allowances Act
Sept. 6, 1960, P.L. 86-707, 74 Stat. 792 (See 5 U.S. Code §§ 5509 , 5721, 5724, 5726, 5727, 5912, 5913, 5921 to 5925, 6301 to 6305, 6310); 22 U.S. Code §§ 287e, 1131, 1136, 1138, 2669; 26 U.S. Code § 912; 50 U.S. Code §§ 403a, 403e

Overseas Private Investment Corporation Amendments Act of 1978
April 24, 1978, P.L. 95-268, 22 U.S. Code §§ 2151, 2191 et seq.

Overseas Private Investment Corporation Amendments Act of 1981
Oct. 16, 1981, P.L. 97-65, 22 U.S. Code § 2151 nt.

Overseas Private Investment Corporation Amendments Act of 1985
Dec. 23, 1985, P.L. 99-204, 22 U.S. Code §§ 2151 nt., 2191, 2191a , 2194, 2194b, 2195, 2197, 2199, 2200a, 2200a nt.

Overseas Private Investment Corporation Amendments Act of 1988
Oct. 1, 1988, P.L. 100-461, 22 U.S. Code § 2151 nt.

Overseas Residents Federal Election Absentee Voting Act
N.J. Stat. Ann., 19:59-1 et seq.

Overstreet Brain or Spinal Cord Injuries Act (Charlie Mack)
Fla. Stat. Ann., 413.465 et seq.

Overthrow Act
Ill. Rev. Stat. 1991, Ch. 38, § 30-1 et seq.

Overtime Wage Act
Conn. Gen. Stat. Ann., § 31-76b et seq.

Overton County Road Superintendent Act
Tenn. Private Acts 1971, Ch. 164

Overton-Whittington Flood Control Act
See Flood Control Act

Owego Parking Authority Act
N.Y. Public Authorities Law (Consol. Laws Ch. 43A) § 1595a et seq.

Owen-Carr State Parks Development Act
Ala. Code 1975, §§ 40-25-2, 40-25-23

Owner Resident Relations Act
See Uniform Owner-Resident Relations Act

Owner's Liability Act (Motor Vehicles)
Cal. Vehicle Code, § 17150
Cal. Vehicle Code 1959, § 17000 et seq., § 17150 et seq.
Ga. Code 1933, 68-301
Iowa Code Ann., 321.493
Mich. Comp. Laws Ann., 257.401
Minn. Stat. Ann., 170.54
N.Y. Vehicle and Traffic Law 1959 (Consol. Laws Ch. 71) § 388

Ownership Act (Common Interest)
Conn. Gen. Stat. Ann., § 47-200

Ownership Act (Cooperative Housing)
Vt. Stat. Ann., Title 11, § 1581 et seq.

Ownership Act (Employee)
Cal. Government Code §§ 15330, 15332

Ownership Act (Unit)
Me. Rev. Stat. Ann. 1964, Title 33, § 560 et seq.
Wis. Stat. Ann., 703.01 et seq.

Ownership Certificate Act (Boat)
N.J. Stat. Ann., 12:7A-1 et seq.

Ownership Disclosure Act (Building Law Violation)
Ill. Rev. Stat. 1991, Ch. 80, § 80 et seq.

Ownership Disclosure Law (Building Law Violations)
Ill. Comp. Stat. 1992, Ch. 765, § 425/0.01 et seq.

Ownership Opportunity Act (Employee)
Mont. Laws 1989, Ch. 671

Ownership Transfer Act (Dies and Molds)
Ill. Comp. Stat. 1992, Ch. 765, § 1053/1 et seq.

Oxford Refuse Disposal Law
N.Y. Local Laws 1972, Town of Oxford, p. 2464

Oyster Act
La. Rev. Stat. Ann., 56:421 et seq.
Md. Ann. Code 1974, Art. NR. § 4-1001 et seq.
N.J. Stat. Ann., 24:14-1 et seq., 50:1-1 et seq.
Va. Code 1950, § 28.1-82

Oyster Act (Bush)
Wash. Laws 1895, Ch. 24

Oyster Act (Town of Islip)
N.Y. Laws 1874, Ch. 549

Oyster Bay Code of Ethics
N.Y. Local Laws 1973, Town of Oyster Bay, p. 2723

Oyster Bay Comptroller Office Law
N.Y. Local Laws 1972, Town of Oyster Bay, p. 2489

Oyster Bay Executive Department Law
N.Y. Local Laws 1972, Town of Oyster Bay, p. 2483

Oyster Bay General Services Law
N.Y. Local Laws 1972, Town of Oyster Bay, p. 2480

Oyster Bay Planning and Development Law
N.Y. Local Laws 1972, Town of Oyster Bay, p. 2486

Oyster Bay Public Works Law
N.Y. Local Laws 1973, Town of Oyster Bay, p. 2476

Oyster Bay Purchasing Law
N.Y. Local Laws 1967, Town of Oyster Bay, p. 1835

Oyster Bay Receiver of Taxes Law
N.Y. Local Laws 1972, Town of Oyster Bay, p. 2474

Oyster Bay Recreation and Community Services Law
N.Y. Local Laws 1972, Town of Oyster Bay, p. 2492

Oyster Bay Town Clerk Office Law
N.Y. Local Laws 1972, Town of Oyster Bay, p. 2471

Oyster Cull Act
Md. Ann. Code 1974, Art. NR, § 4-1015

Oyster Grounds Lease Act
Md. Ann. Code 1974, Art. NR, § 4-11A-05 et seq.

Oyster Inspection Tax Act
Md. Ann. Code 1974, Art. NR, § 4-1020

Oyster Lands Act
Wash. Rev. Code Ann., 79.96.010 et seq.

Oyster Planting and Cultivation Act
Cal. Fish and Game Code 1957, § 6480 et seq.

Oyster Reserves Act
Wash. Rev. Code Ann., 75.24.010 et seq.

Oyster Tax Act
Tex. Penal Code 1925, Art. 937a

Ozark National Scenic Riverways Act
Aug. 27, 1964, P.L. 88-492, 78 Stat. 608, 16 U.S. Code §§ 460m to 460m-7

Ozone Transport Oversight Act
  Ala. Code 1975, § 22-28A-1 et seq.

Ozone Transport Oversight Act (Interstate)
  Ill. Comp. Stat. 1992, Ch. 415, § 130/1 et seq.

P

Pacific Colony Act
Cal. Welfare and Institutions Code, § 7000 et seq.

Pacific Marine Fisheries Compact Act
Alaska Stat. 1962, § 16.45.010 et seq.
Cal. Statutes 1947, Ch. 1447, p. 3014
Ida. Code 1947, 36-2001 et seq.
Wash. Rev. Code Ann., 75.40.030

Pacific Northwest Electric Power Planning and Conservation Act
Dec. 5, 1980, P.L. 96-501, 16 U.S. Code § 839 nt.
Nov. 2, 1994, P.L. 103-437, 16 U.S. Code § 839b
Wash. Rev. Code 1983, 43.52A.010 et seq.

Pacific Railroad Acts
July 1, 1862, Ch. 120, 12 Stat. 489
July 2, 1864, Ch. 216, 13 Stat. 356
July 3, 1866, Ch. 159, 14 Stat. 79
March 3, 1869, Ch. 127, 15 Stat. 324

Pacific Salmon Treaty Act of 1985
March 15, 1985, P.L. 99-5, 16 U.S. Code §§ 3631 nt., et seq.
March 9, 1992, P.L. 102-251, 16 U.S. Code §§ 3631, 3636

Pacific Yew Act
Aug. 7, 1992, P.L. 102-335, 16 U.S. Code §§ 4801, 4801 nt., 4802 to 4807
Nov. 2, 1994, P.L. 103-437, 16 U.S. Code § 4806
Nov. 10, 1998, P.L. 105-362, 16 U.S. Code §§ 4806, 4807

Pack Act (Converted Dwellings)
N.Y. Multiple Dwelling Law 1946 (Consol. Laws Ch. 61A) § 170 et seq.

Pack Act (Reorganization of Guaranty Corporations)
N.Y. Laws 1937, Ch. 926

Pack Act (Single Room Occupancy)
N.Y. Multiple Dwelling Law 1946 (Consol. Laws Ch. 61A) § 248

Package Review Act
Minn. Stat. Ann., 116F.06

Packaged Commodities Sale Act
Conn. Gen. Stat. Ann., § 42-115g et seq.

Packaged Ice Act
Fla. Stat. Ann., 500.509

Packaging and Labeling Act (Fair)
Me. Rev. Stat. Ann. 1964, Title 7, § 521 et seq.
Me. Rev. Stat. Ann. 1964, Title 7, § 521 et seq.

Packaging Food Law
N.J. Stat. Ann., 51:1-13 et seq.

Packers and Stockyards Act
Aug. 15, 1921, Ch. 64, 42 Stat. 159, 7 U.S. Code §§ 181 to 183, 191 to 195, 201 to 203, 205 to 218d, 221 to 229
Aug. 10, 1939, Ch. 663, 53 Stat. 1351, 7 U.S. Code § 211
June 19, 1942, Ch. 421, 56 Stat. 372, 7 U.S. Code § 217a
Aug. 26, 1958, P.L. 85-791, 72 Stat. 944, 7 U.S. Code §§ 193, 194
Sept. 2, 1958, P.L. 85-909, 72 Stat. 1749, 7 U.S. Code §§ 192, 201, 202, 212, 213, 227, 228
July 8, 1963, P.L. 88-61, 77 Stat. 79, 7 U.S. Code § 228
July 31, 1968, P.L. 90-446, 82 Stat. 474, 7 U.S. Code §§ 202, 203 , 205, 208, 213
Sept. 20, 1977, P.L. 95-109, 15 U.S. Code § 1692l
Nov. 23, 1987, P.L. 100-173, 7 U.S. Code §§ 182, 192, 197, 209, 218-218d, 221, 223, 227, 227 nt., 228a, 228b-1 to 228b-4, 228c, 229
Dec. 13, 1991, P.L. 102-237, 7 U.S. Code §§ 192, 227
Oct. 13, 1994, P.L. 103-354, 7 U.S. Code § 228
Nov. 2, 1994, P.L. 103-437, 7 U.S. Code § 228

Oct. 21, 1998, P.L. 105-277, 7 U.S. Code
§ 229a

Packers and Stockyards Act, 1921
Minn. Stat. Ann., 31B.01 et seq.

Packing Act
Ky. Rev. Stat. 1971, 260.040 et seq.

Padavan Law
N.Y. Eminent Domain Procedure Law
(Consol. Laws Ch. 73) § 206 Subd. E
N.Y. Mental Hygiene Law 1972 (Consol.
Laws Ch. 27) §§ 41.18 Subd. e, 41.21,
41.34
N.Y. Social Services Law (Consol. Laws Ch.
55) §§ 463 to 463b

Paddy Creek Wilderness Act of 1981
Jan. 3, 1983, P.L. 97-407, 16 U.S. Code
§ 1132 nt.

Padlocking Act
La. Rev. Stat. Ann., 13:4711 et seq.
Mass. Gen. Laws. Ann., 139:16A
Mich. Comp. Laws Ann., 600.3801 et seq.
Ohio Rev. Code 1953, 4301.73 et seq.

Padre Island National Seashore Act
Sept. 28, 1962, P.L. 87-712, 76 Stat. 650, 16
U.S. Code §§ 459d to 459d-7

Pain Patient's Bill of Rights
Cal. Health and Safety Code § 124960 et seq.

Pain Treatment Act (Intractable)
Cal. Business and Professions Code § 2241.5
Tex. Rev. Civ. Stat., Art. 4495c

Paint Act
S.C. Code Ann. 1976, § 39-45-10 et seq.
Va. Code 1950, § 59.1-177 et seq.

Paint Act (Highway Objects)
Ind. Code Ann., 8-11-4-1, 8-11-4-2

Paint and Varnish Act
Minn. Stat. Ann., 24.131 et seq.

Paint Control Act (Tributyltin Antifoulant)
R.I. Gen. Laws 1956, 46-17.2-1 et seq.

Paint Management Act (Lead-Based)
Mo. Rev. Stat., 334.105, 334.106
Okla. Stat. Ann., Title 27A, § 2-12-101 et
seq.

Paint Sniffer Law
Mont. Code Ann., 45-9-121

Paiute Indian Tribe of Utah Restoration Act
April 3, 1980, P.L. 96-227, 25 U.S. Code
§§ 761 et seq., 761 nt.

**Pajaro Valley Water Management Agency
Act**
Cal. Statutes 1984, Ch. 257

Pakula-Wilson Act (Party Candidates)
N.Y. Election Law 1977 (Consol. Laws Ch.
17) § 6-120

**Paleontological and Archaeological
Resources Protection Act**
Ill. Rev. Stat. 1991, Ch. 127, § 133c.01 et
seq.

Palisades Interstate Park Act
N.Y. Laws 1900, Ch. 170

**Palm Beach County and Municipal
Incinerator System Act**
Fla. Special Laws 1969, Ch. 69-1415

**Palm Beach County Area Planning Board
Act**
Fla. Laws 1965, Ch. 2063

**Palm Beach County Environmental Control
Act**
Fla. Special Laws 1977, Ch. 77-616

**Palm Beach County Firefighters Collective
Bargaining Act**
Fla. Special Laws 1970, Ch. 70-1004

**Palm Beach County Municipal Code
Enforcement Board Act**
Fla. Special Laws 1979, Ch. 79-541

Palm Beach County Solid Waste Act
Fla. Special Laws 1975, Ch. 75-473

Palm Beach County Water and Sewer Act
Fla. Special Laws 1967 Ch. 67-1880

Palm Beach Expressway Authority Law
Fla. Stat. Ann., 348.77 et seq.

Palm Beach Water and Sewer Act
Fla. Laws 1967, Ch. 67-1880

Palmer-Matthews Act (Public Libraries Appropriation)
Mich. Comp. Laws 1948, 397.102 et seq.

Palmer-Schneider Act (Breach of Promise)
Mich. Comp. Laws Ann., 551.301 et seq.

Palmetto Seed Capital Corporation and Partnership Act
S.C. Code Ann. 1976, § 41-44-10 et seq.

Palo Alto Battlefield National Historic Site Act of 1991
June 23, 1992, P.L. 102-304, 16 U.S. Code § 461 nt.

Palo Verde Irrigation District
Cal. Water Code, Appendix, § 33-1 et seq.

Pam Lyncher Sexual Offender Tracking and Identification Act of 1996
Oct. 3, 1996, P.L. 104-236, 42 U.S. Code § 13701 nt.
Nov. 26, 1997, P.L. 105-119, 42 U.S. Code § 14071 nt.

Pan-American Naval Academy Act
July 14, 1941, Ch. 292, 55 Stat. 589, 20 U.S. Code § 221

Panama and Isthmian Canal Act
March 2, 1931, Ch. 375, 46 Stat. 1471

Panama Canal Act Amendments of 1996
Sept. 23, 1996, P.L. 104-201, Title XXXV, Subtitle B, 110 Stat. 2860
Oct. 17, 1998, P.L. 105-261, 22 U.S. Code § 3751 nt.

Panama Canal Act of 1972
Feb. 14, 1984, P.L. 98-217, 22 U.S. Code § 3612

Panama Canal Act of 1979
Sept. 27, 1979, P.L. 96-70, 5 U.S. Code §§ 305, 5102, 5316, 5342, 5343, 5348, 5373, 5404, 5533, 5541, 5583, 5595, 5724a, 6301, 6322, 6323, 8102, 8146, 8336, 8339, 8339 nt., 8348, 8701, 8901w; 8 U.S. Code §§ 1101, 1182; 22 U.S. Code §§ 3601, 3601 nt., 3602, 3611 et seq.; 29 U.S. Code § 213; 39 U.S. Code §§ 403, 3401, 3682; 50 U.S. Code §§ 191, 195, 196
Feb. 14, 1984, P.L. 98-217, 22 U.S. Code § 3612
Oct. 30, 1984, P.L. 98-600, 22 U.S. Code § 3657a
Dec. 23, 1985, P.L. 99-195, 22 U.S. Code §§ 3712, 3793
Dec. 23, 1985, P.L. 99-209, 22 U.S. Code §§ 3771 to 3776, 3779
Dec. 28, 1985, P.L. 99-223, 22 U.S. Code §§ 3612, 3647, 3650, 3731, 3784
Aug. 1, 1986, P.L. 99-368, 22 U.S. Code § 3751
Dec. 22, 1987, P.L. 100-203, 22 U.S. Code § 3714
Nov. 19, 1988, P.L. 100-705, 22 U.S. Code §§ 3612, 3712, 3731
Nov. 5, 1990, P.L. 101-510, 22 U.S. Code §§ 3612, 3614
Oct. 23, 1992, P.L. 102-484, 22 U.S. Code §§ 3712, 3714a, 3731, 3792
Nov. 1, 1993, P.L. 103-160, 22 U.S. Code § 3701
Oct. 5, 1994, P.L. 103-337, 22 U.S. Code § 3731
Oct. 25, 1994, P.L. 103-416, 8 U.S. Code § 1101 nt.
Dec. 21, 1995, P.L. 104-66, 22 U.S. Code § 3722
Feb. 10, 1996, P.L. 104-106, 22 U.S. Code §§ 3611, 3612, 3612a, 3612b, 3645, 3712, 3713, 3723, 3731, 3761, 3775, 3776, 3791, 3794
Sept. 23, 1996, P.L. 104-201, 22 U.S. Code § 3712
Nov. 18, 1997, P.L. 105-85, 22 U.S. Code §§ 3602, 3612, 3612a, 3612b, 3613, 3620, 3622, 3642, 3650, 3652, 3655, 3656, 3657, 3658, 3659, 3661, 3662, 3664, 3665, 3671, 3673, 3681, 3701, 3712, 3714b, 3715c, 3731, 3751, 3752, 3771, 3772, 3776, 3792, 3861, 3862
Oct. 17, 1998, P.L. 105-261, 22 U.S. Code §§ 3612, 3612b, 3620, 3642, 3646, 3647, 3652, 3657, 3657 nt., 3663, 3664, 3671, 3723, 3731, 3751 nt., 3771, 3772, 3776, 3779, 3862

Panama Canal Acts

June 28, 1902, Ch. 1302, 32 Stat. 481, 31 U.S. Code § 744

Aug. 24, 1912, Ch. 390, 37 Stat. 560, 15 U.S. Code § 31; 46 U.S. Code § 11; 49 U.S. Code §§ 5, 6, 51

June 15, 1914, Ch. 106, 38 Stat. 385

Sept. 21, 1922, Ch. 370, 42 Stat. 1004

Oct. 17, 1998, P.L. 105-261, 22 U.S. Code §§ 3642, 3652, 3723, 3771, 3776

Panama Canal Amendments Act of 1995

Feb. 10, 1996, P.L. 104-106, Division C, Title XXXV, Subtitle B, 22 U.S. Code § 3601 nt.

Panama Canal Amendments Acts of 1985

Dec. 23, 1985, P.L. 99-209, 22 U.S. Code §§ 3601 nt., 3771, 3772, 3774 to 3776, 3779

Panama Canal Commission Authorization Act, Fiscal Year 1986

Dec. 28, 1985, P.L. 99-223, 22 U.S. Code §§ 3612, 3647, 3650, 3731, 3784

Panama Canal Commission Authorization Act, Fiscal Year 1987

Aug. 1, 1986, P.L. 99-368, 100 Stat. 775; 22 U.S. Code § 3751 nt., 46 Appx. U.S. Code 1295b

Panama Canal Commission Authorization Act, Fiscal Year 1990

Nov. 29, 1989, P.L. 101-189, 103 Stat. 1688

Panama Canal Commission Authorization Act for Fiscal Year 1991

Nov. 5, 1990, P.L. 101-510, 5 U.S. Code §§ 8336, 8339, 8348

Panama Canal Commission Authorization Act for Fiscal Year 1992

Dec. 5, 1991, P.L. 102-190, 105 Stat. 1586

Panama Canal Commission Authorization Act for Fiscal Year 1993

Oct. 23, 1992, P.L. 102-484, 106 Stat. 2655

Panama Canal Commission Authorization Act for Fiscal Year 1994

Nov. 30, 1993, P.L. 103-160, 106 Stat. 1965

Panama Canal Commission Authorization Act for Fiscal Year 1995

Oct. 5, 1994, P.L. 103-337, 108 Stat. 3111

Panama Canal Commission Authorization Act for Fiscal Year 1996

Feb. 10, 1996, P.L. 104-106, Division C, Title XXXV, Subtitle A, 110 Stat. 637

Panama Canal Commission Authorization Act for Fiscal Year 1997

Sept. 23, 1996, P.L. 104-201, Title XXXV, Subtitle A, 110 Stat 2859

Panama Canal Commission Authorization Act for Fiscal Year 1999

Oct. 17, 1998, P.L. 105-261, Title XXXV, 112 Stat. 2268

Panama Canal Commission Compensation Fund Act of 1988

Nov. 19, 1988, P.L. 100-705, 22 U.S. Code § 3601 nt.

Nov. 5, 1990, P.L. 101-510, 22 U.S. Code § 3715c

Panama Canal Transition Facilitation Act of 1997

Nov. 18, 1997, P.L. 105-85, Title XXXV, Subtitle B, 22 U.S. Code § 3601 nt.

Panama City Civil Service Act

Fla. Special Laws 1941, Ch. 21476

Panama City Downtown Improvement Board Act

Fla. Special Laws 1973, Ch. 73-585, 73-587

Panama City Firemen's Relief and Pension Fund Act

Fla. Special Laws 1973, Ch. 73-587

Panama City Revenue Bond Act

Fla. Special Laws 1949, Ch. 26118

Fla. Special Laws 1963, Ch. 63-1757, § 187 et seq.

Panama Defense Road Act

July 20, 1939, Ch. 335, 53 Stat. 1071

Panama Railroad Company
June 29, 1948, Ch. 706, 62 Stat. 1075
Sept. 26, 1950, Ch. 1049, 64 Stat. 1038

Pandering Act
Ark. Code Ann. 1987, 5-70-104
Cal. Penal Code, § 266i
D.C. Code 1973, § 22-2705 et seq.
Ill. Rev. Stat. 1991, Ch. 38, § 11-16
Md. Ann. Code 1957, Art. 27, § 426 et seq.
Mich. Comp. Laws Ann., 750.455 et seq.
Tex. Penal Code, § 43.01 et seq.
Utah Code Ann. 1953, 76-10-1304

Pandering Law
Dec. 16, 1967, P.L. 90-206, 81 Stat. 645
Aug. 12, 1970, P.L. 91-375, 39 U.S. Code
§ 3008

Panhandle Water Conservation Authority Act
Tex. General and Special Laws 45th Leg.,
1937, p. 507, Ch. 256

Panic and Fire Act
Pa. Purdon's Stat., Title 35, § 1221 et seq.

Paper Purchasing Act
Ill. Rev. Stat. 1991, Ch. 127, § 132.100 et
seq.

Paper Recycling Act
Okla. Stat. Ann., Title 74, § 85.50 et seq.

Paperwork Reduction Act of 1980
Dec. 11, 1980, P.L. 96-511, 44 U.S. Code
§ 101 nt.
Aug. 9, 1989, P.L. 101-73, 44 U.S. Code
§ 3502

Paperwork Reduction Act of 1995
May 22, 1995, P.L. 104-13, 44 U.S. Code
§ 101 nt.

Paperwork Reduction and Information Resources Management Act
Fla. Stat. Ann., 282.003 et seq.

Paperwork Reduction and Simplification Act
Alaska Stat. 1962, Replaced Titles,
§ 37.35.010 et seq.
Tenn. Code Ann., 4-25-101 et seq.

Paperwork Reduction Reauthorization Act of 1986
Oct. 18, 1986, P.L. 99-500, 44 U.S. Code
§§ 101 nt., 3503 nt.
Oct. 30, 1986, P.L. 99-591, 44 U.S. Code
§§ 101 nt., 3503 nt.

Par Value Modification Act
March 31, 1972, P.L. 92-268, 86 Stat. 116,
31 U.S. Code §§ 449, 449a, 449b
Sept. 21, 1973, P.L. 93-110, 87 Stat. 352, 31
U.S. Code §§ 449, 449c

Parade Police Protection Charge Waiver Act
Ill. Rev. Stat. 1991, Ch. 85, §§ 6040, 6041

Parallel Economy Act
P.R. Laws Ann. 1954, Title 3, § 1501 et seq.

Paramedic Act
Cal. Health and Safety Code, § 1480 et seq.
Neb. Rev. Stat. 1943, 71-5501 et seq.
Utah Code Ann. 1953, 26-31-1 et seq.

Paramedic Certification Act
Ky. Rev. Stat. 1971, 311.650 et seq.

Paramedic Services Act
Del. Code of 1974, Title 16, § 9801 et seq.

Paramedics Compensation Act
Ill. Rev. Stat. 1991, Ch. 48, § 281 et seq.

Paramour Act
Tenn. Code Ann., Superseded Vol., 36-831

Paramus Municipal Charter Amendments Law
N.J. Laws 1977, Ch. 100

Paraphernalia Act (Drug)
Ill. Rev. Stat. 1991, Ch. 56 1/2, § 2101 et seq.
Mont. Code Ann., 45-10-101 et seq.
S.C. Code Ann. 1976, § 44-53-110 et seq.

Parcel Carrier Act (Restricted)
Okla. Stat. Ann., Title 47, § 166.1 et seq.

Parcel Identifier Law
See Uniform Parcel Identifier Law

Parcel Post Acts
Aug. 24, 1912, Ch. 389, 37 Stat. 557
July 28, 1916, Ch. 261, 39 Stat. 412

Pardon and Parole Act
Ala. Code 1975, § 15-22-1 et seq.
Cal. Penal Code, § 4800 et seq.
Ill. Rev. Stat. 1991, Ch. 38, § 1003-3-13
Md. Ann. Code 1957, Art. 41, § 4-513
Neb. Rev. Stat. 1943, 29-2246 et seq.
N.H. Rev. Stat. 1955, 4:21 et seq.
N.M. Stat. Ann., 31-21-3 et seq.
Ohio Rev. Code 1953, 2967.01 et seq.
R.I. Gen. Laws 1956, 13-10-1, 13-10-2
Tenn. Code Ann., 40-28-101 et seq.
Tex. Code of Criminal Procedure, Art. 48.01 et seq.
Vt. Stat. Ann., Title 28, § 901 et seq.

Parent Act (Runaway)
N.M. Stat. Ann., 40-6-1 et seq.
Tenn. Code Ann., 36-5-201

Parent Child Act (Adoption)
Wyo. Stat. Ann., § 1-22-114

Parent-Child Legal Relationship Termination Act
Colo. Rev. Stat., 19-11-101 et seq.
Mo. Rev. Stat., 211.441 et seq.
Mont. Code Ann., 41-3-601 et seq.

Parent Educational Participation Act
Tenn. Code Ann., 49-6-7001

Parent Locator Act
Cal. Civil Code, §§ 4604, 4605

Parent Reimbursement Act for Nonpublic Education
Pa. Purdon's Stat., Title 24, § 5701 et seq.

Parent Support Act
R.I. Gen. Laws 1956, 15-10-1 et seq.

Parent-Teacher Conference Leave Law
Tex. Government Code, § 661.151

Parent Tort Liability Act
R.I. Gen. Laws 1956, 9-1-3, 9-1-3.1

Parentage Act
See Uniform Parentage Act

Parentage Act (Acknowledgment of)
Mich. Comp. Laws Ann., 722.1001 et seq.

Parental Consent Act (Abortion)
Mich. Comp. Laws Ann., 722.901 et seq.

Parental Equivalent Instruction Costs Reimbursement Act
Conn. Gen. Stat. Ann. 1983, § 10-281W et seq.

Parental Grant Act (Nonpublic)
Ill. Rev. Stat. 1973, Ch. 122, § 1021 et seq.

Parental Grant Plan for Children of Low Income Families Act (Nonpublic)
Ill. Rev. Stat. 1973, Ch. 122, § 1001 et seq.

Parental Kidnapping Prevention Act of 1980
Dec. 28, 1980, P.L. 96-611, 42 U.S. Code § 1305 nt.

Parental Liability Act
Ariz. Rev. Stat. Ann., § 12-661
Ark. Code Ann. 1987, 9-25-102
Cal. Civil Code, § 1714.1
Colo. Rev. Stat., 13-21-107
Conn. Gen. Stat. Ann., § 52-572
Del. Code of 1974, Title 10, § 3922
Fla. Stat. Ann., 741.24
Haw. Rev. Stat. Ann., § 577-3
Ill. Rev. Stat. 1991, Ch. 70, § 51 et seq.
Kan. Stat. Ann., 38-120
Mich. Comp. Laws Ann., 600.2913
Mont. Code Ann., 40-6-237, 40-6-238
N.D. Cent. Code, 32-03-39
Neb. Rev. Stat. 1943, 43-801
Nev. Rev. Stat. 1979, 41.470
Continued

Ohio Rev. Code 1953, 2151.411
Ore. Rev. Stat., 30.765
S.D. Codified Laws 1967, 25-5-15
Vt. Stat. Ann., Title 15, § 901

Parental Liability Act (Motor Vehicles)
Del. Code of 1974, Title 21, § 6105
Ga. Code Ann., 51-2-3
Ky. Rev. Stat. 1971, Superseded Vols.
  208.235
La. Civil Code, Art. 2318
N.C. Gen. Stat. 1943, § 1-538.1
Tenn. Code Ann., 37-10-101 et seq.
Tex. Family Code, § 33.01 et seq.
Va. Code 1950, §§ 8.01-43, 8.01-44
W. Va. Code 1966, § 55-7A-1 et seq.

Parental Notice of Abortion Act
Del. Code of 1974, Title 24, § 1780 et seq.
Ill. Rev. Stat. 1991, Ch. 38, § 81-61 et seq.
Mont. Code Ann., 50-20-201 et seq.

Parental Notification Act
Ga. Code Ann., 15-11-110 et seq.
Mo. Rev. Stat. 1991 Supp., 210.817 et seq.

Parental Responsibility Act
Ga. Code Ann., 15-11-19, 15-11-26,
  15-11-62
Ida. Code 1947, 32-1301 et seq.
N.M. Stat. Ann., 40-5A-1 et seq.

Parental Responsibility Act (Shared)
Fla. Stat. Ann., 61.13

Parental Right of Recovery Act
Ill. Rev. Stat. 1991, Ch. 70, § 601 et seq.

Parental Rights Act (Termination of)
Utah Code Ann. 1953, 78-3a-101 et seq.

Parental Rights Restoration Act
Mich. Comp. Laws Ann., 722.901 et seq.

Parental Successor Law
Wash. Rev. Code Ann., 72.33.500 et seq.

Parentale Act
Haw. Rev. Stat. Ann., § 584-1 et seq.

Parenting Act
Neb. Rev. Stat. 1943, 43-2901 et seq.
Wash. Rev. Code Ann., 26.09.010 et seq.,
  26.10.010 et seq.

Parenting Act (Off Street)
Haw. Rev. Stat. Ann., § 56-1 et seq.

**Parenting Time and Support Enforcement
Act**
Mich. Comp. Laws Ann., 552.601 et seq.

Parents' Action Act
Ind. Code Ann., 34-1-1-8

Parents Law (Unfit)
Miss. Code Ann. 1972, § 93-15-101 et seq.

Parents Rights to Conscience Act
N.J. Stat. Ann., 18A:35-4.6 et seq.

Pari-Mutuel Betting Act
Cal. Business and Professions Code, § 19590
  et seq.
Fla. Stat. Ann., 550.011 et seq.
Iowa Code Ann., 99D.1 et seq.
Ky. Rev. Stat. 1962, 436.230
Mich. Comp. Laws Ann., 431.72 et seq.
N.M. Stat. Ann., 60-1-1 et seq.
N.Y. Laws 1940, Ch. 254
R.I. Gen. Laws 1956, 41-4-1 et seq.
Utah Laws 1925, Ch. 77
W. Va. Code 1966, § 19-23-9
Wyo. Stat. Ann., § 11-25-101 et seq.

Pari-Mutuel Wagering Act
Fla. Stat. Ann., 550.001 et seq.

Parimutual Tax Act
W. Va. Code 1966, § 19-23-10

Parimutuel Act
Cal. Business and Professions Code, § 19590
  et seq.
Wyo. Stat. Ann., § 11-25-101 et seq.

Parimutuel Betting Law (Off-track)
N.Y. Laws 1973, Ch. 346, § 4

Parimutuel Licensing Simplification Act of 1988
Aug. 22, 1988, P.L. 100-413, 102 Stat. 1101, 28 U.S. Code § 534 nt.

Parimutuel Racing Act
Kan. Stat. Ann., 74-8801 et seq.

Paris Green Act
Pa. 1907 Pamph. Laws 309, No. 235

Parish Court Jurisdiction and Procedure Act
La. Rev. Stat. Ann., 13:1441 et seq.

Parish Fire and Police Civil Service Act
La. Rev. Stat. Ann., 33:2531 et seq.

Parish Industrial District Act (St. Landry)
La. Acts 1986, No. 693

Parish Redevelopment Act
La. Rev. Stat. Ann., 33:4625

Parish Youth Services Act
La. Rev. Stat. Ann., 46:1941.1 et seq.

Parity Act
See Soil Conservation and Domestic Allotment Act

Parity Act (Coinage)
See Currency Acts

Parity Act (State Banks)
N.J. Stat. Ann., 17:13B-1, 17:13B-2

Park Acquisition Law
Cal. Public Resources Code, § 5301 et seq.

Park Act
Cal. Statutes 1927, Ch. 765, p. 1480
Ind. Burns' 1933, 26-1538 et seq.
Mass. Gen. Laws 1984, § 45:2 et seq.
N.J. Laws 1902, Ch. 277
Tenn. Code Ann., 54-17-201 et seq.

Park Act (Authority to Sell)
Ill. Rev. Stat. 1991, Ch. 105, § 112.9, 113

Park Act (Buffalo)
N.Y. Laws 1869, Ch. 165

Park Act (County)
Ark. Stat. 1947, 17-1405 et seq.

Park Act (First Class Cities)
Ind. Code Ann., 36-10-2-2 et seq.

Park Act (Industrial)
See Industrial Park Act

Park Act (Municipal)
Cal. Government Code, § 38000 et seq.

Park Act (Ocean Fronts)
N.J. Stat. Ann., 40:179-98 et seq.

Park Act (Second Class Cities)
Ind. Code Ann., 36-10-7-1 et seq.

Park Act (Westchester County)
N.Y. Laws 1922, Ch. 292

Park Agency Act (Adirondack)
N.Y. Executive Law 1951 (Consol. Laws Ch. 18) § 800 et seq.

Park Airport Act
Ill. Rev. Stat. 1945, Ch. 105, §§ 327b, 327c

Park and City Exchange of Funds Act (Chicago)
Ill. Comp. Stat. 1992, Ch. 70, § 1545/0.01 et seq.

Park and Open Space Act
Colo. Rev. Stat., 29-7.5-101 et seq.

Park and Planning Commission Act (Maryland-National Capital)
Md. Laws 1959, Ch. 780

Park and Playground Act
Cal. Government Code, § 38000 et seq.
D.C. Code Ann., § 8-101 et seq.

Park and Recreation Act (City-County)
Okla. Stat. Ann., Title 19, § 1001 et seq.

Park and Recreation Bond Act (State)
N.M. Stat. Ann., 16-2-20 et seq.

Park and Recreation Improvement Loan Act (North Adams)
Mass. Acts 1964, Ch. 87

Park and Recreation Land Acquisition Bond Act
N.Y. Laws 1960, Ch. 522
N.Y. Laws 1962, Ch. 443
N.Y. Parks and Recreation Law (Consol. Laws Ch. 36b) § 15.01 et seq.

Park and Recreation Land Acquisition Bond Acts
N.Y. Environmental Conservation Law 1972 (Consol. Laws Ch. 43B) 41-0107
N.Y. Unconsolidated Laws, 1601, 1602, 1621, 1622

Park and Recreation Law
Ind. Code Ann., 36-10-3-1 et seq.

Park and Recreation Loan Act (Nantucket)
Mass. Acts 1962, Ch. 15

Park and Recreational Facilities Bond Act
Cal. Public Resources Code, § 5096.225 et seq.
Va. Acts 1977, Ch. 653
Va. Acts 1992, Ch. 781

Park Annuity and Benefit Fund Civil Service Act
Ill. Rev. Stat. 1991, Ch. 24 1/2, § 113.9 et seq.

Park Authorities Act
Ga. Code Ann., 12-3-1 et seq.
Va. Code 1950, § 15.1-1228 et seq.

Park Authority Act (Jekyll Island)
Ga. Code Ann., 12-3-230 et seq.

Park Boards Act
Minn. Stat. 1974, 448.05 et seq.

Park Bond Act (Township)
Ill. Rev. Stat. 1991, Ch. 105, § 224.9 et seq.

Park Bond Act (Z'berg-Collier)
Cal. Public Resources Code, § 5096.71 et seq.

Park Bond Issue Act
N.Y. Laws 1924, Ch. 602

Park Bonds Act
Cal. Statutes 1927, Ch. 765, p. 1480

Park Child Welfare Sanitarium Act
Ill. Rev. Stat. 1991, Ch. 105, §§ 327v9, 327w

Park Civil Service Act
Ill. Rev. Stat. 1991, Ch. 24 1/2, § 77m et seq.

Park Commission Act
Cal. Public Resources Code, § 5001 et seq.
Mich. Comp. Laws Ann., 318.3 et seq.
N.C. Gen. Stat. 1943, § 143-255 et seq.
N.J. Stat. Ann., 40:37-11.1 et seq.
Ohio Rev. Code 1953, 755.01 et seq.

Park Commission Act (Chicopee Woods Area)
Ga. Laws 1988, p. 3783

Park Commission Act (Gainsville)
Ga. Laws 1980, p. 4054

Park Commission Law (Westchester County)
N.Y. Laws 1948, Ch. 852, § 471 et seq.

Park Commissioners Act
Cal. Public Resources Code, § 5181 et seq.
Ill. Rev. Stat. 1991, Ch. 105, § 119.9 et seq.

Park Commissioners Control of Municipal Parks Act
Ill. Rev. Stat. 1991, Ch. 105, § 47.9 et seq.

Park Commissioners Federal Government Conveyance Act
Ill. Rev. Stat. 1991, Ch. 105, §§ 325a.9, 325b

Park Commissioners Land Condemnation Act
Ill. Rev. Stat. 1991, Ch. 105, § 53.9 et seq.

Park Commissioners Land Conveyance Act
Ill. Rev. Stat. 1991, Ch. 105, § 114.9 et seq.

Park Commissioners Land Sale Act
Ill. Rev. Stat. 1991, Ch. 105, § 112.9 et seq.

Park Commissioners Water Control Act
Ill. Rev. Stat. 1991, Ch. 105, § 91.9 et seq.

Park Discontinuance Law
Cal. Government Code, § 38400 et seq.

Park District Act
Ill. Rev. Stat. 1991, Ch. 105, § 1-1 et seq.
Ohio Rev. Code 1953, 1545.01 et seq.

Park District Act (Chicago)
Ill. Comp. Stat. 1992, Ch. 70, § 1505/0.01 et seq.

Park District Airport Site Act
Ill. Rev. Stat. 1991, Ch. 105, § 327c1, 327c1-1

Park District Airport Zoning Act
Ill. Rev. Stat. 1991, Ch. 105, § 327c1.9 et seq.

Park District Aquarium and Museum Act
Ill. Rev. Stat. 1991, Ch. 105, § 325h et seq.

Park District Armory and Airfield Site Act
Ill. Rev. Stat. 1991, Ch. 105, § 327a.1 et seq.

Park District Bond Acts (Chicago)
Ill. Comp. Stat. 1992, Ch. 70, §§ 1520/0.01, 1525/0.01 et seq.

Park District Corporate Note Act (Chicago)
Ill. Comp. Stat. 1992, Ch. 70, § 1530/0.01 et seq.

Park District Debt Assumption Act (Chicago)
Ill. Comp. Stat. 1992, Ch. 70, § 1515/0.01 et seq.

Park District Elevated Highway Act
Ill. Rev. Stat. 1991, Ch. 105, § 327c.9 et seq.

Park District Exposition Authority Lease Act
Ill. Rev. Stat. 1991, Ch. 105, § 327v5.9 et seq.

Park District Historical Museum Act
Ill. Rev. Stat. 1991, Ch. 105, §§ 325a, 325a.1

Park District Immunity Act
Ill. Rev. Stat. 1963, Ch. 105, § 333.2a

Park District Judgment Indebtedness Bond Act (Chicago)
Ill. Comp. Stat. 1992, Ch. 70, §§ 1540/0.01, 1540/1

Park District Police Act
Ill. Rev. Stat. 1991, Ch. 105, §§ 330a, 330a.1

Park District Refunding Bond Act
Ill. Rev. Stat. 1991, Ch. 105, § 255.18a et seq.

Park District Street Car Line Act (Chicago)
Ill. Comp. Stat. 1992, Ch. 70, § 1535/0.01 et seq.

Park District Working Cash Fund Act (Chicago)
Ill. Comp. Stat. 1992, Ch. 70, § 1510/0.01 et seq.

Park Donation and Bequest Law
Cal. Public Resources Code, §§ 5158, 5159

Park Employees' Annuity and Benefit Fund Act
Ill. Rev. Stat. 1991, Ch. 108 1/2, § 12-101 et seq.

Park Highways Law
Cal. Government Code, § 38304

Park Jurisdiction Law
Cal. Government Code, §§ 38300, 38301

Park Land Acquisition Act (Township)
Ill. Rev. Stat. 1991, Ch. 105, § 318.90 et seq.

Park Loan Act (Lake Quinsigamond)
Mass. Acts 1955, Ch. 519

Park Maintenance Act
N.J. Stat. Ann., 40:37-12 et seq.

Park Occupancy Law (Recreational Vehicle)
Cal. Civil Code § 799.20 et seq.

Park Ordinance Violation Incarceration Act
Ill. Rev. Stat. 1991, Ch. 105, § 327z et seq.

Park Ordinance Violation Procedure Act
Ill. Rev. Stat. 1991, Ch. 105, §§ 330h, 331

Park Police Pension Fund Act
Ill. Rev. Stat. 1961, Ch. 105, § 390 et seq.

Park Policemen's Annuity Act
Ill. Rev. Stat. 1961, Ch. 105, § 334 et seq.

Park Preservation Fund Act (Collier)
Cal. Public Resources Code, § 5010

Park, Recreation and Parkway District Law
Cal. Public Resources Code, § 5630 et seq.

Park, Recreation and Wildlife Enhancement Act
Cal. Public Resources Code, § 5096.300 et seq.

Park System Act
Miss. Code Ann. 1972, § 55-3-1 et seq.

Park System Civil Service Act
Ill. Rev. Stat. 1991, Ch. 24 1/2, § 77m et seq.

Park Tax Act
Cal. Government Code, § 50400
Ill. Rev. Stat. 1991, Ch. 24, §§ 11-98-1 et seq., 11-99-1 et seq., 11-100-2

Park Use of Shore Lands Act
Ill. Rev. Stat. 1991, Ch. 105, §§ 324.9, 324.10

Park Water Authority Act (Town of Clifton)
N.Y. Public Authorities Law (Consol. Laws Ch. 43A) § 1120 et seq.

Park Waterworks Improvement Lease Act
Ill. Rev. Stat. 1991, Ch. 105, § 327-9 et seq.

Parker-Watson Act
See Railway Labor Act

Parking Act (Motor Vehicles)
Mich. Comp. Laws Ann., 257.672 et seq.
Mont. Code Ann., 61-8-353 et seq.
N.H. Rev. Stat. 1955, 265:68 et seq.
R.I. Gen. Laws 1956, 31-21-1 et seq.
Vt. Stat. Ann., Title 23, § 1101 et seq.
Wash. Rev. Code Ann., 46.48.575 et seq.
Wis. Stat. Ann., 346.50 et seq.

Parking Act (Municipal)
Ill. Rev. Stat. 1991, Ch. 24, § 11-71-1 et seq.

Parking Act (Off Street)
Haw. Rev. Stat. Ann., § 56-1 et seq.
Mont. Code Ann., 61-8-353 et seq.

Parking and Business Improvement Area Law
Cal. Streets and Highways Code, § 36500 et seq.

Parking and Business Improvement District Act
Utah Code Ann. 1953, 17A-3-401 et seq.

Parking Authority Act
Del. Code of 1974, Title 22, § 501 et seq.
Md. Ann. Code 1957, Art. 41, § 14-301 et seq.
N.C. Gen. Stat. 1943, § 160A-550 et seq.
Neb. Rev. Stat. 1943, 14-1701 et seq.
N.J. Stat. Ann., 40:11A-1 et seq.
Pa. Purdon's Stat., Tite 53, § 341 et seq.
Tenn. Code Ann., 7-65-101 et seq.
Va. Acts 1958, Ch. 383

Parking Authority Act (Albany)
N.Y. Public Authorities Law (Consol. Laws Ch. 43A) § 1493-a et seq.

Parking Authority Act (Alexandria)
Va. Acts 1956, Ch. 406
Va. Acts 1958, Ch. 348

Parking Authority Act (Amsterdam)
N.Y. Public Authorities Law (Consol. Laws Ch. 43A) § 1400 et seq.

Parking Authority Act (Binghamton)
N.Y. Public Authorities Law (Consol. Laws Ch. 43A) § 1599a et seq.

Parking Authority Act (City of North Tonawanda)
N.Y. Public Authorities Law (Consol. Laws Ch. 43A) § 1601 et seq.

Parking Authority Act (City of Yonkers)
N.Y. Public Authorities Law (Consol. Laws Ch. 43A) § 596a et seq.

Parking Authority Act (Cobb County)
Ga. Laws 1957, p. 2744

Parking Authority Act (Cohoes)
N.Y. Public Authorities Law (Consol. Laws Ch. 43A) § 1599a et seq.

Parking Authority Act (Culpeper)
Va. Acts 1976, Ch. 584

Parking Authority Act (Decatur)
Ga. Laws 1968, p. 2892

Parking Authority Act (Elmira)
N.Y. Public Authorities Law (Consol. Laws Ch. 43A) § 1450 et seq.

Parking Authority Act (Endicott)
N.Y. Public Authorities Law (Consol. Laws Ch. 43A) § 1550 et seq.

Parking Authority Act (Fairfax)
Va. Acts 1958, Ch. 536

Parking Authority Act (Fredericksburg)
Va. Acts 1978, Ch. 691

Parking Authority Act (Fulton)
N.Y. Public Authorities Law (Consol. Laws Ch. 43A) § 1525 et seq.

Parking Authority Act (Hampton-Newport News)
Va. Acts 1968, Ch. 20

Parking Authority Act (Harrisonburg)
Va. Acts 1958, Ch. 517

Parking Authority Act (Herndon)
Va. Acts 1991, Ch. 142

Parking Authority Act (Hudson)
N.Y. Public Authorities Law (Consol. Laws Ch. 43A) § 1425a et seq.

Parking Authority Act (Jamestown)
N.Y. Public Authorities Law (Consol. Laws Ch. 43A) § 159aaa et seq.

Parking Authority Act (Johnson City)
N.Y. Public Authorities Law (Consol. Laws Ch. 43A) §§ 1421 to 1421r

Parking Authority Act (Long Beach)
N.Y. Public Authorities Law (Consol. Laws Ch. 43A) § 159aaaa et seq.

Parking Authority Act (Lynchburg)
Va. Acts 1974, Ch. 76

Parking Authority Act (Middletown)
N.Y. Public Authorities Law (Consol. Laws Ch. 43A) § 1621a et seq.

Parking Authority Act (Monroe)
N.Y. Public Authorities Law (Consol. Laws Ch. 43A) § 1420a et seq.

Parking Authority Act (Mount Kisco)
N.Y. Public Authorities Law (Consol. Laws Ch. 43A) § 159aaa et seq.

Parking Authority Act (Mount Vernon)
N.Y. Public Authorities Law (Consol. Laws Ch. 43A) § 1599a et seq.

Parking Authority Act (Municipal)
See Municipal Parking Authority Act

Parking Authority Act (New Rochelle)
N.Y. Public Authorities Law (Consol. Laws Ch. 43A) § 1597a et seq.

Parking Authority Act (New York City)
N.Y. Public Authorities Law (Consol. Laws Ch. 43A) § 1600 et seq.

Parking Authority Act (Niagara Falls)
N.Y. Public Authorities Law (Consol. Laws Ch. 43A) § 1599a et seq.

Parking Authority Act (North Tarrytown)
N.Y. Public Authorities Law (Consol. Laws Ch. 43A) § 1600aa et seq.
N.Y. Public Authorities Law (Consol. Laws Ch. 43A) § 1601 et seq.

Parking Authority Act (North Tonawonda)
N.Y. Public Authorities Law (Consol. Laws, Ch. 43A) § 1601 et seq.

Parking Authority Act (Nyack)
N.Y. Public Authorities Law (Consol. Laws Ch. 43A) § 1622a et seq.

Parking Authority Act (Owego)
N.Y. Public Authorities Law (Consol. Laws Ch. 43A) § 1595a et seq.

Parking Authority Act (Peekskill)
N.Y. Public Authorities Law (Consol. Laws Ch. 43A) § 1500 et seq.

Parking Authority Act (Port Chester)
N.Y. Public Authorities Act (Consol. Laws Ch. 43A) § 1620a et seq.

Parking Authority Act (Port Jervis)
N.Y. Public Authorities Law (Consol. Laws Ch. 43A) § 1585a et seq.

Parking Authority Act (Poughkeepsie)
N.Y. Public Authorities Law (Consol. Laws Ch. 43A) § 1598 et seq.

Parking Authority Act (Rome)
N.Y. Public Authorities Law (Consol. Laws Ch. 43A) § 1470 et seq.

Parking Authority Act (Schenectady)
N.Y. Public Authorities Law (Consol. Laws Ch. 43A) § 1599a et seq.

Parking Authority Act (Suffern)
N.Y. Public Authorities Law (Consol. Laws Ch. 43A) § 1600 et seq.

Parking Authority Act (Syracuse)
N.Y. Public Authorities Law (Consol. Laws Ch. 43A) § 1475 et seq.

Parking Authority Act (Tarrytown)
N.Y. Public Authorities Law (Consol. Laws Ch. 43A) § 1600a et seq.

Parking Authority Act (Tuckahoe)
N.Y. Public Authorities Law (Consol. Laws Ch. 43A) § 1545 et seq.

Parking Authority Act (Vienna)
Va. Acts 1991, Ch. 446

Parking Authority Act (Village of Port Chester)
N.Y. Public Authorities Law (Consol. Laws Ch. 43A) § 1620a et seq.

Parking Authority Act (White Plains)
N.Y. Public Authorities Law (Consol. Laws Ch. 43A) § 1425 et seq.

Parking Board Act (Nashville)
Tenn. Private Acts 1949, Ch. 429

Parking Citation Enforcement Act (Local Government)
Ky. Rev. Stat. 1971, 82.600 et seq.

Parking Commission Act
Mont. Code Ann., 7-14-4601 et seq.

Parking District Act
Cal. Streets and Highways Code, § 35100 et seq.

Parking District Act (Off-Street)
Neb. Rev. Stat. 1943, 19-3301 et seq.
S.C. Code Ann. 1976, § 5-29-10 et seq.

Parking Facilities Act
Ind. Code Ann., 36-9-11.1-1
N.H. Rev. Stat. 1955, 231:114 et seq.
N.J. Stat. Ann., 40:56-1.1 et seq.
S.C. Code Ann. 1976, § 5-29-10 et seq.

Parking Facilities and Project Revenue Bond Act
N.C. Laws 1983, Ch. 168

Parking Facilities Bond Act
Va. Acts 1990, Ch. 863

Parking Facilities Loan Act (Boston)
Mass. Acts 1951, Ch. 625
Mass. Acts 1955, Ch. 450

Parking Facilities Loan Act (Lawrence)
Mass. Acts 1963, Ch. 576

Parking Facilities Revenue Bond Act
N.C. Laws 1975, Ch. 858

Parking Law
Cal. Streets and Highways Code, § 32500 et seq.

Parking Law for Persons with Disabilities
Ga. Code Ann., 40-6-220 to 40-6-228

Parking Meter Act
R.I. Gen. Laws 1956, 31-28-1 et seq.

Parking Offenses Adjudication Act
N.J. Stat. Ann., 39:4-139.2 et seq.
N.J. 39:4-139.2

Parking Station Act (Municipalities)
Okla. Stat. Ann., Title 11. § 32-101 et seq.

Parkinson's Disease Registry Act
Neb. Rev. Stat. 1943, 81-681 to 81-696

Parklands Act
Cal. Public Resources Code, § 5096.141 et seq.

Parklands Payback Pilot Project Act
Pa. Purdon's Stat., Title 50, § 6001 et seq.

Parks Act (Primitive)
Mont. Code Ann., 23-1-115 et seq.

Parks and Recreation Act (Cherokee County)
Ga. Laws 1995, p. 4223

Parks and Recreation Law
N.Y. Consol. Laws Ch. 36B

Parks and Streets Act
Minn. Stat. Ann., 430.01 et seq.

Parks, Recreation and Historic Preservation Law
N.Y. Consol. Laws Ch. 36b

Parkway Act
Cal. Streets and Highways Code, § 885 et seq.

Parkway Authority Act (New York City)
N.Y. Public Authorities Law (Consol. Laws Ch. 43A) § 275 et seq.

Parkway Authority Act (Westchester County)
N.Y. Public Authorities Law (Consol. Laws Ch. 43A) § 400 et seq.

Parochial School Bus Bill
N.Y. Education Law 1947 (Consol. Laws Ch. 16) §§ 1807, 1907, 2021, Subd. 19, 3635

Parol Evidence Act
Iowa Code 1977, 554.2202
La. Rev. Stat. Ann., 15:437
Ore. Rev. Stat. 1953, 41.740

Parole Act
June 25, 1910, Ch. 387, 36 Stat. 819 (See 18 U.S. Code §§ 3570, 4202 to 4207)
Conn. Gen. Stat. 1983, § 54-124a et seq.
Miss. Code Ann. 1972, § 47-7-1 et seq.

Parole Act (County Jail Prisoners)
Cal. Penal Code, § 3075 et seq.

Parole and County Probation Officers' Firearm Education and Training Act
Pa. Purdon's Stat., Title 61, § 332.1 et seq.

Parole and Probation Act
See Probation and Parole Act
Me. Rev. Stat. Ann. 1964, Title 34-A, § 5001 et seq.
S.C. Code Ann. 1976, § 24-21-10 et seq.

**Parole and Probation Compact Act
(Interstate)**
See Interstate Probation and Parole Compact
Act

**Parole and Probation Hearings Act
(Interstate)**
Va. Code 1950, § 53.1-168 et seq.

Parole Board Act (Juvenile)
N.M. Stat. Ann., 32-2-1 et seq.
N.M. Stat. Ann., 37-7-1 et seq.

Parole Commission Phaseout Act of 1996
Oct. 2, 1996, P.L. 104-232, 18 U.S. Code
§ 4201 nt.
Aug. 5, 1997, P.L. 105-33, 18 U.S. Code
§ 4201 nt.

Parole Evidence Act
Ga. Code Ann., 24-6-1 et seq.
La. Rev. Stat. Ann., 15:437
Ore. Rev. Stat. 1953, 41.740

Parole Guidelines Act
Fla. Stat. Ann., 947.001 et seq.

**Parole Reciprocal Agreements Compact Act
(Interstate)**
Ill. Rev. Stat. 1991, Ch. 38, § 1003-3-11 et
seq.

Parole Review Act (Boatwright-Eaves)
Cal. Penal Code, § 3041.2

Parole Violators Return Act (Out of State)
Mich. Comp. Laws Ann., 780.561 et seq.

Parolee Supervision Act (Out-of-State)
See also Uniform Out-of-State Parolee
Supervision Act
Wis. Stat. Ann., 304.13

Parolee Supervision Act (Out of State)
See Uniform Act for Out of State Parolee
Supervision

Paroles and Pardons Reform Act
Tenn. Code Ann., 40-28-101 et seq.

Part-Time Employment Pilot Program Act
Cal. Government Code, § 18030 et seq.

Part-Time School Law
Iowa Code Ann., 289.1 et seq.

Partial-Birth Abortion Ban Act
Ala. Code 1975, § 26-23-1 et seq.
Ariz. Rev. Stat. Ann., § 13-3603.01
Ark. Code 1987, 5-6-201 to 5-6-204
Ill. Comp. Stat. 1992, Ch. 720, § 513/1 et seq.
Iowa Code Ann., 707.8A
Miss. Code Ann. 1972, §§ 41-41-71 to
41-41-73
S.C. Code Ann. 1976, § 44-41-85

Partial Payments Act (Railroads)
Feb. 26, 1921, Ch. 72, 41 Stat. 1145, 49 U.S.
Code § 79

Partial Service Retirement Act
Cal. Government Code, § 19996.30 et seq.

Participation Sales Act of 1966
May 24, 1966, P.L. 89-429, 80 Stat. 164, 7
U.S. Code § 1988; 12 U.S. Code §§ 1717,
1720, 1749, 1757; 20 U.S. Code §§ 743,
745; 31 U.S. Code § 1027 nt.
Aug. 1, 1968, P.L. 90-448, 82 Stat. 545, 12
U.S. Code § 1717 nt.

Particle Accelerator Land Acquisition Act
Ill. Rev. Stat. 1991, Ch. 127, § 47.20 et seq.

Partition Act
Ark. Code Ann. 1987, 18-60-401 et seq.
Cal. Code of Civil Procedure, § 872.010 et
seq.
Conn. Gen. Stat. Ann., § 52-495 et seq.
Fla. Stat. Ann., 64.011 et seq.
Ill. Rev. Stat. 1991, Ch. 110, § 17-101 et seq.
Iowa Code Ann., 557A.4
Mich. Comp. Laws Ann., 600.3301 et seq.
Minn. Stat. Ann., 558.01 et seq.
Mont. Code Ann. 1991, 70-29-101 et seq.
N.H. Rev. Stat. 1955, 538:1 et seq.
N.J. Stat. Ann., 2A:56-1 et seq.
Ohio Rev. Code 1953, 5307.01 et seq.
R.I. Gen. Laws 1956, 34-15-1 et seq.
S.C. Code Ann. 1976, § 15-61-10 et seq.

Tenn. Code Ann., 29-27-101 et seq.

Tex. Property Code, § 23.001 et seq.

Tex. Rules of Civil Procedure as am. 1984, Rule 772 et seq.

Vt. Stat. Ann., Title 12, § 5161 et seq.

Wash. Rev. Code Ann., 7.52.010 et seq.

W. Va. Code 1966, § 37-4-1 et seq.

Partition Fence Act

Ohio Rev. Code 1953, 971.02 et seq.

Partition Law (Personal Property)

Cal. Code of Civil Procedure § 752a

Partnership Act

See Uniform Partnership Act

Partnership Act (Affordable Housing)

Me. Rev. Stat. Ann. 1964, Title 30-A, § 5001 et seq.

Partnership Act (Business Development)

Neb. Rev. Stat. 1943, § 81-1272 et seq.

Partnership Act (Clean Water)

Minn. Stat. Ann., 103F.701 et seq.

Partnership Act (Community Corrections)

Fla. Stat. Ann., 948.50 et seq.

Partnership Act (Education)

Ga. Code Ann., 20-2-1030 et seq.

Partnership Act (Export)

Pa. Purdon's Stat., Title 73, § 399.71 et seq.

Partnership Act (Family-School)

La. Rev. Stat. Ann., 17:406 et seq.

Partnership Act (General)

Mich. Comp. Laws Ann., 449.1 et seq.

Utah Code Ann. 1953, 48-1-1 et seq.

Partnership Act (Home Investment)

Cal. Health and Safety Code § 50896 et seq.

Partnership Act (Job Training)

Md. Ann. Code 1957, Art. 89, § 17 et seq.

Me. Rev. Stat. Ann. 1964, Title 26, § 2001 et seq.

Me. Rev. Stat. Ann. 1964, Title 26, § 2001 et seq.

Partnership Act (Limited)

See also Revised Uniform Limited Partnership Act

Iowa Code Ann., 487.101 et seq.

Partnership Act (New Capital Sources)

N.J. Stat. Ann., 34:1B-107 et seq.

Partnership Act (Private Sector and Education)

Fla. Stat. Ann., 229.602

Partnership Act (Revised Uniform)

Fla. Stat. Ann., 620.81001 et seq.

Partnership Act (Revised)

Tex. Rev. Civ. Stat., Art. 6132b-10.01

Partnership Act (State Housing Initiatives)

Fla. Stat. Ann., 420.907 et seq.

Partnership Act (Technology 2000)

Mass. Gen. Laws Ann., 23F:1 to 23F:9

Partnership Act (Transportation)

Pa. Purdon's Stat., Title 53, § 1621 et seq.

Partnership Act Limited

See Limited Partnership Act

Partnership and Capital Corporation Act

S.C. Code Ann. 1976, § 41-44-10 et seq.

Partnership Association Act

Pa. Purdon's Stat., Title 15, § 12701 et seq.

Partnership Association Act (Limited)

Colo. Rev. Stat., 7-63-101 et seq.

Partnership Certificate Act

Mich. Comp. Laws Ann., 449.101 et seq.

Partnership Fictitious Names Act

Ohio Rev. Code 1953, 1777.01 et seq.

Partnership for Health Amendments of 1967

Dec. 5, 1967, P.L. 90-174, 81 Stat. 533, 42 U.S. Code §§ 201 nt., 217b, 241, 242b, 242c nt., 242g, 243, 244, 246, 249, 251, 254a, 263a, 291m-1, 293e, 295h-4, 296e nt.

Partnership for Health and Human Services Act
Neb. Laws 1996, L.B. 1044

Partnership for Long Term Care Act
Ill. Rev. Stat. 1991, Ch. 23, § 6801-1 et seq.

Partnership for Wildlife Act
Nov. 4, 1992, P.L. 102-587, 16 U.S. Code § 3741 nt.
Oct. 19, 1994, P.L. 103-375, 16 U.S. Code §§ 3742, 3743, 3744
Oct. 30, 1998, P.L. 105-312, 16 U.S. Code § 3744

Partnership Law (Clean Water)
Minn. Stat. 1986, 103F.701 et seq.

Partnership Trust Act (State Archives)
N.Y. Laws 1992, Ch. 758

Partnerships for Economic Development Act
Neb. Rev. Stat. 1943, 81-1288 et seq.

Partnerships in Education for Mathematics, Science, and Engineering Act
Aug. 8, 1984, P.L. 98-377, 20 U.S. Code §§ 3981 et seq., 3981 nt.

Party-Line Act
Ind. Code Ann., 35-28-12-1 et seq.

Party Line Emergency Act
Ill. Rev. Stat. 1991, Ch. 134, § 16.5h et seq.

Party Organization Act
Ind. Code Ann., 3-6-1-1 et seq.

Party Raiding Act
Pa. Purdon's Stat., Title 25, § 2861 et seq.

Party Wall Act
Pa. Purdon's Stat., Title 21, § 15
Pa. Purdon's Stat., Title 53, § 24871 et seq.

Pasco County Expressway Authority Law
Fla. Stat. Ann., 348.80 et seq.

Pasco County Stock Act
Fla. Special Laws 1927, Ch. 13250

Pasco County Uniform Consumer Protection Act
Fla. Special Laws 1974, Ch. 573

Paseo del Este Municipal Utility District Act
Tex. General and Special Laws 1997, Ch. 443

Pasquotank County Peace Officers' Relief Act
N.C. Laws 1959, Ch. 263

PASS Accounts Act (Parents and Students Savings)
N.Y. Tax Law (Consol. Laws Ch. 60) § 612, Subd. k

Pass Act
Ill. Laws 1897, p. 204, No. 1

Pass-On Act (Social Security)
Cal. Welfare and Institutions Code § 11008.1

Passaic River Basin Dredging and Desnagging and Flood Plain Land Acquisition Act
N.J. Laws 1971, Ch. 110

Passaic Valley Sewerage Districts Act
N.J. Stat. Ann., 58:14-1 et seq.

Passenger Act of 1882 (Carriage by Sea)
Aug. 2, 1882, Ch. 374, 22 Stat. 186, 46 U.S. Code §§ 151 to 162, 171

Passenger Air Carriers Act
Cal. Public Utilities Code, § 2739 et seq.

Passenger Carriers Act (Motor)
See Motor Passenger Carrier Act

Passenger Charter Carriers Act
Wash. Rev. Code Ann., 81.70.010 et seq.

Passenger Charter-Party Carriers Act
Cal. Public Utilities Code, § 5351 et seq.

Passenger Elevator Act
Tex. Health and Safety Code, § 754.001 et seq.

Passenger Motor Vehicle Act
Md. Ann. Code 1974, Art. TR, § 13-423 et seq.

Passenger Motor Vehicle Safety Act (Private)
Cal. Vehicle Code 1959, § 27315

Passenger Protection Act (Child)
Ill. Comp. Stat. 1992, Ch. 625, § 25/1 et seq.

Passenger Rail Act (Intercity)
Cal. Government Code §§ 14031.8, 14070 et seq.

Passenger Rail and Clean Air Bond Act of 1990
Cal. Streets and Highways Code § 2701 et seq.

Passenger Rail and Clean Air Bond Act of 1992
Cal. Streets and Highways Code § 2702 et seq.

Passenger Rail and Clean Air Bond Act of 1994
Cal. Streets and Highways Code § 2703 et seq.

Passenger Rail Financing Commission Act
Cal. Government Code, § 92000 et seq.

Passenger Rail Service Act
Me. Rev. Stat. Ann. 1964, Title 23, §§ 7171 et seq., 8001 et seq.

Passenger Rail Service Assistance Program
Tex. Transportation Code, §§ 456.061 to 456.065

Passenger Railroad Commission Act
Tenn. Code Ann., 4-47-101 et seq.

Passenger Railroad Rebuilding Act of 1980
May 30, 1980, P.L. 96-254, 45 U.S. Code §§ 601, 651 et seq., 835, 851 et seq.

Passenger Rate Act
Ill. Rev. Stat. 1983, Ch. 114, § 154 et seq.

Passenger Rate Act (Railroads)
Minn. Stat. Ann., 218.021

Passenger Restraint Devices Act
N.M. Stat. Ann., 66-7-368 et seq.

Passenger Rights on Public Transportation Act
S.C. Code Ann. 1976, § 58-23-1810 et seq.

Passenger Safety Act (Bus)
See Bus Passenger Safety Act
Okla. Stat. Ann., Title 21, § 1901 et seq.

Passenger Tramway Safety Act
N.H. Rev. Stat. 1955, 225-A:1 et seq.

Passenger Transportation Services Act
Tenn. Code Ann., 7-51-1001 et seq.

Passenger Vessel Safety Act of 1993
Dec. 20, 1993, P.L. 103-206, 46 U.S. Code § 2101 nt.

Passing Act (Motor Vehicles)
Ill. Rev. Stat. 1991, Ch. 95 1/2, § 11-702 et seq.

Passport Act
Haw. Session Laws 1852, p. 36, June 24, 1852

Past Consideration Act (Contracts)
N.Y. General Obligations Law (Consol. Laws Ch. 24A) § 5-1105

Pasteurized Milk Law
Colo. Rev. Stat., 13-26-101 et seq.
Ill. Rev. Stat. 1991, Ch. 56 1/2, § 2208 et seq.
Ind. Code Ann., 16-1-23-1 et seq.
Neb. Rev. Stat. 1943, 2-3901 et seq.

Pastoral Counselor Certification Act (Fee-Based)
N.C. Gen. Stat. 1943, § 90-350 et seq.

Pasture Improvement Act (Northeastern Oklahoma)
Okla. Stat. Ann., Title 70, § 3401 et seq.

Pat G. Harden Act
Ala. Acts 1996, p. 837, No. 560

Patent Act (Lands)
Ky. Rev. Stat. 1971, 56.190 et seq.

Patent and Plant Variety Protection Remedy Clarification Act
Oct. 28, 1992, P.L. 102-560, 7 U.S. Code § 2321 nt.

Patent and Trademark Office Authorization Act of 1991
Dec. 10, 1991, P.L. 102-204, 105 Stat. 1636

Patent and Trademark Office Authorization Act of 1993
Dec. 3, 1993, P.L. 103-179, 107 Stat. 2040

Patent Cooperation Treaty
Nov. 14, 1975, P.L. 94-131, 89 Stat. 685, 35 U.S. Code §§ 6, 41, 42, 102, 104, 112, 113, 120, 282, 351 et seq.

Patent Law Foreign Filing Amendments Act of 1988
Aug. 23, 1988, P.L. 100-418, 102 Stat. 1567, 35 U.S. Code § 1 nt.

Patents
July 19, 1952, Ch. 950, 66 Stat. 792, 15 U.S. Code § 1071; 35 U.S. Code §§ 1 to 293
Sept. 6, 1958, P.L. 85-933, 72 Stat. 1793, 35 U.S. Code §§ 3, 7
Sept. 23, 1959, P.L. 86-370, 73 Stat. 650, 35 U.S. Code §§ 3, 7
Oct. 3, 1961, P.L. 87-333, 75 Stat. 748, 35 U.S. Code § 119
Oct. 15, 1962, P.L. 87-831, 76 Stat. 958, 35 U.S. Code § 135
March 26, 1964, P.L. 88-292, 78 Stat. 171, 35 U.S. Code §§ 25, 26
Aug. 14, 1964, P.L. 88-426, 78 Stat. 425, 35 U.S. Code § 3
July 24, 1965, P.L. 89-83, 79 Stat. 259, 35 U.S. Code §§ 41, 112, 151, 154, 282
July 28, 1972, P.L. 92-358, 86 Stat. 501, 35 U.S. Code §§ 102, 119

Paternity Act
See also Uniform Paternity Act
Ala. Code 1975, § 26-12-1 et seq.

Ariz. Rev. Stat. Ann., § 12-841 et seq.
Ark. Code Ann. 1987, 9-10-101 et seq.
Colo. Rev. Stat. Replaced Vols., 19-6-101 et seq.
D.C. Code 1973, § 16-2341 et seq.
Del. Code of 1974, Title 13, § 1321 et seq.
Fla. Stat. 1981, 742.011 et seq.
Ga. Code Ann., 19-7-40 et seq.
Haw. Rev. Stat. Ann., § 579-1 et seq.
Ida. Code 1947, 7-1101 et seq.
Ill. Rev. Stat. 1991, Ch. 40, § 2505 et seq.
Ind. Code Ann., 31-6-6.1-1 et seq.
Iowa Code Ann., 675.1 et seq.
Kan. Stat. Ann., 38-1110 et seq.
Md. Ann. Code 1974, Art. FL, § 5-1001 et seq.
Mich. Comp. Laws Ann., 722.711 et seq.
Mont. Code Ann., 40-6-101 et seq.
N.C. Gen. Stat. 1943, § 49-1 et seq.
N.D. Cent. Code, 14-17-01 et seq.
Neb. Rev. Stat. 1943, 13-101 et seq.
Nev. Rev. Stat. 1979 Reprint, 126.011 et seq.
N.Y. Family Court Act § 511 et seq.
Ohio Rev. Code 1953, 3111.01 et seq.
Okla. Stat. Ann., Title 10, § 71 et seq.
Okla. Stat. 1981, Title 10, § 70 et seq.
S.D. Codified Laws 1967, 25-8-1 et seq.
Tenn. Code Ann., 36-2-101 et seq.
Tex. Family Code, § 13.01 et seq.
Vt. Stat. Ann., Title 15, § 331 et seq.
Wash. Rev. Code Ann., 26.26.010 et seq.
Wis. Stat. Ann., 767.45 et seq.
W. Va. Code 1966, § 48A-6-1 et seq.
Wyo. Stat. 1957, § 14-59 et seq.

Paternity Act (Blood Tests)
See Blood Tests to Determine Paternity Act

Paternity Act (Criminal)
Mont. Rev. Code 1947, 94-9901 et seq.

Paternity and Child Support Amendments Act
D.C. Laws 1977, No. 1-92

Paternity Procedures Clarifying Amendment Act
D.C. Code Ann., § 19-316

Paternity Statute of Limitations
N.Y. Family Court Act, § 517

Paterson-Acker Milk Marketing Act
Mich. Public Acts 1941, No. 369

Pathology and Radiology Services in Hospitals Act
Iowa Code Ann., 135B.19 et seq.

Patient Access to Eye Care Act
Ga. Code Ann., 31-1-20 et seq.

Patient Advocate Law
Mich. Comp. Laws Ann., 700.496

Patient Autonomy Act
Colo. Rev. Stat., 15-14-503 et seq.

Patient Care Act (Appropriate)
Also known as Breast Cancer/Mastectomy Patient Care Act
Ga. Code Ann., 33-24-70 et seq.

Patient Client Protection Act
S.C. Code Ann. 1976, § 43-30-10 et seq.

Patient Cost of Care Act
Ga. Code Ann., 37-9-1 et seq.

Patient Liability Act
Ky. Rev. Stat. 1971, 210.700 et seq.

Patient-Physician Privilege Act
N.Y. Civil Practice Laws and Rules (Consol. Laws Ch. 8) § 4504

Patient Protection Act
Cal. Business and Professions Code § 1680
Ga. Code Ann., 33-20A-1 et seq.
Minn. Stat. 1986, 62J.695 to 62J.76
Miss. Code Ann. 1972, § 83-41-401 et seq.
Mo. Laws 1995, S.B. No. 281, §§ 1 to 7
N.M. Stat. Ann., 59A-57-1 to 59A-57-11
R.I. Gen. Laws 1956, 16-72-1 et seq.

Patient Protection Act (Breast Cancer)
Cal. Health and Safety Code § 1367.635
Cal. Insurance Code § 10123.86

Patient Protection Act (Managed Care)
Neb. Laws 1997, L.B. 279

Patient Records Act (Physicians')
S.C. Code Ann. 1976, § 44-115-10 et seq.

Patient Right to Know Act
Ala. Code 1975, § 27-1-20

Patient Self-Referral Act
Fla. Laws 1992, Ch. 178
Ga. Code Ann., 43-1B-1 et seq.

Patients' Bill of Rights
Mass. Gen. Laws 1984, 111:70E

Patients' Bill of Rights and Responsibilities
Fla. Stat. Ann., 381.026, 381.0261

Patients' Compensation Fund Act
Ill. Rev. Stat. 1991, Ch. 73, § 1065.300 et seq.

Patients Compensation Funds Act
S.C. Code Ann. 1976, § 38-79-410 et seq.

Patient's Right to Independent Review Act
Ga. Code Ann., 33-20A-30 et seq.

Patient's Self-Determination Act of 1990
See 42 U.S. Code §§ 1395i-3, 1395l, 1395cc, 1395bbb

Patrimony Act (Natural)
P.R. Laws Ann. 1954, Title 12, § 1225 et seq.

Patriot's Stadium Enabling Act
Conn. Public Acts 1998, No. 1, Dec. Spec. Sess.

Patrol Act
Wash. Rev. Code 1989, 43.43.010 et seq.

Patrol Act (Counties)
Ky. Rev. Stat. 1971, 70.150 et seq.

Patrol Act (Freeway Service)
Cal. Streets and Highways Code § 2560 et seq.

Patrol Act (Highway)
See Highway Patrol Act

Patrol Act (State)
See State Patrol Act

Patrol Vehicle Act (Electric)
Mich. Comp. Laws Ann., 257.1571 to 257.1577

Pattee Scholarship Act (Surviving Child of Policeman or Fireman)
Cal. Education Code 1976, §§ 68120, 68121

Patterson Act
See Kidnapping Act
May 18, 1934, Ch. 301, 48 Stat. 781

Patterson-Bonine Act (Unemployment Compensation)
Mich. Comp. Laws Ann., 421.3 et seq.

Patuxent River Watershed Act
Md. Ann. Code 1974, Art. NR, § 8-1301 et seq.

Paul Buzzo Act (Highway Litter)
Cal. Vehicle Code 1959, § 23111

Paulding County Airport Authority Act
Ga. Laws 1972, p. 3645

Paulding County Civil Service System Act
Ga. Laws 1980, P. 3119

Paulding County Water Authority Act
Ga. Laws 1961, p. 2837

Pauper Idiot Act
Ky. Rev. Stat. 1962, 203.250 et seq.

Pauper Law (Suits in Forma Pauperis)
Tenn. Code Ann., 20-12-127

Pauper Relief Act (Transient)
Wis. Stat. Ann., 49.02, Subsec. 2m

Paupers Act
Cal. Welfare and Institutions Code, § 200 et seq.
Colo. Rev. Stat. 30-17-101 et seq.
Ill. Rev. Stat. 1991, Ch. 107

La. Code Civil Procedure Art. 5181 et seq.
Me. Rev. Stat. Ann. 1964, Title 22, § 4307 et seq.
Neb. Rev. Stat. 1943, 68-103 et seq.
N.H. Rev. Stat. 1955, 165:1 et seq.
R.I. Gen. Laws 1956, 40-5-1 et seq.
Tenn. Code Ann., 20-12-127
Vt. Acts 1957, No. 299

Paupers Free Transcript Act
W. Va. Code 1966, § 51-7-7

Paving Act
Ark. Acts 1927, p. 1169, No. 359
Kan. Stat. Ann., 12-601 et seq.
La. Rev. Stat. Ann., 33:3381 et seq.
Tex. Rev. Civ. Stat, Art. 1086 et seq.

Paving Bond Act
S.C. Code Ann. 1976, § 5-21-610 et seq.

Pawn Shop Act (Municipal)
Ohio Laws Vol. 102, p. 65

Pawnbrokers Act
Ariz. Rev. Stat. Ann., § 44-1621 et seq.
Cal. Financial Code, § 21000 et seq.
Colo. Rev. Stat. 12-56-101 et seq.
D.C. Code Ann., § 2-1901 et seq.
Del. Code of 1974, Title 24, § 2301 et seq.
Ill. Rev. Stat. 1991, Ch. 17, § 4650 et seq.
Ind. Code Ann., 28-7-5-1 et seq.
Mich. Comp. Laws Ann., 446.201 et seq.
Miss. Code Ann. 1972, § 75-67-1 et seq.
Mo. Rev. Stat., 367.011 et seq.
Mont. Code Ann., 31-1-401 et seq.
N.H. Rev. Stat. 1955, 398:1 et seq.
N.J. Stat. Ann., 45:22-1 et seq.
N.M. Stat. Ann., 56-12-1 et seq.
Ohio Rev. Code 1953, 4727.01 et seq.
Okla. Stat. Ann., Title 59, § 1501 et seq.
Ore. Rev. Stat., 726.010 et seq.
Pa. Purdon's Stat., Title 63, § 281-1 et seq.
R.I. Gen. Laws 1956, 19-26-1 et seq.
S.D. Codified Laws 1967, 37-16-1 et seq.
Tenn. Code Ann., 45-6-101 et seq.
Tenn. Code Ann., 45-6-201 et seq.
Vt. Stat. Ann., title 9, § 3861 et seq.
Wash. Rev. Code Ann., 19.60.010 et seq.

Pawners' Societies Act
Ill. Rev. Stat. 1991, Ch. 17, § 4550 et seq.

Pawnshop Act
Ala. Code 1975, § 5-19A-1 et seq.
La. Rev. Stat. Ann. 37:1781 et seq.
Miss. Code Ann. 1972, § 75-67-301 et seq.
Tex. Finance Code, § 371.001 et seq.

Pawtucket Affordable Residential Housing Act
R.I. Public Laws 1991, Ch. 454

Pawtucket Historic Building Preservation and Affordable Residential Housing Act
R.I. Gen. Laws 1956, 44-4.2-1 et seq.

Pawtucket Minimum Nonresidential Standards Act
R.I. Public Laws 1968, Ch. 70

Pawtucket Minimum Standards Housing Act
R.I. Public Laws 1956, Ch. 3783

Pay Act (Equal)
Ore. Rev. Stat., 652.220 et seq.

Pay Act (State Officers)
Ga. Code 1933, 89-707 et seq.

Pay and Allowances of the Uniformed Services
Sept. 7, 1962, P.L. 87-649, 76 Stat. 451, 10 U.S. Code §§ 101, 142, 517, 555, 564, 701 to 704, 1166, 1167, 1293, 1305, 1405, 3068 to 3071, 3263, 3536 and others; 14 U.S. Code §§ 462a, 485, 755, 758a; 32 U.S. Code §§ 303, 318, 321, 715; 33 U.S. Code §§ 853o, 853o-1, 857a; 37 U.S. Code §§ 101 to 1007; 40 U.S. Code § 491; 42 U.S. Code §§ 207, 210, 210-1, 211; 50 U.S. Code Appx. §§ 2201 to 2204
March 28, 1963, P.L. 88-2, 77 Stat. 4, 37 U.S. Code §§ 302, 303
Oct. 2, 1963, P.L. 88-132, 77 Stat. 210, 37 U.S. Code §§ 201, 203 , 301, 302, 305, 310, 403, 421, 427
Dec. 23, 1963, P.L. 88-238, 77 Stat. 475, 37 U.S. Code § 406a
Aug. 7, 1964, P.L. 88-406, 78 Stat. 383, 37 U.S. Code § 409

Aug. 12, 1964, P.L. 88-422, 78 Stat. 395, 37 U.S. Code § 203
Aug. 14, 1964, P.L. 88-431, 78 Stat. 439, 37 U.S. Code § 406
Oct. 3, 1964, P.L. 88-624, 78 Stat. 1002, 37 U.S. Code § 416
Oct. 13, 1964, P.L. 88-647, 78 Stat. 1070, 37 U.S. Code §§ 205, 209, 415, 416, 422
May 22, 1965, P.L. 89-26, 79 Stat. 116, 37 U.S. Code §§ 405a, 407 , 411, 1006
June 28, 1965, P.L. 89-51, 79 Stat. 173, 37 U.S. Code § 209
July 30, 1965, P.L. 89-101, 79 Stat. 425, 37 U.S. Code § 406
Aug. 21, 1965, P.L. 89-132, 79 Stat. 545, 37 U.S. Code §§ 203, 310, 1008
Aug. 28, 1965, P.L. 89-149, 79 Stat. 585, 37 U.S. Code § 301
Aug. 28, 1965, P.L. 89-151, 79 Stat. 586, 37 U.S. Code § 501
Sept. 17, 1965, P.L. 89-189, 79 Stat. 820, 37 U.S. Code §§ 207, 424
Sept. 21, 1965, P.L. 89-193, 79 Stat. 823, 37 U.S. Code § 1006
Oct. 20, 1965, P.L. 89-278, 79 Stat. 1011, 37 U.S. Code § 301
June 9, 1966, P.L. 89-444, 80 Stat. 198, 37 U.S. Code §§ 402, 415
July 13, 1966, P.L. 89-501, 80 Stat. 276, 37 U.S. Code § 203
Sept. 6, 1966, P.L. 89-554, 80 Stat. 625, 37 U.S. Code §§ 551 to 558
Sept. 30, 1966, P.L. 89-608, 80 Stat. 851, 37 U.S. Code § 405a
Oct. 15, 1966, P.L. 89-680, 80 Stat. 957, 37 U.S. Code §§ 404, 406
Nov. 2, 1966, P.L. 89-718, 80 Stat. 1123, 37 U.S. Code §§ 101, 201, 202, 205, 209, 301, 302, 403 to 407, 409, 415, 416, 419, 422, 501 to 503, 604, 701, 706, 801, 1001, 1006, 1007
June 30, 1967, P.L. 90-40, 81 Stat. 105, 37 U.S. Code §§ 302, 303
Sept. 11, 1967, P.L. 90-83, 81 Stat. 220, 37 U.S. Code §§ 415, 554, 1007
Nov. 8, 1967, P.L. 90-130, 81 Stat. 383, 37 U.S. Code §§ 202, 904
Dec. 1, 1967, P.L. 90-168, 81 Stat. 525, 37 U.S. Code § 404
Dec. 8, 1967, P.L. 90-179, 81 Stat. 548, 37 U.S. Code § 202
Dec. 16, 1967, P.L. 90-207, 81 Stat. 649, 37 U.S. Code §§ 203, 311, 403, 407, 411a
Continued

Jan. 2, 1968, P.L. 90-235, 81 Stat. 757, 37 U.S. Code § 906

Jan. 2, 1968, P.L. 90-236, 81 Stat. 764, 37 U.S. Code § 554

Jan. 2, 1968, P.L. 90-246, 81 Stat. 782, 37 U.S. Code § 409

July 5, 1968, P.L. 90-377, 82 Stat. 288, 37 U.S. Code prec. § 426

Oct. 18, 1968, P.L. 90-603, 82 Stat. 1187, 37 U.S. Code § 311

Oct. 22, 1968, P.L. 90-623, 82 Stat. 1314, 37 U.S. Code §§ 101, 202, 305 to 308, 311, 406, 417, 554, 703, 904, 1001, 1006

June 3, 1969, P.L. 91-20, 83 Stat. 12, 37 U.S. Code § 312

Dec. 30, 1969, P.L. 91-183, 83 Stat. 840, 37 U.S. Code § 404

March 13, 1970, P.L. 91-210, 84 Stat. 53, 37 U.S. Code § 406b

June 12, 1970, P.L. 91-278, 84 Stat. 306, 37 U.S. Code §§ 201, 203, 415

Oct. 21, 1970, P.L. 91-484, 84 Stat. 1083, 37 U.S. Code § 907

Oct. 22, 1970, P.L. 91-486, 84 Stat. 1085, 37 U.S. Code § 405

Dec. 7, 1970, P.L. 91-529, 84 Stat. 1389, 37 U.S. Code § 427

Dec. 7, 1970, P.L. 91-533, 84 Stat. 1392, 37 U.S. Code § 427

Sept. 26, 1972, P.L. 92-436, 86 Stat. 740, 37 U.S. Code § 301

Oct. 2, 1972, P.L. 92-451, 86 Stat. 757, 37 U.S. Code § 202

Oct. 2, 1972, P.L. 92-455, 86 Stat. 761, 37 U.S. Code § 203

Oct. 9, 1972, P.L. 92-477, 86 Stat. 793, 37 U.S. Code § 554

Oct. 12, 1972, P.L. 92-482, 86 Stat. 796, 37 U.S. Code § 552

Oct. 13, 1972, P.L. 92-492, 86 Stat. 810, 37 U.S. Code § 101

Oct. 27, 1972, P.L. 92-581, 86 Stat. 1277, 37 U.S. Code § 312, 312a

Oct. 27, 1972, P.L. 92-596, 86 Stat. 1318, 37 U.S. Code § 501

April 27, 1973, P.L. 93-26, 87 Stat. 26, 37 U.S. Code § 552

July 9, 1973, P.L. 93-64, 87 Stat. 148, 37 U.S. Code §§ 302, 302a , 303, 303a, 401, 403

Nov. 29, 1973, P.L. 93-170, 87 Stat. 689, 37 U.S. Code § 406b

Dec. 28, 1973, P.L. 93-213, 87 Stat. 910, 37 U.S. Code § 411b

May 6, 1974, P.L. 93-274, 88 Stat. 94, 37 U.S. Code §§ 302, 302b, 311, 313

May 10, 1974, P.L. 93-277, 88 Stat. 119, 37 U.S. Code §§ 308, 308a

May 31, 1974, P.L. 93-294, 88 Stat. 177, 37 U.S. Code §§ 301, 301a

Aug. 29, 1974, P.L. 93-394, 88 Stat. 792, 37 U.S. Code § 311

Sept. 19, 1974, P.L. 93-419, 88 Stat. 1152, 37 U.S. Code §§ 101, 203, 402

Pay As You Go Act
N.Y. Laws 1916, Ch. 615, § 2

Pay As You Go Act (Highways)
S.C. Acts 1924, p. 1193, No. 731

Pay-as-you-go Tax Act
See Current Tax Payment Act of 1943

Pay Law (Equal)
N.Y. Labor Law (Consol. Laws Ch. 31) § 194

Pay Law (Polluters)
Mich. Comp. Laws Ann., 299.601 et seq.

Pay Patient Act
Ohio Rev. Code 1953, 5121.02 et seq.

Pay-Per-Call Regulation Act (Intrastate)
Neb. Laws 1993, L.B. 42

Pay-Per-Call Services Consumer Protection Act
Ill. Rev. Stat. 1991, Ch. 134, § 151 et seq.

Pay-Per-Telephone Call Act
Ida. Code 1947, 48-1101 et seq.

Pay Readjustment Act (Army, Navy, etc.)
June 10, 1922, Ch. 212, 42 Stat. 625
March 4, 1923, Ch. 281, 42 Stat. 1507

Pay Readjustment Act of 1942
June 16, 1942, Ch. 413, 56 Stat. 359
Dec. 2, 1942, Ch. 669, 56 Stat. 1037
March 6, 1943, Ch. 11, 57 Stat. 13
June 26, 1943, Ch. 151, 57 Stat. 219
Oct. 18, 1943, Ch. 260, 57 Stat. 571

July 1, 1944, Ch. 372, 58 Stat. 682
Oct. 6, 1945, Ch. 393, 59 Stat. 541
Nov. 24, 1945, Ch. 494, 59 Stat. 587
June 29, 1946, Ch. 523, 60 Stat. 343
May 15, 1947, Ch. 58, 61 Stat. 92
June 20, 1947, Ch. 109, 61 Stat. 134
June 28, 1947, Ch. 162, 61 Stat. 192
July 1, 1947, Ch. 202, 61 Stat. 192
Aug. 5, 1947, Ch. 494, 61 Stat. 776
March 25, 1948, Ch. 157, 62 Stat. 88

Pay Saving Act
See Classification Act of 1949
June 18, 1956, Ch. 402, 70 Stat. 291

Pay While Voting Act
Cal. Elections Code 1976, § 14350
Ill. Rev. Stat. 1991, Ch. 46, § 17-15
Ky. Rev. Stat. 1971, 118.035

Payday Act
Colo. Rev. Stat. 8-4-101 et seq.
Nev. Rev. Stat. 1979 Reprint, 608.060

Payment Acceptance Act (Government Electronics)
N.J. Stat. Ann., 40A:5-43 et seq.

Payment Act (Prompt)
Kan. Stat. Ann., 75-6401 et seq.
N.Y. State Finance Law 1940 (Consol. Laws Ch. 56) § 179d et seq.
Ore. Rev. Stat., 293.462 et seq.

Payment and Collection Law (Wage)
Md. Ann. Code 1974, Art. LE, § 3-501 et seq.

Payment Bond Act (Public Works)
Okla. Stat. Ann., Title 61, §§ 1, 2

Payment Date of Railroad Employees Act
N.Y. Labor Law (Consol. Laws Ch. 31) § 196

Payment Enforcement Act
Ill. Rev. Stat. 1991, Ch. 17, § 605.9 et seq.

Payment for State Lands Act
Cal. Statutes 1945, Ch. 1399, p. 2611

Payment-in-Kind Tax Treatment Act of 1983
July 18, 1984, P.L. 98-369, 98 Stat. 1046, 26 U.S. Code § 61 nt.
Nov. 10, 1988, P.L. 100-647, 26 U.S. Code § 61 nt.

Payment Instruments and Funds Transmission Act
Fla. Stat. Ann., 560.200 to 560.213

Payment Instruments Law
Cal. Financial Code, § 33000 et seq.

Payment of Transfer Taxes in Kind Act
Tenn. Code Ann., 67-8-701 et seq.

Payment of Wages Act
N.M. Stat. Ann., 50-4-1 et seq.

Payment Reauthorization Act (Federal)
D.C. Code Ann., § 47-3406.1

Payments for Governmental Services Act
Ill. Rev. Stat. 1991, Ch. 102, § 36 et seq.

Payments in Lieu of Taxes Act
Sept. 27, 1988, P.L. 100-446, 31 U.S. Code § 6901 nt.
Oct. 22, 1994, P.L. 103-397, 31 U.S. Code §§ 6901 nt., 6902 nt., 6902, 6903 nt., 6903

Payne-Aldrich Act (Tariff)
Aug. 5, 1909, Ch. 6, 36 Stat. 11, 31 U.S. Code §§ 745, 756; 46 U.S . Code §§ 104, 121; 48 U.S. Code § 739

Payroll Development Authority Act (Thomasville)
Ga. Laws 1960, p. 2567

PCB Waste Disposal Act
Ida. Code 1947, 39-6201 et seq.

PE Compact (Post-Secondary Education)
Me. Rev. Stat. Ann. 1964, Title 20A, § 10301 et seq.

Peabody Electric Loan Act
Mass. Acts 1956, Ch. 648

Peabody Hospital Remodeling Loan Act
Mass. Acts 1958, Ch. 636

Peabody School Loan Act
Mass. Acts 1956, Ch. 699

Peace Act
Miss. Code Ann. 1972, §§ 97-35-3, 97-35-5, 97-35-15

Peace Act (Breach of)
La. Rev. Stat. Ann., 14:103
Miss. Code Ann. 1972, § 97-35-13 et seq.

Peace Act (Employment)
Colo. Rev. Stat. 8-3-101 et seq.
Wis. Stat. Ann., 111.01 et seq.

Peace and Safety Act
N.Y. Executive Law 1951 (Consol. Laws Ch. 18) § 63, Subd. 8

Peace and Tranquility Law
Ark. Code Ann. 1987, 5-71-207

Peace Bond Act
Mich. Comp. Laws Ann., 772.1 et seq.
Mont. Rev. Code 1947, 94-5101 et seq.
N.H. Rev. Stat. 1955, 608:1 et seq.
R.I. Gen. Laws 1956, 12-4-1 et seq.
Wash. Rev. Code Ann., 10.13.010 et seq.

Peace Corps Act
Sept. 22, 1961, P.L. 87-293, 75 Stat. 612, 20 U.S. Code § 425; 22 U.S . Code §§ 2501 to 2523; 26 U.S. Code §§ 912, 1303, 1321, 3122, 3401, 6051; 42 U.S. Code §§ 405, 409, 410
April 27, 1962, P.L. 87-442, 76 Stat. 62, 22 U.S. Code § 2502
Oct. 11, 1962, P.L. 87-793, 76 Stat. 865, 22 U.S. Code § 2506
Dec. 13, 1963, P.L. 88-200, 77 Stat. 359, 22 U.S. Code §§ 2501a, 2502, 2504 to 2506, 2509, 2512, 2518
March 17, 1964, P.L. 88-285, 78 Stat. 166, 22 U.S. Code § 2502
Aug. 14, 1964, P.L. 88-426, 78 Stat. 426, 22 U.S. Code § 2503
Aug. 19, 1964, P.L. 88-448, 78 Stat. 490, 22 U.S. Code § 2512

Aug. 24, 1965, P.L. 89-134, 79 Stat. 549, 22 U.S. Code §§ 2502, 2504 to 2506, 2509, 2514
Sept. 13, 1966, P.L. 89-572, 80 Stat. 764, 20 U.S. Code § 425; 22 U.S . Code §§ 2502, 2504, 2509, 2514, 2515 nt., 2522; 26 U.S. Code §§ 912, 1303, 3121, 3122, 3401, 6051; 42 U.S. Code §§ 405, 409, 410
Dec. 5, 1967, P.L. 90-175, 81 Stat. 542, 22 U.S. Code § 2502
June 27, 1968, P.L. 90-362, 82 Stat. 250, 22 U.S. Code § 2502
Oct. 29, 1969, P.L. 91-99, 83 Stat. 166, 22 U.S. Code §§ 2501a, 2502, 2504
July 14, 1970, P.L. 91-352, 84 Stat. 464, 22 U.S. Code §§ 2501a to 2506, 2512, 2513, 2522
July 13, 1972, P.L. 92-352, 86 Stat. 495, 22 U.S. Code §§ 2501a, 2502
June 25, 1973, P.L. 93-49, 87 Stat. 99, 22 U.S. Code §§ 2502, 2509
June 1, 1974, P.L. 93-302, 88 Stat. 191, 22 U.S. Code § 2502
Nov. 14, 1975, P.L. 94-130, 89 Stat. 684, 22 U.S. Code §§ 2502, 2504; 42 U.S. Code § 4955
Aug. 15, 1977, P.L. 95-102, 22 U.S. Code § 2502
Aug. 2, 1978, P.L. 95-331, 22 U.S. Code §§ 2501, 2501 nt., 2502 et seq.
Aug. 14, 1979, P.L. 96-53, 22 U.S. Code §§ 2502, 2506
Dec. 23, 1982, P.L. 97-387, 22 U.S. Code §§ 2505, 2505 nt.
Aug. 8, 1985, P.L. 99-83, 22 U.S. Code §§ 2501 et seq., 2521a et seq.
Aug. 27, 1986, P.L. 99-399, 22 U.S. Code § 2402
Dec. 22, 1987, P.L. 100-202, 22 U.S. Code §§ 2514, 2517
Oct. 24, 1992, P.L. 102-511, 22 U.S. Code § 2507
Oct. 28, 1992, P.L. 102-565, 22 U.S. Code §§ 2502, 2515
Sept. 21, 1993, P.L. 103-82, 22 U.S. Code § 2501-1
Sept. 30, 1996, P.L. 104-208, 22 U.S. Code § 2508
April 30, 1997, P.L. 105-12, 22 U.S. Code § 2504
May 21, 1999, P.L. 106-30, 22 U.S. Code §§ 2502, 2504, 2514

Peace Corps Act Amendment of 1978
Aug. 2, 1978, P.L. 95-331, 22 U.S. Code
§§ 2501, 2501 nt., 2502 et seq.

Peace Corps Fellowship Program Law
Ill. Rev. Stat. 1991, Ch. 122, § 2001 et seq.
N.M. Stat. Ann., 21-21F-5 et seq.

Peace Garden Act
N.D. Cent. Code, 55-05-01 et seq.

**Peace Officer and Fire Fighter Survivors
Scholarship Act**
N.M. Stat. Ann., 21-21F-1 et seq., 21-21F-5

**Peace Officer and Prosecutor Training Fund
Act**
Ga. Code Ann., 15-21-70 et seq.

Peace Officer Discipline Procedures Act
Minn. Stat. Ann., 626.89

Peace Officer Fire Investigation Act
Ill. Rev. Stat. 1991, Ch. 127 1/2, §§ 500, 501

Peace Officer Firearm Training Act
Ill. Rev. Stat. 1991, Ch. 85, § 514 et seq.

Peace Officer Standards and Training Act
Ga. Code Ann., 35-8-1 et seq.
La. Rev. Stat. Ann., 40:2401 et seq.
Utah Code Ann. 1953, 53-6-101 et seq.

Peace Officer Training and Certification Act
Utah Code Ann. 1953, 53-6-201 et seq.

Peace Officer Training Council Act
Ohio Rev. Code 1953, 109.71 et seq.

**Peace Officer Widows and Widowers
Protection Act (Charles Lazzaretto)**
Cal. Government Code § 823

Peace Officers Act (Special)
See Special Peace Officers Act

**Peace Officers Annuity and Benefit Fund
Act**
Ga. Code Ann., 47-17-1 et seq.

**Peace Officers' Benefit Association Act
(Lenoir County)**
N.C. Laws 1961, Ch. 1137

Peace Officers' Disciplinary Act
Ill. Rev. Stat. 1991, Ch. 85, § 2551 et seq.

**Peace Officer's Employer-Employee
Relations Act**
N.M. Stat. Ann., 29-14-1 et seq.

Peace Officers Liability Act
N.M. Stat. Ann. 1953, 39-8-1 et seq.

Peace Officers' Retirement Law (County)
Cal. Government Code, § 31900 et seq.

**Peace Officers' Survivors Supplemental
Benefits Act**
Ga. Code Ann., 49-5-270 et seq.
N.M. Stat. Ann., 29-4A-1 et seq

Peace Officers Training Academy Act
Utah Code Ann. 1953, 67-15-1 et seq.

Peace Studies and Conflict Resolution Act
N.J. Stat. Ann., 18A:3A-1 et seq.

Peaceful Persuasion Act
Mass. Gen. Laws. Ann., 149:24

Peach and Apple Marketing Act
Ill. Rev. Stat. 1991, Ch. 5, § 351 et seq.

**Peach County Water and Sewerage
Authority Act**
Ga. Laws 1986, p. 4664

Peachtree City Airport Authority Act
Ga. Laws 1984, p. 4935

**Peachtree City Water and Sewage Authority
Act**
Ga. Laws 1991, p. 5085

**Peachtree City Water, Sewerage and
Recreational Authority Act**
Ga. Laws 1973, p. 2989

Peanut Act
N.M. Stat. Ann., 76-17-1 et seq.
Okla. Stat. Ann., Title 2, § 1101 et seq.
Continued

Peanut Marketing Act
Fla. Stat. Ann., 573.883 et seq.

Pearl River Bridge Revenue Bond Act
Miss. Code Ann. 1972, § 65-23-301 et seq.

Pearl River Valley Water Supply District Act
Miss. Code Ann. 1972, § 51-9-101 et seq.

Pearl River Valley Water Supply District Security Officer Act
Miss. Code Ann. 1972, § 51-9-171 et seq.

Pearson Industrial Authority Act
Ga. Laws 1969, p. 2905

Pearson-Robertson Act (Prison-Made Goods)
Ala. Code 1975, § 14-7-6 et seq.

Pease Bill (Grading Farm Products)
N.Y. Agriculture and Markets Law (Consol. Laws Ch. 69) § 156c et seq.

Pease Bill (Packaging of Farm Products)
N.Y. Laws 1937, Ch. 309

Peatland Protection Act
Minn. Stat. Ann., 84.035, 84.036

Pecan Industry Act
N.M. Stat. Ann., 76-16-1 et seq.

Pecan Processors and Wholesalers Licensing Act
Ga. Code Ann., 2-14-60 et seq.

Pecan Producers Act
Okla. Stat. Ann., Title 2, § 1551 et seq.

Pecan Promotion and Research Act of 1990
Nov. 28, 1990, P.L. 101-624, 7 U.S. Code §§ 6001 to 6013

Pechan Act (Loyalty)
Pa. Purdon's Stat., Title 65, § 211 et seq.

Pecos National Historical Park Expansion Act of 1990
Nov. 8, 1990, P.L. 101-536, 16 U.S. Code §§ 410 nt., 410rr-7, 410rr-7 nt.

Pecos River Compact Act
N.M. Stat. Ann., 72-15-19 et seq.
Tex. Water Code, § 42.001 et seq.

Peculation Act
N.Y. Penal Law 1909 (Consol. Laws Ch. 40) § 1865

Peddlers and Hawkers Act
Mass. Gen. Laws. Ann., 101:13 et seq.
Mich. Comp. Laws Ann., 445.371 et seq.
N.H. Rev. Stat. 1955, 522:1 et seq.
R.I. Gen. Laws 1956, 5-11-1 et seq.
S.C. Code Ann. 1976, § 40-41-10 et seq.

Peddlers' License Act
Ga. Code Ann., 43-32-1 et seq.
Iowa Code 1981, 332.45 et seq.
Kan. Laws 1901, Ch. 271
Md. Ann. Code 1957, Art. 56, § 21 et seq.
Me. Rev. Stat. Ann. 1964, Title 32, § 4688 et seq.
Ore. Rev. Stat. 1953, 698.010 et seq.
S.D. Codified Laws 1967, 37-13-1 et seq.
Vt. Stat. Ann., Title 32, § 9401 et seq.
Wash. Rev. Code Ann., 36.71.010 et seq.

Peddlers' License Act (Veterans)
Mich. Comp. Laws Ann., 35.441 et seq.

Pedestrian Mall Law
Cal. Streets and Highways Code, § 11000 et seq.
Ore. Rev. Stat., 376.705 et seq.
Utah Code Ann. 1953, 10-15-1 et seq.

Pedestrians Act
Mich. Comp. Laws Ann., 257.655
Mont. Code Ann., 61-8-501 et seq.
R.I. Gen. Laws 1956, 31-18-1 et seq.
S.C. Code Ann. 1976, § 56-5-3110 et seq.

Pedestrians Right of Way Act
Cal. Vehicle Code 1959, § 21950 et seq.
Minn. Stat. Ann., 169.21

N.H. Rev. Stat. 1955, 265:35
Ore. Rev. Stat., 814.010 et seq.
Wash. Rev. Code Ann., 46.61.230 et seq.

Pediatric Medical Practice Act
Ill. Rev. Stat. 1991, Ch. 111, § 4801 et seq.

Peekskill Parking Authority Act
N.Y. Public Authorities Law (Consol. Laws, Ch. 43A) § 1500 et seq.

Peephole Installation Act
Ill. Rev. Stat. 1991, Ch. 67 1/2, § 110 et seq.

Peeping Tom Act
Ark. Code Ann. 1987, 5-71-213
Cal. Penal Code, § 647, Subd. h, Subd. g
Ga. Code Ann., 16-11-61
Ind. Code Ann., 35-45-4-5 et seq.
La. Rev. Stat. Ann., 14:284
Md. Ann. Code 1957, Art. 27, § 580
Miss. Code Ann. 1972, § 97-29-61
N.C. Gen. Stat. 1943, § 14-202
Okla. Stat. Ann., Title 21, § 1171
Ore. Rev. Stat. 1953, 167.165
S.C. Code Ann. 1976, § 16-17-470
Tenn. Code Ann., 39-14-405, 39-14-406

Peer Review Protection Act
Pa. Purdon's Stat., Title 63, § 425.1 et seq.

Peer Review Protection Act (Dental)
N.C. Gen. Stat. 1943, § 90-48.7 et seq.

Peerson Memorial Highway Act
Ill. Rev. Stat. 1991, Ch. 121, §§ 389.9, 390

Pekin and Greenville Federal Correctional Institutions Cession Law
Ill. Comp. Stat. 1992, Ch. 5, § 517/10-1

Pekin and Quad City Civic Centers Act
Ill. Rev. Stat. 1991, Ch. 85, § 3100 et seq.

Pekin Civic Center Authority Law
Ill. Rev. Stat. 1991, Ch. 85, § 3201 et seq.

Pelagic Sealing Act
Aug. 24, 1912, Ch. 373, 37 Stat. 499, 16 U.S. Code § 650

Pelham-Port Chester Parkway Authority Act
N.Y. Public Authorities Law (Consol. Laws Ch. 43A) § 125 et seq.

Pelican Management Act
Utah Code Ann. 1953, 23-21a-1 et seq.

Pembroke Fire Station Loan Act
Mass. Acts 1959, Ch. 258

Pemigewasset River Study Act of 1989
Aug. 10, 1990, P.L. 101-357, 16 U.S. Code § 1271 nt.

Penal and Correctional Code (P. C. C.)
Ida. Code 1947, 20-101 et seq.

Penal and Rehabilitation Authority Act
Ga. Code Ann., 42-3-1 et seq.

Penal Building Authority Act
Ga. Code Ann., 42-3-1 et seq.

Penal Code
See Criminal Code
Conn. Gen. Stat. Ann., § 53a-1 et seq.
Haw. Rev. Stat. Ann., Title 37
Ind. Code Ann., 35-32-1-1 et seq.
Ky. Rev. Stat. 1971, 500.010 et seq.
Mich. Comp. Laws Ann., 750.1 et seq.
Minn. Stat. Ann., 609.01 et seq.
N.Y. Consol. Laws, Ch. 40
Okla. Stat. Ann., Title 21, § 1 et seq.
Pa. Cons. Stat., Title 18, § 101 et seq.
P.R. Laws Ann. 1954, Title 33, § 3001 et seq.
Tex. Penal Code, § 1.01 et seq.
Utah Code Ann. 1953, 76-1-101 et seq.

Penal Limitations Act
N.J. Stat. Ann., 2A:58-1 to 2A:58-9

Penal Obscenity Act
Mo. Rev. Stat. 1969, 563.270 et seq.

Penal Procedure Code
Pa. Cons. Stat., Title 42

Penal Reform Act
Kan. Stat. Ann., 75-5201 et seq.

Penalty Abatement Act
Pa. Purdon's Stat., Title 72, § 5575.1 et seq.

Penalty Act (Death)
S.C. Code Ann. 1976, § 16-3-20 et seq.

Penalty Act (Insurance)
La. Rev. Stat. Ann., 22:656 et seq.

Penalty Act (Limitation of Actions)
Pa. Cons. Stat., Title 42, § 5530 et seq.

Penalty and Interest Act
See Uniform Penalty and Interest Act

Penalty Enforcement Law
N.J. Stat. Ann., 2A:58-1 et seq.

Penalty Mail Act of 1948
June 25, 1948, Ch. 658, 62 Stat. 1048
Aug. 15, 1953, Ch. 511, 67 Stat. 614
March 29, 1956, Ch. 108, 70 Stat. 63
July 14, 1956, Ch. 591, 70 Stat. 536

Pence Act (Public Utilities Rates)
Ohio Rev. Code 1953, 4909.17 et seq.

Pendleton Act (Civil Service)
See Civil Service Act

Pendleton Act (Intoxicating Liquors)
Tenn. Acts 1907, Ch. 17

Penitent-Priest Act
N.Y. Civil Practice Laws and Rules (Consol. Laws Ch. 8) § 4505

Penitentiary Act
March 2, 1831, Ch. 37, 4 Stat. 448
Ill. Rev. Stat. 1991, Ch. 38, § 1001-1-1 et seq.
Wash. Rev. Code Ann., 72.02.015 et seq., 72.09.010 et seq.
W. Va. Code 1966, § 28-5-1 et seq.

Penitentiary Budget Relief Act
Ark. Pope's Digest 1937, §§ 12757 to 12767

Penitentiary-Made Goods Act
Miss. Code Ann. 1972, § 47-5-301 et seq.

Penitentiary Merit System Act
N.M. Stat. Ann. 1953, 42-1-63 et seq.

Penitentiary Work Release Act
Wyo. Stat. Ann., § 7-13-717 et seq.

Penn Serve Act
Pa. Purdon's Stat., Title 71, § 582-1 et seq.

Penn Vest Act
Pa. Purdon's Stat., Title 35, § 751.1 et seq.

Pennies for Progress Act
Va. Code 1950, § 3.1-22.1 et seq.

Pennsylvania Area College Center Act
Pa. Purdon's Stat., Title 24, § 2501.4 et seq.

Pennsylvania Avenue Development Corporation Act of 1972
Oct. 27, 1972, P.L. 92-578; 40 U.S. Code § prec. 871 nt.
Nov. 10, 1978, P.L. 95-629, 40 U.S. Code §§ 872, 874, 875, 877, 885
Oct. 31, 1983, P.L. 98-141, 40 U.S. Code §§ 872, 874, 875, 880, 885
Aug. 22, 1988, P.L. 100-415, 102 Stat. 1104, 40 U.S. Code § 885
Dec. 11, 1991, P.L. 102-219, 40 U.S. Code § 885
Oct. 23, 1992, P.L. 102-439, 40 U.S. Code § 885
Nov. 2, 1994, P.L. 103-437, 40 U.S. Code § 874
April 26, 1996, P.L. 104-134, 40 U.S. Code § 872

Pennsylvania Wilderness Act of 1984
Oct. 30, 1984, P.L. 98-585, 98 Stat. 3100

Pennsylvanians with Disabilities Act
Pa. Cons. Stat., Title 44, § 40

Penny-Dunnigan Pari-mutuel Act
N.Y. Laws 1940, Ch. 254

Penny Stock Reform Act of 1990
Oct. 15, 1990, P.L. 101-429, 15 U.S. Code §§ 78a nt., 78o

Penny Trust Fund Matching Act (John L. Buskey)
Ala. Code 1975, §§ 41-15A-10 to 41-15A-12

Pensacola Downtown Improvement Board Act
Fla. Special Laws 1972, Ch. 72-655

Pensacola-Escambia Charter
Fla. Special Laws 1970, Ch. 70-681

Pensacola-Escambia County Promotion and Development Commission Act
Fla. Special Laws 1967, Ch. 67-1365

Pension Act
Colo. Rev. Stat. 26-2-101 et seq. (WORLD WAR I)
Del. Code of 1974, Title 14, § 3909
Del. Code of 1974, Title 29, §§ 5501, 5502, 5521 to 5524, 5527, 5528, 5531, 5532, 5543, 5544
Fla. Stat. Ann., 409.16 et seq.
Ill. Rev. Stat. 1991, Ch. 108 1/2
Mass. Gen. Laws. Ann., 32:1 et seq.
N.J. Rev. Stat. 1937, 43:1-1 et seq.

Pension Act (Augusta)
Ga. Laws 1925, p. 867
Ga. Laws 1945, p. 813

Pension Act (Blind)
Pa. 1965 Pamph. Laws 400 No. 204
Wyo. Session Laws 1935, Ch. 129

Pension Act (Confederate Soldiers)
Ark. Stat. 1947, 11-1349
Ky. Rev. Stat. 1971, 206.010 et seq.

Pension Act (Confederate)
See Confederate Pension Act

Pension Act (County Employees)
Ga. Laws 1937, p. 738

Pension Act (County)
See County Pension Act

Pension Act (Dalton Police and Firemen)
Ga. Laws 1945, p. 593, § 15 et seq.

Pension Act (De Kalb County)
Ga. Laws 1953 (Nov.-Dec. Sess.), p. 3198

Pension Act (Dothan)
Ala. Acts 1953, p. 145

Pension Act (Firemen and Police)
Mich. Comp. Laws Ann., 38.551 et seq.

Pension Act (Firemen and Policemen)
See Firemen's and Policemen's Pension Act

Pension Act (Highway Patrol)
See Highway Patrol Retirement and Pension Act

Pension Act (Institutional)
N.M. Stat. Ann., 23-1-9 et seq.

Pension Act (Judges)
See Judges Pension Act

Pension Act (Laborers)
Mass. Gen. Laws. Ann., 32:77 et seq.

Pension Act (Mothers)
See Mother's Pension Act

Pension Act (Municipal)
See Municipal Pension Act

Pension Act (Old Age)
See Old Age Pension Act

Pension Act (Policemen)
See Police Pension Act

Pension Act (Public Library Employees)
Mich. Comp. Laws Ann., 38.701 et seq.

Pension Act (Railroads)
See Railway Pension Act

Pension Act (State)
Md. Ann. Code 1957, Art. 73B, § 1 et seq.

Pension Act (Teachers)
See Teachers' Pension Act

Pension Act (Troup County)
Ga. Laws 1951, p. 2637

Pension Act (Veterans)
See Veterans' Pension Act

Pension Acts
July 14, 1862, Ch. 166, 12 Stat. 566
March 3, 1879, Ch. 187, 20 Stat. 469
June 10, 1918, Ch. 96, 40 Stat. 603
June 5, 1920, Ch. 245, 41 Stat. 982

Pension and Retirement Act
Va. Code 1950, § 51-30 et seq.

Pension and Retirement Act (Policemen)
Pa. Purdon's Stat., Title 53, § 761 et seq.

Pension and Retirement System Modification Act (Firefighters)
Okla. Laws 1999, H.B. 1045

Pension Annuitants Protection Act of 1994
Oct. 22, 1994, P.L. 103-401, 29 U.S. Code § 1001 nt.

Pension Benefits Protection Act (Private)
Minn. Stat. Ann., 181B.13

Pension Benefits Protection Tax Act (Private Nonvested)
N.J. Laws 1973, Ch. 124
R.I. Laws 1956, 28-46-1 et seq.

Pension Bond Financing Act
N.J. Stat. Ann., 34:1B-7.45 et seq.

Pension Fund Act (Firemen and Policemen)
See Firemen's and Policemen's Pension Act

Pension Fund Act (Firemen's and Rescue Squad Worker's)
N.C. Gen. Stat. 1943, § 58-86-1 et seq.

Pension Fund Act (First Class Cities)
Pa. Purdon's Stat., Title 53, § 13431 et seq.

Pension Fund Act (Second Class Cities)
Pa. Purdon's Stat., Title 53, § 23561 et seq.

Pension Fund Act (Teachers)
N.J. Stat. Ann., 43:10-18.1 et seq.
N.M. Stat. Ann. 1953, 73-12-16 et seq.

Pension Fund Act (Third Class Cities)
Pa. Purdon's Stat, Title 53, § 39340 et seq.

Pension Fund Tax Act
Neb. Rev. Stat. 1943, 77-730

Pension Funds of Firemen's in Cities Act
See Firemen's and Policemen's Pension Act

Pension Impact Note Act
Ill. Rev. Stat. 1991, CH. 63, § 42.41 et seq.

Pension Increase Act
N.J. Stat. Ann., 43:3B-1 et seq.

Pension Law (Firefighters)
Iowa Code Ann., 410.1 et seq.

Pension Note Act (Confederate)
Ark. Pope's Digest 1937, §§ 10670 to 10672

Pension Plan Funding Standard and Recovery Act (Municipal)
Pa. Purdon's Stat., Title 53, § 895.101 et seq.

Pension Policy Commission Act
May 24, 1979, P.L. 96-14, 29 U.S. Code § 1001 nt.

Pension Portability Act (Interstate)
Fla. Stat. Ann., 121.45 et seq.

Pension Protection Act
Dec. 22, 1987, P.L. 100-203, 26 U.S. Code § 1 nt.
Dec. 19, 1989, P.L. 101-239, 26 U.S. Code §§ 401 nt., 404 nt., 412 nt,. 29 U.S. Code §§ 1021 nt., 1301 nt., 1322nt., 1344 nt., 1341, 1342, 1362

Pension Protection Act (Mrs. Ruth Q. de Prida)
Cal. Education Code 1976, § 22951.5 et seq.

Pension Revocation and Reduction Act (Public Employee)
R.I. Gen. Laws 1956, 36-10.1-1 et seq.

Pension Rights Act (Spousal)
Neb. Rev. Stat. 1943, 42-1101 to 42-1113

Pension Time Credit Transfer Act
Ga. Laws 1953 (Nov.-Dec. Sess.), p. 3000

Pension Transfer Act
N.J. Stat. Ann., 43:2-1 to 43:2-3

Pensioners Complete Supplementation Act
P.R. Acts 1988, No. 39

Peonage Abolition Act
March 2, 1867, Ch. 187, 14 Stat. 546

People Mover Act (St. Paul)
Minn. Stat. 1980, 458B.01 et seq.

Peoples Act (Divorce Residence)
Nev. Rev. Stat. 1979 Reprint, 125.020

People's Utility District Law
Ore. Rev. Stat., 261.005 et seq.

Peoria Civic Center Act
Ill. Rev. Stat. 1991, Ch. 85, § 1441 et seq.

Pepper Act
Also known as Department of Elderly Affairs
Act
Fla. Stat. Ann., 403.01 et seq.
Fla. Stat. Ann., 430.01 et seq.

Pepperell Water Loan Act
Mass. Acts 1950, Ch. 702

Per Capita Act
Aug. 2, 1983, P.L. 98-64, 25 U.S. Code
§ 117a et seq.

Per Capita Tax Act
Minn. Stat. Ann., 275.11 et seq.

Per Diem and Mileage Act
N.M. Stat. Ann., 10-8-1 et seq.

Percent-for-Art Act
Me. Rev. Stat. Ann. 1964, Title 27, § 451 et
seq.
Utah Code Ann. 1953, 9-6-401 et seq.

Percent-or-Art Act
Me. Rev. Stat. Ann. 1964, Title 27, § 451 et
seq.
Mont. Code Ann., 22-2-401 et seq.

Utah Code Ann. 1953, 64-2a-1 et seq.

Percy-Gray Racing Act
N.Y. Laws 1895, Ch. 570

Perfect Tender Rule
Mont. Code Ann. 1987, 30-2-601

**Performance and Accountability Act
(Government)**
Fla. Laws 1994, Ch. 249

Performance and Results Act
Cal. Government Code § 11800 et seq.

**Performance-Based Career Incentive
Program Act**
Ala. Acts 1985, p. 762

Performance-Based Government Act
Wash. Laws 1993, Ch. 406

**Performance Bond Act (Public Works
Contracts)**
Ill. Rev. Stat. 1985, Ch. 29, § 14.9

**Performance Budget and Strategic Planning
Act**
Miss. General Laws 1994, Ch. 602, p. 957

Performance Incentive Program
Ariz. Rev. Stat. Ann., § 15-920

**Performance Management and Recognition
System Amendments of 1991**
March 28, 1991, P.L. 102-22, 5 U.S. Code
§§ 4302a, 4302a nt., 5401 nt., 5406, 5408
nt., 5410

**Performance Management and Recognition
System Reauthorization Act of 1989**
Sept. 30, 1989, P.L. 101-103, 5 U.S. Code
§ 5401 nt.

**Performance Management and Recognition
System Termination Act**
Sept. 30, 1993, P.L. 103-89, 5 U.S. Code
§§ 3372, 3372 nt., 4302a, 4501, 4502, 5301
nt., 5302, 5304 nt., 5332 et seq., 5335
nt., 5361 et seq., 5401 nt., 5410 et seq.,
5948, 8473; 10 U.S. Code §§ 1602, 1732,
1733; 31 U.S. Code § 731

Performance Rating Act of 1950

Sept. 30, 1950, Ch. 1123, 64 Stat. 1098 (See 5 U.S. Code §§ 3502, 4301 to 4308, 5335, 5336)

Sept. 1, 1954, Ch. 1208, 68 Stat. 1115, 2 U.S. Code § 126; See 5 U.S. Code § 4301; 7 U.S. Code § 2262

June 17, 1957, P.L. 85-56, 71 Stat. 159 (See 5 U.S. Code § 4301)

July 11, 1957, P.L. 85-101, 71 Stat. 293 (See 5 U.S. Code § 4301)

Sept. 2, 1958, P.L. 85-857, 72 Stat. 1266 (See 5 U.S. Code § 4301)

March 26, 1964, P.L. 88-290, 78 Stat. 170 (See 5 U.S. Code § 4301)

Perfusionists Act

Tex. Rev. Civ. Stat., Art. 4529e

Perinatal Health Act

Ala. Code 1975, § 22-12A-1 et seq.

Period In Gross Act (Perpetuities)

Mass. Gen. Laws. Ann., 184A:3

Period in Gross Act (Reverter and Rights of Entry)

R.I. Gen. Laws 1956, 34-4-19

Perishable Agricultural Commodities Act Amendments of 1995

Nov. 15, 1995, P.L. 104-48, 7 U.S. Code § 499a nt.

Perishable Agricultural Commodities Act, 1930

June 10, 1930, Ch. 436, 46 Stat. 531, 7 U.S. Code §§ 499a to 499r

Aug. 20, 1937, Ch. 719, 50 Stat. 725, 7 U.S. Code §§ 499a to 499h, 499n

May 14, 1940, Ch. 196, 54 Stat. 214, 7 U.S. Code § 499g

June 29, 1940, Ch. 456, 54 Stat. 696, 7 U.S. Code §§ 499a, 499b

April 6, 1942, Ch. 211, 56 Stat. 200, 7 U.S. Code § 499b

June 15, 1950, Ch. 254, 64 Stat. 217, 7 U.S. Code §§ 499c, 499d, 499o, 499s

July 30, 1956, Ch. 786, 70 Stat. 726, 7 U.S. Code §§ 499b to 499d, 499h, 499m

June 11, 1960, P.L. 86-507, 74 Stat. 200, 7 U.S. Code § 499f

Oct. 1, 1962, P.L. 87-725, 76 Stat. 673, 7 U.S. Code §§ 499a, 499c, 499d, 499f to 499h

Nov. 4, 1969, P.L. 91-107, 83 Stat. 182, 7 U.S. Code §§ 499a, 499c

Oct. 15, 1970, P.L. 91-452, 84 Stat. 928, 7 U.S. Code § 499m

Feb. 15, 1972, P.L. 92-231, 86 Stat. 38, 7 U.S. Code §§ 499f, 499g

Aug. 10, 1974, P.L. 93-369, 88 Stat. 423, 7 U.S. Code § 499b

Nov. 1, 1978, P.L. 95-562, 7 U.S. Code §§ 499a, 499a nt., 499c, 499m

Nov. 6, 1978, P.L. 95-598, 7 U.S. Code § 499

Oct. 18, 1982, P.L. 97-352, 7 U.S. Code §§ 499f, 499f nt.

May 7, 1984, P.L. 98-273, 7 U.S. Code §§ 499b, 499e

Aug. 22, 1988, P.L. 100-414, 102 Stat. 1102, 7 U.S. Code §§ 499c, 499t

Nov. 28, 1990, P.L. 101-624, 7 U.S. Code §§ 499b-1, 499c

Dec. 13, 1991, P.L. 102-237, 7 U.S. Code §§ 499a, 499d, 499e, 499f, 499g, 499h, 499n, 499r

Nov. 15, 1995, P.L. 104-48, 7 U.S. Code §§ 499a et seq.

Perjury Act

Ariz. Rev. Stat. Ann., § 13-2701 et seq.

Cal. Penal Code, § 118 et seq.

D.C. Code 1973, § 22-2501

Ill. Rev. Stat. 1991, Ch. 38, §§ 3-2, 32-3

Ind. Code Ann., 35-44-2-1 et seq.

Md. Ann. Code 1957, Art. 27, § 435 et seq.

Mich. Comp. Laws Ann., 750.422 et seq.

Mont. Code Ann., 45-7-201 et seq.

N.C. Gen. Stat. 1943, § 14-209 et seq.

N.H. Rev. Stat. 1955, 641:1

N.Y. Penal Laws 1965 (Consol. Laws Ch. 40) § 210.00 et seq.

Pa. Cons. Stat., Title 18, § 4901 et seq.

R.I. Gen. Laws 1956, 11-33-1 et seq.

Tex. Penal Code, § 37.01 et seq.

Vt. Stat. Ann., Title 13, § 2901 et seq.

Wash. Rev. Code Ann., 9A.72.090 et seq.

Perkins Act (Indigent Children)

Iowa Laws 1915 (36th G. A.) Ch. 24

Perkins Act (Taxation)
N.J. Laws 1906, p. 571, Ch. 280

Perkins Water Authority Act
Ga. Laws 1972, p. 3604

Permanency Planning Grants to Counties Act
Minn. Stat. Ann., 256F.01 et seq.

Permanent Appropriation Repeal Act of 1934
June 26, 1934, Ch. 756, 48 Stat. 1224, 16 U.S. Code § 514; 21 U.S. Code § 95; 31 U.S. Code §§ 725 to 725h, 725j, 725o, 725p, 725q, 725r, 725s, 725v to 725z; 43 U.S. Code § 863
Aug. 30, 1954, Ch. 1076, 68 Stat. 968, 31 U.S. Code § 725w

Permanent Automobile Licensing Act
Ark. Code Ann. 1987, 27-14-1001 et seq.

Permanent Budget Commission Act
Del. Code of 1974, Title 29, § 6301 et seq.

Permanent Care and Improvement Fund Act (Public Cemetery Districts)
Mont. Code Ann., 7-35-2131 et seq.

Permanent Census Act
See Census Acts

Permanent Improvement and School Book Bond Act
N.C. Public Laws 1939, Ch. 67

Permanent Improvement Appropriation Act
N.C. Laws 1947, Ch. 662
N.C. Laws 1949, Ch. 1248
N.C. Laws 1951, Ch. 995
N.C. Laws 1953, Ch. 873

Permanent Improvement Bond Act
N.C. Laws 1953, Ch. 1149

Permanent Noise Monitoring Act
Ill. Rev. Stat. 1991, Ch. 15 1/2, § 751 et seq.

Permanent Payroll Reduction and Early Retirement Incentive Act
La. Rev. Stat. Ann., 42:541

Permanent Registration Act
Mo. Rev. Stat. 1969, 113.010 et seq.

Permanent Registration Act (Broward County)
Cal. Streets and Highways Code, § 1160.5

Permanent Registration Act (Escambia County)
Fla. Laws 1947, Ch. 23903

Permanent Registration Act (First Class Cities)
Pa. Purdon's Stat., Title 25, § 623-1 et seq.

Permanent Registration Act for Cities of the Second Class, Cities of the Second Class A, Cities of the Third Class, Boroughs, Towns and Townships
Pa. Purdon's Stat., Title 25, § 51.1 et seq.

Permanent Registration Act in Cities of the Second Class
Pa. 1933 Ex. Pamph Laws, 250 No. 62
Pa. 1937 Laws 814, No. 226

Permanent Registration Act in Cities of the Second Class A
Pa. Ex. Pamph. Laws 140, No. 35
Pa. 1937 Pamph. Laws 1132, No. 292

Permanent Registration Act in Cities of the Third Class
Pa. 1935 Pamph, Laws 478, No. 195
Pa. 1937 Pamph. Laws 849, No. 227

Permanent Registration of Voters Act
Ill. Rev. Stat. 1991, Ch.46, § 6-27 et seq.
Ind. Code Ann., 3-7-1-1 et seq.
Iowa Code 1977, 48.1 et seq.
Ky. Rev. Stat. 1971, 116.013 et seq.
La. Rev. Stat. Ann., 18:101 et seq.
Md. Ann. Code 1957, Art. 33, § 3-1 et seq.
N.J. Stat. Ann., 19:31-1 et seq.
R.I. Gen. Laws 1956, 17-9-1 et seq.
Tenn. Code Ann., 2-2-105 et seq.
Wash. Rev. Code Ann., 29.07.010 et seq.
Continued

W. Va. Code 1966, § 3-2-1 et seq.

Permanent Road Division Law
Cal. Streets and Highways Code § 1160.5

Permanent Survey Act
Ill. Rev. Stat. 1991, Ch. 133, § 10.9 et seq.

Permanent Trailer Licensing Act
Cal. Government Code, § 51010 et seq.

Permissive Indemnification Act (Corporations)
Wis. Stat. Ann., 180.0852

Permissive Joinder Act (Parties)
Ohio Civ. Rule 20(A)

Permissive Use Act (Motor Vehicles)
Cal. Vehicle Code 1959, § 17150 et seq.

Permit Act
Ga. Code 1933, 42-1601 et seq.

Permit Act (Intoxicating Liquors)
Conn. Gen. Stat. Ann., § 30-14 et seq.

Permit Act (Water Supply)
Cal. Health and Safety Code, § 1390 et seq.
Tex. Water Code, § 11.121 et seq.

Permit and Health Certificate Act (Importation)
Mont. Code Ann. 1987, 81-2-701 et seq.

Permit and Lease Act (Minerals)
Tex. Natural Resources Code, § 53.061 et seq.

Permit and Lease Act (Oil and Gas)
Tex. Natural Resources Code, § 52.221 et seq.

Permit Extension Act
N.J. Stat. Ann., 40:55D-130 et seq.

Permit Law (Dealer Tag)
See Uniform Dealer Tag Permit Law

Permit Process Facilitation Act
Haw. Session Laws 1985, Act 237

Permit Reform Act
Cal. Government Code, § 15374 et seq.

Permit Reform Act (Environmental Protection)
Cal. Public Resources Code § 71000 et seq.

Permit Reform Act (Wright-Polanco-Lempert)
Cal. Statutes 1992, Ch. 1345

Permit Streamlining Act (Air Pollution)
Cal. Health and Safety Code § 42320 et seq.

Permits and Regulations Administration Act
P.R. Laws Ann. 1954, Title 23, § 71 et seq.

Permitting Act (Geothermal and Cable System Development)
Haw. Rev. Stat. § 196D-1 et seq.

Permitting Reform Act (Water Rights)
Cal. Water Code, § 1228 et seq.

Pernicious Drug Acts
See Natcotics Acts

Pernicious Literature Act
Ind. Burns' 1956 Repl., 10-2805

Perpetual and Restoration of Public Land Act (Survey)
Fla. Stat. Ann., 177.501 et seq.

Perpetual Care and Mill Tailings Licensing Act
Wash. Code 1983, 70.121.010 et seq.

Perpetual Care Fund Act (Cemeteries)
Okla. Stat. Ann., Title 8, § 161 et seq.

Perpetual Trust Act
Ill. Rev. Stat. 1991, Ch. 21, § 63.9 et seq.

Perpetual Trust Act (Burial Lot)
Ill. Comp. Stat. 1992, Ch. 760, § 90/0.01 et seq.
Ill. Rev. Stat. 1991, Ch. 21, § 30.9 et seq.

Perpetually Maintained Cemeteries Act
Ill. Comp. Stat. 1992, Ch. 760, § 95/0.01 et
  seq.
Mont. Code Ann., 37-19-801 et seq.

Perpetuation Act
Neb. Rev. Stat. 1943, 25-1267.08 et seq.

Perpetuation and Filing Act (Corner)
Ida. Code 1947, 55-1601 et seq.

Perpetuation of Evidence Act
Wash. Rev. Code Ann., 10.16.160 et seq.,
  Rules of Court, Pleading, Rule 27a, 69b

Perpetuation of Testimony Act
Neb. Rev. Stat. 1943, 25-1267.08 et seq.
Okla. Stat. 1971, Title 12, § 538.1 et seq.

Perpetuities Act
Ala. Code 1975, § 35-4-4
Ariz. Rev. Stat. Ann., § 33-261
Cal. Civil Code, § 715.2 et seq.
Colo. Rev. Stat. 15-11-1101 et seq.
Conn. Gen. Stat. Ann., § 45-95 et seq.
Ga. Code Ann., 44-6-200 et seq.
Ida. Code 1947, 55-111
Ill. Rev. Stat. 1991, Ch. 30, § 191 et seq.
Ind. Code Ann., 32-1-4-1 et seq.
Iowa Code Ann., 558.68
Ky. Rev. Stat. 1971, 381.215 et seq.
Mass. Gen. Laws. Ann., 184A:1 et seq.
Minn. Stat. Ann., 501H.01 et seq.
N.Y. Estates, Powers and Trusts Law
  (Consol. Laws Ch. 17B) § 9-1.1 et seq.
Ohio Rev. Code 1953, 2131.08
Ore. Rev. Stat.1991, 105.950 et seq.
Pa. Cons. Stat., Title 20, § 6104

Perpetuities Act (Model Rule)
Wyo. Stat. Ann., §§ 34-1-138, 34-1-139

Perpetuities Act (Statutory Rule against)
See Uniform Statutory Rule against Perpetuities

**Perquimans County-Chowan Peace
Officers' Relief Act**
N.C. Laws 1963, Ch. 86

**Perquimans County Peace Officers' Relief
Association Act**
N.C. Laws 1959, Ch. 1283

Perry Act (Suspension of Employees)
Mass. Gen. Laws. Ann., 30:59

**Perry Area Convention and Visitors Bureau
Authority Act**
Ga. Laws 1990, p. 3542

Perry-Fort Valley Airport Authority Act
Ga. Laws 1971, p. 2589

**Perry-Houston County Airport Authority
Act**
Ga. Laws 1994, p. 3885

Perry Telephone Authority Act
Ga. Laws 1973, p. 3776

**Persian Gulf Conflict Higher Education
Assistance Act**
April 6, 1991, P.L. 102-25, 20 U.S. Code
  § 1070 nt.

**Persian Gulf Conflict Supplemental
Authorization and Personnel Benefit Act
of 1991**
April 6, 1991, P.L. 102-25, 10 U.S. Code
  § 101 nt.
Dec. 5, 1991, P.L. 102-190, 37 U.S. Code
  § 302f nt.
Oct. 23, 1992, P.L. 102-484, 106 Stat. 2625
Oct. 5, 1994, P.L. 103-337, 108 Stat. 3057
Dec. 21, 1995, P.L. 104-66, 109 Stat. 712

**Persian Gulf Conflict Veterans'
Compensation and Bond Act**
Pa. Purdon's Stat., Title 51, § 20301 et seq.

Persian Gulf War Veterans Act of 1998
Oct. 21, 1998, P.L. 105-277, Division C,
  Title XVI, 112 Stat. 2681, 38 U.S . Code
  § 101 nt.

Persian Gulf War Veterans' Benefits Act
Oct. 9, 1996, P.L. 104-262, 38 U.S. Code
  § 1117 nt.
Nov. 11, 1998, P.L. 105-368, 38 U.S. Code
  § 1117 nt.

Persian Gulf War Veterans' Benefits Act of 1991

April 6, 1991, P.L. 102-25, 38 U.S. Code § 101 nt.

Nov. 2, 1994, P.L. 103-446, 38 U.S. Code § 101 nt.

Persian Gulf War Veterans' Health Status Act

Nov. 4, 1992, P.L. 102-585, 38 U.S. Code § 527 nt.

Nov. 2, 1994, P.L. 103-446, 38 U.S. Code § 527 nt.

Nov. 11, 1998, P.L. 105-368, 38 U.S. Code § 527 nt.

Persistent Drunk Driver Act

Colo. Rev. Stat., 16-4-403, 42-1-102, 42-2-126, 42-3-130.5, 42-4-1301, Subd. 9, 42-7-406

Persistent Offender Accountability Act

N.J. Stat. Ann., 2C:43-7.1 et seq.

Wash. Rev. Code Ann., 9.94A.392

Persistent School Offender Statute

Mass. Gen. Laws 1932, Ch. 77, § 5

Persistent Violator Act

Ida. Code 1947, 19-5004

Persistent Violators Act (Prohibitory Liquor Act Violations)

Kan. Laws 1911, Ch. 165

Personal and Real Tax Rate Act

D.C. Code Ann., § 47-501 et seq.

Personal Attendant Care Program for Disabled Adults Act

Ga. Code Ann., 30-6-1 et seq.

Personal Attendant Services Act

N.J. Stat. Ann., 30:4G-13 et seq.

Personal Care Facilities Licensing Act

Tex. Health and Safety Code, § 247.001

Personal Care Health Board Act (Griffin-Spalding County)

Ga. Laws 1991, p. 4609

Personal Care Home Act

Tex. Health and Safety Code, § 247.001 et seq.

Personal Care Homes Act (Remedies for Residents of)

Ga. Code Ann., 31-8-130 et seq.

Personal Care or Nursing Home Accountability Act

R.I. Gen. Laws 1956, 23-17.2-1 et seq.

Personal Choice and Living Will Act

Utah Code Ann. 1953, 75-2-1101 et seq.

Personal Custodian Law

Mo. Rev. Stat. 1978, 404.410 et seq.

Personal Identity Abuse Act

Utah Code Ann. 1953, 45-3-1 etseq.

Personal Income Tax Act

Cal. Revenue and Taxation Code, § 17001 et seq.

Del. Code of 1974, Title 30, § 1101 et seq.

N.Y. Tax Law (Consol. Laws Ch. 60) § 601 et seq.

Ore. Rev. Stat., 316.002 et seq.

Pa. Purdon's Stat., Title 72, § 7301 et seq.

R.I. Gen. Laws 1956, 44-30-1 et seq.

Vt. Stat. Ann., Title 32, § 5821 et seq.

W. Va. Code 1966, § 11-21-1 et seq.

Personal Income Tax Act (City)

N.Y. Laws 1975, Ex. Sess., Ch. 881, § 13

N.Y. Tax Law (Consol. Laws Ch. 60) § 1300 et seq.

Personal Income Tax Fairness Simplification and Conformity Act

Cal. Revenue and Taxation Code, §§ 16702, 16704, 16710, 17020.1 to 17020.4, 17020.9, 17020.11, 17021.5, 17024.5

Personal Injuries Act (Seventy-Two Hour)

Wis. Stat. Ann., 904.12

Personal Injuries Act (Suits Against Municipalities)

Ill. Rev. Stat. 1991, Ch. 24, § 1-4-5 et seq.

Personal Injuries Act (Wrongful Death)
See Wrongful Death Act

Personal Injury Representation Agreement Act
Ill. Rev. Stat. 1991, Ch. 29, §§ 70, 71

Personal Interest Act
Tenn. Code Ann., 12-4-101, 12-4-102

Personal Jurisdiction over Nonresidents Act
La. Rev. Stat. Ann., 13:3201 et seq.

Personal Limitation of Actions Act
Mich. Comp. Laws Ann., 600.5813 et seq.

Personal Loan Act
Neb. Rev. Stat. 1943, 8-815 et seq.
P.R. Laws Ann. 1954, Title 10, § 941 et seq.

Personal Net Income Tax Law
Wash. Laws 1935, Ch. 178

Personal Privacy Protection Law
N.Y. Public Officers Law (Consol. Laws Ch. 47) § 91 et seq.

Personal Property Accession Act
Cal. Civil Code, § 1025 et seq.

Personal Property Act
N.J. Stat. Ann., 46:28-1 et seq.
N.Y. Consol. Laws, Ch. 41

Personal Property Act (State Surplus)
Tenn. Code Ann., 12-2-401 et seq.

Personal Property Alternative Custody Act
N.J. Rev. Stat. 1937, 2A:37-29 et seq.

Personal Property and Escheat of Land Act
S.C. Code Ann. 1976, § 27-19-10 et seq.

Personal Property and Self-Service Storage Act (Liens)
Minn. Stat. Ann., 514.970 et seq.

Personal Property Brokers Law
Cal. Financial Code, § 22000 et seq.

Personal Property Disposition Landlord and Tenant Act
Neb. Rev. Stat. 1943, § 69-2301 et seq.

Personal Property Escheat Act
N.J. Stat. Ann., 2A:37-11 et seq.

Personal Property Exemption Act
Ariz. Rev. Stat. Ann., § 33-1121 et seq.
Mass. Gen. Laws. Ann., 235:34
Mich. Comp. Laws Ann., 211.8 et seq.
S.D. Codified Laws 1967, 43-45-1 et seq.

Personal Property Foreclosure Act
Ga. Code Ann., 44-14-230 et seq.

Personal Property Gift Act
W. Va. Code 1966, § 36-1-5

Personal Property Implied Warranty Act
Ga. Code 1933, 96-307

Personal Property Installment Sales Act
Colo. Rev. Stat. 1963, 121-2-1 et seq.

Personal Property Lease Act
P.R. Laws Ann. 1954, Title 10, § 996 et seq.

Personal Property Lien Act
N.C. Gen. Stat. 1943, § 44A-1 et seq.

Personal Property Mortgage Law
P.R. Laws Ann. 1954, Title 30, § 1871 et seq.

Personal Property Owner's Rights and Garnishment Act
Tenn. Code Ann., 26-2-101 et seq.

Personal Property Partition Law
Cal. Code of Civil Procedure § 752a

Personal Property Recording Act
D.C. Code 1973, § 42-102 et seq.
Iowa Code Ann., 556.3, 556.4

Personal Property Storage Act
Ill. Rev. Stat. 1991, Ch. 111 2/3, § 118.9 et seq.

Personal Property Tax Act
Ariz. Laws 1943, Ch. 77
D.C. Code Ann., § 47-1508 et seq.
Haw. Session Laws 1933, Special Session, Act 9
Me. Rev. Stat. Ann. 1964, Title 36, § 601 et seq.
Mich. Comp. Laws Ann., 211.8 et seq.
Ohio Rev. Code 1953, 5711.01 et seq.
Ore. Rev. Stat., 308.250
Pa. Purdon's Stat., Title 72, § 3242 et seq.

Personal Property Tax Act (Business)
N.J. Stat. Ann., 54:11A-1 et seq.

Personal Property Tax Act (First Class School Districts)
Pa. Purdon's Stat., Title 24, § 581.1 et seq.

Personal Property Tax Act (Intangibles)
See Intangible Property Tax Act

Personal Property Tax Act (Limitation on Collection)
Ill. Comp. Stat. 1992, Ch. 35, §§ 225/1, 225/2
Ill. Rev. Stat. 1991, Ch. 120, §§ 2201, 2202

Personal Property Tax Act (Smaller Municipalities)
Pa. 1947 Pamph. Laws 1145, No. 481

Personal Property Tax Act of 1969
Ore. Rev. Stat., 316.002 et seq.

Personal Property Tax Exemption Act
Mich. Comp. Laws Ann., 211.9

Personal Property Tax Lien Act (Cities)
Iowa Code Ann., 420.231

Personal Property Tax Rate Act
D.C. Code Ann., § 47-501 et seq.

Personal Property Taxation Law (Intangible)
Fla. Stat. Ann., 199.012 et seq.

Personal Property Use Tax Act
Iowa Code Ann., 423.1 et seq.

Personal Protection Insurance Law
Mass. Gen. Laws. Ann., 90:34M

Personal Receivership Act
Mich. Comp. Laws Ann., 691.801 et seq.

Personal Registration Act
Pa. 1906 Ex. Pamph. Laws 49, No. 12
Pa. 1913 Pamph. Laws 977, No. 452
Pa. 1919 Pamph. Laws 857, No. 348

Personal Responsibility and Employment Demonstration Program
Colo. Rev. Stat., 26-2-501 et seq.

Personal Responsibility and Public Assistance Reform Act
Ark. Acts 1997, No. 1058

Personal Responsibility and Work Opportunity Reconciliation Act of 1996
Aug. 22, 1996, P.L. 104-193, 42 U.S. Code § 1305 nt.
Sept. 30, 1996, P.L. 104-208, 8 U.S. Code §§ 1183a nt., 1612, 1631, 1632, 1641, 1642
Oct. 19, 1996, P.L. 104-327, 42 U.S. Code § 601 nt.
June 12, 1997, P.L. 105-18, 8 U.S. Code § 1612
Aug. 5, 1997, P.L. 105-33, 8 U.S. Code §§ 1611 to 1613, 1621, 1622, 1625, 1631, 1632, prec. 1641, 1641 to 1643, 1645, 1646; 21 U.S. Code § 862a; 26 U.S. Code §§ 51, 3304, 6103, 6334, 6402, 7523; 42 U.S. Code §§ 601 nt., 613 nt., 618, 622, 624, 625, 628b, 652, 655 nt., 656, 664, 671, 672, 1382c, 9910d
June 23, 1998, P.L. 105-185, 8 U.S. Code §§ 1612, 1613
Oct. 21, 1998, P.L. 105-277, 8 U.S. Code §§ 1183a nt., 1613
Oct. 28, 1998, P.L. 105-306, 8 U.S. Code §§ 1611, 1621

Personal Rights Protection Act
Tenn. Code Ann., 47-25-1101 et seq.

Personal Service Contracts Act
Ky. Rev. Stat. 1971, 45.700 et seq.

Personal Service Wage Refund Act
Ill. Rev. Stat. 1991, Ch. 48, § 216a et seq.

Personal Sports Mobile Business Practices Act
Me. Rev. Stat. Ann. 1964, Title 10, § 1241 et seq.

Personal Watercraft Safety Act
La. Rev. Stat. Ann., 34:855.1 et seq.
Okla. Stat. Ann., Title 63, § 4220 et seq.

Personalized License Plates Act
Utah Code Ann. 1953, 41-1-49.11 et seq.

Personnel Act
Conn. Gen. Stat. 1983, § 5-193 et seq.
Ill. Rev. Stat. 1991, Ch. 127, § 63b101 et seq.
Me. Rev. Stat. Ann. 1964, Title 5, § 7039 et seq.
N.M. Stat. Ann., 10-9-1 et seq.
Okla. Stat. Ann., Title 74, § 840.1 et seq.
Va. Code 1950, § 2.1-110 et seq.

Personnel Act (State)
Alaska Stat. 1962, § 39.25.010 et seq.
Conn. Gen. Stat. Ann., § 15-193 et seq.
Ind. Code Ann., 4-15-2-1 et seq.
Iowa Code Ann., 19A.1 et seq.
Ky. Rev. Stat. 1971, 18A.005 et seq.
Mo. Rev. Stat., 36.010 et seq.
N.C. Gen. Stat. 1943, § 126-1 et seq.
Nev. Rev. Stat. 1979 Reprint, 284.010 et seq.
N.H. Rev. Stat. 1955, 98:1 et seq.
P.R. Laws Ann. 1954, Title 3, § 1301 et seq.

Personnel Administration Act
Ariz. Rev. Stat. Ann., § 41-761 et seq.
Mont. Rev. Code 1947, 59-1201 et seq.
Wyo. Stat. Ann., § 9-2-1001 et seq.

Personnel and Compensation Act (District Attorney)
N.M. Stat. Ann., 36-1A-1 et seq.

Personnel Commission Act
Ida. Code 1947, 67-5301 et seq.

Personnel Files Act (School Employees)
La. Rev. Stat. Ann., 17:1331 et seq.

Personnel Interchange Program
Okla. Stat. Ann., Title 74, § 840.26 et seq.

Personnel Management Act (State)
Utah Code Ann. 1953, 67-19-1 et seq.

Personnel Office Act
Neb. Rev. Stat. 1943, 81-1301 et seq.

Personnel Placement Services Act (Private)
S.C. Code Ann. 1976, § 41-25-10 et seq.

Personnel Practices Act
La. Rev. Stat. Ann., 39:85 et seq.

Personnel Program Assistance Act (Local)
Ill. Rev. Stat. 1991, Ch. 127, §§ 63b119, 63b119.1

Personnel Radiation Monitoring Act
Ill. Rev. Stat. 1991, Ch. 111 1/2, § 230.10 et seq.

Personnel Record Review Act
Ill. Rev. Stat. 1991, Ch. 48, § 2000 et seq.

Personnel Recruiting Services Act
Tenn. Code Ann., 62-31-101 et seq.

Personnel Relations Law
Ore. Rev. Stat., 240.005 et seq.

Personnel System Act
N.H. Rev. Stat. 1955, 21-I:48 et seq.

Personnel System Act (State)
Colo. Rev. Stat., 24-50-101 et seq.

Personnel System Act (Statewide)
Miss. Code Ann. 1972, § 25-9-101 et seq.

Personnel Training Act (Emergency Medical Service)
N.Y. Public Health Law 1953 (Consol. Laws Ch. 45) § 3050 et seq.

Persons of Unsound Mind Extradition Act
See Uniform Act for the Extradition of Persons of Unsound Mind

Persons Responding to Oil Spills Act
Ala. Code 1975, § 6-5-332.2

Persons Responding to Oil Spills Act (Regarding Liability for)
Ala. Code 1975, § 6-5-332.2

Persons with a Serious Mental Illness Act (Family Support for)
N.J. Stat. Ann., 30:177-43 et seq.

Persons with Developmental Disabilities and Traumatic Brain Injury (Bill of Rights for)
Ala. Code 1975, § 38-9C-1 et seq.

Persons with Developmental Disabilities Home and Community-based Services Act
Colo. Rev. Stat., 26-4.5-201 et seq.

Persons with Disabilities (Parking Law for)
Ga. Code Ann., 40-6-220 to 40-6-228

Persons with Health Complexes Related to Acquired Immune Deficiency Syndrome Home and Community-based Services Act
Colo. Rev. Stat., 26-4-641 et seq.

Persons with Mental Retardation Act
Tex. Health and Safety Code, § 591.001 et seq.

Persons with Severe Chronic Disabilities Act (Community Trust for)
N.J. Stat. Ann., 3B:11-19 et seq.

Pertussis Vaccine Act
Ill. Rev. Stat. 1991, Ch. 111 1/2, § 7501 et seq.

Pervasive and Autism Developmental Disorders Act (Interagency Council on)
Tex. Human Resources Code, § 114.001 et seq.

Pervasive Development Disorders and Autism Act
Tex. Human Resources Code, § 114.001 et seq.

Pest Abatement District Law
Cal. Health and Safety Code, § 2800 et seq.

Pest Act
Va. Code 1950, § 3.1-188.20 et seq.

Pest Act (Plant)
Pa. Purdon's Stat., Title 3, § 258.1 et seq.

Pest and Disease Control District Law (Wine Grape)
Cal. Food and Agricultural Code 1967, § 6200 et seq.

Pest and Predatory Animal Control Act
Ill. Rev. Stat. 1991, Ch. 8, § 230 et seq.

Pest and Weed Control Act
Wyo. Stat. Ann., § 11-5-101 et seq.

Pest and Wild Animal Control in Counties Act
Ida. Code 1947, 25-2601 et seq.

Pest Control Act
Ark. Code Ann. 1987, 17-30-101 et seq.
Cal. Business and Professions Code, § 8500 et seq.
Colo. Rev. Stat., 35-4-101 et seq.
Fla. Stat. Ann., 482.011 et seq.
Kan. Laws 1973, Ch. 371
La. Rev. Stat. Ann., 40:1261 et seq.
Mich. Comp. Laws Ann., 286.201 et seq.
N.C. Gen. Stat. 1943, § 106-65.22 et seq.
N.M. Stat. Ann., 76-6-1 et seq.
Pa. Purdon's Stat., Title 3, § 111.21 et seq.
S.D. Codified Laws 1967, 38-20-1 et seq.
Tenn. Code Ann., 62-21-101 et seq.

Pest Control Act (Forests)
Vt. Stat. Ann., Title 10, § 2661 et seq.

Pest Control Act (Plant)
Mass. Gen. Laws. Ann., 128:16 et seq.

Pest Control Act (Structural)
Ga. Code Ann., 43-45-1 et seq.
La. Rev. Stat. Ann., 3:3301 et seq.
Okla. Stat. Ann., Title 2, § 3-171 et seq.

Pest Control Compact Act
See also Structural Pest Control Act
Del. Code of 1974, Title 3, § 9001 et seq.
Ga. Code Ann., 2-7-130 et seq.
Ill. Rev. Stat. 1991, Ch. 5, § 280 et seq.
Md. Ann. Code 1974, Art. AG, § 5-701 et seq.
Me. Rev. Stat. Ann. 1964, Title 12, § 8501 et seq.
Me. Rev. Stat. Ann. 1964, Title 12, § 8501 et seq.
Minn. Stat. Ann., 18.62 et seq.
N.C. Gen. Stat. 1943, § 106-65.55 et seq.
N.D. Cent. Code, 4-32-01 et seq.
N.H. Rev. Stat. 1955, 430:21 et seq.
N.J. Stat. Ann., 32:30-1 et seq.
N.M. Stat. 1978, 76-6-10 et seq.
Ohio Rev. Code 1953, 921.60 et seq.
Ore. Rev. Stat. 1953, 670.650 et seq.
Pa. Purdon's Stat., Tilte 3, § 214-41 et seq.
S.C. Code Ann. 1976, § 46-11-10 et seq.
Tenn. Code Ann., 43-6-301 et seq.
Va. Code 1950, § 3.1-188.1 et seq.
Vt. Stat. Ann., Title 6, § 981 et seq.
Wash. Rev. Code Ann., 17.34.010 et seq.
Wis. Laws 1965, Ch. 583
W. Va. Code 1966, § 19-12B-1 et seq.

Pest Control Districts Act (Cotton)
Ariz. Rev. Stat. Ann., § 48-1301 et seq.

Pest Control Industry Act
Ky. Rev. Stat. 1971, Superseded Vols., 249.250 et seq.

Pest Eradication Law
Cal. Public Resources Code, § 4712 et seq., § 4451

Pest Inspection Act (Entomology)
Colo. Rev. Stat. 35-4-101 et seq.

Pest Management and Quarantine Act
Mont. Code Ann., 80-7-401 et seq.

Pest Research Act (University of California)
Cal. Food and Agriculture Code, § 576 et seq.

Pesticide Act
Ala. Code 1975, § 2-27-1 et seq.
Ariz. Rev. Stat. Ann., §§ 3-341 et seq., 3-371 et seq.
Ark. Code Ann. 1987, 2-16-401 et seq., 2D-20-201 et seq.
Colo. Rev. Stat., 35-9-101 et seq., 35-10-101 et seq.
Conn. Gen. Stat. Ann., § 22a-46 et seq.
D.C. Laws 1978, No. 2-70
Fla. Stat. Ann., 487.011 et seq., 487.151 et seq.
Ga. Code Ann., 2-7-50 et seq.
Haw. Rev. Stat. Ann., § 149A-1 et seq.
Ida. Code 1947, 22-3401 et seq.
Ill. Rev. Stat. 1991, Ch. 5, § 801 et seq., Ch. 1111/2, § 2201 et seq.
Ind. Code Ann., 15-3-3.5-1 et seq.
Iowa Code Ann., 206.1 et seq.
Kan. Stat. Ann., 2-2438a et seq.
Ky. Rev. Stat. 1971, 217.541 et seq., 217B.010 et seq.
La. Rev. Stat. Ann., 3:3201 et seq.
Mass. Gen. Laws. Ann., 132B:1 et seq.
Md. Ann. Code 1974, Art. AG, §§ 5-101 et seq., 5-201 et seq.
Me. Rev. Stat. Ann. 1964, Title 7, § 601 et seq.
Mich. Comp. Laws Ann., 286.551 et seq.
Mich. Comp. Laws Ann., 324.8301 et seq.
Miss. Code Ann. 1972, § 69-23-101 et seq.
Mo. Rev. Stat., 281.010 et seq.
Mont. Code Ann., 80-8-101 et seq.
N.C. Gen. Stat. 1943, § 143-434 et seq.
N.D. Cent. Code, 4-35-01 et seq.
Neb. Laws 1993, L.B. 588, §§ 1 to 34
Nev. Rev. Stat. 1979 Reprint, 586.010 et seq.
N.J. Stat. Ann., 13:1F-1 et seq.
N.M. Stat. Ann., 76-4-1 et seq.
Ore. Rev. Stat., 452.245 et seq., 634.006 et seq.
Pa. Purdon's Stat., Title 3, § 111.21 et seq.
Continued

711

P.R. Laws Ann. 1954, Title 5, § 1001 et seq.

R.I. Gen. Laws 1956, 23-25-1 et seq.

S.C. Code Ann. 1976, § 46-13-10 et seq.

Tenn. Code Ann., 62-21-101 et seq.

Tex. Agriculture Code, § 76-001 et seq.

Utah Code Ann. 1953, 4-14-1 et seq.

Va. Code 1950, §§ 3.1-189 et seq., 3.1-249.1 et seq.

Wash. Rev. Code Ann., 15.58.010 et seq., 17.21.010 et seq.

Wis. Stat. Ann., 94.67 et seq.

W. Va. Code 1966, §§ 19-16A-1 et seq., 19-16B-1 et seq.

Wyo. Stat. Ann., § 35-7-350 et seq.

Pesticide Applicators' Act
Colo. Rev. Stat., 35-10-101 et seq.

Pesticide Brokers Act
Cal. Food and Agricultural Code § 12400 et seq.

Pesticide Committee Act
W. Va. Code 1966, § 19-12C-1 et seq.

Pesticide Monitoring Improvements Act of 1988
Aug. 23, 1988, P.L. 100-418, 102 Stat. 1411, 21 U.S. Code § 1401 nt.

Pesticide Registration Act
Md. Ann. Code 1974, Art. AG, § 5-101 et seq.
Mo. Rev. Stat., 263.269 et seq.

Pesticide Waste Control Law
La. Rev. Stat. Ann., 3:1821 et seq.

Pesticide Waste Disposal Act
Miss. Code Ann. 1972, § 69-23-301 et seq.

Pesticides Research Act
Aug. 1, 1958, P.L. 85-582, 72 Stat. 479, 16 U.S. Code § 742d-1, 742d- 1 nt.
Sept. 16, 1959, P.L. 86-279, 73 Stat. 563, 16 U.S. Code § 742d-1 nt.
Oct. 1, 1965, P.L. 89-232, 79 Stat. 902, 16 U.S. Code § 742d-1 nt.
July 11, 1968, P.L. 90-394, 82 Stat. 338, 16 U.S. Code § 742d-1 nt.

Pests and Diseases Act (Horticulture)
Wash. Rev. Code Ann., 15.08.010 et seq.

Pet and Companion Animal Welfare Act
Minn. Stat. Ann., 346.35 et seq.

Pet Animal Care and Facilities Act
Colo. Rev. Stat., 35-80-101 to 35-80-117

Pet Breeder Warranty Act (Polanco-Lockyer)
Cal. Health and Safety Code, § 25989.500 et seq.

Pet Food Act
Cal. Food and Agricultural Code 1967, § 19200 et seq.

Pet Inoculation Act
S.C. Code Ann. 1976, § 47-5-60 et seq.

Pet Protection Act
Cal. Health and Safety Code § 25995 et seq.

Pet Sterilization Act
N.M. Stat. Ann., 77-1-18 et seq.

Pet Turtle Certification Act
Ark. Stat. 1947, 82-2801 et seq.

Pete Turnham Excellence in Education Bond Act Issue Act
Ala. Acts 1998, No. 373

Peter C. Harris Act (Veterans' Orphans)
Ga. Code 1933, 78-301 et seq.

Petersburg National Battlefield Act
Aug. 24, 1962, P.L. 87-603, 76 Stat. 403, 16 U.S. Code §§ 423h-1 to 423h-3

Petri Act (Deficiency Judgments)
Ohio Rev. Code 1953, 2329.08

Petrified Forest National Park Act
March 28, 1958, P.L. 85-358, 72 Stat. 69, 16 U.S. Code §§ 119, 119a

Petrillo Bill
See Communications Acts

Petris-Gonsalves-Deukmejiam Senior Citizens Property Tax Assistance Law

Cal. Revenue and Taxation Code, § 20501 et seq.

Petris-McAteer Act (San Francisco Bay)

Cal. Government Code, § 66600 et seq.

Petris-Short-Lanterman Act (Community Mental Health)

Cal. Welfare and Institutions Code, § 5000 et seq.

Petroglyph National Monument Boundary Adjustment Act

May 1, 1998, P.L. 105-174, § 3005, 16 U.S. Code § 431 nt.

Petroglyph National Monument Establishment Act of 1990

June 27, 1990, P.L. 101-313, 16 U.S. Code § 431 nt.

May 1, 1998, P.L. 105-174, 16 U.S. Code § 431 nt.

Petroleum Act

See Hot-Oil Act

Petroleum Allocation Act

R.I. Gen. Laws 1956, 42-81-1 et seq.

Petroleum and Coal Mining Act

Pa. Purdon's Stat., Title 58, § 601.101 et seq.

Petroleum and Gas Law (Conservation)

Cal. Public Resources Code, § 3000 et seq.

Petroleum and Liquefied Natural Gas Act

N.Y. Environmental Conservation Law 1972 (Consol. Laws Ch. 43B) § 23-1701 et seq.

Petroleum and Motor Fuel Standards Act

Ill. Rev. Stat. 1991, Ch. 5, § 1701 et seq.

Petroleum Carriers Act

Minn. Stat. Ann., 221.011 et seq.

Petroleum Clean Water Trust Fund Act

Ida. Code 1947, 41-4901 et seq.

Petroleum Conservation Act

Ohio Rev. Code 1953, 1509.01 et seq.

Petroleum Education and Marketing Act

Ill. Comp. Stat. 1992, Ch. 225, § 728/1 et seq.

Petroleum Environmental Response Bank Act

S.C. Code Ann. 1976, § 44-2-10 et seq.

Petroleum Excise Tax Law

Okla. Stat. Ann., Title 68, § 11101 et seq.

Petroleum Fuel Reporting Act

Mass. Gen. Laws Ann., 94:295C et seq.

Petroleum Gas Research, Marketing and Safety Act (Liquefied)

Okla. Stat. 1981, Title 52, § 420.20 et seq.

Petroleum Industry Information Reporting Act

Cal. Public Resources Code, § 25350 et seq.

Haw. Rev. Stat. Ann., § 486J-1 et seq.

Petroleum Market Share Act

Me. Rev. Stat. Ann. 1964, Title 10, § 1671

Petroleum Marketing Practices Act

June 19, 1978, P.L. 95-297, 15 U.S. Code §§ 2801, 2801 nt., 2802 et seq.

Oct. 24, 1992, P.L. 102-486, 15 U.S. Code §§ 2821 to 2824

Oct. 19, 1994, P.L. 103-371, 15 U.S. Code §§ 2801, 2802, 2805, 2806

Petroleum Marketing Practices Act Amendments of 1994

Oct. 19, 1994, P.L. 103-371, 15 U.S. Code § 2801 nt.

Petroleum Oil Severance Tax Act

Ind. Code Ann., 6-8-1-1 et seq.

Petroleum Overcharge Distribution and Restitution Act of 1986

Oct. 21, 1986, P.L. 99-509, 15 U.S. Code § 4501 nt.

Oct. 21, 1998, P.L. 105-277, 15 U.S. Code § 4502

Petroleum Overcharge Restitution Act
N.Y. Energy Law (Consol. Laws Ch. 17A)
§ 5-122
N.Y. Environmental Conservation Law 1972
(Consol. Laws Ch. 43B) §§ 27-0403,
27-0405
N.Y. Laws 1991, Ch. 615, 659
N.Y. Laws 1994, Ch. 722
N.Y. Transportation Law (Consol. Laws Ch.
61a) § 440

Petroleum Pipe Line Act
July 30, 1941, Ch. 333, 55 Stat. 610, 15 U.S.
Code prec. § 715 nt.
Mich. Comp. Laws Ann., 483.1 et seq.

Petroleum Products Accounting Act
Haw. Rev. Stat. Ann., § 486D-1 et seq.

Petroleum Products Act
Iowa Code 1975, 208.1 et seq.
Neb. Rev. Stat. 1943 § 66-1215 et seq.
N.M. Stat. Ann., 57-19-1 et seq.
P.R. Laws Ann. 1954, Title 10, § 481 et seq.

**Petroleum Products Fair Trade Practices
Act**
N.M. Stat. Ann., 57-19A-1 et seq.

Petroleum Products Franchise Act
Va. Code 1950, § 59.1-21.8 et seq.
W. Va. Code 1966, § 47-11C-1 et seq.

Petroleum Products Fraud Prevention Law
Cal. Business and Professions Code, § 20780
et seq.

Petroleum Products Gross Receipts Tax Act
N.J. Stat. Ann., 54:15B-1 et seq.

Petroleum Products Inspection Act
Miss. Code Ann. 1972, § 75-55-1 et seq.
Nev. Rev. Stat. 1979 Reprint, 590.010 et seq.

Petroleum Products Inspection Law
Kan. Stat. Ann., 55-422 et seq.

Petroleum Products Loading Fee Act
N.M. Stat. Ann., 7-13A-1 et seq.

Petroleum Products Special Tax Law
Tenn. Code Ann., 67-3-901 et seq.

Petroleum Products Standards Act
N.M. Stat. Ann., 57-19-25 et seq.

**Petroleum Products Supply Act
(Emergency)**
N.M. Stat. Ann., 70-8-1 et seq.

Petroleum Products Tax Act
Tenn. Code Ann., 67-3-101 et seq.

**Petroleum Products Tax Exemption and
Refund Act**
Tenn. Code Ann., 67-3-201 et seq.

Petroleum Release Remedial Action Act
Neb. Rev. Stat. 1943, 66-1501 et seq.

Petroleum Set-Aside Act (Emergency)
Vt. Stat. Ann., Title 9, § 4131 et seq.

Petroleum Storage Act (Above Ground)
Cal. Health and Safety Code § 25270 et seq.

Petroleum Storage Cleanup Act
N.M. Stat. Ann., 74-4D-1 et seq.

**Petroleum Storage Tank Release Indemnity
Program**
Okla. Stat. Ann., Title 17, § 350 et seq.

Petroleum Storage Tank Trust Fund Act
Ark. Code Ann. 1987, 8-7-901 et seq.

Petroleum Tank Release Cleanup Act
Minn. Stat. Ann., 115C.01 et seq.

Petroleum Tank Truck Carriers Act
Va. Code 1950, § 56-338.19 et seq.

Petroleum Trade Practices Act
Tenn. Code Ann., 47-25-601 et seq.

Petroleum Underground Storage Tank Act
Iowa Code Ann., 455G.1 et seq.
Tenn. Code Ann., 68-215-101 et seq.

Petty Loan Act
Ind. Code 1971, 28-7-4-1 et seq.
Ky. Rev. Stat. 1971, 288.410 et seq.

Md. Ann. Code 1974, Art. CL, § 12-201 et seq.

Petty Theft Act
Cal. Penal Code, § 488

Pharmaceutical Assistance Contract for the Elderly Act
Pa. Purdon's Stat., Title 72, § 3762-301 et seq.

Pharmaceutical Assistance to the Elderly
R.I. Gen. Laws 1956, 42-66.2-1 et seq.

Pharmaceutical Continuing Education Act
Nev. Rev. Stat. 1979 Reprint, 639.217 et seq.
N.J. Stat. Ann., 45:14-11.2 et seq.
Okla. Stat. Ann., Title 59, § 361 et seq.

Pharmaceutical Insurance Coverage
N.Y. Executive Law (Consol. Laws Ch. 18) § 547 et seq.

Pharmaceutical Insurance Coverage Act (Elderly)
N.Y. Executive Law 1951 (Consol. Laws, Ch. 18) § 547 et seq.

Pharmaceutical Product Development and Utilization Act
Miss. Code Ann. 1972, § 57-23-1 et seq.

Pharmaceutical Rebate Act
N.J. Stat. Ann., 40:55D-135 et seq.

Pharmaceutical Service Plan Act
Ill. Rev. Stat. 1991, Ch. 32, § 691.1 et seq.

Pharmacies Act (Hospital)
Ark. Code Ann. 1987, 17-91-601 et seq.

Pharmacist Prescriptive Authority Act
N.M. Stat. Ann., 61-11B-1 et seq.

Pharmacists Act
Ga. Code Ann., 26-4-70 et seq.

Pharmacists' Registration Act
Mass. Gen. Laws. Ann., 112:24 et seq.

Pharmacy Access Act
Del. Code of 1974, Title 18, § 7301 et seq.

Pharmacy Act
Alaska Stat. 1962, § 08.80.010 et seq.
Ariz. Rev. Stat. Ann., § 32-1901 et seq.
Ark. Code Ann. 1987, 17-91-101 et seq.
Cal. Business and Professions Code, § 4000 et seq.
Colo. Rev. Stat., 12-22-101 et seq.
Conn. Gen. Stat. Ann., § 20-163 et seq.
D.C. Code Ann., § 2-2001 et seq.
Fla. Stat. Ann., 465.001 et seq.
Ga. Code Ann., 26-4-100 et seq.
Ida. Code 1947, 54-1701 et seq.
Ill. Rev. Stat. 1991, Ch. 111, § 4121 et seq.
Ind. Code Ann., 25-26-13-1 et seq.
Iowa Code Ann., 155A.1 et seq.
Kan. Stat. Ann., 65-1625 et seq.
Ky. Rev. Stat. 1971, 315.010 et seq.
La. Rev. Stat. Ann., 37:1171 et seq.
Md. Ann. Code 1974, Art. HO, § 12-101 et seq.
Me. Rev. Stat. Ann. 1964, Title 32, § 13701 et seq.
Mich. Comp. Laws Ann., 333.17701 et seq.
Minn. Stat. Ann., 151.01 et seq.
Miss. Code Ann. 1972, § 73-21-71 et seq.
Mo. Rev. Stat., 338.010 et seq.
Mont. Code Ann., 37-7-101 et seq.
N.C. Gen. Stat. 1943, § 90-53 et seq.
N.D. Cent. Code, 43-15-01 et seq.
Neb. Rev. Stat. 1943, 71-1,142 et seq.
Nev. Rev. Stat. 1978 Reprint, 639.001 et seq.
N.H. Rev. Stat. 1955, 318:1 et seq.
N.J. Stat. Ann., 45:14-1 et seq.
N.M. Stat. Ann., 61-11-1 et seq.
N.Y. Education Law 1947 (Consol. Laws Ch. 16) § 6800 et seq.
Ohio Rev. Code 1953, 4729.01 et seq.
Okla. Stat. Ann., Title 59, § 353.1 et seq.
Ore. Rev. Stat., 51.040, 167.203, 414.325, 430.405, 435.010, 453.025, 475.005, 475.015, 475.075, 475.085, 475.135, 475.185, 475.992, 475.995, 616.855, 689.010 et seq.
Pa. Purdon's Stat., Title 63, § 390-1 et seq.
P.R. Laws Ann. 1954, Title 20, § 381 et seq.
R.I. Gen. Laws 1956, 5-19-1 et seq.
S.C. Code Ann. 1976, § 40-43-10 et seq.
S.D. Codified Laws 1967, 36-11-1 et seq.
Continued

Tenn. Code Ann., 63-10-101 et seq.
Tex. Rev. Civ. Stat., Art. 4542a-1 et seq.
Tex. Rev. Civ. Stat. 1974, Art. 4542a-1
Utah Code Ann. 1953, 58-17-1 et seq.
Vt. Stat. Ann., Title 26, §§ 1894, 1897, 2021 et seq.
Vt. Stat. Ann., Title 26, § 1891 et seq.
Wash. Rev. Code Ann., 18.64.001 et seq.
Wis. Stat. Ann., 450.01 et seq.
W. Va. Code 1966, § 30-5-1 et seq.
Wyo. Stat. Ann., § 33-24-101 et seq.

Pharmacy and Drugs Act
Ore. Rev. Stat. 1953, 453.001 et seq.

Pharmacy Licensing Act (Out of State Mail Service)
Ida. Code 1947, 54-1740 et seq.

Pharmacy Ownership Act
Mich. Comp. Laws Ann., 338.481, 338.482

Pharmacy Practice Act
Conn. Public Acts 1995, No. 264

Pharmacy Registration Act (Out-of-State)
La. Rev. Stat. Ann., 44:2701 et seq.

Pharmacy Robbery Act
Ala. Code 1975, § 13A-8-50 et seq.

Pharmacy Service Corporation Act (Non Profit)
Kan. Stat. Ann., 40-19d01 et seq.

Pharmacy Service Corporation Act (Non-Profit)
Kan. Stat. Ann., 40-19d01 et seq.

Pharmacy Technician Act
Wyo. Stat. 1977, § 33-24-301 et seq.

Phelps Act (Seeing Eye Dogs)
N.Y. Civil Rights Law (Consol. Laws, Ch. 6) § 47

Phenylketonuria Testing Act
Ill. Rev. Stat. 1991, Ch. 111 1/2, § 4902.9 et seq.

Philadelphia City Charter Act
Pa. Purdon's Stat., Title 53, § 12101 et seq.

Philadelphia Consolidation Act
Pa. Purdon's Stat., Title 53, § 16251 et seq.

Philadelphia County Court Act
Pa. Purdon's Stat., Title 17, § 681 et seq.

Philadelphia Extension Act (Pennsylvania Turnpike)
Pa. Purdon's Stat., Title 36, § 653 et seq.

Philadelphia Incorporation Act
Pa. Purdon's Stat., Title 53, § 16251 et seq.

Philadelphia Loop Act (Pennsylvania Turnpike)
Pa. Purdon's Stat., Title 36, § 652.1 et seq.

Philadelphia Municipal Court Act
Pa. Cons. Stat., Title 17, § 1121 et seq.

Philadelphia Municipal Utility Inventory and Receivables Financing Act
Pa. Purdon's Stat., Title 53, § 16999.1 et seq.

Philadelphia Regional Port Authority Act
Pa. Purdon's Stat., Title 55, § 697.1 et seq.

Philadelphia School District Taxing Act
Cal. Health and Safety Code, § 1597.80 et seq.

Philadelphia Traffic Court Act
Pa. Purdon's Stat., Title 42, § 1110.1 et seq.

Philanthropy Protection Act of 1995
Dec. 8, 1995, P.L. 104-62, 15 U.S. Code § 80a-51 nt.

Philippine Army, Scouts, and Guerilla Veterans of World War II Naturalization Act of 1997
Nov. 26, 1997, P.L. 105-119, § 112, 8 U.S. Code § 1101 nt.

Philippine Currency Reserve Act
June 16, 1934, Ch. 655, 48 Stat. 1115

Philippine Government Acts
March 2, 1901, Ch. 803, 31 Stat. 910
July 1, 1902, Ch. 1369, 32 Stat. 691
Aug. 29, 1916, Ch. 416, 39 Stat. 545

Philippine Independence Act
Jan. 17, 1933, Ch. 11, 47 Stat. 761
March 24, 1934, Ch. 84, 48 Stat. 456
Aug. 7, 1939, Ch. 502, 53 Stat. 1231
June 29, 1944, Ch. 323, 58 Stat. 626
Sept. 22, 1959, P.L. 86-346, 73 Stat. 622, 22
U.S. Code § 1393

Philippine Property Act of 1946
July 3, 1946, Ch. 536, 60 Stat. 418, 22 U.S.
Code §§ 1381, 1382 to 1386
Dec. 21, 1950, Ch. 1144, 64 Stat. 1116, 22
U.S. Code § 1382

Philippine Rehabilitation Act of 1946
April 30, 1946, Ch. 243, 60 Stat. 128
Aug. 2, 1946, Ch. 741, 60 Stat. 805
Jan. 26, 1948, Ch. 16, 62 Stat. 4
July 2, 1948, Ch. 810, 62 Stat. 1224
Sept. 7, 1949, Ch. 545, 63 Stat. 692

Philippine Tariff Acts
March 8, 1902, Ch. 140, 32 Stat. 54
March 3, 1905, Ch. 1408, 33 Stat. 928
Feb. 26, 1906, Ch. 509, 34 Stat. 24
Aug. 5, 1909, Ch. 6, 36 Stat. 84

Philippine Trade Act of 1946
April 30, 1946, Ch. 244, 60 Stat. 141, 22 U.S.
Code §§ 1251 to 1255, 1261 to 1266, 1271
to 1274, 1281, 1291, 1301 to 1305, 1311 to
1313, 1321, 1322, 1331, 1332, 1334, 1341
to 1348, 1351 to 1360; 48 U.S. Code § 734

Philippine Trade Agreement Revision Act of 1955
Aug. 1, 1955, Ch. 438, 69 Stat. 413, 22 U.S.
Code §§ 1371, 1372, 1373, 1374 to 1378;
48 U.S. Code § 734

Philippine Travel Pay Act
May 2, 1940, Ch. 182, 54 Stat. 176

Phillips-Cox Act (Labor Injunctions)
Mass. Gen. Laws. Ann., 214:6

Phipps Law
May 9, 1924, Ch. 150, 43 Stat. 116, 43 U.S.
Code § 384

Phoenix City Civil Service System Act
Ala. Local Acts 1947, p. 14, No. 15

Phosphate Detergent Act
Pa. Purdon's Stat., Title 35, § 722.1 et seq.

Phosphate Land Reclamation Act
Fla. Stat. Ann., 378.201 et seq.

Phosphate Research Competitive Negotiation Act (Institute of)
Fla. Stat. Ann., 378.102

Photographers Fraudulent Practices Act
N.C. Gen. Stat. 1943, § 66-59 et seq

Photographers Licensing Act
See Photography Act

Photographic and Microfilm Records Act
Tex. Rules of Criminal Evidence, Rule 901 et
seq.

Photographic Copies as Evidence Act
See also Uniform Photographic Copies as
Evidence Act
Conn. Gen. Stat. Ann., § 1-7 et seq.
Va. Code 1950, § 8.01-391

Photographic Copies of Business and Public Records as Evidence Act
See also Uniform Photographic Copies of
Business and Public Records as Evidence
Act
See Uniform Photographic Copies of
Business and Public Records as Evidence
Act
Alaska Comp. Laws Ann. 1949, § 58-1-21 et
seq.
Del. Code of 1974, Title 10, § 4309
Fla. Stat. Ann., 92.33
Haw. Rev. Stat. Ann., § 622-4
Mont. Code Ann. 1947, 93-801-5 et seq.
Nev. Rev. Stat. Ann., 52.245 et seq.
N.M. Stat. Ann. 1953, 20-2-20 et seq.
Okla. Stat. Ann., Title 12, § 521 et seq.
Wyo. Session Laws 1977, Ch. 188, § 1,
Subsecs. 1-12-501, 1-12-502
Continued

Photographic Examiners Act
Va. Acts 1938, Ch. 342

Photography Act
Fla. Laws 1939, Ch. 19317
N.C. Public Laws 1935, Ch. 155
N.D. Laws 1939, Ch. 188

Physical and Occupational Therapy Practice Act
Tenn. Code Ann., 63-13-101 et seq.

Physical and Sexual Abuse Victim Protection Act (Child)
Ala. Code 1975, § 15-25-30 et seq.

Physical Education Act
Cal. Education Code 1976, §§ 3350 et seq., 51222, 52518

Physical Examination of Injured Claimant Act
Wash. Rev. Code Ann., Rules of Court, Rule 35

Physical Fitness and Wellness Act
Cal. Government Code § 12040 et seq.

Physical Fitness Services Act
Ill. Rev. Stat. 1991, Ch. 29, § 51 et seq.
La. Rev. Stat. Ann., 51:1575 et seq.
S.C. Code Ann. 1976, § 44-79-10 et seq.

Physical Therapist Good Samaritan Law
N.Y. Education Law 1947 (Consol. Laws Ch. 16) § 6737

Physical Therapist Lien Act
Ill. Rev. Stat. 1991, Ch. 82, § 601 et seq.
Mont. Code Ann. 1987, 71-3-1111 et seq.

Physical Therapist Practice Act
Mo. Rev. Stat., 334.500 to 334.620
Utah Code Ann. 1953, 58-24a-101 et seq.

Physical Therapists Practice Act
Ala. Code 1975, § 34-24-190 et seq.
Alaska Stat. 1962, § 08.84.010 et seq.
Ark. Code Ann. 1987, 17-92-101 et seq.
Ark. Stat. 1947, 72-1301 et seq.
Cal. Business and Professions Code, §§ 2600 et seq., 2650 et seq.

Colo. Rev. Stat. 1973, 12-41-101 et seq.
D.C. Code Ann., § 2-1703.1 et seq.
Fla. Stat. 1983, 486.011 et seq.
Ga. Code Ann., 43-33-1 et seq.
Haw. Stat. § 461J-1 et seq.
Ida. Code 1947, 54-2201 et seq.
Ill. Rev. Stat. 1991, Ch. 111, §§ 4201 et seq., 4220.1 et seq., 4251 et seq.
Ind. Code Ann., 25-27-1-1 et seq.
Iowa Code Ann., 148A.1 et seq.
Ky. Rev. Stat. 1971, 327.010 et seq.
La. Rev. Stat. Ann., 37:2401 et seq.
Mass. Gen. Laws. Ann., 112:23A et seq.
Md. Ann. Code 1974, Art. HO, § 13-101 et seq.
Me. Rev. Stat. Ann. 1964, Title 32, § 3111 et seq.
Miss. Code Ann. 1972, § 73-23-31 et seq.
Mo. Rev. Stat., 334.500 et seq.
Mont. Code Ann., 37-77-101 et seq.
N.C. Gen. Stat. 1943, § 90-270.24 et seq.
N.D. Cent. Code, 43-26-01 et seq.
Nev. Rev. Stat. 1979 Reprint, 640.011 et seq.
N.H. Rev. Stat. 1955, 328-A:1 et seq.
N.J. Stat. Ann., 45:9-37.11 et seq.
N.M. Stat. Ann., 61-12-1 et seq.
Okla. Stat. Ann., Title 59, § 887.1 et seq.
Pa. Purdon's Stat., Title 63, § 1301 et seq.
S.C. Code Ann. 1976, § 40-45-10 et seq.
S.D. Codified Laws 1967, 36-10-18 et seq.
Tenn. Code Ann., 63-13-101 et seq.
Utah Code Ann. 1953, 58-24-1 et seq.
Vt. Stat. Ann., Title 26, § 2071 et seq.
Wash. Rev. Code Ann., 18.74.003 et seq.
Wis. Stat. Ann., 448.03 to 448.05

Physical Therapy Act
N.M. Stat. Ann., 61-12D-1 to 61-12D-19

Physical Therapy Assistant Act
Nev. Rev. Stat. 1979 Reprint, 640.230 et seq.

Physical Therapy Corporations Act
Cal. Business and Professions Code, § 2690 et seq.

Physical Valuation of Property Act
See Valuation Act (Interstate Commerce)

Physically Disabled Persons Special Identification-Registration- Parking Regulations Act
Ark. Stat. 1947, 75-266.19 et seq.

Physically Handicapped Act
N.Y. Education Law 1947 (Consol. Laws Ch. 16) § 1001 et seq.

Physically Handicapped Act (Second Injury)
N.C. Gen. Stat. 1943, § 97-35

Physically Handicapped or Developmentally Disabled Persons Act (Group Homes)
Okla. Stat. Ann., Title 63, § 1-818.1 et seq.

Physically or Developmentally Disabled Persons Community Residential Living Act
Okla. Stat. Ann., Title 60, § 860 et seq.

Physician Assistant Act
Md. Ann. Code 1974, Art. HO, § 15-101 et seq.
N.M. Stat. Ann., 61-6-7 to 61-6-10
Okla. Stat. Ann., Title 39, § 519.1 et seq.

Physician Assistant Good Samaritan Law
N.Y. Education Law 1947 (Consol. Laws Ch. 16) § 6547

Physician Assistant Licensing Act
Tex. Laws 1993, Ch. 214

Physician Assistant Practice Act
Ga. Code Ann., 43-34-100
Ill. Rev. Stat. 1991, Ch. 111, § 4601 et seq.
Iowa Code Ann., 148C.1 et seq.
N.M. Stat. Ann., 61-6-7 et seq.
Tenn. Code Ann., 63-19-101 et seq.
Utah Code Ann. 1953, 58-12-70 et seq.

Physician-Dentist Loan Redemption Program
N.J. Stat. Ann., 18A:72D-1 et seq.

Physician-Dentist Loan Redemption Program Act
N.J. Stat. Ann., 18A:72D-1 et seq.

Physician-Dentist Scholarship Act
N.J. Stat. Ann., 18A:72J-1 et seq.

Physician Education Loan Repayment Act (Rural)
Utah Code Ann. 1953, 26-9a-101 et seq.

Physician Law (Disabled)
Miss. Code Ann. 1972, § 73-25-51

Physician Licensing Act
Conn. Gen. Stat. Ann., § 20-8 et seq.

Physician, Nurse, and Hospital Lien Act
Mont. Code Ann., 71-3-1111 et seq.

Physician, Nurse, Physical Therapist, Occupational Therapist, Chiropractor, Dentist and Hospital Lien Act
Mont. Code Ann., 71-3-1111 et seq.

Physician, Nurse, Physical Therapist, Occupational Therapist, Chiropractor, Dentist, Psychologist, Licensed Social Worker, Licensed Professional Counselor, and Hospital Lien Act
Mont. Code Ann., 71-3-1111 et seq.

Physician-Patient Privileged Communication Act
Cal. Evidence Code, § 990 et seq.
Ill. Rev. Stat. 1991, Ch. 110, § 8-802
Ky. Rev. Stat. 1971, 213.200
La. Rev. Stat. Ann., 15:476
Mich. Comp. Laws Ann., 600.2157
Minn. Stat. Ann., 595.02, Subd. 4
N.C. Gen. Stat. 1943, § 8-53
N.M. Stat. Ann., 38-6-6, Subd. d
N.Y. Civil Practice Law and Rules (Consol. Laws Ch. 8) § 4504
Ohio Rev. Code 1953, 2317.02, Subd. B
Pa. Cons. Stat., Title 42, § 5929
S.D. Codified Laws 1967, 19-2-3
Va. Code 1950, § 8.01-399
W. Va. Code 1931, § 50-6-10, Subd. e
Wyo. Stat. Ann., § 1-12-101

Physician/Medical Practitioner Provider Medicaid Act
W. Va. Code 1966 § 9-4B-1 et seq.

Physicians and Hospital Mutual Insurance Association Act
Neb. Rev. Stat. 1943, 44-2901 et seq.

Physicians and Physicians Assistants Grant and Scholarship Program
Utah Code Ann. 1953, 26-9-201 et seq.

Physicians and Surgeons Medical Practice Act
Cal. Business and Professions Code, § 2000 et seq.

Physicians and Surgeons Practice Act
Mich. Comp. Laws Ann., 333.17001 et seq.
N.H. Rev. Stat. 1955, 329:1 et seq.
P.R. Laws Ann. 1954, Title 20, § 72 et seq.
R.I. Gen. Laws 1956, 5-37-1 et seq.
Tex. Rev. Civ. Stat., Art. 4495b
Vt. Stat. Ann., Title 26, § 1311 et seq.
Wash. Rev. Code Ann., 18.71.010 et seq.
W. Va. Code 1966, § 30-3-1 et seq.

Physicians and Surgeons Practice Act (Podiatric)
Wash. Rev. Code Ann., 18.22.005 et seq.

Physicians' and Surgeons Registration Act
N.M. Stat. Ann., 61,6,22 et seq.

Physician's Assistants Act (Osteopathic)
N.M. Stat. 1978, 61-10A-1 et seq.

Physician's Assistants Practice Act
Cal. Business and Professions Code, § 3500 et seq.
Ill. Rev. Stat. 1991, Ch. 111, § 4601 et seq.
Mich. Comp. Laws Ann., 333.17008 et seq.

Physicians' Conflict of Interest Disclosure Act
Tenn. Code Ann., 63-6-501 et seq.

Physicians for Rural Areas Assistance Act
Ga. Code Ann., 31-34-1 et seq.

Physicians' Lien Act
Ill. Rev. Stat. 1991, Ch. 82, §§ 101.1 et seq., 101.01 et seq.
Mont. Code Ann. 1987, 71-3-1111 et seq.

Physicians Mutual Insurance Association Act
Neb. Rev. Stat. 1943, 44-2901 et seq.

Physicians' Patient Records Act
S.C. Code Ann. 1976, § 44-115-10 et seq.

Physician's Practice Act
Wyo. Stat. Ann., § 33-26-101 et seq.

Physicians' Reciprocity Act
Ohio Rev. Code 1953, 4731.29

Physicians' Registration Act
Mass. Gen. Laws. Ann., 112:2 et seq.

Physicians' Service Act
N.M. Stat. Ann. 1953, 58-16-1 et seq.

Physician's Trained Assistants Act
Tenn. Code Ann., 63-19-101 et seq.

Physics Practice Act (Medical)
Tex. Rev. Civ. Stat., Art. 4512n

Pickens County Water and Sewer Act
Ga. Laws 1969, p. 2764

Picketing Act
Ala. Code 1975, § 13A-11-122 et seq.
Ark. Code Ann. 1987, 11-3-401 et seq.
Ga. Code Ann., 34-6-5
Mich. Comp. Laws Ann., 423.9f
Ore. Laws 1939, Ch. 2
S.D. Codified Laws 1967, 60-10-4 et seq.
Tex. Rev. Civ. Stat., Art. 5154d
Va. Code 1950, § 40.1-53
Wis. Stat. Ann., 103.535

Picketing Act (Public Places)
Miss. Code Ann. 1972, § 97-7-63

Picketing Act (Residential)
Conn. Gen. Stat. Ann., § 31-120
Ill. Rev. Stat. 1991, Ch. 38, § 21.1-1 et seq.

Pickett Act
June 25, 1910, Ch. 421, 36 Stat. 847, 16 U.S. Code § 471; 43 U.S. Code §§ 141 to 143

Pickle Card and Bingo Regulatory Act
Neb. Rev. Stat. 1943, 9-201 et seq.

Pickle Card Lottery Act
Neb. Rev. Stat. 1943, § 9-301 et seq.

Pickup Truck and Automobile Acquisition Act
Ark. Code Ann. 1987, 22-8-201 et seq.

Picture Film Act (Motion Picture Censorship)
Kan. Laws 1917, Ch. 308

Pictured Rocks National Lakeshore Act
Oct. 15, 1966, P.L. 89-668, 80 Stat. 922, 16 U.S. Code §§ 460s to 460s-13

Pier End Statute
N.Y. Laws 1901, Ch. 466, § 879

Pier Guard Act
N.Y. Laws 1942, Ch. 881

Pier Loan Act (Rockport Granite Company)
Mass. Acts 1956, Ch. 604

Pier Protection Act (Bridge)
Ill. Comp. Stat. 1992, Ch. 605, §§ 110/1, 110/1.1
Ill. Rev. Stat. 1991, Ch. 121, §§ 193a, 193a.1

Pierson Act (Municipal Waterworks)
N.J. Laws 1917, C 240

Pierson Bond Act
N.J. Stat. Ann., 40A:2-1 et seq.

Pierson Budget Act
N.J. Stat. Ann., 40A:4-1 et seq.

Pigeon River Country State Forest Hydrocarbon Development Act
Mich. Comp. Laws Ann., 319.121 et seq.

Pike County Water and Sewerage Authority Act
Ga. Laws 1991, p. 4180

Pillow Tax Act
Iowa Code Ann., 422A.1, 422A.2

Pilot Commission Act
Ore. Rev. Stat., 776.010 et seq.

Pilot Family Assessment Intervention and Resource Act
Cal. Welfare and Institutions Code § 1400 et seq.

Pilot Land Development and Disposal Act (Lincoln County)
Nev. Rev. Stat. 1973 Reprint, 321.540 et seq.

Pilot Pension Plan Law (San Francisco)
Cal. Harbors and Navigation Code § 1160 et seq.

Pilot Program Feeder Road Act
Miss. Code Ann. 1972, § 65-10-1 et seq.

Pilot Program for Selected Paroled Juvenile Offenders
Ill. Comp. Stat. 1992, Ch. 730, § 5/3-16-5

Pilot Project Act (Mental Illness Services)
Ill. Rev. Stat. 1991, Ch. 91 1/2, § 1400 et seq.

Pilot Records Improvement Act of 1996
Oct. 9, 1996, P.L. 104-264, Title V, 49 U.S. Code § 40101 nt.

Pilot Schools Act
Colo. Rev. Stat., 22-38-101 et seq.

Pilotage Act
Alaska Stat. 1962, Replaced Titles, § 08.62.010 et seq.
Del. Code of 1974, Title 23, § 100 et seq.
Haw. Rev. Stat. Ann., § 462A-1 et seq.
La. Rev. Stat. Ann., 34:941 et seq.
Md. Ann. Code 1974, Art. BP, § 11-201 et seq., BO, § 11-101 et seq.
N.C. Gen. Stat. 1943, §§ 76-13, 76-33, 76-69
N.H. Rev. Stat. 1955, 271-A:5 et seq.
Ore. Rev. Stat., 776.015 et seq.
Pa. Purdon's Stat., Title 55, § 31 et seq.
R.I. Gen. Laws 1956, 46-9-1 et seq.
Tex. Rev. Civ. Stat., Art. 8278
Tex. Rev. Civ. Stat. 1925, Arts 8248 to 8257, 8264 to 8280
Wash. Rev. Code Ann., 88.16.005 et seq.

Pilotage Act (Marine)
Alaska Stat. 1962, § 08.62.010 et seq.

Pilotage Commission Act
Ala. Code 1975, § 33-4-1 et seq.

Pilotage Fee Commission Act
La. Rev. Stat. Ann., 34:1121 et seq.

Pilots Licensing and Regulatory Act
Tex. Rev. Civ. Stat., Art. 8280c

Pilots Licensing and Regulatory Act (Brazoria County)
Tex. General and Special Laws 1991, p. 1162, Ch. 246
Tex. Transportation Code, § 68.001 et seq.

Pilots Licensing and Regulatory Act (Galveston County)
Tex. Rev. Civ. Stat., Art. 8280b, §§ 1.01 to 6.05
Tex. Transportation Code, § 67.001 et seq.

Pilots Licensing and Regulatory Act (Houston)
Tex. Transportation Code, § 66.001 et seq.

Pimping Act
Cal. Penal Code, § 266i

Pinball Arcade and Pinball Machine Ordinance (Smithfield)
R.I. Public Laws 1982, Ch. 119

Pinball Machine Act
Vt. Stat. Ann., Tile 13, § 2135 et seq.

Pinball Machines Tax Act
Wash. Rev. Code Ann., 82.28.010 et seq.

Pinchot Road Act
Pa. Purdon's Stat., Title 36, § 1738-1 et seq.

Pine Barrens Maritime Reserve Act (Long Island)
N.Y. Environmental Conservation Law (Consol. Laws Ch. 43B) § 57-0101 et seq.

Pine Barrens Protection Act (Long Island)
N.Y. Environmental Conservation Law 1972 (Consol. Laws Ch. 43B) § 57-0103 et seq.
N.Y. Public Officers Law (Consol. Laws Ch. 47) § 17
N.Y. State Finance Law 1940 (Consol. Laws Ch. 56) § 97o

Pine Creek Scenic Rivers Act
Pa. Purdon's Stat., Title 32, § 820.171 et seq.

Pine Hill Water and Sewerage Authority Act
Ga. Laws 1972, p. 2003

Pinelands Development Credit Bank Act
N.J. Stat. Ann., 13:18A-30 et seq.

Pinelands Environmental Council Act
N.J. Laws 1985, Ch. 302

Pinelands Municipal Property Tax Stabilization Act
N.J. Stat. Ann., 54:1-68 et seq.
N.J. 54:1-82, 54:1-83

Pinelands Protection Act
N.J. Stat. Ann., 13:18A-1 et seq.

Pinellas County Air Quality Management Act
Fla. Special Laws 1978, Ch. 78-601

Pinellas County Industry Council Act
Fla. Special Laws 1969, Ch. 69-1490

Pinellas County Municipal Code Enforcement Boards Act
Fla. Special Laws 1980, Ch. 80-588

Pinellas County Salt Water Fishing Law
Fla. Special Laws 1953, Ch. 29432

Pinellas County Solid Waste Disposal and Resource Recovery Act
Fla. Special Laws 1975, Ch. 75-487

Pinellas County Teachers Professional Negotiations Act
Fla. Special Laws 1971, Ch. 71-875

Pinellas County Transportation Authority Law
Fla. Stat. 1975, 348.012 et seq.

Pinellas County Uniform Consumer Protection Act
Fla. Special Laws 1973, Ch. 73-602
Fla. Special Laws 1976, Ch. 76-471

Pinellas Park Water Management District Law
Fla. Special Laws 1975, Ch. 491

Pinellas Suncoast Transit Authority Law
Fla. Special Laws 1970, Ch. 70-907

Pinellas Sundown Act
Fla. Special Laws 1977, Ch. 637

Pinellas Sundown II Act
Fla. Special Laws 1978, Ch. 596

Pink Bollworm Eradication Act
Tex. Agriculture Code, § 74.051 et seq.

Pinon Nut Act
N.M. Stat. Ann., 25-10-1 et seq.

Pioneers' Monument Law
Cal. Public Resources Code, § 5101 et seq.

Pipe Line Carriers Act
Wash. Rev. Code Ann., 81.88.020 et seq.

Pipeline Act
Alaska Stat. 1962, § 42.06.140 et seq.
Ga. Code Ann., 46-4-20 et seq.
Iowa Code Ann., 479.1 et seq.
N.D. Cent. Code, 49-19-01 et seq.
Neb. Rev. Stat. 1943, 75-501 et seq.
Pa. Purdon's Stat., Title 15, § 3351 et seq.

Pipeline Common Carrier Law
Ill. Comp. Stat. 1992, Ch. 220, § 5/15-100 et seq.

Pipeline Intrastate Regulatory Act (Natural Gas Transmission)
Fla. Laws 1992, Ch. 284, § 2 et seq.

Pipeline Law (Hazardous Liquid)
La. Rev. Stat. Ann., 30:751 et seq.

Pipeline Safety Act
Ark. Code Ann. 1987, 23-15-201 et seq.
Cal. Government Code, § 51010 et seq.
Ill. Rev. Stat. 1991, Ch. 111 2/3, § 551 et seq.
Neb. Rev. Stat. 1943, 81-542 et seq.
N.M. Stat. Ann., 70-3-11 et seq.
S.D. Codified Laws 1967, Miscellaneous Superseded Code Provisions, § 34-41-1 et seq.

Pipeline Safety Act of 1979
Nov. 30, 1979, P.L. 96-129, 18 U.S. Code § 831 nt.; 49 U.S. Code §§ 1671 et seq., 2001, 2001 nt., 2002 et seq.

Pipeline Safety Act of 1992
Oct. 24, 1992, P.L. 102-508, 49 U.S. Code Appx. § 1671 nt.

Pipeline Safety Reauthorization Act of 1988
Oct. 31, 1988, P.L. 100-561, 49 U.S. Code Appx. § 1671 nt.
Oct. 31, 1994, P.L. 103-429, 49 U.S. Code Appx. § 1680 nt.

Pipeline Siting Act (Natural Gas Transmission)
Fla. Stat. Ann., 403.9401 et seq.

Pipeline Utilities Law
Cal. Public Utilities Code, § 10201 et seq.

Pipelines Act (Interstate Gas)
Miss. Code Ann. 1972, § 77-11-301 et seq.

Piper Act (Practice of Law)
N.Y. Judiciary Law (Consol. Laws Ch. 90) § 750, Subd. 7

Piper-Livingston Act (Savings Bank Life Insurance)
N.Y. Insurance Law (Consol. Laws Ch. 28) § 2201 et seq.

Piracy Act (Video)
N.M. Stat. Ann., 30-16B-1 et seq.

Piracy and Counterfeiting Amendments Act of 1982
May 24, 1982, P.L. 97-180, 17 U.S. Code § 506(a), 18 U.S. Code §§ 2311, 2318, 2319

Piracy Law (Record)
N.Y. Penal Law 1965 (Consol. Laws Ch. 40) § 275.00 et seq.

Pisani Act (School District Voters;
N.Y. Education Law 1947, (Consol. Laws Ch. 16) § 2012 Subd. 4

Piscataway Park Expansion Act of 1994
Oct. 6, 1994, P.L. 103-350, 108 Stat. 3146

Pistol Act
Md. Ann. Code 1957, Art. 27, § 441 et seq.
Mich. Comp. Laws Ann., 28.421 et seq.
N.H. Rev. Stat. 1955, 159:1 et seq.
N.Y. Penal Law 1965 (Consol. Laws Ch. 40) § 265.01 et seq.
S.D. Codified Laws 1967, 23-7-1 etseq.
Tex. Penal Code, § 46.01 et seq.

Pistol Registration Law
Ark. Acts 1923, p. 379, No. 430

Pistol Sale Registration Law
Cal. Penal Code, §§ 12350, 12351

Pistols Act
S.C. Code Ann. 1976, §§ 16-23-10 et seq., 22-9-180 et seq.

Pistols or Other Firearms Local Tax Law
Mich. Comp. Laws Ann., 123.1101 et seq.

Pitman-Bloom Act
Nov. 4, 1939, Ch. 2, 54 Stat. 4, 22 U.S. Code §§ 441, 444, 445, 447 to 451, 453 to 457

Pitt County Peace Officers' Relief Act
N.C. Laws 1953, Ch. 903

Pittman Act
April 23, 1918, Ch. 63, 40 Stat. 535

Pittman Embassy Picketing Act
Feb. 15, 1938, Ch. 29, 52 Stat. 30

Pittman-Robertson Act
See Wild Life Restoration

Pittman-Robertson Enabling Act (Wildlife Restoration)
Mich. Comp. Laws Ann., 299.201

Pittman Underground Water Act
Oct. 22, 1919, Ch. 77, 41 Stat. 293

Pittsburg School District Taxing Act
Pa. Purdon's Stat., Title 24, §§ 582.1 et seq., 584.1 et seq.

Pittsburgh Commission Act (Port)
Pa. Purdon's Stat., Title 55, § 698.21 et seq.

Pittsburgh Ripper Act (City Government)
Pa. Purdon's Stat., Title 53, § 22181 et seq.

Pittsburgh Tax Act
Pa. 1877 Pamph. Laws 16, No. 14

Pittsfield Off-Street Parking Facilities Loan Act
Mass. Acts 1955, Ch. 694

Pittsfield School Building Loan Act
Mass. Acts 1949, Ch. 535

Placement Act (Homeless Family)
Ill. Comp. Stat. 1992, Ch. 310, § 85/1 et seq.

Placement Act (Pupil)
Ark. Code Ann. 1987, 6-18-301 et seq.

Placement Act (Schools)
Ala. Code 1958, Title 52, 61(1) et seq.

Placement and Unemployment Insurance Law
Neb. Rev. Stat. 1943, 48-601 et seq.

Placement of Children Compact Act
See Interstate Compact on Placement of Children Act

Placement of Pupils Act
See Pupil Placement Act

Placer County Flood Control and Water Conservation District Act
Cal. Water Code, Appendix § 126-1 et seq.

Placer County Water Agency Act
Cal. Water Code, Appendix, § 81-1 et seq.

Placer Law
Colo. Rev. Stat., 34-43-112 et seq.

Placer Mining Act
Alaska Stat. 1962, § 27.10.090 et seq.

Placer Mining District Law
Cal. Public Resources Code, § 2401 et seq.

Placer Mining Protection Act
Ida. Code 1947, 47-1312 et seq.

Placer Mining Water Pollution Act
Cal. Public Resources Code, § 2551 et seq.

Places of Refuge Act
Wash. Rev. Code Ann., 74.32.010 et seq.

Plagiarism Act
Ill. Rev. Stat. 1991, Ch. 144, §§ 218.9, 219

Plagiarism Act (Academic)
Ill. Comp. Stat. 1992, Ch. 110, §§ 5/0.01, 5/1

Plain Act (Initiative Petitions)
N.D. Laws 1911, Ch. 86

Plain Language Act (Insurance)
Conn. Gen. Stat. Ann., § 38-486 et seq.

Plain Language Consumer Contract Act
Pa. Purdon's Stat., Title 73, § 2201 et seq.

Plain Language Contract Act
Minn. Stat. Ann., 325G.29 et seq.
Mont. Laws 1985, Ch. 615
N.J. Stat. Ann., 59:12-1 et seq.
N.Y. General Obligations Law (Consol. Laws Ch. 24A) § 5-702
N.Y. Insurance Law 1984 (Consol. Laws Ch. 28) § 3102

Plainfield Charter
N.J. Laws 1968, Ch. 159

Plan of Exchange Act (Insurance Companies)
Neb. Rev. Stat. 1943, 44-133.01 et seq.

Plank-Fuller Act (Town Highways)
N.Y. Laws 1898, Ch. 351

Planned Community Act
See also Uniform Planned Community Act
Ore. Rev. Stat., 94.550 et seq., 95.550 to 94.783

Planned Community Development Act
Mont. Code Ann., 7-2-4701 et seq.

Planned Growth and Development Act
Ga. Code Ann., 12-5-41, 20-2-553, 32-5-24, 32-10-4, 45-12-190

Planned Industrial Expansion Law
Mo. Rev. Stat., 100.300

Planned Real Estate Development Full Disclosure Act
N.J. Stat. Ann., 45:22A-21 et seq.

Planned Unit Development Act
Colo. Rev. Stat., 24-67-101 et seq.
Nev. Rev. Stat. 1979 Reprint, 278A.010 et seq.
N.J. Rev. Stat. 1937, 40:55-54 et seq.

Planning Act
See Zoning Act, Zoning and Planning Act

Planning Act (Cities)
Mass. Gen. Laws. Ann., 41:70 et seq.
Okla. Stat. Ann., Title 11, § 47-101 et seq.
Ore. Rev. Stat., 227.010 et seq.
S.D. Codified Laws 1967, 11-6-1 et seq.

Planning Act (City-County)
Ind. Code Ann., 36-7-4-201 et seq.
Mont. Rev. Code 1947, 11-3801 et seq.

Planning Act (Comprehensive Family)
Fla. Stat. Ann., 381.0051

Planning Act (Counties)
Colo. Rev. Stat., 30-28-101 et seq.
Mich. Comp. Laws Ann., 125.101 et seq.
N.J. Rev. Stat. 1937, 40:27-1 et seq.
Ore. Rev. Stat., 215.010 et seq.
S.C. Code Ann. 1976, § 4-27-10 et seq.
S.D. Codified Laws 1967, 11-2-1 et seq.

Planning Act (Energy and Transportation)
Miss. Code Ann. 1972, § 57-39-1 et seq.

Planning Act (Local)
See Local Planning Act

Planning Act (Municipal)
Ga. Code 1933, 69-801 et seq.
Mich. Comp. Laws Ann., 125.31 et seq.
N.J. Stat. Ann., 40:55-1 et seq.
S.D. Codified Laws 1967, 11-4-1 et seq.
Wyo. Stat. Ann., § 15-1-601 et seq.

Planning Act (Municipalities)
La. Rev. Stat. Ann., 33:101 et seq.

Planning Act (Nuclear Emergency)
Me. Rev. Stat. Ann. 1964, Title 37-B, § 951
et seq.

Planning Act (Post-War)
Pa. 1943 Pamph. Laws 90, No. 51

Planning Act (Regional)
See Regional Planning Act

Planning Act (State)
See State Planning Act
N.J. Stat. Ann., 52:18A-197 et seq.

Planning Act (Townships)
Ind. Code Ann., 18-7-6-1 et seq.

Planning Act (Water Resource)
Kan. Stat. Ann., 82a-901 et seq.

Planning Act for Educational Excellence (Strategic)
Utah Code Ann. 1953, 53A-1a-101 et seq.

Planning Aid Fund Act
Colo. Rev. Stat., 24-66-101 et seq.

Planning and Analysis Act (Manpower)
Ill. Rev. Stat. 1991, Ch. 144, § 178 et seq.

Planning and Budget Act
P.R. Laws Ann. 1954, Title 23, § 62 et seq.

Planning and Budgeting Act (Capital Facilities)
Fla. Stat. Ann., 216.015 et seq.

Planning and Community Right to Know Act (Emergency)
Kan. Stat. Ann., 65-5701 et seq.

Planning and Development Act
Mo. Rev. Stat., 251.150 et seq.
Vt. Stat. Ann., Title 24, § 4301 et seq.
W. Va. Code 1966, § 8-25-1 et seq.

Planning and Economic Development Act
Miss. Code Ann. 1972, § 57-63-1 et seq.
Mont. Code Ann., 90-1-101 et seq.

Planning and Economic Development Policy Act
Mo. Rev. Stat. 1978, 620.600

Planning and Land Use Regulation Act (Comprehensive)
Me. Rev. Stat. Ann. 1964, Title 30-A, § 4311
et seq.
R.I. Gen. Laws 1956, 45-22.2-1 et seq.

Planning and Management Act (Data Processing)
Okla. Stat. Ann., Title 74, § 118.1 et seq.

Planning and Notification Act (Hazardous Materials)
Okla. Stat. Ann., Title 27A, § 4-2-101 et seq.

Planning and Programming Act
Neb. Rev. Stat. 1943, 84-131 et seq.

Planning and Programming Bureau Act
Ga. Code Ann., 45-12-173 et seq.

Planning and Zoning Act
See Zoning Act, Zoning and Planning Act

Planning and Zoning Act (Cobb County)
Ga. Laws 1956, p. 2006

Planning and Zoning Act (Counties)
See County Planning and Zoning Act

Planning and Zoning Commission Act
Md. Ann. Code 1957, Art. 66B, §§ 1.00 et seq., 3.01 et seq.

Planning and Zoning District Act (Counties)
Mont. Code Ann., 76-2-101 et seq.

Planning and Zoning Enabling Act
Ga. Code 1933, 69-1201 et seq.
Md. Ann. Code 1957, Art. 66B, § 3.01 et seq.
Mo. Rev. Stat., 89.010 et seq.

Planning Board Act
Ark. Code Ann. 1987, 14-17-203 et seq.
Pa. Purdon's Stat., Title 71, § 1050.9 et seq.
Tex. Rev. Civ. Stat. 1925, Art. 8197e

Planning Board Act (Broward County)
Fla. Special Laws 1959, Ch. 59-1154
Fla. Special Laws 1972, Ch. 72-497

Planning Board Act (Cities)
Mont. Code Ann., 76-1-101 et seq.

Planning Board Organic Act
Md. Ann. Code 1957, Art. 66B, § 3.01 et seq.
P.R. Laws Ann. 1954, Title 23, § 62 et seq.

Planning by Local Governments Act
S.C. Code Ann. 1976, § 6-7-10 et seq.

Planning Code (Municipalities)
Pa. Purdon's Stat., Title 53, § 10101 et seq.

Planning Commission Act
Ark. Code Ann. 1987, 14-56-402 et seq., 14-56-410
Ga. Code 1933, 69-1201 et seq.
Iowa Code Ann., 28I.1 et seq.
Md. Ann. Code 1957, Art. 66B. § 3.01 et seq.
Nev. Rev. Stat. 1979 Reprint, 278.030 et seq.
N.M. Stat. Ann. 1953, 14-18-1 et seq.
Vt. Stat. Ann., Title 24, § 4321 et seq.
Wis. Stat. 1989, 66.945

Planning Commission Act (Capital City)
Ill. Comp. Stat. 1992, Ch. 20, § 3920/0.01 et seq.

Planning Commission Act (Cities and Towns)
Wash. Rev. Code Ann., 35.63.010 et seq.

Planning Commission Act (Cobb County)
Ga. Laws 1943, p. 902

Planning Commission Act (De Kalb County)
Ga. Laws 1956, p. 3332

Planning Commission Act (Metropolitan Area)
Okla. Stat. Ann., Title 19, § 863.1 et seq.

Planning Commission Act (Municipal)
See Municipal Planning Commission Act

Planning Commission Act (Regional)
See Regional Planning Commission Act

Planning Council Act
Conn. Gen. Stat. Ann., § 4-60a et seq.
Vt. Acts 1967, No. 167, §§ 1 to 5

Planning Council on Developmental Disabilities Law
Ill. Rev. Stat. 1991, Ch. 91 1/2, § 1951 et seq.

Planning Council on Mental Health Law
Ill. Rev. Stat. 1991, Ch. 91 1/2, § 1901 et seq.

Planning Development and Research Act
Minn. Stat. 1988, 126.81

Planning District Act
N.M. Stat. Ann., 4-58-1 et seq.

Planning Enabling Act
Ill. Rev. Stat. 1991, Ch. 24, § 11-12-4 et seq.
N.J. Stat. Ann., 40:55-1 et seq.
Utah Code Ann. 1953, 10-9-19 et seq.
Wash. Rev. Code Ann., 36.70.010 et seq.

Planning Enabling Act (Comprehensive)
S.C. Code Ann. 1976, § 6-29-310 et seq.

Planning Enabling Act (Regional)
Ill. Rev. Stat. 1991, Ch. 34, § 5-14001 et seq.

Planning Law (Regional)
Mass. Gen. Laws 1984, 40B:1 et seq.

Planning, Research and Development Act
S.C. Code Ann. 1976, § 13-3-10 et seq.

Plant Act
Ark. Code Ann. 1987, 2-16-201 et seq.
Fla. Stat. Ann., 581.011 et seq.
Mo. Rev. Stat., 263.010 et seq.

Plant Analysis Laboratory Act
Neb. Rev. Stat. 1943, 2-3101 et seq.

Plant and Seed Certification Act
Ida. Code 1947, 22-1101 et seq.
Ida. Code 1947, 22-1511 et seq.
N.H. Rev. Stat. 1955, 433:10 et seq.
Tex. Agriculture Code, § 62.001 et seq.

Plant and Soil Amendment Act
Ida. Code 1947, 22-1101 et seq.
Me. Rev. Stat. Ann. 1964, Title 7, § 775 et seq.
Miss. Code Ann. 1972, § 69-24-1 et seq.

Plant Board Act
Ark. Code Ann. 1987, 2-16-201 et seq.

Plant Board Building Act
Ark. Acts 1969, p. 331, No. 117

Plant Certification Act (Creameries)
Ida. Code 1947, 22-1501 et seq.

Plant City Urban Renewal Act
Fla. Special Laws 1961, Ch. 61-2693

Plant Closing Act
Mass. Gen. Laws 1984, 128:16 et seq.

Plant Disease Act
Ga. Code Ann., 2-12-1 et seq.
Mich. Comp. Laws Ann., 286.201 et seq.
N.M. Stat. Ann., 76-5-11 et seq.
W. Va. Code 1966, § 19-12-1 et seq.

Plant Disease and Insect Pest Act
Mo. Rev. Stat., 263.010 et seq.

Plant Food Act
Ga. Code Ann., 2-12-1 et seq.

Plant Inspection Act
Ill. Laws 1917, p. 37

Plant Patent Amendments Act of 1998
Oct. 27, 1998, P.L. 105-289, 112 Stat. 2780, 35 U.S. Code § 1 nt.

Plant Pest Act
Kan. Stat. Ann., 2-2112 et seq.
Minn. Stat. Ann., 18.44 et seq.
Pa. Purdon's Stat., Title 3, § 258.1 et seq.
R.I. Gen. Laws 1956, 2-16-1 et seq.
Tenn. Code Ann., 43-6-101 et seq.
Va. Code 1950, § 3.1-135 et seq.
W. Va. Code 1966, § 19-12-1 et seq.

Plant Pest Control Act
Mass. Gen. Laws. Ann., 128:16 et seq.
N.D. Cent. Code, 4-33-01 et seq.

Plant Protection Act
N.M. Stat. Ann., 76-5-2 et seq.

Plant Protection Act (Native)
N.H. Rev. Stat. 1955, 217-A:1 et seq.

Plant Protection and Conservation Act
N.C. Gen. Stat. 1943, § 106-202.12 et seq.

Plant Protection and Plant Pest Act
Neb. Rev. Stat. 1943, § 2-1072 et seq.

Plant Quarantine Act
See Nursery Stock Quarantine Act
July 31, 1947, Ch. 405, 61 Stat. 680, 7 U.S. Code § 154
Haw. Rev. Stat. Ann., § 150A-1 et seq.
P.R. Laws Ann. 1954, Title 5, § 613 et seq.
S.D. Codified Laws 1967, 38-24A-1 et seq.

Plant Quarantine Inspection Act
Cal. Food and Agricultural Code 1967, § 5341 et seq.

Plant Quarantine, Inspection and Protection Act (Maritime and Airport)
Cal. Statutes 1990, Ch. 1612

Plant Recognition Act (Rare)
Ky. Acts 1994, Ch. 164, §§ 1 to 4

Plant Species List Act (Endangered)
N.J. Stat. Ann., 13:1B-15.151 et seq.

Plant Variety Protection Act
Dec. 24, 1970, P.L. 91-577, 84 Stat. 1542, 7 U.S. Code §§ 1562, 1611, 2321 to 2331, 2351 to 2357, 2371, 2372, and others; 28 U.S. Code §§ 1338, 1498, 1545, 2343
Dec. 22, 1987, P.L. 100-203, 7 U.S. Code § 2371
Oct. 28, 1992, P.L. 102-560, 7 U.S. Code §§ 2541, 2570
Oct. 6, 1994, P.L. 103-349, 7 U.S. Code §§ 2327, 2330, 2353, 2354, 2357, 2401, 2401 nt., 2402, 2404, 2422 to 2425, 2442, 2461 to 2463, 2482, 2483, 2486, 2501 to 2504, 2532, 2541 to 2543, 2561, 2566, 2568, 2570
April 4, 1996, P.L. 104-127, 7 U.S. Code §§ 2402, 2483

Plant Variety Protection Act Amendments of 1994
Oct. 6, 1994, P.L. 103-349, 7 U.S. Code § 2321 nt.

Plant Worker Safety Act (Refinery and Chemical)
Cal. Labor Code, § 7850 et seq.

Plants Law (Genetically Engineered)
Minn. Stat. Ann., 18F.01 et seq.

Plastic Act (Degradable)
Ill. Rev. Stat. 1991, Ch. 111 1/2, § 7901 et seq.

Plastic Container Coding Act
Neb. Laws 1993, L.B. 63, § 1

Plastic Container Labeling Act
Okla. Stat. Ann., Title 27A, § 2-11-501 et seq.

Plastic Recycling and Litter Act
R.I. Gen. Laws 1956, 21-27.1-1 et seq.

Plastics Development Act (Agricultural Commodity-Based)
Ill. Rev. Stat. 1991, Ch. 5, § 2601 et seq.

Plastics Dies and Molds Ownership Transfer Act
Ill. Rev. Stat. 1981, Ch. 140, § 201 et seq.

Plastics Recycling Development Fund Act
Mich. Comp. Laws Ann., 299.471 et seq.

Plateau Underground Water Conservation and Supply District Act
Tex. General and Special Laws 59 th Leg., 1965, p. 1054, Ch. 517

Platinum Sales Act
Ill. Rev. Stat. 1991, Ch. 121 1/2, § 137.90 et seq.

Plats Act
Alaska Stat. 1962, § 40.15.010 et seq.
Fla. Stat. Ann., 177.011 et seq.
Ill. Rev. Stat. 1991, Ch. 109
Mich. Comp. Laws Ann., 560.101 et seq.
Mont. Code Ann., 76-3-101 et seq.
Ohio Rev. Code 1953, 711.001 et seq.
Va. Code 1950, § 15.1-475 et seq.
Wash. Rev. Code Ann., 58.08.010 et seq.
Wis. Stat. Ann., 236.01 et seq.

Platt Amendment (Cuba)
March 2, 1901, Ch. 803, 31 Stat. 897

Plawecki-Bullard Employee Right to Know Act
Mich. Comp. Laws Ann., 423.501 et seq.

Playground Act
Mass. Gen. Laws. Ann., 45:14 et seq.
N.M. Stat. Ann., 5-4-1 et seq.

Playground and Park Act
Cal. Government Code, § 38000 et seq.

Playground Equipment Safety Act
Mich. Comp. Laws Ann., 408.681 et seq.

Playground Improvement Loan Act (Westminster)
Mass. Acts 1957, Ch. 208

Playgrounds Loan Act (Gloucester)
Mass. Acts 1956, Ch. 627

Playland Authorities Act (Westchester County)
N.Y. Laws 1940, Ch. 826

Playland Commission Act
N.Y. Laws 1983, Ch. 601

Playland Commission Act (Westchester County)
N.Y. Laws 1941, Ch. 777

Pleading and Practice Act
Ark. Stat. 1947, 16-63-201 et seq.
La. Code Civil Procedure Art. 852 et seq.
Md. Ann. Code 1957, Art. 75, § 1 et seq.
Okla. Stat. 1981, Title 12, § 2001

Pleading and Practice Act (Neel Act)
Ga. Code 1933, 81-103

Pleading Code
Okla. Stat. Ann., Title 12, § 2001

Pleasure Boating Act
Ida. Code 1947, 67-7001 et seq.
La. Rev. Stat. Ann., 34:851.1 et seq.

Pleasure Riding Tax Law
Cal. Government Code, § 53940 et seq.

Plebiscite Act
P.R. Laws Ann. 1954, Title 16, § 844 et seq.

Pledge of Goods or Sale by Minors Act
Ill. Rev. Stat. 1991, Ch. 23, § 2365.9 et seq.

Pledges Act
Mont. Code Ann., 71-2-101 et seq.

PLO Commitments Compliance Act of 1989
Feb. 16, 1990, P.L. 101-246, 104 Stat. 76
April 30, 1994, P.L. 103-236, 108 Stat. 473
Oct. 25, 1994, P.L. 103-415, 108 Stat. 4303

Ployhar-Doyle Act (Constitutional Amendments)
N.D. Laws 1911, Ch. 94

Plumage Act (Fishing Lures)
N.Y. Environmental Conservation Law 1972 (Consol. Laws Ch. 43B) § 11-1729 et seq.

Plumas County Flood Control and Water Conservation District Act
Cal. Statutes 1959, Ch. 2114, p. 4912

Plumbers and Steam Fitters Act
Ga. Code Ann., 43-14-1 et seq.
Ga. Laws 1937, p. 748

Plumbers Licensing Law
Colo. Rev. Stat., 12-58-101 et seq.
Fla. Stat. Ann., 553.01 et seq.
Ill. Rev. Stat. 1991, Ch. 111, § 1101 et seq.
Ky. Rev. Stat. 1971, 318.010 et seq.
La. Rev. Stat. Ann., 37:1361 et seq.
Mass. Gen. Laws. Ann., 142:1 et seq.
Md. Ann. Code 1974, Art. BO, § 12-101 et seq.
Me. Rev. Stat. Ann. 1964, Title 32, § 3301 et seq.
Mich. Comp. Laws Ann., 338.901 et seq.
Mo. Rev. Stat., 341.010 et seq.
Mont. Code Ann., 37-69-101 et seq.
N.D. Cent. Code, 43-18-01 et seq.
N.H. Rev. Stat. 1955, 329-A:1 et seq.
N.J. Stat. Ann., 45:14C-1 et seq.
N.M. Stat. Ann., 60-13-1 et seq.
Ohio Rev. Code 1953, 3703,01 et seq.
Okla. Stat. Ann., Title 59, § 1001 et seq.
Ore. Rev. Stat., 693.010 et seq.
Pa. Purdon's Stat., Title 53, § 4591 et seq.
R.I. Gen. Laws 1956, 5-20-1 et seq.
S.C. Code Ann. 1976, § 40-49-10 et seq.
S.D. Codified Laws 1967, 36-25-1 et seq.
Tex. Rev. Civ. Stat., Art. 6243-101
Utah Code Ann. 1953, 58-55-1 et seq.
Vt. Stat. Ann., Title 26, § 2171 et seq.
Wash. Laws 1905, Ch. 66
Wis. Stat. Ann., 145.01 et seq.

Plumbing and Drainage Law
Cal. Health and Safety Code, § 800 et seq.

Plumbing and Heating Contractors' License Act
N.C. Gen. Stat. 1943, § 87-16 et seq.

Plumbing Code
Mo. Rev. Stat., 341.090 et seq.

Plumbing Code Act (New Castle County)
Del. Code of 1974, Title 16, § 8101 et seq.

Plumbing Code For Cities of The First Class
Pa. Purdon's Stat., Title 53, § 14791 et seq.

Plumbing Control Act
Fla. Stat. Ann., 553.01 et seq.

Plumbing Control Act (Sarasota County)
Pa. Purdon's Stat., Title 35, § 723.1

Plumbing Inspection Act
D.C. Code Ann., § 1-1023 et seq.
Pa. Purdon's Stat., Title 53, § 4599

Plumbing License Law
Tex. Rev. Civ. Stat., Art. 6243-101

Plumbing System Lead Ban and Notification Act
Pa. Purdon's Stat., Title 35, § 723.1 et seq.

Plymouth County Court House Loan Act
Mass. Acts 1961, Ch. 336

Plymouth County Hospital Loan Act
Mass. Acts 1939, Ch. 262

Plymouth County-Marshfield Riprap Loan Act
Mass. Acts 1957, Ch. 341

Plymouth County Registry of Deeds Loan Act
Mass. Acts 1952, Ch. 475

Plymouth County Shore Protection Loan Act
Mass. Acts 1951, Ch. 396
Mass. Acts 1952, Ch. 531
Mass. Acts 1955, Ch. 381

Mass. Acts 1957, Ch. 239
Mass. Acts 1961, Ch. 366
Mass. Acts 1962, Ch. 464

Pocket of Poverty Program
Fla. Stat. Ann., 420.801 et seq.

Podiatric Medical Practice Act
Ill. Rev. Stat. 1991, Ch. 111, § 4801 et seq.

Podiatric Medicine Practice Act
Okla. Stat. Ann., Title 59, § 135.1 et seq.

Podiatric Physicians and Surgeons Practice Act
Wash. Rev. Code Ann., 18.22.005 et seq.

Podiatrist Good Samaritan Law
N.Y. Education Law 1947 (Consol. Laws Ch. 16) § 7006, Subd. 3

Podiatrist Licensing Act
Okla. Stat. Ann., Title 59, § 136 et seq.
Utah Code Ann. 1953, 58-5a-101 et seq.

Podiatry Licensing Act
Ala. Code 1975, 34-24-230
D.C. Code Ann., § 2-2201 et seq.
Ind. Code Ann., 25-29-1-1 et seq.
Iowa Code Ann., 149.1 et seq.
Kan. Stat. Ann., 65-2001 et seq.
Mass. Gen. Laws. Ann., 112:13 et seq.
Md. Ann. Code 1974, Art. HO. § 16-101 et seq.
Nev. Rev. Stat. 1979 Reprint, 635.010 et seq.
N.H. Rev. Stat. 1955, 315:1 et seq.
N.M. Stat. Ann., 61-8-1 et seq.
Okla. Stat. Ann., Title 59, § 136 et seq.
Pa. Purdon's Stat., Title 63, § 42.1 et seq.
S.C. Code Ann. 1976, § 40-43-150 et seq.
S.C. Code Ann. 1976, § 40-51-10 et seq.
S.D. Codified Laws 1967, 36-8-1 et seq.
Vt. Stat. Ann., Title 26, § 321 et seq.

Point Revocation Act (Drivers' License)
Mo. Rev. Stat., 302.302 et seq.

Point Reyes National Seashore Act
Sept. 13, 1962, P.L. 87-657, 76 Stat. 538, 16 U.S. Code §§ 459c to 459c-7
Oct. 15, 1966, P.L. 89-666, 80 Stat. 919, 16 U.S. Code §§ 459c-1, 459c-7
Continued

April 3, 1970, P.L. 91-223, 84 Stat. 90, 16 U.S. Code §§ 459c-2, 459c-7

Point Shaving Act

Miss. Code Ann. 1972, § 97-29-17

Point Shaving Act (Sports Bribery)

N.Y. Penal Law 1965 (Consol. Laws Ch. 40) § 180.35 et seq.

Point System Act (Drivers of Motor Vehicles)

Ohio Rev. Code 1953, 4507.021

S.C. Code Ann. 1976, § 56-1-710 et seq.

Point System Act (Fish and Game)

S.C. Code Ann. 1976, § 50-9-1010 et seq.

Points of Light Foundation Act

Nov. 16, 1990, P.L. 101-610, 42 U.S. Code §§ 12501, 12661 to 12664

Poison Act (Caustic)

Wash. Rev. Code Ann., 69.36.010 et seq.

Poison Act (Economic)

N.M. Stat. Ann., 76-4-1 et seq.

Poison Act (Sale Regulation)

Cal. Business and Professions Code, § 4160 et seq. ibfe Poison Control Network Act

N.Y. Laws 1986, Ch. 70, § 1

N.Y. Public Health Law 1953 (Consol. Laws Ch. 45) § 2500d

Poison Control Act

Okla. Stat. Ann., Title 63, § 2654.1 et seq.

Poison Labeling Act

Pa. 1917 Pamph. Laws 208, No. 119, § 17

Poison Pill Defense Act

N.Y. Business Corporation Law (Consol. Laws Ch. 4) § 505, Subd. a

Poison Prevention Act

Wash. Rev. Code Ann., 70.106.010 et seq.

Poison Prevention Packaging Act

Cal. Health and Safety Code, § 30000 et seq.

Haw. Rev. Stat. Ann., § 330C-1 et seq.

Ill. Rev. Stat. 1991, Ch. 111 1/2, § 291 et seq.

Md. Ann. Code 1974, Art. HG, § 22-301 et seq.

R.I. Gen. Laws 1956, 23-24.1-1 et seq.

Poison Prevention Packaging Act of 1970

Dec. 30, 1970, P.L. 91-601, 84 Stat. 1670, 7 U.S. Code § 135; 15 U.S. Code §§ 1261, 1471 to 1476; 21 U.S. Code §§ 343, 352, 353, 362

Oct. 21, 1972, P.L. 92-516, 86 Stat. 998, 15 U.S. Code § 1471

Jan. 4, 1983, P.L. 97-414, 15 U.S. Code § 1472

Poison Protection Act (Children's)

Cal. Health and Safety Code, § 30050 et seq.

Poisoning Act (Childhood Lead)

Minn. Stat. Ann., 144.9501 et seq.

Poisoning Act (Domestic Animals)

Ohio Rev. Code 1953, 959.03

Poisoning Control Act (Lead)

Me. Rev. Stat. Ann. 1964, Title 22, § 1314 et seq.

Poisoning Prevention Act (Lead)

Ga. Code Ann., 31-40-1 et seq.

Ill. Rev. Stat. 1991, Ch. 111 1/2, § 1301 et seq.

N.Y. Public Health Laws 1953 (Consol. Laws Ch. 45) § 1370a et seq.

R.I. Gen. Laws 1956, 23-24.6-1 et seq.

Poisons Act

Cal. Business and Professions Code, § 4160 et seq.

Iowa Code Ann., 205.1 et seq.

Md. Ann. Code 1974, Art. HG, § 22-201 et seq.

Mich. Comp. Lawa 1979, 286.201 et seq., 750.431 et seq.

Mont. Code Ann., 37-7-401, 37-7-402

N.H. Rev. Stat. 1955, 430:28 et seq.

R.I. Gen. Laws 1956, 21-30-6 et seq.

Poisons Act (Caustic)

See Caustic Poison Act

N.Y. Agriculture and Markets Law (Consol. Laws Ch. 69) § 170 et seq.

Poisons Act (Economic)
See Economic Poisons Act

Poker Act
Cal. Penal Code, § 337s

Poker Devices Control Law (Video Draw)
La. Rev. Stat. Ann., 33:4862.1 et seq.

Polanco-Bates License Plates for the Arts Act
Cal. Vehicle Code 1959, § 5074

Polanco-Deddeh Anti-Obscenity Act
Cal. Penal Code, § 311 et seq.

Polanco-Ferguson Anti-Child Pornography Act
Cal. Penal Code, § 311.11

Polanco-Ferguson Housing Assistance Act
Cal. Health and Safety Code, §§ 33080.7, 33334.10, 33334.12, 34312.5

Polanco-Lempert-Wright Hazardous Waste Treatment Permit Reform Act
Cal. Statutes 1992, Ch. 1345

Polanco-Lockyer Pet Breeder Warranty Act
Cal. Health and Safety Code, § 25989.500 et seq.

Polanco Mentor-Protege Program
Cal. Government Code § 14136

Police Academy Act
Ga. Code Ann., 35-4-1 et seq.

Police Act
D.C. Code 1973, § 4-101 et seq.
Mich. Comp. Laws Ann., 28.1 et seq.
N.H. Rev. Stat. 1955, 106-B:1 et seq.
Ore. Rev. Stat., 181.010 et seq.
P.R. Laws Ann. 1954, Title 25, § 1001 et seq.

Police Act (Kansas City)
Mo. Rev. Stat., 84.350 et seq.

Police Act (Metropolitan)
See Metropolitan Police Act

Police Act (Park District)
Ill. Rev. Stat. 1991, Ch. 105, §§ 330a, 330a.1

Police Act (State Railroad)
Me. Rev. Stat. Ann. 1964, Title 23, § 6071 et seq.

Police and Bystander Protection and Safe Pursuit Act (Royce-Thompson)
Cal. Vehicle Code 1959, § 14602.1

Police and Fire Alarm System Loan Act (Salem)
Mass. Acts 1952, Ch. 75

Police and Fire Commission Act
Wis. Stat. Ann., 62.13

Police and Fire Department Civil Service Act for Cities of the Second Clas
Mo. Rev. Stat. 1969, 85.360 et seq.

Police and Fire Department Organization Act (Dalton)
Ga. Laws 1945, p. 593

Police and Fire Departments Act
Ky. Rev. Stat. 1971, 95.010 et seq.

Police and Fire Employee Relations Act
Tex. Local Government Code, § 174.001 et seq.

Police and Fire Fighters Compulsory Arbitration Act
Mich. Comp. Laws Ann., 423.231 et seq.

Police and Fire Public Interest Arbitration Reform Act
N.J. Stat. Ann., 34:13A-1 et seq.

Police and Fire Retirement System Act (Local)
Ark. Code Ann. 1987, 24-10-101 et seq.

Police and Firefighter Postretirement Adjustment Act (Special Ad Hoc Municipal)
Pa. Purdon's Stat., Title 53, § 896.101 et seq.

**Police and Firefighter's Salary Act
Amendment**
D.C. Code Ann., § 4-406

Police and Firemen's Civil Service Act
Ark. Code Ann. 1987, 14-51-101 et seq.
Mich. Comp. Laws Ann., 38.501 et seq.
N.C. Laws 1947, Ch. 83
Pa. Purdon's Stat., Title 53, § 46171 et seq.
Tex. Local Government Code, § 143.001 et
seq.
Tex. Rev. Civ. Stat., Art. 1269m

Police and Firemen's Pension Act
Mich. Comp. Laws Ann., 38.551 et seq.
Miss. Code Ann. 1972, § 21-29-101 et seq.
Neb. Rev. Stat. 1943, 15-1001 et seq.
Tex. Rev. Civ. Stat.,Art. 6243a et seq.

Police and Firemen's Pension Act (Dalton)
Ga. Laws 1945, p. 593, § 15 et seq.

Police and Firemen's Pension Act (Tampa)
Fla. Special Laws 1941, Ch. 21590

**Police and Firemen's Pension Fund Act
(Macon)**
Ga. Laws 1939, p. 1149

**Police and Firemen's Relief Association
Guidelines Act**
Minn. Stat. Ann., 69.77

**Police and Firemen's Relief Fund Act of
1887**
Ill. Rev. Stat. 1961, Ch. 24, § 870 et seq.

Police and Firemen's Retirement System Act
Mich. Comp. Laws Ann., 38.551 et seq.
N.J. Rev. Stat. 1937, 43:16A-1 et seq.
N.Y. Retirement and Social Security Law
(Consol. Laws Ch. 51A) § 290 et seq.

**Police and Firemen's Salary Act
Amendments of 1970 - 1975**
D.C. Code Ann., § 4-406, 4-411

Police Authorization and Expansion Act
D.C. Code Ann., §§ 33-552, 47-3406

Police Civil Service Act
Minn. Stat. Ann., 419.01 et seq.
Pa. Purdon's Stat., Title 53, § 53251 et seq.
Wash. Rev. Code Ann., 41.12.010 et seq.
W. Va. Code 1966, § 8-14-6 et seq.
Wyo. Stat. Ann., § 15-1-101 et seq.

Police Compact Act
N.H. Rev. Stat. 1955, 106-D:1 et seq.

Police Compact Act (Mid-Atlantic)
N.J. Stat. Ann., 53:6-1 et seq.

Police Compact Act (New England)
See New England State Police Compact Act

Police Compact Act (Southern)
La. Rev. Stat. Ann., 40:1312.1 et seq.

Police Corps Act
Sept. 13, 1994, P.L. 103-322, 42 U.S. Code
§§ 13701 nt., 14091 et seq.
Oct. 7, 1998, P.L. 105-244, 42 U.S. Code
§ 14092
Oct. 21, 1998, P.L. 105-277, 42 U.S. Code
§§ 14097, 14101

Police Court Act
D.C. Code Ann., §§ 22-1101, 22-2722
Ill. Rev. Stat. 1991, Ch. 125, § 51 et seq.
Kan. Stat. Ann., 12-4101 et seq.
Mont. Code Ann., 3-11-101 et seq.

Police Court Act (Grand Rapids)
Mich. Comp. Laws Ann., 729.1 et seq.

**Police Department Reorganization Law
(Jacksonville)**
Fla. Special Laws 1965, Ch. 65-1747

**Police Departments Nomenclature Act
(Municipal and County)**
Ga. Code Ann., 35-10-1 et seq.

**Police, Fire, and Emergency Officers
Educational Assistance Act of 1998**
Nov. 13, 1998, P.L. 105-390, 112 Stat. 3495,
42 U.S. Code § 3711 nt.

Police Forty Hour Week Law (First and Second Class Cities)
N.Y. Laws 1956, Ch. 764

Police Indemnification Act
Mich. Comp. Laws 1948, 124.101

Police Insurance and Annuity Act
S.C. Code Ann. 1962, § 61-301 et seq.

Police Matrons Act
D.C. Code 1973, § 4-116 et seq.
Mich. Comp. Laws Ann., 123.891 et seq.

Police Mutual Aid Act
D.C. Code Ann., § 1-1125 et seq.

Police Mutual Aid Agreement Act
Del. Code of 1974, Title 11, § 1941 et seq.

Police of Puerto Rico Act
P.R. Laws Ann. 1954, Title 25, § 221 et seq.

Police Officer Enforcement Act (Humane Society)
Pa. Purdon's Stat., Title 3, § 456.1 et seq.

Police Officers and Firefighters Employment Relations Act
Del. Code of 1974, Title 19, § 1601 et seq.

Police Officer,s and Firefighter's Survivor's Educational Assistance Act
Ala. Acts 1991, p. 1058

Police Officer's Cancer Protection Act
Cal. Labor Code, § 3212.1

Police Officers Insurance and Annuity Fund
Fla. Laws 1941, Ch. 20916

Police Officers' Relief Act (Pasquotank County)
N.C. Laws 1959, Ch. 263

Police Officers Retirement Trust Fund (Municipal)
Fla. Stat. Ann., 185.01 et seq.

Police Officers' Survivors Supplemental Benefits Act
N.M. Laws 1995, Ch. 59

Police Pension Act
Ariz. Rev. Stat. Ann. § 9-911 et seq.
Ill. Rev. Stat. 1959, Ch. 24, § 880 et seq.
Mass. Gen. Laws. Ann., 32:83 et seq.
Minn. Stat. Ann., 69.011 et seq., 423.075 et seq.
Wyo. Stat. Ann., § 15-5-220 et seq.

Police Pension Act (500,000 and under)
Ill. Rev. Stat. 1991, Ch. 108 1/2, § 3-101 et seq.

Police Pension Act (Over 500,000)
Ill. Rev. Stat. 1991, Ch. 108 1/2, § 5-101 et seq.

Police Pension Act (St. Louis)
Mo. Rev. Stat., 86.010 et seq.

Police Pension Act (West Palm Beach)
Fla. Special Laws 1947, Ch. 24981

Police Pension and Retirement Act
Ariz. Rev. Stat. Ann., § 9-911 et seq.
Del. Code of 1974, Title 11, § 1947 et seq.
Fla. Stat. Ann., 185.01 et seq.
Ga. Laws 1933, p. 213
Ind. Code Ann., 36-8-8-1 et seq.
Iowa Code Ann., 410.1 et seq.
La. Rev. Stat. Ann., 11:1312 et seq.
Mass. Gen. Laws. Ann., 32:83 et seq.
Minn. Stat. Ann., 69.011 et seq., 423.075 et seq.
Mo. Rev. Stat., 86.010 et seq.
Mont. Code Ann., 19-9-101 et seq.
N.D. Cent. Code, 40-45-01 et seq.
N.H. Rev. Stat. 1955, 103:1 et seq.
N.J. Stat. Ann., 43:16-1 et seq.
Ohio Rev. Code 1953, 741.01 et seq.
Okla. Stat. Ann., Title 11, § 50-101 et seq.
Pa. Purdon's Stat., Title 53, §§ 790.1, 39301 et seq.
P.R. Laws Ann. 1954, Title 25, § 376 et seq.
Tex. Rev. Civ. Stat., Art. 6243j
Wyo. Stat. Ann., § 15-5-301 et seq.

Continued

Police Pension Fund Act (New Rochelle)
N.Y. Laws 1904, Ch. 268

Police Pension Fund Act (Newburgh)
N.Y. Laws 1907, Ch. 205

Police Power Act (Second Class Townships)
Pa. Purdon's Stat., Title 53, § 67001 et seq.

Police Powers Act (Chicago Sanitary District)
Ill. Rev. Stat. 1991, Ch. 42, §§ 359.9, 360

Police Protection Charge Waiver Act (Parade)
Ill. Rev. Stat. 1991, Ch. 85, §§ 6040, 6041

Police Protection District Act
Cal. Health and Safety Code, § 20000 et seq.

Police Radio Dispatcher Training Act
N.M. Stat. Ann., 29-7A-1 et seq.

Police Relief and Pension Act
Ark. Code Ann. 1987, 24-11-403 et seq.
Cal. Government Code, § 50800 et seq.
Ohio Rev. Code 1953, 741.31 et seq.
Pa. Purdon's Stat., Title 53, § 23644 et seq.
Wash. Rev. Code Ann., 41.20.005 et seq.

Police Relief Fund Act 1887
Ill. Rev. Stat. 1961, Ch. 24, § 880 et seq.

Police Retirement Act
S.C. Code Ann. 1976, § 9-11-10 et seq.

Police Retirement Act (Kansas City)
Mo. Rev. Stat., 86.370 et seq.

Police Retirement System Act (State)
Me. Rev. Stat. Ann. 1964, Title 25, § 1592 et seq.

Police Salary Act
D.C. Code Ann., § 4-406 et seq.

Police Search Cost Recovery Act
Ill. Rev. Stat. 1991, Ch. 70, §§ 850, 851

Police Services to Elderly Persons Law (Committee for the Coordination of)
La. Rev. Stat. Ann., 15:1231 to 15:1236

Police Station Loan Act (North Adams)
Mass. Acts 1954, Ch. 571

Police Tenure Act
Ky. Rev. Stat. 1971, 95.440
N.J. Stat. Ann., 40A:14-147
Pa. Purdon's Stat., Title 53, § 811 et seq.

Police Training Act
Del. Code of 1974, Title 11, § 8401 et seq.
Ill. Rev. Stat. 1991, Ch. 85, § 501 et seq.

Police Training Institute Act
Ill. Rev. Stat. 1991, Ch. 144, § 63.9 et seq.

Policeman's Bill of Rights
Fla. Stat. Ann., 112.532 et seq.

Policeman's Survivor Tuition Act
Ala. Code 1975, § 36-21-95 et seq.

Policemen and Firemen Arbitration Act (Labor Disputes)
Okla. Stat. Ann., Title 11, § 151-101 et seq.
Pa. Purdon's Stat., Title 43, § 217.1 et seq.
R.I. Gen. Laws 1956, 28-9.2-1 et seq.

Policemen and Firemen Pension Act
Miss. Code Ann. 1972, § 21-29-101 et seq.

Policemen and Firemen Tenure Act
Ind. Code Ann., 36-8-3.5-1 et seq.

Policemen and Firemens Heart and Lung Act
Pa. Purdon's Stat., Title 53, § 637

Policemen and Firemens Relief Fund Act
D.C. Code Ann., §§ 4-125, 4-160, 4-161

Policemen and Firemens Retirement and Disability Act
D.C. Code Ann., § 4-607 et seq.

Policemen and Firemens Retirement and Disability Act Amendments
D.C. Code Ann., § 4-607 et seq.

Policemen and Firemens Salary Act Amendments
D.C. Code Ann., §§ 4-406, 4-412

Policemen and Firemens Special Compensation Act (Disability)
Pa. Purdon's Stat., Title 53, §§ 637, 638

Policemen,s and Firemens Pension Reform Act
Colo. Rev. Stat., 31-30-801 et seq.

Policemen's and Firemens Relief Act
Minn. Stat. Ann., 69.011 et seq.

Policemen's and Firemen's Retirement System Act
N.Y. Retirement and Social Security Law (Consol. Laws Ch. 51A) § 290 et seq.

Policemen's Annuity and Benefit Fund Act (Over 500,000)
Ill. Rev. Stat. 1991, Ch. 108 1/2, § 5-101 et seq.

Policemen's Annuity and Benefit Fund Act of 1921
Ill. Rev. Stat. 1959, Ch. 24, § 945 et seq.

Policemen's Indemnification Act
See Indemnification Act (Policemen)

Policemen's Minimum Wage Act
Ill. Rev. Stat. 1991, Ch. 24, § 10-3-1 et seq.

Policemen's Relief Act (Fourth Class Cities)
Minn. Stat. Ann., 423.41 et seq.

Policemen's Relief and Retirement Fund Act
Tex. Rev. Civ. Stat., Arts. 6243d-1

Policemen's Retirement Act
See Retirement Act (Police)

Policies Act (Family Support Personnel)
Fla. Stat. Ann., 110.1521 et seq.

Policies and Contracts Act (Insurance)
Ohio Rev. Code 1953, 3902.01 et seq.

Policies Misrepresentation Law
Cal. Insurance Code, § 780 et seq.

Policies Misrepresentations Law (Insurance)
Cal. Insurance Code § 780 et seq.

Policy Act
N.Y. Penal Law 1965 (Consol. Laws Ch. 40) §§ 225.00, Subd. 11; 225.10, Subd. 2; 225.15, 225.20

Policy Act (Valued)
Miss. Code Ann. 1972, § 83-13-1 et seq.

Policy Advisory and Sentencing Commission Act
N.C. Laws 1990, Ch. 1076

Policy Council for Children and Families Act
Ga. Code Ann., 49-5-250 to 49-5-264

Policy Game Act
Tex. Penal Code 1925, Art. 642c

Policy Language Simplification Act
Ore. Rev. Stat., 734.750 et seq.

Policy Language Simplification Law (Health Insurance)
N.M. Stat. Ann., 59A-19-1 et seq.
Okla. Stat. Ann., Title 36, § 3641 et seq.

Polio Vaccine Act
Ill. Rev. Stat. 1991, Ch. 111 1/2, § 22.99 et seq.

Poliomyelitis Vaccination Assistance Act of 1955
Aug. 12, 1955, Ch. 863, 69 Stat. 704
Feb. 15, 1956, Ch. 39, 70 Stat. 18

Political Accountability and Disclosure Act
Neb. Rev. Stat. 1943, 49-1401 et seq.

Political Action Disclosure Act
Utah Code Ann. 1953, 20-14a-1 et seq.

Political Activities Act (Relief Administration)
Ill. Rev. Stat. 1991, Ch. 24 1/2, § 38n.9 et seq.

Political Activity Act
N.Y. Election Law 1976 (Consol. Laws Ch. 17) § 11-1729 et seq.

Political Activity Act (State Employees)
Ill. Rev. Stat. 1991, Ch. 24 1/2, § 38r.9 et seq.
N.C. Gen. Stat. 1943, § 126-13 et seq.

Political Advertisement Act
S.D. Codified Laws 1967, 12-25-4.1

Political Contributions and Expenditures Act
Cal. Government Code, § 9900 et seq.
N.H. Rev. Stat. 1955, 664:1 et seq.
Okla. Stat. Ann., Title 26, § 15-101 et seq.
Wis. Stat. Ann., 11.38

Political Disabilities Removal Act
May 22, 1872, Ch. 193, 17 Stat. 142

Political Freedom Act (Public Employee)
Tenn. Code Ann., 8-50-601 et seq.

Political Headquarters Act
Ark. Stat. 1947, 3-1406 et seq.

Political Issues Disclosure Act
Utah Code Ann. 1953, 20-14b-1 et seq.

Political Participation Act
D.C. Laws 1978, No. 2-101

Political Practices Act
Ark. Code Ann. 1987, 7-6-101 et seq.

Political Reform Act
Cal. Government Code, § 81000 et seq.

Political Subdivision Bond Election Law
Wyo. Stat. Ann., § 22-21-101 et seq.

Political Subdivision Budget Limit Act
Neb. Rev. Stat. 1943, 77-3412 et seq.

Political Subdivision Employees Uniform Group Benefits Act
Tex. Local Government Code, § 172.001 et seq.

Political Subdivision Veteran's Preference Enforcement Act
Colo. Rev. Stat., 29-5.5-101 et seq.

Political Subdivisions, Local Option Tax Control Act
Neb. Rev. Stat. 1943, 77-3401 et seq.

Political Subdivisions Procurement Interest Payment Act
Pa. Purdon's Stat., Title 72, § 1601-C et seq.

Political Subdivisions Self-Funding Benefits Act
Neb. Rev. Stat. 1943, § 13-1601 et seq.

Political Subdivisions Telecommunications and Data Processing Procurement Law
La. Rev. Stat. Ann., 38:2234 et seq.

Political Subdivisions Telecommunications Procurement Law
La. Rev. Stat. Ann., 38:2234 et seq.

Political Subdivisions Tort Claims Act
Neb. Rev. Stat. 1943, 23-2401 et seq.
Okla. Stat. Ann., Title 51, § 151 et seq.
Pa. Purdon's Stat., Title 53, § 5311.101 et seq.

Political Subdivisions Unfunded Mandates Act
Tex. Government Code, § 320.001 et seq.

Polk County City Court Juvenile Act
Ga. Laws 1947, p. 1245

Polk County Municipal Utility District Act
Tex. General and Special Laws 1997, Ch. 814

Polk County Water, Sewerage, and Solid Waste Authority Act
Ga. Laws 1967, p. 3108
Ga. Laws 1994, p. 3876
Ga. Laws 1996, p. 4052

Polk County Watershed Improvement Act
Fla. Special Laws 1969, Ch. 69-1509

Poll Tax Act
Ala. Code 1958, Title 51, § 237 et seq.
Alaska Laws 1913, Ch. 54
Miss. Code 1942, § 3160 et seq.
Mont. Laws 1891, p. 73
Nev. Rev. Stat. 1957, 363.010 et seq.
N.H. Rev. Stat. 1955, 72:1
Tenn. Code Ann. 1955, Superseded Vol.,
   67-401 et seq.
Tex. Election Code, Art. 5.09
Tex. Tax Code, § 251.001 et seq.
Wash. Laws 1893, Ch. 69, § 6 et seq.
Wash. Laws 1903, Ch. 119
Wash. Laws 1905, Ch. 156
Wash. Laws 1921, Ch. 174

Poll Tax Act (Roads)
Iowa Laws 1872 (14th G. A.), Ch. 31

Poll Tax Amendment
Tex. Const. 1876, Art. 6, § 2

Polling Place Act (Police Officers)
La. Rev. Stat. Ann., 18:428

Pollock-Lewis Act (Mining)
Ohio Laws Vol. 114, p. 603

Pollock-Yoder Act (Elections)
Ohio Laws Vol. 114, p. 679

Pollutant Discharge Act (Water)
Ill. Rev. Stat. 1991, Ch. 85, § 1700 et seq.

Pollutant Discharge Elimination System Act
Okla. Stat. Ann., Title 27A, § 2-6-201 et seq.

Pollutant Discharge Prevention and Control Act
Fla. Stat. Ann., 376.011 et seq.

Pollutant Spill Prevention and Control Act
Fla. Stat. Ann., 376.011 et seq.

Polluters Pay Act (Hazardous Materials)
Mich. Comp. Laws Ann., 299.601 et seq.

Polluters Pay Law
Mich. Comp. Laws Ann., 324.20101 et seq.

Pollution Abatement Act (Drainage District)
Ill. Rev. Stat. 1991, Ch. 42, §§ 472.9, 473

Pollution Abatement and Industrial Facilities Financing Act
N.C. Gen. Stat. 1943, § 159A-1 et seq.

Pollution Abatement Authority Act (Whey)
Vt. Stat. Ann., Title 10, § 1701 et seq.

Pollution Abatement Enforcement Act
Ill. Rev. Stat. 1991, Ch. 14, § 10 et seq.

Pollution Abatement Facilities and Waste Disposal Financing Act
Ark. Code Ann. 1987, 15-22-701 et seq.

Pollution Act
Pa. Purdon's Stat., Title 35, § 691.1 et seq.

Pollution Act (Schuylkill River)
Pa. Purdon's Stat., Title 32, § 751.1 et seq.

Pollution Act (Water)
See Water Pollution Act

Pollution and Waste Disposal Act
N.H. Rev. Stat. 1955, 485-A:1 et seq.

Pollution and Water Disposal Act
N.H. Rev. Stat. 1955, 485-1:1 et seq.

Pollution Control Act
Ala. Code 1975, 22-28-1 et seq.
Colo. Rev. Stat. 1963, 25-7-101 et seq.
Miss. Code Ann. 1972, § 49-17-1 et seq.
N.Y. Environmental Conservation Law
   (Consol. Laws, Ch. 43B) § 17-0101 et seq.
S.C. Code Ann. 1976, § 48-1-10 et seq.

Pollution Control Act (Air and Water)
See Air and Water Pollution Control Act

Pollution Control Act (Air)
See Air Pollution Control Act

Pollution Control Act (Hardee County)
Fla. Special Laws 1967, Ch. 67-1436

Pollution Control Act (Hillsborough County)
Fla. Special Laws 1967, Ch. 67-1504

Pollution Control Act (Manatee County)
Fla. Special Laws 1967, Ch. 67.1671

Pollution Control Act (Motor Vehicle)
Cal. Health and Safety Code, § 43000 et seq.

Pollution Control Act (Oil and Hazardous Substances)
Fla. Stat. Ann., 376.011 et seq.
N.C. Gen. Stat. 1943, § 143-215.75 et seq.

Pollution Control Act (Sediment)
N.C. Gen. Stat. 1943, § 113A-50 et seq.

Pollution Control Act (Water and Sewage Treatment and Plant Grant)
Fla. Stat. Ann., 403.1821

Pollution Control Act (Water)
See Water Pollution Control Act

Pollution Control Act (Watercraft)
Mich. Comp. Laws Ann., 323.331 et seq.

Pollution Control Agency Law
Minn. Stat. Ann., 116.01 et seq.

Pollution Control and Industrial Facilities Financing Act
N.C. Gen. Stat. 1943, § 159C-1 et seq.

Pollution Control and Industrial Facilities Pool Program Financing Act
N.C. Gen. Stat. 1943, § 159D-1 et seq.

Pollution Control and Sewage Treatment Plant Grant Act (Water)
Fla. Stat. Ann., 403.1821 et seq.

Pollution Control Compact (New England Interstate Water)
Me. Rev. Stat. Ann. 1964, Title 38, § 491 et seq.

Pollution Control Compact (Water)
Tex. Water Code, § 26.043

Pollution Control Compact Act (New England Interstate Water)
Conn. Gen. Stat. Ann., § 22a-308 et seq.
Me. Rev. Stat. Ann. 1964, Title 38, § 491 et seq.

Pollution Control Coordinating Act
Okla. Stat. Ann., Title 82, § 931 et seq.

Pollution Control Facilities Financing Authority Act
P.R. Laws Ann. 1954, Title 12, § 1251 et seq.

Pollution Control Financing Act
Ida. Code 1947, 31-4501 et seq.
N.J. Stat. Ann., 40:37C-1 et seq.

Pollution Control Financing Act (Industrial)
See Industrial Pollution Control Financing Act

Pollution Control Financing Authority Act
Cal. Health and Safety Code, § 44500 et seq.

Pollution Control Revenue Bond Act
N.M. Stat. Ann., 3-59-1 et seq.

Pollution Control Revenue Bond Act (County)
N.M. Stat. 1978, 4-60-1 et seq.

Pollution Disclosure Act
Wash. Rev. Code Ann., 90.52.010 et seq.

Pollution Liability Protection Act (Heating Oil)
Wash. Rev. Code Ann., 70.149.010 et seq.

Pollution Management and Control Act (Nonpoint Source)
Haw. Session Laws 1993, Act 345

Pollution of Waters Act
Fla. Stat. Ann., 387.01 et seq.

Pollution Phase-Out Compact
La. Rev. Stat. Ann., 30:1099.1 et seq.

Pollution Prevention Act
Colo. Rev. Stat., 25-16.5-101 et seq.
Fla. Stat. Ann., 403.072 et seq.
N.J. Stat. Ann., 13:1D-35 et seq.

Pollution Prevention Act (Multimedia)
Miss. Code Ann. 1972, § 49-31-1 et seq.

Pollution Prevention Act (Toxic)
Ill. Rev. Stat. 1991, Ch. 111 1/2, § 7951 et seq.

Pollution Prevention Act of 1990
Nov. 5, 1990, P.L. 101-508, 42 U.S. Code § 13101 nt., 13101 to 13109

Pollution Prevention/Waste Minimization Act
Del. Code of 1974, Title 7, § 7801 et seq.

Pollution Prosecution Act of 1990
Nov. 16, 1990, P.L. 101-593, 42 U.S. Code § 4321 nt.

Pollution Reciprocal Access Act (Transboundary)
Mich. Comp. Laws Ann., 3.871 et seq.

Polygraph Act
S.C. Code Ann. 1976, § 40-53-10 et seq.

Polygraph Act (Sex Offense Victim)
Ill. Rev. Stat. 1991, Ch. 38, §§ 1550, 1551

Polygraph Examiners Act
Ala. Code 1975, § 34-25-1 et seq.
Ark. 1947, 17-32-101 et seq.
Cal. Business and Professions Code, § 9300 et seq.
Ga. Code Ann., 43-36-1 et seq.
La. Rev. Stat. Ann., 37:2831 et seq.
Me. Rev. Stat. Ann. 1964, Title 32, § 7151 et seq.
Mich. Comp. Laws Ann., 338.1701 et seq.
Miss. Code Ann. 1972, § 73-29-1 et seq.
N.D. Cent. Code, 43-31-01 et seq.
N.M. Stat. Ann., 61-26-1 et seq.
Okla. Stat. Ann., Title 59, § 1451 et seq.
Ore. Rev. Stat., 703.010 et seq.
S.C. Code Ann. 1976, § 40-53-10 et seq.
Tenn. Code Ann., 62-27-101 et seq.

Tex. Rev. Civ. Stat., Art. 4413(29cc)

Polygraph Licensing Act
N.D. Cent. Code, 43-31-01 et seq.

Polygraph Protection Act
Mich. Comp. Laws Ann., 37.201 et seq.
Vt. Stat. Ann., Title 21, § 494 et seq.

Polygraph Protection Act of 1988
June 27, 1988, P.L. 100-347, 102 Stat. 656, 29 U.S. Code §§ 2001 nt., 2001 to 2009

Polygraphers and Private Investigators Act
N.M. Stat. Ann., 61-27A-1 et seq.

Polygraphist Act
La. Rev. Stat. Ann., 37:2831 et seq.

Polygraphy Act
N.M. Stat. Ann., 61-26-1 et seq.

Pomerene Bills of Lading Act (Interstate Commerce)
See Bill of Lading Act (Interstate and Foreign Commerce)

Pomeroy-Metcalf Act (Laboratory)
N.Y. Public Health Law 1953 (Consol. Laws Ch. 45) § 570 et seq.

Ponca Creek and Lower Niobrara River Compact Act
S.D. Codified Laws 1967, 46-32-1, 46-32-2

Ponca Restoration Act
Oct. 31, 1990, P.L. 101-484, 25 U.S. Code §§ 983 nt., 983-983h
Oct. 24, 1992, P.L. 102-497, 25 U.S. Code § 983h
Feb. 12, 1996, P.L. 104-109, 25 U.S. Code § 983c

Ponce Port Commission Act
P.R. Laws Ann. 1954, Title 23, § 521 et seq.

Pond Act (Liquor Tax)
Ohio Laws Vol. 79, p. 66

Pontiac Civic Center Law
Ill. Rev. Stat. 1991, Ch. 85, § 7008-1 et seq.

Pontiac, Randolph County, Carbondale, Riverside, Matteson, Ottawa, Illinois Valley, and Waukegan Civic Centers Act
Ill. Rev. Stat. 1991, Ch. 85, § 7000-1 et seq.

Pony Express Act
Mo. Rev. Stat., 390.030

Poochigian and Davis Special Education Reform Act
Cal. Statutes 1997, Ch. 854

Pool Act (Municipal Group-Funded)
Kan. Stat. Ann., 12-2616 et seq.

Pool and Trust Law
Iowa Code Ann., 553.1 et seq.

Pool Hall Act (Local Option)
Tex. General Laws 33rd Leg., 1913, p. 136, Ch. 74

Pool Hall Act (Prohibition)
Tex. Penal Code 1925, Art. 653
Tex. Rev. Civ. Stat., Art. 4668

Pool Room Act
Ky. Rev. Stat. 1962, 528.030, 528.070 et seq.
Wash. Rev. Code Ann., 67.12.021 et seq.

Pool Room License Act
Wash. Rev. Code Ann., 67.12.021 et seq.

Pool Selling Act (Criminal)
Conn. Gen. Stat. Ann., § 53-295
Ill. Rev. Stat. 1991, Ch. 38, § 28-1

Poole Act (Rural Electrification)
Ala. General Acts 1935, p. 110

Poole-Langley Act (Confederate Veterans)
Ala. Code 1975, § 31-8-1 et seq.

Pooling Act (Cooperatives)
Ky. Rev. Stat. 1971, 272.101 et seq.

Pooling Act (Oil and Gas)
Ill. Rev. Stat. 1991, Ch. 96 1/2, § 5436
Okla. Stat. Ann., Title 52, § 87.1
Pa. Purdon's Stat., Title 58, § 401 et seq.

Pooling Act (Restraint of Trade)
Ala. Code 1975, § 8-10-1

Pools, Trusts and Combines Act
Ill. Rev. Stat. 1959, Ch. 121 1/2, § 301 et seq.

Poor Act
Colo. Rev. Stat., 30-17-101 et seq.
Conn. Gen. Stat. 1958, § 17-262 et seq.
Iowa Code Ann., 252.1 et seq.
Mass. Gen. Laws. Ann., 117:1 et seq.
Mich. Comp. Laws Ann., 401.1 et seq.
N.J. Stat. Ann., 44:1-1 et seq.
Ore. Rev. Stat., 411.010 et seq.
Pa. 1835-36 Pamph. Laws 539, No. 168
R.I. Gen. Laws 1956, 40-5-1 et seq.

Poor Debtors Relief Act
Mich. Comp. Laws 1948, 643.1 et seq.
R.I. Gen. Laws 1956, 10-13-1 et seq.
Va. Code 1950, § 34-26 et seq.

Poor Persons Law
N.Y. Civil Practice Law and Rules (Consol. Laws Ch. 8) § 1102

Poor Persons Transportation Act
Conn. Gen. Stat. Ann., § 17-293

Poor Relief Act
Ill. Rev. Stat. 1991, Ch. 23, § 6-1 et seq.
Ind. Code Ann., 12-2-1-1 et seq.
Minn. Stat. Ann., 261.001 et seq.
N.Y. Civil Practice Law and Rules (Consol Laws Ch. 8) § 1102
Ohio Rev. Code 1953, 5113.01 et seq.
Pa. 1925 Pamph. Laws 762, No. 413

Poor Relief Act (Municipal)
Vt. Acts 1957, No. 299

Poor Working Families Assistance Act
N.J. Laws 1971, Ch. 209

Popcorn Promotion, Research, Consumer Information Act
April 4, 1996, P.L. 104-127, Title V, Subtitle E, 7 U.S. Code 7401 nt.

Population Advisory Council Act
Colo. Rev. Stat., 24-40-101 et seq.

Population Management Act (Prison)
Okla. Stat. Ann., Title 57, § 610 et seq.

Population of Waters Control Act(Air and Water)
Fla. Laws 1961, Ch. 61-577

Population Research and Family Planning Services Law
Nev. Rev. Stat. 1967 Reprint, 439.273 et seq.

Pork Producers Act
Okla. Stat. Ann., Title 2, § 1201 et seq.

Pork Promotion Assessment Act
Ida. Code 1947, 25-3401 et seq.
N.C. Gen. Stat. 1943, § 106-790 et seq.

Pork Promotion, Research, and Consumer Information Act of 1985
Dec. 23, 1985, P.L. 99-198, 7 U.S. Code §§ 4801 et seq., 4801 nt.

Pork Research and Marketing Act
Mont. Code Ann., 81-8-601 et seq.

Pornographic Nuisance Act
Ind. Code Ann., 34-1-52.5-1 et seq.

Pornography Act
Ark. Code Ann. 1987, 5-68-501
Colo. Rev. Stat. 1963, 40-27-1 et seq.
Ill. Rev. Stat. 1991, Ch. 38, § 11-20, 11-20.1
N.Y. Penal Law 1965 (Consol. Laws Ch. 40) § 235.00 et seq.

Pornography Act (Child)
S.C. Code Ann. 1976, § 16-3-80 et seq.

Pornography and Child Exploitation Prevention Act (Computer)
Fla. Stat. Ann., 847.0135

Pornography Prevention Act (Child)
Neb. Rev. Stat. 1943, § 28-1463.01 et seq.

Port and River Development Commission Act
Ky. Rev. Stat. 1971, 65.510 et seq., 139.483, 154.310 et seq.

Port and Tanker Safety Act of 1978
Oct. 17, 1978, P.L. 95-474, 33 U.S. Code § 41221, 1221 nt., 1222 et seq.; 46 U.S. Code §§ 214, 391a

Port Authorities Act (Municipal)
N.J. Stat. Ann., 40:68A-29 et seq.

Port Authority Act
Mich. Comp. Laws Ann., 120.101 et seq.
N.J. Stat. Ann., 40:68A-1 et seq.
Ohio Rev. Code 1953, 4582.01 et seq.
Tenn. Code Ann., 7-87-101 et seq.

Port Authority Act (Brunswick)
Ga. Laws 1945, p. 1023

Port Authority Act (Dade County)
Fla. Laws 1945, Ch. 22963

Port Authority Act (Deepwater)
Tex. Water Code, § 19.001 et seq.

Port Authority Act (Fort Pierce)
Fla. Special Laws 1961, Ch. 61-2754

Port Authority Act (Greater Orlando)
Fla. Special Laws 1957, Ch. 57-1658

Port Authority Act (Hillsborough County)
Fla. Special Laws 1945, Ch. 23338

Port Authority Act (Manatee County)
Fla. Special Laws 1967, Ch. 67-1681

Port Authority Act (Metropolitan Government)
Tenn. Code Ann., 7-5-101 et seq.

Port Authority Act (Municipal)
Alaska Stat. 1962, § 29.35.600 et seq.

Port Authority Act (New York and New Jersey)
N.J. Rev. Stat. 1937, 40:68A-1 et seq.
N.Y. Unconsol. Laws § 6401 et seq.

Port Authority Act (Ogdensburg)
N.Y. Public Authorities Law (Consol. Laws Ch. 43A) § 1375 et seq.

Port Authority Act (Philadelphia)
Pa. Purdon's Stat., Title 55, § 697.1

Port Authority Act (Rochester-Monroe County)
N.Y. Public Authorities Law (Consol. Laws Ch. 43A) § 1349a et seq.

Port Authority Act (Savannah)
Ga. Laws 1925, p. 1451

Port Authority Act (Second Class Counties)
Pa. Purdon's Stat., Title 55, § 551 et seq.

Port Authority Act (Third Class Cities)
Pa. Purdon's Stat., Title 55, § 571 et seq.

Port Authority and Economic Development Corporation Act
R.I. Gen. Laws 1956, 42-64-1 et seq.

Port Authority of New York and New Jersey Act
N.Y. Unconsolidated Law, § 6401 et seq.

Port Chester Parking Authority Act
N.Y. Public Authorities Act (Consol. Laws Ch. 43A) § 1620a et seq.

Port Chester Police Justice's Court Act
N.Y. Laws 1949, Ch. 851

Port Chicago National Memorial Act of 1992
Oct. 28, 1992, P.L. 102-562, 16 U.S. Code § 431 nt.

Port Commission Act
Ind. Code Ann., 8-10-1-1 et seq.

Port Commission Act (Alexandria)
Va. Acts 1962, Ch. 392

Port Commission Act (Tar River)
N.C. Laws 1951, Ch. 593

Port Commissioners Act
Wash. Rev. Code Ann., 53.12.010 et seq.

Port Development Act (Baltimore City)
Md. Laws 1951, Ch. 200

Port Development Assistance Law
Minn. Stat. Ann., 457A.01 et seq.

Port Development Project Act
N.Y. Laws 1962, Ch. 209

Port Development Revolving Loan Program
Ill. Comp. Stat. 1992, Ch. 30, § 750/9-11

Port District Act
Ida. Code 1947, 70-1101 et seq.

Port District Act (Albany)
N.Y. Laws 1925, Ch. 192

Port District Act (Chicago)
Ill. Rev. Stat. 1991, Ch. 19, § 152 et seq.

Port District Act (Havana)
Ill. Rev. Stat. 1991, Ch. 19, § 600 et seq.

Port District Act (Illinois Valley)
Ill. Rev. Stat. 1991, Ch. 19, § 801 et seq.

Port District Act (Joliet)
Ill. Rev. Stat. 1991, Ch. 19, § 251 et seq.

Port District Act (Seneca)
Ill. Rev. Stat. 1991, Ch. 19, § 351 et seq.

Port District Act (Shawneetown)
Ill. Rev. Stat. 1991, Ch. 19, § 401 et seq.

Port District Act (Tri-City)
Ill. Rev. Stat. 1991, Ch. 19, § 284 et seq.

Port District Act (Waukegan)
Ill. Rev. Stat. 1991, Ch. 19, § 179 et seq.

Port District Act (White County)
Ill. Rev. Stat. 1991, Ch. 19, § 750 et seq.

Port District Economic Development Financing Act
Ida. Code 1947, 70-2101 et seq.

Port District Marine Construction Act (Hillsborough County)
Fla. Special Laws 1978, Ch. 78-527, 1984, Ch. 84-447

Port District Revenue Bond Act
Ida. Code 1947, 70-1801 et seq.

Port Districts Act
Cal. Harbors and Navigation Code, § 6200 et seq.
Mich. Comp. Laws Ann.,120.51 et seq.
Wash. Rev. Code Ann., 53.04.010 et seq.

Port Districts Report Act
Mich. Comp. Laws 1948, 120.24b

Port Districts Trade Center Act
Wash. Rev. Code Ann., 53.29.900

Port Facilities Bond Act
Va. Acts 1977, Ch. 654

Port Facilities Development Act
Alaska Stat. 1962, § 30.15.010 et seq.

Port Facilities Financing Act
Fla. Stat. Ann., 315.01 et seq.

Port Industrial Development Act
Wash. Rev. Code Ann., 53.25.010 et seq.

Port Jervis City Court Act
N.Y. Laws 1958, Ch. 270

Port Jervis Parking Authority Act
N.Y. Public Authorities Law (Consol. Laws Ch. 43A) § 1585a et seq.

Port of Corpus Christi Pilots Licensing and Regulatory Act
Tex. Transportation Code, § 70.001 et seq.

Port of New Jersey Revitalization, Dredging, Environmental Cleanup, Lake Restoration, and Delaware Bay Area Economic Development Act
N.J. Laws 1996, Ch. 70

Port of New York Authority Act
N.Y. Laws 1921, Ch. 154
N.Y. Laws 1922, Ch. 43

N.Y. Laws 1926, Ch. 279
N.Y. Laws 1927, Ch. 700
N.Y. Laws 1928, Ch. 486
N.Y. Laws 1934, Ch. 251

Port of Oswego Authority Act
N.Y. Public Authorities Law (Consol. Laws Ch. 43A) § 1350 et seq.

Port of Pittsburgh Commission Act
Pa. Purdon's Stat., Title 55, § 698.21 et seq.

Port Orange Water and Sewer Revenue Act
Fla. Special Laws 1951, Ch. 27832

Port Procedures Act (Deepwater)
Tex. Rev. Civ. Stat., Art. 5415i
Tex. Transportation Code, § 52.001 et seq.

Port Revolving Fund Act
Ore. Rev. Stat., 777.850 et seq.

Port Unification and Financing Act
N.J. Stat. Ann., 34:1B-144 et seq.

Portability Act (Interstate Pension)
Fla. Stat. Ann., 121.45 et seq.

Portability and Accountability Act (Health Insurance)
Ill. Comp. Stat. 1992, Ch. 215, § 97/1 et seq.

Portability of Benefits for Nonappropriated Fund Employees Act of 1990
Nov. 5, 1990, P.L. 101-508, 5 U.S. Code §§ 2101 nt., 2105, 2105 nt., 3502, 5334, 5335, 5365, 5551, 6308, 6312, 8331, 8347, 8401, 8461, 8901

Portability, Rating and Renewability Health Insurance Act (Small Employer)
Ill. Comp. Stat. 1992, Ch. 215, § 95/1-1 et seq.

Portable Fire Extinguisher Law
Cal. Health and Safety Code, § 13190.1 et seq.

Portable Retirement Benefit Program
Ill. Comp. Stat. 1992, Ch. 40, § 5/15-136.4 et seq.

Portage County Court Act
Wis. Laws 1891, Ch. 357

Portal-to-Portal Act of 1947
May 14, 1947, Ch. 52, 61 Stat. 84, 29 U.S. Code §§ 216, 251 to 262
Sept. 23, 1966 P.L. 89-601, 80 Stat. 844, 29 U.S. Code § 255
Aug. 20, 1996, P.L. 104-188, 29 U.S. Code § 254

Porter Act
See Foreign Service Buildings Act of 1926

Porter-Burns Act (Water Resources Development Bonds)
Cal. Water Code, § 12930 et seq.

Porter-Byrne Act
Cal. Water Code, § 12930 et seq.

Porter-Cobey Federal Water Project Recreation Act
Cal. Public Resources Code, § 5094 et seq.

Porter-Cobey Saline Water Conversion Act
Cal. Water Code, § 12945 et seq.

Porter-Collier Act (Vehicles)
Cal. Vehicle Code 1959, § 35551

Porter-Cologne Water Quality Control Act
Cal. Water Code, § 13000 et seq.

Porter-Diehl Act (Port Districts Report)
Mich. Comp. Laws 1948, 120.24b

Porter-Dolwig Ground Water Basin Protection Law
Cal. Water Code, § 12920 et seq.

Porter-Post Act (Hunting and Trapping Licenses)
Mich. Comp. Laws Ann., 316.303, 316.305

Porter-Rayburn Act (Teachers' Retirement System)
Ky. Rev. Stat. 1971, 161.220 et seq.

Porter Resolution (Narcotic Drugs)
March 2, 1923, Ch. 190, 42 Stat. 1431

Porter-Taft Act (County Library Districts)
Ohio Rev. Code 1953, 3375.19 et seq.

Portland Reincorporation Act
Ore. Special Laws 1903, p. 3

Ports and Harbors Act
Miss. Code Ann. 1972, § 59-5-1 et seq.

Ports and Waterways Safety Act of 1972
July 10, 1972, P.L. 92-340, 86 Stat. 424, 33 U.S. Code §§ 1221 to 1227; 46 U.S. Code § 391a
Oct. 17, 1978, P.L. 95-474, 33 U.S. Code §§ 1221, 1221 nt., 1222 et seq.
Oct. 15, 1982, P.L. 97-322, 33 U.S. Code § 1231a
Oct. 30, 1984, P.L. 98-557, 33 U.S. Code § 1229
Aug. 27, 1986, P.L. 99-399, 33 U.S. Code § 1226
Aug. 18, 1990, P.L. 101-380, 33 U.S. Code §§ 1223, 1228, 1232
Nov. 16, 1990, P.L. 101-599, 33 U.S. Code § 1232a
Oct. 19, 1996, P.L. 104-324, 33 U.S. Code §§ 1223, 1226, 1232
Nov. 13, 1998, P.L. 105-383, 33 U.S. Code §§ 1222, 1230

Ports Authority Act
Conn. Gen. Stat. Ann., § 7-329a et seq.
Ga. Code Ann., 52-2-1 et seq.
Md. Ann. Code 1974, Art. TR, § 6-101 et seq.
N.H. Rev. Stat. 1955, 271-A:1 et seq.
P.R. Laws Ann. 1954, Title 23, § 331 et seq.
Va. Code 1950, § 62.1-128 et seq.

Ports Bond Act
N.C. Laws 1949, Ch. 820

Ports of Entry Act (Motor Vehicles)
Ida. Code 1947, 67-2926 et seq.
Kan. Stat. Ann., 66-1301 et seq.
N.M. Stat. Ann., 65-5-1 et seq.

Portsmouth-Kittery Bridge Compact
N.H. Rev. Stat. 1955, 234:43 et seq.

Position Classification Act
Tex. Government Code, § 654.001 et seq.

Posse Comitatus Act (Use of Army)
June 18, 1878, Ch. 263, 20 Stat. 152 (See 18
U.S. Code § 1385)

Possession Affidavit Act (Real Estate Claims)
Iowa Code Ann., 614.17

Possession of Stolen Property Act
Ill. Rev. Stat. 1991, Ch. 38, § 16-1

Possessory Act (Title to Public Lands)
Cal. Statutes 1850, Ch. 83, p. 203
Cal. Statutes 1852, Ch. 82, p. 158

Possessory Interest Holder Property Tax Postponement Act (Senior Citizens)
Cal. Revenue and Tax Code, § 206.040 et seq.

Possessory Lien Act
Minn. Stat. Ann., 514.18 et seq.

Post-Attack Resource Management Act
Ida. Code 1947, 67-5501 et seq.
Mont. Rev. Code 1947, 77-1501 et seq.
Mont. Rev. Code 1947, 77-2401 et seq.
Ore. Rev. Stat. 1953, 401.410 et seq.
Va. Code 1950, § 44-146.2 et seq.

Post-Conviction Act
Neb. Rev. Stat. 1943, 29-3001 et seq.

Post-Conviction Defender Commission Act
Tenn. Code Ann., 40-30-301 et seq.

Post-Conviction Determination of Constitutional Rights Act
Ohio Rev. Code 1953, 2953.21 et seq.

Post-Conviction Hearing Act
Ill. Rev. Stat. 1991, Ch. 110A, § 651 et seq.
N.C. Gen. Stat. 1943, § 15A-1411 et seq.
Ohio Rev. Code 1953, 2953.21 et seq.
Ore. Rev. Stat., 138.510 et seq.
Pa. Cons. Stat., Title 42, § 9541 et seq.

Post-Conviction Procedure Act
See also Uniform Post-Conviction Procedure Act
Ark. Act 1957, No. 419
Ida. Code 1947, 19-4901 et seq.
Iowa Code Ann., 663A.1 et seq.
Md. Ann. Code 1957, Art. 27, § 645A et seq.
Me. Rev. Stat. Ann. 1964, Title 14 § 5502 et seq.
Minn. Stat. Ann., 590.01 et seq.
Mont. Code Ann., 46-21-101 et seq.
N.D. Cent. Code 29-32.1-01 et seq.
Nev. Rev. Stat. 1979 Reprint, 177.315 et seq.
Okla. Stat. Ann., Title 22, 1080 et seq.
S.C. Code Ann. 1976, § 17-27-10 et seq.
S.D. Codified Laws 1967, 23A-34-1 et seq.
Tenn. Code Ann., 40-30-101 et seq.

Post-Conviction Relief Act
Kan. Stat. Ann., 60-1507
Ore. Rev. Stat., 138.510 et seq.
Vt. Stat. Ann., Title 13, § 7131 et seq.
Wyo. Stat. Ann., § 7-14-101 et seq.

Post-Enemy Attack Continuity in Government Act
Mont. Code Ann. 1947, 82-3801 et seq.

Post Mortem Examination Act
Ga. Code Ann., 45-16-20 et seq.
Md. Ann. Code 1974, Art. HG, § 5-301 et seq.
N.C. Gen. Stat. 1943, § 130A-377
Okla. Stat. Ann., Title 63, § 931 et seq.
Tenn. Code Ann., 38-7-101 et seq.

Post Office Department Appropriation Acts
March 25, 1940, Ch. 71, 54 Stat. 55
May 31, 1941, Ch. 156, 55 Stat. 227
March 10, 1942, Ch. 178, 56 Stat. 163
June 30, 1943, Ch. 179, 57 Stat. 263
April 22, 1944, Ch. 175, 58 Stat. 195
April 24, 1945, Ch. 92, 59 Stat. 68
July 20, 1946, Ch. 588, 60 Stat. 581
July 1, 1947, Ch. 186, 61 Stat. 228
June 14, 1948, Ch. 466, 62 Stat. 416
June 30, 1949, Ch. 286, 63 Stat. 367
Sept. 6, 1950, Ch. 896, 64 Stat. 640
Aug. 11, 1951, Ch. 301, 65 Stat. 186
Continued

June 30, 1952, Ch. 523, 66 Stat. 292

June 18, 1953, Ch. 132, 67 Stat. 73

May 28, 1954, Ch. 242, 68 Stat. 147

June 11, 1959, P.L. 86-39, 73 Stat. 69, 12 U.S. Code § 364

June 30, 1960, P.L. 86-561, 1960, 74 Stat. 287, 12 U.S. Code § 364

Aug. 21, 1961, P.L. 87-159, 75 Stat. 396, 12 U.S. Code § 364

Aug. 6, 1962, P.L. 87-575, 76 Stat. 313, 12 U.S. Code § 364

June 13, 1963, P.L. 88-39, 77 Stat. 61, 12 U.S. Code § 364

Aug. 1, 1964, P.L. 88-392, 78 Stat. 371, 12 U.S. Code § 364

June 30, 1965, P.L. 89-57, 79 Stat. 199, 12 U.S. Code § 364

June 29, 1966, P.L. 89-474, 80 Stat. 225, 12 U.S. Code § 364

July 7, 1967, P.L. 90-47, 81 Stat. 116, 12 U.S. Code § 364

June 19, 1968, P.L. 90-350, 82 Stat. 192, 12 U.S. Code § 364

Sept. 29, 1969, P.L. 91-74, 83 Stat. 119, 12 U.S. Code § 364

Sept. 26, 1970, P.L. 91-422, 84 Stat. 875, 12 U.S. Code § 364

Post Office Department Financial Control Act of 1950
Aug. 17, 1950, Ch. 735, 64 Stat. 460

Post Office Department Property Act of 1954
July 22, 1954, Ch. 560, 68 Stat. 521
July 9, 1956, Ch. 525, 70 Stat. 510

Post-Porter Act (Hunting and Trapping Licenses)
Mich. Comp. Laws Ann. 316.303, 316.305

Post Roads Act
Ore. Laws 1917, Ch. 175

Post-Roads Act
March 3, 1877, Ch. 103, 19 Stat. 319

Post-Secondary Education Act (Coordinating Commission on)
Neb. Rev. Stat. 1943, 85-1401 et seq.

Post Secondary Education and Security Information Act
Fla. Stat. Ann., 240.2682 et seq.

Post-Secondary Education Articulation Act
N.M. Stat. Ann., 21-1B-1 et seq.

Post-Secondary Education Financial Assistance Law
Miss. Code Ann. 1972, § 37-106-1 et seq.
Miss. Code Ann. 1972, § 37-106-1 et seq.

Post-Secondary Educational Institution Act
N.M. Stat. Ann., 21-23-1 et seq.

Post Secondary Educational Institutions Act
N.M. Stat. Ann., 21-23-1

Post-Secondary Educational Planning Act
N.M. Stat. Ann., 21-2-1 et seq.

Post-Secondary Enrollment Options Act-
Me. Rev. Stat. Ann. 1964, Title 20-A, § 4751 et seq.

Post-Secondary Institution License Act (Nonpublic)
S.C. Code Ann. 1976, § 59-58-10 et seq.

Post-Secondary Review Program Act
Kan. Stat. Ann., 76-3101 et seq.

Post-Separation Family Violence Relief Act-
La. Rev. Stat. Ann., 9:361 et seq.

Post War Aid and Recovery Act (County)
Tenn. Code Ann., 5-11-101 et seq.

Post War Aid and Recovery Act (Municipal)
Tenn. Code Ann., 7-36-101 et seq.

Post War Planning Law
Pa. 1943 Pamph. Laws 90, No. 51

Post War Projects Act
Pa. Purdon's Stat., Title 53, § 1431 et seq.

Post-War Reserve Fund Act
N.C. Gen. Stat. 1943, § 143-191 et seq.

Post War Reserve Fund and Planning Act (Municipal)

Fla. Laws 1943, Ch. 21893

Postage Stamp Vending Machine Act

Ill. Comp. Stat. 1992, Ch. 35, §§ 815/1 to 815/3

Ill. Rev. Stat. 1991, Ch. 121 1/2, § 910 et seq.

Postal Convention (Hawaii and United States, 1870)

Haw. Session Laws 1872, p. 41, June 20, 1870

Postal Employees Hours Act

See McKellar-Mead 40-Hour Mail Act

Postal Employees Safety Enhancement Act

Sept. 28, 1998, P.L. 105-241, 112 Stat. 1572, 39 U.S. Code § 101 nt.

Postal Employees Salary Adjustment Act of 1962

Oct. 11, 1962, P.L. 87-793, 76 Stat. 850

Postal Employees Salary Increase Act of 1960

July 1, 1960, P.L. 86-568, 74 Stat. 296

Postal Field Service Classification Act of 1955

See Postal Field Service Compensation Act of 1955

Postal Field Service Compensation Act of 1955

June 10, 1955, Ch. 137, 69 Stat. 88
July 31, 1956, Ch. 804, 70 Stat. 741
May 14, 1958, P.L. 85-399, 72 Stat. 107
May 27, 1958, P.L. 85-426, 72 Stat. 143
May 29, 1958, P.L. 85-432, 72 Stat. 151
June 20, 1958, P.L. 85-462, 72 Stat. 215
Aug. 25, 1958, P.L. 85-751, 72 Stat. 844
Sept. 2, 1958, P.L. 85-914, 72 Stat. 1761
July 31, 1959, P.L. 86-122, 73 Stat. 268
July 1, 1960, P.L. 86-568, 74 Stat. 296

Postal Pay Act of 1945

July 6, 1945, Ch. 274, 59 Stat. 435
Oct. 29, 1949, Ch. 785, 63 Stat. 984

Postal Policy Act of 1958

May 27, 1958, P.L. 85-426, 2 Stat. 134

Postal Rate Increase Act, 1958

May 27, 1958, P.L. 85-426, 72 Stat. 138
Sept. 2, 1958, P.L. 85-893, 72 Stat. 1713

Postal Rate Revision and Federal Employees Salary Act of 1948

July 3, 1948, Ch. 830, 62 Stat. 1260
April 28, 1950, Ch. 121, 64 Stat. 91
July 20, 1953, Ch. 233, 67 Stat. 183
May 27, 1958, P.L. 85-426, 72 Stat. 138
July 14, 1960, P.L. 86-644, 74 Stat. 479

Postal Reorganization Act

Aug. 12, 1970, P.L. 91-375, 84 Stat. 719, 2 U.S. Code § 356; 3 U.S. Code § 19; 5 U.S. Code §§ 2104, 2105, 3104, 4301, 5102 to 5104, 5312, 5314 to 5316, 5541, 6301, 6323, 7101, 8344; 12 U.S. Code §§ 24, 1701; 15 U.S. Code § 537; 16 U.S. Code § 460; 17 U.S. Code § 8; 18 U.S . Code §§ 12, 440, 441, 500, 501, 612, 876, 877, 1114, 1303, 1341, 1342, 1463, 1696, 1699, 1703 and others; 22 U.S. Code § 611; 31 U.S. Code §§ 72, 129, 724a; 39 U.S. Code §§ 101, 102, 201 to 208, 401 to 412, 601 to 606, 1001 to 1011, 1201 to 1209, 2001 to 2010, 2201, 2401 and others; 40 U.S. Code §§ 356, 474, 615, 723, 724; 42 U.S. Code § 2942

Oct. 14, 1970, P.L. 91-448, 84 Stat. 921, 18 U.S. Code § 501

Postal Revenue and Federal Salary Act of 1967

Dec. 16, 1967, P.L. 90-206, 81 Stat. 613, 2 U.S. Code §§ 60e-14, 60j, 61-1, 61-2, 74a-2, 136a, 136a-1, 293c, 351 to 361; 3 U.S. Code § 102 nt.; 5 U.S. Code §§ 3110, 4101, 5303, 5304 nt., 5314 to 5316 and others; 16 U.S. Code § 590h nt.; 22 U.S. Code §§ 867, 870; 28 U.S. Code §§ 548 nt., 603, 604 nt., 753 nt., 792; 31 U.S. Code §§ 42a, 51a; 38 U.S. Code § 4107; 40 U.S. Code §§ 162a, 166b, 166b-1, 166b-3

Nov. 2, 1994, P.L. 103-437, 2 U.S. Code § 74a-2

Postal Salary Act of 1945

July 6, 1945, Ch. 274, 59 Stat. 435
July 10, 1952, Ch. 650, 66 Stat. 548
Continued

Postal Salary Classification Act of 1925
See Reclassification Act of 1925

Postal Savings Depositaries Act
June 25, 1910, Ch. 386, 36 Stat. 814

Postal Savings System Accounts Escheat Act
Ark. Stat. 1947, 50-613 et seq.
Iowa Code 1983, 556.30 et seq.
Md. Ann. Code 1957, Art. 95c, § 27 et seq.
N.D. Laws 1971, Ch. 518
Nev. Rev. Stat. 1979 Reprint, 40.500 et seq.
Okla. Stat. Ann., Title 60, § 701 et seq.
R.I. Gen. Laws 1956, 33-21A-1 et seq.

Postal Savings System Statute of Limitations Act
July 13, 1984, P.L. 98-359, 31 U.S. Code §§ 1301 nt., 1322

Postal Service
Sept. 2, 1960, P.L. 86-682, 74 Stat. 578
Sept. 21, 1961, P.L. 87-270, 75 Stat. 569
Oct. 4, 1961, P.L. 87-367, 75 Stat. 795
June 15, 1962, P.L. 87-484, 76 Stat. 102
June 19, 1962, P.L. 87-487, 76 Stat. 103
June 19, 1962, P.L. 87-491, 76 Stat. 106
June 25, 1962, P.L. 87-496, 76 Stat. 109
Sept. 7, 1962, P.L. 87-646, 76 Stat. 442
Oct. 11, 1962, P.L. 87-793, 76 Stat. 832
Oct. 23, 1962, P.L. 87-865, 76 Stat. 1144
Dec. 21, 1963, P.L. 88-219, 77 Stat. 462
Dec. 23, 1963, P.L. 88-239, 77 Stat. 476
Aug. 14, 1964, P.L. 88-426, 78 Stat. 402
Aug. 19, 1964, P.L. 88-448, 78 Stat. 492
Aug. 22, 1964, P.L. 88-480, 78 Stat. 593
Aug. 9, 1965, P.L. 89-116, 79 Stat. 499
Oct. 29, 1965, P.L. 89-301, 79 Stat. 1113
Nov. 1, 1965, P.L. 89-315, 79 Stat. 1163
March 28, 1966, P.L. 89-377, 80 Stat. 92
July 5, 1966, P.L. 89-492, 80 Stat. 262
July 12, 1966, P.L. 89-500, 80 Stat. 274
July 18, 1966, P.L. 89-504, 80 Stat. 289
Sept. 6, 1966, P.L. 89-554, 80 Stat. 631
Sept. 20, 1966, P.L. 89-593, 80 Stat. 815
Oct. 8, 1966, P.L. 89-632, 80 Stat. 878
Oct. 10, 1966, P.L. 89-637, 80 Stat. 882
Nov. 2, 1966, P.L. 89-725, 80 Stat. 1154

May 8, 1967, P.L. 90-15, 81 Stat. 14
Oct. 11, 1967, P.L. 90-105, 81 Stat. 274
Oct. 21, 1967, P.L. 90-109, 81 Stat. 278
Dec. 16, 1967, P.L. 90-206, 81 Stat. 613
June 20, 1968, P.L. 90-353, 82 Stat. 240
June 29, 1968, P.L. 90-368, 82 Stat. 278
Aug. 2, 1968, P.L. 90-449, 82 Stat. 611
Oct. 12, 1968, P.L. 90-560, 82 Stat. 997
Oct. 17, 1968, P.L. 90-590, 82 Stat. 1153
Aug. 12, 1970, P.L. 91-375, 84 Stat. 719, 39 U.S. Code §§ 101 to 5605
Jan. 8, 1971, P.L. 91-656, 84 Stat. 1955, 39 U.S. Code § 410
Jan. 8, 1971, P.L. 91-662, 84 Stat. 1973, 39 U.S. Code §§ 3001, 4001
July 9, 1971, P.L. 92-51, 85 Stat. 132, 39 U.S. Code §§ 3210, 3216
May 1, 1972, P.L. 92-286, 86 Stat. 133, 39 U.S. Code § 5005
Oct. 6, 1972, P.L. 92-469, 86 Stat. 782, 39 U.S. Code § 3401
Dec. 18, 1972, P.L. 93-191, 87 Stat. 737, 39 U.S. Code §§ 3206, 3210, 3212, 3214 to 3216, 3218, 3219
March 27, 1974, P.L. 93-255, 88 Stat. 52, 39 U.S. Code § 3216
June 30, 1974, P.L. 93-328, 88 Stat. 287, 39 U.S. Code §§ 2009, 3626
July 10, 1974, P.L. 93-340, 88 Stat. 294, 5 U.S. Code § 5520
July 12, 1974, P.L. 93-349, 88 Stat. 354, 39 U.S. Code § 1005

Postal Service and Federal Employees Salary Act of 1962
Oct. 11, 1962, P.L. 87-793, 76 Stat. 832, 2 U.S. Code §§ 60a nt., 60f nt.; See 5 U.S. Code §§ 5101 et seq.; 7 U.S. Code § 1857; 10 U.S. Code § 1581; 16 U.S. Code §§ 590h nt., 742; 21 U.S. Code § 113a; 22 U.S. Code §§ 290a, 867, 870, 1017, 2385, 2454, 2506; 28 U.S. Code §§ 508, 603 nt., 604 nt., 753 nt.; 42 U.S. Code §§ 2201, 2473, 2521; 49 U.S. Code § 1343; 50 U.S. Code 402 nt.

Postal Service and Federal Salary Act of 1967
April 12, 1977, P.L. 95-19, 2 U.S. Code § 359 et seq.

Postal Service Appropriation Act
July 9, 1971, P.L. 92-49, 85 Stat. 110

Postal Service Appropriation Act, 1976
Aug. 9, 1975, P.L. 94-91, 89 Stat. 444, 26
U.S. Code §§ 7443 nt.; 31 U.S. Code
§§ 638c nt., 699b; 33 U.S. Code § 776; 40
U.S. Code § 490

Postal Service Appropriation Act, 1989
Sept. 22, 1989, P.L. 100-440, 3 U.S. Code
§ 102 nt.; 26 U.S. Code § 7443 nt.; 33 U.S.
Code § 776; 40 U.S. Code §§ 490a, 490d

Postal Service Appropriations Act, 1987
Oct. 18, 1986, P.L. 99-500, 18 U.S. Code
§ 2254
Oct. 30, 1986, P.L. 99-591, 18 U.S. Code
§ 2254

Postal Service Appropriations Act, 1988
Dec. 22, 1987, P.L. 100-202, 101 Stat. 1329

Postal Service Appropriations Act, 1990
Nov. 3, 1989, P.L. 101-136, 103 Stat. 790

Postal Service Appropriations Act, 1991
Nov. 5, 1990, P.L. 101-509, 39 U.S. Code
§§ 403 nt., 2401, 2401 nt., 3626, 3626 nt.

Postal Service Appropriations Act, 1992
Oct. 28, 1991, P.L. 102-141, 105 Stat. 842

Postal Service Appropriations Act, 1993
Oct. 6, 1992, P.L. 102-393, 39 U.S. Code
§ 403 nt.

Postal Service Appropriations Act, 1994
Oct. 28, 1993, P.L. 103-123, 107 Stat. 1234

Postal Service Appropriations Act, 1996
Nov. 19, 1995, P.L. 104-52, Title II, 109 Stat.
476

Postal Service Appropriations Act, 1998
Oct. 10, 1997, P.L. 105-61, Title II, 111 Stat.
1290

Postal Service Appropriations Act, 1999
Oct. 21, 1998, P.L. 105-277, 101(h), Title II,
112 Stat. 2681

Postconviction Relief Act
Pa. Cons. Stat., Title 42, § 9541 et seq.

Posted Property Act
Cal. Penal Code, § 552 et seq.

**Postgovernment Employment Restrictions
Act (Milton Marks)**
Cal. Government Code § 87406

**Posthumous Citizenship for Active Duty
Service Act of 1989**
March 6, 1990, P.L. 101-249, 8 U.S. Code
§ 1101 nt.

Posting Law
N.J. Stat. Ann., 48:8-16
N.Y. Environmental Conservation Law 1972
(Consol. Laws Ch. 43B) § 11-2101 et seq.

Posting Property Act
N.M. Stat. Ann. 1953, 40A-14-6 et seq.

Postmark Prompt Payment Act
R.I. Gen. Laws 1956, 6-42.1-1 et seq.

Postsecondary Drug-Free Education Act
Ga. Code Ann., 20-1-20 et seq.

**Postsecondary Education Act (Equal
Opportunities in)**
Neb. Laws 1996, L.B. 900

Postsecondary Education Authorization Act
Ga. Code Ann., 20-3-100 et seq.
N.D. Cent. Code, 15-20.4-01 et seq.
Nev. Rev. Stat. 1979 Reprint, 394.361 et seq.
Tenn. Code Ann., 49-7-2001 et seq.

**Postsecondary Education Facilities
Authority Act**
Colo. Rev. Stat. 1973, 23-15-101 et seq.

**Postsecondary Education Security
Information Act**
Fla. Stat. Ann., 240.2682 et seq.

Postsecondary Education Technology Revenue Bond Act (Archie-Hudson and Cunneen)
Cal. Education Code 1976, § 67359.10 et seq.

Postsecondary Educational Facilities Authority Act
Colo. Rev. Stat., 10-4-701 et seq.

Postsecondary Educational Institutions Act (Nonpublic)
Ga. Code Ann., 20-3-250.1 et seq.

Postsecondary Enrollment Options Act
Colo. Rev. Stat., 22-35-101 et seq.
Iowa Code Ann., 261C.1 et seq.
Me. Rev. Stat. Ann. 1964, Title 20-A, § 4751 et seq.
Minn. Stat. Ann., 123.3514

Postsecondary Proprietary School Act
Utah Code Ann. 1953, 53B-5-101 et seq.

Postsecondary Student Assistance Amendments of 1981
Aug. 13, 1981, P.L. 97-35, 20 U.S. Code § 1001 nt.

Postwar Construction Law
Cal. Government Code, § 15750 et seq.

Postwar Planning and Acquisition Aid Act
Cal. Statutes 1944, 4th Ex. Sess., Ch. 47, p. 196

Postwar Unemployment and Construction Act
Cal. Statutes 1945, Ch. 647, p. 1301

Potable Water Safeguard Law
N.Y. Local Laws 1972, Town of Richmond, p. 2716

Potato Act
Mich. Comp. Laws Ann., 290.151 et seq.

Potato Certification and Grading Act
Ore. Rev. Stat., 632.306 et seq.

Potato Dealers Act (Wholesale)
Mich. Comp. Laws Ann., 290.451 et seq.

Potato Development Act
Neb. Rev. Stat. 1943, 2-1801 et seq.

Potato Disease Act (Golden Nematode)
N.Y. Laws 1947, Ch. 663

Potato Improvement, Marketing, and Advertising Act
Minn. Stat. 1965, 30.31 et seq.

Potato Industry Act
Wis. Stat. Ann., 100.39 et seq.

Potato Industry Promotion Act
Minn. Stat. Ann., 30.461 et seq.
N.D. Cent. Code, 4-10.1-01 et seq.

Potato Inspection Act
Mo. Rev. Stat. 1929, p. 104
Neb. Rev. Stat. 1943, 2-1813 et seq.
Tex. Agriculture Code, § 91.141 et seq.
Va. Code 1950, § 3.1-285 et seq.

Potato Inspection Law (Carlots)
Neb. Rev. Stat. 1943, 89-142 et seq.

Potato Labeling Act
N.D. Cent. Code, 19-22-01 et seq.

Potato Lien Law
Me. Rev. Stat. Ann. 1964, Title 10, § 3321 et seq.

Potato Marketing Act
Me. Rev. Stat. Ann. 1964, Title 7, § 991 et seq.

Potato Research and Promotion Act
Jan. 11, 1971, P.L. 91-670, 84 Stat. 2041, 7 U.S. Code §§ 2611 to 2627
Aug. 26, 1982, P.L. 97-244, 7 U.S. Code §§ 2611 nt., 2617, 2621, 2623
Nov. 29, 1983, P.L. 98-171, 7 U.S. Code § 2617
Nov. 28, 1990, P.L. 101-624, 7 U.S. Code §§ 2611 to 2614, 2617 to 2619, 2622 to 2624, 2625 nt.
Dec. 13, 1991, P.L. 102-237, 7 U.S. Code § 2619

Potato Research and Promotion Act Amendments of 1990
Nov. 28, 1990, P.L. 101-624, 7 U.S. Code § 2611 nt.

Potato Seed Act
Minn. Stat. Ann., 30.01 et seq.
N.C. Gen. Stat. 1943, § 106-284.5 et seq.

Potato Seed Labeling Act
Iowa Code Ann., 199.7
Md. Ann. Code 1974, Art. AG, § 9-301 et seq.

Potato Tax Act
Me. Rev. Stat. Ann. 1964, Title 36, § 4601 et seq.

Potomac Highlands Airport Authority Compact Act
Md. Ann. Code 1974, Art. TR, § 10-103

Potomac River Basin Compact Act
D.C. Code Ann., §§ 7-1301, 7-1302
Md. Ann. Code 1974, Art. NR, § 8-301
Va. Code 1950, § 62.1-69.1 et seq.

Potomac River Compact Act
Md. Ann. Code 1974, Art. NR, § 4-306
Va. Code 1950, § 28.1-203

Potomac River Fisheries Act
Md. Ann. Code 1957, Superseded Vol., Art. 66C, § 306 et seq.

Potomac River Riparian Rights Act
Va. Code 1950, § 62.1-44.113 et seq.

Potter Act (Railroads)
Wis. Laws 1874, Ch. 273

Poughkeepsie Parking Authority Act
N.Y. Public Authorities Law (Consol. Laws Ch. 43A) (Consol. Laws Ch. 43A) § 1598 et seq.

Poultry Act
Ky. Rev. Stat. 1971, 257.320 et seq.

Poultry and Egg Resources Act
Neb. Rev. Stat. 1943, 2-3401 et seq.

Poultry and Livestock Disease Control Board Act
Ga. Code Ann., 4-4-1.1 et seq.

Poultry and Livestock Raising Law (Cooperative)
Miss. Code Ann. 1972, § 79-19-1 et seq.

Poultry and Meat Byproducts Disposal Act
Miss. Code Ann. 1972, § 41-51-1 et seq.

Poultry and Meat Inspection Act
Conn. Gen. Stat. Ann., § 22-392 et seq.
Del. Code of 1974, Title 3, § 8701 et seq.
Ill. Rev. Stat. 1991, Ch. 56 1/2, § 301 et seq.
Mass. Gen. Laws 1984, 94:146 et seq.
Mont. Laws 1991, Ch. 577, §§ 1 to 16
Neb. Rev. Stat. 1943, 54-1901 et seq.
N.J. Stat. Ann., 24:16B-1 et seq.
Tex. Health and Safety Code, § 433.001 et seq.
Va. Code 1950, § 3.1-884.17 et seq.

Poultry and Meat Inspection and Humane Slaughter Act
Ind. Code Ann., 16-6-5-1 et seq.

Poultry and Meat Products Inspection and Licensing Act
See Meat and Poultry Products Inspection and Licensing Act

Poultry and Poultry Products for Human Consumption Act
P.R. Laws Ann. 1954, Title 24, § 741 et seq.

Poultry and Rabbit Products Inspection Act
Ky. Rev. Stat. 1971, Superseded Vol., 217A.010 et seq.

Poultry and Stock Act
S.C. Code Ann. 1976, § 46-27-820

Poultry and Stock Act (Preparations)
S.C. Code Ann. 1976, § 46-27-810 et seq.

Poultry Bonding Act
Mass. Gen. Laws. Ann., 94:152A et seq.

Poultry By-Products Disposal Act
Miss. Code Ann. 1972, § 41-51-1 et seq.

Poultry Dealers License Act
Ill. Rev. Stat. 1967, Ch. 8, § 127 et seq.

Poultry Disease Control Act
Kan. Stat. Ann., 2-908 et seq.
Neb. Rev. Stat. 1943, 2-3001 et seq.

Poultry, Egg and Livestock Production Assistance Act
Miss. Code 1942, § 4435-51 et seq.

Poultry Hygiene Law
Pa. Purdon's Stat., Title 31, § 483.1 et seq.

Poultry Improvement Act
Cal. Food and Agricultural Code 1967, § 1101 et seq.

Poultry Industry Act
N.C. Gen. Stat. 1943, § 106-539 et seq.

Poultry Inspection Act
Cal. Food and Agricultural Code 1967, § 18650 et seq.
Haw. Rev. Stat. Ann., § 161-1 et seq.
Ill. Rev. Stat. 1991, Ch. 8, § 130.9 et seq.
Iowa Code Ann., 189A.1 et seq.
Neb. Rev. Stat. 1943, 54-1901 et seq.
Ore. Rev. Stat., 619.410 et seq.
Tex. Rev. Civ. Stat., Art. 4476-7
Vt. Stat. Ann., Title 6, § 3191 et seq.

Poultry Labeling Act
Haw. Rev. Laws 1955, § 22C-11 et seq.

Poultry, Meat and Meat-Food Regulation and Inspection Law
Miss. Code Ann. 1972, § 75-33-1 et seq.

Poultry Producers Financial Protection Act of 1987
Nov. 23, 1987, P.L. 100-173, 7 U.S. Code §§ 181 nt., 182, 192, 197, 209, 218 to 218d, 221, 223, 227, 227 nt., 228a, 228b-1 to 228b-4, 228c, 229

Poultry Products Act
Wash. Rev. Code Ann., 16.74.010 et seq.

Poultry Products and Meat Products Inspection Act
Conn. Gen. Stat. § 22-392 et seq.
Md. Ann. Code 1974, Art. AG, § 4-201 et seq.
N.C. Gen. Stat. 1943, § 106-549.49
Okla. Stat. Ann., Title 2, § 6-251 et seq.
S.C. Code Ann. 1976, § 47-19-10 et seq.
Utah Code Ann. 1953, 4-32-1 et seq.

Poultry Products Inspection Act
Aug. 28, 1957, P.L. 85-172, 71 Stat. 441, 21 U.S. Code §§ 451 to 469
June 25, 1962, P.L. 87-498, 76 Stat. 110, 21 U.S. Code § 453
Aug. 18, 1968, P.L. 90-492, 82 Stat. 791, 21 U.S. Code §§ 451 to 461, 463 to 465, 467, 467a to 467f, 470
June 30, 1982, P.L. 97-206, 21 U.S. Code § 464(c)(3), (4)
Oct. 17, 1984, P.L. 98-487, 21 U.S. Code § 454
Dec. 23, 1985, P.L. 99-198, 21 U.S. Code § 466
Dec. 7, 1989, P.L. 101-205, 21 U.S. Code § 467b
Dec. 13, 1991, P.L. 102-237, 21 U.S. Code § 464
Oct. 29, 1992, P.L. 102-571, 21 U.S. Code § 453
Dec. 8, 1993, P.L. 103-182, 21 U.S. Code § 466
Nov. 2, 1994, P.L. 103-437, 21 U.S. Code §§ 454, 470
Dec. 8, 1994, P.L. 103-465, 21 U.S. Code § 466
Md. Ann. Code 1974, Art. AG, § 4-201 et seq.
N.C. Gen. Stat. 1943, § 106-549.49 et seq.

Poultry Products Promotion Council and Tax Act
N.J. Rev. Stat. 1937, 54:47A-1 et seq.

Poultry Racket Act
Aug. 14, 1935, Ch. 532, 49 Stat. 648, 7 U.S. Code §§ 192, 218 to 218d, 221 to 224

Poultry Waste Management Program
Va. Code 1950, § 62.1-44.17:1.1

Poundage Fees Act
Md. Ann. Code 1974, Art. CJ, § 7-402

Poundmaster Fee Act
D.C. Laws 1977, No. 2-26

Poundstone Amendment
Colo. Constitution, Art. 20, § 1

Pour-Over Act
Ala. Code 1975, § 43-8-140
Ariz. Rev. Stat. Ann., § 14-2511
Ark. Code Ann. 1987, 28-27-101 et seq.
Cal. Probate Code, § 170 et seq.
Colo. Rev. Stat. 1963, 153-5-44
Conn. Gen. Stat. Ann., § 45a-260
D.C. Code 1973, § 18-306
Del. Code of 1974, Title 12, § 211
Fla. Stat. Ann., 732.513
Ida. Code 1947, 15-2-511
Ill. Rev. Stat. 1991, Ch. 110 1/2, § 4-4
Ind. Code Ann., 29-1-6-1, Subd. j
Kan. Stat. Ann., 59-3101 et seq.
Md. Ann. Code 1974, Art. ET, §§ 4-411, 4-412
Mich. Comp. Laws Ann., 555.461 et seq.
Miss. Code Ann. 1972, § 91-5-11
Mont. Rev. Code 1947, 91-312
N.C. Gen. Stat. 1943, § 31-47
N.D. Cent. Code, 30.1-08-11
Neb. Rev. Stat. 1943, 30-2336
N.J. Stat. Ann., 3B:4-1 et seq.
N.M. Stat. Ann., 45-2-511, 46-5-1 et seq.
Ohio Rev. Code 1953, 2107.63
Okla. Stat. Ann., Title 84, § 301 et seq.
Pa. 1957 Pamph. Laws 793, No. 378
R.I. Gen. Laws 1956, 33-6-33
S.C. Code Ann. 1976, Superseded Vols., § 21-33-20
Tenn. Code Ann., 32-3-106
Tex. Probate Code, § 58a
Utah Code Ann. 1953, 75-2-511
Va. Code 1950, § 64.1-73
Vt. Stat. Ann., Title 14, § 2329
Wis. Stat. Ann., 701.07 et seq.

Wyo. Stat. Ann., § 2-6-103

Poverty Pocket Program
Fla. Stat. Ann., 420.801 et seq.

POW Homecoming Act
Cal. Statutes 1973, Ch. 19

POW/MIA Family Relief Act
Cal. Probate Code, § 1776 et seq.

POW/MIA Scholarship Act
Ida. Code 1947, 33-4301, 33-4302

Powell Act (Highway Funds)
N.C. Gen. Stat. 1943, § 136-41.1 et seq.

Power Act
Ore. Laws 1933, Ch. 357

Power Act (Bone)
Wash. Rev. Code Ann., 54.04.020 et seq.

Power Act (Hydroelectric)
See Hydroelectric Power Act

Power Act (Public)
Wash. Rev. Code Ann., 54.04.010 et seq.

Power and Energy Authority
La. Rev. Stat. Ann., 33:4545.1 et seq.

Power and Energy Law (Electric)
Miss. Code Ann. 1972, § 77-5-701 et seq.

Power and Water Board Act
Utah Code Ann. 1953, 73-10-1 et seq.

Power Authority Act
Alaska Stat. 1962, § 44.83.010 et seq.
Ariz. Rev. Stat. Ann., § 48-1501 et seq.
La. Rev. Stat. Ann., 33:4545.1 et seq.
N.Y. Public Authorities Law (Consol. Laws Ch. 43A) § 1000 et seq.
Okla. Stat. 1981, Title 11, § 24-101

Power Authority Act (Green Island)
N.Y. Public Authorities Law (Consol. Laws Ch. 43A) § 1020 et seq.

Power Authority Act (Long Island)
N.Y. Public Authorities Law (Consol. Laws Ch. 43A) § 1020 et seq.

Power Commission Act
Wash. Rev. Code Ann., 43.52.250 et seq.

Power Companies Act
Mich. Comp. Laws Ann., 486.251 et seq.

Power Companies Condemnation Act
Mich. Comp. Laws Ann., 486.252a et seq.

Power Development Authority Act
Colo. Rev. Stat. 1973, 37-95-101 et seq.

Power District Act
Ariz. Rev. Stat. Ann., § 48-1501 et seq.
Miss. Code Ann. 1972, § 77-5-101 et seq.
Nev. Rev. Stat. 1957, 312.010 et seq.
S.D. Codified Laws 1967, 49-35-1 et seq.
Tenn. Code. Ann., 7-83-101 et seq.
Wyo. Stat. Ann., § 37-7-101 et seq.

Power Equipment Dealership Act (Outdoor)
Kan. Stat. Ann., 16-1301 et seq.

Power Equipment Manufacturers, Distributors, Wholesalers, and Servicing Dealers Act (Outdoor)
Fla. Stat. Ann., 686.601 to 686.614

Power Line and Safety Act (Overhead)
Mo. Rev. Stat. 1978, 319.075

Power of Appointment Exercise Act
Ill. Rev. Stat. 1991, Ch. 30, §§ 176.50, 176.51

Power of Appointment Law (Release of)
Miss. Code Ann. 1972, § 91-15-1 et seq.

Power of Attorney Act
See Uniform Statutory Form Power of Attorney Act
Ill. Rev. Stat. 1991, Ch. 110 1/2, § 801-1 et seq.

Power of Attorney Act (Durable)
See also Uniform Durable Power of Attorney Act
Haw. Rev. Stat. Ann., § 551D-1 et seq.
Ill. Rev. Stat. 1991, Ch. 110 1/2, § 802-1 et seq.
Ind. Code Ann., 30-2-11-1 et seq.
Tex. Probate Code, § 481 et seq.
W. Va. Code 1966, § 20-5A-1 et seq.

Power of Attorney Act (Medical)
W. Va. Code 1966 § 16-30A-1 et seq.

Power of Attorney Act (Military Member)
Ariz. Rev. Stat. Ann., § 14-5104.01

Power of Attorney Act (Service of Process)
Tex. Bus Corp. Act, Art. 8.10

Power of Attorney Act (Statutory Form)
Conn. Gen. Stat. Ann., § 1-42 et seq.
La. Rev. Stat. Ann., 9:3861 et seq.

Power of Attorney Act (Water)
W. Va. 1966, § 39-4-1 et seq.

Power of Attorney for Health Care Act
Ga. Code Ann., 31-36-1 et seq.
Ill. Rev. Stat. 1991, Ch. 110 1/2, § 804-1 et seq.
N.J. Stat. Ann., 12:7-23.1 et seq.

Power of Attorney for Health Care Act (Durable)
Miss. Code Ann. 1972, § 41-41-151 et seq.

Power of Attorney for Property Law (Statutory Short Form)
Ill. Rev. Stat. 1991, Ch. 110 1/2, § 803-1 et seq.

Power of Cities Act
Ind. Code Ann., 36-4-4-1 et seq.

Power of Sale Mortgage Foreclosure Act
Okla. Stat. Ann., Title 46, § 40 et seq.

Power or Train Brakes Safety Appliance Act of 1958
April 11, 1958, P.L. 85-375, 72 Stat. 86, 45 U.S. Code § 9

Power Planning and Conservation Act (Pacific Northwest Electric)
Wash. Rev. Code 1983, 43.52A.010 et seq.

Power Plant and Industrial Fuel Use Act of 1978
Nov. 9, 1978, P.L. 95-620, 15 U.S. Code § 796; 42 U.S. Code §§ 8301 et seq.; 45 U.S. Code §§ 821, 822, 825; 49 U.S. Code § 26b

Dec. 21, 1982, P.L. 97-375, 42 U.S. Code § 8452

May 21, 1987, P.L. 100-42, 42 U.S. Code § 8301 et seq., 8411, 8412, 8431 et seq., 8441, 8471

Oct. 24, 1992, P.L. 102-486, 42 U.S. Code § 8373

Dec. 21, 1995, P.L. 104-66, 42 U.S. Code §§ 8421, 8482, 8455

Power Plant Dam Act
Kan. Stat. Ann., 82a-101 et seq.

Power Plant Siting Act
Minn. Stat. Ann., 116C.51 et seq.

Power Production Act (Small)
Me. Rev. Stat. Ann. 1964, Title 35-A, § 3301 et seq.

Power Production Facilities Act
Me. Rev. Stat. Ann. 1964, Title 35, § 2321 et seq.

Power Pumping District Act (County)
Cal. Statutes 1915, Ch. 745, p. 1483

Power Supply Cooperatives Act
Va. Code 1950, § 56-231.1 et seq.

Power System Revenue Bond Law (Mineral County)
Nev. Statutes 1961, Ch. 169, p. 256

Power Tax Act
S.C. Code Ann. 1976, § 12-23-10 et seq.

Power Vessel Act
N.J. Stat. Ann., 12:7-1 et seq.

Power Vessel Noise Control Act
N.J. Stat. Ann., 12:7-23.1 et seq.

Powerplant Communities Information Act (Nuclear)
Cal. Public Utilities Code, §§ 8301 et seq.

Powerplant Siting Coordination Act
Cal. Public Utilities Code, § 2851 et seq.

Powers Act (City)
N.Y. General City Law (Consol. Laws Ch. 21) § 19 et seq.

Powers Act (Estates)
N.Y. Estates, Powers and Trust Law (Consol. Laws Ch. 17 B) § 10-1-1 et seq.

Powers Act (Trustees)
Minn. Stat. Ann., 501 B.76 et seq.
Neb. Rev. Stat. 1943, 30-2819 et seq.

Powers and Trusts Act
Kan. Stat. Ann., 58-2401 et seq.

Powers in Trust Instruments Act
Conn. Gen. Stat. Ann., § 45-100a et seq.

Powers of Appointment Act
Colo. Rev. Stat., 15-2-101 et seq.
Mich. Comp. Laws Ann., 556.111 et seq.

Powers of Appointment Act (Estates)
N.Y. Estates, Powers and Trusts Law (Consol. Laws Ch. 17B) § 10-1.1 et seq.
Wis. Stat. Ann., 702.01 et seq.

Powers of Appointment Act of 1951
June 28, 1951, Ch. 165, 65 Stat. 91

Powersville Water Authority Act
Ga. Laws 1972, p. 3724

PPBES Act (Program Planning, Budgeting, and Evaluating System)
Colo. Rev. Stat., 22-44-201 et seq.

Practical Nurse Act

Mo. Rev. Stat., 335.046 et seq.

N.D. Cent. Code, 43-12.1-01 et seq.

N.H. Rev. Stat. 1955, 326:17 et seq., 326-B:1 et seq.

Pa. Purdon's Stat., Title 63, § 651 et seq.

S.D. Codified Laws 1967, 36-9-1 et seq.

Practical Nurse Licensing Act

Colo. Rev. Stat., 12-38-101 et seq.

Colo. Rev. Stat. 1963, 97-2-1 et seq.

D.C. Code Ann., § 2-1702.1 et seq.

W. Va. Code 1966, § 30-7A-1 et seq.

Practical Nurse Training Extension Act of 1961

April 24, 1961, P.L. 87-22, 75 Stat. 44, 20 U.S. Code §§ 15aa to 15cc, 15jj

Practical Nurses Practice Act

Ga. Code Ann., 43-26-30 et seq.

Practical Technician and Technologist Licensing Act (Radiology)

Utah Code Ann. 1953, 58-54-1 et seq.

Practice Act

Ala. Code 1958, Title 7, § 182 et seq.

Conn. Gen. Stat. Ann., § 52-1 et seq.

Ga. Code Ann., 9-11-1 et seq.

Ill. Rev. Stat. 1991, Ch. 110, § 1 et seq.

Ind. Code Ann., 34-1-1-1 et seq.

Mass. Gen. Laws. Ann., 231:6 et seq.

Md. Ann. Code 1957, Art. 75, § 1 et seq.

Mont. Rev. Code 1947, 93-101 et seq.

N.C. Gen. Stat. 1943, § 1-1 et seq.

Nev. Rev. Stat. 1979 Reprint, 10.010 et seq.,

N.J. Stat. Revised 1937, 2:27-1 et seq.

Pa. 1887 Pamph. Laws 271, No. 158

R.I. Gen. Laws 1956, 9-1-1 et seq.

Vt. Acts 1915, No. 90

Wash. Rev. Code Ann., 4.04.010 et seq.

W. Va. Code 1966, § 56-1-1 et seq.

Practice Act (Athletic Training)

N.J. Stat. Ann., 45:9-37.35 et seq.

Practice Act (Chancery)

Miss. Code Ann. 1972, § 9-5-3 et seq.

Practice Act (Criminal)

See Criminal Practice Act

Practice Act (Dental)

See Dental Practice Act

Practice Act (Dietetics)

Ga. Code Ann., 43-11A-1 et seq.

Practice Act (Jefferson County)

Ala. General Acts 1888-89, p. 797

Practice Act (Medical Physics)

Tex. Rev. Civ. Stat., Art. 4512n

Practice Act (Medical)

See Medical Practice Act

Practice Act (Nurse)

See Nurse Practice Act

Utah Code Ann. 1953, 58-31-1 et seq.

Practice Act (Nursing)

Cal. Business and Professions Code § 2700 et seq.

Tex. Rev. Civ. Stat., Art. 4513 et seq.

Practice Act (Occupational Therapy)

See Occupational Therapy Act

Practice Act (Optometry)

Utah Code Ann. 1953, 58-16a-101 et seq.

Practice Act (Physical Therapist)

Mo. Rev. Stat., 334.500 to 334.620

Utah Code Ann. 1953, 58-24a-101 et seq.

Practice Act (Physical Therapists)

See Physical Therapists Practice Act

Practice Act (Real Estate)

N.H. Rev. Stat. 1955, 331-A:1 et seq.

Practice Act (Respiratory Care)

Miss. Code Ann. 1972, § 73-59-1 et seq.

Okla. Stat. Ann., Title 59, § 2026 et seq.

Practice Act (Uniform Administrative Agencies)
N.D. Cent. Code, 28-32-01 et seq.

Practice Act (Veterinary)
See Veterinary Practice Act

Practice Act of the Public Utilities Commissioner
Ore. Rev. Stat., 756.500 et seq.

Practice and Licensure Act (Optometric)
Pa. Purdon's Stat., Title 63, § 244.1 et seq.

Practice and Pleading Act (Neel Act)
Ga. Code 1933, 81-103

Practice Conformity Act
June 1, 1872, Ch. 255, 17 Stat. 197

Practice of Nursing in Expanded Role Act
Neb. Rev. Stat. 1943, 71-1704 et seq.

Practice of Occupational Therapy Act
See Occupational Therapy Practice Act

Practice of Psychology Act
Jan. 8, 1971, P.L. 91-657, 84 Stat. 1955
D.C. Code Ann., § 2-1704.1 et seq.

Practicing Marriage and Family Therapy Act
N.J. Stat. Ann., 45:8B-1 et seq.

Prairie Fire Act
Okla. Stat. Ann., Title 2, § 741 et seq.

Prairie Grass Act
Ill. Rev. Stat. 1991, Ch. 1, § 2901-55

Prairie State 2000 Fund Act
Ill. Rev. Stat. 1991, Ch. 48, § 1501 et seq.

Prairie Trail Authority Act
Ill. Rev. Stat. 1991, Ch. 96 1/2, § 9601 et seq.

Prairie Week Act
Ill. Rev. Stat. 1991, Ch. 1, § 3051-75

Pre-audit Law
Ark. Stat. 1947, 13-301 et seq.

Pre-emption Act (Public Lands)
La. Rev. Stat. Ann., 41:171 et seq.

Pre-emption Acts
May 29, 1830, Ch. 208, 4 Stat. 420
Jan. 23, 1832, Ch. 9, 4 Stat. 496
June 19, 1834, Ch. 54, 4 Stat. 678
June 22, 1838, Ch. 119, 5 Stat. 251
Sept. 4, 1841, Ch. 16, 5 Stat. 453
March 3, 1843, Ch. 86, 5 Stat. 619
March 3, 1873, Ch. 266, 17 Stat. 602
March 3, 1873, Ch. 283, 17 Stat. 609
April 21, 1876, Ch. 72, 19 Stat. 35
May 23, 1876, Ch. 104, 19 Stat. 55
March 3, 1879, Ch. 192, 20 Stat. 472, 43 U.S. Code § 251

Pre-emptive Rights Act (Corporate Shares)
Ohio Rev. Code 1953, 1701.15

Pre-Filing of Bills Act
Ill. Rev. Stat. 1991, Ch. 63, § 42.21 et seq.

Pre-Hospital Emergency Medical Services Act
Ill. Rev. Stat. 1979, Ch. 111 1/2, § 4101 et seq.

Pre-Internship Teaching Program
Cal. Education Code 1976, § 44305 et seq.

Pre-judgment Garnishment Act
Wis. Stat. Ann., 812.01 et seq.

Pre-K-16 Mathematics, Science, and Technology Improvement Act
Colo. Rev. Stat., 22-81-101 et seq

Pre-Lien Notice Act
Cal. Civil Code, §§ 3097, 3114

Pre-Need Cemetery Sales Act
Ill. Rev. Stat. 1991, Ch. 21, § 201 et seq.

Pre-Need Funeral Service Contract Act
Ga. Code Ann., 43-18-90 et seq.
N.M. Stat. Ann., 59A-49-1 et seq.
Utah Code Ann. 1953, 58-58-1 et seq.

Pre-Need Sales Act (Burial)
Neb. Rev. Stat. 1943, 12-1101 et seq.

Pre-Primary Convention Act
N.M. Stat. Ann. 1953, Superseded Vol.,
3-11-3 et seq.

Preadjudication Act
Ill. Rev. Stat. 1939, Ch. 120, § 812 et seq.

Prebankruptcy Statute (Cities)
N.Y. Local Finance Law (Consol. Laws Ch.
33A) § 85.00 et seq.

Precautions Act
Tenn. Code Ann., 65-12-108, 65-12-109

Precinct Boundary Adjustment Act
N.M. Stat. Ann., 1-3-10 et seq.

Precious Metal and Gem Dealer Act
Mich. Comp. Laws Ann., 445.481 et seq.
Okla. Stat. Ann., Title 59, § 1, 521 et seq.

**Precious Metal Object Dealers and
Pawnbrokers Act (Secondhand)**
Md. Ann. Code 1974, Art. BR, § 12-601 et
seq.

Precursor Substances Act
Okla. Stat. 1981, Title 63, § 2-321

**Precursors to Controlled Substances Act
(Regulation of)**
Haw. Rev. Stat. Ann., §§ 329-81 to 329-91
Haw. Rev. Stat. 1985, §§ 329-81 to 329-91

Predator Act (Sexually Violent)
Iowa Code Ann., 709C.1 et seq.

Predator Control Act (Counties)
N.M. Stat. Ann., 77-15-1 et seq.

Predators Act (Sexual)
Fla. Stat. Ann., 775.21 et seq.

Predatory Animal and Pest Control Act
Ill. Rev. Stat. 1991, Ch. 8, § 230 et seq.

Predatory Animal Bounty Act
Ore. Rev. Stat., 610.205 et seq.

Predatory Animal Control Act
Mont. Code Ann., 81-7-101 et seq.
S.D. Codified Laws 1967, 40-36-1 et seq.

Predatory Fish and Animal Law
Cal. Fish and Game Code 1957, §§ 3803,
4153, 5501

Predevelopment Assistance Act (Housing)
Fla. Stat. Ann., 420.303 et seq.

Predevelopment Loan Program Act
Fla. Stat. Ann., 420.521 et seq.

Preference Act (Laborers)
Wyo. Stat. Ann., § 16-6-201 et seq.

Preference Act (State Commerce)
Cal. Government Code, § 4330 et seq.

Preference Act (Veterans')
See Veterans' Preference Act

Preference Act (Water Rights)
Wyo. Stat. Ann., § 41-3-102

Preference in Employment Laws (Veterans)
S.D. Codified Laws 1967, 3-3-1 et seq.

Preference of Claims for Wages Act
Ill. Rev. Stat. 1991, Ch. 82, § 62.9 et seq.

Preference Procurement Act
P.R. Laws Ann. 1954, Title 3, § 918d et seq.

**Preference Procurement Policy Act of the
Government of Puerto Rico**
P.R. Acts 1989, No. 42

Preferences by Insolvent Corporations Act
Wash. Rev. Code Ann., 23.72.010 et seq.

**Preferential Assessment Act (Agricultural
Land)**
Fla. Stat. 1969, 193.071
Iowa Code Ann., 426.1 et seq.
Md. Ann. Code 1974, Art. TP, § 8-209 et seq.
Minn. Stat. Ann., 273.111
N.J. Stat. Ann., 54:4-23.2 et seq.
Ore. Rev. Stat., 308.370 et seq.

Preferential Assessment Act (Industries)
Ala. Code 1975, § 40-9-40 et seq.

Preferential Primary Election Act
Ark. Code Ann. 1987, § 7-8-306 et seq.

Preferential Voting Act
N.J. Stat. Ann., 40:75-1 et seq.

Preferred Provider Agreements Act
Me. Rev. Stat. Ann. 1964, Title 24-A, § 2670 et seq.
Mont. Laws 1991, Ch. 638

Preferred Provider Arrangement Act (Nonprofit Service Organizations)
Me. Rev. Stat. Ann. 1964, Title 24, § 2333 et seq.

Preferred Provider Arrangements Act
Ga. Code Ann., 33-30-20 et seq.

Preferred Provider Arrangements Law
N.M. Stat. Ann., 59A-22A-1 et seq.

Preferred Provider Organization Act
N.Y. Worker's Compensation Law (Consol. Laws Ch. 67) § 350 et seq.

Preferred Provider Organization and other Prepaid Health Benefits Plans Protection Act (HMO)
Miss. Code Ann. 1972, § 83-41-301 et seq.

Preferred Surety Bond Guarantee Program Act of 1988
Nov. 3, 1988, P.L. 100-590, 15 U.S. Code § 661 nt.

Pregnancy Birthing Center Licensing Act
Tex. Rev. Civ. Stat., Art. 244.001 et seq.

Pregnancy Discrimination Act
Oct. 31, 1978, P.L. 95-555, 42 U.S. Code § 2000e
D.C. Code Ann., § 46-111

Pregnancy Freedom of Choice Act
Cal. Statutes 1977, Ch. 1190

Pregnancy Prevention Act (Adolescent)
S.C. Code Ann. 1976, § 44-122-10 et seq.

Pregnancy Prevention Act (Teenage)
Cal. Penal Code § 261.5

Pregnancy Prevention and Services Act
N.Y. Social Services Law (Consol. Laws Ch. 55) § 465 et seq.

Pregnant and Parenting Womens Alternative Sentencing Program Act
Cal. Penal Code § 1174 et seq.

Prehistoric and Historic Sites Preservation Act
N.M. Stat. Ann., 18-8-1 et seq.

Prehospital Emergency Medical Care Personnel Act
Cal. Health and Safety Code, § 1797 et seq.

Prehospital Emergency Medical Care Personnel and Medical Services System Act
Cal. Health and Safety Code § 1797 et seq.

Prejudgment Attachment Act
Mont. Code Ann. 1991, 27-18-101 et seq.
N.C. Gen. Stat. 1943, § 1-440.1 et seq.
Wash. Rev. Code Ann., 6.25.010 et seq.

Prejudgment Remedies Act
Conn. Gen. Stat. Ann., § 52-278a et seq.

Prejudgment Replevin Act
Fla. Stat. Ann., 78.068

Premarital Agreement Act
See Uniform Premarital Agreement Act

Premarital Medical Examination Act
Mont. Code Ann., 40-1-203 et seq.

Premarital Medical Examination Act (Venereal Disease)
Ala. Code 1975, §§ 22-16-5, 22-16-6
Ark. Stat. 1947, 55-237 et seq.
Cal. Civil Code, § 4300 et seq.
Ga. Code Ann., 19-3-40 et seq.
Ill. Rev. Stat. 1991, Ch. 40, § 204
Continued

Mich. Comp. Laws Ann., 551.151 et seq.
Mont. Code Ann., 40-1-203 et seq.
Va. Code 1950, § 20-1 et seq.

Premises Liability Act
Ill. Rev. Stat. 1991, Ch. 80, § 301 et seq.

Premium Coupons Act
Cal. Business and Professions Code § 17700 et seq.

Premium Finance Company Act
Tenn. Code Ann., 56-37-101 et seq.

Premium Tax Act
Okla. Stat. Ann., Title 36, § 624

Premium Tax Act (Foreign Insurance Companies)
Kan. Stat. Ann., 40-252

Premiums Tax Act (Insurance)
Neb. Rev. Stat. 1943, 77-907 et seq.
Wash. Rev. Code Ann., 48.14.020 et seq.

Prenatal and Newborn Care Act
Ill. Rev. Stat. 1991, Ch. 111 1/2, § 7021 et seq.

Prenatal Blood Test Act (Syphilis)
Cal. Health and Safety Code, § 3220 et seq.
Conn. Gen. Stat. Ann., § 19a-90
Ill. Rev. Stat. 1991, Ch. 111 1/2, § 4800 et seq.
Okla. Stat. Ann., Title 63, §§ 1-515, 1-516
W. Va. Code 1966, § 16-4A-1 et seq.

Prenatal Care Act
N.Y. Public Health Law (Consol. Laws Ch. 45) § 2520 et seq.

Preneed Funeral Arrangement Act
Utah Code Ann. 1953, 58-58-1 et seq.

Preneed Funeral Consumer Protection Act
N.Y. General Business Law (Consol. Laws Ch. 20) § 453
N.Y. Public Health Law 1953 (Consol. Laws Ch. 45) §§ 3428, 3442, 3450

Preowned Home Warranty Service Company Act
Colo. Rev. Stat., 12-61-601 et seq.

Prepaid Affordable College Tuition Program
Miss. Code Ann. 1972, § 37-155-1 et seq.

Prepaid College Tuition Act (Wallace-Folsom)
Ala. Acts 1991, p. 1717

Prepaid Dental Care Plan Act
Colo. Rev. Stat., 10-16.5-101 et seq.
N.M. Stat. Ann., 59A-48-1 et seq.
Okla. Stat. Ann., Title 36, § 6, 141 et seq.

Prepaid Entertainment Contract Act
Ohio Rev. Code 1953, 1345.41 et seq.

Prepaid Funeral Contract Funding Act
Mich. Comp. Laws Ann., 328.211 et seq.

Prepaid Health Care Act
Haw. Rev. Stat. Ann., § 393-1 et seq.

Prepaid Health Clinic Act
Fla. Stat. Ann., 641.40 et seq.

Prepaid Health Plan Act (Waxman-Duffy)
Cal. Welfare and Institutions Code, § 14200 et seq.

Prepaid Legal Services Act
N.D. Cent. Code, 26.1-19-01 et seq.
Tex. Rev. Civ. Stat., Art. 320b

Prepaid Limited Health Service Organization Act
Fla. Stat. Ann., 632.002 et seq.
Neb. Rev. Stat. 1943, 44-4701 et seq.

Prepaid Tuition Act
Ill. Comp. Stat. 1992, Ch. 110, § 979/1 et seq.

Preparation Act (Award for Excellence in Teacher)
Ill. Rev. Stat. 1991, Ch. 40, § 2601 et seq.
Iowa Code Ann., 595A.1 et seq.
Me. Rev. Stat. Ann. 1964, Title 19, § 141 et seq.

N.C. Gen. Stat. 1943, § 52B-1 et seq.

N.D. Cent. Code, 14-03.1-01 et seq.

N.J. Stat. Ann., 34:2-31 et seq.

Ore. Rev. Stat., 108.700 et seq.

Tex. Family Code, § 5.41 et seq.

Va. Code 1950, § 20-147 et seq.

Wash. Rev. Code 1983, 28A.625.350 et seq.

Preparation Evaluation Act (Workforce)
N.Y. Executive Law 1951 (Consol. Laws Ch. 18) § 980 et seq.

Preparations for Stock and Poultry Act
S.C. Code Ann. 1976, § 46-27-820 et seq.

Preparedness Act
See Army Reorganization Acts

Preparedness Act (Emergency)
Kan. Stat. Ann., 48-904 et seq.

Prepayment of Federally Subsidized Mortgage Act (Notice of)
Ill. Rev. Stat. 1991, Ch. 67 1/2, § 901 et seq.

Preprosecution Diversion Act
N.M. Stat. Ann., 31-16A-1 et seq.

Prerogative Court Act
N.J. Stat. Ann., Superseded Vol., 2:30-1 et seq.

Presbyterian Act
N.J. Stat. Ann., 16:11-1 et seq.

Preschool Program Act
Colo. Rev. Stat., 22-28-101 et seq.

Preschool Special Education Act
Ala. Code 1975, § 16-39A-1 et seq.

Prescribed Burning Act
Ala. Code 1975, §   sect9-13-210, 9-13-270 to 9-13-274
Fla. Stat. Ann., 590.026
Ga. Code Ann., 12-6-145 et seq.
Miss. Code Ann. 1972, § 49-19-301 et seq.

Prescribed Child Care Center Regulatory Act
Tenn. Public Acts 1992, Ch. 1030

Prescribed Fire Act
S.C. Code Ann. 1976, § 48-34-10 et seq.

Prescription Act (Adverse Possession)
Tex. Rev. Civ. Stat., Art. 5507 et seq.

Prescription Act (Controlled Substances)
Tenn. Code Ann., 53-10-301 et seq.

Prescription Act (Criminal Prosecutions)
La. Code of Crim. Proc. 1966, Art. 571 et seq.

Prescription Act (Spirituous Liquor)
Del. Rev. Code 1935, § 6203

Prescription Act (Third Party)
Me. Rev. Stat. Ann. 1964, Title 32, § 13771 et seq.
Okla. Stat. Ann., Title 15, § 7, 81 et seq.

Prescription Drug Amendments of 1992
Aug. 26, 1992, P.L. 102-353, 21 U.S. Code § 301 nt.

Prescription Drug Distributors License Act (Wholesale)
Pa. 1992 Pamph. Laws, No. 145

Prescription Drug Marketing Act of 1987
April 22, 1988, P.L. 100-293, 21 U.S. Code §§ 301 nt., 333, 353 and nt., 381

Prescription Drug Payment Assistance Program
Del. Code of 1974, Title 16, § 3001 et seq.

Prescription Drug Price and Quality Stabilization Act
N.J. Stat. Ann., 24:6E-1 et seq.

Prescription Drug Price Information Act
D.C. Code Ann., § 33-701 et seq.

Prescription Drug User Fee Act of 1992
June 25, 1948, Ch. 644, 62 Stat. 672, 3 U.S. Code §§ 1 to 208
Jan. 19, 1949, Ch. 2, 63 Stat. 4, 3 U.S. Code §§ 102, 104, 111
Oct. 15, 1949, Ch. 695, 63 Stat. 880, 3 U.S. Code §§ 105, 106
Aug. 15, 1950, Ch. 715, 64 Stat. 448, 3 U.S. Code § 203
Continued

Oct. 20, 1951, Ch. 521, 65 Stat. 1781, 3 U.S.
Code §§ 102, 111

Oct. 31, 1951, Ch. 655, 65 Stat. 711, 3 U.S.
Code §§ 6, 11 to 13, 301 to 303

June 28, 1952, Ch. 481, 66 Stat. 283, 3 U.S.
Code § 203

June 20, 1953, Ch. 146, 67 Stat. 76, 3 U.S.
Code § 204

Sept. 3, 1954, Ch. 1263, 68 Stat. 1227, 3 U.S.
Code § 18

March 2, 1955, Ch. 9, 69 Stat. 11, 3 U.S.
Code § 104

July 31, 1956, Ch. 804, 70 Stat. 740, 3 U.S.
Code § 105

Aug. 1, 1958, P.L. 85-584, 72 Stat. 485, 3
U.S. Code § 204

Aug. 25, 1958, P.L. 85-745, 72 Stat. 838, 3
U.S. Code § 102 nt.

Oct. 4, 1961, P.L. 87-367, 75 Stat. 794, 3
U.S. Code § 105

Oct. 4, 1961, P.L. 87-389, 75 Stat. 820, 3
U.S. Code § 21; 5 U.S. Code § 2191 nt.

June 8, 1962, P.L. 87-481, 76 Stat. 95, 3 U.S.
Code §§ 202, 203

Aug. 14, 1964, P.L. 88-426, 78 Stat. 422, 3
U.S. Code §§ 104, 105

Sept. 9, 1965, P.L. 89-174, 79 Stat. 669, 3
U.S. Code § 19

Oct. 15, 1966, P.L. 89-670, 80 Stat. 948, 3
U.S. Code § 19

Dec. 23, 1967, P.L. 90-222, 81 Stat. 726, 3
U.S. Code § 105

Jan. 17, 1969, P.L. 91-1, 83 Stat. 3, 3 U.S.
Code § 102

Sept. 15, 1969, P.L. 91-67, 83 Stat. 106, 3
U.S. Code § 104

March 19, 1970, P.L. 91-217, 84 Stat. 74, 3
U.S. Code §§ 202 to 204, 206, 207

April 15, 1970, P.L. 91-231, 84 Stat. 198, 3
U.S. Code § 102 nt.

Aug. 12, 1970, P.L. 91-375, 84 Stat. 775, 3
U.S. Code § 19

Oct. 29, 1992, P.L. 102-571, 21 U.S. Code
§ 301 nt.

Prescription of Actions Act (Torts)
La. Civil Code, Art. 2315

Prescription Program Act (Third Party)
Me. Rev. Stat. Ann. 1964, Title 32, § 13771
et seq.

Prescription Tax Deed Act
Ga. Code 1933, 92-8315

Prescriptive Act (Statute of Limitations)
La. Civil Code, Art. 3457 et seq.

Prescriptive Authority Act (Pharmacist)
N.M. Stat. Ann., 61-11b-2 et seq.

**Prescriptive Right Prohibition Act
(Transmission Line)**
Ill. Rev. Stat. 1991, Ch. 134, §§ 14.9, 15

Prescriptive Teaching Act
Okla. Stat. Ann., Title 70, § 1210.271 et seq.

Preservation Act (Family)
Colo. Rev. Stat., 26-5.5-101 et seq.
Miss. Laws 1994, Ch. 607, §§ 22 to 26

Preservation Act (Historical)
Utah Code Ann. 1953, 9-8-501 et seq.

Preservation Act (Indian Family)
Minn. Stat. Ann., 257.35 et seq.

Preservation Act (Lottery Fund)
Pa. 1991 Pamph. Laws, No. 36

Preservation Act (Natural Areas)
Ill. Rev. Stat. 1991, Ch. 105, § 701 et seq.

Preservation Act (Natural Wild Rice)
Minn. Stat. Ann., 116J.645

Preservation Act (Property Rights)
Mich. Comp. Laws Ann., 24.421 et seq.

Preservation Act (State Rail)
Mo. Rev. Stat. 1978, 680.130 et seq.

Preservation Act (Unmarked Burial Sites)
Kan. Stat. Ann., 75-2741 et seq.

Preservation Act (Wild Flower)
Ga. Code Ann., 12-6-170 et seq.

**Preservation and Assistance Act (State
Railroad)**
Me. Rev. Stat. Ann. 1964, Title 23, § 7101 et
seq.

Preservation and Conservation Easements Act
Neb. Rev. Stat. 1943, 76-2, 111 et seq.

Preservation and Development Authority Act (Canal Place)
Md. Ann. Code 1974, Art. FI, § 13-1031

Preservation and Management of State Records and other Historical Records Act
Tex. Government Code, § 441.180 et seq.

Preservation and Restoration of Water Resources Act
Fla. Laws 1977, Ch. 77-369, § 1
Fla. Stat. Ann., 403.0615

Preservation and Trimming Act (Mangrove)
Fla. Stat. Ann., 403.9321 et seq.

Preservation Bond Act (Open Space)
N.J. Laws 1991, Ch. 183

Preservation District Act
Ga. Code Ann., 44-10-40 et seq.

Preservation Easement Act (Cultural Properties)
N.M. Stat. Ann., 47-12A-1 et seq.

Preservation of Business and Government Records Act
Wash. Rev. Code Ann., 40.20.010 et seq.

Preservation of Essential Records Act
Tex. Government Code, § 441.051 et seq.
W. Va. Code 1966, § 5-8-1 et seq.

Preservation of Essential Records and Records Management Act
W. Va. Code 1966, § 5A-8-1 et seq.

Preservation of Folklife Act
Minn. Stat. Ann., 138.81 et seq.

Preservation of Historical Documents Act
Ill. Rev. Stat. 1991, Ch. 128, § 17.9 et seq.

Preservation of Private Business Records Act
See also Uniform Preservation of Private Business Records Act
Ill. Rev. Stat. 1991, Ch. 116, § 59 et seq.
Md. Ann. Code 1974, Art. BR, § 1-301 et seq.
Md. Ann. Code 1974, Art. BR, § 1-307 et seq.
N.H. Rev. Stat. 1955, 337-A:1 et seq.
Okla. Stat. Ann., Title 67, § 251 et seq.

Preservation of Records Act
Mich. Comp. Laws 1948, 600.2148 et seq.

Preservation of Sheep Act
N.J. Laws 1901, C 160

Preservation 2000 Act
Fla. Stat. Ann., 259.101, Subsec. 3

Preserve Our Heritage Act
Utah Code Ann. 1953, 9-8-801 et seq., 63-11-1 et seq.

Preserved Farmland Tax Stabilization Act
Pa. Purdon's Stat., Title 72, § 5491.1 et seq.

President John F. Kennedy Assassination Records Collection Act of 1992
Oct. 26, 1992, P.L. 102-526, 44 U.S. Code 2107 nt.
Oct. 6, 1994, P.L. 103-345, 44 U.S. Code § 2107 nt.
July 3, 1997, P.L. 105-25, 44 U.S. Code § 2107 nt.

President John F. Kennedy Assassination Records Collection Extension Act of 1994
Oct. 6, 1994, P.L. 103-345, 44 U.S. Code § 2107 nt.

Presidential and Executive Office Accountability Act
Oct. 26, 1996, P.L. 104-331, 3 U.S. Code § 401 nt.

Presidential Ballot Law
N.J. Stat. Ann., 19:58-1 et seq.

Presidential Convention Delegate Act
Tenn. Code Ann., 2-13-301 et seq.

Presidential Election Act

Miss. Code Ann. 1972, § 23-11-1 et seq.

Presidential Election Campaign Fund Act

Dec. 10, 1971, P.L. 92-178, 85 Stat. 497, 26 U.S. Code § 9001

Presidential Election Campaign Fund Act of 1966

Nov. 13, 1966, P.L. 89-809, 80 Stat. 1587, 26 U.S. Code § 6096; 31 U.S. Code §§ 971 to 973

Presidential Elections New Resident Voters Act

See Uniform Act for Voting by New Residents in Presidential Elections

Presidential Electors Act

Ala. Code 1975, § 17-19-1 et seq.

Ga. Code Ann., 21-2-10 et seq.

Presidential Inaugural Ceremonies Act

Aug. 6, 1956, Ch. 974, 70 Stat. 1049, 36 U.S. Code §§ 721 to 729

Jan. 30, 1968, P.L. 90-251, 82 Stat. 4, 36 U.S. Code §§ 722, 723, 728, 730

D.C. Code Ann., § 1-1801 et seq.

Presidential Landmark Commission Act

Tenn. Code Ann., 4-11-301 et seq.

Presidential Libraries Act of 1986

May 27, 1986, P.L. 99-323, 44 U.S. Code § 101 nt.

Presidential Preference Primary Act

Ala. Code 1975, 17-18A-1 et seq.

D.C. Code Ann., §§ 1-1306, Subd. b, 1-1314

Ga. Code Ann., 21-2-190 et seq.

Minn. Laws 1949, Ch. 433

N.C. Gen. Stat. 1943, § 163-213.1 et seq.

Tenn. Public Acts 1971, Ch. 102

Presidential Primary Act

Cal. Elections Code 1976, § 6000 et seq.

Nev. Rev. Stat. 1979 Reprint, 298.095 et seq.

N.M. Stat. Ann., 1-8-53 et seq.

P.R. Laws Ann. 1954, Title 16, § 1321 et seq.

Presidential Primary Act (Open)

Cal. Elections Code 1976, § 6300 et seq.

Presidential Primary Act (Save the)

Cal. Elections Code 1961, §§ 2151, 13203, 13206, 13300 to 13302

Presidential Protection Assistance Act of 1976

Dec. 19, 1985, P.L. 99-190, 18 U.S. Code § 3056 nt.

Nov. 3, 1989, P.L. 101-136, 18 U.S. Code § 3056 nt.

Nov. 5, 1990, P.L. 101-509, 18 U.S. Code § 3056 nt.

Oct. 28, 1991, P.L. 102-141, 18 U.S. Code § 3056 nt.

Nov. 19, 1995, P.L. 104-52, 18 U.S. Code § 3056 nt.

Oct. 19, 1996, P.L. 104-316, 18 U.S. Code § 3056 nt.

Presidential Recordings and Materials Preservation Act

Oct. 19, 1984, P.L. 98-497, 44 U.S. Code §§ 2111 nt. et seq.

Presidential Records Act of 1978

Nov. 4, 1978, P.L. 95-591, 44 U.S. Code §§ 101 nt., 2107, 2108, 2201, 2201 nt., 2202 et seq.

Presidential Science and Technology Advisory Organization Act of 1976

May 11, 1976, P.L. 94-282, 42 U.S. Code §§ 6601 et seq.

Presidential Succession Act

Jan. 19, 1886, Ch. 4, 24 Stat. 1 (See 3 U.S. Code §§ 1, 19)

July 18, 1947, Ch. 264, 61 Stat. 380, 3 U.S. Code § 17

Presidential Transition Act of 1963

Aug. 17, 1963, P.L. 100-398, 102 Stat. 985, 3 U.S. Code § 102 nt.

March 7, 1964, P.L. 88-277, 78 Stat. 153, 3 U.S. Code § 102 nt.

Oct. 14, 1976, P.L. 94-499, 3 U.S. Code §§ 102 et seq.

Presidential Transitions Effectiveness Act

Aug. 17, 1988, P.L. 100-398, 102 Stat. 985, 3 U.S. Code § 102 nt.; 5 U.S. Code prec. §§ 3301, 3345, 3348, 5723

Presidential Voting Act

N.M. Laws 1967, Ch. 125

President's Emergency Food Assistance Act of 1984

Oct. 12, 1984, P.L. 98-473, 7 U.S. Code § 1728 nt., 1728a, 1728b

President's Media Commission on Alcohol and Drug Abuse Prevention Act

Oct. 27, 1986, P.L. 99-570, 21 U.S. Code §§ 1301 et seq., 1301 nt.

Presiding Officer of Educational Institution Act

Ill. Rev. Stat. 1991, Ch. 144, §§ 16m, 17

Presley-Brown Interagency Children's Services Act

Cal. Welfare and Institutions Code, § 18986 et seq.

Presley-Felando-Eaves Wiretap Act

Cal. Penal Code, § 629 et seq.

Presley-Lewis Air Quality Management Act

Cal. Health and Safety Code, § 40400 et seq.

Presley Urban Fishing Program Act

Cal. Public Resources Code § 5670 et seq.

Pressure Vessel and Boiler Safety Act

See Boiler and Pressure Vessel Safety Act

Pressure Vessels and Boilers Act

Me. Rev. Stat. Ann. 1964, Title 26, § 141 et seq.

Prestige License Plates Act

Ga. Code Ann., 40-2-60 et seq.

Preston School of Industry Act

Cal. Statutes 1937, Ch. 369, p. 1005, § 1000 et seq.

Presumed Decedents Act

Ohio Rev. Code 1953, 2121.01 et seq.
Pa. Cons. Stat., Title 51, § 9401

Presumption Act (Intoxicated Drivers)

S.D. Codified Laws 1967, 32-23-7

Presumption Act (Workmen's Compensation)

Mass. Gen. Laws. Ann., 152:7A

Presumptive Evidence Act (Tax Deeds)

Okla. Stat. Ann., Title 68, § 452

Pretended Title Act

Tenn. Code Ann., 66-4-201 et seq.

Preterition Act

N.Y. Estates, Powers and Trusts Law (Consol. Laws Ch. 17B) § 5-3.2

Pretermission Act

N.Y. Estates, Powers and Trusts Law (Consol. Laws Ch. 17B) § 5-3.2

Pretermitted Child Act (Wills)

Ala. Code 1975, § 43-8-91
Ark. Code Ann. 1987, 28-39-407, Subd. b
Cal. Probate Code, §§ 90, 91
Fla. Stat. Ann., 732.302
Ida. Code 1947, 15-2-302
Ky. Rev. Stat. 1971, 394.380
Mass. Gen. Laws. Ann., 191:20
Mo. Rev. Stat., 474.240
Mont. Rev. Code 1947, 91A-2-302
N.M. Stat. Ann., 45-2-301, 47-1-20, 47-1-21
Ohio Rev. Code 1953, 2107.34
Ore. Rev. Stat., 112.405
Tenn. Code Ann., 32-3-103

Pretermitted Heir Act (Wills)

Iowa Code Ann., 633.220, 633.267
Mich. Comp. Laws Ann., 700.127
Mont. Code Ann. 1947, 91-136
Nev. Rev. Stat. 1979 Reprint, 133.160 et seq.
Ore. Rev. Stat. 1953, 114.250
R.I. Gen. Laws 1956, 33-6-23
Wash. Rev. Code Ann., 11.12.090

Pretermitted Spouse Act (Wills)
Fla. Stat. Ann., 732.301

Pretrial Conference Act
Ga. Code 1933, 81-1013, 81-1014

Pretrial Criminal Procedure Act
N.C. Gen. Stat. 1943, § 15A-901 et seq.

Pretrial Examination Act
N.C. Gen. Stat. 1943, § 1-568.t et seq.
N.C. Rules of Civil Procedure, Rules 26-37

Pretrial Intervention Act
Miss. Code Ann. 1972, § 99-15-101 et seq.
S.C. Code Ann. 1976, § 17-22-10 et seq.

Pretrial Procedure Act
Ga. Code Ann., 17-7-1 et seq.
Kan. Stat. Ann., 60-216

Pretrial Services Act
Ill. Rev. Stat. 1991, Ch. 38, § 300 et seq.

Pretrial Services Act of 1982
Sept. 27, 1982, P.L. 97-267, 18 U.S. Code
§§ 3141 nt., 3152, 3152 nt., 3153 to 3155;
28 U.S. Code § 604

Prevailing Rate Equalization Adjustment Act of 1972
May 17, 1972, P.L. 92-298, 86 Stat. 146, 2
U.S. Code § 60a nt.; 5 U.S . Code § 5035 nt.

Prevailing Wage Act
Mich. Comp. Laws Ann., 408.551 et seq.

Prevailing Wage Act (Public Works)
Ohio Rev. Code 1953, 4115.03 et seq.
Ore. Rev. Stat., 279.348 et seq.
Tenn. Code Ann. 1955, 12-406 et seq.
Tex. Rev. Civ. Stat., Art. 5159a
Wash. Rev. Code Ann., 39.12.010 et seq.

Prevailing Wage Act (State Contracts)
Ind. Code Ann., 5-16-7-1 et seq.

Prevailing Wage Act (State Employee)
Ill. Rev. Stat. 1989, Ch. 127, §§ 390.9, 391
La. Rev. Stat. Ann., 38:2301
Mass. Gen. Laws. Ann., 149:26 et seq.

Mo. Rev. Stat., 290.210 et seq.
N.J. Stat. Ann., 34:11-56.25 et seq.
N.Y. Labor Law (Consol. Laws Ch. 31)
§ 220 et seq.
Pa. Purdon's Stat., Title 43, § 165-1 et seq.
Tenn. Code Ann., 12-4-401 et seq.
Wyo. Stat. Ann., § 27-4-401 et seq.

Prevailing Wage Rate Act
Cal. Labor Code, § 1770 et seq.
Ill. Rev. Stat. 1991, Ch. 48, § 39s-0.01 et seq.
Ky. Rev. Stat. 1971, 337.505 et seq.
N.Y. Labor Law (Consol. Laws Ch. 31)
§§ 220, 225-227

Prevent Pollution From Ships
Oct. 19, 1996, P.L. 104-324, 33 U.S. Code
§ 1905

Preventative Health Care Act (Children's)
Ark. Code 1987, 23-79-141

Prevention Act (Dropout)
Fla. Stat. Ann., 230.2316

Prevention and Control Act (Air Pollution)
Colo. Rev. Stat., 25-7-101 et seq.

Prevention and Intervention Act (Domestic Abuse)
P.R. Acts 1989, No. 54

Prevention and Protection Act (William and Budd Bell)
Fla. Stat. Ann., 39.001 et seq.

Prevention and Response Act (Oil Spill)
Cal. Government Code §§ 8574.1 et seq.,
8670.1 et seq.
Cal. Public Resources Code § 8750 et seq.

Prevention and Treatment Act (Osteoporosis)
Ala. Code 1975, § 22-13A-1 et seq.
Miss. Code Ann. 1972, § 41-93-1 et seq.

Prevention and Treatment Act (Substance Abuse)
Me. Rev. Stat. Ann. 1964, Title 5, § 20001 et
seq.

Prevention Code (Fire)
N.Y. Adm. Code '85, § 27-4001 et seq.

Prevention, Early Assistance, and Early Childhood Act
Fla. Stat. Ann., 411.201 et seq.

Prevention Law (Domestic Violence)
Cal. Family Code § 5510 et seq.

Prevention of Access by Children to Tobacco Products Act
Fla. Laws 1992, Ch. 285

Prevention of Child Abuse Act (Trust Fund)
Minn. Stat. Ann., 299A.20 et seq.

Prevention of Child Abuse and Neglect Act
D.C. Code Ann., § 6-2101 et seq.
Ohio Rev. Code 1953, 3109.13 et seq.

Prevention of Chronic Illness Act
N.J. Stat. Ann., 26:1A-92 et seq.

Prevention of Cruelty to Animals Act
Wash. Rev. Code Ann., 16.52.010 et seq.

Prevention of Domestic Violence Act
N.J. Stat. Ann., 2C:25-1 et seq.

Prevention of Homelessness Act
N.J. Stat. Ann., 52:27D-280 et seq.

Prevention of the Administration of Lie Detection Procedures Act
D.C. Code Ann., § 36-801 et seq.

Prevention of Youth Access to Tobacco Act
La. Rev. Stat. Ann., 14:91.8
Miss. Code Ann. 1972, §§ 45-37-1 et seq., 97-5-25, 97-5-43 to 97-5-47, 97-27-35
Okla. Stat. 1981, Title 37, § 600.1 et seq.

Prevention Program Act
Pa. Purdon's Stat., Title 35, § 6029.201 et seq.

Preventive Health Amendments of 1984
Oct. 30, 1984, P.L. 98-555, 42 U.S. Code §§ 201 nt., 247b, 247c, 300w, 300w-5, 300w-9, 300w-10

Preventive Health Amendments of 1992
Oct. 27, 1992, P.L. 102-531, 42 U.S. Code § 201 nt.

Preventive Health Amendments of 1993
Dec. 14, 1993, P.L. 103-183, 42 U.S. Code § 201 nt.

Price Act
Pa. Cons. Stat., Title 20, § 8301 et seq.

Price Act (Real Estate)
Pa. 1853 Pamph. Laws 503, No. 304

Price Adjustment Act of 1938
June 21, 1938, Ch. 554, 52 Stat. 819, 7 U.S. Code § 1302

Price and Hour Act (Barber's)
Utah Code Ann. 1953, Miscellaneous Superseded Code Provisions, 13-3-1 et seq.

Price Anderson Amendments Act of 1988
Aug. 20, 1988, P.L. 100-408, 102 Stat. 1066, 42 U.S. Code §§ 2011 nt., 2014, 2210, 2273, 2282a

Price Control Act
Ga. Code 1933, 106-401 et seq.

Price Control Act (New York City)
N.Y. Local Laws 1945, New York City, No. 34

Price Control Act of 1942
See Emergency Price Control Act of 1942

Price Control Extension Act of 1946
July 25, 1946, Ch. 671, 60 Stat. 664

Price Discrimination Act
See Robinson-Patman Price Discrimination Act
Ida. Code 1947, 48-201 et seq.
La. Rev. Stat. Ann., 51:331 et seq.
Minn. Stat. Ann., 325D.01 et seq.
Mont. Rev. Code 1947, 51-501 et seq.
N.M. Stat. Ann., 57-14-1 et seq.
Okla. Stat. Ann., Title 79, § 81 et seq.
Ore. Rev. Stat., 646.040

Price Fixing Act
Ga. Code 1933, 106-401 et seq.
Haw. Rev. Laws 1955, § 205-25
Mont. Code Ann. 1947, 51-101 et seq.
Wash. Rev. Code 1974, 19.89.010 et seq.

Price Fixing Act (Barbers)
N.M. Stat. Ann. 1953, 67-14-25 et seq.
Ore. Laws 1945, Ch. 198

Price Fixing Act (Fair Trade)
S.C. Code Ann. 1976, § 39-7-10 et seq.

Price Fixing Act (Food)
Ohio Rev. Code 1953, 1331.05

Price Fixing Act (Gasoline)
Tenn. Public Acts 1927, Ch. 22

Price Maintenance Act
Mont. Laws 1937, Ch. 42

Price Maintenance Act (Resale)
Mass. Gen. Laws 1984, 93:14E et seq.
Va. Code 1950, § 59.1-1 et seq.

Price Posting Act
Ill. Rev. Stat. 1977, Ch. 43, § 205 et seq.

Price Posting Act (Gasoline)
Wis. Stat. Ann., 100.18, Subsec. 8

Price Protection Act (Natural Gas)
Kan. Stat. Ann., 55-1401 et seq.

Pricing Law (Item)
N.Y. Agriculture and Markets Law (Consol. Laws Ch. 69) § 214i

Pridham Act (Liability of Public Officers)
See Cal. Government Code, § 1993
Cal. Statutes 1911, p. 1115

Priest Penitent Act
Del. Code of 1974, Title 10, § 4316
N.Y. Civil Practice Law and Rules (Consol. Laws Ch. 8) § 4505

Prieta-Loma Earthquake-Cypress Neighborhood Relief Act
Cal. Streets and Highways Code §§ 227, 227.1

Prima Facie Act (Railroads)
Miss. Code Ann. 1972, § 13-1-119

Prima Facie Evidence Act (Liquor)
Tex. Alcoholic Beverage Code, § 101.32

Prima Facie Speed Act
Ohio Rev. Code 1953, 4511.21

Prima Facie Tort Act
Ga. Code Ann., 51-1-6

Primaries Act
Pa. 1906 Ex. Pamph. Laws 36, No. 10
Pa. 1913 Pamph. Laws 719, No. 400

Primary Act (White)
Tex. Election Code, Art. 13.01 et seq.

Primary Care Capital Funding Act
N.M. Stat. Ann., 24-1C-1 et seq.

Primary Care Education and Training Act
N.Y. Public Health Law 1953 (Consol. Laws Ch. 45) § 900 et seq.

Primary Care Provider Act
Neb. Rev. Stat. 1943, 71-5210 et seq.

Primary Care Support Program Act
W. Va. Code 1966 § 16-2H-1 et seq.

Primary Class Cities Zoning Act
Neb. Rev. Stat. 1943, 15-901 et seq.

Primary Dealers Act of 1988
Aug. 23, 1988, P.L. 100-418, 102 Stat. 1386, 22 U.S. Code § 5341

Primary Election Act
Alaska Stat. 1962, § 15.25.010 et seq.
Ariz. Rev. Stat. Ann., § 16-201 et seq.
Ark. Stat. 1947, 3-101 et seq.
Cal. Elections Code 1961 § 2500 et seq.
Colo. Rev. Stat., 1-4-101 et seq.
Conn. Gen. Stat. Ann., § 9-372 et seq.

Del. Code of 1974, Title 15, § 3101 et seq.

Ga. Code Ann., 21-2-1 et seq.

Haw. Rev. Stat. Ann., § 12-1 et seq.

Ida. Code 1947, 34-701 et seq.

Ill. Rev. Stat. 1991, Ch. 46, § 7-1 et seq.

Ind. Code Ann., 3-10-1-1 et seq.

Iowa Code Ann., 43.1 et seq.

Kan. Stat. Ann., 25-202 et seq.

Ky. Rev. Stat. 1971, Superseded Vols., 119.010 et seq.

Ky. Rev. Stat. 1971, 118.105 et seq.

La. Rev. Stat. Ann., 18:401 et seq.

Mass. Gen. Laws. Ann., 53:23 et seq.

Md. Ann. Code 1957, Art. 33, § 12-1 et seq.

Me. Rev. Stat. Ann. 1964, Title 21-A, § 331 et seq.

Mich. Comp. Laws Ann., 168.531 et seq.

Minn. Stat. Ann., 204D.01 et seq.

Mo. Rev. Stat., 115.341 et seq.

Mont. Code Ann., 13-10-201 et seq.

N.C. Gen. Stat. 1943, § 163-104 et seq.

N.D. Cent. Code, 16.1-11-01 et seq.

Neb. Rev. Stat. 1943, 32-501 et seq.

Nev. Rev. Stat. 1979 Reprint, 293.175 et seq.

N.H. Rev. Stat. 1955, 56:1 et seq.

N.J. Stat. Ann., 19:23-1 et seq.

Ohio Rev. Code 1953, 3513.01 et seq.

Okla. Stat. Ann., Title 26, §§ 8-101 et seq., 5-114 et seq., 6-107 et seq.

Ore. Rev. Stat., 249.011 et seq.

R.I. Gen. Laws 1956, 17-15-1 et seq.

S.D. Codified Laws 1967, 12-6-1 et seq.

Tenn. Code Ann., 2-13-101 et seq.

Tex. Election Code, Art. 13.01 et seq.

Utah Code Ann. 1953, 20-3-1 et seq.

Vt. Stat. Ann., Title 17, § 2351 et seq.

Wash. Rev. Code Ann., 29.18.010 et seq., 29.21.010 et seq.

W. Va. Acts 1915, Ch. 26, § 28

W. Va. Code 1966, § 8-15-14 et seq.

Wyo. Stat. Ann., § 22-5-201 et seq.

Primary Election Act (Brundidge)
Ark. Stat. 1947, 3-204 et seq.

Primary Election Act (Direct)
Cal. Elections Code 1976, § 6400 et seq.

Primary Election Act (Municipalities)
W. Va. Acts 1915, Ch. 26, § 28
W. Va. Code 1966, § 8-15-14 et seq.

Primary Election Act (Presidential)
Cal. Elections Code 1976, § 6000 et seq.

Primary Election Act (Richards)
S.D. Laws 1911, Ch. 201
S.D. Laws 1917, Ch. 234

Primary Election Act (Run-Off)
Ark. Acts 1933, p. 109, No. 38

Primary Election Law
N.M. Stat. Ann., 1-8-10 et seq.

Primary Election Recount Act
Okla. Stat. Ann., Title 26, § 8-111 et seq.

Primary Financing Law (McKool-Stroud)
Tex. Election Code, § 173.001 et seq.

Primary Forest Product Assessment Act
N.C. Gen. Stat. 1943, § 113A-189 et seq.
S.C. Code Ann. 1976, § 48-30-10 et seq.

Primary Health Care Act (Rural)
N.M. Stat. Ann., 24-1A-1 et seq.

Primary Health Care Act of 1978
Nov. 10, 1978, P.L. 95-626, 42 U.S. Code §§ 201 nt., 254a, 254a-1, 254d nt., 256, 294t, 294u, 295h-1

Primary Health Care Practitioners Act
Pa. Purdon's Stat., Title 62, § 5001.1301 et seq.

Primary Health Care Services Act
Tex. Health and Safety Code, § 31.001 et seq.

Primary Highway Routes Act
Wash. Rev. Code Ann., 47.17.005 et seq.

Primary Highway Transportation Improvement District in Individual Localities Act
Va. Code 1950, § 15.1-1372.21 et seq.

Primary Highway Transportation Improvement District in Multi-County Areas Act
Va. Code 1950, § 15.1-1372.1 et seq.

Primary Recount Act
Ga. Code Ann., 21-2-495

Primary Reimbursement Act
Mich. Comp. Laws Ann., 168.624f

Primary Road Improvement Act (County)
Okla. Stat. Ann., Title 69, § 670 et seq.

Primary Road Law
Iowa Code Ann., 313.1 et seq.

Primitive Parks Act
Mont. Code Ann., 23-1-115 et seq.

Prince George's County Underground Storage Act
Md. Ann. Code 1974, Art. NR, § 6-201 et seq.

Principal and Income Act
See also Revised Uniform Principal and Income Act
See also Uniform Principal and Income Act
Conn. Public Acts 1999, No. 164
La. Rev. Stat. Ann., 9:2141 et seq.

Principal and Income Act (Revised)
See also Revised Uniform Principal and Income Act
Ind. Code 1971, 30-4-5-2 et seq.
N.C. Gen. Stat. 1943, § 37-16 et seq.
Neb. Rev. Stat. 1943, 30-3101 et seq.
Okla. Stat. Ann., Title 60, § 175.1 et seq.
Ore. Rev. Stat., 129.005 et seq.
Pa. Cons. Stat., Title 20, § 8101 et seq.
S.D. Codified Laws 1967, 55-13-1 et seq.
Tex. Property Code, § 113.101 et seq.
Utah Code Ann. 1953, 22-3-1 et seq.
Va. Code 1950, § 55-253 et seq.
Wash. Rev. Code Ann., 11.104.010 et seq.
Wis. Stat. Ann., 701.20
W. Va. Code 1966, § 36-6-1 et seq.
Wyo. Stat. Ann., § 2-3-101 et seq.

Principal and Income Act (Tenants and Remaindermen)
Cal. Statutes 1947, p. 2476

Principal Employer Act
Conn. Public Acts 1991, p. 1735, Ch. 138

Principal Liability Act (Workmen's Compensation)
Kan. Stat. Ann., 44-503

Principals' and Teachers' Contracts Termination Act
N.C. Gen. Stat. 1943, § 115-142

Pringle Act (Motor Vehicles)
Ohio Laws Vol. 114, p. 173

Pringle-Roberts Act (Bonds)
Ohio Laws Vol. 114, p. 11

Print Access Aids for Visionary Disabled Persons Law
Tex. Government Code, § 441.111 et seq.

Printers' Ink Act (False Advertising)
Conn. Gen. Stat. Ann., § 42-115a
Fla. Stat. Ann., 817.06
Ga. Code Ann., 10-1-420 et seq.
Ill. Rev. Stat. 1991, Ch. 121 1/2, § 157.21a et seq.
Iowa Code Ann., 714.16
Mass. Gen. Laws. Ann., 266:91
Ohio Rev. Code 1953, 2911.41
Wis. Stat. Ann., 100.18

Printing Act
March 21, 1961, P.L. 87-2, 75 Stat. 5 (See 44 U.S. Code § 906)

Printing Act (State and Public)
Ark. Stat. 1947, 14-301 et seq.
Ind. Code Ann., 4-13-4.1-1 et seq.
Mich. Comp. Laws 1948, 19.151 et seq.
Mo. Rev. Stat. 1969, 34.0170 et seq.
S.C. Code Ann. 1976, § 11-25-10 et seq.

Printing and Binding Acts
Jan. 12, 1895, Ch. 23, 28 Stat. 601, 1 U.S.
Code § 30; 15 U.S. Code § 187; 31 U.S.
Code § 589; 43 U.S. Code § 1457
March 2, 1901, No. 16, 31 Stat. 1464
Jan. 20, 1905, Ch. 50, 33 Stat. 610
March 30, 1906, No. 13, 34 Stat. 825
March 1, 1907, Ch. 2284, 34 Stat. 1012
Jan. 15, 1908, No. 3, 35 Stat. 565
April 19, 1949, Ch. 72, 63 Stat. 48
Sept. 23, 1950, Ch. 1001, 64 Stat. 980
July 10, 1952, Ch. 632, 66 Stat. 540
July 11, 1961, P.L. 87-85, 75 Stat. 202

Printing and Public Documents Act
N.Y. Consol. Laws Ch. 58

Printing Control Act
Mont. Code Ann., 18-7-301 et seq.

Printing Council Act
Wyo. Session Laws 1967, Ch. 235

Priolo-Alquist Earthquake Fault Zoning Act
Cal. Public Resources Code § 2621 et seq.

Priolo-Alquist Geologic Hazard Zones Act
Cal. Public Resources Code, § 2621 et seq.

Priolo-Alquist Special Studies Zones Act
Cal. Public Resources Code, § 2621 et seq.

Prior Conviction Act
Ariz. Rev. Stat. Ann., § 13-604
Mo. Rev. Stat. 1969, 556.280
Nev. Rev. Stat. 1979 Reprint, 207.010

Prior Lien Law (Tenement Houses)
N.Y. Multiple Dwelling Law 1946 (Consol.
Laws Ch. 61A) § 307

Prior Offender Act
Mont. Code Ann. 1947, 94-4713 et seq.

Priorities Act
Fla. Laws 1941, Ch. 20855

Priorities Act (Merchant Ship)
Cal. Probate Code, § 16300 et seq.
Fla. Stat. 1973, 690.01 et seq.
Ida. Code 1947, 68-1001 et seq.

Ill. Rev. Stat. 1991, Ch. 30, § 501 et seq.
Ky. Rev. Stat. 1971, 386.190 et seq.
La. Rev. Stat. Ann., 9:241 et seq.
Mich. Comp. Laws Ann., 555.51 et seq.
Minn. Stat. Ann., 501B.59 et seq.

Priorities and Allocations Act
June 28, 1940, Ch. 440, 54 Stat. 676, 41 U.S.
Code § 40; 42 U.S. Code §§ 1501 to 1505

Priority Act (Claims against Estates)
Ore. Rev. Stat., 115.001

Priority of Shipments Act (Railroads)
Aug. 10, 1917, Ch. 51, 40 Stat. 272

Priority Social Services Act
Me. Rev. Stat. Ann. 1964, Title 22, § 6101 et
seq.

Prison Act
Mich. Comp. Laws Ann., 800.33 et seq.
N.J. Stat. Ann., 30:4-136 et seq.
N.Y. Correction Law (Consol. Laws Ch. 43)

Prison and Jail Authority Act
W. Va. Code 1966, § 31-20-1 et seq.

Prison and Parole Act
Ill. Rev. Stat. 1991, Ch. 38, § 1003-14-2 et
seq.

Prison Board Act (Second Class County)
Pa. Purdon's Stat., Title 61, § 407.1 et seq.

Prison Construction Bond Act (New)
Cal. Penal Code, §§ 7300 et seq., 7400 et
seq., 7420 et seq.

Prison Escape Act
Aug. 3, 1935, Ch. 432, 49 Stat. 513 (See 18
U.S. Code § 751)
Mich. Comp. Laws Ann., 750.193 et seq.
Pa. Cons. Stat., Title 18, § 5121
Wash. Rev. Code Ann., 9A.76.110 et seq.

Prison Facilities Improvement Act
Pa. Purdon's Stat., Title 61, § 390.101 et seq.

Prison Facilities Legislative Bond Act
N.C. Laws 1990, Ch. 933

Prison Farm Act
Ky. Acts 1914, Ch. 52

Prison Farm and Road Camp Act
Cal. Penal Code, § 4100 et seq.

Prison Goods Label Act
Tex. Rev. Civ. Stat., Art. 6166z8

Prison Goods Sales Act
Cal. Penal Code, § 2880 et seq.
Tex. Rev. Civ. Stat., Art. 9007

Prison Industries Act
Ga. Code Ann., 42-10-1 et seq.
Ill. Rev. Stat. 1991, Ch. 38, § 1003-13-1 et seq.
Mich. Comp. Laws Ann., 800.321 et seq.
Miss. Code Ann. 1972, § 47-5-531 et seq.
N.M. Stat. Ann., 33-8-1 et seq.

Prison Industry Enhancement Program
Miss. Code Ann. 1972, § 47-5-1251

Prison Inmate Care and Custody Reimbursement Act (County)
Colo. Rev. Stat., 17-26-201 et seq.

Prison Inmate Care and Custody Reimbursement Act (State)
Colo. Rev. Stat., 17-10-101 et seq.

Prison Inmate Training Reform Act
La. Rev. Stat. Ann., 15:731 to 15:733

Prison Inspection Act
Ill. Rev. Stat. 1991, Ch. 38, § 1101 et seq.

Prison Labor Act
Colo. Rev. Stat., 27-24-101 et seq.
Wis. Stat. Ann., 303.01 et seq.

Prison Literacy Act
Cal. Penal Code § 2053
Ga. Code Ann., 42-12-1 et seq.

Prison Litigation Reform Act of 1995
April 26, 1996, P.L. 104-134, Title VIII, 18 U.S. Code § 3601 nt.

Prison Made Goods Act
Ala. Code 1975, § 14-7-6 et seq.
Ark. Code Ann. 1987, 12-30-202 et seq.
Haw. Rev. Stat. Ann., § 354-1 et seq.
Kan. Stat. Ann., 75-5273 et seq.
La. Rev. Stat. Ann., 51:691 et seq.
Mont. Laws 1953, Ch. 162
R.I. Gen. Laws 1956, 13-7-1 et seq.
Wash. Rev. Code 1979, 19.20.010 et seq.
W. Va. Code 1966, § 28-5B-1 et seq.

Prison-Made Goods Act
Tex. Government Code, § 497.021
Tex. Government Code, § 497.021 et seq.

Prison Medical Services Act
Pa. Purdon's Stat., Title 61, § 1011 et seq.

Prison Overcrowding Emergency Powers Act
Ark. Code Ann. 1987, 12-28-601 et seq.
Mich. Comp. Laws Ann., 800.71 et seq.
Miss. Code Ann. 1972, § 47-5-701 et seq.
Miss. Code Ann. 1972, § 47-5-701 et seq.
Okla. Stat. 1981, Title 57, § 570 et seq.
S.C. Code Ann. 1976, § 24-3-1110 et seq.

Prison Overcrowding Reform Act
Wash. Rev. Code Ann., 9.95.380 et seq.

Prison Population Management Act
Okla. Stat. Ann., Title 57, § 610 et seq.

Prison Program (Special Needs)
Miss. Laws 1994, Ch. 450

Prison Reform Act
Ga. Code Ann., 42-4-6, 42-5-57, 42-5-3, 42-5-4

Prison Reimbursement Act
Mich. Comp. Laws Ann., 800.401 et seq.

Prison Reorganization Act
Cal. Penal Code, § 5000 et seq.

Prison Sentences Good Time Act
Mass. Gen. Laws Ann., 127:129

Prison System Improvement Act
Tex. Rev. Civ. Stat., Art. 6203c, Tex. Government Code, § 496.001 et seq.

Prison Testing Act of 1988
Nov. 4, 1988, P.L. 100-607, 42 U.S. Code §§ 300ee-6, 300ee-6 nt.

Prison Use Act
S.C. Code Ann. 1976, § 24-3-10 et seq.

Prison Visitation Act (Official)
Pa. Purdon's Stat., Title 61, § 1091 et seq.

Prisoner Interchange Act
Ill. Rev. Stat. 1991, Ch. 75, §§ 60, 61

Prisoner Literacy Act
Cal. Penal Code, § 2053

Prisoner Litigation Reform Act
Mo. Rev. Stat., 547.200 et seq.

Prisoner of War Bonus Act
Ill. Rev. Stat. 1991, Ch. 126 1/2, § 57.60 et seq.

Prisoner Production Expense Act
Ill. Rev. Stat. 1991, Ch. 38, §§ 156-10, 156-11

Prisoner Rehabilitation Act
Tenn. Code Ann., 41-21-501 et seq.

Prisoner Reimbursement to the County Act
Mich. Comp. Laws Ann., 801.81 et seq.

Prisoners as Witnesses Extradition Act
Wis. Stat. Ann., 976.01

Prisoners as Witnesses in Criminal Proceedings Act (Rendition of)
See Uniform Rendition of Witnesses in Criminal Proceedings Act
Me. Rev. Stat. Ann. 1964, Title 15, § 1464 et seq.

Prisoners as Witnesses in Criminal Proceedings Act (Rendition)
See also Uniform Rendition of Prisoners as Witnesses in Criminal Proceedings Act
Ida. Code 1947, 19-3013 et seq.

Kan. Stat. Ann., 22-4207 et seq.
Ky. Rev. Stat. 1971, 421.600 et seq.
Mich. Comp. Laws Ann., 780.111 et seq.

Prisoners' Employment Law
Cal. Penal Code, § 2700 et seq.

Prisoners of War Compensation Act (Vietnam Conflict)
Pa. Cons. Stat., Title 51, § 2015 et seq.

Prisoners Public Works Act
Okla. Stat. Ann., Title 57, § 215 et seq.

Prisoners' Road Work Law
Cal. Penal Code, § 2760 et seq.

Prisoner's Statement Act
Ga. Code Ann., 24-9-20

Prisons and Prisoners Treatment and Corrections Act
Neb. Rev. Stat. 1943, 83-170 et seq.

Prisons and Reformations Good Time Act
Ind. Code 1976, 11-7-6.1-1 et seq.

Privacy Act
Cal. Civil Code, §§ 1798.1 et seq., 3344
Conn. Gen. Stat. Ann., § 4-190 et seq.
Ga. Code Ann., 50-32-1 et seq.
Ind. Code 1982, 4-1-6-1 et seq.
Mass. Gen. Laws. Ann., 66A:1 et seq.
Minn. Stat. Ann., 13.01 et seq.
N.Y. Civil Rights Law (Consol. Laws Ch. 6) §§ 50, 51
Ohio Rev. Code 1953, 1347.01 et seq.
Utah Code Ann. 1953, 76-9-401 et seq.
Va. Code 1950, § 8.01-40
Wash. Rev. Code Ann., 9.73.010 et seq.

Privacy Act (Communications Consumer)
Conn. Gen. Stat. Ann., § 53-420 et seq.

Privacy Act (Consumer Communications)
Ill. Rev. Stat. 1991, Ch. 38, § 87-1 et seq.

Privacy Act (Employee)
N.M. Stat. Ann., 50-11-1 et seq.

Privacy Act (Financial Records)
Tenn. Code Ann., 45-10-101 et seq.

Privacy Act (Financial)
N.C. Gen. Stat. 1943, § 53B-1 et seq.

Privacy Act (Library)
Mich. Comp. Laws Ann., 397.601 et seq.
N.M. Stat. Ann., 18-9-1 et seq.

Privacy Act (Omnibus)
Ark. Stat. 1947, 16-801 et seq.

Privacy Act (Reproductive)
Wash. Laws 1992, Ch. 1

Privacy Act (Video Consumer)
N.Y. General Business Law (Consol. Laws Ch. 20) § 670 et seq.

Privacy Act of 1974
June 1, 1977, P.L. 95-38, 5 U.S. Code § 552a nt.

Privacy Impact Statement
N.Y. Public Officers Law (Consol. Laws Ch. 47) § 93

Privacy of Child Victims of Criminal Sexual Offenses Act
Ill. Rev. Stat. 1991, Ch. 38, § 1451 et seq.

Privacy of Communications Act
Minn. Stat. Ann., 626A.01 et seq.

Privacy Protection Act
N.Y. Public Officers Law (Consol. Laws Ch. 47) § 91 et seq.
Va. Code 1950, § 2.1-377 et seq.

Privacy Protection Act (Cable Subscriber)
N.J. Stat. Ann., 48:5A-54 et seq.

Privacy Protection Act of 1980
Oct. 13, 1980, P.L. 96-440, 42 U.S. Code § 2000aa nt.
Sept. 30, 1996, P.L. 104-208, 42 U.S. Code § 2000aa

Privacy Protection for Rape Victims Act of 1978
Oct. 28, 1978, P.L. 95-540, 28 U.S. Code Appx. 412, 412 nt., 1103 nt.

Privacy, Security, and Dissemination of Criminal History Information Act
Neb. Rev. Stat. 1943, 29-3501 et seq.

Private Academic Schools Act
Pa. Purdon's Stat., Title 24, § 6701 et seq.

Private Activity Bond Allocation Act
Ark. Code Ann. 1987, 15-5-501 et seq.
Fla. Stat. Ann., 159.801 et seq.
Ga. Code Ann., 36-82-182 et seq.
Ill. Rev. Stat. 1991, Ch. 17, § 6851 et seq.
Iowa Code Ann., 7C.1 et seq.
Kan. Stat. Ann., 74-5058 et seq.
Miss. Code Ann. 1972, § 31-23-1 et seq.
Mont. Code Ann. 1985, 17-5-1201 et seq.
N.M. Stat. Ann., 60-20-1 et seq.
N.Y. General Municipal Law (Consol. Laws Ch. 24) § 850 nt.
N.Y. Laws 1990, Ch. 47
N.Y. Laws 1991, Chs. 43, 337
N.Y. Laws 1992, Ch. 60
N.Y. Laws 1995, Ch. 127
N.Y. Laws 1996, Ch. 104, § 2
N.Y. Laws 1997, Ch. 115
N.Y. Laws 1998, Ch. 426
Okla. Stat. Ann., Title 62, § 695.21 et seq.
Va. Code 1950, § 15.1-1399.10 et seq.

Private Activity Bond Ceiling Allocation Act
Colo. Rev. Stat., 24-32-1701 et seq.
Utah Code Ann. 1953, 11-17a-1 et seq.

Private Activity Bond Ceiling Redistribution Act
N.Y. Laws 1988, Ch. 772

Private Activity Bond Volume Cap Allocation Act
N.J. Stat. Ann., 49:2A-1 et seq.

Private and Community Mausoleum and Columbarium Law
Cal. Health and Safety Code, § 9501 et seq.

Private and Mutual Water Service Law
Cal. Public Utilities Code, § 2725 et seq.

Private Attorney General Statute
Cal. Code of Civil Procedure § 1021.5

Private Bank License Act
Pa. Purdon's Stat., Title 72, § 2221 et seq.

Private Banking Act
Ind. Code Ann., 28-2-1-1 et seq.
N.Y. Banking Law (Consol. Laws Ch. 2) § 160 et seq.
Pa. Purdon's Stat., Title 7, § 1901 et seq.

Private Bulk Grain Storage Law
Cal. Civil Code, § 1880 et seq.
Nev. Rev. Stat. 1957, 103.010 et seq.

Private Business and Vocational Schools Act
Ill. Rev. Stat. 1991, Ch. 144, § 136 et seq.

Private Business Corporation Act
Wash. Rev. Code Ann., 23A.04.010 et seq.

Private Business Records Preservation Act
Md. Ann. Code 1974, Art. BR, § 1-307 et seq.
Okla. Stat. Ann., Title 67, § 251 et seq.

Private Business Schools Act
Pa. Purdon's Stat., Title 24, § 2751 et seq.

Private Business, Trade and Correspondence School Act
Minn. Stat. Ann., 141.21 et seq.

Private Car Ad Valorem Tax Law
Mo. Rev. Stat., 137.1000 to 137.1030

Private Car Line Company Act (Taxation)
Ill. Rev. Stat. 1981, Ch. 120, § 372.1 et seq.

Private Car Tax Law
Cal. Revenue and Taxation Code, § 11201 et seq.

Private Carriers Act
Colo. Rev. Stat., 40-11-101 et seq.
Tex. Rev. Civ. Stat., Art. 911b, §§ 1a, 1b

Private Carriers' Registration Act
Cal. Public Utilities Code, §§ 4000 to 4002, 4005 to 4008, 4010, 4015, 4020, 4021

Private College Act
Ill. Rev. Stat. 1991, Ch. 144, § 120 et seq.

Private College Campus Police Act
Ill. Rev. Stat. 1991, Ch. 144, §§ 1950, 1951

Private Colleges and Universities Facilities Authority Act
Ala. Code 1975, § 16-18A-1 et seq.
Ga. Code Ann., 20-3-200 et seq.

Private Contractors License Act (Plumbers)
Ida. Code 1947, 54-2601 et seq.

Private Corporations Act
P.R. Laws Ann. 1954, Title 14, § 1101 et seq.

Private Correctional Facility Moratorium Act
Ill. Rev. Stat. 1991, Ch. 38, § 1581 et seq.

Private Detective Agencies and Private Detectives Law
Wash. Rev. Code Ann., 18.165.010 et seq.

Private Detective and Private Security Agencies Act
Cal. Business and Professions Code, § 7500 et seq.
Ga. Code Ann., 43-38-1 et seq.
Ill. Rev. Stat. 1987, Ch. 111, § 2651 et seq.
Ill. Rev. Stat. 1991, Ch. 111, § 2651 et seq.
Md. Ann. Code 1974, Art. BP, § 13-801 et seq.
Mich. Comp. Laws Ann., 338.821 et seq.
N.D. Cent. Code, 43-30-01 et seq.
N.J. Stat. Ann., 45:19-8 to 45:19-27
N.Y. General Business Law (Consol. Laws Ch. 20) § 70 et seq.
Pa. Purdon's Stat., Title 22, § 11 et seq.
P.R. Laws Ann. 1954, Title 25, § 285 et seq.
R.I. Gen. Laws 1956, 5-5-1 et seq.
S.C. Code Ann. 1976, § 40-17-10 et seq.
Tex. Rev. Civ. Stat., Art. 4413(29bb)

Private Detective, Private Alarm and Private Security Act

Ill. Comp. Stat. 1992, Ch. 225, § 446/1 et seq.

Private Detectives' and Private Investigators' Licensing Act

N.Y. General Business Law (Consol. Laws Ch. 20) § 70 et seq.

Private Drainage Rights Act

Mo. Rev. Stat., 244.010 et seq.

Private Dwelling Discrimination and Segregation Act (New York City)

N.Y. City Adm. Code 1938, Ch. 1, § B1-7.0, Subd. 5

Private Elementary and Secondary Education Authorization Act

Nev. Rev. Stat. 1979 Reprint, 394.201 et seq.

Private Employer Alcohol and Drug-Free Workplace Act

Ida. Code 1947, 72-1701 et seq.

Private Employment Agency Act

Ark. Code Ann. 1987, 11-11-201 et seq.

Cal. Business and Professions Code, § 9900 et seq.

Colo. Rev. Stat., 12-24-101 et seq.

Fla. Stat. Ann., 449.01 et seq.

Ga. Code Ann., 34-10-1 et seq.

Ill. Rev. Stat. 1991, Ch. 111, § 900 et seq.

Mich. Comp. Laws Ann., 338.2001 et seq.

Ohio Rev. Code 1953, 4143.01 et seq.

S.C. Code Ann. 1976, § 41-25-10 et seq.

Tenn. Code Ann., 62-31-101 et seq.

Tex. Rev. Civ. Stat., Art. 5221a-7

Private Investigator and Adjuster Act

Cal. Business and Professions Code, § 7500 et seq.

Private Investigators and Detectives Act

Cal. Business and Professions Code § 7512 et seq.

Private Investigators and Polygraphers Act

N.M. Stat. Ann., 61-27A-1 et seq.

Private Investigators and Private Securities Agencies Act

Ark. Code Ann. 1987, 17-33-101 et seq. 3(29bb)

Cal. Business and Professions Code, § 7512 et seq.

Me. Rev. Stat. Ann. 1964, Title 32, § 8101 et seq.

N.M. Stat. Ann., 61-27-1 et seq.

Okla. Stat. Ann., Title 59, § 1750.1 et seq.

Tenn. Code Ann., 62-26-201 et seq.

Tex. Rev. Civ. Stat., Art. 4413(29bb)

Vt. Stat. Ann., Title 26, § 3151 et seq.

Private Investigators and Private Security Agencies Act

Del. Code of 1974, Title 24, § 1301 et seq.

Private Licensed Schools Act

Pa. Purdon's Stat., Title 24, § 6501 et seq.

Private Liquor Club Act

Kan. Stat. Ann., 41-2601 et seq.

Private Medical Scholarship Agreement Act

Ill. Rev. Stat. 1991, Ch. 144, § 2700 et seq.

Private Motor Carrier Act

Ohio Rev. Code 1953, 4923.02 et seq.

Private Non-profit Institutions of Higher Learning Educational Facilities Authority Act

Miss. Code Ann. 1972, § 37-104-1 et seq.

S.C. Code Ann. 1976, § 59-109-10 et seq.

Private Nonvested Pension Benefits Protection Tax Act

N.J. Laws 1973, Ch. 124

R.I. Gen. Laws 1956, 28-46-1 et seq.

Private Nursing Homes and Hospital Act

Pa. 1931 Pamph. Laws 510, No. 165

Private Occupational Certification Act

Conn. Gen. Stat. Ann., § 10-7a et seq.

Private Occupational Education Act

Colo. Rev. Stat., 12-59-101 et seq.

Private Ownership of Special Nuclear Materials Act

Aug. 26, 1964, P.L. 88-489, 78 Stat. 602, 42 U.S. Code §§ 2012, 2013, 2072 nt., 2073 to 2078, 2135, 2153, 2201, 2221, 2233, 2234

Private Partnership Act (Business Relocation Mission)

N.J. Stat. Ann., 34:1B-88 et seq.

Private Passenger Motor Vehicle Safety Act

Cal. Vehicle Code 1959, § 27315

Private Pension Benefits Protection Act

Minn. Stat. Ann., 181B.01 et seq.

Private Personnel Placement Services Act

S.C. Code Ann. 1976, § 41-25-10 et seq.

Private Postsecondary and Vocational Education Reform Act

Cal. Education Code 1976, § 94700 et seq.

Private Prison Contracting Act

Tenn. Code Ann., 41-24-101 et seq.

Private Prison Enabling and Contracting Act

W. Va. Code 1966 § 25-5-1 et seq.

Private Prison Moratorium and Study Act

Pa. Purdon's Stat., Title 61, § 1081 et seq.

Private Probation Provider Licensing Act

Utah Code Ann. 1953, 58-56-1 et seq.

Private Property Assessment Act

Mont. Code Ann., 2-10-101 et seq.

Private Property Protection Act

Kan. Stat. Ann., 77-701 et seq.
Utah Code Ann. 1953, 78-34a-1 et seq.

Private Property Rights Act (Ombudsman for)

Ariz. Rev. Stat. Ann., § 41-1311 et seq.

Private Property Rights Protection Act (Bert J. Harris, Jr.)

Fla. Stat. Ann., 70.001

Private Protective Services Licensing and Regulatory Act

N.C. Gen. Stat. 1943, § 74C-1 et seq.
Tenn. Code Ann., 62-35-101 et seq.

Private Railroad Car Tax Act

Cal. Revenue and Taxation Code, § 11201 et seq.

Private Real Property Protection Act

W. Va. Code 1966, § 22-1A-1 et seq.

Private Real Property Rights Preservation Act

Ga. Code Ann., 22-5-1 et seq.

Private Road Act

Tenn. Code Ann., 54-14-101 et seq.

Private School Corporation Act

Fla. Stat. Ann., 623.01 et seq.

Private School Licensing Act

Wyo. Stat. Ann., § 21-11-101 et seq.

Private Schools Act

Okla. Stat. Ann., Title 70, § 21-101 et seq.

Private Schools Building Safety Act

Cal. Education Code 1976, § 39160 et seq.

Private Schools, Equal Opportunity Education Assistance Act

La. Rev. Stat. Ann., 17:2990.1 et seq.

Private Schools Free Transportation Act

Conn. Gen. Stat. Ann., § 10-281

Private Seal Abolishment Act

Ill. Rev. Stat. 1991, Ch. 30, §§ 153a.9, 153b

Private Sector and Education Partnership Act

Fla. Stat. Ann., 229.602

Private Securities Litigation Reform Act of 1995

Dec. 22, 1995, P.L. 104-67, 15 U.S. Code § 78a nt.

Private Security Guard Act
La. Rev. Stat. Ann., 37:3171 et seq.
Me. Rev. Stat. Ann. 1964, Title 32, § 9401 et seq.
Mich. Comp. Laws Ann., 338.1051 et seq.
R.I. Gen. Laws 1956, 5-5.1-1 et seq.

Private Sewage Disposal Licensing Act
Ill. Rev. Stat. 1991, Ch. 111 1/2, § 116.301 et seq.

Private Shooting Preserve Act
S.D. Codified Laws 1967, 41-10-1 et seq.

Private Technical and Trade School Registration Act
Ind. Code Ann., 20-12-62-1 et seq.

Private Trade Schools Act
Mich. Comp. Laws Ann., 395.101 et seq.
N.Y. Education Law 1947 (Consol. Laws Ch. 16) § 5001 et seq.
Pa. Purdon's Stat., Title 24, § 1725.1 et seq.

Private Vocational Educational Authorization Act
Neb. Rev. Stat. 1943, 79-2801 et seq.

Private Vocational School Act
Colo. Rev. Stat., 12-59-101 et seq.

Private Well Construction Act
Va. Code 1950, § 32.1-176.1 et seq.

Private Works Act
La. Rev. Stat. Ann., 9:4801 et seq.

Privately Operated Colleges Act
Ill. Rev. Stat. 1991, Ch. 144, § 121 et seq.

Privatization Act
Ark. Code Ann. 1987, 8-5-601 et seq.
Ky. Rev. Stat. 1986, 107.770

Priviledge Act (Newsmen)
Ariz. Rev. Stat. Ann., § 12-2237
Mont. Code Ann. 1987, 26-1-901 et seq.

Priviledge Tax Act (Carriers)
W. Va. Code 1966, § 11-12A-1 et seq.

Privilege Act
La. Civil Code, Art. 3182 et seq.

Privilege Act (Newsmen)
See Newsman's Privilege Act (Disclosure)
Ariz. Rev. Stat. Ann., § 12-2237
Mont. Code Ann. 1987, 26-1-901 et seq.
Pa. Cons. Stat., Title 42, § 5942
R.I. Gen. Laws 1956, 9-19.1-1 et seq.

Privilege and Franchise Tax Act (Corporations)
Mich. Comp. Laws Ann., 450.2062 et seq.
Utah Code Ann. 1953, 59-7-101 et seq.

Privilege, Communication, Complacency Act
Wyo. Stat. 1957, § 1-140

Privilege Dividend Tax Act
Wis. Laws 1935, Ch. 505, § 3

Privilege License Tax Act
N.C. Gen. Stat. 1943, § 105-33 et seq.

Privilege Sales Tax Act
Ariz. Rev. Stat. Ann., § 42-1301 et seq.

Privilege Tax Act
N.M. Stat. Ann. 1953, 72-16-4 et seq.
Tenn. Code Ann., 67-4-401 et seq.

Privilege Tax Act (Intoxicating Liquors)
Ore. Rev. Stat., 473.010 et seq.

Privilege Tax Act (Severance and Business)
W. Va. Code 1966 § 11-13A-1 et seq.

Privilege Tax Law (Local)
Miss. Code Ann. 1972, § 27-17-1 et seq.

Privilege Tax Law (State-wide)
Miss. Code Ann. 1972, § 27-15-1 et seq.

Privileged Communication Acts (Disclosure, Privileged Matter)
N.Y. Civil Practice Laws and Rules (Consol. Laws Ch. 8) § 3101

Privileged Communication Acts (Husband-Wife)

N.D. Cent. Code, 31-01-02

N.D. Rules of Evidence 1977, Rule 504

N.Y. Civil Practice Laws and Rules (Consol. Laws Ch. 8) § 4502

Privileged Communication Acts (Priest-Penitent)

N.Y. Civil Practice Laws and Rules (Consol. Laws Ch. 8) § 4505

Privileged Communication Acts (Psychologist-Client)

N.Y. Civil Practice Laws and Rules (Consol. Laws Ch. 8) § 4507

Privileged Communications Act

Cal. Evidence Code, §§ 911 et seq., 930 et seq.

Colo. Rev. Stat., 13-90-107

Ida. Code 1947, 9-203

Ill. Rev. Stat. 1991, Ch. 51, §§ 5.1, 5.2

Ind. Code Ann., 34-1-14-5

Kan. Stat. Ann., 60-426 et seq.

Mich. Comp. Laws Ann., 600.2156 et seq.

Miss. Code Ann. 1972, § 13-1-21

Mont. Code Ann., 26-1-801 et seq.

N.M. Stat. Ann., 38-6-6

Ore. Rev. Stat., 40.225

S.D. Codified Laws 1967, 19-2-1 et seq.

Utah Code Ann. 1953, 78-24-8

Wash. Rev. Code Ann., 5.60.060

Wis. Stat. Ann., 885.205, 905.01 et seq.

W. Va. Code 1931, Ch. 50, Art. 6, § 10

Privileged Communications Act (Attorney and Client)

N.Y. Civ. Prac. Law and Rules (Consol. Laws, Ch. 8) § 4503

Ohio Rev. Code 1953, 2317.02, Subd. A

Privileged Communications Act (Newsmen)

Ark. Stat. 1947, 43-917

Privileged Communications Act (Physician-Patient)

See Physician-Patient Privileged Communications Act

Privileges and Immunities Clause

Va. Code 1950, § 8.01-399

Prize Fights Act (Prohibition)

Cal. Penal Code, § 412 et seq.

Tex. Penal Code 1925, Arts. 610, 611

Prizes and Gifts Act

N.H. Rev. Stat. 1955, 358-O:1 et seq.

S.C. Code Ann. 1976, § 37-15-10 et seq.

Va. Code 1950, § 59-1.406 et seq.

W. Va. Code 1966 § 46A-6D-1 et seq.

Prizes Law (Promotional Advertising of)

Wash. Rev. Code 1983, 19.170.010 et seq.

Pro-Children Act of 1994

March 31, 1994, P.L. 103-227, 20 U.S. Code §§ 6081 et seq.

Pro-Competitive Certificate of Need Act

Utah Code Ann. 1953, Miscellaneous Superseded Code Provisions, 26-22-1 et seq.

Pro-Family Tax Equity Act

Ga. Code Ann., 48-7-20

Pro Rata Act (Insurance)

Wis. Stat. Ann., 631.43

Probate Act

See also Uniform Probate Code

Ala. Code 1975, § 43-8-1 et seq.

Ark. Stat. 1947, 57-601 et seq., 60-201 et seq., 28-25-101 et seq.

Ga. Code Ann., 53-3-1 et seq.

Ill. Rev. Stat. 1991, Ch. 110 1/2, § 1-1 et seq.

Ind. Code Ann., 29-1-1-1 et seq.

Iowa Code Ann., 633.1 et seq.

Kan. Stat. Ann., 59-101 et seq.

La. Rev. Stat. Ann., 9:2421 et seq.

Mo. Rev. Stat., 472.005 et seq.

Nev. Rev. Stat. 1979 Reprint, 136.010 et seq.

N.H. Rev. Stat. 1955, 547:1 et seq.

N.J. Stat. Ann., 3B:3-17

Ohio Rev. Code 1953, 2101.01 et seq., 2129.05 et seq.

Okla. Stat. Ann., Title 58, § 1 et seq.

Ore. Rev. Stat., 111.005 et seq.

Continued

Pa. Cons. Stat., Title 20, § 101 et seq.

S.D. Codified Laws 1967, 29A-1-1 et seq.

Tenn. Code Ann., 32-5-101 et seq.

Tex. Probate Code, §§ 1 et seq., 100 et seq.

Wash. Rev. Code Ann., 11.02.001 et seq.

Wis. Stat. Ann., 851.001 et seq., 868.01 et seq.

W. Va. Code 1966, § 41-1-1 et seq.

Wyo. Stat. Ann., § 2-1-101 et seq.

Probate Act of Foreign Wills

See also Uniform Probate of Foreign Wills Act

Ala. Code 1975, § 43-8-175

Colo. Rev. Stat. 1963, 153-6-1 et seq.

Kan. Stat. Ann., 59-2229, 59-2230

La. Rev. Stat. Ann., 9:2421 et seq.

Ohio Rev. Code 1953, 2129.05 et seq.

Tenn. Code Ann., 32-5-101 et seq.

Tex. Probate Code, § 100 et seq.

Wis. Stat. Ann., 868.01

Wyo. Stat. Ann., § 2-11-101 et seq.

Probate and Guardianship Procedure

S.D. Codified Laws 1967, 30-1-1 et seq.

Probate Appeal Act

Ill. Rev. Stat. 1991, Ch. 110 1/2, §§ 26-1, 26-2

N.H. Rev. Stat. 1955, 567-A:1 et seq.

Probate Claim Act (Limitations)

Fla. Stat. Ann., 733.702

Probate Claims Act

Minn. Stat. Ann., 524.3-104 et seq.

Probate Code

Fla. Stat. Ann., 731.005 et seq.

Probate Code (Revised)

Ariz. Laws 1994, Ch. 290

Probate Court Act

Conn. Gen. Stat. Ann., § 45a-1 et seq.

Ill. Rev. Stat. 1963, Ch. 37, § 299 et seq.

S.C. Code Ann. 1976, § 14-23-10 et seq.

Probate Court and Registry of Deeds Loan Act (Barnstable County)

Mass. Acts 1952, Ch. 472

Probate Court Loan Act (Norfolk County)

Mass. Acts 1959, Ch. 472

Probate Court Reform Act

Conn. Gen. Stat. Ann., § 45a-80 et seq.

Probate Homestead Act

Ariz. Rev. Stat. Ann., § 14-2401 et seq.

Okla. Stat. Ann., Title 58, § 311 et seq.

Probate Judges' Retirement Act

Mich. Comp. Laws Ann., 38.901 et seq.

Probate Mortgage Act

Wash. Rev. Code Ann., 11.56.010 et seq.

Probate Murder Statute

Fla. Stat. Ann., 732.802

Probate Reform Act

Okla. Stat. Ann., Title 58, § 380 et seq.

Probation Act

March 4, 1925, Ch. 521, 43 Stat. 1259 (See 18 U.S. Code §§ 3651, 3653 to 3656)

Ala. Code 1975, § 15-22-50 et seq.

Alaska Stat. 1962, § 33.05.010 et seq.

Ariz. Rev. Stat. Ann., § 13-901 et seq.

Cal. Penal Code, § 1203 et seq.

Conn. Gen. Stat. Ann., § 54-103 et seq.

D.C. Code Ann., § 24-103 et seq.

Ga. Code Ann., 42-8-1 et seq.

Ill. Rev. Stat. 1991, Ch. 38, § 1005-6-1 et seq.

Ind. Code Ann., 35-7-1-1 et seq.

Iowa Code Ann., 907.1 et seq.

La. Code of Crim. Proc. 1966, Art. 893 et seq.

Mass. Gen. Laws. Ann., 276:83 et seq.

Mich. Comp. Laws Ann., 771.1 et seq.

Mo. Rev. Stat., 549.361 et seq.

N.C. Gen. Stat. 1943, § 15A-1341 et seq.

Neb. Rev. Stat. 1943, 29-2209 et seq.

Neb. Rev. Stat. 1943, 29-2246 et seq.

N.H. Rev. Stat. 1955, 504:1 et seq.

Pa. Purdon's Stat., Title 61, § 331.1 et seq.

P.R. Laws Ann. 1954, Title 34, § 1026 et seq.

R.I. Gen. Laws 1956, 12-18-1 et seq., 12-19-8 et seq.

Tenn. Code Ann., 40-35-301 et seq.

Tex. Code of Criminal Procedure, Arts. 42.12, 42.13

Vt. Stat. Ann., Title 28, §§ 401 et seq., 1201 et seq.

Wash. Rev. Code Ann., 9.95.200 et seq.

Probation and Community Justice Act
Ill. Laws 1985, P.A. 84-823

Probation and Parole Act
Ala. Code 1975, § 15-22-1 et seq.

Alaska Stat. 1962, Replaced Titles, § 33.15.010 et seq.

Cal. Penal Code, § 3040 et seq.

Colo. Rev. Stat. 17-2-101 et seq.

Conn. Gen. Stat. Ann., § 54-124a et seq.

D.C. Code 1973, § 24-201a et seq.

Del. Code of 1974, Title 11, § 7701 et seq.

Fla. Stat. Ann., 947.001 et seq., 948.01 et seq., 949.01 et seq.

Haw. Rev. Stat. Ann., § 353-61 et seq.

Ill. Rev. Stat. 1991, Ch. 38, §§ 1003-3-1 et seq., 1003-3-11 et seq., 1003-14-1 et seq.

Iowa Code Ann., 906.1 et seq.

Kan. Stat. Ann., 21-4601 et seq., 22-3717 et seq.

Ky. Rev. Stat. 1971, Superseded Vol., 439.070 et seq.

Ky. Rev. Stat. 1971, 439.250 et seq.

La. Rev. Stat. Ann., 15:574.2 et seq.

Mass. Gen. Laws. Ann., 127:128 et seq.

Md. Ann. Code 1957, Art. 41, § 4.501 et seq.

Me. Rev. Stat. Ann. 1964, Title 34-A, § 5001 et seq.

Mich. Comp. Laws Ann., 791.231 et seq.

Miss. Code Ann. 1972, § 47-7-1 et seq.

Mo. Rev. Stat., 217.650 et seq., 549.361

Mont. Code Ann., 46-23-101 et seq.

N.C. Gen. Stat. 1943, § 148-52.1 et seq.

Neb. Rev. Stat. 1943, 29-2246 et seq.

N.H. Rev. Stat. 1955, 651-A:1 et seq.

N.J. Stat. Ann., 2C:45-1 et seq., 30:4-123.45 et seq.

N.M. Stat. Ann., 31-21-3 et seq., 31-21-22 et seq.

N.Y. Correction Law (Consol. Laws Ch. 43) § 210 et seq.

Ore. Rev. Stat. 1953, 144.005 et seq.

Pa. Purdon's Stat., Title 61, § 291 et seq.

P.R. Laws Ann. 1954, Title 4, § 1501 et seq.

R.I. Gen. Laws 1956, 13-8-1 et seq.

S.C. Code Ann. 1976, § 24-21-10 et seq.

Va. Code 1950, § 53.1-134 et seq.

Vt. Stat. Ann., Title 28, § 401 et seq.

Wash. Rev. Code Ann., 9.95.110 et seq.

Wis. Stat. 1987, 57.13

W. Va. Code 1966, § 62-12-1 et seq.

Wyo. Stat. Ann., § 7-13-401 et seq.

Probation and Parole Compact Act (Interstate)
See Interstate Probation and Parole Compact Act

Probation and Parole Supervision Act (Out-of-State)
Fla. Stat. Ann., 949.07 et seq.

Mass. Gen. Laws. Ann., 127:151A et seq.

Vt. Stat. Ann., Title 28, § 1301

Wash. Rev. Code Ann., 9.95.270

Probation and Parole Support Act
R.I. Gen. Laws 1956, 12-18.1-1 et seq.

Probation and Parolee Act
S.C. Code Ann. 1976, § 24-21-10 et seq.

Probation and Probation Officers Act
Fla. Stat. Ann., 947.001 et seq.

Ga. Code Ann., 42-8-25 et seq.

Ill. Rev. Stat. 1991, Ch. 38, § 204-1a9 et seq.

Probation Challenge Program Act
Ill. Rev. Stat. 1991, Ch. 38, § 1501 et seq.

Probation Community Service Act
Ill. Rev. Stat. 1991, Ch. 38, §§ 204a, 204a-1

Probation, Parole and Executive Clemency Act
Mont. Code Ann., 46-23-101 et seq.

Probation Provider Licensing Act (Private)
Utah Code Ann. 1953, 58-50-1 et seq.

Problem Pregnancy Health Services and Care Act
Ill. Rev. Stat. 1991, Ch. 111 1/2, § 4601-100 et seq.

Procedural Bill of Rights Act (Public Safety Officers)
Cal. Government Code, § 3300 et seq.

Procedural Rules Act
Pa. Purdon's Stat., Title 17, § 61 et seq.

Procedural Support Act
Pa. Cons. Stat., Title 42, § 6701 et seq.

Procedure Act (Civil)
See Civil Procedure Act

Procedure Act (Collegiate Athletic Association Compliance ent Enforcement)
Fla. Stat. Ann., 240.5339 et seq.

Procedure Act (Extraordinary and Equitable Remedies)
Ga. Code Ann., 23-3-1 et seq.

Procedure Act (Federal Court Local Law Certificate)
Wash. Rev. Code 1983, 2.60.900

Procedure Act (Juvenile)
Vt. Stat. Ann., Title 33, § 631 et seq.

Procedure Act (Life-Prolonging)
Fla. Stat. Ann., 765.01 et seq.

Procedure Act (Utilities Commission)
N.C. Gen. Stat. 1943, § 62-60 et seq.

Procedure Law (Criminal)
Fla. Stat. Ann., 900.01 et seq.

Procedures Act (Environmental Coordination)
Wash. Rev. Code 1983, 90.62.010 et seq.

Procedures Act (Mental Hospital Admission)
Okla. Stat. 1981, Title 43A, § 5-301 et seq.

Procedures and Control Act (Revenue)
Utah Code Ann. 1953, 63-38a-101 et seq.

Procedures and Succession Act (Legislative Emergency)
Neb. Rev. Stat. 1943, 50-501 et seq.

Procedures For Families in Conflict Act
Wash. Rev. Code Ann., 13.32A.010 et seq.

Procedures Simplification Act (Ecology)
Wash. Rev. Code 1983, 43.21B.001 et seq.

Process Act
May 8, 1792, Ch. 36, 1 Stat. 275
Ill. Rev. Stat. 1991, Ch. 110, § 2-201 et seq.
Mich. Comp. Laws Ann., 600.1801 et seq.
Mo. Rev. Stat., 506.110 et seq.
S.C. Code Ann. 1976, § 17-13-10 et seq.
Vt. Stat. Ann., Title 12, § 654 et seq.
Wash. Rev. Code Ann., 4.28.080

Process Act (Nonresident Motorist)
See Nonresident Motorist Substituted Service Act

Process Act (Unauthorized Insurers)
See Unauthorized Insurers Process Act

Process Patent Amendments Act of 1988
Aug. 23, 1988, P.L. 100-418, 102 Stat. 1563, 35 U.S. Code § 1 nt.

Process Server Act
Utah Code Ann. 1953, 78-12a-1 et seq.

Process Service Act
See Service of Process Act

Processed Foodstuff Marketing Act
Cal. Statutes 1937, p. 2256

Processes Products Inspection Improvements Act of 1986
Nov. 10, 1986, P.L. 99-641, 21 U.S. Code § 601 nt.

Processing Act (Food)
Wash. Rev. Code 1983, 69.07.920

Processing, Slaughter, and Sale of Meat Animals Act

Colo. Rev. Stat., 35-33-101 et seq.

Processioning Act

Ga. Code Ann., 44-4-5 et seq.

Processors Act

Cal. Food and Agricultural Code 1967, § 55401 et seq. § 55605 et seq.

Processor's Act (Personal Property Act)

Ore. Rev. Stat., 308.250

Processor's Regulation Act (Milk)

Miss. Code Ann. 1972, § 75-31-501 et seq.

Procurement Act

Colo. Rev. Stat., 24-101-101 et seq.

Ky. Rev. Stat. 1971, 45A.005 et seq.

La. Rev. Stat. Ann., 39:1551 et seq.

Mont. Code Ann., 18-4-121 et seq.

S.C. Code Ann. 1976, § 11-35-10 et seq.

Procurement and Contract Act (Small Business)

Cal. Government Code, § 14835 et seq.

Procurement and Service Act

P.R. Laws Ann. 1954, Title 3, § 915 et seq.

Procurement Code

Alaska Stat. 1962, § 36.30.005 et seq.

Ill. Comp. Stat. 1992, Ch. 30, § 500/1-1 et seq.

La. Rev. Stat. Ann., 39:1551 et seq.

N.M. Stat. Ann., 3-1-28 et seq.

Procurement of Architectural and Engineering Services Act-General Using Authorities

Md. Ann. Code 1974, Art. TR, § 13-101 et seq.

Procurement of Architectural and Engineering Services Act-Transportation Agencies

Md. Ann. Code 1974, Art. TR, § 2-301 et seq.

Procurement Stewardship Act

N.Y. Laws 1995, Ch. 83, §§ 31 to 41

Produce Act

Mont. Code Ann., 80-3-301 et seq.

Produce Agency Act

March 3, 1927, Ch. 309, 44 Stat. 1355, 7 U.S. Code §§ 491 to 497

Produce Dealers Act

Cal. Food and Agricultural Code 1967, § 56101 et seq.

Colo. Rev. Stat., 12-16-101 et seq.

Minn. Stat. Ann., 27.01 et seq.

Ore. Rev. Stat., 585.010 et seq.

Utah Code Ann. 1953, 4-7-1 et seq.

Produce Labeling Act

Fla. Stat. Ann., 504.011 et seq.

Ind. Code Ann., 24-6-6-1 et seq.

Produce Market Loan Fund Act

Va. Code 1950, § 3.1-65 et seq.

Produce Marketing Act

Cal. Food and Agricultural Code 1967, § 59501 et seq.

N.M. Stat. Ann., 76-15-10 et seq.

Va. Code 1950, § 3.1-47 et seq.

Produce Preference Law

Iowa Code Ann., 73.1 et seq.

Produce Wholesalers' License Act

Mont. Rev. Code 1947, 84-3401 et seq.

Producer Controlled Insurer Act

Miss. Code Ann. 1972, § 83-59-1 et seq.

Producer Controlled Insurer Act (Business Transacted with)

Cal. Insurance Code § 1216 et seq.

Minn. Stat. 1986, 60J.06 et seq.

Okla. Stat. Ann., Title 36, § 1671 et seq.

Producer Controlled Property and Casualty Insurer Act

Ga. Code Ann., 33-48-1 et seq.

Iowa Code Ann., 510A.1 et seq.

Producer Controlled Property or Casualty Insurer Act (Business Transacted with)
Ala. Code 1975, § 27-6B-1 et seq.
Iowa Code Ann., 510A.1 et seq.
Ky. Rev. Stat. 1971, 304.3-400c et seq.
Neb. Laws 1992, L.B. 1006, §§ 68 to 75
R.I. Gen. Laws 1956, 27-48-1 et seq.

Producer Cooperative Association Act
R.I. Gen. Laws 1956, 7-7-1 et seq.

Producer Licensing Act (Single Insurance)
Colo. Rev. Stat., 10-2-101 et seq.

Producer Pool Act (Beginning Agricultural)
Okla. Stat. Ann., Title 74, § 5063.21 et seq.

Producer's Lien Act
N.M. Stat. Ann., 48-5B-1 et seq.

Producing Facilities Disposal Act of 1953
March 21, 1956, Ch. 89, 70 Stat. 51, 50 U.S. Code Appx. §§ 1941f nt., 1941r nt., 1941y
July 29, 1970, P.L. 91-358, 84 Stat. 571

Product Development Act
Okla. Stat. Ann., Title 74, § 5066.1 et seq.

Product Development Corporation Act
Conn. Gen. Stat. Ann., § 32-32 et seq.

Product Liability Act
Ark. Code Ann. 1987, 16-116-101 et seq.
Ind. Code Ann., 33-1-1.5-1 et seq.
Kan. Stat. Ann., 60-3301 et seq.
Ky. Rev. Stat. 1971, 411.300 et seq.
La. Rev. Stat. Ann., 9:2800.51 et seq.
N.C. Gen. Stat. 1943, § 99B-1 et seq.
N.D. Cent. Code, 28-01.1-01 et seq.
Tenn. Code Ann., 29-28-101 et seq.
Utah Code Ann. 1953, 78-15-1 et seq.

Product Liability Insurance Act
Ill. Rev. Stat. 1991, Ch. 73, §§ 1200, 1201

Product Liability Reform Act
Ida. Code 1947, 6-1401 et seq.

Product Liability Risk Retention Act
Me. Rev. Stat. Ann. 1964, Title 24-A, § 6001 et seq.

Product Liability Risk Retention Act of 1981
See Liability Risk Retention Act of 1986
Sept. 25, 1981, P.L. 97-45, 15 U.S. Code § 3901 nt.
Dec. 1, 1983, P.L. 98-193, 15 U.S. Code § 3901

Product Liability Statute of Repose et seq.
Ala. Code 1957, § 6-5-50 et seq.

Product Procurement Act (Domestic)
Mo. Rev. Stat., 34.350 et seq.

Product Promotion Fair Practices Act (Mail and Telephone Consumers)
Ark. Acts 1991, No. 680

Product Safety Act
Mont. Code Ann., 50-30-101 et seq.

Product Selection Act (Drug)
Mont. Code Ann. 1987, 37-7-501 et seq.

Production Act (Small Power)
Me. Rev. Stat. Ann. 1964, Title 35-A, § 3301 et seq.

Production Agriculture Programs Act
Ill. Rev. Stat. 1991, Ch. 5, § 2550 et seq.

Production and Transportation Act
Okla. Stat. Ann., Title 52, § 21 et seq.

Production Facilities and Animal Research Protection Act
Mo. Laws 1992, S.B. No. 498

Production Facilities Animal Research Protection Act
Ill. Comp. Stat. 1992, Ch. 720, § 215/1 et seq.

Production Incentive Tax Credit for New Coal Act
Mont. Code Ann. 1987, 15-35-201 et seq.

Production Incentives Act (Natural Gas and Crude Oil)
N.M. Stat. Ann., 7-30-1 et seq.

Production Revenue Standards Act
Okla. Stat. Ann., Title 52, § 570.1 et seq.

Productivity and Incentive Act
Tex. General and Special Laws 1991, p. 3890, Ch. 888
Tex. Rev. Civ. Stat., Art. 6252-29a

Products Delivery Guarantee Act (Food)
N.M. Stat. Ann., 57-24-1 et seq.

Products Liability Limitations Act
Ala. Code 1975, § 6-5-500 et seq.

Products License Act (Cigarette or Tobacco)
Vt. Stat. Ann., Title 32, § 7771 et seq.

Products Standards Act (Organic Food)
Pa. Cons. Stat., Title 3, § 5901 et seq.

Profanation Law
N.Y. General Business Law (Consol. Laws Ch. 20) § 136

Professional Accounting Corporations Law
La. Rev. Stat. Ann., 12:1011 et seq.

Professional and Amateur Sports Protection Act
Oct. 28, 1992, P.L. 102-559, 28 U.S. Code §§ 1 nt., 3701 et seq.

Professional and Civil Engineers Act
Cal. Business and Professions Code, § 6700 et seq.

Professional and Executive Liability Fund Act
Md. Ann. Code 1957, Art. 48A, § 557 et seq.

Professional and Licensing Vocational Act
Haw. Rev. Stat. Ann., § 481H-1 et seq.

Professional and Practical Nursing Act
S.D. Codified Laws 1967, 36-9-1- et seq.

Professional and Vocational Licensing Act
See Uniform Professinal and Vocational Licensing Act
Haw. Rev. Stat. Ann., § 436B-1 et seq.

Professional Architectural Corporations Act
La. Rev. Stat. Ann., 12:1086 et seq.

Professional Architectural, Engineering and Land Surveying Services Procurement Act
Wyo. Stat. Ann., § 9-2-1027 et seq.

Professional Assistance Law (Allied Health Care)
Ill. Rev. Stat. 1991, Ch. 144, § 1481 et seq.

Professional Association Act
Ala. Code 1975, § 10-10-1 et seq.
Conn. Gen. Stat. Ann., § 34-82
Ga. Code Ann., 14-10-1 et seq.
Ill. Rev. Stat. 1991, Ch. 106 1/2, § 100 et seq.
N.H. Rev. Stat. 1955, 294-A:1 et seq.
Ohio Rev. Code 1953, 1785.01 et seq.
Pa. Purdon's Stat., Title 15, § 12601 et seq.
S.C. Code Ann. 1976, Superseded Vols., § 33-51-10 et seq.
Tenn. Code Ann., 61-1-105
Tex. Rev. Civ. Stat., Art. 1528f
Va. Code 1950, § 54-873 et seq.

Professional Association Mutual Insurance Company Act
Neb. Rev. Stat. 1943, 44-3101 et seq.

Professional Athletic Competition Act
N.M. Stat. Ann., 60-2A-1 et seq.

Professional Beauticians Act
Pa. Purdon's Stat., Title 63, § 507 et seq.

Professional Bondsmen Act
Nev. Rev. Stat. 1979 Reprint, 697.010 et seq.
N.H. Rev. Stat. 1955, 598-A:1 et seq.
Pa. Cons. Stat., Title 42, § 5741 et seq.

Professional Boxing and Wrestling Act
Ill. Rev. Stat. 1991, Ch. 111, § 5001 et seq.

Professional Boxing Licensing Act
Okla. Stat. Ann., Title 3A, § 500 et seq.

Professional Boxing Safety Act of 1996
Oct. 9, 1996, P.L. 104-272, 15 U.S. Code § 6301 nt.

Professional Certification Act (Property Taxation)
Tex. Rev. Civ. Stat., Art. 8885

Professional Chiropractic Corporations Act
La. Rev. Stat. Ann., 12:1051 et seq.

Professional Community Planners Act
Mich. Comp. Laws Ann., 338.1351 et seq.

Professional Consultants Competetive Negotiations Act
Fla. Stat. Ann., 287.055

Professional Corporation Act
Ala. Code 1975, § 10-4-220 et seq.
Alaska Stat. 1962, § 10.45.010 et seq.
Ariz. Rev. Stat. Ann., § 10-2201 et seq.
Ark. Code Ann. 1987, 4-29-201 et seq.
Cal. Corporations Code, § 13400 et seq.
D.C. Code Ann., § 29-601 et seq.
Ga. Code Ann., 14-7-1 et seq.
Haw. Rev. Stat. Ann., § 415A-1 et seq.
Ind. Code Ann., 23-1-17-1 et seq.
Iowa Code Ann., 496C.1 et seq.
Kan. Stat. Ann., 17-2706 et seq.
Mass. Gen. Laws. Ann., 156A:1 et seq.
Minn. Stat. Ann., 319A.01 et seq.
Miss. Code Ann. 1972, §§ 79-10-1 to 79-10-117
Miss. Code Ann. 1972, § 79-9-1 et seq.
Mo. Rev. Stat., 356.011 et seq.
Mont. Code Ann., 35-4-108 et seq.
N.C. Gen. Stat. 1943, § 55B-1 et seq.
N.D. Cent. Code, 10-31-01 et seq.
Neb. Rev. Stat. 1943, 21-2201 et seq.
N.M. Stat. Ann., 53-6-1 et seq.
N.Y. Business Corporation Law (Consol. Laws Ch. 4) § 1501 et seq.
Okla. Stat. Ann., Title 18, § 801 et seq.
Ore. Rev. Stat., 58.005 et seq.
Pa. Purdon's Stat., Title 15, § 2901 et seq.
Tenn. Code Ann., 48-3-401 et seq.
Tex. Rev. Civ. Stat., Art. 1528e
Utah Code Ann. 1953, 16-11-1 et seq.
Vt. Stat. Ann., Title 11, § 801 et seq.
Wis. Stat. 1987, 180.99

Professional Corporation Act (Attorneys)
Minn. Stat. Ann., 319A.01 et seq.

Professional Corporation Act (Chiropractors)
Minn. Stat. Ann., 319A.01 et seq.

Professional Corporation Act (Dentists)
Minn. Stat. Ann., 319A.01 et seq.

Professional Corporation Act (Medical)
Ind. Code Ann., 23-1.5-1-8 et seq.
S.D. Codified Laws 1967, 47-11-1 et seq.

Professional Corporation Act (Optometrists)
Minn. Stat. Ann., 319A.01 et seq.

Professional Corporation Act (Revised)
Ala. Code 1975, § 10-4-380 et seq.

Professional Corporation Revision Act
D.C. Code Ann., § 29-621

Professional Corporation Supplement Act
S.C. Code Ann. 1976, § 33-19-101 et seq.

Professional Corporations and Associations Act
Nev. Rev. Stat. 1979 Reprint, 89.010 et seq.

Professional Counselor Act
Md. Ann. Code 1974, Art. HO, § 17-101 et seq.
Miss. Code Ann. 1972, § 73-30-1 et seq.
Tex. Rev. Civ. Stat. 1974, Art. 4512g

Professional Counselor, Associate Counselor, and Marital and Family Therapist Licensing Act
S.C. Code Ann. 1976, § 40-75-10 et seq.

Professional Counselor Licensing Act
N.J. Stat. Ann., 45:8B-34 et seq.
Utah Code Ann. 1953, 58-60-401 et seq.

Professional Counselor Licensing Act (Clinical)
Ill. Comp. Stat. 1992, Ch. 225, § 107/1 et seq.

Professional Counselor Registration Act
Kan. Stat. Ann., 65-5801 et seq.

Professional Counselors Act (Licensed)
Okla. Stat. Ann., Title 59, § 1901 et seq.

Professional Counselors, Social Workers, and Marriage and Family Therapists Licensing Act
Ga. Code Ann., 43-7A-1 et seq.

Professional Criminals Act
N.Y. Penal Law 1965 (Consol. Laws Ch. 40) § 70.10

Professional Dental Corporation Act
Ind. Code Ann., 23-1.5-1-8 et seq.
La. Rev. Stat. Ann., 12:981 et seq.

Professional Development and Program Improvement Act
Cal. Education Code 1976, § 44630 et seq.

Professional Driver Training Act
Ariz. Rev. Stat. Ann., § 32-2351 et seq.

Professional Educator Excellence Act
Wash. Rev. Code Ann., 28A.04.122 et seq., 28A.70.010 et seq.

Professional Employer Organization Act
Ga. Code Ann., 45-13-90 et seq.

Professional Employer Recognition Act
Ida. Code 1947, 44-2401 et seq.

Professional Employers, Organizations and Groups Licensing Act
Mont. Code Ann., 39-8-101 et seq.

Professional Engineering Practice Act
Cal. Business and Professions Code, § 6700 et seq.
Del. Code of 1974, Title 24, § 2801 et seq.
Fla. Stat. Ann., 471.001
Ill. Rev. Stat. 1991, Ch. 111, § 5101 et seq., § 5201 et seq.
Mich. Comp. Laws Ann., 338.551 et seq.

Ore. Rev. Stat., 672.002 et seq.

Professional Engineers and Land Surveyors Act
D.C. Code Ann., § 2-2301 et seq.
Md. Ann. Code 1974, Art. BP, § 14-101 et seq.
Mont. Code Ann., 37-67-101 et seq.
Pa. Purdon's Stat., Title 63, § 148 et seq.
Wash. Rev. Code Ann., 18.43.010 et seq.

Professional Engineers and Land Surveyors Licensing Act
Utah Code Ann. 1953, 58-22-101 et seq.

Professional Engineers' and Land Surveyors' Licensing and Registration Act
Ill. Rev. Stat. 1991, Ch. 111, § 5201 et seq.
Ohio Rev. Code 1953, 4733.01 et seq.
Pa. 1921 Pamph. Laws 1131, No. 422
Pa. 1990 Pamph. Laws No. 192
Utah Code Ann. 1953, 58-22-1 et seq.

Professional Engineers' Registration Act
Sept. 19, 1950, Ch. 953, 64 Stat. 854

Professional Engineers Registration Act (Registered)
Mass. Gen. Laws Ann., 112:81D et seq.

Professional Firms Act
Minn. Stat. 1986, 319B.01 to 319B.12

Professional Foresters Law
Cal. Public Resources Code, § 750 et seq.

Professional Geologists Licensing Act
Ala. Code 1975, § 34-41-1 et seq.

Professional Geologists Practice Act (Registered)
Miss. Code Ann. 1972, § 73-63-1 et seq.

Professional Incentive and Rural Health Systems Act
Neb. Rev. Stat. 1943, § 71-5650 et seq.

Professional Land Surveying Practice Act
Ill. Rev. Stat. 1991, Ch. 111, § 3251 et seq.
Md. Ann. Code 1974, Art. BO, § 15-101 et seq.
Continued

Tex. Rev. Civ. Stat., Art. 5282c

Professional Land Surveyors Act
Cal. Business and Professions Code § 8700 et seq.

Professional Landscape Architects Act
Neb. Rev. Stat. 1943, 81-8, 184 et seq.

Professional Law Corporations Act
La. Rev. Stat. Ann., 12:801 et seq.

Professional Liability Fund Act
N.M. Stat. Ann., 41-6-1 et seq.
Ore. Rev. Stat., 752.055 et seq.

Professional Liability Insurance Availability Act
Neb. Rev. Stat. 1943, 44-3001 et seq.

Professional Liability Reciprocal Insurance Law
Tenn. Code Ann., 56-17-101 et seq.

Professional Loan Forgiveness Act (Childhood Education)
Pa. 1993 Pamph. Laws, No. 73

Professional Malpractice Claims Act
N.H. Rev. Stat. 1955, 519-A:1 et seq.

Professional Massage/Bodywork Practitioner Act
Del. Code of 1974, Title 24, § 5301 et seq.

Professional Medical Conduct Reform Act
N.J. Stat. Ann., 2A:84A-22.10, 2C:21-4.1, 2C:21-20, 2C:43-12, 2C:52-2, 17:3-D-17, 26:2H-12.2, 26:2H-12.2a, 45:1-2.5, 45:5-8, 45:9-1, 45:9-16, 45:9-19.3 to 45:9-19.15, 45:9-19.4 et seq.

Professional Medical Corporation Act
La. Rev. Stat. Ann., 12:901 et seq.

Professional Midwifery Practice Act
N.Y. Education Law 1947 (Consol. Laws Ch. 16) § 6950 et seq.

Professional Negotiations Act (School Employees)
Kan. Stat. Ann., 72-5413 et seq.

Professional Negotiations Act for Teachers
Mont. Rev. Code 1947, 75-6115 et seq.

Professional Nursing Corporations Act
La. Rev. Stat. Ann., 12:1071 et seq.

Professional Nursing Law
Pa. Purdon's Stat., Title 63, § 211 et seq.

Professional Occupational Therapy Corporations Act
La. Rev. Stat. Ann., 12:1190 et seq.

Professional Optometry Corporations Law
La. Rev. Stat. Ann., 12:1110 et seq.

Professional Physical Therapy Practice Act
Mo. Rev. Stat., 334.500 et seq.

Professional Planners Licensing Act
N.J. Stat. Ann., 45:14A-1 et seq.

Professional Practice Act
Cal. Education Code 1959, § 44200 et seq.
Iowa Code Ann., 147.1 et seq.

Professional Practice Act (Mental Health)
Utah Code Ann. 1953, 58-60-101 et seq.

Professional Practices Act (Educational)
Utah Code Ann. 1953, 53A-7-101 et seq.

Professional Prosecutors Act
Tex. Rev. Civ. Stat. 1974, Art. 332B-4

Professional Psychologist Practice Act
N.M. Stat. Ann., 61-9-1 et seq.
Pa. Purdon's Stat., Title 63. § 1201.1 et seq.

Professional Psychology Corporation Act
La. Rev. Stat. Ann., 12:1130 et seq.

Professional Responsibility Law
Tenn. Public Acts, 1971, Ch. 161

Professional Review Panel Act
Wyo. Stat. Ann., § 9-2-1701 et seq.

Professional Service Corporation Act
Del. Code of 1974, Title 8, § 601 et seq.
Fla. Stat. Ann., 621.01 et seq.

Ida. Code 1947, 30-1301 et seq.

Ill. Rev. Stat. 1991, Ch. 32, § 415-1 et seq.

Ky. Rev. Stat. 1971, 274.005 et seq.

Md. Ann. Code 1974, Art. CA, § 5-101 et seq.

Me. Rev. Stat. Ann. 1964, Title 13, § 701 et seq.

Mich. Comp. Laws Ann., 450.221 et seq.

Mont. Code Ann. 1981, 35-4-101 et seq.

N.J. Stat. Ann., 14A:17-1 et seq.

R.I. Gen. Laws 1956, 7-5.1-1 et seq.

Wash. Rev. Code Ann., 18.100.010 et seq.

Professional Service Corporation and Limited Liability Company Act

Fla. Stat. Ann., 621.02 et seq.

Professional Service Corporations Act (Attorneys)

S.D. Codified Laws 1967, 47-13A-1 et seq.

Professional Service Incorporation Act

N.Y. Business Corporations Law 1961 (Consol. Laws Ch. 4) § 1501 et seq.

Professional Services Negotiation Act

Del. Code of 1974, Title 29, § 6930 et seq.

Professional Services Procurement Act

Tex. Government Code, § 2254.001 et seq.

Professional Services Selection Act (Local Government)

Ill. Rev. Stat. 1991, Ch. 85, § 6400 et seq.

Professional Social Work Act

Tex. Human Resources Code, § 50.001 et seq.

Professional Soil Classifiers Registration Act

Ala. Code 1975, § 34-32-1 et seq.

Professional Speech Pathologists and Professional Clinical Audiologists Licensure Act

Mo. Rev. Stat., 345.010 et seq.

Professional Standards Act

Ga. Code Ann., 20-2-981 et seq.

Professional Teacher and Administrator Act

Mo. Rev. Stat., 168.400 et seq.

Professional Teaching Practices Act

Alaska Stat. 1962, § 14.20.370 et seq.

Fla. Stat. Ann., 231.545

Ga. Code Ann., 20-2-790 et seq.

Iowa Code 1989, 272A.1 et seq.

Tex. Education Code, § 13.201 et seq.

Professional Thieves Act

Pa. Purdon's Stat., Title 18, § 4821

Professional Tow Truck Act

Mont. Code Ann., 61-8-901 et seq.

Professional Veterinary Medicine Corporations Act

La. Rev. Stat. Ann., 12:1151 et seq.

Professional Wrestling Act

Pa. Purdon's Stat., Title 4, § 24.1

Professions Act (Regulation of Health)

Wash. Rev. Code 1983, 18.120.010 et seq.

Professions and Occupations Act

Md. Ann. Code 1974, Art. BO, § 14-101 et seq.

Professions Practice Act (Mental Health)

Wyo. Stat. 1977, § 33-38-101 et seq.

Profit Corporation Revival Act

Mich. Comp. Laws 1970, 450.431, 450.432

Profiteering Act

P.R. Laws Ann. 1954, Title 13, § 2231 et seq.

Profits, Improvements and Rents Act

Me. Rev. Stat. Ann. 1964, Title 14, § 6951 et seq.

Profits Tax Act

Pa. 1923 Pamph. Laws 876, No. 333

Program Act (Buy Massachusetts)

Mass. Gen. Laws Ann., 23A:10A

Program Act (Clean Fuels Conversion)
Utah Code Ann. 1953, 9-1-701 et seq.

Program Evaluation Act
Md. Ann. Code 1974, Art. SG, § 8-401 et seq.

Program Evaluation Act (Legislative)
Neb. Laws 1992, L.B. 988, §§ 1 to 15

Program for Campus Incentive
S.C. Code Ann. 1976, § 59-21-1210 et seq.

Program for Elderly Pharmaceutical Insurance Coverage
N.Y. Executive Law (Consol. Laws Ch. 18) § 547 et seq.

Program for Work Release Act
S.C. Code Ann. 1976, §§ 24-3-30 et seq., 24-13-610 et seq.

Program Fraud Civil Remedies Act of 1986
Oct. 21, 1986, P.L. 99-509, 31 U.S. Code § 3801 nt.

Program Fund Act (Comprehensive Enforcement)
N.J. Stat. Ann., 2B:19-1 et seq.

Program Improvement Act (Professional Development)
Cal. Education Code 1976, § 44630 et seq.

Program of All-Inclusive Care for the Elderly Act
Colo. Rev. Stat., 26-16-101 et seq.

Program Open Space Act
Md. Ann. Code 1974, Art. NR, § 5-901 et seq.

Program Planning, Budgeting and Evaluating System (PPBES) Act
Colo. Rev. Stat., 22-44-201 et seq.

Prohibited Activities Act (Public Officer)
Ill. Rev. Stat. 1991, Ch. 102, § 0.01 et seq.

Prohibiting Unjust Discrimination in Employment Because of Age Act
Neb. Rev. Stat. 1943, 48-1006 et seq.

Prohibition Act (Fleming County)
Ky. Acts 1885-86 (Local and Private) Ch. 691

Prohibition Act (Hardin County)
Ky. Acts 1883-84 (Local and Private) Ch. 1285

Prohibition Act (Liquor)
Ala. Code 1975, § 28-4-1 et seq.
Ark. Acts 1915, p. 98, No. 30
Ark. Acts 1917, p. 41, No. 13
Ark. Acts 1921, p. 372, No. 324
Fla. Laws 1901, Ch. 4930
Fla. Laws 1918, Ch. 7736
Fla. Laws 1927, Ch. 12257
Ga. Code 1933, 58-101 et seq.
Ill. Laws 1921, p. 681
Ind. Laws 1917, Ch. 4, p. 15
Ind. Laws 1921, Ch. 250, p. 736
Ind. Laws 1923, Ch. 23, p. 70
Ind. Laws 1925, Ch. 48, p. 144
Iowa Code 1971, 125.1 et seq.
Kan. Laws 1881, Ch. 128
Kan. Laws 1917, Ch. 215
Kan. Stat. Ann., 41-101 et seq.
Ky. Acts 1920, Ch. 81
Ky. Acts 1922, Ch. 33
Ky. Rev. Stat. 1971, 244.170
La. Acts 1921, Extra Session, No. 39
Mich. Public Acts 1917, No. 338
Miss. Laws 1908, Ch. 115, p. 116
Mo. Laws 1919, p. 408, No. 2
N.C. Gen. Stat. 1943, § 18A-1 et seq.
N.D. Laws 1890, Ch. 110
N.D. Laws 1921, Ch. 97
Neb. Laws 1917, Ch. 187
Nev. Statutes 1919, Ch. 1, p. 1
Ohio Laws Vol. 108, p. 1182
Okla. Stat. Ann., Title 37
Ore. Laws 1915, Ch. 141
Ore. Rev. Stat., 471.405 et seq.
S.C. Acts 1917, p. 69 No. 38, p. 169 No. 94
S.D. Laws 1890, Ch. 101

S.D. Laws 1917, Ch. 281

Tex. Penal Code 1925, Art. 666 et seq.

Tex. Rev. Civ. Stat. 1925, Art. 5075 et seq.

Utah Laws 1917, Ch. 2

Va. Acts 1918, Ch. 388

Vt. Acts 1921, No. 204

Wash. Laws 1915, Ch. 2

Wash. Laws 1917, Ch. 19

W. Va. Code 1931, § 60-1-1 et seq.

Prohibition Act (Local Option)
Minn. Stat. Ann., 340.20 et seq.

Prohibition Act (Rent Control)
Mass. Gen. Laws Ann., 40Q:1 et seq.

Prohibition Act (Writ)
Mich. Comp. Laws 1948, 636.10 et seq.

Mont. Code Ann., 27-27-101 et seq.

Wash. Rev. Code Ann., 7.16.290 et seq.

Prohibition Acts
See National Prohibition Acts

Prohibition against Rifle and Shotgun Registration Act
Cal. Penal Code § 11106

Prohibition Amendment to Constitution
Dec. 19, 1917, 40 Stat. 1050

Prohibition Conformity Act
N.C. Gen. Stat. 1943, § 18A-1 et seq.

Prohibition Enforcement Act
Cal. Statutes 1921, Ch. 80, p. 79

Mo. Rev. Stat., 311.010 et seq.

Mont. Laws 1917, Ch. 143

N.J. Laws 1922, c 255

N.Y. Laws 1921, Chs. 155, 156

Pa. 1923 Pamph. Laws 34, No. 25

Wis. Laws 1921, Ch. 441

Prohibition of Cigarette Sales to Minors in Federal Buildings and Lands Act
Nov. 19, 1995, P.L. 104-52, Title VI, Sec. 636, 40 U.S. Code § 486 nt.

Prohibition of Female Genital Mutilation Act (New York State)
N.Y. Laws 1997, Ch. 618

Prohibition of Topless Entertainment Law
N.Y. Local Laws 1972, Village of Liberty, p. 3571

Prohibition Reorganization Act of 1930
May 27, 1930, Ch. 342, 46 Stat. 430, 19 U.S. Code §§ 1001, 2071, 2072

Prohibition Repeal Act
See Liquor Law Repeal and Enforcement Act

Project Act (Statewide Accounting)
Tex. Rev. Civ. Stat., Art. 4348f

Project Caanan Act
Tenn. Code Ann., 38-11-101 et seq.

Project DREAM (Dare to Reach for Educational Aspirations and Marks)
Wash. Laws 1991, Ch. 346

Project Early Start
R.I. Gen. Laws 1956, 42-72.3-1 et seq.

Project Even Start
Wash. Rev. Code Ann., 28B.06.010 et seq.

Project Finance Agency Act
N.Y. Laws 1975, Ch. 7

Project Finance Agency Act (New York State)
N.Y. Unconsolidated Law, § 6361 et seq.

Project Financing Community Improvement Districts Act
Ga. Laws 1991, p. 4339

Project Financing Community Improvement Districts Act (Burke County)
Ga. Laws 1991, p. 4136

Project for Human Services Demonstration Act
S.C. Code Ann. 1976, § 1-25-10 et seq.

Project Independence Act
Pa. Purdon's Stat., Title 62, § 3081 et seq.

Project Itemization Act (Capital Budget)
Pa. 1992 Pamph. Laws, No. 188

Project Mainstream Employment Tax Credit Act
N.M. Stat. Ann., 7-1A-1 et seq.

Project Priority List (State Fiscal Year 1990)
N.J. Laws 1991, Ch. 189, § 2; Ch. 190, § 3

Project Self-Reliance
Mich. Public Acts 1985, No. 117, § 136 to 147 et seq.

Project 70 Land Acquisition and Borrowing Act
Pa. Purdon's Stat., Title 72, § 3946.1 et seq.

Projects Act (Industrial Enterprise)
Miss. Code Ann. 1972, § 57-41-1 et seq.

Projects Financing Authority Act (Cambean Basin)
P.R. Acts 1989, First Special Session, No. 9

Promissory Note and Bank Holiday Act
Ill. Rev. Stat. 1991, Ch. 17, § 600 et seq.

Promotion Act (Dairy)
Ala. Code 1975, § 2-13-110 et seq.
N.Y. Agriculture and Markets Law (Consol. Laws Ch. 69) § 258aa

Promotion Act (Tourism)
Ill. Rev. Stat. 1991, Ch. 127, § 200-21 et seq.

Promotion Act (Trade Show)
Kan. Stat. Ann., 74-5075 et seq.

Promotion Coordinating Act (State Export)
Ill. Comp. Stat. 1992, Ch. 20, § 225/1 et seq.

Promotion of Agricultural Development Act
P.R. Laws Ann. 1954, Title 5, § 1551 et seq.

Promotional Advertising of Prizes Law
Wash. Rev. Code 1983, 19.170.010 et seq.

Promotional Scheme Act (Pyramid)
Okla. Stat. Ann., Title 21, § 1071 et seq.

Promotional Schemes Act (Pyramid)
N.M. Stat. Ann., 57-13-1 et seq.

Prompt Arraignment Act
Del. Code of 1974, Title 11, § 1909
N.Y. Criminal Procedure Law (Consol. Laws Ch. 11A) § 120.90

Prompt Disposition of Intrastate Detainers Act
Wis. Stat. Ann., 971.11

Prompt Pay Act
Ga. Code Ann., 13-11-1 et seq.

Prompt Payment Act
May 21, 1982, P.L. 97-177, 31 U.S. Code §§ 1801 et seq., 1981
Cal. Government Code § 926.15
Fla. Stat. Ann., 218.70 et seq.
Ill. Rev. Stat. 1991, Ch. 127, § 132.400 et seq.
Kan. Stat. Ann., 75-6401 et seq.
Neb. Rev. Stat. 1943, § 81-2401 et seq.
N.J. Stat. Ann., 52:32-32 et seq.
Ore. Rev. Stat., 293.462 et seq.
S.D. Codified Laws 1967, 5-26-1 et seq.
Tenn. Code Ann., 12-4-701 et seq.
Utah Code Ann. 1953, 15-6-1 et seq.

Prompt Payment Act (Construction)
Del. Code of 1974, Title 6, § 3501 et seq.

Prompt Payment Act (Debts of State)
N.Y. State Finance Law 1940 (Consol. Laws Ch. 56) § 179d et seq.

Prompt Payment Act (Local Government)
Ill. Rev. Stat. 1991, Ch. 85, § 4301 et seq.

Prompt Payment Act Amendments of 1988
Oct. 14, 1988, P.L. 100-496, 31 U.S. Code §§ 3901 nt., 3901 to 3907, 3903 nt., 3902 nt.; 15 U.S. Code § 644; 39 U.S. Code § 410

Prompt Payment Law (Construction Contract)
Fla. Laws 1992, Ch. 286

Prompt Processing Act (Housing)
N.Y. Laws 1991, Ch. 572
N.Y. Private Housing Finance Law (Consol. Laws Ch. 44B, §§ 1023, 1053

Proof of Foreign Statutes Act
Ariz. Rules of Civil Procedure 1955, Rule 44(d)
Haw. Rev. Stat. 1968, § 622-12
La. Rev. Stat. Ann., 15:424
S.D. Codified Laws 1967, 19-8-1 et seq.

Proof of Statutes Act
See also Uniform Proof of Statutes Act
See Uniform Proof of Statutes Act
Alaska Laws 1923, Ch. 4
Cal. Code of Civil Procedure § 1900
Del. Code of 1974, Title 10, § 4314
Ida. Code 1947, 9-304 et seq.
Ill. Rev. Stat. 1991, Ch. 110, § 8-1101, 8-1102
Ind. Code Ann., 34-3-1-1 et seq.
Kan. Stat. Ann., 1949, 60-2852
La. Rev. Stat. Ann., 13:3717 et seq.
Md. Ann. Code 1974, Art. CJ, § 10-202 et seq.
Mich. Comp. Laws Ann., 600.2114a, 600.2118a
Minn. Stat. Ann., 599.02
Mo. Rev. Stat., 490.010 et seq.
N.D. Cent. Code, 31-09-01 et seq.
Nev. Rev. Stat. 1967 Reprint, Replaced Pages, 49.010 et seq.
Ohio Rev. Code 1953, 2317.08
Ore. Rev. Stat. 1953, 43.310
Pa. Cons. Stat., Title 42, § 5327
S.D. Codified Laws 1967, 19-7-1 et seq.
Tex. Rules of Criminal Evidence, § 901 et seq.
Wash. Rev. Code Ann., 5.44.050

Proof of Statutes Act (Uniform)
Del. Code of 1974, Title 10, § 4314
Ill. Rev. Stat. 1991, Ch. 110, §§ 8-1101, 8-1102

Propaganda Agency Act
June 8, 1938, Ch. 327, 52 Stat. 631, 22 U.S. Code §§ 611 to 621

Propaganda Control Act (Communist)
La. Rev. Stat. Ann., 14:390 et seq.

Propagation of Quail and Pheasant Act (Commercial)
Okla. Stat. Ann., Title 29, § 4-106 et seq.

Propane and Natural Gas Act
Me. Rev. Stat. Ann. 1964, Title 32, § 14801 et seq.

Propane Education and Research Act
Ill. Comp. Stat. 1992, Ch. 430, § 27/1 et seq.
Mo. Laws 1993, S.B. No. 178, § A, Subsecs. 1 to 10

Propane Education and Research Act of 1996
Oct. 11, 1996, P.L. 104-284, 15 U.S. Code § 6401 nt.

Propane Education and Research Fund
Miss. Code Ann. 1972, § 75-57-119

Propane Gas Education, Safety, and Research Act
Fla. Stat. Ann., 527.20 to 527.23

Propane Storage and Safe Handling Act
Cal. Health and Safety Code § 13240 et seq.

Properties Insurance Reserve Fund Act (State)
Utah Code Ann. 1953, 63-9-23 et seq.

Property Acquisition Act (Emergency Archaeological)
Fla. Stat. Ann., 253.027

Property Acquisition Act (State)
Cal. Government Code, § 15850 et seq.
Ga. Code Ann., 22-1-1 et seq.

Property Acquisition Act (Transportation)
Ga. Code Ann., 32-3-1 et seq.

Property Acquisition Act for Management, Construction and Maintenance of Rights-of-Way by the State Highway Department in Advance of Present Need
Ga. Code Ann., 32-3-1

Property Act
Kan. Stat. Ann., 58-501 et seq.
Neb. Rev. Stat. 1943, 76-101 et seq.

Property Act (Abandoned)
See Abandoned Property Act

Property Act (Aliens)
See Alien Property Act

Property Act (Community)
See Community Property Act

Property Act (Condominium)
Haw. Rev. Stat. Ann., § 514A-1 et seq.
Neb. Rev. Stat. 1943, 76-801 et seq.

Property Act (Horizontal)
See Horizontal Property Act

Property Act (Manufactured Home Real)
Wash. Rev. Code 1983, 65.20.010 et seq.

Property Act (Married Women)
See Married Women's Property Act

Property Act (Museum)
Kan. Stat. Ann., 58-4001 et seq.
Mo. Rev. Stat. 1978, 184.101 et seq.

Property Act (Unclaimed)
See Unclaimed Property Act
See Uniform Unclaimed Property Act

Property and Alimony Act (Divorce)
Kan. Stat. Ann., 60-1610

Property and Buildings Commission Act
Ky. Rev. Stat. 1971, 56.440 et seq.

Property and Casualty Guaranty Association Act
Mich. Comp. Laws Ann., 500.7901 et seq.

Property and Casualty Insurance Data Reporting Act
Neb. Rev. Stat. 1943, 44-4601 et seq.

Property and Casualty Insurance Guarantee Act
N.M. Stat. Ann., 59A-43-1 et seq.

Property and Casualty Insurance Guarantee Association Act
Ark. Code Ann. 1987, 23-90-101 et seq.
Fla. Stat. Ann., 631.50
Mo. Rev. Stat. 1978, 375.771 et seq.
N.M. Stat. Ann., 59A-43-1 et seq.
Okla. Stat. Ann., Title 36, § 2001 et seq.
S.C. Code Ann. 1976, § 38-31-10 et seq.
Tex. Insurance Code, Art. 21.28-C
Vt. Stat. Ann., Title 8, § 3611 et seq.

Property and Casualty Insurance Policy Simplification Act
Ark. Code Ann. 1987, 23-80-301 et seq.

Property and Casualty Insurance Rate and Form Act
Neb. Rev. Stat. 1943, § 44-5001 et seq.

Property and Casualty Policy Language Simplification Act
Mont. Code Ann., 33-15-333 et seq.

Property and Contract Emancipation Statute (Married Women)
Iowa Code 1977, 597.1 et seq.

Property and Income Tax Relief Act
Mont. Laws 1979, Ch. 698

Property and Liability Insurance Guaranty Association Act
Neb. Rev. Stat. 1943, 44-2401 et seq.

Property and Mortgage Registry Act
P.R. Laws Ann. 1954, Title 30, § 2001 et seq.

Property and Renunciation of Fiduciary Powers Act
N.C. Gen. Stat. 1943, § 31B-1 et seq.

Property Appraisal Department Act
N.M. Stat. Ann. 1953, 72-25-1 et seq.

Property Assessment Act
Ind. Code Ann., 6-1.1-1-2, 6-1.1-1-3,
6-1.1-2-2, 6-1.1-3-1 et seq.
Ind. Code 1971, 6-1-20-1 et seq.

Property Assessment Administration and Finance Act
Fla. Stat. Ann., 195.0011 et seq.

Property Assessment and Classification Act
Tenn. Code Ann., 67-1-201 et seq.

Property Claims Act of 1943
Oct. 27, 1943, Ch. 287, 57 Stat. 582
Nov. 14, 1945, Ch. 468, 59 Stat. 578

Property Condition Disclosure Act
Ida. Code 1947, 55-2501 et seq.

Property Condition Disclosure Act (Residential)
Okla. Stat. Ann., Title 60, § 831 et seq.

Property Control Act
N.M. Stat. Ann., 15-3-1 et seq.

Property Defacing Control Act
Colo. Rev. Stat. 1963, 40-29-1 et seq.

Property Disposition Act (Unclaimed)
See Uniform Disposition of Unclaimed
Property Act

Property Fire Loss Act
Ill. Rev. Stat. 1991, Ch. 73, §§ 1152.1, 1153

Property in Transit Act (Free Port)
Nev. Rev. Stat. 1979 Reprint, 361.160 et seq.

Property Insurance Act (State)
Cal. Government Code, § 11007

Property Insurance Availability Act
Md. Ann. Code 1974, Art. IN, § 25-401 et seq.

Property Insurance Cancellation Control Act
Me. Rev. Stat. Ann. 1964, Title 24-A, § 3048 et seq.

Property Interests Act (Disclaimer of)
Me. Rev. Stat. Ann. 1964, Title 18-A, § 2-801 et seq.
Mich. Comp. Laws Ann., 554.871 et seq.

Property Interests Disclaimer Act
See Uniform Disclaimer of Property Interest Act

Property Law (Community)
Cal. Civil Code, § 164 et seq.

Property-Liability Insurance Guaranty Association Act
Neb. Rev. Stat. 1943, 44-2401 et seq.
N.J. Stat. Ann., 17:30A-1 et seq.

Property of Absent Persons Act (Curatorship of)
La. Rev. Stat. Ann., 13:3421 et seq.

Property of Unincorporated Associations Act
Ill. Rev. Stat. 1991, Ch. 30, § 182.9 et seq.

Property Owned by Aliens Act
Ill. Rev. Stat. 1991, Ch. 6, § 0.01 et seq.

Property Owners' Association Act
Ga. Code Ann., 44-3-220 et seq.

Property Owners' Improvement District Law
Ark. Code Ann. 1987, 14-93-101, 14-93-102 et seq.

Property Owners Roadside Vegetation Control Information Act
Cal. Food and Agricultural Code 1967, § 5501 et seq.

Property Posting Act
N.M. Stat. Ann. 1953, 40A-14-6 et seq.

Property Protection Act (Buyer)
Del. Code of 1974, Title 6, § 2570 et seq.

Property Recordation Act
N.C. Gen. Stat. 1943, § 47-17 et seq.

Property Recovery Act
Pa. Purdon's Stat., Title 71, § 826.1 et seq.

Property Recovery Act (Commonwealth)
Pa. Purdon's Stat., Title 71, § 826.1 et seq.

Property Redevelopment and Tax Abatement Act
Tex. Tax Code, § 312.001 et seq.

Property Regimes Act (Horizontal)
Wash. Rev. Code 1983, 64.32.010 et seq.

Property Registry Act
P.R. Laws Ann. 1954, Title 30, § 1748 et seq.

Property Relief Act
Ida. Code 1947, Superseded Vol., 63-3001 et seq.
Iowa Code Ann., 422.1 et seq.

Property Requisitioning Act
Oct. 16, 1941, Ch. 445, 55 Stat. 742
March 27, 1942, Ch. 199, 56 Stat. 181

Property Rights Acquisition Act
Mich. Comp. Laws Ann., 3.251 et seq.

Property Rights at Death Act
See Uniform Disposition of Community Property Rights at Death Act

Property Rights Preservation Act
Mich. Comp. Laws Ann., 24.421 et seq.

Property Sale Act (County Officer)
Ill. Comp. Stat. 1992, Ch. 55, § 55/0.01 et seq.

Property Sale Act (Library)
Ill. Rev. Stat. 1991, Ch. 81, § 27.99 et seq.

Property Tax Act
Alaska Laws 1949, Ch. 10
Colo. Rev. Stat. 1963, 137-1-1 et seq.
Ind. Code Ann., 6-1.1-1-1 et seq.
Mich. Comp. Laws Ann., 211.1 et seq.
N.J. Stat. Ann., 54:4-1 et seq.

N.M. Stat. Ann., 7-35-1 et seq.
Ohio Rev. Code 1953, 5701.01 et seq.
Okla. Stat. Ann., Title 68, § 2801 et seq.
Tex. Tax Code, § 1.01 et seq.
Utah Code Ann. 1953, 59-2-101 et seq.
Wash. Rev. Code Ann., 84.04.010 et seq.
Wis. Stat. Ann., 70.01 et seq.

Property Tax Act (Corporations)
Mich. Comp. Laws Ann., 211.5, 211.11

Property Tax Act (Exemption)
S.C. Code Ann. 1976, § 12-37-220

Property Tax Act (Homestead Rebate)
N.J. Stat. Ann., 54:4-8.57 et seq.

Property Tax Act (Intangibles)
See also Intangible Property Tax Act
Ga. Code Ann., 48-6-20 et seq., 48-6-60 et seq.

Property Tax Act (Personal)
See Personal Property Tax Act

Property Tax Act (Real)
See also Real Property Tax Act
Haw. Rev. Stat. Ann., § 246-1 et seq.

Property Tax Allocation Act (County Economic Development Project Area)
Ill. Rev. Stat. 1991, Ch. 34, § 7001 et seq.

Property Tax Alternatives Act (City)
Ida. Code 1947, 50-1043 et seq.

Property Tax Amnesty Program Act
Ga. Code Ann., 48-16A-1 et seq.

Property Tax and Fiscal Disclosure Law
R.I. Gen. Laws 1956, 44-35-1 et seq.

Property Tax Assistance Act (Senior Citizens)
Nev. Rev. Stat. 1979 Reprint, 361.800 et seq.
Pa. Purdon's Stat., Title 72, § 4751-1 et seq.

Property Tax Assistance Law
Cal. Revenue and Taxation Code § 20501 et seq.

Property Tax Code
Ill. Comp. Stat. 1992, Ch. 35, § 200/1-1 et
seq.

Property Tax Collection Act
Ind. Code Ann., 6-1.1-22-1 et seq.

Property Tax Credit Act
Ga. Code Ann., 48-7-29.3

Property Tax Deduction Act
N.J. Stat. Ann., 54A:3A-15 et seq.

Property Tax Deferral Act (Homestead)
Fla. Stat. Ann., 197.242 et seq.

Property Tax Deferral Reform Act
D.C. Code Ann., §§ 47-824, 47-845, 47-846

Property Tax Exemption Act
Ind. Code Ann., 6-1.1-11-1 et seq.
S.C. Code Ann. 1976, § 12-37-220

Property Tax Exemption Act (Homeowners)
Cal. Const. Art. 13, § 3
Cal. Revenue and Taxation Code §§ 218,
218.5, 251 et seq.

**Property Tax Exemption for Lands in
Intensive Agricultural Use Act**
P.R. Laws Ann. 1954, Title 13, § 622 et seq.

Property Tax Extension Limitation Act
Ill. Comp. Stat. 1992, Ch. 35, § 245/1 et seq.
Ill. Rev. Stat. 1989, Ch. 20, § 2501-1 et seq.

**Property Tax Extension Limitation Law
(One-Year)**
Ill. Comp. Stat. 1992, Ch. 35, §§ 18-246 to
18-249.5

Property Tax Levy Limitation Act
Wash. Rev. Code Ann., 84.52.050

Property Tax Limitation Act
Mich. Comp. Laws Ann., 211.201 et seq.

**Property Tax Limitation Act
(Roos-Johnson-Marks)**
Cal. Revenue and Taxation Code, §§ 97.2,
97.65

**Property Tax or Rent Rebate Act (Senior
Citizens)**
Pa. Purdon's Stat., Title 72, § 4751-1 et seq.

**Property Tax Postponement Act (Senior
Citizens Mobile Home)**
Cal. Revenue and Taxation Code, § 20639 et
seq.

**Property Tax Postponement Act (Senior
Citizens)**
Cal. Revenue and Taxation Code, § 20640 et
seq.

Property Tax Refund Act
Minn. Stat. Ann., 290A.01 et seq.

Property Tax Refund Act (Senior Citizen)
Ill. Rev. Stat. 1991, Ch. 24, §§ 1500, 1501

Property Tax Relief Act
Cal. Government Code, § 16100 et seq.
Cal. Revenue and Taxation Code, §§ 218,
401.4
Cal. Statutes 1972, Ch. 1406, p. 2931
Neb. Rev. Stat. 1943, 77-4201 et seq.
Ore. Rev. Stat. 1953, 315.001 et seq.
R.I. Gen. Laws 1956, 44-33-1 et seq.
S.D. Codified Laws 1967, 10-13-1 et seq.

**Property Tax Relief Act (Energy Tax
Receipts)**
N.J. Stat. Ann., 52:27D-438 et seq.

**Property Tax Relief Act (First and Second
Class County)**
Pa. Purdon's Stat., Title 72, § 4749.1 et seq.

Property Tax Relief Act (Homeowners)
Wash. Rev. Code Ann., 84.09.080,
84.33.040, 84.33.077, 84.33.078,
84.36.473, 84.36.475, 84.36.477,
84.40.405, 84.52.015, 84.55.005, 84.55.090

**Property Tax Relief Act (Senior Citizens and
Disabled Persons)**
Ill. Rev. Stat. 1991, Ch. 67 1/2, § 401 et seq.

**Property Tax Relief and Replacement Act
(Omnibus)**
R.I. Gen. Laws 1956, 44-45-1 et seq.

Property Tax Stabilization Act (Pinelands Municipal)
N.J. Stat. Ann., 54:1-68 et seq.

Property Tax Stabilization and Relief Act (Westchester County)
N.Y. Tax Law (Consol. Laws Ch. 60) § 1262b

Property Taxation and Professional Certification Act
Tex. Rev. Civ. Stat., Art. 8885

Property Taxes of Alien Landlords Act
Ill. Rev. Stat. 1991, Ch. 6, §§ 8.9, 9

Property Taxpayers Information Act
Mont. Code Ann., 15-10-202 et seq.

Property Transfer Act (Responsible)
Ill. Rev. Stat. 1991, Ch. 30, § 901 et seq.

Property Transfer Tax Act
Vt. Stat. Ann., Title 32, § 9601 et seq.

Prophylactic and Contraceptive Act
Ore. Rev. Stat., 435.010 et seq.

Prophylactic Control Act
Neb. Rev. Stat. 1943, 71-1104 et seq.

Proportional Registration
Wash. Rev. Code Ann., 46.87.010 et seq.

Proposed Ad Valorem Tax Increases Act (Advertisement of)
Miss. Laws 1994, Ch. 414

Proposition 13 (Jarvis-Gann Initiative)
Cal. Const. Art. 13A, § 1 et seq.

Proposition 13 Initiative (Jarvis-Gann)
Cal. Const. Art. 13A, § 1 et seq.

Proposition 218 Omnibus Implementation Act
Cal. Statutes 1997, Ch. 38

Proprietary Function Act (Municipal)
Neb. Rev. Stat. 1943, 18-2801 et seq.

Proprietary School Act
Colo. Rev. Stat., 12-59-101 et seq.
Ga. Code Ann., 20-4-60 et seq.
Kan. Stat. Ann., 72-4916 et seq.
Ky. Acts 1972, Ch. 340
Ky. Rev. Stat. 1971, Superseded Vols., 163.310 et seq.
S.C. Code Ann. 1976, § 40-60-70 et seq., § 59-59-10 et seq.
Tex. Education Code, § 32.01 et seq.
Wash. Rev. Code Ann., 18.82.010 et seq.

Proprietary School Act (Out-of-State)
N.M. Stat. Ann., 21-24-2

Proprietary School Act (Postsecondary)
Utah Code Ann. 1953, 53B-5-101 et seq.

Proprietary School and College Registration Law
Miss. Code Ann. 1972, § 75-60-1 et seq.

Proprietary School Education Assurance Act
Mich. Comp. Laws Ann., 395.251

Proraters, Check Sellers and Bill Payers Law
Cal. Financial Code, § 12000 et seq.
Cal. Food and Agriculture Code 1967, § 59501 et seq. § 59513 et seq.

Proration Act (Estate Taxes)
Conn. Gen. Stat. Ann., § 12-400 et seq.
Del. Code of 1974, Title 12, § 2901 et seq.
Fla. Stat. Ann., 733.817
Pa. 1937 Pamph. Laws 2762, No. 565

Proration Act (Federal Estate Tax)
Cal. Probate Law § 970 et seq.

Proration Act (Oil and Gas)
Okla. Laws 1933, p. 278
Tex. Natural Resources Code, § 85.053 et seq.

Proration Agreement (Bus Taxation)
Vt. Stat. Ann., Title 23, § 561 et seq.

Proration Prevention Act
Ala. Acts 1988, 2d Sp. Sess., No. 981

Proration Reciprocity and Taxation Agreement (Bus)
Me. Rev. Stat. Ann. 1964, Title 29, § 431 et seq.

Proration Reciprocity and Taxation Agreement Act (Bus)
Me. Rev. Stat. Ann. 1964, Title 36, § 1492 et seq.

Prosecuting Attorneys Coordinating Office Act
Mich. Comp. Laws Ann., 49.101 et seq.

Prosecuting Attorneys Salary Act
Ind. Code Ann., 33-14-7-1 et seq.

Prosecuting Attorneys Training Coordinator Act
Iowa Code Ann., 13A.1 et seq.

Prosecutor and Peace Officer Training Fund Act
Ga. Code Ann., 15-21-70 et seq.

Prosecutor Coordinator Act
Ark. Code Ann. 1987, 16-21-201 et seq.

Prosecutor's Advisory Council Act
Ill. Rev. Stat. 1991, Ch. 14, § 101 et seq.

Prosecutors Supersession Act
Pa. Purdon's Stat., Title 71, § 297

Prospective New Community Certification Act
Tenn. Code Ann., Superseded Vol., 13-1501 et seq.

Prosser Act (Contributory Negligence)
Ark. Stat. 1947, 27-1730.1 et seq.

Prosthetics and Orthodontics Act
Tex. Rev. Civ. Stat., Art. 8920

Prostitution Act
Haw. Rev. Stat. Ann., § 712-1200 et seq.
Ill. Rev. Stat. 1991, Ch. 38, § 11-14
Mich. Comp. Laws Ann., 750.448 et seq.

Minn. Stat. 1986, 617.33 et seq.
N.C. Gen. Stat. 1943, § 14-203 et seq.
N.Y. Penal Law 1965 (Consol. Laws Ch. 40) § 230.00 et seq.

Prostitution Coercion Liability Act
Haw. Session Laws 1999, Act 203

Prostitution Solicitation Act
Mich. Comp. Laws Ann., 750.448 et seq.

Prostrate Cancer Act
Cal. Health and Safety Code § 104310 et seq.

Prostrate Cancer Detection Act (Grace H. Kenyon)
Cal. Business and Professions Code § 2248

Protected Facilities for Housing Government Witnesses Act
N.J. Stat. Ann., 2A:18-61.22 et seq.

Protected Rivers Act
Conn. Public Acts 1994, No. 150

Protected Tenancy Act (Senior Citizens and Disabled)
N.J. Stat. Ann., 2A:18-61.22 et seq.

Protection Act (Battered Women)
Cal. Health and Safety Code § 300.5

Protection Act (Capitol View)
Cal. Government Code § 8162.5 et seq.

Protection Act (Consumer)
See also Uniform Consumer Protection Act
N.Y. Adm. Code '85, § 20-700 et seq.

Protection Act (Credit Services)
Mich. Comp. Laws Ann., 445.1821 et seq.

Protection Act (Groundwater and Freshwater)
Mich. Comp. Laws Ann., 286.851 et seq.

Protection Act (Insurance Fraud)
Mont. Code Ann., 33-1-1201 et seq.

Protection Act (Natural Areas)
R.I. Gen. Laws 1956, 42-122-1 et seq.

Protection Act (Radiation)

Miss. Code Ann. 1972, § 45-14-7 et seq.

Protection Act (Telephone Sales)

N.Y. Personal Property Law (Consol. Laws Ch. 41) § 440 et seq.

Protection Act (Volunteer)

Fla. Stat. 1992, 768.1355

Protection and Advocacy for Developmentally Disabled Persons Act

Ill. Rev. Stat. 1991, Ch. 91 1/2, §§ 1150, 1151

Protection and Advocacy for Mentally Ill Individuals Act of 1986

May 23, 1986, P.L. 99-319, 42 U.S. Code § 10801 nt.

Oct. 18, 1988, P.L. 100-509, 42 U.S. Code §§ 10802, 10804 to 10806, 10821, 10822, 10825, 10827, 10827 nt.

Nov. 27, 1991, P.L. 102-173, 42 U.S. Code §§ 10801 et seq.

July 10, 1992, P.L. 102-321, 42 U.S. Code §§ 10821, 10826

April 30, 1997, P.L. 105-12, 42 U.S. Code § 10805

Protection and Advocacy for Mentally Ill Individuals Amendments Act of 1988

Oct. 18, 1988, P.L. 100-509, 42 U.S. Code § 10801 nt.

Protection and Advocacy for Mentally Ill Individuals Amendments Act of 1991

Nov. 27, 1991, P.L. 102-173, 42 U.S. Code § 10801 nt.

Protection and Advocacy for Mentally Ill Persons Act

Ill. Rev. Stat. 1991, Ch. 91 1/2, § 1350 et seq.

Protection and Indemnity Club, and Commercial Fishermen's Hull Insurance Act

N.C. Gen. Stat. 1943, § 58-340.1 et seq.

Protection and Preservation of the Caves, Caverns or Sinkholes Act

P.R. Laws Ann. 1954, Title 12, § 1143 et seq.

Protection and Reduction of Government Secrecy Act

April 30, 1994, P.L. 103-236, 50 U.S. Code § 401 nt.

Protection and Safe Pursuit Act (Police and Bystander)

Cal. Vehicle Code § 14602.1

Protection and Use of Intellectual Property Act

Tex. Health and Safety Code, § 12.020

Protection Association Act (Health and Life Insurance)

Colo. Rev. Stat., 10-20-101 et seq.

Protection District Act

Cal. Statutes 1880, Ch. 63, p. 55

Cal. Statutes 1895, Ch. 201, p. 247

Cal. Statutes 1907, Ch. 25, p. 16

Protection District Act (Flood Control)

Cal. Water Code, Appendix §§ 4-1 et seq., 6-1 et seq., 11-1 et seq.

Protection from Abuse Act

Ala. Code 1975, § 30-5-1 et seq.

Kan. Stat. Ann., 60-3101 et seq.

Pa. Cons. Stat., Title 23, § 6101 et seq.

Protection from Domestic Abuse Act

La. Rev. Stat. Ann., 46:2121 et seq.

Miss. Code Ann. 1972, § 93-21-1 et seq.

Neb. Rev. Stat. 1943, 42-901 et seq.

N.M. Stat. Ann., 40-13-1 et seq.

Okla. Stat. Ann., Title 22, § 60 et seq.

S.C. Code Ann. 1976, § 20-4-10 et seq.

S.D. Codified Laws 1967, 25-10-1 et seq.

Protection Fund Act (Great Lakes)

Pa. Purdon's Stat., Title 32, § 817.11

Protection Island National Wildlife Refuge Act

Oct. 15, 1982, P.L. 97-333, 16 U.S. Code § 668dd nt.

Mich. Comp. Laws Ann., 3.671 et seq.

Protection Law (Consumer)
La. Rev. Stat. Ann., 51:1401 et seq.

Protection of Children Against Exploitation Act
Ark. Code Ann. 1987, 5-27-301 et seq.

Protection of Children against Sexual Exploitation
Tenn. Code Ann., 39-17-1001 et seq.

Protection of Children Against Sexual Exploitation Act of 1977
Feb. 6, 1978, P.L. 95-225, 18 U.S. Code §§ 2423, 2251 et seq. 2251 nt.

Protection of Children From Sexual Predators Act of 1998
Oct. 30, 1998, P.L. 105-314, 112 Stat. 2974, 18 U.S. Code § 1 nt.

Protection of Copyrights Act
See Copyright Act

Protection of Foreign Officials and Official Guests of the United States Act
Oct. 24, 1972, P.L. 92-539, 86 Stat. 1070, 18 U.S. Code §§ 112, 970, 1116, 1117, 1201

Protection of Groundwater Act
N.M. Stat. Ann., 74-6B-1 et seq.

Protection of Highways Law (County)
Cal. Streets and Highways Code, § 1480 et seq.

Protection of Highways Law (State)
Cal. Streets and Highways Code, § 660 et seq.

Protection of Home Buyers from Loss of Contract Deposits Law (Village of Spring Valley)
N.Y. Local Laws 1969, Village of Spring Valley, p. 2915

Protection of Human Subjects in Medical Experimentation Act
Cal. Health and Safety Code, § 24170 et seq.

Protection of Minors Act
D.C. Code Ann., § 22-2011 et seq.

Protection of Minors from Harmful Materials Act
N.C. Gen. Stat. 1943, § 19-9 et seq.
Tex. Penal Code, § 43.24

Protection of Persons from Restraint Act
Colo. Rev. Stat., 26-20-101 et seq.

Protection of Public Employee Retirement Benefits Act
Fla. Stat. Ann., 112.60 et seq.

Protection of Public Employees Act
Ida. Code 1947, 6-2103 et seq.
Utah Code Ann. 1953, 67-21-1 et seq.

Protection of Public Water Supply Act
Wyo. Stat. Ann., § 35-4-201 et seq.

Protection of the Abused, Neglected, or Exploited Disabled Adult Act
N.C. Gen. Stat. 1943, § 108A-99 et seq.

Protection of the Abused or Neglected Elderly Act
N.C. Gen. Stat. 1943, § 108A-40 et seq.

Protection of Tidewaters Act
Ga. Code Ann., 52-1-1 et seq.

Protection Orders Act (Child)
Mo. Laws 1991, H.B. No. 598

Protection to Motor Vehicle Buyers Act
P.R. Laws Ann. 1954, Title 23, § 1021 et seq.

Protective Act (Livestock Sellers)
Neb. Rev. Stat. 1943, 54-1801 et seq.

Protective and Guardianship Proceedings Act
Ala. Acts 1991, p. 975

Protective Committee Act
Mich. Comp. Laws Ann., 451.302 et seq.

Protective Services Act (Adult)
Fla. Stat. Ann., 415.101 et seq.
Me. Rev. Stat. Ann. 1964, Title 22, § 3470 et seq.
N.J. Stat. Ann., 52:27D-406 et seq.
N.M. Stat. Ann., 27-7-14 et seq.
Continued

N.Y. Social Services Law (Consol. Laws Ch. 55) §§ 473a, 473b

Protective Services Act (Children)
Cal. Welfare and Institutions Code, § 16500 et seq.

Protective Services Act (Older Adults)
Pa. Purdon's Stat., Title 35, § 10229.101 et seq.

Protective Services Act for Aged Persons or Disabled Adults
Mont. Code Ann., 52-3-201 et seq.
Okla. Stat. Ann., Title 43A, § 10-101 et seq.
Pa. Purdon's Stat., Title 35, § 10211 et seq.

Protective Services for Mentally Retarded Persons Act
Vt. Stat. Ann., Title 33, § 3601 et seq.

Protest Fund Act (State Treasury)
Ill. Rev. Stat. 1991, Ch. 127, § 172, 172a

Providence Charter Act
R.I. Public Laws 1940, Ch. 832

Providence Finance Act
R.I. Public Laws 1945, Ch. 1665

Providence Hospital Commemorative Plaque Act
May 28, 1986, P.L. 99-325, 100 Stat. 501

Providence Minimum Standards Housing Act
R.I. Public Laws 1956, Ch. 3715

Providence Mobile Home Parks and Trailer Camps Local Law
N.Y. Local Laws 1972, Town of Providence, p. 2616

Providence Retirement Act
R.I. Public Laws 1923, Ch. 489

Provider Act (Primary Care)
Neb. Rev. Stat. 1943, 71-5210 et seq.

Provider Agreements Act (Preferred)
Mont. Laws 1991, Ch. 638

Provider Assessment Act (Health Care)
R.I. Gen. Laws 1956, 44-50-1 et seq.

Provider Assessment Act (Nursing Facility)
R.I. Gen. Laws 1956, 44-51-1 et seq.

Provider Assessment Act (Outpatient Health Care Facility)
R.I. Gen. Laws 1956, 44-52-1 et seq.

Provider Cooperation Act (Health Care Facility)
Neb. Rev. Stat. 1943, 71-7701 et seq.

Provider Cooperation Act (Health Care)
Kan. Stat. Ann., 65-4955 et seq.

Provider Self-Referral Act
S.C. Code Ann. 1976, § 44-113-10 et seq.

Provider Self-Referral Act (Health Care)
S.C. Code Ann. 1976, § 44-113-30 et seq.

Provider Service Network Act
N.M. Stat. Ann., 59D-42A-1 to 59D-42A-9

Provider Tax Act (Health Care)
W. Va. Code 1966 § 11-27-1 et seq.

Provincetown Water Loan Act
Mass. Acts 1952, Ch. 439

Provincetown Wharf Loan Act
Mass. Acts 1955, Ch. 139

Provisional Convention between Portugal and the Hawaiian Islands
Haw. Session Laws 1882, p. 122, Aug. 26, 1882

Provisional Credit Law (Bank Collections)
N.J. Stat. Ann., Superseded Vol., 17:9A-235

Provisional Governments Resolution (Virginia, Texas, Mississippi)
Feb. 18, 1869, No. 8, 15 Stat. 344

Provisional Legal Status Act
P.R. Laws Ann. 1954, Title 32, § 2871 et seq.

Provisional Order Act (Street Improvement)
N.M. Stat. Ann., 3-33-11 et seq.

Provisional Remedies Act
Ariz. Rev. Stat. Ann., § 12-2401 et seq.

Proxies Act (Health Care)
Mass. Gen. Laws 1984, 201D:1 et seq.

Proximity Act (High-Voltage)
N.Y. Labor Law (Consol. Laws Ch. 31)
§ 202h

Proxmire Act
See Genocide Convention Implementation
Act of 1987

Prudent Investor Act
See also Uniform Prudent Investor Act
Kan. Stat. Ann., 17-5004 et seq.
Mass. Gen. Laws Ann., 203B:1 et seq.
N.J. Stat. Ann., 3B:20-11.1 et seq.

Prudent Man Act
N.H. Rev. Stat. 1955, 564:18, Subd. 5

Prudent Man Act (Investments)
Cal. Civil Code, § 2261
Cal. Probate Code, § 1121 et seq.
Colo. Rev. Stat., 15-1-301 et seq.
Del. Code of 1974, Title 12, §§ 3302, 3526
Ida. Code 1947, 68-501 et seq.
Ill. Rev. Stat. 1991, Ch. 17, § 1675
Iowa Code Ann., 633.123
Kan. Stat. Ann., 17-5004 et seq.
La. Rev. Stat. Ann., 9:2127
Me. Rev. Stat. Ann. 1964, Title 18A, § 7-302
Mich. Comp. Laws Ann., 555.201
N.H. Rev. Stat. 1955, 564:18, Subd. IV
N.J. Stat. Ann., 3A:15-35 et seq.
N.M. Stat. Ann. 1953, 33-1-16
Ohio Rev. Code 1953, 2109.371
Okla. Stat. Ann., Title 60, § 161
Ore. Rev. Stat., 128.057
Tenn. Code Ann., 35-3-117
Tex. Property Code, § 113.056
Utah Code Ann. 1953, 75-7-402 et seq.
Va. Code 1950, § 26-45.1
Wis. Stat. Ann., 881.01

Prudent Purchaser Act
Mich. Comp. Laws Ann., 550.51 et seq.

Prune Commission Act
Ida. Code 1947, 22-3001 et seq.

Pseudorabies and Swine Brucellosis Control and Eradication Act
Mich. Comp. Laws Ann., 287.801 et seq.

Pseudorabies Control Act
Ill. Rev. Stat. 1991, Ch. 8, § 801 et seq.
Neb. Rev. Stat. 1943, 54-2201 et seq.
S.C. Code Ann. 1976, § 47-6-10 et seq.

Psychiatric and Chemical Dependency Facility Certificate of Need Act
Okla. Stat. Ann., Title 63, § 1-871 et seq.

Psychiatric Inpatient Treatment of Minors Act
Va. Code 1950, § 16.1-335 et seq.

Psychiatric Technician Certification Act
Cal. Business and Professions Code, §§ 4500 et seq., 4510 et seq.

Psychiatrist-Patient Privileged Communication Act
Conn. Gen. Stat. Ann., § 52-146d
Ga. Code Ann., 24-9-21, 24-9-40
Utah Code Ann. 1953, 58-25A-9

Psychiatrists Act (Mental Examination of Defendants)
Pa. 1933 Pamph. Laws 224, No. 78

Psychiatry and Neurology Service Act (University Hospital)
Okla. Stat. 1961, Title 70, § 3301 et seq.

Psychological Corporations Act
Cal. Business and Professions Code, § 2995 et seq.

Psychological Services Act
Fla. Stat. Ann., 490.001 et seq.

Psychologist Act
Cal. Business and Professions Code, § 2900 et seq.
Colo. Rev. Stat., 12-43-101 et seq.

Continued

Conn. Gen. Stat. Ann., § 20-186 et seq.

D.C. Code Ann., §§ 2-1704.1 et seq., 2-1704.12, 2-1704.13, 2-1704.14, 2-1704.7

Fla. Stat. Ann., 490.001 et seq.

Ga. Code Ann., 43-39-1 et seq.

Ill. Rev. Stat. 1991, Ch. 82, § 550 et seq.

Ill. Rev. Stat. 1991, Ch. 111, § 5351 et seq.

Kan. Stat. Ann., 74-5301 et seq.

Mass. Gen. Laws. Ann., 112:118 et seq.

Md. Ann. Code 1974, Art. HO, § 18-101 et seq.

Mich. Comp. Laws Ann., 333.18201 et seq., 333.18211 et seq.

Minn. Stat. Ann., 148.88 et seq.

Mo. Rev. Stat., 337.010 et seq.

N.C. Gen. Stat. 1943, § 90-270.1 et seq.

N.D. Cent. Code, 43-32-01 et seq.

Neb. Rev. Stat. 1943, 71-3801 et seq.

N.H. Rev. Stat. 1955, 330-A:1 et seq.

N.M. Stat. Ann., 61-9-1 et seq.

Okla. Stat. Ann., Title 59, § 1351 et seq.

Pa. Purdon's Stat., Title 63, § 1201 et seq.

P.R. Laws Ann. 1954, Title 20, § 3201 et seq.

Tex. Rev. Civ. Stat., Art. 4512c

Wash. Rev. Code Ann., 18.83.005 et seq.

Psychologist Licensing Act
Utah Code Ann. 1953, 58-61-101 et seq.

Psychologist Lien Act (Clinical)
Ill. Comp. Stat. 1992, Ch. 770, § 10/0.01 et seq.

Psychologist's Certification and Licensing Act
Tex. Rev. Civ. Stat., Art. 4512c

Psychologists Licensing Act (Clinical)
Ill. Comp. Stat. 1992, Ch. 225, § 15/1 et seq.

Psychologist's Lien Act
Mont. Code Ann., 71-3-1111 et seq.

Psychology Licensing Law
Cal. Business and Professions Code § 2900 et seq.

Psychopathic Act (Criminal Sexual)
Ill. Rev. Stat. 1991, Ch. 38, § 105-1.01 et seq.

Psychopathic Delinquents Act
Cal. Welfare and Institutions Code, § 7050 et seq.
Wash. Rev. Code Ann., 71.06.010 et seq.

Psychopathic Offender Act
Ohio Rev. Code 1953, 2947.24 et seq.

Psychopathic Parole Act
Cal. Welfare and Institutions Code, § 5075 et seq.

Psychopathic Personality Act
Mass. Gen. Laws. Ann., 123A:1 et seq.
Minn. Stat. Ann., 526.09 et seq.

Psychotherapist Regulation Act (Social)
Tex. Rev. Civ. Stat., Art. 4512f

Psychotherapy Sexual Exploitation Act
Ill. Rev. Stat. 1991, Ch. 70, § 800 et seq.

Psychotropic Substances Act of 1978
Nov. 10, 1978, P.L. 95-633, 21 U.S. Code §§ 352, 801 nt., 801a, 802, 811, 812, 823, 827, 830, 841 to 843, 852, 872, 881, 952, 953, 965

Public Accommodations Act (Civil Rights)
Alaska Stat. 1962, § 18.80.230
Cal. Civil Code, §§ 51, 52
Colo. Rev. Stat., 24-34-601 et seq.
Conn. Gen. Stat. Ann., § 46a-64
Del. Code of 1974, Title 24, § 1501
Ida. Code 1947, 18-7301 et seq.
Ill. Rev. Stat. 1991, Ch. 68, § 5-101 et seq.
Ind. Code Ann., 22-9-1-1 et seq.
Iowa Code Ann., 601A.1 et seq.
Kan. Stat. Ann., 44-1001 et seq.
Ky. Rev. Stat. 1971, 344.120 et seq.
Mass. Gen. Laws. Ann., 272:98
Md. Ann. Code 1957, Art. 49B, § 11 et seq.
Me. Rev. Stat. Ann. 1964, Title 5, § 4591 et seq.
Me. Rev. Stat. Ann. 1964, Title 17, § 1301-A
Mich. Comp. Laws Ann., 750.146 et seq.
Minn. Stat. Ann., 363.03
Mo. Rev. Stat., 213.065 et seq.
Neb. Rev. Stat. 1943, 20-302 et seq.
Nev. Rev. Stat. 1979 Reprint, 651.050 et seq.

N.H. Rev. Stat. 1955, 354-A:8, Subd. IV

N.J. Stat. Ann., 10:1-2 et seq.

N.M. Stat. Ann., 28-1-7 et seq.

N.Y. Civil Rights Law (Consol. Laws Ch. 6) § 40 et seq.

Ohio Rev. Code 1953, 4112.01 et seq.

Ore. Rev. Stat., 30.670 et seq.

Pa. Purdon's Stat., Title 18, § 4654

R.I. Gen. Laws 1956, 11-24-1 et seq.

S.D. Codified Laws 1967, 20-13-23 et seq., 20-12-1 et seq.

Vt. Stat. Ann., Title 9, § 4501 et seq.

Wash. Rev. Code Ann., 9.91.010, 49.60.215

Wis. Stat. Ann., 942.04

Public Accomodations Act

Alaska Stat. 1962, § 11.60.230

N.H. Rev. Stat. 1955, 353:1 et seq.

Ore. Rev. Stat., 30.670 et seq.

Public Accountancy Act

Md. Ann. Code 1974, Art. BO, § 2-101 et seq.

Neb. Rev. Stat. 1943, 1-105 to 1-171

N.M. Stat. Ann., 61-28A-1 et seq.

Public Accountants Act

Ala. Code 1975, § 34-1-1 et seq.

Alaska Stat. 1962, § 08.04.005 et seq.

Ark. Code Ann. 1987, 17-12-101, 17-12-102 et seq.

Cal. Business and Professions Code, § 5000 et seq.

Colo. Rev. Stat., 12-2-101 et seq.

D.C. Code Ann., § 2-101 et seq.

Fla. Stat. Ann., 473.301 et seq.

Ga. Code Ann., 43-3-1 et seq.

Haw. Rev. Stat. Ann., § 466-1 et seq.

Ida. Code 1947, 54-201 et seq.

Ill. Rev. Stat. 1991, Ch. 111, § 5500.01 et seq.

Ind. Code Ann., 25-2-1-1 et seq.

Iowa Code Ann., 116.1 et seq.

Ky. Rev. Stat. 1971, 325.220 et seq.

Md. Ann. Code 1974, Art. BO, § 2-101 et seq.

Md. Ann. Code 1974, Art. BP, §§ 2-701, 2-702

Mich. Comp. Laws Ann., 338.2101 et seq.

Miss. Code Ann. 1972, § 73-33-1 et seq.

Mont. Code Ann., 37-50-101 et seq.

N.C. Gen. Stat. 1943, § 93-1 et seq.

N.D. Cent. Code, 43-02.1-01 et seq.

Neb. Rev. Stat. 1943, 1-106 et seq.

Nev. Rev. Stat. 1979 Reprint, 628.015 et seq.

N.H. Rev. Stat. 1955, 309A:1 et seq.

N.J. Stat. Ann., 45:2B-1 et seq.

N.M. Stat. Ann., 61-28-1 et seq.

N.Y. Education Law 1947 (Consol. Laws Ch. 16) § 7400 et seq.

Okla. Stat. Ann., Title 59, § 15.1 et seq.

P.R. Laws Ann. 1954, Title 20, § 771 et seq.

R.I. Gen. Laws 1956, 5-3-1 et seq.

S.C. Code Ann. 1976, § 40-1-10 et seq.

S.D. Codified Laws 1967, 36-20-1 et seq.

Tenn. Code Ann., 62-1-101 et seq.

Tex. Rev. Civ. Stat. Art. 41a-1

Utah Code Ann. 1953, 58-26-1 et seq.

Vt. Stat. Ann., Title 26, § 13 et seq.

Wash. Rev. Code Ann. 18.04.015 et seq.

Wis. Stat. Ann., 442.01 et seq.

Wyo. Stat. Ann., § 33-3-101 et seq.

Public Accounting Act (Public Funds—Supervision)

Ind. Code Ann., 5-11-1-1 et seq.

Public Adjuster Regulatory Act

Ill. Rev. Stat. 1983, Ch.111, § 751 et seq.

Md. Ann. Code 1957, Art. 48A, § 181

Public Adjusters' Licensing Act

N.J. Stat. Ann., 17:22B-1 et seq.

Public Administrator Act

Mich. Comp. Laws Ann., 720.201 et seq.

Public Advocate Act

N.J. Stat. Ann., 52:27E-1 et seq.

Public Advocate Restructuring Act

N.J. Stat. Ann., 52:27E-50 et seq.

Public Agencies Joint Exercise of Powers Act

Mass. Gen. Laws Ann., 40:4A

Public Agencies Joint Powers Act

Cal. Government Code, § 6500 et seq.

Public Agencies Meeting Act
Ill. Rev. Stat. 1991, Ch. 102, § 41.01 et seq.

Public Agencies Roster Act
Cal. Government Code, § 53050 et seq.

Public Airport Authority Act
Colo. Rev. Stat., 41-3-101 et seq.

Public Airports Act
Utah Code Ann. 1953, 2-5-1 et seq.

Public and Assisted Housing Drug Elimination Act of 1990
Nov. 28, 1990, P.L. 101-625, 42 U.S. Code §§ 11901 to 11909
Oct. 26, 1996, P.L. 104-330, 42 U.S. Code §§ 11902 to 11905
Oct. 21, 1998, P.L. 105-276, 42 U.S. Code §§ 11902 to 11905

Public and Assisted Housing Drug Elimination Program Amendments of 1998
Oct. 21, 1998, P.L. 105-276, § 586, 112 Stat. 2646, 42 U.S. Code § 11901 nt.

Public and Business Records as Evidence Act
Me. Rev. Stat. Ann. 1964, Title 16, § 451 et seq.
Pa. Cons. Stat., Title 42, §§ 6108, 6109

Public and Community Service Programs Act
Ill. Comp. Stat. 1992, Ch. 745, § 10/6A-101 et seq.

Public and Private Sector Copartnership for the New Housing Operation
P.R. Laws Ann. 1954, Title 17, § 891 et seq.

Public and School Employees' Health Benefits Act
N.J. Rev. Stat. 1937, 52:14-17.25 et seq.

Public Assembly Act
N.Y. City Adm. Code '38, Ch. 26, § C26-1437.0 et seq.

Public Assembly Act (Segregation)
Va. Code 1950, §§ 18.1-356, 18.1-357

Public Assistance Act
Colo. Rev. Stat., 26-2-101 et seq.
D.C. Code Ann., § 3-201.1 et seq.
Del. Code of 1974, Title 31, § 501 et seq.
Ga. Code Ann., 49-4-1 et seq.
Ida. Code 1947, 56-201 et seq.
Ill. Rev. Stat. 1991, Ch. 23, § 1-1 et seq.
Ky. Rev. Stat. 1971, 205.010 et seq.
Mich. Comp. Laws Ann., 400.1 et seq.
N.H. Rev. Stat. 1955, 167:1 et seq.
N.M. Stat. Ann., 27-2-1 et seq.
Ore. Rev. Stat., 411.010 et seq.
Pa. Purdon's Stat., Title 62, § 401 et seq.
R.I. Gen. Laws 1956, 40-6-1 et seq.
Utah Code Ann. 1953, 55-15-1 et seq.
Wash. Rev. Code Ann., 74.04.005 et seq.
Wis. Stat. Ann., 49.001 et seq.
Wyo. Stat. Ann., § 42-1-101 et seq.

Public Assistance Appeals Act
N.M. Stat. Ann., 27-3-1 et seq.

Public Assistance Home Repair, Weatherization and Shutoff Protection Act
Mich. Comp. Laws Ann., 400.1151 et seq.

Public Assistance Payment Increase Act
D.C. Code Ann., § 3-205.25

Public Assistance Payments Cycling Act
N.J. Laws 1985, Ch. 501
N.J. Stat. Ann., 44:10-5.1 et seq.

Public Assistance Productivity Act
Fla. Stat. Ann., 409.027

Public Assistance Programs Act (State)
Md. Ann. Code 1974, Department of Human Resources, § 63

Public Assistance Records Non Disclosure Act
Alaska Stat. 1962, § 47.05.030

Public Assistance Regulation Revising the Definition of Certain Terms of the Financial and Medical Assistance Programs
D.C. Laws 1977, No. 1-108

Public Assistance Reserve Fund Act
R.I. Gen. Laws 1956, Superseded Vol., 40-10-1 et seq.

Public Assistance Technical Clarification, Administration of Oaths, and Police Service and Fire Service Schedule Approval Act
D.C. Code Ann., §§ 1-338.1, 3-205.52

Public Auction Act
Mich. Comp. Laws Ann., 446.51 et seq.
Mont. Code Ann., 30-11-501 et seq.
Neb. Laws 1955, Ch. 266
Okla. Stat. Ann., Title 59, § 981 et seq.

Public Auction Act (New Goods)
Kan. Stat. Ann., 58-1014 et seq.

Public Auction Sales Act
Ohio Rev. Code 1953, 1318.01 et seq.

Public Audit Act
Colo. Rev. Stat. 1963, 110-1-1 et seq.

Public Auditorium Authorities Law
Pa. Purdon's Stat., Title 53, § 23841 et seq.

Public Authorities Act
N.Y. Consol. Laws, Ch. 43A

Public Bathing Act
Pa. Purdon's Stat., Title 35, § 672 et seq.

Public Benefit Corporation Act (Nonprofit)
Cal. Corporations Code, § 5110 et seq.

Public Bid Act
La. Rev. Stat. Ann., 38:2181 et seq.

Public Bid Disclosure Act
Fla. Stat. Ann., 218.80

Public Bidder Act
Iowa Code Ann., 446.19, 446.21

Public Bidding Act (Municipal Contracts)
N.J. Stat. Ann., 40A:11-4 et seq.

Public Bodies Purchasing Act
Miss. Code Ann. 1972, § 31-7-301 et seq.

Public Bond Sale Act
Iowa Code Ann., 75.1 et seq.

Public Borrowing Act
Va. Code 1950, § 15-605.1 et seq.

Public Bridge Authority Act (Buffalo and Fort Erie)
N.Y. Laws 1933, Ch. 824

Public Broadcasting Act
Cal. Government Code, § 8800 et seq.
Haw. Rev. Stat. Ann., § 314-1 et seq.
N.J. Stat. Ann., 48:23-1 et seq.
Tenn. Public Acts 1984, Ch. 514

Public Broadcasting Act of 1967
Nov. 7, 1967, P.L. 90-129, 81 Stat. 365, 47 U.S. Code §§ 390 to 399
April 26, 1968, P.L. 90-294, 82 Stat. 108, 47 U.S. Code § 396

Public Broadcasting Amendments Act of 1981
Aug. 13, 1981, P.L. 97-35, 47 U.S. Code § 609 nt.
Jan. 3, 1983, P.L. 97-410, 47 U.S. Code § 396 nt.

Public Broadcasting Council Act
Kan. Stat. Ann., 75-4912 et seq.

Public Broadcasting Financing Act of 1970
Oct. 7, 1970, P.L. 91-437, 84 Stat. 888, 47 U.S. Code § 396
Dec. 31, 1975, P.L. 94-192, 89 Stat. 1099, 47 U.S. Code §§ 396, 397

Public Broadcasting Financing Act of 1975
Dec. 31, 1975, P.L. 94-192, 47 U.S. Code §§ 396 et seq.

Public Building Act (Construction and Repair)
Mass. Gen. Laws. Ann., 149:29

Public Building and Housing Project Assistance Act
Alaska Stat. 1962, § 18.55.010 et seq.

Public Building Authority (Jefferson)
Ga. Laws 1999, H.B. 833

Public Building Authority Act
Ark. Stat. 1947, 5-1001 et seq.
Ill. Rev. Stat. 1991, Ch. 127, § 213.01 et seq.
Ind. Code Ann., 19-8-4-1 et seq.
Tenn. Code Ann., 12-10-101 et seq.
Tex. Rev. Civ. Stat. 1974, Art. 601c
Va. Code 1950, § 2.1-234.10 et seq.

Public Building Bond Act
Wash. Rev. Code Ann., 43.83.010 et seq.

Public Building Commission Act
Ill. Rev. Stat. 1991, Ch. 85, § 1031 et seq.

Public Building Construction and Planning Act
Okla. Stat. Ann., Title 61, § 201 et seq.

Public Building Construction Bond Act
N.J. Laws 1968, Ch. 128

Public Building Contracts Act
N.C. Gen. Stat. 1943, § 143-128 et seq.

Public Building Egress Act
Ill. Rev. Stat. 1991, Ch. 111 1/2, § 3500 et seq.

Public Building Energy Efficiency and Water Conservation Act
N.M. Stat. Ann., 6-23-1 et seq.

Public Building Safety Law
Va. Code 1950, § 27-63 et seq.

Public Buildings Accessibility Act
Tenn. Code Ann., 68-18-201 et seq.

Public Buildings Act
May 25, 1926, Ch. 380, 44 Stat. 630, 40 U.S. Code §§ 341, 342, 344 to 347
June 16, 1949, Ch. 218, 63 Stat. 199, 40 U.S. Code § 345
Sept. 2, 1958, P.L. 85-886, 72 Stat. 1710, 40 U.S. Code § 345

June 16, 1972, P.L. 92-313, 86 Stat. 216, 40 U.S. Code §§ 175 nt. , 490, 602a, 603, 606, 611
Oct. 21, 1972, P.L. 92-520, 86 Stat. 1019, 40 U.S. Code § 616
July 10, 1973, P.L. 93-72, 87 Stat. 169, 40 U.S. Code § 607
Ariz. Rev. Stat. Ann., § 34-101 et seq.
La. Rev. Stat. Ann., 49:131 et seq.
N.Y. Consol. Laws, Ch. 44

Public Buildings Act of 1949
June 16, 1949, Ch. 218, 63 Stat. 176, 40 U.S. Code §§ 297, 297a, 298 to 298d, 345, 352 to 355
July 22, 1954, Ch. 560, 68 Stat. 518, 40 U.S. Code § 352 nt.
July 12, 1955, Ch. 331, 69 Stat. 297, 40 U.S. Code §§ 352 nt., 356a
Aug. 9, 1955, Ch. 629, 69 Stat. 552, 40 U.S. Code § 37a
July 9, 1956, Ch. 525, 70 Stat. 510, 40 U.S. Code § 356
July 18, 1956, P.L. 85-542, 72 Stat. 399, 40 U.S. Code § 298d
Aug. 12, 1970, P.L. 91-375, 84 Stat. 782, 40 U.S. Code § 356

Public Buildings Act of 1959
Sept. 9, 1959, P.L. 86-249, 73 Stat. 479, 40 U.S. Code §§ 341 nt. , 490, 601 to 615
June 8, 1962, P.L. 87-476, 76 Stat. 92, 40 U.S. Code § 607
Aug. 1, 1968, P.L. 90-448, 82 Stat. 544, 40 U.S. Code § 612
Aug. 12, 1970, P.L. 91-375, 84 Stat. 782, 40 U.S. Code § 615
Nov. 17, 1988, P.L. 100-678, 40 U.S. Code §§ 603, 606, 617 to 619
Aug. 9, 1989, P.L. 101-73, 40 U.S. Code § 612
June 13, 1991, P.L. 102-54, 40 U.S. Code § 612
Nov. 2, 1994, P.L. 103-437, 40 U.S. Code §§ 606, 610
Sept. 30, 1996, P.L. 104-208, 40 U.S. Code § 612

Public Buildings Amendments of 1972
Nov. 2, 1994, P.L. 103-437, 40 U.S. Code § 602a

Public Buildings Amendments of 1988
Nov. 17, 1988, P.L. 100-678, 40 U.S. Code § 601 nt.

Public Buildings and Earthquake Safety Rehabilitation Bond Act
Cal. Government Code, § 8878.50 et seq.

Public Buildings Arts Inclusion Act
N.J. Laws 1978, Ch. 117

Public Buildings Authorities Law (Municipal)
R.I. Gen. Laws 1956, 45-50-1 et seq.

Public Buildings Purchase Contract Act of 1954
July 22, 1954, Ch. 560, 68 Stat. 518, 40 U.S. Code §§ 356, 357
July 12, 1955, Ch. 331, 69 Stat. 297, 40 U.S. Code §§ 352 nt., 356a

Public Campaign Fund Act
Mont. Code Ann., 13-37-301 et seq.

Public Cemetery District Act
Cal. Health and Safety Code, § 8890 et seq.
Mont. Code Ann., 7-35-2101

Public Cemetery District Permanent Care and Improvement Fund Act
Mont. Code Ann., 7-35-2101 et seq., 7-35-2131 et seq.

Public Charter Schools Act
Ida. Code 1947, 33-5201 et seq.

Public College Auxilary Organization Act
N.J. Stat. Ann. 18A:64-26 et seq.

Public Community College Act
Ill. Rev. Stat. 1991, Ch. 122, § 101-1 et seq.

Public Competitive Bidding Act
Okla. Stat. Ann., Title 61, § 101 et seq.

Public Concessions Act
Haw. Rev. Stat. Ann., § 102-1 et seq.

Public Construction Bond Act
Ill. Rev. Stat. 1991, Ch. 29, § 14.9 et seq.

Public Construction Cost Accounting
Cal. Public Contract Code, § 21000 et seq.

Public Construction Flexibility Demonstration Project Act (Ithaca City School District)
N.Y. Laws 1997, Ch. 500

Public Contract and Bond Law
Iowa Code Ann., 23.1 et seq.

Public Contract Bond Act
Ida. Code 1947, 54-1925 et seq.
Md. Ann. Code 1957, Art. 90, § 11

Public Contract Fraud Act
Ill. Rev. Stat. 1991, Ch. 127, § 132.50 et seq.
La. Rev. Stat. Ann., 14:140

Public Contractors Bonds Act
Alaska Stat. 1962, §§ 36.25.010, 36.25.020

Public Contractors' License Act
Mont. Code Ann., 37-71-101 et seq.

Public Contracts Act
June 30, 1936, Ch. 881, 49 Stat. 2036, 29 U.S. Code § 557; 41 U.S. Code §§ 35 to 45
La. Rev. Stat. Ann., 38:2211 et seq.
N.C. Gen. Stat. 1943, § 143-128 et seq.

Public Contracts Act (Local)
N.J. Stat. Ann., 40A:11-1 et seq.

Public Contracts Bidding Act
N.Y. General Municipal Law (Consol. Laws Ch. 24) § 101 et seq.

Public Contracts Emergency Termination Act
Cal. Government Code, § 4400 et seq.

Public Contracts Prevailing Wage Act
Tenn. Code Ann., 12-4-401 et seq.

Public Contracts Termination Act
Utah Code Ann. 1953, Miscellaneous Superseded Code Provisions, 63-14-1 et seq.

Public Contracts, Works and Improvements Act
La. Rev. Stat. Ann., 38:1 et seq.

Public Control Act (Boston Elevated Railway)
Mass. Special Acts 1918, Ch. 159

Public Convenience and Necessity Act (Certificate of)
Miss. Code Ann. 1972, § 77-3-1 et seq.

Public Convenience Stations Act
D.C. Code Ann., §§ 8-132, 8-133

Public Conveyance Notice Act
Ill. Rev. Stat. 1991, Ch. 100, §§ 30, 31

Public Corporation Debt Management Act
R.I. Gen. Laws 1956, 35-18-1 et seq.

Public Corporation Financial Integrity and Accountability Act
R.I. Gen. Laws 1956, 35-20-1 et seq.

Public Costs Savings Act
Tenn. Code Ann., 68-11-1201 et seq.

Public Cotton Classers Act
Tex. Agriculture Code, § 112.001 et seq.

Public Counsel Act
Neb. Rev. Stat. 1943, 81-8,240 et seq.

Public Counsel Act (Ombudsman)
Neb. Rev. Stat. 1943, 81-8, 240 et seq.

Public Counsel Services Act (Committee for)
Mass. Gen. Laws Ann., 211D:1 et seq.

Public Country Warehouse Act
Ind. Burns' 1933, 67-501 et seq.

Public Credit Act
March 18, 1869, Ch. 1, 16 Stat. 1

Public Crossing Act
Ga. Code Ann., 46-8-190

Public Dance Halls Act
S.D. Codified Laws 1967, 42-4-1 et seq.

Public Debt Act
July 20, 1939, Ch. 336, 53 Stat. 1071, 31 U.S. Code § 757b

Public Debt Act of 1941
Feb. 19, 1941, Ch. 7, 55 Stat. 7, 31 U.S. Code §§ 742a, 755 to 757 nts., 757b, 757c
March 28, 1942, Ch. 205, 56 Stat. 190, 31 U.S. Code § 742a
June 25, 1947, Ch. 147, 61 Stat. 180, 31 U.S. Code § 742
Sept. 22, 1959, P.L. 86-346, 73 Stat. 624, 31 U.S. Code § 742a

Public Debt Act of 1942
March 28, 1942, Ch. 205, 56 Stat. 189, 31 U.S. Code §§ 742a, 754a, 754b, 757b

Public Debt Act of 1943
April 11, 1943, Ch. 52, 57 Stat. 63, 31 U.S. Code §§ 757b, 757c
April 3, 1945, Ch. 51, 59 Stat. 47, 31 U.S. Code § 757c

Public Debt Act of 1944
June 9, 1944, Ch. 240, 58 Stat. 272 (See 26 U.S. Code §§ 4001, 4011, 4021, 4471) 31 U.S. Code § 757b

Public Debt Act of 1945
April 3, 1945, Ch. 51, 59 Stat. 47, 31 U.S. Code §§ 741a, 757b, 757c, 757d, 757c

Public Debt Act of 1946
June 26, 1946, Ch. 501, 60 Stat. 316, 31 U.S. Code § 757b and nt.

Public Debt Act of 1959
June 30, 1959, P.L. 86-74, 73 Stat. 156, 31 U.S. Code § 757b

Public Debt and Tax Rate Extension Act of 1960
June 30, 1960, P.L. 86-564, 74 Stat. 290, 26 U.S. Code §§ 11, 162 nt., 613, 821, 4061, 4251, 4261, 5001, 5022, 5041, 5051, 5063, 5701, 5707, 6412 ; 31 U.S. Code § 757b
Sept. 14, 1960, P.L. 86-781, 74 Stat. 1018, 26 U.S. Code § 613 nt.

Public Debt Commission Act
Mich. Comp. Laws Ann., 132.1 et seq.

Public Defender Act
Alaska Stat. 1962, § 18.85.010 et seq.
Ariz. Rev. Stat. Ann., § 11-581 et seq.
Ark. Code Ann. 1987, 16-87-101 et seq.
Cal. Government Code, § 27700 et seq.
Colo. Rev. Stat., 21-1-101 et seq.
Conn. Gen. Stat. Ann., § 51-289 et seq.
D.C. Code Ann., § 1-2701 et seq.
Del. Code of 1974 Title 29, § 4601 et seq.
Fla. Stat. Ann., 27.50 et seq.
Ill. Rev. Stat. 1991, Ch. 34, § 3-4001 et seq.
Ind. Code Ann., 33-1-7-1 et seq.
Minn. Stat. Ann., 611.12
Neb. Rev. Stat. 1943, 29-1805.01 et seq.
N.J. Stat. Ann., 2A:158A-1 et seq.
N.M. Stat. Ann., 31-15-1 et seq.
Ore. Rev. Stat., 151.010 et seq.
Pa. Purdon's Stat., Title 16, § 9960.1 et seq.
R.I. Gen. Laws 1956, 12-15-1 et seq.
Wyo. Stat. Ann., § 7-1-107 et seq.

Public Defender System Act (Statewide)
Miss. Code Ann. 1972, §§ 25-32-31 to 25-32-65

Public Defenders Act (State Appellate)
Ida. Code 1947, 19-867 to 19-872

Public Deposit Insurance Act
S.D. Codified Laws 1967, 4-6A-1 et seq.

Public Deposit Protection Act
Colo. Rev. Stat., 11-10.5-101 et seq.
Conn. Gen. Stat. Ann., § 36-382 et seq.

Public Deposit Protection Act (Savings and Loan Association)
Colo. Rev. Stat., 11-47-101 et seq.

Public Deposits Act
Ida. Code 1947, 57-101 et seq.
Ind. Code Ann., 5-13-4-1 et seq., 5-13-5-1 et seq.
Ore. Rev. Stat., 295.005 et seq.
Wis. Stat. Ann., 34.01 et seq.

Public Deposits Act (Collateral Pool)
Tenn. Code Ann., 9-4-501 et seq.

Public Deposits Act (Collateral)
R.I. Gen. Laws 1956, 35-10.1-1 et seq.

Public Deposits Insurance Fund Act
Ind. Code Ann., 5-13-4-1 et seq., 5-13-5-1 et seq.

Public Deposits Security Act
Fla. Stat. Ann., 280.01 et seq.
Okla. Stat. Ann., Title 62, § 72.1 et seq.
Va. Code 1950, § 2.1-359 et seq.

Public Disbursements Voucher Act
Wash. Rev. Code Ann., 42.24.035 et seq.

Public Disclosure Act
Wash. Rev. Code Ann., 42.17.010 et seq.

Public Display of Offensive Sexual Material Law
N.Y. Penal Law 1965 (Consol. Laws Ch. 40) §§ 245.10, 245.11

Public Documents Act
P.R. Laws Ann. 1954, Title 3, § 1001 et seq.

Public Domain Act
Mich. Comp. Laws Ann., 322.202 et seq.

Public Domain Range Act
Colo. Rev. Stat., 35-45-101 et seq.

Public Drainage Act
Minn. Stat. 1988, 106A.005 et seq.

Public Drinking Water Protection Act
R.I. Gen. Laws 1956, 46-15.3-1 et seq.

Public Drunkenness Act
Cal. Penal Code, § 647, Subd. f
Ga. Code Ann., 16-11-41
N.C. Gen. Stat. 1943, § 14-443 et seq.
N.Y. Local Laws 1971, Town of Orangetown, p. 3020
N.Y. Local Laws 1973, Village of Suffern, p. 3806

Public Eating and Drinking Places Act
Pa. Purdon's Stat., Title 53, § 13201 et seq.

Public Education Act
Ark. Code 1987, 6-15-1001 et seq.
Fla. Stat. Ann., 228.001 et seq.
Md. Ann. Code 1974, Art. ED, § 1-101 et seq.

Public Education Act (Demonstration of Restructuring in)
Cal. Education Code 1976, § 58900 et seq.

Public Education Governance Reform Act
Tenn. Public Acts 1984, Ex. Sess., Ch. 6

Public Education Incentive Program Act
Colo. Rev. Stat., 22-21-101 et seq.

Public Education Lottery Act
Fla. Stat. Ann., 24.101 et seq., 159.801 et seq.

Public Education Revenue Bond Act
Utah Code Ann. 1953, 53A-20a-101 et seq.

Public Education Trust Fund Act (Volunteer)
Tenn. Code Ann., 49-3-401 et seq.

Public Educational Grants Program Act
Tex. Education Code, § 56.031 et seq.

Public Election Act
Me. Rev. Stat. Ann. 1964, Title 21-A, § 1121 et seq.

Public Elementary and Secondary School Self-Insurance Act
Ark. Code Ann. 1987, 6-20-1501 et seq.

Public Elevator Act (Warehouses)
Minn. Stat. 1961, 610.01 et seq.

Public Elevator Air Act (Clean)
Ill. Comp. Stat. 1992, Ch. 720, § 560/1 et seq.

Public Employee Armed Services Rights Act
Ill. Rev. Stat. 1991, Ch. 126 1/2, § 801 et seq.

Public Employee Bargaining Act
Ind. Code Ann., 22-6-4-1 et seq.
N.M. Stat. Ann., 10-70-1 et seq.
Ore. Rev. Stat., 243.650 et seq.

Public Employee Charitable Fund-Raising Act
N.J. Stat. Ann., 52:14-15.9cl et seq.

Public Employee Collective Bargaining Act
Ore. Rev. Stat., 243.650 et seq.

Public Employee Community Right-to-Know Act
Tex. Health and Safety Code, § 506.001 et seq.

Public Employee Disability Act
Ill. Rev. Stat. 1991, Ch. 70, §§ 90.9, 91

Public Employee Fair Share Fee Law
Pa. Purdon's Stat., Title 43, § 1102.1 et seq.

Public Employee Hazardous Chemical Protection and Right to Know Act
Ga. Code Ann., 45-22-1 et seq.

Public Employee Labor Relations Act
Ga. Code Ann., 34-6-40 et seq.
N.H. Rev. Stat. 1955, 273-A:1 et seq.

Public Employee No Strike Act
N.Y. Civil Service Law (Consol. Laws, Ch. 7) 210

Public Employee Organization Act
Cal. Government Code, § 3500 et
Ga. Code Ann., 16-11-41 et seq.

Public Employee Pension Forfeiture
Pa. Purdon's Stat., Title 43, § 1311 et seq.

Public Employee Pension Revocation and Reeducation Act
R.I. Gen. Laws 1956, 36-10.1-1 et seq.

Public Employee Political Freedom Act
Tenn. Code Ann., 8-50-601 et seq.

Public Employee Relations Act
Mich. Comp. Laws Ann., 423.1 et seq.
Minn. Stat. 1969, 179.50 et seq.

Ore. Rev. Stat., 240.060 et seq.
Pa. Purdon's Stat., Title 43, § 1101.101 et
seq.

Public Employee Representation Act
Mich. Comp. Laws Ann., 423.201 et seq.

**Public Employee Retirement Benefits
Forfeiture Act**
Mich. Comp. Laws Ann., 38.2701 et seq.

**Public Employee Retirement Benefits
Protection Act**
Fla. Stat. Ann., 112.60 et seq.

**Public Employee Retirement Study
Commission Act**
Pa. Purdon's Stat., Title 43, § 1401 et seq.

**Public Employee Workers' Compensation
Act**
Ark. Code Ann. 1987, 21-5-601 et seq.

**Public Employees' and Teachers'
Reciprocal Service Credit Act**
W. Va. Code 1966, § 5-13-1 et seq.

Public Employees' Antistrike Act
Mich. Comp. Laws Ann., 423.201 et seq.
Minn. Stat. 1969, 179.50 et seq.
Ohio Rev. Code 1953, 4117.15 et seq.
Pa. Purdon's Stat., Title 43, § 215.1 et seq.

Public Employees Charitable Campaign Act
P.R. Laws Ann. 1954, Title 3, § 2051 et seq.

**Public Employees' Chemical Right to Know
Act**
Ark. Acts 1991, No. 556

**Public Employees' Collective Bargaining
Act**
Haw. Rev. Stat. Ann., § 89-1 et seq.
Mont. Code Ann., 39-31-101 et seq.
Ore. Rev. Stat., 243.650 et seq.
Wash. Rev. Code Ann., 41.56.010 et seq.

Public Employees' Compensation Act
Haw. Rev. Stat. Ann., § 77-1 et seq.

**Public Employees Contributory Retirement
Act**
Mass. Gen. Laws Ann., 32:1 et seq.

Public Employees' Disability Act
Utah Code Ann. 1953, 49-9-101 et seq.

Public Employees Eight Hour Labor Act
Okla. Stat. 1981, Title 61, § 3

Public Employees' Enabling Act
Kan. Stat. Ann., 40-2301 et seq.

Public Employees' Fair Employment Act
N.Y. Civil Service Law 1958 (Consol. Laws
Ch. 7) § 200 et seq.
N.Y. Local Laws 1967, Town of Putnam
Valley, p. 1888
N.Y. Local Laws 1969, Village of Freeport,
p.2510

Public Employees Health Benefits Act
P.R. Laws Ann. 1954, Title 3, § 729a et seq.

Public Employees' Health Insurance Act
S.D. Codified Laws 1967, 3-12A-1 et seq.

Public Employees' Insurance Act
Cal. Government Code, § 53200 et seq.
W. Va. Code 1966, § 5-16-1 et seq.

Public Employees Labor Relations Act
Kan. Stat. Ann., 44-801 et seq.
Mass. Gen. Laws. Ann., 150E:1 et seq.
Minn. Stat. 1969, 179.50 et seq.
N.H. Rev. Stat. 1955, 273-A:1 et seq.
S.D. Codified Laws 1967, 3-18-1 et seq.
Tex. Rev. Civ. Stat., Art. 5154c
Wis. Stat. Ann., 111.70 et seq.

**Public Employees' Labor Relations Act
(Chatham County)**
Ga. Laws 1968, p. 2953

**Public Employees Labor Relations Act
(Municipal)**
Me. Rev. Stat. Ann. 1964, Title 26, § 961 et
seq.

Public Employees Labor Union Act
Ala. Code 1958, Title 55, § 317(1) et seq.

Public Employees' Liability Law (Operation of Motor Vehicles)
Cal. Vehicle Code 1959, § 17000 et seq.

Public Employees' Long-Term Care Act
Cal. Government Code, § 21410 et seq.

Public Employees' Loyalty Oath Act
N.H. Rev. Stat. 1955, 92:2, 648:15

Public Employees Mediation Act
N.D. Cent. Code, 34-11-01 et seq.

Public Employees Medical and Hospital Care Act
Cal. Government Code, § 22751 et seq.

Public Employees' Noncontributory Retirement Act
Utah Code Ann. 1953, 49-3-101 et seq.

Public Employees Oath Act (Levering)
Cal. Government Code, § 3100 et seq.
N.J. Laws 1983, Ch. 516

Public Employees Occupational Safety and Health Act
N.J. Laws 1983, Ch. 516
N.J. Stat. Ann., 34:6A-25 et seq.

Public Employees Pension Act (Noncontributory)
N.J. Rev. Stat. 1937, 43:8B-1 et seq.

Public Employees Protection Act
Ida. Code 1947, 6-2103 et seq.
Utah Code Ann. 1953, 67-21-1 et seq.

Public Employees' Retirement Act
Alaska Stat. 1962, § 39.35.010 et seq.
Ariz. Rev. Stat. Ann., § 38-741 et seq.
Colo. Rev. Stat., 24-51-201 et seq.
Ind. Code Ann., 5-10-1-1 et seq.
Iowa Code Ann., 97B.1 et seq.
Mass. Gen. Laws. Ann., 32:1 et seq.
Minn. Stat. Ann., 353.01 et seq.
Miss. Code Ann. 1972, § 25-11-1 et seq.
Mont. Code Ann., 19-3-101 et seq.

Mont. Code Ann. 1947, 68-101 to 68-1313
Nev. Rev. Stat. 1979 Reprint, 286.010 et seq.
N.M. Stat. Ann., 10-11-1 et seq.
Ohio Rev. Code 1953, 145.01 et seq.
Okla. Stat. Ann., Title 74, § 901 et seq.
Ore. Rev. Stat., 237.001 et seq.
S.D. Codified Laws 1967, 3-12-46 et seq.
Wis. Stat. Ann., 40.20 et seq.
W. Va. Code 1966, § 5-10-1 et seq.

Public Employees' Retirement Act II
Utah Code Ann. 1953, 49-2-101 et seq.
W. Va. Code 1966 § 5-10D-1 et seq.

Public Employees Retirement Reciprocity Act
N.M. Stat. Ann., 10-13A-1 et seq.

Public Employees' Retirement-Social Security Integration Act
N.J. Stat. Ann., 43:15A-1 et seq.

Public Employees' Retirement System Act
Cal. Government Code, § 20000 et seq.
Colo. Rev. Stat., 24-51-101 et seq.
Mont. Code Ann., 19-3-101 et seq.
N.J. Stat. Ann., 43:15A-1 et seq.
Okla. Stat. 1981, Title 74, § 901 et seq.

Public Employees Retirement System Act
Wash. Rev. Code Ann., 41.40.005 et seq.

Public Employees Retirement System School Employees Alternative System
Cal. Government Code §§ 21700 to 21703

Public Employees Social Security Act
Colo. Rev. Stat., 24-51-701 et seq.
Wash. Rev. Code Ann., 41.48.010 et seq.

Public Employees' Social Security Coverage Act
Mich. Comp. Laws Ann., 38.851 et seq.

Public Employees Social Security Integration and Supplemental Retirement Benefits Act
Ind. Code Ann., 5-10-3-1 et seq.

Public Employees Subversive Activities Law
N.Y. Civil Services Law (Consol. Laws Ch. 7) § 105

Public Employees Subversive Conduct Law
N.Y. Laws 1951, Ch. 233

Public Employer Community Right-to-Know Act
Tex. Health and Safety Code, § 506.001 et seq.

Public Employer-Employee Relations Act
Kan. Stat. Ann., 75-4321 et seq.

Public Employment Antidiscrimination Act
Ariz. Rev. Stat. Ann., § 41-1461 et seq.

Public Employment Labor Relations Act
Minn. Stat. Ann., 179A.01 et seq.

Public Employment Office Act
Ill. Rev. Stat. 1991, Ch. 48, § 172.90 et seq.

Public Employment Relations Act
Alaska Stat. 1962, § 23.40.070 et seq.
Haw. Rev. Stat. Ann., § 89-1 et seq.
Iowa Code Ann., 20.1 et seq.
Mich. Comp. Laws Ann., 423.1 et seq.
Neb. Rev. Stat. 1943, 48-801 et seq.

Public Employment Relations Act (Antistrike)
Mich. Comp. Laws Ann., 423.201 et seq.

Public Employment Service Act
Ida. Code 1947, 72-1345
P.R. Laws Ann. 1954, Title 29, § 551 et seq. .

Public Enemy Act (Disorderly Persons)
Mich. Comp. Laws Ann., 750.167, 750.168
N.J. Laws 1934, Ch. 155
N.Y. Penal Law 1909 (Consol. Laws Ch. 40) § 722, Subds. 11, 12

Public Energy Authority Act
W. Va. Code 1966 § 5D-1-1 et seq.

Public Entities Liability Act
Cal. Government Code, § 815 et seq.

Public Entity Construction Grant Anticipation Note Act
La. Rev. Stat. Ann., 39:1801 et seq.

Public Ethics Law
Md. Ann. Code 1974, Art. SG, § 15-1001 et seq.

Public Facilities Art Allocation Act
R.I. Gen. Laws 1956, 42-75.2-1 et seq.

Public Facilities Authority Act (Athens-Clarke County)
Ga. Laws 1996, p. 3746

Public Facilities Authority Act (Athens)
Ga. Laws 1960, p. 2531

Public Facilities Authority Act (Fayette County)
Ga. Laws 1978, p. 3377

Public Facilities Authority Act (Gwinnett County)
Ga. Laws 1975, p. 4463

Public Facilities Authority Act (Sparta-Hancock)
Ga. Laws 1991, p. 4394

Public Facilities Authority Act (Tyrone)
Ga. Laws 1979, p. 3938

Public Facilities Authority Act (Winder)
Ga. Laws 1998, H.B. 1768

Public Facilities Boards Act
Ark. Stat. 1947, 14-137-101 et seq.

Public Facilities Concession Regulation Act
Pa. Cons. Stat., Title 62, § 4301 et seq.
Pa. Purdon's Stat., Title 69, § 2501 et seq.

Public Facilities Department Act (Boston)
Mass. Acts 1966, Ch. 642

Public Facilities District Act
Va. Acts 1946, Ch. 93

Public Facilities Finance Act
Ark. Code Ann. 1987, 22-3-1201 et seq.

Public Facility Corporation Act
Tex. Rev. Civ. Stat., Art. 717s

Public Fallout Shelter Act
Ariz. Rev. Stat. Ann., § 34-441 et seq.

Public Finance Act
Utah Code Ann. 1953, 63-1-12 et seq.
Va. Code 1950, § 15.1-227.1 et seq.

Public Finance Authority Act
Tex. Rev. Civ. Stat., Arts. 601c, 601d

Public Financing Campaign Act
Ky. Rev. Stat. 1971, 121A.010c et seq.

Public Fire Safety Buildings Act
Ohio Rev. Code 1953, 737.34 et seq.

Public Freight Motor Vehicle Act
Md. Ann. Code 1957, Art. 56, § 181 et seq.

Public Funds Accounting Act
Ill. Rev. Stat. 1991, Ch. 102, § 19.9 et seq.

Public Funds Authority Act
Minn. Stat. Ann., 446A.01 et seq.

Public Funds Collateral Act
Tex. Government Code, § 2257.001 et seq.

Public Funds Deposit Act
Ill. Rev. Stat. 1991, Ch. 102, § 33.9 et seq.
Mich. Comp. Laws Ann., 129.11 et seq.

Public Funds Deposit Security Act
Neb. Laws 1996, L.B. 1274

Public Funds Direct Deposit Act
Fla. Stat. Ann., 215.85

Public Funds in Failed Banks Act
Ill. Rev. Stat. 1991, Ch. 102, §§ 18.9, 19

Public Funds Investment Act
Ill. Rev. Stat. 1991, Ch. 85, § 900 et seq.
Tex. Government Code, § 2256.001 et seq.

Public Funds Investment and Local Government Investment Pool Act
Va. Code 1950, § 2.1-234.1 et seq.

Public Funds Statement Publication Act
Ill. Rev. Stat. 1991, Ch. 102, § 4.90 et seq.

Public General Hospital Assistance Act
N.J. Stat. Ann., 30:19-12.29 et seq.

Public Good Act (Condemnation)
Vt. Stat. Ann., Title 30, § 110 et seq.

Public Grain Warehouse Act
Ark. Stat. 1987, 2-17-201 et seq.
Ill. Rev. Stat. 1991, Ch. 114, § 214.1 et seq.
Miss. Code Ann. 1972, § 75-44-1 et seq.
Neb. Rev. Stat. 1943, 88-501 et seq.
S.D. Codified Laws 1967, 49-43-1 et seq.

Public Graveyards Act
Ill. Rev. Stat. 1991, Ch. 21, § 12.9 et seq.

Public Ground Waters Act
Wash. Rev. Code Ann., 90.44.020 et seq.

Public Guardian for Elderly Adults Act
N.J. Stat. Ann., 52:27G-20 et seq.

Public Guardian Law
Cal. Welfare and Institutions Code, § 8000 et seq. § 5175 et seq.

Public Guardianship Act
Fla. Stat. Ann., 744.701 et seq.
Wyo. Stat. 1977, § 3-7-101 et seq.

Public Guardianship for Adults with Mental Retardation Act
Minn. Stat. Ann., 252A.01 et seq.

Public Guardianship for the Elderly Law
Tenn. Code Ann., 34-7-101 et seq.

Public Health Act (Boston)
Mass. Gen. Laws Ann., 111 Appendix:2-1 et seq.

Public Health Act (Local)
Minn. Stat. Ann., 145A.01 et seq.

Public Health Act (Native American)
Neb. Rev. Stat. 1943, 71-7615 to 71-7622

Public Health and Environmental Protection Act (MTBE)
Cal. Health and Safety Code §§ 25299.37.1, 116366
Cal. Water Code § 13285

Public Health and Human Services Act
Sept. 13, 1994, P.L. 103-322, 42 U.S. Code § 300w-10

Public Health and Marine-Hospital Service Act
July 1, 1902, Ch. 1370, 32 Stat. 712, 46 U.S. Code § 654

Public Health and Safety Act
La. Rev. Stat. Ann., 40:1 et seq.

Public Health Board Act
Ill. Rev. Stat. 1991, Ch. 24, § 11-17-1 et seq.

Public Health Care Trust Fund Act
Miss. Laws 1999, H.B. 70

Public Health Cigarette Smoking Act of 1969
April 1, 1970, P.L. 91-222, 84 Stat. 87, 15 U.S. Code §§ 1331 to 1340

Public Health Code
Ala. Code 1975, § 22-1-1 et seq.
Alaska Stat. 1962, § 18.05.010 et seq.
Colo. Rev. Stat., 25-1-101 et seq.
Ind. Code Ann., 16-1-1-1 et seq.
Kan. Stat. Ann., 65-101 et seq.
Ky. Rev. Stat. 1971, 211.005 et seq.
Mich. Comp. Laws Ann., 333.1101 et seq.
Mont. Code Ann., 50-1-101 et seq.
N.C. Gen. Stat. 1943, § 130-1 et seq.
N.D. Cent. Code, 23-01-01 et seq.
N.J. Stat. Ann., 26:1-1 et seq.
N.M. Stat. Ann., 24-1-1 et seq.
N.Y. Consol. Laws, Ch. 45
Okla. Stat. Ann., Title 63, § 1-101 et seq.
Vt. Stat. Ann., Title 18, § 1 et seq.
W. Va. Code 1966, § 16-1-1 et seq.

Public Health Dental Program Act
Fla. Stat 1991, 381.0052

Public Health Department Act
Ill. Rev. Stat. 1991, Ch. 111 1/2, § 21.1 et seq.

Public Health Department Reorganization Act
Colo. Rev. Stat., 25-1-101 et seq.

Public Health Departments Act (Counties)
Ill. Rev. Stat. 1991, Ch. 111 1/2, § 20c et seq.

Public Health District Act
Ill. Rev. Stat. 1991, Ch. 111 1/2, § 0.01 et seq.

Public Health, Education and Welfare Tax Act
Conn. Gen. Stat. Ann., § 12-406 et seq.

Public Health Improvement Act
Mont. Code Ann., 50-1-401 et seq.

Public Health, Insurance-Federal Portability and Accountability Act
N.Y. Laws 1997, Ch. 661

Public Health Laboratories Act (Municipal; County)
Cal. Health and Safety Code, § 1000 et seq.

Public Health Law
N.C. Gen. Stat. 1943, § 130A-1 et seq.

Public Health Licensure Law
Neb. Rev. Stat. 1943, 71-101 et seq.

Public Health Nuisance Act
N.J. Stat. Ann., 26:3B-1 et seq.

Public Health Nursing Act
Ill. Rev. Stat. 1959, Ch. 111 1/2, § 35g et seq.

Public Health Priority Funding Act
N.J. Stat. Ann., 26:2F-1 et seq.

Public Health Reorganization Act (Local)
Tex. Health and Safety Code, § 121.001 et seq.

Public Health Service Act

Aug. 14, 1912, Ch. 288, 37 Stat. 309, 31 U.S. Code §§ 583, par 6, 711

July 1, 1944, Ch. 373, 58 Stat. 682, 42 U.S. Code §§ 201 to 207, 209 to 229, 241 to 272, 281 to 286

Feb. 25, 1946, Ch. 35, 60 Stat. 30, 42 U.S. Code § 225

July 3, 1946, Ch. 538, 60 Stat. 421, 42 U.S. Code §§ 201, 209, 210, 215, 218, 219, 241, 242a, 244, 246

Aug. 13, 1946, Ch. 958, 60 Stat. 1041, 42 U.S. Code §§ 201 nt., 209, 291 to 291m

Feb. 28, 1948, Ch. 83, 62 Stat. 38, 31 U.S. Code §§ 72, 583, 711; 42 U.S. Code §§ 2, 16, 98 nts., 201, 201 nt., 204, 206, 207, 209 to 212a, 218a, 230; 46 U.S. Code § 654; 48 U.S. Code § 508; 49 U.S. Code §§ 177, 181

June 16, 1948, Ch. 481, 62 Stat. 464, 42 U.S. Code §§ 201, 203, 206, 210, 218, 219, 241, 246, prec. §§ 281, 283, 284, 286, 287, 287a to 287d

June 19, 1948, Ch. 544, 62 Stat. 531, 42 U.S. Code § 291i

June 19, 1948, Ch. 554, 62 Stat. 536, 42 U.S. Code § 291f

June 24, 1948, Ch. 621, 62 Stat. 598, 42 U.S. Code §§ 201, 210, 218, 241, 288 to 288e, 291k

June 25, 1948, Ch. 654, 62 Stat. 1017, 42 U.S. Code §§ 222, 227, 241, 248, 249, 255, 260

June 29, 1948, Ch. 728, 62 Stat. 1103, 42 U.S. Code § 291g, 291g nt.

Oct. 26, 1949, Ch. 722, 63 Stat. 898, 42 U.S. Code §§ 291, 291 nt., 291d, 291f, 291h, 291i, 291j, 291n

Aug. 15, 1950, Ch. 714, 64 Stat. 444, 42 U.S. Code §§ 210, 218, 286, prec. 289, 289a to 289c

Oct. 31, 1951, Ch. 653, 65 Stat. 700, 42 U.S. Code § 207

June 25, 1952, Ch. 460, 66 Stat. 157, 42 U.S. Code § 255

July 17, 1952, Ch. 931, 66 Stat. 758, 42 U.S. Code § 207

July 27, 1953, Ch. 243, 67 Stat. 196, 42 U.S. Code § 291d

May 8, 1954, Ch. 195, 68 Stat. 79, 42 U.S. Code §§ 257, 260a, 261, 261a

July 12, 1954, Ch. 471, 68 Stat. 461, 42 U.S. Code §§ 291, 291h, 291i, 291j, 291m, 291o, 291p, 291q, 291r, 291s, 291t, 291u, 291v

July 15, 1954, Ch. 507, 68 Stat. 481, 42 U.S. Code §§ 213, 224

Aug. 31, 1954, Ch. 1158, 68 Stat. 1025, 42 U.S. Code § 244a

July 28, 1955, Ch. 417, 69 Stat. 382, 42 U.S. Code § 242b

April 27, 1956, Ch. 211, 70 Stat. 116, 42 U.S. Code §§ 209, 211, 212, 214, 217, 218a

April 30, 1956, Ch. 223, 70 Stat. 121, 42 U.S. Code § 211c

June 29, 1956, Ch. 477, 70 Stat. 430, 42 U.S. Code § 210

July 3, 1956, Ch. 510, 70 Stat. 490, 42 U.S. Code §§ 241, 242c

July 24, 1956, Ch. 676, 70 Stat. 622, 42 U.S. Code §§ 257, 260, 260a

July 28, 1956, Ch. 772, 70 Stat. 709, 42 U.S. Code §§ 273, 274

July 30, 1956, Ch. 779, 70 Stat. 717, 42 U.S. Code §§ 2 nt., 16 nt., 98 nt., 201 nt., 211a nt., 212a nt., 214 nt., 222 nt., 230 nt., 249 nt., 292 to 292i

July 31, 1956, Ch. 804, 70 Stat. 741, 42 U.S. Code § 210

Aug. 1, 1956, Ch. 837, 70 Stat. 881, 42 U.S. Code § 213

Aug. 1, 1956, Ch. 852, 70 Stat. 910, 42 U.S. Code §§ 246, 291g, 291i, 291t

Aug. 2, 1956, Ch. 871, 70 Stat. 923, 42 U.S. Code §§ 242a, 242b, 242d, 242e, 291d, 291s

Aug. 3, 1956, Ch. 907, 70 Stat. 960, 42 U.S. Code §§ 275 to 281

Aug. 10, 1956, Ch. 1041, 70A Stat. 619, 42 U.S. Code §§ 212, 213a

June 21, 1957, P.L. 85-58, 71 Stat. 181, 42 U.S. Code § 267

June 20, 1958, P.L. 85-462, 72 Stat. 214, 42 U.S. Code § 210

July 22, 1958, P.L. 85-544, 72 Stat. 400, 42 U.S. Code § 246

Aug. 1, 1958, P.L. 85-580, 72 Stat. 467, 42 U.S. Code § 267

Aug. 1, 1958, P.L. 85-589, 72 Stat. 489, 42 U.S. Code §§ 291w to 291z

Aug. 14, 1958, P.L. 85-664, 72 Stat. 616, 42 U.S. Code §§ 291d, 291s

Aug. 27, 1958, P.L. 85-777, 72 Stat. 933, 42 U.S. Code §§ 292c, 292d

Sept. 2, 1958, P.L. 85-861, 72 Stat. 1547, 42 U.S. Code § 213a

Sept. 2, 1958, P.L. 85-881, 72 Stat. 1704, 42 U.S. Code § 262

Sept. 6, 1958, P.L. 85-929, 72 Stat. 1789, 42 U.S. Code § 210

June 25, 1959, P.L. 86-70, 73 Stat. 148, 42 U.S. Code §§ 201, 273 nt., 274, 291i

July 23, 1959, P.L. 86-105, 73 Stat. 239, 42 U.S. Code §§ 242d, 242e

Aug. 14, 1959, P.L. 86-158, 73 Stat. 349, 42 U.S. Code §§ 291n-1, 291v

Aug. 14, 1959, P.L. 86-160, 73 Stat. 359, 42 U.S. Code § 213a

April 8, 1960, P.L. 86-415, 74 Stat. 32, 42 U.S. Code §§ 201, 209 , 210 to 212, 253

July 12, 1960, P.L. 86-610, 74 Stat. 364, 42 U.S. Code § 242f

July 12, 1960, P.L. 86-624, 74 Stat. 419, 42 U.S. Code §§ 201, 255, 264, 291i

Sept. 2, 1960, P.L. 86-703, 74 Stat. 764, 42 U.S. Code § 210

Sept. 8, 1960, P.L. 86-720, 74 Stat. 819, 42 U.S. Code §§ 242d, 242g

Sept. 15, 1960, P.L. 86-798, 74 Stat. 1053, 42 U.S. Code § 241

Oct. 5, 1961, P.L. 87-395, 75 Stat. 824, 42 U.S. Code §§ 246, 247a, 289c nt., 291i, 291n, 291s, 291t, 291w, 292c to 292g

July 27, 1962, P.L. 87-555, 76 Stat. 244, 42 U.S. Code § 213a

Sept. 7, 1962, P.L. 87-649, 76 Stat. 497, 42 U.S. Code §§ 207, 210, 210-1, 211

Sept. 25, 1962, P.L. 87-688, 76 Stat. 587, 42 U.S. Code §§ 246, 291g, 291i, 201t

Sept. 25, 1962, P.L. 87-692, 76 Stat. 592, 42 U.S. Code § 242h

Oct. 11, 1962, P.L. 87-793, 76 Stat. 864, 42 U.S. Code § 210

Oct. 17, 1962, P.L. 87-838, 76 Stat. 1072, 42 U.S. Code §§ 217a, 241, 289d to 289h, 292c, 292d

Oct. 23, 1962, P.L. 87-868, 76 Stat. 1155, 42 U.S. Code § 247b

July 19, 1963, P.L. 88-71, 77 Stat. 83, 42 U.S. Code § 253

Sept. 24, 1963, P.L. 88-129, 77 Stat. 164, 42 U.S. Code §§ 292 to 292b, 292d to 294e

Oct. 2, 1963, P.L. 88-132, 77 Stat. 214, 42 U.S. Code § 213a

Oct. 31, 1963, P.L. 88-164, 77 Stat. 282, 42 U.S. Code §§ 291k, 295 to 295e

Aug. 13, 1964, P.L. 88-424, 78 Stat. 398, 42 U.S. Code § 249

Aug. 14, 1964, P.L. 88-431, 78 Stat. 440, 42 U.S. Code § 213a

Aug. 18, 1964, P.L. 88-443, 78 Stat. 447, 42 U.S. Code §§ 247c, 291 to 291o

Aug. 27, 1964, P.L. 88-497, 78 Stat. 613, 42 U.S. Code §§ 242d, 242g

Sept. 4, 1964, P.L. 88-581, 78 Stat. 908, 42 U.S. Code §§ 291c, 291o, 293, 293a, 293e, 293h, 296 to 298b

Oct. 13, 1964, P.L. 88-654, 78 Stat. 1086, 42 U.S. Code §§ 294, 294a

Aug. 5, 1965, P.L. 89-109, 79 Stat. 435, 42 U.S. Code §§ 242h, 246, 247a, 247b

Aug. 9, 1965, P.L. 89-115, 79 Stat. 448, 42 U.S. Code §§ 241, 292c, 292d

Oct. 6, 1965, P.L. 89-239, 79 Stat. 926, 33 U.S. Code § 763c; 42 U.S. Code §§ 201 nts., 211a, 212a, 214 nt., 222 nt., 299 to 299i

Oct. 22, 1965, P.L. 89-290, 79 Stat. 1052, 42 U.S. Code §§ 293, 293a, 293d, 294 to 294d, 295f to 295f-4, 295g, 297b, 298b

Oct. 22, 1965, P.L. 89-291, 79 Stat. 1059, 42 U.S. Code §§ 277,

Aug. 14, 1966, P.L. 89-538, 80 Stat. 348, 42 U.S. Code § 213a

Nov. 2, 1966, P.L. 89-709, 80 Stat. 1103, 42 U.S. Code §§ 293, 293a, 293d, 293e, 294 to 294b

Nov. 3, 1966, P.L. 89-749, 80 Stat. 1181, 42 U.S. Code §§ 242g, 243, 246

Nov. 3, 1966, P.L. 89-751, 80 Stat. 1222, 42 U.S. Code §§ 293e, 294a to 294d, 295h, 295h-1 to 295h-5, 297c to 297f, 298c, 298c-1 to 298c-8

Nov. 8, 1966, P.L. 89-793, 80 Stat. 1449, 42 U.S. Code §§ 257, 3402

June 24, 1967, P.L. 90-31, 81 Stat. 79, 42 U.S. Code § 225a

Dec. 5, 1967, P.L. 90-174, 81 Stat. 533, 42 U.S. Code §§ 217b, 241, 242b, 242g, 243, 244, 246, 249, 251, 254a, 263a, 291m-1, 293e, 295h-4, 296e

Aug. 16, 1968, P.L. 90-489, 82 Stat. 771, 42 U.S. Code §§ 289a nt., 289l to 289k

Aug. 16, 1968, P.L. 90-490, 82 Stat. 773, 42 U.S. Code §§ 242d, 242g, 292b to 292e, 293 to 293d, 294 to 294d, 294f, 295f to 295h-3, 295h-6, 295h-7, 296 to 296b, 296d to 297f, 297h, 298b to 298c-1

Oct. 15, 1968, P.L. 90-574, 82 Stat. 1005, 42 U.S. Code §§ 210, 219, 242h, 291a, 291b, 299a to 299e, 299j

Oct. 18, 1968, P.L. 90-602, 82 Stat. 1173, 42 U.S. Code §§ 263b to 263n

Continued

March 12, 1970, P.L. 91-208, 84 Stat. 52, 42 U.S. Code §§ 242d, 242g

March 12, 1970, P.L. 91-209, 84 Stat. 52, 42 U.S. Code § 242h

March 13, 1970, P.L. 91-212, 84 Stat. 63, 42 U.S. Code §§ 201, 275 to 280a-1, 280b to 280b-12

May 14, 1970, P.L. 91-253, 84 Stat. 216, 42 U.S. Code § 212

June 30, 1970, P.L. 91-296, 84 Stat. 336, 42 U.S. Code §§ 229b, 242b, 242g, 246, 291a to 291f, 291i, 291j-1 to 291j-10, 291o, 291o-1, 299a

July 29, 1970, P.L. 91-358, 84 Stat. 572, 42 U.S. Code § 260a

Oct. 16, 1970, P.L. 91-464, 84 Stat. 988, 42 U.S. Code § 247b

Oct. 27, 1970, P.L. 91-513, 84 Stat. 1240, 42 U.S. Code §§ 201, 225a, 242, 242a, 257 to 261a

Oct. 30, 1970, P.L. 91-515, 84 Stat. 1297, 42 U.S. Code §§ 210, 217a, 218, 241, 242b to 242f, 242i, 242j, 243 to 247b, 262, 263f, 277, 289a to 289c, 289e, and others

Nov. 2, 1970, P.L. 91-519, 84 Stat. 1343, 42 U.S. Code §§ 295f-1, 295f-2, 295h to 295h-2, 295h-3a to 295h-3d, 295h-7 to 295h-9

Dec. 24, 1970, P.L. 91-572, 84 Stat. 1506, 42 U.S. Code §§ 201 nt., 300 to 300a-6

Dec. 31, 1970, P.L. 91-616, 84 Stat. 1853, 42 U.S. Code §§ 218, 246

Dec. 31, 1970, P.L. 91-623, 84 Stat. 1868, 42 U.S. Code §§ 233, 254b

July 9, 1971, P.L. 92-52, 85 Stat. 144, 42 U.S. Code §§ 294b to 294d, 295g, 297, 297c, 297e, 297f, 298c

March 21, 1972, P.L. 92-255, 86 Stat. 77, 42 U.S. Code §§ 218, 246, 257

May 11, 1972, P.L. 92-293, 86 Stat. 136, 42 U.S. Code § 259

May 16, 1972, P.L. 92-294, 86 Stat. 137, 42 U.S. Code §§ 300b to 300b-5

May 19, 1972, P.L. 92-305, 86 Stat. 162, 43 U.S. Code §§ 289a, 289c-1

Aug. 29, 1972, P.L. 92-414, 86 Stat. 650, 42 U.S. Code §§ 300b, 300b-2, 300b-3, 300b-5, 300c to 300c-4

Sept. 19, 1972, P.L. 92-423, 86 Stat. 680, 42 U.S. Code §§ 218, 241, 287 to 287i

Sept. 21, 1972, P.L. 92-425, 86 Stat. 713, 33 U.S. Code § 857a; 42 U.S. Code § 213a

Sept. 30, 1972, P.L. 92-449, 86 Stat. 748, 42 U.S. Code §§ 247b, 247c, 300

Oct. 27, 1972, P.L. 92-585, 86 Stat. 1290, 42 U.S. Code §§ 234, 254b, 294a

June 18, 1973, P.L. 93-45, 87 Stat. 91, 42 U.S. Code §§ 280b-9, 291a, 291j-1, 291j-5, 295h-1, 295h-2, 295h-3a, 299a, 300, 300a-1, 300a-2, 300a-3

Nov. 9, 1973, P.L. 93-151, 87 Stat. 568, 42 U.S. Code § 246

Nov. 16, 1973, P.L. 93-154, 87 Stat. 594, 33 U.S. Code § 763c; 42 U.S . Code §§ 201 nt., 211a, 212a, 222 nt., 295f-2, 295f-4, 295f-6, 300d to 300d-9

Dec. 29, 1973, P.L. 93-222, 87 Stat. 914, 42 U.S. Code §§ 280c, 300e to 300e-14

April 22, 1974, P.L. 93-270, 88 Stat. 90, 42 U.S. Code §§ 289d, 289g, 300c-11

May 14, 1974, P.L. 93-282, 88 Stat. 132, 42 U.S. Code §§ 242a, 289k-1, 289l

May 31, 1974, P.L. 93-296, 88 Stat. 185, 42 U.S. Code §§ 289dk-2 to 289k-5

July 12, 1974, P.L. 93-348, 42 U.S. Code §§ 218, 241, 242a, 282, 286a, 286b, 287a, 287b, 287d, 288a, 289c, 289c-1, 289g, 289k, 289l, 289l-1 to 289l-3, 295f-2

July 23, 1974, p. L. 93-353, 88 Stat. 362, 42 U.S. Code §§ 235, 236, 242b, 242c, 242k to 242o, 244-1, 245a, 247d, 253b

July 23, 1974, P.L. 93-352, 88 Stat. 358, 42 U.S. Code §§ 241, 282, 286a to 286d, 286g, 289l, 289l-4

July 23, 1974, P.L. 93-354, 88 Stat. 376, 42 U.S. Code §§ 247b, 289c-1 to 289c-3

Aug. 23, 1974, P.L. 93-385, 88 Stat. 341, 42 U.S. Code §§ 234, 294, 294b, 297a, 297c

June 23, 1976, P.L. 94-317, 42 U.S. Code § 201 et seq.

Aug. 1, 1977, P.L. 95-83, 42 U.S. Code § 201 et seq.

Nov. 16, 1977, P.L. 95-190, 42 U.S. Code § 300j-1 et seq.

Dec. 19, 1977, P.L. 95-215, 42 U.S. Code § 295f-1 et seq.

Nov. 1, 1978, P.L. 95-559, 42 U.S. Code § 300e et seq.

Nov. 8, 1978, P.L. 95-613, 42 U.S. Code §§ 300, 300a-1 to 300a-4, 300c-11

Nov. 9, 1978, P.L. 95-619, 42 U.S. Code §§ 300h-2, 300n-1

Nov. 9, 1978, P.L. 95-622, 42 U.S. Code §§ 246, 300v et seq.

Nov. 9, 1978, P.L. 95-623, 42 U.S. Code §§ 210, 229c, 242b et seq., 289k, 289l-1, 292e et seq.

Nov. 10, 1978, P.L. 95-626, 42 U.S. Code §§ 201 nt., 218, 246 et seq., 254a to 256a, 294t, 294u, 295h-1, 300d-2 et seq., 300u-5 et seq.

Nov. 10, 1978, P.L. 95-633, 42 U.S. Code § 242a

July 10, 1979, P.L. 96-32, 42 U.S. Code § 210 et seq.

Sept. 6, 1979, P.L. 96-63, 42 U.S. Code §§ 300j to 300j-2

Sept. 29, 1979, P.L. 96-76, 42 U.S. Code §§ 201, 201 nt., 204, 206, 206 nt., 207 et seq., 254k, 294b et seq.

Oct. 4, 1979, P.L. 96-79, 42 U.S. Code §§ 201, 201 nt., 246, 300k -1, 300k-1 nt, 300k-2 et seq.; 42 U.S. Code §§ 300p to 300p-3, 300o to 300o-3§ repealed

Dec. 12, 1979, P.L. 96-142, 42 U.S. Code §§ 256, 295g-9, 300c-11, 300c-12, 300d-1 to 300d-3, 300d-6, 300d-8, 300d-21

Jan. 2, 1980, P.L. 96-180, 42 U.S. Code § 218

Jan. 2, 1980, P.L. 96-181, 42 U.S. Code §§ 218, 300l-2, 300m-3

Sept. 8, 1980, P.L. 96-342, 42 U.S. Code §§ 211 et seq.

Dec. 1, 1982, P.L. 98-194, 42 U.S. Code § 254g

Dec. 21, 1982, P.L. 97-375, 42 U.S. Code §§ 254b, 254i

Jan. 4, 1983, P.L. 97-414, 42 U.S. Code §§ 209, 236, 242k, 243, 254c, 255, 255 nt., 287 nt., 294j, 297-1, 300w-300y

July 18, 1984, p. L. 98-369, 98 Stat. 1112 et seq.

Oct. 12, 1984, P.L. 98-473, 42 U.S. Code § 257

Oct. 19, 1984, P.L. 98-509, 42 U.S. Code §§ 290aa et seq., 300x et seq.

Oct. 30, 1984, P.L. 98-551, 42 U.S. Code § 254r, 300u, 300u-5 to 300u-9

Oct. 30, 1984, P.L. 98-555, 42 U.S. Code §§ 247b, 247c

Nov. 8, 1984, P.L. 98-620, 42 U.S. Code § 300j-9

Aug. 15, 1985, P.L. 99-91, 42 U.S. Code § 295g-1

Aug. 16, 1985, P.L. 99-92, 42 U.S. Code §§ 296 et seq., 297, 297- 1, 297a-297e, 297i

Oct. 22, 1985, P.L. 99-129, 42 U.S. Code §§ 254l, 292 et seq., 295 et seq., 296k to 296m, 297a, 298b-5, 300aa-14

Nov. 8, 1985, P.L. 99-145, 10 U.S. Code § 2172

Nov. 20, 1985, P.L. 99-158, 42 U.S. Code §§ 218, 241, 275 et seq. , 280b et seq., 281 et seq., 290aa-5

April 7, 1986, P.L. 99-272, 42 U.S. Code §§ 210 prec. 295i, 300w-9, 300aa-15, 300bb-1 to 300bb-8

May 23, 1986, P.L. 99-339, 42 U.S. Code §§ 300f, 300g-1 et seq., 300h et seq., 300i, 300i-1, 300j et seq.

July 1, 1986, P.L. 99-348, 42 U.S. Code § 211

July 2, 1986, P.L. 99-349, 100 Stat. 737

Aug. 27, 1986, P.L. 99-401, 42 U.S. Code § 290dd-3

Oct. 22, 1986, P.L. 99-514, 42 U.S. Code §§ 300bb-2, 300bb-5, 300bb-6

Oct. 27, 1986, P.L. 99-570, 42 U.S. Code § 290dd-1

Nov. 10, 1986, P.L. 99-646, 42 U.S. Code §§ 257, 300w-3

Nov. 10, 1986, P.L. 99-649, 42 U.S. Code prec. § 280b

Nov. 14, 1986, P.L. 99-654, 42 U.S. Code §§ 300w-3, 300w-4

Nov. 14, 1986, P.L. 99-660, 42 U.S. Code §§ 218, 241, 242c, 262, 262 nt., 286, 289, 290aa-3, 295g-8, 300e-1, 399k-1 nt., prec. 300x, 300x et seq. prec. 300aa et seq., prec. 300cc, 300cc et seq.

July 22, 1987, P.L. 100-77, 42 U.S. Code §§ 254e, 256, 256a, 290bb-1a, 290bb-2, 290cc-21 et seq.

Aug. 18, 1987, P.L. 100-97, 42 U.S. Code § 295g-8a

Nov. 29, 1987, P.L. 100-175, 42 U.S. Code §§ 280c to 280c-5

Dec. 1, 1987, P.L. 100-177, 42 U.S. Code §§ 242a, 242c, 242k, 242m, 242n, 242p, 247b, 254d to 254g, 254h-1, 254k, 254l-1, 254m to 254r, 295g-8, 300aa-2 nt.

Dec. 22, 1987, P.L. 100-203, 42 U.S. Code § 254o

July 1, 1988, P.L. 100-360, 102 Stat. 808, 42 U.S. Code §§ 300a- 12, 300aa-21

Oct. 4, 1988, P.L. 100-471, 42 U.S. Code § 247

Oct. 24, 1988, P.L. 100-517, 102 Stat. 2578

Continued

Oct. 28, 1988, P.L. 100-553, 42 U.S. Code §§ 281, prec. 285j, 285j prec. 285m, 285m, 285m-1-285m-6

Oct. 31, 1988, P.L. 100-572, 42 U.S. Code § 247b-1

Oct. 31, 1988, P.L. 100-578, 42 U.S. Code § 263a

Nov. 4, 1988, P.L. 100-607, 42 U.S. Code generally §§ 201 et seq.

Nov. 7, 1988, P.L. 100-628, 42 U.S. Code §§ 256, 290aa-3 nt., 290bb-2, 290cc-29, 290cc-35

Nov. 10, 1988, P.L. 100-647, 42 U.S. Code § 300bb-8

Nov. 18, 1988, P.L. 100-690, 42 U.S. Code §§ 242a, 242c, 286, 289 prec. 290aa, 290aa, 290aa-3 et seq., 290bb-2, 290cc, 290cc-1, 290cc-2, prec. 290ff, 290ff, 300x et seq. prec. 300y, 300y-300y-2, 300x-9a, 300x-9b

Nov. 23, 1988, P.L. 100-713, 42 U.S. Code §§ 254r, 254r nt., 254s

Aug. 16, 1989, P.L. 101-93, 42 U.S. Code §§ 207, 256, 285a-2 et seq.

Nov. 29, 1989, P.L. 101-190, 42 U.S. Code § 289e Dec. 19, 1989, P.L. 101-239, generally 42 U.S. Code §§ 201 et seq.

Aug. 10, 1990, P.L. 101-354, 42 U.S. Code §§ 300k-300n-5

Aug. 15, 1990, P.L. 101-368, 42 U.S. Code § 247b

Aug. 15, 1990, P.L. 101-374, 42 U.S. Code §§ 290aa-12, 290cc-2, 300x-4

Aug. 18, 1990, P.L. 101-381, 42 U.S. Code §§ 284a, 286, 287a, 287c-2, 289f, 290aa-3a, 299c-5, 300ff-11 to 300ff-18, 300ff-21 to 300ff-30, 300ff-41, 300ff-55, 300ff-61 to 300ff-67, 300ff-71 to 300ff-76, 300ff-80 to 300ff-90, 300aaa to 300aaa-13

Nov. 3, 1990, P.L. 101-502, 37 U.S. Code §§ 201, 201 nt., 42 U.S . Code §§ 207, 247b, 300aa-2 nt., 300aa-6, 300aa-11 to 300aa-13, 300aa- 15, 300aa-16, 300aa-21, 300ff-13, 300ff-47, 300ff-49

Nov. 5, 1990, P.L. 101-508, 42 U.S. Code § 299c-1

Nov. 5, 1990, P.L. 101-509, 42 U.S. Code §§ 212, 212 nt., 237, 254l

Nov. 6, 1990, P.L. 101-527, 42 U.S. Code §§ 242k nt., 242k, 242m , 251c, 254b, 254c, 254c-1, 254u, 256a, 292h nt., 292m, 294o, 294bb, 294cc, 295g-2, 300u-6

Nov. 15, 1990, P.L. 101-557, 42 U.S. Code §§ 280c, 280c-2, 280c- 3, 280c-5, 285e-2, 285e-3, 300u-6, 300u-6 nt.

Nov. 15, 1990, P.L. 101-558, 42 U.S. Code §§ 280b, 280b-1-280b-3

Nov. 16, 1990, P.L. 101-590, 42 U.S. Code §§ 300d et seq. generally, 300w-4, 300w-9

Nov. 16, 1990, P.L. 101-597, 42 U.S. Code §§ 242a, 254d et seq. generally, 294h, 294n, 294aa, 295g-1, 296m

Nov. 16, 1990, P.L. 101-613, 42 U.S. Code §§ 285g-4, 285g-4 nt.

Nov. 16, 1990, P.L. 101-616, 42 U.S. Code §§ 273 et seq. generally, prec. 275, 280b, 280c

Nov. 28, 1990, P.L. 101-629, 42 U.S. Code § 263b et seq.

Nov. 28, 1990, P.L. 101-639, 42 U.S. Code §§ 290cc-13, 299a, 300x-3, 300x-11, 300x-12

Nov. 29, 1990, P.L. 101-644, 42 U.S. Code § 254s

Nov. 29, 1990, P.L. 101-645, 42 U.S. Code §§ 256, 290bb-2, 290cc -21 to 290cc-35

Nov. 29, 1990, P.L. 101-647, 42 U.S. Code § 290aa-6

April 6, 1991, P.L. 102-25, 42 U.S. Code § 294d

June 13, 1991, P.L. 102-54, 42 U.S. Code §§ 213, 242k, 246, 257, 287c-2, 290dd-3, 290ee-3

Aug. 14, 1991, P.L. 102-96, 42 U.S. Code § 300cc-13

Nov. 26, 1991, P.L. 102-168, 42 U.S. Code §§ 300u, 300u-5, 300aa -11, 300aa-12, 300aa-15, 300aa-16, 300aa-19, 300aa-21

Nov. 26, 1991, P.L. 102-170, 42 U.S. Code § 290b

Dec. 12, 1991, P.L. 102-229, 42 U.S. Code § 300aaa-12

Dec. 17, 1991, P.L. 102-239, 42 U.S. Code § 300aaa-12

June 16, 1992, P.L. 102-300, 42 U.S. Code § 262

July 10, 1992, P.L. 102-321, 42 U.S. Code §§ 201 nt., 236, 242a, 247d, 280d, 280d nt., 280c et seq., 281, 282, 284d, 285n et seq., 285o et seq., 285p et seq., 288, 288b, 289c-1, 290b, 290aa et seq., 290bb et seq., 290cc et seq., 290dd et seq., 290ee et seq., 290ff et seq., 299gg, 300d et seq., 300cc-2 , 300dd et seq., 300x et seq., 300y, 300y-11

July 23, 1992, P.L. 102-325, 42 U.S. Code § 295g-8

Aug. 26, 1992, P.L. 102-352, 42 U.S. Code §§ 285n, 285n-2, 285o, 285o-2, 285p, 290aa-1, 290aa-3, 300x-7, 300x-27, 300x-33, 300x-53, 300y

Oct. 13, 1992, P.L. 102-408, 106 Stat. 1994

Oct. 13, 1992, P.L. 102-409, 42 U.S. Code § 283a

Oct. 13, 1992, P.L. 102-410, 42 U.S. Code §§ 299, 299aa to 299a- 2, 299b to 299b-3, 299c to 299c-3, 299c-5, 300w-9

Oct. 24, 1992, P.L. 102-501, 42 U.S. Code § 233

Oct. 24, 1992, P.L. 102-507, 42 U.S. Code § 285e-5

Oct. 24, 1992, P.L. 102-515, 42 U.S. Code §§ prec. 280e, 280e to 280e-4

Oct. 27, 1992, P.L. 102-531, 42 U.S. Code §§ 236, 242b, 247b-1, 247b-3 to 247b-5, 247c-1, 247d, 254b, 254c, 256, 256a, prec. 256c, 256c, 280b, 280b-1, 280b-2, prec. 280d-11, 280d-11, 285c-4, 285d-7, 285m-4, 289c, 290aa-9, 292y, 293j, 293l, 294n, 295j, 295l, 295n, 295o, 296k, 298b-7, 300l-1, 300u, 300u-1, 300u-5, 300u-7, 300w et seq., 300aa-2, 300aa-15, 300aa-19, 300aa-26, 300cc, 300cc-2, 300cc-15, 300cc-17, 300cc-20, 300cc-31, 300ee-31, 300ee-32, 300ee-34, 300ff-11, 300ff-12, 300ff-17, 300ff-27, 300ff-28, 300ff-41, 300ff-43 300ff-49, 300ff-75

Oct. 27, 1992, P.L. 102-539, 42 U.S. Code §§ prec. 263b, 263b

Nov. 4, 1992, P.L. 102-585, 42 U.S. Code §§ prec. 256b, 256b

June 10, 1993, P.L. 103-43, 42 U.S. Code §§ 201 et seq.

Aug. 10, 1993, P.L. 103-66, 42 U.S. Code §§ 300aa-12, 300aa-14 to 3000aa-16

Dec. 14, 1993, P.L. 103-183, 42 U.S. Code §§ 233, 238j, 242b, 242k, 242l, 242m, 247b, 247b-1, 247b-5, 247b-6, 247b-7, 247c, 247c-1, 254j, 256d, 280b et seq., 280e-4, 285f-2, 300d, 300d-1, 300d-2, 300d-3, 300d-12, 300d -13, 300d-16, 300d-22, 300d-31 et seq., 300k, 300m, 300n, 300n-1, 300n-4, 300n- 4a, 300n-5, 300u-5, 300u-8, 300aa-26

Oct. 25, 1994, P.L. 103-417, 42 U.S. Code §§ 281, 287c-11

Nov. 2, 1994, P.L. 103-437, 42 U.S. Code §§ 300c-12, 300j-9

Nov. 2, 1994, P.L. 103-446, 42 U.S. Code §§ 290aa-1, 290dd-1, 300ff-14

Nov. 2, 1994, P.L. 103-448, 42 U.S. Code §§ 280c-6, 300c-12, 300j-9

Dec. 21, 1995, P.L. 104-66, 42 U.S. Code §§ 238h, 289c-1, 298b-6 , 300a-6a, 300h-5, 300h-6, 300j-1, 300u-4

April 26, 1996, P.L. 104-134, 42 U.S. Code §§ 238n, 262

May 20, 1996, P.L. 104-146, 5 U.S. Code § 4103 nt.; 42 U.S. Code §§ 294n, 300cc nt., 300ff-11 et seq.

July 29, 1996, P.L. 104-166, 42 U.S. Code §§ 280b-1b, 300d-52, 300d-61, 300ff-34, 300ff-111

Aug. 20, 1996, P.L. 104-188, 42 U.S. Code § 300bb-2

Aug. 21, 1996, P.L. 104-191, 42 U.S. Code §§ 233, 242k, 300e, 300bb-2, 300bb-6, 300bb-8, prec. 300gg, 300gg, 300gg-1, prec. 300gg-11, 300gg- 11 to 300gg-13, prec. 300gg-21, 300gg-21 to 300gg-21, prec. 300gg-41, 300gg-41 to 300gg-47, prec. 300gg-91, 300gg-91, 300gg-92

Sept. 23, 1996, P.L. 104-201, 42 U.S. Code §§ 207, 290aa, 299c-4

Sept. 26, 1996, P.L. 104-204, 42 U.S. Code §§ prec. 300gg, prec. 300gg-4, 300gg-4, 300gg-5, prec. 300gg-11, prec. 300gg-21, 300gg-21, 300gg-23, prec. 300gg-41, 300gg-44, prec. 300gg-51, 300gg-51, 300gg-61 to 300gg-63

Oct. 11, 1996, P.L. 104-299, 42 U.S. Code §§ 233, prec. 254b, 254b, 254c, 256c

Oct. 19, 1996, P.L. 104-316, 42 U.S. Code §§ 284c, 290b, 290cc- 28, 300d-16, 300x-52

April 30, 1997, P.L. 105-12, 42 U.S. Code §§ 238o, 295

Aug. 5, 1997, P.L. 105-33, 42 U.S. Code §§ 254c-2, 254c-3

Nov. 13, 1997, P.L. 105-78, 42 U.S. Code § 247e

Nov. 18, 1997, P.L. 105-85, 42 U.S. Code § 213a

Nov. 21, 1997, P.L. 105-115, 42 U.S. Code §§ 247b-8, 262, 263a, 282, 299a-3

April 21, 1998, P.L. 105-168, 42 U.S. Code § 247b-4

May 1, 1998, P.L. 105-174, 42 U.S. Code § 254c-3

July 16, 1998, P.L. 105-196, 42 U.S. Code §§ 274g, 274k, 274l, 274m

Oct. 7, 1998, P.L. 105-244, 42 U.S. Code § 292d

Oct. 7, 1998, P.L. 105-245, 42 U.S. Code § 284a

Oct. 9, 1998, P.L. 105-248, 42 U.S. Code § 263b

Continued

Oct. 21, 1998, P.L. 105-277, 42 U.S. Code §§ 281, 283g, 287c-21, 300x-7, 300x-33, 300aa-11, 300gg-6, 300gg-52

Oct. 31, 1998, P.L. 105-340, 42 U.S. Code §§ 242k, 280e-4, 283a, 284e, 285a-8, 285b-7a, 285e-10, 287d, 300k, 300n-4a, 300n-5, 300u-5, 300u-9

Nov. 10, 1998, P.L. 105-362, 42 U.S. Code §§ 282, 284c, 285c-4, 285d-4, 285g-3, 289c-1, 300a-6a, 300aa-4

Nov. 13, 1998, P.L. 105-392, 42 U.S. Code §§ 213, 218a, 242a, 242k, 242m, 247b, 247b-1, 247b-6, 247b-7, 247c, 254l-1, 254q-1, 254r, 280c-3, 280c-4, 280c-5, 280f, 280f-1 to 280f-3, 282, 285f-2, 287a-2, 287a-3, 288-1 to 288-3, 288-5, 290b, 290aa-3, 290dd-2, 292b, 292d to 292f, 292h, 292i, 292o, 292r to 292t, 292y, 293, 293a to 293d, 293j to 293p, 294, 294a to 294g, 294n, 295, 295a to 295e, 295j to 295l, 295n, 295n-1, 295n-2, 295o, 295o-1, 295o-2, 295p, prec. 296, 296, 296a to 296g, 296j, 296k to 296m, prec. 296p, 296p, 296r, 297, 297-1, prec. 297a to 297c, 297e, 297n, prec. 297q, 297q, prec. 297t, 297t, 298, 298a, 298b, 298b-1 to 298b-5, 298b-7, 300d-13, 300d-32, 300k, 300n-1, 300u, 300u-6, 300w-9, 300ff-28

Public Health Service Act Technical Amendments Act

Aug. 26, 1992, P.L. 102-352, 42 U.S. Code § 201 nt.

Public Health Service Amendments of 1987

Dec. 1, 1987, P.L. 100-177, 42 U.S. Code §§ 201 nt., 242a, 242c, 242k, 242m, 242n, 242p, 247b, 245d to 254g, 254h-1, 254k, 254-1, 254m to 254r, 295g-8, 300aa-2 nt., 11137

Dec. 19, 1989, P.L. 101-239, 42 U.S. Code §§ 11111, 11115, 11137 nt.

Public Health Service Commissioned Corps Personnel Act of 1960

April 8, 1960, P.L. 86-415, 74 Stat. 32, 42 U.S. Code §§ 201, 209 , 210, 211, 212, 253, 415

Public Health Services Act (Community)

Neb. Laws 1992, L.B. 1019, §§ 101 to 121

Public Health Statistics Act

Haw. Rev. Stat. Ann., § 338-1 et seq.

Public Higher Education Act

D.C. Code Ann., § 31-1401 et seq.

Public Highway Authority Law

Colo. Rev. Stat., 43-4-501 et seq.

Public Highways Act

Minn. Stat. Ann., 160.01 et seq.

Public Hospital Act

N.C. Gen. Stat 1943, § 131E-5 et seq.

Public Hospital Act (Counties)

Mo. Rev. Stat., 205.160 et seq.

Public Hospital Board Act (Sarasota County)

Fla. Laws 1949, Ex. Sess., Ch. 26468

Public Hospital Districts Act

Mont. Code Ann., 7-34-2101 et seq.

S.D. Codified Laws 1967, 34-10-1 et seq.

Wash. Rev. Code Ann., 70.44.003 et seq.

Public Housing Act

N.J. Stat. Ann., 55:15-1 et seq.

N.Y. Consol. Laws, Ch. 44A

Public Housing Act (Baker-Metcalf)

N.Y. Civil Rights Law (Consol. Laws, Ch. 6) § 18b, Subd. 3

Public Housing Administration Organic Act

P.R. Acts 1989, No. 66

Public Housing Anti-Discrimination Act

Vt. Stat. Ann., Title 9, § 4500 et seq.

Public Housing Discrimination Act

Cal. Health and Safety Code, § 35700 et seq.

Public Housing Discrimination Act (Austin-Wicks)

N.Y. Civil Rights Law (Consol. Laws Ch. 6) § 18a et seq.

Public Housing Drug Elimination Act
N.Y. Public Housing Law (Consol. Laws Ch. 44A) § 301 et seq.

Public Housing Drug Elimination Act of 1988
See Public and Assisted Housing Drug Elimination Act of 1990
Nov. 18, 1988, P.L. 100-690, 42 U.S. Code § 11901 nt.

Public Housing Limited Dividend Act
N.Y. Private Housing Finance Law (Consol. Laws Ch. 44B) § 76 et seq.
N.Y. Public Housing Law (Consol. Laws Ch. 44A) § 173

Public Housing Security Demonstration Act of 1978
Oct. 31, 1978, P.L. 95-557, 12 U.S. Code §§ 1701z-6 nt.
Oct. 17, 1984, P.L. 98-479, 12 U.S. Code § 1701z-6
Sept. 21, 1993, P.L. 103-82, 12 U.S. Code § 1701z-6 nt.

Public Housing Tenant Manager Training Act
Ill. Rev. Stat. 1991, Ch. 67 1/2, § 1201 et seq.

Public Improvement Act (Counties)
Mich. Comp. Laws Ann., 46.171 et seq.

Public Improvement Act (Municipalities)
Ind. Code Ann., 19-8-16-1 et seq.

Public Improvement Bonds Act
Ala. Code 1975, 11-81-160 et seq.

Public Improvement by Special Assessment Act
Ariz. Rev. Stat. Ann., § 48-572 et seq.

Public Improvement District Act (County)
Colo. Rev. Stat., 30-20-501 et seq.

Public Improvement District Assessment Act
Tex. Local Government Code, § 372.001 et seq.

Public Improvements Act
Del. Code of 1974, Title 29, § 6901 et seq.
Ind. Code Ann., 5-16-1-1.1 et seq.
N.Y. Local Laws 1972, Town of Evans, p. 1380

Public Improvements Act (Municipal)
Ala. Code 1975, 11-48-1 et seq.

Public Improvements Act (Townships)
Mich. Comp. Laws Ann., 41.411 et seq.

Public Improvements Authority Act (Harris County)
Ga. Laws 1995, p. 4052

Public Improvements Contractor's Bond Act
Cal. Government Code, § 4200 et seq.

Public Improvements Loan Act
R.I. Public Laws 1938, Ch. 2610

Public Improvements Trust Act
Okla. Stat. Ann., Title 60, § 381 et seq.

Public Indebtedness Act
Minn. Stat. Ann., 475.51 et seq.

Public Indecency Act
Pa. Cons. Stat., Title 18, § 5901 et seq.

Public Information and Education Act (Diethylstilbestrol)
Pa. Purdon's Stat., Title 35, § 6211 et seq.

Public Infrastructure Loan and Grant Program Act
Ill. Rev. Stat. 1991, Ch. 127, § 2708-1 et seq.

Public Initiatives, Referendums and Measures Disclosure Act
Ark. Code Ann. 1987, 7-9-401 et seq.

Public Initiatives, Referendums and Measures Referred to Voters by the General Assembly Disclosure Act
Ark. Code 1987, 7-9-401 et seq.

Public Institutional Building Authority Act
Ohio Rev. Code 1953, 151.01 et seq.

Public Instruction Code
Wash. Rev. Code Ann., 28A.01.010 et seq.

Public Insurance Adjusters Act
Cal. Insurance Code, § 15000 et seq.

Public Interest Arbitration Reform Act (Police and Fire)
N.J. Stat. Ann., 34:13A-1 et seq.

Public Interest Energy Research, Demonstration, and Development Program
Cal. Public Resources Code § 25620 et seq.

Public Internship Program (Carl Albert)
Okla. Stat. Ann., Title 74, § 840-3.2 et seq.

Public Intoxication Act
D.C. Code 1973, § 25-128

Public Irrigation District Law
Colo. Rev. Stat., 37-41-101 et seq.

Public Irrigation Law
P.R. Laws Ann. 1954, Title 22, § 251 et seq.

Public Irrigation Law (Lajas Valley)
P.R. Laws Ann. 1954, Title 22, § 341 et seq.

Public Junior College Act
Ill. Rev. Stat. 1991, Ch. 122, § 101-1 et seq.

Public Labor Relations Act
Ill. Rev. Stat. 1991, Ch. 48, § 1601 et seq.
Pa. Purdon's Stat., Title 43, § 211.1 et seq.

Public Land Act (Survey Restoration and Perpetuation of)
Fla. Stat. Ann., 177.501 et seq.

Public Land Administration Act
July 14, 1960, P.L. 86-649, 74 Stat. 506, 43 U.S. Code §§ 1361 to 1364, 1371 to 1374, 1381 to 1383

Public Land Management Act (Coastal)
Tex. Natural Resources Code, § 33.001 et seq.

Public Land Survey Restoration and Perpetuation Act
Fla. Stat 1983, 177.501 et seq.

Public Lands Abatement Act
Miss. Code Ann. 1972, § 29-1-117

Public Lands Act
Alaska Stat. 1962, § 38.05.005 et seq.
Cal. Public Resources Code § 6001 et seq.
Colo. Rev. Stat., 36-2-101 et seq.
La. Rev. Stat. Ann., 41:1 et seq.
N.Y. Consol. Laws, Ch. 46
Pa. Purdon's Stat., Title 64, § 601 et seq.
Wash. Rev. Code Ann., 79.01.004 et seq.

Public Lands Act (Defense of Title)
Cal. Statutes 1850, Ch. 83, p. 203
Cal. Statutes 1852, Ch. 82, p. 158

Public Lands and National Parks Act of 1983
Oct. 31, 1983, P.L. 98-141, 16 U.S. Code § 1 nt.

Public Lands Assessment Act
Wash. Rev. Code Ann., 79.44.003 et seq.

Public Lands Corps Act of 1993
Sept. 21, 1993, P.L. 103-82, 16 U.S. Code §§ 1701 nt.; 1721 et seq.

Public Lands Easement Act
Wash. Rev. Code Ann., 79.36.230 et seq.

Public Lands Lease Act
Wash. Rev. Code Ann., 79.01.088 et seq., 79.01.242 et seq., 79.12.570 et. seq.

Public Lands Management Act (Coastal)
Tex. Natural Resources Code, § 33.001 et seq.

Public Lands Preemption Act
La. Rev. Stat. Ann., 41:171 et seq.

Public Lands Sales Act
Alaska Stat. 1962, § 38.05.045 et seq.
Tex. Natural Resources Code, § 51.001 et seq.
Wash. Rev. Code Ann., 79.01.088 et seq.

Public Lands Sales Acts
Aug. 3, 1846, Ch. 78, 9 Stat. 51, 43 U.S. Code § 1171
Feb. 26, 1895, Ch. 133, 28 Stat. 687, 43 U.S. Code § 1171
June 27, 1906, Ch. 3554, 34 Stat. 517, 43 U.S. Code § 1171
March 28, 1912, Ch. 67, 37 Stat. 77, 43 U.S. Code § 1171
March 9, 1928, Ch. 164, 45 Stat. 253, 43 U.S. Code § 1171
June 28, 1934, Ch. 865, 48 Stat. 1274, 43 U.S. Code § 1171
July 30, 1947, Ch. 383, 61 Stat. 630, 43 U.S. Code § 1171
Sept. 19, 1964, P.L. 88-607, 78 Stat. 986, 43 U.S. Code §§ 1411 to 1418
Sept. 19, 1964, P.L. 88-608, 78 Stat. 988, 43 U.S. Code §§ 1421 to 1427
Sept. 26, 1968, P.L. 90-516, 82 Stat. 870, 43 U.S. Code §§ 1431 to 1435

Public Liability Act (Municipal)
See Municipal Liability Act

Public Liability and Property Damage Insurance Act (StateVehicles)
N.M. Stat. Ann. 1953, 64-25-8, 64-25-9

Public Liability Moratorium Act
Cal. Civil Code, § 22.3

Public Libraries Act (State Aid)
Mich. Comp. Laws Ann., 397.551 et seq.

Public Libraries Appropriation Act
Mich. Comp. Laws 1948, 397.102 et seq.

Public Libraries Tax Act
Okla. Stat. Ann., Title 65, § 1-104

Public Library Act
D.C. Code Ann., § 37-101 et seq.
Ga. Code Ann., 20-5-1 et seq.
Ill. Rev. Stat. 1991, Ch. 81, § 1001-1 et seq.
Ind. Code Ann., 20-14-1-1 et seq.
Md. Ann. Code 1974, Art. ED, § 23-101 et seq.
Mo. Rev. Stat., 182.010 et seq.
N.H. Rev. Stat. 1955, 202-A:1 et seq.
Ohio Rev. Code 1953, 3375.01 et seq.

Wash. Rev. Code Ann., 27.12.010 et seq.

Public Library Act (Chicago)
Ill. Comp. Stat. 1992, Ch. 75, § 20/0.01 et seq.

Public Library Act (Manatee County)
Fla. Special Laws 1971, Ch. 71-760

Public Library Act (North Shore)
N.Y. Laws 1968, Ch. 856

Public Library Act (Shelter Rock)
N.Y. Laws 1962, Ch. 972

Public Library Aid Act
Mich. Comp. Laws Ann., 397.551 et seq.

Public Library Construction Assistance Act
Del. Code of 1974, Title 29, § 6601A et seq.

Public Library District Act
Ill. Laws 1992, P.A. 87-1277

Public Library Employees' Pension Act
Mich. Comp. Laws Ann., 38.701 et seq.

Public Library Financial Assistance Act
N.M. Stat. Ann. 1953, 4-11-19 et seq.

Public Library Service Act
Ky. Rev. Stat. 1971, 171.201 et seq.

Public Livestock Market Charter Act
La. Rev. Stat. Ann., 3:661 et seq.
Tenn. Code Ann., 44-12-101 et seq.

Public Livestock Market Development Act
Ida. Code 1947, 25-1719 et seq.

Public Livestock Marketing Business Act
Ala. Code 1975, § 2-15-115 et seq.

Public Mall Act
Colo. Rev. Stat., 31-25-401 et seq.

Public Marketing Act
N.J. Stat. Ann., 4:25-1 et seq.
S.D. Codified Laws 1967, 37-4-1 et seq.
W. Va. Code 1966, § 19-2A-1 et seq.

Public Markets Act
S.D. Codified Laws 1967, 37-4-1 et seq.

Public Mass Transportation Act
N.M. Stat. Ann., 67-3-67 et seq.

Public Medical Assistance Act
Fla. Stat. Ann., 154.301 et seq.

Public Meeting Law
La. Rev. Stat. Ann., 44:4 et seq.

Public Meeting Law (Local Agencies)
Cal. Government Code, § 54950 et seq.

Public Meeting Law (State Agencies)
Cal. Government Code, § 11120 et seq.

Public Meetings Act (Open)
See also Open Public Meetings Act
Ill. Rev. Stat. 1991, Ch. 102, § 41.01 et seq.
Minn. Stat. Ann., 471.705
Neb. Rev. Stat. 1943, 84-1408 et seq.
N.J. Stat. Ann., 10:4-6 et seq.
Utah Code Ann. 1953, 52-4-1 et seq.

Public Meetings Act (Ralph M. Brown)
Cal. Government Code, § 54950 et seq.

Public Meetings Notice Act
Wash. Rev. Code Ann., 42.32.030

Public Money Act
Ill. Rev. Stat. 1991, Ch. 102, § 33.9 et seq.
Mich. Comp. Laws Ann., 750.489 et seq.

Public Money Deposit Law (County and Municipal Corporations)
Cal. Financial Code, §§ 856, 860, 1203

Public Money Deposit Law (State Funds)
Cal. Government Code, § 16500 et seq.

Public Morals Act (Guilford County)
N.C. Public-Local Laws 1913, Ch. 761

Public Motor Carrier Act
Kan. Stat. Ann., 66-1, 108 et seq., 66-1302 et seq.

Public Movers Act
N.J. Laws 1968, Ch. 375

Public Movers and Warehousemen Licensing Act
N.J. Stat. Ann., 45-14D-1 et seq.

Public Museum Law
Cal. Government Code, § 37541 et seq.

Public Nonsectarian Hospital Act
Ill. Rev. Stat. 1991, Ch. 34, § 5-7001 et seq.

Public Nuisance Act
Colo. Rev. Stat., 16-13-301 et seq.

Public Nuisance Act (Lewdness)
Ill. Rev. Stat. 1991, Ch. 100 1/2, § 0.01 et seq.

Public Nuisances Act
Colo. Rev. Stat., 16-13-301 et seq.
Ill. Rev. Stat. 1991, Ch. 100 1/2, § 0.01 et seq.
Ind. Code Ann., 35-1-102-1 et seq.
Minn. Stat. Ann., 609.705 et seq.
Wash. Rev. Code Ann., 9.66.010 et seq.

Public Obligations Registration Act
Fla. Stat. Ann., 279.01 et seq.
Ida. Code 1947, 57-901 et seq.
Mont. Code Ann., 17-5-1101 et seq.
N.C. Gen. Stat. 1943, § 159E-1 et seq.
N.J. Stat. Ann., 49:2-2 et seq.
Okla. Stat. Ann., Title 62, § 581 et seq.
R.I. Gen. Laws 1956, 35-13-1 et seq.
Tenn. Code Ann., 9-19-101 et seq.
Utah Code Ann. 1953, 15-7-1 et seq.
W. Va. Code 1966 § 13-2F-1 et seq.

Public Off-Street Parking Act
Haw. Rev. Stat. Ann., § 56-1 et seq.

Public Offenses Act
Ind. Code Ann., 35-45-1-1 et seq.

Public Office Succession Act (Emergency Interim)
Tex. Government Code, § 616.001 et seq.

Public Officer Prohibited Activities Act
Ill. Rev. Stat. 1991, Ch. 102, § 0.01 et seq.

Public Officer Simultaneous Tenure Act
Ill. Rev. Stat. 1991, Ch. 102, § 4.9 et seq.

Public Officers Act
N.Y. Consol. Laws, Ch. 47
Wash. Rev. Code Ann., 42.04.020 et seq.

Public Officers and Employees' Absence on Military Duty Act
N.Y. Military Law (Consol. Laws Ch. 36) §§ 242, 243

Public Officers and Employees Act
La. Rev. Stat. Ann., 42:1 et seq.

Public Officers and Employees Code of Ethics Act
Fla. Stat. Ann., 112.311 et seq.

Public Officers' and Employees' Ethics Act
Utah Code Ann. 1953, 67-16-1 et seq.

Public Officers and Employees Liability Act
N.M. Stat. Ann. 1953, 5-13-1 et seq.

Public Officers and Employees Relations Act
Kan. Stat. Ann., 75-4301 et seq.

Public Officers and Employees' Retirement System Act
N.H. Rev. Stat. 1955, 100-A:1 et seq.

Public Officers and Employees Salary Act
Ky. Rev. Stat. 1971, 64.480 et seq.

Public Officers Bond Act
Wash. Rev. Code Ann., 42.08.005 et seq.

Public Officers Financial Disclosure
Cal. Government Code, § 3700 et seq.

Public Officers Liability Law
Cal. Government Code, §§ 820 et seq., 1950 et seq.

Public Officers Recall Act
Ga. Code Ann., 21-4-1 et seq.

Public Officers Resistance and Obstruction Act
Okla. Stat. 1981, Title 21, § 540

Public Official Compensation Law
Pa. Purdon's Stat., Title 65, § 366.1 et seq.

Public Officials Act
Iowa Code Ann., 68B.1 et seq.

Public Officials Bribery Act
Pa. Purdon's Stat., Title 65, § 401 et seq.
Wis. Stat. Ann., 946.10 et seq.

Public Officials Conduct and Lobbyist Disclosure Act
Ga. Laws 1992, p. 1075

Public Officials Facsimile Signature Act
See also Uniform Facsimile Signature of Public Officials Act
Colo. Rev. Stat., 11-55-101 et seq.
Del. Code of 1974, Title 29, § 5401 et seq.
Fla. Stat. 116.34
Ida. Code 1947, 59-1018 et seq.
Nev. Rev. Stat. Ann., 351.010 et seq.
Okla. Stat. Ann., Title 62, § 601 et seq.
Tex. Rev. Civ. Stat., Art. 717j-1

Public Open Meetings Act
Wash. Rev. Code Ann., 42.30.010 et seq.

Public Outdoor Recreation Plan Act
Cal. Public Resources Code, § 8750 et seq.

Public Park Condemnation Act
Va. Code 1950, § 25-46.2:1

Public Park Preservation Act
Cal. Public Resources Code, § 5400 et seq.

Public Parking Act (Warren)
R.I. Public Laws 1968, Ch. 204

Public Parking Areas Regulation Act
P.R. Laws Ann. 1954, Title 23, § 805 et seq.

Public Parking Loan Act (Beverly)
Mass. Acts 1963, Ch. 139

Public Parking Loan Act (Holyoke)
Mass. Acts 1955, Ch. 663

Public Parking Loan Act (Lowell)
Mass. Acts 1955, Ch. 362

Public Parking Loan Act (Lynn)
Mass. Acts 1956, Ch. 655

Public Parking Loan Act (Malden)
Mass. Acts 1954, Ch. 600

Public Parking Loan Act (New Bedford)
Mass. Acts 1958, Ch. 242

Public Parks Act
Mass. Gen. Laws. Ann., 45:2 et seq.

Public Parks Act (Wilmington)
Del. Laws Vol. 17, p. 404, Ch. 204

Public Participation and Enforcement Act
Ga. Code Ann., 12-17-1 et seq.

Public Participation in Parole Act
Cal. Penal Code, § 3043.5

Public Passages Act (Obstructed)
La. Rev. Stat. Ann., 14:100.1

Public Passenger Motor Vehicle Act
Md. Ann. Code 1957, Art. 56, § 181 et seq.

**Public Passenger Motor Vehicle Responsi-
bility Law**
La. Rev. Stat. Ann., 45:200.1 et seq.

Public Pay Roll Fraud Statute
La. Rev. Stat. Ann., 14:138, 14:139

Public Pension Review Act
Tenn. Code Ann., 3-9-201 et seq.

Public Places Naming Act
D.C. Code Ann., §§ 1-337, Subd. f, 7-454,
7-451

Public Policy Environmental Act
P.R. Laws Ann. 1954, Title 12, § 1121 et seq.

Public Policy Questions Act
Ill. Rev. Stat. 1991, Ch. 46, § 28-1 et seq.

**Public Postsecondary Education Reorgani-
zation Act**
D.C. Code Ann., § 31-1501 et seq.

Public Power Act
Wash. Rev. Code Ann., 54.04.010 et seq.

Public Power Act (Grid System)
Neb. Laws 1965, Ch. 404

Public Power District Act
Neb. Rev. Stat. 1943, 70-601 et seq.
Wyo. Stat. Ann., § 41-7-801 et seq.

Public Power Supply Authority Act
Vt. Stat. Ann., Title 30, § 5001 et seq.

Public Printing Act
S.C. Code Ann. 1976, § 11-25-10 et seq.

Public Printing and Documents
Oct. 22, 1968, P.L. 90-620, 82 Stat. 1238, 44
U.S. Code §§ 101 to 3703
Dec. 26, 1969, P.L. 91-167, 83 Stat. 453, 44
U.S. Code § 305
June 12, 1970, P.L. 91-276, 84 Stat. 303, 44
U.S. Code § 906
June 23, 1970, P.L. 91-287, 84 Stat. 320, 44
U.S. Code §§ 2909, 3303a, 3308, 3309
July 31, 1970, P.L. 91-359, 84 Stat. 668, 44
U.S. Code § 317
July 31, 1970, P.L. 91-369, 84 Stat. 693, 44
U.S. Code § 305
June 6, 1972, P.L. 92-310, 86 Stat. 204, 44
U.S. Code §§ 301, 308
Aug. 10, 1972, P.L. 92-368, 86 Stat. 507, 44
U.S. Code § 1915
Aug. 10, 1972, P.L. 92-373, 83 Stat. 528, 44
U.S. Code § 906
Oct. 25, 1972, P.L. 92-546, 86 Stat. 1155, 44
U.S. Code §§ 2501, 2503, 2504
Nov. 16, 1973, P.L. 93-153, 87 Stat. 593, 44
U.S. Code §§ 3502, 3512
Dec. 18, 1973, P.L. 93-191, 87 Stat. 745, 44
U.S. Code §§ 733, 907
March 27, 1974, P.L. 93-255, 88 Stat. 52, 44
U.S. Code §§ 733, 907
June 8, 1974, P.L. 93-314, 88 Stat. 239, 44
U.S. Code §§ 906, 910

Public-Private Contracting Act (Wastewater Treatment)
N.J. Stat. Ann., 58:27-19 et seq.

Public-Private Contracting Act (Water Supply)
N.J. Stat. Ann., 58:26-10 et seq.

Public-Private Partnership Act
Md. Ann. Code 1974, Art. SG, § 15-523

Public-Private Regional Field Offices Act
N.J. Laws 1995, Ch. 205

Public Procurement Act
Va. Code 1950, § 11-35 et seq.

Public Property Finance Act
Tex. Local Government Code, § 271.001 et seq.

Public Property Lead Elimination Act
D.C. Code Ann., §§ 9-302, 9-303

Public Purchase Act
Ind. Code Ann., 5-17-1-1 et seq.
Miss. Code Ann. 1972, § 31-7-1 et seq.
N.M. Stat. Ann., 13-1-21 et seq.

Public Purchases in Other States Act
Ill. Rev. Stat. 1989, Ch. 29, § 39.9 et seq.

Public Purpose Buildings and Community-Based Facilities Construction Bond Act
N.J. Laws 1991, Ch. 184

Public Purpose Buildings Construction Bond Act
N.J. Laws 1980, Ch. 119

Public Radio and Television Grant Act
Ill. Rev. Stat. 1991, Ch. 127, § 1550 et seq.

Public Rail Corporation Act
R.I. Gen. Laws 1956, 42-64.2-1 et seq.

Public Rangelands Improvement Act of 1978
Oct. 25, 1978, P.L. 95-514, 16 U.S. Code §§ 1332, 1333; 43 U.S. Code §§ 1751 et seq., 1901, 1901 nt., 1902 et seq.

Public Records Act
Cal. Government Code, § 6250 et seq.
Colo. Rev. Stat., 24-72-201 et seq.
Fla. Stat. Ann., 119.01 et seq.
Ga. Code Ann., 50-18-90 et seq.
Kan. Stat. Ann., 45-201 et seq.
La. Rev. Stat. Ann., 44:1 et seq.
Miss. Code Ann. 1972, § 25-61-1 et seq.
N.H. Rev. Stat. 1955, 91-A:1 et seq.
N.M. Stat. Ann., 14-3-1 et seq.
Va. Code 1950, § 42.1-76 et seq.
Wyo. Stat. Ann., § 16-4-201 et seq.

Public Records Act (Destroyed)
Ill. Rev. Stat. 1991, Ch. 116, § 4.9 et seq.

Public Records Act (Enhanced Access to)
Mich. Comp. Laws Ann., 15.441 et seq.

Public Records Act (Evidence)
Nev. Rev. Stat. 1979 Reprint, 52.085 et seq.

Public Records Administration Act
R.I. Gen. Laws 1956, 38-3-1 et seq.

Public Records Commission Act
Ind. Code Ann., 5-15-5.1-1 et seq.

Public Records Evidence Act
N.Y. Civil Practice Laws and Rules (Consol. Laws Ch. 8) § 4518

Public Records Inspection Act
N.D. Cent. Code, 44-04-18
N.M. Stat. Ann., 14-2-4 et seq.

Public Records Inspection by Citizens Act
Pa. Purdon's Stat., Title 65, § 66.1 et seq.

Public Records Management Act
Mont. Code Ann., 2-6-201 et seq.

Public Records Management and Archives Act
Ark. Code Ann. 1987, 13-4-101 et seq.

Public Records Management and Preservation Act
W. Va. Code 1966, § 5-8-1 et seq.

Public Records Photographic Copies as Evidence Act
N.C. Gen. Stat. 1943, § 8-45.1 et seq.

Public Records Preservation Act
Mich. Comp. Laws Ann., 600.2137

Public Records Recovery Act
N.M. Stat. Ann., 14-5-1 et seq.

Public Records Sunshine Law (Access to)
Vt. Stat. Ann., Title 1, § 315 et seq.

Public Recreation Act
Okla. Stat. Ann., Title 11, § 33-101 et seq.

Public Recreation Facilities Act
Cal. Statutes 1945, Ch. 1422, p. 2676

Public Recreational Facilities Authorities Act
Va. Code 1950, § 15.1-1271 et seq.

Public Registry Act
La. Rev. Stat. Ann., 9:2721 et seq.

Public Regulation Commission Act
N.M. Stat. Ann., 8-8-1 to 8-8-21

Public Regulation Commission Apportionment Act
N.M. Stat. Ann., 8-7-1 to 8-7-10

Public Residential Conveyance Act
P.R. Laws Ann. 1954, Title 17, § 701 et seq.

Public Resources Code
Cal. Statutes 1939, Ch. 93, p. 1067

Public Retirement System Reporting and Disclosure Act
N.Y. Retirement and Social Security Law (Consol. Laws Ch. 51A) § 150 et seq.

Public Retirement Systems Standards Law
Ga. Code Ann., 47-20-1 et seq.

Public Revenue Code
Ga. Code Ann., 48-1-1 et seq.

Public Revenue Service Tax Act
Colo. Laws 1937, p. 1144, Ch. 240

Public Road Act
Tenn. Code Ann., 54-10-101 et seq.

Public Roads and Highways Bond Act
N.J. Stat. Ann., Superseded Vol., 27:5C-1 et seq.

Public Safety Act
Me. Rev. Stat. Ann. 1964, Title 37-B, § 701 et seq.
N.J. Laws 1991, Ch. 78

Public Safety and Recreational Firearms Use Protection Act
Sept. 13, 1994, P.L. 103-322, 18 U.S. Code §§ 921 nt., 921 et seq.

Public Safety Code
Utah Code Ann. 1953, 53-1-101 et seq.

Public Safety Commission Ordinance (Dalton)
Ga. Laws 1992, p. 7205

Public Safety Communications Act
Ark. Code Ann. 1987, 12-10-301 et seq.

Public Safety Department Act
Ga. Code Ann., 35-2-1 et seq.
Iowa Code Ann., 80.1 et seq.
N.M. Stat. Ann., 9-19-1 et seq.
Tex. Government Code, § 411.001 et seq.

Public Safety Department Fund Act
Mich. Comp. Laws Ann., 28.101 et seq.

Public Safety Department Reorganization Act
W. Va. Code 1966, § 15-2-1 et seq.

Public Safety Emergency Telephone Act
Pa. Purdon's Stat., Title 35, § 7011 et seq.

Public Safety Employee Benefits Act
Ill. Comp. Stat. 1992, Ch. 820, § 320/1 et seq.

Public Safety Nomenclature Act (Department of)
Ga. Code Ann., 35-2-80 to 35-2-88

Public Safety Noncontributory Retirement Act
Utah Code Ann. 1953, 49-4a-101 et seq.

Public Safety Officers' Benefits Act of 1976
Sept. 29, 1976, P.L. 94-430, 42 U.S. Code § 3701 et seq.

Public Safety Officers Procedural Bill of Rights Act
Cal. Government Code, § 3300 et seq.

Public Safety Partnership and Community Policing Act of 1994
Sept. 13, 1994, P.L. 103-322, 42 U.S. Code §§ 3711 nt., 3793, 3796dd et seq.

Public Safety Personnel Retirement Act
Ariz. Rev. Stat. Ann., § 38-841 et seq.

Public Safety Radio Services Act
Ga. Code Ann., 50-5-180 et seq.

Public Safety Retirement Act
Utah Code Ann. 1953, 49-11-1 et seq., 49-4-101 et seq.

Public Safety Solicitation Act
Mich. Comp. Laws Ann., 14.301 et seq.

Public Safety Telephone Act
N.C. Gen. Stat. 1943, § 62A-1 et seq.

Public Safety Training Center Act
Ga. Code Ann., 35-5-1 et seq.

Public Salary Tax Act of 1939
April 12, 1939, Ch. 59, 53 Stat. 574 (See 4 U.S. Code § 111)

Public Scales License Act
Iowa Code Ann., 214.1 et seq.

Public School Act
D.C. Code 1973, § 31-101 et seq.
N.C. Gen. Stat. 1943, § 115C-1 et seq.
N.H. Rev. Stat. 1955, 186:1 et seq.
N.J. Stat. Ann. 18A:1-1 et seq.

Pa. Purdon's Stat., Title 24, § 1-101 et seq.
S.D. Codified Laws 1967, 13-1-1 et seq.

Public School Audit Law
Okla. Stat. Ann., Title 70, § 22-101 et seq.

Public School Authority Act
Va. Code 1950, § 22.1-162 et seq.

Public School Building Authority Act
Pa. Purdon's Stat., Title 24, § 791.1 et seq.

Public School Buildings Act
N.M. Stat. Ann., 22-26-1 et seq.

Public School Capital Finance Assistance Act
N.J. Stat. Ann., 34:1B-7.20 et seq.

Public School Capital Improvements Act
N.M. Stat. Ann., 22-25-1 et seq.

Public School Capital Outlay Act
N.M. Stat. Ann., 22-24-1 et seq.

Public School Code
N.M. Stat. Ann., 22-1-1 et seq.

Public School Code (Greensboro)
N.C. Laws 1949, Ch. 385

Public School Contracts Law
N.J. Stat. Ann. 18A:18A-1 et seq.

Public School Disciplinary Tribunal Act
Ga. Code Ann., 20-2-750 et seq.

Public School Education Act
N.J. Stat. Ann., 18A:7A-1 et seq.

Public School Educational Cooperative Act
Ark. Code Ann. 1987, 6-13-901 et seq.

Public School Emergency Capital Outlay Act
N.M. Stat. Ann., 22-24-1 et seq.

Public School Employee Fair Hearing Act
Ark. Acts 1991, No. 631

Public School Employees' Retirement Act
Ga. Code Ann., 47-4-1 et seq.
Mich. Comp. Laws Ann., 38.201 et seq., 38.1301 et seq.
Continued

835

Pa. Cons. Stat., Title 24, § 8101 et seq.

Public School Employees' Retirement System Act
Ga. Code Ann., 47-4-1 et seq.

Public School Employment Relations Act
Del. Code of 1974, Title 14, § 4001 et seq.

Public School Facilities Funding Act
Tex. Rev. Civ. Stat., Art. 717t

Public School Fair Dismissal Act
Miss. Code Ann. 1972, § 37-9-101 et seq.
Pa. Cons. Stat., Title 24, § 8101 et seq.

Public School Fair Employment and Dismissal Practices Act
Ark. Stat. 1947, 80-1243 et seq.

Public School Fee Act
Minn. Stat. Ann., 120.71 et seq.

Public School Finance Act
Colo. Rev. Stat., 22-50-101 et seq.,
22-53-101 et seq., 22-54-101 et seq.
Colo. Rev. Stat., 22-54-101 et seq.
N.M. Stat. Ann., 22-8-1 et seq.

Public School Finance Act of the State of Colorado
Colo. Laws 1952, p. 153, Ch. 59

Public School Food Services Act
D.C. Code Ann., § 31-801 et seq.

Public School Foundation Act
Colo. Rev. Stat. 1963, 123-6-1 et seq.

Public School Foundation Act of 1969
Colo. Rev. Stat. 1963, 123-38-1 et seq.
Okla. Stat. Ann., Title 70, § 18-101 et seq.

Public School Foundation Program Act
See also Foundation Program Act (Schools)
Ohio Rev. Code 1953, 3317.01 et seq.
Wyo. Stat. Ann., § 21-13-305 et seq.

Public School Health Service Act
Ark. Code Ann. 1987, 6-1-201 et seq. .

Public School Improvement Act
Okla. Stat. Ann., Title 70, § 1210.51 et seq.

Public School Insurance Authority Act
N.M. Stat. Ann., 22-2-6.1 et seq.

Public School Land Sales Act
Tex. Natural Resources Codes, § 51.001 et seq.

Public School Law Revision Act
S.D. Codified Laws 1967, 13-1-1 et seq.

Public School Library Protection Act
Cal. Education Code 1976, § 18175

Public School Professional Practices Act
Ida. Code 1947, 33-1251 et seq.

Public School Reform Act
N.J. Laws 1993, Ch. 7

Public School Retired Employees Group Insurance Act
Tex. Insurance Code, Art. 3.50-4

Public School Retirement Systems Act (St. Louis)
Mo. Rev. Stat., 169.410 et seq.

Public School Safety Act
N.J. Stat. Ann., 18A:17-42 et seq.

Public School Student Services Act
Ark. Acts 1991, No. 908

Public School Support Act
Neb. Laws 1974, L. B. 772

Public School Teacher Tenure Act for Cities over 300,000 Population
Ga. Laws 1968, p. 3697

Public School Teachers' Retirement Act
Cal. Education Code 1976, § 22000 et seq.
Utah Code Ann. 1953, 49-2-101 et seq.

Public Schools Act (Meditation in)
N.M. Stat. Ann., 22-27-1 et seq.

Public Securities Act
N.M. Stat. Ann., 6-14-1 et seq.

Public Securities Act (Supplemental)
N.M. Stat. Ann., 6-14-8 et seq.

Public Securities Information Reporting Act
Colo. Rev. Stat., 11-58-101 et seq.

Public Securities Limitation of Action Act
N.M. Stat. Ann., 6-14-4 et seq.

Public Securities Recording Act (Municipal-ities)
N.C. Gen. Stat. 1943, § 160-406 et seq.

Public Securities Refunding Act
Colo. Rev. Stat., 11-56-101 et seq.
S.D. Codified Laws 1967, 6-8A-1 et seq.
Wyo. Stat. Ann., § 16-5-101 et seq.

Public Securities Short-Term Interest Rate Act
N.M. Stat. Ann., 6-18-1 et seq.

Public Securities Validation Act
Mich. Comp. Laws Ann., 600.2942
Nev. Statutes 1965, Ch. 278, p. 595
Nev. Statutes 1966, Sp. Sess., Ch. 19, p. 37
Nev. Statutes 1967, Ch. 27, p. 56
Nev. Statutes 1971, Ch. 17, p. 14
Nev. Statutes 1973, Ch. 219, p. 275
Nev. Statutes 1975, Ch. 283, p. 364
Nev. Statutes 1977, Ch. 54, p. 127
N.M. Laws 1977, Ch. 125
N.M. Laws 1979, Ch. 68
N.M. Laws 1979, Ch. 83
N.M. Laws 1979, Ch. 111
N.M. Stat. Ann., 6-16-1 et seq.
N.M. Stat. Ann., 60-8A-18
N.M. Stat. Ann. 1953, 11-8-1 et seq., 11-8-10 et seq., 11-8-5 et seq.
Wyo. Stat. Ann., § 16-5-201 et seq.

Public Service Act
Conn. Gen. Stat. Ann., § 16-1 et seq.
Ill. Rev. Stat. 1991, Ch. 111 2/3, § 1-101 et seq.
Ky. Rev. Stat. 1971, 278.010 et seq.
Minn. Stat. Ann., 216A.01 et seq.

N.Y. Consol. Laws Ch. 48
Ore. Rev. Stat., 756.010 et seq.
P.R. Laws Ann. 1954, Title 27, § 1001 et seq.

Public Service Authority Act (Camden County)
Ga. Laws 1990, p. 4273

Public Service Commission Act
Ala. Code 1975, § 37-1-1 et seq.
Alaska Stat. 1962, § 42.05.010 et seq.
D.C. Code Ann., § 43-101 et seq.
Del. Code of 1974, Title 26, § 101 et seq.
Fla. Stat. Ann., 350.01 et seq.
Ind. Code Ann., 8-1-1-1 et seq.
Ky. Rev. Stat. 1971, 278.010 et seq.
Md. Ann. Code 1957, Art. 78
Mich. Comp. Laws Ann., 460.1 et seq.
Miss. Code Ann. 1972, § 77-1-1 et seq.
Mo. Rev. Stat., 386.010 et seq.
Mont. Code Ann., 69-1-101 et seq.
Neb. Rev. Stat. 1943, 75-101 et seq.
Nev. Rev. Stat. 1979 Reprint, 703.010 et seq.
N.Y. Public Service Law (Consol. Laws Ch. 48) § 1 et seq.
Ohio Rev. Code 1953, 4905.01 et seq.
Utah Code Ann. 1953, 54-1-1 et seq.
Vt. Stat. Ann., Title 30, § 1 et seq.
Wash. Rev. Code Ann., 80.01.010 et seq.
W. Va. Code 1966, § 24-1-1 et seq.

Public Service Commission Revolving Fund Act
Nev. Rev. Stat. 1957, 703.230

Public Service Commissioners' Retirement Act
Tenn. Code Ann. 1955, 65-151 et seq.

Public Service Companies Act
Md. Ann. Code 1957, Art. 78, § 23 et seq.
Pa. 1913 Pamph. Laws 1374, No. 854

Public Service Company Tax Act
Haw. Rev. Stat. Ann., § 239-1 et seq.

Public Service Corporation Act
Ariz. Rev. Stat. Ann., § 40-201 et seq.

Public Service Corporation Assessment Act
Okla. Stat. Ann., Title 68, § 2442 et seq.

Public Service Corporation Tax Act
R.I. Gen. Laws 1956, 44-13-1 et seq.

Public Service District Act (New Ellenton)
S.C. Acts 1951, p. 854, No. 452

Public Service Easements Vacation Law
Cal. Government Code, § 50430 et seq.

Public Service Letter Act (Employment)
Okla. Stat. Ann., Title 40, § 171

Public Service Personnel Act
P.R. Laws Ann. 1954, Title 3, § 1301 et seq.

Public Services Act (Suspension of Essential Services and Establishment of Minimal Procedural Requirements)
P.R. Laws Ann. 1954, Title 27, § 1301 et seq.

Public Services Districts for Water and Sewage Services Act (Water Districts Act)
W. Va. Code 1966, § 16-13A-1 et seq.

Public Services Protection Act
Conn. Public Acts 1991, p. 512, No. 452

Public Space Rental Act
D.C. Code Ann., § 7-1001 et seq.

Public Space Utilization Act
D.C. Code Ann., § 7-1031 et seq.

Public Streets Highways, and Service Easements Vacation Law
Cal. Streets and Highways Code, § 8300 et seq.

Public Support Act
Pa. Purdon's Stat., Title 62, § 1971 et seq.

Public Support of Children Act
Utah Code Ann. 1953, 62A-11-301 et seq.

Public Sureties Relief Act
Ind. Code Ann., 5-4-4-1 et seq.

Public Swimming Pool Inspection and Hotel Service Establishment Act
Tenn. Code Ann., 68-14-301 et seq.

Public Swimming Pools Act
Mich. Comp. Laws Ann., 333.12521 et seq.

Public Telecommunications Act
Va. Code 1950, § 22-344.4 et seq.

Public Telecommunications Act of 1988
Nov. 7, 1988, P.L. 100-626, 47 U.S. Code § 609 nt.

Public Telecommunications Act of 1992
Aug. 26, 1992, P.L. 102-356, 47 U.S. Code § 609 nt.

Public Telecommunications Financing Act of 1978
Nov. 2, 1978, P.L. 95-567, 5 U.S. Code § 5316 nt.; 47 U.S. Code §§ 390 et seq., 609 nt.

Public Telecommunications Utility Law
Utah Code Ann. 1953, 54-8b-1 et seq.

Public Telephone Information Act
Va. Code 1950, § 59.1-424 et seq.

Public Television and Radio Act
N.Y. Education Law 1947 (Consol. Laws Ch. 16) § 236

Public Terminal Grain Warehouse Act
S.D. Codified Laws 1967, 49-44-1 et seq.

Public Transit Act
Fla. Stat. Ann., 341.011 et seq.
Utah Code Ann. 1953, 11-20-1 et seq.

Public Transit Employee Training Programs Act
Ark. Stat. 1947, 14-334-101
Ill. Rev. Stat. 1991, Ch. 111 2/3, § 801 et seq.

Public Transit System Act
Ark. Code Ann. 1987, 20-2201 et seq.

Public Transportation Act
Ga. Code Ann., 32-1-1 et seq.
Neb. Rev. Stat. 1943, 13-1201 to 13-1212

N.J. Stat. Ann. 27:25-1 et seq.

Pa. Cons. Stat., Title 74, § 1101 et seq.

Public Transportation Act (Rural Highway)

Cal. Streets and Highways Code, § 2500 et seq.

Public Transportation and Public Utilities Act

Ga. Code Ann., 46-1-1 et seq.

Public Transportation Assistance Act

Ill. Rev. Stat. 1977, Ch. 111 2/3, § 611 et seq.

Public Transportation Assistance Act (Elderly and Handicapped Coordinated)

Kan. Stat. Ann., 75-5032 et seq.

Public Transportation Authorities Act

N.C. Gen. Stat. 1943, § 160A-575 et seq.

Public Transportation Authority Act

Mich. Comp. Laws Ann., 124.451 et seq.

N.C. Gen. Stat. 1943, § 160A-575 et seq.

Public Transportation Authority Act (Regional)

Ida. Code 1947, 40-2101 et seq.

Public Transportation Coordination Assistance Program

N.Y. Transportation Law (Consol. Laws Ch. 61A) § 73a et seq.

Public Transportation Loan Act

Ill. Rev. Stat. 1983, Ch. 111 2/3, § 621 et seq.

Public Transportation Passenger Rights Act

S.C. Code Ann. 1976, § 58-23-1810 et seq.

Public Trust Act

Okla. Stat. Ann., Title 60, § 176 et seq.

Public Trust Fund Act

Vt. Stat. Ann., Title 24, § 2431 et seq.

Public Trust Fund Act (Municipal Improvements)

N.J. Rev. Stat. 1937, 2A:44-148

Public Trustee Act

Colo. Rev. Stat., 38-37-101 et seq.

Public Trustee Act (Estates)

N.H. Rev. Stat. 1955, 564:2-a et seq.

Public University Energy Conservation Act

Ill. Comp. Stat. 1992, Ch. 110, § 62/1 et seq.

Public Utilities Act

Ala. Code 1975, § 37-1-1 et seq.

Cal. Public Utilities Code, § 201 et seq.

Colo. Rev. Stat., 40-1-101 et seq.

Conn. Gen. Stat. Ann., § 16-1 et seq.

D.C. Code Ann., § 43-509 et seq.

D.C. Code 1967, § 43-101 et seq.

Del. Code of 1974, Title 26, § 101 et seq.

Haw. Rev. Stat. Ann., § 269-1 et seq.

Ida. Code 1947, 61-101 et seq.

Ill. Rev. Stat. 1991, Ch. 111 2/3, § 1-101 et seq.

Ind. Code Ann., 8-1-1-1 et seq.

Kan. Stat. Ann., 66-101 et seq.

Ky. Rev. Stat. 1971, 278.010 et seq.

Me. Rev. Stat Ann. 1964, Title 35A § 103

Mich. Comp. Laws Ann., 460.51 et seq.

Minn. Stat. Ann., 216B.01 et seq.

Miss. Code Ann. 1972, § 77-3-1 et seq.

Mo. Rev. Stat., 386.010 et seq.

N.C. Gen. Stat. 1943, § 62-1 et seq.

N.D. Cent. Code, 49-01-01 et seq.

Nev. Rev. Stat. 1979 Reprint, 704.005 et seq.

N.H. Rev. Stat. 1955, 362:1 et seq.

N.J. Stat. Ann., 48:1-1 et seq.

N.M. Stat. Ann., 62-3-1 et seq.

N.Y. Public Service Law (Consol. Laws Ch. 48)

Ohio Rev. Code 1953, 4901.01 et seq.

Ore. Rev. Stat., 757.005 et seq.

Pa. Cons. Stat., Title 66, § 101 et seq.

R.I. Gen. Laws 1956, 39-1-1 et seq.

S.D. Codified Laws 1967, 49-1-1 et seq.

Utah Code Ann. 1953, 54-1-1 et seq.

Va. Code 1950, § 56-265.13:1 et seq.

Wash. Rev. Code Ann., 80.01.010 et seq.

Wis. Stat. Ann., 196.01 et seq.

Wyo. Stat. Ann., § 37-1-101 et seq.

Public Utilities Affiliates Act

Va. Code 1950, § 56-76 et seq.

Public Utilities and Carriers Act
La. Rev. Stat. Ann., 45:1 et seq.

Public Utilities Antistrike Act
Mo. Rev. Stat., 295.010 et seq.
N.J. Stat. Ann., 34:13B-1 et seq.
Pa. Purdon's Stat., Title 43, § 213.1 et seq.
Wis. Stat. Ann., 111.50 et seq.

Public Utilities Commission Act
Alaska Stat. 1962, § 42.05.010 et seq.
Colo. Rev. Stat., 40-2-101 et seq.
D.C. Code Ann., § 43-401 et seq.
N.C. Gen. Stat. 1943, § 62-10 et seq.
N.H. Rev. Stat. 1955, 363:1 et seq.

Public Utilities Commission Enforcement Act
Cal. Public Utilities Code, §§ 1033.7, 1042, 3710, 3774.5, 3942, 5229, 5285.5, 5374.5, 5378.5

Public Utilities Commission Procedure Act
N.C. Gen. Stat 1943, § 62-60 et seq.

Public Utilities Commissioner's Practice Act
Ore. Rev. Stat., 756.500 et seq.

Public Utilities Compulsory Arbitration Act
Mo. Rev. Stat., 295.010 et seq.
Wis. Stat. Ann., 111.50 et seq.

Public Utilities Construction Antiduplication Law
Colo. Rev. Stat., 40-5-101 et seq.

Public Utilities Department Act
N.J. Stat. Ann., 48:2-1 et seq.

Public Utilities Franchise Tax Act
Ky. Rev. Stat. 1971, 136.120

Public Utilities Labor Disputes Act
Ind. Code Ann., 22-6-2-1 et seq.
Md. Ann. Code 1957, Art. 89, § 14 et seq.
N.J. Stat. Ann., 34:13B-1 et seq.
Wis. Stat. Ann., 111.50 et seq.

Public Utilities Labor Relations Act
Va. Code 1950, § 40-75 et seq.

Public Utilities Mediation Act
Mo. Rev. Stat., 295.010 et seq.

Public Utilities Regulation Act
Iowa Code Ann., 476.1 et seq.
Md. Ann. Code 1957, Art. 78, § 51 et seq.

Public Utilities Regulatory Policies Act of 1978
Nov. 8, 1984, P.L. 98-620, 43 U.S. Code § 2011
Oct. 16, 1986, P.L. 99-495, 16 U.S. Code § 824a-3

Public Utilities Reimbursement Act
D.C. Code Ann., § 7-135, 5-804, 5-806

Public Utilities Relocation Act
Minn. Stat. Ann., 161.46

Public Utilities Revenue Act
Ill. Comp. Stat. 1992, Ch. 35, § 620/1 et seq.
Ill. Rev. Stat. 1991, Ch. 120, § 468 et seq.

Public Utilities Review Act
May 14, 1934, Ch. 283, 48 Stat. 775 (See 28 U.S. Code § 1342)

Public Utilities Securities Act
Mich. Comp. Laws Ann., 460.301 et seq.
Va. Code 1950, § 56-55 et seq.

Public Utilities Seizure Act
Mass. Gen. Laws. Ann., 150B:1 et seq.
Mo. Rev. Stat., 295.010 et seq.
N.D. Cent. Code, 37-01-06, 37-01-07
Va. Code 1950, § 56-509 et seq.

Public Utilities Tax Act
Haw. Rev. Stat. Ann., § 239-1 et seq.
Ill. Rev. Stat. 1991, Ch. 111 2/3, § 2-202 et seq.
Ind. Code Ann., 6-1.1-8-1 et seq.
Wash. Rev. Code Ann., 82.16.010 et seq.
Wis. Stat. Ann., 76.01 et seq.

Public Utility Accident Fault Determination Act
N.J. Stat. Ann. 48:2-21.4 et seq.

Public Utility Act

Miss. Code Ann. 1972, § 77-3-1 et seq.

Mont. Code Ann., 69-1-101 et seq.

N.M. Stat. Ann., 62-13-1 et seq.

Pa. Cons. Stat., Title 66, § 101 et seq.

Tenn. Code Ann., 65-4-101 et seq.

Wash. Rev. Code Ann., 80-01.010 et seq.

Wyo. Stat. Ann., § 37-1-101 et seq.

Public Utility Act (Wilmington)

Del. Laws Vol. 26, p. 466, Ch. 206

Public Utility Act of 1935

See Federal Power Act and Public Utility Holding Company Act

Public Utility Anti-Gambling Act

N.J. Stat. Ann., 2A:146-3

Public Utility Arbitration Law

Fla. Stat. Ann., 453.01 et seq.

Public Utility Assessment Act

Wash. Rev. Code Ann., 84.12.200 et seq.

Public Utility Authority Act (Oconee County)

Ga. Laws 1980, p. 3429

Public Utility Bond Financing Act

N.H. Rev. Stat. 1955, 374-C:1 et seq.

Public Utility Company Act

Okla. Stat. Ann., Title 17, § 151 et seq.

Public Utility District Act

Cal. Public Utilities Code § 15501 et seq.

Public Utility District Act (Donner Summit)

Cal. Statutes 1950, 1st Ex. Sess., Ch. 15, p. 450

Cal. Water Code, Appendix, § 58-1 et seq.

Public Utility District Act (Joint)

Cal. Public Utilities Code, § 16873

Public Utility District Act (Mono County)

Cal. Statutes 1957, Ch. 1413, p. 2747

Public Utility District Act (Municipal)

Cal. Public Utilities Code, § 11501 et seq.

Public Utility District Act (Olivehurst)

Cal. Statutes 1950, 1st Ex. Sess., Ch. 12, p. 446

Cal. Water Code, Appendix, § 56-1 et seq.

Public Utility District Act (Unincorporated Territory)

Cal. Public Utilities Code, § 15701 et seq.

Public Utility Districts Act

Alaska Stat. 1962, Replaced Titles, § 42.35.010 et seq.

Wash. Rev. Code Ann., 54.04.010 et seq.

Public Utility Districts Tax Act

Wash. Rev. Code Ann., 54.28.010 et seq.

Public Utility Employees Arbitration Act

Pa. Purdon's Stat., Title 43, § 213.1 et seq.

Public Utility Environmental Standards Act

Conn. Gen. Stat. Ann., § 16-50g et seq.

Public Utility Fee Act

Wash. Rev. Code Ann., 80.24.010 et seq., 81.24.010 et seq.

Public Utility Financing Bank Act

Me. Rev. Stat. Ann. 1964, Title 35-A, § 2901 et seq.

Public Utility Franchise Act

R.I. Gen. Laws 1956, 39-17-1 et seq.

Public Utility Holding Company Act

Aug. 26, 1935, Ch. 687, 49 Stat. 803, 15 U.S. Code §§ 79 to 79z-6

Aug. 28, 1958, P.L. 85-791, 72 Stat. 946, 15 U.S. Code § 79x

Oct. 15, 1970, P.L. 91-452, 84 Stat. 929, 15 U.S. Code § 79r

Nov. 6, 1978, P.L. 95-598, 15 U.S. Code § 79k

Dec. 4, 1987, P.L. 100-181, 15 U.S. Code §§ 79h, 79r, 79x, 79y, 79z-4

Nov. 15, 1990, P.L. 101-550, 15 U.S. Code § 79z-5

Oct. 24, 1992, P.L. 102-486, 15 U.S. Code §§ 79, 79z-5a, 79z-5b, 79z-6

Continued

Feb. 8, 1996, P.L. 104-104, 15 U.S. Code
§§ 79, 79z-5c, 79z-6
Kan. Stat. Ann., 66-1401 et seq.
N.J. Stat. Ann., 48:3-7.1

Public Utility Labor Disputes Act
Ind. Code Ann., 22-6-2-1 et seq.

Public Utility Property Tax Act
Mich. Comp. Laws Ann., 207.1 et seq.

Public Utility Realty Tax Act
Pa. Purdon's Stat., Title 72, § 8101-A et seq.

Public Utility Regulation Act
Tex. Rev. Civ. Stat., Art. 1446c

Public Utility Regulatory Act
Tex. Rev. Civ. Stat., Art. 1446c-0
Tex. Utility Code, § 11.001 et seq.

Public Utility Regulatory Policies Act
Kan. Stat. Ann., 66-1, 185

Public Utility Regulatory Policies Act of 1978
Nov. 9, 1978, P.L. 95-617, 15 U.S. Code
§§ 717f, 717x to 717z, 3201 et eq.; 16 U.S.
Code §§ 791a nt., 796, 824 et seq., 2601 et
seq.; 30 U.S. Code §§ 1311, 1312, 1314 to
1316; 42 U.S. Code § 6801 et seq.; 43 U.S.
Code § 2001 et seq.
June 30, 1980, P.L. 96-294, 16 U.S. Code
§§ 824a-3 et seq., 2705 et seq.
Nov. 15, 1990, P.L. 101-575, 16 U.S. Code
§ 824a-3
Oct. 24, 1992, P.L. 102-486, 16 U.S. Code
§§ 2602, 2621, 2622, 3202, 3203

Public Utility System Improvement District Law (Consolidated)
Ark. Code Ann. 1987, 14-217-101 et seq.

Public Vessels Act
March 3, 1925, Ch. 428, 43 Stat. 1112, 46
U.S. Code §§ 781 to 790
Aug. 30, 1954, Ch. 1076, 68 Stat. 968, 46
U.S. Code § 790

Public Wage Rate Act
Cal. Labor Code, § 1770 et seq.

Public Warehouse Act
Ala. Code 1975, § 8-15-1 et seq.
Minn. Stat. 1961, 230.01 et seq.
Mo. Rev. Stat., 415.010 et seq.
Ore. Rev. Stat., 586.210 et seq.
S.D. Codified Laws 1967, 49-42-1 et seq.
Tex. Agriculture Code, § 14.201 et seq.

Public Warehouse Act (Grain)
Ill. Rev. Stat. 1991, Ch. 114, § 214.1 et seq.
Kan. Stat. Ann., 34-223 et seq.

Public Warehouse and Commodity Indemnity Act
Okla. Stat. Ann., Title 2, § 9-20 et seq.

Public Water and Wastewater Environmental Health Act
Tenn. Code Ann., 68-221-101 et seq.

Public Water District Act
Ill. Rev. Stat. 1991, Ch. 111 2/3, § 187.9 et seq.

Public Water Supply Act
Ill. Rev. Stat. 1991, Ch. 111 1/2, § 121a1 et seq.
Iowa Code 1971, 136A.1 et seq.
Pa. Purdon's Stat., Title 35, § 691.1 et seq.
Wash. Rev. Code Ann., 70.116.010 et seq.

Public Water Supply Operations Act
Ill. Rev. Stat. 1991, Ch. 111 1/2, § 500 et seq.

Public Water System Coordination Act
Wash. Rev. Code Ann., 70.116.010 et seq.

Public Water System Investment and Consolidation Act
Cal. Public Utilities Code § 2718

Public Waters Act
N.D. Cent. Code, 61-01-01 et seq.

Public Waterways Act
Wash. Rev. Code Ann., 91.08.010 et seq.

Public Weigher Law (Model State)
Conn. Gen. Stat. Ann., § 43-16a et seq.

Public Weighers Act
Ga. Code Ann., 10-2-40 et seq.
Tex. Agriculture Code, § 13.251 et seq.

Public Weighmasters Act
Cal. Business and Professions Code, § 12700 et seq.
Nev. Rev. Stat. 1979 Reprint, 582.010 et seq.
Pa. Purdon's Stat., Title 73, § 1771 et seq.
S.C. Code Ann. 1976, § 39-11-10 et seq.

Public Welfare Act
Ala. Code 1975, 38-1-1 et seq.
Alaska Stat. 1962, § 47.05.010 et seq.
Ark. Code Ann. 1987, 20-76-101 et seq.
Ga. Code Ann., 49-1-1 et seq.
Ind. Code Ann., 12-1-1-1 et seq.
Md. Ann. Code 1957, Art. 88A, § 1 et seq.
Minn. Stat. Ann., 256.01 et seq.
Miss. Code Ann. 1972, § 43-1-1 et seq.
Mont. Code Ann., 53-1-101 et seq.
N.M. Stat. Ann., 27-1-1 et seq.
N.Y. Social Services Law (Consol. Laws Ch. 55)
Pa. Purdon's Stat., Title 62, § 101 et seq.
P.R. Laws Ann. 1954, Title 8, § 1 et seq.
S.C. Code Ann. 1976, § 43-1-10 et seq.
Tex. Human Resources Code, § 11.001 et seq.
Wash. Rev. Code Ann., 74.04.005 et seq.
W. Va. Code 1966, §§ 9-1-1 et seq., 49-1-1 et seq.
Wyo. Stat. Ann., § 42-1-101 et seq.

Public Welfare Amendments of 1962
July 25, 1962, P.L. 87-543, 76 Stat. 172, 42 U.S. Code §§ 301 to 303, 306, 601 to 609, 721 to 723, 726 to 728, 906, 1201 to 1203, 1206, 1301, 1308 and others
June 29, 1963, P.L. 88-48, 77 Stat. 70, 42 U.S. Code § 608 nt.
June 30, 1964, P.L. 88-345, 78 Stat. 235, 42 U.S. Code § 608 nt.
Oct. 13, 1964, P.L. 88-641, 78 Stat. 1042, 42 U.S. Code § 608 nt.

Public Welfare and Assistance Act
La. Rev. Stat. Ann., 46:1 et seq.
Va. Code 1950, § 63.1-86 et seq.

Public Welfare Board Act
D.C. Code 1973, § 3-101 et seq.

Public Welfare Facilities Survey and Construction Act
P.R. Laws Ann. 1954, Title 24, § 332 et seq.

Public Welfare Institutions Use System of Industries Act
R.I. Gen. Laws 1956, 13-7-1 et seq.

Public Welfare Licensing Act
Minn. Stat. 1986, 245.781 et seq.

Public Welfare Loan Act (New Bedford)
Mass. Acts 1952, Ch. 547

Public Welfare Transfer of Funds Act
Ill. Rev. Stat. 1991, Ch. 127, §§ 167b.9, 167c

Public Welfare Work Incentive Program Act
N.C. Gen. Stat 1943, § 108-39.1

Public Wholesale Water Supply District Act
Kan. Stat. Ann., 19-3545 et seq.

Public Work Force Act (Drug-Free)
Ga. Code Ann., 45-23-1 et seq.
Mo. Laws 1993, S.B. No. 67

Public Work Procedure Act
N.D. Laws 1937, Ch. 198

Public Work Relief Compensation Act
Ohio Rev. Code 1953, 4127.01 et seq.

Public Works Acceleration Act
Sept. 14, 1962, P.L. 87-658, 76 Stat. 541, 40 U.S. Code § 462; 42 U.S . Code §§ 1492, 2641 to 2643

Public Works Act
Alaska Stat. 1962, § 35.10.010 et seq.
D.C. Code Ann., §§ 7-132, 43-1513, 43-1524 et seq., 43-1601 et seq.
Fla. Laws 1935, Ch. 17174
La. Rev. Stat. Ann., 24:61 et seq.
Mass. Gen. Laws. Ann., 149:44A et seq.
Md. Ann. Code 1974, Art. SF, § 10-101 et seq.
Continued

N.C. Gen. Stat. 1943, § 133-1 et seq.

N.M. Stat. Ann. 1953, 6-8-1 et seq.

N.Y. Consol. Laws, Ch. 75

Ore. Laws 1935, Sp. Sess. Ch. 64

Tenn. Public Acts 1935, Ex. Sess., Ch. 10

Utah Code Ann. 1953, 55-3-1 et seq.

Wash. Rev. Code Ann., 39.04.010 et seq.

Public Works Act (Bonds of Contractors)
See Miller Act

Public Works Act (Brevard County)
Fla. Special Laws 1967, Ch. 67-1145

Public Works Act (Contractors' Bond)
Cal. Labor Code, § 4200 et seq.

Public Works Act (Contracts)
La. Rev. Stat. Ann., 38:2181 et seq.

Public Works Act (County)
Fla. Laws 1967, Ch. 67-664
Fla. Laws 1968, Extra Session, Ch. 68-74
Mich. Comp. Laws Ann., 123.731 et seq.

Public Works Act (Defense)
R.I. Public Laws 1942, Ch. 1203

Public Works Act (Employment of Illinois Workers)
Ill. Rev. Stat. 1991, Ch. 48, § 2200 et seq.

Public Works Act (Fayette County)
Tenn. Private Acts 1974, Ch. 234

Public Works Act (Municipal)
S.C. Code Ann. 1976, § 5-31-10 et seq.

Public Works Act (Navy)
See Navy Public Works Act

Public Works Act (Oyster Bay)
N.Y. Local Laws 1966, Town of Oyster Bay, p. 1476
N.Y. Local Laws 1972, Town of Oyster Bay, p. 2476

Public Works Act (Prisoners)
Okla. Stat. Ann., Title 57, § 215 et seq.

Public Works Act (Syracuse)
N.Y. Laws 1905, Ch. 684

Public Works Act Onondaga County
N.Y. Laws 1949, Ch. 816
N.Y. Local Laws 1961, Onondago County, No. 2, § 11.01 et seq.

Public Works Administration Act
June 16, 1933, Ch. 90, 48 Stat. 195

Public Works Administration Appropriation Act of 1938
June 21, 1938, Ch. 554, 52 Stat. 817
April 5, 1941, Ch. 40, 55 Stat. 92, 31 U.S. Code § 42 nt.; 49 U.S. Code § 305a
June 26, 1943, Ch. 145, 57 Stat. 180, 12 U.S. Code §§ 1439a, 1463 nt.; 29 U.S. Code §§ 48 to 48g nt.; 31 U.S. Code § 42 nt.; 49 U.S. Code § 305a

Public Works Administration Extension Act of 1937
June 29, 1937, Ch. 401, 50 Stat. 358

Public Works Alien Employment Law
Cal. Labor Code, § 1850 et seq.

Public Works and Atomic Energy Commission Appropriation Act of 1968
Nov. 20, 1967, P.L. 90-147, 81 Stat. 471, 31 U.S. Code § 638c; 43 U.S . Code § 377a

Public Works and Economic Development Act Amendments of 1971
Aug. 5, 1971, P.L. 92-65, 85 Stat. 166, 42 U.S. Code § 3131 nt.

Public Works and Economic Development Act Amendments of 1976
May 23, 1977, P.L. 95-31, 42 U.S. Code § 3121 nt.

Public Works and Economic Development Act of 1965
Aug. 26, 1965, P.L. 89-136, 79 Stat. 552, 42 U.S. Code §§ 3121, 3131 to 3136, 3141 to 3143, 3151, 3152, 3161, 3162, 3171, 3181 to 3189, 3201 to 3203, 3211 to 3266
Nov. 8, 1966, P.L. 89-794, 80 Stat. 1477, 42 U.S. Code § 3161
Oct. 11, 1967, P.L. 90-103, 42 U.S. Code §§ 3183, 3185, 3188a, 3189, 3204

Nov. 25, 1969, P.L. 91-123, 83 Stat. 216, 42 U.S. Code §§ 3131, 3151, 3152, 3161, 3181, 3185, 3186, 3188a, 3190 to 3192

May 21, 1970, P.L. 91-258, 84 Stat. 235, 42 U.S. Code § 3188a

July 6, 1970, P.L. 91-304, 84 Stat. 375, 42 U.S. Code §§ 3135, 3141, 3152, 3171

Aug. 5, 1971, P.L. 92-65, 85 Stat. 166, 42 U.S. Code §§ 3131, 3135, 3141, 3152, 3161, 3162, 3171, 3188a, 3191

June 18, 1972, P.L. 93-46, 87 Stat. 96, 42 U.S. Code §§ 3135, 3141, 3151, 3152, 3171, 3188a

Dec. 31, 1975, P.L. 94-188, 89 Stat. 1079, 42 U.S. Code §§ 3181, 3182, 3188a, 3192, 3194 to 3196

Nov. 23, 1988, P.L. 100-707, 42 U.S. Code §§ 3231, 3232

Nov. 13, 1998, P.L. 105-393, 7 U.S. Code § 2204b-1; 33 U.S. Code § 2220; 42 U.S. Code §§ 3121, 3121 nt., 3122, 3123, 3131 to 3133, 3135 to 3137, 3141, 3142, 3142a, 3143 to 3151, 3151a, 3152, 3153, 3161, 3162, 3171 to 3175, 3191 to 3197, 3201 to 3204, 3211 to 3222, 3223 to 3226, 3231 to 3235, 3241 to 3246, 3246a to 3246c, 4246e to 4246h

Public Works Apprentice and Training Act
N.M. Stat. Ann., 13-4D-1 et seq.

Public Works Appropriation Act of 1956
July 15, 1955, Ch. 370, 69 Stat. 354 (See 10 U.S. Code § 3535 nt.) 43 U.S. Code § 377a

Public Works Appropriation Act of 1957
July 2, 1956, Ch. 490, 70 Stat. 478, 43 U.S. Code § 377a

Public Works Appropriation Act of 1958
Aug. 26, 1957, P.L. 85-167, 71 Stat. 421, 43 U.S. Code § 377a
Oct. 4, 1961, P.L. 87-367, 75 Stat. 788

Public Works Appropriation Act of 1959
Sept. 2, 1958, P.L. 85-863, 72 Stat. 1572, 43 U.S. Code § 377a

Public Works Appropriation Act of 1960
Sept. 10, 1959, P.L. 86-254, 73 Stat. 491, 43 U.S. Code § 377a

Public Works Appropriation Act of 1961
Sept. 2, 1960, P.L. 86-700, 74 Stat. 743, 43 U.S. Code § 377a

Public Works Appropriation Act of 1962
Sept. 30, 1961, P.L. 87-330, 75 Stat. 727, 16 U.S. Code § 832a-1; 43 U.S. Code § 377a

Public Works Appropriation Act of 1963
Oct. 24, 1962, P.L. 87-880, 76 Stat. 1216, 31 U.S. Code § 638c; 43 U.S. Code §§ 373a-1, 377a

Public Works Appropriation Act of 1964
Dec. 31, 1963, P.L. 88-257, 77 Stat. 844, 31 U.S. Code § 638c; 43 U.S . Code § 377a

Public Works Appropriation Act of 1965
Aug. 30, 1964, P.L. 88-511, 78 Stat. 682, 31 U.S. Code § 638c; 43 U.S . Code § 377a

Public Works Appropriation Act of 1966
Oct. 28, 1965, P.L. 89-299, 79 Stat. 1096, 31 U.S. Code § 638c; 43 U.S. Code § 377a

Public Works Appropriation Act of 1967
Oct. 15, 1966, P.L. 89-689, 80 Stat. 1002, 31 U.S. Code § 638c; 43 U.S. Code § 377a

Public Works Arbitration Act
R.I. Gen. Laws. 1956, 37-16-1 et seq.

Public Works Authority Act (Catoosa County)
Ga. Laws 1998, H.B. 1734

Public Works Bond Act
Fla. Stat. Ann., 255.05
Mich. Comp. Laws Ann., 570.101 et seq.
Mo. Rev. Stat., 107.170
N.J. Rev. Stat. 1937, 2A:44-143 et seq.

Public Works Building Loan Act (Northhampton)
Mass. Acts 1953, Ch. 598

Public Works Contractor Bond Act
Mo. Rev. Stat., 107.170
Pa. Purdon's Stat., Title 8, § 191 et seq.

Public Works Contractors License Act
Ida. Code 1947, 54-1901 et seq.
Nev. Statutes 1931, Ch. 212, p. 365

Public Works Contractors' Surety Bond Law
Me. Rev. Stat. Ann. 1964, Title 14, § 871

Public Works Contracts Act
Mich. Comp. Laws Ann., 123.501 et seq.

Public Works Contracts Act (Deposits)
N.Y. Public Works Law (Consol. Laws Ch. 75) § 14 et seq.

Public Works Department Act
Mass. Gen. Laws. Ann., 16:1 et seq.

Public Works Eight Hour Act
Ore. Rev. Stat., 279.338

Public Works Eminent Domain Law
N.C. Gen. Stat. 1943, § 40A-40 et seq.
Nev. Rev. Stat. 1979 Reprint, 340.010 et seq.
S.C. Code Ann. 1976, Superseded Vols.,
§ 28-5-10 et seq.

Public Works Employment Act of 1976
July 22, 1976, P.L. 94-369, 42 U.S. Code
§§ 6701 et seq.
May 23, 1977, P.L. 95-30, 42 U.S. Code
§§ 6722 et. seq.
Dec. 21, 1995, P.L. 104-66, 42 U.S. Code
§ 6733

Public Works Employment Act of 1977
May 13, 1977, P.L. 95-28, 42 U.S. Code
§§ 6701 et seq.

Public Works Employment Discrimination Act
Ill. Rev. Stat. 1991, Ch. 29, § 16.9 et seq.

Public Works Federal Aid Act
Alaska Comp. Laws Ann. 1949, Supp. 1957,
§ 14A-3-11 et seq.

Public Works Finance Act
Ill. Rev. Stat. 1991, Ch. 29, § 33a.1 et seq.

Public Works Fiscal Responsibility Accounting Act
Colo. Rev. Stat., 24-16-101 et seq.

Public Works for Water and Power Development and Energy Research Appropriation Act, 1978
Aug. 7, 1977, P.L. 95-96, 43 U.S. Code
§ 377a

Public Works for Water and Power Resources Development and Atomic Energy Commission Appropriation Act of 1969
Aug. 12, 1968, P.L. 90-479, 82 Stat. 705, 31
U.S. Code § 638c; 43 U.S . Code § 377a
Aug. 25, 1972, P.L. 92-405, 86 Stat. 621, 43
U.S. Code § 377a
Aug. 16, 1973, P.L. 93-97, 87 Stat. 318, 43
U.S. Code § 377a
Aug. 28, 1974, P.L. 93-393, 88 Stat. 782, 43
U.S. Code § 377a
Dec. 26, 1975, P.L. 94-180, 89 Stat. 1035, 43
U.S. Code § 377a

Public Works for Water, Pollution Control, and Power Development and Atomic Energy Commission Appropriation Act of 1970
Dec. 11, 1969, P.L. 91-144, 83 Stat. 323, 31
U.S. Code § 638c; 43 U.S . Code § 377a

Public Works for Water, Pollution Control, and Power Development and Atomic Energy Commission Appropriation Act of 1971
Oct. 7, 1970, P.L. 91-439, 84 Stat. 890, 31
U.S. Code § 638c; 43 U.S. Code § 377a

Public Works Grant-in-Aid Act
N.M. Stat. 1978, 6-11-7 et seq.

Public Works Improvement Act of 1984
Oct. 19, 1984, P.L. 98-501, 42 U.S. Code
§ 3121 nt.

Public Works Lien Act
La. Rev. Stat. Ann., 38:2241 et seq.
Wash. Rev. Code Ann., 60.28.010 et seq.

Public Works Mediation Act
N.M. Stat. Ann., 13-4C-1 et seq.

Public Works Minimum Wage Act
Ind. Code Ann., 5-16-7-1 et seq.
N.M. Stat. Ann., 13-4-10 et seq.

Public Works Payment Bond Act
Okla. Stat. Ann., Title 61, §§ 1, 2

Public Works Preference Act
Ill. Rev. Stat. 1991, Ch. 48, § 268.9 et seq.

Public Works Wage Rate Act
Cal. Labor Code, § 1770 et seq.
Tex. Rev. Civ. Stat., Art. 5159a

Public Works Wages Law
Fla. Stat. 1983, 215.19

Publication Act (Summons)
N.Y. Civil Practice Law and Rules (Consol. Laws Ch. 8) § 315

Publication of Sample Ballots Act
D.C. Code Ann., § 1-1306, Subd. a, + 6

Publication Service Act
Fla. Stat. Ann., 49.011 et seq.

Publications and Forms Management Act
Pa. Purdon's Stat., Title 71, § 2011 et seq.

Publicity Act
Nev. Statutes 1937, Ch. 177, p. 382

Publicity Act (County Claims)
Ark. Code Ann. 1987, 1-3-102

Publicity Act (Regional Port District)
Ill. Rev. Stat. 1991, Ch. 19, §§ 491.9, 492

Publicity in Taking Evidence Act (Anti-Trust)
March 3, 1913, Ch. 114, 37 Stat. 731, 15 U.S. Code § 30

Publicity of Political Contributions Act
See Federal Corrupt Practices Acts

Publicity Tax Act
N.M. Stat. Ann. 1953, Superseded Vol., 14-44-1 et seq.

Publicly Owned Treatment Works Act (State Beneficiary Public Trusts)
Okla. Stat. Ann., Title 27A, §§ 1011 to 1017

Publicly Owned Treatment Works Penalty Law
Pa. 1992 Pamph. Laws, No. 9

Public's Right to Know Act
Wis. Stat. Ann., 19.81 et seq.

Pueblo Depot Activity Development Authority Act
Colo. Rev. Stat., 29-23-101 et seq.

Puerto Rican Federal Relations Act
March 2, 1917, Ch. 145, 39 Stat. 951, 48 U.S. Code §§ 731, 733, 734, 737, 741, 742, 745, 747 to 749, 751, 794, 795, 863, 864, 867, 868, 872, 874, 891 to 893

Puerto Rican Rehabilitation Act
Feb. 11, 1936, Ch. 51, 49 Stat. 1135

Puerto Rico and the Caribbean Cardiovascular Center Corporation Act
P.R. Laws Ann. 1954, Title 24, § 343 et seq.

Puerto Rico Civil Code
April 12, 1900, Ch. 191, 31 Stat. 77, 11 U.S. Code §§ 1, 11; 48 U.S. Code §§ 733, 736, 738 to 740, 744, 866

Puget Sound Ferry System Act
Wash. Rev. Code Ann., 47.60.010 et seq.

Puget Sound Pilotage Act
Wash. Rev. Code Ann., 88.16.005 et seq.

Puget Sound Water Quality Protection Act
Wash. Rev. Code Ann., 90.71.900

Pulaski and Wytheville Parking Authority Act
Va. Acts. 1968, Ch. 682

Pulaski, Casimir, Holiday Act
Ill. Comp. Stat. 1992, Ch. 5, § 490/20

Pulaski Charter
Tenn. Private Acts 1949, Ch. 711

Pull Tabs and Jar Games Act
Ill. Rev. Stat. 1991, Ch. 120, § 1051 et seq.

Pulpwood Scaling and Practices Act
Miss. Code Ann. 1972, § 75-79-1 et seq.

Pump Installers Act (Water Well)
Tex. General and Special Laws 1991, Ch. 697
Tex. Rev. Civ. Stat., Art. 8905

Punishment and Community Corrections Act
Ala. Code 1975, § 15-18-170

Punishment and Corrections Act (Community)
Ala. Code 1975, § 15-18-170 et seq.

Punishment for Attempts Act
Cal. Penal Code, § 664

Punitive Damages Act
N.J. Stat. Ann., 2A:15-5.9 et seq.

Punta Borinquen Administration and Development Authority Act
P.R. Laws Ann. 1954, Title 23, § 692 et seq.

Pupil Assignment Act
Ark. Stat. 1947, 80-1519 et seq., 6-18-301 et seq.
Fla. Stat. Ann., 230.232
La. Rev. Stat. Ann., 17:101 et seq.
Miss. Code Ann. 1972, § 37-15-13 et seq.
N.C. Gen. Stat. 1943, § 115C-364 et seq.
Tenn. Code Ann., 49-6-3102 et seq.

Pupil Enrollment Act
Ark. Stat. 1947, 80-1519 et seq.
N.C. Gen. Stat. 1943, § 115C-364 et seq.

Pupil Fair Dismissal Act
Minn. Stat. Ann., 127.26 et seq.

Pupil Integration Act (Voluntary)
Cal. Education Code 1976, §§ 42248, 42249

Pupil Motivation and Maintenance Program and Dropout Recovery Act
Cal. Education Code 1976, § 54720 et seq.

Pupil Placement Act
Ala. Code 1958, Title 52, § 61(1) et seq.
Ark. Code Ann. 1987, 6-18-301 et seq.
La. Rev. Stat. Ann., 17:101 et seq.
N.C. Gen. Stat. 1943, § 1156-364 et seq.
S.C. Code Ann. 1976, § 59-19-510 et seq.
Tex. Education Code, § 21.074 et seq.
Va. Code 1950, § 22-232.1 et seq.

Pupil Textbook and Instructional Materials in Center Program Act
Cal. Education Code 1976, § 60117

Pupil Transfer Act
Ind. Code Ann., 20-8.1-6.1-1 et seq.

Pupil Transportation Act
Mich. Comp. Laws Ann., 257.1801 et seq.

Purchase Act (Lease)
La. Rev. Stat. Ann., 39:1761 et seq., 39:1780 et seq.

Purchase Age Law (Sale of Liquor)
N.Y. Alcoholic Beverage Law (Consol. Laws Ch. 3B) §§ 65 to 65b
N.Y. General Obligations Law (Consol. Laws Ch. 24A) § 11-100
N.Y. Penal Law 1965 (Consol. Laws Ch. 40) § 260.20

Purchase Agreement Act (Consumer Rental)
Neb. Rev. Stat. 1943, 69-2101 et seq.

Purchase Agreement Act (Rental)
N.M. Stat. Ann., 57-26-1 et seq.

Purchase Agreement Act (Rentals)
La. Rev. Stat. Ann., 9:3351 et seq.
Mo. Rev. Stat. 1978, 407.660 et seq.

Purchase and Contract Act
N.C. Gen. Stat. 1943, § 143-48 et seq.

Purchase First Program Act
N.J. Stat. Ann., 34:1B-101 et seq.

Purchase-Lease Agreement Act
Wash. Laws 1992, Ch. 134

Purchase Money Attachment Act
S.C. Code Ann. 1976, § 15-19-510 et seq.

Purchase Money Lien Law
Miss. Code 1942, § 337

Purchase Money Mortgage Act
N.C. Gen. Stat. 1943, § 45-21.38

Purchase Money Priority Act
Cal. Civil Code, § 2898

Purchase or Assignment of Wages Act
N.J. Stat. Ann., 34:11-25

Purchase Order Act
Okla. Stat. Ann., Title 62, § 310.4

Purchase-Rental Agreement Act
Fla. Stat. Ann., 559.9231 et seq.
Kan. Stat. Ann., 50-680 et seq.
Minn. Stat. Ann., 325F.84 et seq.

Purchaser and Vender Risk Act
Cal. Civil Code § 1662
Tex. Property Code, § 5.007

Purchaser and Vendor Risk Act
See also Uniform Vendor and Purchaser Risk Act
Cal. Civil Code, § 1662
Ill. Rev. Stat. 1991, Ch. 29, § 8.1 et seq.
Okla. Stat. Ann., Title 16, § 201 et seq.
Tex. Property Code, § 5.007
Wis. Stat. Ann., 706.12

Purchasers' Quieting Title Law
Cal. Statutes 1939, Ch. 896, p. 2504

Purchasers' Relief Law
Cal. Statutes 1937, Ch. 689, p. 1955

Purchases Act (Public)
See Public Purchase Act

Purchases Agreement Act (Consumer Rental)
Iowa Code Ann., 537.3601 et seq.

Purchasing Act (County)
Ga. Laws 1941, p. 408

Purchasing Act (Public Bodies)
Miss. Code Ann. 1972, § 31-7-301 et seq.

Purchasing Act (State)
Alaska Stat. 1962, § 36.30.005 et seq.
Ariz. Rev. Stat. Ann., § 41-729 et seq.
Ark. Code Ann. 1987, 19-11-201 et seq.
Cal. Government Code, § 14780 et seq.
Ga. Code Ann., 50-5-50 et seq.
Ill. Rev. Stat. 1991, Ch. 127, § 132.1 et seq.
Mo. Rev. Stat., 34.010 et seq.
Mont. Code Ann., 18-4-121 et seq.
Nev. Rev. Stat. 1979 Reprint, 333.010 et seq.
N.M. Stat. Ann., 13-1-1 et seq.
N.Y. Local Laws 1967, Town of Oyster Bay, p. 1835
N.Y. Local Laws 1972, County of Monroe, p. 677
Okla. Stat. Ann., Title 74, § 85.1 et seq.
Tex. Rev. Civ. Stat., Art. 601b, § 3.01 et seq.
W. Va. Code 1966, § 5A-3-1 et seq.

Purchasing Act (Township)
Ill. Rev. Stat. 1991, Ch. 139, § 190 et seq.

Purchasing Agent Act
Kan. Stat. Ann., 19-260a, et seq.
Mich. Comp. Laws Ann., 17.21 et seq.
Mo. Rev. Stat., 34.010 et seq.
N.M. Stat. Ann., 13-1-21 et seq.

Purchasing Agent Act (County)
Mich. Comp. Laws Ann., 45.81 et seq.

Purchasing Agent Act (Onondaga County)
N.Y. Laws 1906, Ch. 20

Purchasing Agent Act (State)
Mich. Comp. Laws Ann., 17.21 et seq.
N.M. Stat. Ann., 13-1-1 et seq.

Purchasing and General Services Act
Tex. Rev. Civ. Stat. 1974, Art. 601b

Purchasing Commission Act
Ky. Rev. Stat. 1971, 45.360 et seq.
Tenn. Private Acts 1951, Ch. 16

Purchasing Cooperative Act (Health Care)
Fla. Stat. Ann., 408.001

Purchasing Discount Act
N.M. Stat. Ann., 13-1A-1 et seq.

Purchasing Group Act (Health Care)
Ill. Comp. Stat. 1992, Ch. 215, § 123/1 et seq.

Purchasing Group and Risk Retention Act
N.M. Stat. Ann., 59A-55-1 et seq.

Purchasing Pool Act (Health Care)
Neb. Rev. Stat. 1943, 44-6701, 44-6702

Purchasing Reform Act
Ga. Code Ann., 50-5-51 et seq.

Pure Air Act
Cal. Health and Safety Code, § 39080 et seq.

Pure Drugs Act
Cal. Health and Safety Code, § 26200 et seq.
Pa. 1897 Pamph. Laws 85, No. 68
Pa. 1917 Pamph. Laws 758, No. 282

Pure Feed Act
Tex. Agriculture Code, § 141.001 et seq.

Pure Food Act
Ariz. Rev. Stat. Ann., § 36-901 et seq.
Cal. Health and Safety Code, § 26450 et seq.
Colo. Rev. Stat., 25-5-401 et seq.
Haw. Rev. Stat. Ann., § 328-1 et seq.
Ill. Rev. Stat. 1963, Ch. 56 1/2, § 1 et seq.
Ind. Code Ann., 16-1-28-1 et seq.
Ky. Rev. Stat. 1971, 217.005 et seq.
Me. Rev. Stat. Ann. 1964, Title 7, § 481 et seq.
Mich. Comp. Laws Ann., 289.111 et seq.
Minn. Stat. Ann., 31.01 et seq.
Mo. Rev. Stat., 196.010 et seq.
N.C. Gen. Stat. 1943, § 106-120 et seq.
N.D. Cent. Code, 19-02-01 et seq.
Neb. Rev. Stat. 1943, 81-216.01 et seq.
N.J. Stat. Ann., 24:1-1 to 24:17-8
Okla. Stat. Ann., Title 63, § 1-1101 et seq.
Ore. Rev. Stat., 616.005 et seq.
Pa. Purdon's Stat., Title 31, § 1 et seq.
S.C. Code Ann. 1962, § 32-1511 et seq.
Tex. Rev. Civ. Stat., Art. 4465a et seq.
Va. Code 1950, § 3.1-361 et seq.

Pure Food and Drugs Act
See Food and Drugs Acts
Ark. Stat. 1987, 20-57-101 et seq., 20-56-201 et seq.
Fla. Stat. Ann., 500.01 et seq.
Ga. Code Ann., 26-1-1 et seq.
La. Rev. Stat. Ann., 40:601 et seq.
Mass. Gen. Laws. Ann., 94:186 et seq.
Md. Ann. Code 1974, Art. HG, § 21-101 et seq.
Mont. Rev. Code 1947, 27-701 et seq.
Ohio Rev. Code 1953, 3715.01 et seq.
R.I. Gen. Laws 1956, 21-31-1 et seq.
S.C. Code Ann. 1976, § 44-53-10 et seq.
S.D. Codified Laws 1967, 39-1-1 et seq.
Tenn. Code Ann. 1955, 52-101 et seq.
Wis. Stat. Ann., 97.01 et seq.
W. Va. Code 1966, § 16-7-1 et seq.

Pure Food, Drug and Cosmetics Act
N.H. Rev. Stat. 1955, 146:1 et seq.
Tex. Rev. Civ. Stat., Art. 4476-5

Pure Liquor Law
N.D. Cent. Code, 19-08-01 et seq.

Pure Milk Law
Cal. Food and Agricultural Code, § 35601 et seq.

Pure Pet Food Act
Cal. Health and Safety Code, § 27000 et seq.

Pure Seed Act
Ark. Code Ann. 1987, 2-18-101 et seq.
Ida. Code 1947, 22-414 et seq.
Ky. Rev. Stat. 1971, 250.010 et seq.
Minn. Stat. 1982, 21.47 et seq.
Miss. Code Ann. 1972, § 69-3-1 et seq.
Mo. Rev. Stat., 266.011 et seq.

N.D. Cent. Code, 4-09-06 et seq.

Okla. Stat. Ann., Title 2, § 8-21 et seq.

Tenn. Code Ann., Superseded Vol., 43-901 et seq.

Wyo. Stat. Ann., § 11-12-101 et seq.

Pure Seed Labeling Act

Fla. Stat. Ann., 578.011 et seq.

Pure Stream Act

Pa. Purdon's Stat., Title 35, § 691.1 et seq.

Pure Water Law

Cal. Health and Safety Code, § 4010 et seq.

Pa. Purdon's Stat., Title 35, § 721.1 et seq.

Pure Water Sewer Use Law

N.Y. Local Laws 1972, County of Monroe, p. 690

Pure Waters Authority Act

N.Y. Public Authorities Law (Consol. Laws 43A) § 1280 et seq.

Pure Waters Bond Act

N.Y. Laws 1965, Ch. 176

N.Y. Unconsolidated Laws, §§ 7371 et seq.

Purebred Paso Fino Horse Agro-Industry Act

P.R. Laws Ann. 1954, Title 5, § 2001 et seq.

Purgation Act (Voters' Registration)

Ky. Rev. Stat. 1971, 116.115 et seq.

Purity of Drinking Water Act

P.R. Laws Ann. 1954, Title 12, § 1551 et seq.

Purity of Election Act

Cal. Elections Code 1976, § 11500 et seq.

Purnell Act

Feb. 24, 1925, Ch. 308, 43 Stat. 970

N.M. Stat. Ann., 21-8-13

Purnell Act (Agricultural Experiment Stations)

Me. Rev. Stat. Ann. 1964, Title 36, § 3201 et seq.

Purnell Act (Corn Borer Eradication)

Feb. 9, 1927, Ch. 90, 44 Stat. 1065, 7 U.S. Code § 146

Pursuit Act

See Uniform Act on Fresh Pursuit

Putnam County and Municipality Tax Collection Act

Fla. Special Laws 1969, Ch. 69-1517

Putnam County Development Authority Act

Fla. Special Laws 1961, Ch. 61-2727

Putnam County-Eaton Charter Commission Act

Ga. Laws 1972, p. 2665

Putnam County Road Law

Tenn. Private Acts 1974, Ch. 208

Putnam Valley Collapsed Structures and Unsafe Building Law

N.Y. Local Laws 1967, Town of Putnam Valley, p. 1869

Putnam Valley Highway Opening and Crossing Law

N.Y. Local Laws 1967, Town of Putnam Valley, p. 1886

Putnam Valley Public Employees' Fair Employment Law

N.Y. Local Laws 1967, Town of Putnam Valley, p. 1888

Puyallup Tribe of Indians Settlement Act of 1989

June 21, 1989, P.L. 101-41, 25 U.S. Code §§ 1773 et seq., 1773 nt., 1773a nt.

Pyramid and Multilevel Distributorship Act

Wyo. Stat. Ann., § 40-3-101 et seq.

Pyramid or Multilevel Sales Act

N.M. Stat. Ann., 57-13-1 et seq.

Utah Code Ann. 1953, 76-6a-1 et seq.

Pyramid Promotional Scheme Act

Okla. Stat. Ann., Title 21, § 1071 et seq.

Pyramid Promotional Schemes Act
N.M. Stat. Ann., 57-13-1 et seq.

Pyramid Sales Act
N.D. Cent. Code, 51-16.1-01 et seq.

Pyrotechnic Safety Board Act
S.C. Code Ann. 1976, § 23-8-10 et seq.

Q

Quad Cities Interstate Metropolitan Authority Compact Act

May 10, 1990, P.L. 101-288, 104 Stat. 178 lfe Ill. Rev. Stat. 1991, Ch. 85, § 6241 et seq.

Quad Cities Regional Economic Development Authority Act

Ill. Rev. Stat. 1991, Ch. 85, §§ 6201 et seq., 6501 et seq.

Quad City and Pekin Civic Centers Act

Ill. Rev. Stat. 1991, Ch. 85, § 3100 et seq.

Quad City Civic Center Authority Law

Ill. Laws 1984, P.A. 83-1435

Ill. Rev. Stat. 1991, Ch. 85, § 3101 et seq.

Quad-County Peace Officers' Relief Association Act

N.C. Laws 1951, Ch. 1097

Quadrennial Assessment Law

N.M. Stat. Ann. 1953, 72-2-15 et seq.

Quadrennial Elections Act

Kan. Stat. Ann., 13-1702a

Quadrennial Re-registration Act for Monroe County

Fla. Laws 1945, Ch. 22708

Quahog Tax Act

Me. Rev. Stat. Ann. 1964, Title 12, § 6624;Title 36, § 4631 et seq.

Quail Act

Miss. Code Ann. 1972, § 49-13-1 et seq.

Quail and Squirrel Act (Garrett)

Ark. Special Acts 1923, p. 565, No. 267

Quaker Marriages Act

D.C. Code 1973, §§ 30-106, 30-112, 30-113

Qualification of Educational Personnel Act (Interstate Agreement)

See Interstate Agreement on Qualification of Educational Personnel Act

Qualifications Based Selection Act (Architectural, Engineering, and Land Surveying)

Ill. Comp. Stat. 1992, Ch. 30, § 535/1 et seq.

Qualified Thrift Lender Reform Act of 1991

Dec. 19, 1991, P.L. 102-242, 12 U.S. Code § 1461 nt.

Qualifying Income Interest for Life Act (Estate Taxes)

Mass. Gen. Laws Ann., 65A:5, 65A:5A

Quality Act (Environmental)

Okla. Stat. Ann., Title 27A, § 1-1-101 et seq.

Quality Assurance Act (Lawyers Referral Service)

Tex. Rev. Civ. Stat., Art. 320d

Quality Assurance Act (Mammogram)

Utah Code Ann. 1953, 26-21a-201

Quality Assurance Act (Mammography)

Pa. Purdon's Stat., Title 35, § 5651 et seq.

Quality Basic Education Act

Ga. Code Ann., 20-2-130 et seq.

Quality Control Center Act

P.R. Laws Ann. 1954, Title 23, 248 et seq.

Quality Education Act

Ark. Code Ann. 1987, 6-15-201 et seq.

N.J. Stat. Ann., 18A:7D-1 et seq.

Quality Health Care Act (Long Term)

Ala. Code 1975, § 22-6-20 et seq.

Haw. Rev. Stat. Ann., § 671D-1 et seq.

Quality Housing and Work Responsibility Act of 1998

Oct. 21, 1998, P.L. 105-276, Title V, 112 Stat. 2518, 42 U.S. Code § 1437 nt.

Oct. 21, 1998, P.L. 105-277, 42 U.S. Code § 1437n

Quality Improvement Act
Haw. Rev. Stat. Ann., § 671D-1 et seq.
Pa. Purdon's Stat., Title 73, § 399.91 et seq.

Quality Improvement Act (State Government)
Tenn. Public Act 1992, Ch. 774

Quality Jobs Act
Neb. Laws 1995, L.B. 829

Quality Jobs Act (Saving)
Okla. Stat. Ann., Title 68, § 3701 et seq.

Quality Jobs Program Act
Okla. Stat. Ann., Title 68, § 3601 et seq.

Quality Joint Development Act (Water)
Wash. Rev. Code Ann., 70.150.010 et seq.

Quality Label Act
Va. Code 1950, § 3.1-349 et seq.

Quality Performance and School District Finance Act
Kan. Stat. Ann., 72-6405

Quality Program Act
Kan. Stat. Ann., 75-37,115

Quality Water Act
Utah Code Ann. 1953, 19-5-101 et seq.

Quarantine Act (Animals)
Ark. Code Ann. 1987, 2-40-102 et seq.
Cal. Food and Agricultural Code 1967, § 9501 et seq.
La. Rev. Stat. Ann., 3:2091 et seq.
Mich. Comp. Laws Ann., 287.1 et seq., 287.101 et seq.
Pa. Purdon's Stat., Title 3, § 341 et seq.
Tex. Agriculture Code, § 161.001 et seq.
Wash. Rev. Code Ann., 16.36.005 et seq.

Quarantine Act (Dower)
Ky. Rev. Stat. 1971, 392.050

Quarantine Act (Persons)
Iowa Code Ann., 139.1 et seq.
Mont. Rev. Code 1947, 69-4112
N.C. Gen. Stat. 1943, §§ 130-80 et seq., 130A-145

N.H. Rev. Stat. 1955, 141-C:11 et seq.
R.I. Gen. Laws 1956, 23-8-1 et seq.
Tex. Health and Safety Code, § 81.001 et seq.
Wash. Rev. Code 1985, 70.20.040 et seq.

Quarantine Act (Plants)
Cal. Food and Agricultural Code 1967, § 5001 et seq.
Ore. Rev. Stat., 570.005 et seq.
P.R. Laws Ann. 1954, Title 5, § 613 et seq.

Quarantine Act (Ships)
Wash. Rev. Code Ann., 70.16.010 et seq.

Quarantine Acts
Feb. 15, 1893, Ch. 114, 27 Stat. 449
June 19, 1906, Ch. 3433, 34 Stat. 299
July 10, 1940, Ch. 566, 54 Stat. 747

Quarantine and Pest Management Act
Mont. Code Ann., 75-11-501 et seq.

Quarry and Pit Safety Act (Aggregate)
Tex. Natural Resources Code, § 133.001 et seq.

Quarry Operation, Reclamation and Safe Closure Act
Ark. Code Ann. 1987, 15-57-401 et seq.

Quart-a-Month Act (Intoxicating Liquor)
S.C. Laws 1917, p. 69, No. 38, § 2

Quarter Horse Racing Act
Ill. Rev. Stat. 1975, Ch. 8, § 401 et seq.

Quartz Miners' Protection Act
Cal. Labor Code § 7400 et seq.

Quasi-Community Property Act
Cal. Civil Code § 4803 et seq.

Quasi-Criminal and Misdemeanor Bail Act
Ill. Rev. Stat. 1991, Ch. 16, § 80 et seq.

Quasi Garnishment Act (City Employees)
Wis. Stat. Ann., 812.23

Quasi-Public Corporations Act
Tenn. Code Ann. 1955, 48-601 et seq.

Queens Boundary Act
N.Y. Laws 1928, Ch. 802

Queens-Mid-Town Tunnel Authority Act
N.Y. Laws 1935, Ch. 681

Quentin L. Kopp Conflict of Interest Act
Cal. Government Code § 15626

Quequechan River Improvement Loan Act
Mass. Acts 1957, Ch. 607

Questions of Law Certification Act
See also Uniform Certification of Questions
of Law Act
Conn. Gen. Stat. Ann., § 51-199a
Mass. Ann. Code 1974, CJ, § 12-601 et seq.

Quick Taking Act (Eminent Domain)
Ariz. Rev. Stat. Ann., § 12-1116
Conn. Gen. Stat. Ann., § 8-129
Ill. Rev. Stat. 1991, Ch. 110 § 7-101 et seq.
La. Rev. Stat. Ann., 19:141 et seq., 48:441 et
seq.
Md. Ann. Code 1974, Art. TR, § 8-334 et
seq.
Miss. Code Ann. 1972, § 11-27-81 et seq.
N.C. Gen. Stat. 1943, § 40A-1 et seq.
Nev. Rev. Stat. 1979 Reprint, 37.100 et seq.

Quickie Divorce Act
Nev. Rev. Stat. 1979 Reprint, 125.020

Quiet Communities Act of 1978
Nov. 8, 1978, P.L. 95-609, 42 U.S. Code
§§ 4901 nt., 4905, 4910, 4913, 4918, 6901
et seq.; 49 U.S. Code § 1431

Quiet Title Act
Ala. Code 1975, § 6-6-540 et seq.
Ariz. Rev. Stat. Ann., § 12-1101 et seq.
Ark. Code Ann. 1987, 18-60-501 et seq.
Cal. Code of Civil Procedure § 738 et seq.
D.C. Code 1973, § 16-3301
Iowa Code Ann., 649.1 et seq.
Mass. Gen. Laws Ann., 240:6 et seq.
Mo. Rev. Stat., 527.150 et seq.
Mont. Code Ann. 1991, 70-28-101 et seq.
N.C. Gen. Stat. 1943, § 41-10
N.J. Rev. Stat. 1937, 2A:62-1 et seq.

N.M. Stat. Ann., 42-6-1 et seq.
N.Y. Real Property Actions and Proceedings
Law (Consol. Laws Ch. 81) §§ 1941 to
1946
Pa. 1949 Pamph. Laws 1692, No. 512
R.I. Gen. Laws 1956, 34-16-1 et seq.
Utah Code Ann. 1953, 78-40-1 et seq.
Wash. Rev. Code Ann., 7.28.010 et seq.

**Quilted Clothing, Bedding and Upholstered
Furniture Act**
Utah Code Ann. 1953, 4-10-1 et seq.

Quimby-Marler Instructional Television Act
Cal. Education Code 1976, § 51870 et seq.

Quimby-Walsh Act (Indecent Exposure)
Cal. Penal Code § 318.5

Quincy Civic Center Act
Ill. Rev. Stat. 1989, Ch. 85, § 2801 et seq.

**Quincy, Herrin, and Jefferson County Civic
Centers Act**
Ill. Rev. Stat. 1991, Ch. 85, § 2700 et seq.

Quincy Hoffman-Gary Corbin Act
Mich. Comp. Laws Ann., 205.202 et seq.

Quincy Veterans Home Act
Ill. Rev. Stat. 1991, Ch. 23, § 5050 et seq.

**Quinebaug and Shetucket Rivers Valley
National Heritage Corridor Act of 1994**
Nov. 2, 1994, P.L. 103-449, 16 U.S. Code
§ 461 nt.

Quinlan-Merritt Act (Marriage Licenses)
Mich. Comp. Laws Ann., 551.103a

Quinn District of Columbia Barber Act
D.C. Code Ann., § 2-401 et seq.

**Quinn District of Columbia Cosmetology
Act**
D.C. Code Ann., § 2-901 et seq.

Quinn-Ives Act (Anti Discrimination)
N.Y. Executive Law 1951 (Consol. Laws Ch.
18) § 290 et seq.

Quinn-Neustein Act (Labor Injunctions)
N.Y. Labor Law (Consol. Laws Ch. 31)
§ 807

Quit Claim Deeds Act
N.M. Stat. Ann., 47-1-30 et seq.

**Quitman County Water and Sewerage
      Authority Act**
Ga. Laws 1998, H.B. 1574

Quo Warranto Act
Cal. Code of Civil Procedure § 802 et seq.
D.C. Code 1973, § 16-3501 et seq.
Ga. Code Ann., 9-6-60 et seq.
Haw. Rev. Stat. Ann., § 659-1 et seq.
Ill. Rev. Stat. 1991, Ch. 110, § 18-101 et seq.
Mass. Gen. Laws Ann., 249:6 et seq.
Mich. Comp. Laws Ann., 600.4501 et seq.
Mo. Rev. Stat., 531.010 et seq.
Mont. Code Ann. 1991, 27-28-101 et seq.
N.J. Stat. Ann., Superseded Vol., 2A:66-5 et
seq.
Pa. Cons. Stat., Title 42 § 721
R.I. Gen. Laws 1956, 10-14-1 et seq.
Tenn. Code Ann., 29-35-101 et seq.
Tex. Civil Prac. and Rem. Code, § 66.001 et
seq.
Vt. Acts 1876, No. 74
Wash. Rev. Code Ann., 7.56.010 et seq.

Quogue Fire Prevention Code
N.Y. Local Laws 1972, Village of Quogue, p.
3717

Quota Act (Intoxicating Liquor)
Wis. Stat. Ann., 125.51 Subsec. 4

Quota Act (Liquor Licenses)
Mont. Code Ann. 1991, 16-4-201
Pa. 1939 Pamph. Laws 806, No. 358

Quota Law (Immigration)
May 19, 1921, Ch. 8, 42 Stat. 5
May 26, 1924, Ch. 190, 43 Stat. 153

R

R. F. C. Extension Act
March 4, 1939, Ch. 4, 53 Stat. 510, 15 U.S. Code § 609

R. F. C. Lending Act
June 5, 1942, Ch. 352, 56 Stat. 326

R. F. C. Lending Authority Act
Oct. 23, 1941, Ch. 454, 55 Stat. 744

R. F. C. Relief Obligations Act
See Reconstruction Finance Corporation Act

R. M. S. Titanic Maritime Memorial Act of 1986
Oct. 21, 1986, P.L. 99-513, 16 U.S. Code §§ 450rr nt., 450rr to 450rr-6

Rabbit and Rabbit Products Inspection Act
Okla. Stat. Ann., Title 2, § 6-280.1 et seq.

Rabbits and Poultry Products Inspection Act
Ky. Rev. Stat. 1971, Superseded Vol., 217A.010 et seq.

Rabies Act
Ala. Code 1975, § 3-7-1 et seq.
Ark. Code Ann. 1987, 20-19-301 et seq.
Cal. Health and Safety Code § 1900 et seq.
Ill. Comp. Stat. 1992, Ch. 510, § 5/1 et seq..
La. Rev. Stat. Ann., 40:1275 et seq.
Mich. Comp. Laws 1970, 329.101 et seq.
Miss. Code Ann. 1972, § 41-53-1 et seq.
N.C. Gen. Stat. 1943, § 130A-184 et seq.
Neb. Rev. Stat. 1943, 71-4401 et seq.
Pa. Purdon's Stat., Title 3, § 455.1 et seq.
Vt. Stat. Ann., Title 20, §§ 3801, 4003 et seq.

Rabin Law (School Salaries)
N.Y. Education Law 1947 (Consol. Laws Ch. 16) § 3106, Subd. 3

Rabun County Airport Authority Act
Ga. Laws 1975, p. 3003

Rabun County-Clayton Water and Sewer Authority Act
Ga. Laws 1992, p. 6403

Rabun County Economic Development Authority Act
Ga. Laws 1992, p. 4912

Race Defamation Act
Ill. Rev. Stat. 1961, Ch. 38, § 471

Race Horse Industry Reform Act
Pa. Purdon's Stat., Title 4, § 325.101 et seq.

Race Segregation Act
La. Rev. Stat. Ann., 45:521 et seq.

Race Track Act
Fla. Stat. Ann., 550.011 et seq.

Races Act (Motor Vehicle)
Vt. Stat. Ann., Title 31, § 301 et seq.

Racetrack Video Lottery Act
W. Va. Code 1966, § 29-22A-1 et seq.

Racial Harassment Act
R.I. Gen. Laws 1956, 42-80-1 et seq.

Racial Imbalance Act (Schools)
Conn. Gen. Stat. Ann., § 10-226a et seq.
Mass. Gen. Laws Ann., 15:1I et seq., 71:37C, 71:37D

Racial Integrity Act
Va. Code 1950, § 20-50 et seq.

Racial Justice Act
Ga. Code Ann., 17-10-80 et seq.

Racine Municipal Court Act
Wis. Laws 1951, Ch. 177

Racing Act
Colo. Rev. Stat., 12-60-100.2 et seq.
Ida. Code 1947, 54-2501 et seq.
Mass. Gen. Laws Ann., 128A:1 et seq.
Mich. Comp. Laws Ann., 431.61 et seq.
Nev. Rev. Stat. 1979 Reprint, 466.010 et seq.
N.J. Stat. Ann., 5:5-22 et seq.
Ore. Rev. Stat., 462.010 et seq.
Continued

P.R. Laws Ann. 1954, Title 15, § 181 et seq.
R.I. Gen. Laws 1956, 41-3-1 et seq.
Tex. Rev. Civ. Stat., Art. 179e, § 1.01 et seq.
Vt. Stat. Ann., Title 31, § 601 et seq.

Racing Act (Bicycle)
N.M. Stat. Ann., 60-2D-1 et seq.

Racing Act (Harness)
Me. Rev. Stat. Ann. 1964, Title 8, §§ 261 et seq.,261-A et seq.

Racing Act (Hillsborough County)
Fla. Laws 1953, Ch. 28499

Racing Act (Horse and Dog)
Vt. Stat. Ann., Title 31, § 601 et seq.

Racing Act (Horse)
See Horse Racing Act

Racing Act (Motor Vehicles)
N.C. Gen. Stat. 1943, § 20-141.3

Racing Act (Municipal Motor Vehicle)
Fla. Stat. Ann., 549.08

Racing Act (Parimutuel)
Kan. Stat. Ann., 74-8801 et seq.

Racing Act (Simulcasting)
N.H. Rev. Stat. 1955, 436:99 et seq.
N.J. Stat. Ann., 4:19-15.1 et seq.
N.J. Stat. Ann., 5:5-110 et seq.
S.C. Code Ann. 1976, § 47-5-10 et seq.
Tex. Health and Safety Code, § 826.001 et seq.
Tex. Rev. Civ. Stat. 1974, Art. 4477-6a

Racing and Wagering Board Act
N.Y. Laws 1973, Ch. 346, § 3

Racing Bets Act
Mont. Rev. Code 1947, 94-2425 et seq.

Racing Commission Act
La. Rev. Stat. Ann., 4:141 et seq.
Md. Ann. Code 1974, Art. BR, § 11-201 et seq.
N.H. Rev. Stat. 1955, 284:6 et seq.
N.M. Stat. Ann., 60-1-1 et seq.
Ohio Rev. Code 1953, 3769.01 et seq.

Tex. Penal Code 1925, Art. 655a
Va. Code 1950, § 59.1-216 et seq.

Racing Commission Act (Currituck County)
N.C. Laws 1949, Ch. 541

Racing Control Act
Tenn. Code Ann., 4-36-101 et seq.

Racing, Hobby, Carrier, and Show Pigeon Act
Ill. Comp. Stat. 1992, Ch. 510, § 45/1 et seq.

Racing Law (Greyhound)
Ark. Code Ann. 1987, 23-111-101 et seq.

Racing, Pari-Mutuel Wagering and Breeding Law
N.Y. Consol. Laws Ch. 47A, § 101 et seq.

Racing Profits Charity Act
Fla. Stat. Ann., 550.03

Racketeer Influenced and Corrupt Organizations Act
Del. Code of 1974, Title 11, § 1501 et seq.
Fla. Stat. Ann., 895.01 et seq.
Ga. Code Ann., 16-14-1 et seq.
Miss. Code Ann. 1972, § 97-43-1 et seq.
N.C. Gen. Stat. 1943, § 75D-1 et seq.
N.D. Cent. Code, 12.01-06.1-01 et seq.
Ore. Rev. Stat., 161.705, 166.715 et seq.
Tenn. Code Ann., 39-12-201 et seq.

Racketeer Influenced and Corrupt Organizations Act (RICO)
Oct. 15, 1970, P.L. 91-452, 18 U.S. Code §§ 1961 to 1968
Nov. 2, 1978, P.L. 95-575, 18 U.S. Code § 1961
Dec. 22, 1995, P.L. 104-67, 18 U.S. Code § 1964

Racketeering Act
Ida. Code 1947, 18-7801 et seq.
La. Rev. Stat. Ann., 15:1351 et seq.
N.M. Stat. Ann., 30-42-1 et seq.

Racketeering Act (Drug)
La. Rev. Stat. Ann., 15:1351 et seq.

Racketeering Activities and Corrupt Organizations Act
Conn. Gen. Stat. Ann., § 53-393 et seq.

Racketeering Influences and Criminal Enterprise Act
Utah Code Ann. 1953, 76-10-1601 et seq.

Radar Act (Motor Vehicles)
Ohio Rev. Code 1953, 4511.091
Pa. Cons. Stat., Title 75, § 3368

Radiation Accident Response Act
N.J. Stat. Ann., 26:2D-37 et seq.

Radiation Control Act
Cal. Health and Safety Code § 25800 et seq.
Ga. Code Ann., 31-13-1 et seq.
Ind. Code Ann., 13-1-2-1 et seq.
Kan. Stat. Ann., 48-1601 et seq.
Ky. Acts 1978, Ch. 279
Ky. Rev. Stat. 1971, 211.840 et seq.
La. Rev. Stat. Ann., 30:1101 et seq.
Md. Ann. Code 1974, Art. EN, § 8-101 et seq.
Neb. Rev. Stat. 1943, 71-3501 et seq.
Pa. Purdon's Stat., Title 73, § 1001 et seq.
S.C. Code Ann. 1976, § 13-7-10 et seq.
Tex. Health and Safety Code, § 401.005 et seq.
Utah Code Ann. 1953, 19-3-101 et seq.

Radiation Control and Nuclear Energy Development Act
Kan. Stat. Ann., 48-1601 et seq.

Radiation Control for Health and Safety Act of 1968
Oct. 18, 1968, P.L. 90-602, 82 Stat. 1173, 42 U.S. Code §§ 263b to 263n

Radiation-Exposed Veterans Compensation Act of 1988
May 20, 1988, P.L. 100-321, 102 Stat. 485, 38 U.S. Code § 102 nt.

Radiation Exposure Compensation Act
Oct. 15, 1990, P.L. 101-426, 42 U.S. Code § 2210 nt.
Nov. 5, 1990, P.L. 101-510, 42 U.S. Code § 2210 nt.
Oct. 24, 1992, P.L. 102-486, 42 U.S. Code § 2210 nt.

Radiation Exposure Control Act
S.D. Codified Laws 1967, 34-21-1 et seq.

Radiation Health and Safety Act (Medical)
Me. Rev. Stat. Ann. 1964, Title 32, § 9851 et seq.

Radiation Installation Act
Ill. Rev. Stat. 1991, Ch. 111 1/2, § 193.9 et seq.

Radiation Management Act
Okla. Stat. Ann., Title 27A, § 2-9-101 et seq.

Radiation Monitoring Act (Personnel)
Ill. Rev. Stat. 1991, Ch. 111 1/2, § 230.10 et seq.

Radiation Operators Act
Ky. Acts 1972, Ch. 339
Ky. Rev. Stat. 1971, 211.870, 211.890

Radiation Protection Act
Alaska Stat. 1962, §§ 46.03.250 et seq., 46.03.250 et seq.
Cal. Health and Safety Code §§ 25572 et seq., 25700 et seq.
Fla. Stat. Ann., 404.011 et seq.
Ill. Rev. Stat. 1991, Ch. 111 1/2, § 210-1 et seq.
Md. Ann. Code 1974, Art. EN, § 8-101 et seq.
Me. Rev. Stat. Ann. 1964, Title 22, § 671 et seq.
Miss. Code Ann. 1972, § 45-14-1 et seq.
N.C. Gen. Stat. 1943, § 104E-1 et seq.
N.J. Stat. Ann., 26:2D-1 et seq.
N.M. Stat. Ann., 74-3-1 et seq.
Pa. Purdon's Stat., Title 35, § 7110.101
Tex. Health and Safety Code, § 401.001 et seq.
Utah Code Ann. 1953, 26-1-27 et seq.
Wis. Stat. Ann., 140.50 et seq.

Radio Act (State Police)
Ill. Rev. Stat. 1991, Ch. 121, § 307.20 et seq.

Radio Act of 1927
Feb. 23, 1927, Ch. 169, 44 Stat. 1162

Radio and Television Grant Act (Public)
Ill. Rev. Stat. 1991, Ch. 127, § 1550 et seq.

Radio and Television Licensing Act
Ind. Code Ann., 25-36-1-1 et seq.

Radio and Television Technician Act
P.R. Laws Ann. 1954, Title 20, § 2401 et seq.

Radio Astronomy Zoning Act
W. Va. Code 1966, § 37A-1-1 et seq.

Radio-Astronomy Zoning Act
P.R. Laws Ann. 1954, Title 23, § 211 et seq.

Radio Broadcasting Act
Mich. Comp. Laws Ann., 484.301 et seq.
N.J. Stat. Ann., 48:11-1 et seq.

Radio Broadcasting Legal Notices Act
Wash. Rev. Code Ann., 65.16.130 et seq.

Radio Broadcasting Liability Act
Wash. Rev. Code Ann., 19.64.010 et seq.

Radio Broadcasting to Cuba Act
Oct. 4, 1983, P.L. 98-111, 22 U.S. Code §§ 1465 et seq.
Feb. 16, 1990, P.L. 101-246, 22 U.S. Code § 1465c
April 30, 1994, P.L. 103-236, 22 U.S. Code §§ 1465b, 1465c, 1465g
Oct. 21, 1998, P.L. 105-277, 22 U.S. Code §§ 1465a to 1465f

Radio Common Carrier Act
Ga. Code Ann., 46-6-1 et seq.
Tenn. Code Ann., 65-30-101 et seq.

Radio-Communications Acts
June 24, 1910, Ch. 379, 36 Stat. 629
Aug. 13, 1912, Ch. 287, 37 Stat. 302

Radio, Cosmetics and Playing Cards Tax Act
Tex. Tax Code, § 151.001 et seq.

Radio Defamation Act
Ga. Code Ann., 51-5-10
Minn. Stat. Ann., 544.043
Neb. Rev. Stat. 1943, 86-601 et seq.
Nev. Rev. Stat. 1979 Reprint, 41.340 et seq.

Radio Dispatcher Training Act
N.M. Stat. Ann., 29-7A-1 et seq.

Radio Free Asia Act of 1998
Oct. 17, 1998, P.L. 105-261, Title XXXIX, 112 Stat. 2277

Radio Services Act (Public Safety)
Ga. Code Ann., 50-5-180 et seq.

Radio Telephone Privacy Act (Cordless and Cellular)
Cal. Penal Code § 632.5

Radio Utility Act
Ala. Code 1975, § 37-4-100 et seq.
Ga. Code Ann., 46-6-1 et seq.

Radioactive and Hazardous Materials Act
N.M. Stat. Ann., 74-4A-1 et seq.

Radioactive Material Disposal Act
N.M. Laws 1977, Ch. 122, §§ 1 et seq.

Radioactive Waste Act
Wash. Rev. Code Ann., 43.200.010 et seq.

Radioactive Waste Act (High Level)
N.H. Rev. Stat. 1955, 125-G:1 et seq.

Radioactive Waste Authority Act (Low-Level)
Me. Rev. Stat. Ann. 1964, Title 38, § 1501 et seq.
Mich. Comp. Laws Ann., 333.26201 et seq.

Radioactive Waste Compact (Central Midwest)
Ill. Comp. Stat. 1992, Ch. 45, §§ 140/0.01, 140/1

Radioactive Waste Compact (Midwest Interstate Low-Level)
Iowa Code Ann., 457B-1

**Radioactive Waste Compact Act
(Low-Level)**
Colo. Rev. Stat., 24-60-2201 et seq.
Wis. Stat. Ann., 16.10 et seq.

Radioactive Waste Consultation Act
N.H. Rev. Stat. 1955, 127:77-b et seq.

Radioactive Waste Disposal Act (Low-Level)
Me. Rev. Stat. Ann. 1964, Title 38, § 1481 et
seq.
Neb. Rev. Stat. 1943, 81-1578 et seq.
Pa. Purdon's Stat., Title 35, § 7130.101 et
seq.

**Radioactive Waste Disposal Authority Act
(Low-Level)**
Tex. Health and Safety Code, § 402.001 et
seq.
Tex. Rev. Civ. Stat. 1974, Art. 4590f-1

**Radioactive Waste Disposal Facility Siting
Act (Regional Low-Level)**
N.J. Stat. Ann., 13:1E-177 et seq.

**Radioactive Waste Disposal Regional
Facility Act (Low-Level)**
Pa. Purdon's Stat., Title 35, § 7131.101 et
seq.

**Radioactive Waste Management Act
(Low-Level)**
Mass. Gen. Laws Ann., 111H:1 to 111H:48
N.Y. Environmental Conservation Law 1972
(Consol. Laws Ch. 43B) § 29-0101 et seq.
N.Y. Public Authorities Law (Consol. Laws
Ch. 43A) §§ 1851, 1854b et seq.
N.Y. Public Health Law 1953 (Consol. Laws
Ch. 45) § 2485

**Radioactive Waste Management Authority
Act (Low-Level)**
N.C. Gen. Stat. 1943, § 104G-1 et seq.

**Radioactive Waste Management Compact
(Low-Level)**
Ga. Code Ann., 12-8-120 et seq.

**Radioactive Waste Management Compact
(Northeast Interstate)**
Conn. Gen. Stat. Ann., § 22a-161

**Radioactive Waste Management Compact
(Southeast Interstate Low-Level)**
S.C. Code Ann. 1976, § 48-47-10 et seq.

**Radioactive Waste Management Compact
Act**
N.J. Stat. Ann., 32:31-1

Radioactive Waste Storage Act
Ill. Rev. Stat. 1991, Ch. 111 1/2, § 230 et seq.

**Radioactive Waste Storage and Transpor-
tation Act**
Wash. Rev. Code Ann., 70.99.010 et seq.

**Radioactive Waste Tracking and Permitting
Act**
Ill. Comp. Stat. 1992, Ch. 420, § 37/1

Radioactive Waste Transportation Act
Miss. Code Ann. 1972, § 45-14-51 et seq.

**Radioactive Waste Transportation and
Disposal Act**
S.C. Code Ann. 1976, §§ 13-7-110 et seq.,
48-48-10 et seq.

Radiologic Technologist Certification Act
Fla. Stat. Ann., 468.3001 et seq.
N.J. Stat. Ann., 26:2D-24 et seq.
Tex. Rev. Civ. Stat., Art. 4512m, §§ 2.01 et
seq.
Wash. Rev. Code Ann., 18.84.010 et seq.
Wyo. Stat. Ann., § 33-37-101 et seq.

Radiological Health Protection Compact Act
Conn. Gen. Stat. Ann., §§ 22a-159, 22a-160
Mass. Acts 1967, Ch. 801
Me. Rev. Stat. Ann. 1964, Title 22, § 751 et
seq.
N.H. Rev. Stat. 1955, 125-B:1 et seq.
R.I. Gen. Laws 1956, 23-12.5-1 et seq.

Radiological Health Service Act
Tenn. Code Ann., 68-202-201 et seq.
Vt. Stat. Ann., Title 18, § 1601 et seq.

**Radiology and Pathology Services in
Hospitals Act**
Iowa Code 1977, 135B.19 et seq.

Radiology Technologist and Radiology Practical Technician Licensing Act
Utah Code Ann. 1953, 58-54-1 et seq.

Radon Certification Act
Pa. Purdon's Stat., Title 63, § 2001 et seq.

Radon Control Act
Mont. Code Ann., 75-3-601 et seq.

Radon Gas and Indoor Air Quality Research Act of 1986
Oct. 17, 1986, P.L. 99-499, 42 U.S. Code § 7401 nt.

Radon Gas Demonstration Project and Home Improvement Loan Act
Pa. Purdon's Stat., Title 35, § 7501

Radon Industry Licensing Act
Ill. Comp. Stat. 1992, Ch. 420, § 44/1 et seq.

Radon Mitigation Act
Ill. Rev. Stat. 1991, Ch. 111 1/2, § 243-1 et seq.

Radon Registration Act
Me. Rev. Stat. Ann. 1964, Title 22, § 771 et seq.

Radon Testing Act
Ill. Rev. Stat. 1989, Ch. 111 1/2, § 242 et seq.

Rafferty Bill (Race Hatred)
N.J. Stat. Revised 1937, Superseded Vol., 2:157B-1 to 2:157B-8

Raffle and Gambling Act (Charitable)
Tex. Rev. Civ. Stat., Art. 179f

Raffle and Lottery Act
Neb. Rev. Stat. 1943, 9-401 et seq.

Raffle Control Act
Wis. Stat. Ann., 163.90 et seq.

Raffle Enabling Act (Charitable)
Tex. Rev. Civ. Stat., Art. 179f

Raffles Act
Ill. Rev. Stat. 1991, Ch. 85, § 2300 et seq.
N.H. Rev. Stat. 1955, 287-A:1 et seq.

Raffles and Bingo Law
Colo. Rev. Stat., 12-9-101 et seq.
Mont. Code Ann., 87, 23-5-401 et seq.
N.M. Stat. Ann., 60-2B-1 et seq.

Raffles, Bingo and Keno Licensing Act
La. Rev. Stat. Ann., 33:4861.1 et seq.

Raffles Licensing Law
N.J. Stat. Ann., 5:8-50 et seq.

Rail Act (High-Speed)
Tex. Rev. Civ. Stat., Art. 6674v.2

Rail and Bus-Passenger Safety Act
Ga. Code Ann., 16-12-121

Rail Authority Act (State)
W. Va. Code 1966, § 29-18-1 et seq.

Rail Corporation Act (Public)
R.I. Gen. Laws 1956, 42-64.2-1 et seq.

Rail District Act
Colo. Rev. Stat., 32-12-101 et seq.

Rail Freight Preservation and Improvement Act
Pa. Purdon's Stat., Title 55, § 696.1 et seq.

Rail Improvement Authority Law
Mo. Rev. Stat., 620.950 et seq.

Rail Line Revitalization Act (Agriculture and Industrial Branch)
Neb. Rev. Stat. 1943, 74-1401 et seq.

Rail Passenger Authority Law
Ga. Code Ann., 46-9-270 et seq.

Rail Passenger Service Act
Ill. Rev. Stat. 1991, Ch. 114, § 850 et seq.

Rail Passenger Service Act of 1970
Oct. 30, 1970, P.L. 91-518, 84 Stat. 1327, 26 U.S. Code § 250; 45 U.S. Code §§ 501, 502, 521, 522, 541 to 548, 561 to 565, 581 to 583, 601, 602, 621, 622, 641 to 645
June 22, 1972, P.L. 92-316, 86 Stat. 227, 45 U.S. Code §§ 543, 545, 546, 548, 562, 563, 565, 601, 602, 644, 645
Nov. 3, 1973, P.L. 93-146, 87 Stat. 518, 45 U.S. Code §§ 502, 543 , 545, 546, 548, 561 to 564, 601, 602, 641

May 26, 1975, P.L. 94-25, 89 Stat. 90, 45 U.S. Code §§ 543, 545, 548, 563, 564, 601, 602, 621

Sept. 29, 1979, P.L. 96-73, 45 U.S. Code §§ 501-502, 545 et seq.

May 30, 1980, P.L. 96-254, 45 U.S. Code §§ 562, 601, 651 et seq.

April 7, 1986, P.L. 99-272, 45 U.S. Code §§ 502, 544-546, 548, 562, 562 nt., 563-565, 601, 621, 622, 644, 645, 659, 650

June 22, 1988, P.L. 100-342, 102 Stat. 636, 45 U.S. Code §§ 541, 543, 548, 602

Sept. 30, 1988, P.L. 100-457, 45 U.S. Code § 581

July 6, 1990, P.L. 101-322, 45 U.S. Code §§ 601, 649

Nov. 16, 1990, P.L. 101-610, 45 U.S. Code §§ 546, 546 nt.

Nov. 28, 1990, P.L. 101-641, 45 U.S. Code §§ 562, 562 nt.

Oct. 27, 1992, P.L. 102-533, 45 U.S. Code §§ 502, 544, 546, 563, 601, 602, 650, 650b, 650c, 650d, 650e

Oct. 31, 1994, P.L. 103-429, 26 U.S. Code §§ 250, 250 nt.; 45 U.S. Code §§ 564, 650d, 650e

Rail Preservation Act

Ala. Code 1975, § 37-10-1 et seq.

Mo. Rev. Stat., 620.992 et seq.

Rail Preservation Act (State)

Mo. Rev. Stat., 680.130 et seq.

Rail Preservation Bond Act

N.Y. Laws 1974, Ch. 118, § 2

N.Y. Transportation Law (Consol. Laws Ch. 61a) § 6

Rail Safety and Service Improvement Act

Nov. 8, 1984, P.L. 98-620, 45 U.S. Code § 1205

Oct. 21, 1986, P.L. 99-509, 45 U.S. Code § 825a

Rail Safety Enforcement and Review Act

Sept. 3, 1992, P.L. 102-365, 45 U.S. Code § 421 nt.

Rail Safety Improvement Act of 1988

June 22, 1988, P.L. 100-342, 102 Stat. 624, 45 U.S. Code §§ 1-14, 16, 22 to 24, 28, 29, 32, 34, 38 to 40, 43, 43a, 61 to 64a, 401 nt., 421 nt., 431, 431 nt., 437, 438, 438 nt., 440, 441, 444, 445, 541, 543, 543 nt., 548, 602, 650a, 650a nt., 854; 49 U.S. Code Appx. § 26

Sept. 3, 1992, P.L. 102-365, 45 U.S. Code § 431 nt.

Rail Service Act (Passenger)

Me. Rev. Stat. Ann. 1964, Title 23, § 7171 et seq.; Title 32, § 8001 et seq.

Rail Service Assistance Program Act

Kan. Stat. Ann., 75-5040 et seq.

Rail Service Improvement Act

Minn. Stat. Ann., 222.46 et seq.

Rail Services Preservation Bond Act

N.J. Laws 1974, Ch. 113

Rail Transportation Act (High Speed)

Fla. Stat. Ann., 341.3201 et seq.

Rail Transportation Commission Act (High Speed)

Fla. Laws 1984, Ch. 84-207

Rail Transportation Improvement Act

Oct. 19, 1976, P.L. 94-555, 45 U.S. Code § 501 et seq.

Rail Transportation Improvement Act (Costa)

Cal. Streets and Highways Code §§ 2701 to 2701.02, 2701.05 to 2701.08, 2701.10 to 2701.23, 2702 to 2702.02, 2702.05 to 2702.08, 2702.10 to 2702.22, 2703 to 2703.02, 2703.05 to 2703.08, 2703.10 to 2703.22

Railroad Act

Alaska Comp. Laws Ann. 1949, §§ 47-2-91 et seq., 47-2-179, 49-3-1 et seq.

Haw. Rev. Stat. Ann., § 273-1 et seq.

Ill. Rev. Stat. 1991, Ch. 114, § 0.01 et seq.

Kan. Stat. Ann., 66-201 et seq.

La. Rev. Stat. Ann., 45:321 et seq.

Mich. Comp. Laws Ann., 463.1 et seq.

Continued

N.H. Rev. Stat. 1955, 367:1 et seq.
N.J. Stat. Ann., 48:12-1 et seq.
N.Y. Consol. Laws, Ch. 49
Okla. Stat. Ann., Title 66, § 1 et seq.
Pa. Purdon's Stat., Title 15, § 3901 et seq.
R.I. Gen. Laws 1956, 39-6-1 et seq.
S.C. Code Ann. 1976, § 58-17-10 et seq.
Vt. Stat. Ann., Title 30, § 701 et seq.
Wash. Rev. Code Ann., 81.36.010 et seq.
Wis. Stat. Ann., 190.001 et seq.

Railroad Act (Alaska)
See Alaska Railroad Acts

Railroad Act (Formation of Corporations)
Pa. Purdon's Stat., Title 15, § 3904 et seq.

Railroad Act (Organization)
Ark. Stat. 1947, 73-301.1 et seq.
Mo. Rev. Stat., 388.010 et seq.

Railroad Act (Regulations)
Mo. Rev. Stat., 389.010 et seq.

Railroad and Bridge Capital Budget Supplemental Act for 1991-1992
Pa. 1992 Pamph. Laws, No. 143

Railroad and Canal Tax Act
N.J. Stat. Ann., 54:29A-1 et seq.

Railroad and Public Utilities Commission Act
Tenn. Code Ann., 65-1-101 et seq.

Railroad and Telegraph Seizure Act (Civil War)
Jan. 31, 1862, Ch. 15, 12 Stat. 334

Railroad Anti-Featherbedding Law
Ariz. Rev. Stat. Ann., § 40-886.01 et seq.
Cal. Labor Code § 6900 et seq.

Railroad Antipass Act
Neb. Rev. Stat. 1943, 74-815 et seq.

Railroad Approval Act (Elevated)
Ill. Rev. Stat. 1991, Ch. 131 1/4, § 12.9 et seq.

Railroad Assessment Act
June 13, 1934, Ch. 498, 48 Stat. 954
Ill. Rev. Stat. 1991, Ch. 120, § 560 et seq.

Railroad Authorities Act (Regional)
S.D. Codified Laws 1967, 49-17A-1 et seq.

Railroad Authority (Heber Valley Historic)
Utah Code Ann. 1953, 9-3-301 et seq.

Railroad Authority Act
Colo. Rev. Stat., 24-43-101 et seq.
Miss. Code Ann. 1972, § 19-29-1 et seq.
N.M. Stat. Ann. 1953, 69-11-1 et seq.
S.D. Codified Laws 1967, 49-16B-1 et seq.

Railroad Authority Act (North Coast)
Cal. Government Code § 93000 et seq.

Railroad Authority Compact (Mississippi-Alabama)
Miss. Code Ann. 1972, § 77-9-531 et seq.

Railroad Bell and Whistle Act
See Bell and Whistle Act (Railroads)

Railroad Bond Guarantee Act
Ill. Rev. Stat. 1991, Ch. 114, § 49a.9 et seq.

Railroad Borrowing Act
Ill. Rev. Stat. 1991, Ch. 114, § 34.9 et seq.

Railroad Bridge Act
Ill. Rev. Stat. 1991, Ch. 114, § 44.9 et seq.

Railroad Car Company Tax Act
N.M. Stat. Ann., 7-11-1 et seq.

Railroad Car Supply Law
Neb. Rev. Stat. 1943, 74-503 et seq.

Railroad Clearance Act
Mo. Rev. Stat., 389.580 et seq.

Railroad Code
Mich. Comp. Laws Ann., 462.101 et seq.

Railroad Commission Act
Ark. Code Ann. 1987, 23-2-101 et seq.
Cal. Statutes 1915, p. 115
Colo. Stat. Ann. 1935, Ch. 29 § 11 et seq.

Fla. Stat. Ann., 350.01 et seq.
Ind. Code Ann., 8-3-1-1 et seq.
Ky. Rev. Stat. 1971, 276.010 et seq.
Mont. Code Ann., 69-14-101 et seq.
Neb. Rev. Stat. 1943, 75-101 et seq.
Nev. Statutes 1907, Ch. 44, p. 73
Ore. Rev. Stat., 760.005 et seq.
Pa. 1907 Pamph. Laws 337, No. 250
Tex. Rev. Civ. Stat., Arts. 6444 et seq.,
    6559i-1 et seq.
Wash. Laws 1905, Ch. 81

Railroad Commission Fee Law
Cal. Public Utilities Code § 5001 et seq.

Railroad Company Charter Change Act
Ill. Rev. Stat. 1991, Ch. 114, § 29.90 et seq.

Railroad Comparative Negligence Act
Ark. Code Ann. 1987, 23-12-904
Fla. Stat. Ann., 768.06
Ga. Code Ann., 46-8-291
Iowa Code Ann., 327D.188

Railroad Condemnation Act
Ky. Rev. Stat. 1971, 416.010 et seq.
Md. Ann. Code 1957, Art. 23, § 193 et seq.
Mich. Comp. Laws Ann., 464.15 et seq.

Railroad Conditional Sale Act
La. Rev. Stat. Ann., 45:1241 et seq.

Railroad Consolidation Act
Ill. Rev. Stat. 1991, Ch. 114, § 38.9 et seq.
Pa. Purdon's Stat., Title 15, § 4252 et seq.

Railroad Contributory Negligence Statute
Ark. Code Ann. 1987, 23-12-904

Railroad Control Acts
March 21, 1918, Ch. 25, 40 Stat. 451
June 16, 1933, Ch. 91, 48 Stat. 211, 49 U.S.
    Code §§ 5, 5a, 15a, 15b, 19a

Railroad Corporation Act
Ind. Code Ann., 8-4-1-1 et seq.
Md. Ann. Code 1957, Art. 23, § 184 et seq.
S.C. Code Ann. 1976, § 58-17-10

Railroad Crossing Stop Act
Ark. Code Ann. 1987, 23-12-411
Ill. Rev. Stat. 1983, Ch. 114, § 131, 132
Mich. Comp. Laws Ann., 469.1 et seq.
Minn. Stat. Ann., 219.16 et seq.
Mont. Code Ann., 69-14-601 et seq.
N.J. Stat. Ann., 48:12-49 et seq.
Okla. Stat. Ann., Title 66, § 121 et seq.
S.C. Code Ann. 1976, §§ 58-15-910,
    58-17-1390, 58-17-3380 et seq.
Tex. Rev. Civ. Stat., Art. 6701d, § 86
Va. Code 1950, § 56-414 et seq.
Wash. Rev. Code Ann., 81.53.010 et seq.,
    81.54.010 et seq.

**Railroad Demolition, Removal and
    Relocation Act**
N.Y. Laws 1937, Ch. 929, § I41-1.0 et seq.

Railroad Demurrage Act
Minn. Laws, 1907. Ch. 23

Railroad Depot Act
Ill. Rev. Stat. 1991, Ch. 114, § 47.9 et seq.

Railroad Director Residence Act
Ill. Rev. Stat. 1991, Ch. 114, § 51.9 et seq.

Railroad Employee Equity Act
Me. Rev. Stat. Ann. 1964, Title 26, § 2071 et
    seq.

Railroad Employees' Act
Colo. Rev. Stat., 40-33-101 et seq.
Ohio Rev. Code 1953, 4973.09
Ore. Rev. Stat., 764.110 et seq.

Railroad Employees Payment Act
N.Y. Labor Law (Consol. Laws Ch. 31)
    § 190 et seq.

Railroad Employees Wrongful Death Act
Ga. Code Ann., 34-7-41 et seq.

Railroad Employers' Liability Act
See Employers' Liability Act (Railroads)

Railroad Equipment Conditional Sales Law
Cal. Public Utilities Code § 7576 et seq.

Railroad Equipment Mortgage Act
Mont. Rev. Code 1947, 72-303 et seq.
Ohio Rev. Code 1953, 1701.66

Railroad Fare Act
Mich. Comp. Laws Ann., 468.31 to 468.38
W. Va. Acts 1907, Ch. 41

Railroad Fellow Servant Act
Ark. Code Ann. 1987, 11-8-109
Minn. Stat. Ann., 219.77
N.C. Gen. Stat. 1943, § 62-242

Railroad Fencing Act
Cal. Public Utilities Code § 7626 et seq.
Colo. Rev. Stat., 40-27-102 et seq.
Fla. Stat. Ann., 356.01 et seq.
Ill. Rev. Stat. 1991, Ch. 95 1/2, § 18c-7504 et
  seq.
Iowa Code Ann., 327G.1 et seq.
Kan. Stat. Ann., 66-308 et seq.
Ky. Rev. Stat. 1971, 256.100 et seq.
La. Rev. Stat. Ann., 45:503
Minn. Stat. Ann., 219.31 et seq.
Neb. Rev. Stat. 1943, 74-601 et seq.
N.Y. Railroad Law (Consol. Laws Ch. 49)
  § 52b
Tenn. Code Ann., 44-8-101 et seq.

Railroad Fire Act
Colo. Rev. Stat., 40-30-101 et seq.
S.C. Code Ann. 1976, § 58-17-3920

Railroad Franchise Tax Act
N.J. Stat. Ann., 54:29A-13 et seq.

Railroad Full Crew Act
Ariz. Rev. Stat. Ann. 1956, § 40-881 et seq.
Ark. Stat. 1947, 73-720 et seq.
Ind. Code Ann., 8-9-2-1 et seq.
Mass. Gen. Laws Ann., 160:185
Miss. Code 1942, § 7759 et seq.
Neb. Rev. Stat. 1943, 75-421, 75-424,
  75-425, 74-532
Nev. Rev. Stat. 1979 Reprint, 705.390 et seq.
N.Y. Railroad Law (Consol. Laws Ch. 49)
  § 54a et seq.
Ohio Rev. Code 1953, 4999.06
Tex. Rev. Civ. Stat., Art. 6380

Wash. Rev. Code Ann., 81.40.010 et seq.

Railroad Hazards Act
Ark. Code Ann. 1987, 23-12-503 et seq.
Ga. Code Ann., 46-8-170

Railroad Headlight Act
Ark. Code Ann. 1987, 23-12-402

**Railroad Holding Company Dissolution Act
(Boston)**
Mass. Acts 1946, Ch. 518

Railroad Hours of Service Act
Wash. Rev. Code Ann., 81.40.040 et seq.

Railroad Incorporation Act
Ark. Code Ann. 1987, 23-11-201 et seq.
Ill. Rev. Stat. 1991, Ch. 114, § 0.01 et seq.

Railroad Injuries Act
Ark. Code Ann. 1987, 23-12-902 et seq.

Railroad Intangible Tax Act
Tex. Tax Code, §§ 21.07, 24.01, 24.07

Railroad Interstate Line Consolidation Act
Ill. Rev. Stat. 1991, Ch. 114, § 41.9 et seq.
Neb. Rev. Stat. 1943, 74-101 et seq.

Railroad Intoxicating Liquor Act
Ill. Rev. Stat. 1991, Ch. 114, § 100d.9 et seq.

Railroad Land Grant Forfeiture Act
Sept. 29, 1890, Ch. 1040, 26 Stat. 496, 43
  U.S. Code §§ 904 to 907

Railroad Lessees Act
Ill. Rev. Stat. 1991, Ch. 114, § 45.9 et seq.

Railroad Liability Act
Fla. Stat. Ann., 768.05 et seq.
Minn. Stat. Ann., 219.01 et seq.

Railroad Liability Act (Employees)
Tex. Rev. Civ. Stat., Art. 6432 et seq.

Railroad Lien Act
Ark. Code Ann. 1987, 18-44-401 et seq.
Ill. Rev. Stat. 1991, Ch. 82, § 48.9 et seq.
Tenn. Code Ann., 65-10-101 et seq.

Railroad Livestock Protection Law
Iowa Code Ann., 327G.1 et seq.

Railroad Livestock Transportation Act
Wash. Rev. Code Ann., 81.56.120

Railroad Lookout Act
Ark. Code Ann. 1987, 23-12-907
Tenn. Code Ann., 65-12-108

Railroad Maximum Passenger Rate Act
Ala. General Acts 1907, p. 104

Railroad Mooring Act
Ill. Rev. Stat. 1991, Ch. 114, § 104.01 et seq.

Railroad Mortgage Act
La. Rev. Stat. Ann., 45:381 et seq.

Railroad Motive Power and Equipment Act
Nov. 19, 1919, Ch. 116, 41 Stat. 359

Railroad Motor and Aerial Transport Act
Ill. Rev. Stat. 1991, Ch. 114, § 49.90 et seq.

Railroad Obstructed Crossing Act
Ind. Burns' 1933, 55-2016 et seq.

Railroad Obstruction Act
Ill. Rev. Stat. 1991, Ch. 114, § 100m et seq.

Railroad Operative Contract Act
Ill. Rev. Stat. 1991, Ch. 114, § 42.9 et seq.

Railroad Overhead Bridge Act
N.J. Stat. Ann., 27:5G-5 et seq.

Railroad Pass Act
Ky. Rev. Stat. 1971, 276.240 et seq.

Railroad Passenger Removal Act
Ill. Rev. Stat. 1989, Ch. 114, § 86.9 et seq.

Railroad Passenger Service Contract Act
N.J. Stat. Ann., 27:1A-15 et seq.

Railroad Passenger Transportation Compact Act
Conn. Gen. Stat. Ann., § 16-343

Railroad Planning and Projects Act
N.M. Stat. Ann., 63-3A-1 et seq.

Railroad Police Act
Ill. Rev. Stat. 1991, Ch. 114, § 97.9 et seq.
Md. Ann. Code 1957, Art. 23, § 256 et seq.
Me. Rev. Stat. Ann. 1964, Title 23, § 6071 et seq.
Miss. Code Ann. 1972, § 77-9-501 et seq.

Railroad Powers Act
Ill. Rev. Stat. 1991, Ch. 114, § 49b.9 et seq.

Railroad Precautions Law
Tenn. Code Ann., 65-12-108 et seq.

Railroad Preservation Act
R.I. Gen. Laws 1956, 39-6.1-1 et seq.

Railroad Preservation and Assistance Act
Me. Rev. Stat. Ann. 1964, Title 23, § 7101 et seq.

Railroad Prima Facie Act
Miss. Code Ann. 1972, § 13-1-119

Railroad Rate Act
See Interstate Commerce Acts

Railroad Rate Adjustment Act of 1973
July 10, 1973, P.L. 93-69, 87 Stat. 166, 49 U.S. Code § 15a

Railroad Rates Act
Iowa Code Ann., 327D.1 et seq.
Ky. Acts 1914, Ch. 68
Minn. Stat. Ann., 218.011 et seq.
Neb. Rev. Stat. 1943, 74-801 et seq.
Ore. Rev. Stat., 760.105 et seq.
Pa. Purdon's Stat., Title 66, § 2171 et seq.

Railroad Rates Act (Freight)
Minn. Stat. Ann., 218.041 et seq.

Railroad Rates Act (Passenger)
Minn. Stat. Ann., 218.021

Railroad Redevelopment Corporation Act
N.Y. Railroad Law (Consol. Laws Ch. 49) § 300 et seq.

Railroad Regulation Act

Mich. Comp. Laws Ann., 462.2 et seq.

S.D. Codified Laws 1967, 49-16A-1 et seq.

Railroad Relocation Authority Act (Capital City)

Ill. Comp. Stat. 1992, Ch. 70, § 1910/1 et seq.

Railroad Reorganization Act

N.Y. Railroad Law (Consol. Laws Ch. 49) § 140 et seq.

Railroad Reorganization Acts

March 3, 1933, Ch. 204, 47 Stat. 1470, 11 U.S. Code §§ 101a, 203, 205

Aug. 27, 1935, Ch. 774, 49 Stat. 911, 11 U.S. Code § 205

Railroad Retirement Acts

June 27, 1934, Ch. 868, 48 Stat. 1283

Aug. 29, 1935, Ch. 812, 49 Stat. 967

June 24, 1937, Ch. 382, 50 Stat. 307, 45 U.S. Code §§ 228a to 228c, 228e to 228p, 228r, 228s

June 11, 1940, Ch. 307, 54 Stat. 264, 45 U.S. Code § 228a

Aug. 13, 1940, Ch. 664, 54 Stat. 785, (See 26 U.S. Code §§ 3231, 7701), 45 U.S. Code §§ 151, 228a, 351

Oct. 8, 1940, Ch. 757, 54 Stat. 1014, 45 U.S. Code § 228c-1

Oct. 10, 1940, Ch. 842, 54 Stat. 1100, 45 U.S. Code §§ 228a, 228i

April 8, 1942, Ch. 227, 56 Stat. 204, 45 U.S. Code §§ 228a, 228c-1, 228e, 228-s

July 31, 1946, Ch. 709, 60 Stat. 722 (See 26 U.S. Code §§ 323, 7701) 45 U.S. Code §§ 228a, 351

June 23, 1948, Ch. 608, 62 Stat. 576, 45 U.S. Code §§ 228c, 228e

Oct. 30, 1951, Ch. 632, 65 Stat. 683, 45 U.S. Code §§ 228a to 228c-1, 228e, 228q

July 18, 1952, Ch. 945, 66 Stat. 777, 45 U.S. Code §§ 228a, 228e

June 16, 1954, Ch. 300, 68 Stat. 250, 45 U.S. Code § 228c

Aug. 31, 1954, Ch. 1164, 68 Stat. 1038, 45 U.S. Code §§ 228a to 228c, 228e, 228s-1

Sept. 1, 1954, Ch. 1206, 68 Stat. 1081, 45 U.S. Code §§ 228a, 228b, 228e

Aug. 12, 1955, Ch. 869, 69 Stat. 715, 45 U.S. Code §§ 228b, 228e, 228j, 228l

Aug. 1, 1956, Ch. 836, 70 Stat. 836, 45 U.S. Code §§ 228a, 228e

Aug. 1, 1956, Ch. 837, 70 Stat. 876, 45 U.S. Code §§ 228a, 228c-1

Aug. 7, 1956, Ch. 1022, 70 Stat. 1077, 45 U.S. Code §§ 228c, 228e, 228l

Aug. 30, 1957, P.L. 85-238, 71 Stat. 520, 45 U.S. Code §§ 228a, 228e

Aug. 28, 1958, P.L. 85-840, Title VII, § 703, 72 Stat. 1056, 45 U.S. Code § 228a

Sept. 6, 1958, P.L. 85-927, 72 Stat. 1778, 45 U.S. Code §§ 228c, 228e, 228j, 228m

May 19, 1959, P.L. 86-28, 73 Stat. 25, 45 U.S. Code §§ 228b, 228c , 228e, 228s-1

Aug. 29, 1959, P.L. 86-211, 73 Stat. 436, 45 U.S. Code § 228s-1

Sept. 22, 1959, P.L. 86-346, 73 Stat. 622, 45 U.S. Code §§ 228o, 228c, 228e

June 30, 1961, P.L. 87-64, 75 Stat. 142, 45 U.S. Code § 228a

Sept. 22, 1961, P.L. 87-285, 75 Stat. 585, 45 U.S. Code §§ 228b, 228e

Oct. 5, 1963, P.L. 88-133, 77 Stat. 219, 45 U.S. Code §§ 228c, 228c-1, 228e, 228o

July 30, 1965, P.L. 89-97, 79 Stat. 335, 45 U.S. Code §§ 228a, 228e, 228s-2

Sept. 29, 1965, P.L. 89-212, 79 Stat. 858, 45 U.S. Code §§ 228a to 228c, 228e

Oct. 30, 1966, P.L. 89-699, 80 Stat. 1073, 45 U.S. Code §§ 228b, 228c, 228e, 228o

Oct. 30, 1966, P.L. 89-700, 80 Stat. 1079, 45 U.S. Code §§ 228a to 228c-1, 228e, 228h, 228i, 228j, 228s, 228s-1

Jan. 2, 1968, P.L. 90-248, 81 Stat. 860, 45 U.S. Code § 228e

Feb. 15, 1968, P.L. 90-257, 82 Stat. 16, 45 U.S. Code §§ 228a to 228c, 228e, 228j

Oct. 22, 1968, P.L. 90-624, 82 Stat. 1316, 45 U.S. Code § 228a

March 17, 1970, P.L. 91-215, 84 Stat. 70, 45 U.S. Code §§ 228c, 228o

Aug. 12, 1970, P.L. 91-377, 84 Stat. 791, 45 U.S. Code §§ 228b, 228c, 228e, 228o

July 2, 1971, P.L. 92-46, 85 Stat. 101, 45 U.S. Code §§ 228b, 228c, 228e

Oct. 4, 1972, P.L. 92-460, 86 Stat. 765, 45 U.S. Code §§ 228b, 228c, 228e

Oct. 30, 1972, P.L. 92-603, 86 Stat. 1373, 45 U.S. Code § 228s-3

July 6, 1973, P.L. 93-58, 87 Stat. 141, 45 U.S. Code §§ 228c, 28e

July 10, 1973, P.L. 93-69, 87 Stat. 162, 45 U.S. Code §§ 228b, 228c, 228e

Oct. 16, 1974, P.L. 93-445, 45 U.S. Code §§ 231 et seq.

Aug. 9, 1975, P.L. 94-92, 89 Stat. 464, 45 U.S. Code §§ 231 nt., 231n

Oct. 18, 1976, P.L. 94-547, 45 U.S. Code §§ 231 et seq.

Nov. 4, 1979, P.L. 96-101, 45 U.S. Code § 231f

May 30, 1980, P.L. 96-254, 45 U.S. Code § 231f

July 18, 1984, P.L. 98-369, 98 Stat. 1097, 45 U.S. Code § 231f

Oct. 18, 1988, P.L. 100-504, 45 U.S. Code § 231v

Nov. 10, 1988, P.L. 100-647, 45 U.S. Code §§ 231, 231a, 231e

Dec. 21, 1995, P.L. 104-66, 45 U.S. Code § 231u

Dec. 29, 1995, P.L. 104-88, 45 U.S. Code § 231

Oct. 21, 1998, P.L. 105-277, 45 U.S. Code § 231e

Railroad Retirement Board Appropriation Acts

June 26, 1940, Ch. 428, 54 Stat. 596

July 1, 1941, Ch. 269, 55 Stat. 496

July 2, 1942, Ch. 475, 56 Stat. 590

July 12, 1943, Ch. 221, 57 Stat. 516

June 28, 1944, Ch. 302, 58 Stat. 569

July 3, 1945, Ch. 263, 59 Stat. 379

July 26, 1946, Ch. 672, 60 Stat. 699

July 8, 1947, Ch. 210, 61 Stat. 277

June 14, 1948, Ch. 465, 62 Stat. 405

June 29, 1949, Ch. 275, 63 Stat. 297

Sept. 6, 1950, Ch. 896, 64 Stat. 656

Aug. 31, 1951, Ch. 373, 65 Stat. 222

July 5, 1952, Ch. 575, 66 Stat. 371

July 31, 1953, Ch. 296, 67 Stat. 258

Aug. 16, 1954, Ch. 736, 68A Stat. 431, 26 U.S. Code §§ 3201, 3202, 3211, 3212, 3221, 3231 to 3233

Aug. 31, 1954, Ch. 1164, 68 Stat. 1040, 26 U.S. Code §§ 3201, 3202, 3211, 3221, 3231

Railroad Retirement Revenue Act of 1983

Aug. 12, 1983, P.L. 98-76, 97 Stat. 419

April 7, 1986, P.L. 99-272, 45 U.S. Code § 231 nt.

Nov. 10, 1988, P.L. 100-647, 45 U.S. Code § 231n nt.

Nov. 5, 1990, P.L. 101-508, 45 U.S. Code § 231n nt.

Railroad Retirement Solvency Act of 1983

Aug. 12, 1983, P.L. 98-76, 97 Stat. 411, 45 U.S. Code § 231t nt.

Dec. 22, 1987, P.L. 100-203, 45 U.S. Code § 231n nt.

Dec. 19, 1989, P.L. 101-239, 45 U.S. Code § 231n nt.

Nov. 5, 1990, P.L. 101-508, 45 U.S. Code § 231n nt.

Aug. 15, 1994, P.L. 103-296, 45 U.S. Code § 231m nt.

Dec. 21, 1995, P.L. 104-66, 45 U.S. Code § 231f-1

Railroad Retirement Tax Act

July 31, 1946, Ch. 709, 60 Stat. 722 (See 26 U.S. Code §§ 3201 to 3233, 3501 to 3503, 6011, 6071, 6081, 6091, 6151, 6205, 6303, 6313, 6513, 7701) 45 U.S. Code §§ 228a, 351

Aug. 16, 1954, Ch. 736, 68A, Stat. 431, 26 U.S. Code §§ 3201, 3202, 3211, 3212, 3221, 3231 to 3233

Aug. 31, 1954, Ch. 1164, 68 Stat. 1040, 26 U.S. Code §§ 3201, 3202, 3211, 3221, 3231

May 19, 1959, P.L. 86-28, 73 Stat. 28, 26 U.S. Code §§ 3201, 3202 , 3211, 3221

Oct. 5, 1963, P.L. 88-133, 77 Stat. 221, 26 U.S. Code §§ 3201, 3202, 3211, 3221

July 30, 1965, P.L. 89-97, 79 Stat. 335, 26 U.S. Code §§ 3201, 3211, 3221

Oct. 30, 1966, P.L. 89-699, 80 Stat. 1078, 26 U.S. Code §§ 3201, 3211, 3221

Oct. 30, 1966, P.L. 89-700, 80 Stat. 1088, 26 U.S. Code §§ 3201, 3202, 3211, 3221

Oct. 22, 1968, P.L. 90-624, 82 Stat. 1316, 26 U.S. Code § 3231

March 17, 1970, P.L. 91-215, 84 Stat. 70, 26 U.S. Code §§ 3211, 3221

Aug. 9, 1975, P.L. 94-93, 89 Stat. 466, 26 U.S. Code §§ 3201, 3211, 3221, 3231

Railroad Revitalization Act

Okla. Stat. Ann., Title 66, § 302.1 et seq.

Railroad Revitalization and Regulatory Reform Act of 1976

Feb. 5, 1976, P.L. 94-210, 45 U.S. Code §§ 801 et seq.

Nov. 1, 1978, P.L. 95-565, 45 U.S. Code § 825

Nov. 8, 1978, P.L. 95-607, 45 U.S. Code §§ 825, 827, 829

Nov. 9, 1978, P.L. 95-620, 45 U.S. Code §§ 821, 822, 825

Sept. 29, 1979, P.L. 96-73, 45 U.S. Code §§ 825, 827, 829

Nov. 4, 1979, P.L. 96-101, 45 U.S. Code §§ 821, 825

May 30, 1980, P.L. 96-254, 45 U.S. Code §§ 825, 835, 851 et seq.

Dec. 21, 1982, P.L. 97-375, 45 U.S. Code § 835

April 7, 1986, P.L. 99-272, 45 U.S. Code § 853

July 2, 1986, P.L. 99-349, 45 U.S. Code § 827 nt.

Oct. 21, 1986, P.L. 99-509, 45 U.S. Code §§ 821, 825, 829, 831

June 22, 1988, P.L. 100-342, 45 U.S. Code § 854

Dec. 18, 1991, P.L. 102-240, 45 U.S. Code § 831

Oct. 27, 1992, P.L. 102-533, 45 U.S. Code §§ 838, 856

Oct. 31, 1994, P.L. 103-429, 45 U.S. Code § 856

Dec. 29, 1995, P.L. 104-88, 45 U.S. Code §§ 802, 825, 829, 830

June 9, 1998, P.L. 105-178, 45 U.S. Code §§ 821 to 824

Railroad Right of Way Act (Fences)

N.Y. Railroad Law (Consol. Laws Ch. 49) § 52b

Railroad Right of Way Acts

March 3, 1875, Ch. 152, 18 Stat. 482, 43 U.S. Code §§ 934 to 939

March 2, 1899, Ch. 374, 30 Stat. 990, 25 U.S. Code §§ 312 to 318

Railroad Right-of-Way Conveyance Validation Act of 1985

Oct. 27, 1986, P.L. 99-543, 100 Stat. 3040

Railroad Right-of-Way Preservation and Bridge Rehabilitation and Improvement Bond Act

N.J. Laws 1991, Ch. 180

Railroad Right of Way Reversion Act

Iowa Code Ann., 327G.77

Railroad Safety Act

Me. Rev. Stat. Ann. 1964, Title 23, § 7301 et seq., Title 35, § 771 et seq.

Railroad Safety Appliance Act

Wash. Rev. Code Ann., 81.44.031 et seq.

Railroad Sanitation Act

Ill. Rev. Stat. 1991, Ch. 114, § 100.9 et seq.

Railroad Settlement Act

N.J. Stat. Ann., App. A:4-7.1 et seq., App. A:4-7.14 et seq.

Railroad Speed Act

Miss. Code Ann. 1972, § 77-9-237

Railroad Standard Clearance Act

Minn. Stat. Ann., 219.45 et seq.

Railroad Station Blackboard Act

Ind. Code 1971, 8-2-26-1, 8-2-26-2

Railroad Stock Liability Act (Livestock)

Kan. Stat. Ann., 66-265, 66-295 et seq., 66-317, 66-318

Railroad Stock Transfer Act

Ill. Rev. Stat. 1991, Ch. 114, § 29m et seq.

Railroad Subscription Act

Tenn. Code Ann., 65-7-101 et seq.

Railroad Tax Act

Mo. Rev. Stat., 151.010 et seq.

Neb. Rev. Stat. 1943, 77-601 et seq.

N.J. Stat. Ann., 54:29A-1 et seq.

Tenn. Code Ann., 67-5-1301 et seq.

Railroad Tax Act (Central)

Ill. Comp. Stat. 1992, Ch. 35, § 605/0.01 et seq.

Railroad Tax Moratorium Act
N.Y. Real Property Tax Law (Consol. Laws Ch. 50A) § 489a et seq.

Railroad Terminal Authority Act
Ill. Rev. Stat. 1991, Ch. 114, § 361 et seq.

Railroad Transportation of Hazardous Materials Act
Ill. Rev. Stat. 1991, Ch. 114, § 501 et seq.

Railroad Unemployment Insurance Act
June 25, 1938, Ch. 680, 52 Stat. 1094, 42 U.S. Code §§ 503, 1104, 1107; 45 U.S. Code §§ 351 to 364, 366, 367

June 20, 1939, Ch. 227, 53 Stat. 845, 42 U.S. Code § 503; 45 U.S. Code §§ 351 to 354, 356, 360 to 363, 366a

July 2, 1940, Ch. 530, 54 Stat. 741, 45 U.S. Code § 363

Oct. 10, 1940, Ch. 842, 54 Stat. 1094, 45 U.S. Code §§ 351 to 356, 361, 362

April 8, 1942, Ch. 227, 56 Stat. 210, 45 U.S. Code § 351, 351 nt.

June 30, 1942, Ch. 463, 56 Stat. 465, 45 U.S. Code § 363

July 31, 1946, Ch. 709, 60 Stat. 722 (See 26 U.S. Code §§ 3231, 7701) 45 U.S. Code §§ 228a, 351 to 356, 358, 362, 363

June 23, 1948, Ch. 608, 62 Stat. 577, 45 U.S. Code §§ 358, 360, 361

Oct. 30, 1951, Ch. 632, 65 Stat. 691, 45 U.S. Code §§ 351, 354

May 15, 1952, Ch. 290, 66 Stat. 73, 45 U.S. Code §§ 352, 353

Aug. 31, 1954, Ch. 1164, 68 Stat. 1041, 45 U.S. Code §§ 351, 352, 358

Aug. 12, 1955, Ch. 869, 69 Stat. 716, 45 U.S. Code §§ 352, 362

Aug. 28, 1958, P.L. 85-791, 72 Stat. 948, 45 U.S. Code § 355

Sept. 6, 1958, P.L. 85-927, 72 Stat. 1782, 45 U.S. Code §§ 351, 354, 358, 361, 362

May 19, 1959, P.L. 86-28, 73 Stat. 30, 45 U.S. Code §§ 351 to 354, 358, 360

June 11, 1960, P.L. 86-507, 74 Stat. 202, 45 U.S. Code § 362

Oct. 5, 1963, P.L. 88-133, 77 Stat. 222, 45 U.S. Code §§ 353, 354 , 358, 360

Oct. 30, 1966, P.L. 89-700, 80 Stat. 1087, 45 U.S. Code §§ 351, 352, 356, 358, 360, 362

Feb. 15, 1968, P.L. 90-257, 82 Stat. 23, 45 U.S. Code §§ 351 to 354, 360, 362, 363

Oct. 22, 1968, P.L. 90-624, 82 Stat. 1316, 45 U.S. Code § 351

Oct. 15, 1970, P.L. 91-452, 84 Stat. 930, 45 U.S. Code § 362

Aug. 9, 1975, P.L. 94-92, 89 Stat. 461, 45 U.S. Code §§ 351 to 353, 358, 360, 361

Nov. 8, 1984, P.L. 98-620, 45 U.S. Code § 355

Sept. 30, 1985, P.L. 99-107, 45 U.S. Code § 360

Nov. 14, 1985, P.L. 99-155, 45 U.S. Code § 360

Dec. 13, 1985, P.L. 99-181, 45 U.S. Code § 360

Dec. 18, 1985, P.L. 99-189, 45 U.S. Code § 360

April 7, 1986, P.L. 99-272, 45 U.S. Code § 360

Nov. 10, 1988, P.L. 100-647, 45 U.S. Code §§ 351 et seq., 360 et seq.

July 6, 1990, P.L. 101-322, 45 U.S. Code §§ 358, 358 nt.

Dec. 29, 1995, P.L. 104-88, 45 U.S. Code §§ 351, 352

Oct. 9, 1996, P.L. 104-251, 45 U.S. Code §§ 352, 368

Railroad Unemployment Insurance Amendments Act of 1996
Oct. 9, 1996, P.L. 104-251, 45 U.S. Code § 367 nt.

Railroad Unemployment Insurance and Retirement Improvement Act of 1988
Nov. 10, 1988, P.L. 100-647, 45 U.S. Code § 367 nt.

Railroad Union Depot Act
N.C. Gen. Stat. 1943, § 62-231

Railroad Water Craft Act
Ill. Rev. Stat. 1991, Ch. 114, § 46.9 et seq.

Railroad Widening Act
Pa. Purdon's Stat., Title 15, § 4081 et seq.

Railroads Income Tax Act
Alaska Comp. Laws Ann. 1949, §§ 48-8-1, 48-8-2

Railroads Rate Law
Neb. Rev. Stat. 1943, 74-801 et seq.

Rails to Trails Act
Pa. Purdon's Stat., Title 32, § 5611 et seq.

Rails to Trails Program
W. Va. Code 1966, § 5B-1A-1 et seq.

Railway Construction Promotion Act (Oahu)
Haw. Session Laws 1888, Ch. 62

Railway Employees Water Act
Ill. Rev. Stat. 1991, Ch. 111 2/3, § 370 et seq.

Railway Finance Authority Act
Iowa Code Ann., 307B.1 et seq.

Railway Franchise Act
Haw. Session Laws 1898, Act 69

Railway Joint Rates Act
Minn. Stat. Ann., 218.031 et seq.

Railway Labor Act
May 20, 1926, Ch. 347, 44 Stat. 577 (See 15 U.S. Code §§ 21, 45) 18 U.S. Code § 373; 28 U.S. Code §§ 1291 to 1294; 45 U.S. Code §§ 151 to 163, 181 to 188
June 21, 1934, Ch. 691, 48 Stat. 1185, 45 U.S. Code §§ 151 to 158, 160 to 162
April 10, 1936, Ch. 166, 49 Stat. 1189, 45 U.S. Code §§ 181 to 188
Jan. 10, 1951, Ch. 1220, 64 Stat. 1238, 45 U.S. Code § 152
Aug. 31, 1964, P.L. 88-542, 78 Stat. 748, 45 U.S. Code § 154
June 20, 1966, P.L. 89-456, 80 Stat. 208, 45 U.S. Code § 153
April 23, 1970, P.L. 91-234, 84 Stat. 199, 45 U.S. Code § 153
Oct. 15, 1970, P.L. 91-452, 84 Stat. 930, 45 U.S. Code § 157
Aug. 4, 1988, P.L. 100-380, 102 Stat. 896
Oct. 19, 1994, P.L. 103-380, 108 Stat. 3512
Dec. 29, 1995, P.L. 104-88, 45 U.S. Code § 151
Oct. 9, 1996, P.L. 104-264, 45 U.S. Code § 151
Minn. Stat. Ann., 219.79

Railway Mail Service Pay Act
July 28, 1916, Ch. 261, 39 Stat. 412

Railways Services at Cost Act (Street)
Mass. Gen. Laws Ann., 161:115 et seq.

Rain Control Act (Acid)
N.H. Rev. Stat. 1955, 125-D:1 et seq.

Raines Law (Liquor Tax)
N.Y. Laws 1896, Ch. 112

Rains-Levine Community Crime Prevention Act
Cal. Penal Code § 13840 et seq.

Raised Check Act
Conn. Gen. Stat. Ann., § 42a-4-406

Raker Act (Reclamation and Irrigation)
May 15, 1922, Ch. 190, 42 Stat. 541, 12 U.S. Code § 773; 43 U.S. Code §§ 511 to 513

Raleigh Charter
N.C. Laws 1949, Ch. 1184

Raleigh Civil Service Act
N.C. Laws 1981, Ch. 241

Ralph C. Dills Act
Cal. Government Code § 3524

Ralph Civil Rights Act
Cal. Civil Code §§ 51.7, 52
Cal. Labor Code § 1419

Ralph M. Brown Act (Public Meetings)
Cal. Government Code § 54950 et seq.

Ralph Sewer Act
Mo. Laws 1927, p. 439

Ram Act
Kan. Stat. Ann., 47-111

Ramapo Consumer Protection Law
N.Y. Local Laws 1972, p. 2670

Ramapo Contract Deposit and Maintenance Law
N.Y. Local Laws 1967, pp. 1911, 1915

Ramapo Department of Finance Law
N.Y. Local Laws 1968, p. 2927

Ramapo Department of Parks and Recreation Law
N.Y. Local Laws 1967, p. 1920

Ramapo Department of Public Works Law
N.Y. Local Laws 1968, p. 2944

Ramapo Development Easement Acquisition Law
N.Y. Local Laws 1967, p. 1895

Ramapo Interim Development Law
N.Y. Local Laws 1966, p. 1520
N.Y. Local Laws 1971, p. 3173

Ramapo Management and Maintenance Law of Parking, Accessory and Other Areas
N.Y. Local Laws 1969, p. 2013

Ramapo Peddler and Solicitor Law
N.Y. Local Laws 1971, p. 3176

Ramapo Refuse Removal Law
N.Y. Local Laws 1969, p. 2005

Ramapo Sewer Rent Law
N.Y. Local Laws 1969, p. 2017

Ramapo Sewer System Licensing and Use Law
N.Y. Local Laws 1967, p. 1899

Ramapo Soil and Excavation Law
N.Y. Local Laws 1968, p. 2938

Ramapo Traffic Violations Bureau Law
N.Y. Local Laws 1969, p. 2016

Ramapo Village Incorporation Law
N.Y. Local Laws 1967, p. 1908

Ramapo Visual Road Obstruction Law
N.Y. Local Laws 1971, p. 3161

Ramey Act (County Sewers)
Ohio Laws Vol. 110, p. 338

Ramey-McCarthy Old Age Assistant Act
Ky. Rev. Stat. 1971, 205.010 et seq.

Ramon Turnquest School Crossing Guard Act
Fla. Laws 1992, Ch. 194

Ramsey County Civil Service Act
Minn. Laws 1941, Ch. 513

Ramspeck Act
Nov. 26, 1940, Ch. 919, 54 Stat. 1211 (See 5 U.S. Code §§ 2102, 3304)
Dec. 19, 1995, P.L. 104-65, 5 U.S. Code §§ 3304, 3304 nt.

Ramspeck-Mead Act
Aug. 1, 1941, Ch. 346, 55 Stat. 613

Ranch and Farm Heritage Museum Act
N.M. Stat. Ann., 18-11-1 et seq.

Randall, Stacey and Bennett Shareholder Equity Act
Mich. Comp. Laws Ann., 450.1790 et seq.

Randolph Act (Uniform Act on Fresh Pursuit)
D.C. Code Ann., § 23-901 et seq.

Randolph County, Carbondale, Riverside, Matteson, Ottawa, Illinois Valley, Waukegan, and Pontiac Civic Centers Act
Ill. Rev. Stat. 1989, Ch. 85, § 7000-1 et seq.

Randolph County Civic Center Law
Ill. Rev. Stat. 1991, Ch. 85, § 7001-1 et seq.

Randolph County Salary Act
Ark. 1948 Initiated Act No. 2 of Randolph County

Randolph-Cuthbert Airport Authority Act
Ga. Laws 1971, p. 2837

Randolph Sewerage Loan Act
Mass. Acts 1955, Ch. 273
Mass. Acts 1960, Ch. 278

Randolph-Sheppard Act
Aug. 7, 1998, P.L. 105-220, 20 U.S. Code § 107a

Randolph-Sheppard Act Amendments of 1974
Nov. 21, 1974, P.L. 93-651, 5 U.S. Code § 5108; 20 U.S. Code §§ 107 to 107b-3, 107d to 107d-4, 107e

Randolph-Sheppard Vending Stand Act
June 20, 1936, Ch. 638, 49 Stat. 1559, 20 U.S. Code §§ 107 to 107f
Aug. 3, 1954, Ch. 655, 68 Stat. 663, 20 U.S. Code §§ 107 to 107f

Range Act (Fences)
Mont. Code Ann., 81-4-101 et seq.

Range Act (Public Domain)
Colo. Rev. Stat., 35-45-101 et seq.

Range Clearance and Revegetation Act
Cal. Public Resources Code §§ 4771, 4861 et seq.

Range Code
Nev. Rev. Stat. 1979 Reprint, 568.010 et seq.

Range Court Act
Minn. Stat. Ann., 484.01 et seq.

Range Levy Act
N.M. Stat. Ann., 39-6-1 et seq.

Rangeland Grasshopper Control Act (Insect Pests and Plant Diseases)
Neb. Rev. Stat. 1943, 2-1066 et seq.

Rangeland Protection Act
N.M. Stat. Ann., 76-7B-1 et seq.

Rangeland Renewable Resources Planning Act
Aug. 17, 1974, P.L. 93-378, 16 U.S. Code § 1600 et seq.

Rangeland Resources Act
Mont. Code Ann., 76-14-101 et seq.

Rankin Act
See Gold Star Mothers Act

Rankin Veterans Act
May 3, 1939, Ch. 109, 53 Stat. 652

Rankin Veterans Pension Act
June 10, 1942, Ch. 402, 56 Stat. 350

Rankin World War Widows Act
May 13, 1938, Ch. 214, 52 Stat. 352

Ransdell Act
May 26, 1930, Ch. 320, 46 Stat. 379

RAP Act (Rural Access Program)
Ala. Code 1975, § 23-1-330 et seq.

Rape Act
Ark. Code Ann. 1987, 5-14-101
Cal. Penal Code § 261 et seq.
D.C. Code 1973, § 22-2801
Ill. Rev. Stat. 1991, Ch. 38, § 12-12 et seq.
Mich. Comp. Laws Ann., 750.520
Mo. Rev. Stat., 566.030, Subsec. 3
Mont. Code Ann., 45-5-501 et seq.
N.C. Gen. Stat. 1943, §§ 14-21 et seq., 14-27.1
N.H. Rev. Stat. 1955, 632-A:1 et seq.
Ohio Rev. Code 1953, 2907.02, Subd. A, 2
R.I. Gen. Laws 1956, 11-37-1 et seq.
Tenn. Code Ann., 39-13-502 et seq.
Wash. Rev. Code Ann., 9A.44.010 et seq.

Rape Shield Act
N.H. Rev. Stat. 1955, 632-A:6
N.M. Stat. Ann., 30-9-16
Wash. Rev. Code Ann., 9A.44.020
Wis. Stat. Ann., 972.11, Subsec. 2

Rape Victims Assistance Act
N.C. Gen. Stat. 1943, § 143B-480.1 et seq.

Rape Victims Emergency Treatment Act
Ill. Rev. Stat. 1991, Ch. 111 1/2, § 87-1 et seq.

Rapid Rail Transit Compact (Mississippi-Louisiana-Alabama-Georgia)
Ala. Code 1975, § 37-11-1
Ga. Code Ann., 46-9-300
Miss. Code Ann. 1972, § 57-45-1

Rapid Transit Act
N.Y. Consol. Laws, Ch. 48A
N.Y. Railroad Law (Consol. Laws Ch. 49) § 220 et seq.

Rapid Transit Authority Act (Atlanta)
Ga. Laws 1965, p. 2243

Rapid Transit Authority Act (West Bay)
Cal. Public Utility Code Appendix 2, § 1.1 et seq.

Rapid Transit District Act (San Francisco Bay Area)
Cal. Public Utilities Code § 28500 et seq.

Rapid Transit Franchise Act
Haw. Session Laws 1898, Act 69

Rapid Transit Noise Code Act
N.Y. Public Authorities Law (Consol. Laws Ch. 43A) § 1204

Rare Plant Protection and Conservation Act
Tenn. Code Ann., 70-8-301 et seq.

Rare Plant Recognition Act
Ky. Acts 1994, Ch. 164, §§ 1 to 4

Rash Gullion Act
Ky. Acts 1922, Ch. 33

Rate Act
See Interstate Commerce Acts

Rate Act (Negotiated)
Minn. Stat. Ann., 256I.01 et seq.

Rate Law (Railroads)
Neb. Rev. Stat. 1943, 74-801 et seq.

Rate of Prevailing Wage Act
N.Y. Labor Law (Consol. Laws Ch. 31) § 220 et seq.

Rate Reduction and Tax Reform Act (Business)
N.Y. Laws 1991, Ch. 817

Rate Reform Act (Electric)
Me. Rev. Stat. Ann. 1964, Title 35-A, § 3151 et seq.

Rate Regulation Act (Casualty and Surety Insurance)
See Casualty and Surety Rate Regulatory Act

Rate Regulation Act (Insurance)
Ark. Code Ann. 1987, 23-67-101 et seq.
Ark. Stat. 1947, 66-401 et seq.
N.M. Stat. Ann., 59A-17-1 et seq.
Pa. Purdon's Stat., Title 40, § 1181 et seq.

Rate Regulatory Act (Fire, Marine and Inland Marine Insurance)
Mass. Gen. Laws Ann., 174A:1 et seq.
Pa. Purdon's Stat., Title 40, § 1221 et seq.

Rate Regulatory Act (Insurance)
Ga. Code Ann., 33-9-1 et seq.

Rate Regulatory Act (Railroads)
Pa. Purdon's Stat., Title 66, § 2171 et seq.

Rate Regulatory Act (Title Insurance)
Pa. 1953 Pamph. Laws 1312, No. 372

Rate Regulatory Law (Casualty and Surety)
Mass. Gen. Laws Ann., 175A:1 et seq.

Rate Revision and Modification Act
See Uniform Rate Revision and Modification Act

Ratemaking Act
Mont. Code Ann., 33-16-103
Mont. Laws 1991, Ch. 400

Rates of Interest Act
Wis. Stat. Ann., 138.01 et seq.

Rating Act
Fla. Stat. Ann., 627.011 et seq.

Rating Act (Casualty)
Wis. Stat. Ann., 204.37 et seq.

Rating Act (Fire Insurance)
See Fire Insurance Rating Act

Rating Act (Insurance Other Than Life)
Mo. Rev. Stat., 379.316 et seq.

Rating Act (Insurance)
Ala. Code 1975, § 27-13-1 et seq.
Cal. Insurance Code § 11730 et seq.

Rating Act (Workers' Compensation)
Me. Rev. Stat. Ann. 1964, Title 24-A, § 2361 et seq.

Rating Bureau Act (Insurance)
Ind. Code Ann., 27-1-22-1 et seq.

Rating Law (Insurance)
Fla. Stat. Ann., 627.011 et seq.

Rating Organization Act
Mich. Comp. Laws Ann., 500.2436 et seq., 500.2630 et seq.

Rating, Renewability and Portability Health Insurance Act (Small Employer)
Ill. Comp. Stat. 1992, Ch. 215, § 95/1-1 et seq.

Ratio Act
N.Y. Laws 1910, Ch. 494

Ratliff-Ward Textbook Act
Ky. Rev. Stat. 1971, 156.405, 156.447, 156.474, 156.475, 157.100, 157.110

Rattigan-Burton Act (Medical Assistance for Aged)
Cal. Welfare and Institutions Code §§ 4700 et seq., 14500

Rattlesnake National Recreation Area and Wilderness Act of 1980
Oct. 19, 1980, P.L. 96-476, 16 U.S. Code § 460ll nt.
Oct. 31, 1983, P.L. 98-140, 16 U.S. Code § 460ll-3

Rawson-McCallum Act (Statutes of Limitations)
Mich. Comp. Laws Ann., 600.2915, 600.5805, 600.5807, 600.5809, 600.5813, 600.5821

Ray-Fitzpatrick-Lowman-Rayburn Act (Teachers' Retirement)
Ky. Rev. Stat. 1971, 161.220, 161.260, 161.290, 161.340, 161.400, 161.410, 161.430, 161.470, 161.515, 161.540, 161.550, 161.600, 161.620,

Rayburn, Lyon, Hayes, Cline, Lowman Act (Workmen's Compensation)
Ky. Rev. Stat. 1971, 342.121, 342.185, 342.315, 342.316

Rayburn-Porter Act (Teachers' Retirement System)
Ky. Rev. Stat. 1971, 161.220 et seq.

Rayburn-Ray-Fitzpatrick-Lowman Act (Teachers' Retirement)
Ky. Rev. Stat. 1971, 161.220, 161.260, 161.290, 161.340, 161.400, 161.410, 161.430, 161.470, 161.515, 161.540, 161.550, 161.600, 161.620

Raymond B. Stewart Career Achievement Program Act
Fla. Stat. Ann., 231.5335 et seq.

Raymond H. Alexander, M.D., Emergency Medical Transportation Services Act
Fla. Stat. Ann., 401.2101 et seq.

Re-enrollment Act
Ky. Public Acts 1865, Ch. 1300

Re-entry or Entry Rights Act
Ill. Rev. Stat. 1991, Ch. 30, § 37a.9 et seq.

Re-inspection of Motor Vehicles following Accidents Act
N.Y. Vehicle and Traffic Law 1959 (Consol. Laws Ch. 71) § 301a

R.E. Van Norstrand Neighborhood Assistance Act
Conn. Gen. Stat. Ann., § 12-631 et seq.

Reach and Apply Act (Insurance Proceeds)
Me. Rev. Stat. Ann. 1964, Title 24-A, § 2904

Reach Program Act
N.J. Stat. Ann., 44:10-12 et seq.

Readability of Insurance Policies Act
Minn. Stat. Ann., 72C.01 et seq.

Readable Insurance Certificate Act (Hospital, Medical and Dental Service Corporation)
N.C. Gen. Stat. 1943, § 58-66-1 et seq.

Readable Insurance Policies Act
N.C. Gen. Stat. 1943, § 58-38-1 et seq.

Reading Education Act (Remedial)
Fla. Laws 1971, Ch. 71-273

Reading Initiative Program
Cal. Education Code 1976, §§ 19335, 19336

Reading Study Act
Cal. Education Code 1959, § 9775 § 54100 et seq.

Ready to Learn Act
Oct. 27, 1992, P.L. 102-545, 20 U.S. Code § 2701 nt.

Reagan-De la Garza Act
Tex. Natural Resources Code, § 33.001 et seq.

Real Actions Statute of Limitations
Tenn. Code Ann., 28-2-101 et seq.

Real and Personal Tax Rate Act for Tax Year 1978
D.C. Code Ann., § 47-501 et seq.

Real Estate Agency Corporation Act of 1915
Ill. Laws 1915, p. 330

Real Estate and Business Brokers Act
La. Rev. Stat. Ann., 37:1431 et seq.

Real Estate and Business Brokers License Act
D.C. Code Ann., § 45-1901 et seq.

Real Estate Appraisal Act
Neb. Rev. Stat. 1943, 77-1301 et seq.

Real Estate Appraisal Licensing and Certification Act
Me. Rev. Stat. Ann. 1964, Title 32, § 13961 et seq.

Real Estate Appraisal Voluntary Certification Act
Ky. Rev. Stat. 1971, 324A.010 et seq.

Real Estate Appraiser Act
Ala. Code 1975, § 34-27A-1 et seq.
Ida. Code 1947, 54-4101 et seq.
Md. Ann. Code 1974, Art. BO, § 16-101 et seq.
Wash. Rev. Code Ann., 18.140.900 et seq.

Real Estate Appraiser Act (Certified)
Ida. Code 1947, 54-4101 et seq.
Okla. Stat. Ann., Title 59, §§ 858-700 et seq.
Wash. Rev. Code Ann., 18.140.005 et seq.
Wyo. Stat. Ann., § 33-39-101 et seq.

Real Estate Appraiser Certification Act
Pa. Purdon's. Stat., Title 63, § 457.1 et seq.
R.I. Gen. Laws 1956, 5-20.7-1 et seq.

Real Estate Appraiser Licensing Act
Ill. Comp. Stat. 1992, Ch. 225, § 457/1 et seq.

Real Estate Appraiser Licensing and Certification Act
Cal. Business and Professions Code § 11300 et seq.
Ga. Code Ann., 43-39A-1 et seq.
Miss. Code Ann. 1972, § 73-34-1 et seq.
Mont. Laws 1991, Ch. 409, §§ 1, 2, 4 to 28
Neb. Rev. Stat. 1943, 76-2201 et seq.
W. Va. Code 1966 § 37-14-1 et seq.

Real Estate Appraiser Registration and Certification Act
Utah Code Ann. 1953, 61-2b-1 et seq.

Real Estate Appraiser Registration, License, and Certification Act
S.C. Code Ann. 1976, § 40-60-10 et seq.

Real Estate Appraisers Act

Ala. Code 1975, § 34-27A-1

N.C. Gen. Stat., § 93A-70 et seq.

N.J. Stat. Ann., 45:14F-1 et seq.

N.M. Stat. Ann., 61-30-1 et seq.

Okla. Stat. 1981, Title 59, § 858-700 et seq.

Real Estate Board Act

N.H. Rev. Stat. 1955, 331-A:1-a et seq.

Real Estate Bond Act

N.D. Cent. Code, 54-30-01 et seq.

Real Estate Broker and Salesperson Licensing Act

Ga. Code Ann., 43-40-1 et seq.

Ind. Code Ann., 25-34.1-1-1 et seq.

Kan. Stat. Ann., 58-3034 et seq.

Real Estate Broker Lien Law (Commercial)

Ill. Comp. Stat. 1992, Ch. 770, § 15/1 et seq.

Pa. 1998 Pamph. Laws, No. 34

Real Estate Brokerage Representation Act

Ida. Code 1947, 54-2060 et seq.

Real Estate Brokers' Act

Ida. Code 1947, 54-2021 et seq.

Iowa Code Ann., 117.1 et seq.

Mass. Gen. Laws Ann., 112:87 PP et seq.

Md. Ann. Code 1957, Art. 56, § 212 et seq.

Md. Ann. Code 1974, Arts. BO, § 17-101 et seq., RP, § 14-105

Mont. Code Ann., 37-51-101 et seq.

N.C. Gen. Stat. 1943, § 93A-1 et seq.

Neb. Rev. Stat. 1943, 81-885.01 et seq.

Nev. Rev. Stat. 1979 Reprint, 645.001 et seq.

N.H. Rev. Stat. 1955, 331-A:1 et seq.

N.M. Stat. Ann., 61-29-1 et seq.

Ohio Rev. Code 1953, 4735.01 et seq.

Ore. Rev. Stat., 696.010 et seq.

S.C. Code Ann. 1976, § 40-57-10 et seq.

Tex. Rev. Civ. Stat., Art. 6573a

Utah Code Ann. 1953, 61-2-1 et seq.

Va. Code 1950, § 54.1-2100 et seq.

Vt. Stat. Ann., Title 26, § 2211 et seq.

Wash. Rev. Code Ann., 18.85.010 et seq.

Wis. Stat. Ann., 452.01 et seq.

Real Estate Brokers' Advance Fee Act

Conn. Gen. Stat. Ann., § 20-320

Real Estate Brokers and Salesman Act

Cal. Business and Professions Code § 1000 et seq.

Real Estate Brokers' and Salesmen's License Act

Colo. Rev. Stat., 12-61-101 et seq.

Ill. Rev. Stat. 1991, Ch. 111, § 5801 et seq.

N.Y. Real Property Law (Consol. Laws Ch. 50) § 440a

Wyo. Stat. Ann., § 33-28-101 et seq.

Real Estate Brokers' Escrow Accounts Act

Miss. Code Ann. 1972, § 73-35-101 et seq.

Real Estate Brokers' License Act

Kan. Stat. Ann., 58-3034 et seq.

Mich. Comp. Laws Ann., 451.201 et seq.

Minn. Stat. Ann., 82.17 et seq.

Miss. Code Ann. 1972, § 73-35-1 et seq.

Mo. Rev. Stat., 339.010 et seq.

N.J. Rev. Stat. Ann., 45:15-1 et seq.

N.M. Stat. Ann., 61-29-1 et seq.

Pa. Purdon's Stat., Title 63, § 455.101 et seq.

Tenn. Code Ann., 62-13-101 et seq.

Real Estate Brokers' License Act (Nonresident)

Ind. Burns' 1933, 42-1001 et seq.

Real Estate Brokers Regulating Act

P.R. Laws Ann. 1954, Title 20, § 3001 et seq.

Real Estate Claims Act (Forty Year Limitations)

Ill. Rev. Stat. 1991, Ch. 110, § 13-118 et seq.

Real Estate Commission Act

Ala. Code 1975, § 34-27-1 et seq.

Conn. Gen. Stat. Ann., § 20-311 et seq.

Ind. Code Ann., 25-34.1-2-1 et seq.

Ky. Rev. Stat. Ann., 324.010 et seq.

Mo. Rev. Stat., 339.120 et seq.

N.J. Stat. Ann., 45:15-1 et seq.

Real Estate Commissioners Act
Ore. Rev. Stat., 696.375 et seq.

Real Estate Consumer's Agency and Disclosure Act
Ala. Code 1975, § 34-27-80 et seq.

Real Estate Contract Forfeiture Act
Wash. Rev. Code Ann., 61.30.010 et seq.

Real Estate Contract under Seal Act
Ill. Rev. Stat. 1991, Ch. 29, § 0.01 et seq.

Real Estate Conveyance Tax Act
Conn. Gen. Stat. Ann., § 12-494 et seq.
R.I. Gen. Laws 1956, 44-25-1 et seq.

Real Estate Cooperative Act
Pa. Cons. Stat., Title 68, § 4101 et seq.
Va. Code 1950, § 55-424 et seq.

Real Estate Cooperative Marketing Act
Utah Code Ann. 1953, 57-23-6 et seq.

Real Estate Dealers License Act
Tex. Rev. Civ. Stat., Art. 6573a

Real Estate Deed Recordation Tax Act
D.C. Code Ann., § 45-921 et seq.

Real Estate Development Full Disclosure Act
N.J. Stat. Ann., 45:22A-21 et seq.

Real Estate Disclosure Act
N.M. Stat. Ann., 47-13-1 et seq.

Real Estate Holding Act (Nonprofit Associations)
Cal. Corporations Code §§ 20001, 21200 et seq.

Real Estate Investment Board Act
Ga. Code 1933, 40-2801 et seq.

Real Estate Investment Trust (REIT) Act
Ala. Code 1975, § 10-13-1 et seq.
Md. Ann. Code 1974, Art. CA, §§ 2-310, Subd. a, 8-203, Subd. h, 8-206, 8-801

Real Estate Investment Trust Act
Ill. Rev. Stat. 1991, Ch. 30, § 250 et seq.
La. Rev. Stat. Ann., 12:491 et seq.

Tex. Rev. Civ. Stat., Art. 6138A
Utah Code Ann. 1953, 16-12-1 et seq.
Va. Code 1950, § 6.1-343 et seq.

Real Estate Land Development Act
Wash. Rev. Code Ann., 58.19.940

Real Estate Law
Cal. Business and Professions Code § 10000 et seq.

Real Estate Leasing Act
Ill. Comp. Stat. 1992, Ch. 30, § 563/1 et seq.

Real Estate License Act
Ala. Code 1975, § 34-27-1 et seq.
Ark. Code Ann. 1987, 17-35-301 et seq.
D.C. Code Ann., § 45-1921 et seq.
Fla. Stat. Ann., 475.01 et seq.
Ga. Code Ann., 43-40-1 et seq.
Ill. Rev. Stat. 1991, Ch. 111, § 5801 et seq.
Ind. Code Ann., 25-34.1-3-1 et seq.
Ky. Rev. Stat. Ann., 324.010 et seq.
La. Rev. Stat. Ann., 37:1430 et seq.
Mont. Code Ann., 37-51-102 et seq.
Neb. Rev. Stat. 1943, 81-885.01 et seq.
N.J. Stat. Ann., 45:15-1 et seq.
Okla. Stat. Ann., Title 59, § 858-101 et seq.
Ore. Rev. Stat., 696.010 et seq.
S.C. Code Ann. 1976, § 40-57-10 et seq.
Tex. Rev. Civ. Stat., Art. 6573a
Utah Code Ann. 1953, 61-2-1 et seq.
Wyo. Stat. Ann., § 33-28-101 et seq.

Real Estate Licensing and Registration Act
Pa. Purdon's Stat., Title 63, § 455.101 et seq.

Real Estate Loan Act
Cal. Business and Professions Code § 10240 et seq.

Real Estate Mortgage Redemption Act
Kan. Stat. Ann., 60-2414

Real Estate Mortgage Tax Act
Okla. Stat. Ann., Title 68, § 1901 et seq.

Real Estate Practice Act
N.H. Rev. Stat. 1955, 331-A:1 et seq.

Real Estate Property Tax Act
Ohio Rev. Code 1953, 319.28 et seq.

Real Estate Ratio Study Act
Kan. Stat. Ann., 79-1485 et seq.

Real Estate Recording Act
Minn. Stat. Ann., 507.01 et seq.
Pa. Purdon's Stat., Title 53, § 16951 et seq.
Vt. Stat. Ann., Title 27, § 341 et seq.

Real Estate Recovery Fund Act
Fla. Stat. Ann., 475.482 et seq.
N.M. Stat. Ann., 61-29-20 et seq.
Utah Code Ann. 1953, 61-2a-1 et seq.

Real Estate Sale Discrimination Act
Ill. Rev. Stat. 1991, Ch. 38, § 70-50 et seq.

Real Estate Sale Validation Act
Ill. Rev. Stat. 1991, Ch. 110 1/2, §§ 100, 101

Real Estate Sales Excise Tax Act
Wash. Rev. Code Ann., 82.45.010 et seq.

Real Estate Sales Full Disclosure Act
N.J. Stat. Ann., 45:15-16.27 et seq.

Real Estate Sales Regulating Act
N.J. Stat. Ann., 45:15-1 et seq.

Real Estate Settlement Procedures Act Amendments of 1975
Jan. 2, 1976, P.L. 94-205, 89 Stat. 1157, 12 U.S. Code §§ 2601 to 2607, 2609, 2616, 2617

Real Estate Settlement Procedures Act of 1974
Dec. 22, 1974, P.L. 93-533, 12 U.S. Code §§ 2601 et seq.
Nov. 30, 1983, P.L. 98-181, 12 U.S. Code §§ 2602, 2607
Feb. 5, 1988, P.L. 100-242, 12 U.S. Code § 2607
Nov. 28, 1990, P.L. 101-625, 12 U.S. Code §§ 2605, 2609, 2610
April 10, 1991, P.L. 102-27, 12 U.S. Code § 2605
June 13, 1991, P.L. 102-54, 12 U.S. Code § 2607

Oct. 28, 1992, P.L. 102-550, 12 U.S. Code §§ 2602, 2604
Sept. 23, 1994, P.L. 103-325, 12 U.S. Code §§ 2605, 2606
Sept. 30, 1996, P.L. 104-208, 12 U.S. Code §§ 2602, 2603, 2605 to 2607, 2609, 2611 to 2614, 2617

Real Estate Subdivision Law
Cal. Business and Professions Code § 11000 et seq.

Real Estate Syndicate Act
Cal. Business and Professions Code, § 10250 et seq.
N.Y. General Business Law (Consol. Laws Ch. 20) § 352e et seq.

Real Estate Syndication Offerings Act
N.J. Stat. Ann., 49:3-27 et seq.

Real Estate Tax Act
D.C. Code Ann., § 47-801 et seq.

Real Estate Tax Exemption Act
Mich. Comp. Laws Ann., 211.7

Real Estate Tax Lien Act
Iowa Code Ann., 445.28

Real Estate Tax Sale Law
Pa. Purdon's Stat., Title 72, § 5860.101 et seq.

Real Estate Time-Share Act
Fla. Stat. Ann., 721.01 et seq.
Ill. Rev. Stat. 1991, Ch. 30, § 701 et seq.
Mass. Gen. Laws Ann., 183B:1 et seq.
Md. Ann. Code 1974, Art. RP, § 11A-101 et seq.
R.I. Gen. Laws 1956, 34-41-1.01 et seq.
Va. Code 1950, § 55-360 et seq.

Real Estate Time-Share Act (Model)
Wis. Stat. Ann., 707.02 et seq.

Real Estate Transaction Recovery Act
Va. Code 1950, § 54.1-2112 et seq.

Real Estate Transactions Act (Brokerage Relationships in)
Ga. Code Ann., 10-6A-1 et seq.
Ill. Comp. Stat. 1992, Ch. 225, § 455/38.1 et seq.
Kan. Stat. Ann., 58-30,101 et seq.

Real Estate Transfer Tax Act
Ill. Rev. Stat. 1991, Ch. 120, § 1001 et seq.
N.Y. Tax Law (Consol. Laws Ch. 60) § 1400 et seq.

Real Estate Transfer Tax Act (State)
Mich. Comp. Laws Ann., 207.521 et seq.

Real Estate Trust Act
N.M. Stat. Ann., 47-2-1 et seq.

Real Limitations of Actions Act
Mich. Comp. Laws Ann., 600.5801 et seq.

Real Party in Interest Act
Kan. Stat. Ann., 60-217, Subd. a
Ky. Rev. Stat. Ann., 304.14-290
Mo. Rev. Stat., 507.010
N.Y. Civil Practice Law and Rules (Consol. Laws Ch. 8) § Prec.1001
Ohio Civil Rules, Rule 17, Subd. A
Ore. Rules of Civil Procedure, Rule 26A
S.C. Code Ann. 1976, § 15-5-70 et seq.

Real Property Acquisition Act
Ida. Code 1947, 58-1101 et seq.

Real Property Acquisition Policies Act
Miss. Code Ann. 1972, § 43-37-1 et seq.

Real Property Acquisition Policies and Relocation Assistance Act
See Uniform Relocation Assistance and Real Property Acquisition Policies Act

Real Property Act
N.J. Stat. Ann., 46:1-1 et seq.
N.Y. Consol. Laws, Ch. 50

Real Property Act (Manufactured Home)
Wash. Rev. Code Ann., 65.20.010 et seq.

Real Property Actions and Proceedings Law
N.Y. Consol. Laws, Ch. 81

Real Property Betterment Act
S.C. Code Ann. 1976, § 27-27-10 et seq.

Real Property Charges Act (Local Agencies)
Cal. Government Code § 50303 et seq.

Real Property Conservation Rights Act
Ill. Rev. Stat. 1991, Ch. 30, § 400 et seq.

Real Property Descent Act
Mich. Comp. Laws Ann., 700.104 et seq.

Real Property Elevation Act
N.Y. Real Property Law (Consol. Laws Ch. 50) § 149

Real Property Foreclosure Act
Ga. Code Ann., 44-14-180 et seq.

Real Property Gains Tax Act
N.Y. Tax Law (Consol. Laws Ch. 60) § 1440 et seq.

Real Property Improvement Assessment Act
Ill. Comp. Stat. 1992, Ch. 35, §§ 210/1 to 210/4
Ill. Rev. Stat. 1991, Ch. 120, § 900 et seq.

Real Property Leasing Act (State)
Ill. Comp. Stat. 1992, Ch. 30, § 562/1

Real Property Loan Brokers Act
Cal. Civil Code § 3081.01 et seq.

Real Property Marketable Title Act
N.C. Gen. Stat. 1943, § 47B-1 et seq.

Real Property Ownership Declaration Act
Alaska Laws 1945, Ch. 49

Real Property Recording Act
See Recording Act (Real Property)

Real Property Rental Control Act (Commercial)
Cal. Civil Code § 1954.25 et seq.

Real Property Repair and Deduct Act
Okla. Stat. Ann., Title 41, § 101 et seq.

Real Property Securities Dealers Act
Cal. Business and Professions Code § 10237 et seq.

Real Property Tax Act
Haw. Rev. Stat. Ann., § 246-1 et seq.
N.Y. Consol. Laws, Ch. 50A

Real Property Tax Act (Circuit Breaker Tax Credit)
N.Y. Tax Law (Consol. Laws Ch. 60) § 606, Subd. e

Real Property Tax Appellate Provisions Act
D.C. Code Ann., § 47-825

Real Property Tax Exemption Law
N.Y. Local Laws 1973, County of Yates, p. 1328

Real Property Tax Increment Allocation Redevelopment Act
Ill. Rev. Stat. 1991, Ch. 24, § 11-74.4-1 et seq.
Mo. Rev. Stat., 99.800 et seq.

Real Property Tax Revision Act
D.C. Code Ann., § 47-801 et seq.

Real Property Taxation Exemption (Age Sixty Five and Older)
N.Y. Local Laws 1973, Village of East Bloomfield, p. 3321

Real Property Transfer Tax Act
N.H. Rev. Stat. 1955, 78-B:1 et seq.

Realignment and Efficiency Act (Trial Court)
Cal. Government Code § 12419.10
Cal. Statutes 1991, Ch. 90

Realtors Act (License)
Tenn. Code Ann., 62-13-101 et seq.
Tex. Rev. Civ. Stat., Art. 6573a

Realty Improvement Sewerage and Facilities Act
N.J. Rev. Stat. 1937, 58:11-23 et seq.

Realty Interest Transfer Tax Law
Miss. Code 1942, § 9426-11 et seq.

Realty Purchasers' Relief Law
Cal. Statutes 1858, Ch. 121, p. 95

Realty Recording Act
Colo. Laws 1957, p. 611, Ch. 211

Realty Redemption Act
See Redemption Act (Realty)

Realty Transfer Act
Mont. Code Ann., 15-7-301 et seq.

Realty Transfer Tax Act
Pa. Purdon's Stat., Title 72, § 3283 et seq.
S.D. Codified Laws 1967, 43-4-20 et seq.

Reapportionment Act
Minn. Stat. Ann., 2.02 et seq.
N.M. Stat. Ann. 1953, 2-7-1 et seq., 2-9-13 et seq.
Wis. Stat. Ann., 4.001 et seq.

Reapportionment Act (Assembly Districts)
Cal. Government Code §§ 490, 491

Reapportionment Act (Congressional Districts)
Cal. Government Code § 470
Ga. Code Ann., 21-2-4
Ill. Rev. Stat. 1991, Ch. 46, § 156.f1

Reapportionment Act (House of Representatives)
R.I. Gen. Laws 1956, 22-2-1 et seq.

Reapportionment Act (Legislative)
Ala. Code 1975, §§ 29-1-1.2, 29-1-2.3
Ark. Stat. 1947, 3-401 et seq.
Cal. Elections Code 1976, § 30010 et seq.
Colo. Laws 1964 Second Extra Session, Ch. 2
Del. Code of 1974, Title 29, § 801 et seq.
Fla. Laws 1965, Extra Session, Ch. 65-2440
Fla. Stat. Ann., 10.001 et seq.

Ga. Code Ann., 28-1-1 et seq.

Ill. Rev. Stat. 1991, Ch. 46, §§ 156f.1 et seq., 158-1, 158.2 et seq., 801 et seq.

Ind. Code Ann., 2-1-1.2-1 et seq.

Iowa Code Ann., 41.1, 41.2

Kan. Stat. Ann., 4-101 et seq.

La. Rev. Stat. Ann., 24:35, 24:35.1

Mass. Gen. Laws Ann., 57:4

Neb. Rev. Stat. 1943, 5-103.01 et seq.

N.J. Stat. Ann., 52:10-1 et seq.

N.M. Laws 1966, Ch. 27

N.M. Stat. Ann., 2-7-1 et seq., 2-8-1 et seq.

N.Y. Laws 1802, Ch. 79

N.Y. Laws 1808, Ch. 90

N.Y. Laws 1822, Ch. 209

N.Y. Laws 1826, Ch. 289

N.Y. Laws 1836, Ch. 436

N.Y. Laws 1846, Ch. 94

N.Y. Laws 1857, Ch. 339

N.Y. Laws 1866, Ch. 805

N.Y. Laws 1879, Ch. 208

N.Y. Laws 1892, Ch. 397

N.Y. Laws 1906, Ch. 431

N.Y. Laws 1907, Ch. 727

N.Y. Laws 1916, Ch. 373

N.Y. Laws 1917, Ch. 798

N.Y. State Law (Consol. Laws Ch. 57) §§ 110 et seq., 120 et seq.

Ore. Rev.Stat., 188.235, 188.245

Pa. 1963 Ex. Pamph. Laws 1419, No. 1

Pa. 1963 Ex. Pamph. Laws 1432, No. 2

Tenn. Code Ann., 3-1-101 et seq.

Utah Code Ann. 1953, Miscellaneous Superseded Code Provisions, 36-1-11 et seq.

Va. Code 1950, §§ 24.1-12.3, 24.1-14.2

Vt. Stat. Ann., Title 17, § 1881

Wyo. Stat. Ann., § 28-2-101 et seq.

Reapportionment Act (Local Government)
Nev. Rev. Stat. 1979 Reprint, 237.015 et seq.

Reapportionment Act (Municipal)
Pa. Purdon's Stat., Title 53, § 11601 et seq.

Reapportionment Act (Senate)
R.I. Gen. Laws 1956, 22-1-1 et seq.

Reapportionment Act (Senatorial Districts)
Cal. Government Code § 480

Reapportionment Act of 1901
Jan. 16, 1901, Ch. 93, 31 Stat. 733

Reapportionment Act of 1911
Aug. 8, 1911, Ch. 5, 37 Stat. 13

Reapportionment Act of 1929
June 18, 1929, Ch. 28, 46 Stat. 21, § 22

Reapportionment Compliance Act
N.Y. Laws 1964, 2nd Ex. Sess., Ch. 976
N.Y. State Law (Consol. Laws Ch. 57) §§ 121, 124
Vt. Stat. Ann., Title 17, § 1891 et seq.

Reapportionment House of Representatives Act
S.C. Code Ann. 1976, §§ 1-1-730 et seq., 2-1-10 et seq.

Reapportionment Implementation Act
Minn. Stat. Ann., 2A.01 et seq.

Reapportionment Reform Act
Del. Code of 1974, Title 29, § 871 et seq.

Rear End Collision Act
Mich. Comp. Laws Ann., 257.402

Rear End Presumption Act
Mich. Comp. Laws Ann., 257.402

Reasonable Doubt Act
N.Y. Criminal Procedure Law (Consol. Laws Ch. 11A) § 70.20
Ohio Rev. Code 1953, 2945.04

Reasonable Insanity Test Act
Ala. Code 1975, § 13A-3-1 et seq.

Reasonable Rents Act
P.R. Laws Ann. 1954, Title 17, § 181 et seq.

Reasonable Speed Act (Motor Vehicles)
Iowa Code Ann., 321.285
N.H. Rev. Stat. 1955, 265:60

Reassessment Act
Wash. Rev. Code Ann., 84.24.010 et seq.

Rebate Act
Me. Rev. Stat. Ann. 1964, Title 36, § 6301 et seq.

Rebate Act (Common Carriers)
Wash. Rev. Code Ann., 81.28.210 et seq.

Rebate Act (Insurance)
Ark. Stat. 1947, 66-326 et seq.
N.C. Miscellaneous Superceded Code Provisions, § 58-44.5
Ore. Rev. Stat., 744.655
Pa. Purdon's Stat., Title 40, §§ 275, 276
Wash. Rev. Code Ann., 48.30.140, 48.30.170

Rebate Act (Pharmaceutical)
N.J. Stat. Ann., 40:55D-135 et seq.

Rebate Act (Senior Citizens Rent or Property)
Pa. Purdon's Stat., Title 72, § 4751-1 et seq.

Rebel Correspondence Act (Civil War)
Feb. 25, 1863, Ch. 60, 12 Stat. 696

Rebuild New York Through Transportation Infrastructure Renewal Bond Act
N.Y. State Finance Law 1940 (Consol. Laws Ch. 56) § 61
N.Y. Transportation Law (Consol. Laws Ch. 63) § 420 et seq.

Rebuilding Communities and Neighborhood Preservation Act
Mo. Rev. Stat., 135.535, Subsecs. 1 to 5

Recalcitrant Tuberculosis Act (Removal)
Ohio Rev. Code 1953, 339.52

Recall Act
D.C. Code Ann., § 1-291 et seq.
Mont. Code Ann., 2-16-601 et seq.

Recall Election Act
La. Rev. Stat. Ann., 42:341 et seq.
Mich. Comp. Laws Ann., 168.951 et seq.
Wash. Rev. Code Ann., 29.82.010 et seq.

Recall Election Act (County and Township Officers)
Cal. Elections Code 1961, § 27200 et seq.

Recall Election Act (Municipal Officers)
Cal. Elections Code 1961, § 27500 et seq.

Recall Election Act (State Officers)
Cal. Elections Code 1976, § 27000 et seq.

Recall Election Law
See Uniform Recall Election Law

Receipt of Federal Moneys Act (Appropriation and Budgeting)
R.I. Gen. Laws 1956, 42-41-1 et seq.

Receipted Bill Act (Motor Vehicle Damages)
Pa. 1929 Pamph. Laws 905, No. 403, § 1208

Receiver of Taxes Law
N.Y. Local Laws 1972, Town of Oyster Bay, p. 2474

Receivers Act
Cal. Code of Civil Procedure, § 564 et seq.
La. Rev. Stat. Ann., 12:151 et seq.
Mont. Code Ann., 27-20-101 et seq.
Tex. Rev. Civ. Stat., Art. 2293 et seq.
Tex. Rules of Civil Procedure Rules 695, 695a
Wash. Rev. Code Ann., 7.60.010 et seq.

Receivership Act
N.M. Stat. Ann., 44-8-1 et seq.

Receivership Act (Alternative)
R.I. Gen. Laws 1956, 19-15.1-1 et seq.

Receivership Act (Corporations)
Ky. Rev. Stat. 1971, 271B.1-010

Receivership Act (Disorderly Houses)
N.Y. Multiple Dwelling Law (Consol. Laws Ch. 61A) § 359

Receivership Fee Act (Building and Loan)
Ill. Comp. Stat. 1992, Ch. 705, §§ 230/0.01, 230/1
Ill. Rev. Stat. 1991, Ch. 17, §§ 3620, 3621

Receivership Law (Long-Term Care Facility)
Ark. Code Ann. 1987, 20-10-901 et seq.

Receptacle Identification Law
Neb. Rev. Stat. 1943, 28-1329 et seq.

Reception Act (Common Law)
Ala. Code 1975, § 1-3-1
Mo. Rev. Stat., 1.010
Va. Code 1950, §§ 1-10, 1-11
Wyo. Stat. Ann., § 8-1-101

Reception Act (Escheats)
Ark. Code Ann. 1987, 62-1801 et seq.

Reception Center Law (Penal Institutions)
N.Y. Correction Law (Consol. Laws Ch. 43) § 60 et seq.

Recharge and Recovery Act (Groundwater)
Utah Code Ann. 1953, 73-3b-101 et seq.

Rechargeable Battery Recycling Act
May 13, 1996, P.L. 104-142, Title I, 42 U.S. Code § 14301 nt.

Recidivist Act (Habitual Criminal)
Alaska Stat. 1962, § 12.55.040 et seq.
Ariz. Rev. Stat. Ann., §§ 13-604
Cal. Penal Code §§ 644, 666, 667.5
Conn. Gen. Stat. Ann., § 53a-40
D.C. Code 1973, § 22-104
Del. Code of 1974, Title 11, § 4214
Fla. Stat. Ann., 775.084
Ga. Code Ann., 17-10-7
Kan. Stat. Ann., 21-4504
La. Rev. Stat. Ann., 15:529.1
Me. Rev. Stat. Ann. 1964, Title 15, § 1742
Mich. Comp. Laws Ann., 769.10 et seq.
Minn. Stat. 1978, 609.155
Mo. Rev. Stat., 558.016
Mont. Code Ann., 46-18-501 et seq.
N.C. Gen. Stat. 1943, §§ 14-19, 15A-645, 15A-928
Neb. Rev. Stat. 1943, 29-2221
N.Y. Penal Law 1965 (Consol. Laws Ch. 40) § 70.10
Ohio Rev. Code 1953, 2929.11
Pa. Cons. Stat., Title 18, § 1103 et seq.

S.C. Code Ann. 1976, § 17-25-40 et seq.
Tenn. Code Ann., 39-1-801 et seq.
Tex. Penal Code, §§ 12.42, 12.43
Va. Code 1950, § 53-296
Wis. Stat. Ann., 939.62, 973.12

Reciprocal Access Law (Transboundary Pollution)
N.J. Stat. Ann., 2A:58A-1 et seq.

Reciprocal Agreement for Collection of Wages Act of 1977
Mont. Code Ann., 39-3-301 et seq.

Reciprocal Banking Act
Fla. Stat. Ann., 658.295
N.C. Gen. Stat. 1943, § 53-209 et seq.

Reciprocal Banking Act (Regional)
Ark. Code Ann. 1987, 23-32-1801 et seq.
Fla. Stat. Ann., 658.295

Reciprocal Demurrage Act
Kan. Stat. Ann., 66-168, 66-201 et seq.

Reciprocal Discovery Law
N.Y. Criminal Procedure Law (Consol. Laws Ch. 11A) § 240.10 et seq.

Reciprocal Enforcement of Support Act
See Uniform Reciprocal Enforcement of Support Act

Reciprocal Enforcement of Support Act (Revised)
See Revised Uniform Reciprocal Enforcement of Support Act

Reciprocal Enforcement of Tax Act
Tex. Tax Code, § 151.615

Reciprocal Foreign Trustees Act
Ill. Rev. Stat. 1985, Ch. 17, § 2801 et seq.

Reciprocal Full Faith and Credit Taxation Act
Ind. Code Ann., 6-8-8-1 et seq.

Reciprocal Hunting and Fishing Licenses Act (California-Arizona)
Cal. Fish and Game Code 1957, § 375

Reciprocal Inheritance Act (Alien)
N.C. Gen. Stat. 1943, §§ 64-3 to 64-5

Reciprocal Inheritance Act (Aliens)
N.C. Gen. Stat. 1943, § 64-3 et seq.

Reciprocal Inheritance Tax Exemption Act
Kan. Stat. Ann., 79-1501e

Reciprocal Insurance Act
Cal. Insurance Code § 1280 et seq.
Ga. Code Ann., 33-17-1 et seq.
Ill. Rev. Stat. 1991, Ch. 73, § 673 et seq.
Ind. Code Ann., 27-6-6-1 et seq.
Ky. Rev. Stat. 1971, 304.27-010 et seq.
Mich. Comp. Laws Ann., 500.7200 et seq.
Wash. Rev. Code Ann., 48.10.010 et seq.

Reciprocal Insurers Liquidation Act
Ala. Code 1958, Title 28, § 339 et seq.
Ill. Rev. Stat. 1991, Ch. 73, § 833.1 et seq.
Ohio Rev. Code 1953, 3903.24 et seq.

Reciprocal Interstate Banking Act
Minn. Stat. Ann., 48.90 et seq.
N.C. Gen. Stat. 1943, § 53-209 et seq.

Reciprocal Limitations Act
Pa. Purdon's Stat., Title 73, § 1645.1 et seq.

Reciprocal Nonsupport Act
Ala. Code 1975, § 30-4-80 et seq.
Colo. Rev. Stat., 14-5-101 et seq.

Reciprocal or Exchange Insurance Act
Tenn. Code Ann., 56-16-201 et seq.

Reciprocal Regional Banking Act
Ala. Code 1975, § 5-13A-1 et seq.

Reciprocal Retirement Act
Mich. Comp. Laws Ann., 38.1101 et seq.

Reciprocal Rights Act (Foreign Heirs)
Cal. Probate Code § 259 et seq.
Iowa Code Ann., 567.8
Mont. Rev. Code 1947, 91-520, 91-521
Ore. Rev. Stat., 111.070

Reciprocal Rights Act (Inheritance)
Cal. Probate Code § 259 et seq.

Reciprocal Savings and Loan Acquisition Act
N.C. Gen. Stat. 1943, § 54B-48.1 et seq.

Reciprocal Savings Institutions Act (Regional)
Ala. Acts 1987, p. 207, No. 152

Reciprocal Sporting Fishing Licenses Act
Cal. Fish and Game Code 1957, § 390

Reciprocal Tariff Act
June 12, 1934, Ch. 474, 48 Stat. 943, 19 U.S. Code §§ 1351 to 1354

Reciprocal Tax Act (McLinn-Bates)
Ind. Code Ann., 6-2-2-1 et seq.

Reciprocal Tax Collection Act
D.C. Code Ann., § 47-431 et seq.

Reciprocal Tax Enforcement Act
Va. Code 1950, § 58.1-2

Reciprocal Trade Relations Act
July 26, 1911, Ch. 3, 37 Stat. 4

Reciprocal Transfer Tax Act
See also Uniform Reciprocal Transfer Tax Act
Cal. Revenue and Taxation Code §§ 13851, 15451
Haw. Rev. Stat. Ann., § 236-11
Ill. Rev. Stat. 1991, Ch. 120, § 375
Ind. Code 1971, 6-4-1-26
Pa. Purdon's Stat., Title 72, §§ 2306, 2307
Wyo. Stat. Ann., § 39-6-801

Reciprocal Transfer Tax Act (Nonresidents)
N.Y. Tax Law (Consol. Laws Ch. 60) § 248p

Reciprocal Trust Act (Foreign Corporations)
Ill. Rev. Stat. 1985, Ch. 17, § 2801 et seq.

Reciprocity Act
Ind. Code Ann., 9-7-7-1 et seq.
Minn. Stat. Ann., 290.081

P.R. Laws Ann. 1954, Title 3, § 806

Reciprocity Act (Decedents' Estates)
Wis. Stat. Ann., 72.11, Subsec. 2

Reciprocity Act (Insurance)
Tenn. Code Ann., 56-4-218

Reciprocity Act (Motor Vehicles)
Cal. Vehicle Code 1959, § 8000 et seq.
Ida. Code 1947, 49-206 et seq.
Kan. Stat. Ann., 74-4302
N.J. Stat. Ann., 39:3-15 et seq.
Okla. Stat. Ann., Title 47, § 22.31 et seq.
S.D. Codified Laws 1967, 32-10-1 et seq.
Va. Code 1950, § 46.2-106 et seq.

Reciprocity Act (Physicians)
Ohio Rev. Code 1953, 4731.29

Reciprocity Act (Retirement System)
P.R. Laws Ann. 1954, Title 3, § 797 et seq.

Reciprocity Act (Tax Collection)
Me. Rev. Stat. Ann. 1964, Title 36, § 174
Miss. Code Ann. 1972, § 27-75-1 et seq.
Pa. 1963 Pamph. Laws 1052, No. 456

Reciprocity Taxation and Proration Agreement Act (Bus)
Me. Rev. Stat. Ann. 1964, Title 36, § 1492 et seq.

Reciprocity Treaty (United States Export-Import)
Haw. Session Laws 1876, p. 161, Jan. 30, 1875

Reckless Driver Act (Guest)
Iowa Code 1983, 321.494

Reckless Driving Act
Ariz. Rev. Stat. Ann., § 28-693
Cal. Vehicle Code 1959, § 23103
La. Rev. Stat. Ann., 14:99
Mich. Comp. Laws Ann., 257.626
Minn. Stat. Ann., 169.11
Mont. Code Ann., 61-8-301
N.C. Gen. Stat. 1943, § 20-140
N.D. Cent. Code, 39-08-03
N.J. Stat. Ann., 39:4-96

N.M. Stat. Ann. 1953, 64-22-3
Ohio Rev. Code 1953, 4511.20
Okla. Stat. Ann., Title 47, § 121.3
Ore. Rev. Stat., 811.140
R.I. Gen. Laws 1956, 31-27-1 et seq.
Tenn. Code Ann., 55-10-205
Vt. Stat. Ann. 1959, Title 23, § 1181 et seq.
Wash. Rev. Code Ann., 46.61.500
Wis. Stat. Ann., 346.62

Reckless Flying Act
Wis. Stat. Ann., 114.09, 114.095

Reckless Homicide Act
Ill. Rev. Stat. 1991, Ch. 38, § 9-3
Me. Rev. Stat. Ann. 1964, Title 29, § 1315
S.C. Code Ann. 1976, § 56-5-2910

Reclamation Act
Neb. Rev. Stat. 1943, 46-501 et seq.
P.R. Laws Ann. 1954, Title 28, § 71 et seq.
Wash. Rev. Code Ann., 89.16.005 et seq.

Reclamation Act (Abandoned Mine)
N.M. Stat. Ann., 69-25B-1 et seq.

Reclamation Act (Abandoned Mined Lands and Water)
Ill. Rev. Stat. 1991, Ch. 96 1/2, § 8001.01 et seq.

Reclamation Act (Coal)
Okla. Stat. 1981, Title 45, § 742.1 et seq.

Reclamation Act (Land-Surface Mining)
Ala. Code 1975, § 9-16-107 et seq.
S.D. Codified Laws 1967, 45-6A-1 et seq.

Reclamation Act (Mining Lands)
Okla. Stat. Ann., Title 45, § 721 et seq.
Utah Code Ann. 1953, 40-8-1 et seq.

Reclamation Act (Open Cut Land)
Okla. Stat. Ann., Title 45, § 721 et seq.

Reclamation Act (Open Pit Mines)
Pa. Purdon's Stat., Title 52, § 1396.1 et seq.

Reclamation Act (Settlers)
Wis. Laws 1935, Ch. 550, Subch. 96

Reclamation Act (Strip Mining)
Ky. Rev. Stat. 1971, 350.010 et seq.
Md. Ann. Code 1974, Art. NR, § 7-501 et seq.
Ohio Rev. Code 1953, 1513.01 et seq.

Reclamation Act (Surface Mining)
Ill. Rev. Stat. 1991, Ch. 96 1/2, § 7901.01 et seq.

Reclamation Acts
Feb. 2, 1911, Ch. 32, 36 Stat. 895, 43 U.S. Code § 374
Feb. 24, 1911, Ch. 155, 36 Stat. 930, 43 U.S. Code § 522
Aug. 13, 1914, Ch. 247, 38 Stat. 686, 43 U.S. Code §§ 373, 414, 418, 435 to 437, 440, 443 to 465, 469, 471 to 481, 492 to 497, 499
Aug. 4, 1939, Ch. 418, 53 Stat. 1198, 43 U.S. Code § 485k
May 10, 1956, Ch. 256, 70 Stat. 151, 43 U.S. Code § 419

Reclamation Acts (Irrigation of Arid Lands)
June 17, 1902, Ch. 1093, 32 Stat. 388, 43 U.S. Code §§ 372, 373, 381, 383, 391, 392, 411, 414, 419, 421, 431, 432, 434, 439, 461, 491, 498, 1457
May 20, 1920, Ch. 192, 41 Stat. 605, 43 U.S. Code § 375
Oct. 1, 1982, P.L. 97-275, 42 U.S. Code § 502

Reclamation and Abandoned Mine Lands Act
W. Va. Code 1966 § 22-3-1 et seq.

Reclamation and Development Grants Program Act
Mont. Code Ann., 90-2-1101 et seq.

Reclamation and Improvement Authority Act (Land)
Mich. Comp. Laws Ann., 125.2451 et seq.

Reclamation and Irrigation Act
See Irrigation and Reclamation Act

Reclamation and Surface Mining Conservation Act
Pa. Purdon's Stat., Title 52, § 1396.1 et seq.

Reclamation Authorization Act of 1975
March 11, 1976, P.L. 94-228, 43 U.S. Code § 615kkkk
Oct. 24, 1988, P.L. 100-516, 43 U.S. Code § 615llll-6

Reclamation Authorization Act of 1976
Oct. 4, 1976, P.L. 94-455, 90 Stat. 1824
Dec. 18, 1987, P.L. 100-196, 101 Stat. 1313

Reclamation Board Law
Cal. Water Code § 8520 et seq.

Reclamation Board Law (Bonds)
Cal. Water Code § 9250 et seq.

Reclamation Contract Act (Conservancy District)
N.M. Stat. Ann., 73-18-1 et seq.

Reclamation Development Act of 1974
Oct. 31, 1994, P.L. 103-434, 108 Stat. 4538

Reclamation District Dissolution Law
Cal. Water Code § 53700 et seq.

Reclamation Districts Act
Cal. Water Code § 50000 et seq.
Wash. Rev. Code Ann., 89.30.001 et seq.

Reclamation Fund Act
June 25, 1910, Ch. 407, 36 Stat. 835, 43 U.S. Code §§ 397, 398, 400, 413, 436, 437

Reclamation Project Act of 1939
Aug. 4, 1939, Ch. 418, 53 Stat. 1198, 43 U.S. Code §§ 375a, 387 to 389, 485 to 485k
April 24, 1945, Ch. 94, 59 Stat. 75, 43 U.S. Code §§ 485b nt., 485c, 485f
Aug. 18, 1950, Ch. 752, 64 Stat. 463, 43 U.S. Code § 387
Aug. 8, 1958, P.L. 85-611, 72 Stat. 542, 43 U.S. Code §§ 485a, 485b nt., 485h
Sept. 21, 1959, P.L. 86-308, 73 Stat. 584, 43 U.S. Code § 485b-1.
Aug. 28, 1962 P.L. 87-613, 76 Stat. 407, 43 U.S. Code § 485h

Reclamation Project Authorization Act of 1972

Oct. 30, 1984, P.L. 98-570, 43 U.S. Code §§ 615aaa, 615ddd, 615eee

Oct. 24, 1988, P.L. 100-516, 43 U.S. Code §§ 615aaa, 615bbb, 615ddd, 615iii

Reclamation Projects Authorization and Adjustment Act of 1992

Oct. 20, 1972, P.L. 92-514, 86 Stat. 964, 43 U.S. Code §§ 615aaa to 615zzz

Oct. 12, 1982, P.L. 97-293, 43 U.S. Code § 485h(f)

Oct. 30, 1992, P.L. 102-575, 43 U.S. Code § 371 nt.

Nov. 2, 1994, P.L. 103-437, 43 U.S. Code §§ 371 nt., 390h-4, 390h-6 to 390h-14

Oct. 9, 1996, P.L. 104-266, 43 U.S. Code §§ 390h-1 to 390h-3, 390h-9, 390h-13 to 390h-15

Oct. 30, 1998, P.L. 105-321, 43 U.S. Code § 390h-16

Reclamation Recreation Management Act of 1992

Oct. 30, 1992, P.L. 102-575, 16 U.S. Code §§ 4601-31 et seq., 460l-31 nt.

Reclamation Recycling and Water Conservation Act of 1996

Oct. 9, 1996, P.L. 104-266, 43 U.S. Code § 390h nt.

Reclamation Reform Act of 1982

Oct. 12, 1982, P.L. 97-293, 42 U.S. Code §§ 390aa et seq.

Dec. 22, 1987, P.L. 100-203, 43 U.S. Code §§ 390nn, 390ww

Nov. 2, 1994, P.L. 103-437, 43 U.S. Code § 390ww

Dec. 21, 1995, P.L. 104-66, 43 U.S. Code § 390ww

Reclamation Safety of Dams Act Amendments of 1984

Aug. 28, 1984, P.L. 98-404, 43 U.S. Code §§ 506 nt., 508, 509

Reclamation Safety of Dams Act of 1978

Nov. 2, 1978, P.L. 95-578, 43 U.S. Code §§ 506, 506 nt., 507 to 509, 511, 1511

Aug. 28, 1984, P.L. 98-404, 43 U.S. Code §§ 506 nt., 508, 509

Reclamation States Drought Assistance Act of 1988

Aug. 11, 1988, P.L. 100-387, 102 Stat. 957, 43 U.S. Code § 502 nt.

Reclamation States Emergency Drought Relief Act of 1991

March 5, 1992, P.L. 102-250, 43 U.S. Code §§ 2201 et seq., 2201 nt.

Nov. 2, 1994, P.L. 103-437, 43 U.S. Code § 2213

Sept. 30, 1996, P.L. 104-206, Title II, 43 U.S. Code § 2241

Reclamation Wastewater and Groundwater Act

Oct. 13, 1997, P.L. 105-62, 43 U.S. Code § 390h-12g

Reclamation Wastewater and Groundwater Study and Facilities Act

Oct. 30, 1992, P.L. 102-575, 43 U.S. Code §§ 390h nt., 390h et seq.

Reclassification Act

See Classification Act of 1923

Reclassification Act (Cities)

Ky. Rev. Stat. 1971, 81.010, 81.026

Reclassification Act of 1925

Feb. 28, 1925, Ch. 368, 43 Stat. 1053

Oct. 18, 1943, Ch. 261, 57 Stat. 572

Recodification Act

N.D. Laws 1939, Ch. 110

Recodification Acts (Wildlife)

S.C. Code Ann. 1976, §§ 50-11-10 et seq., 50-17-10 et seq.

Recognition Act (Divorce)

Neb. Rev. Stat. 1943, 42-341 et seq.

Recognition Act (Foreign Country Money-Judgments)

See Foreign Money-Judgments Recognition Act

Recognition of Acknowledgements Act
See also Uniform Recognition of Acknowledgements Act
Alaska Stat. 1962, Replaced Titles, §§ 43.30.200, 43.30.210
Del. Code of 1974, Title 29, § 4321 et seq.
Kan. Stat. Ann., 53-301 et seq.
Minn. Stat. Ann., 358.32 et seq.
Okla. Stat. Ann., Title 49, § 101 et seq.
Ore. Rev. Stat. Ann., 194.500 et seq.
Utah Code Ann. 1953, 57-2a-1 et seq.
Wis. Stat. Ann., 706.07

Recognition of International Treaties Act
Fla. Stat. Ann., 260.011

Recognizance Act
Ohio Rev. Code 1953, 2947.16
S.C. Code Ann. 1976, § 17-15-10 et seq.

Recognized Normal School Act
Ill. Rev. Stat. 1991, Ch. 122, § 734.9 et seq.

Reconciliation Act (Family)
Wash. Rev. Code Ann., 13.32A.010 et seq.

Reconciliation Act (Norfolk County)
Mass. Acts 1961, Ch. 620

Reconciliation Act (Worcester County)
Mass. Acts 1961, Ch. 620

Reconstruction Act (Disaster Recovery)
Cal. Government Code § 8877.1 et seq.

Reconstruction Acts
March 2, 1867, Ch. 152, 14 Stat. 428
March 23, 1867, Ch. 6, 15 Stat. 2
July 19, 1867, Ch. 30, 15 Stat. 14
March 11, 1868, Ch. 25, 15 Stat. 41
Dec. 22, 1869, Ch. 3, 16 Stat. 59

Reconstruction and Reemployment Law
Cal. Government Code § 15530 et seq.

Reconstruction Finance Corporation Act
Jan. 22, 1932, Ch. 8, 47 Stat. 5
June 19, 1934, Ch. 653, 48 Stat. 1112
Feb. 24, 1938, Ch. 32, 52 Stat. 79
April 13, 1938, Ch. 140, 52 Stat. 212
June 25, 1940, Ch. 427, 54 Stat. 572
Sept. 16, 1940, Ch. 721, 54 Stat. 897
Sept. 18, 1940, Ch. 722, 54 Stat. 898
Sept. 26, 1940, Ch. 734, 54 Stat. 961
June 10, 1941, Ch. 190, 55 Stat. 248
June 11, 1942, Ch. 404, 56 Stat. 355
Aug. 7, 1946, Ch. 811, 60 Stat. 901
June 30, 1947, Ch. 166, 61 Stat. 202
May 25, 1948, Ch. 334, 62 Stat. 261
June 29, 1948, Ch. 723, 62 Stat. 1101
July 1, 1948, Ch. 784, 62 Stat. 1209
July 19, 1949, Ch. 351, 63 Stat. 446
Oct. 25, 1949, Ch. 729, 63 Stat. 906
April 20, 1950, Ch. 94, 64 Stat. 80
Oct. 24, 1951, Ch. 555, 65 Stat. 615
July 30, 1953, Ch. 282, 67 Stat. 230, 15 U.S. Code §§ 603
June 29, 1954, Ch. 410, 68 Stat. 320, 15 U.S. Code §§ 603, 609
Aug. 19, 1964, P.L. 88-448, 78 Stat. 494, 15 U.S. Code § 603 nt.

Reconstruction Finance Corporation Appropriation Act of 1952
Nov. 1, 1951, Ch. 664, 65 Stat. 740

Reconstruction Finance Corporation Disaster Loan Act
April 17, 1936, Ch. 234, 49 Stat. 1232, 12 U.S. Code § 1703; Title 15 U.S. Code § 605k

Reconstruction Finance Corporation Exports Resolution
March 26, 1934, Ch. 90, 48 Stat. 500, 15 U.S. Code § 616a

Reconstruction Finance Corporation Extension Act
Jan. 20, 1934, Ch. 3, 48 Stat. 318.
Jan. 28, 1935, Ch. 1, 49 Stat. 1

Reconstruction Finance Corporation Liquidation Act
July 30, 1953, Ch. 282, 67 Stat. 230, 15 U.S. Code §§ 603, 609 nt.; 40 U.S. Code § 459; 50 U.S. Code §§ 98 nt., 544 nt.; 50 U.S. Code Appx. §§ 1929 nt., 2094 nt., 2261 nt.
June 29, 1954, Ch. 410, 68 Stat. 320, 15 U.S. Code § 603 nts.
Aug. 2, 1954, Ch. 649, 68 Stat. 643, 40 U.S. Code § 459

Reconstruction Finance Corporation Tax Exemption Act
March 20, 1936, Ch. 160, 49 Stat. 1185

Reconstruction Proclamation
July 8, 1864, No. 18, 13 Stat. 744

Reconstruction Transportation Appropriation Act (Anthracite Coal)
Pa. 1939 Pamph. Laws 1113, No. 393

Reconstruction Transportation Appropriation Act (Bituminous Coal)
Pa. 1939 Pamph. Laws 1115, No. 394

Reconveyance Act (Tax Titles)
Ill. Rev. Stat. 1991, Ch. 120, § 736 et seq.

Record Act (Criminal Convictions)
Cal. Evidence Code §§ 452.5, 1280, 1500.5
Cal. Government Code §§ 69844.5, 71280.5

Record Carrier Competition Act of 1981
Dec. 29, 1981, P.L. 97-130, 47 U.S. Code § 609 nt.

Record Information Act (Criminal History)
Me. Rev. Stat. Ann. 1964, Title 16, § 611 et seq.

Record on Appeal Fee Act
Ill. Rev. Stat. 1991, Ch. 53, §§ 80.9, 81

Record Piracy Law
N.Y. Penal Law 1965 (Consol. Laws Ch. 40) § 275.00 et seq.

Record Program (Archaeological)
N.C. Gen. Stat. 1943, § 70-46 et seq.

Record Rental Amendment of 1984
Oct. 4, 1984, P.L. 98-450, 98 Stat. 1727, 17 U.S. Code §§ 101 nt., 109, 109 nt., 115
Nov. 5, 1988, P.L. 100-617, 17 U.S. Code § 109 nt.
Dec. 8, 1993, P.L. 103-182, 17 U.S. Code § 109 nt.

Record Retention Act (Banks)
S.C. Code Ann. 1976, § 34-3-510 et seq.

Record Review Act (Personnel)
Ill. Rev. Stat. 1991, Ch. 48, § 2000 et seq.

Record Title Act
Iowa Code Ann., 614.17

Recordation Act
La. Rev. Stat. Ann., 44:1 et seq.

Recordation Act (Land)
Mont. Code Ann., 70-21-201 et seq.

Recordation Act (Property)
N.C. Gen. Stat. 1943, § 47-17 et seq.

Recordation Law (Real Property)
Cal. Civil Code § 1213 et seq.

Recordation Tax Act
Md. Ann. Code 1974, Art. TG, § 12-101 et seq.
Va. Code 1950, § 58.1-800 et seq.

Recorders Act
Ill. Rev. Stat. 1991, Ch. 115, § 1 et seq.

Recorder's Court Act (Counties)
N.C. Gen. Stat. 1943, §§ 7A-109 et seq., 7-215 et seq.

Recorder's Court Act (Detroit)
Mich. Comp. Laws Ann., 726.1 et seq.

Recorder's Court Act (Municipal)
N.C. Gen. Stat. 1943, § 7A-109 et seq., 7-185 et seq.

Recorder's Court Jury Act
Mich. Comp. Laws Ann., 600.1301 et seq.

Recorders Fee Act
Ind. Code Ann., 36-2-7-10
Pa. Purdon's Stat., Title 16, § 11411 et seq.

Recorders' Registration Act
Tex. Rev. Civ. Stat., Art. 6591 et seq.

Recording Act
Ark. Code Ann. 1987, 14-15-402 et seq.
La. Rev. Stat. Ann., 44:1 et seq.
N.M. Stat. Ann., 14-9-1 et seq.
Continued

R.I. Gen. Laws 1956, 34-13-1 et seq.
S.C. Code Ann. 1976, § 30-5-10 et seq.

Recording Act (Accounts Receivable)
Ala. Code 1958, Title 39, § 207 et seq.
Ga. Code 1933, 85-1806 et seq.
Mo. Rev. Stat. Ann., 410.010 et seq.

Recording Act (Agricultural Liens)
Va. Code 1950, § 43-53

Recording Act (Chattel Mortgages)
Ala. Code 1958, Title 47, § 110
Kan. Stat. Ann., 84-9-101 et seq.
Md. Ann. Code 1974, Art. CL, § 9-301 et seq.
Me. Rev. Stat. Ann. 1964, Title 11, § 9-401
Mich. Comp. Laws Ann., 440.9101 et seq.
N.C. Gen. Stat. 1943, § 47-20
Okla. Stat. Ann., Title 46, § 57 et seq.
Wis. Stat. Ann., 409.101 et seq.

Recording Act (Conditional Sales)
Ala. Code 1958, Title 47, § 131
Md. Ann. Code 1974, Art. CL, § 9-301 et seq.
Okla. Stat. Ann., Title 60, § 318
Wis. Stat. Ann., 409.101 et seq.

Recording Act (Conveyances)
Colo. Rev. Stat., 38-35-101 et seq.
Haw. Rev. Stat. Ann., § 502-1 et seq.
Ky. Rev. Stat. 1971, 382.080 et seq.
Mich. Comp. Laws Ann., 565.29
Minn. Stat. Ann., 507.01 et seq.
Utah Code Ann. 1953, 57-3-1 et seq.

Recording Act (Cooperative)
N.J. Stat. Ann., 46:8D-1 et seq.

Recording Act (Deeds)
Me. Rev. Stat. Ann. 1964, Title 33, § 201 et seq.

Recording Act (Depositions)
Me. Rev. Stat. Ann. 1964, Title 16, § 551 et seq.

Recording Act (Homestead)
Me. Rev. Stat. Ann. 1964, Title 14, § 4552

Recording Act (Instruments)
Tenn. Code Ann., 66-24-101 et seq.

Recording Act (Mining Claims)
Alaska Stat. 1962, §§ 27.10.050, 27.10.060
Me. Rev. Stat. Ann. 1964, Title 12, § 547

Recording Act (Personal Property)
D.C. Code Ann., § 42-101 et seq.
Iowa Code Ann., 556.3, 556.4

Recording Act (Real Property)
Ala. Code 1975, § 35-4-90 et seq.
Ariz. Rev. Stat. Ann., § 33-411 et seq.
Cal. Government Code § 27280 et seq.
D.C. Code 1973, § 45-801 et seq.
Fla. Stat. Ann., 695.01 et seq.
Ind. Code Ann., 32-1-2-16 et seq.
Kan. Stat. Ann., 58-2221
Mass. Gen. Laws Ann., 183: 4
Me. Rev. Stat. Ann. 1964, Title 33, § 201 et seq.,
Miss. Code Ann. 1972, § 89-5-1 et seq.
Mo. Rev. Stat., 442.380 et seq.
Mont. Code Ann., 70-21-201 et seq.
N.D. Cent. Code, 47-19-01 et seq.
N.J. Rev. Stat. Ann., 46:15-1 et seq.
N.Y. Real Property Law (Consol. Laws Ch. 50) § 290 et seq.
Ohio Rev. Code 1953, 317.08, 5301.01, 5301.23, 5301.25, 5301.331
Pa. Purdon's Stat., Title 21, § 351
S.D. Codified Laws 1967, 43-28-1 et seq.
Tex. Property Code, § 12.001 et seq.
Vt. Stat. Ann., Title 27, § 341
Wash. Rev. Code Ann., 65.08.060 et seq.
Wyo. Stat. Ann., § 34-1-101 et seq.

Recording Act (Unauthorized)
N.M. Stat. Ann., 30-16B-1 et seq.

Recording Act of 1955
Aug. 5, 1955, Ch. 573, 69 Stat. 534, 43 U.S. Code § 274 nt.
Va. Code 1950, § 55-95 et seq.
W. Va. Code 1966, § 39-1-1 et seq.

Recording Acts (Mortgage Tax Law)
N.Y. Tax Law (Consol. Laws Ch. 60) § 253

Recording Affidavits Act
Conn. Gen. Stat. Ann., § 47-12a

Records Act (County)
Me. Rev. Stat. Ann. 1964, Title 30, § 344 et seq.

Records Act (Documents)
Ga. Code Ann., 50-18-90 et seq.

Records Act (Marriage, Dissolution, and Invalidity)
Ill. Rev. Stat. 1991, Ch. 40, § 900 et seq.

Records Act (Medical)
Tenn. Code Ann., 68-11-301 et seq.

Records Act (Military Compensation)
Ill. Rev. Stat. 1991, Ch. 126 1/2, §§ 61m, 62

Records Act (Missing Children)
Ill. Rev. Stat. 1991, Ch. 23, § 2280 et seq.

Records Act (Municipal)
Me. Rev. Stat. Ann. 1964, Title 30, § 2211 et seq.
Pa. Purdon's Stat., Title 53, § 9001 et seq.

Records Act (Preservation of Private Business)
N.H. Rev. Stat. 1955, 337-A:1 et seq.

Records Act (Public)
Colo. Rev. Stat., 24-72-101 et seq.

Records Act (State and Local)
Mo. Rev. Stat., 109.200 et seq.

Records and Archives Act
Okla. Stat. 1981, Title 67, § 305 et seq.

Records and Archives Management Act
Me. Rev. Stat. Ann. 1964, Title 5, § 91 et seq.

Records and Archives Service and Information Practices Act
Utah Code Ann. 1953, 63-2-59 et seq.

Records and Codes Act (Municipal Adoption)
Ill. Rev. Stat. 1991, Ch. 85, § 1000 et seq.

Records as Evidence Act
W. Va. Code 1966, § 57-1-1 et seq.

Records as Evidence Act (Business and Public)
Me. Rev. Stat. Ann. 1964, Title 16, § 451 et seq.

Records as Evidence Act (Business)
See Uniform Business Records as Evidence Act

Records as Evidence Act (Photographic Copies)
See also Uniform Photographic Copies of Business and Public Records as Evidence Act
Alaska Comp. Laws Ann. 1949, Supp. 1957, § 58-1-21 et seq.
Me. Rev. Stat. Ann. 1964, Title 46 § 456
Ohio Rev. Code 1953, 2317.41
Wis. Stat. Ann., 889.29

Records Certification Act (Filmed)
Ill. Rev. Stat. 1989, Ch. 116, § 34.3 et seq.

Records Confidentiality Act
Mont. Code Ann., 22-1-1101 et seq.

Records Destruction Act (Filmed)
Ill. Rev. Stat. 1991, Ch. 116, §§ 47.01, 47.1

Records Disclosure Act
Tex. Transportation Code, § 730.001 et seq.

Records for Veterans Administration Act
Ill. Rev. Stat. 1991, Ch. 116, § 28.9 et seq.

Records Law (Local Government)
Me. Rev. Stat. Ann. 1964, Title 30-A, § 1701 et seq.

Records Management Act
Cal. Government Code §§ 14740, 14741
Iowa Code Ann., 304.1 et seq.
Miss. Code Ann. 1972, § 25-59-1 et seq.
N.D. Cent. Code, 54-46-01 et seq.
Continued

Neb. Rev. Stat. 1943, 84-1201 et seq.
Utah Code Ann. 1953, 63-27-1 et seq.

Records Management Act (Public)
Mont. Code Ann., 2-6-201 et seq.

Records Management Act (State)
Cal. Government Code § 14740 et seq.

Records Management and Archives Act
N.H. Rev. Stat. 1955, 5:25 et seq.

Records Management and Preservation of Essential Records Act
W. Va. Code 1966, § 5A-8-1 et seq.

Records Media Act
Mich. Comp. Laws Ann., 24.401 et seq.

Records Open to Public Act
Kan. Stat. Ann., 45-201 et seq.

Records Preservation Act
Mich. Comp. Laws Ann., 600.2148 et seq.
Tex. Government Code, § 441.051 et seq.

Records Reproduction Act (Filmed)
Ill. Rev. Stat. 1991, Ch. 116, § 34.9 et seq.

Records Retention Act
See Uniform Records Retention Act

Records Screening Act (Children's and Juvenile Facility Criminal)
N.M. Stat. Ann., 24-18-1 et seq.

Records Transfer Act (Service Compensation)
Ill. Rev. Stat. 1991, Ch. 126 1/2, §§ 62a, 62a.1

Recount Act (Election)
Ga. Code Ann., 21-2-495
Ind. Code Ann., 3-12-6-1 et seq., 3-12-10-1 et seq.
Ky. Rev. Stat. 1971, 120.015 et seq.
Okla. Stat. Ann., Title 26, § 8-101 et seq.

Recovery Act
N.Y. Laws 1933, 1st Ex. Sess., Ch. 781
Ohio Laws Vol. 115, p. 603

Recovery Act (Small Business)
Conn. Gen. Stat. Ann., 32-347 to 32-349

Recovery and Resource Conservation Act
Neb. Rev. Stat. 1943, 81-1140

Recovery and Solid Waste Planning Act
Tenn. Code Ann., 68-31-601 et seq.

Recovery District Act
La. Acts 1988 First Ex. Sess., No. 15
La. Rev. Stat. Ann., 39:2001 et seq.

Recovery for Retail Theft Act (Civil)
Me. Rev. Stat. Ann. 1964, Title 14, § 8301 et seq.

Recovery Fund Act (Economic)
N.J. Laws 1992, Ch. 16

Recovery of Real Property Act (Actions for)
Cal. Code of Civil Procedure § 315 et seq.

Recreation Act
Minn. Stat. Ann., 471.15 et seq.

Recreation Act (Community)
Cal. Education Code 1976, § 10900 et seq.

Recreation Act (Nassau County)
Fla. Special Laws 1961, Ch. 61-2525

Recreation Act (Outdoor)
N.M. Stat. Ann. 1978, 16-1-1 et seq.

Recreation Act (Public)
Okla. Stat. Ann., Title 11, § 33-101 et seq.

Recreation Act of 1926
June 14, 1926, Ch. 578, 44 Stat. 741, 43 U.S. Code § 869
June 4, 1954, Ch. 263, 68 Stat. 173, 43 U.S. Code §§ 869 to 869-3
June 20, 1966, P.L. 89-457, 80 Stat. 210, 43 U.S. Code § 869-1

Recreation and Campground Area Licensing Act
Ill. Comp. Stat. 1992, Ch. 210, § 95/1 et seq.

Recreation and Community Services Law
N.Y. Local Laws 1972, Town of Oyster Bay, p. 2492

Recreation and Conservation Act
Fla. Stat. Ann., 375.011 et seq.

Recreation and Development Act
Okla. Stat. Ann., Title 74, § 1901 et seq.

Recreation and Fish and Wildlife Enhancement Bond Act
Cal. Water Code § 11922 et seq.

Recreation and Park Bond Act (State)
N.M. Stat. Ann., 16-2-20

Recreation and Park District Act (Lake Cuyamaca)
Cal. Statutes 1961, Ch. 1654

Recreation and Park Law
Ind. Code Ann., 36-10-3-1 et seq.

Recreation and Park Loan Act
Mass. Acts 1962, Ch. 15

Recreation and Public Purposes Act
See also Recreation Act of 1926
July 8, 1986, P.L. 99-350, 100 Stat. 763

Recreation and Public Purposes Amendment Act of 1988
Nov. 10, 1988, P.L. 100-648, 43 U.S. Code § 869 nt.

Recreation and Sports Development Organic Act
P.R. Laws Ann. 1954, Title 3, § 442 et seq.

Recreation and Tourism Act
Okla. Stat. Ann., Title 74, § 1801 et seq.

Recreation and Water Conservation and Control Act (Bradford County)
Fla. Special Laws 1967, Ch. 67-1130

Recreation and Water Conservation and Control Act (Citrus County)
Fla. Special Laws 1967, Ch. 67-1205

Recreation and Water Conservation and Control Act (Lafayette County)
Fla. Special Laws 1967, Ch. 67-1598

Recreation Authorities Law (Veterans)
N.C. Gen. Stat. 1943, § 165-23 et seq.

Recreation Authority Act
Me. Rev. Stat. Ann. 1964, Title 10, § 5001 et seq.

Recreation Authority Act (Atlanta and Fulton County)
Ga. Laws 1960, p. 2810

Recreation Authority Act (Calhoun)
Ga. Laws 1992, p. 6750

Recreation Authority Act (Chatham County)
Ga. Laws 1995, p. 4281

Recreation Authority Act (Cobb County)
Ga. Laws 1958, p. 2004

Recreation Authority Act (Dublin-Laurens County)
Ga. Laws 1999, H.B. 378, No. 1

Recreation Authority Act (First Class Counties)
N.J. Rev. Stat. Ann., 40:37B-1 et seq.

Recreation Authority Act (Franklin County)
Ga. Laws 1997, p. 4033

Recreation Authority Act (Gwinnett County)
Ga. Laws 1975, p. 3108

Recreation Authority Act (Hartwell)
Ga. Laws 1996, p. 3998

Recreation Authority Act (Lincoln County)
Ga. Laws 1997, p. 4566

Recreation Authority Act (Richmond Hill Area)
Ga. Laws 1996, p. 3646

Recreation Authority Act (Twiggs County)
Ga. Laws 1996, p. 4015

Recreation Board Act
D.C. Code 1973, § 8-201 et seq.

Recreation Bond Authorization Act
Mich. Comp. Laws Ann., 318.551 et seq.

Recreation Bond Implementation Act
Mich. Comp. Laws Ann., 318.571 et seq.

Recreation Development Act (Outdoor)
N.Y. Navigation Law 1941 (Consol. Laws Ch. 37) § 140 et seq.
N.Y. Stat. Finance Law 1940 (Consol. Laws Ch. 56) § 61
N.Y. Tax Law (Consol. Laws Ch. 60) § 289c

Recreation District Act
Colo. Rev. Stat., 32-2-101 et seq.
Fla. Stat. Ann., 418.20 et seq.
Ida. Code 1947, 31-4301 et seq.
Miss. Code Ann. 1972, § 55-9-21 et seq.

Recreation District Act (Counties)
Cal. Public Resources Code § 5431

Recreation District Act (Metropolitan)
Colo. Rev. Stat., 32-2-101 et seq.

Recreation District and Metropolitan Culture Compact Act
Mo. Rev. Stat., 70.445 et seq.

Recreation Districts Act for Class AA Counties and for Counties of the Second, Fourth, Eighth or Ninth Class
Wash. Rev. Code Ann., 36.69.010 et seq.

Recreation Districts Act for Counties
Wash. Rev. Code Ann., 36.69.900

Recreation Enabling Law
N.C. Gen. Stat. 1943, § 160A-350 et seq.

Recreation Facilities Act
N.M. Stat. Ann., 5-4-1 et seq.

Recreation Improvement Fund Act
Mich. Comp. Laws Ann., 318.531 et seq.

Recreation Initiative Program of 1995
Tenn. Code Ann., 11-9-201 to 11-9-203

Recreation Land Preservation Act
Colo. Rev. Stat., 25-13-101 et seq.

Recreation Lands and State Wildlife Management Act
Wash. Rev. Code Ann., 43.98A.010 et seq.

Recreation Liability Act
Neb. Rev. Stat. 1943, 37-1001 et seq.

Recreation, Park and Conservation Fund Act (Keystone)
Pa. 1993 Pamph. Laws, No. 50

Recreation Trails System Act
Colo. Rev. Stat., 33-42-101 et seq.
Ida. Code 1947, 67-4223, 67-4232 et seq.
Ore. Rev. Stat., 390.950 et seq.
Wash. Rev. Code Ann., 67.32.010 et seq.

Recreational Act (Arkansas River)
Colo. Rev. Stat., 33-12.5-101 et seq.

Recreational Advisory Council Act
Miss. Code Ann. 1972, § 55-1-1 et seq.

Recreational and Park Facilities Act
Cal. Public Resources Code § 5096.225 et seq.

Recreational and Park Facilities Bond Act
Va. Acts 1992, Ch. 781

Recreational Boating Safety Act of 1986
Nov. 7, 1986, P.L. 99-626, 46 U.S. Code § 13101 nt.

Recreational Corporations Act
Ala. Code 1975, § 11-60-1 et seq.

Recreational Development Company Act
P.R. Laws Ann. 1954, Title 15, § 501 et seq.

Recreational District Act
Miss. Code Ann. 1972, § 55-9-21 et seq.

Recreational Entrant Act (Landowner's Liability)
Wis. Stat. Ann., 29.68

Recreational Facilities and Park Act
Cal. Public Resources Code § 5096.225 et seq.

Recreational Facilities Authority Act
Va. Code 1950, § 10.1-1600 et seq., 15.1-1271 et seq.

Recreational Facilities Authority Act (Rome)
Ga. Laws 1999, H.B. 711

Recreational Facilities Revenue Bond Act (Tampa)
Fla. Special Laws 1949, Ch. 26255

Recreational Fisheries Conservation and Management Act
S.C. Code Ann. 1976, § 50-20-10 et seq.

Recreational Harbor District Act
Cal. Harbors and Navigation Code § 6400 et seq.

Recreational Highway Act
Wash. Rev. Code Ann., 47.39.010 et seq.

Recreational Hunting Safety and Preservation Act of 1994
Sept. 13, 1994, P.L. 103-322, 16 U.S. Code §§ 5201 nt., 5201 et seq.

Recreational Improvement and Rehabilitation Act
Pa. Purdon's Stat., Title 32, § 5401 et seq.

Recreational Land Act
Miss. Code Ann. 1972, § 55-3-3 et seq.

Recreational Land Liability Act
Miss. Code Ann. 1972, § 89-2-21 et seq.

Recreational Land Trust Fund Act
Mich. Comp. Laws Ann., 318.401 et seq.

Recreational Loan Act (Metropolitan District Commission)
Mass. Acts 1957, Ch. 627

Recreational Loan Act (Metropolitan District)
Mass. Acts 1955, Ch. 731

Recreational Opportunities Act (Handicapped Persons)
N.J. Stat. Ann., 52:27D-170 et seq.

Recreational System Act (County)
Mo. Rev. Stat., 67.781 et seq.

Recreational Therapy Practice Act
Utah Code Ann. 1953, 58-40-1 et seq.

Recreational Trails Act
Cal. Public Resources Code § 5070 et seq.
Colo. Rev. Stat., 33-11-101 et seq.
Fla. Stat. Ann., 260.011 et seq.

Recreational Trails of Illinois Act
Ill. Comp. Stat. 1992, Ch. 20, § 862/1 et seq.

Recreational Trespass Act
Mich. Comp. Laws Ann., 317.171 et seq.
N.M. Stat. Ann., 17-4-7 et seq.

Recreational Use of Land and Water Act
Pa. Purdon's Stat., Title 68, § 477-1 et seq.

Recreational Vehicle and Mobile Home Park Act
Ky. Rev. Stat. 1971, 219.310 et seq.

Recreational Vehicle and Trailer Law
Cal. Civil Code § 800 et seq.

Recreational Vehicle Park and Camping Ground
N.Y. Local Laws 1971, Town of Lewiston, p. 2599

Recreational Vehicle Park Occupancy Law
Cal. Civil Code § 799.20 et seq.

Recreational Vehicles and Factory-
Manufactured Structures Standards
Code
Tenn. Code Ann., 68-126-101 et seq.

Recreational Vehicles and Manufactured
Homes Uniform Standard Code
Neb. Rev. Stat. 1943, 71-4601 et seq.

Recreational Waters Act
S.C. Code Ann. 1976, § 44-55-2320 et seq.

Recrimination Act (Divorce)
Cal. Civil Code §§ 122, 123
Ill. Rev. Stat. 1991, Ch. 40, § 408
N.Y. Domestic Relations Law (Consol. Laws
Ch. 14) § 171, Subd. 4
Wyo. Stat. Ann., § 20-55

Rector Anti-Trust Act
Ark. Stat. 1987, 4-75-309 et seq.

Rector Dam Authority Law
Cal. Statutes 1935, Ch. 413, p. 1463

Recusation Act
Colo. Rev. Stat., 39-9-2 et seq.

Recycled Newsprint Use Act
Ill. Rev. Stat. 1989, Ch. 96 1/2, § 9751 et seq.

Recycling Act
N.J. Stat. Ann., 13:1E-92 et seq.
R.I. Gen. Laws 1956, 23-18.8-1 et seq.
W. Va. Code 1966 § 20-11-1 et seq.

Recycling Act (Land)
Minn. Laws 1992, Ch. 512
Okla. Stat. Ann., Title 27A, § 2-11-401 et
seq.

Recycling Act (Tire)
N.M. Stat. Ann., 74-11-1 et seq.

Recycling Act (Used Motor Oil)
Ill. Rev. Stat. 1991, Ch. 96 1/2, § 7751 et seq.

Recycling Act (Used Oil)
Pa. Purdon's Stat., Title 58, § 471 et seq.
Wash. Rev. Code Ann., 70.95I.005 et seq.

Recycling Act (Waste Tire)
Cal. Public Resources Code § 42860 et seq.
Okla. Stat. Ann., Title 68, § 53001 et seq.
Utah Code Ann. 1953, 26-32a-101 et seq.

Recycling and Chlorofluorocarbon
Reduction Act
Minn. Stat. Ann., 116.70 et seq.

Recycling and Clear Communities Act
N.J. Stat. Ann., 13:1E-92 et seq.

Recycling and Litter Reduction Act
Neb. Rev. Stat. 1943, 81-1534 et seq.

Recycling and Litter Reduction Incentive
Act (Beverage Container)
Ga. Code Ann., 12-17-1 et seq.

Recycling and Recycled Materials
Procurement Act
Okla. Stat. Ann., Title 74, § 85.50 et seq.

Recycling and Reduction Law (Solid Waste)
La. Rev. Stat. Ann., 30:2411 et seq.

Recycling and Solid Waste Management
Fund Act
Ark. Code Ann. 1987, 8-6-601 et seq.

Recycling, Collection and Management of
Used Oil Act
Tex. Health and Safety Code, § 371.001 et
seq.

Recycling Development Fund Act (Plastics)
Mich. Comp. Laws Ann., 299.471 et seq.

Recycling Enhancement Act (Oil)
Cal. Public Resources Code § 48600 et seq.

Recycling Fund Transfer Act (Vehicle)
Ill. Rev. Stat. 1991, Ch. 95 1/2, §§ 239.40,
239.41

Recycling Incentive Act (Manufacturer)
Okla. Stat. Ann., Title 68, § 2357.51 et seq.

Recycling Law (New York City)
N.Y. Adm. Code '85, § 16-301 et seq.

Recycling, Litter Control, and Resource Recovery Assessment Act
Cal. Revenue and Taxation Code § 42000 et seq.

Recycling Makes Cents, Office Paper Recovery Act
Mich. Comp. Laws Ann., 299.461 et seq.

Recycling Management Act (State Government)
Neb. Rev. Stat. 1943, 81-1642 et seq.

Recycling, Reuse and Source Reduction Incentive Act
Okla. Stat. Ann., Title 27A, 2-11-301 et seq.

Recycling, Reuse, and Ultimate Destruction Incentive Act
Okla. Stat. Ann., Title 68, §§ 2357.14 to 2357.20

Recycling, Waste Planning and Waste Reduction (Municipal)
Pa. Purdon's Stat., Title 53, § 4000.101 et seq.

Red Can Act
Mich. Comp. Laws Ann., 750.502

Red Cross Act
See American National Red Cross Act

Red Flag Act
Cal. Military and Veterans Code § 616
Colo. Rev. Stat., 40-23-4 et seq.
Iowa Code Ann., 689.5 et seq.

Red Hook Unsafe Buildings and Collapsed Structures Law
N.Y. Local Laws 1971, Village of Red Hook, p. 4368

Red Light Abatement Act
Ala. Code 1975, § 6-5-140 et seq.
Cal. Penal Code § 11225 et seq.
Colo. Rev. Stat. 1963, 39-15-1 et seq.
D.C. Code 1973, § 22-2713 et seq.
La. Rev. Stat. Ann., 13:4711 et seq.
Mich. Comp. Laws Ann., 600.3801 et seq.
Wash. Rev. Code Ann., 7.48.050 et seq.

Red Light Abatement Act (District of Columbia)
Feb. 7, 1914, Ch. 16, 38 Stat. 280

Red Light Injunction and Abatement Act
Iowa Code Ann., 99.1 et seq.
Ky. Rev. Stat. 1971, 233.010 et seq.

Red River Compact Act
Ark. Stat. 1987, 15-23-501 et seq.
La. Acts 1978, No. 71
Okla. Stat. Ann., Title 82, §§ 1431, 1432
Tex. Water Code, § 46.001 et seq.

Red River Designation Act of 1993
Dec. 2, 1993, P.L. 103-170, 16 U.S. Code §§ 1271 nt., 1274

Red River Redevelopment Authority Act
Tex. General Laws 1997, Ch. 831

Red Rock Canyon National Conservation Area Establishment Act of 1990
Nov. 16, 1990, P.L. 101-621, 16 U.S. Code § 460ccc et seq.
Nov. 2, 1994, P.L. 103-437, 16 U.S. Code § 460ccc-3
Nov. 2, 1994, P.L. 103-450, 16 U.S. Code §§ 460ccc-1, 460ccc-3, 460ccc-5, 460ccc-8
Oct. 19, 1998, P.L. 105-263, 16 U.S. Code § 460ccc-1

Red Scale Eradication Act
Cal. Statutes 1947, Ch. 629, p. 1635

Redd Racing Act (Pari-mutuel Betting)
Utah Laws 1925, Ch. 77

Redeemable Coupon Law
Cal. Business and Professions Code § 17700 et seq.

Redemption Act (Mortgage Moratorium)
Kan. Laws 1933, Ch. 232
Kan. Laws 1934, Special Session, Ch. 3
Kan. Laws 1935, Ch. 226

Redemption Act (Realty)
Ariz. Rev. Stat. Ann., § 12-1281 et seq.
Cal. Revenue and Taxation Code § 4101 et seq.
Continued

Ill. Rev. Stat. 1991, Ch. 110, § 12-122
Ind. Code Ann., 34-1-4-7
Iowa Code Ann., 447.1 et seq.
Kan. Stat. Ann., 60-2414
Md. Ann. Code 1974, Art. TP, § 14-827
Ohio Rev. Code 1953, 5723.03
Ore. Rev. Stat., 23.530 et seq.
Pa. Purdon's Stat., Title 72, §§ 5876 et seq.,
6071 et seq., 6105.1 et seq.
Tenn. Code Ann., 66-8-101 et seq.
Wash. Rev. Code Ann., 6.23.010 et seq.

Redemption Act (Taxation)
Cal. Revenue and Taxation Code § 4101 et
seq.

Redemption and Bank Note Act
See Bank Nt. and Redemption Act

Redemption and Execution Sales Law
Wash. Rev. Code Ann., 6.21.010, 6.23.010 et
seq.

Redevelopment Act
Ga. Code Ann., 8-4-1 et seq.
Neb. Rev. Stat. 1943, 58-501 to 58-533

Redevelopment Act (Blighted Areas)
Ill. Comp. Stat. 1992, Ch. 315, § 5/1 et seq.

Redevelopment Act (Housing)
Mass. Gen. Laws Ann., 121A:1 et seq.,
121B:1 et seq.

Redevelopment Act (Municipal)
Minn. Stat. 1986, 462.411 et seq.

Redevelopment Act (Parish)
La. Rev. Stat. Ann., 33:4625

Redevelopment Act (Urban)
Cal. Health and Safety Code § 33000 et seq.
Colo. Rev. Stat., 29-4-301 et seq.
Conn. Gen. Stat. Ann., § 8-124 et seq.
D.C. Code Ann., § 5-801 et seq.
Ga. Code Ann., 36-61-1 et seq.
Ind. Code Ann., 18-7-8-1 et seq.
Kan. Stat. Ann., 17-4742 et seq.
Ky. Rev. Stat. 1971, 99.330 et seq.
Minn. Stat. Ann., 462.411 et seq.
N.C. Gen. Stat. 1943, § 160A-500 et seq.

Nev. Rev. Stat. 1979 Reprint, 279.382 et seq.
R.I. Gen. Laws 1956, 45-31-1 et seq.
S.C. Code Ann. 1976, Superseded Vols.,
§ 31-7-10 et seq.
Wis. Stat. Ann., 66.405 et seq.

Redevelopment Agencies Law
N.J. Stat. Ann., 40:55C-1 et seq.

Redevelopment Agency Act
La. Acts 1968, No. 179 (Shreveport)
La. Acts 1968, No. 215 (Monroe)
La. Acts 1968, No. 272 (Lake Charles)
La. Acts 1968, No. 439 (DeRidder, Golden
Meadow, Houma, Junction City, Minden,
Opelousas, Thibodaux, West Monroe)
La. Acts 1970, No. 525 (Lake Providence
and Rayville)
La. Acts 1972, No. 90 (Bossier City)
La. Acts 1972, No. 673 (Alexandria and
Bogaluse)
La. Acts 1972, No. 762 (Ferriday)

**Redevelopment and Housing Cooperation
Law**
N.J. Stat. Ann., 55:14B-1 et seq.

Redevelopment and Housing Law
P.R. Laws Ann. 1954, Title 17, § 101 et seq.

Redevelopment and Housing Law (Local)
N.J. Stat. Ann., 40A:12A-1 et seq.

Redevelopment and Revitalization Act
Nev. Statutes 1975, Ch. 702, p. 1428

Redevelopment and Slum Clearance Act
Alaska Stat. 1962, § 18.55.480 et seq.
N.J. Stat. Ann., 40:55-21.1 et seq.

Redevelopment and Voluntary Cleanup Act
Mont. Code Ann., 75-10-730 et seq.

**Redevelopment Area Economic Cooperation
and Implementation Act**
Pa. Purdon's Stat., Title 73, § 331 et seq.

Redevelopment Assistance Act
N.J. Stat. Ann., 13:1B-15.13 et seq.
Pa. Purdon's Stat., Title 35, § 1661 et seq.

Redevelopment Authority Act
Wis. Stat. Ann., 66.431

Redevelopment Authority Act (Land Clearance)
Del. Code of 1974, Title 31, § 4501 et seq.
Kan. Laws 1953, Ch. 106
Mo. Rev. Stat., 99.300 et seq.
Pa. Purdon's Stat., Title 35, § 1701 et seq.
Wis. Stat. Ann., 66.431

Redevelopment Authority Act (Portland)
Me. Private and Special Laws 1951, Ch. 217

Redevelopment Bond Act
Md. Ann. Code 1957, Art. 41, § 14-801 et seq.

Redevelopment Bonding Law
N.M. Stat. Ann., 3-60A-26 et seq.

Redevelopment Companies Act
N.J. Stat. Ann., 55:14D-1 et seq.
N.Y. Private Housing Finance Law (Consol. Laws Ch. 44B) § 100 et seq.

Redevelopment Cooperation Law (Urban)
Pa. Purdon's Stat., Title 35, § 1741 et seq.

Redevelopment Corporation Act
N.J. Stat. Ann., 52:9Q-9 et seq.

Redevelopment Corporation Act (Urban)
Mich. Comp. Laws Ann., 125.901 et seq.
Mo. Rev. Stat., 353.010 et seq.
N.J. Rev. Stat. Ann, 55:14D-1 et seq.
N.Y. Private Housing Finance Law (Consol. Laws Ch. 44B) § 100 et seq.
Va. Acts 1946, Ch. 190

Redevelopment Financing Act (Brownfield)
Mich. Comp. Laws Ann., 125.2651 et seq.

Redevelopment Housing Projects Act
La. Rev. Stat. Ann., 40:381 et seq.

Redevelopment Law (Municipal)
N.Y. General Municipal Law (Consol. Laws Ch. 24) § 970a et seq.

Redevelopment Law (Urban)
N.M. Stat. Ann., 3-60A-5 et seq.

Redevelopment Limited Dividend Act (Urban)
Mass. Gen. Laws Ann., 121A:9

Redevelopment of Cities and Towns Act
Ind. Code Ann., 18-7-7-1 et seq.

Redevelopment Powers Act
Ga. Code Ann., 36-44-1 et seq.

Redevelopment Project Rehousing Act
Ill. Rev. Stat. 1991, Ch. 67 1/2, § 91.990 et seq.

Redevelopment Projects Act
Ala. Code 1975, § 24-2-1 et seq.
N.H. Rev. Stat. 1955, 205:1 et seq.

Redevelopment Urban Renewal Act
Md. Laws 1975, Ch. 380
Md. Laws 1976, Chs. 79 to 81, 410

Redhibition Act
La. Civil Code, Art. 2520 et seq.

Redistricting Act
Wash. Rev. Code Ann., 44.05.010 et seq.

Redistricting Act (Congress)
N.Y. State Law (Consol. Laws Ch. 57) § 110 et seq.

Redistricting Act (Congressional)
Miss. Code Ann. 1972, § 23-5-223
Va. Code 1950, § 24.1-4.3

Redistricting Act (House of Representatives)
Okla. Stat. Ann., Title 14, § 121 et seq.

Redistricting Act (Judicial Districts)
Okla. Stat. Ann., Title 20, § 92a

Redistricting Act (Legislative)
Ala. Code 1975, §§ 29-1-1.2, 29-1-2.3
Fla. Stat. Ann., 10.001 et seq.
Ill. Rev. Stat. 1991, Ch. 46, § 156f.1 et seq.
Kan. Stat. Ann., 4-120 et seq.
Ky. Rev. Stat. 1971, 6.011 et seq., 118.485
Continued

Mich. Comp. Laws Ann., 3.51
Minn. Stat. 1985, 2.02 et seq.
Miss. Code Ann. 1972, § 23-5-223
N.Y. State Law (Consol. Laws Ch. 57) § 120 et seq.
Tenn. Code Ann., 3-1-101 et seq.
Va. Code 1950, § 24.1-4
Wash. Rev. Code Ann., 44.05.010 et seq.

Redlining Law (Insurance)
N.Y. Insurance Law 1984 (Consol. Laws Ch. 28) §§ 3429, 3431, 3433 3431, 3433

Redlining Law (Mortgages)
N.Y. Banking Law (Consol. Laws Ch. 2) § 9f

Reduced Fare Law (Prohibition)
Ky. Rev. Stat. 1971, 276.240

Reduced Speed Act (Motor Vehicles)
Ariz. Rev. Stat. Ann., § 28-701

Reduced Transit Fares for Elderly Act
Ill. Rev. Stat. 1977, Ch. 111 2/3, § 641 et seq.

Reduced Transit Fares for Students Act
Ill. Rev. Stat. 1977, Ch. 122, § 791 et seq.

Reduced Tuition Act (Senior Citizens)
N.M. Stat. Ann., 21-21D-5 et seq.

Reduced Worktime Act
Cal. Government Code § 18041 et seq.
Cal. Government Code § 19996.20 et seq.

Reduction Act (International Dispute)
Colo. Rev. Stat., 13-22-501 et seq.

Reduction Act (Salaries)
Iowa Laws 1933 (45th G. A.), Ch. 89

Reduction Act (Trial Court Delay)
Cal. Government Code § 68600 et seq.

Reduction Act (Waste)
La. Rev. Stat. Ann., 30:2291 et seq.

Reduction and Recycling Act (Comprehensive Chloroflourocarbon)
Minn. Stat. Ann., 116.731 et seq.

Reduction and Recycling Act (Solid Waste)
La. Rev. Stat. Ann., 30:2411 et seq.

Reduction and Revocation Act (Public Employee Pension)
R.I. Gen. Laws 1956, 36-10.1-1 et seq.

Reduction and Simplification of Paperwork Act
Tenn. Code Ann., 4-25-101 et seq.

Reduction Assessment Act (Demand)
Ala. Code 1975, § 13A-12-280 et seq.

Reduction of Flood Damage Act
Va. Code 1950, § 62.1-44.108 et seq.

Reduction, Recycling, Treatment Research and Demonstration Act (Hazardous Waste)
Cal. Health and Safety Code § 25244 et seq.

Redwood Empire Parks Development Act
Cal. Statutes 1982, Ch. 1164

Reed Amendment
March 3, 1917, Ch. 162, 39 Stat. 1069
Feb. 24, 1919, Ch. 18, 40 Stat. 1151

Reed-Bulwinkle Act
June 17, 1948, P.L. 80-662, Ch. 491, 62 Stat. 472, 49 U.S. Code § 10706
Feb. 5, 1976, P.L. 94-210, 49 U.S. Code § 10706

Reed-Jenkins Act
May 29, 1928, P.L. 70-574, Ch. 864, 45 Stat. 954 (See 8 U.S. Code §§ 1101 nt., 1103, 1353)

Reed-Johnson Act
Also known as World War Veterans' Act of 1924 June 7, 1924, P.L. 68-242, 43 Stat. 607

Reef Act (Artificial)
La. Rev. Stat. Ann., 56:2021 et seq.

Reelfoot Lake Control Act
Tenn. Public Acts 1931, Ch. 56
Tenn. Public Acts 1935, Ch. 164

Reemployment Act (Injured Worker)
Utah Code Ann. 1953, 35-10-1 et seq.

Reemployment Act (Veterans)
See Veterans' Reemployment Act

Reemployment Insurance Act
Wis. Stat. Ann., 108.01 et seq.

Reemployment of Merchant Marine Members Act
June 23, 1943, P.L. 78-87, Ch. 142, 57 Stat. 162

Rees-Doyle Health and Welfare Program Supervision Act
Cal. Insurance Code § 10640 et seq.

Rees-Levering Motor Vehicle Sales Finance Act
Cal. Civil Code § 2981 et seq.

Rees-Richards Act (Air Pollution)
Cal. Health and Safety Code § 426.5

Referees Act
Wash. Rev. Code Ann., 2.24.060, 4.48.010 et seq.

Referees Salary and Expense Fund Act of 1984
July 10, 1984, P.L. 98-353, 11 U.S. Code § 101 nt.

Reference Act
Mich. Comp. Laws Ann., 618.67 et seq.
Pa. Cons. Stat., Title 42, §§ 7361, 7362
R.I. Gen. Laws 1956, 9-15-1 et seq.
Wash. Rev. Code Ann., 4.48.010 et seq.

Reference Act (Bradford County)
Pa. 1869 Pamph. Laws 725, No. 698

Reference Act (Trial by Referees)
Mont. Code Ann., 25-7-701 et seq.

Reference and Arbitration Act
Pa. Cons. Stat., Title 42, §§ 7361, 7362

Referendum Act
Mont. Code Ann., 13-27-101 et seq.
P.R. Acts 1950, 6th Sp. Sess. No. 27
Wash. Rev. Code Ann., 29.79.010 et seq.

Referendum Act (Advisory)
N.M. Stat. Ann., 22-4A-1 et seq.

Referendum Act (Beer)
Okla. Laws 1933, p. 338

Referendum Act (Bonds)
Ill. Rev. Stat. 1991, Ch. 24, §§ 8-4-1, 8-4-2

Referendum Act (Special Method)
Ala. Code 1975, § 28-2-20 et seq.

Referendum and Initiative Act
Colo. Rev. Stat., 1-40-101 et seq,
D.C. Code Ann., § 1-281 et seq.
Mich. Comp. Laws Ann., 168.471 et seq.
Minn. Stat. Ann., 3B.01 et seq.
Wyo. Stat. Ann., § 22-24-101 et seq.

Referendum and Initiative Act (Municipalities)
Iowa Laws 1907 (32d G. A.), Ch. 48, § 19

Referendum and Initiative Enabling Act (County Measures)
Ark. Stat. 1947, 2-301 et seq.

Referendum, Initiative, and Recall Charter Amendments Act
D.C. Code Ann., §§ 1-281 to 1-287, 1-291 to 1-295

Referendums, Measures and Public Initiatives Referred to Voters by the General Assembly Disclosure Act
Ark. Code Ann. 1987, 7-9-401 et seq.

Refinancing Act (Revenue Bonds)
Miss. Code Ann. 1972, § 31-27-7 et seq.
Mont. Code Ann., 7-7-4601 et seq.
S.C. Code Ann. 1976, § 6-17-10 et seq.

Refinery and Chemical Plant Worker Safety Act
Cal. Labor Code § 7850 et seq.

Reforestation Act
Cal. Public Resources Code § 4691 et seq.
Ida. Code 1947, 38-201 et seq.
N.H. Rev. Stat. 1955, 221:1 et seq.
Continued

Ore. Rev. Stat. 1953, 321.255 et seq.
Wash. Rev. Code 1951, 76.08.010 et seq.,
76.12.020 et seq.

Reforestation Fund Act
Mich. Comp. Laws Ann., 320.71

Reforestation Lands Tax Act
Wash. Rev. Code Ann., 84.28.005 et seq.

Reforestation Relief Act
March 31, 1933, Ch. 17, 48 Stat. 22

Reform Act (Antitrust)
Mich. Comp. Laws Ann., 445.771 et seq.

Reform Act (Boating Safety)
Ala. Code 1975, § 33-5-50 et seq.

Reform Act (Congressional Campaign)
Minn. Stat. Ann., 10A.40 et seq.

Reform Act (County)
Ind. Code Ann., 17-1-24-1 et seq.

Reform Act (Credit)
Mich. Comp. Laws Ann., 445.1851 et seq.

Reform Act (Dartmouth)
N.H. Laws 1816, June Session, Ch. 35

Reform Act (Education)
Ky. Rev. Stat. 1971, 158.010 et seq.
Mass. Laws 1993, Ch. 71, § 95
Miss. Code Ann. 1972, § 37-1-1 et seq.

Reform Act (Electric Rate)
Me. Rev. Stat. Ann. 1964, Title 35-A, § 3151
et seq.

Reform Act (Executive Branch)
Okla. Stat. Ann., Title 74, §§ 10.1 to 10.3

Reform Act (Health Care)
Fla. Stat. Ann., 408.0015 et seq.
Ky. Rev. Stat. 1971, 216.900 et seq.
Wash. Rev. Code Ann., 41.05.006 et seq.

Reform Act (Professional Medical Conduct)
N.J. Stat. Ann., 45:9-19.4 et seq.

Reform Act (Rent Regulation)
N.Y. General Business Law (Consol. Laws
Ch. 20) §§ 352eee, 352eeee
N.Y. Real Property Actions and Proceedings
Law (Consol. Laws Ch. 81) §§ 421a, 467b
N.Y. Tax Law (Consol. Laws Ch. 60) § 171b
N.Y. Unconsol. Laws, § 8581 et seq.

Reform Act (Sentence)
Ga. Laws 1994, p. 1959

Reform Act (State Funds)
Tex. Government Code, § 404.091 et seq.

Reform Act (Tort)
Minn. Stat. Ann., 60A.06 et seq.
Mo. Rev. Stat., 408.040, 490.715, 509.050,
510.263, 537.067, 537.068, 537.117,
537.760 et seq., 538.300
Wash. Rev. Code Ann., 4.16.160, 4.16.300,
4.16.310, 4.24.005, 4.24.264, 4.24.420,
4.56.250, 4.56.260, 5.40.050, 5.40.060,
5.60.060, 7.70.090, 48.19.450, 48.22.050,
51.24.060

Reform Act (Welfare)
Neb. Rev. Stat. 1943, 68-1708 et seq.
N.H. Rev. Stat. 1955, 520:1 et seq.

Reform Act for Divorce
N.Y. Domestic Relations Law (Consol. Laws
Ch. 14) §§ 210, 211, 230 and 235

**Reform Act for the Provision of Health Care
for the Medically Indigent**
Colo. Rev. Stat. 1973, 26-15-101 et seq.

Reform of Juvenile Justice Act
Fla. Stat. Ann., 39.0205 et seq.

Reform School Act
Ill. Private Laws 1863, p. 40, Ch. 14
Ky. Rev. Stat. 1971, 198.010 et seq.

Reformation Act (Perpetuities)
Ky. Rev. Stat. 1971, 381.216

Reformatories and Prisions Good Time Act
Ind. Code Ann., 11-7-6.1-1 et seq.

Reformatory Act
Colo. Rev. Stat., 27-22-101 et seq.
Ill. Rev. Stat. 1991, Ch. 38, § 1003-1-1 et
  seq.
Ind. Code Ann., 11-2-3-1 et seq.
Ky. Rev. Stat. 1971, 198.010 et seq.
Neb. Rev. Stat. 1943, 83-465 et seq.

Reformatory Creation Act
Me. Rev. Stat. Ann. 1964, Title 34A, § 3401
  et seq.

Reformatory for Women Act
Ill. Rev. Stat. 1977, Ch. 23, § 2801 et seq.

Reformatory Sentence Act
Me. Rev. Stat. Ann. 1964, Title 17-A, § 1251
  et seq.

Refrigerated Locker Act
Colo. Rev. Stat., 35-33-101 et seq.
Conn. Gen. Stat. Ann., § 21a-60

Refrigerated Warehouses Act
Ill. Rev. Stat. 1991, Ch. 56 1/2, § 79.1 et seq.

Refrigeration and Air Conditioning Contractor License Law
Tex. Rev. Civ. Stat., Art. 8861

Refrigeration Code
N.Y. Adm. Code '85, § 27-4109

Refrigeration, Heating, Ventilation, and Air Conditioning Contractors Act
Md. Ann. Code 1974, Art. BR, § 9A-601 et
  seq.

Refrigeration Law (Egg)
Pa. 1991 Pamph. Laws, No. 32

Refrigerator Act (Abandoned)
Ill. Rev. Stat. 1991, Ch. 23, §§ 2355.9, 2356

Refuge Places Act
Wash. Rev. Code 1951, 74.32.010 et seq.

Refuge Recreation Act
Sept. 28, 1962, P.L. 87-714, 76 Stat. 653, 16
  U.S. Code §§ 460k to 460k-4

Refugee Act of 1980
March 17, 1980, P.L. 96-212, 8 U.S. Code
  §§ 1101 nt., 1151 et seq., 1521 et seq.
April 30, 1994, P.L. 103-236, 8 U.S. Code
  § 1525
Sept. 30, 1996, P.L. 104-208, 8 U.S. Code
  § 1522 nt.

Refugee and Migration Assistance Act of 1962
Nov. 29, 1975, P.L. 94-141, 89 Stat. 771, 22
  U.S. Code § 2601

Refugee Assistance Amendments Act of 1982
Oct. 25, 1982, P.L. 97-363, 8 U.S. Code
  §§ 1101 nt., 1522 to 1524

Refugee Assistance Extension Act of 1986
Nov. 6, 1986, P.L. 99-605, 8 U.S. Code
  § 1101 nt.

Refugee Education Assistance Act of 1980
Oct. 10, 1980, P.L. 96-422, 8 U.S. Code
  § 1522 nt.
Oct. 20, 1994, P.L. 103-382, 8 U.S. Code
  § 1522 nt.
Sept. 30, 1996, P.L. 104-208, 8 U.S. Code
  § 1522 nt.
Aug. 7, 1998, P.L. 105-220, 8 U.S. Code
  § 1522 nt.
Oct. 21, 1998, P.L. 105-277, 8 U.S. Code
  § 1522 nt.

Refugee Relief Act of 1953
Aug. 7, 1953, P.L. 83-203, Ch. 336, 67 Stat.
  400
Aug. 31, 1954, Ch. 1169, 68 Stat. 1045

Refund Act (Motor Fuel Tax)
N.M. Stat. Ann. 1953, 64-26-31 et seq.

Refund Act (Taxes)
Ala. Code 1975, §§ 40-1-11, 40-1-12
Ind. Code Ann., 6-1.1-26-1 et seq.
Neb. Rev. Stat. 1943, 77-1734 et seq.
Okla. Stat. Ann., Title 68, § 227 et seq.
Pa. Purdon's Stat., Title 72, §§ 5566b, 5566c

Refund Anticipation Loan Act
N.C. Gen. Stat. 1943, § 53-245 et seq.

Refund Intercept Program Act (Tax)
N.M. Stat. Ann., 7-2C-1 et seq.

Refund Law (Bottle)
Ore. Rev. Stat., 459A.700 et seq.

Refund Policy Disclosure Act
N.J. Stat. Ann., 56:8-2.14 et seq.

Refund Tax Act
Okla. Stat. Ann., Title 68, § 227 et seq.

Refunding Act
Fla. Stat. Ann., 132.01 et seq.
Miss. Code Ann. 1972, § 31-15-1 et seq.
S.C. Code Ann. 1976, § 11-15-410 et seq.

Refunding Act (County Indebtedness)
Colo. Rev. Stat., 30-26-401 et seq.

Refunding Act (Highway Bonds)
Ark. Act 1947, p. 7, No. 4

Refunding Act (Municipal)
Mich. Comp. Laws Ann., 136.1 et seq.
Neb. Rev. Stat. 1943, 18-1101, 18-1102
Ohio Laws Vol. 116, p. 57

Refunding Act (Public Securities)
Wyo. Stat. Ann., § 9-7-1301 et seq.

Refunding Act (State Bonds)
Mont. Code Ann., 17-5-301 et seq.

Refunding Act (Street Improvement Bonds)
Okla. Stat. Ann., Title 11, § 36-310 et seq.

Refunding Act for Special Obligation Bonds Act
S.C. Code Ann. 1976, § 11-15-600 et seq.

Refunding Act of 1984 for 1915 Improvement Act Bonds
Cal. Streets and Highways Code § 9500 et seq.

Refunding Acts
July 14, 1870, Ch. 256, 16 Stat. 272
Jan. 20, 1871, Ch. 23, 16 Stat. 399

Refunding and Reassessment Act
Cal. Statutes 1931, Ch. 877, p. 1861

Refunding Assessment Bond Act
Cal. Statutes 1935, p. 2023

Refunding Bond Act
N.C. Gen. Stat. 1943, § 142-29.1 et seq.
N.J. Laws 1985, Ch. 74
Utah Code Ann. 1953, 11-27-1 et seq.
Wash. Rev. Code Ann., 39.53.010 et seq.

Refunding Bond Act (Forest Preserve District)
Ill. Rev. Stat. 1991, Ch. 96 1/2, § 6550 et seq.

Refunding Bond Act (Municipal)
Okla. Stat. Ann., Title 62, § 421 et seq.

Refunding Bond Act (State)
W. Va. Code 1966 § 13-2G-1 et seq.

Refunding Bond Act (Township)
Ill. Rev. Stat. 1991, Ch. 139, § 173.9 et seq.

Refunding Bond Authority Act
R.I. Gen. Laws 1956, 35-8.1-1 et seq.

Refunding Bond Authorization Act
D.C. Laws 1975, No. 1-41

Refunding Bond Validation Law (Municipal)
Cal. Statutes 1935, Ch. 92, p. 443

Refunding Revenue Securities Law
Colo. Rev. Stat., 11-54-101 et seq.

Refundments Act
Minn. Stat. Ann., 16A.48

Refuse Collection and Disposal Act (Townships)
Ill. Rev. Stat. 1991, Ch. 139, § 331 et seq.

Refuse Collection Law
N.Y. Local Laws 1969, Town of New Castle, p. 1693
N.Y. Local Laws 1970, Town of New Castle, p. 2134

Refuse Collector Licensing and Regulating Law
N.Y. Local Laws 1969, Town of Richmond, p. 2024

Refuse Disposal Act
Ind. Code Ann., 36-9-6-19
N.M. Stat. Ann., 4-52-1 et seq.

Refuse Disposal Districts Act
N.H. Rev. Stat. 1955, 53-B:1 et seq.

Refuse Disposal Enabling Act (Regional)
Me. Rev. Stat. Ann. 1964, Title 38, § 1701 et seq.

Refuse Disposal Law
N.Y. Local Laws 1967, Town of Webster, p. 2005
N.Y. Local Laws 1969, Town of Hamburg, p. 1310
N.Y. Local Laws 1969, Town of Ramapo, p. 2005
N.Y. Local Laws 1969, Town of Richmond, p. 2021
N.Y. Local Laws 1970, Village of Spring Valley, p. 4166
N.Y. Local Laws 1972, Town of Greene, p. 1574
N.Y. Local Laws 1972 Town of Oxford, p. 2464
N.Y. Local Laws 1972, Town of Skaneateles, p. 2864
N.Y. Local Laws 1973, Village of Greene, p. 3385

Regan-Dills Act (Narcotics)
Cal. Health and Safety Code §§ 11350 et seq., 11500

Regarding Liability for Persons Responding to Oil Spills Act
Ala. Code 1975, § 6-5-332.2

Regents' Academic Scholars Act (State)
Okla. Stat. Ann., Title 70, § 2401 et seq.

Regents College of Law Act
Ill. Rev. Stat. 1991, Ch. 144, §§ 330, 331

Regents Retirement Plan Act
Ga. Code Ann., 47-21-1 et seq.

Regimes Act (Horizontal Property)
Wash. Rev. Code Ann., 64.32.010 et seq.

Regina Mae Armstrong Act
Fla. Stat. Ann., 777.04 et seq.

Regional Action Planning Commission Amendments of 1969
Nov. 25, 1969, P.L. 91-123, 83 Stat. 216, 42 U.S. Code §§ 3181, 3185, 3186, 3188a, 3190 to 3192

Regional Action Planning Commission Improvement Act of 1975
Dec. 31, 1975, P.L. 94-188, 89 Stat. 1087, 42 U.S. Code §§ 3181 et seq.,3182, 3183 nt., 3188a, 3192, 3194 to 3196

Regional Advisory Council Act
N.J. Stat. Ann., 32:25-1 et seq.

Regional Airport Act
Ark. Code Ann. 1987, 14-362-101, 14-362-102 et seq.

Regional Airport Authority Act (Heart of Georgia)
Ga. Laws 1995, p. 4448

Regional Airport Authority Act (Winchester)
Va. Acts 1991, Ch. 687

Regional Airport Authority at Blackstone Act (Southside)
Va. Acts 1992, Ch. 371

Regional Airport Commission Act (Roanoke)
Va. Acts 1986, Ch. 140

Regional Ambulance Services Law
Ill. Rev. Stat. 1989, Ch. 111 1/2, § 8301 et seq.

Regional and County Housing Commission Act
Ky. Rev. Stat. 1971, 80.310 et seq.

Regional and Metropolitan Planning Act (Southwestern Illinois)
Ill. Rev. Stat. 1991, Ch. 85, § 1151 et seq.

Regional and State Planning Act
Fla. Stat. Ann., 186.001 et seq.

Regional Centers of Artistic Excellence Act
N.J. Stat. Ann., 52:16A-26.1 et seq.

Regional Community Colleges Act
Mass. Gen. Laws Ann., 15:27 et seq.

Regional Computer Resource Center Law
Pa. Purdon's Stat., Title 24, § 6001 et seq.

Regional Cooperative Education Act
N.M. Stat. Ann., 22-2B-1 et seq.

Regional Correctional Facilities Act
Ill. Rev. Stat. 1991, Ch. 5, § 2203-1

Regional Correctional Facility Act
Mont. Code Ann., 53-30-501 et seq.

Regional Council Act
Ill. Rev. Stat. 1991, Ch. 85, § 1010 et seq.

Regional County Solid Waste Management District Act (Sacramento)
Cal. Public Resources Code § 60000 et seq.

Regional Development Act
Dec. 19, 1973, P.L. 99-190, 45 U.S. Code § 711
Feb. 28, 1975, P.L. 94-5, 89 Stat. 7, 45 U.S. Code §§ 701 nt., 712, 715 to 717
Dec. 31, 1975, P.L. 94-188, 89 Stat. 1079, 40 U.S. Code Appx. §§ 2 nt., 31 nt., 32, 101, 102, 105 to 107, 201, 202, 205, 207, 211, 214, 223 to 225, 302, 303, 320, 401, 405; 42 U.S. Code §§ 3121, 3181 et seq., 3182, 3183 nt., 3188a, 3192, 3194 to 3196;
Nov. 23, 1977, P.L. 95-199, 45 U.S. Code §§ 712 et seq.
Nov. 1, 1978, P.L. 95-565, 45 U.S. Code §§ 726, 747
Nov. 4, 1978, P.L. 95-597, 45 U.S. Code §§ 743, 743 nt.
Nov. 8, 1978, P.L. 95-607, 45 U.S. Code § 744
Nov. 8, 1978, P.L. 95-611, 45 U.S. Code §§ 711, 716, 721, 724

Sept. 29, 1979, P.L. 96-73, 45 U.S. Code §§ 712, 721, 724, 743
Nov. 4, 1979, P.L. 96-101, 45 U.S. Code § 721
May 30, 1980, P.L. 96-254, 45 U.S. Code § 726
Dec. 21, 1982, P.L. 97-365, 45 U.S. Code § 792
Nov. 8, 1984, P.L. 98-620, 45 U.S. Code § 745
April 7, 1986, P.L. 99-272, 45 U.S. Code §§ 797b nt., 797c
Oct. 21, 1986, P.L. 99-509, 45 U.S. Code §§ 702, 726, 727, 741, 797, 797i
June 27, 1988, P.L. 100-352, 102 Stat. 663, 45 U.S. Code §§ 719, 743
Dec. 29, 1995, P.L. 104-88, 45 U.S. Code §§ 702, 741, 744, 748, 797I
Oct. 19, 1996, P.L. 104-317, 45 U.S. Code §§ 719, 743, 745
June 9, 1998, P.L. 105-178, 45 U.S. Code § 721
Minn. Stat. Ann., 462.381 et seq.
Minn. Stat. 1986, 462.383

Regional Development Act (Appalachian)
Md. Ann. Code 1957, Art. 41A, § 6-401 et seq.

Regional Development Authority Law (Will-Kankakee)
Ill. Rev. Stat. 1991, Ch. 85, § 7451 et seq.

Regional Diagnostic Center Act
Mich. Comp. Laws 1970, 330.21

Regional Disposal Authority Act (Hamilton County)
Tenn. Private Acts 1972, Ch. 420

Regional District Act (Maryland-Washington)
Md. Laws 1943, Ch. 992

Regional Economic Development Act
Conn. Public Acts 1993, No. 382, §§ 23 to 28
Ore. Rev. Stat., 285.630

Regional Economic Development Authority Act (Quad Cities)
Ill. Rev. Stat. 1991, Ch. 85, §§ 6201 et seq., 6501 et seq.

Regional Education Compact Act (Southern)
Ky. Acts 1950, Ch. 252
Md. Ann. Code 1974, Art. ED, § 25-201 et seq.

Regional Education Service Agencies Act (Voluntary)
Va. Code 1950, § 22-351 et seq.

Regional Education Service Center Act
Okla. Stat. Ann., Title 70, § 1210.271 et seq.

Regional Educational Compact Act
Tex. Education Code, § 160.01 et seq.

Regional Employment Assessment, Job Search Assistance, and Placement Services for Displaced Workers Act
Cal. Unemployment Insurance Code § 9970 et seq.

Regional Field Offices Act (Public-Private)
N.J. Laws 1995, Ch. 205

Regional Forest Fire Protection Compact Act
Ga. Code Ann., 12-10-61 et seq.

Regional Fuel Tax Agreement Act
N.H. Rev. Stat. 1955, 260:65-b to 260:65-d

Regional Health Authority Act (Santa Barbara)
Cal. Health and Safety Code § 1175 et seq.

Regional Health Services Districts Act
S.C. Code Ann. 1976, § 44-7-2010 et seq.

Regional Housing Act
N.M. Stat. Ann., 11-3A-1 et seq.

Regional Housing Authority Act
Ga. Code Ann., 8-3-100 et seq.
Tex. Local Government Code, § 392.001 et seq.

Regional Intermodal Facilities Act
Ark. Code Ann. 1987, 14-143-101 et seq.

Regional Interstate Banking Act
Ga. Code Ann., 7-1-620 et seq.

Regional Jail and Jail Facility Authority Act
W. Va. Code 1966 § 31-20-1 et seq.

Regional Jail Authorities Act
Ga. Code Ann., 42-4-90 to 42-2-105

Regional Jail Authority Act
Va. Acts 1990, Ch. 725

Regional Jail Capital Expenditures Act (Grants to Counties for)
Ga. Code Ann., 42-4-120 et seq.

Regional Juvenile Services Act
N.M. Stat. Ann., 33-12-1 et seq.

Regional Library Act
Mich. Comp. Laws Ann., 397.151 et seq.

Regional Library Facilities and Services Act (Shasta County)
Cal. Government Code § 26170 et seq.

Regional Low-Level Radioactive Waste Disposal Facility Siting Act
N.J. Stat. Ann., 13:1E-177 et seq.

Regional Market Authority Act (Albany)
N.Y. Public Authorities Law (Consol. Laws Ch. 43A) § 850 et seq.

Regional Market Authority Act (Central New York)
N.Y. Public Authorities Law (Consol. Laws Ch. 43A) § 825 et seq.

Regional Market Authority Act (Genesee Valley)
N.Y. Public Authorities Law (Consol. Laws Ch. 43A) § 875 et seq.

Regional Market Authority Act (Lower Hudson)
N.Y. Public Authorities Law (Consol. Laws Ch. 43A) § 800 et seq.

Regional Mental Health Services Act
Ida. Code 1947, 39-3123 et seq.

Regional Off-track Betting Corporation Law
N.Y. Laws 1973, Ch. 346, § 5

Regional Park Districts Law
Cal. Public Resources Code § 5500 et seq.

Regional Parking Authority Act (Village of Monroe)
N.Y. Public Authorities Law (Consol. Laws Ch. 43A) § 1420a et seq.

Regional Planning Act
Cal. Government Code § 65000 et seq.
Ind. Code Ann., 18-7-1.1-1 et seq.
La. Rev. Stat. Ann., 33:131 et seq.
Mass. Gen. Laws Ann., 40B:1 et seq.
Mich. Comp. Laws Ann., 125.11 et seq.
N.M. Stat. Ann., 3-56-1 et seq.
Pa. Cons. Stat., Title 53, § 2341 et seq.
Pa. Purdon's Stat., Title 53, § 491 et seq.
S.C. Code Ann. 1976, § 6-7-110 et seq.

Regional Planning and Community Development Act
Mo. Rev. Stat., 251.150 et seq.

Regional Planning Commission Act
Ill. Rev. Stat. 1991, Ch. 85, §§ 1020, 1021
Iowa Code Ann., 473A.1 et seq.
Okla. Laws 1943, p. 26
Wis. Stat. Ann., 66.945

Regional Planning Compact Act (Bi-State)
N.Y. Laws 1965, Ch. 413

Regional Planning Compact Act (Interstate)
N.H. Rev. Stat. 1955, 36-B:1, 36-B:2

Regional Planning Compact Act (Tri-State)
N.Y. Unconsol. Laws § 8301 et seq.

Regional Planning Council Act
Fla. Stat. Ann., 186.501 et seq.

Regional Planning Enabling Act
Ill. Rev. Stat. 1991, Ch. 34, § 5-14001 et seq.

Regional Port District Act (Havana)
Ill. Rev. Stat. 1991, Ch. 19, § 600 et seq.

Regional Port District Act (Illinois Valley)
Ill. Rev. Stat. 1991, Ch. 19, § 801 et seq.

Regional Port District Act (Jackson-Union Counties)
Ill. Rev. Stat. 1991, Ch. 19, § 851 et seq.

Regional Port District Act (Joliet)
Ill. Rev. Stat. 1991, Ch. 19, § 251 et seq.

Regional Port District Act (Kaskaskia)
Ill. Comp. Stat. 1992, Ch. 70, § 1830/1.1 et seq.

Regional Port District Act (Mt. Carmel)
Ill. Rev. Stat. 1991, Ch. 19, § 701 et seq.

Regional Port District Publicity Act
Ill. Rev. Stat. 1991, Ch. 19, §§ 491.9, 492

Regional Public Transportation Authority Act
Ida. Code 1947, 40-2101 et seq.
N.C. Gen. Stat. 1943, § 160A-600 et seq.

Regional Rail Reorganization Act of 1973
Jan. 2, 1974, P.L. 93-236, 87 Stat. 985, 31 U.S. Code § 856; 45 U.S. Code §§ 701, 711 to 725, 741 to 744, 761 to 763, 771 to 779, 791 to 793

Regional Railroad Authorities Act
Minn. Stat. Ann., 398A.01 et seq.
N.D. Cent. Code, 49-17.2-01 et seq.
S.D. Codified Laws 1967, 49-17A-1 et seq.

Regional Reciprocal Banking Act
Ala. Code 1975, § 5-13A-1 et seq.
Ark. Code Ann. 1987, 23-32-1801 et seq.
Fla. Stat. Ann., 658.295
N.C. Gen. Stat. 1943, § 53-209 et seq.
Tenn. Code Ann., 45-12-101 et seq.

Regional Reciprocal Savings and Loan Acquisition Act
N.C. Gen. Stat. 1943, § 54B-48.1 et seq.

Regional Reciprocal Savings Institutions Act
Ala. Acts 1987, p. 207, No. 152
Tenn. Code Ann., 45-3-1401 et seq.

Regional Refuse Disposal Districts Act
N.H. Rev. Stat. 1955, 53-B:1 et seq.

Regional Renaissance Initiative Act (Southwestern Pennsylvania)
Pa. Purdon's Stat., Title 16, § 3011 et seq.

Regional Ride Share Services Matching Fund Program
Me. Rev. Stat. Ann. 1964, Title 10, § 1461 et seq.

Regional Sanitary Sewer Districts Act
Minn. Stat. Ann., 115.61 et seq.

Regional Savings and Loan Act
Ark. Code Ann. 1987, 23-37-801 et seq.

Regional School District Act
Mass. Gen. Laws Ann., 71:14 et seq.

Regional School District Act (Chariho)
R.I. Public Laws 1958, Ch. 55, § 20
R.I. Public Laws 1992, Ch. 479

Regional School District Athletic Field Loan Act (Wachusett)
Mass. Acts 1967, Ch. 84

Regional Sewage Disposal District Act
Cal. Health and Safety Code § 5900 et seq.

Regional Sewage Disposal Planning Act
N.C. Gen. Stat. 1943, § 162A-26 et seq.

Regional Solid Waste Management Authorities Act
Ga. Code Ann., 12-8-50 et seq.
Miss. Code Ann. 1972, § 17-17-301 et seq.

Regional Tollway Authority Act
Tex. Transportation Code, § 366.001 et seq.

Regional Tourism Marketing Act
Mich. Comp. Laws Ann., 141.891 et seq.

Regional Transit Authority Act
La. Rev. Stat. Ann., 48:1651 et seq.

Regional Transit District Act (Sacramento)
Cal. Public Utilities Code § 102000 et seq.

Regional Transit Districts Act
Vt. Stat. Ann., Title 24, § 5121 et seq.

Regional Transportation and Regional Planning Act
Ind. Laws 1965, Ch. 349, p. 1034

Regional Transportation Authority Act
Del. Code of 1974. Title 2, § 1301 et seq.
Fla. Stat. Ann., 163.565 eq seq.
Ill. Rev. Stat. 1991, Ch. 111 2/3, § 701.01 et seq.
Mass. Gen. Laws Ann., 161B:1 et seq.
S.C. Code Ann. 1976, § 58-25-10 et seq.
Va. Stat. Ann., Title 29, § 701 et seq.

Regional Transportation Authority Act (Central Florida)
Fla. Stat. Ann., 343.61 et seq.

Regional Transportation Commission Act (San Diego County)
Cal. Public Utilities Code § 132000 et seq.

Regional Transportation District Act
Colo. Rev. Stat., 32-9-101 et seq.

Regional Universities Act
N.C. Gen. Stat. 1943, § 116-44.10 et seq.

Regional Vocational and Trade School Act
Ala. Code 1975, § 16-60-190 et seq.

Regional Waste Disposal Act
Tex. Water Code, § 30.001 et seq.

Regional Water and Sewer Districts Act
Ohio Rev. Code 1953, 6119.01 et seq.

Regional Water Authority Act (West Georgia)
Ga. Laws 1988, p. 4926

Regional Water Board (Upper Mohawk Valley)
N.Y. Public Authorities Law (Consol. Laws Ch. 43A) § 1226aa et seq.

Regional Water Distribution District Act
Ark. Code Ann. 1987, 14-116-101 et seq.

Regional Water Supply Planning Act
N.C. Gen. Stat. 1943, § 162A-20 et seq.

Register Act
See also Federal Register Act
Pa. 1945 Pamph. Laws 1392, No. 443
Va. Code 1950, § 9-6.15 et seq.
Wash. Rev. Code Ann., 34.08.010 et seq.

Register Act (Court)
S.C. Code Ann. 1976, § 14-3-940 et seq.

Register Act (State)
S.C. Code Ann. 1976, § 1-23-10 et seq.

Register and Administrative Procedure Act
Tex. Rev. Civ. Stat., Art. 6252-13a

Register for Missing Children (Central)
Mass. Gen. Laws Ann., 22A:1 et seq.

Register of Critical Areas Act (State)
Me. Rev. Stat. Ann. 1964, Title 5, § 3310 et seq.

Register of Historic Places Act
Okla. Stat. Ann., Title 53, § 351 et seq.

Register of Wills Act
Pa. Purdon's Stat., Title 20, § 1840.101 et seq.
Pa. 1917 Pamph. Laws 415, No. 191

Register of Wills Fee Bill Act (First Class County)
Pa. 1982 Pamph. Laws 11, No. 5

Register Publication Act
D.C. Code Ann., § 1-1505

Registered Agent Act
S.D. Codified Laws 1967, 47-2-27 et seq.

Registered Agent Act (Corporation)
Neb. Rev. Stat. 1943, 21-20,113 et seq.

Registered Architects Act
Pa. Purdon's Stat., Title 63, § 34.1 et seq.

Registered Bond Act
Ill. Rev. Stat. 1991, Ch. 17, § 6651 et seq.
Miss. Code Ann. 1972, § 31-21-1 et seq.

Registered Construction Inspectors Law
Cal. Business and Professions Code § 9100 et seq.

Registered Container Trade Mark Act
Ill. Rev. Stat. 1991, Ch. 140, § 121 et seq.

Registered Electrologist Act
Okla. Stat. Ann., Title 59, § 536.1 et seq.

Registered Land Surveyors Act
Nev. Rev. Stat. 1979 Reprint, 625.250 et seq.

Registered Limited Liability Partnership Act
Ariz. Rev. Stat. Ann., § 29-244 et seq.

Registered Nurse Practitioner Student Scholarship Program (Advanced)
Kan. Stat. Ann., 74-32,131 et seq.

Registered Nurses Act
Mo. Rev. Stat., 335.011 et seq.
N.H. Rev. Stat. 1955, 326-B:1 et seq.
Tenn. Code Ann., 63-7-101 et seq.
Wash. Rev. Code Ann., 18.88.005 et seq.

Registered Nurses and Licensed Attendants Act
Pa. 1927 Pamph. Laws 988, No. 477

Registered Nurses Baccalaureate Assistance Law
Ill. Comp. Stat. 1992, Ch. 110, § 915/1 et seq.
Ill. Rev. Stat. 1991, Ch. 144, § 1401 et seq.

Registered Physical Therapists Law
Mass. Gen. Laws Ann., 112:23A et seq.

Registered Professional Geologists Practice Act
Miss. Code Ann. 1972, § 76-63-1 et seq.

Registered Professional Nurse Practice Act
Ga. Code Ann., 43-26-1 et seq.

Registered Public Obligations Act
Ark. Code Ann. 1987, 19-9-401 et seq.
Cal. Government Code §§ 5050 to 5062
Fla. Stat. Ann., 279.01 et seq.
Ida. Code 1947, 57-901 et seq.
N.C. Gen. Stat. 1943, § 159E-1 et seq.
Okla. Stat. Ann., Title 62, § 581 et seq.
R.I. Gen. Laws 1956, 35-13-1 et seq.
Utah Code Ann. 1953, 15-7-1 et seq.

Registered Public Surveyors Act
Tex. Rev. Civ. Stat., Art. 5282a

Registered Sanitarians Act
Ky. Rev. Stat. 1971, 223.010 et seq.
Utah Code Ann. 1953, 58-20-0.5 et seq.

Registered Titles Act (Torrens)
Ill. Rev. Stat. 1991, Ch. 30, § 44h et seq.

Registered Volunteers Program Act
Ark. Code Ann. 1987, 6-22-101 et seq.

Registers of Deeds Supplemental Pension Fund Act
N.C. Gen. Stat. 1943, § 161-50 et seq.

Registrars of Property Appeals Act
P.R. Laws Ann. 1954, Title 30, § 2271 et seq.

Registration Act
Ind. Code Ann., 3-7-1-1 et seq.
P.R. Laws Ann. 1954, Title 16, § 391 et seq.

Registration Act (Absentee Voters)
Fla. Laws 1935, Ch. 16987

Registration Act (Accountants')
Mass. Gen. Laws Ann., 112:87A et seq.

Registration Act (Aircraft)
Fla. Stat. Ann., 329.10

Registration Act (Architects')
Mass. Gen. Laws Ann., 112.60A et seq.
N.H. Rev. Stat. 1955, 310-A:28 et seq.

Registration Act (Athletic Trainers)
Kan. Stat. Ann., 65-6901 et seq.

Registration Act (Auctioneer)
Wash. Rev. Code Ann., 18.11.050 et seq.

Registration Act (Automobiles)
See Automobile Registration Act

Registration Act (Bee Keepers)
Ore. Rev. Stat., 602.010 et seq.

Registration Act (Boroughs, Towns and Townships)
Pa. Purdon's Stat., Title 25, § 951-1 et seq.

Registration Act (Business Names)
Mass. Gen. Laws Ann., 110:5
Vt. Stat. Ann., Title 11, § 1621 et seq.

Registration Act (Conveyances)
Haw. Rev. Stat. Ann., § 502-1 et seq.
Ill. Rev. Stat. 1991, Ch. 30, § 29

Registration Act (Corporations)
Mo. Rev. Stat., 351.120 et seq.

Registration Act (Dade County)
Fla. Laws 1945, Ch. 22971

Registration Act (Dentists)
Mass. Gen. Laws Ann., 112:43 et seq.

Registration Act (Elections)
Ala. Code 1975, § 17-4-120 et seq.
Colo. Rev. Stat. 1-2-201 et seq.
Mich. Comp. Laws Ann., 168.491 et seq.
Miss. Code Ann. 1972, § 23-5-301 et seq.
Mo. Rev. Stat., 115.132 et seq.
Mont. Code Ann., 13-2-102 et seq.
R.I. Gen. Laws 1956, 17-9-1 et seq.
S.D. Codified Laws 1967, 12-4-1 et seq.
Utah Code Ann. 1953, 20-2-1 et seq.
Wash. Rev. Code Ann., 29.07.010 et seq.

Registration Act (Engineers)
Mont. Code Ann., 37-67-101 et seq.
Nev. Rev. Stat. 1979 Reprint, 625.010 et seq.
N.M. Stat. Ann. 1953, 67-21-1 et seq.
Pa. 1921 Pamph. Laws 1131, No. 422
Pa. 1927 Pamph. Laws 820, No. 415
Pa. 1945 Pamph. Laws 913, No. 367

Registration Act (Environmental Specialist and Sanitarian)
Okla. Stat. Ann., Title 59, § 1150.1 et seq.

Registration Act (Family Day Care Provider)
N.J. Stat. Ann., 30:5B-16 et seq.

Registration Act (Federal Tax Lien)
See Federal Tax Lien Registration Act

Registration Act (First Class Cities)
Ky. Rev. Stat. 1971, Superseded Vols., 117.675
Pa. Purdon's Stat., Title 25, § 623.1 et seq.

Registration Act (Foreign Corporation)
Ala. Code 1975, § 10-2A-220 et seq.
Colo. Rev. Stat., 38-25-101 et seq.
Md. Ann. Code 1974, Art. CA, § 7-201 et seq.
Me. Rev. Stat. Ann. 1964, Title 33, § 1801 et seq.
N.Y. Business Corporations Law 1961 (Consol. Laws Ch. 4) §§ 1301 et seq., 1304
Pa. Pamph. Laws 1874, 108, No. 33

Registration Act (General)
P.R. Laws Ann. 1954, Title 16, § 391 et seq.

Registration Act (Health Care Assistant)
Utah Code Ann. 1953, 58-60-101 et seq.

Registration Act (Hotels)
N.H. Rev. Stat. 1955, 353:3

Registration Act (Land Surveying)
N.M. Stat. Ann. 1953, 67-21-1 et seq.

Registration Act (Land)
Alaska Stat. 1962, § 34.10.010 et seq.
Colo. Rev. Stat., 38-36-101 et seq.
Ga. Code Ann., 44-2-40 et seq.

Haw. Rev. Stat. Ann., § 501-1 et seq.
Mass. Gen. Laws Ann., 185:1 et seq.
Minn. Stat. Ann., 508.01 et seq.
S.D. Codified Laws 1967, 43-30-1 et seq.
Utah Code Ann. 1953, 58-20-0.5 et seq.
Wash. Rev Code Ann., 65.12.005 et seq.

Registration Act (Legal Instruments)
N.C. Gen. Stat. 1943, § 47-17 et seq.

Registration Act (Lobbyists)
Vt. Stat. Ann., Title 2, § 251 et seq.

Registration Act (Medical)
Md. Ann. Code 1974, Art. HO, § 14-301 et seq.

Registration Act (Missing Children)
Ill. Rev. Stat. 1991, Ch. 23, § 2270 et seq.
Pa. Purdon's Stat., Title 35, § 401-A et seq.

Registration Act (Mortgages)
See Mortgage Registration Act

Registration Act (Motor Vehicles)
See Motor Vehicle Registration Act

Registration Act (Motor)
Mont. Code Ann., 61-3-301 et seq.

Registration Act (Nurses)
Mass. Gen. Laws Ann., 112.108 et seq.
Md. Ann. Code 1974, Art. HO, § 8-301 et seq.
N.Y. Education Law 1947 (Consol. Laws Ch. 16) § 6900 et seq.

Registration Act (Nursing Home Administration)
Mass. Gen. Laws Ann., 112:108 et seq.

Registration Act (Optometrists)
Mass. Gen. Laws Ann., 112:66 et seq.

Registration Act (Organizations)
Ark. Stat. 1947, 6-817 et seq.

Registration Act (Permanent)
Md. Ann. Code 1957, Art. 33, § 3-3 et seq.

Registration Act (Pharmacists)
Mass. Gen. Laws Ann., 112:24 et seq.

Registration Act (Physical Therapy)
Cal. Business and Professions Code § 2601

Registration Act (Physicians and Surgeons)
N.M. Stat. Ann., 61-6-22 et seq.

Registration Act (Physicians)
Mass. Gen. Laws Ann., 112:2 et seq.

Registration Act (Podiatrists')
Mass. Gen. Laws Ann., 112:13 et seq.

Registration Act (Professional Engineers and Land Surveyors)
Pa. Purdon's Stat., Title 63, § 148 et seq.

Registration Act (Professional Engineers)
Mass. Gen. Laws Ann., 112:81D et seq.

Registration Act (Proprietary School and College)
Miss. Code Ann. 1972, § 75-60-1 et seq.

Registration Act (Psychologists')
Mass. Gen. Laws Ann., 112:118 et seq.

Registration Act (Public Obligations)
W. Va. Code 1966 § 13-2F-1 et seq.

Registration Act (Racial Integration)
Va. Code 1950, Misc. Superseded Code Provisions, § 18.1-380

Registration Act (Recording)
S.C. Code Ann. 1976, § 30-5-10 et seq.

Registration Act (Records)
Tenn. Code Ann., 66-24-101 et seq.
Tex. Rev. Civ. Stat., Art. 6591 et seq.

Registration Act (Sanitarian and Environmental Specialist)
Okla. Stat. Ann., Title 59, § 1150.1 et seq.

Registration Act (Sanitarians)
Fla. Stat. Ann., 491.01 et seq.

Registration Act (School and College)
Miss. Code Ann. 1972, § 75-60-1 et seq.

Registration Act (Second Class Cities)
Pa. Purdon's Stat., Title 25, § 951-1 et seq.

Registration Act (Securities)
Minn. Stat. Ann., 80A.01 et seq.

Registration Act (Sex Offenders)
Ida. Code 1947, 18-8301 et seq.
Me. Rev. Stat. Ann. 1964, Title 34-A, § 11001
Mich. Comp. Laws Ann., 28.721 et seq.
Minn. Stat. Ann., 243.166
Mont. Laws 1991, Ch. 293
N.M. Stat. Ann., 29-11A-1 et seq.
Okla. Stat. Ann., Title 57, § 581 et seq.
W. Va. Code 1966 § 61-8F-1 et seq.

Registration Act (Sexual or Violent Offender)
Mont. Code Ann., 46-18-254, 46-18-255, 46-23-501 et seq.

Registration Act (Subversive Organizations)
Cal. Corporations Code § 35000 et seq.
Mont. Rev. Code 1947, 94-4411 et seq.

Registration Act (Third Class Cities)
Pa. Purdon's Stat., Title 25, § 951-1 et seq.

Registration Act (Torrens)
See Torrens Land Title Registration Act

Registration Act (Trade Names)
See Trade Names Registration Act

Registration Act (Trademarks)
See also Trade Names Registration Act
Neb. Rev. Stat. 1943, 87-111 et seq.

Registration Act (Trailers)
Wis. Stat. Ann., 341.25, Subsec. 1

Registration Act (Trustees)
Minn. Stat. Ann., 507.35

Registration Act (Tulsa County)
Okla. Stat. Ann., Title 26, § 4-101 et seq.

Registration Act (Used Car Dealers)
Ga. Code Ann., 43-47-1 et seq.

Registration Act (Vehicles)
Cal. Vehicle Code 1959, § 4000 et seq.

Registration Act (Vessel and Motor)
Okla. Stat. Ann., Title 63, §§ 4001 to 4043

Registration Act (Veterinarians)
Mass. Gen. Laws Ann., 112:54 et seq.

Registration Act (Vital Statistics)
Ky. Rev. Stat. 1971, Superseded Vols., 213.010 et seq.

Registration Act (Vocational)
Mont. Code Ann. 1947, 41-801 et seq.

Registration Act (Voter)
Fla. Stat. Ann., 97.032

Registration Act (Voters')
See Voters' Registration Act

Registration Acts (Vehicles)
N.Y. Vehicle and Traffic Laws 1959 (Consol. Laws Ch. 71) § 401

Registration and Disclosure Act (Continuing Care Provider)
La. Rev. Stat. Ann., 51:2171 et seq.
Pa. Purdon's Stat., Title 40, § 3201 et seq.

Registration and Disclosure Act (Lobbyist)
Tenn. Code Ann., 3-6-101 et seq.

Registration and Investigation Act (Charitable)
N.J. Stat. Ann., 45:17A-18 et seq.

Registration and License Fee Exemption Act (Special Equipment)
Cal. Vehicle Code 1959, § 4010

Registration and License Tax Act (Aircraft)
Ohio Rev. Code 1953, 4561.17 et seq.

Registration and Licensing Act (Motor Vehicles)
S.C. Code Ann. 1976, § 56-3-10 et seq.

Registration and Licensing Fees Act
D.C. Code Ann., § 1-346, 1-347

Registration and Professional Certification Act (Tax Assessors)
Tex. Rev. Civ. Stat., Art. 8885

Registration and Purgation Act
Ky. Rev. Stat. 1971, 116.015.

Registration and Voting of Electors Act (Military Services)
Utah Code Ann. 1953, 20-17-1 et seq.

Registration by Mail Act (Voter)
S.C. Code Ann. 1976, § 7-5-155 et seq.

Registration Date Act (Motor Vehicles)
D.C. Code 1973, § 40-102

Registration Law
Miss. Code Ann. 1972, § 23-5-301 et seq.
Pa. Purdon's Stat., Title 63, § 151.1

Registration Law (Engineer, Land Surveyor and Geologist)
Pa. 1992 Pamph. Laws, No. 151

Registration Law (Vehicles)
N.Y. Vehicle and Traffic Law 1959 (Consol. Laws, Ch. 71), § 401

Registration of Athletes Agents Act
Iowa Code Ann., 9A.1 et seq.
Wash. Rev. code. Ann., 18.175.010 et seq.

Registration of Birth Act
D.C. Code Ann., § 6-201 et seq.

Registration of Foreign Business Trusts Act
Miss. Code Ann. 1972, § 79-16-1 et seq.

Registration of Foreign Limited Liability Companies Act
Miss. Code Ann. 1972, § 79-6-1 et seq.

Registration of Foreign Limited Liability Partnerships Act
Miss. Code Ann. 1972, § 79-31-1 et seq.

Registration of Geologists Act
Ark. Code Ann. 1987, 17-45-101 et seq.
Del. Code of 1974, Title 24, § 3601 et seq.
Ga. Code Ann., 43-19-1 et seq.

Registration of Insurance Holding Companies Act
Del. Code of 1974, Title 18, § 5001 et seq.

Registration of State Administrative Rules Act
N.C. Gen. Stat. 1943, §§ 150A-58 et seq., 150B-18

Registration of Title Act
Minn. Stat. Ann., 508.01 et seq.

Registration of Vehicles Act
Haw. Rev. Stat. § 286-41 et seq.

Registration of Voters Act
See Voters' Registration Act

Registration Requirements Act for Certain Makers of Mortgages and Deeds of Trust on Residential Real Property
N.C. Gen. Stat. 1943, § 53-233 et seq.

Registration Requirements for Mortgage Loan Brokers Act
S.C. Code Ann. 1976, § 40-58-10 et seq.

Registration Tax Act (Business Franchises)
W. Va. Code 1966, § 11-12-1 et seq.

Registration Tax Act (Vehicles)
S.D. Codified Laws 1967, 32-5-1 et seq.

Registration under False Pretenses Act (Animal)
Ill. Comp. Stat. 1992, Ch. 720, §§ 720/0.01, 720/1

Registry Act (Cancer)
Miss. Code Ann. 1972, § 41-9-1 et seq.

Registry Act (Chattel Mortgages)
Ark. Stat. 1947, 16-201

Registry Act (Conveyances)
Ky. Rev. Stat. 1971, 382.080 et seq.
La. Civil Code Art. 2251 et seq.
N.J. Stat. Ann., 46:15-1 et seq.
S.C. Code Ann. 1962, § 60-1 et seq.

Registry Act (Corporations)
Pa. Purdon's Stat., Title 15, § 1 et seq.

Registry Act (Instruments of Debt)
Ga. Code Ann., 44-14-140 et seq.

Registry Act (Opticians)
Tex. Rev. Civ. Stat., Art. 4551-1

Registry Act (Real Estate)
Pa. Purdon's Stat., Title 53, § 16951 et seq.

Registry Act (Vital Statistics)
P.R. Laws Ann. 1954, Title 24, § 1041

Registry of Deeds Loan Act (Norfolk County)
Mass. Acts 1959, Ch. 472

Registry of Deeds Loan Act (Plymouth County)
Mass. Acts 1952, Ch. 475

Registry of Election Finance Act
Tenn. Code Ann., 2-10-201 et seq.

Registry of Powers of Attorney Act
P.R. Laws Ann. 1954, Title 4, § 921 et seq.

Regular Life Act (Insurance)
Mo. Rev. Stat., 376.010 et seq.

Regular Pay Day Law
Cal. Labor Code § 200 et seq.

Regular Salary Procedures and Restrictions Act
Ark. Acts 1973, No. 284

Regular School Attendence Law
S.C. Code Ann. 1976, § 59-65-10 et seq.

Regulated Certified Bank Act
Ga. Code 1933, 13-2301 et seq.

Regulated Loan Act
Iowa Code Ann., 536.1 et seq.
Minn. Stat. Ann., 56.001 et seq.

Regulated Medical Waste Management Act
N.J. Stat. Ann., 13:1E-48.1 et seq.

Regulated Shooting Preserve Act
N.M. Stat. Ann., 17-3-35 et seq.

Regulating Traffic on Highways Act
Ga. Code Ann., 40-1-1 et seq.
Ind. Code Ann., 9-4-1-1 et seq.
Mont. Code Ann., 61-8-101 et seq., 61-9-101
et seq.
S.C. Code Ann. 1976, § 56-5-10 et seq.

Regulation Act (Aboveground Tank)
Okla. Stat. Ann., Title 17, § 401 et seq.

Regulation Act (Boat)
See Boat Regulation Act

Regulation Act (Coal Mines)
Ill. Rev. Stat. 1991, Ch. 96 1/2, § 3801 et seq.

Regulation Act (Collection Agency)
La. Rev. Stat. Ann., 9:3576.1 et seq.

Regulation Act (Credit)
Mass. Gen. Laws Ann., 140D:1 et seq.

Regulation Act (Hospitals)
Ga. Code Ann., 31-7-1 et seq.

Regulation Act (Milk Processors')
Miss. Code Ann. 1972, § 75-31-501 et seq.

Regulation Act (Tanning Facility)
Iowa Code Ann., 136D.1 et seq.

Regulation Act (Water Service)
Neb. Rev. Stat. 1943, 75-1001 et seq.

Regulation Act (Wine)
Ga. Code Ann., 3-6-20 et seq.

**Regulation and Integral Development of
Artisanry Act**
P.R. Laws Ann. 1954, Title 18, § 1205 et seq.

Regulation and Licensing Department Act
N.M. Stat. Ann., 9-16-1 et seq.

**Regulation of Agreements and Practices
(Consumer Credit Code)**
Iowa Code Ann., 537.3101 et seq.
Me. Rev. Stat. Ann. 1964, Title 9-A, § 3-101
et seq.

**Regulation of Agreements and Practices
(Revised Uniform Consumer Credit
Code)**
See Revised Uniform Consumer Credit
Code—Regulation of Agreements and
Practices

Regulation of Birds and Mammals Act
Ind. Code Ann., 14-2-4-1 et seq.

**Regulation of Burglar Alarm System
Businesses Act**
S.C. Code Ann. 1976, § 40-79-10 et seq.

**Regulation of Business Practice and
Consumer Protection Act**
Mass. Gen. Laws Ann., 93A:1 et seq.

**Regulation of Business Practices between
Vehicle Manufacturers, Distributors and
Dealers**
Me. Rev. Stat. Ann. 1964, Title 10, § 1431 et
seq.

Regulation of Chiropractors Act
Ind. Code Ann., 25-10-1-1 et seq.

**Regulation of Credit Accident and Health
Insurance (Model Act)**
Nev. Rev. Stat. 1967 Reprint, 692.500 et seq.

**Regulation of Credit Life Insurance and
Credit Accident and Health Insurance
Act**
See Credit Life Insurance and Credit
Accident and Health Insurance Act

Regulation of Credit Life Insurance and Credit Health Insurance Act
N.M. Stat. Ann., 59A-25-1 et seq.

Regulation of Dentistry Act
Mont. Code Ann., 37-4-101 et seq.

Regulation of Escrow Businesses Act
Mont. Laws 1991, Ch. 651

Regulation of Health Professions Act
Neb. Rev. Stat. 1943, 71-6201 et seq.
Wash. Rev. Code Ann., 18.120.010 et seq.

Regulation of Hospitals Act
Alaska Stat. 1962, § 18.20.010 et seq.

Regulation of Invention Development Services Act
Tex. Rev. Civ. Stat. 1974, Art. 9020

Regulation of Lobbying Act
Alaska Stat. 1962, § 24.45.011 et seq.
N.Y. Laws 1977, Ch. 937, § 1

Regulation of Materials Used in Mattresses and Bedding Act
Ind. Code Ann., 16-1-33-1, 16-9-4-1 et seq.

Regulation of Precursors to Controlled Substances Act
Haw. Rev. Stat. Ann., §§ 329-81 to 329-91

Regulation of Reserves Ceded to Nonadmitted Reinsurers Act
Ark. Code Ann. 1987, 23-62-302 et seq.

Regulation of Unauthorized Insurance Act
Colo. Rev. Stat., 10-3-901 et seq.

Regulations and Permits Administration Organic Act
P.R. Laws Ann. 1954, Title 23, § 71 et seq.

Regulations for Pedestrian Act
S.C. Code Ann. 1976, § 56-5-3110 et seq.

Regulatory Accountancy Act
Iowa Code Ann., 116.1 et seq.

Regulatory Act (Check Cashers)
N.J. Stat. Ann., 17:15A-30 et seq.

Regulatory Act (Medical Waste)
Mich. Comp. Laws Ann., 333.13801 et seq.

Regulatory Act (Public Utility)
Tex. Rev. Civ. Stat., Art. 1446c-0

Regulatory Act (Scrap Tire)
Mich. Comp. Laws Ann., 299.561 et seq.

Regulatory Agency Review Act
Ga. Code Ann., 43-2-1 et seq.

Regulatory Agency Sunset Act
Ill. Rev. Stat. 1991, Ch. 127, § 1901 et seq.

Regulatory and Licensing Act (Pilots)
Tex. Rev. Civ. Stat., Art. 8280c

Regulatory and Reclamation Act (Coal Mining)
Mass. Gen. Laws Ann., 21B:1 et seq.

Regulatory Authorization Act (Telecommunications)
Del. Code of 1974, Title 26, § 701 et seq.

Regulatory Fairness Act
Wash. Rev. Code 1983, 19.85.010 et seq.

Regulatory Fee Law (Environmental)
N.Y. Environmental Conservation Law 1972 (Consol. Laws Ch. 43B) § 72-0101 et seq.

Regulatory Flexibility Act
Sept. 19, 1980, P.L. 96-354, 5 U.S. Code § 601 nt.
Del. Code of 1974, Title 29, § 10401 et seq.
N.J. Stat. Ann., 52:14B-16 et seq.

Regulatory Impact Statement
N.Y. State Administrative Procedure Act (Consol. Laws Ch. 82) §§ 202, 202

Regulatory Jurisdiction Act
See Uniform Regulatory Jurisdiction Act

Regulatory Labor Unions
Fla. Stat. 477.01 et seq.

Regulatory Law (Water and Wastewater Sysytems)
Fla. Stat. Ann., 367.011 et seq.

Regulatory Licensing Reform Act
Haw. Rev. Stat. Ann., § 26H-1 et seq.

Regulatory Loan Act
Mich. Comp. Laws Ann., 493.1 et seq.
Tex. Rev. Civ. Stat., Art. 5069-3.01 et seq.

Regulatory Programs Evaluation Act
Md. Ann. Code 1974, Art. SG, § 10-130 et seq.

Regulatory Reform Act
Fla. Stat. Ann., 11.61
Ga. Laws 1998, S.B. 416
Ill. Rev. Stat. 1991, Ch. 127, § 1951 et seq.

Regulatory Reform Act (Insurance)
N.C. Gen. Stat. 1943, § 58-41-1 et seq.

Regulatory Reform Act (Solid Waste Disposal)
Cal. Public Resources Code § 43100 et seq.

Regulatory Reform Act (Utility)
Okla. Laws 1991, Ch. 17

Regulatory Reform and Business Assistance Act
Ill. Comp. Stat. 1992, Ch. 20, § 608/1 et seq.

Regulatory Review Act
Pa. Purdon's Stat., Title 71, § 745.1 et seq.

Regulatory Review and Evaluation Act
Md. Ann. Code 1974, Art. SG, § 10-130 et seq.

Regulatory Sunset Act
Fla. Stat. Ann., 11.61

Regulatory Takings Act
Ida. Code 1947, 67-8001 et seq.
Wyo. Stat. 1977, §§ 9-5-301 to 9-5-305

Rehabilitation Act
Ark. Code Ann. 1987, 20-79-201 et seq.
Colo. Rev. Stat., 29-4-301 et seq.

Me. Rev. Stat. Ann. 1964, Title 26, § 1411 et seq.
Mich. Comp. Laws Ann., 395.81 et seq.
N.J. Stat. Ann., 34:16-20
N.Y. Education Law 1947 (Consol. Laws Ch. 16) § 1001 et seq.
Pa. Purdon's Stat., Title 43, § 681.1 et seq.

Rehabilitation Act (Blighted Areas)
Mich. Comp. Laws Ann., 125.71 et seq.

Rehabilitation Act (Endowment for Vocational)
Fla. Stat. Ann., 413.615

Rehabilitation Act (Family Farm)
Kan. Stat. Ann., 2-3401 et seq.

Rehabilitation Act (Housing)
Tex. Rev. Civ. Stat., Art. 12691-5

Rehabilitation Act (Juvenile Offender)
N.J. Stat. Ann., 30:8-61 et seq.
W. Va. Code 1966 § 49-5B-1 et seq.

Rehabilitation Act (Narcotics)
La. Rev. Stat. Ann., 40:1051 et seq.

Rehabilitation Act (Prisoner)
Tenn. Code Ann., 14-29-101 et seq.

Rehabilitation Act (Residential)
Cal. Health and Safety Code § 37910 et seq.

Rehabilitation Act (Resort District)
Mich. Comp. Laws Ann., 125.2201 et seq.

Rehabilitation Act (Rural)
N.C. Public Laws 1935, Ch. 459

Rehabilitation Act (State Office)
Utah Code Ann. 1953, 53A-24-101 et seq.

Rehabilitation Act (Vocational)
See Vocational Rehabilitation Act

Rehabilitation Act Amendments of 1984
Feb. 22, 1984, P.L. 92-221, 29 U.S. Code §§ 701 nt.; 720, 732, 761a, 762, 774, 777a, 781, 783, 791, 795g, 1901 et seq.; 42 U.S. Code §§ 6001, 6012, 6033, 6061, 6081

Rehabilitation Act Amendments of 1986
Oct. 21, 1986, P.L. 99-506, 29 U.S. Code § 701 nt.

Rehabilitation Act Amendments of 1991
June 6, 1991, P.L. 102-52, 29 U.S. Code § 701 nt.

Rehabilitation Act Amendments of 1992
Oct. 29, 1992, P.L. 102-569, 29 U.S. Code § 701 nt.
Aug. 11, 1993, P.L. 103-73, 29 U.S. Code §§ 701 nt., 706, 721, 761a

Rehabilitation Act Amendments of 1993
Aug. 11, 1993, P.L. 103-73, 29 U.S. Code § 701 nt.
Aug. 7, 1998, P.L. 105-220, 29 U.S. Code § 701 nt.

Rehabilitation Act of 1973
Sept. 26, 1973, P.L. 93-112, 87 Stat. 355, 29 U.S. Code §§ 701 to 709, 720 to 724, 730 to 732, 740, 741, 750, 760 to 764, 770 to 776, 780 to 787, 790 to 794
March 27, 1978, P.L. 95-251, 29 U.S. Code § 792
Nov. 6, 1978, P.L. 95-602, 29 U.S. Code §§ 701 et seq.
Oct. 17, 1979, P.L. 96-88, 29 U.S. Code §§ 761b, 794c
Dec. 21, 1982, P.L. 97-375, 29 U.S. Code § 732
Feb. 22, 1984, P.L. 98-221, 29 U.S. Code §§ 720, 732, 761a, 762, 774, 777a, 781, 783, 791, 795g
Oct. 19, 1984, P.L. 98-524, 29 U.S. Code § 721
July 2, 1986, P.L. 99-349, 100 Stat. 740
Oct. 21, 1986, P.L. 99-506, 20 U.S. Code §§ 1681 to 1686; 29 U.S. Code §§ 203, 701 to 796g; 2000c, 2000c-6, 2000c-9, 2000d to 2000d-4, 3001 et seq., 3056 et seq., 6101 et seq.
March 22, 1988, P.L. 100-259, 102 Stat. 29, 29 U.S. Code §§ 706, 794
Nov. 7, 1988, P.L. 100-630, 29 U.S. Code §§ 702 et seq., 731 nt., 777c nt.
July 26, 1990, P.L. 101-336, 29 U.S. Code § 706
June 6, 1991, P.L. 102-52, 29 U.S. Code §§ 720, 732, 741, 761, 771, 772, 774, 775, 777, 777a, 777f, 785, 792, 795f, 795i, 795q, 796i

June 13, 1991 P.L. 102-54, 29 U.S. Code §§ 721, 761a, 761b, 791, 792
Oct. 7, 1991, P.L. 102-119, 29 U.S. Code §§ 721, 774, 777a, 795m , 796d
Oct. 29, 1992, P.L. 102-569, 29 U.S. Code §§ 701, 706, 712, 713, 718, 718a, 718b, 721 to 723, 796 et seq., prec. 797, 797a, 797b
Aug. 11, 1993, P.L. 103-73, 29 U.S. Code §§ 706, 718 et seq., 721 et seq., 725, 730 et seq., 744, 753, 753a, 761a, 762, 771a, 777, 777a, 777f, 783, 791, 792, 794e, 795l, 796, 796c et seq., 796k
March 9, 1994, P.L. 103-218, 29 U.S. Code §§ 706, 761a, 771a
Oct. 20, 1994, P.L. 103-382, 29 U.S. Code §§ 708, 761a, 794
Dec. 21, 1995, P.L. 104-66, 29 U.S. Code §§ 712, 732, 771a, 777a , 781
Feb. 10, 1996, P.L. 104-106, 29 U.S. Code § 721
April 30, 1997, P.L. 105-12, 29 U.S. Code § 794e
Aug. 7, 1998, P.L. 105-220, 29 U.S. Code §§ 701, 701 nt., 702 to 718, 718a, 718b, 720 to 728a, 730 to 732, 741, 751, 760 to 765, 771 to 776, 780 to 785, 791, 795, 795a, 795g to 795n, 796, 796a to 796d, 796d-1, 796e, 796e-1 to 796e-3, 796f, 796f-1 to 796f-6, 796j to 796l, 797, 797a, 797b
Oct. 7, 1998, P.L. 105-244, 29 U.S. Code § 705
Oct. 21, 1998, P.L. 105-277, 29 U.S. Code §§ 701, 701 nt., 705 to 718, 721, 722, 725, 730, 731, 732, 741, 765, 795g to 795n, 796d
Oct. 31, 1998, P.L. 105-332, 29 U.S. Code § 796f-4
Nov. 13, 1998, P.L. 105-394, 29 U.S. Code §§ 705, 763, 764, 781, 792, 794b, 794e

Rehabilitation and Betterment Act of 1949
Oct. 7, 1949, Ch. 650, 63 Stat. 724, 43 U.S. Code § 504, 504 nt.
Mar 3, 1950, Ch. 47, 64 Stat. 11, 43 U.S. Code § 504
Oct. 3, 1975, P.L. 94-102, 89 Stat. 485, 43 U.S. Code §§ 392, 422k, 504

Rehabilitation and Disclosure Act (Continuing Care Facility)
Tex. Health and Safety Code, § 246.001 et seq.

Rehabilitation and Liquidation Act (Insurance)
See also Insurers Rehabilitation and Liquidation Act
Ky. Rev. Stat. 1971, 304.33-010 et seq.
Me. Rev. Stat. Ann. 1964, Title 24-A, § 4351 et seq.
Mo. Rev. Stat. 1978, 375.1150

Rehabilitation and Liquidation Act (Insurers)
Miss. General Laws 1991, Ch. 417, p. 298
R.I. Gen. Laws 1956, 27-14.3-1 et seq.

Rehabilitation and Liquidation Act (Life and Health Insurers)
N.J. Stat. Ann., 17B:32-31 et seq.

Rehabilitation and Penal Authority Act
Ga. Code Ann., 42-3-1 et seq.

Rehabilitation and Support Mental Health Services Incentive Act
Neb. Rev. Stat. 1943, 71-5042 to 71-5052

Rehabilitation and Treatment Act (Alcoholism)
Mass. Gen. Laws Ann., 111B:1 et seq.

Rehabilitation and Welfare Services Planning Act
Ill. Rev. Stat. 1991, Ch. 127, § 951 et seq.

Rehabilitation Center Act
Cal. Penal Code § 6550 et seq.
Cal. Welfare and Institutions Code § 3300 et seq.

Rehabilitation Commission Act
Tex. Human Resources Code, § 111.01 et seq.

Rehabilitation, Comprehensive Services, and Developmental Disabilities Amendments Act
Nov. 6, 1978, P.L. 95-602, 29 U.S. Code §§ 701 et seq.; 38 U.S. Code § 1904; 42 U.S. Code §§ 6000 et seq., 6031 to 6033, 6061 et seq., 6081
July 10, 1979, P.L. 96-32, 42 U.S. Code §§ 6009, 6081
Oct. 30, 1990, P.L. 101-476, 20 U.S. Code § 1400 nt.

Rehabilitation Corporation Act (Rural)
Ill. Rev. Stat. 1991, Ch. 127, § 42a2.9 et seq.

Rehabilitation Counseling Act
P.R. Laws Ann. 1954, Title 20, § 2651 et seq.

Rehabilitation Counselor Licensing Act
La. Rev. Stat. Ann., 37:3441 et seq.

Rehabilitation Facilities Set-Aside Act
N.J. Stat. Ann., 2C:46-5 et seq.

Rehabilitation Loan Act (Veterans)
Wis. Stat. Ann., 45.35

Rehabilitation Mortgage Insurance Corporation Act (New York City)
N.Y. Private Housing Finance Law (Consol. Laws Ch. 44B) § 700 et seq.

Rehabilitation of Alcoholics Act
D.C. Code Ann., § 24-521 et seq.

Rehabilitation of Disabled Persons Act
Ill. Rev. Stat. 1991, Ch. 23, § 3429 et seq.

Rehabilitation Practitioner Registration Act
Md. Ann. Code 1974, Art. LE, § 9-6A-20 et seq.

Rehabilitation, Supervision and Liquidation Act (Insurers)
S.C. Code Ann. 1976, § 38-27-10 et seq.

Rehabilitative and Health Services Reorganization Act
Fla. Laws 1992, Ch. 58

Rehousing Act (Redevelopment Project)
Ill. Rev. Stat. 1991, Ch. 67 1/2, § 91.990 et seq.

Reid-Jurkiewicz Act (Home Rule Cities—Supervisors)
Mich. Comp. Laws Ann., 46.401 et seq.

Reid-Schneider Act (Public Library Employees' Pensions)
Mich. Comp. Laws Ann., 38.706

Reimbursement Act

Minn. Laws 1957, Extra Session, Ch. 4 et seq.

Reimbursement Act (Correctional Facility)

Mich. Comp. Laws Ann., 800.401 et seq.

Reimbursement Act (Fines and Forfeitures)

Pa. Cons. Stat., Title 42, § 5702

Reimbursement Act (Habeas Corpus)

Ill. Rev. Stat. 1991, Ch. 65, § 36.9 et seq.

Reimbursement Act (Highway Construction)

S.C. Acts 1926, p. 1001, No. 559
Tenn. Code Ann., 54-4-401 et seq.

Reimbursement Act (Incarceration)

Mo. Rev. Stat. 1978, 217.825

Reimbursement Act (Legislature)

Ariz. Rev. Stat. Ann., §§ 41-1103, 41-1104

Reimbursement Act for Nonpublic Education

Pa. Purdon's Stat., Title 24, § 5701 et seq.

Reimbursement for Health Care Reform Act

Wyo. Stat. Ann., § 26-22-501 et seq.

Reimbursement Grants for Parental Equivalent Instruction

Conn. Gen. Stat. Ann., § 10-281w et seq.

Reimbursement to County Act (Inmate)

Tenn. Code Ann., 41-11-101 to 41-11-112

Reincorporation Act

Ore. Special Laws 1903, p. 3

Reindeer Industry Act of 1937

Sept. 1, 1937, Ch. 897, 25 U.S. Code §§ 500 to 500n
Oct. 22, 1986, P.L. 99-514, 25 U.S. Code § 500g

Reinsurance Act

Iowa Code Ann., 521.1 et seq.
Minn. Stat. 1965, 61.13 et seq.

Reinsurance Act (Assumption)

Neb. Rev. Stat. 1943, 44-6201 et seq.

Reinsurance Act (Credit for)

Okla. Stat. Ann., Title 36, § 5121 et seq.

Reinsurance Credit Act

Iowa Code Ann., 521B.1 et seq.

Reinsurance Intermediary Act

Ala. Code 1975, § 27-5A-1 et seq.
Alaska Stat. 1962, 21.27.010 et seq.
Ariz. Rev. Stat. Ann., 20-486.01 et seq
Ark. Code 1987, 23-62-401 et seq.
Cal. Insurance Code § 1781.1 et seq.
Colo. Rev. Stat., 10-2-301 et seq.
Conn. Gen. Stat. 1983, § 38a-760 et seq.
D.C. Code Ann., § 35-3101 et seq.
Del. Code of 1974, Title 18, § 1601 et seq.
Fla. Stat. Ann., 626.7492
Ga. Code Ann., 33-49-1 et seq.
Haw. Rev. Stat. Ann., § 431:9B-101 et seq.
Ida. Code 1947, 41-5101 et seq.
Ill. Rev. Stat. 1991, Ch. 73, § 1601 et seq.
Ind. Code Ann., § 27-6-9-1 et seq.
Iowa Code Ann., 521C.1 et seq.
Kan. Stat. Ann., 40-4501 et seq.
Ky. Rev. Stat. 1971, 304.9-700c et seq.
La. Rev. Stat. Ann., 22:1210.20 et seq.
Mass. Gen. Laws Ann., 175:177M to 175:177W
Md. Ann. Code 1974, Art. 8-501i
Me. Rev. Stat. Ann. 1964, Title 24-A, § 750 et seq.
Mich. Comp. Laws Ann., 500.1151 et seq.
Minn. Stat. Ann., 60A.70 et seq.
Miss. Code Ann. 1972, § 83-19-201 et seq.
Mo. Rev. Stat. 1978, 375.001 et seq.
Mont. Code Ann., 33-2-1701 et seq.
N.C. Gen. Stat. 1943, 58-9-1 lfe.N.D. Cent. Code, 26-1-31.1-01
Neb. Laws 1992, L.B. 1006, §§ 55 to 67
Nev. Rev. Stat. Ann., 681A.010
N.H. Rev. Stat. 1935, 402-F:1
N.J. Stat. Ann., 17:22E-1
N.M. Stat. Ann., 59A-12D-1 et seq.
N.Y. Insurance Law 1984 (Consol. Laws Ch. 28) § 2101 et seq.
Continued

Ohio Rev. Code 1953, 39.01

Okla. Stat. Ann., Title 36, § 5101 et seq.

Ore. Rev. Stat., 744.801

Pa. Purdon's Stat., Title 40,321.1

R.I. Gen. Laws 1956, 42-80.1-1 et seq.

S.C. Code Ann. 1976, § 38-46-10 et seq.

Tenn. Code Ann., § 56-6-801 et seq.

Tex. Insurance Code, Art. 21.07-7

Utah code Ann., 31A-23-701

Va. Code 1950, § 38.2-1850

Vt. Stat. Ann., Title 8, § 4801

Wash. Rev. Code Ann., 48.94.900

W. Va. Code 1966 § 33-38-1 et seq.

Wyo. Stat. Ann., § 26-47-101 et seq.

Reintegration and Stabilization Act

N.J. Stat. Ann., 52:17B-181 et seq.

Reinvest in Minnesota Resources Law

Minn. Stat. 1986, 103F.505 et seq.

Reinvestment Act (Community)

N.Y. Banking Law (Consol. Laws Ch. 4) § 28b

REIT (Real Estate Investment Trust) Act

Md. Ann. Code 1974, Art. CA, §§ 2-310, Subd. a, 8-203, Subd. h, 8-206, 8-801

Rejected Vehicle Inspection Extension Act

D.C. Laws 1976, No. 1-84

Relations Act (Municipal Employees)

Mass. Gen. Laws Ann., 150E:1 et seq.

Relative Custody Assistance Act

Minn. Stat. 1986, 257.85

Relatives Responsibility Act (Welfare)

Ala. Acts 1951, p. 1195

Ore. Rev. Stat., 416.010 et seq.

Wis. Stat. Ann., 49.90

Relay Telecommunications System Act

Neb. Rev. Stat. 1943, 86-1301 et seq.

Release From Custody and Bail Reform Act

D.C. Code 1973, § 24-406

Tenn. Code Ann., 40-11-101 et seq.

Release of Genetically Engineered Organisms Act

Ill. Rev. Stat. 1991, Ch. 111 1/2, § 7600 et seq.

Release of Power of Appointment Law

Miss. Code Ann. 1972, § 91-15-1 et seq.

Release of Record Act (Mineral Lease)

Ill. Rev. Stat. 1991, Ch. 96 1/2, § 4400 et seq.

Release Program Act (Conditional)

Fla. Stat. Ann., 947.141

Released Time Act (Religious Instruction)

Ind. Code Ann., 20-8.1-3-22

N.Y. Education Law 1947 (Consol. Laws Ch. 16) § 3210

Ore. Rev. Stat. 1953, 336.260

Reliable and Stable Source of Revenues for WMATA Act

D.C. Code Ann., §§ 1-2466, 1-2467

Relief Act

Cal. Welfare and Institutions Code § 18450 et seq.

Mass. Gen. Laws Ann., 117:1 et seq.

Wash. Rev. Code Ann., 74.04.005 et seq., 74.08.025 et seq.

Relief Act (Emergency Unemployment)

Wis. Laws 1931-1932, Special Session, Ch. 29

Relief Act (Emergency)

N.Y. Laws 1931, Ex. Sess., Ch. 798

N.Y. Laws 1932, Chs. 545, 567

N.Y. Laws 1933, Chs. 2, 9, 34, 44, 69, 259, 646

N.Y. Laws 1933, 1st Ex. Sess., Ch. 782

N.Y. Laws 1934, Chs. 15, 65, 71, 273, 303

N.Y. Laws 1935, Chs. 25, 239, 264

N.Y. Laws 1936, Chs. 13, 210

Relief Act (Firemen)

Minn. Stat. Ann., 69.011 et seq., 424.01 et seq.

Relief Act (Hunger)
Ore. Rev. Stat., 411.851 et seq.

Relief Act (Policemen)
Minn. Stat. Ann., 423A.01 et seq.

Relief Act (Revaluation)
N.J. Stat. Ann., 54:1-35.39 et seq.

Relief Act (Spanish War Veterans)
Minn. Laws 1931, Ch. 405

Relief Act (Sureties on Public Depository Bonds)
Ind. Code Ann., 5-4-4-1 et seq.

Relief Act (Taxing Districts)
Wash. Rev. Code Ann., 39.64.005 et seq.

Relief Act (Transient Pauper)
Wis. Stat. Ann., 49.02, Subsec. 2m

Relief Aid for War-Devastated Countries
May 31, 1947, Ch. 90, 61 Stat. 125

Relief and Pension Act (Firemen and Policemen)
Ohio Rev. Code 1953, 741.01 et seq.

Relief and Pension Act (Firemen)
Pa. Purdon's Stat., Title 53, § 23601 et seq.

Relief and Pension Act (Policemen)
Ark. Code Ann. 1987, 24-11-403 et seq.
Pa. Purdon's Stat., Title 53, § 23644 et seq.

Relief and Pension Fund Act (Firemen)
See Firemen's Relief and Pension Act

Relief Assistance Act
Pa. Purdon's Stat., Title 62, § 1971 et seq.

Relief Bond Act
Tex. Rev. Civ. Stat., Arts. 842b to 842f

Relief Commission Act
Ohio Laws Vol. 116, pp. 133, 240
Ohio Laws Vol. 117, p. 13
Tex. General Laws 43rd Leg., 1933, p. 365, Ch. 141

Relief Deficiency Acts
Feb. 4, 1939, Ch. 1, 53 Stat. 507
April 13, 1939, Ch. 62, 53 Stat. 578

Relief from Judgments Act
Wis. Stat. Ann., 806.07

Relief Fund Act (Firemen)
N.H. Rev. Stat. 1955, 402:66 et seq.

Relief Loan Act (Hurricanes)
Mass. Acts 1954, Ch. 689

Relief Loan Act (Municipalities)
Mass. Acts 1943, Ch. 44
Mass. Acts 1951, Ch. 108
Mass. Acts 1955, Ch. 18
Mass. Acts 1959, Ch. 329
Mass. Acts 1962, Ch. 502

Relief of Indigent Act (Alaska)
Alaska Comp. Laws Ann. 1949, § 35-1-51

Relief Organization Law
Colo. Rev. Stat., 119-1-1 et seq.

Relief-Recovery Act of 1938
See Work Relief and Public Works Appropriation Act of 1938

Relief Sales Tax Act
Pa. Purdon's Stat., Title 72, § 3282

Relief Tax Act (County-City)
Nev. Rev. Stat. 1979 Reprint, 377.010 et seq.

Relief Tax Act (Unemployment)
N.Y. Laws 1933, 1st Ex. Sess., Ch. 815

Relief Tax Authorization Act
Ill. Rev. Stat. 1991, Ch. 107, §§ 46.9, 47

Relief Worker's Compensation Act
Ind. Code 1982, 12-2-12-1 et seq.

Religious and Charitable Risk Pooling Trust Act
Ill. Rev. Stat. 1991, Ch. 148, § 201 et seq.

Religious Associations Act
Neb. Laws 1949, Ch. 31

Religious Charitable and Benevolent Association Act
Mo. Rev. Stat., 352.010

Religious Corporation Law (Nonprofit)
Cal. Corporations Code § 9110 et seq.

Religious Corporation Sole Act
Mont. Code Ann., 35-3-101 et seq.

Religious Corporation Validation Act
Ill. Rev. Stat. 1991, Ch. 32, §§ 188.3, 188.4

Religious Corporations Act
Ill. Rev. Stat. 1991, Ch. 32, § 163 et seq.
Md. Ann. Code 1974, Art. CA, § 5-301 et seq.
N.Y. Consol. Laws, Ch. 51

Religious, Educational or Charitable Corporation Dissolution Act
Ill. Rev. Stat. 1991, Ch. 32, §§ 200.9, 201

Religious Exemption Act (Tax)
Ga. Code Ann., 48-5-41

Religious Freedom Act
Mass. Gen. Laws Ann., 119:33
Va. Code 1950, § 57-1

Religious Freedom Restoration Act
Fla. Stat. Ann., 761.01 et seq.
R.I. Gen. Laws 1956, 42-80.1-1 et seq.

Religious Freedom Restoration Act of 1993
Nov. 16, 1993, P.L. 103-141, 5 U.S. Code § 504; 42 U.S. Code §§ 1988, 2000bb nt., 2000bb et seq.

Religious Liberty and Academic Freedom Act (Nation's Capital)
D.C. Code Ann., § 1-2520

Religious Liberty and Charitable Donation Protection Act of 1998
June 19, 1998, P.L. 105-183, 11 U.S. Code § 101 nt.

Religious Observance Act
N.Y. Education Law 1947 (Consol. Laws Ch. 16) § 3210

Religious Observances Act (University)
Ill. Rev. Stat. 1991, Ch. 144, §§ 2100, 2101

Religious Protection Act (Adoptions)
Ill. Rev. Stat. 1991, Ch. 40, § 1519
Mass. Gen. Laws Ann., 210:5B

Religious, Racial and Ethnic Harassment Commission Act
R.I. Gen. Laws 1956, 42-80-1 et seq.

Religious Societies Act
Del. Code of 1974, Title 27, § 101 et seq.
N.J. Stat. Ann., 16:1-1 et seq.

Religious Societies, Religious Organizations and Churches Act
Ind. Code 1971, 23-11-1-1 et seq.

Religious Toleration Act
N.H. Laws 1819, Ch. 76, § 3

Relinquishment Act
Tex. General Laws 4th Leg., 1851-52, p. 63, Ch. 71
Tex. General Laws 42nd Leg., 1931, p. 28, Ch. 23

Relinquishment Act (Lands across or under Streams)
Tex. Rev. Civ. Stat., Art. 5414a

Relinquishment Act (Oil and Gas Lands)
Tex. Natural Resources Code, § 52.171 et seq.

Relinquishment and Adoption Act
Kan. Stat. Ann., 59-2111 et seq.

Relinquishment of Children Act
Colo. Rev. Stat. 1963, 22-5-1 et seq.

Relocation Act
Haw. Rev. Stat. § 111-1 et seq.
Wash. Rev. Code Ann., 8.26.010 et seq.

Relocation Act (Airport)
Haw. Rev. Stat. Ann., § 261-31 et seq.

Relocation Act (Displaced Person)
Ill. Rev. Stat. 1991, Ch. 67 1/2, § 107 et seq.

Relocation Act (Emergency Government)
Ill. Rev. Stat. 1991, Ch. 85, § 50 et seq.

Relocation Act (Government)
Ida. Code 1947, 67-102 et seq.

Relocation Act (Highway)
Cal. Streets and Highways Code § 170 et seq.

Relocation Act (House)
Ill. Rev. Stat. 1991, Ch. 67 1/2, § 102.9 et seq.

Relocation Act (Utilities)
See Utilities Relocation Act

Relocation Act Amendments of 1991
See Uniform Relocation Act Amendments of 1991

Relocation and Land Acquisition Policy Act (Highways)
Ga. Code Ann., 32-8-1 et seq.

Relocation Assistance Act
See also Uniform Relocation Assistance Act
Ala. Code 1975, § 23-1-200 et seq.
Ariz. Rev. Stat. Ann., § 28-1841 et seq.
Cal. Government Code § 7260 et seq.
Conn. Gen. Stat. Ann., § 8-266 et seq.
Ga. Code Ann., 32-8-1 et seq.
Haw. Rev. Stat. Ann., § 111-1 et seq.
Ind. Code Ann., 8-13-18.5-1 et seq.
La. Rev. Stat. Ann., 38:3101 et seq.
Mass. Gen. Laws Ann., 79A:1 et seq.
Me. Rev. Stat. Ann. 1964, Title 23, § 241 et seq.
Miss. Code Ann. 1972, § 43-39-1 et seq.
Mont. Code Ann., 70-31-101 et seq.
N.D. Cent. Code, 54-01.1-01 et seq.
Neb. Rev. Stat. 1943, 76-1214 et seq.
N.J. Stat. Ann., 20:4-1 et seq., 52:31B-1 et seq.
N.M. Stat. Ann., 42-3-1 et seq.

Okla. Stat. Ann., Title 63, § 1092.1 et seq.
S.C. Code Ann. 1976, § 28-11-10 et seq.
Utah Code Ann. 1953, 57-12-1 et seq.
Wyo. Stat. Ann., § 16-7-101 et seq.

Relocation Assistance Act (Highways)
See Highway Relocation Assistance Act

Relocation Assistance Act (Utility)
Wyo. Stat. Ann., § 24-13-101 et seq.

Relocation Assistance and Land Acquisition Policy Act
Ga. Code Ann., 22-4-1 et seq.

Relocation Assistance and Real Property Acquisition Policies Act
See also Uniform Relocation Assistance and Real Property Acquisition Policies Act
N.C. Gen. Stat. 1943, § 133-5 et seq.
Nev. Rev. Stat. 1979 Reprint, 342.010 et seq.
Ohio Rev. Code 1953, 163.51 et seq.
Va. Code 1950, § 25-235 et seq.

Relocation of Trespassing Vehicles Law (Commercial)
Ill. Comp. Stat. 1992, Ch. 625, § 5/18a-100 et seq.

Relocation of Utility Facilities Act
Ind. Code Ann., 8-1-9-1 et seq.
Minn. Stat. Ann., 161.46
N.D. Cent. Code, 24-01-41

Relocation Regulation Payment Increase Amendment Act
D.C. Code Ann., § 5-833

Remaindermen and Tenants Income Law
Cal. Civil Code § 730 et seq.

Remand Act (District Courts)
Mass. Gen. Laws Ann., 231:102C

Remedial Action Act (Petroleum Release)
Neb. Rev. Stat. 1943, 66-1501 et seq.

Remedial Action Reform Act (Expedited)
Cal. Health and Safety Code § 25396.1 et seq.

Remedial Drainage Improvement Act
Minn. Stat. 1988, 106A.005 et seq.

Remedial Education Act
La. Rev. Stat. Ann., 17:394 et seq.
Miss. Code Ann. 1972, 37-20-1 et seq.

Remedial Reading Education Act
Fla. Stat. Ann., 233.051

Remedial Trust Fund Action Reform Act
Ark. Code Ann. 1987, 8-7-501 to 8-7-522

Remediation Standards Act (Environmental and Land Recycling)
Pa. Purdon's Stat., Title 35, § 6026.101 et seq.

Remedies and Penalties (Consumer Act)
Wis. Stat. Ann., 425.101 et seq.

Remedies and Penalties (Consumer Credit Code)
Iowa Code Ann., 537.5101 et seq.
Kan. Stat. Ann., 16a-5-101 et seq.
Me. Rev. Stat. Ann. 1964, Title 9-A, § 5.101 et seq.
S.C. Code Ann. 1976, § 37-5-101 et seq.
Wyo. Stat. Ann., § 40-14-501 et seq.

Remedies and Penalties (Revised Uniform Commercial Code)
See Revised Uniform Consumer Credit Code—Remedies and Penalties

Remedies for Criminal Practices Act (Civil)
Fla. Stat. Ann., 772.101 et seq.

Remedies for Residents of Personal Care Homes Act
Ga. Code Ann., 31-8-130 et seq.

Remission Act (Bail)
Cal. Penal Code § 1305 et seq.

Remodeling and Reconstruction Loan Act (Lynn)
Mass. Acts 1951, Ch. 359

Remodeling and Reconstruction Loan Act (Revere)
Mass. Acts 1952, Ch. 573

Remonumentation and Survey Act (State)
Mich. Comp. Laws Ann., 54.261 et seq.

Remote Financial Service Unit Act
N.M. Stat. Ann., 58-16-1 et seq.

Removal Act
Tenn. Code Ann., 8-47-101 et seq.
Utah Code Ann. 1953, 77-6-1 et seq.

Removal Act (Appellate Court; Public Officials)
Ind. Acts 1982, P.L. 3
Ind. Code 1976, 34-4-18-2 et seq.

Removal Act (Equitable Claims)
Ala. Code 1958, Title 13, § 153

Removal from Office Act (Public Officers)
N.C. Gen. Stat. 1943, § 128-16 et seq.

Removal of Brush, Grass, Rubbish or Weeds and Spraying of Poisonous Shrubs or Weeds Law (Greece)
N.Y. Local Laws 1971, Town of Greece, p. 1847

Removal of Causes Act
See Judiciary Acts

Removal of Fire and Health Hazards and Weeds Law
N.Y. Local Laws 1973, Village of Orchard Park, p. 3656

Removal of Health Hazards and Weeds Law (Castleton-on-Hudson)
N.Y. Local Laws 1966, Village of Castleton-on-Hudson, p. 1917

Removal of Judges Act
Neb. Rev. Stat. 1943, 24-715 et seq.

Removal of Regulatory Barriers to Affordable Housing Act of 1992
Oct. 28, 1992, P.L. 102-550, 42 U.S. Code §§ 12705a et seq., 12705 nt.

Removal of Restrictions on Service Act
Dec. 13, 1941, Ch. 571, 55 Stat. 799

Removal of Sand and Gravel Act
Conn. Gen. Stat. Ann., § 22a-383 et seq.

Remove or Repair Unsafe Buildings and Collapsed Structures Act
N.Y. Local Laws 1973, Town of Lloyd, p. 2474

Removing Cloud on Title Act
Ga. Code Ann., 23-3-42

Renaissance Act (Rural)
Cal. Government Code § 15373 et seq.

Renaissance Zone Act
Mich. Comp. Laws Ann., 125.2681 et seq.

Renal Disease Act
Mich. Comp. Laws Ann., 333.5401 et seq.

Renal Disease Treatment Act
Ill. Rev. Stat. 1991, Ch. 111 1/2, § 22.30 et seq.

Rend Lake Dam and Reservoir on the Big Muddy River Act
Ill. Comp. Stat. Ann., Ch. 70, § 2115/0.01.

Rend Lake Dam and Reservoir Operation and Maintenance Act
Ill. Comp. Stat. Annn., Ch. 20, §§ 879/0.01

Render, Nichols, Hahn, Frymeier, Ashby, and Hale Act (Mosquito Control)
Ky. Rev. Stat. 1971, 249.510 et seq.

Renderers' Licensing Act
Tex. Health and Safety Code, § 144.001 et seq.

Rendering Act
W. Va. Code 1966, § 47-22-10 et seq.

Rendition Act (Extradition)
Md. Ann. Code 1957, Art. 41, § 2-201 et seq.

Rendition Amendment to the Interstate Compact on Juveniles
Ala. Acts 1986, No. 419

Rendition and Extradition Act (Uniform)
N.D. Cent. Code, 29-30.3-01 et seq.

Rendition of Accused Persons Act
See Uniform Rendition of Accused Persons Act

Rendition of Prisoners as Witnesses in Criminal Proceedings Act
See Uniform Rendition of Prisoners as Witnesses in Criminal Proceedings Act

Rendition of Prisoners in Criminal Proceedings Act
Tex. Code of Criminal Procedure 1965, Art. 24.29

Renegotiation Act
April 28, 1942, Ch. 247, 56 Stat. 245, 50 U.S. Code Appx. § 1191
Oct. 21, 1942, Ch. 619, 56 Stat. 982, 50 U.S. Code Appx. § 1191
Feb. 25, 1944, Ch. 63, 58 Stat. 78, 50 U.S. Code Appx. § 1191, 1
June 30, 1945, Ch. 210, § 1, 59 Stat. 294, 50 U.S. Code Appx. § 1191
June 14, 1947, Ch. 105, 61 Stat. 133, 50 U.S. Code Appx. § 1191
June 28, 1949, Ch. 268, 63 Stat. 280, 50 U.S. Code Appx. § 1191
March 23, 1951, Ch. 15, 65 Stat. 23, 50 U.S. Code Appx. § 1191
July 17, 1952, Ch. 924, 66 Stat. 752, 50 U.S. Code Appx. § 1191
July 9, 1973, P.L. 93-66, 87 Stat. 152, 50 U.S. Code Appx. § 1212
June 30, 1974, P.L. 93-329, 88 Stat. 288, 50 U.S. Code Appx. § 1212
Dec. 31, 1975, P.L. 94-185, 89 Stat. 1061, 50 Appx. U.S. Code § 1212

Renegotiation Act of 1948
April 21, 1948, Ch. 333, 62 Stat. 259, 50 U.S. Code Appx. § 1193

Renegotiation Act of 1951

March 23, 1951, Ch. 15, 65 Stat. 7 (See 26 U.S. Code § 1481) 50 U.S. Code Appx. §§ 1191, 1211 to 1233

July 17, 1952, Ch. 924, 66 Stat. 753, 50 U.S. Code Appx. § 1231

Sept. 1, 1954, Ch. 1209, 68 Stat. 1116, 50 U.S. Code Appx. §§ 1202, 1215, 1216, 1231

Aug. 3, 1955, Ch. 499, 69 Stat. 447, 50 U.S. Code Appx. §§ 1212, 1216

Aug. 1, 1956, Ch. 821, 70 Stat. 786, 50 U.S. Code Appx. §§ 1212, 1213, 1215 to 1218a, 1223, 1224

July 13, 1959, P.L. 86-89, 73 Stat. 210, 50 U.S. Code Appx. §§ 1211nt., 1212, 1213, 1217

June 11, 1960, P.L. 86-507, 74 Stat. 202, 50 U.S. Code Appx. §§ 1215, 1217

July 3, 1962, P.L. 87-520, 76 Stat. 134, 50 U.S. Code Appx. §§ 1212, 1215, 1218, 1218a

June 30, 1964, P.L. 88-339, 78 Stat. 233, 50 U.S. Code Appx. §§ 1212, 1213

Aug. 14, 1964, P.L. 88-426, 78 Stat. 426, 50 U.S. Code Appx. § 1217

June 30, 1966, P.L. 89-480, 80 Stat. 232, 50 U.S. Code Appx. § 1212

Oct. 24, 1968, P.L. 90-634, 82 Stat. 1345, 50 U.S. Code Appx. §§ 1212, 1215, 1216

July 1, 1971, P.L. 92-41, 85 Stat. 97, 50 U.S. Code Appx. §§ 1212, 1213, 1215, 1216, 1218, 1218a, 1224

Renegotiation Amendments Act of 1956

Aug. 1, 1956, Ch. 821, 70 Stat. 786, 50 U.S. Code Appx. §§ 1212, 1213, 1215 to 1218a, 1223, 1224

Renegotiation Amendments Act of 1968

Oct. 24, 1968, P.L. 90-634, 82 Stat. 1345, 19 U.S. Code §§ 160 nt., 1356f to 1356j; 26 U.S. Code § 103; 50 U.S. Code Appx. §§ 1212, 1215, 1216

Renewable and Small Group Rate Act

N.M. Stat. Ann., 59A-23C-1 et seq.

Renewable Energy and Energy Efficiency Technology Competitiveness Act of 1989

Dec. 11, 1989, P.L. 101-218, 42 U.S. Code §§ 12001 to 12007, 12001 nt.

Oct. 24, 1992, P.L. 102-486, 42 U.S. Code §§ 12001 to 12006

Renewable Energy, Energy Efficiency, and Coal Resources Development Law

Ill. Comp. Stat. 1992, Ch. 20, § 687/6-1 et seq.

Renewable Energy Industry Development Act of 1983

July 18, 1984, P.L. 98-370, 42 U.S. Code §§ 6201 nt., 6276, 6276 nt.

Renewable Energy Resource Finance Act

Ark. Code Ann. 1987, 14-167-201 et seq.

Renewable Energy Resources Act of 1980

June 30, 1980, P.L. 96-294, 42 U.S. Code § 7371 et seq., 7371 nt.

Renewable Natural Resources Research Act

Miss. Code Ann. 1972, § 57-18-1 et seq.

Renewable Resource Development Act

Mont. Code Ann., 90-2-101 et seq.

Renewable Resources Extension Act Amendments of 1987

Jan. 5, 1988, P.L. 100-231, 16 U.S. Code § 1600 nt.

Renewable Resources Extension Act of 1978

June 30, 1978, P.L. 95-306, 16 U.S. Code §§ 1600 nt., 1671 et seq.

Jan. 5, 1987, P.L. 100-231, 16 U.S. Code §§ 1671 nt., 1674, 1675

Nov. 28, 1990, P.L. 101-624, 16 U.S. Code §§ 1672, 1674, 1674a

Dec. 13, 1991, P.L. 102-237, 16 U.S. Code § 1672

April 4, 1996, P.L. 104-127, 16 U.S. Code § 1673

June 23, 1998, P.L. 105-185, 16 U.S. Code § 1675

Renewal Act (Actions)

Del. Code of 1974, Title 10, § 8118

Ga. Code Ann., 9-2-61

Renewal Act (Deferred Building)
Neb. Rev. Stat. 1943, 81-173

Renewal Act (Limitations)
Ga. Code Ann., 9-2-61
Mo. Rev. Stat., 516.230

Reno Charter
Nev. Statutes 1903, Ch. 102, p. 184
Nev. Statutes 1905, Ch. 71, p. 98
Nev. Statutes 1971, Ch. 662, p. 1962

Rensselaer County Charter
N.Y. Local Laws 1972, County of
Rensselaer, p. 777

Rensselaer County Medical Examiner Law
N.Y. Local Laws 1971, County of
Rensselaer, p. 792

Rensselaer County Sheriffs Compensation Law
N.Y. Local Laws 1970, County of
Rensselaer, p. 922

Rensselaer County Water and Sewer Authority Act
N.Y. Public Authorities Law (Consol. Laws
Ch. 43A) § 1199 et seq.

Rensselaerville Housing and Mobile Home Law
N.Y. Local Laws 1972, Town of Rensselaerville, p. 2690

Rent Act (Double)
Ill. Rev. Stat. 1991, Ch. 110, § 9-203

Rent Administrator Delegation Act
D.C. Code Ann., § 45-2514

Rent and Rehabilitation Law (City)
N.Y. Adm. Code '85, § 26-402

Rent and Rehabilitation Law (New York City)
N.Y. City Adm. Code '38, Ch. 51, § Y51-1.0
et seq.
N.Y. Unconsolidated Laws, § 26-401 et seq.

Rent Ceiling Act
D.C. Code Ann., § 45-2516 et seq.

Rent Collection by Distraint Act
S.C. Code Ann. 1976, § 27-39-210

Rent Concession Act
Ill. Rev. Stat. 1991, Ch. 80, § 40.9 et seq.

Rent Control Act
Conn. Public Acts 1991, p. 350, No. 394
D.C. Code Ann., § 45-1501 et seq.
Mass. Acts 1953, Ch. 434
Minn. Laws 1947, Ch. 632
Mo. Laws 1947, Vol. I, p. 474
N.J. Stat. Ann., 2A:42-11 et seq.
N.Y. Laws 1945, Ch. 314 (Business)
N.Y. Laws 1945, Chs. 3, 315 (Commercial)
N.Y. Laws 1946, Ch. 274 (Housing)
N.Y. Laws 1948, Ch. 679 (Business)
N.Y. Laws 1949, Ch. 534 (Commercial
Space)
N.Y. Laws 1949, Ch. 535 (Business Space)
N.Y. Laws 1949, Ch. 591 (Housing)
N.Y. Laws 1950, Ch. 326 (Business)
N.Y. Laws 1950, Ch. 327 (Commercial)
N.Y. Laws 1951, Ch. 430 (Business)
N.Y. Laws 1951, Ch. 431 (Commercial)
N.Y. Local Laws 1947, New York City, Nos.
54, 66 to 68 (Housing)
Va. Code 1950, § 44-160 et seq.

Rent Control Act (Commercial)
Haw. Session Laws 1945, Act 69

Rent Control Act (Emergency)
Wis. Laws 1947, Ch. 442

Rent Control Act (Optional)
N.J. Stat. Ann., 2A:42-74

Rent Control Law (Residential)
N.Y. City Adm. Code 1938, Ch. 51,
§ Y51-1.0 et seq.

Rent Control Law (State Housing)
N.Y. Unconsol. Laws, § 8581 et seq.

Rent Control Law for New York State (Emergency Housing)
N.Y. Unconsol. Laws, § 8581 et seq.

Rent Control Notification Act
D.C. Laws 1976, No. 1-88

Rent Control Preemption Act
Ill. Comp. Stat. 1992, Ch. 50, § 825/1 et seq.

Rent Control Prohibition Act
Mass. Gen. Laws Ann., 40Q:1 et seq.

Rent Distress Act
Md. Ann. Code 1974, Art. RP, § 8-301 et seq.

Rent Escrow Law
Md. Ann. Code 1974, Art. RP, § 8-211

Rent Impairing Violations Act
N.Y. Multiple Dwelling Law 1946 (Consol. Laws Ch. 61A) § 302a

Rent Law (Emergency)
N.Y. Laws 1920, Chs. 130-139
N.Y. Laws 1920, Ex. Sess., Chs. 942-945, 947-952
N.Y. Laws 1922, Chs. 663, 664
N.Y. Laws 1923, Ch. 892

Rent Lien Law
Wash. Rev. Code Ann., 60.72.010 et seq.

Rent or Property Tax Rebate Act (Senior Citizens)
Pa. Purdon's Stat., Title 72, § 4751-1 et seq.

Rent Regulation Reform Act
N.Y. General Business Law (Consol. Laws Ch. 20) §§ 352eee, 352eeee
N.Y. Real Property Tax Law (Consol. Laws Ch. 50A) §§ 421a, 467b
N.Y. Tax Law (Consol. Laws Ch. 60) § 171b
N.Y. Unconsol. Laws § 8581a et seq.

Rent Stabilization Law
N.Y. City Adm. Code '85, § 26-501 et seq.

Rent Stabilization Law (New York)
N.Y. Unconsol. Laws, § 26-501 et seq.

Rent Strike Law (New York City)
N.Y. Real Property Actions and Proceedings Law (Consol Ch. 81) § 769 et seq.

Rent-to-Own Agreement Act
N.H. Rev. Stat. 1955, 358-P:1 et seq.

Rent to Own Program Law
N.Y. Personal Property Law (Consol. Laws Ch. 41) § 500 et seq.

Rent Withholding Act
Pa. Purdon's Stat., Title 35, § 1700-1

Rental Accomodations Act
D.C. Code Ann., § 45-1638 et seq.

Rental Accomodations Act Amendments
D.C. Laws 1977, No. 1-122

Rental Act (Automobiles)
Conn. Gen. Stat. Ann., § 14-154a

Rental Act (Moderate Cost Housing)
Conn. Gen. Stat. Ann., § 8-69 et seq.

Rental Assistance Act
Mass. Gen. Laws Ann., 121B:42 et seq.

Rental Assistance and Self-Sufficiency Program Act
Colo. Rev. Stat., 29-4-901 et seq.

Rental Dwellings Repair Act
Haw. Rev. Stat. Ann., § 666-41 et seq.

Rental Horse Licensing and Protection Law
N.Y. Adm. Code '85, § 17-326 et seq.

Rental Housing Act
D.C. Code Ann., § 5-835

Rental Housing Act Amendment
D.C. Code Ann., § 45-1699.6

Rental Housing Incentive Guarantee Program
N.J. Stat. Ann., 55:14K-64 et seq.

Rental Industry Act (Motor Vehicle)
Haw. Rev. Stat. Ann., § 437D-1 et seq.

Rental Location Agent Act
Tenn. Code Ann., 62-25-101 et seq.

Rental Premises Standards Law (Town of Evans)
N.Y. Local Laws 1967, Town of Evans, p. 1532

Rental Proptery Utility Service Act
Ill. Comp. Stat. Ann., Ch. 765, Ch. § 735/0.01 et seq.

Rental Protection Act (Consumer Goods)
W. Va. Code 1966 § 46B-1-1 et seq.

Rental Purchase Act
Ark. Code Ann. 1987, 4-92-101 et seq.
Okla. Stat. Ann., Title 59, § 1950 et seq.

Rental Purchase Act (Karnette)
Cal. Civil Code § 1812.620 et seq.

Rental Purchase Agreement Act
Md. Ann. Code 1974, Art. CL, § 12-1101 et seq.
Miss. Code Ann. 1972, §§ 75-24-151 to 75-24-175
N.M. Stat. Ann., 57-26-1 et seq.
Utah Code Ann. 1953, 15-8-1 et seq.

Rental Purchase Agreements-Consumer Credit Code
Me. Rev. Stat. Ann. 1964, Title 9-A, § 11-101 et seq.

Rental Purchases Agreement Act
Colo. Rev. Stat., 5-10-101 et seq.
Fla. Stat. Ann., 559.9231 et seq.
Ill. Comp. Stat. Ann., Ch. 815, § 655/0.01
Iowa Code Ann., 537.3601 et seq.
La. Rev. Stat. Ann., 9:3351 et seq.
Minn. Stat. Ann., 325F.84 et seq.
Mo. Rev. Stat. 1978, 407.660 et seq.
R.I. Gen. Laws 1956, 6-44-1 et seq.
Tenn. Public Acts 1991, Ch. 225

Rental Vehicle Tax Reform Act
D.C. Code Ann., § 40-111 et seq.

Renter's Financial Responsibility and Protection Act
Ill. Comp. Stat. 1992, Ch. 625, § 27/1 et seq.

Renter's Lien Act
N.J. Stat. Ann., 2A:44-165 et seq.

Renters Property Tax Assistance Law
Cal. Revenue and Taxation Code § 20501 et seq.

Rents Act
P.R. Laws Ann. 1954, Title 17, § 181 et seq.

Rents, Profits and Improvements Act
Me. Rev. Stat. Ann. 1964, Title 14, § 6951 et seq.

Renunciation Act (Dower)
Mont. Rev. Code 1947, 22-107 et seq.

Renunciation Act (Wills)
Ky. Rev. Stat. 1971, 392.080
Me. Rev. Stat. Ann. 1964, Title 18-A, § 2-201

Renunciation of Fiduciary Powers and Property Act
N.C. Gen. Stat. 1943, § 31B-1 et seq.

Reorganization Act (Administrative Departments)
Tenn. Code Ann., 4-3-101 et seq.

Reorganization Act (Administrative)
Miss. Code Ann. 1972, § 7-13-1 et seq.
Ohio Laws Vol. 109, p. 105

Reorganization Act (Agriculture Department)
N.J. Rev. Stat. Ann., 4:1-1, 4:1-2, 4:1-4.1, 4:1-24 et seq.

Reorganization Act (Banks)
Minn. Laws 1933, Ch. 55
S.D. Codified Laws 1967, 51-27-1 et seq.

Reorganization Act (Consular)
See Consular Reorganization Act

Reorganization Act (Coroner)
Miss. Code Ann. 1972, § 19-21-101 et seq.

Reorganization Act (Court of Appeals)
Tenn. Code Ann., 16-4-101 et seq.

Reorganization Act (Courts)
Kan. Laws 1975, Ch. 178

Reorganization Act (District Court)
Mass. Gen. Laws Ann., 218:6, 218:79 et seq.
Mich. Comp. Laws Ann., 600.8101 et seq.

Reorganization Act (Environmental)
Fla. Stat. Ann., 403-801 et seq.

Reorganization Act (Executive)
See Executive Reorganization Act

Reorganization Act (Finance)
Mass. Gen. Laws Ann., 7:2 et seq.

Reorganization Act (Land Offices)
Alaska Comp. Laws Ann. 1949, § 47-2-41 et
seq.

Reorganization Act (Legislative)
Tex. Government Code, § 301.011 et seq.

Reorganization Act (Military Forces)
Ga. Code Ann., 38-2-1 et seq.

Reorganization Act (Mutual Life Insurance Company)
Pa. Purdon's Stat., Title 40, § 1010.21 et seq.

Reorganization Act (Navy Department)
See Navy Department Reorganization Act

Reorganization Act (Railroads)
N.Y. Railroad Law (Consol. Laws Ch. 49)
§ 140 et seq.

Reorganization Act (Schools)
See also School Reorganization Act
Del. Code of 1974, Title 14, §§ 1001 et seq.,
1101 et seq., 4004A
Ga. Code Ann., 20-2-61 et seq.
Ida. Code 1947, 33-301 et seq.
Ind. Code Ann., 20-4-1-1 et seq.
Kan. Stat. Ann., 72-5625 et seq.

Mich. Comp. Laws Ann., 388.681 et seq.
Minn. Stat. Ann., 122.41 et seq.
Mo. Rev. Stat. 1959, 165.657 et seq.
Neb. Rev. Stat. 1943, 79-426.01 et seq.
S.D. Codified Laws 1967, 13-6-1 et seq.
Wyo. Stat. 1957, § 21-224 et seq.

Reorganization Act (State Agencies)
Ind. Code Ann., 4-3-6-1 et seq.
R.I. Public Laws 1969, Ch. 134
S.C. Code Ann. 1976, § 1-19-10 et seq.

Reorganization Act (State Departments)
Minn. Stat. Ann., 15.01 et seq.
S.D. Laws 1943, Ch. 257

Reorganization Act (State Government)
Colo. Laws 1955, p. 861, Ch. 291

Reorganization Act Amendments of 1984
Nov. 8, 1984, P.L. 98-614, 5 U.S. Code
§§ 901 nt., 905, 906, 908, 910 to 912

Reorganization Act of 1939
April 3, 1939, Ch. 36, 53 Stat. 561 (See 3
U.S. Code § 106) 31 U.S. Code § 2

Reorganization Act of 1939-1949
Alaska Laws 1951, Ch. 133
Conn. Gen. Stat. Ann., § 3-1 et seq.
Fla. Stat. Ann., 20.02 et seq.
Haw. Rev. Stat. § 26-1 et seq.
La. Acts 1940, No. 47
N.H. Laws 1950, Sp. Sess., Ch. 5
N.J. Stat. Ann., 17:9A-124 et seq.,
17:9A-157 et seq.
N.M. Laws 1951, Ch. 140
Pa. Purdon's Stat., Title 71, § 750-1 et seq.
P.R. Laws Ann. 1954, Title 3, § 1151
Tenn. Code Ann., 4-3-101 et seq., 8-23-101,
10-1-101, 10-1-102, 59-4-101, 63-1-102

Reorganization Act of 1945
Dec. 20, 1945, Ch. 582, 59 Stat. 613

Reorganization Act of 1949
June 20, 1949, Ch. 226, 63 Stat. 203 (See 5
U.S. Code §§ 901 to 913)
Feb. 11, 1953, Ch. 3, 67 Stat. 4 (See 5 U.S.
Code § 905)
March 25, 1955, Ch. 16, 69 Stat. 14 (See 5
U.S. Code 905)

Sept. 4, 1957, P.L. 85-286, 71 Stat. 611 (See 5 U.S. Code §§ 905, 906)

April 7, 1961, P.L. 87-18, 75 Stat. 41 (See 5 U.S. Code § 905)

July 2, 1964, P.L. 88-351, 78 Stat. 240 (See 5 U.S. Code § 905)

June 18, 1965, P.L. 89-43, 79 Stat. 135 (See 5 U.S. Code § 905)

Reorganization Act of 1974 (State Omnibus)
Mo. Rev. Stat., Appendix B

Reorganization Act of 1977
April 6, 1977, P.L. 95-17, 5 U.S. Code §§ 901 et seq.

Reorganization Effective Date Act
June 7, 1939, Ch. 193, 53 Stat. 813
June 4, 1940, Ch. 231, 54 Stat. 230

Reorganization of Districts into Improvement Acts
Wash. Rev. Code Ann., 85.20.010 et seq., 85.22.010 et seq.

Reorganization of Executive Agencies Act
Mich. Comp. Laws 1948, 16.1 et seq.

Reorganization of Government Act
Va. Acts 1927, Ch. 33

Reorganization of Judiciary Act
Haw. Session Laws 1892, Ch. 57

Reorganization of School Districts Act
Iowa Code Ann., 275.1 et seq.

Reorganization Plan No. 3 of 1979
Dec. 21, 1982, P.L. 97-377, 5 U.S. Code Appx. § 2; 19 U.S. Code § 2171 nt.

Reorganization Plan No. 4 of 1970
Dec. 28, 1977, P.L. 95-219, 5 U.S. Code Appx. § 2

Repair Act (Motor Vehicle)
Fla. Stat. Ann., 559.901 et seq.

Repair and Deduct Act (Real Property)
Cal. Civil Code §§ 1941, 1942
Mont. Code Ann., 70-26-203
N.D. Cent. Code, 47-16-13, 47-16-13.1

Okla. Stat. Ann., Title 41, § 101
S.D. Codified Laws 1967, 43-32-8, 43-32-9

Repair Study Act (Auto Body)
Cal. Statutes 1992, Ch. 479

Repairmen's Lien Act
Miss. Code Ann. 1972, § 85-7-101

Reparation Act (Motor Vehicles)
R.I. Gen. Laws 1956, 31-47-1 et seq.

Reparation Motor (Vehicle Act)
Ky. Rev. Stat. 1971, 304.39-010 et seq.

Reparation Reform Act (No-Fault Act)
N.J. Stat. Ann., 39:6A-1 et seq.

Reparations Act
Kan. Stat. Ann., 66-154a et seq.

Reparations Act (Crime Victims')
La. Rev. Stat. Ann., 46:1801 et seq.
N.M. Stat. Ann., 31-22-1 et seq.
Utah Code Ann. 1953, 63-63-1 et seq.

Reparations Act (No-Fault Insurance, Automobile Injury)
Kan. Stat. Ann., 40-3101 et seq.

Reparations Act (Standard Auto Accident)
Colo. Rev. Stat., 10-4-701 et seq.

Reparations Act (Watersheds)
Cal. Water Code § 1245 et seq.

Repatriation Act
Oct. 5, 1917, Ch. 68, 40 Stat. 340

Repeater Act (Habitual Criminal)
Wis. Stat. Ann., 939.62, 973.12

Replacement Housing and Relocation Act
N.J. Stat. Ann., 27:7-72 et seq.

Replacement Parts Act (Model Quality)
Colo. Rev. Stat., 10-3-1301 et seq.

Replevin Act
Ark. Code Ann. 1987, 18-60-809 et seq.
Haw. Rev. Stat. 1968, § 654-1 et seq.
Ill. Comp. Stat. Ann., Ch. 735, § 5/19-101 et seq.
Continued

Ky. Rev. Stat. 1971, 426.450 et seq.
Mich. Comp. Laws Ann., 600.7301 et seq.
Miss. Code Ann. 1972, § 11-37-1 et seq.
Mont. Code Ann., 27-17-101 et seq.
Nev. Rev. Stat. 1979 Reprint, 31.840 et seq.
N.H. Rev. Stat. 1955, 536-A:1 et seq.
N.J. Stat. Ann., 2A:59-1 et seq.
N.M. Stat. Ann., 42-8-1 et seq.
Pa. Cons. Stat., Title 42, § 323
R.I. Gen. Laws 1956, 34-21-1 et seq.
Vt. Stat. Ann., Title 12, § 5321 et seq.
Wash. Rev. Code Ann., 7.64.010 et seq.

Report Cards Act (School)
Ark. Code Ann. 1987, 6-15-801 et seq.

Reporters' Confidence Act
Mont. Code Ann., 26-1-901 et seq.

Reporters' Privilege Act
Del. Code of 1974, Title 10, § 4320 et seq.

Reporters' Shield Law
Mont. Code Ann., 26-1-901 et seq.

Reporting Act
N.J. Stat. Ann., 34:1-70, 34:15-96 et seq.

Reporting Act (Arson Information)
Colo. Rev. Stat., 10-4-1001 et seq.

Reporting Act (Child Abuse)
Ohio Rev. Code 1953, 2151.421

Reporting Act (Cocaine Baby)
Minn. Stat. Ann., 626.5562

Reporting Act (Domestic Abuse)
Okla. Stat. Ann., Title 22, § 40.5, 40.6

Reporting Act (Economic Development)
R.I. Gen. Laws 1956, 42-64.4-1 et seq.

Reporting and Disclosure Act (Retirement System)
N.Y. Retirement and Social Security Law (Consol. Laws Ch. 51A) § 150 et seq.

Reporting and Registration Act (Noncontrolled Substances)
Pa. Purdon's Stat., Title 35, § 881 et seq.

Reporting Automobile Accident Act
N.D. Cent. Code, 39-08-04 et seq.

Reporting Immunity Act (Arson and Theft)
Okla. Stat. Ann., Title 36, § 6301 et seq.

Reporting Immunity Act (Arson)
Me. Rev. Stat. Ann. 1964, Title 25, § 2411 et seq.

Reporting Law (Child-Support Delinquency)
Cal. Family Code § 4700 et seq.

Reporting of Improper Governmental Activities Act
Cal. Government Code § 8547 et seq.

Reporting Practices Act (Shorthand)
Wash. Rev. Code Ann., 18.145.005 et seq.

Reports to Legislative Research Unit Act
Ill. Comp. Stat. Ann., §§ 110/0.01, 110/1

Repossession Act (Conditional Sales)
Mo. Rev. Stat. 1959, 428.110

Repossession Security Act (Manufactured Homes)
Minn. Stat. Ann., 327.61 et seq.

Repossessors Act
Cal. Business and Professions Code § 7544 et seq.

Representation Agreement Act (Fire Damage)
Ill. Comp. Ann., Ch. 815, §§ 625/0.01, 625/1

Representation Agreement Act (Personal Injury)
Ill. Comp. Ann., Ch. 815, §§ 640/0.01, 640/1

Representative Apportionment Act
Pa. Purdon's Stat., Title 25, §§ 2215, 2216

Representative Districts Act
Ky. Rev. Stat. 1971, 6.031

Representative Districts Validation Act
Mich. Comp. Laws Ann., 565.651 et seq.

Representative Town Meeting Act
Mass. Gen. Laws Ann., 43A:1 et seq.

Representatives Act
Wash. Rev. Code Ann., 44.07B.001 et seq.

Representatives Election Act
July 14, 1862, Ch. 170, 12 Stat. 572

Reprieves, Pardons and Commutations Law
Cal. Penal Code § 4800 et seq.

Reproductive Privacy Act
Wash. Rev. Code Ann., 9.02.902

Republic of the Philippines Military Assistance Act
June 26, 1946, Ch. 500, 60 Stat. 315

Republican River Compact Act
Colo. Rev. Stat., 37-67-101, 37-67-102

Repurchase Act (Tax Sales)
N.M. Stat. Ann. 1953, 72-8-31, 72-8-32

Request for Admissions Act
Ga. Code 1933, 70-207, 81-1012

Reregistration Act (Brevard County)
Fla. Laws 1949, Ch. 25453

Reregistration Act (Election)
Fla. Stat. Ann., 97.011 et seq.

Reregistration Act (Monroe County)
Fla. Laws 1945, Ch. 22708

Resale Act (Unredeemed Lands)
Okla. Stat. Ann., Title 68, § 3125 et seq.

Resale Broker Act (Time-Share)
Tenn. Code Ann., 66-32-102 et seq.

Resale of Tickets Act
Mass. Gen. Laws Ann., 140:185A et seq.

Resale Price Maintenance Act
Ariz. Rev. Stat. Ann., § 44-1421 et seq.
Del. Code of 1974, Title 6, § 1901 et seq.
Haw. Rev. Laws 1955, § 205-20 et seq.
La. Rev. Stat. Ann., 51:421 et seq.

Mass. Gen. Laws Ann., 93:14A et seq.
Miss. Code 1942, § 1108
N.J. Stat. Ann., 56:4-3 et seq.
Pa. Purdon's Stat., Title 73, § 7 et seq.
Va. Code 1950, § 59.1-1 et seq.

Resale Royalties Act
Cal. Civil Code § 986

Rescue Act (Urban Heavy)
Cal. Government Code §§ 8584, 8584.1

Rescue Squad District Act
Ill. Rev. Stat. 1991, Ch. 85, § 6851 et seq.

Rescue Squad, Fire Company and Ambulance Service Assistance Act (Volunteer)
Pa. Purdon's Stat., Title 72, § 3943.1 et seq.

Rescue Squad Workers' and Firemen's Pension Fund Act
N.C. Gen. Stat. 1943, § 58-86-1 et seq.

Rescue Squads Assistance Act
Va. Code 1950, § 32.1-115 et seq.

Research Act
Miss. General Laws 1960, Ch. 389, p. 608

Research Act (Controlled Substances Therapeutic)
Mass. Gen. Laws Ann., 94D:1 et seq.

Research Act (County or Historical)
Ill. Rev. Stat. 1991, Ch. 81, § 69.9 et seq.

Research and Academic Excellence Initiatives Act
S.C. Code Ann. 1976, § 59-104-10 et seq.

Research and Cancer Control Act
Fla. Stat. Ann., 240.5121

Research and Consulting Act (University Faculty)
Ill. Rev. Stat. 1991, Ch. 144, § 215.9 et seq.

Research and Control Act (Cancer)
Fla. Stat. Ann., 385.201

Research and Development Act
Miss. Code Ann. 1972, § 57-13-1 et seq.
N.M. Stat. Ann., 9-15-16 et seq.

Research and Development Act (Energy)
N.M. Stat. Ann., 71-4-1 et seq.

Research and Development Act (Trucking Industry)
Okla. Stat. Ann., Title 47, § 1161 et seq.

Research and Development Authority Act
Neb. Rev. Stat. 1943, 58-401 et seq.

Research and Development Commission Act
Fla. Stat. Ann., 23.140 et seq.

Research and Development Incentives Act
Okla. Stat. Ann., Title 68, § 54001 et seq.

Research and Development Tax Credit Law
Pa. Purdon's Stat., Title 72, § 8701-B et seq.

Research and Economic Development Act (University-Based)
Iowa Code Ann., 262B.1 et seq.

Research and Education Act (Sustainable Agriculture)
Mont. Laws 1991, Ch. 659

Research and Training for Eastern Europe and the Independent States of the Former Soviet Union Act of 1983
Nov. 22, 1983, P.L. 98-164, 22 U.S. Code §§ 4501, 4501 nt., 4509
Oct. 28, 1991, P.L. 102-138, 22 U.S. Code § 4509
Dec. 17, 1993, P.L. 103-199, 22 U.S. Code § 4501 et seq.

Research Authority Act (Mississippi University)
Miss. Code Ann. 1972, § 37-141-1 et seq.

Research Corporation Act (University of Rhode Island)
R.I. Gen. Laws 1956, 35-12-1 et seq.

Research, Development, Demonstration and Commercialization Act (Energy)
Cal. Public Resources Code § 25645 et seq.

Research Equipment Act (Science and Technology)
Okla. Stat. Ann., Title 74, §§ 2013 to 2016

Research Facilities Act
July 23, 1963, P.L. 88-74, 7 U.S. Code §§ 390 et seq.
Dec. 23, 1985, P.L. 99-190, 7 U.S. Code §§ 390 et seq., 390 nt.
Nov. 28, 1990, P.L. 101-624, 7 U.S. Code § 390c
Dec. 21, 1995, P.L. 104-66, 7 U.S. Code § 390i
April 4, 1996, P.L. 104-127, 7 U.S. Code §§ 390 nt., 390, 390a to 390d
June 23, 1998, P.L. 105-185, 7 U.S. Code §§ 390a, 390b, 390d

Research Facilities and Farm Animal Protection Act
Ga. Code Ann., 4-11-30 et seq.
Kan. Stat. Ann., 47-1825 et seq.
Mont. Laws 1991, Ch. 205
S.C. Code Ann. 1976, § 47-21-10 et seq.
Tenn. Public Acts 1992, Ch. 782

Research Fairness Act (Health)
Cal. Health and Safety Code § 439.900 et seq.

Research Foundation Act
Kan. Laws 1963, Ch. 416

Research Indemnity Trust and Ground Water Assessment Act
Mont. Code Ann., 15-38-101 et seq.

Research Information Act (Confidential)
Mich. Comp. Laws Ann., 390.1551 et seq.

Research Investment Act
La. Rev. Stat. Ann., 51:2201 et seq.

Research, Marketing and Safety Act (Liquefied Petroleum Gas)
Okla. Stat. 1981, Title 52, § 420.20 et seq.

Research Mitigation Banking Act
Colo. Rev. Stat., 37-85.5-101 et seq.

Research on Aging Act of 1974
May 31, 1974, P.L. 93-296, 88 Stat. 184, 42
U.S. Code §§ 289k-2 to 289k-5

Research or Exhibiting Facilities Protection Act (Animal)
Miss. Code Ann. 1972, § 69-29-301 et seq.

Research Park Act (University)
N.M. Stat. Ann., 21-28-1 et seq.

Research, Planning, and Development Act
Minn. Laws 1990, 1st Sp. Sess., Ch. 12, Art.
8, § 27
Minn. Stat. 1988, 126.81
S.C. Code Ann. 1976, § 13-3-10 et seq.

Research Policy Act
Alaska Stat. 1962, § 44.19.251 et seq.
Ore. Rev. Stat., 351.865 et seq.

Research Promotion Act (Small Business Innovation)
N.Y. Public Authorities Law (Consol. Laws
Ch. 43A) § 3102c

Research School Act (Developmental)
Okla. Stat. Ann., Title 70, §§ 1210.571 to
1210.579

Reservation (Mineral Rights)
Okla. Stat. Ann., Title 12A, § 5-110

Reservation Act (Horseneck Beach)
Mass. Acts 1955, Ch. 583

Reserve Act (Military)
Cal. Military and Veterans Code § 550 et seq.

Reserve Corps Compensation Act
July 15, 1939, Ch. 284, 53 Stat. 1042

Reserve Forces Act of 1955
Aug. 9, 1955, Ch. 665, 69 Stat. 598 (See 10
U.S. Code §§ 268 to 272, 275, 279, 511,
1162) 50 U.S. Code Appx. §§ 454, 456

Reserve Forces Bill of Rights and Vitalization Act
Dec. 1, 1967, P.L. 90-168, 81 Stat. 521, 10
U.S. Code §§ 133 nt., 136, 175, 262, 264,
266, 269, 270, 270, 511, 3013, 3019, 3033,
5034, 8013, 8019, 8033, 8212 nt., 8850; 32
U.S. Code § 502; 37 U.S. Code § 404

Reserve Forces Facilities Act of 1958
Aug. 20, 1958, P.L. 85-685, 72 Stat. 664, 10
U.S. Code §§ 2233, 2233a

Reserve Forces Facilities Act of 1959
Aug. 10, 1959, P.L. 86-149, 73 Stat. 324

Reserve Forces Facilities Act of 1960
June 8, 1960, P.L. 86-500, 74 Stat. 188

Reserve Forces Facilities Act of 1961
June 27, 1961, P.L. 87-57, 75 Stat. 112

Reserve Forces Facilities Authorization Acts
Nov. 7, 1963, P.L. 88-174, 77 Stat. 329
Aug. 1, 1964, P.L. 88-390, 78 Stat. 365
Sept. 16, 1965, P.L. 89-188, 79 Stat. 820
Sept. 12, 1966, P.L. 89-568, 80 Stat. 757
Oct. 21, 1967, P.L. 90-110, 81 Stat. 309
July 21, 1968, P.L. 90-408, 82 Stat. 392
Dec. 5, 1969, P.L. 91-142, 83 Stat. 318
Oct. 26, 1970, P.L. 91-511, 84 Stat. 1227
Oct. 25, 1972, P.L. 92-545, 86 Stat. 1154
Nov. 29, 1973, P.L. 93-166, 87 Stat. 661, 10
U.S. Code §§ 2674, 2676, 2684, 4774,
9774; 42 U.S. Code §§ 1594k, 3374

Reserve Forces Revitalization Act of 1996
Sept. 23, 1996, P.L. 104-201, Title XII, 10
U.S. Code § 10001 nt.

Reserve Fund Act (Federal Facilities)
Mass. Gen. Laws Ann., 29:2X

Reserve Fund Act (Taxing District)
Ill. Comp. Stat. 1992, Ch. 35, §§ 725/1 to
725/4

Reserve General Fund Act
S.C. Constitution, Article 3, § 36

Reserve Officer Personnel Act of 1954
  Sept. 3, 1954, Ch. 1257, 68 Stat. 1147
  June 30, 1955, Ch. 247, 69 Stat. 218

Reserve Officer Personnel Management Act
  Oct. 5, 1994, P.L. 103-337, 10 U.S. Code
    10001 nt.
  Feb. 10, 1996, P.L. 104-106, 10 U.S. Code
    §§ 113, prec. 501, 620, 741, 3853 nt.,
    12102, 12201, 12203, 12320, 12645, 14310
    nt.

Reserve Officers Training Corps Law
  Ill. Rev. Stat. 1991, Ch. 122, § 30-16.1 et seq.

**Reserve Officers' Training Corps
Vitalization Act of 1964**
  Oct. 13, 1964, P.L. 88-647, 78 Stat. 1063, 10
    U.S. Code §§ 1475, 1478, 1481, 2031, 2101
    to 2111, 3201, 4348, 5404, 5504, 5652b,
    6023, 6387, 6959, 8201, 9348, 9385 nt.; 37
    U.S. Code §§ 205, 209, 415, 422

Reserved Fund Act (Five Percent)
  S.C. Constitution, Article III, § 36

Reserved Shore Spaces Act
  Alaska Comp. Laws Ann. 1949, § 47-2-52

Reservist Acts
  June 29, 1918, Ch. 112, 40 Stat. 634
  Oct. 19, 1918, Ch. 190, 40 Stat. 1014

Reservist Relief Act (Military)
  Cal. Statutes 1991, Ch. 49

Reservoir Act (Big Kincaid Creek)
  Ill. Comp. Stat. 1992, Ch. 615, § 80/0.01 et
    seq.
  Ill. Rev. Stat. 1991, Ch. 19, §§ 1130, 1131

Reservoir Act (Lincoln)
  Ill. Rev. Stat. 1991, Ch. 19, §§ 1110, 1111

Reservoir Loan Act (Cleveland)
  Mass. Acts 1962, Ch. 405

Reservoir Loan Act (Hamilton)
  Mass. Acts 1956, Ch. 561

Reservoir Safety Act
  Colo. Rev. Stat., 37-87-105 et seq.

Reservoir Site Acquisition Act
  R.I. Public Laws 1967, Ch. 197

Reservoirs and Dams Safety Act
  S.C. Code Ann. 1976, § 49-11-110 et seq.

Resettlement Act (Veterans)
  Ga. Laws 1945, p. 170

Residence Act (New York City)
  N.Y. Adm. Code 1938, §§ B40-4.0 tp
    F41-41.0

Residence Act (Servicemen)
  Ala. Code 1975, § 6-7-20

**Residence Lien Restriction and Lien
Recovery Fund Act**
  Utah Code Ann. 1953, 38-11-101 et seq.

**Residence Location Planning Act
(Community)**
  Ill. Rev. Stat. 1989, Ch. 91 1/2, § 921 et seq.

Residence of Minors for Tuition Act
  Ill. Rev. Stat. 1991, Ch. 144, § 40a.9 et seq.

Residences Picketing Act
  Conn. Gen. Stat. 1983, § 31-120

Residency Law (Floating Home)
  Cal. Civil Code § 800 et seq.

Resident Abuse and Neglect Act
  N.M. Stat. Ann., 30-47-1 et seq.

**Resident Abuse Prevention Training Act
(Nurse Aid)**
  Pa. Purdon's Stat., Title 63, § 671 et seq.

Resident Agent Act
  Fla. Stat. Ann., 626.912
  S.D. Codified Laws 1967, 47-2-27, 47-2-58

Resident Alien Course Act
  Ill. Rev. Stat. 1991, Ch. 111, § 8050 et seq.

Resident Motorists' Law
Cal. Vehicle Code 1959, § 17461

Resident-Owner Relations Act
N.M. Stat. Ann., 47-8-1 et seq.

Resident Process Act (Corporations)
N.C. Gen. Stat. 1943, §§ 55-5-04, 55-16-02
to 55-16-04, 55-16-20

Resident Student Financial Assistance Program Act
Mont. Code Ann., 20-26-101 et seq.

Residential Alternative Licensing Act (Community)
Ill. Comp. Stat. 1992, Ch. 210, § 140/1 et seq.

Residential Builders Act
Mich. Comp. Laws Ann., 338.1501 et seq.

Residential Building Contractors Law
Minn. Stat. Ann., 326.83 et seq.

Residential Building Energy Conservation Act
Colo. Rev. Stat., 6-7-101 et seq.

Residential Care Act
Okla. Stat. Ann., Title 63, § 1-819 et seq.

Residential Care Administrators Act
Ida. Code 1947, 54-4201 et seq.

Residential Care and Assisted Living Facility Licensing Act
R.I. Gen. Laws 1956, 23-17.4-1 et seq.

Residential Care Facilities for the Elderly Act
Cal. Health and Safety Code § 1569 et seq.

Residential Care Facilities for the Elderly Authorities Act
Ga. Code Ann., 31-7-110 et seq.

Residential Care Licensing Law (Adult)
La. Rev. Stat. Ann., 40:2151 et seq.

Residential Conservation Service Act
Ga. Code Ann., 31-7-110 et seq.

Residential Conveyance Act
P.R. Laws Ann. 1954, Title 17, § 701 et seq.

Residential Earthquake Recovery Act (Green, Hill, Areias, Farr)
Cal. Insurance Code § 5000 et seq.

Residential Energy Conservation Act
Ore. Rev. Stat., 469.631 et seq.

Residential Finance Authorities Act for Large Municipalities (Urban)
Ga. Code Ann., 36-41-1 et seq.

Residential Finance Authority Act
Ga. Code Ann., 8-3-170 et seq.

Residential Ground Rent Act
Tenn. Code Ann., 66-30-101 et seq.
Va. Code 1950, § 55-79.01 et seq.

Residential Health Care Recipient Ombudsman Act
Ala. Acts 1985, p. 1029

Residential Home Loan Act
N.M. Stat. Ann., 56-8-22 et seq.

Residential Home Notification Act (Child)
Miss. Code Ann. 1972, § 43-16-1 et seq.

Residential Housing Act (Group)
Minn. Stat. Ann., 256I.01 to 256I.06

Residential Housing Finance Law (Local)
Kan. Stat. Ann., 12-5219 et seq.

Residential Housing Rent Regulation and Control Act
Alaska Stat. 1962, Replaced Title,
§ 34.06.010 et seq.

Residential Improvement Loan Act
Ill. Rev. Stat. 1991, Ch. 17, § 5800 et seq.

Residential Landlord and Tenant Act
See also Uniform Residential Landlord and
Tenant Act
Miss. Code Ann. 1972, 89-8-1 et seq.
Mont. Code Ann., 70-24-101 et seq.
Mont. Code Ann., 70-24-101 et seq.
Nev. Rev. Stat. Ann., 118A.010 et seq.
Continued

N.H. Rev. Stat. 1955, 613-A:1 et seq.
Okla. Stat. Ann., Title 41 § 101 et seq.
Pa. Cons. Stat., Title 42, § 5971 et seq.
Utah Code Ann. 1953, 77-33-1 et seq.
Wash. Rev. Code Ann., 59.18.010
Wis. Stat. Ann., 976.01

Residential Landlord and Tenant Act (Mobile Home Parks)
Ariz. Rev. Stat. Ann., § 33-1401 et seq.
Kan. Laws 1992, Ch. 306

Residential Landlord and Tenant Act (Uniform)
Ariz. Rev. Stat. Ann., § 33-1301 et seq.

Residential Landlord-Tenant Code
Haw. Rev. Stat. § 521-1 et seq.

Residential Lead-Based Paint Hazard Reduction Act of 1992
Oct. 28, 1992, P.L. 102-550, 42 U.S. Code §§ 4851, et seq., 4851 nt.
April 26, 1996, P.L. 104-134, 42 U.S. Code § 4852

Residential Lending, Brokerage and Servicing Act
Tenn. Code Ann., 45-13-101 et seq.

Residential Living Act (Disabled Persons)
Okla. Stat. Ann., Title 60, § 860 et seq.

Residential Modular Building Act
Tenn. Code Ann., 68-126-301 et seq.

Residential Mortgage License Act
Ill. Rev. Stat. 1991, Ch. 17, § 2321-1 et seq.

Residential Mortgage Originator and Servicer Licensing Act
Minn. Stat. 1986, 58.01 et seq.

Residential Mortgage Practices Act
Ida. Code 1947, 26-3101 et seq.

Residential Parking Tax Exemption Act
D.C. Code Ann., § 47-2001

Residential Picketing Act
Ill. Rev. Stat. 1991, Ch. 38, § 21.1-1 et seq.

Residential Property Condition Disclosure Act
Okla. Stat. Ann., Title 60, § 831 et seq.

Residential Property Sale Subject to Land Trust Act
Ill. Rev. Stat. 1991, Ch. 29, § 8.30 et seq.

Residential Property Tax Relief Act
D.C. Code Ann., § 47-849 et seq.

Residential Real Property Registration Requirements Act for Certain Makers of Mortgages and Deeds of Trust
N.C. Gen. Stat. 1943, § 53-233 et seq.

Residential Real Property Transfer Excise Tax Act
D.C. Code Ann., § 47-1401 et seq.

Residential Rehabilitation Act
Cal. Health and Safety Code § 37910 et seq.
Utah Code Ann. 1953, 11-25-1 et seq.

Residential Rent Control Law
N.Y. City Adm. Code 1938, Ch. 51, § Y51-1.0 et seq.

Residential Rent Law
N.Y. Laws 1946, Ch. 274
N.Y. Laws 1949, Ch. 591

Residential Service Company Act
Tex. Rev. Civ. Stat., Art. 6573b

Residential Student Financial Assistance Program Act
Mont. Code Ann., 20-26-101 et seq.

Residential Telephone Equipment Consumer Protection Act
N.Y. General Business Law (Consol. Laws Ch. 20) § 349b

Residential Truth in Construction Act
La. Rev. Stat. Ann., 9:4851 et seq.

Residential Youth Care Facility Licensing Act (Secure)
Ill. Comp. Stat. 1992, Ch. 730, § 175/45-1

Residents' Bill of Rights (Long-Term Care)
Mont. Laws 1991, Ch. 582

Residents of Long-Term Care Facilities Bill of Rights
S.C. Code Ann. 1976, § 44-81-10 et seq.

Residents Property Tax Program
Me. Rev. Stat. Ann. 1964, Title 36, § 6201-A et seq.

Residents' Tax Relief Act
Fla. Laws 1998, Ch. 341, §§ 1 to 4

Residents Transfer Tax Law
N.Y. Tax Law (Consol. Laws Ch. 60) § 220 et seq.

Residual Market Deficit Resolution and Recovery Act (Workers Compensation)
Me. Rev. Stat. Ann. 1964, Title 24-A, § 2391 et seq.

Resign-to-Run Law (Elections)
Fla. Stat. Ann., 99.012, Subsec. 2

Resistance and Obstruction Act (Public Officers)
Okla. Stat. Ann., Title 21, § 540

Resisting Arrest Law
Mich. Comp. Laws Ann., 750.479

Resocialization Furlough Act
D.C. Laws 1977, No. 1-130

Resolution Dispute Act
Colo. Rev. Stat., 13-22-301 et seq.

Resolution of Dispute Act
Neb. Rev. Stat. 1943, 25-2901 et seq.

Resolution of Interposition
Miss. General Laws 1956, Ch. 466, p. 741

Resolution Trust Corporation Completion Act
Dec. 17, 1993, P.L. 103-204, 12 U.S. Code § 1421
July 29, 1998, P.L. 105-216, 12 U.S. Code § 1831q

Resolution Trust Corporation Funding Act of 1991
March 23, 1991, P.L. 102-18, 12 U.S. Code § 1421 nt.
Dec. 12, 1991, P.L. 102-233, 12 U.S. Code § 1441a nt.

Resolution Trust Corporation Refinancing, Restructuring, and Improvement Act of 1991
Dec. 12, 1991, P.L. 102-233, 12 U.S. Code § 1421 nt.
Oct. 28, 1992, P.L. 102-550, 12 U.S. Code §§ 1441a, 3345, 3348

Resolution Trust Corporation Thrift Depositor Protection Reform Act of 1991
Dec. 12, 1991, P.L. 102-233, 12 U.S. Code § 1421 nt.

Resort Act (Camping Membership)
Tex. Property Code, § 222.001

Resort District Law
Cal. Public Resources Code § 10000 et seq.

Resort District Rehabilitation Act
Mich. Comp. Laws Ann., 125.2201 et seq.

Resort Improvement District Law
Cal. Public Resources Code § 13000 et seq.

Resort Owners Corporation Act (Summer)
Mich. Comp. Laws Ann., 455.201 et seq.

Resource and Reference Center Act (Agricultural Law)
Pa. 1998 Pamph. Laws, No. 11

Resource and Transportation Development Act
N.M. Stat. Ann., 7-23-1

Resource Center Law (Computer)
Pa. Purdon's Stat., Title 24, § 6001 et seq.

Resource Conservation Act (Wild)
Pa. Purdon's Stat., Title 32, § 5301 et seq.

Resource Conservation and Recovery Act of 1976

Oct. 21, 1976, P.L. 94-580, 42 U.S. Code §§ 6901 et seq.

Nov. 2, 1984, P.L. 98-616, 42 U.S. Code §§ 6901 et seq.

Neb. Rev. Stat. 1943, 81-1140 et seq.

Resource Conservation, Recovery and Beautification Act

Ky. Rev. Stat. 1971, Superseded Vols., 224.905 et seq.

Resource Development Act (Central Nevada)

Nev. Statutes 1969, Ch. 615, p. 1180

Resource Development and Outdoor Recreation Act

Wis. Stat. Ann., 23.30, 23.31

Resource Development Fund Act (Forest and Mineral)

Mich. Comp. Laws Ann., 299.251 et seq.

Resource Directory Act (Central Disability)

Mich. Comp. Laws Ann., 395.321 et seq.

Resource Extraction Reclamation Act

Fla. Stat. Ann., 378.401 et seq.

Resource Grant Program (School and Community)

Fla. Stat. Ann., 232.258

Resource Indemnity and Groundwater Assessment Act

Also known as Resource Indemnity Trust Act

Mont. Code Ann., 15-38-101 et seq.

Resource Inventory Act

Mich. Comp. Laws Ann., 321.201 et seq.

Resource Mitigation Bank Act

Colo. Rev. Stat., 37-85.5-101 et seq.

Resource Planning Act (Water)

Kan. Stat. Ann., 82a-901 et seq.

Resource Reclamation Act

Ark. Code Ann. 1987, 8-7-301 et seq.

Resource Recovery Act

La. Rev. Stat. Ann., 30:1121 et seq.

Mich. Comp. Laws Ann., 299.301 et seq.

Resource Recovery Act (Ulster County)

N.Y. Public Authorities Law (Consol. Laws Ch. 43A) § 2050a et seq.

Resource Recovery Act of 1970

Oct. 26, 1970, P.L. 91-512, 84 Stat. 1227, 42 U.S. Code §§ 3251 to 3254f, 3256 to 3259

Resource Recovery Agency Act (Brookhaven)

N.Y. Public Authorities Law (Consol. Laws Ch. 43A) § 2051a et seq.

Resource Recovery Agency Act (Broome County)

N.Y. Public Authorities Law (Consol. Laws, Ch. 43A), § 2047a et seq.

Resource Recovery Agency Act (Dutchess County)

N.Y. Public Authorities Law (Consol. Laws Ch. 43A) § 2047a et seq.

Resource Recovery Agency Act (Islip)

N.Y. Public Authorities Law (Consol. Laws Ch. 43A) § 2046a et seq.

Resource Recovery Agency Act (Onondaga County)

N.Y. Public Authorities Law 43A, § 2045a et seq.

Resource Recovery and Development Act

La. Rev. Stat. Ann., 30:1150.1 et seq.

Resource Recovery and Energy Facility Finance Act

N.C. Gen. Stat. 1943, § 159F-1 et seq.

Resource Recovery and Management Act

Fla. Stat. Ann., 403.702 et seq.

Resource Recovery and Solid Waste Disposal Act
N.J. Stat. Ann., 13:1E-136 et seq.

Resource Recovery and Solid Waste Disposal Act (Bay County)
Fla. Laws 1983, Ch. 83-370

Resource Recovery and Solid Waste Disposal Act (Hillsborough County)
Fla. Laws 1983, Ch. 83-415

Resource Recovery and Solid Waste Disposal Authority Act
W. Va. Code 1966, § 16-26-1 et seq.

Resource Recovery and Solid Waste Disposal Facility Bond Act
N.J. Laws 1985, Ch. 330

Resource Recovery and Waste Management Finance Act
Mich. Comp. Laws Ann., 123.311 et seq.

Resource Recovery, Conservation, and Solid Waste Management Act (Municipal)
Tex. Health and Safety Code, § 363.001 et seq.
Tex. Rev. Civ. Stat., Art. 4477-7c

Resource Recovery Development Act (Solid Waste)
Pa. Purdon's Stat., Title 35, § 755.1 et seq.

Resource Recovery Development Authorities Act
Ga. Code Ann., 36-63-1 et seq.

Resource Recovery Policy Act
Tex. Health and Safety Code, § 362.001 et seq.

Resource Rivers Act
Fla. Laws 1985, Ch. 347

Resource Sharing through Distance Learning Act (Educational)
Pa. 1993 Pamph. Laws, No. 45

Resource Trust Act (Indemnity)
Mont. Code Ann., 15-38-101 et seq.

Resources Act
Fla. Stat. Ann., 282.318

Resources Authority Act
S.C. Code Ann. 1976, § 11-37-10 et seq.
Va. Code 1950, § 62.1-197 et seq.

Resources Commission Act
Ga. Laws 1957, p. 264

Resources Cost Share Finance Act (Water)
Ark. Code Ann. 1987, 15-22-801 et seq.

Resources Development Act
Alaska Stat. 1962, § 44.37.010 et seq.
Okla. Stat. Ann., Title 74, § 1801 et seq.

Resources Excise Tax Act
N.M. Stat. Ann., 7-25-1 et seq.

Resources Extraction Reclamation Act
Fla. Stat. Ann., 378.401 et seq.

Resources Law (Reinvest in Minnesota)
Minn. Stat. Ann., 103F.501 et seq.

Resources Law (Water)
Mo. Rev. Stat., 640.400 et seq.

Resources Management Act (Information)
Tex. General and Special Laws 1991, p. 3569, Ch. 788, § 2 et seq.
Tex. Government Code, § 2054.001 et seq.
Tex. Rev. Civ. Stat., Art. 4413(32j)

Resources Management Act (Ocean)
Cal. Public Resources Code § 36000 et seq.
Wash. Rev. Code Ann., 43.143.005 et seq.

Resources Management Act (Weather)
Cal. Water Code § 400 et seq.

Resources Management Act (Wildland Fire Protection)
Cal. Public Resources Code § 4461 et seq.

Resources Management and Paperwork Reduction Act (Information)
Fla. Stat. Ann., 282.003 et seq.

Resources Protection Act (Archaeological and Paleontological)
Ill. Comp. Stat. 1992, Ch. 20, § 3435/0.01 et seq.

Resources Surcharge Law (Energy)
Cal. Revenue and Taxation Code § 40001 et seq.

Respiratory Care Act
Fla. Stat. Ann., 468.35 et seq.
N.M. Stat. Ann., 61-12B-1 et seq.
R.I. Gen. Laws 1956, 23-39-1 et seq.

Respiratory Care Practice Act
Cal. Business and Professions Code § 3700 et seq.
Ga. Code Ann., 43-34-140 et seq.
Ida. Code 1947, 54-4301 et seq.
Miss. Code Ann. 1972, § 73-59-1 et seq.
Okla. Stat. Ann., Title 59, § 2026 et seq.
S.C. Code Ann. 1976, § 40-47-500 et seq.
Utah Code Ann. 1953, 58-57-1 et seq.

Respiratory Care Practices Regulation Act
P.R. Laws Ann. 1954, Title 20, § 3401 et seq.

Respiratory Care Practitioner Act
Tenn. Code Ann., 63-6-401 et seq.

Respiratory Care Practitioner Licensing Act
N.J. Stat. Ann., 45:14E-1 to 45:14E-15

Respiratory Care Practitioners Act
Md. Ann. Code 1974, Art. HO, § 14-5A-01 et seq.

Respiratory Enabling Act
D.C. Laws 1977, No. 1-105

Respiratory Therapy Practice Act
Kan. Stat. Ann., 65-5501 et seq.
La. Rev. Stat. Ann., 37:3301 et seq.

Respite Care Services Act
Ida. Code 1947, 39-4701 et seq.

Respite Demonstration Program Act
Ill. Rev. Stat. 1985, Ch. 23, § 1601 et seq.

Responders Liability Act (Oil Spill)
Ala. Code 1975, § 6-5-332.2
Ill. Comp. Stat. 1992, Ch. 740, § 113/1
Pa. Purdon's Stat., Title 35, § 6023.1 et seq.
S.C. Code Ann. 1976, § 48-44-10 et seq.

Response Act (Emergency)
Okla. Stat. Ann., Title 27A, § 4-1-101 et seq.

Response Act (Environmental)
Kan. Stat. Ann., 65-3452a et seq.

Response Action Contractor Indemnification Act
Ill. Rev. Stat. 1991, Ch. 111 1/2, § 7201 et seq.

Response and Liability Act (Environmental)
Minn. Stat. Ann., 115B.01 et seq.

Response and Notification Act (Emergency)
Okla. Stat. Ann., Title 63, § 689 et seq.

Response and Prevention Act (Oil Spill)
Tex. Natural Resources Code, § 40.001 et seq.

Response to Hazardous Material Incidents Act
Mont. Code Ann., 10-3-1201 et seq.

Responsibilities and Bill of Rights (Patients)
Fla. Stat. Ann., 381.026, 381.0261

Responsibility Act (Aircraft Financial)
N.H. Rev. Stat. 1955, 422-A:1 et seq.

Responsibility Act (Financial and Safety)
Iowa Code Ann., 321A.1 et seq.

Responsibility Act (Motor Vehicles)
See Motor Vehicle Financial Responsibility Act

Responsibility Act (Parental)
N.M. Stat. Ann.,40-5A-1 et seq.

Responsibility Act (Parents)
See Parental Liability Act

Responsibility Act (Union)
Ga. Code Ann., 9-2-24 et seq.
Ga. Code 1933, 3-117 et seq.

Responsibility Act (Unitary Residence and Financial)
Minn. Stat. Ann., 256G.01 et seq.

Responsibility Act (Vehicles)
N.C. Gen. Stat. 1943, § 20-309 et seq.

Responsibility in Pensions Act
Cal. Government Code § 31515 et seq.

Responsible Property Transfer Act
Ill. Rev. Stat. 1991, Ch. 30, § 901 et seq.

Responsible Relative Act (Poor Relief)
Mich. Comp. Laws Ann., 401.1 et seq.

Responsible Vendor Act
Ala. Code 1975, § 28-10-1
Ala. Code 1975, § 28-10-1
Fla. Stat. Ann., 561.701 et seq.

Responsive Verdict Act
La. Code of Crim. Proc., Art. 814

Rest Period for Women Act
Ky. Rev. Stat. 1971, Superseded Vols., 337.365

Restaurant Act
Cal. Health and Safety Code § 28600 et seq.
Colo. Rev. Stat., 12-44-201 et seq.
Iowa Code Ann., 137A.1 et seq.
Pa. Purdon's Stat., Title 35, § 655.1 et seq.

Restaurant and Hotel Act
Ohio Rev. Code 1953, 3731.01 et seq.
S.C. Code Ann. 1976, § 45-1-10 et seq.
Wis. Stat. Ann., 50.50 et seq.

Restaurant and Hotel Commission Act
Fla. Stat. Ann., 509.013 et seq.

Restaurant and Hotel Worker's Lien Law
Wash. Rev. Code Ann., 60.34.010 et seq.

Restaurant, Bar, and Tavern Wage Protection Act
Mont. Code Ann., 39-3-601 et seq.

Restaurant Health Act
W. Va. Code 1966, § 16-6-1 et seq.

Restaurants, Boardinghouses, Hotels and Motels Act
S.C. Code Ann. 1976, § 45-1-10 et seq.

Restaurants Maximum Hours Act
N.M. Stat. Ann. 1978, 50-4-13

Restitution Act
S.C. Code Ann. 1976, §§ 17-22-10 et seq., 24-3-20 et seq.

Restitution Act (Community Service)
Miss. Code Ann. 1972, § 99-20-1 et seq.

Restitution Centers Act
Cal. Penal Code § 6220 et seq.
Tenn. Code Ann., 41-6-101 et seq.

Restitution Withholding Act
Ala. Acts 1984, p. 859

Restitutionary Act (Oil Overcharge)
Tex. Government Code, § 2305.001 et seq.
Tex. Rev. Civ. Stat., Art. 4413(56) § 1 et seq.

Restoration Act (Grave and Cemetery)
Ill. Rev. Stat. 1991, Ch. 21, § 60.9 et seq.

Restoration Act (Oilfield Site)
La. Rev. Stat. Ann., 30:80 et seq.

Restoration Act (Property-Divorce)
Ky. Rev. Stat. 1971, Superseded Vol., 403.065

Restoration Acts (Representation in Congress)
June 22, 1868, Ch. 69, 15 Stat. 72
June 25, 1868, Ch. 70, 15 Stat. 73
Jan. 26, 1870, Ch. 10, 16 Stat. 62
July 15, 1870, Ch. 298, 16 Stat. 363

Restoration and Perpetuation of Public Land Act (Survey)
Fla. Stat. Ann., 177.501 et seq.

Restoration and Preservation of Water Resources Act
Fla. Stat. Ann., 403.0615

Restoration Financing Authority Act (Urban Waterfront Area)
Cal. Public Resources Code § 32000 et seq.

Restoration Fund Act
Ore. Rev. Stat., 278.011 et seq.

Restoration Jobs Act (Environmental)
Wash. Rev. Code Ann., 43.21J.900

Restoration Project Act (Fish)
Ill. Rev. Stat. 1991, Ch. 56, § 249, 250 et seq.

Restoration Trust Fund Act (Critical State Concern)
Fla. Stat. Ann., 380.0558

Restraint Law (Railroad Cattle Guards)
Iowa Code Ann., 327G.1 et seq.

Restraint of Trade Act
See also Anti-Trust Acts
Cal. Business and Professions Code § 16600 et seq.
Fla. Stat. Ann., 542.15 et seq.
Kan. Stat. Ann., 50-101 et seq.
Mich. Comp. Laws Ann., 445.701 et seq.
Neb. Rev. Stat. 1943, 59-801 et seq.
Wis. Stat. Ann., 133.01 et seq.

Restraint of Trade Act (Monopolies)
N.Y. General Business Law (Consol. Laws Ch. 20) § 340 et seq.

Restraint of Trade and Conspiracy Act
Mo. Rev. Stat., 416.040 et seq.

Restricted Employment Driving Privilege Act
Cal. Vehicle Code 1959, §§ 16076, 16080 et seq.

Restricted Parcel Carriers Act
Okla. Stat. Ann., Title 47, § 166.1 et seq.

Restriction Act (Chinese)
Haw. Session Laws 1887, Special Session, Ch. 28

Restrictions Act (Title XX)
S.C. Code Ann. 1976, § 43-1-230 et seq.

Restrictions Removal Act (Oklahoma)
May 27, 1908, Ch. 199, 35 Stat. 312

Restructuring Act (Higher Education)
N.J. Stat. Ann., 18A:3B-1 et seq.

Restructuring Act (Public Advocate)
N.J. Stat. Ann., 52:27E-50 et seq.

Restructuring Program Act (Welfare)
Miss. Code Ann. 1972, § 43-49-1 et seq.

Resumption Act (Currency)
See Specie Payment Resumption Act

Resuscitate Act (Do Not)
W. Va. Code 1966 § 16-30C-1 et seq.

Retail Credit Accounts Law
Md. Ann. Code 1974, CL, § 12-501 et seq.

Retail Credit Sales Act
Mo. Rev. Stat., 408.250 et seq.

Retail Drug Control Act
Conn. Gen. Stat. Ann., § 21a-126 et seq.
La. Rev. Stat. Ann., 37:1194 et seq.

Retail Electric Supplier Certified Territory Act
Okla. Stat. Ann., Title 17, § 158.21 et seq.

Retail Electric Supplier Unincorporated Area Certified Territory Act
Pa. Cons. Stat., Title 15, §§ 7301 et seq., 7351

Retail Food Facilities Law (Uniform)
See Uniform Retail Food Facilities Law

Retail Food Store Inspection Act
Tenn. Public Act 1986, Ch. 633

Retail Food Store Sanitation Act
Colo. Rev. Stat., 25-4-1301 et seq.

Retail Franchising Act
Va. Code 1950, § 13.1-557 et seq.

Retail Gross Receipts Tax Act
N.J. Stat. Ann., 54:11C-1 et seq.

Retail Installment and Home Solicitation Sales Act
Ga. Code Ann., 10-1-1 et seq.

Retail Installment Sales Act
Alaska Stat. 1962, § 45.10.010 et seq.
Cal. Civil Code § 1801 et seq.
Colo. Rev. Stat., 121-2-1 et seq.
Conn. Gen. Stat. Ann., § 42-83 et seq.
Del. Code of 1974, Title 6, § 4301 et seq.
Fla. Stat. Ann., 520.30 et seq.
Haw. Rev. Stat. Ann., § 476-1 et seq.
Ill. Rev. Stat. 1991, Ch. 17, § 5201 et seq.
Ind. Code Ann., 26-1-2-612 et seq.
Kan. Laws 1958, Ch. 9
Mass. Gen. Laws Ann., 255B:1 et seq.
Md. Ann. Code 1974, CL, § 12-601 et seq.
Mich. Comp. Laws Ann., 445.851 et seq.
Mont. Code Ann., 31-1-201 et seq.
N.C. Gen. Stat. 1943, § 25A-1 et seq.
N.D. Cent. Code, 51-13-01 et seq.
Neb. Rev. Stat. 1943, 45-334 et seq.
Nev. Rev. Stat. 1979 Reprint, 97.015 et seq.
N.J. Stat. Ann., 17:16C-1 et seq.
N.Y. Personal Property Law (Consol. Laws Ch. 41) § 401 et seq.
Ohio Rev. Code 1953, 1317.01 et seq.
Okla. Stat. Ann., Title 14A, § 1-101 et seq.
Okla. Stat. Ann., Title 15, § 652 et seq.
Ore. Rev. Stat., 83.010 et seq.
P.R. Laws Ann. 1954, Title 10, § 731 et seq.
Tenn. Code Ann., 47-11-101 et seq.
Tex. Rev. Civ. Stat., Art. 5069-6.01 et seq.
Va. Code 1950, § 46.1-545
Vt. Stat. Ann., Title 9, § 2401 et seq.
Wash. Rev. Code Ann., 63.14.010 et seq.
Wis. Stat. Ann., 218.01, Subsec. 6

Retail Installment Sales Act (Door to Door)
N.J. Stat. Ann., 17:16C-61.1 et seq.

Retail Installment Sales Act (Motor Vehicles)
Colo. Rev. Stat., 13-16-1 et seq.
Ill. Rev. Stat. 1991, Ch. 121 1/2, § 561 et seq.
Ky. Rev. Stat. 1971, 190.090 et seq.
Me. Rev. Stat. Ann. 1964, Title 9, § 3401 et seq.
Mich. Comp. Laws Ann., 566.301 et seq.
Minn. Stat. Ann., 168.66 et seq.
N.H. Rev. Stat. 1955, 361-A:1 et seq.
N.M. Stat. Ann. 1978, 58-19-1 et seq.
N.Y. Personal Property Law (Consol. Laws Ch. 41) § 301 et seq.
Vt. Stat. Ann., Title 9, § 2351 et seq.

Retail Installment Sales and Financing Companies Act
P.R. Laws Ann. 1954, Title 10, § 731 et seq.

Retail Installment Sales and Services Act
Mass. Gen. Laws Ann., 255D:1 et seq.

Retail Installment Sales Finance Act (Motor Vehicle)
Vt. Stat. Ann., Title 9, § 2351 et seq.

Retail Leasing Act (Motor Vehicle)
N.Y. Personal Property Law (Consol. Laws Ch. 41) § 330 et seq.

Retail License Act (Cigarettes)
Md. Ann. Code 1957, Art. 56, § 65 et seq.

Retail Liquor License Act
Mont. Code Ann., 16-4-101 et seq.
W. Va. Code 1966 § 60-3A-1 et seq.

Retail Liquor License Quota Act
Mont. Code Ann., 16-4-201
Pa. Purdon's Stat., Title 47, § 4-461

Retail Liquor Sales Enforcement Tax Act
Kan. Stat. Ann., 79-4101 et seq.

Retail Merchants' Gross Sales Tax Act
Ky. Acts 1930, Ch. 149

Retail Merchants' License Act (Transient)
Mont. Code Ann., 7-21-2401 et seq.

Retail Merchants' License Tax Law
Ky. Acts 1930, Ch. 149

Retail Motor Fuel Marketing Act
Mont. Laws 1991, Ch. 499

Retail Sale of Liquor by the Drink Act
Ida. Code 1947, 23-901 et seq.

Retail Sale of Motor Fuels Act
N.J. Stat. Ann., 56:6-1 et seq.

Retail Sales Act (University)
Ill. Rev. Stat. 1991, Ch. 144, §§ 251.9, 252

Retail Sales and Use Tax Act
Va. Code 1950, § 58.1-600 et seq.

Retail Sales Tax Act
Ark. Code Ann. 1987, 26-52-101 et seq.
Cal. Revenue and Taxation Code § 6001 et seq.
Colo. Rev. Stat., 39-26-101 et seq.
Fla. Stat. Ann., 212.01 et seq.
Ill. Rev. Stat. 1991, Ch. 120, § 440 et seq.
Iowa Code Ann., 422.42 et seq.
Kan. Stat. Ann., 79-3601 et seq.
Md. Ann. Code 1974, Art. TG, § 11-101 et seq.
Mo. Rev. Stat., 144.010 et seq.
N.D. Cent. Code, 57-39.2-01 et seq.
Ohio Rev. Code 1953, 5739.01 et seq.
S.D. Codified Laws 1967, 10-45-1 et seq.
Wash. Rev. Code Ann., 82.08.010 et seq.

Retail Sales Tax Act (Temporary)
Mass. Acts 1966, Ch. 14, § 1

Retail Sales Tax Law (City of New York)
N.Y. City Adm. Code 38, Ch. 46, § M46-15.0 et seq.

Retail Sales Taxation Fairness Act
Fla. Stat. Ann., 212.215

Retail Service Station Act
D.C. Code Ann., § 10-201 et seq.

Retail Stores Eight Hour Labor Act
Mont. Code Ann.,, 39-4-105

Retail Theft Act
Ill. Rev. Stat. 1991, Ch. 38, § 16A-1 et seq.
N.D. Cent. Code, 51-21-01 et seq.

Retail Theft Act (Civil Recovery for)
Me. Rev. Stat. Ann. 1964, Title 14, § 8301 et seq.

Retailers' and Consumers' Sales and Use Tax Act
Ga. Code Ann., 48-8-1 et seq.

Retailers' Occupation Tax Act
Ill. Comp. Stat. 1992, Ch. 35, § 120/1 et seq.
Ill. Rev. Stat. 1991, Ch. 120, § 440 et seq.

Retailers Occupation Tax Act (Counties)
Ill. Rev. Stat. 1987, Ch. 34, § 409.1

Retailers' Occupation Tax Act (Municipal)
Ill. Rev. Stat. 1991, Ch. 24, § 8-11-1.3

Retailers' Sales Tax Act
Kan. Stat. Ann., 79-3601 et seq.
Tenn. Code Ann., 67-6-101 et seq.

Retaliation Act
Mo. Laws 1937, p. 536

Retaliation Act (Foreign Corporations)
N.J. Stat. Ann., 14A:13-2

Retaliatory Eviction Act
Ill. Rev. Stat. 1991, Ch. 80, §§ 70, 71
N.Y. Real Property Law (Consol. Laws Ch. 50) § 223b

Retaliatory Insurance Tax Act
Ariz. Rev. Stat. Ann., § 20-230
Cal. Insurance Code § 1560
Ill. Rev. Stat. 1991, Ch. 73, §§ 1056, 1056.1
Ind. Code Ann., 27-1-20-12
Ky. Rev. Stat. 1971, 304.3-270, 304.8-160
Md. Ann. Code 1957, Art. 48A, § 61
Minn. Stat. Ann., 71.23
Ore. Rev. Stat., 731.854
Tex. Rev. Civ. Stat., Art. 4758

Retaliatory Liquor Act
Del. Code of 1974, Title 4, § 728

Retardation Act (Mental)
Tex. Rev. Civ. Stat., Art. 591.001 et seq.

Retardation Law
R.I. Gen. Laws 1956, 40.1-22-1 et seq.

Retardation Prevention and Community Services Act
Fla. Stat. Ann., 393.061 et seq.

Retarded Citizens Sexual Protection Act
Ala. Code 1975, §§ 13A-6-62, 13A-6-64

Retarded Defendant Act
Ala. Acts 1985, p. 1020

Retarded Persons Bill of Rights
Fla. Stat. Ann., 393.13, 393.14

Retention Act (Business)
N.J. Stat. Ann., 54:4-1.13 et seq.

Retention Act (Mold Lien)
S.C. Code Ann. 1976, § 39-69-10 et seq.

Retention of Assessors Local Law
N.Y. Local Laws 1971, Town of Victor, p. 3637

Retired Employees Group Insurance Act (Public School)
Tex. Insurance Code, Art. 3.50-4

Retired Federal Employees Health Benefits Act
Sept. 8, 1960, P.L. 86-724, 74 Stat. 849 (See 5 U.S. Code §§ 8901 to 8913)
June 22, 1965, P.L. 89-45, 79 Stat. 170

Retired Judge Service Act
D.C. Code Ann., §§ 11-1504, 11-1565

Retired Teachers' Minimum Pension Act
Ind. Code Ann., 21-6.1-6-1 et seq.

Retired Teachers' Week Act
Ill. Rev. Stat. 1991, Ch. 1, § 3051-80

Retiree Benefits Bankruptcy Protection Act of 1988
June 16, 1988, P.L. 100-334, 11 U.S. Code §§ 101 nt., 1106, 1114, 1114 nt., 1129

Retiree Health Care Act
N.M. Stat. Ann., 10-7C-1 et seq.

Retiree Refund Act (Federal)
Ga. Code Ann., 48-2-101 et seq.

Retirement Account Act (Judicial)
Wash. Rev. Code Ann., 2.14.010 et seq.

Retirement Act
Cal. Government Code § 20000 et seq.
Mass. Gen. Laws Ann., 32:1 et seq.
N.Y. Retirement and Social Security Law (Consol. Laws Ch. 51A) § 1 et seq.
Okla. Stat. Ann., Title 74, § 901 et seq.
S.D. Codified Laws 1967, 3-12-46 et seq.
Va. Code 1950, § 51-30 et seq.

Retirement Act (Attorneys-General)
Tenn. Code Ann., 8-618 et seq.

Retirement Act (Boston)
Mass. Acts 1922, Ch. 521

Retirement Act (Civil Service)
See Civil Service Retirement Acts

Retirement Act (County Employees)
Cal. Government Code §§ 31250 et seq., 31450 et seq.
Neb. Rev. Stat. 1943, 23-2331 et seq.

Retirement Act (County Fire Service)
Cal. Government Code § 32200 et seq.

Retirement Act (County Officers and Employees)
Fla. Stat. Ann., 122.01 et seq.

Retirement Act (Criminal Investigator)
Wyo. Stat. Ann., § 9-3-601 et seq.

Retirement Act (District Attorneys)
Ga. Code Ann., 47-13-1 et seq.

951

Retirement Act (Educational)
N.M. Stat. Ann. 1978, 22-11-1 et seq.

Retirement Act (Employees' Contributing)
Me. Rev. Stat. Ann. 1964, Title 5, § 17001 et seq.

Retirement Act (Employees' Contributory)
Me. Rev. Stat. Ann. 1964, Title 5, § 17001 et seq.

Retirement Act (Fay Kirtland)
Fla. Stat. Ann., 112.363

Retirement Act (Fifth Class Counties)
Pa. Purdon's Stat., Title 16, § 11621 et seq.

Retirement Act (Firemen and Police)
Iowa Code Ann., 411.1 et seq.

Retirement Act (Firemen)
See Firemen's Retirement Act

Retirement Act (Fourth Class Counties)
Pa. Purdon's Stat., Title 16, § 11561 et seq.

Retirement Act (Game and Fish Warden)
Wyo. Stat. Ann., § 9-3-610 et seq.

Retirement Act (Game Wardens')
Mont. Code Ann., 19-8-105 et seq.

Retirement Act (Higher Education)
Wyo. Stat. Ann., § 21-19-101 et seq.

Retirement Act (Highway Employees)
Ark. Code Ann. 1987, 24-5-101 et seq.

Retirement Act (Highway Patrol Officers')
Mont. Code Ann., 19-6-106 et seq.

Retirement Act (Highway Patrolmen)
Mont. Rev. Code 1947, 31-201 et seq.

Retirement Act (Judges)
See Judges Retirement Act

Retirement Act (Judicial)
N.M. Stat. Ann., 10-12B-1 et seq.

Retirement Act (Kent County)
Del. Code of 1974, Title 9, § 4301 et seq.

Retirement Act (Law Enforcement Officers)
N.C. Gen. Stat. 1943, § 143-166.1 et seq.

Retirement Act (Legislative)
Cal. Government Code § 9350 et seq.
Ga. Code Ann., 47-6-1 et seq.
Mich. Comp. Laws Ann., 38.1001 et seq.
Mo. Rev. Stat. 1969, 104.630 et seq.
Nev. Rev. Stat. 1979 Reprint, 218.2371 et seq.

Retirement Act (Magistrate)
N.M. Stat. Ann., 10-12C-1 et seq.

Retirement Act (Municipal Employees)
See Municipal Employees' Retirement Act

Retirement Act (Municipal Police)
Mont. Code Ann., 19-9-101 et seq.
Pa. Purdon's Stat., Title 53, § 881.101 et seq.

Retirement Act (Newton)
Mass. Acts 1928, Ch. 355

Retirement Act (Police)
Fla. Stat. Ann., 185.01 et seq.
Mass. Gen. Laws Ann., 32:83 et seq.
Pa. Purdon's Stat., Title 53, § 761 et seq.

Retirement Act (Probate Judges)
Ga. Code Ann., 47-11-20 et seq.
Mich. Comp. Laws Ann., 38.901 et seq.

Retirement Act (Providence)
R.I. Public Laws 1923, Ch. 489

Retirement Act (Public Employees')
Ariz. Rev. Stat. Ann., § 38-841 et seq.
Mont. Code Ann., 19-3-101 et seq.
Ore. Rev. Stat., 237.001 et seq. bfe
Retirement Act (Public Safety Employees)

Retirement Act (Public Employees)
See Public Employees' Retirement Act

Retirement Act (Public Safety Noncontributory)
Utah Code Ann. 1953, 49-4a-101 et seq.

Retirement Act (Public School Employees)
See Public School Employees' Retirement Act

Retirement Act (School Employees)
See School Employees' Retirement Act
Neb. Rev. Stat. 1943, 79-1501 to 79-1566

Retirement Act (School Teachers)
Wash. Rev. Code Ann., 41.32.005 et seq.

Retirement Act (Sheriffs')
Mont. Code Ann., 19-7-105 et seq.

Retirement Act (State Board of Accounts)
Ind. Code Ann., 4-26-3-1 et seq.

Retirement Act (State Employees and Teachers)
Wyo. Stat. Ann., § 9-3-401 et seq.

Retirement Act (State Employees)
See State Employees' Retirement System Act

Retirement Act (State Highway Patrol)
Wyo. Stat. Ann., § 9-3-601 et seq.

Retirement Act (State)
Utah Code Ann. 1953, 49-1-101 et seq.

Retirement Act (Statewide Volunteer Firefighters)
Tex. Rev. Civ. Stat., Art. 6243e.3

Retirement Act (Supplemental)
Va. Code 1950, § 51-111.9 et seq.

Retirement Act (Sussex County)
Del. Code of 1974, Title 9, § 7008 et seq.

Retirement Act (Teachers and School Employees)
Mo. Rev. Stat., 169.010 et seq.

Retirement Act (Teachers and State Employees)
See Teachers' and State Employees' Retirement Act

Retirement Act (Teachers)
See Teachers' Retirement Act

Retirement Act (Veterans)
N.J. Stat. Ann., 43:4-1 et seq.

Retirement Act (Worcester)
Mass. Acts 1923, Ch. 410

Retirement Act for Retired Members of State Retirement Systems
Fla. Stat. Ann., 112.351 et seq.

Retirement Act II (Public Employees)
W. Va. Code 1966 § 5-10D-1 et seq.

Retirement and Pension Act (Fulton County Teachers)
Ga. Laws 1937, p. 892

Retirement and Pension Act (Police)
Fla. Stat. Ann., 185.01 et seq.
La. Rev. Stat. Ann., 40:1421 et seq.
Mass. Gen. Laws Ann., 32:83 et seq.
Me. Rev. Stat. Ann. 1964, Title 5, § 17001 et seq.
Mo. Rev. Stat., 86.010 et seq.
N.H. Rev. Stat. 1955, 103:1 et seq.

Retirement and Pension System Act (Highway Patrol)
Kan. Laws 1947, Ch. 409

Retirement and Relief Act
Ala. Code 1958, App., § 1543 et seq.

Retirement and Social Security Act
N.Y. Consol. Laws, Ch. 51A
S.C. Code Ann. 1976, § 9-5-10 et seq.

Retirement and Survivors' Annuities for Bankruptcy Judges and Magistrates Act of 1988
Nov. 15, 1988, P.L. 100-659, 28 U.S. Code § 1 nt.

Retirement Benefits Act (Public Employees)
Ind. Code Ann., 5-10.2-4-1 et seq., 5-10.3-8-1 et seq.

Retirement Benefits Forfeiture Act (Public Employee)
Mich. Comp. Laws Ann., 38.2701 et seq.

Retirement Code (State Employees)
Pa. Cons. Stat., Title 71, § 5101 et seq.

Retirement Community for Continuing Care Act
S.C. Code Ann. 1976, § 37-11-10 et seq.

Retirement Community Full Disclosure Act
N.J. Stat. Ann., 45:22A-1 et seq.

Retirement Community Provider Registration Act (Continuing Care)
Ore. Rev. Stat., 101.010 et seq.

Retirement Community Regulation and Financial Disclosure Act
N.J. Stat. Ann., 52:27D-330 et seq.

Retirement Equity Act of 1984
Aug. 23, 1984, P.L. 98-397, 26 U.S. Code §§ 72, 401, 402, 410, 411, 414, 417, 1054, 6052, 6057; 29 U.S. Code §§ 1001 nt., 1025, 1052 to 1056, 1144
Oct. 21, 1986, P.L. 99-514, 26 U.S. Code §§ 401 nt.; 29 U.S. Code § 1001 nt.
Dec. 19, 1989, P.L. 101-239, 29 U.S. Code § 1001 nt.

Retirement Fund Act (Common)
N.Y. Retirement and Social Security Law (Consol. Laws Ch. 51A) § 120 et seq.

Retirement Fund Act (Gainesville)
Ga. Laws 1941, p. 1453

Retirement Fund Act (Municipalities)
Wis. Stat. Ann., 40.20 et seq.

Retirement Fund Act (Solicitor General)
Ga. Code Ann., 47-10-1 et seq.

Retirement Fund Act (State Police)
La. Rev. Stat. Ann., 40:1421 et seq.

Retirement Fund Act (Superior Court Clerks)
Ga. Code Ann., 47-14-1 et seq.

Retirement Fund Act (Teachers)
Ind. Code Ann., 21-6.1-1-1 et seq.
N.D. Cent. Code, 15-39.1-01 et seq.
N.M. Stat. Ann. 1953, 73-12-16 et seq.

Retirement Fund Act (Trial Judges and Solicitors)
Ga. Code Ann., 47-10-1 et seq.

Retirement Incentive Act (Universities)
N.Y. Laws 1992, Ch. 494, §§ 1 to 14

Retirement Income Act (Supplemental)
N.C. Gen. Stat. 1943, § 135-90 et seq.

Retirement Income Protection Act (Morrissey)
Cal. Revenue and Taxation Code § 17952.5

Retirement Law (Public Employees)
N.Y. Retirement and Social Security Law (Consol. Laws Ch. 51A) § 2 et seq.

Retirement Law (Teachers)
Ark. Stat. 1947, 80-14-12 et seq.

Retirement of Judges Act (Compulsory)
Ill. Comp. Stat. 1992, Ch. 705, §§ 55/0.01, 55/1

Retirement Pensions Act (Griffin)
Ga. Laws 1941, p. 1474

Retirement Plan Act (Regents)
Ga. Code Ann., 47-21-1 et seq.

Retirement Protection Act of 1994
Dec. 8, 1994, P.L. 103-465, 26 U.S. Code § 1 nt.
Aug. 5, 1997, P.L. 105-34, 26 U.S. Code § 412 nt.

Retirement Reciprocity Act
N.M. Stat. Ann. 1978, 10-13-1 et seq.

Retirement Reciprocity Act (Public Employees)
N.M. Stat. Ann., 10-13A-1 et seq.

Retirement Reform Act
D.C. Code Ann., § 1-701 et seq.

Retirement Reform Act (Teacher's)
W. Va. Code 1966, § 18-7B-1 et seq.

Retirement Regulations Adoption Act
D.C. Code Ann., § 1-751 et seq.

Retirement Savings Act
Ill. Rev. Stat. 1991, Ch. 127, § 3751 et seq.

Retirement Savings Protection Act
Ga. Code Ann., 10-5-14.1

Retirement-Straight Line Adjustment Act of 1958
Sept. 2, 1958, P.L. 85-866, 72 Stat. 1669, 26 U.S. Code [IRC 1954], § 1016 nt.

Retirement Study Commission Act (Public Employee)
Pa. Purdon's Stat., Title 43, § 1401 et seq.

Retirement System Act
Fla. Stat. Ann., 121.011 et seq.

Retirement System Act (Americus)
Ga. Laws 1950, p. 2230

Retirement System Act (Charlotte Firefighters)
N.C. Laws 1991, Ch. 506

Retirement System Act (Fireman)
N.H. Rev. Stat. 1955, 102:1 et seq.

Retirement System Act (Judicial)
N.J. Stat. Ann., 43:6A-1 et seq.
Okla. Stat. Ann., Title 20, § 1101 et seq.
Wash. Rev. Code Ann., 2.10.010 et seq.

Retirement System Act (Law Enforcement Officers and Fire Fighters)
Wash. Rev. Code Ann., 41.26.005 et seq.

Retirement System Act (Local Government Employees)
N.C. Gen. Stat. 1943, § 128-21 et seq.

Retirement System Act (Municipal Employees)
Vt. Stat. Ann., Title 24, § 5051 et seq.

Retirement System Act (Policemen's and Firemen's)
N.Y. Retirement and Social Security Law (Consol. Laws Ch. 51A) § 290 et seq.

Retirement System Act (Public Employees)
Mont. Rev. Code 1947, 68-1501 et seq.
N.J. Stat. Ann., 43:15A-1 et seq.
Ohio Rev. Code 1953, 145.01 et seq.
Okla. Stat. Ann., Title 74, § 901 et seq.
Wash. Rev. Code Ann., 41.40.005 et seq.

Retirement System Act (School Employees)
Ohio Rev. Code 1953, 3309.01 et seq.

Retirement System Act (State Employees)
Ala. Code 1975, 36-27-1 et seq.
Ga. Code Ann., 47-2-1 et seq.
Md. Ann. Code 1957, Art. 73B, § 1 et seq.
R.I. Gen. Laws 1956, 36-8-1 et seq.
Tex. Public Retirement System, Title 110B, § 21.001 et seq.

Retirement System Act (State Police)
Me. Rev. Stat. Ann. 1964, Title 25, § 1592 et seq.
N.J. Stat. Ann., 53:5A-1 et seq.
Vt. Stat. Ann., Title 3, § 501 et seq.
W. Va. Code 1966, § 15-2A-1 et seq.

Retirement System Act (State)
Me. Rev. Stat. Ann. 1964, Title 5, § 17001 et seq.

Retirement System Act (Superior Court Judges)
Ga. Code Ann., 47-9-1 et seq.

Retirement System Act (Teachers)
Ga. Code Ann., 47-3-1 et seq.
Vt. Stat. Ann., Title 16, § 1934

Retirement System and Pension Act (Troup County)
Ga. Laws 1951, p. 2637

Retirement System for Justices and Judges Act
See Uniform Retirement System for Justices and Judges Act
Okla. Stat. Ann., Title 20, § 1101 et seq.

Retirement System Law (Judicial)
Iowa Code Ann., 602.9101 et seq.
Wash. Rev. Code Ann., 2.10.010

Retirement System Law (Public Employees)
Iowa Code Ann., 97B.1 et seq.

Retirement System Reporting and Disclosure Act
N.Y. Retirement and Social Security Law (Consol. Laws, Ch. 51A), § 150 et seq.

Retirement Systems Act (Private Employees)
Cal. Statutes 1945, § p. 1996

Retirement Systems Act Cafeteria Plan
S.C. Code Ann. 1976, §§ 9-1-60 et seq., 12-7-775 et seq.

Retirement Systems Actuarial Note Act
N.C. Gen. Stat. 1943, § 120-112 et seq.

Retirement Systems Disclosure Law
Cal. Corporations Code § 28000 et seq.
N.H. Rev. Stat. 1955, 100-A:1 et seq.

Retirement Systems Reciprocal Act
Ill. Rev. Stat. 1991, Ch. 108 1/2, § 20-101 et seq.

Retirement Systems Reciprocity Act
P.R. Laws Ann. 1954, Title 3, § 797 et seq.

Retirement Trust Fund (Municipal Police Officers)
Fla. Stat. Ann., 185.01 et seq.

Retraction Act (Defamation)
Ore. Rev. Stat., 30.150 et seq.

Retraction Act (Libel)
Cal. Civil Code § 48a
Conn. Gen. Stat. Ann., § 52-237
Fla. Stat. Ann., 770.02
Ga. Code Ann., 51-5-11
Ind. Code Ann., 34-4-15-1 et seq.
Iowa Code Ann., 659.2 et seq.
Mass. Gen. Laws Ann., 231.93
Minn. Stat. Ann., 548.06
Ore. Rev. Stat., 30.150 et seq.
Wis. Stat. Ann., 895.05

Retraining and Reemployment Act (Occupational)
N.Y. Labor Law (Consol. Laws Ch. 31) § 820 et seq.

Retrocession Act (Boesche's Division)
Ill. Comp. Stat. 1992, Ch. 5, §§ 550/0.01, 550/1
Ill. Rev. Stat. 1991, Ch. 1, §§ 4450, 4451

Retrocession Act (Chain of Rocks)
Ill. Comp. Stat. 1992, Ch. 5, §§ 565/0.01, 565/1

Retrocession Act (Chanute Air Force Base)
Ill. Comp. Stat. 1992, Ch. 5, § 537/5-1

Retrocession Act (Colville Indian Reservation Criminal Jurisdiction)
Wash. Rev. Code Ann., 37.12.100 et seq.

Retrocession Act (Fort Sheridan)
Ill. Rev. Stat. 1991, Ch. 1, §§ 4350, 4351

Retrocession Act (Granite City Depot)
Ill. Rev. Stat. 1991, Ch. 1, §§ 4601.9, 4602

Retrocession Act (Higgins Road)
Ill. Rev. Stat. 1991, Ch. 1, §§ 4400, 4401

Retrocession Act (Veteran's Administration)
Ill. Rev. Stat. 1991, Ch. 1, § 4550 et seq.

Return Act (Corporate Surplus)
Me. Rev. Stat. Ann. 1964, Title 36, § 6501 et seq.

Return Act (Individual Surplus)
Me. Rev. Stat. Ann. 1964, Title 36, § 6401 et seq.

Returnable Container Act
N.Y. Environmental Conservation Law 1972, (Consol. Laws Ch. 43B) § 27-1001 et seq.

Reuse and Recycling Access Act (Solid Waste)
Cal. Public Resources Code § 42900 et seq.

Reuse and Redevelopment Act (Hazardous Site)
Ga. Code Ann., 12-8-200 et seq.

Reuse, Recyling and Ultimate Destruction Incentive Act
Okla. Stat. Ann., Title 68, §§ 2357.14 to 2357.20

Reutilization of Land Act
Neb. Rev. Stat. 1943, 77-3201 et seq.

Revaluation of Property Act
Wash. Rev. Code Ann., 84.41.010 et seq.

Revaluation Relief Act
N.J. Stat. Ann., 54:1-35.39 et seq.

Revenue Act
Ark. Code Ann. 1987, 26-27-301 et seq.
D.C. Code Ann., §§ 25-124, 25-138, 47-1701 et seq., 47-2001 et seq., 47-2201 et seq., 47-2301 et seq., 47-2401 et seq., 47-2601 et seq., 47-3301 et seq., 47-3401 et seq., 47-3701 et seq
Fla. Stat. Ann., 212.01 et seq.
Ga. Code Ann., 48-1-1 et seq.
Ill. Comp. Stat. 1992, Ch. 35, § 205/1 et seq.
Ill. Rev. Stat. 1991, Ch. 120
Ind. Code Ann., 6-8-3-1 et seq.
Ky. Rev. Stat. 1971, 131.010 et seq.
Md. Ann. Code 1974, Art. SF, § 6-101 et seq.
Minn. Laws 1973, Ch. 650
Miss. Code Ann. 1972, § 27-65-1 et seq.
Miss. Code 1942, § 9219.5-01 et seq.
Mo. Rev. Stat., 137.010 et seq.
Mont. Laws 1971, 2nd Ex. Sess., Ch. 9
N.C. Gen. Stat. 1943, § 105-1 et seq. seq.

Neb. Rev. Stat. 1943, 77-101 et seq.
Pa. 1879 Pamph. Laws 112, No. 122
Pa. 1889 Pamph. Laws 420, No. 332
S.D. Codified Laws 1967, 10-1-1 et seq.
Tenn. Code Ann., 67-4-201 et seq.
Wash. Rev. Code Ann., 82.01.050 et seq.

Revenue Act (Brewers and Distillers)
Pa. 1897 Pamph. Laws 464, No. 408

Revenue Act (Brokers)
Pa. 1907 Pamph. Laws 175, No. 139

Revenue Act (District of Columbia)
D.C. Code Ann., § 47-2501 et seq. seq., 47-2501 et seq.
D.C. Laws 1975, No. 1-23
D.C. Laws 1976, No. 1-70
D.C. Laws 1977, No. 1-124

Revenue Act (Drainage District)
Wash. Rev. Code Ann., 85.32.010 et seq.

Revenue Act (Emergency)
Miss. Code Ann. 1972, § 27-65-1 et seq.

Revenue Act (Income Tax)
N.C. Gen. Stat. 1943, § 105-130 et seq.

Revenue Act (Public Utilities)
Ill. Comp. Stat. 1992, Ch. 35, § 620/1 et seq.

Revenue Act (Sales Tax)
Utah Code Ann. 1953, 59-12-101 et seq.

Revenue Act of 1948
April 2, 1948, Ch. 168, 62 Stat. 110

Revenue Act of 1950
Sept. 23, 1950, Ch. 994, 64 Stat. 906, 42 U.S. Code § 411
July 23, 1951, Ch. 238, 65 Stat. 124
July 21, 1952, Ch. 951, 66 Stat. 820

Revenue Act of 1951
Oct. 20, 1951, Ch. 521, 65 Stat. 452, 2 U.S. Code §§ 31b, 31b nt.; 3 U.S. Code §§ 102, 111, 111 nt.; 12 U.S. Code § 1464; 42 U.S. Code § 302 nt.; 50 U.S. Code Appx. § 1191
March 31, 1954, Ch. 126, 68 Stat. 46
March 30, 1955, Ch. 18, 69 Stat. 15
March 29, 1956, Ch. 115, 70 Stat. 67

Continued

March 29, 1957, P.L. 85-12, 71 Stat. 10

June 30, 1958, P.L. 85-475, 72 Stat. 260

June 30, 1959, P.L. 86-75, 73 Stat. 158, 26 U.S. Code § 5701 nt.

June 30, 1960, P.L. 86-564, 74 Stat. 291, 26 U.S. Code § 5701 nt.

June 30, 1961, P.L. 87-72, 75 Stat. 193, 26 U.S. Code § 5701 nt.

June 28, 1962, P.L. 87-508, 76 Stat. 114, 26 U.S. Code § 5701 nt.

June 29, 1963, P.L. 88-52, 77 Stat. 73, 26 U.S. Code § 5701 nt.

June 30, 1964, P.L. 88-348, 78 Stat. 237, 26 U.S. Code § 5701 nt.

Revenue Act of 1962

Oct. 16, 1962, P.L. 87-834, 76 Stat. 960, 12 U.S. Code § 1464; 26 U.S. Code §§ 38, 39, 46 to 48, 72, 78, 162, 167, 170, 179, 181, 182, 216, 245, 263, 274, and others

Revenue Act of 1964

Feb. 26, 1964, P.L. 88-272, 78 Stat. 19, 26 U.S. Code §§ 1 to 5, 11, 12, 21, 34, 35, 37, 38 nt., 46, 48, 62, 72, 79, 105, 116, 121, 122, 141, 144, 163 to 165, 170, 172, 213, 214, 217, 218, 242 to 244, 246, and others; 26 U.S. Code [IRC 1939] §§ 43, 925; 42 U.S. Code §§ 409, 411

Revenue Act of 1971

Dec. 10, 1971, P.L. 92-178, 15 U.S. Code § 1232 nt., 26 U.S. Code § 1 nt.

Jan. 3, 1975, P.L. 93-625, 26 U.S. Code § 167 nt.

July 18, 1984, P.L. 98-369, 98 Stat. 818, 1000, 26 U.S. Code §§ 38nt., 991 nt.

Revenue Act of 1978

Nov. 6, 1978, P.L. 95-600, 26 U.S. Code §§ 1 et seq.

April 1, 1980, P.L. 96-222, 26 U.S. Code §§ 1 et seq.

April 2, 1980, P.L. 96-223, 26 U.S. Code §§ 306, 6031 et seq.

July 18, 1984, P.L. 98-369, 98 Stat. 494

Oct. 22, 1986, P.L. 99-514, 26 U.S. Code § 3401 nt.

Aug. 20, 1996, P.L. 104-188, 26 U.S. Code § 3401

Revenue Act of 1987

Dec. 22, 1987, P.L. 100-203, 26 U.S. Code § 15 nt.

Nov. 10, 1988, P.L. 100-647, 26 U.S. Code §§ 21 nt., 301 nt., 304 nts., 453 nt., 1503 nt.

Dec. 19, 1989, P.L. 101-239, generally 26 U.S. Code § 1 et seq.

Nov. 5, 1990, P.L. 101-508, 26 U.S. Code § 7801 nt.

Dec. 8, 1994, P.L. 103-465, 26 U.S. Code § 7801 nt.

March 20, 1996, P.L. 104-117, 26 U.S. Code § 7801 nt.

Revenue Acts

Sept. 8, 1916, Ch. 463, 39 Stat. 756, 15 U.S. Code §§ 71-77; 19 U.S. Code §§ 1333, 1335

March 3, 1917, Ch. 159, 39 Stat. 1000

Oct. 3, 1917, Ch. 63, 40 Stat. 300

Feb. 24, 1919, Ch. 18, 40 Stat. 1057, 2 U.S. Code §§ 271, 272, 273 -277; 6 U.S. Code § 15; 19 U.S. Code § 460

Nov. 23, 1921, Ch. 136, 42 Stat. 227, 6 U.S. Code § 15; 31 U.S. Code §§ 753, 757

June 2, 1924, Ch. 234, 43 Stat. 253, 2 U.S. Code §§ 271 to 277; 6 U.S . Code § 15; 48 U.S. Code § 845

Feb. 26, 1926, Ch. 27, 44 Stat. 9, 6 U.S. Code § 15; 48 U.S. Code § 845

May 29, 1928, Ch. 852, 45 Stat. 791

June 6, 1932, Ch. 209, 47 Stat. 169

May 10, 1934, Ch. 277, 48 Stat. 683, 19 U.S. Code § 1617; 31 U.S. Code §§ 192, 195, 475, 506, 514; 40 U.S. Code §§ 301, 302, 306, 308

Aug. 30, 1935, Ch. 829, 49 Stat. 1014

June 22, 1936, Ch. 690, 49 Stat. 1652, 7 U.S. Code §§ 610, 615, 616, 617, 623, 641 to 656, 658, 659

March 13, 1937, Ch. 40, 50 Stat. 29

June 29, 1937, Ch. 402, 50 Stat. 358

Aug. 26, 1937, Ch. 815, 50 Stat. 813

Aug. 29, 1937, Ch. 871, 50 Stat. 870

May 28, 1938, Ch. 289, 52 Stat. 447

June 15, 1938, Ch. 439, 52 Stat. 699

June 29, 1939, Ch. 247, 53 Stat. 862, 7 U.S. Code § 645

June 24, 1940, Ch. 414, 54 Stat. 505

June 25, 1940, Ch. 419, 54 Stat. 516, 31 U.S. Code § 757b

Feb. 19, 1941, Ch. 7, 55 Stat. 7

Sept. 20, 1941, Ch. 412, 55 Stat. 687

Oct. 21, 1942, Ch. 619, 56 Stat. 798, 7 U.S. Code §§ 644, 648; 15 U.S. Code § 80a-3; 50 U.S. Code Appx. §§ 527, 573 nt., 1013 nt., 1191

Feb. 25, 1944, Ch. 63, 58 Stat. 26, 19 U.S. Code § 1201; 42 U.S. Code § 401; 50 U.S. Code Appx. §§ 1191, 1192

June 29, 1945, Ch. 200, 59 Stat. 264

June 30, 1945, Ch. 210, 59 Stat. 294, 50 U.S. Code Appx. § 1192 nt.

June 30, 1945, Ch. 211, 59 Stat. 295

Nov. 8, 1945, Ch. 453, 59 Stat. 556, 31 U.S. Code § 738a

June 25, 1947, Ch. 143, 61 Stat. 178

June 12, 1948, Ch. 459, 62 Stat. 387

June 28, 1949, Ch. 268, 63 Stat. 280

Sept. 23, 1950, Ch. 994, 64 Stat. 962

Revenue Adjustment Act of 1975

Dec. 23, 1975, P.L. 94-164, 89 Stat. 970, 26 U.S. Code §§ 1 nt., 11, 21, prec. 31, 42, 43, 103, 141, 883, 1561, 3402, 6012, 6153, 6154

May 23, 1977, P.L. 95-30, 26 U.S. Code §§ 42 nt., 43 nt.

Nov. 6, 1978, P.L. 95-600, 26 U.S. Code § 43 nt.

Revenue and Expenditure Control Act of 1968

June 28, 1968, P.L. 90-364, 82 Stat. 251, 26 U.S. Code §§ 51, 103, 243, 276, 501, 963, 3402, 4061, 4251, 6020, 6154, 6412, 6425, 6651, 6655, 7203, 7502, 7701; 31 U.S. Code §§ 11 nt., 757b nt.; 42 U.S. Code §§ 603, 607, 1396b

Dec. 31, 1970, P.L. 91-614, 84 Stat. 1843, 26 U.S. Code § 4251 nt.

Revenue and Taxation Act

Cal. Statutes 1939, Ch. 154, p. 1274

La. Rev. Stat. Ann., 47:1 et seq.

Revenue and Taxation Department Act

N.M. Stat. 1978, 9-11-1 et seq.

Revenue Anticipation Act

Ga. Code Ann., 36-82-60 et seq.

Ill. Rev. Stat. 1991, Ch. 85, § 831 et seq.

Revenue Board Act (Franklin County)

Ala. General Acts 1951, p. 1288, No. 735

Revenue Bond Act

Ark. Code Ann. 1987, 19-9-601 et seq.

Cal. Government Code § 54300 et seq.

Fla. Stat. Ann., 159.01 et seq.

Ga. Code Ann., 36-82-60 et seq.

Haw. Rev. Stat. Ann., § 49-1 et seq.

Ida. Code 1947, 50-1027 et seq.

Mich. Comp. Laws Ann., 141.101 et seq.

N.C. Gen. Stat. 1943, § 160-413 et seq.

N.C. Public Laws 1935, Ch. 473

N.D. Cent. Code 40-35-01 et seq.

N.M. Stat. Ann., 6-14-1 et seq.

N.M. Stat. Ann. 1953, Superseded Vol., 11-10-1 et seq.

Ore. Rev. Stat., 288.805 et seq.

P.R. Laws Ann. 1954, Title 21, § 661 et seq.

S.D. Laws 1935, Ch. 163

Tenn. Code Ann., 7-34-101 et seq.

Va. Code 1950, § 33.1-267 et seq.

Revenue Bond Act (Bay County)

Fla. Special Laws 1951, Ch. 27397

Revenue Bond Act (Board of Regents)

Ill. Comp. Stat. 1992, Ch. 110, § 710/1 et seq.

Revenue Bond Act (Bradenton Civic Center)

Fla. Special Laws 1951, Ch. 27412

Revenue Bond Act (Bridges)

Miss. Code Ann. 1972, § 65-21-1 et seq.

N.C. Gen. Stat. 1943, § 136-89.31 et seq.

Revenue Bond Act (Chesapeake Bay Ferry)

Va. Acts 1954, Ch. 693

Revenue Bond Act (Clewiston)

Fla. Special Laws 1961, Ch. 61-2018

Revenue Bond Act (Community College)

Cal. Education Code 1976, § 81900 et seq.

Revenue Bond Act (County and Municipality Development)

Colo. Rev. Stat., 29-3-101 et seq.

Revenue Bond Act (County Industrial)
N.M. Stat. Ann., 4-59-1 et seq.

Revenue Bond Act (County Pollution Control)
N.M. Stat. Ann., 4-60-1 et seq.

Revenue Bond Act (Eustis)
Fla. Special Laws 1949, Ch. 25822

Revenue Bond Act (Higher Education)
S.C. Code Ann. 1976, § 59-147-10 et seq.

Revenue Bond Act (Industrial Building)
Tenn. Code Ann., 7-37-101 et seq.

Revenue Bond Act (Industrial Development)
Neb. Rev. Stat. 1943, 18-1614 et seq.

Revenue Bond Act (Irrigation and Agricultural Improvement District)
Ariz. Rev. Stat. Ann., § 48-141 et seq.

Revenue Bond Act (Live Oak)
Fla. Special Laws 1949, Ch. 25987

Revenue Bond Act (Mascotte)
Fla. Special Laws 1955, Ch. 30977

Revenue Bond Act (Municipal Parking)
Cal. Statutes 1949, Ch. 1484, p. 2581

Revenue Bond Act (Municipal Utility)
Okla. Stat. Ann., Title 11, § 22-150 et seq.

Revenue Bond Act (Municipal)
Ala. Code 1975, § 11-81-140 et seq.
Alaska Stat. 1962, § 29.47.240 et seq.
Ariz. Rev. Stat. Ann., § 9-521 et seq.
Mont. Code Ann., 7-7-4401 et seq.
N.M. Stat. Ann. 1953, 14-30-1 et seq.

Revenue Bond Act (National Guard Member)
Cal. Military and Veterans Code § 480 et seq.

Revenue Bond Act (Panama City)
Fla. Special Laws 1949, Ch. 26118
Fla. Special Laws 1963, Ch. 63-1757,

Revenue Bond Act (Pollution Control)
N.M. Stat. Ann. 1978, 3-59-1 et seq.

Revenue Bond Act (Public Education)
Utah Code Ann. 1953, 53A-20a-101 et seq.

Revenue Bond Act (San Francisco Harbor)
Cal. Harbors and Navigation Code § 3300 et seq.

Revenue Bond Act (Sanitary District)
Ill. Rev. Stat. 1991, Ch. 42, § 319.1 et seq.

Revenue Bond Act (State College)
Cal. Education Code 1976, § 90010 et seq.

Revenue Bond Act (Turnpike System)
N.H. Rev. Stat. 1955, 237-A:1 et seq.

Revenue Bond Act (University of California Dormitory)
Cal. Education Code 1976, § 92400 et seq.
Cal. Statutes 1947, Ch. 1027, p. 2289

Revenue Bond Act (University of Illinois)
Ill. Rev. Stat. 1991, Ch. 144, § 70.90 et seq.

Revenue Bond Act (Utility)
S.C. Code Ann. 1976, § 6-21-10 et seq.
S.D. Codified Laws 1967, 9-40-1 et seq.

Revenue Bond Act (Water and Sewer District)
Ida. Code 1947, 42-4101 et seq.

Revenue Bond Financing Act (University Auxiliary Facilities)
Ill. Rev. Stat. 1991, Ch. 144, § 48.1 et seq.

Revenue Bond Financing Act of 1959
See Tennessee Valley Authority Bond Limitation Acts

Revenue Bond Guaranty Law (Industrial)
Ark. Code Ann. 1987, 15-4-601 et seq.

Revenue Bond Law of Unincorporated Towns
Nev. Rev. Stat. 1979 Reprint, 350.350 et seq.

Revenue Bond Refinancing Act
Ark. Code Ann. 1987, 14-231-101 et seq.
Fla. Stat. Ann., 159.01 et seq.
Ind. Code Ann., 5-1-6-1 et seq.
Mont. Code Ann., 7-7-4601 et seq.
N.D. Cent. Code, 40-36-01 et seq.
Ore. Rev. Stat., 287.302 et seq.
S.C. Code Ann. 1976, § 6-17-10 et seq.
Tenn. Code Ann., 9-12-101 et seq.
W. Va. Code 1966, § 13-2A-1 et seq.

Revenue Bond Refunding Act
W. Va. Code 1966, § 13-2E-1 et seq.

Revenue Bonding Jobs Protection Act
Wis. Stat. Ann., 66.521, 108.04

Revenue Certificate Law
Ga. Code Ann., 36-82-60 et seq.

Revenue Classification Law
Ark. Code Ann. 1987, 19-6-101 et seq.

Revenue Deficiency Reserve Fund Act
Cal. Government Code § 16410 et seq.

Revenue Department Act
Mich. Comp. Laws Ann., 205.1 et seq.

Revenue Department Building Act
Ark. Acts 1961, 1st Ex. Sess., No. 38

Revenue Department Building Expansion Act
Ark. Acts 1977, p. 1898, No. 749

Revenue Distribution Act
Ky. Rev. Stat. 1971, 47.010, 47.020

Revenue Financing Act (Arcadia)
Fla. Special Laws 1941, Ch. 21102

Revenue Financing Act (Chipley)
Fla. Special Laws 1941, Ch. 21145

Revenue Forgone Reform Act
Oct. 28, 1993, P.L. 103-123, 39 U.S. Code
§§ 101 nt., 410, 2401, 2401 nt., 3202, 3621,
3625 to 3627, 3642, 3683

Revenue Funds Availability Act
D.C. Laws 1976, No. 1-42

Revenue Law
Colo. Stat. Ann. 1935, Ch. 142

Revenue Law-Cities of the First Class
Ky. Rev. Stat. 1971, Superseded Vol., 91.020
et seq.

Revenue Machinery Act
N.C. Gen. Stat. 1943, § 105-271 et seq.

Revenue Procedures Act
S.C. Code Ann. 1976, § 12-60-10 et seq.

Revenue Procedures and Control Act
Utah Code Ann. 1953, 63-38a-101 et seq.

Revenue Procedures and Taxpayers' Bill of Rights Act
Ala. Code 1975, § 40-2A-1 et seq.

Revenue Producing Buildings and Structures Act (Southern Illinois University)
Ill. Rev. Stat. 1991, Ch. 144, § 641 et seq.

Revenue Producing Commercial Paper Act
Ill. Rev. Stat. 1991, Ch. 17, § 6801 et seq.

Revenue Producing Municipal Facilities Act
Me. Rev. Stat. Ann. 1964, Title 30-A, § 5401
et seq.

Revenue Producing Undertaking Law
N.Y. General Municipal Law (Consol. Laws
Ch. 23) § 400 et seq.

Revenue Recapture Act
Minn. Stat. Ann., 270A.01 et seq.

Revenue Reconciliation Act of 1989
Dec. 19, 1989, P.L. 101-239, 26 U.S. Code
§ 1 nt.
Nov. 5, 1990, P.L. 101-508, 26 U.S. Code
§§ 41 nt., 42 nt., 108 nt., 120 nt., 127 nt.,
162 nt., 2040 nt., 6302 nt.

Revenue Reconciliation Act of 1990
 Nov. 5, 1990, P.L. 101-508, 26 U.S. Code § 1 nt.
 Aug. 20, 1996, P.L. 104-188, 26 U.S. Code §§ 42, 56, 168, 247, 261 nt.,, 593, 832, 1016, 1042, 1253, 6038, 6302, 6724, 9507 nt.

Revenue Reconciliation Act of 1993
 Aug. 10, 1993, P.L. 103-66, 26 U.S. Code § 1 nt.
 Aug. 20, 1996, P.L. 104-188, 26 U.S. Code §§ 38 nt., 42 nt., 197 nt., 1258 nt.; 42 U.S. Code § 401 nt.

Revenue Recovery Act
 D.C. Code Ann., § 47-421 et seq.

Revenue Sharing Act
 Fla. Stat. Ann., 218.20 et seq.
 N.J. Stat. Ann., 54A:10-1 et seq.

Revenue Sharing Trust Fund Supplement to the General Appropriation Act of 1973 (Federal)
 Pa. 1974 Pamph. Laws 1334, No. 4 A

Revenue Stabilization Act
 Ark. Code Ann. 1987, 19-5-101 et seq.

Revenue Standards Act (Production)
 Okla. Stat. Ann., Title 52, § 570.1 et seq.

Revenue Tax Act to Legalize and Control Alcoholic Beverages and Liquors
 Ga. Code 1933, 58-1001 et seq.

Revenues Distribution Act (Motor Vehicles)
 Ohio Rev. Code 1953, 4501.04

Revere Funding Loan Act
 Mass. Acts 1955, Ch. 543

Revere Remodeling and Reconstruction Loan Act
 Mass. Acts 1952, Ch. 573

Reverse Annuity and Alternative Mortgage Loan Act
 Iowa Code Ann., 528.1 et seq.
 Mich. Comp. Laws Ann., 141.901 et seq.

Reverse Annuity Mortgage Loan Act
 Mont. Code Ann., 90-6-501 et seq.

Reverse Condemnation Act
 Mo. Rev. Stat., 523.090
 Tenn. Code Ann., 29-16-123

Reverse Mortgage Act
 Mo. Rev. Stat., 443.901 et seq.
 N.C. Gen. Stat. 1943, § 53-255 et seq.
 S.C. Code Ann. 1976, § 29-4-20 et seq.

Reverse Mortgage Enabling Act
 W. Va. Code 1966, § 47-24-1 et seq.

Reverse Mortgage Loan Act
 S.D. Codified Laws 1967, 54-12-1 et seq.

Reversion Act (Railroad Right of Way)
 Iowa Code Ann., 327G.77

Reversion Act (School Site)
 Iowa Code Ann., 297.15

Reversion Act (Surrender or Merger)
 Ill. Rev. Stat. 1991, Ch. 30, §§ 38.9, 39

Reversions Act (State Claims)
 Iowa Code Ann., 614.24

Reverter Act
 Fla. Stat. Ann., 689.18
 Ill. Rev. Stat. 1991, Ch. 30, § 37b et seq.
 Neb. Rev. Stat. 1943, 76-299 et seq.

Review Act (Administrative Procedure)
 Mo. Rev. Stat., 536.010 et seq.

Review Act (Utilization)
 Minn. Stat. 1986, 62M.01 et seq.

Review and Prevention Act (Child Fatality)
 S.C. Acts 1993, p. 1263, No. 164

Review Board Pilot Program Act (Local Citizen)
 Mont. Code Ann., 41-3-1001 et seq.

Review Committee of the Joint Appropriation Act (JARC)
S.C. Code Ann. 1976, § 2-65-10 et seq.

Review, Continuation, Reestablishment or Termination of Regulatory Agencies Act
Ga. Code Ann., 43-2-1 et seq.

Review Enabling Act (Land and Subdivision Development)
R.I. Gen. Laws 1956, 45-23-25 et seq.

Review Organization Act (Utilization)
Kan. Stat. Ann., 40-22a01 et seq.

Review Organization Immunity Act
N.M. Stat. 1978, 41-9-1 et seq.

Review Team Act (Child Death)
Ill. Comp. Stat. 1992, Ch. 20, § 515/1

Revised Airports Act
Del. Code of 1974, Title 2, § 901 et seq.
Neb. Rev. Stat. 1943, 3-201 et seq., 18-1502
Wash. Rev. Code Ann., 14.08.010 et seq.

Revised Article 5 (Letters of Credit)
See also Uniform Commercial Code—Letters of Credit (Revised Article 6).
Miss. Code Ann. 1972, § 75-5-101 et seq.
Pa. Cons. Stat., Title 13, § 5101 et seq.

Revised Business Corporation Act
See also Uniform Business Corporation Act
Utah Code Ann. 1953, 16-10a-101 et seq.

Revised Cities and Villages Act
Ill. Rev. Stat. 1989, Ch. 24, § 21-0.1 et seq.
Ill. Rev. Stat. 1991, Ch. 24, § 1-1-1 et seq.

Revised Judicature Act
Mich. Comp. Laws Ann., 600.101 et seq.

Revised Limited Partnership Act
See also Uniform Revised Limited Partnership Act
See Revised Uniform Limited Partnership Act
Alaska Stat. 1962, § 10.50.070 et seq.
Cal. Corporations Code § 15611 et seq.

N.Y. Partnership Law (Consol. Laws Ch. 39) § 121-101 et seq.

Revised Maine Securities Act
Me. Rev. Stat. Ann. 1964, Title 32, § 10101 et seq.

Revised Model State Administrative Procedure Act
Mont. Code Ann., 2-4-101 et seq.

Revised Organic Act of the Virgin Islands
July 22, 1954, Ch. 558, 68 Stat. 497, 21 U.S. Code §§ 104, 111 (see 26 U.S. Code § 7652; 48 U.S. Code §§ 1541 to 1545, 1561, 1571 et seq.,)
Sept. 1, 1954, Ch. 1213, 68 Stat. 1140, 48 U.S. Code § 1644
Aug. 30, 1957, P.L. 85-224, 71 Stat. 510, 48 U.S. Code § 1597
Sept. 16, 1959, P.L. 86-289, 73 Stat. 568, 48 U.S. Code §§ 1572, 1573, 1597, 1617
March 16, 1962, P.L. 87-419, 76 Stat. 35, 48 U.S. Code § 1596
March 20, 1962, P.L. 87-421, 76 Stat. 43, 48 U.S. Code § 1599
Nov. 19, 1963, P.L. 88-180, 77 Stat. 335, 48 U.S. Code § 1574
July 30, 1965, P.L. 89-98, 79 Stat. 423, 48 U.S. Code § 1572.
Aug. 30, 1966, P.L. 89-548, 80 Stat. 371, 48 U.S. Code § 1571
Oct. 13, 1966, P.L. 89-643, 80 Stat. 890, 48 U.S. Code § 1574
Aug. 23, 1968, P.L. 90-496, 82 Stat. 837, 48 U.S. Code §§ 1541, 1561, 1572 to 1575, 1591, 1593, 1595, 1597, 1599, 1641
June 2, 1970, P.L. 91-272, 84 Stat. 296, 48 U.S. Code § 1614
Oct. 16, 1970, P.L. 91-460, 84 Stat. 978, 48 U.S. Code § 1542
June 2, 1971, P.L. 92-24, 85 Stat. 76, 48 U.S. Code § 1617
Aug. 17, 1972, P.L. 92-389, 86 Stat. 563, 48 U.S. Code § 1572
Oct. 19, 1973, P.L. 93-130, 87 Stat. 460, 48 U.S. Code § 1572
May 27, 1975, P.L. 94-26, 89 Stat. 94, 48 U.S. Code § 1596
Oct. 15, 1977, P.L. 95-132, 48 U.S. Code §§ 1599 et seq.
Nov. 6, 1978, P.L. 95-598, 48 U.S. Code §§ 1612, 1615
Continued

March 12, 1980, P.L. 96-205, 48 U.S. Code
§§ 1545, 1642

Oct. 19, 1982, P.L. 97-357, 48 U.S. Code
§§ 1574, 1591

Dec. 8, 1983, P.L. 98-213, 48 U.S. Code
§§ 1543, 1561

Oct. 5, 1984, P.L. 98-454, 98 Stat. 1732,
1737, 48 U.S. Code §§ 1561, 1574, 1611,
1612, 1613, 1613a, 1614

Aug. 27, 1986, P.L. 99-396, 48 U.S. Code
§ 1593

Dec. 12, 1989, P.L. 101-219, 48 U.S. Code
§ 1615

Nov. 2, 1994, P.L. 103-437, 48 U.S. Code
§ 1613

Aug. 20, 1996, P.L. 104-186, 48 U.S. Code
§ 1596

Nov. 10, 1998, P.L. 105-362, 48 U.S. Code
§ 1591

Revised Partnership Act
See also Revised Uniform Limited
Partnership Act
Tex. Rev. Civ. Stat., Art. 6132b-11.01 et seq.

Revised Price Act (Real Estate)
Pa. Cons. Stat., Title 20, § 8301 et seq.

Revised Probate Code
Ariz. Laws 1994, Ch. 290
Ga. Code Ann., 53-1-1 et seq.
Mich. Comp. Laws Ann., 700.1 et seq.

Revised Professional Corporation Act
Ala. Code 1975, § 10-4-380 et seq.

Revised School Code
Mich. Comp. Laws Ann., 380.1 et seq.

Revised Securities Act
Me. Rev. Stat. Ann. 1964, Title 32, § 10101
et seq.

Revised Statutes Amending Acts
Feb. 18, 1875, Ch. 80, 18 Stat. 316
Feb. 27, 1877, Ch. 69, 19 Stat. 240
July 11, 1940, Ch. 580, 54 Stat. 751, 5 U.S.
Code § 56
July 12, 1940, Ch. 618, 54 Stat. 758, 22 U.S.
Code §§ 1175 to 1177

Revised Uniform Adoption Act
Ark. Code Ann. 1987, 9-9-201 et seq.
N.D. Cent. Code, 14-15-01 et seq.

Revised Uniform Airports Act
Minn. Stat. Ann., 360.031 et seq.

Revised Uniform Consumer Credit Code
Kan. Stat. Ann., 16a-1-101 et seq.

Revised Uniform Consumer Credit Code-Finance Charges and Related Provisions
Kan. Stat. Ann., 16a-2-101 et seq.

Revised Uniform Consumer Credit Code-Insurance
Kan. Stat. Ann., 16a-4-101 et seq.

Revised Uniform Consumer Credit Code-Regulation of Agreements and Practices
Kan. Stat. Ann., 16a-3-101 et seq.

Revised Uniform Consumer Credit Code-Remedies and Penalties
Kan. Stat. Ann., 16a-5-101 et seq.

Revised Uniform Enforcement of Support Act
Mich. Comp. Laws Ann., 780.151 et seq.

Revised Uniform Estate Tax Apportionment Act
Haw. Rev. Stat. Ann., § 236A-1 et seq.
Ida. Code 1947, § 15-3-916
Md. Code Ann. 1974, Art. ET, § 11-109
N.D. Cent. Code, 30.1-20-16
Ore. Rev. Stat., 116.303 et seq.
R.I. Gen. Laws 1956, 44-23.1-1 et seq.
Vt. Stat. Ann., Title 32, § 7301 et seq.
Wash. Rev. Code Ann., 83.110.010 et seq.

Revised Uniform Federal Tax Lien Registration Act
Md. Ann. Code 1974, Art. RP, § 3-401 et seq.
Mont. Code Ann., 71-3-201 et seq.
Pa. 1963 Pamph. Laws 523, No. 279
S.D. Codified Laws 1967, 44-7-1 et seq.

Revised Uniform Gift to Minors Act

Mont. Code Ann., 72-26-101 et seq.
N.D. Cent. Code, 47-24-01 et seq.

Revised Uniform Limited Partnership Act

Ala. Code 1975, § 10-9A-1 et seq.
Ariz. Rev. Stat. Ann., § 29-301 et seq.
Ark. Code Ann. 1987, 4-43-101 et seq.
Colo. Rev. Stat., 7-62-101 et seq.
Conn. Gen. Stat. Ann., § 34-9 et seq.
Del. Code of 1974, Title 6, § 17-101 et seq.
Fla. Stat. Ann., 620.101 et seq.
Ga. Code Ann., 14-9-100 et seq.
Ida. Code 1947, 53-201 et seq.
Ill. Rev. Stat. 1991, Ch. 106 1/2, § 151-1 et seq.
Iowa Code Ann., 545.101 et seq.
Kan. Stat. Ann., 56-1a01 et seq.
Ky. Rev. Stat. 1971, 362.401 et seq.
Mass. Gen. Laws Ann., 109:1 et seq.
Md. Ann. Code 1974, Art. CA, § 10-101 et seq.
Me. Rev. Stat. Ann. 1964, Title 31, § 401 et seq.
Mich. Comp. Laws Ann., 449.1101 et seq.
Minn. Stat. Ann., 322A.01 et seq.
Mo. Rev. Stat. 1978, 359.011 et seq.
Mont. Code Ann., 35-12-501 et seq.
N.C. Gen. Stat. 1943, § 59-101 et seq.
N.D. Cent. Code, 45-10-01 et seq.
Neb. Rev. Stat. 1943, 67-233 et seq.
N.J. Stat. Ann., 42:2A-1 et seq.
N.Y. Partnership Law (Consol. Laws Ch. 39) § 121-101 et seq.
Okla. Stat. Ann., Title 54, § 301 et seq.
S.C. Code Ann. 1976, § 33-42-10 et seq.
Tenn. Code Ann., 61-2-101 et seq.
Tex. Rev. Civ. Stat., Art. 6132a-1, § 1.01
Utah Code Ann. 1953, 48-2a-1102 et seq.
Va. Code 1950, § 50-73.1 et seq.
Wash. Rev. Code Ann., 25.10.010 et seq.
Wyo. Stat. Ann., § 17-14-201 et seq.

Revised Uniform Partnership Act

Fla. Stat. Ann., 620.81001 et seq.
Md. Ann. Code 1974, Art. CA, § 9A-1001 et seq.

Revised Uniform Principal and Income Act

Ariz. Rev. Stat. Ann., § 14-7401 et seq.
Ark. Code Ann. 1987, 28-70-101 et seq.
Cal. Probate Code § 16300 et seq.
Haw. Rev. Stat. Ann., § 557-1 et seq.
Ind. Code Ann., 30-2-3-1 et seq.
Kan. Stat. Ann., 58-901 et seq.
Ky. Rev. Stat. 1971, 386.191 to 386.349
Md. Ann. Code 1974, Art. ET, § 14-201 et seq.
Mich. Comp. Laws Ann., 555.51 et seq.
Minn. Stat. Ann., 501.48 et seq.
Miss. Code Ann. 1972, § 91-17-1 et seq.
Mont. Code Ann. 1987, 72-25-101 et seq.
N.D. Cent. Code, 59-04.1-01 et seq.
Nev. Rev. Stat. 1979 Reprint, 164.140 et seq.
N.J. Stat. Ann., 3B:19A-1 et seq.
N.M. Stat. Ann. 1978, 46-3-1 et seq.
N.Y. Estates, Powers and Trusts Law (Consol. Laws Ch. 17B) § 11-2.1
S.C. Code Ann. 1976, § 62-7-401 et seq.

Revised Uniform Reciprocal Enforcement of Support Act

Ariz. Rev. Stat. Ann., § 12-1651 et seq.
Ark. Code Ann. 1987, 9-14-301 et seq.
Cal. Code of Civil Procedure, § 1650 et seq.
Colo. Rev. Stat., 14-5-101 et seq.
Fla. Stat. Ann., 88.011 et seq.
Ga. Code Ann., 19-11-40 et seq.
Haw. Rev. Stat. Ann., § 576-1 et seq.
Ida. Code 1947, 7-1048 et seq.
Ill. Rev. Stat. 1991, Ch. 40, § 1201 et seq.
Iowa Code Ann., 252A.1 et seq.
Kan. Stat. Ann., 23-451 et seq.
Ky. Rev. Stat. 1971, 407.010 et seq.
La. Rev. Stat. Ann., 13:1641 et seq.
Me. Rev. Stat. Ann. 1964, Title 19, § 395 et seq.
Mich. Comp. Laws Ann., 780.151 et seq.
Minn. Stat. Ann., 518C.01 et seq.
Mont. Code Ann., 40-5-101 et seq.
N.C. Gen. Stat. 1943, § 52A-1 et seq.
N.D. Cent. Code, 14-12.1-01 et seq.
Neb. Rev. Stat. 1943, 42-762 et seq.
Nev. Rev. Stat. 1979 Reprint, 130.010 et seq.
N.H. Rev. Stat. 1955, 546:1 et seq.
N.J. Stat. Ann., 2A:4-30.24 et seq.

Continued

N.M. Stat. Ann., 40-6-1 et seq.
Ohio Rev. Code 1953, 3115.01 et seq.
Okla. Stat. Ann., Title 43, § 301 et seq.
Ore. Rev. Stat., 110.005 et seq.
Pa. Cons. Stat., Title 23, § 4501 et seq.
Pa. Cons. Stat., Title 42, § 6741 et seq.
R.I. Gen. Laws 1956, 15-11-1 et seq.
S.C. Code Ann. 1976, § 20-7-960 et seq.
S.D. Codified Laws 1967, 25-9A-1 et seq.,
Tex. Family Code, § 21.01 et seq.
Va. Code 1950, § 20-88.12 et seq.
Vt. Stat. Ann., Title 15, § 385 et seq.
Wis. Stat. Ann., 767.65
W. Va. Code 1966 § 48A-7-1 et seq.
Wyo. Stat. Ann., § 20-4-101 et seq.

Revision of Statutes Acts
June 27, 1866 Ch. 140, 14 Stat. 74
March 3, 1901, Ch. 853, 31 Stat. 1181

Revisory Act
Ill. Laws 1973, P.A. 78-255
Ill. Laws 1974, P.A. 78-1297
Ill. Laws 1976, P.A. 79-1454
Ill. Laws 1982, P.A. 82-783, 86-1057
Ill. Laws 1984, P.A. 83-1362
Ill. Laws 1985, P.A. 84-832
Ill. Laws 1986, P.A. 84-1308
Ill. Laws 1989, P.A. 85-1440, 86-820
Ill. Laws 1990, P.A. 86-1028

Revitalization Act (Agriculture and Industrial Brand Rail Line)
Neb. Rev. Stat. 1943, 74-1401 et seq.

Revitalization Act (Apparel Industry)
Cal. Government Code § 15317

Revitalization Act (Neighborhood)
Kan. Stat. Ann., 12-17,114 et seq.

Revitalization Act (Rural Pennsylvania)
Pa. Purdon's Stat., Title 71, § 1190.101 et seq.

Revitalization and Leadership Development Act (Rural)
Ore. Rev. Stat., 285.678 et seq.

Revitalization and Redevelopment Law
Nev. Statutes 1975, Ch. 702, p. 1428

Revitalization Authority Act (Agricultural)
Neb. Rev. Stat. 1943, 2-4701 et seq.

Revitalization of Employment Act
S.C. Code Ann. 1976, § 59-54-10 et seq.

Revival Act (Corporations)
Md. Ann. Code 1974, Art. CA, § 3-508 et seq.

Revival Act (Nonprofit Corporations)
Mich. Comp. Laws Ann., 450.441 et seq.

Revival Act (Profit Corporations)
Mich. Comp. Laws 1970, 450.431, 450.432

Revival Act (Wills)
Kan. Stat. Ann., 59-612

Revival of Actions Act
Ala. Code 1975, § 6-5-460 et seq.
Miss. Code Ann. 1972, § 11-3-17
Ohio Rev. Code 1953, 2311.21

Revocable Permit Act (Franchises)
Okla. Laws 1925, p. 150

Revocation Act (Wills)
Ga. Code Ann., 53-2-70 et seq.
Mich. Comp. Laws Ann., 700.149
N.Y. Estates, Powers and Trusts Law (Consol. Laws Ch. 17B) §§ 3-4.1 et seq., 5-1.3

Revocation and Reduction Act (Public Employee Pension)
R.I. Gen. Laws 1956, 36-10.1-1 et seq.

Revocation of License Act (Nursing)
N.Y. Education Law 1947 (Consol. Laws Ch. 16) § 6510

Revocation of Licenses Procedure Act
N.C. Gen. Stat. 1943, § 150-9 et seq.

Revolutionary War and War of 1812 Historic Preservation Study Act of 1996
Nov. 12, 1996, P.L. 104-333, § 603, 16 U.S. Code § 1a-5 nt.

Revolving Charge Account Act
S.C. Code Ann. 1976, § 37-2-207 et seq.

Revolving Charge Agreements Act
Neb. Rev. Stat. 1943, 45-204 et seq.

Revolving Charge Billing Act
Ill. Rev. Stat. 1991, Ch. 17, § 5100 et seq.

Revolving Credit Act
Fla. Stat. Ann., 520.30 et seq.
N.D. Cent. Code, 51-14-01 et seq.

Revolving Fund Act (Emergency Medical Services)
Ark. Code Ann. 1987, 20-13-101 et seq.

Revolving Fund Act (Public Service Commission)
Nev. Rev. Stat. 1979 Reprint, 703.230

Revolving Fund Act (Rural Health Services)
Ark. Code Ann. 1987, 20-12-401 et seq.

Revolving Fund Authority Act (Water Quality)
S.C. Code Ann. 1976, § 48-5-10 et seq.

Revolving Fund Safe Drinking Water Treatment Act
Mont. Code Ann., 75-6-201 et seq.

Revolving Loan and Grant Act (Clean Water)
N.C. Gen. Stat. 1943, § 159G-1 et seq.

Revolving Loan Fund (Historic Preservation)
N.J. Stat. Ann., 13:1B-15.115a to 13:1B-15.115d

Revolving Loan Fund Act (Schools)
Ark. Code Ann. 1987, 6-20-801 et seq.

Reward Act (Fugitive Apprehensions)
Ill. Rev. Stat. 1991, Ch. 60, § 11.9 et seq.

Rewards Act
Wash. Rev. Code Ann., 10.85.030 et seq.

Reye's Syndrome Reporting Act
Ill. Rev. Stat. 1991, Ch. 111 1/2, § 5701 et seq.

Reynolds Act (Labor)
Ohio Rev. Code 1953, 4109.10 et seq., 4113.10 et seq.

Reynolds Act (State Employees Retirement)
Ky. Rev. Stat. 1971, 61.510 et seq.

Reynolds Aviation Training Act
See Army Aviation Cadet Act

Reynolds-Sanders Act (Taxation)
Ky. Rev. Stat. 1971, 132.485

Rhea County Road Act
Tenn. Private Acts 1927, Ch. 38

Rheumatic Diseases Treatment Act
Ill. Rev. Stat. 1991, Ch. 111 1/2, § 7251 et seq.

Rheumatic Fever and Heart Disease Medicine Act
Ill. Rev. Stat. 1991, Ch. 111 1/2, § 22.09 et seq.

Rhinebeck Halloween Curfew Law
N.Y. Local Laws 1971, Town of Rhinebeck, p. 3257

Rhinoceros and Tiger Conservation Act of 1994
Oct. 22, 1994, P.L. 103-391, 16 U.S. Code §§ 5301 nt., 5301 et seq.
Oct. 30, 1998, P.L. 105-312, 16 U.S. Code §§ 5302, 5303,5305a, 5305b, 5306

Rhinoceros and Tiger Conservation Act of 1998
Oct. 30, 1998, P.L. 105-312, Title IV, 112 Stat. 2959, 16 U.S. Code § 5301 nt.

Rhode Island Challenge Grants Act
R.I. Gen. Laws 1956, 16-72-1 et seq.

Rhode Island Indian Claims Settlement Act
　Sept. 30, 1996, P.L. 104-208, 25 U.S. Code
　　§ 1708

Rhode Island Rivers Council
　R.I. Gen. Laws 1956, 46-28-1 et seq.

Rice Development Act
　Tex. General & Special Laws 47th Leg.,
　　1941, p. 695, Ch. 434

Rice Development Commission Act
　Ark. Acts 1941, p. 59, No. 29

Rice Production Act of 1975
　Feb. 16, 1976, P.L. 94-214, 7 U.S. Code
　　§§ 428c et seq.
　Sept. 29, 1977, P.L. 95-113, 7 U.S. Code
　　§§ 1352, 1352 nt., 1428, 1428 nt.

Rice Research and Promotion Act
　Ark. Code Ann. 1987, 2-20-501 et seq.

**Rice Straw Burning Reduction Act
(Connelly-Areias-Chandler)**
　Cal. Health and Safety Code § 41865

Rice Straw Demonstration Project
　Cal. Health and Safety Code §§ 39750 et
　　seq., 41865, 44535, 44537.5

**Richard B. Russell Development Authority
Act (Elbert County)**
　Ga. Laws 1991, p. 3587

Richard R. Renick Act (Marine Corals)
　Fla. Stat. Ann., 370.114

Richards Primary Law
　S.D. Laws 1911, Ch. 201
　S.D. Laws 1917, Ch. 234

Richards-Rees Act (Air Pollution)
　Cal. Health and Safety Code § 426.5

**Richland County-City of Columbia Study
Commission Act**
　S.C. Acts 1971, p. 1682, No. 832

Richmond Ambulance Authority Act
　Va. Acts 1991, Ch. 431

**Richmond County-Augusta Building
Authority Act**
　Ga. Laws 1952, p. 338

**Richmond County-Augusta Charter
Commission Act**
　Ga. Laws 1974, p. 2324

**Richmond County-Augusta Coliseum
Authority Act**
　Ga. Laws 1973, p. 3042

**Richmond County Employees Pension Fund
Act**
　Ga. Laws 1945, p. 748

Richmond County Peace Officers' Relief Act
　N.C. Laws 1963, Ch. 824

Richmond County Tenure Act
　Ga. Laws 1937-38 Ex. Sess., p. 875

**Richmond Hill Area Convention and
Visitors Bureau Authority Act**
　Ga. Laws 1996, p. 4442

Richmond Hill Recreation Authority Act
　Ga. Laws 1996, p. 3646

**Richmond Officers' and Employees' Tenure
Act**
　Ga. Laws 1937-38 Ex. Sess., p. 875

Richmond Potable Water Safeguard Law
　N.Y. Local Laws 1972, Town of Richmond,
　　p. 2716

**Richmond Refuse Collectors Licensing &
Regulating Law**
　N.Y. Local Laws 1969, Town of Richmond,
　　p. 2024

Richmond Refuse Disposal Law
　N.Y. Local Laws 1969, Town of Richmond,
　　p. 2021

Ricky Ray Hemophilia Relief Fund Act of 1998
Nov. 11, 1998, P.L. 105-369, 112 Stat. 3368, 42 U.S. Code § 3006-22 nt.

RICO
See Racketeer Influenced and Corrupt Organizations Act

Rider Safety Act
Me. Rev. Stat. Ann. 1964, Title 8, § 801 et seq.

Rides and Amusement Attractions Safety Act
W. Va. Code 1966 § 21-10-1 et seq.

Rideshare Support and Improvement Act
Cal. Government Code § 15925 et seq.

Ridesharing Act
Neb. Rev. Stat. 1943, 60-2501 et seq.
N.J. Stat. Ann., 27:26-1 et seq.
Okla. Stat. Ann., Title 47, § 1001 et seq.
S.C. Code Ann. 1976, § 58-23-18 et seq.
Tenn. Code Ann., 65-19-201

Ridesharing Arrangements Act
Ill. Rev. Stat. 1991, Ch. 95 1/2, § 901 et seq.

Riding and Hiking Trails Law
Cal. Public Resources Code § 5070 et seq.

Riegle Community Development and Regulatory Improvement Act of 1994
Sept. 23, 1994, P.L. 103-325, 12 U.S. Code § 4701 nt.
Sept. 30, 1996, P.L. 104-208, 12 U.S. Code § 4803

Riegle-Neal Amendments Act of 1997
July 3, 1997, P.L. 105-24, 12 U.S. Code § 1811 nt.

Riegle-Neal Interstate Banking and Branching Efficiency Act of 1994
Sept. 29, 1994, P.L. 103-328, 12 U.S. Code § 1811 nt.

Rifle Act (Air)
Ill. Rev. Stat. 1991, Ch. 38, § 82 et seq.

Rifle and Shotgun Registration Act
Cal. Statutes 1990, Ch. 177

Rifle and Shotgun Registration Act (Prohibition against)
Cal. Penal Code § 11106

Riggs Act (Tubercular Cattle)
Ohio Rev. Code 1953, 941.51 et seq.

Right of Conscience Act
Ill. Rev. Stat. 1991, Ch. 111 1/2, § 5301 et seq.

Right of Conscience Act (Health Care)
Ill. Comp. Stat. 1992, Ch. 745, § 7-/1 et seq.

Right of Election Act (Surviving Spouse)
N.Y. Estates, Powers and Trusts Law (Consol. Laws Ch. 17B) § 5-1.1 et seq.

Right of Passage Act (Health Care)
Ga. Code Ann., 52-1-30 et seq.
Ill. Comp. Stat. 1992, Ch. 745, § 70/1 et seq.

Right of Privacy Act
N.Y. Civil Rights Law (Consol. Laws Ch. 6) § 50 et seq.
Utah Code Ann. 1953, 76-9-401 et seq.
Va. Code 1950, § 8.01-40 et seq.
Wash. Rev. Code Ann., 9.73.010 et seq.

Right of Way Act (Alaska)
Alaska Comp. Laws Ann. 1949, § 47-2-91 et seq.

Right of Way Act (Emergency Vehicles)
Wash. Rev. Code Ann., 46.61.210

Right of Way Act (Motor Vehicles)
Cal. Vehicle Code 1959, § 21800 et seq.
Conn. Gen. Stat. Ann., § 14-245 et seq.
Ill. Rev. Stat. 1991, Ch. 95 1/2, § 11-901 et seq.
Iowa Code Ann., 321.319 et seq.
Md. Ann. Code 1974, TR, § 21-401 et seq.
Mich. Comp. Laws Ann., 257.649 et seq.
Minn. Stat. Ann., 169.20
Mo. Rev. Stat., 304.022
N.D. Cent. Code, 39-10-22
N.Y. Vehicle and Traffic Law 1959 (Consol. Laws Ch. 71) § 1140 et seq.

Continued

Okla. Stat. Ann., Title 47, § 11-401 et seq.
R.I. Gen. Laws 1956, 31-17-1 et seq.
Wash. Rev. Code Ann., 46.61.180 et seq.

Right of Way Act (Pedestrians)
Cal. Vehicle Code 1959, § 21950 et seq.
N.H. Rev. Stat. 1955, 265:35
Ore. Rev. Stat., 814.010 et seq.
Wash. Rev. Code Ann., 46.61.230 et seq.

Right of Way Act (Railways)
See Railroad Right of Way Act

Right of Way Act (Street Railroad)
Ill. Rev. Stat. 1991, Ch. 131 1/4 § 0.01 et seq.

Right of Way Act (Telephone Line)
Ill. Rev. Stat. 1991, Ch. 134, § 11.9 et seq.

Right of Way Act (Traffic)
Alaska Laws 1966, Ch. 92
Ga. Code Ann., 40-6-70 et seq.
Ind. Code Ann., 9-4-1-81 et seq.
Mich. Comp. Laws Ann., 257.649 et seq.
Mont. Code Ann., 61-8-339 et seq.
N.C. Gen. Stat. 1943, § 20-155 et seq.
Ohio Rev. Code 1953, 4511.41 et seq.
Va. Code 1950, § 46.2-822 et seq.
Wis. Stat. Ann., 346.18 et seq.

Right of Way Act of 1891
March 3, 1891, Ch. 561, 26 Stat. 1101, 16
U.S. Code §§ 471, 607, 611, 611a, 613; 25
U.S. Code § 495; 30 U.S. Code §§ 35, 36,
48, 52 ; 43 U.S. Code §§ 161, 162, 173,
174, 185, 212, 262, 321, 323, 325, 327 to
329 and others

Right of Way Designation Law
N.Y. Local Laws 1972, County of Onondaga,
p. 755

Right-of-Way Leasing Act (1930)
Alaska Stat. 1962, § 38.35.010 et seq.

Right-of-Way Naming Act (Monroe County)
N.Y. Laws 1991, Ch. 769

Right of Way Reversion Act (Railroads)
Iowa Code Ann., 327G.77

Right to Bargain Act (Employees)
Mass. Gen. Laws Ann., 150A:3

Right to Bargain Act (Labor Relations)
Mass. Gen. Laws Ann., 150A:3

Right to Compete Act
Cal. Business and Professions Code §§ 651,
651.3, 1320, 1680, 2556, 3129, 4333,
17500.1

Right to Counsel Act
Tenn. Code Ann., 40-14-102

Right to Die Act
Colo. Rev. Stat., 15-14-403 to 15-14-409
Kan. Stat. Ann., 65-28,101 et seq.
N.M. Stat. Ann., 24-7-1 et seq.

Right to Employment Act
P.R. Laws Ann. 1954, Title 29, § 1101 et seq.

Right to Farm Act
Fla. Stat. Ann., 823.14
Haw. Rev. Stat. Ann., § 165-1 et seq.
La. Rev. Stat. Ann., 3:3601 et seq.
Mich. Comp. Laws Ann., 286.471 et seq.
Neb. Rev. Stat. 1943, 2-4401 et seq.
N.J. Stat. Ann., 4:1C-1 et seq.
N.M. Stat. Ann., 47-9-1 et seq.
R.I. Gen. Laws 1956, 2-23-1 et seq.
S.C. Code Ann. 1976, § 46-45-10 et seq.
Tenn. Code Ann., 43-26-101 et seq.
Va. Code 1950, §§ 3.1-22.28, 3.1-22.29

Right to Farm and Ranch Act
Wyo. Stat. Ann., § 11-44-101 et seq.

Right to Financial Privacy Act
Nov. 10, 1978, P.L. 95-630, 12 U.S. Code
§§ 3401 et seq.
Oct. 15, 1982, P.L. 97-320, 12 U.S. Code
§§ 3412, 3414
Oct. 27, 1986, P.L. 99-569, 12 U.S. Code
§ 3414
Oct. 27, 1986, P.L. 99-570, 12 U.S. Code
§§ 3403, 3413, 3414
Nov. 18, 1988, P.L. 100-690, 12 U.S. Code
§§ 3403, 3412, 3413, 3417, 3420
Aug. 9, 1989, P.L. 101-73, 12 U.S. Code
§§ 3401, 3412, 3413, 3420

Nov. 29, 1990, P.L. 101-647, 12 U.S. Code §§ 3401, 3413

Dec. 19, 1991, P.L. 102-242, 12 U.S. Code § 3412

Oct. 28, 1992, P.L. 102-550, 12 U.S. Code §§ 3412, 3420

Oct. 29, 1992, P.L. 102-568, 12 U.S. Code § 3413

Dec. 21, 1995, P.L. 104-66, 12 U.S. Code § 3421

Oct. 19, 1998, P.L. 105-264, 12 U.S. Code § 3413

Cal. Government Code § 7460 et seq.

Mo. Rev. Stat., 408.675 et seq.

Right to Fish Law
La. Rev. Stat. Ann., 56:640.1 et seq.

Right to Garnish Law
Fla. Stat. Ann., 77.01 et seq.

Right to Inspect Personnel Files Act
Del. Code of 1974, Title 19, § 719 et seq.

Right to Know Act
Mass. Gen. Laws Ann., 111F:1 et seq.
Me. Rev. Stat. Ann. 1964, Title 1, § 401 et seq.
Neb. Rev. Stat. 1943, 84-712 et seq.
Vt. Stat. Ann., Title 1, § 311 et seq.

Right to Know Act (Civil)
Vt. Stat. Ann., Title 13, § 1451 et seq.

Right to Know Act (Community)
Ga. Code Ann., 12-17-1 et seq.
Me. Rev. Stat. Ann. 1964, Title 22, § 1696-A et seq.
N.Y. Adm. Code '85, § 24-701 et seq.
W. Va. Code 1966 § 16-31-1 et seq.

Right to Know Act (Employees)
Mich. Comp. Laws Ann., 423.501 et seq.
Minn. Laws 1983, Ch. 316

Right-to-Know Act (Fisherman's)
Ala. Acts 1998, H.B. 72

Right to Know Act (Hazardous Chemicals)
N.C. Gen. Stat. 1943, § 95-173 et seq.

Right to Know Act (Hazardous Substances)
N.M. Stat. Ann., 50-9-2.1, 50-9-3, 50-9-5.1

Right to Know Act (Manufacturing Facilities Community)
Tex. Health and Safety Code, § 505.001 et seq.

Right to Know Act (Meetings)
N.J. Stat. Ann., 10:4-6 et seq.

Right to Know Act (Public Employees' Chemical)
Ark. Acts 1991, No. 556

Right to Know Act (Public Records)
Conn. Gen. Stat. Ann., § 1-19 et seq.
N.H. Rev. Stat. 1955, 91-A:1 et seq.
N.J. Stat. Ann., 47:1A-1 et seq.
Pa. Purdon's Stat., Title 65, § 66.1 et seq.

Right-to-Know Act (Women's)
Ga. Code Ann., 16-12-150 et seq.
Mont. Code Ann., 50-20-301 et seq.
S.C. Code Ann. 1976, § 44-41-310 et seq.

Right to Know Act (Worker and Community)
Pa. Purdon's Stat., Title 35, § 7301 et seq.
Wash. Rev. Code Ann., 49.70.010 et seq.

Right to Know Act (Worker's)
N.H. Rev. Stat. 1955, 277-A:1 et seq.

Right to Know Law (Sale of Student Loans)
N.Y. Banking Law (Consol. Laws Ch. 2) § 9k
N.Y. Education Law 1947 (Consol. Laws Ch. 16) § 683a

Right to Know Law (Student Borrower)
N.Y. Banking Law (Consol. Laws Ch. 2) § 9i
N.Y. Education Law 1947 (Consol. Laws Ch. 16) § 683a

Right to Know Law (Toxic Substances in the Workplace)
Also known as Workers' Right to Know Law
N.Y. Labor Law (Consol. Laws Ch. 31) § 875 et seq.
Continued

N.Y. Public Health Law 1953 (Consol. Laws Ch. 45) § 4800 et seq.

Right-to-Life Act
R.I. Gen. Laws 1956, 23-4.13-1 et seq.

Right to Natural Death Act
Tenn. Code Ann., 32-11-101 et seq.

Right to Organize Act (Labor)
Mass. Gen. Laws Ann., 150A:1 et seq.
Mich. Comp. Laws Ann., 423.1 et seq.
N.J. Stat. Ann., 34:12-1 et seq.

Right to Privacy Act
N.H. Rev. Stat. 1955, 359-C:1 et seq.

Right to Privacy in the Workplace Act
Ill. Rev. Stat. 1991, Ch. 48, § 2851 et seq.

Right to Work Act
July 5, 1935, Ch. 372, 49 Stat. 457, 29 U.S. Code § 164
June 23, 1947, Ch. 120, 61 Stat. 151, 29 U.S. Code § 164
Ala. Code 1975, § 25-7-30 et seq.
Ariz. Rev. Stat. Ann., § 23-1301 et seq.
Ark. Code Ann. 1987, 11-3-301 et seq.
Fla. Const. 1885, Declaration of Rights § 6
Ga. Code Ann., 34-6-20 et seq.
Ida. Code 1947, 44-2001
Ind. Burns' 1933, 40-2701 et seq.
Iowa Code Ann., 731.1 et seq.
Kan. Const. 1859, Art. 15, § 12
La. Rev. Stat. Ann., 23:881 et seq.
Miss. Code Ann. 1972, § 71-1-47
Mont. Code Ann., 39-33-101 et seq.
N.C. Gen. Stat. 1943, § 95-78 et seq.
N.D. Cent. Code, 34-01-14
Neb. Rev. Stat. 1943, 48-217
Nev. Rev. Stat. 1979 Reprint, 613.230 et seq.
S.C. Code Ann. 1976, § 41-7-10 et seq.
S.D. Codified Laws 1967, 60-8-3 et seq.
Tenn. Code Ann., 50-1-201 et seq.
Tex. Labor Code, § 101.051 et seq.
Utah Code Ann. 1953, 34-34-1 et seq.
Va. Code 1950, § 40.1-58 et seq.
Wyo. Stat. Ann., § 27-7-108 et seq.

Right to Work Law (Agricultural Laborers')
La. Rev. Stat. Ann., 23:881 et seq.

Right-Turn on Red Act
S.C. Code Ann. 1976, § 56-5-970 et seq.

Rights and Responsibilities Act (Taxpayers')
Wash. Rev. Code Ann., 82.32A.002 et seq.

Rights for Persons with Developmental Disabilities Act
R.I. Gen. Laws 1956, 40.1-26-1 et seq.

Rights for Persons with Developmental Disabilities in Community Residences Act
R.I. Gen. Laws 1956, 40.1-22.1-1 et seq.

Rights of Action Survival Act
Wis. Stat. Ann., 895.01 et seq.

Rights of Crime Victims Act
Utah Code Ann. 1953, 77-38-1 et seq.

Rights of Entry or Re-entry Act
Ill. Rev. Stat. 1991, Ch. 30, § 37a.9 et seq.

Rights of Married Women Act
Ill. Rev. Stat. 1991, Ch. 40, § 1000 et seq.

Rights of People Act
P.R. Laws Ann. 1954, Title 1, § 9 et seq.

Rights of the Terminally Ill Act
See also Uniform Rights of the Terminally Ill Act
Ark. Code Ann. 1987, 20-17-202 et seq.
Mont. Code Ann., 50-9-101 et seq.
Neb. Laws 1992, L.B. 671, §§ 1 to 16
Okla. Stat. Ann., Title 63, § 3101.1 et seq.
R.I. Gen. Laws 1956, 23-4.11-1 et seq.

Rights-of-Way Across Federal Lands Act
Utah Code Ann. 1953, 27-16-101 et seq.

Rights Restoration Act (Parental)
Mich. Comp. Laws Ann., 722.901 et seq.

Rights to Cable Services Act (Tenants')
W. Va. Code 1966 § 5-18A-1 et seq.

Riley Act (Earthquake Protection)
Cal. Health and Safety Code § 19100 et seq.

Rio Grande American Canal Extension Act of 1990
Oct. 18, 1990, P.L. 101-438, 104 Stat. 1001

Rio Grande Compact Act
N.M. Stat. Ann., 72-15-3
Tex. Water Code, § 41.001 et seq.

Rio Grande Designation Act of 1994
May 4, 1994, P.L. 103-242, 16 U.S. Code §§ 1271 nt., 1274, 1276

Rio Grande Pollution Correction Act of 1987
Oct. 3, 1988, P.L. 100-465, 22 U.S. Code §§ 277 nt., 277g, 277g-1 to 277g-3

Rio Grande Valley State Park Act
N.M. Stat. Ann., 16-4-9 et seq.

Riot Act
Ala. Code 1975, § 13A-11-3
D.C. Code 1973, § 22-1122
Ga. Code Ann., 16-11-30 et seq.
Md. Ann. Code 1957, Art. 82, § 1 et seq.
Mich. Comp. Laws Ann., 750.523 et seq.
Miss. Code 1942, § 2361.5-01 et seq.
Mont. Code Ann., 45-8-103, 45-8-104
N.H. Rev. Stat. 1955, 644:1 et seq.
Va. Code 1950, § 18.1-247 et seq.
Wash. Rev. Code Ann., 9A.84.010
Wis. Stat. Ann., 66.091

Riot Act (Liability)
Cal. Government Code § 50140 et seq.
N.H. Rev. Stat. 1955, 31:53 et seq.
N.J. Stat. Ann., 2A:48-8, 2A:48-9
N.Y. General Municipal Law (Consol. Laws Ch. 24) § 71

Riot Control Act
N.M. Stat. Ann. 1978, 30-20-4 et seq.

Riot Control and Prevention Act
Okla. Stat. Ann., Title 21, § 1321.1 et seq.

Riot Damage Act
Ill. Rev. Stat. 1991, Ch. 38, § 25-1

Riparian Act
Fla. Stat. Ann., 271.02 et seq.
N.J. Rev. Stat. 1937, 12:3-2 et seq.

Riparian Habitat Conservation Act
Cal. Fish and Game Code 1957, § 1385 et seq.

Ripe Olive Standardization Act
Cal. Food and Agricultural Code 1967, § 41521 § 41361

Ripon Municipal Court Act
Wis. Laws 1951, Ch. 179

Ripper Act (Boulevard and Park Commissioners)
N.J. Laws 1930, p. 1092, Chs. 260 to 262

Riprap Loan Act (Marshfield)
Mass. Acts 1957, Ch. 341

Risk Act (Vendor and Purchaser)
Tex. Property Code, § 5.007

Risk-Based Capital (RBC) for Insurers Act
Ala. Code 1975, § 27-2B-1 et seq.
Ida. Code 1947, 41-5401 et seq.

Risk-Based Capital Act
Ill. Comp. Stat. 1992, Ch. 215, § 5/35A-1 et seq.
N.M. Stat. Ann., 59A-5A-1 et seq.

Risk-Based Capital Act (Insurers)
Mont. Code Ann., 33-2-1901 et seq.
Neb. Rev. Stat. 1943, 44-6001 et seq.

Risk-Based Capital for Life or Health Insurers Act
Ariz. Rev. Stat. Ann., § 20-488 et seq.

Risk Indemnification Trust Act (Nonprofit)
La. Rev. Stat. Ann., 22:1521 et seq., 22:2001 et seq.
Minn. Stat. Ann., 60A.29

Risk Management Act
Ark. Code Ann. 1987, 23-61-602 et seq.

Risk Management Act (Intergovernmental)
Neb. Rev. Stat. 1943, 44-4301 et seq.

Risk Management Planning and Accidental Release Prevention Act
Fla. Stat. Ann., 252.934 to 252.945

Risk Pool Act (Local Government)
N.C. Gen. Stat. 1943, § 58-23-1 et seq.

Risk Retention Act
Ala. Code 1975, § 27-31A-1 et seq.
Cal. Insurance Code § 125 et seq.
Md. Ann. Code 1974, Art. IN, § 25-101 et seq.
Miss. Code Ann. 1972, § 83-55-1 et seq.
Neb. Rev. Stat. 1943, 44-4401 et seq.
N.J. Stat. Ann., 17:47A-1 et seq.
Okla. Stat. Ann., Title 36, § 6451 et seq.
W. Va. Code 1966 § 33-24-1 et seq.
W. Va. Code 1966 § 33-32-1 et seq.

Risk Retention Act (Liability)
Ida. Code 1947, 41-4801 et seq.
Me. Rev. Stat. Ann. 1964, Title 24-A, § 6091 et seq.

Risk Retention Act (Model)
Colo. Rev. Stat., 10-3-1401 et seq.

Risk Retention Act (Product Liability)
Me. Rev. Stat. Ann. 1964, Title 24-A, § 6001 et seq.

Risk Retention Amendments of 1986
Oct. 27, 1986, P.L. 99-563, 15 U.S. Code § 3901 nt.

Risk Retention Groups Act
La. Rev. Stat. Ann., 22:2071 et seq.
Utah Code Ann. 1953, 31A-15-201 et seq.

Risk Retention Groups and Purchasing Groups Act
N.M. Stat. Ann., 59A-55-1 et seq.
N.Y. Insurance Law 1984 (Consol. Laws Ch. 28) § 5901 et seq.

River Act (Natural)
Mich. Comp. Laws Ann., 281.761 et seq.

River and Harbor Act
July 3, 1930, Ch. 847, 46 Stat. 918, 33 U.S. Code §§ 426, 465, 569a, 584a, 607a; 48 U.S. Code § 1399
Oct. 17, 1940, Ch. 895, 54 Stat. 1198, 33 U.S. Code § 603
Aug. 18, 1941, Ch. 377, 55 Stat. 638, 33 U.S. Code §§ 701b, 701b- 2, 701c nt., 701c-2, 701c-3, 701f nt., 701f-1 nt., 701g, 701j nt., 701m, 701n 702a-1, 702-12
July 14, 1960, P.L. 86-645, 74 Stat. 484, 33 U.S. Code § 426
D.C. Code 1973, § 7-526

River and Harbor Act of 1945
March 2, 1945, Ch. 19, 59 Stat. 10, 33 U.S. Code §§ 544b, 603a

River and Harbor Act of 1948
June 30, 1948, Ch. 771, 62 Stat. 1172, 22 U.S. Code § 275a; 33 U.S. Code § 572
Oct. 27, 1965, P.L. 89-298, 79 Stat. 1094, 22 U.S. Code § 275a

River and Harbor Act of 1950
May 17, 1950, Ch. 188, 64 Stat. 163, 33 U.S. Code §§ 534, 569a, 573

River and Harbor Act of 1954
Sept. 3, 1954, Ch. 1264, 68 Stat. 1248, 16 U.S. Code § 460d; 33 U.S. Code §§ 701b-8, 701g, 702a-12 nt., 706
Aug. 9, 1955, Ch. 674, 69 Stat. 612

River and Harbor Act of 1958
July 3, 1958, P.L. 85-500, 72 Stat. 300, 33 U.S. Code §§ 545a, 610, 633
Oct. 27, 1965, P.L. 89-298, 79 Stat. 1092, 33 U.S. Code §§ 610, 633
Oct. 12, 1996, P.L. 104-303, 33 U.S. Code § 610

River and Harbor Act of 1960
July 14, 1960, P.L. 86-645, 74 Stat. 480, 33 U.S. Code §§ 426, 577, 578
Oct. 27, 1965, P.L. 89-298, 79 Stat. 1095, 33 U.S. Code § 577
Dec. 31, 1970, P.L. 91-611, 84 Stat. 1821, 33 U.S. Code § 577

River and Harbor Act of 1962
Oct. 23, 1962, P.L. 87-874, 76 Stat. 1173, 33 U.S. Code §§ 426c to 426g

River and Harbor Act of 1965
Oct. 27, 1965, P.L. 89-298, 79 Stat. 1089, 22 U.S. Code § 275a; 33 U.S. Code §§ 59c, 59d, 426g, 540 nt., 577, 610, 633

River and Harbor Act of 1966
Nov. 7, 1966, P.L. 89-789, 80 Stat. 1405

River and Harbor Act of 1968
Aug. 13, 1968, P.L. 90-483, 82 Stat. 731, 33 U.S. Code §§ 59c-1, 59g to 59i, 426i, 562a

River and Harbor Act of 1970
Dec. 31, 1970, P.L. 91-611, 84 Stat. 1818, 33 U.S. Code §§ 426g, 569a, 577, 577a, 595a, 1161, 1165a

Nov. 17, 1988, P.L. 100-676, 33 U.S. Code § 1293a

Oct. 31, 1992, P.L. 102-580, 106 Stat. 4809

River Basin Act (Altamaha)
Ga. Code Ann., 12-5-420 et seq.

River Basin Act (Chattahoochee)
Ga. Code Ann., 12-5-400 et seq.

River Basin Compact (Arkansas-Oklahoma)
Ark. Code Ann. 1987, 15-23-401

River Basin Monetary Authorization Acts
May 12, 1967, P.L. 90-17, 81 Stat. 15
Aug. 13, 1968, P.L. 90-483, 82 Stat. 750

River Bed Act
Tex. Rev. Civ. Stat., Art. 5421c

River Bridge Construction Compact (Arkansas-Mississippi)
Miss. Code Ann. 1972, § 65-25-121 et seq.

River Conservancy Act (San Joaquin)
Cal. Public Resources Code § 32500 et seq.

River Conservancy District Validation Act
Ill. Rev. Stat. 1991, Ch. 42, §§ 410.01, 410.1

River Conservancy Districts Act
Ill. Rev. Stat. 1991, Ch. 42, § 383 et seq.

River Drainage and Flood Control Act (Neponset)
Mass. Acts 1955, Ch. 743

River Flood Control Compact Act
Conn. Gen. Stat. Ann., § 25-99 et seq.

River Forest Civic Center Act
Ill. Rev. Stat. 1991, Ch. 85, § 3301 et seq.

River Improvement Act
N.Y. Environmental Conservation Law (Consol. Laws Ch. 43B) § 15-2501 et seq.

River Improvement Loan Act (Quequechan)
Mass. Acts 1957, Ch. 607

River Loan Act (Hoosic)
Mass. Acts 1950, Ch. 649

River Management Act
Mich. Comp. Laws Ann., 485.101 et seq.

River Parishes Transit Authority Act
La. Rev. Stat. Ann., 48:1601 et seq.

River Port District Law
Cal. Harbors and Navigation Code § 6800 et seq.

River Protection Act (Wekiva)
Fla. Stat. Ann., 369.301 et seq.

River Valley Development Authority Act (Upper Illinois)
Ill. Rev. Stat. 1991, Ch. 85, § 7151 et seq.

Riverboat Economic Development and Gaming Control Act
La. Rev. Stat. Ann., 4:501 et seq.

Riverhead Housing Code
N.Y. Local Laws 1968, Town of Riverhead, p. 2955

Riverport and Airport Financing Act (Multicounty)
Ark. Acts 1991, No. 738

Riverport Authority Act
Ky. Rev. Stat. 1971, 65.510 et seq.

Rivers Act (Des Plaines and Illinois)
Ill. Rev. Stat. 1991, Ch. 19, § 40.9 et seq.

Rivers Act (Multiple Use)
Conn. Public Acts 1995, No. 333

Rivers Act (Scenic)
S.C. Code Ann. 1976, § 49-29-10 et seq.

Rivers Improvement Act (Ohio and Wabash)
Ill. Rev. Stat. 1991, Ch. 1, § 3550 et seq.

Rivers, Lakes and Streams Act
Ill. Rev. Stat. 1991, Ch. 19, § 51.9 et seq.

Riverside Civic Center Law
Ill. Rev. Stat. 1991, Ch. 85, § 7003-1 et seq.

Riverside County Flood Control and Water Conservation Act
Cal. Water Code Appendix, 48-1 et seq.

Riverside County Transportation Sales Tax Act
Cal. Public Utilities Code § 240000 et seq.

Riverside, Matteson, Ottawa, Illinois Valley, Waukegen, Pontiac, Randolph County, and Carbondale Civic Centers Act
Ill. Rev. Stat. 1991, Ch. 85, § 7000-1 et seq.

Riverside Regional Jail Authority Act
Va. Acts 1990, Ch. 725

Rives-Robinson Registration Law
Ky. Rev. Stat. 1962, 117.010 et seq.
Ky. Rev. Stat. 1971, Superseded Vol., 117.600 et seq.

Road Act (Alexander)
Ark. Acts 1915, p. 1400, No. 338

Road Act (Anderson County)
Tenn. Private Acts 1963, Ch. 232

Road Act (Campbell County)
Tenn. Private Acts 1947, Ch. 159

Road Act (Cotton)
Ark. Pope's Digest 1937, § 7062 et seq.

Road Act (County Bonds)
Mo. Laws 1907, p. 411

Road Act (County)
Mich. Comp. Laws Ann., 224.1 et seq.
Neb. Rev. Stat. 1943, 39-1401 et seq.
N.Y. Laws 1890, Ch. 555
Pa. 1911 Pamph. Laws 244

Road Act (Dallas County)
Tex. Laws 52nd Leg., 1951, p. 563, Ch. 328

Road Act (De Kalb County)
Tenn. Private Acts 1931, Ch. 558

Road Act (Fayette County)
Tenn. Private Acts 1941, Ch. 454

Road Act (Grainger County)
Tenn. Private Acts 1945, Ch. 476

Road Act (Harrelson)
Ark. Acts 1923, Ex. Sess., p. 11, No. 5

Road Act (Harris County)
Tex. Local and Special Laws 33rd Leg., 1913, p. 64, Ch. 17

Road Act (Henry County)
Tenn. Private Acts 1972, Ch. 326

Road Act (Johnson County)
Tenn. Private Acts 1949, Ch. 567

Road Act (Macon County)
Tenn. Private Acts 1947, Ch. 249

Road Act (Martineau)
Ark. Acts 1927, p. 17, No. 11

Road Act (Putnam County)
Tenn. Private Acts 1974, Ch. 208

Road Act (Rhea County)
Tenn. Private Acts 1927, Ch. 38

Road Act (Sevier County)
Tenn. Private Acts 1933, Ch. 10

Road Act (State)
Ky. Rev. Stat. 1971, 177.010 et seq.

Road Act (Stewart County)
Tenn. Private Acts 1951, Ch. 171

Road Act (Tipton County)
Tenn. Private Acts 1943, Ch. 120

Road Act (Toll)
Ky. Rev. Stat. 1971, 177.390 et seq.

Road Acts
Alaska Stat. 1962, § 19.05.010 et seq.
Colo. Rev. Stat., 43-2-201 et seq.
Ind. Code Ann., 8-11-1-1 et seq.
Kan. Stat. Ann., 68-401 et seq.
Md. Ann. Code 1974, Art. TR, § 8-210 et seq.
Mich. Comp. Laws Ann., 220.1 et seq.
Minn. Stat. Ann., 160.01 et seq.
N.C. Gen. Stat. 1943, § 136-4 et seq.
N.J. Rev. Stat. 1937, 27:1-1 et seq., 40:128-1 et seq., 40:150-1 et seq., 40:153-1 et seq., 40:178-1 et seq.
Ohio Rev. Code 1953, 5501.02 et seq.
Pa. Purdon's Stat., Title 36, § 1761 et seq.
Tenn. Code Ann., 54-10-101 et seq.
W. Va. Code 1966, § 17-1-1 et seq.
Wyo. Stat. Ann., § 24-1-101 et seq.

Road and Bridge Act
Ill. Rev. Stat. 1991, Ch. 121, § 1-101 et seq.
Mo. Rev. Stat., 228.010 et seq.

Road and Bridge Act (Alachua County Subdivision)
Fla. Special Laws 1953, Ch. 28872

Road and Bridge Act (Bexar County)
Tex. Special Laws 42nd Leg., 1931, p. 259, Ch. 137

Road and Bridge Repair Act (Franklin County)
Ala. General Acts 1951, p. 378, No. 143

Road and Highway Bonding Act (State)
Ore. Rev. Stat., 367.105 et seq.

Road and Trail Act
Alaska Stat. 1962, § 19.30.111 et seq.

Road Bond Act
Iowa Laws 1928 (42nd G. A.), Ch. 2

Road Bond Act (County and District)
Tex. Rev. Civ. Stat., Art. 6702-1, § 4.411 et seq.

Road Bond Act (York County)
S.C. Acts 1955, p. 1493, No. 604

Road Bond Assumption Act
Tex. Rev. Civ. Stat., Art. 6674q-1 et seq.

Road Bond Issue Act
Ill. Rev. Stat. 1957, Ch. 121, § 266 et seq.

Road Bonding Act (County)
Ore. Rev. Stat., 370.010 et seq.

Road Bonding Act (Six Million Dollars)
Ore. Code 1930, §§ 44-501 to 44-513

Road Bonding Act (Ten Million Dollars)
Ore. Code 1930, §§ 44-601 to 44-615

Road Camp Act
Cal. Penal Code § 4100 et seq.

Road Camp Act (Convicts)
Cal. Penal Code § 2760 et seq.

Road Camp Act (Joint County)
Cal. Penal Code § 4200 et seq.

Road Commission Act
Utah Code Ann. 1953, 27-12-27 et seq.

Road Construction and Bonding Act
Ore. Code 1930, §§ 44-801 to 44-810

Road Department Act
Fla. Stat. Ann., 334.01 et seq.

Road District Act
Mo. Rev. Stat., 233.010 et seq.

Road District Improvement Act
Cal. Statutes 1907, p. 806
Cal. Statutes 1921, p. 311

Road District Maintenance Act
Cal. Streets and Highways Code § 1550.1 et seq.

Road Districts or Counties General Bond Act
S.C. Acts 1926, p. 1001, No. 559

Road Division Law (Permanent)
Cal. Streets and Highways Code § 1160.5

Road Fund Transfer Act (Township)
Ill. Rev. Stat. 1991, Ch. 139, § 167.01 et seq.

Road Improvement Act
N.J. Laws 1903, Ch. 97
N.Y. Laws 1926, Ch. 549

Road Improvement Act (County Primary)
Okla. Stat. Ann., Title 69, § 670 et seq.

Road Improvement Act (County)
Okla. Stat. Ann., Title 69, § 685 et seq.

Road Improvement Districts Act (Counties)
Wash. Rev. Code Ann., 36.88.010 et seq.

Road Improvement Impact Fee Law
Ill. Rev. Stat. 1991, Ch. 121, § 5-901 et seq.

Road Law (Feeder)
Miss. Code Ann. 1972, § 65-10-1 et seq.

Road Maintenance District Act
Ark. General Acts 1919, p. 47, No. 69
Cal. Streets and Highways Code § 1550.1 et seq.

Road Plan Act (Federal-Aid Combined)
Cal. Streets and Highways Code § 2220 et seq.

Road Poll Tax Law
Iowa Laws 1872 (14th G. A.), Ch. 31
Wash. Laws 1893, Ch. 69, § 6 et seq.
Wash. Laws 1903, Ch. 119
Wash. Laws 1905, Ch. 156

Road Program Act (Industrial)
Wyo. Stat. Ann., § 24-5-101 et seq.

Road, Street and Highway Classification Act
Mich. Comp. Laws Ann., 247.651 et seq.

Road Superintendent Act (Kershaw County)
S.C. Code of Laws 1952, § 33-1729 et seq.

Road Superintendent Act (Overton County)
Tenn. Private Acts 1971, Ch. 164

Road System Act (State Aid)
N.J. Stat. Ann., 27:13A-1 et seq.

Road Tax Act
S.C. Code Ann. 1976, § 12-27-230 et seq.

Road Tax Act (Gross Receipts)
Va. Code 1950, § 58-638 et seq.

Road Tax Act (Motor Carriers)
N.J. Stat. Ann., 54:39A-1 et seq.
Pa. Cons. Stat., Title 75, § 9601 et seq.

Road Tax Act (Motorbus)
Pa. Cons. Stat., Title 75, § 9801 et seq.

Road Toll Act (Motor Vehicles)
N.H. Rev. Stat. 1955, 260:30 et seq.

Road Vacation Act (Counties)
Wash. Rev. Code Ann., 36.87.010 et seq.

Road Worker Safety Act
Ill. Rev. Stat. 1991, Ch. 121, § 314.01 et seq.

Roads Act (Dirt)
Conn. Gen. Stat. Ann., § 13-56 et seq.

Roads Act (Safe)
Mass. Gen. Laws Ann., 90:23, 90:24 et seq., 90C:2, 218:26, 258A:1

Roads Act (Towns)
Minn. Stat. Ann., 164.01 et seq.

Roads and Highways Act
Nev. Rev. Stat. 1979 Reprint, 408.010 et seq.
Ore. Rev. Stat., 366.005 et seq.

Roads Development Amendment
W. Va. Acts 1968, Ch. 16

Roads Employment Act
June 18, 1934, Ch. 586, 48 Stat. 995 (See 23 U.S. Code § 126)

Roads Program (Gateway)
Mass. Gen. Laws Ann., 90H:1 et seq.

Roadside Advertising Act
Mich. Comp. Laws Ann., 247.275 et seq.

Roadside Menagerie Act
Pa. 1936 Ex. Pamph. Laws 18, No. 8

Roadside Sign Act
Colo. Rev. Stat. Replaced Vols., 43-1-401 et seq.

Roadside Sign Control and Outdoor Advertising Act
N.J. Stat. Ann., 43:10-46 et seq.

Roadside Vegetation Control Information Act (Property Owners')
Cal. Food and Agricultural Code 1967, § 5501 et seq.

Roanoke Regional Airport Commission Act
Va. Acts 1986, Ch. 140

Robbery Act
Ala. Code 1975, § 13A-8-41 et seq.
Ariz. Rev. Stat. Ann., § 13-1901 et seq.
Cal. Penal Code § 211 et seq.
Ga. Code Ann., 16-8-40, 16-8-41
Ill. Rev. Stat. 1991, Ch. 38, §§ 18-1, 18-2
Md. Ann. Code 1957, Art. 27, § 486 et seq.
Mich. Comp. Laws Ann., 750.529 et seq.
Mont. Code Ann., 45-5-401
Neb. Rev. Stat. 1943, 28-324
N.H. Rev. Stat. 1955, 636:1
N.J. Rev. Stat. 2C:15-1
Okla. Stat. Ann., Title 21, § 791 et seq.
R.I. Gen. Laws 1956, 11-39-1
S.C. Code Ann. 1976, § 16-11-310 et seq.
Tenn. Code Ann., 39-13-401, 39-13-402, 39-2-502
Wash. Rev. Code Ann., 9A.56.190 et seq.

Wis. Stat. Ann., 943.32
W. Va. Code 1966, § 61-2-12

Robbery Act (Pharmacy)
Ala. Code 1975, § 13A-8-50 et seq.

Robbery, Housebreaking and Burglary Act
S.C. Code Ann. 1976, § 16-11-310 et seq.

Robbery with Firearms Act
Miss. Code Ann. 1972, § 97-3-79

Robbins-Brown Insurance Consumer Reform Act
Cal. Insurance Code §§ 675.5, 676, 676.2, 676.5, 677.2, 678.1

Robbins-Katz Los Angeles Transportation Act
Cal. Statutes 1990, Ch. 95

Robbins-McAlister Financial Responsibility Act
Cal. Statutes 1991, Ch. 946

Robbins-Nielson-Bergeson-Costa County Revenue Stabilization Act
Cal. Government Code § 16265 et seq.

Robbins-Roos-La Follette Long-Term Care Insurance Act
Cal. Insurance Code § 10230 et seq.

Robbins-Rosenthal Fair Debt Collection Practices Act
Cal. Civil Code § 1788 et seq.

Robbins-Seastrand Health Insurance Guaranty Association Act
Cal. Insurance Code § 1066 et seq.

Robbins-Vulch-Calderon Financial Institutions Act
Cal. Financial Code § 22

Roberson-Archer Act
Ala. Code 1975, § 33-5-50 et seq.

Robert A. Aft Institute Assistance Act
Oct. 3, 1980, P.L. 96-374, 94 Stat. 1502

Robert F. Kennedy Memorial Stadium and National Guard Armory Public Safety Act

D.C. Code Ann., § 2-341 et seq.

Robert H. McCabe CLAST and Other Skills Act

Fla. Laws 1995, Ch. 411

Robert J. Pierce Act

D.C. Code Ann., § 1-1202

Robert Louis Stevenson Park Act

Cal. Statutes 1945, Ch. 1453, p. 2735

Robert T. Stafford Disaster Relief and Emergency Assistance Act

May 22, 1974, P.L. 93-288, 88 Stat. 143, 12 U.S. Code §§ 1706c, 1709, 1715l; 20 U.S. Code §§ 241-1, 646, 758; 26 U.S. Code §§ 165, 5064, 5708; 31 U.S. Code § 1264; 38 U.S. Code § 1820; 40 U.S. Code § 461; 42 U.S. Code §§ 3231 to 3236; 4401 nts., 5121, 5122, 5131, 5132, 5141 to 5158, 5171 to 5184, 5186 to 5189, 5201, 5202; 48 U.S. Code § 1681 nt.

June 20, 1977, P.L. 95-51, 42 U.S. Code § 5202

July 2, 1986, P.L. 99-349, 7 U.S. Code § 1441-1 nt.

Nov. 23, 1988, P.L. 100-707, 12 U.S. Code § 5121 nt.; 42 U.S. Code § 5121 nt.

Nov. 16, 1990, P.L. 101-591, 16 U.S. Code § 3505 nt.

Feb. 24, 1992, P.L. 102-247, 42 U.S. Code § 5122

Dec. 3, 1993, P.L. 103-181, 42 U.S. Code §§ 5170c, 5170c nt.

Sept. 23, 1994, P.L. 103-325, 42 U.S. Code § 5154

Oct. 5, 1994, P.L. 103-337, 12 U.S. Code §§ 1706c, 1709, 1715l; 20 U.S. Code §§ 241-1, 646; 26 U.S. Code §§ 165, 5064, 5708; 38 U.S. Code § 3720; 42 U.S. Code §§ 5132, 5201, 4401 nt., 5121 nt.

Dec. 21, 1995, P.L. 104-66, 42 U.S. Code § 5196

Robert W. Crown Children's Services Act

Cal. Health and Safety Code § 248 et seq.

Roberti-Greene Home Purchase Assistance Program

Cal. Health and Safety Code § 51341 et seq.

Roberti-Imbrecht-Rains-Goggin Child Sexual Abuse Prevention Act

Cal. Statutes 1981, Ch. 1064

Roberti Intergenerational Education Act

Cal. Education Code 1976, § 33470 et seq.

Roberti-Roos Assault Weapons Control Act

Cal. Penal Code § 12275 et seq.

Roberti-Rosenthal Item Pricing Act

Cal. Civil Code § 7100 et seq.

Roberti-Z'berg-Harris Urban Open-Space and Recreation Program Act

Cal. Public Resources Code § 5620 et seq.

Roberts Act

Aug. 30, 1964, P.L. 88-515, 40 U.S. Code §§ 701 to 703

Roberts Act (Minimum Wage)

Ohio Rev. Code 1953, 4115.03 et seq.

Roberts-Burke Employers' Liability Act

La. Rev. Stat. Ann., 23:1021 et seq.

Roberts-Gillen Act (State Insurance Fund)

Ohio Laws Vol. 114, p. 26

Roberts-Goodwin Act (Gasoline Tax)

Ohio Rev. Code 1953, 4501.04, 5735.23

Roberts-Pringle Act (Bonds)

Ohio Laws Vol. 114, p. 11

Robertson Act (Insurance Company Investments)

Tex. Insurance Code, Art. 3.33

Robertson County Jury Commission Act

Tenn. Private Acts 1925, Ch. 169

Robertson-Fitzhugh Liquor Act

Tex. Bus. and Commerce Code, § 15.01 et seq.

Tex. Penal Code 1911, Art. 611 et seq.

Robertson-Pearson Act (Prison-Made Goods)
Ala. Code 1975, § 14-7-6 et seq.

Robertson-Pittman Act
See Wild Life Restoration Act

Robertson-Pittman Enabling Act (Wildlife Restoration)
Mich. Comp. Laws 1979, 299.201

Robin Hood Law
Tex. Education Code, Art. 16.001 et seq.

Robins Rape Evidence Law
Cal. Evidence Code §§ 782, 1103

Robinson-Embry Act (Intoxicating Liquors)
Ky. Rev. Stat. 1971, 244.290, 244.480

Robinson Farm Bureau Act
Ky. Rev. Stat. 1971, 247.240 et seq.

Robinson Jury Law
Ala. Code 1958, Title 62, § 207 et seq.

Robinson-Patman Act
May 26, 1938, Ch. 283, 52 Stat. 446, 15 U.S. Code § 13c

Robinson-Patman Anti-Discrimination Act
June 19, 1936, Ch. 592, 15 U.S. Code §§ 13 to 13b, 21a
May 26, 1938, Ch. 283, 15 U.S. Code § 13c

Robinson-Patman Price Discrimination Act
June 19, 1936, Ch. 592, 49 Stat. 1526, 15 U.S. Code §§ 13 to 13b, 21a

Robinson, Vance and Blake Act (Soil Conservation)
Ky. Rev. Stat. 1971, 262.010 et seq.

Rochester City Court Act
N.Y. Laws 1918, Ch. 495, § 10
N.Y. Laws 1950, Ch. 771

Rochester-Genesee Regional Transportation Authority Act
N.Y. Public Authorities Law (Consol. Laws Ch. 43A) § 1299aa et seq.

Rochester-Monroe County Port Authority Act
N.Y. Public Authorities Law (Consol. Laws Ch. 43A) § 1349a et seq.

Rock and Coal Dust Act
Ind. Code Ann., 22-10-8-1, 22-10-8-2

Rock Creek Park Act
D.C. Code Ann., § 8-140 et seq.

Rock Island Railroad Transition and Employee Assistance Act
May 30, 1980, P.L. 96-254, 45 U.S. Code §§ 1001 et seq.
Nov. 8, 1984, P.L. 98-620, 45 U.S. Code § 1018
April 7, 1986, P.L. 99-272, 45 U.S. Code § 797b nt.
Dec. 29, 1995, P.L. 104-88, 45 U.S. Code §§ 1003, 1015

Rock Mining Act
Mont. Code Ann., 82-4-301 et seq.

Rock Road Act
Kan. Stat. Ann., 68-701 et seq.

Rockdale County-Conyers Charter Commission Act
Ga. Laws 1988, p. 3899

Rockdale County Water and Sewerage Authority Act
Ga. Laws 1995, p. 3994

Rockford Civic Center Act
Ill. Rev. Stat. 1991, Ch. 85, § 1331 et seq.

Rockford Off Street Parking Act
Ill. Rev. Stat. 1991, Ch. 127, §§ 3470, 3471

Rockland County Stream Control Act
N.Y. Laws 1975, Ch. 846

Rockland-Westchester Hudson River Crossing Authority Act
N.Y. Public Authorities Law (Consol. Laws Ch. 43A) § 600 et seq.

Rockport Granite Company Pier Loan Act
Mass. Acts 1956, Ch. 604

Rockwell-Anderson Environmental Protection Act
Mich. Comp. Laws Ann., 691.1201 et seq.

Rocky Mountain Arsenal National Wildlife Refuge Act of 1992
Oct. 9, 1992, P.L. 102-402, 16 U.S. Code § 668dd nt.

Rocky Mountain Low-level Radioactive Waste Compact
Jan. 15, 1986, P.L. 99-240, 99 Stat. 1902

Rocky Mountain Low-Level Radioactive Waste Compact Act
Colo. Rev. Stat., 24-60-2201 et seq.
N.D. Cent. Code 23-20.5-01 et seq.
Nev. Rev. Stat. 1979 Reprint, 459.007, 459.008
N.M. Stat. Ann., 11-9A-1 et seq.
Wyo. Stat. Ann., § 9-6-201 et seq.

Rocky Mountain National Park Act
Jan. 26, 1915, Ch. 19, 38 Stat. 798, 16 U.S. Code §§ 191, 193 to 195

Rodda Act (Collective Bargaining)
Cal. Government Code § 3540 et seq.

Rodda-Montoya Act (Education)
Cal. Statutes 1976, Ch. 323

Rodda-Moretti-Lewis-Brown Child Development Act
Cal. Education Code 1976, § 8200 et seq.

Rodent Control Act
R.I. Gen. Laws 1956, 23-7.1-1 et seq.
S.D. Codified Laws 1967, 38-20-1 et seq.

Rodent Extermination Law
Cal. Health and Safety Code § 1800 et seq.

Rodenticide Act
N.C. Gen. Stat. 1943, § 143-434 et seq.

Rodenticide, Insecticide and Fungicide Act
Colo. Rev. Stat. 35-9-101 et seq.
Mich. Comp. Laws Ann., 286.557 et seq.

Miss. Code Ann. 1972, §§ 69-23-3, 69-23-107
Mont. Rev. Code 1947, 27-201 et seq.
N.C. Gen. Stat. 1943, § 143-434 et seq.
N.D. Cent. Code, 19-18-01 et seq.
S.D. Codified Laws 1967, 38-20A-1 et seq.
Tenn. Code Ann., 43-8-101 et seq.
Tex. Agricultural Code, § 76.001 et seq.
Utah Code Ann. 1953, 4-14-1 et seq.
Va. Code 1950, § 3.1-189 et seq.
Vt. Stat. Ann., Title 6, § 911 et seq.

Rogan Act (Reapportionment)
Wis. Stat. Ann., 4.01, 4.02

Roger Wells Act (Park City)
Ky. Acts 1938, Ch. 64

Rogers Act (Firemen and Policemen)
Ala. Code 1958 Title 29, § 9

Roger's Act (Foreign Service)
See Foreign Service Act

Rogers Act (Public Utilities)
Ohio Rev. Code 1953, 745.01 et seq.

Rogers-Allen Act (Milk Control)
N.Y. Agriculture and Markets Law (Consol. Laws Ch. 69) § 258k et seq.

Rogers-Allen Act (Milk Pricing)
N.Y. Agriculture and Markets Law (Consol. Laws Ch. 69) § 258m

Rogue River Closing Act
Ore. Rev. Stat., 511.205 et seq.

Rogues and Vagabonds Act
Md. Ann. Code 1957, Art. 27, § 490

Roll Back Act (Millage Tax)
Fla. Stat. Ann., 236.251

Roll Back Act (Taxation)
Ky. Rev. Stat. 1971, 132.010 et seq.

Roller Skating Rink Safety and Fair Liability Act
N.J. Stat. Ann., 5:14-1 to 5:14-7

Roller Skating Safety Act
Ga. Code Ann., 51-1-43
Me. Rev. Stat. Ann. 1964, Title 8, § 603 et seq.
Mich. Comp. Laws Ann., 445.1721 et seq.

Rolling Store Tax Act (Motor Vehicle)
Ga. Code 1933, 92-2950 et seq.

Romano-Cihak-Montgomery Act (Charter Townships)
Mich. Comp. Laws Ann., 42.1 et seq.

Rome City Court Act
N.Y. Laws 1954, Ch. 579

Rome Development Authority Act (Historic)
N.Y. Public Authorities Law (Consol. Laws Ch. 43A) § 1900 et seq.

Ron Ennis Memorial Act
Fla. Stat. Ann., 553.482

Ronald McCurdy and Walter Thomas Act
Ala. Acts 1990, No. 339

Roofing Industry Licensing Act
Ill. Rev. Stat. 1991, Ch. 111, § 7501 et seq.

Room and Board Home Care Act
Okla. Stat. Ann., Title 63, § 1-820 et seq.

Room Occupancy Excise Tax Act
Mass. Gen. Laws Ann., 64G:1 et seq.

Rooming and Boarding House Act
N.J. Stat. Ann., 55:13B-1 et seq.

Rooms and Meals Tax Act
N.H. Rev. Stat. 1955, 78-A:1 et seq.
Vt. Stat. Ann., Title 32, § 9201 et seq.

Roos-Johnson-Marks Property Tax Limitation Act
Cal. Revenue and Tax Code §§ 97.2, 97.65

Roos-Marks Local Bond Pooling Act
Cal. Government Code § 6584 et seq.

Roos-Roberti Assault Weapons Control Act
Cal. Penal Code § 12275 et seq.

Roosevelt Campobello International Park Act
July 7, 1964, P.L. 88-363, 78 Stat. 299, 16 U.S. Code § 1101 to 1113

Roosevelt-Hamilton Act (Mortgage Moratorium)
Mich. Public Acts 1937, No. 1

Roosevelt Highway Bill
Ore. Code 1930, §§ 44-1101 to 44-1109

Roosevelt Library Act
July 18, 1939, Ch. 324, 53 Stat. 1062

Roosevelt-Watson Act (Land Contract Moratorium)
Mich. Public Acts 1937, No. 2

Root-Jarvis Act (Pari-Mutuel Horse Racing)
Mich. Comp. Laws Ann., 431.1 et seq.

Root-Jarvis-Mosier-Case Act (Fresh Fruit)
Mich. Comp. Laws Ann., 286.341 et seq.

Rope Act (Fire Escapes)
Okla. Stat. Ann., Title 63, § 172

Rose-Blanford Long-Term Policy Act
Ky. Rev. Stat. 1971, 7B.010 et seq.

Rose-Knuckles Teachers' Refund Measure
Ky. Acts 1934 (Ex. Sess.) Ch. 12

Roseberry Act (Employers' Liability)
Cal. Labor Code § 2801
Cal. Statutes 1911, p. 796

Rosemary Elebash Call Before You Dig Act
Ala. Acts 1994, p. 922, No. 489

Rosenberry Act (Reapportionment)
Wis. Stat. Ann., 4.001, 4.002

Rosenman Act (Emergency Rent Law)
N.Y. Laws 1923, Ch. 892

Rosenthal-Farr Motion Picture Marketing Act
Cal. Government Code § 15335.22

Rosenthal-Naylor Act
Cal. Public Resources Code § 25680 et seq.

Rosenthal-Robbins Auto Insurance Nondescription Law
Cal. Insurance Code § 11628

Rosenthal-Roberti Item Pricing Act
Cal. Civil Code § 7100 et seq.

Rose's Law
Ala. Code 1975, § 27-48-2

Rossmoor Special Community Services District Law
Cal. Government Code § 60400 et seq.

Rossville Charter
Tenn. Private Acts 1972, Ch. 289

Roster of Public Agencies Act
Cal. Government Code § 53050 et seq.

Roswell Park Cancer Institute Corporation Act
N.Y. Public Authorities Law (Consol. Laws Ch. 43A) § 3550 et seq.

Roth Act (Conversions to Condominium)
Fla. Stat. Ann., 718.604 et seq.

Roth Cooperative Conversion Act
Fla. Stat. Ann., 719.604 et seq.

Rotterdam Burglar, Fire, and Other Emergency Alarms Law
N.Y. Local Laws 1973, Town of Rotterdam, p. 2871

Rotterdam Dangerous Buildings and Structures Law
N.Y. Local Laws 1969, Town of Rotterdam, p. 2041

Rotterdam Motorcycle Law
N.Y. Local Laws 1972, Town of Rotterdam, p. 2807

Rotterdam Snowmobiles Law
N.Y. Local Laws 1972, Town of Rotterdam, p. 2808

Rough Cull Law
N.J. Stat. Ann., 50:2-7 to 50:2-9

Round Lake Local Law Relating to Zoning
N.Y. Local Laws 1971, Village of Round Lake, p. 4458

Round Valley Act
N.J. Stat. Ann., 58:20-1 et seq.

Rout Act
Ind. Code 1971, 35-1-77-9 et seq.

Route 66 Study Act of 1990
Sept. 28, 1990, P.L. 101-400, 104 Stat. 861

Rowell-Smith Martin-Hittle-Burke Act (Occupational Disease)
Mich. Comp. Laws Ann., 418.401 et seq.

Rowlett Municipal Courts of Record Act
Tex. Government Code, § 30.01291 et seq.

Rowley Water Loan Act
Mass. Acts 1954, Ch. 204

Roy E. Campbell Trauma Act
Fla. Stat. Ann., 395.0146, 395.031, 395.033 to 395.037

Royalty Adjustment Act of 1942
Oct. 31, 1942, Ch. 634, 56 Stat. 1013

Royalty Tax Act (Mining)
Minn. Stat. 1986, 299.01 et seq.

Royce-Thompson Police and Bystander Protection and Safe Pursuit Act
Cal. Statutes 1991, Ch. 1048
Cal. Vehicle Code 1959, § 14602.1

Royer Act (Taxation)
Ohio Laws Vol. 94, p. 336

Rubber Act of 1948
March 31, 1948, Ch. 166, 62 Stat. 101, 50 U.S. Code Appx. §§ 1921, 1921 nt., 1922, 1938
June 24, 1950, Ch. 357, 64 Stat. 256, 50 U.S. Code Appx. §§ 1928, 1938
June 23, 1952, Ch. 453, 66 Stat. 154, 50 U.S. Code Appx. §§ 1928, 1938

Aug. 7, 1953, Ch. 338, § 22, 67 Stat. 415, 50 U.S. Code Appx. §§ 1941t, 1938

Rubber Producing Facilities Disposal Act of 1953

Aug. 7, 1953, Ch. 338, 67 Stat. 408, 50 U.S. Code Appx. § 1941 nt.

March 31, 1955, Ch. 19, 69 Stat. 15, 50 U.S. Code Appx. § 1941w

Aug. 9, 1955, Ch. 696, 69 Stat. 628, 50 U.S. Code Appx. §§ 1938 nt., 1941r nt., 1941x

Rubenstein Act (County Probation Department)

Ohio Laws Vol. 111, p. 423

Rudee Inlet Authority Act

Va. Acts 1990, Ch. 227

Rugby Historic Preservation Act

Tenn. Public Acts 1972, Ch. 821

Ruh Act (Functions and Resources)

Ky. Acts 1950, Ch. 124

Rule against Perpetuities

See also Uniform Statutory Rule against Perpetuities

See Perpetuities Act

Mass. Gen. Laws Ann., 184A:1 et seq.

Me. Rev. Stat. Ann. 1964, Title 33, § 101 et seq.

Rule for Practical Training of Law Students

Nev. Supreme Court Rule 49.5

Rule in Shelley's Case Abolishment Act

Ill. Rev. Stat. 1991, Ch. 30, § 185.9 et seq.

Iowa Code Ann., 557.20

Rule in Shelley's Case Act

Conn. Gen. Stat. Ann., § 51-14

Ind. Code Ann., 34-5-2-1, 34-5-2-2

Tex. Government Code, § 22.003

Rule Making Act (Bar Examination)

Ga. Code Ann., 15-19-3

Rule Making Act (State Boards)

Ind. Code Ann., 4-22-2-1 et seq.

Rule Making Enabling Act (Supreme Court)

Ga. Code Ann., 15-2-18

Rule of the Road at Sea

See International Rules (Collisions at Sea)

Rulemaking Act (Negotiated)

Mont. Code Ann., 2-5-101 et seq.

Rules Act (State Agencies)

N.M. Stat. Ann. 1978, 14-4-1 et seq.

Rules and Regulations Act

P.R. Laws Ann. 1954, Title 3, § 1041 et seq.

Rules and Regulations Filing Act

Ala. Code 1958, Title 13, § 17(2)

Kan. Stat. Ann., 77-415 et seq.

Me. Rev. Stat. Ann. 1964, Title 4, § 8

Rules for Administration of Assets Held by the Commissioners of the Land Office

Okla. Stat. Ann., Title 64, § 161

Rules for Legislative Investigations

Me. Rev. Stat. Ann. 1964, Title 3, § 401 et seq.

Rules of Appellate Procedure

Mont. Code Ann., Title 25, Ch. 21

Rules of Civil Appellate Procedure

S.D. Codified Laws 1967, 15-26A-1 et seq.

Rules of Civil Procedure

Kan. Stat. Ann., 60-201 et seq.

Mont. Code Ann., Title 25, Ch. 20

Rules of Civil Procedure for Limited Actions

Kan. Stat. Ann., 61-1701 et seq.

Rules of Construction Act

Kan. Stat. Ann., 77-201

Rules of Criminal Procedure

Iowa Code Ann., 813.1 et seq.

S.D. Codified Laws 1967, 23A-1-1 et seq.

Rules of Decisions Act
June 25, 1948, Ch. 646, 62 Stat. 944, 28 U.S. Code § 1652

Rules of Evidence
Wis. Stat. Ann., 901.01 et seq.

Rules of Evidence Act
Ark. Code Ann. 1987, 16-41-101
Mont. Code Ann., Title 26, Ch. 10
Neb. Rev. Stat. 1943, 27-101 et seq.
N.J. Stat. Ann., 2A:84A-1 et seq.
S.D. Codified Laws 1967, 19-9-1 et seq.

Rules of Navigation Act
Wash. Rev. Code Ann., 88.04.005 et seq.

Rules of Practice Act
Tex. Government Code, § 22.003

Rules of the Road Act (Motor Vehicles)
Ala. Code 1975, § 32-5A-1 et seq.
Cal. Vehicle Code 1959, § 21000 et seq.
Del. Code of 1974, Title 21, § 4101 et seq.
Ga. Code Ann., 40-6-1 et seq.
Iowa Code 1977, 321.1 et seq.
Kan. Stat. Ann., 8-1501 et seq.
Me. Rev. Stat. Ann. 1964, Title 29, § 941 et seq.
Mich. Comp. Laws Ann., 257.634 et seq.
Neb. Rev. Stat. 1943, 39-601 et seq.
R.I. Gen. Laws 1956, 31-15-1 et seq.
Tenn. Code Ann., 55-8-101 et seq.
Wash. Rev. Code Ann., 46.61.005 et seq.

Rumanian Declaration of War
June 5, 1942, Ch. 325, 56 Stat. 307, 50 U.S. Code Appx. nt. prec. § 1

Rumford Fair Housing Act
Cal. Health and Safety Code § 35700 et seq.

Run of Mine Act
Ohio Laws Vol. 104, p. 181

Runaway and Homeless Youth Act
La. Rev. Stat. Ann., 46:1351 et seq.
N.Y. Executive Law 1951 (Consol. Laws Ch. 18) § 532 et seq.

Runaway and Homeless Youth Act of 1974
Sept. 7, 1974, P.L. 93-415, 88 Stat. 1129, 42 U.S. Code §§ 5701, 5702, 5711 to 5716, 5731, 5732, 5751
Oct. 3, 1977, P.L. 95-115, 91 Stat. 1058, 42 U.S. Code §§ 5711 to 5713, 5731, 5732 nt., 5741, 5751
Dec. 8, 1980, P.L. 96-509, 94 Stat. 2750, 2761, 42 U.S. Code §§ 5601 nt., 5711 to 5713, 5715, 5751
Oct. 12, 1984, P.L. 98-473, 42 U.S. Code § 5702
Nov. 18, 1988, P.L. 100-690, 42 U.S. Code § 5711 et seq.
Dec. 7, 1989, P.L. 101-204, 42 U.S. Code § 5715
Nov. 4, 1992, P.L. 102-586, 42 U.S. Code §§ 5711, 5712a, 5712b, 5712c, 5713, 5714, prec. 5714a, 5714a, 5714b, prec. 5714-11, 5714-11, 5714-21, 5714-22, 5714-23, 5714-24, prec. 5715, 5715, 5716, 5731, 5732, 5733, 5751
Sept. 13, 1994, P.L. 103-322, 42 U.S. Code § 5712d

Runaway Father Law
Ind. Code Ann., 31-2-1-1 et seq.

Runaway Pappy Act
Ala. Code 1975, § 30-4-80 et seq.
Ark. Code Ann. 1987, 9-14-301 et seq.
Ind. Code Ann., 31-2-1-1 et seq.
Kan. Stat. Ann., 23-451 et seq.
Mich. Comp. Laws Ann., 780.151 et seq.
Minn. Stat. Ann., 518.41 et seq.
Miss. Code Ann. 1972, § 93-11-1 et seq.
N.C. Gen. Stat. 1943, § 52A-1 et seq.
Pa. Cons. Stat., Title 23, § 4501 et seq.
Tex. Family Code, § 21.01 et seq.

Runaway Parent Act
N.M. Stat. Ann., 40-6-1 et seq.
Tenn. Code Ann., 36-5-201

Runaway Youth Act
Sept. 7, 1974, P.L. 93-415, 88 Stat. 1129, 42 U.S. Code §§ 5701, 5702, 5711 to 5716, 5731, 5732, 5751
Tenn. Code Ann., 37-2-501 et seq.
Wash. Rev. Code Ann., 13.30.010 et seq.

Runaway Youth and Family Act
Fla. Stat. Ann., 409.441

Runners and Cappers Act (Attorneys)
Cal. Business and Professions Code § 6150 et seq.
Va. Code 1950, § 54.1-3939 et seq.

Runners and Cappers Law (Dentists)
Cal. Business and Professions Code § 1680, Subd. a

Runners and Cappers Law (Embalmers and Funeral Directors)
Cal. Business and Professions Code § 7695 et seq.

Runners and Cappers Law (Optometrists)
Cal. Business and Professions Code § 3100

Runners and Cappers Law (Physicians)
Cal. Business and Professions Code § 2399

Runoff Primary Election Act
Ark. Acts 1933, p. 109, No. 38
Okla. Laws 1929, Special Session, p. 303

Runoff Primary Law (New York City)
N.Y. Election Law 1976 (Consol. Laws Ch. 17) §§ 6-162, 8-100, 16-116

Rural Access Program (RAP) Act
Ala. Code 1975, § 23-1-330 et seq.

Rural Affairs Act
N.Y. Executive Law 1951 (Consol. Laws Ch. 18) § 480 et seq.

Rural Aid Act (Schools)
Tex. General and Special Laws 47th Leg., 1941, p. 880, Ch. 549
Tex. General Laws 43rd Leg., 1933, p. 627, Ch. 211

Rural Air Service Survival Act
Oct. 9, 1996, P.L. 104-264, § 278, 49 U.S. Code § 40101 nt.

Rural Ambulance Service Districts Act
Okla. Stat. 1981, Title 19, § 1201 et seq.

Rural and Agricultural Youth Development Act
Pa. 1991 Pamph. Laws, No. 33

Rural and Community Development Loan Program
Iowa Code Ann., 15.281 et seq.

Rural and Intercity Common Carrier Surface Transportation Surface Transportation Assistance Act
Pa. Purdon's Stat., Title 55, §§ 651 et seq.

Rural and Municipal Electrification Cooperative Agency Act
Me. Rev. Stat. Ann. 1964, Title 35-A, § 4101 et seq.
Me. Rev. Stat. Ann. 1964, Title 35-A, § 4101 et seq.

Rural and Urban Enterprise Zone Act
Colo. Rev. Stat. Ann., 39-30-101 et seq.

Rural and Urban Teacher Loan Forgiveness Act
Pa. Purdon's Stat., Title 24, § 5191 et seq.

Rural and Urban Transit Districts Act
Tex. Transportation Code, § 458.001 et seq.

Rural Bond Bank Act
Ill. Rev. Stat. 1991, Ch. 17, § 7201-1 et seq.

Rural Cemetery Act
Mich. Comp. Laws Ann., 456.101 et seq.
N.Y. Laws 1847, Ch. 133

Rural Cemetery Associations Act
Ida. Code 1947, 27-201 et seq.
N.J. Stat. Ann., 8A:1-1 et seq.

Rural Cemetery District Act
Neb. Rev. Stat. 1943, 12-909 et seq.

Rural Community Development Act
Iowa Code Ann., 387.1 et seq.

Rural Credit Union Act
Tex. Rev. Civ. Stat., Art. 2461-1.01 et seq.

Rural Credits Act
Minn. Stat. Ann., 41.51 et seq.
Miss. Code Ann. 1972, § 81-15-1 et seq.
Ore. Code 1930, §§ 60-1101 to 60-1111
S.D. Code 1939, 55.3201 et seq.

Rural Credits Acts
See Federal Farm Loan Acts

Rural Crisis Recovery Program Act of 1987
Dec. 29, 1987, P.L. 100-219, 7 U.S. Code
§§ 2661 nt., 2662

Rural Development Act
Alaska Stat. 1962, § 44.47.130 et seq.
La. Rev. Stat. Ann., 3:291 et seq.
S.C. Acts 1996 Ex. Sess., p. 3818, No. 462

Rural Development Act of 1972
Aug. 30, 1972, P.L. 92-419, 86 Stat. 657, 5
U.S. Code § 5315; 7 U.S. Code §§ 1006,
1010a, 1011, 1921 nt., 1924 to 1927, 1929,
1929a, 1931 to 1933, 1941 to 1943; 16 U.S.
Code §§ 590g, 590h, 590o, 1001 to 1005;
42 U.S. Code § 3122
Aug. 10, 1973, P.L. 93-86, 87 Stat. 240, 7
U.S. Code §§ 2651, 2654
Sept. 29, 1977, P.L. 95-113, 7 U.S. Code
§§ 2662 et seq., 2269
July 1, 1978, P.L. 95-313, 16 U.S. Code
§§ 2651 to 2654
Dec. 23, 1985, P.L. 99-198, 7 U.S. Code
§§ 2662, 2663
Dec. 29, 1987, P.L. 100-219, 7 U.S. Code
§ 2662
Nov. 28, 1990, P.L. 101-624, 7 U.S. Code
§§ 2662, 2662 nt., 2663
Dec. 13, 1991, P.L. 102-237, 7 U.S. Code
§§ 2662, 2663
Oct. 13, 1994, P.L. 103-354, 7 U.S. Code
§ 2212a
April 4, 1996, P.L. 104-127, 7 U.S. Code
§§ 2204b, 2662, 2663

**Rural Development, Agricultural, And
Related Agencies Appropriations Act,
1987**
Oct. 18, 1986, P.L. 99-500, 7 U.S. Code
§ 940a
Dec. 22, 1987, P.L. 100-202, 101 Stat. 1329
Dec. 22, 1987, P.L. 100-203, 7 U.S. Code
§§ 940b, 940c, 946, 948

**Rural Development, Agricultural and
Related Agencies Appropriations Act,
1989**
Oct. 1, 1988, P.L. 100-460, 102 Stat. 2267

**Rural Development, Agriculture, and
Related Agencies Appropriations Act,
1990**
Nov. 21, 1989, P.L. 101-161, 103 Stat. 951

**Rural Development, Agriculture, and
Related Agencies Appropriations Act,
1991**
Nov. 5, 1990, P.L. 101-506, 104 Stat. 1315
April 10, 1991, P.L. 102-27, 105 Stat. 133

**Rural Development, Agriculture, and
Related Agencies Appropriations Act,
1997**
Oct. 19, 1996, P.L. 104-316, 7 U.S. Code
§ 2207a

Rural Development Authority Act
Ark. Code Ann. 1987, 14-188-101 et seq.
N.C. Laws 1965, Ch. 988

Rural Development Corporation Act
P.R. Laws Ann. 1954, Title 5, § 1701 et seq.

Rural Development Finance Authority Act
Minn. Stat. Ann., 362A.01 et seq.

Rural Development Loan Act
La. Rev. Stat. Ann., 51:951 et seq.

Rural Development Policy Act of 1980
Sept. 24, 1980, P.L. 96-355, 7 U.S. Code
§ 2201 nt.
Oct. 13, 1994, P.L. 103-354, 7 U.S. Code
§ 2211b

Rural Diversification Act
Ill. Rev. Stat. 1991, Ch. 5, § 2251 et seq.

Rural Economic Action Plan
Okla. Stat. Ann., Title 62, § 2001 et seq.

Rural Economic Development Act
Cal. Government Code § 15373 et seq.
Ga. Code Ann., 50-8-120 et seq.
Ill. Rev. Stat. 1991, Ch. 5, § 2201-1 et seq.
Tex. Government Code, § 481.081 et seq.

Rural Economic Development Act of 1990

Nov. 28, 1990, P.L. 101-624, 7 U.S. Code §§ 141 nt., 411a, 950aaa to 950aaa-4, 1421 nt., 1421b to 1421d, 1921 nts., 1926-1, 1926b nt., 1932 nt., 2001a nt., 2007 nt., 2007 to 2007e, 2204d, 2279, 2262, 2262a, 2263, 3125b, 6601, 13 U.S. Code §§ 141 nt., 142 nt., 15 U.S. Code § 714 nt., 18 U.S. Code §§ 657, 658, 1006, 1014, 21 U.S. Code §§ 114a, 114b, 114i, 136, 136a, 147a

Rural Economic Development Program Act

Pa. Purdon's Stat., Title 73, § 392.101 et seq.

Rural Education Research Program Act

N.Y. Education Law 1947 (Consol. Laws Ch. 16) § 1201 et seq.

Rural Electric and Community Services Cooperative Act

Tenn. Code Ann., 65-26-101 et seq.

Rural Electric and Telephone Cooperative Act

Mont. Code Ann., 35-18-101 et seq.

Rural Electric Cooperative Act

Conn. Gen. Stat. Ann., § 33-218 et seq.

Fla. Stat. Ann., 425.01 et seq.

Mo. Rev. Stat., 394.010 et seq.

N.M. Stat. Ann. 1978, 62-15-1 et seq.

N.Y. Consol. Laws, Ch. 77A

Okla. Stat. 1981, Title 18, § 437 et seq.

S.C. Code Ann. 1976, § 33-49-10 et seq.

S.D. Codified Laws 1967, 47-21-1 et seq.

Rural Electric Cooperative Corporation Act

Ky. Rev. Stat. 1971, 279.010 et seq.

Rural Electric Membership Corporation Act

Ind. Code Ann., 8-1-13-1 et seq.

Rural Electrification Act

Ariz. Rev. Stat. Ann., § 10-751 et seq.

Ga. Code Ann., 46-3-170

La. Rev. Stat. Ann., 45:121 et seq.

N.C. Gen. Stat. 1943, § 117-1 et seq.

N.D. Cent. Code, 10-13-01 et seq.

Neb. Rev. Stat. 1943, 70-701 et seq.

N.H. Rev. Stat. 1955, 301:53 et seq.

S.C. Acts 1933, p. 362, No. 275

Va. Code 1950, § 56-209 et seq.

Rural Electrification Act (Cooperative Corporation)

Ark. Code Ann. 1987, 23-18-301 et seq.

Rural Electrification Act of 1936

May 20, 1936, Ch. 432, 49 Stat. 1363, 7 U.S. Code §§ 901 to 914

Sept. 21, 1944, Ch. 412, 58 Stat. 739, 7 U.S. Code §§ 903 to 905

Dec. 23, 1944, Ch. 725, 58 Stat. 925, 7 U.S. Code § 904

Oct. 28, 1949, Ch. 776, 63 Stat. 948, 7 U.S. Code §§ 901 to 924

June 15, 1955, Ch. 139, 69 Stat. 131, 7 U.S. Code §§ 903, 904

Oct. 23, 1962, P.L. 87-862, 76 Stat. 1140, 7 U.S. Code § 924

May 7, 1971, P.L. 92-12, 85 Stat. 29, 7 U.S. Code §§ 903, 922, 931, 932, 941 to 950b

June 30, 1972, P.L. 92-324, 86 Stat. 390, 7 U.S. Code § 947

May 11, 1973, P.L. 93-32, 87 Stat. 65, 7 U.S. Code §§ 903, 906a, 930 to 940, 945 to 948

Nov. 4, 1975, P.L. 94-124, 89 Stat. 677, 7 U.S. Code §§ 906, 936, 938

July 2, 1986, P.L. 99-349, 7 U.S. Code § 936 nt.

Oct. 21, 1986, P.L. 99-509, 7 U.S. Code § 936a

Oct. 30, 1986, P.L. 99-591, 7 U.S. Code § 940a

Nov. 5, 1990, P.L. 101-508, 7 U.S. Code § 940d

Nov. 28, 1990, P.L. 101-624, 7 U.S. Code §§ 911a, 912, 917, 918, 924 to 928, 932, 932b, 939, 945 to 948, 950, 950aa, 950aa-1

Dec. 13, 1991, P.L. 102-237, 7 U.S. Code §§ 911a, 917, 950aa, 950aa-1

Oct. 21, 1992, P.L. 102-428, 7 U.S. Code § 936b

Aug. 10, 1993, P.L. 103-66, 7 U.S. Code §§ 936c

Nov. 1, 1993, P.L. 103-129, 7 U.S. Code §§ 901 nt., 902, 904, 913, 924, 935, 936c to 936e, 937, 939, 940d, 946, 948, 1926, 2006f, 2008e

Dec. 8, 1993, P.L. 103-182, 7 U.S. Code § 903 nt.

Dec. 17, 1993, P.L. 103-201, 7 U.S. Code § 936e

Continued

Oct. 13, 1994, P.L. 103-354, 7 U.S. Code
§§ 901 et seq.

Dec. 21, 1995, P.L. 104-66, 7 U.S. Code
§ 948

April 4, 1996, P.L. 104-127, 7 U.S. Code
§§ 902 et seq., 917, 931, 932, 939, 940a,
946, 950aa, 950aa-1

Rural Electrification Act of 1938

June 21, 1938, Ch. 554, 52 Stat. 818, 7 U.S.
Code § 903

Oct. 13, 1994, P.L. 103-354, 7 U.S. Code
§ 903 nt.

Dec. 8, 1994, P.L. 103-465, 7 U.S. Code
§ 903 nt.

**Rural Electrification Administration
Improvement Act of 1992**

Oct. 21, 1992, P.L. 102-428, 7 U.S. Code
§§ 901 nt., 936b

**Rural Electrification Administration
Technical Amendments Act of 1976**

Oct. 20, 1976, P.L. 94-570, 7 U.S. Code
§§ 901 et seq.

Rural Electrification Authority Act

Ala. General Acts 1935, p. 110
Miss. Code Ann. 1972, § 77-5-1 et seq.
N.M. Stat. Ann., 45-3-1 et seq.
S.C. Code Ann. 1976, § 58-29-10 et seq.
Tenn. Code Ann., 65-23-101 et seq.

**Rural Electrification Cooperative Enabling
Act**

Me. Rev. Stat. Ann. 1964, Title 35-A, § 3701
et seq.

Rural Electrification Transfer Act

S.C. Acts 1940, p. 2059, No. 1030

Rural Energy Conservation Act

Ill. Rev. Stat. 1991, Ch. 5, § 2202-1 et seq.

Rural Finance Administration Act

Minn. Stat. Ann., 41B.01 et seq.

Rural Fire Districts Act

Mont. Code Ann., 7-33-2101 et seq.
Neb. Rev. Stat. 1943, 35-501 et seq.

Rural Fire Protection Districts Act

N.D. Cent. Code, 18-10-01 et seq.
Ore. Rev. Stat., 478.002 et seq.
S.D. Codified Laws 1967, 34-31A-1 et seq.

Rural Fire Protection Program Fund Act

Okla. Stat. Ann., Title 19, § 901.55 et seq.

**Rural Health and Safety Education Act of
1990**

Nov. 28, 1990, P.L. 101-624, 7 U.S. Code
§ 2661 nt.

Rural Health Care System Act (Statewide)

Tex. Insurance Code, Art. 20C.01 et seq.

Rural Health Clinics Act of 1983

Dec. 1, 1983, P.L. 98-194, 42 U.S. Code
§ 201 nt.

Rural Health Initiative Act

W. Va. Code 1966, § 18B-16-1 et seq.

Rural Health Opportunities Loan Act

Neb. Rev. Stat. 1943, 71-5671 et seq.

Rural Health Services Revolving Fund Act

Ark. Code Ann. 1987, 20-12-401 et seq.

**Rural Health Systems and Professional
Incentive Act**

Neb. Rev. Stat. 1943, 44-5650 et seq.

Rural High School Act

Kan. Stat. Ann., 72-3501 et seq.
Tex. Education Code, § 25.01 et seq.

Rural Highway Funds Act

Ky. Acts 1964, Ch. 17, Part 2, Art. 1, § 2

Rural Highway Public Transportation Act

Cal. Streets and Highways Code § 2500 et
seq.

Rural Highway System Act

Kan. Stat. Ann., 68-591 et seq.

Rural Highways Act

Minn. Stat. Ann., 163.01 et seq.

Rural Hospital Act
Fla. Stat. Ann., 395.102

Rural Hospital Authorities Assistance Act
Ga. Code Ann., 31-7-94.1

Rural Hospital Flexibility Act
Miss. Code Ann. 1972, § 41-9-201 et seq.

Rural Housing Amendments of 1983
Nov. 30, 1983, P.L. 98-181, 42 U.S. Code § 1441 nt.

Rural Housing Authority Law
Fla. Stat. Ann., 421.27 et seq.
Nev. Rev. Stat. Ann., 315.960 et seq.

Rural Housing Land Acquisition and Site Development Act
Fla. Stat. Ann., 420.20 et seq.

Rural Human Services Networking Program
N.Y. Social Services Law (Consol. Laws Ch. 55) § 464 et seq.

Rural Improvement Districts Act
Mont. Code Ann., 7-12-2101 et seq.

Rural Industrial Assistance Act of 1986
Aug. 28, 1986, P.L. 99-409, 7 U.S. Code § 1921

Rural Industrial Development Act
Tex. Government Code, § 481.081 et seq.

Rural Infrastructure Act
N.M. Stat. Ann., 75-1-1 et seq.

Rural Issues Task Force Act
Pa. Purdon's Stat., Title 71, § 1190.51 et seq.

Rural Leadership Training Act
Pa. Purdon's Stat., Title 53, § 897.1 et seq.

Rural Mail Route Act
Neb. Rev. Stat. 1943, 39-1001 et seq.

Rural Manpower Services Act
Fla. Stat. Ann., 446.40 et seq.

Rural Medical Access Program
Me. Rev. Stat. Ann. 1964, Title 24-A, § 6301 et seq.

Rural Medical Act
Ore. Rev. Stat., 352.165 et seq.

Rural Medical Scholarship Fund Act
Ky. Rev. Stat. 1971, Superseded Vols., 211.290 et seq.

Rural Pennsylvania Revitalization Act
Pa. Purdon's Stat., Title 71, § 1190.101 et seq.

Rural Physician Education Loan Repayment Act
Utah Code Ann. 1953, 26-9a-101 et seq.

Rural Physician Scholarship Act
Utah Code Ann. 1953, 26-9b-101 et seq.

Rural Police Act (Kershaw County)
S.C. Code of Laws 1952, § 53-561 et seq.

Rural Post-Roads Act
See Federal Aid Acts

Rural Primary Care and Emergency Medical Services Act
Okla. Stat. Ann., Title 63, § 1-706.1 et seq.

Rural Primary Health Care Act
N.M. Stat. Ann., 24-1A-1 et seq.

Rural Public Transportation Coordination Assistance Program
N.Y. Transportation Law (Consol. Law, Ch. 61a), § 73a et seq.

Rural Rehabilitation Act
N.C. Public Laws 1935, Ch. 459
Wash. Rev. Code Ann., 15.70.010 et seq.

Rural Rehabilitation Corporation Act
Ill. Rev. Stat. 1991, Ch. 127, § 42a2.9 et seq.
Ind. Code Ann., 15-7-2-1 et seq.
Utah Code Ann. 1953, 4-19-1 et seq.

Rural Rehabilitation Corporation Assets Act
Pa. Purdon's Stat., Title 71, § 751-24 et seq.

Rural Rehabilitation Corporation Trust Liquidation Act
May 3, 1950, Ch. 152, 64 Stat. 98, 7 U.S. Code § 1001 nt.; 40 U.S. Code §§ 440 to 444

Rural Rehabilitation Trust Liquidation Act
Cal. Statutes 1949, Ch. 414, p. 762

Rural Relief Act
La. Rev. Stat. Ann., 51:3000 et seq.

Rural Renaissance Act
Cal. Government Code § 15373 et seq.

Rural Revitalization and Leadership Development Act
Ore. Rev. Stat., 285.678 et seq.

Rural Risk Underwriting Association Law
Miss. Code Ann. 1972, § 83-38-1 et seq.

Rural Road Improvement District Act
Neb. Rev. Stat. 1943, 39-1638 et seq.
Okla. Stat. Ann., Title 19, § 902.1 et seq.

Rural Roads Authority Act
Ga. Code Ann., 32-10-1 et seq.

Rural Roads Inventory Act
Okla. Stat. 1981, Title 69, § 677 et seq.

Rural School District Act
Ore. Rev. Stat., 334.005 et seq.

Rural Services Act
Ark. Code Ann. 1987, 6-11-118 et seq.

Rural Small Business Enhancement Act of 1990
Nov. 15, 1990, P.L. 101-574, 15 U.S. Code § 631 nt.

Rural Telecommunications Improvements Act of 1990
Nov. 28, 1990, P.L. 101-624, 7 U.S. Code §§ 901 nt., 946 nt.

Rural Telephone Act
Ala. Code 1975, § 37-6-40 et seq.
N.C. Gen. Stat. 1943, § 117-30 et seq.
Va. Code 1950, § 56-485 et seq.

Rural Telephone Bank Act
May 7, 1971, P.L. 92-12, 85 Stat. 29, 7 U.S. Code §§ 931 to 950b

Rural Telephone Cooperative Act
Ark. Code Ann. 1987, 23-17-201 et seq.
Ga. Code Ann., 46-5-60 et seq.
Ind. Code Ann., 8-1-17-1 et seq.
Ky. Rev. Stat. 1971, 279.310 et seq.
Okla. Stat. Ann., Title 18, § 438.1 et seq.

Rural Telephone Cooperative Association ERISA Amendments Act of 1991
Aug. 14, 1991, P.L. 102-89, 29 U.S. Code § 1001 nt.

Rural Virginia Development Foundation Act
Va. Code 1950, § 3.1-27.37 et seq.

Rural Water Act
Ky. Rev. Stat. 1971, 42.200

Rural Water Districts Act
Neb. Rev. Stat. 1943, 46-1001 et seq.

Rural Water Improvement District Bond Guaranty Act
Ark. Stat. 1947, 20-2101 et seq.

Rural Water, Sewer, Gas and Solid Waste Management Districts Act
Okla. Stat. 1981, Title 82, § 1324.1 et seq.

Rural Zoning Act
Mont. Code Ann., 76-2-101 et seq., 76-2-201 et seq.
Ohio Rev. Code 1953, 303.01 et seq.
S.D. Code 1939, 12.20A.01 et seq.

Rural Zoning Act (County)
S.D. Codified Laws 1967, 11-2-1 et seq.

Rural Zoning Act (Township)
Mich. Comp. Laws Ann., 125.271 et seq.

Rural Zoning Enabling Act (County)
Mich. Comp. Laws Ann., 125.201 et seq.

Rural/Downstate Health Act
Ill. Rev. Stat. 1991, Ch. 111 1/2, § 8051 et seq.

Rush Unsafe Buildings Law
N.Y. Local Laws 1973, Town of Rush, p. 2878

Russell Act (Business Licenses)
Ohio Laws Vol. 80, p. 129

Russell Amendment.
June 27, 1944, Ch. 286, 58 Stat. 387, 31 U.S. Code § 696

Russell-Overton Amendment.
Sept. 16, 1940, Ch. 720, 54 Stat. 892, 50 U.S. Code Appx. § 1158

Russian Friendship Treaty
Haw. Session Laws 1870, p. 83, June 19, 1869

Russian Roulette Act (Taxation)
Fla. Stat. Ann., 194.101

Rutgers, The State University Act
N.J. Stat. Ann., 18A:65-1 et seq.

Ryan Act (Drug Users)
Mich. Comp. Laws Ann., 335.201 et seq.

Ryan Act (Teacher Preparation and Licensing)
Cal. Education Code 1976, § 44200 et seq.

Ryan Liquor Control Act
N.Y. Alcoholic Beverage Control Law (Consol. Laws Ch. 3B) § 101b

Ryan Master Teacher Act
Cal. Education Code 1976, § 44490 et seq.

Ryan White Comprehensive AIDS Resources Emergency Act of 1990
Aug. 18, 1990, P.L. 101-381, 42 U.S. Code § 201 nt.
May 20, 1996, P.L. 104-146, 42 U.S. Code § 201 nt.

Ryder Act (Revaluation of Property)
Wash. Rev. Code Ann., 84.41.010 et seq.

Rye Park Act
N.Y. Laws 1907, Ch. 711

Effective Computer

User Documentation

Effective Computer

User Documentation

James Crown

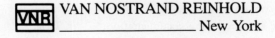

VAN NOSTRAND REINHOLD
_____ New York

Library of Congress Catalog Card Number 91-46610
ISBN 0-442-00863-5

Printed in the United States of America.

Van Nostrand Reinhold
115 Fifth Avenue
New York, New York 10003

Chapman and Hall
2-6 Boundary Row
London, SE1 8HN, England

Thomas Nelson Australia
102 Dodds Street
South Melbourne 3205
Victoria, Australia

Nelson Canada
1120 Birchmount Road
Scarborough, Ontario MIK 5G4, Canada

16 15 14 13 12 11 10 9 8 7 6 5 4 3 2 1

Library of Congress Cataloging-in-Publication Data

Crown, James.
     Effective computer user documentation / by James Crown.
        p.   cm.
     Includes index.
     ISBN 0-442-00863-5
     1. Electronic data processing documentation.   I. Title.
QA76.9.D6C76   1992
005.1'5—dc20   91-46610
                                         CIP

CONTENTS

☞ The masculine pronoun to mean two sexes is a space and time saver as well as a rhetorical convention. Most things males can do, females can do as well. One that both would do well to avoid is unproductive wordplay.

Preface

User documentation is the weak link of the computer industry. It is largely ignored by those who design applications and systems. It is an afterthought. When it is done, it is often done poorly. And yet user documentation is the vital link between the technicians and the largely nontechnical users.

The vast majority of computer users have no idea how these complex computer systems work — and they need not know. What the user does need to understand is how to call information to the screen, how to manipulate that information, and how to store it away. Effective user documentation shows the user how to do that.

Effective Computer User Documentation has been written for those who have to produce and manage a documentation project. It is a step-by-step guide to a set of processes and a concept methodology that has been tried and improved on over a number of years. This is a how-to-do-it book that steps the documentation writer/editor from creation to finished product introduced to the users.

This book does not spend a lot of time discussing theories. It takes a practical approach — reflecting the fact that it has been written by a writer and editor who spends a large part of his time responding to the user documentation needs of large corporations and government bodies. This is a book for those busy individuals who are either dedicated documentation staff or who are suddenly thrown into the task with little or no background in writing, editing, designing, producing, or managing the documentation project.

The first time you work through this book, start from the beginning and move on in the order of the processes. After this first pass, the book can then be used as a reference manual. Consult topics as you need them. Review examples for new ways to handle old problems.

As with many instructional books, this was in many ways a collaborative effort which gained considerably because of its exposure to a tight-knit group of highly skilled professionals. Thanks is due to each of them.

Primary thanks must go to the man who found me writing spy novels and television drama, a disgruntled ex-newspaper editor, and taught me the basics of documentation and instructional writing. His name is Rob McKilliam. He is a fine documentation practitioner and teacher.

My staff at Communications Publishing Corporation has made a distinct contribution. Particular thanks must go to Jeff Junee, my colleague and friend, who has joined me in teaching this course in Australia and the United States. He has contributed greatly to the fine tuning of many of the practical conclusions in this book. Denise Bush, colleague and co-conspirator, is a fine artist and designer. Her contribution to our documentation, and hence this book, is significant. Barbara Hall, my secretary, is the calming influence so necessary in a creative environment. Without her, there would be anarchy — the antithesis of creativity. To my other editors and writers, my thanks.

A special note of thanks to the hundreds of students who have passed through my documentation seminars at the National Computer Center and the College of Computer Management and Information Technology at the Polytechnic University of the Philippines. Their enthusiasm and questioning have helped me refine my ideas, and have made each of my frequent trips to Manila a new adventure.

One must never overlook an enthusiastic editor and Van Nostrand Reinhold's Dianne Littwin has been a great help keeping my nose to the grindstone. My agent, Richard Deutch, continues his warmly appreciated role as mentor, confessor, slave driver, and good friend.

Finally, there are my three women, wife Norma, and my daughters Danielle and Vanessa, who make it all worthwhile and without whose support very little of this would be possible. Love you all.

Style and layout of this Book

A few words of explanation are needed about how this book is structured and written because a problem was identified early in its preparation. Like all publishers, Van Nostrand Reinhold has a set style guide for how its books should look and how they should be written. However, this book is about the writing of computer user documentation and thus many of the rules associated with book editing don't apply.

To avoid confusing the reader who might read an instruction on how to do something on one page and then turn the page to see the exact opposite done, Van Nostrand Reinhold's editors have been gracious enough to allow the author to break away from book style and follow manual documentation style in many places.

I thank the editors for this privilege and I fully accept responsibility for any inconsistencies that might appear from their normal book style, such as short paragraphs, pages that fall short of the last line on the page, extra capitalization, and other such devices that mark documentation as different from other forms of text. The reason for these variations will become obvious as you read the text.

James Crown
Sydney, Australia

Effective Computer

User Documentation

CHAPTER 1

Getting started

What are we going to accomplish?

Let me tell you a little story.

Imagine that you have just completed writing and editing six manuals for a major tire company. Because the manuals will be used across the nation, you want to make sure they work so you have moved into a useability lab to put the documentation to a practical test.

Fred, manager of one of 200 tire stores across the country and picked because he knows nothing about computers, has agreed to help you check out the manuals. He is in the small television studio unpacking the seven boxes of equipment, unaware you and your documentation team are watching him on the camera monitors and from behind the one-way mirror.

The first manual in the first box is the Installation Manual. Fred follows your instructions and diagrams to the letter. Everything is hooked up and it is time to go to the first disk. It's a 5 1/4-inch disk in its black case. It was originally in a plain white envelope taped inside the front cover of the manual. But when Fred opened the manual for the first time, he took the black disk out of the white envelope and put the disk on the table beside him.

Now, having read through the introductory material, Fred is ready to start. He picks up the disk from the table and looks down at the first instruction:

- **Take the disk out of the envelope**

Fred smiles. He can do this. He starts to peel away the black envelope in which he knows there must be a disk because he can see the round center. He has considerable difficulty and he can't understand why you have made the task so hard for him.

Inside the observation room, you are having a mild heart attack. How could Fred be so dumb, you ask? Everyone knows the *disk* is a black *square*!

Finally Fred extracts the disk from the black envelope. He is now holding the round disk. He looks at the next instruction:

- **Holding the disk by the bottom right corner....**

Which corner? At this point, Fred is in trouble, and so are you. What seems straightforward isn't. Your user is lost because of what you took for granted. Disks aren't necessarily round in this context and bottom right corners are hard to find on a round object.

Writing effective user documentation is not an easy task.

What we're going to accomplish in this book is simply put: We're going to tackle the topic of user documentation in such a way as to make sure we never end up with a user finding himself in the position of our friend Fred. We're going to learn a set of processes that match documentation to a user profile.

We're going to develop a set of rules, a set of standards, a set of milestones that can be applied to any kind of documentation you may be required to produce — documentation processes that can be used in a computer environment or in a noncomputer environment.

This may be print-based documentation, the common manual, on-line electronic documentation, or one of a myriad of other forms of effective user documentation.

Technical versus user documentation

I also want to break you free of the old belief that a manual is always the best form of documentation. For most projects, the manual is best. But not always.

We are looking at user documentation, not technical documentation. User documentation documents the system from the user's point of view looking inward. Technical documentation documents the system from the point of view of the technical system looking outwards. From a user perspective we don't care, for example, about the methods employed to store, process, and retrieve data. We are concerned with how to call up and manipulate that data, and how to send it away either for storage or for some kind of printout.

There is a world of difference between documenting from a user's perspective, and documenting the technical aspects of a system or individual application. Technical documentation is another topic, for another time and place. It bears little relationship to our subject.

(This concept is basic to this book. It is why we refuse, in my company, to define ourselves as technical writers. We are user writers. Technical writers tend to see issues from the perspective of technical detail rather than from the perspective of the user. IBM manuals tend to be fine examples of this inability of the documentation writer to communicate effectively with the common user.)

Internal and external documentation

The kind of documentation we produce may be labeled in two ways: internal documentation and external documentation.

Internal documentation is produced for in-house use. It is commissioned and used by the same organization that develops it, although it may be developed by outside consultants. External documentation, on the other hand, is produced for outside use, for users outside the organization within which the documentation is being produced. The most common examples of documentation of this type are manuals and reference cards that accompany commercially available software and hardware.

It is important to recognize the difference because invariably external documentation is produced to a higher standard and has a larger budget than internal documentation. The reason for this is more a management problem than a documentation problem. External documentation is often used as a marketing tool to help sell a product. A direct link can then be made between the quality of the documentation and the profit the organization makes.

Internal documentation is used inside the organization and its linkage to the product and to the profit line is often difficult for senior management to see. Internal documentation is usually something someone *has* to do after everything else has been done. It is a prime candidate for cost-cutting and is often subjected to the time-squeeze.

Total documentation

One of the key aspects of effective documentation is a concept called *total documentation*. This involves development of a documentation set, that is, an acknowledgement that documentation does not necessarily consist of only a manual, and that the total organization workflow — those tasks that involve computer use, as well as noncomputer tasks — should be documented together.

The discussion below is summarized in the chart on the next page. My task was to provide documentation for a government department. There were five systems in place. The basic problems were that:

❏ no single division of the department knew what other divisions were doing

❏ no documentation had been done of the physical systems and their operation

❏ almost all policy and business rules had been handed down by word of mouth

❏ no formal training structure existed

My first task was to develop all the possibilities and then cut those possibilities down to a recommendation of what the documentation set should include.

The physical systems

The physical systems included the five systems and covered procedure and operations. Form and content were to be standardized across the whole department. Manuals, reference cards, and help screens would be the user tools.

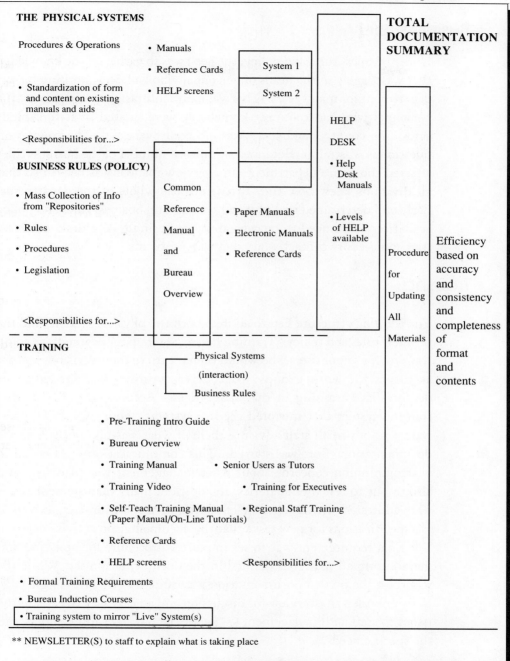

THE PHYSICAL SYSTEMS

Procedures & Operations

- Manuals
- Reference Cards
- HELP screens

- Standardization of form and content on existing manuals and aids

<Responsibilities for...>

BUSINESS RULES (POLICY)

- Mass Collection of Info from "Repositories"
- Rules
- Procedures
- Legislation

<Responsibilities for...>

TRAINING

- Pre-Training Intro Guide
- Bureau Overview
- Training Manual
- Training Video
- Self-Teach Training Manual (Paper Manual/On-Line Tutorials)
- Reference Cards
- HELP screens

- Senior Users as Tutors
- Training for Executives
- Regional Staff Training

<Responsibilities for...>

- Formal Training Requirements
- Bureau Induction Courses
- Training system to mirror "Live" System(s)

System 1

System 2

Common Reference Manual and Bureau Overview

- Paper Manuals
- Electronic Manuals
- Reference Cards

Physical Systems (interaction)

Business Rules

HELP DESK

- Help Desk Manuals
- Levels of HELP available

TOTAL DOCUMENTATION SUMMARY

Procedure for Updating All Materials

Efficiency based on accuracy and consistency and completeness of format and contents

** NEWSLETTER(S) to staff to explain what is taking place

Business rules

Under business rules and policy, the need was to gather all the knowledge that was largely in the heads of personnel who had been working for the department for many years. This was a difficult task because some of the personnel who had the most knowledge were located in state capitals across the country, and some were located overseas. (The country in question is Australia). Because a significant number of the business rules affected the entire department, an overview manual was needed so that all divisions knew how they fitted into the whole of the department. Early on I determined that physical systems and business rules and policy activities would need to be centralized on a single help desk which all staff could easily contact when they had problems.

Training

The training structure had to address both the physical systems and the business rules and policy. Training had to be set up for new staff, ongoing training for senior users who would then return to their divisions and act as tutors for work groups. Executive training was needed, plus decentralized training in the state offices. Accordingly, we set up a training system that mirrored the live systems. Four-page newsletters were sent out to all staff advising them of what was taking place as the documentation effort was started. This communication was needed to overcome union concerns about what management was planning, and also to put to rest user anxieties. In addition, many management issues were addressed with a schedule of additional responsibilities, as well as job specifications for new tasks that the documentation activity defined. The final requirement was to set in place a procedure for updating and maintaining all materials defined in the documentation set. While the report on the needed documentation was quite lengthy, the single page chart provided an overview for discussion and an easy way to explain the issues to staff and management — people who really didn't understand the specific needs.

On one page, we had the total documentation picture. And that's what we're going to address in this book. We need a methodology to follow and a set of skills to carry out that methodology.

Perhaps you have been involved in this little scenario.

The project team meets often as a system is being designed and developed. A group of earnest young men and women are trying their best to address all the issues. They talk of a system development life cycle, modules, hardware, networking, security and so forth. There is a cursory mention of user training, but the topic is quickly passed over. Training has to do with experienced *users* and ordinary users — generally people with little or no knowledge of computers — are outsiders to this technically oriented team.

Perhaps one of the team members remembers another topic that received only the briefest of mentions in the multitude of texts written about systems, system development and implementation. The team member asks about documentation. What kind of documentation will accompany the new system?

There is little enthusiasm for the topic. Documentation has to do with computer users whereas this is a project meeting. The project is seen as highly technical and the technical environment is a world far removed from the world of clerks, managers, and other frontline staff out there somewhere in the offices and warehouses.

A programmer offers his solution. "There will be some on-line help. I'll write it as I go," he says. Others agree, perhaps one of them adding that the system is "quite simple to operate".

The team member who brought up the subject of documentation in the first place suggests that a user guide will be necessary, perhaps even a training manual. A system administrator's guide would also be useful for the major interstate branch offices.

At this point there are yawns, raised eyebrows, and silence. The project manager, noticing the lack of enthusiasm, dismisses the whole topic by putting it off to a future meeting, adding that documentation will be done according to the standards necessary. Once again, documentation has been bypassed.

This is not only the case at project meetings. It takes place in seminars about systems, in textbooks and in classrooms. Everything is discussed in detail and documentation is explained away in a paragraph or two.

For example, in one well-known text about system concepts, structures, and applications, the word "documentation" does not appear in the index, even though many minor topics are indexed.

If you search long enough, you find a paragraph after a short discussion of user training. The paragraph reads:

> Next to training, course documentation is vital in initiating a system. Reliability and ease of use are key factors in the success of documentation. Optimally, end users should be able to open the documentation two months after class, quickly find a description of a process, read it and understand it.

Full stop, period — and nothing more.

Another well known text, consisting of 327 pages but no index, dismisses documentation with these words: "The importance of user manuals and user training programs cannot be overemphasised." This is followed by three sentences which describe a disaster at a department store because of poor documentation. But there is no discussion about how to produce effective documentation.

The need for effective documentation

Why is documentation needed? If you can't answer that question, then you will undoubtedly fail when you attempt to prepare documentation.

There are always reasons that can be cited for *not* preparing documentation:

❑ It costs money, time, and resources — and there is never enough money, time, or resources to go around.

❑ Documentation is seldom done well, so why waste time doing it.

❑ Documentation is never used.

❑ A training course will suffice.

❑ On-line help has been written by the programmers who programmed the system.

In a perfect world, documentation might not be necessary. But we don't live in a perfect world. Systems are seldom well designed (from a user's point of view); systems always seem to have problems, or are being updated; and there is very little standardization of key usage or command usage. If the perfect system (and the perfect user) were possible, then documentation could be ignored.

Of course, some systems are so poorly designed that even documentation won't help the user. If you come across one of those, the answer might be to conduct a training course at some Club Med. It may turn out financially cheaper, and do wonders for the tan and morale of the users.

User/management concerns

There is no such thing as a perfect world, or a perfect system — just as there is no such thing as a perfect user.

A group of perfect users would mean a group of individuals who all know the same thing, who all see their work task the same way, who all see the same images for the same words, who are identical in thought, word and deed. Such a group does not exist, thank goodness.

Documentation must take into consideration the differences between users.

For example, the 22-year-old clerk, and the 45-year-old marketing executive may both be using the same system. But they do not think the same way, they probably don't process thoughts or arrive at conclusions in the same manner, and yet they both have to navigate through the system.

Consider documentation like a transport system. A bus carries many passengers, a dump truck carries a load of dirt, and a Porsche carries two people very quickly. You cannot design a single mode of transport to be all things to all users.

Documentation must be prepared for the differing needs of users and for the differing needs of management.

Why some documentation fails

One of the most efficient ways of moving toward a definition of what makes an effective piece of documentation is to review why documentation often fails and suggest some of the many consequences of producing ineffective documentation.

The failure of some documentation can be categorized under three headings: user attitudes, management attitudes, and the documentation writer's attitude.

User attitudes

Users reject documentation for many reasons:

❏ they've tried to find the information before, but they couldn't find what they wanted — so they're not going to waste time trying again

❏ they've found the information they wanted, but it was written in such a way that they couldn't understand it

❏ they found the information, but they know the information is old and that revisions have been made to the system

❏ they're too lazy to go looking for the information

❏ they're turned off because the manual, for example, is 500 pages thick

❏ there's only one copy of the manual and it's locked in the supervisor's desk

Management attitudes

Sometimes the problem rests with management, not only management of the organization, but also system management:

❏ Time-squeeze.

Management has been waiting for the system for some time. The system is now ready. But while documentation can be planned, it cannot be effectively done until after the system is locked in. (Developmental changes can easily destroy many hours of documentation planning and writing.) It is often difficult to sell the fact you need time to properly document the system. The writer finds himself under siege.

❏ Refusal to acknowledge the value of documentation.

This is often a problem if documentation is left to the technical staff. Programmers have been known to be the main culprits of this attitude. They've finished the system, they want to get on with the next task. They don't live in the world of the users and they don't relate easily to the user's needs. They see documentation as the "armpit of the computer industry".

❏ Failure to communicate.

If management and the technical staff failed to come to a complete agreement about the scope and design of a system, the documentation often reflects that indecision and the user will inherit the confusion.

❏ Budget constraints.

Time and cost constraints may mean that a writer has to write a single manual that is expected to serve too many audiences and accomplish too much. The most effective effective manual usually has a single group of users and a single purpose.

The writer's attitude

Sometimes it is the writer who causes the problems.

❏ The writer doesn't take enough time to understand the system before starting to write.

❏ The writer becomes more concerned about the look of the manual, the design factors, than about the content.

❏ The writer believes that truth is more important than clarity. Factual statements are made but without the explanation that results in the user understanding the factual statement. If there is any doubt about the factual statement the writer leaves it out, rather than taking the time to further define the facts.

Effects of ineffective documentation

The effects of ineffective documentation can be quite wide-ranging, from low productivity through to legal proceedings.

❏ Errors made by operators can reduce efficiency and waste resources.

❏ The costs of training can increase substantially. (A survey of Fortune 500 companies shows that the single most underbudgeted systems cost for implementation is training, and that the weakest link in most projects is documentation.)

While some organizations have full-fledged training departments, the documentation writer can make a significant contribution if involved in the production of training materials to be used by professional trainers.

❏ Users may reject a system they don't understand, or find difficult to use. And if it is the first system of a number of systems to be implemented, that failure casts a pall of gloom and doom over the next system to be installed.

A survey shows that help calls to software service desks, and equipment returned to retailers, are often linked to users who claim they don't understand how to use the application or equipment. They can't understand the documentation.

❏ It is conceivable that poor documentation could lead to legal action. The potential for an error of this scale exists on many systems. Training and documentation have to cover the possibilities.

Defining effective documentation

This brings us to the obvious question: What is an effective piece of documentation?

Put simply: Documentation is effective if its target audience — its set of users — makes use of it.

Five characteristics

Let's define five characteristics of effective documentation:

❏ the documentation is available in a form and in a place that users can refer to it when it is needed

❏ the information in the documentation is easy to find

❏ the information in the documentation is easy to comprehend

❏ the information is up-to-date, reflecting latest changes and revisions to the system

❏ the information is reliable and convincing.

Perhaps the most important words here are:

Reliable and Comprehend

Reliable and comprehend go straight to the heart of all effective documentation.

Reliable means: trustworthy, able to be relied on

Comprehend means: the ability of the mind to understand, power to grasp ideas, ability to know

The connection between *reliable* and *comprehend* is better understood if we work through a typical scenario.

In **Scenario** 1, our user is working on Inventory. Everything is going smoothly until he reaches the option 'Masterfile Records Lock'. He can't remember how to use the option. The only other user in this particular office is away sick and the manager is new and hasn't used the system yet.

Our user looks up at the shelf containing the user manuals for the system. He shakes his head and ignores them. Two weeks ago he looked up a procedure for Stock Records by Item in Stores Enquiries and could find no reference to the option even though it appears on his Stores Enquiries Menu.

Our user now logs off the system because that is the normal procedure if he is going to leave his desk. He walks down the corridor to the elevator and takes the elevator to the basement where the computer department is located.

In the computer room everyone is busy but someone finally tells him the technician who can answer his questions is on a coffee break. He can wait 10 minutes or go to the coffee shop on the fifth floor and see if the technician is there. Eventually, the user gets the information he needs, but it has taken him half an hour.

The problem is that the user has lost confidence in his manuals because he questions their reliability. He once searched for information he knows should be there and he didn't find it. Now he assumes it is a waste of time to count on the manuals.

Consider **Scenario 2**. Same user. Same problem with that Inventory option. Once again he looks up at the manuals gathering dust on the bookshelf. And once again he shakes his head, logs off the system and goes in search of someone from the computer department. But this time he ignored the manuals for a different reason.

Two weeks ago he looked up a procedure for Stock Records by Item in Stores Enquiries. He found it but it was written in technical terms far beyond his level of understanding — or need. It took him half an hour to make sense of it.

The user has lost confidence in the manual because he believes the manual is incomprehensible. It doesn't matter that the writer who wrote it understands how it works. If the user believes he won't understand it, he won't bother opening the manual.

Consider **Scenario 3**. Same user. Same problem with that Inventory option. Once again he looks up at the manuals. Once again he shakes his head, logs off the system, and goes in search of someone from the computer department. But this time he ignored the manual for another reason.

In this case he realizes that his problem is that there has been a system change since he did Inventory last year. He ignores the manuals because no updates or revisions have ever been sent out since the original documentation was issued three years ago. Once again our user is rejecting the documentation because he cannot rely on it for the solution to his problem.

In these scenarios the manuals are on the shelf gathering dust. Other documentation that is unreliable or incomprehensible can usually be found propping open a door, piled under a monitor to bring the screen up to eye level, or under someone's feet as a portable footrest. Often a filing cabinet in an infrequently used corner of the office contains the manuals, piled high with plastic shrink-wrapped updates. It's a sad commentary on an organization's inability to properly confront the weaknesses in its documentation effort. The image of the cobweb-shrouded filing cabinet should haunt every manager. Productivity and efficiency suffer. The bottomline suffers.

Comprehension, reliability, and let's add availability — if any of these are missing, the user will go looking elsewhere and your documentation will have failed.

While there are five characteristics of effective documentation, each of these characteristics does not command equal weight in every type of manual. The reason a manual exists, its mission, will determine which of the characteristics is primary and which are secondary.

Primary versus secondary emphasis

If you were about to build a house, one of the first steps would be to hire an architect. You must sit down with the architect, and show him some rough sketches. You need four bedrooms and a study. A living room, kitchen, bathroom, garage, dining room are on your must-have list. To those basics you'd like to have a swimming pool, a second bathroom, and a workshop joined to the garage.

Then you and the architect look at the budget. There are limitations to what you can really do. Sometimes those limitations are defined by the size of the block on which you plan to build your house. More often, the limitation is financial. So you plan around your financial realities — what you can afford. An area is set aside for the swimming pool, but for the time being it will be covered with a flower bed. The second bathroom goes in, but the workshop has to be forgotten.

The architect takes all the items on your must-have list and your wish list and tries to develop a plan that will give you as much as possible for your money. Documentation works the same way.

Like the architect, the documentation designer (often the writer) has to balance the varied needs of the groups of users with the budget for the documentation project and the time constraints to produce the documentation. The must-have items receive primary emphasis and the wish-list items are given secondary emphasis.

Both primary and secondary concerns are important and must receive due consideration. However, in our imperfect world, compromises often have to be made and the documentation writer must be able to identify what is most important and what is of lesser importance.

For example, consider the User Reference Manual that is designed to help more experienced users operate the system efficiently.

❏ The primary concern is that the users can quickly locate the information they need.

❏ A secondary concern is that the users be able to immediately understand that information.

❏ A secondary concern is that the information is accurate and up to date.

Now consider the Training Manual designed to introduce beginners to the system.

❏ Finding information is a secondary concern because, as beginners, these users may not know what they are looking for.

❏ The primary emphasis is that when the beginner finds information, that information is easily understood.

❏ A secondary concern is that the information be complete.

Next consider the Systems Maintenance Manual, designed to assist maintenance programmers solve occasional operational problems.

❏ A secondary concern is the ease with which information can be found. While this is important, the maintenance staff will search until they find the answers.

❏ A secondary concern is the ease with which they can understand the information. Most likely they'll spend time sorting it out.

❏ The primary emphasis is that the information is complete, accurate, and up-to-date.

The documentation designer must balance the needs of the user with the resources on hand. Ideally, everything is treated with primary emphasis. Realistically, it might not be that easy. Getting the emphasis right can make or break the whole project.

CHAPTER 2

The users

What do users really need?

Before we start building documentation, we must do what every writer must do at the beginning of a documentation project — we must examine the users.

There are a couple of foundations on which every piece of effective documentation rests: one of those foundations is an understanding of the system you are documenting, another is an understanding of the users that this particular piece of documentation is being prepared for. The users are the target audience and you are courting disaster if you fail to define completely that target audience.

You start to understand your users by addressing the following topics:

❏ How do users understand?

❏ How do users read?

❏ How do users decide what's worthwhile reading?

❏ How do users approach documentation?

Some of these topics are more important to one group of users than to others; some of these topics are common to all users quite irrespective of education and background.

Let's examine the topics one by one:

How do users understand?

When a user is confronted by a new word or phrase, a new idea, or a new concept, that user will interpret what is new and unknown in terms of what the user already knows, or has experienced.

How this process actually works is important to understand because it is a central issue for the documentation writer. If the role of the writer is to make an issue understandable, then the writer must recognize what steps a user will go through when confronted by something that is not readily understandable. This is one of the critical concerns in almost all communications.

Know your user's mindset

For our purposes, let's define our particular use of *mindset* as the information you have stored away over the length of your life about any given subject. Let's consider the television set. This is a subject where the mindset develops at an early age. Even before we can walk or talk, most babies have focused on the television set and have developed a mindset about this marvellous box in the corner of the room. It is pure entertainment, strange, somewhat frightening at times, and so forth.

As we get older, we start adding other descriptions to the television set. Physical descriptions change. We know we can have little ones and big ones, color or black-and-white, stereo or mono, plug them into the electrical outlet in the wall, run them on batteries, run them using the power from the lighter socket in the car.

This mindset expands rapidly when the description reaches out beyond the physical television set to the content of television programming, the related subject of videotape and video recorders, to satellite broadcasts, and on and on.

An emotional part of the mindset develops as well as physical and practical aspects. The critics of television chastise us for wasted hours watching what some label as mindless soap operas. Others talk of biased news telecasts, of endless repeats of commercials, and of all the other negative and positive labels that help develop our mindset about the television set.

When someone mentions the word *television*, or the phrase *television set*, you have an immediate picture of what is being talked about. Your mindset takes over. If you are told that the television set is made of plastic, you have no trouble because you also have a mindset for *plastic*.

But if you were told the television set cabinet was made of maligmium, you'd be in trouble because it is highly unlikely you'll have any mindset for the word "maligmium". In the massive database that is your mind, you have no files on maligmium, no indexed entries, no instant glossary entry for that word.

However, the word maligmium has already been filed away and you have started a collection of information. So far there are only a few basic inferences. If a television set is made of maligmium, it's obvious the material is not too heavy, probably not too expensive, probably easy to manufacture and to mold into a box shape. It's obviously a solid because you can't make a television set out of a gas or a liquid.

In our subject of user documentation, you will constantly come upon words and concepts which will be unknown to the users. As you develop your profile of the users, think carefully about the mindset of the group. It helps set the level of language you employ, determines how much scene-setting you do, and how you handle technical jargon — all are topics we'll deal with later in this book.

Matching the level of technical detail and the level of language to the level of the user is one of the key ingredients of effective documentation. Can there be any value in providing a computer illiterate with the kind of instructions found in the passage below? Unfortunately, too many computer professionals fail to realize the gap between their knowledge and the knowledge of the average user.

Options   This allows you to specify particular options to compile programs, suppress symbol table, include code, and append heading to show generated code being executed. Options are:

C Compile programs after they are generated.

S Suppress Symbol Table. The Symbol Table is used if you wish to debug the program by looking at contents of variables used in the program. If you do not intend to use the Pick DEBUG, it is suggested that you use this option as the generated object code will be smaller.

I Include Code. If you specify this option, then all **I**, **O**, **R**, and **P** processes will include the code for all **P**, **A**, **C**, and **V** processes that they reference within the main program.

The purpose of this option is to increase performance of the generated program. It will reduce the number of external subroutines that are required. Use it where you have a number of Paragraphs called from an Input process, particularly if those Paragraphs are small. The disadvantage of this option is that the generated program will become larger and may reach the limit determined by the Operating System. For most Pick systems, the maximum program size is 32K and thus you may be forced to forgo this option.

H Append **(G)** to the Heading displayed when the program is running to show that generated code is being executed.

You may enter a combination of options:

* Type: `CI   <ENTER>`

How do users read?

While whole books have been written on this subject, the basics must be covered here because of the impact the topic has on the final acceptability of the documentation.   There are some basic conclusions for the documentation process that develop straight out of scientific findings about how we read.

Words and phrases are not read character by character until a word is formed, and then a word becomes part of a phrase. The combination of the eye and the brain work much more quickly and, quite remarkably, with a lot less information.

A reader scans a line and picks up the shapes of words and groups of words. What is being taken in and processed by the brain are the external and internal shapes, the outlines, of words and phrases. The eye jumps and stops, jumps and stops, as it moves across a line. It is as if the eye takes in a piece of the line and then stops to process what it has just seen, arrives at a conclusion, stores that conclusion away, and then jumps on and repeats the process.

Scientists who measure such things claim the pauses, called fixations, take up about 94 percent of reading time. These fixations last about a quarter of a second. The processing, the conclusions, and the storing away all take place during the fixation pauses.

When the eye reaches the end of a sentence, it swings back to the start of the next line like the old typewriter carriage return. The speed with which this process takes place depends on the reader, on how well he has learned to read, on his ability to comprehend, and on how the reading material has been written and laid out on the page. A less skilled reader may be reduced to processing a single word at a time. When this happens, there is a further loss of time while the reader is forced to go back over words already read in order to form them together into a sentence.

The aim of effective documentation is to reduce the number of fixations, and cut down the number of times the reader has to stop new processing and return to form the comprehension link between words or groups of words.

One of the implications of this reading process is the problem of errors, both factual and typographical. The practiced reader recognizes shapes and patterns, so a certain amount of the processing is left to the brain rather than the eye. As a result, sentence structure, the reader's experience, and the context, all come into play. A common example that we all face is where we read a word that we *expect* to be there into a sentence, rather than the word that is *actually* printed. While this can have an affect in general reading, it has a more specific implication in documentation. In editing and proofreading, people make mistakes involving simple words and phrases, or words that are missing are supplied by the brain rather than with the eye.

From a documentation viewpoint, there are four practical conclusions to this brief explanation of how we read. These will be dealt with in detail later in this book, but for now we provide this summary.

❏ If the unity of words is important, then the space relationship between letters in words must be appropriate for the eye. Too much space between letters makes the words hard to read and slows up the reading process.

For example:

> R e a d i n g   t h i s   q u i c k l y   i s   d i f f i c u l t

> Reading this is much easier

❏ If the shape of letters is important, along with their ascenders and descenders, then lowercase letters should be used in preference to capital letters. Studies show that reading time increases about four times when text is set all in capital letters. The eye and mind must both slow down to understand what is being read.

For example: READING PAGES OF THIS IS DIFFICULT

> Reading pages of this is much easier

❏ If the upper parts of letters have more distinctive patterns than the lower half of letters, it is important to maintain adequate distance between lines. This distance is called *leading*, sometimes referred to as ledding.

For example:

> lower half of the letter, it is important to maintain

> lower half of the letter, it is important to maintain

> lower half of the letter, it is important to maintain

Leading is discussed in more detail later in this book.

While the issues involved in typography are discussed later in this book, consider the readability (and legibility) of the following passages:

Throughout this guide, we use certain symbols, typestyles and conventions to help you. For example, you might find a line that looks like this:

- *Type: ATI9 <E>*

  What you actually type appears in a special typeface:

  ATI9

  Whatever appears on your screen will also be displayed in this manual in this special typeface, for example messages:

  CONNECT

Throughout this guide, we use certain symbols, typestyles, and conventions to help you. For example, you might find a line that looks like this:

- Type: ATI9 <E>

  What you actually type appears in a special typeface:

  ATI9

  Whatever appears on your screen will also be displayed in this manual in this special typeface, for example messages:

  CONNECT

THROUGHOUT THIS GUIDE, WE USE CERTAIN SYMBOLS, TYPESTYLES, AND CONVENTIONS TO HELP YOU. FOR EXAMPLE, YOU MIGHT FIND A LINE THE LOOKS LIKE THIS:

- TYPE: ATI9 <E>

  WHAT YOU ACTUALLY TYPE APPEARS IN A SPECIAL TYPEFACE.

  ATI9

  WHATEVER APPEARS ON YOUR SCREEN WILL ALSO BE DISPLAYED IN THIS MANUAL IN THIS SPECIAL TYPEFACE, FOR EXAMPLE

  CONNECT

Throughout this guide, we use certain symbols, typestyles, and conventions to help you. For example, you might find a line that looks like this:

- Type: `ATI9` `<E>`

What you actually type appears in a special typeface:

`ATI9`

Whatever appears on your screen will also be displayed in this manual in this special typeface, for example messages:

`CONNECT`

Throughout this guide, we use certain symbols, typestyles, and conventions to help you. For example, you might find a line that looks like this:

- Type: `ATI9` `<E>`

What you actually type appears in a special typeface:

`ATI9`

Whatever appears on your screen will also be displayed in this manual in this special typeface, for example messages:

`CONNECT`

Throughout this guide, we use certain symbols, typestyles, and conventions to help you. For example, you might find a line that looks like this:

- Type: `ATI9`   `<E>`

What you actually type appears in a special typeface:

`ATI9`

Whatever appears on your screen will also be displayed in this manual in this special typeface, for example messages:

`CONNECT`

Deciding what's worthwhile reading

One of the major problems facing the documentation writer is that the documentation being produced has to struggle with all the other competitors demanding the user's time. If the documentation is difficult to use and demands too much of the user's time, the user will set it aside and that documentation will not be used. Let's put this topic in perspective.

Consider that if you were to read a book a week for your entire life — and very few people read a book a month, much less one a week — you'd read about 4000 books if you lived to a reasonable age. Now consider that a reasonable university library or major city library has in excess of 1,000,000 books. Consider the percentage 4000 out of 1,000,000 makes. Ever since the first time I thought this concept through, I have found myself questioning the time allotment every time I pick up a book. Is this a book I can really afford the time to read?

Those critical first reactions

Hand users a new manual and watch what they do with it. (This little play takes place in countless book stores too!) They pick up the manual and flick through it, usually starting somewhere near the middle of the manual and working toward the back. They pause occasionally if something attracts their attention. When they reach the back, they use the thumb to flick through the pages toward the front. Perhaps at this point they may look at the contents page, or the index.

The process doesn't make sense, does it? So, what are these users doing? What they are doing is trying to decide whether this manual is going to be useful. This is their first impression and as with a lot of decisions made in life, the first impression is critical.

From this first reaction flows another reaction which colors how well your documentation is accepted (and, hence, used). Human beings make snap judgments and then stick with those judgments, in some cases even if they can be proven wrong. This is not restricted to documentation. This is common across a whole range of human endeavor.

The effect of this in manual writing is that unless your manual looks attractive and feels attractive, the user may reject it before he even gets a chance to really use it. And once rejected, it is likely to stay rejected. Many of the suggestions in this book are aimed at avoiding this initial rejection.

As a side note, which we'll develop later, almost all of the internal documentation produced by my company is accompanied by a short training course run with the users (or a small group of representative users from across a company) on the day the documentation is handed out for the first time. This course shows the users how to use the manual, explains what the manual covers, and does not cover. Manuals introduced properly are used more extensively than manuals merely dropped on a user's desk.

The rational review

If the manual makes it past the first reaction successfully, the user will then start making what might be called a more rational review of the documentation. His decisions now are based on what we have already discussed as the definition of effective documentation. The user asks:

❏ Is the information easy to find?

❏ Is the information easy to understand?

❏ Is the information up-to-date, reflecting the latest changes and revisions to the system?

So, there are two considerations in that first meeting of manual and user. The user might ask himself:

❑ Does the manual *look* and *feel* good enough to warrant my spending valued time with it?

❑ Does the manual have the information in it that I need, and can I count on its reliability?

If your user is an average reader, one of the first parts of the manual that will catch his eye is the level of the language used in the text.

Dealing with computer jargon

Remember that computers are merely tools, like the telephone, the fax machine, and the photocopier. The language that computer professionals employ is not the language of the average user and must either be avoided or, if there is no way to avoid this language, then the terms that make computer language difficult to understand must be explained.

This topic is discussed in more detail later in chapter 4, but it is important enough to be introduced here as we develop our understanding of the users.

Most dictionaries deal with jargon in a negative way. For example, *Webster's New Ideal Dictionary* 1978, page 279, defines jargon as "confused, unintelligible language; a hybrid language or dialect used for communication between peoples of different speech; the special vocabulary or idiom of a particular activity or group; obscure and often pretentious language marked by circumlocutions and abstract words". That, in itself, should be enough to make you want to avoid it.

Computer manuals filled with computer jargon — the language of the computer professional, rather than the language of the user — are everywhere. As I stated before, IBM produces manuals that are excellent examples of jargon-filled documentation. Whenever I make this statement at one of my documentation courses, heads around the classroom all nod knowingly.

One of the weaknesses of the computer industry is that this new industry has spawned a whole new language and the people who make use of that language have failed to recognize the gap between themselves and the rest of us. And yet they are constantly producing hardware and software tools they expect us to use.

This is a problem that has been with us throughout history. Consider trying to explain the modern airplane to Julius Caesar. Aviation jargon like attitude, airspeed, thrust, and so forth would mean little to the man who rides a horse or a chariot.

How does the documentation writer tackle the problem of jargon? If he can ignore it, which is almost impossible in most cases, he should, and if he can't ignore it then he must make sure the jargon problem disappears. Jargon ceases to be a problem when the writer explains the jargon word or phrase in words the user can understand. When the user has a mindset available to cover the term, then the term is no longer a barrier to understanding.

Be careful when deciding what qualifies as jargon. In the example on aviation, "attitude" is a jargon word. It has a very specific meaning. But consider a teacher to whom "attitude" is also a jargon word, but with a different meaning. To a computer programmer, "security" has a specific meaning. To a stock market analyst, a "security" has another meaning. While digital, analog, and firmware are common words in a computer environment, they all need explanation to the 19-year-old clerk or the 35-year-old warehouse worker. And the mindset of a 19-year-old might differ from that of a 35-year-old. Abbreviations such as ASCII (American Standard Code for Information Interchange) must also be defined.

Your early definition of the user will help you determine what words the user will likely understand. If you have any doubts about whether a word falls into the category of jargon — define it.

Let's look at how jargon might be handled. Your profile of the user and the context in which the documentation will be used will tell you whether a word like "data" needs to be treated as jargon. In most cases I would avoid using data and use information instead. Of course, the purist would argue that there is a difference between data and information, but if the user is not going to need to know the difference why not use the more recognizable word? The user is going to have enough on his mind, without adding more.

An alternative is to conclude that data is a rather common term these days and your users might be expected to know what data is. If your users fall into this category, use data and provide a definition in the glossary.

On some occasions the user might know what it's all about, but not recognize the jargon label. For example, in word processing there are numerous words used to designate the action a typist used to take to move from the end of one line to the beginning of the next line. Sometimes it's called a carriage return, or ENTER, or RETURN or some symbol. Most users understand the concept, but need to have the label explained.

A related weakness of the computer industry is the way some jargon words have more than one meaning. For example, portable. One definition of portable is a program that can be easily run on many different computers. Another is a computer that can be tucked under your arm and carried around. Or consider "procedure", which can often have the same meaning as "subroutine". I'd use procedure. Users don't have much need to know about subroutines.

A significant problem is the user who has a different definition for the jargon word. Attitude in aviation, and attitude in education, security as a computer concept, and security as a financial concept are all examples.

The safest way to handle this problem is to avoid the use of the jargon word or phrase. This is important if you are writing a reference manual where the user might enter the manual at any point and not have the advantage of introductory text. An alternative is to provide pointers on pages that might cause problems. The pointers should either be a glossary entry or to the place in the manual where the appropriate explanation has been made.

If the user does not know the concept behind a jargon word, then the writer must find a way to explain that concept. This is difficult, because concepts are often hard to describe in words. A diagram might work better. For example, consider the simple concept of a window, as shown below. This simple drawing makes it quite clear.

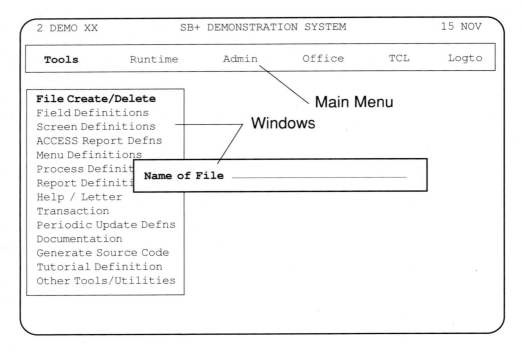

If the concept is difficult to explain with text or a drawing, consider introducing it in a training session, or in a hands-on tutorial.

Related to jargon is the need to make sure the user starts and remains on the same wavelength as the writer. It is very common to hear two people arguing and for one of them to finally say: "Now I understand. What I thought you meant was. . ." To help avoid this problem, the writer must provide the context, the environment.

For example, the phrase

```
Check your baggage
```

only takes on its true meaning when it is placed in its proper context or environment. If you are at the airport, you are handing over your baggage to be stored on the airplane. If you are at home, you might be checking to see if you've packed everything you will need in your suitcase.

The word "Documentation" itself might cause problems. Consider these environments:

❑ To the academic, documentation has to do with identifying sources, usually in footnotes and endnotes in a term paper.

❑ To the computer user, it usually means a manual.

❑ To the computer programmer, it usually means input and output requirements, notes on the algorithm, or data structure used.

How do users approach documentation?

Each piece of documentation must have a philosophy about it. Put another way, the writer must establish the exact context in which a piece of documentation is going to be used. Not only is knowledge of the user important, but also knowledge of the environment in which the user will be operating is critical.

As an example, consider on-line help. We'll cover this topic in detail later, but for now consider the amount of help needed and how that help should be written for the following two environments:

The first environment is a situation where a clerk is dealing with a customer and that clerk is filling in a form on a computer. Ten questions have to be answered and at question number five, the clerk forgets the procedure.

In some systems, the on-line help might produce four screens of information and what the clerk needs to know would be mixed in with a number of topics on screen three. While the clerk desperately searches for the information, the customer becomes frustrated by the delay.

If the help has been constructed with the right philosophy, the environment in which the clerk is using the help would be taken into consideration.

The help screen would come up and the basic "do this" information would be displayed. Do this, do this, do this, thank the customer. After the customer has gone, the clerk could then turn to a more detailed version of on-line help to understand why he was required to do this and do this, or he could turn to the manual for a complete discussion of the procedure.

Taking this need for a philosophy one step further, the on-line help for this procedure might be displayed on the screen in such a way that the prompt remains active so the help line can be read and the proper information typed in at the same time. This is when you are producing truly effective documentation.

On the other hand, if the need for help is in an environment where a more leisurely approach can be taken, there is no need for the short, no commentary approach. In an office setting, the help can include both "Do This" and "Understand This" material.

A philosophy is necessary and the writer must understand the appropriate philosophies available, and then match them to the user and the user's environment.

CHAPTER 3

The writer and documentation tools

The documentation writer

The documentation writer differs from other kinds of writers in many ways. The documentation writer does not create in the same way as most of us think writers create. For the documentation writer, the creation has already taken place in the notes and actions of the programmers and analysts who have come before. While there is room for creativity in documentation writing, it is not a literary type of creativity.

The documentation writer is almost always in the instructional mode. He is concerned with getting across a clear, concise message to the users of his documentation. As a result, the documentation writer must have a very clear understanding on the users. (I have used the phrase "the documentation writer" over and over again in the last two paragraphs. This is intentional. For this exercise, you are only a documentation writer, not a screen writer or a novel writer or a poetry writer. It is a concept many writers have trouble recognizing. They continually want to be literary, and literary is not particularly appropriate here.)

In many ways, the writer may be the only link on the entire project between the technical side (which is often overwhelming) and the non-technical user. In some cases, the writer may be the only true *user* who has hands-on activity with a new system.

The writer must set aside whatever technical knowledge he has, if he has any, and see everything from the user's point of view. It is the only effective way to approach documentation. Writers with no formal technical training often make the best documentation writers. They ask the questions the user wants answered.

When should the writer become involved?

In too many cases, the documentation writer becomes involved in the project right at the end. On the flow chart of the work to be done, documentation is a little box after testing, usually just before training and installation. Often there is very little you can do to influence this scheduling. If that's where you find yourself, grin and bear it — and hope for a better break next time.

However, I firmly believe the documentation writer should be a member of the project team right from the beginning of the project. This does not mean the writer will have much to do, but he can attend regular meetings and provide some user input.

The most effective documentation produced by my company has been documentation where we have been involved early on, have attended enough meetings to keep up to date with the system's development, and have had opportunities to represent the users — contributing on screen design and layout, on the choice of words used for screen prompts, and so forth. When it came time to document the system, we were well ahead in terms of research and the manuals needed were delivered much earlier than normal, to management's delight.

Of course — and contrary to some advice I've heard — the writer should not start documenting until development is finished. To start while programmers are still making changes to the programming is to court disaster. You are inviting trouble. A programming change, to menu structure for example, that the technical team calls minor could easily result in a major change to your documentation.

The documentation set

The documentation writer is armed with an impressive set of tools and a large collection of strategies with which to tackle any documentation task. When confronted by something that needs documenting, the writer's initial thoughts must turn to deciding what strategies and tools will be deployed. Will there be a manual for this project? A reference card, on-line help, and so forth?

The documentation set is defined as the collection of documentation tools that a user will have available when being introduced to, or when using the new system. Sometimes the manual is the only tool you will need. On other occasions, a manual is wholly inappropriate. A short case history should put this topic into perspective.

Case history: when manuals won't work

The problem was simple. A large maintenance hangar, about the size of two football fields and located in a remote area, handled maintenance service for large earth-movers. All these earth-movers were the same size and make and each was worth in excess of $100,000 so the maintenance side of operations was important. These machines must be kept operational.

Management had decided to put in a new computer system to keep track of the maintenance program, the supply of parts, and so forth. The assignment was, according to management, to write manuals that could be used by the maintenance workers, mostly mechanics and engineers. Unfortunately, the senior management, who commissioned the new documentation, was located in a big city a long way away from the actual work site. Before leaving for the site I was warned that the workers on the site were making trouble. They didn't want the computer system installed. A senior manager confided to me that he thought the union was just using the computer system as a ploy to demand more money. I wasn't convinced. I'd heard the argument too many times.

This kind of project demonstrates the different levels of users the documentation writer comes into contact with and how the writer might respond. Take the following examples from a project I worked on. For meeting with senior management, I wore a shirt and tie. For meeting with supervisors and foremen on site, I wore a khaki work-shirt and slacks. For mess hall talk sessions with the workers, I wore their unique uniform: shorts and blue undershirt.

As far as transportation, from the head office in the big city I took an airplane ride to a small airport in the country, then a smaller airplane into the desert, and then a four-wheel jeep across the desert to the actual site. It was desolate and hot, an ugly place to work. Not a woman was in sight (a point important to remember given the final solutions to the documentation problems posed here). The workers labored from dawn to dusk for a couple of weeks and then enjoyed a week's rest and recreation in the big city. Off-duty hours were spent drinking and playing games in a staff canteen. These were tough men. After a few hours with them, I knew manuals would be a problem. These guys were not going to take time out to read.

There was also another problem. There was little consistency among the terms they applied when talking about the parts of their earth-movers. One mechanic would talk of an RJ72, another called it a Gizmo, another called it an Are-Jay. Terminology would have to be cleaned up if the system was going to do its job.

In the first few hours I confirmed my suspicions. The furor over the computer system had more to do with worker insecurity about the computer system in terms of their job security. Management was not listening properly — a common problem. A newsletter or a head office visitor could easily take some of the pressure off.

The supervisors and foremen were not much help. They were suffering most from the management problem created by the imminent arrival of the unwelcome computer system. They felt sandwiched between management and workers. It was my job to find solutions, they pointed out politely. Leave them out of it as much as possible.

So the problem was quickly defined. What would work in an environment where no one wanted to spend time reading? As I toiled to understand the user, and wrestled with the problem of developing a common terminology, I noticed that taking pride of place in most work areas were *Playboy* and *Penthouse* centerfolds. While I admired the obvious charms that were on display and noted the reverence and affection the workers displayed toward these posters, the answer to this site's documentation problems became obvious.

I planned a set of huge wall charts and because all the equipment being maintained was the same height, I could also use charts suspended from the roof. The terminology problem was also solved. Blown up drawings could be made and displayed in a similar style. Thus, from any computer location around the hangar, simple instructions and drawings would always be near by. I added to this basic plan a detailed training session for each employee during one of their breaks in the city and the work force would be covered.

To keep the workers' attention, I had those centerfolds blown up to the same height as the charts (somewhat larger than lifesize) and tacked on each side of the display panels. And once a year the centerfolds would be replaced. As an extra, two-fold reference cards were also prepared, laminated, and made available at each computer workstation.

The solutions worked well. Of course, management back in the big city still wanted a manual, so I wrote one for them based on the training materials that would be used at the training sessions.

The lesson here, of course, is that manuals are not always the best solution even though they are the most common documentation tool. Knowledge of the user will determine the best tool and the best strategy. Take the time to do your research. It always pays off in the end.

Documentation tools come in many sizes and shapes. The following table shows some of their appropriate applications. The role of each tool must be weighed against the needs of the user.

✔ = useful   ✗ = not useful

Documentation Tools	Training		Reference	How-To
	Formal	*Self-Teach*		
Technical reference manual	✗	✗	✔	✗
Installation manual	✔	✔	✔	✔
User operations manual	✗	✗	✔	✔
Leader's (Training) manual	✔	✗	✗	✗
Student's (Training) workbook	✔	✔	✔	✗
Quick reference cards	✗	✗	✔	✔
Wall charts	✔	✔	✔	✔
Keyboard overlays	✗	✗	✔	✔
Terminal stickers	✗	✗	✔	✔
Screen prompts/messages	✗	✗	✔	✔
On-Line Help	✗	✔	✔	✔
On-Line tutorials	✔	✔	✗	✔
On-Line manuals	✗	✗	✗	✗
Video	✔	✔	✗	✔
Overheads	✔	✗	✗	✗
Slides (with script or sound)	✔	✗	✗	✗

The tools: advantages and disadvantages

Mastering the tools is a prerequisite of a good documentation writer, as it is with any professional or skilled worker. Each tool has advantages and disadvantages. The documentation set often becomes a balance between what works best and what you can afford — the classic tradeoff.

MANUALS

- Convenient to use, easy to personalize, tangible, relatively inexpensive, can be all-inclusive
- Difficult to update in quantity, passive, never used if poorly produced

QUICK REFERENCE CARDS

- Quick to prepare, inexpensive, easy to update, users tend to use them
- Limited room for information and explanations

WALL CHARTS

- Attractive, easy to find the information, can get a lot of information in one place
- Can be difficult to design and prepare, expensive, difficult to update, usually not suitable for complex instructions

KEYBOARD OVERLAYS AND TERMINAL STICKERS

- Inexpensive in quantity, information always available
- Expensive in small quantities, little room for information/explanation

SCREEN PROMPTS/MESSAGES

- Inexpensive and easy to prepare, used extensively
- Often poorly done leaving user confused

ON-LINE HELP

- Easy to update, can be context sensitive

- Not satisfactory for new computer users, little information on screen, expensive on disk space/system resources

ON-LINE TUTORIALS

- Consistency with training, can be fun, encourage interactive involvement = more effective learning

- Difficult and expensive to prepare, difficult and expensive to update

ON-LINE DOCUMENTATION

- Information always on hand, easily updated if on a mainframe system

- Difficult for users to access when experiencing a problem, twice as many pages (screens) than a manual to allow for clarity, difficult to locate solutions to individual problems, generally not user friendly

VIDEO

- Can show it happening, light relief for a training course, will get attention if well produced

- Expensive, a waste of time if amateur production, impossible to update

OVERHEADS

- Inexpensive to produce, easy to update, can add interest to training sessions if well produced

- Limited room for information/explanations, not suitable for reference material

SLIDES (with script or sound)

- Inexpensive to produce, easy to update, can add interest to training sessions if well produced

- Only useful for short interest sessions or demonstrations where real situation or equipment is not available

The two-fold reference card

The two-fold reference card (or quick reference card) needs a special comment because it is a tool that users find very practical, and yet it is often overlooked by those producing internal documentation, although common in external documentation. The two-fold reference card is merely an 8.5 by 11 inch piece of paper (sometimes made of a stiffer card), folded twice horizontally to produce six faces.

Those six faces provide a considerable amount of room on which to place the answers to user's most commonly asked questions. The card replaces all those little pieces of paper stuck to the edges of terminals and keyboards which remind a user how or when to carry out certain tasks, or what to do in a crisis.

I usually produce the artwork for these cards immediately after finishing a manual, while everything is fresh in my mind. If the system has been in place and the users are working with it, I wander around and make notes of those items users have chosen to write down on those little pieces of papers and on desk pads and blotters.

A colleague of mine carried out a study that suggested a well designed two-fold card will satisfy 80 percent of the questions, asked by 75 percent of the users.

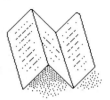

In defense of the manual

There has been some criticism of the manual as a documentation tool. Considerable debate goes on as to whether or not the manual is still a viable documentation form. The argument is based on the fact that the computer should be the center of all activity.

We treat that argument as an academic exercise. Granted, the documentation of the future will be more centered on the computer itself. However, talk about how paper manuals will disappear is just that — mere talk.

For the foreseeable future, we will all be working with paper-based manuals and thus, as documentation writers, we must learn how to build these tools even better. This is not just our opinion, it is the opinion of some of the largest companies in the world.

The growing debate about electronic manuals — where the printed manual is available on-line — is extremely misleading. A solid case can be made that on-line Manuals do not work, and cannot be made to work, as mere electronic versions of the printed page. The screen and the printed page to are too dissimilar to ever consider that one will totally replace the other.

We will deal with this problem in more detail in the chapter discussing on-line help.

Different types of manuals

However, to be constructive, let's look at a number of different kinds of manuals.

System specification

A well prepared system specifications manual always helps highlight weaknesses in the design of any computer system. If written prior to system development (as it should be) it will direct the analysts to design a system within strict guidelines.

System awareness guide

This gives an overview of a system that is about to be introduced to management and staff. It usually shows how the system will make everyone's job easier, more effective, and more enjoyable.

Computer system procedure

This manual is for a wider use. It probably includes details of management policy and office procedures, as well as an explanation of how to use the system.

User reference

This assumes the user understands the basics of the system, but occasionally needs a quick reference to details. There may be any number of user reference manuals. For example, one user reference manual may contain details needed by the system administrator, while another contains those needed by the desk clerk. (Note that user reference manuals are very different from training and installation guides.)

System maintenance reference

This type of manual contains very different information from that found in a user reference manual. For example, it may explain what to do if the system crashes, how each program is structured, which variables are used in each program, and so on.

Installation

This manual emphasizes the "how to set it up" aspect.

Installation training service

Suppliers of software packages often provide an installation training service for their customers. This manual is designed to help the training staff to work more efficiently with the customers and reduce the overall costs of installation training.

Tutorial support

These manuals are produced as working documents to assist a user training on a system. They are usually designed to work with some form of on-line tutorial.

Post installation support

Suppliers of software packages often provide "post installation" support services for their customers. This manual would be designed to help the support staff solve customer problems and reduce the overall support costs.

Contractual obligation

Sometimes the only reason for documentation is that the legal contract for the supply of the system insists that documentation be provided. This is a reasonable requirement. But if the contract does not stipulate the content, the documentation is usually hastily done and incomplete. Unfortunately, providers of systems often believe there is no profit in doing this kind of manual well.

Marketing tool

This type of manual aims at convincing a potential buyer of the benefits of the system. It presents its information more persuasively and less technically than the user manual.

Training

This manual also tries to sell the system, but it usually emphasizes "how to use it" rather than "why to use it" information.

Policy

This manual contains all the company rules, codes of business practices, methodologies, and instructions to be applied in given situations. It supplies rules and guidelines rather than "how to do it" information.

Operations and procedure

These manuals supply the "how to do it" information by setting out complete procedures in line with company policy.

Often the *only* reason for documentation is that only one or two people within an organization are familiar with the behind the scenes detail of the system. If they leave, the organization may face real difficulties unless something is documented.

Any large system might make use of all or a combination of manuals from this list. Each manual would have a separate mission to perform and, perhaps, an entirely different group of users. The key is that the manuals would be structured so that each meets a particular need for a particular user or group of users. Each manual's blueprint will be different as will the level of language.

In summary, see once again the link between knowledge of the users and the actual piece of documentation you finally write.

CHAPTER 4

10 documentation processes — how to

An introduction to the 10 processes

Having set the scene by examining the role of documentation, the different types of documentation, and the leading role played by the writer, it is time to turn to the actual mechanics of the documentation task.

Ten processes have been set in place to act as a guide to preparing a documentation item. Depending on what particular item you need — perhaps a manual, a reference card, or a wall chart — certain processes will become more important than others. However, as you will quickly see, some processes are common to whatever item you choose from the available documentation set.

For the purposes of introducing the 10 processes, we will assume we're working on a manual. This is the most common form of documentation and will no doubt remain so for some time to come. While on-line help and electronic manuals (which we look at later in this book) are becoming more important members of the set, there are still problems with execution and, particularly, with acceptance by most computer users who remain computer illiterates, even though they may spend a large part of their working day in front of a keyboard and terminal.

These processes represent key points along the way. As with any kind of campaign, be it military or business, we must have a clear objective or mission. We must have a sense of strategy about how we are going to carry out the mission, and a definitive set of tactics to execute the strategy.

I use these processes daily, and the writers, artists, and editors who work with me use these processes as well. When I first started out, there were fewer processes. More have been added, all have undergone revision and continue to do so in order to change with the times. As the technical programmer must keep abreast of changes in his profession, so it is equally important for the documentation writer to keep up with the latest developments in the use of words, graphics, design, and so forth.

Effective documentation requires patience,
time, and a certain set of skills

The first ground rule that needs to be set in granite is that documentation takes time and patience. Documentation is not creative writing. Very few documentation writers have the luxury to await the arrival of the muse, and even fewer will find corporate sympathy for that much abused condition known as writer's block.

It is highly unlikely you will get it absolutely right the first time. Heavy editing and rewriting should be expected. There is also a significant amount of subjectivity involved. Learn to accept others' idea, but also recognize that you are the expert and no matter how well meaning colleagues and superiors may be — the responsibility remains with *you* to produce a piece of documentation that meets the needs of the users.

Another ground rule is that you are writing to instruct, to inform; your primary purpose is not to entertain or to prove your creativity. Avoid flights of fancy.

An order for the task

The 10 processes provide an order for the task. They can be viewed as individual missions you need to accomplish on your way to your objective. Those missions, and the order in which you must tackle them, are:

Process 1	Name and Definition
Process 2	Understanding the User
Process 3	Research and Organization
Process 4	Designing
Process 5	Blueprinting
Process 6	Writing
Process 7	Editing
Process 8	Proofreading
Process 9	Producing
Process 10	Maintaining

How to get started

To get started, let's borrow another phrase from the technical people and talk about using the top-down development approach. Top-down programming, or structured programming, means writing programs where the whole system is divided into simple tasks, then each task is written and tested before proceeding to the next one.

We can look at each of our processes as a single task, with various subtasks. In documentation, we execute the whole process and avoid the temptation to move on before finishing the task at hand.

But we also need to keep the whole structure clearly in mind and ensure a sense of balance throughout. Thus we will start at the beginning and progress steadily to the end — without undue emphasis on certain chapters or sections merely because we might happen to be better versed in certain topics.

This lack of balance is a common problem for many writers and conscious steps need to be taken to avoid falling into the obvious structural crevices it creates in the finished documentation.

Let me tell you a little story

Consider the young, enthusiastic mural painter who has finally been given the chance to create a masterpiece. The city council of a seaside resort wants a mural painted on the side of half-block-long factory wall. It was an eyesore and the mural painter works cheaply and is very enthusiastic. The city leaders want three elements in the mural: the city, the seashore, and the sea. They're not very creative so their only instruction is that each of the three elements should get about equal space.

The mural painter is excited and eager and gets right down to work. He can see the whole image in his head, he tells onlookers. It will be a grand vision. First, he starts to paint the city.

He climbs his ladder and starts painting. Vivid detail, brilliant colors, fine execution. The city comes alive in his painting. Every street is complete, every house looks as though it is lived in, every man and woman and child seems almost alive. He paints on and on, never leaving his ladder, never pausing. He is reproducing what is indelibly printed on his mind. Already, as he works on a fire hydrant's detail in front of a massive firehouse, he can see every grain of sand, and every white-capped wave to come.

Finally, his city portion is finished. He climbs down from his ladder and steps back. His face crumbles, his shoulders sag. He has used up 70 percent of the whole wall for the city. The seashore and sea will be out of proportion, the project a failure. He was so busy on the details, he forgot to *see* the whole picture in its finished form.

That is what the documentation writer must guard against. It is often easy to get started, but without proper planning, with a blueprint to work from, the whole manual is likely to lack proportion. It will be out of balance, with emphasis usually in sections where the writer is secure in his knowledge of the subject, and those areas about which the writer knows less will be short and sparse on detail.

The documentation writer must address his mural in the same way that a professional mural painter, with experience and knowledge of his craft, would tackle the city-beach-sea assignment.

First there would be a blueprint and a thoroughly defined specification of what is to be accomplished. There would be some painting. And then the painter would come down off the ladder, stand back, and take a look. The blueprint would be constantly referred to. Everything would stay in proportion, everything would be in balance. Perhaps the mural painter would even sketch in the whole wall before starting to fill in the detail.

That's the key for these documentation processes. The manual is written in a series of complete start-to-finish motions. No single part gets extra emphasis, unless that part is singled out in the specification.

While we have 10 processes to step through to provide the foundations for effective documentation, it is also important at this stage that you see the project broken down into phases, as shown on the next page. The table shows the entire project from start to finish. The 10 processes are shown in this table as a methodology to follow. The 12-phase table is discussed in detail later when we look at time management of documentation tasks.

Phase 1	Research and Organization	
	Learning System and Users	
	Developing Format	
	Setting Style Guide	
	Writing Contents Blueprint	

Phase 2	Getting Approval To Proceed	

Phase 3	Research/Writing the 1st Draft	
	Writer's Edit of 1st Draft	
	Print out 1st Draft	

Phase 4	Technical Accuracy	
	and Completeness Check	

Phase 5	Writing the 2nd Draft	
	Writer's Edit of 2nd Draft	
	Print out 2nd Draft	

Phase 6	1st Full Proofreading	

Phase 7	Writing the 3rd Draft	
	Writer's Edit of 3rd Draft	
	Print out 3rd Draft	

Phase 8	Final Proofreading	

Phase 9	Minor Edits	
	Print out Acceptance Copy	

Phase 10	Acceptance	

Phase 11	Production	

Phase 12	Distribution	
	Introducing to Users	

Process 1: Name and Define

PROCESS ONE

Clearly name and define each item of documentation. Recognize that the name and definition are the focal points of the documentation task.

Clearly name and provide a definition for each item of documentation. The name and definition are the focal points of the documentation task.

It is very easy to start writing one manual and end up halfway through the task finding yourself writing a different kind of manual, and then by the time you've written the last third, finding yourself with an entirely different manual.

To avoid this common problem, you need to take two steps right at the beginning. These are very concrete steps. At this point you are actually on the verge of doing something, rather than just thinking about doing something.

Provide a name

The first step is to name the item of documentation, and then to start thinking of the item by that name. This name will provide a major part of the definition of the manual.

> Welcome to the *JumpMaster Reference Manual*, your guide to XYZ International's JumpMaster product - Batch Version.

> Welcome to the *NetComm FaxNet User's Guide*. FaxNet enables you to use your network of IBM PCs (XT, AT, or compatible) to send and receive faxes.

Welcome to Concept's *Personnel Administration User Manual...*

There is no need here for fancy names. These are all acceptable and they all provide some form of definition:

❏ New Employee Training Manual

❏ System Administration Guide

❏ Installation Manual

❏ On-Line Tutorial Workbook

Work on the title until you feel a commitment to that title. A self-test is to ask yourself: Could I go to management with this title and ask them to run off 10,000 four-color brochures announcing the impending arrival of this manual? If you have that kind of commitment, then you have found a good title.

Provide a definition

The next stage demands that you create a working definition for the item of documentation. At this point, you need the answers to two very specific questions:

1   Why is this system being installed?

2   Why is this item of documentation required?

Armed with the answers to these questions, you can start defining the mission of your item of documentation. In the case of a manual, you will have some idea of why you need to prepare the manual, and what you want the manual to accomplish when it is finally opened by the users. As with any major task, it is useless to start thinking about the strategy and tactics of how you will go about your task until you have a clear understanding of your final objective.

While you are carrying out this process, be sure to avoid flights of fancy. This activity requires having both feet firmly on the ground. Think in concrete terms. Avoid abstracts. Be explicit and definite.

The *JumpMaster Reference Manual* has been designed to serve a number of purposes, including:

❑ providing details about the various options available for configuring JumpMaster to your specific requirements

❑ providing an on-going reference guide for the efficient operation of JumpMaster

The aim of the *SB+ Reference Manual* is to:

❑ provide an introduction to the facilities within SB+

❑ act as a companion to the extensive on-line help available within SB+

❑ provide technical information and tips for more efficient use of SB+

A problem starts to surface if you cannot find a clear focus during the definition stage. Occasionally, the problem might appear even earlier, during the search for an appropriate name.

You know you need a user's guide, a procedural guide to the how to do it aspect of the task. But part of what you have been asked for is a trainer's manual. There is a conflict here that needs to be resolved immediately.

During the definition process, that conflict becomes even more obvious. The structure of a procedural manual and the structure of a training manual are somewhat different. They might be for the same groups of users, and for the same system, but the way they will be used, and what they will be used for, are different.

What do you do when there are competing claims on the mission or objective of the manual? The easiest answer is:

☞ When there are competing claims, it is easier to write two manuals, one to satisfy each claim. One manual will address each definition.

The more difficult answer — which we'll deal with later in this book — is to adapt the single manual to cover more than one purpose.

Process 1 is not easy. While, at first glance, choosing a name may not prove difficult, defining the mission of the documentation requires careful thought and a clear understanding of what you are trying to accomplish.

Process 1 is also important because you will want to return to it over and over again as you work through the task. It will become a signpost. Am I still addressing the definition? Am I still on track?

Process 2: Define the User

> ## PROCESS TWO
>
> **Know your user's needs and point of view. Put yourself into the mindset of the user.**

Know your user's needs and point of view. Put yourself into the mindset of the user.

In the discussion we've already been through, we've established the need to understand the user — to get inside the user's mindset — so that your approach, your choice of words, your choice of format and design, represents the most effective way of communicating to your defined user group.

That's the purpose of Process 2 — through researching the user, you will build up a profile of the group you will be writing for.

The action you need to take consists of two distinct parts:

1 You must get to know your user.

2 You must write down a definitive description of that user.

Once again, be explicit and definite. You need a thorough view of the average user of the system, if that is the person you are writing for. The average user can be very different depending on where you look. If the average user for the manual you have defined is a 19-year-old clerk, that 19-year-old will be very different when compared with the 48-year-old marketing manager who might also be your defined user.

Out of your findings will come decisions on how you will structure your approach to such concerns as the use of jargon, the amount of detail on topics like how to use the keyboard, and some basic decisions including the level of language to be used.

If you've written a number of manuals, you may already have considerable experience in defining users. You will still need to confirm your assumptions about any specific group. Spend time with the users. Join them in the workplace. Sit with them. See how they carry out their job tasks.

If the users are not operational yet, then watch how they carry out the noncomputerized version of their tasks. Think through the problems they might face in making the step from manual to computerized operations.

Seeing the user at work is an important aspect of defining that user. It is also important to get to know even more about the users. The following are usually key indicators:

❏ educational background

❏ leisure time interests

❏ what radio station they listen to

❏ what television shows they watch

❏ what do they think about the impending installation of the system

❏ what do they think the manual should tell them

Once I was given a documentation assignment by a large national company. Management said they wanted a policy-procedure manual, definitely not a how to do it manual. During this definition stage, I traveled to many locations where users were hard at work. The message on the shop floor, was emphatic: the users wanted how to do it manuals.

They wanted to know what key to press, what information to fill in for each field, how to respond to every prompt. If I had listened to management only, I would have written the wrong manual. All this information will help you form a definition of the user and, as a result, a definition of the documentation.

Tying the first two processes together

While you need to carry out the first two processes in some detail, rest assured you are not wasting any time. While there is a very practical first-stage application to what you are doing, you are also taking out a long-term insurance policy against writing the wrong manual.

Before I developed and followed these processes, I found myself too often in this scenario. The first draft of the manual — three months of writing — lands on the desk of management, is distributed for reading, and criticisms start to flow:

❑ "I thought you were writing a training manual that I can use with small classes in our training classroom," moans the training manager.

❑ "I thought you were writing an operational guide they could use at their work stations," complains the dispatch supervisor.

❑ "I thought you were writing a detailed reference manual for my maintenance staff," argues the chief engineer.

And, of course, I thought I was writing a manual covering only the system inquiries and reports module.

It is far better to find out that someone thinks you are doing something different from what you think you are doing at this stage rather than after you have put in a lot of work. Competing claims should be defined now, not later.

When Process 1 and Process 2 are finished, you have actually started writing the first part of the manual. With a little reworking, and the addition of some extra pieces which will quickly fall into place, you will have the foreword or preface.

A little hint here: Be sure to include the foreword in the package of materials you will put forward for management approval before you start writing. This approval step will be discussed in more detail after we review the blueprinting — table of contents process (Process 5).

Another hint: If you have any doubts about users reading the foreword page, apply a useful contribution made by programmers. Put a big message at the top of the page which says:

> Read Me First!

The user must read this foreword page. There is information here that will not be repeated.

Let's look at an example to see how Process 1 and Process 2 create a foreword page on a project I wrote. There was a further complication that developed on this project and because it is a common problem, it is worthwhile detailing here.

The project was to write documentation for a commercial package called FaxNet. This is an example of external documentation. The manual is part of the package.

Here are the notes under the headings of the processes:

Process 1: Name and Definition

The FaxNet User's Guide

The guide will be used as a complete reference manual, with the emphasis being on how to do it from user configuration, through chronological operations of creating, sending, receiving, printing, storing, retrieving, deleting fax messages.

To consider: There are many useful utilities and special functions which will need to be covered including such diverse topics as how to create your own fonts for your faxes. These will break the chronological flow if inserted in the main body text.

Process 2: Define the Users

A substantial number of users have never worked on a facsimile network. However, all are experienced in operating a computer and working on a network.

Problem: There will also be some advanced users who will have had substantial experience on other kinds of facsimile networks or related systems.

Having complete these two processes, I started to look at the system. In my first major discussion with the technical people who created FaxNet, it became obvious that the system administrator had a distinct role quite separate from the user. As well, the system administrator had significant knowledge and experience that most users would not have.

The complication was that FaxNet management wanted a single manual for both users and the system administrator.

Back to the processes. In addition to what was already defined, I had to add:

Process 1 - Name and Definition

The FaxNet Supervisor's Guide

This guide will be used by supervisors experienced in networks and communications to install and configure the networking aspects of FaxNet.

Process 2 - Define the Users

The system administrators will be experienced in networking and communications. In most respects they will be similar to the more experienced users defined in the user's guide.

The dilemma here is one that has to be faced by writers on many documentation assignments. There is no average user. There is a need, in its most elementary form, to produce three manuals — one for the beginning user, one for the experienced user, and another for experienced system administrators.

On some occasions, the answer is to pick the most average, or the largest group of users, and write to them. Other groups of users will still be able to use the manual, but they may find it more difficult.

On the FaxNet project, I researched the system (which we'll discuss later) and then came up with the following solution. Publish a single manual in three distinct parts: 1. Users, 2. Supervisors, 3. Appendices. Break Part 1 into two subparts: For New Users *and* For Experienced Users.

Part 2 will have a new title page, and its own contents page and, if the supervisor wished, it could be taken out and put in another three-ring binder. (This met the management requirement for a single manual, but provided some flexibility when the documentation was actually put to use.)

The finished foreword is shown on the next page.

FOREWORD

The *Fax Net User's Guide* and the accompanying *FaxNet Supervisor's Guide* have been structured so they can be used easily by both experienced and new users.

Of course, the supervisor will be responsible for installing and configuring the network and the workstations and thus will require additional knowledge about networks and communications.

There are four sections in the *User's Guide:*

1   Introduction

2   Quick Start for Experienced Users

3   For New Users

4   Appendices

The *Supervisor's Guide* has additional information on installation and configuration, which must be carried out by the system supervisor before FaxNet can be used.

All users and supervisors should read the ***Introduction***. It provides an overview to this guide and acquaints you with FaxNet.

Experienced users will find the section ***Quick Start for Experienced Users*** useful. It provides a stripped down operating guide to routine FaxNet procedures and assumes you have knowledge and experience in using networks and communications systems.

If this is your first experience with this sort of system, the section ***For New Users*** provides step-by-step instructions so you can make maximum use of FaxNet's extensive features at your workstation.

The ***Appendices*** contain useful utilities as well as additional information, including an extensive glossary to help improve your productivity.

As you can see, the foreword comes directly out of the work you did on the first two processes, along with a few more details which become obvious as you start researching the system you are documenting. The development of the table of contents, and the actual writing, will also be made easier by the time and effort you have put in so far.

Defining the possibilities also helps in defining limitations. If you are writing a training manual, you won't tackle the task the same way as you would a maintenance manual.

Defining how much the user already knows about computers, or about the job they are already doing, will help you determine whether you have to explain what a keyboard is, or how much jargon you can use from the industry your users are a part of. For example, if you are writing a manual for use by private security guards, you will have to be careful in defining the computer system's security menu. Security to you might mean one thing (passwords, log on Ids), but something quite different to the professional *security* guard.

This definition also helps the user. Reading through the foreword of the manual will provide the user with some indication of whether they are reading the right manual. If the user is not part of the profiled group, then the user is forewarned. They may have some difficulty understanding what has been written.

The next two pages show an example of another Read Me First document.

Read This First

CONGRATULATIONS — and welcome to SB+. You have just purchased an outstanding product.

SB+ is an applications generator, which includes a runtime environment together with all administrative and office functions expected of a complete package.

Whatever the system you wish to write, you have already bought the right tools. But as with any tradesman or professional, taking the time to learn to use the tools properly now will pay off handsomely in the future.

If you are already an experienced programmer, you will find a wealth of features which can be used to create a system as complex and polished as any handwritten code.

We have tried to make SB+ and its documentation easy and attractive to use for total novices and for competent, experienced programmers.

The aim of this *SB+ Reference Manual*, and the accompanying *SB+ Administration Manual* is to:

❑ provide an introduction and reference to the facilities of SB+

❑ act as a companion to the extensive On-Line Help available within SB+

❑ provide technical information and tips for the more efficient use of SB+

The *SB+ Reference Manual* and *SB+ Administration Manual* are for:

❑ the user who wishes to develop or maintain an application within SB+

❑ the administrator of the SB+ environment

How to Use These Manuals

The *SB+ Reference Manual* guides you through the complete installation, application building, running, and maintenance of a system. The manual also provides detailed technical information allowing maximum functionality to be achieved within your application(s).

The *SB+ Administration Manual* guides you through the administration of the SB+ environment.

Immediately after the Introduction section in the *SB+ Reference Manual*, there are important notes on efficient ways to learn SB+. We recommend you read these notes fully.

The Operating Environment

The operating environment is the underlying database structure and language/commands that SB+ is dependent on to run. This operating environment may be the actual operating system or the software between the operating system and SB+.

For example, Pick is both an operating system and an operating environment. It can also be an operating environment running on UNIX or DOS operating systems. Universe and UniData are operating environments which run on the UNIX operating system.

When we refer to operating environment in these SB+ manuals, we are referring to Universe, UniData, Pick, Prime, or McDonnell Douglas.

Process 3: Organize and Research

PROCESS THREE

Organize your research so that you truly understand
the system you are documenting. Know
the size and shape of the task.

Gathering your material and interviewing

The time has now come to gather the material you will need to write
your manual. This will be difficult or easy, depending on a number of
factors, some of which you may not be able to influence.

I have had the dubious pleasure of accepting a rather large contract from
a rather large and well known corporation, only to be told during contract
discussions that the reason we were being asked to document the 10 new
systems was that the in-house people were all very busy. They hoped we
would be able to get on with the task without taking up very much of
their time.

To do documentation properly, you have to become part of the team
putting together the system, and part of the team of users you are writing
for.

I have already discussed why you have to relate to the users. Suffice it to
say in summary that you will not get very far in terms of writing an
efficient piece of documentation if you do not know your users.

Knowing the users and knowing the system go hand in hand. I don't
particularly care which one you learn first, although I personally tend
toward understanding my users first.

I want to assume here that you take my tack on learning a new system. I go in as a dumb user. I get someone to show me around the system for, say, an hour or two and then I ask to be alone and I "play" with the system, making notes and talking into a tape recorder.

I then go back to my office and make a question list of all those things I want more information about. I also jot down under various headings all those things I think I know because of my first "play session".

In almost every project we've worked on, we've found it hard to pin down technical people to answer our questions. The best method is to formally schedule a time for your technical interviews and then go into those meetings with your homework done.

We talk each point through. I don't make notes. I rely on my tape recorder and all the extra commentary I throw in during the question and answer period. It's too easy to miss something that happens as a response to a pressed function key. As the programmer answers prompts, and so forth, I talk continually into my recorder, trying to note everything that happens.

I break these sessions up so that no single session is too long. A couple of hours with a programmer can be a daunting task at best — they are not usually the greatest conversationalists — and the amount of material I get on tape in a couple of hours can often keep me going for a couple of days.

While I am listening to my tape and making my notes, I am also keeping a second sheet of paper beside me with new questions that develop from each session. I do not pick up the phone every time I have a query. There is nothing that will upset corporate executives, users or technical people faster than a writer who calls them two or three times a day with queries. (I maintain this rule even when I am writing a draft. If I've got a problem I put in two ?? and move on. I save all the questions for another one of my scheduled meetings.)

Most programmers probably think I am a real dummy because I have no guilt or anxiety about asking the most simple of questions. Often, even if I think I know the answer, I ask it anyway. There might be something new, at least new to you, and the programmer is so close to his subject that he might overlook telling you about it because he knows it so well he starts to believe everyone else knows about it too.

Every time the programmer lapses into jargon and uses a new term, question him about that term. An infuriating aspect of documentation is that often programmers develop new jargon to label something that already has an industry-accepted label. It's also important to make sure that your understanding of a jargon term is the same as that of the programmer who is showing you the system.

When the programmer has taken you through various steps in the system, let him get on with something he needs to do while you check what he has told you. I have seen programmers step through a procedure in a way that makes perfect sense to them, but that would not work in the user's environment.

For example, one efficient programmer I worked with early on in my documentation career moved from task to task by typing in a set of unique commands. I duly recorded those commands and almost wrote them into my first draft until I realized those commands would not be available to the user.

The live system and the training system

Make sure when you are playing with the system that you know whether you are in a test system, a training system, or in the live system. I once added a number of new clients to a system, and created sales and work orders, before someone told me I was working in the live system. Great difficulties were experienced trying to erase my phony entries.

The downside is that I have worked in a number of test and training systems and have done a considerable amount of work before someone finally pointed out:

> "Oh, that feature has been dropped and we haven't got around to taking it out of the test system!"

> OR

> "We've changed all those screens in the live system. Didn't anyone tell you?"

> OR

> "We've added new function keys for that part of the system."

When you're sure you know how the system works, it's time to move on to the next process.

Process 4: Design

```
┌─────────────────────────────────────────────┐
│                                              │
│              PROCESS FOUR                    │
│                                              │
│     Design the page format, type and graphics with │
│       the user firmly in mind.  Make sure the design │
│            will accommodate the entire task. │
│                                              │
└─────────────────────────────────────────────┘
```

Introduction

Now that you understand the user and the system you are documenting, it is time to make some decisions as to how best to organize the material so it will be most useful to the user.

What we are talking about here is the way you are going to present your message. Involved in this process are topics such as the physical size of the page, the format or layout of the page, the use of graphics, typography, and display of text blocks.

This design process is important. Take your time. You will have to consider topics that might require some outside help. For example, what size and style of type? What family of typefaces? What typeface to use inside screens layouts? How long should a single line of text be, given the typesize of that text? How much space between lines?

The questions might include: What tables and illustrations will be used? What about color? What about page numbering? Will production be done on single-sided pages or double-sided pages?

Another basic question is: Will I use a word processing package for the whole project, or will I need to go to a desktop publishing package to finish it? For example, some of my manuals are done totally in Microsoft Word™. Others are done in Aldus Pagemaker™ because of design requirements. For example, the layout shown on the next page needed PageMaker, or its equivalent.

3. Getting Started

Introduction   This section provides details to help you get started with the RADS system. It also tells you about the layout of the screens and windows, and how to log on and off. You will also be shown how to access the Master Menu to begin your work.

Screen Layout   The layout of the screen is similar for menus, screens and windows. If you study the example below, you'll understand the areas of the screen referred to in later sections of this manual.

A menu is a list of activities — or options — you can perform. To select an activity:

- Type in the number displayed beside that option — and press ENTER

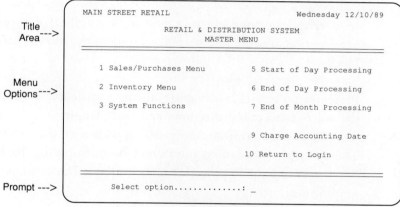

```
MAIN STREET RETAIL                          Wednesday 12/10/89

                    RETAIL & DISTRIBUTION SYSTEM
                            MASTER MENU
    ========================================================

      1 Sales/Purchases Menu        5 Start of Day Processing

      2 Inventory Menu              6 End of Day Processing

      3 System Functions           7 End of Month Processing


                                   9 Charge Accounting Date

                                  10 Return to Login
    ========================================================

          Select option.............:  _
```

Title Area --->

Menu Options --->

Prompt --->

The Master Menu

All RADS menus are divided into three sections:

❏ The TITLE area displays the name of your location, the current date and day, as well as the name of the menu.

❏ The MENU OPTIONS area in the middle of the screen. This area lists the options you can select, and their respective numbers.

❏ The PROMPT area, where messages and instructions appear. These messages will guide you while you are using RADS. It is also where you type in the number representing your selection from the menu.

Presenting the message

There are a number of ways we could handle the issues involved in design and presentation. For our purposes, let's talk about the look. I choose this way of tackling the task because that is the way most of the users approach their documentation. The first impression will be how the documentation looks.

Initial impression is critical, both the exterior packaging and the interior page layouts. If it looks difficult, the user will undoubtedly grit his teeth. If the layout is clean and easy on the eye, the user will be more relaxed, no matter how difficult the concepts or operational procedures.

In getting the look right, there are a number of topics. First is presentation, leading into graphics, typography, and the handling of text blocks.

Presentation has its counterparts in the way people communicate with the voice, with raised eyebrows and body language. The tone of voice one adopts can convey an impression at odds with the words themselves. The so-called pregnant pause cannot be mirrored in the written word but there are equally powerful tools available to the writer, editor, and graphic designer.

In the past, the issue of presentation was often separated from the writing task. Even today, some organizations separate their writers, editors, and graphic designers, which is unfortunate.

It is fundamental to the way I think documentation should be done that the design is developed prior to the words being written, and that the words, even as early as first draft, be written into the same finished format that the user will see.

In times past, writers of documentation would often write in longhand and then pass the words on to a typing pool where some typist laid out the pages in a most elementary of styles. In theory this was a simple system but in practice it led to layouts that defied understanding. The writer would scribble headings in the margin with a sort of layered approach. Often, the result was something like this:

1.   THIS IS THE MAIN HEADING IN CAPITAL LETTERS
1.1 NEXT LEVEL HEADINGS ARE INDENTED
1.1.1. Next Level Headings were further indented
1.1.1.1 Next Level headings were about as far as you could go
1.1.1.1.a   Until Someone Added a Character
1.1.1.1.a.i   And Someone Else Added a Roman Numeral

There are a couple of ludicrous devices at work here. As the headings march across the page, there is less and less room in which to put the body text. In many cases you end up writing down the far side of the page in very short sentences. This still goes on. I recently saw a military alumni magazine page laid out this way.

The second problem with this kind of layout is the numbering, which we'll deal with in more detail later on. Suffice to say here: Do you look up an item by its heading, or by looking for a reference such as 1.1.2.3.a.iv? (I'd look up Logging Off on page 22. I certainly would find it difficult to wrestle with Logging Off as section 1.2.3.a)

This may sound foolish to dwell upon in such detail, and we will discuss it again later, but I am amazed at the number of companies and organizations who still have procedures, policy, and training manuals with this old-fashioned form of layout.

Let's do away with such anachronistic ideas. They do not help the user. They allow the writer and editor to ignore a large part of the presentation responsibility. I maintain that presentation is critical to the act of communicating information. The responsibility must be shouldered by the writer and editor.

The writer armed with a good word processor and/or a good desktop publishing package, like PageMaker™, now has the tools to try out new ideas, or to refine old ideas. Of course, commercial documentation tasks rarely allow a lot of time for "creative" experimentation, but proper design can now be an integral part of every page.

Many topics will be covered in this section of the book and some of those topics deal with very subjective issues. Put five designers around a table and you'll often get five different opinions. In addition, some topics are difficult to place in a given section.

For example, if we are looking at typography should we discuss color there or under the heading of graphics. And the issue of handling text blocks could be placed under typography or our section on the look. Consult the table of contents or the index to find a specific subject.

Using an artist

The question is often asked: Should I make use of an art director or a graphic artist at this point?

The answer is not easy because it depends on the project and how it is to be used, and also on how much experience you have as a designer, quite a different set of skills from the skills needed as a writer.

For example: if you are designing a manual for external documentation, possibly to go into a fancy package to be sold over the counter, a graphic artist or art director will be valuable (and probably part of the budget).

If there is a graphic artist on staff, you might want to consult him during the design stage, no matter how much experience you have. I make that comment because the staff artist is no doubt accessible and you are not going to increase the cost of your manual with a mere consultation. Two heads are better than one.

However, if you are doing internal documentation and there is no staff artist on hand, you must decide whether it is worth the extra cost to engage an artist, even for a short period of time.

If you are a writer or an editor, it is incumbent on you to learn the basic principles of design. With desktop publishing as the natural route to many finished manuals, it is foolish to have a desktop publishing tool without developing the layout and design skills necessary for effectively using that tool.

Off-the-shelf formats

After you have written a few manuals you will notice that a number of them are starting to have common characteristics. Some formats are transportable from one documentation task to another. You soon start to develop what I like to call off-the-shelf formats.

Just as you can buy an off-the-shelf application and then tinker with it to tailor-make it to your needs, so too you can develop off-the-shelf documentation formats.

The key here is to recognize when something you have developed for one project will REALLY work on a new project. The danger is that you will accept a previous format because it means you don't have to take time to think up a more appropriate one.

The advantages in using the off-the-shelf format are:

❑ it will save you time (and thus money)

❑ it will feel comfortable if it truly is compatible with the new material

❑ it will provide you with the opportunity to fine-tune a format that you have already worked on

That fine-tuning might come in handy when you come to write a new version of the old manual that produced the original format.

Custom design

Bear in mind that off-the-shelf formats do not always work and that you must be very sure before selecting a predetermined format that it will encompass all the problems you are about to face as you start the documentation processes.

If the off-the-shelf format won't work, then you have to move to a custom design. Recognize that you will need more time and more money because you will be starting from scratch.

There are many excellent books available on custom design. I recommend you browse through these, making notes and thinking through how some of these designs could be used in the documentation task. Don't wait until you have a specific task in mind. Browse to learn, browse to be ready with a solution when you finally do encounter a problem task.

Standard page layouts

The standard page layout is a very useful tool if the design is done carefully, if it is used only where it really belongs, and if it can make a contribution. Used incorrectly it can quickly confuse the user.

A definition: a standard page layout is a convenient way of laying out a number of pages in a similar manner because the material to be presented has similar characteristics. For example, there may be similarities in the way options are handled in a system. Perhaps there are four options on each menu and most of the actions you carry out in these options are similar. A standard page layout would be a way of presenting information about these options in a standardized way that the user would easily understand and, having understood the first page, would find subsequent pages easy to follow.

The characteristics of a standard page layout are simple, The page is usually divided up and the same type of information is presented in the same way and in the same place on each page, as shown below. The example on page 93 gives you an idea.

| The options available are always displayed here. |
| When to use this option is always displayed here. |
| Procedure is always displayed here. |

You do not have to use a standard page layout for an entire manual. Trying to do that has resulted in many poor manuals. You use a standard page layout for a chapter or two, or for a section of a chapter where the material suits standardization.

There are many ways a page can be broken up. That decision is made in light of the material. One of the most common is this layout:

The function of the command

    A brief description of the function.

The action of the command

    A detailed description of how the user uses the command.

Messages

    A description of messages that may appear as a result of using the command.

Added detail

    Extra information that may be of use to the user, such as shortcuts.

Advantages of standard page layouts

Standard page layouts — and example of which is shown on the next page — are excellent tools for the following reasons:

❑ The page is easy to use.

The user only needs to be shown how one of the pages works in order to understand how the whole section works.

❑ The information is easy to find.

With the page divided into labeled sections, and with the sections understood by the user, the user can go straight to the information that is needed. He doesn't need to spend time reading and searching.

❑ The information is easy to understand.

The information the user is searching for has been labeled and placed in a certain part of the page and thus is already set into a certain context.

As an aside, this becomes quite clear if you consider on-line help as set inside a standard page layout. For example, warning messages might appear on the help screen in a certain location, say, bottom right corner with a flashing box around the message. This standard location for all warning messages tells the user a lot even before the user reads the message.

For the documentation writer, standard page layouts make the manual:

❑ Easier to write

Once the format for the standard page layout has been set in place, it is easier for the writer to fill in the blanks and decide what is important and what is not important for display and explanation.

❑ Easier to train

When introducing the standard page layout to new users, the trainer can concentrate on a single page. Once the users understand a single page, all other pages follow the same format.

The Inventory Menu
STOCK TRANSFERS

This option allows you to record the movement of stock in and out of your location.

These options are available:

1　Transfers Out
2　Transfers In (Goods & Transfer Record Received)
3　Transfers In (Goods Received before Transfer Record)
4　Match Unreconciled Transfers

Option	How to use the option

1　TRANSFERS OUT

Use this option to produce the delivery docket, so goods can be moved from one location to another.

- Type in location number
- Change delivery address (if required)
- Type in your User ID
- Type in Product/Search code
- Select product
- Type in transfer quantity
- Type <P> to print docket and update files
  You will be returned to the Stock Transfers Transactions screen.

2　TRANSFERS IN
(Goods & Transfer Record Received)

Use this option to record the transfer details of stock that has arrived at your location — and the system has transmitted details from the sending location.

- Type in your User ID
- Type in your higher-level password
- Type in stock transfer number
- Select the transfer
- Type in quantities received
- Type <U> to update files
  You will be returned to the Stock Transfers Transactions screen.

Of course, the most obvious location for standard page layouts is the reference manual where the user will go to a specific topic for specific information. If the pages are standard and the topics are arranged alphabetically, the user will have little trouble finding what he needs to know.

Standard page layout techniques

It is difficult to lay down too many strict rules for the development of standard page layouts because you must take into consideration the system design and how it interacts with the user, the purpose of the manual, and so forth.

However, there are three general rules worthy of discussion.

- Use the standard only where appropriate

- Avoid complicated layouts

- Keep the user in mind

Let's have a look at these rules.

Use the standard only where appropriate

It is highly unlikely that a standard page layout will work for an entire manual. For example, a standard page layout might work well to cover 50 options across a system. But that layout cannot be stretched to fit the introductory sections of the manual — use of function keys, installation, daily backup, and so forth.

Don't try to write material into a standard page layout if it is obvious that the message is not going to be communicated properly.

It is quite correct to have more than one standard page layout in a single manual. Explain clearly at the beginning of each new section how that section is laid out, if giving that explanation will assist the user.

The use of the keys on the keyboard, for example, often fits into a neat, concise standard page layout. However, there are other subjects that cannot be standardized, and there is no need to try.

Use the standard page layout where it really works best — in an area where there are a great number of pages that can be handled as a single design layout. This does not necessarily mean these pages are the most important; it merely means that the information can be standardized to make understanding easier.

Often only minor changes are needed to adapt a standard for, say, report functions, to be appropriate for explaining enquiry functions. Procedures involved in Inventory functions often lend themselves to standardization.

One of the advantages of breaking away from the standard page layout, when you find a function that doesn't lend itself to standardization, is that you are alerting the user to the fact that something has changed, that this particular function doesn't operate like others already explained.

Avoid complicated layouts

The basic requirement for a standard page layout is to have a system that has been put together in an orderly way in the first place.

If the programmer has been kind, the system will be neat and will lend itself to orderly documentation. If this is the case you may be able to develop standard page layouts that are quite sophisticated. Avoid the temptation to create complicated layouts. It is not necessary and as with so many other rules about presentation, the design should not attract attention. It is the information the design has been created to contain that should attract the attention of the user.

Design for the user, not to impress other documentation writers and designers. Keep it simple is a rule that works here very well.

The ultimate test of a standard page layout is the amount of explanation you have to give to a user before he can follow the information flow. If your explanation on how to use the standard page layout needs more than a short paragraph of explanation, then you are probably making the design too complicated.

A well-designed standard page layout, with a simple explanation, substantially reduces the amount of time a training officer might need to get a user actually working on the system.

Keep the user in mind

As with all documentation activity, you must keep the user firmly in mind while you are creating the standard page layout. How will he use the page? What will he be looking for? Can your user turn the page and have his eye go exactly to the information he is searching for because he knows where he will find the solution to his particular problem?

The type of manual will also influence the type of standard page layout you develop. If the manual is a reference manual, the user will be searching for something specific — most likely something *exceptional*. Highlight the exceptional.

In the typical training or procedure manual, it is probably the step-by-step information that is important. Develop a format that allows easy movement from one step to another.

In the Error Message section of a manual, make it easy to find the message that appears on the screen. The solution to the error is secondary in the *finding* process. In too many manuals, it is difficult to find the right spot to start reading. Make the right spot your key design point.

Three-part technique

The three-part technique has advantages in two areas of documentation. It can provide you with a standard page layout that works very well, and it can provide you with the solution when you have a diverse group of users and, for reasons of budget or time, can only produce one manual.

First, let's deal with the three-part technique's relationship to the standard page layout.

We can break the three-part technique down this way:

> Introduction Part
>> What is it?
>> What's it for?
>> What does it do?
>> Why is it needed?
> Information Part
>> How does it work?
> Technical Part
>> More detailed information

Adopting this standardized layout helps the writer focus on asking similar questions to fill similar holes in the manual's format. This is advantageous because the user feels comfortable knowing how the structure works and recognizes that the answers to questions can be found under convenient labels.

But the three-part technique becomes even more useful when we are presented with a less than perfect world, where we find ourselves confronted with different groups of users, with different backgrounds and abilities, and we only have enough budget or time to prepare one manual.

The first two documentation processes — name and define the manual, and understand the user — suggests the manual is going to only have one mission for one group of people. We now understand why that is necessary and how to go about it.

The three-part technique permits us to carry out what we know is a compromise — the preparation of a manual for more than one level of user experience. Let's look at a simple example.

The manual must address users with little experience, as well as those with considerable experience. Experienced users would be bored reviewing all the introductory notes needed by the beginner; and the beginner would be lost in the detail which the experienced user would understand.

So we split the manual into three parts and use the same approach we discussed in how the page might become a standard page layout. Part 1 is the beginner's guide, the introductory section. Part 2 is the information section. Part 3 is the technical detail or experienced user's section. Of course, the beginner will graduate and later become an experienced user, so there is actually more in this manual for the beginner than for the experienced user. That's as it should be.

In Part 1 — the introduction or getting started section — explain the jargon, explain what everything is for, and how it works. Tell the user to read this section carefully and then continue as though the beginner will do as you suggested. (Do not make the mistake of repeating introductory materials in Part 2 and Part 3, although pointers in Part 2 to ancillary material in Parts 1 and 3 will be very helpful.)

Part 2 is the actual manual. It is the reason the manual exists. Here you address the definition of the manual for the defined user group. Write for one user group. The definition of that group is likely to be the "most number of users" (a commercial reality). With appropriate pointers to Parts 1 and 3, you should be able to cater for the fringe areas — the experienced user and the beginner.

Graphics

We live in a world of graphics. We tend to think in graphic form. To do documentation well you need to be able to see where graphics will work. You need to expand your abilities beyond being only a wordsmith. Think of your words and your graphics as partners in the communication process.

Five reasons for graphics

There are at least five good reasons for introducing graphics into documentation:

❏ Graphics can emphasize important points.

❏ Graphics can increase a reader's interest in the text. Boring material can often be made interesting by developing the point in graphic form.

❏ Graphics may be able to simplify, and thus better explain, new concepts and difficult ideas. Response time in understanding is often shortened when information is presented in tabular or graphic formats.

❏ Graphics are better acknowledged by our brains. One side of our brain is better able to assess text blocks, the other side is better able to take in graphic representation of information. The side that assesses text is often overused in our society. The side that takes in graphics is underused. By using graphics, we are actually expanding the use of the reader's mind, by allowing the two sides of the brain to be used in the communication process.

❏ Graphics are also useful in allowing the user to scan and skip, searching for particular information. Used as headings or as Spot Art, they aid the eye in finding what it is looking for.

For example, in the documentation example on the following page, note the graphic of the Print menu.

Printing a Fax

You can print a copy of a fax that has been received by using the FaxNet menu system, or from your DOS prompt.

To print a fax using the FaxNet menu system:

① Ensure you have correctly selected your printer in the configuration window.

If the printer you want to use is connected to your network:

- Set printer to NETWORK and printer port to the name of your network print queue

If the printer is connected to your workstation only:

- Set printer to LOCAL and printer port to the name of your network printer queue

- Select your printer using the Printer Type field

② Select the Print option from the Main Menu.

The Print menu will be displayed.

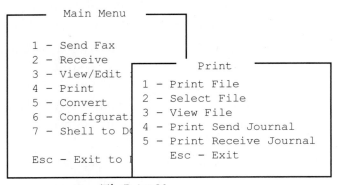

The Print Menu

③ Use the Select File option to choose the fax you want to print.

④ Select the Print option from the Print menu, after making sure the printer is connected.

The selected fax will be converted to printable form and printed immediately.

Remember that reports and screens are graphics. Some manuals show reports that look like they have been copied straight from the output of the printer. These can be improved as graphic representations for your manuals by drawing in the outline of the report. If the entire report is not going to be shown, you can show a cut line at the bottom of the report representation.

The screen is another issue. In my company we don't use screen dumps very often, but we do draw a lot of screens. These are graphics and the size and use of, for example, the Courier typeface, is a graphics decision made to ensure that the screen drawing represents something similar to what the user will actually see.

Business art can be imported into your manual to dress it up. We often use a hand, with a finger pointing at something we want to make sure the user doesn't miss. Although we have a scanner we don't use it very often. We have a large library of commercial or business art which more than satisfies our needs.

A strong word of caution: You are designing a piece of communication. You are not trying to see how many diagrams and pictures you can crowd into the manual. Try to avoid the three-ring circus approach. Keep the page clean and minimize the graphics. Use them only when you can really justify them. When you do use a graphic, keep it simple like the example below.

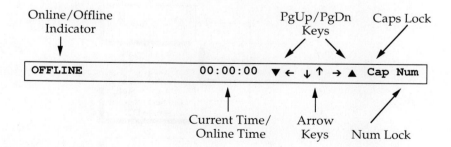

Diagrams and pictures

"A picture is worth a thousand words" may be true sometimes, but it's not always true for diagrams in computer manuals. It may take a thousand words just to explain how to use the diagram. And sometimes the information in a diagram could be explained better in 10 words.

So use diagrams with care. They can be useful, especially in introductions, to help explain general concepts such as the connection details (shown below) in a modem software manual. They are not so useful for explaining the detailed facts in a user reference guide or a program maintenance manual. They can be essential for defining wiring diagrams, circuit board layouts, and explaining how to change ribbons in a new printer.

Line drawings are best, since they are relatively easy to prepare and duplicate satisfactorily during final production. The example below was used in one of my modem operating manuals. This was a case of using a picture plus 10 words to explain a concept.

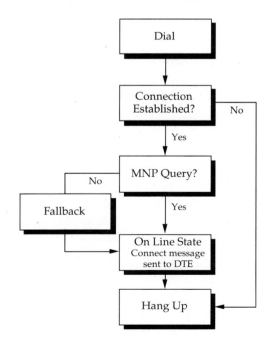

Cartoons are a special type of diagram. They have the advantage that they attract attention to the information. However, take care the information doesn't get lost in the humor. *We are not dealing with entertainment here.*

Flow charts can help the user see the overall picture in a complicated time-sequence or space-sequence procedure. But in most cases, they should only be considered as a support tool to a well-written narrative. If flow charts are used, they must be well captioned. Avoid technical flow charts. The little symbols programmers use mean little to a user.

Screen dumps are a useful technique in introductory or training manuals. (Screen dumps, like the one shown below, are 'snapshot' diagrams of what appears on the screen at a particular stage.) They can help the inexperienced user gain confidence by checking that what's on the screen agrees with what is in the manual.

They can also help an experienced computer user get a broad overview of a system without having to operate it. However, screen dumps are bulky, contain limited information, are difficult to update, and can be misleading or confusing when an interactive system becomes complex.

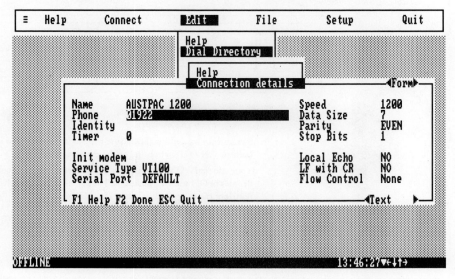

Once you have a suitable modem cable, follow the instructions set out below:

- Connect the modem cable between the modem's RS-232 socket and your computer.

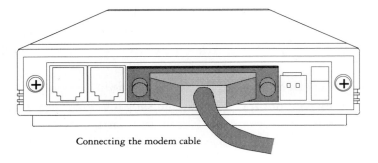

Connecting the modem cable

- Connect the modem to its plug pack power supply and connect the plug pack to a 240 volt wall socket.

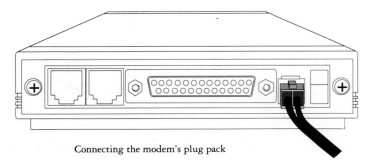

Connecting the modem's plug pack

- Switch your modem on. Make sure the modem is switched on at both its ON/OFF switch and at the mains wall socket.

Your modem's ON/OFF switch uses international symbols to denote the ON and OFF positions. The I symbol indicates the ON position; the O symbol indicates the OFF position.

Icons

Icons or spot art should be used. They are superior to either commands or menus as a system control device. The reason is that icons decrease the burden on the user's memory by making everything that is relevant to the task visible. Objects can be understood purely in terms of their visible characteristics. Those who work in the world of the Macintosh computer with its icon representations will know exactly what we are getting at here. The new Windows environment works well too.

Keep spot art in mind when looking for appropriate icons. Use icons that look like the action they represent and that are readily recognizable to your target users. And avoid any attempt at humor — especially with icons that will be used over and over again.

And once again, do not overdo the use of icons. Too many and you start to lose the impact.

Some general guidelines

Almost everything we've said about text and users — about the need to know your users — holds true for the use of graphics.

As you develop your table of contents, keep graphics in the mind and plan for their use right from the beginning. Make notes in your contents lists of possible graphics and places where graphics might be effective. As you develop your contents list you are thinking about the most important topics. Graphics should only be used with important topics. Graphics must be limited — on the grounds of space, time to prepare them, and the cost — so graphics are probably best used with the most important topics.

Whatever graphics you choose to use, be sure to keep them simple. Cut out all unnecessary details that might tend to distract from the primary focus or message.

Make sure your graphic stands out from its background. Box it, shade it, color it — if you've taken time to create a graphic make sure it is not lost in the middle of the text. A shadow box, as shown in the example below, works well.

Take the time to read a few books on graphic illustration. I don't mean go out and plagiarize material — but the best stimulation in this area is to study what others have done.

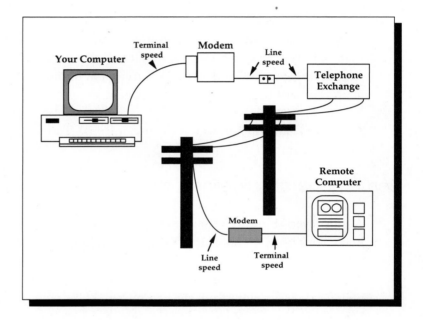

Typography

A key factor in the look of the manual is the effect of the single pages, and then the effect of a series of pages. This is important because few users look at only one page and the confidence they feel grows as they view a number of pages.

Good typography, set off by well thought out use of white space, and the appropriate use of graphics (for example, screens, message boxes, windows, and so forth) will make your page eminently readable.

The measure of good typography is its ease of readability. No matter how decorative the typography is, if it is not easy to read, then it is poor typography. There is a place for tricky typography, for the three-ring circus approach (often found in European newspapers) and for upside down headings, but documentation is not the place. At the risk of being old-fashioned, the traditional typefaces, used in a traditional manner work best for modern manuals. The user should consider the content, not the way it is displayed.

In the world of typography, another word is often used: legibility. When legibility is considered, it is the ease with which the reader can discern each letter that is important. The issue of readability is wider, and the criterion is how the reader "sees" the entire column of type on a page. How the text is written is also a factor in readability.

During this design stage, the following typography factors should be considered as important to the readability of your manual.

Typeface style

There are some proven rules here. Stick with traditional faces. Body copy should be a serif face, such as Times or Garamond. If you are producing advertising brochures or annual reports or comic books, then you should spend time experimenting with typefaces. If you are producing instructional manuals, stick with typefaces that have a proven track record. Hundreds of newspapers and magazines can't be wrong. They use various versions of Times. A number of successful manuals have moved from Times to Garamond. We will provide a couple of examples, and then some explanations.

This is a common Times face in 11 point.

In the world of typography, another word is often used: legibility. When legibility is considered, it is the ease with which the reader can discern each letter that is important. The issue of readability is wider, with the measurement having to do with how the reader "sees" the entire column of type on a page.

This is a common Garamond face called Garamond 3 in 11 point.

In the world of typography, another word is often used: legibility. When legibility is considered, it is the ease which with the reader can discern each letter that is important. The issue of readability is wider, with the measurement having to do with how the reader "sees" the entire column of type on a page.

(This book is Garamond 3 in 12 point.)

This is a common Garamond face in 11 point.

In the world of typography, another word is often used: legibility. When legibility is considered, it is the ease with which the reader can discern each letter that is important. The issue of readability is wider, with the measurement having to do with how the reader "sees" the entire column of type on a page.

Serif or sans serif?

For our purposes, we should always use a serif face. Sans serif has its place, but it should not be used for body text.

Times and Garamond are serif typefaces.

Helvetica is a common sans serif face.

Serif faces have a couple of distinguishing characteristics. They have thick and thin strokes and they have serifs, which are circled below.

TIMES   TIMES

Typeface designers claim that the serifs tend to unite the letters into words, thus making them easier to read and help readers identify the shapes as words.

The sans serif typeface has strokes of the same thickness, and does not have any serifs.

HELVETICA

The problem with sans serif is that certain letter combinations produce problems for the eye. For example:

Illinois and Illegibility   (Illinois and Illegibility)

These problems are not as obvious when a sans serif face is used more for effect than in a long passage of body text. More concentration is required on the part of the user. With all strokes having the same thickness, there is lack of what is called type color and used in a block, as is common in body text, the effect can become quite tiring.

Compare these two examples:

As with many trends in the modern world, there is a school of thought which suggests that sans serif is more modern, somewhat trendy. As a result, manuals are being produced in sans serif. Avoid the temptation. Help the user by making the body text as easy as possible to read. Use a serif face. (Helvetica - 10 pt)

As with many trends in the modern world, there is a school of thought which suggests that sans serif is more modern, somewhat trendy. As a result, manuals are being produced in sans serif. Avoid the temptation. Help the user by making the body text as easy as possible to read. Use a serif face. (Garamond 3 - 12 pt)

Typeface consistency

Once you have chosen a typeface for your body copy, stick with it. Avoid the circus mentality common in many European newspapers, magazines, and, unfortunately, in computer manuals. The circus mentality is a label that is applied to a page in which the designer (writer, or editor) has mixed different typefaces — typefaces from different families.

The easiest way to avoid the circus mentality is to pick a body text, then define the bold and italic versions as part of the standard for your manual. To this set of standards, you need to add additional typefaces for special uses, such as boxes, warnings, and high-level headings. Beginners tend to mix too many typefaces. The effect is to clutter the page and confuse the reader. The fewer typefaces, the more traditional the approach, the easier the material will be to read.

Let's assume your basic typeface is going to be Times. To this you can add *Times Italic* and **Times Bold** for emphasis. Unless you have a very good reason, there is no reason to mix any other typefaces in the body text section of your manual.

(Be careful with the use of **boldface type**. Don't overuse it. Comprehension of the typeface Times drops from 89 percent to 50 percent in its bold form. Other typefaces suffer even more severely in boldface.)

However, careful use of an additional typestyle will help dress up those parts of your manual requiring something more than a mere body text style. The justification for this is the word "special".

Special typefaces for special needs

While common or normal headings should be in the same typeface as the body text, main section or chapter headings require special treatment. One nice mix is a typeface called Avant Garde. It works well as a level 1 heading, for section or chapter headings.

Chapter 1 - The JumpMaster System

or

CHAPTER 1 - THE JUMPMASTER SYSTEM

or, perhaps, set to the right margin (flush right):

1. THE JUMPMASTER SYSTEM

(We'll look at the question of type sizes later in this section.)

Another special need is the breakaway box, most often used for warnings. The key here is to make sure the user is stopped short by any warning. The best way to do this is to break the text block with a breakaway box like this:

```
┌──────────── WARNING ────────────┐
│                                  │
│  If you proceed past this point, you risk losing  │
│  all the information you have been entering.       │
│                                  │
└──────────────────────────────────┘
```

A screen typeface

Besides a body text typeface, and a special typeface for special needs, most computer manuals require an additional typeface to handle the requirements of "mirroring" information displayed on your computer screen, as well as screen messages that need to be mixed with the body text.

Most computer screens use a nonproportional typeface. To match that screen face, the most useful typeface is Courier.

```
Courier is a nonproportional typeface.  This means that
each letter occupies the same amount of space.  An I
and a M occupy the same width.  As well as mirroring
what the user will see on the screen, the Courier typeface
also provides some additional variety for the page.
```

Let's look at some examples:

When you reach the end of the report, a message is displayed:

```
END OF REPORT  Press <Spacebar> to continue
```

OR

The Scan Menu shows six options:

```
1 - Scan
2 - Add
3 - Select File
4 - View File
5 - Rename
6 - Scanner Setup
```

Further examples of Courier as a screen typeface are shown on the next page.

```
    OUTGOING FACSIMILE  till Monday 15/10/90 12:19:46

DATE      TIME    DUR    PHONE No     SYS FILE P   Result
06/09/90  10:35  00:45  1234567      0A230219 00 no answer
                                     24 1D N 0000 010 1

JANE {plans.fax}
----------------------------------------------------------
06/09/90  11:00  01:10  2345678      0A230219 00 no answer
                                     24 1D N 0000 010 1

JANE {logo.fax}
----------------------------------------------------------
08/09/90  18:15  01:03  3456789      0A29134B 00 no answer
                                     24 1D N 0000 010 1

JANE {meeting.fax}
```

Sample of a Faxout Journal

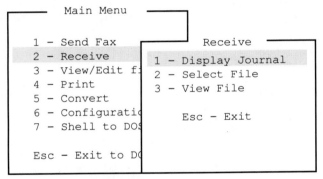

```
┌──── Main Menu ────┐
│                   │
│  1 - Send Fax     │
│  2 - Receive ──────────┬──── Receive ────┐
│  3 - View/Edit f│      │ 1 - Display Journal │
│  4 - Print      │      │ 2 - Select File  │
│  5 - Convert    │      │ 3 - View File    │
│  6 - Configurati│      │                  │
│  7 - Shell to DO│      │    Esc - Exit    │
│                 │      │                  │
│  Esc - Exit to D│      │                  │
└─────────────────┴──────┴──────────────────┘
```

The Receive Menu

```
┌──── File Info ────┐
│ name  D:FAX_OUT\HEADER.FAX │
│ date  16/8/1990 9:13:0 │
│ size  5393  bytes │
│ type  FAX 1D      │
│ lines 243         │
│ resol NORMAL      │
└───────────────────┘
```

The File Info Window

Use of all CAPS

The use of all caps should be avoided as much as possible. For example, the text below (which deals with the greater readability of text set in upper and lower case) is much less readable when set in all caps (immediately following).

RESEARCH SHOWS THAT PART OF THE PROCESS OF READING INVOLVES SEEING THE SHAPES THAT WORDS MAKE. THOSE SHAPES ARE CAUSED NOT ONLY BY THE NUMBER OF LETTERS IN A WORD, BUT ALSO BY THE ASCENDERS (L,T,B, ETC) AND DESCENDERS (P,G,Y, ETC). STATISTICS SHOW THAT A SENTENCE WRITTEN IN UPPER AND LOWERCASE IS MUCH EASIER TO READ THAN ONE WRITTEN IN ALL CAPS. READABILITY OF TEXT THAT IS SET IN ALL CAPS IS REDUCED BY ABOUT 33 PERCENT. ALSO A CONSIDERATION IS THE STATISTIC THAT ALL CAPS OCCUPIES ABOUT 40 TO 50 PERCENT MORE SPACE. WHILE YOU WOULD THINK IT OBVIOUS THAT THESE KIND OF STATISTICS WOULD RESULT IN NO ONE USING ALL CAPS, WRITERS CONTINUE TO PUT IMPORTANT FACTS IN ALL CAPS TO EMPHASIZE THEM. WARNINGS THAT MUST NOT BE IGNORED ARE PUT IN ALL CAPS AND BOXED. THIS DOES NOT WORK.

Research shows that part of the process of reading involves seeing the shapes that words make. Those shapes are caused not only by the number of letters in a word, but also by the ascenders (l, t, b, etc.) and descenders (p, g, y, etc.). Statistics show that a sentence written in upper and lower case is much easier to read than one written in all caps. Readability of text that is set in all caps is reduced by about 33 percent. Also a consideration is the statistic that all caps occupies about 40 to 50 percent more space. While you would think it obvious that these kind of statistics would result in no one using all caps, writers continue to put important facts in all caps to emphasize them. Warnings that must not be ignored are put in all caps and boxed. This does not work.

Use of *Italics*

Again, the text below is much more readable when set in Roman letters.

Italics are not as easy to read as Roman letters. Roman are up and down, Italics are designed on the diagonal. There is a sense of movement in Italics that make them useful for emphasis — to highlight a single word, or a short phrase. However, that sense of movement is wearying to the eye after a very short time. Italics have their place. The names of books, of ships, for emphasis, in a questions and answer format to set the shorter questions off against the longer answers. They should be avoided in any context longer than a sentence and certainly should never become the style for paragraph after paragraph of body text. An associate who once had to read an entire manual written in Italics said that when he was finished, everything he read for the next few days seems to have type that was falling over!

Italics are not as easy to read as Roman letters. Roman are up and down, Italics are designed on the diagonal. There is a sense of movement in Italics that make them useful for emphasis — to highlight a single word, or a short phrase. However, that sense of movement is wearying to the eye after a very short time. Italics have their place. The names of books, of ships, for emphasis, in a question and answer format to set the shorter question off against the longer answer. They should be avoided in any context longer than a sentence and certainly should never become the style for paragraph after paragraph of body text. An associate who once had to read an entire manual written in italics said that when he was finished, everything he read for the next few days seems to have type that was falling over!

Typeface size

The choice of body text typeface size is dictated by a number of factors, including:

❏ the size of the page

❏ the width of the text block column(s)

❏ the characteristics of the chosen body text typeface

Choosing the type size will impact on the read. This paragraph is written in 12 point Garamond 3. While it might seem logical that the larger the point size (within reason), the easier it is to read, there are other considerations.

If your page is 5.5 inches by 9 inches, 12 point type will probably be too large. You'll end up with a lot more pages than you need. The choice of 11 point or 10 point will be more suitable. However, if you are working on an 8.5 inch by 11 inch page, 12 point type will work well. It is unlikely your text block will occupy the entire width of the page, so the width of the text block will dictate the point size.

Avoid body text below 9 point. It might be suitable to set sports results in 5 point, but the manual reader will quickly give up.

Let's look at some examples:

This user's guide assumes you are familiar with the operation of the keyboard and screen of the personal computer or terminal to which you will connect your modem. If you don't know how to use your PC or terminal, read the operating manual that came with it. (Times 9 point)

This user's guide assumes you are familiar with the operation of the keyboard and screen of the personal computer or terminal to which you will connect your modem. If you don't know how to use your PC or terminal, read the operating manual that came with it. (Times 10 point)

This user's guide assumes you are familiar with the operation of the keyboard and screen of the personal computer or terminal to which you will connect your modem. If you don't know how to use your PC or terminal, read the operating manual that came with it. (Times 11 point)

This user's guide assumes you are familiar with the operation of the keyboard and screen of the personal computer or terminal to which you will connect your modem. If you don't know how to use your PC or terminal, read the operating manual that came with it. (Times 12 point)

Line leading

Leading (also known as ledding) is the white space between lines. Normal leading is at least two points. For most manual writing, with traditional typefaces, a word processor setting of Auto produces appropriate leading. However, adding extra leading between lists and procedure steps helps to isolate those instructions, making them easier to follow.

Let's look at some examples:

This user's guide assumes you are familiar with the operation of the keyboard and screen of the personal computer or terminal to which you will connect your modem. If you don't know how to use your PC or terminal, read the operating manual that came with it. (Times 11 point, Auto leading)

This user's guide assumes you are familiar with the operation of the keyboard and screen of the personal computer or terminal to which you will connect your modem. If you don't know how to use your PC or terminal, read the operating manual that came with it. (Times 11 point, 10 point leading)

This user's guide assumes you are familiar with the operation of the keyboard and screen of the personal computer or terminal to which you will connect your modem. If you don't know how to use your PC or terminal, read the operating manual that came with it. (Times 11 point, 15 point leading)

This user's guide assumes you are familiar with the operation of the keyboard and screen of the personal computer or terminal to which you will connect your modem. If you don't know how to use your PC or terminal, read the operating manual that came with it. (Times 11 point, 20 point leading)

Leading can be effectively increased with lists of information. Consider these examples, where there is Auto leading in the first example, and an extra 2 points of leading added between items in the list in the second example:

When you have typed in your identity number:
- Press **F2**
  The Connection Details form will disappear.
- Press **ESC**
  The program will ask whether you want to save the change you have made.
- Press **Y**
  The dialing directory will appear.
  You have now entered and saved your ID number.

When you have typed in your identity number:

- Press **F2**
  The Connection Details form will disappear.

- Press **ESC**
  The program will ask whether you want to save the change you have made.

- Press **Y**
  The dialing directory will appear.

  You have now entered and saved your ID number.

Line length

The fundamental rule is that columns should not be too wide nor too long and the deciding factor will be the page size — or more accurately, the text block width — and the size of your typeface.

When I was foreign editor of a metropolitan daily newspaper, I used to write a daily foreign affairs commentary. I would often type it out at home before going to work. It never ceased to amaze me that it seemed much easier to read in the newspaper than it did in mere manuscript form straight out of the typewriter. The reason was simple: placed in columns designed for ease of reading, in a traditional face of the appropriate size, the words were easier to read than across the wide column that the typewriter manuscript produced.

If the line is too long, the eyes tire as they make their way back and forth across the page. The maximum and minimum number of characters in a column for best comprehension is not less than 20 and not more than 60. About 9 or 10 words in the line is usually best. If your character count approaches 75, you are well over the limit and should reconsider your design — shorten the width of the text block, or lift the type size.

If the line is too short, the eye has to change course too many times and the read is disrupted.

Given what we have already said about typeface sizes, you can see how that discussion relates to line length. When you decide the width of your body text, the decision to use 10 point, 11 point or 12 point type might be based on the character count. This same discussion might also impact on your choice of typeface. Times is a condensed face and, for example, New Century Schoolbook is not condensed. So over the same line length, and in the same point size, you will get significantly more words in Times than you will in New Century Schoolbook. For economy of space, you might fall back on Times as your typeface choice.

Every six months or so, my documentation writers and editors go on a search for a better body text typeface. "Times is boring," I am told. So we turn to the typefaces available and start experimenting. After a few hours and lots of examples through the laser printer, we keep coming back to Times. Nobody can really come up with a typeface that betters Times.

Occasionally a client for whom we are writing a manual has an idea of his own about typeface. Garamond 3 was a typeface we accepted because a client said he liked the look of it. Originally the client showed us a sample. It was Garamond. It looked nice, but it wasn't condensed enough to be economical for large manuals. In searching for an alternative we came across Garamond 3. It met our criteria, so we went with it. The client, by the way, couldn't see the difference between Garamond and Garamond 3 until it was explained to him.

We have also been faced with a client who showed us a sample of Helvetica and said he would like his manuals written in that typeface. His sample was a short paragraph in a box surrounded by a more traditional serif face. I convinced the client that Helvetica was not a good typeface for a whole manual by producing three pages in Helvetica, by producing those same three pages in Times, and by using the arguments you are reading in this book. The client grinned, said that he was paying us good money to make the right decision, and told us to get on with the job using Times. I was relieved. If he had insisted on Helvetica, I would have terminated the contract and walked away. Doing a manual the wrong way is not our style — and, hopefully, is not your style.

Justified or ragged right

There was a time when it was dangerous to try justifying text across the widths that are most effective for documentation. Great white rivers would appear within the text blocks, breaking up the sentences and causing confusion to the eye and the mind.

This problem has been largely overcome by the presence of the micro-justification feature in most word processing and desktop publishing packages.

As with most rules, there are times when they can be ignored to achieve a special effect. But in the absence of the need for something special, justified text works better than ragged right. While there is no evidence to make a claim that there is an increase in comprehension for justified text, it does look better in terms of the overall page design.

(Ragged left margins should never be used for reasons linked to our earlier discussion of how the eye moves across a sentence and back to the next sentence. It needs an anchor point to return to each time it moves down one line, and that anchor point is the straight-edged left margin.)

On the next three pages the same page has been displayed in three modes:

❏ with justification on and hyphenation control off, so no words are broken at the end of the line

❏ with alignment to the left and hyphenation control off, so no words are broken at the end of the line

❏ with alignment to the left and hyphenation control on, so words are broken, where appropriate, at the end of the line

There's room for subjective opinion here, but I prefer the first example.

1. INTRODUCTION

Welcome to the Avtek MegaPlus and MegaPlus V.32 User's Guide. This user's guide explains the installation and operation of the Avtek MegaPlus and MegaPlus V.32 modems.

With your MegaPlus modems and communications software you will be able to access a wide variety of public and private information services, including bulletin board systems, electronic mail, on-line databases and videotext services. You will be able to communicate with friends who have a modem and a computer, talking electronically and exchanging programs and information.

To Use This Guide

This user's guide assumes you are familiar with the operation of the keyboard and screen of the personal computer or terminal to which you will connect your modem. If you don't know how to use your PC or terminal, read the operating manual that came with it.

This user's guide also assumes that you know how to use your communications program. The MegaPlus modems work with a wide variety of communications software packages.

You won't need to know all the features of the program to start using your modem, but you will need to know how to:

❏ load the communications software

❏ enter on-line (terminal) mode

❏ set the data format (number of data bits, start and stop bits and parity)

❏ log in to the particular service you want to use

1. INTRODUCTION

Welcome to the Avtek MegaPlus and MegaPlus V.32 User's Guide. This user's guide explains the installation and operation of the Avtek MegaPlus and MegaPlus V.32 modems.

With your MegaPlus modems and communications software you will be able to access a wide variety of public and private information services, including bulletin board systems, electronic mail, on-line databases, and videotext services. You will be able to communicate with friends who have a modem and a computer, talking electronically and exchanging programs and information.

To Use This Guide

This user's guide assumes you are familiar with the operation of the keyboard and screen of the personal computer or terminal to which you will connect your modem. If you don't know how to use your PC or terminal, read the operating manual that came with it.

This user's guide also assumes that you know how to use your communications program. The MegaPlus modems work with a wide variety of communications software packages.

You won't need to know all the features of the program to start using your modem, but you will need to know how to:

❑ load the communications software

❑ enter on-line (terminal) mode

❑ set the data format (number of data bits, start and stop bits and parity)

❑ log in to the particular service you want to use

1. INTRODUCTION

Welcome to the Avtek MegaPlus and MegaPlus V.32 User's Guide. This user's guide explains the installation and operation of the Avtek MegaPlus and MegaPlus V.32 modems.

With your MegaPlus modems and communications software you will be able to access a wide variety of public and private information services, including bulletin board systems, electronic mail, on-line databases and videotext services. You will be able to communicate with friends who have a modem and a computer, talking electronically and exchanging programs and information.

To Use This Guide

This user's guide assumes you are familiar with the operation of the keyboard and screen of the personal computer or terminal to which you will connect your modem. If you don't know how to use your PC or terminal, read the operating manual that came with it.

This user's guide also assumes that you know how to use your communications program. The MegaPlus modems work with a wide variety of communications software packages.

You won't need to know all the features of the program to start using your modem, but you will need to know how to:

❑ load the communications software

❑ enter on-line (terminal) mode

❑ set the data format (number of data bits, start and stop bits and parity)

❑ log in to the particular service you want to use

Color

The use of color is a vexing question. In order to keep you on the right track, let's make sure we're both thinking about the same issues as we talk about color.

First of all, a comment on color as it applies to external and internal documentation. There can be no question that color should be used for external documentation, particularly on the packaging and manual cover — and even more particularly if the external documentation is to be sold. But this use of color has more to do with marketing than documentation. Perhaps the use of color here, and the question of design, should be left to those designers and artists who specialize in packaging. As with most documentation projects, there will probably be more budget available for external documentation as well.

Second, what about color inside the manual being produced for external documentation? If the budget allows, you can use color. But use it sparingly. Some very well-known companies have made their manuals unworthy of their products by producing garish color spreads that detract from the words, concepts, and instructional material. Bright red rules top and bottom of the page, heavy blue boxes, headlines in red surrounded by heavy black panels do nothing but disrupt the read.

Another well-known company produced an excellent manual, but then printed all the screens with a sort of silver background and a similar silvery color for the screen text. Sitting at a desk reading the manual required tilting the page every time you wanted to look at a screen so the light touched the page in a certain way. Without tilting the page, the screen seemed to disappear into the paper. Most annoying to the user and a problem easily avoided.

However, muted colors for main section headings do work well, as do muted shadings.

Headlines in color attract attention, but they are harder to read than black headlines on white paper. The same applies to body text. Comprehension drops off even for black body text when it is printed on color. The level of comprehension decay increases as the intensity of the background color increases. Print black body text on white paper. If you have to use colored paper, make sure it is very muted, very pale.

White text on a black background should be avoided at all costs. All you have to do is try to read some popular magazine where the art director has printed a large block of text on a black background. It might look good to the art director, but the reader gets eye strain after the first paragraph. Another reason for avoiding white on black is that unless the printing process is carefully supervised, any overinking might result in some of the white letters losing their crispness, thus increasing the problem of legibility and readability.

Black type on white paper reads some 40 percent faster than white type on black (or the darker shades of grey). This will influence your use of shaded boxes. As a rule of thumb, if you are going to put text in a box and then provide a grey shade in the background of the box, keep it to about 10 percent grey.

As an aside, the highest legibility is produced with black type on a yellow background — but who ever saw a manual printed on yellow paper. And the poorest legibility comes from black type on red, or red type on black.

We all learn from our mistakes. When I was a magazine editor I printed a whole story using white text on a black background. It didn't work. I also put red headlines over a picture of a blue sky. That didn't work either — the shimmer effect was so severe I got a nasty memo from the publisher. Learn from my mistakes, please.

That brings us to the issue of color on internal documentation. First, if you do go to color for your internal documentation, the rules above apply. However, I don't think you need to go to color on internal documentation and if you have the budget to do it, think carefully about using the budget for other purposes.

Perhaps the money might be better spent on increasing the quality of the final production process, or buying better binders, or using a better quality paper, or getting help from a graphic designer on your layouts, or a multitude of other things you can spend money on. Consider producing a two-fold reference card with the extra money. I'm not sure the reader will miss the color and if that is true, then you really don't need it.

Column headings

Headings are very important. They provide the labels that help the user navigate through the manual. They provide the encapsulated view of the topic to show users they are in the right place. The typographic rules for headings are not difficult, certainly not as difficult as the writing rules governing what to say in a heading.

For typography, the basic rules are to stay with the same family of type you used for the body copy except in certain cases, such as the main section or chapter headings or in some places where you actually want to disrupt the reader's view of the page. This latter activity might occur on a warning, or on some subsidiary topic. (A box and a change in typeface usually suffice to break the reader away from the thoughts encompassed in body text.)

Earlier I said that you should avoid large sections of boldface type because it reduces comprehension. This is also true for body text. It is not accurate for headings. In headlines there is no comprehension falloff when boldface type is used. In fact, boldface should be used because it increases the impact and makes the words stand out.

The same might be said of a sans serif headline. However, while the impact will be there, the use of a sans serif headline clashes with our rule of trying to maintain the same typeface family as used in the body text. Because you would never use sans serif for body text, it follows that sans serif would not be considered for headlines.

Most rules can be broken. The sign of the professional is to know when to break the rules. In this book, for example, we use Avant Garde for chapter headings (covered by our discussion of section and chapter headings) but I have also chosen to use it for signifying more minor sections. It is used, for example, in this chapter for starting the discussions of typography, graphics and handling text blocks. I think it works well there.

Be wary of using all caps or italics for long headlines. While they are used by a lot of writers, I believe they are not as effective as upper and lowercase letters. I have a suspicion that they are used because the writer thinks he needs them to help establish the hierarchy of headings.

Hierarchy helps the reader determine what's more important as you work through any given topic. Setting aside the issue of section and chapter headings — where caps or italics might be used as long as the heading is not too long — using upper and lowercase headings can be efficiently done through about four levels of hierarchy. Four levels should be enough for most manuals. If you need more than four levels, you should probably rethink your design. I'll have more to say about hierarchy when we look at text blocks and page design. Consider these examples:

Using serif Times bold 14 point:

How to use the wildcard in supply modules

How To Use The Wildcard In Supply Modules

How to use the wildcard in supply modules

HOW TO USE THE WILDCARD IN SUPPLY MODULES

Using sans serif Helvetica bold 14 point:

How to use the wildcard in supply modules

How To Use The Wildcard In Supply Modules

How to use the wildcard in supply modules

HOW TO USE THE WILDCARD IN SUPPLY MODULES

White space

White space is often talked about when the topics are commercial art, magazine pages, and the like, but for some reason it is largely ignored in textbooks, various instructional materials, and documentation. This is unfortunate because white space is one of the most powerful tools available to a page designer.

White space is all that space on the page that is free of ink. It is not, as some misguided writers have argued, *wasted* space. It has a specific role to play in the design of the page in the same way that your choice of headline typeface has a job to do.

We'll have more to say about white space when we discuss the Look, but bear in mind that white space is a flexible component that can be manipulated to assist in meeting your goals in much the same way as you use typefaces and typesizes.

The Look

The Look is a big topic. To make our discussion easier, we'll break it into two distinct sections.

Section 1 will examine:

❏ The Look of the page

Section 2 will examine:

❏ The Look of the manual

As has been explained earlier, the Look plays an important role in the user's initial reaction to the documentation. If the documentation looks like it has been thrown together, or the design elements confuse the user in the first few moments he spends scanning the pages, it will be rejected with all the consequences of that action. If the Look is attractive, the pages are well laid out, the headings in place, and the text blocks neat and orderly, the user will move from a favorable initial reaction to the more logical question of how the manual will serve his needs.

All the elements discussed under graphics and typography now come into play in putting together the Look of the page, and then the combined Look of the entire manual. A structure needs to be added, not only for the page but also for the total manual.

The starting point is the page. A vital ingredient is the research you have done on the system and the research you have done on the user. Although we are discussing the processes of documentation one after the other, some of these processes overlap. For example, preliminary work on the table of contents (covered in Process 5 - Blueprint) will already have been done as a result of Process 3 - Organize and Research. Process 4 - Design draws on this entire introductory collection of Processes 1 through 5.

The Look of the page

There are many different ways to lay out a page but for effective documentation there is a movement toward what we call the A-B column format. This modern format meets the demands we have encountered in typography and meets the demands of users who, traditionally, search for information in a certain way. It also meets the demands of ease of use for the writer.

The A-B column format is easy to define. It consists of two columns on the page, the first labeled A where the headings are located, and the second column labeled B where the body text goes.

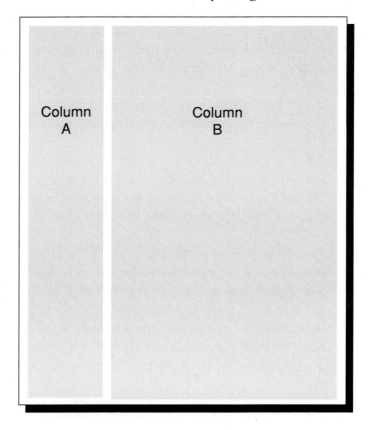

Column
A

Column
B

There is no great mystery attached to the labeling of A and B. We do it because all our editors and writers refer to the columns as A and B, and all styles in our documentation unit are set as style A for column A and style B for column B. This makes it easy to move from word processed copy to page display applications. It makes it easy for discussions between staff members.

As an aside, this kind of standardization is taken a step further when we define further styles. For example:

- Style BB is an indented form of style B, which is main body text, and is called "B with a bullet." Other styles are given names that relate to which column they appear in. This makes it easy for both writers and editors, and for the computer.

❑ Sometimes the bullet changes from • to ❑

  - Style BBB is style BB with an extra indent

  You may choose something slightly different: B1 - B2 - B3.

  A common style in my manuals is to start action statements in a list with a bullet (•), and non-action statements in a list with a box (❑).

Let's work through the list of topics that need to be defined as we start to establish the Look of the page.

Page size

Page size is related to utility, which means taking into consideration:

- ❏ the ultimate size (in numbers of pages, single-sided or double-sided printing, thickness of the paper)
- ❏ the environment in which the manual will be used
- ❏ the production method (printing and binding)
- ❏ the budget
- ❏ marketing requirements

There are three basic sizes that work well, given the appropriate conditions:

- ❏ 5.5 inches by 9 inches
- ❏ 7.5 inches by 9 inches
- ❏ 8.5 inches by 11 inches

The number of pages affects the page size if the manual is going to exceed 200-300 pages. A 300-page manual printed double-sided means 150 sheets of paper. That's getting quite thick for the 5.5 inch by 9 inch page, a page size that has grown in popularity in recent years.

The 5.5 inch by 9 inch page works well to about 200 pages (100 sheets of paper, printed on both sides). Beyond that you should look to a larger size. However, there are some restrictions to the use of the A-B column format on this small page. We'll discuss how to overcome those restrictions later in this section.

The 7.5 inch by 9 inch page size is similar to the style of the Macintosh manual and this size works well to 300 pages, and beyond if necessary. The Macintosh manuals are spiral bound. They open flat on the desk and the size is easy to use in the normal cluttered environment. If they go beyond 300 pages, a D-ring (with three rings) binder works much better than the spiral binding.

The 8.5 inch by 11 inch is most common for in-house documentation. They can be bound in common ring binders (D-ring binders, please). While they are not as easy to use on a cluttered desk, budget concerns often force their use. Paper comes in that size and does not need to be cut to the smaller sizes. This size of paper can also be easily photocopied if production numbers are low, thus contributing to the ease of maintaining updates and revisions. Considerable more information can be placed in the 8.5 inch by 11 inch page format, thus cutting down the total number of pages. With the wide range of inexpensive, commercially available binders, large manuals can be more easily accommodated.

Some thought should be given to the environment in which the manual is going to be used. A group of users passing back and forth a thick 8.5 inch by 11 inch page manual means making life difficult and the documentation is likely to be ignored. However, passing a smaller 5.5 inch by 9 inch manual is much easier. I favor the 7.5 inch by 9 inch manual for cluttered offices and environments where space is at a premium.

External documentation — perhaps manuals written for applications to be sold over the counter — often have a dual role to play. As well as being a user tool, they may be used as part of the marketing of the package. As such, they will usually include features not found in internal documentation. For example, color is often seen as a marketing necessity. The budget usually includes such necessities. Size plays an important role in marketing. The 8.5 inch by 11 inch manual is usually rejected as too large to fit into the external packaging of the product, so one of the two smaller sizes is used.

The three common sizes shown below at 50% size give a quick indication of how much information each page can hold.

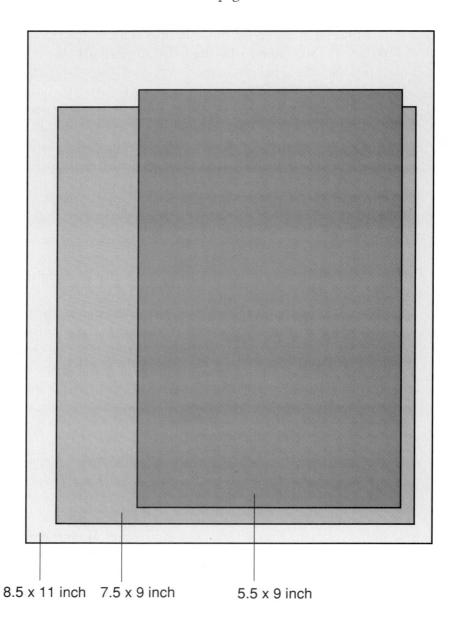

8.5 x 11 inch   7.5 x 9 inch   5.5 x 9 inch

Paper choice

Without getting into too much detail, paper comes with certain characteristics. It can be rough or smooth, with a dull flat or a glossy finish. The initial reaction might be to go for the glossy finish. Certainly the glossy papers reproduce photographs well, but they reflect light easily and thus can irritate the user.

One well-known product has a manual that combines a glossy paper with a text ink that also shines. The result is that the user wastes time tilting the page in various directions trying to read the text through the shine. It looks pretty, but is far from useful. Another concern is how much of what is printed on the other side of the paper shows through. This can be quite disconcerting and can destroy a well laid out page.

Paper weights are usually expressed in grams per square meter (gsm) and you will want a weight which minimizes show-through, has a pleasant feel to it (not too stiff, not too flimsy), and meets your budget. Copying paper is usually in the 70-90 gsm range and writing paper in the 80-100 gsm range. A 40-page manual works well on 120 gsm with a cover of about 250-300 gsm. Common newsletters are usually about 100 gsm.

Your budget will determine some of the parameters on paper choice but bear in mind that paper cost differences for printing small numbers (a couple of hundred copies) of manuals will not vary significantly. The easiest way to handle the question of paper choice is to talk to a printer. Ask for samples and his advice, particularly if the final printing is going to be done by a commercial printing company.

Page element styles

Having decided on the paper and the page size, the next step is to decide on the styles for the text and other elements that will make up the finished page. This includes typefaces, typesizes, positioning, use of graphics, and so forth. Considerable work has to be done here because the style has to work for the entire manual. In other words, the decisions made now will be with you daily as you work through the project. Take your time, do samples and print them out.

Style decisions have to be made:

❑ width of A-B columns

❑ headers and footers

❑ A column headings for all levels of hierarchy

❑ B column main body text

❑ B column text extras, such as lists of information, special introductory section, table of contents, index

❑ special typefaces for special purposes

❑ notes

❑ warnings

❑ screen dumps

❑ tables of information

❑ captions

Let's work through the possibilities for a sample page (7.5 inches by 9 inches). After you make all your style decisions, print a page and write all the styles on that single printout. Use it as a ready reference guide for the rest of the project.

Width of A-B columns, headers, and footers

In our sample, we are working with a page size of 7.5 inches by 9 inches. The pages will be double-sided. A suitable set of measurements include:

Page trim size = 7.5 by 9 inches

Margins (top and bottom) = .50 inch

Margins (each side) = .25 inch

A column = 1.75 inches

B column = 4.5 inches

Gutter between A and B columns = .25 inch

Headers and Footers

Chapter name header = 10 pt Times Italic

Company name footer = 10 pt Times Italic

Page number = 11 pt Times Bold

Position of Headers and Footers

A hairline rule will be drawn the width of the A-B columns, top and bottom of the page on the .75 margin line. Chapter name headers will sit on this line on the outside of the page. Company name footer will sit on this line on the inside of the page, with the page number on the outside of the page.

Headers Go Here

Footers Go Here   **XX**

A column heading

These will be the main topic and subtopic headings in the A column and thus will need a hierarchical structure. Let's assume that your research and the work you have done on the table of contents suggests you will need four levels of hierarchy, plus a chapter heading level.

You can treat the chapter heading separately because it is a special case: it only happens once in each chapter and it might best be displayed in a different typeface from the other headings. A suitable list includes:

- ❏ chapter headings = 18 point Avant Garde (flush right in Column B)

- ❏ level one headings = 14 point Times bold (style A1, flush right)

- ❏ level two headings = 12 point Times bold (style A2, flush right)

- ❏ level three headings = 11 point Times bold (style A3, flush right)

- ❏ level four headings = 11 point Times bold (style A4, flush left) To be used in Column B

Headers Go Here

Chapter Heading Here

Level One Heading

Level Two Heading

Lvl Three Heading

Level Four Heading

B column main body text

For our sample page example, we'll choose a typeface universally acknowledged as one of the finest for body text — Times. Another typeface that works almost as well is Garamond 3. (The main body text of this book is Garamond 12 point.) While the description is not very scientific, one of our major international clients chose Garamond 3 over Times because "Garamond 3 has a Southern California look about it."

While I am choosing Times 11 point for the 7.5 inch by 9 inch page, I'd probably go up to 12 point for 8.5 inch by 11 inch and down to 10 point for 5.5 inch by 9 inch. At the least, I would run a sample page of each.

The body copy used for our sample page (and this paragraph) is in Times 11 point, with automatic leading and some minor variations in the default settings for better word spacing. It has an acceptable character count across the B column body text of about 65 characters. It is justified.

(For the users of PageMaker, we set our tracking at Loose and change the Word Spacing dialog box settings to Minimum 80%, Desired 100%, Maximum 150%.)

B column text extras

The purpose of these styles is to accommodate all the other B column items that will appear on the page as part of body copy. Times will remain the primary body text typeface. These items might include:

- Special introductory material used after the chapter heading

- Special lists

- Action statements

- Table of contents

- Index

Introductory material

After each chapter heading there will be an introductory paragraph summarizing the content of the coming chapter. It will be indented on both sides by .5 inch, and separated from the body text by a .5 point rule.

> In Chapter 6 we will look at how to write a manual, including rules of grammar, punctuation, and spelling. As clear, concise writing is the key to all forms of written communications, you should spend some time studying this section.

Special lists and action statements

Lists should be used as often as possible in effective documentation. They spell out a set of points in an easy-to-read form. They should be used to separate all actions from the rest of the text, as in the examples on the next page.

Listed items should be started with a bullet (•) when they are action statements and with a box (❏) when they are not action statements.

A simple list looks like this:

This is the lead-in line to a simple list of information:

❑ this is the B with a Bullet style (Style BB)

❑ simple lists will have no initial caps, no punctuation

❑ a space before of .05 inch will be inserted between the lines and the wrap-around will have the second line indented like this

❑ space from bullet to text will be .2 inch

A more complicated list looks like this:

This is the lead-in line to a more complicated list of information:

❑ These statements are full sentences and thus start with an initial capital letter and finish with a period.

❑ Each statement should be complete. It is possible to use a second sentence in a single list item if it is necessary.

❑ Make sure that the text in a list is not too long.

Listed action statements looks like this:

This is the lead-in line to a simple set of action statements:

• Start each action statement with an action word

  Follow the action statement with a comment on what will happen as a result of the action statement, like the next listed item.

• Press the ESC key

  You will be returned to the Master Menu.

Note that in the action statements there are no periods or full stops at the end of any action statement. This is to avoid confusion when asking a user to type something and it turns out to be a command. If you put periods at the end of the action statement — and this happens to be at the end of the command — some users will type the period, thinking it is part of the command.

Table of contents and index

The table of contents, for our sample, should remain Times, as should the Index. However, the Index can probably be reduced to 10 point and, depending on its final size, perhaps even to 9 point.

The table of contents will appear totally within the B column. The Index will be broken into two equal columns across the page.

Special typefaces for special purposes

You will need to make decisions about any other typefaces you plan to use on the page. For example, for our sample we will choose to display anything the user must type into the computer in Courier typeface. This same typeface will be used to show anything that appears on the screen, such as menus and options, and messages. For example:

- Type in your user name: `CROWN`

  A message will appear:

      Now type in your Password

Courier typeface can usually be reduced by a point size so that it does not dominate the page. For example, with Times 11 point, use Courier 10 point. With Times 12 point, use Courier 11 point.

In our sample page, we will choose not to use any other typefaces. However, one successful combination we have used is to place certain predetermined words or options or keys in Avant Garde and reduce the point size by 1 point. There is an example on the next page.

In this example, Avant Garde 9 point has been mixed with Times 11 point and Courier 10 point:

To use the Select Phone option:
- Log on to your network
- Type: `FaxNet`

  Your Main Menu will be displayed.
- Press 1

  The Send Fax menu will be displayed.
- Press 5

  The Select Phone window will be displayed.
- Type in the destination phone number <ENTER>

  You will be returned to the Send Fax menu and the destination phone number will appear in the bottom right of the screen.

One of the advantages of designing your page with this kind of care is that it moves you well away from wall-to-wall writing, the kind most associated with university term papers. In wall-to-wall writing, there is little white space and the eyes get tired quickly as they try to wade through all the text. Another danger in wall-to-wall writing is that when your eye leaves the page to type something on your keyboard, it is very difficult to find your place when you return to the text. Consider the difficulty of following the instructions in the example below in a wall-to-wall format:

To make use of the Select Phone option, log on to your network, and then type FaxNet. Your Main Menu will be displayed. Press 1. The Send Fax menu will be displayed. Press 5. The Select Phone window will be displayed. Type in the destination phone number and press ENTER. You will be returned to the Send Fax menu and the destination phone number will appear in the bottom right of the screen.

Notes and warnings

A style needs to be set for your notes and warnings. Remember that warnings should be used sparingly, so that when they do appear the user will take notice of them. When used too often, they suffer the same problem as the little boy who cried wolf.

Notes can be used more often than warnings, but even notes suffer if more than one appears on a page.

For our sample page, we'll use these styles.

For notes, we'll use the typeface Zapf Dingbat and the character of a pointing finger. The note text will be in style BB (B with a bullet) and the pointing finger will be lifted one point size to 12 point.

☞ This is an example of a note. It should contain information of a nature that demands that it be singled out from the main body text. The note should not be too long.

The warning must demand attention and have a strong visual impact on the page. The box approach works well and breaks up the text. Make sure the box is indented on both sides. The text looks good centered. Use Avant Garde for the word WARNING.

┌─────────── WARNING ───────────┐

This is a warning and as such it must be heeded.
We will not waste your time or scare you
by putting information that is not
important in this warning box.

└───────────────────────────────┘

Screen drawings or screen dumps

A decision must be made whether you will use screen dumps, or whether you will draw your screens (or portions of screens) yourself. We use both methods, depending on the number of screens or windows that will be needed in the manual. Another consideration is the complexity of the screen that needs reproducing. It takes time to draw a screen.

One argument for drawing a screen is that you can choose to only show that portion of the screen that you are talking about at the time. For example, take the following screen dump:

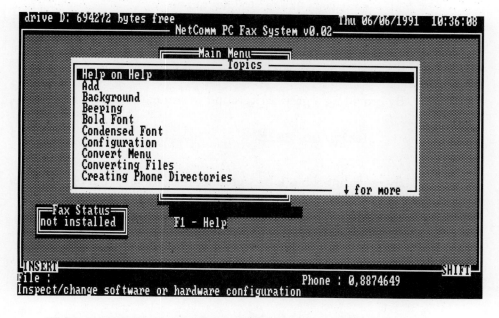

This screen dump looks good and shows a lot of information. It would be difficult to draw from scratch. However, its complexity may be its downfall. If the discussion is only about the topics showing in the window, do we really need all the other detail?

Here's the drawing we might make of the Topic window, using Courier 10 point.

```
┌─────────────────────────  Topics  ─────────────────────┐
│ Help on Help                                            │
│ Add                                                     │
│ Background                                              │
│ Beeping                                                 │
│ Bold Font                                               │
│ Condensed Font                                          │
│ Configuration                                           │
│ Convert Menu                                            │
│ Converting Files                                        │
│ Creating Phone Directories                              │
│                                                         │
└─────────────────────────────────────────────────────────┘
```

The highlighting can be done in one of three ways:

By making the item bold, as done above.

By providing a grey background to simulate the highlighting.

Help on Help

By providing a black background, making it even more realistic.

Help on Help

Tables and captions

If tables are used, it is helpful to set the style design for those tables at this point. For our sample, we'll use tables made up of .05 point lines. The text will be Helvetica, as in the example below.

Captions will be in 10 point Times Italic, centered below the illustration. There are no specific references to table or figure. All illustrations will be placed on the page where the body text describes the illustration (or on the page before or after and referred to as such).

Mnemonics	Work Order	Purchase Order
	WKORD	PRORD

The Mnemonics for the Orders Window

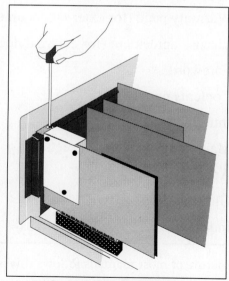

Securing the InModem

The Look of the manual

Now that we have looked at some of the elements that make up the page, such as the typeface, sentence length, and the use of heads, let's start looking at the manual as a whole — as part of the total design criteria.

What are we going to have in this manual, and how is it going to be structured? This is a fundamental question and it must be addressed at this point, although final details cannot be locked in until you have researched the system enough to ensure that everything you have to document will fit within the design you are starting to put in place.

Let's start at the front and list the items you might logically expect to find in an average manual.

Title page

Copyright, disclaimers, trademarks

Warranty page (for external documentation)

License agreement (for external documentation)

Foreword

Contents page

Introduction

Main body chapters (or sections)

Appendices

Glossary

Index

The structure of most manuals follows this pattern. The structure of the main body chapters will come as you start to research the users and the system.

(As already discussed, avoid the temptation to start off with installation, followed by configuration, and finally moving on to operations. Installation and configuration are usually only done once. Put them in the back of the book out of the way, and get right into operations.)

The table of contents forces you to formalize your plan. But also remember that it is not necessary to have all your contents listed on the contents page. What you must have listed are your top two or three levels of hierarchy.

Some writers get carried away with dividing the manual into multiple sections and then dividing those sections into chapters. One modem manual I reviewed had seven sections divided into 20 chapters. It seems that the writer felt that the challenge was to write as many chapters as possible. The user would have been well served with either the 20 chapter headings alone, or — even better — the seven sections with a well-thought-out hierarchy inside those individual sections.

In some cases I do away completely with chapters; in other cases I do away with sections. It is not often that you need both. Whatever choice you make, be sure to keep the hierarchical headings somewhat equal. For example, if your manual was about a fax facility that works with a modem, your section headings might be:

Using the PC Fax System

Phone Directories

Creating Faxes

Sending Faxes

Receiving and Printing Faxes

Viewing and Editing Faxes

There is a natural progression here. This list of sections can be worked through one after the other, or can be used for reference with the user turning to the specific section. Software installation and configuration sections came later — but with a pointer up front which says:

> Before doing anything, turn to the Installation and
> Configuration Section, Appendix A, page 180

The following topics need to be addressed to ensure the standardization of the Look.

❏ Section summaries

❏ Numbering systems

❏ Conventions

❏ Future revision and maintenance needs

❏ Section dividers

Section summaries

Not all manuals need section or chapter summaries. They usually come in one of two forms — on a section title page that contains only the title of the section and the summary, or as the first topic on a page. In either case, the summary should be short and to the point.

The summary should provide the user with the contents of the section in a nutshell. The summary aids the user by confirming that he has actually turned to the section he needs or, equally as important, suggests to the user that he has not found the section he needs.

Let's look at a couple of examples:

> ### Appendix A: DOS SERVICES & FAX UTILITIES
>
> The NetComm PC Fax System provides full access to normal DOS functions, such as renaming, deleting, and copying files. It also has a full range of utilities to increase the power and flexibility of your fax operations.
>
> In this appendix, you'll learn how to run DOS programs and utilities from within the PC Fax System, how to include a variety of fonts within a fax, how to create your own fonts, and how to convert faxes from 2D to 1D compression formats.

The example I have chosen here covers an appendix, which has some special considerations.

This summary above supported a 28-page section in the manual. On the table of contents it was a single line entry because of its status as an appendix and thus the summary had the added value of explaining the contents of the section.

Normally, the material contained in the appendices can be dealt with in the table of contents with single line entries and a more complete summary included on the opening page of the appendix. In some cases, where the appendix is large and the topics diverse, you might want to include a contents list on the first page of that appendix. The decision about which route to take should be weighed against the knowledge of the user and the complexity of the material. All other considerations being equal, always find in favor of assisting the user.

Let's look at another example, this time for a section summary that starts at the top of the first page of the section text.

---

2 GETTING STARTED

AutoSoft has been designed to be easy to use. There are only a few keystrokes you need to remember. This section explains:

❑ how to make a working copy of AutoSoft

❑ how to install the program on your computer

❑ how to use the pull-down menus and forms

In this example I have chosen to use a Zapf Dingbat box (❑) rather than the bullet (•) because I reserve bullets for "do this" action statements.

Section summaries can produce a number of bonuses. For example, I often write the section summaries first — as part of my blueprinting when I am developing the table of contents. These summaries help confirm in my own mind that I have the correct structure in place and that the flow of the manual from one section to the next is appropriate.

Another bonus is that the section summaries can be copied and perhaps reformatted as an overview of the entire manual. This feature is useful when introducing the manual(s) to new users.

A further bonus is that if the manual grows large and must be broken into more than one binder, the section summaries can be reorganized to show what topics are covered in each binder(s).

Be consistent throughout the entire manual. It is disconcerting for the user to find one kind of summary on one section and another kind of summary on the next section. It is even more disconcerting to find section summaries on some sections and not on others. Use the summary to set the scene — to lay out the geography of what comes next — and to orient the user on the course to be followed.

Of course the ultimate summary is the Read Me First or foreword page, which we've already looked at. The foreword page has summarized not only the manual but also the user and who we expect that user to be. While the foreword has other roles to play it is, in its simple form, another kind of summary.

The numbering dilemma

It is truly unfortunate that manuals continue to be written with numbering systems that follow archaic rules about numbering. Numbers should never be used to set one item off from another item unless there is a specific reason to use a number.

Traditionally, numbers have been used everywhere. You might find page numbers, section numbers, paragraph numbers, item or list numbers, figure and table numbers, and so forth. Each time you consider the use of numbering you must question the reason. For example, page numbering. All manuals need page numbering. But what format should the page number take?

A general rule

Numbers (or alpha characters, A, B, C) should only be used if they:

❑ Determine an order of importance

   1 is more important than 2, 2 is more important than 3

❑ Determine a hierarchy not obvious in any other way

   For headings, where you cannot control the size of type.

❑ Show the order in which multi step activity should take place

   Do step 1, then do step 2, then do step 3

❑ Are needed as a point of reference later on

   Repeat from step 5 on page 20.

Page numbers

When we look at the structure of the table of contents in Process 5, we will see how the user moves down the contents list to the major heading, then moves down the subheadings until he finds the topic he wants, and then he moves to the page number.

The page number then becomes the most important pointer to where information is located in the manual. As the user moves through the manual to find the page, he must remember the page number. Obviously, then, the page number should be kept as simple as possible.

Page numbers are often used in the text to refer users to other parts of the manual. The same rule applies — keep it simple.

Therefore, we should avoid a page number like: 5.6/132

The 5.6/132 usually results when the writer thinks it is helpful to provide not only the page reference, but the item or paragraph number as well. Users do not identify topics by these artificial numbering structures. If they are looking for a topic on a page, they need the number of the page and the *name* of the topic.

Number pages sequentially from 1 to the end of the manual, if possible. This is the easiest for the writer and the user. However, there will be times when sections will have to be numbered so that each section starts with Page 1. When this happens, the page number should be accompanied by the number of the section as well. This may be in the form:

Section 5 Page 20

It is even more helpful to name the section:

5 Work Order Inquiries - Page 20

The user then knows he is in the correct section and can concentrate on the page number.

Section numbering

Section numbers are useful, particularly if they are used in the page headers, or in the footers. Section numbers decrease in value (and become more difficult for both writer and user to make use of) as they become more complicated.

Thus the ideal is to use a single number for an entire section and not to break it into any kind of subnumbering system. Asking a user to refer to Section 5.2 or, as is commonly seen, Section 5.2.2 is nowhere near as helpful as referring the user to Section — Page — Topic:

Section 5, Page 7 — Masterfile Updates

I like providing the user with the name (Masterfile Updates) of whatever is being referenced. It ensures that the user has truly found the reference.

Paragraph numbers

Paragraph numbering has little use in user manuals. It may be of use in technical manuals where analysis needs to numbered, but that is outside the scope of the manuals we are studying here. Paragraph numbering is like encountering a bureaucracy. It gets in the way of clear thinking and tends to confuse rather than guide.

Use paragraph numbers only after careful review shows it is absolutely necessary, and there is no other way around it.

Numbering items in a list

Items in a list should only be numbered if they meet one of the requirements under the general rule explained earlier in this section. Short lists of action statements are better served by using a bullet (•). If there are only three steps, there is no need to number those steps.

However, if a procedure requires eight steps then numbering those steps will help the user remember where he is. (In this case, use numbers and not A, B, C alpha characters. Most users are more comfortable with 1, 2, 3. . . 6, 7, 8 than with A, B, C. . .F, G, H.)

Try to keep the steps to 8 or less. If the list of items exceeds eight, try to break the list up in such a way that you can take the user through eight or less, then break the list and start the numbering again. Quite often, long procedures can be broken into subsets.

I once edited a manual with a procedure that ran for 28 steps. Users were having trouble following the list. I divided the 28 steps into four groups of six and one group of four with a couple of sentences between each group. The users found it much easier to follow. The sentences merely explained what had happened, or was happening, as the steps were followed.

Numbering items in a list is also useful if the procedure can be broken into a number of steps and each step has a number of action statements or alternative action statements. An example is shown on the next page.

To use the *Select Phone* option to edit phone directories, follow these steps:

1   Choose the *Select Phone* option from the Send Menu

    A window will appear on the screen.

2   Type: ?

    The default directory will be displayed.

    If you want to display another directory, instead of default:

    • Type: ?DIRECTORY_NAME <E>

       The Phone Directory Window will be displayed.

3   Highlight the entry you want to Edit

    • Press F2

    • Press E

       The Phone Directory Edit Window will appear.

Notice how, in the example above, the numbered steps (there are seven steps in the full procedure) each have an action, and steps 2 and 3 have additional actions within the step.

Figure and table numbering

The numbering of figures and tables only needs to be done if the user is going to be referred to those tables and figures from elsewhere in the manual. There is no need to provide Figure 5.3 labels if the figure only appears once. Telling a user to see Table 2.3 is nowhere near as useful as telling the users to:

Refer to the Function Key table on Page 25

Tables or figures should be located as near as possible to the text that explains or refers to them. Asking a user to go to "the next page" or "the previous page" is quite legitimate, as is the use of the words "above" or "below" when referring to a table or figure on the same page. (Avoid referring to anything on a previous page as "above". It not only looks funny, it's physically incorrect.)

If a table or a figure is not too large and is referred to more than once, consider repeating the table or figure at the appropriate place in the text so the user doesn't have to move too far away from where he is reading.

Revisions, maintenance, and numbering

The larger topic of revision and maintenance is dealt with later in this book, but page numbering must be thought about early on. If revisions and updates are going to be added regularly, then the page numbering might be best by section. It is unlikely the entire manual will the subject of updating. It is more likely you will be adding pages here and there.

Most users have no trouble with inserts labeled with the page number and A, B, C. The user will be able to find Page 75A. If it is a new topic, then the table of contents should also be reissued. At a certain point, as the inserts grow larger, consideration will have to be given to updating the entire manual in a new version.

Section dividers

On manuals with more than 80 pages, the user will be well served if you consider dividing the sections (or chapters), and making that division obvious. They become a physical signposting to the manual, helping the user get quickly to the section he is searching for. There are at least four practical methods.

Card with tab

Each section has a card (colored or plain) with a full tab sticking out beyond the edge of the page. On the tab is the name of the section. The tabs run one after the other down the side of the manual, allowing a quick flick of the finger to take the user to the section. A cheaper version of this is to purchase commercially available numbered tabs and show only the section number.

Solid black block

A solid black (or grey) block tab marker can be printed on the outside edge of the page. When the manual is viewed from the side the black mark on the edge of each page becomes a black marker the depth of the number of pages in the section. This allows quick rifling of the pages with the thumb to reach the needed section. Like the tabs, the black markers run one after another down the side of the manual's outside pages.

Change page color

Print each section of the manual on a different color paper. While this certainly makes the section stand out, you must carefully consider the colors and make sure they provide good black color contrast. Only the most pale colors work.

Section page color

A variation on the above method would have only the first page of each section in color. This is effective if the page is printed on a card slightly heavier than the text page.

If you use one of these methods, be sure to:

- Use the method only for sections which have the same hierarchy. For example, between chapters or major sections. Do not separate Level 2 hierarchy topics on some occasions and not on others. Be consistent throughout.

- Ensure the manual has enough pages in each section to make the section dividers worthwhile. Too few pages and the appearance will be more comical than useful.

Conventions and style

Near the front of your manual, explain to the reader any of the special symbols, typestyles, or other devices you plan to use. This procedure is quite straight-forward, but often overlooked. The example below shows a number of style conventions that assist the user.

To use the *Select Phone* option to edit phone directories, follow these steps:

1   Choose the *Select Phone* option from the Send Menu

A window will appear on the screen.

2   Type: ?

The default directory will be displayed.

If you want to display another directory, instead of default:

- Type: `?DIRECTORY_NAME` <E>

The Phone Directory Window will be displayed.

3   Highlight the entry you want to edit

- Press F2

- Press E

The Phone Directory Edit Window will appear.

Some of these conventions, such as the <E>, the use of special typefaces for the main body text, the screen words `?DIRECTORY_NAME`, and the keys F2 and E, need to be explained to the user. Others, such as the use of initial capped letters for Send Menu and Phone Directory Window need to be determined in the writer's Style Guide which we'll look at later in this book. A typical conventions section is shown on the next three pages.

Conventions and Style

Throughout this guide, we use certain symbols, typestyles and conventions to help you. For example, you might find a line that looks like this:

- Type: ATI9 <E>

  What you actually type appears in a special typeface:

  ATI9

  Whatever appears on your screen will also be displayed in this manual in this special typeface, for example, messages:

  CONNECT

When we want you to press the ENTER key, we use a symbol:

    <E> (which means "and press ENTER")

On some keyboards the ENTER key is labelled RETURN. You press RETURN or ENTER, as appropriate for your keyboard. The same is true for keyboards showing a symbol, rather than RETURN or ENTER.

    RETURN = ENTER = ⏎

In some cases where the <E> symbol might be confusing, we will tell you to "Press the ENTER key".

Another typeface is used to highlight program names, directory names, and so forth. For example, you might find this line:

'The FAXSYS.COM program is loaded into your computer's memory.'

When you see the bullet (•), it usually starts an action statement. We want you to take some specific action, such as:

• Switch your computer on

• Type: ATI9 <E>

Note that we do use a (.) full stop after an action statement. We do that to avoid confusion when you are asked to type commands and other information. For example, the command AT&F1. actually includes a full stop (.) as part of the command.

When we list general information, we use a box (❏), like this:

❏ How to begin dialing.

❏ Using MNP® for error-free communication.

When we have special information we want you to take NOTE of, we use a pointing finger (☞), like this:

☞ Your modem's ON/OFF switch uses international symbols to show the ON and OFF positions. The **I** symbol indicates the ON position; the **O** symbol indicates the OFF position.

Information we want you to pay special attention to is placed in a WARNING box, like this:

```
┌──────────── WARNING ────────────┐
│   Telecom regulations require that the modem,   │
│   when operating in originate mode, waits no    │
│   longer than 30 seconds for a carrier to be    │
│       detected from a remote modem.             │
└─────────────────────────────────┘
```

Sometimes you will need to press a single key; other times you will have to press two keys. In this guide, the following convention is used to help make the combinations clear.

• Press ESC

  This means press only the ESC key.

• Press Shift-F7

  The use of the hyphen (-) between the keys means that you press both keys together. In this case, the Shift key and the F7 key.

DEFAULTS are settings that are preset in the factory. The default settings are indicated in this guide by the symbol: ■ For example: If the default was AT&G0 in this list:

■ AT&G0 Do not generate guard tones
 AT&G1 Generate guard tones of 550Hz
 AT&G2 Generate guard tones of 1800Hz

There is a glossary at the back of this guide to assist you with unfamiliar words.

Process 5: Blueprint the Contents

> ## PROCESS FIVE
>
> **Design the table of contents as the blueprint for the manual. The table of contents is not complete until it is reviewed and approved.**

Do not start writing until the contents have been "locked in".

By this point in your task you have given your manual a name and a reason for existing. You understand your user, you have researched the system and you have looked at the physical design of your manual.

It is now time to take your knowledge about the system and your understanding of the user and merge them together into the blueprint you will use to actually write the manual.

By now you might be facing management pressure because you do not have a lot to show for the time you have spent, and this blueprinting process is going to take even more time. But don't shortcut it. Don't start writing the manual until the table of contents — your Blueprint — is finished right down to being laid out in its page format.

As part of this process we would also do an estimated page count for each section of the manual as part of the documentation management task. This is difficult to do without experience, but it is a worthwhile exercise. (This task is explained in detail later in this book in chapter 6, Managing the Documentation Project.)

There are a number of different ways to tackle the table of contents or contents listings. After reviewing some generalities, we'll look at some alternatives to the traditional contents listings.

Some generalities

Carrying out this process is going to take some time. Recognize that and don't rush. It is here you can almost guarantee the success of your manual; this is also the place where you can doom the whole project.

You blueprint your manual by preparing the table of contents because you will need the blueprint to follow during writing and editing, much as a builder follows the architect's blueprint in constructing a house. It would be foolish to launch any detailed construction without a plan to follow, and writing a manual requires lots of detail and thus lots of planning.

None of the time you are spending on these early processes is being wasted. It may seem so to outsiders, or superiors who don't understand your task, but they are wrong. What are you are doing now is guaranteeing your work. Without these preliminaries, it is highly likely you will arrive at the end of your project with a manual or another item of documentation that will not do the job.

Get your users involved

Getting users involved at this stage has distinct advantages. They will feel they are part of the decision-making process for a system which they will soon be a part of. We often meet with a representative sample of users, explain what we are trying to accomplish, and then ask the users for their ideas.

Listen to their ideas carefully. If you are receptive to some of their ideas (and some of their ideas will equal your own — so give the users the credit for thinking of them), you will be creating a positive environment for the introduction of the system and of your documentation. You will be helping create a positive initial reaction.

Finish your table of contents

There are a number of reasons for finishing your table of contents, all the way through to finished layout. Many writers write out their contents as a mere list on a scrap of paper, by hand. This is dangerous because the list is too easy to change, and changing the list might change your structure and send you off into some box canyon you can't get out of without retracing your steps. If you end up retracing your steps, you inevitably waste time and resources.

Second, you will want to gain approval for the design and contents list, and presenting a properly formatted table of contents will make it easier for outsiders to understand your plan.

Third, you are going to be referring to this blueprint daily for a long time while you write, edit and proofread your manual. A neatly finished blueprint is much easier to follow.

A fourth reason for finishing the table of contents is that you want to make it easy for the users to find things. At the same time you don't want the table of contents to be too long. Ideally, it will be one page. Two pages are okay, three only if you have no choice. But any table of contents that runs to four or more pages is hard to use and is liable to be rejected by the user. You won't know how much space your table of contents will take up until you've dropped it into its page format.

If you find your table of contents reaching beyond two pages, have a good look at the way you are constructing your manual. Go back and look at the hierarchy of headings and ask if all those levels are necessary to get the user to the part of the manual he needs to reach.

Users have trouble navigating through multiple levels of hierarchy. Try to keep it to three levels maximum.

> MAIN SECTION
>> Sub-Section
>>> Sub-Sub-section (lowest level)

If extra levels of hierarchical headings are necessary, consider whether some of those levels of headings could be more usefully placed at the beginning of the Section or Chapter inside the manual, in order to get them off the table of contents page.

Try to visualize each part of the manual as you write the contents list. Weigh various topic areas against each other to see that undue attention has not been given to one subject over another. One thing to watch for is extra headings in areas where you have additional knowledge versus a few headings in areas where your knowledge is weak.

Rules are made to be broken, of course, but a rule of thumb suggests most topics in a manual should not exceed about five pages. This means frequent headings to help guide the user. If the text for a topic stretches for more than five pages, then look for some logical break to divide it or search for subtopics which might be broken out with an additional lower-level heading. However, if you review the section and it still needs seven pages — then go with the seven pages.

I try not to write a manual of more than 300 pages. That's 300 double-sided pages, 150 sheets of paper. There are manuals that are thicker that work, but not often. If it looks like it is going to be more than 300 pages, go back to the blueprint and study it. Is it really one manual, or is it trying to do the work of two manuals. At the same time, if the manual needs more than 300 pages and you have questioned the length and can live with it, then go ahead and break the rule.

If you do the table of contents the right way using this process, you will theoretically not have to make any changes as you proceed through the writing and editing processes. However, in reality, you'll always find headings you want to add or subtract. There is no problem with this. Minor changes shouldn't hurt your project.

While you have put some thought into standard page layouts during your format and design stage, now is the time to match your standard page layout ideas against the table of contents. Review the rules of standard page layouts. Remember the need to design for the majority of topics. The table of contents provides this information.

The table of contents can also be tested against the Reliability and comprehension criteria we laid down when we discussed what the user needs in a manual. Will the information be easy to find? Will the user be confident that the manual is complete?

Gain approval for your plan

Now is the time to gain approval for your plan. With the blueprint neatly locked into a finished page format, with standard page layouts designed, with a title and a solid purpose, it is time to lay the project out in front of those who will use it, and those who will judge it when you are finished.

This is the time to make sure you are writing the manual everyone is expecting. It is also the time for anyone who has a valid case against the page size you have chosen, or the typefaces, or some other element, to speak up. These discussions may well ruin weeks of good work if they are brought up after you have finished the first draft. Format changes, and the like, are difficult to implement successfully after the writing has been done.

Before moving to variations on the traditional table of contents, and a newer concept — the activity index — let's summarize the role of the contents listing.

To meet the requirements of effective documentation, a table of contents must meet the following standards:

Information is in a form and a place where users can refer to it when it is needed.

❑ at the front of the manual, directly after title page, legal and warranty pages, and the foreword (or Read Me First) page

Information is easy to find.

❑ topics are grouped in a logical order, with a simple page or section numbering system

Information is easy to comprehend.

❑ the logical order of the topics helps the user understand the structure of the system

Information is up-to-date.

❑ the structure of the contents listings allows for updates and revisions (usually through reissuing the table of contents with the revision handouts)

Information is reliable and convincing.

❑ all topics needed are covered in a way that will make the manual useful to the user, with design characteristics in place to make the table of contents easy to read

Two typical first pages from the tables of contents are shown on the next two pages. Note how the 300-page rule had to be set aside in the second example.

Contents

CONTENTS

The Activities Index

Most of my manuals now have what we call an activities index. The topic needs to be introduced here because it is a flow-on from the contents listing and often is placed directly after the table of contents page.

The question you need to ask is, How does my user look up information? The traditional index might become quite complicated if the user wanted to, for example:

View Inventory Transfers Not Recorded Onto the System.

An index entry at the back of the book might show it this way:

Inventory
    Transfers, View
        Not Recorded On System 30

Whereas, an activity index entry might record it this way:

Inventory Transfers
    View Transfers Not Recorded Onto System 30

The key here is to make life easy for the user. Ask yourself how the user wants to look up information and then display the information in a format that meets the user's needs.

On the next two pages are examples of activities indexing. Note the page numbering is mixed up. The user goes for the page number only after finding the topic so there is no need for the numbering to be sequential. What is needed is a logic to the display of topics. The first example shows the information the way a user will actually use it. The second example, maintenance enquiries, lists menus as well as options. It is located later in the manual (page 121) and points back at topics covered in an enquiries section.

While the traditional index has a place (and is discussed in detail later in this book), the activities index has proven itself across a number of our manuals.

Activity Index

MAINTENANCE ENQUIRIES

Menus & Activities Index

These are the Enquiry menus and Enquiry options available in the Maintenance module.

MAINTENANCE

⌐— *Menus* —┐		⌐— *Options* —┐
➤ **Plant Catalogue**	➤ **Enquiries**	Plant Enquiry 71
		Part Where Used Enquiry 75
		Drawings of Plant Enquiry 89
		Drawings of Area Enquiry 92
		Drawings of Section Enquiry 95
		Drawings of Unit Enquiry 98
		Drawings Enquiry 86
		Specification Enquiry 74
		Bill of Material Enquiry 80
		Process Line Enquiry 68
➤ **Work Orders**	➤ **Enquiries**	Backlog Enquiry 67
		Work Order Projection Enquiry 96
		Job Request Enquiry 48
		Main Work Order Enquiry 53
		Trade Enquiry 77
		Job Procedures Enquiry 45
		History Question Sets Enquiry 36
		Job Description Enquiry 42
		Isolation Permits Enquiry 39
		Special Requirements Enquiry 55
		Departments Enquiry 83
		Frequency Enquiry 23
		Operations Data Enquiry 51
➤ **Equipment History**	➤ **Enquiries**	History Enquiry 26

Contents by sections

One of the more productive ways of handling the contents page is to list the major headings at the front of the manual, keeping the list short and to the point. At the start of each major section or chapter, a more detailed contents list is displayed. For example, the following entry in a modem reference manual is found at the front of the manual in the traditional contents listings:

At the start of section 8, the following contents list is displayed:

(and so forth through listings to page 153)

This works well and is recommended, particularly in reference manuals. If the section has some kind of tab marking or can be turned to directly, the user will usually go straight to the section he needs.

Contents and Emphasis

Another technique which will come in handy is to forget the traditional structure of the table of contents page — which starts at page 1 and works its way sequentially to the last page — and think, once again, about how the user will be using the manual. In other words, instead of making the focus the page numbers, forget the page numbers and put the focus where it really belongs — back on the user and his needs.

Most of us use a table of contents page this way:

① we scan down the page looking for a major heading for the topic we are searching for (or a heading directly related to our topic)

② we scan the sub-headings beneath the major heading looking for the most specific reference we can find

③ having found that heading we scan to the right and find the page number

For example, to find Logging On in the example below:

The logic behind this approach suggests that if the page number is only searched for after the reference has been found, the order in which items are placed in a table of contents has very little to do with the page numbering.

An extension of this thinking allows a tremendous flexibility in the way we handle the table of contents. A single manual can be made to cater for different emphases.

In its simple form, consider the needs of an experienced user and an inexperienced user and a budget that only allows for the writing of one manual. The inexperienced user needs the following sections at the top of his table of contents:

The experienced user is more likely to find the table of contents useful if it gets right to the point, with the kind of information the inexperienced user needs tucked away at the bottom of the last page of the contents listings. The experienced user may find his listing starting this way:

This is only a simple example but it starts to show some of the possibilities. If you have to accommodate more than one group of users, or if you have to use a single manual across a number of different functional tasks, consider using different tables of contents to handle each definition.

☞ An immediate word of warning. The manual must be written to a single blueprint — a single table of contents — and then the second or third or fourth table of contents imposed on that single manual. Never try to write the manual with more than one emphasis. It won't work. The power comes from pointing different types of user in different ways to the same basic text.

This simple structure suggests that you could develop a table of contents for a manual which would be used in a training course for new users, another table of contents for inexperienced users, and a third table of contents for the user who has been using the system for some time and only needs a ready reference guide.

The same approach could be used to cover installation and configuration, two topics that often only occur once. Too often, these topics might clutter up the first 30 pages of a manual. They can be safely tucked away at the back of the manual — perhaps as an appendix — and a table of contents can be included which starts with the headings Installation and Configuration. It makes no difference if the first page number on the contents listing is page 225.

So far, our simple example only moved sections around. We can extend our thinking to moving topics around even more dramatically if that will help the users. Remember, the user wants a logical pattern to follow. Therefore we might assemble the table of contents with any logical emphasis. Perhaps we might use one of these:

Who does the task:

> In this listing, the emphasis is on the operator and the table of contents reflects the tasks the operator does, no matter where those tasks are found in the manual.

By location:

> An example here might concentrate on tasks done by the national office, or by state offices, or by city offices, or by branch offices within cities. If there are tasks common to all offices, this is reflected in the tables of contents for each office. However, tasks carried out only by a city office would not appear on the table of contents for the other offices.

> This same approach could also be used within a large organization under such headings as warehouse, or engineering, or accounts, maintenance, and so forth.

While there may seem to be an endless list of emphases that can be placed on a table of contents, remember that the manual must be written with one emphasis clearly in mind and the additional emphases are created strictly within the table of contents.

It follows that the ideal situation would be to write different manuals for each emphasis. However, time and budget constraints allows few of us that privilege and what you are attempting to do here is to find a way of accommodating as many users as possible with one manual.

The Contents as a guide

The listings on the contents page do more than just point you at a section in the manual. They also work independently as a guide to what the system or application actually does. A user should be able to tell a lot from reading the contents page. There should also be a link between the contents listings and the beginning of each chapter or section.

For example, on a manual describing a product called the PC Fax System which provides an IBM or compatible computer with fax capability, the table of contents listed the following headings for chapter 4.

4   Using the PC Fax System
        Background Operation
        Getting to Know the Menu System
        Using the On-Line Help System
            Cross-Reference Topics
            The Help Index
        Selecting Files
            Speed Selecting Files
            Changing Directories in the File Selection Window
        Selecting a Phone Number
            Using the Select Phone Option

Inside the manual, at the beginning of chapter 4, is this comment:

This chapter describes how to:
❏ Run and the PC Fax System
❏ Summon Help on-line
❏ Select files to work with
❏ Select a destination phone number

Working from these headings, it would not be difficult to create a small training guide that could be used to introduce new users to the system. Under each of the headings used to explain what is in the chapter, and working from the information you know is important because it is listed on the contents listings, the training guide could be produced quite easily.

For example, under the heading: Summon Help On-Line

Summon Help On-Line

Using the On-Line Help System

The Fax Menu System provides extensive, context-sensitive Help. This means that when you call Help, the information displayed is appropriate to the activity you are doing at the time.

Cross-Referenced Topics

When you are in a Help screen, you will often see words highlighted. This highlighted text indicates a cross-reference where you can find out more about the highlighted topic. If only one word on the screen is highlighted, press ENTER to call up information about that word.

The Help Index

The Help Index provides information on a range of topics about the PC Fax System and its use. This can be used for browsing or to answer specific questions when you are not in an area where you can access context sensitive Help.

For comparison, the actual pages in the manual looked like this:

Using the On-Line Help System

The Fax Menu System provides extensive, context-sensitive Help. This means that when you call up Help, the information displayed is appropriate to the activity you are doing at the time.

To call for Help:

- Press F1

  Help information will be displayed. If there is more than one screen of Help available, use the PgUp and PgDn keys to move backward and forward through the screens.

To leave the Help screens:

- Press ESC

  The Help Window will close.

Cross-Referenced Topics

When you are in a Help screen, you will often see words highlighted. This highlighted text indicates a cross-reference where you can find out more about the highlighted topic. If only one word is highlighted:

- Press ENTER

  Information about the highlighted word will appear.

If more than one word is highlighted:

- Press the Right-Arrow key to move from one highlighted word to the next

- Press ENTER to call information on the selected word

The Help Index   The Help Index provides information on any topic. To use the Help Index:

- Press F1

  The current Help Window will be displayed.

- Press F1 again

  The Help Index will be displayed. The Help Index is accessible from any Help screen.

- Move around the Index using the PgDn, PgUp, HOME, END and the cursor control (Arrow) keys to find the topic you want

- Highlight the topic by moving the cursor to it

- Press ENTER

  The relevant Help Window will be displayed.

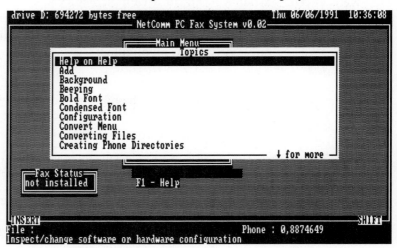

To leave the Help Index:

- Press ESC

  You will be returned to the screen you were at when you entered Help.

Fleshing out the blueprint

In keeping with the philosophy of passing through the manual in complete sweeps, the next step is to put some flesh on the Blueprint skeleton. The object here is not to fill in all the words but to get on paper the headings and a rough idea about what will be covered under each heading.

The best way to see this is by studying an example. The manual is a guide to a communications software package named AutoSoft. The table of contents for Section 1 looked like this:

> 1   Introduction
>   Features and Benefits
>   How to Use This Guide
>   Conventions and Style
>   Computer Requirements
>   Entering Terminal Mode
>   Fast-track to Text Services
>   Fast-track to Discovery
>   Fast-track for Manual Modems

Fleshing out the blueprint went like this:

Introduction

Welcome to the AutoSoft User's Guide. AutoSoft is an easy-to-use versatile communications package for IBM and IBM compatible computers.

Features and Benefits

AutoSoft has extensive features to assist your communications' tasks.

How to Use This Guide

This guide has been designed in three sections, followed by the appendices.

Conventions and Style

Throughout this guide, we use certain symbols, typestyles, and conventions to help you.

Computer Requirements

To use AutoSoft your computer must have:

Entering Terminal Mode

Some modems require that you enter "full-duplex terminal mode" in order to test your modem. Here's how to do this with AutoSoft:

Fast-Track to Text Services

This section shows you how to log on to a text service quickly with AutoSoft.

Fast-Track to Discovery

This section shows you how to log on to Discovery 40 or Discovery 80 videotex system with AutoSoft.

Fast-Track for Manual Modems

This section shows you how to log on to remote services when you are using a manual modem. (The manual modem is controlled by front panel switches and requires you to manually dial the number you require.)

The table of contents for Section 2 looked like this:

The first pass filled in the headings this way:

Getting Started

This section explains how to make a working copy of AutoSoft, how to install the program on your computer, and how to use the pull-down menus and forms.

Making a Work Disk

Before you begin investigating the uses of AutoSoft, make a working copy of your master disk.

Installing: Floppy Drive Computers

AutoSoft may be run from a single 5.25 inch or 3.5 inch disk. Here's how to make a working copy.

Installing: Hard Disk Computers

Follow this procedure if you are using AutoSoft with a hard disk drive:

Path Support

AutoSoft is fully compatible with the DOS path searching convention. Thus, if the directory in which AutoSoft resides is included in the file search path you will be able to run AutoSoft from any directory on your computer.

Running AutoSoft

AutoSoft has been designed to be easy to use. There are only a few keystrokes you need to remember.

Finding Help

AutoSoft provides you with on-screen help, if you need it. To see AutoSoft's Help screens:

Using AutoSoft

There are four main features of the AutoSoft main screen: the status line, the menus, the scrolling window, and the forms. This section looks at each of these features.

The Status Line

At the bottom of the screen is the status line.

The Menus

The menus are lists of options which allow you to control the operation of AutoSoft. Topics here are: Opening Menus, Choosing Menu Options, and Closing a Menu.

Scrolling Windows

Scrolling windows allow you to select the name of a communications service you wish to connect to, a file to print, the type of modem you are using, and other features. Topics here are: Selecting Entries, Searching, and Scrolling Window Options,

Forms

AutoSoft's forms contain detailed information about the configuration of AutoSoft, communications services in the dialling directory, the types of modem you are using, and other information. Topics include Moving About the Forms, Field Types, Changing Forms, and Saving Changes.

Special Keys

It is sometimes necessary to send an Escape character to a remote system (some bulletin boards require you to press ESC when you first connect).

Using a Mouse

If you have a Microsoft mouse (or compatible mouse) attached to your computer, you may use it to open menus and choose options.

Configuring AutoSoft

Configuration is a term referring to the way AutoSoft is set up to run on your computer. AutoSoft comes ready to run on most computers. You may want to perform this quick check of AutoSoft's configuration to ensure that it is configured properly for your computer.

Tone or Pulse Dialing

AutoSoft permits your modem to tone dial or pulse dial.

The Table of Contents for Section 3 looked like this:

The first pass filled in the headings this way:

Basic Communications

This section shows how to use AutoSoft to connect to public bulletin boards and videotex services, and how to transfer files between your computer and other computers.

Text Communications

AutoSoft makes your computer act as a terminal connected to other computers. This allows you to log on to bulletin boards, electronic mail services, and even mainframe computers.

Dialing and Connecting

AutoSoft comes complete with its own dialing directory, containing a list of remote services that you may call immediately.

Hanging Up the Modem

When you are ready to log off a service, once the modem hangs up, AutoSoft's main screen will reappear.

Transferring Files

Often users of computers want to exchange information or programs with a communications service or with each other. Topics here: Receiving Files, Sending Files, ZModem Multiple File Uploads, Sending Messages, and Prepared Text

Capturing Text

AutoSoft allows you to capture all the text received from remote systems and save it to a text file on your disk.

Videotex Communications

Videotex communications allow you to log on to Discovery 40 and other Prestel-compatible services, such as Market Advantage, Elderlink, and Westpac. This section shows you how to log on to Discovery 40. (This section is a step-by-step guide to using Discovery 40.)

The appendices and end matter in this manual include:

- A Glossary
- B Technical Details
- C ASCII Table
- Index

Process 6: Write

> ## PROCESS SIX
>
> **Write the entire manual from beginning to end in a relaxed, conversational and personal style.**

The writing of all the words is the hard part, made easier by the processes you've already made your way through. The writing takes the most time and requires patience and an enthusiasm that is likely to wane as the pile of pages slowly grows and the procedures seem to grind on in a seemingly endless collection of steps and instructions.

The most effective way to get through this process is to start at the beginning, on page 1, and write all the way to what will be the final page before the Index. Make this first draft one complete pass through the manual. If you don't have enough information on some aspect, write what you do know and then pass on to the next topic. At least, put some words on paper under every heading.

Some writers start writing the sections they know the most about first. The danger with this approach is that the manual can become unbalanced. What we want to achieve is a sense of balance and the easiest way to do this is to keep the whole picture in view as we write each part of it.

Handle the areas where you don't know information in a consistent manner. For example, place two questions marks (??) wherever you have a problem. Later, a simple search for ?? will take you to the problem areas.

Unlike the creative writer working on a novel, the documentation writer is spending most of his time in an organizing mode. Armed with research, printouts, the contents as a blueprint, and knowledge of the user, the writer organizes the words on the paper as much as writes them.

Getting organized

Before getting into the rules and standards of good writing, let's spend a few moments getting organized. It is unlikely you will get very far with this writing task if you can't organize the top of your desk. (When I start a new manual writing project, I get a box and take everything off my desk except my notes and my computer. Pictures of wife and kids, clock, calculator, letters, ashtray, lighter — everything into the box. I want my huge desktop uncluttered except for the task at hand.)

I have a couple of three D-ring binders on hand, with colored section dividers and adhesive labels. One of those binders holds the latest draft of the pages. (I like to print out pages as I finish each section. That way I can see some progress.)

The second binder holds my notes and research material. It's organized in the same order as the first binder with the same color dividers separating sections and the same adhesive labels identifying the contents of each section. I can move back and forth between latest draft of the manuscript and the research materials quite easily.

The contents page takes pride of place on my desktop. It's my guide and my lifeline to the sanity of knowing that with every heading that I tick off I am one heading closer to finishing that mind-boggling first draft.

Another sheet of paper that I keep handy is my control sheet, neatly ruled with columns for the name of the computer file, and the folder, the start and end page numbers for that file, and a space for comments and problems. Later, as the manual grows to a dozen sections and maybe as many as three or four files in each section, this control sheet tells me where I am, and where various pages can be found.

These are all practical matters, but they must be dealt with before the writing begins. It might be a cliche to talk about a cluttered desk leading to a cluttered mind, but I don't mind using a cliche if it helps make the point. In documentation, a cluttered mind can destroy a project.

Some notes on writing

Write the manual all the way through and then go back and write what you couldn't write the first pass through. And in between those two passes, make sure you gather the information that gave you trouble on the first pass.

While the first complete pass is important, there are some parts that you can purposely set aside until you've got the bulk of the pages written. These include:

❑ section introductions

❑ examples that further illustrate

❑ graphics (although be sure to note where they are needed and, perhaps, draw in a box to show position and allow some room on the page)

❑ tables

❑ summaries

The approach here might be likened to a military offensive where the the hard parts can be bypassed to be dealt with at a later time (another pass through) when the objective (the first pass through) has been met.

Don't try to edit and write at the same time. Editing is a special function you carry out later. Of course, write as well as you can all the time but always remember that no one is going to see the draft you are writing until after you have cleaned it up so keep pushing ahead. Wordiness, run-on sentences, and incorrect punctuation can all be dealt with later. Right now you've got to get the steps in order, the explanations in place, and make sure each section has enough words in it so you can step back at the end of the first pass and see the shape of what you are trying to create.

A word of warning

You will be working from your research notes and you will be dealing with topics that require accuracy and precision. Right from the first word, be accurate. If you are dealing with figures, check them as you go along. If the cable is an RJ11 in your notes, be sure it is an RJ11 on your page.

As your manual grows larger, the distance to your original research notes will seem to grow. Details written early will be harder to find. So make sure your research findings are accurately portrayed in your first draft.

The second pass

After you have made your first pass, you will undoubtedly need to take a break from the keyboard (or the yellow legal pad, depending on your preference for dealing with those first words) and return to research. If you think better with a pencil and a notebook for the first pass, then now is the time to type it out.

The first pass is not complete until the pages are printed out in a format that looks somewhat like the final pages. In other words, you aren't ready for a second pass until you've got headings in place and text blocks where they belong. You can't add much until the pages actually start to look like finished pages — formatted and with those elements of design we've looked at earlier.

Pages should be printed because it is virtually impossible to add, amend, edit or proofread effectively from a computer screen. (I use a 21-inch screen so I can see a double-page spread all laid out in PageMaker and I still am more effective editing a hardcopy printout. You are creating a manual, so work with a page as close to the final product as possible. Conversely, if I am writing on-line help or an on-line tutorial, I stay as far away from hard-copy printouts as possible. It's very difficult to match the attributes of the screen to paper and vice versa.)

Before the second pass writing starts, review the first draft on the hard-copy printout marking minor corrections with a red pen. Don't worry about making the corrections now. What you want to accomplish now is a list of what's missing so you can go find the answers. This is also the time when you can note additional screen printouts you might need, as well as areas where additional examples would be helpful.

Throughout all of this, keep the user firmly in mind. Imagine the user sitting by your arm, reading with you. Pay attention to your imaginary user. If he looks like he is confused, find a way to help him. Mark an area that needs revision. Don't do the revision yet, but mark it clearly.

After you have gathered the missing information, start from page 1 and write again, working through every page and expanding the text. Make minor adjustments to the contents list if required.

Writer's block syndrome

Much has been made of a syndrome called writer's block. Personally, I've never experienced the syndrome. My writing includes years of newspaper and magazine stories, a few novels, television drama, a couple of nonfiction books, and I've never had writer's block. Perhaps it was because of my newspaper training. There was always a deadline coming up.

I can imagine the reaction of my editors had I looked up blankly and claimed I couldn't think of what to write next. It would have been short and to the point: "Young man, if you want to keep getting a paycheck, you'd better start finding the right words!"

Having admitted never having experienced writer's block, I also have to add that there are times when the words do not come easily. And that is the heart of the problem. If the words are not coming easily, it is usually a sign that you don't know enough about your subject. That's not writer's block, that's poor or incomplete research, or trying to write to a blueprint that's not designed properly.

If you are having trouble writing, step back and review the whole picture. It may be that the section you are having trouble with really belongs somewhere else and would flow more easily if it was moved.

Do you really understand the subject? The sign of a professional documentation writer is the ability to write constructively about any subject. And the only way to do that is to understand each new subject through research.

When one of my documentation writers has trouble explaining something on paper, I ask him to explain it to me. I ask questions, I probe, I argue. The writer explains, repeats it over again, makes me understand. If he can't make me understand, he goes back and does more research. If he can make me understand, then he can write that explanation on paper. That straightforward explanation that works in a face-to-face encounter is usually exactly the explanation that works best on paper.

Sir Arthur Conan Doyle (1859-1930), the creator of Sherlock Holmes, once said: "It has long been an axiom of mine that the little things are infinitely the most important." Sir Arthur was right, and as you write keep him in mind. The word processor and desktop publishing tools now available mean we can turn out reams of paper and countless numbers of words, but fast production of poor documentation doesn't help anyone.

Before we turn to review some of mechanics of writing, let's summarize where we are. The purpose of the first pass was to add some flesh to the skeleton represented by the contents blueprint. The second pass gave us the opportunity to provide some tone and color to that flesh. To go beyond that, to add some beauty, we need to consider poise and balance and, in documentation, that requires paying close attention to how we structure our words into sentences, our sentences into paragraphs, and our pages into useful tools for the user.

Writing technique

It is impossible to cover all the mechanics of good writing in this book. However, some basic topics must be included. The following section addresses issues that are important in documentation. Remember that documentation is a kind of writing just as novel writing, or screenplay writing, or poetry are all kinds of writing. Not every writing rule the documentation writer must follow is a rule appropriate to the novelist.

For example:

❏ An indicator light might be on or off, for the documentation writer. It does not need to shine, glow, twinkle, or sparkle as it might for the poet.

❏ An inept documentation writer might tell a user to *strike* a key, whereas an enlightened writer would tell the user to *press* a key.

❏ A technical writer (or countless programmers who should know better) might write — "Press Any Key to Continue" — leaving the new user searching the keyboard for a key labeled "Any Key". (Of course, that user will undoubtedly choose to press one of the few keys on the keyboard that will not respond to that message.) The user-oriented documentation writer will write: Press the spacebar to continue.

The following list covers the most important issues in a random order. Following the list are examples covering each of these topics.

• Be concise, write tightly

• Cut words and phrases

• Cut irrelevant text

• Cut repetition

• Watch for tautology

• Write for the user

- Personalize your writing
- Provide users with benefits
- Keep your writing positive
- Use contractions
- Use subjective opinion
- Be specific (see topic below: Use specific examples)
- Use provable facts and figures
- Choose verbs that convey action
- Keep it active
- Which tense?
- Action for verbs, not nouns
- Action for verbs, not infinitives
- Choose words that build images
- Use comparisons
- Use concrete nouns
- Write clearly
- Use simple words
- Use simple sentences and paragraphs

Be concise, write tightly

Writing in a concise manner saves time for the writer and saves time for the user. Being concise means writing what needs to be said in the fewest number of words. When you write concisely you are able to emphasize the important points. Remember, though, that while you want to write tightly, you must ensure you are still getting the entire message across. Writing incomplete instructions can be very annoying to the user.

The main rules for concise, tight writing are:

- Cut all words and phrases that do not contribute to the point you want to make.

- Cut all repetition, unless that repetition is needed to make your point.

Cut words and phrases

Phrases should be replaced with single words. In replacing a phrase, be careful not to change your original meaning.

WORDY	CONCISE
a number of	many
at this time	now
be an indication of	indicate, show
consensus of opinion	consensus
date of the policy	policy date
due to the fact that	because
during the time that	while
few and far between	seldom, scarce
during the year of 1990	for 1990
for the purpose of	for; to
for the reason that	since; because
from the point of view of	as
give consideration to	consider

have need for	need
in a manner similar to	like
in accordance with	according to (following)
in an effort to improve	to improve
in due course	soon
in many cases	often; frequently
in most cases	usually
in order to	to
in some cases	sometimes
in spite of the fact that	although
in (for) the amount of	for
interface with	meet, work with
in the city of	in
in the event that	if
in the vicinity of $60	about $60
in reference to	about, regarding
in view of the fact that	because
subsequent to	after
under date of	dated
under the circumstances	because
the majority of	most
with regard to	regarding (about)
with the result that	so

There are many phrases you can eliminate that have no contribution to make. For example:

- ❏ allow us to say
- ❏ please be advised
- ❏ considering the facts
- ❏ at the present time
- ❏ let me say this about that

Clauses using the words *that* and *which* can often be cut.

Poor: The supervisor provided disks that are of the 5 1/4 inch size.

Better: The supervisor provided 5 1/4 inch disks.

The following should be avoided at the beginning of sentences:

    It is, It was, There is, There was, There were

Poor: It was known by the supervisor that keyboard operation must start the program. . .

Better: The supervisor knew the keyboard operators must start the program. . .

Poor: There are five steps that should be carried out.

Better: Five steps should be carried out.

Cut irrelevant text

Concise documentation comes not only from cutting words to an effective minimum but also from ruthlessly eliminating text that is irrelevant to the activity. Some basic rules include:

- Define your point and then write to that point.
- Watch for sentences that ramble.
- Don't spend too much time on issues that are obvious.
- Avoid writing introductions that try to cover too many topics.
- Avoid pompous phrases.
- Don't spend too much time trying to be overly polite.
- Cut excessive use of adjectives
- Cut excessive use of prepositions.
- Get to the real issues as quickly as possible.

Examples:

Poor: Should your computer appear to be malfunctioning. . .

Better: If your computer isn't working. . .

Poor: Such examples would include those like. . .

Better: For example. . .

Poor: In order to commence the procedure. . .

Better: Start the procedure by. . .

Poor: The report can be stopped by depressing the <N> key

Better: Press the <N> key to stop the report

Better: Press N — the report will stop

Poor: At this point in time. . .

Better: Now. . .

Poor: We want to call your attention to the fact that. . .

Better: We want to remind you. . .

Cut repetition

One justification for repeating a point is to further emphasize that point. Unless the point is worth the emphasis, repetition can become boring and divert the attention of the user.

- Use a shorter form of the manual's title. For example if the manual is the *NetComm Modem Reference Guide*, make most of the references to this guide.

- Avoid: noun clusters, such as *structured learning environment* instead of tutorial, prepositional phrases (using: *as a result of* instead of *because*); redundancies (using: *repeat again*); unnecessary words (using: *really and truly* instead of *truly*).

USE	AVOID
problems	design constraint considerations
mistake	quality reduction factor
good, excellent, newest	state of the art

Watch for tautology

A tautology is an unnecessary repetition of words. They are very common in everyday speech. However, they should be avoided when writing. An effective writer or editor will watch for these common occurrences:

AVOID	USE
• advancing ahead	advance
• important essentials	important, essential
• basic fundamentals	basic, fundamental
• brief in duration	brief
• cooperate together	cooperate
• mutual cooperation	cooperate
• plan in advance	plan

- final ending   end, conclusion
- final conclusion   end, conclusion
- in the same way as described   as described
- merge together   merge
- reduce down   reduce
- still continue   continue
- resume again   resume

Poor: It is immediately obvious that the disk is full.

Better: It is obvious the disk is full.

Poor: Before shutting down the computer, first make a back-up.

Better: Before shutting down the computer, make a back-up.

Watch out for:

AVOID	USE
• absolutely essential	essential
• square in shape	square
• small in size	small
• spell out in detail	spell out, explain
• eliminate completely	eliminate, end
• currently existing	current, existing

Write clearly

Writing clearly means making sure the user gets your message. You must ensure that you and your users are on the same wavelength. The words you choose must have the same meaning to the user when he needs them as they had to you when you wrote them.

These are the basic rules:

• Use simple words
• Use simple sentences and paragraphs

Use simple words

Use simple, familiar words that are readily understandable. Avoid Latin terms, even if they are short. If you must use jargon or technical terms, make sure they are well defined either before the user comes across them or the first time they are mentioned.

USE	*AVOID*
about	circa (L)
after	subsequent
but	nevertheless
think	deem
end	terminate
error	inadvertency
for example	e.g. (L)
help	assistance, facilitate
home, house	domicile
issue	promulgate
method	methodology
pay	remuneration
send	forward
show	implement
show, uncover	disclose (indicate)
talk	converse

tell, say, write	advise, communicate
that is	i.e. (L)
use	utilization (utilize)

The same rules, of course, apply to phrases.

USE	*AVOID*
because	for the reason that
believe	are of the opinion
for, to	for the purpose of
before	prior to
after	subsequent to
about	with reference to
use	make use of
near	close proximity
consider	give consideration to
begin (start)	initiate, or commence
more	in excess of

For example:

Poor: Attempt this procedure. . .

Better: Try this procedure. . .

Poor: Prioritize your tasks. . .

Better: Rank your tasks. . .

Poor: It is essential that you back up your daily work.

Better: You must back up your daily work.

Use simple sentences and paragraphs

When you write a sentence, and arrange those sentences into paragraphs, keep in mind the length of the sentence, the unity of the thoughts you are expressing the clarity of those thoughts, and the emphasis various parts of the sentence are being given.

Short sentences are always best. A short sentence should not have more than about 20 words. A 30-word sentence can be used, but not too many of them and certainly you should avoid two or three 30-word sentences in a row. A very short sentence (fewer than 10 words) is fine, but too many very short sentences will make the read choppy and difficult to read.

For documentation, short paragraphs are essential. Long paragraphs are uninviting and if they are filled with facts can be daunting to understand.

Unity in a sentence is critical. Unity means not mixing unrelated facts together in the same sentence.

Unity in a paragraph means not mixing unrelated facts in a paragraph. Pick your main fact or point, write your topic or first sentence to that point, develop that point, and conclude that point with additional sentences in the same paragraph. (In some cases, your main point, or the topic, might come later in the paragraph, particularly if you need supporting information to help make the presentation of the topic sentence absolutely clear.)

Coherence means that the words are arranged in such an order that the meaning is clear, that the ideas have clarity. If you are using modifiers, the modifiers should be close to the word being modified. A real danger in documentation writing is writing that lacks clarity.

Be specific

If you want to write in a convincing manner, you need to show that you know something the user needs to know. The user will recognize this if your writing is specific, definite, and concrete. Avoid vague terms and generalizations. Three rules are:

- Keep to provable facts and figures
- Choose verbs that convey action
- Choose words that build images

Use provable facts and figures

Whenever you are about to use a general word, search for a more specific word. Provable facts and figures are more convincing.

Poor: This word processor prints letters quickly.

Better: This word processor prints 500 personalized 100 word letters in 30 minutes.

Poor: JumpMaster has won several prizes.

Better: JumpMaster has won first prize in four international contests in the past year.

Vague, general words are often *opinion* words. Vague words may have different meanings to the writer and the user. For example: how fast is fast?

A man walking along the street might think a motorcycle passing by is moving fast. The man on the motorcycle might think the airplane passing by overhead is moving fast.

How big is *big?* Compared to what?

The following words often cause problems because of their lack of definition:

a few	high	low	more	quick	soon
early	long	many	most	slow	tall

There are times when you may need to avoid being specific. They should be exceptions to the rule.

❑ When you do not have access to provable figures or facts

❑ When being too specific might be offensive or undiplomatic

❑ When specific facts or figures are not important to the procedure or operation

Choose verbs that convey action

Definitive sentences can be constructed from strong action verbs. The keys to concrete writing are to use active rather than passive verbs, and to put the action in the verbs and not in the infinitives or the nouns.

Keep it active

The verb is in the active voice when the subject performs the action that the verb expresses. For example:

Active: The cow jumped over the moon.

              The subject (the cow) did the jumping; the verb jumped is active.

Passive: The moon was jumped over by the cow.

Passive: The installation program should be loaded.

Active: Load the installation program.

You should write your documentation in the active voice because it will bring interest and a sense of activity to text which, if written in the passive voice, may become dull and lifeless.

One significant advantage to the active voice is that it calls for specifics.

* The installation program should be loaded. (passive)

  By whom? When?

* Enter the installation program. (active)

  Suggests now — by the user!

The active voice is easier to read, easier to understand, and easier to execute. Do this! *not* This should be done. The active voice means tighter writing. It requires fewer words.

The active voice also requires that you, the writer, must be sure of your facts and figures. It is difficult to give an order, or make a definitive statement if you are not sure of the details that make up that order or statement.

A documentation writer must be prepared to take responsibility for what is written. Those who are unwilling to take responsibility will write: "It is recommended," rather than: "We recommend. . ."

Writing in the active voice is not easy, but master it because the reward is a much more effective piece of documentation.

In our previous discussion about the personal style — the use of *we* and *you*, we left out a major advantage. The use of *we* and *you* helps keep your writing active. It is difficult to write in the passive voice when using *you* and *we*. "We recommend you do this!"

For example:

"You should now connect your modem to your computer." There is no question what the writer wants you (the user) to do.

"The modem should now be connected to the computer" leaves a question as to who should make the connection, and which modem and which computer is meant.

Use an active verb to make your sentences more:

Specific   "The supervisor decided" is more explicit than "A decision has been made."

Personal   "You should note" is both personal and specific; "It should be noted" is impersonal.

Concise	The passive needs extra words. Writing and the reading are slower. For example: "The facts prove" versus "It is proven by facts."
Emphatic	Passive verbs dull action. "Enter your password" versus "A password should be entered."

There may be occasions when you will need to use the passive voice. For example:

- To avoid issuing a specific command.

  "You must clean the keyboard with a damp cloth." is better written: "The keyboard must be cleaned with a damp cloth."

- To place emphasis on the object of the action.

  "Your computer is insured up to $15,000," you have intentionally placed emphasis on "your computer."

- When the user isn't the key to the sentence.

  In "Four reports were run before the end of the month procedure was run," the emphasis is on the four reports, not on the end of month procedure.

Which tense?

Picking the right tense is important. Of the three — past, present and future — the most useful for our purpose is the present. You use the present tense for instructions and to describe information; the past tense is used to report results or to provide historical anecdote; and the future tense for what will or might happen in the future.

The main advantage to the present tense is that it provides a sense of immediacy. For example:

"When you use a new floppy disk, first format the disk. This prepares it for use in your computer."

This example in the future tense would be:

"If you are going to use a new floppy disk, your first step will be to format the disk. This will prepare the disk for use in your computer."

Action for verbs, not nouns

There are seven verbs you should use with care.

They are: *be, give, have, hold, make, put,* and *take* (in any tense). They cause problems when the action they introduce is hidden in a 'quiet noun.'

Action Hiding in a "Quiet Noun"
Poor: (action in noun)   The function of this program is the collection of data and the running of statements.

Action in the Verb
Better: (action in verb)   This program collects data and runs reports.

Poor: EDP will give consideration to the report.

Better: EDP will consider the report.

Poor: The module has a requirement for. . .

Better: The module requires that. . .

Poor: The uses held the meeting in the office.

Better: The uses met in the office.

Poor: The user puts his trust in his manual.

Better: The user trusts his manual.

Poor: Take a look at your database records.

Better: Look at your database records.

Action for verbs, not infinitives

Infinitives can also hide action. In the example below the main verb in the poor sentence follows 'is' (or some form of 'to be') and the preposition 'to,' and doesn't show much action.

Poor: (action in infinitive)   The responsibility of the database operators is *to check* all incoming records and *to enter* them. In addition it is their responsibility *to keep* the database logbook up to date.

Better: (action in the verb)   Database operators must *check* and *enter* all incoming records and *keep* the database logbook up to date.

Write for the user

Always remember that you are writing for a person, for a user who needs your support. You are not writing to show off your literary ability, or your command of big words. Write in a clear, concise, complete, and correct manner, but never lose sight of the user — the reader. The rules are not difficult:

- Personalize your writing. Use *you* and *we*.
- Provide the users with features and benefits.
- Keep your writing positive.

Personalize your writing

When you personalize your writing, you make your words more relevant to the user. In some case you might use *I*; more often you can make effective use of *we*.

For example:

Poor: It is recommended a back-up be made after each work session.

Better: We recommend a back-up be made after each work session.

Try to get your user involved in the first paragraph. "This section shows you how to install your new modem." You can maintain the support relationship with your user by often referring to the user. *Use* you and *your*. Equally important is to not overdo the use of *we*. The user should take precedence over the organization.

A user manual that uses *you* and *we* is often more interesting to use because people find people more interesting than they do inanimate objects such as computers, printers, and cables.

The use of *you* will become even more important when we discuss active versus passive writing later in this section.

You may want to avoid using *you* in certain cases.

❏ In the Troubleshooting section, where the user may have made a mistake:

Poor:	You failed to check the amount of available memory before starting.
Better:	The amount of available memory was insufficient for. . .
Poor:	Your user guide tells you clearly how to. . .
Better:	The user guide explains how to. . .

❏ When the manual is to be used by someone who may not want to be addressed in an informal manner, such as you and I (or we). A management policy and procedure manual is not an appropriate place for such informality.

❏ When the manual will be used by different groups of users. For example, a storeman might have trouble with a manual that uses *you* and is addressing a procedure used mostly by an accounts clerk.

Write like you talk

Many of us can speak well, and can explain concepts and instructions without difficulty as long as we are facing the user. And many of us, when we sit down to write, suddenly can't find the right words, or write stiffly or without color. Sometimes our words, sentences and paragraphs read more like a piece of late nineteenth century prose rather than twentieth or twenty-first century communication. In his day Ben Franklin was understood by his readers. Today, many of us would have trouble following his prose.

One of the advantages of writing like you talk is that you won't force the user to keep reaching for a dictionary. Imagine the user sitting beside you. While the basic rules of grammar can still be in place, there is no need for you to stick to every rules you learned at high school or in college. The great Winston Churchill said that short words are the best. He was once criticized for putting a preposition at the end of a sentence. His response: "That is the kind of nonsense up with which I shall not put."

And what of split infinitives. One of the best-known phrases of our time, from that gallant television series, *Star Trek*, says: "To *boldly go* where no man has gone before." If the writer who coined that phrase had stuck to the rules, the sentence would have lost its impact. Who can get excited by: "To *go boldly* where no man has gone before."

A good test is to read your words out loud. If your writing is stilted or out of touch with the ear, you'll hear it quickly.

Use contractions

To write as we talk means that you can use contractions. They aid in communication because they are what we are most used to hearing. They'll take the stiffness out of your sentences. Use them:

- you'll
- don't
- can't

Provide users with benefits

Providing the user with a benefit for performing a procedure helps keep the user on track. Users will respond more favorably — even to complicated procedures — if some specific benefit will come out of persevering with the procedure.

The feature-benefit is often used in sales proposals. You explain a feature and then you explain the benefit that comes from using the feature. When you explain a feature, make sure you say what it does, and what's good about using it. Users understand better when they know what something does, how it works, and how it will *help them* do their work more effectively (and more easily). At its most basic, you might explain the feature. Then move to *this means,* finally then moving to *what this really means*. For example:

The JumpMaster program includes a wildcard facility. *This means* that if you do not know the whole name or a customer, or the correct spelling of the customer's name, you can type in a part of the name and the program will display all the names that match the part of the name you typed. *What this really means* is that the program will help you find customers quickly and efficiently.

Another example:

This word processor has a built-in thesaurus. *This means* that a single keystroke will bring up a list of words that can be substituted for the word highlighted. *What this really means* is that your word processor will help you write more effectively.

You can also use the feature-benefit approach to make sure you are not providing the user with information that is irrelevant. After you've made your opening statement, you might look at the sentence and see it as the user might see it. Okay, I understand that, but *so what? How does that help me?* Here's an example — and notice how using *you* in this example doesn't make it any more meaningful to the user. "You will be glad to know that we are now doing our computer housekeeping from 5 AM to 7 AM and from 8 PM to 9 PM each day."

The user shrugs and asks: So what? What should have been written is: "We are now doing our computer housekeeping from 5 AM to 7 AM and from 8 PM to 9 PM each day instead of between 11 PM and 2 PM. This means users will not be inconvenienced during the working day as has been the case in the past." (What is implied in this paragraph is that workers will now be able to get through all their work without excessive overtime which had been demoralizing to the users and expensive for management.)

Another advantage is that you can check that what you are writing is relevant to the user you are writing for. For example, if you write a paragraph that explains how data is stored in the hard disk, you might want to test the relevance by putting yourself in the place of your users and asking: So what? For an accounts clerk, it is of little or no relevance. For a programmer of Management Information Systems manager, it is probably very relevant. Who is the manual for? If it is for the accounts clerk, you can cut the paragraph out or at least reduce it to a short comment.

Keep your writing positive

Provide the user with additional support by accenting the positive. While in terms of "Do this" not "Don't do this".

The user wants to know what can be done and how to do it. Avoid words such as: *no, won't, cannot, never, impossible.* Writing what can be done often makes clear what cannot be done without the need for negative words and phrases. However, be sure to use a negative word when spelling out a warning. For example, Do *not* press ESC-R when loading JumpMaster data files. All data will be erased from the master databank. (Not only should you use a negative, but also this warning should be boxed and displayed prominently.)

Negative: It is impossible to offer customer support for JumpMaster if you do not sign and send us the attached warranty card ...

Positive: As soon as your signed warranty card reaches us, we will be able to offer customer support for JumpMaster ...

Negative: We don't refund if the seal of the package containing the program disks is broken.

Positive   We refund when the package containing the program disks is returned with the seal unbroken.

Use subjective opinion

Too much of anything can hurt, and subjective opinion can only be used occasionally. However, it is a valuable tool and it will assist the user. For example: If a report takes a long time to run, tell the user that fact. The user now knows not to start running the report five minutes before lunch hour starts.

Subjective opinion can be useful when there is more than one way to do a task. "This is the simplest way to review the files..." tells the user that there are other ways, but this is the way we recommend. If you tell the user the most difficult way and then that user finds the simpler way, he is not going to be very pleased. Remember, you are writing this documentation to *help* the user.

One of the characteristics of computer documentation is the constant parade of facts. Some subjective opinion helps break the monotony.

A word of warning. If you use subjective opinion, make sure you are absolutely right. If you offer an opinion and the user finds out you are wrong, the credibility of the whole manual will suffer. Also, don't overuse subjectivity. Facts are what procedures are built upon. Too much subjectivity can get in the way of where you are taking the user.

Choose words that build images

Words and how well you use them are one of the keys to successful documentation. Word tools include: comparisons, specific examples, concrete rather than abstract nouns, and appropriate adjectives and adverbs.

Use comparisons

Using a comparison can provide the user with some measure with which to view a more difficult concept. For example:

Vague: The Z88 notebook computer has a large memory.

Vivid: The two RAM packs in the Z88 notebook computer have enough memory to hold three complete Robert Ludlum spy novels.

Use specific examples

It would be difficult to use too many examples. This does not mean filling the pages with a series of mind-numbing screen dumps. Users profit from examples if the examples are short, relevant, and easy for the users to understand. Bear in mind how much the user may or may not know at the point where you insert the example.

Depending on the format of your manual you may want to set your example off from the main text. This is particularly useful in a training manual where you may have lots of examples. A box around the example or a rule above or below the example works well.

Whenever possible, the structure for examples should be consistent throughout the documentation. For example:

- Type in the text `<ENTER>`

   as in: `Report Heading`   **`Stock Code`**

- Type in the field description `<ENTER>`

   as in: `Field Description`   **`Customer Name`**

Use concrete nouns

A concrete noun represents a subject the user can touch, see, smell, feel, hear, or taste. An abstract noun as a subject designates intangible concepts. These concepts are difficult to "see" and do not help the user visualize anything.

Abstract: Termination of the service contract will be in June.

Concrete: The service *contract* ends in June.

A note of caution: when referring to an *inanimate object,* avoid using the abstract word *thing.* Use a more specific word related to the *thing,* such as *event, element, fact, condition, method, plan, purpose, principle.*

The Fog Index

There are a number of guides that measure readability. Among the easiest to apply is Robert Gunning's popular Fog Index. (This is also available in a computer version, where the computer does all the calculations. However it is interesting to understand the formula.)

It is based on two factors: sentence length and percentage of difficult words. This index is structured to assist you find the educational grade level of your writing, based on the American educational system.

The steps:

1 Find average sentence length. Use an example at least 100 words long, beginning with the first word of a paragraph.

   Divide the total number of words in this passage by the number of complete thoughts.

   (A simple or complex sentence has one complete thought; a compound sentence contains two complete thoughts.)

   Your quotient gives the average sentence length.

2 Figure the percentage of "difficult" words. Count the number of words of three syllables or more. Include any unexplained abbreviations (CMD, BSD), but don't count words:

   ❏ that are (correctly) capitalized

   ❏ that are combinations of short, easy words (like shopkeeper, salesman)

   ❏ that are verb forms made into three syllables by adding *ed* or *es* (like *deleted*)

Divide the number of difficult words by the total number of words. Your quotient is the percentage of difficult words.

3 Add the average sentence length and the percentage of difficult words and multiply by 0.4.

The product, called the Fog Index, is the reading level (number of years of education) needed.

An example:

❑ If a paragraph has 120 words in 7 sentences, the average sentence length is 17.1 words. If 15 of the 120 words are considered hard words, the percentage is 12.5. From these figures you can compute the Gunning Fog Index — 11.8.

Words in example	120.0
Sentences	7.0
Average sentence length (120/7)	17.1
Percentage of hard words (15/120)	12.5
	———
Total	29.6
Multiplier	0.4
	———
Fog Index (grade level, high school senior)	11.8

Additional notes:

- Count anything as a word that has spaces around it. For example: June 1, 1991 is three words; two thousand dollars (spelled out) is three words. 6 1/2 is one word. Two words with a hyphen between counts as one word. (Consider hyphenated words as polysyllables if one part is a word of three syllables or more. For example: seventy-two is four syllables.) $8555.75 is counted as one word.

- Don't count 1, 2, 3 or A, B, C before paragraphs as words.

- Don't consider numerals as polysyllables, regardless of pronunciation. For example: $886,753,550.75 is one syllable.

The most appropriate reading level is between 8 and 12 — grade 8 to grade 12. *Reader's Digest* and *Time* magazine have indices between 9 and 10; *Scientific American* averages 11 or 12. If your writing level approached 13, the average user will probably have trouble with your text. Many legal and insurance documents have Fog Index of about 26, at least 14 school years beyond a typical grade 12 student.

Use these kind of measurements as a guide only. The words you write will still not mean much if they have poor grammar or weak style. Incomplete thoughts, abstract words, too many short sentences, and too many long words will all contribute to unreadable text, no matter what the index reveals.

Process 7: Editing

```
PROCESS SEVEN

Do the edit yourself.  Edit for clarity,
brevity and accuracy.
```

The editing process is one of the most critical tasks in the preparation of effective documentation. It is a task where poor writing can be improved. It is also a time when good writing can be destroyed, so it requires a clear understanding of what editing is all about.

While the editing process requires you to edit your own manuscript, and that is what this section will deal with, it is important to explain a second dimension of editing. If multiple writers are working on a documentation project, one writer should be appointed editor.

The appointment of an editor in a multiwriter environment does not absolve each writer from editing his own work. The role of the editor is in this circumstance is to ensure that all the manuals look and read as though they were written by a single writer. The editor in a multiwriter project polices the style guide as the primary guide to how the documentation reads, and then imposes his own style on the finished manuscripts.

This single editor imprint on a group of manuals assists the user as he moves from one manual to another. The tone, the style, the look, everything about the manuals is similar. The user feels comfortable and confidence built by using one manual is transferred to the next. Picture a family of manuals with similar physical structure.

While the role of the editor in a multiwriter workplace is important, the most common documentation tasks are handled by a single writer who is also the editor.

Editing must be done by the writer (or the editor in a multiwriter environment) because it is an extension of the writing task. The first edit is also the writer's task because it is unlikely that the manual is ready for anyone else to read at this point. There will be too many things left to fix.

Wherever possible, avoid letting anyone else read your manual until after you have had the opportunity to edit the manuscript all the way from the first page to the last. Put off those demands that often arise to let someone read the first couple of chapters.

Holding off interested onlookers (and do-gooders) may turn out being more of a management problem than a documentation problem. I usually fall back on the fact that I let them review and approve the task at the end of the blueprint (Process 5) stage. The next time they look at the manuscript is the first proofreading stage.

Edit each draft

An editing pass should follow each writing pass. At the start of the discussion of the 10 processes, I argued that the writer should always make a complete pass through the documentation. The same holds true for the editing. Start at the beginning and work through to the end. It helps keep all the topics in perspective.

Editing occurs when you step out of your position as writer and assume a number of roles:

❑ the critic, who questions everything

❑ the new user, who is reading each phrase and paragraph in a quest for knowledge

❑ the grammarian, who is concerned with the use of grammar and the correctness of language form and structure

❑ the artist, who views the whole page more as a graphic than a collection of words and pictures and who is looking for balance and design

❏ the technician (be he programmer or analyst) who is searching for technical accuracy

❏ the boss who is concerned that he is getting quantity and quality for his money

A few basics

A few basics that need to be defined:

• Don't assume that editing requires massive rewriting. Editing is usually best accomplished by moving text around, deleting text, and picking words which better express the information. Rewriting usually takes longer than editing.

• Don't try to edit on the screen. You need to see the whole page in a representation as close to the finished product as possible. The screen does not produce such a finished product. Only a paper printout can approximate the finished paper page. (This holds true even if you are working on a double-page layout screen.)

• Make sure your printed page for editing is as high quality as possible. Don't use a dot matrix printer if a laser printer is available. Don't print out your pages on extra wide computer paper, if you can print on paper more closely representing the page size of the finished manual. For example, printing on 8.5 by 11-inch paper is superior to printing on 13-inch-wide computer paper.

• Edit the Look as well as the content. Place your work in its finished format as you proceed. If you are writing in a word processing package (like Word) and then dumping the text into a desktop publishing package (like PageMaker), you are not ready to edit until the format and the design elements are all in place in the PageMaker version.

• Accept that you are going to cut words and phrases. The most effective edits are those that tighten up wordy passages. Most writers find this difficult to do after they have labored to write all those words. But it must be done. Be ruthless on the first edit.

Before you start your edit:

- Review Process 1

  Pay particular attention to the definition you gave your documentation. Constantly ask yourself if you have remained true to that definition. Is the mission of the manual being accomplished?

- Review Process 2

  You are writing to meet the needs of a particular group of users. Have you met those needs? Will your user understand what you have written?

- Review your style guide

  Consistency throughout your documentation is important. It is also difficult to maintain across a large manual written over many days or weeks. Have your style guide close at hand so you can easily check the styles you originally set in place.

- Read the foreword or Read Me First page(s) thoroughly

  Weigh each chapter, as you edit it, against the claims you made in the foreword. The foreword defines the aim of the manual, who the manual is written for, and how to use the manual.

The editing priorities

While the comments above form a backdrop to the editing process, there are some specific chores to be done as you read through the pages:

- Change the order of words, sentences, paragraphs, and sections to bring the key points to the top.

  A common problem in the first draft is that the key point (of sentences, paragraphs, sections) is often buried. As you wrote the first draft you were probably more concerned about getting words on paper. Often you will find you write *around* the subject. During this edit, find the subject and bring it to the top.

- Rewrite sentences that go beyond 20 words.

  This is too specific a rule to be obeyed without question. There are times when you will want a long sentence, but that should be the exception. Short sentences are easier to understand and remember. Be wary of too many commas, or the use of semicolons. Too often these punctuation marks are merely used to string two or three ideas together in the same sentence. Question them. Two short sentences are usually better than one long sentence. Having said that, don't end up with a manual filled with five-word sentences. That will defeat the purpose. The read will be too choppy. Vary the length and build a rhythm.

- Cut sentences that are unnecessary.

  The first draft will often be filled with duplications. You'll tend to say the same thing more than once. If you need to repeat yourself for emphasis, do so. But if that emphasis is not absolutely needed, cut the second explanation.

- Cut unnecessary words

  Be ruthless here. There are very few manuscripts in first draft that would suffer from a one-third reduction in the number of words. Edit that last sentence to read: With first drafts cut one out of every three words.

- Tighten up the examples

  As with the main text, first draft examples tend to be longer than necessary to make a point. Review each example.

- Add examples where necessary

  As you read the text, add examples where necessary. It may have been perfectly clear to you at the time you wrote it. Will an example make it clearer to the user?

- Move a topic to another section

  Although you have followed your table of contents in writing the first draft, the edit may reveal how a topic may be better located somewhere else.

- Watch for holes in the information

  A common problem in the first draft is missing information. You detailed five steps and six were needed. Often it is a phrase that is missed. Your mind is already at work composing the next sentence, and it drops the critical phrase off the previous sentence or paragraph.

- Edit the Look as well as the words

  As you work through the words, review the layout. Improve it. Ensure that it is consistent. Presentation is a key to effective communication. You'll lose the opportunity to strength the whole documentation if you fail to edit the look and the words together.

The most common errors

There is no easy way to edit. After spending many years doing this onerous task in newspapers, magazines, books, and now documentation, I find the most effective way is to lock myself in my office, take the telephone off the hook, and read the whole manuscript out loud, even pronouncing each punctuation mark. This is not the time to try out the latest techniques in speed reading. Take it slow and pay attention to the task at hand.

The most common errors you'll face include:

- ❑ spelling mistakes
- ❑ punctuation mistakes
- ❑ typing mistakes
- ❑ jargon inconsistencies
- ❑ hierarchical heading inconsistencies
- ❑ grammar mistakes
- ❑ factual mistakes and inconsistencies
- ❑ cross-referencing omissions

Take frequent breaks

Allow yourself enough time to break up the editing task into shorter rather than longer periods. Manuals are not exciting to read, nor should they be. They are not meant to be entertaining. As a result it is usually difficult to concentrate for more than about 45 minutes at a time. Error rates increase dramatically after 60 minutes of sustained editing, unless you are a professional editor.

Keep your user clearly in mind as you edit. Try to assume the role of user. Question the manual. Many manuals introduce more questions than they answer because they introduce new topics, without explaining those new topics, while answering an unrelated query.

Keep the purpose of the manual clearly in mind. If it is a reference manual, edit sections at random. A reference guide should stand up to this kind of scrutiny. A training manual, on the other hand, needs to be edited from start to finish. Random reading of a training guide usually won't work because each chapter builds upon knowledge learned in the previous chapter.

If you find that your mind refuses to read the words on the page — a frequent problem — and introduces its own words, try reading the manuscript into a tape recorder and then playing the tape and following the manuscript. It's a simple but effective trick.

Always make sure you are working on the correct version. With the editing being done on a hard copy printout, it is easy to end up working on an earlier version. Clearly number each draft and file away old copies.

Research shows that you will need two passes through the first edit. If the editor concentrates on the task, about 85-90 percent of the edits will be done in these two passes. A third pass is usually not cost-effective. It is better to stop editing, start making the corrections on the screen, and move on to the second draft.

After you have made the first draft corrections, and checked those corrections to make sure they have been done properly, it is time to print out a clean copy of the manual and send it to a proofreader for a technical accuracy and completeness check.

Editing the Look

Those who will be looking at your manual before it is distributed — supervisors, fellow documentation colleagues, proofreaders — will, as will the users, form an initial opinion from that first Look. Therefore, part of the editing chore on the first draft will be to check the presentation.

The difference between adequate and excellent often has to do with the finish of a product. The *finish* has two definable qualities. The first is straightforward and has to do with all those elements on the page that readers will actually see, such as typeface and typesize consistency and the use of bold and italics for emphasis.

The second part of *finish* is more difficult to describe. It represents those elements on the page that, if correct, will often never be noticed by the reader. If they are incorrect or missing altogether, the user will only notice that the finish is missing and that the presentation is less than complete. The following items include some of those elements which contribute to this finished look.

- Ensure that your text or heading always starts the same distance from the top of the page. (Headers and footers should also be checked to ensure they print out in the same position on every page.)

- Ensure that page breaks are appropriate. (For example, I always try to finish a paragraph on a page. I dislike reading a sentence that breaks and continues to the next page. My style accommodates that.)

- Ensure that a new topic starts on a new page.

- Ensure that tabbing and margins are the same throughout.

- Ensure there is proper word-spacing across the entire text.

- Ensure high-quality printing from your laser printer and photocopier when making the initial editing and proofreading copies. Watch the contrast so the early readers can truly distinguish bold face words and characters from "overinked" toner cartridges.

- Put your printed out manuscript in a clean binder with a slip in cover and spine so the product looks like a finished job. Do this right from the first printout you make for yourself.

- Ensure that the holes punched for the binding are all equal so the pages have a finished look. Nothing destroys the look faster than unequal hold punching and ragged page sections bound in a binder.

There is no substitute for accuracy in editing. You are refining and polishing. You are checking that the text is complete and that the presentation, or Look, is as professional as you can make it. By now you will have put in considerable effort. Carrying out the editing process is no time to let your guard down. Many manuals are lifted from mere mediocre products to products of excellence during editing.

Process 8: Proofreading

PROCESS EIGHT
Provide guidelines for proofreaders. Be sure the proofreaders are qualified to pass judgement.

The fundamental fact to remember during this process is that your page layout and design, typefaces and typesizes, definitions of user, the emphasis of the manual, and the table of contents have already been reviewed and passed upon long before you reach this process. This activity was done at the end of Process Five - Blueprinting.

This is fundamental because proofreaders have a bad habit of wanting to tamper with the basics. And tampering with the basics now can undo all the hard work the writer has accomplished.

The writer who did not take the time to have someone in authority pass judgment on the first five processes at the end of Process Five is asking for trouble during the proofreading process.

The task of the proofreader is to check your manual to ensure:

❑ accuracy

❑ consistency

❑ completeness

❑ (in some cases) usability

To carry out this task the proofreader should:

- mark factual errors
- mark errors of spelling
- indicate missing information
- indicate errors of emphasis
- comment on style and grammar
- comment on layout and design

You will notice that I have used three different words in the list of tasks the proofreader should carry out: *mark*, *indicate*, and *comment*. When a proofreader finds a mistake he should *mark* the mistake clearly and provide the correction or, at the least, tell the writer where the correct answer might be found.

There is nothing more aggravating than having a proofreader write "WRONG" in the margin without adding what is "RIGHT". If the proofreader knows enough to say it is wrong, then it logically follows that he knows enough to tell you what is right.

Indicating what is missing is important because there will be times when the proofreader might be the only one who can tell you something is missing. Indicating the content and position of what is missing can become critical to the success of the manual. This does not mean that the proofreader has to write the missing text. All he needs do is indicate to the writer that more work is needed at a certain spot and that he, or someone else, has the information.

Errors of emphasis have to be handled carefully. The proofreader should indicate where he believes there is an error of emphasis, and then you must weigh that indication against your profile of the user and your definition of the type of manual. Quite often, the emphasis you choose is correct for your user and your definition but is misinterpreted by the proofreader.

Not providing corrections and not indicating the location and source of missing information are two common weaknesses in the proofreading process. Your need for this information should be highlighted in a cover sheet that goes to the proofreader with the manuscript. As for the fifth item, choosing the word *comment* was intentional. Most proofreaders are not qualified to correct style, grammar, layout and design. That is the province of the writer/editor/artist, and thus you are best positioned to have the final say in this area.

I usually ask proofreaders to mark errors and indicate missing information directly on the manuscript (in red ink). I then provide a sheet of paper with a heading: For Comments On Style, Grammar, Layout, Design. The degree to which you use the comments made here by the proofreader will be determined by the qualifications of the proofreader.

Who should proofread?

Finding a suitable proofreader is often difficult, and sometimes becomes a management problem as much as a documentation problem. The worst scenario is for the manual to end up on the desk of a busy executive who does not possess the detailed knowledge of the system being documented to catch the errors and omissions.

Equally difficult to handle is the proofreader who has so much technical knowledge and so little knowledge of the actual users that he immediately starts turning the manual into a technical reference handbook.

The two examples above are the most common problems. Perhaps a definition of the ideal proofreader is someone with enough technical knowledge but who is busy enough to only have the time to check the technical accuracy and completeness.

What to tell the proofreader

The cover sheet accompanying the manual should reflect what the writer knows about the proofreader. The technical proofreader should be asked to remember the user, while the nontechnical proofreader should be asked to remember the importance of technical accuracy.

The definition of the manual and a short version of the user profile should be included, as well as a brief commentary on the words *mark*, *indicate,* and *comment*.

Ask the proofreader to make his marks in red ink. I have never provided a list of copyediting or proofreading marks to be used, as is common practice in most books on the subject. I find that most proofreaders ignore the official marks you ask them to use. I also find that proofreaders generally correct and mark errors quite clearly.

Be sure to tell the proofreader how long he has for proofreading. Discuss this with him. As you will see later when we discuss management of the documentation project, proofreading time has to be allocated and policed if the project is to stay on schedule.

I also tell the proofreader that proofreading is a demanding process and should not be attempted in one session. As with the editing process, frequent breaks during proofreading are needed. Make sure the proofreader understands this.

Proofreading by committee

Perhaps the worst scenario a writer can be confronted with is proofreading by committee. The manual is to be photocopied and sent to a number of proofreaders, often representing totally different constituencies. I have faced a difficult client who wanted seven proofreaders at each stage: technical, research, validation, marketing, manufacturing, customer service, and the chief executive.

This scenario produces many problems, not the least of which is that the writer is faced with seven proofread manuals. Not only does the writer have to take time to collate all the corrections into one manual, but the proofreaders will have wasted considerable time all marking the same error. And should a chief executive be wasting his valuable time reading successive drafts?

Worse still, some proofreaders will, for example, tell you that the correct number is 22, while others will say it is 20. More time will be wasted trying to determine the correct number.

If you are faced with this problem, suggest that the first proofread for technical accuracy and completeness be done by only one or two proofreaders and that the second draft,— which should be error-free compared with the first draft, be circulated more widely. This will save everyone a lot of time.

If you cannot overcome the problem of multiple proofreaders — and, unfortunately, the practice is widespread — then try to restrict the number of copies distributed. Marketing can proofread Customer Support's copy after it has been read by Technical.

Be sure to control the number of copies sent out and returned. Put them all in binders and number the binders. The last thing you want to have happen is for the first draft to end up in the hands of users. It's too early for that.

Final comments

Some proofreaders are very industrious. They start rewriting the whole manual. This is difficult to ignore if the proofreader is someone in a position of authority. But this practice must be faced and discussed with the proofreader as soon as it becomes apparent that it is taking place.

The style of the manual must be consistent throughout. It is unlikely the proofreader's style is the same as the writer's. If the rewriting is to correct errors, then have the proofreader indicate the error and let the writer do the rewriting. If the rewriting is being done merely because the proofreader would prefer to see the text the way he would have written it, the writer must be firm and insist on the text being left intact.

If major problems are found in the structure of the manual, or in the definition of its user, then the writer may be forced to go back to the beginning and step through each of the processes again.

If, after careful proofreading, a conclusion is reached that there are major problems with the manual — perhaps the approvals after Process Five are no longer valid — it is often easier to set the draft aside and start again. Step through the processes and write a new manual. Trying to patch up a manual with basic flaws seldom works.

The index

Earlier in this book I argued in favor of replacing the traditional index with an activity index, where the user would look up information by activity rather than by a single word. Its works well and has more utility than the traditional single-word index. However, I recognize that most writers and users will feel uneasy about not having the single-word index.

Realize that creating an effective index is not a small task that can be quickly run through when the final manual pages have been printed out. And, of course, it is a waste of time to create an index until the page numbering is locked in place.

Preparing an index takes time and thought. Many publishing companies employ indexers, rather than leaving the task to the writer. I believe that the writer should compile the index because the writer is the person who knows the subject the best, having just completed the manuscript.

Role of the index

The index has a number of functions, including:

❑ guiding a user to specific topic, beyond what the table of contents might provide

❑ providing the user with some of the natural links between widespread topics

❑ indicating what is *not* in the manual

❑ labeling the terminology used in the manual

Considering the functions of the manual's index, the same definition of completeness can be used to judge its effectiveness as has been used to define the entire documentation project: ease of use, reliability, accuracy, and so forth.

The profile of the user and the definition of the manual will both assist in determining what to put into the index. The problem with indexing is that there are a lot of rules and yet no really perfect way to handle every case. Some manuals require all keywords to be handled strictly alphabetical, while other manuals with a pure alphabetical listing of all words would be useless.

For example, a manual I recently wrote detailed the information to be typed in at every prompt. Across the entire manual, the prompt File Name appears 200 times. Listing each appearance under an entry called File Name would be useless because the user needs references within a specific usage. The solution was to point the user from an entry called File Name to the appropriate heading, such as Periodic Update Screen.

Getting started

Think like a user and anticipate how the user will look up information, and then construct the index in that manner.

I like to tailor the index myself, ignoring the automatic index generators now found in most word processors. I want total control of this important task. To do the job properly, you will still have to override the automatic index generator at some point and I find it much faster to do the indexing myself.

Never start indexing until the manuscript is finished. Consider it a separate unit of work. Page numbering can change too easily as you are writing, editing, and proofreading. Time spent working on an index too early can easily become time wasted.

Let's work through a typical, relatively simple index example.

I print out the entire manuscript, put it in a binder and then work through the manuscript, underlining every word I want in the index. Every time I underline a word, I note in the margin any cross-references. For example:

In reading page 23 of a manual, I find an entry for Changing Directories.

I underline:

Changing Directories

In the margin I write:

Directories Changing 23

Later, I find a reference Creating Directories. I underline it and write in the margin: Directories Creating 25

As I find them, I follow the same procedure for other entries, such as Phone Directories, Editing Directories, Sorting Directories.

After a complete pass has been made through the entire manual, I type all my underlined entries and the margin entries into my word processor, followed by a straight alphabetical sort.

The list in my example would now look like this:

Changing Directories 23
Creating Directories 25
Directories Changing 23
Directories Creating 25
Directories Editing 30
Directories Phone 25-34
Directories Sorting 33
Editing Directories 30
Phone Directories 25-34
Sorting Directories 33

This example list now needs cleaning up, to provide this finished list:

> **C**
>
> Changing Directories 23
> Creating Directories 25
> **D**
> Directories
>   Changing 23
>   Creating 25
>   Editing 30
>   Phone 25-34
>   Sorting 33
> **E**
> Editing Directories 30
> **P**
> Phone Directories 25-34
> **S**
> Sorting Directories 33

The user may then look for Phone Directories under P for Phone, or under D for Directories. Of course, there are many more entries than merely those shown above. In this example, Phone Directory entry has the following subentries:

> Phone Directories 25-34
>   Directory Edit Window 26, 30, 31
>   Selecting 25

> You also find Directory Edit Window under **D**
> and Selecting Phone Directories under **S**

Another common format is to combine the index and glossary together so that you get a short definition, where appropriate, beside the index entry. This has to be handled carefully otherwise your index-glossary can get out of control. But with the world of computers so filled with jargon, this approach can be helpful in letting the user know he has found the right entry.

I do not index glossary entries. Many manuals do and I believe it is personal preference which route you take. I consider the table of contents, the index, and the glossary as three separate tools. My users are well aware, from the foreword (Read Me First), and the table of contents that all three tools exist and I expect the user to utilize each tool. Indexing the glossary adds extra entries to the index, which is already too long!

Subdividing an entry

Once again, there are no clear rules. The look of the entry will give you some ideas. If you are indexing the word Printer and you end up with 40 references, then take a look and see if the word Printer could, or should, be broken down into subheadings such as:

Printer,
    Imagewriter
    LaserWriter
    Muffler
    Port
    Ribbon

(Use the singular, rather than the plural. Thus: port instead of ports, printer instead of printers.)

Make life easy for the user. If you are indexing a manual on a payroll system and you have three distinct categories such as:

> setting up a salary
> viewing a salary
> amending a salary

Set your index up this way:

> Salary
> > Setting up
> > Amending
> > Viewing

Using SEE and SEE ALSO

There are often a number of ways to look up the same information. For example: how would you look up floppy disk drives or hard disk drives? Some users might start with floppy, others with disk, and still others with drive. You have to make a choice and then direct the users to your choice.

There is a school of thought that suggests providing a reference for each of the possibilities, but that could produce a much longer index. There is no hard and fast rule, though.

The words to use when directing users to another entry are: See and See Also. The widely accepted practice is to use:

See — to direct a reader to the standard entry you have chosen, from the nonstandard entry the user might have referred to first

See Also — to direct a user to a related topic

The significant reference

Care should be taken not to index every reference that exists throughout the manual. Search for the significant references, those that provide explanation and information about an entry.

Nothing is more frustrating, or more common, than to turn to a reference only to find nothing can be learned from that reference.

One useful method is to boldface or italicize the most significant reference (be it a page or a group of pages) so the user can see quickly where to go for a discussion of the reference. If your manual has many screens or reports, you might bold face or italicize the page on which appears the screen or report appears. If you use these methods be sure to tell the user at the top of the index the relevance of the bold or italic and perhaps repeat that note at the top or bottom of each page of the index. Few users will turn to the first page of the index. They'll go with the alphabet. They know that indices are alphabetical.

Your manual may have more than one index. You may choose to index tables or screens or reports separately from the main index. If you do this, be sure to provide a clear pointer in the main index to the secondary indices.

Punctuating the entry

The most important rule for punctuation is to be consistent throughout. For example, the rules might be:

- Capitalize the first letter of each entry, no matter what sublevel you are on

- Do not use punctuation between the entry and the page number unless you are qualifying the initial word, as in:

    Function Keys, Editing 8

    On-Line Help 10

- Use a comma and a space between page numbers as in:

    Editing a Schedule 34, 40, 66

- Use a hyphen and the first and last page numbers where the entry is discussed across a number of pages as in:

    Print Faxes 79-83

- Don't use a hyphen, but do mention each page number if the reference is significant but within another topic area as in a discussion about
    Printers: Keyboard 30, 31, 32

- Don't use periods, semicolons or colons.

Process 9: Production

> ## PROCESS NINE
>
> **To capitalize on first impressions, always maintain as high a level of professional finish as the budget allows.**

The documentation writer may be finished with his task after preparing the index and having the manual accepted as complete. Production may be a chore undertaken by others. However, it is important that the writer understand the production process for two reasons:

❏ the production method has to be kept in mind during the opening processes because many of the decisions made then will impact upon the method of production

❏ the writer may be asked to supervise the production process

The initial planning will have decided page size which will impact on whether or not you can use common commercially available binders, on whether or not you will print on one side of the page (single-sided) or both sides (double-sided) which will dictate the style of your left-right page layouts, and so forth.

The revision and maintenance problems will also have been discussed during the early planning and they, too, will play a role in determining the production method.

For example, if there are updates to be sent out then production of a perfect bound (as in a typical novel) book form for your manual will create the problem of what to do with the new inserts.

The writer may have to play a supervising role in the production process. While you may be able to run half a dozen copies through a laser printer, or 10 copies through the office photocopier, anything beyond that will require a new set of professional skills — those of the printer. If you are not knowledgeable in print production, ask for help, both at the start of the project and at printing time.

There is also the need to consider the way the finished manuals will be bound. These range from using binders already in the office, through having special size binders (and boxes) made up, through a whole range of various kinds of combs and coils, and finally to perfect-bound hard and soft covered books.

I have stressed repeatedly the need for the best presentation possible of your finished manual. You have put in a tremendous effort, considerable money has already been spent before you reach production, and it is a tragedy that many documentation projects collapse at this point because of a lack of attention to the final print production.

Sending the manual to an outside printer will show up as a direct cost. Don't fall into the common trap that because the designing, writing, editing, and proofreading were all undertaken internally, the costs are covered in payroll and don't show up as easily. The costs are considerable to this point and all this cost could be for nothing if the production is not carried out well.

Remember those initial user reactions.

Production possibilities - printing and binding

There are a number of print production possibilities and we'll review the most common to the documentation task.

- ❏ laser printing

- ❏ high-quality photocopying

- ❏ commercial (offset) printing

Once the pages have been printed, they need to be bound in some form and we'll look at:

- ❏ standard ring binders

- ❏ special size ring binders (and boxes)

- ❏ comb and coil binding

- ❏ perfect-bound soft and hardcover books

Print production

The decision about which of the available print options to use is based on two criteria: the budget you have to work with, and the number of copies of each manual that you need to distribute.

Laser printing

The common office 300 dpi (dot per inch) laser printer works best if you:

- ❏ want one or two copies

- ❏ are printing only one side of the paper (single-sided)

- ❏ don't have too many pages

It is not often that the option of the office laser printer is chosen. Seldom will you be producing documentation to these standards. In fact, your original definitions back in Process 1 and 2 would probably have suggested that documentation of the kind we are discussing in this book would be uneconomical for these quantities and this number of users. Reproduction using the 300 dpi machine is suitable for most internal documentation manuals. Using 600 dpi is even better.

The common office photocopier can be added to the laser printer to lift the number of copies to about 10, but beyond that even this combination becomes uneconomical. Printing on both sides (double-sided) of the paper with a common office photocopier demands a lot of time and a certain amount of precision in positioning the page.

High-quality photocopying

The next step is high-quality, commercial photocopying. This works best for:

❑ printing up to 100 copies

❑ printing either single-sided or double-sided pages

❑ when you have budget problems preventing full commercial printing

This production method usually requires going to an outside printer. In dealing with the printer, you will have to provide specifications about you want done. This includes:

❑ what paper you want the pages printed on

❑ whether you want single-sided or double-sided printing

❑ whether the printed pages are to be collated into finished manuals

You will need to provide the printer with:

❑ a printer's reference copy of the finished manual

This is usually made up by printing a laser printer copy of the manual and then pasting the pages back to back to simulate the finished manual.

The pages the high-quality photocopying uses as the masters to copy may come from your laser printer. If the printer is going to produce these master pages, he will need:

❑ a copy of your manual on disk

❑ a control sheet showing what desktop publishing system (and version number) was used to produce the pages, and what typefaces are used in the manual

Commercial (offset) printing

Of the methods discussed so far, this is the most expensive, the most demanding, and, as might be expected, the most effective for high print runs. Usually commercial printing is used for print runs in excess of 100 copies and where the page numbers exceed 100 pages.

The rule to remember here is that it takes time to prepare and set up the presses, and thus the unit cost for manuals is very high for small print runs, but that unit cost decreases rapidly when the number of copies increases. For example, it may cost you $3.00 a manual for a 150-page manual for 5000 copies, but it may only cost you $1.50 for each additional copy for every 1000 copies you print as the press continues beyond 5000.

This is not the place to discuss the mechanics of offset printing. Suffice to say it is the most common method for large documentation projects.

In addition to the printer's reference copy discussed under high quality photocopy, you will need to provide the printer with bromides. Bromides are also referred to as camera-ready art. For documentation purposes, everything you need to complete your pages should already be in your computer. Normally, there will be no holes left where outside artwork has to be pasted in.

The easiest way to have bromides made is to deliver your disk containing your manual to a bureau and to explain your needs. You will need a control sheet listing the files, and a list of the appropriate typefaces you have used in preparing your pages. If the bureau does not have the typefaces you'll have to supply the screen and downloadable fonts on a disk. The bureau will then print out the bromides on a special paper with appropriate cropping marks on each corner.

If you have additional artwork that requires pages to be pasted onto board and photographed before being printed, I recommend you get outside assistance from a pasteup artist. The work is highly skilled and the final presentation will be directly related to how well this task is done.

When your bromides have been made, check them to make sure everything is as you planned including the correct typefaces, then deliver them to your printer.

Along with the printer's reference copy, you'll need to tell the printer:

- ❏ what paper you want the pages printed on
- ❏ whether you want single-sided or double-sided printing
- ❏ whether the printed pages are to be collated into finished manuals
- ❏ print run numbers

Binder production

There are not many possibilities for binding manuals. Like the printing processes, there are cheap ways and expensive ways. However, the method of binding must be decided back at the beginning of the project.

A key consideration is how the revisions and maintenance of the manuals are to be carried out. If there are frequent updates expected during the lifetime of the manual, then a standard ring binder with standard size pages output from a local laser printer might be the best answer.

However, if the production method has been a unique size page in a specially made binder, then the updates will be handled by the same production process, perhaps high-quality photocopying.

Another key consideration in binding is that the manual, to be most useful, should lie flat on a desktop. Few things can be as frustrating as trying to hold a manual open to a page while typing at a keyboard. Many external documentation producers, in an attempt to make a finished book look good, produce what is known as *perfect binding* where the pages are clamped together and glued along the spine. They look great but the pages only lie flat at the center.

Standard ring binders

Most internal documentation is printed to fit the standard page (8.5 by 11 inches) in a standard three-ring binder. There is nothing wrong with this approach up to about 200 pages. Try to use D-ring binders, and a minimum of three rings. Less than three rings and the page flops around too much. The standard O-ring is inferior to the D-ring. The D provides a much better hold on the pages.

I prefer the standard binders with the clear plastic sheet on the cover and spine. This allows a cover and spine sheet to be printed and inserted, provided a professional finish to the outside of the binder.

Special size binders (with boxes)

The next step beyond the standard binder is to have a special binder made to the size you require. This is usually needed when you design a nonstandard page. Once again, the same rules apply as for a standard binder. Use D-rings and so forth.

If the binder is being made up specially, you will usually have the choice of having your spine and cover printed directly on the binder or having a clear sheet behind which you can place your own paper-produced cover and spine.

Those who make binders may also want to have a box made in which to keep the binder. This is common with external documentation. If this is the case, consult with your binder-box maker about the needed specifications and be guided by the professional maker. It is a specialized task requiring considerable skill.

Comb and coil binding

Comb and coil bindings provide an alternative to the binder. Whether made of plastic or metal, they allow the manual to lie flat. I like them for small training manuals. Used with the right-sized coil or comb, and a clear cover allowing a nice cover page to be designed and printed, they can make an effective presentation.

However, they do have a couple of disadvantages. The coil provides no opportunity to label the spine. They are limited to about 100 pages maximum. Beyond that and the pages wear easily, tearing at the coil. They are also difficult to store. They do not stand upright easily without extra-firm card backcovers, and the comb or coil is often wider than the pages, providing an annoying interlocking of coils if placed side-by-side with similarly bound manuals.

Lastly, comb and coil bound manuals are not easy to update. The comb is easier than the coil, but neither of them matches the ease with which a ring binder can be updated.

Perfect-bound soft and hardcover books

As already mentioned, these look wonderful until you open them up and start to use them and then they keep trying to close up on you, unless you break their spines as I regularly do. They are normally cheaper to produce in large numbers than custom making binders and boxes.

For the purposes of the kind of documentation we are talking about here, I would recommend that you stay away from this production method. Unless your manual is to be read with both hands holding it, you don't have to refer to it while using your hands for another task, and you are not going to want to update it with new pages.

Some companies are addressing the problem of producing a perfect bound book which lies flat on the desk. I have seen nothing produced so far to get excited about. (I know it's heresy to publishers, but I cut the spines off my perfect bound reference books and then three-hole punch or coil bind the loose pages.)

A special problem — dirty environments

Having produced a number of manuals used above and below the ground in mine sites, I recommend that you use some kind of plastic-coated paper for manual pages being used in dirty environments.

In the case of our mining manuals, a key requirement was that once every couple of weeks someone could take a damp cloth and clean up the pages. This method is expensive, but over the life of the manual it is usually less expensive than having to constantly replace the manual as the pages become too dirty to use.

Process 10: Maintain and Revise

> ## PROCESS TEN
>
> **Plan maintenance and revision procedures at the beginning of the task so design and production allows easy up-dating.**

Maintenance and revision procedures — the ability to prepare and send out an update page or pages — will extend the life of a manual. If no provision is made for maintenance and revision, the manual starts to lose its usefulness with the first change that was not recorded.

As has been made clear right from the start of this book, a manual that is not updated is a manual the user cannot have confidence in. And if the user loses confidence in the documentation, it will not be used and thus it was a waste of time and money preparing it.

Manuals can be updated in two ways:

- The entire manual can be scrapped and another version written, incorporating the old text that has not changed and the new changes.

- A structure can be put in place to send update pages, plus changes in the tables of contents, and the index, to the users.

Writing a new version

If the system undergoes radical change, then revision is usually the only way to go. However, this is expensive and time consuming.

If, in the original planning, it can be defined that some aspect of the system is going to change, make provision for those changes in the original design. Instead of writing a single large manual, try designing two or three smaller manuals covering the same ground. Then, when the changes are finally made, it may only mean revising one of the two or three manuals originally written. This will have little impact on the users. They merely replace the old version with the new version and continue on.

Update pages

The alternative is to produce update pages. This will extend the life of the manual and, done with care, will act to continually encourage users to use their documentation knowing that it contains the latest revisions and updates.

To develop a strategy whereby revisions and maintenance can be done through updates, the process must start with the original design. Page numbering must be thought about in terms of the numbers of potential updates. If most updates are scattered through the manuals in groups of less than five pages, I'd consider using a sequential page numbering from 1 to the end. The updates would then take A. . .B. . .C. . .D. . .E. Users are not going to get lost finding page 75A or 101B.

If the number of updates after a certain page number is going to be more than five, or perhaps might include a whole new chapter about some new application or function, I would drop the sequential page numbering of the whole manual back to page numbering a chapter at a time.

We have already looked at how to number pages and chapters for both whole manual page numbering and chapter or section numbering. Slight variations can be made to accommodate these revisions.

When the pages are updated, ensure that a new table of contents and a new index are sent out to replace the out-of-date ones. Consider sending out a new title page which lists the date of the latest revisions. This will help reinforce to the users that the manual is being kept up-to-date. Put the revision date on each new page and on the revised title page.

Make sure the users actually get the updates. I have seen situations where the updates, in their neatly shrink-wrapped covers, went straight into the supervisor's desk drawer and never made it to the manuals.

Make sure that old pages are taken out of the manuals and the new pages are put in. A snap audit — or the mere announcement that such an audit is likely — will quickly drive the message home. If this becomes too severe a problem, you can resort to having the users sign and receipt that they have received and inserted the new pages, or in the extreme, require that the old pages be returned to you. (These suggestions are somewhat extreme, but this is an important issue worthy of such steps if they are required.)

Set a schedule for updates, perhaps quarterly, and then keep to that schedule. If you have no updates for a particular quarter, then send a memo around advising everyone that no updates are being made.

If you have a number of updates, send a covering memo explaining the most important of the changes. This is also the opportunity to bring to the user's attention any changes which might result in problems if the user continued to use the old procedure.

Lastly, make the changes important. Don't waste the valuable time of the user change "there" to "their" or "who" to "whom". Do nothing to trivialize the importance of revision and maintenance.

CHAPTER 5

Introducing documentation to users

Introducing documentation to users

Too often finished user documentation is, more or less, thrown at the users. If users have had bad experiences with previous documentation, they may respond to the new documentation by merely opening a desk drawer and tossing it in. So much for all your hard work!

Properly designed documentation, with a fine Look, may go part way to eliciting the appropriate response from users. If they like the Look, they may take the next step and start reading. If they like what they read, then the documentation will be used.

However, there are ways of eliminating the uncertainty. Designing a short introductory training program that explains the new documentation will ensure that the users "get inside" the covers. Done properly, this training program proves to the user the worth of the documentation. The user gains confidence and the documentation becomes a useful tool.

A well-designed, well-written, well-introduced and well-accepted manual:

❑ reduces user help requests

❑ reduces training and support time

❑ ensures that users gain the maximum potential benefits from the system

The two most valuable benefits from well produced and introduced documentation are:

❑ Users will use the manual as a self-training aid to help themselves step through the more difficult options. This reduces the amount of option specific training required.

❑ As users gain confidence in the manuals and the system, they will use the system to its full potential.

The approach will vary slightly depending on whether the documentation has been produced in-house — whether by a consultant or a staff writer — or it is external documentation that accompanies a package or system purchased complete with documentation.

One early question that needs to be addressed is whether the documentation should be introduced to the users by the writer of the documentation or by the organization's training department. Some writers make excellent trainers, know how to handle a group, and make maximum use of the training session. Other writers will find this very difficult. Whichever approach is taken, the training program must be structured and carefully thought out in advance.

If the documentation is being prepared in-house, then the introduction can start while the documentation is still in its planning stage. Users can be consulted about their needs and can be made to feel that they are making a contribution to both form and content.

I usually do this by having a representative group of users join an early planning session where we discuss the layout and the reasons for choosing certain designs and ways of presenting information. To be honest, most users cannot contribute greatly at this point. But the astute writer will let them have their say and, hopefully, hear some of his own ideas coming from the users. It's basic psychology at work. The users feel they have had some say in how it is all going together and when the documentation is finally delivered, will feel a proprietary ownership of the finished product.

Whichever approach is taken, it is important not to release documentation into an organization without putting all of the users, or at least a representative group, through the introductory training program.

Objectives of introducing documentation

The objectives to be met during this introduction are simple:

- Build enthusiasm for the forthcoming release of the documentation
- Establish user ownership of the documentation
- Establish user pride in the documentation
- Build user confidence in the documentation
- Familiarize users with the design, layout, conventions, and style

Prior to release

As well as meeting with the users during the early processes, while you are preparing your user profile, and any meetings you might have to ask the opinion of the users as to the approach you are going to take, you should always be looking for ways of selling the documentation.

I have always argued that a newsletter should be distributed to staff whenever new technology is being introduced. It helps cut down the fear that many users feel when confronted with the myriad of rumors that accompany change. The newsletter is an excellent vehicle for putting across the intention to introduce new documentation. Documentation is the interface between system and user, as we've already established. The more confidence the users have in that interface, the more efficient and trouble-free will be the actual implementation of the system.

This selling of the documentation varies from site to site, and depends on many factors, not all of which we can address here. But it is well worth the effort.

Selling the new documentation

The size and scope of the selling process depends on your budget considerations and the anticipated user acceptance (or resistance) to the documentation. Not all of these will be appropriate, but the intention here is to be creative and innovative.

- Prepare commonly used and inexpensive give-aways to be distributed among users. These could include pens, pencils, rulers, notepads, desk accessories and so forth. These might have the program or system name and include a comment such as "Watch for the manuals" or "Coming soon to a workstation near you".

- Place regular articles in widely read internal information media such as staff newsletters, bulletins, or electronic mail. These articles should be short and aimed at attracting attention with headings such as "Help is on the Way". Articles should always refer to the value of the users' input. It is also helpful to identify key users who have helped in the documentation process.

  These key users must be well respected and have a high profile within their group. They do not have to be experts in the use of the system.

- Present basic progress reports at staff meetings as the deadline draws near. Of course this should only be done if the project is on schedule and never promise more than you intend to deliver. This has the effect of arousing the interest of users so that they will all want to open and read the documentation when it arrives.

The training course

The aim of the training course is to build user confidence in both the content and structure of the documentation so they will return to their workstations enthusiastic about the new tool.

The introduction should take about two hours. (If you need a day to learn how to use a manual, then there's something seriously wrong with the manual.)

The training course should be structured in six stages

1   Explain the history

Explain the background to why the documentation is necessary, and what prompted management to prepare the documentation.

2   Explain the methodology

Explain the methodology behind the documentation processes and use this to show that the needs of users have been paramount in the planning and production of the documentation.

3   Explain the process

Explain the documentation process in brief so that users will understand the various steps that were taken to produce the manuals. Emphasis should be placed on the value of any user input in helping to prepare the documentation.

4   Introduce the documentation

If it is a manual, make sure you have enough copies so that each user in the training session gets one. How was it produced, how will it be updated, why the size and color was chosen, why the page layout looks like it does, and so forth.

5   Introduce the layout

Introduce the layout of the manual and take the users step-by-step through the key areas. Take particular care to explain:

❏ the use of the foreword: why it is there, what it contains

❏ the introduction: what is said in the introduction

❏ the page numbering system: how it is used in the manual

❏ the table of contents: how it is used, what it contains

❏ the index: where it is located, how it is used

❏ the glossary: what it contains, how to use it

❏ the standards and conventions: what are they, how are they used in the manual

❏ the standard page layouts: how is each option structured, how do you use the structure

An exercise should be introduced to take users from the table of contents through a general option, and a second exercise which starts from the Index and then leads to an option. Both these exercises should familiarize the users with ways of navigating around the manual. If you have an activity index, as described earlier in this book, another exercise should concentrate on the ease of use of this particular tool.

6   Introduce an option

Step through a specific option so users are comfortable with the sequence and layout. It is not necessary for users to have hands-on practice. You are not teaching anyone how to use the system during this training program. The emphasis must remain the manual.

The whole purpose of this training and introduction is to make the user feel confident. Both the user, and the writer, can feel confident if the definition of an effective piece of documentation has been met.

CHAPTER 6

Managing the documentation project

Documentation management

Managing a documentation project poses a number of problems. This section attempts to address those problems and to provide a set of phases by which the project can be reduced to a manageable group of activities.

After breaking the task into blocks or units of work, we will look at various methods by which estimates can be made of the amount of time that might be needed to carry out each phase. These estimates are based on case studies carried out across a number of documentation projects.

Time is the basis of all planning and most budgeting. From the time estimates can come cost estimates — documentation is very labor intensive — and then the resource allocation.

Later in this book there will be a discussion of the documentation strategy report which is a preliminary piece of work done when an organization is not sure what documentation is needed, or when the organization wants accurate costing and time scheduling before committing to the actual writing of the documentation. That strategy report constitutes most of what we will call phase 1.

For this section we will focus on a single manual as being the correct piece of documentation to solve the defined needs. If you have more than one manual to write, do all the early planning at once. Often, by planning all the manuals at one time, it is possible to merge requirements and cut down the number of different manuals. Perhaps the most important statement to be made under the topic of management is that the more experience a documentation writer has, the more accurate will be the estimates. This is true of many pursuits but is particularly true for documentation development.

While we have argued that there is little room for literary-type creativity in the documentation process, there are still a number of creative tasks that often defy traditional time-scheduling.   Documentation is not a treadmill activity, or some kind of production line assignment.

The time involved in writing and editing varies greatly from one writer to the next and by keeping track of your own progress across a number of documentation tasks, you will be able to make more accurate estimates when confronted with a new task.

Another unknown, which will vary greatly from one assignment to the next, is the time allotment that must be estimated for tasks that are not controlled directly by the writer, such as:

❏ technical changes that might be made to a system after the writer has completed planning and/or writing, forcing the writer to backtrack over ground already covered

❏ time taken for various approvals and proofreading

❏ common interruptions to the daily schedule that draw the writer away from the task at hand

In order to estimate and budget time for the documentation task, the writer must provide some figure for those time slots he does not control. The most effective way to handle this is to write the time slots and their allocations into the initial agreement or contract (for the consultant) or into the terms of reference (for the staff writer).

While this agreement serves many functions, it also focuses the attention of those commissioning the documentation to the role they must play, and the time they will have to carry out that role.

The typical documentation project includes the following phases:

Phase 1	Research and Organization Learning System and Users Developing Format Setting Style Guide Writing Contents Blueprint	
Phase 2	Getting Approval To Proceed	
Phase 3	Research/Writing the 1st Draft Writer's Edit of 1st Draft Print out 1st Draft	
Phase 4	Technical Accuracy and Completeness Check	
Phase 5	Writing the 2nd Draft Writer's Edit of 2nd Draft Print out 2nd Draft	
Phase 6	1st Full Proofreading	
Phase 7	Writing the 3rd Draft Writer's Edit of 3rd Draft Print out 3rd Draft	
Phase 8	Final Proofreading	
Phase 9	Minor Edits Print out Acceptance Copy	
Phase 10	Acceptance	
Phase 11	Production	
Phase 12	Distribution Introducing to Users	

Phase 1: the preliminaries

This is the most difficult phase to assign time to because it is in this phase that you will see the full extent of the documentation task that lies ahead. As has been pointed out earlier in this book, these preliminaries represent a significant amount (about 20 percent) of the total documentation time. Don't try to take any shortcuts. Try to resist the pressure of supervisors who believe that because the clock is ticking on the project, there should automatically be an ever-growing pile of manual pages appearing in a tray on your desk. Effective documentation doesn't work that way.

Research and organization

This topic has been covered in detail in the processes discussed earlier in this book. In many ways, this phase is self-management. It involves clearing the decks and receiving the initial brief of what might be needed to document the system properly. The terms of reference (or the letter of agreement or contract for the outside documentation consultant) need to be spelled out clearly to avoid misunderstandings during the execution of the project.

Learning the system and users

The time allotted to these tasks will vary with your knowledge of the system you are about to document and your knowledge of the users you will be writing for. If you are working in-house as a staff writer, you may already have been briefed on the system while it was in development, and you may have already written documentation for the same target groups of users. If this is the case, the time allotment for these two tasks should be short.

However, if you are an outsider to the organization or have not been exposed to either the system or the users, it is important you do not try to short circuit the needs here.

Developing the format

Once you have researched the system and the users, you may decide that an existing "off-the-shelf" format might suffice. This will cut the time down for this task. However, guard against trying to put a square peg in a round hole by forcing the new task into a format that doesn't really work. If you don't get this right, it will cause problems later and each problem will require additional time to solve.

The same comment as above applies to standard page layouts. Don't try to force non-standard material into a standard form. It won't work. Make sure that the format you decide to use will accommodate all the requirements of the project. Costly time problems will surface later if you suddenly find yourself confronted with a section that doesn't work in the format you've chosen.

Your choice of paper, the method of printing, the binding method, are all topics that should be addressed here. For example, your binding method will impact on how you will handle revisions and maintenance of the manual in the future, and this will effect issues such as page and section numbering, style of index, and so forth.

Setting the style guide

Deciding the style and usage in advance will save considerable time during the writing and editing stages. If a corporate style guide is in place — and, unfortunately, very few organizations have a style guide in place — then the time for this task will be minimal, limited to checking that it covers the requirements for the project being undertaken.

If the style guide is not in place, one needs to be done based on the chapter in this book dealing with this topic. The complexity of the project will determine the time needed.

Writing the contents blueprint

This task is fundamental to everything that comes after. The topic is well covered in this book. It requires the preliminaries of knowing your user and having researched the system you are documenting. The more detailed your headings in every area, the more time you will save later.

Do not short track this task. The value of a good blueprint cannot be overestimated. Trying to patch up a faulty or incomplete blueprint after the writing phase is under way will cost you a lot of time.

The amount of detail you physically note during this phase 1 activity will depend on your own style and needs. The minimum should be:

❏ a written summary of the objective and purpose of the manual

❏ a written summary of the user(s) profile

❏ two or three finished pages, showing:

- physical layout, typefaces, screen dumps, and so forth

- some written text to show level of language and technicality, as well as the way action statements and examples will be laid out

❏ a style guide for usage and definition

❏ the full contents list for use as a blueprint

Phase 2: initial approval

While gaining approval for all decisions you have made so far is critical to the final success of the project, it is a task that remains difficult to budget for time because it usually involves a number of people. These people are often decision makers in an organization with their own priorities to meet and thus are not able to (or willing to) fit into your schedule.

If you are acting as a consultant and have an agreement or contract with the organization for which you are providing the documentation, you might consider writing clauses into the agreement covering those time sequences you don't directly control.

If you are a staff writer, they could be added into the terms of reference that should be prepared for all documentation projects. The purpose is to draw the attention of others, such as supervisors and proofreaders, to the question of the time schedule. For example, I handle this initial approval by inserting words similar to those below into our agreement with the client.

Initial Approval

The client shall approve the following:

- ❏ physical layout and design of the manual (from sample pages)
- ❏ level of language (from sample pages)
- ❏ style guide (from the document that will serve as the style guide)
- ❏ contents list detailed headings

The nominated individual shall have three working days to review this material

It works best if the client organization appoints a *nominated individual* to work with the documentation writer. This speeds things up because it requires the nominated individual to decide how wide the distribution of the various drafts will be.

For example, on one of my projects the proofreading was done by seven proofreaders from various divisions within the company. The company's nominated individual handled distribution of the initial material and the various drafts as I provided them, arranged to get the proofread copies back and then transferred the changes into one master copy. The discrepancies (and there inevitably will be discrepancies in detail when there are multiple proofreaders) were arbitrated by the nominated individual.

This initial approval may take some time and it may require some changes in the basic scheme, but it is better for everyone to agree now than to try to make changes later. This is the time for the objective or the mission of the manual to be firmly implanted in the minds of those who will accept the finished product. Now is the opportunity for the training department to realize that the manual will be a reference guide, and not a training document, or for the operations department to recognize that this is a training manual and not a detailed step-by-step procedural document.

In some cases, the documentation writer will need to justify his decisions. For example, choice of typeface and physical layout are quite subjective issues. There are numerous ways a manual page can be laid out, and there are a number of workable typefaces. Your choices, however, should be based on the rules you understand (perhaps those in this book) and you should have little difficulty defining the reasons behind your choices.

Justifying the style guide is mainly a matter of correct versus incorrect usage. However, there are some subjective decisions to be made here and the writer should listen carefully to any advice offered. However, once the style guide is approved, it should be tampered with as little as possible.

The level of language is based on an analysis of the target users and the writer should be able to explain his choice. Be careful here to recognize that the users may be a very different group from the decision makers and care should be taken that the decision makers don't try to change the level of language away from the users to their own level. Remember that if the bulk of users are 19-year-old clerks and the *nominated individual* is a 55-year-old finance director, the level of language must match that of the clerks.

Most of the time devoted to this initial approval phase should be spent on the contents list. The structure of the documentation must receive approval now, so that it is not in question later. The next time the organization has a time to review (and thus to tamper) with the structure will be after the first draft has been written and the time consequences involved in extensive structural changes then can be devastating.

Technical system changes

The most effective documentation does not get under way until after a system has finished the development stages. The reason for this is obvious — even the most minor change to the system can have a tremendous impact on the form and content of the documentation.

A 10-minute "minor" technical change by a programmer could lead to the documentation writer throwing out a week's worth of writing.

This "system change" problem needs to be addressed constantly, and can be highlighted by adding a comment into the agreement or terms of reference developed for the project. The wording we use goes like this:

> In the event the client makes any significant changes to the system or procedures, or cannot supply information at the time it is needed, the spirit of cooperation on which this agreement is based will allow for both parties to mutually agree on variations to the progress and completion deadlines.

Adding this paragraph allows for everyone to recognize the existence of a potential problem. Sometimes that problem becomes obvious when documentation reveals a design weakness. If technical changes are to be made to a system, careful consideration should also be given to the impact of those changes on the documentation effort and schedule.

Estimating phases 3, 5, 7, and 9

Phase 3	Research/Writing the 1st Draft Writer's Edit of 1st Draft Print out 1st Draft	
Phase 5	Writing the 2nd Draft Writer's Edit of 2nd Draft Print out 2nd Draft	
Phase 7	Writing the 3rd Draft Writer's Edit of 3rd Draft Print out 3rd Draft	
Phase 9	Minor Edits Print out Acceptance Copy	

Phases 4, 6, and 8 can be ignored for the moment because they are phases outside the control of the writer.

Armed with an approved contents list, time estimates can be made for the phases covering the writing and editing of each of the drafts. Most of the figures are based on the most difficult phase — researching and writing the first draft. There are two estimates to be made, and then combined:

❏ the speculative estimate

❏ the mathematical estimate

When these two estimates have been completed, the figures can be combined and assessed to provide a guide to how long the first draft of the project will take.

Phases 5, 7, and 9 can then be added working from percentages based on a number of projects undertaken by my company's editors and writers.

❑ Phase 5:   20 percent of the total writer-controlled time

❑ Phase 7:   10 percent of the total writer-controlled time

❑ Phase 9:   5 percent of the total writer-controlled time

Remember that writer-controlled time does not include those phases where *outsiders*, such as proofreaders, are working with the manuscript.

Two qualifications need to be made immediately.

❑ The accuracy of the estimates will improve with the experience of the person doing the estimating.

❑ The final figure from these estimates represents how long it will take to do the actual project and does not include all the interruptions, weekends, staff meeting, holidays, social chattering, "urgent other tasks", and so forth that invariably break up a working schedule. (To accommodate these interruptions, declare your real working time in any given week as 30 hours — or whatever is appropriate for your circumstances: your normal working hours minus the interruptions.)

The speculative estimate

The speculative estimate requires working through the contents list noting as many factors as possible which will influence the time it will take you to write what is needed. This requires a certain amount of imagination and is thus difficult for many writers who spend a lot of time working on technical subjects.

The key requirement is to set aside a couple of hours when you will not be disturbed. This kind of speculation is most successful when you can immerse yourself in the subject.

Address each heading on the contents list with these kinds of questions:

1 What subject(s) will I write about here?

2 What do my users really want (need) to know?

3 What do I already know about this subject, and do I really understand that information?

4 Is this subject easy to explain?

5 Are there any difficult topics in this subject?

6 Which areas of this subject will need examples?

7 Who will I need to talk with to find the answers to my questions?

8 Have I written about this subject before and, if so, can I adapt the material and use it here?

9 Has anyone else written about this subject before and, if so, can I adapt that material and use it here?

10 What illustrations or graphics (screen dumps) will be needed and, if so, can I prepare them myself, or will I need assistance?

11 How many pages will it take to make these explanations?

On the contents list, write down the number of hours you think you will need to research and write the first draft of the section. Don't worry about the time for editing. That comes later. All we're interested in here is in getting the first words on paper.

Go through this question and thinking exercise for each section on the contents list. When you have worked your way through the entire manual, add up all the hours. You now have a total number of hours for the research and writing of the first draft of your manual.

SECTION	# of PAGES	HRS/SECTION	
Section 1			
Section 2			
Section 3			
Section 4			
Section 5			
Section 6			

The mathematical estimate

Set aside your speculative estimate. The mathematical estimate is a simple numbers game, based on figures we've worked out across a great number of projects. Once again, it is necessary to stress that the more experience you gain, the more accurate will be your estimates.

Turn your contents list into a matrix something like this:

SECTION	# of PAGES	MIN/PAGE	TOTAL
Section 1			
Section 2			
Section 3			
Section 4			
Section 5			
Section 6			

Transfer the estimated number of pages from the figures you developed during the speculative estimate.

Do some simple calculations based on these figures:

Research and writing: 90 minutes per page

(It often works out that you will spend about 45 minutes researching and 45 minutes writing for each page.)

The first draft research and writing represents about 45 percent of the total project, and the initial phase of definition, design, and contents blueprint takes about 20 percent of the total project time.

The next step is to combine the speculative and mathematical estimates and review each chapter, questioning any area where the two estimates differ greatly.

SECTION	Mathematical Estimate	Speculative Estimate	Final Estimate
Section 1			
Section 2			
Section 3			
Section 4			
Section 5			
Section 6			

There are a number of reasons why your mathematical estimate and speculative estimate will vary. Some sections may have a number of topics that don't fill a page. For example, Using the New Topic, New Page rule — these kinds of pages will not take as long to research and write. The section may include concepts which you know will be difficult to explain. Some pages may have screen dumps and will not take as long to write.

If you work through the manual, section by section, checking the variations and making adjustments, you will be able to fill in the final estimates quite accurately.

You now have an estimate of the time it will take to research and write the first draft in numbers of hours and we know this represents about 45 percent of the project. You can now fill in the rest of this table. (The shaded areas require further explanation before they can be filled in. While they are part of the project, they are not directly controlled by the writer.)

Percentage of Writer-controlled Project Time

Phase 1	Research and Organization Learning System and Users Developing Format Setting Style Guide Writing Contents Blueprint	20 %
Phase 2	Getting Approval To Proceed	
Phase 3	Research/Writing the 1st Draft Writer's Edit of 1st Draft Print out 1st Draft	45 %
Phase 4	Technical Accuracy and Completeness Check	
Phase 5	Writing the 2nd Draft Writer's Edit of 2nd Draft Print out 2nd Draft	20 %
Phase 6	1st Full Proofreading	
Phase 7	Writing the 3rd Draft Writer's Edit of 3rd Draft Print out 3rd Draft	10 %
Phase 8	Final Proofreading	
Phase 9	Minor Edits Print out Acceptance Copy	5 %
Phase 10	Acceptance	
Phase 11	Production	
Phase 12	Distribution Introducing to Users	

Let's look at an example, where our speculative estimates show 81 pages as the total needed to meet the needs. The writer also estimates he'll be able to devote about 30 hours a week to this particular project.

An example: 81 pages, 30 hours a week

		%	Days	Hours
Phase 1	Research and Organization Learning System and Users Developing Format Setting Style Guide Writing Contents Blueprint	20	9	54
Phase 2	Getting Approval To Proceed			
Phase 3	Research/Writing the 1st Draft Writer's Edit of 1st Draft Print out 1st Draft	45	20.2	121
Phase 4	Technical Accuracy and Completeness Check			
Phase 5	Writing the 2nd Draft Writer's Edit of 2nd Draft Print out 2nd Draft	20	9	54
Phase 6	1st Full Proofreading			
Phase 7	Writing the 3rd Draft Writer's Edit of 3rd Draft Print out 3rd Draft	10	4.5	27
Phase 8	Final Proofreading			
Phase 9	Minor Edits Print out Acceptance Copy	5	2.2	13.5
Phase 10	Acceptance			
Phase 11	Production			
Phase 12	Distribution Introducing to Users			

Phase 4: an early check

The technical and accuracy check is a special kind of proofreading. It provides the writer with the opportunity to make sure the manual includes all the necessary bits and pieces. This is not a check for grammar, or style. It is a check on the basic accuracy of the technical detail and on the overall completeness. It is the first opportunity the writer has to check the exactness of the contents blueprint.

From this point on, the writer can concentrate on fine-tuning the manual, on strengthening weak areas with rewriting, and on adding examples where they are needed to ensure user understanding.

While the writer may find it difficult to control the time involved in this early technical accuracy proofreading, the consultant writer might help his planning by including this kind of guidance in the initial agreement.

> The first draft will be provided for proofreading for technical accuracy. This draft should be in the hands of the proofreader for a maximum of five working days.

The five working days will allow the writer to fill in an estimated time for phase 4.

Phase 6: the formal proofreading

By the time of the formal proofreading, the manuscript will already have been through a preliminary accuracy and technical check (phase 4). It has then been rewritten through second draft stage (phase 5) and fine tuned.

Once again, the writer may find it difficult to control the time taken by the proofreaders, particularly if the writer is part of an in-house staff and the proofreaders are higher up the management ladder.

One approach is to write into the agreement, or some other terms of reference, this kind of qualification.

> The second draft will be provided for formal proofreading. The manuscript should be in the hands of the proofreader for five working days.

If more than one proofreader is involved, time must also be allotted for collating the proofreading comments into a single master copy that can then be used with the third draft. In some cases, a meeting might be needed to resolve disputes that often arise when more than one proofreader is involved.

Phase 8: the final proofreading

The final proofreading should go smoothly and in many ways should be a formality. Technical accuracy has been checked on the two earlier proofreadings and the writer has been checking for typos and grammar each time he makes a pass through the manuscript.

The writer can exert some control over the time of this final proofreading by noting in the agreement, or in the terms of reference:

> The third draft will be provided for final proofreading. The manuscript should be in the hands of the proofreader for three working days.

In some cases, this final proofreading will result in acceptance of the manual. If this is the case, the manual can move into phase 11: production. However, it is more likely that some minor edits will be needed.

Phase 10: acceptance

If the manual requires additional work after the final proofreading, those edits (phase 9) should be executed quickly and the manuscript returned to the nominated individual for formal acceptance.

This phase 10 acceptance is important because it is my belief that while the writer must take all due care with the documentation, it is the responsibility of the client or the senior project manager to take over that responsibility at the time of acceptance. Again, the writer must be able to budget time to this phase.

Final acceptance of the manual should take place within three days of delivery.

Production should never start until formal acceptance of the manuscript has taken place.

Let's expand our earlier example by adding in the times for those tasks not controlled directly by the writer.

An example: 81 pages, 30 hours a week

		%	Days	Hours
Phase 1	Research and Organization Learning System and Users Developing Format Setting Style Guide Writing Contents Blueprint	20	9	54
Phase 2	Getting Approval To Proceed		3	
Phase 3	Research/Writing the 1st Draft Writer's Edit of 1st Draft Print out 1st Draft	45	20.2	121
Phase 4	Technical Accuracy and Completeness Check		5	
Phase 5	Writing the 2nd Draft Writer's Edit of 2nd Draft Print out 2nd Draft	20	9	54
Phase 6	1st Full Proofreading		5	
Phase 7	Writing the 3rd Draft Writer's Edit of 3rd Draft Print out 3rd Draft	10	4.5	27
Phase 8	Final Proofreading		3	
Phase 9	Minor Edits Print out Acceptance Copy	5	2.2	13.5
Phase 10	Acceptance		3	
Phase 11	Production			
Phase 12	Distribution Introducing to Users			

Our example, an 81-page manual, now has a start and finish and an allotment of hours and days. To summarize the table on the previous page:

Total days (phases 1 to 10):   63.9 days (64)

This works out at 4.7 hours per page.

Total writer-controlled days: 44.9 (45)

This works out at 3.3 hours per page.

These days are 6-hour work days, allowing 2 hours a day for routine interruptions — a work week of 30 hours.

The uncontrollable factor remains the time when the manuscript is out of the hands of the writer during proofreading. These time slots have been defined in the terms of reference and the impact should be clearly spelled out in those same terms of reference if these times are exceeded. This simple paragraph should suffice:

If the nominated individual takes longer to proofread (or to carry out phases 2, 4, 6, 8, or 10) than the allotted time in the schedule, the extra time shall be added on to the project schedule.

While this paragraph covers the writer, it often creates problems on its own, particularly in the production phases and eventual distribution to users. It is better to increase the proofreading time during planning. What must not be done is to try and cut the writer's phases short in order to make up lost time in proofreading.

While it may seem obvious, it is important to note that these days and hours we have been working with are actual working days. They do not take into consideration weekends and holidays. To get a calendar date for the finish of our project, these *other* days must be taken into consideration. The table on the next page provides a sample schedule for a project started on August 1.

An example: 81 pages, 30 hours a week

		%	Days	Hours	Dates
Phase 1	Research and Organization Learning System and Users Developing Format Setting Style Guide Writing Contents Blueprint	20	9	54	Sept 16 Sept 27
Phase 2	Getting Approval To Proceed		3		Sept 30 Oct 2
Phase 3	Research/Writing the 1st Draft Writer's Edit of 1st Draft Print out 1st Draft	45	20.2	121	Oct 3 Nov 4
Phase 4	Technical Accuracy and Completeness Check		5		Nov 5 Nov 12
Phase 5	Writing the 2nd Draft Writer's Edit of 2nd Draft Print out 2nd Draft	20	9	54	Nov 13 Nov 26
Phase 6	1st Full Proofreading		5		Nov 27 Dec 4
Phase 7	Writing the 3rd Draft Writer's Edit of 3rd Draft Print out 3rd Draft	10	4.5	27	Dec 5 Dec 11
Phase 8	Final Proofreading		3		Dec 12 Dec 16
Phase 9	Minor Edits Print out Acceptance Copy	5	2.2	13.5	Dec 17 Dec 19
Phase 10	Acceptance		3		Dec 20 Dec 24

For the purpose of this example, the year was 1991 and the holidays considered were Columbus Day (Oct 14), Veterans Day (Nov 11), and Thanksgiving Day (Nov 28). Note how many *calendar* days the project takes when compared with the *working* days.

Phase 11: production

Planning for production, if the writer is controlling production, can start in phase 1 with decisions about the method of production and binding. More serious work can start after phase 4. By this phase, the size and shape of the manuscript is usually well understood, and outside printing and binding firms can be asked to provide time and cost quotes to complete the job.

Production time is often underestimated. There are a number of stages to the production process, and each should be blocked out and added to the schedule. These time commitments can then be added into the schedule.

Phase 12: distribution to users

Whenever possible, in-house documentation should not be distributed to users without some form of introductory training session.

The training session should not take more than a couple of hours and, depending on the number of users, might take place with all users or a group of representative users who can then repeat the key points to others in their immediate work area.

The "overlooked" storage problem

After the manuals have been printed and bound and perhaps put into boxes, they usually have to be stored before distribution. This can create a space and weight problem and is often overlooked. One of my company's clients asked us to produce 10,000 manuals in binders in boxes for distribution worldwide. Consider a normal boxed manual in a binder, with dimensions like this:

9 inches long x 7 inches wide x 2 inches deep

To avoid crushing, each pile of manuals is made up of 20 manuals.

The company ordered 10,000 binders in boxes — that's 500 piles.

The 10,000 manuals will occupy floor space of about 219 square feet, or about the size of an average car garage.

And, consider the weight: 10,000 x 2 pounds/unit = 20,000 pounds

CHAPTER 7

On-line help

Developing on-line help

The subject of on-line documentation is far too vast to be dealt with in this book. It covers an array of topics including, but certainly not limited to, help messages, tutorials, menus, prompts, error messages, on-line manuals, reference books, and so on. On-line documentation works best when the documents being referenced can be seen and understood in small chunks. It works least well when the read is long and involved, and the content requires critical thought and perhaps linkage to other topics.

On-line documentation is held on a computer system and displayed to the screen rather than being printed on the paper page. For example, a telephone directory is an ideal candidate for on-line display. Each entry is a separate topic, linked only by commonality of names and then separated by addresses and telephone numbers. Turning this documentation textbook into an on-line document would not be in the best interests of the user. Too many of the topics covered here cannot be seen as single units. There is too much subjectivity involved in decision making here.

For our purposes we will deal with two forms of on-line documentation:

❑ on-line help

❑ on-line tutorials

Before we start, it is important to put into context the argument between paper-based documentation and the on-line variety. There has been much talk of the paperless office. While some offices now have less paper and computer terminals allow for the exchange of written (and spoken) memos through electronic mail and the like, other offices are finding that the amount of paper is growing as the computer systems grow.

One institution which has more than 20,000 pages of on-line reference materials shows a marked increase in the number of printouts. Users find what they want, then print out the page to use it. There also remains some legal questions about the legality of documents on media other than paper, for example, legal disclaimers, warranties, and the like.

While the paper-based page is unlikely to disappear within the next couple of generations, the power and usability of on-line documentation have made it a valuable tool that the documentation writer/editor can no longer ignore.

At the same time, the programmer and system designer must recognize the role of the documentation writer in developing effective on-line documents. The difficulty is that traditionally the computer and screen have been the exclusive property of the programmer. Because on-line activity has required programming of some sort, the technical side of the industry has jealously guarded its territory. This has resulted in the ludicrous situation where paper-based documentation has been written by the documentation writer with a distinct user bias, while the on-line documentation has a technical bias because the programmer failed to make the mental transition to user while documenting the system.

I have written on-line documentation in response to both these situations — straight into the system, and as a hard copy printout showing text and layout which a programmer then turned into program lines for display. Within the 4GL world, the writer has no difficulty designing an on-line structure that works well, and then writing the needed documentation directly into the computer.

Why consider on-line documentation?

On-line documentation has increased in popularity during the past few years for a number of reasons.

❏ System memories have been constantly growing, eliminating early fears that on-line documents took up too much space.

❏ Systems and applications often grow faster than documentation can keep up. By the time the manual is finished, it must be revised. On-line documents, carefully constructed initially, are faster to revise and update. (Production and distribution of a single on-line system is often less expensive and faster than multiple copies of paper-based manuals as well.)

❏ Large paper-based manuals tend to frighten users. When using an on-line help system, the user only sees a small portion at a time. The user may never see the full extent of the help system.

❏ Paper-based manuals require maximum effort from the user with little if any interaction between user and page. Well-designed help systems involve the user.

❏ On-line documentation is part of the whole look and feel of the computer package. There is no third element (the paper-based manual) in the way. The user interacts with the computer.

Many users believe that everything they need to know is in the computer. Why should I read the manual when everyone tells me how sophisticated the computer is?

On-line versus paper-based

On-line documentation has not been successful in many cases because the documentation writer failed to come to grips with the fundamental differences between the on-line document and the paper-based document. Recognizing the differences is the first step toward designing an effective on-line document.

The fundamental difference is that while the on-line page has some of the general characteristics of the paper page, it is generally smaller and shaped differently.

The standard screen displays 24 lines of 80 characters, about 320 words. To turn that screen into something the user can comprehend (with blank space and design elements), those 320 words will be reduced to less than 200. The entire screen page will equal about 20 percent of a well-designed paper page. Put another way: consider that the screen page is a series of 3 x 5 inch blank cards. That's the amount of primary space you have to work with.

The misuse of the screen space has been one of the main reasons for user rejection of on-line documents. Until recently, it was common to find wall-to-wall writing in on-line documents prepared by programmers. With studies showing that users often believe that a screen has more on it than really exists, it is easy to conclude that users reject most on-line documents as less than helpful.

Legibility

Screen text is much less legible than text on a printed page. The maximum density on a printed page should be about 40 percent. On the screen, the maximum density should not exceed 25 percent. Some studies suggest that 15 percent is an even better density figure, allowing maximum user acceptance of screen-displayed information.

Consider what this means in terms of work space. If all the elements on the screen page were placed together, they should not exceed the 25 percent in the center of this square. Of course, the elements will be spread across the page, providing lots of blank space to set each individual element apart from the others.

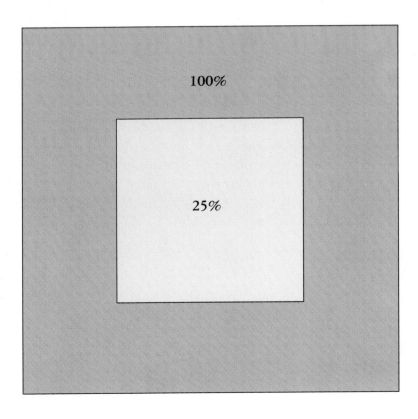

It is difficult to remember that the screen does not equal a blank sheet of paper. The eye does not respond to the elements on the screen in the same way as it does to elements on paper. The screen lacks many of the devices that aid the eye on paper. For example, we already know the value of ascenders and descenders in helping the eye define shapes and thus the meaning of words and phrases. But on the screen the descenders are often nonexistent or squashed. On many screens, we still find all caps as the text style.

What we have called leading — the space between horizontal lines of text — in our discussions about layout of text on the printed page plays an even more important role with screen text. Too often text lines on the screen have less leading than on the printed page. The characters of one line of text blur into the characters of the text line above and below. Screen text needs even more leading. Screen leading should not be less than 50 percent the height of the character. To make it easy, consider type of 12 points — the leading should not be less 6 points. For 14-point text, use 7 points or more leading.

While microjustification and kerning controls exist to allow justified text blocks on the printed page, there is no equivalent control for screen displays and thus justified text blocks should be avoided. Text should be justified left with ragged right.

Resolution

The screen has very poor resolution compared with the output of a laser printer, or a professionally typeset page. The screen's resolution might be measured at 100 dots per inch (dpi), while a standard laser printer is at 300 or 600 dpi and professional typesetting is about 2000 dpi.

Background

The question of what background color and what color the text will be displayed in also has to be addressed. The normal printed page comes in black and white — acknowledged as the best color combination possible. Users prefer dark text on a light background, most likely because it reminds them of the printed page. Research indicates the actual difference between dark text/light background (negative contrast) and light text/ dark background (positive contrast) is minimal. Additional studies show that legibility increases as contrast between text and background increases. Because of the ability to call on various color combinations, this background and text combination becomes important. I'll have more to say about color later.

While different studies show different conclusions and it is not our task here to say who is right and who is wrong, the characteristics of the screen tend to slow down both the reading and the comprehension speed of the user. (One study suggests by as much as 28.5 percent.)

The active prompt

One problem that needs to be addressed is to beat the old problem of losing contact with the active screen when on-line help is called. The user needs help to fill in a field, asks for help, pages through a couple of screens to find what he needs, then has to put the help away and try to remember what is necessary.

The answer is to place the help information on the screen in a place where the user can still see the prompt or the area of the screen where he is working. (One of the advantages of the manual is that it can be open on your desk while you are working on the screen.)

Techniques for on-line help

The documentation writer/editor must learn the techniques of writing On-Line documentation. While the paper manual will continue, there will be a natural growth in accompanying on-line documentation. As well, knowledge about the strengths and weaknesses of using on-line documentation is important when discussing the topic with programmers, clients, and so forth who often mistakenly believe that anything that can be done on paper can be duplicated on the screen.

Structure

There are many structures, but the one I have found most successful is based on the philosophy that not all users need the same level of help. For some users (and for some prompts) a mere reminder is all that is needed. Some users need more information (perhaps a couple of paragraphs), and other users need more extensive information (perhaps a couple of screens).

Thus we could think of help as a series of levels you can pass through until you find the information you need.

❏ **Level** 1: the reminder (press F1 to access). This level provides a sentence or two, plus an indicator if more help is available.

❏ **Level** 2: the paragraph (press F1 from level 1 help to access). This level expands on level 1, plus an indicator if more help is available.

❏ **Level** 3: full screen (press F1 from level 2 help to access). This level is the traditional help screen.

❏ **Level** 4: system help (Press /? from anywhere to access). This level allows access from anywhere in the system. The help is made up of level 3 help, plus special topics (level 5).

Structure of on-line help

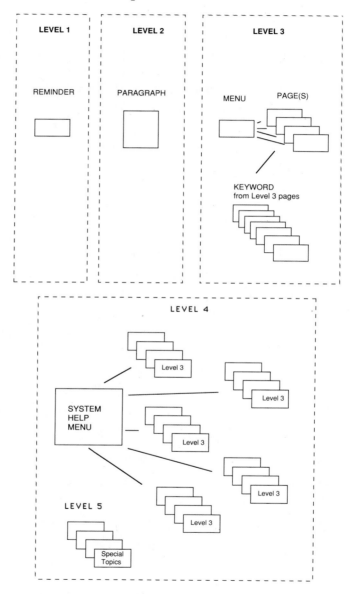

The following pages show how this works in practice.

SB+ offers a number of Help levels, accessed by pressing the F1 key to step through each level.

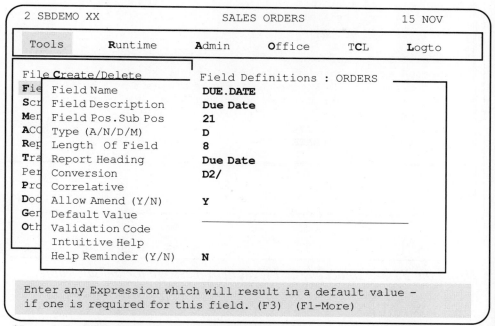

```
2 SBDEMO XX                  SALES ORDERS               15 NOV

  Tools      Runtime      Admin      Office      TCL      Logto

 File Create/Delete            Field Definitions : ORDERS
 Fie   Field Name            DUE.DATE
 Scr   Field Description     Due Date
 Men   Field Pos.Sub Pos     21
 Acc   Type (A/N/D/M)        D
 Rep   Length Of Field       8
 Tra   Report Heading        Due Date
 Per   Conversion            D2/
 Pro   Correlative
 Doc   Allow Amend (Y/N)     Y
 Gen   Default Value
 Oth   Validation Code
       Intuitive Help
       Help Reminder (Y/N)   N


 Enter any Expression which will result in a default value -
 if one is required for this field. (F3)  (F1-More)
```

Use of the F1 key to access 1st level help message for default value.

1st - Reminder

Press F1 to see a short one or two line Help message displayed at the bottom of the screen.

If additional F1 Help is available it will be indicated at the end of 1st level Help message. The message will remain on the screen for the duration of the input.

F3 indicates that Intuitive Help is also available.

```
  2 SBDEMO XX                   SALES ORDERS                   15 NOV

 ┌─────────────────────────────────────────────────────────────────┐
 │ Enter — if required — the default value this field is most likely  │
 │ to contain.  If a default is used, less key strokes are required to│
 │ enter data into the field.  The default value should be the most   │
 │ likely value to be used.                                          │
 │                                                                    │
 │ A default may be any Expression resulting in a value which can then│
 │ be presented as a default.  The default code expression will be    │
 │ executed immediately before the field is accessed on a screen —    │
 │ unless the default is executed on screen entry. (See Screen prompt │
 │ 'Defaults (0/1)')                                                  │
 │                                                                    │
 │ Eg:  Default Value  @DATE + 10             (F3)                    │
 └─────────────────────────────────────────────────────────────────┘
  Oth  Validation Code
       Intuitive Help
       Help Reminder (Y/N)


 F2-Save F4-Del F5-Review F6-Prnt F7-Copy F8-Addit F9-NewFile F10-More
```

Using the F1 key to access 2nd level help message for default value.

2nd - Window

Pressing the F1 key again (after accessing Reminder Help) will open a window on the screen, if available. The window will contain additional Help.

The window will remain on the screen for the duration of the input.

```
 DEFAULT


        If a field is always to have its default value taken, that is
        — the operator is not given the opportunity to amend the field
        — then a [S] may be appended immediately after the default
          code.  It becomes a skip field.

        This is useful in conditional expressions where, depending on
        a condition being true, certain value must always be taken,
        else another value is offered as a default and may be
        overridden.

        Eg:  IF (TYPE= "D", 25[S],"")

        If the field called TYPE is equal to D, then the default value
        is always 25, else there is no default and the value will be
        prompted for.



                                                              1/2
```

Using the F1 key to access 3rd level help message for default value.

3rd - Full Page

Pressing the F1 key again (after accessing Window Help) will open a full page of Help, where available.

The presence of more than one page of Help text is indicated by the current page number in the bottom right corner.

It is possible to print any full page Help text by entering the letter **P** and pressing the <ENTER> key.

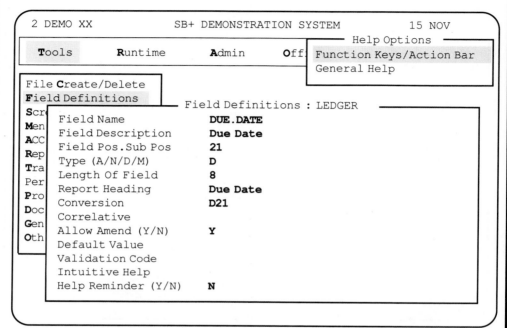

```
 2 DEMO XX              SB+ DEMONSTRATION SYSTEM              15 NOV
                                                    ┌─ Help Options ─────────┐
   Tools        Runtime        Admin        Off│   Function Keys/Action Bar  │
                                                │   General Help             │
 ┌─────────────────────────────┐               └────────────────────────────┘
 │ File Create/Delete           │
 │ Field Definitions            │  ┌─ Field Definitions : LEDGER ─────────────┐
 │ Scr│                            │    Field Name           DUE.DATE          │
 │ Men│                            │    Field Description    Due Date          │
 │ ACC│                            │    Field Pos.Sub Pos    21                │
 │ Rep│                            │    Type (A/N/D/M)       D                 │
 │ Tra│                            │    Length Of Field      8                 │
 │ Per│                            │    Report Heading       Due Date          │
 │ Pro│                            │    Conversion           D21               │
 │ Doc│                            │    Correlative                            │
 │ Gen│                            │    Allow Amend (Y/N)    Y                 │
 │ Oth│                            │    Default Value                          │
 │                                 │   Validation Code                        │
 │                                 │   Intuitive Help                         │
 │                                 │   Help Reminder (Y/N)   N                 │
 │                                 └──────────────────────────────────────────┘
```

Using the F1 key to access 4th level help message for default value.

4th - Help Menu

Pressing the F1 key again (after accessing Full page Help) will provide you with a Help menu specific to the screen you are on. You will find Help on Function Keys and the Action Bar here.

☞ In most cases all levels of help are not necessary and therefore are not represented. For example, after a Level 1 Reminder you may not find a Level 2 Window, but be taken directly to a higher level of help.

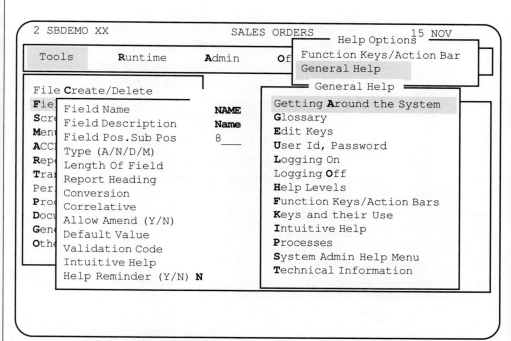

Accessing General Help menu from a SB+ Tool.

5th - General Help

General Help on a number of topics is available at this level.

Glossary   *For example*, a Glossary is available at this level.
If you ask for Glossary Help, the letters of the alphabet will appear. Choose the first letter of the entry you are interested in. Glossary definitions appear in alphabetical order. You may also access the Glossary from any prompt within SB+ by typing:

/GLOSS

Intuitive Help

On most prompts SB+ provides a guide to help you enter the required input. If Intuitive Help is available, a (F3) will appear in the F1 Help message. The type of Help provided by pressing F3 (or the key defined for Intuitive Help for your terminal) will depend upon the input.

For example: the following screen shows F3 Intuitive Help called from the *Conversion* prompt. It is offering a selection of valid responses to the prompt — recognising that the field is a date field.

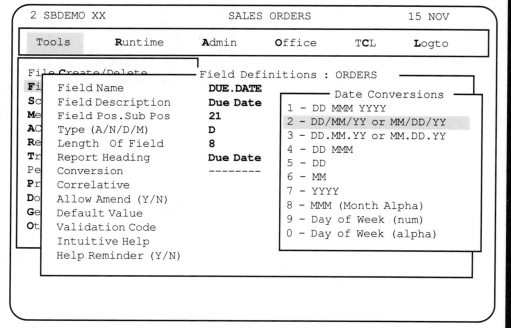

Choice available when pressing F3 at Conversion prompt

For example: If entering a field name, pressing F3 will display all field names currently available and provide the option to select a field name(s) for amendment.

When entering a validation, the F3 key will display a template to assist you in defining your validation step by step.

Intuitive Help differs from F1 On-Line Help in that this Help is not textual help, but a process where the result is the actual response required for the prompt. It is *doing* as opposed to *finding out.* We recommend you try the F3 wherever it is available. It is an excellent way to learn what options/inputs are available within SB+.

Remember that the facilities and functionality available through Intuitive Help within SB+ will also be available within the applications you build using SB+. This is also true of F1 On-line Help.

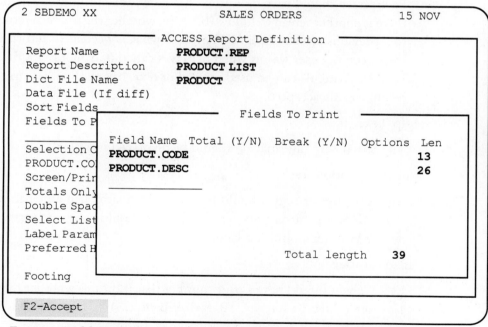

Entering Fields To Print using F3, while defining an ACCESS report.

Screen Layout

The screen layout should be well thought out before you start. Placing the various elements in certain locations across the screen, and then maintaining those positions throughout the help system will aid the user. On-line documentation should be seen as primarily a graphics environment, and thus design and balance must be carefully considered.

Most traditional help screens need the following minimum elements:

Title

Each screen should have a title so the user can immediately confirm he has reached the correct help screen.

Navigation

Each screen should have indicators that show, at a minimum, whether there is another screen to follow (NEXT), whether the user can return to a previous screen (PREVIOUS), and what is needed to return to the screen the user was in when help was called (CANCEL or QUIT HELP). Symbols can be used instead of text, but the symbols must be universally accepted.

Help Text

The actual help information should be displayed in a block.

Warnings and Notes

Any warnings or notes should be treated in a similar manner in all screens. Special attention-getting devices should be used (perhaps reverse video or a blinking label).

Page Number

Every screen should have a page number that indicates whether there are more follow-on screens. (Page 1 or page 1/3)

The screen should always be balanced. There are many possibilities. The following examples work well.

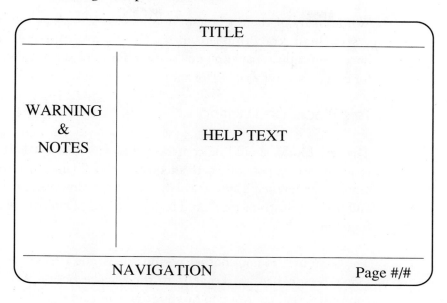

Some specific guidelines

While many of the documentation processes, such as researching the system and knowing the users, are as appropriate for on-line documentation as paper manuals, there are some specific considerations for designing and writing for the screen.

Text Blocks and Writing

The text blocks should be constructed to say what needs to be said as economically as possible, with adequate white (blank) space to make the sentence or paragraph appear as a distinct unit. However, proper sentence and paragraph structure should be maintained. Don't write in sentence fragments.

The computer is not another person. It is not a friend or an enemy. Don't personalize it. Leave it to the science fiction writers to have computers that address you by your first name, or tell you that you have done well, or display messages such as: "I'm searching for the answer to your query".

Many users are still wary of computers. Bear in mind that few people like being "put down" and the computer should not be seen as showing the characteristics of intellectual superiority. The ultimate poor-taste message is anything that suggests: "You should know the answer to that. What are you — a dummy?"

Avoid the use of negative words. Common words such as INVALID and ERROR are often found on the screen. As with all documentation writing, the simple word remains best. For example, use END rather than TERMINATE, as in: "To end this activity, press ESC".

Keep the tone of the writing the same as found in any accompanying paper manual. The ideal is to have the same writer write both the manual and the on-line help.

Don't scroll, or at least restrict the scrolling to the help text area of the screen. The format of the screens — the way you have displayed the various elements that make up the screen — is important to the user's ability to understand. If the whole screen scrolls, formatting becomes useless. If you must scroll, then scroll only within that section of the screen containing the help text. Place a scrolling bar on the right side of the help text area so the user can control the scrolling. Users read and comprehend at different speeds, so avoid any mechanism that automates the scrolling.

Limit the number of screens. Break the main subject into subtopics and provide a menu to let the user access the subtopic necessary. Alternatively, provide a short overview of the subject at the end of which there is a short menu allowing the user to more accurately choose where to go next. I would question the structure of the help if the user was required to page through more than three screens on a single topic. Providing 10 or 15 screen pages only burdens the user.

Provide each subtopic with a page reference to the paper manual, if appropriate. This allows a more succinct presentation on the screen and points the user to secondary information.

Be sure that the user can easily find instructions on how to use the help system, either in the paper manual or in a general help section that can be easily accessed.

I have seen users trapped by an on-line help system that included "How to Log On" as part of the help but also required the user to be logged on before he could access help. (A neat way around this problem is to provide an early prompt that responds to a /HELP before Log On — password and user ID — takes place. The /HELP calls up a single screen showing the user how to formally log on.) However, a caution note is needed here. Some computer operation managements may consider any access to computer capabilities before formal log on as creating the potential for possible security problems.

Graphics, attention-getters, color

Certain kinds of graphics requiring high-resolution display fail on the low-resolution screen. The resolution of the screen determines the smallest acceptable text size and the amount of detail available for the display of drawings and the like.

One of the advantages of the screen over the printed page is the ability of the documentation writer to take advantage of the unique attributes of the screen. Many of these can be used to develop emphasis, as an attention getter. They include the many colors usually available to the screen display, the blinking ability, highlighting, and reverse video. The same warning applies here as applies with the overuse of emphasis devices on the paper page. Too much emphasis ultimately results in no emphasis at all. Only emphasize what truly needs to be emphasized. Draw attention only when attention is warranted.

For example, a warning that a certain action will lead to a system crash should be emphasized and labeled with an attention-getting device. One of the advantages of placing the warning element in a fixed position on the screen is that its presence alone will alert the user. The addition of a special color, used only for warnings, will also help as will a reverse video or blinking warning label.

Color is powerful if used judiciously. The first determination to be made is whether all users will be using color screens. If some users may be working with monochrome screens, color combinations must be tested to make sure the display remains effective when color is removed. Remember, too, that the most legible color combination remains black and white.

Avoid using color merely to make everything look pretty. Too many color combinations reduce the speed and the accuracy of the read. Use color to:

❏ help emphasize elements of importance

❏ help separate the blocks of elements

Be consistent with the use of color. If you are using color to help separate various elements, such as warnings from notes, or title from navigation, maintain the same colors through all screens.

Use a neutral background and check each color combination to ensure that any single color does not dominate on its own in such a way that the eye is attracted merely by the color.

An example from HyperCard

There are many fine examples of on-line help (and many examples of very poor help) available with applications and systems now in use. Perhaps two of the best are found with Microsoft's Excel™ and Apple Computer's HyperCard™.

The following pages provide a short example of the power in HyperCard's help structure. Documentation writers would do well to explore this powerful help system. Recognize that it is virtually impossible to do justice to this help structure within the confines of the flat paper page. You need to use a computer to see the magic.

The opening screen is accessed by:

• Clicking on the Help icon

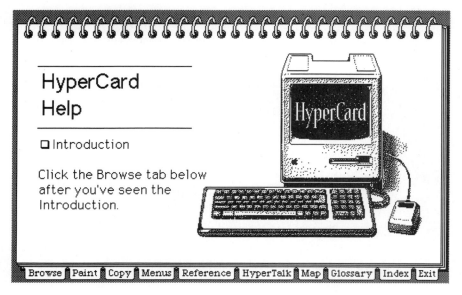

- Click on the map tab

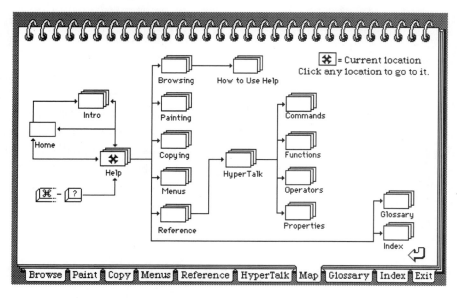

- Click on the glossary tab (or the glossary location icon)

  You can also go straight to the glossary by clicking on the glossary tab from the HyperCard help screen.

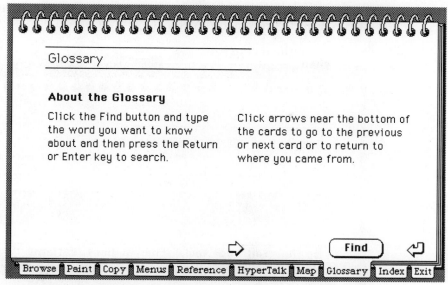

- Click on the Find Button

- Type: tool

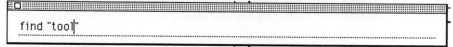

find "tool"

- Press RETURN

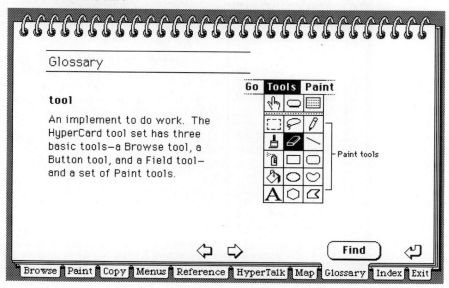

If you want to know about menus

- Click on the menus tab

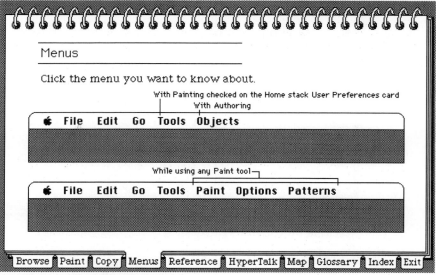

- Click on the edit keyword

Clicking on any keyword here will bring up information

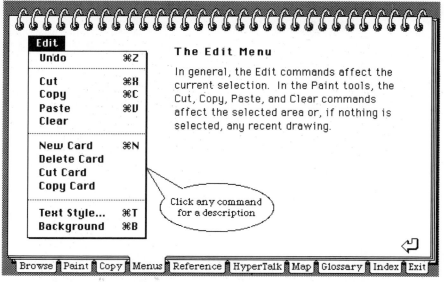

- Click on Copy Card

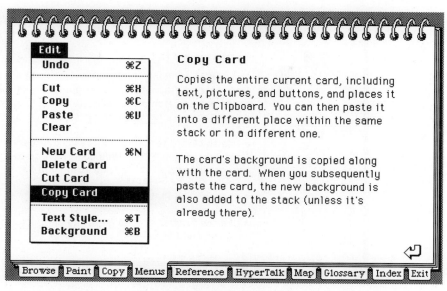

- Let's assume you want information on copying

- Click the Copy Tab

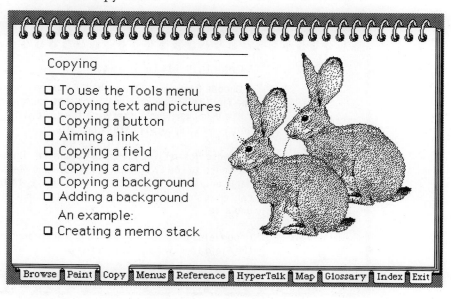

- Click on Copying a Field

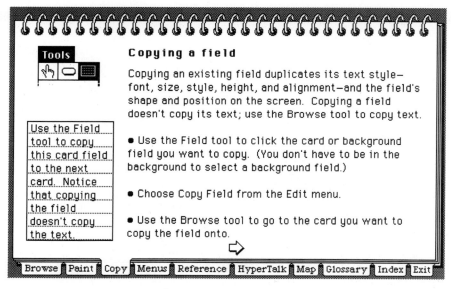

The arrow at the bottom of the screen indicates there's more information

- Click on the arrow.

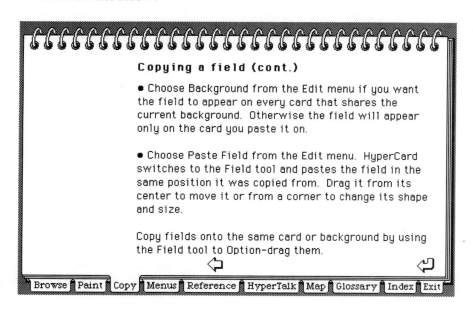

The screen below shows the context sensitive help screen for Microsoft Excel's excellent help display. It is a powerful help system well worth exploring. (While this example was taken from a MacIntosh, an almost identical view is found in the DOS Windows environment.)

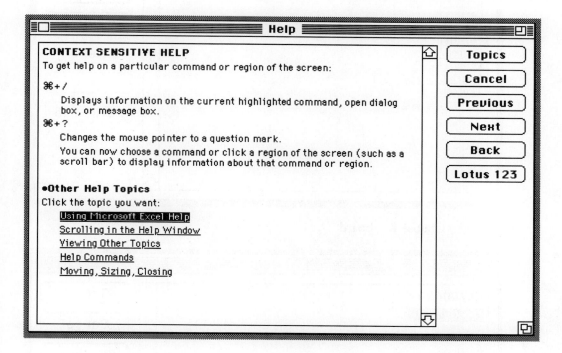

The Back Button remembers where you've been so you can step back along the help path you've been taking.

Let's step through some Excel screens.

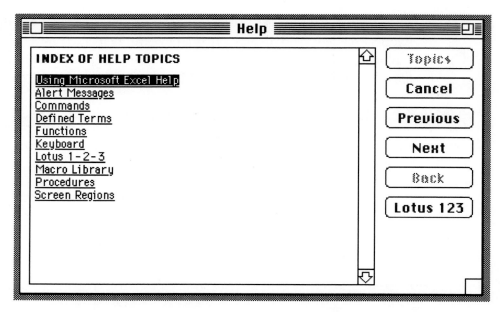

- Choose Keyboard

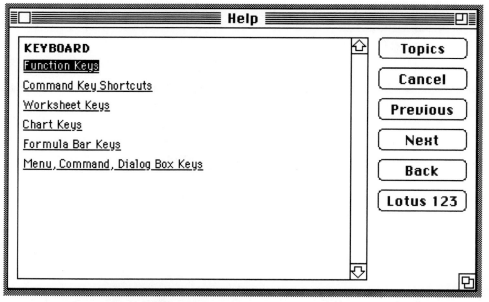

- Choose Worksheet Keys

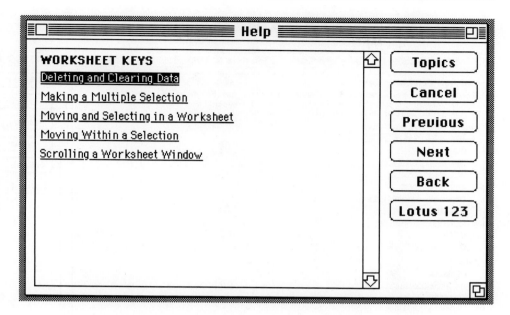

• Choose Moving Within a Selection

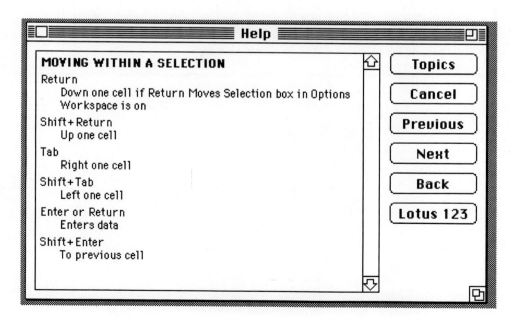

Excel provides this help index explanation:

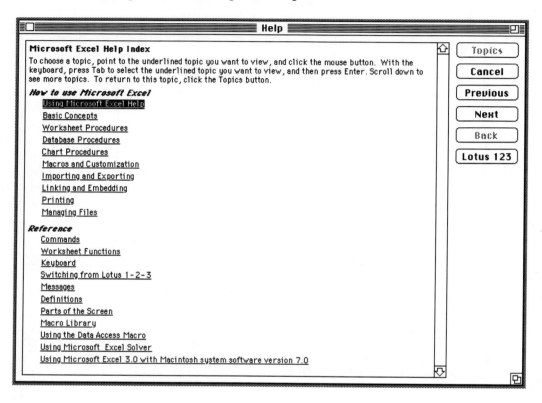

CHAPTER 8

On-line tutorials

Defining the on-line tutorial

An *on-line tutorial* is a learning tool.

A good tutorial is short and direct and allows a user to use the application in the way he would do in a real, live environment. It provides the basics. It's an introduction. It allows the user to make mistakes, knowing there is no risk to company operations. A tutorial takes the user through a part of an application in a step-by-step manner. It does not attempt to teach the user how to use the whole application. A tutorial may only explain the basics, or it may go further and cover advanced topics. It may include sample data and specially created tutorial files so the user accesses information as he would do on a live system.

Some tutorials have extensive text available on-screen, and some have a printed manual to be used with the on-screen tutorial. We can join tutorials and the subject of computer-assisted instruction together. If you want to get more specific, you might claim it's a tutorial if it has a printed manual accompanying it, and it's computer-aided instruction if it doesn't have a manual. Good definitions are hard to find here.

Whatever your definition, you are looking for much the same end result — a learning/teaching method based on interaction between user and the program. It should be very personal, almost like user and teacher working one-on-one together. (However, this does not mean that you should personalize the computer. The computer remains an IT.)

There are many fine examples of tutorials accompanying existing commercial products. However, the quality of tutorials produced for internal documentation is generally quite poor. This is unfortunate because the techniques and tools are available. What is usually missing in the in-house produced tutorials is the creativity needed to make the learning experience meaningful.

The key points

The key aspects of a tutorial can be covered by these points:

❑ The user must be taken through the tutorial in a series of steps.

❑ Explain what each step means, not only the how-to, but the why. If this means introducing a little corporate policy in order to explain a step, include that policy.

❑ Anticipate anywhere where the user might get off the track, and devise a way to bring the user back on track. If a user gets into trouble in a tutorial, it's your job to provide the steps necessary to get him out of trouble and back on course.

❑ Be sure to show — early on — how to exit the tutorial. Make it very clear where the user is going when he exits.

❑ Make extensive use of screens. The user should be able to look at the screen exactly as it exists in a live system. If there is a printed manual with the tutorial, use screen dumps or recreate the screen exactly as it appears. If windows appear within the screen, or overlapping background information, make sure this information is shown. Don't show the window alone.

❑ Be sure that any teaching text which appears on the tutorial screen is neatly set off from the screen itself so there is no question in the user's mind about what the real screen looks like.

❑ Define everything as you go along. If it is possible to have a glossary on standby, which can be accessed by a keystroke then use a glossary and make its availability obvious. Jargon must be dealt with early.

❏ Don't be too tough on the user. Coax the user along, rather than hitting him with a stick. Remember that the user is usually new to this subject and may be having difficulty understanding. Try to determine in advance what those difficulties may be and address them.

❏ Write the tutorial to a specific user profile and be consistent with that profile. At the same time recognize that if there is more than one profile group of users, there may be a need for more than one form of the same tutorial — using differing levels of language, or simpler or more complex design.

Length of the tutorial

Twenty minutes is about right. More than 30 minutes is hard to sustain. Less than 10 minutes and you are probably not making enough impact, although that's a subjective view.

Users prefer a number of small operations to a single large operation because they are following what is known as closure leading to relief. The mind likes to exercise memory, complete a task, reduce the memory load, and gain relief. *Closure* is the completion of a task leading to relief. The pressure for closure means preference is given to completing multiple small operations rather than a single, large operation.

The tutorial's printed manual

If possible, don't plan on using a printed manual with the tutorial, at least not with the actual teaching/learning activity. The reason for this is that you want to avoid a situation where the user is looking at a printed manual, then to the screen, then to the keyboard, then back to the screen, then back to the manual, and so forth. Most beginners have to look at the keyboard repeatedly.

Try to eliminate the manual so the user is going back and forth between keyboard and screen only.

Creating the tutorial

The first task in creating a tutorial is to write a scenario. It is important that the user be carrying out a task rather than be seen merely learning what certain keys do. The best tutorial develops the scenario so it includes a number of tutorials in an entire task.

One approach is to develop a storyboard, such as used in the movies. Each frame on the board shows a single action to be taken by the user, followed by a frame that shows the result of that action. Additional frames above and below the main story line accommodate wrong decisions taken by the user, and the appropriate frame showing the action of how to move back to the main storyline. The advantage of the storyboard is that you can quickly see if any steps have been omitted.

Keep the commentary strictly to the point. No asides or discussions or peripheral matters. For a new user, what is actually happening may be mysterious enough without introducing peripheral topics.

Be consistent in your approach. Pick a way of doing something and stick to it. Don't introduce some kind of advanced keystroking as an alternative. You don't need to show everything. You need to keep it simple so the user builds up his confidence in the system and his own skills in using that system.

If there are stretches of activity where the user would have to fill in a lot of information, repeating over and over what he has just learned, do it for him.

A good example is a spreadsheet. Let the user fill in a few cells, then let the computer fill in the rest. Explain to the user that you are helping by filling in the rest of the cells so that you can move on to the next activity to be done with the spreadsheet.

If you don't tell the user that you are filling in the cells for him, some day some clerk is going to fill in the first three cells because that's what was done in the tutorial, and then sit there waiting for the computer to fill in the rest of the cells.

Introduce the tutorial

Like a manual, a tutorial needs to be introduced before the user actually starts work with it. This introduction may either be on-screen or in printed form, but it should cover the following:

❏ What the user can expect to learn.

❏ How the tutorial is structured.

❏ Where to start.

  The tutorial may offer one starting point for a beginner, and a second starting point for more advanced users.

❏ If necessary, there should be discussion of what the basic configuration of the user's computer system should be, and what additional materials might be needed — extra backup disk, notepad.

❏ Point out the topics not included in the tutorial and where that information can be found — in other words, point at the reference and any other manuals, two-fold reference cards, and so forth.

❏ If the tutorial has more than one part, have a table of contents covering the whole tutorial.

  This assists in the teaching process by providing anticipation about where the tutorial is taking the user.

❑ Each section of a tutorial should have its own introduction, much as would be done in a manual

However, it is important to remember that a computer screen — if you are writing directly to screen — is not a page in a manual. The characteristics are different and the way a user reads a screen is different. (Review the commentary in chapter 7.)

❑ Of course, there should also be a summary at the end of the exercise. The summary can be a list, or in the form of a quiz. The summary helps reinforce what the user has learned.

Test the tutorial

Always test the tutorial with a select group of users before releasing it for general use. The testing process allows you to refine the flow of the tutorial and to discover if there are any areas where users can go off course.

What next?

When the user is finished the tutorial, he should be told where to go next. Has the tutorial prepared the user to move to the live system? Has the tutorial prepared the user for some intermediate training stage on the way to the live system?

An example

Microsoft Excel calls its tutorial a tour. It is a fine example of what can be done to assist the user. The following pages step through only one part of this excellent example. It is a model worth studying. Space here does not permit a full showing, but the screens will provide an indication of what can be done by documentation writers and designers working with creativity and an obvious knowledge of how the application works.

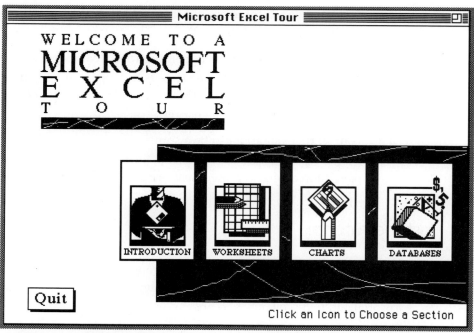

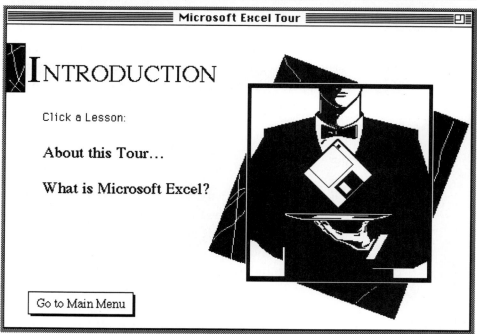

ABOUT THIS TOUR...

Welcome to this tour of Microsoft Excel.

The three buttons below appear throughout the tour.
Clicking them will move you through the tour in various ways.

The Previous Arrow   **The Help Button**   **The Next Arrow**

Click the Next arrow to move forward.

Microsoft Excel Tour

Clicking the Next arrow, as you've already
discovered, moves you forward one step.

Similarly, clicking the Previous arrow moves
you back a step if you wish to review.

The Help button displays a set of Course Controls.

Click the Help button to proceed.

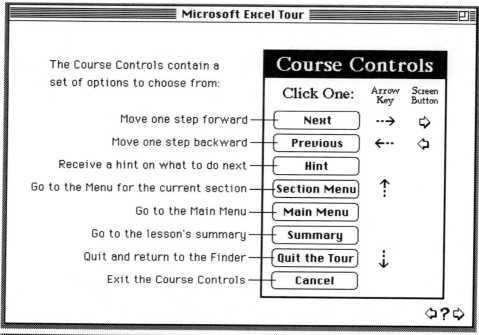

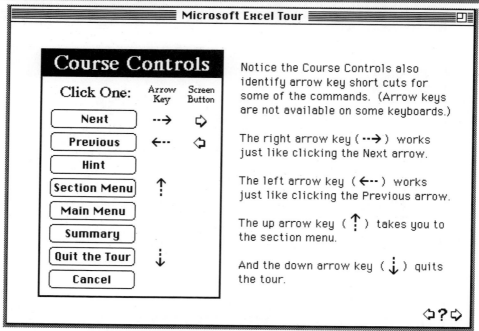

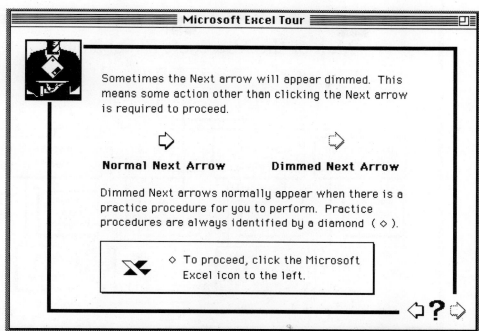

Sometimes the Next arrow will appear dimmed. This means some action other than clicking the Next arrow is required to proceed.

Normal Next Arrow   **Dimmed Next Arrow**

Dimmed Next arrows normally appear when there is a practice procedure for you to perform. Practice procedures are always identified by a diamond (◇).

◇ To proceed, click the Microsoft Excel icon to the left.

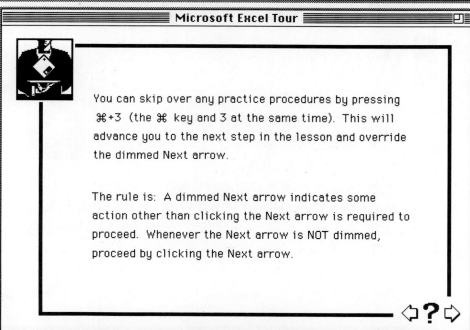

You can skip over any practice procedures by pressing ⌘+3 (the ⌘ key and 3 at the same time). This will advance you to the next step in the lesson and override the dimmed Next arrow.

The rule is: A dimmed Next arrow indicates some action other than clicking the Next arrow is required to proceed. Whenever the Next arrow is NOT dimmed, proceed by clicking the Next arrow.

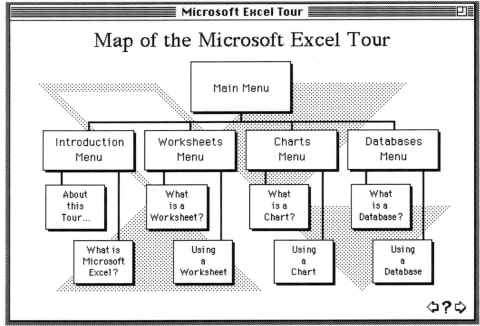

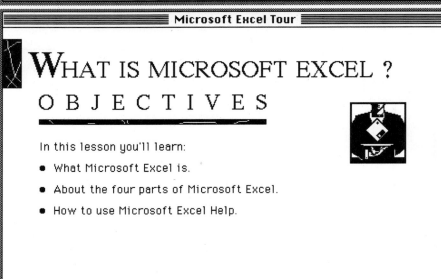

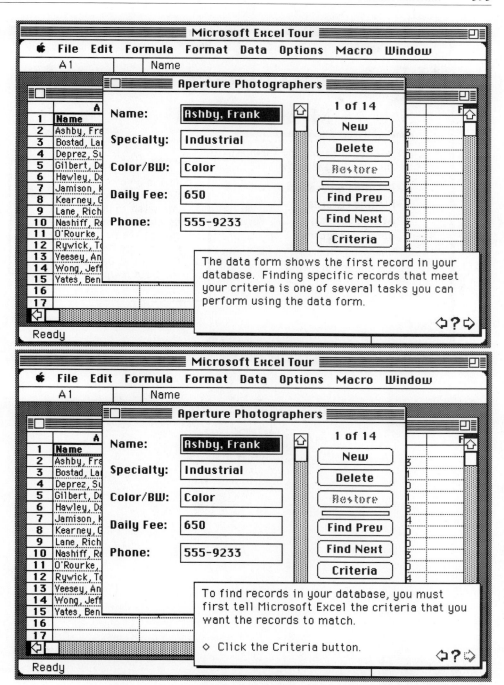

Microsoft Excel Tour

File Edit Formula Format Data Options Macro Window

A1   Name

Aperture Photographers

Name:	Ashby, Frank
Specialty:	Industrial
Color/BW:	Color
Daily Fee:	650
Phone:	555-9233

1 of 14

New
Delete
Restore
Find Prev
Find Next
Criteria

	A
1	**Name**
2	Ashby, Fra
3	Bostad, La
4	Deprez, Su
5	Gilbert, De
6	Hawley, Da
7	Jamison, K
8	Kearney, G
9	Lane, Rich
10	Nashiff, Re
11	O'Rourke,
12	Rywick, Te
13	Yeesey, An
14	Wong, Jeff
15	Yates, Ben
16	
17	

The data form shows the first record in your database. Finding specific records that meet your criteria is one of several tasks you can perform using the data form.

Ready

Microsoft Excel Tour

File Edit Formula Format Data Options Macro Window

A1   Name

Aperture Photographers

Name:	Ashby, Frank
Specialty:	Industrial
Color/BW:	Color
Daily Fee:	650
Phone:	555-9233

1 of 14

New
Delete
Restore
Find Prev
Find Next
Criteria

	A
1	**Name**
2	Ashby, Fra
3	Bostad, La
4	Deprez, Su
5	Gilbert, De
6	Hawley, Da
7	Jamison, K
8	Kearney, G
9	Lane, Rich
10	Nashiff, Re
11	O'Rourke,
12	Rywick, Te
13	Yeesey, An
14	Wong, Jeff
15	Yates, Ben
16	
17	

To find records in your database, you must first tell Microsoft Excel the criteria that you want the records to match.

◇ Click the Criteria button.

Ready

≡ **Microsoft Excel Tour** ≡

Using a Database

S U M M A R Y

Click a topic to see its summary
in the summary window:

✓ Defining a database
  Finding records
  Adding records
  Deleting records
  Changing records
  Saving and printing

——— DEFINING A DATABASE ———

To define a database:
1) Select the worksheet data
   you wish to define as a
   database. (Include an empty
   row at the bottom for an
   expandable database.)
2) Choose Set Database from
   the Data menu.

⇦ **?** ⇨

CHAPTER 9

The style guide

An indispensable guide

Documentation should never read like a mystery novel with secrets that will be revealed later in the story. The user faces enough problems without having to try to understand those unknowns that the documentation writer could have assisted with.

Developing a style guide is critical to the final success of effective documentation. I remain mystified why more organizations don't have style guides already in place. The use of a style guide goes far beyond documentation. It can be used across the whole organization, in administration, in marketing, and within information technology documentation.

The style guide merely provides guidelines for usage, and includes the organization's chosen styles for each of the following.

- ❏ terminology — for consistency in using jargon
- ❏ spelling — of hard words, and words where there is a choice
- ❏ company and product names
- ❏ problem words
- ❏ abbreviations — first mention, subsequent mentions
- ❏ acronyms — first mention, subsequent mentions
- ❏ quotations marks — single or double
- ❏ italics
- ❏ numbers and symbols
- ❏ punctuation
- ❏ lists — punctuation, capitalization
- ❏ headings
- ❏ captions, figures, and tables

A style guide may be created for a single documentation project, or you might have a corporate style guide, to which you add specific problems of documentation where styles are required, such as:

❏ special typefaces for screen representation and screen messages

❏ function key description (F1 or f1 or Func 1 or Fk 1)

❏ warnings

❏ header and footer style

❏ steps in procedures (• or Step 1 or 1 or ①)

With the style guide playing such an important role, I have chosen to provide a number of pages from a relatively simple style guide we use for the development of a new client's documentation.

This guide, shown on the following pages, is meant as an example only. The sign of the professional documentation writer is to know when to vary from the style guide. Unless you have a good reason, stick to the published version.

XYZ Company

Style and Standards Guide

for

User Documentation

Read Me First

The XYZ Company Style and Standards Guide is meant to provide a base document against which XYZ Company documentation can be prepared and measured. This guides provides some rules to assist in the design, writing, and management of documentation.

When you have a question about the style of some aspect of documentation, this guide should be able to provide an answer. If you have a question that isn't answered here, then record the decision that is made and incorporate it into this guide to assist the next person who asks the same question. In other words, this guide is meant to be a growing, maturing document. No style guide can cover every eventuality. Sooner or later, you'll come across something not covered here which requires a unique solution. Don't feel constrained by the rules here to the detriment of your own creativity. However, these are the basics and unless you have a good reason to do otherwise, stick to these basics.

This guide assumes that you are, at the least, a technical writer who wants to become a user documentation writer. There is a significant difference between the two. One interprets technical details for technical readers; the second interprets technical detail for non-technical readers. Writing for nontechnical users requires careful judgment and choice in terms of language and layout.

This guide is in two parts:

Part One takes you through the primary concerns you must have in order to get started.

Part Two consists of an alphabetical listing of general considerations such as special spellings, hyphenated words, common grammatical mistakes and so forth.

Contents

Steps in a Procedure
  Simple procedures
  Numbering steps

Screens and Windows
  Captions

Structure of Manuals
  Introduction
  Title page
  Legal pages
  Foreword
  Contents page(s)
  Introduction section
  Body sections
  Appendices
  Index

PART TWO

Introduction

General Considerations
  An alphabetical listing of common questions
  and concerns encountered in the preparation of
  documentation.

Keys

Miscellaneous
  Acronyms
  "Affect and Effect"
  Enter, type, and press
  Hardware and software
  Hyphenation for words
  Mode

PART ONE

Introduction

XYZ Company products work well, look good, and command respect in the marketplace. The minimum requirement of XYZ Company documentation must be to match the physical product. Documentation must work well, look good, and command respect in the marketplace.

Objectives of XYZ Company documentation

The objective of XYZ Company documentation is to meet these basic requirements of effective documentation:

❏ the information in the documentation is easy to find

❏ the information in the documentation is easy to comprehend

❏ the information is up-to-date, reflecting the latest changes and revision

❏ the information is reliable (as in "able to be relied upon") and convincing

Definition of the user

It is important to have an image of the user of the product in mind when the manual is written. We might define the manual in two ways, with priority on the first:

❏ users who are nontechnical, who use the computer as *just another tool* in carrying out their daily tasks

❏ users who are technically minded, who use the computer as more than a mere tool, or perhaps as their main tool

Which user is the manual for?

If marketing defines the market-target user as primarily nontechnical, then the emphasis of the manual should match. If the product is marketed to computer professionals, then the manual may be technically oriented.

There is an important difference between technical writing and user writing. The easiest way to lose a nontechnical user is to produce a technical manual for that user. Defining the users is important in terms of deciding the style of writing and level of jargon to be used in the manual.

The Page

This section describes the physical dimensions of the page and the physical size of the main elements that make up the page.

Introduction

A basic requirement is that the writing and layout proceed together. It is extremely difficult to create an effective piece of documentation if the layout features are not put in place as the writing is proceeding. The writer does not need to worry about not being a layout artist, or a graphic artist. By following this style guide, those decisions have been made for you.

Modern word processing and desktop publishing applications such as PageMaker provide an environment in which the art director and writer function can be combined. It is not time consuming to do the two tasks together. In fact, the contribution made to the overall effectiveness of the documentation is far outweighed by any minor inconvenience.

At the editing and proofreading stages, the entire manual can be reviewed. The Look needs to be edited and proofed as well as the actual words. All XYZ Company manuals should have pages that look like they have been designed by the same designer — in the same way that the text should appear to have been written by the same writer.

Physical dimensions

The physical dimensions of the page should be:

Outside Trim (for Production)

   19 cm wide x 23 cm deep

Heading Text Area (A column)

   4.5 cm wide x 18.7 cm deep

Body Text Area (B column)

   10 cm wide x 18.7 cm deep

Boxes

The most effective box is placed in B column and indented 2 cm on each side.

Screens and Windows

Screens should be sized as most appropriate to contain the information needed. A 10 cm-wide screen in B column is most effective, but often too small to be useful. Expanding that screen size to 12 cm or 13 cm works well. In this case, the right side of the screen should line up with the right margin of B column and the screen allowed to "hang into" the A column. The least effective screen is the one that cuts the page in half by stretching the full width of the A and B columns.

Tables

Wherever possible tables should be made to fit within the B column. If necessary to go outside the B column, the same thoughts apply as discussed in Screens.

Tables should be consistent throughout the manual. If they are all within the B column and centered, then make sure they are *all* centered. If they are flush right within the B column, then have them *all* flush right.

White space

The page must never look too dense, dark, or complicated. The easiest way to avoid this problem is to make sure there is adequate white space on the page.

This white space comes between headings and body text, between lines and paragraphs. It comes from not *cramming* too much on a page.

Fonts and Styles

In this section is information about font (typefaces) and the styles of various headings, body text, notes, and warnings.

Section headings

Section Headings: Avant Garde 18 point caps (not bold) B column, flush right

FOR NEW USERS

Text headings (A column)

Text Headings: Garamond 3 bold (A column, flush right)

$$\text{Heading level 1 - 14 point}$$

$$\text{Heading level 2 - 12 point}$$

$$\text{Heading level 3 - 11 point}$$

If it is necessary to use a level 4 and level 5 heading, they should be placed in the B column as a single line, flush left, still as Garamond 3 Bold.

Heading level number 4 - 12 point

Heading level number 5 - 11 point

The hierarchy of headings can be easily determined from the contents page (which acts as your architect's blueprint for the building of the manual).

Body text (B column)

Body text: Garamond 3, 11 point (Justified)

After installing FaxNet, you have computer fax capabilities on your local area network — for text and graphics. You can install one, two or three FaxNet cards and be licensed to connect more than 50 user workstations to your FaxNet network.

Style: Garamond 3, 11 point, auto leading

Body (bullet •) text

Action statements and lists make use of the bullet style.

To send a fax using a network processor:

• Log on to your network

• Load WordPerfect

• Display the document you want to fax

• This is body bullet text style and shows the indent for the second and subsequent lines.

Style: Garamond 3, 11 point, auto leading, second line is indented 5 mm. The bullet is set (Option-8 in Times and Garamond 3), then tab (5 mm) to start of sentence. Space before is 3 point.

Further tabs can be set at 5 mm intervals to provide a stepped hierarchy if needed. For example:

- Use the Up/Dn arrow keys to highlight the file you want in the file window — <R>

    - Press Esc to exit without making a selection

Key words

Key words: Avant Garde 9 point

Some discretion should be shown here. The intent is to make sure the user picks up on key words, commands, options, and so forth that appear in the body copy. However, overuse will nullify the effect.

Be careful not to repeat your header and footer information. This will occur if you use both the Letter To Fax option and the INCLUDE statement.

Be careful not to use Avant Garde when Courier is called for, as discussed next.

Screen text

Words on the Screen/in a Window: Courier 10 point

Courier has been chosen to represent, in the manual, words appearing on the screen or in a window. What is needed is a typeface that most closely matches the nonproportional typeface used on the screen. Courier is the most common nonproportional typeface and works well for this purpose. Courier should be used:

❑ where you type word(s)

❑ where you show a screen message

❑ on all screens and windows

For example:

To do this, follow these steps:

- Type: `FaxNet — <R>`

A message will be displayed:

```
Phone directory changed, save Y/N?
```

Or with a menu:

```
1 - Send Fax

2 - Receive

3 - View/Edit file

4 - Print

5 - Convert

6 - Configuration

7 - Shell to DOS

Esc - Exit to DOS
```

Or with a window:

```
F:\USERS\JANE\FAX_OUT\PLANS.FAX
```

Notes

Notes are in Garamond 3, in Style BB+, with a 12 point Zapf Dingbat in place of the normal bullet.

The Zapf Dingbat is produced by pressing the Shift-+ keys, which creates a ☞

☞ Although it is recommended, you do not have to include the filename. However, you *must* include the phone number in your document.

The use of the 12 point Zapf Dingbat requires a change to Style BB by placing the TAB at 7 mm, rather than the normal 5 mm. This is to accommodate the 12 point Zapf Dingbat.

Warnings

While notes can be used as often as needed — subject to the rules of overuse — warnings should be used only when it is truly needed to WARN the user. Overuse of the warning has the same effect as the little boy who cried wolf once too often.

The style for a warning is a box and Avant Garde 10 point, as in this example:

WARNING

Handle the FaxNet Card by its edges only.

Many of the components in the FaxNet Card are sensitive to static electricity.

Discharge any static electricity in your body by touching a metal object such as a metal filing cabinet or metal door handle.

Headers and Footers

The header should contain the name of the section. It should be set in Garamond 3 Italic 10 point. The footer should contain the name of the manual and the page number:

- set the name in Garamond bold italic 10 point
- set the page number in Garamond bold 12 point

Italics

As a general rule, italic typeface should be used in body text for emphasis. Overuse should be avoided. A rule of thumb is that any more than two uses of italics for emphasis on a single page should be questioned carefully.

Bold

Boldface type should be kept for headings and occasional uses as defined in this guide, such as the name of the manual and page number. Use of boldface in body text should be avoided.

Captions

Captions should be set in Garamond 3 italics 11 point and centered under the graphic — be it a menu, screen, table, or drawing. It should be a simple descriptive note and, wherever possible, should be only a single line, with no full stop. For example:

Fax Server Configuration Showing Default

Fax Server Main Menu

The Text

This section covers capitalization and page numbering.

Need for consistency

The need here is for XYZ Company documentation to look and read as if it has all been written by one super writer. While the style of expression and choice of words has some bearing on this, it is most important that the writing be consistent.

That consistency comes from word choice, sentence structure, grammar and spelling, and the method of explaining things. After the first few pages of a manual, the user should feel quite at home and there should be no sudden changes in the ways things are being done. Or, if there is a change— such as a section of Standard Page Layouts, an example of which is shown on the facing page — then this change should be signaled and explained as early as the Foreword where some comment has been made on the structure of the manual.

The feeling in XYZ Company user guides should be: "You (the user) and Me (the writer)".

Capitalization

The intent is to use capital letters as seldom as possible. However, where lowercase letters may be confusing to the reader, a capped letter should be used. Different parts of the manual have slightly different rules. For example, the rules covering the use of caps and lowercase may vary from body text to headings. The primary requirement is *understanding* by the user.

Body Text

The names of things specific

Initial caps should be used on specific entities which could be misinterpreted by the user if not capped. This is particularly important in the case of options, commands and so forth which, if left in lowercase, may convey the wrong sense For example:

Local Command State

Escape Sequence

the fourth Number Directory entry

the Answer Tone Sequence command enables you

the DTR (Data Terminal Ready) signal is

the S Register setting

(but "this register is the")

will disable the Inactivity Timer

(but "the inactivity time expired")

Local Analog Loopback test

A style must also be set for *computer* words, thus our style is all CAPS for words of this type:

\USERS\USERNAME\FAX_OUT

\USERS\USERNAME\FAX_IN

\USERS\USERNAME\TEMP

CAPTURE L=2 Q=QFAX TI=5

ENDCAP

COMPANY.FAX

PHONE.DIR

```
?DIRECTORY_NAME
NPRINT NEWONE.DOC Q=QFAX
F:\USERS\JANE\FAX_OUT\LOGO.FAX
```
in the fax server's FAX_OUT directory

in FAXNET, FAX_OUT, FAXMAIL subdirectories

Headings

Key words have initial cap letter, even if they are lowercase in the main body text. For example:

"the FaxNet menu system is used to"

but the A column heading would be:

"Using the FaxNet Menu System"

Some rules:

Capitalize prepositions of four letters or more:

About, With, From, Between

Don't capitalize coordinating conjunctions:

and, but, or, for, nor, yet, so, or articles: a, an, the

Captions:

Same as for Headings

Some examples:

How FaxNet Software Works

Receiving and Printing Faxes

Using Phone Directories

Introduction

Quick Start for Experienced Users

For New Users

Appendices   (plural is not Appendixes)

Appendix A

Contents page

The rules for capitalization on the Contents page follow the same rules as laid down for headings.

Page numbering

Page numbering should be as simple as possible. Very seldom is there a good enough reason to break the straightforward 1, 2, 3, 4, 5 and so forth straight from front to back of the manual.

No page numbers should be placed on foreword, legal or contents pages. Normally, page 1 should be the first page of section one, which is usually the introduction. However, with a special manual like the XYZ Company Reference Guide, page numbering can be done by section. In this case the name of the section should be repeated in the footer close to the page number.

Steps in a Procedure

Careful attention must be given to the writing and display of steps in a procedure. Clarity is essential and the easiest way to produce clarity is to break procedures down to their most basic parts.

Simple Procedures

For a simple three-step procedure, the bullet style is the most simple. For more complicated procedures, the steps should be numbered and the bullets used to clarify activity within the numbered step.

Each action statement should be set on a line by itself, and any discussion needed should be set on an indented line below the action statement.

For example:

To use the Select Phone option:

- Log on to your network

- Type: `FaxNet`

  Your Main Menu will be displayed.

- Press 1

  The Send Fax menu will be displayed.

- Press 5

  The Select Phone window will be displayed.

- Type in the destination phone number — <R>

  You will be returned to the Send Fax menu and the destination phone number will appear in the bottom right of the screen.

Note the use of Courier 10 point font to indicate something typed, and the use of Avant Garde 9 point font to define key words.

Note also that there is no punctuation (no full stop) at the end of the action statements. Leaving out the punctuation avoids any confusion about what must be typed. There are a number of occasions when a full stop could be confused with a character or number sequence to be typed. For example:

- Include the following line at the end of your document:

  `<*INC:D:\PBRUSH\SIGNED.FAX.>`

Numbering steps

When there are a number of steps, or steps have substeps within them, use a numbering system. To make the numbers stand out, we use Zapf Dingbat 12 point numbers:

Option U	①
Option =	②
Sh-Op '	③
Sh-Op O	④
Option 5	⑤
Sh-Op =	⑥
Option ,	⑦
Option .	⑧
Option Y	⑨
Option M	⑩
Shift +	☞
Shift S	✳

Screens and Windows

Screens, or parts of screens, should represent what the user truly sees. However, if the topic being dealt with is merely a window on a screen, it should be referred to as a window and only the window needs to be shown. Details covering the use of the Courier typeface are found in Screen Text above.

Captions (for screens and windows)

Captions for screens and windows should be specific.

Avoid using figure and table, unless there is a specific need for such a reference. If the graphic is used on a page, or on the previous or next page, then the reference should say so.

Using the words "in the screen below" is more user-friendly than a reference to Fig. 1.

As discussed earlier, captions should be set in Garamond 3 italics 11 point and centered under the graphic — be it menu, screen, drawing, or table.

The caption should be a simple descriptive note and, wherever possible, should be only a single line, with no full stop. For example:

Fax Server Configuration Showing Default

Fax Server Main Menu

Structure of Manuals

The structure of manuals for XYZ Company should follow a similar pattern wherever possible. Of course, the content often determines the structure. For example, the structure of the XYZ Company Reference Guide both in design and writing is quite different from the FaxNet guide.

However, the following basic structure should be used as a guide:

Title page

Copyright/disclaimer/trademarks page

Warranty registration page

Legal page

Foreword (Read Me First) page

Contents page(s)

Introduction (or first section)

Body sections

Appendices (general topics as needed)

Appendix: Specifications

Appendix: the ASCII table

Appendix: the glossary

Index

Title

The title should be straightforward and straight to the point. The word "guide" is preferred over "manual".

FaxNet User's Guide   (in italics when complete reference, but "this guide" when general reference)

Legal pages

Copyright/trademarks page
Warranty registration page
Legal (disclaimer) page

These pages are quite uniform, but must be reviewed from time to time to make sure they are up to date. The legal (disclaimer) page must not be changed without senior management approval because of the legal implications of the wording.

Foreword

Every manual should have a foreword or preface. If you have doubts that it will be read, put a major heading on the page: "Read Me First".

The foreword briefly introduces the product and the manual. It tells the user what he can expect from the manual. It should tell the user who the writer expects the user to be. In other words, if installation and configuration require a significant level of computer knowledge beyond what the normal user will be expected to have, the foreword will make this clear so the user does not become turned off as he reads the installation and configuration procedures. The foreword should be short — one page maximum.

Contents page(s)
Use Contents (not Table of Contents)

The contents page(s) is the blueprint of the manual. It is not complete until it has been reviewed and approved. Do not start writing until the contents page is locked in.

The initial contents at the front of the manual should be kept to three pages or less. If it is necessary to go over three pages, then consideration should be given to inserting a sectional contents at the beginning of each section, or major section, throughout the manual.

For example: In the XYZ Company Reference Guide, we put the Contents at the beginning of the manual but it was running long so we decided to list all the commands and S registers in a separate contents page at the start of the relevant sections on commands and S registers.

Try to keep the hierarchy to three levels or less:

Level 1 topics 22
Level 2 topics 24
Level 3 topics 26

Introduction section

The first section of the manual should be introductory. It should introduce the product, provide some features and benefits, a list of needed equipment, any special details about the rest of the manual, a list of conventions or symbols, and perhaps a list of Acronyms if required. The section should be short and to the point. There is no need to provide a detailed overview of every section of the manual, unless the manual is to be used as a formal textbook. It is unlikely that any XYZ Company manual will be used as a textbook.

Body sections

Body sections should flow smoothly as a result of getting the Contents structure in place. Be sure to unveil the story in a logical form. Talk about creating, before you worry about saving. If there is a log in procedure, be sure to follow it immediately with details about logging out.

Do not start the manual with installation, which is usually only done once. It should be contained in an appendix at the back of the manual so users will not have to wade through it every time they open the manual.

Appendices

The appendices should be made up of subjects that are important enough to be included but which will break the flow of information if included in the body sections of the manual. For example, in the FaxNet manual there is a discussion of how to create personalized fonts for use in faxes. One place to put that is in the manual under preparing faxes for sending. However, it is not a subject that *must* be dealt with in the normal flow of preparing and sending faxes and thus it is better off as an extra.

Other appendices include:

- ❏ specifications
- ❏ glossary
- ❏ the ASCII table

Index

A manual without an index is next to useless, but a manual with an index that is not complete is both useless and frustrating. Be sure to do the index as one of the last tasks. To do it earlier is a waste of time because of the risk of page numbering changes.

Avoid sending the user on a trail of references in order to come up with a workable definition. Avoid referring the user to other places in the manual if it is possible to include the definition where the user first looks.

Punctuation of index entries:

- Cap the first letter
- No comma after an entry (unless entry is qualified)
- No period or other punctuation

For example:

Disk 15

Key, Security 56

Use *see* to refer the user to an entry you have chosen as the *standard* entry from a *nonstandard* entry.

Use *see also* to refer a user to a topic that is related to the standard entry.

Be sure to budget time to do the index well. It is not a small task, and it is not an easy task.

PART TWO

Introduction
This section covers some of the more common questions that arise in documentation preparation.

The standard for XYZ Company spelling is the *Webster's New Ideal Dictionary*.

General considerations

A

all right (not alright)

alter   (change things, don't alter them)

any time (not anytime)

appendices (not appendixes)

Arrow keys

auto-reliable

auto-repeat (with hyphenation)

B

back panel (not backpanel)

back up (when used as a verb)

Backspace key (use DELETE)

backup (when used as a noun or adjective)

backward (not backwards)

BAT

because (use instead of *since* in cause-effect relationship)

bit (as in "then bit 7 of S Register 39 must be")

black-and-white

bps (bits per second)

built-in (hyphenate when used as an adjective)

C

Capture command

Card (as in specific reference to PC Fax Card...)

card (as in peripheral card; the card)

carrier signal

change (change things, don't alter them)

COM1 (not com1 or Com1)

command (the Find command; the View command)

configuration (no cap)

Contents   (not Table of Contents)

cursor control keys

D

d/Bm

database (one word)

Delete key (*see* backspace key)

different from (not "different than")

differently than (not "differently from")

DIR

Down-Arrow key

dpi (dots per inch)

drive D: (not Drive D:)

due to (use "because of")

due to the fact that (use "because")

E

e.g. (use "for example")

enable (don't overuse: use allow, permit)

enter (as in enter data; see enter, type and press under "Miscellaneous")

Error codes

Esc key

Etc. (use "and so forth", or "and so on")

EXE

F

facilitate (avoid; use help, make easier)

Family (as in "the SmartModem Family of products")

family (as in "the modem family is made up of")

fax (not facsimile)

Faxin Journal

FaxNet menu system

FaxNet Supervisor

Faxout Journal

fewer (use with individual items; less with quantity/bulk)

Fig. (as in Figure 3 — avoid using)

file *type* (two words: data file, source file, work file)

filename (one word)

finish (used by people: people *finish*, things *are done*) following (adj., n., v.; not preposition — use "after")

G

guide (lowercase when not in the formal full title)

this guide (preferable form over "the guide")

H

hex (not Hex, use hexadecimal in first reference)

highlight (in action statement: • highlight the option.)

highlighted (as in "the option will be highlighted")

I

IBM PCs (no apostrophe)

ID (not Id or id)

implement (avoid; use "do", "use")

in order to   (use: "to")

input (don't use as verb; use enter or type)

installation (no cap)

inverse (as in screen display; not inverted)

Issue commands (see enter, type, and press under "Miscellaneous")

it (avoid; use a specific word or phrase)

K

Keys

L

left corner (upper left corner, not left *hand* corner)

Left-Arrow key

less (use with quantity/bulk; *fewer* with individual items)

licensed

line feed (two words)

logo (not LOGO)

low resolution (as a noun)

low-resolution (as an adjective)

lowercase (not lower-case or lower case)

M

MAKEFAX

minimize (avoid; use "lower", "reduce", "decrease")

MNP

motherboard (avoid; use "main logic board")

N

XYZ Company Customer Support Department

O

off-line

on-line

on-line Help (not On-Line Help)

operating system (no caps in general reference)

option (not Option)

output (n., adj; never use as a verb)

owing to the fact that (use "because of")

P

page (as in "see page 2")

PageMaker

PEP (Packetized Ensemble Protocol)

percent (in data use % sign)

percent (in text, write out "percent")

PgDn key

port (as in "the communications port is used to")

power cord (not power cable)

press keys   (nonprintable keys; *see* enter, type, and press under
  "Miscellaneous")

product name (caps, no quotation marks, as WordStar)

Protocol Convertor (in reference to specific device)

protocol (as in "the protocol is needed to")

Q

QFAX

quotation marks (avoid wherever possible, use italics)

R

random access memory (use RAM after first reference)

read-only memory (use ROM after first reference)

reappear

redial

redialing

reloaded (no hyphen)

replicate (avoid; use copy)

retransmit (no hyphen)

RETURN key (preferred over ENTER key)

RETURN key (usually as — <R> in 'and press Return')

right corner (upper right corner, not right *hand* corner)

Right-Arrow key

S

semicolon (;)

SENDFAX

since (use "because")

standalone (one word)

subdirectory

submenu

symbol (do not use to mean character, letter, digit)

T

Tab key

table (as in Table 1; avoid wherever possible)

table of contents (*see* Contents)

this (avoid, use a specific word or phrase)

throughput

toward (not towards)

troubleshoot (as a verb, one word)

troubleshooting (as a noun, one word)

type characters/words (*see* enter, type, and press in "Miscellaneous")

U

Up-Arrow key

uppercase (n., adj.; not upper case or upper-case)

user's (not User's)

utility (not Utility)

W

word processing (two words)

WordPerfect

WordStar

work file (two words)

wrap around (verb)

wraparound (noun, adjective)

X

X scale (not X-scale)

Z

zero (as in "contain a zero value")

zeros (zeroes)

Miscellaneous

9-pin connector (better than DB-9)

Keys

The style for the use of keys is as follows:

Arrow keys

Down-Arrow key

Esc key

Left-Arrow key

PgDn key

PgUp key

RETURN and ENTER keys (use <R> in action line)

Right-Arrow key

Spacebar

Tab key

Up-Arrow key

When two keys are pressed together:

Control-D

When three keys are pressed together:

Control-Shift-D

When two keys are pressed, but not necessarily together:

Esc N

Miscellaneous

Some general comments on issues that surface from time to time.

Acronyms

When forming the plural of an acronym without full stops inserts, do not add an apostrophe before the **s**, as in: PABX and PABXs, or PC and PCs.

"Affect" and "Effect"

When used as a verb, *affect* means to influence. As a noun, *affect* is best avoided. *Effect* as a verb is rarely used and means to cause. *Effect* as a noun is more common and means result.

Enter, type, and press

Enter data

Type words and characters

Press keys

Issue commands

Hardware and software

If a printer is the only peripheral outside of normal hardware/software needs, then list the printer under hardware and avoid a special heading of "peripheral".

Hyphenation for words

The general acceptance is to hyphenate two words when those words modify the noun as a unit, when confusion might result if the hyphen was left out, or when one of the words is a past or present participle, or when the two modifiers include a number or single letter, as in the following examples:

read-only memory

machine-language program

D-shaped connector

80-column display

Do not hyphenate two words when one is *very* or an adverb that ends in *ly*, as in:

newly completed program

very good response time

Mode

A state of the system that determines the system's response to users' actions. Avoid when not absolutely necessary. *High-resolution graphics* is preferred to *high-resolution graphics mode.* You enter or leave a mode, not turn on or turn off a mode.

CHAPTER 10

The corporate strategy report

The corporate strategy report

A documentation strategy report is a document that provides the answers to all the questions that need to be answered before the documentation task can be efficiently undertaken.

Unless you are an experienced documentation writer, you will need to go through the exercise of preparing a documentation strategy report. If this is done properly, you will not be wasting any time because the strategy report will save time (and money) as you set about the task.

You do not need a strategy report if:

❏ you, and your supervisor, have a clear definition of the documentation you need

❏ the task is small enough to be seen as a whole

❏ the costing and time resources are clearly understood and accepted

❏ the production method is clearly understood

Where the task requires a number of manuals, or a mix of documentation tools in a documentation set, the strategy report becomes even more important.

Let's look at a real example. The material that follows comes from a strategy report prepared for a large mining company. There were numerous sites across the country, and many users split into specific user groups. Each user group required manuals specific to its job functions. There were dozens of menus and hundreds of options that had to be documented.

Summary of Recommendations and Suggestions

The page reference following the recommendation or suggestions refers to the page in the report where it is discussed in more detail. We recommend:

That manuals be produced in accordance with the site by site lists produced in this report and with the physical characteristics as defined in this report. (Part 2, page 5; Part 5, page 25)

That manuals be produced in a page size of 22 cm deep by 19 cm wide, in a three-D-ring binder, with two types of paper — one for use in dirty locations and one for use in clean work areas. (Part 3, page 16)

That a guide be prepared, as part of the documentation task, covering the topic of interfaces between the system and other applications. (Part 2, page 7)

That a guide be prepared, as part of the documentation task, covering an introduction to the system and serving as a Getting Acquainted reference tool for new employees. (Part 2, page 7)

That manuals be written and finished in a priority order based on the following:
❏ specific site requests in order to meet urgent needs
❏ to provide manuals for the most numbers of users
(Part 2, page 8)

That all manuals include, as part of their contents, the how to function, as well as policy and procedure. (Part 2, page 9)

That, where necessary, system housekeeping be done to bring user groups in line with the user groups necessary to match the manuals. Furthermore, those users who now have menus and options they cannot access should have those menus and options deleted from their screens through rearrangement of user groups. (Part 2, page 9; Appendix 1)

That the documentation task include a guide for training new system users, as well as an on-line tutorial covering the basic operations of the system. (Part 2, page 11)

That the following items be prepared as part of the documentation suite:
    ❏ three-fold reference cards
    ❏ plastic wall charts
    ❏ on-line help
      (Part 2, page 12)

PART 1

PART 2

PART 3

PART 4

Explanation of part 1

The amount of detail you put into Part 1 — following this real example — depends on the formality of the strategy report. In this example, the strategy report would be used to help sell the project to those who have to find the money to carry out the entire task.

The headings used here are:

Introduction

This part of the report contains a description of the task undertaken by the documentation consultants, and the methodology behind the recommendations.

The Task Undertaken

Here we defined the task as defined by the company

Our task was to investigate and make recommendations on the following points:

- to define all documentation needed for the efficient use of the System
- to report on user groups and their specific needs
- to provide an overview of comments from users as to their documentation needs

Our Methodology

Here we defined how we tackled the task — how we went about understanding the system, the users and the role the system played within each site.

Those Interviewed

We listed visits to sites and the names and positions of those we interviewed to gather our facts.

Explanation of Part 2

In this part of the strategy report we present the recommendations and — where appropriate — a commentary on those recommendations.

We also added this paragraph:

"Where we have formed conclusions in areas not directly related to documentation, such as in system implementation, system response time, and housekeeping, those conclusions are expressed as suggestions, because they fall outside the scope of our terms and reference."

The headings used here:

The Manuals

Manuals By Location

The manuals were defined for each site by name. For example: Site ABC needed the following manuals:

- ❏ Accounts
- ❏ Administration
- ❏ Auditing
- ❏ Catalogue (equipment)
- ❏ Catalogue (supply)
- ❏ Creditors
- ❏ Engineering 1
- ❏ Engineering 2
- ❏ Enquiries
- ❏ Marketing
- ❏ Operations
- ❏ Projects
- ❏ Purchasing
- ❏ Reports

- ❏ Stores
- ❏ Supply
- ❏ System reference manual
- ❏ Transport and safety

Lists were written for each site.

A commentary was written to justify each manual's existence.

Additional Manuals

Here we defined the need for a guide to explain how the system interfaced with other applications, such as the payroll system.

We also recommended a guide for new users that would provide an overview to the entire system.

Priorities

Here we listed the priorities for the writing and production of the manuals. The criteria here was to get the manuals done that would cover the most users, as well as special needs defined by the individual sites.

The commentary here included needs defined by specific users so that competing claims could be ruled on by the company.

The How-to function

This heading was needed because the original contention by the company was that the How-to function was not a high priority — that definition of fields and policy were more important. The Commentary points out that almost every user expressed the need for How-To information. One user expressed it this way:

"How-to procedures are written on the backs of envelopes, on desk blotters, and on pieces of paper stuck to terminals and walls — and this is not good enough!"

Housekeeping

Here we documented the need to bring the user group lists in line with the manuals. All sites recognized the need to carry out housekeeping. The Commentary stated that housekeeping would not delay the start of documentation because the early period of the task would require the writers to learn the system and write basic options. Housekeeping must be completed before the final collation of the options into manuals takes place.

Training

Here we recommended and justified the need for a training manual, as well as an on-line tutorial covering basic operations of the system.

Other Documentation

Here we recommended the need for a two-fold reference card to cover the extensive list of mnemonics used by the System. We also recommended a plastic wall chart for use in the many dirty areas involved in mining operations. On-line help was recommended, to be written by the same writers to ensure consistency in language and style.

Miscellaneous Observations

In this area we suggested that the company look at the topics of system down time (which was serious at some sites), system implementation (at some sites, because of the lack of documentation, users had found shortcuts that were impacting negatively on the whole system's integrity); and failure to use the system (some users were ignoring the system because without documentation, they could not figure out how to use the system effectively).

Other Documentation

Manuals, as have been outlined, are but one aspect of the successful documentation of a system. Given our review of the system, we feel there are additional items that would make up a successful documentation suite.

Recommendations: That the following items be prepared as part of the documentation suite:
- ❏ three-fold reference cards
- ❏ plastic wall charts
- ❏ on-line help

Two-fold Card

At all sites, the need was expressed for legitimate shortcuts. For example, using the codes (mnemonics) to go straight to the work area. Almost all users acknowledged they were not using the system efficiently because they did not know the shortcuts. These, plus other commonly required functions, are best produced on a two-fold reference card which is kept at the terminal.

There would need to be a number of cards produced because of the array of mnemonics available to be used in the system. This task should take place after the manuals have been completed.

Plastic Wall Chart

Many of the dirty areas would be better served by having the functionality and mnemonics listed on plastic wall charts for ready reference by workshop staff. This task should take place after the manuals have been completed.

There was also a need to catalogue some criticisms of the accounting staff who felt the system "was engineering oriented, without appropriate accounting modules, even though we are expected to use it".

Explanation of part 3

In this part of the strategy report, recommendations and comments were made on the physical format of the manuals, their binders and the boxes.

The headings used here:

❏ **The Page**

Describes the trim size of the page and the actual text area sizes.

❏ **The Typefaces**

Describes the typefaces and typesizes.

❏ **Menus, Options, Screens, and Prompts**

Describes how these items will be shown on the page. Special typefaces to be used, and so forth.

❏ **Length of Text Lines**

The main body text must meet certain criteria for maximum readability. These criteria are described under this heading.

❏ **The Paper**

Describes the quality of paper to be used. In this case we picked one paper for clean areas and another paper for the dirty areas.

❏ **Updates and Revisions**

A fundamental consideration in designing the format on manuals is how often will there be revisions or updates. This also impacts on the method of page numbering and on the way the finished manuals will be bound.

❏ **Modules, Page Titles, Numbering Systems**

Describes some of the fundamental labeling decisions that have to be made to ensure consistency and standardization. When you have multiple manuals, as in this case, it is necessary to make sure each manual has a clear, simple title. Header labels for the top of the page have to be clearly thought out here to ensure the user can find his way around the manual easily.

❏ **Sample Page Layouts**

At least one example of each different kind of layout should be done at this stage. For example: menu pages are different from option pages and field definition pages are different again. Screen layout should be shown. These page layouts also provide the opportunity to show the structure of the writing and how the option is to be broken down for clear explanation of the steps.

Explanation of part 4

In this part of the strategy report, we discuss the time and cost parameters of carrying out the total documentation task. In this example, we separated the activity into three parts: the manuals and reference cards, the training manual and on-line tutorial, and on-line help. The activity here follows the same pattern as described in chapter 6, Managing the Documentation Project.

Explanation of part 5

In this part of the report, the contents of each individual manual are detailed. There are two parts to Part 5 when the system is as large as the one covered by this example.

First there is discussion of what material might be common to all manuals. With each user seeing only those options permitted by virtue of their user ID and password combination, the individual options become the lowest common denominator — the option becomes the chapter.

At the same time, the core material about how to use the system, how to use the manuals, troubleshooting, glossary, and so forth, will appear in every manual. The structure of the manual is described in detail.

The second concern is to list all the users and arrange the options into manuals so that the total table of contents for each manual to be written can be described.

THE CONTENTS

The core chapters for all manuals identified for site A will be the same — with minor editing to provide each manual with identification to its own site.

The sites outside of Brisbane will also have a short section discussing the structure of the system and how the linkage to Brisbane works so that users will understand the relationship of the terminal they are working at and the main computer at Brisbane.

Core Contents I

The core contents for all manuals will include:

- Foreword
- Table of Contents (specific to each manual)
- The System
- Using the System
  - Introduction
  - Some Useful Definitions (Glossary)
  - The Keyboard and Its Use
  - Passwords, User Names
    Logging On, Logging Off
- Menus, Options, Screens, Reports and Prompts

Contents Specific to Each Manual

- Introduction
- When and Why to Use
- How to Use, Including Off-computer Procedures
- Definitions for All Menus (by Option)
- Definitions for All Screens (by Prompt)
- Definitions for All Reports
- Definitions for All Report (headings)
  The contents specific for each manual are detailed in the following pages.

Core Contents II

- System Administration and You
  - How to Summon Help
  - Error Messages and What They Mean
    Errors You Can Correct Yourself
    Errors You Can Correct, but Must Report
    Errors You Can Do Nothing About, Except Report
  - Index (Activity)

The appendices

The appendices in this example consisted of a database printout we prepared listing every user, their user group, the user's job title, department, location and the name of the manual. As a result of this database, we were able to make recommendations to tighten up the user groups. The most common problem was user groups that had only a couple of users. Those users could be moved to larger user groups, thus cutting down the total number of manuals that had to be written.

Glossary

A-column

in this book, defined as the format area of a page in which the headings for topics and subtopics are placed

Activities index

in this book, an index arranged by tasks and activities rather than the traditional single word index

Application

a computer program enabling the user to create, enter and design information, such as word processing, spreadsheet and drawing programs

Artwork (see Mechanicals, Bromides)

Ascender

the vertical stroke on a lower case letter, as in b, h, d, extending above the x-height (the height of the letter x)

Baseline

the horizontal line that specifies the bottom of a lowercase letter, excluding the descenders

B-column

in this book, defined as the format area of a page in which the body text, graphic elements, and so forth are placed

Body (text)

the main text on the page, excluding headings, normally described as column B text in this book

Bold

the heavier, blacker version of a given typeface

Box

❏ in this book, a Zapf Dingbat typeface character used to set list items apart

Braces (see also Brackets, Parentheses)

{ }

Brackets (see also Braces, Parentheses)

[ ] often referred to as square brackets

Bromides (see Mechanicals)

Bullets (blobs, cannon balls)

• in this book, a character used to signal an action statement and created by pressing option-8 keys in Times and Garamond 3 typefaces

Camera-ready art (see Mechanicals)

Caption

text used under or near an illustration to describe that illustration

Character

a letter, number or other character

Coated paper

a paper with a smooth finish

Color separations

pieces of film, each representing a particular color used in offset printing

Condensed type

a typeface where the characters have been compressed vertically to give a tall, slim appearance; compressed typefaces occupy less space on a line than their normal counterparts

Data

in this book, information processed by the computer

Descender

> the vertical stroke on a lower case letter, as in g, p, y, extending below the baseline

Desktop publishing

> an application or program that is a tool for the writer, editor, artist and printer, integrating page layout, graphics, text entry and printing

Documentation set

> a combination of documentation tools such as a manual, quick reference card and on-line help needed to properly explain a system to users

Dots per inch (dpi)

> a measure of screen or printer resolution, with the higher number of dots resulting in a higher level of resolution

Drop-Shadow (also Shadow Box)

> a black or tinted background placed behind and slightly offside to create a shadow effect

Electronic documentation

> a more accurate description of on-line documentation

Em

> a measurement unit determined as the width of the letter M in a given typeface

En

> a measurement unit half the width of an em; often determined as the width of the letter N in a given typeface

External documentation

> documentation produced for commercial purchases, such as a manual with software for sale, as opposed to internal or in-house documentation

Family (type)

> a group of typefaces with common designs, but which have different forms, such as Garamond, Garamond Bold and Garamond Bold Italic which all belong to the Garamond family

Folio

> the page number

Font

> the total set of characters (including letters, punctuation marks, numbers and symbols) in a typeface; in this book referred to as the typeface

Foot (Footer)

> the margin area at the bottom (foot) of the page, often used for page number or name of the manual

Form (see Window)

Format

> the arrangement of the elements on a page or, more widely, the arrangement of elements making up an entire manual

Gate fold

> a sheet of paper folded twice vertically to create six faces, in this book referred to as a quick reference card or two-fold card

Gutter

> the space between columns of text placed side-by-side on the page; also the space between the text and the inside edge of the page

Head (Header)

> the margin area at the top (head) of the page, often used for page number or name of the manual

Highlight

> to set some page element so that it appears different to the other elements on the page, as in boxing, bolding, reversing

Hyphenation

> a break in a text line, followed by a hyphen (-); used to produce even word spacing on the line

Initial cap

> using a capital letter to start a word

Internal documentation

> documentation produced for in-house use, usually produced by an organization for use within that organization, as opposed to external documentation

Italic

> the slightly slanted or sloped version of a typeface

Justification

> the arrangement of word spacing so that all lines are of equal length; that is they all start at the same margin on the left and end at the same margin on the right

Layout

> the way in which text and graphic elements are placed in relation to one another on a page

Leading (also Ledding)

> the vertical space in points between the baselines of lines of type

Letter spacing

> the spacing between type characters

Line illustration

> a graphic composed of lines

Lowercase

the smaller version of letters, as in a, b, c as opposed to uppercase letters, A, B, C

Margins

the space on the page between the text areas and the edges of the page

Measure

the width of a column of text

Mechanicals (Bromides, Camera-ready art)

complete, assembled art, ready to be photographed to produce printing plates; in this book, pages ready to go to the commercial printer

Mindset

in this book, the information an individual has stored away over the length of his life about any given subject and which is then used to form an opinion about that subject or related or new subjects

Offset printing

a method of commercial printing suitable for large print runs

On-line documentation

in this book, the use of the computer to provide information similar to that found in paper-based documentation; such as on-line help and on-line tutorials

Overmatter

text that is too long to fit in the required text area

Page

one side of a sheet of paper

Page depth

usually measures the length of the available text area on the page; as opposed to trim size

Parentheses (see also Braces, Brackets)

( )

Perfect binding

a binding method where pages are glued together along one edge; not an appropriate method for user documentation

Pica

a typographical measurement unit, equals 12 points or about 1/6th of an inch

Point

the basic typographic measurement unit defining the size of a line of type; 72 points equals an inch

Printed both sides

pages printed on both sides, as in normal book printing; as opposed to printing on a single side as is common in in-house documentation

Proportional typefaces

in typography, the condition in which certain letters take up more space than other letters, as in Times and Garamond; as opposed to nonproportional typefaces, as in Courier, where each letter occupies the same space

Range left

text aligned to the left side of the column with right side ragged

Range right

text aligned to the right side of the column with left side ragged

Recto

a right-hand page

Resolution

the sharpness of definition of an image, determined by the number of dots per inch (dpi) on a screen or printer

Reversing out

> printing white text or white graphic on a black or darkly toned background

Revise

> in this book, updating or maintaining a finished manual

Ring binder

> a stiff folder, with spine and metal binding rings; can be purchased in commercial sizes, or made to size

Run

> usually used to define the number of copies to be printed, as in print run

Running head

> a minor headline repeated at the top of pages, often used for the name of the manual

Saddle-stitch

> a binding method using staples placed in the gutter to hold the pages together; suitable only for small numbers of pages

Sanserif

> typefaces without serifs, such as Helvetica and Avant Garde

Screen dump

> a picture of the screen image, or a portion of the image, that can be used as an illustration in a manual

Serif

> small strokes at the end of the significant strokes in a typeface, such as Times or Garamond

Spine

> the bound edge of a manual; no spine on coil or spiral bound manuals

Square brackets (see Brackets)

Technical documentation

> in this book, documentation produced usually by technical writers for a technical audience as opposed to user documentation prepared for a nontechnical audience

Title page

> first page of a manual with minimum information being the name of the manual

Total documentation

> in this book, the preparation of documentation across many levels of activities including, but not limited to, the physical systems, business rules and policy, and training requirements for those areas

Trim

> the act of cutting the edges of a page to the final trim size

Trimmed size

> the final size of the page from one edge of the paper to the other

Typeface (see font)

Typography

> the subject of arranging and studying type forms

Unjustified

> a text block ranged to the left with the right edge of the block left uneven (ragged)

Upper case

> the larger version of letters, as in A, B, C as opposed to lowercase letters, a, b, c

User documentation

> in this book, documentation produced for a nontechnical audience written in a user friendly manner

Verso

a left-hand page

White space

the blank areas of a page; vitally important as a design element in the final look of the page

Widow

a short line at the end of a paragraph that appears at the top of the next page, looking out of place

Window

in this book, a pop-up box that appears on a computer screen, sometimes referred to as a form

Word space

the space appearing between words in a text line

x-height

in type, the height of the lowercase letter x in a given typeface

Index